LANGENSCHEIDT
STANDARD DICTIONARIES

LANGENSCHEIDT'S
STANDARD
ITALIAN DICTIONARY

Italian-English
English-Italian

by

R. C. MELZI

LANGENSCHEIDT

*Neither the presence nor the absence of a designation that any
entered word constitutes a trademark
should be regarded as affecting the legal status of any trademark.*

AUG 1 7 2006

PREFACE

Inasmuch as the basic function of a bilingual dictionary is to provide semantic equivalences, syntactical constructions are shown in both the source and the target languages on both sides of the Dictionary. In performing this function, a bilingual dictionary must fulfill six purposes. That is, an Italian and English dictionary must provide (1) Italian words which an English-speaking person wishes to use in speaking and writing (by means of the English-Italian part), (2) English meanings of Italian words which an English-speaking person encounters in listening and reading (by means of the Italian-English part), (3) the spelling, pronunciation, and inflection of Italian words and the gender of Italian nouns which an English-speaking person needs in order to use Italian words correctly (by means of the Italian-English part), (4) English words which an Italian-speaking person wishes to use in speaking and writing (by means of the Italian-English part), (5) Italian meanings of English words which an Italian-speaking person encounters in listening and reading (by means of the English-Italian part), and (6) the spelling, pronunciation, and inflection of English words which an Italian-speaking person needs in order to use English words correctly (by means of the English-Italian part).

It may seem logical to provide the pronunciation and inflection of English words and the pronunciation and inflection of Italian words and the gender of Italian nouns where these words appear as target words inasmuch as target words, according to (1) and (4) above, are sought for the purpose of speaking and writing. Thus the user would find not only the words he seeks but all the information he needs about them in one and the same place. But this technique is impractical because target words are not alphabetized and could, therefore, be found only by the roundabout and uncertain way of seeking them through their translations in

PREFAZIONE

Dato che la funzione principale di un dizionario bilingue è quella di fornire all'utente equivalenze semantiche, le costruzioni sintattiche sono indicate in entrambe le lingue, quella di partenza e quella di arrivo, in entrambe le parti del Dizionario. Per compiere questa funzione, un dizionario bilingue deve raggiungere sei scopi differenti. Cioè, un dizionario italiano e inglese deve fornire (1) nella parte inglese-italiano, le parole italiane che la persona anglofona vuole adoperare parlando e scrivendo l'italiano; (2) nella parte italiano-inglese, il significato in inglese delle parole italiane che tale persona oda nella lingua parlata o legga in libri o giornali; (3) nella parte italiano-inglese, l'ortografia, la pronunzia, la flessione delle parole italiane e il genere dei nomi italiani che la persona anglofona deve conoscere per servirsi correttamente della lingua italiana; (4) nella parte italiano-inglese, le parole inglesi che la persona italofona vuole adoperare parlando o scrivendo l'inglese; (5) nella parte inglese-italiano, il significato in italiano delle parole inglesi che tale persona oda nella lingua parlata o legga in libri o giornali; (6) nella parte inglese-italiano, l'ortografia, la pronunzia figurata e la flessione delle parole inglesi che la persona italofona deve conoscere per servirsi correttamente della lingua inglese.

A prima vista potrebbe sembrare logico che la pronunzia e la flessione delle parole inglesi e la pronunzia e la flessione delle parole italiane e il genere dei nomi italiani fossero indicati dove queste parole si trovano nella lingua d'arrivo, dato che le parole della lingua d'arrivo, secondo i punti (1) e (4) enunciati più sopra, sono consultate da coloro che vogliono parlare e scrivere in lingua straniera. In questa maniera l'utente troverebbe non solo le parole che cerca, ma tutte le informazioni che gli sono necessarie, nello stesso luogo. Questa tecnica, peraltro, non è pratica poiché le parole della lingua d'arrivo non si trovano in ordine

the other part of the dictionary. And this would be particularly inconvenient for persons using the dictionary for purposes (2) and (5) above. It is much more convenient to provide immediate alphabetized access to pronunciation and inflection where the words appear as source words.

alfabetico e potrebbero quindi essere trovate solo in maniera complicata nella parte opposta del dizionario. E ciò sarebbe specialmente scomodo per coloro che usano il dizionario per gli scopi (2) e (5) menzionati più sopra. È molto più semplice aggiungere la pronunzia e la flessione nella serie alfabetica in cui le parole si trovano nella loro lingua di partenza.

Since Italian is an almost perfectly phonetic language, IPA transcription of Italian words has been omitted. The only elements of pronunciation not shown by standard spelling are the values of tonic e and o (§1; pp. 3, 4) the stress of words stressed on the third syllable from the end (§3,3; p. 5), the value of intervocalic s when unvoiced, and the values of z and zz when voiced (§1; p. 4); these are shown in the entry words themselves.

Dato che l'italiano è una lingua quasi perfettamente fonetica, non si è data la trascrizione delle parole italiane nell'alfabeto dell'Associazione Fonetica Internazionale. Considerando che l'ortografia comune non mostra il vario timbro della e (§1, p. 3) e della o (§1, p. 4) quando esse sono toniche, l'accento delle parole sdrucciole (§3,3, p. 5), la pronunzia della s sorda (§1, p. 4) e la pronunzia delle z e zz sonore (§1, p. 4), si è data tale informazione nell'esponente stesso.

All words are treated in a fixed order according to the parts of speech and the functions of verbs, as follows: adjective, article, substantive, pronoun, adverb, preposition, conjunction, transitive verb, intransitive verb, reflexive verb, auxiliary verb, impersonal verb, interjection.

Ogni singola voce è trattata secondo uno schema fisso che si riferisce alle parti del discorso o alle funzioni del verbo, nel seguente ordine: aggettivo, articolo, sostantivo, pronome, avverbio, preposizione, congiunzione, verbo transitivo, verbo intransitivo, verbo riflessivo, verbo ausiliare, verbo impersonale e interiezione.

Meanings with labels come after more general meanings. Labels (printed in roman and in parentheses) refer to the preceding entry or phrase (printed in boldface).

I significati accompagnati da sigle si trovano dopo quelli di accezione più generale. Tali sigle (che sono sempre stampate in carattere romano e in parentesi) si riferiscono all'esponente precedente, stampato in grassetto, o alla frase precedente, ugualmente stampata in grassetto.

In view of the fact that the users of this Italian and English bilingual dictionary are for the most part English-speaking people, definitions and discriminations are provided in English. They are printed in italics and in parentheses and refer to the English word which they particularize:

Dato che gli utenti di questo dizionario bilingue italiano e inglese sono per lo più anglofoni, definizioni e locuzioni esplicative sono apportate in inglese. Sono stampate in corsivo e in parentesi e si riferiscono sempre alla parola inglese il cui significato cercano di spiegare:

porter ['portər] *s (doorman)* portiere *m; (man who carries luggage)* facchino; . . .
órdine *m* order; . . . series (*e.g., of years*); college (*e.g., of surgeons*); . . .

English adjectives are always translated by the Italian masculine form

Gli aggettivi inglesi sono sempre tradotti in maschile italiano, anche se il

regardless of whether the translation of the exemplary noun modified would be masculine or feminine:

nome che qualificano sia un femminile italiano:

tough [tʌf] *adj* duro; . . . ; *(luck)* cattivo; . . .

In order to facilitate the finding of the meaning and use sought for, changes within a vocabulary entry in part of speech and function of verb, in irregular inflection, in the use of an initial capital, in the gender of Italian nouns, and in the pronunciation of English words are marked with parallels: ||, instead of the usual semicolons.

Per facilitare l'uso del Dizionario, i raggruppamenti sono stati fatti secondo le parti del discorso, la funzione del verbo, la flessione irregolare, l'uso della maiuscola iniziale, il genere dei nomi italiani e la pronunzia delle parole inglesi e sono separati da sbarrette verticali: ||, invece del punto e virgola che è stato generalmente usato.

Since vocabulary entries are not determined on the basis of etymology, homographs are included in a single entry. When the pronunciation of an English homograph changes, this is shown in the proper place after parallels:

Dato che gli esponenti in questo Dizionario non sono stati selezionati su base etimologica, tutti gli omografi sono inclusi sotto il medesimo esponente. Il cambio di pronunzia di un omografo inglese è indicato al posto adatto dopo sbarrette verticali:

frequent [ˈfrikwənt] *adj* frequente || [friˈkwɛnt]
or [ˈfrikwənt] *tr* . . .

However, when the pronunciation of an Italian homograph changes, the words are entered separately:

Però, quando la pronunzia di un omografo italiano cambia, si hanno esponenti separati:

retina *f* small net
rètina *f* (anat) retina
tóc‧co ‧ca (-chi ‧che) *adj* . . . || *m* touch; . . .
tòc‧co *m* (-chi) chunk, piece; . . .

Periods are omitted after labels and grammatical abbreviations and at the end of vocabulary entries.

Il punto è stato omesso dopo sigle, abbreviazioni grammaticali, ed alla fine di ogni articolo.

Proper nouns are listed in their alphabetical position in the main body of the Dictionary. Thus **Svezia** and **svedese** do not have to be looked up in two different sections of the book. And all subentries are listed in strictly alphabetical order.

Tutti i nomi propri sono posti nella loro posizione alfabetica nel corpo del Dizionario: quindi **Svezia** e **svedese** non si trovano in sezioni separate di questo libro. Per la medesima ragione di semplicità d'uso, le parole e frasi contenute sotto ogni esponente sono poste in ordine alfabetico.

The gender of Italian nouns is shown on both sides of the Dictionary, except that the gender of masculine nouns ending in **-o**, feminine nouns ending in **-a** and **-ione**, masculine nouns modified by an adjective ending in **-o**, and feminine nouns modified by an adjective

Il genere dei nomi italiani è indicato in entrambe le parti del Dizionario, eccezion fatta nella parte inglese-italiano, per le parole maschili che terminano in **-o**, per le parole femminili che terminano in **-a** e in **-ione**, per i nomi maschili accompagnati da un

ending in -a is not shown on the English-Italian side.

aggettivo che termina in -o e per i nomi femminili accompagnati da un aggettivo che termina in -a.

The feminine form of an Italian adjective used as a noun (or an Italian feminine noun having identical spelling with the feminine form of an adjective) which falls alphabetically in a separate position from the adjective is treated in that position and is listed again as a cross reference under the adjective:

Quando un nome femminile italiano ha la medesima grafia della forma femminile di un aggettivo o quando tale forma femminile di aggettivo è usata come nome, lo si trova elencato nella sua posizione alfabetica come nome e poi di nuovo come rinvio interno sotto l'aggettivo:

> **nòta** *f* mark, score, . . .
> **nò·to -ta** *adj* . . . ‖ *m* . . . ‖ *f* see **nota**

The centered period is used in vocabulary entries of inflected words to mark off, according to standard orthographic principles in the two languages, the final syllable that has to be detached before the syllable showing the inflection is added:

Qualora l'esponente italiano o inglese sia un vocabolo a flessione, un punto leggermente elevato sopra il rigo è stato usato per separare, secondo le regole ortografiche di ciascuna delle due lingue, la sillaba finale che dev'essere rimossa prima che la nuova desinenza di flessione possa essere attaccata al corpo dell'esponente, per es.:

> **vèc·chio -chia (-chi -chie)** *adj* . . .
> **put·ty** ['pʌti] *s* (-ties) . . . ‖ *v* (*pret & pp* -tied) . . .
> **hap·py** ['hæpi] *adj* (-pier; -piest) . . .

If the entry word cannot be divided by a centered period the full form is given in parentheses:

Se l'esponente non può essere scisso a mezzo del suddetto punto, la forma completa è indicata in parentesi:

> **mouse** [maʊs] *s* (**mice** [maɪs]) . . .
> **mouth** [maʊθ] *s* (**mouths** [maʊðz]) . . .
> **die** [daɪ] *s* (**dice** [daɪs']) . . . ‖ *s* (**dies**) . . . ‖ *v* (*pret & pp* **died**; *ger* **dying**) *intr* . . .

Many Italian verbs which take an indirect object have, as their equivalent, English verbs which take a direct object. This is shown on both sides of this Dictionary by the insertion of (with *dat*) after the Italian verb, e.g.,

Molti verbi italiani che reggono un oggetto indiretto hanno come equivalente inglesi verbi che reggono un oggetto diretto. Questa equivalenza è indicata in entrambe le parti del Dizionario con l'aggiunta di (with *dat*) dopo il verbo italiano, per es.:

> **ubbidire §176** *intr* . . . ; (with *dat*) to obey
> **obey** [o'be] *tr* ubbidire (with *dat*)

On the Italian-English side inflection is shown by: a) numbers that refer to the grammatical tables of articles, pronouns, etc., and to the tables of model verbs; they are placed before the abbreviation indicating the part of speech:

Nella parte italiano-inglese la flessione si indica: a) con numeri che si riferiscono alle tavole grammaticali degli articoli, dei pronomi, ecc., e alle tavole dei verbi modello; questi numeri sono posti innanzi all'abbreviazione indicante la parte del discorso:

> **mì·o -a §6** *adj & pron poss*
> **lui §5** *pron pers*
> **congiùngere §183** *tr & ref*

b) the first person singular of the present indicative of verbs in which the stess falls on either an **e** or an **o** not stressed in the infinitive or on the third syllable from the end, whatever the vowel may be:

b) con la prima persona singolare del presente dell'indicativo dei verbi non sdruccioli all'infinito in cui l'accento tonico cade o su una **e** o su una **o**, o su qualsiasi vocale di una parola sdrucciola:

ritornare (ritórno) *tr* . . .
visitare (vìsito) *tr* . . .

c) the feminine endings of all adjectives which end in **-o**:

c) con la desinenza femminile di tutti gli aggettivi che terminano in **-o** nel maschile:

laborió•so -sa [s] *adj* . . .

d) the plural endings of nouns and adjectives which are formed irregularly:

d) con la desinenza plurale dei nomi e aggettivi che si formano in maniera irregolare:

bràc•cio *m* (**-cia** *fpl*) . . . || *m* (**-ci**) . . .
cit•tà *f* (**-tà**) . . .
dià•rio -ria (**-ri -rie**) *adj* . . . || *m* . . . || *f* . . .
fotogram•ma *m* (**-mi**) . . .
fràn•gia *f* (**-ge**) . . .
laburi•sta (**-sti -ste**) *adj* . . . || *mf* . . .
la•go *m* (**-ghi**) . . .
òr•co *m* (**-chi**) . . .
òtti•co -ca (**-ci -che**) *adj* . . . || *m* . . . || *f* . . .

e) the full plural forms of all nouns that cannot be divided by a center period or whose plural cannot be shown by such division:

e) con la completa forma plurale di quei nomi che non possono essere scissi col suddetto punto o che hanno mutamenti interni:

re *m* (**re**) . . .
caporeparto *m* (**capireparto**) . . .

Labels and abbreviations

Sigle ed abbreviazioni

abbr abbreviation—abbreviazione
(acronym) word formed from the initial letters or syllables of a series of words—parola costituita dalle lettere o sillabe iniziali di una serie di parole
adj adjective—aggettivo
adv adverb—avverbio
(aer) aeronautics—aeronautica
(agr) agriculture—agricoltura
(alg) algebra—algebra
(anat) anatomy—anatomia
(archaic) arcaico
(archeol) archeology—archeologia
(archit) architecture—architettura
(arith) arithmetic—aritmetica
art article—articolo
(astr) astronomy—astronomia
(astrol) astrology—astrologia
(aut) automobile—automobile
aux auxiliary verb—verbo ausiliare
(bact) bacteriology—batteriologia
(baseball) baseball
(basketball) pallacanestro
(bb) bookbinding—legatoria
(Bib) Biblical—biblico
(billiards) biliardo
(biochem) biochemistry—biochimica
(biol) biology—biologia
(bot) botany—botanica
(bowling) bowling
(boxing) pugilato
(bridge) bridge
(Brit) British—britannico
(cards) carte da gioco
(carp) carpentry—falegnameria
(checkers) gioco della dama
(chem) chemistry—chimica
(chess) scacchi
(coll) colloquial—familiare
(com) commercial—commerciale
comb form elemento di parola composta
comp comparative—comparativo
cond conditional—condizionale
conj conjunction—congiunzione
(cricket) cricket
(culin) cooking—cucina
dat dative—dativo
def definite—determinativo, definito
dem demonstrative—dimostrativo
(dentistry) medicina dentaria
(dial) dialectal—dialettale
(dipl) diplomacy—diplomazia

(disparaging) sprezzante
(eccl) ecclesiastical—ecclesiastico
(econ) economics—economia
(educ) education—istruzione
e.g., or *e.g.,* per esempio
(elec) electricity—elettricità
(electron) electronics—elettronica
(ent) entomology—entomologia
(equit) horseback riding—equitazione
f feminine noun—nome femminile
(fa) fine arts—belle arti
fem feminine—femminile
(fencing) scherma
(fig) figurative—figurato
(fin) financial—finanziario
(football) football americano
fpl feminine noun plural—nome femminile plurale
fut future—futuro
(geog) geography—geografia
(geol) geology—geologia
(geom) geometry—geometria
ger gerund—gerundio
(golf) golf
(gram) grammar—grammatica
(herald) heraldry—araldica
(hist) history—storia
(hort) horticulture—orticoltura
(hunt) hunting—caccia
(ichth) ichthyology—ittiologia
i.e., cioè
imperf imperfect—imperfetto
impers impersonal verb—verbo impersonale
impv imperative—imperativo
ind indicative—indicativo
indef indefinite—indefinito, indeterminativo
inf infinitive—infinito
(ins) insurance—assicurazione
interj interjection—interiezione
interr interrogative—interrogativo
intr intransitive verb—verbo intransitivo
invar invariable—invariabile
(Italian cards) carte italiane
(jewelry) gioielleria
(joc) jocular—faceto
(journ) journalism—giornalismo
(law) diritto, legge
(letterword) word in the form of an abbreviation which is pronounced by sounding the names of its letters in

succession and which functions as a part of speech—parola in forma di abbreviazione che si ottiene pronunziando consecutivamente la denominazione di ciascuna lettera e che funziona come parte del discorso

(lexicography) lessicografia
(ling) linguistics—linguistica
(lit) literary—letterario
(log) logic—logica
m masculine noun—nome maschile
(mach) machinery—macchinario
masc masculine—maschile
(math) mathematics—matematica
(mech) mechanics—meccanica
(med) medicine—medicina
(metallurgy) metallurgia
(meteor) meteorology—meteorologia
mf masculine or feminine noun according to sex—nome maschile o nome femminile secondo il sesso
m & f see below between (mythol) and (naut)
(mil) military—militare
(min) mining—lavorazione delle miniere
(mov) moving pictures—cinematografo
mpl masculine noun plural—nome maschile plurale
(mus) music—musica
(mythol) mythology—mitologia
m & f masculine and feminine noun without regard to sex—nome maschile e femminile senza distinzione di sesso
(naut) nautical—nautico
(nav) naval—navale
neut neuter—neutro
num number—numero
(obs) obsolete—in disuso
(obstet) obstetrics—ostetricia
(opt) optics—ottica
(orn) ornithology—ornitologia
(painting) pittura
(pathol) pathology—patologia
(pej) pejorative—peggiorativo
perf perfect—perfetto, passato
pers personal—personale; person—persona
(pharm) pharmacy—farmacia
(philately) filatelia
(philol) philology—filologia
(philos) philosophy—filosofia
(phonet) phonetics—fonetica
(phot) photography—fotografia
(phys) physics—fisica
(physiol) physiology—fisiologia
pl plural—plurale
(poet) poetical—poetico
(poker) poker
(pol) politics—politica
pp past participle—participio passato
poss possessive—possessivo
pref prefix—prefisso
prep preposition—preposizione

prep phrase prepositional phrase—frase preposizionale
pres present—presente
pret preterit—passato remoto
pron pronoun—pronome
(pros) prosody—prosodia
(psychoanal) psychoanalysis—psicanalisi
(psychol) psychology—psicologia
(psychopath) psychopathology—psicopatologia
qlco or *qlco* qualcosa—something
qlcu or *qlcu* qualcuno—someone
(racing) corse
(rad) radio—radio
ref reflexive verb—verbo riflessivo o pronominale
rel relative—relativo
(rel) religion—religione
(rhet) rhetoric—retorica
(rok) rocketry—studio dei razzi
(rowing) canottaggio
(rr) railroad—ferrovia
(rugby) rugby
s substantive—sostantivo
(scornful) sprezzante
(Scot) Scottish—scozzese
(sculp) sculpture—scultura
(sew) sewing—cucito
sg singular—singolare
(slang) gergo
s.o. or *s.o.* someone—qualcuno
(soccer) calcio
spl substantive plural—sostantivo plurale
(sports) sport
ssg substantive singular—sostantivo singolare
s.th or *s.th* something—qualcosa
subj subjunctive—congiuntivo
suf suffix—suffisso
super superlative—superlativo
(surg) surgery—chirurgia
(surv) surveying—agrimensura, topografia
(taur) bullfighting—tauromachia
(telg) telegraphy—telegrafia
(telp) telephone—telefonia
(telv) television—televisione
(tennis) tennis
(tex) textile—tessile
(theat) theater—teatro
(theol) theology—teologia
tr transitive verb—verbo transitivo
(trademark) marchio di fabbrica
(typ) printing—tipografia
(U.S.A.) S.U.A.
v verb—verbo
var variant—variante
(vet) veterinary medicine—medicina veterinaria
(vulg) vulgar—volgare, ordinario
(wrestling) lotta
(zool) zoology—zoologia

PART ONE

Italian-English

Contents

Indice

	page
Italian Spelling and Pronunciation	3
Grammatical Tables	7
Model Italian Verbs	17
Italian-English Vocabulary – *Vocabolario Italiano-Inglese*	37–364

Italian Spelling and Pronunciation

§1. The Italian Alphabet. 1. The twenty-one letters of the Italian alphabet are listed below with their names and their sounds in terms of approximate equivalent English sounds. Their gender is masculine or feminine.

LETTER	NAME	APPROXIMATE SOUND
a	a	Like *a* in English *father*, e.g., **facile, padre.**
b	bi	Like *b* in English *boat*, e.g., **bello, abate.**
c	ci	When followed by **e** or **i**, like *ch* in English *cherry*, e.g., **cento, cinque;** if the **i** is unstressed and followed by another vowel, its sound is not heard, e.g., **ciarla, cieco.** When followed by **a, o, u,** or a consonant, like *c* in English *cook*, e.g., **casa, come, cura, credere.** The digraph **ch,** which is used before **e** and **i,** has likewise the sound of *c* in English *cook*, e.g., **chiesa, perché.**
d	di	Like *d* in English *dance*, e.g., **dare, madre.**
e	e	Has two sounds. One like *a* in English *make*, shown on stressed syllables in this DICTIONARY by the acute accent, e.g., **séra, trénta;** and one like *e* in English *met*, shown on stressed syllables in this DICTIONARY by the grave accent, e.g., **fèrro, fèsta.**
f	effe	Like *f* in English *fool*, e.g., **farina, efelide.**
g	gi	When followed by **e** or **i**, like *g* in English *general*, e.g., **gelato, ginnasta;** if the **i** is unstressed and followed by another vowel, its sound is not heard, e.g., **giallo, giorno.** When followed by **a, o, u,** or a consonant, like *g* in English *go*, e.g., **gamba, goccia, gusto, grado.** The digraph **gh,** which is used before **e** and **i,** has likewise the sound of *g* in English *go*, e.g., **gherone, ghisa.** When the combination **gli** (a) is a form of the definite article or the personal pronoun, (b) is final in a word, or (c) is intervocalic, it has the sound of Castilian *ll*, which is somewhat like *lli* in English *million*, e.g., (a) **gli uomini, gli ho parlato ieri,** (b) **battagli,** (c) **figlio, migliore.** When it is (a) initial (except in the word **gli,** above), (b) preceded by a consonant, or (c) followed by a consonant, it is pronounced like *gli* in English *negligence*, e.g., (a) **glioma,** (b) **ganglio,** (c) **negligenza.** The combination **gl** followed by **a, e, o,** or **u** is pronounced like *gl* in English *globe*, e.g., **glabro, gleba, globo, gluteo, inglese, poliglotto.** The digraph **gn** has the sound of Castilian *ñ*, which is somewhat like *ni* in English *onion*, e.g., **signore, gnocco.**
h	acca	Always silent, e.g., **ah, hanno.** See **ch** under **c** above and **gh** under **g** above.
i	i	Like *i* in English *machine*, e.g., **piccolo, sigla.** When unstressed and followed by another vowel, like *y* in English *yes*, e.g., **piatto, piede, fiore, fiume.** For **i** in **ci,** see **c** above, in **gi,** see **g** above, and in **sci,** see **s** below.

3

LETTER	NAME	APPROXIMATE SOUND
l	elle	Like *l* in English *lamb*, e.g., **labbro, lacrima.**
m	emme	Like *m* in English *money*, e.g., **mano, come.**
n	enne	Like *n* in English *net*, e.g., **nome, cane.**
o	o	Has two sounds. One like *o* in English *note*, shown on stressed syllables in this DICTIONARY by the acute accent, e.g., **dópo, sóle;** and one like *ou* in English *ought*, shown on stressed syllables in this DICTIONARY by the grave accent, e.g., **còsa, dònna.**
p	pi	Like *p* in English *pot*, e.g., **passo, carpa.**
q	cu	This letter is always followed by the letter **u** and the combination has the sound of *qu* in English *quart*, e.g., **quanto, questo.**
r	erre	Like *r* in English *rubber*, with a slight trill, e.g., **roba, carta.**
s	esse	Has two sounds. When initial and followed by a vowel, when preceded by a consonant and followed by a vowel, and when followed by **c** [k] **f, p, q,** or **t,** like *s* in English *see*, e.g., **sale, falso, scappare, spazio, stoffa;** and when standing between two vowels and when followed by **b, d, g** [g], **l, m, n, r** or **v,** like *z* in English *zero*, e.g., **paese, sbaglio, svenire.** However, **s** standing between two vowels in some words and initial **s** followed by **b, d, g** [g], **l, m, n, r,** or **v** in some foreign borrowings are pronounced like *s* in *see*, e.g., **casa*, tesa, smoking, slam** In this DICTIONARY this is indicated by the insertion of [s] immediately after the entry word. However, when initial **s** stands between two vowels in a compound, its pronunciation remains that of initial **s,** e.g., **autoservizio** and this is not indicated. The digraph **sc,** when followed by **e** or **i** has the sound of *sh* in English *shall*, e.g., **scelta, scimmia;** if the **i** is unstressed and followed by another vowel, its sound is not heard, e.g., **sciame, sciopero.** The trigraph **sch** has the sound of *sc* in English *scope*, e.g., **scherzo, schiavo.**
t	ti	Like *t* in English *table*, e.g., **terra, pasto.**
u	u	Like *u* in English *rule*, e.g., **luna, mulo.** When followed by a vowel, like *w* in English *was*, e.g., **quanto, guerra, nuovo.**
v	vu	Like *v* in English *vain*, e.g., **vita, uva.**
z	zeta	Has two sounds. One like *ts* in English *nuts*, e.g., **grazia, zucchero;** and one like *dz* in English *adze*, e.g., **zero, mezzo.** In this DICTIONARY the sound of *dz* in *adze* is indicated by the insertion of [dz] immediately after the entry word. If the sound is long, [ddzz] is inserted

* Intervocalic **s** is generally voiced in the north of Italy.

2. The following five letters are found in borrowings from other languages.

LETTER	NAME	EXAMPLES
j	i lunga	**jazz, jingo**
k	cappa	**kiosco, kodak**
w	doppia vu	**water-polo, whisky**
x	ics	**xenofobo, xilofono**
y	ipsilon	**yacht, yoghurt**

3. Consonants written double are longer than consonants written single, that is, it takes a longer time to pronounce them, e.g., **camino** *chimney* and **cam-**

mino *road,* **capello** *hair* and **cappello** *hat.* Special attention is called to the following double consonants: **cc** followed by **e** or **i** has the sound of *ch ch* in English *beach chair,* that is, a lengthened *ch* (not the sound of *ks*), e.g., **accento; cch** has the sound of *kk* in English *bookkeeper,* e.g., **becchino; cq** has the sound of *kk* in English *bookkeeper,* e.g., **acqua; gg** followed by **e** or **i** has the sound of *ge j* in English *carriage joiner,* e.g., **peggio; ggh** has the sound of *g g* in English *tag game,* e.g., **agghindare.**

§2. Division of Syllables. In the application of the following rules for the syllabic division of words, the digraphs **ch, gh, gl, gn,** and **sc** count as single consonants.

(a) When a single consonant stands between two vowels it belongs to the following syllable, e.g., **ca·sa, fu·mo, ami·che, la·ghi, fi·glio, biso·gno, la·sciare.**

(b) When a consonant group consisting of two consonants of which the second is **l** or **r** stands between two vowels, the group belongs to the following syllable, e.g., **nu·cleo, so·brio, qua·dro.**

(c) When a consonant group consisting of two or more consonants of which the first or the second is **s** stands between two vowels, that part of the group beginning with **s** belongs to the following syllable, e.g., **ta·sca, bo·schi, fine·stra, super·sti·zione, sub·strato.**

(d) When a consonant group consisting of two or three consonants of which the first is **l, m, n,** or **r** stands between two vowels, the **l, m, n,** or **r** belongs to the preceding syllable, the other consonant or consonants to the following syllable, e.g., **al·bero, am·pio, prin·cipe, mor·te, in·flazione, com·pleto.**

(e) When a double consonant stands between two vowels or between a vowel and **l** or **r,** the first belongs to the preceding syllable, the second to the following syllable, e.g., **bab·bo, caval·lo, an·no, car·ro, mez·zo, sup·plica, lab·bro, quat·tro.**

§3. Stress and Accent Marks. 1. Whenever stress is shown as part of regular spelling, it is shown on **a, i,** and **u** by the grave accent mark, e.g., **libertà, giovedì, gioventù,** on close **e** and **o** by the acute accent mark, e.g., **perché,** and on open **e** and **o** by the grave accent mark, e.g., **caffè, parlò.** This occurs (a) in words ending in a stressed vowel, as in the above examples, (b) in stressed monosyllables in which the vocalic element is a diphthong of which the first letter is unstressed **i** or **u,** e.g., **già, più, può,** and (c) on the stressed monosyllable of any pair of monosyllables of which one is stressed and the other unstressed, in order to distinguish one from the other, e.g., **dà** *he gives* and **da** *from,* **è** *is* and **e** *and,* **sé** *himself* and **se** *if,* **sì** *yes* and **si** *himself.*

2. Whenever stress is not shown as part of regular spelling, it is often difficult to determine where it falls.

(a) In words of two syllables, the stress falls on the syllable next to the last, e.g., **ca'sa, mu'ro, ter'ra.** If the syllable next to the last contains a diphthong, that is, a combination of a strong vowel (**a, e,** or **o**) and a weak vowel (**i** or **u**), the strong vowel is stressed, regardless of which vowel comes first, e.g., **da'ino, ero'ico, ne'utro, fia'to, dua'le, sie'pe, fio're, buo'no.**

(b) In words of more than two syllables, the stress may fall on the syllable next to the last, e.g., **anda'ta, canzo'ne, pasto're** or on a preceding syllable, e.g., **fis'sile, gon'dola, man'doria.** In these positions also the stressed syllable may contain a diphthong, e.g., **inca'uto, idra'ulico, fio'cina.**

(c) If a weak vowel in juxtaposition with a strong vowel is stressed, the two vowels constitute two separate syllables, e.g., **abba·i'no, ero·i'na, pa·u'ra, miri'ade, vi'a.**

(d) Two strong vowels in juxtaposition constitute two separate syllables, e.g., **pa·e'se, aure'ola, ide'a, oce'ano.**

(e) Two weak vowels in juxtaposition generally constitute a diphthong in which the first vowel is stressed in some words, e.g., **flu'ido** and the second vowel in others, e.g., **piu'ma.**

(f) If a word ends in a diphthong, the diphthong is stressed, e.g., **marina'i, paria'i, ero'i.**

3. In this DICTIONARY, stress is understood or shown on all words that do not bear an accent mark as part of regular spelling according to the following principles. In the application of these principles, individual vowels and not diphthongs are counted as units. In some words in which it is not necessary to show stress, an accent mark is used to show the quality of the stressed vowels **e** and **o.**

As in regular Italian spelling, stress is shown on **a, i,** and **u** by the grave accent mark, on close **e** and **o** by the acute accent mark, and on open **e** and **o** by the grave accent mark.

(a) It is understood that in words of more than one syllable in which no accent mark is shown, the stress falls on the vowel next to the last, e.g., **casa,**

5

fiato, duale, abbaino, paura. In such words as slèpe, fióre, buòno, paése, fluènte, eròe, nói, pòi, the accent mark is used to show the quality of the vowel.

(b) An accent mark is placed on the stressed vowel if the word is stressed on the third vowel from the end, e.g., mùsica, slmbolo, dàino, incàuto, marinàio, contìnuo, infànzia. If this vowel is e or o, the acute or grave accent mark must correspond to the quality of the vowel, e.g., flòcina, rómpere, nèutro, eròico, assèdio, filatóio.

(c) Contrary to the above-mentioned principle of counting vowels, an accent mark is placed on the strong vowel of a final diphthong, e.g., marinài, assài.

(d) Contrary to the above-mentioned principle of counting vowels, an accent mark is placed on the i of final ia, ie, il, and io, e.g., farmacìa, scìa, farmacìe, mormorìi, gorgoglìo, fìo.

(e) An accent mark is placed on some borrowings ending in a consonant, e.g., hàrem, revòlver.

(f) The loss of the last vowel or last syllable of a word does not alter the position of the stress of the word, e.g., la maggior parte, in alcun modo, fan bene.

Grammatical Tables

84. The Definite Article and Combinations with Prepositions.

		MASC BEFORE CONSONANT	MASC BEFORE S IMPURE OR Z[1]	MASC BEFORE VOWEL	FEM BEFORE CONSONANT	FEM BEFORE VOWEL
	SG	il	lo	l'	la	l'[3]
	PL	i	gli	gli[2]	le	le[3]
WITH a	SG	al	allo	all'	alla	all'[3]
	PL	ai	agli	agli[2]	alle	alle[3]
WITH di	SG	del	dello	dell'	della	dell'[3]
	PL	dei	degli	degli[2]	delle	delle[3]
WITH con	SG	col	collo	coll'	colla	coll'[3]
	PL	coi	cogli	cogli[2]	colle	colle[3]
WITH da	SG	dal	dallo	dall'	dalla	dall'[3]
	PL	dai	dagli	dagli[2]	dalle	dalle[3]
WITH in	SG	nel	nello	nell'	nella	nell'[3]
	PL	nei	negli	negli[2]	nelle	nelle[3]
WITH su	SG	sul	sullo	sull'	sulla	sull'[3]
	PL	sui	sugli	sugli[2]	sulle	sulle[3]

[1] Other letters and groups of letters, which occur in a few words, are **gn**, **pn**, **ps**, **sc**, **x**, and **i** before a vowel, sometimes spelled **j** or **y**.

[2] These forms may drop the **i** before words beginning with **i**, e.g., **gl'Inglesi**.

[3] The **e** of these forms is not elided, e.g., **le erbe**.

7

85. Personal and Reflexive Pronouns.

PERSONS	SUBJECT	PERSONAL DIRECT OBJECT	PERSONAL INDIRECT OBJECT	REFLEX. & RECIPROCAL DIRECT & INDIRECT OBJECT	PERSONAL PREPOSITIONAL OBJECT	REFLEX. & RECIPROCAL PREPOSITIONAL OBJECT
SG						
1	io *I*	**mi** *me*	**mi** *to me*	**mi** *myself; to myself*	**me** *me*	**me** *myself*
2	tu *you*	**ti** *you*	**ti** *to you*	**ti** *yourself; to yourself*	**te** *you*	**te** *yourself*
3 MASC	egli, lui *he*	**lo** *him or it*	**gli** *to him*	**si** *himself; to himself*	**lui** *him*	**sé** *himself*
3 FEM	lei, essa *she*	**la** *her or it*	**le** *to her*	**si** *herself; to herself*	**lei, essa** *her*	**sé** *herself*
2 FORMAL	Lei *you*	**La** *you*	**Le** *to you*	**si** *yourself; to yourself*	**Lei** *you*	**sé** *yourself*
PL						
1	noi *we*	**ci** *us*	**ci** *to us*	**ci** *ourselves; to ourselves; to each other*	**noi** *us*	**noi** *ourselves; each other*
2	voi *you*	**vi** *you*	**vi** *to you*	**vi** *yourself; yourselves; to yourself; to yourselves; to each other*	**voi** *you*	**voi** *yourself; yourselves; each other*
3 MASC	loro, essi *they*	**li** *them*	**loro** *to them*	**si** *themselves; to themselves; to each other*	**loro, essi** *them*	**sé** *themselves; each other*
3 FEM	loro, esse *they*	**le** *them*	**loro** *to them*	**si** *themselves; to themselves; to each other*	**loro, esse** *them*	**sé** *themselves; each other*
2 FORMAL	Loro *you*	**Li** } *you* **Le** }	**Loro** *to you*	**si** *yourselves; to yourselves; to each other*	**Loro** *you*	**sé** *yourselves; each other*

ci and **vi** both mean also *here, there, to it, in it, to them, in them, about it.*
ne means *of, from,* or *with him, her, it, them; some, any; from here, from there, thence, about it.*

meco *with me,* **teco** *with you,* and **seco** *with him, with himself; with her, with herself; with you, with yourself, with yourselves; with them, with themselves; with each other* may be used instead of **con me, con te,** and **con sé** respectively.

8

COMBINATION OF DIRECT AND INDIRECT OBJECT

PERSONS		PERSONS		
1 SG & 3 SG	me lo / me la } him, her, it to me	1 PL & 3 SG	ce lo / ce la } him, her, it to us	
1 SG & 3 PL	me li / me le } them to me	1 PL & 3 PL	ce li / ce le } them to us	
2 SG & 3 SG	te lo / te la } him, her, it to you	2 PL & 3 SG	ve lo / ve la } him, her, it to you	
2 SG & 3 PL	te li / te le } them to you	2 PL & 3 PL	ve li / ve le } them to you	
3 SG & 3 SG	glielo / gliela } him, her, it to him gliela } him, her, it to her	3 SG & 3 PL	lo / la } VERB loro him, her, it to them	
3 SG & 3 PL	glieli / gliele } them to him gliele } them to her	3 PL & 3 PL	li / le } VERB loro them to them	
2 SG FORMAL & 3 SG	Glielo / Gliela } him, her, it to you	3 SG & 2 PL FORMAL	lo / la } VERB Loro him, her, it to you	
2 SG FORMAL & 3 PL	Glieli / Gliele } them to you	3 PL & 2 PL FORMAL	li / le } VERB Loro them to you	

The form **si** (third singular and plural reflexive and reciprocal indirect object) changes to **se** before one of the direct objects **lo, la, li,** and **le,** and before **ne,** e.g., **se lo mette** he puts it on; **se n'è andato** he went away.

In combinations, **ne** occupies the same position as **lo, la, li,** and **le,** and forms one word with **gli,** namely, **gliene.**

86 Possessive Adjectives and Pronouns

PERSON, NUMBER & SEX OF POSSESSOR	GENDER & NUMBER OF POSSESSIVE ADJECTIVE OR PRONOUN ACCORDING TO THE GENDER & NUMBER OF THE PERSON OR THING POSSESSED				MEANING OF ADJECTIVE	MEANING OF PRONOUN
SG	MSG	MPL	FSG	FPL		
1	il mio	i miei	la mia	le mie	my	mine
2	il tuo	i tuoi	la tua	le tue	your	yours
3 MASC	il suo	i suoi	la sua	le sue	his	his
3 FEM	il suo	i suoi	la sua	le sue	her	hers
3 NEUT	il suo	i suoi	la sua	le sue	its	its
2 FORMAL	il Suo	i Suoi	la Sua	le Sue	your	yours
PL						
1	il nostro	i nostri	la nostra	le nostre	our	ours
2	il vostro	i vostri	la vostra	le vostre	your	yours
3	il loro	i loro	la loro	le loro	their	theirs
2 FORMAL	il Loro	i Loro	la Loro	le Loro	your	yours

The definite article, shown here, is not generally used (a) in direct address, e.g., **mio caro amico** *my dear friend,* (b) after the verb **essere,** e.g., **la casa è nostra** *the house is ours,* and (c) when a singular form modifies the name of a relative, e.g., **sua sorella** *his sister.* With forms of the indefinite article, the possessive adjective, whether standing before or after the noun, is translated by *of*

plus the possessive pronoun, e.g., **un amico mio** *a friend of mine;* **una sua zia** *an aunt of his* (or *of hers*). The forms of the possessive pronouns also have the force of nouns, e.g., **il mio** *my property, my belongings;* **i suoi** *his people, relatives, followers, troops, retinue,* etc.; **la mia** *my letter;* **la sua** *his opinion.*

10

87. The Demonstrative Adjective.

	MASC BEFORE CONSONANT	MASC BEFORE s IMPURE OR z (see note 1, p. 7)	MASC BEFORE VOWEL	FEM BEFORE CONSONANT	FEM BEFORE VOWEL
SG	quel *that*	quello	quell'	quella	quell'
PL	quei *those*	quegli	quegli	quelle	quelle
SG	questo *this*	questo	questo or quest'	questa	questa or quest'
PL	questi *these*	questi	questi	queste	queste

§8. The Demonstrative Pronoun.

	MASC	FEM	MASC
SG	**quello** *that one*	**quella**	**quegli** *that one; the former*
PL	**quelli** *those*	**quelle**	
SG	**questo** *this one*	**questa**	**questi** *this one; the latter*
PL	**questi** *these*	**queste**	

The demonstrative pronoun **quello** is often followed by **che, di,** or **da** and the masculine singular form may be shortened to **quel** before these words.

SG	**colui** *that one*	**colei**
PL	**coloro** *those*	**coloro**
SG	**costui** *this one*	**costei**
PL	**costoro** *these*	**costoro**

code·sto -sta -sti -ste and **cote·sto -sta -sti -ste** are demonstrative adjectives and demonstrative pronouns and mean *that (of yours)*.

12

89. Indefinite Article and Numeral Adjective.

MASC	MASC	MASC	FEM	FEM
BEFORE CONSONANT	BEFORE S IMPURE OR Z (see note 1, p. 7)	BEFORE VOWEL	BEFORE CONSONANT	BEFORE VOWEL
un *a, an; one*	uno	un	una	un'

§10. Indefinite Pronoun uno.

MASC	FEM
uno *one*	una

§11. Correlative Indefinite Pronoun.

	MASC	FEM
SG	l'uno . . . l'altro *one . . . the other*	l'una . . . l'altra
PL	gli uni . . . gli altri *some . . . the others*	le une . . . le altre

§12. Reciprocal Indefinite Pronoun.

	MASC	FEM
SG	l'un l'altro *each other, one another*	l'una l'altra
PL	gli uni gli altri	le une le altre

Table of Regular Endings of Italian Verbs

The stem to which the endings of the gerund, past participle, present participle, imperative, present indicative, present subjunctive, imperfect indicative, preterit indicative, and imperfect subjunctive are attached is obtained by dropping the ending of the infinitive, viz., **-are, -ere, -ire**.

The stem to which the endings of the future indicative and present conditional are attached is obtained by dropping the **-e** of the ending of the infinitive of all conjugations and changing the **a** of the ending of the infinitive of the first conjugation to **e**.

The letters before the names of some of the tenses of this table correspond to the designation of the tenses shown on the following page.

Letters printed in italics have a written accent that is not part of the regular spelling.

TENSE	FIRST CONJUGATION	SECOND CONJUGATION	THIRD CONJUGATION
inf	**-are**	**-ére** (or **-ere**)	**-ire**
ger	-ando	-*è*ndo	-*è*ndo
pp	-ato	-uto	-ito
pres part	-ante	-*è*nte	-*è*nte
(a) *impv*	-a -ate	-i -*é*te	-i -ite
(b) *pres ind*	-o -i -a -iamo -ate -ano	-o -i -e -iamo -*é*te -ono	-o -i -e -iamo -ite -ono
(c) *pres subj*	-i -i -i -iamo -iate -ino	-a -a -a -iamo -iate -ano	-a -a -a -iamo -iate -ano
(d) *imperf ind*	-avo -avi -ava -avamo -avate -*à*vano	-*é*vo -*é*vi -*é*va -evamo -evate -*é*vano	-ivo -ivi -iva -*í*vamo -ivate -*í*vano
(e) *pret ind*	-*à*i -asti -*ò* -ammo -aste -*à*rono	-*é*i -*é*sti -*è* -*é*mmo -*é*ste -*é*rono	-*ì*i -isti -*ì* -immo -iste -*í*rono
imperf subj	-assi -assi -asse -*à*ssimo -aste -*à*ssero	-*é*ssi -*é*ssi -*é*sse -*é*ssimo -*é*ste -*é*ssero	-issi -issi -isse -*ì*ssimo -iste -*í*ssero
(f) *fut ind*	-er-*ò* -er-*à*i -er-à -er-*é*mo -er-*é*te -er-anno	-*ò* -*à*i -à -*é*mo -*é*te -anno	-*ò* -*à*i -à -*é*mo -*é*te -anno

TENSE	FIRST CONJUGATION	SECOND CONJUGATION	THIRD CONJUGATION
pres cond	-er-èi -er-ésti -er-èbbe -er-émmo -er-éste -er-èbbero	-èi -ésti -èbbe -émmo -éste -èbbero	-èi -ésti -èbbe -émmo -éste -èbbero

MODEL VERBS
ORDER OF TENSES

(a) imperative
(b) present indicative
(c) present subjunctive

(d) imperfect indicative
(e) preterit indicative
(f) future indicative

In addition to the infinitive, gerund, and past participle, which are shown in line one of these tables, all simple tenses are shown if they contain at least one irregular form, except (1) the present conditional, which is always formed on the stem of the future indicative, (2) the imperfect subjunctive, which is always formed on the stem of the *2nd sg* of the preterit indicative, and (3) the present participle, which is generally formed by changing the final -**do** of the gerund to -**te** (exceptions being shown in parentheses after the gerund).

Letters printed in italics have a written accent that is not part of the regular spelling.

§100 ACCÈDERE—accedèndo—acceduto
  (e) accedètti *or* accedéi *or* accèssi; accedésti; accedètte *or* accedé *or* accèsse; accedémmo; accedéste; accedèttero *or* accedérono *or* accèssero

§101 ACCÈNDERE—accendèndo—accéso
  (e) accési, accendésti, accése, accendémmo, accendéste, accésero

§102 ADDURRE—adducèndo—addótto
  (b) adduco, adduci, adduce, adduciamo, adducéte, addùcono
  (c) adduca, adduca, adduca, adduciamo, adduciate, addùcano
  (d) adducévo, adducévi, adducéva, adducevamo, adducevate, adducévano
  (e) addussi, adducésti, addusse, adducémmo, adducéste, addùssero

§103 AFFÌGGERE—affiggèndo—affisso
  (e) affissi, affiggésti, affisse, affiggémmo, affiggéste, affissero

§104 AFFLÌGGERE—affliggèndo—afflitto
    (e) afflissi, affliggésti, afflisse, affliggémmo, affliggéste, afflìssero

§105 ALLÙDERE—alludèndo—alluso
    (e) allusi, alludésti, alluse, alludémmo, alludéste, allùsero

§106 ANDARE—andando—andato
    (a) va *or* va' *or* vai, andate
    (b) vò *or* vado, vai, va, andiamo, andate, vanno
    (c) vada, vada, vada, andiamo, andiate, vàdano
    (f) andrò, andrài, andrà, andrémo, andréte, andranno

§107 ANNÈTTERE—annettèndo—annèsso *or* **annèttere,** annetténdo, annésso
    (e) annettéi *or* annèssi *or* annéssi; annettésti; annetté *or* annèsse *or* annésse; annettémmo; annettéste; annettérono *or* annèssero *or* annéssero

§108 APPARIRE—apparèndo—apparso
    (a) apparisci *or* appari; apparite
    (b) apparisco *or* appàio; apparisci *or* appari; apparisce *or* appare; appariamo; apparite; apparìscono *or* appàiono
    (c) apparisca *or* appàia; apparisca *or* appàia; apparisca *or* appàia; appariamo; appariate; apparìscano *or* appàiano
    (e) apparvi *or* apparìi *or* apparsi; apparisti; apparve *or* apparì *or* apparse; apparimmo; appariste; appàrvero *or* apparìrono *or* appàrsero

§109 APPÈNDERE—appendèndo—appéso
    (e) appési, appendésti, appése, appendémmo, appendéste, appésero

§110 APRIRE—aprèndo—apèrto
    (e) aprìi *or* apèrsi; apristi; aprì *or* apèrse; aprimmo; apriste; aprìrono *or* apèrsero

§111 ÀRDERE—ardèndo—arso
    (e) arsi, ardésti, arse, ardémmo, ardéste, àrsero

§112 ASPÈRGERE—aspergèndo—aspèrso
    (e) aspèrsi, aspergésti, aspèrse, aspergémmo, aspergéste, aspèrsero

§113 ASSÌDERE—assidèndo—assiso
    (e) assisi, assidésti, assise, assidémmo, assidéste, assìsero

§114 ASSÌSTERE—assistèndo—assistito
    (e) assistéi *or* assistètti; assistésti; assisté *or* assistètte; assistémmo; assistéste; assistérono *or* assistèttero

§115 ASSÒLVERE—assolvèndo—assòlto *or* assoluto
    (e) assolvéi *or* assolvètti *or* assòlsi; assolvésti; assolvé *or* assolvètte *or* assòlse; assolvémmo; assolvéste; assolvérono *or* assolvèttero *or* assòlsero

§116 ASSÙMERE—assumèndo—assunto
    (e) assunsi, assumésti, assunse, assumémmo, assuméste, assùnsero

§117 ASSÙRGERE—assurgèndo—assurto
    (e) assursi, assurgésti, assurse, assurgémmo, assurgéste, assùrsero

§118 AVÈRE—avèndo—avuto
    (a) abbi, abbiate
    (b) ho, hai, ha, abbiamo, avete, hanno
    (c) àbbia, àbbia, àbbia, abbiamo, abbiate, àbbiano
    (e) èbbi, avésti, èbbe, avémmo, avéste, èbbero
    (f) avrò, avrài, avrà, avrémo, avréte, avranno

§119 AVVIARE—avviando—avviato
    (b) avvìo, avvìi, avvìa, avviamo, avviate, avvìano
    (c) avvìi, avvìi, avvìi, avviamo, avviate, avvìino

§120 BÉRE—bevèndo—bevuto
    (a) bévi, bevéte
    (b) bévo, bévi, béve, beviamo, bevéte, bévono
    (c) béva, béva, béva, beviamo, beviate, bévano
    (d) bevévo, bevévi, bevéva, bevevamo, bevevate, bevévano
    (e) bévvi *or* bevéi *or* bevètti; bevésti, bévve *or* bevé *or* bevètte; bevémmo; bevéste; bévvero *or* bevérono *or* bevèttero
    (f) berrò, berrài, berrà, berrémo, berréte, berranno

§121 CADÉRE—cadèndo—caduto
    (e) caddi, cadésti, cadde, cadémmo, cadéste, càddero
    (f) cadrò, cadrài, cadrà, cadrémo, cadréte, cadranno

§122 CECARE—cecando—cecato
    (a) cièca *or* cèca; cecate
    (b) cièco *or* cèco; cièchi *or* cèchi; cièca *or* cèca; cechiamo; cecate; ciècano *or* cècano
    (c) cièchi *or* cèchi; cièchi *or* cèchi; cièchi *or* cèchi; cechiamo; cechiate; cièchino *or* cèchino
    (f) cecherò, cecherài, cecherà, cecherémo, cecheréte, cecheranno

§123 CÈDERE—cedèndo—ceduto
    (e) cedéi *or* cedètti; cedésti; cedé *or* cedètte; cedémmo; cedéste; cedérono *or* cedèttero

19

§124 CHIÈDERE—chiedèndo—chièsto
(e) chièsi, chiedésti, chièse, chiedémmo, chiedéste, chièsero

§125 CHIÙDERE—chiudèndo—chiuso
(e) chiusi, chiudésti, chiuse, chiudémmo, chiudéste, chiùsero

§126 CÌNGERE—cingèndo—cinto
(e) cinsi, cingésti, cinse, cingémmo, cingéste, cìnsero

§127 CÒGLIERE—coglièndo—còlto
(a) còlgi, cogliéte
(b) còlgo, còlgi, còglie, cogliamo, cogliéte, còlgono
(c) còlga, còlga, còlga, cogliamo, cogliate, còlgano
(e) còlsi, cogliésti, còlse, cogliémmo, cogliéste, còlsero

§128 COMINCIÀRE—cominciando—cominciato
(b) comìncio, cominci, comìncia, cominciamo, cominciate, comìnciano
(c) cominci, cominci, cominci, cominciamo, cominciate, comìncino
(f) cominceròm, cominceràm, comincerà, cominceràm, cominceràte, cominceranno

§129 COMPÈTERE—competèndo—*pp* missing

§130 CÒMPIERE—compièndo—compiuto
(a) cómpi, compite
(b) cómpio, cómpi, cómpie, compiamo, compite, cómpiono
(c) cómpia, cómpia, cómpia, compiamo, compiate, cómpiano
(d) compivo, compivi, compiva, compivamo, compivate, compìvano
(e) compiéi *or* compìi; compiésti *or* compisti; compié *or* compì; compiémmo *or* compimmo; compiéste *or* compiste; compiérono *or* compìrono

§131 COMPRÌMERE—comprimèndo—comprèsso
(e) comprèssi, comprimésti, comprèsse, comprimémmo, compriméste, comprèssero

§132 CONCÈDERE—concedèndo—concèsso
(e) concedéi *or* concèssi *or* concedétti; concedésti; concedé *or* concèsse *or* concedètte; concedémmo; concedéste; concedérono *or* concèssero *or* concedèttero

§133 CONCÈRNERE—concernèndo—*pp* missing
(e) concernéi *or* concernètti; concernésti; concerné *or* concernètte; concernémmo; concernéste; concernérono *or* concernèttero

20

§134 **CONÓSCERE**—conoscèndo—conosciuto
(e) conóbbi, conoscésti, conóbbe, conoscémmo, conoscéste, conóbbero

§135 **CONQUÌDERE**—conquidèndo—conquiso
(e) conquisi, conquidésti, conquise, conquidémmo, conquidéste, conquìsero

§136 **CONSÙMERE**—*ger* missing—consunto
(a) missing
(b) missing
(c) missing
(d) missing
(e) consunsi, consunse, consùnsero
(f) missing

§137 **CONVÈRGERE**—convergèndo—convèrso
(e) convèrsi *or* convergéi; convergésti; convèrse *or* convergé; convergémmo; convergéste; convèrsero *or* convergérono

§138 **CONVERTIRE**—convertèndo—convertito
(e) convertìi *or* convèrsi; convertisti; convertì or convèrse; convertimmo; convertiste; convertìrono *or* convèrsero

§139 **CÓRRERE**—corrèndo—córso
(e) córsi, corrésti, córse, corrémmo, corréste, córsero

§140 **COSTRUIRE**—costruèndo—costruito
(a) costruisci, costruite
(b) costruisco, costruisci, costruisce, costruiamo, costruite, costruìscono
(c) costruisca, costruisca, costruisca, costruiamo, costruiate, costruìscano
(e) costruìi *or* costrussi; costruisti; costruì *or* costrusse; costruimmo; costruiste; costruìrono *or* costrùssero

§141 **CRÉDERE**—credèndo—creduto
(e) credéi *or* credètti; credésti; credé *or* credètte; credémmo; credéste; credérono *or* credèttero

§142 **CRÉSCERE**—crescèndo—cresciuto
(e) crébbi, crescésti, crébbe, crescémmo, crescéste, crébbero

§143 **CUCIRE**—cucèndo—cucito
(b) cùcio, cuci, cuce, cuciamo, cucite, cùciono
(c) cùcia, cùcia, cùcia, cuciamo, cuciate, cùciano

§144a **CUÒCERE**—cuocèndo *or* cocèndo (cocènte)—còtto *or* cociuto

(a) cuòci, cocéte
(b) cuòcio, cuòci, cuòce, cociamo, cocéte, cuòciono
(c) cuòcia, cuòcia, cuòcia, cociamo, cociate, cuòciano
(d) cocévo, cocévi, cocéva, cocevamo, cocevate, cocévano
(e) còssi, cocésti, còsse, cocémmo, cocéste, còssero
(f) cocerò, coceràì, cocerà, cocerémo, coceréte, coceranno

§144b DARE—dando—dato
(a) dà or dàì or da'; date
(b) dò or dò; dàì; dà; diamo; date; danno
(c) dìa, dìa, dìa, diamo, diate, dìano
(e) dièdi or dètti; désti; diède or dètte or diè; démmo; déste; dièdero or dèttero
(f) darò, daràì, darà, darémo, daréte, daranno

§145 DECÌDERE—decidèndo—deciso
(e) decisi, decidésti, decise, decidémmo, decidéste, decìsero

§146 DELÌNQUERE—delinquèndo—*pp* missing
(a) missing
(c) missing
(e) missing

§147 DEVÒLVERE—devolvèndo—devoluto
(e) devolvéi or devolvètti; devolvésti; devolvé or devolvètte; devolvémmo; devolvéste; devolvérono or devolvèttero

§148 DIFÈNDERE—difendèndo—diféso
(e) difési, difendésti, difése, difendémmo, difendéste, difésero

§149 DILÌGERE—diligèndo—dilètto
(a) missing
(b) missing
(c) missing
(d) missing
(e) dilèssi, diligésti, dilèsse, diligémmo, diligéste, dilèssero
(f) missing

§150 DIPÈNDERE—dipendèndo—dipéso
(e) dipési, dipendésti, dipése, dipendémmo, dipendéste, dipésero

§151 DIRE—dicèndo—détto
(a) di' or dì; dite
(b) dico, dici, dice, diciamo, dite, dìcono
(c) dica, dica, dica, diciamo, diciate, dìcano
(d) dicévo, dicévi, dicéva, dicevamo, dicevate, dicévano
(e) dissi, dicésti, disse, dicémmo, dicéste, dìssero
(f) dirò, diràì, dirà, dirémo, diréte, diranno

§152 DIRÌGERE—dirigèndo—dirètto
    (e) dirèssi, dirigésti, dirèsse, dirigémmo, dirigéste, dirèssero

§153 DISCÈRNERE—discernèndo—*pp* missing
    (e) discernéi; discernésti; discerné *or* discernètte; discernémmo; discernéste; discernérono *or* discernèttero

§154 DISCÙTERE—discutèndo—discusso
    (e) discussi, discutésti, discusse, discutémmo, discutéste, discùssero

§155 DISSÒLVERE—dissolvèndo—dissòlto
    (e) dissòlsi *or* dissolvéi *or* dissolvètti; dissolvésti; dissòlse *or* dissolvé *or* dissolvètte; dissolvémmo; dissolvéste; dissòlsero *or* dissolvérono *or* dissolvèttero

§156 DISTÌNGUERE—distinguèndo—distinto
    (e) distinsi, distinguésti, distinse, distinguémmo, distinguéste, distìnsero

§157 DIVÈRGERE—divergèndo—*pp* missing
    (é) obsolete

§158 DIVÌDERE—dividèndo—diviso
    (e) divisi, dividésti, divise, dividémmo, dividéste, divìsero

§159 DOLÉRE—dolèndo—doluto
    (a) duòli, doléte
    (b) dòlgo, duòli, duòle, doliamo, doléte, dòlgono
    (c) dòlga, dòlga, dòlga, doliamo, doliate, dòlgano
    (e) dòlsi, dolésti, dòlse, dolémmo, doléste, dòlsero
    (f) dorrò, dorrài, dorrà, dorrémo, dorréte, dorranno

§160 DOVÉRE—dovèndo—dovuto
    (b) dèbbo *or* dèvo; dèvi; dève; dobbiamo; dovéte; dèbbono *or* dèvono
    (c) dèva *or* dèbba; dèva *or* dèbba; dèva *or* dèbba; dobbiamo; dobbiate; dèvano *or* dèbbano
    (e) dovéi *or* dovètti; dovésti; dové *or* dovètte; dovémmo; dovéste; dovérono *or* dovèttero

§161 ELÌDERE—elidèndo—eliso
    (e) elisi, elidésti, elise, elidémmo, elidéste, elìsero

§162 EMÈRGERE—emergèndo—emèrso
    (e) emèrsi, emergésti, emèrse, emergémmo, emergéste, emèrsero

§163 ÉMPIERE & EMPIRE—empièndo—empito *or* empiuto
    (a) émpi, empite

(b) émpio, émpi, émpie, empiamo, empite, émpiono
(c) émpia, émpia, émpia, empiamo, empiate, émpiano
(d) empivo, empivi, empiva, empivamo, empivate, em-
    pìvano
(e) empiéi or empìi; empiésti; or empisti; empié or empì;
    empiémmo or empimmo; empiéste or empiste;
    empiérono or empìrono
(f) empirò, empirài, empirà, empirémo, empiréte, em-
    piranno

§164 **ÈRGERE**—ergèndo—èrto
     (e) èrsi, ergésti, èrse, ergémmo, ergéste, èrsero

§165 **ESÌGERE**—esigèndo—esatto
     (e) esigéi or esigètti; esigésti; esigé or esigètte; esigémmo;
         esigéste; esigérono or esigèttero

§166 **ESÌMERE**—esimèndo—pp missing
     (e) esiméi or esimètti; esimésti; esimé or esimètte;
         esimémmo; esiméste; esimérono or esimèttero

§167 **ESPÀNDERE**—espandèndo—espanso
     (e) espandéi or espandètti or espansi; espandésti; espandé
         or espandètte or espanse; espandémmo; espandéste;
         espandérono or espandèttero or espànsero

§168 **ESPÈLLERE**—espellèndo—espulso
     (e) espulsi, espellésti, espulse, espellémmo, espelléste,
         espùlsero

§169 **ESPLÒDERE**—esplodèndo—esplòso
     (e) esplòsi, esplodésti, esplòse, esplodémmo, esplodéste,
         esplòsero

§170 **ÈSSERE**—essèndo—stato
     (a) sii, siate
     (b) sóno, sèi, è, siamo, siète, sóno
     (c) sìa, sìa, sìa, siamo, siate, sìano
     (d) èro, èri, èra, eravamo, eravate, èrano
     (e) fui, fósti, fu, fummo, fóste, fùrono
     (f) sarò, sarài, sarà, sarémo, saréte, saranno

§171 **ESTÒLLERE**—estollèndo—pp missing
     (e) missing

§172 **EVÀDERE**—evadèndo—evaso
     (e) evasi, evadésti, evase, evadémmo, evadéste, evàsero

§173 **FARE**—facèndo—fatto
     (a) fa or fài or fa'; fate

24

(b) fàccio *or* fò; fài; fa; facciamo; fate; fanno
(c) fàccia, fàccia, fàccia, facċiamo, facciate; fàcciano
(d) facévo, facévi, facéva, facevamo, facevate, facévano
(e) féci, facésti, féce, facémmo, facéste, fécero
(f) farò, farài, farà, farémo, faréte, faranno

§174 FÈNDERE—fendèndo—fenduto *or* fésso
(e) fendéi *or* fendètti; fendésti; fendé *or* fendètte; fendémmo; fendéste; fendérono *or* fendèttero

§175 FÈRVERE—fervèndo—*pp* missing
(e) fervéi *or* fervètti; fervésti; fervé *or* fervètte; fervémmo; fervéste; fervérono *or* fervèttero

§176 FINIRE—finèndo—finito
(a) finisci, finite
(b) finisco, finisci, finisce, finiamo, finite, finìscono
(c) finisca, finisca, finisca, finiamo, finiate, finìscano

§177 FLÈTTERE—flettèndo—flèsso
(e) flettéi *or* flèssi; flettésti; fletté *or* flèsse; flettémmo; flettéste; flettérono *or* flèssero

§178 FÓNDERE—fondèndo—fuso
(e) fusi, fondésti, fuse, fondémmo, fondéste, fùsero

§179 FRÀNGERE—frangèndo—franto
(e) fransi, frangésti, franse, frangémmo, frangéste, frànsero

§180 FRÌGGERE—friggèndo—fritto
(e) frissi, friggésti, frisse, friggémmo, friggéste, frìssero

§181 GIACÉRE—giacèndo—giaciuto
(b) giàccio; giaci; giace; giacciamo *or* giaciamo; giacete; giàcciono
(c) giàccia, giàccia, giàccia, giacciamo, giacciate, giàcciano
(e) giàcqui, giacésti, giàcque, giacémmo, giacéste, giàcquero

§182 GIOCARE—giocando—giocato
(a) giuòca *or* giòca; giocate
(b) giuòco *or* giòco; giuòchi *or* giòchi; giuòca *or* giòca; giochiamo; giocate; giuòcano *or* giòcano
(c) giuòchi *or* giòchi; giuòchi *or* giòchi; giuòchi *or* giòchi; giochiamo; giochiate; giuòchino *or* giòchino
(f) giocherò, giocherài, giocherà, giocherémo, giocheréte, giocheranno

§183 GIÙNGERE—giungèndo—giunto
(e) giunsi, giungésti, giunse, giungémmo, giungéste, giùnsero

25

§184 GODÉRE—godèndo—goduto
    (e) godéi *or* godètti; godésti; godé *or* godètte; godémmo;
        godéste; godérono *or* godèttero
    (f) godrò, godrài, godrà, godrémo, godréte, godranno

§185 IMBÉVERE—imbevèndo—imbevuto
    (e) imbévvi, imbevésti, imbévve, imbevémmo, imbevéste,
        imbévvero

§186 INCÓMBERE—incombèndo—*pp* missing
    (e) incombéi *or* incombètti; incombésti; incombé *or* in-
        combètte; incombémmo; incombéste; incombérono
        or incombèttero

§187 INDÙLGERE—indulgèndo—indulto
    (e) indulsi, indulgésti, indulse, indulgémmo, indulgéste,
        indùlsero

§188a INFERIRE—inferèndo—inferito *or* infèrto
    (a) inferisci, inferite
    (b) inferisco, inferisci, inferisce, inferiamo, inferite, in-
        ferìscono
    (c) inferisca, inferisca, inferisca, inferiamo, inferiate, infe-
        rìscano
    (e) inferìi *or* infèrsi; inferisti; inferì *or* infèrse; inferimmo;
        inferiste; inferìrono *or* infèrsero

§188b INSTARE—instando—*pp* missing

§189 INTRÌDERE—intridèndo—intriso
    (e) intrisi, intridésti, intrise, intridémmo, intridéste, in-
        trìsero

§190 INTRÙDERE—intrudèndo—intruso
    (e) intrusi, intrudésti, intruse, intrudémmo, intrudéste, in-
        trùsero

§191 IRE—*ger* missing—ito
    (a) *sg* missing, ite
    (b) missing
    (c) missing
    (d) ivo, ivi, iva, ivamo, ivate, ìvano
    (e) *1st sg* missing, isti, *3rd sg* missing, *1st pl* missing, iste,
        ìrono

§192 LÈDERE—ledèndo—léso *or* lèso
    (e) lési, ledésti, lése, ledémmo, ledéste, lésero

§193 LÈGGERE—leggèndo—lètto
    (e) lèssi, leggésti, lèsse, leggémmo, leggéste, lèssero

§194 LIQUEFARE—liquefacèndo—liquefatto
  (a) liquefà, liquefate
  (b) liquefò or liquefàccio; liquefài; liquefà liquefacciamo; liquefate; liquefanno
  (c) liquefàccia, liquefàccia, liquefàccia, liquefacciamo, liquefacciate, liquefàcciano
  (d) liquefacévo, liquefacévi, liquefacéva, liquefacevamo, liquefacevate, liquefacévano
  (e) liqueféci, liquefacésti, liqueféce, liquefacémmo, liquefacéste, liquefécero
  (f) liquefarò, liquefaràì, liquefarà, liquefarémo, liquefaréte, liquefaranno

§195 MALEDIRE—maledicèndo—maledétto
  (a) maledici, maledite
  (b) maledico, maledici, maledice, malediciamo, maledite, maledìcono
  (c) maledica, maledica, maledica, malediciamo, malediciate, maledìcano
  (d) maledicévo or maledivo; maledicévi or maledivi; maledicéva or malediva; maledicevamo or maledivamo; maledicevate or maledivate; maledicévano or maledìvano
  (e) maledìi or maledissi; maledisti or maledicésti; maledì or maledisse; maledimmo or maledicémmo; malediste or maledicéste; maledìrono or maledìssero
  (f) maledirò, maledirài, maledirà, maledirémo, malediréte, malediranno

§196 MALVOLÉRE—*ger* missing—malvoluto
  (a) missing
  (b) missing
  (c) missing
  (d) missing
  (e) missing
  (f) missing

§197 MANCARE—mancando—mancato
  (b) manco, manchi, manca, manchiamo, mancate, màncano
  (c) manchi, manchi, manchi, manchiamo, manchiate, mànchino
  (f) mancherò, mancheràì, mancherà, mancherémo, mancheréte, mancheranno

§198 MÉTTERE—mettèndo—mésso
  (e) misi, mettésti, mise, mettémmo, mettéste, mìsero

§199 MÌNGERE—mingèndo—minto
  (e) minsi, mingésti, minse, mingémmo, mingéste, mìnsero

27

§200 MÒRDERE—mordèndo—mòrso
(e) mòrsi, mordésti, mòrse, mordémmo, mordéste, mòrsero

§201 MORIRE—morèndo—mòrto
(a) muòri, morite
(b) muòio, muòri, muòre, moriamo, morite, muòiono
(c) muòia, muòia, muòia, moriamo, moriate, muòiano
(f) morrò *or* morirò; morràì *or* moriràì; morrà *or* morirà;
  morrémo *or* morirémo; morréte *or* moriréte; mor-
  ranno *or* moriranno

§202 MUÒVERE—muovèndo *or* movèndo (movènte)—mòsso
(a) muòvi, movéte
(b) muòvo, muòvi, muòve, moviamo, movéte, muòvono
(c) muòva, muòva, muòva, moviamo, moviate, muòvano
(d) movévo, movévi, movéva, movevamo, movevate,
  movévano
(e) mòssi, movésti, mòsse, movémmo, movéste, mòssero
(f) moverò, moveràì, moverà, moverémo, moveréte, move-
  ranno

§203 NÀSCERE—nascèndo—nato
(e) nàcqui, nascésti, nàcque, nascémmo, nascéste, nàcquero

§204 NASCÓNDERE—nascondèndo—nascósto
(e) nascósi, nascondésti, nascóse, nascondémmo, nas-
  condéste, nascósero

§205 NEGLÌGERE—negligèndo—neglètto
(a) missing
(b) missing
(c) missing
(e) neglèssi, negligésti, neglèsse, negligémmo, negligéste,
  neglèssero

§206 NUÒCERE—nuocèndo—nociuto
(a) nuòci, nocéte
(b) nuòccio *or* nòccio; nuòci; nuòce; nociamo; nocéte;
  nuòcciono *or* nòcciono
(c) nòccia, nòccia, nòccia, nociamo, nociate, nòcciano
(d) nocévo, nocévi, nocéva, nocevamo, nocevate, nocévano
(e) nòcqui, nocésti, nòcque, nocémmo, nocéste, nòcquero
(f) nocerò, noceràì, nocerà, nocerémo, noceréte, noceranno

§207 OFFRIRE—offrèndo (offerènte)—offèrto
(e) offrìi *or* offèrsi; offristi; offrì *or* offérse; offrimmo;
  offriste; offrìrono *or* offèrsero

§208 OTTÙNDERE—ottundèndo—ottuso
(e) ottusi, ottundésti, ottuse, ottundémmo, ottundéste,
  ottùsero

§209 PAGARE—pagando—pagato
(b) pago, paghi, paga, paghiamo, pagate, pàgano
(c) paghi, paghi, paghi, paghiamo, paghiate, pàghino
(f) pagherò, pagherài, pagherà, pagherémo, pagheréte, pagheranno

§210 PARÉRE—parèndo (parvènte)—parso
(a) missing
(b) pàio; pari; pare; pariamo or paiamo; paréte; pàiono
(c) pàia; pàia; pàia; pariamo or paiamo; pariate or paiate; pàiano
(e) parvi, parésti, parve, parémmo, paréste, pàrvero
(f) parrò, parrài, parrà, parrémo, parréte, parranno

§211 PÀSCERE—pascèndo—pasciuto
(a) pascéi or pascètti; pascésti; pascé or pascètte; pascémmo; pascéste; pascérono or pascèttero

§212 PÈRDERE—perdèndo—pèrso or perduto
(e) perdéi or pèrsi or perdètti; perdésti; perdé, or pèrse or perdètte; perdémmo; perdéste; perdérono or pèrsero or perdèttero

§213 PERSUADÉRE—persuadèndo—persuaso
(e) persuasi, persuadésti, persuase, persuadémmo, persuadéste, persuàsero

§214 PIACÉRE—piacèndo—piaciuto
(b) piàccio, piaci, piace, piacciamo, piacéte, piàcciono
(c) piàccia, piàccia, piàccia, piacciamo, piacciate, piàcciano
(e) piàcqui, piacésti, piàcque, piacémmo, piacéste, piàcquero

§215 PIÀNGERE—piangèndo—pianto
(e) piansi, piangésti, pianse, piangémmo, piangéste, piànsero

§216 PIÒVERE—piovèndo—piovuto
(e) piòvvi, piovésti, piòvve, piovémmo, piovéste, piòvvero

§217 PÒRGERE—porgèndo—pòrto
(e) pòrsi, porgésti, pòrse, porgémmo, porgéste, pòrsero

§218 PÓRRE—ponèndo—pósto
(a) póni, ponéte
(b) póngo, póni, póne, poniamo, ponéte, póngono
(c) pónga, pónga, pónga, poniamo, poniate, póngano
(d) ponévo, ponévi, ponéva, ponevamo, ponevate, ponévano
(e) pósi, ponésti, póse, ponémmo, ponéste, pósero

§219 POTÉRE—potèndo (potènte or possènte)—potuto
(a) missing
(b) pòsso, puòi, può, possiamo, potéte, pòssono

(c) pòssa, pòssa, pòssa, possiamo, possiate, pòssano

(e) potéi or potètti; potésti, poté or potètte; potémmo; potéste; potérono or potèttero

(f) potrò, potrài, potrà, potrémo, potréte, potranno

§220 **PRÈNDERE**—prendèndo—préso

(e) prési, prendésti, prése, prendémmo, prendéste, présero

§221 **PROVVEDÉRE**—provvedèndo—provveduto or provvisto

(e) provvidi, provvedésti, provvide, provvedémmo, provvedéste, provvìdero

§222 **PRÙDERE**—prudèndo—*pp* missing

(e) *1st sg* missing; *2nd sg* missing; prudé or prudètte; *1st pl* missing; *2nd pl* missing; prudérono or prudèttero

§223 **RÀDERE**—radèndo—raso

(e) rasi, radésti, rase, radémmo, radéste, ràsero

§224 **REDÌGERE**—redigèndo—redatto

(e) redassi, redigésti, redasse, redigémmo, redigéste, redàssero

§225 **REDÌMERE**—redimèndo—redènto

(e) redènsi, redimésti, redènse, redimémmo, rediméste, redènsero

§226 **RÈGGERE**—reggèndo—rètto

(e) rèssi, reggésti, rèsse, reggémmo, reggéste, rèssero

§227 **RÈNDERE**—rendèndo—réso

(e) rési or rendéi or rendètti; rendésti; rése or rendé or rendètte; rendémmo; rendéste; résero or rendérono or rendèttero

§228 **RETROCÈDERE**—retrocedèndo—retrocèsso or retroceduto

(e) retrocèssi or retrocedéi or retrocedètti; retrocedésti; retrocèsse or retrocedé or retrocedètte; retrocedémmo; retrocedéste; retrocèssero or retrocedérono or retrocedèttero

§229 **RIAVÉRE**—riavèndo—riavuto

(a) riabbi, riabbiate

(b) riò, riài, rià, riabbiamo, riavéte, rianno

(c) riàbbia, riàbbia, riàbbia, riabbiamo, riabbiate, riàbbiano

(e) rièbbi, riavésti, rièbbe, riavémmo, riavéste, rièbbero

(f) riavrò, riavrài, riavrà, riavrémo, riavréte, riavranno

§230 **RIDARE**—ridando—ridato

(a) ridài or ridà; ridate

(b) ridò, ridài, ridà, ridiamo, ridate, ridanno

(c) ridìa, ridìa, ridìa, ridiamo, ridiate, ridìano

(e) ridièdi *or* ridètti; ridésti; ridiède *or* ridètte; ridémmo; ridéste; ridièdero *or* ridèttero

(f) ridarò, ridarài, ridarà, ridarémo, ridaréte, ridaranno

§231 RÌDERE—ridèndo—riso
(e) risi, ridésti, rise, ridémmo, ridéste, rìsero

§232 RIFLÈTTERE—riflettèndo—riflèsso *or* riflettuto

§233 RIFÙLGERE—rifulgèndo—rifulso
(e) rifulsi, rifulgésti, rifulse rifulgémmo, rifulgéste, rifùlsero

§234 RILÙCERE—rilucèndo—*pp* missing

§235 RIMANÉRE—rimanèndo—rimasto
(b) rimango, rimani, rimane, rimaniamo, rimanéte, rimàngono
(c) rimanga, rimanga, rimanga, rimaniamo, rimaniate, rimàngano
(e) rimasi, rimanésti, rimase, rimanémmo, rimanéste, rimàsero
(f) rimarrò, rimarrài, rimarrà, rimarrémo, rimarréte, rimarranno

§236 RINCORARE—rincorando—rincorato
(a) rincuòra, rincorate
(b) rincuòro, rincuòri, rincuòra, rincoriamo, rincorate, rincuòrano
(c) rincuòri, rincuòri, rincuòri, rincoriamo, rincoriate, rincuòrino

§237 RISOLARE—risolando—risolato
(a) risuòla, risolate
(b) risuòlo, risuòli, risuòla, risoliamo, risolate, risuòlano
(c) risuòli, risuòli, risuòli, risoliamo, risoliate, risuòlino

§238 RISPÓNDERE—rispondèndo—rispósto
(e) rispósi, rispondésti, rispóse, rispondémmo, rispondéste, rispósero

§239 RÓDERE—rodèndo—róso
(e) rósi, rodésti, róse, rodémmo, rodéste, rósero

§240 RÓMPERE—rompèndo—rótto
(e) ruppi, rompésti, ruppe, rompémmo, rompéste, rùppero

§241 ROTARE—rotando—rotato
(a) ruòta, rotate
(b) ruòto, ruòti, ruòta, rotiamo, rotate, ruòtano
(c) ruòti, ruòti, ruòti, rotiamo, rotiate, ruòtino

§242 **SALIRE**—salèndo—salito
   (b) salgo, sali, sale, saliamo, salite, sàlgono
   (c) salga, salga, salga, saliamo, saliate, sàlgano

§243 **SAPÉRE**—sapèndo (sapiènte)—saputo
   (a) sappi, sappiate
   (b) sò, sai, sa, sappiamo, sapéte, sanno
   (c) sàppia, sàppia, sàppia, sappiamo, sappiate, sàppiano
   (e) sèppi, sapésti, sèppe, sapémmo, sapéste, sèppero
   (f) saprò, saprài, saprà, saprémo, sapréte, sapranno

§244 **SCÉGLIERE**—sceglièndo—scélto
   (a) scégli, scegliéte
   (b) scélgo, scégli, scéglie, scegliamo, scegliéte, scélgono
   (c) scélga, scélga, scélga, scegliamo, scegliate, scélgano
   (e) scélsi, scegliésti, scélse, scegliémmo, scegliéste, scélsero

§245 **SCÉNDERE**—scendèndo—scéso
   (e) scési, scendésti, scése, scendémmo, scendéste, scésero

§246 **SCÈRNERE**—scernèndo—*pp* missing
   (e) scernéi *or* scernètti; scernésti; scerné *or* scernètte; scer-
     némmo; scernéste; scernérono *or* scernèttero

§247 **SCÌNDERE**—scindèndo—scisso
   (e) scissi, scindésti, scisse, scindémmo, scindéste, scìssero

§248 **SCOIARE**—scoiando—scoiato
   (a) scuòia, scoiate
   (b) scuòio, scuòi, scuòia, scoiamo, scoiate, scuòiano
   (c) scuòi, scuòi, scuòi, scoiamo, scoiate, scuòino

§249 **SCÒRGERE**—scorgèndo—scòrto
   (e) scòrsi, scorgésti, scòrse, scorgémmo, scorgéste, scòrsero

§250 **SCRÌVERE**—scrivèndo—scritto
   (e) scrissi, scrivésti, scrisse, scrivémmo, scrivéste, scrìssero

§251 **SCUÒTERE**—scotèndo—scòsso
   (a) scuòti, scotéte
   (b) scuòto, scuòti, scuòte, scotiamo, scotéte, scuòtono
   (c) scuòta, scuòta, scuòta, scotiamo, scotiate, scuòtano
   (d) scotévo, scotévi, scotéva, scotevamo, scotevate, scoté-
     vano
   (e) scòssi, scotésti, scòsse, scotémmo, scotéste, scòssero

§252 **SEDÉRE**—sedéndo—seduto
   (a) sièdi, sedéte
   (b) sièdo *or* sèggo; sièdi; siède; sediamo; sedéte; sièdono
     or sèggono
   (c) sièda *or* sègga; sièda *or* sègga; sièda *or* sègga; sediamo;
     sediate; sièdano *or* sèggano
   (e) sedéi *or* sedètti; sedésti; sedé *or* sedètte; sedémmo;
     sedéste; sedérono *or* sedèttero

§253 **SEPPELLIRE**—seppellèndo—sepólto *or* seppellito
  (a) seppellisci, seppellite
  (b) seppellisco, seppellisci, seppellisce, seppelliamo, seppel-
      lite, seppellìscono
  (c) seppellisca, seppellisca, seppellisca, seppelliamo, seppel-
      liate, seppellìscano

§254 **SODDISFARE**—soddisfacèndo—soddisfatto
  (a) soddisfa *or* soddisfài *or* soddisfa'
  (b) soddisfàccio *or* soddisfò *or* soddisfo; soddisfài *or*
      soddisfi; soddisfà *or* soddisfa; soddisfacciamo; sod-
      disfate; soddisfanno *or* soddìsfano
  (c) soddisfàccia *or* soddisfi; soddisfàccia *or* soddisfi; soddi-
      sfàccia *or* soddisfi; soddisfacciamo; soddisfacciate;
      soddisfàcciano *or* soddìsfino
  (d) soddisfacévo, soddisfacévi, soddisfacéva, soddisface-
      vamo, soddisfacevate, soddisfacévano
  (e) soddisféci, soddisfacésti, soddisféce, soddisfacémmo,
      soddisfacéste, soddisfécero
  (f) soddisfarò, soddisfarài, soddisfarà, soddisfarémo, soddi-
      sfaréte, soddisfaranno

§255 **SOLÉRE**—solèndo—sòlito
  (a) missing
  (b) sòglio, suòli, suòle, sogliamo, soléte, sògliono
  (c) sòglia, sòglia, sòglia, sogliamo, sogliate, sògliano
  (e) missing
  (f) missing

§256 **SÒLVERE**—solvèndo—soluto
  (e) solvéi *or* solvètti; solvésti; solvé *or* solvètte; solvémmo;
      solvéste; solvérono *or* solvèttero

§257 **SONARE**—sonando—sonato
  (a) suòna, sonate
  (b) suòno, suòni, suòna, soniamo, sonate, suònano
  (c) suòni, suòni, suòni, soniamo, soniate, suònino

§258 **SÓRGERE**—sorgèndo—sórto
  (e) sórsi, sorgésti, sórse, sorgémmo, sorgéste, sórsero

§259 **SOSPÈNDERE**—sospendèndo—sospéso
  (e) sospési, sospendésti, sospése, sospendémmo, sospendéste,
      sospésero

§260 **SPÀNDERE**—spandèndo—spanto
  (e) spandéi *or* spandètti *or* spansi; spandésti; spandé *or*
      spandètte *or* spanse; spandémmo; spandéste; spandé-
      rono *or* spandèttero *or* spànsero

§261 **SPÀRGERE**—spargèndo—sparso
  (e) sparsi, spargésti, sparse, spargémmo, spargéste, spàrsero

33

§262 SPÈGNERE—spegnèndo—spènto
  (b) spéngo *or* spèngo; spégni *or* spègni; spégne *or* spègne;
      spegniamo; spegnéte; spéngono *or* spèngono
  (c) spénga *or* spènga; spénga *or* spènga; spénga *or* spènga;
      spegniamo; spegniate; spéngano *or* spèngano
  (e) spènsi, spegnésti, spènse, spegnémmo, spegnéste, spèn-
      sero

§263 STARE—stando—stato
  (a) sta *or* stai *or* sta'; state
  (b) stò, stài, sta, stiamo, state, stanno
  (c) stìa, stìa, stìa, stiamo, stiate, stìano
  (e) stètti, stésti, stètte, stémmo, stéste, stèttero
  (f) starò, starài, starà, starémo, staréte, staranno

§264 STRÌDERE—stridèndo—*pp* missing
  (e) stridéi *or* stridètti; stridésti; stridé *or* stridètte; stri-
      démmo; stridéste; stridérono *or* stridèttero

§265 STRÌNGERE—stringèndo—strétto
  (e) strinsi, stringésti, strinse, stringémmo, stringéste, strìn-
      sero

§266 STRÙGGERE—struggèndo—strutto
  (e) strussi, struggésti, strusse, struggémmo, struggéste,
      strùssero

§267 SVÈLLERE—svellèndo—svèlto
  (b) svèllo *or* svèlgo; svèlli; svèlle; svelliamo; svelléte;
      svèllono *or* svèlgono
  (c) svèlla *or* svèlga; svèlla *or* svèlga; svèlla *or* svèlga;
      svelliamo; svelliate; svèllano *or* svèlgano
  (e) svèlsi, svellésti, svèlse, svellémmo, svelléste, svèlsero

§268 TACÉRE—tacèndo—taciuto
  (b) tàccio, taci, tace, taciamo, tacéte, tàcciono
  (c) tàccia, tàccia, tàccia, taciamo, taciate, tàcciano
  (e) tàcqui, tacésti, tàcque, tacémmo, tacéste, tàcquero

§269 TÀNGERE—tangèndo—pp missing
  (a) missing
  (b) *1st sg* missing; *2nd sg* missing; tange; *1st pl* missing;
      2nd pl missing; tàngono
  (c) *1st sg* missing; *2nd sg* missing; tanga; *1st pl* missing;
      2nd pl missing; tàngano
  (d) *1st sg* missing; *2nd sg* missing; tangéva; *1st pl* missing;
      2nd pl missing; tangévano
  (e) missing
  (f) *1st sg* missing; *2nd sg* missing; tangerà; *1st pl* missing;
      2nd pl missing; tangeranno

§270 **TÈNDERE**—tendèndo—téso
 (e) tési, tendésti, tése, tendémmo, tendéste, tésero

§271 **TENÉRE**—tenèndo—tenuto
 (a) tièni, tenéte
 (b) tèngo, tièni, tiène, teniamo, tenéte, tèngono
 (c) tènga, tènga, tènga, teniamo, teniate, tèngano
 (e) ténni, tenésti, ténne, tenémmo, tenéste, ténnero
 (f) terrò, terrài, terrà, terrémo, terréte, terranno

§272 **TÒRCERE**—torcèndo—tòrto
 (e) tòrsi, torcésti, tòrse, torcémmo, torcéste, tòrsero

§273 **TRARRE**—traèndo—tratto
 (a) trài, traéte
 (b) traggo, trài, trae, traiamo, traéte, tràggono
 (c) tragga, tragga, tragga, traiamo, traiate, tràggano
 (d) traévo, traévi, traéva, traevamo, traevate, traévano
 (e) trassi, traésti, trasse, traémmo, traéste, tràssero

§274 **UCCÌDERE**—uccidèndo—ucciso
 (e) uccisi, uccidésti, uccise, uccidémmo, uccidéste, uccìsero

§275 **UDIRE**—udèndo or udièndo—udito
 (a) òdi, udite
 (b) òdo, òdi, òde, udiamo, udite, òdono
 (c) òda, òda, òda, udiamo, udiate, òdano
 (f) udirò or udrò; udirài or udrài; udirà or udrà; udirémo
  or udrémo; udiréte or udréte; udiranno or udranno

§276 **ÙRGERE**—urgèndo—*pp* missing
 (a) missing
 (e) missing

§277 **USCIRE**—uscèndo—uscito
 (a) èsci, uscite
 (b) èsco, èsci, èsce, usciamo, uscite, èscono
 (c) èsca, èsca, èsca, usciamo, usciate, èscano

§278 **VALÉRE**—valèndo—valso
 (b) valgo, vali, vale, valiamo, valéte, vàlgono
 (c) valga, valga, valga, valiamo, valiate, vàlgano
 (e) valsi, valésti, valse, valémmo, valéste, vàlsero
 (f) varrò, varrài, varrà, varrémo, varréte, varranno

§279 **VEDÉRE**—vedèndo—veduto or visto
 (e) vidi, vedésti, vide, vedémmo, vedéste, vìdero
 (f) vedrò, vedrài, vedrà, vedrémo, vedréte, vedranno

§280 **VEGLIARE**—vegliando—vegliato
 (b) véglio, végli, véglia, vegliamo, vegliate, végliano
 (c) végli, végli, végli, vegliamo, vegliate, véglino

§281 **VÉNDERE**—vendèndo—venduto
    (e) vendéi *or* vendètti; vendésti; vendé *or* vendètte; ven-
        démmo; vendéste; vendérono *or* vendèttero

§282 **VENIRE**—venèndo (veniènte)—venuto
    (a) vièni, venite
    (b) vèngo, vièni, viène, veniamo, venite, vèngono
    (c) vènga, vènga, vènga, veniamo, veniate, vèngano
    (e) vénni, venisti, vénne, venimmo, veniste, vénnero
    (f) verrò, verrài, verrà, verrémo, verréte, verranno

§283 **VÈRTERE**—vertèndo—*pp* missing

§284 **VÌGERE**—vigèndo—*pp* missing
    (a) missing
    (b) *1st sg* missing; *2nd sg* missing; vige; *1st pl* missing;
        2d pl missing; vìgono
    (c) *1st sg* missing; *2d sg* missing; viga; *1st pl* missing;
        2d pl missing; vìgano
    (d) *1st sg* missing; *2d sg* missing; vigéva; *1st pl* missing;
        2d pl missing; vigévano
    (e) missing

§285 **VÌNCERE**—vincèndo—vinto
    (e) vinsi, vincésti, vinse, vincémmo, vincéste, vìnsero

§286 **VÌVERE**—vivèndo—vissuto
    (e) vissi, vivésti, visse, vivémmo, vivéste, vìssero
    (f) vivrò, vivrài, vivrà, vivrémo, vivréte, vivranno

§287 **VIZIARE**—viziando—viziato
    (b) vìzio, vizi, vìzia, viziamo, viziate, vìziano
    (c) vizi, vizi, vizi, viziamo, viziate, vìzino

§288 **VOLÉRE**—volèndo—voluto
    (a) vògli, vogliate
    (b) vòglio, vuòi, vuòle, vogliamo, voléte, vògliono
    (c) vòglia, vòglia, vòglia, vogliamo, vogliate, vògliano
    (e) vòlli, volésti, vòlle, volémmo, voléste, vòllero
    (f) vorrò, vorrài, vorrà, vorrémo, vorréte, vorranno

§289 **VÒLGERE**—volgèndo—vòlto
    (e) vòlsi, volgésti, vòlse, volgémmo, volgéste, vòlsero

§290 **VOLTEGGIARE**—volteggiando—volteggiato
    (b) voltéggio, voltéggi, voltéggia, volteggiamo, volteggiate,
        voltéggiano
    (c) voltéggi, voltéggi, voltéggi, volteggiamo, volteggiate,
        voltéggino
    (f) volteggerò, volteggerài, volteggerà, volteggerémo, vol-
        teggeréte, volteggeranno

A

A, a [α] *m & f* first letter of the Italian alphabet

a *prep* (**ad** in front of a vowel) to, e.g., **diede il libro a Giovanni** he gave the book to John; in, e.g., **a Milano** in Milan; at, e.g., **a casa** at home; within, e.g., **a tre miglia da qui** within three miles (from here); on, e.g., **portare una catena al collo** to wear a chain on one's neck; e.g., **al sabato** on Saturdays; for, e.g., **a vita** for life; by, e.g., **fatto a mano** made by hand; with, e.g., **una gonna a pieghe** a skirt with pleats; as, e.g., **eleggere a presidente** to elect as chairman; into, e.g., **fu gettato a mare** he was thrown into the sea; of, e.g., **un quarto alle due** fifteen minutes of two

àba·co *m* (**-chi**) (archit) abacus

abate *m* abbot

abbacchiare §287 *tr* to knock down (e.g., *olives*); to sell too cheap || *ref* to lose courage; to be dejected

abbacchia·to -ta *adj* (coll) dejected

abbàc·chio *m* (**-chi**) baby lamb (*slaughtered*)

abbacinare (**abbàcino**) *tr* to dazzle; to deceive

abbadéssa *f* var of **badessa**

abbagliante *adj* dazzling || *m* (aut) bright light, high beam

abbagliare §280 *tr* to dazzle; to deceive; to blind (*with the lights of a car*)

abbà·glio *m* (**-gli**) error; **prendere abbaglio** to make a mistake

abbaiamento *m* bark (*of dog*)

abbaiare §287 *intr* to bark; to yelp

abbaino *m* dormer window; skylight; attic

abbambinare *tr* to walk (*a heavy piece of furniture*)

abbandonare (**abbandóno**) *tr* to abandon; to give up; to let go (e.g., *the reins*); to let fall; (sports) to withdraw from || *ref* to yield; to lose courage

abbandóno *m* abandon, abandonment; desertion; neglect; relaxation; renunciation (*of a right*); cession (*of property*); withdrawal (*from a fight*)

abbarbicare §197 (**abbàrbico**) *intr & ref* to cling; to hold on

abbassalin·gua *m* (**-gua**) tongue depressor

abbassaménto *m* lowering; reduction; drop, fall

abbassare *tr* to lower; to dim (*lights*); to turn (*the radio*) lower; **abbassare le armi** to surrender; **abbassare la cresta** to yield || *ref* to lower oneself; to drop

abbas·so *m* (**-so**) angry shout (*of a crowd*) || *adv* down, below; downstairs || *interj* down with!

abbastanza *adj invar* enough || *adv* enough; rather, fairly

abbàttere *tr* to demolish; to fell; to shoot down; to refute (*an argument*); to depress || *ref* to be depressed, be downcast

abbattiménto *m* demolition; felling; shooting down; chill; (fig) depression; **abbattimento alla base** (econ) basic exemption (*from taxes*)

abbattu·to -ta *adj* dejected, downcast || *f* clearing (*of trees*)

abbazìa *f* abbey; abbacy

abbeceda·rio *m* (**-ri**) speller, primer

abbelliménto *m* embellishment, ornamentation

abbellire §176 *tr* to embellish, adorn; to landscape

abbeverare (**abbévero**) *tr* to water (*animals*) || *ref* to quench one's thirst

abbevera·tóio *m* (**-tói**) watering trough

abbic·cì *m* (**-cì**) alphabet; speller; primer; ABC's, rudiments

abbiènte *adj* well-to-do || *m*—**gli abbienti** the haves; **gli abbienti e nullatenenti** the haves and the have-nots

abbiettézza or **abiettézza** *f* abjectness, baseness

abbièt·to -ta or **abièt·to -ta** *adj* abject, base, low

abbiezióne or **abiezióne** *f* wretchedness, baseness

abbigliaménto *m* attire, wear

abbigliare §280 *tr & ref* to dress; to dress up

abbinaménto *m* coupling; merger

abbinare *tr* to couple; to join, merge

abbindolare (**abbìndolo**) *tr* to dupe, deceive

abbiosciare §128 *ref* to fall down; to lose heart, be downcast

abbisognare (**abbisógno**) *intr* to be in need

abboccamento *m* interview, conversation

abboccare §197 (**abbócco**) *tr* to swallow (*the hook*); to fit (*pipes*) || *intr* to bite (*said of fish*); to fall; to fit (*said of pipes*) || *ref* to confer

abbocca·to -ta *adj* palatable; slightly sweet (*wine*)

abbonacciare §128 *ref* to calm down, abate (*said of weather*)

abbonaménto *m* subscription; **abbonamento postale** mailing permit

abbonare (**abbòno**) *tr* to take out a subscription for (*s.o.*) || *ref* to subscribe || §257 *tr* to remit (*a debt*); to forgive

abbona·to -ta *mf* subscriber; commuter

abbondante *adj* abundant, plentiful; heavy (*rain*)

abbondanza *f* abundance, plenty

abbondare (**abbóndo**) *intr* (ESSERE & AVERE) to abound; to exceed; **abbondare di** or **in** to abound in

abbonire §176 *tr* to calm; to placate || *ref* to calm down

abbordàbile *adj* accessible, approachable; negotiable (*curve*)

abbordàg·gio *m* (-gi) boarding (*of an enemy ship*); **andare all'abbordaggio di** to board

abbordare (**abbórdo**) *tr* to board (*an enemy ship*); to negotiate (*a curve*); to face (*a problem*); (fig) to button-hole

abborracciare §128 *tr* to botch, bungle

abborracciatura *f* botch, bungle

abbottonare (**abbottóno**) *tr* to button ‖ *ref* (coll) to keep to oneself

abbottonatura *f* buttoning; row of buttons

abbozzare (**abbòzzo**) *tr* to sketch; to hew (*e.g., a statue*); (naut) to tie up ‖ *intr* (coll) to take it

abbòzzo *m* sketch, draft

abbracciabò·sco *m* (-schi) (bot) woodbine

abbracciare *m* embrace, embracing ‖ §128 *tr* to embrace, hug; to seize (*an opportunity*); to become converted to (*e.g., Christianity*); to enter (*a profession*); to span, encompass ‖ *ref* to cling; to embrace one another

abbràc·cio *m* (-ci) embrace, hug

abbrancare §197 *tr* to grab; to herd ‖ *ref* to cling; to join a herd

abbreviaménto *m* abbreviation, shortening

abbreviare §287 (**abbrèvio**) *tr* to abbreviate, shorten, abridge

abbreviatura *f* shortening, abridgment

abbreviazióne *f* abbreviation

abbrivo or **abbrivio** *m* headway (*of a ship*); **prendere l'abbrivio** to gather momentum

abbronzante [dz] *adj* suntanning ‖ *m* suntan lotion

abbronzare [dz] (**abbrónzo**) *tr* & *ref* to bronze; to tan

abbronza·to -ta [dz] *adj* tanned, suntanned

abbronzatura [dz] *f* tan, suntan

abbruciacchiare §287 *tr* to singe

abbrunare *tr* to brown; to hang crepe on ‖ *ref* to wear mourning

abbrunire §176 *tr* to turn brown; to tan; to burnish

abbrustolire §176 *tr* to toast; to singe ‖ *ref* to tan; to become sunburned

abbrutiménto *m* degradation, brutishness

abbrutire §176 *tr* to degrade; to brutalize ‖ *intr* & *ref* to become brutalized

abbuiare §287 *tr* to darken; to hush up, hide ‖ *ref* to grow dark; to become gloomy ‖ *impers*—**abbuia** it's growing dark

abbuòno *m* allowance, discount; handicap (*in racing*)

abburattaménto *m* sifting

abburattare *tr* to sift, bolt

abdicare §197 (**àbdico**) *tr* & *intr* to abdicate; **abdicare a** to give up, renounce; to abdicate (*e.g., the throne*)

abdicazióne *f* abdication

aberrare (**abèrro**) *intr* to deviate

aberrazióne *f* aberration

abéte *m* fir

abetina *f* forest of fir trees

abiàti·co *m* (-ci) (coll) grandson

abièt·to -ta *adj* abject, base, low

abigeato *m* (law) cattle rustling

àbile *adj* able, clever, capable; (mil) fit

abili·tà *f* (tà) ability, skill

abilitare (**abìlito**) *tr* to certify (*e.g., a teacher*); to qualify, license

abilita·to -ta *adj* certified (*teacher*)

abilitazióne *f* qualification; certification (*of teachers*)

abissale *adj* abysmal

Abissìnia, l' *f* Abyssinia

abissi·no -na *adj* & *mf* Abyssinian

abisso *m* abyss; fountain (*of knowledge*); slough (*of degradation*)

abitàbile *adj* inhabitable

abitàcolo *m* (aer) cockpit; (aut) cab, interior; (naut) compass bowl; **abitacolo eiettàbile** (aer) ejection capsule

abitante *mf* inhabitant; resident

abitare (**àbito**) *tr* to inhabit; to occupy ‖ *intr* to dwell, live, reside

abitati·vo -va *adj* living, e.g., **condizioni abitative** living conditions

abita·to -ta *adj* inhabited, populated ‖ *m* built-up area

abita·tóre -trice *mf* dweller

abitazióne *f* dwelling; housing

àbito *m* suit (*for men*); dress (*for women*); garb, attire; habit; **abiti** clothes; **abito da ballo** evening gown; **abito da cerimonia** formal dress; **abito da inverno** winter suit; winter clothes; **levarsi l'abito** to doff the cassock; **prender l'abito** to enter the Church

abituale *adj* habitual

abituare (**abìtuo**) *tr* to accustom ‖ *ref* to grow accustomed

abitudinà·rio -ria *adj* (-ri -rie) set in his ways

abitùdine *f* habit, custom

abituro *m* (poet) shanty, hut

abiura *f* abjuration

abiurare *tr* to abjure

ablati·vo -va *adj* & *m* ablative

ablazióne *f* (med) removal; (geol) erosion

abluzióne *f* ablution

abnegare §209 (**abnégo** & **abnègo**) *tr* to renounce, abnegate

abnegazióne *f* abnegation, self-denial

abnòrme *adj* abnormal

abolire §176 *tr* to abolish

abolizióne *f* abolition

abominàbile *adj* abominable

abominare (**abòmino**) *tr* to abominate, detest

abominazióne *f* abomination

abominévole *adj* abominable

aborìge·no -na *adj* aboriginal ‖ *m* aborigine; **aborigeni** aborigines

aborrire §176 & (**abòrro**) *tr* to abhor, loathe ‖ *intr*—**aborrire da** to shun, shrink from

abortire §176 *intr* to abort

abòrto *m* abortion, miscarriage; **aborto di natura** monstrosity

abrasióne *f* abrasion; erosion

abrasi·vo -va *adj* & *m* abrasive

abrogare §209 (**àbrogo**) *tr* to abrogate

abrogazióne *f* abrogation

abruzzése *adj* of the Abruzzi ‖ *mf* person of the Abruzzi ‖ *m* dialect of the Abruzzi

àbside *f* (archit) apse

abusare *intr*—**abusare di** to go to excesses in (*e.g., smoking*); to take advantage of; to impose on

abusi·vo -va *adj* illegal, abusive; unwarranted

abuso *m* abuse, excess

acà·cia *f* (**-cie**) acacia

acanto *m* acanthus

àcaro *m* (ent) acarus, mite, tick; **acaro della scabbia** itch mite

ac·ca *m* & *f* (**-ca** or **-che**) h (*letter*); **non valere un'acca** (coll) to not be worth a fig

accadèmia *f* academy

accadèmi·co -ca (**-ci -che**) *adj* academic ‖ *mf* academician

accadére §121 *intr* (ESSERE) to happen, occur

accadu·to -ta *adj* happened, occurred ‖ *m* fact, event; what has taken place

accagliare §280 *tr, intr* (ESSERE) & *ref* to curdle, coagulate

accalappiaca·ni *m* (**-ni**) dogcatcher

accalappiare §287 *tr* to catch (*a dog*); to snare; (fig) to fool

accalcare §197 *tr* to crowd ‖ *ref* to throng

accaldare *ref* to get hot; to become flushed

accalda·to -ta *adj* hot; perspired

accalorare (**accalóro**) *tr* to excite ‖ *ref* to get excited

accalora·to -ta *adj* excited, animated

accampaménto *m* encampment, camp; camping

accampare *tr* to encamp; to advance, lay (*a claim*) ‖ *ref* to camp, encamp

accanimento *m* animosity, bitterness; obstinacy, stubbornness

accanìre §176 *ref* to persist; to work doggedly; **accanirsi contro** to harass

accani·to -ta *adj* obstinate, persistent; furious; fierce, ruthless, bitter (*fight*)

accanto *adv* near, nearby; **accanto a** near

accantonaménto *m* tabling (*e.g., of a discussion*); reserve (*of money*); (mil) billeting; (sports) camping

accantonare (**accantóno**) *tr* to set aside (*money*); (mil) to billet

accaparraménto *m* cornering (*of market*)

accaparrare *tr* to corner (*merchandise*); to hoard; to put a down payment on (*e.g., a house*); (coll) to gain (*somebody's affection*)

accaparra·tóre -trice *mf* monopolizer; hoarder

accapigliare §280 *ref* to pull each other's hair; to scuffle; to come to blows

accapo or **a capo** *m* paragraph

accappa·tóio *m* (**-tói**) bathrobe

accapponare (**accappóno**) *tr* to castrate (*a rooster*) ‖ *ref* to wrinkle; **mi si accappona la pelle** I get gooseflesh

accarezzare (**accarézzo**) *tr* to caress, fondle; to pet; to nurture (*e.g., a*

hope); **accarezzare le spalle di** to strike; to club

accartocciare §128 (**accartòccio**) *tr* to wrap up in a cone ‖ *ref* to curl up

accartoccia·to -ta *adj* curled up

accasare [s] *tr* & *ref* to marry

accasciaménto *m* dejection

accasciare §128 *tr* to weaken, enfeeble; to depress ‖ *ref* to weaken; to lose heart

accasermare [s] (**accasèrmo**) *tr* to quarter, billet

accatastare *tr* to register (*real estate*); to pile, heap up

accattabrì·ghe *mf* (**-ghe**) quarrelsome person, scrapper

accattare *tr* to beg for; to borrow (*e.g., ideas*) ‖ *intr* to beg

accattonàg·gio *m* (**-gi**) begging, mendicancy

accattó·ne -na *mf* mendicant, beggar

accavalcare §197 *tr* to straddle; to go over

accavalciare §128 *tr* to bestride

accavallare *tr* to superimpose; to cross (*one's legs*) ‖ *ref* to pour forward, run high (*said of waves*)

accecaménto *m* blinding

accecare §122 *tr* to blind; to countersink *tr* *intr* (ESSERE) to become blind ‖ *ref* to blind oneself

acceca·tóio *m* (**-tói**) countersink

accèdere §100 *intr* (ESSERE) to enter, approach; to accede

acceleraménto *m* acceleration

accelerare (**accèlero**) *tr* & *intr* to accelerate

accelera·to -ta *adj* accelerated; intensive (*course*); local (*train*) ‖ *m* local train

acceleratóre *m* accelerator

accelerazióne *f* acceleration

accèndere §101 *tr* to kindle; to turn on (*e.g., the light*); to light (*e.g., a match, a cigar*) ‖ *ref* to catch fire; to become lit; **accendersi in viso** to become flushed

accendisìgaro *m* lighter

accendi·tóio *m* (**-tói**) candle lighter

accenditóre *m* lighter

accennare (**accénno**) *tr* to nod; to point at; to sketch ‖ *intr* to refer; to hint

accénno *m* nod; sign; allusion

accensióne *f* lighting, kindling; (aut) ignition; (law) contraction (*of a debt*); **accensione improvvisa** spontaneous combustion

accentare (**accènto**) *tr* to accent

accènto *m* accent; stress; (poet) accent (*word*); **accento tonico** stress accent

accentraménto *m* centralization

accentrare (**accèntro**) *tr* to concentrate, centralize

accentuare (**accèntuo**) *tr* to accentuate ‖ *ref* to become aggravated

accentuazióne *f* accentuation

accerchiaménto *m* encirclement

accerchiare §287 (**accérchio**) *tr* to encircle, surround

accertàbile *adj* verifiable

accertaménto *m* ascertainment, verification; determination (*e.g., of taxes*)

accertare (accèrto) *tr* to assure; to ascertain, verify; to determine (*the tax due*) || *ref* to make sure

accé·so -sa [s] *adj* lit; turned on; on (*e.g., radio*); excited, aroused; bright (*color*)

accessìbile *adj* accessible; moderate (*price*)

accessióne *f* accession

accèsso *m* access, approach; admittance, entry; fit (*of anger, of coughing*)

accessò·rio -ria (-ri -rie) *adj* accessory || *m* accessory; (mach) accessory, attachment

accétta *f* hatchet, axe, cleaver; **tagliato con l'accetta** rough-hewn

accettàbile *adj* acceptable

accettare (accètto) *tr* to accept

accettazióne *f* acceptance; receiving room; (econ) acceptance

accèt·to -ta *adj* agreeable; welcome; **male accetto** unwelcome

accezióne *f* meaning, acceptation

acchiappafarfal·le *m* (-le) butterfly net

acchiappamó·sche *m* (-sche) fly catcher

acchiappare *tr* to grab, seize; (coll) to catch in the act

acchito *m* (billiards) break; **di primo acchito** at first

acciaccare §197 *tr* to crush; to trample upon; (coll) to lay low (*e.g., by illness*)

acciac·co *m* (-chi) illness, infirmity, ailment

acciaiare §287 *tr* to convert into steel; to strengthen with steel

acciaierìa *f* steel mill, steelworks

ac·ciàio *m* (-ciài); **acciaio inossidàbile** stainless steel

acciaiòlo *m* whetstone

acciambellare (acciambèllo) *tr* to shape in the form of a doughnut || *ref* to curl up

acciarino *m* flintlock; linchpin; (nav) war nose (*of a torpedo*)

accidèmpoli *interj* (slang) darn it!

accidentale *adj* accidental

accidenta·to -ta *adj* paralyzed; uneven, rough (*road*); broken (*ground*)

accidènte *m* accident; crack-up; (coll) paralytic stroke; (coll) hoot, fig; (coll) pest, menace (*child*); (mus) accidental; **accidentì!** (coll) darn!, damn!; **correre come un accidente** to run like the devil; **mandare un accidente a** to wish ill luck to; **per accidente** perchance

accìdia *f* sloth

accidió·so -sa [s] *adj* slothful

acciglìare §280 *ref* to frown, knit one's brow

accìngere §126 *ref*—**accingersi a** to get ready to

-àccio -àccia *suf* *adj* & *mf* (-acci -acce) no good, e.g., **gentàccia** no good people; good-for-nothing, e.g., **ragazzàccio** good-for-nothing boy

acciò *or* **acciocché** *conj* (poet) so that

acciottolare (acciòttolo) *tr* to pave with cobblestones

acciottola·to -ta *adj* cobblestone || *m* cobblestone pavement

acciottollì·o *m* (-ì) clatter (*e.g., of dishes*)

accipìcchia *interj* (coll) darn it!

acciuffare *tr* to seize, grab, pinch (*a thief*)

acciu·ga *f* (-ghe) anchovy

acclamare *tr* to acclaim || *intr* to voice one's approval

acclamazióne *f* acclamation

acclimatare (acclìmato) *tr* & *ref* to acclimate

acclimatazióne *f* acclimatation

acclìve *adj* (poet) steep

acclivi·tà *f* (-tà) acclivity

acclùdere §105 *tr* to enclose

acclu·so -sa *adj* enclosed

accoccare §197 (accòcco & accòcco) *tr* (poet) to nock (*the arrow*)

accoccolare (accòccolo) *ref* to squat down

accodare (accòdo) *tr* to line up || *ref* to line up, queue

accogliènte *adj* cozy, hospitable, inviting

accogliènza *f* reception, welcome

accògliere §127 *tr* to receive; to welcome; to grant (*a request*) || *ref* (poet) to gather

accoglitrice *f* receptionist

accòlito *m* acolyte, altar boy; follower

accollare (accòllo) *tr* to overload (*a cart*); **accollare qlco a qlcu** to charge s.o. with s.th || *intr* to go up to the neck (*said of a dress*) || *ref* to assume, take upon oneself

accolla·to -ta *adj* high-necked (*dress*); high-cut (*shoes*) || *f* accolade

accollatura *f* neck, neckhole

accòlta *f* (poet) gathering

accoltellare (accoltèllo) *tr* to knife

accomandante *m* limited partner

accomandatà·rio *m* (-ri) (law) general partner

accomàndita *f* (law) limited partnership

accomiatare *tr* to dismiss || *ref* to take leave

accomodaménto *m* arrangement; compromise; settlement

accomodante *adj* accommodating, obliging

accomodare (accòmodo) *tr* to arrange; to fix; to settle || *intr* to be convenient || *ref* to adapt oneself; to agree; to sit down; **si accomodi** have a seat, make yourself comfortable

accomodatura *f* arrangement; repair

accompagnaménto *m* retinue; cortege; (mus) accompaniment; (law) writ of mandamus; (mil) softening-up (*by gunfire*)

accompagnare *tr* to accompany; to escort; to follow; to match || *ref*—**accompagnarsi a** *or* **con** to join

accompagna·tóre -trice *mf* escort; guide; (mus) accompanist

accomunare *tr* to mingle, mix; to unite, associate; to share

acconciaménto *m* arrangement

acconciare §128 (accòncio) *tr* to prepare for use; to arrange; to set (*e.g., the hair*) || *ref* to adorn oneself; to dress one's hair; to adapt oneself

acconcia·tóre -trice *mf* hairdresser

acconciatura *f* hairdo; headdress
accón·cio -cia *adj* (**-ci -ce**) proper, fitting
accondiscendènte *adj* acquiescing, acquiescent
accondiscendènza *f* acquiescence
accondiscéndere §245 *intr* to acquiesce, consent; to yield
acconsentire (**acconsènto**) *intr* to consent, acquiesce
acconsenziènte *adj* consenting, acquiescing
accontentare (**accontènto**) *tr* to satisfy, please || *ref* to be satisfied, be please !
accónto *m* installment
accoppare (**accòppo**) *tr* (coll) to kill; (coll) to beat to death || *ref* (coll) to get killed
accoppiaménto *m* pairing; mating; (mach) parallel operation
accoppiare §287 (**accòppio**) *tr* to couple, pair, cross (*e.g., animals*) || *ref* to mate, copulate
accoppiata *f* daily double (*in races*)
accoraménto *m* sadness, sorrow
accorare (**accòro**) *tr* to stab to death; to sadden || *ref* to sadden, grieve
accora·to -ta *adj* saddened, grieving
accorciare §128 (**accórcio**) *tr* & *ref* to shorten; to shrink
accorciatura *f* shortening; shrinking
accordare (**accòrdo**) *tr* to harmonize (*colors*); to reconcile (*people*); to tune up; to grant; (gram) to make agree || *ref* to agree; to match
accorda·to -ta *adj* tuned up || *m* (econ) credit limit
accorda·tóre -trice *mf* (mus) tuner
accordatura *f* tuning
accòrdo *m* agreement, accordance; (law) mutual consent; (mus) harmony; **d'accordo** O.K., agreed; **d'accordo con** in accord with; **di comune accordo** with one accord; **essere d'accordo** to agree; **mettersi d'accordo** to come to an agreement
accòrgere §249 *ref* to perceive, notice; **accorgersi di** to become aware of, realize; **senza accorgersi** inadvertently
accorgiménto *m* smartness; device, trick
accórrere §139 *intr* (ESSERE) to run up, rush up
accortézza *f* alertness; shrewdness, perspicacity
accòr·to -ta *adj* alert; shrewd, perspicacious
accosciare §128 (**accòscio**) *ref* to squat
accostàbile *adj* approachable
accostaménto *m* approach; combination (*e.g., of colors*)
accostare (**accòsto**) *tr* to approach; to bring near; to leave (*a door*) ajar || *intr* to be near; to cling, adhere; (naut) to come alongside; (naut) to maneuver alongside a pier; (naut) to change direction, haul || *ref* to approach, come near; to cling (*e.g., to a faith*)
accosta·to -ta *adj* ajar
accò·sto -sta *adj* (coll) near || *m* ap-

proach; help || **accosto** *adv* near; **accosto a** near, close to
accovacciare §128 *ref* to crouch
accovonare (**accovóno**) *tr* to sheave
accozzàglia *f* hodgepodge; motley crowd
accozzare (**accòzzo**) *tr* to jumble up; to collect, gather (*people*) together || *ref* to collect, congregate
accòzzo *m* jumble, medley
accreditàbile *adj* chargeable (*e.g., account*); creditable
accreditaménto *m* crediting
accreditare (**accrédito**) *tr* to credit, believe; to accredit (*an ambassador*); to credit (*one's account*)
accredita·to -ta *adj* confirmed (*news*); accredited
accréscere §142 *tr* & *ref* to increase
accresciménto *m* increase
accucciare §128 *ref* to curl up (*said of dogs*)
accudire §176 *tr* (coll) to attend (*a sick person*) || *intr*—**accudire a** to take care of
acculturazióne *f* acculturation
accumulare (**accùmulo**) *tr*, *intr* & *ref* to accumulate; to gather
accumulatóre *m* storage battery
accumulazióne *f* accumulation
accuratézza *f* care, carefulness
accura·to -ta *adj* careful, painstaking
accusa *f* accusation, charge; **pubblica accusa** (law) public prosecutor
accusare *tr* to accuse, charge; to betray; to acknowledge (*receipt*); (cards) to declare, bid
accusati·vo -va *adj* & *m* accusative
accusa·to -ta *adj* accused || *mf* defendant
accusatóre -trice *mf* accuser; **pubblico accusatore** (law) public prosecutor, district attorney
accusatò·rio -ria *adj* (**-ri -rie**) accusatory, accusing
acèfa·lo -la *adj* headless; without the first page (*said of a manuscript*)
acèr·bo -ba *adj* unripe, green, sour
àcero *m* maple tree, sugar maple
acèrri·mo -ma *adj* bitter, fierce
acetato *m* acetate
acèti·co -ca *adj* (**-ci -che**) acetic
acetificare §197 (**acetìfico**) *tr* to acetify
acetilène *m* acetylene
acéto *m* vinegar; **aceto aromatico** aromatic spirits; **sotto aceto** pickled
acetóne *m* acetone
acetósa [s] *f* (bot) sorrel
acetosèlla [s] *f* wood sorrel
acetó·so -sa [s] *adj* vinegarish || *f* see **acetosa**
Acherónte *m* Acheron
Achille *m* Achilles
acidificare §197 (**acidìfico**) *tr* to acidify
acidi·tà *f* (**-tà**) acidity; **acidità di stomaco** heartburn
àci·do -da *adj* acid, sour || *m* acid; **sapere d'acido** to taste sour
acidu·lo -la *adj* acidulous
àcino *m* berry (*of grapes*); bead (*of rosary*)
acme *f* acme; crisis
acne *f* acne

acònito *m* (bot) monkshood

àcqua *f* water; rain; purity (*e.g., of a diamond*); **acqua a catinelle** pouring rain; **acqua alta** high water; **acqua corrente** running water; **acqua dolce** fresh water; drinking water; **acqua in bocca!** mum's the word!; **acqua morta** stagnant water; **acqua ossigenata** hydrogen peroxide; **acqua potabile** drinking water; **acqua salata** salt water; **acqua viva** spring; **all'acqua di rose** very mild; **avere l'acqua alla gola** to be in dire straits; **bell'acqua** of the first water; **fare acqua** to leak (*said of a boat*); **fare un buco nell'acqua** to waste one's efforts; **portare acqua al mare** to carry coals to Newcastle; **prendere l'acqua** to get wet; **sott'acqua** (fig) underhand; **tirare l'acqua al proprio mulino** to be grist to one's mill; **versare acqua in un cesto** to waste one's efforts

acquaforte *f* (acquefòrti) etching

acquaforti·sta *mf* (-sti -ste) etcher

ac·quàio -quàia (-quài -quàie) *adj* watering (*trough*) || *m* sink

acquaiò·lo -la *adj* water || *m* water carrier; (sports) water boy

acquamarina *f* (acquemarine) aquamarine

acquaplano *m* aquaplane

acquaràgia *f* turpentine

acquarèllo *m* var of acquerello

acquà·rio *m* (-ri) aquarium || **Acquario** *m* (astr) Aquarius

acquartierare (acquartièro) *tr* (mil) to quarter || *ref* to be quartered

acquasanta *f* holy water

acquasantièra *f* (eccl) stoup

acquàti·co -ca *adj* (-ci -che) aquatic, water

acquattare *ref* to crouch, squat

acquavite *f* brandy; liquor, rum

acquazzóne *m* downpour, heavy shower

acquedótto *m* aqueduct

àcque·o -a *adj* aqueous, watery

acquerelli·sta *mf* (-sti -ste) watercolorist

acquerèllo *m* watercolor; watered-down wine

acquerùgiola *f* fine drizzle

acquiescènte *adj* acquiescent

acquietare (acquiéto) *tr* to pacify, placate || *ref* to quiet down

acquirènte *mf* buyer, purchaser; **il miglior acquirente** the highest bidder

acquisire §176 *tr* to acquire

acquisi·tóre -trice *mf* salesperson, agent || *m* salesman || *f* saleswoman

acquistare *tr* to purchase, buy; to acquire; to gain (*e.g., ground*) || *intr* to improve

acquisto *m* buy, purchase; acquisition

acquitrino *m* marsh

acquitrinó·so -sa [s] *adj* marshy

acquolina *f*—**far venire l'acquolina in bocca a** to make one's mouth water

acquó·so -sa [s] *adj* watery

àcre *adj* sour; pungent; acrid; bitter (*words*)

acrèdine *f* acrimony, sourness

acrimònia *f* acrimony

acro *m* acre

acròba·ta *mf* (-ti -te) acrobat

acrobàti·co -ca (-ci -che) *adj* acrobatic || *f* acrobatics

acrobatismo *m* acrobatics

acrobazìa *f* acrobatics; stunt, feat

acrocòro *m* plateau

acrònimo *m* acronym

acròpo·li *f* (-li) acropolis

acròsti·co·m (-ci) acrostic

acuire §176 *tr* to sharpen, whet

acuità *f* acuity

acùle·o *m* (-i) quill; prickle, thorn; stinger (*of an insect*)

acume *m* acumen

acuminare (acùmino) *tr* to sharpen, whet

acumina·to -ta *adj* pointed, sharp

acùsti·co -ca (-ci -che) *adj* acoustic(al) || *f* acoustics

acutézza *f* acuteness, sharpness

acutizzare [ddzz] *tr & ref* to sharpen

acu·to -ta *adj* acute, sharp || *m* high note

ad *prep* var of **a** before words beginning with a vowel

adagiare §290 *tr* to lay down gently; to lower gently || *ref* to lie down; to stretch out

adà·gio *m* (-gi) adage; (mus) adagio || *adv* slowly; gently; (mus) adagio

Adamo *m* Adam

adattàbile *adj* adaptable

adattaménto *m* adaptation; adaptability

adattare *tr* to adapt, fit || *ref* to adapt oneself; to become adapted; **adattarsi a** to go with; to match; to be becoming

adat·to -ta *adj* suitable, adequate

addebitaménto *m* debiting

addebitare (addèbito) *tr* to debit; **addebitare una spesa a qlcu** to debit s.o. with an expense

addèbito *m* charge; (com) debit; **elevare l'addebito di qlco a qlcu** (law) to charge s.o. with s.th

addènda *mpl* addenda

addèndo *m* (math) addend

addensare (addènso) *tr* to thicken || *ref* to thicken; to gather, throng

addentare (addènto) *tr* to bite || *ref* (mach) to mesh

addentatura *f* bite; (carp) tongue (*of tongue and groove*)

addentella·to -ta *adj* toothed, notched || *m* chance, occasion; (archit) toothing

addentrare (addéntro) *tr* to penetrate || *ref* to penetrate; to proceed

addéntro *adv* inside; **addentro in** into; inside of

addestraménto *m* training

addestrare (addèstro) *tr & ref* to train

addestra·tóre -trice *mf* trainer

addét·to -ta *adj* assigned; attached; pertaining || *m* attaché; **addetto stampa** press secretary

addì *adv* the (+ *a certain date*), e.g., **addì 27 gennaio** the 27th of January

addiàc·cio *m* (-ci) sheepfold; bivouac

addiètro *m* (naut) stern; **per l'addietro** in the past || *adv* behind; ago; **dare**

addietro to back up; **lasciarsi addietro** to delay; **tempo addietro** some time ago; **tirarsi addietro** to back away

addì·o m (-i) farewell; **dare l'addio to** say good-bye; **dare l'estremo addìo** to pay one's last respects; **fare gli addìi** to say good-bye || *interj* farewell!, good-bye!

addìre §151 *tr* (poet) to consecrate || *ref* to be suitable, be becoming; **addirsi a** to be becoming to

addirittura *adv* directly; even, without hesitation; absolutely, positively

addirizzare *tr* to straighten up; **addirizzare le gambe ai cani** to try the impossible

additare *tr* to point out

additi·vo -va *adj* & *m* additive

addivenìre §282 *intr* (ESSERE)—**addivenìre a** to come to, reach (*e.g., an agreement*)

addizionale *adj* additional || *f* supplementary tax

addizionare (**addizióno**) *tr* & *intr* to add

addizionatrice *f* adding machine

addizióne *f* addition

addobbaménto *m* adornment, decoration

addobbare (**addòbbo**) *tr* to adorn, bedeck, decorate

addobba·tóre -trice *mf* decorator

addòbbo *m* adornment, decoration; hangings (*in a church*)

addocilire §176 *tr* to soften up

addolcire §176 *tr* to sweeten; to calm down || *ref* to mellow, soften

addolorare (**addolóro**) *tr* & *ref* to grieve; **addolorarsi per** to grieve over, lament

addolora·to -ta *adj* sorrowful || **l'Addolorata** *f* (eccl) Our Lady of Sorrows

addòme *m* abdomen

addomesticàbile *adj* tamable

addomesticaménto *m* taming

addomesticare §197 (**addomèstico**) *tr* to tame; to accustom || *ref* to become accustomed

addomestica·to -ta *adj* tame, domesticated

addominale *adj* abdominal

addormentare (**addorménto**) *tr* to put to sleep; to numb || *ref* to fall asleep; to be asleep (*said of a limb*)

addormenta·to -ta *adj* asleep; numbed

addossare (**addòsso**) *tr* to put on; **addossare qlco a qlco** to lean s.th against s.th; **addossare qlco a qlcu** to put s.th on s.o.; (fig) to entrust s.o. with s.th || *ref* to take upon oneself; to crowd together; **addossarsi a** to lean against; to crowd

addossa·to -ta *adj* leaning

addòsso *adv* on; on oneself, on one's back; about oneself; **addosso a** on, upon; against; **avere la sfortuna addosso** to be always unlucky; **dare addosso a qlcu** to assail s.o.; **levarsi d'addosso** to get rid of; **levarsi i panni d'addosso** to take the shirt off one's back

addót·to -ta *adj* adduced, alleged

addottorare (**addottóro**) *tr* to confer the doctor's degree on || *ref* to receive the doctor's degree

addurre §102 *tr* to adduce; to allege; (poet) to bring

Ade *m* Hades

adeguare (**adéguo**) *tr* to equalize; to bring in line || *ref* to conform, adapt oneself

adegua·to -ta *adj* adequate

adeguazióne *f* equalization

adémpiere §163 *tr* to fulfill, accomplish || *ref* to come true

adempiménto *m* fulfillment, discharge (*of one's duty*)

adempire §176 *tr* to fulfill, accomplish || *ref* to come true

adenòide *adj* adenoid || **adenoidi** *fpl* adenoids

adèpto *m* follower; initiate

aderènte *adj* adherent || *mf* adherent, supporter

aderènza *f* adherence; (mach) friction; (pathol) adhesion; **aderenze** connections

aderìre §176 *intr* to adhere; to stick; **aderìre a** to grant (*e.g., a request*); to concur with; to subscribe to

adescare §197 (**adésco**) *tr* to lure, bait, entice; (mach) to prime (*a pump*)

adesióne *f* adhesion; support; (phys) adherence

adesi·vo -va *adj* & *m* adhesive

adèsso *adv* now, just now; **da adesso in poi** from now on; **per adesso** for the time being

adiacènte *adj* adjacent

adiacènza *f* adjacency; **adiacenze** vicinity

adianto *m* (bot) maidenhair

adibire §176 *tr* to assign; to use

àdipe *m* fat

adipó·so -sa [s] *adj* adipose

adirare *ref* to get angry

adira·to -ta *adj* angry, mad

adire §176 *tr* to apply to (*the court*); to enter into possession of (*an inheritance*)

adocchiare §287 (**adòcchio**) *tr* to eye; to ogle; to spot

adolescènte *adj* & *mf* adolescent

adolescènza *f* adolescence

adombrare (**adómbro**) *tr* to shade; to hide, veil || *ref* to shy (*said of a horse*); (fig) to take umbrage

Adóne *m* Adonis

adontare (**adónto**) *tr* (obs) to offend || *ref* to take offense

adoperare (**adòpero** & **adópero**) *tr* to use, employ || *ref* to exert oneself; to do one's best

adoràbile *adj* adorable

adorare (**adóro**) *tr* to adore; to worship || *intr* (archaic) to pray

adora·tóre -trice *mf* worshiper || *m* (joc) admirer, suitor

adorazióne *f* adoration, worship

adornare (**adórno**) *tr* to adorn || *ref* to bedeck oneself

adór·no -na *adj* adorned, bedecked; (poet) fine, beautiful

adottante *mf* (law) adopter

adottare (adòtto) *tr* to adopt
adotti·vo -va *adj* adoptive; foster *(child)*
adozióne *f* adoption
Adrìàti·co -ca *adj* (**-ci -che**) Adriatic || **Adriatico** *m* Adriatic
adulare (àdulo) *tr* to flatter; to fawn on
adula·tóre -trice *mf* flatterer
adulatò·rio -ria *adj* (**-ri -rie**) flattering; fawning
adulazióne *f* adulation; fawning
adulterante *adj* & *m* adulterant
adulteri·no -na *adj* bastard; adulterated
adultè·rio *m* (**-ri**) adultery
adùlte·ro -ra *adj* adulterous || *m* adulterer || *f* adulteress
adul·to -ta *adj* & *mf* adult
adunanza *f* assembly
adunare *tr* & *ref* to assemble, gather
adunata *f* reunion, meeting; (mil) muster
adun·co -ca *adj* (**-chi -che**) hooked, crooked
adunghiare §287 *tr* (poet) to claw
adu·sto -sta *adj* skinny; (poet) burnt
aerare (àero) *tr* to air, ventilate
aerazióne *f* aeration; airing
àère·o -a *adj* aerial; air; overhead; high, lofty; airy, fanciful || *m* airplane; (rad & telv) aerial
aerobrigata *f* (mil) wing
aerocistèrna *f* (aer) tanker
aerodinàmi·co -ca (**-ci -che**) *adj* aerodynamic(al); streamlined || *f* aerodynamics
aeròdromo *m* airfield, airdrome
aerofaro *m* airport beacon
aerofotogram·ma *m* (**-mi**) aerial photograph
aerogiro *m* helicopter
aerògrafo *m* spray gun *(for painting)*
aerolìnea *f* airline; **aerolinea principale** trunkline
aeròlite *m* aerolite, meteorite
aeromarìtti·mo -ma *adj* air-sea
aeròmetro *m* aerometer
aeromòbile *m* aircraft; **aeromobile senza pilota** drone, pilotless aircraft
aeromodellismo *m* model-airplane building
aeromodelli·sta *mf* (**-sti -ste**) model-airplane builder
aeromodèllo *m* model airplane
aeromotóre *m* windmill; aircraft motor
aeronàu·ta *m* (**-ti**) aeronaut
aeronàuti·co -ca (**-ci -che**) *adj* aeronautic(al) || *f* aeronautics
aeronave *f* airship, aircraft
aeroplano *m* airplane
aeropòrto *m* airport, airfield
aeroportuale *adj* airport
aerorazzo [ddzz] *m* rocket spaceship
aeroriméssa *f* hangar
aerosbar·co *m* (**-chi**) landing of airborne troops
aeroservì·zio [s] *m* (**-zi**) air service
aerosilurante [s] *f* torpedo plane
aerosiluro [s] *m* aerial torpedo
aerosòl [s] *m* aerosol
aerosostenta·to -ta [s] *adj* airborne
aerospaziale *adj* aerospace
aerospà·zio *m* (**-zi**) aerospace

aerostàti·co -ca (**-ci -che**) *adj* aerostatic(al) || *f* aerostatics
aeròstato *m* aerostat
aerostazióne *f* air terminal
aerotas·sì *m* (**-sì**) taxiplane
aerotrasportare (aerotraspòrto) *tr* to airlift
aerotrasporta·to -ta *adj* airlifted; airborne
aerovìa *f* (aer) beam *(course indicated by a radio beam)*; (aer) air lane
afa *f* sultriness; **fare afa a** (coll) to be a pain in the neck to
afèresi *f* apheresis
affàbile *adj* affable, agreeable
affaccendare (affaccèndo) *tr* to busy || *ref* to busy oneself, bustle
affaccenda·to -ta *adj* busy, bustling; occupied with busywork
affacciare §128 *tr* to show or display at the window; to bring forward (*e.g.*, an objection); to raise (a doubt) || *ref* to show oneself (at the door or window); to present itself (said of a doubt)
affaccia·to -ta *adj* facing
affagottare (affagòtto) *tr* to bundle || *ref* to bundle up; to dress sloppily
affamare *tr* to starve
affama·to -ta *adj* starved, ravenous || *mf* starveling; hungry person; wretch
affannare *tr* to worry, to afflict || *intr* to pant; to be out of breath || *ref* to worry; to bustle around
affanna·to -ta *adj* panting; out of breath; worried
affanno *m* shortness of breath; grief, sorrow
affannó·so -sa [s] *adj* panting; wearisome
affardellare (affardèllo) *tr* to bundle together; (mil) to pack
affare *m* affair, matter; business; condition, quality; deal; **affari** business; **affari esteri** foreign affairs; **un buon affare** a good deal; a bargain
affarismo *m* sharp business practice
affari·sta *mf* (**-sti -ste**) unscrupulous operator
affarìsti·co -ca *adj* (**-ci -che**) sharp
affascinante *adj* fascinating, charming
affascinare (affàscino) *tr* to fascinate, charm; to seduce; to spellbind || (affascìno) *tr* to bundle, to sheave
affascina·tóre -trice *adj* fascinating, charming || *mf* charmer, spellbinder
affastellare (affastèllo) *tr* to fagot (*twigs*): to sheave, bundle (*e.g.*, hay); to pile, heap (*wood, crops, etc*); (fig) to jumble up
affaticare §197 *tr* to fatigue, tire, weary || *ref* to get tired; to weary; to toil
affatica·to -ta *adj* weary, tired
affatto *adv* quite, entirely; **niente affatto** not at all; **non . . . affatto** not at all
affatturare *tr* to bewitch; to adulterate (*e.g.*, food)
affermare (affèrmo) *tr* to affirm, assert || *intr* to nod assent || *ref* to take hold (said, e.g., of a new product)
affermati·vo -va *adj* & *f* affirmative
affermazióne *f* affirmation; assertion,

statement; success (e.g., of a new product); (sports) victory

afferrare (afferro) tr to grab, grasp; to catch, nab || ref to cling

affettare (affetto) tr to slice; to cut up || **(affètto)** tr to affect

affetta·to -ta adj affected || m cold cuts

affettatrice f slicing machine

affettazióne f affectation

affetti·vo -va adj emotional

affèt·to -ta adj afflicted, burdened || m affection, love; feeling

affettuosi·tà [s] f (-tà) love, affection

affettuó·so -sa [s] adj affectionate, loving, tender

affezionare (affezióno) tr to inspire affection in || ref—**affezionarsi a** to become fond of

affeziona·to -ta adj affectionate, loving; **Suo affezionatissimo** best regards; **tuo affezionatissimo** love, as ever

affezióne f affection

affiancare §197 tr to place next; to favor, help; (mil) to flank

affiataménto m harmony; teamwork

affiatare tr to harmonize

affibbiare §287 tr to buckle, fasten; to deliver (a blow); to play (a trick); to slap (a fine)

affidaménto m consignment, delivery; trust, confidence; **dare affidamento** to be trustworthy; **fare affidamento su** to rely upon

affidare tr to entrust; to commit (to memory); **affidare qlco a qlcu** to entrust s.o with s.th || ref to trust; **affidarsi a** to trust in

affievoliménto m weakening

affievolire §176 tr to weaken || ref to grow weaker

affiggere §103 tr to post; to fix (one's eyes or glance) || ref to gaze, stare

affigliare §280 tr & ref var of affiliare

affilacoltèl·li m (-ll) steel (for sharpening knives)

affilara·sólo m (-sól) strop

affilare tr to sharpen, hone, whet; to make thin || ref to become thin

affila·to -ta adj sharp, sharpened; thin || f sharpening

affila·tóio m (-tói) sharpener

affilatrice f grindstone

affiliare §287 tr to affiliate || ref to become affiliated; **affiliarsi a** to become a member of

affilia·to -ta adj affiliated || mf affiliate; foster child; member of a secret society

affiliazióne f affiliation

affinare tr to sharpen; to refine, purify; to improve (e.g., one's style) || ref to improve

affinché conj so that, in order that; **affinché non** lest

affine adj akin, related; similar || mf in-law || m kinsman f kinswoman || adv—**affine di** in order to

affini·tà [s] f (-tà) affinity

affiochire §176 tr to make hoarse; to weaken || ref to become hoarse; to grow dim (said of a candle)

affioraménto m surfacing; (min) outcrop

affiorare (affióro) intr to surface, emerge; to appear, to show

affissare tr (poet) to fix || ref to concentrate; (poet) to gaze

affissióne f posting, bill posting

affis·so -sa adj fixed; posted || m bill, poster; door or window; (gram) affix

affittacàme·re m (-re) landlord || f landlady

affittanza f rent

affittare tr to rent || ref—**si affitta** for rent

affitto m rent, rental; **dare in affitto** to rent (to grant by lease); **prendere in affitto** to rent (to take by lease)

affittuà·rio -ria mf (-ri -rie) renter; tenant

affliggènte adj tormenting, distressing

affliggere §104 tr to afflict, distress || ref to grieve

afflit·to -ta adj afflicted, grieving || mf afflicted person, wretch

afflizióne f affliction, distress

afflosciare §128 (afflòscio) tr to cause to sag; to weaken || ref to droop; to sag; to be deflated; to faint

affloscire §176 tr & ref var of afflosciare

affluènte adj & m confluent

affluènza f confluence; abundance; crowd

affluire §176 intr (ESSERE) to flow (said of river); to flock (said of people); to pour in (said of earnings)

afflusso m flow

affogaménto m drowning

affogare §209 (affógo) tr to drown; to smother || intr (ESSERE) to drown

affoga·to -ta adj drowned; poached (egg)

affollaménto m crowd, throng

affollare (affóllo & affòllo) tr to crowd; to overcome || ref to crowd

affolla·to -ta adj crowded

affondaménto m sinking

affondami·ne m (-ne) mine layer

affondare (affóndo) tr to sink; to stick || ref to sink

affondata f (aer) nosedive

affóndo m (fencing) lunge || adv deeply

afforestare (afforèsto) tr to reforest

affossare (affòsso) tr to ditch; (fig) to table (e.g., a proposal); to hollow out || ref to become sunken or hollow (said, e.g., of cheeks)

affossatóre m ditchdigger; gravedigger

affrancare §197 tr to set free; to free; to redeem (a property); to stamp || ref to free oneself; to take heart

affrancatrice f postage meter

affrancatura f stamp, stamping

affràngere §179 tr to weary; (obs) to break down (the spirit)

affran·to -ta adj weary; broken down, broken-hearted

affratellaménto m fraternization

affratellare (affratèllo) tr to bind in brotherly love || ref to fraternize

affrescare §197 (affrésco) tr to fresco; to paint in fresco

affré·sco m (-schi) fresco
affrettare (**affrétto**) tr & ref to hurry, hasten
affretta· to -ta adj hurried
affrontare (**affrónto**) tr to face, confront ‖ ref to meet in combat; to come to blows
affronta·to -ta adj—**affrontati** (herald) combattant
affrónto m affront, offense
affumicare §197 (**affùmico**) tr to smoke; to blacken; to smoke out; to smoke (meat or fish)
affumica·to -ta adj smoked; dark (glasses)
affusolare [s] (**affùsolo**) tr & ref to taper
affusola·to -ta [s] adj tapered; slender
affusto m gun carriage
afga·no -na adj & mf Afghan
àfo·no -na adj voiceless
afori·sma m (-smi) aphorism
afó·so -sa [s] adj sultry
Africa, l' f Africa
africa·no -na adj & mf African
afrodisìa·co -ca adj & m (-ci -che) aphrodisiac
afta m mouth ulcer; **afta epizootica** (vet) foot-and-mouth disease
àgata f agate ‖ **Agata** f Agatha
agènda f notebook; agenda
agènte adj active ‖ m agent; broker; merchant; officer; **agente delle tasse** tax collector; **agente di cambio** stockbroker; money changer; **agente di commercio** broker, commission merchant; **agente di custodia** jailer; **agente di polizia** police officer, policeman; **agente di spionaggio** informer; **agente provocatore** agent provocateur
agenzia f agency; office, branch; **agenzia immobiliare** real-estate office
agevolare (**agévolo**) tr to facilitate, help
agevolazióne f facility; **agevolazione di pagamento** easy terms
agévole adj easy
agevolézza f facility
aggallare intr to come to the surface
agganciaménto m docking (in space); (rr) coupling
agganciare §128 tr to hook; (rr) to couple; (mil) to engage (the enemy)
aggàn·cio m (-ci) docking (in space); (rr) coupling
aggég·gio m (-gi) gadget
aggettivale adj adjectival
aggettivo m adjective
agghiacciaménto m freezing
agghiacciante adj hair-raising, frightful
agghiacciare §128 tr to freeze ‖ ref to freeze; to be horrified
agghiaccia·to -ta adj frozen, icy
agghindare tr & ref to preen, primp
àg·gio m (-gi) agio; **fare aggio** to be at a premium
aggiogare §209 (**aggiógo**) tr to yoke
aggiornaménto m adjournment (e.g., of a meeting); bringing up to date
aggiornare (**aggiórno**) tr to bring up to date; to adjourn ‖ ref to keep up with the times

aggiraménto m surrounding, outflanking
aggirare tr to surround, outflank; to swindle ‖ ref to roam, wander; **aggirarsi su** to approximate; to be almost
aggiudicare §197 (**aggiùdico**) tr to adjudicate, award ‖ ref to win
aggiudicazióne f adjudication, award
aggiùngere §183 tr to add; to join, connect ‖ ref to be added; to join
aggiunta f addition
aggiuntare tr to attach, join
aggiun·to -ta adj & m associate, assistant, deputy ‖ f see **aggiunta**
aggiustàbile adj repairable
aggiustaménto m settlement; adjustment; (mil) correction (of fire)
aggiustare tr to fix, repair; to adjust; (mil) to correct (cannon fire); **aggiustare per le feste** (coll) to fix; (coll) to give a good beating to ‖ ref (archaic) to come closer; (coll) to manage; (coll) to come to an agreement
aggiusta·tóre -trice mf repairer, fixer ‖ m repairman
aggiustatura f fixing, repairing, repair
agglomerare (**agglòmero**) tr & ref to pile up; to crowd together
agglomerato m built-up area; **agglomerato urbano** urban center
agglutinare (**agglùtino**) tr & ref to agglutinate
agglutinazióne f agglutination
aggobbire §176 tr to bend, bend over ‖ intr (ESSERE) & ref to hunch over
aggomitolare (**aggomìtolo**) tr to coil ‖ ref to curl up
aggradare intr (with dat) (poet) to please; **come Le aggrada** as you please
aggradire §176 tr to appreciate ‖ intr (poet) (with dat) to please
aggraffare tr to hook; to grab; to join (metal sheets) with a double seam; to stitch, staple
aggraffatrice f folding machine; (mach) can sealer
aggranchire §176 tr to benumb; to deaden, stupefy ‖ intr to become numb
aggrappare tr to grab; to clamp ‖ ref to cling
aggravaménto m aggravation
aggravante adj (law) aggravating (circumstances)
aggravare tr to aggravate; to overload (e.g., one's stomach) ‖ ref to get worse
aggrà·vio m (-vi) burden (e.g., of taxes); **fare aggravio a qlcu di qlco** to impute s.th to s.o.
aggraziare §287 tr to embellish; to render graceful ‖ ref to win, gain; to ingratiate oneself
aggrazia·to -ta adj graceful; polite
aggredire §176 tr to assail, attack, assault
aggregare §209 (**aggrègo**) tr & ref to join, unite
aggrega·to -ta adj adjunct ‖ m aggregation
aggressióne f aggression

aggressi·vo -va *adj* aggressive ‖ *m* (mil) poison gas

aggressóre *m* aggressor

aggricciare §128 *tr* to wrinkle; (slang) to knit (*e.g., the brow*) ‖ *ref* (poet) to shiver

aggrinzare *tr & ref* to wrinkle

aggrinzire §176 *tr & ref* var of **aggrinzare**

aggrondare (**aggróndo**) *tr* to knit (*the brow*)

aggrottare (**aggròtto**) *tr* to knit (*the brow*)

aggrovigliare §280 *tr* to tangle, entangle ‖ *ref* to become entangled

aggrumare *tr & ref* to clot; to coagulate

aggruppare *tr* to group

agguagliare §280 *tr* to level; to equalize; to compare

agguantare *tr* to grab; to nab; (coll) to hit; **agguantare per il collo** to grab by the neck ‖ *ref*—**agguantarsi a** to get hold of

agguato *m* ambush; **cadere in un agguato** to fall into a trap; **stare in agguato** to wait in ambush

agguerrire §176 *tr* to train for war; to inure to war; to inure

aghétto *m* shoestring; (mil) lanyard

agiatézza *f* comfort, wealth; **vivere nell'agiatezza** to live in comfort

agia·to -ta *adj* well-to-do, comfortable

àgile *adj* agile, nimble; prompt

agili·tà *f* (**-tà**) agility, nimbleness; promptness

à·gio *m* (**-gi**) comfort; opportunity; ease; **agi** conveniences, comforts; **a Suo agio** at your convenience; **aver agio** to have time; **stare a proprio agio** to feel at ease; to be comfortable; **vivere negli agi** to live comfortably

agiografia *f* hagiography

agiògrafo *m* hagiographer

agire §176 *intr* to act; to work; (theat) to act, perform

agitare (**àgito**) *tr* to agitate, shake; to stir; to stir up; to discuss (*e.g., a problem*) ‖ *ref* to toss; to shake; to stir; to get excited

agita·to -ta *adj* rough, choppy (*sea*); troubled, upset ‖ *mf* violently insane person

agita·tóre -trice *mf* agitator ‖ *m* shaker

agitazióne *f* agitation

agli §4

agliàce·o -a *adj* garlicky

à·glio *m* (**-gli**) garlic

agnellino *m* little lamb, lambkin

agnèllo *m* lamb

agnizióne *f* recognition

agnòsti·co -ca *adj & mf* (**-ci -che**) agnostic

a·go *m* (**-ghi**) needle; pointer (*of scales*); stem (*of valve*)

agognare (**agógno**) *tr* to covet

agóne *m* contest; arena

agonia *f* agony, death struggle; anguish

agonìsti·co -ca *adj* (**-ci -che**) competitive, aggressive (*spirit*); athletic (*competition*) ‖ *f* athletics

agonizzare [ddzz] *intr* to agonize, be in agony; (fig) to die out

agopuntura *f* acupuncture

ago·ràlo *m* (**-ràl**) needle case

agosta·no -na *adj* August, e.g., **pomeriggio agostano** August afternoon

agósto *m* August

agostinia·no -na *adj & m* Augustinian

agòsto *m* August

agrà·rio -ria (**-ri -rie**) *adj & m* agrarian ‖ *m* landlord ‖ *f* agriculture

agrèste *adj* country

agrìco·lo -la *adj* agricultural

agricoltóre *m* farmer; agriculturist

agricoltura *f* agriculture

agrifò·glio *m* (**-gli**) holly

agrimensóre *m* surveyor

agrimensura *f* surveying

a·gro -gra *adj* sour, bitter ‖ *m* citrus juice; sourness, bitterness; surrounding country

agrodólce *adj* sweet and sour; (fig) acidulous (*tone*)

agronomia *f* agronomy

agrònomo *m* agronomist

agrume *m* citrus (*tree and fruit*); **agrumi** citrus fruit

agucchiare §287 *intr* to knit or sew idly

agùglia *f* spire; top; (ichth) gar; (poet) eagle; (obs) needle

aguzzare *tr* to sharpen; to whet (*the appetite*)

aguzzino [ddzz] *m* slave driver; jailer

aguz·zo -za *adj* sharp, pointed

ah *interj* ah!, aha!; ha!

ahi *interj* ouch!

ahimè *interj* alas!

àia *f* yard, barnyard; threshing floor; governess ‖ **L'Aia** *f* the Hague

Aiace *m* Ajax

àio *m* (**-ài**) tutor

aiòla *f* lawn; flower bed

àire *m* push; short run (*preparing for a jump*); **dare l'aire a** to start off; **prendere l'aire** to take off

airóne *m* heron

aitante *adj* robust, stalwart

aiuòla *f* (poet) var of **aiola**

aiutante *adj* helping ‖ *mf* assistant ‖ *m* (mil) adjutant; **aiutante di campo** aide-de-camp; **aiutante di sanità** orderly

aiutare *tr* to help ‖ *ref* to strive; to help oneself; to help one another

aiutato *m* first assistant (*e.g., of a surgeon*)

aiuto *m* aid, help; assistant; first assistant (*of a surgeon*)

aizzare (**aizzo**) *tr* to incite, to incite to riot; to sic (*a dog*)

al §4

a·la *f* (**-li** & **-le**) wing; sail, vane (*of windmill*); blade (*e.g., of fan*); brim (*of hat*); (football) end; **ala a freccia** backswept wing; **ala di popolo** throng; **fare ala a** to line up along

alabarda *f* halberd

alabardière *m* halberdier

alabastri·no -na *adj* alabaster; white as alabaster

alabastro *m* alabaster

àlacre *adj* eager, lively

alacrità *f* alacrity

alàg·gio *m* (-gi) hauling, towing
alamaro *m* braid, gimp
alambic·co *m* (-chi) still
alano *m* Great Dane
alare *adj* wing (*e.g.*, *span*) ‖ *m* andiron ‖ *tr* to haul
Alasca, l' *f* Alaska
ala·to -ta *adj* winged, sublime
alba *f* dawn, daybreak
albagìa *f* haughtiness
albanése [s] *adj & mf* Albanian
Albania, l' *f* Albania
àlbatro *m* (orn) albatross
albeggiaménto *m* dawning
albeggiare §290 (**albéggio**) *intr* (ESSERE) to dawn; (poet) to sparkle (*said, e.g., of ice*) ‖ *impers* (ESSERE)—**albeggia** the day dawns
alberare (**àlbero**) *tr* to plant (*trees*); to reforest; to hoist (*a mast*); to mast (*a ship*)
albera·to -ta *adj* tree-lined; (naut) masted
alberèllo *m* small tree; apothecary's jar
albergare §209 (**albèrgo**) *tr* to lodge; to put up at a hotel; (fig) to harbor ‖ *intr* to lodge; to put up
alberga·tóre -trice *mf* hotelkeeper
alberghiè·ro -ra *adj* hotel
albèr·go *m* (-ghi) hotel; refuge; hospitality; **albergo diurno** day hostel; **albergo per la gioventù** youth hostel
àlbero *m* tree; poplar; (mach) shaft; (naut) mast; **albero a camme** (aut) camshaft; **albero a gomito** (aut) crankshaft; **albero di distribuzione** (aut) camshaft; **albero di Natale** Christmas tree; **albero di trasmissione** (aut) transmission; **albero genealogico** family tree
albicòc·ca *f* (-che) apricot
albicòc·co *m* (-chi) apricot tree
al·bo -ba *adj* (poet) white ‖ *m* album; bulletin board; (law) roll; comic book; **albo d'onore** honor roll ‖ *f see* alba
albóre *m* (poet) whiteness; (poet) dawn
album *m* (**album**) album, scrapbook
albume *m* albumen
albumina *f* albumin
àlca·li *m* (-li) alkali
alcali·no -na *adj* alkaline
alce *m* moose; elk
alchìmia *f* alchemy
alchimi·sta *m* (-sti) alchemist
alcióne *m* halcyon
alciò·nio -nia *adj* (-ni -nie) halcyon
àlco·le *m* alcohol
alcolici·tà *f* (-tà) alcoholic content
alcòli·co -ca *adj* (-ci -che) alcoholic ‖ *m* alcoholic beverage
alcolismo *m* alcoholism
alcolizzare [ddzz] *tr* to intoxicate ‖ *ref* to become intoxicated
alcolizza·to -ta [ddzz] *adj* intoxicated ‖ *mf* alcoholic
alcool *m* (**alcool**) var of **alcole**
alcoolici·tà *f* (-tà) var of **alcolicità**
alcoòli·co -ca (-ci -che) *adj & m* var of **alcolico**
alcoolismo *m* var of **alcolismo**
alcoolizzare [ddzz] *tr* var of **alcolizzare**

alcoolizza·to -ta [ddzz] *adj & mf* var of **alcolizzato**
alcòva *f* bedroom; bed; alcove
alcunché *pron* something, anything
alcu·no -na *adj & pron* some; **alcu·ni -ne** some; quite a few, several, a good many
aldilà *m* life beyond, afterlife
àlea *f* chance, hazard; **correre l'alea to** try one's luck
aleggiare §290 (**aléggio**) *intr* to flutter; to flap the wings; to hover
aleróne *m* var of **alettone**
alesàg·gio *m* (-gi) (mach) bore
alesare (**aléso**) *tr* (mach) to bore
alesatóre *m* reamer
alesatrice *s* boring machine
Alessandria d'Egitto *f* Alexandria
alessandri·no -na *adj & mf* Alexandrian ‖ *m* Alexandrine (*verse*)
Alessandro *m* Alexander; **Alessandro Magno** Alexander the Great
alétta *f* small wing; fin (*of fish*); (aer) tab; **aletta di compensazione** trim tab; **aletta parasole** (aut) sun visor
alettóne *m* (aer) aileron, flap
Aleuti·no -na *adj*—**Isole Aleutine** Aleutian Islands
al·fa *m* (-fa) alpha ‖ *f* esparto
alfabèti·co -ca *adj* (-ci -che) alphabetical
alfabetizzazióne [ddzz] *f* teaching to read; learning to read
alfabèto *m* alphabet; code (*e.g., Morse*)
alfière *m* flagbearer, standardbearer; (chess) bishop
alfine *adv* finally, at last
al·ga *f* (-ghe) alga; **alga marina** seaweed
àlgebra *f* algebra
algèbri·co -ca *adj* (-ci -che) algebraic
Algèri *f* Algiers
Algerìa, l' *f* Algeria
algeri·no -na *adj & mf* Algerian
aliante *m* (aer) glider
alianti·sta *mf* (-sti -ste) glider pilot
àli·bi *m* (-bi) alibi
alice *f* anchovy
alienàbile *adj* alienable
alienare (**alièno**) *tr* to alienate; to transfer, convey ‖ *ref*—**alienarsi dalla ragione** to go out of one's mind
aliena·to -ta *adj* alienated ‖ *mf* insane person; dispossessed person
alienazióne *f* alienation
alieni·sta *mf* (-sti -ste) alienist
alièno -na *adj* disinclined; (poet) foreign, alien
alimentare *adj* alimentary ‖ **alimentari** *mpl* food, foodstuff ‖ *v* (**aliménto**) *tr* to feed; to fuel
alimentari·sta *mf* (-sti) food merchant; food-industry worker
alimenta·tóre -trice *mf* stoker ‖ *m* (mach) stoker, feeder
alimentazióne *f* nourishment; feeding; (mil) loading; **alimentazione artificiale** intravenous feeding
aliménto *m* food, nourishment; feed; **alimenti** alimony (*maintenance*)
allmònia *f* alimony
alìnea *f* (law) paragraph, section

alìquota f share; parcel, quota

aliscafo m hydrofoil

alisè·o -a adj trade (wind) ‖ m trade wind

alitare (àlito) intr to breathe; to blow gently; **non alitare** to not breathe a word

àlito m breath; (fig) breeze

alìvo·lo -la adj (poet) winged; (fig) swift

alla §4

allacciaménto m binding; connection, linking

allacciare §128 tr to bind, tie; to connect; to buckle; (fig) to deceive

allacciatura f lacing; buckling

allagare §209 tr to flood, overflow

allampana·to -ta adj tall and lean, lanky

allargare §209 tr to broaden, widen; **allargare la mano** to be lenient; to be liberal; **allargare il freno** to give free rein ‖ ref to widen, spread out; **mi si allarga il cuore** I feel relieved

allargatura f widening

allarmante adj alarming

allarmare tr to alarm ‖ ref to worry, become alarmed

allarme m alarm; **allarme aereo** air-raid warning; **cessato allarme** all clear; **falso allarme** false alarm; **stare in allarme** to be alarmed

allascare §197 tr (naut) to ease, slacken (a rope)

allato adv (poet) near; **allato a** near; beside; in comparison with

allattaménto m nursing, feeding; **allattamento artificiale** bottle feeding

allattare tr to nurse (at the breast); to feed (with a bottle)

alle §4

alleanza f alliance

alleare (allèo) tr to ally ‖ ref to become allied; to be connected

allea·to -ta adj allied ‖ mf ally

allegare §209 tr to enclose; to adduce; to allege; **allegare i denti** to set the teeth on edge ‖ intr (hort) to ripen

allega·to -ta adj enclosed ‖ m enclosure

alleggeriménto m lightening, easing

alleggerire §176 tr to lighten; to alleviate ‖ ref to put on lighter clothes; **alleggerirsi di** (naut) to jettison

allegorìa f allegory

allegòri·co -ca adj (-ci -che) allegorical

allegraménte adv cheerfully, merrily; thoughtlessly

allegrézza f joy, cheerfulness

allegrìa f cheer, gaiety; **stare in allegria** to be merry ‖ interj good cheer!

allé·gro -gra adj cheerful, merry, gay ‖ m (mus) allegro

alleluia m hallelujah

allenaménto m training

allenare (allèno) tr & ref to train

allena·tóre -trice adj training ‖ mf trainer, coach

allentare (allènto) tr to loosen, slacken; to mitigate; (coll) to deliver (a blow); **essere allentato** to have a hernia ‖ ref to slow up; to loosen up; to diminish

allergìa f allergy

allèrgi·co -ca adj (-ci -che) allergic

allérta f alert ‖ adv alert, on the alert

allessare (allèsso) tr to boil

allés·so -sa adj boiled ‖ m boiled meat, boiled beef

allestire §176 tr to prepare, make ready; to rig (e.g., a ship); to produce (e.g., a play)

allettaménto m allure, fascination

allettante adj alluring, enticing

allettare (allètto) tr to allure, entice; to confine to bed; to bend (plants) to the ground ‖ ref to be confined to bed

allevaménto m raising, breeding; flock

allevare (allèvo) tr to raise, breed; to rear

alleva·tóre -trice mf raiser, breeder

alleviare §287 (allèvio) tr to alleviate, lighten

allibire §176 intr (ESSERE) to turn pale; to be astonished, be dismayed

allibraménto m registration, entry; booking (of bets)

allibrare tr to register, enter; to book (a bet) on a horse

allibratóre m bookmaker (at races)

allietare (allièto) tr to cheer, enliven

alliè·vo -va mf pupil, student; follower, disciple ‖ m trainee; **allievo ufficiale** cadet

alligatóre m alligator

allignare intr to take root; to do well, prosper

allineaménto m alignment; falling in line

allineare (allìneo) tr to align; (typ) to justify ‖ ref to align oneself, be aligned

allinea·to -ta adj aligned; **non allineato** nonaligned, uncommitted

allitterazióne f alliteration

allo §4

allòc·co m (-chi) horned owl; (fig) dolt, nincompoop

allocu·tóre -trice mf (poet) speaker

allocuzióne f (poet) speech, address

allòdola f lark, skylark

allogare §209 (allògo) tr to place; to let, lease; to find employment for; to invest (money); to marry off (a daughter)

allòge·no -na adj minority ‖ mf member of an ethnic minority

alloggiaménto m (mil) lodging, quarters; (carp, mach) housing

alloggiare §290 (allòggio) tr to lodge, put up ‖ intr to lodge, stay

allòg·gio m (-gi) lodging, living quarters; accommodations

allontanaménto m removal; estrangement

allontanare tr to remove; to send away; to exonerate; to dismiss; to alienate ‖ ref to go away; to withdraw; to become estranged

allóra adj then ‖ adv then; at that time; in that case; **da allora** ever since; **da allora in poi** from that time on; **fino allora** until then; **per allora** at that time

allorché conj when

allòro m laurel; **riposare sugli allori** to rest on one's laurels

allorquando conj (poet) when

àlluce m big toe

allucinante adj hallucinating; dazzling; deceptive

allucinare (**allùcino**) tr to hallucinate; to dazzle; to deceive

allucinazióne f hallucination

allùdere §105 intr to allude

allume m alum

alluminare (**allùmino**) tr to illuminate (a manuscript); (poet) to light

alluminio m aluminum

allunàg·gio m (-gi) lunar landing; **allunaggio morbido** soft lunar landing

allunare intr to land on the moon

allunga f (mach) adapter

allungàbile adj extensible; extension (table)

allungaménto m lengthening

allungare §209 tr to lengthen; to stretch out (e.g., the hand); to dilute (e.g., wine); (coll) to deliver (e.g., a slap); (sports) to pass (the ball); **allungare il collo** to crane the neck; **allungare il passo** to walk faster || ref to grow longer; to stretch; to grow taller

allun·go m (-ghi) (sports) sprint; (sports) forward pass

allusióne f allusion

alluvióne m flood

almanaccare §197 tr to dream of || intr to dream, muse

almanac·co m (-chi) almanac

alméno adv at least; if only

alno m (bot) alder

àloe m & f aloe

alògeno m halogen

alogenuro m halide

alóne m halo

alòsa f (ichth) shad

alpacca f German silver

alpe f high mountain, alp || **le Alpi** the Alps

alpèstre adj mountainous; (fig) uncouth

alpigia·no -na adj mountain, mountainous; (fig) uncouth || mf mountaineer

alpinismo m mountain climbing

alpini·sta mf (-sti -ste) mountain climber

alpinìsti·co -ca adj (-ci -che) mountain-climbing

alpi·no -na adj alpine; Alpine || m alpine soldier

alquan·to -ta adj & pron some; **alquanti -te** some; quite a few, several, a good many || **alquanto** adv somewhat, rather

Alsàzia, l' f Alsace

alsazia·no -na adj & mf Alsacian

alt m (alt) halt, stop || interj halt!, stop!

altaléna f seesaw; swing; (fig) ups and downs; **altalena a bilico** seesaw; **altalena sospesa** swing

altalenare (**altaléno**) intr to seesaw; to swing

altana f roof terrace

altare m altar

altarino m small altar; **svelare gli alta-**

rini (joc) to expose the skeleton in the closet

altèa f marsh mallow

alterare (**àltero**) tr to alter; to falsify; to adulterate; to anger || ref to alter; to become adulterated; to get angry

altera·to -ta adj altered; adulterated; feverish; angry

alterazióne f change, alteration; adulteration; slight fever

altercare §197 (**altèrco**) intr to dispute, quarrel

altèr·co m (-chi) altercation; **venire a un alterco** to get into a quarrel

alterìgia f haughtiness

alternare (**altèrno**) tr & ref to alternate

alternati·vo -va adj alternating || f alternative; choice

alterna·to -ta adj alternate; alternating (current)

alternatóre m (elec) alternator

altèr·no -na adj alternate

altè·ro -ra adj proud, haughty

altézza f height; width (of cloth); depth (of water); pitch (of sound); (astr, geom) altitude; (fig) loftiness, nobility; (naut) latitude; (typ) size; **essere all'altezza di** to be up to, be equal to; (naut) to be off || **Altezza** f Highness

altezzó·so -sa [s] adj haughty

altìc·cio -cia adj (-ci -ce) tipsy

altimetro m altimeter

altipiano m var of **altopiano**

altisonante [s] adj high-sounding

altìssi·mo -ma adj very high, highest || **l'Altissimo** m the Most High

altitùdine f altitude

al·to -ta adj high; tall; wide (cloth); deep (water); upper; full (day); late (e.g., Easter); deep (sleep); early (Middle Ages); loud (voice); lofty (peak) || m top; upper part; high quarters; **alti e bassi** ups and downs; **fare alto e basso** to be the undisputed boss; **guardare qlcu dall'alto in basso** to look down one's nose at s.o.; **in alto** up || **alto** adv up

altofórno m (altifórni) blast furnace

altoloca·to -ta adj high-placed, high-ranking

altoparlante m loudspeaker

altopiano m (altipiani) plateau

altrettan·to -ta adj & pron as much; the same; **altrettanti -te** as many || **altrettanto** adv as much; the same

altri indef pron invar someone; someone else; **non altri che** no one else but

altrièri m & adv day before yesterday

altriménti adv otherwise

al·tro -tra adj other; next (world); **altro ieri** day before yesterday; **chi altro?** who else?; **domani l'altro** the day after tomorrow; **fra l'altro** among other things; **ieri l'altro** the day before yesterday; **l'altro anno** last year; **l'altro giorno** the other day; **noi altri** we; **qualcun altro** somebody else; anybody else; **quest'altro** (**giorno, mese, anno**) next (day, month, year) || pron other; anything else; **altro che!** why yes! || **l'altro §11** correlative *indef pron* || **l'altro §12** reciprocal *pron*

altrónde *adv* (poet) somewhere else; **d'altronde** besides; on the other hand

altróve *adv* elsewhere, somewhere else

altrui *adj invar* somebody else's, other people's || *pron invar* somebody else || *m*—**l'altrui** what belongs to someone else

altrui·sta (-**sti** -**ste**) *adj* altruistic || *mf* altruist

altura *f* height; (naut) high seas

alun·no -na *mf* pupil, student

alveare *m* beehive

àlveo *m* bed (*of a river*)

alvèolo *m* alveolus; socket (*of tooth*); cell (*of honeycomb*)

alzabandiè·ra *m* (-**ra**) raising of the flag

alzacristal·li *m* (-**li**) (aut) crank (*to raise a window*)

alzàia *f* tow line; towpath

alzare *tr* to lift, raise; to cut (*cards*); to shrug (*one's shoulders*); to set (*sail*); **alzare al cielo** to praise to the sky; **alzare i tacchi** to show a clean pair of heels; **alzare la cresta** to get cocky || *ref* to rise; to get up; **alzarsi in piedi** to stand up

alzata *f* raising, lifting; shrugging (*of shoulders*); standing up; riser (*of step*); three-tier candy tray; **alzata di scudi** rebellion; **alzata di testa** whim, caprice

alzavàlvo·le *m* (-**le**) (aut) valve lifter

alzo *m* gunsight

amàbile *adj* amiable; sweetish (*wine*)

amabili·tà *f* (-**tà**) amiability, kindness

ama·ca *f* (-**che**) hammock

amàlga·ma *m* (-**mi**) amalgam

amalgamare (**amàlgamo**) *tr* to amalgamate || *ref* to amalgamate; to blend

amalgamazióne *f* amalgamation

amante *adj* loving, fond || *m* lover || *f* mistress

amanuènse *m* amanuensis, scribe

amare *tr* to love; to like || *ref* to love one another

amareggiare §290 (**amaréggio**) *tr* to make bitter; to sadden || *ref* to become bitter; to sadden

amarèna *f* sour cherry

amarétto *m* macaroon

amarézza *f* bitterness

ama·ro -ra *adj* bitter || *m* bitters; bitterness

amarógno·lo -la *adj* bitterish

amarra *f* (naut) hawser

amarrare *tr & intr* var of **ammarrare**

ama·tóre -trice *mf* lover; amateur

amató·rio -ria *adj* (-**ri** -**rie**) amatory, of love

amàzzone [ddzz] *f* horsewoman; female jockey; (obs) riding habit; **cavalcare all'amazzone** to ride sidesaddle || **Amazzone** *f* (myth) Amazon

ambage *f* winding path; **ambagi** circumlocutions; **senz'ambagi** without beating about the bush

ambasceria *f* embassy

ambà·scia *f* (-**sce**) shortness of breath; grief, sorrow

ambasciata *f* embassy; ambassadorship; errand, mission

ambasciatóre *m* ambassador

ambasciatrice *f* ambassadress

ambedùe *adj invar*—**ambedue i** or **le** both || *pron invar* both

ambiare §287 *intr* to amble, pace (*said of a horse*)

ambiatura *f* pacing (*said of a horse*)

ambidè·stro -stra *adj* ambidextrous

ambidùe *adj & pron invar* var of **ambedue**

ambientare (**ambiènto**) *tr* to accustom; to place (*a story in a certain period*) || *ref* to get accustomed to one's surroundings; to orient oneself

ambienta·tóre -trice *mf* interior decorator; (theat) decorator

ambiènte *adj* room, e.g., **temperatura ambiente** room temperature || *m* environment; habitat; milieu; room; **trovarsi fuori del proprio ambiente** to be out of one's element

ambigui·tà *f* (-**tà**) ambiguity

ambi·guo -gua *adj* ambiguous

àm·bio *m* (-**bi**) amble, pacing

ambire §176 *tr* to be eager for || *intr* to be ambitious; **ambire a** to be ambitious for

àmbito *m* range, circle; (mus) range; **nell'ambito di** within

ambizióne *f* ambition

ambizióso -sa [s] *adj* ambitious || *mf* ambitious person

ambo or **am·bi -be** *adj pl*—**ambo i, ambo le, ambi i, ambe le** both

ambosèssi *adj invar* of both sexes, e.g., **giovani ambosessi** young people of both sexes

ambra *f* amber; **ambra grigia** ambergris

ambròsia *f* ambrosia; (bot) ragweed

ambulante *adj* itinerant; circulating; ambulant || *m* mail car

ambulanza *f* ambulance

ambulare (**àmbulo**) *intr* (coll) to ambulate

ambulatò·rio -ria (-**ri** -**rie**) *adj* ambulatory || *m* clinic, first-aid department

Amburgo *m* Hamburg

amèba *f* amoeba

a·men *m* (-**men**) amen || *interj* amen!

ameni·tà *f* (-**tà**) *f* amenity; pleasantry

amèno -na *adj* pleasant, agreeable; amusing (*fellow*)

Amèrica, l' *f* America; **l'America del Nord** North America; **l'America del Sud** South America

americana *f* bicycle race between pairs

americanismo *m* Americanism

americanizzare [ddzz] *tr* to Americanize || *ref* to become Americanized

america·no -na *adj & mf* American || *m* vermouth with bitters || *f* see **americana**

ametista *f* amethyst

amianto *m* asbestos

amicale *adj* (poet) friendly

amichévole *adj* friendly; (sports) noncompetitive

amicìzia *f* friendship; **stringere amicizia con** to make friends with

ami·co -ca (-ci -che) *adj* friendly || *mf* friend; beloved || *m* boy friend; lover, paramour; **amico del cuore** bosom friend || *f* girl friend; mistress

amidàce·o -a *adj* starchy

amidatura *f* starching

àmido *m* starch

Amlèto *m* Hamlet

ammaccare §197 *tr* to crush; to pound; to bruise; to dent

ammaccatura *f* bruise; dent

ammaestraménto *m* instruction, teaching; training

ammaestrare (ammaèstro & ammaéstro) *tr* to teach, to educate; to train (*animals*)

ammainare (ammàino) *tr* to lower (*e.g., a flag*)

ammalare *intr* (ESSERE) to fall ill || *ref* to fall ill; **ammalarsi di** to come down with

ammala·to -ta *adj* ill, sick || *mf* patient

ammaliare §287 *tr* to cast a spell on; to charm, enchant, fascinate; to bewitch

ammalia·tóre -trice *adj* charming, enchanting || *mf* charmer || *m* enchanter, sorcerer || *f* enchantress, sorceress

amman·co *m* (-chi) shortage

ammanettare (ammanétto) *tr* to handcuff

ammaniglia·to -ta *adj* shackled; (fig) closely bound, closely tied

ammannare *tr* to sheave (*grain*)

ammannire §176 *tr* to prepare (*a dish*); to dish up (*a meal*)

ammansare *tr & ref* var of **ammansire**

ammansa·tóre -trice *mf* (poet) tamer

ammansire §176 *tr* to tame; to calm || *ref* to become tamed; to calm down

ammantare *tr* to mantle, clothe; to cover; to hide (*the truth*)

ammanto *m* mantle, cloak; (fig) authority

ammaràg·gio *m* (-gi) landing on water; splashdown (*of a space vehicle*)

ammaraménto *m* var of **ammaraggio**

ammarare *intr* (aer) to land on water; (rok) to splash down

ammarrare *tr* (naut) to moor

ammassare *tr* to amass || *ref* to crowd, throng

ammasso *m* heap, pile; cluster (*of stars*); government stockpile

ammattiménto *m* worry, nuisance

ammattire §176 *intr* (ESSERE) to go crazy; **fare ammattire** to drive crazy

ammattonare (ammattóno) *tr* to floor with bricks

ammattona·to -ta *adj* floored with bricks || *m* brick floor; bricklaying

ammazzare *tr* to kill || *ref* to kill oneself; to get killed

ammazzasèt·te *m* (-te) braggart

ammazza·tóio *m* (-tói) slaughterhouse

ammènda *f* fine; satisfaction (*for injury*); **fare ammenda** to make amends

ammendaménto *m* emendation: improvement (*of land*)

ammendare (ammèndo) *tr* to emendate; to improve (*land*)

ammennicolo *m* excuse; trifle; **ammennicoli** extras

ammés·so -sa *adj* admitted; **ammesso che** supposing that; **ammesso e non concesso** for the sake of argument

amméttere §198 *tr* to admit; to accept, suppose

ammezzare [ddzz] (ammèzzo) *tr* to leave half-finished (*a piece of work*); to fill halfway; to empty halfway

ammezzato [ddzz] *m* mezzanine

ammiccare §197 *intr* to wink; to cock one's eye

amministrare *tr* to administer, manage

amministra·tóre -trice *mf* administrator, manager; **amministratore delegato** chairman of the board

amministrazióne *f* administration, management; **ordinaria amministrazione** run-of-the-mill business

ammiràbile *adj* admirable

ammiràglia *f* (nav) flagship

ammiragliato *m* admiralty

ammirà·glio *m* (-gli) admiral; **ammiraglio d'armata** admiral; **ammiraglio di divisione** rear admiral; **ammiraglio di squadra** vice admiral; **grande ammiraglio** admiral of the fleet

ammirare *tr* to admire || *intr* to wonder

ammirati·vo -va *adj* admiring; exclamation (*mark*)

ammira·tóre -trice *mf* admirer || *m* suitor

ammirazióne *f* admiration

ammirévole *adj* admirable

ammissibile *adj* admissible; permissible

ammissióne *f* admission; (mach) intake; **ammissione comune** consensus

ammobiliaménto *m* furnishing; furniture

ammobiliare §287 *tr* to furnish

ammodernare (ammodèrno) *tr* to modernize

ammòdo *adj invar* well-mannered, polite || *adv* properly

ammogliare §280 (ammóglio) *tr* to marry, give in marriage || *ref* to marry, get married

ammoglia·to *adj* married || *m* married man

ammollare (ammòllo) *tr* to soften; to soak; to slacken (*e.g., a hawser*); to deliver (*a slap*) || *ref* to get soaked

ammollire §176 *tr* to soften; to weaken || *ref* to soften; to mellow

ammoniaca *f* ammonia

ammoniménto *m* warning

ammonire §176 *tr* to admonish, reprimand

ammoni·tóre -trice *adj* warning

ammonizióne *f* admonition, warning

ammontare *m* amount, total || *v* (ammónto) *tr* to pile up || *intr* (ESSERE) to amount

ammonticchiare §287 *tr* to pile up, heap up

ammorbare (ammòrbo) *tr* to infect, contaminate

ammorbidènte *m* softener

ammorbidire §176 *tr* to soften; to mitigate || *ref* to soften

ammortaménto *m* amortization; payment, redemption (*of a loan*)

ammortare (ammòrto) *tr* to amortize
ammortire §176 *tr* to deaden; to weaken, soften
ammortizzaménto [ddzz] *m* amortization, amortizzement
ammortizzare [ddzz] *tr* to amortize; (aut) to absorb (*shocks*)
ammortizzatóre [ddzz] *m* (aut) shock absorber
ammosciare §128 (ammóscio) *tr, intr & ref* var of **ammoscire**
ammoscia·to -ta *adj* (coll) downcast
ammoscire §176 *tr* to make sag; to make flabby ‖ *intr & ref* to sag; to become flabby; to droop
ammucchiare §287 *tr* to heap up, pile up ‖ *ref* to crowd together
ammuffire §176 *intr* (ESSERE) to become moldy
ammusare *tr & intr* to nuzzle
ammutinaménto *m* mutiny, riot
ammutinare (ammùtino & ammutino) *tr* to incite to riot ‖ *ref* to mutiny
ammutinato *m* mutineer
ammutolire §176 *intr* (ESSERE) to become silent; to be dumfounded
amnesìa *f* amnesia
amnistìa *f* amnesty
amnistiare §287 or §119 *tr* to amnesty
amo *m* hook; **abboccare all'amo** to bite, to swallow the hook
amorale *adj* immoral; amoral
amorali·tà *f* (-tà) immorality; amorality
amóre *m* love; eagerness; **amor proprio** amour-propre, self-esteem; **con amore** with pleasure; **d'amore e d'accordo** in perfect agreement; **fare all'amore** to make love; **fare l'amore** to flirt; **per amor del cielo** for heaven's sake; **per amore di** for the sake of; **un amore di bambino** a charming child; **un amore di cappello** a darling hat
amoreggiare §290 (amoréggio) *intr* to flirt; to play around
amorévole *adj* loving; kindly
amòr·fo -fa *adj* amorphous; safety (*match*)
amorino *m* cupid; cute child; love seat; (bot) mignonette
amoró·so -sa [s] *adj* loving; kindly; amorous; love (*e.g., life*) ‖ *mf* lover ‖ *m* fiancé ‖ *f* fiancée
amovìbile *adj* removable
amperàg·gio *m* (-gi) amperage
ampère *m* ampere
amperòmetro *m* ammeter
amperóra *m* ampere-hour
ampiézza *f* width, breadth; trajectory (*of a missile*); amplitude; **ampiezza di vedute** open-mindedness
àm·pio -pia *adj* (-pi -pie) ample; wide; roomy
amplèsso *m* (poet) embrace
ampliaménto *m* amplification, extension
ampliare §287 *tr* to enlarge, widen ‖ *ref* to widen
amplificare §197 (amplìfico) *tr* to amplify; to widen; to exaggerate
amplifica·tóre *m* (rad & telv) amplifier
amplificazióne *f* amplification
amplitùdine *f* amplitude
ampólla *f* cruet; (eccl) ampulla
ampollièra *f* cruet stand

ampollosi·tà [s] *f* (-tà) grandiloquence, turgidity
ampolló·so -sa [s] *adj* grandiloquent, turgid
amputare (àmputo) *tr* to amputate
amputazióne *f* amputation
amulèto *m* amulet, charm
anabbagliante *m* (aut) low beam; **anabbaglianti** (aut) dimmers
anacàr·dio *m* (-di) cashew
ànace *m* var of **anice**
anacorè·ta *m* (-ti) anchorite, hermit
anacronismo *m* anachronism
anacronisti·co -ca *adj* (-ci -che) anachronistic(al)
anàgrafe *m* bureau of vital statistics; registry of births, deaths, and marriages
anagram·ma *m* (-mi) anagram
analcòli·co -ca (-ci -che) *adj* nonalcoholic; soft (*drink*) ‖ *m* soft drink
analfabè·ta *mf* (-ti -te) illiterate
analfabèti·co -ca *adj* (-ci -che) unalphabetized, unalphabetic
analfabetismo *m* illiteracy
analgèsi·co -ca *adj & m* (-ci -che) analgesic
anàli·si *f* (-si) analysis; breakdown; **analisi grammaticale** parsing; **analisi dell'urina** urinalysis
anali·sta *mf* (-sti -ste) analyst; **analista finanziario** financial analyst; **analista tempi e metodi** efficiency expert, efficiency engineer
analiti·co -ca *adj* (-ci -che) analytic(al)
analizzare [ddzz] *tr* to analyze; to assay (*ores*); (telv) to scan
analogìa *f* analogy
anàlo·go -ga *adj* (-ghi -ghe) analogous; similar
anamnè·si *f* (-si) (med) case history
ananasso *m* pineapple
anarchìa *f* anarchy
anàrchi·co -ca (-ci -che) *adj* anarchical ‖ *m* anarchist
anatè·ma or **anàte·ma** *m* (-mi) anathema
anatomìa *f* anatomy
anatòmi·co -ca *adj* (-ci -che) anatomic(al)
ànatra *f* duck; drake
anatròccolo *m* duckling
an·ca *f* (-che) hip; (coll) thigh (*e.g., of a chicken*); **dare d'anche** to run away; **menare anca** to walk
ancèlla *f* maidservant
ancestrale *adj* ancestral
anche *adv* also, too; even; (poet) yet; **anche a** + *inf* even if + *ind*
anchilosare (anchilòso) *tr* to paralyze ‖ *ref* to become paralyzed
anchilòsto·ma *m* (-mi) hookworm
àn·cia *f* (-ce) (mus) reed
ancillare *adj* servant
ancòra *adv* still, yet; again; more e.g., **ancora cinque minuti** five minutes more
àncora *f* anchor; keeper (*of magnet*); armature (*of buzzer or electric bell*); **ancora di salvezza** last hope; **gettar l'ancora** to cast anchor; **salpare** or **levar l'ancora** to weigh anchor
ancoràg·gio *m* (-gi) anchorage, berth

ancorare (àncoro) *tr* to anchor; to tie (*e.g., a currency to gold*) ‖ *ref* to anchor; to hold fast

ancorché *conj* although

andalu·so -sa *adj & mf* Andalusian

andaménto *m* course, progress

andante *adj* ordinary, common; continuous

andare *m* going; gait; **a lungo andare** in the long run ‖ §106 *intr* (ESSERE) to go; to spread (*said of news*); to be (*e.g., proud*); to work (*said of machinery*); (with *dat*) to fit, e.g., **quel vestito non gli va** that suit does not fit him; (with *dat*) to please, e.g. **quel vestito non le va** that dress does not please her; **andare a cavallo** to go horseback riding; **andare a finire** to wind up; **andare a male** to spoil; **andare a picco** to sink; **andare d'accordo** to agree; **andare in cerca di** to seek; **andare in macchina** to be in press; **andare in onda** (rad & telv) to go on the air; **andare per i vent'anni** to be bordering on twenty years; **andare pazzo per** to be crazy about; **andare soldato** to be drafted; **andare via** to go away; **come va?** how are things?; **mi va il vino dolce** I like sweet wine; **ne va della vita** life is at stake; **va da sé** it goes without saying ‖ *ref*—**andarsene** to go away, leave

anda·to -ta *adj* gone, past; finished; (coll) spoiled (*e.g., meat*) ‖ *f* going; journey, trip; **a lunga andata** in the long run; **andata e ritorno** round trip; **dare l'andata a** to give the go-ahead to

andatura *f* gait; pace; **fare l'andatura** to set the pace

andazzo *m* bad practice, bad habit; fad

Ande, le the Andes

andicappare *tr* to handicap

andi·no -na *adj* Andean

andiriviè·ni *m* (-ni) coming and going; maze; ado

àndito *m* corridor, hallway

andróne *m* hall, lobby

aneddòti·co -ca *adj* (-ci -che) anecdotal

anèddoto *m* anecdote

anelante *adj* panting

anelare (anèlo) *tr* to long for ‖ *intr* to yearn; (poet) to pant

anèlito *m* last breath; yearning; (poet) panting; **mandare l'ultimo anelito** to breathe one's last

anellino *m* ringlet

anèllo *m* ring; link (*of a chain*); traffic circle; segment (*of a worm*); (sports) track; **ad anello** ring-shaped; **anello di congiunzione** (fig) link; **anello di fidanzamento** engagement ring ‖ **anella** *fpl* (poet) ringlets; (archaic) rings

anemia *f* anemia

anèmi·co -ca *adj* (-ci -che) anemic

anestesia *f* anesthesia

anestesi·sta *mf* (-sti -ste) anesthetist

anestèti·co -ca *adj & m* (-ci -che) anesthetic

anestetizzare [ddzz] *tr* to anesthetize

aneuri·sma *m* (-smi) aneurysm

anfi·bio -bia (-bi -bie) *adj* amphibian; (fig) ambiguous ‖ *m* amphibian

anfiteatro *m* amphitheater

anfitrióne *m* (lit) generous host

anfratto *m* ravine; narrow, winding, rugged spot

anfrattuosi·tà [s] *f* (-tà) rough broken ground; winding, rough spot

anfrattuó·so -sa [s] *adj* winding, rough, craggy

angariare §287 *tr* to pester, oppress

angèli·co -ca *adj* (-ci -che) angelic(al)

àngelo *m* angel; **angelo custode** guardian angel

angheria *f* vexation; outrage; imposition

angina *f* quinsy; **angina pectoris** angina pectoris

angipòrto *m* blind alley; narrow lane

anglica·no -na *adj & mf* Anglican

anglicismo *m* Anglicism

anglicizzare [ddzz] *tr* to Anglicize ‖ *ref* to become Anglicized

anglòfo·no -na *adj* English-speaking ‖ *m* English-speaking person

anglosàssone *adj & mf* Anglo-Saxon

angolare *adj* angular; corner (*stone*) ‖ *m* angle iron ‖ *v* (àngolo) *tr* to take an angle shot of; (sports) to kick (*the ball*) into the corner of the goal

angolazióne *f* (mov) angle shot

angolièra *f* corner shelving; corner cupboard

àngolo *m* angle; corner

angoló·so -sa [s] *adj* angular

àngora *f* Angora cat; Angora goat

angò·scia *f* (-sce) anxiety, distress, anguish

angosciare §128 (angòscio) *tr* to distress

angoscia·to -ta *adj* tormented, distressed

angosció·so -sa [s] *adj* agonizing

anguilla *f* eel

anguillé·sco -sca *adj* (-schi -sche) as slippery as an eel

angùria *f* watermelon

angùstia *f* narrowness; scarcity; **stare in angustia** to be worried

angustiare §287 *tr* to distress, grieve ‖ *ref* to worry

angu·sto -sta *adj* narrow

ànice *m* anise

anicino *m* anise cookie

anidride *f* anhydride

àni·dro -dra *adj* anhydrous

anilina *f* aniline

ànima *f* soul; life (*e.g., of the party*); core; kernel; bore (*of gun*); mold (*of button*); mind; enthusiasm; pith (*of fruit*); sounding post (*of violin*); web (*of rail*); **anima dannata** evil counselor; **anima mia!** darling!; **anima nera** villain; **anima viva** living soul; **buon'anima** late, e.g., **mio padre, buon'anima** my late father; **dannare l'anima** to lose patience; **la buon'anima di** the late; **rompere l'anima a** to annoy

animale *adj* animal; (poet) of the soul; (poet) animate ‖ *m* animal; (fig) boor, lout

animalé·sco -sca *adj* (**-schi -sche**) animal, bestial

animare (**ànimo**) *tr* to animate, to enliven; to promote ‖ *ref* to become lively or heated

anima·to -ta *adj* animated (*cartoon*); animated, lively; animal

anima·tóre -trice *adj* animating ‖ *m* moving spirit; (*mov*) animator

animazióne *f* animation

animèlla *f* sweetbread

ànimo *m* mind; heart, affection; courage; **aprire l'animo** to open one's heart; **avere in animo di** to have a mind to; **mal animo** ill will; **mettersi l'animo in pace** to resign oneself; **perdersi d'animo** to lose heart; **serbare nell'animo** to keep in mind

animosi·tà [s] *f* (**-tà**) animosity, ill will

animó·so -sa [s] *adj* bold; spirited (*animal*); hostile

anióne *m* anion

anisétta *f* anisette

ànitra *f* var of **anatra**

anitròccolo *m* var of **anatroccolo**

annacquare (**annàcquo**) *tr* to water; to water down

annaffiare §287 *tr* to sprinkle; to water (*wine*)

annaffia·tóio *m* (**-tói**) sprinkling can

annaffia·tóre -trice *adj* watering, sprinkling

annali *mpl* annals *spl*

annaspare *tr* to reel ‖ *intr* to gesticulate; to grope; to flounder

annata *f* year; year's activity; year's rent; year's issues (*of a magazine*)

annebbiare §287 (**annébbio**) *tr* to befog; to dim ‖ *ref* to become foggy; to become dim

annegaménto *m* drowning

annegare §209 (**annégo**) *tr* & *intr* (**ESSERE**) to drown

anneriménto *m* blackening

annerire §176 *tr* to blacken ‖ *ref* to turn black

annessióne *f* annexation

annès·so -sa *adj* united, attached ‖ *m* annex; **con tutti gli annessi e connessi** everything included

annèttere §107 *tr* to annex; to attach, enclose; to unite; to ascribe (*importance*)

annichilante *adj* annihilating; devastating (*e.g., reply*)

annichilare (**annichilo**) *tr* to annihilate ‖ *ref* to destroy oneself; (fig) to humble oneself

annichilire §176 *tr* & *ref* var of **annichilare**

annidare *tr* to nest; (fig) to nourish, cherish ‖ *ref* to nest; to hide; (fig) to settle

annientaménto *m* annihilation

annientare (**anniènto**) *tr* to annihilate; to knock down, demolish; (fig) to crush ‖ *ref* to humble oneself

anniversà·rio -ria *adj* & *m* (**-ri -rie**) anniversary

anno *m* year; **anno bisestile** leap year; **anno luce** light-year; **anno nuovo** New Year; **anno scolastico** school year; **avere . . . anni** to be . . . years old; **l'anno che viene** next year; **l'anno corrente** this year; **quest'altr'anno** next year; **un anno dopo l'altro** year in, year out

annobilire §176 *tr* to ennoble

annodare (**annòdo**) *tr* to knot, tie; (fig) to tie up ‖ *ref* to get entangled

annoiare §287 (**annòio**) *tr* to bore ‖ *ref* to become bored

annòna *f* food; food-control agency

annonà·rio -ria *adj* (**-ri -rie**) food; rationing (*card*)

annó·so -sa [s] *adj* old, aged

annotare (**annòto**) *tr* to jot down; to chalk up; to annotate; to comment

annotazióne *f* note; notation, annotation

annottare (**annòtta**) *impers* (**ESSERE**) & *ref* to grow dark, get dark; **si annotta** it's growing dark; **è annottato** it grew dark

annoverare (**annòvero**) *tr* to count, number

annuale *adj* annual ‖ *m* anniversary

annuà·rio *m* (**-ri**) annual, yearbook

annuire §176 *intr* to nod assent; to consent

annullaménto *m* nullification, annulment

annullare *tr* to annul, nullify, cancel; to call off ‖ *ref* to cancel one another

annunciare §128 *tr* var of **annunziare**

Annunciazióne *f* Annunciation

annunziare §287 *tr* to announce; (fig) to forecast, foreshadow

annunzia·tóre -trice *mf* announcer, newscaster

annùn·zio *m* (**-zi**) announcement, notice; **annunzio economico** classified ad; **annunzio pubblicitario** advertisement; **annunzio pubblicitario radiofonico** (rad) commercial

ànnu·o -a *adj* yearly, annual

annusare [s] *tr* to smell; to snuff (*tobacco*)

annuvolaménto *m* cloudiness

annuvolare (**annùvolo**) *tr* to cloud, becloud ‖ *ref* to become cloudy; to turn somber

anòdi·no -na *adj* pain-relieving; ineffective; weak, colorless (*person*)

ànodo *m* anode

anomalìa *f* anomaly

anòma·lo -la *adj* anomalous

anonimia *f* anonymity

anòni·mo -ma *adj* anonymous ‖ *m* anonymous author; **serbare l'anonimo** to preserve one's anonymity

anormale *adj* abnormal ‖ *m* queer fellow

anormali·tà *f* (**-tà**) abnormality

ansa *f* handle (*of vase*); pretext; bend (*of a river*)

ansante *adj* panting

ansare *intr* to pant

ànsia *f* anxiety; **essere in ansia** to be worried

ansie·tà *f* (**-tà**) anxiety

ansimare (**ànsimo**) *intr* to pant

ansió·so -sa [s] *adj* anxious

antagonismo *m* antagonism

antagoni·sta (-sti -ste) *adj* antagonistic || *mf* antagonist, opponent

antagonisti·co -ca *adj* (-ci -che) antagonistic

antàrti·co -ca *adj* (-ci -che) antarctic || Antartico *m* Antarctic

antecedènte *adj* preceding || *m* antecedent

antecedènza *f* antecedence

antecessóre *m* predecessor

antefatto *m* background, antecedents

anteguèr·ra (-ra) *adj* prewar || *m* prewar period

anteluca·no -na *adj* (poet) predawn

antenato *m* ancestor

antènna *f* lance; (naut) yard; (rad & telv) aerial, antenna; (zool) antenna

antepórre §218 *tr* to prefer; to place before

anteprima *f* (mov & theat) preview

anteriόre *adj* fore, front; previous; earlier

antesignano [s] *m* forerunner

anti- *pref adj* anti-, e.g., **anticomunistico** anticommunist; un-, e.g., **antieconomico** uneconomical || *pref mf* anti-, e.g., **anticomunista** anticommunist

antiabbagliante *adj* antiglare || *m* low beam

antiàci·do -da *adj* & *m* antacid

antiaère·o -a *adj* antiaircraft || *f* antiaircraft defense

antibattèri·co -ca (-ci -che) *adj* antibacterial || *m* bactericide

antibiòti·co -ca *adj* & *m* (-ci -che) antibiotic

anticà·glia *f* (-glie) antique, curio; rubbish, junk

anticàmera *f* waiting room, anteroom; **fare anticamera** to cool one's heels

anticarro *adj invar* antitank

antichi·tà *f* (-tà) antiquity; **antichità** *fpl* antiques

anticipare (antìcipo) *tr* to advance; to speed up; to pay in advance; to leak (*news*); to expect, anticipate || *intr* to be early

anticipa·to -ta *adj* in advance (*e.g., payment*)

anticipazióne *f* advance; collateral loan; expectation, anticipation

anticipo *m* advance; loan (*on accounts receivable*); **in anticipo** in advance

anti·co -ca *adj* (-chi -che) antique, ancient, old; **all'antica** in the old-fashioned manner; **gli antichi** the ancients; the forefathers; **in antico** in olden times

anticoncezionale *adj* & *f* contraceptive

anticonformi·sta *mf* (-sti -ste) nonconformist

anticonformisti·co -ca *adj* (-ci -che) unconventional

anticongelante *adj* & *m* antifreeze

anticongiunturale *adj* crisis, emergency

anticòrpo *m* antibody

anticristo *m* Antichrist

antidatare *tr* to predate

antiderapante *adj* nonskid

antidetonante *adj* antiknock || *m* antiknock compound

antidiluvia·no -na *adj* antediluvian

antidoto *m* antidote

antievanescènza *f* (rad) antifading device

antifecondati·vo -va *adj* & *m* contraceptive

antifona *f* antiphon; **capire l'antifona** (fig) to get the message

antifurto *adj invar* antitheft || *m* antitheft device

antigàs *adj invar* gas (*e.g., mask*)

antigièni·co -ca *adj* (-ci -che) unsanitary

antilope *f* antelope

antimeridia·no -na *adj* antemeridian, A.M.

antimissile *adj invar* antimissile

antimònio *m* antimony

antincèndio *adj invar* fire-fighting; fire, e.g., **scala antincendio** fire escape

antinéb·bia *adj invar* fog || *m* (-bia) fog light

antinéve *adj invar* snow, e.g., **catena antineve** snow chain

antiorà·rio -ria *adj* (-ri -rie) counterclockwise

antipatìa *f* antipathy, dislike

antipàti·co -ca *adj* (-ci -che) antipathetic; disagreeable; uncongenial

antipièga *adj invar* crease-resistant, wrinkle-proof

antipodi *mpl* antipodes

antipòlio *adj invar* polio (*e.g., vaccine*)

antipòrta *f* stormdoor; corridor

antiquà·rio -ria (-ri -rie) *adj* antiquarian || *m* antiquary, antiquarian

antiqua·to -ta *adj* obsolete; antiquated

antireligió·so -sa [s] *adj* antireligious, irreligious

antirùggine *adj invar* antirust

antirumóre *adj invar* antinoise

antisala [s] *f* anteroom, waiting room

antisassi [s] *adj invar* protecting against falling stones

antischiavi·sta *adj* & *mf* (-sti -ste) abolitionist

antisemi·ta [s] (-ti -te) *adj* anti-Semitic || *mf* anti-Semite

antisemìti·co -ca [s] *adj* (-ci -che) anti-Semitic

antisemitismo [s] *m* anti-Semitism

antisètti·co -ca [s] *adj* & *m* (-ci -che) antiseptic

antisociale [s] *adj* antisocial

antisóle [s] *adj invar* sun (*glasses*); suntan (*lotion*)

antisommergibile [s] *adj* antisubmarine

antistatale *adj* antigovernment

antitàrmi·co -ca *adj* (-ci -che) mothproof

antitèmpo *adv* early, prematurely

antìte·si *f* (-si) antithesis

antitèti·co -ca *adj* (-ci -che) antithetic(al)

antitossina *f* antitoxin

antiuòmo *adj invar* (mil) antipersonnel

antivigìlia *f*—**l'antivigilia di** two days before

antologìa *f* anthology

antònimo *m* antonym

antrace *m* anthrax

antracite *f* anthracite

antro *m* cave; den, hovel
antròpi·co -ca *adj* (-ci -che) human
antropofagìa *f* cannibalism
antropòfa·go -ga (-gi -ghe) *adj* cannibalistic || *m* cannibal
antropòlde *adj* anthropoid
antropologìa *f* anthropology
antropomòrfi·co -ca *adj* (-ci -che) anthropomorphic
antropomòr·fo -fa *adj* see **scimmia**
anulare *adj* ring-shaped, annular || *m* ring finger
Anvèrsa *f* Antwerp
anzi *adv* on the contrary, rather; **anzi che no** rather || *prep* (poet) before
anziani·tà *f* (-tà) seniority
anzia·no -na *adj* old, elderly; senior || *m* senior
anziché *conj* rather than
anzidét·to -ta *adj* aforesaid
anzitutto *adv* above all, first of all
apatìa *f* apathy
apàti·co -ca *adj* (-ci -che) apathetic
ape *f* bee; **ape operaia** worker; **ape regina** queen bee
aperitìvo *m* apéritif
apèr·to -ta *adj* open; frank, candid || *m* open space; **all'aperto** in the open
apertura *f* opening; aperture; approach; **ad apertura di libro** at sight; **apertura alare** (*of a bird*) wingspread; (aer) wingspan
apià·rio *m* (-ri) apiary
àpice *m* apex, top; climax
apicol·tóre -trice *mf* beekeeper, apiarist
apicoltura *f* beekeeping, apiculture
Apocalisse *f* Apocalypse, Revelation
apocalìtti·co -ca *adj* (-ci -che) apocalyptic(al)
apòcri·fo -fa *adj* apocryphal
apofonìa *f* ablaut
apogèo *m* apogee
apòlide *adj* stateless || *m* man without a country
apolìti·co -ca *adj* (-ci -che) nonpolitical, nonpartisan
apologè·ta *m* (-ti) apologist
apologèti·co -ca *adj* (-ci -che) apologetic
apologìa *f* apology
apòlo·go *m* (-ghi) apologue
apoplessìa *f* apoplexy
apoplètti·co -ca *adj & m* (-ci -che) apoplectic
apostasìa *f* apostasy
apòsta·ta *mf* (-ti -te) apostate
apostolato *m* apostolate
apostòli·co -ca *adj* (-ci -che) apostolic(al)
apòstolo *m* apostle
apostrofare (**apòstrofo**) *tr* to write with an apostrophe; to apostrophize
apòstrofe *f* apostrophe (*to a person*)
apòstrofo *m* (gram) apostrophe
apoteò·si *f* (-si) apotheosis
appagare §209 *tr* to satisfy, gratify || *ref*—**appagarsi di** to be content with
appaiare §287 *tr* to pair, couple; to match || *ref* to match (*said, e.g., of colors*)
appallottolare (**appallòttolo**) *tr* to

crumple into a ball || *ref* to become lumpy
appaltare *tr* to contract for
appalta·tóre -trice *mf* contractor
appalto *m* contract; state monopoly; **appalto di sali e tabacchi** tobacco shop
appannàg·gio *m* (-gi) appanage; (fig) prerogative
appannare *tr* to tarnish; to befog, becloud || *ref* to become clouded (*said, e.g., of one's eyesight*)
apparato *m* decoration; display; appliance; leadership (*of political party*); (rad, telv) set
apparecchiare §287 (**apparécchio**) *tr* to prepare; to set (*the table*) || *ref* to get ready
apparecchiatura *f* sizing (*of paper; of a wall*); preparation (*of a canvas*); apparatus
apparéc·chio *m* (-chi) apparatus; sizing; preparation; gadget; (rad, telv) set; airplane; **apparecchio da caccia** fighter plane; **apparecchio telefonico** telephone
apparentare (**apparènto**) *tr* to tie, unite (*through marriage*) || *ref* to become related; to become intimate; (pol) to form a coalition
apparènte *adj* apparent, seeming
apparènza *f* appearance; **in apparenza** seemingly
appariglìare §280 *tr* to pair, team (*horses*)
apparìre §108 *intr* (ESSERE) to appear, seem; to look
appariscènte *adj* showy, flashy, gaudy
apparizióne *f* apparition; appearance
appartaménto *m* apartment
appartare *tr* to set aside || *ref* to withdraw, retire
apparta·to -ta *adj* secluded, solitary
appartenènza *f* belonging, membership; **appartenenze** accessories; annexes
appartenére §271 *intr* (ESSERE & AVERE) to belong; to pertain || *impers* (ESSERE & AVERE)—**appartiene a** it behooves, it is up to
appassionaménto *m* excitement, interest, enthusiasm
appassionare (**appassióno**) *tr* to move; to interest; to excite || *ref* to be deeply interested
appassiona·to -ta *adj* impassioned; deep, ardent || *m* fan, amateur
appassìre §176 *intr* (ESSERE) to wilt, wither; to decay; to dry up (*said, e.g., of grapes*)
appellare (**appèllo**) *tr* (law) to appeal; (poet) to call || *ref* to appeal; **appellarsi da** or **contro** (law) to appeal
appèllo *m* call, roll call; **fare appello a** to summon (*e.g., one's strength*); **fare l'appello** to call the roll; **mancare all'appello** to be absent
appéna *adv* hardly, scarcely; only; just || *conj* as soon as; **non appena as** soon as, no sooner
appèndere §109 *tr* to hang
appéndice *f* appendix; feuilleton
appendicectomìa *f* appendectomy

appendicite *f* appendicitis
Appennino, l' *m* the Appennines
appesantire [s] §176 *tr* to make heavy; to burden, overwhelm ‖ *ref* to get heavy; to get fat
appestare (**appèsto**) *tr* to infect; to stink up
appesta·to -ta *adj* plague-ridden ‖ *m* plague victim
appetire §176 *tr* to crave, long for ‖ *intr* (ESSERE & AVERE) to be appetizing
appetito *m* appetite
appetitó·so -sa [s] *adj* appetizing, tempting
appètto *adv* opposite; **appetto a** opposite; in comparison with
appezzaménto *m* plot, parcel (*of land*)
appianare *tr* to smooth, level; to settle (*a dispute*); to get around (*a difficulty*)
appiana·tólo *m* (**-tói**) road grader
appiattare *tr* & *ref* to hide
appiattiménto *m* leveling; equalization
appiattire §176 *tr* & *ref* to flatten, to level
appiccare §197 *tr* to hang; **appiccare il fuoco a** to set on fire; **appiccare una lite** to pick a fight
appicciare §128 *tr* (coll) to string together; (coll) to kindle, light
appiccicare §197 (**appiccico**) *tr* to stick, glue; **appiccicare uno schiaffo a** to slap ‖ *ref* to stick, adhere
appiccicatíc·cio -cia *adj* (**-ci -ce**) sticky
appíc·co *m* (**-chi**) grip; steep wall (*of mountain*); (fig) pretext
appiè *adv*—**appiè di** at the foot of; at the bottom of
appiedare (**appièdo**) *tr* to order (*a cavalryman*) off a horse; to order (*e.g., troops*) off a vehicle; to force out of a car (*said, e.g., of motor trouble*)
appièno *adv* (poet) fully
appigionare (**appigióno**) *tr* to rent ‖ *ref*—**appigionasi** for rent
appigiónasi [s] *m* for-rent sign
appigliare §280 *ref* to cling, adhere; **appigliarsi a un pretesto** to seize a pretext
appí·glio *m* (**-gli**) grip; (fig) pretext
appiómbo *m* perpendicular ‖ *adv* plumb, perpendicularly
appioppare (**appiòppo**) *tr* to plant with poplar trees; to tie (*a vine*) to a poplar tree; (coll) to deliver (*a blow*); (coll) to pass off (*e.g., inferior goods*)
appisolare (**appisolo**) *ref* to snooze, doze
applaudire §176 & (**applàudo**) *tr* to applaud ‖ *intr* to applaud, clap the hands; (with *dat*) to applaud
applàuso *m* applause; **applausi** applause
applicàbile *adj* applicable
applicare §197 (**àpplico**) *tr* to apply; to attach; to give (*e.g., a slap*); to put into effect (*a law*); to assign ‖ *ref* to apply oneself
applica·to -ta *adj* applied; appliqué ‖ *m* clerk
applicazióne *f* application; appliqué

applique *m* (elec) wall fixture
appoggiaca·po *m* (**-po**) headrest; tidy (*on back of chair*)
appoggiagómi·ti *m* (**-ti**) elbowrest
appoggiama·no *m* (**-no**) mahlstick
appoggiare §290 (**appòggio**) *tr* to lean; to rest; to prop, support; to raise (*the tone of voice*); to give (*a slap*); to second (*a motion*); (fig) to back, support ‖ *intr* to lean; to rest ‖ *ref*—**appoggiarsi a** or **su** to lean on
appoggia·tólo *m* (**-tói**) support, rest; banister
appoggiatura *f* (mus) grace note
appòg·gio *m* (**-gi**) support, prop; backer; backing, support; grip; (mach) bearing
appollaiare §287 *ref* to roost
appórre §218 *tr* to affix, append
apportare (**appòrto**) *tr* to cause; to presage; (poet) to carry
appòrto *m* carrying; contribution; (law) share
appositaménte *adv* expressly, on purpose
appòsi·to -ta *adj* proper, fitting
apposizióne *f* apposition
appòsta *adj invar* suitable ‖ *adv* on purpose, expressly, intentionally
appostaménto *m* ambush
appostare (**appòsto**) *tr* to ambush ‖ *ref* to lie in ambush
apprèndere §220 *tr* to learn ‖ *ref* (poet) to take hold
apprendi·sta *mf* (**-sti -ste**) apprentice
apprendistato *m* apprenticeship
apprensióne *f* apprehension, fear
apprensí·vo -va *adj* apprehensive
appressare (**apprèsso**) *tr* (poet) to approach ‖ *ref* to come near
apprèsso *adj invar* next, following ‖ *adv* near; later on; **appresso a** near; after
apprestare (**apprèsto**) *tr* to prepare; to supply, provide (*e.g., help*) ‖ *ref* to prepare, get ready
apprettare (**apprètto**) *tr* to dress (*leather*); to size (*cloth*)
apprètto *m* tan (*for leather*); sizing (*for cloth*)
apprezzàbile *adj* appreciable
apprezzaménto *m* appreciation; estimation
apprezzare (**apprèzzo**) *tr* to appreciate
apprezza·to -ta *adj* esteemed
appròc·cio *m* (**-ci**) approach; **approcci** advances
approdare (**appròdo**) *intr* (ESSERE & AVERE) to land; (with *dat*) (poet) to benefit; **approdare a** to come to
appròdo *m* landing
approfittare *intr*—**approfittare di** to capitalize on ‖ *ref*—**approfittarsi di** to take advantage of
approfondire §176 *tr* to make deep; to study thoroughly ‖ *ref*—**approfondirsi in** to go deep into
approntare (**apprónto**) *tr* to prepare, make ready
appropriare §287 (**appròprio**) *tr* to adapt; to bestow ‖ *ref*—**appropriarsi a** to befit; **appropriarsi di** to appropriate; to embezzle

appropria•to -ta *adj* appropriate
appropriazióne *f* appropriation; **appropriazione indebita** fraudulent conversion, embezzlement
approssimare (appròssimo) *tr* to bring near || *ref* to approach, come near
approssimati•vo -va *adj* approximate
approssimazióne *f* approximation
approvàbile *adj* laudable
approvare (appròvo) *tr* to approve, countenance; to subscribe to (*an opinion*); to pass (*a student; a law*); to confirm
approvazióne *f* approval; confirmation; passage (*of a law*)
approvvigionaménto *m* supply
approvvigionare (approvvigióno) *tr* to supply || *ref* to be supplied
appuntaménto *m* appointment; date; **appuntamento amoroso** assignation
appuntare (appùnto) *tr* to sharpen; to fasten, pin; to stick (*a pin*) in; to point; to jot down, take note of; to prick up (*one's ears*); (fig) to reproach || *ref* to be turned; to aim
appunta•to -ta *adj* sharpened || *m* corporal (*of Italian police*)
appuntellare (appuntèllo) *tr* to shore up, prop up
appuntellatura *f* shoring up, propping up
appuntino *adv* precisely, meticulously
appuntire §176 *tr* to sharpen
appunti•to -ta *adj* sharp, pointed
appunto *m* note; blame, charge; **muovere un appunto** to blame; **per l'appunto** just, precisely || *adv* exactly, precisely
appurare *tr* to ascertain
appuzzare *tr* to befoul, pollute
apribottì•glie *m* (-**glie**) bottle opener
apri•co -ca *adj* (-**chi -che**) (poet) sunny, bright
aprile *m* April
apripì•sta *m* (-**sta**) blade (*of bulldozer*); bulldozer
aprire §110 *tr* to open; to turn on; to dig (*e.g., a grave*) || *ref* to open; to clear up (*said of the weather*); **aprirsi con** to open one's heart to; **aprirsi il varco tra** to press through
apriscàto•le *m* (-**le**) can opener
aquà•rio *m* (-**ri**) aquarium || **Aquario** *m* (astr) Aquarius
aquàti•co -ca *adj* (-**ci -che**) aquatic
àquila *f* eagle; genius
aquili•no -na *adj* aquiline
aquilóne *m* north wind; kite
aquilòtto *m* eaglet; cadet (*in Italian Air Force Academy*)
Aquinate, l' *m* Saint Thomas Aquinas
ara *f* (poet) altar; are (*100 square meters*)
arabé•sca *f* (-**sche**) (mus) arabesque
arabesca•to -ta *adj* arabesque
arabé•sco -sca (-**schi -sche**) *adj* arabesque || *m* arabesque; doodle || *f* see **arabesca**
Aràbia, l' *f* Arabia
aràbi•co -ca *adj* (-**ci -che**) Arabic
aràbile *adj* tillable

àra•bo -ba *adj* Arabic, Arabian || *mf* Arab (*person*) || *m* Arabic (*language*)
aràchide *f* peanut (*vine*)
aragonése [s] *adj* & *mf* Aragonese
aragósta *f* (*Palinurus vulgaris*) lobster
aràldi•co -ca (-**ci -che**) *adj* heraldic || *f* heraldry
araldo *m* herald
arancéto *m* orange grove
aràn•cia *f* (-**ce**) orange
aranciata *f* orangeade
aràn•cio *adj* *invar* orange (*in color*) || *m* (-**ci**) orange tree
arancióne *adj* & *m* orange (*color*)
arare *tr* to plow; (naut) to drag (*the anchor*)
aratro *m* plow
arazzo *m* tapestry, arras
arbitràg•gio *m* (-**gi**) (sports) umpiring; (com) arbitrage
arbitrale *adj* judge's, umpire's
arbitrare (àrbitro) *tr* to umpire, referee || *intr* to arbitrate || *ref*—**arbitrarsi di** to take the liberty to
arbitrà•rio -ria *adj* (-**ri -rie**) arbitrary; wanton
arbitrato *m* arbitration
arbì•trio *m* (-**tri**) will; abuse, violation; **libero arbitrio** free will
àrbitro *m* arbiter; judge, referee, umpire
arboscèllo *m* small tree
arbusto *m* shrub, bush
ar•ca *f* (-**che**) sarcophagus; ark; chest; **arca di Noè** Noah's Ark; **arca di scienza** (fig) fountain of knowledge
àrcade *adj* & *m* Arcadian
Arcàdia *f* Arcadia, Arcady
arcài•co -ca *adj* (-**ci -che**) archaic
arcaismo *m* archaism
arcàngelo *m* archangel
arca•no -na *adj* mysterious, arcane || *m* mystery
arcata *f* arch; arcade
archeologia *f* archaeology
archeològi•co -ca *adj* (-**ci -che**) archaeological
archeòlo•go -ga *mf* (-**gi -ghe**) archaeologist
archètipo *m* archetype
archétto *m* (archit) small arch; (elec) trolley pole; (mus) bow
archi- *pref adj* archi-, e.g., **architettonico** architectonic || *pref m* & *f* archi-, e.g., **architettura** architecture
archibù•gio *m* (-**gi**) harquebus
Archimède *m* Archimedes
architettare (architétto) *tr* to plan (*a building*); (fig) to contrive, plot
architétto *m* architect
architettòni•co -ca *adj* (-**ci -che**) architectural
architettura *f* architecture
architetturale *adj* architectural
architrave *m* architrave; doorhead, lintel
archiviare §287 *tr* to file; to lay aside, shelve; (law) to throw out
archì•vio *m* (-**vi**) archives; record office; chancery, public records
archivi•sta *mf* (-**sti -ste**) archivist, file clerk

arci- *pref adj* archi-, e.g., **arcivescovile** archiepiscopal ‖ *pref m & f* arch-, e.g., **arciprete** archpriest

arcicontèn·to -ta *adj* (coll) very glad

arcidiàcono *m* archdeacon

arcidu·ca *m* (**-chi**) archduke

arciduchéssa *f* archduchess

arcière *m* archer, bowman

arci·gno -gna *adj* gruff, surly

arcióne *m* saddlebow; **montare in arcioni** to mount, to mount a horse

arcipèla·go *m* (**-ghi**) archipelago

arciprète *m* archpriest; dean

arcivescovado *m* archbishopric

arcivéscovo *m* archbishop

ar·co *m* (**-chi**) bow; (archit) arch; (geom, elec) arc; **arco rampante** flying buttress

arcobaléno *m* rainbow

arco·làio *m* (**-lài**) reel; **girare come un arcolaio** to spin like a top

arcuare (**àrcuo**) *tr* to arch; to bend; to camber

arcua·to -ta *adj* bent, curved; bow (e.g., legs); **avere le gambe arcuate** to be bowlegged

ardènte *adj* burning; hot; ardent, impassioned

àrdere §111 *tr* to burn ‖ *intr* to burn; to be in full swing (said, e.g., of a war)

ardèsia *f* slate

ardiménto *m* boldness, daring

ardire *m* boldness; presumption; impudence ‖ §176 *intr*—**ardire** + *inf* or **ardire di** + *inf* to dare to + *inf*

arditézza *f* daring; temerity

ardi·to -ta *adj* daring; rash ‖ *m* (hist) shock trooper

ardóre *m* intense heat; ardor

àr·duo -dua *adj* arduous

àrea *f* area, surface; group, camp; **area arretrata** backward area

àrem *m* (**àrem**) harem

arèna *f* arena; **scendere nell'arena** to throw one's hat in the ring

aréna *f* sand

arenare (**aréno**) *intr* (ESSERE) & *ref* to run aground

arenària *f* sandstone

arén·go *m* (**-ghi**) (hist) town meeting

arenile *m* sandy beach

arenó·so -sa [s] *adj* sandy

areòmetro *m* hydrometer

aeronàuti·co -ca *adj & f* (**-ci -che**) var of **aeronautico**

areoplano *m* var of **aeroplano**

areopòrto *m* var of **aeroporto**

areòstato *m* var of **aerostato**

àrgano *m* winch; (naut) capstan

argentare (**argènto**) *tr* to silver; to silver-plate; to back (a mirror) with foil

argenta·to -ta *adj* silver; silvery; silver-plated

argentatura *f* silver plating; silver plate; foil (of mirror)

argènte·o -a *adj* silver, silvery

argenterìa *f* silverware

argentière *m* silversmith; jeweler

argenti·no -na *adj* silver, silvery; Argentine ‖ *mf* Argentine ‖ *f* high-necked sweater ‖ **l'Argentina** *f* Argentina

argènto *m* silver; (archaic) money; **argenti** silverware; **argento vivo** quicksilver

argentóne *m* German silver

argilla *f* clay

argilló·so -sa [s] *adj* clayey

arginare (**àrgino**) *tr* to dam, dike; to hold back, check

àrgine *m* embankment, dam; (fig) defense

ar·go *m* (**-ghi**) (chem) argon; (orn) grouse ‖ **Argo** *m* Argus

argomentare (**argoménto**) *tr & intr* to argue

argomentazióne *f* argumentation, discussion

argoménto *m* argument; pretext; subject; **fuori dell'argomento** beside the point

argonàu·ta *m* (**-ti**) Argonaut

arguire §176 *tr* to deduce, infer; (archaic) to denote

argutézza *f* wit; witty remark

argu·to -ta *adj* keen, acute; witty

argùzia *f* keenness; wit

ària *f* air; climate; look; mien; aria, tune; poem; **all'aria aperta** in the open air; **a mezz'aria** in midair; halfway; **andare all'aria** to fail; **aria condizionata** air conditioning; **avere l'aria di** to seem to; to look like; **dare aria a** to air; **in aria** in the air; **tira un'aria pericolosa** a mean wind is blowing

aria·no -na *adj & mf* Aryan

aridi·tà *f* (**-tà**) dryness, aridity; dearth

àri·do -da *adj* arid, dry, barren; (fig) dry

arieggiare §290 (**arièggio**) *tr* to air; to imitate ‖ *ref*—**arieggiarsi a** to give oneself the airs of

ariète *m* ram; (mil) battering ram ‖ **Ariete** *m* (astr) Aries

ariétta *s* breeze; (mus) short aria

arin·ga *f* (**-ghe**) herring; **aringa affumicata** kippered herring, kipper

arin·go *m* (**-ghi**) assembly; field; joust; **scendere nell'aringo** to throw one's hat in the ring

arió·so -sa [s] *adj* airy, breezy; (fig) of wide scope

àrista *f* loin of pork

arista *f* (bot) awn

aristocràti·co -ca (**-ci -che**) *adj* aristocratic ‖ *m* aristocrat

aristocrazìa *f* aristocracy

Aristòtele *m* Aristotle

aristotèli·co -ca *adj & m* (**-ci -che**) Aristotelian

aritmèti·co -ca (**-ci -che**) *adj* arithmetical ‖ *m* arithmetician ‖ *f* arithmetic

arlecchino *adj invar* harlequin; fiesta (e.g., dishes) ‖ **Arlecchino** *m* Harlequin

ar·ma *f* (**-mi**) arm, weapon; (fig) army; (mil) corps, service; **alle prime armi** at the beginning; **arma bianca** steel blade; **arma da taglio** cutting weapon; **arma delle trasmissioni** signal corps

armacòllo *m*—**ad armacollo** slung across the shoulders (said of a rifle)

armà·dio *m* (**-di**) cabinet; closet; **armadio a muro** built-in closet; **armadio**

d'angolo corner cupboard; **armadio farmaceutico** medicine cabinet; **armadio guardaroba** armoire

armaiòlo *m* gunsmith

armamentà·rio *m* (**-ri**) outfit, set (*of tools*)

armaménto *m* armament; crew; gun crew; crew (*of rowboat*); outfit, equipment

armare *tr* to arm; to dub (*s.o. a knight*); to outfit, commission (*a ship*); to cock (*a gun*); to brace, shore up (*a building*); (rr) to furnish with track || *ref* to arm oneself; to outfit oneself

arma·to -ta *adj* armed; reinforced (*concrete*) || *m* soldier || *f* army; navy; fleet; (nav) task force

arma·tóre -trice *adj* outfitting || *m* shipowner; (min) carpenter; (rr) trackwalker

armatura *f* armor; scaffold; framework; support; reinforcement (*for concrete*); (elec) plate (*of condenser*)

armeggiare §290 (**arméggio**) *intr* to fumble, fool around; to scheme; (archaic) to handle arms; (archaic) to joust

armeggì·o *m* (**-i**) fooling around; scheming, intriguing

armè·no -na *adj* & *mf* Armenian

arménto *m* herd

armeria *f* armory

armière *m* (aer) gunner

armìge·ro -ra *adj* warlike, bellicose || *m* warrior; bodyguard

armistiziale *adj* armistice

armistì·zio *m* (**-zi**) *m* armistice

armonìa *f* harmony; **in armonia con** according to

armòni·co -ca (**-ci -che**) *adj* harmonic; resonant; harmonious || *f* harmonica; **armonica a bocca** mouth organ

armonió·so -sa [*s*] *adj* harmonious

armonizzare [ddzz] *tr* & *intr* to harmonize

arnése [*s*] *m* tool, implement; garb, dress; (coll) gadget; **bene in arnese** well-heeled; **male in arnese** down at the heels

àrnia *f* beehive

arò·ma *m* (**-mi**) aroma, odor; zest

aromàti·co -ca *adj* (**-ci -che**) aromatic

aromatizzare [ddzz] *tr* to flavor; to spice

arpa *f* harp

arpeggiare §290 (**arpéggio**) *intr* to play arpeggios; to play a harp; to strum

arpég·gio *m* (**-gi**) arpeggio

arpìa *f* Harpy; (coll) harpy

arpionare (**arpióno**) *tr* to harpoon

arpióne *m* hinge (*of door*); hook; harpoon; spike (*for mountain climbing*)

arpionismo *m* ratchet

arpi·sta *mf* (**-sti -ste**) harpist

arrabattare *ref* to exert oneself, to strive, to endeavor

arrabbiare §287 *intr* (ESSERE) to go mad (*said of dogs*) || *ref* to become angry (*said of people*)

arrabbia·to -ta *adj* mad (*dog*); angry; obstinate; confirmed

arrabbiatura *f* rage; **prendersi un'arrabbiatura** to burn up (*with rage*)

arraffare *tr* to snatch

arrampicare §197 (**arràmpico**) *ref* to climb, climb up

arrampicata *f* climbing

arrampica·tóre -trice *mf* climber; mountain climber; **arrampicatore sociale** social climber

arrancare §197 *intr* to hobble, limp; to struggle, work hard; to row hard

arrangiaménto *m* agreement; (mus) arrangement

arrangiare §290 *tr* to arrange; to fix; (coll) to steal || *ref* to manage, get along

arrecare §197 (**arrèco**) *tr* to cause; to carry, deliver

arredaménto *m* furnishing; furnishings; equipment

arredare (**arrèdo**) *tr* to furnish; to equip

arreda·tóre -trice *mf* interior decorator; upholsterer; (mov) property man

arrèdo *m* furnishings, furniture; piece of furniture; **arredi sacri** church supplies

arrembàg·gio *m* (**-gi**) boarding (*of a ship*)

arrenare (**arréno**) *tr* to sand

arrèndere §227 *tr* (archaic) to surrender || *ref* to surrender; **arrendersi a discrezione** to surrender unconditionally

arrendévole *adj* yielding, compliant, flexible

arrendevolézza *f* suppleness; compliance

arrestare (**arrèsto**) *tr* to stop; to arrest || *ref* to stop, stay

arrèsto *m* arrest; stop; pause; (mach) stop, catch; arresti (mil) house arrest; **in stato d'arresto** under arrest

arretrare (**arrètro**) *tr* to withdraw || *intr* (ESSERE & AVERE) & *ref* to withdraw

arretra·to -ta *adj* withdrawn; backward; back (*issue*); overdue || **arretrati** *mpl* arrears

arricchiménto *m* enrichment

arricchire §176 *tr* to enrich || *intr* (ESSERE) & *ref* to get rich

arricchi·to -ta *mf* nouveau riche

arricciacapé·li *m* (**-li**) curler

arricciare §128 *tr* to curl; to wrinkle; to screw up (*one's nose*); **arricciare il pelo** to bristle (*said of a person*); to bristle up (*said of an animal*) || *ref* to curl up

arriccia·to -ta *adj* curled up || *m* first coat (*of cement*)

arricciatura *f* curling (*of hair*); pleating (*of a skirt*); kink (*in a rope*)

arridere §231 *tr* (poet) to grant || *intr* to smile

arrin·ga *f* (**-ghe**) harangue; (law) lawyer's plea

arringare §209 *tr* to harangue; (law) to plead

arrischiare §287 *tr* to endanger; to risk || *ref* to dare, venture

arrischia·to -ta *adj* risky; daring

arrivare *tr* to reach || *intr* (ESSERE) to arrive; to happen; to get along, be successful; **arrivare a** to reach; to succeed in

arriva·to -ta *adj* arrived; successful; **ben arrivato** welcome

arrivedér·ci *m* (**-ci**) good-bye || *interj* good-bye!, so long!

arrivedéria *interj* good-bye!

arrivismo *m* social climbing, ruthless ambition

arrivi·sta *mf* (**-sti -ste**) social climber

arrivo *m* arrival; (sports) goal line; (sports) finishing·line

arroccare §197 (**arrócco**) *tr* to put (*e.g.*, *flax*) on the distaff || §197 (**arròcco**) *tr* to shelter; (chess) to castle || *ref* to seek shelter; (chess) to castle

arròc·co *m* (**-chi**) castling

arrochire §176 *tr* to make hoarse || *intr* (ESSERE) to become hoarse

arrogante *adj* arrogant, insolent

arroganza *f* arrogance, insolence

arrogare §209 (**arrògo**) *tr*—**arrogare a sé** to arrogate to oneself || *ref* to arrogate to oneself

arrolare §237 *tr* var of **arruolare**

arrossare (**arrósso**) *tr* to redden

arrossire §176 *intr* (ESSERE) to blush; to change color

arrostire §176 *tr* to roast; to toast; **arrostire allo spiedo** to barbecue on the spit || *intr* (ESSERE) & *ref* to roast

arrò·sto *m* (**-sto & -sti**) roast

arrotare (**arròto**) *tr* to grind, hone; to smooth; to strike, run over; to spit (*one's teeth*) || *ref* to grind (*to work hard*); to sideswipe

arrotatrice *f* floor sander

arrotatura *f* sharpening

arrotino *m* grinder

arrotolare (**arròtolo**) *tr* to roll

arrotondaménto *m* rounding; rounding out; increase (*in salary*)

arrotondare (**arrotóndo**) *tr* to make round; to round out; to supplement (*a salary*) || *ref* to round out, become plump

arrovellare (**arrovèllo**) *tr* to vex || *ref* to become angry; to strive, endeavor; **arrovellarsi il cervello** to rack one's brains

arroventare (**arrovènto**) *tr* to make red-hot || *ref* to become red-hot

arroventire §176 *tr* & *ref* var of **arroventare**

arruffapòpo·li *m* (**-li**) rabble-rouser

arruffare *tr* to tangle; to muss, rumple; to confuse

arruf·fìo *m* (**-fìi**) tangle; confusion, mess

arruffó·ne -na *mf* blunderer; swindler

arrugginire §176 *tr*, *intr* (ESSERE) & *ref* to rust

arruolaménto *m* enlistment; draft

arruolare (**arruòlo**) *tr* to recruit; to draft || *ref* to enlist

arruvidire §176 *tr* to make rough, roughen || *intr* (ESSERE) to become rough

arsenale *m* arsenal; navy yard

arsèni·co -ca (**-ci -che**) *adj* arsenic, arsenical || *m* arsenic

ar·so -sa *adj* burnt; dry, parched; **arso di** consumed with

arsura *f* sultriness; dryness

arte *f* art; ability; guile; **ad arte** on purpose; **arti e mestieri** arts and crafts

artefare §173 *tr* to adulterate

artefat·to -ta *adj* adulterated; artificial

artéfice *m* craftsman; creator

artèria *f* artery

arterioscleròsi *m* arteriosclerosis

arterió·so -sa [s] *adj* arterial

artesia·no -na *adj* artesian

àrti·co -ca *adj* (**-ci -che**) arctic || **Artico** *m* Arctic

articolare *adj* articular || *v* (**artìcolo**) *tr* & *ref* to articulate

articola·to -ta *adj* articulated; articulate; (gram) combined; jagged (*coastline*)

articolazióne *f* articulation

articoli·sta *mf* (**-sti -ste**) columnist; feature writer

articolo *m* article; item; paragraph; **articolo di fondo** editorial; **articolo di spalla** comment

artificiale *adj* artificial

artificière *m* pyrotechnist; (mil) demolition expert

artifì·cio *m* (**-ci**) artifice; sophistication, affectation; **artificio d'illuminazione** (mil) flare

artificiosi·tà [s] *f* (**-tà**) artfulness, craftiness; artificiality

artific ió·so -sa [s] *adj* artful, crafty; artificial, affected

artigianato *m* craftsmanship

artigia·no -na *adj* of craftsmen || *m* craftsman

artigliare §280 *tr* (poet) to claw

artiglière *m* artilleryman

artiglieria *f* artillery; **artiglieria a cavallo** mounted artillery

artì·glio *m* (**-gli**) claw; **cadere negli artigli di** to fall into the clutches of

arti·sta *mf* (**-sti -ste**) artist; actor

artìsti·co -ca *adj* (**-ci -che**) artistic

ar·to -ta *adj* (poet) narrow || *m* limb

artrite *f* arthritis

artrìti·co -ca *adj* & *mf* (**-ci -che**) arthritic

arturia·no -na *adj* Arthurian

arzigogolare [dz] (**arzigògolo**) *intr* to muse; to cavil

arzigògolo [dz] *m* fantasy; cavil

arzìl·lo -la [dz] *adj* lively, sprightly; (coll) sparkling (*wine*)

arzin·ga *f* (**-ghe**) tong (*of a blacksmith*)

asbèsto *m* asbestos

ascèlla *f* armpit

ascendènte *adj* ascendant || *m* upper hand, ascendancy; **ascendenti** forefathers

ascendènza *f* ancestry, lineage

ascéndere §245 *tr* to climb || *intr* (ESSERE & AVERE) to ascend, climb

ascensionale *adj* rising; lifting

ascensióne *f* ascent, climb || **Ascensione** *f* Ascension, Ascension Day

ascensóre *m* elevator

ascésa [s] *f* ascent

ascèsso *m* abscess

ascè·ta *mf* (**-ti -te**) ascetic

ascèti·co -ca *adj* (**-ci -che**) ascetic

ascetismo *m* asceticism

à·scia *f* (**-sce**) adze

asciugacapél·li *m* (**-li**) hair drier
asciugamano *m* towel; **asciugamano spugna** Turkish towel
asciugante *adj* drying; blotting; soaking ‖ *m* dryer
asciugare §209 *tr* to dry, dry up; to wipe; to drain (*e.g.*, *a glass of wine*) ‖ *ref* to dry oneself; to dry, dry up
asciuga·tólo *m* (**-tói**) towel; bath towel
asciugatrice *f* dryer
asciut·to -ta *adj* dry; skinny; blunt (*in speech*) ‖ *m* dry land; dry climate; **all'asciutto** pennyless
ascoltare (**ascólto**) *tr* to listen to ‖ *intr* to listen
ascolta·tóre -trice *mf* listener
ascólto *m* listening; **stare in ascolto** to listen
ascòrbi·co -ca *adj* (**-ci -che**) ascorbic
ascrit·to -ta *adj* ascribed; belonging ‖ *m* member
ascrivere §250 *tr* to inscribe, register; to ascribe, attribute
ascultare *tr* to sound (*s.o.'s chest*)
asèpsi [s] *f* asepsis
asètti·co -ca [s] *adj* (**-ci -che**) aseptic
asfaltare *tr* to tar, pave
asfalto *m* asphalt
asfissia *f* asphyxia
asfissiante *adj* asphyxiating; poison (*gas*); boring
asfissiare §287 *tr* to asphyxiate; to bore ‖ *intr* (ESSERE) to be asphyxiated
asfodèlo *m* asphodel
Àsia, l' *f* Asia; **l'Asia Minore** Asia Minor
asiàti·co -ca *adj* & *mf* (**-ci -che**) Asian, Asiatic
asilo *m* shelter; asylum; home; **asilo di mendicità** poorhouse; **asilo infantile** kindergarten; **asilo per i vecchi** old-age home, nursing home
asimmetria [s] *f* asymmetry
asimmètri·co -ca [s] *adj* (**-ci -che**) asymmetric(al)
asinàggine [s] *f* stupidity, asininity
asi·nàio [s] *m* (**-nài**) donkey driver
asinata [s] *f* stupidity, folly
asiné·sco -sca [s] *adj* (**-schi -sche**) asinine
asini·no -na [s] *adj* asinine
àsino [s] *m* ass, donkey; **fare l'asino a** (slang) to play up to; **qui casca l'asino** here is the rub
asma *f* asthma
asmàti·co -ca *adj* & *mf* (**-ci -che**) asthmatic
àsola *f* buttonhole; buttonhole hem
aspàra·go *m* (**-gi**) asparagus; piece of asparagus; **asparagi** asparagus (*as food*)
aspèrgere §112 *tr* to sprinkle
aspersióne *f* aspersing, sprinkling
aspettare (**aspètto**) *tr* to wait for, await; to expect; **aspettare al varco** to be on the lookout for ‖ *intr* to wait; **fare aspettare** to keep waiting ‖ *ref* to expect
aspettativa *f* expectancy, expectation; leave of absence without pay
aspètto *m* waiting; aspect, look; **al primo aspetto** at first sight

àspide *m* asp
aspirante *adj* suction (*pump*) ‖ *m* aspirant; applicant, candidate; suitor; upperclassman (*in naval academy*)
aspirapólve·re *m* (**-re**) vacuum cleaner
aspirare *tr* to inhale, breathe in; to suck (*e.g.*, *air*); (phonet) to aspirate ‖ *intr* to aspire
aspiratóre *m* exhaust fan
aspirazióne *f* aspiration; (aut) intake
aspirina *f* aspirin
aspo *m* reel
asportàbile *adj* removable
asportare (**aspòrto**) *tr* to remove, take away
asportazióne *f* removal
asprézza *f* sourness; roughness, harshness
a·spro -spra *adj* sour; rough, harsh
assaggiare §290 *tr* to taste; to sample, test; **assaggiare il terreno** (fig) to see how the land lies
assaggia·tóre -trice *mf* taster
assàg·gio *m* (**-gi**) taste, sample; tasting; test, trial
assài *adj invar* a lot of ‖ *m* much ‖ *adv* enough; fairly; very
assale *m* axle
assalire §242 *tr* to attack, assail; (fig) to seize
assali·tóre -trice *mf* assailant
assaltare *tr* to assault; **assaltare a mano armata** to stick up
assalto *m* assault, attack; (law) battery; **cogliere d'assalto** to catch unawares; **prendere d'assalto** to assault
assaporare (**assapóro**) *tr* to taste; to relish, enjoy
assassinare *tr* to assassinate; (fig) to murder
assassì·nio *m* (**-ni**) assassination, murder
assassì·no -na *adj* murderous ‖ *mf* assassin, murderer
asse *m* axle; shaft, spindle; (geom, phys) axis; **asse ereditario** estate; **asse stradale** median strip ‖ *f* plank; **asse da stiro** ironing board
assecondare (**assecóndo**) *tr* to help; to second; to uphold
assediante *adj* besieging ‖ *m* besieger
assediare §287 (**assèdio**) *tr* to lay siege to, besiege
assè·dio *m* (**-di**) siege; **assedio economico** economic sanctions; **cingere d'assedio** to besiege
assegnaménto *m* awarding; allowance; faith, reliance; **fare assegnamento su** to rely upon
assegnare (**asségno**) *tr* to assign; to prescribe; to distribute; to award
assegnatà·rio -ria *mf* (**-ri -rie**) assignee
assegnazióne *f* assignment; awarding
asségno *m* allowance; check; **assegni fringe** benefits; **assegni familiari** family allowance; **assegno a copertura garantita** certified check; **assegno a vuoto** worthless check; **assegno di studio** (educ) stipend; **assegno turistico** traveler's check; **assegno vademecum** certified check; **contro assegno** C.O.D.

assemblàg·gio *m* (-gi) (mach) assembling, assembly

assemblèa *f* assembly

assembraménto *m* gathering

assembrare (assémbro) *tr* & *ref* to gather

assennatézza *f* good judgment, discretion

assenna·to -ta *adj* sensible, prudent

assènso *m* approval, consent

assentare (assènto) *ref* to be absent, to absent oneself

assènte *adj* absent ‖ *mf* absentee

assenteìsmo *m* absenteeism

assentire (assènto) *tr* (poet) to grant ‖ *intr* to assent, acquiesce; **assentire con un cenno** to nod assent

assènza *f* absence

assenziènte *adj* consenting, approving

assèn·zio *m* (-zi) absinthe; (bot) wormwood

asserire §176 *tr* to affirm, assert

asserragliare §280 *tr* to barricade ‖ *ref* to barricade oneself

assèrto *m* (poet) assertion

asser·tóre -trice *mf* advocate, supporter

asserviménto *m* enslavement

asservire §176 *tr* to enslave; to subjugate

asserzióne *f* assertion

assessóre *m* councilman; alderman

assestaménto *m* arrangement; settling (*of a building*)

assestare (assèsto) *tr* to arrange; to adapt, regulate; to deliver, deal (*a blow*) ‖ *ref* to become organized; to settle (*said of a building*)

assesta·to -ta *adj* sensible, prudent

assetare (asséto) *tr* to make thirsty; (fig) to inflame

asseta·to -ta *adj* thirsty; parched; eager ‖ *mf* thirsty person

assettare (assètto) *tr* to tidy, straighten up ‖ *ref* to straighten oneself up

assetta·to -ta *adj* tidy

assètto *m* arrangement; order; (naut) trim; **assetto longitudinale** (aer) pitch, attitude; **in assetto di guerra** ready for war; **male in assetto** in poor shape

asseverare (assèvero) *tr* to asseverate, assert

assicèlla *f* roofing board, lath; batten

assicuràbile *adj* insurable

assicurare *tr* to assure; to insure; to protect; to fasten; to deliver (*e.g., a thief*) ‖ *ref* to make sure; to take out insurance

assicura·to -ta *adj* & *mf* insured ‖ *f* insured letter

assicura·tóre -trice *mf* insurer

assicurazióne *f* assurance; insurance; **assicurazione contro gli infortuni sul lavoro** workman's compensation insurance; **assicurazione contro i danni** casualty insurance; **assicurazione incendio** fire insurance; **assicurazione infortuni** accident insurance; **assicurazione per la vecchiaia** old age insurance; **assicurazione sociale** social security; **assicurazione sulla vita** life insurance

assideraménto *m* freezing; frostbite

assiderare (assìdero) *ref* to freeze; to become frostbitten

assìdere §113 *ref* (poet) to take one's seat (*e.g., on the throne*)

assì·duo -dua *adj* assiduous, diligent

assième *m* ensemble ‖ *adv* together; **assieme a** together with

assiepare (assièpo) *tr* & *ref* to crowd

assillante *adj* disturbing, troublesome

assillare *tr* to beset, trouble

assillo *m* gadfly; (fig) stimulus, goad

assimilare (assìmilo) *tr* to assimilate; to compare

assimilazióne *f* assimilation

assiòlo *m* horned owl

assiò·ma *m* (-mi) axiom

assiomàti·co -ca *adj* (-ci -che) axiomatic

assi·ro -ra *adj* & *mf* Assyrian

assisa *f* (poet) uniform, livery; (geol) layer; (archaic) duty, tax; **assise** criminal court; assembly, session; (hist) assises

assistènte *mf* assistant; **assistente sanitario** practical nurse; **assistente sociale** social worker ‖ *m*—**assistente ai lavoro** foreman ‖ *f*—**assistente di volo** (aer) hostess

assistènza *f* assistance, help; intervention; **assistenza pubblica** relief

assistenziale *adj* welfare, charity

assistere §114 *tr* to assist, help ‖ *intr*—**assistere a** to attend, be present at

assito *m* flooring, boarding

assiuòlo *m* var of **assiolo**

asso *m* ace; **asso del volante** speed king; **piantare in asso** to walk out on

associare §128 (assòcio) *tr* to associate; **associare alle carceri** to take to prison ‖ *ref* to associate; to become a member; to subscribe; to participate

associa·to -ta *adj* associate ‖ *mf* associate, partner

associazióne *f* association; union; subscription; membership

assodare (assòdo) *tr* to solidify; to strengthen; to ascertain ‖ *ref* to solidify; to strengthen

assoggettare (assoggètto) *tr* to subject, subdue ‖ *ref* to submit

assola·to -ta *adj* sunny, exposed to the sun

assolcare §197 (assòlco) *tr* to furrow

assoldare (assòldo) *tr* to hire, recruit

assólo *m* (mus) solo

assolutismo *m* absolutism

assolutisti·co -ca *adj* (-ci -che) absolutist, despotic

assolu·to -ta *adj* & *m* absolute

assoluzióne *f* absolution

assòlvere §115 *tr* to absolve; to fulfill

assomigliare §280 *tr* to compare; to make similar, make equal ‖ *intr* (ESSERE & AVERE) (with *dat*) to resemble, to look like; to be like ‖ *ref* to resemble each other, look alike; **assomigliarsi a** to resemble

assommare (assòmmo) *tr* to add; to be the epitome of; (archaic) to complete ‖ *intr* (ESSERE) to amount

assonna·to -ta *adj* sleepy

assopire §176 *tr* to lull to sleep; to

soothe || *ref* to drowse, to nod; to calm down
assorbènte *adj* absorbent || *m* sanitary napkin
assorbiménto *m* absorption
assorbire §176 & (**assòrbo**) *tr* to absorb
assorbì·to -ta *adj* absorbed; **assorbito da** consumed with
assordare (**assórdo**) *tr* to deafen || *ref* to become deaf; to dim; to lessen
assortiménto *m* assortment; **avere in assortimento** (com) to carry, stock
assortire §176 *tr* to assort, sort out; to stock
assortì·to -ta *adj* assorted; **bene assortito** well matched
assòr·to -ta *adj* engrossed, absorbed
assottigliare §280 *tr* to thin; to sharpen; to reduce || *ref* to grow thinner
assuefare §173 *tr* to accustom || *ref* to become accustomed
assuefazióne *f* habit, custom
assùmere §116 *tr* to assume; to hire; to raise, elevate; (law) to accept in evidence
Assunta *f* Assumption
assunto *m* thesis, argument; (poet) task
assun·tóre -trice *mf* contractor
assunzióne *f* assumption; hiring; (law) examination || **Assunzione** *f* Assumption
assurdi·tà *f* (**-tà**) absurdity
assur·do -da *adj* absurd || *m* absurdity
assùrgere §117 *intr* (ESSERE) (poet) to rise
asta *f* staff; rod; arm (*e.g., of scale*); lance; leg (*of compass*); stroke (*in handwriting*); shaft (*of arrow*); auction; (naut) boom; (naut) mast; (elec) trolley pole; **a mezz'asta** half-mast; **vendere all'asta** to auction, auction off
astante *mf* bystander || *m* physician on duty (*in a hospital*)
astanterìa *f* receiving ward
astato *m* (chem) astatine
astè·mio -mia *adj* abstemious, temperate || *mf* teetotaler
astenére §271 *ref* to abstain
astensióne *f* abstension
astenuto *m* person who abstains from voting; abstention (*vote withheld*)
astèrgere §164 (*pp* **astèrso**) *tr* to wipe
asterì·sco *m* (**-schi**) asterisk
asticciòla *f* penholder; rib (*of umbrella*); temple (*of eyeglasses*)
àstice *m* (*Hommarus vulgaris*) lobster
asticèlla *f* (sports) bar
astinènte *adj* abstinent
astinènza *f* abstinence
à·stio *m* (**-sti**) grudge, rancor
astió·so -sa [s] *adj* full of malice, spiteful
astóre *m* goshawk
stràgalo *m* astragalus, anklebone
astrakàn *m* Persian lamb
astrarre §273 *tr* to abstract || *intr*—**astrarre da** to leave aside, overlook
astrat·to -ta *adj* abstract || *m* abstract
astrazióne *f* abstraction
astringènte *adj* & *m* astringent
-astro -astra *suf* *adj* -ish, e.g., **verdastro**

greenish || *suf* *mf* -aster, e.g., **poetastro** poetaster
astro *m* star, heavenly body; (bot) aster; (fig) star
astrologìa *f* astrology
astrològi·co -ca *adj* (**-ci -che**) astrological
astròlo·go *m* (**-gi** or **-ghi**) astrologer
astronàu·ta *mf* (**-ti -te**) astronaut
astronàuti·co -ca *adj* (**-ci -che**) astronautic(al) || *f* astronautics
astronautizzare [ddzz] *intr* (ESSERE) to be an astronaut
astronave *f* spaceship, spacecraft
astronomìa *f* astronomy
astrònomo *m* astronomer
astronòmi·co -ca *adj* (**-ci -che**) astronomic(al)
astruserìa *f* abstruseness
astrusi·tà *f* (**-tà**) abstruseness
astru·so -sa *adj* abstruse
astùc·cio *m* (**-ci**) case, box
astu·to -ta *adj* astute, crafty
astùzia *f* astuteness, craftiness
àta·vo -va *mf* ancestor
ateismo *m* atheism
atei·sta *mf* (**-sti -ste**) atheist
Atène *f* Athens
atenèo *m* athenaeum; university
ateniése [s] *adj* & *mf* Athenian
àte·o -a *adj* atheistic || *mf* atheist
atlante *m* atlas || **Atlante** *m* Atlas
atlànti·co -ca *adj* (**-ci -che**) Atlantic || **Atlantico** *m* Atlantic
atlè·ta *mf* (**-ti -te**) athlete
atletéssa *f* female athlete
atlèti·co -ca *adj* (**-ci -che**) *adj* athletic || *f* athletics; **atletica leggera** track and field
atmosfèra *f* atmosphere
atmosfèri·co -ca *adj* (**-ci -che**) atmospheric
atòllo *m* atoll
atòmi·co -ca *adj* (**-ci -che**) atomic; (coll) stunning
atomizzare [ddzz] *tr* to atomize
atomizzatóre [ddzz] *m* atomizer
àtomo *m* atom
atòni·co -ca *adj* (**-ci -che**) (pathol) weak
àto·no -na *adj* (gram) atonic
atout *m* (atouts) trump
à·trio *m* (**-tri**) entrance hall, lobby
atróce *adj* atrocious
atroci·tà *f* (**-tà**) atrocity
atrofìa *f* atrophy
atròfi·co -ca *adj* (**-ci -che**) atrophied
atrofizzare [ddzz] *tr* & *ref* to atrophy
attaccabottó·ni *mf* (**-ni**) bore, pest, buttonholer
attaccabri·ghe *mf* (**-ghe**) (coll) quarrelsome person, scrapper
attaccaménto *m* attachment, affection
attaccapan·ni *m* (**-ni**) coathanger
attaccare §197 *tr* to attach; to bind, unite; to sew on; to stick; to hitch (*a horse*); to hang; to attack; to strike up (*a conversation*); to begin; to communicate (*a disease*); **attaccare un bottone a** (fig) to buttonhole || *intr* to stick; to gain a foothold, take root; to begin || *ref* to stick; to

cling; to spread (*said of a disease*); (fig) to become attached

attaccatìc·cio -cia *adj* (**-ci -ce**) sticky

attacchino *m* billposter

attac·co *m* (**-chi**) attachment; onslaught; fastening; seizure (*e.g., of epilepsy*); spell (*e.g., of coughing*); (elec) plug; (rad) jack; (sports) forward line; **attacco cardiaco** heart attack

attagliare §280 *ref*—**attagliarsi a** to fit, become

attanagliare §280 *tr* to grip; to seize; to hold (*e.g., with tongs*)

attardare *ref* to tarry, delay

attecchire §176 *intr* to take root; to take hold

atteggiaménto *m* attitude

atteggiare §290 (**attéggio**) *tr* to compose (*e.g., one's face*); to place ‖ *ref* to pose; to strike an attitude

attempa·to -ta *adj* elderly

attendaménto *m* camping; jamboree (*of Boy Scouts*)

attendare (**attèndo**) *ref* to encamp; to pitch one's tent

attendènte *m* (mil) orderly

attèndere §270 *tr* to await; (archaic) to keep; **attèndere l'ora propizia** to bide one's time ‖ *intr*—**attèndere a** to attend to

attendìbile *adj* reliable

attendismo *m* wait-and-see attitude

attendi·sta (**-sti -ste**) *adj* wait-and-see ‖ *mf* fence-sitter

attenére §271 *tr* (poet) to keep (*a promise*) ‖ *intr*—**attenére** (with *dat*) to concern, e.g., **ciò non gli attiene** this does not concern him ‖ *ref*—**attenersi a** to conform to

attentare (**attènto**) *intr*—**attentare a** to attempt (*s.o.'s life*) ‖ *ref* to make an attempt, dare

attentato *m* attempt

attenta·tóre -trice *mf* would-be murderer; attacker

attèn·ti *m* (**-ti**) attention ‖ *interj* (mil) attention!

attèn·to -ta *adj* attentive; careful

attenuare (**attènuo**) *tr* to extenuate, play down; to attenuate; to mitigate

attenzióne *f* attention; **fare attenzione** to take care; **prestare attenzione** to pay attention

atterràg·gio *m* (**-gi**) landing; **atterraggio di fortuna** emergency landing; **atterraggio senza carrello** crash-landing

atterraménto *m* landing; pinning, pin (*in wrestling*); (boxing) knocking down; **atterramento frenato** (aer) arrested landing

atterrare (**attèrro**) *tr* to fell; to knock down; to pin (*in wrestling*); (fig) to humiliate ‖ *intr* to land; **atterrare scassando** or **atterrare senza carrello** to crash-land

atterrire §176 *tr* to frighten, terrify ‖ *ref* to become frightened

atté·so -sa [s] *adj* awaited, expected; **atteso che** considering that ‖ *f* waiting; expectation; **in attesa (di)** waiting (for)

attestare (**attèsto**) *tr* to certify, attest; to prove; to join; (mil) to deploy ‖ *ref* (mil) to take a stand

attestato *m* certificate

attestazióne *f* testimony; affidavit; attestation, proof

àtti·co -ca (**-ci -che**) *adj & mf* Attic ‖ *m* attic

attì·guo -gua *adj* adjacent, contiguous

attillare *tr & ref* to preen

attilla·to -ta *adj* tight, close-fitting; tidy, all dressed up

àttimo *m* moment, split second; **di attimo in attimo** any moment

attinènte *adj* related, pertinent

attinènza *f* relation; **attinenze** appurtenances; annexes

attìngere §126 *tr* to draw (*water*); to get; (poet) to attain (*e.g., glory*)

attingi·tóio *m* (**-tói**) ladle

attitùdine *f* aptitude; attitude

attirare *tr* to draw, attract

attivare *tr* to activate; to expedite

attivazióne *f* activation; reassessment

attivi·tà *f* (**-tà**) activity; **attività** *fpl* assets

attì·vo -va *adj* active; profit-making ‖ *m* assets

attizzare *tr* to stir, poke (*a fire*); (fig) to stir up

attizza·tóio *m* (**-tói**) poker

at·to -ta *adj* apt, fit ‖ *m* act, action; gesture; (law) instrument; **all'atto pratico** in reality; **atti** proceedings (*of a learned society*); **atti notarili** legal proceedings; **atto di nascita** birth certificate; **fare atto di presenza** to put in a brief formal appearance; **atto di vendita** bill of sale; **nell'atto** o **sull'atto** in the act

attòni·to -ta *adj* astonished

attorcigliare §280 *tr* to twist ‖ *ref* to wind; to coil up

attóre *m* actor; (law) plaintiff; **attore giovane** (theat) juvenile; **primo attore** (theat) lead

attorniare §287 (**attórnio**) *tr* to surround; (fig) to dupe

attórno *adv* around; **andare attorno a** walk around; **attorno a** around, near; **darsi d'attorno** to busy oneself; **levarsi qlcu d'attorno** to get rid of s.o.

attortigliare §280 *tr* to twist ‖ *ref* to wind; to coil up

attraccare §197 *tr & intr* to moor, dock

attrac·co *m* (**-chi**) mooring, docking

attraènte *adj* attractive

attrarre §273 *tr* to attract, draw

attrattì·vo -va *adj* attractive; alluring ‖ *f* attraction, charm

attraversaménto *m* crossing; **attraversamento pedonale** pedestrian crossing

attraversare (**attravèrso**) *tr* to cross; to go through; to thwart; **attraversare il passo a** to stand in the way of

attravèrso *adv* across; crosswise; **andare attraverso** to go down the wrong way (*said of food or drink*); (fig) to go wrong; **attraverso a** through, across ‖ *prep* through, across

attrazióne *f* attraction

attrezzare (**attrèzzo**) *tr* to outfit, equip

attrezzatura *f* outfit; gear, equipment; **attrezzatura di una nave** rigging; **attrezzature** facilities

attrezzi·sta (**-sti -ste**) *mf* gymnast ‖ *m* toolmaker; (theat) property man

attrézzo *m* tool, utensil; **attrezzi** gymnastic equipment

attribuire §176 *tr* to award; to attribute; **attribuire qlco a qlcu** to credit s.o. with s.th ‖ *ref* to ascribe to oneself, claim for oneself

attributo *m* attribute

attribuzióne *f* attribution

attrice *f* actress; (law) plaintiff; **prima attrice** (theat) lead

attristare *tr* (poet) to sadden ‖ *ref* to become sad

attri·to -ta *adj* worn, worn-out ‖ *m* attrition; disagreement

attruppare *tr* to band, group ‖ *ref* to mill about, throng

attuàbile *adj* feasible

attuale *adj* present; present-day, current

attuali·tà *f* (**-tà**) timeliness; reality; **attualità** *fpl* current events; **di viva attualità** newsworthy; timely; in the news

attualizzare [ddzz] *tr* to bring up to date ‖ *ref* to become a reality

attuare (**àttuo**) *tr* to carry out, make come true ‖ *ref* to come true

attuà·rio -ria (**-ri -rie**) *adj* (hist) transport (*e.g., ship*) ‖ *m* actuary

attuazióne *f* realization

attutire §176 *tr* to mitigate; to deaden (*a sound, a blow*) ‖ *ref* to diminish (*said of a sound*)

audace *adj* audacious

audàcia *f* audacity

audiofrequènza *f* audio frequency

audiovisi·vo -va *adj* audio-visual

auditi·vo -va *adj* var of **uditivo**

auditóre *m* var of **uditore**

auditò·rio *m* (**-ri**) auditorium

audizióne *f* program; audition; (law) hearing

àuge *f* acme; **essere in auge** to enjoy a great reputation; to be in vogue; to be on top of the world

augurale *adj* well-wishing; salutatory

augurare (**àuguro**) *tr* to wish; to bid (*good day*) ‖ *intr* to augur ‖ *ref* to hope; to expect

àugure *m* augur

augù·rio *m* (**-ri**) wish; augury, omen

augustè·o -a *adj* Augustan

augu·sto -sta *adj* august, venerable

àula *f* hall; classroom; (poet) chamber (*of a palace*)

àuli·co -ca *adj* (**-ci -che**) courtly; noble, elevated

aumentare (**auménto**) *tr* to augment, increase ‖ *intr* (ESSERE) to increase, rise

auménto *m* increase

àura *f* (poet) breeze; (poet) breath

àure·o -a *adj* golden, gold

aurèola *f* halo

auricolare *adj* ear; first-hand ‖ *m* (telp) receiver; (rad) earphone

auròra *f* dawn; (fig) aurora

ausiliare *adj* auxiliary ‖ *m* collaborator, helper

ausilià·rio -ria (**-ri -rie**) *adj* auxiliary; (mil) supply ‖ *m* helper; (mil) reserve officer ‖ *f* female member of the armed forces

ausì·lio *m* (**-li**) (poet) help

auspicare §197 (**àuspico**) *tr* to wish, augur

àuspice *m* sponsor; (hist) augur

auspì·cio *m* (**-ci**) sponsorship; (hist, poet) augury, omen; **sotto gli auspici di** under the auspices of

austeri·tà *f* (**-tà**) austerity

austè·ro -ra *adj* austere

australe *adj* austral, southern

Austràlia, l' *f* Australia

australia·no -na *adj & mf* Australian

Austria, l' *f* Austria

austrì·aco -ca *adj & mf* (**-ci -che**) Austrian

autarchìa *f* autarky; autonomy (*of an administration*)

autàrchi·co -ca *adj* (**-ci -che**) autonomous, independent

autènti·ca *f* (**-che**) authentication of a signature or a document

autenticare §197 (**autèntico**) *tr* to authenticate

autentici·tà *f* (**-tà**) authenticity

autènti·co -ca (**-ci -che**) *adj* authentic, genuine ‖ *f* see **autentica**

autière *m* (mil) driver

auti·sta *mf* (**-sti -ste**) (aut) driver

au·to *f* (**-to**) auto

autoabbronzante [dz] *adj* tanning ‖ *m* tanning lotion

autoaffondaménto *m* scuttling

autoambulanza *f* ambulance

autobiografìa *f* autobiography

autobiogràfi·co -ca *adj* (**-ci -che**) autobiographical

autoblinda·to -ta *adj* armored

autoblin·do *m* (**-do**) armored car

autobótte *f* tank truck

àuto·bus *m* (**-bus**) bus

autocarro *m* truck, motor truck

autocèntro *m* (mil) motor pool

autocistèrna *f* tank truck

autocivétta *f* unmarked police car

autocolónna *f* row of cars

autocombustióne *f* spontaneous combustion

autocontròllo *m* self-control

autocorrièra *f* intercity bus, highway bus

autocrazìa *f* autocracy

autocrìti·ca *f* (**-che**) self-criticism

autòcto·no -na *adj* autochthonous, independent

autodecisióne *m* free will

autodeterminazióne *f* self-determination

autodidat·ta *mf* (**-ti -te**) self-taught person

autodidàtti·co -ca *adj* (**-ci -che**) self-instructional

autodifésa [s] *f* self-defense

autodisciplìna *f* self-discipline

autòdromo *m* automobile race track

autoemotè·ca *f* (**-che**) bloodmobile

autofilettante *adj* self-threading

autofurgóne *m* van; **autofurgone cellu-**

lare police van; **autofurgone funebre** hearse

autogiro m autogyro

autogovèrno m self-government

autògra·fo -fa adj autographic(al) ‖ m autograph

auto·grù f (-grù) tow truck

autolesioni·sta mf (-sti -ste) person who wounds himself to avoid the draft or collect insurance

autoletti·ga f (-ghe) ambulance

autolibro m bookmobile

autolìnea f bus line

autò·ma m (-mi) automaton, robot

automàti·co -ca (-ci -che) adj automatic ‖ m snap

automatizzare [ddzz] tr to automate

automazióne f automation

automèzzo [ddzz] m motor vehicle

automòbile f automobile, car; **automobile da corsa** racing car; **automobile di serie** stock car; **automobile fuori serie** custom-made car

automobilismo m motoring

automobili·sta mf (-sti -ste) motorist

automobilìsti·co -ca adj (-ci -che) car, automobile

automo·tóre -trice adj self-propelled ‖ f (rr) automotive rail car

autonolég·gio m (-gi) car rental agency

autonomìa f autonomy; (aer, naut) cruising radius

autonomi·sta adj (-sti -ste) autonomous

autòno·mo -ma adj autonomous, independent

autoparchég·gio m (-gi) parking; parking lot

autopar·co m (-chi) parking; parking lot

autopiano m player piano

autopilò·ta m (-ti) (aer) automatic pilot

autopómpa f fire engine

autopsìa f autopsy

autorà·dio f (-dio) car radio

autóre m author; perpetrator; creator, maker

autoreattóre m ramjet engine

autorespiratóre m aqualung

autorévole adj authoritative

autoriméssa f garage

autori·tà f (-tà) authority

autorità·rio -ria adj (-ri -rie) authoritarian

autoritratto m self-portrait

autorizzare [ddzz] tr to authorize

autorizzazióne [ddzz] f authorization

autoscala f hook and ladder; ladder (of hook and ladder)

autoscuòla f driving school

autoservi·zio m (-zi) bus service, bus line; self-service

autosilo m parking garage

autostazióne f bus station

autostèllo m roadside motel

auto·stòp m (-stòp) hitchhiking; **fare l'autostop** to hitchhike

autostoppi·sta mf (-sti -ste) hitchhiker

autostrada f highway, turnpike

autosufficiènte adj self-sufficient

autote·làio m (-lài) (aut) frame

autotrasportare (**autotras.pòrto**) tr to truck

autotrasportatóre m trucker

autotreni·sta m (-sti) truck driver, teamster

autotrèno m tractor trailer

autoveìcolo m motor vehicle

autovettura f car, automobile

autrice f authoress

autunnale adj autumnal, fall

autunno m autumn, fall

avallare tr to endorse (a promissory note); to guarantee

avallo m endorsement (of a promissory note)

avambràc·cio m (-ci) forearm

avampósto m outpost

avancàrica f—**ad avancarica** muzzleloading

avanguàrdia f vanguard; avant-garde

avanguardismo m avant-garde

avanguardi·sta m (-sti) avant-gardist; (hist) member of Fascist youth organization

avannòtto m small fry (young freshwater fish)

avanti adj preceding ‖ m forward ‖ adv forward, ahead; **andare avanti** to proceed, to go ahead; **andare avanti negli anni** to be up in years; **avanti a** in front of; **avanti che** rather than; **avanti di** before; **essere avanti** to be advanced (in work or study); **in avanti** ahead ‖ prep—**avanti Cristo** before Christ; **avanti giorno** before daybreak ‖ interj come in!

avantièri adv day before yesterday

avantrèno m (aut) front-axle assembly; (mil) limber

avanzaménto m advancement

avanzare tr to advance; to overcome; to be creditor for, e.g., **avanza cento dollari da suo fratello** he is his brother's creditor for one hundred dollars; to save ‖ intr (mil) to advance ‖ intr (ESSERE) to advance; to stick out; to be abundant; to be left over, e.g., **avanzano due polpette** two meatballs are left over; **avanzare negli anni** to grow older ‖ ref to advance, come forward

avanza·to -ta adj advanced; progressive ‖ f (mil) advance

avanzo m remainder; **avanzi** remains

avarìa f damage, breakdown; (naut) average

avariare §287 tr to damage, spoil ‖ intr to spoil

avarìa·to -ta adj damaged, spoiled

avarizìa f avarice, greed

ava·ro -ra adj avaricious, stingy ‖ mf miser

avellana f filbert

avellano m filbert tree

avèllo m (poet) tomb

avéna f oats

avére m belongings, property; assets, credit; amount due ‖ §118 tr to have; to hold; to wear; to receive, get; to stand (a chance); to be, e.g., **avere . . . anni** to be . . . years old; **avere caldo** to be hot; to be warm; **avere fame** to be hungry; **avere freddo** to be cold; **avere fretta** to be in a hurry;

avere paura to be afraid; avere ragione to be right; avere sete to be thirsty; avere sonno to be sleepy; avere torto to be wrong; avere vergogna to be ashamed; avere voglia di to be anxious to; avere qlco da + inf to have s.th to + inf, e.g., ho molto lavoro da fare I have a lot of work to do; averla con to be angry at; non avere niente a che fare con to have nothing to do with ‖ impers—v'ha there is ‖ aux to have, e.g., ha letto il giornale he has read the newspaper; avere da + inf to have to + inf, e.g., avevo da lavorare I had to work; to be to + inf, e.g., ha da venire alle cinque he is to arrive at five o'clock

avià·rio -ria (-ri -rie) adj bird ‖ m aviary

avia·tóre -trice mf aviator ‖ f aviatrix

aviazióne f aviation

avicoltóre m bird raiser; poultry farmer

avidi·tà f (-tà) avidity, greediness

àvi·do -da adj avid, greedy

avière m airman

aviogètto m jet plane

aviolìnea f airline

aviopista f (aer) airstrip

avioriméssa f (aer) hangar

aviotraspor·ta·to -ta adj airborne

avi·to -ta adj ancestral

a·vo -va mf grandparent; ancestor ‖ m grandfather ‖ f grandmother

avocare §197 (àvoco) tr to demand (jurisdiction); to expropriate

avò·rio m (-ri) ivory

avul·so -sa adj (poet) torn, uprooted; (poet) separated

avvalére §278 ref—avvalersi di to avail oneself of

avvallaménto m sinking, settling

avvallare tr (poet) to lower (e.g., one's eyes) ‖ ref to sink; (lit) to humiliate oneself

avvalorare (avvalóro) tr to strengthen, confirm ‖ ref to gain strength

avvampare tr (poet) to inflame ‖ intr (ESSERE) to burn

avvantaggiare §290 tr to be profitable to; to benefit ‖ ref to profit; avvantaggiarsi su to overcome; to beat

avvedére §279 ref—avvedersi di to notice, become aware of

avvedutézza f discernment; shrewdness

avvedu·to -ta adj prudent; shrewd; fare qlcu avveduto di to inform s.o. of

avvelenaménto m poisoning

avvelenare (avveléno) tr to poison ‖ ref to take poison; to be poisoned

avveniménto m happening, event

avvenire adj invar future, to come ‖ m future; in avvenire in the future ‖ §282 intr (ESSERE) to happen, occur; avvenga quel che vuole come what may

avventare (avvènto) tr to hurl; to deliver (a blow); to venture (an opinion) ‖ ref to throw oneself

avventatézza f thoughtlessness, heedlessness

avventa·to -ta adj thoughtless, heedless; all'avventata heedlessly

avventì·zio -zia adj (-zi -zie) outside, exterior; temporary, occasional

avvènto m advent; elevation, rise

avven·tóre -tóra mf customer, consumer

avventura f adventure

avventuriè·ro -ra adj adventurous ‖ m adventurer ‖ f adventuress

avventuró·so -sa [s] adj adventurous, adventuresome

avverare (avvéro) tr to make true ‖ ref to come true

avvèr·bio m (-bi) adverb

avversà·rio -ria (-ri -rie) adj opposing, contrary ‖ mf adversary, opponent

avversióne f aversion

avversi·tà f (-tà) adversity

avvèr·so -sa adj adverse; (obs) opposite ‖ avverso prep (law) against

avvertènza f prudence, caution; advice; avvertenze instructions, directions

avvertiménto m caution, warning; advice

avvertire (avvèrto) tr to caution, warn; to notice

avvezzare (avvézzo) tr to accustom; to inure; to train; avvezzar male to spoil ‖ ref to get accustomed

avvéz·zo -za adj accustomed

avviaménto m starting; introduction; trade school; good shape (of a business); (mach) starting; (typ) adjustment (of printing press)

avviare §119 tr to start, set in motion; to introduce; to initiate; to begin ‖ ref to set out

avvia·to -ta adj going, thriving (concern)

avvicendaménto m alteration, rotation (of crops)

avvicendare (avvicèndo) tr & ref to alternate

avvicinaménto m approach; rapprochement

avvicinare tr to bring near or closer; to approach, go or come near to ‖ ref to approach, come near; avvicinarsi a to come closer, approach

avviliménto m discouragement, dejection

avvilire §176 tr to degrade; to deject ‖ ref to become dejected, become discouraged

avviluppare tr to entangle, snarl; to wrap

avvinazza·to -ta adj & mf drunk

avvincènte adj fascinating

avvìncere §285 tr to fascinate, charm; (poet) to twine

avvinghiare §287 tr to claw; to clasp, clutch ‖ ref to grip one another

avvì·o m (-i) beginning

avviságlia f skirmish; prime avvisaglie onset; first signs

avvisare tr to inform, advise; (archaic) to observe, notice

avvisa·tóre -trice mf announcer, messenger ‖ m alarm; (theat) callboy; avvisatore acustico (aut) horn; avvisatore d'incendio fire alarm

avviso m advise; notice, poster; opinion; avviso di chiamata alle armi notice of induction; **sull'avviso** on one's guard

avvistare *tr* to sight

avvitaménto *m* (aer) tailspin

avvitare *tr* to screw; to fasten ‖ *ref* (aer) to go into a tailspin

avviticchiare §287 *tr* to entwine ‖ *ref* to cling

avvivare *tr* to revive; to stir up

avvizzire §176 *tr* & *intr* (ESSERE) to wither

avvocatéssa *f* woman lawyer

avvocato *m* lawyer, attorney

avvocatura *f* law, legal profession

avvòlgere §289 *tr* to wind; to wrap up; to spread over, surround ‖ *ref* to wind around; to wrap oneself up

avvolgiménto *m* winding; wrapping; (elec) coil; (mil) envelopment

avvol·tólo *m* (-tóli) vulture

avvoltolare (avvòltolo) *tr* to roll up ‖ *ref* to roll around, wallow

aziènda [dz] *f* business, firm

azionare (azióno) *tr* to start; to drive, propel

aziona·rio -ria *adj* (-ri -rie) (com) stock

azióne *f* action, act; (law) suit; (com) share (*of stock*); **azione legale** prosecution; **azione privilegiata** preferred stock

azioni·sta *mf* (-sti -ste) stockholder, shareholder

azòto [dz] *m* nitrogen

azoturo [dz] *m* nitride

aztè·co -ca *adj* & *mf* (-chi -che) Aztec

azzannare *tr* to seize with the fangs

azzardare [ddzz] *tr* to risk; to advance ‖ *ref* to dare

azzarda·to -ta [ddzz] *adj* daring

azzardo [ddzz] *m* chance, hazard

azzardó·so -sa [ddzz] [s] *adj* hazardous, risky

azzeccagarbu·gli *m* (-gli) shyster

azzeccare §197 (azzécco) *tr* to hit; to deliver; to pass off (*counterfeit money*); **azzeccarla** (coll) to hit the mark

azzimare [ddzz] (àzzimo) *tr* & *ref* to spruce up

àzzi·mo -ma [ddzz] *adj* unleavened (*bread*)

azzittare & **azzittire** §176 *tr* to hush ‖ *ref* to keep quiet

azzoppare (azzòppo) *tr* to cripple ‖ *ref* to become lame or crippled

Azzòrre [ddzz] *fpl* Azores

azzuffare *ref* to come to blows; to scuffle

azzur·ro -ra [ddzz] *adj* blue ‖ *m* blue; Italian athlete (*in international competition*)

azzurrógno·lo -la [ddzz] *adj* bluish

B

B, b [bi] *m* & *f* second letter of the Italian alphabet

ba·bàu *m* (-bàu) bogey, bugbear

babbè·o -a *adj* foolish ‖ *mf* fool

babbo *m* (coll) daddy, father

babbù·cia *f* (-ce) babouche; bedroom slipper

babbuino *m* baboon

babèle *f* babel ‖ **Babele** *f* Babel

babilònia *f* confusion ‖ **Babilònia** *f* Babylon

babórdo *m* (naut) port

bacare §197 *ref* to become worm-eaten

baca·to -ta *adj* worm-eaten; rotten

bac·ca *f* (-che) berry

bacca·là *m* (-là) dried codfish; (coll) skinny person; (coll) lummox

baccalaureato *m* baccalaureate, bachelor's degree

baccanale *m* bacchanal

baccano *m* noise, hubbub; **fare baccano** to carry on

baccante *f* bacchant

baccellière *m* (hist) bachelor

baccèllo *m* pod

baccellóne *m* simpleton, fool

bacchétta *f* rod, wand, baton; **bacchetta magica** magic wand; **bacchette del tamburo** drumsticks

bacchétto *m* stick; handle (*of a whip*)

bacchettó·ne -na *mf* bigot

bàcchi·co -ca *adj* (-ci -che) Bacchic

Bacco *m* Baccus

bachè·ca *f* (-che) showcase

bachelite *f* bakelite

bacheròzzo *m* worm; earthworm; (coll) cockroach

bachicoltura *f* silkworm raising

baciama·no *m* (-ni) kissing of the hand

baciapi·le *mf* (-le) bigot

baciare §128 *tr* to kiss; **baciare la polvere** to bite the dust ‖ *ref* to kiss one another

bacia·to -ta *adj* kissed; rhymed (*couplet*)

bacile *m* basin

bacillo *m* bacillus

bacinèlla *f* small basin; (phot) tray

bacino *m* basin; reservoir; cove; (anat) pelvis; **bacino carbonifero** coal field; **bacino di carenaggio** drydock; **bacino fluviale** river basin

bà·cio *m* (-ci) kiss; **a bacio** with a northern exposure

baciucchiare §287 *tr* to keep on kissing ‖ *ref* to pet

ba·co *m* (-chi) worm; **baco da seta** silkworm

bacuc·co -ca *adj* (-chi -che)—**vecchio bacucco** dotard

bada *f*—**tenere a bada** to stave off; to delay

badare *tr* to tend, take care of ‖ *intr* to attend; to take care; to pay attention; **badare a** to mind; to watch over; to attend to; **badare alla salute** to take care of one's health

badéssa f abbess

badìa f abbey

badilata f shovelful

badile m shovel

baffo m whiskers; whisker; **baffi** mustache; whiskers; **baffo di gatto** (rad) cat's whiskers; **leccarsi i baffi** to lick one's chops; **sotto i baffi** up one's sleeve

baga·gliàio m (-gliài) (rr) baggage car; (rr) baggage room; (aut) baggage rack

bagaglièra f baggage room

bagaglière m baggage master

bagà·glio m (-gli) baggage, luggage; (of knowledge) fund

bagagli·sta m (-sti) porter (in a hotel)

bagarinàg·gio m (-gi) profiteering; (theat) scalping

bagarino m profiteer; scalper

bagà·scia f (-sce) harlot, prostitute

bagattèlla f trifle, bauble

baggiano m nitwit, simpleton

bà·glio m (-gli) (naut) beam

baglióre m shine, gleam

bagnante mf bather, swimmer; vacationer at the seashore

bagnare tr to bathe; to wet; to soak; to water, sprinkle; to moisten; (fig) to celebrate || ref to bathe; to wet one another

bagnaròla f (coll) bathtub

bagnasciu·ga f (-ghe) (naut) waterline

bagnino m lifeguard

bagno m bath; bathroom; bathtub; **bagno di luce** diathermy; **bagno di schiuma** bubble bath; **bagno di sole** sun bath; **bagno di vapore** steam bath; **bagno turco** Turkish bath; **essere in un bagno di sudore** to be soaked with perspiration; **fare il bagno** to take a bath

bagnomaria m (bagnimarìa) double boiler; bain-marie; **a bagnomaria** in a double boiler

bagórdo m carousal, revelry; **far bagordi** to carouse, revel

bàio bàia (bài bàie) adj & m bay || f bay; jest; trifle; **dare la baia a** to make fun of, tease

baionétta f bayonet; **baionetta in canna** with fixed bayonet

bàita f mountain hut

balaustrata f balustrade

balaùstro m baluster

balbettaménto m stammering

balbettare (balbétto) tr to stammer; to speak poorly (a foreign language) || intr to stammer; to babble (said of a baby)

balbettì·o m (-i) babble (of a baby); stammering

balbùzie f stammering

balbuziènte adj stammering || mf stammerer

Balcani, i the Balkans

balcàni·co -ca adj (-ci -che) Balkan

balconata f balcony; (theat) upper gallery

balcóne m balcony

baldacchino m canopy, baldachin

baldanza f boldness; aplomb, assurance

baldanzó·so -sa [s] adj bold; self-assured

bal·do -da adj bold; self-assured

baldòria f carousal, revelry; **fare baldoria** to carouse, revel

baldrac·ca f (-che) harlot, prostitute

baléna f whale

balenare (baléno) intr to stagger || intr (ESSERE) to flash, e.g., **gli balena un pensiero** a thought flashes through his mind || impers (ESSERE)—**balena,** it is lightning

balenièra f whaler, whaleboat

baléno m flash; flash of lightning; **in un baleno** in a flash

balenòttera f rorqual

balèstra f crossbow; (aut) spring, leaf spring

balestrière m crossbowman

bàlia f wet nurse; **balia asciutta** dry nurse; **prendere a balia** to wet-nurse

balìa f power; **in balia di** at the mercy of

balìsti·co -ca (-ci -che) adj ballistic || f ballistics

balla f bale; (vulg) lie

ballàbile adj dancing || m dance tune

ballare tr to dance || intr to dance; to shake; to be loose; to wobble (said, e.g., of a chair)

ballata f ballad; (mus) ballade

balla·tóio m (-tói) gallery; perch (in birdcage)

ballerì·no -na adj dancing || m ballet dancer; dancer; dancing partner || f dancing girl; ballerina; chorus girl; ballet slipper; (orn) wagtail

ballétto m ballet; chorus

ballo m dance; chorus; ball; stake; **ballo di San Vito** Saint Vitus's dance; **ballo in maschera** masked ball; **in ballo** at stake; in question; **tirare in ballo** to drag in

ballonzolare (ballónzolo) intr to hop around

ballottàg·gio m (-gi) runoff

ballottare (ballòtto) tr to ballot (e.g., a candidate)

balneare adj bathing; water, watering

baloccare §197 (balòcco) tr to amuse with toys || ref to play; to trifle, to fool around

balòc·co m (-chi) toy; hobby

balordàggine f silliness

balór·do -da adj silly, foolish

balsàmi·co -ca adj (-ci -che) balmy; antiseptic

balsamina f balsam

bàlsamo m balm, balsam

bàlti·co -ca adj (-ci -che) Baltic

baluardo m bastion, bulwark

baluginare (balùgino) intr (ESSERE) to flicker; to flash (through one's mind)

balza f crag, cliff; flounce (on dress); fringe (on curtains, bedspreads, etc.)

balza·no -na adj white-footed (horse); odd, funny || f flounce; fringe; white mark (on horse's foot)

balzare tr to throw (a rider; said of a horse) || intr (ESSERE) to jump, leap;

to bounce; **balzare in mente a** to suddenly dawn on

balzellare (balzèllo) *intr* to hop

balzèllo *m* hop; tribute; tax; toll; **stare a balzello** to lie in wait

balzellóni *adv*—**a balzelloni** leaping, skipping

balzo *m* leap; bounce; **pigliare la palla al balzo** to take time by the forelock

bambàgia *f* cotton wool

bambinàggine *f* childishness

bambinàia *f* nursemaid; **bambinaia ad ore** baby sitter

bambiné·sco -sca *adj* (**-schi -sche**) childish

bambi·no -na *adj* childish ‖ *mf* child

bambòc·cio *m* (**-ci**) fat baby; doll; rag doll

bàmbola *f* doll; **bambola di pezza** rag-doll

bam·bù *m* (**-bù**) bamboo

banale *adj* banal, commonplace

banali·tà *f* (**-tà**) banality, commonplaceness, triviality

banana *f* banana; hair with curls shaped as rolls

bananièra *f* banana boat

banano *m* banana plant

ban·ca *f* (**-che**) bank; embankment

bancàbile *adj* negotiable

bancarèlla *f* cart, pushcart; stall

bancà·rio -ria (**-ri -rie**) *adj* bank, banking ‖ *m* bank clerk

bancarótta *f* bankruptcy; **fare bancarotta** to go bankrupt

banchettare (banchétto) *intr* to feast, banquet

banchétto *m* banquet

banchière *m* banker

banchina *f* garden bench; bicycle path; sidewalk; shoulder (*of highway*); dock, pier; (**rr**) platform; (**mil**) banquette

ban·co *m* (**-chi**) bench; seat; bank; witness stand; school (*of fish*); **banco di coralli** coral reef; **banco di ghiaccio** ice pack; **banco di nebbia** fog bank; **banco di prova** (**mach**) bench; **banco di sabbia** sandbar; **banco d'ostriche** oyster bed; **banco lotto** lottery office

bancogiro *m* (**com**) transfer of funds

bancóne *m* counter; bench

banconòta *f* banknote

banda *f* band; **andare alla banda** (**naut**) to list; **da ogni banda** from every side; **mettere da banda** to put aside

bandèlla *f* hinge (*of door or window*); hinged leaf (*of table*)

banderuòla *f* banderole; weather vane

bandièra *f* flag; banner; **battere la bandiera** (*e.g.,* **italiana**) to fly the (*e.g* *Italian*) flag; **mutar bandiera** to change sides

bandierare (bandièro) *tr* (**aer**) to feather

bandire §176 *tr* to announce (*e.g., a competitive examination*); to banish

bandìsti·co -ca *adj* (**-ci -che**) (**mus**) band

bandi·to -ta *adj* announced; open (*house*) ‖ *m* bandit ‖ *f* preserve (*for hunting or fishing*)

bandi·tóre -trice *mf* town crier; auctioneer; barker

bando *m* announcement; banishment; **bandi matrimoniali** (**eccl**) banns; **mandare in bando** to exile, banish

bandolièra *f* bandoleer; **a bandoliera** slung across the shoulders

bàndolo *m* end of a skein; **perdere il bandolo** to lose the thread (*e.g., of a story*)

bara *f* bier, coffin

barac·ca *f* (**-che**) hut, cabin; (**fig**) household; **fare baracca** to carouse around

baracca·to -ta *adj* lodged in a hut or a cabin; slum (*e.g., section*) ‖ *m* dweller in a hut or a cabin; slum dweller

baraccóne *m* big circus tent

baraónda *f* hubbub; mess

barare *intr* to cheat (*e.g., at cards*)

bàratro *m* abyss, chasm

barattare *tr* to barter; **barattare le carte in mano a uno** to distort someone's words; **barattar parole** to chat, talk ‖ *intr* to barter

barattière *m* grafter

baratto *m* barter

baràttolo *m* can, canister, jar

barba *f* beard; whiskers; barb, vane (*of feather*); (**naut**) line; **barba a punta** imperial, goatee; **barba (e.g. la barba (a)** to shave; **farla in barba a qlcu** to act in spite of s.o.; to dupe s.o.; **mettere barbe** to take root; **radersi la barba** to shave

barbabiètola *f* beet; sugar beet

barbafòrte *m* horseradish

barbagian·ni *m* (**-ni**) owl; (**fig**) jackass

barbà·glio *m* (**-gli**) glitter, dazzle

barbaré·sco -sca (**-schi -sche**) *adj* Barbary ‖ *m* inhabitant of the Barbary States

barbàri·co -ca *adj* (**-ci -che**) barbaric

barbà·rie *f* (**-rie**) barbarism, barbarity

barbarismo *m* barbarism

bàrba·ro -ra *adj* barbarous, barbaric ‖ *m* barbarian

barbazzale *m* curb (*of bit*)

Barberia, la Barbary States

barbétta *f* fetlock (*tuft of hair on horse*); goatee; (**mil**) barbette; (**naut**) painter

barbière *m* barber

barbierìa *f* barbershop

barbì·glio *m* (**-gli**) barb (*of arrow*)

barbi·no -na *adj* shoddy; botched; stingy

bàr·bio *m* (**-bi**) (**ichth**) barbel

barbiturato *m* barbiturate

barbitùri·co -ca (**-ci -che**) *adj* barbituric ‖ *m* barbiturate

barbo *m* var of **barbio**

barbò·gio -gia *adj* (**-gi -gie**) senile

barbóne *m* long beard, thick beard; poodle; (**coll**) bum, hobo

barbó·so -sa [s] *adj* boring

barbugliare §280 *tr* to stutter (*e.g., a word*) ‖ *intr* to stutter; to bubble, gurgle

barbu·to -ta *adj* bearded

bar·ca *f* (**-che**) boat; heap; (**fig**) family

affairs; **barca a motore** motorboat; **barca da pesca** fishing boat; **barca a remi** rowboat

barcàc·cia *f* (**-ce**) (theat) stage box

barcaiòlo *m* boatman

barcamenare (**barcaméno**) *ref* to manage, get along

barcarizzo *m* (naut) gangway

barcaròla *f* barcarole

barcata *f* boatful

barchéssa *f* tool shed

barchétta *f* small boat; (naut) log chip

barcollare (**barcòllo**) *intr* to totter, stagger

barcollóni *adv* staggering, tottering

barcóne *m* barge

bardare *tr* to harness || *ref* to get dressed

bardatura *f* harnessing; harness

bardo *m* bard

bardòsso *m* —**a bardosso** (archaic) bareback

barèlla *f* stretcher

barellare (**barèllo**) *tr* to carry on a stretcher || *intr* to totter, stagger

barenatura *f* (mach) boring

bargèllo *m* (hist) chief of police; (hist) police headquarters

bargi·glio *m* (**-gli**) wattle

baricèntro *m* center of gravity; (fig) essence, gist

barile *m* barrel, cask

barilòtto *m* keg

bàrio *m* barium

bari·sta *mf* (**-sti -ste**) bartender, barkeeper || *m* barman || *f* barmaid

baritonale *adj* baritone

barito·no -na *adj* barytone || *m* baritone

barlume *m* glimmer, gleam

baro *m* cheat, cardsharp

baròc·co -ca *adj & m* (**-chi -che**) baroque

baròmetro *m* barometer

baróne *m* baron

baronéssa *f* baroness

barra *f* bar; link; rod; sandbar; **andare alla barra** to plead a case; **barra del timone** (naut) tiller; **barra di torsione** (aut) torsion bar; **barra spaziatrice** space bar (*of typewriter*)

barrare *tr* to cross, draw lines across (*a check*)

barrétta *f* bar (*e.g., of chocolate*)

barricare §197 (**bàrrico**) *tr* to barricade || *ref* to barricade oneself

barricata *f* barricade

barrièra *f* barrier; bar; **barriera corallina** barrier reef

barrire §176 *intr* to trumpet (*said of elephant*)

barrito *m* trumpeting, cry of an elephant

barroc·ciàio *m* (**-ciài**) cart driver

barròc·cio *m* (**-ci**) cart

baruffa *f* fight, quarrel

barzellétta [dz] *f* joke

basale *adj* basal

basalto *m* basalt

basaménto *m* foundation (*of building*); baseboard; base (*of column*)

basare *tr* to base || *ref*—**basarsi su** to be based on; to rest on

ba·sco -sca *adj & mf* (**-schi -sche**) Basque

basculla *f* balance, scale

base *f* base, foundation; (fig) basis; **a base di** composed of, made of; **base navale** naval base, naval station; **in base a** according to

ba:étta *f* sideburns

bàsi·co -ca *adj* (**-ci -che**) (chem) basic

basilare *adj* basic, fundamental

Basilèa *f* Basel

basìli·ca *f* (**-che**) basilica

basìli·co *m* (**-ci**) basil

basilissa *f* (fig) queen bee

bàsolo *m* large paving stone

bassacórte *f* barnyard

bassézza *f* baseness

bas·so -sa *adj* low; shallow; late (*e.g., date*); (fig) base, vile; **basso di statura** short || *m* bottom; hovel (*in Naples*); (mus) basso || **basso** *adv* low; down; **a basso, da basso** or **in basso** downstairs

bassofóndo *m* (**bassifóndi**) (naut) shallows, shallow water; **bassifondi** underworld, slums

bassopiano *m* lowland

bassorilièvo *m* bas-relief

bassòt·to -ta *adj* stocky || *m* basset hound

bassotuba *m* bass horn

bassura *f* (fig) baseness

basta *f* hem; basting (*with long stitches*) || *interj* enough!

bastante *adj* sufficient, adequate; comfortable (*income*)

bastar·do -da *adj* bastard; irregular || *m* bastard

bastare *intr* to suffice, be enough; **basta!** enough!; **basta che** + *subj* as long as + *ind*; **bastare a sé stesso** to be self-sufficient; **non basta che** + *subj* not only + *ind*

bastévole *adj* sufficient

bastiménto *m* ship; shipload

bastióne *m* bastion; (fig) defense, rampart

basto *m* packsaddle; (fig) burden

bastonare (**bastóno**) *tr* to club, cudgel; **bastonare di santa ragione** to give a good thrashing to

bastonata *f* clubbing, cudgeling; **darsi bastonate da orbi** to thrash one another soundly

bastoncino *m* small stick; roll; (anat) rod

bastóne *m* stick, cane; pole; club; baton; staff; French bread; **bastone a leva** crowbar; **bastone animato** sword cane; **bastone da golf** club; **bastone da montagna** alpenstock; **bastone da passeggio** walking stick; **bastone da sci** ski pole; **bastoni** suit in Neapolitan cards corresponding to clubs; **mettere il bastone tra le ruote** to throw a monkey wrench into the machinery

batàc·chio *m* (**-chi**) clapper (*of bell*); cudgel

batata *f* sweet potato

batisfèra *f* bathysphere
batista *f* batiste, cambric
batòsta *f* blow; (fig) blow
bàtrace or **batrace** *m* batrachian
battà·glia *f* (**-glie**) battle; campaign
battagliare §280 *intr* to fight
battagliè·ro -ra *adj* fighting, warlike
battà·glio *m* (**-gli**) clapper (*of bell*); knocker
battaglióne *m* battalion
battèllo *m* boat; **battello di salvataggio** lifeboat; **battello pneumatico** rubber raft
battènte *m* leaf (*e.g., of door*); knocker; tapper (*of alarm clock*)
bàttere *m*—**in un batter d'occhio** in the twinkling of an eye ‖ *tr* to beat; to hit; to strike; to strike (*the hour; said of a clock*); to click (*teeth, heels*); to clap (*hands*); to stamp (*one's foot*); to mint (*coins*); to fly (*a flag*); to beat (*time*); to scour (*the countryside*); to flap (*the wings*); (sports) to bat; (sports) to kick (*a penalty*); **battere a macchina** to type; **battere il naso in** to chance upon; **battere la fiacca** to goof off; **battere la grancassa per** to ballyhoo; **battere la strada** to be a streetwalker; **senza batter ciglio** without batting an eye ‖ *intr* (ESSERE) to be beaten down (*said, e.g., of rain*); to beat (*said of the heart*); to chatter (*said of teeth*); to knock (*at the door*); **battere in ritirata** to beat a retreat; **battere in testa** to knock (auto) to knock
batteria *f* battery; set (*of utensils*); (sports) heat
batterici·da (**-di -de**) *adj* bactericidal ‖ *m* bactericide
battèri·co -ca *adj* (**-ci -che**) bacterial
battè·rio *m* (**-ri**) bacterium
batteriologìa *f* bacteriology
batteriòlo·go -ga *mf* (**-gi -ghe**) bacteriologist
batteri·sta *mf* (**-sti -ste**) jazz drummer
battesimale *adj* baptismal
battésimo *m* baptism; **tenere a battesimo** to christen
battezzare (**battézzo**) [*ddzz*] *tr* to christen ‖ *ref* to receive baptism; to assume the name of
battibaléno *m*—**in un battibaleno** in the twinkling of an eye
battibéc·co *m* (**-chi**) squabble
batticuòre *m* palpitation; (fig) trepidation
battilò·ro *m* (**-ro**) goldsmith; silversmith
battimano *m* applause
battimuro *m*—**giocare a battimuro** to pitch pennies (against a wall)
battipalo *m* pile driver
battipan·ni *m* (**-ni**) clothes beater
battira·me *m* (**-me**) coppersmith
battiscó·pa *m* (**-pa**) washboard, baseboard
batti·sta *adj & mf* (**-sti -ste**) Baptist
battistèro *m* baptistry
battistra·da *m* (**-da**) outrider; (sports) leader; (aut) tread
battitappéto *m* carpet sweeper
bàttito *m* beating; palpitation; ticking;

wink; pitter-patter (*of rain*)
batti·tóio *m* (**-tói**) leaf (*e.g., of door*); casement; cotton beater
battitóre *m* (hunt) beater; (baseball) batter
battitrice *f* threshing machine
battitura *f* thrashing, whipping; threshing (*e.g., of wheat*)
battu·to -ta *adj* beaten; hammered ‖ *m* pavement ‖ *f* beat; stroke, keystroke; meter (*in poetry*); witticism, quip; (hunt) battue; (mus) bar; (tennis) service; (theat) line; (theat) cue; **battuta d'aspetto** (mus) pause; **dare la battuta** to give the cue
batùffolo *m* wad; (fig) bundle
baule *m* trunk; **baule armadio** wardrobe trunk; **fare i bauli** to be on one's way; **fare il baule** to pack one's trunk
baulétto *m* small trunk; handbag; jewel case
bava *f* slobber; foam, froth; burr (*on metal edge*); **avere la bava alla bocca** to be frothing at the mouth; **bava di vento** breath of air, soft breeze
bavaglino *m* bib
bavà·glio *m* (**-gli**) gag
bavarése [*s*] *adj & mf* Bavarian ‖ *f* Bavarian cream; chocolate cream
bàvero *m* collar
bavièra *f* beaver (*of helmet*) ‖ **la Baviera** Bavaria
bavó·so -sa [*s*] *adj* slobbering, slobbery
bazza [*ddzz*] *f* protruding chin; windfall
bazzana [*ddzz*] *f* sheepskin
bazzècola [*ddzz*] *f* trifle, bauble
bazzicare §197 [*bàzzico*] *tr* to frequent
bazzòt·to -ta [*ddzz*] *adj* soft-boiled; uncertain (*weather*)
beare (**bèo**) *tr* to delight ‖ *ref* to be delighted, be enraptured
beatificare §197 [*beatìfico*] *tr* to beatify
beatitùdine *f* beatitude, bliss
bea·to -ta *adj* blissful, happy; blessed ‖ *mf* blessed
be·bè *m* (**-bè**) baby
beccàc·cia *f* (**-ce**) woodcock
beccaccino *m* snipe
beccafi·co *m* (**-chi**) figpecker, beccafico
bec·càio *m* (**-cài**) butcher
beccamòr·ti *m* (**-ti**) gravedigger
beccare §197 (**bécco**) *tr* to peck; to pick; (coll) to catch ‖ *ref* to peck one another; to quarrel
beccata *f* peck
beccheggiare §290 (**becchéggio**) *intr* (naut) to pitch
becchég·gio *m* (**-gi**) (naut) pitching
beccherìa *f* butcher shop
becchìme *m* food for poultry
becchino *m* gravedigger
béc·co *m* (**-chi**) beak, bill; tip, point; nozzle (*e.g., of teapot*); billy goat; (vulg) cuckold; **bagnarsi il becco** (joc) to wet one's whistle; **mettere il becco in** (coll; joc) to stick one's nose into; **non avere il becco di un quattrino** to not have a red cent
beccùc·cio *m* (**-ci**) small bill; lip, spout
beccuzzare *tr* to peck ‖ *ref* to bill (*said of doves*)

béce·ro -ra *adj* (coll) boorish ‖ *m* (coll) boor

beduì·no -na *adj & m* Bedouin

befana *f* (coll) Epiphany; old hag

bèffa *f* jest, mockery; **farsi beffa di** to make fun of

beffar·do -da *adj* mocking

beffare (**bèffo**) *tr* to mock, deride ‖ *ref* —**beffarsi di** to make fun of

beffeggiare §290 (**beffèggio**) *tr* to scoff at, deride

bè·ga *f* (**-ghe**) quarrel; trouble

beghìna *f* Beguine; bigoted woman

begònia *f* begonia

bèl *adj* apocopated form of **bello**, used only before masculine singular nouns beginning with a consonant except impure **s, z, gn, ps,** and **x,** e.g., **bel ragazzo**

belare (**bèlo**) *tr* to croon ‖ *intr* to bleat, baa; to moan

belato *m* bleat, baa

bèl·ga *adj & mf* (**-gi -ghe**) Belgian

Bèlgio, il Belgium

bèll' *adj* apocopated form of **bello**, used only before singular nouns of both genders beginning with a vowel, e.g., **bell'amico; bell'epoca**

bèlla *adj fem* of **bello** ‖ *f* belle; girl-friend; final draft; (sports) final game; (sports) rubber match; **alla bell'e meglio** the best one could; **bella di notte** (bot) four-o'clock

belladònna *f* belladonna

bellétto *m* rouge, makeup

bellézza *f* beauty; **che bellezza!** how lovely!; **la bellezza di** as much as

bellici·sta *adj* (**-sti -ste**) bellicose

bèlli·co -ca *adj* (**-ci -che**) war, warlike

bellicó·so -sa [s] *adj* bellicose

belligerante *adj & m* belligerent

belligeranza *f* belligerence

bellimbusto *m* fop, dandy, beau

bèl·lo -la (declined like **quello** §7) *adj* beautiful; lovely; handsome; good-looking; pleasing; fine; quite a, e.g., **una bella cifra** quite a sum; fair; pretty; **bell'e fatto** ready-made; taken care of; **farla bella** to start trouble; (coll) to do it, e.g., **l'hai fatta bella** you've done it; **farsi bello** to dress up; **farsi bello di** to appropriate ‖ *m* beauty; beautiful; climax; fine weather; beau; **il bello è** the funny thing is; **sul più bello** just then; **sul più bello che** just when ‖ *f* see **bella** ‖ *bello adv*—**bel bello** slowly

bellospirito *m* (**begli spiriti**) wit, bel-esprit

bellui·no -na *adj* wild, fierce

bellumóre *m* (**begli umori**) jolly fellow

bel·tà *f* (**-tà**) beauty (*woman*); (lit) beauty

bélva *f* wild beast

belvedére *m* (**rr**) observation (*car*) ‖ *m* belvedere; (naut) topgallant

Belzebù *m* Beelzebub

bemòlle *m* (mus) flat

benama·to -ta *adj* beloved

benarriva·to -ta *adj* welcome

benché *conj* although, albeit

bènda *f* bandage; band; blindfold; **benda gessata** cast, surgical dressing

bendàg·gio *m* (**-gi**) bandage

bendare (**bèndo**) *tr* to bandage; **bendare gli occhi a** to blindfold

bendispó·sto -sta *adj* well-disposed

bène *adj* well; well-born ‖ *m* goal, aim; good; love; sake; **bene dell'anima** profound affection; **beni** (econ) assets, goods; **beni di consumo** consumer goods; **beni immobili** real estate; **beni mobili** personal property, chattels; **beni rifugio** hedge (*e.g., against inflation*); **è un bene** it is a blessing; **fare del bene** to do good; **per il Suo bene** for your sake; **voler bene a** to love, like; **to care for** ‖ *adv* well; all right; properly; **ben bene** quite carefully; **star bene** to be well; **va bene** O.K., all right

benedetti·no -na *adj & m* Benedictine

benedét·to -ta *adj* blessed; holy

benedire §195 *tr* to bless; to praise; **andare a farsi benedire** (coll) to go to wrack and ruin; **mandare a farsi benedire** (coll) to get rid of, dump

benedizióne *f* benediction; boon

beneduca·to -ta *adj* well-behaved

benefattóre *m* benefactor

benefattrice *f* benefactress

beneficare §197 (**benèfico**) *tr* to benefit, help

beneficènza *f* welfare; charity, benefi-cence

beneficiale *adj* beneficial

beneficiare §128 *intr* to benefit

beneficià·rio -ria *adj & mf* (**-ri -rie**) beneficiary

beneficiata *f* benefit performance; streak of good luck; streak of bad luck

benefì·cio *m* (**-ci**) benefice; profit; favor; benefit

benèfi·co -ca *adj* (**-ci -che**) beneficial; beneficent

benemerènte *adj* deserving, well-deserving

benemèri·to -ta *adj* worthy, deserving ‖ *m*—**benemerito della patria** national hero ‖ *f*—**la Benemerita** the Carabinieri

beneplàcito *m* approval, consent; **a beneplacito di** at the pleasure of

benèssere *m* well-being, comfort; prosperity

benestante *adj* well-to-do ‖ *mf* well-to-do person

benestare *m* approval; prosperity; **dare il benestare a** to approve

benevolènte *adj* benevolent

benevolènza *f* benevolence

benèvo·lo -la *adj* well-meaning; benevolent

benfat·to -ta *adj* well-done; well-favored; shapely

benga·la *m* (**-li & -la**) fireworks

benga·lì *adj & m* (**-lì**) Bengalese

beniami·no -na *mf* favorite child; favorite

benigni·tà *f* (**-tà**) benignity; graciousness; mildness (*of climate*)

beni‧gno **-gna** *adj* benign; gracious; mild (*climate*)

benintenziona‧to **-ta** *adj* well-meaning

benintéso [s] *adv* of course, naturally

bènna *f* bucket, scoop (*e.g., of dredge*)

benna‧to **-ta** *adj* (lit) well-born

benpensante *m* sensible person; conformist

benportante *adj* well-preserved

benservito *m* testimonial, recommendation; **dare il benservito a** to dismiss, fire

bensì *adv* indeed ‖ *conj* but

bentorna‧to **-ta** *adj & m* welcome ‖ *interj* welcome back!

benvenu‧to **-ta** *adj & m* welcome; **dare il benvenuto a** to welcome

benvi‧sto **-sta** *adj* well-thought-of

benvolére *tr*—**farsi benvolere da qlcu** to enter the good graces of s.o.; **prendere a benvolere qlcu** to be well-disposed toward s.o.

benvolu‧to **-ta** *adj* liked, loved

benzina *f* gasoline, gas; benzine; **far benzina** (coll) to get gas

benzi‧nàio *m* **(-nài)** gasoline dealer; gas-station attendant

benzòlo *m* benzene

beóne *m* drunkard, toper

bequadro *m* (mus) natural

berciare §197 **(bèrcio)** *intr* (coll) to yell

bére *m* drink, drinking ‖ §120 *tr* to drink; (fig) to swallow; **bere come una spugna** to drink like a fish; **darla a bere** to make believe

bergamòt‧to **-ta** *adj* bergamot ‖ *m* bergamot orange ‖ *f* bergamot pear

berillio *m* beryllium

berlina *f* pillory; berlin, coach; (aut) sedan; **mettere alla berlina** to pillory

berlinése [s] *adj* Berlin ‖ *mf* Berliner

Berlino *m* Berlin

bermuda *mpl* Bermuda shorts ‖ **le Bermude** Bermuda

bernòccolo *m* bump, protuberance; (fig) knack

berrétta *f* biretta

berrétto *m* cap; **berretto a sonagli** cap and bells; **berretto da notte** nightcap; **berretto gogliardico** student cap

bersagliare §280 *tr* to harass, pursue; to bomb, bombard

bersà‧glio *m* **(-gli)** target; butt (*of a joke*); target (*of criticism*)

bèrta *f* pile driver; **dar la berta a** to ridicule

bertùc‧cia *f* **(-ce)** Barbary ape; **fare la bertuccia di** to ape

bestémmia *f* blasphemy

bestemmiare §287 **(bestémmio)** *tr* to blaspheme, curse

bestemmia‧tóre **-trice** *adj* blasphemous ‖ *mf* blasphemer

béstia *f* beast, animal; **andare in bestia** to fly into a rage; **bestia da soma** beast of burden; **bestia nera** pet aversion, bête noire; **bestie grosse** cattle

bestiale *adj* beastly, bestial

bestiali‧tà *f* **(-tà)** beastliness; blunder

bestiame *m* livestock; **bestiame da cortile** barnyard animals; **bestiame grosso** cattle

bestino *m* gamy odor; stench of perspiration

bestiòla *f* tiny animal; pet

bestsèl‧ler *m* **(-ler)** best seller

Betlèmme *f* Bethlehem

betonièra *f* cement mixer

béttola *f* tavern

bettolière *m* tavern keeper

bettònica *f* betony; **conosciuto più della bettonica** very well-known

betulla *f* birch

bèuta *f* flask

bevanda *f* drink, beverage

beveràg‧gio *m* **(-gi)** beverage, potion

bevìbile *adj* drinkable

bevi‧tóre **-trice** *mf* drinker

bevuta *f* drink, drinking

bezzicare §197 **(bézzico)** *tr* to peck; to vex ‖ *ref* to fight one another

biacca *f* white lead

biada *f* feed; **biade** harvest

bianca‧stro **-stra** *adj* whitish

biancheria *f* laundry; linen; underwear; **biancheria da letto** bed linen; **biancheria da tavola** table linen; **biancheria di bucato** freshly laundered clothes; **biancheria intima** underclothes

bianchézza *f* whiteness

bianchire §176 *tr* to blanch; to bleach; to polish

bian‧co **-ca** **(-chi -che)** *adj* white; clean; **bianco come un cencio lavato** as white as a ghost ‖ *m* white; **dare il bianco a** to whitewash; **in bianco** blank (*paper*); **mangiare in bianco** to eat a bland or non-spicy diet; **ricamare in bianco** to embroider

biancóre *m* whiteness

biancospino *m* hawthorn

biascicare §197 **(biàscico)** *tr* to chew with difficulty; to peck at (*one's food*); to mumble

biasimare **(biàsimo)** *tr* to blame

biasimévole *adj* blamable, censurable

biàsimo *m* blame, censure; **dare una nota di biasimo a** to censure

biauricolare *adj* binaural

Bìbbia *f* Bible

bibe‧rón *m* **(-rón)** nursing bottle

bibita *f* soft drink

bìbli‧co **-ca** *adj* **(-ci -che)** Biblical

biblio‧bus *m* **(-bus)** bookmobile

bibliòfi‧lo **-la** *mf* bibliophile

bibliografìa *f* bibliography

bibliotè‧ca *f* **(-che)** library; bookshelf, stack; collection (*of books*); **biblioteca ambulante** walking encyclopedia

bibliotecà‧rio **-ria** *mf* **(-ri -rie)** librarian

bìbu‧lo **-la** *adj* absorbent (*e.g., paper*)

bì‧ca *f* **(-che)** pile of sheaves

bicarbonato *m* bicarbonate; **bicarbonato di soda** bicarbonate of soda, baking soda

bicchierata *f* glassful; wine party

bicchière *m* glass

bicchierino *m* small glass, liquor glass; **bicchierino da rosolio** whiskey glass, jigger

biciclétta *f* bicycle

bicilìndri‧co **-ca** *adj* **(-ci -che)** two-cylinder

bicìpite adj two-headed ‖ m biceps
bicòc·ca f (-che) castle built on a hill; shanty, hut
bicolóre adj two-color
bicòrno m two-cornered hat
bidèllo m school janitor, caretaker
bidènte m two-pronged pitchfork
bidimensionale adj two-dimensional
bidóne m can (for milk); drum (for gasoline or oil); jalopy; (slang) fraud
bidon·ville f (-ville) shantytown
biè·co -ca adj (-chi -che) awry; sullen; cross; fierce; **guardar bieco** to look askance (at)
bièlla f connecting rod
biennale adj biennial ‖ f biennial show
biènne adj biennial
bièn·nio m (-nl) biennium
biètola f Swiss chard
biétta f wedge, chock; (naut) batten
bifase adj diphase
biffa f (surv) rod
biffare tr to cross out; (surv) to level
bifi·do -da adj bifurcate
bifocale adj bifocal
bifól·co m (-chi) ox driver; clodhopper, boor
biforcaménto m bifurcation
biforcare §197 (bifórco) tr to bifurcate
biforcazióne f bifurcation, branching off; fork (of a road)
biforcu·to -ta adj forked; cloven (e.g., hoof)
bifrónte adj two-faced
bi·ga f (-ghe) chariot
bigamìa f bigamy
bìga·mo -ma adj bigamous ‖ mf bigamist
bighellonare (**bighellóno**) intr to idle, dawdle, dally
bighelló·ne -na mf idler, dawdler
bigino m (slang) pony (used to cheat)
bi·gio -gia adj (-gi -gie) gray, grayish; (fig) undecided
bigiotterìa f costume jewelry; costume jewelry store
bigliardo m billiards
bigliet·tàio m (-tài) ticket agent; (rr) conductor
biglietterìa f ticket office; (theat) box office
bigliétto m note; card; ticket; **biglietto d'abbonamento** commutation ticket; season ticket; **biglietto d'andata e ritorno** round-trip ticket; **biglietto di banca** banknote; **biglietto di lotteria** lottery ticket, chance; **biglietto d'invito** invitation; **biglietto di visita** calling card; business card; **biglietto di Stato** banknote; **mezzo biglietto** half fare
bigné m (bigné) puff, creampuff
bigodino m curler; roller
bigón·cia f (-ce) vat; bucket; **a bigonce** abundantly
bigón·cio m (-ci) vat; tub; (theat) ticket box (for stubs)
bigottismo m bigotry
bigòt·to -ta adj bigoted ‖ mf bigot
bilàn·cia f (-ce) balance, scale; **bilancia commerciale** balance of trade; **bilan-**

cia dei pagamenti balance of payments ‖ **Bilancia** f (astr) Libra
bilanciare §128 tr & ref to balance
bilancière m balance; balance wheel; rope-walker's balancing rod
bilàn·cio m (-ci) balance; **bilancio consuntivo** balance sheet; **bilancio preventivo** budget; **fare il bilancio** to balance; to strike a balance
bile f bile; **rodersi dalla bile** to burn with anger
bìlia f billiard ball; marble; (billiards) pocket
biliardino m pocket billiards; pinball machine
biliardo m billiards
biliare adj bile; gall (stone)
bili·co m (-chi) balance, equipoise; **in bilico** in balance; **tenere in bilico** to balance
bilingue adj bilingual
bilióne m billion; trillion (Brit)
bilió·so -sa [s] adj bilious
bim·bo -ba mf child
bimensile adj bimonthly
bimèstre m period of two months
bimotóre adj twin-engine ‖ m twin-engine plane
binà·rio -ria (-ri -rie) adj binary ‖ m (rr) track; **binario morto** (rr) siding; **uscire dai binari** (rr) to run off the track; (fig) to go astray
bina·to -ta adj binary; twin (e.g., guns)
binda f (aut) jack
binòcolo m binoculars; **binocolo da teatro** opera glasses
binò·mio -mia (-mi -mie) adj binomial ‖ m binomial; couple, pair
biòccolo m wad (of cotton); flake (of snow); flock (of wool)
biochimi·co -ca (-ci -che) adj biochemical ‖ m biochemist ‖ f biochemistry
biodegradàbile adj biodegradable
biofisica f biophysics
biografìa f biography
biogràfi·co -ca adj (-ci -che) biographic(al)
biògra·fo -fa mf biographer
biologìa f biology
biòlo·go m (-gi) biologist
biondeggiare §290 (biondéggio) intr to be or become blond; to ripen (said of grain)
bión·do -da adj blond, fair ‖ m blond; blondness ‖ f blonde
biopsìa f biopsy
biòssido m dioxide
bipartìti·co -ca adj (-ci -che) two-party, bipartisan
biparti·to -ta adj bipartite ‖ m two-party government
bìpede adj & m biped
bipènne f double-bitted ax
biplano m biplane
bipósto adj invar having seats for two ‖ m two-seater
birba f rascal, rogue
birbante m scoundrel, rascal; (joc) madcap, wild young fellow
birbanterìa f knavery; trick
birbonata f trick

birbó·ne -na *adj* wicked || *mf* rascal, rogue, scoundrel

bireattóre *m* twin jet

birichinata *f* prank

birichi·no -na *adj* prankish; spirited || *mf* rogue; urchin

birillo *m* pin; **birilli** ninepins; tenpins

Birmània, la Burma

birra *f* beer; **birra chiara** light beer; **birra scura** dark beer

bir·ràio *m* (**-rài**) brewer; beer distributor

birrerìa *f* brewery; tavern; beer saloon

bis *adj invar*—**treno bis** (rr) second section || *m* (**bis**) encore || *interj* encore!

bisàc·cia *f* (**-ce**) knapsack; saddlebag; bag (*of mendicant friar*)

Bisànzio *m* Byzantium

bisa·vo -va *mf* great-grandparent; ancestor || *m* great-grandfather || *f* great-grandmother

bisbèti·co -ca (**-ci -che**) *adj* shrewish; crotchety; cantankerous || (fig) shrew

bisbigliare §280 *tr* & *intr* to whisper

bisbì·glio *m* (**-gli**) whisper

bisbòccia *f*—**fare bisboccia** to revel

bisboccióne *m* reveler

bis·ca *f* (**-che**) gambling house

Biscàglia *f* Biscay, e.g., **Baia di Biscàglia** Bay of Biscay; **la Biscàglia** Biscay

biscaglina *f* (naut) Jacob's ladder

biscazzière *m* gaming-house operator; habitué of a gaming house; marker (*at billiards*)

bìschero *m* (mus) peg

bì·scia *f* (**-sce**) snake; **biscia d'acqua** water snake

biscottare (**biscòtto**) *tr* to toast

biscotterìa *f* cookie factory; cookie store

biscottièra *f* cookie jar

biscottifì·cio *m* (**-ci**) cookie factory

biscòt·to -ta *adj* twice-baked || *m* cookie

biscròma *f* (mus) demisemiquaver

bisdòsso *m*—**a bisdosso** bareback

bisecare [s] §197 (**bìseco**) *tr* to bisect

bisènso [s] *m* double meaning

bisessuale [s] *adj* bisexual

bisestile *adj* leap (*year*)

bisettimanale [s] *adj* biweekly

bisettrice [s] *f* bisector

bisezióne [s] *f* bisection

bisìlla·bo -ba [s] *adj* disyllabic

bislac·co -ca *adj* (**-chi -che**) queer, extravagant

bislun·go -ga *adj* (**-ghi -ghe**) oblong

bismuto *m* bismuth

bisnòn·no -na *mf* great-grandparent; **bisnonni** ancestors || *m* great-grandfather || *f* great-grandmother

bisógna *f* (lit) task, job

bisognare (**bisógna**) *intr* (with *dat*) to need, e.g., **gli bisognavano tre litri di benzina** he needed three liters of gasoline || *impers*—**bisogna** + *inf* it is necessary to, e.g., **bisogna partire** it is necessary to leave; **bisogna che** + *subj* must, to have to, e.g., **bisogna che me ne vada** I must go,

I have to go; **bisognando** if need be; **non bisogna** one should not; **più che non bisogna** more than necessary

bisognévole *adj* needy

bisógno *m* need; want, lack; **aver bisogno di** to need; **c'è bisogno di** there is need of; **se ci fosse bisogno** if need be

bisognó·so -sa *adj* needy || **i bisognosi** the needy

bisolfato [s] *m* bisulfate

bisolfito [s] *m* bisulfite

bisolfuro [s] *m* bisulfide

bisónte *m* bison

bistec·ca *f* (**-che**) beefsteak, steak; **bistecca al sangue** rare steak

bisticciare §128 *intr* & *ref* to quarrel, bicker

bistìc·cio *m* (**-ci**) quarrel, bickering; play on words, pun

bistrattare *tr* to mistreat

bistu·rì *m* (**-rì**) bistouri, surgical knife

bisul·co -ca [s] *adj* (**-chi -che**) cloven

bisun·to -ta *adj* greasy

bitagliènte *adj* double-edged

bitórzolo *m* wart (*on humans, plants, or animals*); pimple (*on human face*)

bitta *f* (naut) bollard

bitume *m* bitumen, asphalt

bituminó·so -sa [s] *adj* bituminous

bivaccare §197 *intr* to bivouac; to spend the night

bivac·co *m* (**-chi**) bivouac

bi·vio *m* (**-vi**) fork (*of road*); **essere al bivio** (fig) to be at the crossroads

bizanti·no -na [dz] *adj* Byzantine

bizza [ddzz] *f* tantrum; **fare le bizze** to go into a tantrum

bizzarrìa [ddzz] *f* extravagance, oddity

bizzar·ro -ra [ddzz] *adj* bizarre, odd; skittish (*e.g., horse*)

bizzèffe [ddzz] *adv*—**a bizzeffe** plenty, in abundance

bizzó·so -sa [ddzz] [s] *adj* irritable

blandire §176 *tr* to blandish, coax; to soothe, mitigate

blandìzie *fpl* blandishment

blan·do -da *adj* bland

blasfemare (**blasfèmo**) *tr* & *intr* to blaspheme

blasfè·mo -ma *adj* blasphemous

blasona·to -ta *adj* emblazoned

blasóne *m* coat of arms, blazon

blaterare (**blàtero**) *intr* to babble

blatta *f* water bug, cockroach

blenoraggìa *f* gonorrhea

blè·so -sa *adj* lisping

blindàg·gio *m* (**-gi**) armor

blindare *tr* to armor

bloccare §197 (**blòcco**) *tr* to block; to blockade; to stop; to jam; to close up; to freeze (*e.g., prices*); (sports) to block || *intr*—**bloccare su** to vote as a block for || *ref* to stop

blòc·co *m* (**-chi**) block; blockade; notebook, pad; freezing (*e.g., of wages*); **in blocco** in bulk

bloc-notes *m* (**-notes**) notebook

blu *adj invar* & *m* blue

blua·stro -stra *adj* bluish

bluffare *intr* to bluff

blusa *f* blouse; smock

bò·a *m* (-a) boa ‖ *f* buoy
boà·rio -ria *adj* (-ri -rie) cattle
boa·ro -ra *adj & m* stable boy
boato *m* roar; **boato sonico** sonic boom
bobina *f* spool (*of thread*); coil (*of wire*); reel (*of movie film*; *of magnetic tape*); roll (*of film*); cylinder, bobbin; (elec) coil; **bobina d'accensione** spark coil
bóc·ca *f* (-che) mouth; nozzle; muzzle (*of gun*); pit (*of the stomach*); opening; straits; pass; **a bocca aperta** agape; **bocca da fuoco** cannon; **di buona bocca** easily pleased; **in bocca al lupo!** good luck!; **per bocca** orally; **rimanere a bocca asciutta** to be foiled; to be left high and dry; **tieni la bocca chiusa!** shut up!
boccaccé·sco -sca *adj* (-schi -sche) written by or in the style of Boccaccio; bawdy, licentious
boccàc·cia *f* (-ce) ugly mouth; grimace; **fare le boccacce** to make faces
boccà·glio *m* (-gli) nozzle (*of hose or pipe*); mouthpiece (*of megaphone*)
boccale *adj* oral ‖ *m* jug, tankard
boccapòrto *m* hatch; port; mouth (*of oven or furnace*); **chiudere i boccaporti** to batten the hatches
boccascè·na *m* (-na) proscenium, front (*of stage*)
boccata *f* mouthful; **andare a prendere una boccata d'aria** to go out for a breath of fresh air
boccétta *f* small bottle, vial; small billiard ball
bocchéggio *m* gasping; moribund
boccheggiare §290 (bocchéggio) *intr* to gasp
bocchétta *f* nozzle (*of sprinkling can*); mouthpiece (*of wind instrument*); opening (*of drainage or ventilation system*); **bocchetta stradale** manhole
bocchino *m* cigarette holder; mouthpiece (*of cigarette or of musical instrument*)
bòc·cia *f* (-ce) decanter; ball (*for bowling*); **bocce** bowls
bocciare §128 (bòccio) *tr* to score (*at bowling*); to reject (*a proposal*); to flunk (*a student*)
bocciatura *f* failure
boccino *m* jack (*at bowls*)
bocciòlo *m* bud
bóccola *f* buckle; earring; (mach) bushing
bocconcino *m* morsel; (culin) stew
boccóne *m* mouthful; piece; morsel; **buttar giù un boccone amaro** to swallow a bitter pill; **levarsi il boccone di bocca** to take the bread out of one's mouth (to help someone); **mangiare un boccone** to have a bite ‖ **bocconi** *adv* flat on one's face
boè·mo -ma *adj & mf* Bohemian
boè·ro -ra *adj & m* Boer
bofonchiare §287 (bofónchio) *intr* to snort, grumble
bò·ia *m* (-ia) hangman, executioner
boiata *f* (vulg) infamy; (slang) trash
boicottàg·gio *m* (-gi) boycott
boicottare (boicòtto) *tr* to boycott

bòl·gia *f* (-ge) pit (*in hell*)
bólide *m* (astr) bolide, fireball; (aut) racer; (joc) lummox; **andare come un bolide** to go like a flash
bolina *f* (naut) bowline; **di bolina** (naut) close-hauled
bolivia·no -na *adj & mf* Bolivian
bólla *f* bubble; blister; ticket; **bolla di consegna** receipt; **bolla di spedizione** delivery ticket; **bolla di sapone** soap bubble; **bolla papale** papal bull
bollare (bóllo) *tr* to stamp; to brand
bolla·to -ta *adj* stamped; sealed
bollatura *f* stamp; brand; postage
bollènte *adj* boiling, scalding hot
bollétta *f* ticket; receipt; bill; **essere in bolletta** (coll) to be broke
bollettà·rio *m* (-ri) receipt book
bollettino *m* bulletin; receipt; **bollettino dei prezzi correnti** price list; **bollettino di versamento** (com) deposit ticket; **bollettino meteorologico** weather forecast
bollire (bóllo) *tr & intr* to boil
bolli·to -ta *adj* boiled ‖ *m* boiled beef
bollitura *f* boiling
bóllo *m* mark, cancellation; revenue stamp; postmark; seal; **bollo a freddo** seal (*embossed*); **bollo postale** cancellation, postmark
bollóre *m* boiling; sultriness; (fig) passion, excitement; **alzare il bollore** to begin to boil
bollió·so -sa [s] *adj* blistery
bolscevi·co -ca *adj & mf* (-chi -che) Bolshevik
bolscevismo *m* Bolshevism
ból·so -sa *adj* broken-winded (*horse*); asthmatic
bòma *f* (naut) boom
bómba *f* bomb; bubble gum; fireworks; (aer) double loop; (journ) scandal; **bomba a idrogeno** hydrogen bomb; **bomba a mano** hand grenade; **bomba antisommergibile** depth charge; **bomba a orologeria** time bomb; **bomba atomica** atom bomb; **bomba H** (acca) H bomb; **tornare a bomba** (fig) to get back to the point
bombàggio *m* swelling (*of a spoiled can of food*)
bombardaménto *m* bombing, bombardment
bombardare *tr* to bomb, bombard; to besiege (*with questions*)
bombardière *m* (aer) bomber; (mil) artilleryman
bombétta *f* derby (*hat*)
bómbola *f* bottle, cylinder; **bombola d'ossigeno** oxygen tank
bombonièra *f* candy box
bomprèsso *m* (naut) bowsprit
bonàc·cia *f* (-ce) calm, calm sea; (fig) normalcy; (com) stagnation
bonacció·ne -na *adj* good-hearted, good-natured
bonarie·tà *f* (-tà) kindheartedness, good nature
bonà·rio -ria *adj* (-ri -rie) kindhearted, good-natured
boncinèllo *m* hasp
bonìfi·ca *f* (-che) reclamation; re-

claimed land; improvement (e.g., of morals); clearing of mines; (metallurgy) hardening and tempering

bonificare §197 (**bonìfico**) tr to reclaim; to discount, make a reduction of; to clear of mines

bonìfi·co m (-**ci**) discount

bonomìa f good nature; simple-heartedness

bon·tà f (-**tà**) goodness; kindness; **avere la bontà di** to be kind enough to; **bontà mia** (**sua**, etc.) through my (his, her, etc.) kindness; **per mia** (**sua**, etc.) **bontà** through my (his, her, etc.) efforts

bòra f northeast wind

borace m borax

borbogliare §280 (**borbóglio**) intr to gurgle; to rumble

borbòni·co -ca (-**ci** -**che**) adj Bourbon ‖ m Bourbonist

borbottare (**borbòtto**) tr to mutter ‖ intr to mutter; to gurgle; to rumble (said, e.g., of thunder)

borbottìo m (-**i**) mutter; gurgle; rumble

bòrchia f upholsterer's nail; boss, stud

bordare (**bórdo**) tr to border, hem

bordata f (naut) tack; (nav) broadside

bordatura f border, hem

bordeggiare §290 (**bordéggio**) intr (naut) to tack

bordèllo m brothel

borde·rò m (-**rò**) list; note; (theat) box office, receipts

bórdo m side (of ship); border, hem; edge, rim; (naut) tack; (naut) board; **a bordo** on board; **a bordo di** on board; on, in; **bordo d'entrata** (aer) leading edge; **bordo d'uscita** (aer) trailing edge; **d'alto bordo** (naut) big, sea-going; (fig) high-toned; **virare di bordo** (naut) to change course

bordóne m staff; bass stop (of organ); drone (of insect); **tener bordone a** (mus) to accompany; (fig) to hold the bag for

bordura f hem, edge; rim

boreale adj northern, boreal

borgata f hamlet, village

borghése [s] adj middle-class ‖ mf bourgeois, person of the middle class; civilian; **in borghese** in civilian clothes; in plainclothes

borghesìa f bourgeosie, middle class; **alta borghesia** upper middle class

bór·go m (-**ghi**) borough; small town; suburb

borgógna m Burgundy (wine) ‖ **la Borgogna** Burgundy

borgognóne m iceberg

borgomastro m burgomaster

bòria f haughtiness, vainglory

bòri·co -ca adj (-**ci** -**che**) boric

borió·so -sa [s] adj haughty, puffed-up; blustery

bòro m boron

borotal·co m (-**chi**) talcum powder

bórra f flock (for pillows); (fig) rubbish, filler

borràc·cia f (-**ce**) canteen (e.g., for carrying water)

bórro m gully

bórsa f bag; pouch; bourse, exchange; (sports) purse; **borsa da viaggio** traveling bag; **borsa dell'acqua** hot-water bag; **borsa della spesa** shopping bag; **borsa di ghiaccio** ice bag; **borsa di studio** scholarship; **borsa merci** commodity exchange; **borsa nera** black market; **borsa valori** stock exchange; **essere di borsa larga** to be generous; **o la borsa o la vita!** your money or your life!; **pagare di borsa propria** to pay out of one's own pocket

borsaiòlo m pickpocket

borsanéra f black market

borsaneri·sta mf (-**sti** -**ste**) black marketeer

borseggiare §290 (**borséggio**) tr to pick the pocket of; to rob

borseggia·tóre -trice mf pickpocket

borsellino m purse

borsétta f handbag, pocketbook

borsétto m man's purse

borsi·sta mf (-**sti** -**ste**) recipient of a scholarship; stockbroker

borsìsti·co -ca adj (-**ci** -**che**) stock-exchange

borsite f bursitis

boscàglia f thicket, underbrush

boscaiòlo m woodcutter

boscheréc·cio -cia adj (-**ci** -**ce**) wood, woodland; rustic; pastoral

boschétto m coppice, copse

boschi·vo -va adj wooded, wood

bò·sco m (-**schi**) woods, forest; **bosco ceduo** or **da taglio** tree farm

boscó·so -sa [s] adj wooded, woody

bòsforo m (lit) straits ‖ **Bosforo** m Bosphorus

bòsso m boxwood

bòssolo m box; cartridge case

botàni·co -ca adj (-**ci** -**che**) botanic(al) ‖ m botanist ‖ f botany

bòtola f trap door

bòtolo m small snarling dog

bòtta f hit; bump; rumble (e.g., of an explosion); thrust, lunging (in fencing); (fig) disaster; **botta dritta** (fencing) lunge; **botta e risposta** give-and-take; **botte da orbi** severe beating

bot·tàio m (-**tài**) cooper

bótte f barrel, cask, casket

botté·ga f (-**ghe**) store, shop; **chiudere bottega** to close up shop

botte·gàio -gàia (-**gài** -**gàie**) adj store, shop ‖ mf storekeeper, shopkeeper

botteghino m box office; lottery agency

bottìglia f bottle; **bottiglia Molotov** Molotov cocktail

bottiglierìa f wine store, liquor store

bottino m booty, spoil; capture; cesspool; sewage

bòtto m hit, bump; explosion; noise; toll (of bell); **di botto** all of a sudden

bottoncino m small button; cuff button; **bottoncino di rosa** rosebud

bottóne m button; stud; bud; **attaccare un bottone a** (fig) to buttonhole; **botton d'oro** (bot) buttercup; **bottone automatico** snap; **bottone della**

luce (elec) pushbutton; **bottoni gemelli** cuff links; **bottoni gustativi** taste buds

bottonièra *f* row of buttons; buttonhole; (elec) panel (*with buttons*)

bova·ro -ra *adj & m* var of **boaro**

bovile *m* ox stable

bovi·no -na *adj* cattle, cow; bovine || *m* bovine

box *m* (**box**) locker (*e.g., in a station*); box stall (*for a horse*); pit (*in auto racing*); garage (*on the ground floor of a split-level*); play pen

boxare (**bòxo**) *intr* to box

boxe *f* boxing

bòzza *f* stud, boss; bump (*caused by blow*); rough copy, draft; **bozze** (typ) galleys, galley proof

bozzèllo *m* (mach) block and tackle

bozzétto *m* sketch

bòzzolo *m* cocoon; lump (*of flour*)

bra·ca *f* (**-che**) safety belt; (naut) sling; **brache** (archaic) breeches; (joc) trousers

braccare §197 *tr* to stalk; to hunt out

braccétto—a braccetto arm in arm

bracciale *m* armlet, armband; arm rest

braccialétto *m* bracelet

bracciante *m* laborer

bracciata *f* armful; stroke (*in swimming*); **bracciata a rana** breaststroke; **bracciata sul dorso** backstroke

bràc·cio *m* (**-cia** *fpl*) arm (*of body*; unit of length (*about 60 centimeters*); **a braccia aperte** with open arms; **avere le braccia legate** to have one's hands tied; **braccia** laborers; **braccio destro** right-hand man; **braccio di ferro** Indian wrestling; **fare a braccio di ferro** to play at Indian wrestling; **sentirsi cascare le braccia** to lose courage || *m* (**-ci**) arm (*e.g., of sea, chair, lamp, etc.*); beam (*of balance*); **braccio diretto** cutoff (*of river*)

bracciòlo *m* arm; arm rest; banister

brac·co *m* (**-chi**) hound, beagle

bracconàg·gio *m* (**-gi**) poaching

bracconière *m* poacher

brace *f* embers; (coll) charcoal; **farsi di brace** to blush

brachétta *f* flap (*of trousers*); (bb) joint; **brachette** shorts

brachière *m* truss (*for hernia*)

bracière *m* brazier

braciòla *f* chop, cutlet

bra·do -da *adj* wild, untamed

bra·go -ghi (lit) mud, slime

brama *f* ardent desire; covetousness; longing

bramare *tr* to desire intensely; to covet; to long for

bramino *m* Brahmin

bramire §176 *intr* to roar; to bell (*said of a deer*)

bramito *m* bell (*of deer*)

bramosia [s] *f* covetousness; greed

bramó·so -sa [s] *adj* (lit) covetous, greedy

bran·ca *f* (**-che**) branch (*of tree*); flight (*of stairs*); **branche** (poet) clutches

brànchia *f* gill

brancicare §197 (**bràncico**) *tr* to finger, handle || *intr* to grope

bran·co *m* (**-chi**) flock, herd; (pej) crowd

brancolare (**bràncolo**) *intr* to grope

branda *f* cot

brandèllo *m* tatter, shred

brandire §176 *tr* to brandish

brando *m* (lit) sword

brano *m* shred, bit; excerpt; **cadere a brani** to fall apart; **fare a brani** to tear apart

brasare *tr* to braze (*to solder with brass*); (culin) to braise

brasile *m* brazil (*nut*) || **il Brasile** Brazil

brasilia·no -na *adj & mf* Brazilian

bravàc·cio *m* (**-ci**) braggart, swaggerer

bravare *tr* to challenge; to threaten || *intr* to brag

bravata *f* swagger, bluster; boast; stunt

bra·vo -va *adj* good, able; honest; goodhearted; brave; **alla brava** rapidly; **bravo ragazzo** good boy; **fare il bravo** to boast, be a braggart || *m* mercenary soldier; bravo, hired assassin || **bravo!** *interj* well done!, bravo!

bravura *f* ability; bravery; bravura

brèc·cia *f* (**-ce**) breach, gap; crushed stone

brefotrò·fio *m* (**-fi**) foundling hospital

Bretagna, la Britanny

bretèlla *f* suspenders; strap, shoulder strap

brètone *adj* Breton; Arthurian

brève *adj* brief, short; **in breve** in a nutshell; **per farla breve** in short || *m* (eccl) brief || *adv* (lit) in short

brevettare (**brevétto**) *tr* to patent

brevétto *m* patent; (aer) license; (obs) commission

brevià·rio *m* (**-ri**) compendium; handbook, vade mecum; (eccl) breviary

brevi·tà *f* (**-tà**) brevity

brézza [ddzz] *f* breeze

brezzare (**brézzo**) [ddzz] *tr* to winnow || *intr* to blow gently

bricchétta *f* briquet

bric·co *m* (**-chi**) kettle, pot

bricconata *f* rascality

briccó·ne -na *mf* rascal

bricconeria *f* rascality

briciola *f* crumb; **ridurre in briciole** to crumb, crumble

briciolo *m* bit, fragment; (fig) least bit; **andare in bricioli** to crumble; **mandare in bricioli** to crumble

bri·ga *f* (**-ghe**) worry, trouble; **attaccar briga** to pick a fight; **darsi la briga di** to worry about; **trovarsi in una briga** to be in trouble

brigadière *m* noncommissioned officer (*in carabinieri*); (hist) brigadier

brigantàg·gio *m* (**-gi**) brigandage

brigante *m* brigand

brigantino *m* (naut) brig, brigantine; **brigantino goletta** (naut) brigantine

brigare §209 *tr* to plot; to scheme to get || *intr* to plot, scheme

brigata *f* company; (mil) brigade

bri·glia *f* (**-glie**) bridle; harness (*for holding baby*); (naut) bobstay; **a briglia sciolta** at full speed; **tirare le briglie a** to bridle

brillante *adj* brilliant || *m* cut diamond

brillare *tr* to husk, hull (*rice*); to explode (*e.g.*, *a mine*) || *intr* to shine, sparkle; **far brillare** to explode, blow up

brilli·o *m* (**-i**) shine, sparkle

bril·lo -la *adj* tipsy

brina *f* frost

brinare *tr* to frost; to turn (*e.g.*, *hair*) gray || *impers* (ESSERE)—**è brinato** there was frost; **brina** there is frost

brinata *f* frost

brindare *intr* to toast; **brindare alla salute di** to toast

brindisi *m* (**-si**) toast; pledge; **fare un brindisi a** to toast

brì·o *m* (**-i**) sprightliness, liveliness, verve, spirit

briò·scia *f* (**-sce**) brioche

briò·so -sa [s] *adj* sprightly, lively

briscola *f* briscola (*game*); trump (*card*)

britànni·co -ca *adj* (**-ci -che**) British, Britannic

britan·no -na *adj* British || *mf* Briton

brivido *m* shake, shiver; thrill; **brivido di freddo** chill, shiver

brizzola·to -ta *adj* grizzled

bròc·ca *f* (**-che**) pitcher; pitcherful; shoot, bud; hobnail

broccatèllo *m* brocatel

broccato *m* brocade

bròc·co *m* (**-chi**) twig; shoot; center pin (*of shield or target*); (coll) nag; **dar nel brocco** to hit the bull's eye

bròccolo *m* (bot) broccoli; **bròccoli** broccoli (*as food*)

bròda *f* slop, thin or tasteless soup; mud

brodàglia *f* slop

brodétto *m* fish soup

bròdo *m* broth; **andar in brodo di giuggiole** (fig) to swoon with joy; **brodo in dadi** cube bouillon; **brodo ristretto** consommé

brodó·so -sa [s] *adj* thin, watery (*soup*)

brogliàc·cio *m* (**-ci**) (com) daybook, first draft; (naut) first draft of logbook

bròglio *m* (**-gli**) plot, intrigue; maneuver; **broglio elettorale** political maneuver

bròlo *m* (archaic) garden; (lit) garland

bromìdri·co -ca *adj* (**-ci -che**) hydrobromic

bròmo *m* bromine

bromuro *m* bromide

bronchite *f* bronchitis

brón·cio *m* (**-ci**) pout, pouting; **fare il broncio** to sulk; **tenere il broncio a** to harbor a grudge against

brón·co *m* (**-chi**) bronchial tube; thorny branch; ramification (*of antlers*)

brontolare (**bróntolo**) *tr* to grumble (*to express with a grumble*); to grumble at || *intr* to grumble, mutter; to rumble; to gurgle (*said of water*)

brontolì·o *m* (**-i**) grumble, mutter; rumble; gurgle

brontoló·ne -na *m* grumbler; curmudgeon

bronzare [dz] (**brónzo**) *tr* to bronze

brónze·o -a [dz] *adj* bronze; tanned

bronzina [dz] *f* little bell; (mach) bearing; (mach) bushing

brónzo [dz] *m* bronze

brossura *f* brochure; **in brossura** paperback

brucare §197 *tr* to browse, graze

bruciacchiare §287 *tr* to singe

bruciante *adj* burning

bruciapélo *m*—**a bruciapelo** point-blank

bruciare §128 *tr* to burn; to burn down; to singe; to scorch; to cauterize (*a wound*); (sports) to overcome with a burst of speed; **bruciare le tappe** to go straight ahead; to press on || *intr* (ESSERE) to burn; to smart, sting || *ref* to burn (*e.g.*, *one's fingers*); to get burnt; to blow (*one's brains*) out; to burn out (*said of an electric light or fuse*); **bruciarsi i vascelli alle spalle** to burn one's bridges behind one

bruciatìc·cio *m* (**-ci**) burnt material; **sapere di bruciaticcio** to taste burnt

brucia·to -ta *adj* burnt; burnt out || *f* burnt taste or smell || *f* roast chestnut

bruciatóre *m* burner; heater; **bruciatore a gas** gas burner; **bruciatore a nafta** oil burner

bruciatori·sta *m* (**-sti**) oil burner mechanic

bruciatura *f* burn

brucióre *m* burning; burn; inflammation; **bruciore agli occhi** eye inflammation; **bruciore di stomaco** heartburn

bru·co *m* (**-chi**) caterpillar; worm

brùffolo *m* (coll) small boil

brughièra *f* waste land; heath

brulicare §197 (**brùlico**) *intr* to crawl; to swarm (*e.g.*, *with bees*); to teem (*with people*)

brulichì·o *m* (**-i**) crawling; swarming; teeming

brul·lo -la *adj* barren, bare

bruma *f* shipworm; (lit) fog; (lit) winter

bruna·stro -stra *adj* brownish

brunire §176 *tr* to burnish

bru·no -na *adj* brown; dark (*bread; complexion*) || *m* brown; dark; brunet; **vestire a bruno** to dress in black || *f* brunette

bru·sca *f* (**-sche**) horse brush; **con le brusche** curtly

bruschézza *f* brusqueness

bruschino *m* scrub brush

bru·sco -sca (**-schi -sche**) *adj* sour; curt, gruff; sharp (*weather*); dangerous; sudden || *m* twig || *f* see **brusca**

brùscolo *m* speck, mote; **fare di un bruscolo una trave** to make a mountain out of a molehill

brusì·o *m* (**-i**) buzz, buzzing; (fig) whispering (*gossip*)

brutale *adj* brutal

brutali·tà *f* (**-tà**) brutality

brutalizzare [ddzz] *tr* to brutalize

bru·to -ta *adj* & *m* brute

brutta *f* rough copy

bruttare *tr* (lit) to soil

bruttézza *f* ugliness; (fig) lowliness

brut·to -ta *adj* ugly, homely; foul (*weather*); bad (*news*); **alle brutte** at the worst; **con le brutte** harshly; **farla brutta a** to play a mean trick on;

guardare brutto to look irritated; **vedersela brutta** to foresee trouble ‖ *m* worst; bad weather ‖ *f* see **brutta**

bruttura *f* ugliness

bùbbola *f* lie; trifle

bùbbolo *m* jingle bell (*on horse*)

bubbòni·co -ca *adj* (**-ci -che**) bubonic

bu·ca *f* (**-che**) hole; pit; hollow; **buca cieca** trap (*for hunting*); **buca del biliardo** pocket; **buca delle lettere** mailbox; **buca del suggeritore** prompter's box; **buca sepolcrale** grave

bucané·ve *m* (**-ve**) snowdrop

bucanière *m* buccaneer

bucare §197 *tr* to pierce; to prick; to puncture (*a tire*)

bucato *m* wash; laundry; **di bucato** freshly laundered; **fare il bucato in famiglia** (fig) to not air one's family affairs, to not wash one's dirty linen in public

bucatura *f* piercing; puncturing; puncture; **bucatura di una gomma** flat tire

bùc·cia *f* (**-ce**) rind, peel; skin (*of a person; of fruit and vegetables*); tender bark; **fare le bucce a** (coll) to thwart, frustrate

bucherellare (**bucherèllo**) *tr* to riddle

bu·co *m* (**-chi**) hole; **fare un buco nell'acqua** to fail miserably

bucòli·co -ca *adj* (**-ci -che**) bucolic, pastoral

Budda *m* Buddha

buddismo *m* Buddhism

buddi·sta *mf* (**-sti -ste**) Buddhist

budèl·lo *m* (**-la** *fpl*) bowel; **budella** bowels; guts ‖ *m* (**-li**) casing (*for salami*); pipe; blind alley

budino *m* pudding

bùe *m* (**buòi**) ox (*for draft*); steer (*for meat*); **bue muschiato** musk ox

bùfalo *m* buffalo

bufèra *f* storm; **bufera di neve** snowstorm; **bufera di pioggia** rainstorm; **bufera di vento** windstorm

buffa *f* cowl; gust of wind; (archaic) trick, jest

buffare *tr* to huff (*at checkers*) ‖ *intr* to joke; (archaic) to blow

buffetteria *f* (mil) accouterments

buffétto *m* tap, slight blow

buf·fo *adj* funny, comical ‖ *m* gust of wind; comic ‖ *f* see **buffa**

buffonata *f* buffoonery; antics

buffóne *m* buffoon, clown; (hist) jester; **buffone di corte** court jester

buffoneria *f* buffoonery

buffoné·sco -sca *adj* (**-schi -sche**) clownish

bugìa *f* lie; candlestick; **bugia ufficiosa** white lie

bugiar·do -da *adj* lying, false ‖ *mf* liar

bugigàttolo *m* cubbyhole

bugna *f* ashlar; (naut) clew

bugnato *m* ashlar; (archit) boss

bù·io -ia (*pl* **-i -ie**) *adj* dark ‖ *m* darkness; **buio pesto** pitch dark

bulbo *m* bulb

bùlga·ro -ra *adj & mf* Bulgarian ‖ *m* Russian leather

bulinare *tr* to engrave

bulino *m* burin

bullétta *f* tack

bullonare (**bullóno**) *tr* to bolt

bullóne *m* bolt

buon *adj* apocopated form of **buono,** used before masculine singular nouns except those beginning with impure s, z, gn, ps, and x

buon' *adj* apocopated form of **buona** used before feminine singular nouns beginning with a vowel, e.g., **buon'ora**

buonagràzia *f* (**buonegràzie**) courtesy, good manners; **con Sua buonagrazia** with your permission

buonamano *f* (**buonemani**) tip, gratuity

buonànima *f* departed; **la buonanima di** the late lamented

buonavò·glia *m* (**-glia**) intern (*in a hospital*); (coll) lazybones ‖ *f* good will

buoncostume *m* morals

buongu·stàio *m* (**-stài**) gourmet; connoisseur

buò·no -na *adj* good; kind; high (*society*); cheap (*price*); **alla buona** plainly; without ceremony; **buono a nulla** good-for-nothing; **con le buone** kindly, gently; **che Dio la mandi buona a** may God be kind with; **essere in buona con** to be on good terms with ‖ *m* good person; bond; ticket; **buono a nulla** ne'er-do-well; **buono del tesoro** government bond; **buono di consegna** delivery order; **buono premio** trading stamp

buonsènso *m* common sense

buontempó·ne -na *adj* jolly ‖ *m* playboy ‖ *f* fun-loving girl; playgirl

buonumóre *m* good humor, good cheer

buonuscìta *f* indemnity; bonus; severance pay

burattare *tr* to sift

buratti·nàio *m* (**-nài**) puppeteer; puppet maker

burattinata *f* clowning

burattino *m* puppet

buratto *m* sifter, sifting machine

burbanza *f* haughtiness, arrogance

burbanzó·so -sa [s] *adj* haughty, arrogant

bùrbe·ro -ra *adj* gruff, surly

bùr·chio *m* (**-chi**) (naut) lighter

burgun·do -do *adj & mf* Burgundian

burla *f* joke, jest; prank; **mettere in burla** to ridicule; **fuori di burla** joking aside

burlare *tr* to ridicule ‖ *intr* to be joking ‖ *ref*—**burlarsi di** to make fun of

burlé·sco -sca (**-schi -sche**) *adj* funny; mocking; burlesque; jocose ‖ *m* burlesque; mock-heroic

burlétta *f* joke, jest; **mettere in burletta** to ridicule

burló·ne *m/f* joker, jester

burócrate *m* bureaucrat

burocràti·co -ca *adj* (**-ci -che**) bureaucratic; clerical (*error*)

burocrazìa *f* bureaucracy; red tape

burra·sca *f* (**-sche**) storm

burrascó·so -sa [s] *adj* stormy

burrièra *f* butter dish

burrifi·cio *m* (**-ci**) butter factory, dairy

burro *m* butter

burróne *m* canyon, ravine

burró·so -sa [s] *adj* buttery

buscare §197 *tr* to get; to catch ‖ *intr* to be damaged ‖ *ref*—**buscarsi un malanno** to catch a cold

busécchia *f* casing (*for sausage*)

busillis *m*—**qui sta il busillis** here's the rub, that's the trouble

bussa *f* hit, blow; **venire alle busse** to come to blows

bussare *intr* to knock; **bussare a quattrini** (fig) to hit somebody for a loan

bussata *f* knock (*at the door*)

bussa-tòlo *m* (**-tòli**) knocker

bùssola *f* sedan chair; door; revolving door; swinging door; ballot box; (mach) bushing; (aer & naut) compass; **perdere la bussola** to lose one's bearings

bussolòtto *m* dice box

busta *f* envelope; briefcase; **busta a finestrella** window envelope; **busta primo giorno** first-day cover; **in busta a parte** under separate cover

bustapa·ga *f* (**-ga**) pay envelope

bustarèlla *f* bribery; kickback

bustina *f* powder, dose; small envelope; (mil) cap, fatigue cap

busto *m* chest, trunk; bust; corset

butirró·so -sa [s] *adj* buttery

buttafuò·ri *m* (**-ri**) bouncer (*in a night club*); (theat) callboy; (naut) outrigger

buttare *tr* to throw; to waste (*e.g., time*); to give off (*e.g., smoke*); **buttar giù** to demolish; to swallow; (fig) to discredit; to jot down; **buttar via** to throw away; to cast aside ‖ *intr* to secrete, ooze ‖ *ref* to throw oneself; to let oneself fall; **buttarsi giù** (fig) to become downcast

butterare (**bùttero**) *tr* to pock, pit

bùttero *m* pockmark; cowboy

buzzo [ddzz] *m* (vulg) belly; **di buzzo buono** with energy; willingly

C

C, c [t/i] *m & f* third letter of the Italian alphabet

càbala *f* cabala; cabal, intrigue

cabina *f* cabin, stateroom; car, cage (*of elevator*); cockpit (*of airplane*); booth (*of telephone*); cab (*of locomotive*)

cablàg·gio *m* (**-gi**) (elec) cable (*in auto or radio*)

cablare *tr* to cable

cablografare (**cablògrafo**) *tr* to cable

cablogram·ma *m* (**-mi**) cablegram, cable

cabotàg·gio *m* (**-gi**) coasting trade, coastal traffic

cabrare *intr* to zoom

cabrata *f* zoom

cacào *m* cocoa

cacasènno *m* (slang) wiseacre

cacatò·a *m* (**-a**) cockatoo

càc·cia *m* (**-cia**) pursuit plane, fighter; (nav) destroyer ‖ *f* chase, hunt; pursuit; **caccia alle streghe** witch hunt

cacciagióne *f* small game; venison; kill (*e.g., of game birds*)

cacciapiè·tre *m* (**-tre**) (rr) cowcatcher

cacciare §128 *tr* to hunt; to chase; to rout; to send out; to stick, thrust; to utter (*e.g., a cry*); **cacciar fuori** to pull out; **cacciar via** to chase away ‖ *ref* to hide; to intrude; to get; to wind up; to thrust oneself; **cacciarsi negli affari di** to butt into the affairs of

cacciasommergìbi·li *m* (**-li**) subchaser, submarine chaser

cacciata *f* hunting party; expulsion

cacciatóra *f* hunting jacket; **alla cacciatora** (culin) stewed with herbs

cacciatóre *m* hunter; (aer) fighter pilot; **cacciatore di frodo** poacher; **cacciatore di teste** headhunter

cacciatorpediniè·re *m* (**-re**) destroyer

cacciatrice *f* huntress

cacciavì·te *m* (**-te**) screwdriver

càccola *f* gum (*on edge of eyelid*); (slang) snot

caccoló·so -sa [s] *adj* gummy (*eyelid*); (slang) snotty

ca·chi (**-chi**) *adj* khaki ‖ *m* Japanese persimmon; khaki

cacic·co *m* (**-chi**) Indian chief; boss (*in Latin America*)

cà·cio *m* (**-ci**) cheese; **come il cacio sui maccheroni** (coll) at the right moment

cacofóni·co -ca *adj* (**-ci -che**) cacophonous

cac·tus *m* (**-tus**) cactus

cadau·no -na *adj* each ‖ *pron* each one

cadàvere *m* corpse, cadaver

cadavèri·co -ca *adj* (**-ci -che**) cadaverous

cadènte *adj* falling (*star*); rickety (*house*); run-down, decrepit (*person*)

cadènza *f* cadence, rhythm; accent (*peculiar to a region*)

cadére §121 *intr* (ESSERE) to fall; to sink; to slough (*said, e.g., of crust*); to fail; (gram) to end; **cadere a proposito** to come in handy; to come at the right moment; **cadere dalle nuvole** to be dumfounded

cadétto *m* cadet

càdmio *m* cadmium

caducità *f* transiency, brevity

cadu·co -ca *adj* (**-ci -che**) fleeting; deciduous

cadu·no -na *adj & pron* var of **cadauno**

cadu·to -ta *adj* fallen; lost, gone astray; **i caduti** the fallen, the dead ‖ *f* fall; crash (*of stock market*); slump (*of prices*)

caf·fè *m* (**-fè**) coffee; café

caffeina *f* caffeine

caffetteria *f* cafeteria

caffettièra *f* coffeepot

cafó·ne -na *adj* loud, gaudy ‖ *m* boor, lout

cagionare (cagióno) *tr* to cause, produce

cagióne *f* cause, reason; **a cagione di** because of

cagionévole *adj* sickly, delicate

cagliare §280 *tr*, *intr* (ESSERE) & *ref* to curdle, curd

cagliata *f* curd

cà·glio *m* (-**gli**) rennet

cagna *f* bitch

cagnara *f* barking (*of dogs*); uproar, confusion

cagné·sco -sca (-**schi -sche**) *adj* dog-like, doggish ‖ *m*—**guardare in cagnesco** to look askance at; **stare in cagnesco con** to be angry with

Caino *m* Cain

Càiro, il Cairo

cala *f* cove; (naut) hold

calabrése [s] *adj* & *mf* Calabrian

calabróne *m* hornet

calafatare *tr* (naut) to caulk

cala·màio *m* (-**mài**) inkwell

calamaro *m* squid

calamita *f* magnet; (*mineral*) loadstone; (fig) magnet, attraction

calami·tà *f* (-**tà**) calamity, disaster

calamitare *tr* to magnetize

calamitó·so -sa [s] *adj* calamitous

càlamo *m* reed, quill

calandra *f* calender; (aut) grille

calante *adj* waning (*moon*)

calàp·pio *m* (-**pi**) snare; noose

calapran·zi *m* (-**zi**) dumbwaiter

calare *tr* to lower; to strike (*sails*) ‖ *intr* (ESSERE) to fall, sag (*said, e.g., of prices*); to grow shorter (*said of days*); to come down; to shrink (*said, e.g., of meat*); to lose weight; to set (*said, e.g., of the sun*); to wane (*said of the moon*); (mus) to drop in pitch ‖ *ref* to let oneself down; to dive

calata *f* lowering; descent; invasion; fall; wharf; (coll) intonation; **calata del sole** sunset

cal·ca *f* (-**che**) crowd, throng

calca·gno *m* (-**gni**) heel ‖ *m* (-**gna** *fpl*) (fig) heel; **alle calcagna di** at the heels of

calcare *m* limestone ‖ §197 *tr* to trample; to trace (*on paper*); to tread (*the boards*); to emphasize; **calcare la mano** to exaggerate; **calcare le orme di** to follow in the footsteps of

calce *m*—**in calce** at the foot of the page; **in calce a** at the foot of ‖ *f* lime; **calce viva** quicklime

calcedònio *m* chalcedony

calcestruzzo *m* concrete

calciare §128 *tr* & *intr* to kick

calciatóre *m* soccer player; football player

calcificare §197 (**calcifico**) *tr* & *ref* to calcify

calcificazióne *f* calcification

calcina *f* mortar; lime

calcinàc·cio *m* (-**ci**) flake of plaster; **calcinacci** ruins, rubble

calci·nàio *m* (-**nài**) lime pit

calcinare *tr* to calcine; to lime (*e.g., a field*)

càl·cio *m* (-**ci**) kick; soccer; calcium; (*e.g., of rifle*) butt; **calcio d'inizio** (sports) kickoff

calciocianamide *m* calcium cyanamide

cal·co *m* (-**chi**) tracing; cast; imprint

calcografia *f* copper engraving

calcolare (**càlcolo**) *tr* to calculate; to estimate, reckon; to compute; to consider

calcola·tóre -trice *adj* calculating ‖ *m* calculator; computer; schemer ‖ *f* calculating machine, adding machine

càlcolo *m* calculation; estimate; planning; calculus; (pathol) calculus, stone; **calcolo biliare** gallstone; **calcolo errato** miscalculation; **fare calcolo su** to count upon

calcolò·si *f* (-**si**) (pathol) stones

calcomania *f* decalcomania

caldàia *f* boiler

cal·dàio *m* (-**dài**) cauldron, boiler

caldalléssa *f* boiled chestnut

caldana *f* flush

caldano *m* brazier

caldarròsta *f* roast chestnut

caldeggiare §290 (**caldéggio**) *tr* to favor, support; to recommend

calde·ràio *m* (-**rài**) coppersmith; boilermaker

calderóne *m* cauldron

cal·do -da *adj* warm; hot; rich (*voice*); **caldo, caldo** quite recent ‖ *m* heat; warmth; **aver caldo** to be warm (*said of people*); to be hot (*said of people*); **fa caldo** it is warm; it is hot; **non mi fa nè caldo nè freddo** it leaves me cold, it does not move me

calefazióne *f* heating

caleidoscò·pio *m* (-**pi**) kaleidoscope

calendà·rio *m* (-**ri**) calendar

calènde *fpl*—**calende greche** Greek calends

calendimàggio *m* May Day

calèsse *m* buggy, gig

calére *impers*—**non mi cale** (lit) I don't care

calettare (**calétto**) *tr* to dovetail, mortise ‖ *intr* to fit

calibrare (**càlibro**) *tr* to gauge, calibrate

càlibro *m* caliber; (mach) calipers; (fig) quality, importance

càlice *m* wine cup; (bot) calyx; (eccl) chalice

cali·cò *m* (-**cò**) calico

califfo *m* caliph

caligine *f* fog, mist; (fig) darkness

caliginó·so -sa [s] *adj* foggy, misty; (fig) dark, gloomy

calla *f*—**calla dei fioristi** calla lily

calle *f* lane, alley

callifu·go *m* (-**ghi**) corn remedy

calligrafia *f* penmanship; handwriting

calli·sta *mf* (-**sti -ste**) chiropodist

callo *m* corn; callus; **fare il callo a** to get used to; **pestare i calli a qlcu** to step on s.o.'s feet

callosi·tà [s] *f* (-**tà**) callosity; callus

calló·so -sa [s] *adj* corny; callous; hard

calma *f* calm, tranquillity

calmante adj sedative, calming, soothing || m sedative

calmare tr to calm, soothe, appease || ref to calm down; to subside, abate

calmierare (calmièro) tr to fix the price of

calmière m ceiling price; price control

cal·mo -ma adj calm, quiet, still || f see **calma**

calo m decrease; shrinkage

calomelano m calomel

calóre m heat; warmth; fervor, ardor; (pathol) rash, inflammation; (vet) rut, mating season

caloria f calorie

calòri·co -ca adj (-ci -che) caloric

calorífero m heater, radiator

caloró·so -sa [s] adj warm; hot; cordial; heated

calò·scia f (-sce) var of **galoscia**

calòtta f skullcap; case (e.g., of watch); (aut) hubcap; (mach) cap; **calotta cranica** skull

calpestare (calpésto) tr to trample

calpestí·o m (-í) trampling

calúgine f down (of bird)

calùnnia f calumny, slander

calunniare §287 tr to calumniate, slander

calunnia·tóre -trice mf slanderer

calunnió·so -sa [s] adj slanderous

Calvàrio m (Bib) Calvary

calvizie f baldness

cal·vo -va adj bald

calza f sock; stocking; wick; **calza da donna** stocking; **calze** hose, hosiery; **fare la calza** to knit

calzamàglia f tights

calzare m footwear || tr to wear, put on (shoes, gloves, or socks) || intr to fit (said of any garment); to suit

calzascar·pe m (-pe) shoehorn

calza·tóio m (-tói) shoehorn

calzatura f footwear; **calzature** footwear

calzaturière m shoe manufacturer

calzaturiè·ro -ra adj shoe (e.g., industry) || m shoe worker

calzaturifí·cio m (-ci) shoe factory

calzeròtto m woolen sock

calzet·tàio m (-tài) hosier

calzettóne m knee-high woolen sock (for mountain boots)

calzifí·cio m (-ci) hosiery mill

calzino m sock; **calzini corti** socks; half hose; **calzini lunghi** knee-high socks

calzo·làio m (-lài) shoemaker; cobbler

calzoleria f shoemaker's shop; shoe store

calzoncini mpl shorts

calzóne m trouser leg; **calzoni** trousers, pants; slacks; **calzoni a zampe d'elefante** bell-bottom trousers, flares

camaleònte m chameleon

camarilla f cabal, clique

cambiadí·schi m (-schi) record changer

cambiale f promissory note, IOU

cambiaménto m change, modification

cambiare §287 tr to change, exchange; to shift (gears) || intr to change, switch || ref to change (clothing); **cambiarsi in** to turn into

cambiavalu·te m (-te) moneychanger

càm·bio m (-bi) change; switch; rate of exchange; (mil) relief; **cambio a cloche** shift lever, stick; **cambio di velocità** gearshift; **in cambio di in** exchange for, in place of

cambrètta f staple (to hold a wire)

cam·brì m (-brì) cambric

cambusa f (naut) galley

cambusière m steward

càmera f room; bedroom; chamber; **camera ardente** funeral parlor; **Camera dei comuni** House of Commons; **Camera dei deputati** House of Representatives; **camera d'aria** inner tube; **camera di sicurezza** detention cell; vault (of bank)

camera·ta m (-ti) friend, comrade || f dormitory; barracks; roomful (of students or soldiers)

cameratismo m comradeship

camerièra f waitress; maid, chambermaid

camerière m waiter; steward; valet

camerino m small room; toilet, lavatory; (nav) noncommissioned officer's quarters; (theat) dressing room

càmice m gown (of physician); smock (of painter); (eccl) alb

camiceria f shirt store; shirt factory

camicétta f blouse

camicia f shirt; casing, jacket (e.g., of boiler); lining (e.g., of furnace); vest (of sailor); folder; **camicia da giorno** chemise; **camicia da notte** nightgown; **camicia di forza** strait jacket; **camicia di maglia** coat of mail; **camicia nera** black shirt (Fascist); **camicia rossa** red shirt (Garibaldine); **dare la camicia** to give the shirt off one's back; **essere nato con la camicia** to be born with a silver spoon in one's mouth; **perdere la camicia** to lose one's shirt

cami·ciàio -ciàia mf (-ciài -ciàie) shirtmaker, haberdasher

camiciòla f sport shirt; undershirt; T-shirt; (obs) vest

camiciòtto m smock (of mechanic); jumper; sport shirt

caminétto m small fireplace; fireplace

camino m fireplace; chimney, smokestack; shaft (in mountain); mouth (of volcano); (naut) funnel

cà·mion m (-mion) truck

camionale f highway

camioncino m small truck; panel truck, pickup truck

camionétta f small truck; van (e.g., of police)

camioní·sta m (-sti) truckdriver, teamster

camma f (mach) cam; (mach) wiper

cammellière m camel driver

cammèllo m camel

cammèo m cameo

camminaménto m (mil) communication trench

camminare intr to walk; to go, run

camminata f walk; gait; (obs) hall with fireplace

cammina·tóre -trice mf walker; runner

cammino *m* road, way, route; path (*e.g., of the moon*); course; journey; **cammin facendo** on the way; **cammino battuto** beaten path; **cammino coperto** (mil) covered way; **mettersi in cammino** to set out, start out

camomilla *f* camomile

camòrra *f* underworld

camò·scio *m* (-**sci**) chamois

campagna *f* country; countryside; country property; season (*for harvesting*); campaign; **andare in campagna** to go on vacation (in the country)

campagnò·lo -la *adj* country, rural ‖ *mf* peasant

campale *adj* field (*artillery*); pitched, decisive (*battle*)

campana *f* bell; bell glass, bell jar; lamp shade; (archit) bell; **a campana** bell-bottomed; **campana a martello** alarm bell, tocsin; **campana di vetro** bell glass; **campana pneumatica** caisson

campanàc·cio *m* (-**ci**) cowbell

campanaro *m* bell ringer; (archaic) bell founder

campanèlla *f* small bell; door knocker; curtain ring; (bot) bluebell

campanèllo *m* bell; small bell; doorbell, chimes; **campanello d'allarme** alarm bell

campanile *m* steeple, belfry; native city or town

campanilismo *m* parochialism

campano *m* cowbell

campare *tr* to keep alive; to save; to bring out the details of ‖ *intr* (ESSERE) to live; to survive; **si campa** one ekes out a living

campa·to -ta *adj*—**campato in aria** without any foundation ‖ *f* span

campeggiare §290 (**campéggio**) *intr* to camp, encamp; to stand out

campeggiatóre -trice *mf* camper

campég·gio *m* (-**gi**) camping, outing; campground; (bot) logwood

campeggi·sta *mf* (-**sti -ste**) camper

campèstre *adj* field, country; (sports) cross-country

campidò·glio *m* (-**gli**) capitol ‖ **Campidoglio** *m* Capitoline (*hill*); Capitol (*temple*)

campionare (**campióno**) *tr* to sample

campionà·rio -ria (-**ri -rie**) *adj* of samples; trade (*exposition*) ‖ *m* sample book, catalogue, pattern book

campionato *m* championship, title

campióne *m* champion; sample; specimen; standard; **campione senza valore** uninsured parcel, sample post

campionéssa *f* championess

campionissimo *m* world champion, ace

campo *m* field; camp; ground; tennis court; golf course; center (*e.g., for refugees*); **campo addestramento** training camp; **campo d'aviazione** airfield, airport; **campo di battaglia** battlefield; **campo petrolifero** oil field; **lasciare il campo** to retreat; **mettere in campo** to bring up, adduce; **piantare il campo** to pitch camp

camposanto *m* cemetery, churchyard

camuffare *tr* to disguise, mask; to camouflage ‖ *ref* to disguise oneself

camu·so -sa *adj* snub-nosed

Canadà, il Canada

canadése [*s*] *adj & mf* Canadian

canàglia *f* scoundrel; rabble

canagliata *f* knavery, mean trick

canale *m* canal; irrigation ditch; network (*of communications*); pipe, drain; (anat) duct, tract; (rad, telv) channel; (theat) aisle; **Canale della Manica** English Channel; **Canale di Panama** Panama Canal; **Canale di Suez** Suez Canal

canalizzare [**ddzz**] *tr* to channel; to install pipes in; (elec) to wire

canalizzazióne [**ddzz**] *f* channeling; piping; ductwork; (elec) wiring

canalóne *m* ravine

cànapa *f* hemp

cana·pè *m* (-**pè**) sofa, couch; (culin) canapé

cànapo *m* rope, cable

Canàrie, le the Canaries

canarino *m* canary

cancàn *m* noise, racket

cancellare (**cancèllo**) *tr* to cancel, erase; to obliterate; to write off (*a debt*); to scratch (*a horse*) ‖ *ref* to vanish, fade

cancellata *f* railing

cancellatura *f* erasure

cancellazióne *f* cancellation; erasure (*of a tape*)

cancelleria *f* chancellery; stationery

cancellière *m* chancellor; court clerk; registrar, recorder

cancèllo *m* gate, railing, grating

canceró·so -sa [*s*] *adj* cancerous ‖ *mf* cancer victim

cànchero *m* trouble; troublesome person; (coll) cancer

cancrèna *f* gangrene; **andare in cancrena** to become gangrenous

cancrenó·so -sa [*s*] *adj* gangrenous

cancro *m* cancer; (bot) canker ‖ **Cancro** *m* (astr) Cancer

candeggiante *adj* bleaching ‖ *m* bleaching agent, bleach

candeggiare §290 (**candéggio**) *tr* to bleach

candeggina *f* bleach

candég·gio *m* (-**gi**) bleaching

candéla *f* candle; candlestick; candlepower; (aut) spark plug; **studiare a lume di candela** to burn the midnight oil; **tenere la candela a** to favor the love affair of

candelabro *m* candelabrum

candelière *m* candlestick

candelòra *f* Candlemas

candelòtto *m* big wax candle; **candelotto lacrimogeno** tear-gas canister

candida·to -ta *mf* candidate

candidatura *f* candidature, candidacy

càndi·do -da *adj* white; candid

candire §176 *tr* to candy

candi·to -ta *adj* candied ‖ *m* candied fruit

candóre *m* whiteness; candor

cane *m* dog; hound; hammer, cock (*of gun*); ham actor; **cane barbone**

poodle; **cane bastardo** mongrel; **cane da ferma** setter; **cane da guardia** watchdog; **cane da presa** retriever; **cane da punta** pointer; **cane grosso** big shot; **cane guida per ciechi** seeing eye dog; **cane sciolto** (pol) lone wolf; **come un cane** all alone; **come un cane in chiesa** as an unwelcome guest; **da cani** poorly; **menare il can per l'aia** to beat around the bush; **non c'è un cane** there is nobody there; **raddrizzare le gambe ai cani** to perform an impossible task

canèstro m basket

cànfora f camphor

cangiante adj changeable (color); changing, iridescent

canguro m kangaroo

canìcola f dog days

canile m doghouse, kennel

canino adj canine || m canine tooth

canìzie f gray hair; head of gray hair; old age

canna f cane, reed; rod (for fishing or measuring); pipe (of organ); barrel (of gun); **canna da zucchero** sugar cane; **canna di caduta** disposal chute; **canna fumaria** chimney; **canna della gola** (coll) windpipe

cannèlla f small tube; tap (of barrel); cinnamon

cannèllo m pipe, tube; stick (e.g., of licorice); (chem) pipette; **cannello ossiacetilènico** acetylene torch; **cannello ossidrico** oxyhydrogen blowpipe

cannellóni mpl cannelloni

cannéto m cane field

cannibale m cannibal

cannìc·cio m (-ci) wicker frame; shade made out of rushes

cannocchiale m spyglass; **cannocchiale astronòmico** telescope

cannonata f cannonade, cannon shot; (slang) hit

cannoncino m small gun; **cannoncino antiaèreo** antiaircraft gun

cannóne m gun, cannon; pipe, stovepipe; box pleat; shin (of cattle); **è un cannone** (coll) he's the tops

cannoneggiare §290 (**cannonéggio**) tr to cannonade, shell

cannonièra f gunboat

cannonière m gunner, artilleryman; kicker (in soccer)

cannùc·cia f (-ce) reed; thin tube; stem (e.g., of pipe); straw (for drinking); (chem) pipette

canòa f canoe; launch

canòcchia f mantis shrimp

cànone m canon; rule; rent; fee, charge (for use of radio)

canonicato m canonry

canòni·co -ca (-ci -che) adj canonical, canon (law) || m canon; priest || f parsonage, rectory

canonizzare [ddzz] tr to canonize

canò·ro -ra adj song (bird); melodious

canottàg·gio m (-gi) boating, rowing

canottièra f undershirt, T-shirt; skimmer, boater

canottière m oarsman

canòtto m skiff, scull, shell

canovàc·cio m (-ci) dishcloth; embroidery cloth; plot (of novel or play)

cantàbile adj singable; songlike; cantabile || m song

cantamban·co m (-chi) jongleur, wandering minstrel; mountebank

cantante adj singing, song || mf singer

cantare m song; chant; laisse, epic strophe || tr to sing; to chant || intr to sing; to chant; (coll) to squeal

cantàride f Spanish fly

càntaro m urn

cantastò·rie mf (-rie) minstrel

canta·tóre -trice adj singing || mf singer

cantau·tóre -trice mf singer composer

canterano m chest of drawers

canterellare (**canterèllo**) tr & intr to sing in a low voice, hum

canterì·no -na adj singing, warbling; decoy (bird) || mf songster, singer

càntero m urinal

canticchiare §287 tr & intr to hum

cànti·co m (-ci) canticle

cantière· m shipyard, dockyard; navy yard; undertaking, work in progress; **avere in cantiere** to have in hand, be working at; **cantiere edile** building site; builder's yard

cantilèna f singsong; **la stessa cantilena** the same old tune

cantimban·co m (-chi) var of **cantambanco**

cantina f cellar; wine cellar; wine shop, canteen

cantinière m cellarman; butler; wineshop keeper; sommelier

canto m song, singing; chant; canto; crow (of rooster); chirping (of grasshopper); corner, edge; (mus) voice part; **canto del cigno** swan song; **dal canto mio** for my part; **d'altro canto** on the other hand; **da un canto** on the one hand

cantonata f corner (of street); **prendere una cantonata** to make a blunder

cantóne m corner (of room or building); canton

cantonièra f corner cupboard; (rr) section worker's house

cantonière m road laborer; (rr) section hand

cantóre m choir singer; cantor; (poet) singer

cantùc·cio m (-ci) nook, niche

canutézza f hoariness

canutiglia f gold thread

canu·to -ta adj gray-haired; white-haired; (poet) white

canzonare (**canzóno**) tr to mock, ridicule

canzonatò·rio -ria adj (-ri -rie) mocking

canzonatura f mockery, gibe

canzóne f song; canzone

canzonétta f canzonet; popular song

canzonetti·sta mf (-sti -ste) singer (e.g., in a nightclub) || m songster || f songstress

canzonière m songbook; collection of poems; song writer

caolino m kaolin

caos *m* chaos
caòti·co -ca *adj* (**-ci -che**) caotic
capace *adj* capacious; capable, intelligent; legally qualified; **capace di** with a capacity of (*e.g., fifty people*); **essere capace di** to be able to; **fare capace di** to convince of
capaci·tà *f* (**-tà**) capacity; capability
capacitare (**capàcito**) *tr* to persuade || *ref* to become convinced
capanna *f* hut, cabin; thatched cottage; bathhouse
capannèllo *m* group, crowd
capanno *m* hunting box; cabana, bathhouse
capannóne *m* large shed; hangar
caparbiàggine *f* var of **caparbietà**
caparbie·tà *f* (**-tà**) obstinacy, stubborness
capàr·bio -bia *adj* (**-bi -bie**) stubborn, hard-headed
caparra *f* down payment, deposit; performance bond
capatina *f* short visit
capeggiare §290 (**capéggio**) *tr* to lead
capeggia·tóre -trice *mf* leader
capellini *mpl* small vermicelli
capéllo *m* hair; **averne fin sopra i capelli** to have one's fill; **capelli** hair; **capelli a spazzola** crew cut; **c'è mancato un capello che** + *subj* he came close to + *ger*; **far rizzare i capelli a qlcu** to make s.o.'s hair stand on end
capellóne *m* hippie, beatnik
capellu·to -ta *adj* hairy; long-haired
capelvènere *m* maidenhair
capèstro *m* halter; gallows
capezzale *m* bolster; (fig) bedside
capézzolo *m* nipple, teat; udder
capidò·glio *m* (**-gli**) var of **capodoglio**
capiènza *f* capacity (*e.g., of bus*)
capigliatura *f* head of hair
capillare *adj* capillary; (fig) far-reaching
capinéra *f* (orn) blackcap
capintè·sta *m* (**-sta**) boss; (sports) head, leader
capire §176 *tr* to understand; **capire a volo** to grasp immediately || *intr*—**non capire dalla contentezza** to be bursting with joy || *ref* to understand each other; to agree
capitale *adj* capital; mortal (*sin*) || *m* capital; principal; **capitale sociale** capital stock || *f* capital (*of country*)
capitalismo *m* capitalism
capitali·sta *mf* (**-sti -ste**) capitalist
capitalisti·co -ca *adj* (**-ci -che**) capitalistic
capitalizzare [ddzz] *tr* to capitalize; to compound (*interest*)
capitana *f* flagship
capitanare *tr* to lead, captain
capitaneria *f* (hist) captaincy; **capitaneria di porto** harbor-master's office; coast guard office; port authority's office
capitano *m* captain; skipper, master (*of ship*); commander (*in air force*); **capitano di corvetta** or **capitano di fregata** (nav) lieutenant commander;

capitano di gran cabotaggio master; **capitano di lungo corso** master; **capitano di porto** harbor master; **capitano di vascello** (nav) commander
capitare (**càpito**) *intr* (ESSERE) to arrive; to happen, occur; to happen to get, *e.g.,* **capitò a casa mia alle tre** he happened to get to my house at three; **capitare bene** to be lucky; **dove capita** at random
capitazióne *f* poll tax
capitèllo *m* (archit) capital; (bb) headband
capitolare *adj & m* capitular || *v* (**capitolo**) *intr* to capitulate, surrender
capitolato *m* (com) specifications
capitolazióne *f* capitulation
capitolo *m* chapter; article, paragraph (*of contract*)
capitombolare (**capitómbolo**) *intr* to tumble
capitómbolo *m* tumble; **fare un capitombolo** (fig) to collapse
capitóne *m* big eel
capitozzare (**capitòzzo**) *tr* to poll (*a tree*)
capo *m* head; chief; boss, leader; top; (geog) cape; (nav) chief petty officer; **a capo scoperto** bareheaded; **capo d'accusa** (law) charge; **capo del governo** prime minister; **capo dello stato** president, chief of state; **capo di vestiario** garment; **capo scarico** scatterbrain; **col capo nel sacco** (fig) heedlessly; **da capo** all over (again); **fare capo a** to flow into; **in capo a** at the end of (*e.g., one month*); **in capo al mondo** at the end of the world; **per sommi capi** briefly; **rompersi il capo** to rack one's brain; **scoprirsi il capo** to take one's hat off; **senza capo né coda** without rhyme or reason; **venire a capo di** to come to the end of
capobanda *m* (**capibanda**) bandmaster; ringleader
capocamerière *m* headwaiter
capocannonière *m* (**capicannonièri**) petty gunnery officer; (soccer) leader in number of goals
capòcchia *f* head (*e.g., of a match*)
capòc·cia *m* (**-ci & -cia**) head of household; foreman, boss (*e.g., of road-workers or farmers*)
capocòmi·co *m* (**-ci**) head of dramatic company
capocòr·da *m* (**capicòrda**) (elec) binding post, terminal
capocrònaca *m* (**capicrònaca**) leading article
capocronista *m* (**capicronisti**) city editor
capocuòco *m* (**capocuòchi & capicuòchi**) chef
capodanno *m* (**capodanni & capi d'anno**) New Year's Day
capodò·glio *m* (**-gli**) sperm whale
capofàbbrica *m* (**capifàbbrica**) foreman, superintendent
capofabbricato *m* (**capifabbricato**) air-raid warden

capofamìglia *m* (**capifamìglia**) head of the family

capofila *m* (**capifila**) head of a line ‖ *f* (**capofila**) head of a line

capofitto *adj invar*—a capofitto headlong

capogiro *m* vertigo, dizziness; **da capogiro** dizzying, e.g., **prezzi da capogiro** dizzying prices

capolavó·ro *m* (**-ri**) masterpiece

capolèttera *m* (**capilèttera**) letterhead; (typ) first large bold letter of a paragraph

capolìnea *m* (**capilìnea**) terminal, terminus

capolino *m*—fare capolino to peep

capolista *m* (**capilista**) first (*of a list*); (sports) leader ‖ *f* (**capolista**) first (*of a list*)

capoluò·go *m* (**-ghi**) capital (*of province*); county seat

capomacchìni·sta *m* (**-sti**) chief engineer

capomastro *m* (**capomastri & capimastri**) foreman; building contractor

capomùsica *m* (**capimùsica**) bandmaster

capoofficina *m*: (**capiofficina**) superintendent (*of shop*)

capopàgina *m* (**capipàgina**) heading (*of newspaper*)

capopèzzo *m* (**capipèzzo**) gunnery sergeant

capopòpolo *m* (**capipòpolo**) demagogue

caporale *m* corporal

caporeparto *m* (**capireparto**) department manager, floor walker; shop foreman

capórione *m* ringleader

caposaldo *m* (**capisaldi**) (fig) main point, basis; (mil) stronghold; (surv) datum

caposezióne *m* (**capisezióne**) department head

caposquadra *m* (**capisquadra**) group leader; (sports) team captain

capostazióne *m* (**capistazióne**) station master

capostìpite *m* founder (*of family*); prototype, archetype

capotaménto *m* var of **cappottamento**

capotare (**capòto**) *intr* var of **cappottare**

capotasto *m* nut (*of violin*)

capotàvola *m* (**capitàvola**) head of the table, honored guest

capòte *f* (aut) top

capotrèno *m* (**capitrèno & capotrèni**) (rr) conductor

capottaménto *m* var of **cappottamento**

capottare (**capòtto**) *intr* var of **cappottare**

capoufficio *m* (**capiufficio**) office manager

capovèrso *m* paragraph; (typ) indentation

capovòlgere §289 *tr* to overturn; (fig) to upset ‖ *ref* to overturn; (fig) to be or become reversed

capovolgiménto *m* upset; (fig) reversal

capovòlta *f* overturn; turn (*in swimming*)

cappa *f* cape, cloak; mantle; letter K; shroud (*of clouds*); (naut) trysail;

cappa del cielo vault of heaven; **navigare alla cappa** (naut) to lay to

cappèlla *f* chapel; **cappella mortuaria** undertaker's parlor ‖ **Cappella Sistina** Sistine Chapel

cappel·làio *m* (**-lài**) hatter, hat maker or dealer

cappellano *m* chaplain

cappellata *f* hatful

cappelleria *f* hat store

cappellièra *f* hatbox

cappèllo *m* hat; bonnet; cap (*of mushroom*); head (*of nail*); cowl (*of chimney*); preamble (*of newspaper article*); **cappello a cencio** slouch hat; **cappello a cilindro** top hat; **cappello a cono** dunce cap; **cappello a due punte** cocked hat; **cappello a tre punte** three-cornered hat; **cappello del lume** lampshade; **cappello di feltro** felt hat; **cappello di paglia** straw hat; **cappello floscio** fedora; **fare di cappello** to take one's hat off; **prendere cappello** to take offense

cappellóne *adj invar* Western (*movie*) ‖ *m* big hat; (coll) recruit; (mov) Western character

càppero *m* (bot) caper; **capperi!** (coll) wow!

càp·pio *m* (**-pi**) bow; noose; loop

capponàia *f* chicken coop

cappóne *m* capon

cappòtta *f* cape; navy coat; hood (*of car*)

cappottaménto *m* upset, rolling over

cappottare (**cappòtto**) *intr* to upset, roll over

cappottatura *f* (aer) cowl

cappòtto *m* overcoat; lurch (*at the close of game*); (cards) slam; **cappotto da mezza stagione** lightweight coat

cappuccino *m* espresso with cream; Capuchin (*friar*)

Cappuccétto *m*—**Cappuccetto Rosso** Little Red Ridinghood

cappùc·cio *m* (**-ci**) hood, cowl; cabbage; cap (*of fountain pen*)

capra *f* goat; nanny goat; tripod

ca·pràio -pràia *mf* (**-prài -pràie**) goatherd

caprétto -ta *mf* kid

capriata *f* truss (*to support roof*)

capric·cio *m* (**-ci**) whim, fancy, caprice; tantrum; flirting; (mus) capriccio

capricció·so -sa [*s*] *adj* whimsical, capricious; naughty; fanciful, bizarre

Capricòrno *m* (astr) Capricorn

caprifò·glio *m* (**-gli**) honeysuckle

caprimul·go *m* (**-gi**) (orn) goatsucker

capri·no -na *adj* goatlike, goatish ‖ *m* smell of goat

capriòla *f* female roe deer; caper, somersault; **fare capriole** to cut capers, to caper

capriòlo *m* roe deer; roebuck

capro *m* he-goat, billy goat; **capro espiatorio** scapegoat

capróne *m* he-goat, billy goat

càpsula *f* capsule; percussion cap; cap (*of bottle*); (rok) capsule

captare *tr* to captivate; to catch, intercept; to harness (*a waterfall*); (rad, telv) to pick up (*a signal*)

captazióne *f* undue influence (*to secure an inheritance*)

capzió·so -sa [s] *adj* insidious, treacherous

carabàttola *f* (coll) trifle

carabina *f* carbine

carabinière *m* carabineer; Italian military policeman, carabiniere; (*hist*) cavalryman

caracollare (**caracòllo**) *intr* to caracole, caper; (coll) to trot along

caracòllo *m* caracole, caper

caraffa *f* carafe, decanter

caràmbola *f* carom

carambolare (**caràmbolo**) *intr* to carom

caramèlla *f* piece of hard candy; taffy; (coll) monocle; **caramelle** hard candy

caramellare (**caramèllo**) *tr* to caramel; to candy

caramèllo *m* caramel (*burnt sugar*)

caraménte *adv* affectionately

carati·sta *m* (-sti) shareholder (*in ship or business*)

carato *m* carat; share (*of ship*)

caràttere *m* character; type; handwriting; characteristic; disposition; **carattere corsivo** (typ) italic; **carattere maiuscolo** capital; **carattere minuscolo** small letter, lower case; **carattere neretto** or **grassetto** (typ) boldface

caratteri·sta *m* (-sti) character actor ‖ *f* (-ste) character actress

caratteristi·co -ca (-ci -che) *adj* & *f* characteristic

caratterizzare [ddzz] *tr* to characterize

caratura *f* share (*in business or ship*)

cara·vàn *m* (-vàn) trailer, mobile home

caravanserrà·glio *m* (-gli) caravansary

caravèlla *f* caravel; carpenter's glue

carbo·nàio -nàia (**-nài -nàie**) *adj* coal ‖ *m* coal man, coal dealer ‖ *f* charcoal pit; coalbin, bunker; coal yard

carbonato *m* carbonate

carbón·chio *m* (-chi) (agr) smut (*on wheat*); (jewelry) carbuncle

carboncino *m* charcoal (*pencil and drawing*)

carbóne *m* coal; charcoal; carbon (*of arc light or primary battery*); **carbone bianco** hydroelectric power; **carbone dolce** charcoal; **carbone fossile** coal; **fare carbone** to coal

carbòni·co -ca *adj* (-ci -che) carbonic

carbonièra *f* coal yard; (naut) collier; (rr) tender

carbonile *m* (naut) bunker

carbònio *m* (chem) carbon

carbonizzare [ddzz] *tr* to carbonize; to char

carbùncolo *m* boil, carbuncle; (archaic) ruby

carburante *m* fuel

carburatóre *m* carburetor

carburazióne *f* (aut) mixture

carburo *m* carbide

carcassa *f* carcass; framework; (aut) jalopy; (fig) wreck

carcerare (**càrcero**) *tr* to jail

carcerà·rio -ria *adj* (-ri -rie) jail, prison

carcera·to -ta *adj* imprisoned ‖ *mf* prisoner

càrce·re *m* (-ri *fpl*) jail, prison

carcerière *m* jailer, prison guard

carciòfo *m* artichoke

cardàni·co -ca *adj* (-ci -che) universal (*e.g., joint*)

cardano *m* universal joint

cardatrice *f* carding machine

cardellino *m* goldfinch

cardìa·co -ca (-ci -che) *adj* heart, cardiac ‖ *m* heart patient

cardinale *adj* cardinal ‖ *m* (eccl, orn) cardinal

cardinalì·zio -zia *adj* (-zi -zie) cardinal, cardinal's

càrdine *m* hinge; (fig) pivot, mainstay (*e.g., of theory*)

càr·dio *m* (-di) cockle (*mollusk*)

cardiochirurgia *f* heart surgery

cardiogram·ma *m* (-mi) cardiogram

cardiòlo·go *m* (-gi) cardiologist

cardiopalmo *m* tachycardia

cardiopatìa *f* heart disease

cardo *m* (bot) thistle; (bot) cardoon

carèna *f* ship's bottom; (aer) outer cover (*of airship*); (bot) rib

carenàg·gio *m* (-gi) careening a ship; careen

carenare (**carèno**) *tr* to careen (*a ship*)

carenatura *f* streamlining; **carenatura di fusoliera** (aer) turtleback

carènza *f* lack, want

carestìa *f* famine; scarcity (*e.g., of manpower*)

carézza *f* caress; **fare una carezza a** to caress

carezzare (**carézzo**) *tr* to caress

carezzévole *adj* caressing, fondling; sweet, suave; blandishing

cariare §287 *tr* to cause (*a tooth*) to decay; to corrode ‖ *ref* to decay; to rot

cariàtide *f* caryatid

caria·to -ta *adj* decayed

càri·ca *f* (-che) office, appointment; charge; (fig) insistence

caricaménto *m* loading

caricare §197 *tr* to load; to burden; to wind (*a watch*); to fill (*a pipe*); to charge (*a battery*); to deepen (*a color*); **caricare la mano** to exceed; **caricare le dosi** to exaggerate ‖ *ref* to burden oneself

carica·to -ta *adj* exaggerated, affected

carica·tóre -trice *adj* loading ‖ *m* clip, magazine (*for rifle*); loader (*of gun*); cassette (*of tape recorder*); charger (*of battery*); longshoreman; (phot) cartridge, cassette

caricatura *f* caricature, cartoon; **mettere in caricatura** to ridicule

caricaturi·sta *mf* (-sti -ste) cartoonist, caricaturist

càrice *m* (bot) sedge

càri·co -ca *adj* (-chi -che) loaded; burdened; vivid (*color*); strong (*tea*); charged (*battery*) ‖ *m* loading; load, burden; charge; cargo ‖ *f* see **carica**

càrie *f* caries, decay

cari·no -na *adj* nice, pretty, cute; **questa è carina!** this is funny!

cari·tà *f* **(-tà)** charity; alms; (poet) love; **per carità** please

caritévole *adj* charitable

caritati·vo -va *adj* (obs) charitable

carlin·ga *f* **(-ghe)** fuselage

Carlo *m* Charles

Carlomagno *m* Charlemagne

carlóna *f*—**alla carlona** carelessly, haphazardly

carlòtta *f* charlotte ‖ **Carlotta** Charlotte

carme *m* poem, lyric poem

carmì·nio *m* **(-ni)** carmine

carnagióne *f* complexion

car·nàio *m* **(-nài)** carnage; slaughter house; mass of humanity

carnale *adj* carnal, sensual; full (*e.g., brother, cousin*)

carname *m* carrion

carne *f* flesh; meat; **bene in carne** plump; **carne da macello** cannon fodder; **carne suina** pork; **carne viva** open wound; **essere solo carne ed ossa** to be nothing but skin and bones; **in carne ed ossa** in person, in the flesh; **troppa carne al fuoco** too many irons in the fire

carnéfice *m* executioner

carneficina *f* slaughter, carnage

càrne·o -a *adj* fleshy, meaty; flesh-colored

carnet *m* **(carnet)** notebook; check-book; backlog

carnevale *m* carnival

carnièra *f* hunting jacket; gamebag

carnière *m* gamebag

carnivo·ro -ra *adj* carnivorous ‖ *mpl* carnivores; Carnivora

carnò·so -sa [s] *adj* fleshy

ca·ro -ra *adj* dear (*beloved; high in price*) ‖ **caro** *adv* dear ‖ *m* high price; beloved; **i miei cari** my parents; my relatives; my friends

carógna *f* carcass; cad, rotter; **carogne** carrion

carosèllo *m* tournament; carousel, merry-go-round

caròta *f* carrot; (fig) lie

caròtide *f* carotid artery

carovana *f* caravan; group, crowd; union of longshoremen; apprenticeship; (naut, nav) convoy; **far carovana** to join a tour; **fare la carovana** to be an apprentice

carovaniè·ro -ra *adj* caravan ‖ *f* desert trail

carovi·ta *m* **(-ta)** high cost of living; cost-of-living increase

carovive·ri *m* **(-ri)** high cost of living; cost-of-living increase

carpa *f* (ichth) carp

carpentière *m* carpenter

carpire §176 *tr* to snatch, seize; to extract, worm (*a secret*)

carpóni *adv* on all fours; **avanzare carponi** to crawl

carradóre *m* cart maker, wheelwright

car·ràio -ràia **(-rài -ràie)** *adj* passable for vehicles ‖ *f* cart road

carrarèc·cia *f* **(-ce)** country road; rut

carreggiata *f* paved road; track (*of vehicles*); (fig) right path

carrellare **(carrèllo)** *intr* (mov, telv) to dolly

carrellata *f* (mov) dolly shot, tracking shot

carrèllo *m* car (*for narrow-gauge track*); carriage (*of typewriter*); cart (*for shopping*); (aer) landing gear; (mach, rr) truck; (mov, telv) dolly; **carrello d'atterraggio** (aer) undercarriage, landing gear; **carrello elevatore** fork-lift truck

carrétta *f* cart; tramp steamer

carrettata *f* cartful; **a carrettate** abundantly

carrettière *m* cart driver, drayman; teamster

carrétto *m* small cart; **carretto a mano** pushcart

carriàg·gio *m* **(-gi)** wagon; **carriaggi** (mil) baggage train

carrièra *f* career; **di gran carriera** at top speed

carrieri·sta *mf* **(-sti -ste)** unscrupulous go-getter

carriòla *f* wheelbarrow

carro *m* wagon; cart; wagonload; cartload; carload; (rr) car; (astr) Plough; (poet) chariot; **carri armati** (mil) armor; **carro allegorico** float (*in a pageant*); **carro armato** (mil) tank; **carro attrezzi** (aut) tow truck, wrecker; **carro bestiame** (rr) cattle car; **carro botte** or **carro cisterna** (aut) tank truck; (rr) tank car; **carro di Tespi** traveling show; **carro funebre** hearse; **carro gru** (rr) wrecking crane; **carro marsupio** (rr) double decker (*used to transport automobiles*); **carro merci** (rr) freight car; **Gran Carro** (astr) Big Dipper; **mettere il carro innanzi ai buoi** to put the cart before the horse; **Piccolo Carro** (astr) Little Dipper ‖ *m* **(carra** *fpl*) carload; wagonload; cartload

carròzza *f* wagon carriage; **carrozza letti** (rr) sleeping car; **carrozza ristorante** (rr) dining car; **carrozza salone** (rr) club car; **con la carrozza di S. Francesco** on shank's mare; **signori, in carrozza!** (rr) all aboard!

carrozzàbile *adj* open to vehicular traffic ‖ *f* road open to vehicular traffic

carrozzèlla *f* small wagon; baby carriage; wheelchair; hackney

carrozzino *m* baby carriage; sidecar

carrozzóne *m* wagon; hearse; caravan (*e.g., of gypsies*); (rr) car

carruba *f* carob

carrubo *m* carob tree

carrùcola *f* pulley

carta *f* paper; document (*e.g., of identification*); **alla carta** à la carte; **carta assorbente** blotter; **carta astronomica** astronomical map; **carta bianca** carte blanche; **carta bollata** stamped paper (*for official documents*); **carta carbone** carbon paper; **carta catramata** tar paper; **carta da disegno** drawing paper; **carta da gioco** playing card; **carta da giornale** newsprint; **carta da imballaggio** or **da impacco** wrapping paper; **carta da lettera** or **da lettere** writing paper; **carta geografica** map, chart; **carta igienica** toilet paper; **carta oleata** wax paper; **carta torna-**

sole litmus paper; **carta velina** India paper; tissue paper; **carta vetrata** sandpaper; **carte papers,** writings; **carte francesi** cards in the four suits spades, hearts, diamonds, and clubs; **carte napoletane** cards in the four suits gold coins, cups, swords, and clubs; **fare le carte** to shuffle the cards; **fare le carte a qlcu** to tell s.o.'s fortune with cards

cartacarbóne *f* (**cartecarbóne**) carbon paper

cartàc·cia *f* (**-ce**) waste paper

cartàce·o *-a adj* (**-i -e**) paper

Cartàgine *f* Carthage

car·tàio *m* (**-tài**) papermaker; paper dealer; (cards) dealer

cartamonéta *f* paper money

cartapècora *f* parchment

cartapésta *f* papier-mâché

cartà·rio -ria *adj* (**-ri -rie**) paper

cartastràccia *f* (**cartestracce**) wrapping paper; wastepaper

cartég·gio *m* (**-gi**) correspondence; (aer, naut) reckoning

cartèlla *f* lottery ticket; card (*e.g., of bingo*); page of manuscript; Manila folder; schoolbag; briefcase; binding (*of book*); **cartella clinica** clinical chart; **cartella di rendita** government bond; **cartella esattoriale** tax bill; **cartella fondiaria** bond certificate

cartellino *m* label; nameplate (*on door*); file; (sports) contract; **cartellino di presenza** timecard; **cartellino signaletico** criminal record

cartèllo *m* poster; sign (*on store*); (com) cartel, trust; **cartello di sfida** challenge; **cartello stradale** traffic sign

cartellóne *m* show bill, theater poster; bill (*for advertising*); **tenere il cartellone** to find public favor, make a hit, be the rage

car·ter *m* (**-ter**) chain guard (*of bicycle*); (aut) crankcase

cartièra *f* papermill

cartilàgine *f* cartilage, gristle

cartina *f* dose; cigarette paper; small map

cartòc·cio *m* (**-ci**) paper cone; charge (*of gun*); cornhusk; (archit) scroll

cartògrafo *m* cartographer

carto·làio *m* (**-lài**) stationer

cartoleria *f* stationery store

cartolina *f* card, post card; **cartolina precetto** induction notice

cartomante *mf* fortuneteller

cartoncino *m* light cardboard, calling card; **cartoncino natalizio** Christmas card

cartóne *m* cardboard, carton; **cartone animato** (mov) animated cartoon

cartùc·cia *f* (**-ce**) cartridge; shot, shell; **mezza cartuccia** (fig) half pint

cartuccièra *f* cartridge belt

casa [s] *f* house; dwelling; home; household; **andare a casa** to go home; **casa base** (baseball) home base; **casa colonica** farm house; **casa da gioco** gambling house; **casa del diavolo** faraway place; **casa di bambole** playhouse, doll's house; **casa di correzione** reform school; **casa di cura**

sanatorium, private clinic; **casa di riposo** convalescent home, nursing home; **casa di spedizione** shipping agency; **casa di tolleranza** bawdyhouse; **casa madre** home office, headquarters; **esser di casa** to be intimate; **fuori casa** (sports) away; **in casa** (sports) home; **metter su casa** to set up housekeeping; **sentirsi a casa** to feel at home; **stare a casa** to stay at home; **star di casa** to dwell, live

casac·ca *f* (**-che**) coat; **voltar casacca** to be a turncoat

casàccio *m*—**a casaccio** at random; heedlessly

casalin·go -ga (**-ghi -ghe**) [s] *adj* home, domestic; stay-at-home; home-made ‖ **casalinghi** *mpl* household articles ‖ *f* housewife

casamatta [s] *f* casemate, bunker

casaménto [s] *m* apartment house, tenement; tenants

casata [s] *f* house, lineage

casato [s] *m* birth, family; (obs) family name

cascame *m* waste; remnants (*e.g., of silk*)

cascante *adj* flabby, loose; (poet) languid, dull

cascare §197 *intr* (ESSERE) to fall, droop; to fit (*said of clothes*); **cascare dalla noia** to be bored to death; **cascare dal sonno** to be overwhelmed with sleep; **cascare diritto** to escape unscathed; **non casca il mondo** the world is not coming to an end

cascata *f* fall, waterfall; necklace (*e.g., of pearls*); **a cascata** flood of, e.g., telefonate **a cascata** flood of telephone calls ‖ **le Cascate del Niagara** Niagara Falls

cascina *f* farm house; dairy barn

ca·sco *m* (**-schi**) helmet, crash helmet; electric hairdrier; cluster (*e.g., of bananas*)

caseggiato [s] *m* built-up zone; block, row of houses; apartment house

caseifi·cio *m* (**-ci**) dairy, creamery, cheese factory

casèlla [s] *f* pigeonhole; square (*of paper*); **casella postale** post-office box

casellante [s] *mf* gatekeeper ‖ *m* (rr) trackwalker

casellà·rio [s] *m* (**-ri**) filing cabinet; row of post-office boxes; **casellario giudiziale** criminal file

casèllo [s] *m* tollgate (*on turnpike*); (rr) trackwalker's house

casèrma *f* barracks; fire station

casino [s] *m* country house; clubhouse; (slang) whorehouse; (slang) noise, racket

casisti·ca *f* (**-che**) case study; (eccl) casuistry

caso *m* case; chance; fate; vicissitude; opportunity; **a caso** inadvertently; **al caso** eventually; **caso fortuito** (law) act of God; **caso mai** assuming that, in the event that; **è il caso** it is the moment; **far caso a qlco** to notice s.th; **in ogni caso** in any event; **mettere il caso che** suppose; **mi fa caso** I am surprised; **non fare caso a** to make nothing of, pay no attention to; **per caso** perchance

casolare [s] *m* hut, hovel; isolated farmhouse

casòtto [s] *m* cabana, bathhouse; sentry box

Càspio *adj* Caspian

càspita *interj* you don't say!

cassa *f* box; chest; case; stock (*of rifle*); cash; cash register; desk (*e.g., in hotel*); check-out (*in a supermarket*); **a pronta cassa** by cash; **cassa acustica** loudspeaker; **cassa di risparmio** savings bank; **cassa malattia** health insurance; **cassa rurale** farmers' credit cooperative; **in cassa** in hand (*said of money*)

cassafórma *f* (**casseforme**) (archit) form (*for cement*)

cassafòrte *f* (**cassefòrti**) safe

cassapanca *f* (**cassapanche & casse-panche**) wooden chest

cassare *tr* to erase, cancel; to cross off; (law) to annull

cassata *f* Neapolitan ice cream with soft core; Sicilian cake

cassazióne *f* annulment, abolition; cancellation

casserétto *m* (naut) poop

càssero *m* (naut) quarterdeck; **cassero di poppa** (naut) cockpit

casseruòla *f* saucepan

cassétta *f* small box; coach box; (theat) box office; **cassetta dei ferri** work-box; **cassetta delle lettere** mail box; **cassetta di cottura** dish warmer; **cassetta di sicurezza** safe-deposit box; **cassetta per ugnature** miter box

cassettièra *f* chest of drawers

cassétto *m* drawer; **cassetto di distri-buzione** (mach) slide valve

cassettóne *m* chest of drawers; (archit) coffer, caisson

cassiè·re -ra *mf* cashier; teller

cassóne *m* large case, large box; chest; caisson (*for underwater construction*); body (*of truck*); (mil) caisson

cassonétto *m* cornice

cast *m* cast (*of actors*)

casta *f* caste

castagna *f* chestnut; **castagna d'India** horse chestnut

castagnéto *m* chestnut grove

castagno *m* chestnut tree; chestnut (*lumber*); **castagno d'India** horse chestnut tree

casta·no -na *adj* chestnut (*color*)

castellana *f* chatelaine

castellano *m* lord of the castle, squire

castellétto *m* scaffold; (min) gallows, headframe

castèl·lo *m* castle; works (*e.g., of watch*); scaffold; jungle gym; hydrau-lic boom, bucket lift (*on truck*); (naut) forecastle; **castello di men-zogne** pack of lies; **castello in aria** castle in Spain ‖ *m* (**-la** *fpl*) (archaic) castle

castigare §209 *tr* to punish; (poet) to correct, castigate

castigatézza *f* purity (*e.g., of style*)

castiga·to -ta *adj* decent, modest; pure (*language*)

Castìglia, la Castile

castiglia·no -na *adj & mf* Castilian

casti·go *m* (**-ghi**) punishment; (fig) scourge; **mettere in castigo** (coll) to punish

casti·tà *f* (**-tà**) chastity; (fig) purity

ca·sto -sta *adj* chaste; pure, elegant (*language or style*)

castóne *m* setting (*of stone*)

castòro *m* beaver

castrare *tr* to castrate; to spay; (fig) to expurgate

castra·to -ta *adj* castrated; spayed; (fig) effeminate ‖ *m* mutton (*of castrated sheep*); eunuch

castróne *m* wether (*sheep*); gelding (*horse*); (fig) nincompoop

castroneria *f* (vulg) stupidity

casuale *adj* fortuitous, casual; sundry (*e.g., expenses*)

casuali·tà *f* (**-tà**) chance, accident

casùpola [s] *f* hut, hovel

cataclì·sma *m* (**-smi**) cataclysm

catacómba *f* catacomb

catafal·co *m* (**-chi**) catafalque

catafàscio *adv*—**a catafascio** topsy-turvy

catalès·si *f* (**-si**) catalepsy

catàli·si *f* (**-si**) catalysis

catalizza·tóre -trice [ddzz] *adj* catalytic ‖ *m* catalyst

catalogare §209 (**catàlogo**) *tr* to cata-logue

catàlo·go *m* (**-ghi**) catalogue

catapècchia *f* hovel

catapla·sma *m* (**-smi**) poultice, plaster; (fig) bore

catapulta *f* catapult

catapultare *tr* to catapult

cataratta *f* cataract; sluice (*of canal*)

catarro *m* catarrh

catar·si *f* (**-si**) catharsis

catàrti·co -ca *adj* (**-ci -che**) cathartic

catasta *f* pile, heap

catastale *adj* land (*office*)

catasto *m* real-estate register; land office

catàstrofe *f* catastrophe; wreck

catastròfi·co -ca *adj* (**-ci -che**) cata-strophic

catechismo *m* catechism

catechizzare [ddzz] *tr* to catechize

categoria *f* category; weight (*in box-ing*); (sports) class

categòri·co -ca *adj* (**-ci -che**) categori-cal; classified (*telephone directory*)

caténa *f* chain; range (*of mountains*); (archit) tie beam; **catene da neve** tire chains; **mordere la catena** to champ the bit

catenàc·cio *m* (**-ci**) bolt; (fig) jalopy; (journ) giant-size headline

catenèlla *f* chain

cateratta *f* var of **cataratta**

catèrva *f* great quantity, large number

catetère *m* catheter

cateterizzare [ddzz] *tr* to catheterize

catinèlla *f* water basin; **piovere a cati-nelle** (coll) to rain cats and dogs

catino *m* basin

càtodo *m* cathode

Catóne *m* Cato; **Catone il Maggiore** Cato the Elder

catòr·cio *m* (**-ci**) (coll) piece of junk

catramare *tr* to tar
catramatrice *f* asphalt-paving machine
catrame *m* tar, coal tar
càttedra *f* desk (*of teacher*); chair, professorship
cattedrale *adj & f* cathedral
cattedràti·co **-ca** (**-ci -che**) *adj* pedantic || *m* professor
catte·gù *m* (**-gù**) catgut
cattivare *tr* to captivate
cattivèria *f* wickedness; piece of wickedness
cattivi·tà *f* (**-tà**) captivity
catti·vo **-va** *adj* bad; wicked; vicious (*animal*); worthless; poor (*reputation; condition*); nasty; naughty; (*archaic*) cowardly || *mf* wicked person || *m* bad taste; **sapere di cattivo** to taste bad
cattolicità *f* catholicity
cattòli·co **-ca** (**-ci -che**) *adj* catholic || *adj & mf* Catholic
cattura *f* capture, seizure; arrest
catturare *tr* to capture, seize; to arrest
caucàsi·co **-ca** *adj & mf* (**-ci -che**) Caucasian
caucciù *m* (**caucciù**) rubber
càusa *f* cause, motive; fault; lawsuit, action; **a causa di** on account of; **causa civile** civil suit; **causa penale** criminal suit; **fare causa** to take legal action; **intentare causa a** to bring suit against
causale *adj* causal || *f* cause
causare (**càuso**) *tr* to cause
causìdi·co *m* (**-ci**) amicus curiae; (*joc*) pettifogger
càusti·co **-ca** *adj* (**-ci -che**) caustic
cautèla *f* caution; precaution, care
cautelare *adj* guaranteeing, protecting || *v* (**cautèlo**) *tr* to guarantee, protect || *ref* to take precautions
cauterizzare [ddzz] *tr* to cauterize
càu·to **-ta** *adj* cautious, prudent; cagey
cauzióne *f* security, bail; **dare cauzione** to give bail
cava *f* quarry; cave; (*fig*) mine
cavadènti *m* (**-ti**) (coll) tooth puller, poor dentist
cavagno *m* (coll) basket
cavalcare §197 *tr* to ride; to cross over (*e.g., a river*) || *intr* to ride; **cavalcare a bisdosso** to ride bareback; **cavalcare all'amazzone** to ride sidesaddle
cavalcata *f* ride; cavalcade
cavalcatura *f* mount
cavalca·vìa *m* (**-vìa**) bridge (*between two buildings*); overpass
cavalióni *adj*—**a cavalcioni** (**di**) astride
cavalierato *m* knighthood
cavalière *m* rider (*on horseback*); knight; cavalier; chevalier; **a cavaliere** astride; **cavaliere d'industria** adventurer; **cavaliere errante** knight errant; **essere a cavaliere di** to overlook (*e.g., a valley*); to stretch over (*e.g., two centuries*)
cavalla *f* mare
cavalleggièro *m* cavalryman
cavalleré·sco **-sca** *adj* (**-schi -sche**) chivalrous, knightly

cavallerìa *f* cavalry; chivalry, knighthood; (fig) chivalry
cavallerizza *f* manège, riding school; horsemanship; horsewoman
cavallerizzo *m* horseman; riding master
cavallétta *f* grasshopper
cavallétto *m* tripod; easel; trestle (*of ski lift*); scaffold (*e.g., of stonemason*); sawhorse, sawbuck
cavalli·no **-na** *adj* horse, horse-like || *m* foal, colt || *f* foal, filly; **correre la cavallina** to be on the loose; to sow one's wild oats
cavallo *m* horse; knight (*in chess*); crotch (*of pants*); **a cavallo** on horseback; **a cavallo di** astride; **andare col cavallo di San Francesco** to ride shank's mare; **cavallo a dondolo** hobbyhorse; **cavallo di battaglia** battle horse; (fig) specialty, forte; **cavallo da corsa** race horse; **cavallo da tiro** draft horse; **cavallo di Frisia** cheval-de-frise; **cavallo di ritorno** confirmed news; **cavallo vapore** metric horsepower; **essere a cavallo** (fig) to have turned the corner
cavallóne *m* big horse; billow
cavallùc·cio *m* (**-ci**) little horse; **a cavalluccio** on one's shoulders; **cavalluccio marino** (ichth) sea horse
cavare *tr* to dig; to extract (*e.g., a tooth*); to pull out (*e.g., money*); to draw; **cavare il cuore a** to move s.o. to compassion; **cavare una spina dal cuore a qlcu** to ease so.o.'s mind || *ref* to take off (*e.g., one's hat*); **cavarsela** to overcome an obstacle; to get out of trouble; **cavarsi la camicia di dosso** to give the shirt off one's back; **cavarsi la fame** to eat one's fill; **cavarsi la voglia** to satisfy one's wishes
cavastiva·li *m* (**-li**) bootjack
cavatap·pi *m* (**-pi**) corkscrew
cavaturàccio·li *m* (**-li**) corkscrew
cavèrna *f* cave, cavern
cavernó·so **-sa** [s] *adj* cavernous; deep (*voice*)
cavézza *f* halter; (fig) check
càvia *f* guinea pig; **cavia umana** (fig) guinea pig
caviale *m* caviar
cavìc·chio *m* (**-chi**) peg
cavì·glia *f* (**-glie**) ankle; bolt; pin, dowel, peg
caviglièra *f* ankle support
cavillare *intr* to cavil, quibble
cavillo *m* quibble
cavilló·so **-sa** [s] *adj* quibbling, captious
cavi·tà *f* (**-tà**) cavity
ca·vo **-va** *adj* hollow || *m* hollow; cable; trough (*between two waves*); (naut) hawser; **cavo di rimorchio** towline; **cavo telefonico** telephone cable || *f* see cava
cavolfióre *m* cauliflower
càvolo *m* cabbage; **cavolo di Bruxelles** Brussels sprouts (*food*); (bot) Brussels sprout; **non capire un cavolo** (vulg) to not understand a blessed thing
cazzòtto *m* (vulg) punch, sock
cazzuòla *f* trowel

ce §5

cecare §122 *tr* to blind

cèc·ca *f* (**-che**) magpie; **fare cecca** to misfire

cecchino *m* sniper

céce *m* chickpea

ceci·tà *f* (**-tà**) blindness

cè·co **-ca** *adj* & *mf* (**-chi -che**) Czech

Cecoslovàcchia, la Czechoslovakia

cecoslovac·co **-ca** *adj* & *mf* (**-chi -che**) Czechoslovak

cèdere §123 *tr* to cede; to give up; to sell at cost; **cedere il passo** to let s.o. through; **cedere la strada** to yield the right of way; **non cederla** to be second to none ‖ *intr* to give in, yield; to give way, succumb; to sag

cedévole *adj* yielding; soft; pliable

cedìglia *f* cedilla

cediménto *m* cave-in; (fig) yielding

cèdola *f* slip; coupon

cedri·no **-na** *adj* citron; citron-like; cedar, cedar-like

cèdro *m* (*Citrus medica*) citron; (*Cedrus*) cedar; **cedro del Libano** cedar of Lebanon

CEE *m* (letterword) (**Comunità Economica Europea**) EEC (*European Economic Community-Common Market*)

cefalèa *f* slight headache; headache

cèfalo *m* (ichth) mullet

cèffo *m* snout; (pej) face; **brutto ceffo** ugly mug

ceffóne *m* slap in the face

celare (**cèlo**) *tr* to hide, conceal

cela·to **-ta** *adj* hidden ‖ *f* sallet

celebèrri·mo **-ma** *adj* very famous, renowned

celebrare (**cèlebro**) *tr* & *intr* to celebrate

celebrazióne *f* celebration

cèlebre *adj* famous, renowned, celebrated

celebri·tà *f* (**-tà**) celebrity

cèlere *adj* swift, rapid; express (*train*); short, quick; prompt ‖ **Celere** *f* special police

celeri·tà *f* (**-tà**) swiftness, rapidity; speed (*e.g., of a machine gun*)

celèste *adj* heavenly, celestial; blue, sky-blue ‖ *m* blue, sky blue; **celesti** heavenly spirits; (mythol) gods

celestiale *adj* celestial, heavenly

cèlia *f* jest; **mettere in celia** to deride; **per celia** in jest

celiare §287 (**cèlio**) *intr* to jest, joke

celibà·rio **-ria** (**-ri -rie**) *adj* single ‖ *m* old bachelor

celibato *m* celibacy; bachelorhood

cèlibe *adj* single, unmarried ‖ *m* bachelor

cèlla *f* cell; **cella frigorifera** walk-in refrigerator; **cella campanaria** belfry

cèllofan or **cellofàn** *m* cellophane

cèllula *f* cell; **cellula fotoelettrica** photoelectric cell

cellulare *adj* cellular; ventilated (*fabric*); solitary (*confinement*)

celluloìde *f* celluloid

cellulò·so **-sa** [*s*] *adj* cell-like, cellular ‖ *f* cellulose

cèl·ta *mf* (**-ti -te**) Celt

cèlti·co **-ca** *adj* (**-ci -che**) Celtic; venereal (*disease*)

cementare (**ceménto**) *tr* to cement

ceménto *m* cement, concrete; **cemento armato** reinforced concrete

céna *f* supper; **Ultima Cena** Last Supper

cenàcolo *m* cenacle

cenare (**céno**) *intr* to sup, have supper

cenciaiò·lo **-la** *mf* ragpicker

cén·cio *m* (**-ci**) rag, duster (*for cleaning*)

cenció·so **-sa** [*s*] *adj* tattered, ragged

cénere *adj* ashen ‖ *f* ash; cinder; **andare in cenere** to go up in smoke; **ceneri** ashes (*of a person*); **ridurre in cenere** to burn to ashes ‖ **le Ceneri** Ash Wednesday

cenerèntola *f* (fig) Cinderella ‖ **Cenerèntola** *f* Cinderella (*of the fable*)

cén·gia *f* (**-ge**) ledge (*of a mountain*)

cénno *m* sign; wave (*with hand*); nod; wag; wink; gesture; hint; notice; **al cenni di** at the orders of; **fare cenno a** or **di** to mention; **fare cenno di no** to shake one's head; **fare cenno di sì** to nod assent

cenò·bio *m* (**-bi**) monastery

cenobi·ta *m* (**-ti**) monk, cenobite

censiménto *m* census

censire §176 *tr* to take the census of

cènso *m* wealth, income; census (*in ancient Rome*)

censóre *m* censor; faultfinder; (educ) proctor

censuà·rio **-ria** (**-ri -rie**) *adj* income; tax (*register*) ‖ *m* taxpayer

censura *f* censure; censorship; faultfinding

censurare *tr* to censure; to criticize, find fault with

centàuro *m* centaur

centellinare *tr* to sip; to take a nip of

centellino *m* sip, nip

centenà·rio **-ria** (**-ri -rie**) *adj* & *mf* centenary, centennial ‖ *m* centenary, centennial (*anniversary*)

centèsi·mo **-ma** *adj* hundredth ‖ *m* hundredth; centime; cent; penny

centìgrado *m* centigrade

centigrammo *m* centigram

centìmetro *m* centimeter; tape measure

cèntina *f* (archit) centering; (aer) rib

centi·nàio *m* hundred; **un centinaio di** about a hundred ‖ *m* (**-nàia** *fpl*)—**a centinaia** by the hundreds

cènto *adj, m & pron* a hundred, one hundred; **per cento** per cent

centomila *adj, m & pron* a hundred thousand, one hundred thousand

centóne *m* cento

centopièdi·di *m* (**-di**) centipede

centrale *adj* central ‖ *f* headquarters, home office; powerhouse, generating station; telephone exchange; **centrale di conversione** (elec) transformer station; **centrale telefonica** central

centralini·sta *mf* (**-sti -ste**) telephone operator

centralino *m* telephone exchange

centralizzare [*ddzz*] *tr* to centralize

centrare (**cèntro**) *tr* to center; to hit the center of

centrattac·co *m* (-**chi**) (sports) center forward

centrìfu·go -ga *adj* (-**ghi -ghe**) centrifugal ‖ *f* centrifuge

centrìno *m* centerpiece

centrìpe·to -ta *adj* centripetal

centri·sta *mf* (-**sti -ste**) (pol) centrist

cèntro *m* center; **al centro** downtown; **far centro** to hit the mark

centrocampo *m* (soccer) midfield

centuplicare §197 (**centùplico**) *tr* to multiply a hundredfold

cèntu·plo -pla *adj* & *m* hundredfold

céppo *m* trunk, stump; log; block (*for beheading*); brake shoe; stock (*of anchor*); **ceppi** stocks, fetters ‖ **il Ceppo** (coll) Christmas

céra *f* wax; face, aspect, air, look; **di cera** waxen; pale; **cera da scarpe** shoe polish; **avere buona cera** to look well; **fare buona cera a** to welcome

ceralac·ca *f* (-**che**) sealing wax

ceràmi·co -ca (-**ci -che**) *adj* ceramic ‖ *f* ceramics

cerare (**céro**) *tr* to wax

Cèrbero *m* Cerberus

cerbiatto *m* fawn

cerbottana *f* blowgun, peashooter

cer·ca *f* (-**che**) search, quest; **in cerca di** in search of

cercare §197 (**cérco**) *tr* to seek, look for; to desire, yearn for; **cercare il pelo nell'uovo** to be a faultfinder, to nitpick ‖ *intr* to try

cerca·tóre -trice *adj* seeking ‖ *mf* seeker; mendicant ‖ *m* prospector

cérchia *f* coterie; compass, limits (*of a wall*); circle (*of friends*)

cerchiare §287 (**cérchio**) *tr* to hoop (*a barrel*); to circle, encircle

cér·chio *m* (-**chi**) circle; hoop; loop; **fare il cerchio della morte** (aer) to loop the loop; **in cerchio** in a circle ‖ *m* (-**chia** *fpl*) (archaic) circle

cerchióne *m* rim; tire (*of metal*)

cereale *adj* & *m* cereal

cerebrale *adj* cerebral

cère·o -a *adj* waxen; wax-colored, pale

cerfò·glio -gli (-**gli**) chervil

cerimònia *f* ceremony; **fare cerimonie** to stand on ceremony; to make a fuss

cerimoniale *adj* & *m* ceremonial

cerimonière *m* master of ceremonies (*at court*)

cerimonió·so -sa [s] *adj* ceremonious

cerino *m* wax match; taper

cernéc·chio *m* (-**chi**) tuft (*of hair*)

cernièra *f* hinge; clasp (*of handbag*); **a cerniera** hinged; **cerniera lampo** zipper

cèrnita *f* sorting, selection, grading

céro *m* church candle; **offrire un cero** to light a candle

ceróne *m* make-up (*of actor*)

ceròtto *m* adhesive tape; (fig) bore; **cerotto per i calli** corn plaster

certame *m* (poet) combat; competition, contest (*of poets*)

certézza *f* certitude, assurance, conviction, certainty

certificare §197 (**certìfico**) *tr* to certify, certificate

certificato *m* certificate

cèr·to -ta *adj* such, some; convinced; certain; real, positive ‖ *m* certainty; **di certo** or **per certo** for certain ‖ **certi** *pron* some ‖ **certo** *adv* undoubtedly

certósa *f* Carthusian monastery, charterhouse

certosi·no *m* Carthusian monk; chartreuse (*liquor*); **da certosino** with great patience

certu·no -na *adj* (obs) some ‖ **certuni** *pron* some

cerùle·o -a *adj* cerulean

cerume *m* ear wax

cervellétto *m* cerebellum

cervelli·no -na *adj* & *mf* scatterbrain

cervèllo *m* (**cervèlli** & **cervèlla** *fpl*) brain; head; mind; **dare al cervello** to go to one's head

cervellòti·co -ca *adj* (-**ci -che**) queer, extravagant

cervice *f* (anat) cervix; (poet) nape of the neck

cerviè·ro -ra *adj* lynx-like; ‖ *m* lynx

cervi·no -na *adj* deer-like ‖ **Cervino** *m* Matterhorn

cèrvo *m* deer; (ent) stag beetle; **cervo volante** kite

Cèsare *m* Caesar

cesàre·o -a *adj* Caesarean; (poet) courtly

cesellare (**cesèllo**) *tr* to chase, chisel; to carve, engrave; to polish (*e.g., a poem*)

cesella·tóre -trice *mf* chaser, engraver, chiseler

cesellatura *f* chasing, engraving; polished writing

cesèllo *m* burin, graver

cesóla *f* shears, metal shears; **cesole** shears (*for gardening*)

cesoiatrice *f* shearing machine

cèspite *m* source (*of income*); (poet) tuft

cèspo *m* tuft

cespù·glio *m* (-**gli**) bush, shrub, thicket

cèssa *f*—**senza cessa** without letup

cessare (**cèsso**) *tr* to stop, interrupt ‖ *intr* to cease, stop; **cessare di** + *inf* to stop + *ger*

cessazióne *f* cessation, discontinuance; **cessazione d'esercizio** going out of business

cessionà·rio *m* (-**ri**) assignee

cèsso *m* (vulg) privy, outhouse

césta *f* basket, hamper

cestinare *tr* to throw into the wastebasket; to reject (*a book, article, etc.*)

césto *m* basket; tuft; head (*e.g., of lettuce*)

cesura *f* caesura

cetàceo *m* cetacean

cèto *m* class; **ceto medio** middle class

cétra *f* lyre; cither; inspiration

cetriolino *m* gherkin

cetriòlo *m* cucumber; (fig) dolt

che *adj* what; which; what a, e.g., **che bella giornata!** what a beautiful day! ‖ *pron interr* what ‖ *pron rel* who; whom; that; which; (coll) in which ‖ *m*—**essere un gran che** to be a big

shot, to be somebody || *adv* how,
e.g., **che bello!** how nice!; **non . . .
che** only, e.g., **non venne che Luigi**
only Luigi came; no one but, e.g.,
non restò che mio cugino no one but
my cousin stayed || *conj* that; (*after
comparatives*) than, as

ché *adv* (coll) why || *conj* (coll) because; (coll) so that

checché *pron* (lit) whatever, no matter
what

checchessìa *pron* (lit) anything, everything

chèla *f* claw

che•pì *m* (**-pì**) kepi

cherubino *m* cherub

chetare (**chéto**) *tr* to quiet; to placate ||
ref to quiet down, become quiet

chetichèlla *f*—**alla chetichella** surreptitiously, stealthily

ché•to -ta *adj* quiet, still

chi *pron interr* who; whom || *pron rel*
who; whom; **chi . . . chi** some . . .
some

chiàcchiera *f* chatter, idle talk; gossip;
glibness; **fare quattro chiacchiere** to
have a chat

chiacchierare (**chiàcchiero**) *intr* to chat;
to gossip

chiacchierata *f* talk, chat; **fare una
chiacchierata** to visit

chiacchieri•no -na *adj* talkative, loquacious

chiacchieri•o *m* (**-ì**) chattering, jabbering (*of a crowd*)

chiacchieró•ne -na *adj* talkative, loquacious || *mf* chatterbox

chiama *f* roll call; **fare la chiama** to call
the roll; **mancare alla chiama** to be
absent at the roll call

chiamare *tr* to call; to hail (*a cab*);
to invoke, call upon; **chiamare al
telefono** to call up; **esser chiamato a**
to have the vocation for || *ref* to be
named; **si chiama Giovanni** his name
is John

chiamata *f* call; (law) designation (*of
an heir*); (telp) ring; (theat) curtain
call; (typ) catchword

chiappa *f* (vulg) buttock; (slang) catch
(*e.g., of fish*)

chiarét•to -ta *adj & m* claret

chiarézza *f* clarity, clearness

chiarificare §197 (**chiarifico**) *tr* to
clarify

chiarificazióne *f* clarification

chiariménto *m* explanation

chiarire §176 *tr* to clear up, explain;
to unravel || *intr* (ESSERE) to clear,
become clear || *ref* to make oneself
clear; to assure oneself

chia•ro -ra *adj* clear; bright; light
(*color*); honest; clear-cut; plain (*language*); illustrious, famous || *m* light;
bright color; brightness; **chiaro di
luna** moonlight; **con questi chiari di
luna** in these troubled times; **mettere
in chiaro** to clarify, explain || **chiaro**
adv plainly; **chiaro e tondo** bluntly,
frankly

chiaróre *m* light, glimmer

chiaroveggènte *adj & mf* clairvoyant

chiaroveggènza *f* clairvoyance

chiassata *f* uproar, disturbance, racket;
noisy scene

chiasso *m* noise; uproar; alley; **fare
chiasso** to cause a sensation

chiassó•so -sa [s] *adj* noisy; gaudy

chiatta *f* barge; pontoon

chiavarda *f* bolt

chiave *f* key; wrench; (archit) keystone;
(mus) clef; **avere le chiavi di** to own;
chiave a rollino adjustable wrench;
chiave a tubo socket wrench; **chiave
di volta** keystone; **chiave inglese**
monkey wrench; **fuori chiave** off
key; **sotto chiave** under lock and key

chiavétta *f* key; cock; cotter pin

chiàvi•ca *f* (**-che**) sewer

chiavistèllo *m* bolt

chiazza *f* spot, blotch

chiazzare *tr* to spot, blotch; to mottle

chiazza•to -ta *adj* spotted, mottled

chic•ca *f* (**-che**) sweet, candy

chìcchera *f* cup

chicchessìa *pron indef* anyone, anybody

chicchirichì *m* cock-a-doodle-doo

chic•co *m* (**-chi**) grain, seed; bead (*of
rosary*); bean (*of coffee*); **chicco di
grandine** hailstone; **chicco d'uva**
grape

chièdere §124 *tr* to ask; to ask for; to
beg (*pardon*); to require; to sue (*for
damages or peace*); **chiedere a qlcu
di** + *inf* to ask s.o. to + *inf*; **chiedere
in prestito** to borrow; **chiedere qlco
a qlcu** to ask s.o. for s.th || *ref* to
wonder

chiéri•ca *f* (**-che**) tonsure; priesthood

chiéri•co *m* (**-ci**) clergyman; altar boy;
(archaic) clerk

chièsa *f* church

chiesuòla *f* small church; clique, set
(*e.g., of artists*); (naut) binnacle

chì•glia *f* (**-glie**) keel; **chiglia mobile**
(naut) centerboard

chilo *m* kilo, kilogram; **fare il chilo** to
take a siesta

chilociclo *m* kilocycle

chilogrammo *m* kilogram

chilohèrtz *m* kilohertz

chilomètrag•gio *m* (**-gi**) distance in
kilometers

chilomètri•co -ca *adj* (**-ci -che**) kilometric; interminable (*e.g., speech*)

chilòmetro *m* kilometer

chilo•watt *m* (**-watt**) kilowatt

chimèra *f* chimera; daydream, utopia

chimèri•co -ca *adj* (**-ci -che**) chimerical

chìmi•co -ca *adj* (**-ci -che**) chemical ||
m chemist || *f* chemistry

chimòno *m* kimono

china *f* slope, decline; India ink; cinchona

chinare *tr* to bend; to lower (*one's
eyes*); **chinare il capo** to nod assent;
chinare la fronte to yield, give in ||
ref to bend, stoop

china•to -ta *adj* bent, lowered; bitter;
with quinine, e.g., **vino chinato** wine
with quinine

chincàglie *fpl* notions, knickknacks, sundries

chincaglière *m* notions or knicknack dealer
chincaglierìa *f* knicknack; **chincaglierie** knicknacks, notions
chinina *f* quinine (*alkaloid*)
chinino *m* quinine (*salt of the alkaloid*)
chi·no -na *adj* bent, lowered || *f* see **china**
chiòc·cia *f* (-ce) brooding hen
chiocciare §128 (**chiòccio**) *intr* to cluck; to sit, brood; to crouch
chiocciata *f* brood
chiòc·cio -cia (-ci -ce) *adj* hoarse || *f* see **chioccia**
chiòcciola *f* snail; (anat) cochlea; (mach) nut
chioccolì·o *m* (-i) cackle (*of hen*); gurgle (*of water*)
chiodare (**chiòdo**) *tr* to nail
chioda·to -ta *adj* nailed shut; hobnailed
chiòdo *m* nail; spike; obsession; craze; (coll) debt; **chiodi** climbing irons; **chiodo a espansione** expansion bolt; **chiodo da cavallo** horseshoe nail; **chiodo di garofano** clove; **chiodo ribattino** rivet
chiòma *f* hair; mane; foliage; (astr) coma
chioma·to -ta *adj* hairy, long-haired; leafy
chiòssa *f* gloss
chiosare (**chiòso**) *tr* to gloss, comment on
chiò·sco *m* (-schi) kiosk, stand, newsstand; pavilion, bandstand
chiòstra *f* circular range (*of mountains*); (poet) enclosure; (poet) set (*of teeth*); (poet) zone, region
chiòstro *m* cloister
chiòt·to -ta *adj* quiet, still; **chiotto chiotto** still as a mouse
chiromante *mf* palmist
chiromanzìa *f* palmistry
chiropràtica *f* chiropractice
chirurgìa *f* surgery
chirùrgi·co -ca *adj* (-ci -che) surgical
chirur·go *m* (-ghi & -gi) surgeon
chissà *adv* maybe
chitarra *f* guitar; **chitarra hawaiana** ukulele
chitarri·sta *mf* (-sti -ste) guitar player
chiùdere §125 *tr* to shut, close; to lock; to turn off; to fasten; to block (*a road*); to fence in; to nail shut (*a box*); to strike (*a balance*); to conclude, wind up; **chiudere a chiave** to lock; **chiudere bottega** to go out of business; **chiudere il becco** (slang) to shut up || *intr* to shut, close; to lock || *ref* to shut, close; to lock; to withdraw; to cloud over
chiùnque *pron indef invar* anybody, anyone || *pron rel invar* whoever, whomever; anyone who, anyone whom
chiurlo *m* (orn) curlew
chiusa [s] *f* fence; lock (*of canal*); end, conclusion (*e.g., of letter*)
chiusino [s] *m* manhole
chiu·so -sa [s] *adj* shut, closed, locked; stuffy (*air*); high-bodiced (*dress*);

close (*vowel*) || *m* enclosure, corral; close || *f* see **chiusa**
chiusura [s] *f* closing, end; fastener; lock; **chiusura lampo** zipper, slide fastener
ci §5
ciabatta *f* slipper; old shoe
ciabat·tàio *m* (-tài) cobbler
ciabattare *intr* to shuffle along
ciabattino *m* cobbler, shoemaker
ciàc *f* (mov) clappers
cialda *f* wafer; thin waffle
cialdóne *m* cone (*for ice cream*)
cialtró·ne -na *mf* rogue, scoundrel; slovenly person
ciambèlla *f* doughnut; **ciambella di salvataggio** life saver
ciambellano *m* chamberlain
ciampicare §197 (**ciàmpico**) *intr* to stumble along
ciana *f* (slang) fishwife
cianamide *f* cyanamide
ciàn·cia *f* (-ce) chatter, prattle, idle gossip
cianciare §128 (**ciàncio**) *intr* to chatter, prattle
cianciafrùscola *f* trifle, bagatelle
cianfrusà·glia *f* (-glie) trifle, trinket; rubbish, trash, junk
cianìdri·co -ca *adj* (-ci -che) hydrocyanic
cianògeno *m* cyanogen
cianuro *m* cyanide
ciao *interj* (coll) hi!, hello!; (coll) goodbye!, so long!
ciarla *f* chatter, prattle, idle talk; gossip
ciarlare *intr* to chatter, prattle
ciarlatanata *f* charlatanism, quackery
ciarlatanerìa *f* charlatanism
ciarlatané·sco -sca *adj* (-schi -sche) charlatan
ciarlatano *m* charlatan, quack
ciarliè·ro -ra *adj* talkative, garrulous
ciarpame *m* rubbish, junk
ciaschedu·no -na *adj indef* each || *pron indef* each one, everyone
ciascu·no -na *adj indef* each || *pron indef* each one, everyone
cibare *tr* & *ref* to feed
cibà·rio -ria (-ri -rie) *adj* alimentary || **cibarie** *fpl* foodstuffs, victuals
cibo *m* food; meal; (fig) dish
cicala *f* cicada; grasshopper; locust; (fig) chatterbox; (naut) anchor ring
cicalare *intr* to prattle, babble; to chatter
cicalé·ccio *m* (-ci) prattle, babble; chatter
cicatrice *f* scar
cicatrizzare [ddzz] *tr* to heal (*a wound*) || *intr* (ESSERE) & *ref* to heal, scar
cicatrizzazióne [ddzz] *f* closing, healing (*of a wound*)
cìc·ca *f* (-che) butt (*of cigar or cigarette*); (slang) chewing gum
ciccare §197 *intr* to chew tobacco; (coll) to boil with anger
cicchettare (**cicchétto**) *tr* (slang) to prime (*a carburetor*); (slang) to dress down, reprimand || *intr* to tipple
cicchétto *m* nip (*of liquor*); (slang) dressing down

cìc·cia *f* (-ce) (joc) flesh; (joc) fat
cicció·ne -na *mf* fatty
ciceróne *m* guide ‖ **Cicerone** *m* Cicero
ciclàbile *adj* open to bicycles; bicycle, e.g., **pista ciclabile** bicycle trail
cìcli·co -ca *adj* (-ci -che) cyclic(al)
cicli·sta *mf* (-sti -ste) cyclist, bicyclist
ciclo *m* cycle; (coll) bicycle; **ciclo operativo** (econ) turnover
ciclomotóre *m* motorbike
ciclomotori·sta *mf* (-sti -ste) driver of motorbike
ciclóne *m* cyclone
ciclòpe *m* cyclops
ciclòpi·co -ca *adj* (-ci -che) cyclopean, gigantic
ciclopista *f* bicycle trail
ciclostilare *tr* to mimeograph
ciclostile *or* ciclostilo *m* mimeograph
ciclotróne *m* cyclotron
cicógna *f* stork
cicòria *f* chicory; endive
cicuta *f* hemlock
ciè·co -ca (-chi -che) *adj* blind; **alla cieca** blindly ‖ *mf* blind person ‖ *m* blind man; **i ciechi** the blind
cièlo *m* sky; heaven; weather, climate; roof (e.g., of wagon); **a ciel sereno** in the open air; **cielo a pecorelle** mackerel or fleecy sky; **dal cielo** from above; **non stare né in cielo né in terra** to be utterly absurd; **per amor del cielo** for heaven's sake; **portare al cielo** to praise to the skies; **santo cielo!** good heavens!; **volesse il cielo che . . . !** would that . . . !
cifra *f* number, figure; Arabic numeral; sum, total; digit; initial, monogram; cipher, code; **cifra d'affari** amount of business, turnover; **cifra tonda** round number
cifrare *tr* to cipher, code; to embroider (a monogram)
cifrà·rio *m* (-ri) code, cipher
ci·glio *m* (-glia *fpl*) eyelash; eyebrow; **a ciglio asciutto** with dry eyes; **ciglia** (zool) cilia; **senza batter ciglio** without batting an eye ‖ *m* (-gli) (fig) edge, brow
ciglióne *m* bank, embankment
cigno *m* swan; cob
cigolante *adj* creaky, squeaky
cigolare (cìgolo) *intr* to squeak, creak
cigolì·o *m* (-ìi) squeak, creak
Cile, il Chile
cilécca *f*—**fare cilecca** to misfire
cileccare §197 (cilécco) *intr* to goof, blunder; to fail
cilè·no -na *adj* & *mf* Chilean
cilè·stro -stra *adj* (poet) azure, blue
cili·cio *m* (-ci) sackcloth
ciliè·gia *f* (-gie & -ge) cherry
ciliè·gio *m* (-gi) cherry tree
cilindrare *tr* to calender (e.g., paper); to roll (a road)
cilindrata *f* (aut) cylinder capacity, piston displacement
cilìndri·co -ca *adj* (-ci -che) cylindric(al)
cilindro *m* cylinder; top hat; roll, roller
cima *f* top, summit; tip (e.g., of a pole); peak (of mountain); edge, end; rope, cable; head (e.g., of let-

tuce); (coll) genius; **da cima a fondo** from top to bottom
cimare *tr* to cut the tip off; to shear; (agr) to prune
cimasa *f* (archit) coping
cìmbalo *m* gong; (obs) cymbal; **in cimbali** tipsy; in a tizzy
cimè·lio *m* (-li) relic, souvenir, memento
cimentare (ciménto) *tr* to risk (e.g., one's life); to provoke; (archaic) to assay ‖ *ref* to expose oneself; to venture
ciménto *m* risk, danger; (archaic) assay
cìmice *f* bug; bedbug; (coll) thumbtack
cimièro *m* crest; (poet) helmet
ciminièra *f* chimney (of factory); smokestack (of locomotive); funnel (of steamship)
cimitèro *m* cemetery, graveyard; (fig) ghosttown
cimósa [s] *or* cimóssa *f* selvage; blackboard eraser
cimurro *m* distemper; (joc) cold
Cina, la China
cinabro *m* cinnabar; crimson; red ink
cìn·cia *f* (-ce) titmouse
cinciallégra *f* great titmouse
cincilla *f* chinchilla
cincischiare §287 *tr* to shred; to wrinkle, crease; to waste (time); to mumble (words) ‖ *intr* to wrinkle, crease
cine *m* (coll) cinema
cineamatóre *m* amateur movie maker
cine·asta *m* (-sti) motion-picture producer; movie fan; movie actor ‖ *f* movie actress
cinecàmera *f* movie camera
cinedilettante *mf* amateur movie maker
cinegiornale *m* newsreel
cinelàndia *f* movieland
cìne·ma *m* (-ma) movies; movie house
cinematografare (cinematògrafo) *tr* to film, shoot
cinematografìa *f* cinema, motion pictures, movie industry
cinematogràfi·co -ca *adj* (-ci -che) movie, motion-picture; movie-like
cinematògrafo *m* motion picture; movie theater; (fig) hubbub; (fig) funny sight
cineparchég·gio *m* (-gi) drive-in movie
cinepar·co *m* (-chi) drive-in movie
cineprésa [s] *f* movie camera
cinère·o -a *adj* ashen
cinescò·pio *m* (-pi) kinescope, TV tube
cinése [s] *adj* & *mf* Chinese
cineteatro *m* movie house; **cineteatro all'aperto** outdoor movie
cinetè·ca *f* (-che) film library
cinèti·co -ca (-ci -che) *adj* kinetic ‖ *f* kinetics
cingallégra *f* var of cinciallegra
cìngere §181 *tr* to surround; to gird (e.g., the head); to gird on (e.g., the sword); **cingere cavaliere** to dub a knight; **cingere d'assedio** to besiege
cinghia *f* belt, strap; **tirare la cinghia** to tighten one's belt
cinghiale *m* wild boar
cinghiata *f* lash
cingola·to -ta *adj* track-driven, caterpillar

cìngolo *m* endless metal belt, track; girdle, belt (*of a priest*)

cinguettare (cinguétto) *intr* to chirp, twitter; to babble

cinguettì·o *m* (-**i**) chirp, twitter; (fig) babble

cìni·co -ca (-**ci** -**che**) *adj* cynical || *m* cynic

ciniglia *f* chenille

cinismo *m* cynicism

cinòfilo *m* dog lover

cinquanta *adj, m & pron* fifty

cinquantenà·rio -ria (-**ri** -**rie**) *adj* fifty-year-old; occurring every fifty years || *m* fiftieth anniversary

cinquantènne *adj* fifty-year-old || *mf* fifty-year-old person

cinquantèn·nio *m* (-**ni**) period of fifty years, half century

cinquantèsi·mo -ma *adj, m & pron* fiftieth

cinquantina *f* about fifty; **sulla cinquantina** about fifty years old

cìnque *adj & pron* five; **le cìnque** five o'clock || *m* five; fifth (*in dates*)

cinquecenté·sco -sca *adj* (-**schi** -**sche**) sixteenth-century

cinquecènto *adj, m & pron* five hundred || *f* small car || **il Cinquecento** the sixteenth century

cinquina *f* set of five; five numbers (*drawn at Italian lotto*); (mil) pay

cinta *f* fence, wall; circuit, enclosure; circumference (*of a city*)

cintare *tr* to surround; to fence in; to hold (*in wrestling*)

cìn·to -ta *adj* surrounded, girded || *m* belt; girdle; **cinto erniario** truss || *f* see **cinta**

cìntola *f* waist; belt; **con le mani alla cintola** idling, loafing

cintura *f* belt; waist; waistband; lock (*in wrestling*); **cintura di salvataggio** life preserver; **cintura di sicurezza** safety belt

cinturare *tr* to surround

cinturino *m* strap (*of watch or shoes*); hem (*e.g., of cuffs*)

cinturóne *m* belt; Sam Browne belt

ciò *pron* this; that; **a ciò** for that purpose; **a ciò che** so that; **ciò nondimeno** or **ciò nonostante** though, nevertheless; **con tutto ciò** in spite of everything; **per ciò** therefore

ciòc·ca *f* (-**che**) lock (*of hair*); cluster (*e.g., of cherries*)

ciòc·co *m* (-**chi**) log; **dormire come un ciocco** to sleep like a log

cioccolata *adj invar* chocolate || *f* chocolate (*beverage*)

cioccolatino *m* chocolate candy

cioccolato *m* chocolate; **cioccolato al latte** milk chocolate

cioè *adv* that is to say, namely; to wit; rather

ciondolare (cióndolo) *tr* to dangle || *intr* to dawdle; to stroll, saunter

cióndolo *m* pendant, charm

ciondolóne *m* idler || *adv* dangling

ciòtola *f* bowl

ciòttolo *m* pebble, small stone; cobblestone

ciottoló·so -sa [s] *adj* pebbly

cip *m* (**cip**) chip (*in gambling*)

cipi·glio *m* (-**gli**) frown

cipólla *f* onion; bulb (*e.g., of a lamp*); nozzle (*of sprinkling can*)

cippo *m* column; bench mark

ciprèsso *m* cypress

cipria *f* face powder; **cipria compatta** compact

cipriò·ta *adj & mf* (-**ti** -**te**) Cypriot

Cipro *m* Cyprus

circa *adv* about, nearly || *prep* concerning, regarding, as to

cìr·co *m* (-**chi**) circus; **circo equestre** circus; **circo glaciale** cirque; **circo lunare** walled plain

circolante *adj* circulating; lending (*library*) || *m* available cash (*of a corporation*)

circolare *adj* circular; cashier's (*check*) || *f* circular (*letter*); (rr) beltline || *v* (**cìrcolo**) *intr* to circulate

circolazióne *f* circulation; traffic; currency; **circolazione sanguigna** bloodstream; circulation of blood

cìrcolo *m* circle; circulation (*of blood*); reception (*e.g., at court*); club, set, group

circoncidere §145 *tr* to circumcise

circoncisióne *f* circumcision

circonci·so -sa *adj* circumcised

circondare (circóndo) *tr* to surround, encircle; to overwhelm (*e.g., with kindness*) || *ref* to surround oneself; to be surrounded

circondà·rio *m* (-**ri**) district; surrounding territory

circonduzióne *f* rotation (*e.g., of the body in calisthenics*)

circonferènza *f* circumference

circonflès·so -sa *adj* circumflex

circonlocuzióne *f* circumlocution

circonvallazióne *f* city-line road; (rr) beltline

circonvenire §282 *tr* to circumvent; to outwit

circonvenzióne *f* circumvention

circonvici·no -na *adj* neighboring, nearby

circoscrit·to -ta *adj* circumscribed

circoscrivere §250 *tr* to circumscribe

circoscrizióne *f* district; circuit

circospèt·to -ta *adj* circumspect, cautious

circospezióne *f* circumspection

circostante *adj* neighboring, surrounding, nearby || **circostanti** *mpl* neighbors; bystanders, onlookers

circostanza *f* circumstance

circostanziale *adj* circumstantial

circostanziare §287 *tr* to describe in detail; to circumstanciate

circostanzia·to -ta *adj* detailed, circumstantial

circuire §176 *tr* to circumvent

circùito *m* circuit; race (*of automobiles or bicycles*); **circuito stampato** (rad, telv) printed circuit

circumnavigare §209 (**circumnàvigo**) *tr* to circumnavigate

circumnavigazióne *f* circumnavigation

cirìlli·co -ca *adj* (-**ci** -**che**) Cyrillic

Ciro m Cyrus
cirro m cirrus
cirrò·si f (-si) cirrhosis
cispa f gum (on edge of eyelids)
cisposità [s] f gum; gumminess
cispó·so -sa [s] adj gummy
ciste f cyst
cistèrna f cistern; tank
cisti f cyst
cistifèllea f gall bladder
citante mf (law) plaintiff
citare tr to cite, quote; to mention; (law) to summon, subpoena
citazióne f citation, quotation; mention; (law) summons, subpoena; (mil) commendation
citillo m (zool) gopher
citòfono m intercom
citostàti·co -ca adj (-ci -che) (biochem) cancer-inhibiting
citrato m citrate
citri·co -ca adj (-ci -che) citric
citrul·lo -la adj simple, foolish || mf simpleton, fool
cit·tà f (-tà) city, town || **Città del Capo** Cape Town; **Città del Messico** Mexico City; **Città del Vaticano** Vatican City; **città fungo** boom town
cittadèlla f citadel
cittadinanza f citizenship
cittadi·no -na adj city, town, civic || mf citizen; city dweller, urbanite || m townsman
ciù·co m (-chi) (coll) donkey, ass
ciuffo m lock, forelock; tuft; (bot) tassel
ciuffolòtto m (orn) bullfinch
ciurlare intr—**ciurlare nel manico** to play fast and loose
ciurma f crew, gang, mob
ciurmare tr (archaic) to charm; (archaic) to trick, inveigle
ciurmatóre m swindler, charlatan
civétta f barn owl, little owl; unmarked police car; ship used as decoy; (fig) coquette, flirt
civettare (**civétto**) intr to flirt
civetterìa f coquettishness, coquetry
civettuò·lo la adj coquettish; attractive
cìvi·co -ca adj (-ci -che) civic; town, city
civile adj civil; civilian || mf civilian
civili·sta mf (-sti -ste) attorney, solicitor
civilizzare [ddzz] tr to civilize || ref to become civilized
civilizzazióne [ddzz] f civilizing (e.g., of barbarians); civilization
civil·tà f (-tà) civilization; civility
civismo m good citizenship
clac·son m (-son) horn (of a car)
claire f (claire) grating (in front of a store window)
clamóre m clamor, uproar
clamoró·so -sa [s] adj noisy; clamorous
clan m (clan) clan; clique
clandesti·no -na adj clandestine
clangóre m clangor, clang
clarinetti·sta mf (-sti -ste) clarinet player
clarinétto m clarinet
clarino m clarion
classe f class

classicheggiante adj classicistic
classicismo m classicism
classici·sta mf (-sti -ste) classicist
classici·tà f (-tà) classical spirit; classical antiquity
clàssi·co -ca (-ci -che) adj classic(al) || m classic
classifi·ca f (-che) rank, rating (in competitive testing); classification; (sports) rating
classificare §197 (**classìfico**) tr to classify; to rate, rank || ref to score
classificazióne f classification
claudicante adj lame, limping
claudicare (**clàudico**) intr to limp
clauné·sco -sca adj (-schi -sche) clownish
clàusola f provision, proviso; clause; close, conclusion (e.g., of a speech); **clausola rossa** instructions for payment (in bank-credit documents); **clausola verde** shipping instructions (in bank-credit documents)
clausura f (eccl) seclusion; (fig) secluded place
clava f club, bludgeon
clavicémbalo m harpsicord
clavìcola f clavicle, collarbone
clemàtide f clematis
clemènte adj clement, indulgent; mild (climate)
clemènza f clemency; mildness
cleptòmane adj & mf kleptomaniac
clericale adj clerical || m clericalist
clericalismo m clericalism
clèro m clergy
clessidra f water clock; sandglass
clicchetti·o m (-ii) clicking, click-clack (e.g., of a typewriter)
cli·ché m (-ché) cliché; stereotype (plate)
cliènte m client, customer, patron
clientèla f clientele, customers; practice (of a professional man)
cli·ma m (-mi) climate
climatèri·co -ca adj (-ci -che) climacteric; crucial
climatè·rio m (-ri) climacteric; crucial period
climàti·co -ca adj (-ci -che) climatic
climatizzazióne [ddzz] f air conditioning
clìni·co -ca (-ci -che) adj clinic || m clinician; highly skilled physician || f clinic; private hospital
cli·sma m (-smi) enema
clistère m enema; **clistere a pera** fountain syringe
cloa·ca f (-che) sewer
cloche f (cloche) woman's wide-brimmed hat; (aer) stick; (aut) floor gearshift
clorare (**clòro**) tr to chlorinate
clorato m chlorate
cloridri·co -ca adj (-ci -che) hydrochloric
clòro m chlorine
clorofilla f chlorophyll
clorofòr·mio m (-mi) chloroform
cloroformizzare [ddzz] tr to chloroform
cloruro m chloride

coabitare (coàbito) *intr* to live together; to cohabit

coabitazióne *f* sharing (*of an apartment*)

coaccusà·to -ta *adj* jointly accused ‖ *m* codefendant

coacèrvo *m* accumulation (*e.g., of interest*)

coadiutóre *m* coadjutor

coadiuvànte *adj* helping ‖ *m* helper

coadiuvare (coàdiuvo) *tr* to assist, advise

coagulare (coàgulo) *tr & ref* to coagulate, clot

coagulazióne *f* coagulation, clotting

coàgulo *m* clot

coalescènza *f* coalescence

coalizióne *f* coalition

coalizzare [ddzz] *tr & ref* to unite, rally

coartare *tr* to coerce, force

coartazióne *f* coercion, forcing

coatti·vo -va *adj* forceful, compelling

coat·to -ta *adj* coercive

coautóre *m* coauthor

coazióne *f* coercion

cobalto *m* cobalt

cocaina *f* cocaine

cocainòmane *mf* cocaine addict

coc·ca *f* (**-che**) notch (*of arrow*); corner, edge (*e.g., of a handkerchief*); three-mast galley

coccarda *f* cockade

cocchière *m* coachman, cab driver

còc·chio *m* (**-chi**) coach; chariot

cocchiume *m* bung

còc·cia *f* (**-ce**) sword guard; (coll) head, noggin

còccige *m* coccyx

coccinèlla *f* ladybug

cocciniglia *f* cochineal

còc·cio *m* (**-ci**) earthenware; broken piece of pottery

cocciutàggine *m* stubborness

cocciu·to -ta *adj* stubborn

còc·co *m* (**-chi**) coconut (*tree and nut*); (bact) coccus; (coll) egg; (coll) darling, favorite

cocco-dè *m* (**-dè**) cackle

coccodrillo *m* crocodile

còccola *f* berry (*of cypress*); darling girl

coccolare (còccolo) *tr* to fondle, cuddle ‖ *ref* to nestle, cuddle up; to bask

còcco-lo -la *adj* (coll) nice, darling ‖ *m* darling boy ‖ *f* see **coccola**

coccolóne or **coccolóni** *adv* squatting

cocènte *adj* burning

cocktail *m* (**cocktail**) cocktail; cocktail party

còclea *f* dredge; (anat) cochlea

cocómero *m* watermelon; (coll) simpleton

cocorita *f* parakeet

cocuzza *f* (coll) pumpkin; (coll) head, noggin

cocùzzolo *m* crown (*of hat*); peak (*of mountain*)

códa *f* tail; train (*of skirt*); pigtail (*of hair*); **coda di paglia** (coll) uneasy conscience; **con la coda dell'occhio** out of the corner of the eye; **con la coda tra le gambe** with its tail between its legs; (fig) crestfallen; **di** **coda** last; **fare la coda** to stand in line; **in coda** in a row; at the tail end

codardìa *f* (lit) cowardice

codar·do -da *adj* cowardly ‖ *mf* coward

codazzo *m* (pej) trail (*of people*)

codeina *f* codein

codé·sto -sta §7 *adj* ‖ §8 *pron*

còdice *m* code; codex; **codice della strada** traffic laws; **codice di avviamento postale** zip code

codicillo *m* codicil

codificare §197 (**codìfico**) *tr* to codify

codi·no -na *adj* reactionary; conformist ‖ *m* pigtail (*of a man*); (fig) reactionary; conformist ‖ *f* small tail

códolo *m* tang, shank (*e.g., of knife*); handle (*of spoon or knife*); head (*of violin*)

coeducazióne *f* coeducation

coefficiènte *m* coefficient

coerciti·vo -va *adj* coercive

coercizióne *f* coercion

coerède *mf* coheir

coerènte *adj* coherent; consistent

coerènza *f* coherence; consistency

coesióne *f* cohesion

coesistènza *f* coexistence

coesìstere §114 *intr* to coexist

coesi·vo -va *adj* cohesive

coetàne·o -a *adj & m* contemporary

coè·vo -va *adj* contemporaneous, coeval

cofanétto *m* small chest, small coffer

còfano *m* chest, coffer; box, case (*for ammunition*); (aut) hood

còffa *f* masthead, crow's-nest

cofirmatà·rio -ria *adj & mf* (**-ri -rie**) cosigner

cogitabón·do -da *adj* (poet & joc) thoughtful, meditative

cogitare (còglto) *tr & intr* (poet & joc) to cogitate

cógli §4

cògliere §127 *tr* to gather; to hit (*the target*); to pluck (*flowers*); to grab, seize; (fig) to guess; **cogliere in flagrante** to catch in the act; **cogliere la palla al balzo** to seize time by the forelock; **cogliere nel giusto** to hit the nail on the head; **cogliere qlcu alla sprovvista** to catch s.o. napping; **cogliere sul fatto** to catch in the act

coglióne *m* (vulg) testicle; (vulg) simpleton, fool

coglioneria *f* (vulg) great stupidity

cognata *f* sister-in-law

cognato *m* brother-in-law

cògni·to -ta *adj* (poet & law) wellknown

cognizióne *f* cognition, knowledge

cognóme *m* surname, family name

coguaro *m* cougar

cói §4

coibènte *adj* nonconducting ‖ *m* nonconductor

coincidènza *f* coincidence; harmony, identity; transfer (*from one streetcar or bus to another*); (rr) connection

coincìdere §145 *intr* to coincide

coinquilino *m* fellow tenant

cointeressare (cointerèsso) *tr* to give a share (*of profit*) to

cointeressa·to -ta *adj* jointly interested ‖ *mf* party having a joint interest

cointeressènza *f* interest, share

coinvòlgere §289 *tr* to involve

còito *m* coitus, intercourse

cól §4.

colà *adv* over there

colabròdo *m* colander, strainer

colàg·gio *m* (-**gi**) loss, leak

colapa·sta *m* (-**sta**) colander

colare (cólo) *tr* to filter, strain; to sift (*wheat*); to cast (*metals*); **colare a picco** to sink ‖ *intr* to leak, drip; to flow (*said of blood*); **colare a picco** to sink

colata *f* casting (*of metal*); stream of lava; slide (*of snow or rocks*)

colatíc·cio *m* (-**ci**) drip, dripping

cola·tóio *m* (-**tói**) colander, strainer

colazióne *f* breakfast; lunch; **colazione al sacco** picnic; **prima colazione** breakfast; **seconda colazione** lunch

colbac·co *m* (-**chi**) busby

colèi §8 *pron dem*

colèn·do -da *adj* (archaic) honorable

colè·ra *m* (-**ra**) cholera

colesterina *f* cholesterol

coli·brì *m* (-**brì**) hummingbird

còli·co -ca *adj & f* (-**ci -che**) colic

colino *m* strainer

cólla §4

còlla *f* glue; paste; **colla di pesce** isinglass

collaborare (collàboro) *intr* to collaborate; to contribute (*to newspaper or magazine*)

collaboratóre -tríce *mf* collaborator; contributor (*to newspaper or magazine*)

collaborazióne *f* collaboration

collaborazioni·sta *mf* (-**sti -ste**) collaborationist

collana *f* necklace; series, collection (*of literary works*)

collante *adj & m* adhesive

collare *m* collar ‖ *v* (**còllo**) *tr* to lift or lower (*with a rope*)

collasso *m* collapse

collaterale *adj & m* collateral

collaudare (collàudo) *tr* to test; to approve; to pass

collauda·tóre -tríce *mf* tester

collàudo *m* test

collazionare (collazióno) *tr* to collate

cólle §4

còlle *m* hill; low peak; mountain pass

collè·ga *mf* (-**ghi -ghe**) colleague, associate

collegaménto *m* connection, telephone connection; contact; (mil) liaison

collegare §209 (collégo) *tr* to join, connect ‖ *intr* to agree, be in harmony ‖ *ref* to become allied; to make contact, make connection (*e.g., by phone*)

collegiale *adj* collegiate ‖ *mf* boarding-school student

collegiata *f* collegiate church

collè·gio *m* (-**gi**) college (*e.g., of surgeons*); boarding school, academy

còllera *f* anger, wrath; **montare in collera** to become angry

collèri·co -ca *adj* (-**ci -che**) hot-tempered, choleric

collètta *f* collection; collect (*in church*)

collettivismo *m* collectivism

collettivi·tà *f* (-**tà**) collectivity, community

collettí·vo -va *adj* collective ‖ *m* party worker (*of leftist party*)

collétto *m* collar; flank (*of a tooth*)

collet·tóre -tríce *adj* connecting; collecting (*pipe*) ‖ *m* collector; tax collector; manifold; (elec) commutator (*of D.C. device*); (elec) collector (*of A.C. device*); **collettore d'ammissione** intake manifold; **collettore di scarico** exhaust manifold

collettoria *f* tax office; small post office

collezionare (collezióno) *tr* to collect (*e.g., stamps*)

collezióne *f* collection; collection, series (*of literary works*)

collezioni·sta *mf* (-**sti -ste**) collector

collídere §135 *intr* to collide

collimare *tr* to point (*a telescope*) ‖ *intr* to coincide, match; to dovetail

collina *f* hill; **in collina** in the hill country

collinó·so -sa [*s*] *adj* hilly

collì·rio *m* (-**ri**) eyewash

collisióne *f* collision; (fig) conflict: **entrare in collisione** to collide

cóllo §4

còllo *m* neck; piece (*of baggage*); package, parcel; **al collo** in a sling; (fig) downhill; **collo del piede** instep; **collo d'oca** crankshaft; **in collo** in one's arms (*said of a baby*)

collocaménto *m* placement, employment; **collocamento a riposo** retirement; **collocamento in aspettativa** leave of absence without pay; **collocamento in malattia** sick leave

collocare §197 (còlloco) *tr* to place; to find employment for; to sell; **collocare a riposo** to retire; **collocare in aspettativa** to give a leave of absence without pay to; **collocare in malattia** to grant sick leave to

collocazióne *f* location (*of a book in a library*); catalogue card

colloidale *adj* colloidal

collòide *m* colloid

colloquiale *adj* colloquial

collò·quio *m* (-**qui**) talk, conference; colloquy; colloquium, symposium

collló·so -sa [*s*] *adj* gluey, sticky

collotòrto *m* (**collitòrti**) bigot, hypocrite

collòttola *f* nape or scruff of the neck

collúdere §105 *intr* to be in collusion

collusióne *f* collusion

collutó·rio *m* (-**ri**) mouthwash

colluttare *intr* to scuffle, fight

colluttazióne *f* scuffle, fight

cólma *f* high-water level (*during high tide*)

colmare (cólmo) *tr* to fill, fill up; to fill in (*with dirt*); to overwhelm; **colmare una lacuna** to bridge a gap

colmata *f* silting; reclaimed land; sand bank

cól·mo -ma *adj* full, filled up ‖ *m* top, peak, summit; (archit) ridgepole; (fig) acme; **al colmo di** at the height of; **è il colmo** that's the limit ‖ *f* see **colma**

colofóne *m* colophon

colofònia *f* rosin

colombàia *f* dovecot

colombèlla *f* ingenue; **a colombella** vertically

colóm·bo -ba *mf* pigeon, dove ‖ **Colombo** *m* Columbus

colònia *f* colony; cologne; settlement; summer camp; **colonia penale** penal colony; penitentiary ‖ **Colonia** *f* Cologne

coloniale *adj* colonial ‖ *m* colonial; colonist; **coloniali** imported foods

colòni·co -ca *adj* (**-ci -che**) farm (*e.g., house*)

colonizzare [ddzz] *tr* to colonize; to settle

colonizzazióne [ddzz] *f* colonization

colonna *f* column; row; **colonna sonora** sound track; **Colonne d'Ercole** Pillars of Hercules

colonnato *m* colonnade

colonnèllo *m* colonel

colonnétta *f* small column; gasoline pump

colò·no -na *mf* sharecropper; colonist; settler; (poet) farmer

colorante *adj* coloring ‖ *m* dye; stain

colorare (**colóro**) *tr* & *ref* to color; to stain

colora·to -ta *adj* colored; stained (*glass*)

colorazióne *f* coloring

colóre *m* color; paint; suit (*of cards*); flush (*at poker*); shade; character (*of a deal*); **di colore** colored (*man*); **farne di tutti i colori** to be up to all kinds of deviltry; **farsi di tutti i colori** to change countenance

colorifi·cio *m* (**-ci**) paint factory; dye factory

colorire §176 *tr* to color

colori·to -ta *adj* colored, flushed; expressive ‖ *m* color, complexion; (fig) expression

coloritura *f* coloring; characteristic; political complexion

colóro §8

colossale *adj* colossal

Colossèo *m* Coliseum

colòsso *m* colossus

cólpa *f* fault; sin; guilt; (law) injury; **avere la colpa** to be guilty; to be wrong; **essere in colpa** to be guilty

colpévole *adj* guilty ‖ *mf* guilty person, culprit

colpevoli·sta *mf* (**-sti -ste**) person who prejudges s.o. guilty

colpire §176 *tr* to hit, strike; to harm; to impress; **colpire nel segno** to hit the mark

cólpo *m* hit, blow; strike; tip, rap; knock; shot; round (*of gun*); cut, slash (*of knife*); thrust (*e.g., of spear*); lash (*of animal's tail*); toot (*of car's horn*); **andare a colpo sicuro** to know where to hit; **colpo apoplettico** stroke; **colpo da maestro** master stroke; **colpo d'aria** draft; **colpo d'ariete** water hammer; **colpo di fortuna** stroke of luck; **colpo di fulmine** love at first sight; **colpo di**

grazia coup de grâce; **colpo di mano** surprise attack; **colpo di scena** dramatic turn of events; **colpo di sole** sunstroke; **colpo di spugna** wiping the slate clean; **colpo di stato** coup d'état; **colpo di telefono** telephone call; **colpo di testa** sudden decision, inconsiderate action; **colpo di vento** gust of wind; **colpo d'occhio** view; glance, look; **di colpo** at once; **fallire il colpo** to miss the mark; **fare colpo** to make a hit; **sul colpo** then and there; **tutto in un colpo** all at once

colpó·so -sa [s] *adj* unpremeditated; involuntary (*e.g., manslaughter*)

coltèlla *f* butcher knife; (elec) knife switch

coltellàc·cio *m* (**-ci**) hunting knife; butcher knife; (naut) studding sail

coltellata *f* stab, gash, slash; **fare a coltellate** to fight with knives

coltelleria *f* cutlery

coltelli·nàio *m* (**-nài**) cutler

coltèllo *m* knife; **a coltello** edgewise (*said of bricks*); **avere il coltello per il manico** to have the upper hand; **coltello a serramanico** switchblade knife; pocketknife

coltivare *tr* to cultivate

coltiva·to -ta *adj* cultivated

coltivatóre *m* farmer

coltivazióne *f* cultivation

cól·to -ta *adj* cultivated; learned (*word*) ‖ *m* garden; (archaic) worship

cóltre *f* blanket; comforter; (fig) pall; **coltri** bedclothes

coltróne *m* quilt

coltura *f* cultivation; crop; culture (*e.g., of silkworms, bacteria*)

colubrina *f* culverin

colùi §8 *pron dem*

comandaménto *m* commandment

comandante *m* commanding officer; commandant; (nav) captain; **comandante del porto** harbor master; **comandante in seconda** (naut) first mate

comandare *tr* to command, order; to direct (*employees*); to register (*a letter*); (mach) to regulate; (mach) to control; (poet) to overlook, command the view of (*e.g., a valley*); **comandare a bacchetta** to command in a dictatorial manner ‖ *intr* to command; **comandi!** (mil) at your orders!

comando *m* command, order

comare *f* godmother; (coll) friend, neighbor; (coll) gossip

combaciare §128 *tr* (archaic) to gather ‖ *intr* to fit closely together; to tally, dovetail; to coincide

combattènte *adj* fighting ‖ *m* combatant

combàttere *tr* & *intr* to combat ‖ *ref* to fight one another

combattiménto *m* combat; fight; battle; **fuori combattimento** knockout, K.O.; **fuori combattimento tecnico** technical knockout, T.K.O.; **mettere fuori combattimento** to knock out; (fig) to weaken

combatti·vo -va adj pugnacious, combative

combattu·to -ta adj heated (discussion); overcome (by doubt); torn (between two opposing feelings)

combinare tr to combine; to match (e.g., colors); to organize || intr to agree; **combinare a** to succeed in || ref to agree; to chance, happen; to combine

combinazióne f combination; chance; coverall (for mechanics or flyers)

combriccola f gang

combustìbile adj combustible || m fuel, combustible

combustióne f combustion; (poet) upheaval

combutta f gang, band; **essere in combutta** to be in cahoots

cóme m manner, way; **il come e il perché** the why and the wherefore || adv as; like; as for; how; **come mal?** why?; **e come!** and how!; **ma come?** what?, how is it? || conj as; as soon as; while; how; because; since; **come se** as if

comecché conj (lit) although; (poet) wherever

comedóne m blackhead

cométa f comet

comici·tà f (-tà) comicalness

còmi·co -ca (-ci -che) adj comic(al) || m comic; author of comedies; comic actor

comìgnolo m chimney pot; ridge (of roof)

cominciare §128 tr & intr to begin, start, commence

comitato m committee

comitiva f group, party; (poet) retinue

comi·zio m (-zi) (pol) meeting, rally; (hist) comitia

còm·ma m (-mi) paragraph, article (of law or decree)

commèdia f comedy; play, drama; (fig) farce; **commedia di carattere** comedy of character; **commedia d'intreccio** comedy of intrigue; **far la commedia** to pretend, feign; **finire in commedia** to end ludicrously; **finire la commedia** to stop faking

commediànte mf actor; comedian (amusing person); (fig) hypocrite

commediògra·fo -fa mf playwright, comedian

commemorare (commèmoro) tr to commemorate

commemorati·vo -va adj commemorative, memorial

commemorazióne f commemoration

commènda f commandership (of an order); (eccl) commendam

commendàbile adj commendable

commendare (commèndo) tr (lit) to commend, praise; (obs) to entrust

commendati·zio -zia (-zi -zie) adj introductory || f letter of introduction; recommendation

commendatóre m commander (of an order)

commendévole adj commendable

commensale mf guest; table companion

commensurare (commènsuro & commènsuro) tr to compare; to proportion, prorate

commentare (commènto) tr to comment, comment on

commentà·rio m (-ri) commentary; diary, journal

commenta·tóre -trice mf commentator

commènto m comment; **fare commenti** to criticize; **non far commenti!** don't waste your time talking!

commerciàbile adj marketable

commerciale adj commercial; common, ordinary

commerciali·sta mf (-sti -ste) business-administration major; attorney specializing in commercial law

commerciante mf merchant, dealer

commerciare §128 (commèrcio) tr to deal in; to buy and sell || intr to deal

commèr·cio m (-ci) commerce, trade; illegal traffic; (poet) intercourse; **commercio all'ingrosso** wholesale (trade); **commercio al minuto** retail (trade); **fuori commercio** not for sale; **in commercio** for sale

commés·so -sa adj committed || mf clerk (in a store) || m salesman; clerk (in a court); janitor (in a school); **commesso viaggiatore** traveling salesman || f saleslady; order (of merchandise)

commestìbile adj edible || **commestìbili** mpl staples, groceries; foodstuffs

commèttere §198 tr to join, connect; to commit; to charge, commission; to peg; (poet) to entrust || intr to join, fit

commettitura f joint, seam

commiato m leave; **dare commiato a** to dismiss; **prender commiato** to take one's leave

commilitóne m comrade, comrade in arms

comminare tr (law) to determine, fix (a penalty)

comminatò·rio -ria adj threatening

commiserare (commisero) tr to pity, feel sorry for

commiserazióne f commiseration

commissariale adj commissioner's, e.g., **funzioni commissariali** commissioner's functions; commissar's functions

commissariato m commissary; inspector's office

commissà·rio m (-ri) commissary; inspector; commissioner; **commissario del popolo** commissar; **commissario di bordo** purser; **commissario di pubblica sicurezza** police inspector; **commissario tecnico** (sports) soccer commissioner

commissionare (commissióno) tr to commission, order

commissionà·rio -ria (-ri -rie) adj commission || m commission merchant

commissióne f commission, agency; order (of merchandise); committee; errand; commitment (of an act)

commisurare tr to proportion (e.g., crime to punishment)

committènte mf buyer, customer

commodòro *m* commodore

commòs·so -sa *adj* moved; moving

commovènte *adj* moving, touching

commozióne *f* commotion; emotion; **commozione cerebrale** (pathol) concussion

commuòvere §202 *tr* to move; to touch; to stir ‖ *ref* to be moved; to be touched

commutare *tr* to commute; to switch ‖ *ref* to turn

commuta·tóre -trice *adj* commutative ‖ *m* (elec) change-over switch; (elec) commutator (*switch*); (telp) plugboard ‖ *f* converter

commutatori·sta *mf* (-**sti** -**ste**) (telp) operator

commutazióne *f* commutation; (telp) selection; (elec) switchover

co·mò *m* (-**mò**) chest; chest of drawers

còmoda *f* commode

comodare (**còmodo**) *tr* to lend ‖ *intr* (with *dat*) to please, e.g., **non le comoda** it doesn't please her

comodino *m* night table; (theat) bit player; **fare il comodino a** (coll) to follow sheepishly

comodi·tà *f* (-**tà**) comfort; convenience; opportunity

còmo·do -da *adj* comfortable; convenient; easy; loose-fitting; calm ‖ *m* convenience; ease; advantage; comfort; opportunity; **a Suo comodo** at your convenience; **comodo di cassa** credit (*at the bank*); **con comodo** without hurrying; **fare comodo** to come in handy; (with *dat*) to please, e.g., **non gli fa comodo** it doesn't please him; **fare il proprio comodo** to think only of oneself; **stia comodo!** make yourself at home! ‖ *f* see **comoda**

compaesa·no -na *mf* fellow citizen ‖ *m* fellow countryman ‖ *f* fellow countrywoman

compàgine *f* strict union; connection; assemblage; (fig) cohesion

compagna *f* companion, mate; (archaic) company

compagnìa *f* company; **Compagnia di Gesù** Society of Jesus; **compagnia stabile** (theat) stock company

compa·gno -gna *adj* like, similar ‖ *m* fellow; companion, comrade; mate; partner; **compagno d'armi** comrade in arms; **compagno di viaggio** fellow traveler ‖ *f* see **compagna**

companàti·co -ca *m* (-**ci**) food to eat with bread

comparàbile *adj* comparable

comparati·vo -va *adj* & *m* comparative

compara·to -ta *adj* comparative

comparazióne *f* comparison

compare *m* godfather; best man (*at wedding*); fellow; confederate

comparire §108 *intr* to appear; to be known; to cut a figure

comparizióne *f* appearance (*in court*)

comparsa *f* appearance; (theat) extra, supernumerary; (law) petition, brief; **far comparsa** to cut a figure

compartecipare (**compartécipo**) *intr* to share

compartecipazióne *f* sharing; **compartecipazione agli utili** profit sharing

compartécipe *adj* sharing

compartiménto *m* circle, clique; district; (naut, rr) compartment

compartire §176 & (**comparto**) *tr* to divide up, distribute

compassa·to -ta *adj* measured; stiff, formal; reserved; self-controlled

compassionare (**compassióno**) *tr* to pity

compassióne *f* compassion, pity

compassionévole *adj* compassionate; pitiful

compasso *m* compass; **compasso a grossezza** calipers

compatibile *adj* excusable; compatible

compatiménto *m* compassion; condescension

compatire §176 *tr* to pity; to forgive, overlook; to bear with; **farsi compatire** to become an object of ridicule ‖ *intr* to pity

compatriò·ta *mf* (-**ti** -**te**) compatriot

compattézza *f* compactness

compat·to -ta *adj* compact, tight

compendiare §287 (**compèndio**) *tr* to epitomize, summarize

compèn·dio *m* (-**di**) compendium, summary; **fare un compendio di** to abstract

compendió·so -sa [s] *adj* compendious, brief, succinct

compenetràbile *adj* penetrable

compenetrabilità *f* penetrability

compenetrare (**compènetro**) *tr* to penetrate; to permeate; to pervade ‖ *ref* to be overcome; **compenetrarsi di** to be conscious of

compensare (**compènso**) *tr* to compensate, pay; to balance, offset; to clear (*checks*)

compensa·to -ta *adj* compensated; laminated ‖ *m* laminate; plywood

compensazióne *f* compensation; offset; (com) clearing (*of checks*)

compènso *m* reward; retribution; pay; **in compenso** on the other hand

cómpera *f* var of **compra**

comperare (**cómpero**) *tr* & *intr* var of **comprare**

competènte *adj* competent

competènza *f* competence; jurisdiction; **competenze honoraria**

compètere §129 *intr* to compete; to concern; to have jurisdiction

competiti·vo -va *adj* competitive

competi·tóre -trice *mf* competitor, contender

competizióne *f* competition, contest

compiacènte *adj* complaisant, obliging

compiacènza *f* complaisance, kindness; pleasure

compiacére §214 *tr* to gratify ‖ *intr* (with *dat*) to please, e.g., **non posso compiacere a tutti** I cannot please everybody ‖ *ref* to be pleased; **compiacersi con** to congratulate; **compiacersi di** to be kind enough to

compiaciménto *m* pleasure; congratulation; approval

compiaciu·to -ta *adj* pleased, satisfied

compiàngere §215 *tr* to pity ‖ *ref* to feel sorry

compian·to -ta *adj* lamented (*departed person*) ‖ *m* sympathy; (*poet*) sorrow; (*poet*) lament

compiegare §209 (**compiègo**) *tr* to enclose (*in a letter*)

cómpiere §130 *tr* to complete, finish; to fulfill, accomplish; **compiere . . . anni to be . . . years old; compiere gli anni** to have a birthday ‖ *ref* to happen; to come true

compilare *tr* to compile

compila·tóre -trice *mf* compiler

compilazióne *f* compilation

compiménto *m* fulfillment, accomplishment

compire §176 *tr* to complete, finish; to fulfill, accomplish; **per compir l'opera** as if it weren't enough ‖ *ref* to happen; to come true

compitare (**cómpito**) *tr* to syllabify; to read poorly; to spell, spell letter by letter

compitazióne *f* spelling letter by letter

compitézza *f* courtesy, politeness

cómpito *m* task; exercise; homework

compi·to -ta *adj* courteous, polite; (*poet*) adequate

compiu·to -ta *adj* accomplished

compleanno *m* birthday; **buon compleanno** happy birthday

complementare *adj* complementary; additional (*tax*) ‖ *f* graduated income tax

compleménto *m* complement; (*mil, nav*) reserve

complessióne *f* build, physique

complessi·tà *f* (**-tà**) complexity

complessi·vo -va *adj* total, aggregate

complès·so -sa *adj* complex, complicated; compound (*fracture*) ‖ *m* whole; complex; **in complesso** in general

completare (**complèto**) *tr* to complete, carry through; to supplement, round off

complè·to -ta *adj* complete, full; overall, thoroughgoing; **al completo** full (*e.g., bus*) ‖ *m* set (*of matching items*); suit of clothes; **completo femminile** lady's tailor-made suit; **completo maschile** man's suit

complicare §197 (**còmplico**) *tr* to complicate ‖ *ref* to become complicated

complica·to -ta *adj* complicated, complex

complicazióne *f* complication

còmplice *mf* accomplice, accessory

complici·tà *f* (**-tà**) complicity

complimentare (**compliménto**) *tr* to compliment ‖ *ref*—**complimentarsi con** to congratulate

compliménto *m* compliment; congratulation; favor; **complimenti** regards; **complimenti!** congratulations!; **fare complimenti** to stand on ceremony; **senza complimenti** without ceremony; without any further ado

complimentó·so -sa [s] *adj* ceremonious; complimentary

complottare (**complòtto**) *intr* to plot

complòtto *m* plot, machination

compliù·vio *m* (**-vi**) valley (*of roof*)

componènte *adj* component ‖ *mf* member ‖ *m* component (*component part*) ‖ *f* component (*force*)

componìbile *adj* sectional (*e.g., bookcase*)

componiménto *m* composition, settlement (*of a dispute*)

compórre §218 *tr* to compose; to arrange; to settle (*a quarrel*); to lay out (*a corpse*); (*typ*) to set

comportaménto *m* behavior

comportare (**compòrto**) *tr* to allow, tolerate; to entail ‖ *ref* to behave; to handle (*said, e.g., of a motor*); **comportarsi male** to misbehave

compòrto *m* (*com*) delay

compòsi·to -ta *adj* composite ‖ **composite** *fpl* (*bot*) Compositae

composi·tóio *m* (**-tói**) (*typ*) composing stick

composi·tóre -trice *mf* compositor, typesetter; composer ‖ *f* typesetting machine

composizióne *f* composition; settlement

compósta *f* compote; **composta di frutta** stewed fruit

compostézza *f* neatness, tidiness; good behavior; orderliness

compostièra *f* compote, compotier

compó·sto -sta *adj* compound; neat, tidy; well-behaved ‖ *m* compound ‖ *f* see **composta**

cómpra *f* purchase; shopping; **compre** shopping

comprare (**cómpro**) *tr* to buy, purchase; to buy off ‖ *intr* to buy, shop; to trade

compra·tóre -trice *mf* buyer, purchaser

compravéndere §281 *tr* to make a deal in, to transfer (*e.g., a house*)

compravéndita *f* transaction; transfer (*e.g., of real estate*)

comprèndere §220 *tr* to comprehend, include, comprise; to overwhelm; to understand; to forgive

comprendò·nio *m* (**-ni**) (*joc*) understanding

comprensìbile *adj* understandable, comprehensible

comprensióne *f* comprehension, understanding

comprensi·vo -va *adj* comprehensive; understanding

comprensò·rio *m* (**-ri**) land to be reclaimed; area, zone, e.g., **comprensorio turìstico** tourist area

comprè·so -sa *adj* comprised, included; understood; deeply touched; immersed

comprèssa *f* compress

compressióne *f* compression

comprès·so -sa *adj* compressed; (*fig*) repressed; (*aut*) supercharged ‖ *f* see **compressa**

compressóre *m* compressor; **compressore stradale** road roller

comprimà·rio *m* (**-ri**) (*med*) associate chief of staff; (*theat*) second lead

comprìmere §131 *tr* to compress; to repress, restrain; to tamp

compromés·so -sa *adj* jeopardized, in danger ‖ *m* compromise; referral (*to arbitration*)

compromettènte *adj* compromising

compromèttere §198 *tr* to compromise; to endanger; to involve, commit; (law) to refer (*to arbitration*)

comproprie·tà *f* (**-tà**) joint ownership

comproprietà·rio -ria *mf* (**-ri -rie**) joint owner

compròva *f* confirmation

comprovare (compròvo) *tr* to confirm; to circumstantiate

compulsare *tr* to consult, peruse; to summon (*to appear in court*)

compulsi·vo -va *adj* compulsive

compun·to -ta *adj* contrite, repentant

compunzióne *f* compunction

computàbile *adj* computable

computare (còmputo) *tr* to compute

computi·sta *mf* (**-sti -ste**) bookkeeper

computisterìa *f* bookkeeping

còmputo *m* computation, reckoning

comunale *adj* municipal, town (*e.g., hall*); community-owned; (poet) common

comunanza *f* community; **in comunanza** in common

comune *adj* common ‖ *m* normalcy; commune, municipality; town; town hall; (hist) guild; (nav) common seaman; **in comune** in common ‖ *f* commune (*in communist countries*); (theat) main stage entrance; **andare per la comune** to follow the crowd; **per la comune** commonly

comunèlla *f* cabal, clique; passkey (*in a hotel*); (law) mutual insurance (*of cattlemen*); **fare comunella con** to consort with

comunicàbile *adj* communicable

comunicante *adj* communicant; communicating ‖ *m* priest who gives communion

comunicare §197 (**comùnico**) *tr* to communicate; to administer communion to ‖ *intr* to communicate ‖ *ref* to spread; to receive communion, to commune

comunicati·vo -va *adj* communicable, spreading; communicative

comunicato *m* communiqué; **comunicato commerciale** advertisement, ad; **comunicato stampa** press release

comunicazióne *f* communication; statement; (telp) connection; **comunicazioni** communications

comunióne *f* community; (law) community property ‖ **Comunione** *f* Communion

comunismo *m* communism

comuni·sta (**-sti -ste**) *adj* communist ‖ *mf* communist; (law) joint tenant

comunisti·co -ca *adj* (**-ci -che**) communistic

comuni·tà *f* (**-tà**) community

comunità·rio -ria *adj* (**-ri -rie**) community, e.g., **interessi comunitari** community interests

comùnque *adv* however, nevertheless ‖ *conj* however, no matter how

cón §4 *prep* with; by (*e.g., boat*); **con + art + inf** by **+ ger**, e.g., **col leggere** by reading

conato *m* effort, attempt

cón·ca *f* (**-che**) washbowl, washbasin; copper water jug; valley, hollow; (poet) shell; **conca idràulica** drydock

concatenaménto *m* (poet) concatenation

concatenare (concatèno) *tr* to link ‖ *ref* to unfold, ensue

concatenazióne *f* concatenation

concàusa *f* joint cause; (law) aggravation

cònca·vo -va *adj* concave; hollow ‖ *m* hollow

concèdere §132 *tr* to grant, concede; to stretch (*a point*) ‖ *ref* to let oneself go, give oneself over

concènto *m* harmony; (fig) agreement

concentraménto *m* concentration

concentrare (concèntro) *tr* to concentrate; to center ‖ *ref* to concentrate, focus; to center

concentra·to -ta *adj* concentrated; condensed (*e.g., milk*) ‖ *m* purée (*e.g., of tomatoes*)

concentrazióne *f* concentration; (chem) condensation

concèntri·co -ca *adj* (**-ci -che**) concentric

concepìbile *adj* conceivable

concepiménto *m* conception; (fig) formulation

concepire §176 *tr* to conceive; (fig) to nurture

concerìa *f* tannery

concèrnere §133 *tr* to concern

concertare (concèrto) *tr* to scheme, concert; (mus) to orchestrate, arrange ‖ *ref* to agree

concerta·to -ta *adj* agreed upon; (mus) with accompaniment ‖ *m* ensemble (*of orchestra, soloists, and chorus*)

concerta·tóre -trice *mf* arranger ‖ *m* plotter, schemer

concertazióne *f* (mus) arrangement

concerti·sta *mf* (**-sti -ste**) concert performer, soloist

concèrto *m* concert; concerto; (fig) choir

concessionà·rio *m* (**-ri**) sole agent, concessionaire; dealer; lessee (*of business establishment*)

concessióne *f* concession; dealership; admission

concessi·vo -va *adj* concessive

concès·so -sa *adj* granted, admitting

concètto *m* concept; opinion

concettó·so -sa [*s*] *adj* concise; full of ideas; full of conceits

concettuale *adj* conceptual

concezióne *f* conception; formulation

conchìglia *f* shell, conch; (sports) jock guard, protective cup

conchiùdere §125 *tr*, *intr* & *ref* var of **concludere**

cón·cia *f* (**-ce**) tanning

conciapèl·li *m* (**-li**) tanner

conciare §128 (**cóncio**) *tr* to tan; to cure (*e.g., tobacco*); to arrange; to straighten up; to reduce; to cut (*a precious stone*); **conciare per le feste** (coll) to give a good beating to ‖ *ref* to get messed up, get dirty

conciatét·ti *m* (**-ti**) roofer

conciató·re -trice *mf* tanner

conciliàbile *adj* reconcilable

conciliàbolo *m* conventicle, secret meeting

conciliante *adj* conciliatory

conciliare *adj* council ‖ *m* member of an ecclesiastical council ‖ §287 *tr* to conciliate, reconcile; to settle (*a fine*); to promote (*e.g., sleep*); to obtain (*a favor*) ‖ *ref* to become reconciled

concilia·tóre -trice *adj* conciliatory ‖ *mf* conciliator, peacemaker ‖ *m* justice of the peace

conciliazióne *f* conciliation ‖ **la Conciliazione** the Concordat (*of 1929 between Italy and the Vatican*)

conci·lio *m* (**-li**) council; church council

concimàia *f* manure pit

concimare *tr* to manure

concimazióne *f* spreading of manure; chemical fertilization

concime *m* manure; fertilizer

cón·cio -cia (**-ci -ce**) *adj* tanned ‖ *m* ashlar; dung, manure; (archaic) agreement; **concio di scoria** cinder block ‖ *f* see **concia**

conciofossecosaché *conj* (archaic) since

concionare (**concióno**) *intr* (archaic) to harangue

concióne *f* (archaic) harangue; (archaic) assembly

conciossiacosaché *conj* (archaic) since

concisióne *f* concision, brevity

conci·so -sa *adj* concise, brief

concistòro *m* consistory; (fig) assembly

concitare (**cóncito**) *tr* to excite, stir up

concita·to -ta *adj* excited; (poet) decisive

concitazióne *f* impetus; excitement

concittadi·no -na *mf* fellow citizen

conclave *m* conclave

conclùdere §105 *tr* to conclude ‖ *intr* to conclude; to be convincing ‖ *ref* to conclude, end; **concludersi con** to end with; to result in

conclusionale *adj* (law) summary

conclusióne *f* conclusion; **conclusioni** (law) summation

conclusi·vo -va *adj* conclusive

conclu·so -sa *adj* concluded; terminated; (poet) closed

concomitante *adj* concomitant

concordanza *f* concordance, agreement; (gram) concord; **concordanze** concordance (*e.g., to the Bible*)

concordare (**concòrdo**) *tr* to agree on; to make agree ‖ *intr & ref* to come to an agreement

concordato *m* agreement; concordat; settlement (*with creditors*)

concòrde *adj* in agreement

concòrdia *f* concord, harmony

concorrènte *adj* competitive ‖ *m* (com) competitor; (sports) contestant

concorrènza *f* competition

concorrenziale *adj* competitive (*e.g., price*)

concórrere §139 *intr* to converge; to concur; to compete

concórso *m* attendance; concurrence; combination (*of circumstances*); competition; competitive examination; contest; **concorso di bellezza** beauty contest; **concorso di pubblico** turnout; **fuori concorso** not entering the competition; in a class by itself

concretare (**concrèto**) *tr* to realize (*e.g., a dream*); to conclude, accomplish ‖ *ref* to come true

concretézza *f* concreteness, consistency

concrè·to -ta *adj* concrete, real; practical ‖ *m* practical matter; **in concreto** really, in reality

concubina *f* concubine

concubinàg·gio *m* (**-gi**) concubinage

concubinato *m* var of **concubinaggio**

conculcare §197 *tr* (lit) to trample under foot; (lit) to violate

concupire §176 *tr* (poet) to lust for

concupiscènza *f* concupiscence, lust

concussióne *f* extortion, shakedown; **concussione cerebrale** (pathol) concussion

condanna *f* conviction; sentence; (fig) blame, condemnation

condannare *tr* to condemn; to find guilty, convict; to sentence; to damn (*to eternal punishment*); to declare incurable; to wall up

condanna·to -ta *adj* condemned ‖ *m* convict

condensare (**condènso**) *tr & ref* to condense

condensa·to -ta *adj* condensed (*e.g., milk*)

condensatóre *m* condenser

condensazióne *f* condensation

condiménto *m* condiment, seasoning

condire §176 *tr* to season

condiret·tóre -trice *mf* associate manager

condiscendènte *adj* condescending

condiscendènza *f* condescension

condiscéndere §245 *intr* to condescend

condiscépo·lo -la *mf* schoolmate, school companion

condivídere §158 *tr* to share

condizionale *adj & m* conditional ‖ *f* (law) suspended sentence

condizionare (**condizióno**) *tr* to condition; to treat (*to prevent spoilage*)

condizionatóre *m* air conditioner

condizióne *f* condition; term (*of sale*); **a condizione che** provided that; **condizioni** condition, shape (*e.g., of a shipment*); **essere in condizione di** to be in a position to

condoglianza *f* condolence; **fare le condoglianze a** to extend one's sympathy to

condolére §159 *ref* to condole

condomì·nio *m* (**-ni**) condominium

condòmi·no -na *mf* joint owner (*of real estate*)

condonare (**condóno**) *tr* to condone; to remit

condóno *m* pardon, parole

condót·to -ta *adj* country (*doctor*) ‖ *m* duct, canal; conduit ‖ *f* behavior, conduct; district (*of country doctor*); transportation; pipeline; (theat) baggage; **condotta forzata** flume

conducènte *m* driver; bus driver; motorman

condù·plex *mf* (**-plex**) (telp) party-line user

condurre §102 *tr* to lead; to drive (*a car*); to round up (*cattle*); to pipe (*e.g., gas*); to conduct; to trace (*a line*); to take; to bring; to manage; **condurre a termine** to bring to fruition, realize || *intr* to lead || *ref* to behave; to betake oneself, go; **condursi a** (poet) to be reduced to (*e.g., poverty*)

conduttivi·tà *f* (**-tà**) conductivity

condutti·vo -va *adj* conductive

condut·tóre -trice *adj* guiding, leading || *m* operator (*of a bus*); driver (*of a car*); (rr) engineer; (rr) ticket collector; (phys) conductor

conduttura *f* conduit, pipeline

conduzióne *f* conduction; leasing

conestàbile *m* constable (*keeper of a castle*)

confabulare (**confàbulo**) *intr* to confabulate, commune; to connive, scheme

confacènte *adj* suitable, appropriate; helpful

confare §173 *ref*—**confarsi a** to agree with, e.g., **le uova non gli si confanno** eggs do not agree with him

confederare (**confèdero**) *tr & ref* to confederate

confedera·to -ta *adj & m* confederate

confederazióne *f* confederation

conferènza *f* conference; lecture; **conferenza illustrata** chalk talk; **conferenza stampa** press conference

conferenziè·re -ra *mf* speaker, lecturer

conferiménto *m* conferring, bestowal

conferire §176 *tr* to confer, bestow; to add; to contribute || *intr* to confer; to contribute; **conferire alla salute** to be healthful

confèrma *f* confirmation; **a conferma di** (com) in reply to, confirming

confermare (**confèrmo**) *tr* to confirm; to verify; to retain (*in office*) || *ref* to become more sure of oneself; to prove to be; to remain (*in the conclusion of a letter*)

confessare (**confèsso**) *tr & ref* to confess

confessionale *adj* confessional; church; church-related, parochial (*e.g., school*) || *m* confessional

confessióne *f* confession

confès·so -sa *adj* acknowledged, self-admitted; **confesso e comunicato** having made one's confession and taken communion

confessóre *m* confessor

confetteria *f* candy store, confectioner's shop

confettièra *f* candy box

confettière *m* candy maker; candy dealer, confectioner

confètto *m* sugar-covered nut, sweetmeat; losenge, drop

confettura *f* candy; preserves, jam; **confetture** confectionery

confezionare (**confezióno**) *tr* to make; to tailor (*a suit*)

confezióne *f* preparation, manufacturing; packaging; **confezioni** ready-made clothes

confezioni·sta *mf* (**-sti -ste**) ready-made clothier

conficcare §197 *tr* to drive (*a nail*); to thrust (*a knife*) || *ref* to become embedded

confidare *tr* to trust (*a secret*) || *intr* to trust || *ref* to confide

confidènte *adj* confident || *mf* confident; informer

confidènza *f* confidence; secret; familiarity

confidenziale *adj* confidential; friendly

configgere §104 *tr* to plunge, thrust

configurazióne *f* configuration

confinante *adj* bordering || *mf* neighbor

confinare *tr* to exile; to confine || *intr* to border

confinà·rio -ria *adj* (**-ri -rie**) border (*e.g., zone*)

Confindùstria *f* (acronym) **Confederazione Nazionale degli Industriali** National Confederation of Industrialists

confine *m* border, boundary line; boundary mark, landmark

confino *m* exile (*in a different town*)

confi·sca *f* (**-sche**) confiscation

confiscare §197 *tr* to confiscate

confit·to -ta *adj* nailed; bound; tied; **confitto in croce** nailed to the cross

conflagrazióne *f* conflagration

conflitto *m* conflict

conflittualità *f* confrontation; belligerent attitude

confluènte *m* confluent

confluènza *f* confluence

confluire §176 *intr* to flow together, join; to converge

confóndere §178 *tr* to confuse; to overwhelm (*with kindness*); to humiliate; **confondere con** to mistake for || *ref* to mix; to become confused

conformare (**confórmo**) *tr* to shape; to conform || *ref* to conform

conformazióne *f* conformation

confórme *adj* faithful, exact; in agreement; true (*copy*)

conformeménte *adv* in conformity

conformi·sta *mf* (**-sti -ste**) conformist

conformi·tà *f* (**-tà**) conformity; **in conformità di** in conformity with, in accord with

confortante *adj* comforting

confortare (**confórto**) *tr* to comfort

confortévole *adj* comforting, consoling; comfortable

confòrto *m* comfort, solace; convenience; corroboration; **conforti religiosi** last rites

confratèllo *m* brother, confrere

confratèrnita *f* brotherhood

confricare §197 *tr* to rub

confrontare (**confrónto**) *tr* to compare, confront; to consult || *intr* to correspond

confrónto *m* comparison; (law) cross examination; **a confronto di** or **in confronto a** in comparison with; with regard to

confusaménte *adv* vaguely, hazily

confusionale *adj* confusing; confused

confusionà·rio -ria (-ri -rie) *adj* blundering; scatterbrain ‖ *mf* blunderer; scatterbrain

confusióne *f* confusion, disorder; noise; error; embarrassment; shambles

confu·so -sa *adj* confused, mixed; vague, hazy; **in confuso** indistinctly

confutare (cònfuto) *tr* to confute

confutazióne *f* confutation

congedare (congèdo) *tr* to dismiss; to let (*a tenant*) go; (mil) to discharge ‖ *ref* to take leave

congeda·to -ta *adj* discharged ‖ *m* discharged soldier

congèdo *m* dismissal; leave; permission to leave; (mil) discharge; envoy, envoi; **congedo per motivi di salute** sick leave; **dare il congedo a** to discharge; **prender congedo** to take leave

congegnare (congégno) *tr* to assemble (*machinery*); to contrive, cook up

congégno *m* contrivance, gadget; mechanism; design (*of a play*)

congelaménto *m* freezing; frostbite

congelare (congèlo) *tr & ref* to freeze, congeal

congela·tóre -trice *adj* freezing ‖ *m* freezer; freezer unit; freezing compartment (*of a refrigerator*)

congènere *adj* similar, alike

congeniale *adj* congenial

congèni·to -ta *adj* congenital

congèrie *f* congeries

congestionare (congestióno) *tr* to congest

congestióne *f* congestion

congettura *f* conjecture

congetturare *tr* to conjecture

congiùngere §183 *tr & ref* to unite, join

congiuntiva *f* (anat) conjunctiva

congiuntivite *f* (pathol) conjunctivitis

congiunti·vo -va *adj* conjunctive; subjunctive ‖ *m* subjunctive ‖ *f* see **congiuntiva**

congiun·to -ta *adj* joined; joint ‖ *m* relative

congiuntura *f* juncture; joint; circumstance, situation; **bassa congiuntura** (econ) unfavorable circumstance; (econ) crisis

congiunzióne *f* conjunction

congiura *f* conspiracy, plot

congiurare *intr* to conspire, plot

congiura·to -ta *adj* & *m* conspirator

conglobare (conglòbo) *tr* to lump together

conglomerare (conglòmero) *tr & ref* to pile up, conglomerate

conglomera·to -ta *adj* & *m* conglomerate

congratulare (congràtulo) *intr* to rejoice ‖ *ref*—**congratularsi con** to congratulate

congratulazióne *f* congratulation

congrèga *f* gang; cabal; religious brotherhood

congregare §209 (congrègo) *tr & ref* to congregate

congregazióne *f* congregation

congressi·sta *mf* (-sti -ste) delegate ‖ *m* congressman ‖ *f* congresswoman

congrèsso *m* congress, assembly; conference; convention

congruènte *adj* congruous

congruènza *f* congruence

còn·gruo -grua *adj* congruous; congruent

conguagliare §280 *tr* to adjust; to make up (*what is owed*)

conguà·glio *m* (-gli) balance; adjustment (*of wages*)

coniare §287 (cònio) *tr* to mint, coin

coniatura *f* mintage, coinage

còni·co -ca (-ci -che) *adj* conic(al) ‖ *f* conic section

conìfera *f* conifer

coniglièra *f* warren, rabbit hutch

coni·glio *m* (-gli) rabbit

cò·nio *m* (-ni) die (*to mint coins*); mintage; wedge; **dello stesso conio** (fig) of the same feather; **di nuovo conio** newly-minted; new-fangled

coniugale *adj* conjugal

coniugare §209 (cònjugo) *tr* to conjugate ‖ *ref* to marry, get married

coniuga·to -ta *adj* coupled, paired ‖ *mf* spouse, consort

coniugazióne *f* conjugation

cònjuge *mf* spouse; **coniugi** *mpl* husband and wife

connaturale *adj* inborn, innate

connatura·to -ta *adj* deep-seated, deep-rooted; congenital

connazionale *mf* fellow countryman

connessióne *f* connection

connès·so -sa & connès·so -sa *adj* connected, tied

connèttere & connèttere §107 *tr* to connect, link ‖ *ref* to refer

connetti·vo -va *adj* connective

connivènte *adj* conniving

connivènza *f* connivance

connotare (connòto) *tr* to connote

connotato *m* personal characteristic

connù·bio *m* (-bi) wedding, union

còno *m* cone

conòcchia *f* distaff

conoscènte *mf* acquaintance

conoscènza *f* knowledge; acquaintance; understanding; consciousness; **conoscenza di causa** full knowledge; **essere a conoscenza di** to be acquainted with; **prendere conoscenza di** to take cognizance of

conóscere §134 *tr* to know; to recognize; **conoscere i propri polli** to know one's onions; **conoscere per filo e per segno** to know thoroughly; **conoscere ragioni** to listen to reason; **darsi a conoscere** to make oneself known; to reveal oneself ‖ *intr* to reason ‖ *ref* to acknowledge oneself to be; to know one another

conoscìbile *adj* knowable

conosci·tóre -trice *mf* connoisseur, expert

conosciu·to -ta *adj* known, well-known; proven

conquìdere §135 *tr* (poet) to conquer

conquista *f* conquest
conquistare *tr* to conquer, win
conquista·tóre -trice *adj* conquering ‖ *m* conqueror; lady killer
consacrare *tr* to consecrate ‖ *ref* to dedicate oneself
consacrazióne *f* consecration
consanguineità *f* consanguinity
consanguíne·o -a *adj* consanguineous; **fratello consanguineo** half brother on the father's side ‖ *m* kin
consapévole *adj* aware, conscious
consapevolézza *f* awareness, consciousness
cón·scio -scia *adj* (**-sci -see**) conscious
consecuti·vo -va *adj* consecutive
conségna *f* delivery; (mil) order; (mil) confinement (*to barracks*); **in consegna** (com) on consignment
consegnare (conségno) *tr* to deliver; to entrust; (mil) to confine (*to barracks*)
consegnatà·rio *m* (**-ri**) consignee
conseguènte *adj* consequent; consistent; **conseguente a** resulting from; consistent with
conseguènza *f* consequence; consistency; **in conseguenza di** as a result of
conseguíbile *adj* attainable
conseguiménto *m* attainment
conseguíre (conséguo) *tr* to attain; to obtain ‖ *intr* to ensue, result
consènso *m* consent, approval; consensus
consensuale *adj* mutual-consent (*e.g., agreement*)
consentiménto *m* consent
consentíre (consènto) *tr* to allow, permit ‖ *intr* to agree, consent; to yield; to admit
consenziènte *adj* consenting
consèr·to -ta *adj* intertwined; folded (*arms*); **di conserto** in agreement
consèrva *f* preserve, purée (*e.g., of tomatoes*); tank (*for water*); sauce (*e.g., of cranberries*); **conserve alimentari** canned goods; **di conserva** together, in a group; **far conserva di** to preserve
conservare (consèrvo) *tr* to preserve; to keep; to cure (*e.g., meat*); to cherish (*a memory*) ‖ *ref* to keep; to remain; to keep in good health
conservati·vo -va *adj* preserving; conservative ‖ *m* conservative
conserva·tóre -trice *adj* preserving; conservative ‖ *mf* keeper, curator; conservative
conservatòria *f* registrar's office (*in a court house*)
conservatò·rio *m* (**-ri**) conservatory; girl's boarding school (*run by nuns*)
conservatorismo *m* conservatism
conservazióne *f* conservation; preservation; self-preservation; canning
consèsso *m* assembly
consideràbile *adj* considerable; large, important
considerare (considero) *tr* to consider; to rate; (law) to provide for
considera·to -ta *adj* considered; **considerato che** considering that, since;

tutto considerato all in all, considering
considerazióne *f* consideration
considerévole *adj* considerable
consigliare *adj* council, councilmanic ‖ §280 *tr* to advise, counsel ‖ *ref* to consult
consigliè·re -ra *mf* counselor, advisor ‖ *m* chancellor (*of embassy*); councilman; **consigliere delegato** chairman of the board
consí·glio *m* (**-gli**) advice, counsel; will (*of God*); decision, idea; council; **consiglio d'amministrazione** (com) board of directors; **consiglio dei ministri** cabinet; **consiglio municipale** city council; **l'eterno consiglio** the will of God; **venire a più miti consigli** to become more reasonable
consimile *adj* similar
consistènte *adj* consistent, solid; trustworthy
consistènza *f* consistency, resistance; foundation, grounds
consistere §114 *intr* to consist; **consistere in** to consist of
consociare §128 (**consòcio**) *tr* to syndicate, unite
consocia·to -ta *adj* syndicated, united
consociazióne *f* syndicate, association, group
consò·cio -cia *mf* (**-ci -cie**) fellow shareholder; associate, partner
consolare *adj* consular ‖ *v* (**consólo**) *tr* to console, cheer, comfort ‖ *ref* to rejoice; to take comfort
consolato *m* consulate
consola·tóre -trice *adj* comforting ‖ *mf* comforter
consolazióne *f* consolation
còsole *m* consul
consò·le *f* (**-le**) console
consòlida *f*—**consolida maggiore** comfrey; **consolida reale** field larkspur
consolidaménto *m* consolidation
consolidare (consòlido) *tr* to consolidate ‖ *ref* to consolidate; to harden
consolida·to -ta *adj* consolidated; joint (*e.g., balance sheet*); hardened ‖ *m* funded public debt; government bonds
consonante *adj & f* consonant
consonànti·co -ca *adj* (**-ci -che**) consonant
consonanza *f* consonance; agreement; (mus) harmony
còso·no -na *adj* consonant
consorèlla *adj* sister (*e.g., company*) ‖ *f* sister of charity; sister branch; sister firm
consòrte *adj* (poet) equally fortunate; (poet) united ‖ *mf* consort, mate, spouse
consortería *f* political clique
consòr·zio *m* (**-zi**) syndicate, consortium; (poet) society
constare (cònsto) *intr* to consist ‖ *impers* to be known; to be proved; to understand, e.g., **gli consta che Lei ha torto** he understands that you are wrong
constatare (constato & cònstato) *tr* to verify, ascertain, establish

constatazióne *f* ascertainment, verification

consuè·to -ta *adj* usual, customary; **consueto a** accustomed to, used to || *m* manner, custom; **di consueto** generally

consuetudinà·rio -ria *adj* (-ri -rie) customary; common (*law*)

consuetùdine *f* custom; common law; (poet) familiarity

consulènte *adj* advising, consulting || *mf* adviser, expert

consulènza *f* expert advice

consulta *f* council

consultare *tr* to consult || *ref* to take counsel; to counsel with one another; **consultarsi con** to take counsel with

consultazióne *f* consultation; reference; **consultazione popolare** referendum

consulti·vo -va *adj* advisory

consulto *m* consultation (*of physicians*); legal conference

consul·tóre -trice *mf* adviser, expert || *m* councilman

consultò·rio *m* (-ri) clinic, dispensary

consumare *tr* to consume; to perform, to consummate || *ref* to be consumed, to waste away

consuma·to -ta *adj* consummate, accomplished; consummated (*marriage*); consumed, worn out

consuma·tóre -trice *adj* consuming || *mf* consumer; customer (*of a restaurant*)

consumazióne *f* consummation (*e.g., of a crime*); consumption (*of food*); food or drink

consumismo *m* consumerism

consumo *m* consumption; wear

consunti·vo -va *adj* end-of-year (*e.g., report*); (econ) consumption || *m* balance sheet

consun·to -ta *adj* worn-out

consunzióne *f* consumption

contàbile *adj* bookkeeping || *mf* accountant; bookkeeper, clerk; **esperto contabile** certified public accountant

contabili·tà *f* (-tà) accounting, bookkeeping; accounts

contachìlòme·tri *m* (-tri) odometer; (coll) speedometer

contadiné·sco -sca *adj* (-schi -sche) farm, farmer; rustic

contadí·no -na *adj* rustic || *mf* peasant, farmer

contado *m* country, countryside

contagiare §290 *tr* to infect

contà·gio *m* (-gi) contagion

contagió·so -sa [s] *adj* contagious

contagi·ri *m* (-ri) tachometer

contagóc·ce *m* (-ce) dropper, eyedropper

contaminare (contàmino) *tr* to contaminate; to pollute

contaminazióne *f* contamination; pollution

contante *adj & m* cash; **in contanti** cash

contare (cónto) *tr* to count; to limit; to regard, value; to propose; **contarie grosse** (coll) to tell tall tales || *intr* to count; **contare su** to count on

contasecón·di *m* (-di) watch with second hand

conta·to -ta *adj* limited; numbered (*e.g., days*)

conta·tóre -trice *adj* counting || *mf* counter || *m* meter; **contatore dell'acqua** water meter; **contatore della luce** electric meter

contattare *tr* to contact

contatto *m* contact

cónte *m* count

contèa *f* county

conteggiare §290 (contéggio) *tr* to charge (*e.g., a bill*) || *intr* to count

contég·gio *m* (-gi) reckoning, calculation; (sports) count; **conteggio alla rovescia** countdown

contégno *m* behavior; reserve, reserved attitude; air

contegnó·so -sa [s] *adj* reserved, dignified

contemperare (contèmpero) *tr* to adapt; to mitigate, moderate

contemplare (contèmplo) *tr* to contemplate

contemplati·vo -va *adj* contemplative

contemplazióne *f* contemplation

contèmpo *m*—**nel contempo** meanwhile

contemporaneaménte *adv* at the same time

contemporàne·o -a *adj* contemporaneous || *mf* contemporary

contendènte *adj* fighting || *m* contender, fighter; (law) contestant

contèndere §270 *tr* to contest, oppose || *intr* to contend, fight || *ref* to fight

contenére §271 *tr* to contain || *ref* to restrain oneself; to behave

conteniménto *m* containment

contenitóre *m* container

contentare (contènto) *tr* to satisfy, content || *ref* to be satisfied

contentézza *f* gladness, contentedness, contentment

contentino *m* gratuity, makeweight, gift to a customer

contèn·to -ta *adj* contented, glad, happy; satisfied || *m* (poet) happiness, contentedness

contenuto *m* content; contents

contenzióne *f* contention

contenzióso [s] *m* legal matter; legal department (*of a corporation*)

conterie *fpl* beads, sequins

conterrà·neo -nea *adj* from the same country || *m* fellow countryman || *f* fellow countrywoman

conté·so -sa [s] *adj* coveted || *f* contest; dispute; **venire a contesa** to dispute

contéssa *f* countess

contestare (contèsto) *tr* to serve (*e.g., a summons*); to deny; to challenge, contest; **contestare qlco a qlcu** to charge s.o. with s.th

contestazióne *f* notification, summons; dispute, confrontation; challenge

contè·sto -sta *adj* (poet) intertwined || *m* context

contì·guo -gua *adj* contiguous

continentale *adj* continental

continènte *adj & m* continent

continènza *f* continence

contingentaménto *m* import quota

contingentare (contingènto) *tr* to assign a quota to (*imports*)

contingènte *adj* possible, contingent; (obs) due ‖ *m* contingent; import quota; **contingente di leva** draft quota

contingènza *f* contingency

continuare (continuo) *tr* to continue ‖ *intr* to last, continue; **continuare a +** *inf* to keep on + *ger*

continuazióne *f* continuation

continui·tà *f* (-tà) continuity

conti·nuo -nua *adj* continuous; direct (*current*); **di continuo** continuously

cón·to -ta *adj* (archaic) well-known; (poet) gentle; (poet) narrated ‖ *m* figuring; account; bill, invoice; check (*in a restaurant*); opinion; worth, value; **a conti fatti** everything considered; **chiedere conto di** to call to account; **conto all'indietro** countdown; **di conto** valuable; **estratto conto** (com) statement; **fare conto di +** *inf* to intend to + *inf*; **fare conto su** to count on; **fare di conto** to count; **fare i conti senza l'oste** to reckon without one's host; **il conto non torna** the sums do not jibe; **in conto** on account; **in conto di** in one's position as; **per conto di** in the name of; **per conto mio** as far as I am concerned; **render conto di** to give an account of; **rendersi conto di** to realize, be aware of; **tener conto di** to reckon with; **tener di conto** to treat with care; **torna conto** it is worthwhile

contòrcere §272 *tr* to twist ‖ *ref* to writhe

contorciménto *m* contortion, writhing

contornare (contórno) *tr* to surround

contórno *m* outline; contour; circle (*of people*); side dish (*of vegetables*)

contorsióne *f* contorsion; gyration (*e.g., of a dancer*); squirm

contòr·to -ta *adj* twisted (*e.g., face*)

contrabbandare *tr* to smuggle

contrabbandiè·re -ra *adj* smuggling ‖ *mf* smuggler; bootlegger

contrabbando *m* contraband; smuggling; **di contrabbando** by smuggling; (fig) without paying

contrabbasso *m* contrabass, bass viol

contraccambiare §287 *tr* to reciprocate, return ‖ *intr* to reciprocate

contraccàm·bio *m* (-bi) exchange; **in contraccambio di** in exchange for, in return for

contraccólpo *m* shock, rebound; recoil (*of a rifle*); backlash (*of a machine*)

contrada *f* road; (poet) region

contraddire §151 (*impv sg* **contraddici**) *tr* to contradict ‖ *ref* to contradict oneself; to contradict one another

contraddistinguere §156 *tr* to earmark ‖ *ref* to stand out

contraddittò·rio -ria (-ri -rie) *adj* contradictory; incoherent ‖ *m* open discussion, debate

contraddizióne *f* contradiction

contraènte *adj* contracting; acting ‖ *mf* contractor (*person who makes a contract*); (law) party

contrarè·o -a *adj* antiaircraft

contraffare §173 *tr* to counterfeit; to

fake, sham ‖ *intr* (archaic) to disobey ‖ *ref* to camouflage oneself, disguise oneself

contraffat·to -ta *adj* counterfeit; adulterated; apocryphal

contraffat·tóre -trice *mf* counterfeiter; falsifier

contraffazióne *f* forgery; fake; imitation; piracy (*of book*); mockery (*of justice*)

contraffòrte *m* spur (*of mountain*); crossbar (*to secure door*); (archit) buttress

contraggènio *m*—**a contraggenio** against one's will

contral·to (-to) *adj* alto ‖ *m* contralto (*voice*) ‖ *f* contralto (*singer*)

contrammirà·glio *m* (-gli) rear admiral

contrappasso *m* retributive justice

contrappesare [s] (**contrappéso**) *tr* to counterweight, counterbalance

contrappéso [s] *m* counterweight, counterpoise

contrappórre §218 *tr* to oppose; to compare ‖ *ref*—**contrapporsi a** to oppose

contrappó·sto -sta *adj* opposing ‖ *m* opposite, antithesis

contrappunto *m* counterpoint

contrare (cóntro) *tr* (boxing) to counter; (bridge) to double

contrariare §287 *tr* to oppose, counter; to thwart; to contradict; to bother, vex

contrarie·tà *f* (-tà) contrariety, vexation; setback

contrà·rio -ria (-ri -rie) *adj* contrary, opposite ‖ *m* opposite; **al contrario** on the contrary; **al contrario di** unlike; **avere qlco in contrario** to have some objection, object

contrarre §273 *tr & ref* to contract

contrassegnare (contrasségno) *tr* to earmark, mark

contrasségno *m* earmark; proof

contrastare *tr* to oppose; to obstruct; to prevent ‖ *intr* to contrast; to disagree; (poet) to quarrel ‖ *ref* to contend

contrasto *m* contrast; fight, dispute; (telv) contrast knob

contrattàbile *adj* negotiable

contrattaccare §197 *tr* to counterattack

contrattac·co *m* (-chi) counterattack

contrattare *tr* to contract for, negotiate a deal for ‖ *intr* to bargain

contrattèmpo *m* mishap

contrat·to -ta *adj* contracted ‖ *m* contract

contrattuale *adj* contractual

contravveléno *m* antidote

contravvenire §282 *intr* (with *dat*) to contravene; **contravvenire a** to infringe upon

contravvenzióne *f* violation; ticket, fine; **in contravvenzione** in the wrong; **intimare una contravvenzione a** to give a ticket to

contrazióne *f* contraction

contribuènte *mf* taxpayer

contribuire §176 *intr* to contribute

contributo *m* contribution

contribu·tóre -trice *mf* contributor

contribuzióne *f* contribution
contristare *tr* & *ref* to sadden
contri·to *-ta adj* contrite
contrizióne *f* contrition
cóntro *m* con, contrary opinion || *adv* —**contro di** against, versus; **dar contro a** to oppose; **di contro** opposite, facing; **per contro** on the other hand || *prep* against, versus; at; **contro pagamento** upon payment; **contro vento** into the wind; **contro voglia** unwillingly
controbàttere *tr* (mil) to counterattack; (fig) to contest
controbilanciare §128 *tr* to counterpoise, counterbalance
controcanto *m* (mus) counterpoint
controcarro *adj invar* antitank
controchìglia *f* keelson
controcorrènte *f* countercurrent; undertow; (fig) undercurrent || *adv* upstream
controdado *m* lock nut
controffensiva *f* counteroffensive
controfigura *f* (mov) stand-in; (mov) stuntman
controfilo *m*—**a controfilo** against the grain
controfinèstra *f* storm window
controfirma *f* countersign
controfirmare *tr* to countersign
controfòdera *f* inner facing (*of a suit, between lining and cloth*)
controfuò·co *m* (-**chi**) backfire (*to check the advance of a forest fire*)
controindicare §197 (**controìndico**) *tr* to contraindicate
controllare (**contròllo**) *tr* to control, check || *ref* to control oneself
contròllo *m* control, check; restraint; (rad, telv) knob
controllóre *m* (com) comptroller; (rr) ticket collector, conductor
controluce *f* picture taken against the light || *adv* against the light
contromano *adv* against traffic
contromar·ca *f* (-**che**) check, stub (*e.g., of ticket*)
contromàr·cia *f* (-**ce**) countermarch; (aut) reverse, reverse gear
contromezzana [ddzz] *f* (naut) topsail
contronòta *f* countermanding note
contropalo *m* strut
controparte *f* (law) opponent
contropedale *m* foot brake (*of a bicycle*)
contropélo *m* close shave (*in the opposite direction of hair's growth*) || *adv* against the grain; the wrong way (*said of the hair*); against the nap; **accarezzare contropelo** to stroke the wrong way
contropiède *m* counterattack; **cogliere in contropiede** to catch off balance
contropòrta *f* storm door
controproducènte *adj* counterproductive, self-defeating
contropropósta *f* counterproposition
contropròva *f* proof; second balloting
contrórdine *m* countermand
controrèplica *f* retort; (law) rejoinder
controrifórma *f* Counter Reformation

controrivoluzióne *f* counterrevolution
controsènso *m* nonsense; mistranslation
controspallina *f* (mil) epaulet
controspionàg·gio *m* (-**gi**) counterespionage
controvalóre *m* equivalent
controvènto *m* (archit) strut; (archit) crossbrace || *adv* windward
controvèrsia *f* controversy
controvèr·so *-sa adj* controversial, moot
controvòglia *adv* unwillingly
contumace *adj* (archaic) contumacious; (law) absent from court; (law) guilty of nonappearance
contumàcia *f* quarantine; (archaic) contumacy; (law) nonappearance; **in contumacia** (law) in absentia
contumèlia *f* contumely
contundènte *adj* blunt
conturbante *adj* disturbing, upsetting
conturbare *tr* to disturb, upset || *ref* to become perturbed
contusióne *f* bruise, contusion
contu·so *-sa adj* bruised
contuttoché *conj* although
contuttociò *conj* although
convalescènte *adj* convalescent
convalescènza *f* convalescence
convalescenzià·rio *m* (-**ri**) convalescent home
convàlida *f* validation; confirmation
convalidare (**convàlido**) *tr* to validate; to confirm; to strengthen (*e.g., a suspicion*)
convégno *m* meeting, convention
conveniènte *adj* convenient; adequate; useful; profitable (*business*); cheap, reasonable
conveniènza *f* convenience; suitability, fitness; propriety; profit; **convenienze** conventions
convenire §282 *tr* to fix (*e.g., a price*); (law) to summon || *intr* (ESSERE) to convene; to agree; to fit, be appropriate; (poet) to flow together || *ref* to be proper; (with *dat*) to behoove, befit, *e.g.*, **gli si conviene** it behooves him || *impers*—**conviene** it is necessary
convènto *m* convent; monastery
convenu·to *-ta adj* agreed upon || *m* agreement; (law) defendant; **convenuti** conventioners, delegates
convenzionale *adj* conventional
convenzióne *f* convention
convergènte *adj* converging, convergent
convergènza *f* convergence
convèrgere §137 *intr* to converge
convèrsa *f* lay sister; flashing (*on a roof*)
conversare (**convèrso**) *intr* to converse
conversazióne *f* conversation
conversióne *f* conversion; change of heart; (mil) wheeling
convèrso *m* lay brother
convertìbile *adj* convertible || *m* (aer) fighter-bomber || *f* (aut) convertible
convertibili·tà *f* (-**tà**) convertibility
convertire §138 *tr* to convert, change; to translate || *ref* to convert, change; (poet) to address oneself

converti•to -ta *adj* converted || *mf* convert

convertitóre *m* converter

convès•so -sa *adj* convex

convincènte *adj* convincing

convìncere §285 *tr* to convince; to convict || *ref* to become convinced

convincimento *m* conviction

convìn•to -ta *adj* convinced, confirmed; convicted

convinzióne *f* conviction

convita•to -ta *adj* invited || *mf* guest (*at a banquet*)

convìto *m* banquet

convìtto *m* boarding school

convit•tóre -trice *mf* boarding-school student

convivènte *adj* living together

convivènza *f* living together; **convivenza illecita** cohabitation; **convivenza umana** human society

convìvere §286 *intr* to live together; to cohabit

conviviale *adj* convivial

convì•vio *m* (-vi) banquet

convocare §197 (cònvoco) *tr* to summon, convoke; to convene

convocazióne *f* convocation

convogliare §280 (convòglio) *tr* to convoy, escort; to convey, carry

convò•glio *m* (-gli) convoy; cortege; (rr) train

convolare (convólo) *intr*—**convolare a nozze** to get married

convòlvolo *m* (bot) morning-glory

convulsióne *f* convulsion

convul•so -sa *adj* convulsive; convulsed; choppy (*style*)

coonestare (coonèsto) *tr* to justify, palliate

cooperare (coòpero) *intr* to cooperate

cooperati•vo -va *adj & f* cooperative

coopera•tóre -trice *adj* coadjutant, co-operating || *m* coadjutor

cooperazióne *f* cooperation

coordinaménto *m* coordination

coordinare (coórdino) *tr* to coordinate; to collect (*ideas*)

coordinati•vo -va *adj* (gram) coordinate

coordina•to -ta *adj & f* coordinate

coordinazióne *f* coordination

coòrte *f* cohort

copèr•chio *m* (-chi) lid, cover; top (*of box*)

copertìna *f* small blanket, child's blanket; cover (*of book*)

copèr•to -ta *adj* covered; protected; cloudy; obscure || *m* cover; shelter; **al coperto** under cover; indoors; secure || *f* blanket, cover; seat cover; case, sheath; (naut) deck; **coperta da viaggio** steamer rug, lap robe; **far coperta a** to cover up for

copertóne *m* canvas; casing, shoe (*of tire*); **copertone cinturato** belted tire

copertura *f* covering; cover; coverage; whitewash; (boxing) defensive stance; (archit) roof

còpia *f* copy; (poet) abundance; (archaic) opportunity; **brutta copia** first draft; **copia a carbone** carbon copy; **copia dattiloscritta** typescript; **per copia conforme** certified copy (*formula appearing on a document*)

copialètte•re *m* (-re) letter file; copying press

copiare §287 (còpio) *tr* to copy

copiati•vo -va *adj* indelible; copying

copiatura *f* copying; copy; plagiarism

copiglia *f* cotterpin

copilò•ta *mf* (-ti -te) copilot

copióne *m* (theat) script

copiosi•tà [s] *f* (-tà) copiousness

copió•so -sa [s] *adj* copious

copi•sta *mf* (-sti -ste) scribe; copyist

copisterìa *f* copying office; public typing office

còppa *f* cup, goblet; bowl; pan (*of balance*); trophy; (aut) crankcase; (aut) housing; **coppe** suit of Neapolitan cards corresponding to hearts

coppàia *f* chuck (*of lathe*)

còppia *f* couple; pair; **a coppie** two by two; **far coppia fissa** to go steady

coppière *m* cupbearer

coppìglia *f* var of **copiglia**

cóppo *m* earthenware jar (*for oil*); roof tile

copribu•sto *m* (-sto) bodice

copricapo *m* headgear

copricaté•na *m* (-na) chain guard (*on bicycle or motorcycle*)

coprifuò•co *m* (-chi) curfew

coprinu•ca *m* (-ca) havelock

coprìre §110 *tr* to cover; to occupy (*a position*); to coat (*e.g., a wall*); to drown (*a noise*) || *ref* to cover oneself; (econ) to hedge

copritelè•ra *m* (-ra) cozy

coprivivan•de *m* (-de) dish cover

cò•pto -pta *adj* Coptic || *mf* Copt

còpula *f* copulation; (gram) copula

coque *f* see **uovo**

corà•gio *m* (-gi) courage; effrontery; (obs) heart; **fare coraggio a** to hearten, encourage; **prendere il coraggio a quattro mani** to screw up one's courage

coraggió•so -sa [s] *adj* courageous

corale *adj* choral; (archaic) cordial; (fig) unanimous || *m* chorale

coralli•no -na *adj* coral

corallo *m* coral

corame *m* engraved leather

coramèlla *f* razor strop

Corano *m* Koran

corata *f* haslet

coratèlla *f* giblets

corazza *f* breastplate, cuirass; shoulder pad (*in football*); armor plate; carapace, shell

corazzare *tr* to armor || *ref* to armor, protect oneself

corazza•to -ta *adj* armor-plated, armored; plated; protected || *f* battleship, dreadnought

corazzière *m* cuirassier; mounted carabineer

còrba *f* basket

corbellerìa *f* (coll) blunder

corbèllo *m* basket; basketful

corbézzolo *m* (bot) arbutus; **corbezzoli!** gosh!

còrda *f* rope; tightrope; string (*of an*

instrument); chord; woof; cord; plumbline; **dare la corda a** to wind *(a clock)*; **essere con la corda al collo** to have a rope around one's neck; **mostrare la corda** to be threadbare; **tagliare la corda** to take off, leave; **tenere sulla corda** to keep in suspense

cordame *m* cordage

cordata *f* group of climbers tied together

cordellina *f* (mil) braided cord, braid; (mil) lanyard

cordiale *adj & m* cordial

cordialità *f* (-tà) cordiality

cordièra *f* (mus) tailpiece

cordò·glio *m* (-gli) sorrow, grief

cordonata *f* gradient

cordóne *m* cordon; (anat, elec) cord; curbstone; **cordone litorale** sandbar; **cordone sanitario** sanitary cordon

corèa *f* St. Vitus's dance ‖ **Corea** *f* Korea

corea·no -na *adj & mf* Korean

coréggia *f* leather strap

coreografia *f* choreography

coreògrafo *m* choreographer

coriàce·o -a *adj* tough, leathery

coriàndolo *m* (bot) coriander; **coriandoli** confetti

coricare §197 **(còrico)** *tr* to put to bed ‖ *ref* to lie down, go to bed

corindóne *m* corundum

corìn·zio -zia *adj & mf* (-zi -zie) Corinthian

cori·sta *mf* (-sti -ste) choir singer, choirmaster ‖ *m* chorus man; (mus) tuning fork; (mus) pitch pipe

coriza [dz] or **corizza** [ddzz] *f* coryza

cormorano *m* cormorant

cornàcchia *f* rook, crow

cornamusa *f* bagpipe

cornata *f* butt; hook, goring *(by bull)*

còrne·o -a *adj* horn, horn-like ‖ *f* cornea

cornétta *f* (mus) cornet; (mus) cornet player; (telp) receiver; (hist) pennon *(of cavalry)*

cornétto *m* little horn; amulet *(in shape of horn)*; crescent *(bread)*; ear trumpet

cornìce *f* cornice; frame; (typ) box; (archit) pediment

cornicióne *m* (archit) ledge; (archit) cornice

cornificare §197 **(cornìfico)** *tr* (joc) to cuckold

cornìòla *f* carnelian

còrniola *f* (bot) dogberry

còrniolo *m* (bot) dogwood

còrno *m* horn; wing *(of army)*; edge, end; (mus) horn; **corno da caccia** hunting horn; **corno da scarpe** shoe horn; **corno dell'abbondanza** horn of plenty; **corno dogale** (hist) Doge's hat; **corno inglese** (mus) English horn; **non capire un corno** to not understand a blessed thing; **non valere un corno** to not be worth a fig; **un corno!** (slang) heck no! ‖ *m* **(còrna** *fpl)* horn *(of animal)*; **alzare le corna** to raise one's head; to become rambunctious; **dire corna di** to speak evil of; **fare le corna** to make horns, to touch wood *(to ward off the evil eye)*; **mettere le corna a** to cuckold *(one's husband)*; to be unfaithful to *(one's wife)*; **portare le corna** to be cuckolded; **rompersi le corna** to get the worst of it

cornu·to -ta *adj* horny; horn-shaped; (vulg) cuckolded

còro *m* choir; chorus; chancel

corollà·rio *m* (-ri) corollary

coróna *f* crown; coronet; wreath, garland; range *(of mountains)*; collection *(e.g., of sonnets)*; stem *(of watch)*; felloe *(of wheel)*; (astr) corona; (rel) string *(of beads)*; (mus) pause; **fare corona a** to surround

coronaménto *m* crowning; (archit) capstone; (naut) taffrail

coronare (coróno) *tr* to crown; to top, surmount

coronà·rio -ria *adj* (-ri -rie) coronary; (hist) rewarded with a garland

corpétto *m* baby's shirt; waistcoat, vest

corpino *m* bodice; vest

còrpo *m* body; substance; staff *(of teachers)*; (mil) corps; (typ) em quad; **a corpo a corpo** hand-to-hand *(fight)*; (sports) in a clinch; **a corpo morto** heavily; doggedly; **andare di corpo** to have a bowel movement; **avere in corpo** (fig) to have inside; **corpo del reato** corpus delicti; **corpo di Bacco!** good Heavens!; **corpo di ballo** ballet; **corpo di commissariato** (mil) supply corps; **corpo di guardia** guard, guardhouse; **corpo semplice** (chem) simple substance; **prendere corpo** to materialize

corporale *adj* bodily, body ‖ *m* (eccl) corporal, Communion cloth

corporativismo *m* corporatism *(e.g., of Fascist Italy)*

corporati·vo -va *adj* corporative, corporate

corpora·to -ta *adj* corporate

corporatura *f* size, build

corporazióne *f* corporation

corpòre·o -a *adj* corporeal

corpó·so -sa [s] *adj* heavy-bodied

corpulèn·to -ta *adj* corpulent

corpùscolo *m* particle; (phys) corpuscle

Corpus Dòmini *m* (eccl) Corpus Christi

corredare (corrèdo) *tr* to provide, furnish; to annotate, accompany

corredino *m* layette

corrèdo *m* trousseau; outfit, garb; actor's kit; furniture; equipment; apparatus *(e.g., footnotes)*

corrèggere §226 *tr* to correct; to straighten *(e.g., a road)*; to rewrite, revise *(news)*; to touch up the flavor of ‖ *ref* to reform

corrég·gia *f* (-ge) leather strap

corregionale *adj* fellow ‖ *mf* person of the same section of the country

correità *f* complicity

correlare (corrèlo) *tr* to correlate

correlati·vo -va *adj* correlative

correla·tóre -trice *mf* second reader *(of a doctoral dissertation)*

correlazióne *f* correlation; (gram) sequence

corrènte *adj* current; running; fluent; recurring; run-of-the-mill || *m*—**essere al corrente di** to be acquainted with; to be abreast of; **mettere al corrente di** to acquaint with || *f* current; draft (*of air*); stream (*of water*); mass (*of lava*); (elec) current; (fig) tide; **contro corrente** upstream; **corrente alternata** (elec) alternating current; **corrente continua** (elec) direct current; **corrente di rete** (elec) house current

córrere §139 *tr* to travel; to run (*a risk; a race*); **correre la cavallina** to sow one's wild oats || *intr* (ESSERE & AVERE) to run; to speed; to race; to flow; to fly (*said of time*); to elapse; to be (e.g., *the year 1820*); to be current (*said of coins*); to spread (*said of gossip*); to mature (*said of interest*); to intervene (*said of distance*); to have dealings; **ci corre!** there is quite a difference!; **ci corre poco che cadesse** he narrowly escaped falling; **correre a gambe levate** to run at breakneck speed; **corre l'uso** it is the fashion; **corrono parole grosse** they are having words; **non corre buon sangue fra loro** there is bad blood between them

corresponsàbile *adj* jointly responsible

corresponsióne *f* payment; (fig) gratitude

correttézza *f* correctness

corretti·vo -va *adj* corrective || *m* flavoring

corrét·to -ta *adj* correct; flavored; spiked

corret·tóre -trice *mf* corrector; **correttore di bozze** proofreader

correzionale *adj* correctional

correzióne *f* correction

córri còrri *m* rush

corri·dólo *m* (-dól) corridor; hallway; (tennis) alley; (theat) aisle

corridóre *adj* running || *m* racer; runner (*in baseball*)

corrièra *f* mail coach; bus

corrière *m* courier; mail; carrier (*of merchandise*)

corrispetti·vo -va *adj* equivalent, proportionate || *m* requital, compensation

corrispondènte *adj* corresponding, equivalent || *mf* correspondent

corrispondènza *f* correspondence

corrispóndere §238 *tr* to pay, compensate || *intr* to correspond

corri·vo -va *adj* rash; indulgent

corroborante *adj* corroborating || *m* tonic

corroborare (**corròboro**) *tr* to corroborate; to invigorate

corroborazióne *f* corroboration

corródere §239 *tr* to corrode; to erode

corrómpere §240 *tr* to spoil; to corrupt; to suborn || *ref* to putrefy, rot

corrosióne *f* corrosion

corrosi·vo -va *adj* & *m* corrosive

corró·so -sa *adj* corroded; eroded

corrót·to -ta *adj* corrupted, corrupt; putrefied, rotten || *m* (archaic) lament

corrucciare §128 *tr* to anger, vex || *ref* to get angry

corrùc·cio *m* (-ci) anger, vexation

corrugaménto *m* wrinkling; (geol) fold

corrugare §209 *tr* to wrinkle, knit (*one's brow*) || *ref* to frown

corruscare §197 *intr* (poet) to shine

corruttèla *f* corruption

corruttìbile *adj* corruptible

corrut·tóre -trice *adj* corrupting, depraving || *m* seducer; briber

corruzióne *f* corruption; putrefaction, decomposition

córsa *f* race; run; trip; fare; (mach) stroke; (hist) privateering; **a tutta corsa** at full speed; **corsa al galoppo** flat race; **corsa al trotto** harness racing; **corsa semplice** one-way ticket; **corse** horse racing; **da corsa** race, for racing, e.g., **cavallo da corsa** race horse; **di corsa** running, in a hurry; **fare una corsa** to run an errand; **prendere la corsa** to begin to run

corsalétto *m* corselet

corsa·ro -ra *adj* privateering || *m* privateer, corsair, pirate

corsétto *m* corset

corsìa *f* aisle; ward (*in hospital*); runner (*of carpet*); lane (*of highway*); **corsia d'accesso** entrance lane; **corsia d'uscita** exit lane

Còrsica, la Corsica

corsivi·sta *mf* (-sti -ste) (journ) political writer

corsi·vo -va *adj* cursive; (poet) running; (poet) current || *m* cursive handwriting; (typ) italics

córso *m* course; navigation (*by sea*); path (*of stars*); parade; large street; boulevard; tender (*of currency*); current rate, current price (*of stock at the exchange*); **corso d'acqua** watercourse; **fuori corso** (coin) no longer in circulation; **in corso** in circulation; in progress; **in corso di** in the course of; **in corso di stampa** in press

còr·so -sa *adj* & *mf* Corsican

cor·sóio -sóia (-sói -sóie) *adj* running (*knot*); (mach) on rollers || *m* slide (*of slide rule*); (mach) slide

córte *f* court; **corte bandita** open house; **Corte d'appello** appellate court; **Corte di cassazione** Supreme Court; **fare la corte a** to pay court to, woo

cortéc·cia *f* (-ce) bark; crust (*of bread*); (fig) appearance; (anat) cortex

corteggiaménto *m* courtship

corteggiatóre *m* wooer, suitor

cortég·gio *m* (-gi) retinue; cortege

cortèo *m* procession; parade; funeral train; wedding party

cortése *adj* courteous, polite; (lit) liberal; (poet & hist) courtly

cortesìa *f* courtesy, politeness; (lit) liberality; (poet & hist) courtliness; **per cortesia** please

còrtice *m* cortex

cortigia·no -na *adj* flattering; courtly || *mf* courtier; flatterer || *f* courtesan

cortile *m* courtyard; barnyard

cortina _f_ curtain; **cortina di ferro** iron curtain; **cortina di fumo** smoke screen; **oltre cortina** behind the iron curtain

cortisóne _m_ cortisone

cór·to -ta _adj_ short; close (_haircut_); **alle corte** in short; **essere a corto di** to be short of; **per farla corta in** short

cortocircùito _m_ short circuit

cortometràg·gio _m_ (**-gi**) (mov) short

cor·vè _f_ (**-vè**) tiresome task, drudgery; **corvè di cucina** kitchen police

corvétta _f_ corvette

corvi·no -na _adj_ raven-black

còrvo _m_ raven; crow

còsa [s] _f_ thing; **belle cose!** or **buone cose!** regards!; **che cosa** what; **cosa da nulla** a mere trifle, nothing at all; **cos'ha?** what's the matter with you (him, her)?; **cosa pubblica** commonweal; **cosa strana** no wonder; **cose** belongings; **per la qual cosa** wherefore; **per prima cosa** first of all; **sopra ogni cosa** above all; **tante belle cose!** best regards!; **una cosa** something; **una cosa nuova** a piece of news

cosac·co -ca (**-chi -che**) _adj_ Cossack's ‖ _mf_ Cossack

cò·scia _f_ (**-sce**) thigh; haunch; leg (_of gun_); (archit) abutment; **coscia di montone** leg of lamb

cosciènte _adj_ conscious; sensible; aware

cosciènza _f_ conscience; consciousness; conscientiousness; awareness

coscienzió·so -sa [s] _adj_ conscientious

cosciòtto _m_ leg; leg of lamb

coscrit·to -ta _adj_ conscript ‖ _m_ conscript, recruit, draftee

coscrìvere §250 _tr_ to conscript

coscrizióne _f_ conscription, draft

così [s] _adj invar_—**un così...** or **un... così** such a ‖ _adv_ thus; like this; so; **così ... come** as ... as; **così così** so so; **e così via** and so on, and so forth; **per così dire** so to speak

cosicché [s] _conj_ so that

cosiddét·to -ta [s] _adj_ so-called

cosiffat·to -ta [s] _adj_ such, similar

cosino [s] _m_ (coll) little fellow

cosmèti·co -ca _adj & m_ (**-ci -che**) cosmetic

còsmi·co -ca _adj_ (**-ci -che**) cosmic; outer (_space_)

còsmo _m_ cosmos; outer space

cosmòdromo _m_ space center

cosmologìa _f_ cosmology

cosmonàu·ta _mf_ (**-ti -te**) cosmonaut, astronaut

cosmopoli·ta _adj & mf_ (**-ti -te**) cosmopolitan

còso [s] _m_ (coll) thing, what-d'you-call-it

cospàrgere §261 _tr_ to spread; to sprinkle

cospèrgere §112 _tr_ (poet) to wet, sprinkle

cospètto _m_ presence; **al cospetto di** in the presence of

cospì·cuo -cua _adj_ distinguished, outstanding; huge, immense; (poet) conspicuous

cospirare _intr_ to conspire, plot

cospira·tóre -trice _mf_ conspirator

cospirazióne _f_ conspiracy, plot

còsta _f_ side; rib; coast, seashore; slope; welt (_along seam_); wale (_in fabric_); (naut) frame

costà _adv_ there; over there

costaggiù _adv_ down there

costante _adj & f_ constant

Costantinòpoli _f_ Constantinople

costanza _f_ constancy ‖ **Costanza** _f_ Constance

costare (**còsto**) _intr_ (ESSERE) to cost; to be expensive; **costare caro** to cost dear; **costare un occhio della testa** to cost a fortune

costarica·no -na or **costaricènse** _adj & mf_ Costa Rican

costassù _adv_ up there

costata _f_ rib roast; side

costeggiare §290 (**costéggio**) _tr_ to sail along; to run along; to border on ‖ _intr_ to coast

costèi §8 _pron dem_

costellare (**costèllo**) _tr_ to stud, star

costellazióne _f_ constellation

costernare (**costèrno**) _tr_ to dismay, cause consternation to

costernazióne _f_ consternation

costì _adv_ there

costiè·ro -ra _adj_ coast, coastal; offshore ‖ _f_ coastline; gentle slope

costipare _tr_ to constipate; to heap, pile ‖ _ref_ to become constipated

costipazióne _f_ constipation

costituènte _adj_ constituent; constituting ‖ _m_ member of constituent assembly; (chem) constituent

costituire §176 _tr_ to constitute; to form ‖ _ref_ to form; to become; to appoint oneself; to give oneself up (_to justice_); **costituirsi in giudizio** (law) to sue (_in civil court_); **costituirsi parte civile** (law) to appear as a plaintiff (_in civil court_)

costituto _m_ (law) pact, agreement; (naut) master's declaration (_to health authorities_)

costituzionale _adj_ constitutional

costituzióne _f_ constitution; charter; composition; (law) appearance; surrender (_to justice_)

còsto _m_ cost; **a costo di** at the price of; **ad ogni costo** at any cost; **a nessun costo** by no means; **a tutti i costi** at any cost, in any event; **costo della vita** cost of living; **sotto costo** below cost

còstola _f_ rib; spine (_of book_); back (_of knife_); **avere qlcu alle costole** to have s.o. at one's heels; **rompere le costole a** (fig) to break the bones of; **stare alle costole di** to be at the back of

costolétta _f_ chop, cutlet

costolóne _m_ (archit) groin

costóro §8 _pron dem_

costó·so -sa [s] _adj_ costly

costrìngere §265 _tr_ to force, constrain; (poet) to compress

costritti·vo -va _adj_ constrictive

costrizióne _f_ constriction

costruire §140 _tr_ to construct, build

costrut·to -ta *adj* constructed ‖ *m* profit; sense; (gram) construction; **dov'è il costrutto?** what's the point?
costruttóre *m* builder
costruzióne *f* construction; building
costùi §8 *pron dem*
costumanza *f* custom
costumare *intr* (+ *inf*) to be in the habit of (+ *ger*) ‖ *intr* (ESSERE) to be the custom; to be in use
costumatézza *f* good manners
costuma·to -ta *adj* polite, well-bred
costume *m* custom, manner; costume, dress; bathing suit
costumi·sta *mf* (-sti -ste) (theat) costumer
costura *f* seam
cotale *adj & pron* such ‖ *adv* (archaic) thus
cotan·to -ta *adj & pron* (poet) so much ‖ **cotanto** *adv* (poet) such a long time
còte *f* flint
coténna *f* pigskin; rind; (coll) hide, skin
coté·sto -sta §7 *adj dem* ‖ **§8** *pron dem*
cóti·ca *f* (-che) (coll) hide, skin (*of porker*)
cotógna *f* quince (*fruit*)
cotognata *f* quince jam
cotógno *m* quince (*tree*)
cotolétta *f* chop, cutlet
cotóne *m* cotton; thread; **cotone fulminante** guncotton; **cotone idrofilo** absorbent cotton; **cotone silicato** mineral wool
cotonière *m* cotton manufacturer
cotoniè·ro -ra *adj* cotton ‖ *mf* cotton worker
cotonifi·cio *m adj* (-ci) cotton mill
cotonó·so -sa [s] *adj* cotton; cottony
còtta *f* cooking; baking; drying (*of bricks*); (sports) exhaustion; (coll) drunkenness; (joc) infatuation, love; (eccl) surplice; **cotta d'armi** coat of mail
cottimi·sta *mf* (-sti -ste) pieceworker
còttimo *m* piecework
còt·to -ta *adj* cooked; baked; burnt; suntanned; (joc) half-baked; (joc) in love; (sports) exhausted ‖ *m* brick ‖ *f* see **cotta**
cottura *f* cooking; **a punto di cottura** (culin) done just right
coutènte *mf* (law) joint user; (telp) party-line user
cóva *f* brooding; nest
covare (*cóvo*) *tr* to brood, to hatch; to harbor or nurse (*an enmity*); to nurture (*a disease*); **covare con gli occhi** to look fondly at; **covare le lenzuola** to loll around ‖ *intr* to smolder (*said of fire or passion*)
covata *f* brood, covey
covile *m* doghouse; den
cóvo *m* shelter; den, lair; **farsi il covo** (fig) to gather a nestegg; **uscire dal covo** to stick one's nose out of the house
covóne *m* sheaf; cock (*of hay*)
còzza *f* cockle
cozzare (*còzzo*) *tr* to hit; to butt (*one's head*) ‖ *intr* to butt; (fig) to clash;

cozzare contro to bump into ‖ *ref* to hit one another; to fight
còzzo *m* butt; clash, conflict
crac *m* crash
crampo *m* cramp
crà·nico -ca *adj* (-ci -che) cranial
crà·nio *m* (-ni) cranium, skull
cràpula *f* excess (*in eating and drinking*)
cras·so -sa *adj* crass, gross; large (*intestine*)
cratère *m* crater; bomb crater
cràuti *mpl* sauerkraut
cravatta *f* tie, necktie; **cravatta a farfalla** bow tie; **fare cravatte** to be a usurer
creanza *f* politeness; **buona creanza** good manners
creare (*crèo*) *tr* to create; to name, elect
creati·vo -va *adj* creative
crea·to -ta *adj* created ‖ *m* creation, universe
crea·tóre -trice *adj* creative ‖ *mf* creator
creatura *f* creature; baby; **povera creatura!** poor thing!
creazióne *f* creation; (poet) election
credènte *adj* believing ‖ *mf* believer
credènza *f* credence, faith, belief; sideboard, buffet; (coll) credit
credenziale *f* letter of credit; **credenziali** credentials
credenzière *m* butler
crédere §141 *tr* to believe; to think; **lo credo bene!** I should say so! ‖ *intr* to believe; to trust; **credere a** to believe in; **credere in Dio** to believe in God ‖ *ref* to believe oneself to be
credibile *adj* credible
credibilità *f* credibility
crédito *m* credit
credi·tóre -trice *mf* creditor
crèdo *m* credo, creed
credulità *f* credulity
crèdu·lo -la *adj* credulous
crèma *f* cream; custard; **crema da scarpe** shoe polish; **crema di bellezza** beauty cream; **crema di pomodoro** cream of tomato soup; **crema evanescente** vanishing cream; **crema per barba** shaving cream
cremaglièra *f* rack; cogway, cograil
cremare (*crèmo*) *tr* to cremate
crema·tóio *m* (-tói) crematory
cremató·rio *m* (-ri) crematory
cremazióne *f* cremation
cremerìa *f* creamery
crèmisi *adj & m* crimson
Cremlino *m* Kremlin
cremlinologìa *f* Kremlinology
cremortàrtaro *m* cream of tartar
cremó·so -sa [s] *adj* creamy
crèn *m* horseradish
creolina *f* creolin
crèo·lo -la *adj & mf* Creole
creosòto *m* creosote
crèpa *f* crack, crevice; rift
crepàc·cio *m* (-ci) crevasse; fissure
crepacuòre *m* heartbreak
crepapància *m*—**mangiare a crepapancia** to burst from eating too much
crepapèlle *m*—**ridere a crepapelle** to split one's sides laughing

crepare (**crèpo**) *intr* to burst; to crack; to chip; (slang) to croak; **crepare dalla sete** to die of thirst; **crepare dalle risa** to die laughing; **crepare d'invidia** to be green with envy

crepitare (**crèpito**) *intr* to crackle (*said of fire or weapons*); to rustle (*said of leaves*)

crepìt·o *m* (**-i**) crackle; rustle; pitter-patter (*of rain*)

crepuscolare *adj* twilight; (fig) dim

crepùscolo *m* twilight

crescènte *adj* rising, growing; crescent (*moon*) ‖ *m* (astr & heral) crescent

crescènza *f* growth

créscere §142 *tr* to grow, raise; to increase ‖ *intr* (ESSERE) to grow; to increase; to rise (*said, e.g., of prices*); to wax (*said of the moon*); **farsi crescere** to grow (*a beard*)

crescióne *m* watercress

créscita *f* growth; outgrowth; rise (*of water*)

crèsima *f* confirmation

cresimare (**crèsimo**) *tr* to confirm

Crèso *m* (mythol) Croesus

cré·spo -spa *adj* crispy, kinky; (archaic) wrinkled ‖ *m* crepe ‖ *f* wrinkle; ruffle

crésta *f* comb (*of chicken*); crest; **abbassare la cresta** to come down a peg or two; **alzare la cresta** to become insolent

crestàia *f* (coll) milliner

créta *f* clay

cretése [s] *adj & mf* Cretan

cretinerìa *f* idiocy

creti·no -na *adj & mf* idiot, cretin

cribro *m* (poet) sieve

cric·ca *f* (**-che**) clique, gang; group; crevice

cric·co *m* (**-chi**) (aut) jack

cricéto *m* hamster

cri cri *m* chirping (*of crickets*)

criminale *adj* criminal; (law) penal ‖ *mf* criminal

criminali·sta *mf* (**-sti -ste**) penal lawyer, criminal lawyer

criminalità *f* criminality

crìmine *m* crime

criminologìa *f* criminology

criminòlo·go *m* (**-gi**) criminologist

criminó·so -sa [s] *adj* criminal

crinale *adj* (poet) hair ‖ *m* ridge (*of mountains*)

crine *m* horsehair; (poet) hair; (poet) sunbeam

crinièra *f* mane

crinolina *f* crinoline

cripta *f* crypt

criptocomuni·sta *mf* (**-sti -ste**) fellow traveler

crisàlide *f* chrysalis

crisantèmo *m* chrysanthemum

cri·si *f* (**-si**) crisis; shortage (*of houses*); attack (*e.g., of fever*); outburst (*of tears*); (econ) slump; **crisi ancillare** or **domestica** servant problem; **in crisi** in difficulties

cristallerìa *f* glassware; crystal service; glassware shop; glassworks

cristallièra *f* china closet

cristalli·no -na *adj* crystalline ‖ *m* crystalline lens

cristallizzare [ddzz] *tr & ref* to crystallize

cristallo *m* crystal; glass; pane (*of glass*); windshield; **cristallo di rocca** rock crystal; **cristallo di sicurezza** (aut) safety glass

cristianaménte *adv* in a Christian manner, like a Christian; (coll) decently; **morire cristianamente** to die in the faith

cristianésimo *m* Christianity

cristianità *f* Christendom

cristia·no -na *adj & mf* Christian

Cristo *m* Christ; **avanti Cristo** before Christ (B.C.); **dopo Cristo** after Christ (A.D.); **un povero cristo** (slang) a poor guy

critè·rio *m* (**-ri**) criterion; judgment

crìti·ca *f* (**-che**) criticism; critique; slur

criticare §197 (**crìtico**) *tr* to criticize, censure; to find fault with

crìti·co -ca (**-ci -che**) *adj* critical ‖ *mf* critic; (coll) faultfinder ‖ *f* see **critica**

crittografìa *f* cryptography

crittogram·ma *m* (**-mi**) cryptogram

crivellare (**crivèllo**) *tr* to riddle

crivèllo *m* sieve, riddle

croa·to -ta *adj & mf* Croatian

Croàzia, la Croatia

croccante *adj* crisp, crunchy ‖ *m* almond brittle, peanut brittle

crocchétta *f* croquette

cròcchia *f* chignon, topknot

crocchiare §287 (**cròcchio**) *intr* to crackle; to sound cracked or broken; to cluck (*said of a hen*); to crack (*said of joints*)

cròc·chio *m* (**-chi**) group (*of people*); **far crocchio** to gather around

cróce *f* cross; x (*mark made by illiterate person*); tail (*of coin*); (fig) trial; **Croce del Sud** Southern Cross; **croce di Malta** Maltese cross; **Croce Rossa** Red Cross; **croce uncinata** swastika; **fare una croce sopra** to forget about; **gettare la croce addosso** (fig) to put the blame on; **mettere in croce** to crucify

crocefisso *m* crucifix

crocerossìna *f* Red Cross worker

croceségno *m* cross, x (*mark made instead of signature*)

crocétta *f* (naut) crosstree

croce·vìa *m* (**-via**) crossroads, intersection

crocia·to -ta *adj* crossed; crusading; see **parola** ‖ *m* crusader ‖ *f* crusade

crocièra *f* cruise; (archit) cross (*vault*); (mach) cross (*of universal joint*)

crocière *m* (orn) crossbill

crocifìggere §104 *tr* to crucify

crocifissióne *f* crucifixion

crocifìs·so -sa *adj* crucified ‖ *m* crucifix

crò·co *m* (**-chi**) crocus

crogiolare (**crògiolo**) *tr* to cook on a low fire; to simmer; to temper (*glass*) ‖ *ref* to bask; to snuggle (*e.g., in bed*)

crogiolo *m* cooking on a low fire; simmering; tempering (*of glass*)

crogiòlo *m* crucible; (fig) melting pot

crollare (**cròllo**) *tr* to shake (*e.g., one's head*) ‖ *intr* (ESSERE) to fall down, collapse ‖ *ref* to shake

cròllo *m* shake; fall, collapse

cròma *f* (mus) quaver

cromare (**cròmo**) *tr* to plate with chromium

croma·to -ta *adj* chromium-plated; chrome ‖ *m* chrome yellow

cromatura *f* chromium plating

cròmo *m* chrome, chromium

cromosfèra *f* chromosphere

cromosò·ma [s] *m* (**-mi**) chromosome

cròna·ca *f* (**-che**) chronicle; report, news; **cronaca bianca** news of the day; **cronaca giudiziaria** court news; **cronaca mondana** social column; **cronaca nera** police and accident report; **cronaca rosa** wedding column; stork news

cròni·co -ca (**-ci -che**) *adj* chronic ‖ *mf* incurable

croni·sta *mf* (**-sti -ste**) reporter; chronicler

cronistòria *f* chronicle

cronologìa *f* chronology

cronològi·co -ca *adj* (**-ci -che**) chronologic(al)

cronometrare (**cronòmetro**) *tr* to time

cronomètri·co -ca *adj* (**-ci -che**) chronometric(al); split-second

cronometri·sta *m* (**-sti**) (sports) timekeeper

cronòmetro *m* stopwatch; chronometer

crosciare §128 (**cròscio**) *tr* (archaic) to heave, throw ‖ *intr* to rustle (*said of dry leaves*); to pitter-patter (*said of rain*)

cròsta *f* crust; bark (*of tree*); scab; slough; shell (*of crustacean*); poor painting

crostàceo *m* crustacean

crostata *f* pie

crostino *m* toast

crostó·so -sa [s] *adj* crusty

croupier *m* (**croupier**) croupier

crucciare §128 *tr* to worry, vex; to chagrin ‖ *ref* to worry; to become angry

cruccia·to -ta *adj* afflicted; worried; angry; chagrined

crùc·cio *m* (**-ci**) sorrow; (obs) anger; **darsi cruccio** to fret

cruciale *adj* crucial

crucivèr·ba *m* (**-ba**) crossword puzzle

crudèle *adj* cruel

crudel·tà *f* (**-tà**) cruelty

crudézza *f* crudity; harshness

cru·do -da *adj* raw; rare (*meat*); (poet) cruel

cruèn·to -ta *adj* (lit) bloody

crumiro *m* scab (*in strikes*)

cruna *f* eye (*of a needle*)

cru·sca *f* (**-sche**) bran; (coll) freckles

cruscante *adj* Della-Cruscan; affected ‖ *m* member of the Accademia della Crusca

cruschèllo *m* middlings

cruscòtto *m* (aut) dashboard; (aer) instrument panel

cuba·no -na *adj* & *mf* Cuban

cubatura *f* volume

cùbi·co -ca *adj* (**-ci -che**) cubic; cube (*root*)

cubitale *adj* very large (*handwriting or type*)

cùbito *m* cubit; (poet) elbow

cubo *m* cube

cuccagna *f* plenty; windfall; Cockaigne

cuccétta *f* berth

cucchiàia *f* large spoon; ladle; trowel; bucket (*of power shovel*); **cucchiaia bucata** skimmer

cucchiaiàta *f* spoonful; tablespoonful

cucchiaino *m* teaspoon; teaspoonful; spoon (*lure*)

cuc·chiàio *m* (**-chiài**) spoon; spoonful; tablespoon; **cucchiaio da minestra** soupspoon

cucchiaióne *m* ladle

cùc·cia *f* (**-ce**) dog's bed; **a cuccia!** lie down!

cucciare §128 *intr* (ESSERE) & *ref* to lie down (*said of a dog*)

cucciolata *f* litter (*e.g., of puppies*)

cùcciolo *m* puppy; cub; (fig) greenhorn

cuc·co *m* (**-chi**) cuckoo; simpleton; darling (*child*)

cuccuru·cù *m* (**-cù**) cock-a-doodle-doo

cucina *f* kitchen; cuisine; kitchen range; **cucina componibile** kitchen with sectional cabinets; **cucina economica** kitchen range; **fare da cucina** to prepare a meal

cucinare *tr* to cook; (fig) to fix

cucinétta *f* kitchenette

cuciniè·re -ra *mf* cook

cucire §143 *tr* to sew; to stitch ‖ *ref*— **cucirsi la bocca** to keep one's mouth shut

cucirino *m* sewing thread

cuci·tóre -trice *adj* sewing ‖ *mf* sewing machine operator ‖ *f* seamstress; sewing machine (*for bookbinding*); **cucitrice a grappe** stapler

cuci·to -ta *adj* sewn ‖ *m* sewing; needle work

cucitura *f* seam; sewing; stitches

cu·cù *m* (**-cù**) cuckoo

cuculo or **cùculo** *m* cuckoo

cùffia *f* bonnet (*for baby*); coif; (rad) headset; (telp) headpiece; (theat) prompter's box

cugi·no -na *mf* cousin

cui *pron invar* whose; to which; whom; which; of whom; of which; **per cui** (coll) therefore

culatta *f* breech (*of a gun*)

culinà·rio -ria (**-ri -rie**) *adj* culinary ‖ *f* gastronomy

cuila *f* cradle

cullare *tr* to rock (*a baby*); (fig) to delude ‖ *ref* to have delusions

culminante *adj* highest; culminating

culminare (**cùlmino**) *intr* to culminate

cùlmine *m* top, summit

culo *m* (vulg) behind; (slang) bottom (*of glass or bottle*): **culi di bicchiere** (coll) fake diamonds

cul·to -ta *adj* cultivated; learned (*e.g., word*) ‖ *m* cult, worship

cul·tóre -trice *mf* devotee

cultura *f* culture; **cultura fisica** physical culture

culturale *adj* cultural

cumino *m* (bot) caraway seed; (bot) cumin

cumulati·vo -va *adj* cumulative

cùmulo m heap, pile; concurrence (of penal sentences); cumulus

cuna f cradle

cùneo m wedge; chock; (archit) voussoir

cunétta f ditch; gutter

cunìcolo m small tunnel; burrow

cuòcere §144a tr to cook; to bake (bricks); to burn, dry up; (fig) to stew || intr to cook; to burn; to dry up; (with dat) to grieve, to pain

cuò·co -ca mf (-chi -che) cook

cuòio m (cuòi) leather; **avere il cuoio duro** to have a tough hide; **cuoio capelluto** scalp || m (cuoia fpl) (archaic) leather; **tirare le cuoia** (slang) to croak, to kick the bucket

cuòre m heart; **avere il cuore da coniglio** to be chicken-hearted; **avere il cuore da leone** to be lion-hearted; **cuori** (cards) hearts; **di cuore** gladly; heartily; **fare cuore a** to encourage; **stare a cuore** to be important

cupidìgia f cupidity, greed, covetousness

Cupido m Cupid

cùpi·do -da adj greedy, covetous

cu·po -pa adj dark; deep (color, voice); sad, gloomy

cùpola f dome, cupola; crown (of hat)

cura f care; interest; cure; ministry; (poet) anxiety; **a cura di** edited by (e.g., text)

curare tr to take care of; to heed || intr to see to it || ref to take care of oneself; to care; to deign; **curarsi di** to care for

curatèla f (law) guardianship

curatì·vo -va adj curative

cura·to -ta adj cured; healed || m curate

cura·tóre -trice mf curator; trustee; editor (of critical edition); receiver (in bankruptcy)

curculióne m (ent) weevil

cur·do -da adj & mf Kurd

cùria f curia; bar

curiale adj curia; legal

curialé·sco -sca adj (-schi -sche) hairsplitting, legalistic

curiosare [s] (curióso) intr to pry around, snoop; to browse around

curiosi·tà [s] f (-tà) curiosity; whim; curio

curió·so -sa [s] adj curious; bizarre, quaint

curro m roller

cursóre m process server; court messenger; slide (of slide rule)

curva f curve; bend; sweep; **curva di livello** contour line

curvare tr to curve, bend; **curvare la fronte** to bow down, yield || intr to curve (said of a road); to take a curve, negotiate a curve || ref to curve, bend; to bow; to become bent; to warp

curvatura f curving, bending; warp; stoop, curvature; camber

cur·vo -va adj bent, curved || f see curva

cuscinétto m small pillow; pad (for ink); buffer (zone); (mach) bearing; **cuscinetto a rulli** roller bearing; **cuscinetto a sfere** ball bearing

cuscino m pillow; cushion

cùspide f point (e.g., of arrow); (archit) steeple

custòde adj guardian (angel) || m custodian; janitor; warden; guard; (coll) policeman, cop

custòdia f safekeeping, custody; case (e.g., of violin); trust; (mach) housing

custodire §176 tr to keep; to protect, guard; to be in charge of (prisoners); to take care of; to cherish (a memory)

cutàne·o -a adj cutaneous

cute f (anat) skin

cuticagna f (joc) nape of the neck

cutìcola f epidermis; cuticle; dentine

cutireazióne f skin test (for allergic reactions)

cutréttola f (orn) wagtail

D

D, d [di] m & f fourth letter of the Italian alphabet

da prep from; to; at; on; through; between; since; with; by, e.g., **è stato arrestato dalla polizia** he was arrested by the police; worth, e.g., **un libro da mille lire** a book worth a thousand lire; worthy of, e.g., **azione da gentiluomo** action worthy of a gentleman; at the house, office, shop, etc., of, e.g., **dal pittore** at the house of the painter; **da Giovanni** at John's; **dall'avvocato** at the lawyer's office; **d'altro lato** on the other hand; **d'ora in poi** from now on

dabbasso adv downstairs; down below

dabbenàggine f simplicity, foolishness

dabbène adj invar honest, upright, e.g., **un uomo dabbene** an honest man;

simple, foolish, e.g., **un dabben uomo** a Simple Simon

daccanto adv near, nearby

daccapo adv again, all over again; **andar daccapo** to begin a new paragraph; **daccapo a piedi** from top to bottom

dacché conj since

dado m cube; pedestal (of column); (mach) nut; (mach) die (to cut threads); **dadi** dice; **giocare ai dadi** to shoot craps; **il dado è tratto** the die is cast

daffare m things to do; bustle; **darsi daffare** to bustle, bustle about

da·ga f (-ghe) dagger

dagli §4 || interj—**dagli al ladro!** stop thief!; **e dagli!** cut it out!

dài §4

dài·no -na *mf* fallow deer ‖ *m* fallow deer; buckskin

dal §4

dàlia *f* dahlia

dalla §4

dallato *adv* aside; sideways

dalle §4

dalli *interj*—**dalli al ladro!** stop thief!; **e dalli!** cut it out!

dallo §4

dàlma·ta *adj & mf* (**-ti -te**) Dalmatian

Dalmàzia, la Dalmatia

daltòni·co -ca *adj* (**-ci -che**) color-blind

daltonismo *m* color blindness

dama *f* lady; dancing partner; checkers; **andare a dama** (checkers) to be crowned; **dama di compagnia** companion; **dama di corte** lady-in-waiting

damare *tr* (checkers) to crown

damascare §197 *tr* to damask

damaschinare *tr* to damascene

dama·sco -schi *m* (**-schi**) damask ‖ **Damasco** *f* Damascus

damerino *m* fop, dandy

damigèlla *f* (lit) damsel; (orn) demoiselle; **damigella d'onore** bridesmaid

damigiana *f* demijohn

danaro *m* var of **denaro**

danaró·so -sa [s] *adj* wealthy, rich

dande *fpl* leading strings

danése [s] *adj* Danish ‖ *mf* Dane ‖ *m* Danish (*language*); Great Dane

Danimarca, la Denmark

dannare *tr* to damn; to bedevil ‖ *ref* to be damned; to fret

danna·to -ta *adj* damned; wicked; terrible (*e.g., fear*) ‖ *m* damned soul

dannazióne *f* damnation

danneggiare §290 (**dannéggio**) *tr* to damage; to injure, impair

danneggia·to -ta *adj* damaged; injured, impaired ‖ *mf* victim

danno *m* damage; injury; (ins) loss; **chiedere i danni** to ask for indemnification; **far danni a** to damage; **rifare i danni a** to indemnify; **tuo danno** so much the worse for you

dannó·so -sa [s] *adj* damaging, harmful

dante *m*—**pelle di dante** buckskin

danté·sco -sca *adj* (**-schi -sche**) Dantean, Dantesque

danti·sta *mf* (**-sti -ste**) Dante scholar

Danùbio *m* Danube

danza *f* dance; dancing

danzare *tr & intr* to dance

danza·tóre -trice *mf* dancer

dappertutto *adv* everywhere

dappiè *adv*—**dappiè di** at the foot of

dappiù *adv*—**dappiù di** more than

dappòco *adj invar* worthless

dappòi *adv* (obs) afterwards, after

dapprèsso *adv* near, nearby, close

dapprima *adv* first, in the first place

dapprincipio *adv* first, in the beginning; over again

dardeggiare §290 (**dardéggio**) *tr* to hurl darts at; to beat down on; to look daggers at ‖ *intr* to hurl darts; to beat down

dardo *m* dart, arrow; tip (*of blowtorch*)

da·re *m* (**-re**) (com) debit; **dare e avere** debit and credit ‖ §144b *tr* to give; to set (*fire*); to hand over; to lay down (*one's life*); to render (*e.g., unto Caesar*); to give away (*a bride*); to take (*an examination*); to tender (*one's resignation*); to say (*good night*); to shed (*tears*); **dare acqua a** to water; **dare alla luce** to give birth to; to bring out (*e.g., a book*); **dare aria a** to air; **dare ... anni a qlcu** to think that s.o. is ... years old; **dare a ridire** to give rise to complaint; **dare da intendere** to lead to believe; **dare fastidio a** to bother, annoy; **dare fondo a** to use up; **dare gli otto giorni a** to dismiss, fire; **dare il benvenuto a** to welcome; **dare il via a** to start (*e.g., a race*); **dare la colpa a** to declare guilty; to put the blame on; **dare la mano a** to shake hands with; **dare l'assalto a** to assault; **dare luogo a** to give rise to; **dare noia a** to bother; **dare per certo a** to assure; **dare ragione a** to agree with; **dare torto a** to disagree with; **dare via** to give away ‖ *intr* to burst; to begin; to beat down (*said of the sun*); **dare a** to verge on; to face, overlook; **dare addosso a** to attack, persecute; **dare al or sui nervi di** to irritate, irk; **dare alla testa** to go to one's head, e.g., **il vino gli dà alla testa** wine goes to his head; **dare contro a** to disagree with; **dare del ladro a** to call (s.o.) a thief; **dare del Lei a** to address formally; **dare del tu a** to address familiarly; **dare di volta il cervello** to go raving mad, e.g., **gli ha dato di volta il cervello** he went raving mad; **dare già** to abate; **dare in** to hit; **dare in affitto** to rent, lease; **dare nell'occhio** to attract attention; to hit the eye; **dare nel segno** to hit the target ‖ *ref* to put on, e.g., **darsi la cipria** to put powder on; **darsela a gambe** to take to one's heels; **darsela per intesa** to become convinced; to take for granted; **darsele** to strike one another; **darsi a** to give oneself over to; **darsi delle arie** to put on airs; **darsi il vanto di** to boast of; **darsi un bacio** to kiss one another; **darsi la mano** to shake hands; **darsi la morte** to commit suicide; **darsi pace** to resign oneself; **darsi pensiero** to worry; **darsi per malato** to declare oneself ill; to fall ill; **darsi per vinto** to give in, submit; **può darsi** it's possible, maybe; **si dà il caso** it happens

dàrsena *f* dock; basin

data *f* date; deal (*of cards*); **a ... data** (com) ... days hence, on or before ... days; **di fresca data** new (*e.g., friend*); **di vecchia data** old (*e.g., friend*)

datare *tr* to date ‖ *intr*—**a datare da** beginning with

datà·rio *m* (**-ri**) date stamp

dati·vo -va *adj & m* dative

da·to -ta *adj* inclined, bent; addicted; given; appointed (*date*); **dato e non concesso** assumed for the sake of argument; **dato che** since ‖ *m* datum ‖ *f* see **data**

da·tóre -trice *mf* giver, donor; **datore di lavoro** employer; **datore di sangue** blood donor; **datori di lavoro** management

dàttero *m* date; (zool) date shell

dattilografare (dattilògrafo) *tr* to typewrite, type

dattilografìa *f* typewriting

dattilògra·fo -fa *mf* typist

dattiloscopìa *f* examination of fingerprints

dattiloscrit·to -ta *adj* typewritten ‖ *m* typescript

dattórno *adv* near, nearby; **darsi dattorno** to strive; **stare dattorno a** to cling to; **togliersi dattorno qlcu** to get rid of s.o.

davanti *adj invar* fore, front ‖ **davan·ti** *m* (-ti) front, face ‖ *adv* ahead, in front; **davanti a** in front of; **levarsi davanti a qlcu** to get out of someone's way; **passare davanti a** to pass, outstrip

davanzale *m* window sill

davanzo *adv* more than enough

davvéro *adv* indeed; **dire davvero** to speak in earnest

daziare §287 *tr* to levy a duty on

dà·zio *m* (-zi) duty, custom; custom office

dèa *f* goddess

debellare (debèllo) *tr* (lit) to crush

debilitare (debìlito) *tr* to debilitate

debilitazióne *f* debilitation

débi·to -ta *adj* due ‖ *m* debit; debt; **debito pubblico** national debt

debi·tóre -trice *mf* debtor

débole *adj* weak; faint; gentle (*sex*); **debole di mente** feeble-minded ‖ *m* weakness, weak point; weakness, foible; weakling

debolézza *f* weakness, debility

debordare (debórdo) *intr* (ESSERE & AVERE) to overflow

debòscia *f* debauchery

deboscia·to -ta *adj* debauched ‖ *mf* debauchee

debuttante *adj* beginning ‖ *mf* beginner ‖ *f* debutante

debuttare *intr* to come out, make one's debut; (theat) to perform for the first time; (theat) to open

debutto *m* debut; (theat) opening night, opening

dècade *f* ten; period of ten days; (mil) ten days' pay

decadènte *adj* & *m* decadent

decadènza *f* decadence; lapse (*of insurance policy*); (law) forfeiture

decadére §121 *intr* (ESSERE) to decline; to lose one's standing; (ins) to lapse; **decadere da** (law) to forfeit

decadiménto *m* decadence; (law) forfeiture

decadu·to -ta *adj* fallen upon hard times

decaffeinizzare [ddzz] *tr* to decaffeinate

decalcificatóre *m* water softener

decalcomanìa *f* decalcomania

decàlo·go *m* (-ghi) decalogue

decampare *intr* to decamp; **decampare da** to abandon (*a plan*)

decano *m* dean

decantare *tr* to praise, extol; to decant; (lit) to purify ‖ *intr* to undergo decantation

decapàggio *m* (metallurgy) pickling

decapitare (decàpito) *tr* to behead, decapitate

decapitazióne *f* beheading

decappottàbile *adj* & *f* (aut) convertible

decèdere §123 *intr* (ESSERE) to die; to decease

decelerare (decèlero) *tr* & *intr* to decelerate

decennale *adj* & *m* decennial

decènne *adj* & *mf* ten-year-old

decèn·nio *m* (-ni) decade

decènte *adj* decent; proper

decentralizzare [ddzz] *tr* to decentralize

decentrare (decèntro) *tr* to decentralize

decènza *f* decency; propriety

decèsso *m* decease, demise

decìdere §145 *tr* to decide; to persuade ‖ *intr* & *ref* to decide; **deciditi!** make up your mind!

decifràbile *adj* decipherable

decifrare *tr* to decipher, decode; (fig) to puzzle out (*e.g., somebody's intentions*); (mus) to sight-read

dècima *f* tithe

decimale *adj* & *m* decimal

decimare (dècimo) *tr* to decimate

decìmetro *m* decimeter; **doppio decimetro** ruler

dèci·mo -ma *adj, m* & *pron* tenth ‖ *f* see **decima**

decisionale *adj* decision-making

decisióne *f* decision

decisì·vo -va *adj* decisive, conclusive

deci·so -sa *adj* determined, resolute; appointed (*time*)

declamare *tr* to declaim ‖ *intr* to declaim; to inveigh

declamazióne *f* declamation

declaratò·rio -ria *adj* (-ri -rie) declarative

declinare *tr* to decline; to declare, show; (gram) to decline; (lit) to bend ‖ *intr* to set (*said, e.g., of a star*); to slope; to diminish

declinazióne *f* declination; (gram) declension

declino *m* decline

decli·vio *m* (-vi) declivity, slope

decollàg·gio *m* (-gi) take-off; lift-off

decollare (decòllo) *tr* to decapitate ‖ *intr* (aer) to take off; (rok) to lift off

decòllo *m* take-off; lift-off

decolorante *adj* bleaching ‖ *m* bleach

decompórre §218 *tr, intr* & *ref* to decompose

decomposizióne *f* decomposition

decompressióne *f* decompression

decongelare (decongèlo) *tr* to thaw; (com) to unfreeze

decontaminare (decontàmino) *tr* to decontaminate

decorare (decòro) *tr* to decorate

decorati·vo -va *adj* decorative

decora·tóre -trice *mf* decorator

decorazióne *f* decoration
decòro *m* decorum, propriety; decor; dignity; decoration
decoró·so **-sa** [s] *adj* fitting, decorous, proper; dignified
decorrènza *f* beginning, effective date; lapse
decórrere §139 *intr* (ESSERE) to elapse; to begin; (lit) to run; **a decorrere da** effective, beginning with
decór·so **-sa** *adj* past ‖ *m* period, span; course; development; **nel decorso di** in the course of
decòt·to **-ta** *adj* (com) insolvent ‖ *m* decoction
decozióne *f* (com) insolvency
decrèpi·to **-ta** *adj* decrepit
decréscere §142 *intr* (ESSERE) to decrease
decretare (decréto) *tr* to decree
decréto *m* decree; **decreto legge** decree law
decùbito *m* recumbency
decuplicare §197 **(decùplico)** *tr* to multiply tenfold
dècu·plo **-pla** *adj* tenfold ‖ *m* tenfold part
decurtare *tr* to diminish, decrease
decurtazióne *f* decrease
dèda·lo **-la** *adj* (lit) ingenious ‖ *m* maze, labyrinth
dèdi·ca *f* (-che) dedication; inscription (*in a book*)
dedicare §197 **(dèdico)** *tr* to dedicate; to inscribe (*a book*) ‖ *ref* to devote oneself
dèdi·to **-ta** *adj* devoted; addicted
dedizióne *f* devotion; (obs) surrender
dedurre §102 *tr* to deduce; to deduct; to derive; (hist) to found (*a colony*)
deduzióne *f* deduction
defalcàbile *adj* deductible
defalcare §197 *tr* to deduct, withhold
defal·co *m* (**-chi**) deduction, withholding
defecare §197 **(defèco)** *tr* (chem) to purify ‖ *intr* to defecate
defenestrare (defenèstro) *tr* to throw out of the window; (fig) to fire; (pol) to unseat
defenestrazióne *f* defenestration; (fig) firing, dismissal
deferènte *adj* deferential; (anat) deferent
deferènza *f* deference
deferire §176 *tr* to submit; (law) to commit; **deferire il giuramento a qlcu** to put s.o. under oath ‖ *intr* to defer
defezionare (defezióno) *intr* to desert, defect
defezióne *f* defection
deficiènte *adj* deficient, lacking ‖ *mf* idiot
deficiènza *f* deficiency; idiocy
dèfi·cit *m* (**-cit**) deficit
deficità·rio **-ria** *adj* (**-ri -rie**) lacking; deficit (*e.g., budget*)
defilare *tr* to defilade ‖ *ref* to protect oneself
denfinìbile *adj* definable
definire §176 *tr* to define; to settle (*an argument*)

definiti·vo **-va** *adj* definitive; **in definitiva** after all
defini·to **-ta** *adj* definite
definizióne *f* definition; settlement (*of an argument*)
deflagrare *intr* to burst into flame; (fig) to burst out
deflazionare (deflazióno) *tr* (com) to deflate
deflazióne *f* deflation
deflèttere §177 *intr* to deflect
deflettóre *m* (aut) vent window; (mach) baffle
deflorare (deflòro) *tr* to deflower
defluire §176 *intr* (ESSERE) to flow down; (fig) to pour out
deflusso *m* flow; outflow, outpour; ebbtide
deformare (defórmo) *tr* to deform; to cripple; to alter (*a word*)
defórme *adj* deformed, crippled
deformi·tà *f* (**-tà**) deformity
defraudare (defràudo) *tr* to defraud, bilk
defun·to **-ta** *adj* dead; deceased; defunct; late ‖ *mf* dead person, deceased ‖ *m* deceased; **i defunti** the deceased
degenerare (degènero) *intr* (ESSERE & AVERE) to degenerate; to worsen
degenera·to **-ta** *adj* degenerate, perverted ‖ *mf* degenerate, pervert
degenerazióne *f* degeneracy, degeneration
degènere *adj* degenerate
degènte *adj* bedridden; hospitalized ‖ *mf* patient; inpatient
degènza *f* confinement; hospitalization
dégli §4
deglutire §176 *tr* to swallow
degnare (dégno) *tr* to honor ‖ *ref* to deign, condescend
degnazióne *f* condescension
dé·gno **-gna** *adj* worthy; **degno di nota** noteworthy
degradante *adj* degrading
degradare *tr* to degrade; to downgrade; (mil) to break ‖ *ref* to become degraded
degradazióne *f* degradation
degustare *tr* to taste
degustazióne *f* tasting
dèh *interj* oh!
déi §4
deiezióne *f* excrement; (geol) detritus
deificare §197 **(deìfico)** *tr* to deify
dei·tà *f* (**-tà**) deity
dél §4
dela·tóre **-trice** *mf* informer
delazióne *f* informing; (law) administration of an oath
dèle·ga *f* (**-ghe**) proxy, power of attorney
delegare §209 **(dèlego)** *tr* to delegate
delega·to **-ta** *adj* delegated ‖ *m* delegate; (eccl) legate
delegazióne *f* delegation
deletè·rio **-ria** *adj* (**-ri -rie**) deleterious
delfino *m* dolphin; (hist) dauphin
delibare *tr* to relish; to touch on; to ratify (*a foreign decree*)

delibazióne *f* ratification (*of a foreign decree*)
deliberare (**delìbero**) *tr* to deliberate; to decide; to award (*at auction*) || *intr* to deliberate
delibera·to -ta *adj* deliberate; resolved
deliberazióne *f* deliberation; decision
delicatézza *f* delicacy; gentleness; tactfulness; luxury
delica·to -ta *adj* delicate; gentle; tactful
delimitare (**delìmito**) *tr* to delimit
delineare (**delìneo**) *tr* to outline, sketch || *ref* to take shape; to appear
delinquènte *m* criminal
delinquènza *f* delinquency; **delinquenza minorile** juvenile delinquency
delinquere §146 *intr* to commit a crime
defì-quio *m* (**-qui**) fainting spell, swoon; **cadere in deliquio** to faint
delirare *intr* to be delirious; to rave; (*lit*) to stray
defì-rio *m* (**-ri**) delirium; frenzy; **andare in delirio** to go wild; **cadere in delirio** to become delirious
delitto *m* crime
delittuó·so -sa [*s*] *adj* criminal
delizia *f* delight; (*hort*) Delicious (*variety of apple*)
deliziare §287 *tr & ref* to delight
delizió·so -sa [*s*] *adj* delicious; delightful
délla §4
délle §4
déllo §4
dèl·ta *m* (**-ta**) delta
delucidare (**delùcido**) *tr* to elucidate; to remove the sheen from
delucidazióne *f* elucidation; removal of sheen
delùdere §105 *tr* to disappoint; to deceive; to foil
delusióne *f* disappointment; deception
delu·so -sa *adj* disappointed; deceived
demagnetizzare [*ddzz*] *tr* to demagnetize
demagogìa *f* demagogy
demagò·go *m* (**-ghi**) demagogue
demandare *tr* (*law*) to commit
demà·nio *m* (**-ni**) state land, state property
demarcare §197 *tr* to demarcate
demarcazióne *f* demarcation
demènte *adj* demented, crazy; idiotic || *mf* insane person; idiot
demènza *f* insanity, madness; idiocy
demèrito *m* demerit
demilitarizzare [*ddzz*] *tr* to demilitarize
democràti·co -ca (**-ci -che**) *adj* democratic || *mf* democrat
democrazìa *f* democracy || **Democrazia Cristiana** Christian Democratic Party
democristia·no -na *adj* Christian Democratic || *mf* Christian Democrat
demogràfi·co -ca *adj* (**-ci -che**) demographic
demolìre §176 *tr* to demolish
demoli·tóre -trice *adj* wrecking; destructive || *mf* wrecker
demolizióne *f* demolition
dèmone *m* demon
demonìa·co -ca *adj* (**-ci -che**) fiendish; demoniacal

demò·nio *m* (**-ni**) demon; **avere il demonio addosso** to be full of the devil
demoralizzare [*ddzz*] *tr* to demoralize || *ref* to become demoralized
demoralizza·to -ta [*ddzz*] *adj·* demoralized, dejected
denaro *m* money; denier (*of nylon thread*); **avere il denaro contato** to be short of money; **denari** suit of Neapolitan cards corresponding to diamonds
denatura·to -ta *adj* denatured
denegare §209 (**dènego** or **denégo**) *tr* to deny
denigrare *tr* to denigrate; to backbite
denominare (**denòmino**) *tr* to call, designate
denomina·tóre -trice *adj* designating || *m* denominator
denominazióne *f* denomination; designation
denotare (**denòto**) *tr* to denote
densi·tà *f* (**-tà**) density
dèn·so -sa *adj* dense, thick
dentale *adj & f* dental
dentare (**dènto**) *tr* to notch, scallop || *intr* to teethe
dentaruòlo *m* teething ring
denta·to -ta *adj* toothed
dentatura *f* set of teeth; teeth (*of gear*)
dènte *m* tooth; peak (*of mountain*); pang (*of jealousy*); fluke (*of anchor*); prong (*of fork*); **battere i denti** to shiver; **dente canino** canine tooth; **dente del giudizio** wisdom tooth; **dente di latte** baby tooth; **dente di leone** (bot) dandelion; **mettere i denti** to teethe
dentellare (**dentèllo**) *tr* to notch, scallop; to perforate (*stamps*)
dentellatura *f* notch; perforation (*of postage stamps*); (*archit*) denticulation
dentèllo *m* notch, scallop; lace; (*archit*) dentil
dentièra *f* denture, plate; cog
dentifrì·cio -cia (**-ci -cie**) *adj* tooth || *m* dentifrice
denti·sta *mf* (**-sti -ste**) dentist
dentizióne *f* teething
déntro *adv* inside, in; **dentro di** inside of; within; **essere dentro** (coll) to be behind bars; **in dentro** inward || *prep* inside of
denuclearizzare [*ddzz*] *tr* to denuclearize
denudare *tr* to denude; to strip; (*lit*) to unveil
denunciare §128 *tr* var of **denunziare**
denùnzia *f* denunciation; announcement; report
denunziare §287 *tr* to denounce; to accuse; to announce; to report
denutri·to -ta *adj* undernourished
denutrizióne *f* undernourishment
deodorante *adj & m* deodorant
deodorare (**deodóro**) *tr* to deodorize
depauperare (**depàupero**) *tr* to impoverish
depennare (**depénno**) *tr* to strike out, expunge
deperìbile *adj* perishable

deperiménto *m* deterioration; decline

deperire §176 *intr* (ESSERE) to deteriorate; to perish; to decay

depilatò·rio -ria *adj & m* (**-ri -rie**) depilatory

deplorare (deplòro) *tr* to deplore; to reproach

deploŕévole *adj* deplorable; reproachable

depolarizzare [ddzz] *tr* to depolarize

depórre §218 *tr* to lay; to lay down (*crown, arms*); to depose (*e.g., a king*); to take off (*clothes*); to give up (*hope*); to renounce; **deporre l'àbito talare** to doff the cassock

deportare (depòrto) *tr* to deport

deporta·to -ta *adj* deported ǁ *mf* deportee

deportazióne *f* deportation

depositare (depòsito) *tr* to deposit; to register, check ǁ *intr* to settle (*said, e.g., of sand*)

deposità·rio -ria (**-ri -rie**) *adj* deposit ǁ *mf* depositary

depòsito *m* deposit; checking (*e.g., of a suitcase*); registration; heap (*e.g., of refuse*); warehouse; morgue; receiving ward; (mil) depot; **deposito bagagli** baggage room

deposizióne *f* deposition; Descent from the Cross

deprava·to -ta *adj* depraved

depravazióne *f* depravation

deprecare §197 (**deprèco**) *tr* to deprecate

depredare (deprèdo) *tr* to plunder

depredazióne *f* depredation

depressióne *f* depression

deprès·so -sa *adj* depressed

deprezzaménto *m* depreciation

deprezzare (deprèzzo) *tr* to depreciate; to underestimate ǁ *intr* (ESSERE) to depreciate

deprimènte *adj* depressing

deprìmere §131 *tr* to humble, discourage; to depress

depurare *tr* to purify

deputare (dèputo) *tr* to deputize, delegate

deputa·to -ta *mf* deputy, delegate; representative

deputazióne *f* deputation, delegation

deragliaménto *m* derailment

deragliare §280 *intr* to be derailed, to run off the track

derapàg·gio *m* (**-gi**) skidding

derapare *intr* to skid

derelit·to -ta *adj & mf* derelict

derelizióne *f* dereliction

dereta·no -na *adj & m* posterior

deridere §231 *tr* to deride, mock

derisióne *f* derision, ridicule

derisò·rio -ria *adj* (**-ri -rie**) derisory, derisive

deriva *f* (aer) vertical stabilizer; (aer, naut) leeway; (naut) drift; **alla deriva** adrift

derivare *tr* to derive; to branch off (*e.g., a canal*) ǁ *intr* (ESSERE) to be derived, arise; to drift

deriva·to -ta *adj* derivative ǁ *m* derivative (*word*) ǁ *f* (math) derivative

derivazióne *f* derivation; (elec) shunt; (telp) extension

dermatòlo·go *m* (**-gi**) dermatologist

dermòide *f* imitation leather

dèro·ga *f* (**-ghe**) exception; **in deroga a** deviating from

derogare §209 (**dèrogo**) *intr* to transgress; **derogare a** to deviate from

derrata *f* foodstuff; **derrate** foodstuff, produce

derubare *tr* to rob

dèr·vis *m* (**-vis**) or **dervì·scio** *m* (**-sci**) dervish

desalazióne [s] *f* desalinization

desalificare [s] §197 (**desalìfico**) *tr* to desalt

dé·sco *m* (**-schi**) dinner table; meal

descritti·vo -va *adj* descriptive

descrìvere §250 *tr* to describe

descrizióne *f* description

desegregazióne [s] *f* desegregation

desensibilizzare [s] [ddzz] *tr* to desensitize

desèrti·co -ca *adj* (**-ci -che**) desert, wild

desèr·to -ta *adj* deserted; **andare deserto** to be unattended ǁ *m* desert

desideràbile [s] *adj* desirable

desiderare (desìdero) [s] *tr* to desire; **farsi desiderare** to make oneself scarce; to be dilatory

desidè·rio [s] *m* (**-ri**) desire; craving; lust; **lasciar desiderio di sé** to be greatly missed

desideró·so -sa [s] *adj* desirous

designare [s] *tr* to designate

designazióne [s] *f* designation

desinare *m* dinner ǁ *intr* to dine

desinènza *f* (gram) ending

desì·o *m* (**-i**) (lit) desire

desìstere [s] §114 *intr* to desist

desolante *adj* distressing

desolare (dèsolo) *tr* to distress; (lit) to devastate

desola·to -ta *adj* desolate; distressed

desolazióne *f* desolation; distress

dèspo·ta *m* (**-ti**) despot

despòti·co -ca *adj* (**-ci -che**) var of **dispotico**

despotismo *m* var of **dispotismo**

des·sèrt *m* (**-sèrt**) dessert

destare (désto) *tr* to awaken; to stir up ǁ *ref* to wake up

destinare *tr* to destine; to assign; to address

destinatà·rio -ria *mf* (**-ri -rie**) consignee; addressee

destinazióne *f* destination; assignment

destino *m* destiny; (com) destination

destituire §176 *tr* to demote; to dismiss; to deprive

destituzióne *f* demotion; dismissal

dé·sto -sta *adj* awake; (fig) wide-awake

dèstra *f* right, right hand

destreggiare §290 (**destréggio**) *intr* to maneuver ǁ *ref* to manage shrewdly

destrézza *f* skill, dexterity

destrière or **destrìero** *m* (lit) steed

dè·stro -stra *adj* right; skillful ǁ *f* see **destra**

destròr·so -sa *adj* clockwise; right-hand; (bot) dextrorse

destròsio *m* dextrose

desùmere [s] §116 *tr* to obtain; to infer

detectì·ve *m* (-ve) detective

detèc·tor *m* (-tor) (rad) detector

detenére §271 *tr* to hold; to detain

deten·tóre -trìce *m/f* holder; receiver (*of stolen goods*)

detenu·to -ta *m/f* prisoner

detenzióne *f* illegal possession; detention

detergènte *adj & m* detergent

detèrgere §164 (*pp* **detèrso**) *tr* to cleanse; to wipe

deterioràbile *adj* perishable

deteriorare (**deterióro**) *tr* to spoil || *intr* (ESSERE) & *ref* to deteriorate, spoil

determinare (**detèrmino**) *tr* to determine; to fix; to decide; to cause || *ref* to decide; to happen

determinatézza *f* determination; precision

determinatì·vo -va *adj* (gram) definite

determina·to -ta *adj* given; resolved, determined

determinazióne *f* determination

deterrènte *adj & m* deterrent

detersì·vo -va *adj* cleansing || *m* cleanser; detergent

detestàbile *adj* detestable

detestare (**detèsto**) *tr* to detest

detettóre *m* detector; **detettore di bugie** lie detector

detonare (**detòno**) *intr* to explode, detonate

detonatóre *m* blasting cap, detonator

detonazióne *f* detonation; report

detrarre §273 *tr* to take away; (lit) to detract

detrat·tóre -trìce *m/f* detractor

detrazióne *f* detraction; deduction

detriménto *m* detriment

detrito *m* debris; detritus; (fig) outcast, outlaw

detronizzare [ddzz] *tr* to dethrone

détta *f*—**a detta di** according to

dettagliante *m* retailer

dettagliare §280 *tr* to tell in detail; to itemize; to retail || *intr*—**pregasi dettagliare** please send detailed information

dettà·glio *m* (-gli) detail; retail

dettame *m* (lit) law, norm

dettare (**détto**) *tr* to dictate; (lit) to compose, write; **dettar legge** to impose one's will

dettato *m* dictation; (lit) style

dettatura *f* dictation

dét·to -ta *adj* called, named; **detto (e) fatto** no sooner said than done || *m* saying || *f* see **detta**

deturpare *tr* to disfigure, mar

deturpazióne *f* disfigurement, disfiguration

devalutazióne *f* devaluation

devastare *tr* to devastate, lay waste; (fig) to disfigure

devasta·tóre -trìce *adj* devastating || *m* devastator

devastazióne *f* devastation

deviaménto *m* switching; derailment; (fig) straying

deviare §119 *tr* to turn aside; to lead astray; (rr) to switch; (rr) to derail

|| *intr* to deviate; to wander; to go astray; (rr) to run off the track

deviatóre *m* (rr) switchman; (elec) two-way switch

deviazióne *f* deviation; detour; curvature (*of the spine*); (phys) declination; (phys) deflection; (rr) switching

deviazionismo *m* deviationism

deviazioni·sta *m/f* (-sti -ste) deviationist

devoluzióne *f* transfer

devòlvere §147 *tr* to transfer || *intr & ref* (lit) to roll down

devò·to -ta *adj* devoted; devout, pious || *m* devout person; worshiper

devozióne *f* devotion

di §4 *prep* of; in, e.g., **la più bella della famiglia** the prettiest one in the family; (*with definite article*) some, e.g., **mi occorrono dei fiammiferi** I need some matches; than, e.g., **più veloce del baleno** faster than lightning; from, e.g., **è di Milano** he is from Milan; off, e.g., **smontare di sella** to get off the saddle; about, e.g., **discutere di politica** to talk about politics; with, e.g., **ornare di fiori** to adorn with flowers; made of, e.g., **una casa di mattoni** a house made of bricks; by, e.g., **di notte** by night; for, e.g., **amor di patria** love for one's country; worth, e.g., **casa di dieci milioni** house worth ten million; in the amount of, e.g., **multa di mille lire** fine in the amount of one thousand lire; son of, e.g., **Carlo Giovannini di Filippo** Carlo Giovannini son of Philip; daughter of, e.g., **Anna Ponti di Antonio** Anna Ponti daughter of Anthony; **di corsa** running; **di gran lunga** greatly; by far; **di . . . in** from . . . to; **di là da** beyond; **di nascosto** stealthily; **di qua da** on this side of; **di quando in quando** from time to time; **di tre metri** three meters long or wide or high

dì *m* (**dì**) day; **a dì** (e.g., **ventisei**) this (e.g., twenty-sixth) day; **conciare per il dì delle feste** (coll) to beat up

diabète *m* diabetes

diabèti·co -ca *adj & m/f* (-ci -che) diabetic

diabòli·co -ca *adj* (-ci -che) diabolic(al)

diàcono *m* deacon

diadè·ma *m* (-mi) diadem (*of king*); tiara (*of lady*)

diàfa·no -na *adj* diaphanous

diafonia *f* (telp) cross talk

diafram·ma *m* (-mi) diaphragm; (fig) partition

diàgno·si *f* (-si) diagnosis

diagnosticare §197 (**diagnòstico**) *tr* to diagnose

diagonale *adj & f* diagonal

diagram·ma *m* (-mi) diagram; chart

diagrammare *tr* to diagram

dialettale *adj* dialectal

dialètti·co -ca (-ci -che) *adj* dialectic(al) || *m* dialectician || *f* dialectic; (philos) dialectics

dialètto *m* dialect

dialettòfo·no -na *adj* dialect-speaking || *m* dialect-speaking person

dialogare §209 (**diàlogo**) *intr* to carry on a dialogue

dialoga·to -ta *adj* written in the form of a dialogue || *m* dialogue

diàlo·go *m* (**-ghi**) dialogue

diamante *m* diamond; **diamante tagliavetro** glass cutter

diametrale *adj* diametric(al)

diàmetro *m* diameter

diàmine *interj* good heavens!; the devil!; sure!

diana *f* (mil) reveille || **Diana** *f* Diana

dianzi *adv* (lit) a short while ago

diàpa·son *m* (**-son**) (mus) pitch; (mus) tuning fork

diapositiva *f* (phot) slide, transparency

dià·rio -ria (**-ri -rie**) *adj* daily || *m* diary; journal; **diario scolastico** homework book || *f* per diem

diarrèa *f* diarrhea

diascò·pio *m* (**-pi**) slide projector

diaspro *m* jasper

diàstole *f* diastole

diatermìa *f* diathermy

diatriba *f* diatribe

diavolàc·cio *m* (**-ci**) devil; **buon diavolaccio** good fellow

diavolerìa *f* deviltry; devilment; evil plot

diavolè·rio *m* (**-ri**) hubbub, uproar

diavoléto *m* hubbub, uproar

diavolétto *m* little devil, imp

diàvolo *m* devil; **avere il diavolo in corpo** to be nervous; **avere un diavolo per capello** to be in a horrible mood; **buon diavolo** good fellow; **essere come il diavolo e l'acqua santa** to be at opposite poles; **fare il diavolo a quattro** to make a racket; to try very hard

dibàttere *tr* to debate || *ref* to struggle; to writhe

dibattiménto *m* debate; (law) pleading, trial

dibàttito *m* debate

dicastèro *m* department, ministry

dicèmbre *m* December

dicerìa *f* rumor, gossip

dichiarare *tr* to declare, state; to find (*guilty*); to proclaim; to nominate, name || *ref* to declare oneself to be; to declare one's love; to plead (*e.g., guilty*)

dichiarazióne *f* declaration; avowal (*of love*); return (*of income tax*); **dichiarazioni** representations

diciannòve *adj & pron* nineteen; **le diciannove** seven P.M. || *m* nineteen; nineteenth (*in dates*)

diciannovèsi·mo -ma *adj, m & pron* nineteenth

diciassètte *adj & pron* seventeen; **le diciassette** five P.M. || *m* seventeen; seventeenth (*in dates*)

diciassettèsi·mo -ma *adj, m & pron* seventeenth

diciottèsi·mo -ma *adj, m & pron* eighteenth

diciòtto *adj & pron* eighteen; **le diciotto** six P.M. || *m* eighteen; eighteenth (*in dates*)

dici·tóre -trice *mf* reciter

dicitura *f* caption, legend; (lit) wording, language

dicotomìa *f* dichotomy

didascalìa *f* note, notice; caption; legend (*e.g., on coin*); (mov) subtitle

didascàli·co -ca *adj* (**-ci -che**) didactic

didàtti·co -ca (**-ci -che**) *adj* didactic; elementary school (*director, principal*) || *f* didactics

didéntro *m* (coll) inside

didiètro *m* behind; back (*of house*) || *adv* behind

dièci *adj & pron* ten; **le dieci** ten o'clock || *m* ten; tenth (*in dates*)

diecimila *adj, m & pron* ten thousand

diecina *f* about ten

dière·si *f* (**-si**) dieresis

diè·sis *m* (**-sis**) (mus) sharp

dièta *f* diet; **dieta idrica** fluid diet

dietèti·co -ca (**-ci -che**) *adj* dietetic || *f* dietetics

dieti·sta *mf* (**-sti -ste**) dietitian

diètro *adj invar* back, rear || *m* back, rear || *adv* back, behind; **dal di dietro** from behind; **di dietro** hind (*legs*); back (*side*); behind, back (*e.g., of cupboard*) || *prep* behind; beyond; after; upon; **dietro a** behind; beyond; after; according to; **dietro consegna** on delivery; **dietro domanda** upon application; **dietro versamento** upon payment; **essere dietro a** to be in the process of

dietrofrónt *m* (mil) about face

difatti *adv* indeed

difèndere §148 *tr* to defend, protect || *ref* to protect oneself; (coll) to get along

difensi·vo -va *adj & f* defensive

difen·sóre -sóra or **difenditrice** *adj* defense || *mf* defender

difésa [s] *f* defense; bulwark; protection; **legittima difesa** self-defense; **pigliare le difese di** to defend, back up; **venire in difesa di** to go to the defense of

difettare (**difètto**) *intr* to be lacking; to be defective; **difettare di** to lack

difetti·vo -va *adj* defective

difètto *m* lack; blemish; fault; defect; **essere in difetto** to be at fault; **far difetto a** to lack, e.g., **gli fa difetto il denaro** he lacks money

difettó·so -sa [s] *adj* defective

diffamare *tr* to defame, slander

diffama·tóre -trice *mf* defamer, slanderer

diffamazióne *f* defamation, slander

differènte *adj* different

differènza *f* difference; spread; variance; **a differenza di** unlike; **c'è una bella differenza** it's a horse of another color

differenziale *adj & m* differential

differenziare §287 (**differènzio**) *tr* to differentiate

differiménto *m* deferment

differire §176 *tr* to postpone, defer || *intr* to be different; to differ

difficile *adj* hard, difficult; awkward (*situation*); hard-to-please; unlikely

|| *mf* hard-to-please person || *m—* **fare il difficile** to be hard to please; **qui sta il difficile!** here's the trouble!

difficol·tà *f* (**-tà**) difficulty; defect; obstacle; objection

difficoltó·so -sa [*s*] *adj* difficult, troublesome; fastidious

diffida *f* notice; warning

diffidare *tr* to give notice to; to warn || *intr* to mistrust

diffidènte *adj* distrustful

diffidènza *f* mistrust

diffóndere §178 *tr* to spread; to circulate; to broadcast || *ref* to spread; to dwell at length

diffórme *adj* unlike; (obs) deformed

diffrazióne *f* diffraction

diffusióne *f* spreading; circulation (*of a newspaper*); diffusion; (rad) broadcast

diffu·so -sa *adj* diffuse; widespread

diffusóre *m* diffuser (*to soften light*); baffle (*of loudspeaker*); (mach) choke

difilato *adv* forthwith, right away

difrónte *adj invar* in front

difterite *f* diphtheria

di·ga *f* (**-ghe**) dike; dam

digerènte *adj* alimentary (*canal*), digestive (*tube*)

digeribile *adj* digestible

digerire §176 *tr* to digest; to tolerate, stand

digestióne *f* digestion

digesti·vo -va *adj* digestive

digèsto *m* digest

digitale *adj* digital || *f* (bot) digitalis

digitalina *f* (pharm) digitalin

digiunare *intr* to fast

digiu·no -na *adj* without food; deprived; **digiuno di cognizioni** ignorant; **tenere digiuno** to keep in ignorance || *m* fast; **a digiuno** on an empty stomach; **fare digiuno** to fast

digni·tà *f* (**-tà**) dignity; **dignità** *fpl* dignitaries

dignità·rio *m* (**-ri**) dignitary

dignitó·so -sa [*s*] *adj* dignified

digradare *tr* to shade (*colors*) || *intr* to slope; to fade

digredire §176 *intr* to digress

digressióne *f* digression

digrignare *tr* to show (*one's or its teeth*); to grit (*one's teeth*)

digrossare (**digròsso**) *tr* to rough-hew; to whittle down; (fig) to refine || *ref* to become refined

diguazzare *tr* to beat (*a liquid*) || *intr* to wallow; to splash

dilagare §209 *intr* to flood, to overflow; to spread abroad

dilaniare §287 *tr* to tear to pieces || *ref* to slander one another

dilapidare (**dilàpido**) *tr* to squander

dilatare *tr* to expand; to dilate || *ref* to expand; to spread

dilatazióne *f* expansion; dilation

dilatò·rio -ria *adj* (**-ri -rie**) delaying; dilatory

dilavare *tr* to wash away, erode

dilava·to -ta *adj* dull, flat; wan

dilazionare (**dilazióno**) *tr* to delay, put off; (com) to extend

dilazióne *f* delay; (com) extension

dileggiare §290 (**diléggio**) *tr* to mock

dicòg·gio *m* (**-gi**) mockery, scoffing; **mettere in dileggio** to scoff at

dileguare (**diléguo**) *tr* to scatter || *intr* (ESSERE) to disappear, vanish; to melt

dilèm·ma *m* (**-mi**) dilemma

dilettante *mf* amateur; dilettante

dilettanté·sco -sca *adj* (**-schi -sche**) amateurish

dilettare (**dilètto**) *tr* to delight || *ref* to delight; **dilettarsi a** + *inf* to delight in + *ger*; **dilettarsi di** to pursue as a hobby, e.g., **si diletta di pittura** he pursues painting as a hobby

dilettévole *adj* delectable, delightful

dilèt·to -ta *adj* beloved || *m* loved one; pleasure; hobby

diligènte *adj* diligent

diligènza *f* diligence; stagecoach

dilucidare (**dilùcido**) *tr* to elucidate

diluire §176 *tr* to dilute

dilungare §209 *tr* (archaic) to stretch || *ref* to expatiate; to be ahead by several lengths (*said of a race horse*)

dilungo *m*—**a un dilungo** more or less

diluviare §287 *tr* to devour || *intr* (ESSERE & AVERE) to rain (*said, e.g., of bullets*) || *impers* (ESSERE)—**diluvia** it is pouring

dilù·vio *m* (**-vi**) deluge, flood; **diluvio universale** Flood

dimagrante *adj* reducing

dimagrare *tr* to thin down || *intr* (ESSERE) to become thin; to lose weight; to become exhausted (*said of land*); (fig) to become meager

dimagrire §176 *intr* (ESSERE) to become thin; to lose weight, reduce

dimanda *f* var of **domanda**

dimane *adv* (coll) tomorrow

dimani *m* & *adv* var of **domani**

dimenare (**diméno**) *tr* to wag (*the tail*); to beat (*eggs*); to wave (*one's arms*); to stir up (*a question*) || *ref* to toss; to busy oneself

dimensióne *f* dimension; (fig) nature

dimenticanza *f* oversight, neglect; **andare in dimenticanza** to be forgotten

dimenticare §197 (**diméntico**) *tr* to forget; to forgive || *ref* to forget; **dimenticarsi di** to forget; to neglect

dimenticatóio *m*—**mettere nel dimenticatoio** (coll) to forget

diménti·co -ca *adj* (**-chi -che**) forgetful; neglectful

dimés·so -sa *adj* humble, modest (*demeanor*); low (*voice*); shabby (*clothes*)

dimestichézza *f* familiarity

dimèttere §198 *tr* to dismiss; to release || *ref* to resign

dimezzare [*ddzz*] (**dimèzzo**) *tr* to halve

diminuire §176 *tr* to lessen, reduce; to lower (*prices*) || *intr* (ESSERE) to diminish

diminuti·vo -va *adj* & *m* diminutive

diminuzióne *f* diminution

dimissionare (**dimissióno**) *tr* to dismiss, discharge || *ref* to resign

dimissionà·rio -ria *adj* (**-ri -rie**) resigning, outgoing

dimissióne *f* resignation; **dare le dimissioni** to resign

dimól·to -ta *adj & m* (coll) much ‖ **dimolto** *adv* (coll) much

dimòra *f* stay; residence; (lit) delay; **mettere a dimora** to install; to plant (*trees*); **senza dimora** (lit) without delay; **senza fissa dimora** vagrant

dimorare (dimòro) *intr* to stay; to reside; (lit) to delay

dimostràbile *adj* demonstrable

dimostrante *m* demonstrator

dimostrare (dimóstro) *tr* to demonstrate; to register (*e.g., anger*); **dimostrare trent'anni** to look thirty ‖ *intr* to demonstrate ‖ *ref* to prove oneself to be

dimostrati·vo -va *adj* demonstrative; (mil) diverting

dimostra·tóre -trice *mf* demonstrator

dimostrazióne *f* demonstration

dinàmi·co -ca (-ci -che) *adj* dynamic ‖ *f* dynamics

dinamismo *m* dynamism

dinamite *f* dynamite

dìna·mo *f* (-mo) generator, dynamo

dinanzi *adj invar* front, e.g., **la porta dinanzi** the front door; preceding, e.g., **il mese dinanzi** the preceding month ‖ *adv* ahead; beforehand; (lit) before; **dinanzi a** before, in front of

dina·sta *m* (-sti) dynast

dinastìa *f* dynasty

dinàsti·co -ca *adj* (-ci -che) dynastic

dindo *m* (coll) turkey

dindòn *m* ding-dong ‖ *interj* ding-dong!

diniè·go *m* (-ghi) denial

dinoccola·to -ta *adj* gangling; clumsy (*gait*)

dinosàuro [s] *m* dinosaur

dintórno *m*—**dintorni** surroundings, neighborhood ‖ *adv* around; **dintorno a** around

dì·o -a *adj* (-i -e) (poet) godly ‖ *m* (**dèi**) god; **gli dei the gods** ‖ **Dio** *m* God; **che Dio la manda** cats and dogs (*said of rain*); **come Dio volle** at long last; **come Dio vuole** botched (*piece of work*); **Dio ci scampi!** God forbid!; **Dio santo!** good heavens!; **grazie a Dio** God willing; thank God; **voglia Dio** God grant

diòce·si *f* (-si) diocese

diodo *m* (electron) diode

diomedèa *f* (orn) albatross

diottrìa *f* (opt) diopter

dipanare *tr* to unravel, unwind

dipartiménto *m* department

dipartire §176 *tr* (archaic) to divide ‖ *intr* (**diparto**) (ESSERE) & *ref* (lit) to depart

dipartita *f* (lit) departure; (lit) demise

dipendènte *adj* dependent ‖ *mf* employee

dipendènza *f* dependence; employment; annex; (com) branch; **in dipendenza di** as a consequence of

dipèndere §150 *intr* (ESSERE) to depend; **dipendere da** to depend on

dipingere §126 *tr* to paint; **dipingere a olio** to paint in oils; **dipingere a tempera** to distemper ‖ *ref* to paint one-

self; to put make-up on; to appear, e.g., **gli si dipinse in volto la paura** fear appeared on his face

dipìn·to -ta *adj* painted ‖ *m* painting, picture

diplò·ma *m* (-mi) diploma, certificate

diplomare (diplòmo) *tr* to grant a degree to; to graduate ‖ *ref* to receive a degree; to graduate

diplomàti·co -ca (-ci -che) *adj* diplomatic; true, faithful (*copy*) ‖ *m* diplomat ‖ *f* diplomatics

diploma·to -ta *adj* graduated ‖ *mf* graduate ‖ *m* alumnus ‖ *f* alumna

diplomazìa *f* diplomacy

dipòi *adv* after, thereafter

diportare (dipòrto) *ref* (lit) to behave; (obs) to have a good time

dipòrto *m* recreation; (obs) sport; **andare a diporto** to go on an outing; to go for a walk

dipresso *adv*—**a un dipresso** about, approximately

diradare *tr* to thin out (*vegetation*); to disperse; to space out (*one's visits*) ‖ *intr* (ESSERE) & *ref* to diminish; to disperse

diramare *tr* to prune; to circulate (*notices*); to issue (*a communiqué*) ‖ *ref* to branch out; to spread

diramazióne *f* branch; ramification; issuance

dire *m* talk; **per sentito dire** by hearsay; **stando al dire** according to his words ‖ §151 *tr & intr* to say; to tell; to call (*e.g., s.o. a genius*); to talk; **detto (e) fatto** no sooner said than done; **dica pure!** go ahead!; speak up!; **dire bene di** to speak well of; **dire di no** to say no; **dire di sì** to say yes; **direi quasi** I dare say; **dire la sua** to have one's say; **dire male di** to speak ill of; **dirla grossa** to make a blunder; to tell a tall tale; **dirlo chiaro e tondo** to speak bluntly; **dirne un sacco e una sporta a** to pour insults upon; **è tutto dire** that's all; **non c'è che dire** it's a fact; **non fo per dire** I do not want to boast; **per così dire** so to speak; **per meglio dire** rather; **trovarci a dire** to find fault with; **trovare da dire con** to have words with; **voler ben dire** to be sure; **voler dire** to mean ‖ *ref*—**dirsela con** to connive with; **si dice** it is said

dirètro *m & adv* (archaic) behind, back

direttissima *f* (rr) high-speed line; **per direttissima** straight up (*in mountain climbing*)

direttissimo *m* express train

diretti·vo -va *adj* managerial ‖ *m* board of directors ‖ *f* directive; direction; guideline

dirèt·to -ta *adj* direct; directed a; addressed to; directed at; bound for ‖ *m* through train

diret·tóre -trice *mf* manager; principal ‖ *m* director; **direttore di macchina** (naut, nav) chief engineer; **direttore di tiro** (nav) gunnery officer; **direttore di un giornale** editor; **direttore d'or-**

chestra orchestra leader; **direttore responsabile** publisher; **direttore tecnico** (sports) manager ‖ *f* see **direttrice**

direttò·rio **-ria** (**-ri -rie**) *adj* directorial ‖ *m* directory

direttrice *adj fem* directing; guiding; front (*wheels*) ‖ *f* directress; line of action

direzionale *adj* directional; managerial

direzióne *f* direction; management; run (*of events*)

dirigènte *adj* leading; managerial ‖ *m* employer; boss; leader; executive

dirigere §152 *tr* to direct; to turn; to lead ‖ *ref* to address oneself; **dirigersi verso** to head for

dirigibile *adj & m* dirigible

dirimpètto *adj invar & adv* opposite; **dirimpetto a** opposite to; in comparison with

dirit·to **-ta** *adj* straight; right; unswerving; (coll) smart ‖ *m* law; obverse, face (*of coin*); fee, dues; (fin) right; **a buon diritto** rightly so; **di diritto** by law; **diritti d'autore** copyright; **diritti di segreteria** registration fee; **diritti doganali** customs duty; **diritti speciali di prelievo** (econ) special drawing rights; **diritto canonico** canon law; **diritto consuetudinario** common law; **diritto internazionale** international law; **in diritto** according to law ‖ *f* right, right hand ‖ **diritto** *adv* straight; **tirare diritto** to go straight ahead

dirittura *f* direction; uprightness; (sports) straightaway, home stretch

dirizzóne *m* blunder

diroccare §197 (**diròcco**) *tr* to knock down ‖ *intr* (ESSERE) (archaic) to fall down

dirocca·to **-ta** *adj* dilapidated, rickety

dirompènte *adj* fragmentation (*bomb*)

dirottaménto *m* hijacking; skyjacking (*of an airplane*)

dirottare (**diròtto**) *tr* to detour (*traffic*); to hijack (*e.g., a ship*); to skyjack (*an airplane*) ‖ *intr* to change course

dirottatóre *m* hijacker; skyjacker (*of a plane*)

diròt·to **-ta** *adj* copious, heavy (*rain, tears*); (lit) craggy; **a dirotto** cats and dogs (*said of rain*)

dirozzare [ddzz] (**diròzzo**) *tr* to roughhew; to refine ‖ *ref* to become polished

dirugginire §176 *tr* to take the rust off; to limber up; to gnash (*one's teeth*); to clear (*one's mind*)

dirupa·to **-ta** *adj* rocky, craggy

dirupo *m* rock; crag, cliff

disabbigliare §280 *tr & ref* to undress, disrobe

disabita·to **-ta** *adj* uninhabited

disabituare (**disabituo**) *tr* to disaccustom ‖ *ref* to become unaccustomed

disaccenta·to **-ta** *adj* unaccented

disaccòrdo *m* disagreement

disadat·to **-ta** *adj* unfit

disadór·no **-na** *adj* unadorned, bare

disaffezionare (**disaffezióno**) *tr* to alien-

ate the affection of; to estrange ‖ *ref* to become estranged

disaffezióne *f* dislike

disagévole *adj* troublesome, uncomfortable

disagiare §290 *tr* to trouble, inconvenience

disagia·to **-ta** *adj* uncomfortable; needy

disà·gio *m* (**-gi**) discomfort; need

disalberare (**disàlbero**) *tr* to dismast

disambienta·to **-ta** *adj* bewildered, strange

disàmina *f* examination, scrutiny

disaminare (**disàmino**) *tr* to scrutinize; to weigh

disamorare (**disamóro**) *tr* to alienate the affection of; to estrange ‖ *ref* to become estranged

disancorare (**disàncoro**) *intr* to weigh anchor; to leave port ‖ *ref* to weigh anchor; (fig) to free oneself

disanimare (**disànimo**) *tr* to dishearten

disappetènza *f* loss of appetite

disapprovare (**disappròvo**) *tr* to disapprove

disapprovazióne *f* disapproval

disappunto *m* disappointment

disarcionare (**disarcióno**) *tr* to unsaddle, unhorse; to kick out

disarmare *tr* to disarm; to dismantle (*a scaffold*); to ship (*oars*); (naut) to unrig ‖ *ref* to disarm; (fig) to give up

disarma·to **-ta** *adj* unarmed, defenseless

disarmo *m* disarmament; dismantling; unrigging

disarmonìa *f* discord; contrast

disarmòni·co **-ca** *adj* (**-ci -che**) discordant

disarticolare (**disartìcolo**) *tr* to limber up; to disjoint ‖ *ref* to become dislocated

disassociare §128 (**disassòcio**) *tr* to disassociate

disastra·to **-ta** *adj* damaged ‖ *mf* victim

disastro *m* disaster, calamity; wreck

disastró·so **-sa** [s] *adj* disastrous

disattèn·to **-ta** *adj* inattentive; careless

disattenzióne *f* inattention; carelessness

disattivare *tr* to deactivate (*e.g., a mine*)

disavanzo *m* (com) deficit

disavedu·to **-ta** *adj* heedless

disaventura *f* misfortune

disavvertènza *f* inadvertence

disavvezzare (**disavvézzo**) *tr* to break (*s.o.*) of a habit ‖ *ref*—**disavvezzarsi da** to give up or lose the habit of

disavvéz·zo **-za** *adj* unaccustomed

disbórso *m* disbursement, outlay

disboscare §197 (**disbòsco**) *tr* to deforest

disbrigare §209 *tr* to dispatch ‖ *ref* to extricate oneself

disbri·go *m* (**-ghi**) prompt execution, dispatch

discacciare §128 *tr* (lit) to chase away

discanto *m* (mus) harmonizing

discàpito *m* damage; **tornare a discapito di** to be detrimental to

discàri·ca *f* (**-che**) discharge (*e.g., of pollutants*); dumping (*of refuse*); unloading (*of a ship*)

discàri•co *m* (-chi) exculpation; **a discarico di** in defense of
discatóre *m* hockey player; discus thrower
discendènte *adj* descending; sloping; down (*train*) ‖ *mf* descendant
discendènza *f* descent; pedigree
discéndere §245 *tr* to go down ‖ *intr* (ESSERE & AVERE) to descend, go down; to slope; to fall (*said, e.g., of thermometer*); to get off; **discendere in picchiata** (aer) to nose-dive
discènte *mf* student, pupil
discépo•lo -la *mf* disciple
discèrnere §153 *tr* to discern
discernibile *adj* discernible
discerniménto *m* discernment
discésa [s] *f* descent; slope; drop
discettare (**discètto**) *tr* (lit) to discuss
dischiodare (**dischiòdo**) *tr* to take the nails out of
dischiùdere §125 *tr* to open; to reveal
discin•to -ta *adj* scantily dressed; untidy; in disarray
disciògliere §127 *tr* to dissolve, melt; (lit) to untie ‖ *ref* to dissolve, melt
disciplina *f* discipline; whip, scourge
disciplinare *adj* disciplinary ‖ *m* regulation ‖ *tr* to discipline
disciplina•to -ta *adj* obedient
di•sco *m* (-schi) disk; (phonograph) record; bob (*of pendulum*); (ice hockey) puck; (sports) discus; (rr) signal; (pharm) tablet; **disco combinatore** (telp) dial; **disco microsolco** microgroove record; **disco volante** flying saucer
discòfilo *m* record lover
discòide *m* (pharm) tablet, pill
disco•lo -la *adj* undisciplined, wild ‖ *m* rogue, rascal
discolorare (**discolóro**) *tr* to discolor ‖ *ref* to pale
discolorazióne *f* discoloration; paleness
discólpa *f* defense
discolpare (**discólpo**) *tr* to defend
disconnèttere §107 *tr* to disconnect
disconóscere §134 *tr* to ignore, to disregard; to be ungrateful for
discontinuare (**discontìnuo**) *tr* to perform sporadically ‖ *intr* to lose continuity
disconti•nuo -nua *adj* uneven
disconvenire §282 *intr* (ESSERE) (lit) to disagree ‖ *impers* (ESSERE) (lit) to be improper
discoprire §110 (**discòpro**) *tr* to discover
discordante *adj* discordant
discordare (**discòrdo**) *intr* (ESSERE) to disagree, differ
discòrde *adj* discordant; opposing
discòrdia *f* discord, dissension
discórrere §139 *intr* to talk, chat; (coll) to keep company; **discorrere del più e del meno** to make small talk; **e via discorrendo** and so forth
discórso *m* discourse; conversation; speech; **pochi discorsi!** (coll) cut it out!
discostare (**discòsto**) *tr* to remove ‖ *ref* to withdraw; to differ

discò•sto -sta *adj* distant ‖ **discosto** *adv* far
discotè•ca *f* (-che) record library; discotheque
discreditare (**discrédito**) *tr* to discredit
discrédito *m* discredit
discrepanza *f* discrepancy
discretaménte *adv* rather; fairly well
discré•to -ta *adj* discreet; fairly large; fair
discrezióne *f* discretion
discriminante *adj* discriminatory; extenuating ‖ *m* (math) discriminant
discriminare (**discrìmino**) *tr* to discriminate; to extenuate
discriminazióne *f* discrimination
discussióne *f* discussion; argument
discus•so -sa *adj* controversial
discùtere §154 *tr* to discuss ‖ *intr* to discuss; to argue
discutibile *adj* moot, debatable
disdegnare (**disdégno**) *tr* to disdain, scorn ‖ *ref* (obs) to be angry
disdégno *m* disdain, scorn
disdegnó•so -sa [s] *adj* disdainful
disdétta *f* ill luck; (law) notice
disdicévole *adj* unbecoming, unseemly
disdire §151 *tr* to retract; to belie; to cancel; to countermand; to terminate the contract of ‖ *ref* to retract; **disdire a** to be unbecoming to
disdòro *m* shame; **tornare a disdoro di** to bring shame on
disegnare [s] (**diségno**) *tr* to draw; to sketch; to design; (obs) to elect
disegna•tóre -trice [s] *mf* cartoonist; designer ‖ *m* draftsman
diségno [s] *m* drawing; sketch; outline; plan; design; **disegno animato** (mov) cartoon; **disegno di legge** (law) bill
disellare [s] (**disèllo**) *tr* var of **dissellare**
diserbante *adj* weed-killing ‖ *m* weed-killer
diseredare (**diserèdo**) *tr* to disinherit
disereda•to -ta *adj* disinherited ‖ **i diseredati** the underprivileged
disertare (**disèrto**) *tr* to desert; (lit) to lay waste ‖ *intr* to desert
disertóre *m* deserter
diserzióne *f* desertion
disfaciménto *m* disintegration
disfare §173 *tr* to undo; to defeat; to melt; to unknit; to break up (*housekeeping*); **disfare il letto** to remove the bedclothes ‖ *ref* to spoil (*said, e.g., of meat*); **disfarsi di** to get rid of
disfatta *f* defeat
disfattismo *m* defeatism
disfatti•sta *mf* (-sti -ste) defeatist
disfat•to -ta *adj* undone; defeated; melted; broken up; ravaged ‖ *f* see **disfatta**
disfida *f* (lit) challenge
disfunzióne *f* malfunction
disgelare (**disgèlo**) *tr & intr* to thaw
disgèlo *m* thaw
disgiùngere §183 *tr & ref* to separate
disgiunti•vo -va *adj* disjunctive
disgràzia *f* disfavor; bad luck, misfortune; accident; **per disgrazia** unfortunately

disgrazia·to -ta *adj* unlucky; wretched
disgregaménto *m* disintegration
disgregare §209 (disgrègo) *tr* & *ref* to disintegrate
disgregazióne *f* disintegration
disguido *m* miscarriage, missending (*of a letter*)
disgustare *tr* to disgust, sicken || *ref* to become disgusted, sicken; to have a falling-out, to part company
disgusto *m* disgust, repugnance
disgustó·so -sa [s] *adj* disgusting
disidratare *tr* to dehydrate
disilla·bo -ba *adj* disyllabic || *m* disyllable
disillùdere §105 *tr* to delude, deceive || *ref* to become disillusioned
disillusióne *f* disillusion
disimboscare §197 (disimbòsco) *tr* to put back in circulation
disimparare *tr* to unlearn, forget
disimpegnare (disimpégno) *tr* to release; to free, to open; to loosen; to redeem (*a pledge*); to clear; to perform || *ref* to succeed
disimpégno *m* release; redemption; performance; disengagement; di disimpegno for every day (*e.g., a suit*); main (*e.g., hallway*)
disimpiè·go *m* (-ghi) unemployment; (mil) withdrawal
disincagliare §280 *tr* to set afloat; (fig) to disentangle
disincantare *tr* disenchant
disinfestare (disinfèsto) *tr* to exterminate
disinfestazióne *f* extermination
disinfettante *adj* & *m* disinfectant
disinfettare (disinfètto) *tr* to disinfect
disingannare *tr* to disillusion || *ref* to become disillusioned
disinganno *m* disillusion
disinnescare §197 (disinnésco) *tr* to defuse
disinnestare (disinnèsto) *tr* to disconnect; to throw out, disengage
disinserire §176 *tr* (elec) to disconnect; (aut) to disengage
disintasare [s] *tr* to unclog
disintegrare (disintégro) *tr* & *ref* to disintegrate
disintegrazióne *f* disintegration
disinteressare (disinterèsso) *tr* to make (*s.o.*) lose interest || *ref* to lose interest; to take no interest
disinteressa·to -ta *adj* selfless, unselfish
disinterèsse *m* disinterest; unselfishness
disintossicare §197 (disintòssico) *tr* to free of poison; (fig) to clean the air in || *ref* to shake the drug habit
disinvòl·to -ta *adj* free and easy; fresh, forward
disinvoltura *f* naturalness, ease of manners, offhandedness; freshness; impudence
disi·o *m* (-i) (poet) desire
disistima *f* scorn, low regard, disesteem
disistimare *tr* to scorn, hold in low regard
dislivèllo *m* difference of level; disparity
dislocaménto *m* transfer of troops; (naut) displacement

dislocare §197 (dislòco) *tr* to transfer (*troops*); to post (*sentries*); (naut) to displace
dislocazióne *f* (mil) transfer; (geog, naut, psychol) displacement
dismisura *f* excess; a dismisura excessively
disobbedire §176 *intr* var of disubbidire
disobbligare §209 (disòbbligo) *tr* to free from an obligation || *ref* to repay a favor
disoccupa·to -ta *adj* unemployed, jobless; idle; unoccupied || *m* unemployed person; i disoccupati the jobless
disoccupazióne *f* unemployment
disone·stà *f* (-stà) dishonesty; shamelessness
disonè·sto -sta *adj* dishonest; shameless; immoral
disonorante *adj* disgraceful
disonorare (disonóro) *tr* to dishonor, disgrace; to seduce
disonóre *m* dishonor, shame
disonorévole *adj* dishonorable; shameful
disoppilare (disòppilo) *tr* to clear of obstructions
disópra *adj invar* upper || *m* (disópra) upper part, top; prendere il disopra to have the upper hand || *adv* above; al disopra di above
disordinare (disórdino) *tr* to cancel, countermand; to confuse; to mess up || *intr* to indulge || *ref* to become disorganized
disordina·to -ta *adj* confused; messy; untidy; intemperate
disórdine *m* confusion; mess; disarray; disorder; intemperance
disorganizzare [ddzz] *tr* to disorganize; to disrupt
disorganizzazióne [ddzz] *f* disorganization, disorder; disruption
disorientaménto *m* disorientation; confusion, bewilderment
disorientare (disoriènto) *tr* to cause (*s.o.*) to lose his way; to confuse; to disorient || *ref* to be bewildered; to lose one's bearings
disorienta·to -ta *adj* disoriented; confused, bewildered; lost, astray
disormeggiare §290 (disorméggio) *tr* to unmoor
disossare (disòsso) *tr* to bone || *ref* (lit) to lose weight
disótto [s] *adj invar* below || *m* (disótto) lower part, bottom || *adv* below; al disotto di below, underneath
disotturare *tr* to unclog
dispàc·cio *m* (-ci) dispatch; urgent letter; dispaccio telegrafico telegram
dispara·to -ta *adj* disparate
disparére *m* disagreement
dìspari *adj invar* odd, uneven
dispari·tà *f* (-tà) disparity
dispàrte *adv*—in disparte apart, aside; starsene in disparte to keep aloof
dispèn·dio *m* (-di) expenditure; waste
dispendió·so -sa [s] *adj* expensive; wasteful

dispènsa *f* cupboard; pantry; distribution; number (*of magazine*); installment (*of book*); dispensation; (naut) storeroom; (coll) store

dispensare (dispènso) *tr* to exempt, free; to distribute ‖ *ref*—**dispensarsi da** to get out of

dispensà·rio *m* (**-ri**) dispensary

dispensa·tóre -trice *mf* dispenser

dispensiè·re -ra *mf* dispenser ‖ *m* steward

dispepsìa *f* dyspepsia

dispèpti·co -ca *adj* & *mf* (**-ci -che**) dyspeptic

disperare (dispèro) *intr* to despair; **fare disperare** to drive crazy ‖ *ref* to despair

dispera·to -ta *adj* hopeless ‖ *m* poor wretch; **come un disperato** desperately ‖ *f*—**alla disperata** with all one's might

disperazióne *f* desperation, despair

dispèrdere §212 *tr* to scatter; to waste ‖ *ref* to disperse; (fig) to waste one's energies

dispersióne *f* dispersion; loss; (elec) leakage

dispersività *f* tendency toward disorganization

dispersi·vo -va *adj* dispersive; disorganized

dispèr·so -sa *adj* scattered; lost; dispersed; missing in action

dispersóre *m* (elec) leakage conductor

dispètto *m* spite; (lit) haughtiness; **a dispetto di** in spite of; **far dispetto a** to provoke

dispettó·so -sa [s] *adj* pestiferous; spiteful, resentful

dispiacènte *adj* sorry; distressing

dispiacére *m* sorrow, displeasure ‖ §214 *intr* (ESSERE) to be displeasing; to be sorry, e.g., **mi dispiace** I am sorry; (with *dat*) to displease; (with *dat*) to dislike, e.g., **le mie parole gli dispiacciono** he dislikes my words; **Le dispiace?** would you please?; **se non Le dispiace** if you don't mind

dispiegare §209 (**dispiègo**) *tr* to manifest; (lit) to unfurl ‖ *ref* to spread out; to flow out

displù·vio *m* (**-vi**) divide, watershed; ridge (*of roof*)

disponìbile *adj* available; open-minded

disponibili·tà *f* (**-tà**) availability; inactive status; **disponibilità** *fpl* available funds

dispórre §218 *tr* to dispose; to prepare ‖ *intr* to provide; to dispose; **disporre di** to have (*available*) ‖ *ref* to get ready

dispositivo *m* gadget; device; (mil) deployment

disposizióne *f* arrangement; inclination, disposition; disposal; instruction; (law) provision

dispó·sto -sta *adj* arranged; disposed; provided; willing; **ben disposto** disposed ‖ *m* (law) proviso

dispòti·co -ca *adj* (**-ci -che**) despotic

dispotismo *m* despotism

dispregiatì·vo -va *adj* disparaging; (gram) pejorative

disprè·gio *m* (**-gi**) contempt; disrepute

disprezzàbile *adj* contemptible; negligible

disprezzare (disprèzzo) *tr* to despise

disprèzzo *m* contempt, scorn

dìsputa *f* dispute; debate

disputàbile *adj* debatable

disputare (dìsputo) *tr* to contest; to discuss; to vie for (*victory*) ‖ *intr* to dispute, debate; to vie ‖ *ref* to vie for

disqualificare §197 (**disquàlifico**) *tr* to disqualify

disquisizióne *f* disquisition

dissacrare *tr* to desecrate

dissacrazióne *f* ¹esecration

dissaldare *tr* to unsolder

dissanguare (dissànguo) *tr* to bleed ‖ *ref* to bleed; to ruin oneself

dissangua·to -ta *adj* bled white; **morire dissanguato** to bleed to death

dissapóre *m* disagreement

disseccare §197 (**dissécco**) *tr* to dry ‖ *ref* to dry; to dry up

disselciare §128 (**dissélcio**) *tr* to remove the cobblestones from

dissellare (dissèllo) *tr* to unsaddle

disseminare (dissémino) *tr* to disseminate; to scatter

dissennà·to -ta *adj* foolish, unwise; crazy, mad

dissensióne *f* dissension

dissènso *m* dissent; disagreement

dissenterìa *f* dysentery

dissentire (dissènto) *intr* to dissent

dissenziènte *adj* dissenting ‖ *mf* dissenter

disseppellire §176 *tr* to exhume

dissertare (dissèrto) *intr* to discourse

dissertazióne *f* dissertation

disservì·zio *m* (**-zi**) poor service

dissestare (dissèsto) *tr* to unsettle; to disarrange

dissesta·to -ta *adj* financially embarrassed; mentally deranged

dissèsto *m* financial embarrassment; mental derangement

dissetante *adj* thirst-quenching

dissetare (disséto) *tr* to quench the thirst of ‖ *ref* to quench one's thirst

dissezióne *f* dissection

dissidènte *adj* & *m* dissident

dissidènza *f* dissent

dissì·dio *m* (**-di**) dissent; disagreement

dissigillare *tr* to unseal ‖ *ref* (lit) to melt

dissìmile *adj* unlike

dissimulare (dissìmulo) *tr* to dissimulate, disguise ‖ *intr* to dissimulate

dissimulazióne *f* dissimulation

dissipare (dìssipo) *tr* to dissipate; to squander; to clear up (*a doubt*) ‖ *ref* to dissipate

dissipa·to -ta *adj* & *mf* profligate

dissipa·tóre -trice *mf* squanderer

dissipazióne *f* dissipation

dissociare §128 (**dissòcio**) *tr* to dissociate, disassociate ‖ *ref* to dissociate or disassociate oneself

dissociazióne *f* dissociation

dissodare (dissòdo) tr to cultivate
dissolutézza f profligacy
dissolu·to -ta adj & mf profligate
dissoluzióne f dissolution
dissolvènza f (mov) fade-out; **dissolvenza incrociata** (mov) lap dissolve
dissòlvere §155 tr to dissolve; to clear up (a doubt); (obs) to untie ‖ ref to dissolve
dissomiglianza f dissimilarity
dissonanza f dissonance
dissotterrare (dissottèrro) tr to exhume; to unearth
dissuadére §213 tr to dissuade
dissuè·to -ta adj (lit) unaccustomed
dissuggellare (dissuggèllo) tr to unseal
distaccamento m (mil) detachment
distaccare §197 tr to detach; to remove; to transfer; to outdistance ‖ ref to stand out; to withdraw, become separated
distacca·to -ta adj detached; branch (office)
distac·co m (-chi) detachment; separation; (sports) spread (in points)
distante adj distant; aloof; different ‖ adv far away
distanza f distance; **mantenere le distanze** to keep one's distance; **tenere a distanza** to keep at arm's length
distanziare §287 tr to outdistance
distare intr to be distant
distèndere §270 tr to stretch; to spread; to unfurl; to relax; to knock down; to write ‖ ref to stretch; to spread out; to relax
distensióne f relaxation; relaxation of tension
disté·so -sa [s] adj stretched out; full (voice); lank (hair) ‖ m—**per disteso** in full ‖ f expanse; row; **a distesa** with full voice; at full peal
distillare tr to distill; to exude; to pour; to trickle ‖ intr (ESSERE) to trickle ‖ ref—**distillarsi il cervello** to rack one's brain
distilla·to -ta adj distilled ‖ m distillate
distilla·tóre -trice mf distiller ‖ m still
distillerìa f distillery
distinguìbile adj distinguishable
distinguere §156 tr to distinguish; to make out; to tell (one thing from another); to divide
distinta f note, list; **distinta di versamento** deposit slip
distintaménte adv distinctly; sincerely yours
distinti·vo -va adj distinctive ‖ m emblem, insignia, badge
distin·to -ta adj distinct; distinguished; sincere (greetings); reserved (seat); **Distinto Signor . . .** (on an envelope) Mr. . . . ‖ f see **distinta**
distinzióne f distinction
distògliere §127 tr to dissuade; to deter; to distract; to turn (one's eyes) away
distòrcere §272 tr to distort; to twist ‖ ref to become distorted; to sprain (e.g., one's ankle)
distorsióne f distortion; sprain; **distorsione acustica** wow
distrarre §273 tr to distract; to divert;

to amuse; to pull (a muscle) ‖ ref to become distracted; to relax
distrat·to -ta adj absent-minded
distrazióne f absent-mindedness; distraction; diversion (of money); pull (of muscle)
distrét·to -ta adj (obs) close; (obs) hard-pressed ‖ m district; precinct (e.g., of police); circuit (of court); ward (in city); **distretto militare** draft board; **distretto postale** postal zone ‖ f stricture; necessity
distrettuale adj district
distribuire §176 tr to distribute; to pass out; to allot; to deploy (troops); (theat) to cast (roles); (mov) to release; (mil) to issue (e.g., clothing)
distribu·tóre -trice adj distributing, dispensing ‖ mf distributor, dispenser ‖ m distributor; **distributore automatico** vending machine; **distributore di benzina** gasoline pump
distribuzióne f distribution; issue; delivery; (aut) timing gears; (mov) release; (fig) dispensation
districare §197 tr to unravel ‖ ref to extricate oneself
distrofìa f dystrophy
distruggere §266 tr to destroy; to ruin
distrutti·vo -va adj destructive
distruzióne f destruction
disturbare tr to disturb, bother; **disturbo?** may I come in? ‖ ref to bother; to go out of one's way
disturba·tóre -trice mf disturber; **disturbatore della quiete pubblica** disturber of the peace
disturbo m trouble, bother; disturbance; (rad) interference; **disturbi atmosferici** static, atmospherics; **togliere il disturbo a** to take leave of
disubbidiènte adj disobedient
disubbidiènza f disobedience
disubbidire §176 intr to disobey; (with dat) to disobey
disuguaglianza f inequality; disparity
disuguale adj uneven; unequal
disuma·no -na adj inhumane; unbearable
disunióne f disunion
disunire §176 tr to disunite
disusa·to -ta adj obsolete, out of use
disuso m disuse; **in disuso** obsolete
disùtile adj useless; burdensome ‖ m worthless fellow; (com) loss
disvì·o m (-i) miscarriage, missending (of a letter)
ditale m thimble; fingerstall
ditata f poke with a finger; finger mark; dab (with a finger)
dito m (dita fpl) finger; toe; **avere le dita d'oro** to have a magic touch; **dita della mano** fingers; **dita del piede** toes; **legarsela al dito** to never forget ‖ m (diti) finger, e.g., **dito indice** index finger; **dito anulare** ring finger; **dito medio** middle finger; **dito mignolo** little finger; **dito pollice** thumb
ditta f firm, house; office
dittàfono m intercom; dictaphone
dittatóre m dictator

dittatura *f* dictatorship
dittongare §209 (**dittòngo**) *tr* to diphthongize
dittòn·go *m* (**-ghi**) diphthong
diurèti·co -ca *adj & m* (**-ci -che**) diuretic
diur·no -na *adj* daily; daytime || *f* (theat) matinée
diutur·no -na *adj* long-lasting
diva *f* diva; (mov) star; (lit) goddess
divagare §209 *tr* to amuse; to distract || *intr* to digress || *ref* to relax
divagazióne *f* distraction; digression; relaxation
divampare *intr* (ESSERE & AVERE) to blaze, flare
divano *m* divan; couch, sofa
divaricare §197 (**divàrico**) *tr* to spread (*one's legs*); to open up (*an incision*)
divà·rio -ria *m* (**-ri**) difference
divèllere §267 *tr* to eradicate, uproot
diveni·re *m* (**-re**) (philos) becoming || §282 *intr* (ESSERE) (lit) to become; (archaic) to come
diventare (**divènto**) *intr* (ESSERE) to become; **diventare di tutti i colori** to blush; to be embarrassed; **diventare grande** to grow up; **diventare matto** to go mad; **diventare pallido** to turn pale; **diventare piccolo** to grow smaller; **diventare rosso** to blush
divèr·bio *m* (**-bi**) argument; **venire a diverbio** to have an altercation
divergènza *f* divergency
divèrgere §157 *intr* to diverge
diversificare §197 (**diversìfico**) *tr* to diversify || *ref* to be diversified; to differ
diversióne *f* diversion
diversi·tà *f* (**-tà**) diversity
diversi·vo -va *adj* diverting || *m* diversion
diver·so -sa *adj* different; **diver·si -se** several, e.g., **diverse ragazze** several girls || **diver·si -se** *pron* several
divertènte *adj* diverting, amusing
divertiménto *m* amusement, pastime; fun; (mus) divertimento
divertire (**divèrto**) *tr* to amuse, entertain; (lit) to turn aside || *ref* to have fun, enjoy oneself; (lit) to go away
diverti·to -ta *adj* amused; amusing
divétta *f* starlet
divezzare (**divézzo**) *tr* to wean || *ref*— **divezzarsi da** to get out of the habit of
dividèndo *m* dividend
dividere §158 *tr* to divide; to partition; to split; to share in (*e.g., s.o.'s grief*) || *ref* to be divided; to become separated; **dividersi fra** to divide one's time between
divièto *m* prohibition; **divieto d'affissione** post no bills; **divieto di parcheggio** no parking; **divieto di sosta** no stopping; **divieto di svolta** no turns; **divieto di transito** no thoroughfare
divinare *tr* (lit) to divine
divina·tóre -trice *adj* divining || *m* diviner

divinazióne *f* divination
divincolare (**divìncolo**) *tr & ref* to wriggle
divini·tà *f* (**-tà**) divinity
divinizzare [ddzz] *tr* to deify
divi·no -na *adj* divine
divisa *f* uniform; motto; part (*in hair*); **divise foreign** exchange
divisare *tr* (lit) to intend
divisìbile *adj* divisible
divisióne *f* division; partition; (sports) league
divisionismo *m* (painting) divisionism; (pol) separatism
divismo *m* (mov) star system; (mov) adulation of stars
divisóre *m* (math) divisor
divisò·rio -ria (**-ri -rie**) *adj* dividing || *m* partition; (math) divisor
di·vo -va *adj* (lit) divine || *m* (theat, mov) star; (lit) god || *f* see **diva**
divolgare §209 (**divólgo**) *tr & ref* var of **divulgare**
divorare (**divóro**) *tr* to devour; to gulp down; to consume; **divorare la via** to burn up the road
divora·tóre -trice *adj* consuming || *mf* consumer (*e.g., of food, books*)
divorziare §287 (**divòrzio**) *intr* to become divorced; **divorziare da** to divorce
divorzia·to -ta *adj* divorced || *m* divorcé || *f* divorcée
divòr·zio *m* (**-zi**) divorce
divulgare §209 *tr* to divulge; to publicize; to popularize || *ref* to spread; to become popular
divulga·tóre -trice *adj* popularizing || *mf* popularizer; **divulgatore di calunnie** scandalmonger; **divulgatore di notizie** telltale
divulgazióne *f* publicizing; popularization
divulsióne *f* (surg) dilation
dizionà·rio *m* (**-ri**) dictionary; **dizionario geografico** gazetteer
dizióne *f* diction; reading (*of poetry*)
do [dɔ] *m* (**do**) (mus) do; (mus) C
dóc·cia *f* (**-ce**) shower; gutter (*on roof*); spout; (fig) dash of cold water; **fare la doccia** to take a shower
docciare §128 (**dóccio**) *tr, intr* (ESSERE) & *ref* to shower
doccióne *m* trough, gutter; gargoyle
docènte *adj* teaching || *m* teacher; **libero docente** certified university teacher
docènza *f* teaching post; **libera docenza** lectureship
dòcile *adj* docile; tame; amenable (*person*); workable (*material*)
documentare (**documénto**) *tr* to document || *ref* to gather information
documentà·rio -ria *adj & m* (**-ri -rie**) documentary
documénto *m* document; paper; **documenti di bordo** ship's papers
dodecafonìa *f* twelve-tone system
dodecasìlla·bo -ba *adj* twelve-syllable, dodecasyllable
dodicèsi·mo -ma *adj, m & pron* twelfth
dódici *adj & pron* twelve; **le dódici**

twelve o'clock || *m* twelve; twelfth (*in dates*)

dó·ga *f* (**-ghe**) stave

dogale *adj* (hist) of the doge

dogana *f* duty; customs; custom house

doganière *m* customs officer

dòge *m* (hist) doge

dò·glia *f* (**-glie**) (lit) pain, pang; **doglie** labor pains

dò·glio *m* (**-gli**) barrel; (lit) large jar

doglió·so -sa [s] *adj* (lit) sorrowful

dòg·ma *m* (**-mi**) dogma

dogmàti·co -ca (**-ci -che**) *adj* dogmatic || *mf* dogmatist

dogmatismo *m* dogmatism

dólce *adj* sweet; soft; gentle; fresh (*water*); mild (*climate*); delicate (*feet*); **dolce far niente** sweet idleness || *m* sweet; sweet dish; **dolci** candy

dolceama·ro -ra *adj* bittersweet

dolcézza *f* sweetness; mildness; gentleness

dolcia·stro -stra *adj* sweetish

dolcière *m* candy maker; pastry baker

dolcificare §197 (**dolcifico**) *tr* to sweeten

dolciume *m* sweet; **dolciumi** candy

dolènte *adj* aching; sorrowful; sorry

dolére §159 *intr* (ESSERE & AVERE) to ache, e.g., **gli dolgono i denti** his teeth ache || *ref* to grieve || *impers* (ESSERE) to be sorry, e.g., **mi duole che Lei non possa venire** I am sorry that you won't be able to come

dolicònice *m* bobolink

dòllaro *m* dollar

dòlo *m* fraud, malice, guile

dolomite *f* dolomite || **Dolomiti** *fpl* Dolomites

dolorante *adj* aching

dolorare (**dolóro**) *intr* (lit) to ache

dolóre *m* ache; sorrow; contrition

doloró·so -sa [s] *adj* painful; sorrowful

doló·so -sa [s] *adj* intentional, fraudulent; (law) felonious

domàbile *adj* tamable

domanda *f* question; application; appeal; (econ) demand; **domanda suggestiva** (com) leading question; **fare una domanda** to ask a question

domandare *tr* to ask; to ask for; **domandare la parola** to ask for the floor || *intr* to inquire || *ref* to wonder; (lit) to be called

doma·ni *m* (**-ni**) tomorrow || *adv* tomorrow; **a domani** until tomorrow; **domani a otto** a week from tomorrow; **domani l'altro** the day after tomorrow

domare (**dómo**) *tr* to tame; to extinguish; to quell

doma·tóre -trice *mf* tamer

domattina *adv* tomorrow morning

doméni·ca *f* (**-che**) Sunday

domenicale *adj* Sunday (*e.g., rest*)

domenica·no -na *adj* & *m* Dominican (*e.g., order*)

domesticare §197 (**domèstico**) *tr* to domesticate

domèsti·co -ca (**-ci -che**) *adj* family; household; familiar; domestic || *mf* domestic, servant || *f* maid; **alla**

domestica family style; **domestica a mezzo servizio** part-time domestic

domiciliare *adj* house || §287 *tr* (com) to draw || *ref* to dwell; to settle

domicilia·to -ta *adj* residing

domici·lio *m* (**-li**) domicile, residence; principal office; **domicilio coatto** imprisonment; **franco domicilio** free delivery

dominare (**dòmino**) *tr* to dominate, rule; to master; to overlook || *intr* to prevail; to reign || *ref* to control oneself

domina·tóre -trice *mf* ruler

dominazióne *f* domination; rule

domineddìo *m* *invar* (coll) the Lord God

dominica·no -na *adj* & *mf* Dominican (*e.g., Republic*)

domì·nio *m* (**-ni**) dominion; domain

dòmi·no *m* (**-no**) domino (*cloak*); dominoes (*game*)

dòn *m* (used only before singular Christian name) don (*Spanish title*); Don (*priest*); uncle (*familiar title of elderly man*)

donare (**dóno**) *tr* to donate; to give as a present || *intr*—**donare a** to be becoming to

dona·tóre -trice *mf* donor; **donatore di sangue** blood donor

donazióne *f* gift, donation

donchisciotté·sco -sca *adj* (**-schi -sche**) quixotic

dónde *adv* wherefrom, whence

dondolare (**dóndolo**) *tr* to swing, rock || *ref* to swing, rock; to loaf around

dondolì·o *m* (**-i**) swinging, rocking

dóndolo *m*—**a dondolo** rocking (*chair, horse*); **andare a dondolo** to loaf around

dondoló·ne -na *mf* idler, loafer

dongiovan·ni *m* (**-ni**) Don Juan

dònna *f* woman; ladyship; (lit) lady; (coll) Mrs.; (coll) maid; (cards) queen; **da donna** woman's, e.g., **scarpe da donna** woman's shoes; **donna cannone** fat lady (*of circus*); **donna di casa** housewife; **Nostra Donna** Our Lady

donnaiòlo *m* ladies' man, philanderer

donné·sco -sca *adj* (**-schi -sche**) womanly, feminine

dònnola *f* weasel

dóno *m* gift; **in dono** as a gift

donzèlla [dz] *f* (lit) damsel

donzèllo [dz] *m* (coll) doorman; (lit) page

dópo *adv* afterwards, later; **dopo che** after; **dopo di** after || *prep* after; **dopo + pp** after having + *pp*

dopobar·ba *adj invar* after-shaving || *m* (**-ba**) after-shaving lotion

dopodomani *m* & *adv* the day after tomorrow

dopoguèr·ra *m* (**-ra**) postwar era

dopolavóro *m* government office designed to organize workers' leisure time

dopopranzo *m* afternoon || *adv* in the afternoon

doppiàg·gio *m* (**-gi**) (mov) dubbing

doppiare §287 (dóppio) *tr* to double; (mov) to dub

doppière *m* candelabrum

doppiétta *f* double-barreled shotgun; (aut) double shift

doppiézza *f* duplicity

dóp·pio -pia (-pi -pie) *adj* double; coupled; double-dealing ‖ *adv* twice, twofold ‖ *m* double; twice as much; (tennis) doubles; (theat) understudy

doppióne *m* duplicate; (philol) doublet

doppiopèt·to *adj invar* double-breasted ‖ *m* (-to) double-breasted suit

dorare (dòro) *tr* to gild; (culin) to brown; **dorare la pillola** to sugar-coat the pill

dora·to -ta *adj* gilt, golden

doratura *f* gilding

dormicchiare §287 *intr* to doze

dormiènte *adj* sleeping ‖ *mf* sleeper

dormigliό·ne -na *mf* sleepyhead

dormire (dòrmo) *tr & intr* to sleep; **dormire a occhi aperti** to be overcome with sleep; **dormire della grossa** to sleep profoundly; **dormire tra due guanciali** to be safe and secure

dormita *f* long sleep; **fare una bella dormita** to have a long sleep

dormitò·rio *m* (-ri) dormitory

dormivé·glia *m* (-glia) drowsiness

dorsale *adj* dorsal; back (*bone*) ‖ *m* head (*of bed*); back (*of chair*) ‖ *f* (geog) ridge

dòrso *m* back; (sports) backstroke

dosàg·gio *m* (-gi) dosage

dosare (dòso) *tr* to dose

dosatura *f* dosage

dòse *f* dose

dòsso *m* back; (lit) summit; **levarsi di dosso** to take off; **mettersi in dosso** to put on

dotare (dòto) *tr* to provide with a dowry; to endow; to bless

dotazióne *f* dowry; endowment; supply

dòte *f* dowry; gift; endowment

dòt·to -ta *adj* learned, erudite ‖ *m* scholar; (anat) duct

dottorale *adj* doctoral

dottó·re -réssa *mf* doctor

dottrina *f* doctrine; Christian doctrine

dóve *m* where; **per ogni dove** everywhere ‖ *adv* where; **da dove** or **di dove** from where; which way; **fin dove** up to what point; **per dove** which way ‖ *conj* where; whereas

dovere *m* duty, obligation; homework; **a dovere** properly; **doveri** regards; **farsi un dovere di** to feel duty-bound to; **mettere qlcu a dovere** to put s.o. in his place; **più del dovere** more than one should; **sentirsi in dovere di** to feel duty-bound to ‖ §160 *tr & intr* to owe ‖ *aux* (ESSERE & AVERE) must, e.g., **deve farlo** you must do it; to have to, e.g., **dovei partire** I had to leave; ought to, e.g., **dovrebbe lucidare la macchina** he ought to polish the car; should, e.g., **dovresti immaginarti** you should imagine; to be to, e.g., **il treno doveva arrivare alle sei** the train was to arrive at six; to be supposed to, e.g., **deve aver**

fatto un lungo viaggio he is supposed to have taken a long journey

doveró·so -sa [s] *adj* proper, right

dovìzia *f* (lit) abundance, wealth

dovunque *adv* wherever, anywhere; everywhere

dovu·to -ta *adj & m* due

dozzina [ddzz] *f* dozen; room and board; **da** or **di dozzina** common, ordinary; **tenere a dozzina** to board

dozzinale [ddzz] *adj* common, ordinary

dozzinante [ddzz] *mf* boarder

dra·ga *f* (-ghe) dredge

dragàg·gio *m* (-gi) dredging

dragami·ne *m* (-ne) minesweeper

dragare §209 *tr* to dredge

dràglia *f* (naut) stay

dra·go *m* (-ghi) dragon; **drago volante** kite

dragóna *f* sword strap

dragoncèllo *m* (bot) tarragon

dragóne *m* dragon; dragoon

dram·ma *m* (-mi) drama, play; **dramma musicale** (hist) melodrama ‖ *f* drachma; dram

drammàti·co -ca (-ci -che) *adj* dramatic ‖ *f* drama, dramatic art

drammatizzare [ddzz] *tr* to dramatize

drammatur·go *m* (-ghi) playwright, dramatist

drappég·gio *m* (-gi) drape; pleats

drappeggiare §290 (drappéggio) *tr* to drape ‖ *ref* to be draped

drappèlla *f* pennon (*on bugler's trumpet*)

drappèllo *m* squad, platoon

drapperìa *f* dry goods; dry-goods store

drappo *m* cloth, silk cloth; (billiards) green cloth, baize

dràsti·co -ca *adj* (-ci -che) drastic

drenàg·gio *m* (-gi) drainage

drenare (drèno) *tr* to drain

dressàg·gio *m* (-gi) *m* training (*of animals*)

dribblare *tr & intr* (sports) to dribble

drit·to -ta *adj* straight; (lit) correct; **dritto come un fuso** straight as a ramrod ‖ *m* (fig) old fox ‖ *f* right; (naut) starboard

drizza *f* (naut) halyard

drizzare *tr* to straighten; to address; to erect; to cock (*the head*); to direct (*a blow*); **drizzare le gambe ai cani** to do the impossible; **drizzare le orecchie** to prick up one's ears ‖ *intr* (naut) to hoist the halyard ‖ *ref* to stand erect

drò·ga *f* (-ghe) drug; spice; seasoning

drogare §209 (drògo) *tr* to drug; to spice, season

drogherìa *f* grocery (store)

droghière *m* grocer

dromedà·rio *m* (-ri) dromedary

dru·do -da *adj* (archaic) faithful; (lit) strong ‖ *m* (obs) vassal; (lit) lover

drùi·da *m* (-di) druid

drupa *f* (bot) drupe, stone fruit

duale *adj & m* dual

dualismo *m* dualism

dualità *f* duality

dùb·bio -bia (-bi -bie) *adj* doubtful ‖ *m* doubt; misgiving; **mettere in dub-**

bio to question; to risk; **senza dubbio** no doubt

dubbió·so -sa [s] *adj* dubious; doubtful; (*lit*) dangerous

dubitare (dùbito) *intr* to doubt; to suspect; **dubitare di** to mistrust; to doubt; **non dubitare!** don't worry!

du·ca *m* (**-chi**) duke; (*lit*) leader

ducato *m* duchy; ducat

duce *m* leader; duce

duchéssa *f* duchess

duchessina *f* young duchess

duchino *m* young duke

due *adj* & *pron* two; **le due** two o'clock ‖ *m* two; second (*in dates*) ‖ *f*—**fra le due** between two alternatives

duecenté·sco -sca *adj* (**-schi -sche**) thirteenth-century

duecentèsi·mo -**ma** *adj, m* & *pron* two hundredth

duecènto *adj, m* & *pron* two hundred ‖ **il Duecento** the thirteenth century

duellante *adj* dueling ‖ *m* duelist

duellare (duèllo) *intr* to duel

duèllo *m* duel; contest; debate; **sfidare a duello** to challenge to a duel

duemila *adj, m* & *pron* two thousand ‖ **Duemila** *m* twenty-first century

duepèz·zi *m* (**-zi**) two-piece bathing suit

duétto *m* (*mus*) duet

dulcamara *f* (*bot*) bittersweet

dulcina *f* artificial sweetening

duna *f* dune

dunque *m*—**venire al dunque** to come

to the point ‖ *adv* then ‖ *conj* therefore, hence ‖ *interj* well!

duodèno *m* (anat) duodenum

duòlo *m* (*lit*) grief

duòmo *m* cathedral; dome (*e.g., of a boiler*)

du·plex *m* (**-plex**) (telp) party line

duplicare §197 (dùplico) *tr* to duplicate

duplica·to -ta *adj* & *m* duplicate

duplicatóre *m* duplicator

dùplice *adj* twofold, double ‖ *f* (racing) daily double

duplici·tà *f* (**-tà**) duplicity

duràbile *adj* durable, lasting

duràci·no -na *adj* clingstone ‖ *f* clingstone peach

duralumínio *m* duralumin

durare *tr* to endure, bear ‖ *intr* to last; **durare a** + *inf* to keep on + *ger*; **durare in carica** to remain in office

durata *f* duration; lasting quality; **di lunga durata** long-lasting

durante *prep* during; throughout

duratu·ro -ra *adj* enduring, lasting

durévole *adj* lasting, durable

durézza *f* hardness; toughness; rigidity

du·ro -ra *adj* hard; hard-boiled (*egg*); durum (*wheat*); tough (*skin*); harsh; (phonet) voiceless ‖ *m* hard part; hard floor; hard soil; **il duro sta che . . .** the trouble is that **. . .** ; **tener duro** to hold out

duróne *m* callousness, callosity

dùttile *adj* ductile; tractable

E

E, e [e] *m* & *f* fifth letter of the Italian alphabet

e *conj* and

ebani·sta *m* (**-sti**) cabinetmaker

ebanisteria *f* cabinetmaking; cabinetmaker's shop

ebanite *f* ebonite, vulcanite

èbano *m* ebony

ebbène *interj* well!

ebbrézza *f* intoxication, drunkenness

èb·bro -bra *adj* intoxicated ‖ *mf* drunk

ebdomadà·rio -ria *adj* & *m* (**-ri -rie**) weekly

èbete *adj* stupid, dull, dumb

ebollizióne *f* boil, boiling

ebrài·co -ca (**-ci -che**) *adj* Hebrew, Hebraic ‖ *m* Hebrew (*language*)

ebrè·o -a *adj* & *mf* Hebrew ‖ *m* Hebrew (*language*); Jew; **ebreo errante** Wandering Jew

è·bro -bra *adj* & *mf* var of ebbro

ebùrne·o -a *adj* (*lit*) ivory

ecatòmbe *f* hecatomb, slaughter

eccedènte *adj* exceeding ‖ *m* excess

eccedènza *f* excess, surplus

eccèdere §123 *tr* to exceed ‖ *intr* to go too far

eccellènte *adj* excellent

eccellènza *f* excellence ‖ **Eccellenza** *f* Excellency

eccèllere §162 *intr* (ESSERE) to excel

eccèl·so -sa *adj* unexcelled; very high ‖ —**l'Eccelso** *m* the Most High

eccentrici·tà *f* (**-tà**) eccentricity

eccèntri·co -ca (**-ci -che**) *adj* eccentric; suburban ‖ *mf* vaudeville performer ‖ *m* (mach) eccentric

eccepìbile *adj* objectionable

eccepire §176 *tr* (law) to take exception to ‖ *intr* (law) to object

eccessi·vo -va *adj* excessive; overweening (*opinion*)

eccèsso *m* excess; **all'eccesso** excessively; **andare agli eccessi** to go to extremes; **dare in eccessi** to fly into a rage; **eccesso di peso** excess weight

eccètera *adv* and so forth, et cetera

eccètto *prep* except, but; **eccetto che** except that; unless

eccettuare (eccèttuo) *tr* to except

eccettua·to -ta *adj* excepted ‖ **eccettuato** *prep* except

eccezionale *adj* exceptional

eccezióne *f* exception; objection; **ad eccezione di** with the exception of; **d'eccezione** extraordinary; **sollevare un'eccezione** (law) to take exception

ecchimò·si *f* (**-si**) bruise

eccì·dio *m* (**-di**) massacre

eccitàbile *adj* excitable

eccitaménto *m* instigation; excitement
eccitante *adj* stimulating ‖ *m* stimulant
eccitare (**èccito**) *tr* to excite ‖ *ref* to become excited or aroused; (sports) to warm up
eccitazióne *f* excitement; (elec) excitation
ecclesiàsti•co **-ca** (**-ci -che**) *adj* ecclesiastical ‖ *m* clergyman
ècco *tr invar* here is (are), there is (are); **ecco che** here, e.g., **ecco che viene** here he comes; **eccoci** here we are; **ecco fatto** that's it; **eccola** here she is; here it is; **eccomi** here I am: **eccone** here are some ‖ *intr invar* here I am; here it is; **quand'ecco** suddenly ‖ *interj* look!
eccóme *interj* and how!, indeed!
echeggiare §290 (**echéggio**) *intr* (ESSERE & AVERE) to echo
eclètti•co **-ca** *adj & mf* (**-ci -che**) eclectic
eclissare *tr* to eclipse ‖ *ref* to be eclipsed; (coll) to vanish, sneak away
eclis•sì *f* (**-sì**) eclipse
eclìtti•ca *f* (**-che**) ecliptic
èclo•ga *f* (**-ghe**) var of **egloga**
è•co *m & f* (**-chi** *mpl*) echo; **far eco a** to echo
ecogonìòmetro *m* sonar
ecologìa *f* ecology
economato *m* comptroller's or administrator's office
economìa *f* administration; management; economy; economics; **economìa aziendale** business management; **economia di mercato** free enterprise; **economia domestica** home economics; **economia politica** political economy; economics; **economìe** savings; **fare economìa** to save
economì•co **-ca** *adj* (**-ci -che**) economic(al); cheap
economì•sta *mf* (**-sti -ste**) economist
economizzare [ddzz] *tr & intr* to economize, save
ecòno•mo **-ma** *adj* thrifty ‖ *m* comptroller; administrator
ecosistè•ma [s] *m* (**-mi**) ecosystem
ecumèni•co **-ca** *adj* (**-ci -che**) ecumenical
eczè•ma [dz] *m* (**-mi**) eczema
édera *f* ivy
edìcola *f* shrine; newsstand
edificante *adj* edifying
edificare §197 (**edìfico**) *tr* to build; to edify ‖ *intr* to build
edifica•tóre **-trice** *adj* building ‖ *mf* builder
edificazióne *f* building; edification
edifi•cio *m* (**-ci**) building, edifice; pack (*e.g., of lies*); structure
edìle *adj* building, construction ‖ *m* builder, construction worker
edilì•zio **-zia** (**-zi -zie**) *adj* building, construction ‖ *f* building trade
edìpi•co **-ca** *adj* (**-ci -che**) Oedipus (*e.g., complex*)
Edipo *m* Oedipus
èdi•to **-ta** *adj* published
edi•tóre **-trice** *adj* publishing ‖ *mf* publisher; editor (*e.g., of a text*)
editorìa *f* publishing; publishers

editoriale *adj* editorial; publishing ‖ *m* editorial
editoriali•sta *mf* (**-sti -ste**) editorial writer
editto *m* edict
edizióne *f* edition; performance; (fig) vintage
edonismo *m* hedonism
edoni•sta *mf* (**-sti -ste**) hedonist
edòt•to **-ta** *adj* (lit) informed, acquainted; **rendere qlcu edotto su qlco** (lit) to inform s.o. of s.th
edredóne *m* eider, eider duck
educanda *f* boarding-school girl; convent-school girl
educandato *m* (convent) boarding school for girls
educare §197 (**èduco**) *tr* to educate; to rear, bring up; to train; to accustom, inure; (lit) to grow
educati•vo **-va** *adj* educational
educa•to **-ta** *adj* educated; polite, well-bred
educa•tóre **-trice** *mf* educator
educazióne *f* education; breeding, manners; **educazione civica** civics
edule *adj* edible
efèbo *m* (coll) sissy
efèlide *f* freckle
effeminatézza *f* effeminacy
effemina•to **-ta** *adj* effeminate; frivolous
efferatézza *f* savagery
effervescènte *adj* effervescent
effervescènza *f* effervescence
effettivaménte *adv* really
effetti•vo **-va** *adj* real, true; effective; full (*e.g., member*); regular (*e.g., army officer*) ‖ *m* effective; total amount; (mil) manpower
effètto *m* effect, result; (com) promissory note; (billiards) English; (sports) spin; **a questo effetto** for this purpose; **effetti** effects, belongings; **effetto di luce** play of light; **effetto ottico** optical illusion; **fare effetto** to make a sensation; **fare l'effetto di** to give the impression of; **in effetto** in fact; **mandare a effetto** to carry out; **porre in effetto** to put into effect
effettuàbile *adj* feasible
effettuare (**effèttuo**) *tr* to bring about; to contrive; to actuate; **effettuare** (**una corsa, un servizio**) to run, e.g., **l'autobus effettua una corsa ogni mezz'ora** the bus runs every half hour
efficace *adj* effective; forceful (*writer*)
efficà•cia *f* (**-cie**) effectiveness, efficacy; (law) validity
efficiènte *adj* efficient
efficiènza *f* efficiency; **in piena efficienza** in full working order; in top condition
effigiare §290 *tr* to portray, represent
effi•gie *f* (**-gie** or **-gi**) effigy; image
effìme•ro **-ra** *adj* ephemeral
efflusso *m* flow, outflow
efflù•vio *m* (**-vi**) effluvium; emanation (*e.g., of light*)
effrazióne *f* (law) burglary
effusióne *f* effusion; outflow; shedding (*of blood*); effusiveness
egemonìa *f* hegemony

egè·o -a *adj* Aegean
ègida *f* aegis
Egitto, l' *m* Egypt
egizia·no -na *adj & mf* Egyptian
eglantina *f* sweetbrier
eglefino *m* haddock
égli §5 *pron pers* he
èglo·ga *f* (-ghe) eclogue
egocèntri·co -ca *adj & mf* (-ci -che) egocentric
egoismo *m* egoism, selfishness
egoi·sta (-sti -ste) *adj* selfish || *mf* egoist
egoìsti·co -ca *adj* (-ci -che) egoistic(al)
egotismo *m* egotism
egoti·sta (-sti -ste) *adj* egotistic || *mf* egotist
egrè·gio -gia *adj* (-gi -gie) (lit) outstanding; Egregio Signore Mr. (*before a man's name in an address on a letter*); Dear Sir
eguaglianza *f* equality
eguale *adj* var of uguale
egualità·rio -ria *adj & m* (-ri -rie) equalitarian
éhi *interj* hey!
él *pron* (lit) he; (archaic) they
eiaculazióne *f* ejaculation
eiettàbile *adj* ejection (*seat*)
eiezióne *f* ejection
él *pron* (archaic) he
elaborare (elàboro) *tr* to elaborate; to digest; to secrete
elabora·to -ta *adj* elaborate || *m* written exercise
elaboratóre *m* computer
elaborazióne *f* elaboration; data processing
elargire §176 *tr* to donate
elargizióne *f* donation
elastici·tà *f* (-tà) elasticity; agility; (com) oscillation; (com) range
elàsti·co -ca *adj* (-ci -che) *adj* elastic || *m* rubber band; bedspring
élce *m & f* holm oak
elefante *m* elephant; elefante marino sea elephant
elefantéssa *f* female elephant
elegante *adj* elegant, fashionable
elegantó·ne -na *mf* fashion plate || *m* dandy, dude
eleganza *f* elegance, stylishness
elèggere §193 *tr* to elect
eleggìbile *adj* eligible
elegia *f* elegy
elegìa·co -ca *adj* elegiac
elementare *adj* elementary || elementari *fpl* elementary schools
eleménto *m* element; rudiment; member; cell (*of battery*); elementi personnel, e.g., elementi femminili female personnel
elemòsina *f* alms; (eccl) collection; chiedere l'elemosina to beg; vivere d'elemosina to live on charity
elemosinare (elemòsino) *intr* to beg
Elèna *f* Helen
elencare §197 (elènco) *tr* to list; to enumerate
elèn·co *m* (-chi) list; elenco telefonico telephone directory
eletti·vo -va *adj* elective
elèt·to -ta *adj* elect; distinguished

(*audience*); precious (*metal*); chosen (*people*) || *mf* elect
elettorato *m* electorate, constituency
elet·tóre -trice *mf* voter; elector
elettràuto *m* automobile electrician; automotive electric shop
elettrici·sta *mf* (-sti -ste) electrician
elettrici·tà *f* (-tà) electricity
elèttri·co -ca *adj* (-ci -che) *adj* electrical || *m* electrical worker
elettrificare §197 (elettrìfico) *tr* to electrify
elettrizzare [ddzz] *tr* to electrify (*e.g., a person*) || *ref* to become electrified
ellètro *m* amber
elettrocalamita *f* electromagnet
elettrocardiògrafo *m* electrocardiograph
elettrocardiogram·ma *m* (-mi) electrocardiogram
elettrodinàmi·co -ca (-ci -che) *adj* electrodynamic || *f* electrodynamics
elèttrodo *m* electrode
elettrodomèsti·co -ca (-ci -che) *adj* electric household || *m* electric household appliance
elettroesecuzióne *f* electrocution
elettròge·no -na *adj* generating (*unit*)
elettròli·si *f* (-si) electrolysis
elettrolìti·co -ca *adj* (-ci -che) electrolytic
elettròlito *m* electrolyte
elettromagnèti·co -ca *adj* (-ci -che) electromagnetic
elettromo·tóre -trice *adj* electromotive || *m* electric motor || *f* electric train; electric railcar
elettróne *m* electron
elettròni·co -ca (-ci -che) *adj* electronic || *f* electronics
elettropómpa *f* electric pump
elettrosquasso *m* electroshock
elettrostàti·co -ca (-ci -che) *adj* electrostatic || *f* electrostatics
elettrotècni·co -ca (-ci -che) *adj* electrotechnical || *m* electrician; electrical engineer || *f* electrical engineering
elettrotrèno *m* electric train
elevaménto *m* elevation
elevare (èlevo & elèvo) *tr* to lift, elevate; (math) to raise || *ref* to rise
elevatézza *f* loftiness, dignity
eleva·to -ta *adj* high, lofty
eleva·tóre -trice *adj* elevating || *m* elevator
elevazióne *f* elevation; (sports) jump; (math) raising
elezióne *f* election; choice
èlfo *m* elf
èli·ca *f* (-che) propeller; (geom) helix
elicoidale *adj* helicoidal
elicòttero *m* helicopter
elìdere §161 *tr* to annul; to elide || *ref* to neutralize one another
eliminare (elìmino) *tr* to eliminate
eliminatò·rio -ria (-ri -rie) *adj* eliminating || *f* (sports) heat
eliminazióne *f* elimination; extermination
èlio- *comb form adj* helio-, e.g., eliocentrico heliocentric || *comb form*

m & f helio-, e.g., **elioterapìa** heliotherapy

èlio *m* helium

eliocèntri·co -ca *adj* (**-ci -che**) heliocentric

eliògrafo *m* heliograph

elioteràpi·co -ca *adj* (**-ci -che**) sunshine (*treatment*); sunbathing (*establishment*)

eliotrò·pio *m* (**-pi**) heliotrope; bloodstone

elipòrto *m* heliport

elisabettia·no -na *adj* Elizabethan

elì·sio -sia *adj* (**-si -sie**) Elysian

elisióne *f* elision

elì·sir *m* (**-sir**) elixir

èlitra *f* elytron, shard

élla *pron* (lit) she ‖ **Ella** *pron* (lit) you

ellèboro *m* hellebore

ellèni·co -ca *adj* (**-ci -che**) Hellenic

ellisse *f* ellipse

ellìs·si *f* (**-si**) (gram) ellipsis

ellìtti·co -ca *adj* (**-ci -che**) elliptical

-èllo -èlla *suf adj* little, e.g., **poverello** poor little

elmétto *m* helmet; tin hat

élmo *m* helmet

elogiare §290 (**elògio**) *tr* to praise

elò·gio *m* (**-gi**) praise, encomium; write-up; **elogio funebre** eulogy

eloquènte *adj* eloquent

eloquènza *f* eloquence

elò·quio *m* (**-qui**) (lit) speech, diction

élsa *f* hilt

elucidare (**elùcido**) *tr* to elucidate

elùdere §105 *tr* to elude, evade

elusì·vo -va *adj* elusive

elvèti·co -ca *adj & mf* (**-ci -che**) Helvetian

elzevì·ro -ra [dz] *adj* Elzevir ‖ *m* Elzevir book; (journ) literary article

emacia·to -ta *adj* emaciated, lean

emanare *tr* to send forth; to issue ‖ *intr* (ESSERE) to emanate; to come forth

emanazióne *f* emanation; issuance

emancipare (**emàncipo**) *tr* to emancipate ‖ *ref* to become emancipated

emancipazióne *f* emancipation

emarginare (**emàrgino**) *tr* to note in the margin; (fig) to put aside, neglect

emarginato *m* marginal note

emàti·co -ca *adj* (**-ci -che**) blood, hematic

ematite *f* hematite

embar·go *m* (**-ghi**) embargo

emblè·ma *m* (**-mi**) emblem

emblemàti·co -ca *adj* (**-ci -che**) emblematic

embolìa *f* embolism

èmbrice *m* flat roof tile; shingle

embriologìa *f* embryology

embrionale *adj* embryonic

embrióne *m* embryo

emendaménto *m* emendation (*of a text*); amendment (*to a law*)

emendare (**emèndo**) *tr* to correct; to emend; to amend (*a law*) ‖ *ref* to reform

emergènza *f* emergence; emergency

emèrgere §162 *intr* (ESSERE) to emerge;

to surface (*said of a submarine*); to loom; to stand out

emèri·to -ta *adj* emeritus (*professor*); famous

emerotè·ca *f* (**-che**) periodical library

emersióne *f* emersion; surfacing

emèr·so -sa *adj* emergent

emèti·co -ca *adj & m* (**-ci -che**) emetic

eméttere §198 *tr* to emit, send forth; to utter (*a statement*); (com) to issue

emiciclo *m* hemicycle; floor (*of legislative body*)

emicrània *f* migraine, headache

emigrante *adj & mf* emigrant

emigrare *intr* (ESSERE & AVERE) to emigrate

emigra·to -ta *adj & mf* emigrant

emigrazióne *f* emigration; migration (*e.g., of birds*)

eminènte *adj* eminent

eminènza *f* eminence; (eccl) Eminence

emisfèro *m* hemisphere

emissà·rio *m* (**-ri**) emissary; outlet (*river or lake*); drain

emissióne *f* emission; issuance; (rad) broadcast

emistì·chio *m* (**-chi**) hemistich

emittènte *adj* emitting; issuing; (rad) broadcasting ‖ *f* (rad) transmitting set; broadcasting station

emofilìa *f* hemophilia

emoglobina *f* hemoglobin

emolliènte *adj & m* emollient

emoluménto *m* fee, emolument

emorragìa *f* hemorrhage

emorròidi *fpl* hemorrhoids, piles

emostàti·co -ca *adj* (**-ci -che**) hemostatic ‖ *m* hemostat

emotè·ca *f* (**-che**) blood bank

emotivi·tà *f* (**-tà**) emotionalism

emoti·vo -va *adj* emotional ‖ *mf* emotional person

emottìsi *f* (pathol) hemoptysis

emozionante *adj* emotional, moving

emozionare (**emozióno**) *tr* to move, stir; to thrill

emozióne *f* emotion

empiastro *m* var of **impiastro**

émpiere §163 *tr & ref* var of **empire**

empie·tà *f* (**-tà**) impiety; cruelty

ém·pio -pia *adj* (**-pi -pie**) impious; pitiless, wicked

empìre §163 *tr* to fill; (lit) to fulfill; **empire qlcu di insulti** to heap insults on s.o. ‖ *ref* to get full

empìre·o -a *adj* heavenly, sublime ‖ *m* empyrean

empìri·co -ca *adj* (**-ci -che**) empirical ‖ *mf* empiricist

empirismo *m* empiricism

empirì·sta *mf* (**-sti -ste**) empiricist

émpito *m* (lit) rush; fury

empò·rio *m* (**-ri**) emporium, mart

emulare (**èmulo**) *tr* to emulate

emulazióne *f* emulation, rivalry; (law) evil intent

èmu·lo -la *adj* emulous ‖ *mf* emulator

emulsionare (**emulsióno**) *tr* to emulsify

emulsióne *f* emulsion

encefalite *f* encephalitis

encìcli·ca *f* (**-che**) encyclical

enciclopedìa *f* encyclopedia

enciclopèdi·co -ca *adj* (-ci -che) encyclopedic

enclave *f* enclave

enclìti·co -ca *adj & f* (-ci -che) enclitic

encomiàbile *adj* praiseworthy

encomiare §287 (encòmio) *tr* to praise

encò·mio *m* (-mi) encomium, praise

endecasìlla·bo -ba *adj* hendecasyllabic || *m* hendecasyllable

endemia *f* endemic

endèmi·co -ca *adj* (-ci -che) endemic

èndice *m* nest egg; (obs) souvenir

endocàr·dio *m* (-di) (anat) endocardium

endocarpo *m* (bot) endocarp

endòcri·no -na *adj* endocrine

endourba·no -na *adj* inner-city

endoveno·so -sa [s] *adj* intravenous

energèti·co -ca *adj* (-ci -che) energy (*e.g., crisis*); (med) tonic || *m* (med) tonic

energìa *f* energy, power

enèrgi·co -ca *adj* (-ci -che) energetic

energùme·no -na *mf* wild or mad person

ènfa·si *f* (-si) emphasis; forcefulness

enfàti·co -ca *adj* (-ci -che) emphatic

enfiare §287 (énfio) *tr & ref* to swell

enfisè·ma *m* (-mi) emphysema

enfitèu·si *f* (-si) lease (*of land*)

enig·ma *m* (-mi) enigma, riddle, puzzle

enigmàti·co -ca *adj* (-ci -che) enigmatic, puzzling

-ènne *suf adj* -year-old, e.g., **ragazzo diciassettenne** seventeen-year-old boy || *suf mf* -year-old person, e.g., **diciassettenne** seventeen-year-old person

ennèsi·mo -ma *adj* nth

-èn·nio *suf m* (-ni) period of . . . years, e.g., **ventennio** period of twenty years

enòlo·go -ga *mf* (-gi -ghe) oenologist

enórme *adj* enormous

enormeménte *adv* enormously

enormi·tà *f* (-tà) enormity; outrage; absurdity

Enrico *m* Henry

ènte *m* being; entity; corporation; agency, body

enteroclìsma *m* (-smi) enema

enti·tà *f* (-tà) entity; value, importance

entomologìa *f* entomology

entram·bi -be *adj*—**entrambi i** both || *pron* both

entrante *adj* next (*e.g., week*)

entrare (éntro) *intr* (ESSERE) to enter; to go (*said of numbers*); to get (*into one's head*); **entrarci** to make it, e.g., **con questi soldi non c'entro** I can't make it with this money; **entrarci come i cavoli a merenda** to be completely out of line; **entrare a** to begin to; **entrare in** to enter (*e.g., a room*); to fit in; to go in (*said of a number*); to get into (*one's head*); **entrare in amore** to be in heat (*said of animals*); **entrare in ballo** to come into play; **entrare in carica** to take up one's duties; **entrare in collera** to get angry; **entrare in collisione** to collide; **entrare in contatto** to establish contact; **entrare in gioco** to come into play; **entrare in guerra** to go to war; **entrare in società** to make one's debut; **entrare nella parte di** (theat)

to play the role of; **entrare in vigore** to become effective; **Lei non c'entra** this is none of your business; **questo non c'entra** this is beside the point

entrata *f* entry; entrance; **entrata di favore** (theat) complimentary ticket; **entrate** income

entratura *f* entry; entrance; assumption (*of a position*); familiarity

éntro *adv* inside || *prep* within; **entro di** within, inside of

entrobórdo *m* inboard motorboat

entrotèrra *m* inland, hinterland

entusiasmare *tr* to carry away, enthuse || *ref* to be carried away, to become enthused

entusiasmo *m* enthusiasm

entusia·sta (-sti -ste) *adj* enthusiastic || *mf* enthusiast, devotee

entusiàsti·co -ca *adj* (-ci -che) enthusiastic

enucleare (enùcleo) *tr* to elucidate; (surg) to remove

enumerare (enùmero) *tr* to enumerate

enumerazióne *f* enumeration

enunciare §128 *tr* to enunciate, state

enunciati·vo -va *adj* (gram) declarative

enunciazióne *f* enunciation, statement

enzi·ma [dz] *m* (-mi) enzyme

èpa *f* (lit) belly; paunch

epàti·co -ca *adj* (-ci -che) hepatic, liver

epatite *f* (pathol) hepatitis

epènte·si *f* (-si) epenthesis

eperlano *m* (ichth) smelt

èpi·co -ca *adj & f* (-ci -che) epic

epicurè·o -a *adj & m* epicurean

epidemia *f* epidemic

epidèmi·co -ca *adj* (-ci -che) epidemic (al)

epidèrmi·co -ca *adj* (-ci -che) epidermal; (fig) superficial, skin-deep

epidèrmide *f* epidermis

Epifanìa *f* Epiphany

epiglòttide *f* (anat) epiglottis

epìgono *m* follower; descendant

epìgrafe *f* epigraph

epigram·ma *m* (-mi) epigram

epigrammàti·co -ca *adj* (-ci -che) epigrammatic

epilessìa *f* (pathol) epilepsy

epilètti·co -ca *adj & m* (-ci -che) epileptic

epìlo·go *m* (-ghi) epilogue; conclusion

episcopale *adj* episcopal

episcopalia·no -na *adj & mf* Episcopalian

episcopato *m* episcopate, bishopric

episòdi·co -ca *adj* (-ci -che) episodic

episò·dio *m* (-di) episode

epìstola *f* epistle

epistolà·rio *m* (-ri) letters, correspondence

epitàf·fio *m* (-fi) epitaph

epitè·lio *m* (-li) epithelium

epìteto *m* epithet; insult

epitomare (epìtomo) *tr* to epitomize

epìtome *f* epitome

èpo·ca *f* (-che) epoch; period; moment; **fare epoca** to be epoch-making

epopèa *f* epic

eppure *conj* yet, and yet

epsomite *f* Epsom salt

epurare *tr* to cleanse; to purge
epurazióne *f* purification; purge
equànime *adj* calm, composed; impartial
equanimità *f* equanimity; impartiality
equatóre *m* equator
equatoriale *adj* & *m* equatorial
equazióne *f* equation
equèstre *adj* equestrian
equilàte·ro -ra *adj* equilateral
equilibrare *tr* to balance; (aer) to trim ‖ *ref* to balance one another
equilibra·to -ta *adj* level-headed
equilibra·tóre -trice *adj* stabilizing ‖ *m* (aer) horizontal stabilizer
equilì·brio *m* (**-bri**) equilibrium, balance; (fig) proportion; **equilibrio politico** balance of power
equilibrì·sta *mf* (**-sti -ste**) acrobat, equilibrist
equi·no -na *adj* & *m* equine
equinoziale *adj* equinoctial
equinò·zio *m* (**-zi**) equinox
equipaggiaménto *m* equipment, outfit
equipaggiare §290 *tr* to equip, outfit; (naut) to fit out; (naut) to man
equipàg·gio *m* (**-gi**) equipage; (naut) crew, complement; (sports) team; (rowing) crew
equiparare *tr* to equalize (*e.g., salaries*)
équipe *f* team
equipollènte *adj* equivalent
equi·tà *f* (**-tà**) equity, fair-mindedness
equitazióne *f* horsemanship
equivalènte *adj* & *m* equivalent
equivalére §278 *intr* (ESSERE & AVERE) —**equivalere a** to be equivalent to ‖ *ref* to be equal
equivocare §197 (**equìvoco**) *intr*—**equivocare su** to mistake, misunderstand
equìvo·co -ca (**-ci -che**) *adj* equivocal; ambiguous ‖ *m* misunderstanding
è·quo -qua *adj* equitable, fair
èra *f* era, age; **era spaziale** space age
erà·rio *m* (**-ri**) treasury
èrba *f* grass; **erba limoncina** lemon verbena; **erba medica** alfalfa; **erbe** vegetables; **erbe aromatiche** herbs; **far l'erba** to cut the grass; **in erba** (fig) budding; **metter a erba** to put to pasture
erbàc·cia *f* (**-ce**) weed
erbaggi *mpl* vegetables
erbaiò·lo -la *mf* fresh vegetable retailer
erbici·da *m* (**-di**) weed-killer
erbivéndo·lo -la *mf* fresh fruit and vegetable retailer
erbìvo·ro -ra *adj* herbivorous
erborì·sta *mf* (**-sti -ste**) herbalist
erbó·so -sa [s] *adj* grassy
Èrcole *m* Hercules
ercù·leo -a *adj* Herculean
erède *m* heir ‖ *f* heiress
eredi·tà *f* (**-tà**) inheritance; heredity
ereditare (**erèdito**) *tr* to inherit
eredità·rio -ria *adj* (**-ri -rie**) hereditary; crown (*prince*)
ereditièra *f* heiress
eremì·ta *m* (**-ti**) hermit
eremitàg·gio *m* (**-gi**) hermitage
èremo *m* hermitage
eresìa *f* heresy

eresiar·ca *m* (**-chi**) heretic
erèti·co -ca (**-ci -che**) *adj* heretical ‖ *mf* heretic
erèt·to -ta *adj* erect, straight
erezióne *f* erection
ergastola·no -na *mf* lifer
ergàstolo *m* life imprisonment; prison for persons sentenced to life imprisonment
èrgere §164 *tr* (lit) to erect; (lit) to lift ‖ *ref* to rise (*said, e.g., of a mountain*)
èrgo *m invar*—**venire all'ergo** to come to a conclusion ‖ *adv* thus, hence
èri·ca *f* (**-che**) heather
erìgere §152 *tr* to erect, build ‖ *ref* to rise; **erigersi a** to set oneself up as
eritrè·o -a *adj* & *mf* Eritrean
ermafrodi·to -ta *adj* & *m* hermafrodite
ermellino *m* ermine
ermèti·co -ca *adj* (**-ci -che**) airtight; watertight; hermetic
èrnia *f* hernia; **ernia del disco** (pathol) herniated disk
eródere §239 *tr* to erode
eròe *m* hero
erogare §209 (**èrogo**) *tr* to distribute; to bestow
erogazióne *f* distribution; bestowal
eròi·co -ca *adj* (**-ci -che**) heroic
eroicòmi·co -ca *adj* (**-ci -che**) mock-heroic
eroìna *f* heroine; (pharm) heroin
eroismo *m* heroism
erómpere §240 *intr* to erupt, burst out
erosióne *f* erosion
eròti·co -ca *adj* (**-ci -che**) erotic
erotismo *m* eroticism
èrpete *m* (pathol) herpes, shingles
erpicare §197 (**èrpico**) *tr* to harrow
érpice *m* harrow
errabón·do -da *adj* (lit) wandering
errante *adj* errant; wandering
errare (**èrro**) *intr* to wander; to err; (lit) to stray
erra·to -ta *adj* mistaken, wrong
errò·ne·o -a *adj* erroneous
erróre *m* error, mistake; fault; (lit) wandering; **errore di lingua** slip of the tongue; **errore di scrittura** slip of the pen; **errore di stampa** misprint; **errore giudiziario** miscarriage of justice; **salvo errore od omissione** barring error or omission
ér·to -ta *adj* arduous, steep; erect ‖ *f* arduous ascent; **all'erta** on the alert
erudire §176 *tr* to educate, instruct
erudi·to -ta *adj* erudite, learned ‖ *m* scholar, savant
erudizióne *f* erudition, learning
eruttare *tr* to belch forth (*e.g., lava*); to utter (*obscenities*) ‖ *intr* to belch
erutti·vo -va *adj* eruptive
eruzióne *f* eruption
esacerbare (**esacèrbo**) *tr* to embitter; to exacerbate ‖ *ref* to become embittered
esagerare (**esàgero**) *tr* & *intr* to exaggerate
esagera·to -ta *adj* exaggerated, excessive ‖ *mf* exaggerator
esagerazióne *f* exaggeration

esagitare (esàgito) *tr* to perturb

esàgono *m* hexagon

esalare *tr* to exhale; **esalare l'ultimo respiro** to breathe one's last ‖ *intr* to spread (*said of odors*)

esalazióne *f* exhalation; fume, vapor

esaltare *tr* to exalt; to excite ‖ *ref* to glorify oneself; to become excited

esalta·to -ta *adj* frenzied, excited ‖ *mf* hothead

esame *m* examination; checkup, test; **dare gli esami** to take an examination; **esame attitudinale** aptitude test; **esame del sangue** blood test; **esame di riparazione** make-up test; **fare gli esami** to prepare a test (*for a student*); **prendere in esame** to take in consideration

esàmetro *m* hexameter

esaminan·do -da *mf* candidate; examinee

esaminare (esàmino) *tr* to examine; to test

esamina·tóre -trice *mf* examiner

esàngue *adj* bloodless; (fig) pale

esànime *adj* lifeless

esasperante *adj* exasperating

esasperare (esàspero) *tr* to exasperate ‖ *ref* to become exasperated

esasperazióne *f* exasperation

esattézza *f* exactness; punctuality

esat·to -ta *adj* exact; punctual

esattóre *m* tax collector; bill collector

esattorìa *f* tax collector's office; bill collector's office

esaudire §176 *tr* to grant

esauriènte *adj* exhaustive; convincing

esaurimento *m* depletion (*e.g., of merchandise*); (pathol) exhaustion; (naut) drainage

esaurire §176 *tr* to exhaust; to play out (*e.g., a hooked fish*); to use up ‖ *ref* to be exhausted; to be depleted; to be sold out

esauri·to -ta *adj* exhausted; depleted; sold out; out of print

esau·sto -sta *adj* exhausted; empty

esautorare (esàutoro) *tr* to deprive of authority; to discredit (*a theory*)

esazióne *f* exaction; collection

é·sca *f* (-sche) bait; punk (*for lighting fireworks*); tinder (*for lighting powder*); **dare esca a** to foment

escandescenza *f*—**dare in escandescenze** to fly off the handle

escava·tóre -trice *mf* excavator, digger ‖ *m* excavator; **escavatore a vapore** steam shovel ‖ *f* (mach) excavator

escavazióne *f* excavation

eschimése [s] *adj* & *mf* Eskimo

esclamare *tr* & *intr* to exclaim

esclamati·vo -va *adj* exclamatory; exclamation (*mark*)

esclùdere §105 *tr* to exclude; to keep or shut out

esclusióne *f* exclusion; **a esclusione di** with the exception of

esclusiva *f* sole right, monopoly; (journ) scoop

esclusivi·sta (-sti -ste) *adj* clannish; bigoted ‖ *mf* bigot; (com) sole agent

esclusi·vo -va *adj* exclusive; intolerant, bigoted ‖ *f* see **esclusiva**

esclu·so -sa *adj* excluded, excepted

escogitare (escògito) *tr* to think up, invent; to think out

escoriare §287 (escòrio) *tr* & *ref* to skin

escoriazióne *f* abrasion

escreménto *m* excrement

escrescènza *f* excrescence

escrè·to -ta *adj* excreted ‖ *m* excreta

escursióne *f* excursion; (mach) sweep; (mil) transfer; **escursione termica** (meteor) temperature range

escursioni·sta *mf* (-sti -ste) excursionist, sightseer

escussióne *f* (law) examination, cross-examination

esecrare (esècro) *tr* to execrate

esecrazióne *f* execration

esecuti·vo -va *adj* & *m* executive

esecu·tóre -trice *mf* (mus) performer ‖ *m* executor; **esecutore di giustizia** executioner ‖ *f* executrix

esecuzióne *f* accomplishment, completion; performance; execution; **esecuzione capitale** capital punishment

esegè·si *f* (-si) exegesis

eseguire (eséguo) & §176 *tr* to execute, carry out; to perform

esèm·pio m (-pi) example; **a mo' d'esempio** as an illustration; **dare il buon esempio** to set a good example; **per esempio** for instance

esemplare *adj* exemplary ‖ *m* copy; specimen ‖ *v* (esèmpio) *tr* (lit) to copy

esemplificare §197 (esemplìfico) *tr* to exemplify

esentare (esènto) *tr* to exempt

esènte *adj* exempt, free

esenzióne *f* exemption

esèquie *fpl* obsequies, funeral rites

esercènte *adj* practicing ‖ *mf* dealer, merchant

esercire §176 *tr* to practice; to run (*a store*)

esercitare (esèrcito) *tr* to exercise; to tax (*e.g., s.o.'s patience*); to practice, ply (*a trade*); to wield (*e.g., power*) ‖ *ref* to practice

esercitazióne *f* exercise, training; **esercitazioni militari** drilling

esèrcito *m* army; (fig) flock; **Esercito della Salvezza** Salvation Army

esercì·zio *m* (-zi) exercise; practice; training; homework; occupation; drill; **d'esercizio** (com) administrative (*expenses*); **esercizio finanziario** fiscal year; **esercizio provvisorio** (law) emergency appropriation; **esercizio pubblico** establishment open to the public; **esercizio spirituale** (eccl) retreat

esibire §176 *tr* to exhibit ‖ *ref* to show oneself, appear; **esibirsi di** to offer to

esibizióne *f* exhibition

esigènte *adj* demanding, exigent

esigènza *f* demand, requirement, exigency

esìgere §165 *tr* to demand; to require; to exact; to collect

esigìbile *adj* due; collectable

esigui·tà *f* (-tà) meagerness, scantiness

esì·guo -gua *adj* meager, scanty

esilarante *adj* exhilarating; laughing (*gas*)

esilarare (**esìlaro**) *tr* to amuse ‖ *ref* to be amused

èsile *adj* slender, thin; weak

esiliare §287 *tr* to exile ‖ *ref* to go into exile; to withdraw

esilia·to -ta *adj* exiled ‖ *m* exile (*person*)

esì·lio *m* (**-li**) exile, banishment

esìmere §166 *tr* to exempt ‖ *ref*—**esimersi da** to avoid (*an obligation*)

esì·mio -mia *adj* (**-mi -mie**) distinguished, eminent

-èsi·mo -ma *suf adj & pron* -eth, e.g., **ventesimo** twentieth; -th, e.g., **diciannovesimo** nineteenth

esistènte *adj* existent; extant

esistènza *f* existence

esistenzialismo *m* existentialism

esìstere §114 *intr* (ESSERE) to exist

esitante *adj* hesitant

esitare (**èsito**) *tr* to retail ‖ *intr* to hesitate; (med) to resolve itself

esitazióne *f* hesitation; haw (*in speech*)

èsito *m* result, outcome; sale; outlet; (philol) late form; **dare esito a** (com) to reply

esiziale *adj* ruinous, fatal

èsodo *m* exodus, flight

esòfa·go *m* (**-gi**) esophagus

esonerare (**esònero**) *tr* to exempt, release

esònero *m* exemption, release

Esòpo *m* Aesop

esorbitante *adj* exorbitant

esorbitare (**esòrbito**) *intr*—**esorbitare da** to go beyond

esorcismo *m* exorcism

esorcizzare [ddzz] *tr* to exorcise

esordiènte *adj* beginning, budding ‖ *mf* beginner ‖ *f* debutante

esòr·dio *m* (**-di**) beginning

esordire §176 *intr* to make a start; (theat) to debut; (theat) to open

esortare (**esòrto**) *tr* to exhort

esortazióne *f* exhortation

esò·so -sa *adj* greedy, avaricious; hateful; exorbitant (*price*)

esòti·co -ca *adj* (**-ci -che**) exotic

esotismo *m* exoticism; borrowing (*from a foreign language*)

espàndere §167 *tr* to expand ‖ *ref* to spread out; to confide

espansióne *f* expansion; effusiveness

espansionismo *m* expansionism

espansivi·tà *f* (**-tà**) effusiveness

espansi·vo -va *adj* expansive; effusive

espan·so -sa *adj* flared; expanded, dilated

espatriare §287 *intr* to emigrate

espà·trio *m* (**-tri**) emigration

espediènte *m* expedient, makeshift; ruse; **vivere di espedienti** to live by one's wits

espedire §176 *tr* to expedite ‖ *ref*—**espedirsi di** to get rid of

espèllere §168 *tr* to expel, eject

esperiènza *f* experience; experiment

esperiménto *m* experiment; test

espèr·to -ta *adj & m* expert

espettorare (**espèttoro**) *tr & intr* to expectorate

espiare §119 *tr* to expiate; to placate (*the gods*); **espiare una pena** to serve a sentence

espiatò·rio -ria *adj* (**-ri -rie**) expiatory

espiazióne *f* expiation

espirare *tr & intr* to breath out, to exhale

espirazióne *f* exhaling

espletare (**esplèto**) *tr* to dispatch, complete

esplicare §197 (**èsplico**) *tr* to carry out; (lit) to explain

esplicati·vo -va *adj* explanatory

esplìci·to -ta *adj* explicit

esplòdere §169 *tr* to shoot; to fire (*a shot*) ‖ *intr* (ESSERE & AVERE) to explode; to burst forth

esploratóre -trice *mf* explorer ‖ *m* (nav) gunboat; **giovane esploratore** boy scout

esplorazióne *f* exploration; (telv) scanning

esplosióne *f* explosion, blast; (fig) outburst

esplosi·vo -va *adj & m* explosive

esponènte *adj* (typ) superior ‖ *m* spokesman; dictionary entry; catchword (*of dictionary*); (math) exponent; (naut) net weight

espórre §218 *tr* to expose, show; to expound; to abandon (*a baby*); to lay out (*a corpse*); to lay open (*to danger*) ‖ *intr* to show, exhibit ‖ *ref* to expose oneself

esportare (**espòrto**) *tr* to export

esporta·tóre -trice *mf* exporter

esportazióne *f* export, exportation

esposimetro *m* exposure meter

esposi·tóre -trice *mf* commentator; exhibitor

esposizióne *f* exposition; abandonment (*of a baby*); exhibit, fair; line (*of credit*); exposure (*of a house*); (phot) exposure

espó·sto -sta *adj* exposed; aforementioned ‖ *m* petition, brief; foundling

espressióne *f* expression; feeling

espressi·vo -va *adj* expressive

esprès·so -sa *adj* manifest; express; prepared on the spot ‖ *m* espresso; messenger; special-delivery letter; special-delivery stamp

esprìmere §131 *tr* to express; to convey (*an opinion*); (lit) to squeeze ‖ *ref* to express oneself

espropriare §287 (**espròprio**) *tr* to expropriate ‖ *ref* to deprive onself; **espropriarsi di** to divest oneself of

esprò·prio *m* (**-pri**) expropriation

espugnare *tr* to take by storm

espulsióne *f* expulsion; (mach) ejection

espulsóre *m* ejector

espurgare §209 *tr* to expurgate

éssa §5 *pron pers* she; it

ésse §5 *pron pers* they

essènza *f* essence

essenziale *adj* essential ‖ *m* main point

èssere *m* being; existence; condition; (coll) character; **in essere** in good shape ‖ §170 *intr* (ESSERE) to be;

c'è there is; **ci sono** there are; **ci sono!** I get it!; **come sarebbe a dire?** what do you mean?; **come se nulla fosse** as if nothing had happened; **esserci** to have arrived, to be there; **essere di** to belong to; **essere per** to be about to; **può essere** maybe; **sarà** maybe; **sia . . . sia** both . . . and; whether . . . or || *aux* (ESSERE) (to form passive) to be, e.g., **fu investito da un tassametro** he was run over by a taxi; (to form the compound tenses of certain intransitive verbs and all reflexive verbs) to have, e.g., **sono arrivati** they have arrived; **mi sono appena alzato** I have just got up || *impers* (ESSERE) to be, e.g., **è giusto** it is fair

éssi §5 *pron pers* they
essiccare §197 *tr* to dry || *ref* to dry up
essiccatóio *m* (-tói) drier
essiccazióne *f* drying
èsso §5 *pron pers* he; it; **chi per esso** his representative
essudare *intr* to exude
èst *m* east
èstasi *f* (-si) ecstasy; **andare in estasi** to become enraptured
estasiare §287 *tr* to enrapture, delight || *ref* to become enraptured
estate *f* summer
estàtico -ca *adj* (-ci -che) ecstatic, enraptured
estemporàneo -a *adj* extemporaneous
estèndere §270 *tr* to extend; to broaden (*e.g., one's knowledge*); to draw up (*a document*) || *ref* to extend
estensibile *adj* applicable; **inviare saluti estensibili a** to send greetings to be extended to (*e.g., another person*)
estensióne *f* extension; extent; expanse (*e.g., of water*); (*mus*) compass, range
estensivo -va *adj* extensive
estènso -sa *adj*—**per esteso** fully
estensóre *adj* extensible || *m* compiler (*e.g., of a dictionary*); (*sports*) exerciser, chest expander
estenuante *adj* exhausting
estenuare (estènuo) *tr* to exhaust || *ref* to become exhausted
esterióre *adj* exterior || *m* outside appearance
esteriorità *f* (-tà) appearance
esternare (estèrno) *tr* to reveal, manifest || *ref* to confide
estèrno -na *adj* external; outside; day (*student*) || *m* exterior, outside; (baseball) outfielder; **all'esterno** outside; **in esterno** (*mov*) on location
èstero -ra *adj* foreign || *m* foreign countries; **all'estero** abroad
esterrefatto -ta *adj* terrified
estéso -sa [s] *adj* extended, wide; **per esteso** in full
estèta *mf* (-ti -te) aesthete
estètico -ca (-ci -che) *adj* aesthetic || *f* aesthetics
estetista *mf* (-sti -ste) beautician
estimatóre -trice *mf* appraiser; admirer
èstimo *m* appraisal; assessment
estìnguere §156 *tr* to extinguish; to quench (*thirst*); to pay off (*a debt*) || *ref* to die out

estinguìbile *adj* extinguishable; payable
estìnto -ta *adj* extinguished; extinct || *m* deceased, dead person
estintóre *m* fire extinguisher
estìrpare *tr* to uproot; to eradicate; to pull (*a tooth*)
estirpatóre -trice *mf* eradicator || *m* (*agr*) weeder
estivare *tr & intr* to summer
estivo -va *adj* summer; summery
estòllere §171 *tr* to extol
èstone *adj & mf* Estonian
estòrcere §272 *tr* to extort; **estorcere qlco a qlcu** to extort s.th from s.o.
estorsióne *f* extortion
estradare *tr* (law) to extradite
estradizióne *f* extradition
estràneo -a *adj* extraneous, foreign; aloof || *mf* outsider
estrapolare (estràpolo) *tr* to extrapolate
estrarre §273 *tr* to extract, draw; to pull (*a tooth*)
estratto -ta *adj* extracted || *m* extract; abstract; certified copy; (*typ*) off-print; **estratto conto** bank statement; **estratto dell'atto di nascita** copy of one's birth certificate
estrazióne *f* extraction; drawing (*of lottery*)
estrèma *f* (sports) wing, end
estremista *adj & mf* (-sti -ste) extremist
estremità *f* (-tà) end; tip, top; extremity; **le estremità** the extremities
estrèmo -ma *adj* extreme; **esalare l'estremo respiro** to breath one's last || *m* extremity; end, extreme; **essere agli estremi** to be near the end; **estremi essenziali** || *f* see **estrema**
estrìnseco -ca *adj* (-ci -che) extrinsic
èstro *m* horsefly; whim, fancy; inspiration; **estro venereo** heat (*of female animal*)
estrométtere §198 *tr* to oust, expel
estróso -sa [s] *adj* fanciful, whimsical; inspired
estrovèrso -sa or **estrovertito -ta** *adj & mf* extrovert
estrùdere §190 *tr* to extrude
estuàrio *m* (-ri) estuary
esuberante *adj* exuberant; buoyant
esuberanza *f* exuberance; buoyancy; **a esuberanza** abundantly
esulare (èsulo) *intr* (ESSERE & AVERE) to go into exile; **esulare da** to be alien to
esulcerare (esùlcero) *tr* to ulcerate on the surface; (fig) to exacerbate
esulcerazióne *f* superficial ulceration; (fig) exasperation, exacerbation
èsule *mf* exile (*person*)
esultante *adj* exultant, jubilant
esultare *intr* to exult
esumare *tr* to exhume; to revive (*e.g., a custom*)
esumazióne *f* exhumation; revival
età *f* (-tà) age; **che età ha?** how old is he (or she)?; **ha la sua età** he (or she) is no longer a youngster; **l'età di mezzo** Middle Ages; **maggiore età** majority; **mezza età** middle age; **minore età** minority
etamine *f* cheesecloth
ètere *m* ether

etère·o -a *adj* ethereal
eternare (**etèrno**) *tr* to immortalize ‖ *ref* to become immortal
eterni·tà *f* (**-tà**) eternity
etèr·no -na *adj* eternal, everlasting ‖ *m* eternity; **in eterno** forever
eterodòs·so -sa *adj* heterodox
eterogène·o -a *adj* heterogeneous
èti·ca *f* (**-che**) ethics
etichétta *f* label; card (*e.g., of a library*); etiquette; **etichetta gommata** sticker
etichettare (**etichétto**) *tr* to label
èti·co -ca (**-ci -che**) *adj* ethical; consumptive ‖ *m* consumptive ‖ *f* see **etica**
etile *m* ethyl
etilène *m* ethylene
etili·co -ca *adj* (**-ci -che**) ethyl
ètimo *m* etymon
etimologìa *f* etymology
etìope *adj & mf* Ethiopian
Etiòpia, l' *f* Ethiopia
etiòpi·co -ca *adj* (**-ci -che**) Ethiopian
etisìa *f* tuberculosis
ètni·co -ca *adj* (**-ci -che**) ethnic(al)
etnografìa *f* ethnography
etnologìa *f* ethnology
etru·sco -sca *adj & mf* (**-schi -sche**) Etruscan
ettàgono *m* heptagon
èttaro *m* hectare
ètte *m* (coll) particle, jot, whit, tittle
ètto or **ettogrammo** *m* hectogram
-étto -étta *suf adj* rather, e.g., **piccoletto** rather small; -ish, e.g., **rotondetto** roundish
ettòlitro *m* hectoliter
eucalipto *m* eucalyptus
eucaristìa *f* Eucharist
eufemismo *m* euphemism
eufonìa *f* euphony
eufòni·co -ca *adj* (**-ci -che**) euphonic
euforìa *f* euphoria
eufòri·co -ca *adj* (**-ci -che**) euphoric
eufuismo *m* euphuism
eugenèti·co -ca (**-ci -che**) *adj* eugenic ‖ *f* eugenics
eunu·co *m* (**-chi**) eunuch
europè·o -a *adj & mf* European
Euròpa, l' *f* Europe
eurovisióne *f* European television chain
eutanasìa *f* euthanasia
Èva *f* Eve
evacuaménto *m* evacuation
evacuare (**evàcuo**) *tr* to evacuate ‖ *intr* to evacuate; to have a bowel movement
evacuazióne *f* evacuation; bowel movement

evàdere §172 *tr* to evade; to complete (*a deal*); to answer (*a letter*); to execute (*orders*) ‖ *intr* (ESSERE) to flee, escape
evanescènza *f* evanescence; (rad) fading
evanescènte *adj* evanescent; vanishing
evangèli·co -ca *adj* (**-ci -che**) evangelic (al)
evangeli·sta *m* (**-sti**) evangelist
evangelizzare [ddzz] *tr* to evangelize; to campaign for; to subject to political propaganda
evaporare (**evapóro**) *tr & intr* to evaporate
evaporatóre *m* evaporator; humidifier
evaporazióne *f* evaporation
evasióne *f* evasion, escape; (com) reply; **dare evasione a** to complete (*an administrative matter*)
evasì·vo -va *adj* evasive
eva·so -sa *adj* escaped ‖ *m* escapee
evasóre *m* tax dodger
eveniènza *f* eventuality, contingency; **nell'evenienza che** in the event (that); **per ogni evenienza** just in case
evènto *m* event; **eventi correnti** current events; **fausto** or **lieto evento** happy event
eventuale *adj* contingent
eventuali·tà *f* (**-tà**) eventuality
eversì·vo -va *adj* upsetting; destructive
evidènte *adj* evident; clear
evidènza *f* evidence; clearness; **mettersi in evidenza** to make oneself conspicuous; **tenere in evidenza** (com) to keep active
evirare *tr* to emasculate
evitare (**èvito**) *tr* to avoid, shun; **evitare qlco a qlcu** to spare s.o. s.th, to save s.o. from s.th
èvo *m* age, era; **evo antico** ancient times; **evo moderno** modern times; **medio evo** Middle Ages
evocare §197 (**èvoco**) *tr* to evoke
evoluìre §176 *intr* (aer, nav) to maneuver
evolu·to -ta *adj* developed; progressive; modern
evoluzióne *f* evolution
evòlvere §115 *tr* to develop ‖ *ref* to evolve
evvi·va *m* (**-va**) cheer ‖ *interj* long live!, hurrah!
èx *adj invar* ex-, e.g., **la sua ex moglie** his ex-wife; ex, e.g., **ex dividendo** ex dividend
ex li·bris *m* (**-bris**) bookplate
extraconiugale *adj* extramarital
extraeuropè·o -a *adj* non-European
ex vó·to *m* (**-to**) votive offering
eziologìa *f* etiology

F

F, f ['effe] *m & f* sixth letter of the Italian alphabet
fa *m* (**fa**) (mus) F, fa
fabbisógno *m invar* need; requirement
fàbbri·ca *f* (**-che**) building, construction; factory, plant

fabbricante *mf* builder, manufacturer
fabbricare §197 (**fàbbrico**) *tr* to manufacture; to fabricate
fabbrica·to -ta *adj* built ‖ *m* building
fabbricazióne *f* building; erection; manufacturing; fabrication (*invention*)

fabbro m blacksmith; locksmith; (fig) master; **fabbro ferraio** blacksmith

faccènda f business, matter; **faccende domestiche** household chores

faccendiè·re -ra mf operator, schemer

faccétta f small face; face, facet

facchinàg·gio m (-gi) porterage; (fig) drudgery

facchino m porter; **lavorare come un facchino** to work like a slave

fàc·cia f (-ce) face; countenance; **avere la faccia di** to have the gall to; **di faccia a** opposite; **faccia da galeotto** (coll) gallows bird; **faccia tosta** cheek, gall; **in faccia a** in front of

facciale adj facial

facciata f façade; page; (fig) surface appearance

face f (lit) torch

facè·to -ta adj facetious

facèzia f pleasantry, banter; **scambiar facezie** to banter with each other

fachiro m fakir

fàcile adj easy; inclined; loose (morals); glib (tongue); **è facile** it is probable ‖ m something easy

facili·tà f (-tà) facility, ease; inclination; **facilità di pagamento** easy payments, easy terms; **facilità di parola** glibness

facilitare (**facìlito**) tr to facilitate; to grant (credit); to give (easy terms)

facilitazióne f facilitation; easy terms; cut rate

facinoró·so -sa [s] adj criminal ‖ m hoodlum, thug

facoltà f (-tà) faculty; power; school (of a university); **facoltà** fpl means, wealth

facoltati·vo -va adj optional

facoltó·so -sa [s] adj wealthy, affluent

facóndia f loquacity, gift of gab

facón·do -da adj loquacious

facsìmi·le m (-le) facsimile

faènza f faïence ‖ **Faenza** f Faenza

fàg·gio m (-gi) (bot) beech

fagia·no -na mf pheasant

fagiolino m string bean

fagiò·lo m bean; (coll) sophomore; **andare a fagiolo a** (coll) to fit perfectly; **fagiolo bianco** lima bean

fà·glia f (-glie) (geol) fault

fagòtto m bundle; (mus) bassoon; **far fagotto** (coll) to pack up

fàida f vengeance, vendetta

faìna f stone marten

falange f phalanx

fal·bo ·ba adj tawny

falcata f step, stride; bucking

falce f scythe; crescent (of moon); **falce messoria** sickle

falcétto m sickle

falciare §128 tr to mow

falcia·tóre ·trice mf mower ‖ f mowing machine

falcidiare §287 tr to reduce; to cut down

fal·co m (-chi) hawk; **falco pescatore** osprey

falcóne m falcon

falconeria f falconry

falconière m falconer

falda f band, strip; flake (of snow); gable (of roof); brim (of hat); foot (of mountain); slab (of stone); waist plate (of armor); hem (of suit); flounce (of dress); layer (of rock); flap, coattail; **falda della camicia** shirttail; **falde** straps (to hold a baby); **mettersi in falde** to wear tails

falegname m carpenter; cabinetmaker

falegnameria f carpentry; cabinetmaking; carpenter shop; woodworker shop

falèna f moth

falla f hole, leak; (archaic) fault

fallace adj fallacious, deceptive

fallà·cia f (-cie) fallacy

fallare intr & ref (lit) to be mistaken

fallìbile adj fallible

fallimentare adj bankrupt; ruinous

falliménto m bankruptcy; (fig) collapse, failure

fallire §176 tr to miss (the target) ‖ intr (ESSERE) to go bankrupt; to fail ‖ intr (AVERE) to be mistaken

falli·to -ta adj & mf bankrupt

fallo m error, fault; sin; flaw; phallus; (sports) penalty; (sports) foul; **cadere in fallo** to make the wrong move; to be mistaken; **cogliere in fallo** to catch in the act; **far fallo a** to fail, e.g., **gli faccio fallo** I fail him; **senza fallo** without fail

fa·lò m (-lò) bonfire

falpa·là f (-là) flounce, furbelow

falsare tr to falsify, alter; (lit) to forge

falsari·ga f (-ghe) guideline (for writing); model, pattern; **seguire la falsariga di** to follow in the footsteps of

falsà·rio m (-ri) forger; counterfeiter

falsétto m falsetto

falsificare §197 (**falsìfico**) to falsify; to forge, fake

falsificazióne f falsification; forgery; misrepresentation

falsi·tà f (-tà) falsehood; falsity

fal·so ·sa adj false; wrong (step); assumed (name); bogus, counterfeit, fake (money); phony ‖ m falsehood; perjury; forgery; **commettere un falso** to perjure oneself; to commit forgery; **giurare il falso** to bear false witness; to perjure oneself

fama f fame; reputation; **cattiva fama** notoriety

fame f hunger; dearth; **aver fame** to be hungry; **avere una fame da lupo** to be as hungry as a wolf, to be as hungry as a bear; **morire di fame** to starve to death; to be ravenous

famèli·co ·ca adj (-ci -che) starving, famished

famigera·to ·ta adj notorious

famìglia f family; community; **di famiglia** intimate; **in famiglia** at home

famì·glio m (-gli) beadle, usher; hired man

familiare adj family; familiar, intimate; homelike ‖ m member of the family

familiari·tà f (-tà) familiarity; **avere familiarità con** to be familiar with

familiarizzare [ddzz] *tr* to familiarize

famó•so -sa [s] *adj* famous, illustrious

fanale *m* lamp, lantern; (rr) headlight; **fanale di coda** taillight

fanalino *m* small light; (aut) parking light; (aut) tail light

fanàti•co -ca (-ci -che) *adj* fanatic, fanatical ‖ *mf* fanatic

fanatismo *m* fanaticism

fanatizzare [ddzz] *tr* to make a fanatic of

fanciulla *f* girl; spinster; bride

fanciullé•sco -sca *adj* (-schi -sche) childish; children's

fanciullézza *f* childhood; (fig) infancy

fanciullo•lo -la *adj* childish; childlike ‖ *mf* child ‖ *m* boy ‖ *f* see **fanciulla**

fandònia *f* fib, tale, yarn

fanèllo *m* (orn) linnet; (orn) finch

fanfara *f* military band; fanfare

fanfaróne *m* braggart

fangatura *f* mud bath

fanghìglia *f* mud, slush

fan•go *m* (-ghi) mud; **fare i fanghi** to take mud baths

fangó•so -sa [s] *adj* muddy

fannullo•ne -na *mf* idler, loafer

fanóne *m* whalebone

fantaccino *m* infantryman, foot soldier

fantascientìfi•co -ca *adj* (-ci -che) science-fiction

fantasciènza *f* science fiction

fantasia *f* fantasy, fancy, whim; (mus) fantasia; **di fantasia** fancy

fantasió•so -sa [s] *adj* fanciful; imaginative

fanta•sma *m* (-smi) ghost, spirit; phantom; **fantasma poetico** poetic fancy

fantasticare §197 (fantàstico) *tr* to imagine, dream up ‖ *intr* to daydream

fantasticherìa *f* imagination, daydreaming

fantàsti•co -ca *adj* (-ci -che) fantastic ‖ **fantastico** *interj* unbelievable!

fante *m* infantryman, foot soldier; (cards) jack; (obs) youth

fanteria *f* infantry

fanté•sca *f* (-sche) (joc, lit) housemaid

fantino *m* jockey

fantòc•cio *m* (-ci) puppet

fantomàti•co -ca *adj* (-ci -che) ghostly; mysterious

farabutto *m* scoundrel, heel

faraóna *f* guinea fowl

faraóne *m* Pharaoh; (cards) faro

farcire §176 *tr* to stuff

fardèllo *m* bundle; burden; **far fardello** to pack one's bags

fare *m* doing; break (*of day*); way (*of acting*); **sul far della sera** at nightfall ‖ §173 *tr* to do; to make; to work; to take (*e.g., a walk, a step*); to give (*a sigh*); to deal (*cards*); to suffer (*hunger*); to lead (*a good or bad life*); to render (*service*); to log (*e.g., 15 m.p.h.*); to be, e.g., **tre volte tre fa nove** three times three is nine; to build (*e.g., a house*); to put together (*a collection*); to prepare (*dinner*); to say, utter (*a word*); to have (*a dream*); to give (*fruit*); to pay (*atten-*

tion); to play (*a role*); to stir up (*pity*); to mention (*a name*); **fare il** (or **la**) to be a (*e.g., carpenter*); **fare + inf** to have + *inf*, e.g., **gli ho fatto . . . I** had him . . . ; to make + *inf*, e.g., **il medico mi fece . . .** the doctor made me . . . ; to have + *pp*, e.g., **farò fare . . . I** shall have . . . done; **fare acqua** to leak, to take in water; to get a supply of water; (coll) to urinate; **fare a metà** to divide in half; **fare a pugni** to come to blows; **fare a tempo** to be on time; **fare benzina** to buy gasoline; **fare caldo a** to keep warm, e.g., **questa coperta gli fa caldo** this blanket keeps him warm; **fare carbone** to coal; **fare . . . che** to have been . . . since, e.g., **fanno tre mesi che siamo in questa città** it has been three months since we have been in this city; **fare che + subj** to see to it that + *ind*, e.g., **faccia che comincino a lavorare subito** see to it that they begin to work at once; **fare colpo** to make an impression; **fare corona a** to crown; **fare cuore a** to encourage; **fare del male a** to harm; **fare di + inf** to see to it that + *ind*; **fare di tutto** to do one's best; **fare festa a** to cheer; **fare fiasco** to fail; **fare finta di** to pretend to; **fare fronte a** to face, meet; **fare fuoco su** to fire upon; **fare il gioco di** to play into the hands of; **fare il pappagallo** to parrot, ape; **fare il pieno** to fill up (*with gasoline*); **fare la bocca a** to get used to; **fare la calza** to knit; **fare la coda** to queue up, line up; **fare la festa a** to kill; **fare la guardia** to stand guard; **fare la mano a** to get used to; **fare le cose in famiglia** to wash one's dirty linen at home; **fare le cose in grande stile** to splurge; **fare legna** to gather firewood; **fare l'occhio** to become accustomed; **fare mente** to pay attention; **fare onore a** to do honor to; **fare paura a** to frighten; **fare sangue** to bleed; **fare sapere a qlcu** to let s.o. know; **fare scalo** (aer, naut) to make a call; **fare sì che** to act in such a way that; to see to it that; **fare silenzio** to keep silent; **fare specie a** to amaze, e.g., **il tuo comportamento gli fa specie** your behavior amazes him; **fare tesoro di** to prize; **fare una bella figura** to look good; to make a fine appearance; **fare una mala figura** to look bad; to make a bad showing; **fare una malattia** (coll) to get sick; **fare vela** to set sail; **fare venire** to send for; **fare vigilia** to fast; **farla corta** to cut it short; **farla franca** to get off scot-free; **farla grossa** to commit a blunder; **farla in barba a** to outwit; **farne di cotte e di crude, farne di tutti i colori,** or **farne più di Carlo in Francia** to engage in all sorts of mischief; to paint the town red; **non fare che + ind** to do nothing but + *inf* ‖ *intr*—**averla a che fare con** to have words with; to have to deal with; **fare a coltellate** to have a fight with knives; **fare a girotondo** to play ring-around-the-rosy; **fare al caso di** to fit; to suit; **fare a meno di** to do without; **fare da** to serve as, e.g., **fare da cuscino** to serve as a pillow; **fare da cena** to fix dinner; **fare di cappello** to take one's hat off; **fare presto** to hurry; **fare per** to be just the thing for; **fare tardi** to be late || *ref* to become; to cut (*e.g., one's hair*); to move, e.g., **farsi in là** to move farther; **farsi avanti** to come forward; **farsi beffe di** to make fun of; **farsi bello** to bedeck oneself; to dress up; **farsi bello di** to boast about; to appropriate; **farsi gioco di** to make fun of; **farsi le labbra** to put lipstick on; **farsi strada** to make one's way; **farsi una ragione di** to rationalize, explain to oneself; **farsi un baffo** to not give a hoot; **si fa giorno** it is getting light; **si fa tardi** it is getting late || *impers*—**che tempo fa?** what's the weather like?; **fa** ago, e.g., **alcune settimane fa** a few weeks ago; **fa estate** it is like summer; **fa fino** it is smart; **fa freddo** it is cold; **fa luna** there is moonlight, the moon is out; **fa nebbia** it is foggy; **fa notte** it is nighttime; it is dark; it is getting dark; **fa sole** it is sunny, the sun is out; **fa tipo** or **fa tono!** that's classy!; **non fa nulla** it doesn't matter, never mind

farètra *f* quiver
farfalla *f* butterfly; bow tie; (mach) butterfly valve; (coll) promissory note
farfallóne *m* large butterfly; blunder; Don Juan
farfugliare §280 *intr* to mumble, mutter
farina *f* flour; **farina d'avena** oatmeal; **farina di legno** sawdust; **farina di ossa** bone meal; **farina gialla** yellow corn meal
farinàce·o -a *adj* farinaceous || **farinacei** *mpl* flour-yielding cereals
farinata *f* porridge
faringe *f* pharynx
faringite *f* pharingitis
farinó·so -sa *s* *adj* floury; powdery (*snow*); crumbly, friable
farisèo *m* Pharisee; (fig) pharisee
farmacèuti·co -ca *adj* (-ci -che) pharmaceutical, drug
farmacia *f* pharmacy; drugstore; medicine cabinet; **farmacia di guardia** or **di turno** drugstore open all night and Sunday
farmaci·sta *mf* (-sti -ste) pharmacist, druggist
fàrma·co *m* (-ci or -chi) remedy, medicine
farneticare §197 (farnètico) *intr* to rave
farnèti·co -ca (-chi -che) *adj* raving || *m* delirium; craze
faro *m* lighthouse, beacon; (aut) headlight; **faro retromarcia** (aut) back-up light
farràgine *f* hodgepodge
farraginó·so -sa *s* *adj* confused, mixed

farsa *f* farce; burlesque
farsè·sco -sca *adj* (-schi -sche) farcical, ludicrous
farsétto *m* sweater; (hist) doublet
fascétta *f* girdle; band; wrapper; clamp; **fascetta editoriale** advertising band (*of book*)
fà·scia *f* (-sce) band; belt; bandage; newspaper wrapper; **fascia del cappello** hatband; **fascia di garza** gauze bandage; **fascia elastica** abdominal supporter; (aut) piston ring; **fasce del neonato** swaddling clothes; **in fasce** newborn; **sotto fascia** in a wrapper
fasciame *m* (naut) planking; (naut) plating
fasciare §128 to bind; to bandage; to wrap; to surround
fasciatura *f* bandaging, dressing
fascìcolo *m* number, issue; pamphlet; file, dossier; (bb) fasciculus
fascina *f* fagot
fascina·tóre -trice *mf* charmer
fàscino *m* fascination, charm
fà·scio *m* (-sci) bundle; sheaf; bunch (*of flowers*); pencil or beam (*of rays*); fascist party
fascismo *m* fascism
fasci·sta *adj* & *mf* (-sti -ste) fascist
fase *f* phase, stage; (aut) cycle; (astr, elec, mach) phase
fastèllo *m* bundle, fagot
fasti *mpl* records, annals; notable events; (hist) Roman calendar
fasti·dio *m* (-di) annoyance; (coll) loathing, nausea; **avere in fastidio** to loathe; **dar fastidio a** to annoy; **fastidi** troubles, worries
fastidió·so -sa *s* *adj* annoying, irksome; irritable; (obs) disgusting
fasti·gio *m* (-gi) top, summit
fa·sto -sta *adj* (lit) propitious || *m invar* pomp, display || *mpl* see **fasti**
fastó·so -sa *s* *adj* pompous, ostentatious
fata *f* fairy; **buona fata** fairy godmother; **Fata Morgana** Fata Morgana (*mirage; Morgan le Fay*)
fatale *adj* fatal; inevitable; irresistible (*woman*)
fatalismo *m* fatalism
fatali·sta *mf* (-sti -ste) fatalist
fatali·tà *f* (-tà) fatality, fate
fatalóna *f* vamp
fata·to -ta *adj* fairy, enchanted; (lit) predestined
fati·ca *f* (-che) fatigue, weariness; labor; **a fatica** with difficulty; **da fatica** draft (*e.g., horse*); of burden (*beast*); **durar fatica a** + *inf* to have trouble in + *ger*
faticare §197 *intr* to toil; **faticare a** to be hardly able to
faticó·so -sa *s* *adj* burdensome, heavy; (lit) weary
fatìdi·co -ca *adj* (-ci -che) fatal
fato *m* fate, destiny
fatta *f* kind, sort; **essere sulla fatta di** to be on the trail of
fattàc·cio *m* (-ci) (coll) crime
fattézze *fpl* features

fattìbile *adj* feasible, possible
fattispècie *f*—**nella fattispecie** in this particular case
fat·to -ta *adj* made, e.g., **fatto a mano** handmade; broad (*daylight*); deep (*night*); ready-made (*e.g., suit*); **ben fatto** well-done; shapely; **esser fatto per** to be cut out for; **fatto di** made of; **venir fatto a** to happen, chance, e.g., **gli venne fatto d'incontrarmi** he happened to meet me ‖ *m* fact; act, deed; feat; action; business, affair; **badare ai fatti propri** to mind one's own business; **cogliere sul fatto** to catch in the act; **dire a qlcu il fatto suo** to give s.o. a piece of one's mind; **fatto compiuto** fait accompli; **fatto d'arme** feat of arms; **fatto sì è** the fact remains that; **in fatto di** concerning; as of; **sapere il fatto proprio** to know one's business; **venire al fatto** to come to the point ‖ *f* see **fatta**
fat·tóre -tóra or **-toréssa** *mf* farm manager ‖ *m* maker; factor; steward ‖ *f* stewardess; manager's wife
fattorìa *f* farm; stewardship
fattorino *m* delivery boy, messenger boy; conductor (*of streetcar*)
fattrice *f* (zool) dam
fattucchiè·re -ra *mf* magician ‖ *m* sorcerer ‖ *f* sorceress, witch
fattura *f* preparation; workmanship; bill, invoice; (coll) witchcraft; (lit) creature
fatturare *tr* to adulterate; to invoice, bill
fattura·to -ta *adj* adulterated ‖ *m* (com) turnover
fatturi·sta *mf* (**-sti -ste**) billing clerk
fà·tuo -tua *adj* fatuous
fàuci *fpl* jaws; (fig) mouth
fàuna *f* fauna
fàuno *m* faun
fàu·sto -sta *adj* propitious, lucky
fau·tóre -trice *mf* supporter, promoter
fava *f* broad bean; **pigliare due piccioni con una fava** to catch two birds with one stone
favèlla *f* speech; (lit) tongue
favilla *f* spark; **far** or **mandare faville** to sparkle
favo *m* honeycomb
fàvola *f* fable; tale; **favola del paese** talk of the town
favoló·so -sa [s] *adj* fabulous; mythical
favóre *m* favor; help; cover (*e.g., of night*); **a favore di** for the benefit of; **di favore** special (*price*); complimentary (*ticket*); **favore politico** patronage; **per favore** please; **per favore di** courtesy of
favoreggiaménto *m* abetting, support
favoreggiare §290 (**favoréggio**) *tr* to abet, support
favoreggia·tóre -trice *mf* abettor, supporter, backer
favorévole *adj* favorable; propitious
favorire §176 *tr* to favor; to accept; to oblige, accommodate; **favorire qlcu di qlco** to oblige s.o. with s.th; **favorisca** + *inf* please + *inf*, be kind

enough to + *inf;* **favorisca alla cassa** please pay the cashier; **favorisca uscire!** please leave!; **tanto per favorire** just to keep you company; **vuol favorire?** won't you please join us (*at a meal*)?; please help yourself!
favorita *f* royal mistress
favoritismo *m* favoritism
favori·to -ta *adj* & *mf* favorite ‖ *m* protegé; **favoriti** sideburns ‖ *f* see **favorita**
fazióne *f* faction; **essere di fazione** to be on guard duty
fazió·so -sa [s] *adj* factious ‖ *m* partisan
fazolétto *m* handkerchief; **fazzoletto da collo** neckerchief
fé *f* var of **fede**
feb·bràio *m* (**-brài**) February
fèbbre *f* fever; fever blister; **febbre da cavallo** (coll) very high fever; **febbre da fieno** hay fever; **febbre dell'oro** gold fever
febbricitante *adj* feverish
febbrile *adj* feverish
Fèbo *m* Phoebus
féc·cia *f* (**-ce**) dregs; (fig) dregs (*of society*); **fino alla feccia** to the bitter end
fèci *fpl* feces
fècola *f* starch
fecondare (**fecóndo**) *tr* to fecundate
fecondazióne *f* fecundation; **fecondazione artificiale** artificial insemination
fecondi·tà *f* (**-tà**) fecundity
fecón·do -da *adj* fecund, prolific
féde *f* faith; certificate; wedding ring; faithfulness; **far fede** to bear witness; **in fede di che** in testimony whereof; **in fede mia!** upon my word! **prestar fede a** to put one's faith in; **tener fede alla parola data** to keep one's word
fedecommésso *m* fideicommissum; trusteeship
fedéle *adj* faithful, devoted ‖ *mf* faithful person; **i fedeli** the faithful
fedel·tà *f* (**-tà**) faithfulness, allegiance; fidelity; **ad alta fedeltà** hi-fi
fèdera *f* pillowcase
federale *adj* federal
federali·sta *mf* (**-sti -ste**) federalist
federati·vo -va *adj* federative
federa·to -ta *adj* federate, federated
federazióne *f* federation; (sports) league
Federico *m* Frederick
fedifra·go -ga *adj* (**-ghi -ghe**) unfaithful, treacherous
fedina *f* police record; **avere la fedina sporca** to have a bad record; **fedine** sideburns
fégato *m* liver; courage; **fegato d'oca** pâté de foie gras; **rodersi il fegato** to be consumed with rage
félce *f* fern
feldspato *m* feldspar
felice *adj* happy; blissful; glad; felicitous
felici·tà *f* (**-tà**) happiness; bliss
felicitare (**felìcito**) *tr* to make happy; **che Dio vi feliciti!** God bless you! ‖

ref to rejoice; **felicitarsi con qlcu per qlco** to congratulate s.o. for or on s.th

felicitazióne f congratulation
feli·no -na adj & m feline
fellóne m (lit) traitor
félpa f plush
felpa·to -ta adj covered with plush; soft (e.g., step)
féltro m felt; felt hat
felu·ca f (-che) two-cornered hat; (naut) felucca
fémmina adj & f female
femminile adj feminine, female || m feminine gender
femminili·tà f (-tà) femininity, womanliness
femminismo m feminism
fèmore m femur; thighbone
fendènte m slash with a sword
fèndere §174 tr to split, cleave; to plow (water); to rend (air); to make one's way through (a crowd) || ref to split; to come apart
fenditura f split, breach, fissure
fenice f phoenix
feni·cio -cia (-ci -cie) adj & mf Phoenician || **la Fenicia** Phoenicia
fèni·co -ca adj (-ci -che) carbolic
fenicòttero m flamingo
fenòlo m phenol
fenomenale adj phenomenal
fenòmeno m phenomenon; freak, monster; **essere un fenomeno** to be unbelievable
ferace adj (lit) fertile
ferale adj (lit) mortal, deadly
fèretro m bier, coffin
feriale adj working (day); weekday
fèrie fpl vacation; **ferie retribuite** vacation with pay
ferire §176 tr to wound; to strike; **senza colpo ferire** without striking a blow || ref to wound oneself
feri·to -ta adj wounded, injured || m wounded person; injured person; **i feriti** the wounded; the injured || f wound, injury
feritóia f loophole; embrasure
feri·tóre -trice mf assailant
férma f setting (of setter or pointer); (mil) service; (mil) enlistment
fermacarro m (rr) buffer
fermacar·te m (-te) paperweight; large paper clip
fermacravat·ta m (-ta) tiepin
fermà·glio m (-gli) clasp; buckle; clip; brooch
fermare (férmo) tr to stop; to pay (attention); to fasten; to close, shut; to detain (in police station); to set (game); to reserve (seats) || ref to stop; to stay
fermata f stop; **fermata a richiesta** or **facoltativa** stop on signal
fermentare (ferménto) tr & intr to ferment
fermentazióne f fermentation
ferménto m ferment
fermézza f firmness; steadfastness
fér·mo -ma adj firm; stopped; quiet (water); (fig) steadfast; **fermo in**

posta general delivery; **fermo restando che** seeing that; **stare fermo** to be quiet || m stop; detention; **mettere il fermo a** to stop (a check)
fermopòsta m general delivery || adv care of general delivery
feróce adj fierce; wild
ferò·cia f (-cie) ferocity, ferociousness, fierceness
feròdo m (aut) brake lining
ferragósto m Assumption; mid-August holiday
ferrame m ironware
ferramén·to m (-ti) iron or metal bracket; iron or metal trimming || m (-ta fpl)—**ferramenta** hardware
ferrare (fèrro) tr to shoe (a horse); to hoop (a barrel)
ferra·to -ta adj iron; ironclad; shod (horse); spiked (shoe); well-versed || f pressing, ironing; mark or burn (caused by ironing); (coll) iron grate
ferravèc·chio m (-chi) scrap-iron dealer, junkman
fèrre·o -a adj iron; ironclad
ferrièra f ironworks; (obs) iron mine
fèrro m iron; tool; anchor; sword; **ai ferri** on the grill, broiled (e.g., steak); **essere sotto i ferri del chirurgo** to go under the knife; **ferri** shackles; **ferri del mestiere** tools of the trade; **ferro battuto** wrought iron; **ferro da arricciare** curling iron; **ferro da calza** knitting needle; **ferro da cavallo** horseshoe; **ferro da stiro** iron, flat-iron; **ferro fuso** cast iron; **ferro grezzo** pig iron; **mettere a ferro e fuoco** to put to fire and sword; **venire ai ferri corti** to get into close quarters
ferromodellismo m hobby of model railroads
ferrotranvièri mpl transport workers
ferrovia f railroad; **ferrovia a dentiera** rack railway; **ferrovia sopraelevata** elevated railroad
ferrovià·rio -ria adj (-ri -rie) railroad
ferrovière m railroader
fèrtile adj fertile
fertilizzante [ddzz] adj fertilizing || m fertilizer
fertilizzare [ddzz] tr to fertilize
fervènte adj fervent
fèrvere §175 intr to be fervent; to rage (said, e.g., of a battle); to go full blast
fèrvi·do -da adj fervent
fervóre m fervor; (fig) heat
fervorino m lecture, sermon
fesseria f (slang) stupidity, nonsense; (slang) trifle
fés·so -sa adj cracked; cleft; (slang) dumb || m (lit) cranny; **fare fesso qlcu** (slang) to play s.o. for a sucker
fessura f crack; cranny
fèsta f feast; holiday; birthday; saint's day; **a festa** festively; **buone feste!** happy holiday!; **conciare per le feste** to drub the daylights out of; **fare festa a** to welcome; **fare le feste** to spend the holidays; **far festa** to celebrate; to take the day off; **far la festa**

a to do in, kill; **festa del ceppo** Christmas; **festa da ballo** or **danzante** dancing party; **festa della mamma** Mother's Day; **festa del papà** Father's Day; **festa di precetto** (eccl) day of obligation; **festa nazionale** national holiday; **mezza festa** half holiday

festante *adj* cheerful

festeggiaménto *m* celebration

festeggiare §290 (**festéggio**) *tr* to celebrate, fete; to cheer

festi·no -na *adj* (lit) rapid || *m* party

festivi·tà *f* (-**tà**) festivity

festi·vo -va *adj* festive, holiday

festóne *m* festoon

festó·so -sa [s] *adj* cheerful, merry

festu·ca *f* (-**che**) straw; (fig) mote

fetènte *adj* stinking; stink (*bomb*) || *mf* (fig) stinker, louse

fetíc·cio *m* (-**ci**) fetish

feticismo *m* fetishism

fèti·do -da *adj* stinking, fetid

fèto *m* fetus

fetóre *m* stench

fétta *f* slice; **tagliare a fette** to slice

fettina *f* thin slice; twist (*of lemon*); **fettina di vitello** veal cutlet

fettùc·cia *f* (-**ce**) tape, ribbon

fettuccíne *fpl* noodles

feudale *adj* feudal

feudalismo *m* feudalism

feudatà·rio -ria (-**ri -rie**) *adj* feudatory || *m* feudal vassal

fèudo *m* fief

fiaba *f* fairy tale; tale, yarn

fiacca *f* tiredness; sluggishness; **batter la fiacca** to loaf, to goof off

fiaccare §197 *tr* to weaken; to weary; to break || *ref* to weaken; to break (*e.g., one's neck*)

fiacche·ràio *m* (-**rài**) (coll) hackman, cabman

fiacchézza *f* weakness; sluggishness

fiac·co -ca *adj* (-**chi -che**) weak; sluggish; slack || *f* see **fiacca**

fiàccola *f* torch; **fiaccola della discordia** firebrand

fiaccolata *f* torchlight procession

fiala *f* vial, phial

fiamma *f* flame; blaze; (mil) insignia; (nav) pennant; **alla fiamma** (culin) flaming; **dare alle fiamme** to set on fire; **diventare di fiamma** to blush; **in fiamme** afire

fiammante *adj* blazing; **nuovo fiammante** brand-new

fiammata *f* blaze; flare-up

fiammeggiante *adj* flaming, blazing; (archit) flamboyant

fiammeggiare §290 (**fiamméggio**) *tr* to singe || *intr* to flame, blaze

fiammífero *m* match

fiammin·go -ga (-**ghi -ghe**) *adj* Flemish; Dutch (*e.g., master*) || *mf* Fleming || *m* Flemish (*language*); (orn) flamingo

fiancata *f* blow with one's hip; dig, sarcastic remark; side, flank; (nav) broadside

fiancheggiare §290 (**fianchéggio**) *tr* to flank; to border (*a road*); to support

fiancheggia·tóre -trice *mf* supporter, backer

fian·co *m* (-**chi**) flank, side; hip; **di fianco** sideways; **fianco a fianco** side by side; **fianco destr'!** (mil) right face!; **fianco destro** (naut) starboard; **fianco sinistr'!** (mil) left face!; **fianco sinistro** (naut) port; **prestare il fianco a** to leave oneself wide open to; **tenersi i fianchi dal ridere** to split one's sides laughing

Fiandre, le *fpl* Flanders

fia·sca *f* (-**sche**) flask

fiaschetteria *f* tavern, wine shop

fia·sco *m* (-**schi**) straw-covered wine bottle; flask; fiasco

fiata *f* (archaic) time

fiatare *intr* to breathe; **senza fiatare** without breathing a word

fiato *m* breath; (archaic) stench; **avere il fiato grosso** to be out of breath; **bere d'un fiato** to gulp down; **col fiato sospeso** holding one's breath; **dare fiato a** to blow, sound (*a trumpet*); **d'un fiato** or **in un fiato** without interruption; in one gulp; **fiati** (mus) winds; **senza fiato** out of breath

fiatóne *m*—**avere il fiatone** to be out of breath

fibbia *f* clasp, buckle

fibra *f* fiber

fibró·so -sa [s] *adj* fibrous

ficcana·so [s] *mf* (-**si** *mpl* -**so** *fpl*) (coll) busybody, meddler; nosy person

ficcare §197 *tr* to stick; to drive (*e.g., a nail*); to push; **ficcare gli occhi addosso a** to gaze at, stare at; **ficcare il naso negli affari degli altri** to poke one's nose in other people's business || *ref* to hide; to butt in; to get involved

fi·co *m* (-**chi**) fig; fig tree

ficodíndia *m* (*pl* **fichidíndia**) prickly pear

fidanzaménto *m* engagement, betrothal

fidanzare *tr* to betroth || *ref* to become engaged

fidanza·to -ta *adj* engaged || *m* fiancé || *f* fiancée

fidare *tr* to entrust || *intr* to trust || *ref* to have confidence; **fidarsi a** (coll) to dare to; **fidarsi di** to trust, rely on

fida·to -ta *adj* trustworthy, reliable

fi·do -da *adj* (lit) faithful, trusted || *m* loyal follower; credit; **far fido** to extend credit

fidùcia *f* faith, confidence; (com) credit; **di fiducia** trustworthy

fiducià·rio -ria (-**ri -rie**) *adj* fiduciary || *mf* fiduciary, trustee

fidució·so -sa [s] *adj* confident, hopeful

fièle *m* *invar* gall, bile; acrimony

fienile *m* hayloft

fièno *m* hay

fierís·ti·co -ca *adj* (-**ci -che**) of a fair, *e.g.*, **attività fieristica** activity of a fair

fiè·ro -ra *adj*.fierce; dignified; proud || *f* fair; exhibit; wild beast

fièvole *adj* feeble, weak

fifa *f* (coll) scare; **avere la fifa** (coll) to be chicken; **avere una fifa blu** (coll) to be scared stiff

fifó·ne -na *mf* (coll) scaredy-cat

figgere §104 *tr* (lit) to drive, thrust || *ref*—**figgersi in capo** to get into one's head

figlia *f* daughter; (com) stub; **figlia consanguinea** stepdaughter on the father's side

figliare §280 *tr & intr* to whelp (*said of animals*)

figlia·stro -stra *mf* stepchild || *m* stepson || *f* stepdaughter

figliata *f* litter (*e.g., of pigs*)

fi·glio -glia *mf* child, offspring || *m* son; **figli** children; **figlio consanguineo** stepson on the father's side || *f* see **figlia**

figliòc·cio -cia (**-ci -ce**) *mf* godchild || *m* godson || *f* goddaughter

figliolanza *f* children, offspring

figliò·lo -la *mf* child || *m* son, boy || *f* daughter, girl

figura *f* figure; illustration; figurehead; face card; **far bella figura** to make a good showing; **far cattiva figura** to make a poor showing; **far figura** to look good; **figura retorica** figure of speech

figurante *mf* (theat) extra, super

figurare *tr* to feign; to represent || *intr* to figure; to appear; to make a good showing || *ref* to imagine; **si figuri!** imagine!

figurati·vo -va *adj* (fa) figurative

figura·to -ta *adj* figurative (*speech*); transcribed (*pronunciation*); illustrated (*book*)

figurina *f* figurine; card, picture (*of a series of athletes or entertainment celebrities*)

figurini·sta *mf* (**-sti -ste**) dress designer; costume designer

figurino *m* fashion plate; fashion magazine

figuro *m* scoundrel; gangster

figuróne *m*—**fare un figurone** to make a very good showing

fila *f* row; file, line; series; **di fila** in a row; **fare la fila** to wait in line; **file** ranks

filàc·cia *f* (**-ce**) lint

filacció·so -sa [*s*] or **filacció·so -sa** [*s*] *adj* thready, stringy

filamento *m* filament

filamentó·so -sa [*s*] *adj* thready, stringy; thread-like

filanda *f* spinning mill; silk spinning mill

filante *adj* spinning; shooting (*star*); thready; flowing (*e.g., line*)

filantropia *f* philanthropy

filantròpi·co -ca *adj* (**-ci -che**) philanthropic

filàntro·po -pa *mf* philanthropist

filare *m* row, line || *tr* to spin; to drip; ooze; to rest on (*one's oars*); to make (*e.g., ten knots*); (naut) to pay out; (mus) to hold (*a note*); **filare l'amore** to be in love || *intr* to spin (*said of a spider*); to rope, thread (*said of wine*

or *syrup*); to make sense; to drip; **fare filare dritto qlcu** to keep s.o. in line; **filare a** to do (*e.g., twenty miles an hour*); **filare all'inglese** to take French leave; **fila via!** (coll) get out!

filармòni·co -ca (**-ci -che**) *adj* philharmonic || *f* philharmonic society

filastròc·ca *f* (**-che**) rigmarole; nursery rhyme

filatelìa *f* philately

filatèli·co -ca (**-ci -che**) *adj* philatelic(al) || *mf* philatelist

fila·to -ta *adj* spun; well-constructed (*speech*) || *m* yarn

fila·tóio *m* (**-tói**) spinning wheel

filatura *f* spinning; spinning mill

filettare (**filétto**) *tr* to fillet; (mach) to thread

filettatura *f* stripe (*on a cap*); (mach) thread

filétto *m* fillet; stripe; snaffle (*on a horse's bit*); fine stroke (*in handwriting*); (mach) thread; (typ) ornamental line, headband; (typ) rule

filiale *adj* filial || *f* branch office

filiazióne *f* filiation

filibustière *m* filibuster, buccaneer; adventurer

filièra *f* (mach) drawplate; (mach) die (*to cut threads*)

filigrana *f* filigree; watermark (*in paper*)

filippi·no -na *adj* Philippine || *m* Filippino || **le Filippine** the Philippines

Filippo *m* Philip

filistè·o -a *adj & m* philistine; Philistine

Fillide *f* Phyllis

film *m* (film) film; movie, motion picture; **film parlato** or **sonoro** talking picture

filmare *tr* to film

filmina *f* filmstrip

filmìsti·co -ca *adj* (**-ci -che**) movie, motion-picture

filmotè·ca *f* (**-che**) film library

fi·lo *m* (**-li**) thread; wire; yarn; blade (*of grass*); breath (*of air*); string (*of pearls*); edge (*of razor*); **dare del filo da torcere** to cause trouble; **essere ridotto a un filo** to be only skin and bones; **fil di voce** thin voice; **filo a piombo** plumb line; **filo d'acqua** thin stream; **filo della schiena** or **delle reni** spine; **filo spinato** barbed wire; **passare a fil di spada** to put to the sword; **per filo e per segno** in detail; from beginning to end; **senza fili** wireless; **stare a filo** to stand upright; **tenere i fili** (fig) to pull wires; **tenere in filo** to keep in line; **un filo di** a bit of || *m* (**-la** *fpl*) string (*e.g., of cooked cheese*); (archaic) file, row

filo·bus *m* (**-bus**) trolley bus

filodiffusióne *f* wired wireless; cable TV

filodrammàti·co -ca *adj & mf* (**-ci -che**) (theat) amateur

filogovernati·vo -va *adj* on the government side

filologia *f* philology

filòlo·go -ga (**-gi -ghe**) *adj* philologic(al) || *m* philologist

filóne *m* vein (*of ore*); ripple (*of a cur-*

rent); stream; loaf (*of bread*); (lit) mainstream; **filone d'oro** gold lode

filó·so -sa [s] *adj* stringy

filosofìa *f* philosophy

filosòfi·co -ca *adj* (**-ci -che**) philosophic(al)

filòso·fo -fa *mf* philosopher

filovìa *f* trolley bus line

filtrare *tr* to filter; to percolate (*coffee*) || *intr* to filter, permeate

filtrazióne *f* filtering, filtration

filtro *m* filter; philter

filugèllo *m* silkworm

filza *f* string (*of pearls*); series (*of errors*); row; dossier, file; basting (*of dress*)

finale *adj* final, last; consumer (*goods*) || *m* end, ending; (mus) finale; (sports) finish || *f* end, ending; (sports) finals

finali·sta *mf* (**-sti -ste**) finalist

finali·tà *f* (**-tà**) end, purpose

finanche *adv* even

finanza *f* finance

finanziaménto *m* financing

finanziare §287 *tr* to finance

finanzià·rio -ria (**-ri -rie**) *adj* finance, financial || *f* (com) holding company

finanzia·tóre -trice *mf* financial backer

finanzièra *f* frock coat; **alla finanziera** with giblet gravy

finanzière *m* financier; (coll) customs officer

fin·ca *f* (**-che**) column, row (*of ledger*)

finché *conj* until, as long as; **finché non** until

fine *adj* fine, thin; choice, nice || *m* end, purpose; conclusion; (lit) limit, border; **a fine di bene** to good purpose, for the best; **secondo fine** ulterior motive || *f* end, conclusion; **condurre a fine** to bring to fruition; **fine di settimana** weekend; **in fin dei conti** after all; **senza fine** endless

fine-settima·na *m* or *f* (**-na**) weekend

finèstra *f* window; (lit) gash, wound; **finestra a ghigliottina** sash window; **finestra a ghigliottina** sash window; **finestra panoramica** picture window; **finestre** (lit) eyes

finestrino *m* (aut, rr) window

finézza *f* thinness; delicacy; finesse; kindness

fìngere §126 *tr* to feign, pretend; (lit) to invent || *intr* to feign, pretend || *ref* to pretend to be

finiménto *m* finishing touch; **finimenti** harness

finimóndo *m* fracas, uproar

finire §176 *tr* to end; to put an end to; **finiscila!** cut it out! || *intr* (ESSERE) to end, to be over; to abut; to wind up; **finire con** + *inf* to wind up + *ger*; **finire di** + *inf* to finish + *ger*, e.g., **ho finito di farmi la barba** I have finished shaving

fini·to -ta *adj* finished; accomplished; finite; exhausted; spent; **aver finito** to be through; **falla finita!** cut it out!; **farla finita con** to be through with; **farla finita con la vita** to end one's life

finitura *f* finish, finishing touch

finlandése [s] *adj* Finnish || *mf* Finlander, Finn || *m* Finnish (*language*)

Finlàndia, la Finland

finni·co -ca *adj* & *mf* (**-ci -che**) Finnic

fi·no -na *adj* fine, thin; refined; pure; sheer; **fare fino** (coll) to be refined || *adv* even; **fin a quando?** till when?; **fin da domani** beginning tomorrow; **fin da ora** beginning right now; **fin dove?** how far?; **fin in cima** up to the top; **fino a** until; down to; up to; as far as; **fin qui** up to now; up to this point

finòc·chio *m* (**-chi**) fennel; (vulg) fairy, queer

finóra *adv* up to now, heretofore

finta *f* pretense; fly (*of trousers*); (sports) feint; **far finta di** + *inf* to pretend to + *inf*, to feign + *ger*

fintantoché *conj* until

fin·to -ta *adj* false (*teeth*); fake; fictitious; sham (*battle*) || *mf* hypocrite || *f* see **finta**

finzióne *f* pretense; fiction; figment

fio *m*—**pagare il fio** to pay the piper; **pagare il fio di** to pay the penalty for

fioccare §197 (**fiòcco**) *intr* (ESSERE) to fall (*said of snow*); to flow (*said, e.g., of complaints*) || *impers* (ESSERE) —**fiocca** it is snowing

fiòc·co *m* (**-chi**) bow, knot; flake (*of snow*); flock, tuft (*of wool*); (naut) jib; **coi fiocchi** excellent; made to perfection; **fiocco pallone** (naut) spinnaker

fioccó·so -sa [s] *adj* flaky

fiòcina *f* harpoon

fiò·co -ca *adj* (**-chi -che**) feeble, faint

fiónda *f* sling; slingshot

fio·ràio -ràia (**-rài -ràie**) *mf* florist || *f* flower girl

fiorami *mpl*—**a fiorami** with flower design

fiordaliso *m* fleur-de-lis; (bot) iris; (lit) lily

fiòrdo *m* fjord

fióre *m* flower; prime (*of life*); best, pick; bloom; **a fior d'acqua** on the surface; skimming the water; **a fior di labbra** in a low tone, sottovoce; **a fior di pelle** skin-deep, superficial; **fior di** (coll) a lot of; **fiore di latte** cream; **fiori** (cards) clubs; **primo fiore** down (*soft hairy growth*)

fiorènte *adj* flourishing, thriving

fiorenti·no -na *adj* & *mf* Florentine

fiorettare (**fiorétto**) *tr* (fig) to overembellish

fiorétto *m* little flower; choice, pick; overembellishment; choice passage (*from life of saint*); foil; button of foil

fioricoltóre *m* var of **floricoltore**

fioricoltùra *f* var of **floricoltura**

fiorino *m* florin

fiorire §176 *tr* to cause to flower; to adorn with flowers || *intr* (ESSERE) to flower, bloom; to flourish; to break out (*said of skin eruption*); to get moldy

fiori·sta *mf* (**-sti -ste**) florist

fiori·to -ta *adj* flowering; flowery;

mottled; moldy; studded (e.g., with errors)

fioritura f flowering; flourish; mold; (pathol) eruption

fiorrancino m (orn) kinglet, firecrest

fiorràn·cio m (-ci) marigold

fiòtto m gush, surge; (obs) wave

Firènze f Florence

firma f signature; power of attorney; good reputation; (mil) enlisted man; **buona firma** famous writer; **farci la firma** (coll) to accept quite willingly; **firma di favore** guarantor's signature

firmaiòlo m (mil) enlisted man

firmaménto m firmament

firmare tr to sign

firmatà·rio -ria (**-ri -rie**) adj signatory ‖ mf signer, signatory

fisarmòni·ca f (**-che**) accordion

fiscale adj fiscal, tax

fischiare §287 tr to whistle; to boo ‖ intr to whistle; to ring (said of ears); to blow (said, e.g., of a factory whistle)

fischiettare (**fischiétto**) tr & intr to whistle

fischiétto m whistle (instrument)

fi·schio m (**-schi**) whistle; hiss, boo; blow (of whistle); ringing (in the ears)

fi·sciù m (**-sciù**) kerchief, fichu

fisco m invar treasury; internal revenue service

fisi·co -ca (**-ci -che**) adj physical; bodily ‖ m physicist; physique; (obs) physician ‖ f physics

fisima f whim, fancy, caprice

fisiologia f physiology

fisiològi·co -ca adj (**-ci -che**) physiological

fisionomia or **fisonomia** f physiognomy; countenance, face; appearance

fisionomi·sta mf (**-sti -ste**) person good at faces; physiognomist

fi·so -sa adj (lit) fixed

fissàg·gio m (**-gi**) (phot) fixing

fissare (**fìsso**) tr to fix; to fasten; to gaze at; to reserve; to hire; **fissare lo sguardo** to gaze ‖ ref to gaze, stare; to become obsessed; to settle down

fissati·vo -va adj fixing

fissa·to -ta adj fixed; (coll) cracked ‖ mf (coll) crackpot

fissa·tore -trice adj (phot) fixing ‖ m fixer; **fissatore per capelli** hair spray; hair dressing

fissazióne f fixation; fixed idea

fissile adj fissionable

fissionàbile adj fissionable

fissióne f fission

fis·so -sa adj fixed; regular ‖ m pay

fistola f (pathol) fistula; (lit) pipe

fitta f pang, stitch; crowd; great amount; (coll) blow; (obs) quagmire

fittàvolo m tenant farmer

fitti·zio -zia adj (**-zi -zie**) fictitious

fit·to -ta adj fixed, dug in; thick, dense; pitch (dark) ‖ m thick; rent; tenancy ‖ f see **fitta**

fittóne m (bot) taproot

fiuma·no -na adj river; from Fiume ‖ m person from Fiume ‖ f flood, stream

fiumara f torrent

fiume m river; **a fiumi** like a river

fiutare tr to snuff, sniff; to smell

fiutata f snuff, sniff

fiuto m sense of smell; snuff; flair

flàcci·do -da adj flabby

flacóne m flacon

flagellare (**flagèllo**) tr to scourge, lash, flagellate

flagèllo m whip, scourge; pest, plague; (coll) mess

flagrante adj flagrant; **in flagrante** (delitto) in the act

flan m (flan) pudding; (typ) mat

flanèlla f flannel

flàn·gia f (**-ge**) flange

flato m gas, flatus

flatulènza f flatulence

flautino m flageolet

flauti·sta mf (**-sti -ste**) flutist

flàuto m flute; **flauto diritto** or **dolce** (mus) recorder

fla·vo -va adj (lit) blond, golden

flèbile adj mournful

flebite f phlebitis

flèmma f apathy; coolness; phlegm

flemmàti·co -ca adj (**-ci -che**) phlegmatic(al)

flessibile adj flexible, pliable

flessióne f bending; (com) fall, drop; (gram) inflection

flessuó·so -sa [s] adj lithe, willowy; winding; flowing (style)

flèttere §177 tr to flex; (gram) to inflect

flirtare intr to flirt

flòra f flora

floreale adj floral

floricoltóre m floriculturist

floricoltura f floriculture

flòri·do -da adj florid; flourishing

flò·scio -scia adj (**-sci -sce**) flabby; soft (hat)

flòtta f fleet

flottante adj floating ‖ m (com) floating stock

flottare (**flòtto**) tr & intr to float

flottiglia f flottilla

fluènte adj flowing

fluidità f fluidity

flùi·do -da adj & m fluid; fluent (style)

fluire §176 intr (ESSERE) to flow; to pour

fluitazióne f log driving

fluorescènte adj fluorescent

fluorescènza f fluorescence

fluorìdri·co -ca adj (**-ci -che**) hydrofluoric

fluorite f fluor, fluorite

fluorizzazióne [ddzz] f fluoridation

fluòro m fluorine

fluoruro m fluoride

flusso m flow; flood (of tide); high tide; (pathol) flow (e.g., of blood); (phys) flux

flutto m (lit) wave

fluttuare (**flùttuo**) intr to fluctuate; to bob, toss; to waver; to surge, stream

fluviale adj fluvial, river

fobìa f phobia

fò·ca f (**-che**) seal; sealskin

focàc·cia f (**-ce**) flat, rounded loaf; cake

focaccina f bun

fo·càia *adj fem* (**-càie**) flint
focale *adj* focal
fóce *f* mouth (*of river*)
focèna *f* porpoise
fochi·sta *m* (**-sti**) fireman, stoker; fireworks manufacturer
foco·làie *m* (**-lài**) (pathol) focus; (fig) hotbed
focolare *m* hearth; firebox; fireside, home
focó·so -sa [s] *adj* fiery, high-spirited
fòdera *f* lining (*of suit*); cover, case
foderare (**fòdero**) *tr* to line; to cover
fòdero *m* sheath, scabbard; raft
fó·ga *f* (**-ghe**) ardor, impetus
fòg·gia *f* (**-ge**) fashion, shape; **a foggia di** shaped like
foggiare §290 (**fòggio**) *tr* to shape, fashion
fòglia *f* leaf; petal; foil (*of gold*); **mangiare la foglia** (fig) to get wise, catch on
fogliame *m* foliage
fò·glio *m* (**-gli**) sheet; bill, banknote; folio; newspaper; permit; **foglio d'avviso** notice; **foglio di congedo** (mil) discharge; **foglio d'iscrizione** application; **foglio di via** (mil) travel orders; **foglio modello** blank form; **foglio rosa** (aut) permit; **foglio volante** flier, handbill
fógna *f* sewer, drain
fognatura *f* sewerage
fòla *f* tale, fable
fola·ga *f* (**-ghe**) (zool) coot
folata *f* gust; (lit) flight (*of birds*)
folclóre *m* folklore
folgorante *adj* striking; flashing; meteoric (*career*)
folgorare (**fólgoro**) *tr* to strike (with lightning) ‖ *intr* to flash by ‖ *impers* —**folgora** it is thundering
fólgore *m* (lit) thunderbolt ‖ *f* flash of lightning; thunderbolt
fólla *f* crowd; (fig) flock
follare (**fóllo**) *tr* to full
fòlle *adj* mad, crazy; (aut) neutral; (mach) loose (*pulley*)
folleggiare §290 (**follèggio**) *intr* to act foolishly; to frolic
follemènte *adv* desperately, madly
follétto *m* elf; little imp
follìa *f* madness, lunacy; folly; **alla follia** madly; **far follie per** to be crazy about
follicolo *m* follicle
fól·to -ta *adj* thick; beetle (*brow*); deep (*night*) ‖ *m* depth (*e.g., of the night*); thick (*e.g., of the battle*)
fomentare (**foménto**) *tr* to foment
fòmite *m* (lit) instigation; impetus
fónda *f* anchorage; lowland; saddlebag; **alla fonda** at anchor
fónda·co *m* (**-chi**) (hist) warehouse
fondale *m* depth (*of river, sea*); (theat) backdrop
fondamentale *adj* fundamental, basic
fondamén·to *m* (**-ti**) ground, foundation; basis; **fare fondamento su** to count on; **fondamenti** elements; **senza fondamento** baseless; without getting anywhere ‖ *m* (**-ta** *fpl*)—**fondamenta** foundations (*of a building*)

fondare (**fóndo**) *tr* to found; to build; to charter ‖ *ref*—**fondarsi su** to rely on; to be based upon
fondatézza *f* basis, ground, foundation
fonda·to -ta *adj* well-founded
fonda·tóre -trice *mf* founder
fondazióne *f* foundation
fondèllo *m* bottom, base
fondènte *m* flux
fóndere §178 *tr* to smelt; to melt; to blow (*a fuse*); to cast (*a statue*); to blend (*colors*) ‖ *intr* to melt; to blend ‖ *ref* to melt; to blend; to burn out
fonderìa *f* foundry
fondià·rio -ria (**-ri -rie**) *adj* real-estate, land ‖ *f* real-estate tax
fondìna *f* holster; (coll) soup dish
fondi·sta *mf* (**-sti -ste**) editorialist; (sports) long-distance runner
fóndita *f* (typ) font
fonditóre *m* smelter, founder
fón·do -da *adj* deep ‖ *m* bottom; fund; innermost nature; seat; end; background; land, property; **a doppio fondo** with a false bottom; **a fondo** thoroughly; **a fondo perduto** as an outright grant; **dar fondo** (naut) to cast anchor; **dar fondo a** to exhaust; **di fondo** (journ) editorial; (sports) long-distance; **fondi** funds; lees; **fondi di bottega** remnants; **fondi di caffè** coffee grounds; **fondo comune d'investimento** mutual fund; **fondo d'ammortamento** sinking fund; **fondo di beneficenza** community chest; **fondo tinta** foundation (*in make-up*); **in fondo** in the end; at the bottom; after all
fonè·ma *m* (**-mi**) phoneme
fonèti·co -ca (**-ci -che**) *adj* phonetic ‖ *f* phonetics
fonògeno *m* pickup (*of record player*)
fonògrafo *m* phonograph, Gramophone
fonogram·ma *m* (**-mi**) telegram delivered by telephone
fonologìa *f* phonology
fonorivelatóre *m* pickup (*of record player*)
fonovalìgia *f* portable phonograph
fontana *f* fountain; spring; source
fónte *m* (lit) spring, source; **fonte battesimale** font ‖ *f* spring; fountain; source; **da fonte autorevole** on good authority
foraggiare §290 *tr* to subsidize ‖ *intr* to forage
forag·gio *m* (**-gi**) forage, provender, fodder
foràne·o -a *adj* rural; outer; (naut) outer (*dock*)
forare (**fóro**) *tr* to pierce; to bore; to puncture ‖ *intr* to have a flat tire ‖ *ref* to be punctured
foratura *f* puncture
fòrbice *f*—**a forbice** (sports) scissors (*e.g., kick*); **forbici** scissors; clippers; **forbici per le unghie** nail clippers
forbìre §176 *tr* to wipe; to polish; to shine
fór·ca *f* (**-che**) fork; pitchfork; gallows; mountain pass; **fare la forca a qlcu** (slang) to betray s.o.; (slang) to do s.o. dirt; **fatto a forca** V-shaped

forcèlla 162 foschìa

forcèlla *f* fork (*of bicycle or motorcycle*); mountain pass; fork-shaped pole; hairpin; cradle (*of handset*); (coll) wishbone (*of chicken*)
forchétta *f* fork; (coll) wishbone (*of chicken*); **alla forchetta** (culin) cold (*e.g., lunch*)
forchettàta *f* forkful; blow with a fork
forchettóne *m* carving fork
forcina *f* hairpin
fòrcipe *m* forceps
forcóne *m* pitchfork
forellino *m* pinhole
forèsta *f* forest
forestale *adj* forest, park
foresterìa *f* guest quarters (*in college or monastery*)
forestierismo *m* borrowing (*from another language*)
forestiè·ro -ra *adj* foreign ‖ *mf* foreigner; stranger; outsider
forfètta·rio -ria *adj* (**-ri -rie**) job, e.g., **contratto forfettario** job contract; all-inclusive, e.g., **combinazione forfettaria** all-inclusive price agreement
fórfora *f* dandruff
fòr·gia *f* (**-ge**) forge; smithy
forgiare §290 (**fòrgio**) *tr* to forge
foriè·ro -ra *adj* forerunning ‖ *mf* forerunner, harbinger
fórma *f* shape; form; mold (*e.g., for cakes*); wheel (*of cheese*); (typ) form; **forma da cappelli** hat block; **forma da scarpe** shoe tree; shoe last (*used by shoemaker*); **forme** shape, body; good manners; **salvare le forme** to save face
formaggièra *f* dish for grated cheese
formàg·gio *m* (**-gi**) cheese
formaldèide *f* formaldehyde
formale *adj* formal; prim
formalismo *m* formality
formali·tà *f* (**-tà**) formality
formalizzare [ddzz] *tr* to scandalize ‖ *ref* to be shocked
formare (**fórmo**) *tr & ref* to form
forma·to -ta *adj* formed ‖ *m* format
formazióne *f* formation
fòrmica *f* (trademark) Formica
formì·ca *f* (**-che**) ant
formi·càio *m* (**-cài**) anthill; (fig) swarm
formichière *m* anteater
formicolare (**formìcolo**) *intr* to swarm; to crawl ‖ *intr* (ESSERE) to creep (*said, e.g., of a leg*)
formicolì·o *m* (**-ì**) swarm; creeping sensation, numbness
formidàbile *adj* formidable
formó·so -sa [s] *adj* shapely, buxom
fòrmula *f* formula; (aut) category, class; **formula dubitativa** (law) lack of evidence; **formula piena** (law) acquittal
formulare (**fòrmulo**) *tr* to formulate
formulà·rio *m* (**-ri**) formulary; form
fornace *f* furnace, kiln
for·nàio -nàia *mf* (**-nài -nàie**) baker
fornèllo *m* stove, range; (*of boiler*) firebox; bowl (*of pipe*); (min) shaft; **fornello a gas** gas range; **fornello a spirito** kerosene stove; chafing dish
fornire §176 *tr* to furnish, supply

forni·tóre -trice *mf* supplier, purveyor
fornitura *f* supply; order; delivery
fórno *m* oven; furnace; kiln; bakery; (theat) empty house; **al forno or in forno** baked; **alto forno** blast furnace; **forno crematorio** crematorium; **far forno** (theat) to play before an empty house
fóro *m* hole
fòro *m* forum; (law) bar
forosétta [s] *f* (lit) peasant girl
fórse *m* doubt; **mettere in forse** to endanger; to put in doubt ‖ *adv* perhaps, maybe
forsenna·to -ta *adj* mad, insane ‖ *mf* lunatic
fòrte *adj* strong; firm; bad (cold); fat, hefty; fast (color); offensive (joke); hard (smoker); main (dish); (lit) thick ‖ *m* strong person; fortress; bulk, main body; forte; (lit) thick; **sapere di forte** to have a strong flavor; **farsi forte** to bear up; **farsi forte di** to appropriate, use; to be cocksure of ‖ *adv* hard, strong; much; loud; openly; a lot; fast; swiftly
fortézza *f* fortress; strength; fortitude
fortificare §197 (**fortìfico**) *tr* to fortify ‖ *ref* to be strengthened; to dig in
fortificazióne *f* fortification
fortino *m* blockhouse, redoubt
fortùi·to -ta *adj* fortuitous
fortuna *f* fortune; luck; good luck; fate, destiny; (lit) storm; **avere fortuna** to be lucky; to be a hit; **buona fortuna!** good luck!; **di fortuna** makeshift, emergency; **non aver la fortuna di** to not be fortunate enough to; **per fortuna** luckily
fortunale *m* storm, tempest
fortuna·to -ta *adj* fortunate, lucky
fortunó·so -sa [s] *adj* eventful
forùncolo *m* boil; pimple
forviare §119 *tr* to mislead, lead astray ‖ *intr* to go astray
fòrza *f* strength; force; power; police; (phys) force; **a forza di** by dint of; **a tutta forza** at full speed; **bassa forza** (mil) enlisted personnel; **di forza** by force; **di prima forza** first-rate; **far forza a** to encourage; to force; **fare forza a sé stesso** to restrain oneself; **forza!** courage!; **forza di corpo** (typ) height-to-paper; **forza maggiore** force majeure, act of God; **forza muscolare** brawn; **forza pubblica** police; **forza viva** kinetic energy; **per forza** of course; under duress
forzare (**fòrzo**) *tr* to force; to strain; to rape; to tamper with (a lock); **forzare il passo** to hasten one's step; **forzare la consegna** (mil) to violate orders
forza·to -ta *adj* forced; force (e.g., feed) ‖ *m* convict
forzière *m* chest, coffer
forzó·so -sa [s] *adj* compulsory; imposed by law
forzu·to -ta *adj* husky, robust
foschìa *f* smog; mist; haze

fó•sco -sca *adj* **(-schi -sche)** dark; gloomy; misty

fosfato *m* phosphate

fosforeggiare §290 **(fosforéggio)** *intr* to phosphoresce; to glow

fosforescènte *adj* phosphorescent

fòsforo *m* phosphorus

fòssa *f* grave; hollow; hole; ditch; moat; pit; den (*of lions*); **fossa biologica** sewage-treatment plant; **fossa di riparazione** (aut) pit; **fossa settica** septic tank

fossato *m* ditch; moat

fossétta *f* dimple

fòssile *adj & m* fossil

fossilizzare [ddzz] *tr* to fossilize || *ref* to become fossilized

fòsso *m* ditch; moat

fò•to *f* **(-to)** photo

fotocòpia *f* photocopy

fotocopiare §287 **(fotocòpio)** *tr* to photocopy

fotoelèttri•co -ca (-ci -che) *adj* photoelectric || *f* (mil) searchlight

fotogèni•co -ca *adj* **(-ci -che)** photogenic

fotogiornale *m* pictorial magazine

fotografare (fotògrafo) *tr* to photograph

fotografìa *f* photography; photograph

fotogràfi•co -ca *adj* **(-ci -che)** photographic

fotògrafo *m* photographer

fotogram•ma *m* **(-mi)** (phot) frame

fotoincisióne *f* photoengraving

fotolampo *m* flashlight

fotòmetro *m* exposure meter

fotomontàg•gio *m* **(-gi)** photomontage

fototubo *m* phototube

fra *m invar* brother, e.g., **fra Cristoforo** Brother Christopher || *prep* among; between; in, within

frac *m* (frac) swallow-tailed coat

fracassare *tr* to crash, smash || *ref* to crash

fracasso *m* crash; uproar; (coll) slew

fràdi•cio -cia (-ci -cie) *adj* rotten; soaked || *m* rotten part; decay; wet ground

fràgile *adj* fragile; brittle; frail

fragilità *f* fragility, frailty

fràgola *f* strawberry

fragóre *m* din; peal; roar

fragoró•so -sa *adj* noisy

fragrante *adj* fragrant

fraintèndere §270 *tr* to misunderstand

frammassóne *m* Freemason

frammassonerìa *f* Freemasonry

frammentare (framménto) *tr* to fragment

frammentà•rio -ria *adj* **(-ri -rie)** fragmentary

framménto *m* fragment

framméttere §198 *tr* to interpose || *ref* to meddle; **frammettersi in** to intrude in, to butt into

frammèzzo [ddzz] *adv* in the middle || *prep* in the midst of

frammischiare §287 *tr* to mix || *ref* to concern oneself

frana *f* landslide; (fig) collapse

franare *intr* to slide; to collapse

francesca•no -na *adj & mf* Franciscan

francé•sco -sca (-schi -sche) *adj* (archaic) French || **Francesco** *m* Francis || **Francesca** *f* Frances

francése *adj* French || *m* French (*language*); Frenchman (*person*); **i francesi** the French || *f* Frenchwoman

francesismo *m* gallicism

francesizzare [ddzz] *tr* to Frenchify

franchézza *f* frankness

franchi•gia *f* **(-gie)** franchise; exemption; deductible insurance; (naut) shore leave; **franchigia postale** franking privilege

Frància, la France

fran•co -ca (-chi -che) *adj* free; frank; Frankish; **farla franca** to get off scot free; **franco di porto** prepaid, postpaid; **franco domicilio** home delivery, free delivery || *m* franc || **Franco** *m* Frank

francobóllo *m* postage stamp, stamp

frangènte *m* breaker, surf; **essere nei frangenti** to be in bad straits

fràngere §179 *tr* to crush; (lit) to break || *ref* to break, comb (*said of waves*)

frangétta *f* bangs

fràn•gia *f* **(-ge)** fringe; embellishment; shoreline; bangs; **frangia di corallo** coral reef

frangìbile *adj* breakable

frangiflut•ti *m* **(-ti)** breakwater

frangi-vènto *m* **(-vènto)** windbreak

frangizòl•le *m* **(-le)** disc harrow

Frankfur•ter *m* **(-ter)** hot dog

fran•tóio *m* **(-tói)** crusher; **frantoio a mascelle** jawbreaker

frantumare *tr* to crush; to break to pieces || *ref* to be crushed; to go to pieces

frantume *m* fragment; **andare in frantumi** to go to pieces

frappé *m* **(frappé)** shake; frappé; **frappé alla menta** mint julep; **frappé di latte** milk shake

frappórre §218 *tr* to interpose || *ref* to interfere; to intervene

frasà•rio *m* **(-ri)** language, speech

fra•sca *f* **(-sche)** branch; bush; ornament; whim; frivolous woman, flirt

frase *f* sentence; (mus) phrase; **frase fatta** cliché; **frase idiomatica** idiom; **frasi** words; **frasi di commiserazione** condolences

fraseggiare §290 **(fraséggio)** *intr* to use phrasing; to use big words; (mus) to phrase

fraseologìa *f* phraseology

fràssino *m* ash tree

frastagliare §280 *tr* to cut out (*e.g., paper*)

frastaglia•to -ta *adj* indented, jagged; ornamented

frastornare (frastórno) *tr* to disturb; (lit) to prevent

frastuòno *m* din, roar

frate *m* friar, monk, brother

fratellanza *f* brotherhood

fratellastro *m* stepbrother; half brother

fratèllo *m* brother; **fratelli** brothers and sisters; **fratello consanguineo** half brother on the father's side; **fratello**

dì latte foster brother; **fratello ge- mello** twin

fraterni·tà f (-tà) fraternity

fraternizzare [ddzz] intr to fraternize

fratèr·no -na adj fraternal, brotherly

fratrici·da (-dì -de) adj fratricidal ‖ mf fratricide

fratrici·dio m (-dì) fratricide

fratta f brushwood; (coll) hedge

frattàglie fpl giblets, chitterlings, offal

frattanto adv meantime, meanwhile

frattèmpo m—**nel frattempo** meanwhile

frattura f fracture; break; breach

fratturare tr & ref to fracture, break

fraudolènto adj fraudulent

frazionare (fraziόno) tr to fractionate; to break up

frazionà·rio -ria adj (-ri -rie) fractional

frazióne f fraction; hamlet; (eccl) breaking of the host

fréc·cia f (-ce) arrow, bolt; steeple, spire; clock (on hosiery); (archit) rise; (fig) aspersion; **freccia consen- siva** arrow (on traffic light); **freccia direzionale** (aut) turn signal

frecciata f arrow shot; taunt, gibe; **dare una frecciata a** to hit for a loan

freddare (fréddo) tr to chill; to kill

freddézza f chill; cold, coldness; cool- ness, cold shoulder; sang-froid

fréd·do -da adj cold; cool, chilly; frigid ‖ m cold, cold weather; chill; **a freddo** cold; cooly; **avere freddo** to be cold (said of people); **fare freddo** to be cold (said of weather); **freddo cane** biting cold; **sentire freddo** to feel cold; **sudare freddo** to be in a cold sweat

freddolό·so -sa [s] adj chilly (person)

freddura f joke, pun; cold weather

freddurì·sta mf (-stì -ste) punster

fregagióne f rubbing, rubdown, mas- sage

fregare §209 (frégo) tr to rub; to strike (a match); (slang) to steal; (slang) to cheat, dupe; (vulg) to make love with ‖ ref to rub (e.g., one's hands); **fregarsene di** (vulg) to not give a hoot about

fregata f rubbing; (nav) frigate; (orn) frigate bird; (slang) cheating

fregatura f (slang) cheating; (slang) hitch, halt

fregiare §290 (frégio) tr to decorate; to fret

fré·gio m (-gi) decoration; insignia (on cap of officer); (archit) frieze

fré·go m (-ghi) line, stroke

frégola f rut, heat; (slang) mania, craze

fremènte adj throbbing; thrilling

frèmere §123 tr (lit) to beg insistently ‖ intr to throb; to be thrilled; to shake, tremble, rustle; to shudder (with horror); (fig) to boil; (fig) to fret

frèmito m throb; thrill; shudder; roar; quiver

frenare (fréno) tr to brake, stop; to bridle (a horse); to curb (passions); to restrain (e.g., laughter); **frenare la corsa** to slow down ‖ intr to put the brakes on ‖ ref to control oneself

frenatόre m (rr) brakeman

frenesìa f frenzy; (fig) craze, fever; (lit) thought

frenèti·co -ca adj (-ci -che) frenzied; frantic; crazy, enthusiastic

fréno m bit, bridle; brake; (fig) check; (mach) lock; **freno ad aria compressa** air brake; **mordere il freno** to champ the bit; **senza freno** wild, unbridled; **tenere a freno** to keep in check

frenologìa f phrenology

frequentare (frequènto) tr to frequent; to attend ‖ intr to associate

frequenta·tóre -trice mf patron, cus- tomer; frequenter, habitué

frequènte adj frequent; rapid (pulse); (lit) crowded

frequènza f frequency; attendance; **fre- quenza ultraelevata** ultrahigh fre- quency

frèsa f milling cutter; burr (of dentist's drill)

fresatrice f milling machine

fresatura f (mach) milling

freschézza f freshness; coolness

fré·sco -sca (-schi -sche) adj fresh; cool; **fresco di malattia** just recov- ered; **fresco di stampa** fresh off the press; **fresco di studi** fresh out of school; **star fresco** to be in a fix; to be all wrong ‖ m cool weather; tropi- cal fabric; **di fresco** recently; **fare fresco** to be cool (said of weather); **mettere al fresco** (coll) to put in the clink; **per il fresco** in cool weather

frescό·ne -na mf (slang) dumbell

frescura f coolness, freshness

frétta f hurry, haste; **avere fretta** to be in a hurry; **in fretta** in a hurry; **in fretta e furia** in a rush

frettazzo m plasterer's wooden trowel; steel brush

frettolό·so -sa [s] adj hurried, hasty

freudismo m Freudianism

friàbile adj friable, crumbly

friabilità f friableness

fricassèa f fricassee

frìggere §180 tr to fry; **mandare qlcu a farsi friggere** to tell s.o. to go to the devil ‖ intr to fry; to sizzle; to fret

friggitoria f fried-food shop

frigidézza f frigidity

frigidi·tà f (-tà) coldness; frigidity

frigi·do -da adj cold; frigid

frì·gio -gia adj (-gi -gie) Phrygian

frignare intr to whimper

frigorìfe·ro -ra adj refrigerating ‖ m refrigerator; (journ) morgue

fringuèl·lo -la mf chaffinch, finch

frinire §176 intr to chirp

frisata f gunnel

frittata f omelet; **fare la frittata** (coll) to make a mess of it

frittèlla f fritter; pancake; (coll) grease spot

frit·to -ta adj fried; cooked, ruined ‖ m fry, fried platter

frittura f frying; fry, fried platter

frivolézza f frivolity

frìvo·lo -la adj frivolous; flighty

frizionare (friziόno) tr to massage

frizióne *f* friction; massage; (aut) clutch

frizzante [ddzz] *adj* crisp, brisk (*weather*); sparkling (*wine*)

frizzare [ddzz] *intr* to tingle; to sparkle, fizz (*said of wine*); (fig) to sting

frizzo [ddzz] *m* jest, witticism; gibe, dig

frodare (**fròdo**) *tr* to cheat, swindle

fròde *f* fraud; **frode fiscale** tax evasion or fraud

fròdo *m invar* customs evasion; **di frodo** smuggled

fró-gia *f* (-**ge** or -**gie**) nostril (*of horse*)

fròl-lo -**la** *adj* high (*meat*); soft, tender; (fig) weak

frónda *f* branch, bough; political opposition; **fronde** foliage; ornaments

frondó-so -**sa** [s] *adj* leafy

frontale *adj* front; frontal

frónte *m* (mil, pol) front; **far fronte a** to face; to face up to; to meet (*expenses*); **tenere fronte a** to face, resist || *f* forehead, brow; countenance; title page; headline; (fig) face; **a fronte** opposite, facing; **a fronte di** (com) in reference to; **dietro fronte!** (mil) about face!; **di fronte a** in the face of; facing; **di fronte a tutti** in plain view; **fronte destr'!** (mil) right face!; **mettere a fronte** to compare; **tenere a fronte** to have in front of one's eyes

fronteggiare §290 (**frontéggio**) *tr* to face, front || *ref* to face one another

frontespi-zio *m* (-**zi**) title page

frontièra *f* border, frontier

frontóne *m* (archit) pediment; (archit) gable

frónzolo *m* bauble, gewgaw; **fronzoli** finery, frippery

fròtta *f* crowd; swarm; flock

fròttola *f* fib; popular poem; **frottole** humbug

frugale *adj* frugal (*meal*; *life*); temperate (*in eating or drinking*)

frugare §209 *tr* to rummage through; to search (*a person*) || *intr* to rummage, poke around

frùgo-lo -**la** *my* restless child, imp

fruire §176 *tr* to enjoy || *intr*—**fruire di** to enjoy

fruitóre *m* user

frullare *tr* to beat, whip || *intr* to flutter; to spin; **frullare per il capo a** to get into the head of, e.g., **cosa gli è frullato per il capo?** what got into his head?

frulla-to -**ta** *adj* whipped || *m* shake (*drink*)

frullatóre *m* electric beater

frullino *m* egg beater

fruménto *m* wheat

frumentóne *m* corn

frusciare §128 *intr* to rustle

frusci-o *m* (-**i**) rustle, rustling

frusta *f* whip; egg beater

frustare *tr* to whip, lash; (fig) to censure; (coll) to wear out (*clothes*)

frustata *f* lash; (fig) censure

frustino *m* whip, crop

fru-sto -**sta** *adj* worn out, threadbare || *f* see **frusta**

frustrare *tr* to frustrate, baffle; to discomfit

frut-ta *f* (-**ta** & -**te**) fruit; **essere alle frutta** to be at the end of the meal, to be having one's dessert

fruttare *tr* & *intr* to yield

fruttéto *m* orchard

frutticoltóre *m* fruit grower

fruttièra *f* fruit dish

fruttìfe-ro -**ra** *adj* fruit-bearing; fruitful, profitable; (lit) fecund

fruttificare §197 (**fruttìfico**) *intr* to fructify; to yield

fruttivéndo-lo -**la** *mf* fruit dealer

frutto *m* fruit; **frutti di mare** shellfish; **mettere a frutto** to make yield

fruttuó-so -**sa** [s] *adj* fruitful, profitable

fu *adj invar* late (*deceased*); son of the late . . . ; daughter of the late . . .

fucilare *tr* to shoot

fucilata *f* rifle shot

fucilazióne *f* execution by a firing squad

fucile *m* rifle, gun; **fucile ad aria compressa** air gun; **fucile da caccia** shotgun; **un buon fucile** a good shot

fucileria *f* fusillade

fucilière *m* rifleman

fucina *f* forge, smithy

fu-co *m* (-**chi**) (bot) rockweed; (zool) drone

fùcsia *f* fuchsia

fu-ga *f* (-**ghe**) flight; leak; row (*e.g., of rooms*); spurt (*in bicycle race*); (mus) fugue; **di fuga** hastily; **prendere la fuga** to take flight; **volgere in fuga** to put to flight; to take flight

fugace *adj* passing, fleeting

fugare §209 *tr* (lit) to avoid; (lit) to put to flight; (lit) to dispel

fuggènte *adj* passing, fleeting

fuggévole *adj* fleeting

fuggia-sco -**sca** (-**schi** -**sche**) *adj* fleeing, fugitive || *mf* fugitive; refugee

fuggi fug-gi *m* (-**gi**) stampede

fuggire *tr* to flee; to avoid || *intr* (ESSERE) to flee, run away; (sports) to take the lead; **fuggire a** to flee from

fuggiti-vo -**va** *adj* & *mf* fugitive

fulcro *m* fulcrum; (fig) pivot

fulgènte *adj* (lit) resplendent

fùlgi-do -**da** *adj* resplendent

fulgóre *m* resplendency, radiance

fuliggine *f* soot

fuligginó-so -**sa** [s] *adj* sooty

fulmicotóne *m* guncotton

fulminante *adj* crushing (*illness*); withering (*look*); explosive || *m* exploding cap; (coll) match

fulminare (**fùlmino**) *tr* to strike by lightning; to strike down; to confound, dumfound || *ref* (elec) to burn out, to blow out || *impers* (ESSERE)—**fulmina** it is lightning

fùlmine *m* lightning, thunderbolt; **fulmine a ciel sereno** bolt out of the blue

fulmìne-o -**a** *adj* swift, instant

ful-vo -**va** *adj* tawny

fumaiòlo *m* chimney; smokestack; (naut) funnel

fumante *adj* smoking; steaming; dusty
fumare *tr* to smoke; (lit) to exhale ǁ *intr* to smoke; to steam; to fume; **fumare come un turco** to smoke like a chimney
fumata *f* smoking; smoke signal; **fare una fumata** to have a smoke
fuma·tóre -trice *mf* smoker
fumetti·sta *mf* (-sti -ste) cartoonist
fumétto *m* cartoon; **fumetti** comics
fumigare §209 (**fùmigo**) *tr* (obs) to fumigate ǁ *intr* to steam, smoke
fumigazióne *f* fumigation
fumi·sta *m* (-sti) heater man; joker, hoaxer
fumisterìa *f* fondness for practical jokes; bamboozling
fumo *m* smoke; vapor, steam; smoking; (coll) hot air; **andare in fumo** to go up in smoke; **fumi** vapors, fumes; **mandare in fumo** to squander; to thwart; **sapere di fumo** to taste smoky; **vedere qlcu come il fumo negli occhi** to not be able to stand s.o.; **vender fumo** to peddle influence
fumòge·no -na *adj* smoke, e.g., **cortina fumogena** smoke curtain
fumó·so -sa [s] *adj* smoky; obscure
funambolismo *m* tightrope walking; (fig) acrobatics
funàmbo·lo -la *mf* tightrope walker; (fig) acrobat
fune *f* rope, cable; **fune portante** suspension cable
fùnebre *adj* funeral; funereal, gloomy
funerale *adj & m* funeral
funerà·rio -ria *adj* (-ri -rie) funeral
funère·o -a *adj* funereal; funeral
funestare (**funèsto**) *tr* to afflict
funè·sto -sta *adj* baleful; mournful
fungàia *f* mushroom farm; mushroom bed; flock, swarm
fùngere §183 *intr*—**fungere da** to act as
fun·go *m* (-ghi) mushroom; fungus; **fungo atomico** mushroom cloud; **venir su come i funghi** to mushroom
fungó·so -sa [s] *adj* fungous
funicolare *adj* cable, cable-driven ǁ *f* funicular railway
funìvia *f* cableway
funzionale *adj* functional
funzionalità *f* functionalism
funzionaménto *m* working order; functioning
funzionare (**funzióno**) *intr* to work; to function; **funzionare da** to act as
funzionà·rio -ria *mf* (-ri -rie) functionary, official; public official
funzióne *f* function; office; duty; (eccl) service; **facente funzione** acting; **mettere in funzione** to make (*s.th*) work
fuò·co *m* (-chi) fire; burner (*of gas range*); focus; (fig) home; (lit) thunderbolt; **al fuoco!** fire! (*warning*); **andare per il fuoco** (culin) to boil over; **cuocere a fuoco lento** (culin) to simmer; **dar fuoco a** to set fire to; **di fuoco** fiery; blushing; **far fuoco** to fire; **fuochi artificiali** fireworks; **fuoco di fila** enfilade; **fuoco!** (mil) fire!; **fuoco di paglia** (fig) flash in the pan; **fuoco di segnalazione** flare; **fuoco fatuo** will-o'-the-wisp; **fuoco**

incrociato cross fire; **fuoco nutrito** drumfire; **mettere a fuoco** to focus; **mettere una mano sul fuoco** to be absolutely sure, to swear by it
fuorché *prep* except; **fuorché di** except to
fuòri *adv* outside, out; aside; e.g., **lasciar fuori** to leave aside; **andar di fuori** (culin) to boil over; **dar fuori** to do away with; to squander; **di fuori** outside; **far fuori** to publish; **fuori di** out of; outside of; beyond (*a doubt*); off (*the road*); beside (*oneself*); **fuori d'uso** out of style; obsolete; **il di fuori** the outside; **in fuori** protruding; forward; **mettere fuori** to throw out; to spread; to exhibit ǁ *prep* beyond; out of; outside; **fuori commercio** not for sale; **fuori concorso** in a class by itself (himself, etc.); **fuori luogo** untimely, out of place; **fuori (di) mano** far away; solitary; **fuori testo** inserted, tipped in
fuoribór·do *m* (-do) outboard; outboard motor
fuoricombattimén·to (-to) *adj* knocked out ǁ *m* knockout
fuorigiò·co *m* (-co) (sports) offside
fuorilég·ge *mf* (-ge) outlaw
fuorisè·rie (-rie) *adj* custom-built ǁ *m & f* custom model ǁ *f* custom-built car
fuoristra·da *m* (-da) land rover
fuoriuscì·to -ta *adj* exiled ǁ *mf* political exile ǁ *f* leak; flow; protrusion
fuorvia·to -ta *adj* mislead, misguided
furbacchió·ne -na *mf* slippery person
furberìa *f* slyness, cunning
fur·bo -ba *adj* sly, cunning ǁ *mf* knave; **furbo di tre cotte** slicker
furènte *adj* furious
furerìa *f* (mil) company headquarters
furétto *m* ferret
furfante *m* sharper, scoundrel
furfanterìa *f* rascality
furgoncino *m* small delivery van
furgóne *m* truck; patrol wagon; hearse; **furgone cellulare** prison van
furgoni·sta *mf* (-sti -ste) truck driver, teamster
fùria *f* fury; strength, violence; hurry; **a furia di** by dint of; **con furia** in a hurry; **far furia a** to urge; **montare in furia** to go berserk; to fly off the handle
furibón·do -da *adj* furious, wild
furière *m* soldier attached to company headquarters
furió·so -sa [s] *adj* furious; fierce; mad
furóre *m* furor, frenzy; violence; longing; **far furore** to be a hit, to be all the rage
fororeggiare §290 (**furoréggio**) *intr* to be a hit, be all the rage
furti·vo -va *adj* stealthy; furtive; stolen (*e.g., goods*)
furto *m* theft; stolen goods; **di furto** stealthily; **furto con scasso** burglary
fusa [s] *fpl*—**fare le fusa** to purr
fuscèllo *m* twig
fusciac·ca *f* (-che) sash (*around the waist*)

fusèllo [s] *m* spindle; axle, shaft
fusibile *adj* fusible || *m* (elec) fuse
fusióne *f* fusion; melting; merger; blending (*of colors*)
fu·so -sa *adj* melted; molten
fuso [s] *m* spindle; shank (*of anchor*); shaft (*of column*); (aut) axle; **fuso orario** time zone
fusolièra *f* (aer) fuselage
fustagno *m* fustian
fustàia *f* adult forest, full-grown forest
fustèlla *f* (perforating) punch; (pharm) price stub

fustigare §209 (fùstigo) *tr* to whip
fusto *m* trunk (*of tree*); stalk; stem (*of key*); beam (*of balance*); butt (*of gun*); trunk, body; frame (*of armchair*); tank (*for holding liquids*); drum (*metal receptacle*); holding stick (*of umbrella*); shaft (*of column*); **d'alto fusto** full-grown (*tree*)
fùtile *adj* futile, trifling
futilità *f* futility
futurismo *m* futurism
futuri·sta *mf* (-sti -ste) futurist
futu·ro -ra *adj* & *m* future

G

G, g [dʒi] *m* & *f* seventh letter of the Italian alphabet
gabardi·ne *f* (-ne) gabardine; gabardine raincoat or topcoat
gabbamón·do *m* (-do) cheat, sharper
gabbanèlla *f* gown (*of physician or patient*); robe
gabbano *m* cloak; frock; **mutare gabbano** to be a turncoat
gabbare *tr* to dupe, cheat || *ref*—**gabbarsi di** to make fun of
gàbbia *f* cage; ox muzzle; dock (*in courtroom*); (mach) housing; (naut) top; (naut) topsail; **gabbia d'imballaggio** crate; **gabbia toracica** rib cage
gabbiano *m* sea gull
gabbo *m*—**farsi gabbo di** to make fun of; **prendere a gabbo** to make light of
gabèlla (gabèllo) *tr* to palm off; to swallow (*e.g., a tall story*); (obs) to tax
gabellare (gabèllo) *tr* to palm off; to swallow (*e.g., a tall story*); (obs) to tax
gabinétto *m* office (*of doctor, dentist, lawyer*); cabinet; chamber (*of judge*); toilet; closet; laboratory; **gabinetto da bagno** bathroom; **gabinetto di decenza** toilet, bathroom
ga·gà *m* (gà) fop, dandy; lounge lizard
gaggia *f* acacia
gagliardétto *m* pennon; pennant
gagliardia *f* (lit) vigor; (lit) prowess
gagliar·do -da *adj* vigorous; stalwart; hearty (*e.g., voice*)
gagliòf·fo -fa *adj* loutish; rascal || *mf* lout; rascal
galézza *f* gaiety, vivacity
gàio gàia *adj* (gài gàie) gay, vivacious
gala *m* & *f* gala; gala affair; **di gala** formal; **mettersi in gala** to dress up || *f* frill; bow tie (*for formal attire*); (naut) bunting
galalite *f* casein plastic, galalith
galante *adj* gallant, courtly; amorous; pretty, graceful
galanteria *f* gallantry, courtliness
galantuò·mo *m* (-mini) honest man; (coll) my good fellow
galàssia *f* galaxy
galatèo *m* good manners
galèna *f* (min) galena
galeóne *m* galleon
galeòt·to -ta *adj* (archaic) intermediary

(*in love affairs*) || *m* galley slave; convict; (archaic) procurer
galèra *f* galley; forced labor
gali·lèo -lèa (-lèi -lèe) *adj* & *m* Galilean
galla *f* (bot) gall; (pathol) blister; **a galla** afloat; **tenersi a galla** (fig) to keep alive; to manage; **venire a galla** to come to the surface
galleggiante *adj* floating || *m* float
galleggiare §290 (galléggio) *intr* to float
galleria *f* tunnel; gallery; balcony; mall, arcade; wind tunnel
Galles, il Wales
gallése [s] *adj* Welsh || *m* Welshman; Welsh (*language*) || *f* Welsh woman
gallétta *f* cracker; hardtack; (naut) ball on top of flagpole
gallétto *m* cockerel; (fig) gallant; (fig) whippersnapper; (mach) wing nut; **fare il galletto** to swagger
gàlli·co -ca *adj* & *m* (-ci -che) Gallic
gallina *f* hen; **gallina faraona** guinea fowl
gal·lo -la *adj* Gallic; (sports) Bantam (*weight*) || *m* rooster, cock; weathercock; Gaul; Gallic (*language*); **fare il gallo** to strut; **gallo cedrone** wood grouse; **gallo d'India** turkey
gallòc·cia *f* (-ce) (naut) cleat
gallóne *m* braid; stripe; chevron; gallon
galoppare (galòppo) *intr* to gallop; (fig) to rush around
galoppata *f* gallop
galoppa·tóio *m* (-tói) bridle path
galoppino *m* errand boy; **galoppino elettorale** ward heeler
galòppo *m* gallop; **andare al piccolo galoppo** to canter; **di gran galoppo** at full speed; **piccolo galoppo** canter
galò·scia *f* (-sce) overshoe, rubber
galvanizzare [ddzz] *tr* to electroplate; (fig) to galvanize
galvanoplàsti·ca *f* (-che) electroplating
gamba *f* leg; stem; (aer) shock strut; **a gambe all'aria** upside down; **a gambe levate** at top speed; upside down; **darsela a gambe** to take to one's heels; **essere in gamba** to be in good shape; to be on the ball; **essere male in gamba** to be in bad shape; **gamba di legno** peg leg; **gambe a ciambella** bowlegs; **le gambe mi fanno giacomo** my knees shake;

prendere qlcu sotto gamba to make light of s.o.; **raddrizzare le gambe ai cani** to try the impossible

gambale *m* legging, gaiter; boot last; leg (*of boot*)

gamberétto *m* shrimp

gàmbero *m* (*Astacus, Cambarus*) crawfish

gambétto *m* stumble; trip; (chess) gambit

gambo *m* stem

gamèlla *f* (mil) mess kit, mess tin

gamma *f* gamut; range; **gamma d'onda** (rad) wave band

ganà·scia *f* (-sce) jaw; (aut) brake shoe; **mangiare a quattro ganasce** to eat like a horse

gàn·cio *m* (-ci) hook; clasp; hanger

gan·ga *f* (-ghe) gang; (min) gangue

gànghero *m* hinge; clasp; **uscire dai gangheri** to fly off the handle

gàn·glio *m* (-gli) ganglion

ganzo [dz] *m* (slang) lover; (coll) slicker

gara *f* competition, match; **fare a gara** to compete; **gara d'appalto** competitive bidding

garagi·sta *m* (-sti) garage man

garante *adj* responsible ‖ *m* guarantor; **farsi garante per** to vouch for

garantire §176 *tr* to guarantee; to secure (*a mortgage*)

garanti·to -ta *adj* guaranteed, warranted; downright; absolute (*liar*)

garanzia *f* guarantee, warranty; insurance, assurance

garbare *tr* (naut) to shape (*a hull*) ‖ *intr* (ESSERE) (with *dat*) to like, e.g., **non gli garbano le Sue parole** he does not like your words

garbatézza *f* politeness, courtesy

garba·to -ta *adj* polite, courteous

garbo *m* politeness, good manners; gesture; act; shape (*of a hull*); good cut (*of clothes*); elegance (*in painting or writing*); **a garbo** correctly

garbù·glio *m* (-gli) tangle, confusion; mess

gardènia *f* gardenia

gareggiare §290 (garéggio) *intr* to compete, vie

garétta *f* var of **garitta**

garétto *m* var of **garretto**

garganèlla *f*—**bere a garganella** to gulp down

gargarismo *m* gargling; gargle

gargarizzare [ddzz] *intr* & *ref* to gargle

gargaròzzo *m* throat, gullet

garitta *f* railroad-crossing box; (mil) sentry box; (rr) brakeman's box

garòfano *m* carnation, pink

garrése [s] *m* withers

garrétto *m* ankle (*of man*); hock (*of horse*)

garrire §176 *intr* to chirp, twitter; to flap; (archaic) to quarrel

garrito *m* chirp, twitter

garròtta *f* garrote

gàrru·lo -la *adj* garrulous

garza [dz] *f* gauze

garzonato [dz] *m* apprenticeship

garzó·ne -na [dz] *mf* helper ‖ *m* helper, boy; apprentice; (archaic) bachelor; **garzone di stalla** stableboy

gas *m* (gas) gas; gasoline; **gas asfissiante** poison gas; **gas delle miniere** firedamp; **gas esilarante** laughing gas; **gas illuminante** illuminating gas; **gas lacrimogeno** tear gas

gasdótto *m* gas pipeline

gasificare §197 (gasìfico) *tr* var of **gassificare**

gasòlio *m* Diesel oil

gasòmetro *m* var of **gassometro**

gassificare §197 (gassìfico) *tr* to gasify

gassi·sta *m* (-sti) gasworker; gas fitter; gas-meter reader

gassòmetro *m* gasholder, gas tank

gassó·so -sa [s] *adj* gaseous, gassy ‖ *f* soda, pop

gastronomia *f* gastronomy

gatta *f* she-cat, tabby; **comprare la gatta nel sacco** to buy a pig in a poke; **gatta ci cova** something is rotten in Denmark; **pigliare una gatta da pelare** to take on a heavy burden, to get a tiger by the tail

gattabùia *f* (coll) clink, lockup

gattamòrta *f* (gattemòrte) hypocrite

gattino *m* kitten; (bot) catkin

gat·to -ta *m* (-ti) *m* tomcat; tamper, pile driver; **gatto a nove code** cat-o'-nine-tails; **gatto soriano** tortoiseshell cat; **quattro gatti** a handful of people ‖ *f* see **gatta**

gattóni *adv* on all fours

gattopardo *m* (zool) serval; **gattopardo americano** ocelot

gattùc·cio *m* (-ci) compass saw; (ichth) small dotted dogfish

gaudènte *adj* jovial ‖ *m* bon vivant

gàu·dio *m* (-di) joy, happiness

gavazzare *intr* (lit) to revel

gavétta *f* mess kit, mess gear; **venire dalla gavetta** to come up through the ranks

gavitèllo *m* buoy

gazza [ddzz] *f* magpie

gazzarra [ddzz] *f* racket, uproar

gazzèlla [ddzz] *f* gazelle

gazzétta [ddzz] *f* newspaper; gazette; newsmonger, gossip; **Gazzetta Ufficiale** Official Gazette (*in Italy*); Congressional Record (*U.S.A.*)

gazzettino [ddzz] *m* small newspaper; column, e.g., **gazzettino rosa** social column; newsmonger, gossip

gazzósa [ddzz] *f* var of **gassosa**

gèl *m* gel

gelare (gèlo) *tr* to freeze; to nip ‖ *intr* (ESSERE) & *ref* to freeze ‖ *impers* (ESSERE & AVERE)—**gela** it is freezing

gelata *f* frost

gela·tàio -tàia *mf* (-tài -tàie) ice-cream dealer

gelateria *f* ice-cream parlor

gelatièra *f* ice-cream freezer

gelatière *m* ice-cream dealer

gelatina *f* gelatin; jelly; **gelatina di frutta** fruit jelly; gum drop

gelatinizzare [ddzz] *tr* & *ref* to gelatinize; to jell

gela·to -ta *adj* frozen ‖ *m* ice cream;

gelato da passeggio ice cream on a stick, popsicle

gèli·do -da adj icy, ice-cold

gèlo m frost; ice; cold; **diventare di gelo** to remain dumfounded; **farsi di gelo** to be cold or aloof; **sentirsi il gelo addosso** to get a chill

gelóne m chilblain

gelosìa [s] f jealousy; great care; shutter

geló·so -sa [s] adj jealous; solicitous

gèlso m mulberry

gelsomino m jasmine

gemebón·do -da adj (lit) moaning

gemellàggio m sisterhood (of two cities)

gemèl·lo -la adj twin; sister (ship) mf twin ‖ **gemelli** mpl cufflinks ‖ **Gemelli** mpl (astr) Gemini

gèmere §123 tr (lit) to lament ‖ intr (ESSERE & AVERE) to moan, groan; to suffer; to squeak (said of a wheel); to ooze; to coo (said of a dove)

gèmito m moan; howl (of wind)

gèmma f gem; (bot) bud

gemma·to -ta adj gemmate; jeweled

gendarme m gendarme, policeman

genealogìa f genealogy

generalato m generalship

generale adj general ‖ m general; **generale d'armata** (mil) general; **generale di brigata** brigadier general; **generale di corpo d'armata** lieutenant general; **generale di divisione** major general ‖ f (mil) assembly; **stare sulle generali** to speak in vague generalities

generali·tà f (-tà) generality; majority; **generalità** fpl personal data

generalizzare [ddzz] tr to generalize; to bring into general use ‖ intr to generalize, deal in generalities

generare (gènero) tr to beget; to generate ‖ ref to occur

genera·tóre -trice adj generating ‖ m generator ‖ f generatrix

generazióne f generation

gènere m genus; kind, type; genre; (gram) gender; **del genere** similar, alike; **farne di ogni genere** to commit all sorts of mischief; **genere umano** mankind; **generi alimentari** foodstuffs; **generi diversi** sundries, assorted articles; **in genere** generally

genèri·co -ca (-ci -che) adj generic; vague; all-round; general (e.g., practitioner) ‖ mf (theat) actor playing bit parts ‖ m vagueness, imprecision

gènero m son-in-law

generosi·tà [s] f (-tà) generosity

generó·so -sa [s] adj generous; rich (wine)

gène·si f (-si) genesis ‖ **il Gènesi** Genesis

genèti·co -ca (-ci -che) adj genetic(al) ‖ f genetics

genetlìa·co -ca (-ci -che) adj birth ‖ m birthday

gengìva f (anat) gum

genìa f set, gang; (lit) breed

geniale adj clever; genial; inspired, genius-like

geniali·tà f (-tà) cleverness, ingeniousness; genius; (lit) geniality

genière m (mil) engineer

gè·nio m (-ni) genius; (mil) corps of engineers; **andare a genio** (with dat) to like, e.g., **la musica moderna non gli va a genio** he does not like modern music; **fare qlco di genio** to do s.th willingly

genitale adj genital ‖ **genitali** mpl genitals

geniti·vo -va adj & m genitive

geni·tóre -trice mf parent

gen·nàio m (-nài) January

genocìdio m genocide

genovése [s] adj & mf Genoese

gentàglia f riffraff, rabble, scum

gènte adj (archaic) gentle ‖ f people; nation; family; (nav) crew; **gente d'arme** soldiers; **gente di mal affare** riffraff; **gente di mare** sailors

gentildònna f gentlewoman

gentile adj gentle; nice; genteel ‖ **Gentili** mpl heathen

gentilézza f gentleness; kindness; **per gentilezza** kindly, please

gentilì·zio -zia adj (-zi -zie) of noble family; (lit) ancestral

gentiluò·mo m (-mini) gentleman, nobleman

genuflèttere §177 ref to kneel down

genuì·no -na adj genuine

genziana f gentian

geofìsi·co -ca (-ci -che) adj geophysical ‖ f geophysics

geografìa f geography

geogràfi·co -ca adj (-ci -che) geographic(al)

geògra·fo -fa mf geographer

geologìa f geology

geòlo·go -ga mf (-gi -ghe) geologist

geòme·tra m (-tri) geometrician; land surveyor

geometrìa f geometry

gerà·nio m (-ni) geranium

gerar·ca m (-chi) leader

gerarchìa f hierarchy

geràrchi·co -ca adj (-ci -che) hierarchical; **per via gerarchica** through proper channels

Geremìa f Jeremiah

geremìade f jeremiad

gerènte m manager, director; **gerente responsabile** (journ) managing editor

gèr·go m (-ghi) jargon

geriatrìa f geriatrics

Gèrico f Jericho

gèrla f pannier (carried on the back)

Germània, la Germany

germàni·co -ca adj (-ci -che) Germanic

germànio m germanium

germanizzare [ddzz] tr to Germanize

germa·no -na adj german, e.g., **fratello germano** brother-german; Germanic ‖ m (lit) brother-german; **germano nero** (orn) coot; **germano reale** (orn) mallard

gèrme m germ; (lit) offspring

germici·da (-di) adj germicidal ‖ m germicide

germinare (gèrmino) *intr* (ESSERE & AVERE) to germinate

germogliare §280 (germóglio) *tr* to put forth || *intr* (ESSERE & AVERE) to bud, sprout

germó·glio *m* (-gli) bud, sprout

gerogliì·co -ca *adj* & *m* (-ci -che) hieroglyphic

Geròlamo *m* Jerome

gerontocò·mio *m* (-mi) or **gerotrò·fio** *m* (-fi) old people's home, nursing home

gerùn·dio *m* (-di) gerund

Gerusalèmme *f* Jerusalem

gessare (gèsso) *tr* to plaster; to lime (*a field*)

gèsso *m* gypsum; plaster; chalk; (sculp) plaster cast

gessó·so -sa [s] *adj* plastery, chalky; chalklike

gèsta *f* (archaic) army; **gesta** *fpl* deeds, exploits

gestante *f* pregnant woman

gestazióne *f* gestation

gesticolare (gesticolo) *intr* to gesticulate

gestióne *f* management, operation; data processing

gestire §176 *tr* to manage, operate || *intr* to gesticulate; (theat) to make gestures

gèsto *m* gesture; attitude; act, deed

ge·stóre -strice *mf* manager, operator; **gestore di stazione** (rr) station agent

gestualità *f* bodily movements (*e.g., of an actor*)

Gesù *m* Jesus; **Gesù Cristo** Jesus Christ

gesuì·ta *m* (-ti) Jesuit

gesuìti·co -ca *adj* (-ci -che) Jesuitic(al)

gettare (gètto) *tr* to throw; to cast; to pour; to lay (*e.g., a floor*); to send forth; to yield; to broadcast (*seed*); to risk (*one's life*); **gettare la colpa addosso a qlcu** to lay the blame on s.o.; **gettare le armi** to lay down one's arms; **gettar giù** to fell, knock down; **gettar sangue** to bleed || *ref* to throw oneself; to plunge; to flow, empty (*said of a river*)

gettata *f* pour, pouring; jetty; shoot, sprout; cast; range (*of a gun*); **gettata cardìaca** (med) rate of flow of blood

gèttito *m* yield; waste; **far gettito di** to waste

gètto *m* throw; gush; shoot, sprout; cast; precast concrete slab; (aer) jet; **a getto** (aer) jet; **a getto continuo** continuously; **di getto** spontaneously; **far getto di** to waste; **primo getto** first draft

gettonare (gettóno) *tr* (coll) to call up from a pay station; (coll) to make the selection of (*a record in a jukebox*)

gettóne *m* counter, token; attendance fee; (cards) chip

gettopropulsióne *f* jet propulsion

ghepardo *m* cheetah

ghép·pio *m* (-pi) kestrel

gherì·glio *m* (-gli) kernel, meat (*of nut*)

gherlino *m* (naut) warp, line

gherminèlla *f* trick, sleight of hand; trickery

ghermire §176 *tr* to claw; to seize

gheróne *m* gusset

ghétta *f* gaiter; **ghette** spats

ghétto *m* ghetto

ghiacciàia *f* icebox, cooler

ghiac·ciàio *m* (-ciài) glacier; **ghiacciaio continentale** polar cap

ghiacciare §128 *tr* to freeze || *intr* (ESSERE) to freeze || *impers* (ESSERE) —**ghiaccia** it is freezing

ghiaccia·to -ta *adj* iced; ice-cold; frozen || *f* flavored crushed ice

ghiàc·cio -cia (-ci -ce) *adj* icy, ice-cold || *m* ice; **ghiaccio secco** dry ice

ghiacciò·lo -la *adj* crumbly, breakable || *m* icicle; popsicle

ghiàia *f* gravel, crushed stone

ghianda *f* fringe (*on a curtain*); (bot) acorn; **ghiande** mast (*for swine*)

ghiandàia *f* (orn) jay

ghiàndola *f* gland

ghibellì·no -na *adj* & *m* Ghibelline

ghièra *f* ferrule; ring

ghigliottina *f* guillotine; **a ghigliottina** sash (*window*)

ghigliottinare *tr* to guillotine

ghigna *f* (coll) grimace

ghignare *intr* to grimace; to sneer

ghigno *m* sneer, smirk; grin

ghinèa *f* guinea

ghìngheri *m invar*—**in ghingheri** dressed up

ghiót·to -ta *adj* fond; gluttonous; eager; dainty (*food*) || *f* (culin) dripping pan

ghiottó·ne -na *mf* glutton; (zool) glutton, wolverine

ghiottoneria *f* gluttony; tidbit; (fig) rarity

ghiòzzo [ddzz] *m* dolt; (ichth) gudgeon

ghirba *f* jar; (coll) skin, life

ghiribizzo [ddzz] *m* (coll) whim, caprice

ghirigòro *m* doodle, curlicue

ghirlanda *f* garland, wreath

ghiro *m* dormouse; **dormire come un ghiro** to sleep like a log

ghisa *f* cast iron

già *adv* already; once upon a time; formerly || *interj* indeed!

giac·ca *f* (-che) jacket, coat; **giacca a due petti** double-breasted coat; **giacca a vento** windbreaker

giacché *conj* since

giacènte *adj* lying; idle (*capital*); unclaimed (*letter*); in abeyance

giacènza *f* lying; stay, abeyance; **giacenze di capitali** idle capital; **giacenze di magazzino** unsold stock of merchandise

giacére §181 *intr* (ESSERE) to lie; to be in abeyance; (lit) to be prostrate

giacì·glio *m* (-gli) pallet, cot

giacimento *m* field, bed; **giacimento petrolifero** oil field

giacinto *m* hyacinth

Giàcomo *m* James

giaculatòria *f* ejaculation (*prayer*); litany (*monotonous account*); curse

giada *f* jade

giaggiòlo *m* (bot) iris

giaguaro m jaguar
giaiétto m jet (black coal)
gialappa f (pharm) jalap
gialla·stro -stra adj yellowish
gial·lo -la adj yellow; detective (book or picture); white (with fear) ‖ m yellow; detective story, whodunit; suspense movie; **giallo dell'uovo** egg yolk
giamaica·no -na adj & mf Jamaican
giàmbi·co -ca adj (-ci -che) iambic
giambo m iamb
giammài adv never
giansenismo m Jansenism
Giappóne, il Japan
giapponése [s] adj & mf Japanese
giara f crock, jar
giardinàg·gio m (-gi) gardening
giardinétta f station wagon
giardiniè·re -ra f gardener ‖ f jardiniere; mixed pickles; mixed salad; wagonette; station wagon
giardino m garden; **giardino d'infanzia** kindergarten; **giardino pensile** roof garden; **giardino zoologico** zoological garden
giarrettièra f garter
Giasóne m Jason
giavanése [s] adj & mf Javanese
giavellòtto m javelin
gibbó·so -sa [s] adj gibbous, humped; humpbacked; rough (ground)
gibèrna f cartridge box; cartridge belt
gi·bus m (-bus) opera hat
gi·ga f (-ghe) gigue, jig
gigante adj & m giant
giganté·sco -sca adj (-schi -sche) gigantic
gigantéssa f giantess
gigióne m ham actor
gi·glio m (-gli) Madonna lily; fleur-de-lys
gilda f guild
gi·lè f (-lè) vest, waistcoat
gimnòto m electric eel
ginecología f gynecology
ginecòlo·go -ga m f (-gi -ghe) gynecologist
gine·pràio m (-prài) juniper thicket; (fig) mess
ginépro m juniper
ginèstra f (bot) Spanish broom
Ginèvra f Geneva
ginevri·no -na adj & mf Genevan
gingillare ref to trifle; to idle
gingillo m trifle, bauble
ginnà·sio m (-si) secondary school; gymnasium
ginna·sta mf (-sti -ste) gymnast
ginnàsti·co -ca adj (-ci -che) gymnastic ‖ f gymnastics; **ginnastica a corpo libero** or **ginnastica da camera** calisthenics
gìnni·co -ca adj (-ci -che) gymnastic
ginocchiata f blow with the knee; blow on the knee
ginocchièra f kneepad; elastic bandage (for knee); kneepiece (of armor)
ginòc·chio m (-chi) knee; **avere il ginocchio valgo** to be bowlegged; **avere il ginocchio varo** to be knock-kneed; **in ginocchio** on one's knees

‖ m (-chia fpl) knee; **fino alle ginocchia** knee-deep; **gettarsi alle ginocchia di** to go down on one's knees to; **mettere qlcu in ginocchio** to bring s.o. to his knees
ginocchióni adv on one's knees
giocare §182 tr to play; to stake, bet, risk, gamble; to make a fool of ‖ intr to play; to gamble; to circulate (said of air); (fig) to play a role; **giocare a** to play; to wager; **giocare a mosca cieca** to play blindman's buff; **giocare con** to risk; **giocare d'armi** to fence; **giocare d'azzardo** to gamble; **giocare di** to use (e.g., one's wits); **giocare di gomiti** to elbow one's way; **giocare di mano** to steal; **giocare sulle parole** to play on words; to pun ‖ ref to risk (e.g., one's life); to gamble away
giocata f wager, stake; game, play
gioca·tóre -trice m f player; gambler; speculator
giocàttolo m toy, plaything
giocherellare (giocherèllo) intr to play, trifle
giochétto m children's game; child's play; dirty trick
giò·co m (-chi) game; gambling; play; wager, stake; set; joke; (cards) hand; **entrare in gioco** to come into play; **fare gioco a** to come in handy to; **fare il doppio gioco** to be guilty of duplicity; **fare il gioco di** to play into the hands of; **giochi di equilibrio** balancing act; **gioco da ragazzi** child's play; **gioco d'azzardo** gambling; game of chance; **gioco del bussolotti** (fig) jugglery; **gioco di destrezza** game of skill; **gioco di parole** play on words, pun; **gioco di prestigio** sleight of hand; **gioco di società** parlor game; **metter in gioco** to risk; to stake; **per gioco** for fun; **prendersi gioco di** to make fun of
giocofòrza m—è **giocofòrza** + inf it is necessary + inf
giocolière m juggler
giocón·do -da adj merry, joyful
giocó·so -sa [s] adj jocose, jolly
giogàia f dewlap; chain of mountains
gió·go m (-ghi) yoke; beam (of balance); rounded peak; pass
giòia f joy, happiness; darling; jewel; **darsi alla pazza gioia** to have a wild time
gioiellería f jewelry; jewelry store
gioiellière m jeweler
gioièllo m jewel
gioió·so -sa [s] adj joyful
gioire §176 (pres part missing) intr to rejoice
Giòna m Jonas
Giordània, la Jordan (country)
giorda·no -na adj & mf Jordanian ‖ **Giordano** m Jordan (river)
Giórgio m George
giorna·làio -làia m f (-lài -làie) newsdealer
giornale m newspaper; magazine; (com) journal; **giornale di bordo** log, logbook; **giornale murale** poster; **giornale radio** newscast

giornaliè·ro -ra *adj* daily || *mf* day laborer

giornalismo *m* journalism

giornali·sta *mf* (**-sti -ste**) journalist; **giornalista pubblicista** free-lance writer || *m* newspaperman || *f* newspaperwoman

giornalménte *adv* daily

giornata *f* day; day's work; birthday; pay, salary; battle; day's march; **giornata campale** pitched battle; **giornata della mamma** Mother's Day; **giornata lavorativa** workday; **vivere alla giornata** to live from hand to mouth

giórno *m* day; **a giorni** within the next few days; **a giorni . . . a giorni** some days . . . others; **a giorno** open, openwork (*needlework*); full (*light*); **ai giorni nostri** nowadays; **al giorno d'oggi** nowadays; **buon giorno** good day; good morning; good-bye; **dare gli otto giorni a** to dismiss, fire; **di ogni giorno** everyday (*e.g., clothes*); **essere a giorno** to be up to date; **giorno dei morti** All Souls' Day; **giorno di lavoro** workday; **giorno di paga** payday; **giorno fatto** broad daylight; **giorno feriale** weekday; **giorno festivo** holiday; **mettere a giorno** to bring up to date; **otto giorni oggi** one week from today; **passare un brutto giorno** to have a bad time; **un giorno o l'altro** one of these days

giòstra *f* joust; merry-go-round

giostrare (**giòstro**) *intr* to joust; to get along, manage; to idle, loiter

Giosuè *m* Joshua

Giotté·sco -sca *adj* (**-schi -sche**) of the school of Giotto

giovaménto *m* benefit, advantage

gióvane *adj* young; youthful; fresh (*e.g., cheese*); Younger, e.g., **Plinio il Giovane** Pliny the Younger || *m* young man; boy, apprentice; **i giovani** the young || *f* young woman

giovanile *adj* youthful

Giovanni *m* John; **Giovanni Battista** John the Baptist

giovanòtta *f* young woman

giovanòtto *m* young man; (coll) bachelor

giovare (**gióvo**) *tr* (lit) to help || *intr* (with *dat*) to help, to be of use to || *ref* to avail oneself || *impers* (ESSERE) —**non giova** it's no use

Giòve *m* Jupiter

giove·dì *m* (**-dì**) Thursday; **giovedì santo** Maundy Thursday

giovèn·ca *f* (**-che**) heifer

gioventù *f* youth

giovévole *adj* helpful, beneficial

gioviale *adj* jovial

giovinézza *f* youth

gip *f* (**gip**) jeep

gippóne *m* large jeep, panel truck

giràbile *adj* endorsable

giradi·schi *m* (**-schi**) record player

giradito *m* (pathol) felon

giraffa *f* giraffe; (mov, telv) boom, crane

girafilièra *f* diestock

giramà·schio *m* (**-schi**) tap wrench

giraménto *m*—**giramento di testa** vertigo, dizziness

giramón·do *m* (**-do**) globetrotter

giràndola *f* girandole; pinwheel; (fig) weathercock

girandolare (**giràndolo**) *intr* to stroll, sauter

girante *mf* endorser || *f* blade (*e.g., of fan*)

girare *tr* to turn; to tour; to go around, travel over; to switch (*the conversation*); to film, shoot; to transfer (*a phone call*); to endorse; (mil) to surround || *intr* to turn; to circulate; to spin (*said of one's head*) || *ref* to turn; to toss and turn

girarròsto *m* turnspit; **girarrosto a motore** rotisserie

girasóle *m* sunflower

girata *f* turn; walk, ramble; (com) endorsement; (cards) deal; (coll) tongue-lashing

giratà·rio -ria *mf* (**-ri -rie**) endorsee

giravòlta *f* turn, pirouette; bend; sudden change of mind

girellare (**girèllo**) *intr* to stroll, wander around

girèllo *m* rump; go-cart, walker

girévole *adj* revolving

girino *m* tadpole; bicycle rider competing on the Tour of Italy

giro *m* periphery; turn, revolution; ride; size (*of hat*); edge (*of glass*); round (*of a doctor*); (sports) tour; (sports) lap; (com) transfer; (cards) hand; (theat) tour; **a giro di posta** by return mail; **andare in giro** to poke along; **giro collo** neckline; **giro d'affari** volume of business, turnover; **giro di parole** circumlocution; **fare il giro di** to tour; **mettere in giro** to spread (*news, gossip*); **nel giro di** within (*a period*); **prendere in giro** to poke fun at

girobùssola *f* gyrocompass

girondolare (**giróndolo**) *intr* var of girandolare

giróne *m* (sports) conference; (sports) division; (sports) league; (archaic) circle

gironzolare [dz] (**girónzolo**) *intr* to stroll, saunter

giropilò·ta *m* (**-ti**) gyropilot

giroscò·pio *m* (**-pi**) gyroscope

girotóndo *m* ring-around-a-rosy

giròtta *f* weather vane

girovagare §209 (**giròvago**) *intr* to roam, wander

giròva·go -ga (**-ghi -ghe**) *adj* wandering; strolling (*player*) || *m* vagrant, hobo

gita *f* trip, excursion, outing

gita·no -na *adj* & *mf* Gypsy

gitante *mf* excursionist, vacationist

gittata *f* range (*of gun*)

giù *adv* down; **andar giù** to go down; to deteriorate; to get worse; **buttar giù** to throw down; (culin) to start to cook, e.g., **buttar giù gli spaghetti** to start to cook the spaghetti; (fig) to jot down; **da . . . in giù** for the past . . .; **dar giù** to look worse (*said *of a sick person*); **esser già** to be downcast; **giù dì lì** thereabouts; **in giù** down; downstream; **mandar giù** to swallow; **non andar giù** to not be able to stomach or swallow, e.g., **non gli vanno giù i bugiardi** he cannot stomach liars; **venire giù** to come down; to crumble; to collapse

giubba *f* coat, jacket; mane

giubbétto *m* small coat; bodice; jerkin

giubbòtto *m* jacket (*e.g., of a motorcyclist*); **giubbotto salvagente** (aer, naut) life jacket

giubilare (giùbilo) *tr* to retire, to pension ‖ *intr* to rejoice

giubilèo *m* jubilee

giùbilo *m* jubilation, exultation

giuda *m* Judas ‖ **Giuda** *m* Judas

giudài·co -ca *adj* (-ci -che) Judaic

giudaismo *m* Judaism

giudè·o -a *adj* Judean; Jewish ‖ *mf* Judean; Jew

giudicare §197 **(giùdico)** *tr* to judge; to find (*e.g., s.o. innocent*); to try (*a case*) ‖ *intr* to judge, deem

giudicato *m* (hist) Sardinian region; **passare in giudicato** (law) to become final

giùdice *m* judge; magistrate, justice; **giudice conciliatore** justice of the peace; **giudice popolare** member of the jury

giudizià·rio -ria *adj* (-ri -rie) judicial, judiciary

giudì·zio *m* (-zi) judgment; wisdom; trial; sentence; **giudizio di Dio** (hist) ordeal; **giudizio finale** Last Judgment; **metter giudizio** to mend one's ways

giudizió·so -sa [s] *adj* judicious, wise

giùggiola *f* jujube; (joc) trifle; **andare in brodo di giuggiole** to swoon, become ecstatic

giugno *m* June

giugulare *adj* jugular ‖ *v* **(giùgolo)** *tr* to cut the throat of

giulèbbe *m* julep

giuliana *f* (culin) julienne ‖ **Giuliana** Juliana

giuli·vo -va *adj* gay

giullare *m* jongleur; (pej) mountebank

giumén·to -ta *mf* beast of burden ‖ *f* female saddle horse

giun·ca *f* (-che) (naut) junk

giunchiglia *f* (bot) jonquil

giun·co *m* (-chi) (bot) rush

giùngere §183 *tr* to join (*e.g., one's hands*) ‖ *intr* (ESSERE) to arrive; **giungere a** or **in** to arrive at, reach; **giungere a + inf** to succeed in + *ger*; **mi giunge nuovo** it's news to me

giungla *f* jungle

Giunóne *f* Juno

giunòni·co -ca *adj* (-ci -che) Junoesque

giunta *f* addition; makeweight; strip (*of cloth*); junta; committee; **dì prima giunta** at the very beginning; **per giunta** in addition

giuntare *tr* to join

giuntatrice *f* (mov) splicer

giunto *m* (mach) joint, coupling;

giunto a sfere ball-and-socket joint; **giunto cardanico** universal joint

giuntura or **giunzióne** *f* joint; juncture, seam

giuò·co *m* (-chi) var of **gioco**

giuraménto *m* oath; **deferire il giuramento a** to put under oath

giurare *tr* to swear, pledge ‖ *intr* to swear

giura·to -ta *adj* sworn ‖ *m* juror

giuria *f* committee; jury

giurìdi·co -ca *adj* (-ci -che) juridical

giurisdizióne *f* jurisdiction

giurisprudènza *f* jurisprudence

giurì·sta *mf* (-sti -ste) jurist

Giusèppe *m* Joseph

Giuseppina *f* Josephine

giusta *prep* according to; in accordance with

giustappórre §218 *tr* to juxtapose

giustézza *f* correctness, justness; (typ) measure

giustificàbile *adj* justifiable

giustificare §197 **(giustifico)** *tr* to justify ‖ *ref* to excuse oneself

giustificazióne *f* justification

giustizia *f* justice; **far giustizia a** to execute; **farsi giustizia da sé** to take the law into one's own hands; **render giustizia a** to do justice to

giustiziare §287 *tr* to execute

giustizière *m* executioner; (obs) judge

giu·sto -sta *adj* just; opportune ‖ *m* just man; just price; rights, due ‖ **giusto** *adv* just, justly

gla·bro -bra *adj* smooth (*face*)

glaciale *adj* glacial; (fig) icy

gladiatóre *m* gladiator

gladiòlo *m* gladiolus

glàndola *f* var of **ghiandola**

glassa *f* glaze, icing

glassare *tr* to glaze, ice

glèba *f* clod, lump of earth

gli §4 *art* ‖ §5 *pers pron*

glicerina *f* glycerin

glìcine *m* wistaria

gliéla; gliéle; gliéli; gliélo; gliéne §5

globale *adj* total, aggregate

glòbo *m* globe; **globo oculare** eyeball

globulare *adj* globular, global

glòbulo *m* globule; (physiol) corpuscle

gloglottare (gloglòtto) *intr* to gobble; to gurgle

gloglottì·o *m* (-i) gobble, gobbling; gurgle

glòria *f* glory

gloriare §287 **(glòrio)** *tr* (lit) to exalt ‖ *ref* to boast; to glory

glorificare §197 **(glorifico)** *tr* to glorify

glorió·so -sa [s] *adj* glorious; proud

glòssa *f* gloss

glossà·rio *m* (-ri) glossary

glòttide *f* glottis

glottòlo·go -ga *mf* (-gi -ghe) linguist

glucòsio *m* glucose

glùtine *m* gluten

gnòc·co *m* (-chi) potato dumpling

gnòmo *m* gnome

gnòrri *m invar*—**fare lo gnorri** to feign ignorance

gòb·bo -ba *adj* hunchbacked ‖ *mf*

hunchback ‖ *f* hump; hunch; hump (*of gibbous moon*); hook (*of nose*)

góc·cia *f* (-ce) drop; bead; **avere la goccia al naso** to have a runny nose; **goccia d'acqua** raindrop

góc·cio *m* (-ci) drop, swallow

gócciola *f* drop; bead

gocciolare (**gócciolo**) *tr & intr* to drip

gocciola·tólo *m* (-tói) dripstone

goccioll·o·m (-i) drip, trickle

godére §184 *tr* to enjoy ‖ *intr* to take pleasure; to revel; to profit ‖ *ref* to enjoy; **godersela** to have a good time

godìbile *adj* enjoyable

godiménto *m* enjoyment, pleasure

goffàggine *f* clumsiness

gòf·fo -fa *adj* awkward; ill-fitting

gógna *f* pillory; **mettere alla gogna** to pillory

góla *f* throat; neck; gluttony; gorge (*of mountain*); mouth (*of cannon*); flue (*of chimney*); (archit) ogee; **far gola a** to tempt; **mentire per la gola** to lie shamelessly; **tornare a gola** to repeat (*said of food*)

golétta *f* neck (*of shirt*); (naut) schooner

gòlf *m* (**gòlf**) sweater, cardigan; (sports) golf

gólfo *m* gulf; **golfo mistico** orchestra pit ‖ **Golfo Persico** Persian Gulf

Gòlgota, il Golgotha

goliardo *m* goliard; university student

golosi·tà [s] *f* (-tà) gluttony; tidbit

goló·so -sa [s] *adj* gluttonous; appetizing

gómena *f* hawser

gomitata *f* blow with the elbow; nudge

gómito *m* elbow; bend; **alzare il gomito** to crook the elbow; **dare di gomito a** to nudge

gomìtolo *m* skein, clew

gómma *f* gum; rubber; eraser; tire; **bucare una gomma** to have a flat tire; **gomma arabica** gum arabic; **gomma a terra** flat tire; **gomma da masticare** chewing gum; **gomma lacca** shellac

gommapiuma *f* foam rubber

gomma·to -ta *adj* gummed; with tires

gommatura *f* gumming; (aut) tires

gommi·sta *m* (-sti) tire dealer; tire repairman

gommó·so -sa [s] *adj* gummy

góndola *f* gondola; (aer) pod

gonfalóne *m* gonfalon

gonfiare §287 (**gónfio**) *tr* to inflate, blow up; to bloat; to swell; to exaggerate; to puff up ‖ *intr* (ESSERE) to swell ‖ *ref* to swell; to puff up; to bulge, balloon

gonfiatura *f* inflation; exaggeration

gonfiézza *f* swelling; grandiloquence

gón·fio -fia (-fi -fie) *adj* inflated, swollen; conceited ‖ *m* swelling, bulge

gonfióre *m* swelling

gongolare (**góngolo**) *intr* to rejoice; to be elated

goniòmetro *m* goniometer; protractor

gònna *f* skirt; **gonna pantaloni** culottes

gonnèlla *f* skirt; (fig) petticoat

gonnellino *m* kilt; ballerina skirt

gón·zo -za [dz] *mf* simpleton, fool

gòra *f* millpond; marsh; (coll) spot

górbia *f* tip (*of umbrella*)

gorgheggiare §290 (**gorghéggio**) *tr & intr* to warble; to trill

gorghég·gio *m* (-gi) warbling; trill

gór·go *m* (-ghi) whirlpool; (lit) river

gorgogliare §280 (**gorgóglio**) *intr* to gurgle

gorgó·glio *m* (-gli) gurgle

gorgogli·o·m (-i) gurgling

goril·la *m* (-la) gorilla

gòta *f* cheek; (lit) side

gòti·co -ca *adj & m* (-ci -che) Gothic

Gòto *m* Goth

gótta *f* (pathol) gout

gottazza *f* (naut) scoop

gottó·so -sa [s] *adj* gouty

governale *m* fin (*of bomb*); (obs) rudder

governante *adj* governing ‖ *m* ruler ‖ *f* governess; housekeeper

governare (**govèrno**) *tr* to rule, govern; to steer (*a ship*); to tend (*animals*); to wash and dry (*dishes*); to run (*e.g., a bank*) ‖ *intr* to steer

governati·vo -va *adj* government

govèrno *m* government; tending (*e.g., of animals*); running (*of household*); cleaning (*of house*); blending (*of wine*); (archaic) steering

gózzo *m* crop, craw (*of bird*); (pathol) goiter

gozzovigliare §280 *intr* to go on a spree

gracchiare §287 *intr* to caw

gràc·chio *m* (-chi) caw; (orn) chough

gracidare (**gràcido**) *intr* to croak; to honk (*said, e.g., of a goose*)

gràcile *adj* weak, frail; thin, delicate

gradasso *m* swaggerer, braggadocio

grada·to -ta *adj* graded; gradual

gradazióne *f* gradation; alcoholic proof; **gradazione vocalica** (phonet) ablaut

gradévole *adj* pleasant

gradiménto *m* pleasure; acceptance (*of a product*)

gradinata *f* steps; tier (*of seats*)

gradino *m* step; (fig) stepping stone

gradire §176 *tr* to like; to welcome

gradi·to -ta *adj* agreeable; welcome (*guest*); kind (*letter*)

grado *m* degree; rank; (nav) rating; (archaic) step; **a buon grado o a mal grado** willy-nilly; **a grado a grado** little by little; **a Suo grado** according to your wishes; **di buon grado** willingly; **di secondo grado** secondary (*school*); **essere in grado di** to be in a position to; **saper grado a** (lit) to be grateful to

graduale *adj & m* gradual

graduare (**gràduo**) *tr* to graduate

gradua·to -ta *adj* graduated ‖ *m* noncommissioned officer

graduatòria *f* ranking; rank

graffa *f* clamp; brace; bracket

graffiare §287 *tr* to scratch; (coll) to swipe

graffiétto *m* tiny scratch; marking gage

gràf·fio *m* (-fi) scratch

grafia *f* writing, spelling; (gram) graph

gràfi·co -ca (-ci -che) *adj* graphic ‖ *m* graph, diagram; designer (*for printing industry*); member of printers' union ‖ *f* graphic arts

grafite *f* graphite

grafologia *f* graphology

gragnòla *f* hail

gramàglia *f* crepe; widow's weeds; **in gramàglie** in mourning

gramigna *f* couch grass; weed

grammàti·co -ca (-ci -che) *adj* grammatical ‖ *m* grammarian ‖ *f* grammar

grammo *m* gram

grammofòni·co -ca *adj* (**-ci -che**) phonograph, recording

grammòfono *m* phonograph, record player

gra·mo -ma *adj* poor, sad; wretched, miserable; frail, sickly

gran *adj* apocopated form of **grande**, used before singular and plural nouns beginning with a consonant sound other than *gn, pn, ps*, impure *s, x,* and *z*

gra·na *m* (**-na**) Parmesan cheese ‖ *f* (**-ne**) cochineal; grain (*of wood, metal, etc*); (slang) dough; (coll) trouble

granàglie *fpl* grain, cereals

gra·nàio *m* (**-nài**) granary, barn

granata *adj invar* & *m* garnet (*color*) ‖ *f* pomegranate (*fruit*); garnet; broom; grenade

granatière *m* grenadier

granatina *f* grenadine

Gran Bretagna, la Great Britain

grancassa *f* bass drum

grancèvola *f* spider crab

gràn·chio *m* (**-chi**) crab; claw (*of hammer*); (coll) cramp; **prendere un granchio** to make a blunder

grandangolare *adj* wide-angle

grande *adj* big, large; great; tall; high (*mass; voice*); long (*time*); capital (*letter*); full (*speed*); grown-up ‖ *m* grownup; grandeur; grandee; **fare il grande** to show off; **i grandi** the great; **in grande** on a large scale; lavishly

grandézza *f* size; enormity; greatness; quantity; **in grandezza naturale** lifesize; **grandezze** ostentatiousness

grandezzó·so -sa [s] *adj* ostentatious

grandiloquènza *f* grandiloquence

grandinare (gràndino) *tr* (obs) to hail ‖ *intr* to hail ‖ *impers* (ESSERE & AVERE)—**grandina** it is hailing

grandinata *f* hailstorm

gràndine *f* hail

grandiosi·tà [s] *f* (**-tà**) grandeur, magnificence

grandió·so -sa [s] *adj* grandiose, grand

grandu·ca *m* (**-chi**) grand duke

granduchéssa *f* grand duchess

granèllo *m* grain, seed; speck

gxànfia *f* clutch

granìco·lo -la *adj* grain, wheat

granire §176 *tr* to grain; to stipple; (mus) to make (*the notes*) clear-cut ‖ *intr* to teethe

granita *f* sherbet, water ice

granito *m* granite

granitura *f* knurl, milled edge

grano *m* wheat; grain of wheat; grain; speck; **grano duro** durum wheat; **grano saraceno** buckwheat; **grano turco** corn

granturco *m* corn

granulare *adj* granular ‖ *v* (**grànulo**) *tr* to granulate

granulatóre *m* crusher

grànulo *m* granule, pellet, bud

granuló·so -sa [s] *adj* granular; lumpy; gritty; friable, crumbly

grappa *f* eau de vie; clamp, brace

grappétta *f* staple; crampon

grappino *m* (naut) grapnel

gràppolo *m* bunch, cluster

grassàg·gio *m* (**-gi**) (aut) lubrication

grassatóre *m* highwayman

grassazióne *f* holdup

grassétto *m* boldface

grassézza *f* fatness; richness

gras·so -sa *adj* fat; rich; greasy; risqué ‖ *m* fat, suet; grease; shortening

grassòc·cio -cia *adj* (**-ci -ce**) pudgy, plump

grata *f* grate, grating

gratèlla *f* strainer; sieve; broiler

gratic·cia *f* (**-ce**) (theat) gridiron

gratíc·cio *m* (**-ci**) lattice, trellis

gratìcola *f* gridiron; grating; graticule

gratifi·ca *f* (**-che**) bonus

gratificare §197 (**gratìfico**) *tr* to give a bonus to; (fig) to pelt (*with insults*)

gratificazióne *f* bonus

gratis *adv* gratis, free, for nothing

gratitùdine *f* gratitude

gra·to -ta *adj* grateful, appreciative ‖ *f* see **grata**

grattacapo *m* trouble, worry

grattacièlo *m* skyscraper

grattare *tr* to scratch; to scrape; to grate; (slang) to snitch ‖ *intr* to scratch; to grate

grattùgia *f* grater

grattugiare §290 *tr* to grate

gratùi·to -ta *adj* gratuitous, free

gravame *m* burden; tax; (law) appeal; **fare gravame a qlcu di qlco** to impute s.th to s.o.

gravare *tr* to burden, oppress; (obs) to seize ‖ *intr* (ESSERE & AVERE) to weigh; to lie; to be sorry, e.g., **gli grava d'avermi disturbato** he is sorry to have bothered me ‖ *ref*—**gravarsi di** to take upon oneself

grave *adj* heavy; burdensome; grave, serious ‖ *m* (phys) body; **stare sul grave** to put on airs

graveolènte *adj* stinking

gravézza *f* heaviness; burden; oppression; (obs) taxation

gravidanza *f* pregnancy

gràvi·do -da *adj* pregnant; fraught

gravi·tà *f* (**-tà**) gravity

gravitare (gràvito) *intr* ṭo gravitate; to weigh, lie

gravitazióne *f* gravitation

gravó·so -sa [s] *adj* heavy; hard, burdensome; oppressive

gràzia *f* grace; pardon, mercy; delicacy; kindness; **di grazia!** please!;

essere nelle grazie di qlcu to be in s.o.'s good graces; fare grazia di qlco a qlcu to spare s.o. s.th; grazia di Dio abundance, bounty; grazie! thank you!; grazie tante! thanks a lot!; in grazia di thanks to; male grazie bad manners; per grazie as a favor; render grazia a to thank; saper grazia a to be thankful to

graziare §287 tr to pardon; graziare qlcu di qlco to grant s.th to s.o.

grazió·so -sa [s] adj graceful, pretty; gracious; (lit) free, gratuitous

Grècia, la Greece

grè·co -ca (-ci -che) adj & mf Greek || f fret, fretwork; bullion (on Italian general's hat); tunic

gregà·rio -ria (-ri -rie) adj gregarious || m private; follower

grég·ge m (-gi or -ge fpl) flock, herd

grég·gio -gia (-gi -ge) adj coarse; raw, unrefined || m crude oil

gregoria·no -na adj Gregorian

grembiale m var of grembiule

grembiule m apron; frock; smock

grembiulino m pinafore

grèmbo m lap; womb; bosom

gremire §176 tr to crowd || ref to become crowded

gremi·to -ta adj overcrowded

gréppia f manger, crib

gréto m dry gravel bed of a river

grettézza f stinginess; narrow-mindedness

grét·to -ta adj stingy; narrow-minded

grève adj heavy; uncouth; (lit) grievous

gréz·zo -za [ddzz] adj raw, crude; coarse

gridare tr to cry out; to cry for (help); (coll) to scold || intr to cry out, shout

grido m cry (of animal) || m (grida fpl) cry; scream; shout; yell; fame; di grido famous; grido di guerra war cry; ultimo grido latest fashion

grifa·gno -gna adj rapacious, fierce

griffa f hobnail; (mov, phot) sprocket

grifo m snout (of pig); (pej) snoot; (lit) griffin

grifóne m vulture; (mythol) griffin

grigia·stro -stra adj grayish

gri·gio -gia adj & m (-gi -gie) grey

grigiovérde adj invar olive-drab || m olive-drab uniform

griglia f gridiron, broiler; grate, grille; (elec) grid (of vacuum tube)

grillare tr to grill, broil || intr to sizzle; to bubble (said of fermenting wine); to have a sudden whim

grillétto m trigger

grillo m cricket; whim, fancy

grimaldèllo m picklock

grinfia f claw, clutch; grinfie clutches

grinta f grim or forbidding face

grinza f wrinkle; crease; non fare una grinza to be perfect

grinzó·so -sa [s] adj wrinkled; creased

grippare intr & ref to bind, jam

grisèlla f (naut) ratline

gri·sou m (-sou) firedamp

grissino m breadstick

Groenlàndia, la Greenland

grómma f incrustation, deposit

grónda f eaves; slope (of ground)

grondàia f gutter (of roof)

grondare (gróndo) tr to drip || intr (ESSERE) to ooze (said, e.g., of perspiration); to drip; grondare di sangue to stream with blood

gròppa f back (of animal); top (of mountain); restare sulla groppa a to be stuck with, e.g., gli sono restati sulla groppa cento esemplari he is stuck with one hundred copies

groppata f bucking (of horse)

gróppo m knot, tangle; lump (in throat); squall

groppóne m back, rump

gròssa f gross; dormire della grossa to sleep like a log

grossézza f bigness; thickness; density; swelling (of river); (fig) coarseness; grossezza d'udito hardness of hearing

grossi·sta mf (-sti -ste) wholesaler

gròs·so -sa adj big, large; thick; heavy (seas); swollen (river); hard (breathing); offensive (words); coarse (e.g., salt); pregnant; deep (voice); (coll) important; alla grossa approximately; di grosso a lot, very much; dirla grossa to talk nonsense; farla grossa to make a blunder; grosso d'udito hard of hearing; in grosso wholesale; sparare grosse to tell tall tales || m bulk; main body (e.g., of an army) || f see grossa

grossola·no -na adj coarse; boorish, uncouth; big (blunder)

gròtta f grotto; (coll) inn

grotté·sco -sca (-schi -sche) adj & m grotesque || f (hist) grotesque painting

grovièra f Gruyère cheese

grovì·glio m (-gli) tangle, snarl

gru f (gru) (orn, mach) crane

grùc·cia f (-ce) crutch; clothes hanger; (obs) wooden leg

grufolare (grùfolo) intr to nuzzle || ref to wallow (in mud)

grugnire §176 tr & intr to grunt

grugnìto m grunt

grugno m snout; (pej) snoot; fare il grugno to sulk

grui·sta m (-sti) crane operator

grulleria f foolishness

grul·lo -la adj silly, simple

gruma f deposit, incrustation

grumo m lump; clot

grùmolo m heart (e.g., of lettuce); small lump

grumó·so -sa [s] adj lumpy; incrusted, scaly

gruppo m group; main body (e.g., of runners); club; gruppo elettrogeno generating unit; gruppo motore (aut) power plant

grùzzolo m hoard, pile; farsi il gruzzolo to feather one's nest

guadagnare tr to earn; to win; to gain; to pick up (speed); to reach (port) || intr to win; to look better || ref to win; to win over; guadagnarsi il pane or la vita to earn one's living

guadagno m earnings; profit; a basso

guadagno (rad, telv) low-gain; **ad alto guadagno** (rad, telv) high-gain
guadare *tr* to wade, ford
guado *m* ford; (bot) woad; **passare a guado** to ford
guài *interj* woe!
guaina *f* case; scabbard, sheath; corset; (aut) seat cover
guàio *m* (**guài**) trouble ‖ *interj* see **guài**
guaire §176 *intr* to yelp; to whine
guaito *m* yelp, whine
gualcire §176 *tr* to crumple
gualdrappa *f* saddlecloth
Gualtièro *m* Walter
guàn·cia *f* (**-ce**) cheek; moldboard; cheek side (*of gunstock*)
guanciale *m* pillow; **dormire tra due guanciali** to sleep safe and sound
guan·tàio -tàia *mf* (**-tài -tàie**) glove maker; glove merchant
guanterìa *f* glove factory
guantièra *f* glove case; tray
guanto *m* glove; **gettare il guanto** to fling down the gauntlet; **raccogliere il guanto** to take up the gauntlet; **trattare con i guanti gialli** to handle with kid gloves
guantóne *m* big glove; **guantoni da pugilato** boxing gloves
guardabarriè·re *m* (**-re**) (rr) gatekeeper, crossing watchman
guardabò·schi *m* (**-schi**) forester
guardacàc·cia *m* (**-cia**) gamekeeper
guardacò·ste *m* (**-ste**) coast guard; coast-guard cutter
guardafì·li *m* (**-li**) (elec) lineman
guardalì·nee *m* (**-nee**) (rr) trackwalker; (sports) linesman
guardama·no *m* (**-no**) guard (*of sabre or rifle*); work glove; (naut) handrail
guardaportó·ne *m* (**-ne**) doorman
guardare *tr* to look at; to protect, watch; to pay attention to; to face, overlook; (obs) to keep to (*one's bed*); (obs) to keep to (*a holiday*); **guardare a vista** to keep under close watch; **guardare dall'alto in basso** to look down one's nose at; **guardare di sotto in su** to leer at ‖ *intr* to look; to pay attention; **Dio guardi!** God forbid!; **guardare a** to face (*said, e.g., of a room*); **guardare di non + inf** to be careful not to + *inf*; **guardare in faccia** to face (*e.g., danger*); **stare a guardare** to keep on the sidelines ‖ *ref* to look at one another; to look at oneself; **guardarsi da** to keep from; to guard against
guardarò·ba *m* (**-ba**) wardrobe; linen closet; checkroom, cloakroom
guardarobiè·re -ra *mf* hatcheck attendant ‖ *f* hatcheck girl
guardasigìl·li *m* (**-li**) minister of justice (*in Italy*); (Brit) Lord Privy Seal; (U.S.A.) attorney general; (hist) keeper of the seals
guardaspal·le *m* (**-le**) bodyguard
guardata *f* quick look, glance
guarda·vìa *m* (**-via**) guardrail; median strip
guàrdia *f* watch; guard; top water level; flyleaf; **di guardia** on duty;

fare la guardia a to watch; **guardia campestre** forester; **guardia carceraria** prison guard; **guardia del corpo** guard, body guard; **guardia di finanza** customs officer; **guardia d'onore** honor guard; **guardia forestale** forester; park guard; **guardia giurata** private policeman; **guardia medica** emergency clinic; **guardia municipale** police officer; **guardia notturna** night watch; **mettere qlcu in guardia** to warn s.o.; **montare la guardia** to be on guard duty, keep guard; **stare in guardia** to be on one's guard
guardiamari·na *m* (**-na**) (nav) ensign
guardiano *m* keeper; warden; watchdog; (eccl) superior; **guardiano notturno** night watchman
guardìna *f* lockup; **in guardina** in jail
guardinfante *m* bustle (*worn under the back of a woman's skirt*)
guardìn·go -ga *adj* (**-ghi -ghe**) wary
guàrdolo *m* welt (*in shoe*)
guardóne *m* peeping tom
guarentì·gia *f* (**-gie**) guarantee
guarìbile *adj* curable
guarigióne *f* cure, recovery
guarire §176 *tr* to cure; to heal ‖ *intr* (ESSERE) to recover; to heal
guaritóre *m* healer; quack
guarnigióne *f* (mil) garrison
guarnire §176 *tr* to equip; to rig; to trim; (naut) to rig; (culin) to garnish ‖ *intr* to add beauty
guarnizióne *f* decoration; trimming; lining; (culin) garniture; (mach) gasket; (mach) washer
Guascógna, la Gascony
guascó·ne -na *adj* & *mf* Gascon
guastafè·ste *mf* (**-ste**) kill-joy
guastare *tr* to ruin, spoil; to undo; to wreck; (obs) to lay waste; **guastare le uova nel paniere a** to spoil the plans of (*ref* to spoil; to worsen (*said, e.g., of the weather*); (mach) to break down; **guastarsi con qlcu** to quarrel with s.o.; **guastarsi il sangue** to blow one's top
guastatóre *m* commando
gua·sto -sta *adj* ruined, spoiled; wrecked ‖ *m* breakdown; corruption; discord
guatare *tr* (lit) to look askance or with fear at
Guayana, la Guyana
guazza *f* dew
guazzabù·glio *m* (**-gli**) muddle, mess
guazzare *tr* to make (*an animal*) wade in a river ‖ *intr* to wallow
guazzétto *m* stew, ragout
guazzo *m* puddle, pool; gouache
guèl·fo -fa *adj* & *mf* Guelph
guèr·cio -cia (**-ci -ce**) *adj* cross-eyed; one-eyed; almost blind ‖ *mf* cross-eyed person; one-eyed person
guèrra *f* war; warfare; **guerra a coltello** internecine feud; **guerra di Troia** Trojan war; **guerra fredda** cold war; **guerra lampo** blitzkrieg; **guerra mondiale** world war

guerrafon·dàio **-dàia** (**-dài** **-dàie**) *adj* warmongering ‖ *mf* warmonger

guerreggiare *tr* §290 (**guerréggio**) *tr* to fight, war against ‖ *intr* to fight ‖ *ref* to make war on one another

guerré·sco **-sca** *adj* (**-schi** **-sche**) warlike

guerriè·ro **-ra** *adj* war, warlike ‖ *mf* fighter ‖ *m* warrior

guerriglia *f* guerrilla

guerriglièro *m* guerrilla (*soldier*)

gufo *m* misanthrope; (orn) horned owl

gùglia *f* spire; peak

gugliata *f* needleful

Guglièlmo *m* William

guida *f* guide; guidance; driving; runner (*rug*); guidebook; manual (*of instruction*); (aut) steering; **guida a destra** right-hand drive; **guide reins** (*of horse*); (mach) slide

guidaiòlo *m* leader (*among animals*)

guidare *tr* to guide, lead; to steer; to drive ‖ *intr* to drive ‖ *ref* to restrain oneself

guida·tóre **-trice** *mf* driver

guilderdóne *m* (lit) premium, prize

guidóne *m* pennant, pennon

guidoslitta *f* bobsled

guidovia *f* ski lift

Guinèa, la Guinea

guinzà·glio *m* (**-gli**) leash; (fig) fetter, shackle

guisa *f* way, manner; **in guisa che** so that; **in guisa di** under the guise of

guit·to **-ta** *adj* miserly, niggardly ‖ *m* strolling player

guizzare *intr* to dart; to wriggle; to flash (*said of lightning*); (naut) to yaw ‖ *intr* (ESSERE) to slip away

guizzo *m* dart; wriggle; flash

gù·scio *m* (**-sci**) shell; pod (*of pea*); tick (*of mattress*); **guscio di noce** nutshell; **guscio d'uovo** eggshell

gustare *tr* to taste; to relish ‖ *intr* (ESSERE & AVERE) to please; to like, e.g., **gli gustano le gite in barca** he likes boat rides

gusto *m* taste; pleasure, fun; whim; style; **di cattivo gusto** tasteless; **di gusto** gladly, with gusto; **prendere gusto per** to take a liking for; **prendersi il gusto di** to relish; **provar gusto** to have fun

gustó·so **-sa** [s] *adj* tasty

guttapèrca *f* gutta-percha

gutturale *adj & f* guttural

H

H, h [ˈakkɑ] *m & f* eighth letter of the Italian alphabet

handicappare *tr* var of **andicappare**

hangar *m* (**hangar**) hangar

havaia·no **-na** *adj & mf* Hawaiian

henné *m* henna

hertz *m* hertz

hertzia·no **-na** *adj* Hertzian

hi-fi *f* (coll) hi-fi

hockei·sta *m* (**-sti**) hockey player

hollywoodia·no **-na** *adj* Hollywood, Hollywood-like

hurrà *interj* hurrah!

I

I, i, [i] *m & f* ninth letter of the Italian alphabet

i §4 *def art* the

iarda *f* yard

iato *m* hiatus

iattanza *f* boasting, bragging

iattura *f* misfortune, calamity

ibèri·co **-ca** *adj* (**-ci** **-che**) Iberian

ibernare (**ibèrno**) *intr* to hibernate

ibi·sco *m* (**-schi**) hibiscus

ibridare (**ìbrido**) *tr & intr* to hybridize

ìbri·do **-da** *adj & m* hybrid

icàsti·co **-ca** *adj* (**-ci** **-che**) figurative; realistic

-ìccio **-ìccia** *suf adj* -ish, e.g., **gialliccio** yellowish

iconocla·sta *mf* (**-sti** **-ste**) iconoclast

iconografia *f* iconography

iconoscò·pio *m* (**-pi**) iconoscope

iddì·o *m* (**-i**) god ‖ **Iddio** *m* God

idèa *f* idea; goal, purpose; bit, touch; **avere idea di** to have a mind to; **dare l'idea di** to seem; **farsi un'idea di** to grasp the notion of; **idea fissa** fixed idea; **neanche per idea** not in the least

ideale *adj & m* ideal

idealismo *m* idealism

ideali·sta *mf* (**-sti** **-ste**) idealist

idealìsti·co **-ca** *adj* (**-ci** **-che**) idealistic

idealizzare [ddzz] *tr* to idealize

ideare (**idèo**) *tr* to conceive

idea·tóre **-trice** *mf* inventor

idem *adv* ditto

idènti·co **-ca** *adj* (**-ci** **-che**) identical

identificare §197 (**identìfico**) *tr* to identify ‖ *ref* to resemble each other; **identificarsi con** to identify with

identificazióne *f* identification

identi·tà *f* (**-tà**) identity

ideologia *f* ideology

idi *mpl & fpl* ides

idìlli·co **-ca** *adj* (**-ci** **-che**) idyllic

idìl·lio *m* (**-li**) idyll; romance

idiò·ma *m* (**-mi**) language, idiom

idiomàti·co **-ca** *adj* (**-ci** **-che**) idiomatic

idiosincrasìa f aversion; (med) idiosyncrasy

idiò·ta (-ti -te) adj idiotic ‖ mf idiot

idiotismo m idiom; idiocy

idiozìa f idiocy

idolatrare tr & intr to idolize

idolatrìa f idolatry

idolo m idol

idonei·tà f (-tà) fitness, aptitude; qualification

idòne·o -a adj fit; qualified; opportune

idra f hydra

idrante m hydrant, fireplug

idratante adj moisturizing

idratare tr & ref to hydrate

idrato m hydrate

idràuli·co -ca (-ci -che) adj hydraulic ‖ m plumber ‖ f hydraulics

idrì·co -ca adj (-ci -che) water, e.g., forza idrica water power

idrocarburo m hydrocarbon

idroelèttri·co -ca adj (-ci -che) hydroelectric

idròfi·lo -la adj absorbent

idrofobìa f hydrophobia, rabies

idròfo·bo -ba adj hydrophobic, rabid

idròfu·go -ga adj (-ghi -ghe) waterproof

idrogenare (idrògeno) tr to hydrogenate

idrògeno m hydrogen

idròpi·co -ca (-ci -che) adj dropsical ‖ mf patient suffering from dropsy

idropisìa f dropsy

idroplano m hydroplane (boat)

idropòrto m seaplane airport

idrorepellènte adj water-repellent

idroscalo m seaplane airport

idro·scì m (-scì) water ski

idroscivolante m (naut) hydroplane

idrosilurante m torpedo plane

idròssido m hydroxide

idroterapìa f hydrotherapy

idrovìa f inland waterway

idrovolante m seaplane, hydroplane

idròvo·ro -ra adj suction (pump) ‖ f suction pump

ièna f hyena

ièri m & adv yesterday; ieri l'altro the day before yesterday; ieri notte last night; ieri sera last evening, last night, yesterday evening

ietta·tóre -trice mf hoodoo

iettatura f evil eye; bad luck, jinx

igiène f hygiene; sanitation

igièni·co -ca adj (-ci -che) hygienic, sanitary

igname m yam

igna·ro -ra adj unaware; inexperienced

igna·vo -va adj (lit) slothful

ignizióne f ignition

ignòbile adj (lit) ignoble

ignominìa f ignominy; outrage

ignominió·so -sa [s] adj ignominious

ignorante adj ignorant; illiterate ‖ mf ignoramus

ignoranza f ignorance

ignorare (ignòro) tr to not know; to ignore

ignò·to -ta adj & m unknown

ignu·do -da adj (lit) naked ‖ m (lit) naked person

il §4 def art the

ilare adj cheerful

ilari·tà f (-tà) cheerfulness; laughter

ilice f (lit) ilex, holm oak

ilio m (anat) ilium

illanguidire §176 tr to weaken ‖ intr (ESSERE) to get weak

illazióne f inference

illéci·to -ta adj illicit, unlawful ‖ m unlawful act

illegale adj illegal

illeggiadrire §176 tr to embellish

illeggìbile adj illegible

illegìtti·mo -ma adj illegitimate

illé·so -sa adj unhurt, unharmed

illettera·to -ta adj & mf illiterate

illìba·to -ta adj spotless, pure

illimita·to -ta adj unlimited

illìri·co -ca adj (-ci -che) Illyrian

illògi·co -ca adj (-ci -che) illogical

illùdere §105 tr to delude

illuminare (illùmino) tr to illuminate; to brighten; to enlighten ‖ ref to grow bright

illumina·to -ta adj illuminated; enlightened; educated

illuminazióne f illumination; enlightenment

illuminismo m Age of Enlightenment

illusióne f illusion; delusion; farsi illusioni to indulge in wishful thinking

illusionismo m sleight of hand; magic

illusioni·sta mf (-sti -ste) magician

illu·so -sa adj deluded ‖ mf deluded person

illusò·rio -ria adj (-ri -rie) illusory, illusive

illustrare tr to illustrate; to explain, elucidate ‖ ref to become famous

illustra·to -ta adj illustrated, pictorial

illustra·tóre -trice mf illustrator

illustrazióne f illustration; illustrious person

illustre adj illustrious, famous

illustrìssi·mo -ma adj distinguished; honorable; **Illustrissimo Signore** Dear Sir; Mr. (addressing a letter)

imbacuccare §197 tr & ref to muffle up; to wrap up

imbaldanzire §176 tr to embolden ‖ intr (ESSERE) & ref to grow bold

imballàg·gio m (-gi) wrapping, packaging

imballare tr to wrap up, package; to bale; to race (the motor); **imballare in una gabbia** to crate ‖ ref to race (said of a motor)

imballa·tóre -trice mf packer

imballo m packing; packaging, wrapping; racing (of motor)

imbalsamare (imbàlsamo) tr to embalm; to stuff (animals)

imbambola·to -ta adj gazing, staring; stunned, dumfounded; sleepy-eyed; sluggish

imbandierare (imbandièro) tr to bedeck with flags

imbandire §176 tr to prepare (food, a meal, a table) lavishly

imbarazzante adj embarrassing, awkward

imbarazzare tr to embarrass; to encumber, hamper; to upset (the stomach)

imbarazza·to -ta *adj* embarrassed, perplexed; upset (*stomach*); ill-at-ease

imbarazzo *m* embarrassment, annoyance; **imbarazzo di stomaco** upset stomach

imbarbarire §176 *tr & ref* to make barbarous; to corrupt (*a language*)

imbarcadèro *m* landing pier

imbarcare §197 *tr* to ship; to load, embark; to ship (*water*) ‖ *ref* to sail; to embark; to curve (*said of furniture*)

imbarca·tóio *m* (-**tói**) landing pier

imbarcazióne *f* boat; **imbarcazione di salvataggio** lifeboat

imbar·co *m* (-**chi**) embarkation; port of embarkation

imbardare *intr & ref* (aer) to yaw; (aut) to swerve, lurch

imbardata *f* (aer) yaw; (aut) swerve, lurch

imbarilare *tr* to barrel

imbastardire §176 *tr* to corrupt ‖ *ref* to become corrupt

imbastire §176 *tr* (sew) to baste; (fig) to sketch out

imbastitura *f* (sew) basting

imbàttere *ref*—**imbattersi bene** to be lucky; **imbattersi in** to come across; **imbattersi male** to have bad luck

imbattibile *adj* unbeatable

imbavagliare §280 *tr* to gag

imbeccare §197 (**imbécco**) *tr* to feed (*a fledgling*); (fig) to prompt

imbeccata *f* beakful; (fig) prompting

imbecillàggine *f* imbecility

imbecille *adj & mf* imbecile

imbecilli·tà *f* (-**tà**) imbecility

imbèlle *adj* unwarlike; cowardly

imbellettare (**imbellétto**) *tr* to apply rouge, to apply make-up on ‖ *ref* to put on make-up

imbellire §176 *tr* to embellish

imbèrbe *adj* beardless; callow

imbestialire §176 *tr* to enrage ‖ *intr* (ESSERE) & *ref* to become enraged

imbévere §185 *tr* to soak; to soak up; to imbue ‖ *ref* to become soaked; to become imbued

imbiancare §197 *tr* to whiten; to bleach; to whitewash ‖ *intr* (ESSERE) & *ref* to turn white (*said, e.g., of hair*); to clear up (*said of weather*)

imbiancatura *f* bleaching (*of laundry*); whitening; whitewashing

imbianchimento *m* bleaching

imbianchino *m* whitewasher; house painter; (pej) dauber

imbianchire §176 *tr* to whiten; to bleach ‖ *ref* to turn white

imbiondire §176 *tr* to bleach (*hair*) ‖ *intr* to become blond; to ripen (*said of wheat*)

imbizzarrire [ddzz] *intr* (ESSERE) & *ref* to become skittish (*said of a horse*); to become infuriated

imbizzire [ddzz] §176 *intr* (ESSERE) to get angry

imboccare §197 (**imbócco**) *tr* to feed by mouth; to put (*an instrument*) in one's mouth; to take, enter (*a road*); to prompt ‖ *intr* (ESSERE) to

flow; to open (*said of a road*); (mach) to fit

imboccatura *f* entrance (*of street*); inlet; opening, top (*e.g., of bottle*); bit (*of bridle*); (mus) mouthpiece; **avere l'imboccatura a** to be experienced in

imbóc·co *m* (-**chi**) entrance; inlet; opening

imbonimento *m* claptrap

imbonire §176 *tr* to lure, entice (*s.o. to buy or enter*)

imbonitóre *m* barker

imborghesire §176 *tr* to render middle-class ‖ *intr* (ESSERE) to become middle-class

imboscare §197 (**imbòsco**) *tr* to hide; to hide (*s.o.*) underground ‖ *ref* to shirk; to be a slacker

imbosca·to -ta *adj* (mil) shirking, draft-dodging ‖ *m* (mil) slacker; (mil) goldbrick ‖ *f* ambush; **tendere un'imboscata** to set an ambush

imboscatóre *m* accomplice of a draft dodger; hoarder (*of scarce items*)

imboschire §176 *tr* to forest

imbottare (**imbótto**) *tr* to barrel

imbottigliare §280 *tr* to bottle; to bottle up ‖ *ref* to get bottled up (*said of traffic*)

imbottire §176 *tr* to pad, fill; to stuff; to pad (*a speech*)

imbottita *f* bedspread, quilt

imbottitura *f* padding

imbra·ca *f* (-**che**) breeching strap (*of harness*); safety belt; (naut) sling

imbracare §197 *tr* to sling

imbracciare §128 *tr* to fasten (*shield*); to level (*gun*)

imbrancare §197 *tr & ref* to herd

imbrattacar·te *mf* (-**te**) scribbler

imbrattamu·ri *mf* (-**ri**) dauber

imbrattare *tr* to soil, dirty; to smudge, smear

imbrattaté·le *mf* (-**le**) dauber

imbratto *m* dirt; smudge, smear; daub; scribble; swill

imbrigliare §280 *tr* to bridle

imbroccare §197 (**imbròcco**) *tr* to hit (*the target*); to guess right

imbrodare (**imbròdo**) *tr* to soil

imbrogliare §280 (**imbròglio**) *tr* to cheat; to mix up; to tangle; to confuse; **imbrogliare le vele** (naut) to take in the reef ‖ *ref* to get tangled up; to get confused; to turn bad (*said of weather*)

imbrò·glio *m* (-**gli**) cheat; tangle; (naut) reef; **cacciarsi in un imbroglio** to get involved in a mess

imbroglió·ne -na *mf* swindler

imbronciare §128 (**imbróncio**) *intr* (ESSERE) & *ref* to pout, sulk ‖ *ref* to lower (*said of the weather*)

imbroncia·to -ta *adj* sulky, surly; cloudy, overcast

imbrunire *m*—**sull'imbrunire** at nightfall ‖ *intr* (ESSERE) to turn brown ‖ *impers* (ESSERE)—**imbrunisce** it is growing dark

imbruttire §176 *tr* to mar; to make ugly ‖ *intr* (ESSERE) & *ref* to grow ugly

imbucare §197 *tr* to mail; to put in a hole ‖ *ref* to hide

imburrare *tr* to butter
imbuto *m* funnel
imène *m* (anat) hymen, maidenhead
imitare (**ìmito**) *tr* to imitate
imita·tóre -trice *mf* imitator; (theat) mimic
imitazióne *f* imitation
immacola·to -ta *adj* immaculate
immagazzinare [ddzz] *tr* to store, store up
immaginare (**immàgino**) *tr* to imagine; to guess; to invent || *ref*—**sì immaginì!** of course!; not at all!
immaginà·rio -ria *adj* (-**ri -rie**) imaginary
immaginativa *f* imagination
immaginazióne *f* imagination
immàgine *f* image; picture
immaginó·so -sa (-**sa**) *adj* imaginative
immalinconire §176 *tr* to sadden || *intr* (ESSERE) & *ref* to become melancholy
immancàbile *adj* unfailing; certain
immane *adj* monstruous; gigantic
immangiàbile *adj* uneatable, inedible
immantinènte *adv* (lit) immediately
immarcescìbile *adj* incorruptible
immateriale *adj* immaterial
immatricolare (**immatrìcolo**) *tr* to matriculate
immatricolazióne *f* matriculation
immatu·ro -ra *adj* immature; premature
immedesimare (**immedésimo**) *tr* to identify; to blend || *ref* to identify oneself
immediataménte *adv* immediately
immediatézza *f* immediacy
immedia·to -ta *adj* immediate
immemoràbile *adj* immemorial
immèmore *adj* forgetful
immèn·so -sa *adj* immense, huge
immèrgere §162 *tr* to immerse; to plunge || *ref* to plunge; to become absorbed
immerita·to -ta *adj* undeserved
immeritévole *adj* undeserving
immersióne *f* immersion; submersion (of a submarine); (naut) draft
imméttere §198 *tr* to let in; **immettere qlcu nel possesso di** (law) to grant s.o. possession of
immigrante *adj* & *mf* immigrant
immigrare *intr* (ESSERE) to immigrate
immigrazióne *f* immigration; (biol) migration
imminènte *adj* imminent
imminènza *f* imminence
immischiare §287 *tr* to involve || *ref* to meddle; to become involved
immiserire §176 *tr* to impoverish || *intr* (ESSERE) & *ref* to become impoverished; to become debased
immissà·rio *m* (-**ri**) tributary
immissióne *f* letting in, introduction; intake; insertion (in lunar orbit)
immòbile *adj* motionless, immobile; real (property) || **immobili** *mpl* real estate
immobiliare *adj* real, e.g., **proprietà immobiliare** real estate; real-estate, e.g., **imposta immobiliare** real-estate tax
immobilizzare [ddzz] *tr* to immobilize; to pin down; to tie up (capital)

immodè·sto -sta *adj* indecent; immodest
immolare (**immòlo**) *tr* to immolate
immondézza *f* filth; impurity
immondez·zàio *m* (-**zài**) rubbish heap, dump; garbage can
immondìzia *f* trash; garbage; filth
immón·do -da *adj* filthy, dirty; unclean
immorale *adj* immoral
immorali·tà *f* (-**tà**) immorality
immortalare *tr* to immortalize
immortale *adj* immortal
immortalità *f* immortality
immò·to -ta *adj* (lit) motionless
immune *adj* immune
immunizzare [ddzz] *tr* to immunize
immutàbile *adj* immutable
immuta·to -ta *adj* unchanged
i·mo -ma *adj* (lit) bottom, lowest || *m* (lit) bottom; (lit) depth
impaccare §197 *tr* to pack, wrap up
impacchettare (**impacchétto**) *tr* to pack, bundle
impacciare §128 *tr* to hamper; to embarrass || *ref* to meddle
impaccia·to -ta *adj* hampered; clumsy
impàc·cio *m* (-**ci**) embarrassment; hindrance; trouble; **essere d'impaccio** to be in the way
impac·co *m* (-**chi**) wrapping; (med) compress
impadronire §176 *ref*—**impadronirsi di** to seize; to take possession of; to master (a language)
impagàbile *adj* invaluable, priceless
impaginare (**impàgino**) *tr* (typ) to make up (in pages), paginate
impaginato *m* (typ) page proof
impagliare §280 *tr* to cane (a chair); to stuff (an animal; a doll); to pack in straw
impalare *tr* to impale; to tie to a pole or stake || *ref* to stiffen up
impala·to -ta *adj* stiff, rigid
impalcatura *f* scaffold; frame, framework
impallidire §176 *intr* to turn pale; to blanch; to grow dim (said of a star); (fig) to wane
impalmare *tr* (lit) to wed
impalpàbile *adj* impalpable
impaludare *tr* to make swampy or marshy || *intr* to become marshy
impanare *tr* to bread; to thread (a screw) || *intr* to screw in
impaniare §287 *tr* to trap, ensnare || *ref* to fall into the trap
impantanare *tr* to turn into a swamp || *ref* to get stuck, to sink (in vice)
impaperare (**impàpero**) *ref* to fluff, make a slip
impappinare *tr* to confuse || *ref* to blunder; to stammer
imparare *tr* to learn; **imparare a memoria** to learn by heart || *intr* **imparare a** to learn to, to learn how to
impareggiàbile *adj* peerless, unmatched
imparentare (**imparènto**) *tr* to bring into the family || *ref*—**imparentarsi con** to marry into
ìmpari *adj* odd, uneven
imparrucca·to -ta *adj* bewigged
impartire §176 *tr* to impart
imparziale *adj* impartial

impasse *f* blind alley; deadlock; (cards) finesse

impassìbile *adj* impassible, impassive

impastare *tr* to knead; to mix; to smear with paste

impasta·to -ta *adj* kneaded; smeared; **impastato di** tainted with; overwhelmed with (*sleep*)

impasto *m* paste; pastiche

impastoiare §287 (**impastóio**) *tr* to fetter, hamstring

impataccare §197 *tr* to besmear, soil

impattare *tr* to even up; to tie (*a game*); **impattarla con** to tie (*a person*)

impatto *m* impact

impaurire §176 *tr* to scare || *ref* to get scared

impàvi·do -da *adj* fearless

impazlènte *adj* impatient

impazientire §176 *intr* (ESSERE) & *ref* to get impatient

impazlènza *f* impatience

impazzare *intr* (ESSERE) to be wild with excitement; to go mad; (culin) to curdle

impazzata *f*—**all'impazzata** at top speed; berserk

impazzire §176 *intr* (ESSERE) to go crazy; **fare impazzire** to drive crazy

impeccàbile *adj* impeccable

impeciare §128 (**impécio**) *tr* to tar

impedènza *f* impedance

impediménto *m* hindrance, obstacle, impediment

impedire §176 *tr* to impede, hinder; to obstruct || *intr* to prevent; **impedire** (with *dat*) **di** + *inf* or **che** + *subj* to prevent from + *ger*

impegnare (**impégno**) *tr* to pawn; to reserve (*a room*); to engage (*the enemy*); to keep occupied; to pledge || *ref* to obligate oneself; to go all out; to become entangled

impegnatì·vo -va *adj* demanding (*activity*); binding (*promise*)

impegna·to -ta *adj* pawned; pledged; occupied; committed

impégno *m* commitment; obligation; task; zeal; **senza impegno** without promising

impegolare (**impégolo**) *tr* to tar || *ref* to become entangled

impelagare §209 (**impèlago**) *ref* to bog down; to become entangled

impelliccíare §128 *tr* to fur; to veneer

impenetràbile *adj* impenetrable

impenitènte *adj* impenitent; confirmed

impennàg·gio *m* (**-gi**) (aer) empennage

impennare (**impénno**) *tr* to feather; (fig) to give wings to || *ref* to rear (*said of a horse*); to take umbrage; (aer) to zoom

impennata *f* rearing (*of horse*); (aer) zoom

impensàbile *adj* unthinkable

impensa·to -ta *adj* unexpected

impensierire §176 *tr* & *ref* to worry

imperante *adj* prevailing

imperare (**impèro**) *intr* to rule, reign; to prevail; **imperare su** to rule over

imperatì·vo -va *adj* & *m* imperative

imperatóre *m* emperor

imperatrice *f* empress

impercettìbile *adj* imperceptible

imperdonàbile *adj* unforgivable

imperfèt·to -ta *adj* & *m* imperfect

imperfeziòne *f* imperfection

imperiale *adj* imperial || *m* upper deck (*of bus or coach*); **imperiali** imperial troops

imperiali·sta *adj* & *mf* (**-sti -ste**) imperialist

impè·rio *m* (**-ri**) empire; rule

imperió·so -sa [s] *adj* imperious; imperative

imperì·to -ta *adj* (lit) inexperienced

imperitu·ro -ra *adj* immortal; everlasting, imperishable

imperìzia *f* inexperience

imperlare (**impèrlo**) *tr* to bead; to cover with beads (*of perspiration*)

impermalire §176 *tr* to provoke || *ref* to become provoked

impermeàbile *adj* waterproof || *m* raincoat

imperniare §287 (**impèrnio**) *tr* to pivot; (fig) to base

impèro *adj invar* Empire || *m* empire; control, sway

imperscrutàbile *adj* inscrutable

impersonale *adj* impersonal

impersonare (**impersóno**) *tr* to impersonate || *ref*—**impersonarsi in** to be the embodiment of; (theat) to impersonate

impertèrri·to -ta *adj* undaunted

impertinènte *adj* impertinent, pert

impertinènza *f* impertinence

imperturbàbile *adj* imperturbable

imperturba·to -ta *adj* unperturbed

imperversare (**impervèrso**) *intr* to storm, rage; to be the rage

impèr·vio -via *adj* (**-vi -vie**) impassable

impeto *m* impetus; onslaught; violence; outburst; **d'impeto** rashly

impetrare (**impètro**) *tr* to beg for; to obtain by entreaty || *intr* (ESSERE) (lit) to turn to stone

impetti·to -ta *adj* puffed up with pride

impetuó·so -sa [s] *adj* impetuous

impiallacciare §128 *tr* to veneer

impiallacciatura *f* veneer, veneering

impiantare *tr* to install (*a machine*); to set up (*a business*); to open (*an account*)

impiantito *m* floor, flooring

impianto *m* installation; plant; system

impiastrare *tr* to plaster; to dirty

impiastricciare §128 *tr* to plaster; to daub; to soil

impiastro *m* (med) plaster; (fig) bore

impiccagióne *f* hanging

impiccare §197 *tr* to hang

impicciare §128 *tr* to hinder; to bother || *ref* to meddle, butt in; **impicciarsi degli affari propri** to mind one's own business

impìc·cio *m* (**-ci**) hindrance; trouble; **essere d'impiccio** to be in the way

impicció·ne -na *mf* meddler

impiccolire §176 *tr* to reduce in size || *ref* to shrink in size

impiegare §209 (**implègo**) *tr* to employ;

to use; to devote (*one's energies*); to spend (*time*); to invest (*capital*); to take (*time*) || *ref* to have a job
impiegatì·zio -zia *adj* (*-zi -zie*) employee, white-collar
impiega·to -ta *mf* employee; clerk
impiè·go *m* (*-ghi*) employment; use; job; place of business; investment
impietosire [s] §176 *tr* to move to pity || *ref* to be moved to pity
impietrire §176 *tr, intr* (ESSERE) & *ref* to turn to stone
impigliare §176 *tr* to entangle || *ref* to become entangled
impigrire §176 *tr* to make lazy || *intr* (ESSERE) & *ref* to get lazy
impinguare (**impìnguo**) *tr* & *ref* to fatten
impinzare *tr* to stuff || *ref* to stuff oneself; **impinzarsi il cervello** to stuff one's brain (*with knowledge*)
impìombare (**impìombo**) *tr* to lead; to plumb, seal with lead; to fill (*a tooth*); (naut) to splice (*a cable*)
impìombatura *f* seal; filling (*of tooth*); (naut) splicing
impipare *ref*—**impiparsi di** (slang) to not give a hoot about
implacàbile *adj* implacable
implicare §197 (**ìmplico**) *tr* to implicate; to imply
implìci·to -ta *adj* implicit, implied
implorare (**implòro**) *tr* to implore
implume *adj* unfledged, featherless
impolìti·co -ca *adj* (*-ci -che*) unpolitical; impolitic, injudicious
impollinare (**impòllino**) *tr* to pollinate
impoltronire §176 *tr* to make lazy || *ref* to get lazy
impolverare (**impòlvero**) *tr* to cover with dust || *ref* to get covered with dust
impomatare *tr* to pomade; to smear with pomade
imponderàbile *adj* imponderable; weightless
imponderabilità *f* imponderability; weightlessness
imponènte *adj* imposing; stately
imponìbile *adj* taxable || *m* taxable income
impopolare *adj* unpopular
impopolarità *f* unpopularity
imporre §218 *tr* to place, put; to impose; to order; to compel; to give (*a name*) || *intr* (ESSERE) to be imposing; (with *dat*) to order, command || *ref* to command respect; to win favor; to be necessary
importante *adj* important; sizable || *m* important thing
importanza *f* importance; size; **darsi importanza** to assume an air of importance
importare (**impòrto**) *tr* to import; to imply; to involve || *intr* (ESSERE) to be of consequence || *impers* (ESSERE)—**importa** it matters; **non importa** never mind
importa·tóre -trice *mf* importer
importazióne *f* importation; import
impòrto *m* amount

importunare *tr* to bother, importune
importu·no -na *adj* importunate, bothersome || *mf* bore
imposizióne *f* imposition; giving (*of a name*); order, command; taxation
impossessare (**impossèsso**) *ref*—**impossessarsi di** to seize; to master (*a language*)
impossìbile *adj* & *m* impossible
impossìbili·tà *f* (*-tà*) impossibility
impossibilitare (**impossibìlito**) *tr* to make impossible; to make unable or incapable
impossibilita·to -ta *adj* unable
impòsta *f* tax; shutter; (archit) impost; **imposta complementare** surtax; **imposta sul valore aggiunto** value-added tax
impostare (**impòsto**) *tr* to start, begin; to state (*a problem*); to mail; to lay (*a stone*); to open (*an account*); to attune (*one's voice*); to lay the keel of (*a ship*) || *ref* to take one's position, get ready
impostazióne *f* beginning, starting; laying; mail, mailing; (com) posting
impo·stóre -stóra *mf* impostor
impostura *f* imposture
impotènte *adj* weak; impotent
impotènza *f* impotence
impoverimento *m* impoverishment
impoverire §176 *tr* to impoverish || *intr* (ESSERE) & *ref* to become impoverished
impraticàbile *adj* impracticable; impassable
impratichire §176 *tr* to train, familiarize || *ref* to become familiar (*e.g., with a task*)
imprecare §197 (**imprèco**) *tr* to wish (*e.g., s.o.'s death*) || *intr* to curse
imprecazióne *f* imprecation, curse
imprecisàbile *adj* undefinable
imprecisióne *f* inexactness, inaccuracy
impreci·so -sa *adj* vague, inexact
impregnare (**imprégno**) *tr* to impregnate
impremedita·to -ta *adj* unpremeditated
imprendìbile *adj* impregnable
imprendi·tóre -trice *mf* contractor || *m*—**imprenditore di pompe funebri** undertaker
imprenditoriale *adj* managerial
imprepara·to -ta *adj* unprepared
impreparazióne *f* unpreparedness
imprésa [s] *f* enterprise; undertaking; achievement; firm, concern; (theat) management; **impresa (di) pompe funebri** undertaking establishment
impresà·rio [s] *m* (*-ri*) manager; (theat) impresario
imprescindìbile *adj* essential, indispensable; unavoidable
impresentàbile *adj* unpresentable
impressionàbile *adj* impressionable
impressionante *adj* striking, impressive; frightening
impressionare (**impressióno**) *tr* to impress; (phot) to expose || *ref* to become frightened; (phot) to be exposed
impressióne *f* impression
imprestare (**imprèsto**) *tr* (coll) to lend

imprèstito *m* (philol) borrowing
imprevedibile *adj* unforeseeable
imprevedu·to -ta *adj* unforeseen
imprevidènte *adj* improvident
imprevi·sto -sta *adj* unforeseen, unexpected ‖ **imprevisti** *mpl* unforeseen events
imprigionare (**imprigióno**) *tr* to imprison
imprìmere §131 *tr* to impress; to imprint; to impart (*e.g., motion*)
improbàbile *adj* improbable, unlikely
impro·bo -ba *adj* dishonest; laborious
improdutti·vo -va *adj* unproductive
imprónta *f* print, imprint; mark; **impronta digitale** fingerprint
improntare (**imprónto**) *tr* to impress, imprint; to mark
improntitùdine *f* audacity, impudence
impronunziàbile *adj* unpronounceable
impropè·rio *m* (**-ri**) insult
improprie·tà *f* (**-tà**) impropriety; error
imprò·prio -pria *adj* (**-pri -prie**) improper, inappropriate; (math) improper
improrogàbile *adj* unextendible
improvvi·do -da *adj* improvident
improvvisare *tr* to improvise ‖ *ref* to suddenly decide to become
improvvisa·to -ta *adj* improvised; impromptu ‖ *f* surprise; surprise party
improvvisazióne *f* improvisation
improvvi·so -sa *adj* sudden ‖ *m* (mus) impromptu; **all'improvviso** or **d'improvviso** suddenly
imprudènte *adj* imprudent; rash
imprudènza *f* imprudence; rashness
impudènte *adj* shameless; brazen; impudent
impudènza *f* shamelessness; impudence
impudicizia *f* immodesty
impudi·co -ca *adj* (**-chi -che**) immodest, indecent
impugnare *tr* to grip, seize; to take up (*arms*); to impugn, contest
impugnatura *f* handle; grip, hold; hilt, haft
impulsi·vo -va *adj* impulsive
impulso *m* impulse; **dare impulso a** to promote, foment
impunemènte *adv* with impunity
impunità *f* impunity
impuni·to -ta *adj* unpunished
impuntare *intr* to stumble, trip; to stutter ‖ *ref* to stutter; to balk; to be stubborn; **impuntarsi a** or **di** + *inf* to stubbornly insist on + *ger*
impuntigliare §280 *ref* to persist, insist
impuntire §176 *tr* to tuft (*e.g., a pillow*)
impuntura *f* backstitch
impuri·tà *f* (**-tà**) impurity; unchastity
impu·ro -ra *adj* impure; unchaste
imputàbile *adj* attributable
imputare (**ìmputo**) *tr* to impute; to charge, accuse; (com) to post
imputa·to -ta *mf* accused, defendant
imputazióne *f* imputation; charge, accusation; (com) posting
imputridire §176 *tr & intr* (ESSERE) to rot
in *prep* in; at; into; to; on, upon; through; during; married to, e.g.,

Maria Roberti in Bianchi Marie Roberti married to Bianchi; as, e.g., **in premio** as a prize; by, e.g., **in automobile** by car; of, e.g., **studente in legge** student of law; **essere in quattro** to be four; **in alto** up; **in breve** soon; in a word; **in giù** down; **in là** there; **in qua** here; **in realtà** really; **in seguito a** because of; **-ina** *suf fem* about, e.g., **cinquantina** about fifty
inabbordàbile *adj* unapproachable
inàbile *adj* unfit; ineligible; awkward
inabili·tà *f* (**-tà**) unfitness; awkwardness; inability
inabilitare (**inabìlito**) *tr* to incapacitate; to render unfit; to disqualify
inabilitazióne *f* disqualification
inabissare *tr* to plunge ‖ *ref* to sink
inabitàbile *adj* uninhabitable
inabita·to -ta *adj* uninhabited
inaccessìbile *adj* inaccessible; unfathomable
inaccettàbile *adj* unacceptable
inacerbire §176 *tr* to exacerbate ‖ *ref* to grow bitter
inacidire §176 *tr & ref* to sour
inadattàbile *adj* unadaptable; maladjusted
inadat·to -ta *adj* inadequate
inadegua·to -ta *adj* inadequate
inadempiènte *adj* not fulfilling; **inadempiente agli obblighi di leva** draft-dodging
inafferràbile *adj* that cannot be caught or captured; incomprehensible; elusive
inalare *tr* to inhale
inalatóre *m* inhaler
inalberare (**inàlbero**) *tr* to hoist ‖ *ref* to rear; to fly into a rage
inalteràbile *adj* unalterable
inamidare (**inàmido**) *tr* to starch
inamida·to -ta *adj* starched; pompous, starchy
inammissìbile *adj* inadmissible
inamovìbile *adj* irremovable
inamovibili·tà *f* (**-tà**) irremovability; tenure
inane *adj* inane; futile
inanella·to -ta *adj* curly; beringed
inanima·to -ta *adj* inanimate; lifeless
inanizióne *f* starvation
inappagàbile *adj* unquenchable
inappaga·to -ta *adj* unsatisfied
inappellàbile *adj* definitive, final
inappetènza *f* lack of appetite
inapprezzàbile *adj* inappreciable, imperceptible; inestimable
inappuntàbile *adj* faultless, impeccable
inarcare §197 *tr* to arch; to raise (*one's eyebrows*)
inargentare (**inargènto**) *tr* to silver
inaridire §176 *tr* to dry; to parch ‖ *ref* to dry up
inarrestàbile *adj* irresistible
inarrivàbile *adj* unattainable; inimitable
inarticola·to -ta *adj* indistinct, inarticulate
inascolta·to -ta *adj* unheeded
inaspetta·to -ta *adj* unexpected
inasprimènto *m* exacerbation

inasprire §176 *tr* to aggravate ‖ *ref* to sour; to become embittered; to become sharper; to become fierce or furious

inastare *tr* to hoist (*flag*); to fix (*bayonets*)

inattaccàbile *adj* unattackable; unassailable; **inattaccàbile da** resistant to

inattendìbile *adj* unreliable

inatté·so -sa [s] *adj* unexpected

inatti·vo -ta *adj* inactive

inaudi·to -ta *adj* unheard-of

inaugurale *adj* inaugural; maiden (*voyage*)

inaugurare (**inàuguro**) *tr* to inaugurate; to usher in (*the New Year*); to open (*e.g., an exhibit*); to unveil (*a statue*); to sport for the first time

inaugurazióne *f* inauguration

inauspica·to -ta *adj* (lit) inauspicious

inavvedu·to -ta *adj* careless, rash

inavvertènza *f* inadvertence, oversight

inavverti·to -ta *adj* unnoticed; inadvertent, thoughtless

inazióne *f* inaction

incagliare §280 *tr* to hamper; to run aground ‖ *intr* (ESSERE) & *ref* to run aground; (fig) to get stuck

incà·glio *m* (-**gli**) running aground; hindrance, obstacle

incalcinare *tr* to whitewash; to lime (*a field*)

incalcolàbile *adj* incalculable

incallire §176 *tr* to make callous ‖ *intr* (ESSERE) to become callous; to become inured

incalli·to -ta *adj* callous; inveterate

incalzante *adj* pressing

incalzare *tr* to press, pursue ‖ *intr* to be imminent; to be pressing ‖ *ref* to follow one another in rapid succession

incamerare (**incàmero**) *tr* to confiscate

incamminare *tr* to launch; to guide, direct ‖ *ref* to set out; to be on one's way

incanagli·to -ta *adj* vile, despicable

incanalare *tr* to channel ‖ *ref* to flow

incancrenire §176 *tr* to affect with gangrene ‖ *ref* to become gangrenous; (fig) to become callous

incandescènte *adj* incandescent; (fig) red-hot

incandescènza *f* incandescence

incannare *tr* to reel, wind

incantare *tr* to bewitch; to auction off ‖ *ref* to become enraptured; to be spellbound; to jam, get stuck (*said of machinery*)

incanta·tóre -trice *adj* enchanting ‖ *m* enchanter ‖ *f* enchantress

incantésimo *m* enchantment, spell

incantévole *adj* enchanting, charming

incanto *m* enchantment; bewitchery; auction; **d'incanto** marvelously well

incanutire §176 *tr, intr* (ESSERE) & *ref* to turn gray-headed, to turn gray (*said of a person*)

incanuti·to -ta *adj* hoary

incapace *adj* incapable; (law) incompetent ‖ *mf* oaf; (law) incompetent

incapaci·tà *f* (-**tà**) incapacity; (law) incompetence

incaparbire §176 *intr* (ESSERE) & *ref* to be obstinate; to be determined

incaponire §176 *ref* to get stubborn; to be determined

incappare *intr* (ESSERE) to stumble

incappottare (**incappòtto**) *tr* to cover with a coat ‖ *ref* to wrap oneself in a coat

incappucciare §128 *tr* to cover with a hood

incapricciare §128 *ref*—**incapricciarsi di** to take a fancy to; to become infatuated with

incapsulare (**incàpsulo**) *tr* to encapsulate; to cap

incarcerare (**incàrcero**) *tr* to jail, incarcerate; (fig) to confine

incaricare §197 (**incàrico**) *tr* to charge ‖ *ref*—**incaricarsi di** to take charge of; to take care of

incarica·to -ta *adj* in charge; visiting (*professor*) ‖ *mf* deputy; **incaricato d'affari** chargé d'affaires

incàri·co *m* (-**chi**) task; appointment, position; **per incarico di** on behalf of

incarnare *tr* to incarnate, embody

incarna·to -ta *adj* incarnate ‖ *m* pink complexion

incarnazióne *f* incarnation

incarnire §176 *intr* (ESSERE) & *ref* to grow in (*said of a toenail*)

incarni·to -ta *adj* ingrown (*toenail*)

incartaménto *m* file, dossier

incartapecori·to -ta *adj* shriveled up

incartare *tr* to wrap up (*in paper*)

incasellare [s] (**incasèllo**) *tr* to file; to sort out

incasellatóre [s] *m* post-office file clerk

incassare *tr* to box up; to put (*a watch*) in a case; to mortise (*a lock*); to channel (*a river*); to cash (*a check*); (fig) to take (*e.g., blows*) ‖ *intr* to fit; to take it

incasso *m* receipts

incastellatura *f* scaffolding

incastonare (**incastóno**) *tr* to set, mount (*a gem*); **incastonare citazioni in un discorso** to stud a speech with quotations

incastrare *tr* to insert; to mortise; (fig) to corner ‖ *intr* to fit ‖ *ref* to fit; to become imbedded; to telescope (*said, e.g., of a train in a collision*)

incastro *m* joint; insertion; (carp) tenon; (carp) mortise

incatenare (**incaténo**) *tr* to chain, put in chains; to tie down, restrain

incatramare *tr* to tar

incàu·to -ta *adj* unwary, careless

incavallatura *f* truss (*to support roof*)

incavare *tr* to hollow out; to groove

incava·to -ta *adj* hollow

incavatura *f* hollow

incavicchiare §287 *tr* to peg

incavigliare §280 *tr* to peg

incavo *m* hollow; cavity; **incavo dell'ascella** armpit

incazzottare (**incazzòtto**) *tr* (naut) to furl

incèdere *m* stately walk ‖ §123 *intr* to walk stately

incendiare §287 (**incèndio**) *tr* to set on fire; (fig) to inflame ‖ *ref* to catch fire

incendià·rio -ria *adj* & *mf* (**-ri -rie**) incendiary

incèn·dio *m* (**-di**) fire; **incendio doloso** arson

incenerire §176 *tr* to reduce to ashes; to wither (*e.g., with a look*) ‖ *ref* to turn to ashes

inceneritóre *m* incinerator

incensare (**incènso**) *tr* (eccl) to incense; (fig) to flatter

incensa·tóre -trice *mf* incense burner; (fig) flatterer

incensière *m* incense burner

incènso *m* incense

incensura·to -ta *adj* uncensored; (law) having no previous record

incentivo *m* incentive

inceppare (**incéppo**) *tr* to hinder; to shackle ‖ *ref* to jam (*said of firearm*)

incerare (**incéro**) *tr* to wax

incerata *f* oilcloth; (naut) raincoat

incernierare (**incernièro**) *tr* to hinge

incertézza *f* uncertainty, incertitude

incèr·to -ta *adj* uncertain; irresolute ‖ *m* uncertainty; **incerti** extras; **incerti del mestiere** cares of office, occupational annoyances, occupational hazards

incespicare §197 (**incéspico**) *intr* to stumble

incessàbile *adj* (lit) ceaseless

incessante *adj* unceasing, incessant

incèsto *m* incest

incestuó·so -sa [s] *adj* incestuous

incètta *f* cornering (*of market*)

incettare (**incètto**) *tr* to corner (*market*)

incetta·tóre -trice *mf* monopolizer

inchiavardare *tr* to key, bolt

inchièsta *f* probe, inquest; (journ) inquiry

inchinare *tr* to bend; to bow (*the head*) ‖ *intr* (lit) to go down (*said of stars*); *ref* to bow; to yield

inchi·no -na *adj* bent; bowing ‖ *m* bow; curtsy

inchiodare (**inchiòdo**) *tr* to nail; to spike; to rivet; to tie, bind; to stop (*a car*) unable; to transfix ‖ *ref* to freeze (*said, e.g., of brakes*); (fig) to be tied down; (fig) to go into debt

inchiostrare (**inchiòstro**) *tr* (typ) to ink

inchiòstro *m* ink; **inchiostro di china** India ink, Chinese ink

inciampare *intr* to trip, stumble

inciampo *m* stumbling block, obstacle; **essere d'inciampo a** to be in the way of

incidentale *adj* incidental

incidente *adj* incidental ‖ *m* incident; accident; argument, question

incidènza *f* incidence

incìdere §145 *tr* to engrave; to cut; to record (*a record, a tape; a song*); **incidere all'acqua forte** to etch ‖ *intr*—**incidere su** to weigh heavily on (*expenses, a budget*); to leave a mark on

incinerazióne *f* incineration; cremation

incinta *adj fem* pregnant

incipiènte *adj* incipient

incipriare §287 *tr* to powder ‖ *ref* to powder oneself

incirca *adv* about; **all'incirca** more or less

incisióne *f* engraving; cutting (*of a record*); recording (*of a tape; of a song*); incision; **incisione all'acquaforte** etching

incisi·vo -va *adj* incisive; sharp (*photograph*) ‖ *m* incisor

inciso *m* (gram) parenthetical clause; (mus) theme; **per inciso** incidentally

incisóre *m* engraver, etcher

incitare *tr* to incite, provoke

incivile *adj* uncivilized; uncouth

incivilire §176 *tr* to civilize ‖ *ref* to become civilized

inclemènte *adj* inclement, harsh

inclemènza *f* inclemency, harshness

inclinare *tr* to tilt; to bow, bend; to incline ‖ *intr* (fig) to lean ‖ *ref* to bend

inclinazióne *f* inclination; slope; **inclinazione laterale** (aer) bank; **inclinazione magnetica** magnetic dip

incline *adj* inclined

incli·to -ta *adj* famous; noble

inclùdere §105 *tr* to enclose, include

inclusi·vo -va *adj* including; **inclusivo di** including

inclu·so -sa *adj* enclosed; included; inclusive ‖ *f* enclosed letter

incoerènte *adj* incoherent

incògliere §127 *tr* (lit) to catch in the act ‖ *intr*—**incògliere a** to happen to

incògni·to -ta *adj* unknown ‖ *m* incognito; unknown; **in incognito** incognito ‖ *f* (math) unknown quantity; (fig) puzzle

incollare (**incòllo**) *tr* to glue, paste; to size (*paper*) ‖ *intr* to stick ‖ *ref* to stick; to take on one's shoulders

incollatura *f* neck (*of horse*); glueing, sticking

incollerire §176 *intr* & *ref* to get angry

incolloca·to -ta *adj* unemployed

incolonnare (**incolónno**) *tr* to set up in columns

incolonnatore *m* tabulator

incolóre *adj* colorless

incolpàbile *adj* blamable; (lit) guiltless

incolpare (**incólpo**) *tr*—**incolpare di** to charge with

incól·to -ta *adj* uncultivated; unkempt

incòlume *adj* unharmed, unhurt

incolumità *f* safety, security

incombènte *adj* (*danger*) impending; (*duty*) incumbent

incombènza *f* task, charge, incumbency

incómbere §186 *intr* (ESSERE) to be impending; to be incumbent

incombustìbile *adj* incombustible

incominciare §128 *tr* & *intr* (ESSERE) to begin

incommensuràbile *adj* immeasurable; (math) incommensurable

incomodare (**incòmodo**) *tr* to bother, disturb ‖ *ref* to bother; **non s'incomodi!** don't bother!

incòmo·do -da *adj* bothersome, inconvenient ‖ *m* inconvenience; ailment;

levare l'incomodo a to get out of the way of

incomparàbile *adj* incomparable

incompatìbile *adj* incompatible; unforgivable

incompetènte *adj & mf* incompetent

incompiu·to -ta *adj* unfinished

incomplè·to -ta *adj* incomplete

incompó·sto -sta *adj* untidy; unkempt; unbecoming (*behavior*)

incomprensìbile *adj* incomprehensible

incomprensióne *f* lack of understanding

incompré·so -sa [s] *adj* misunderstood

incomprimìbile *adj* irrepressible; incompressible

inconcepìbile *adj* inconceivable

inconciliàbile *adj* irreconcilable

inconcludènte *adj* inconclusive; insignificant

inconcus·so -sa *adj* (lit) unshaken

incondizióna·to -ta *adj* unconditional

inconfessàbile *adj* unspeakable, vile

inconfessa·to -ta *adj* unavowed

inconfondìbile *adj* unmistakable

inconfutàbile *adj* irrefutable

incongruènte *adj* inconsistent

incòn·gruo -grua *adj* incongruous

inconoscìbile *adj* unknowable

inconsapèvole *adj* unaware, unconscious

incòn·scio -scia *adj & m* (-sci -sce) unconscious

inconseguènte *adj* inconsistent, inconsequential

inconsidera·to -ta *adj* inconsiderate

inconsistènte *adj* flimsy; inconsistent

inconsistènza *f* flimsiness; inconsistency

inconsolàbile *adj* inconsolable

inconsuè·to -ta *adj* unusual

inconsul·to -ta *adj* ill-advised, rash

incontamina·to -ta *adj* uncontaminated

incontenìbile *adj* irrepressible

incontentàbile *adj* insatiable; hard to please; exacting

incontinènza *f* incontinence

incontrare (incóntro) *tr* to meet; to encounter, meet with || *intr* (ESSERE) to catch on (*said, e.g., of fashions*) || *ref* to meet; to agree || *impers* (ESSERE) to happen

incontrastàbile *adj* indisputable

incontrasta·to -ta *adj* undisputed

incóntro *m* meeting; encounter; success; meet; game, fight, match; occasion, opportunity; **all'incontro** on the other hand; opposite; **andare incontro a** to go towards; to go to meet; to face; to meet (*expenses*); to accommodate; **farsi incontro a** to advance toward

incontrollàbile *adj* uncontrollable

incontrolla·to -ta *adj* unchecked

incontrovertìbile *adj* incontrovertible

inconveniènte *adj* inconvenient || *m* inconvenience, disadvantage

incoraggiante *adj* encouraging

incoraggiare §290 *tr* to encourage

incorare §257 (incuòro) *tr* to hearten

incordare (incòrdo) *tr* to string (*e.g., a racket*); to tie up (*with a cord*) || *ref* to stiffen (*said of a muscle*)

incornare (incòrno) *tr* (taur) to gore

incorniciare §128 *tr* to frame; (journ) to border; (slang) to cuckold

incoronare (incoróno) *tr* to crown

incoronazióne *f* coronation

incorporàbile *adj* absorbable; adaptable

incorporare (incòrporo) *tr* to incorporate; to absorb || *ref* to incorporate

incorpòre·o -a *adj* incorporeal

incorreggìbile *adj* incorrigible

incórrere §139 *intr* (ESSERE)—**incorrere in** to incur

incorrót·to -ta *adj* uncorrupt

incosciènte *adj* unconscious; unaware; irresponsible || *mf* irresponsible person

incosciènza *f* unconsciousness; irresponsibility; madness

incostante *adj* inconstant, fickle

incredìbile *adj* incredible, unbelievable

incrèdu·lo -la *adj* incredulous || *mf* disbeliever; doubter

incrementare (increménto) *tr* to increase, boost

increménto *m* increase, increment, boost

incresció·so -sa [s] *adj* disagreeable, unpleasant

increspare (incréspo) *tr* to ripple; to wrinkle; to knit (*the brow*); to pleat || *ref* to ripple

incretinire §176 *tr* to make stupid; (fig) to deafen || *intr* (ESSERE) to become stupid; to lose one's mind

incriminare (incrìmino) *tr* to incriminate

incrinare *tr* to flaw; to ruin

incrinatura *f* crack, flaw

incrociare §128 (incròcio) *tr* to cross || *intr* (naut) to cruise || *ref* to cross one another; to interbreed

incrociatóre *m* (nav) cruiser

incró·cio *m* (-ci) crossing; cross; crossroads; crossbreed

incrollàbile *adj* unshakable

incrostare (incròsto) *tr* to incrust; to inlay (*e.g., with mosaic*) || *ref* to become incrusted

incrostazióne *f* incrustation

incrudelire §176 *tr* to enrage || *intr* to commit cruelties || *intr* (ESSERE) to become cruel; **incrudelire su** to commit cruelties upon

incruèn·to -ta *adj* bloodless

incubare (ìncubo & incùbo) *tr* to incubate

incubatrice *f* incubator; brooder

incubazióne *f* incubation; **in incubazione** brewing (*said of an infectious disease*)

ìncubo *m* nightmare

incùdine *f* anvil; **essere tra l'incudine e il martello** to be between the devil and the deep blue sea

inculcare §197 *tr* to inculcate

incunàbolo *m* incunabulum

incuneare (incùneo) *tr & ref* to wedge

incuràbile *adj & mf* incurable

incurante *adj* careless, indifferent

incùria *f* malpractice; neglect

incuriosire [s] §176 *tr* to intrigue || *ref* to be intrigued

incursióne *f* incursion; **incursione aerea** air raid

incurvare *tr* to bend; (lit) to lower ‖ *intr* (ESSERE) & *ref* to bend; to warp

incurvatura *f* bend, curve

incustodì·to -ta *adj* unguarded, unwatched

incùtere §154 *tr* to inspire; **incutere terrore a** to strike with terror

ìndaco *adj* & *m* indigo

indaffara·to -ta *adj* busy

indagare §209 *tr* & *intr* to investigate; **indagare su** to investigate

indaga·tóre -trice *adj* probing, searching ‖ *mf* investigator

indàgine *f* investigation, inquiry

indarno *adv* (lit) in vain

indebitare (**indébito**) *tr* to burden with debts ‖ *ref* to run into debt

indebita·to -ta *adj* indebted

indébi·to -ta *adj* undue; unjust; fraudulent (*conversion*) ‖ *m* what one does not owe; excess payment

indebolimènto *m* weakening

indebolire §176 *tr*, *intr* (ESSERE) & *ref* to weaken

indecènte *adj* indecent

indecènza *f* indecency; outrage

indecifràbile *adj* indecipherable

indecisióne *f* indecision

indecì·so -sa *adj* uncertain; undecided; indecisive

indecoró·so -sa *adj* indecorous, unseemly

indefès·so -sa *adj* indefatigable

indefinìbile *adj* indefinable

indefinì·to -ta *adj* indefinite; undefined

indegnì·tà *f* (-**tà**) indignity

indé·gno -gna *adj* unworthy; disgraceful

indelèbile *adj* indelible

indelica·to -ta *adj* indelicate

indemagliàbile *adj* runproof

indemonia·to -ta *adj* possessed by the devil; restless

indènne *adj* undamaged, unscathed; **tener indenne** to guarantee against harm or damage

indennì·tà *f* (-**tà**) indemnity; indemnification; **indennità di carica** special emolument; bonus; **indennità di carovita** cost-of-living allowance; **indennità di preavviso** severance pay; **indennità di trasferta** per diem

indennizzare [ddzz] *tr* to indemnify

indennizzo [ddzz] *m* indemnification; indemnity

inderogàbile *adj* inescapable

indescrivìbile *adj* indescribable

indesideràbile *adj* undesirable

indesidera·to -ta *adj* unwished-for; undesirable

indeterminatì·vo -va *adj* indefinite

indetermina·to -ta *adj* indeterminate; (gram) indefinite

indi *adv* (lit) then; (lit) thence; **da indi innanzi** (lit) from that moment on

India, l' *f* India; **le Indie Occidentali** the West Indies; **le Indie Orientali** the East Indies

india·no -na *adj* & *mf* Indian; **fare l'indiano** to feign ignorance ‖ *f* printed calico

indiavola·to -ta *adj* devilish, fierce; impish (*child*)

indicare §197 (**ìndico**) *tr* to indicate; to show

indicatì·vo -va *adj* & *m* indicative

indica·to -ta *adj* appropriate, fitting; recommended, advisable

indica·tóre -trice *adj* indicating, pointing ‖ *m* indicator; **indicatore di direzione** (aut) turn signal; **indicatore di livello** gauge; **indicatore di pressione** pressure gauge; **indicatore di velocità** (aut) speedometer; **indicatore stradale** road sign; **indicatore telefonico** telephone directory

indicazióne *f* indication; direction; **indicazioni per l'uso** instructions

ìndice *m* index finger; pointer, gauge; indicator; sign, indication; index; (typ) fist; **indice delle materie** table of contents ‖ **Indice** *m* Index; **mettere all'Indice** to put on the Index; to ban, index

indicìbile *adj* inexpressible, unspeakable

indietreggiare §290 (**indietréggio**) *intr* (ESSERE & AVERE) to withdraw

indiètro *adv* back; behind; **all'indietro** backwards; **dare indietro** to return, give back; **domandare indietro** to ask back; **essere indietro** to be slow (*said of a watch*); to be behind; to be backward, be slow; **tirarsi indietro** to withdraw; to step back

indifendìbile *adj* indefensible

indifé·so -sa [s] *adj* defenseless

indifferènte *adj* indifferent; **essere indifferente a** to be the same to; **lasciare indifferente** to leave cold

indifferènza *f* indifference

indìge·no -na *adj* indigenous ‖ *m* native

indigènte *adj* indigent, poor

indigestìbile *adj* indigestible

indigestióne *f* indigestion

indigè·sto -sta *adj* indigestible; (fig) dull, boring

indignare *tr* to anger, shock ‖ *ref* to be aroused, be indignant

indigna·to -ta *adj* indignant, outraged

indignazióne *f* indignation

indignì·tà *f* (-**tà**) indignity

indimenticàbile *adj* unforgettable

indipendènte *adj* & *m* independent

indipendènza *f* independence

indìre §151 *tr* to announce publicly; (lit) to declare (*war*)

indirèt·to -ta *adj* indirect

indirizzare *tr* to direct; to address

indirizzà·rio *m* (-**ri**) mailing list

indirizzo *m* address; direction

indiscernìbile *adj* indiscernible

indisciplìna *f* lack of discipline

indisciplina·to -ta *adj* undisciplined

indiscré·to -ta *adj* indiscreet; tactless

indiscrezióne *f* indiscretion; gossip; news leak

indiscus·so -sa *adj* unquestioned

indiscutìbile *adj* indisputable

indispensàbile *adj* indispensable ‖ *m* essential

indispettire §176 *tr* to annoy ‖ *ref* to get annoyed

indisponènte *adj* vexing, irritating

indispórre §218 *tr* to indispose; to disgust

indisposizióne *f* indisposition

indispó·sto -sta *adj* indisposed

indissolùbile *adj* indissoluble

indistin·to -ta *adj* indistinct

indistruttìbile *adj* indestructible

indisturba·to -ta *adj* undisturbed

indìvia *f* endive

individuàbile *adj* distinguishable

individuale *adj* individual

individuali·tà *f* (-**tà**) individuality

individuare (**individuo**) *tr* to individuate; to outline; to single out

individuo *m* individual; fellow

indivisìbile *adj* indivisible

indivi·so -sa *adj* undivided

indiziare §287 *tr* to cast suspicion on

indizià·rio -ria *adj* (-**ri** -**rie**) circumstancial

indì·zio *m* (-**zi**) clue; token; symptom

indòcile *adj* indocile, unteachable

Indocina, l' *f* Indochina

indocinése [s] *adj* & *mf* Indochinese

indoeuropè·o -a *adj* & *m* Indo-European

indolcire §176 *tr* to sweeten ‖ *ref* to become sweet

ìndole *f* temper, disposition; nature

indolènte *adj* indolent

indolenziménto *m* soreness, stiffness; numbness

indolenzire §176 *tr* to make sore or stiff; to benumb ‖ *ref* to become sore or stiff

indolenzi·to -ta *adj* sore, stiff; numb

indolóre *adj* painless

indomàbile *adj* indomitable

indoma·ni *m* (-**ni**) morrow, next day; **l'indomani di . . .** the day after . . .

indoma·to -ta *adj* (lit) indomitable, untamed

indòmi·to -ta *adj* (lit) indomitable, untamed

Indonèsia l' *f* Indonesia

indonesia·no -na *adj* & *mf* Indonesian

indorare (**indòro**) *tr* to gild; (culin) to brown; (fig) to sugar-coat

indoratura *f* gilding

indossare (**indòsso**) *tr* to wear; to put on

indossatrice *f* mannequin, model

indòsso *adv* on, on one's back; **avere indosso** to have on, wear

Indostàn, l' *m* Hindustan

indosta·no -na *adj* & *mf* Hindustani

indòtto *m* (elec) armature (*of motor*)

indottrinare *tr* to indoctrinate

indovinare *tr* to guess; **indovinarla** to guess right; **non indovinarne una** to never hit the mark

indovina·to -ta *adj* felicitous

indovinèllo *m* puzzle, riddle

indovi·no -na *mf* soothsayer, fortuneteller

indù *adj invar* & *mf* Hindu

indùb·bio -bia *adj* (-**bi** -**bie**) undoubted, undisputed

indubita·to -ta *adj* undeniable

indugiare §290 *tr* to delay ‖ *intr* to linger; to hesitate ‖ *ref* to linger

indù·gio *m* (-**gi**) delay; **rompere gli**

indugi to come to a decision; **senza ulteriore indugio** without further delay

indulgènte *adj* indulgent

indulgènza *f* indulgence

indùlgere §187 *tr* to grant; to forgive ‖ *intr* to be indulgent; **indulgere a** to indulge; to yield to

indulto *m* (law) pardon

induménto *m* garment; **indumenti ìntimi** undergarments, unmentionables

indurire §176 *tr* to harden ‖ *intr* (ESSERE) to harden; to get stiff

indurre §102 *tr* to induce

indùstria *f* industry; **grande industria** heavy industry

industriale *adj* industrial ‖ *m* industrialist

industrializzare [ddzz] *tr* to industrialize

industriare §287 *ref* to try, try hard; **industriarsi a** or **per** + *inf* to try to + *inf*, to do one's best to + *inf*

industrió·so -sa [s] *adj* industrious

indut·tóre -trice *adj* inducing, provoking ‖ *m* (elec) field (*of motor*)

induzióne *f* induction

inebetire §176 *tr* to dull; to stun ‖ *intr* (ESSERE) & *ref* to become dull; to be stunned

inebriare §287 (**inèbrio**) *tr* to intoxicate ‖ *ref* to get drunk

inebriante *adj* intoxicating

ineccepìbile *adj* unexceptionable

inèdia *f* starvation, inanition; boredom

inèdi·to -ta *adj* unpublished; new, novel

ineduca·to -ta *adj* uneducated; ill-mannered

ineffàbile *adj* ineffable

inefficace *adj* ineffectual, ineffective

inefficàcia *f* inefficacy

inefficiènte *adj* inefficient

ineguale *adj* unequal; uneven

ineleggìbile *adj* ineligible

ineluttàbile *adj* inevitable, inescapable

inenarràbile *adj* unspeakable

inerènte *adj* inherent

inèrme *adj* unarmed, defenseless

inerpicare §197 (**inèrpico**) *ref* to clamber

inèrte *adj* inert

inèrzia *f* inertia; inactivity

inesattézza *f* inaccuracy

inesat·to -ta *adj* inaccurate, inexact; uncollected

inesaudi·to -ta *adj* unanswered

inesaurìbile *adj* inexhaustible

inescusàbile *adj* inexcusable

inesigìbile *adj* uncollectable

inesistènte *adj* inexistent

inesoràbile *adj* inexorable

inesperiènza *f* inexperience

inespèr·to -ta *adj* inexperienced; unskilled

inesplicàbile *adj* inexplicable

inesplica·to -ta *adj* unexplained

inesplora·to -ta *adj* unexplored

inesplò·so -sa *adj* unexploded

inespressi·vo -va *adj* inexpressive

inesprimìbile *adj* inexpressible

inespugnàbile *adj* impregnable; incorruptible
inespugna·to -ta *adj* unconquered
inestimàbile *adj* priceless, invaluable
inestinguìbile *adj* inextinguishable
inestirpàbile *adj* ineradicable
inestricàbile *adj* inextricable
inèt·to -ta *adj* inept
ineva·so -sa *adj* unfinished (*business*); unanswered (*mail*)
inevitàbile *adj* unavoidable, inevitable
inèzia *f* trifle, bagatelle
infagottare (infagòtto) *tr & ref* to bundle up
infallìbile *adj* infallible
infamante *adj* shameful, disgraceful
infamare *tr* to disgrace; to slander
infame *adj* infamous; villainous; (coll) horrible || *mf* villain
infàmia *f* infamy; (coll) botch, bungle
infangare §209 *tr* to splash with mud; (fig) to stain, spot
infante *adj & mf* infant, baby || *m* infante || *f* infanta
infantile *adj* infantile, childish
infànzia *f* infancy, childhood
infarcire §176 *tr* to cram; (culin) to stuff
infarinare *tr* to sprinkle with flour; to powder; (fig) to cram || *ref* to be covered with flour
infarinatura *f* sprinkling with flour; (fig) smattering
infastidire §176 *tr* to annoy || *ref* to be annoyed, lose one's patience
infaticàbile *adj* indefatigable, tireless
infatti *adv* indeed; really
infatuare (infàtuo) *tr* to infatuate || *ref* to become infatuated
infatua·to -ta *adj* infatuated
infàu·sto -sta *adj* unlucky, fatal
infecón·do -da *adj* barren
infedéle *adj* unfaithful; inaccurate || *mf* infidel
infedel·tà *f* (-tà) unfaithfulness; inaccuracy; infidelity
infelice *adj* unhappy, unfortunate; unfavorable || *mf* wretch
infelici·tà *f* (-tà) unhappiness
inferióre *adj* inferior; lower; inferiore a lower than; less than; smaller than
inferioritá *f* inferiority
inferire §188a *tr* to inflict; to infer; (naut) to bend (*a sail*)
infermare (infèrmo) *tr* (lit) to weaken || *intr* (ESSERE) to get sick
infermerìa *f* infirmary
infermiè·re -ra *adj* nursing || *m* male nurse || *f* nurse; **infermiera diplomata** trained nurse
infermierìsti·co -ca *adj* (-ci -che) nursing
infermi·tà *f* (-tà) infirmity
infér·mo -ma *adj* infirm; sick || *m* patient
infernale *adj* infernal
infèr·no -na *adj* (lit) lower (*region*) || *m* hell; inferno
inferocire §176 *tr* to infuriate || *intr—* **inferocire su** to be pitiless to || *intr* (ESSERE) to become infuriated
inferriata *f* grating, grill

infervorare (infèrvoro & infervóro) *tr* to excite, stir up || *ref* to get excited; to become absorbed
infestare (infèsto) *tr* to infest
infettare (infètto) *tr* to infect
infetti·vo -va *adj* infectious
infèt·to -ta *adj* infected; corrupted
infezióne *f* infection
infiacchire §176 *tr* to weaken || *intr* (ESSERE) & *ref* to grow weak
infiammàbile *adj* inflammable
infiammare *tr* to inflame; to ignite || *ref* to catch fire, ignite
infiamma·to -ta *adj* burning; aflame; inflamed, excited
infiammazióne *f* inflammation
infi·do -da *adj* untrustworthy
infierire §176 *intr* to become cruel; to be merciless to; to rage (*said, e.g., of a disease*)
infievolire §176 *tr* to weaken
infìggere §103 *tr* to thrust, stick, sink || *ref—***infìggersi in** to creep in; to work in
infilare *tr* to thread (*a needle*); to insert (*a key*); to transfix (*with a sword*); to put on (*e.g., a coat*); to pull on (*one's pants*); to slip on (*a dress*); to slip (*e.g., one's arm into a sleeve*); to string (*beads*); to hit (*the target*); to take (*a road*); to enter through (*a door*); **infilare l'uscio** to slip away; **infilarle tutte** to succeed all the time; **non infilarne mai una** to never succeed || *ref* to slip; to sink; to slide (*e.g., through a crowd*)
infilata *f* row; string (*e.g., of insults*); (mil) enfilade; **d'infilata** lengthwise
infiltrare *ref* to infiltrate; to seep; (fig) to creep
infilzare *tr* to pierce; to string; (sew) to baste
infilzata *f* string (*of pearls, of lies, etc.*)
infi·mo -ma *adj* lowest, bottom
infine *adv* finally
infingar·do -da *adj* lazy, slothful
infini·tà *f* (-tà) infinity
infinitèsi·mo -ma *adj & m* infinitesimal
infiniti·vo -va *adj* (gram) infinitive
infini·to -ta *adj* infinite || *m* infinite; infinity; (gram) infinitive; (math) infinity; **all'infinito** ad infinitum
infino *adv* (lit)—**infino a** until; **as far as**; **infino a che** as long as
infinocchiare §287 (**infinòcchio**) *tr* (coll) to fool, bamboozle
infioccare §197 (**infiòcco**) *tr* to adorn with tassels
infiorare (infióro) *tr* to adorn with flowers; (fig) to sprinkle; (fig) to embellish || *ref* to be covered with flowers
infiorescènza *f* inflorescence
infirmare *tr* to weaken; to invalidate
infischiare §287 *ref—***infischiarsi di** to not care a hoot about
infisso *m* frame (*e.g., of door*); fixture
infittire §176 *tr, intr* (ESSERE) & *ref* to thicken
inflazionare (inflazióno) *tr* to inflate
inflazióne *f* inflation
inflessìbile *adj* inflexible

inflessióne *f* inflection
inflèttere §177 *tr* (lit) to inflect
infliggere §104 *tr* to inflict
influènte *adj* influential
influènza *f* influence; (pathol) influenza
influenzare (**influènzo**) *tr* to influence, sway
influire §176 *intr* to have an influence; **influire su** to influence || *intr* (ESSERE) —**influire in** to flow into
influsso *m* influence; (lit) plague
infocare §182 *tr* to make glow with heat || *ref* to catch fire; to get excited
infoca·to -ta *adj* red-hot; sultry
infognare (**infógno**) *ref* (coll) to sink (e.g., **in vice**); (coll) to get stuck (e.g., **in debt**)
infoltire §176 *tr* & *intr* (ESSERE) to thicken
infonda·to -ta *adj* unfounded, groundless
infóndere §178 *tr* to infuse, instill
inforcare §197 (**infórco**) *tr* to pitch (hay); to bestride; to mount (a horse or bicycle); to put on (one's eyeglasses)
inforcatura *f* pitching with a fork; crotch
informare (**infórmo**) *tr* to inform; (fig) to mold || *ref* to conform; to inquire; **informarsi da** to seek or get information from; **informarsi di** or **su** to inquire about; to find out about
informatì·vo -va *adj* informative, informational
informa·tóre -trice *adj* underlying || *mf* informer; (journ) reporter || *m* informant (of a foreign language)
informazióne *f* piece of information; **chiedere informazioni sul conto di** to inquire about; **informazioni** information
infórme *adj* shapeless
informicolíre §176 *ref* to tingle; **informicolirsi a** to go to sleep, e.g., **gli si è informicolita la gamba** his leg went to sleep
infornare (**infórno**) *tr* to put in the oven; to bake
infornata *f* batch (of bread); (coll) flock
infortunare *ref* to get hurt
infortuna·to -ta *adj* injured || *mf* casualty, victim
infortù·nio *m* (-ni) accident, mishap; **infortunio sul lavoro** job-connected injury
infossare (**infòsso**) *tr* to bury || *ref* to cave in, settle; to become sunken (said of eyes or cheeks)
infracidare (**infràcido**) *tr* var of **infradiciare**
infracidíre §176 *intr* to rot
infradiciare §128 (**infràdicio**) *tr* to drench || *ref* to get drenched; to rot (said of fruit)
inframmettènza *f* interference, meddling
inframméttere §198 *tr* to interpose || *ref* to meddle, interfere
inframmezzare [ddzz] (**inframmèzzo**) *tr* to intersperse

infràngere §179 *tr* & *ref* to break
infrangìbile *adj* unbreakable
infran·to -ta *adj* broken, shattered
infrarós·so -sa *adj* & *m* infrared
infrascrit·to -ta *adj* mentioned below
infrastruttura *f* underpinning; infrastructure; (rr) roadbed
infrazióne *f* infraction, breach
infreddatura *f* mild cold
infreddolíre §176 *ref* to feel cold, to be chilled
infrenàbile *adj* irrepressible
infrequènte *adj* infrequent
infrollíre §176 *tr* to make (meat) high || *intr* (ESSERE) & *ref* to get high (said of meat); (fig) to soften
infruttuó·so -sa [s] *adj* unprofitable
infuòri *adv* out; **all'infuori** outward; **all'infuori di** except
infuriare §287 *tr* to infuriate, enrage || *intr* to get blustery; to rage || *intr* (ESSERE) to lose one's temper
infusióne *f* infusion; sprinkling (of holy water)
infuso *m* infusion
ingabbiare §287 *tr* to cage; to jail; to corner; to build the framework of
ingabbiatura *f* frame, framework
ingaggiare §290 *tr* to hire; to engage || *ref* to sign up; to get tangled up
ingàg·gio *m* (-gi) engagement; (sports) bonus (for signing up)
ingagliardíre §176 *tr* to strengthen || *ref* to become strong
ingannare *tr* to deceive; to cheat; to elude; to beguile || *ref* to be mistaken
inganna·tóre -trice *adj* deceptive || *mf* impostor
ingannévole *adj* deceitful; deceptive
inganno *m* deception; illusion
ingarbugliare §280 *tr* to entangle; to jumble || *ref* to get mixed up; to become embroiled
ingegnare (**ingégno**) *ref* to manage; to scheme
ingegnère *m* engineer
ingegneria *f* engineering; **ingegneria civile** civil engineering; **ingegneria meccanica** mechanical engineering
ingégno *m* brain, intelligence; talent; genius; expediency; (lit) machinery
ingegnosità [s] *f* ingeniousness
ingegnó·so -sa [s] *adj* ingenious; euphuistic
ingelosíre [s] §176 *tr* to make jealous || *intr* (ESSERE) & *ref* to become jealous
ingemmare (**ingèmmo**) *tr* to adorn or stud with gems
ingenerare (**ingènero**) *tr* to engender
ingèni·to -ta *adj* inborn
ingènte *adj* huge, vast
ingentilíre §176 *tr* to refine
ingenui·tà *f* (-tà) ingenuousness; ingenuous act
ingè·nuo -nua *adj* ingenuous, artless || *m* (theat) artless character || *f* (theat) ingénue
ingerènza *f* interference
ingerire §176 *tr* to ingest, swallow || *ref* to meddle

ingessare (ingèsso) *tr* to put in a plaster cast; to plaster up

ingessatura *f* (surg) plaster cast

inghiaiare §287 *tr* to gravel, cover with gravel

Inghilterra, l' *f* England; **la Nuova Inghilterra** New England

inghiottire (inghiótto) & §176 *tr* to swallow; to swallow up; to pocket (*one's pride*)

inghirlandare *tr* to bedeck with garlands; (lit) to encircle

ingiallire §176 *tr* & *intr* (ESSERE) to turn yellow

ingigantire §176 *tr* to exaggerate || *intr* (ESSERE) to grow larger, increase

inginocchiare §287 **(inginòcchio)** *ref* to kneel down

inginocchia·tóio *m* (-tói) prie-dieu

ingioiellare (ingioièllo) *tr* to bejewel; (fig) to stud

ingiù *adv* down; **all'ingiù** downwards

ingiùngere §183 *tr* to order, command || *intr* (with *dat*) to order, command, e.g., **il giudice ingiunse all'imputato di rispondere** the judge ordered the accused to answer

ingiunzióne *f* order; (law) injunction

ingiùria *f* insult, abuse; damage, wear

ingiuriare §287 *tr* to insult

ingiurió·so -sa [s] *adj* insulting

ingiustificàbile *adj* unjustifiable

ingiustifica·to -ta *adj* unjustified

ingiustìzia *f* injustice

ingiù·sto -sta *adj* unjust, unfair || *m* unjust person

inglése [s] *adj* English; **all'inglese** in the English fashion; **andarsene all'inglese** to take French leave || *m* Englishman; English (*language*) || *f* Englishwoman

ingoiare §287 **(ingóio)** *tr* to swallow; to gulp down; **ingoiare un rospo** (fig) to swallow one's pride

ingolfare (ingólfo) *tr* (aut) to flood || *ref* to form a gulf; to get involved; (aut) to flood

ingollare (ingóllo) *tr* to swallow, gulp down

ingolosire [s] §176 *tr* to make the mouth of (*s.o.*) water || *intr* (ESSERE) & *ref* to have a craving

ingombrante *adj* cumbersome

ingombrare (ingómbro) *tr* to clutter

ingóm·bro -bra *adj* encumbered, cluttered || *m* encumbrance; **essere d'ingombro** to be in the way

ingommare (ingómmo) *tr* to glue

ingordìgia *f* greed

ingór·do -da *adj* greedy, covetous

ingorgare §209 **(ingórgo)** *ref* to get clogged up

ingór·go *m* (-ghi) blocking, congestion; **ingorgo stradale** traffic jam

ingovernàbile *adj* uncontrollable

ingozzare (ingózzo) *tr* to gobble, gulp down; to swallow; to cram (*e.g., a goose for fattening*)

ingranàg·gio *m* (-gi) gear, gearwheel; (fig) meshes; **ingranaggio di distribuzione** (aut) timing gear; **ingranaggio elicoidale** worm gear

ingranare *tr* to engage (*a gear*); **ingranare la marcia** to throw into gear || *intr* to be in gear; to succeed

ingrandiménto *m* enlargement; increase

ingrandire §176 *tr* to enlarge; to increase; || *intr* (ESSERE) & *ref* to increase, get larger

ingrassare *tr* to fatten; to lubricate || *intr* (ESSERE) & *ref* to get fat; to get rich

ingrassa·tóre -trice *mf* greaser, lubricator || *f* grease gun; lubricating machine

ingratitùdine *f* ingratitude

ingra·to -ta *adj* ungrateful; thankless || *mf* ingrate

ingraziare §287 *ref* to ingratiate oneself with

ingrediènte *m* ingredient

ingrèsso *m* entrance; admittance, entry; **ingressi** hallway furniture; **primo ingresso** debut

ingrossaménto *m* enlargement; swelling

ingrossare (ingròsso) *tr* to enlarge; to swell; to make bigger; to dull (*the mind*); to raise (*one's voice*) || *intr* (ESSERE) & *ref* to swell; to thicken; to become fat; to become pregnant; to become important

ingròsso *m*—**all'ingrosso** wholesale; approximately, more or less

ingrullire §176 *tr* to drive crazy || *intr* (ESSERE) & *ref* to become silly; **fare ingrullire** to drive crazy

inguadàbile *adj* not fordable

inguainare (inguaìno) *tr* to sheathe

ingualcìbile *adj* wrinkle-free, wrinkle-proof

inguanta·to -ta *adj* with gloves on; **con le mani inguantate** with gloves on

inguarìbile *adj* incurable

inguine *f* (anat) groin

ingurgitare (ingùrgito) *tr* to swallow, gulp down

inibire §176 *tr* to inhibit

inibi·tóre -trice *adj* inhibiting || *m* inhibitor

inidòne·o -a *adj* unfit, unqualified

iniettare (iniètto) *tr* to inject || *ref* to become bloodshot; **iniettarsi di sangue** to become bloodshot

iniezióne *f* injection

inimicare §197 *tr* to make an enemy of; to alienate || *ref*—**inimicarsi con** to fall out with

inimicìzia *f* enmity

inimitàbile *adj* inimitable, matchless

ininterrót·to -ta *adj* uninterrupted

iniqui·tà *f* (-tà) injustice; iniquity

inì·quo -qua *adj* unjust; wicked

iniziale *adj* & *f* initial

iniziare §287 *tr* to initiate || *ref* to begin

iniziativa *f* initiative; sponsorship; **iniziativa privata** private enterprise

inizia·tóre -trice *adj* initiating || *mf* initiator, promoter

iniziazióne *f* initiation

inì·zio *m* (-zi) beginning, start

innaffiare §287 *tr* var of **annaffiare**

innaffia·tóio *m* (-tói) var of **annaffiatoio**

innalzaménto *m* elevation

innalzare *tr* to raise; to elevate; **innalzare al cielo** to praise to the sky || *ref* to rise; to tower

innamorare (innamóro) *tr* to charm, fascinate; to inspire with love || *ref* to fall in love

innamora·to *-ta adj* in love, enamored; fond || *mf* sweetheart || *m* boyfriend || *f* girl friend

innanzi *adj invar* previous, prior (*e.g., day*) || *adv* ahead, before; **innanzi a** in front of; **innanzi di** + *inf* before + *ger*; **mettere innanzi** to prefer; to place before; to advance (*an excuse*); **per l'innanzi** before, in the past; **tirare innanzi** to get along || *prep* before; above; **innanzi tempo** ahead of time; **innanzi tutto** above all

innà·rio *m* (*-ri*) hymnal

inna·to *-ta adj* inborn, innate

innegàbile *adj* undeniable

inneggiare §290 **(innéggio)** *intr*—**inneggiare a** to sing the praises of

innervosire [s] §176 *tr* to make nervous

innescare §197 **(innésco)** *tr* to bait (*a hook*); to prime (*a bomb*)

inné·sco *m* (*-schi*) primer; detonator

innestare (innèsto) *tr* (hort & surg) to graft; (surg) to implant; (med) to inoculate (*a vaccine*); (mach) to engage; (elec) to plug in (*e.g., a plug*); **innestare la marcia** (aut) to throw into gear || *ref* to be grafted; **innestarsi in** to merge with; **innestarsi su** to connect with

innèsto *m* (hort & surg) graft; (surg) implant; (med) inoculation; (mach) engagement; (mach) coupling; (elec) plug

inno *m* hymn; **inno nazionale** national anthem

innocènte *adj* innocent || *m* innocent; **innocenti** foundlings

innocènza *f* innocence

innò·cuo *-cua adj* innocuous, harmless

innominàbile *adj* unmentionable

innomina·to *-ta adj* unnamed

innovare (innòvo) *tr* to innovate

innovazióne *f* innovation

innumerévole *adj* countless, innumerable

-ino *-ina suf adj* little, e.g., **poverino** poor little; hailing from, e.g., **fiorentino** hailing from Florence, Florentine || *suf f* see **-ina**

inoccupa·to *-ta adj* unoccupied || *m* person looking for his first job

inoculare (inòculo) *tr* to inoculate

inoculazióne *f* inoculation

inodó·ro *-ra adj* odorless

inoffensi·vo *-va adj* inoffensive

inoltrare (inóltro) *tr* (com) to forward (*e.g., a request*) || *ref* to advance

inóltre *adv* besides, in addition

inóltro *m* (com) forwarding

inondare (inóndo) *tr* to inundate, flood; to swamp

inondazióne *f* flood, inundation

inoperosità [s] *f* idleness

inoperó·so *-sa* [s] *adj* idle

inopina·to *-ta adj* (lit) unexpected

inopportu·no *-na adj* inopportune, untimely

inoppugnàbile *adj* incontestable; indisputable

inorgàni·co *-ca adj* (*-ci -che*) inorganic

inorgoglire §176 *tr* to make proud || *intr* (ESSERE) & *ref* to grow proud

inorridire §176 *tr* to horrify || *intr* (ESSERE) to be horrified

inospitale *adj* inhospitable

inosservante *adj* unobservant

inosserva·to *-ta adj* unnoticed; unperceived

inossidàbile *adj* stainless

inquadrare *tr* to frame; to arrange

inquadratura *f* framing; (mov, phot) frame

inqualificàbile *adj* unspeakable

inquietante *adj* disquieting

inquietare (inquièto) *tr* to worry || *ref* to worry; to get angry

inquiè·to *-ta adj* worried; restless; angry; (lit) stormy

inquietùdine *f* worry; restlessness; preoccupation

inquili·no *-na mf* tenant

inquinaménto *m* pollution

inquinare *tr* to pollute

inquirènte *adj* investigating

inquisi·tóre *-trice adj* inquiring || *m* inquisitor

inquisizióne *f* inquisition

insabbiare §287 *tr* to cover with sand; to pigeonhole; to shelve || *ref* to get covered with sand; to bury oneself in sand; to get stuck

insaccare §197 *tr* to bag; to stuff (*e.g., salami*); (mil) to hem in; (fig) to bundle up; (coll) to gulp down || *ref* to be packed in; to crumple up; to disappear behind a thick bank of clouds (*said, e.g., of the sun*)

insaccato *m* participant in a sack race; **insaccati** cold cuts, lunch meat

insalata *f* salad; (fig) mess

insalatièra *f* salad bowl

insalubre *adj* unhealthy

insaluta·to *-ta adj* unsaluted; **andarsene insalutato ospite** to take French leave

insanàbile *adj* incurable; implacable

insanguinare (insànguino) *tr* to bloody; to cover with blood; to bathe in blood

insa·no *-na adj* insane

insaponare (insapóno) *tr* to soap; to lather; (fig) to soft-soap

insaporire §176 *tr* to flavor || *intr* (ESSERE) to become tasty

insaputa *f*—**all'insaputa di** without the knowledge of, unbeknown to

insaziàbile *adj* insatiable

insazia·to *-ta adj* insatiate, unsatisfied

inscatolare (inscàtolo) *tr* to can

inscenare (inscèno) *tr* to stage

inscindìbile *adj* inseparable

inscrivere §250 *tr* (geom) to inscribe

inscrutàbile *adj* inscrutable

inscurire §176 *tr, intr* (ESSERE) & *ref* to darken

insecchire §176 *tr* to dry || *intr* (ESSERE) & *ref* to dry up

insediaménto *m* installation (*into an office*); assumption (*of an office*)

insediare §287 (**insèdio**) *tr* to install || *ref* to be installed; to take one's seat; to settle

inségna *f* badge, insignia, emblem; ensign, flag; coat of arms; motto; sign (*e.g., on a restaurant*): traffic sign

insegnaménto *m* education, instruction

insegnante *adj* teaching || *mf* teacher

insegnare (**inségno**) *tr* to teach; to show || *intr* to teach

inseguiménto *m* pursuit

inseguire (**inséguo**) *tr* to pursue, chase; to chase after

insellare (**insèllo**) *tr* to saddle; to put on (*e.g., one's glasses*); to bend

insellatura *f* saddling; bending

insenatura *f* inlet, cove

insensatézza *f* nonsense, folly

insensa·to -ta *adj* nonsensical, foolish || *mf* scatterbrain

insensibile *adj* insensible; unresponsive; insensitive

inseparàbile *adj* inseparable || *m* (orn) lovebird

insepól·to -ta *adj* unburied

inserire §176 *tr* to insert; to plug in || *ref* to slip in; to butt in

inseri·tóre -trice *adj* (elec) connecting || *m* (elec) connector, plug || *f* sorter (*of punch cards*)

insèrto *m* file, folder; insert; spliced film

inservibile *adj* useless, worthless

inserviènte *m* attendant, porter; (eccl) server

inserzionare (**inserzióno**) *intr* to advertise

inserzióne *f* insertion; advertisement

inserzioni·sta (**-sti -ste**) *adj* advertising || *mf* advertiser

insetticì·da *adj & m* (**-di -de**) insecticide

insettìfu·go m (**-ghi**) insect repellent

insètto *m* insect; **insetti** vermin

insìdia *f* trap, ambush; **insidie** lure

insidiare §287 *tr* to ensnare; to try to trap; to try to seduce; to attempt (*someone's life*)

insidió·so -sa [s] *adj* insidious

insième *m* whole, entirety; harmony; ensemble; set; **d'insieme** general, comprehensive; **nell'insieme** as a whole || *adv* together

insigne *adj* famous; notable; arrant (*knave*)

insignificante *adj* insignificant; petty

insignire §176 *tr* to decorate; **insignire qlcu di un titolo** to bestow a title upon s.o.

insignorire §176 *tr* (lit) to invest with a fief || *intr* (ESSERE) to enrich oneself || *ref* to enrich oneself; **insignorirsi di** to seize; to take possession of

insilare *tr* to silo, ensile

insilato *m* ensilage

insincè·ro -ra *adj* insincere

insindacàbile *adj* final, indisputable

insino *adv* (lit)—**insino a** until; as far as; **insino a che** as long as

insinuante *adj* insinuating

insinuare (**insìnuo**) *tr* to stick, thrust;

to insinuate; (law) to register || *ref* to creep, filter; to ingratiate oneself; **insinuarsi in** to worm one's way into

insinuazióne *f* insinuation, hint

insìpi·do -da *adj* insipid, vapid

insistènte *adj* insistent

insistere §114 *intr* to insist

ìnsi·to -ta *adj* inborn, inherent

insociévole *adj* unsociable

insoddisfat·to -ta *adj* dissatisfied

insofferènte *adj* intolerant

insoffrìbile *adj* unbearable, insufferable

insolazióne *f* sunning; sun bath; sunstroke; sunny exposure

insolènte *adj* insolent

insolentire §176 *tr* to insult, abuse || *intr* to be insolent

insolènza *f* insolence; insult

insòli·to -ta *adj* unusual

insolùbile *adj* insoluble

insolu·to -ta *adj* unsolved; not dissolved; unpaid

insolvènza *f* insolvency

insolvìbile *adj* insolvent; bad (*debt*)

insómma *adv* in conclusion || *interj* well!

insommergìbile *adj* unsinkable

insondàbile *adj* unfathomable

insònne *adj* sleepless

insònnia *f* insomnia

insonnolì·to -ta *adj* sleepy, drowsy

insonorizzazióne [ddzz] *f* soundproofing

insopportàbile *adj* unbearable

insorgènte *adj* appearing || *mf* insurgent

insorgènza *f* appearance (*of illness*)

insórgere §258 *intr* (ESSERE) to rise up, revolt; to appear

insormontàbile *adj* unsurmountable, insurmountable

insór·to -ta *adj & m* insurgent

insospettàbile *adj* above suspicion; unexpected

insospetta·to -ta *adj* not suspect; unexpected

insospettire §176 *tr* to make suspicious || *intr* (ESSERE) & *ref* to become suspicious

insostenibile *adj* indefensible; unbearable

insostituìbile *adj* irreplaceable

insozzare (**insózzo**) *tr* to soil, sully

inspera·to -ta *adj* unexpected; unhopedfor

inspiegàbile *adj* unexplainable

inspirare *tr* to inhale, breathe in

inspirazióne *f* inhalation

instàbile *adj* unstable

installare *tr* to install; to set up, settle; to induct (*in an office*) || *ref* to settle

installatóre *m* plumber; erector

installazióne *f* installation; plumbing

instancàbile *adj* untiring

instante *adj* insistent; impending || *m* petitioner

instare (*pp* missing) *intr* to insist; to threaten, be imminent

instaurare (**instàuro**) *tr* to establish

instaurazióne *f* establishment

instigare §209 *tr* var of **istigare**

instillare *tr* var of **istillare**

instituire §176 *tr* var of **istituire**

instruire §176 *tr* var of **istruire**
instrumento *m* var of **istrumento**
instupidire §176 *tr* var of **istupidire**
insù *adv* up; **all'insù** up
insubordina·to -ta *adj* insubordinate
insuccèsso *m* failure
insudiciare §128 (**insùdicio**) *tr* to soil, dirty; to sully || *ref* to get dirty
insufficiènte *adj* insufficient; failing (*in school*)
insufficiènza *f* insufficiency; failure (*in school*)
insulare *adj* insular
insulina *f* insulin
insulsàggine *f* silliness, nonsense
insul·so -sa *adj* insipid; simple, silly
insultante *adj* insulting
insultare *tr* to insult || *intr* (with *dat*) to insult
insulto *m* insult; (pathol) attack
insuperàbile *adj* insuperable; unparalleled
insupera·to -ta *adj* unsurpassed
insuperbire §176 *tr, intr* (ESSERE) & *ref* to swell with pride
insurrezióne *f* insurrection
insussistènte *adj* nonexistent, unfounded
intabarrare *tr* to wrap up
intaccare §197 *tr* to notch; to corrode; to scratch; to attack (*said of a disease*); to damage (*e.g., a reputation*); to cut into (*capital*) || *intr* to stutter
intaccatura *f* notch; (carp) mortise
intagliare §280 *tr* to carve; to engrave
intà·glio *m* (**-gli**) carving; intaglio
intanare *ref* to hide
intangìbile *adj* intangible; inviolable
intanto *adv* meanwhile; (coll) yet; (coll) finally; **intanto che** while; **per intanto** at present; in the meantime
intarsiare §287 *tr* to inlay; (fig) to stud
intarsia·to -ta *adj* inlaid
intàr·sio *m* (**-si**) inlay; inlaid work
intasare [s] *tr* to clog; to tie up (*traffic*); to stop up || *ref* to be clogged up; to be tied up; to be stopped up (*said of nose*)
intascare §197 *tr* to pocket
intat·to -ta *adj* intact, untouched
intavolare (**intàvolo**) *tr* to start (*a conversation*); to broach (*a subject*); to launch (*negotiations*)
intavolato *m* boarding, planking
integèrri·mo -ma *adj* of the utmost honesty
integrale *adj* integral; whole; wholewheat (*bread*); built-in || *m* integral
integralismo *m* policy of the complete absorption of the body politic by an ideology
integrante *adj* constituent, integral
integrare (**intègro**) *tr* to integrate || *ref* to complement each other
integrazióne *f* integration
integrità *f* integrity
ìnte·gro -gra *adj* whole, complete; honest, upright; intact
intelaiatura *f* frame; framework
intellètto *m* intellect, mind; understanding
intellettuale *adj* & *mf* intellectual

intellettuali·tà *f* (**-tà**) intellectuality; intelligentsia
intellettualòide *mf* highbrow
intelligènte *adj* intelligent; clever
intelligènza *f* intelligence; understanding; **essere d'intelligenza con** to be in collusion with
intellighènzia *f* intelligentsia
intelligìbile *adj* intelligible
intemera·to -ta *adj* pure, spotless || *f* reprimand, scolding; long, boring speech
intemperante *adj* intemperate
intemperanza *f* intemperance
intempèrie *fpl* inclement weather
intempesti·vo -va *adj* untimely
intendènte *m* district director; **intendente di finanza** director of customs office; **intendente militare** commissary, quartermaster
intendènza *f* office of the district director; intendance; **intendenza militare** quartermaster corps
intèndere §270 *tr* to understand; to hear; to intend; to turn (*e.g., one's eyes*); to mean; **dare ad intendere a** to lead (*s.o.*) to believe (*s.th*); **far intendere** to give to understand; **farsi intendere** to force obedience; to make oneself understood; **intender dire che** to hear that; **intendere a rovescio** to misunderstand; **intendere a volo** to catch on quickly (to); **intendere ragione** to listen to reason; **lasciare intendere** to give to understand || *intr* to aim (*toward a goal*) || *ref* to come to an agreement; **intendersela con** to be in collusion with; to have an affair with; **intendersi di** to be a good judge of; to be an expert in
intendimènto *m* understanding, comprehension; aim, goal
intendi·tóre -trice *mf* connoisseur, expert; **a buon intenditore poche parole** a word to the wise is sufficient
intenerire §176 *tr* to soften; (fig) to move || *ref* to soften; (fig) to be moved
intensificare §197 (**intensìfico**) *tr* & *ref* to intensify
intensi·tà *f* (**-tà**) intensity
intensi·vo -va *adj* intensive
intèn·so -sa *adj* intense
intentare (**intènto**) *tr* (law) to bring (*action*)
intenta·to -ta *adj* unattempted
intèn·to -ta *adj* intent || *m* intent, goal; **coll'intento di** with the purpose of
intenzionale *adj* intentional
intenziona·to -ta *adj*—**bene intenzionato** well-meaning; **essere intenzionato di** to intend to
intenzióne *f* intention; purpose; **con intenzione** on purpose
intepidire §176 *tr* & *ref* var of **intiepidire**
interbase *f* (baseball) shortstop
intercalare *m* refrain; pet word or phrase || *tr* to intercalate; to inset
intercalazióne *f* intercalation; inset
intercapèdine *f* air space
intercèdere §123 *tr* to seek, get (*a par-

don for s.o.) || *intr* to intercede || *intr* (ESSERE)—**intercedere tra** to intervene or elapse between; to extend between; to exist between

intercettare (**intercètto**) *tr* to intercept; to tap (*a phone*)

intercetta·tóre -trice *mf* interceptor

intercettóre *m* (aer) interceptor

intercomunale *adj* long-distance (**call**)

intercórrere §139 *intr* (ESSERE) to elapse; to happen; to be, to stand

interdét·to -ta *adj* dumfounded; forbidden || *m* interdict; (coll) dumbell

interdire §151 *tr* to prohibit; (eccl) to interdict; (law) to disqualify

interessaménto *m* interest, concern

interessante *adj* interesting; **in stato interessante** in the family way

interessare (**interèsso**) *tr* to interest; to concern || *intr* to be of interest || *ref*—**interessarsi a** to take an interest in; **interessarsi di** to concern oneself with

interessa·to -ta *adj* interested; selfish || *m* interested party

interèsse *m* interest; self-interest

interessènza *f* (com) share, interest

interferènza *f* interference

interferire §176 *intr* to interfere

interfogliare §280 (**interfòglio**) *tr* to interleave

interiezióne *f* interjection

interinato *m* temporary office or tenure

interi·no -na *adj* acting || *m* temporary appointee

interióra *fpl* entrails

interióre *adj* interior || **interiori** *mpl* entrails

interlínea *f* interlining; (typ) leading

interlineare *adj* interlinear || *v* (**interlíneo**) *tr* (typ) to lead

interlocu·tóre -trice *mf* participant (*in a discussion*); person speaking

interloquire §176 *intr* to take part in a discussion; to chime in

interlù·dio *m* (**-di**) interlude

intermedià·rio -ria (**-ri -rie**) *adj* & *mf* intermediary || *m* middleman

intermè·dio -dia (**-di -die**) *adj* intermediate || *mf* supervisor

intermèzzo [ddzz] *m* intermezzo; entr'acte; interval

interminàbile *adj* interminable, endless

intermissióne *f* intermission

intermittènte *adj* intermittent

internaménto *m* internment

internare (**intèrno**) *tr* to intern; to confine; to commit (*an insane person*) || *ref* to go deep (*into a problem*)

interna·to -ta *adj* interned || *m* internee; inmate; boarder; boarding school

internazionale *adj* international

internazionalizzare [ddzz] *tr* to internationalize

interni·sta *mf* (**-sti -ste**) internist

intèr·no -na *adj* inside, internal; inland; interior; boarding (*student*) || *m* inside; interior; (med) intern; lining (*of coat*); **all'interno** inside; **interni** (mov) indoor shots || **gli Interni** the Italian Ministry of Internal Affairs

inté·ro -ra *adj* entire, whole; full (*price*); (lit) upright, honest || *m* whole; **per intero** completely

interpellare (**interpèllo**) *tr* to interpellate; to question; to consult

interpetrare (**intèrpetro**) *tr* var of **interpretare**

interplanetà·rio -ria *adj* (**-ri -rie**) interplanetary

interpolare (**intèrpolo**) *tr* to interpolate

interpolazióne *f* interpolation

interpónte *m* (naut) between-deck

interpórre §218 *tr* to interpose || *ref* to intervene

interpretare (**intèrpreto**) *tr* to interpret

interpretazióne *f* interpretation

intèrprete *mf* interpreter

interpunzióne *f* punctuation

interrare (**intèrro**) *tr* to bury, inter; to fill in (*e.g., a marsh*) || *ref* to become silted

interra·to -ta *adj* underground; **piano interrato** basement

interrogare §209 (**intèrrogo**) *tr* to question; to interrogate

interrogati·vo -va *adj* interrogative || *m* why; question

interrogatò·rio -ria (**-ri -rie**) *adj* questioning || *m* (law) interrogatory; **interrogatorio di terzo grado** third degree

interrogazióne *f* interrogation; quiz, examination; **interrogazione retorica** rhetorical question

interrómpere §240 *tr* to interrupt

interruttóre *m* (elec) switch; **interruttore di linea** (elec) controller

interruzióne *f* interruption

interscàm·bio *m* (**-bi**) interchange

interscolàsti·co -ca *adj* (**-ci -che**) interscholastic; intercollegiate

intersecare §197 (**intèrseco**) *tr & ref* to intersect

intersezióne *f* intersection

interstellare *adj* interstellar

interstì·zio *m* (**-zi**) interstice

interurba·no -na *adj* interurban, intercity; (telp) long-distance || *f* (telp) long-distance call

intervallo *m* interval; pause; (educ) recess; (theat) intermission

intervenire §282 *intr* (ESSERE) to intervene; (surg) to operate; **intervenire a** to take part in

interventi·sta *mf* (**-sti -ste**) interventionist

intervènto *m* intervention; attendance; (surg) operation

intervenzióne *f* intervention

intervista *f* interview; **fare un'intervista a** to interview

intervistare *tr* to interview

inté·so -sa [s] *adj* understood; intended, designed; **bene inteso** of course; **non darsene per inteso** to not pay attention; **rimanere inteso** to agree || *f* understanding, agreement; entente

intèssere (**intèsso**) *tr* to interweave; to wreathe (*a garland*)

intestardire §176 *ref* to get obstinate; to be determined

intestare (intèsto) *tr* to caption; to label; (typ) to head (*a page*); **intestare qlco a qlcu** to register s.th in the name of s.o.; **intestare una fattura a** to issue a bill in the name of || *ref* to become obstinate; to take it into one's head

intesta·to -ta *adj* headed; registered (*stock*); obstinate; (law) intestate

intestazióne *f* heading; registration (*of stock*)

intestinale *adj* intestinal

intesti·no -na *adj & m* intestine; **intestino crasso** large intestine; **intestino tenue** small intestine

intiepidire §176 *tr & ref* to warm up; to cool off

intiè·ro -ra *adj & m* var of **intero**

intimare (**intimo & intimo**) *tr* to intimate; to order, command; to declare (*war*); to impose (*a fine*); (law) to enjoin

intimazióne *f* intimation; order; (law) injunction

intimidazióne *f* intimidation

intimidire §176 *tr* to intimidate; to threaten || *ref* to become bashful

intimi·tà *f* (-tà) intimacy; privacy

ìnti·mo -ma *adj* intimate; inmost; **biancheria intima** underwear, lingerie || *m* intimate friend; depth (*of one's heart*)

intimorire §176 *tr* to frighten

intingere §126 *tr* to dip || *intr*—**intingere in** to dip in || *ref*—**intingersi in un affare** to have a finger in the pie

intingolo *m* sauce, gravy; fancy dish

intirizzire [ddzz] §176 *tr* to benumb || *intr* (ESSERE) *& ref* to become numb or stiff; to become stiff and frostbitten

intirizzi·to -ta [ddzz] *adj* numb

intisichire §176 *tr* to make tubercular; (fig) to weaken || *intr* (ESSERE) to become tubercular; to wither

intitolare (intìtolo) *tr* to title; to dedicate || *ref* to be named; to assume the title of

intoccàbile *adj & m* untouchable

intolleràbile *adj* intolerable

intollerante *adj* intolerant

intonacare §197 (intònaco) *tr* to plaster; to whitewash; to cover (*e.g.*, *with tar*) || *ref*—**intonacarsi la faccia** (joc) to put on one's warpaint

intòna·co m (-chi) plaster; roughcast

intonare (intòno) *tr* to intone; to harmonize; (mus) to tune || *ref* to harmonize, go

intonazióne *f* intonation; harmony

intòn·so -sa *adj* uncut; (lit) unsheared

intontire §176 *tr* to stun || *intr* (ESSERE) *& ref* to become stunned

intoppare (intòppo) *tr* to stumble upon || *intr* (ESSERE) *& ref* to stumble

intòppo *m* obstacle, hindrance

intorbidare (intórbido) *tr* to cloud; to muddy; to obfuscate; to upset (*friendship*); to stir up (*passions*) || *ref* to become cloudy or muddy; to become obfuscated

intorbidire §176 *tr & ref* to cloud; to muddy

intormentire §176 *tr* to benumb || *intr* (ESSERE) to become numb

intórno *adv* around, about; **all'intorno** all around; **intorno a** around; about; **levarsi qlcu d'intorno** to get rid of s.o.

intorpidire §176 *tr* to benumb || *ref* to become numb

intossicare §197 (intòssico) *tr* to poison, intoxicate

intossicazióne *f* poisoning, intoxication

intraducìbile *adj* untranslatable; inexpressible

intrafèrro *m* spark gap; air gap

intralciare §128 *tr* to hamper; to intertwine || *ref* to become hampered

intràl·cio m (-ci) hindrance; **essere d'intralcio** to be in the way; **intralcio del traffico** traffic congestion

intralicciatura *f* lattice truss (*of high-tension tower*)

intrallazzare *intr* to deal in the black market

intrallazza·tóre -trice *mf* black marketeer

intrallazzo *m* black-market dealing; kickback

intramezzare [ddzz] (intramèzzo) *tr* to alternate

intramontàbile *adj* undying, immortal

intransigènte *adj & mf* intransigent, die-hard

intransitàbile *adj* impassable

intransiti·vo -va *adj* intransitive

intrappolare (intràppolo) *tr* to entrap

intraprendènte *adj* enterprising

intraprendènza *f* enterprise, initiative

intraprèndere §220 *tr* to undertake

intrattàbile *adj* unmanageable, intractable

intrattenére §271 *tr* to entertain || *ref* to linger; **intrattenersi su** to dwell upon

intratteniménto *m* entertainment

intravedére §279 *tr* to glimpse, catch a glimpse of; to foresee

intravenó·so -sa [s] *adj* intravenous

intrecciare §128 (intréccio) *tr* to braid; to twine; to cross (*one's fingers*); (fig) to weave; to begin (*a dance*) || *ref* to become embroiled; to become intertwined; to crisscross

intréc·cio m (-ci) knitting; intertwining; plot (*of novel*); (theat) intrigue

intrepidézza *f* intrepidness, intrepidity

intrèpi·do -da *adj* intrepid

intricare §197 *tr* (lit) to entangle

intrica·to -ta *adj* tangled; intricate

intrì·co m (-chi) tangle, jumble

intrìdere §189 *tr* to soak; to knead

intrigante *adj* intriguing || *mf* schemer

intrigare §209 *tr* to tangle || *intr* to intrigue || *ref* (coll) to meddle

intrì·go m (-ghi) intrigue; trouble

intrìnse·co -ca (-ci -che) *adj* intrinsic; intimate || *m* intimate nature, core

intrì·so -sa *adj* soaked || *m* mash

intristire §176 *intr* (ESSERE) to wither; to waste away

introdót·to -ta *adj* introduced; well-known; knowledgeable, expert

introdurre §102 *tr* to introduce; to insert; to open (*a speech*); to show in || *ref* to slip in

introdutti·vo -va *adj* introductory

introduzióne *f* introduction

introitare (intròito) *tr* to collect, take in

intròito *m* receipts, collection; (eccl) introit

introméttere §198 *tr* to insert; to introduce; to involve || *ref* to meddle; to pry

intromissióne *f* meddling; intrusion; intervention

intronare (intròno) *tr* to deafen; to stun

intronizzare [ddzz] *tr* to enthrone

introspetti·vo -va *adj* introspective

introspezióne *f* introspection

introvàbile *adj* unobtainable; inaccessible

introvèr·so -sa *adj & mf* introvert

intrùdere §190 *tr* (lit) to slip in || *ref* to intrude; to trespass

intrufolare (intrùfolo) *tr* (coll) to slip (*e.g., one's hand into somebody's pocket*) || *ref* to slip in, intrude

intrù·glio *m* (-gli) concoction, brew; hodgepodge; imbroglio; mess

intrusióne *f* intrusion

intru·so -sa *adj* intrusive || *mf* intruder

intuire §176 *tr* to know by intuition; to guess; to sense

intuiti·vo -va *adj* intuitive; obvious

intùito *m* intuition; insight

intuizióne *f* intuition

inturgidire §176 *intr* (ESSERE) & *ref* to swell

inuma·no -na *adj* inhuman; inhumane

inumare *tr* to bury, inhume

inumazióne *f* burial, inhumation

inumidire §176 *tr* to moisten || *ref* to get wet

inurbaménto *m* migration to the city

inurba·no -na *adj* uncouth, unmannerly

inurbare *ref* to move into the city; to become citified

inusa·to -ta *adj* unused; unusual

inusita·to -ta *adj* unusual; out-of-the-way

inùtile *adj* useless; worthless

inutilizzàbile [ddzz] *adj* unusable

inutilizzare [ddzz] *tr* to waste (*e.g., time*)

inutilizza·to -ta [ddzz] *adj* unused

inutilménte *adv* needlessly, to no purpose || *interj* no use!

invadènte *adj* meddlesome, intrusive

invàdere §172 *tr* to invade; to encroach on; to spread over; to overcome

invaghire §176 *tr* to charm || *ref* to fall in love

invalére §278 *intr* (ESSERE) to become established; to prevail

invalicàbile *adj* impassable, unsurmountable

invalidàbile *adj* voidable

invalidaménto *m* invalidity; invalidation

invalidare (invàlido) *tr* to void, invalidate; to negate (*e.g., evidence*)

invalidi·tà *f* (-tà) invalidity; invalidation; sickness, disability

invàli·do -da *adj* void, invalid; sick, disabled || *m* disabled person; invalid

inval·so -sa *adj* prevailing

invano *adv* in vain, vainly

invariàbile *adj* invariable

invaria·to -ta *adj* unchanging; unchanged

invasare *tr* to pot (*a plant*); to fill up (*a reservoir*); to possess, obsess

invasa·to -ta *adj* possessed, obsessed

invasióne *f* invasion

inva·so -sa *adj* invaded || *m* potting (*of plant*); capacity (*of reservoir*)

inva·sóre -ditrice *adj* invading || *m* invader

invecchiaménto *m* aging

invecchiare §287 (invècchio) *tr & intr* (ESSERE) to age

invéce *adv* on the contrary, instead; invece di instead of

inveire §176 *intr* to inveigh, rail

invelenire §176 *tr* to envenom; to embitter || *intr* (ESSERE) & *ref* to grow bitter

invendibile *adj* unsalable

invendica·to -ta *adj* unavenged

invendu·to -ta *adj* unsold

inventare (invènto) *tr* to invent

inventariare §287 *tr* to inventory

inventà·rio *m* (-ri) inventory

inventi·vo -va *adj* inventive || *f* inventiveness

inven·tóre -trice *adj* inventive || *mf* inventor

invenzióne *f* invention; (lit) find

inverdire §176 *intr* (ESSERE) to turn green

inverecóndia *f* immodesty

inverecón·do -da *adj* immodest

invernale *adj* winter; wintry

inverniciare §128 *tr* to paint; to varnish

invèrno *m* winter

invéro *adv* (lit) truly, indeed

inverosimiglianza [s] *f* unlikelihood

inverosimile [s] *adj* unlikely

inversióne *f* inversion

invèr·so -sa *adj* inverse, opposite; (coll) cross || *m* inverse

inversóre *m* inverter; inversore di spinta (aer) thrust reverser

invertebra·to -ta *adj & m* invertebrate

invertire §176 & (invèrto) *tr* to invert; to reverse

inverti·to -ta *adj* inverted || *m* invert

investigare §209 (invèstigo) *tr* to investigate

investiga·tóre -trice *adj* investigating || *mf* investigator; detective

investigazióne *f* investigation

investiménto *m* investment; collision

investire (invèsto) *tr* to invest; to collide with; investire di insulti to cover with insults || *ref*—investirsi di to become conscious of (*e.g., one's authority*); (theat) to become identified with (*a character*)

investi·tóre -trice *mf* investor

investitura *f* investiture

invetera·to -ta *adj* inveterate, confirmed

invetrià·to -ta *adj* glazed || *f* window; window pane
invettiva *f* invective
inviare §119 *tr* to send
invia·to -ta *mf* envoy; correspondent
invidia *f* envy
invidiàbile *adj* enviable
invidiare §287 *tr* to envy; to begrudge; **non aver niente da invidiare a** to be just as good as
invidió·so -sa [s] *adj* envious
invigorire §176 *tr* to strengthen, invigorate || *intr* (ESSERE) & *ref* to grow stronger
invilire §176 *tr* to dishearten; to vilify; to lower (*prices*) || *intr* (ESSERE) & *ref* to lose heart; to lose one's reputation
inviluppare *tr* to envelop; to wrap up
invincibile *adj* invincible
invì·o m (-ì) dispatch; shipment; remittance; envoy (*of a poem*)
inviolàbile *adj* inviolable
inviperire §176 *ref* to become enraged
invischiare §287 *tr* to smear with birdlime; to ensnare || *ref* to become ensnared
invisìbile *adj* invisible
invì·so -sa *adj* disliked, hated
invitante *adj* attractive, inviting
invitare *tr* to invite; to summon; (*cards*) to bid; (*cards*) to open; (*mach*) to screw (*e.g., a light bulb*) in; to screw (*e.g., a lid*) on
invità·to -ta *adj* invited || *m* guest
invito *m* invitation; inducement; bottom of stairway; (*cards*) opening
invìt·to -ta *adj* unvanquished
invocare §197 (invòco) *tr* to invoke
invocazióne *f* invocation
invogliare §280 (invòglio) *tr* to induce, entice || *ref* to yearn, long
involare (invòlo) *tr* to steal; to abduct || *intr* (ESSERE) (aer) to take off || *ref* to disappear; to fly away
invòlgere §289 *tr* to wrap, envelop; to involve || *ref* to become entangled
invòlo *m* (aer) take-off
involontà·rio -ria *adj* (-ri -rie) involuntary
invòlto *m* bundle; wrapper
invòlucro *m* wrapping; shell (*of boiler*); (aer) envelope
involù·to -ta *adj* (fig) involved; (lit) enveloped
invòlvere §147 (*pret* missing; *pp* also invòlto) *tr* (lit) to envelop
invulneràbile *adj* invulnerable
inzaccherare (inzàcchero) *tr* to bespatter
inzeppare (inzéppo) *tr* to cram, stuff
inzuccherare (inzùcchero) *tr* to sweeten
inzuppare *tr* to soak || *ref* to get drenched
io m ego; self || §85 *pron pers*
iòdio *m* iodine
iodìdri·co -ca *adj* (-ci -che) hydriodic
ioduro *m* iodide
iògurt *m* yogurt
iò·le *f* (-le) (naut) yawl; (sports) shell
ióne *m* ion
iòni·co -ca *adj* & *m* (-ci -che) Ionic

ionizzare [ddzz] *tr* to ionize
iòsa [s] *f*—**a iosa** in abundance
iperacidità *f* hyperacidity
ipèrbole *f* (geom) hyperbola; (rhet) hyperbole
iperbòli·co -ca *adj* (-ci -che) hyperbolic(al)
ipereccità·to -ta *adj* overexcited
ipermercato *m* shopping center
ipersensìbile *adj* hypersensitive; supersensitive
ipersostentatóre *m* landing flap
ipertensióne *f* hypertension
ipnò·si *f* (-si) hypnosis
ipnòti·co -ca *adj* & *m* (-ci -che) hypnotic
ipnotismo *m* hypnotism
ipnotizzare [ddzz] *tr* to hypnotize
ipnotizza·tóre -trice [ddzz] *adj* hypnotizing || *m* hypnotizer
ipocondrìa·co -ca *adj* & *mf* (-ci -che) hypochondriac
ipocrisìa *f* hypocrisy
ipòcri·ta (-ti -te) *adj* hypocritical || *mf* hypocrite
ipodèrmi·co -ca *adj* (-ci -che) hypodermic
iposolfìto [s] *m* hyposulfite
ipotè·ca *f* (-che) mortgage
ipotecare §197 (ipotèco) *tr* to mortgage
ipotecà·rio -ria *adj* (-ri -rie) mortgage
ipotenusa *f* hypotenuse
ipòte·si *f* (-si) hypothesis; **nella miglior delle ipotesi** at best; **nell'ipotesi che** in the event; **per ipotesi** by supposition
ipotèti·co -ca *adj* (-ci -che) hypothetic(al)
ipotizzare [ddzz] *tr* to hypothesize
ìppi·co -ca *adj* (-ci -che) horse, horseracing || *f* horse racing
ippocampo *m* sea horse
ippocastano *m* horse chestnut tree
ippòdromo *m* race track
ippoglòsso *m* (ichth) halibut
ippopòtamo *m* hippopotamus
iprite *f* mustard gas
ira *f* wrath, anger, ire
irachè·no -na *adj* & *mf* Iraqi
iracóndia *f* wrath, anger
iracón·do -da *adj* wrathful
irania·no -na *adj* & *mf* Iranian
irascìbile *adj* irascible
ira·to -ta *adj* irate, angry
ire §191 *intr* (ESSERE) (lit) to go
irida·to -ta *adj* rainbow-hued || *m* world bicycle champion
iride *f* rainbow; (anat, bot) iris
Irlanda, l' *f* Ireland
irlandése [s] *adj* Irish || *m* Irishman; Irish (*language*) || *f* Irishwoman
ironìa *f* irony
iròni·co -ca *adj* (-ci -che) ironic(al)
iró·so -sa [s] *adj* angry, wrathful
irradiare §287 *tr* to illuminate; to irradiate, radiate; to brighten; (rad) to broadcast || *intr* to radiate || *ref* to radiate; to spread
irraggiare §290 *tr* to illuminate; to irradiate, radiate, beam; to brighten; (rad) to broadcast || *intr* to radiate || *ref* to radiate; to spread

irraggiungìbile *adj* unattainable
irragionévole *adj* unreasonable
irrancidire §176 *intr* (ESSERE) & *ref* to get rancid
irrazionale *adj* irrational
irreale *adj* unreal
irreconciliàbile *adj* irreconcilable
irrecuperàbile *adj* irretrievable, irrecoverable
irredentismo *m* irredentism
irredenti·sta *mf* (-sti -ste) irredentist
irredèn·to -ta *adj* not yet redeemed
irredimìbile *adj* irredeemable
irrefrenàbile *adj* unrestrainable
irrefutàbile *adj* irrefutable
irregimentare (**irregiménto**) *tr* to regiment
irregolare *adj* irregular
irregolari·tà *f* (-tà) irregularity
irreligió·so -sa [s] *adj* irreligious
irremovìbile *adj* irremovable; obstinate
irreparàbile *adj* irreparable; unavoidable
irreperìbile *adj* not to be found; unaccounted for (*e.g.*, soldier)
irreprensìbile *adj* irreproachable
irreprimìbile *adj* irrepressible
irrequiè·to -ta *adj* restless, restive
irresistìbile [s] *adj* irresistible
irresolùbile [s] *adj* unbreakable (bond; contract); insoluble; unsolvable
irresolu·to -ta [s] *adj* irresolute
irrespiràbile *adj* unbreathable
irresponsàbile *adj* irresponsible
irrestringìbile *adj* unshrinkable
irretire §176 *tr* to ensnare, entrap
irrevocàbile *adj* irrevocable
irriconoscìbile *adj* unrecognizable
irriducìbile *adj* irreducible; stubborn
irriflessì·vo -va *adj* thoughtless, rash
irrigare §209 *tr* to irrigate
irrigazióne *f* irrigation
irrigidire §176 *tr* to chill || *intr* & *ref* to stiffen, harden; to get cool
irri·guo -gua *adj* well-watered; irrigating
irrilevante *adj* irrelevant
irrilevanza *f* irrelevance
irrimediàbile *adj* irremediable
irripetìbile *adj* unrepeatable
irrisióne *f* (lit) derision, mockery
irrisò·rio -ria *adj* (-ri -rie) mocking; paltry
irritàbile *adj* peevish; irritable
irritante *adj* irritating || *m* irritant
irritare (**irrito**) *tr* to irritate; to anger; to chafe || *ref* to become irritated
irritazióne *f* irritation
irriverènte *adj* irreverent
irrobustire §176 *tr* & *ref* to strengthen
irrómpere §240 (*pp* missing) *intr* to burst
irrorare (**irròro**) *tr* to sprinkle; to bathe, wet; to spray
irroratrice *f* sprayer; **irroratrice a zaino** portable sprayer
irruènte *adj* impetuous, rash
irruzióne *f* foray, raid; irruption
irsu·to -ta *adj* hairy, bristling
ir·to -ta *adj* prickly; shaggy (hair); **irto di** bristling with
iscrìvere §250 *tr* to inscribe; to register || *ref* to register; to sign up

iscrizióne *f* inscription; registration
Islam, l' *m* Islam
Islanda, l' *f* Iceland
islandése [s] *adj* Icelandic || *mf* Icelander || *m* Icelandic (language)
ìsola *f* island; block; **isola spartitraffico** traffic island
isolaménto *m* isolation; (elec) insulation
isola·no -na *adj* island || *mf* islander
isolante *adj* insulating || *m* (elec) insulation
isolare (**ìsolo**) *tr* to isolate; (elec) to insulate || *ref* to keep apart
isola·to -ta *adj* isolated; (elec) insulated || *m* city block; (sports) independent
isolatóre *m* (elec) insulator
isolazionismo *m* isolationism
isolazioni·sta *mf* (-sti -ste) isolationist
isolétta *f* isle
isòscele *adj* isosceles
isòto·po -pa *adj* isotopic || *m* isotope
ispani·sta *mf* (-sti -ste) Hispanist
ispa·no -na *adj* Hispanic
ispanoamerica·no -na *adj* & *mf* Spanish-American
ispessire §176 *tr* & *ref* to thicken
ispettorato *m* inspectorship
ispet·tóre -trice *mf* inspector; **ispettore di produzione** (mov) production manager
ispezionare (**ispezióno**) *tr* to inspect
ispezióne *f* inspection
ìspi·do -da *adj* bristly
ispirare *tr* to inspire || *ref* to be inspired
ispirazióne *f* inspiration
Israèle *m* Israel
israelia·no -na *adj* & *mf* Israeli
israeli·ta *adj* & *mf* (-ti -te) Israelite
issare *tr* to hoist
issòpo *m* hyssop
istallare *tr* & *ref* var of **installare**
istantàne·o -a *adj* instantaneous || *f* snapshot
istante *m* instant, moment; petitioner
istanza *f* petition; request, application; (law) instance; **in ultima istanza** as a final decision
istèri·co -ca (-ci -che) *adj* hysteric(al) || *mf* hysteric
isterilire §176 *tr* to make barren || *ref* to become barren
isterismo *m* hysteria, hysterics
istigare §209 *tr* to instigate, prompt
istiga·tóre -trice *mf* instigator
istillare *tr* to instill, implant; **istillare il collirio negli occhi** to put drops in the eyes
istinti·vo -va *adj* instinctive
istinto *m* instinct
istituire §176 *tr* to institute, found; (lit) to decide
istituto *m* institute; institution; bank; **istituto di bellezza** beauty parlor
istitu·tóre -trice *mf* founder; teacher, instructor || *m* tutor || *f* governess; nurse
istituzionalizzare [ddzz] *tr* to institutionalize
istituzióne *f* institution
istmo *m* isthmus
istologìa *f* histology

istoriare §287 (istòrio) *tr* to adorn with historical figures

istradare *tr* to direct || *ref* to wend one's way

istrice *m & f* (European) porcupine

istrióne *m* ham actor; buffoon

istrióni·co -ca *adj* (-ci -che) histrionic

istrionismo *m* histrionics

istruire §176 *tr* to instruct; to train; (law) to draw up, prepare (*a case*) || *ref* to learn

istruì·to -ta *adj* learned, educated

istruménto *m* (law) instrument

istruttì·vo -va *adj* instructive

istrut·tóre -trice *mf* instructor; (sports) coach

istruttò·rio -ria (-ri -rie) *adj* investigating, preliminary || *f* (law) preliminary investigation

istruzióne *f* instruction; (law) preliminary investigation; **istruzioni** instructions; directions

istupidire §176 *tr* to make dull; to stupefy

Itàlia, l' *f* Italy

itàlia·no -na *adj & mf* Italian

itàli·co -ca *adj* (-ci -che) italic; Italic; (lit) Italian || *m* italics

italòfo·no -na *adj* Italian-speaking || *m* Italian-speaking person

itinerante *adj* itinerant

itinerà·rio *m* (-ri) itinerary

ittèri·co -ca *adj* (-ci -che) jaundiced

itterizia *f* jaundice

ittiologìa *f* ichthiology

Iugoslàvia, la Yugoslavia

iugosla·vo -va *adj & mf* Yugoslav

iugulare *adj & tr* var of **giugulare**

iuta *f* jute

ivi *adv* (lit) there

J
K
L

L, l ['elle] *m & f* tenth letter of the Italian alphabet

la §4 *def art* the || *m* (mus) la, A; **dare il la** to set the tone || §5 *pers pron*

là *adv* there; **al di là da venire** to come, future; **al di là (di)** beyond; **andare di là** to go in the next room; **andare troppo in là** to go too far; **farsi in là** to move aside; **l'al di là** the life beyond; **più in là** further; **più in là di** beyond; **va' là!** come on!

lab·bro *m* (-bri) edge (*of wound*); (lit) lip || *m* (-bra *fpl*) lip; **labbro leporino** harelip

labiale *adj & f* labial

làbile *adj* (coll) weak; (lit) fleeting

labiolettura *f* lip reading

labirinto *m* labyrinth, maze

laboratò·rio *m* (-ri) laboratory; workshop; **laboratorio linguistico** language laboratory

laborió·so -sa [s] *adj* hard-working, laborious; labored (*e.g., digestion*)

laburì·sta (-sti -ste) *adj* Labour || *mf* Labourite

lac·ca *f* (-che) lacquer

laccare §197 *tr* to lacquer; to japan; to polish (*nails*)

lac·chè *m* (-chè) lackey

lac·cio *m* (-ci) lasso; snare; noose; string; (fig) bond; **laccio delle scarpe** shoelace; **laccio emostatico** tourniquet

lacciòlo *m* snare

lacerare (làcero) *tr* to lacerate; to tear || *ref* to tear

làce·ro -ra *adj* torn; tattered

lacèrto *m* (lit) shred of flesh; (lit) biceps

lacòni·co -ca *adj* (-ci -che) laconic

làcrima *f* tear; drop

lacrimare (làcrimo) *tr* (lit) to weep over || *intr* to water (*said of the eyes*); (lit) to weep

lacrima·to -ta *adj* (lit) lamented

lacrimévole *adj* pitiful

lacrimòge·no -na *adj* tear (*e.g., gas*)

lacrimó·so -sa [s] *adj* teary, watery (*eyes*); tearful; lachrymose

lacuna *f* gap, lacuna; blank (*in one's mind*); **colmare una lacuna** to bridge a gap

lacustre *adj* lake

laddóve *conj* while, whereas

ladré·sco -sca *adj* (-schi -sche) thievish

la·dro -dra *adj* thieving; foul (*weather*); bewitching (*eyes*) || *mf* thief; **ladro di strada** highwayman || *f* inside pocket (*of suit*)

ladróne *m* thief; highwayman; **ladrone di mare** pirate

ladrùncolo *m* petty thief, pilferer

laggiù *adv* down there

lagnanza *f* complaint

lagnare *ref* to complain; to moan

lagno *m* complaint, lament

la·go *m* (-ghi) lake; pool (*of blood*)

làgrima *f* var of **lacrima**

laguna *f* lagoon

lai *m* (lai) lay; **lai** *mpl* (lit) lamentations

laicato *m* laity

là·ico -ca *adj* (-ci -che) lay || *m* layman

làì·do -da *adj* foul; obscene

la·ma *m* (-ma) llama; lama || *f* (-me) blade (*of knife*); marsh; (lit) lowland

lambiccare §197 *tr* to distill || *ref* to strive; **lambiccarsi il cervello** to rack one's brains

lambì·co -ca *m* (-chi) still

lambire §176 *tr* to lap; to graze, to touch lightly

lamèlla *f* thin sheet

lamentare (laménto) *tr* to bemoan, lament || *ref* to moan; to complain

lamentazióne *f* lamentation

lamentévole *adj* plaintive; lamentable

laménto *m* complaint, lament; moan

lamentó·so -sa [s] *adj* plaintive, doleful

lamétta *f* razor blade

lamièra *f* plate; armor plate

lamierino *m* sheet metal, lamina

làmina *f* sheet, lamina

laminare (**làmino**) *tr* to laminate; to roll (*steel*)

lamina·tóio *m* (**-tói**) rolling mill

làmpada *f* lamp, light; **lampada al neon** neon lamp; **lampada a petrolio** oil lamp; **lampada a stelo** pole lamp; **lampada di sicurezza** (min) safety lamp; **lampada fluorescente** fluorescent lamp; **lampada lampo** (phot) flash bulb

lampadà·rio *m* (**-ri**) chandelier

lampadina *f* bulb; **lampadina tascabile** flashlight

lampante *adj* shiny; clear; lamp (*oil*)

lampeggiare §290 (**lampéggio**) *tr* (lit) to flash (*a smile*) || *intr* to flash; (aut) to blink; (coll) to flash the turn signals || *impers* (ESSERE & AVERE)— **lampeggia** it lightens, it is lightning

lampeggiatóre *m* (aut) turn signal; (phot) flashlight

lampio·nàio *m* (**-nài**) lamplighter

lampióne *m* street lamp

lampíride *f* glowworm

lampo *m* lightning; flash of lightning; (fig) flash

lampóne *m* raspberry

lana *f* wool; **buona lana** (coll) rogue, rascal; **lana d'acciaio** steel wool; **lana di vetro** fiberglass, glass wool

lancétta *f* lancet; hand (*of watch*); pointer (*of instrument*)

làn·cia *f* (**-ce**) lance, spear; nozzle (*of fire hose*); launch; **lancia di salvataggio** lifeboat

lanciabóm·be *m* (**-be**) trench mortar

lanciafiam·me *m* (**-me**) flamethrower

lanciamíssi·li (**-li**) *adj* missile-launching || *m* missile launcher

lanciaraz·zi [ddzz] *m* (**-zi**) rocket launcher

lanciare §128 *tr* to throw, hurl; to drop (*from an airplane*); to launch (*e.g., an advertising campaign*) || *ref* to hurl oneself; (rok) to blast off; **lanciarsi col paracadute** to parachute, bail out

lanciasilu·ri *m* (**-ri**) torpedo tube

lància·to -ta *adj* hurled, flung; flying, e.g., **partenza lanciata** flying start

lancia·tóre -trice *mf* hurler, thrower; (baseball) pitcher

lancière *m* lancer

lancinante *adj* piercing

làn·cio *m* (**-ci**) throw; publicity campaign; (aer) drop; (aer) release (*of bombs*); (baseball) pitch; (rok) launch; **lancio del peso** shot put

landa *f* moor; wasteland

lanerie *fpl* woolens

languidézza *f* languidness, languor

làngui·do -da (làngui) *adj* sad (*eyes*)

languire (**lànguo**) & §176 *intr* to languish

languóre *m* languor; languishing; weakness; tenderness

laniè·ro -ra *adj* wool (*industry*)

lanifí·cio *m* (**-ci**) woolen mill

lanó·so -sa [s] *adj* woolly; kinky (*hair*); bushy (*face*)

lantèrna *f* lantern

lanùgine *f* down

lanzichenéc·co *m* (**-chi**) landsknecht

laónde *conj* (lit) wherefore

laotia·no -na *adj* & *mf* Laotian

lapalíssia·no -na *adj* self-evident

lapidare (**làpido**) *tr* to stone (to death); (fig) to pick to pieces

làpide *f* stone tablet; tombstone

lapillo *m* lapillus

là·pis *m* (**-pis**) pencil

lappare *intr* to lap

làppola *f* (bot) burdock; (bot) bur

lappóne *adj* Lappish || *mf* Lapp || *m* Lapp (*language*)

Lappònia, la Lapland

lardellare (**lardèllo**) *tr* to lard; to stuff with bacon

lardo *m* lard; **nuotare nel lardo** to live on easy street

largheggiare §290 (**larghéggio**) *intr* to be liberal; to be lavish

larghézza *f* width; liberality; abundance; **larghezza di vedute** broadmindedness

largire §176 *tr* (lit) to bestow liberally

largizióne *f* bestowal; donation

làr·go -ga (**-ghi -ghe**) *adj* broad, wide; ample; liberal; abundant; (phonet) open; **prenderla larga** to keep away || *m* buono; open sea; square; (mus) largo; **al largo di** (naut) off; **fare largo a** to open the way to; **farsi largo** to elbow one's way; **prendere il largo** to run away; (naut) to put to sea; **tenersi al largo** to keep at a distance || *f*—**alla larga!** keep away! || *largo adv*—**girare largo** to keep away

làrice *m* larch

laringe *f* larynx

laringite *f* laryngitis

laringoià·tra *mf* (**-tri -tre**) laryngologist

laringoscò·pio *m* (**-pi**) laryngoscope

larva *f* (ent) larva; (lit) ghost; (lit) skeleton; (lit) sham

lasagne *fpl* lasagne

lasciapassa·re *m* (**-re**) safe-conduct; permit

lasciare §128 *tr* to leave; to let; to let go of; **lasciar cadere** to drop; **lasciarci le penne** (coll) to die; (coll) to be skinned alive; **lasciar correre** to let go; **lasciar detto** to leave word; **lasciar fare** to leave alone; **lasciare in pace** to leave alone; **lasciare libero** to let go; **lasciare scritto** to leave in writing || *ref* to abandon oneself; to abandon one another

làscito *m* (law) bequest

lascívia *f* lasciviousness

lascí·vo -va *adj* lascivious

lassatí·vo -va *adj* mildly laxative || *m* mild laxative

lassismo *m* laxity

làs·so -sa *adj* lax || *m* lasso; **lasso di tempo** period of time

lassù *adv* up there, up above

lastra *f* slab; paving stone; (phot)

plate; exposed X-ray film; **farsi le lastre** (coll) to be X-rayed
lastricare §197 (làstrico) *tr* to pave
lastricato *m* paving, pavement
làstri·co *m* (-ci or -chi) pavement; road-way; **ridursi sul lastrico** to fall into abject poverty
lastróne *m* slab; plate glass
latènte *adj* latent
laterale *adj* lateral || *m* (soccer) half-back
lateri·zio -zia (-zi -zie) *adj* brick || **laterizi** *mpl* bricks, tiles
làtice *m* latex
latifondi·sta *mf* (-sti -ste) rich land-owner
latifóndo *m* large landed estate
lati·no -na *adj* Latin; lateen (*sail*) || *m* Latin
latitante *adj* hiding || *mf* fugitive
latitanza *f* flight from justice
latitùdine *f* latitude
la·to -ta *adj* wide; broad (*meaning*) || *m* side; **d'altro lato** on the other hand
la·tóre -trice *mf* bearer
latrare *intr* to bark
latrato *m* bark
latrina *f* toilet, lavatory, washroom
latta *f* tin; can
lattàia *f* milkmaid
lat·tàio *m* (-tài) milkman, dairyman
lattante *adj & m* suckling
latte *m* milk; **latte detergente** cleansing cream; **latte di gallina** flip; (bot) star-of-Bethlehem; **latte in polvere** powdered milk; **latte magro** or **scremato** skim milk
lattemièle *m* whipped cream
làtte·o -a *adj* milky
latterìa *f* dairy; creamery
làttice *m* var of **latice**
latticèllo *m* buttermilk
latticì·nio *m* (-ni) dairy product
lattigìnó·so -sa [s] *adj* milky
lattonière *m* tinsmith
lattu·ga *f* (-ghe) lettuce; head of let-tuce; frill
làudano *m* paregoric, laudanum
laudati·vo -va *adj* laudatory
làurea *f* wreath; doctorate; doctoral examination
laurean·do -da *mf* candidate for the doctorate
laureare (làureo) *tr* to confer the doc-torate on; to award (*s.o.*) the title of; (lit) to wreathe || *ref* to receive the doctorate; (sports) to get the tile of
laurea·to -ta *adj* laureate || *m* alumnus, graduate
làuro *m* laurel
làu·to -ta *adj* sumptuous, rich
lava *f* lava
lavabianche·rìa *f* (-rìa) washing ma-chine
lavàbile *adj* washable
lavabo *m* washstand; lavatory
lavacristallo *m* windshield washer
lavacro *m* washing; font; purification; **santo lavacro** baptism
lavàg·gio *m* (-gi) washing; **lavaggio a secco** dry cleaning; **lavaggio del cer-vello** brainwashing

lavagna *f* slate; blackboard; **lavagna di panno** felt board; **lavagna luminosa** overhead projector
lavama·no *m* (-no) washstand
lavanda *f* washing; pumping (*of stom-ach*); lavender
lavandàia *f* laundrywoman; **lavandaia stiratrice** laundress (*woman who washes and irons*)
lavan·dàio *m* (-dài) laundryman; **lavan-daio stiratore** launderer
lavanderìa *f* laundry; **lavanderia a get-tone** laundromat; **lavanderia a secco** dry-cleaning establishment
lavandino *m* sink
lavapiat·ti *mf* (-ti) dishwasher (*person*)
lavare *tr* to wash; to cleanse; **lavare a secco** to dry-clean; **lavare il capo a** to scold || *ref* to wash oneself; **lavarsi le mani** to wash one's hands
lavastovi·glie *mf* (-glie) dishwasher || *m & f* dishwasher (*machine*)
lavata *f* washing; **lavata di capo** scold-ing
lavativo *m* (coll) enema; (coll) bore; (coll) goldbricker
lava·tóio *m* (-tói) laundry room; wash-tub
lava·tóre -trice *mf* washer || *m* washer-man; (mach) purifier || *f* washer-woman; washing machine
lavatura *f* washing; **lavatura a secco** dry cleaning; **lavatura di piatti** dish-water; washing of dishes; (fig) watery soup
lavèllo *m* wash basin; sink
lavoràbile *adj* workable
lavorante *mf* helper, apprentice
lavorare (lavóro) *tr* to work; to till || *intr* to work; to perform; to be busy; to trade; **lavorare ai ferri** to knit; **lavorare di fantasia** to daydream; **lavorare di ganasce** to eat vora-ciously; **lavorare di gomiti** to elbow one's way; **lavorare di mano** to pilfer; **lavorare di traforo** to work with a jig saw
lavorati·vo -va *adj* working; workable
lavora·to -ta *adj* wrought; tilled
lavora·tóre -trice *mf* worker || *m* work-man; workingman || *f* workingwoman
lavorazióne *f* working; manufacturing; tilling
lavorì·o *m* (-ì) bustle; steady work; scheming
lavóro *m* work; labor; steady work; homework; piece of work; (coll) trouble; **a lavori ultimati** when the work is finished; **lavori forzati** hard labor; **lavori in economia** time and material contract work; **lavori tea-trali** theatrical productions; **lavoro a cottimo** piecework; **lavoro a maglia** knitting; **lavoro di cucito** needle-work; **mettere al lavoro** to press into service
lazzarétto [ddzz] *m* lazaretto
lazzaróne [ddzz] *m* cad; (coll) gold-bricker
le §4 *def art* the || §5 *pers pron*
leale *adj* loyal; sincere
leali·sta *mf* (-sti -ste) loyalist
leal·tà *f* (-tà) loyalty; sincerity

lébbra f leprosy
lebbró·so -sa [s] adj leprous || mf leper
lécca-léc·ca m (-ca) (coll) lollypop
leccapiat·ti m (-ti) glutton; sponger
leccapiè·di mf (-di) bootlicker
leccarda f dripping pan
leccare §197 (lécco) tr to lick; to fawn on; (fig) to polish || ref to make oneself up
lecca·to -ta adj affected; polished || f licking
léc·cio m (-ci) holm oak
leccornia f dainty morsel, delicacy
léci·to -ta adj licit, permissible; **mi sia lecito** may I || m right
lèdere §192 tr to damage, injure
lé·ga f (-ghe) league; alloy; **di bassa lega** poor, in poor taste; **fare lega** to unite
legale adj legal; lawyer's; official || m lawyer
legali·tà f (-tà) legality, lawfulness
legalità·rio -ria adj (-ri -rie) (pol) observing the rule of law
legalizzare [ddzz] tr to legalize; to authenticate
legame m bond; connection; relationship
legaménto m tie, bond; ligament; (phonet) liaison
legare §209 (légo) tr to tie; to bind; to unite; to set (a stone); to bequeath; to alloy; (bb) to bind || intr to bond; to mix (said of metals); to go together || ref to unite; **legarsela al dito** to never forget
legatà·rio -ria mf (-ri -rie) legatee
lega·to -ta adj muscle-bound || m legate; bequest; (mus) legato
lega-tóre -trice mf bookbinder
legatoria f bookbindery
legatura f typing; binding; ligature; bookbinding; (mus) tie
legazióne f legation
légge f law; act; **dettar legge** to lay down the law; **è fuori della legge** he is an outlaw; **legge stralcio** emergency law
leggènda f legend; story, tall tale; (journ) caption
leggendà·rio -ria adj (-ri -rie) legendary
lèggere §193 tr, intr & ref to read
leggerézza f lightness; nimbleness; thoughtlessness; fickleness
leggè·ro -ra adj light; nimble; thoughtless; slight; fickle; **alla leggera** lightly || **leggero** adv lightly
leggia·dro -dra adj graceful, lovely
leggìbile adj legible, readable
leggì·o m (-ì) lectern; music stand
legiferare (legìfero) intr to legislate
legionà·rio -ria adj & m (-ri -rie) legionary
legióne f legion
legislati·vo -va adj legislative
legisla·tóre -trice mf legislator
legislatura f legislature
legittimare (legìttimo) tr to legitimize
legittimi·tà f (-tà) legitimacy
legìtti·mo -ma adj legitimate; pure; just, right || f (law) legitim
lé·gna f (-gna & -gne) firewood; (fig) fuel

legnàia f woodpile; woodshed
legname m timber, lumber
legnata f clubbing, thrashing
légno m wood; stick; ship; coach; timber; **legno compensato** plywood; **legno dolce** softwood; **legno forte** hardwood
legnò·lo m ply (e.g., of a cable)
legnó·so -sa [s] adj wooden; tough (meat); dry (style)
legu·lèio m (-lèi) pettifogger
legume m legume; beans || **legumi** vegetables; legumes
leguminósa [s] f leguminous plant; **leguminose** legumes
lèi §5 pron pers; **dare del Lei a** to address formally
lèmbo m edge, border; patch (of land)
lèm·ma m (-mi) entry (in a dictionary)
lèmme lèmme adv (coll) slowly
léna f energy; enthusiasm; (lit) breath
lèndine m nit
lène adj (lit) light, soft, gentle; (phonet) voiced
lenire §176 tr to soothe, assuage
lenóne m panderer, procurer
lenóna f procuress
lènte f lens; bob, pendulum bob; **lente d'ingrandimento** magnifying glass; **lenti glasses**
lentézza f slowness
lenticchia f lentil
lentìggine f freckle
lentigginó·so -sa [s] adj freckly
lèn·to -ta adj slow; slack; (lit) loose (hair); (lit) loose-fitting (garment) || **lento** adv slowly
lènza f fishline
lenzuò·lo m (-li) sheet; (fig) blanket; **lenzuolo a due piazze** double sheet; **lenzuolo funebre** winding sheet, shroud || m (-la fpl) sheet; **lenzuola** pair of sheets (in a bed)
leoncino m lion cub
leóne m lion; **leone d'America** cougar; **leone marino** sea lion || **Leone** m (astr) Leo
leonéssa f lioness
leopardo m leopard
lepidézza f wit; witticism
lèpi·do -da adj witty, facetious
lepisma f (ent) silverfish
lèpre adj invar rendezvous, e.g., **razzo lepre** rendezvous rocket || f hare
leprotto m leveret, young hare
lèr·cio -cia adj (-ci -ce) filthy
lerciume m filth, dirt
lèsbi·co -ca (-ci -che) adj & mf Lesbian || f Lesbian (female homosexual)
lésina f awl; stinginess; miser
lesinare (lésino & lèsino) tr to begrudge || intr to be miserly
lesionare (lesióno) tr to damage; to crack open
lesióne f damage; injury; lesion
lé·so -sa adj damaged; injured
lessare (lésso) tr to boil
lessicale adj lexical
lèssi·co m (-ci) lexicon
lessicografia f lexicography
lessicogràfi·co -ca adj (-ci -che) lexicographic(al)
lessicògrafo m lexicographer

lessicologìa f lexicology

lés·so -sa adj boiled ‖ m boiled meat; soup meat

lè·sto -sta adj swift; nimble; quick; **alla lesta** hastily; **lesto di lingua** ready-tongued; **lesto di mano** light-fingered

lestofante m swindler

letale adj lethal, deadly

leta·màio m (-mài) dunghill

letame m manure, dung

letàrgi·co -ca adj (-ci -che) lethargic

letar·go m (-ghi) lethargy; hibernation

letìzia f happiness, joy

lèttera f letter; **alla lettera** literally; **lettera morta** unheeded, e.g., **le sue parole rimasero lettera morta** his words remained unheeded; **lettere** literature; **lettere credenziali** credentials; **scrivere in tutte lettere** to spell out

letterale adj literal

letterà·rio -ria adj (-ri -rie) literary; learned (word)

lettera·to -ta adj literary; literate ‖ m man of letters; (coll) literate, learned person

letteratura f literature

lettièra f litter, bedding

letti·ga f (-ghe) sedan chair; stretcher

lètto m bed; bedding; **di primo letto** born of the first marriage; **letti gemelli** twin beds; **letto a castello** bunk bed; **letto a due piazze** double bed; **letto a scomparsa** Murphy bed; **letto a una piazza** single bed; **letto bastardo** oversize bed; **letto caldo** hotbed; **letto di morte** deathbed; **letto operatorio** operating table

lèttone or **lettòne** adj Lettish ‖ mf Lett ‖ m Lett, Lettish (language)

Lettónia, La Latvia

let·tóre -trice mf reader; lecturer; meter reader ‖ m reader (e.g., for microfilm); **lettore perforatore** reader (of punch cards)

lettura f reading; lecture; **lettura del pensiero** mind reading

letturi·sta m (-sti) meter reader

leucemìa f leukemia

leucorrèa f leucorrhea

lèva f lever; (mil) draft; (mil) class; **essere di leva** to be of draft age; **fare leva su** to use (s.o.'s emotions)

levachio·di m (-di) claw hammer

levante adj rising ‖ m east; Levant

levanti·no -na adj & mf Levantine

levare (lèvo) tr to lift, raise; to weigh (anchor); to pull (a tooth); to break (camp); to collect (mail); to remove, take away; to subtract; **levare alle stelle** to praise to the sky; **levare il disturbo a** to take leave of ‖ ref to arise; to get up; to take off; to satisfy (e.g., one's hunger); to rise (said of wind); **levarsi dai piedi** to get out of the way; **levarsi dai piedi** or **di mezzo qlcu** to get rid of s.o.

levata f rise; reveille; collection (of mail); withdrawal (of merchandise from warehouse); **levata di scudi** uprising

levatàc·cia f (-ce) getting up at an impossible hour; **ho dovuto fare una levataccia** I had to get up way too early

leva·tóio -tóia adj (-tói -tóie)—**ponte levatoio** drawbridge

levatrice f midwife

levatura f intellectual breadth

leviatano m leviathan

levigare §209 (lèvigo) tr to polish

levigatrice f sander; buffer

levi·tà f (-tà) (lit) levity

levitazióne f levitation

levrière m greyhound

lezióne f lesson; lecture; reading

lezió·so -sa [s] adj affected, mincing

lézzo [ddzz] m stench; filth

lì def art masc plur (obs) the; **li tre novembre** the third of November (in official documents) ‖ §5 pers pron

lì adv there; **di lì** that way; **di lì a un anno** a year hence; **essere lì lì per** to be about to; **fin lì** up to that point; **giù di lì** more or less; **lì per lì** on the spot

libanése [s] adj & mf Lebanese

Libano, il Lebanon

libare tr to toast; to taste ‖ intr to toast

libazióne f libation

libbra f pound

libéc·cio m (-ci) southwest wind

libèllo m libel; (law) brief

libèllula f dragonfly

liberale adj & m liberal

liberali·tà f (-tà) liberality

liberare (lìbero) tr to free; to pay in full for; to open into (said, e.g., of a hall opening into a room); to clear, empty (a room) ‖ ref—**liberarsi da** or **di** to get rid of

libera·tóre -trice adj liberating ‖ mf liberator

liberismo m free trade

libe·ro -ra adj free; vacant; without a revenue stamp (document); open (syllable; heart); outspoken

liber·tà f (-tà) freedom; release (e.g., from mortgage); **libertà provvisoria** bail, parole; **libertà vigilata** probation; **mettersi in libertà** to put comfortable house clothes on; **rimettere in libertà** to set free

liberti·no -na adj & mf libertine

Libia, la Libya

libi·co -ca adj & mf (-ci -che) Libyan

libidine f lust; greed

libidinó·so -sa [s] adj lustful

libido f libido

li·bràio m (-brài) bookseller

librare ref to balance; to soar; (aer) to glide

libratóre m (aer) glider

libreria f bookstore; library (room); bookshelf; book collection

libré·sco -sca adj (-schi -sche) bookish

librétto m booklet; card; (mus) libretto; **libretto di banca** passbook; **libretto degli assegni** checkbook; **libretto di circolazione** car registration; **libretto ferroviario** railroad pass; **libretto di risparmio** passbook (of savings bank)

libro m book; ledger; register (e.g., of births); **a libro** folding; **libro di**

bordo log; **libro in brossura** paperback; **libro mastro** ledger; **libro paga** (com) payroll

liceale *adj* high-school ‖ *mf* high-school student

licènza *f* permit; license; diploma; (mil) leave; **con licenza parlando!** excuse my language!; **dar licenza a** to dismiss; **prender licenza da** to take leave of

licenziaménto *m* dismissal; **licenziamento in tronco** firing on the spot

licenziare §287 (**licènzio**) *tr* to dismiss; to O.K. (*a book to be published*); to graduate ‖ *ref* to take leave; to give notice, resign; to graduate

licenzió·so -sa [s] *adj* licentious

licèo *m* high school; lycée

lichène *m* lichen

licitazióne *f* auction; (bridge) bidding

lido *m* shore; sand bar

liè·to -ta *adj* glad; blessed (*event*)

lève *adj* light; slight

lievitare (**lièvito**) *tr* to leaven ‖ *intr* (ESSERE & AVERE) to rise; to ferment

lièvito *m* yeast; leaven; **lievito in polvere** baking powder

ll-gio -gia *adj* (**-gi -gie**) devoted

lignàg·gio *m* (**-gi**) ancestry, lineage

ligustro *m* privet

lil·la (**-la**) *adj invar* & *m* lilac

lillipuzia·no -na *adj* & *mf* Lilliputian

lima *f* file; **lima per le unghie** nail file

limaccló·so -sa [s] *adj* miry, muddy

limare *tr* to file; to polish (*e.g., a speech*); to gnaw, plague

limatura *f* filing; filings

limbo *m* (lit) edge; (fig) limbo ‖ **Limbo** *m* (theol) Limbo

limétta *f* nail file; (bot) lime

limitare *m* threshold ‖ *v* (**lìmito**) *tr* to limit; to bound

limitazióne *f* limitation

lìmite *m* limit; boundary; check; (soccer) penalty line; **limite di carico** maximum weight; **limite di età** retirement age; **limite di velocità** speed limit; **senza limiti** limitless

limìtro·fo -fa *adj* neighboring (*country*)

limo *m* mud, mire

limonare (**limóno**) *intr* (coll) to spoon

limonata *f* lemonade; (med) citrate of magnesia

limóne *m* lemon tree; lemon

limó·so -sa [s] *adj* slimy

lìmpi·do -da *adj* limpid, clear

lince *f* lynx, wildcat

linciàg·gio *m* (**-gi**) lynching

linciare §128 *tr* to lynch

lin·do -da *adj* neat; clean

linea *f* line; degree (*of temperature*); **conservare la linea** to keep one's figure; **in linea** abreast; (telp) connected; **in linea d'aria** as the crow flies; **linea del fuoco** firing line; **linea del cambiamento di data** international date line; **linea di circonvallazione** (rr) beltline; **linea di condotta** policy; **linea di partenza** starting line; **linea laterale** (sports) side line

lineaménti *mpl* lineaments; elements

lineare *adj* linear ‖ *v* (**lìneo**) *tr* to delineate

lineétta *f* dash; hyphen

linfa *f* (anat) lymph; (bot) sap; **dar linfa** (bot) to bleed

lingòtto *m* (metallurgy) pig, ingot; **lingotto d'oro** bullion

lingua *f* tongue; language; strip (*of land*); **essere di due lingue** to speak with a forked tongue; **lingua in** the correct language; **lingua di gatto** ladyfinger; **lingua lunga** backbiter; **lingua sciolta** glib tongue; **mala lingua** wicked tongue

linguacciu·to -ta *adj* talkative; sharp-tongued

linguàg·gio *m* (**-gi**) language

linguèlla *f* (philately) gummed strip

linguétta *f* tongue (*of shoe*); (mach) pin; (mus) reed

linguìsti·co -ca (**-ci -che**) *adj* linguistic ‖ *f* linguistics

linifi·cio *m* (**-ci**) flax-spinning mill

linimento *m* liniment

lino *m* flax; linen

linósa [s] *f* flaxseed, linseed

linotipi·sta *mf* (**-sti -ste**) linotypist

liocòrno *m* unicorn

liofilizzare [ddzz] *tr* to freeze-dry

liquefare §194 *tr* & *ref* to liquefy

liquefazióne *f* liquefaction

liquidare (**lìquido**) *tr* to liquidate; to close out; to dismiss; to settle

liquidazióne *f* liquidation; clearance; **liquidazione del danno** (ins) adjustment

liquidità *f* liquidity

lìqui·do -da *adj* liquid; (com) due ‖ *m* liquid; cash ‖ *f* liquid

liqui·gàs *m* (**-gàs**) liquid gas

liquirizia *f* licorice

liquóre *m* liqueur; (pharm) liquor

liquorì·sta *mf* (**-sti -ste**) liqueur manufacturer or dealer

lira *f* lira; pound; (mus) lyre ‖ **Lira** *f* (astr) Lyra

lìri·co -ca (**-ci -che**) *adj* lyric; (mus) operatic ‖ *m* lyric poet ‖ *f* lyric; lyric poetry; opera

lirismo *m* lyricism

Lisbóna *f* Lisbon

li·sca *f* (**-sche**) fishbone; lisp

lisciare §128 *tr* to smooth; **lisciare il pelo a** to butter up, flatter; to beat up ‖ *ref* to preen

lì·scio -scia *adj* (**-sci -sce**) smooth; straight (*drink*); black (*coffee*); **passarla liscia** to get away scot-free

liscìvia *f* lye; bleach

lisciviatrice *f* washing machine

lì·so -sa *adj* worn-out, threadbare

lista *f* list; strip, band; stripe; **lista delle spese** shopping list; **lista delle vivande** bill of fare; **lista elettorale** slate (*of candidates*)

listare *tr* to border; to stripe

listèllo *m* lath; (archit) listel

listino *m* price list; market quotation

litanìa *f* litany

lìte *f* quarrel; lawsuit

litigante *adj* quarreling ‖ *mf* quarreler; (law) litigant

litigare §209 (lìtigo) *tr*—**litigare qlco a qlcu** to fight with s.o. for s.th || *intr* to quarrel; to litigate || *ref*—**litigarsi qlco** to strive for s.th
liti·gio *m* (-gi) quarrel, litigation
litigió·so -sa [s] *adj* quarrelsome
lìtio *m* lithium
litografia *f* lithography
litògrafo *m* lithographer
litorale *adj* littoral || *m* seashore, coast-line
litro *m* liter
Lituània, la Lithuania
litua·no -na *adj & mf* Lithuanian || *m* Lithuanian (*language*)
liturgìa *f* liturgy
litùrgi·co -ca *adj* (-ci -che) liturgical
liu·tàio *m* (-tài) lute maker
liuto *m* lute
livèlla *f* level; **livella a bolla d'aria** spirit level
livellaménto *m* leveling; equalization
livellare (livèllo) *tr* to level; to equalize; to survey || *intr* (ESSERE) *& ref* to become level
livella·tóre -trice *adj* leveling || *mf* surveyor || *f* bulldozer
livellazióne *f* leveling
livèllo *m* level; **livello delle acque** sea level
lìvi·do -da *adj* livid, black-and-blue || *m* bruise
lividóre *m* bruise
livóre *m* grudge; hatred
Livórno *f* Leghorn
livrèa *f* livery
lizza *f* tilting ground; **entrare in lizza** to enter the lists
lo §4 *def art* the || §5 *pers pron*
lòb·bia *m & f* (-bia *mpl & fpl*) homburg
lòbo *m* lobe
locale *adj* local || *m* room; place (*of business*); (naut) compartment; **locale notturno** night spot
locali·tà *f* (-tà) locality, spot
localizzare [ddzz] *tr* to localize; to locate || *ref* to become localized
localizzazióne [ddzz] *f* localization; **localizzazióne dei guasti** troubleshooting
locanda *f* inn
locandiè·re -ra *mf* innkeeper
locandìna *f* playbill; flyer; small poster
locare §197 (lòco) *tr* to rent, lease
locatà·rio -ria *mf* (-ri -rie) lessee, renter
loca·tóre -trice *mf* lessor
locazióne *f* rent; lease; **dare in locazione** to rent
locomotìva *f* locomotive, engine
locomo·tóre -trice *adj* locomotive || *m & f* (rr) electric locomotive
locomotorì·sta *m* (-sti) (rr) engineer
locomozióne *f* locomotion; transportation
lòculo *m* burial niche
locùsta *f* locust
locuzióne *f* locution, expression; phrase; idiom
lodàbile *adj* praiseworthy
lodare (lòdo) *tr* to praise || *ref* to praise oneself, brag; **lodarsi di** (poet) to be pleased with

lodatì·vo -va *adj* laudatory
lòde *f* praise; **con la lode cum laude; con lode** plus (*on a report card*)
lodévole *adj* praiseworthy, commendable
lòdo *m* arbitration
logarìtmo *m* logarithm
lòg·gia *f* (-ge) lodge; (archit) loggia
loggióne *m* (theat) upper gallery
lògi·co -ca (-ci -che) *adj* logical; **esser logico** to think logically || *m* logician || *f* logic
logìsti·co -ca (-ci -che) *adj* logistic || *f* logistics
lò·glio *m* (-gli) cockle
logoraménto *m* wear; attrition
logorare (lógoro) *tr* to wear out; to fray || *ref* to wear away; to become threadbare
logorì·o *m* (-ì) wear and tear
lógo·ro -ra *adj* worn out; threadbare
lòlla *f* chaff
lombàggine *f* lumbago
lombar·do -da *adj & mf* Lombard
lombata *f* loin, sirloin
lómbo *m* loin; hip; (lit) ancestry
lombrì·co *m* (-chi) earthworm
londinése [s] *adj* London || *mf* Londoner
Londra *f* London
longànime *adj* patient, forbearing
longanimi·tà *f* (-tà) patience, forbearance
longevità *f* longevity
longè·vo -va *adj* long-lived
longherìna *f* beam, girder
longheróne *m* (aer) longeron; (aer) spar; (aut) main frame member
longitùdine *f* longitude
longobar·do -da *adj & mf* Lombard
lontananza *f* distance
lonta·no -na *adj* distant, remote; vague; indirect || *m* (lit) far-away place || *f*—**alla lontana** from a distance; vaguely; distant (*e.g., relative*) || *lontano adv* far; **da lontano** from afar; **lontano da** away from; far from; **rifarsi da lontano** to start from the very beginning
lóntra *f* otter
lónza *f* pork loin; (poet) leopard
lòppa *f* chaff; skin (*of plant*); slag, dross
loquace *adj* loquacious; (fig) eloquent
loquèla *f* (lit) tongue; (lit) style
lordare (lórdo) *tr* to soil, dirty
lór·do -da *adj* soiled, dirty; **gross** (*weight*)
lordùme *m* dirt, filth
lordùra *f* dirt, filth; soil
lóro §5 *pron pers* || §6 *adj poss & pron*
losan·ga *f* (-ghe) rhombus; (herald) lozenge
ló·sco -sca *adj* (-schi -sche) squint-eyed; cross-eyed; (fig) shady
lóto *m* mud
lòto *m* lotus
lòtta *f* fight; struggle; wrestling; **essere in lotta** to be at war; **lotta libera** catch-as-catch-can
lottare (lòtto) *intr* to fight; to quarrel; to struggle; to wrestle

lotta·tóre -trice *mf* fighter; wrestler

lotteria *f* lottery

lottizzare [ddzz] *tr* to divide into lots

lòtto *m* lotto; parcel, lot

lozióne *f* lotion

lùbri·co -ca *adj* (-ci -che) lewd; (lit) slippery

lubrificante *adj & m* lubricant

lubrificare §197 (**lubrifico**) *tr* to lubricate

lucchétto *m* padlock

luccicare §197 (**lùccico**) *intr* to sparkle; to shine

luccichì·o *m* (-ì) glittering; shining; sparkle

luccicóne *m* big tear

lùc·cio *m* (-ci) pike

lùcciola *f* firefly; usherette (*in movie*); **prendere lucciole per lanterne** to make a blunder; to be seeing things

luce *f* light; sunlight; opening; glass (*of mirror*); leaf (*e.g., of door*); (archit) span; (coll) electricity; **alla luce del sole** in plain view; **fare luce** to shed light; **luce degli occhi** eyesight; **luce del giorno** daylight; **luce della luna** moonlight; **luce di arresto** (aut) stoplight; **luce di incrocio** (aut) dimmer, low beam; **luce di posizione** (aut) parking light; **luce di profondità** (aut) high beam; **luci** (poet) eyes; **luci della ribalta** (fig) stage, boards; **mettere alla luce** to give birth to; **mettere in luce** to reveal; to publish; **venire alla luce** to be born; to come to light

lucènte *adj* shiny, shining

lucentézza *f* brightness; sheen

lucèrna *f* lamp; light; **lucerne** (lit) eyes ‖ **Lucerna** *f* Lucerne

lucernà·rio *m* (-ri) skylight

lucèrtola *f* lizard

lucherino *m* (orn) siskin

Lucia *f* Lucy

lucidare (**lùcido**) *tr* to shine, polish; to trace (*a figure*)

lucida·tóre -trice *mf* polisher (*person*) ‖ *f* (mach) floor polisher

lucidatura *f* polish; tracing (*on paper*)

lucidi·tà *f* (-tà) polish; lucidity

lùci·do -da *adj* bright; lucid ‖ *m* shine; tracing; **lucido per le scarpe** shoe polish

lucìfe·ro -ra *adj* (poet) light-bringing ‖ **Lucifero** *m* Lucifer, morning star

lucignolo *m* wick

lucrare *tr* to win, acquire

lucrati·vo -va *adj* lucrative

lucro *m* gain, earnings, lucre; **lucro cessante** (law) loss of earnings

lucró·so -sa [s] *adj* lucrative

ludì·brio *m* (-bri) mockery; laughingstock

lù·glio *m* (-gli) July

lùgubre *adj* gloomy, dismal

lui §5 *pron pers*

luigi *m* louis ‖ **Luigi** *m* Louis

luma·ca *f* (-che) snail

lume *m* light; lamp; **lume degli occhi** eyesight; **lume delle stelle** starlight; **lumi** eyesight; **lumi di luna** hard times; **perdere il lume degli occhi** to lose one's self-control; **reggere il lume a** to close one's eyes to; **studiare al lume di candela** to burn the midnight oil

lumeggiare §290 (**luméggio**) *tr* to illuminate, to shed light on

lumicino *m* faint light; **essere al lumicino** to be on one's last legs

luminare *m* star; luminary

luminària *f* illumination

lumino *m* night light; votive light; rush light

luminó·so -sa [s] *adj* luminous; bright (*idea*)

luna *f* moon; **andare a lune** to be fickle; **avere la luna di traverso** to be in a bad mood; **luna calante** waning moon; **luna crescente** crescent moon; **luna di miele** honeymoon

lunare *adj* lunar, moon

lunària *f* (min) moonstone; (bot) honesty

lunà·rio *m* (-ri) almanac; **sbarcare il lunario** to live from hand to mouth

lunàti·co -ca *adj* (-ci -che) moody; whimsical

lune·dì *m* (-dì) Monday

lunétta *f* lunette; fanlight

lunga *f*—**alla lunga** in the long run; **alla più lunga** at the latest; **andare per le lunghe** to last a long time, drag on; **di gran lunga** by far; **farla lunga** to dillydally

lungàggine *f* delay, procrastination

lunghézza *f* length; **lunghezza d'onda** wave length; **prendere la lunghezza di** to measure

lungi *adv* (lit) far

lungimirante *adj* (fig) far-sighted

lun·go -ga (-ghi -ghe) *adj* long; sharp (*tongue*); nimble (*fingers*); tall; thin (*soup*); (coll) slow; **a lungo** for a long time; at length; **a lungo andare** in the long run; **lungo disteso** sprawling ‖ *m* length; **in lungo e in largo** far and wide; **per il lungo** lengthwise ‖ *f* see **lunga** ‖ **lungo** *prep* along; during

lungofiume *m* river road

lungola·go *m* (-ghi) lakeshore road

lungomare *m* seashore road

lungometràg·gio *m* (-gi) full-length movie, feature film

lunòtto *m* (aut) rear window

luò·go *m* (-ghi) place; passage; site; (geom) locus; **aver luogo** to take place; **aver luogo in** to be laid in (*e.g., a certain place*); **dar luogo a** to give rise to; **del luogo** local; **far luogo** to make room; **fuori luogo** inopportune(ly); **in alto luogo** high-placed; **in luogo di** instead of; **luogo comune** commonplace; **luogo di decenza** toilet; **luogo di nascita** birthplace; **luogo di pena** penitentiary; **non luogo a procedere** (law) no ground for prosecution; (law) **nolle prosequi; sul luogo** on the spot; **on the premises**

luogotenènte *m* lieutenant

lupa *f* she-wolf

lupanare *m* (lit) brothel

lupé·sco -sca *adj* (**-schi -sche**) wolfish
lupétto *m* young wolf; cub (*in Boy Scouts*)
lupinèlla *f* sainfoin
lupi·no -na *adj* wolfish
lu·po -pa *mf* wolf; **lupo cerviero** lynx; **lupo di mare** seadog; **lupo mannaro** werewolf || *f* see **lupa**
lùppolo *m* hops
lùri·do -da *adj* filthy, dirty
lusco *m*—**tra il lusco e il brusco** at twilight
lusin·ga *f* (**-ghe**) flattery; illusion
lusingare §209 *tr* to flatter || *ref* to be flattered; to hope
lusinghiè·ro -ra *adj* flattering; promising
lussare *tr* to dislocate
lussazióne *f* dislocation

lusso *m* luxury; **di lusso** de luxe; **lusso di** abundance of
lussuó·so -sa [s] *adj* luxurious, sumptuous
lussureggiante *adj* luxuriant
lussùria *f* lust
lussurió·so -sa [s] *adj* lustful, lecherous
lustrare *tr* to polish, shine; to lick (*s.o.'s boots*) || *intr* to shine, be shiny
lustrascar·pe *m* (**-pe**) bootblack
lustrino *m* sequin; tinsel
lu·stro -stra *adj* shiny, polished || *m* shine, polish; period of five years; **dare il lustro a** to shine, polish
lutto *m* mourning; bereavement; **a lutto** black-edged (*e.g., stationery*); **lutto stretto** deep mourning
luttuó·so -sa [s] *adj* mournful

M

M, m ['emme] *m & f* eleventh letter of the Italian alphabet
ma *m* but; **ma e se** ifs and buts || *conj* but; yet || *interj* who knows?; too bad!
màca·bro -bra *adj* macabre
maca·co *m* (**-chi**) macaque; (fig) dumbbell
macadàm *m* macadam
macadamizzare [ddzz] *tr* to macadamize
mac·ca *f* (**-che**) abundance; **a macca** (coll) abundantly; (coll) without paying
maccarèllo *m* mackerel
maccheróni *mpl* macaroni
màcchia *f* spot, stain; brushwood; thicket; (fig) blot; **alla macchia** clandestinely; (painting) done in pointillism; **darsi alla macchia** to join the underground; to escape the law; **macchia solare** sunspot; **senza macchia** spotless
macchiare §287 *tr* to stain, soil || *ref* to become stained; **macchiarsi d'infamia** to soil one's reputation
macchiétta *f* caricature; comedian; **fare la macchietta di** to impersonate, to parody
macchiettare (**macchiétto**) *tr* to speckle
macchietti·sta *mf* (**-sti -ste**) cartoonist; comedian; impersonator
màcchina *f* machine; engine; car, automobile; machination; **andare in macchina** to go to press; **fatto a macchina** machine-made; **macchina da presa** (mov) camera; **macchina da proiezione** projector; **macchina fotografica** camera; **macchina per** or **da cucire** sewing machine; **macchina per** or **da scrivere** typewriter; **scrivere a macchina** to typewrite
macchinale *adj* mechanical
macchinare (**màcchino**) *tr* to plot
macchinà·rio *m* (**-ri**) machinery
macchinazióne *f* machination

macchinétta *f* gadget; **macchinetta del caffè** coffee maker
macchini·sta *m* (**-sti**) engineer; (theat) stagehand
macchinó·so -sa [s] *adj* heavy, ponderous; complicated
macedònia *f* fruit salad, fruit cup
macel·làio *m* (**-lài**) butcher
macellare (**macèllo**) *tr* to butcher
macelleria *f* butcher shop
macèllo *m* slaughterhouse; butchering; carnage; disaster
macerare (**màcero**) *tr* to soak; to mortify (*the flesh*) || *ref* to waste away
macèria *f* low wall; **macerie** ruins
màce·ro -ra *adj* emaciated; skinny || *m* soaking vat (*for papermaking*)
machiavèlli·co -ca *adj* (**-ci -che**) Machiavellian
macigno *m* boulder
macilèn·to -ta *adj* emaciated, pale, wan
màcina *f* millstone; (coll) grind
macinacaf·fè *m* (**-fè**) coffee grinder
macinapé·pe *m* (**-pe**) pepper mill
macinare (**màcino**) *tr* to grind, mill; to burn up (*e.g., the road*)
macina·to -ta *adj* ground || *m* grindings; ground meat || *f* grinding
macinino *m* grinder; (coll) jalopy
mà·cis *m & f* (**-cis**) mace (*spice*)
maciste *m* strong man (*in circus*)
maciullare *tr* to brake (*flax or hemp*); to crush
macrocòsmo *m* macrocosm
màdia *f* bread bin; kneading trough
màdi·do -da *adj* wet, perspiring
madònna *f* lady || **Madònna** *f* Madonna
madornale *adj* huge; gross (*error*)
madre *f* mother; stub; mold; **madre nubile** unwed mother
madreggiare §290 (**madréggio**) *intr* to take after one's mother
madrelingua *f* mother tongue
madrepàtria *f* mother country
madrepèria *f* mother-of-pearl
madresélva *f* (coll) honeysuckle

madrevite f (mach) nut; die; **madrevite ad alette** wing nut

madrigna f stepmother

madrina f godmother; **madrina di guerra** war mother

mae·stà f (-stà) majesty; **lesa maestà** lese majesty

maestó·so -sa [s] adj majestic, stately

maèstra f teacher; (fig) master; **maestra giardiniera** kindergarten teacher

maestrale m northwest wind (in Mediterranean)

maestranze fpl workmen

maestria f skill, mastery

maè·stro -stra adj masterly; main || m teacher; master; instructor; northwester (in Mediterranean); **maestro di cappella** choirmaster || f see **maestra**

mafió·so -sa [s] adj Mafia || mf member of the Mafia; gaudy dresser

ma·ga f (-ghe) sorceress

magagna f fault, weak spot

magagna·to -ta adj spoiled (fruit)

magari adv even, maybe || conj even if || interj would that . . . !

magazzinàg·gio [ddzz] m (-gi) storage

magazziniè·re -ra [ddzz] mf stock-room attendant || m warehouseman

magazzino [ddzz] m warehouse; store; inventory; (phot, journ) magazine; **grandi magazzini** department store

maggése [s] adj May || m (agr) fallow

màg·gio m (-gi) May; May Day

maggiolino m cockchafer

maggiorana f sweet marjoram

maggioranza f majority

maggiorare (**maggióro**) tr to increase

maggiorazióne f increase, appreciation

maggiordòmo m butler; majordomo

maggióre adj bigger; greater; major; main; higher (bidder); older, elder; (mil) master (e.g., sergeant); biggest, greatest; highest; oldest, eldest; **andare per la maggiore** to be all the rage; **maggiore età** majority || m (mil) major; oldest one; **maggiori** ancestors

maggiorènne adj of age || mf grown-up, adult

maggiorènte mf notable

maggiori·tà f (-tà) (mil) C.O.'s office

maggiorità·rio -ria adj (-ri -rie) majority

magìa f magic

màgi·co -ca adj (-ci -che) magic

Magi mpl Magi, Wise Men

magióne f (lit) home, dwelling

magistèro m education, teaching; mastery; (chem) precipitation

magistrale adj teacher's; masterly || f teacher's college

magistrato m magistrate

magistratura f judiciary

màglia f knitting; stitch; link; under-shirt; sports shirt; (hist) mail; (fig) web; **lavorare a maglia** to knit

maglieria f knitting mill; yarn shop; knitwear store

maglietta f polo shirt, T-shirt; buckle (to secure rifle strap); picture hook; buttonhole

maglifi·cio m (-ci) knitwear factory

mà·glio m (-gli) sledge hammer; mallet; drop hammer

maglióne m heavy sweater, jersey

magnàni·mo -ma adj magnanimous

magnano m (coll) locksmith

magnate m (lit) magnate, tycoon

magnèsio m magnesium

magnète m magnet; magneto

magnèti·co -ca adj (-ci -che) magnetic

magnetismo m magnetism

magnetite f loadstone

magnetizzare [ddzz] tr to magnetize

magnetòfono m tape recorder

magnificare §197 (**magnìfico**) tr to extol, praise; to magnify (to exaggerate)

magnificènza f magnificence

magnìfi·co -ca adj (-ci -che) magnificent; munificent; wonderful, splendid

ma·gno -gna adj (lit) great; the Great, e.g., **Alessandro Magno** Alexander the Great

magnòlia f magnolia

ma·go m (-ghi) magician; wizard

magóne m (coll) gizzard; (coll) grief; **avere il magone** (coll) to be in the dumps

magra f low water; (fig) dearth, want

magrézza f leanness; scarcity

ma·gro -gra adj lean, thin; meager || m lean meat; meatless day || f see **magra**

mài adv never; ever; **non . . . mai** never, not ever; **come mai?** how come?

mala·le -la mf pig; hog || m pork || f sow

maialé·sco -sca adj (-schi -sche) piggish

malòli·ca f (-che) majolica

maionése [s] f mayonnaise

mà·is m (-is) corn, maize

maiuscolétto m (typ) small capital

maiùsco·lo -la adj capital || m—**scrivere in maiuscolo** to capitalize || f capital letter

Malacca, la Malay Peninsula

malaccèt·to -ta adj unwelcome

malaccòr·to -ta adj imprudent; awkward

malacreanza f (**malecreanze**) instance of bad manners; **malecreanze** bad manners

malafatta f (**malefatte**) defect; **malefatte** evildoings

malaféde f (**malefédi**) bad faith

malaffare m—**donna di malaffare** prostitute; **gente di malaffare** underworld

malagévole adj rough (road); hard (work)

malagràzia f (**malegràzie**) rudeness, uncouthness

malalingua f (**malelingue**) slanderer, backbiter

malanda·to -ta adj run-down; shabby

malandri·no -na adj dishonest; bewitching (eyes) || m highwayman

malànimo m ill will; **di malanimo** reluctantly

malanno m misfortune; illness; (joc) menace

malaparata f (coll) danger, dangerous situation

malapéna f—**a malapena** hardly

malària *f* malaria
malatìc•cio -cia *adj* (-ci -ce) sickly
mala•to -ta *adj* sick, ill; **essere malato agli occhi** to have sore eyes; **fare il malato** to play sick || *mf* patient; **i malati** the sick
malattìa *f* sickness; illness; disease; **malattie del lavoro** occupational diseases
malaugura•to -ta *adj* unfortunate; ill-omened
malaugù•rio *m* (-ri) ill omen
malavita *f* underworld
malavòglia *f* (**malevòglie**) unwillingness; **di malavoglia** reluctantly
malcapita•to -ta *adj* unlucky || *m* unlucky person
malcàu•to -ta *adj* rash, heedless
malcón•cio -cia *adj* (-ci -ce) battered
malcontèn•to -ta *adj* dissatisfied, malcontent || *mf* malcontent || *m* dissatisfaction
malcostume *m* immorality; bad practice
malcrea•to -ta *adj* ill-bred
maldè•stro -stra *adj* clumsy, awkward
maldicènte *adj* gossipy, slanderous || *mf* gossip, slanderer, backbiter
maldicènza *f* gossip, slander
male *m* evil; ill; trouble; **andare a male** to go to pot; **aversela a male** to take offense; **di male in peggio** from bad to worse, worse and worse; **fare del male** to do ill; **fare male** to be in error; **fare male a** to hurt; **farsi male** to get hurt; to hurt oneself; **far venire il mal di mare a** to make seasick; (fig) to nauseate; **Lei fa male** you should not; **mal d'aereo** airsickness; **mal di capo** headache; **mal di cuore** heart disease; **mal di denti** toothache; **mal di gola** sore throat; **mal di mare** sea-sickness; **mal di montagna** mountain sickness; **mal di pancia** bellyache; **mal di schiena** backache; **mandare a male** to spoil; **mettere male** to sow discord; **prendere a male** to take amiss; **voler male a** to bear a grudge against || *adv* badly, poorly; **male educato** ill-bred; **meno male!** fortunately!; **restar male** to be disappointed; **sentirsi male** to feel sick; **stare male** to be ill; **star male a** to not fit, e.g., **questo vestito gli sta male** this suit does not fit him; **veder male** qlco to disapprove of s.th; **veder male** qlcu to dislike s.o.
maledettaménte *adv* (coll) damned
maledét•to -ta *adj* cursed, damned
maledire §195 *tr* to curse
maledizióne *f* malediction, curse || *interj* damn it!, confound it!
maleduca•to -ta *adj* ill-bred || *mf* boor
malefatta *f* var of **malafatta**
malefì•cio *m* (-ci) curse, spell; witchcraft; wickedness
malèfi•co -ca *adj* (-ci -che) maleficent
maleolènte *adj* (lit) malodorous
malèrba *f* weed, weeds
malése *adj* & *mf* Malay
Malésia, la Malaysia
malèssere *m* malaise; uneasiness; worry

malevolènza *f* malevolence; malice
malèvo•lo -la *adj* malevolent; malicious
malfama•to -ta *adj* ill-famed; notorious
malfat•to -ta *adj* botched; misshapen || *m* misdeed
malfat•tóre -trice *mf* malefactor
malfér•mo -ma *adj* wobbly, unsteady
malfi•do -da *adj* untrustworthy
malgarbo *m* bad manners, rudeness
malgovèrno *m* misrule; mismanagement; neglect
malgrado *prep* in spite of; **mio malgrado** in spite of me || *conj* although
malìa *f* spell, charm
maliar•do -da *adj* enchanting, charming || *mf* magician || *f* enchantress, witch
malignare *intr* to gossip
malignì•tà *f* (-tà) maliciousness; malevolence; malignancy
mali•gno -gna *adj* malicious, evil; unhealthy; malignant || **il Maligno** the Evil One
malinconìa *f* melancholy; melancholia
malincòni•co -ca *adj* (-ci -che) melancholy, wistful
malincuòre *m*—**a malincuore** unwillingly, against one's will
malintenziona•to -ta *adj* evil-minded || *mf* evildoer
malinté•so -sa [s] *adj* misunderstood; misapplied || *m* misunderstanding
maliò•so -sa [s] *adj* malicious; cunning; mischievous; bewitching
malìzia *f* malice; trick; mischief
maliziò•so -sa [s] *adj* malicious; clever, artful; mischievous
malleàbile *adj* malleable; manageable
malleva•dóre -drice *mf* guarantor
mallevería *f* surety
mallo *m* hull, husk
mallòppo *m* bundle; (aer) trail cable; (coll) lump (*in one's throat*); (slang) swag, booty
malmenare (**malméno**) *tr* to manhandle
malmés•so -sa *adj* shabby, seedy; tasteless
malna•to -ta *adj* uncouth; unfortunate; harmful
malnutri•to -ta *adj* undernourished
malnutrizióne *f* malnutrition
ma•lo -la *adj* (lit) bad
malòc•chio *m* (-chi) evil eye
malóra *f* ruin; **mandare in malora** to ruin; **va in malora!** go to the devil!
malóre *m* malaise; fainting spell
malpràti•co -ca *adj* (-ci -che) inexperienced
malsa•no -na *adj* unhealthy; unsound
malsicu•ro -ra *adj* unsafe; insecure
malta *f* mortar; plaster; (obs) mud
maltèmpo *m* bad weather
malto *m* malt
maltòlto *m* ill-gotten gains
maltrattaménto *m* mistreatment
maltrattare *tr* to mistreat, maltreat
malumóre *m* bad humor; **di malumore** in a bad mood
malva *f* mallow
malvà•gio -gia (-gi -gie) *adj* wicked || *mf* wicked person || **il Malvagio** the Evil One

malversare (malvèrso) *tr* to embezzle; to misappropriate

malversazióne *f* embezzlement; misappropriation

malvestì·to -ta *adj* shabby, seedy

malvi·sto -sta *adj* disliked; unpopular

malvivènte *mf* criminal; (lit) profligate

malvolentièri *adv* unwillingly

malvolére *m* malevolence; indolence || §196 *tr* to dislike

mamma *f* mother, mom; (lit) breast; **mamma mìa** dear me!

mammaluc·co *m* (-**chi**) simpleton

mammèlla *f* breast; udder

mammìfe·ro -ra *adj* mammalian || *m* mammal

màmmola *f* violet; (fig) shrinking violet

mam·mùt *m* (-**mut**) mammoth

manàta *f* slap; handful; **dare una manata a** to slap

man·ca *f* (-**che**) left hand, left

mancante *adj* missing, lacking; unaccounted for

mancanza *f* lack; absence; defect; mistake; **in mancanza di** for lack of

mancare §197 *tr* to miss || *intr* (AVERE) to be at fault; **mancare a** to break (*e.g., one's word*); **mancare di** to be wanting; to lack; **mancare di parola** to break one's word || *intr* (ESSERE) to fail (*said, e.g., of electric power*); to be lacking, e.g., **manca il sale nell'arrosto** salt is lacking in the roast; to be missing; to be absent, e.g., **mancano tre soci** three members are absent; to be, e.g., **mancano dieci minuti alle quattro** it is ten minutes to four; (with *dat*) to lack, e.g., **gli mancano le forze** he lacks the strength; to miss, e.g., **mi manca la sua compagnia** I miss his company; **mancare a** to be absent from (*e.g., the roll call*); to be ... from, e.g., **mancano dieci chilometri all'arrivo** we are ten kilometers from the journey's end; **mancare ai vivi** (lit) to pass away; **sentirsi mancare** to feel faint || *impers*—**mancare poco che** + *subj* to narrowly miss + *ger*, e.g., **ci mancò poco che fosse investito da un'automobile** he narrowly missed being hit by a car; **non ci mancherebbe altro!** that would be the last straw!, I should say not!

manca·to -ta *adj* unsuccessful; missed (*opportunity*); abortive (*attempt*), e.g., **omicidio mancato** abortive attempt to murder; manqué, e.g., **un poeta mancato** a poet manqué

manchévole *adj* faulty

manchevolézza *f* fault, shortcoming

màn·cia *f* (-**ce**) tip, gratuity; **mancia competente** reward

manciata *f* handful

manci·no -na *adj* left-handed; underhanded || *mf* left-handed person *f* left hand, left; (mach) floating crane

man·co -ca (-**chi -che**) *adj* left; sinister, ill-omened; (lit) lacking || *m* (lit) lack; **senza manco** (coll) without fail || **manco** *adv*—**manco male!**

(coll) at least!; **manco per idea!** (coll) not at all! || *f* see **manca**

mandaménto *m* jurisdiction

mandante *m* (law) principal

mandare *tr* to send; to condemn (*to death*); to commit (*to memory*); to send forth (*e.g., smoke, buds*); to operate (*a machine*); **che Dio ce la mandi buona!** may God help us!; **mandare ad effetto** to carry out; **mandare all'altro mondo** to dispatch, kill; **mandare a monte** to ruin; **mandare a picco** to sink; **mandare a quel paese** to send to the devil; **mandare a spasso** to fire, dismiss; to get rid of; **mandar giù** to swallow; **mandare in malora** to ruin; **mandare in pezzi** to break to pieces; **mandare per le lunghe** to delay || *intr*—**mandare a chiamare** to send for; **mandare a dire** to send word

mandarino *m* mandarin; (*Citrus nobilis*) tangerine; (*Citrus reticulata*) mandarin orange

mandata *f* sending; delivery (*of merchandise*); group; gang (*e.g., of thieves*); turn (*of key*); **chiudere a doppia mandata** to double-lock

mandatà·rio *m* (-**ri**) mandatary, trustee

mandato *m* mandate; order; **mandato di cattura** arrest warrant; **mandato di comparizione** subpoena; **mandato di perquisizione** search warrant

mandìbola *f* jaw

mandolino *m* mandolin

màndorla *f* almond; kernel (*of fruit*)

mandorla·to -ta *adj* almond || *m* nougat

màndorlo *m* almond tree

mandràgola *f* mandrake

màndria *f* herd

mandriano *m* herdsman

mandrillo *m* mandrill

mandrino *m* (mach) mandrel; (mach) driftpin

mandritta *f*—**a mandritta** to the right

mane *f*—**da mane a sera** from morning till night

maneggévole *adj* usable; manageable; accessible to small craft (*sea*)

maneggiare §290 (**manéggio**) *tr* to work (*e.g., clay*); to handle; to wield (*a sword*); to knead (*dough*); to manage; (equit) to train

manég·gio *m* (-**gi**) handling; intrigue; horsemanship; management; riding school; manège

mané·sco -sca *adj* (-**schi -sche**) ready-fisted; hand (*e.g., weapons*)

manétta *f* throttle (*on a motorcycle*); **manette** handcuffs, manacles

manfòrte *f*—**dar manforte a** to help

manganèllo *m* bludgeon, cudgel

manganése [s] *m* manganese

màngano *m* calender; mangle

mangeréc·cio -cia *adj* (-**ci -ce**) edible

mangerìa *f* graft, peculation

mangiàbile *adj* edible

mangiana·stri *m* (-**stri**) tape recorder

mangia·pane *m* (-**pane**) idler

mangia·prèti *m* (-**prèti**) priest hater

mangiare *m* eating; food || *v* §290 *tr*

to eat; to bite, gnaw; to erode; to embezzle, graft; (cards, chess) to take; **mangiar la foglia** to get wise ‖ *intr* to eat; **mangiare alle spalle di qlcu** to eat at the expense of s.o. ‖ *ref* to eat up; **mangiarsi il fegato** to be green with envy; **mangiarsi la parola** to break one's promise; **mangiarsi le unghie** to bite one's nails; **mangiarsi una promessa** to break one's promise

mangiasòldi *adj invar* money-eating, e.g., **macchina mangiasoldi** money-eating contraption

mangiata *f* (coll) fill, hearty meal, bellyful

mangiatóia *f* manger, crib

mangia·tóre -trice *mf* eater

mangime *m* fodder; feed; poultry feed

mangimìsti·co -ca *adj* (**-ci -che**) feed, e.g., **attrezzature mangimistiche** feed machinery

mangió·ne -na *mf* great eater, glutton

mangiucchiare §287 (**mangiùcchio**) *tr* to nibble

mangusta *f* mongoose

mania *f* mania, craze; complex; whim; **mania di grandezza** delusions of grandeur

mania·co -ca (**-ci -che**) *adj* maniacal; enthusiastic ‖ *m* maniac; fan, enthusiast

màni·ca *f* (**-che**) sleeve; hose; (coll) crowd, bunch; **essere di manica larga** to be broad-minded; **essere nelle maniche di qlcu** to be in the favor of s.o.; **è un altro paio di maniche** this is a horse of another color; **in maniche di camicia** in shirt sleeves; **manica a vento** air sleeve, windsock; **manica per l'acqua** hose ‖ **la Manica** the English Channel

manicarétto *m* dainty, delicacy

manichino *m* mannequin; cuff; (obs) handcuff; **fare il manichino** to model

màni·co *m* (**-chi & -ci**) handle; stock (*of rifle*); shaft (*of golf club*); stem (*of spoon*); (mus) neck; **manico di scopa** broomstick

manicò·mio *m* (**-mi**) insane asylum, madhouse

manicòtto *m* muff; (mach) collar; (mach) nipple; (mach) sleeve

manicu·re *mf* (**-re**) manicure, manicurist (*person*) ‖ *f* (**-re**) manicure (*treatment*)

manicuri·sta *mf* (**-sti -ste**) manicurist

manièra *f* manner, fashion, way; **belle maniere** good manners; **di maniera** (lit, painting) Manneristic; **di maniera che** so that; **in nessuna maniera** by no means; **maniere** bad manners

manièra·to -ta *adj* mannered, affected; genteel

maniè·ro -ra *adj* tame, gentle ‖ *m* manor house, mansion ‖ *f* see **maniera**

manieró·so -sa [s] *adj* genteel; mannered

manifattura *f* manufacture; factory; product; ready-made wear

manifestare (**manifèsto**) *tr* to manifest ‖ *intr* to demonstrate ‖ *ref* to turn out to be

manifestazióne *f* manifestation; demonstration

manifestino *m* leaflet, handbill

manifè·sto -sta *adj* manifest, clear ‖ *m* poster, placard; manifest; (pol) manifesto; **manifesto di carico** (naut) manifest

manìglia *f* handle; knob; (naut) link (*of chain*)

manigóldo *m* criminal; scoundrel

manipolare (**manìpolo**) *tr* to concoct; to adulterate; (telg) to transmit

manipola·tóre -trice *mf* schemer ‖ *m* telegraph key

manìpolo *m* sheaf; (eccl; hist) maniple; (fig) handful

maniscal·co *m* (**-chi**) blacksmith

manna *f* manna; godsend

mannàia *f* axe; knife (*of guillotine*)

mano *f* hand; way (*in traffic*); coat (*of paint*); (lit) handful; (fig) finger; fingertip; **alla mano** plain, affable; **a mani nude** barehanded; **a mano** by hand; **a mano a mano** little by little; **a mano armata** armed (*e.g., robbery*); at gunpoint; **andare contro mano** to buck traffic; **a quattro mani** four-handed; **avere le mani bucate** to be a spendthrift; **avere le mani in pasta** to have one's fingers in the pie; **avere le mani lunghe** to be light-fingered; **battere le mani** to clap; **con le mani in mano** idle; **dare la mano a** to shake hands with; **dare man forte a** to help; **dare una mano** to pitch in; **dare una mano a** to lend a hand to; **di lunga mano** beforehand; **essere colto con le mani nel sacco** to be caught red-handed; **essere svelto di mano** to be light-fingered; **far man bassa (su)** to plunder; **fuori mano** out of the way; **mani di burro** butterfingers; **mani in alto!** hands up!; **man mano (che)** as; **mettere mano a** to begin; **mettere le mani sul fuoco** to guarantee; to swear; **per mano di** at the hands of; **prendere la mano** to balk; to get out of hand; **tenere la mano a** to abet; **venire alle mani** to come to blows

manodòpera *f* labor, manpower; **manodopera qualificata** skilled labor

manòmetro *m* manometer

manométtere §198 *tr* to tamper with

manomissióne *f* tampering

manomòrta *f* (law) mortmain

manòpola *f* mitten; handgrip; strap (*to hold on to*); (rad, telv) knob; (hist) gauntlet

manoscrit·to -ta *adj & m* manuscript

manoscrìvere §250 *intr* to write in one's own handwriting

manovale *m* laborer, helper; hod carrier

manovèlla *f* handle, crank; lever

manòvra *f* maneuver; (rr) shifting; **fare manovra** to maneuver; (rr) to shift

manovrare (**manòvro**) *tr* to maneuver; to handle, drive; (rr) to shift ‖ *intr* to maneuver; (rr) to shunt, shift; (fig) to plot

manovratóre _m_ motorman; driver; (rr) brakeman; (rr) flagman

manrovè·scio _m_ (-**sci**) backhanded slap

mansalva _f_—rubare a mansalva to help oneself freely (_e.g., to the till_)

mansarda _f_ mansard

mansióne _f_ duty, function

mansuè·to -**ta** _adj_ tame; meek

mansuetùdine _f_ tameness; meekness

mantèlla _f_ coat; (mil) cape

mantellina _f_ (mil) cape

mantèllo _m_ woman's coat; coat (_of animal_); (fig) cloak; (mil) cape; (mach) casing

mantenére §271 _tr_ to keep; to maintain; to hold (_e.g., a position_) ‖ _ref_ to stay alive; to last; to remain, stay, continue

mantenimènto _m_ keeping; maintenance

mantenu·to -**ta** _adj_ kept ‖ _m_ gigolo ‖ _f_ kept woman

màntice _m_ bellows; folding top (_of carriage_); (aut) convertible top

manto _m_ mantle; coat; cloak

Màntova _f_ Mantua

mantovana _f_ valance

manuale _adj & m_ manual

manualizzare [ddzz] _tr_ to make (_e.g., a machine_) hand-operated; to include in a manual; to prepare a manual of

manù·brio _m_ (-**bri**) handlebar; handle; dumbbell

manufat·to -**ta** _adj_ manufactured ‖ _m_ manufactured product; manufacture

manutèngolo _m_ accomplice

manutenzióne _f_ maintenance, upkeep

manza [dz] _f_ heifer

manzo [dz] _m_ steer; beef

maometta·no -**na** _adj & mf_ Mahometan, Mohammedan

maomettismo _m_ Mahometanism, Mohammedanism

Maomètto _m_ Mahomet

maóna _f_ barge

mappa _f_ map; bit (_of key_)

mappamóndo _m_ globe; map of the world

marachèlla _f_ mischief

maramèo _m_—fare marameo to thumb one's nose

mara·sma _m_ (-**smi**) utter confusion; (pathol) decrepitude, feebleness

maratóna _f_ marathon

maratonè·ta _m_ (-**ti**) Marathon runner

mar·ca _f_ (-**che**) mark, label; make, brand; token; ticket; (hist, geog) march; **di marca** of quality; **marca da bollo** revenue stamp; **marca di fabbrica** trademark

marcare §197 _tr_ to mark; to label; to brand; to keep the score of; to score (_e.g., a goal_); to accentuate

marcatèm·po _m_ (-**po**) timekeeper

marca·to -**ta** _adj_ marked, pronounced

marchésa _f_ marchioness, marquise

marchése _m_ marquess, marquis

marchia·no -**na** _adj_ gross (_error_)

marchiare §287 _tr_ to brand

màr·chio _m_ (-**chi**) brand; initials; characteristic; trademark

màr·cia _f_ (-**ce**) march; operation; pus; (aut) gear, speed; (mil) hike; (sports) walk; **far marcia indietro** to back up; (naut) to back water; **marcia indietro** (aut) reverse; **marcia nuziale** wedding march

marciapiède _m_ sidewalk; (rr) platform

marciare §128 _intr_ to march; (mil) to advance; (sports) to walk; (coll) to function; **far marciare qlcu** to keep s.o. in line

màr·cio -**cia** (-**ci** -**ce**) _adj_ rotten; infected; corrupt ‖ _m_ rotten part; decayed part; corruption ‖ _f_ see **marcia**

marcire §176 _intr_ (ESSERE) to rot

marciume _m_ rot; pus; decay

mar·co _m_ (-**chi**) mark

marconigram·ma _m_ (-**mi**) radiogram

marconi·sta _mf_ (-**sti** -**ste**) radio operator

mare _m_ sea; bunch, heap; **al mare** at the seashore; **alto mare** high sea; **fa mare** the sea is rough; **gettare a mare** to throw overboard; **mare grosso** rough sea; **mare territoriale** territorial waters; **promettere mari e monti** to promise the moon; **tenere il mare** to be seaworthy

marèa _f_ tide; sea (_e.g., of mud_); **alta marea** high tide; **bassa marea** low tide; **marea di quadratura** neap tide; **marea di sizigia** spring tide

mareggiata _f_ coastal storm

maremòto _m_ seaquake

mareògrafo _m_ tide-level gauge

maresciallo _m_ marshall; warrant officer

marétta _f_ choppy sea; instability

margarina _f_ margarine

margherita _f_ daisy; **margherite beads**

marginale _adj_ marginal

marginatóre _m_ margin stop (_of typewriter_); (typ) try square

màrgine _m_ margin; edge; **margine a scaletta** thumb index

marijuana _f_ marijuana, marihuana

marina _f_ seashore; seascape; navy; **marina mercantile** merchant marine

mari·nàio _m_ (-**nài**) seaman, sailor

marinara _f_ middy blouse

marinare _tr_ to marinate; **marinare la scuola** to cut school, play truant

marinaré·sco -**sca** _adj_ (-**schi** -**sche**) sailor, seamanlike

marina·ro -**ra** _adj_ sea, sailor; seamanlike; nautical ‖ _m_ (coll) sailor ‖ _f_ see **marinara**

mari·no -**na** _adj_ marine, nautical ‖ _f_ see **marina**

mariòlo _m_ rascal

marionétta _f_ puppet, marionette

maritale _adj_ marital

maritare _tr_ to marry ‖ _ref_ to get married

marito _m_ husband

marìtti·mo -**ma** _adj_ maritime, sea ‖ _m_ merchant seaman

marmàglia _f_ riffraff, rabble

marmellata _f_ jam, preserves; **marmellata di arancia** orange marmalade

marmi·sta _m_ (-**sti**) marble worker; marble cutter

marmitta _f_ pot, kettle; (aut) muffler

marmittóne _m_ (coll) sad sack

marmo _m_ marble

marmòc·chio _m_ (-**chi**) brat

marmòre•o -a *adj* marble
marmorizzare [ddzz] *tr* to marble
marmòtta *f* marmot; woodchuck; (fig) sluggard; (rr) switch signal
marmottina *f* salesman's sample case
marna *f* marl
marnare *tr* to marl
marocchi•no -na *adj & mf* Moroccan || *m* morocco leather
Maròcco, il Morocco
maróso [s] *m* billow, surge
marra *f* hoe; fluke (*of anchor*)
marrano *m* Marrano; (fig) scoundrel; (lit) traitor
marronata *f* (coll) blunder, boner
marróne *adj invar* maroon, tan || *m* chestnut; (coll) blunder
Marsiglia *f* Marseille
marsigliése [s] *adj* Marseilles || *m* native or inhabitant of Marseilles || *f* Marseillaise
marsina *f* swallow-tailed coat
Marte *m* Mars
marte•dì *m* (-dì) Tuesday; martedì grasso Shrove Tuesday
martellare (martèllo) *tr* to hammer; to pester (*with questions*) || *intr* to throb; (fig) to insist
martellata *f* hammer blow
martellétto *m* hammer (*of piano or bell*); lever (*of typewriter*)
martèllo *m* hammer; martello dell'uscio knocker; martello perforatore jackhammer
martinétto *m* jack; martinetto a vite screw jack
martingala *f* half belt (*sewn in back of sports jacket*); martingale (*of harness*)
martìnic•ca *f* (-che) wagon brake
martìn pescatóre *m* kingfisher
màrtire *m* martyr
martì•rio *m* (-ri) martyrdom
martirizzare [ddzz] *tr* to martyrize
màrtora *f* marten
martoriare §287 (martòrio) *tr* to torment
marxì•sta *adj & mf* (-sti -ste) Marxist
marzapane *m* marzipan
marziale *adj* martial
marzia•no -na *adj & mf* Martian
marzo *m* March
mas *m* (mas) torpedo boat
mascalzóne *m* cad, rascal
mascèlla *f* jaw; jawbone
màschera *mf* usher || *f* mask; masque; maschera antigas gas mask; maschera di bellezza beauty pack; maschera respiratoria oxygen mask; maschera subacquea diving helmet
mascheraménto *m* camouflage
mascherare (màschero) *tr, intr & ref* to mask; to camouflage
mascherata *f* masquerade
mascherina *f* little mask, loup; tip (*of shoe*); (aut) grille; (phot) mask
maschiare §287 *tr* (mach) to tap
maschiétta *f* tomboy; alla maschietta bobbed (*hair*); tagliare i capelli alla maschietta to bob the hair
maschiétto *m* baby boy; pintle
maschile *adj* masculine; manly; men's;

male (*sex*); boys' (*school*) || *m* masculine
mà•schio -schia *adj* manly, virile; male || *m* male; keep, donjon; tenon; (mach) tap; (carp) tongue
mascolinizzare [ddzz] *tr* to make masculine or mannish || *ref* to act like a man
mascoli•no -na *adj* masculine; mannish (*woman*)
masnada *f* mob, gang; (obs) group
masnadière *m* highwayman
massa *f* mass; body (*of water*); (elec) ground; mettere a massa (elec) to ground; in massa in a body; massa ereditaria (law) estate
massacrante *adj* killing, fatiguing
massacrare *tr* to massacre; to ruin; to wear out, fatigue
massacro *m* massacre
massaggiare §290 *tr* to massage
massaggiatóre *m* masseur
massaggiatrice *f* masseuse
massàg•gio *m* (-gi) massage
massàia *f* housewife
massèllo *m* block (*of stone*); (metallurgy) pig, ingot
masseria *f* farm
masserizie *fpl* household goods
massicciata *f* roadbed; (rr) ballast
massic•cio -cia (-ci -ce) *adj* massive; bulky; heavy; (fig) gross || *m* massif
màssi•mo -ma *adj* maximum; top || *m* maximum, limit; al massimo at the most || *f* maxim; maximum temperature
massì•vo -va *adj* massive
masso *m* rock, boulder
Massóne *m* Mason
Massoneria *f* Masonry
mastèllo *m* washtub
masticare §197 (màstico) *tr* to chew, masticate; to mumble (*words*); to speak (*a language*) poorly; masticare amaro to grumble
masticazióne *f* mastication
màstice *m* mastic; glue; putty
mastino *m* mastiff
mastodònti•co -ca *adj* (-ci -che) mammoth
ma•stro -stra *adj* master || *m* ledger; master, e.g., mastro meccanico master mechanic
masturbare *tr & ref* to masturbate
matassa *f* skein; trouble
matemàti•co -ca *adj* (-ci -che) *adj* mathematical || *m* mathematician || *f* mathematics
materassino *m* (sports) mat; materassino pneumatico air mattress
materasso *m* mattress; (boxing) sparring partner
matèria *f* matter; substance; subject; (coll) pus; dare materia a to give ground for; materia grigia gray matter; materie coloranti dyestuffs; materie prime raw materials
materiale *adj* material; rough, bulky || *m* material; equipment, supplies; (fig) makings, stuff; materiale ferroviario (rr) rolling stock; materiale stabile (rr) permanent way

maternì·tà *f* (-tà) maternity; maternity hospital; maternity ward

matèr·no -na *adj* maternal; mother (*tongue, country*)

matita *f* pencil; **matita per gli occhi** eye-shadow pencil; **matita per le labbra** lipstick; cosmetic pencil

matrice *f* matrix; stub

matrici·da *mf* (-di -de) matricide

matrici·dio *m* (-di) matricide

matricola *f* register, roll; registration (*number*); registry; beginner, novice; freshman (*in university*); **far la matricola a** to haze

matricola·to -ta *adj* notorious, arrant

matrigna *f* stepmother

matrimoniale *adj* matrimonial; double (*bed*); married (*life*)

matrimonialménte *adv* as husband and wife

matrimò·nio *m* (-ni) matrimony, marriage; wedding

matròna *f* matron

matronale *adj* matronly

matta *f* joker, wild card

mattacchió·ne -na *mf* jester, prankster

mattana *f* tantrum; fit of laughter

matta·tóio *m* (-tói) slaughterhouse

matterèllo *m* rolling pin

mattina *f* morning; **di prima mattina** early in the morning; **la mattina in the morning**

mattinale *adj* morning || *m* morning report

mattinata *f* morning; (theat) matinée

mattinìe·ro -ra *adj* early-rising

mattino *m* morning; **di buon mattino** early in the morning

mat·to -ta *adj* crazy; whimsical; dull; false (*jewelry*); wild (*desire*); **andare matto per** to be crazy about; **da matti** unbelievable; **fare il matto** to cut a caper; **matto da legare** raving mad || *f see* **matta**

mattòide *adj & mf* madcap

mattonare (mattóno) *tr* to pave with bricks

mattonato *m* brick floor; **restare sul mattonato** to be utterly destitute

mattóne *m* brick; (fig) bore

mattonèlla *f* tile; cushion (*of billiard table*)

mattutì·no -na *adj* morning || *m* matins

maturan·do -da *mf* lycée student who has to take the baccalaureate examination

maturare *tr* to ripen; to ponder; to pass (*a lycée pupil*) || *intr* (ESSERE) to ripen, mature; to fall due

maturazióne *f* ripening

maturi·tà *f* (-tà) maturity; ripening; lycée final

matu·ro -ra *adj* ripe; mature; due

Matusalèmme *m* Methuselah

mausolèo *m* mausoleum

mazza *f* club; mallet; sledge hammer; cane; mace; golf club; (baseball) bat

mazzacavallo *m* well sweep

mazzapìc·chio *m* (-chi) mallet; sledge

mazzata *f* heavy blow, wallop (*with club*)

mazzeran·ga *f* (-ghe) (mach) tamper

mazzière *m* macer; (cards) dealer

mazzo *m* bunch; bouquet; deck (*of cards*); **fare il mazzo** to shuffle the cards

mazzuòla *f* sledge hammer

mazzuòlo *m* sledge; mallet; wedge (*of golf club*); drumstick (*for bass drum*)

me §5 *pron pers*

meandro *m* meander; labyrinth

MEC *m* (letterword) (**Mercato Europeo Comune**) European Economic Community, Common Market

Mècca, la Mecca; (fig) the Mecca

meccàni·co -ca (-ci -che) *adj* mechanical || *m* mechanic || *f* mechanics; process (*e.g., of digestion*); machinery

meccanismo *m* machinery; mechanism; movement (*of watch*)

meccanizzare [ddzz] *tr* to mechanize || *ref* to become mechanized

mecenate *m* patron (*of the arts*)

méco §5 *prep phrase* (lit) with me

medàglia *f* medal

medaglióne *m* medallion; locket; biographical sketch

medési·mo -ma *adj & pron* same; -self, e.g., **egli medesimo** he himself; very e.g., **la verità medesima** the very truth

mèdia *f* average; secondary school, middle school; (math) mean; **media oraria** average speed || **mèdia** *mpl* media (*of communication*)

mediana *f* median; (soccer) middle line

mediàni·co -ca *adj* (-ci -che) medium

media·no -na *adj* median || *m* (sports) halfback || *f see* **mediana**

mediante *prep* by means of

mediare §287 (**mèdio**) *tr & intr* (ESSERE) to mediate

media·to -ta *adj* indirect

media·tóre -trice *adj* mediating || *mf* mediator; broker; commission merchant

mediazióne *f* mediation; brokerage; broker's fee, commission

medicaménto *m* medicine

medicamentó·so -sa [s] *adj* medicinal

medicare §197 (**mèdico**) *tr* to medicate; to treat

medicastro *m* quack

medicazióne *f* medication; dressing

medichéssa *f* (pej) lady doctor

medicina *f* medicine

medicinale *adj* medicinal || *m* medicine

mèdi·co -ca (-ci -che) *adj* medical || *m* doctor, physician; healer; **fare il medico** to practice medicine; **medico chirurgo** surgeon; **medico condotto** board-of-health doctor; country doctor; **medico curante** family physician

medievale *adj* medieval

medievali·sta *mf* (-sti -ste) medievalist

mè·dio -dia *adj* (-di -die) *adj* average; median; middle; secondary (*school*); medium || *m* middle finger || *f see* **media**

mediòcre *adj* mediocre

mediocri·tà *f* (-tà) mediocrity

medioèvo *m* Middle Ages

medioleggèro *m* welterweight

mediomàssimo *m* light heavyweight
meditabón·do -da *adj* meditative
meditare (**mèdito**) *tr & intr* to meditate
medita·to -ta *adj* considered
meditazióne *f* meditation
mediterrà·neo -nea *adj* inland (*sea*) ‖ **Mediterraneo** *adj & m* Mediterranean
mè·dium *mf* (**-dium**) medium
medusa *f* jellyfish
mefistofèli·co -ca *adj* (**-ci -che**) Mephistophelian
mefíti·co -ca *adj* (**-ci -che**) mephitic
megaciclo *m* megacycle
megàfono *m* megaphone
megalomania *f* megalomania
megalòpo·li *f* (**-li**) megalopolis
mega·òhm *m* (**-òhm**) megohm
megèra *f* hag, termagant, vixen
mèglio *adj invar* better; (coll) best ‖ *m*—**il meglio** the best; **nel meglio di** (coll) in the middle of ‖ *f*—**avere la meglio** to get the upper hand; **avere la meglio di** to get the better of ‖ *adv* better; best; rather; **stare meglio** to feel better; to be becoming; to fit better; **stare meglio a** to be becoming to; to fit; **tanto meglio!** so much the better!
méla *f* apple; nozzle (*of sprinkling can*); **mela cotogna** quince (*fruit*); **mela renetta** pippin
melagrana *f* pomegranate
melanzana [dz] *f* eggplant
melassa *f* molasses, treacle
mela·to -ta *adj* honey, honeyed
melèn·so -sa *adj* dull, silly
melissa *f* (bot) balm
mellìflu·o -a *adj* mellifluous
mélma *f* mud, slime
melmó·so -sa [s] *adj* muddy, slimy
mélo *m* apple tree
melodìa *f* melody
melòdi·co -ca *adj* (**-ci -che**) melodic
melodió·so -sa [s] *adj* melodious
melodram·ma *m* (**-mi**) melodrama; lyric opera; (fig) melodrama
melodrammàti·co -ca *adj* (**-ci -che**) melodramatic
melograno *m* pomegranate tree
melóne *m* melon; cantaloupe; **melone d'acqua** watermelon
membrana *f* membrane; parchment; diaphragm (*of telephone*); (zool) web
membratura *f* frame
mèm·bro *m* (**-bri**, *considered individually*) limb; member; penis ‖ *m* (**-bra** *fpl, considered collectively*) limb (*of human body*)
membru·to -ta *adj* burly, husky
memoràbile *adj* memorable
memoràn·dum *m* (**-dum**) memorandum; agenda, calendar; note; note paper
mèmore *adj* (lit) mindful, grateful
memòria *f* memory; souvenir; memoir; dissertation; (law) brief
memoriale *m* memoir; memorial
memorizzare [ddzz] *tr* to memorize
ména *f* intrigue
mena·bò *m* (**-bò**) (typ) layout, dummy
menadito *m*—**a menadito** at one's fingertips; perfectly
menare (**méno**) *tr* to lead; to bring

(*luck*); to wag (*the tail*); to deliver (*a blow*); (coll) to hit; **menare a effetto** to carry out; **menare buono di** to approve of; **menare il can per l'aia** to beat around the bush; **menare per le lunghe** to delay; **menare vanto** to boast
mènda *f* (lit) fault, flaw
mendace *adj* lying, false, mendacious
mendà·cio *m* (**-ci**) (law) falsehood
mendicante *adj & m* mendicant
mendicare §197 (**méndico**) *tr & intr* to beg
mendici·tà *f* (**-tà**) indigence, poverty
mendi·co -ca *adj & mf* (**-chi -che**) mendicant
menefreghismo *m* I-don't-care attitude
méno *adj invar* less ‖ *m* less; least; minus (*sign*); **i meno** the few; **per lo meno** at least ‖ *adv* less; least; minus; **a meno che** unless; **da meno** inferior; **fare a meno di** to do without; to spare; **meno . . . di** less . . . than; **meno male** fortunately; **meno . . . meno** the less . . . the less; **non poter fare a meno di** + *inf* to not be able to help + *ger*, e.g., **la conferenza non poteva fare a meno di essere un successo** the conference could not help being a success; **quanto meno** at least; **senza meno** without fail; **venir meno** to swoon, pass out; to fail; to lose, e.g., **gli venne meno il cuore** he lost his courage; **venir meno di** to break (*one's word*) ‖ *prep* except; less, minus; of, e.g., **le sette meno dieci** ten minutes of seven
menomare (**mènomo**) *tr* to lessen, diminish; (fig) to hurt, damage
mèno·mo -ma *adj* least
menopàusa *f* menopause
mènsa *f* (prepared) table; mess, mess hall; (eccl) altar; communion table; (poet) mass; (poet) altar; **mensa aziendale** company cafeteria
mensile *adj* monthly ‖ *m* monthly salary or allowance
mensili·tà *f* (**-tà**) monthly installment
mènsola *f* bracket; corner shelf; neck (*of harp*); mantel (*of chimney*); console
ménta *f* mint
mentale *adj* mental; (anat) chin
mentali·tà *f* (**-tà**) mentality, mind
ménte *f* mind; **a mente di** according to; **avere in mente** to mean; to intend; **di mente** mental; **mente direttiva** mastermind; **scappare di mente a qlcu** to escape s.o.'s mind, e.g., **gli è scappato di mente** it escaped his mind; **uscire di mente** to go out of one's mind; **venire in mente a qlcu** to remember, e.g., **non gli è venuto in mente di spedire la lettera** he did not remember to mail the letter
mentecat·to -ta *adj & mf* lunatic
mentina *f* mint; **mentina digestiva** after-dinner mint
mentire §176 & (**mènto**) *intr* to lie;

mentire per la gola to lie through one's teeth
menti·to -ta *adj* false; disguised
menti·tóre -trice *adj* lying || *mf* liar
ménto *m* chin
mentòlo *m* menthol
méntre *m*—**in quel mentre** at that very moment; **nel mentre che** at the time when || *conj* while; whereas
me·nù *m* (-**nù**) menu
menzionare (**menzióno**) *tr* to mention
menzióne *f* mention
menzógna *f* lie
menzogne·ro -ra *adj* false, deceptive; lying, untruthful
meraviglia *f* marvel, wonder; **a meraviglia** wonderfully; **destare le meraviglie di** to amaze; **dire meraviglie di** to praise to the skies; **fare meraviglia** (with *dat*) to amaze; **far meraviglie** to work wonders
meravigliare §280 (**meravìglio**) *tr* to amaze; to astonish || *ref* to be astonished
meraviglió·so -sa [s] *adj* marvelous, wonderful || *m* (lit) supernatural
mercan·te -téssa *mf* merchant, dealer
mercanteggiare §290 (**mercantéggio**) *tr* to sell || *intr* to deal; to haggle
mercantile *adj* mercantile; merchant (*marine*) || *m* cargo boat, freighter
mercanzìa *f* merchandise; (coll) junk
mercato *m* market; trafficking; **a buon mercato** cheap; **far mercato di** to traffic in; **sopra mercato** besides; into the bargain
mèrce *f* merchandise, goods; commodity
mercé *f* favor, grace; mercy; **alla mercé di** at the mercy of; **mercé** a thanks to; **mercé sua** thanks to him (her, etc.)
mercéde *f* pay; (lit) reward
mercenà·rio -ria *adj* & *m* (-**ri** -**rie**) mercenary
merceria *f* notions store; **mercerie** notions
mercerizzare [ddzz] *tr* to mercerize
mèr·ci *adj invar* freight (*train*, *car*, etc.) || *m* (-**ci**) freight train
mer·ciàlo -ciàia *mf* (-**ciàl** -**ciàie**) notions store owner
mercialòlo *m* small businessman; **mercialolo ambulante** peddler
mercole·dì *m* (-**dì**) Wednesday
mercuriale *f* market report; price ceiling
mercùrio *m* mercury || **Mercurio** *m* Mercury
merènda *f* afternoon snack, bite
meretrice *f* harlot
meridia·no -na *adj* & *m* meridian || *f* sundial
meridionale *adj* meridional, southern || *mf* southerner
meridióne *m* south; South
merig·gio *m* (-**gi**) noon
merin·ga *f* (-**ghe**) meringue
meritare (**mèrito**) *tr* to deserve; to win || *intr* (eccl) to merit; **bene meritare di** to deserve the gratitude of || *impers*—**merita** it is worth while to
meritévole *adj* deserving, worthy

mèrito *m* merit; **in merito a** concerning; **per merito di** thanks to; **render merito a** to reward
merito·rio -ria *adj* (-**ri** -**rie**) meritorious
merlan·go *m* (-**ghi**) whiting
merlatura *f* battlement
merlétto *m* lace, needlepoint
mèrlo *m* blackbird; merlon; (fig) simpleton
merluzzo *m* cod
mè·ro -ra *adj* bare, mere; (poet) pure
merovìngi·co -ca (-**ci** -**che**) *adj* Merovingian || *f* Merovingian script
mesata [s] *f* month's wages
méscere (*pp* **mesciuto**) *tr* to pour (*e.g.*, *wine*); (poet) to mix
meschini·tà *f* (-**tà**) pettiness; narrowmindedness; meanness, stinginess
meschi·no -na *adj* petty; narrowminded; wretched; puny || *mf* wretch
méscita *f* pouring; counter; bar
mescolanza *f* mixture, blend
mescolare (**méscolo**) *tr* to mix, blend; to shuffle (*cards*); to stir (*e.g.*, *coffee*) || *ref* to mix, blend; to mingle; to consort; **mescolarsi in** to mind (*somebody else's business*)
mescolatrice *f* mixer, blender
mése [s] *m* month; month's pay
mesétto [s] *m* short month
mesóne *m* (phys) meson
méssa *f* (eccl & mus) Mass; **messa a fuoco** (phot) focusing; **messa a punto** adjustment; clear statement, outline of a problem; (aut) tune-up; **messa a terra** (elec) grounding; **messa cantata** high mass; **messa in marcia** or **in moto** (mach) starting; **messa in orbita** (rok) orbiting; **messa in piega** waving (*of hair*); **messa in scena** staging; **messa in vendita** putting up for sale
messaggerie *fpl* delivery service
messaggè·ro -ra *mf* messenger; postal clerk
messàg·gio *m* (-**gi**) message
messale *m* missal
mèsse *f* harvest; crop
Messìa *m* Messiah
messiàni·co -ca *adj* (-**ci** -**che**) Messianic
messica·no -na *adj* & *mf* Mexican
Mèssico, il Mexico
messinscèna *f* staging; faking
mésso *m* clerk; (poet) messenger
mestare (**mésto**) *tr* to stir || *intr* to intrigue
mesta·tóre -trice *mf* ringleader; schemer
mèstica *f* (painting) filler
mesticare §197 (**mèstico**) *tr* to prime (*a canvas*); to mix (*colors*)
mestierante *mf* potboiler (*person*); tradesman, craftsman
mestière *m* trade, craft; (archaic) task; **di mestiere** by trade; habitual; **essere del mestiere** to be up in one's line
mestièri *m*—**essere di** or **far mestieri** to be necessary
mestizia *f* sadness
mè·sto -sta *adj* sad
méstola *f* ladle; trowel
méstolo *m* kitchen spoon; **avere il mestolo in mano** to be the boss
mèstruo *m* menses, menstruation

mèta *f* goal, aim; (rugby) goal line
méta *f* heap, stack (*e.g.*, *of hay*)
me•tà *f* (**-tà**) half; middle; halfway; better half; **a metà** halfway, in the middle; **aver qlco a metà con qlcu** to go half and half with s.o.
metabòlismo *m* metabolism
metafìsi•co -ca (**-ci -che**) *adj* metaphysical || *m* metaphysician || *f* metaphysics
metafonèsi *f* umlaut, metaphony
metafonìa *f* umlaut, metaphony
metàfora *f* metaphor
metafòri•co -ca *adj* (**-ci -che**) metaphoric(al)
metàlli•co -ca *adj* (**-ci -che**) metallic
metallizzare [ddzz] *tr* to cover with metal
metallo *m* metal; timbre (*of voice*); (poet) metal object; **il vile metallo** filthy lucre
metallòlde *m* nonmetal
metallurgìa *f* metallurgy
metallùrgi•co -ca (**-ci -che**) *adj* metallurgic(al) || *m* metalworker
metalmeccàni•co -ca (**-ci -che**) *adj* metallurgic(al) and mechanical || *m* metalworker
metamòrfo•si *f* (**-si**) metamorphosis
metanizzare [ddzz] *tr* to provide with methane
metano *m* methane
metanodótto *m* natural gas pipeline
metàte•si *f* (**-si**) metathesis
metèora *f* meteor; atmospheric phenomenon
meteorìte *m* & *f* meteorite
meteorologìa *f* meteorology
meteorològi•co -ca *adj* (**-ci -che**) meteorologic(al); weather (*forecast*)
meteoròlo•go -ga *mf* (**-gi -ghe**) meteorologist
metic•cio -cia *adj* & *mf* (**-ci -ce**) halfbreed
meticoló•so -sa [*s*] *adj* meticulous
metìli•co -ca *adj* (**-ci -che**) methyl
metòdi•co -ca *adj* (**-ci -che**) methodical; subject (*e.g.*, *index*) || *mf* methodical person || *f* methodology
metodi•sta *adj* & *mf* (**-sti -ste**) Methodist
mètodo *m* method
metràg•gio *m* (**-gi**) length in meters; **corto metraggio** short; **lungo metraggio** full-length movie, feature film
metratura *f* length in meters
mètri•co -ca *adj* (**-ci -che**) metric(al) || *f* metrics, prosody
mètro *m* meter; (fig) yardstick; (lit) words
métro *m* (coll) subway
metrònomo *m* (mus) metronome
metronòt•te *m* (**-te**) night watchman
metròpo•li *f* (**-li**) metropolis
metropolità•no -na *adj* metropolitan || *m* policeman, traffic cop || *f* subway
metrovìa *f* subway
méttere §198 *tr* to put, place; to set (*e.g.*, *foot*); to run (*e.g.*, *a nail into a board*); to cause (*fear*; *fever*); to employ; to admit; to put forth; to give out; (coll) to charge; (coll) to install; (aut) to engage (*a gear*); **metterci**

to take (*e.g.*, *an hour*); **mettere a confronto** to compare; **mettere a freno** to check; **mettere a fuoco** (phot) to focus; **mettere al bando** to banish; **mettere all'asta** to auction off; **mettere al mondo** to give birth to; **mettere a nudo** to lay bare; **mettere fuori** to pull out; to give out (*news*); to throw (*s.o.*) out; **mettere giù** to lower; **mettere in onda** to broadcast; **mettere in pericolo** to endanger; **mettere la pulce nell'orecchio a** to put a bug in the ear of; **mettere qlcu alla porta** to show s.o. the door; **mettere su** to set up; (coll) to put (*e.g.*, *a coat*) on; **mettere su qlcu contro qlcu** to excite s.o. against s.o. || *intr* to sprout; to lead (*said*, *e.g.*, *of a road*) || *ref* to put on, to don; to place oneself, put oneself; to take shape; **mettersi a** to begin to; **mettersi al bello** to clear up (*said of weather*); **mettersi a letto** to go to bed; **mettersi a sedere** to sit down; **mettersi con** to start to work with; **mettersi in ferie** to take one's vacation; **mettersi in malattia** to fall ill; **mettersi in mare** to put to sea; **mettersi in maschera** to wear a masked costume; **mettersi in salvo** to get out of danger; to save oneself; **mettersi in viaggio** to set out on a journey; **mettersi in vista** to make oneself conspicuous || *impers*—**mette conto** it is worth while
mettima•le *mf* (**-le**) troublemaker
mezzadrìa [ddzz] *f* sharecropping
mezza•dro -dra [ddzz] *mf* sharecropper
mezzaluna [ddzz] *f* (**mezzelune**) half-moon; crescent (*symbol of Turkey and Islam*); curved chopping knife; lunette (*of fortification*)
mezzana [ddzz] *f* procuress; (naut) mizzen
mezzanave [ddzz] *f*—**a mezzanave** amidships
mezzanino [ddzz] *m* mezzanine
mezza•no -na [ddzz] *adj* median; medium; middle || *m* procurer || *f* see mezzana
mezzanòtte [ddzz] *f* (**mezzenòtti**) midnight
mezzatinta [ddzz] *f* (**mezzetinte**) halftone
méz•zo -za *adj* overripe, rotten
mèz•zo -za [ddzz] *adj* half; middle || *m* half; middle; medium; means; vehicle; **a mezzo (di)** by (*e.g.*, *messenger*); **andar di mezzo** to suffer the consequences; to be the loser; **entrare di mezzo** to interpose oneself; **esserci di mezzo** to be present; to be at stake; **giusto mezzo** happy medium; **in mezzo a** among; in the lap of, e.g., **in mezzo alle delicatezze** in the lap of luxury; **in quel mezzo** meanwhile; **levar di mezzo** to get rid of; **mezzi** means; facilities; **mezzi di comunicazione di massa** mass media; **per mezzo di** by means of
mezzobusto [ddzz] *m* (**mezzibusti**) (sculp) bust; **a mezzobusto** half-length (*e.g.*, *portrait*)

mezzo·dì [ddzz] _m_ (**-dì**) noon; south; South

mezzogiórno [ddzz] _m_ noon; south; South

mezzùc·cio [ddzz] _m_ (**-ci**) expedient

mi §5 _pron_

miagolare (**miàgolo**) _intr_ to meow

miagolì·o _m_ (**-i**) meow, mew

mi·ca _f_ (**-che**) mica; (obs) crumb ‖ _adv_—**mica male** (coll) not too bad!; **non . . . mica** not . . . ever; not at all

mìc·cia _f_ (**-ce**) fuse

michelàc·cio _m_ (**-ci**) (coll) lazy bum

micidiale _adj_ deadly; (fig) unbearable

mì·cio -cia _mf_ (**-ci -cie**) (coll) pussy cat

micrò·bio _m_ (**-bi**) microbe

microbiologìa _f_ microbiology

mìcrobo _m_ microbe

microfà·rad _m_ (**-rad**) microfarad

microferrovìa _f_ model railroad

micro·film _m_ (**-film**) microfilm

microfilmare _tr_ to microfilm

micròfono _m_ microphone

microlettóre _m_ microfilm reader

micromotóre _m_ small motor; motor-cycle

microónda _f_ microwave

microschèda _f_ microcard

microscòpi·co -ca _adj_ (**-ci -che**) microscopic(al)

microscò·pio _m_ (**-pi**) microscope

microsól·co _adj invar_ microgroove ‖ _m_ (**-chi**) microgroove; microgroove, long-playing record

microtelèfono _m_ French telephone, handset

midólla _f_ crumb; (coll) marrow

midól·lo _m_ (**-la** _fpl_) marrow; (bot & fig) pith; **midollo spinale** (anat) spinal cord

mièle _m_ honey

mìètere (**mièto**) _tr_ to reap; (lit) to kill

mietitrebbiatrice _f_ combine

mieti·tóre -trice _mf_ reaper, harvester

mietitura _f_ harvesting

mi·gliàio _m_ (**-gliàia** _fpl_) thousand

mì·glio _m_ (**-glia** _fpl_) mile; milestone; **miglio marino** nautical mile; **miglio terrestre** mile ‖ _m_ (**-gli**) millet

miglioraménto _m_ improvement

migliorare (**miglióro**) _tr, intr_ (ESSERE & AVERE) & _ref_ to improve

miglióre _adj_ better; best

migliorìa _f_ improvement (_e.g., of real estate_)

mignatta _f_ leech

mìgnolo _adj masc_ little (_finger or toe_) ‖ _m_ little finger; little toe

migrare _intr_ to migrate

migra·tóre -trice _adj_ & _m_ migrant

migrazióne _f_ migration

Milano _f_ Milan

miliardà·rio -ria _adj_ & _mf_ (**-ri -rie**) billionaire

miliardo _m_ billion

milionà·rio -ria _adj_ & _mf_ (**-ri -rie**) millionaire

milióne _m_ million

milionèsi·mo -ma _adj_ & _m_ millionth

militante _adj_ & _m_ militant

militare _adj_ military ‖ _m_ soldier ‖ _v_ (**milito**) _intr_ to be a member; to mili-

tate; to be in the armed forces; **militare in** to be a member of (_e.g., a party_)

militaré·sco -sca _adj_ (**-schi -sche**) military, soldierly

militarismo _m_ militarism

militari·sta -sti -ste) _adj_ militaristic ‖ _mf_ militarist

militarizzare [ddzz] _tr_ to militarize; to fortify

mìlite _m_ militiaman; soldier; **milite del fuoco** fireman; **Milite Ignoto** Unknown Soldier

militesènte _adj_ exempt from military service ‖ _m_ man exempt from military service

milìzia _f_ militia; (mil) service; struggle; **milizie celesti** heavenly host

miliziano _m_ militiaman

millantare _tr_ to boast of ‖ _ref_ to brag, boast

millanta·tóre -trice _mf_ braggart

millanterìa _f_ bragging

mille _adj, m_ & _pron_ (**mila**) thousand, a thousand, one thousand ‖ **il Mille** the eleventh century; the year one thousand

millecènto _m_ eleven hundred ‖ _f_ car with a 1100 cc. motor

millefò·glie _m_ (**-glie**) puff-paste cake

millenà·rio -ria (**-ri -rie**) _adj_ millennial ‖ _m_ millennium

millèn·nio _m_ (**-ni**) millennium

millepiè·di _m_ (**-di**) millipede

millèsi·mo -ma _adj_ & _m_ thousandth

milliam·père -i (**-père**) milliampere

milligrammo _m_ milligram

millimetra·to -ta _adj_ divided into squares of one millimeter square

millimetro _m_ millimeter

milli·vòlt _m_ (**-vòlt**) millivolt

milza _f_ spleen

mimare _tr_ & _intr_ to mime

mimetizzare [ddzz] _tr_ (mil) to camouflage

mimetizzazióne [ddzz] _f_ (mil) camouflage

mìmi·co -ca (**-ci -che**) _adj_ mimic; sign (_language_) ‖ _f_ mimicry; (theat) gestures; (theat) miming

mì·mo -ma _mf_ mime ‖ _m_ (orn) mockingbird

mina _f_ lead (_of pencil_); (mil) mine; **mina anticarro** antitank mine; **mina antiuomo** antipersonnel mine

minaccévole _adj_ (lit) threatening

minàc·cia _f_ (**-ce**) threat, menace

minacciare §128 _tr_ to threaten, menace

minacció·so -sa [_s_] _adj_ threatening

minare _tr_ to mine; to undermine

minaréto _m_ minaret

minatóre _m_ miner

minatò·rio -ria _adj_ (**-ri -rie**) threatening

minchionare (**minchióno**) _tr_ (slang) to make a sucker of

minchióne _m_ (slang) sucker

minerale _adj_ mineral ‖ _m_ mineral; ore

mineralogìa _f_ mineralogy

minerà·rio -ria _adj_ (**-ri -rie**) mining

minèr·va _m_ (**-va**) safety match

minèstra _f_ vegetable soup

minestróne _m_ minestrone; hodgepodge

mìngere §199 *intr* to urinate

minghèrli·no -na *adj* frail, thin

miniàre §287 *tr* to paint in miniature; to illuminate

miniatùra *f* miniature

miniaturizzàre [ddzz] *tr* to miniaturize

miniaturizzazióne [ddzz] *f* miniaturization

minièra *f* mine

mini·gòlf *m* (-gòlf) miniature golf

minigònna *f* miniskirt

mìnima *f* lowest temperature; (mus) minim

minimizzàre [ddzz] *tr* to minimize

mìni·mo -ma *adj* smallest, least; minimum || *m* minimum; **al mìnimo** at the least; **girare al mìnimo** or **tenere il mìnimo** (aut) to idle || *f* see **mìnima**

mìnio *m* red lead; rouge

ministeriàle *adj* ministerial

ministèro *m* ministry; cabinet; department; **pùbblico ministèro** public prosecutor

ministra *f* (joc) wife of minister; (joc) female minister; (poet) minister

ministro *m* minister; secretary; administrator; **ministro degli Estèri** foreign minister; (U.S.A.) Secretary of State

minorànza *f* minority

minoràre (minóro) *tr* to lessen; to disable

minorà·to -ta *adj* disabled || *mf* disabled person

minorazióne *f* reduction; disability

minóre *adj* smaller, lesser; minor; smallest, least; younger; youngest || *m* minor

minorènne *adj* underage || *mf* minor

minorìle *adj* juvenile (*e.g.*, *court*)

minori·tà *f* (-tà) minority

minuétto *m* minuet

minù·gia *f* (-gia & -gie) (mus) catgut

minùsco·lo -la *adj* small (*letter*); diminutive || *m* & *f* small letter

minùta *f* first draft, rough copy

minutàglia *f* trifles; small fry

minutànte *m* secretary; retailer

minuterìa *f* trinkets, notions

minu·to -ta *adj* minute; small (*change*); common (*people*) || *m* minute; **al minuto** retail; **di minuto in minuto** at any moment; **minuto secóndo** second; **nel minuto in detail**; **per minuto** minutely || *f* see **minùta**

minùzia *f* trifle; **minùzie minùtiae**

minuzió·so -sa [s] *adj* meticulous

minùzzolo *m* scrap, crumb; small boy

mìo mìa §6 *adj* & *pron poss* (**mièi mìe**)

mìope *adj* nearsighted || *mf* nearsighted person

miopìa *f* nearsightedness

mìra *f* aim; sight; target, goal; **prèndere di mìra** to aim at; to torment

miràbile *adj* admirable || *m* wonder

mirabìlia *fpl* wonders; **far mirabìlia** to perform wonders; **dir mirabìlia di** to speak highly of

mirabolànte *adj* amazing, astonishing

miracolà·to -ta *adj* miraculously cured || *mf* miraculously cured person

miràcolo *m* miracle; wonder; **dir mira-**

còli di to praise to the skies; **per miràcolo** by mere chance

miracoló·so -sa [s] *adj* miraculous; wonderful

miràg·gio *m* (-gi) mirage

miràre *tr* (lit) to look at; (lit) to aim at || *intr* to aim; **miràre a** to aim at; **miràre a + inf** to aim to + *inf*; **to intend to + inf**

mirìade *f* myriad

mirino *m* sight (*of gun*); (phot) finder

mirra *f* myrrh

mirtìllo *m* blueberry; whortleberry, huckleberry

mirto *m* myrtle

misantropìa *f* misanthropy

misàntro·po -pa *adj* misanthropic || *mf* misanthrope

miscèla *f* mixture, blend

miscelàre (miscèlo) *tr* to mix, blend

miscellàne·o -a *adj* miscellaneous || *f* miscellany

mìschia *f* fight; (sports) scrimmage

mischiàre §287 *tr* to mix, blend; **to shuffle** (*cards*) || *ref* to mix

misconóscere §134 *tr* to not appreciate, undervalue

miscredènte *adj* misbelieving || *mf* misbeliever

miscù·glio *m* (-gli) mixture, blend

miseràbile *adj* pitiful, miserable; poor, wretched

miseràn·do -da *adj* pitiable

miserère *m* Miserere; **essere al miserère** to be in one's last hours

miserévole *adj* pitiful; pitiable

misèria *f* destitution, misery; wretchedness; lack, want; trifle; **piàngere misèria** to cry poverty

misericòrdia *f* mercy

misericordió·so -sa [s] *adj* merciful

mìse·ro -ra *adj* unhappy, wretched; poor; meager; mean; too small, too short

misfàtto *m* misdeed, misdoing

misirìz·zi *m* (-zi) tumbler (*toy*); (fig) chameleon

misògi·no -na *adj* misogynous || *m* misogynist

missìle *adj* & *m* missile; **missìle antimissìle** antimissile missile; **missìle intercontinentàle** I.C.B.M.; **missìle teleguidàto** guided missile

missilìsti·co -ca *adj* (-ci -che) missile

missionà·rio -ria *adj* & *m* (-ri -rie) missionary

missióne *f* mission

missìva *f* missive

misterió·so -sa [s] *adj* mysterious

mistèro *m* mystery

mìstica *f* mysticism; mystical literature

misticìsmo *m* mysticism

mìsti·co -ca (-ci -che) *adj* & *mf* mystic || *f* see **mìstica**

mistificàre §197 (mistìfico) *tr* to hoax

mistificazióne *f* hoax

mi·sto -sta *adj* mixed || *m* mixture; mixed train

mistùra *f* mixture

misùra *f* measure; size; bounds; fitting; **a misùra che** in proportion as; **di**

misura (sports) with a narrow margin; **su misura** made-to-order

misuràbile *adj* measurable

misurare *tr* to measure; to deliver (*e.g.,* a slap); to budget (*expenses*); to try on (*clothes*); to weigh (*the outcome*) || *intr* to measure || *ref* to compete; to limit oneself; **misurarsi con** to try conclusions with

misura·to -ta *adj* moderate; scanty

misurino *m* measuring spoon or cup

mite *adj* mild; tame; low (*price*)

mìti·co -ca *adj* (**-ci -che**) mythical

mitigare §209 (**mìtigo**) *tr* to mitigate; to assuage, allay || *ref* to abate

mitilo *m* mussel

mito *m* myth

mitologìa *f* mythology

mitològi·co -ca *adj* (**-ci -che**) mythologic(al)

mitòmane *mf* compulsive liar

mi·tra *m* (**-tra**) submachine gun || *f* miter

mitràglia *f* grapeshot; scrap iron; (coll) machine gun

mitragliare §280 (**mitràglio**) *tr* to machine-gun

mitragliatrice *f* machine gun

mitraglièra *f* heavy machine gun

mitraglière *m* machine gunner

mittènte *mf* sender; shipper

mo' *m*—apocopated form of **modo** by way of; **a mo' d'esempio** as an illustration

mòbile *adj* movable; personal (*property*); (fig) fickle; (rr) rolling (*stock*) || *m* piece of furniture; cabinet; (phys) body; **mobili** furniture

mobìlia *f* furniture

mobiliare *adj* (fin) security; (law) movable || §287 (**mobìlio**) *tr* to furnish

mobilière *m* furniture maker; furniture dealer

mobilità *f* mobility

mobilitare (**mobìlito**) *tr & intr* to mobilize

mobilitazióne *f* mobilization

mò·ca *m* (**-ca**) mocha; **caffè moca** Mocha coffee

mocassino *m* mocassin

moccicare §197 (**móccico**) *intr* (slang) to snivel; (slang) to run (*said of the nose*); (slang) to whimper

moccicó·so -sa [*s*] *adj* (slang) snotty

móc·cio *m* (**-ci**) snot, snivel

mocció·so -sa [*s*] *adj* snotty || *m* brat

mòccolo *m* end of candle, snuff; (joc) snot; (slang) curse word; **reggere il moccolo** a qlcu to be a third party to a couple's necking

mòda *f* fashion, vogue; **andar di moda** to be fashionable; to be all the rage; **fuori moda** outdated

modalità *f* (**-tà**) modality; method

modanatura *f* molding

mòdano *m* mold

modèlla *f* model

modellare (**modèllo**) *tr* to model; to mold || *ref* to pattern oneself

modella·tóre -trice *mf* pattern maker; molder

modellino *m* (archit) model, maquette

modèllo *adj invar* model || *m* model; fashion; style; pattern

moderare (**mòdero**) *tr* to moderate, control

moderatézza *f* moderation

modera·to -ta *adj* moderate; (mus) moderato || *m* middle-of-the-roader

modera·tóre -trice *adj* moderating || *m* moderator

modernizzare [*ddzz*] *tr & ref* to modernize

modèr·no -na *adj & m* modern

modèstia *f* modesty; scantiness, meagerness

modè·sto -sta *adj* modest; humble

mòdi·co -ca *adj* (**-ci -che**) reasonable

modìfi·ca *f* (**-che**) modification; alteration

modificare §197 (**modìfico**) *tr* to modify; to change; to alter

modiglióne *m* (archit) modillion

modista *f* milliner

modisterìa *f* millinery; millinery shop

mòdo *m* manner, mode, way; custom; idiom; (gram) mood; (mus) mode; **ad ogni modo** anyhow; nevertheless; **ad un modo** equally; **a modo** proper; properly; **a suo modo** in his own way; **bei modi** good manners; **di modo che** so that; **in malo modo** poorly; **in modo da** so as to; **in nessun modo** by no means; **in ogni modo** anyhow; **in qualche modo** somehow; **modo di dire** idiom; turn of phrase; **modo di fare** behavior; **modo di vedere** opinion; **per modo di dire** so to speak

modulare (**mòdulo**) *tr* to modulate

modulazióne *f* modulation; **modulazione d'ampiezza** amplitude modulation; **modulazione di frequenza** frequency modulation

mòdulo *m* module; blank, form

moffétta *f* skunk

mògano *m* mahogany

mòg·gio *m* (**-gi**) bushel

mò·gio -gia *adj* (**-gi -gie**) downcast, crestfallen

mó·glie *f* (**-gli**) wife

moìne *fpl* blandishments

mòla *f* grindstone; (coll) millstone

molare *adj* grinding; molar || *m* molar || *v* (**mòlo**) *tr* to grind

molassa *f* molasse, sandstone

molatóre *m* grinder (*person*); sander (*person*)

molatrice *f* grinder (*machine*); sander (*machine*); **molatrice di pavimenti** floor sander

mòle *f* size; pile; bulk, mass; huge structure

molècola *f* molecule

molestare (**molèsto**) *tr* to bother, annoy

molèstia *f* bother, trouble, annoyance

molè·sto -sta *adj* bothersome, troublesome

molibdèno *m* molybdenum

molinétto *m* (naut) winch

mòlla *f* spring; (fig) mainspring; **molla a balestra** leaf spring; **molle** tongs; **molle del letto** bedspring; **prendere**

qlco con le molle to keep at a reasonable distance from s.th

mollare (**mòllo**) *tr* to let go; to slacken; to drop (*anchor*); (coll) to soak || *intr* to give up; (coll) to soak; **molla!** (coll) cut it out!

mòlle *adj* wet, soaked; soft; mild; easy (*life*); weak (*character*); flexible || *m* softness; soft ground; **tenere a molle** to soak

mollécca *f* soft-shell crab

molleggiaménto *m* suspension; springiness

molleggiare §290 (**molléggio**) *tr* to provide with springs, to make elastic; (aut) to provide with suspension || *intr* to be springy, to have bounce || *ref* to bounce along

mollég·gio *m* (**-gi**) springs; (aut) suspension; springiness

mollétta *f* hairpin; clothespin; **mollette** sugar tongs

mollettièra *f* puttee

mollettóne *m* swansdown

mollézza *f* softness

molli·ca *f* (**-che**) crumb (*soft inner portion of bread*); **molliche** crumbs

mollificare §197 (**mollìfico**) *tr & ref* to mollify; to soften

mòl·lo -la *adj* soft || *m*—**mettere a mollo** to soak || *f* see **molla**

mollu·sco *m* (**-schi**) mollusk

mòlo *m* pier, wharf

moltéplice *adj* multiple, manifold

moltilaterale *adj* multilateral, many-sided

moltìpli·ca *f* (**-che**) front sprocket (*of bicycle*)

moltiplicare §197 (**moltìplico**) *tr & ref* to multiply

moltitùdine *f* multitude, crowd

mól·to -ta *adj* much, a lot of; very, e.g., **ho molta sete** I am very thirsty || *pron* much; a lot; **a dir molto** mostly; **ci corre molto** there is a great difference || **mol·ti -te** *adj & pron* many || **molto** *adv* very; quite; much; a lot; widely; long; **fra non molto** before long; **non . . . molto** (coll) not . . . at all

momentàne·o -a *adj* momentary

moménto *m* moment; opportune time; (slang) trifle; (phys) momentum; **dal momento che** since; **per il momento** for the time being; **sul momento** this very moment

mòna·ca *f* (**-che**) nun

monacale *adj* monachal, conventual

monacato *m* monkhood

monachésimo *m* monachism, monasticism

monachina *f* little nun; **monachine** sparks

mòna·co *m* (**-ci**) monk; (archit) king post || **Monaco** *m* Monaco || *f* Munich

monar·ca *m* (**-chi**) monarch

monarchìa *f* monarchy

monàrchi·co -ca *adj* (**-ci -che**) monarchical; monarchist(ic) (*advocating a monarch*) || *mf* monarchist

monastèro *m* monastery

monàsti·co -ca *adj* (**-ci -che**) monastic(al)

moncherino *m* stump (*without hand*)

món·co -ca (**-chi -che**) *adj* one-handed; one-armed; incomplete || *mf* cripple

moncóne *m* stump

mondana *f* prostitute

mondani·tà *f* (**-tà**) worldliness

monda·no -na *adj* mundane; worldly; society; fashionable || *m* playboy || *f* see **mondana**

mondare (**móndo**) *tr* to peel, pare; to thresh; to weed; to prune; (fig) to cleanse

mondari·so *mf* (**-so**) rice weeder

mondez·zàlo *m* (**-zài**) dump

mondiale *adj* world, world-wide; (coll) stupendous

mondìglia *f* chaff; trash; refuse

mondina *f* rice weeder

món·do da *adj* clean-peeled; (lit) pure || *m* world; hopscotch; (coll) heap, bunch; **bel mondo** smart set; **cascasse il mondo!** (coll) come what may!; **da che mondo è mondo** since the world began; **essere nel mondo della luna** to be absent-minded; **mandare all'altro mondo** (coll) to send packing; **mettere al mondo** to give birth to; **mondo della luna** world of fancy; **un mondo** a ton; **venire al mondo** to be born || **Mondo** *m*—**Terzo Mondo** Third World

monega·sco -sca *adj & mf* (**-schi -sche**) Monacan

monellerìa *f* prank

monèl·lo -la *mf* urchin, brat || *f* romp

monéta *f* money; coin; piece of money; purse (*in horse races*); change; **batter moneta** to mint money; **moneta sonante** cash

monetà·rio -ria (**-ri -rie**) *adj* monetary || *m*—**falso monetario** counterfeiter

monetizzare [ddzz] *tr* to express in money; to transform into cash

mòngo·lo -la *adj & mf* Mongolian

monile *m* necklace; jewel

mònito *m* admonition, warning

monitóre *m* monitor

mònna *f* (obs) lady; (coll) monkey

monoàlbero *adj invar* (aut) single-camshaft, valve-in-head (*distribution*)

monoaurale *adj* monaural

monoblòc·co (**-co**) *adj* single-block || *m* (aut) cylinder block

monocilìndri·co -ca *adj* (**-ci -che**) (mach) single-cylinder

monòco·lo -la *adj* one-eyed || *m* monocle

monocolóre *adj invar* one-color; one-party

monofa·se *adj* (**-si & -se**) single-phase

monogamìa *f* monogamy

monòga·mo -ma *adj* monogamous || *m* monogamist

monografìa *f* monograph

monogram·ma *m* (**-mi**) monogram

monolìti·co -ca *adj* (**-ci -che**) monolithic

monolìto *m* monolith

monòlo·go *m* (**-ghi**) monologue

monomanìa *f* monomania

monò·mio *m* (-mi) monomial
monopàttino *m* scooter
monopèt·to (-to) *adj* single-breasted ‖ *m* single-breasted suit
monoplano *m* (aer) monoplane
monopò·lio *m* (-li) monopoly
monopolizzare [ddzz] *tr* to monopolize
monopósto *adj invar* one-man ‖ *m* single-seater
monorotàia *adj invar* single-track ‖ *f* monorail
monoscò·pio *m* (-pi) (telv) test pattern
monosìlla·bo -ba *adj* monosyllabic ‖ *m* monosyllable
monòssido *m* monoxide
monoteìsti·co -ca *adj* (-ci -che) monotheistic
monotipìa *f* monotype
monotipo *m* monotype
monotonìa *f* monotony
monòto·no -na *adj* monotonous
monsignóre *m* monsignor
monsóne *m* monsoon
mónta *f* horseback riding; stud; jockey
montacàri·chi *m* (-chi) freight elevator
montàg·gio *m* (-gi) (mach) assembly; (mov) editing; (mov) montage
montagna *f* mountain; **montagna di ghiaccio** iceberg; **montagne russe** roller coaster
montagnó·so -sa [s] *adj* mountainous
montana·ro -ra *adj* mountain ‖ *mf* mountaineer
monta·no -na *adj* mountain
montante *adj* rising ‖ *m* riser, upright; (football) goal post; (aer) strut; (boxing) uppercut; (com) aggregate amount
montare (**mónto**) *tr* to mount; to go up (*the stairs*); to set (*jewels*); to frame (*a painting*); to whip (*e.g., eggs*); to excite; to exaggerate (*news*); to decorate (*a house*); to cover (*said of a male animal*); (mach) to assemble; (mov) to edit; **montare la testa a** to excite; to give a swell head to ‖ *intr* (ESSERE) to jump; to climb; to go up; to rise; to swell; **montare alla testa a** to go to the head of; **montare in collera** to get angry ‖ *impers*—**non monta** it doesn't matter, never mind
monta·tóre -trice *mf* (mach) assembler; (mov) editor
montatura *f* assembly; frame (*of glasses*); appliqué; setting (*of gem*); (journ) ballyhoo; (mov) editing; **montatura pubblicitaria** publicity stunt
montavivan·de *m* (-de) dumbwaiter
mónte *m* mountain; bank; mount (*in palmistry*); (cards) discard; **a monte** uphill; upstream; **andare a monte** to fail; **mandare a monte** to cause to fail; **monte di pietà** pawnbroker's; **monte di premi** pot (*in a lottery*)
montenegri·no -na *adj & mf* Montenegrin
montessoria·no -na *adj* Montessori
montóne *m* ram; mutton; rounded stone
montuó·so -sa [s] *adj* mountainous
montura *f* uniform

monumentale *adj* monumental
monuménto *m* monument
moquète *f* (**moquette**) wall-to-wall carpeting
mòra *f* mulberry; blackberry; brunette; Moorish woman; arrears; penalty (*for arrears*); (archaic) heap of stones
morale *adj* moral ‖ *m* morale; **giù di morale** downcast; **su di morale** in high spirits ‖ *f* morals, ethics; moral (*of a fable*)
moraleggiare §290 (**moraléggio**) *intr* to moralize
moralismo *m* moralism
moralì·tà *f* (-tà) morality; morals
moralizzare [ddzz] *tr & intr* to moralize
moratòria *f* moratorium
morbidézza *f* softness
mòrbi·do -da *adj* soft; sleek; pliable ‖ *m* soft ground
morbillo *m* measles
mòrbo *m* disease; plague
morbó·so -sa [s] *adj* morbid
mòrchia *f* sediment; dregs of oil
mordace *adj* biting, mordacious
mordènte *adj* biting; (chem) mordant; (mach) interlocking ‖ *s* strength; (chem) mordant
mòrdere §200 *tr* to bite; to grab; to corrode; **mordere il freno** to champ the bit
mordicchiare §287 (**mordìcchio**) *tr* to nibble
morèl·lo -la *adj* blackish; black (*horse*) ‖ *m* black horse
morènte *adj* dying ‖ *mf* dying person
moré·sco -sca (-schi -sche) *adj* Moresque, Moorish ‖ *f* Moorish dance
morét·to -ta *adj* brunet ‖ *m* Negro boy; dark-skinned boy; chocolate-covered ice-cream bar ‖ *f* Negro girl; dark-skinned girl; mask; (orn) scaup duck
morfè·ma *m* (-mi) morpheme
morfina *f* morphine
morfinòmane *mf* morphine addict
morfologìa *f* morphology
morìa *f* pestilence; high mortality
moribón·do -da *adj* moribund
morigera·to -ta *adj* temperate, moderate
morire §201 *intr* (ESSERE) to die; to die out; to end (*said of a street*); **morire di noia** to be bored to death
moritu·ro -ra *adj* about to die, doomed
mormóne *mf* Mormon
mormorare (**mórmoro**) *tr* to murmur; to whisper ‖ *intr* to murmur; to whisper; to babble (*said of a brook*); to rustle; to gossip
mormorì·o *m* (-i) whisper; murmur
mò·ro -ra *adj* Moorish; dark-skinned; dark-brown ‖ *mf* Moor ‖ *m* mulberry tree ‖ *f* see mora
morosi·tà [s] *f* (-tà) delinquency (*in paying one's bills*)
moró·so -sa [s] *adj* delinquent (*in paying one's bills*) ‖ *m* (coll) boyfriend; **i morosi** (coll) the lovers ‖ *f* (coll) girl friend
mòrsa *f* vise; (archit) toothing
morsétto *m* clamp; (elec) binding post

morsicare §197 (mòrsico) *tr* to bite
morsicatura *f* bite
morsicchiare §287 (morsìcchio) *tr* to nibble
mòrso *m* bite; bit
mor·tàio *m* (-tài) mortar
mortale *adj* mortal; deadly ‖ *m* mortal
mortali·tà *f* (-tà) mortality
mortarétto *m* firecracker
mòrte *f* death; end; **averla a morte con** to harbor hatred for; **morte civile** (law) attainder, loss of civil rights
mortèlla *f* myrtle
mortificare §197 (mortìfico) *tr* to mortify ‖ *ref* to feel ashamed
mòr·to -ta *adj* dead; still (*life*); morto di fame dying of hunger; **morto di paura** scared to death ‖ *mf* dead person, deceased ‖ *m* hidden treasure; (cards) dummy, widow; **fare il morto** to float on one's back; to play possum; **morto di fame** ne'er-do-well, good-for-nothing; **suonare a morto** to toll
mortò·rio *m* (-ri) funeral
mortuà·rio -ria *adj* (-ri -rie) mortuary
mosài·co -ca (-ci -che) *adj* Mosaic ‖ *m* mosaic
mó·sca *f* (-sche) fly; imperial (*beard*); **mosca bianca** one in a million; **mosca cieca** blindman's buff; **fare venire la mosca al naso a** to make angry ‖ **Mosca** *f* Moscow
moscaiòla *f* fly netting; flytrap
moscardino *m* dandy; (zool) dormouse
moscatèl·lo -la *adj* muscat ‖ *m* muscatel
moscato *m* muscat grape; muscat wine
moscerino *m* gnat
moschèa *f* mosque
moschettière *m* musketeer; Italian National soccer player
moschétto *m* musket
moschettóne *m* snap hook
moschici·da *adj* (-di -de) fly-killing
mó·scio -scia *adj* (-sci -sce) flabby, soft
moscóne *m* big fly; pesky suitor
moscovi·ta *adj* & *mf* (-ti -te) Muscovite
Mosè *m* Moses
mòssa *f* gesture; movement; move; fake; post; **fare la mossa** to sprout (*said of plants*); **mossa di corpo** bowel movement; **prendere le mosse** to begin; **stare sulle mosse** to be about to begin; to be eager to take off (*said of a horse*)
mossière *m* starter (*in a race*)
mòs·so -sa *adj* moved; in motion; plowed; rough (*sea*); blurred (*picture*); wavy (*hair; ground*) ‖ *f* see mossa
mostarda *f* mustard; candied fruit
mósto *m* must
móstra *f* show; pretense, simulation; exhibit; display window; lapel; face (*of watch*); sample; (mil) insignia; (obs) military parade; **far mostra di sé** to show off; **mettersi in mostra** to show off
mostrare (móstro) *tr* to show; to put on; **mostrare a dito** to point to;

mostrare la corda to be threadbare ‖ *ref* to show up; to show oneself
mostreggiatura *f* lapel; cuff
mostrina *f* (mil) insignia
móstro *m* monster
mostruó·so -sa [s] *adj* monstruous
mòta *f* mud, mire
mo·tèl *m* (-tèl) motel
motivare *tr* to cause; to justify
motivazióne *f* justification, reason
motivo *m* motive, reason; motif; theme; (coll) tune; **a motivo di** because of; **motivo per cui** wherefore
mò·to *m* (-ti) motion; movement; emotion; riot; **mettere in moto** to start ‖ *f* (-to) (coll) motorcycle
motobar·ca *f* (-che) motorboat
motocannonièra *f* gunboat
motocarro *m* three-wheeler (*truck*)
motocarrozzétta *f* three-wheeler (*vehicle with sidecar*)
motociclétta *f* motorcycle
motocicli·sta *mf* (-sti -ste) motorcyclist
motocorazza·to -ta *adj* armored, panzer
motofalciatrice *f* power mower
motofurgóne *m* delivery truck
motolàn·cia *f* (-ce) motorboat, speedboat
motonàuti·co -ca (-ci -che) *adj* motorboat ‖ *f* motorboating
motonave *f* motor ship
motopescheréc·cio *m* (-ci) motor fishing boat
mo·tóre -trice *adj* motive (*power*); (mach) drive ‖ *m* motor; engine; car; **a motore** motorized, motor; **motore rotativo** (aut) rotary engine; **primo motore** prime mover ‖ *f* see motrice
motorétta *f* motor scooter
motorino *m* small motor; motor bicycle; **motorino d'avviamento** (aut) starter
motori·sta *m* (-sti) mechanic
motorìsti·co -ca *adj* (-ci -che) motor
motorizzare [ddzz] *tr* to motorize
motoscafo *m* motorboat; **motoscafo da corsa** speedboat
motosé·ga *f* (-ghe) chain saw
motosilurante *f* torpedo boat
motoveicolo *m* motor vehicle
motovelièro *m* motor sailer
motrice *f* (rr) engine, motor; (aut) tractor; **motrice a vapore** steam engine
motteggiare §290 (mottéggio) *tr* to mock, jeer at ‖ *intr* to jest
mottég·gio *m* (-gi) mockery, jest
mòtto *m* witticism; motto; (lit) word
movènte *m* stimulus, motive
movènza *f* bearing, carriage; flow (*of a sentence*); cadence
movibile *adj* movable
movimenta·to -ta *adj* lively; eventful
moviménto *m* motion, movement; traffic; **movimento di cassa** cash turnover
moviòla *f* (mov) viewer and splicer
mozióne *f* motion; (lit) movement
mozzare (mózzo) *tr* to lop off; to sever; **mozzare la testa a** to cut off the head of

mozzicóne *m* stump; butt (*e.g., of cigar*)

móz·zo **-za** *adj* cut off; truncated; cropped (*ears*); docked (*tail*); hard (*breathing*) ‖ *m* cabin boy; **mozzo di stalla** stable boy

mòzzo [ddzz] *m* hub

muc·ca *f* (**-che**) milch cow

mùc·chio *m* (**-chi**) pile, heap; bunch

mucillàgine *f* mucilage

mu·co *m* (**-chi**) mucus, phlegm

mucó·so **-sa** [s] *adj* mucous ‖ *f* mucous membrane

muda *f* molt

muffa *f* mold; mildew; **fare la muffa** to be musty

muffire §176 *intr* (ESSERE) to be musty

mùffola *f* mitten; muffle (*of furnace*)

muflóne *m* mouflon

mugghiare §287 (**mùgghio**) *intr* to bellow; to roar

mùggine *m* (ichth) mullet

muggire §176 & (**muggo**) *intr* to moo, low; to roar; to howl

muggito *m* bellow; moo, low; roar

mughétto *m* lily of the valley

mu·gnàio **-gnàia** *mf* (**-gnài** **-gnàie**) miller

mugolare (**mùgolo**) *intr* to yelp; to moan

mugolì·o *m* (**-i**) yelp; moan

mugò·lio *m* (**-li**) pine tar

mugugnare *intr* (coll) to mumble; (coll) to grumble

mugugno *m* (coll) grumble

mulattière *m* mule driver, muleteer

mulattié·ro **-ra** *adj* mule ‖ *f* mule track

mulat·to **-ta** *adj* & *mf* mulatto

muliebre *adj* womanly, feminine

mulinare *tr* to twirl; to scheme ‖ *intr* to whirl; to muse; to buzz (*in the mind*)

mulinèllo *m* twirl; whirlpool; whirlwind; fishing reel; whirligig; **fare mulinello con** to twirl

mulino *m* mill; **mulino ad acqua** water mill; **mulino a vento** windmill

mu·lo **-la** *mf* mule; (slang) bastard

multa *f* penalty, fine

multare *tr* to fine

multilaterale *adj* multilateral, many-sided

mùlti·plo **-pla** *adj* & *m* multiple

mùmmia *f* mummy

mummificare §197 (**mummìfico**) *tr* to mummify

mùngere §183 *tr* to milk

mungi·tóre **-trice** *mf* milker ‖ *f* milking machine; milk maid

mungitura *f* milking

municipale *adj* municipal, city

municipalizzazióne [ddzz] *f* municipalization; city management

munici·pio *m* (**-pi**) municipality; city council; city hall

munificènza *f* munificence

munìfi·co **-ca** *adj* (**-ci** **-che**) munificent

munire §176 *tr* to fortify; to provide; **munire di** to equip with ‖ *ref* to provide oneself

munizióne *f* (obs) fortification; **munizioni** ammunition; building supplies

muòvere §202 *tr* to move; to wag; to propel, run; to lift (*one's finger*); to take (*a step*); to pose (*a question*); to stir up (*laughter*); to institute (*a lawsuit*); **muovere accusa a** to reproach ‖ *intr* (ESSERE) to begin; to move, start ‖ *ref* to move; to travel; to stir; to set out; to be moved; **muoviti!** hurry up!

mura *fpl* see **muro**

muràglia *f* wall; (fig) obstacle; **muraglia cinese** Chinese Wall

muraglióne *m* high wall, rampart

murale *adj* & *m* mural

murare *tr* to wall; to wall in ‖ *intr* to build a wall; **murare a secco** to build a dry wall ‖ *ref* to close oneself in

murata *f* (naut) bulwark

muratóre *m* bricklayer, mason

muratura *f* bricklaying, stonework

muriàti·co **-ca** *adj* (**-ci** **-che**) muriatic

mu·ro *m* (**-ri**) wall; **muro del pianto** Wailing Wall; **muro del suono** sound barrier ‖ *m* (**-ra** *fpl*)—**mura** walls (*of a city*)

musa *f* muse

muschia·to **-ta** *adj* musk (*e.g., ox*)

mù·schio *m* (**-schi**) musk; (coll) moss

mu·sco *m* (**-schi**) moss

mùscolo *m* muscle; (fig) sinew; (coll) mussel

muscoló·so **-sa** [s] *adj* muscular

muscó·so **-sa** [s] *adj* (lit) mossy

musèo *m* museum

museruòla *f* muzzle

musétta *f* nose bag

mùsi·ca *f* (**-che**) music; band; **cambiare musica** to change one's tune

musicale *adj* musical

musicante *adj* music-playing (*angels*) ‖ *mf* band player; second-rate musician

musicare §197 (**mùsico**) *tr* to set to music

musicassétta *f* cassette, tape cartridge

music-hall *m* (**-hall**) *m* vaudeville, burlesque

musici·sta *mf* (**-sti** **-ste**) musician

musicologìa *f* musicology

musicòlo·go *m* (**-gi**) musicologist

muso *m* muzzle, snout; (coll) mug; (fig) nose; **avere il muso lungo** to make a long face; **mettere il muso** to pout

musó·ne **-na** *mf* pouter, sulker

mussare *tr* to publish with great fanfare (*a piece of news*) ‖ *intr* to foam (*said of wine*)

mùssola or **mussolina** *f* muslin

mussolinia·no **-na** *adj* of Mussolini

mùssolo *m* mussel

mustàc·chio *m* (**-chi**) shroud (*of bowsprit*); **mustacchi** moustache

musulma·no **-na** [s] *adj* & *mf* Moslem

muta *f* change; shift; molt; set (*of sails*); pack (*of hounds*); (mil) watch

mutàbile *adj* changeable

mutande *fpl* shorts, briefs, drawers

mutandine *fpl* panties; **mutandine da bagno** trunks

mutare *tr, intr* (ESSERE) & *ref* to change

mutazióne *f* mutation; (biol) mutation, sport

mutévole *adj* changeable; fickle

mutilare (mùtilo) *tr* to mutilate, maim
mutila·to -ta *adj* mutilated ‖ *mf* cripple; amputee; **mutilato di guerra** disabled veteran
mutismo *m* silence, willful silence; (pathol) dumbness
mu·to -ta *adj* mute; dumb; silent (*movie*); unexpressed ‖ *mf* mute ‖ *f* see **muta**
mùtria *f* sulking attitude; proud demeanor

mùtua *f* mutual benefit society; medical insurance; **mettersi in mutua** to go on sick leave
mutuali·tà *f* (-tà) mutuality; mutual benefit institutions
mutuare (mùtuo) *tr* to borrow; to lend
mutua·to -ta *mf* person insured by mutual benefit society; person insured by medical insurance
mù·tuo -tua *adj* mutual; borrowing ‖ *m* loan ‖ *f* see **mutua**

N

N, n ['enne] *m & f* twelfth letter of the Italian alphabet
nababbo *m* nabob
Nabucodònosor *m* Nebuchadnezzar
nàcchera *f* castanet
nafta *f* crude oil; naphta; Diesel oil
naftalina *f* naphthalene
nàia *f* cobra; (slang) army discipline; (slang) military service
nàiade *f* naiad
nàilon *m* nylon
nanna *f* sleep (*of child*); **fare la nanna** to sleep (*said of child*)
na·no -na *adj & mf* dwarf
nàpalm *m* napalm
napoleòne *m* napoleon (*gold coin*) ‖ **Napoleone** *m* Napoleon
napoleòni·co -ca *adj* (-ci -che) Napoleonic
napoleta·no -na *adj & mf* Neapolitan ‖ *f* espresso coffee machine
Nàpoli *f* Naples
nappa *f* tassel; tuft; kid (*leather*)
narciso *m* narcissus
narcòti·co -ca *adj & m* (-ci -che) narcotic
narcotizzare [ddzz] *tr* to drug, dope; to anesthetize
narghi·lè *m* (-lè) hookah
narice *f* nostril
narrare *tr* to narrate, tell, recount
narrati·vo -va *adj* narrative; fictional ‖ *f* narrative; fiction
narra·tóre -trice *mf* narrator, storyteller
narrazióne *f* narration; tale, story; narrative
nasale [s] *adj & f* nasal
nascènte *adj* nascent; budding; rising (*sun*); dawning (*day*)
nàscere *m* beginning, origin ‖ §203 *intr* (ESSERE) to be born; to bud; to shoot; to dawn; to rise; to spring up; **nascere con la camicia** to be born with a silver spoon in one's mouth
nàscita *f* birth; birthday; origin
nascitu·ro -ra *adj* unborn, future ‖ *mf* unborn child
nascóndere §204 *tr* to hide; **nascondere a** to hide from ‖ *ref* to hide; to lurk
nascondì·glio *m* (-gli) hiding place; hideout; cache
nascondino *m* hide-and-seek; **giocare a nascondino** to play hide-and-seek
nascó·sto -sta *adj* hidden, concealed; secret; **di nascosto** secretly

nasèllo [s] *m* catch (*of latch*); (ichth) hake
nasièra [s] *f* nose ring
naso [s] *m* nose; (fig) face; **aver buon naso** to have a keen sense of smell; **ficcare il naso negli affari degli altri** to pry into the affairs of others; **menare per il naso** to lead by the nose; **naso adunco** hooknose; **restare con un palmo di naso** to be duped
nassa *f* pot (*for fishing*); **nassa per aragoste** lobster pot
nastrino *m* ribbon; badge
nastro *m* ribbon; band; tape; streamer; tape measure; **nastro del cappello** hatband; **nastro isolante** friction tape; **nastro per capelli** hair ribbon
nastùr·zio *m* (-zi) nasturtium
natale *adj* native, natal ‖ **natali** *mpl* birth; birthday; **dare i natali a** to be the birthplace of ‖ **Natale** *m* Christmas
natali·tà *f* (-tà) birth rate
natali·zio -zia (-zi -zie) *adj* natal; Christmas ‖ *m* birthday
natante *adj* swimming; floating ‖ *m* craft
natatóia *f* fin
natató·rio -ria *adj* (-ri -rie) swimming
nàti·ca *f* (-che) buttock
natì·o -a *adj* (-i -e) (poet) native
nativi·tà *f* (-tà) birth, nativity ‖ **Natività** *f* Nativity
nati·vo -va *adj* native; natural, inborn ‖ *mf* native
N.A.T.O. *f* (acronym) (**North Atlantic Treaty Organization**)—la **N.A.T.O.** NATO
na·to -ta *adj* born; **nata** née; **nato e sputato** the spit and image of; **nato morto** stillborn ‖ *mf* child
natura *f* nature; **natura morta** still life; **in natura** in kind
naturale *adj* natural ‖ *m* nature, disposition; **al naturale** life-size
naturalézza *f* naturalness; spontaneity
naturalismo *m* naturalism
naturali·sta *mf* (-sti -ste) naturalist
naturali·tà *f* (-tà) naturalization
naturalizzare [ddzz] *tr* to naturalize ‖ *ref* to become naturalized
naturalizzazióne [ddzz] *f* naturalization
naturalménte *adv* naturally; of course
naufragare §209 (nàufrago) *intr* (ESSERE

& AVERE) to be shipwrecked; to sink, to fail

naufrà·gio *m* (-gi) shipwreck; failure

nàufra·go -ga (-ghi -ghe) *adj* shipwrecked ‖ *mf* shipwrecked person; (fig) outcast

nàusea *f* nausea; disgust; **avere la nausea** to be sick at one's stomach

nauseabón·do -da *adj* sickening, nauseating; (fig) unsavory

nauseante *adj* sickening, nauseous

nauseare (**nàuseo**) *tr* to nauseate, sicken

nausea·to -ta *adj* sickened, disgusted

nàuti·co -ca (-ci -che) *adj* nautical ‖ *f* sailing, navigation

navale *adj* naval, navy, sea

navata *f* nave; **navata centrale** nave; **navata laterale** aisle

nave *f* ship, vessel, boat; craft; **nave ammiraglia** flagship; **nave a motore** motorboat; **nave appoggio** tender; **nave a vela** sailboat; **nave da carico** freighter; **nave da guerra** warship; **nave petroliera** tanker; **nave portaerei** aircraft carrier; **nave rompighiaccio** icebreaker; **nave traghetto** ferryboat

navétta *f* shuttle; **fare la navetta** to shuttle

navicèlla *f* nacelle, cabin (*of airship*); car (*of balloon*)

navigàbile *adj* navigable

navigabili·tà *f* (-tà) navigability; seaworthiness

navigante *adj* sailing ‖ *m* sailor

navigare §209 (**nàvigo**) *tr* & *intr* to navigate, to sail

naviga·to -ta *adj* seawise; wordly-wise

naviga·tóre -trice *mf* navigator

navigazióne *f* navigation

navì·glio *m* (-gli) ship, craft, boat; fleet; navy; canal; **naviglio mercantile** merchant marine

nazionale *adj* national ‖ *f* national team

nazionalismo *m* nationalism

nazionali·sta *mf* (-sti -ste) nationalist

nazionalisti·co -ca *adj* (-ci -che) nationalistic

nazionali·tà *f* (-tà) nationality

nazionalizzare [ddzz] *tr* to nationalize

nazionalizzazióne [ddzz] *f* nationalization

nazióne *f* nation

nazi·sta *adj* & *mf* (-sti -ste) Nazi

nazzarè·no -na [ddzz] *adj* & *mf* Nazarene ‖ **il Nazzareno** the Nazarene

ne §5 *pron* & *adv*

né *conj* neither, nor; **né . . . né** neither . . . nor

neanche *adv* not even; nor; not . . . either

nébbia *f* fog, haze, mist; **fa nebbia** it is foggy; **nebbia artificiale** smoke screen

nebbióne *m* thick fog, pea soup

nebbió·so -sa [s] *adj* foggy, hazy, misty

nebulare *adj* nebular

nebulizzare [ddzz] *tr* to atomize

nebulizzatóre [ddzz] *m* atomizer

nebulósa [s] *f* nebula

nebulosi·tà [s] *f* (-tà) fogginess, haziness, mistiness

nebuló·so -sa [s] *adj* foggy, hazy, misty ‖ *f* see **nebulosa**

néces·saire *m* (-saire) vanity case; sewing kit

necessariaménte *adv* necessarily

necessà·rio -ria (-ri -rie) *adj* necessary, needed; essential ‖ *m* necessity; necessities (*of life*)

necessi·tà *f* (-tà) necessity; need, want; **di necessità** necessarily

necessitare (**necèssito**) *tr* to require; to force ‖ *intr* to be in want; to be necessary; **necessitare di** to need

necrologìa *f* necrology, obituary

necrològi·co -ca *adj* (-ci -che) obituary

necromanzìa *f* necromancy

necròsi *f* necrosis, gangrene

nefan·do -da *adj* heinous, nefarious

nefa·sto -sta *adj* ill-fated; ominous

nefrite *f* nephritis

negare §209 (**négo** & **nègo**) *tr* to deny, negate; to refuse

negati·vo -va *adj* & *f* negative

nega·to -ta *adj* unfit, unsuited

negazióne *f* negation, denial; (gram) negative

neghittó·so -sa [s] *adj* lazy, slothful

neglèt·to -ta *adj* neglected; untidy

négli §4

negligènte *adj* negligent, careless

negligènza *f* negligence, carelessness; dereliction (*of duty*)

neglìgere §205 *tr* to neglect

negoziàbile *adj* negotiable

negoziante *mf* merchant, shopkeeper; dealer; **negoziante all'ingrosso** wholesaler; **negoziante al minuto** retailer; shopkeeper, storekeeper

negoziare §287 (**negòzio**) *tr* to negotiate, transact ‖ *intr* to negotiate, deal

negoziati *mpl* negotiations

negozia·tóre -trice *mf* negotiator

negò·zio *m* (-zi) business; transaction; store, shop; **negozio di cancelleria** stationery store

negrière *m* slave trader; slave driver

negriè·ro -ra *adj* slave ‖ *m* slave trader; slave driver

né·gro -gra *adj* & *mf* Negro

negromante *m* sorcerer

néi §4

nél §4

nélla §4

nélle §4

néllo §4

némbo *m* rain cloud; cloud (*e.g., of dust*)

Nembròd *m* Nimrod

nèmesi *f invar* nemesis ‖ **Nèmesi** *f* Nemesis

nemi·co -ca (-ci -che) *adj* inimical, hostile, unfriendly; enemy; (fig) adverse ‖ *mf* enemy, foe; **Il Nemico** the Evil One

nemméno *adv* not even; nor; not . . . either

nènia *f* funeral dirge; lamentation

nenùfaro *m* water lily

nèo *m* mole (*on the skin*); flaw, blemish; neon; beauty spot

neoclassicheggiante *adj* in the direction of the neoclassical

neòfi·ta *mf* (**-ti -te**) neophite

neolati·no -na *adj* Neo-Latin, Romance

neologismo *m* neologism

neomicina *f* neomycin

nèon *m* neon

neona·to -ta *adj* newborn || *mf* infant, baby; newborn child

neozelandése [dz][s] *adj* New Zealand || *mf* New Zealander

nepènte *f* nepenthe

Nepóte *m* Nepos

neppure *adv* not even; nor; not . . . either

nequizia *f* iniquity, wickedness

nera·stro -stra *adj* blackish

nerbata *f* heavy blow

nèrbo *m* whip; sinew; bulk; strength (*of an opposing force*)

nerboru·to -ta *adj* muscular, sinewy

nereggiare §290 (**neréggio**) *intr* to look black; to be blackish

nerétto *m* (*typ*) boldface

né·ro -ra *adj* black; dark; gloomy; dark-red (*wine*) || *mf* black; Negro || *m* black

nerofumo *m* lampblack

Neróne *m* Nero

nervatura *f* ribbing

nervi·no -na *adj* nerve (*gas*); nervine (*medicine*)

nèrvo *m* nerve; sinew; **avere i nervi** to be in a bad mood

nervosismo [s] *m* nervousness, irritability

nervó·so -sa [s] *adj* nervous, irritable; sinewy, vigorous (*style*) || *m* bad mood; **avere il nervoso** to be in a bad mood

nèsci *m*—**fare il nesci** to feign ignorance

nèspola *f* medlar; **nespole** (coll) blows

nèspolo *m* medlar tree

nèsso *m* connection, link; **avere nesso** to cohere

nessu·no -na *adj* no, not any || **nessuno** *pron* nobody, no one; none; not anybody; not anyone; **nessuno dei due** neither one

nettapén·ne *m* (**-ne**) penwiper

nettare (**nétto**) *tr* to clean, to cleanse

nèttare *m* nectar

nettézza *f* cleanness, cleanliness; neatness; **nettezza urbana** department of sanitation; garbage collection

nét·to -ta *adj* clean; clear; sharp; net || **netto** *adv* clearly, distinctly

nettùnio *m* neptunium

Nettuno *m* Neptune

netturbino *m* street cleaner

neurologia *f* neurology

neurò·si *f* (**-si**) neurosis

neuròti·co -ca *adj* (**-ci -che**) neurotic

neutrale *adj* & *mf* neutral

neutrali·sta *adj* & *mf* (**-sti -ste**) neutralist

neutrali·tà *f* (**-tà**) neutrality

neutralizzare [ddzz] *tr* to neutralize

nèu·tro -tra *adj* neuter; neutral

neutróne *m* neutron

ne·vàio *m* (**-vài**) snowfield; snowdrift

néve *f* snow; **neve carbonica** dry ice

nevicare §197 (**névica**) *impers* (ESSERE) —**nevica** it is snowing

nevicata *f* snowfall

nevìschio *m* sleet

nevó·so -sa [s] *adj* snowy

nevralgia *f* neuralgia

nevrastèni·co -ca *adj* & *mf* (**-ci -che**) neurasthenic

nevvéro (i.e., **n'è vero** for **non è vero**) see non

niacina *f* niacin

nìb·bio *m* (**-bi**) (orn) kite

nicchia *f* niche; nook, recess

nicchiare §287 (**nicchio**) *intr* to waver

nic·chio *m* (**-chi**) shell; nook

nichel *m* nickel

nichelare (**nìchelo**) *tr* to nickel, to nickel-plate

nichelatura *f* nickel-plating

nichelino *m* nickel (*coin*)

nichèlio *m* var of **nichel**

Nicòla *m* Nicholas

nicotina *f* nicotine

nidiata *f* nestful; brood

nidificare §197 (**nidìfico**) *intr* to build a nest, to nest

nido *m* nest; home; nursery; den (*of thieves*)

niènte *m* nothing; nothingness; **dal niente** from scratch; **di niente** you're welcome || *pron* nothing; not . . . anything; **quasi niente** next to nothing

nientediméno *adv* no less, nothing less

Nilo *m* Nile

ninfa *f* nymph

ninfèa *f* white water lily

ninnananna *f* lullaby, cradlesong

ninnolo *m* toy; trinket

nipóte *mf* grandchild || *m* grandson; nephew; **nipoti** descendants || *f* granddaughter; niece

nippòni·co -ca *adj* (**-ci -che**) Nipponese

nirvana, il nirvana

nìti·do -da *adj* clear, distinct

nitóre *m* brightness; elegance

nitrato *m* nitrate

nitrire §176 *intr* to neigh

nitrito *m* neigh; (chem) nitrite

nitro *m* niter; **nitro del Cile** Chile saltpeter

nitroglicerina *f* nitroglycerin

nitruro *m* nitride

niu·no -na *adj* (poet) var of **nessuno**

nive·o -a *adj* snow-white

Nizza *f* Nice

no *adv* no; not; **come no?** why not; certainly; **dire di no** to say no; **no?** is it not so?; **non dir di no** to consent; **proprio no** certainly not

nòbile *adj* noble; second (*floor*) || *m* nobleman || *f* noblewoman

nobiliare *adj* noble, of nobility

nobilitare (**nobìlito**) *tr* to ennoble

nobil·tà *f* (**-tà**) nobility

nòc·ca *f* (**-che**) knuckle

nocchière *m* or **nocchièro** *m* petty officer; (poet) pilot, helmsman

nocchieru·to -ta *adj* knotty

nòc·chio *m* (**-chi**) knot (*in wood*)

nocciòla *adj invar* hazel (*in color*) || *f* hazelnut; filbert

nocciolina *f* little nut; **nocciolina americana** peanut; roasted peanut

nòcciolo *m* stone, pit, kernel; **il noc-**

ciolo della questione the crux of the matter

nocciòlo m hazel (*tree*); filbert (*tree*)

nóce m walnut tree || *f* walnut (*fruit*); **noce del collo** Adam's apple; **noce di cocco** coconut; **noce di vitello** filet of veal; **noce moscata** nutmeg

nocévole adj harmful

noci·vo -va adj harmful, detrimental

nòdo m knot; crux, gist (*of a question*); junction; lump (*in one's throat*); (naut) knot; (phys) node; **lì è il nodo** there's the rub; **nodo d'amore** true-love knot; **nodo ferroviario** rail center, junction; **nodo scorsoio** noose; **nodo stradale** highway center, cross-roads

nodó·so -sa [s] adj knotty

Noè m Noah

noi §5 pron pers we; us; **noi altri** we, e.g., **noi altri italiani** we Italians

nòia *f* boredom; bother, trouble; bug (*in a motor*); **venire a noia** (*with dat*) to weary; **dar noia** (*with dat*) to bother

noial·tri -tre pron we; us; **noialtri italiani** we Italians

noió·so -sa [s] adj boring, annoying

noleggiare §290 (**noléggio**) *tr* to rent; to hire, to charter || *ref*—**si noleggia, si noleggiano** for rent

noleggiatóre m hirer; lessor (*e.g., of a car*)

nolég·gio m (-gi) rent, lease; car rental; chartering; freightage

nolènte adj unwilling

nòlo m rent, hire; **a nolo** for hire

nòmade adj nomad, nomadic || *mf* nomad

nóme m name; fame; reputation; (gram) noun; **a nome di** on behalf of; **in nome di** in the name of; **nome commerciale** firm name; **nome depositato** registered name; **nome di battesimo** Christian name; **nome e cognome** full name

nomèa *f* name, reputation; notoriety

nomìgnolo m nickname; **affibbiare un nomignolo a** to nickname

nòmina *f* appointment; **di prima nomina** newly appointed

nominale adj nominal; noun

nominare (**nòmino**) *tr* to name, call; to mention; to elect; to appoint

nominati·vo -va adj nominative; with names in alphabetical order; (fin) registered || *m* nominative; name; model number

non adv no, not; none, e.g., **non troppo presto** none too soon; **non appena** as soon as; **non c'è di che** you are welcome; **non . . . che** but, only; **non è vero?** is it not so?, isn't it so? La traduzione in inglese di questa domanda dipende generalmente dalla proposizione che la precede. Se la proposizione sarà affermativa, l'interrogazione sarà negativa, p.es. **Lei mi scriverà, non è vero?** You will write me. Won't you? Se la proposizione è negativa, l'interrogazione sarà positiva, p.es. **Lei non beve birra, non è**

vero? You do not drink beer. Do you? Se il soggetto della proposizione è un nome sostantivo, sarà rappresentato nell'interrogazione da un pronome personale, p.es. **Giovanni ha finito, non è vero?** John has finished. Hasn't he?

nonagenà·rio -ria adj & mf (-ri -rie) nonagenarian

nonagèsi·mo -ma adj, pron & m ninetieth

nonconformi·sta mf (-sti -ste) nonconformist

noncurante adj careless, indifferent

noncuranza *f* carelessness, indifference

nondiméno conj yet, nevertheless

nòn·no -na mf grandparent || m grandfather || *f* grandmother

nonnulla m invar nothing, trifle

nò·no -na adj, m & pron ninth

nonostante prep in spite of, notwithstanding; **nonostante che** although, even though

nonpertanto adv nevertheless, still, yet

non plus ultra m ne plus ultra, acme

nonsènso m nonsense

non so ché adj invar indefinable || m invar something indefinable

nontiscordardi·mé m (-mé) forget-me-not

nòrd m north

nòrdi·co -ca (-ci -che) adj Nordic; northern, north || mf northerner

nòrma *f* rule, regulation; **a norma di legge** according to law; **per Sua norma** for your guidance

normale adj normal; normative; perpendicular || *f* perpendicular line

normali·tà *f* (-tà) normality, normalcy

normalizzare [ddzz] *tr* to normalize, to standardize

Normandìa, la Normandy

norman·no -na adj & mf Norman || m Norseman

normati·vo -va adj normative || *f* normativeness

normògrafo m stencil

norvegése [s] adj & mf Norwegian

Norvègia, la Norway

nosocò·mio m (-mi) hospital

nossignóra (*i.e.,* **no signora**) adv no, Madam

nossignóre (*i.e.,* **no signore**) adv no, Sir

nostalgìa *f* nostalgia, longing; homesickness

nostàlgi·co -ca (-ci -che) adj nostalgic; homesick || m worshiper of the good old days (*esp. of Fascism*)

nostra·no -na adj domestic, national; home-grown; regional

nò·stro -stra §6 adj & pron poss

nòstromo m boatswain

nòta *f* mark; score; memorandum; list; bill, invoice; report (*on a subordinate*); (mus) note; **note caratteristiche** personal folder, efficiency report (*of an employee*); **prender nota di** to take down

notàbile adj notable, noteworthy || m notable

no·tàio m (-tài) notary (public); lawyer

notare (**nòto**) *tr* to mark, check; to note, to jot down; to observe; to bring out; **farsi notare** to attract attention, make oneself conspicuous; **nota bene** note well, take notice

notariale or **notarile** *adj* notarial

notazióne *f* notation; annotation; observation

nò•tes *m* (**-tes**) notebook

notévole *adj* noteworthy, remarkable

notìfi•ca *f* (**-che**) notification, notice; service (*e.g., of a summons*)

notificare §197 (**notìfico**) *tr* to report; to serve (*a summons*); to declare ..(*e.g., one's income*)

notificazióne *f* notification, notice; service (*e.g., of a summons*)

notìzia *f* knowledge; report; piece of news; **aver notizie di** to hear from; **notizie news; una notizia** a news item

notizià•rio *m* (**-ri**) news; news report, news bulletin; (rad) newscast; **notiziario sportivo** sports page; (rad, telv) sports news

nò•to -ta *adj* known, well-known ‖ *m* south wind; (coll) swimming ‖ *f* see **nota**

notorie•tà *f* (**-tà**) general knowledge; affidavit; notoriety

notò•rio -ria *adj* (**-ri -rie**) well-known

nottàmbu•lo -la *adj* nighttime; night-wandering ‖ *mf* nightwalker; night owl

nottata *f* night; **far nottata bianca** to spend a sleepless night

nòtte *f* night; **buona notte** good night; **di notte** at night, by night, in the nighttime; **la notte di lunedì** Sunday night; Monday night; **lunedì notte** Monday night; **notte bianca** sleepless night; **notte di San Silvestro** New Year's Eve; watch night

nottetèmpo *adv*—**di nottetempo** at night, in the nighttime

nòttola *f* wooden latch; (zool) bat

nottolino *m* small wooden latch; ratchet, catch

nottur•no -na *adj* nocturnal, night ‖ *m* nocturne

novanta *adj, m & pron* ninety

novantènne *adj* ninety-year-old ‖ *mf* ninety-year-old person

novantèsi•mo -ma *adj, m & pron* ninetieth

novantina *f* about ninety; **sulla novantina** about ninety years old

nòve *adj & pron* nine; **le nove** nine o'clock ‖ *m* nine; ninth (*in dates*)

novecentismo *m* twentieth-century arts and letters

novecentì•sta (**-sti -ste**) *adj* twentieth-century ‖ *mf* artist of the twentieth century

novecènto *adj, m & pron* nine hundred ‖ **il Novecento** the twentieth century

novèlla *f* short story; (poet) news

novelliè•re -ra *mf* storyteller; short-story writer

novellì•no -na *adj* early, tender; inexperienced, green

novellìstica *f* storytelling; fiction

novèl•lo -la *adj* fresh, young, tender; new ‖ *f* see **novella**

novèmbre *m* November

novenà•rio -ria *adj* (**-ri -rie**) nine-syllable

noverare (**nòvero**) *tr* to count; to enumerate; (poet) to remember

nòvero *m* number; class

novilù•nio *m* (**-ni**) new moon

novìssi•mo -ma *adj* (lit) last, newest

novi•tà *f* (**-tà**) newness, originality; novelty, innovation; latest idea; late news

noviziato *m* novitiate; apprenticeship

novì•zio -zia (**-zi -zie**) *mf* novice; apprentice ‖ *f* novice (*in a convent*)

novocaìna *f* novocaine

nozióne *f* notion, conception

nòzze *fpl* wedding, marriage; **nozze d'argento** silver wedding; **nozze d'oro** golden wedding

nube *f* cloud

nubifrà•gio *m* (**-gi**) cloudburst

nùbile *adj* unmarried, single (*woman*); marriageable ‖ *f* unmarried girl

nu•ca *f* (**-che**) nape of the neck, scruff

nucleare *adj* nuclear

nùcleo *m* nucleus; group; (elec) core

nudismo *m* nudism

nudì•sta *adj & mf* (**-sti -ste**) nudist

nudi•tà *f* (**-tà**) nudity, nakedness

nu•do -da *adj* naked, bare; barren; simple; **mettere a nudo** to lay bare; **nudo e crudo** stark-naked; destitute ‖ *m* nude

nùgolo *m* cloud; throng, swarm

nulla *pron* nothing ‖ *m invar* nothing; nothingness

nulla òsta *m* permission; visa

nullatenènte *adj* poor ‖ *mf* have-not

nullificare §197 (**nullìfico**) *tr* to nullify

nullì•tà *f* (**-tà**) nothingness; nonentity; invalidity (*of a document*)

nul•lo -la *adj* void, worthless ‖ **nullo** *pron* (poet) none, no one ‖ **nulla** *m & pron* see **nulla**

nume *m* divinity, deity

numerare (**nùmero**) *tr* to number

numeratóre *m* numerator; numbering machine

numèri•co -ca *adj* (**-ci -che**) numerical

nùmero *m* number; lottery ticket; size (*of shoes*); **numero dispari** odd number; **numero legale** quorum; **numero pari** even number

numeró•so -sa [s] *adj* numerous, large; harmonious

nùn•zio *m* (**-zi**) nuncio; (poet) news

nuòcere §206 *intr* to be harmful; (with *dat*) to harm

nuòra *f* daughter-in-law

nuotare (**nuòto**) *intr* to swim; to float; to wallow (*in wealth*)

nuotata *f* swim, dip, plunge

nuota•tóre -trice *mf* swimmer

nuòto *m* swimming; **gettarsi a nuoto** to jump into the water; **traversare a nuoto** to swim across

nuòva *f* news; late news

Nuòva York *f* New York
Nuova Zelanda, la [dz] New Zealand
nuòvo *-va adj* new; **di nuovo** again; **nuovo di zecca** brand-new; **nuovo fiammante** brand-new; **nuovo venuto** new arrival ‖ *m*—**il nuovo** the new ‖ *f* see **nuova**
nùtria *f* coypu
nutrice *f* wet nurse; (lit) provider
nutriènte *adj* nourishing
nutriménto *m* nourishment
nutrire §176 & (**nutro**) *tr* to nourish; to nurture; to harbor (*e.g.*, *hatred*) ‖ *ref*—**nutrirsi di** to feed on or upon
nutriti·vo *-va adj* nutritious, nutritive
nutri·to *-ta adj* well-fed; strong; rich (*food*); brisk, heavy (*gunfire*)
nutrizióne *f* nutrition; food
nùvo·lo *-la adj* cloudy ‖ *m* cloudy weather; (lit) cloud; (fig) swarm ‖ *f* cloud
nuvoló·so *-sa* [s] *adj* cloudy
nuziale *adj* wedding, nuptial
nuzialità *f* marriage rate

O

O, o [o] *m & f* thirteenth letter of the Italian alphabet
o *conj* or; now; **o . . . o** either . . . or; whether . . . or ‖ *interj* oh!
òa·si *f* (**-si**) oasis
obbediènte *adj* var of **ubbidiente**
obbediènza *f* obedience
obbedire §176 *tr & intr* var of **ubbidire**
obbiettare (**obbiètto**) *tr & intr* var of **oblettare**
obbligare §209 (**òbbligo**) *tr* to oblige; to compel, to force ‖ *ref* to obligate oneself
obbligatìssi·mo *-ma adj* much obliged
obbligatò·rio *-ria adj* (**-ri -rie**) compulsory, obligatory
obbligazióne *f* obligation; burden; (com) debenture, bond
obbligazioni·sta *mf* (**-sti -ste**) bondholder
òbbli·go *m* (**-ghi**) obligation; duty; **d'obbligo** obligatory, mandatory; **fare d'obbligo a qlcu** + *inf* to be necessary for s.o. to + *inf*, *e.g.*, **gli fa d'obbligo lavorare** it is necessary for him to work
obbrò·brio *m* (**-bri**) opprobrium, disgrace; **obbrobri** insults
obbrobrió·so *-sa* [s] *adj* opprobrious, disgraceful
obeli·sco *m* (**-schi**) obelisk
obera·to *-ta adj* overburdened
obesità *f* obesity
obè·so *-sa adj* obese, stout
òbice *m* howitzer
obiettare (**obiètto**) *tr & intr* to argue; to object
obietti·vo *-va adj & m* objective
obiettóre *m* objector; **obiettore di coscienza** conscientious objector
obiezióne *f* objection
obitò·rio *m* (**-ri**) morgue
oblare (**òblo**) *tr* to willingly pay (*a fine*)
obla·tóre *-trice mf* donor
oblazióne *f* donation; (eccl) oblation; (law) payment of a fine
obliare §119 *tr* (lit) to forget
oblì·o *m* (**-i**) (lit) oblivion
oblì·quo *-qua adj* oblique
obliterare (**oblitero**) *tr to* obliterate, cancel
o·blò *m* (**-blò**) (naut) porthole; **oblò di accesso** door (*of space capsule*)
oblun·go *-ga adj* (**-ghi -ghe**) oblong
òbo·e *m* (**-e**) oboe
oboi·sta *mf* (**-sti -ste**) oboist
òbolo *m* mite
ò·ca *f* (**-che**) goose; gander
ocarina *f* ocarina, sweet potato
occasionale *adj* chance; immediate (*cause*)
occasionare (**occasióno**) *tr* to occasion
occasióne *f* occasion; opportunity; ground, pretext; bargain; **all'occasione** on occasion; **d'occasione** second-hand; occasional (*verses*)
occhiàia *f* eye socket; occhiaie rings under the eyes
occhia·làio *m* (**-lài**) optician
occhiale *adj* eye, ocular ‖ *m* **occhiali** *mpl* glasses; goggles; **occhiali antisole** sunglasses; **occhiali a stringinaso** nose glasses
occhialétto *m* lorgnon; monocle
occhiata *f* glance
occhieggiare §290 (**occhléggio**) *tr* to eye ‖ *intr* to peep
occhièllo *m* buttonhole; boutonniere; eyelet; half title; subhead
occhièra *f* eyecup
òc·chio *m* (**-chi**) eye; speck of grease (*in soup*); handle (*of scissors*); ring (*of stirrup*); (typ) face; (fig) bit; **a occhio e croce** at a rough guess; **a quattr'occhi** in private; **battere gli occhi** to blink; **cavarsi gli occhi** to strain one's eyes; **dar nell'occhio** to attract attention; **di buon occhio** favorably; **fare l'occhio a** to get used to; **fare tanto d'occhi** to be amazed, to open one's eyes wide; **lasciare gli occhi su** to covet; **non chiudere un occhio** not to sleep a wink; **occhio!** watch out!; **occhio della testa** outrageous price; **occhio di bue** (naut) porthole; **occhio di cubia** (naut) hawsehole; **occhio di pavone** (zool) peacock butterfly; **occhio di triglia** sheep's eyes; **occhio pesto** black eye; **occhio pollino** corn (*on toes*); **tenere d'occhio** to keep an eye on
occhiolino *m* small eye; **far l'occhiolino** to wink
occidentale *adj* western, occidental
occidènte *adj* (poet) setting (*sun*) ‖ *m* west, occident

occìpite *m* occipital bone
occlusióne *f* occlusion
occlusì•vo -va *adj* & *f* occlusive
occlu•so -sa *adj* occluded
occorrènte *adj* necessary ‖ *m* necessary; (lit) occurrence
occorrènza *f* necessity; **all'occorrenza** if need be
occórrere §139 *intr* (ESSERE) to happen; (with *dat*) to need, e.g., **gli occorre dell'olio** he needs oil ‖ *impers* (ESSERE)—**occorre** it is necessary
occultaménto *m* concealment
occultare *tr* & *ref* to hide
occul•to -ta *adj* occult; (lit) hidden
occupante *adj* occupying ‖ *m* occupant
occupare (òccupo) *tr* to occupy; to employ ‖ *ref* to take employment; **occuparsi di** to busy oneself with, to mind; to attend to
occupa•to -ta *adj* occupied; busy
occupazionale *adj* occupational
occupazióne *f* occupation
oceàni•co -ca *adj* (-ci -che) oceanic
ocèano *m* ocean
òcra *f* ocher
oculare *adj* ocular; see **testimone** ‖ *m* eyepiece
oculatézza *f* circumspection, prudence
ocula•to -ta *adj* circumspect, prudent
oculì•sta *mf* (-sti -ste) oculist
od *conj* or
odalì•sca *f* (-sche) odalisque
òde *f* ode
odepòri•co -ca (-ci -che) *adj* (lit) travel ‖ *m* (lit) travelogue
odiare §287 (òdio) *tr* to hate
odièr•no -na *adj* today's, current
ò•dio *m* (-di) hatred; **avere in odio** to hate; **essere in odio a** to be hated by
odiò•so -sa [s] *adj* hateful, odious
odissèa *f* odyssey ‖ **Odissea** *f* Odyssey
Odissèo *m* Odysseus
odontoìa•tra *mf* (-tri -tre) doctor of dental surgery, dentist
odontoiatrìa *f* odontology, dentistry
odorare (odóro) *tr* & *intr* to smell
odora•to -ta *adj* (poet) fragrant ‖ *m* smell
odóre *m* smell, odor, scent; **cattivo odore** bad odor; **odori** herbs, spice
odoró•so -sa [s] *adj* odorous, fragrant
offèndere §148 *tr* & *intr* to offend ‖ *ref* to take offense
offensì•vo -va *adj* & *f* offensive
offensóre *m* offender
offerènte *mf* bidder; **miglior offerente** highest bidder
offèrta *f* offer; offering, donation; (*at an auction*) bid; (com) supply
offésa [s] *f* offense; wrongdoing; ravage (*of time*); **da offesa** (mil) offensive; **recarsi a offesa** qlco to regard s.th as offensive
officìna *f* shop, workshop; **officina meccanica** machine shop
officló•so -sa [s] *adj* helpful, obliging
offrìre §207 *tr* to offer; to sponsor (*a radio or TV program*); to dedicate (*a book*); to bid (*at an auction*); (com) to tender ‖ *ref* to offer oneself, to volunteer

offuscare §197 *tr* to darken, obscure; to obfuscate; to dim (*mind; eyes*) ‖ *ref* to grow dark; to grow dim
oftàlmi•co -ca *adj* (-ci -che) opthalmic
oftalmòlo•go -ga *mf* (-gi -ghe) ophthalmologist
oggettività *f* objectivity
oggettì•vo -va *adj* & *m* objective
oggètto *m* object; subject, argument; article; **oggetti preziosi** valuables
òggi *m* today; **dall'oggi al domani** suddenly; overnight ‖ *adv* today; **d'oggi in poi** henceforth; **oggi a otto** a week hence; **oggi come oggi** at present; **oggi è un anno** one year ago
oggidì *m invar* & *adv* nowadays
oggigiórno *m invar* & *adv* nowadays
ogìva *f* ogive, pointed arch; nose cone
ógni *adj indef invar* each; every, e.g., **ogni due giorni** every two days; **ogni cosa** everything; **ogni tanto** every now and then; **per ogni dove** (lit) everywhere
ogniqualvòlta *conj* whenever
Ognissan•ti *m* (-ti) All Saints' Day
ognitèmpo *adj invar* all-weather
-ógno•lo -la *suf adj* -ish, e.g., **giallognolo** yellowish
ognóra *adv* (lit) always
ognu•no -na *adj* (obs) each ‖ *pron* each one, everyone
oh *interj* oh!
òhi *interj* ouch!
ohibò *interj* fie!
ohimè *interj* alas!
ohm *m* (ohm) ohm
olanda *f* Dutch linen ‖ **l'Olanda** *f* Holland
olandése [s] *adj* Dutch ‖ *m* Dutch (*language*); Dutchman; Dutch cheese ‖ *f* Dutch woman
oleandro *m* oleander
oleà•rio -ria *adj* (-ri -rie) oil
olea•to -ta *adj* oiled
oleifì•cio *m* (-ci) oil mill
oleodótto *m* pipeline
oleó•so -sa [s] *adj* oily
olezzare [ddzz] (olézzo) *intr* (lit) to smell sweet
olézzo [ddzz] *m* perfume, fragrance
olfatto *m* smell
oliare §287 (òlio) *tr* to oil
oliatóre *m* oiler, oil can
olièra *f* cruet
olìbano *m* frankincense
oligarchìa *f* oligarchy
olimpiade *f* Olympiad
olìmpi•co -ca *adj* (-ci -che) Olympic; Olympian
olimpiòni•co -ca *adj* (-ci -che) Olympic ‖ *mf* Olympic athlete
ò•lio *m* (-li) oil; **ad olio** oil, e.g., **quadro ad olio** oil painting; **olio di fegato di merluzzo** cod-liver oil; **olio di lino** linseed oil; **olio di ricino** castor oil; **olio solare** sun-tan lotion
olìva *f* olive
olivà•stro -stra *adj* livid; swarthy ‖ *m* wild olive (*tree*)
olivéto *m* olive grove
Olivièro *m* Oliver
olìvo *m* olive tree

ólmo *m* elm tree
olocàu·sto -sta *adj* (lit) burnt; (lit) sacrificed ‖ *m* holocaust; sacrifice
ològra·fo -fa *adj* holographic
olóna *f* sailcloth, canvas
oltracciò *adv* besides
oltraggiare §290 *tr* to outrage; to insult
oltràg·gio *m* (-gi) outrage; offense; ravages (*of time*); oltraggio al pudore offense to public morals; oltraggio al tribunale contempt of court
oltraggió·so -sa [s] *adj* outrageous
oltranza *f*—a oltranza to the bitter end
oltranzi·sta *mf* (-sti -ste) (pol) extremist
óltre *adv* beyond; ahead; further; oltre a apart from; in addition to; troppo oltre too far ‖ *prep* beyond; past; more than
oltrecortina *adj invar* beyond-the-iron-curtain ‖ *m* country beyond the iron curtain
oltremare *m invar* country overseas ‖ *adv* overseas
oltremisura *adv* (lit) beyond measure
oltremòdo *adv* (lit) exceedingly
oltrepassare *tr* to overstep; to cross (*a river*); to be beyond (. . . *years old*); (sports) to overtake
oltretómba *m*—l'oltretomba the life beyond
omàg·gio *m* (-gi) homage; compliment; in omaggio complimentary; rendere omaggio a to pay tribute to
òmaro *m* Norway lobster
ombelì·co *m* (-chi) navel
ómbra *f* shade; shadow; umbrage; form, mass; nemmeno per ombra not in the least
ombreggiare §290 (ombréggio) *tr* to shade
ombrèlla *f* shade (*of trees*); (bot) umbel; (coll) umbrella
ombrel·làio *m* (-lài) umbrella maker
ombrellino *m* parasol
ombrèllo *m* umbrella
ombrellóne *m* beach umbrella
ombró·so -sa [s] *adj* shady; touchy; skittish (*horse*)
omelette *f* (omelette) omelet
omelìa *f* homily
omeopàti·co -ca (-ci -che) *adj* homeopathic ‖ *m* homeopathist
omèri·co -ca *adj* (-ci -che) Homeric
òmero *m* (anat) humerus; (lit) shoulder
omertà *f* code of silence of underworld
omèttere §198 *tr* to omit
omètto *m* little man; (coll) clothes hanger; (billiards) pin; (archit) king post
omici·da (-di -de) *adj* homicidal, murderous ‖ *mf* homicide, murderer
omici·dio *m* (-di) homicide, murder; omicidio colposo (law) manslaughter; omicidio doloso (law) first-degree murder
ominó·so -sa [s] *adj* (lit) ominous
omissióne *f* omission
òmni·bus *m* (-bus) omnibus; way train
omnisciènte *adj* all-knowing, omniscient
omogène·o -a *adj* homogeneous
omologare §209 (omòlogo) *tr* to con-

firm, ratify; to probate (*a will*); (sports) to validate
omòni·mo -ma *adj* of the same name ‖ *m* namesake; homonym
omosessuale [s] *adj & mf* homosexual
ón·cia *f* (-ce) ounce; oncia a oncia little by little
ónda *f* wave; a onde wavy; wavily; essere in onda (rad, telv) to be on the air; farsi le onde to have one's hair waved; mettere in onda (rad, telv) to put on the air; onda crespa whitecap; onda portante (rad, telv) carrier wave
ondata *f* wave, billow; gust (*e.g., of smoke*); rush (*of blood*); wave (*of cold weather*)
ondatra *f* muskrat
ónde *pron* from which; of which ‖ *adv* whereof; hence; (poet) wherefrom ‖ *prep* onde + *inf* in order to ‖ *conj* onde + *subj* so that
ondeggiante *adj* waving, swaying
ondeggiare §290 (ondéggio) *intr* to wave, sway; to waver
ondina *f* mermaid; (mythol) undine; (mythol) mermaid
ondó·so -sa [s] *adj* wavy
ondulare (óndulo & òndulo) *tr* to wave; to corrugate (*e.g., metal*) ‖ *intr* to sway
ondula·to -ta *adj* wavy (*hair*); corrugated (*e.g., metal*); bumpy (*road*)
ondulazióne *f* undulation; ondulazione permanente permanent wave
-óne -óna *suf mf* big, e.g., librone big book; dormigliona big sleeper ‖ -óne *suf m* (applies to both sexes) big, e.g., donnone *m* big woman
ònere *m* (lit) onus, burden
oneró·so -sa [s] *adj* onerous, burdensome
onestà *f* honesty; (poet) modesty
onè·sto -sta *adj* honest; fair; (poet) modest ‖ *m* moderate amount; honest gain; honest person
ònice *m* onyx
onnipossènte & onnipotènte *adj* almighty, omnipotent
onnisciènte *adj* omniscient
onniveggènte *adj* all-seeing
onnìvo·ro -ra *adj* omnivorous
onpmàsti·co -ca (-ci -che) *adj* onomastic ‖ *m* name day ‖ *f* study of proper names
onomatopèi·co -ca *adj* (-ci -che) onomatopeic
onoràbile *adj* honorable
onoranza *f* honor; onoranze homage; onoranze funebri obsequies
onorare (onóro) *tr* to honor ‖ *ref* to deem it an honor
onorà·rio -ria (-ri -rie) *adj* honorary ‖ *m* fee, honorarium
onora·to -ta *adj* honored; honest; honorable
onóre *m* honor; d'onore honest, e.g., uomo d'onore honest man; estremi onori last rites; fare gli onori di casa to receive guests; fare onore a to honor; onore al merito credit where

credit is due; **onor del mento** (lit) beard

onorévole *adj* honorable ‖ *m* honorable member (*of parliament*)

onorificènza *f* dignity; decoration

onorifi·co -ca *adj* (-ci -che) honorific; honorary (*e.g., title*)

ónta *f* dishonor, shame; **a onta di** in spite of; **avere onta** to be ashamed; **fare onta a** to bring shame upon; **in onta a** against

ontano *m* alder

O.N.U. (acronym) *f* (**Organizzazione delle Nazioni Unite**) United Nations, U.N.

onu·sto -sta *adj* (poet) laden

opa·co -ca *adj* (-chi -che) opaque

opale *m* opal

opali·no -na *adj* opaline ‖ *f* shiny cardboard; luster (*fabric*)

òpera *f* work; organization, foundation; day's work; (mus) opera; **mettere in opera** to install; to start work on; to make ready; to begin using; **opera di consultazione** reference work; **opera morta** (naut) upper works; **opera viva** (naut) quickwork; **per opera di** thanks to

ope·ràio -ràia (-rài -ràie) *adj* workman's, worker's; working ‖ *m* workman, worker; **operaio a cottimo** pieceworker; **operaio a giornata** day laborer; **operaio specializzato** craftsman, skilled workman ‖ *f* workwoman

operante *adj* actively engaged; operative

operare (**òpero**) *tr* to operate; to work (*a miracle*); (surg) to operate on ‖ *intr* to operate; to be actively engaged ‖ *ref* to be operated on; to occur, take place

operati·vo -va *adj* operative; operations, e.g., **ricerca operativa** operations research

opera·to -ta *adj* operated; embossed ‖ *m* behavior; patient operated on

opera·tóre -trice *mf* operator ‖ *m* (mov) cameraman

operatò·rio -ria *adj* (-ri -rie) surgical (*operation*); operating (*room*); (math) operational

operazióne *f* operation; transaction

operétta *f* short work; (mus) operetta

operisti·co -ca *adj* (-ci -che) operatic

operosi·tà [s] *f* (-tà) industry

operó·so -sa [s] *adj* industrious; active

opi·mo -ma *adj* (lit) fat; rich, fertile

opinare *intr* to opine, deem

opinióne *f* opinion

opòs·sum *m* (-sum) opossum

oppia·to -ta *adj* opiate (*mixed with opium*); dulled by drugs ‖ *m* opiate (*medicine containing opium*)

òppio *m* opium

oppiòmane *adj* opium-eating; opium-smoking ‖ *mf* opium addict

oppórre §218 *tr* to oppose; to offer, put up (*resistance*) ‖ *ref* to be opposite; **opporsi a** to oppose, to be against

opportuni·sta *mf* (-sti -ste) opportunist

opportuni·tà *f* (-tà) opportunity; opportuneness

opportu·no -na *adj* opportune

opposi·tóre -trice *mf* opponent

opposizióne *f* opposition; (law) appeal; **fare opposizione a** to object to

oppó·sto -sta *adj* opposite; contrary ‖ *m* opposite; **all'opposto** on the contrary

oppressióne *f* oppression

oppressi·vo -va *adj* oppressive

opprès·so -sa *adj* oppressed; overcome, overwhelmed ‖ **oppressi** *mpl* oppressed people

oppressóre *m* oppressor

opprimènte *adj* oppressive

opprimere §131 *tr* to oppress; to overcome, overwhelm; to weigh down

oppugnare *tr* to refute, contradict

oppure *adv* otherwise ‖ *conj* or else; or rather

optare (**òpto**) *intr* to choose; (com) to exercise an option

optometri·sta *mf* (-sti -ste) optometrist

opulèn·to -ta *adj* opulent

opùscolo *m* booklet, brochure, pamphlet; **opuscolo d'informazioni** instruction manual

opzióne *f* option

ór *adv* now; **or ora** right now; **or sono** ago

óra *f* hour; time; period (*in school*); **alla buon'ora!** finally!; **a ore** by the hour; **a tarda ora** late; **che ora è?** or **che ore sono?** what time is it?; **da un'ora all'altra** from one moment to the next; **dell'ultima ora** up-to-date (*news*); **di buon'ora** early; early in the morning; **di ora in ora** at any moment; **d'ora in avanti** from this moment on; **d'ora in poi** from now on; **far l'ora** to kill time; **fin ora** until now; **non vedere l'ora di** + *inf* to be hardly able to wait until + *ind*; **ora di cena** suppertime; **ora di punta** rush hour, peak hour; **ora legale** daylight-saving time; **ore piccole** late hours; **un'ora di orologio** one full hour ‖ *adv* now

oràcolo *m* oracle

òra·fo -fa *adj* goldsmith's ‖ *m* goldsmith

orale *adj & m* oral

oralménte *adv* orally; by word of mouth

oramài *adv* now; already

oran·go *m* (-ghi) orangutan

orà·rio -ria (-ri -rie) *adj* hourly; per hour; clockwise ‖ *m* timetable; schedule; roster; **essere in orario** to be on time; **orario di lavoro** working hours; **orario d'ufficio** office hours

ora·tóre -trice *mf* orator

oratò·rio -ria *adj* (-ri -rie) oratorical ‖ *m* (eccl) oratory; (mus) oratorio ‖ *f* oratory, public speaking

orazióne *f* oration; prayer; **orazione domenicale** Lord's Prayer

orbare (**òrbo**) *tr* (lit) to bereave; (lit) to deprive

òrbe *f* (lit) orb; (lit) world

orbène *adv* well

òrbita *f* orbit; (fig) sphere
orbitare (òrbito) *intr* to orbit
orbitazióne *f* orbiting
òr·bo -ba *adj* bereaved; deprived; blind || *m* blind man
òrca *f* killer whale
Òrcadi *fpl* Orkney Islands
orchèstra *f* orchestra; band; orchestra pit
orchestrale *adj* orchestral || *mf* orchestra player; orchestra performer
orchestrare (orchèstro) *tr* to orchestrate; (fig) to organize
orchestrina *f* dance band; dance-band music
orchidèa *f* orchid
ór·cio *m* (-ci) jar, jug, crock
orciòlo *m—a* orciolo puckered up (*lips*)
òr·co *m* (-chi) ogre
òrda *f* horde
ordàlia *f* (hist) ordeal
ordigno *m* gadget, contrivance; tool; ordigno esplosivo infernal machine
ordinale *adj* & *m* ordinal
ordinaménto *m* disposition; regulation
ordinanza *f* ordinance; (mil) orderly; d'ordinanza regulation (*e.g., uniform*); in ordinanza (mil) in formation
ordinare (órdino) *tr* to order; to straighten up; to range; to regulate; to ordain; to trim
ordinà·rio -ria (-ri -rie) *adj* ordinary; plain; inferior; workday (*suit*) || *m* ordinary; full professor; d'ordinario ordinarily, usually
ordina·to -ta *adj* orderly, tidy; ordained || *f* ordinate; straightening up; (aer) frame; (naut) bulkhead
ordinazióne *f* order; ordination
órdine *m* order; row; tier; series (*e.g., of years*); college (*e.g., of surgeons*); nature (*of things*); (law) warrant, writ; in ordine a concerning; ordine del giorno order of the day; ordine d'idee train of thought
ordire §176 *tr* to warp (*cloth*); to hatch (*a plot*)
ordi·to -ta *adj* plotted || *m* warp (*of fabric*)
orécchia *f* ear; dog-ear; con le orecchie tese all ears
orecchiale *m* earphone (*of sonar equipment*)
orecchiétta *f* (anat) auricle
orecchino *m* earring
oréc·chio *m* (-chi) ear; hearing; dog-ear; moldboard; fare orecchio da mercante to turn a deaf ear || *m* (orécchia *fpl*) (archaic) ear
orecchione *m* long-eared bat; (mil) trunnion; orecchioni (pathol) mumps
oréfice *m* goldsmith; jeweler
oreficeria *f* goldsmith shop; jewelry shop
orfanézza *f* orphanage (*condition*)
òrfa·no -na *adj* orphaned || *mf* orphan
orfanotrò·fio *m* (-fi) orphanage (*institution*)
Orfèo *m* Orpheus
organdi *m* organdy
organétto *m* hand organ; mouth organ; organetto di Barberia hand organ

orgàni·co -ca (-ci -che) *adj* organic || *m* personnel, staff || *f* (mil) organization
organigram·ma *m* (-mi) organization chart
organino *m* hand organ, barrel organ
organismo *m* organism
organi·sta *mf* (-sti -ste) organist
organizzare [ddzz] *tr* to organize
organizza·tóre -trice [ddzz] *mf* organizer
organizzazióne [ddzz] *f* organization; Organizzazione delle Nazioni Unite United Nations
òrgano *m* organ; part (*of a machine*); organo di stampa mouthpiece
orgasmo *m* orgasm; agitation, excitement
òr·gia *f* (-ge) orgy
orgó·glio *m* (-gli) pride
orgoglió·so -sa [s] *adj* proud
orientale *adj* & *mf* oriental; Oriental
orientaménto *m* orientation; bearing; trend; trim (*of sail*); orientamento scolastico e professionale aptitude test; vocational guidance
orientare (orièsto) *tr* to orient; to guide; to trim (*a sail*) || *ref* to find one's bearings
orinalé *m* chamber pot, urinal
orinare *tr* & *intr* to urinate
orina·tóio *m* (-tói) urinal, comfort station
oriolo *m* (orn) oriole
oriun·do -da *adj* native || *m* (sports) native son
orizzontale [ddzz] *adj* horizontal || orizzontali *fpl* horizontal words (*in crossword puzzle*)
orizzontare [ddzz] (orizzónto) *tr* to orient || *ref* to get one's bearings
orizzónte [ddzz] *m* horizon
Orlando *m* Roland
orlare (órlo) *tr* to hem, border; orlare a zigzag to pink
órlo *m* edge; brim; hem, border; (fig) brink; orlo a giorno hemstitch
órma *f* footprint; orme remains, vestiges; calcare le orme di to follow the footsteps of
ormeggiare §290 (orméggio) *tr* & *ref* (naut) to moor
ormég·gio *m* (-gi) mooring; mollare gli ormeggi (naut) to cast off
ormóne *m* hormone

ornamentale *adj* ornamental
ornaménto *m* ornament
ornare (órno) *tr* to adorn
orna·to -ta *adj* adorned; ornate ‖ *m* ornament; ornamental design
ornitòlo·go -ga *mf* (**-gi -ghe**) ornithologist
òro *m* gold; (fig) money; **d'oro** gold, golden; **ori** gold objects; jewels; suit of Neapolitan cards corresponding to diamonds; **oro zecchino** pure gold; **per tutto l'oro del mondo** for all the world
orologerìa *f* watchmaking; clockmaking; watchmaker's shop
orolo·giàio *m* (**-giài**) watchmaker; clockmaker
orolò·gio *m* (**-gi**) watch; clock; **orologio a pendolo** clock; **orologio a polvere** sandglass; **orologio a scatto** digital clock; **orologio da polso** wristwatch; **orologio della morte** deathwatch; **orologio solare** sundial
oròscopo *m* horoscope
orpèllo *m* Dutch gold; (fig) tinsel
orrèndo *m* horrible
orrìbile *adj* horrible
òrri·do -da *adj* horrid ‖ *m* horridness; gorge, ravine
orripilante *adj* bloodcurdling, hairraising
orróre *m* horror; awe; **aver in** or **per orrore** to loath; **fare orrore a** to horrify
órsa *f* she-bear ‖ **Orsa** *f*—**Orsa maggiore** Great Bear; **Orsa minore** Little Bear
orsacchiòtto *m* bear cub; Teddy bear
ór·so -sa *mf* bear; **orso bianco** polar bear; **orso grigio** grizzly bear ‖ *f* see **orsa**
orsù *interj* come on!
ortàg·gio *m* (**-gi**) vegetable
ortàglia *f* vegetable garden; vegetable
ortènsia *f* hydrangea
orti·ca *f* (**-che**) nettle; hives
orticària *f* hives, nettle rash
orticoltóre *m* truck gardener; horticulturist
òrto *m* garden, vegetable garden; (lit) sunrise; **orto botanico** botanical garden; **orto di guerra** Victory garden
ortodòs·so -sa *adj* orthodox ‖ *m* Greek Catholic
ortografìa *f* orthography; spelling
ortola·no -na *adj* garden ‖ *m* truck farmer, gardener
ortopèdi·co -ca (**-ci -che**) *adj* orthopedic ‖ *m* orthopedist
òrza *f* bowline; windward
orzare (òrzo) *intr* to sail close to the wind; to luff
orzaiòlo [dz] *m* (pathol) sty
orzata [dz] *f* orgeat
orzata *f* (naut) luff
òrzo [dz] *m* barley
osannare *intr* to cry or sing hosanna; **osannare a** to acclaim, applaud
osare (òso) *intr* to dare
osceni·tà *f* (**-tà**) obscenity
oscè·no -na *adj* obscene; (coll) horrible
oscillante *adj* oscillating

oscillare *intr* to oscillate; to swing; to wobble; to waver, hesitate
oscillazióne *f* oscillation; fluctuation
oscuraménto *m* darkening, dimming; blackout
oscurare *tr* to darken; to blot out; to dim ‖ *ref* to get dark; **oscurarsi in volto** to frown
oscuri·tà *f* (**-tà**) obscurity; darkness; ignorance
oscu·ro -ra *adj* obscure, dark; opaque (*style*) ‖ *m* obscurity, darkness; **essere all'oscuro di** to be in the dark about
osmòsi *f* osmosis
ospedale *m* hospital
ospedalière *m* hospital worker
ospedaliè·ro -ra *adj* hospital ‖ *m* hospitaler
ospedalizzare [ddzz] *tr* to hospitalize
ospitale *adj* hospitable ‖ *m* hospital
ospitali·tà *f* (**-tà**) hospitality
ospitare (òspito) *tr* to lodge, shelter, accommodate; to entertain; (sports) to play (*an opposing team*) at home
òspite *mf* host; guest; **andarsene insalutato ospite** to take French leave; **ospiti** company (*guests at home*)
ospì·zio *m* (**-zi**) hospice; hostel; (lit) hospitality; **ospizio dei vecchi** nursing home; **ospizio di mendicità** poorhouse
ossatura *f* frame, framework; skeleton
òsse·o -a *adj* bony
ossequènte *adj* (lit) respectful; (lit) reverent
ossequiare §287 (**ossèquio**) *tr* to pay one's respects to; to honor
ossè·quio *m* (**-qui**) respect; reverence; **i miei ossequi** my best regards; **in ossequio a** in conformity with; **porgere i propri ossequi a** to pay one's respects to
ossequió·so -sa [s] *adj* obsequious; respectful
osservante *adj & m* observant
osservanza *f* observance; deference
osservare (ossèrvo) *tr* to observe
osserva·tóre -trice *adj* observing, observant ‖ *mf* observer
osservatò·rio *m* (**-ri**) observatory
osservazióne *f* observation; rebuke
ossessionare (ossessióno) *tr* to obsess; to harass, bedevil
ossessióne *f* obsession
ossès·so -sa *adj* possessed ‖ *mf* person possessed
ossìa *conj* or; to wit
ossidante *adj* oxidizing ‖ *m* oxidizer
ossidare (òssido) *tr & ref* to oxidize
òssido *m* oxide; **ossido di carbone** carbon monoxide
ossìdulo *m* protoxide; **ossidulo di azoto** nitrous oxide
ossificare §197 (**ossìfico**) *tr & ref* to ossify
ossigenare (ossìgeno) *tr* to oxygenate; to bleach (*the hair*); to infuse strength into ‖ *ref* to bleach (*the hair*)
ossìgeno *m* oxygen; (fig) transfusion, shot in the arm
ossìto·no -na *adj & m* oxytone

** òs·so** m (-si) bone (of animal); stone (of fruit); **osso di balena** whalebone; **osso di seppia** cuttlebone; **osso duro da rodere** hard nut to crack; **osso sacro** sacrum; **rimetterci l'osso del collo** to be thoroughly ruined; **rompersi l'osso del collo** to break one's neck || m (-sa fpl) bone (of a person); **avere le ossa rotte** to be dead-tired

ossu·to -ta adj bony; scrawny

ostacolare (ostàcolo) tr to hinder; to obstruct; **ostacolare l'azione** (sports) to interfere

ostàcolo m obstacle; obstruction; (golf) hazard; (sports) hurdle

ostàg·gio m (-gi) hostage

ostare (òsto) intr (lit) to be in the way; (with dat) to hinder; **nulla osta** no objection, permission granted

òste ostèssa mf innkeeper || **oste** m & f (lit) army in the field || m (poet) enemy

ostèllo m hostel; (poet) abode

ostentare (ostènto) tr to show, display; to affect, feign

ostenta·to -ta adj affected, ostentatious

ostentazióne f show, ostentation

osteopatìa f osteopathy

osterìa f tavern, inn, taproom

ostéssa f see oste

ostètri·ca f (-che) midwife

ostetrìcia f obstetrics

ostètri·co -ca (-ci -che) adj obstetrical || m obstetrician || f see ostetrica

òstia f wafer; Host; sacrificial victim

òsti·co -ca adj (-ci -che) hard; (lit) repugnant, distasteful

ostile adj hostile

ostili·tà f (-tà) hostility

ostinare ref to be stubborn; to persist

ostina·to -ta adj obstinate; persistent

ostinazióne f obstinacy

ostracismo m ostracism; **dare l'ostracismo a** to ostracize

ostracizzare [ddzz] tr (poet) to ostracize

òstri·ca f (-che) oyster; **ostrica perlifera** pearl oyster

ostri·càlo m (-càl) oyster bed; oysterman

ostruire §176 tr to obstruct; to stop up

ostruzióne f obstruction

Otèllo m Othello

otorinolaringoia·tra mf (-tri -tre) ear, nose, and throat specialist, otorhinolaryngologist

ótre f wineskin; **otre di vento** windbag (person)

ottàni·co -ca adj (-ci -che) octane

ottano m octane

ottanta adj, m & pron eighty

ottantènne adj eighty-year-old || mf eighty-year-old person

ottantèsi·mo -ma adj, m & pron eightieth

ottantina f about eighty; **essere sull'ottantina** to be about eighty years old

ottava f octave

Ottaviano m Octavian

ottavino m (mus) piccolo; (com) commission of ⅛ of 1%

otta·vo -va adj & pron eighth || m eighth; octavo || f see ottava

ottemperare (ottèmpero) intr (with dat) to obey; **ottemperare a** to comply with

ottenebrare (ottènebro) tr to becloud

ottenére §271 tr to obtain, get

ottétto m octet

òtti·co -ca (-ci -che) adj optic(al) || m optician || f optics

ottimismo m optimism

ottimi·sta mf (-sti -ste) optimist

ottimìsti·co -ca adj (-ci -che) optimistic

òtti·mo -ma adj very good, excellent || m best; highest rating

òtto adj & pron eight; **le otto eight** o'clock || m eight; eighth (in dates); (sports) racing shell with eight oarsmen; **otto giorni** a week; **otto volante** roller coaster

ottóbre m October

ottocenté·sco -sca adj (-schi -sche) nineteenth-century

ottocènto adj, m & pron eight hundred || **l'Ottocento** the nineteenth century

ottoma·no -na adj & m Ottoman || m ottoman (fabric) || f ottoman (sofa)

ottomila adj, m & pron eight thousand

ottoname m brassware

ottonare (ottóno) tr to coat with brass

ottóne m brass; **ottoni** (mus) brasses || **Ottone** m Otto

ottuagenà·rio -ria adj & mf (-ri -rie) octogenerian

ottùndere §208 tr (fig) to deaden; (lit) to blunt

otturare tr to fill; to plug; to stop; to obstruct, stop up (e.g., a channel) || ref to clog up

otturatóre m breechblock; (phot, mov) shutter; (mach) cutoff (of cylinder)

otturazióne f filling (of tooth)

ottu·so -sa adj obtuse; blunt

ovàia f ovary

ovale adj oval || m oval; oval face

ovatta f wadding; absorbent cotton

ovattare tr to pad, wad; to muffle

ovazióne f ovation

óve adv (lit) where || conj (lit) if; (poet) while

òvest m west

Ovìdio m Ovid

ovile m sheepcote, fold

ovì·no -na adj ovine || **ovini** mpl sheep

òvo m var of uovo

ovoidale adj egg-shaped

òvulo m pill shaped like an egg; (biol) ovum; (bot) ovule

ovùnque adv (lit) wherever; (lit) everywhere

ovvéro conj or; to wit

òvvia interj come on!

ovviare §119 intr—(with dat) to obviate

òv·vio -via adj (-vi -vie) obvious

oziare §287 (òzio) intr to idle, loiter

ò·zio m (-zi) idleness; leisure

oziosi·tà f (-tà) idleness

ozió·so -sa [s] adj idle; useless, vain

ozòno [dz] m ozone

P

P, p [pi] *m & f* fourteenth letter of the Italian alphabet

pacare §197 *tr* (poet) to placate

pacatézza *f* tranquillity, serenity

paca·to -ta *adj* serene, tranquil

pac·ca *f* (-che) slap

pacchétto *m* parcel, package; book (*of matches*); pack (*of cigarettes*)

pàcchia *f* (coll) hearty meal; (coll) godsend, windfall

pacchia·no -na *adj* boorish, uncouth ‖ *mf* boor

pacciamantura *f* mulching

pacciame *m* mulch

pac·co *m* (-chi) package; **pacchi postali** parcel post (*service*); **pacco dono** gift package; **pacco postale** parcel by mail

paccottiglia *f* shoddy goods, junk; trinkets

pace *f* peace; **lasciare in pace** to leave alone; **mettersi il cuore in pace** to resign oneself

pachidèr·ma *m* (-mi) pachyderm

pachista·no -na *adj & mf* Pakistani

paclè·re -ra *mf* peacemaker

pacificare §197 (**pacìfico**) *tr* to pacify; to appease; to mediate ‖ *ref* to make one's peace

pacifica·tóre -trice *adj* pacifying ‖ *mf* peacemaker

pacificazióne *f* pacification; appeasement

pacìfi·co -ca (-ci -che) *adj* peaceful, pacific; **è pacìfico che** it goes without saying that ‖ *m* peaceable person ‖ **Pacìfico** *adj & m* Pacific

pacifismo *m* pacifism

pacifi·sta *mf* (-sti -ste) pacifist

pacioccó·ne -na *adj* chubby, easygoing person

padèlla *f* frying pan; bedpan; **cadere dalla padella nella brace** to jump from the frying pan into the fire

padiglióne *m* pavilion; hunting lodge; roof (*of car*); ward (*of a hospital*); (naut) rigging, tackle; **padiglione auricolare** (anat) auricle of the ear

Pàdova *f* Padua

padre *m* father; sire; **padre di famiglia** provider; (law) head of household; **Padre Eterno** Heavenly Father

padreggiare §290 (**padréggio**) *intr* to resemble one's father

padrino *m* godfather; second (*in duel*)

padrona *f* owner, boss, mistress; **padrona di casa** lady of the house

padronale *adj* proprietary; private (*e.g., car*)

padronanza *f* command; **padronanza di sé stesso** self-control

padróne *m* owner, boss, master; **essere padrone di** + *inf* to have the right to + *inf*; **padrone di casa** landlord; **padrone di sé** cool and collected

padroneggiare §290 (**padronéggio**) *tr* to master, control

paesàg·gio *m* (-gi) landscape

paesaggi·sta *mf* (-sti -ste) landscapist

paesa·no -na *adj* country ‖ *mf* villager ‖ *m* countryman ‖ *f* countrywoman; **alla paesana** according to local tradition

paése *m* country; village; **i Paesi Bassi** the Netherlands; (hist) the Low Countries; **mandare a quel paese** to send to blazes

paesi·sta *mf* (-sti -ste) landscapist

paffu·to -ta *adj* chubby, plump

pa·ga *f* (-ghe) salary; wages; repayment; **mala paga** poor pay (*person*)

pagàbile *adj* payable

pagàia *f* paddle

pagaménto *m* payment; **pagamento alla consegna** c.o.d.

paganésimo *m* paganism

paga·no -na *adj & mf* pagan, heathen

pagare §209 *tr* to pay; to pay for; **far pagare** to charge; **pagare di egual moneta** to repay in kind; **pagare il fio per** to pay (the penalty) for; **pagare in natura** to pay in kind; **pagare salato** to pay dearly; **pagare un occhio della testa** to pay through the nose ‖ *intr* to pay

paga·tóre -trice *mf* payer

pagèlla *f* report card

pàg·gio *m* (-gi) page (*boy attendant*)

paghe·rò *m* (-rò) promissory note, I.O.U.

pàgina *f* page (*e.g., of book*)

paginatura *f* pagination

pàglia *f* straw; thatch (*for roof*); **paglia di ferro** steel wool; **paglia di legno** excelsior

pagliacce·sco -sca *adj* (-schi -sche) clownish

pagliaccétto *m* rompers

pagliacciata *f* buffoonery, antics

pagliàc·cio *m* (-ci) clown, buffoon; **fare il pagliaccio** to clown

pa·gliàio *m* (-gliài) heap of straw; haystack

paglieric·cio *m* (-ci) straw mattress

paglieri·no -na *adj* straw-colored

pagliétta *f* skimmer, boater; steel wool; (coll) pettifogger

pagnòtta *f* loaf of bread; (coll) bread

pa·go -ga *adj* (-ghi -ghe) satisfied ‖ *f* see **paga**

paguro *m* (zool) hermit crab

pà·io *m* (-ia *fpl*) pair, couple; **è un altro paio di maniche** this is a horse of another color; **fare il paio** to match perfectly

paiòlo *m* caldron, kettle; (mil) platform

Pakistan, il Pakistan

pala *f* shovel; blade (*e.g., of turbine*); paddle (*of waterwheel*); peel (*of baker*); **pala d'altare** altarpiece

paladi·no -na *m & mf* champion ‖ *m* paladin; **farsi paladino di** to champion

palafitta *f* pile dwelling; piles (*to support a structure*)

palafrenière *m* groom

palaféno *m* palfrey

palan·ca *f* (-che) beam, board; (naut)

gangplank; copper coin; **palanche**
(coll) money
palanchino *m* palanquin; (naut) pulley
palandrana *f* (joc) long, full coat
palata *f* shovelful; stroke (*of oar*); **a
palate** by the bucketful
palatale *adj & f* palatal
palati·no -na *adj* palatine; (anat)
palatal
palato *m* palate
palazzina *f* villa
palazzo *m* palace; large office or government building; mansion; **palazzo
dello sport** sports arena; **palazzo di
città** city hall; **palazzo di giustizia**
courthouse
palchetti·sta (**-sti -ste**) *mf* (theat) box-
holder ‖ *m* person who lays floors
palchétto *m* shelf; (theat) small box;
(journ) box
pal·co *m* (**-chi**) flooring; scaffold;
stand, platform; (theat) box; (theat)
stage
palcoscèni·co *m* (**-ci**) (theat) stage
palesare (**paléso**) *tr* to reveal, manifest
‖ *ref* to show oneself
palése *adj* plain, manifest; **fare palese**
to manifest, reveal
palèstra *f* gymnasium; palestra
palétta *f* small shovel, scoop; blade
(*of turbine*)
palettata *f* shovelful
palétto *m* stake; bolt (*of door*)
palificazióne *f* pile work (*in the ground
for foundation*); line of telephone
poles
pà·lio *m* (**-lii**) embroidered cloth (*given
as prize*); **mettere in palio** to offer as a
prize; **palio di Siena** colorful horse-
race at Siena
palissandro *m* Brazilian rosewood
palizzata *f* palisade; picket fence
palla *f* ball; bullet; sphere; **dar palla
nera a** to blackball; **palla da cannone**
cannon ball; **palla di neve** snowball;
prendere la palla al balzo to seize
the opportunity
pallabase *f* baseball
pallacanè·stro *f* (**-stro**) basketball
pallamuro *m* handball
pallanuòto *f* water polo
pallavó·lo *f* (**-lo**) volleyball
palleggiare §290 (**palléggio**) *tr* to toss
(*e.g., a javelin*); to shift from one
hand to another ‖ *intr* (tennis) to
knock a few balls; (soccer) to dribble
‖ *ref*—**palleggiarsi la responsabilità**
to shift the responsibility
pallég·gio *m* (**-gi**) (tennis) knocking
back and forth; (soccer) dribbling
palliati·vo -va *adj & m* palliative
pallidézza *f* paleness
pàlli·do -da *adj* pale; faint
pallina *f* marble; small ball; **pallina
antitarmica** mothball
pallino *m* little ball; (bowling) jack;
bullet; **a pallini** polka-dot; **avere il
pallino di** to be crazy about; **pallini**
buckshot; polka dots
palloncino *m* child's balloon; Chinese
lantern
pallóne *m* (soccer) ball; (aer) balloon;

pallone di sbarramento barrage balloon; **pallone gonfiato** (fig) stuffed
shirt; **pallone sonda** trial balloon
pallonétto *m* (tennis) lob
pallóre *m* pallor, paleness
pallòttola *f* pellet; ball; bullet
pallottolière *m* abacus
pallovale *f* rugby
palma *f* palm; **tenere in palma di mano**
to hold in the highest esteem
palmare *adj* evident, plain
palménto *m* millstone; **mangiare a quattro palmenti** (coll) to stuff oneself
eating
palméto *m* palm grove
palmipede *adj* palmate, web-footed
palmì·zio *m* (**-zi**) palm
palmo *m* span; palm (*of hand*); foot
(*measure*); **a palmo a palmo** little by
little; **restare con un palmo di naso**
to be disappointed
palo *m* pole (*of wood or metal*); beam;
pile; (soccer, football) goal post;
fare il palo to be on the lookout
(*said of thieves*); **palo indicatore**
signpost; **saltare di palo in frasca**
to digress
palombaro *m* diver
palómbo *m* dogfish
palpàbile *adj* palpable
palpare *tr* to touch; to palpate
pàlpebra *f* eyelid; **battere le palpebre**
to blink
palpeggiare §290 (**palpéggio**) *tr* to
finger, touch repeatedly
palpitante *adj* throbbing; burning
(*question*); fluttering (*e.g., with love*)
palpitare (**pàlpito**) *intr* to palpitate,
pulsate; (fig) to pine
palpitazióne *f* palpitation
pàlpito *m* heartbeat; (fig) throb
pal·tò *m* (**-tò**) overcoat
paltoncino *m* child's winter coat; lady's
topcoat
paludaménto *m* (joc) array, attire
palude *f* marsh, bog
paludó·so -sa [*s*] *adj* marshy
palustre *adj* marshy
pàmpino *m* grape leaf
panacèa *f* panacea, cure-all
pàna·ma *m* (**-ma**) Panama hat
panamé·gno -gna *adj & mf* Panamanian
panamense *adj & mf* Panamenian
panare *tr* (culin) to bread
pan·ca *f* (**-che**) bench; **scaldare le
panche** (coll) to loaf around; (coll)
to waste one's time at school
pancétta *f* potbelly; bacon
panchétto *m* footstool
panchina *f* bench
pàn·cia *f* (**-ce**) belly; **a pancia all'aria**
on one's back; **mangiare a crepa
pancia** to stuff oneself like a pig;
mettere su pancia to grow a potbelly; **salvar la pancia per i fichi**
to not take any chances; **tenersi la
pancia dalle risate** to split one's side
laughing
panciata *f* belly flop
pancièra *f* bellypiece; body girth
panciòlle *m*—**in panciolle** frittering
one's time away

panciòtto *m* waistcoat; vest; **panciotto a maglia** cardigan
panciu·to -ta *adj* potbellied
pàncre·as *m* (-as) pancreas
pandemò·nio *m* (-ni) pandemonium
pane *m* bread; thread (*of screw*); cake (*e.g., of butter*); loaf (*of sugar*); (metallurgy) pig; **a pane di zucchero** conic(al); **dire pane al pane e vino al vino** to call a spade a spade; **essere come pane e cacio** to be hand and glove; **essere pane per i propri denti** to be a match for s.o.; **guadagnarsi il pane** to earn one's living; **pane a cassetta** sandwich bread; **pane azzimo** unleavened bread, matzoth; **pan di Spagna** angel food cake, sponge cake; **pane integrale** graham bread; **render pan per focaccia** to give tit for tat
panegìri·co *m* (-ci) panegyric
panetterìa *f* bakery
panettière *m* baker
panétto *m* pat (*e.g., of butter*)
pànfilo *m* yacht
panfrutto *m* plum cake
pangrattato *m* bread crumbs
pània *f* birdlime; **cadere nella pania** to fall into the trap
pàni·co -ca (-ci -che) *adj* panicky ‖ *m* panic
pani·co *m* (-chi) (bot) Italian millet
panièra *f* basket; basketful
panière *m* basket; basketful
panificazióne *f* breadmaking
panifi·cio *m* (-ci) bakery
panino *m* roll, bun; **panino imbottito** sandwich
panna *f* cream, heavy cream; **essere in panna** (naut) to lie to; (aut) to have a breakdown; **mettere in panna** (naut) to heave to; **panna montata** whipped cream
panne *f* (aut) breakdown; **essere in panne** (aut) to have a breakdown
pannèllo *m* linen cloth; pane; panel (*of machine*); (archit; elec) panel
pannìcolo *m* (anat) membrane, tissue
panno *m* cloth; woolen cloth; film, membrane; **bianco come un panno** as white as a ghost; **mettersi nei panni di** to put oneself in the boots of; **non stare più nei propri panni** to be beside oneself with joy; **panni** clothes; **panno verde** baize
pannòcchia *f* ear (*of corn*)
pannolino *m* linen cloth; diaper; sanitary napkin
panòplia *f* panoply
panora·ma *m* (-mi) panorama
panoràmi·co -ca *adj* (-ci -che) panoramic ‖ *f* panoramic view; (mov) panoramic scene
pantaloncini *mpl* trunks
pantalóni *mpl* trousers; **pantaloni da donna** slacks
pantano *m* bog, quagmire
panteismo *m* pantheism
pànteon *m* pantheon
pantèra *f* panther; (slang) police car
pantòfola *f* slipper
pantomima *f* pantomine, mimicry

panzana *f* (lit) fib, lie
Pàolo *m* Paul
paonaz·zo -za *adj & m* purple
pa·pa *m* (-pi) pope; **ad ogni morte di papa** once in a blue moon; **morto un papa se ne fa un altro** nobody is indispensable
pa·pà *m* (-pà) daddy, papa
papàbile *adj* likely to be elected ‖ *mf* front runner ‖ *m* cardinal likely to be elected to the papacy
papale *adj* papal (*e.g., benediction*); Papal (*States*)
papali·no -na *adj* papal ‖ *m* advocate of papal temporal power ‖ *f* skullcap
paparazzo *m* freelance photographer
papato *m* papacy
papàvero *m* poppy; **alto papavero** (fig) big shot
pàpera *f* young goose; slip of the tongue; spoonerism; **fare una papera** to make a boner
pàpero *m* gander
papiro *m* papyrus
pappa *f* bread soup, farina, pap; **pappa molla** (fig) jellyfish
pappafi·co *m* (-chi) (naut) topgallant; (slang) goatee
pappagallo *m* parrot; bedpan; (slang) masher
pappagòr·gia *f* (-ge) double chin, jowl
pappare *tr* (coll) to gulp; (fig) to gobble up fraudulently
pappata·ci *m* (-ci) gnat
pappina *f* light pap; poultice
pàpri·ca *f* (-che) paprika
para *f* crepe rubber
paràbola *f* parable; (geom) parabola
parabórdo *m* (naut) fender
parabréz·za [ddzz] *m* (-za) windshield
paracadutare *tr* to parachute, airdrop ‖ *ref* to parachute
paracadu·te *m* (-te) parachute
paracadutismo *m* parachute jumping; (sports) sky diving
paracaduti·sta *mf* (-sti -ste) parachutist; skydiver ‖ *m* paratrooper
paracarro *m* spur stone
paracól·pi *m* (-pi) doorstop
paràcqua *m* (paràcqua) umbrella
paradèn·ti *m* (-ti) (sports) mouthpiece
paradisìa·co -ca *adj* (-ci -che) heavenly
paradiso *m* paradise
paradossale *adj* paradoxical
paradòsso *m* paradox
parafa *f* initials
parafan·go *m* (-ghi) fender, mudguard
parafare *tr* to initial
paraffina *f* paraffin
parafiam·ma *f* (-ma) fire-proof partition
parafrasare (paràfraso) *tr* to paraphrase
paràfra·si *f* (-si) paraphrase
parafùlmine *m* lightning rod
parafuò·co *m* (-co) screen, fender (*in front of fireplace*)
paràg·gio *m* (-gi) lineage; **paraggi** neighborhood, vicinity
paragonàbile *adj* comparable
paragonare (paragóno) *tr* to compare
paragóne *m* comparison; **a paragone di**

in comparison with; **mettere a paragone** to compare; **senza paragone** beyond compare

paragrafare (paràgrafo) *tr* to paragraph

paràgrafo *m* paragraph

paraguaia·no -na *adj & mf* Paraguayan

paràli·si *f* (-si) paralysis

paralìti·co -ca *adj & mf* (-ci -che) paralytic

paralizzare [ddzz] *tr* to paralyze

parallè·lo -la *adj & m* parallel || *f* (geom) parallel line; **parallele** (sports) parallel bars

paralume *m* lamp shade

paramano *m* cuff, wristband; (archit) facing brick

paraménto *s* facing (*of a wall*); (eccl) vestment

parami·ne *m* (-ne) (nav) paravane

paramó·sche *m* (-sche) fly net

paran·co m (-chi) tackle

paranìn·fo -fa *mf* matchmaker

paranòi·co -ca *adj & mf* (-ci -che) paranoiac

paraòc·chi *m* (-chi) blinker (*on horse*)

parapètto *m* parapet

parapì·glia m (-glia) hubbub

parapiòg·gia *m* (-gia) umbrella

parare *tr* to adorn; to hang; to protect; to parry (*a thrust*); to offer; to drive (*e.g., cattle*) || *intr*—**dove va a parare?** what are you driving at? || *ref* to protect oneself; (eccl) to don the vestments; **pararsi dinanzi a** to loom up in front of

parasóle *m* parasol; (aut) sun visor

paraspal·le *m* (-le) (sports) shoulder pad

parassi·ta (-ti -te) *adj* parasitic || *m* parasite

parassità·rio -ria *adj* (-ri -rie) parasitic(al)

parassìti·co -ca *adj* (-ci -che) parasitic(al)

parastatale *adj* government-controlled || *mf* employee of government-controlled agency

parastin·chi *m* (-chi) (sports) shin guard

parata *f* fence, bar; (fencing) parry; (soccer) catch; (mil) parade; **mala parata** dangerous situation

paratìa *f* bulkhead

parato *m* hangings; **parati** hangings; (naut) bilgeways

paratóia *f* sluice gate

paraur·ti *m* (-ti) (aut) bumper; (rr) buffer

paravènto *m* screen

Par·ca *f* (-che) Fate

parcare §197 *tr & intr* to park

parcèlla *f* bill, fee, honorarium; parcel, lot (*of land*)

parcheggiare §290 (parchéggio) *tr & intr* to park

parchég·gio *m* (-gi) parking; parking lot

parchìmetro *m* parking meter

par·co -ca (-chi -che) *adj* frugal; parsimonious || *m* park; parking; parking lot; **parco dei divertimenti** amusement park

paréc·chio -chia (-chi -chie) *adj indef* a good deal of, a lot of; **parecchi** several || *pron* a good deal, a lot; **parecchi** several || **parecchio** *adv* a lot; rather

pareggiare §290 (paréggio) *tr* to level; to equal; to match; to balance; to recognize || *intr* (sports) to tie

pareggia·to -ta *adj* accredited (*school*)

parég·gio *m* (-gi) leveling; matching; (sports) tie; **pareggio del bilancio** balancing of the budget

parentado *m* kinsfolk, kindred; relationship; **concludere il parentado di** to arrange for the wedding of

parènte *mf* relative; (lit) parent; **parenti** kin

parentèla *f* relationship; relations

parènte·si *f* (-si) parenthesis; break, interval; **fra parentesi** parenthetically; in parentheses; **parentesi quadra** bracket

parére *m* opinion, mind; advice; **a mio parere** in my opinion || §210 *intr* (ESSERE) to seem; **che Le pare?** what is your opinion?; **ma Le pare!** not at all!; **mi pare che** + *subj* it seems to me that + *ind;* I guess that + *ind;* **non Le pare?** don't you think so?; **non mi pare** vero I can't believe it

paréte *f* wall; **tra le pareti domestiche** within the four walls of the home

pargolét·to -ta *adj* (poet) infantile || *mf* (poet) child

pàrgo·lo -la *adj* (poet) infantile || *mf* (poet) child

pari *adj invar* equal, even; **camminare di pari passo** to walk at the same rate; **essere pari** to be quits; **essere pari al proprio compito** to be equal to the task; **fare un salto a piè pari** to jump with feet together; **pari pari** verbatim; **rimanere pari con** (sports) to be tied with; **saltare a piè pari** to skip (*e.g., a page*); to dodge (*a difficulty*); **trattare da pari a pari** to treat as an equal || *m* peer; **al pari di** as, like; **del pari** also; **in pari** even, leveled; **senza pari** matchless, peerless || *f* -**stare alla pari con** to be an even match for

parìa *f* peerage

pà·ria *m* (-ria) pariah

parificare §197 (parìfico) *tr* to level; to match; to accredit (*a school*); to balance

Parìgi *f* Paris

parigi·no -na *adj & mf* Parisian || *f* slow-burning stove; Parisian woman; (rr) switching spur

parìglia *f* pair, couple; team (*of horses*); (cards) two of a kind; **rendere la pariglia** to give tit for tat

pariménti *adv* likewise

pari·tà *f* (-tà) parity

parìtèti·co -ca *adj* (-ci -che) joint (*e.g., committee*)

parlamentare *adj* parliamentary || *mf* member of parliament || *m* (mil) envoy || *v* (parlaménto) *intr* to parley

parlaménto *m* parliament

parlante *adj* talking; life-like || *mf* speaker

parlantina *f* glibness

parlare *m* talk, speech; dialect ‖ *tr* to speak (*a language*) ‖ *intr* to speak, talk; to discuss; **chi parla?** (telp) hello!; **far parlare di sé** to be talked about; **parlare chiaro** to speak bluntly; **parlare del più e del meno** to make small talk; **parlare tra sé e sé** to talk to oneself ‖ *ref* to talk to one another

parla·to **-ta** *adj* spoken; current (*speech*); talking (*movie*) ‖ *m* talkie; (mov) sound track; (theat) dialogue ‖ *f* speech, talk; dialect

parla·tóre **-trice** *mf* speaker

parlatò·rio *m* (**-ri**) visting room (*e.g., in jail*)

parlottare (**parlòtto**) *intr* to whisper in secret

parmigia·no **-na** *adj* & *mf* Parmesan ‖ *m* Parmesan cheese

parnaso *m* Parnassus (*poetry, poets*) ‖ **il Parnaso** Mount Parnassus

paro *m*—**in un par d'ore** in a couple of hours ‖ *adv*—**andare a paro** to keep abreast; **mettere a paro** to compare

parodìa *f* parody; **fare la parodia di** to parody

parodiare §287 (**paròdio**) *tr* to parody

paròla *f* word; speech; **avere parole con** to have words with; **buttare le mezza parola** to make an allusion; **dare la parola a** to give the floor to; **di poche parole** of few words; **domandare la parola a** to ask for the floor; **essere di parola** to keep one's word; **essere in parola con** to have dealings with; **mangiarsi la parola** to break one's word; **mangiarsi le parole** to slur one's words; **non far parola** to not breathe a word; **parola crociata** crossword puzzle; **parola d'ordine** password; **parola macedonia** acronym **parola sdrucciola** proparoxytone; **parole** lyrics; **parole di circostanza** occasional words; **prendere la parola** to take the floor; **rivolgere la parola a** to address; **venire a parole** to begin to quarrel

parolàc·cia *f* (**-ce**) dirty word; swearword

paro·làia **-làia** (**-lài -làie**) *adj* wordy, verbose ‖ *mf* windbag

parolière *m* lyricist

parossismo *m* paroxysm; climax

parossìto·no **-na** *adj* paroxytone

parotite *f* (pathol) parotitis; **parotite epidemica** (pathol) mumps

parrici·da *mf* (**-di -de**) patricide

parrocchétto *m* parakeet; (naut) fore-topsail; (naut) fore-topmast

parròcchia *f* parish

parrocchia·no **-na** *mf* parishioner

pàrro·co *m* (**-ci**) rector, parson

parruc·ca *f* (**-che**) wig; (fig) old fogey

parsimònia *f* parsimony

parsimonió·so **-sa** [*s*] *adj* parsimonious

partàc·cia *f*—**fare una partaccia** to break one's word; **fare una partaccia a** to make a scene in front of; to rebuke loudly

parte *f* part; share; section; side; party; partiality; (theat) role; **a parte** separately; (theat) aside; **d'altra parte** on the other hand; **da parte** aside; **da parte mia** as for me; **fare le parti** to divide in shares; **gran parte di** a great deal of; **in parte** partially; **la maggior parte di** most of; **parte civile** (law) plaintiff; **parte ... parte some ... some; part ... part; prendere in mala parte** to take amiss

partecipante *adj* participating ‖ *mf* participant; (sports) contestant

partecipare (**partécipo**) *tr* to announce; (lit) to share in ‖ *intr*—**partecipare a** to share in; to participate in; **partecipare di** to partake of (*e.g., the nature of an animal*)

partecipazióne *f* announcement; card; announcement (*of a wedding*); share in a business); participation (*in some action*)

partécipe *adj* sharing, partaking

parteggiare §290 (**partéggio**) *intr* to side; **parteggiare per** to side with

Partenóne *m* Parthenon

partènte *adj* departing ‖ *mf* person departing, traveler; (sports) starter

partènza *f* departure; sailing; (sports) start; **di partenza** or **in partenza** about to leave; **partenza lanciata** (sports) running start

particèlla *f* particle

partici·pio *m* (**-pi**) participle

particolare *adj* particular; private; **in particolare** especially ‖ *m* detail

particolareggiare §290 (**particolaréggio**) *tr* to detail

particolarismo *m* regionalism, particularism

particolarìsti·co **-ca** *adj* (**-ci -che**) particularistic; individualistic

particolari·tà *f* (**-tà**) peculiarity; detail

partigianerìa *f* partisanship, factionalism

partigia·no **-na** *adj* & *mf* partisan

partire §176 *tr* (lit) to divide ‖ *v* (**parto**) *intr* to depart; (fig) to arise; **a partire da** beginning with; **far partire** to start (*e.g., a car*) ‖ *ref* to depart, leave

parti·to **-ta** *adj* parted ‖ *m* match (*in marriage*); (pol) party; **ridotto a mal partito** in bad shape; **mettere la testa a partito** to reform; **partito preso** parti pris; **prendere partito** to take sides; to make up one's mind; **trarre il miglior partito da** to make the best of ‖ *f* panel (*e.g., of door*); lot (*of goods*); game; match; party; round (*of golf*); (com) entry; **partita di caccia** hunting party; **partita doppia** (com) double entry; **partita semplice** (com) single entry

partitura *f* (mus) score

partizióne *f* partition, division

parto *m* birth, childbirth

partorire §176 *tr* to bear, bring forth

parvènza *f* (lit) appearance

parziale *adj* partial, one-sided

parziali·tà *f* (**-tà**) partiality

pàscere §211 *tr, intr* & *ref* to pasture, graze

pa·scià *m* (**-scià**) pasha

pasciu·to **-ta** *adj* well-fed

pascolare (pàscolo) *tr & intr* to pasture

pàscolo *m* pasture

Pàsqua *f* Easter; **contento come una Pasqua** as happy as a lark; **Pasqua fiorita** Palm Sunday

pasquale *adj* paschal (*e.g., lamb*)

passàbile *adj* passable, tolerable

passàg·gio *m* (**-gi**) passage; transfer; crossing; traffic; passageway; ride; promotion; (sports) pass; **aprirsi il passaggio** to make one's way; **di passaggio** in passing; transient (*visitor*); **essere di passaggio** to be passing by; **passaggio a livello** railroad crossing; **passaggio zebrato** zebra crossing; **vietato il passaggio** no thoroughfare

passamano *m* passing from hand to hand; ribbon; (coll) railing, handrail

passante *adj* passing (*shot*) || *mf* passerby || *m* strap

passapòrto *m* passport

passare *tr* to cross; to pass; to undergo (*a medical examination*); to move; to hand; to pay; to send (*word*); to pierce; to spend (*time*); to strain; to go over; to let have (*e.g., a slap*); to overstep (*the bounds*); **passare in rassegna** to pass in review; **passare per le armi** to execute; **passare un brutto quarto d'ora** to have a bad ten minutes; **passare un guaio** to have a hard time; **passarla a qlcu** (coll) to forgive s.o.; **passarla liscia** (coll) to get off unscathed; **passarsela bene** (coll) to have a good time || *intr* (ESSERE) to pass; to go; to filter (*said of air, light*); to move; to spoil (*said of food*); to be overcooked; to be promoted; to become; to enter; (lit) to be over; **fare passare qlcu** to let s.o. come in; **passare a nozze** to get married; **passare a seconde nozze** to remarry; **passare avanti a** to overcome; **passare di mente a** to forget, *e.g.,* **gli è passata di mente la riunione** he forgot the meeting; **passare di moda** to go out of style; **passare in giudicato** (law) to be no longer appealable; **passare per** to pass as; **passare per il rotto della cuffia** to barely make it; **passare sopra** a qlco to overlook s.th; **passi!** come in!; **passo!** (rad) over!; **passo** (cards) pass

passata *f* purée; **dare una passata a** to glance at; **dare una passata di straccio a** to rub lightly with a rag; to give a lick and a promise to; **di passata** hurriedly

passatèmpo *m* pastime; hobby

passatì·sta *mf* (**-sti -ste**) traditionalist

passa·to -ta *adj* past; last; overcooked; **essere passato** (coll) to be no longer in one's prime; **passato di moda** out of fashion || *m* past; purée; **passato prossimo** present perfect; **passato remoto** preterit || *f* see **passata**

passatóia *f* runner (*rug*)

passa·tóio *m* (**-tói**) stepping stone

passeggè·ro -ra *adj* passing || *mf* passenger; **passeggero clandestino** stowaway

passeggiare §290 (**passéggio**) *tr* to walk (*e.g., a horse*) || *intr* to walk, promenade

passeggiata *f* promenade; walk; drive, ride; drive, road; **fare una passeggiata** to take a walk; to take a ride

passeggiatrice *f* streetwalker

passég·gio *m* (**-gi**) walk; promenade; **andare a passeggio** to take a walk

passerèlla *f* gangway; catwalk; footbridge

pàsse·ro -ra *mf* sparrow || *f*—**passera di mare** (ichth) flounder

passibile *adj*—**passibile di** subject to, liable to

passiflòra *f* passionflower

passino *m* colander, strainer

passióne *f* passion

passivi·tà *f* (**-tà**) passivity; (com) deficit

passi·vo -va *adj* passive || *m* (com) liabilities; (com) debit side; (gram) passive

pas·so -sa *adj*—see **uva** || *m* step; passage; pass (*in mountain*); pace; footstep; pitch (*of screw, helix, etc.*); (aut) wheelbase; (phot) tread; (phot) size (*of roll*); **a grandi passi** with great strides; **andare al passo** to march in step; to walk (*said of a horse*); **a passi di gigante** by leaps and bounds; **a passo di corsa** running; **a passo d'uomo** walking, at a walk; **aprire il passo** to open the way; **di buon passo** at a good clip; **di pari passo** at the same rate; **fare quattro passi** to take a stroll; **passo doppio** paso doble; **passo d'uomo** manhole; step; **passo falso** misstep; (fig) stumble; **sbarrare il passo** to block the way; **seguire i passi di** to walk in the footsteps of || *interj* (cards) pass!; over!

pasta *f* paste; dough; **di pasta grossa** uncouth, coarse; **pasta alimentare** pasta, macaroni products; **pasta all'uovo** egg noodles; **pasta asciutta** pasta with sauce and cheese; **pasta dentifricia** toothpaste; **una pasta d'uomo** a good-natured man

pastasciutta *f* pasta with sauce and cheese

pasteggiare §290 (**pastéggio**) *intr* to dine

pastèllo *adj invar & m* pastel || *m* crayon

pastétta *f* batter; (coll) trickery

pastìc·ca *f* (**-che**) lozenge, tablet; **pasticche per la tosse** cough drops

pasticceria *f* pastrymaking; pastry; pastry shop

pasticciare §128 (**pasticcio**) *tr & intr* to bungle; to scribble

pasticciè·re -ra *mf* pastry cook; confectioner

pasticcino *m* cookie; patty

pastìc·cio *m* (**-ci**) pie (*of meat, macaroni, etc*); bungle; mess; **cacciarsi nei pasticci** to wind up in the soup

pasticció·ne -na *mf* bungler

pastifì·cio *m* (**-ci**) spaghetti and macaroni factory

pastiglia *f* lozenge, tablet; **pastiglia per la tosse** cough drop

pastina·ca f (-che) parsnip

pa·sto -sta adj (archaic) fed || m meal; **pasto a prezzo fisso** table d'hôte || f see **pasta**

pastóia f hobble; (fig) shackle

pastóne m mash

pastóra f shepherdess

pastorale adj pastoral

pastóre m shepherd; pastor

pastorí·zio -zia (-zi -zie) adj shepherd || f sheep raising

pastorizzare [ddzz] tr to pasteurize

pastó·so -sa [s] adj pasty; mellow

pastrano m overcoat

pastura f pasture; hay; fodder

patac·ca f (-che) large, worthless coin; fake; (coll) medal; (coll) spot

patata f potato

patatrác m (patatràc) crash

patèlla f kneecap; (zool) limpet

patè·ma m (-mi) affliction; **patema d'animo** anxiety

patenta·to -ta adj licensed; (coll) well-known

patènte adj patent || f license; driver's license; **patente sanitaria** (naut) bill of health

patentino m (aut) permit

pateréc·cio m (-ci) whitlow

paternale adj (obs) paternal || f reprimand

paterni·tà f (-tà) paternity; authorship

patèr·no -na adj paternal; fatherly

paternòstro m Lord's Prayer; **è vero come il paternostro** it is the gospel truth

patèti·co -ca (-ci -che) adj pathetic; mawkish || m pathos; mawkishness

pathos m pathos

patibile adj endurable

patibolare adj gallows

patibolo m executioner's instrument; scaffold

patiménto m suffering

pàtina f patina; coating (on paper); varnish; fur (on tongue)

patinare (pàtino) tr to gloss, glaze (e.g., paper)

patire §176 tr to suffer; (gram) to be the recipient of (an action) || intr to suffer

pati·to -ta adj suffering, sickly || mf fan || m boyfriend || f girlfriend

patòge·no -na adj pathogenic

patologia f pathology

patològi·co -ca adj (-ci -che) pathologic(al)

patos m var of **pathos**

patrasso m—**andare a patrasso** to die; to go to ruin; **mandare a patrasso** to kill; to ruin

pàtria f fatherland, native land

patriar·ca m (-chi) patriarch

patriarcale adj patriarchal

patrigno m stepfather

patrimoniale adj patrimonial; property (tax); capital (e.g., transaction)

patrimò·nio m (-ni) patrimony; estate; fortune; (fig) heritage

pà·trio -tria (-tri -trie) adj paternal; of one's country (e.g., love) || f see **patria**

patriò·ta mf (-ti -te) patriot; (coll) fellow citizen

patriòtti·co -ca adj (-ci -che) patriotic

patriottismo m patriotism

patrí·zio -zia (-zi -zie) adj & m patrician || **Patrizio** m Patrick

patrocinante adj pleading (lawyer)

patrocinare tr to favor, sponsor; to plead

patrocina·tóre -trice mf defender; pleader

patroci·nio m (-ni) support; sponsorship; (law) defense; **patrocinio gratuito** public defense

patronato m patronage; charitable institution, foundation; **patronato scolastico** state aid fund

patronéssa f sponsor; trustee (of charitable institution)

patròno m patron saint; patron; sponsor; trustee (of charitable institution); (law) counsel

patta f flap (of garment); bill (of anchor); (coll) potholder; **essere** or **far patta** to be even, tie

patteggiaménto m negotiation

patteggiare §290 (pattéggio) tr & intr to negotiate

pattinàggio m skating

pattinare (pàttino) intr to skate; to skid (said of a car)

pattina·tóio m (-tói) skating rink

pattina·tóre -trice mf skater

pàttino m skate; guide block (of an elevator); (aer) skid, runner; **pattino a rotelle** roller skate

pattino m racing shell with outrigger floats

patto m pact; **a nessun patto** by no means; **a patto che** provided (that); **patto sociale** social contract; **venire a patti** to come to terms

pattùglia f patrol

pattugliare §280 tr & intr to patrol

pattuire §176 tr & intr to negotiate

pattuì·to -ta adj agreed || m agreement

pattume m litter, garbage

pattumièra f dustpan; trash bin

patùrnie fpl—**avere le paturnie** (coll) to be in the dumps

paura f fear; **aver paura di** to be afraid of; **da far paura** frightful; **dar** or **metter paura a** to frighten; **per paura che** for fear that, lest

pauró·so -sa [s] adj fearful

pàusa f pause

pausare (pàuso) tr (lit) to interrupt || intr (lit) to pause

paventare (pavènto) tr & intr to fear

pavesare (pavéso) tr to deck with flags; to dress (a ship)

pavése [s] adj—see **zuppa** || m pavis (shield); (naut) bunting

pàvi·do -da adj cowardly, timid

pavimentare (paviménto) tr to pave

pavimentazióne f paving, pavement

paviménto m floor; bottom (of sea); paving (of street)

pavoncèlla f lapwing

pavó·ne -na or **-néssa** mf peacock

pavoneggiare §290 (pavonéggio) ref to swagger, strut

pazientare (paziènto) intr to be patient

paziènte *adj & mf* patient
paziènza *f* patience; **fare scappare la pazienza a** to drive mad; **pazienza!** too bad!
pazzé·sco -sca *adj* (**-schi -sche**), crazy, wild
pazzìa *f* madness, insanity; folly; **fare pazzie** to act like a fool
pàz·zo -za *adj* crazy, insane; **andar pazzo per** to be crazy about ‖ *mf* crazy person
pèc·ca *f* (**-che**) imperfection
peccamino·so -sa [s] *adj* sinful
peccare §197 (**pècco**) *intr* to sin; to be lacking; to be at fault
peccato *m* sin; **che peccato!** what a pity!; **è un peccato** it's a shame
pecca·tóre -trice *mf* sinner
pécchia *f* bee
pecchióne *m* drone
péce *f* pitch; **pece greca** rosin
pechinése [s] *adj & mf* Pekingese
Pechino *f* Peking
pècora *f* sheep
peco·ràio *m* (**-rài**) shepherd
pecorèlla *f* small sheep, lamb
pecorì·no -na *adj* sheep; sheepish ‖ *m* sheep-milk cheese ‖ *f* sheep manure
peculato *m* embezzlement, peculation
peculiare *adj* peculiar
peculiari·tà *f* (**-tà**) peculiarity
pecù·lio *m* (**-li**) nest egg, savings; (obs) cattle
pecùnia *m* (lit) money
pecunià·rio -ria *adj* (**-ri -rie**) pecuniary
pedàg·gio *m* (**-gi**) toll
pedagogìa *f* pedagogy, pedagogics
pedagògi·co -ca *adj* (**-ci -che**) pedagogic(al)
pedagò·go -ga *mf* (**-ghi -ghe**) pedagogue
pedalare *intr* to pedal
pedale *m* trunk (*of tree*); pedal; treadle (*e.g., of sewing machine*)
pedalièra *f* pedals, pedal keyboard; (aer) rudder bar
pedalino *m* (coll) sock, short stocking
pedana *f* footrest; platform; bedside rug; hem (*of skirt*); (aut) running board; (sports) springboard
pedante *adj* pedantic ‖ *m* pedant
pedanterìa *f* pedantry
pedanté·sco -sca *adj* (**-schi -sche**) pedantic
pedata *f* kick; footprint; tread (*of step*)
pedèstre *adj* pedestrian
pedià·tra *mf* (**-tri -tre**) pediatrician
pediatrìa *f* pediatrics
pedicù·re *mf* (**-re**) pedicure
pedicu·ro -ra *mf* var of **pedicure**
pedilù·vio *m* (**-vi**) foot bath
pedina *f* (checkers) checker, man; (chess) pawn
pedinare *tr* to shadow, follow about
pedìsse·quo -qua *adj* servile
pedivèlla *f* pedal crank
pedóne *m* pedestrian; (chess) pawn
pedule *m* stocking foot ‖ *fpl* climbing shoes, sneakers
pedùncolo *m* (anat, bot, zool) peduncle
pegamòlde *f* imitation leather
pèggio *adj invar* worse; **il peggio** the worst, e.g., **il peggio ragazzo** the worst boy; ‖ *m* worst; **andare per il peggio** to be getting worse ‖ *f* worst; **alla peggio** if worst comes to worst; **averne la peggio** to get the worst of it ‖ *adv* worse; worst; at worst; **peggio + pp** less + *pp*; least + *pp*; **tanto peggio** so much the worse
peggioraménto *m* deterioration, worsening
peggiorare (**peggióro**) *tr & intr* to worsen
peggió·re (**-ri**) *adj* worse; worst ‖ *m* worst
pégli §4
pégno *m* pledge, pawn
pègola *f* pitch; (coll) bad luck
péi §4
pél §4
pèla·go *m* (**-ghi**) (poet) open sea; (coll) mess; **pelago di guai** sea of trouble
pelame *m* hair, coat
pelandróne *m* (coll) shirker, do-nothing
pelapata·te *m* (**-te**) potato peeler
pelare (**pélo**) *tr* to fleece; to pluck; to pare, peel; to clear (*land*); (fig) to strip; to scald, burn ‖ *ref* (coll) to shed; to become bald
pela·to -ta *adj* peeled; hairless, bald; barren ‖ *m* (coll) baldy; **pelati** peeled tomatoes ‖ *f* fleecing, plucking; (joc) baldness, bald spot
pélla §4
pellàc·cia *f* (**-ce**) tough hide
pellame *m* skins, hides
pèlle *f* skin, hide; **a fior di pelle** slightly, superficially; **essere nella pelle di** to be in the boots of; **fare la pelle a** to bump off; **non stare più nella pelle** to be beside oneself with joy; **pelle di dante** buckskin; **pelle d'oca** goose skin, goose flesh; **pelle d'uovo** mull; **pelle pelle** skin-deep, superficial
pélle §4
pellegrinàg·gio *m* (**-gi**) pilgrimage
pellegrinare *intr* (lit) to go on a pilgrimage
pellegrì·no -na *adj* wandering; (lit) foreign; (lit) strange, quixotic ‖ *mf* pilgrim, traveler
pelleròssa *mf* (**pellirosse**) redskin
pelletterìa *f* leather goods; leather goods store
pellicano *m* pelican
pelliccerìa *f* furrier's store; furrier's trade, fur industry
pellìc·cia *f* (**-ce**) fur
pellic·ciàio -ciàia *mf* (**-ciài -ciàie**) furrier
pelliccióne *m* fur jacket
pellìcola *f* film; **pellicola in rotolo** roll film; **pellicola piana** film pack; **pellicola sonora** sound film; **pellicola vergine** unexposed film
pellirós·sa *mf* (**-se**) var of **pellerossa**
pélo *m* hair (*of beard*); pile (*of carpet*); fur; **avere pelo sul cuore** not to be easily moved; **cercare il pelo nell'uovo** to split hairs; **di primo pelo** green, inexperienced; **non avere peli sulla lingua** to not mince one's words; **pelo dell'acqua** water surface; **per un pelo** by a hair's breadth

peloponnesìa·co -ca *adj* **(-ci -che)** Peloponnesian

pelό·so -sa [s] *adj* hairy; self-serving (*e.g., charity*)

péltro *m* pewter

pelùria *f* down, soft hair

péna *f* penalty; concern; compassion; pain, suffering; grief; **a mala pena** barely; **essere in pena per** to worry about; **fare pena** to arouse compassion; **pena infamante** degrading punishment; loss of civil rights; **sotto pena di** under penalty of; **valere la pena** to be worthwhile

penale *adj* penal ‖ *f* penalty

penali·sta *mf* **(-sti -ste)** criminal lawyer

penali·tà *f* **(-tà)** penalty

penalizzare [ddzz] *tr* (sports) to penalize

penare (péno) *intr* to suffer; to find it difficult

pencolare (pèncolo) *intr* to totter; to waver

pendà·glio *m* **(-gli)** pendant; **pendaglio da forca** gallows bird

pendènte *adj* leaning; hanging; pending ‖ *m* pendant

pendènza *f* inclination, pitch; controversy; balance; **in pendenza** pending

pèndere §123 *intr* to hang; to lean; to slope; to pitch

pendice *f* slope, declivity

pen·dìo *m* **(-dìi)** slant; slope

pèndola *f* clock

pendolare *adj* pendulum-like; commuting; transient (*tourist*) ‖ *mf* commuter ‖ *v* (pèndolo) *intr* to sway back and forth; to waver; (nav) to cruise back and forth

pèndolo *m* pendulum; clock

pèndu·lo -la *adj* (lit) hanging

penetrante *adj* penetrating, piercing

penetrare (pènetro) *tr* to penetrate, pierce ‖ *intr* to penetrate ‖ *ref*—**penetrarsi di** to be convinced of; to become aware of

penicillina *f* penicillin

peninsulare *adj* peninsular

penìsola *f* peninsula

penitènte *adj* & *mf* penitent

penitènza *f* penitence; punishment

penitenzià·rio -ria *adj* & *mf* **(-ri -rie)** penitentiary

pénna *f* feather; pen; peen (*of hammer*); (mus) plectrum; **penna a sfera** ball-point pen; **penna d'oca** quill; **penna stilografica** fountain pen

pennàc·chio *m* **(-chi)** panache; plume, tuft; cloud (*of smoke*)

pennaiòlo *m* hack writer

pennarèllo *m* felt-tip pen

penneliare (pennèllo) *intr* to brush; (med) to pencil

pennellata *f* brush stroke

pennèllo *m* brush; (naut) signal flag; (naut) kedge; **pennello per la barba** shaving brush; **stare a pennello** to fit to a T

pennino *m* pen; penpoint, nib

pennóne *m* flagpole; (naut) yard; (mil) pennant

pennù·to -ta *adj* feathered ‖ **pennuti** *mpl* birds

penόmbra *f* penumbra; semidarkness; faint light; **vivere in penombra** to live in obscurity

penό·so -sa [s] *adj* painful

pensàbile *adj* thinkable

pensante *adj* thinking

pensare (pènso) *tr* to think; to think of ‖ *intr* to think; to worry; **dar da pensare a** to cause worry to, e.g., **suo figlio gli dà da pensare** his son causes him worry; **pensa ai fatti tuoi** (coll) mind your own business; **pensa alla salute** (coll) don't worry!; **pensare a** to think of; **pensare di** to plan, intend to

pensata *f* bright idea, brainstorm

pensa·tóre -trice *mf* thinker

pensièro *m* thought; **dare pensiero a** to cause worry to; **darsi pensiero per** to worry about; **essere sopra pensiero** to be absorbed in thought

pensieró·so -sa [s] *adj* thoughtful, pensive

pènsile *adj* hanging, overhead

pensilina *f* marquee

pensionaménto *m* retirement

pensionante *mf* boarder, paying guest

pensionare (pensióno) *tr* to pension

pensiona·to -ta *adj* pensioned ‖ *mf* pensioner ‖ *m* boarding school

pensióne *f* pension; boarding house; **in pensione** retired; **tenere a pensione** to board (*a lodger*); **vivere a pensione** to board (*said of a lodger*)

pensό·so -sa [s] *adj* thoughtful, pensive

pentàgono *m* pentagon

pentagram·ma *m* **(-mi)** (mus) staff, stave

pentàmetro *m* pentameter

Pentecòste, la Pentecost, Whitsunday

pentiménto *m* repentance; correction (*e.g., in a manuscript*); change of heart

pentire (pènto) *ref* to repent; to change one's mind; **pentirsi di** to repent

penti·to -ta *adj* repentant, repenting; **pentito e contrito** in sackcloth and ashes

péntola *f* pot, kettle; potful; **pentola a pressione** pressure cooker

penùlti·mo -ma *adj* next to the last ‖ *f* penult

penùria *f* shortage, scarcity

penzolare (pènzolo) [dz] *intr* to dangle, hang down

penzolóni [dz] *adv* dangling

peònia *f* peony

pepaiòla *f* pepper shaker; pepper mill

pepare (pépo) *tr* to pepper

pepa·to -ta *adj* peppered; peppery

pépe *m* pepper; **pepe della Giamaica** allspice; **pepe di Caienna** red pepper, cayenne pepper

peperóne *m* (bot) pepper

pepita *f* nugget

per *prep* by; through; throughout; for; because of; to, in order to; in favor of; considering; **essere per** to be about to; **per + adj** or **adv + che + subj** however **+ adj** or **adv + ind**, e.g., **per intelligente che sia** however intelligent he is; **per caso** perchance; **per che cosa?** what for?; **per l'appunto** exactly, just; **per lungo** lengthwise; **per me** as for me; **per ora** now; **per parte mia** as for me; **per poco** hardly, scarcely, **per quanto** + adj or adv + subj however + adj or adv + pres ind, e.g., **per quanto disperatamente provi** however desperately he attempts; **per tempo** early; **per traverso** diagonally; **per via che** (coll) because; **stare per** to be about to

péra f pear (fruit); bulb, light bulb; (joc) head

peraltro adv besides, moreover

peranco adv yet

perbacco interj by Jove!

perbène adj invar nice, well brought up

percalle m percale

percènto m percent; percentage

percentuale adj percentage || f percent; commission, bonus

percepibile adj perceptible

percepire §176 tr to perceive; to receive (a salary)

percettibile adj perceptible

percetti·vo -va adj perceptive

percezióne f perception

perché m why, reason; **il perché e il percome** the why and the wherefore || pron rel for which || adv why || conj because; so that

perciò conj therefore, accordingly

percóme m & conj wherefore

percorrènza f stretch, distance

percórrere §139 tr to cross; to cover, go through

percórso m crossing, distance

percòssa f hit, blow; contusion

percuòtere §251 tr to hit, beat; (fig) to shake || intr to strike

percussióne f percussion

percussóre m firing pin

perdènte adj losing || mf loser

pèrdere §212 tr to lose; to waste; to miss (e.g., a train); to ruin; to leak || intr to lose; to leak; to be inferior || ref to get lost; to waste one's time; **perdersi d'animo** to lose heart; **perdersi in un bicchier d'acqua** to become discouraged for nothing

perdifiato m—**a perdifiato** at the top of one's lungs

perdigiór·no mf (-no) idler

perdinci interj good Heavens!

pèrdita f loss; leak; **a perdita d'occhio** as far as the eye can see; **perdite** (mil) casualties

perditèm·po mf (-po) idler || m waste of time

perdizióne f perdition

perdonàbile adj pardonable

perdonare (perdóno) tr to forgive; to spare; **perdonare a qlcu qlco** or **perdonare qlco di qlco** to forgive s.o. for s.th || intr (with dat) to pardon

perdóno m forgiveness, pardon

perdurare intr (ESSERE & AVERE) to last; to persevere

perdu·to -ta adj lost; **andar perduto** to be desperately in love; to get lost

peregrinare intr to wander

peregrinazióne f wandering

peregri·no -na adj far-fetched, outlandish

perènne adj everlasting; perennial

perentò·rio -ria adj (-ri -rie) peremptory

perequare (perèquo) tr to equalize

perequazióne f equalization

perfèt·to -ta adj & m perfect

perfezionaménto m improvement; (educ) specialization

perfezionare (perfezióno) tr to improve, polish up; to perfect || ref to improve; (educ) to specialize

perfezióne f perfection; **a** or **alla perfezione** to perfection

perfidia f perfidy

pèrfi·do -da adj perfidious, treacherous; (coll) foul, nasty

perfini·re m (-re) punch line

perfino adv even

perforante adj piercing, perforating

perforare (perfóro) tr to pierce; to perforate; to punch; to bore

perfora·tóre -trice mf key-punch operator || m drill || f punch; drill; pneumatic drill, rock drill

perforazióne f perforation

pergamèna f parchment, vellum

pèrgamo m (lit) pulpit

pèrgola f bower, pergola

pergolato m arbor, pergola; grape arbor

pericolante adj tottering, unsafe

pericolo m danger; **non c'è pericolo** don't worry

pericoló·so -sa [s] adj dangerous

periferia f periphery; suburbs

perifèri·co -ca adj (-ci -che) peripheral

perifra·si f (-si) periphrasis

perimetro m perimeter

periodare m writing style || v (periodo) intr to turn a phrase

periòdi·co -ca adj (-ci -che) periodic(al) || m periodical

periodo m period; age; (gram) sentence; (phys) cycle; **il periodo delle feste** holiday time

peripezia f vicissitude

pèriplo m circumnavigation

perire §176 intr (ESSERE) to perish

periscò·pio m (-pi) periscope

peritale adj expert

peritare (pèrito) ref (lit) to hesitate

peri·to -ta adj expert, skilled || mf expert; **perito agrario** land surveyor; **perito calligrafo** handwriting expert; **perito chimico** chemist; **perito industriale** industrial engineer

peritonèo m peritoneum

perizia f skill; survey; appraisal

periziare §287 (perizio) tr to estimate, appraise

pèria f pearl; (med) capsule

perlàce·o -a adj pearly

perla·to -ta adj pearly, smooth

perlife·ro -ra adj pearl-producing

perlina f bead

perlomèno adv at least

perlopiù adv mostly, generally

perlustrare tr to patrol

perlustrazióne f patrol, patrolling

permaló·so -sa [s] *adj* touchy, grouchy
permanènte *adj* permanente ‖ *f* permanent wave
permanènza *f* permanence; stay; continuance (*in office*); duration (*of a disease*); **in permanenza** permanent (*employee*); **buona permanenza!** may your stay be happy!
permanére §235 (*pp* **permaso**) *intr* (ESSERE) to remain, stay
permeàbile *adj* permeable
permeare (**pèrmeo**) *tr* to permeate
permés·so -sa *adj* permitted, allowed; **è permesso?** may I come in? ‖ *m* permit; (mil) pass, leave
permèttere §198 *tr* to permit, allow, let; **permette?** do you mind? ‖ *ref* to take the liberty; to afford
permissìbile *adj* permissible
pèrmuta *f* barter; exchange
permutàbile *adj* tradable, exchangeable
permutare (**pèrmuto**) *tr* to barter; (math) to permute
pernàcchia *f* (vulg) raspberry
pernice *f* partridge
pernició·so -sa [s] *adj* pernicious ‖ *f* pernicious malaria
pèr·nio *m* (-ni) var of **perno**
pèrno *m* pivot; pin; kingbolt; swivel; heart (*of the matter*); kernel (*of the story*); support (*of the family*); (mach) journal; **fare perno** to pivot
pernottare (**pernòtto**) *intr* to spend the night, stay overnight
péro *m* pear tree
però *conj* but, yet; however, nevertheless; **e però** (lit) therefore
peróne *m* fibula
peronòspora *f* downy mildew
perorare (**pèroro**) *tr & intr* to perorate; (law) to plèad
perorazióne *f* peroration; (law) pleading
peròssido *m* peroxide; **perossido d'idrogeno** hydrogen peroxide
perpendicolare *adj & f* perpendicular
perpendìcolo *m* plumb line; **a perpendicolo** perpendicularly
perpetrare (**pèrpetro & perpètro**) *tr* (lit) to perpetrate
perpètua *f* priest's housekeeper
perpetuare (**perpètuo**) *tr* to perpetuate
perpè·tuo -tua *adj* perpetual, life ‖ *f* see **perpetua**
perplessi·tà *f* (-tà) perplexity
perplès·so -sa *adj* perplexed; (lit) ambiguous
perquisire §176 *tr* to search
perquisizióne *f* search
persecu·tóre -trice *mf* persecutor, oppressor
persecuzióne *f* persecution
perseguire (**perséguo**) *tr* to pursue; to persecute; to pester
perseguitare (**perséguito**) *tr* to persecute; to pursue; to pester
perseveranza *f* perseverance
perseverare (**persèvero**) *intr* to persevere
persia·no -na *adj* Persian ‖ *m* Persian; Persian lamb ‖ *f* slatted shutter; **persiana avvolgibile** Venetian blind

pèrsi·co -ca (-ci -che) *adj* Persian ‖ *m* (ichth) perch; (obs) peach ‖ *f* (coll) peach
persino *adv* var of **perfino**
persistènte *adj* persistent
persistènza *f* persistence
persistere §114 *intr* to persist
pèr·so -sa *adj* lost, wasted; (archaic) reddish-brown; **a tempo perso** in one's spare time
persóna *f* person; **per persona** apiece; per capita; **persona di servizio** servant; **persone** people
personàg·gio *m* (-gi) personage; character
personale *adj* personal ‖ *m* figure, body; personnel, staff; crew ‖ *f* oneman show
personali·tà *f* (-tà) personality; personage
personificare §197 (**personìfico**) *tr* to personify
perspicace *adj* perspicacious; farsighted
perspicàcia *f* perspicacity
perspì·cuo -cua *adj* perspicuous
persuadére §213 *tr* to persuade ‖ *ref* to become convinced
persuasióne *f* persuasion
persuasi·vo -va *adj* persuasive; pleasing ‖ *f* persuasiveness
persua·so -sa *adj* convinced; resigned
pertanto *conj* therefore; **non pertanto** nevertheless
pèrti·ca *f* (-che) perch; pole
pertinace *adj* pertinacious, persistent
pertinà·cia *f* (-cie) pertinacity, obstinacy
pertinènte *adj* pertinent, relevant
pertinènza *f* pertinence; competence
pertósse *f* whooping cough
pertù·gio *m* (-gi) hole
perturbare *tr* to perturb ‖ *ref* to be perturbed
perturbazióne *f* perturbation; disturbance
Perù, **il Peru**; **valere un Perù** to be worth a king's ransom
peruvia·no -na *adj & mf* Peruvian
pervàdere §172 *tr* (lit) to pervade
pervenire §282 *intr* (ESSERE) to arrive; to come; **pervenire a** to reach
perversióne *f* perversion
perversi·tà *f* (-tà) perversity
pervèr·so -sa *adj* perverse; wicked
pervertiménto *m* perversion
pervertire (**pervèrto**) *tr* to pervert ‖ *ref* to become perverted
perverti·to -ta *adj* perverted ‖ *mf* pervert
pervicace *adj* (lit) obstinate
pervìn·ca *f* (-che) periwinkle
pésa [s] *f* weighing; scale
pesage *m* (pesage) weigh-in; place for weighing in jockeys
pesalètte·re [s] *m* (-re) postal scale
pesante [s] *adj* heavy
pesantézza [s] *f* heaviness; weight
pesare (**péso**) [s] *tr* to weigh ‖ *intr* to weigh; **pesare a qlcu** to weigh upon s.o.
pesa·tóre -trice [s] *mf* scale or weigh-

bridge operator; **pesatore pubblico** inspector for the department of weights and measures

pesatura [s] *f* weighing

pé•sca *f* (**-sche**) fishing; catch (*of fish*) **pesca alla traina** trawling; **pesca d'altura** deep-sea fishing; **pesca di beneficenza** benefit lottery

pè•sca *f* (**-sche**) peach

pescàg•gio *m* (**-gi**) (*naut*) draft

pescàia *f* dam, weir

pescare §197 (**pésco**) *tr* to fish; to draw (*a card*); to dig up (*a piece of news*); to dive for (*pearls*); **pescare con la lenza** to angle for (*fish*) || *intr* to fish; (*naut*) to displace; **pescare con la lenza** to angle; **pescare di frodo** to poach; **pescare nel torbido** to fish in troubled waters

pesca•tóre -trice *mf* fisher; **pescatore di canna** angler; **pescatore di frodo** poacher

pésce *m* fish; (*typ*) omission; (*coll*) biceps; **a pesce** headlong; **non sapere che pesci pigliare** to not know which way to turn; **pesce d'aprile** April fool; **pesce gatto** catfish; **pesce martello** hammerhead || **Pesci** *mpl* (*astr*) Pisces

pesceane *m* (**pescecani** & **pescicani**) shark; (*fig*) war profiteer

pescheréc•cio -cia (**-ci -ce**) *adj* fishing || *m* fishing boat

pescheria *f* fish market

peschièra *f* fishpond; fishpond (*net*)

pescivéndo•lo -la *mf* fishmonger, fish dealer || *f* fishwife, fishwoman

pè•sco *m* (**-schi**) peach tree

pesi•sta [s] *m* (**-sti**) (*sports*) weight lifter

péso -sa [s] *adj* (*coll*) heavy || *m* weight; burden; bob (*of clock*); (*racing*) weigh-in; (*sports*) shot; **di peso** bodily; **peso lordo** gross weight; **peso massimo** (*sports*) heavyweight; **peso specifico** specific gravity; **rubare sul peso** to give short weight; **usare due pesi e due misure** to have a double standard || *f see* **pesa**

pessimismo *m* pessimism

pessimi•sta *mf* (**-sti -ste**) pessimist

pessimisti•co -ca *adj* (**-ci -che**) pessimistic

pèssi•mo -ma *adj* very bad, very poor

pésta *f* track, footprint; **lasciar nelle peste** to leave in the lurch; **seguir le peste di** to follow in the footsteps of

pestàggio *m* beating, clubbing

pestare (**pésto**) *tr* to pound; to trample; to step on; **pestare le orme di** to follow in the footsteps of; **pestare i piedi** to stamp the feet; **pestare sodo** to beat up

pèste *f* plague, pest

pestèllo *m* pestle

pestife•ro -ra *adj* pestiferous

pestilènza *f* pestilence; stench

pestilenziale *adj* pestilential; pernicious

pé•sto -sta *adj* crushed; thick (*darkness*) || *m* Genoese sauce || *f see* **pesta**

pètalo *m* petal

petardo *m* petard, firecracker

petènte *mf* petitioner

petizióne *f* petition; **petizione di principio** begging the question

péto *m* wind, gas

Petrarca *m* Petrarch

petrarché•sco -sca *adj* (**-schi -sche**) Petrarchan

petrolièra *f* (*naut*) tanker

petrolière *adj* incendiary || *m* petroleum-industry worker; incendiary; oilman (*producer*)

petrolìfe•ro -ra *adj* oil-yielding

petrò•lio *m* (**-li**) petroleum; coal oil, kerosene

petró•so -sa [s] *adj* (*lit*) stony

pettegolare (**pettégolo**) *intr* to gossip

pettegolézzo [dzz] *m* gossip, rumor

pettégo•lo -la *adj* gossipy || *mf* gossip

pettinare (**pèttino**) *tr* to comb; to card; (*coll*) to scold

pettinatóre *m* carder

pettinatrice *f* hairdresser; carding machine

pettinatura *f* coiffure, hairstyling

pèttine *m* comb; (*zool*) scallop; **a pettine** perpendicular (*parking*)

pettino *m* dickey; bib (*of an apron*); plastron

pettirósso *m* robin redbreast

pètto *m* breast, chest; bust; bosom; **a un petto** single-breasted; **avere al petto** to feed at the breast; **a due petti** or **a doppio petto** double-breasted; **stare a petto** to be equal

pettorale *adj* pectoral || *m* pectoral; breast collar (*of horse*)

pettorina *f* var of **pettino**

pettoru•to -ta *adj* strutting, haughty

petulante *adj* importunate; impertinent

petulanza *f* importunity; impertinence

petùnia *f* petunia

pèzza *f* piece (*of cloth*); diaper; patch (*in suit or tire*); bolt (*of paper or cloth*); **pezza d'appoggio** supporting document, voucher; **trattare come una pezza da piedi** to wipe one's boots on

pezza•to -ta *adj* spotted, dappled

pezzatura *f* dapple (*on a horse*); size (*e.g., of a loaf of bread*)

pezzènte *mf* beggar

pezzétto *m* little bit; scrap, snip

pèzzo *m* piece; cut (*of meat*); coin; (*journ*) article; **andare** or **cadere a pezzi** to fall apart; **a pezzi e bocconi** by fits and starts; **fare a pezzi** to break to pieces; to blow to bits; **pezzo di ricambio** spare part; **pezzo d'uomo** hunk of a man; **pezzo duro** brick ice cream; **pezzo forte** forte; **pezzo fuso** cast, casting; **un bel pezzo** a good while; **un pezzo grosso** a big shot

pezzuòla *f* small piece of cloth; (*coll*) handkerchief

phy•lum *m* (**-lum**) phylum

piacènte *adj* attractive, pleasant

piacére *m* pleasure; **a piacere** at will; **a Suo piacere** as you please; **fare piacere a** to do a favor for; to please; **per piacere** please; **piacere!**

pleased to meet you! || §214 *intr* (ESSERE) to please; to be pleasing; (with *dat*) to please, e.g., **come piace a Dio** as it pleases God; to like, e.g., **gli piace il ballo** he likes dancing

piacévole *adj* pleasant, pleasing

piacevolézza *f* pleasantness; off-color joke

pia·ga *f* (-ghe) sore; ulcer; wound; plague; (joc) bore; **piaga di decubito** bedsore

piagare §209 *tr* to make sore, injure

piàg·gia *f* (-ge) (archaic) declivity; (lit) clime, country

piaggiare §290 *tr* (lit) to flatter, blandish || *intr* (archaic) to coast

piagnistèo *m* whining

piagnó·ne -na *mf* (coll) weeper, crybaby

piagnucolare (**piagnùcolo**) *intr* to whimper, whine

piagnucoló·ne -na *mf* whimperer, crybaby

piagnucoló·so -sa [s] *adj* whimpering, whining

pialla *f* (carp) plane

piallàc·cio *m* (-ci) veneer

piallare *tr* (carp) to plane

piallatrice *f* (carp) planer

piallatura *f* (carp) planing

piana *f* plain; wide table

pianale *m* plain; platform; (rr) flatcar, platform car

pianeggiante *adj* plane, level

pianèlla *f* mule (*slipper*); tile

pianeròttolo *m* landing (*of stairs*); ledge

piané·ta *m* (-ti) planet; horoscope || *f* (eccl) chasuble

piàngere §215 *tr* to shed (*tears*); to mourn, lament; **piangere miseria** to cry poverty || *intr* to cry, weep

piangimisè·ria *mf* (-ria) poverty-crying penny pincher

piangiucchiare §287 *intr* to whimper

pianificare §197 (**pianifico**) *tr* to level; (econ) to plan

pianifica·tóre -trice *mf* planner

pianino *m* (coll) barrel organ

piani·sta *mf* (-sti -ste) pianist

pia·no -na *adj* plane; plain, flat || *m* plain; plane; floor; plateau; plan; map; (mus) piano; **di primo piano** first-class; **in piano** horizontal; **piano di coda** (aer) tail assembly; **piano di studio** curriculum; **piano regolatore** building plan; **piano terra** ground floor; **primo piano** (phot) close-up; (theat) foreground || *f* see **piana** || **piano** *adv* slowly; softly

pianofòrte *m* piano; **pianoforte a coda** grand piano

pianòla *f* player piano

pianòro *m* plateau

pianotèr·ra *m* (-ra) ground floor

pianta *f* plant; sole (*of foot*); plan, map; floor plan; **di sana pianta** wholly; **in pianta stabile** permanent (*employee*); **pianta rampicante** (bot) climber

piantagióne *f* plantation

piantana *f* scaffolding

piantare *tr* to plant; to set up (*e.g., a gun emplacement*); to pitch (*a tent*); **piantala!** (slang) cut it out!; **piantare baracca e burattini** (coll) to clear out; **piantar chiodi** (coll) to go into debt; **piantare gli occhi addosso a** to stare at; **piantare in asso** to leave in the lurch || *ref* to place oneself; to abandon one another

pianta·to -ta *adj* planted; stuck; driven; **bien piantato** well-built (*person*)

pianta·tóre -trice *mf* planter

pianterréno *m* ground floor

piantito *m* (coll) floor

pianto *m* weeping, tears; sadness; (bot) sap; (coll) sight, mess

piantonare (**piantóno**) *tr* to watch, guard

piantóne *m* watchman; (mil) orderly; (mil) sentry; (bot) cutting, shoot; **piantone di guida** (aut) steering wheel column

pianura *f* plain

piastra *f* plate; piaster (*coin*)

piastrèlla *f* tile; small flat stone; bounce (*of an airplane on landing*)

piastrellaménto *m* bump, bounce (*of motorboat or airplane*)

piastrelli·sta *m* (-sti) tiler, tile layer

piastrina *f* or **piastrino** *m* small plate; (mil) dog tag; (biol) platelet

piatire §176 *intr* (lit) to argue; (coll) to beg insistently

piattafórma *f* platform; roadbed (*of highway*); (rr) turntable; (pol) plank; **piattaforma di lancio** launching pad

piattèllo *m* small dish; bobêche; clay pigeon

piattina *f* electric cord; metal band; (min) wagon

piattino *m* saucer

piat·to -ta *adj* flat || *m* dish, plate; pan (*of scale*); pot (*in gambling*); course (*of meal*); cover (*of book*); flat (*e.g., of blade*); **piatti** (mus) cymbals; **piatto del grammofono** turntable; **piatto del giorno** plat du jour; **piatto di lenticchie** (Bib & fig) mess of pottage; **piatto fondo** soup dish; **piatto forte** pièce de résistance

piàttola *f* (zool) crab louse; (coll) cockroach; (vulg) bore

piazza *f* square; plaza; crowd; market; fortress; **andare in piazza** (coll) to become bald; **da piazza** common, ordinary; **di piazza** for hire (*e.g., cab*); **fare la piazza** (com) to canvass for customers; **far piazza pulita di** to get rid of; to clean out; **mettere in piazza** to noise abroad; **piazza d'armi** parade ground; **scendere in piazza** to take to the streets

piazzafòrte *f* (**piazzefòrti**) stronghold, fortress

piazzale *m* large square, esplanade, plaza

piazzaménto *m* placement; (sports) position (*of a team*)

piazzare *tr* to place; to sell || *ref* to place; to show (*said of a racing horse*)

piazza·to -ta *adj* placed; arrived (*at a high position*) || *f* row, brawl

piazzi·sta *m* (**-sti**) salesman; traveling salesman

piazzòla *f* court, place; rest area (*off a highway*); (mil) emplacement; **piazzola di partenza** (golf) tee

pi·ca *f* (**-che**) (orn) magpie

picaré·sco -sca *adj* (**-schi -sche**) picaresque

pic·ca *f* (**-che**) pike; pique; **per picca** out of spite; **picche** (cards) spades; **rispondere picche** (fig) to answer no

piccante *adj* piquant, racy

piccare §197 *tr* (obs) to prick || *ref* to become angry; **piccarsi di** to pride oneself on

pic·chè *f* (**-chè**) piqué

picchettaménto *m* picketing

picchettare (**picchétto**) *tr* to stake out; to picket

picchétto *m* stake; picket; (mil) detail

picchiare §287 *tr* to hit, strike || *intr* to knock; to strike; to tap (*said, e.g., of rain*); (aer) to nose-dive; **picchiare in testa** (aut) to knock || *ref* to hit one another

picchiata *f* hit, blow; (aer) nose dive

picchia·tóre -trice *mf* hitter || *m* (boxing) puncher

picchierellare (**picchierèllo**) *tr & intr* to tap

picchiettare (**picchiétto**) *tr* to tap; to scrape; to speckle || *intr* to tap

picchiet·tìo *m* (**-tìi**) patter (*e.g., of rain*)

pìc·chio *m* (**-chi**) knock; (orn) woodpecker; **di picchio** all of a sudden

picchiòtto *m* knocker (*on door*)

piccinerìa *f* pettiness

picci·no -na *adj* little, tiny; petty || *mf* child; baby

picciòlo *m* stem (*e.g., of cherry*); leafstalk, petiole

piccionàia *f* dovecote; loft; attic; (theat) upper gallery

piccióne -na *mf* pigeon; **pigliare due piccioni con una fava** to hit two birds with one stone

pic·co *m* (**-chi**) peak; (naut) gaff; **andare a picco** to sink; to go to ruin; **a picco** vertically; **picco di carico** (naut) derrick

piccolézza *f* smallness; trifle

pìcco·lo -la *adj* small; low (*speed*); short (*distance*); young; petty; **da piccolo** when young; **in piccolo** on a small scale; **nel mio piccolo** with my modest abilities || *mf* child

piccóne *m* pick

piccòzza *f* mattock (*for mountain climbing*)

pidocchierìa *f* stinginess; meanness

pidòc·chio *m* (**-chi**) louse; **pidocchio rifatto** (slang) parvenu

pidocchió·so -sa *adj* lousy; stingy

piè· *m* (**piè**) (lit) foot; **ad ogni piè sospinto** on every occasion; **saltare a piè pari** to skip with the feet together; (fig) to skip over

piède *m* foot; leg (*of table*); stalk (*of salad*); bottom (*of column*); trunk (*of tree*); footing; **alzarsi in piedi** to stand up; **a piede libero** free; **a piedi**

on foot; **a piedi nudi** barefooted; **con i piedi di piombo** cautiously; **essere in piedi** to be up and around; **fare con i piedi** to botch; **mettere un piede in fallo** to stumble; **piede di porco** crowbar; **prendere piede** to take hold; **puntare i piedi** to balk; **su due piedi** offhand; **tenere il piede in due staffe** to carry water on both shoulders

piedestallo or **piedistallo** *m* pedestal

piedritto *m* buttress

piè·ga *f* (**-ghe**) bend; crease; pleat; crimp; wrinkle; (fig) turn; **prendere una cattiva piega** to take a turn for the worse

piegare §209 (**piègo**) *tr* to bend; to wave (*hair*); to fold; to pleat; to bow (*head*) || *intr* to turn || *ref* to bow; to bend; to buckle; to yield

piega·tóre -trice *mf* folder || *f* folding machine

piegatura *f* fold, crease

pieghettare (**pieghétto**) *tr* to pleat

pieghévole *adj* folding; pliant; (fig) versatile || *m* folder

pieghevolézza *f* flexibility

piè·go *m* (**-ghi**) folder; bundle of papers

pièna *f* flood; rise (*of river*); crowd; (fig) overflow; **in piena** overflowing

pienézza *f* plenitude, fullness

piè·no -na *adj* full; solid; broad (*daylight*); full (*honors*); **a pieno** or **in pieno** to the full; **colpire nel pieno** to hit the bull's eye; **pieno di** alive with; **pieno di sé** conceited; **pieno zeppo** replete, chock-full || *m* fullness; height (*e.g., of winter*); **fare il pieno** (aut) to fill up || *f* see **piena**

pie·tà *f* (**-tà**) mercy; pity; (lit) piety

pietanza *f* main course

pietó·so -sa [s] *adj* pitiful, piteous; merciful

piètra *f* stone; rock; **pietra angolare** cornerstone; **pietra da affilare** whetstone; **pietra da sarto** French chalk; **pietra dello scandalo** source of scandal; **pietra di paragone** touchstone; **pietra focaia** flint; **pietra miliare** milestone; **pietra tombale** tombstone; **posare la prima pietra** to lay the cornerstone

pietrificare §197 (**pietrìfico**) *tr & ref* to petrify

pietrina *f* flint (*for lighter*)

pietri·sco *m* (**-schi**) rubble; (rr) ballast

Plètro *m* Peter

pietró·so -sa [s] *adj* (lit) stony

pièvano *m* parish priest

pìffero *m* pipe, fife

pìgia *m*—**pigia pigia** crowd, throng

pigia·ma *m* (**-ma & -mi**) pajamas

pigiare §290 *tr* to squeeze, press || *intr* to insist || *ref* to squeeze

pigia·tóre -trice *mf* presser (*of grapes*) || *f* wine press

pigiatura *f* pressing, squeezing

pigionante *mf* tenant

pigióne *f* rent, rental; **dare a pigione** to rent; to grant the possession of; **prendere a pigione** to rent; to hold for payment

pigliamó·sche *m* (-sche) flypaper; flytrap; (orn) flycatcher
pigliare §280 *tr* to take, catch; to mistake; **che Le piglia?** what's the matter with you? ‖ *ref*—**pigliarsela (con)** to get angry (at)
pì·glio *m* (-gli) hold; countenance; **dar di piglio a** to grab
pigménto *m* pigment
pigmè·o -a *adj & mf* pygmy; Pygmy
pigna *f* strainer (*at the end of a suction pipe*); bunch (*of grapes*); (bot) pine cone
pignatta *f* pot
pignò·lo -la *adj* finicky, fussy ‖ *m* pine nut
pignóne *m* pinion; embankment
pignoraménto *m* (law) seizure
pignorare (**pìgnoro**) *tr* (law) to seize
pigolare (**pìgolo**) *intr* to peep (*said, e.g., of young birds*)
pigolì·o *m* (-ì) peep (*e.g., of a young bird*)
pigrìzia *f* laziness
pi·gro -gra *adj* lazy; (lit) sluggish
pila *f* pier; buttress (*of bridge*); heap; sink; font; (elec) cell; (elec) battery; **pila atomica** atomic pile
pilastro *m* pier, pillar
pillàcchera *f* mud splash; (fig) fault
pìllola *f* pill; (slang) bullet; **addolcire la pillola** to sugar-coat the pill
pilóne *m* pier; pylon
pilò·ta (-ti -te) *adj* pilot ‖ *mf* pilot; (aut) driver
pilotàg·gio *m* (-gi) piloting; steering
pilotare (**pilòto**) *tr* to pilot; to drive
pilotina *f* (naut) pilot boat
piluccare §197 *tr* to pluck (*e.g., grapes one by one*); to nibble, pick at; to scrounge; (lit) to consume
piménto *m* allspice
pinacotè·ca *f* (-che) picture gallery
pinéta *f* pine grove
pìngue *adj* fat; rich
pinguèdine *f* fatness, corpulence
pinguino *m* penguin
pinna *f* fin (*of fish*); flipper; (zool) pen shell (*mussel*)
pinnàcolo *m* pinnacle
pino *m* pine tree; **pino marìttimo** pinaster; **pino silvestre** Scotch fir
pinòlo *m* pine nut
pinta *f* pint
pinza *f* claw (*of lobster*); **pinza emostatica** hemostat; **pinza tagliafili** wire cutter; **pinze clippers**; pliers; pincers
pinzatrice *f* stapler
pinzétte *fpl* tweezers, pliers
pinzòche·ro -ra *mf* bigot
pì·o -a *adj* (-i -e) pious; charitable ‖ **Pio** *m* Pius
piòg·gia *f* (-ge) rain
piòlo *m* peg; rung (*of ladder*); picket, stake
piombàggine *f* graphite
piombare (**piómbo**) *tr* to lead; to seal; to knock down; to fill (*a tooth*) ‖ *intr* to fall; to swoop down
piombatura *f* leading; filling (*of tooth*)
piombino *m* weight; seal; plumb; plumb bob

piómbo *m* lead; **a piombo** perpendicularly; **di piombo** suddenly
pionerìsti·co -ca *adj* (-ci -che) pioneering
pionière *m* pioneer
piòppo *m* poplar; **pioppo tremolo** aspen
piorrèa *f* pyorrhea
piotare (**piòto**) *tr* to sod
piova·no -na *adj* rain (*water*)
piova·sco *m* (-schi) rain squall
piovènte *m* pitch, slope
piòvere §216 *intr* (ESSERE) to rain; to pour; to flock (*said of people*); **piovere addosso a** to rain down on; **piovere su** to flow down over ‖ *impers* (ESSERE & AVERE)—**piove** it is raining; it is leaking (*from rain*); **piove a catinelle** or **a dirotto** it is raining cats and dogs
piovigginare (**piovìggina**) *impers* (ESSERE & AVERE)—**piovìggina** it is drizzling
piovigginó·so -sa [s] *adj* drizzling, drizzly
piovór·no -na *adj* (lit) var of **piovoso**
piovosi·tà [s] *f* (-tà) raininess; rainfall
piovó·so -sa [s] *adj* rainy
piòvra *f* octopus; (fig) leech
pipa *f* pipe; **non valere una pipa di tabacco** to not be worth a tinker's dam
pipare *intr* to smoke a pipe
pipata *f* pipe, pipeful
pipistrèllo *m* (zool) bat
pipita *f* hangnail; (vet) pip
pira *f* (lit) pyre
piràmide *f* pyramid
pira·ta *adj invar* pirate ‖ *m* (-ti) pirate; **pirata dell'aria** skyjacker; **pirata della strada** hit-and-run driver
pirateggiare §290 (**piratéggio**) *intr* to pirate
piraterìa *f* piracy; **pirateria letteraria** piracy of literary works
Pirenèi *mpl* Pyrenees
pìri·co -ca *adj* (-ci -che) fireworks; **polvere pirica** gunpowder
pirite *f* pyrite
piroétta *f* pirouette
pirò·ga *f* (-ghe) pirogue
pirolisi *f* (chem) cracking
piróne *m* (mus) tuning pin
piròscafo *m* steamship; **piroscafo da carico** (naut) freighter; **piroscafo da passeggeri** passenger ship
piroscissióne *f* (chem) cracking
pirotècni·co -ca (-ci -che) *adj* pyrotecnic ‖ *m* pyrotecnist ‖ *f* fireworks, pyrotechnics
pisciare §128 *intr* (vulg) to urinate
piscia·tóio *m* (-tói) (vulg) street urinal
piscina *f* swimming pool
pisèllo [s] *m* pea; **pisello odoroso** sweet pea
pisolare (**pìsolo**) *intr* (coll) to doze
pisolo *m* (coll) nap; **schiacciare un pisolo** (coll) to take a nap
pisside *f* (eccl) pyx; (bot) pyxidium
pista *f* track; ring (*of circus*); race track, speedway (*for car races*); ski run; (aer) runway; **pista ciclàbile** bicycle trail; **pista da ballo** dance

floor; **seguire una pista** to follow a clue

pistàc·chio m (-chi) pistachio

pistillo m (bot) pistil

pistòla f pistol

pistolettata f pistol shot

pistolòtto m lecture, talking-to; theatrical peroration

pistóne m piston; plunger

pitagòri·co -ca adj & m (-ci -che) Pythagorean

pitale m (coll) chamber pot

pitoccare §197 (**pitòcco**) intr to beg

pitòc·co m (-chi) beggar; miser

pitóne m python

pittima f plaster; (fig) bore

pit·tóre -trice mf painter

pittoré·sco -sca adj (-schi -sche) picturesque

pittòri·co -ca adj (-ci -che) pictorial

pittura f painting, picture; (coll) paint

pitturare tr to paint; to varnish || ref to put on make-up

più adj & m invar more; several || m (più) plus; most; **credersi da più** to believe oneself superior; **dal più al meno** about, more or less; **i più** most, the majority; **parlare del più e del meno** (coll) to make small talk || adv more; again; **a più non posso** to the very utmost; **in più** besides; **mai più** never again; **non poterne più** to be exhausted; **per di più** besides; **per lo più** for the most part; **più o meno** more or less; **tanto più** moreover; **tutt'al più** mostly

piuma f feather, plume; **piume** (fig) bed

piumàc·cio m (-ci) feather pillow

piumàg·gio m (-gi) plumage

piumino m down; comforter; puff, powder puff; feather duster

piuttòsto adv rather; somewhat

piva f bagpipe; **tornare con le pive nel sacco** to return bitterly disappointed

pivèllo m greenhorn; whippersnapper

pivière m (orn) plover

pizza f pizza; (mov) canister; (coll) bore

pizzaiò·lo -la mf owner of pizzeria || m pizza baker || f—**alla pizzaiola** prepared with tomato and garlic sauce

pizzardóne m (coll) cop, officer

pizzicàgno·lo -la mf grocer; sausage dealer

pizzicare §197 (**pizzico**) tr to pinch; to pluck; to bite, burn; (mus) to pick, twang

pizzicheria f delicatessen, grocery

pizzi·co m (-chi) pinch

pizzicóre m itch

pizzicòtto m pinch; **dar pizzicotti a** to pinch

pizzo m peak (of mountain); goatee; lace

placare §197 tr to placate || ref to calm down

plac·ca f (-che) plate; plaque; tag, badge; (elec, rad) plate; (pathol) blotch, spot

placcare §197 tr to plate; (sports) to tackle

plàci·do -da adj placid

plafond m (plafond) ceiling; (aer) ceiling; (com) top credit

pla·ga f (-ghe) (lit) clime, region

plagiare §290 tr to plagiarize

plagià·rio -ria (-ri -rie) adj plagiaristic || mf plagiarist

plà·gio m (-gi) plagiarism

planare intr (aer) to glide

planata f (aer) gliding

plàn·cia f (-ce) (naut) gangplank; (naut) bridge

planetà·rio -ria (-ri -rie) adj planetary || m planetarium; (aut) planetary gear

plantare m arch support

pla·sma m (-smi) plasma

plasmare tr to mold, shape

plàsti·ca f (-che) plastic art; plastics; plastic surgery; plastic

plasticare §197 (**plàstico**) tr to mold, shape; to cover with plastic

plàsti·co -ca (-ci -che) adj plastic || m relief map; maquette; plastic bomb || f see **plastica**

plastilina f modeling clay

plastron m (plastron) ascot

plàtano m plane tree; **platano americano** buttonwood tree

platèa f audience; (theat) orchestra; (archit) foundation

plateale adj obvious; plebeian

platina f (typ) platen

platinare (**plàtino**) tr to platinize; to bleach (hair)

plàtino m platinum

Platóne m Plato

plaudènte adj enthusiastic

plàudere (**plàudo**) & **plaudire** (**plàudo**) intr to applaud; (with dat) to applaud, e.g., **plaudere alla generosità** to applaud the generosity

plausìbile adj plausible

plàuso m (lit) applause, praise

plebàglia f rabble

plèbe f populace; (lit) crowd

plebè·o -a adj & mf plebeian

plebiscito m plebiscite

plenà·rio -ria adj (-ri -rie) plenary

plenilù·nio m (-ni) full moon

plenipotenzià·rio -ria adj & m (-ri -rie) plenipotentiary

plètora f plethora

plèttro m (mus) pick, plectrum

pleurite f (pathol) pleurisy

pli·co m (-chi) sealed document; bundle of papers; **in plico a parte** or **in plico separato** under separate cover

plotóne m platoon; **plotone d'esecuzione** firing squad

plùmbe·o -a adj lead, leaden

plurale adj & m plural; **al plurale** in the plural

plurilingue adj multilingual

plurimotóre adj multimotored || m multimotor

pluristàdio adj invar (rok) multistage

plusvalènza f unearned increment

plusvalóre m; surplus value (in Marxist economics)

Plutarco m Plutarch

plutocrazìa f plutocracy

Plutóne m Pluto

plutònio _m_ plutonium

pluviale _adj_ rain ‖ _m_ waterspout

pneumàti·co -ca (**-ci -che**) _adj_ pneumatic, air ‖ _m_ tire; **pneumatico da neve** snow tire

po' _m_ see **poco**

pochézza _f_ lack, scarcity

pò·co -ca (**-chi -che**) _adj_ little; short (_distance_); poor (_health; memory_); (_with collective nouns_) few, e.g., **poca gente** few people; (_with plural nouns_) a few, e.g., **fra pochi mesi** in a few months; (_with plural nouns having singular meaning in English_) little, e.g., **pochi quattrini** little money ‖ _m invar_ little; short distance; short time; **a ogni poco** often; **da poco** a little while ago; of no account; **da un bel po'** quite a while; quite a while ago; **fra poco** in a little while; **manca poco a** it won't be long till; **manca poco che** (_e.g., il ragazzo_) **non** + _subj_ (e.g., the boy) almost + _ind_; **per poco non** almost; **poco di buono** good-for-nothing; **poco fa** a little while ago; **saper di poco** to taste flat; **un poco di** or **un po' di** a little ‖ _f_—**poca di buono** hussy ‖ _poco adv_ little; **poco bene** poorly; **poco dopo** shortly after; **poco male** not too poorly

podagra _f_ gout

podére _m_ farm, country property

poderó·so -sa [s] _adj_ powerful

pode·stà _m_ (**-stà**) (hist) mayor; (hist) podesta

podià·tra _mf_ (**-tri -tre**) chiropodist

pò·dio _m_ (**-di**) podium; platform; (archit) base

podismo _m_ foot racing

podi·sta _mf_ (**-sti -ste**) foot racer

poè·ma _m_ (**-mi**) long poem

poesìa _f_ poetry; poem

poè·ta _m_ (**-ti**) poet

poetéssa _f_ poetess

poèti·co -ca (**-ci -che**) _adj_ poetic(al) ‖ _f_ poetics

pòg·gia _f_ (**-ge**) leeward

poggiare §290 (**pòggio**) _tr_ to lean ‖ _intr_ to be based; (mil) to move; (naut) to sail before the wind; (archaic) to rise

poggiatè·sta _m_ (**-sta**) headrest; (aut) head restrainer

pòg·gio _m_ (**-gi**) hillock, knoll

poggiòlo _m_ balcony

pòi _m_ future ‖ _adv_ then; later; **a poi** until later; **poi dopo** later on

poiana _f_ buzzard

poiché _conj_ since, as; (lit) after

pòker _m_ poker (_game_); four of a kind; **poker di ré** four kings

polac·co -ca (**-chi -che**) _adj_ Polish ‖ _mf_ Pole ‖ _f_ (mus) polonaise

polare _adj_ pole, polar

polarizzare [ddzz] _tr_ to polarize

pòl·ca _f_ (**-che**) polka

polèmi·co -ca (**-ci -che**) _adj_ polemical ‖ _f_ polemics

polemizzare [ddzz] _intr_ to engage in polemics

polèna _f_ (naut) figurehead

polènta _f_ corn mush

polentina _f_ poultice

poliambulanza _f_ clinic, emergency ward

policlìni·co _m_ (**-ci**) polyclinic

polifonìa _f_ polyphony

polìga·mo -ma _adj_ polygamous ‖ _m_ polygamist

poliglòt·ta _adj_ & _mf_ (**-ti -te**) polyglot

poliglòt·to -ta _adj_ & _mf_ polyglot

polìgono _m_ polygon; **poligono di tiro** shooting range

polìgrafo _m_ author skilled in many subjects; multigraph

polinesia·no -na _adj_ & _mf_ Polynesian

polinò·mio _m_ (**-mi**) polynomial

pòlio _f_ (coll) polio

poliomielite _f_ poliomielitis, infantile paralysis

pòlipo _m_ (pathol, zool) polyp

polisìlla·bo -ba _adj_ polysyllabic ‖ _m_ polysyllable

polì·sta _m_ (**-sti**) polo player

polìtea·ma _m_ (**-mi**) theater

politècni·co -ca (**-ci -che**) _adj_ polytechnic ‖ _m_ polytechnic institute

politei·sta (**-sti -ste**) _adj_ polytheistic ‖ _mf_ polytheist

politeìsti·co -ca _adj_ (**-ci -che**) polytheistic

politézza _f_ smoothness

polìti·ca _f_ (**-che**) politics; policy

politicante _mf_ petty politician

polìti·co -ca (**-ci -che**) _adj_ political ‖ _m_ politician ‖ _f_ see **politica**

polìtti·co _m_ (**-ci**) polyptych

polizìa _f_ police; **polizia sanitaria** health department; **polizia stradale** highway patrol; **polizia tributaria** income-tax investigation department

poliziè·sco -sca _adj_ (**-schi -sche**) police (_car_); detective (_story_)

poliziòtto _adj masc_ police (_dog_) ‖ _m_ policeman; detective; **poliziotto in borghese** plain-clothes man

pòlizza _f_ policy; ticket (_e.g., of pawnbroker_); **polizza di carico** bill of lading

pólla _f_ spring (_of water_)

pol·làio _m_ (**-lài**) chicken coop

pollaiò·lo -la _mf_ chicken dealer

pollame _m_ poultry

pollastra _f_ pullet; (coll) chick

pollerìa _f_ poultry shop

pòllice _m_ thumb; big toe; inch

pollicoltura _f_ poultry raising

pòlline _m_ pollen

pollivéndo·lo -la _mf_ poultry dealer

póllo _m_ chicken; (fig) sucker; **conoscere i propri polli** (fig) to know one's onions; **pollo d'India** turkey

pollóne _m_ (bot) shoot; (fig) offspring

polmóne _m_ lung; **a pieni polmoni** at the top of one's lungs; **polmone d'acciaio** iron lung

polmonite _f_ pneumonia

pòlo _m_ pole; polo shirt; (sports) polo

Polònia, la Poland

pólpa _f_ meat; pulp; flesh (_of fruit_); (fig) gist; **in polpe** (hist) in knee breeches

polpàc·cio _m_ (**-ci**) calf (_of leg_); cut of meat; ball of thumb

polpastrèllo *m* finger tip
polpétta *f* meat ball; meat patty, cutlet
polpettóne *m* meat loaf; (fig) hash
pólpo *m* (zool) octopus
polpó·so -sa [s] *adj* pulpy, fleshy
polpu·to -ta *adj* meaty
polsino *m* cuff
pólso *m* pulse; wrist; cuff, wristband; strong hand, energy; **di polso** energetic
poltiglia *f* mash; slush
poltrire §176 *intr* to idle; to loll in bed
poltróna *f* armchair; (theat) orchestra seat; **poltrona a orecchioni** wing chair; **poltrona a sdraio** chaise longue; **poltrona letto** day bed
poltroncina *f* parquet-circle seat
poltró·ne -na *mf* lazybones, sluggard ‖ *f* see **poltrona**
poltroneria *f* laziness
poltronissima *f* (theat) first-row seat
pólvere *f* dust; powder; **in polvere** powdered; **polvere da sparo** gunpowder; **polvere di stelle** stardust; **polvere nera** or **pirica** gunpowder; **polveri** gunpowder
polverièra *f* powder magazine; (fig) tinderbox, trouble spot
polverifi·cio -m (-ci) powder works
polverina *f* (pharm) powder
polverino *m* pounce, sand
polverizzare [ddzz] *tr* to crush, powder; to atomize; to pulverize
polverizza·to -ta [ddzz] *adj* powdered (*sugar*)
polverizzatóre [ddzz] *m* atomizer
polveróne *m* dust cloud
polveró·so' -sa [s] *adj* dusty; powdery (*snow*)
pomata *f* ointment; pomade
pomella·to -ta *adj* dapple-grey
pomèllo *m* cheek; cheekbone; pommel, knob
pomeridia·no -na *adj* afternoon, P.M.
pomerig·gio *m* (-gi) afternoon
pomiciare §128 (pómicio) *tr* to pumice ‖ *intr* (slang) to spoon
pomicióne *m* (slang) spooner
pomidòro *m* var of **pomodoro**
pómo *m* apple; knob; pommel (*of saddle*); **pomo della discordia** apple of discord; **pomo di Adamo** Adam's apple; **pomo di terra** potato
pomodòro *m* tomato; **pomodoro di mare** (zool) sea anemone
pómolo *m* (coll) knob, handle
pómpa *f* pump; pomp; state; **in pompa magna** all dressed up; **pompa aspirante** suction pump; **pompa premente** force pump; see **imprenditore** and **impresa**
pompare (pómpo) *tr* to pump; to pump up
pompèlmo *m* grapefruit
pompière *m* fireman
pompó·so -sa [s] *adj* pompous
pòn·ce *m* (-ci) punch
ponderare (pòndero) *tr* to weigh, ponder; to weight ‖ *intr* to think it over
pondera·to -ta *adj* considerate, careful
ponderó·so·-sa [s] *adj* ponderous

ponènte *m* west; west wind; West; West Wind
pónte *m* bridge; metal scaffolding; (aut) axle; (naut) deck; **fare il ponte** to take the day off between two holidays; **fare ponti d'oro a** to offer a good way out to; **ponte aereo** airlift; **ponte delle segnalazioni** (rr) gantry; **ponte di chiatte** pontoon bridge; **ponte di comando** (naut) bridge; **ponte di volo** flight deck; **ponte levatoio** drawbridge; **ponte radio** radio communication; **ponte sospeso** suspension bridge
pontéfice *m* pontiff; (hist) pontifex
pontéggio *m* scaffolding
ponticèllo *m* small bridge; nosepiece (*of eyeglasses*); (mus) bridge
pontière *m* (mil) engineer
pontificale *adj* pontifical ‖ *m* pontifical mass
pontifi·cio -cia *adj* (-ci -cie) papal
pontile *m* pier
pontóne *m* pontoon, barge
ponzare (pónzo) *tr* (coll) to strain to accomplish ‖ *intr* (coll) to rack one's brains
popeli·ne *f* (-ne) broadcloth
popola·no -na *adj* popular ‖ *mf* commoner
popolare *adj* popular ‖ *v* (pòpolo) *tr* to people, populate ‖ *ref* to be inhabited
popolarità *f* popularity
popola·to -ta *adj* peopled; crowded
popolazióne *f* population
pòpolo *m* people; crowd; **popolo grasso** (hist) rich bourgeoisie; **popolo minuto** (hist) artisans, common people
popoló·so -sa [s] *adj* populous
popóne *m* (coll) melon
póppa *f* breast; (naut) stern; (lit) ship; **a poppa** astern, aft
poppante *adj & mf* suckling
poppare (póppo) *tr* to suckle
poppa·tóio *m* (-tói) nursing bottle
poppavia *f*—**a poppavia** astern, aft
pòr·ca *f* (-che) ridge (*between furrows*); sow
porcacció·ne -na *m* cad, rake ‖ *f* slut
por·càio *m* (-cài) swineherd; pigsty
porcellana *f* porcelain, china; (bot) purslane
porcellino *m* piggy; **porcellino d'India** guinea pig
porcheria *f* dirt; (coll) dirty trick; (coll) botch
porchétta *f* roast suckling pig
porcile *m* pigsty
porci·no -na *adj* pig ‖ *m* (bot) boletus
pòr·co -ca *mf* (-ci -che) pig, hog, swine; pork; **porco mondo!** (slang) heck! ‖ *f* see **porca**
porcospino *m* porcupine
pòrfido *m* porphyry
pòrgere §217 *tr* to hand, offer; to relate; **porgere l'orecchio** to lend an ear ‖ *intr* to declaim ‖ *ref* to appear, show up
pornografia *f* pornography
pòro *m* pore
poró·so -sa [s] *adj* porous
pórpora *f* purple

pórpora·to -ta *adj* purple ‖ *m* purple; cardinal

porpori·no -na *adj* purple

pórre §218 *tr* to put; to repose (*trust*); to set (*a limit; one's foot*); to lay (*a stone*); to pose (*a question*); to pay (*attention*); to suppose; to advance (*the candidacy*); **porre gli occhi addosso a** to lay one's eyes on; **porre in dubbio** to cast doubt on; **porre mano a** to set to work at; **porre termine a** to put an end to; **posto che** since, provided ‖ *ref* to place oneself; **porsi in cammino** to set out or forth; **porsi in salvo** to reach safety

pòrro *m* wart; (bot) leek

pòrta *f* door; gate; (cricket) wicket; (sports) goal; **di porta in porta** door-to-door; **fuori porta** outside the city limits; **mettere alla porta** to dismiss, fire; **porta di servizio** delivery entrance; **porta scorrevole** sliding door; **porta stagna** (naut; theat) safety door

portabagà·gli *m* (**-gli**) porter; baggage rack

portabandiè·ra *m* (**-ra**) standard-bearer

portàbile *adj* portable

portàbi·ti *m* (**-ti**) coat hanger

portabottì·glie *m* (**-glie**) bottle rack

portacar·te *adj invar & m* (**-te**) folder

portacati·no *adj invar* washstand-supporting ‖ *m* (**-no**) washstand

portacéne·re *m* (**-re**) ashtray

portachia·vi *m* (**-vi**) key ring

portaci·pria *m* (**-pria**) compact

portadì·schi *m* (**-schi**) record cabinet, record rack; turntable

portadól·ci *m* (**-ci**) candy dish

portaère·i *f* (**-i**) aircraft carrier

portaferi·ti *m* (**-ti**) (mil) stretcher bearer

portafinèstra *f* (**portefinèstre**) French window

portafió·ri *m* (**-ri**) flower vase

portafò·gli *m* (**-gli**) or **portafò·glio** *m* (**-gli**) billfold, wallet; pocketbook; portfolio

portafortu·na *m* (**-na**) charm, amulet

portafrut·ta *m* (**-ta**) fruit dish

portafusìbi·li *m* (**-li**) fuse box

portagiò·ie *m* (**-ie**) jewel box

portaimmondì·zie *m* (**-zie**) trash can, garbage can

portainsé·gna *m* (**-gna**) standard-bearer

portalàmpa·da *m* (**-da**) (elec) socket

portale *m* portal

portalètte·re *m* (**-re**) *mf* letter carrier ‖ *m* postman, mailman

portamaz·ze *m* (**-ze**) caddie

portaménto *m* posture; gait; (fig) behavior

portami·na *m* (**-na**) mechanical pencil

portamissì·li (**-li**) *adj invar* missile-carrying ‖ *m* missile carrier

portamoné·te *m* (**-te**) purse

portamùsi·ca *m* (**-ca**) music stand

portante *adj* carrying; (archit) weight-bearing; (aer) lifting; (rad) carrier ‖ *m* amble

portantina *f* sedan chair; stretcher

portantino *m* bearer (*of sedan chair*); stretcher bearer

portanza *f* (archit) capacity; (aer) lift

portaombrèl·li *m* (**-li**) umbrella stand

portaórdi·ni *m* (**-ni**) (mil) messenger

portapac·chi *m* (**-chi**) parcel delivery man; basket (*on bicycle*)

portapén·ne *m* (**-ne**) penholder

portapiat·ti *m* (**-ti**) dish rack

portaposa·te [s] *m* (**-te**) silverware chest

portapran·zi [dz] *m* (**-zi**) dinner pail

portaraz·zi (**-zi**) [ddzz] *adj invar* missile-carrying ‖ *m* missile carrier

portare (**pòrto**) *tr* to carry; to bring; to take; to carry along; to lead; to herald; to praise; to wear; to drive (*car*); to run (*a candidate*); to adduce; to nurture (*hatred*); (aut) to hold (*e.g., five people*); **portare a conoscenza di** to let know; **portare avanti** to carry forward; **portare in alto** to lift; **portare via** to steal; to take away ‖ *intr* to carry (*said of a gun*) ‖ *ref* to move; to behave; to be (*a candidate*)

portaritrat·ti *m* (**-ti**) picture frame

portasapó·ne *m* (**-ne**) soap dish

portasigarét·te *m* (**-te**) cigarette case

portasìga·ri *m* (**-ri**) cigar case; humidor

portaspìl·li *m* (**-li**) pincushion

portata *f* course (*of a meal*); capacity; flow (*of river*); compass (*of voice*); range (*of voice or gun*); importance; (naut) burden; (naut) tonnage; **a portata di mano** within reach; **a portata di voce** within call, within earshot

portatèsse·re *m* (**-re**) card case

portàtile *adj* portable

porta·to -ta *adj* worn; **portato a** leaning toward ‖ *m* result, effect ‖ *f* see **portata**

porta·tóre -trice *mf* bearer

portatovagliòlo *m* napkin ring

portauò·vo *m* (**-vo**) eggcup

portavó·ce *m* (**-ce**) megaphone; (fig) mouthpiece

porte-enfant *m* (**porte-enfant**) baby bunting

portèllo *m* wicket; leaf (*of cabinet door*); (naut) porthole

portènto *m* portent

portica·to -ta *adj* arcaded ‖ *m* arcade

pòrti·co *m* (**-ci**) portico, arcade, colonnade; shed

portiè·re -ra *mf* concierge ‖ *m* janitor, doorman; (sports) goalkeeper ‖ *f* portiere (*in church door*); (aut) door

porti·nàio -nàia [s] (**-nài -nàie**) *adj* door, door-keeping ‖ *mf* doorkeeper, concierge

portineria *f* janitor's quarters

pòrto *m* port, harbor; transportation charge; port wine; goal; **condurre a buon porto** to carry to fruition; **franco di porto** prepaid, postpaid; **porto a carico del mittente** postage prepaid; **porto assegnato** charges to be paid by addressee; **porto d'armi** permit to carry arms; **porto franco** free port

Portogallo, il Portugal

portoghése [s] *adj & mf* Portuguese;

fare il portoghese (theat) to crash the gate

portóne *m* portal

portorica·no -na *adj & mf* Puerto Rican

Portorico *m* Puerto Rico

portuale *adj* port, harbor || *m* dock worker, longshoreman

porzióne *f* portion

pòsa [s] *f* laying (*e.g., of cornerstone*); posing (*for portrait*); posture, affectation, pose; dregs; (phot) exposure; (lit) rest; **senza posa** relentless; relentlessly

posami·ne (-**ne**) [s] *adj invar* mine-laying || *f* minelayer

posare [s] (**pòso**) *tr* to lay, put down || *intr* to lie; to settle; to pose; **posare a** to pose as || *ref* to settle; to alight; (lit) to rest

posata [s] *f* cover, place (*at table*); table utensil (*knife, fork or spoon*); **posate** knife, fork and spoon

posaterìa [s] *f* service (*of knives, forks, and spoons*)

posa·to -ta [s] *adj* sedate, quiet; placed || *ref see* **posata**

posa·tóre -trice [s] *mf* poseur || *m* layer, installer (*of cables or pipes*)

pòscia *adv* then, afterwards; **poscia che** after

poscritto *m* postscript

posdatare *tr var of* **postdatare**

posdomani *adv* (lit) day after tomorrow

positivaménte *adv* for sure

positi·vo -va *adj* positive || *f* (phot) positive, print

posizióne *f* position; status; (fig) stand

pospórre §218 *tr* to put off, postpone; to put last; **posporre qlco a qlco** to put or place s.th after s.th

pòssa *f* (lit) strength, vigor

possanza *f* (lit) power

possedére §252 *tr* to possess; to own; to master (*a language*); **essere posseduto da** to be enthralled with; to be possessed by

possediménto *m* possession, property

posseditrice *f* owner, possessor

possènte *adj* (lit) powerful

possessióne *f* possession

possessi·vo -va *adj* possessive

possèsso *m* possession

possessóre *m* owner, possessor

possibile *adj* possible || *m*—**fare il possibile** to do one's best

possibili·sta (-**sti** -**ste**) *adj* pragmatically flexible || *mf* pragmatically flexible person, possibilist

possibili·tà *f* (-**tà**) possibility; opportunity; **possibilità** *fpl* means

possidènte *mf* proprietor, owner; **possidente terriero** landowner

pòsta *f* post; mail; post office; box (*in stable*); ambush; bet; **a giro di posta** by return mail; **a posta** on purpose; **darsi la posta** to set up an appointment; **fare la posta a** to have under surveillance; **fermo in posta** general delivery; **levare la posta** to pick up the mail; **posta aerea** air mail; **posta del lettori** (journ) letters to the editor; **poste** postal department

pósta *f* (archaic) planting; (archaic) footprint

postagi·ro *m* (-**ro** & -**ri**) postal transfer of funds

postale *adj* postal, mail || *m* mail; mail train (boat, bus, or plane)

postare (**pòsto**) *tr* (mil) to post || *ref* (mil) to take a position

postazióne *f* (mil) emplacement

postbèlli·co -ca *adj* (-**ci** -**che**) postwar

postbruciatóre *m* (aer) afterburner

postdatare *tr* to postdate

posteggiare §290 (**postéggio**) *tr & intr* to park

posteggia·tóre -trice *mf* parking-lot attendant; customer (*in a parking lot*); (coll) outdoor merchant; **posteggiatore abusivo** parking violator

postég·gio *m* (-**gi**) parking lot; stand (*in outdoor market*); **posteggio di tassì** cabstand

posterióre *adj* back; subsequent, later

posteri·tà *f* (-**tà**) posterity

pòste·ro -ra *adj* later, subsequent || **posteri** *mpl* posterity, descendants

postìc·cio -cia (-**ci** -**ce**) *adj* artificial; false (*e.g., tooth*); temporary || *m* wiglet, ponytail || *f* row of trees

posticipare (**postìcipo**) *tr* to postpone

posticipa·to -ta *adj* deferred

postièria *f* postern

postiglióne *m* postilion

postilla *f* marginal note

postillare *tr* to annotate

posti·no -na *mf* letter carrier || *m* mailman, postman

pósto *m* place; room; seat; job, position; spot; (mil) post; **a posto in** order; orderly; **al posto di** instead of; **essere a posto** to have a good job; **mettere a posto** to find a good job for; (coll) to keep quiet; **quel posto** (coll) seat of the pants; (coll) toilet; **posto a sedere** seat; **posto di blocco** road block; (rr) signal tower; **posto di guardia** (mil) guardhouse; **posto di medicazione** or **di pronto soccorso** first-aid station; **posto in piedi** standing room; **posto letto** bed (*e.g., in hospital*); **posto telefonico pubblico** public telephone, pay station; **rimettere a posto** to fix, repair; **saper stare al proprio posto** to know one's place; **sul posto** on the spot

postrè·mo -ma *adj* (lit) last

postrìbolo *m* (lit) brothel

postulante *adj* petitioning || *mf* petitioner, applicant; (eccl) postulant

postulare (**pòstulo**) *tr* to postulate

pòstu·mo -ma *adj* posthumous || **postumi** *mpl* sequel; (pathol) sequelae

potàbile *adj* drinkable

potare (**póto**) *tr* to trim, prune

potassa *f* potash

potàssio *m* potassium

potatura *f* pruning, polling

potentato *m* (lit) potentate

potènte *adj* powerful; influential || **i potenti** the powers that be

potènza *f* power, might; (math) power; **all'ennesima potenza** (math) to the nth power; (fig) to the nth degree; **in potenza** potential; potentially

potenziale *adj & m* potential
potère *m* ability; authority, power; **in potere di** in the hands of; **potere d'acquisto** purchasing power; **potere esecutivo** executive; **potere giudiziario** judiciary; **quarto potere** fourth estate ‖ §219 *intr* to be powerful; **non ne posso più** I am at the end of my rope; **si può?** may I come in? ‖ *aux* (ESSERE & AVERE) to be able; **non posso fare a meno di** + *inf* I can't help + *ger*; **non potere fare a meno di** to not be able to do without; **posso**, etc. I can; I may, etc.; **potrei**, etc. I could; I might, etc.
pote·stà *f* (-**stà**) power, authority
poveràc·cio -cia *mf* (-**ci -ce**) poor guy, poor soul
pòve·ro -ra *adj* poor; needy, wretched; lean (*gasoline mixture*); **povero in canna** as poor as a church mouse ‖ *mf* pauper; beggar; poor devil ‖ **i poveri** the poor
pover·tà *f* (-**tà**) poverty; paucity, scantiness
poveruòmo *m* (used only in *sg*) poor devil
poziòne *f* potion, brew
pòzza *f* pool, puddle
pozzànghera *f* puddle
pozzétto *m* small well; manhole; forecastle (*in small boat*)
pózzo *m* well; shaft; **pozzo artesiano** artesian well; **pozzo delle catene** (*naut*) chain locker; **pozzo di scienza** fountain of knowledge; **pozzo di ventilazione** (*min*) air shaft; **pozzo nero** cesspool; **pozzo petrolifero** oil well; **pozzo trivellato** deep well; **un pozzo di** (*fig*) a barrel of
Praga *f* Prague
prammàti·co -ca (-**ci -che**) *adj* pragmatic ‖ *f* social custom; **di prammatica** obligatory, de rigueur
pranzare [dz] *intr* to dine
pranzo [dz] *m* dinner; **dopo pranzo** afternoon
pras·si *f* (-**si**) practice, praxis
pratería *f* prairie
pràti·ca *f* (-**che**) practice; knowledge; matter; file, dossier; business; experience; (*naut*) pratique; **aver pratica con** to be familiar with (*people*); **aver pratica di** to be familiar with (*things*); **far pratica** to be an apprentice; **fare le pratiche** to make an application; **in pratica** practically; **insabbiare una pratica** to pigeonhole a matter
praticàbile *adj* practicable; passable ‖ *m* (*theat*) raised platform
praticante *adj* practicing ‖ *mf* apprentice; novice; churchgoer
praticare §197 (**pràtico**) *tr* to practice; to frequent; to be familiar with; to make (*e.g., a hole*); to grant (*a discount*) ‖ *intr* to practice; **praticare in** to frequent
pratici·tà *f* (-**tà**) utility; practicality
pràti·co -ca (-**ci -che**) *adj* practical; experienced ‖ *f* see **pratica**
praticó·ne -na *mf* (*pej*) old hand
prato *m* meadow

pratolina *f* daisy
pra·vo -va *adj* (*lit*) wicked
preaccennare (**preaccénno**) *tr* to mention in advance
preaccenna·to -ta *adj* aforementioned
preallarme *m* early warning
Prealpi *fpl* foothills of the Alps
preàmbolo *m* preamble
preannunziare §287 (**preannùnzio**) *tr* to foretell, forebode
preannùn·zio *m* (-**zi**) advance information; foreboding
preautunnale *adj* pre-fall
preavvertire (**preavvèrto**) *tr* to forewarn
preavvisare *tr* to give advance notice to; to forewarn
preavviso *m* forewarning; notification of dismissal
prebèlli·co -ca *adj* (-**ci -che**) prewar
prebènda *f* prebend; (*fig*) easy money, sinecure
precà·rio -ria *adj* (-**ri -rie**) precarious
precauzióne *f* precaution
precedènte *adj* preceding ‖ *m* precedent; **precedenti** background; **precedenti penali** previous offenses, record
precedènza *f* precedence; (*aut*) right of way; (*fig*) priority
precèdere §123 *tr & intr* to precede
precettare (**precètto**) *tr* (*mil*) to call back from furlough
precètto *m* precept; (*eccl*) obligation
precettóre *m* tutor
precipitare (**precìpito**) *tr* to precipitate; to hasten; (*chem*) to precipitate ‖ *intr* (ESSERE) to fall; to fail; to rush (*said of events*); (*chem*) to precipitate ‖ *ref* to rush
precipitó·so -sa [*s*] *adj* hasty, headlong
precipì·zio *m* (-**zi**) precipice, cliff; ruin; **a precipizio** headlong
preci·puo -pua *adj* chief, principal, primary
precisare *tr* to say exactly, specify, clarify; to fix (*a date*)
precisazióne *f* clarification
precisióne *f* precision
preci·so -sa *adj* precise, exact; punctilious; identical, same; sharp, edgy; **alle sette precise** at seven o'clock sharp
precla·ro -ra *adj* (*lit*) illustrious
preclùdere §105 *tr* to preclude
precòce *adj* precocious, premature
preconcèt·to -ta *adj* preconceived ‖ *m* preconception; prejudice, bias
preconizzare [ddzz] *tr* to foretell, forecast; (*eccl*) to preconize
precórrere §139 *tr* (*lit*) to precede ‖ *intr* (*lit*) to occur before
precursóre *m* precursor
prèda *f* booty, prize; prey
predace *adj* (*lit*) preying, predatory
predare (**prèdo**) *tr* to pillage; to prey upon
preda·tóre -trice *adj* predacious, rapacious ‖ *m* plunderer
predecessóre *m* predecessor
predèlla *f* dais; altar step; platform
predellino *m* footboard
predestinare (**predestino** & **predèstino**) *tr* to predestine

predét·to -ta *adj* aforementioned
prediale *adj* field, rural || *f* land tax
prèdi·ca *f* (-che) sermon
predicare §197 (**prèdico**) *tr & intr* to preach
predicato *m* predicate; **essere in predicato di** + *inf* to be rumored to + *inf*; **essere predicato per** to be considered for
predica·tóre -trice *mf* preacher
predicazióne *f* preaching; sermon
predicòzzo *m* (coll) lecture, scolding
predilèt·to -ta *adj & m* favorite
predilezióne *f* predilection
prediligere §149 (*pres part* missing) *tr* to prefer; to like best
predire §151 *tr* to foretell
predispórre §218 *tr* to predispose, prearrange || *ref* to prepare oneself
predisposizióne *f* predisposition
predizióne *f* prediction
predominare (**predòmino**) *tr* to overcome || *intr* to predominate; to prevail
predomi·nio *m* (-ni) predominance
predóne *m* marauder; **predone del mare** pirate
preesistere §114 *intr* (ESSERE) to preexist
prefabbricare §197 (**prefàbbrico**) *tr* to prefabricate
prefazióne *f* preface
preferènza *f* preference; **a preferenza** rather; **usar preferenze a** to favor
preferìbile *adj* preferable
preferire §176 *tr* to prefer
preferi·to -ta *adj* preferred, favored || *mf* favorite; pet
prefètto *m* prefect
prefettura *f* prefecture
prèfi·ca *f* (-che) professional mourner, paid mourner; (coll) crybaby
prefiggere §103 *tr* to set, fix; (gram) to prefix || *ref* to plan
prefis·so §appointed; prefixed || *m* (gram) prefix; (telp) area code
prefissòlde *m* prefixed combining form
pregare §209 (**prègo**) *tr* to beg, pray; to ask, request; **farsi pregare** to take a lot of asking; **La prego** please; **prego!** please!; beg your pardon!; you are welcome!
pregévole *adj* valuable
preghièra *f* entreaty; prayer
pregiare §290 (**prègio**) *tr* (lit) to praise, esteem || *ref* to be honored, to have the pleasure
pregia·to -ta *adj* precious; esteemed; **la Sua pregiata (lettera)** your favor, your kind letter; **pregiatissimo Signore** (com) dear Sir; **pregiato Signore** (com) dear Sir
prè·gio *m* (-gi) value, worth; esteem; **avere in pregio** to value
pregiudicare §197 (**pregiùdico**) *tr* to damage, harm, jeopardize
pregiudica·to -ta *adj* prejudged; prejudiced; compromised; bound to fail || *m* previous offender
pregiudiziale *adj* (law) pretrial; (pol) essential || *f* (law) pretrial
pregiudiziévole *adj* prejudicial, detrimental

pregiudì·zio *m* (-zi) prejudice, bias; harm, damage
pregnante *adj* pregnant
prè·gno -gna *adj* pregnant; saturated
prè·go *m* (-ghi) (lit) prayer || *interj* please!; beg your pardon!; you are welcome!
pregustare *tr* to foretaste, anticipate with pleasure
preistòri·co -ca *adj* (-ci -che) prehistoric(al)
prelato *m* prelate
prelazióne *f* (law) preemption; (obs) privilege
prelevaménto *m* (com) withdrawal
prelevare (**prelèvo**) *tr* to withdraw (money); to capture
preliba·to -ta *adj* excellent, delicious
prelièvo *m* withdrawal; (med) specimen
preliminare *adj* preliminary || **preliminari** *mpl* preliminary negotiations
prelùdere §105 *intr* to make an introductory statement; (with *dat*) to precede, usher in
prelù·dio *m* (-di) prelude; (*of an opera*) overture
prematu·ro -ra *adj* premature
premeditare (**premèdito**) *tr* to premeditate
premeditazióne *f* premeditation; **con premeditazione** (law) with malice prepense
prèmere §123 *tr* to press; to push; to squeeze || *intr* (ESSERE & AVERE) to press; to be urgent; **premere a** to matter to, e.g., **gli preme** it matters to him; **premere su** to press, put pressure on
premèssa *f* premise; introduction (*to a book*)
preméttere §198 *tr* to state at the onset; to place at the beginning
premiare §287 (**prèmio**) *tr* to award a prize to, reward
premiazióne *f* awarding of prizes
preminènte *adj* prominent, preeminent
prè·mio *m* (-mi) prize; premium; bonus; award
prèmito *m* straining (*to defecate*)
premolare *adj & m* premolar
premonire §176 *tr* (lit) to foretell
premonizióne *f* premonition
premorire §201 *intr* (ESSERE) (with *dat*) to predecease
premunire §176 *tr* to fortify || *ref—* **premunirsi contro** to provide against; **premunirsi di** to provide oneself with
premura *f* haste; attention, care; **aver premura** (di) to be in a hurry (to); **di premura** hastily; **far premura** (with *dat*) to urge
premuró·so -sa [s] *adj* attentive, careful
prèndere §220 *tr* to take; to catch; to lift; to pick up; to fetch; to get; to receive; **prendere a calci** to kick; **prendere a pugni** to punch; **prendere a servizio** to employ, hire; **prendere commiato** to take leave; **prendere con le buone** to treat with kid gloves; **prendere in castagna** to catch in the act; **prendere il sole** to sun oneself; **prendere la fuga** to take flight;

prendere la mano to run away (*said of a horse*); **prendere le mosse** to begin (*said, e.g., of a story*); **prendere lucciole per lanterne** to commit a gross error; **prender paura** to get scared; **prendere per** to take for; **prendere per il naso** to lead by the nose; **prendere quota** (aer) to gain altitude; **prendere sonno** to fall asleep; **prendere un granchio** to make a blunder || *intr* to take root; to set (*said of cement*); to catch (*said of fire*); to turn (*left or right*); **prendere a** + *inf* to begin to + *inf* || *ref* to grab one another; to get along together; **prendersela con** to become angry with; to lay the blame on; **prendersi a** to take hold of

prendi·tóre -trice *mf* receiver; payee (*of a note*); margin buyer || *m* (baseball) catcher

prenóme *m* first name, given name

prenotare (**prenòto**) *tr* to reserve, book || *ref* to register

prenotazióne *f* reservation, booking

preoccupante *adj* worrisome

preoccupare (**preòccupo**) *tr* to preoccupy; **preoccupare la mente di** to win the favor of || *ref* to worry

preoccupazióne *f* preoccupation, worry

preordinare (**preòrdino**) *tr* to foreordain; to prearrange

preparare *tr* to prepare; to prime; to steep, brew || *ref* to be prepared; to brew (*said, e.g., of a storm*)

preparati·vo -va *adj* preparatory || **preparativi** *mpl* preparations

prepara·to -ta *adj* prepared; wellequipped || *m* patent medicine; (med) preparation; **preparato anatomico** dissection, anatomical specimen

preparatò·rio -ria *adj* (**-ri -rie**) preparatory

preparazióne *f* preparation

preponderante *adj* preponderant, prevailing

preponderanza *f* preponderance

prepórre §218 *tr* to prefix; to place before; to prefer; **preporre (qlcu) a** to place (*s.o.*) at the head of

preposizióne *f* preposition

prepósto *m* chief; (eccl) provost

prepotènte *adj* arrogant, overbearing; urgent (*desire*) || *m* bully

prepotènza *f* arrogance; outrage; **di prepotenza** by force

prerogativa *f* prerogative

présa [s] *f* hold, grip; handle; potholder; capture; pinch (*e.g., of salt*); setting (*of cement*); intake; (cards) trick; (elec) jack; (mov) take; **a pronta presa** quick-setting (*cement*); **dar presa** to give rise to; **essere alle prese** to come to grips; **far presa** to stick (*said of glue*); to set (*said of cement*); to take root; **far presa su** to impress; **mettere alle prese** to pit (*e.g., animals*); **presa d'acqua** spigot, faucet; **presa d'aria** outlet (*of air hose*); air shaft; **presa di corrente** (elec) wall socket, outlet, receptacle; **presa di terra** (elec) ground; presa

in giro kidding, joke; **venire alle prese** to come to grips

presà·gio *m* (**-gi**) forecast; portent

presagire §176 *tr* to forecast; to portend

presalà·rio [s] *m* (**-ri**) (educ) stipend

prèsbite *adj* far-sighted || *mf* far-sighted person

presbiteria·no -na *adj & mf* Presbyterian

prescégliere §244 *tr* to choose, select

prescindere §247 (*pret* **prescindéi & prescissi**) *intr*—**a prescindere da** except for; **prescindere da** to leave out

prescolàsti·co -ca *adj* (**-ci -che**) preschool

prescrit·to -ta *adj* prescribed

prescrivere §250 *tr* to prescribe || *intr* (ESSERE) (law) to prescribe, to lapse

prescrizióne *f* prescription; (law) extinctive prescription

presegnale [s] *m* warning sign

presentàbile *adj* presentable

presentare (**presènto**) *tr* to present; to introduce; **presentare la candidatura di** to nominate; **presentat'arm!** present arms! || *ref* to show up, appear; to come, arise (*said, e.g., of an opportunity*)

presenta·tóre -trice *mf* presenter; (rad, telv) announcer || *m* master of ceremonies

presentazióne *f* presentation; introduction

presènte *adj* present; **avere presente** to have in mind; **fare presente qlco a qlcu** to bring s.th to s.o.'s attention; **tenere presente** to keep in mind || *m* present; bystander, onlooker; **al presente** at present; **di presente** immediately || *interj* here!

presentiménto [s] *m* presentiment, foreboding

presentire [s] (**presènto**) *tr* to have a presentiment of

presènza *f* presence; attendance; **di presenza** in person; **presenza di spirito** presence of mind

presenziare §287 (**presènzio**) *tr* to attend; to witness || *intr*—**presenziare a** to be present at; to witness

presè·pio *m* (**-pi**) Nativity, crèche

preservare [s] (**presèrvo**) *tr* to preserve, protect

preservati·vo -va [s] *adj & m* prophylactic

prèside [s] *m* principal (*of secondary school*); **preside di facoltà** dean

presidènte [s] *m* president; chairman; **presidente del Consiglio** premier

presidentéssa [s] *f* president; chairwoman

presidènza [s] *f* presidency; chairmanship

presi·dio [s] *m* (**-di**) garrison; (fig) defense, help; **presidi medical** aids

presièdere [s] §141 (**presièdo**) *tr* to preside over || *intr* to preside; **presiedere a** to preside over

prèssa *f* crowd; haste; (mach) press; **far pressa** (poet) to urge

pressacar·te [s] *m* (**-te**) paperweight

pressaforàg·gio *m* (**-gio**) baler, hay baler

pressante *adj* pressing, urgent
pressappòco *adv* more or less
pressare (**prèsso**) *tr* to press; to urge
pressióne *f* pressure; **far pressione su** to put pressure on; **pressione sanguigna** blood pressure; **sotto pressione** under steam
prèsso *m*—**nei pressi di** in the neighborhood of || *adv* near, nearby; **a un di presso** approximately; **da presso** close; **press'a poco** more or less || *prep* near; about; at; according to; at the house of; at the office of; care of; with, e.g., **godere fama presso** to enjoy popularity with
pressoché *adv* almost, about, nearly
pressurizzare [ddzz] *tr* to pressurize
prestabilire §176 *tr* to preestablish
prestabili·to -ta *adj* appointed
prestanó·me *m* (**-me**) straw man, figurehead
prestante *adj* strong, vigorous; comely
prestanza *f* vigor; (lit) comeliness
prestare (**prèsto**) *tr* to lend; to loan; to give (*ear; help*); to pay (*attention*); to render (*obedience*); to take (*oath*); to keep (*faith*); **prestar man forte** to give aid; **prestar servizio** to work || *ref* to lend oneself; to be suitable; to be willing; to volunteer
presta·tóre -trice *mf* lender; **prestatore d'opera** worker; **prestatori d'opera** labor
prestazióne *f* service; performance
prestigia·tóre -trice *mf* magician, juggler
prestì·gio *m* (**-gi**) prestige; spell, influence; ledgerdemain
prestigió·so -sa [s] *adj* captivating, spellbinding; illusory
prèstito *m* loan; (philol) borrowing; **dare a prestito** to lend; **prendere a prestito** to borrow
prè·sto -sta *adj* (archaic) quick || *m* (mus) presto || *presto adv* soon; fast; quick, quickly; early; **al più presto** at the earliest possible time; **ben presto** soon; **far presto** to hurry; **più presto che può** as soon as you can; **presto detto** easy to say
presùmere §116 *tr & intr* to presume
presunti·vo -va *adj* presumptive; budgeted, estimated (*expenditure*)
presun·to -ta *adj* alleged, supposed; estimated (*expenditure*)
presuntuó·so -sa [s] *adj* presumptuous; bumptious
presunzióne *f* presumption; conceit
presuppórre §218 *tr* to presuppose
presuppósto [s] *m* assumption
prète *m* priest; minister; wooden frame (*to hold bed warmer*)
pretendènte *m* suitor; pretender
pretèndere §270 *tr* to demand, claim; **pretenderla a** to pretend to be || *intr*—**pretendere a** to be a suitor for; to claim (*e.g., a throne*)
pretensióne *f* demand; pretention; pretense
pretensió·so -sa [s] or **pretenzió·so -sa** [s] *adj* pretentious
preterintenzionale *adj* (law) unintentional; (law) justifiable

pretèri·to -ta *adj & m* preterit
preté·so -sa [s] *adj* alleged, ostensible; assumed (*name*) || *f* pretense; pretension
pretèsto *m* pretext, excuse; **sotto il pretesto di** under pretense of
pretòni·co -ca *adj* (**-ci -che**) pretonic
pretóre *m* judge, magistrate (*of lower court*)
prèt·to -ta *adj* pure, genuine
pretura *f* lower court
prevalènte *adj* prevalent, prevailing
prevalènza *f* prevalence; **essere in prevalenza** to be in the majority; **in prevalenza** for the most part
prevalére §278 *intr* (ESSERE & AVERE) to prevail || *ref* to take advantage
prevaricare §197 (**prevàrico**) *intr* to transgress; to graft
prevarica·tóre -trice *mf* grafter
prevedére §279 *tr* to foresee; to provide for (*said of a statute*)
prevedìbile *adj* foreseeable
prevenire §282 *tr* to precede; to anticipate; to forewarn; to prejudice
preventivi·sta *mf* (**-sti -ste**) estimator
preventi·vo -va *adj* preventive; prior; estimated (*budget*) || *m* estimate
prevenu·to -ta *adj* forewarned; biased, prejudiced || *m* defendant
prevenzióne *f* prevention; prejudice, bias
previdènte *adj* provident, prudent
previdènza *f* providence; foresight; **previdenza sociale** social security
previdenziale *adj* social (e.g., responsibility); social-security (e.g., contribution)
prè·vio -via *adj* (**-vi -vie**) with previous, e.g., **previo accordo** with previous agreement
previsióne *f* foresightedness; **in previsione di** anticipating; **previsioni del tempo** weather forecast
previ·sto -sta *adj* foreseen, expected || *m* expected time; estimated amount
prezió·so -sa [s] *adj* precious, valuable; affected; **fare il prezioso** (coll) to play hard to get || **preziosi** *mpl* valuables, jewels
prezzare (**prèzzo**) *tr* to care about; to price
prezzémolo *m* parsley
prèzzo *m* price; cost; **mettere a prezzo** (fig) to sell; **prezzo di favore** special price; **prezzo d'ingresso** admission; **tenere in gran prezzo** to value highly, to esteem highly; **ultimo prezzo** rock-bottom price
prezzolare (**prèzzolo**) *tr* to hire (e.g., a gunman); to bribe
prigióne *f* prison, jail; (naut) brig
prigionìa *f* imprisonment; bondage
prigioniè·ro -ra *adj* imprisoned || *mf* prisoner || *m* stud bolt
prillare *intr* to spin, whirl
prima *f* first grade (*in school*); (rr) first class; (theat) first night; (aut) first (gear); **alla prima** or **sulle prime** at the outset || *adv* before; first; prior; ahead; **di prima** previous; **prima che** before; **prima di** ahead of; before;

prima o poi sooner or later; **quanto prima** as soon as possible

primàrio -ria (**-ri -rie**) *adj* primary ‖ *m* (elec) primary; (med) chief of staff

primati·sta *mf* (**-sti -ste**) (sports) record holder

primato *m* primacy; (sports) record

primavèra *f* spring; springtime; (bot) primrose

primaverile *adj* spring; spring-like

primeggiare §290 (**priméggio**) *intr* to excel

primiè·ro -ra *adj* (lit) prior; (lit) pristine ‖ *f* (cards) meld

primiti·vo -va *adj & m* primitive

primìzia *f* first fruits; scoop, beat

prì·mo -ma *adj* first; early (*dawn*); prime (*cost*); raw (*material*); **sulle prime** at first ‖ *m* first; minute; **primo arrivato** first comer ‖ *f* see **prima**

primogèni·to -ta *adj* first-born; (fig) beloved ‖ *mf* first-born child

primòrdi *mpl* beginning, origin

primordiale *adj* primordial, primeval

prìmula *f* primrose ‖ **Primula** *f*—**la Primula Rossa** the Scarlet Pimpernel

principale *adj* principal, main ‖ *m* (coll) boss, chief

principalménte *adv* chiefly, mainly

principato *m* principality

prìncipe *adj* princeps ‖ *m* prince; **il principe di Galles** the Prince of Wales; **principe ereditario** crown prince

principé·sco -sca *adj* (**-schi -sche**) princely

principéssa *f* princess

principiante *adj* beginning ‖ *mf* beginner

principiare §287 *tr & intr* (ESSERE & AVERE) to begin; **a principiare da** beginning with

princi·pio *m* (**-pi**) beginning; principle; **in principio** at the beginning, at first

princisbécco *m* pinchbeck; **restare o rimanere di princisbecco** to be dumfounded

prióre *m* prior

priori·tà *f* (**-tà**) priority

priorità·rio -ria *adj* (**-ri -rie**) priority, e.g., **progetto prioritario** priority project

prì·sma *m* (**-smi**) prism

privare *tr* to deprive; to remove

privativa *f* government monopoly; salt and tobacco store; patent

priva·to -ta *adj* private ‖ *m* private individual

privazióne *f* privation, loss

privilegiare §290 (**privilègio**) *tr* to privilege; (fig) to endow

privilegia·to -ta *adj* privileged; preferred (*stock*) ‖ *m* privileged person

privilè·gio *m* (**-gi**) privilege

prì·vo -va *adj* deprived; **privo di** lacking

prò·m (**pro**) profit, advantage; **a che pro?** what's the use?; **buon pro!** good appetite!; **far pro** to be good for the health; **il pro e il contro** the pros and the cons ‖ *prep* pro, in favor of

probàbile *adj* probable

probabili·tà *f* (**-tà**) probability; chance; odds

probante *adj* proving; evidential

probatò·rio -ria *adj* (**-ri -rie**) probative, evidential

problè·ma *m* (**-mi**) problem

prò·bo -ba *adj* (lit) honest

procàc·cia *mf* (**-cia**) messenger; mail carrier

procacciare §128 *tr* to get, procure ‖ *ref* to eke out (*a living*); to get into (*trouble*)

procace *adj* buxom, sexy; saucy, petulant

procèdere §123 (**procèdo**) *intr* to proceed, take action ‖ *intr* (ESSERE) to proceed, go ahead

procediménto *m* procedure; behavior

procedura *f* procedure

procèlla *f* (lit) storm, tempest

procellària *f* (orn) petrel

processare (**procèsso**) *tr* to try, prosecute

processióne *f* procession

procèsso *m* process; trial; **processo verbale** minutes

processuale *adj* trial

procinto *m*—**in procinto di** on the point of

procióne *m* raccoon

procla·ma *m* (**-mi**) proclamation

proclamare *tr* to proclaim

proclamazióne *f* proclamation

proclìti·co -ca *adj & f* (**-ci -che**) proclitic

proclive *adj* inclined, disposed

proclivi·tà *f* (**-tà**) proclivity

procrastinare (**procràstino**) *tr* to procrastinate, put off ‖ *intr* to procrastinate

procreare (**procrèo**) *tr* to procreate

procura *f* agency; power of attorney; **Procura della Repubblica** attorney general's office; district attorney's office

procurare *tr* to procure, to get; to cause; **procurare che** to see to it that; **procurare di** to try to ‖ *ref* to get, acquire

procura·tóre -trice *mf* proxy; agent; attorney-at-law; (sports) manager; **Procuratore della Repubblica** district attorney

pròda *f* shore, bank; (archaic) prow

pròde *adj* brave ‖ *m* brave person, hero

prodézza *f* prowess; accomplishment

prodiè·ro -ra *adj* prow, e.g., **cannone prodiero** prow gun; preceding (*in a row of ships*)

prodigare §209 (**pròdigo**) *tr* to squander, lavish ‖ *ref* to do one's best

prodì·gio *m* (**-gi**) prodigy; wonder

prodigió·so -sa [s] *adj* prodigious; wonderful

pròdi·go -ga *adj* (**-ghi -ghe**) lavish, prodigal; **prodigo di** profuse in

proditò·rio -ria *adj* (**-ri -rie**) traitorous

prodótto *m* product; result; **prodotti in scatola** canned goods; **prodotti** (**ortofrutticoli**) produce

produrre §102 *tr* to produce; to turn out; to yield; to breed; to cause; (lit) to prolong; (law) to exhibit ‖ *ref* (theat) to perform, appear

produtti·vo -va *adj* productive

produttivísti·co -ca *adj* (*-ci -che*) productivity, e.g., **fine produttivístico** productivity policy

produt·tóre -trice *adj* producing ‖ *mf* producer; agent; manufacturer's representative ‖ *m* salesman ‖ *f* saleswoman

produzióne *f* production; output; **produzione in massa** or **in serie** mass production

proè·mio *m* (*-mi*) preamble, proem

profanare *tr* to profane, desecrate

profanazióne *f* profanation, desecration

profa·no -na *adj* profane; lay, uninformed ‖ *m* layman; **il profano** the profane

proferire §176 *tr* (lit) to utter; (lit) to proffer

professare (professo) *tr* to profess; to practice (*e.g., law*) ‖ *intr* to practice ‖ *ref* to profess oneself to be

professionale *adj* professional; occupational (*disease*); trade (*school*)

professióne *f* profession; **fare il ladro di professione** to be a confirmed thief; **fare qlco di professione** to pursue the trade of s.th, e.g., **fa il falegname di professione** he pursues the trade of carpenter

professioni·sta *mf* (*-sti -ste*) professional

professorale *adj* professorial; pedantic

profes·sóre -soréssa *mf* professor; teacher; **professore d'orchestra** orchestra member

profè·ta *m* (*-ti*) prophet

profetéssa *f* prophetess

profèti·co -ca *adj* (*-ci -che*) prophetic

profetizzare [ddzz] *tr* to prophesy

profezìa *f* prophecy

profferire §176 (*pp* **proffèrto;** *pret* **profferìi & proffèrsi**) *tr* to offer; (lit) to utter

profi·cuo -cua *adj* profitable

profilare *tr* to outline; to sketch; to hem; (mach) to shape ‖ *ref* to be outlined; to loom

profilas·si *f* (*-si*) prophylaxis

profila·to -ta *adj* outlined; hemmed; (mach) shaped ‖ *m* structural piece

profilàtti·co -ca *adj* (*-ci -che*) prophylactic

profilatura *f* hemming; (mach) shaping

profilo *m* profile; sketch; outline

profittare *intr* to profit, benefit

profitta·tóre -trice *mf* profiteer

profittévole *adj* (lit) profitable

profitto *m* profit; progress; **profitti e perdite** profit and loss

proflù·vio *m* (*-vi*) overflow; (pathol) discharge

profondare (profóndo) *tr & intr* to sink

profóndere §178 *tr* to squander, lavish ‖ *ref* to be profuse

profondi·tà *f* (*-tà*) depth

profón·do -da *adj* deep; profound; searching (*e.g., investigation*) ‖ *m* bottom; depth; subconscious

pro fórma *adj invar* pro forma; perfunctory ‖ *m* (coll) formality

pròfu·go -ga (*-ghi -ghe*) *adj* fugitive ‖ *mf* refugee

profumare *tr* to perfume ‖ *intr* to smell

profumataménte *adv* lavishly

profuma·to -ta *adj* perfumed, fragrant

profumerìa *f* perfumery; perfume shop

profumo *m* perfume; bouquet (*of wine*)

profusióne *f* profusion; **a profusione** in profusion

profu·so -sa *adj* profuse

progè·nie *f* (*-nie*) progeny, offspring; (pej) breed

progeni·tóre -trice *mf* ancestor

progettare (progètto) *tr* to plan; to design

progetti·sta *mf* (*-sti -ste*) planner; designer; wild dreamer

progètto *m* project; plan; draft (*of law*); **far progetti** to plan; **progetto di scala reale** (cards) possible straight flush

prògno·si *f* (*-si*) prognosis

program·ma *m* (*-mi*) program; plan; curriculum; cycle (*of washing machine*); (mov) feature; (theat) playbill; **programma politico** platform

programmare *tr* to program; to plan

programma·tóre -trice *mf* programmer

programmazióne *f* programming

progredire §176 *intr* (ESSERE & AVERE) to progress, advance

progredi·to -ta *adj* advanced

progressióne *f* progression

progressi·sta *adj & mf* (*-sti -ste*) progressive

progressi·vo -va *adj* progressive

progrèsso *m* progress; progression, advance; **fare progressi** to progress

proibire §176 *tr* to prohibit; to prevent

proibi·to -ta *adj* forbidden; **è proibito entrare** no admission; **è proibito fumare** no smoking

proibizióne *f* prohibition

proibizionismo *m* prohibition

proiettare (proiètto) *tr* to project; to cast (*a shadow*) ‖ *intr* to project ‖ *ref* to be projected, project

proièttile *m* projectile, missile

proiettóre *m* projector, projection machine; searchlight; (aut) headlight; **proiettore acustico** sonar projector

proiezióne *f* projection; **proiezione rallentata** slow motion

pròle *f invar* offspring, progeny

proletariato *m* proletariat

proletà·rio -ria *adj & mf* (*-ri -rie*) proletarian

proliferare (prolìfero) *intr* to proliferate

prolificare §197 (**prolìfico**) *intr* to proliferate

prolìfi·co -ca *adj* (*-ci -che*) prolific

prolis·so -sa *adj* prolix, long-winded; long (*e.g., beard*)

pròlo·go *m* (*-ghi*) prologue; preface

prolun·ga *f* (*-ghe*) extension

prolungaménto *m* prolongation, extension

prolungare §209 *tr* to prolong, extend ‖ *ref* to extend; to speak at great length

prolunga·to -ta *adj* extended, protracted

prolusióne *f* inaugural lecture

promemò·ria or **pro memò·ria** *m* (**-ria**) reminder

promés·so -sa *adj* promised || *mf* betrothed || *f* promise; promising individual

promèttere *adj* promising

promèttere §198 *tr* to promise; to threaten (*e.g., a storm*) || *intr* to promise; **promettere bene** to be very promising || *ref*—**promettersi a Dio** to make a vow to God; **promettersi in matrimonio** to become engaged

prominènte *adj* prominent

promì·scuo -scua *adj* promiscuous; coeducational; mixed (*marriage; races*); (*gram*) epicene

promuntò·rio *m* (**-ri**) promontory, cliff

promo·tóre -trice *adj* promoting || *mf* promoter

promozióne *f* promotion

promulgare §209 *tr* to promulgate

promuòvere §202 *tr* to promote; to pass (*a student*); to initiate (*legal suit*); to induce (*e.g., perspiration*)

pronipóte *mf* great-grandchild || *m* great-grandson; grandnephew; **pronipoti** descendants || *f* great-granddaughter; grandniece

prò·no -na *adj* (*lit*) prone

pronóme *m* pronoun

pronominale *adj* (*gram*) pronominal; (*gram*) reflexive (*verb*)

pronosticare §197 (**pronòstico**) *tr* to prognosticate, forecast

pronòsti·co *m* (**-ci**) prognostication, forecast; sign, omen

prontézza *f* readiness; quickness, promptness

prón·to -ta *adj* ready; first (*aid*); quick; prompt; ready (*cash*) || **pronto** *interj* (*telp*) hello!

prontuà·rio *m* (**-ri**) handbook

pronùn·cia *f* (**-cie**) or **pronunzia** *f* pronunciaton; (*law*) judgment

pronunziare §287 *tr* to pronounce; to utter; to pass (*sentence*); to make (*a speech*) || *ref* to pass judgment

pronunzia·to -ta *adj* pronounced, marked; prominent (*nose, chin, beard*) || *m* (*law*) sentence

propaganda *f* propaganda; advertisement; advertising

propagandì·sta *mf* (**-sti -ste**) propagandist; advertiser; agent; detail man

propagandìsti·co -ca *adj* (**-ci -che**) advertising

propagare §209 *tr* to propagate; to spread || *ref* to spread

propàggine *f* offspring; (*geog*) spur, counterfort; (*hort*) layer

propalare *tr* (*lit*) to spread, divulge

propellènte *adj* & *m* propellent

propèllere §168 *tr* to propel

propèndere §123 (*pp* **propènso**) *intr* to incline, tend

propensióne *f* propensity, inclination

propèn·so -sa *adj* inclined, bent

propinare *tr* to administer (*e.g., poison*); **propinare qlco a qlcu** to put s.th over on s.o.

propìn·quo -qua *adj* (*lit*) near; (*lit*) related

propiziare §287 *tr* to propitiate, appease

propi·zio -zia *adj* (**-zi -zie**) propitious, favorable

proponiménto *m* intention, plan

propórre §218 *tr* to propose, present; to propound; **proporre come candidato** to nominate || *ref*—**proporsi di** to propose to, resolve to

proporzionare (**proporzióno**) *tr* to proportion, prorate

proporzióne *f* proportion

propòsito *m* purpose; **a proposito** opportune; opportunely; proper; by the way; **a proposito di** on the subject of; **di proposito** deliberately; **fuor di proposito** out of place; **parlare a proposito** to speak to the point

proposizióne *f* proposition; (*gram*) clause; **proposizione subordinata** dependent clause

propósta *f* proposal; **proposta di legge** bill

propriaménte *adv* exactly; properly

proprie·tà *f* (**-tà**) propriety; ownership; property; **la proprietà** property owners; **proprietà immobiliare** real estate; **proprietà letteraria** copyright; **sulla proprietà** on the premises

proprietà·rio -ria *mf* (**-ri -rie**) owner, proprietor

prò·prio -pria (**-pri -prie**) *adj* peculiar, characteristic; proper (*e.g., name*); own, e.g., **il mio proprio libro** my own book || *m* one's own; **i propri** one's folks; **lavorare in proprio** to work for oneself || **proprio** *adv* just, really, exactly; **non . . . proprio** not . . . at all; **proprio adesso** just, just now

propugnare *tr* to advocate; (*lit*) to fight for

propugna·tóre -trice *mf* (*lit*) advocate

propulsare *tr* to propel; (*lit*) to repulse

propulsióne *f* propulsion

propulsóre *m* propeller, motor

pròra *f* prow, bow

proravìa *f*—**a proravia** (*naut*) fore

pròro·ga *f* (**-ghe**) delay, extension

prorogare §209 (**pròrogo**) *tr* to extend; to put off, delay

prorómpere §240 *intr* to overflow; to burst (*into tears*)

prosa *f* prose

prosài·co -ca *adj* (**-ci -che**) prose; prosaic

prosàpia *f* (*lit*) ancestry

prosa·tóre -trice *mf* prose writer

prosciògliere §127 *tr* to free; to exonerate

prosciugare §209 *tr* to drain, reclaim || *ref* to dry up

prosciutto *m* ham; **prosciutto cotto** boiled ham; **prosciutto crudo** prosciutto

proscrìvere §250 *tr* to proscribe, outlaw

prosecuzióne [*s*] *f* prosecution, pursuit

proseguiménto [*s*] *m* prosecution, pursuit

proseguire [*s*] (**proséguo**) *tr* to follow, pursue || *intr* (ESSERE & AVERE) to continue

prosèlito m proselyte
prosodìa f prosody
prosopopèa f conceit
prosperare (pròspero) intr to prosper, thrive
prosperi·tà f (-tà) prosperity ‖ interj gesundheit!
pròspe·ro -ra adj prosperous, thriving; flourishing; successful ‖ m (coll) match
prosperó·so -sa [s] adj flourishing; healthy; buxom
prospettare (prospètto) tr to face, overlook; to outline ‖ intr—**prospettare su** to face ‖ ref to look; to appear; to loom up
prospetti·vo -va adj prospective ‖ f perspective; prospect; view
prospètto m prospect, view; front (of building); diagram; outline; prospectus
prospettóre m prospector
prospiciènte adj facing
prossimamènte adv shortly
prossimi·tà f -tà proximity, nearness; **in prossimità di** near
pròssi·mo -ma adj near, close; next; immediate (cause) ‖ m neighbor, fellow man
pròstata f prostate
prosternare (prostèrno) ref to prostrate oneself
prostituire §176 tr to prostitute
prostituta f prostitute
prostituzióne f prostitution
prostrare (pròstro) ref to prostrate oneself
prostrazióne f prostration
protagoni·sta mf (-sti -ste) protagonist
protèggere §193 tr to protect; to help, defend; to favor, promote
proteìna f protein
protèndere §270 tr & ref to stretch
pròte·si f (-si) (philol) prothesis; (surg) prosthesis
protèsta f protest, protestation
protestante adj & mf protestant; Protestant
protestare (protèsto) tr to protest; to reject (faulty merchandise) ‖ intr & ref to protest
protestatà·rio -ria (-ri -rie) adj protesting ‖ m protester
protèsto m (com) protest
protèt·to -ta adj protected ‖ m protegé ‖ f protegée
protettoràto m protectorate
protet·tóre -trice adj patron ‖ mf protector, guardian ‖ m patron ‖ f patroness
protezióne f protection; patronage
pròto m (typ) foreman
protocòllo adj invar commercial (size) ‖ m protocol; **mettere a protocollo** to register, record
protopla·sma m (-smi) protoplasm
protòtipo m prototype; (fig) epitome
protozòi [dz] mpl protozoa
protrarre §273 tr to protract, extend ‖ ref to continue
protrùdere §190 intr to protrude (said, e.g., of a broken bone)

protuberante adj protruding, bulging
pròva f test, examination; proof; try, attempt; probationary period (of employment); trial; token (e.g., of friendship); (sports) competition, event; (theat) rehearsal; **a prova di bomba** bombproof; foolproof; **a tutta prova** thoroughly tested; **in prova** on approval; **mettere a dura prova** to test (e.g., one's patience); **mettere alla prova** to test (e.g., one's ability); **mettere in prova** to fit (a suit); **prova del fuoco** trial by fire; **prova dell'acido** acid test; **prova generale** dress rehearsal; **prova indiziaria** circumstantial evidence
provare (pròvo) tr to test; to try; to try on; to try out; to taste; to prove; to feel (e.g., anger); (theat) to rehearse ‖ intr to try ‖ ref to compete
proveniènza f origin
provenire §282 intr (ESSERE) to stem, originate
provènto m income, proceeds
provenzale adj & mf Provençal
provèr·bio m (-bi) proverb; byword
provétta f test tube
provèt·to -ta adj (lit) masterful
provìn·cia f (-ce) province; **in provincia** outside of the big cities
provinciale adj provincial ‖ mf smalltown person ‖ f provincial highway, state highway
provino m gauge; (mov) screen test
provocare §197 (pròvoco) tr to provoke; to bring about, cause; to arouse; to entice
provoca·tóre -trice adj provoking ‖ mf provoker
provocatò·rio -ria (-ri -rie) provoking, provocative
provocazióne f provocation; challenge
provvedére §221 tr to prepare; to supply; **provvedere che** to see to it that ‖ intr to take the necessary steps; **provvedere a** to provide for; **provvedere a + inf** to provide for + ger; **provvedere nei confronti di** to take steps against
provvedimènto m measure, step
provvedi·tóre -trice mf provider ‖ m superintendent; **provveditore agli studi** superintendent of schools
provvedu·to -ta adj supplied; careful
provvidènza f providence; windfall; **provvidenze** provisions, help
provvidenziale adj providential
pròvvi·do -da adj (lit) provident
provvigióne f (com) commission
provvisò·rio -ria adj (-ri -rie) provisional, temporary
provvi·sto -sta adj supplied ‖ f supply, provision; **fare le provviste** to shop
prozìa f grandaunt
prozì·o m (-i) granduncle
prua f bow, prow
prudènte adj prudent, cautious
prudènza f prudence, discretion
prùdere §222 intr to itch; **sentirsi prudere le mani** to feel like giving s.o. a beating
prugna f plum; **prugna secca** prune

prugno *m* plum tree
prùgnola *f* sloe
prùgnolo *m* sloe, blackthorn
pruno *m* thorn
prurito *m* itch
pseudònimo *m* pseudonym; alias; pen name
psicanàlisi *f* psychoanalysis
psicanali•sta *mf* (-sti -ste) psychoanalyst
psicanalizzare [ddzz] *tr* to psychoanalyze
psiche *f* psyche; cheval glass
psichia•tra *mf* (-tri -tre) psychiatrist
psichiatrìa *f* psychiatry
psìchi•co -ca *adj* (-ci -che) psychic
psicologìa *f* psychology
psicològi•co -ca *adj* (-ci -che) psychological
psicòlo•go -ga *mf* (-gi -ghe) psychologist
psicopàti•co -ca *adj* (-ci -che) psychopathic || *mf* psychopath
psicò•si *f* (-si) psychosis
psicosomàti•co -ca *adj* (-ci -che) psychosomatic
psicotècni•co -ca *adj* (-ci -che) psychotechnical || *m* industrial psychologist || *f* industrial psychology
psicòti•co -ca *adj* (-ci -che) psychotic
pubblicare §197 (pùbblico) *tr* to publish
pubblicazióne *f* publication; **pubblicazioni di matrimonio** marriage banns
pubblicismo *m* communications; advertising
pubblici•sta *mf* (-sti -ste) free-lance newspaper writer; publicist
pubblicìsti•co -ca *adj* (-ci -che) advertising; political-science || *f* newspaper business
pubblicità *f* publicity; advertising
pubblicità•rio -ria (-ri -rie) *adj* advertising || *mf* advertising agent
publicizzare [ddzz] *tr* to publicize
publicizzazióne [ddzz] *f* publicizing
pùbbli•co -ca *adj & m* (-ci -che) public; **mettere in pubblico** to publish
pubertà *f* puberty
pudibón•do -da *adj* (lit) modest, bashful; (lit) prudish
pudicìzia *f* modesty; prudery
pudì•co -ca *adj* (-chi -che) modest, chaste; bashful; (lit) reserved
pudóre *m* modesty; decency; shame
puericoltóre *m* pediatrician
puerile *adj* puerile, childish
puerili•tà *f* (-tà) puerility, childishness
puèrpera *f* lying-in patient
pugilato *m* boxing
pugilatóre *m* boxer, prize fighter
pùgile *m* boxer, prize fighter
pugili•sta *m* (-sti) boxer, prize fighter
pù•glia *f* (-glie) stake (in gambling)
pugnace *adj* (lit) pugnacious
pugnalare *tr* to stab
pugnalata *f* stab
pugnale *m* dagger
pugno *m* fist; fistful; punch; **avere in pugno** to have in one's grasp; **di proprio pugno** in one's own hand; **fare a pugni** to fight; to clash

pula *f* chaff
pulce *f* flea; **mettere una pulce nell'orecchio di** to put a bug in the ear of; **pulce tropicale** jigger, chigger
pulcèlla *f* maid, maiden
pulcinèlla *f*—**pulcinella di mare** (orn) Atlantic puffin || **Pulcinel•la** *m* (-la) buffoon; Punch, Punchinello
pulcino *m* chick
pulédra *f* filly
pulédro *m* colt, foal
pulég•gia *f* (-ge) pulley
pulire §176 *tr* to clean; to shine (shoes); to wipe; to polish
puliscipiè•di *m* (-di) doormat
pulì•to -ta *adj* clean; polished; clear (conscience) || *f*—**dare una pulita a** to give a lick and a promise to
pulitura *f* cleaning; **pulitura a secco** dry cleaning
pulizìa *f* cleaning; cleanliness; **fare le pulizie** to clean house
pullulare (pùllulo) *intr* to swarm
pùlpito *m* pulpit
pulsante *m* knob; push button
pulsare *intr* to throb; to pulsate
pulvìscolo *m* fine dust; haze
pulzèlla *f* var of pulcella
pu•ma *m* (-ma) cougar
pungènte *adj* pungent; bitter (cold)
pùngere §183 *tr* to sting; (fig) to goad
pungiglióne *m* stinger (of bee); (fig) sting; (obs) goad
pungitòpo *m* (bot) butcher's broom
pungolare (pùngolo) *tr* to goad, prod
punire §176 *tr* to punish
punizióne *f* punishment; penalty
punta *f* point, tip; prong; brad; bit, trifle; needle (of phonograph); avantgarde; point (of dog); (lit) wound; (fig) peak; (mach) broach; **averne fino alla punta dei capelli** to be sick and tired; **la punta a** to sharpen; **in punta di penna** elegantly; **prendere di punta** to treat roughly; to face up to; **punta delle dita** fingertip; **punta di piedi** tiptoe
puntale *m* tip, ferrule
puntaménto *m* aiming
puntare *tr* to aim; to aim at; to point; to thrust; to dot; to bet; to stare at; to fix (one's eyes); **puntare i piedi** to stiffen up; (fig) to balk || *intr* to aim; to point; to pin; to bet; **puntare su** to count on; **puntare verso** to march on; to sail toward
puntaspil•li *m* (-li) pincushion
puntata *f* jab (with weapon); excursion; bet; issue, number (of magazine); installment (of story); (mil) incursion
punteggiare §290 (puntéggio) *tr* to dot; (gram) to punctuate
puntéggiatura *f* dotting; punctuation
puntég•gio *m* (-gi) score
puntellare (puntèllo) *tr* to prop, brace; to support
puntèllo *m* prop, brace; support
punterìa *f* aiming; aiming gear; (aut) tappet
punteruòlo *m* punch; awl
puntì•glio *m* (-gli) obstinacy, stubbornness; punctilio

puntiglió·so -sa [s] *adj* punctilious, scrupulous; obstinate, stubborn

puntina *f* brad; needle; thumbtack

puntino *m* small dot; G-string; **a puntino** to a T

punto *m* point; period; dot; place, spot; extent; stitch; **dare dei punti a** to be superior to; **di punto in bianco** all of a sudden; **di tutto punto** thoroughly; **due punti** colon; **essere a buon punto** to be well advanced; **essere sul punto di** + *inf* to be about to + *inf*; **fare il punto** (fig; naut) to take one's bearings; **in punto** on the dot; **in punto franco** in bond; **in un punto** together; **mettere a punto** to get in working order; (aut) to tune up; **mettere i punti sulle i** to dot one's i's; **punto assistenza** service agency; **punto di partenza** starting point; **punto di vista** viewpoint; **punto esclamativo** exclamation point; **punto e virgola** semicolon; **punto fermo** full stop; **punto interrogativo** question mark; **punto morto** (mach) dead center; **punto stimato** (naut) dead reckoning; **qui sta il punto!** here's the rub!; **vincere ai punti** (boxing) to win by points, win by decision ‖ *adv*—**né punto né poco** not at all; **non . . . punto** not at all

puntóne *m* rafter

puntuale *adj* punctual, prompt

puntuali·tà *f* (**-tà**) punctuality, promptness

puntura *f* sting; stitch (*sharp pain*); (coll) injection; **puntura lombare** spinal anesthesia

punzecchiare §287 (**punzécchio**) *tr* to keep on stinging; to tease, torment

punzecchiatura *f* sting, bite

punzonare (**punzóno**) *tr* to mark or stamp with a punch

punzonatrice *f* punch press

punzóne *m* punch; nailset

pupa *f* doll; (zool) pupa

pupazzetti·sta *mf* (**-sti -ste**) cartoonist

pupazzétto *m* caricature; cartoon; **pupazzetto di carta** paper doll

pupazzo *m* puppet; **pupazzo di stoffa** rag doll

pupil·lo -la *mf* pupil; ward, protégé ‖ *f* pupil (*of eye*); protégée

pupo *m* (coll) baby

purché *conj* provided, providing

pure *adv* too, also; indeed; (lit) only; **pur di** only in order to; **quando pure** even if; **se pure** even if ‖ *conj* though, although; but, yet

pu·rè *m* (**-rè**) purée; **purè di patate** mashed potatoes

purézza *f* purity

pur·ga *f* (**-ghe**) laxative; purification; purge

purgante *adj* purging ‖ *m* laxative

purgare §209 *tr* to purge; to purify; to expurgate ‖ *ref* to take a laxative

purgati·vo -va *adj* laxative

purgatò·rio *m* (**-ri**) purgatory

purificare §197 (**puríifico**) *tr* to purify

purismo *m* purism

purità *f* purity

purita·no -na *adj & m* puritan; Puritan

pu·ro -ra *adj* pure; clear; simple, mere

purosàn·gue *adj invar & m* (**-gue**) thoroughbred

purpùre·o -a *adj* (lit) purple

purtròppo *adv* unfortunately

purulèn·to -ta *adj* purulent

pus *m* pus

pusillànime *adj* pusillanimous

pàstola *f* pustule; pimple

puta caso *adv* possibly, maybe

putifè·rio *m* (**-ri**) hubbub

putrefare §173 *intr* (ESSERE) & *ref* to putrefy, rot

putrefazióne *f* putrefaction

putrèlla *f* I beam

pàtri·do -da *adj* putrid ‖ *m* corruption

putta *f* (coll) girl; (lit) prostitute

puttana *f* (vulg) whore

put·to -ta *adj* (archaic) meretricious ‖ *m* figure of a child ‖ *f* see **putta**

puzza *f* var of **puzzo**

puzzare *intr* to stink, smell

puzzo *m* stench, smell, bad odor

pùzzola *f* polecat, skunk

puzzolènte *adj* stinking, smelly

puzzonata *f* (coll) contemptible action; (coll) botch, bungle

puzzóne *m* (coll) skunk (*person*)

Q

Q, q [ku] *m & f* fifteenth letter of the Italian alphabet

qua *adv* here; **da un** (**giorno, mese, anno**) **in qua** for the past (day, month, year); **di qua da** on this side of; **in qua** on this side; here

quàcche·ro -ra or **quàcque·ro -ra** *adj & mf* Quaker; **alla quacquera** in a plain fashion

quadèrno *m* copybook; **quaderno di cassa** cash book

quadràngo·lo -la *adj* quadrangular ‖ *m* quadrangle

quadrante *m* quadrant; dial; face (*of watch*); **quadrante solare** sundial

quadrare *tr* to square ‖ *intr* (ESSERE & AVERE) to square; **quadrare a** to be satisfactory to; **quadrare con** to fit

quadra·to -ta *adj* square; sound (*mind*) ‖ *m* square; diaper; (boxing) ring; (nav) wardroom

quadratura *f* squaring; concreteness; (astr) quadrature

quadrèl·lo *m* (**-li**) square ruler; square tile ‖ *m* (**-la** *fpl*) (lit) bolt, arrow

quadreria *f* picture gallery; collection

quadretta·to -ta *adj* checkered

quadrétto *m* small painting; checker, small square; (fig) picture

quadriennale *adj* four-year ‖ *f* quadrennial

quadrifò·glio *m* (-**gli**) four-leaf clover; **a quadrifoglio** cloverleaf

quadrì·glia *m* (-**gli**) (cards) quadrille

quadrimensionale *adj* four-dimensional

quadrimestrale *adj* four-month

quadrimèstre *m* four-month period; four-month payment

quadrimotóre *adj* four-motor ‖ *m* four-motor plane

quadrireattóre *m* four-motor jet

qua·dro -dra *adj* square; (fig) solid ‖ *m* picture; painting; sight; square; table, summary; panel, switchboard; (theat) scene; **quadri** bulletin board; (mil) cadres; (cards) diamonds

quadrùmane *adj* quadrumanous ‖ *m* monkey; ape

quadruplicare §197 (**quadrùplico**) *tr & ref* to quadruple

quadrùplice *adj* quadruple; **in quadruplice copia** in four copies

quàdru·plo -pla *adj & m* quadruple

quaggiù *adv* down here

quàglia *f* quail

quagliare §280 *tr, intr* (ESSERE) *& ref* var of **cagliare**

qualche *adj invar* some, e.g., **qualche giorno** some day; some, e.g., **qualche elefante è bianco** some elephants are white; any, e.g., **ha qualche libro da vendere?** do you have any books to sell?; a few, e.g., **qualche giorno** a few days

qualchedu·no -na *pron indef* var of **qualcuno**

qualcòsa [s] *m* (fig) something; (fig) somebody ‖ *pron indef* something; anything; **qualcosa di buono** something good

qualcu·no -na *pron indef* some; any; somebody; anybody ‖ *m* somebody

quale *adj* which, what; what a, e.g., **quale onore!** what an honor!; as, e.g., **il pane, quale vedi, è fresco** the bread, as you can see, is fresh; **quale che sia** regardless of it ‖ *pron* which; what; (archaic) who; **il quale** who, whom; **per la quale** o.k.; well-bred; commendable; terrific; **quale . . . quale** some . . . some ‖ *prep* as, e.g., **quale ministro** as a minister

qualìfi·ca *f* (-**che**) rating; position; quality, qualification

qualificare §197 (**qualìfico**) *tr* to qualify; to classify; to rate, give a rating to ‖ *ref* to introduce oneself; to qualify

qualifica·to -ta *adj* aggravated (*assault*); qualified (*personnel*); specialized (*worker*)

qualì·tà *f* (-**tà**) quality; capacity

qualóra *conj* if; (lit) whenever

qualsìasi [s] *adj invar* any; whatever; ordinary

qualunque *adj invar* any; whatever; common, ordinary; **in qualunque modo** anyway, anyhow; **qualunque altro** anybody else; **qualunque cosa** anything; no matter what

qualvòlta *conj* (lit) whenever

quando *m* when ‖ *adv* when; **di quando in quando** from time to time; **quando . . . quando** sometimes . . . sometimes ‖ *conj* when; whenever; while; **da quando** since

quantìsti·co -ca *adj* (-**ci** -**che**) quantum

quantì·tà *f* (-**tà**) quantity; number

quantitativo *m* quantity

quan·to -ta *adj* how much; as much; how great; how great a; what a; what; **quan·ti -te** how many; as many ‖ *m* quantum ‖ *pron* how much; as much; how great; how long; that which; what; whatever; **a quanto si dice** according to what is rumored; **da quanto** from what; for how long; **fra quanto** how soon; **per quanto io ne sappia** as far as I know; **quanto più** (or **meno**) **. . . tanto più** (or **meno**) the more (or the less) . . . the more (or the less); **quan·ti -te** how many; all those; as many as; **quanti ne abbiamo?** what's the date? ‖ *quanto adv* how much; as much as; **in quanto** as; **in quanto che** inasmuch as; **per quanto** although; no matter; nevertheless; **quanto a** as to, as for; **quanto mai** as never before; **quanto meno** at least; **quanto prima** as soon as possible

quantunque *conj* although, though

quaranta *adj, m & pron* forty; **gli anni quaranta** the forties; **i quaranta** the forties (*in age*)

quarantèna *f* quarantine

quarantènne *adj* forty-year-old ‖ *mf* forty-year-old person

quarantèsi·mo -ma *adj, m & pron* fortieth

quarantina *f* about forty; **essere sulla quarantina** to be about forty years old

quarantòtto *adj* forty-eight ‖ *m* forty-eight; (coll) hubbub, uproar

quarésima *f* Lent

quartabuòno *m* triangle (*in drafting*); **tagliare a quartabuono** to miter

quartétto *m* quartet; **quartetto d'archi** string quartet

quartière *m* quarter, district; (mil) quarters; (coll) apartment; **quartier generale** headquarters; **senza quartiere** (*fight*) without quarter

quar·to -ta *adj & pron* fourth ‖ *m* fourth; quarter; quarter of a kilo; quarter of a liter; (naut) watch; **l'una e un quarto** a quarter after one; **l'una meno un quarto** a quarter to one

quarzo *m* quartz

quasi *adv* almost, nearly; **quasi che** as if; **quasi mai** hardly ever; **senza quasi** without any ifs and buts

quassù *adv* up here

quat·to -ta *adj* crouching; squatting; **quatto quatto** stealthy, silent; **starsene quatto quatto** to not make a sound

quattordicènne *adj* fourteen-year-old ‖ *mf* fourteen-year-old person

quattordicèsi·mo -ma *adj, m & pron* fourteenth

quattórdici *adj & pron* fourteen; **le**

quattordici two P.M. ‖ *m* fourteen; fourteenth (*in dates*)

quattrino *m* penny; (fig) bit; **quattrini** money

quattro *adj* four; a few, e.g., **quattro gatti** a few people; **a quattro mani** (mus) for four hands ‖ *pron* four; **dirne quattro a** to upbraid; **farsi in quattro** to go all out; **in quattro e quattr'otto** in a few minutes; **le quattro** four o'clock ‖ *m* four; fourth (*in dates*); racing shell with four oarsmen

quattrocènto *adj*, *m & pron* four hundred ‖ **il Quattrocento** the fifteenth century

quattromila *adj*, *m & pron* four thousand

quégli §7 *adj* ‖ §8 *pron*

quéi §7 *adj*

quél §7 *adj* ‖ §8 *pron*

quéll' §7 *adj*

quél·lo -la §7 *adj* ‖ §8 *pron*—**per quello che so io as** far as I know

quèr·cia *f* (**-ce**) oak tree

querci·no -na *adj* oaken

querèla *f* complaint

querelante *adj* complaining ‖ *mf* plaintiff

querelare (**querèlo**) *tr* to sue ‖ *ref* (law) to sue; (lit) to complain

querela·to -ta *adj* accused ‖ *mf* defendant

quèru·lo -la *adj* (lit) plaintive

quesito *m* question; problem; (lit) request

quésti §7 *pron*

questionare (**questióno**) *intr* to quarrel

questionà·rio *m* (**-ri**) questionnaire

questióne *f* question; (coll) quarrel; **questione di gabinetto** call for a vote of confidence; **venire a questione** to quarrel

què·sto -sta §7 *adj* ‖ §8 *pron*—**e con questo?** so what?; **per questo** therefore; **questa** this matter; **questo . . . quello** the former . . . the latter

questóre *m* police commissioner; sergeant at arms (*of congress*)

quèstua *f* begging; collection of alms; **andare alla questua** to go begging; **vietata la questua** no begging

questura *f* police department; police headquarters

questurino *m* (coll) policeman

què·to -ta *adj* var of **quieto**

qui *adv* here; **di qui** hence, from here; this way; **di qui a un anno** one year hence; **di qui in avanti** from now on; **qui vicino** nearby

quiescènza *f* quiescence; retirement

quietanza *f* receipt

quietanzare *tr* to receipt

quietare (**quièto**) *tr* to quiet, calm; to satisfy (*e.g., thirst*) ‖ *ref* to quiet down

quiète *f* quiet, calmness

quiè·to -ta *adj* quiet, calm; still; **stia quieto!** don't worry! ‖ *m* quiet life

quindi *adv* then; therefore; (archaic) thence, from there

quindicènne *adj* fifteen-year-old ‖ *mf* fifteen-year-old person

quindicèsi·mo -ma *adj*, *m & pron* fifteenth

quindici *adj & pron* fifteen; **le quindici** three P.M. ‖ *m* fifteen; fifteenth (*in dates*)

quindicina *f* about fifteen; two weeks, fortnight; semimonthly pay

quindicinale *adj* fortnightly

quinquennale *adj* five-year

quinta *f* (theat) wing; (mus) fifth; **dietro le quinte** behind the scenes

quintale *m* quintal (*100 kilos*)

quintèrno *m* signature of five sheets; (bb) quire

quintessènza *f* quintessence

quintétto *m* quintet

quin·to -ta *adj*, *m & pron* fifth ‖ *f* see **quinta**

quisquilia *f* trifle

quivi *adv* (lit) over there; (lit) then

quòrum *m* quorum

quòta *f* quota; share; altitude; elevation; level (*of stock market*); market average; odds (*in betting*); subscription (*to club*); **quota zero** (fig) point of departure

quotare (**quòto**) *tr* to quote (*a price*); to value, esteem ‖ *ref* to sign up for, e.g., **si quotò duemila lire** he signed up for two thousand lire

quotazióne *f* quotation

quotidia·no -na *adj & m* daily

quoziènte *m* quotient; (sports) percentage; **quoziente d'intelligenza** I.Q.

R

R, r ['erre] *m & f* sixteenth letter of the Italian alphabet

rabàrbaro *m* rhubarb

rabberciare §128 (**rabbèrcio**) *tr* (coll) to patch up

ràbbia *f* rage, anger; rabies

rabbino *m* rabbi

rabbió·so -sa [s] *adj* furious; rabid

rabbonire §176 *tr* to pacify ‖ *ref* to calm down

rabbrividire §176 *intr* (ESSERE) to shiver, shudder

rabbuffare *tr* to rebuke; to dishevel

rabbuffo *m* rebuke; **fare un rabbuffo a** to rebuke

rabbuiare §287 *ref* to darken, turn dark

rabdomante *m* dowser, diviner

rabé·sco *m* (**-schi**) arabesque; scrawl, scribble

ràbi·do -da *adj* rabid

raccapezzare (**raccapézzo**) *tr* to put together; to gather (*news*); to find (*one's way*); to make out (*what is* *meant*) ‖ *ref*—**non raccapezzarsi** to not be able to get one's bearings

raccapricciante *adj* bloodcurdling

raccaprìc·cio *m* (-ci) horror

raccartocciare §128 (raccartòccio) *tr* & *ref* to shrivel

raccattare *tr* to pick up; to gather

racchétta *f* racket; **racchetta da neve** snowshoe; **racchetta da sci** ski pole

ràc·chio -chia *adj* (-chi -chie) (coll) ugly, homely

racchiùdere §125 *tr* to contain, hold

raccògliere §127 *tr* to pick up; to gather; to collect (*e.g., stamps*); to take up (*the gauntlet*); to receive; to reap; to furl (*sail*); to draw in (*a net*); to fold (*the wings*); to shelter (*e.g., foundlings*); **raccogliere i passi** to stop walking ‖ *ref* to gather; to concentrate

raccoglimento *m* concentration; meditation

raccogli·tóre -trice *mf* collector, compiler ‖ *m* folder

raccòl·to -ta *adj* crouched; collected; engrossed; snug, intimate ‖ *m* harvest ‖ *f* harvest; collection; **chiamare a raccolta** to rally

raccomandàbile *adj* recommendable; **poco raccomandabile** unreliable

raccomandare *tr* to recommend; to secure (*e.g., a boat*); to register (*mail*); to exhort ‖ *ref* to recommend oneself; to entreat; **mi raccomando** please; **raccomandarsi a** to beg, implore; **raccomandarsi alle gambe** to take to one's heels

raccomanda·to -ta *adj* recommended; registered ‖ *m* protégé ‖ *f* protégée; registered letter

raccomandazióne *f* recommendation; registration (*of mail*); exhortation

raccomodare (raccòmodo) *tr* to fix; to mend

racconciare §128 (raccóncio) *tr* to fix; to mend ‖ *ref* to clear up (*said of the weather*); to tidy oneself up

raccontare (raccónto) *tr* to tell; **raccontarla bene** to be good at telling lies

raccónto *m* tale; story; narrative

raccorciaménto *m* shortening

raccorciare §128 (raccòrcio) *tr* to shorten

raccordare (raccòrdo) *tr* to link, connect

raccòrdo *m* link, connection; **raccordo a circolazione rotatoria** traffic circle; **raccordo anulare** (rr) belt line; **raccordo ferroviario** junction; spur; siding; **raccordo stradale** connecting road

raccostare (raccòsto) *tr* & *ref* to draw near

raccozzare (raccòzzo) *tr* to scrape together

ràchide *m* & *f* backbone; midrib (*of leaf*); shaft (*of feather*)

rachìti·co -ca *adj* (-ci -che) stunted; weak; (pathol) rickety

rachitismo *m* rickets

racimolare (racìmolo) *tr* to glean; to scrape together

rada *f* roadstead; cove

ràdar *m* radar

addobbare (raddòbbo) *tr* (naut) to refit

raddolcire §176 *tr* & *ref* to sweeten; to mellow

raddoppiare §287 (raddóppio) *tr, intr* (ESSERE) to double, redouble

raddrizzare *tr* to straighten; (elec) to rectify ‖ *ref* to straighten up

raddrizzatóre *m* (elec) rectifier

ràdere §223 *tr* to shave; to raze; to graze, skim ‖ *ref* to shave

radézza *f* rarity, rareness; thinness; sparsity (*of vegetation*); space, distance (*e.g., between trees*)

radiante *adj* radiating

radiare §287 *tr* to strike off; to expel; to condemn (*a ship*); **radiare dall'albo degli avvocati** to disbar

radiatóre *m* radiator

radiazióne *f* radiation; expulsion

ràdi·ca *f* (-che) brier; (coll) root

radicale *adj* & *mf* radical ‖ *m* & *f* (philol) radical, root ‖ *m* (chem, math) radical

radicare §197 (ràdico) *tr* & *intr* to root ‖ *ref* to take root

radice *f* root; base or foot (*e.g., of a mountain or tower*); **mettere radice** to take root; **svellere dalle radici** to pull up by the roots; to eradicate

rà·dio *adj invar* radio ‖ *m* (-di) (anat) radius; (chem) radium ‖ *f* (-dio) radio; **radio fante** (mil) grapevine

radioabbonato *m* (rad) subscriber (*to radio broadcasting*)

radioama·tóre -trice *mf* radio fan; radio ham

radioannunciatóre *m* radio announcer

radioascolta·tóre -trice *mf* radio listener

radioattì·vo -va *adj* radioactive

radiobùssola *f* radio compass

radiocanale *m* radio channel

radiocomanda·to -ta *adj* radio-controlled

radiocròna·ca *f* (-che) newscast

radiocroni·sta *mf* (-sti -ste) newscaster

radiodiffóndere §178 *tr* to broadcast

radiodiffusióne *f* broadcasting

radiofaro *m* radio beacon

radiofòni·co -ca *adj* (-ci -che) radio

radiofonògrafo *m* radiophonograph

radiofò·to *f* (-to) radiophoto

radiofrequènza *f* radiofrequency

radiologìa *f* radiology

radiomontatóre *m* radio assembler

radioónda *f* radio wave; **radioonde** airwaves

radioricevènte *adj* radio ‖ *f* radio set; radio station

radioriparatóre *m* radio repairman

radiosegnale *m* radio signal

radiosentièro *m* range of a radio beacon

radió·so -sa [s] *adj* radiant

radiosorgènte *f* quasar

radiostazióne *f* radio station

radiostélla *f* quasar

radiotas·sì *m* (-sì) radio-dispatched taxi

radiotelescò·pio *m* (-pi) radiotelescope

radiotrasméttere §198 *tr* & *intr* to broadcast, radio

radiotrasmissióne *f* broadcast

radiotrasmittènte adj broadcasting || f broadcasting station

ra·do -da adj rare; thin; sheer; sparse, scattered; **di rado** seldom, rarely

radunare tr & ref to assemble, gather

radunata f gathering; (mil) assembly; **radunata sediziosa** unlawful assembly

raduno m assembly, gathering

radura f clearing, glade

ràfano m (bot) radish

raffazzonare (raffazzóno) tr to mend, patch up

raffazzonatura f patchwork, hodgepodge

rafférma f confirmation; stay (in office); return to office; (mil) reenlistment

raffermare (rafférmo) tr to reaffirm; to secure; (coll) to reconfirm; to reappoint, reelect; to return (e.g., a mayor) to office || intr (ESSERE) & ref to reenlist; (coll) to harden

ràffer·mo -ma adj stale (bread) || f see **rafferma**

ràffi·ca f (-che) gust; blast; burst (e.g., of machine gun); **a raffiche** gusty

raffigurare tr to represent; to symbolize

raffinare tr to refine; to polish || intr (ESSERE) to become refined

raffinatézza f refinement, polish

raffinatura f refinement (of oil)

raffinazióne f refining

raffineria f refinery

ràf·fio m (-fi) hook; grappling iron

rafforzare (raffórzo) tr to strengthen

raffreddaménto m cooling

raffreddare (raffréddo) tr to make cold; to cool; **raffreddare gli spiriti di qlcu** to dampen s.o.'s enthusiasm || intr (ESSERE) & ref to get cold; to cool

raffreddóre m cold

raffrontare (raffrónto) tr to compare; (law) to bring face to face

raffrónto m comparison; confrontation

ràfia f raffia

raganèlla f rattle; (zool) tree frog

ragazza f girl; spinster; (coll) girl friend; **ragazza copertina** cover girl; **ragazza squillo** call girl

ragazzata f boyish prank

ragaz·zo -za mf youth, young person || m boy; (coll) boyfriend || f see **ragazza**

raggelare (raggèlo) intr (ESSERE) to freeze

raggiante adj radiant; beaming

raggiare §290 tr & intr to radiate

raggièra f rayed halo; **a raggiera** radially

ràg·gio m (-gi) ray; beam; spoke; (geom) radius; **raggio d'azione** radius, range of action; **raggio di sole** sunbeam

raggiornare (raggiórno) tr (coll) to bring up to date || intr (ESSERE) to dawn || impers (ESSERE)—**raggiorna** it is dawning

raggirare tr to trick, swindle || ref to roam, wander; **raggirarsi su** to turn on (e.g., a certain subject)

raggiro m trickery, swindle

raggiungere §183 tr to reach; to catch up with, rejoin

raggiungìbile adj attainable

raggomitolare (raggomìtolo) tr to roll up || ref to curl up; to cuddle

raggranellare (raggranèllo) tr to gather; to scrape together

raggrinzire §176 tr & ref to crease, wrinkle

raggrumare tr & ref to clot, coagulate

raggruppaménto m grouping; group

raggruppare tr & ref to group, assemble

ragguagliare §280 tr to compare; to balance; to inform in detail; to level

ragguà·glio m (-gli) comparison; detailed report

ragguardévole adj considerable, notable

ragionaménto m reasoning; discussion

ragionare (ragióno) intr to reason; to discuss || impers ref—**si ragiona** it is rumored

ragióne f reason; account; rate; justice; (math) ratio; **a maggior ragione** with all the more reason; **a ragione** within reason; **aver ragione** to be right; **aver ragione di** to get the best of; **dar ragione a qlcu** to admit that s.o. is right; **di santa ragione** hard, a great deal; **farsi ragione** to be resigned; **in ragione di** at the rate of; **ragion per cui** and therefore; **ragione sociale** (com) trade name; **rendere di pubblica ragione** to publicize

ragioneria f accounting; bookkeeping

ragionévole adj reasonable

ragioniè·re -ra mf accountant; bookkeeper

ragliare §280 intr to bray

rà·glio m (-gli) bray

ragnatéla f spider web

ragno m spider

ra·gù m (-gù) meat gravy; stew

ràion m rayon

rallegraménto m congratulation, act of congratulating; **rallegramenti** congratulations

rallegrare (rallégro) tr to cheer up; to rejoice, gladden || ref to cheer up; to rejoice; **rallegrarsi con** to congratulate

rallentare (rallènto) tr, intr & ref to slow down; to lessen

rallentatóre m slow-motion projector; **al rallentatore** slow-motion

ra·màio m (-mài) tinker, coppersmith

ramaiòlo m ladle

ramanzina [dz] f reprimand

ramare tr to copperplate; (agr) to spray with copper sulfate

ramarro m green lizard

ramazza f broom; (mil) cleaning detail; (mil) soldier on cleaning detail

rame m copper; etching

ramerino m (coll) rosemary

ramificare §197 (ramìfico) intr & ref to branch; to branch off; to branch out, ramify

ramin·go -ga adj (-ghi -ghe) wandering

ramino m copper pot; rummy (card game)

rammagliare §280 tr to reknit; to mend a run in (a stocking)

rammaricare §197 (rammàrico) tr to afflict || ref to be sorry, regret; **rammaricarsi di** to be sorry for

rammàri•co *m* (-chi) regret
rammendare (rammèndo) *tr* to darn
rammèndo *m* darn
rammentare (ramménto) *tr* to remember; to remind ‖ *ref*—**rammentarsi di** to remember
rammenta•tóre -trice *mf* prompter
rammollire §176 *tr* & *ref* to soften
rammolli•to -ta *adj* soft; soft-headed ‖ *m* dodo, jellyfish
ramo *m* branch; bough; point (*of antler*); **ramo di pazzia** streak of madness
ramoscèllo *m* twig; **ramoscello d'olivo** olive branch
rampa *f* ramp; flight (*of stairs*); launching platform
rampicante *adj* climbing ‖ *m* (ichth) perch; (orn) climber
rampino *m* hook; tine, prong; pretext
rampógna *f* (lit) reprimand
rampóllo *m* spring (*of water*); scion; shoot (*of a plant*); (joc) offspring
rampóne *m* harpoon; crampon
rana *f* frog
rànci•do -da *adj* rancid
ràn•cio -cia (-ci -ce) *adj* (poet) orange ‖ *m* (mil) mess
rancóre *m* rancor; grudge; **serbar rancore** to bear malice
randa *f* (naut) spanker; (obs) edge
randà•gio -gia *adj* (-gi -gie) wandering; stray
randellare (randèllo) *tr* to cudgel; to bludgeon; to blackjack
randèllo *m* cudgel; bludgeon
ran•go *m* (-ghi) rank; station
rannicchiare §287 *tr* to cause to curl up ‖ *ref* to crouch; to cower; to cuddle up
ranno *m* lye; **buttar via il ranno e il sapone** to waste one's time and effort
rannuvolare (rannùvolo) *tr* & *ref* to cloud; to darken
ranòcchia *f* frog
ranòc•chio *m* (-chi) frog
rantolare (ràntolo) *intr* to wheeze
ràntolo *m* wheezing; death rattle
ranùncolo *m* buttercup
rapa *f* turnip; **valere una rapa** to be not worth a fig
rapace *adj* rapacious ‖ **rapaci** *mpl* birds of prey
rapare *tr* to shave (*s.o.'s head*) ‖ *ref* to shave one's head; to have one's head shaved
rapidi•tà *f* (-tà) rapidity, swiftness
ràpi•do -da *adj* rapid, swift ‖ *m* (rr) express ‖ **rapide** *fpl* rapids
rapiménto *m* rape, abduction; rapture
rapina *f* pillage, plunder; misappropriation; prey; (lit) fury; **rapina a mano armata** armed robbery
rapinare *tr* to rob, plunder; to hold up; **rapinare qlco a qlcu** to rob s.o. of s.th
rapina•tóre -trice *mf* robber, plunderer
rapire §176 *tr* to rape, abduct; to kidnap; to enrapture
rapi•tóre -trice *mf* kidnaper
rappacificare §197 (rappacìfico) *tr* to reconcile ‖ *ref* to become reconciled
rappezzare (rappèzzo) *tr* to patch; to

piece; **rappezzarla** to get out of trouble
rappèzzo *m* patch; patchwork
rapportare (rappòrto) *tr* to report; to transfer (*a design*) ‖ *ref* to refer
rapporta•tóre -trice *mf* reporter ‖ *m* protractor
rappòrto *m* report; relation; relationship; (math) ratio; **chiamare a rapporto** to summon; **chiedere di mettersi a rapporto** to ask for a hearing; **fare rapporto** to report; **in rapporto a** concerning; **mettersi a rapporto** to report; **sotto ogni rapporto** in every respect
rapprèndere §220 *tr* & *ref* to coagulate
rappresàglia [s] *f* reprisal; retaliation
rappresentante *adj* representing; representative ‖ *mf* representative; agent; **rappresentante di commercio** agent
rappresentanza *f* delegation; proxy; agency; representation
rappresentare (rappresènto) *tr* to represent; to play; to portray
rappresentati•vo -va *adj* representative
rappresentazióne *f* representation; description; (theat) performance; **rappresentazione teatrale diurna** matinée; **sacra rappresentazione** (theat) mystery, miracle play
rapsodìa *f* rhapsody
raraménte *adv* seldom, rarely
rarefare §173 *tr* to rarefy ‖ *ref* to become rarefied
rari•tà *f* (-tà) rarity
ra•ro -ra *adj* rare; **di raro** seldom
rasare [s] *tr* to shave; to mow; to trim; to smooth ‖ *ref* to shave
raschiare §287 (ràschio) *tr* to scrape; to scratch ‖ *intr* to clear one's throat
raschiétto *m* scraper; erasing knife; footscraper
rà•schio *m* (-schi) clearing one's throat; hoarseness; frog in the throat
rasentare (rasènto) *tr* to graze; to scrape; to border on; to come close to
rasènte *adv* close; **rasente a** close to ‖ *prep* close to
ra•so -sa [s] *adj* shaved; trimmed; brimful; disreputable (*clothes*); flush ‖ *m* satin ‖ *adv*—**raso terra** down-to-earth; **volare raso terra** to skim the ground; to hedgehop
ra•sóio [s] *m* (-sói) razor; **rasoio a mano libera** straight razor; **rasoio di sicurezza** safety razor
raspa *f* rasp
raspare *tr* to rasp; to irritate; to stamp, paw; (coll) to steal ‖ *intr* to rasp; to scratch (*said of a chicken*); to scrawl
raspo *m* grape stalk; scraper; (vet) mange
rasségna *f* review; exposition
rassegnare (rasségno) *tr* to resign; **rassegnare le dimissioni** to resign ‖ *ref* to resign oneself; to submit
rassegnazióne *f* resignation
rasserenare (rasseréno) *tr* & *ref* to brighten; to cheer up
rassettare (rassètto) *tr* & *ref* to tidy up

rassicurare *tr* to reassure ‖ *ref* to be reassured

rassodare (rassòdo) *tr* to harden; to strengthen ‖ *intr* (ESSERE) & *ref* to harden

rassomigliare §280 (rassomiglio) *tr* to compare ‖ *intr* (ESSERE) (with *dat*) to resemble ‖ *ref* to resemble each other

rastrellaménto *m* roundup; mop-up operation

rastrellare (rastrèllo) *tr* to rake; to round up; to mop up; to drag (*e.g., the bottom*)

rastrellièra *f* rack; crib

rastrèllo *m* rake

rastremare (rastrèmo) *tr* to taper

rata *f* installment; quota; **a rate** on time; by installments

rateale *adj* installment

rateizzare [ddzz] *tr* to prorate; to divide (*a payment*) into installments

ratifi•ca *f* (-che) ratification

ratificare §197 (ratifico) *tr* to ratify

rat•to -ta *adj* (lit) swift ‖ *m* rat; (lit) rape ‖ **ratto** *adv* (lit) swiftly

rattoppare (rattòppo) *tr* to patch, patch up

rattrappire §176 *tr* to cramp; to make numb, benumb ‖ *ref* to become cramped; to become numb

rattristare *tr* & *ref* to sadden

raucèdine *f* hoarseness

ràu•co -ca *adj* (-chi -che) hoarse, raucous

ravanèllo *m* radish

ravizzóne *m* (bot) rape

ravvedére §279 (*fut* ravvedrò & ravvederò; *pp* ravveduto) *ref* to repent; to mend one's ways

ravvedu•to -ta *adj* repentant; reformed

ravviare §119 *tr* to arrange, adjust; to poke (*fire*) ‖ *ref* to tidy up; (lit) to reform

ravvicinaménto *m* approach; reconciliation; rapprochement

ravvicinare *tr* to bring up; to reconcile ‖ *ref* to approach; to become reconciled; **ravvicinarsi a** to approach

ravviluppare *tr* to wrap up; to wind up; to bamboozle ‖ *ref* to become tangled

ravvisare *tr* to recognize

ravvivare *tr* to revive; to enliven; to brighten; to stir (*fire*) ‖ *ref* to revive

ravvòlgere §289 *tr* to wrap up

razioci•nio *m* (-ni) reasoning; reason; common sense

razionale *adj* rational

razionalizzare [ddzz] *tr* (com, math) to rationalize

razionaménto *m* rationing

razionare (razióno) *tr* to ration

razióne *f* ration; portion

razza *f* race; breed; kind; **di razza** purebred; **far razza** to reproduce; **passare a razza** to go to stud

razza [ddzz] *f* (ichth) ray; **razza cornuta** manta ray

razzìa *f* raid; foray; insect powder

razziale *adj* racial

razziare §119 *tr* & *intr* to foray

razzismo *m* racism

razzi•sta *mf* (-sti -ste) racist

razzo [ddzz] *m* rocket; (coll) spoke; (mil) flare

razzolare (ràzzolo) *intr* to scratch (*said of chickens*); (coll) to rummage

re [e] *m* (re) king

re [e] *m* (re) (mus) re

reagènte *m* reagent

reagire §176 *intr* to react

reale *adj* real, actual; royal, regal

realismo *m* realism; royalism

reali•sta *mf* (-sti -ste) realist; royalist

realisti•co -ca *adj* (-ci -che) realistic

realizzare [ddzz] *tr* to carry out; to realize; to build ‖ *ref* to come true

realizzazióne [ddzz] *f* realization; **realizzazione scenica** production

realizzo |ddzz] *m* conversion into cash; profit taking; forced sale

realménte *adv* really, indeed

real•tà *f* (-tà) reality; actuality; **realtà romanzesca** truth stranger than fiction

reato *m* crime

reatti•vo -va *adj* reactive

reattóre *m* reactor; jet plane; jet engine

reazionà•rio -ria (-ri -rie) *adj* & *mf* reactionary

reazióne *f* reaction; (mach) backlash; **a reazione** jet-propelled

réb•bio *m* (-bi) prong

recalcitrante *adj* balky, restive; **essere recalcitrante a** to be opposed to, to resist

recalcitrare (recàlcitro) *intr* to be balky; to kick; (with *dat*) to buck, resist

recapitare (recàpito) *tr* to deliver

recàpito *m* address; delivery; **far recapito in** to be domiciled in; **recapiti** (com) notes

recare §197 (rèco) *tr* to bring; to cause; **recare ad effetto** to carry out; **recare qlco alla memoria di qlcu** to remind s.o. of s.th; **recare qlco a lode di qlcu** to praise s.o. for s.th ‖ *ref* to go, betake oneself

recèdere §123 *intr* (ESSERE & AVERE) to recede

recensióne *f* book review; collation

recensire §176 *tr* to review; to collate

recensóre *m* reviewer

recènte *adj* recent; **di recente** recently

recessióne *f* recession

recèsso *m* recess; subsiding (*of fever*); ebb tide

recidere §145 *tr* to cut off; to chop off

recidiva *f* relapse; second offense

recingere §126 *tr* to enclose, pen in

recinto *m* enclosure; pen, yard; compound; playpen; paddock; **recinto delle grida** floor of the exchange

recipiènte *m* container

reciprocità *f* reciprocity

recipro•co -ca *adj* (-ci -che) reciprocal

reci•so -sa *adj* cut off; abrupt

rècita *f* show, performance

recitare (rècito) *tr* to recite; to portray, play; **recitare la commedia** to put on an act ‖ *intr* to perform, play; **recitare a soggetto** (theat) to improvise

recitazióne *f* recitation; diction; acting

reclamare *tr* to claim, demand || *intr* to complain

récla·me *f* (-me) advertising; advertisement; **fare réclame a** to advertise; to boost

reclami·sta *mf* (-sti -ste) advertising agent; show-off || *m* advertising man

reclamisti·co -ca *adj* (-ci -che) advertising

reclamo *m* complaint; **fare reclamo to** complain

reclinare *tr* to bow || *intr* to recline

reclusióne *f* seclusion; imprisonment

reclu·so -sa *adj* recluse || *mf* recluse; prisoner

reclusò·rio *m* (-ri) penitentiary

rècluta *f* recruit; rookie

reclutaménto *m* recruitment

reclutare (**rècluto**) *tr* to recruit

recòndi·to -ta *adj* concealed; inmost; recondite

recriminare (**recrìmino**) *intr* to recriminate

recuperare (**recùpero**) *tr* see **ricuperare**

redarguire §176 *tr* to berate

redat·tóre -trice *mf* compiler; newspaper editor; **redattore capo** managing editor; **redattore pubblicitario** copywriter; **redattore responsabile** publisher; **redattore viaggiante** correspondent

redazionale *adj* editorial, editor's (*e.g.*, *policy*)

redazióne *f* writing; draft; version; (journ) city room

redazza *f* mop; (naut) swab

redditi·zio -zia *adj* (-zi -zie) lucrative

rèddito *m* income, revenue; yield; **reddito nazionale** gross national product

redèn·to -ta *adj* redeemed, set free

reden·tóre -trice *mf* redeemer || **Redentore** *m*—**il Redentore** the Redeemer

redenzióne *f* redemption

redìgere §224 *tr* to compile; to write up, compose

redìmere §225 *tr* to redeem; to ransom; to save

rèdine *f* rein

redivi·vo -va *adj* come back to life

rèduce *adj* back (*from war*) || *mf* veteran

réfe *m* thread

referèn·dum *m* (-dum) referendum; **referendum postale** mail questionnaire

referènza *f* reference

referenziare (**referènzio**) *tr* to give references to; to write references for || *intr* to have good references

referenzia·to -ta *adj* with good references, *e.g.*, **impiegato referenziato** employee with good references

refèrto *m* report (*of a physician*)

refettò·rio *m* (-ri) refectory

refezióne *f* lunch, light meal; **refezione scolastica** school lunch

refrattà·rio -ria *adj* (-ri -rie) refractory

refrigerante *adj* cooling || *m* refrigerator; (chem) condenser

refrigerare (**refrìgero**) *tr* to refrigerate; to cool || *ref* to cool off

refrigè·rio *m* (-ri) relief, comfort

refurtiva *f* stolen goods

refuso *m* misprint

regalare *tr* to present; to deliver (*a slap*); to throw away (*money*); **è regalato** it's a steal

regale *adj* regal; royal; imposing

regalìa *f* gratuity; bonus

regalità *f* regality, royalty

regalo *m* present, gift

regata *f* regatta

reggènte *adj* & *m* regent

reggènza *f* regency

règgere §226 *tr* to hold, hold up; to stand, withstand; to guide; (gram) to govern; **reggere il sacco a** to connive with; **reggere l'animo di** + *inf* to bear or stand + *ger*, e.g., **non gli regge l'animo di vederla piangere** he cannot stand seeing her cry || *intr* to hold; to be valid; to last, hold out (*said of weather*); **reggere** (with *dat*) to withstand (*e.g.*, *the cold*); **reggere al paragone** to bear comparison || *ref* to stand up; to hold; to be ruled; **reggersi a** to hold on to; to be governed as (*e.g.*, *a republic*); **reggersi a galla** to float

règ·gia *f* (-ge) royal palace

reggical·ze *m* (-ze) girdle

reggilibro *m* book end

reggimentale *adj* regimental

reggiménto *m* regiment

reggipètto *m* brassiere

reggisé·no *m* (-ni & -no) brassiere

regìa *f* monopoly; (mov) direction; (theat) production

regici·da *mf* (-di -de) regicide

regici·dio *m* (-di) regicide

regime *m* regime; diet; flow (*e.g.*, *of river*); government; authoritarian government; (mach) rate; **regime secco** total abstinence

regina *f* queen; **regina claudia** greengage; **regina madre** queen mother

reginétta *f* young queen; queen (*of a beauty contest*)

rè·gio -gia *adj* (-gi -gie) royal || **i regi** the king's soldiers

regióne *f* region

regi·sta *mf* (-sti -ste) coordinator; (theat) producer; (mov) director

registrare *tr* to register, record; to enter; to tally, log; to adjust; to tune up (*a musical instrument*) || *ref* to register

registra·tóre -trice *mf* registrar || *m* recorder; **registratore di cassa** cash register

registrazióne *f* registration; record, entry; adjustment; (aut) tune-up; (telv) videotaping; (telv) video-taping studio; (telv) video-taped program

registro *m* register; registration; classbook; regulator (*of watch*); stop (*of organ*); **cambiar registro** to change one's tune; **dar registro a** to regulate (*a watch*)

regnante *adj* reigning; prevailing || **i regnanti** the rulers

regnare (**régno**) *intr* to reign, rule; to prevail; to take hold (*said of a root*)

régno *m* kingdom; reign

règola *f* rule; regulation; moderation; **a regola d'arte** to a T; **di regola** as a rule; **in regola** in good order; **mettere in regola** to put in order; **regole** menstruation; **secondo le regole** by the book

regolamentare *adj* regulation ‖ *v* (**regolaménto**) *tr* to regulate

regolaménto *m* regulation; settlement; **regolamento edilizio** building code

regolare *adj* regular; steady (*employment*); stock (*material* ‖ *v* (**règolo**) *tr* to regulate; to adjust; to set (*a watch*); to focus (*a lens*); to settle (*an account*) ‖ *ref* to behave; to control oneself

regolari-tà *f* (-**tà**) regularity

regolarizzare [ddzz] *tr* to regularize

regolatézza *f* regularity; moderation

regola-to -ta *adj* regular, orderly

regola-tóre -trice *adj* regulating; see **piano** ‖ *m* ruler; regulator (*of watch*); (mach) governor; **regolatore dell'aria** register; **regolatore di volume** (rad, telv) volume control

regolazióne *f* regulation

regolízia *f* (coll) licorice

règolo *m* ruler; slat; (orn, hist) kinglet; **regolo calcolatore** slide rule

regredire §176 (*pres participle* **regrediènte**; *pp* **regredito** & **regrèsso**) *intr* (ESSERE & AVERE) to retrogress

regrèsso *m* regression; abatement (*of fever*); (com) recourse

reièt•to -ta *adj* rejected ‖ *mf* outcast

reimbarcare §197 *tr* & *ref* to reship; to transship

reimbar•co *m* (-**chi**) reshipment; transshipment

reincarnare *tr* to reincarnate ‖ *ref* to become reincarnated

reincarnazióne *f* reincarnation

reinseriménto *m* integration

reintegrare (**reintegro**) *tr* to restore; to reinstate; to indemnify

reità *f* guilt

reiterare (**reitero**) *tr* to reiterate

relativi-tà *f* (-**tà**) relativity

relati•vo -va *adj* relative

rela•tóre -trice *adj* reporting ‖ *mf* relator (*of proceedings*); presenter (*of a bill*); dissertation supervisor

relazióne *f* relation; relationship; report; **relazione amorosa** affair; **relazioni** relations; connections

re•lè *m* (-**lè**) (elec) relay

relegare §209 (**rèlego**) *tr* to banish; to store away

religióne *f* religion

religió•so -sa [s] *adj* religious ‖ *m* clergyman ‖ *f* nun

reliquia *f* relic

relit•to -ta *adj* residual ‖ *m* shipwreck; air crash; derelict; shoal, bar

remare (**rèmo** & **rémo**) *intr* to row

rema•tóre -trice *mf* rower ‖ *m* oarsman

reminiscènza *f* reminiscence

remissióne *f* submissiveness; remission

remissi•vo -va *adj* submissive

rèmo *m* oar; **remo alla battana** paddle

rèmora *f* hindrance; (lit) delay

remò•to -ta *adj* remote; **passato remoto** (gram) preterit

réna *f* sand

Renània, la the Rhineland

Renata *f* Renée

rèndere §227 *tr* to return, give back; to give (*thanks*); to render (*justice*); to yield; to translate; to make (*known*); **render conto di** to give an account of; **rendere di pubblica ragione** to publicize; **rendere l'anima a Dio** to give up the ghost; **rendere pan per focaccia** to give tit for tat ‖ *intr* to pay, yield ‖ *ref* to make oneself; to betake oneself; to become; (lit) to surrender; **rendersi conto di** to realize

rendicónto *m* account; report; **rendiconti** proceedings

rendiménto *m* rendering; yield; output; (mech) efficiency

rèndita *f* private income; yield; Italian Government bond

rène *m* kidney

renèlla *f* (pathol) gravel

renétta *f* pippin

réni *fpl* loins; **spezzare le reni a** to break the back of

renitènte *adj* opposed ‖ *m*—**renitente alla leva** draft dodger

rènna *f* reindeer; reindeer skin

Rèno *m* Rhine

rè•o -a *adj* guilty; (lit) wicked ‖ *m* guilty person; accused

reòstato *m* (elec) rheostat

reparto *m* department; (mil) unit; **reparto d'assalto** shock troops

repèllere §168 *tr* to repel

repentàglio *m* jeopardy; **mettere a repentaglio** to jeopardize

repènte *adj*—**di repente** suddenly

repenti•no -na *adj* sudden

reperìbile *adj* available

reperiménto *m* finding

reperire §176 *tr* to find

repèrto *m* (archeol) find; (law) evidence; (law) exhibit; (med) report

repertò•rio *m* (-**ri**) repertory; catalogue

rèpli•ca *f* (-**che**) repetition; replica; (law) rebuttal; (theat) repeat performance; **in replica** in reply

replicare §197 (**rèplico**) *tr* to repeat; to reply, answer; (theat) to repeat (*a performance*)

reportàg•gio *m* (-**gi**) news coverage; reporting

repòr•ter *m* (-**ter**) reporter

repressióne *f* repression; constraint

repressi•vo -va *adj* repressive; controlling, checking (*e.g., a disease*)

reprimere §131 *tr* to repress; to hold back (*tears*) ‖ *ref* to restrain oneself

rèpro•bo -ba *adj* & *m* reprobate

repùbbli•ca *f* (-**che**) republic

repubblica•no -na *adj* & *mf* republican

repulisti *m*—**fare repulisti** (coll) to make a clean sweep

repulsióne *f* repulsion

repulsi•vo -va *adj* var of **ripulsivo**

reputare (**rèputo**) *tr* to think, esteem, repute

reputazióne *f* reputation

rèquie *m* & *f* (eccl) requiem ‖ *f* rest, respite

Rèquiem *m* & *f* Requiem

requisire §176 *tr* to requisition, commandeer

requisito *m* requisite, requirement

requisitòria *f* scolding, reproach; (law) summation

requisizióne *f* requisition

résa [s] *f* surrender; rendering (*of an account*); delivery (*of merchandise*); return (*e.g., of newspapers*); yield; **resa a discrezióne** unconditional surrender

rescindere §247 *tr* to rescind

resezióne [s] *f* (surg) resection

residènte [s] *adj* & *mf* resident

residènza [s] *f* residence

residenziale [s] *adj* residential

residua·to -ta [s] *adj* residual

resì·duo -dua [s] *adj* residual ‖ *m* residue; remainder; balance

rèsina *f* resin

resipiscènza [s] *f* (lit) repentance

resistènte [s] *adj* resistant; strong; fast (*color*) ‖ *mf* member of the Resistance

resistènza [s] *f* resistance ‖ **Resistènza** *f* Resistance

resistere [s] §114 *intr* to resist; (with *dat*) to withstand; (with *dat*) to endure; (with *dat*) to resist

rèso [s] *m* rhesus

resocónto [s] *m* report, relation

respingènte *m* (rr) bumper, buffer

respingere §126 *tr* to drive back, beat off; to reject; to fail (*a student*); to vote down

respin·to -ta *adj* rejected ‖ *mf* failure (*pupil*)

respirare *tr* & *intr* to breathe, respire

respiratò·rio -ria *adj* (-ri -rie) respiratory

respirazióne *f* breathing

respiro *m* breath; breathing; respite

responsàbile *adj* responsible; responsabile dì responsible for

responsabili·tà *f* (-tà) responsibility

respònso *m* decision (*of an oracle*); report (*of a physician*); return (*of an election*); (lit) response

rèssa *f* crowd; **far ressa** to crowd

rèsta *f* string (*of garlic or onions*); awn (*e.g., of wheat*); (coll) fishbone; (*for a lance*) (hist) rest

restante *adj* remaining ‖ *m* remainder

restare (**rèsto**) *intr* (ESSERE) to remain; to stay; to be located; (lit) to stop; **non restare a...che** to have no alternative but to, e.g., **non gli resta che andarsene** he has no alternative but to go; **non restare a qlcu qlco da** + *inf* to not have s.th + to + *inf*, e.g., **non gli resta molto da finire** he does not have much to finish; **resta a vedere** it remains to be seen; **restare qlco a qlcu** to have s.th left, e.g., **gli restano tre dollari** he has three dollars left; **restare sul colpo** to die on the spot; **resti comodo** please don't get up!

restaurare (**restàuro**) *tr* to restore, renovate

restaurazióne *f* restoration

restàuro *m* restoration (*of a building*)

restì·o -a (-ì -e) *adj* balky, restive ‖ *m* balkiness

restituire §176 *tr* to give back, return; (lit) to restore ‖ *ref* (lit) to return

restituzióne *f* restitution, return

rèsto *m* remainder; change; balance; **del resto** besides, after all; **resti** remains

restringere §265 (*pp* ristrétto) *tr* to narrow down; to shrink; to take in (*a suit*); to limit (*expenses*); to tighten (*a knot*); to bind (*the bowels*); to restrict ‖ *ref* to contract; to narrow

restrizióne *f* restriction

retàg·gio *m* (-gi) (lit) heritage

retata *f* haul; (fig) roundup

réte *f* net; network; (soccer) goal; **rete a strascico** trawl; **rete da pesca** fishing net; **rete del letto** bedspring; **rete metallica** wire mesh; window screen; **rete per i capelli** hair net; **rete viaria** highway network

reticèlla *f* small net; hair net; mantle (*of gas jet*)

reticènte *adj* secretive, dissembling; evasive, noncommittal

reticènza *f* secretiveness; evasiveness

reticolato *m* grid (*on map*); wire entanglement

reticolo *m* grid

retina *f* small net

rètina *f* (anat) retina

retino *m* small net; (typ) screen

retòri·co -ca (-ci -che) *adj* rhetorical ‖ *m* rhetorician ‖ *f* rhetoric

retràttile *adj* retractile

retribuire §176 *tr* to remunerate

retributi·vo -va *adj* retributive; salary (*e.g., conditions*)

retri·vo -va *adj* backward

rètro *m* back; verso; back of store ‖ *adv* (lit) behind; **retro a** (lit) behind

retroatti·vo -va *adj* retroactive

retrobotté·ga *m* & *f* (-ga *mpl* -ghe *fpl*) back of store

retrocàmera *f* back room

retrocàrica *f*—**a retrocarica** breech-loading

retrocèdere §228 *tr* to demote; (com) to return; (com) to give a discount to ‖ *intr* (ESSERE & AVERE) to retreat

retrocessióne *f* demotion; (sports) assignment to a lower division

retrodatare *tr* to antedate, predate

retrògra·do -da *adj* backward; retrograde

retroguàrdia *f* rearguard

retromàr·cia *f* (-ce) (aut) reverse

retrorazzo |ddzz] *m* retrorocket

retrosapóre *m* aftertaste

retroscè·na *m* (-na) intrigue, maneuver ‖ *f* backstage

retrospetti·vo -va *adj* retrospective

retrotèr·ra *m* (-ra) hinterland; (fig) background

retrotrèno *m* rear end (*of vehicle*); (aut) rear assembly

retroversióne *f* retroversion; retranslation

retrovie *fpl* zone behind the front

retrovisi·vo -va *adj* rear-view, e.g., **specchietto retrovisivo** rear-view mirror

retrovisóre m rear-view mirror

rètta f board and lodging; straight line; **dar retta a** to pay attention to

rettangolare adj rectangular

rettàngolo m rectangle

rettifi·ca f (-che) straightening; rectification; (mach) grinding; (mach) reboring

rettificare §197 (rettìfico) tr to straighten; to rectify; (mach) to grind; (mach) to rebore

rettifica·tóre -trice adj rectifying || mf rectifier (person) || m rectifier (apparatus)

rettifilo m straightaway

rèttile m reptile

rettili·neo -nea adj rectilinear || m straightaway || f straight line

rettitùdine f straightness; uprightness; rectitude

rèt·to -ta adj straight; correct; upright; (geom) right || m right; recto; (anat) rectum || f see **retta**

rettóre m rector; president (of university)

reumàti·co -ca adj (-ci -che) rheumatic

reumatismo m rheumatism

reverèn·do -da adj & m reverend

reverènte adj var of **riverente**

reverènza f var of **riverenza**

revisióne f revision; (mach) overhaul

revisionismo m revisionism

revisóre m inspector; **revisore dei conti** auditor; **revisore di bozze** proofreader

reviviscènza f rebirth

rèvo·ca f (-che) revocation; recall; repeal

revocare §197 (rèvoco) tr to revoke; to recall; to repeal

revòl·ver m (-ver) revolver

revolverata f gun shot

revulsióne f (med) revulsion

ri- pref re-, e.g., **rivivere** to relive; again, e.g., **rifare** to do again; back, e.g., **riandare** to go back

riabbonare (riabbòno) tr to renew the subscription of || ref to renew one's subscription

riabbracciare §128 (riabbràccio) tr to embrace again; to greet again

riabilitare (riabìlito) tr to rehabilitate || ref to reestablish one's good name

riaccèndere §101 tr to rekindle || ref to become rekindled

riaccompagnare tr to take home

riaccostare (riaccòsto) tr to bring near; to bring together || ref to draw near

riacquistare tr to buy back; to recover

riaddormentare (riaddorménto) tr to put back to sleep || ref to go back to sleep

riaffacciare §128 (riaffàccio) tr to present again || ref to reappear

riaffermare (riaffèrmo) tr to reaffirm

riaggravare tr to make worse || ref to get worse again

rialesare (rialèso) tr to rebore

riallacciare §128 (riallàccio) tr to tie again || ref to be tied or connected

rialto m knoll, height; **fare rialto** (coll) to eat better than usual

rialzare tr to lift, raise; to increase || ref to rise

rialzi·sta mf (-sti -ste) bull (in stock market)

rialzo m rise; raise; knoll, height; **giocare al rialzo** to bull the market

riammobiliare §287 tr to refurnish

rianimare (riànimo) tr to revive; to encourage || ref to revive; to recover one's spirits, to rally

riapertura f reopening

riapparire §108 intr (ESSERE) to reappear

riapparizióne f reappearance

riaprire §110 tr & ref to reopen

riarmare tr to rearm; to reinforce; to refit || intr & ref to rearm

riarmo m rearmament

riar·so -sa adj dry, parched

riassaporare (riassapóro) tr to relish again

riassettare (riassètto) tr to tidy up

riassicurare tr to reinsure; to fasten again; to reassure

riassorbire §176 & (riassòrbo) tr to reabsorb

riassùmere §116 tr to hire again; to summarize, sum up

riassunto m précis, abstract; résumé

riassunzióne f rehiring; resumption

riattaccare §197 tr to attach again; (coll) to begin again; (telp) to hang up

riattare tr to repair, fix

riattivare tr to reactivate

riavére §229 tr to get again; to recover; to get back || ref to recover

riavvicinaménto m var of **ravvicinamento**

riavvicinare tr & ref var of **ravvicinare**

ribadire §176 tr to clinch (a nail); to rivet; to drive home (an idea); to back up (a statement)

ribaldo m scoundrel, rogue

ribalta f bid with hinge; trap door; (theat) footlights; (theat) forestage; (fig) limelight; **a ribalta** hinged

ribaltàbile adj collapsable (e.g., seat) || m dump-truck lift; dump truck

ribaltare tr & ref to upset, turn over

ribassare tr & intr (ESSERE) to lower

ribassi·sta mf (-sti -ste) bear (in stock market)

ribasso m fall, decline; discount, rebate; **giocare al ribasso** to be a bear

ribàttere tr to clinch (a nail); to return (a ball); to iron smooth; to belabor (a point) || intr to answer back

ribattezzare [ddzz] (ribattézzo) tr to rebaptize

ribattino m rivet

ribellare (ribèllo) tr to rouse to rebellion || ref to rebel; **ribellarsi a** to rebel against

ribèlle adj rebellious || mf rebel

ribellióne f rebellion

ri·bes m (-bes) currant; gooseberry

ribobinazióne f rewind (of a tape)

riboccare §197 (ribócco) intr (ESSERE) & AVERE) to overflow

ribollire (ribóllo) tr to boil again ||

intr to boil over; to simmer; to ferment

ribrézzo [ddzz] *m* repugnance, disgust

ributtare *tr* to return (*a ball*); to throw up; to reject; to push back ‖ *intr* to sprout; (with *dat*) to disgust, nauseate

ricacciare §128 *tr* to drive back ‖ *intr* to sprout ‖ *ref* to sneak away, disappear

ricadére §121 *intr* (ESSERE) to fall back; to fall down; to relapse; **ricadere su** to devolve upon

ricaduta *f* relapse

ricalcare §197 *tr* to transfer (*a design*); to imitate; **ricalcare le orme di** follow in the footsteps of

rical·co *m* (**-chi**) copy, copying; **a ricalco** multiple-copy

ricamare *tr* to embroider

ricambiare §287 *tr* to return; to repay ‖ *ref* to change clothes

ricam·bio *m* (**-bi**) exchange; spare part; refill; metabolism; **di ricambio** spare (*part*)

ricamo *m* embroidery; needlework; **ricami** (*fig*) embellishments

ricapitolare (**ricapitolo**) *tr* to recapitulate

ricaricare §197 (**ricàrico**) *tr* to reload; to wind (*a watch*); to charge (*a battery*)

ricattare *tr* to blackmail

ricatta·tóre -trice *mf* blackmailer

ricatto *m* blackmail

ricavare *tr* to draw, extract; to obtain, derive

ricavato *m* proceeds; (fig) fruit, yield

ricavo *m* proceeds

ricchézza *f* wealth; **ricchezza mobile** income from personal property; **ricchezze** riches

ric·cio -cia (**-ci -ce**) *adj* curly ‖ *m* curl; shaving; burr; scroll (*of violin*); crook (*of crozier*); (zool) hedgehog; **riccio di mare** (zool) sea urchin

ricciolo *m* curl

ricciolu·to -ta *adj* curly

ricciu·to -ta *adj* curly

ric·co -ca *adj* (**-chi -che**) rich ‖ **i ricchi** the rich

ricér·ca *f* (**-che**) search; research; **ricerca operativa** operations research

ricercare §197 (**ricérco**) *tr* to search for again; to seek; to investigate; (poet) to pluck (*a musical instrument*)

ricercatézza *f* affectation; sophistication

ricerca·to -ta *adj* sought after, wanted; affected; sophisticated

ricetrasmettitóre *m* two-way radio

ricètta *f* prescription; recipe

ricettàcolo *m* receptacle; depository

ricettare (**ricètto**) *tr* to receive (*stolen goods*); to prescribe

ricetta·rio *m* (**-ri**) recipe book; prescription pad

ricetta·tóre -trice *mf* fence, receiver of stolen goods

ricetti·vo -va *adj* receptive

ricètto *m* (poet) refuge

ricévere §141 *tr* to receive; to get; to contain; to withstand

riceviménto *m* reception; receipt

ricevi·tóre -trice *mf* addressee ‖ *m* receiver; collector; registrar of deeds; **ricevitore postale** postmaster

ricevitorìa *f* collection office; **ricevitoria postale** post office

ricevuta *f* receipt; **accusare ricevuta di** to acknowledge receipt of

ricezióne *f* (rad, telv) reception; **accusare ricezione** to acknowledge receipt

richiamare *tr* to call back; to recall; to call (*e.g., attention*); to quote; to chide ‖ *ref* to refer

richiamato *m* soldier recalled to active duty

richiamo *m* call; recall; admonition; cross reference; advertisement

richièdere §124 *tr* to ask again; to demand; to require; to apply for ‖ *ref* to be required

richiè·sto -sta *adj*—**essere richiesto** to be in demand ‖ *f* request; demand; petition, application

richiùdere §125 *tr* & *ref* to shut again

riciclare *tr* to recycle (*e.g., in the chemical industry*)

ricino *m* castor-oil plant

ricognitóre *m* scout; reconnaissance plane; (law) recognition

ricognizióne *f* recognition; (mil) reconnaissance

ricollegare §209 (**ricollégo**) *tr* to connect ‖ *ref* to be connected; to refer

ricolmare (**ricólmo**) *tr* to fill to the brim; to overwhelm

ricominciare §128 *tr* & *intr* (ESSERE) to begin again, resume

ricomparire §108 *intr* (ESSERE) to reappear

ricomparsa *f* reappearance

ricompènsa *f* compensation, recompense; reward; (mil) award

ricompensare (**ricompènso**) *tr* to compensate, recompense; to reward

ricomperare (**ricómpero**) *tr* var of **ricomprare**

ricompórre §218 *tr* to recompose; to plan again ‖ *ref* to regain one's composure

ricomprare (**ricómpro**) *tr* to buy again; to buy back

riconcentrare (**riconcèntro**) *tr* to concentrate again; to gather (*one's thoughts*) ‖ *ref* to be withdrawn

riconciliare §287 (**riconcìlio**) *tr* to reconcile ‖ *ref* to become reconciled

ricondurre §102 *tr* to bring back; to take back ‖ *ref* to go back

riconfermare (**riconférmo**) *tr* to reconfirm

riconfortare (**riconfòrto**) *tr* to comfort

ricongiùngere §183 *tr* & *ref* to reunite

riconoscènte *adj* grateful

riconoscènza *f* gratitude

riconóscere §134 *tr* to recognize; (mil) to reconnoiter

riconosciménto *m* recognition; **in riconoscimento di** in recognition of

riconquistare *tr* to reconquer

riconsegnare (**riconségno**) *tr* to give back, to return

riconsiderare (riconsìdero) *tr* to reconsider

ricontare (ricónto) *tr* to recount, count again

riconversióne *f* reconversion

riconvertire §138 *tr* to reconvert; to recycle

ricopèr·to -ta *adj* covered; coated

ricopertura *f* covering; seat cover

ricopiare §287 (ricòpio) *tr* to make a fair copy of; to recopy; to copy

ricoprire §110 *tr* to cover; to coat; to hide ‖ *ref* to become covered

ricordanza *f* (poet) memory

ricordare (ricòrdo) *tr* to remember; to remind; to mention ‖ *ref* to remember; **ricordarsi di** to remember

ricòrdo *m* memory; souvenir; **ricordo marmoreo** marble statue

ricorrènte *adj* recurrent, recurring

ricorrènza *f* recurrence; anniversary

ricórrere §139 *intr* (ESSERE & AVERE) to run again; to run back; to resort; to recur; (law) to appeal; **ricorrere a** to have recourse to

ricórso *m* recurrence; recourse; appeal

ricostituènte *adj* invigorating ‖ *m* tonic

ricostituire §176 *tr* to reconstitute, to reform; to reinvigorate

ricostruire §140 *tr* to rebuild; to reconstruct

ricostruzióne *f* rebuilding; reconstruction

ricòtta *f* Italian cottage cheese; **di ricotta** weak

ricoverare (ricóvero) *tr* to shelter ‖ *ref* to take shelter

ricóvero *m* shelter; nursing home; (med) admission; **ricovero antiaereo** air-raid shelter

ricreare (ricrèo) *tr* to recreate; to refresh ‖ *ref* to relax

ricreati·vo -va *adj* refreshing; recreational

ricreatò·rio -ria (-ri -rie) *adj* recreation, recreational ‖ *m* recreation room; playground

ricreazióne *f* recreation; recess

ricrédere §141 *intr*—**far ricredere qlcu** to make s.o. change his mind ‖ *ref* to change one's mind

ricréscere §142 *intr* (ESSERE) to grow again; to swell

ricucire §143 *tr* to sew up

ricuòcere §144a *tr* to cook again; to anneal

ricuperare (ricùpero) *tr* to recover; (naut) to salvage; (sports) to make up for (*rained-out game*)

ricùpero *m* recovery; salvage; rally; making up for (*for lost time or postponed game*)

ricur·vo -va *adj* bent; bent over

ricusare *tr* to refuse

ridacchiare §287 *intr* to titter, giggle

ridancia·no -na *adj* prone to laughter; amusing

ridare §230 (*1st sg pres ind* ridò) *tr* to give back; to give again; **ridare fuori** to vomit ‖ *intr* (coll) to reappear, e.g., **gli ha ridato il foruncolo** his boil has reappeared ‖ *intr*

(ESSERE)—**ridare giù** to have a relapse

ridda *f* round; confusion; throng

ridènte *adj* laughing; bright, pleasant

rìdere §231 *tr* (poet) to laugh at ‖ *intr* to laugh; (poet) to shine; **far ridere i polli** to be utterly ridiculous; **ridere sotto i baffi** to laugh up one's sleeve ‖ *ref*—**ridersi di** to laugh at

ridestare (ridésto) *tr* & *ref* to reawaken

ridicolizzare [ddzz] *tr* to ridicule; to twit

ridìco·lo -la *adj* ridiculous ‖ *m* ridicule; ridiculousness

ridipingere §126 *tr* to paint again

ridire §151 *tr* to tell again; to repeat; to tell (*to express*); **avere** or **trovare a** or **da ridire (su)** to find fault (with)

ridistribuzióne *f* redistribution

ridivenire §282 or **ridiventare (ridivènto)** *intr* (ESSERE) to become again

ridonare (ridóno) *tr* to give back

ridondante *adj* redundant

ridondare (ridóndo) *intr* (ESSERE & AVERE)· (fig) to overflow; **ridondare a** or **in** to redound to

ridòsso *m* back; shelter; **a ridosso** sheltered; as a shelter; behind, close behind

ridót·to -ta *adj* reduced; **mal ridotto** down at the heel ‖ *m* lounge; (theat) foyer ‖ *f* (mil) redoubt

ridurre §102 *tr* to reduce; to adapt; to translate; to lead; to curtail; (mus) to arrange ‖ *ref* to be reduced; to retire

riduttóre *m* (mach) reduction gear

riduzióne *f* reduction; (mus) arrangement

riecheggiare §290 (riechéggio) *tr* & *intr* to echo

riedificare §197 (riedìfico) *tr* to rebuild

rieducare §197 (rièduco) *tr* to reeducate

rielèggere §193 *tr* to reelect

rielezióne *f* reelection

riemèrgere §162 *intr* to resurface

riempiménto *m* fill

riempire §163 *tr* to fill; to stuff

riempiti·vo -va *adj* expletive ‖ *m* expletive; fill-in

rientrante *adj* hollow (*cheeks*); (mil) reentrant

rientranza *f* recess

rientrare (rièntro) *intr* (ESSERE) to reenter; to come back; to recede; (coll) to shrink; **rientrare in** to recover (*one's expenses*); **rientrare in sé** to come to one's senses

rièntro *m* reentry

riepilogare §209 (riepìlogo) *tr* to sum up, recapitulate

riepilo·go m (-ghi) recapitulation

riesame *m* reexamination

riesaminare (riesàmino) *tr* to reexamine

riesumare *tr* to exhume; (fig) to dig up; (fig) to bring back

rievocare §197 (rièvoco) *tr* to recall

rifaciménto *m* adaptation; recasting

rifare §173 (*3d sg* rifà) *tr* to do again, redo; to remake; to imitate; to indemnify; to prepare again; to repeat;

to make (*a bed*) ‖ *ref* to recover; to become again; to recoup one's losses; to begin; **rifarsi con** to get even with; **rifarsi da** to begin with

rifasciare §128 *tr* to rebind

riferiménto *m* reference

riferire §176 *tr* to wound again; to refer; to relate ‖ *ref*—**riferirsi a** to refer to; to concern

riffa *f* raffle; lottery; (coll) violence; **di riffa o di raffa** by hook or crook

rifilare *tr* to trim; (coll) to reel off (*a list of names*); (coll) to deal (*a blow*); (coll) to palm off

rifinire §176 *tr* to give the finishing touch to; to wear out ‖ *intr* to stop ‖ *ref* to wear oneself out

rifiorire §176 *tr* (lit) to revive ‖ *intr* to bloom again ‖ *intr* (ESSERE) to flourish; to grow better; to reappear

rifischiare §287 *tr* to whistle again; (coll) to report ‖ *intr* to talk, gossip

rifiutare *tr* to refuse; (lit) to reject ‖ *intr* (cards) to renege, renounce ‖ *ref* to refuse, deny

rifiuto *m* refusal; refuse, rubbish; rejection; rebuff, spurn; (fig) wreck; (cards) renege; **di rifiuto** waste, e.g., **materiale di rifiuto** waste material

riflessióne *f* reflexion

riflessi·vo -va *adj* thoughtful; (gram) reflexive

rifles·so -sa *adj* reflex, e.g., **azione riflessa** reflex action ‖ *m* reflection; (physiol) reflex; **di riflesso** vicarious

riflèttere §177 (*pp* **riflettuto** & **riflèsso**) *tr* & *intr* to reflect ‖ *ref* to be reflected

riflettóre *m* searchlight; reflector

rifluire §176 *intr* (ESSERE & AVERE) to flow; to flow back

riflusso *m* flow; ebb, ebb tide

rifocillare *tr* to refresh (*with food*) ‖ *ref* to take refreshment

rifóndere §178 *tr* to melt again; to recast; to refund; to reedit

rifórma *f* reform; (mil) rejection ‖ **Riforma** *f*—**la Riforma** the Reformation

riformare (**rifórmo**) *tr* to reform; to amend; (mil) to reject

riformati·vo -va *adj* reformatory

riforma·tóre -trice *adj* reforming ‖ *mf* reformer

riformatò·rio *m* (-**ri**) reform school, reformatory

riforniménto *m* supply; refueling; **fare rifornimento di** to fill up with; **rifornimenti** supplies

rifornire §176 *tr* to supply; to restock; **rifornire di benzina** to refuel

rifràngere §179 *tr* to crush ‖ *ref* to break (*said of waves*) ‖ §179 (*pp* **rifratto**) *tr* to refract ‖ *ref* to be refracted

rifrat·tóre -trice *adj* refracting ‖ *m* refractor

rifrazióne *f* refraction

rifrìggere §180 *tr* to fry again; to rehash ‖ *intr* to fry too long or in too much oil

rifrit·to -ta *adj* fried again; (fig) hack-

neyed ‖ *m* taste of stale fat; (fig) rehash

rifuggire *tr* to avoid ‖ *intr*—**rifuggire da** to abhor ‖ *intr* (ESSERE) to take refuge

rifugiare §290 *ref* to take refuge, take shelter

rifugiato *m* refugee

rifù·gio *m* (-**gi**) refuge; **rifugio alpino** mountain hut; **rifugio antiaereo** air-raid shelter; **rifugio antiatomico** fall-out shelter

rifùlgere §233 *intr* (ESSERE & AVERE) to shine

rifusióne *f* recast; refund, reimbursement

ri·ga *f* (-**ghe**) line; row; rank; ruler; part (*in hair*); stripe; (fig) quality

rigàglie *fpl* giblets

rigàgnolo *m* rivulet; gutter (*at the side of a road*)

rigare §209 *tr* to rule, line; to stripe; to mark; to rifle (*gun*) ‖ *intr*—**rigare diritto** to toe the line

rigatino *m* gingham

rigattière *m* second-hand dealer

rigatura *f* ruling; rifling (*of gun*)

rigenerare (**rigènero**) *tr* to regenerate; to reclaim; to recycle ‖ *ref* to become regenerate

rigenera·tóre *m*—**rigeneratore per i capelli** hair restorer

rigettare (**rigètto**) *tr* to throw back; to reject; to recast; (slang) to throw up ‖ *intr* to sprout

rigetto *m* rejection

righèllo *m* ruler

rigidi·tà *f* (-**tà**) rigidity; rigor; stiffness; **rigidità cadaverica** rigor mortis

rìgi·do -da *adj* rigid, stiff; severe

rigirare *tr* to keep turning; to dupe; to invest; to encircle ‖ *intr* to ramble ‖ *ref* to turn around; to tumble

ri·go *m* (-**ghi**) line; **rigo musicale** (mus) staff

rigò·glio *m* (-**gli**) luxuriance; bloom; gurgling

rigonfiare §287 (**rigónfio**) *tr* to inflate ‖ *intr* (ESSERE) & *ref* to swell up

rigóre *m* rigor; severity; precision; **a rigor di termini** strictly speaking; **di rigore** de rigueur; (sports) penalty (*e.g., kick*)

rigorismo *m* rigorism, strictness, severity

rigori·sta *mf* (-**sti -ste**) rigorist ‖ *m* (soccer) kicker of penalty goal

rigoró·so -sa [s] *adj* rigorous, strict

rigovernare (**rigovèrno**) *tr* to clean, wash (*dishes*); to groom, tend (*animals*)

riguadagnare *tr* to regain

riguardare *tr* to look again; to look back; to examine; to consider; to take care of; to concern ‖ *intr*—**riguardare a** to look out for; to face (*said of a window*) ‖ *ref* to take care of oneself; **riguardarsi da** to keep away from

riguardo *m* care; esteem; regard; **a questo riguardo** in this regard; **ri-**

guardo a as far as . . . is concerned; **senza riguardo a** irrespective of

riguardó·so -sa [s] *adj* considerate

rigurgitare (**rigùrgito**) *tr & intr* to regurgitate

rilanciare §128 *tr* to toss back; to reestablish (*e.g., fashions*); (*poker*) to raise

rilasciare §128 *tr* to free, let go; to relax; to grant || *ref* to relax

rilà·scio *m* (**-sci**) release; delivery; granting, issue (*of a document*)

rilassante *adj* relaxing

rilassare *tr & ref* to relax

rilassatézza *f* laxity

rilegare §209 (**rilégo**) *tr* to tie again; to bind, rebind (*a book*); to set (*a stone*)

rilega·tóre -trice *mf* binder

rilegatura *f* binding

rilèggere §193 *tr* to reread

rilènto *m*—**a rilento** slowly

rilevaménto *m* survey; (*naut*) bearing

rilevare (**rilèvo**) *tr* to lift again; to observe; to draw; to bring out; to survey; to take over; to pick up; (*mil*) to relieve || *intr* to be delineated; to be of import || *ref* to rise again; to recover

rilevatà·rio *m* (**-ri**) successor; (*law*) assignee

rilièvo *m* relief; survey; remark; assumption (*of debts*); taking over (*of business*); **mettere in rilievo** to bring out; to set off

rilò·ga *f* (**-ghe**) traverse rod

rilucènte *adj* shiny, shining

rilùcere §234 *intr* to shine

riluttante *adj* reluctant

riluttanza *f* reluctance

rima *f* rhyme; slit; crevice; **rispondere per le rime** to answer in kind, to retort

rimandare *tr* to send back; to refer; to dismiss; to put off, postpone; to refer; **rimandare a ottobre** to condition (*a student*)

rimando *m* delay; reference; footnote; repartee; postponement; (*sports*) return

rimaneggiare §290 (**rimanéggio**) *tr* to rearrange; to reshuffle; to shake up (*personnel*); to rewrite (*news*)

rimanènte *adj* remaining || *m* remainder; remnant; **i rimanenti** the rest

rimanènza *f* remainder

rimanére §235 *intr* (ESSERE) to remain, stay; to be in agreement; to have left, e.g., **mi sono rimasti solo tre dollari** I only have three dollars left; to be located; (*poet*) to stop; **rimanerci** (*coll*) to be killed; (*coll*) to be duped; **rimanere da** to depend on, e.g., **questo rimane da Lei** this depends on you

rimangiare §290 *tr* to eat again || *ref*— **rimangiarsi la parola** to go back on one's word

rimarcare §197 *tr* to mark again; to point out

rimar·co *m* (**-chi**) remark, notice

rimare *tr & intr* to rhyme

rimarginare (**rimàrgino**) *tr, intr & ref* to heal

rimaritare *tr & ref* to marry again

rimasù·glio *m* (**-gli**) leftover

rima·tóre -trice *mf* poet; rhymster

rimbalzare *intr* (ESSERE & AVERE) to bounce back, rebound

rimbalzo *m* rebound

rimbambire §176 *intr* (ESSERE) & *ref* to become feeble-minded (*from old age*)

rimbambi·to -ta *adj* feeble-minded || *mf* dotard

rimbeccare §197 (**rimbécco**) *tr* to peck; to retort

rimbecilli·to -ta *adj* feeble-minded

rimboccare §197 (**rimbócco**) *tr* to tuck up; to tuck in; to fill to the brim

rimbombare (**rimbómbo**) *intr* (ESSERE & AVERE) to thunder, boom

rimbómbo *m* thunder, boom

rimborsare (**rimbórso**) *tr* to reimburse, pay back

rimbórso *m* repayment

rimboscare §197 (**rimbòsco**) *tr* to reforest || *ref* to take to the woods

rimboschiménto *m* reforestation

rimboschire §176 *tr* to reforest || *intr* (ESSERE) to become wooded

rimbrottare (**rimbròtto**) *tr* to scold

rimbròtto *m* scolding

rimediare §287 (**rimèdio**) *tr* (*coll*) to scrape together; (*coll*) to patch up || *intr* (with *dat*) to remedy; to make up (*lost time*)

rimè·dio *m* (**-di**) remedy

rimembranza *f* remembrance

rimeritare (**rimèrito**) *tr* to reward

rimescolare (**riméscolo**) *tr* to stir; to shuffle (*cards*)

riméssa *f* remittance; shipment; harvest; store; loss; sprout; carriage house; garage; (*sports*) return; (*sports*) putting in play; **rimessa del tram** carbarn

rimestare (**rimésto**) *tr* to stir

rimèttere §198 *tr* to remit; to put back; to set back; to sprout; to postpone, defer; to ship; to vomit; to recover; to deliver; to straighten up; (*sports*) to return; **rimetterci** to lose; **rimettere a nuovo** to renovate; **rimettere in ordine** to tidy up; **rimettere in piedi** to rebuild, restore || *intr* (*coll*) to sprout; (*coll*) to grow; (*lit*) to abate || *ref* to recover; to quiet down; to defer; to be clearing (*said of weather*); **rimettersi a** to go back to (*e.g., bed*); **rimettersi a** + *inf* to start + *ger* + again; **rimettersi in cammino** to start off again

rimirare *tr* to stare at

rìmmel *m* mascara

rimodellare (**rimodèllo**) *tr* to remodel

rimodernare (**rimodèrno**) *tr* to modernize; to remodel; to bring up to date || *ref* to become modern

rimónta *f* reassembly; return (*of migratory birds*); revamping (*of shoes*); (*mil*) remount

rimontare (**rimónto**) *tr* to rewind; to go up (*a stream*); to vamp (*shoes*); to renovate; to regain; to reassemble (*a machine*); (mil) to remount ‖ *intr* (ESSERE & AVERE) to climb again; to go back (*in time*)

rimorchiare §287 (**rimòrchio**) *tr* to tow; to drag along

rimorchiatóre *m* tugboat; tow car

rimòr·chio *m* (**-chi**) tow; trailer; **prendere a rimorchio** to take in tow

rimòrdere §200 *tr* to bite again; to prick (*said, e.g., of conscience*)

rimòrso *m* remorse

rimostranza *f* remonstrance

rimostrare (**rimóstro**) *tr* to show again ‖ *intr* to remonstrate; **rimostrare a** to remonstrate with

rimozióne *f* removal; demotion

rimpannucciare §128 *tr* to outfit better ‖ *ref* to be better dressed; to be better off

rimpastare *tr* to knead again; to reshuffle, remake

rimpasto *m* reshuffling, rearrangement

rimpatriare §287 *tr* to repatriate ‖ *intr* to be repatriated

rimpà·trio *m* (**-tri**) repatriation

rimpètto *adv* opposite; **di rimpetto a** opposite to; in comparison with

rimpiàngere §215 *tr* to regret; to mourn

rimpianto *m* regret

rimpiattare *tr & ref* to hide; **giocare a rimpiattarsi** to play hide-and-seek

rimpiattino *m* hide-and-seek

rimpiazzare *tr* to replace

rimpiazzo *m* replacement, substitute

rimpiccolire §176 *tr* to make smaller ‖ *intr* (ESSERE) to get smaller

rimpinzare *tr* to stuff, cram

rimproverare (**rimpròvero**) *tr* to chide, reproach; **rimproverare qlco di qlco** or **rimproverare qlco a qlcu** to reproach s.o. for s.th

rimpròvero *m* reproach, rebuke

rimuginare (**rimùgino**) *tr & intr* to rummage; to stir; to ruminate

rimunerare (**rimùnero**) *tr* to reward ‖ *intr* to pay

rimunerati·vo -va *adj* remunerative; rewarding

rimunerazióne *f* remuneration

rimuòvere §202 *tr* to remove; to demote; to move

rinàscere §203 *intr* (ESSERE) to be born again; to grow again; to revive; **far rinascere** to revive

rinasciménto *m* rebirth ‖ **Rinascimento** *m* Renaissance

rinàscita *f* rebirth

rincagna·to -ta *adj* snub (*nose*)

rincalzare *tr* to hill (*plants*); to underpin; to tuck in

rincalzo *m* reinforcement; support

rincantucciare §128 *tr & ref* to hide in a corner

rincarare *tr* to raise the price of; to raise; **rincarare la dose** to add insult to injury ‖ *intr* (ESSERE) to rise, go up (*said of prices*)

rincasare [s] *intr* (ESSERE) to return home

rinchiùdere §125 *tr* to enclose, shut in

rinchiu·so -sa [s] *adj* shut in; musty ‖ *m*—**saper di rinchiuso** to smell musty

rincitrullire §176 *intr* (ESSERE) to grow stupid

rincóntro *m*—**a rincontro** opposite

rincorare §236 *tr* to encourage ‖ *ref* to take heart

rincórrere §139 *tr* to pursue, chase

rincórsa *f*—**prendere la rincorsa** to take off (*for a jump*); to get a running start

rincréscere §142 *intr* (ESSERE) (with *dat*) to displease; to be sorry, e.g., **gli rincresce** he is sorry; to mind, **Le rincresce?** do you mind?

rincresciménto *m* regret

rincrudire §176 *tr* to sharpen; to embitter ‖ *intr* (ESSERE) to become bitter; to get worse

rinculare *intr* (ESSERE & AVERE) to back up; to recoil

rinculo *m* recoil

rinfacciare §128 *tr* to throw in one's face

rinfarcire §176 *tr* to stuff

rinfiancare §197 *tr* to support

rinfocolare (**rinfòcolo**) *tr* to rekindle; to revive

rinfoderare (**rinfòdero**) *tr* sheathe

rinforzare (**rinfòrzo**) *tr* to reinforce; strengthen ‖ *intr* (ESSERE) & *ref* to become stronger

rinfòrzo *m* reinforcement

rinfrancare §197 *tr* to reassure ‖ *ref* to buck up

rinfrescante *adj* refreshing ‖ *m* mild laxative

rinfrescare §197 (**rinfrésco**) *tr* to refresh; to restore; to renew ‖ *intr* (ESSERE & AVERE) to cool off (*said of the weather*) ‖ *ref* to have some refreshments; to cool off

rinfré·sco *m* (**-schi**) refreshment

rinfusa *f*—**alla rinfusa** at random; pell-mell; in bulk

ringalluzzire §176 *tr & ref* to perk up

ringhiare §287 *intr* to growl, to snarl

ringhièra *f* railing

rin·ghio *m* (**-ghi**) growl, snarl

ringiovaniménto *m* rejuvenation

ringiovanire §176 *tr* to rejuvenate ‖ *intr* (ESSERE) to grow or look younger

ringraziaménto *m* thanks

ringraziare §287 *tr* to thank; to dismiss

ringuainare (**ringuaino**) *tr* to sheathe

rinnegare §209 (**rinnègo & rinnégo**) *tr* to forswear; to repudiate

rinnega·to -ta *adj & m* renegade

rinnovaménto *m* renewal; reawakening

rinnovare (**rinnòvo**) *tr* to renew; to renovate; to restore; to replace ‖ *ref* to occur again; to renew

rinnovellare (**rinnovèllo**) *tr* to repeat; (poet) to renew ‖ *intr* (ESSERE) & *ref* to change; to renew

rinnòvo *m* renewal

rinocerónte *m* rhinoceros

rinomanza *f* renown

rinoma·to -ta *adj* renowned, famous

rinsaldare *tr* to starch; (fig) to strengthen ‖ *ref* to become confirmed (*in one's opinion*)

rinsanguare (rinsànguo) *tr* to give new strength to || *ref* to regain strength; to recover

rinsavire §176 *intr* (ESSERE) to return to reason

rintanare *ref* to burrow; to hide

rintóc·co *m* (-chi) toll (*of bell*)

rintontire §176 *tr* to stun, to daze

rintracciare §128 *tr* to track down

rintronare (rintròno) *tr* to deafen; to make rumble || *intr* (ESSERE & AVERE) to thunder; to rumble

rintuzzare *tr* to dull, blunt; to repel; to repress

rinùn·cia *f* (-ce) or **rinùnzia** *f* renunciation

rinunziare §287 *tr* to renounce || *intr* (with *dat*) to give up, renounce, e.g., **rinunziò al trono** he renounced the throne

rinvangare §209 *tr* & *intr* var of **rivangare**

rinvenire §282 *tr* to find || *intr* (ESSERE) to come to; **far rinvenire** to bring to, revive

rinviare §119 *tr* to send back; to postpone; to refer; to adjourn; to remit (*to a lower court*)

rinvigorire §176 *tr* to strengthen || *intr* (ESSERE) & *ref* to regain strength

rinví·o *m* (-í) return; postponement; adjournment; reference; (law) continuance

rí·o *m* (-í) (lit) sin; (lit) brook; (coll) canal

rioccupare (riòccupo) *tr* to reoccupy

rioccupazióne *f* reoccupation

rionale *adj* neighborhood

rióne *m* district; neighborhood

riordinare (riórdino) *tr* to rearrange; to reorganize; to order again

riorganizzare [ddzz] *tr* to reorganize

riottó·so -sa [s] *adj* (lit) quarrelsome; (lit) unruly, rebellious

ripa *f* (lit) bank (*of river*); (lit) escarpment

ripagare §209 *tr* to repay; to pay again

riparare *tr* to protect; to mend, fix, repair; to make up (*an exam*) || *intr* —**riparare a** to make up for || *intr* (ESSERE) & *ref* to take refuge; to betake oneself

riparazióne *f* repair; reparation; redress; (educ) make-up

riparlare *intr* to speak again; **ne riparleremo!** you will see!

riparo *m* repair; shelter

ripartire §176 *tr* to divide; to distribute; to share || (riparto) *intr* (ESSERE) to leave again; to start again || §176 *ref* to split up

ripartizióne *f* division; distribution

riparto *m* division; distribution; allotment

ripassare *tr* to cross again; to brush up, review; to repass; to sift again; to check; to read over; (mach) to overhaul || *intr* (ESSERE) to go by; to come by

ripassata *f* checkup; review; (coll) rebuke

ripassa·tóre -trice *mf* checker

ripasso *m* return (*of birds*); (coll) review

ripensare (ripènso) *intr* to keep thinking; **ripensare a** to think of again; to think over again

ripentire (ripènto) *ref* to repent; **ripentirsi di** to repent

ripercórrere §139 *tr* to retrace

ripercuòtere §251 *tr* to reflect; to strike again || *ref* to reverberate

ripescare §197 (ripésco) *tr* to fish again; (fig) to dig up

ripètere *tr* & *intr* to repeat || *ref* to be repeated

ripeti·tóre -trice *mf* repeater; coach; tutor || *m* (rad, telv) rebroadcasting station; (rad) relay

ripetizióne *f* repetition; review; tutoring; **a ripetizióne** repeating (*firearm*)

ripiano *m* terrace; ledge; shelf; landing; (com) balancing

ripíc·co *m* (-chi) pique; spite

ripí·do -da *adj* steep

ripiegaménto *m* bend; (mil) withdrawal, retreat

ripiegare §209 (ripiègo) *tr* to fold, fold over || *intr* to do better; (mil) to fall back || *ref* to bend over; to withdraw into oneself

ripiè·go *m* (-ghi) expedient

ripiè·no -na *adj* full; stuffed || *m* stuffing; (culin) filling

ripigliare §280 *tr* to reacquire; to catch again; to begin again || *intr* to recover || *ref* to renew a quarrel

ripiombare (ripiómbo) *tr* to make plumb; (fig) to plunge back || *intr* (ESSERE) (fig) to plunge back

ripopolare (ripòpolo) *tr* to repopulate; to restock (*e.g., a pond*)

ripórre §218 *tr* to put back; to place (*one's hope*); to repose (*one's trust*) || *ref* to back down; **riporsi a** + *inf* to start + *ger* again

riportare (ripòrto) *tr* to bring back; to report; to get; to transfer (*a design*); (com) to carry forward; (hunt) to retrieve; (math) to carry || *ref* to go back

ripòrto *m* filler; retrieving; (com) balance carried forward; (math) number carried

riposante [s] *adj* restful

riposare [s] (ripòso) *tr*, *intr* & *ref* to rest

ripòso [s] *m* rest; repose; Requiem; retirement; **buon riposo!** sleep well!; **mettere a riposo** to retire; **riposo!** (mil) at ease

riposti·glio *m* (-gli) closet

ripó·sto -sta *adj* innermost || *m* (coll) pantry

riprèndere §220 *tr* to take back; to take up again; to get back; to take in (*a garment*); to catch (*s.th thrown in the air*); to take up (*arms*); to get; to reconquer; to start again, resume; to reprehend; to recover; (mov, telv) to shoot; **riprendere moglie** to remarry || *intr* to start again; to recover, improve; to pick up (*said of a* *motor*) ‖ *ref* to recover; to catch oneself up

riprésa [s] *f* resumption; (aut) pickup; (theat) revival; (mov) shooting, take; (boxing) round; (soccer) second half; (mus, pros) refrain; **a più riprese** several times

ripresentare (ripresènto) *tr* to present again

ripristinare (ripristino) *tr* to restore; to reestablish

ripristino *m* revival, restoration

riprodurre §102 *tr* to reproduce; to express ‖ *ref* to reproduce; to occur

riprodut·tóre -trice *adj* reproducing ‖ *mf* reproducer ‖ *m* reproducer (*e.g., of sound*)

riproduzióne *f* reproduction; playback (*e.g., of tape*)

ripromèttere §198 *tr* to promise again ‖ *ref* to hope; to propose; to hope for

ripròva *f* new proof; confirmation

riprovare (ripròvo) *tr* to try again; to try on again; to feel, experience again; to flunk; to censure ‖ *ref* to try again

riprovazióne *f* disapproval

ripudiare §287 *tr* to repudiate

ripugnante *adj* repugnant, repulsive

ripugnanza *f* repugnance; aversion

ripugnare *intr* (with *dat*) to disgust, revolt, be repugnant to

ripulire §176 *tr* to clean again; to tidy up; to clean up; to polish ‖ *ref* to be dressed up; to become polished

ripulita *f*—**dare una ripulita a** to give a lick and a promise to; **fare una ripulita** (fig) to clean house

ripulsi·vo -va *adj* repulsive

riquadrare *tr* to square; to decorate (*a room*) ‖ *intr* to measure; to square

riquadro *m* square

risac·ca [s] *f* (-che) undertow; backwash

risàia [s] *f* rice field

risalire [s] §242 *tr* to go up again; to stem (*the tide*); **risalire la corrente** to go upstream ‖ *intr* (ESSERE) to climb again; to reascend; (com) to appreciate; to date back

risaltare [s] *tr* to jump again ‖ *intr* (ESSERE & AVERE) to rebound ‖ *intr* to stand out; **far risaltare** to emphasize

risalto [s] *m* emphasis; prominence; relief; foil

risanare [s] *tr* to heal; to reclaim (*land*); to redevelop (*urban areas*); to reorganize ‖ *intr* (ESSERE) to heal; to improve

risapére [s] §243 *tr* to find out

risapu·to -ta [s] *adj* well-known

risarciménto [s] *m* indemnification, redress

risarcire [s] §176 *tr* to indemnify; to compensate

risata [s] *f* outburst of laughter

risatina [s] *f* chuckle

riscaldaménto *m* heating; inflammation

riscaldare *tr* to heat; to warm up; to inflame ‖ *ref* to warm up; to go in heat; to perspire; to get excited

riscaldo *m* inflammation; prickly heat; padding (*for clothes*)

riscattare *tr* to ransom; to redeem ‖ *intr* (ESSERE) to click again (*said, e.g., of a ratchet*)

riscatto *m* ransom; redemption

rischiarare *tr, intr* (ESSERE) & *ref* to clear, clear up

rischiare §287 *tr* to risk ‖ *intr* to run a risk

ri·schio *m* (-schi) risk

rischió·so -sa [s] *adj* risky

risciacquare (risciàcquo) *tr* to rinse

risciacquatura *f* rinse; swill

risciàcquo *m* rinsing (*of mouth*); mouthwash

riscónto *m* (com) discount

riscontrare (riscóntro) *tr* to compare, collate; to check; to reply to ‖ *intr* to reply; to tally ‖ *ref* to tally

riscóntro *m* comparison; check, control; draft; correspondence; reply; **far riscontro** to correspond; **far riscontro con** to correspond to; **far riscontro di** to check; **mettere a riscontro** to compare; **riscontri** drafts (*of air*); parts (*that fit together*)

riscoprire §110 *tr* to rediscover

riscòssa *f* insurrection; recovery, reconquest; (mil) counterattack

riscossióne *f* collection

riscrivere §250 *tr* to rewrite; to write back

riscuòtere §251 *tr* to shake; to wake up; to collect; to get; to redeem ‖ *ref* to wake up; to come to one's senses

riseccare [s] §197 (risécco) *tr, intr* (ESSERE) & *ref* to dry up

risecchire [s] §176 *intr* (ESSERE) & *ref* to dry up

risentiménto [s] *m* resentment, pique

risentire [s] (risènto) *tr* to hear again; to feel ‖ *intr*—**risentire di** to feel the effects of ‖ *ref* to take offense; to wake up; to come to one's senses; (telp) to talk again; **a risentirci!** (telp) until we talk again!; **risentirsi con** to resent (*a person*); **risentirsi di** to feel the effects of; **risentirsi per** to resent (*an act*)

risenti·to -ta [s] *adj* heard again; resentful; strong; swift; incisive

riserbare [s] (risèrbo) *tr* var of **riservare**

risèrbo [s] *m* var of **risèrvo**

risèrva [s] *f* preservation; exclusive rights; preserve; reserve; supply; backlog; reservation; circumspection; vintage

riservare [s] (risèrvo) *tr* to reserve

riservatézza [s] *f* reservedness

riserva·to -ta [s] *adj* reserved; private; classified

riservista [s] *m* (-sti) reservist

risèrvo [s] *m* discretion

risguardo *m* end paper

risièdere [s] *intr* to reside

risma *f* ream; (fig) type

riso [s] *m* rice ‖ *m* (risa *fpl*) laugh; laughter; jest; cheer; (lit) smile

risolare [s] §257 *tr* to resole

risolino [s] *m* smile; giggle

risollevare [s] (**risollèvo**) *tr* to raise again; to lift ‖ *ref* to rise

risolutézza [s] *f* resoluteness

risolu·to -ta [s] *adj* resolved, determined

risoluzióne [s] *f* resolution; resolve; dissolution

risòlvere [s] §256 (*pret ind* **risolvéi** or **risolvètti** or **risòlsi**; *pp* **risòlto**) *tr* to resolve; to solve; to dissolve; to persuade ‖ *ref* to dissolve; to resolve

risolvìbile [s] *adj* solvable

risonante [s] *adj* resounding

risonanza [s] *f* resonance; (fig) sensation

risonare [s] §257 *tr* to ring again; (lit) to repeat ‖ *intr* (ESSERE & AVERE) to resonate; to resound; to ring again; to echo

risórgere [s] §258 *intr* (ESSERE) to rise again; to revive, to come back to life; to recover

risorgiménto [s] *m* renaissance; resurgence ‖ **Risorgimento** *m* Risorgimento

risórsa [s] *f* resource

risór·to -ta [s] *adj* arisen; reborn

risòtto [s] *m* risotto, rice cooked with broth

risparmiare §287 *tr* to save; to spare

rispàr·mio -mio (**-mi**) saving; sparing; savings; **risparmi** savings; **senza risparmio** lavishly

rispecchiare §287 (**rispècchio**) *tr* to reflect

rispedire §176 *tr* to send back; to forward; to reship

rispedizióne *f* reshipment

rispettàbile *adj* respectable

rispettare (**rispètto**) *tr* to respect; **farsi rispettare** to command respect; **rispettare sé stesso** to have self-respect

rispetti·vo -va *adj* respective

rispètto *m* respect; observance; restriction (*e.g., in building*); comparison; regard; **con rispetto parlando** excuse the word; **di rispetto** (naut) spare (*e.g., parts*); **rispetti** regards; **rispetto di sé medesimo** self-respect; **rispetto umano** fear of what people will say

rispettó·so -sa [s] *adj* respectful; respectable (*distance*)

risplendènte *adj* resplendent

risplèndere §281 *intr* (ESSERE & AVERE) to shine

rispóndere §238 *tr* to answer; **risponder picche** (coll) to say no ‖ *intr* to answer; **rispondere a** to answer (*e.g., a letter*); **rispondere con un cenno del capo** to nod assent; **rispondere di** to be responsible for; **rispondere in** to face, overlook

risposare (**rispòso**) *tr & ref* to marry again, remarry

rispósta *f* answer, reply, response

rissa *f* scuffle, brawl

rissó·so -sa [s] *adj* quarrelsome

ristabilire §176 *tr* to reestablish ‖ *ref* to recover

ristagnare *tr* to tin; to solder ‖ *intr* to stagnate

ristampa *f* reprint

ristampare *tr* to reprint

ristorante *m* restaurant

ristorare (**ristòro**) *tr & ref* to refresh

ristora·tóre -trice *adj* refreshing ‖ *m* restaurant

ristòro *m* refreshment; compensation

ristrettézza *f* narrowness; scarcity; **ristrettezza d'idee** narrow-mindedness

ristrét·to -ta *adj* narrow; limited; in straitened circumstances; concentrated, condensed (*e.g., broth*)

ristrutturazióne *f* restructuring

risùc·chio [s] *m* (**-chi**) whirlpool

risultante [s] *adj* resulting ‖ *m & f* resultant; (phys) resultant

risultare [s] *intr* (ESSERE) to result; to prove to be, turn out to be; to appear

risultato [s] *m* result

risurrezióne [s] *f* resurrection

risuscitare [s] (**risùscito**) *tr* to resurrect; to revive ‖ *intr* to be resurrected; to be revived

risvegliare §280 (**risvéglio**) *tr & ref* to awaken; to reawaken

risvé·glio *m* (**-gli**) awakening, reawakening

risvòlto *m* cuff; lapel; inside flap (*of book*); minor aspect (*of a question*)

ritagliare §280 *tr* to cut again; to clip; to trim

rità·glio *m* (**-gli**) clipping (*of paper*); scrap (*of meat*); cutting (*of fabric*); bit (*of time*); **al ritaglio** retail

ritappezzare (**ritappézzo**) *tr* to repaper

ritardare *tr* to delay; to slow down, retard; ‖ *intr* to tarry; to be late; to be slow (*said of a watch*)

ritardatà·rio -ria *mf* (**-ri -rie**) latecomer; (com) delinquent

ritardo *m* delay; retard; lateness; **essere in ritardo** to be late

ritégno *m* reservation; discretion; **senza ritegno** shamelessly

ritemprare (**ritèmpro**) *tr* to temper again; to invigorate ‖ *ref* to harden

ritenére §271 *tr* to retain; to hold; to withhold; to believe, think ‖ *ref* to restrain oneself; to consider oneself; to be considered

ritentare (**ritènto**) *tr* to try again; (law) to retry

ritirare *tr* to withdraw; to pay (*a note*); to throw back; to shoot again; to accept delivery of; to take back (*a promise*) ‖ *intr* to shrink ‖ *ref* to shrink; to withdraw; to fall back, retreat; to retire

ritirata *f* toilet; (mil) retreat

ritiro *m* withdrawal; retreat; retirement; shrinkage; (metallurgy) shrinking

ritma·to -ta *adj* measured (*step*)

ritmi·co -ca *adj* (**-ci -che**) rhythmic(al)

ritmo *m* rhythm; **a ritmo serrato** at a quick pace

rito *m* rite; (fig) ritual, ceremony; **di rito** customary

ritoccare §197 (**ritócco**) *tr* to retouch; to brush up

ritóc·co *m* (**-chi**) retouch; improvement; change

ritòrcere §272 *tr* to twist, twine; to wring; to retort

ritornare (**ritórno**) *tr* to return, give back || *intr* (ESSERE) to return, go back, come back; **ritornare in sé** to come back to one's senses

ritornèllo *m* refrain; chorus (*of song*)

ritórno *m* return; reoccurrence; **di ritorno** reoccurring; **essere di ritorno** to be back; **far ritorno** to return; **ritorno di fiamma** backfire

ritòr·to -ta *adj* twisted || *m* twist

ritrarre §273 *tr* to retract; to draw; to portray || *intr*—**ritrarre da** to look like || *ref* to retreat; to portray oneself

ritrasméttere §198 *tr* (rad, telv) to retransmit, rebroadcast

ritrattare *tr* to treat again; to retract; (coll) to portray || *ref* to recant

ritrattazióne *f* retraction

ritratti·sta *mf* (-**sti** -**ste**) portrait painter

ritratto *m* portrait, picture; photograph; **ritratto parlante** spit and image

ritri·to -ta *adj* (fig) stale, trite

ritrósa [s] *f* (coll) cowlick

ritrosìa [s] *f* coyness, shyness

ritró·so -sa [s] *adj* coy, shy; **a ritroso** backwards || *f* see **ritrosa**

ritrovare (**ritròvo**) *tr* to discover; to find; to regain; to meet again || *ref* to meet again; to find oneself; to find one's bearings; **non ritrovarcisi** to be out of sorts

ritrovato *m* discovery, find

ritròvo *m* meeting; nightspot; **ritrovo estivo** summer resort; **ritrovo notturno** night club

rit·to -ta *adj* upright; straight; right || *m* face (*of medal*); prop; (sports) post || *f* (lit) right hand

rituale *adj* & *m* ritual

riunióne *f* reunion; meeting; assembly; **riunione alla sommità** summit conference

riunire §176 *tr* to assemble; to reunite; to reconcile || *ref* to gather together; to meet; to be reunited; to rally

riuscire §277 *intr* (ESSERE) to go out again; to turn out, turn out to be; to lead (*said, e.g., of a door*); to succeed; **riuscire a** + *inf* to succeed in + *ger* || *impers*—**riesce** (with *dat*) **di** + *inf* to succeed in + *ger*, e.g., **non gli è riuscito di farsi ricevere** he did not succeed in being received

riuscita *f* success; result; outlet

riva *f* shore; bank; (naut) board

rivale *adj* & *mf* rival

rivaleggiare §290 (**rivaléggio**) *intr* to compete; **rivaleggiare con** to rival

rivalére §278 *ref*—**rivalersi di** to use; **rivalersi su qlcu** to resort to s.o. for compensation; **to fall back on s.o.**, to have recourse to s.o.

rivali·tà *f* (-**tà**) rivalry

rivalsa *f* compensation; revenge; (com) recourse

rivalutare (**rivàluto** & **rivaluto**) *tr* to revalue

rivalutazióne *f* reassessment

rivangare §209 *tr* to rake up; to mull over || *intr* to reminisce

rivedére §279 *tr* to see again; to review; to check; to reread; to revise; to read (*proof*) || *ref* to see one another; **a rivederci!** good-bye!, au revoir!

rivedìbile *adj* deferred (*for draft*)

rivelare (**rivélo**) *tr* to reveal; to detect; (phot) to develop

rivela·tóre -trice *adj* revealing || *m* (phot) developer; (rad) detector; **rivelatore di mine** mine detector

rivelazióne *f* revelation

rivéndere §281 *tr* to resell; (fig) to surpass

rivendicare §197 (**rivéndico**) *tr* to demand; to claim

rivendicazióne *f* demand; claim

rivéndita *f* resale; shop; **rivendita sali e tabacchi** cigar store

rivendi·tóre -trice *mf* seller, dealer, retailer

rivendùgliolo *m* peddler; huckster

rivèrbero *m* reverberation; reflection; glare; echo

riverènte *adj* reverent

riverènza *f* reverence; curtsy, bow

riverire §176 *tr* to revere; to pay one's respects to

riversare (**rivèrso**) *tr* to pour again; to transfer || *ref* to overflow

rivèr·so -sa *adj* on one's back

rivestiménto *m* coating; covering; lining

rivestire (**rivèsto**) *tr* to dress again; to coat; to line; to cover; to wear; to have (*importance*); to hold (*a rank*) || *ref* to get dressed again; to wear; to be covered

rivièra *f* coast || **Riviera** *f* Riviera

riviera·sco -sca *adj* (-**schi** -**sche**) coastal; riverside

rivìncere §285 *tr* to win back

rivincita *f* revenge; return match; **prendersi la rivincita** to get even

rivista *f* review; parade; magazine, journal; revue; proofreading

rivìvere §286 *tr* to relive || *intr* (ESSERE) to live again; to revive

rivo *m* (lit) rivulet, brook

rivolare (**rivólo**) *intr* (ESSERE & AVERE) to fly again

rivolére §288 *tr* to want back

rivòlgere §289 *tr* to turn again; to revolve; to overturn; to train (*a weapon*); to address; to deter || *ref* to turn; to turn around; **rivolgersi a** to apply to

rivolgiménto *m* turn; revolution; upheaval

rivòlta *f* revolt; cuff

rivoltante *adj* revolting

rivoltare (**rivòlto**) *tr* to overturn; to turn inside out; to toss (*salad*); to upset || *ref* to turn around; to revolt; to toss

rivoltèlla *f* revolver; spray gun

rivoltellata *f* revolver shot

rivoltó·so -sa [s] *adj* rebellious || *m* rioter; rebel

rivoluzionare (**rivoluzióno**) *tr* to revolutionize

rivoluzionà·rio -ria adj & mf (-ri -rie) revolutionary

rivoluzióne f revolution

rizza f (naut) rigging

rizzare tr to raise; to hoist; to pay (attention); to build; (naut) to lash || ref to rise; to bristle (said of hair); to rear up (said of a horse)

ròba f things, stuff; property

robinia f locust tree

robivèc·chi m (-chi) junk dealer

robu·sto -sta adj robust; burly

róc·ca f (-che) distaff

ròc·ca f (-che) fortress

roccafòrte f (rocchefòrti) stronghold

rocchétto m spool; reel; coil; roll (of film); pinion, rear sprocket wheel; (eccl) rochet; **rocchetto d'accensione** ignition coil; **rocchetto d'induzione** induction coil

ròc·cia f (-ce) rock; crag; cliff

roccló·so -sa [s] adj rocky

rò·co -ca adj (-chi -che) hoarse; (poet) faint

rodàg·gio m (-gi) breaking in, running in; adjustment period (to a new situation); **in rodaggio** (aut) being run in

Ròdano m Rhone

rodare (ròdo) tr to break in; (aut) to run in

ródere §239 tr to gnaw; to bite; to corrode || ref to worry, to fret

Ròdi f Rhodes

rodì·o m (-i) gnawing

rodi·tóre -trice adj gnawing || mf rodent

rodomónte m braggart

rogare §209 (ròge) tr to draw up (a contract); (law) to request

ròglto m (law) instrument, deed

rógna f mange; itch

rognóne m (culin) kidney

rognó·so -sa [s] adj scabby, mangy

rò·go m (-ghi) pyre; stake

rollì·o m (-i) roll (of ship)

Róma f Rome

romané·sco -sca adj (-schi -sche) Roman (dialect)

Romania, la Rumania

romànl·co -ca adj & m (-ci -che) Romanesque

roma·no -na adj & mf Roman; **pagare alla romana** to go Dutch

romanticismo m romanticism

romànti·co -ca (-ci -che) adj romantic || mf romanticist

romanza f romance; ballad

romanzare tr to fictionalize

romanzé·sco -sca adj (-schi -sche) romantic; of chivalry; novelistic

romanzlère m novelist

roman·zo -za adj Romance (language) || m novel; story; romance; fiction; **romanzi** fiction; **romanzo a fumetti** comic strip; comic book; **romanzo d'appendice** serial story, feuilleton; **romanzo giallo** whodunit; **romanzo rosa** love story

rombare (rómbo) intr to thunder

rómbo m thunder, roar

romè·no -na adj & mf Rumanian

romi·to -ta adj (lit) lonely || m (coll) hermit

rómpere §240 tr to break; to bust; **rompere la testa a** to annoy, pester || intr to overflow; to be wrecked; to break; **rompere in pianto** to burst out crying || ref to fly to pieces; **rompersi la testa** to rack one's brains

rompicapo m annoyance; puzzle; jig-saw puzzle

rompicòllo m madcap; **a rompicollo** headlong, rashly; at breakneck speed

rompighiàc·cio m (-cio) icebreaker; ice pick

rompiscàto·le m (-le) bore, pest

roncl·glio m (-gli) (poet) hook

róncola f pruning hook

rónda f patrol; beat (of policeman)

rondèlla f (mach) washer

róndine f swallow

rondóne m European swift

ronfare (rónfo) intr (coll) to snore; (coll) to purr

ronzare [dz] (rónzo) intr to buzz; to hum

ronzino [dz] m jade, nag

ronzì·o [dz] m (-i) buzzing; humming

ròsa adj invar & m pink || f rose; group; rosette; **rosa dei venti** compass card; **rosa del Giappone** (bot) camelia; **rosa delle Alpi** (bot) rhododendron; **rosa di tiro** (mil) dispersion

ro·sàio m (-sài) rosebush

rosà·rio m (-ri) rosary; **recitare il rosario** to count one's beads

rosa·to -ta adj rosy

ròse·o -a adj rosy

roséto m rose garden

rosétta f rosette; hard roll; (mach) washer

rosicanti [s] mpl rodents

rosicchiare [s] §287 tr to gnaw; to pick (a bone); to bite (one's fingernails)

rosmarino m (bot) rosemary

rosolare (ròsolo) tr (culin) to brown

rosolìa f German measles

rosóne m (archit) rosette; (archit) rose window

ròspo m toad; ugly person; unsociable person; **ingoiare un rospo** to swallow a bitter pill

rossa·stro -stra adj reddish

rossétto m rouge; **rossetto per le labbra** lipstick

rós·so -sa adj red; red-headed; Red; **diventare rosso** to blush || mf red-head; Red (Communist) || m red

rossóre m redness; blush

rosticcerìa f grill; rotisserie

rotàbile adj open to vehicular traffic (road); (rr) rolling (stock) || f road open to vehicular traffic

rotàia f rail; rut; **uscire dalle rotaie** to jump the track; (fig) to go astray

rotare §257 tr & intr to rotate; to circle

rotativa f (typ) rotary press

rotazióne f rotation

roteare (ròteo) tr to roll (the eyes); to flourish (a sword) || intr to circle

rotèlla f small wheel; caster; roller; kneecap; disk (of ski pole); **gli**

manca una rotella he has a screw loose

rotocàl·co *m* (-chi) rotogravure

rotolare (ròtolo) *tr & intr* (ESSERE) to roll || *ref* to turn over; to wallow

ròtolo *m* roll; bolt; coil; **a rotoli** to rack and ruin

rotolóne *m* tumble; **a rotoloni** falling down; to rack and ruin

rotón·do -da *adj* round; rotund || *f* rotunda; terrace

rótta *f* break; rout; (aer, naut) course; **a rotta di collo** at breakneck speed; **mettere in rotta** to rout

rottame *m* fragment; wreck; **rottami** scraps, debris; wreckage; **rottami di ferro** scrap iron

ròt·to -ta *adj* broken; shattered; inured || *m* break, tear; **e rotti** odd, e.g., **duecento e rotti** two hundred odd; **per il rotto della cuffia** hardly; just about || *f* see rotta

rottura *f* break; breakage; rupture; breakdown (*of relations*); crack

ròtula *f* kneecap

rovèllo *m* (lit) anger

rovènte *adj* red-hot

róvere *m & f* oak tree || *m* oak (*lumber*)

rovè·scia *f* (-sce) cuff; **alla rovescia** inside out; upside down; the wrong way

rovesciaménto *m* upset; overturn

rovesciare §128 (rovèscio) *tr* to overturn; to upset; to throw back (*one's head*); to spill (*liquid*); to pour; to hurl (*insults*); to turn inside out || *intr* to throw up || *ref* to spill; to pour; to upset

rovè·scio -scia (-sci -sce) *adj* reverse; inverse; inside out; upside down; backwards || *m* reverse; wrong side; downpour; upset; (com) crash; (tennis) backhand; **a rovescio** upside down; backwards || *f* see rovescia

rovéto *m* bramble; brier patch

rovina *f* ruin; blight; **andare in rovina** to go to ruin; **mandare in rovina** to ruin; **rovine** ruins

rovinare *tr* to ruin || *intr* (ESSERE) to collapse || *ref* to go to ruin

roviní·o *m* (-i) clatter; crash

rovinó·so -sa [s] *adj* ruinous

rovistare *tr* to rummage through

róvo *m* bramble

ròzza [ddzz] *f* nag

róz·zo -za [ddzz] *adj* rough; coarse

ruba *f*—**andare a ruba** to sell like hotcakes; **mettere a ruba** to plunder

rubacchiare §287 *tr* to pilfer

rubacuò·ri (-ri) *adj* ravishing || *m* ladykiller || *f* vamp

rubare *tr* to steal; **rubare a man salva** to pillage, loot || *intr* to steal; **rubare sul peso** to give short measure

rubería *f* thieving, stealing

rubicón·do -da *adj* rubicund

rubinétto *m* faucet; cock

rubino *m* ruby; jewel (*of watch*)

rubiz·zo -za *adj* well-preserved (*person*)

rubri·ca *f* (-che) title, heading; directory; (journ) section

rude *adj* (lit) rough; (lit) rude

ràdere *m* ruin

rudimentale *adj* rudimentary

rudiménto *m* rudiment

ruffia·no -na *mf* go-between || *m* pimp, panderer || *f* bawd, procuress

ru·ga *f* (-ghe) wrinkle; (bot) rocket

rùggine *f* rust; ill-will; (bot) blight

rugginó·so -sa [s] *adj* rusty

ruggire §176 *tr & intr* to roar

ruggito *m* roar

rugiada *f* dew

rugó·so -sa [s] *adj* wrinkled, wrinkly

rullàg·gio *m* (-gi) (aer) taxiing

rullare *tr* to roll || *intr* to roll; to taxi

rulli·o *m* (-i) roll; rub-a-dub

rullo *m* roll; platen (*of typewriter*); pin (*in tenpins*); **rullo compressore** road roller

rumè·no -na *adj & mf* var of **romeno**

ruminare (rùmino) *tr & intr* to ruminate

rumóre *m* noise; rumor; ado; **far molto rumore** to create a stir

rumoreggiare §290 (rumoréggio) *intr* to rumble

rumoró·so -sa [s] *adj* noisy; rumbling; controversial

ruolino *m* roster

ruòlo *m* roll; role; list; **di ruolo** regular, full-time; **fuori ruolo** temporary, part-time

ruòta *f* wheel; paddle wheel; revolving server (*in convent*); **a quattro ruote** four-wheel; **dar la ruota a** to sharpen; **esser l'ultima ruota del carro** to be the fifth wheel to a wagon; **fare la ruota** to spread its tail, strut (*said, e.g., of a peacock*); to turn cartwheels (*said, e.g., of an acrobat*); **ruota dentata** cog, cogwheel; **ruota idraulica** water wheel; **seguire a ruota** to follow closely

rupe *f* cliff

rurale *adj* rural, farm, farmer

ruscèllo *m* brook

ruspa *f* road grader

ruspante *m* barnyard chicken

russare *intr* to snore

Ràssia, la Russia

rus·so -sa *adj & mf* Russian

rustica·no -na *adj* rustic, boorish

rùsti·co -ca (-ci -che) *adj* rustic; coarse || *m* tool shed; cottage; (lit) peasant

rutilante *adj* (lit) shiny

ruttare *tr* (lit) to belch || *intr* (vulg) to belch

rutto *m* (vulg) belch

ruttóre *m* (elec) contact breaker

ruvidézza *f* or **ruvidi·tà** *f* (-tà) coarseness; roughness

rùvi·do -da *adj* coarse; rough

ruzzare [ddzz] *intr* to romp

ruzzolare (rùzzolo) *tr* to roll || *intr* (ESSERE) to tumble down; to roll

ruzzolóne *m* tumble; **a ruzzoloni** tumbling down

s

S, s ['esse] *m & f* seventeenth letter of the Italian alphabet

s- *pref* dis-, e.g., **sleale** disloyal; e.g., **sconto** discount; un-, e.g., **scatenare** to unchain, unleash

sàbato *m* Saturday; (*of Jews*) Sabbath; **sabato inglese** Saturday afternoon off

sabbàti·co -ca *adj* (**-ci -che**) sabbatical

sàbbia *f* sand; **sabbia mobile** quicksand

sabbiatura *f* sand bath; sandblast

sabbièra *f* (**rr**) sandbox

sabbió·so -sa [s] *adj* sandy

sabotàg·gio *m* (**-gi**) sabotage

sabotare (**sabòto**) *tr* to sabotage

sac·ca *f* (**-che**) bag; satchel; (mil) pocket; **sacca d'aria** (aer) air pocket; **sacca da viaggio** traveling bag; duffel bag

saccarina *f* saccharine

saccènte *mf* wiseacre, know-it-all

saccheggiare §197 (**sacchéggio**) *tr* to pillage, plunder

sacchég·gio *m* (**-gi**) pillage, plunder

sacchétto *m* little bag, pouch

sac·co *m* (**-chi**) bag; sack; sackcloth; pouch; (boxing) punching bag; (fig) heap, lot; **fare sacco** to sag; **mettere a sacco** to sack; **mettere nel sacco** to outwit; **sacco alpino** knapsack; **sacco a pelo** or **a piuma** sleeping bag; **sacco postale** mailbag

saccòc·cia *f* (**-ce**) (coll) pocket

sacerdòte *m* priest; (fig) devotee

sacerdotéssa *f* priestess

sacerdòzio *m* priesthood; ministry

sacramentale *adj* sacramental; (joc) habitual, ritual

sacraménto *m* sacrament

sacrà·rio *m* (**-ri**) memorial; sanctuary, shrine

sacresta *f* var of **sagrestia**

sacrificare §197 (**sacrifico**) *tr* to sacrifice; to waste; to force ‖ *ref* to sacrifice oneself

sacrifì·cio *m* (**-ci**) sacrifice

sacrilè·gio *m* (**-gi**) sacrilege

sacrìle·go -ga *adj* (**-ghi -ghe**) sacrilegious

sacri·sta *m* (**-sti**) sexton

sacristia *f* var of **sagrestia**

sa·cro -cra *adj* sacred

sacrosan·to -ta *adj* sacrosanct; sacred (*truth*)

sàdi·co -ca *adj* (**-ci -che**) sadistic ‖ *mf* sadist

sadismo *m* sadism

saétta *f* stroke of lightning; hand (*of watch*); (mach) bit; (lit) arrow

saettare (**saétto**) *tr* to shoot; **saettare sguardi a** to look daggers at

saettóne *m* (archit) strut

sagace *adj* sagacious, shrewd

sagà·cia *f* (**-cie**) sagacity

saggézza *f* wisdom

saggiare §290 *tr* to assay; to test; (dial) to taste

saggia·tóre -trice *mf* assayer ‖ *m* assay balance

saggina *f* sorghum

sàg·gio -gia (**-gi -ge**) *adj* wise ‖ *m* sage; assay; sample; proof; theme; test; rate (*of interest*); display; **di saggio** examination (*copy*)

saggì·sta *mf* (**-sti -ste**) essayist

sagittària *f* (bot) arrowhead

sagittà·rio *m* (**-ri**) (obs) archer ‖ **Sagittario** *m* Sagittarius

sàgola *f* (naut) halyard

sàgoma *f* outline; target; model, pattern; (joc) character

sagomare (**sàgomo**) *tr* to outline; to mold; to shape

sagomato *m* billboard

sagra *f* anniversary consecration (*of church*); festival

sagrato *m* elevated square in front of a church; churchyard; (coll) curse

sagrestano *m* sexton, sacristan

sagrestia *f* sacristy, vestry

sàia *f* serge

sàio *m* (**sài**) habit (*of monk or nun*); doublet; frock coat

sala *f* axletree; hall, room; (bot) cattail, reed mace; **sala da ballo** dance hall; **sala da pranzo** dining room; **sala d'aspetto** waiting room; anteroom; **sala operatoria** operating room

salac·ca *f* (**-che**) (coll) sardine; (coll) shad

salace *adj* salacious; pungent

salamandra *f* salamander

salame *m* salami

salamèlec·co *m* (**-chi**) salaam

salamòia *f* brine

salare *tr* to salt; (coll) to cut (*school*)

salaria·to -ta *adj* wage-earning ‖ *m* wage earner

salà·rio *m* (**-ri**) pay, wages

salassare *tr* to bleed

salasso *m* bloodletting

sala·to -ta *adj* salted; salty; dear, expensive; (fig) sharp ‖ *m* salt pork; cold cuts ‖ *f* salting

salda *f* starch solution (*used in laundering*)

saldacón·ti *m* (**-ti**) bookkeeping department; credit department; ledger; bookkeeping machine

saldare *tr* to solder; to set (*a bone*); to weld; to pay, settle ‖ *ref* to knit (*said of a bone*); (lit) to heal

saldatóre *m* solderer; welder; soldering iron

saldatura *f* soldering; setting (*of bones*); joint; continuity; **saldatura autogena** welding

saldézza *f* firmness

sal·do -da *adj* firm; valid (*reason*); flawless ‖ *m* balance; clearance sale; job lot; payment; **saldi** remnants ‖ *f* see **salda**

saldobrasatura *f* soldering

sale *m* salt; wit; (lit) sea; **restare di sale** to be dumbfounded; **sale inglese** Epsom salts; **sali aromatici** smelling salts; **sali da bagno** bath salts

salgèmma *f* rock salt

sàlice *m* willow tree; **salice piangente** weeping willow

salicilato *m* salicylate

saliènte *adj* projecting; (fig) salient ‖ *m* projection

salièra *f* saltcellar, salt shaker

salini·tà *f* (-**tà**) salinity

sali·no -na *adj* saline; salty ‖ *f* salt bed

salire §242 *tr* to climb ‖ *intr* (ESSERE) to climb; to go up; to rise; **salire in** or **su** to get on (*e.g., a train*)

saliscén·di *m* (-**di**) latch; **saliscendi** *mpl* ups and downs

salita *f* climbing; ascent, rise; slope; **in salita** uphill

saliva *f* saliva

salma *f* corpse, body

salma·stro -stra *adj* briny; saltish ‖ *m*— **sapere di salmastro** to smell or taste salty

salmerìe *fpl* wagon train; (mil) supplies

salmì *m*—**in salmì** (culin) in a stew

salmo *m* psalm

salmodiare §287 (**salmòdio**) *intr* to chant, sing hymns, intone

salmóne *m* salmon

salnitro *m* saltpeter

Salomóne *m* Solomon

salóne *m* hall; salon, drawing room; (naut) saloon; **salone da barbiere** barber shop; **salone dell'automobile** auto show

salòtto *m* drawing room; living room, parlor; reception room

salpare *tr* to weigh (*anchor*) ‖ *intr* (ESSERE) to weigh anchor

salsa *f* sauce

salsapariglia *f* sarsaparilla

salsèdine *f* saltiness

salsìc·cia *f* (-**ce**) sausage

salsièra *f* gravy boat

sal·so -sa *adj* salty; saline ‖ *m* saltiness ‖ *f* see **salsa**

saltabeccare §197 (**saltabécco**) *intr* to hop

saltaleóne *m* coil spring

saltare *tr* to jump; to skip; to sauté; (sports) to vault; hurdle; **far saltare** to kick out; to blow up (*e.g., a mine*); **saltare la sbarra** (coll) to go A.W.O.L. ‖ *intr* (ESSERE & AVERE) to jump; to pop off, e.g., **mi è saltato un bottone** one of my buttons has popped off; to blow out (*said of a fuse*); **saltare agli occhi** to be self-evident; **saltare a piè pari** to skip with both feet; **saltar fuori** to pop out (*said of the eyes*); to appear suddenly; **saltare in mente a** to come to the mind of; **saltare il ticchio a** (**qlcu**) **di** to feel like + *ger*, e.g., **gli è saltato il ticchio di cantare** he felt like singing; **saltare la mosca al naso a** (**qlcu**) to blow one's top, e.g., **le è saltata la mosca al naso** she blew her top; **saltare per aria** to blow up; **saltare su** to start (*to make a sudden jerk*); **saltare su a** + *inf* to begin suddenly to + *inf*

salta·tóre -trice *mf* jumper, hurdler

saltellare (**saltèllo**) *intr* to skip, hop

saltellóni *adv*—**a saltelloni** skipping, hopping

saltimban·co *m* (-**chi**) acrobat, tumbler; mountebank

salto *m* jump; leap; fall; skip; (*of animals*) mating; (fig) step; **a salti** skipping, jumping; **al salto sauté; fare quattro salti** to dance; **fare un salto** to hop, hurry; **salto a pesce** jackknife (*dive*); **salto coll'asta** pole vaulting; **salto in altezza** high jump; **salto in lunghezza** broad jump; **salto mortale** somersault; **salto nel vuoto** leap in the dark

saltuà·rio -ria *adj* (-**ri -rie**) desultory, occasional

salubre *adj* salubrious, healthy, healthful

salume *m* pork product

salumerìa *f* pork butcher shop

salumiè·re -ra *mf* pork butcher

salutare *adj* healthful ‖ *tr* to greet; to salute; (lit) to proclaim

salute *f* health; salvation; safety ‖ *interj* good luck!; to your health!; gesundheit!

saluto *m* salute; greeting; salutation; **distinti saluti** sincerely yours

salva *f* salvo; outburst; **a salve** with blank cartridges, with blanks

salvacondótto *m* safe-conduct

salvada·nàio *m* (-**nài**) piggy bank

salvagèn·te *m* (-**te** & -**ti**) life preserver; fender (*of trolley car*) ‖ *m* (-**te**) safety island

salvaguardare *tr* to safeguard

salvaguàrdia *f* safeguard

salvaménto *m* safety

salvamotóre *m* circuit breaker; fuse box

salvapun·te *m* (-**te**) pencil cap; tap (*on sole of shoe*)

salvare *tr* to save; to spare (*a life*); to rescue ‖ *ref* to save oneself; to be rescued; **si salvi chi può!** every man for himself!

salvatàg·gio *m* (-**gi**) rescue

salvatóre *m* savior, rescuer ‖ **il Salvatore** the Saviour

salvazióne *f* salvation

salve *interj* hello!, hail!

salvézza *f* salvation; safety

sàlvia *f* (bot) sage

salviétta *f* napkin; paper napkin; paper towel

sal·vo -va *adj* safe; saved; secure ‖ *m*—**mettere in salvo** to put in a safe place; **mettersi in salvo** to reach safety ‖ *f* see **salva** ‖ **salvo** *prep* except; **salvo che** unless; **salvo il vero** unless I am mistaken

samarita·no -na *adj* & *mf* Samaritan

sambu·co *m* (-**chi**) elder tree

san *adj* apocopated and unstressed form of **santo**

sanàbile *adj* curable

sanare *tr* to heal; to remedy; to reclaim (*land*); to normalize

sanatò·rio *m* (-**ri**) sanatorium

sancire §176 *tr* to ratify, sanction; to establish

sàndalo *m* sandal; sandalwood; flat-bottom boat

sandolino *m* canoe, skiff, kayak
sangue *m* blood; **agitarsi il sangue** to fret; **all'ultimo sangue** (*duel*) to the death; **al sangue rare** (*meat*); **a sangue freddo** in cold blood; cold-blooded; **cavar sangue da una rapa** to draw blood from a stone; **farsi cattivo sangue** to get angry; **il sangue non è acqua** blood is thicker than water; **puro sangue** thoroughbred; **sangue dal naso** nosebleed; **sangue freddo** calmness, composure
sangui·gno -gna *adj* blood (*circulation*); bloody; sanguine, ruddy || *m* (lit) color of blood
sanguinante *adj* bloody, bleeding
sanguinare (**sànguino**) *intr* to bleed; to be rare (*said of meat*)
sanguinà·rio -ria *adj* (**-ri -rie**) sanguinary
sanguinó·so -sa [s] *adj* bloody; bleeding; (fig) stinging
sanguisu·ga [s] *f* (**-ghe**) leech
sani·tà *f* (**-tà**) health; healthfulness; soundness (*of body*); sanity; health department
sanità·rio -ria *adj* (**-ri -rie**) health; sanitary || *m* physician
sa·no -na *adj* healthy; sound; **sano e salvo** safe and sound
sant' *adj* apocopated form of **santo** and **santa**
santa *f* saint
santabàrbara *f* (**santebàrbare**) (nav) powder magazine
santarellina *f* goody-goody girl
santificare §197 (**santifico**) *tr* to sanctify
santìssi·mo -ma *adj* most holy || *m* Eucharist
santi·tà *f* (**-tà**) sanctity, holiness; sainthood, saintliness
san·to -ta *adj* saintly; holy; sacred; blessed, livelong, e.g., **tutto il santo giorno** all the livelong day || *m* saint; name day; (fig) someone || *f* see **santa**
santorég·gia *f* (**-ge**) (bot) savory
santuà·rio *m* (**-ri**) sanctuary
sanzionare (**sanzióno**) *tr* to sanction; to ratify
sanzióne *f* sanction
sapére *m* knowledge; **sapere fare savoir-faire** || §243 *tr* to know; to find out; to know how to; **far sapere** to let know; **saperla lunga** to know a thing or two; **un certo non so che a certain something**, something vague || *intr*— **sapere di** to know; to taste; to smell; to smack of; **mi sa che** I think that; **non voler più saperne di** to not want to have anything to do with; **sapere male** (with *dat*) to feel sorry, e.g., **gli sa male** he feels sorry || *ref*—**che io mi sappia** as far as I know
sàpido -da *adj* savory; witty
sapiènte *adj* wise; talented; trained (*dog*) || *m* wise man
sapientó·ne -na *mf* wiseacre, know-it-all
sapiènza *f* wisdom; knowledge
saponària *f* (bot) soapwort

saponata *f* soapsuds; lather; (fig) **soft soap**
sapóne *m* soap; **sapone da toletta** toilet soap; **sapone per la barba** shaving soap
saponétta *f* cake of soap
saponière *m* soap maker
saponifi·cio *m* (**-ci**) soap factory
saponó·so -sa [s] *adj* soapy
sapóre *m* taste; savor; flavor
saporire §176 *tr* to savor
saporitaménte *adv* heartily; soundly
sapori·to -ta *adj* tasty; flavorful; salty; expensive
saporó·so -sa [s] *adj* savory; witty
saputèl·lo -la *adj* cocksure || *m* smart aleck
sarac·co *m* (**-chi**) hand saw
saracè·no -na *adj* Saracen, Saracenic || *m* Saracen; quintain
saraciné·sca *f* (**-sche**) metal shutter (*of store*); sluice gate; (hist) portcullis
sarcasmo *m* sarcasm
sarcàsti·co -ca *adj* (**-ci -che**) sarcastic
sarchiare §287 *tr* to weed
sarchia·tóre -trice *mf* weeder || *f* (agr) cultivator
sarchièllo *m* weeding hoe
sàr·chio *m* (**-chi**) hoe
sarcòfa·go *m* (**-gi** & **-ghi**) sarcophagus
sarcràuti *mpl* sauerkraut
Sardégna, la Sardinia
sardèlla *f* pilchard; sardine
sardina *f* pilchard; sardine
sar·do -da *adj* & *mf* Sardinian
sardòni·co -ca *adj* (**-ci -che**) sardonic
sarménto *m* vine shoot, running stem
sarta *f* dressmaker
sàrtie *fpl* (naut) shrouds
sarto *m* tailor
sartorìa *f* dressmaker's shop; tailor shop; dressmaking; tailoring
sassaiòla *f* shower of stones
sassata *f* blow with a stone
sasso *m* stone, rock; pebble; (poet) tombstone; **di sasso** stony; **restare di sasso** to be taken aback; **tirare sassi in colombaia** to cut one's nose to spite one's face
sassòfono *m* saxophone
sàssone *adj* & *mf* Saxon
sassó·so -sa [s] *adj* stony
Sàtana *m* Satan
satanasso *m* Satan; devil
satèllite *m* satellite
sa·tin *m* (**-tin**) sateen
satinare *tr* to gloss
sàtira *f* satire
satireggiare §290 (**satiréggio**) *tr* to satirize, lampoon || *intr* to compose satires
satìri·co -ca *adj* (**-ci -che**) satiric(al) || *m* satirist
sàtiro *m* satyr
satól·lo -la *adj* sated, full
saturare *tr* (**sàturo**) *tr* to saturate; to steep; (fig) to fill; (com) to glut (*a market*)
saturni·no -na *adj* Saturnian; saturnine
Saturno *m* (astr) Saturn
sàtu·ro -ra *adj* saturated; (fig) full; (lit) sated

sàu·ro -ra *adj & m* sorrel (*horse*)

Savèrio *m* Xavier

sà·vio -via (-vi -vie) *adj* wise || *m* wise man, sage

savoiar·do -da *adj & mf* Savoyard || *m* ladyfinger

saxòfono *m* saxophone

saziare §287 *tr* to satisfy; to cloy, satiate

sazietà *f* satiety, surfeit; **mangiare a sazietà** to eat one's fill

sà·zio -zia *adj* (-zi -zie) sated; full; satisfied

sbaciucchiare §287 (sbaciùcchio) *tr* to kiss again and again || *ref* to neck

sbadataggine *f* carelessness; oversight

sbada·to -ta *adj* careless; heedless

sbadigliare §280 *intr* to yawn

sbadì·glio *m* (-gli) yawn

sbafa·tóre -trice *mf* sponger

sbafo *m*—a sbafo sponging; **mangiare a sbafo** to sponge

sbagliare §280 *tr* to miss; to mistake; **sbagliarla** to be sadly mistaken || *intr & ref* to be mistaken; to make a mistake

sbaglia·to -ta *adj* wrong; mistaken

sbà·glio *m* (-gli) error, mistake

sbalestrare (sbalèstro) *tr* to fling with the crossbow; to send (*an employee*) far away || *intr* to speak amiss; to ramble; to blunder

sbalestra·to -ta *adj* unbalanced; ill-at-ease

sballare *tr* to unpack; **sballarle grosse** to tell tall tales || *intr* to overbid

sballa·to -ta *adj* unpacked; absurd, wild

sballottare (sballòtto) *tr* to toss

sbalordire §176 *tr* to stun; to amaze; to bewilder || *intr* to lose consciousness; to be dumfounded

sbalorditì·vo -va *adj* amazing

sbalzare *tr* to upset; to send far away; to overthrow; to emboss || *intr* (ESSERE) to bounce

sbalzo *m* leap, jump; climb; embossment, relief; **a sbalzi** by leaps and bounds; **di sbalzo** all of a sudden

sbancare §197 *tr* to clear (*ground*) of rocks; to ruin; (*cards*) to break (*the bank*)

sbandaménto *m* skid; swerve; disbandment; breaking up; (naut) list

sbandare *tr* to disband; (naut) to cause to list || *intr* to list; to skid; to swerve; to deviate || *ref* to disband; to break up

sbanda·to -ta *adj* disbanded; stray; alienated || *mf* alienated person || *m* straggler || *f* listing (*of ship*); skidding (*of vehicle*); **prendere una sbandata per** to get a crush on

sbandierare (sbandièro) *tr* to wave (*a flag*); to display

sbaragliare §280 *tr* to rout; to crush

sbaraglio *m*—mettere allo sbaraglio to endanger

sbarazzare *tr* to clear out; to free || *ref* —sbarazzarsi di to get rid of

sbarazzi·no -na *adj* mischievous || *mf* scamp; **alla sbarazzina** cocked, at an angle (*said of a hat*)

sbarbare *tr* to shave; to uproot || *ref* to shave

sbarbatèllo *m* greenhorn, fledgling

sbarcare §197 *tr* to unload; to discharge; to disembark; to pass; to strew (*fodder*); **sbarcare il lunario** to make ends meet || *intr* (ESSERE) to come ashore, land

sbarca·tóio *m* (-tói) landing pier

sbar·co *m* (-chi) unloading; landing

sbarra *f* bar; (typ) dash

sbarraménto *m* barrage; obstacle

sbarrare *tr* to bar; to block (*the way*); to open (*one's eyes*) wide, e.g., **sbarrò gli occhi** he opened his eyes wide

sbarrétta *f* bar; **sbarrette verticali** (typ) parallels

sbatacchiare §287 *tr* to slam; to flap || *intr* to slam

sbatàc·chio *m* (-chi) shore, prop

sbàttere *tr* to flap; to fling; to slam; to beat; to toss; to send away; to make pale; **sbatter fuori** to throw out || *intr* to flap; to slam

sbattighiàc·cio *m* (-cio) cocktail shaker

sbattitóre *m* electric mixer

sbattiuò·va *m* (-va) egg beater

sbattu·to -ta *adj* haggard, downcast

sbavare *tr* to slobber over; (mach) to trim || *intr* to drivel, slobber; to run (*said of colors*)

sbavatura *f* drivel; run (*of colors*); burr (*of metal*); deckle edge; verbosity

sbeccare §197 (sbécco) *tr & ref* to chip

sbeffeggiare §290 (sbefféggio) *tr* to make fun of

sbellicare §197 *ref*—sbellicarsi dalle risa to burst with laughter

sbèria *f* (coll) slap

sberlèffo *m* scar; grimace; **fare gli sberleffi a** to make faces at

sbevazzare *intr* to guzzle

sbevucchiare §287 *intr* to tipple

sbiadire §176 *tr & intr* (ESSERE) to fade

sbiadì·to -ta *adj* faded; dull

sbiancare §197 *tr* to whiten || *ref* to become white; to pale

sbianchire §176 *tr* (culin) to blanch

sbiè·co -ca (-chi -che) *adj* oblique; **di sbieco** on the bias; **guardare di sbieco** to look askance at || *m* cloth cut diagonally

sbigottire §176 *tr* to terrify, dismay || *intr* (ESSERE) & *ref* to be dismayed

sbilanciare §128 *tr* to unbalance; to upset || *intr* to lose one's balance || *ref* to commit oneself

sbilàn·cio *m* (-ci) disequilibrium; (com) deficit

sbilèn·co -ca *adj* (-chi -che) twisted, crooked

sbirciare §128 *tr* to leer at, ogle; to eye closely

sbir·ro -ra *adj* (coll) smart || *m* (pej) cop

sbizzarrire [ddzz] §176 *tr* to cure the whims of || *ref* to indulge one's whims

sbloccare §197 (sblòcco) *tr* to unblock; to raise the blockade of; to free

sbòbba *f* slop, dishwater

sboccare §197 (sbócco) *tr* to break the

mouth of (*a bottle*); to remove a few drops from (*a bottle*) || *intr* (ESSERE) to flow; to open (*said of a street*); **sboccare in** to turn out to be

sbocca·to -ta *adj* foulmouthed; foul (*language*); chipped at the mouth (*said of a bottle*)

sbocciare §128 (**sbòccio**) *intr* (ESSERE) to bud, burgeon, bloom

sbóc·co *m* (-**chi**) outlet; **avere uno sbocco di sangue** to spit blood

sbocconcellare (**sbocconcèllo**) *tr* to nibble at; to chip, nick

sbollentare (**sbollènto**) *tr* to blanch

sbollire §176 *intr* to stop boiling; to calm down

sbolognare (**sbológno**) *tr* (coll) to palm off; (coll) to get rid of

sbòrnia *f* (coll) drunk, jag; **smaltire la sbornia** to sober up

sborsare (**sbórso**) *tr* to pay out, disburse

sbórso *m* disbursement, outlay

sbottare (**sbòtto**) *intr*—**sbottare a** + *inf* to burst out + *ger*

sbottonare (**sbottóno**) *tr* to unbutton || *ref* (fig) to unbosom oneself

sbozzare (**sbòzzo**) *tr* to rough-hew; to sketch, outline

sbraca·to -ta *adj* without pants; slovenly; vulgar

sbracciare §128 *intr* to gesticulate || *ref* to roll up one's sleeves; to wear sleeveless clothes; to gesticulate; to do one's best

sbraccia·to -ta *adj* bare-armed

sbraitare (**sbràito**) *intr* to scream

sbraltó·ne -na *mf* bigmouth

sbranare *tr* to tear to pieces

sbrano *m* tear, rent

sbrattare *tr* to clean; to clear

sbreccare §197 (**sbrécco**) *tr* to chip, nick

sbrecciare §128 (**sbréccio**) *tr* to open a gap in

sbréndolo *m* tatter, rag

sbriciolare (**sbrìciolo**) *tr* to crumb || *ref* to crumble

sbrigare §209 *tr* to transact; to take care of || *ref* to hasten, hurry; **sbrigarsela** to get out of trouble; **sbrigarsi di** to get rid of; **sbrigati!** make it snappy!, hurry up!

sbrigativ·o -va *adj* quick, brisk; businesslike

sbrigliare §280 *tr* to unbridle; to reduce (*a hernia*); to lance (*an infected wound*) || *ref* to cut loose

sbrinare *tr* to defrost

sbrindella·to -ta *adj* tattered

sbrodolare (**sbròdolo**) *tr* to soil; (fig) to drag out || *ref* to slobber

sbrogliare §280 (**sbròglio**) *tr* to untangle; to clean up || *ref* to extricate oneself; **sbrogliarsela** to get out of a tight spot

sbronzare (**sbrónzo**) *ref* (coll) to get drunk

sbruffare *tr* to squirt out of the mouth; to spatter; to bribe || *intr* to tell tall tales

sbruffo *m* sprinkle, squirt; bribe

sbruffó·ne -na *mf* braggart

sbucare §197 *intr* (ESSERE) to pop out, come out

sbucciare §128 *tr* to peel; to skin || *ref* to slough (*said of snakes*); **sbucciarsela** (coll) to goldbrick

sbucciatura *f* slight abrasion

sbudellare (**sbudèllo**) *tr* to disembowel || *ref*—**sbudellarsi dalle risa** to burst with laughter, split one's sides laughing

sbuffare *tr* & *intr* to puff

sbuffo *m* puff; gust (*of wind*); **a sbuffo** puffed (*sleeve*)

sbullonare (**sbullóno**) *tr* to unbolt

sc- pref dis-, e.g., **sconto** discount; es-, e.g., **scalare** to escalate; ex-, e.g., **scusare** to excuse

scàbbia *f* scabies

sca·bro -bra *adj* rough; stony; tight (*style*)

scabró·so -sa [*s*] *adj* scabrous

scacchièra *f* checkerboard; chessboard

scacchière *m* (mil) sector; (obs) checkerboard; exchequer

scacciaca·ni *m* & *f* (-**ni**) toy gun; gun shooting only blanks

scacciamó·sche *m* (-**sche**) fly swatter

scacciapensiè·ri *m* (-**ri**) jew's-harp

scacciare §128 *tr* to chase away, drive away; to expel

scaccino *m* sexton, sacristan

scac·co *m* (-**chi**) chessman; checker; check; square; **a scacchi** checkered; **dare scacco matto a** to checkmate; **in scacco** or **sotto scacco** in check; **scacchi** chess; **scacco matto** checkmate

scàccoli *mpl* cement piles

scaccomatto *m* checkmate

scadènte *adj* inferior, poor, shoddy

scadènza *f* term, maturity; obligation; **a breve scadenza** short-term; **a lunga scadenza** long-term

scadére §121 *intr* (ESSERE) to decay, to decline; to fall due; to expire; (naut) to drift

scafandro *m* diving suit; **scafandro astronautico** space suit

scaffale *m* bookcase; shelf

scafo *m* hull

scagionare (**scagióno**) *tr* to exonerate, exculpate

scàglia *f* scale (*of fish*); chip; plate (*of medieval armor*); flake (*of soap*); tile (*of slate roof*)

scagliare §280 *tr* to hurl, fling, throw; to scale (*fish*) || *ref* to dash, to rush; to flake

scaglionare (**scaglióno**) *tr* to echelon; to stagger (*e.g., payments*)

scaglióne *m* terrace (*of mountain*); echelon; scale; **a scaglioni** graded (*e.g., income tax*)

scala *f* stairs; ladder; scale; (cards) straight; (rad) dial; **a scala** scaled, graded; **fare le scale** to climb the stairs; **scala a chiocciola** spiral stairway; **scala a gradini** or **a libretto** stepladder; **scala mobile** escalator; (econ) sliding scale; **scala porta** aerial ladder; **scala reale** (poker) straight flush; **su larga scala** large-scale; **su scala nazionale** on a national scale

scalandróne m (naut) gangway

scalare adj graded, scaled; gradual || m (com) running balance || tr to climb, ascend; to scale, grade; to reduce

scalata f climb, ascent; **dar la scalata a** to climb; to climb up to

scalcagna·to -ta adj down-at-the-heel

scalcare §197 tr to slice, carve

scalciare §128 intr to kick

scalcina·to -ta adj (wall or plaster) that is peeling off; worn-out; down-at-the-heels

scalda·acqua m (-acqua) hot-water heater

scaldaba·gno m (-gno) hot-water heater; **scaldabagno a gas** gas heater

scaldalèt·to m (-ti & -to) bedwarmer

scaldare tr to warm, warm up; to heat, heat up || intr (mach) to become hot || ref to warm up; to heat up; **scaldarsi la testa** to get excited

scaldavivan·de m (-de) hot plate

scaldino m hand warmer

scalèa f flight of stairs, stairway

scalèo m stepladder

scalétta f small ladder; small stairs; (mov) rough draft

scalfire §176 tr to graze, scratch; to cut (e.g., glass)

scalfittura f graze, scratch

scalinata f stairway, perron

scalino m step (of a stair); (fig) ladder

scalmana f chill; flush; **prendere una scalmana per** to take a fancy to

scalmanare ref to hustle, bustle; to fuss

scalmana·to -ta adj panting; hotheaded

scalmo m (naut) oarlock

scalo m pier, dock; (naut) ways; (naut) port of call; **fare scalo** (naut) to call, stop; (aer) to land; **scalo di alaggio** (naut) slip; **scalo merci** (rr) freight yard; **senza scalo** (aer, naut) nonstop

scalógna f (coll) bad luck

scalógno m (bot) scallion

scalòppa f veal chop

scaloppina f veal cutlet, scallop

scalpellare (scalpèllo) tr to chisel

scalpellino m stone cutter

scalpèllo m chisel; (surg) scalpel; **scalpello a taglio obliquo** skew chisel

scalpicciare §128 tr & intr to shuffle

scalpitare (scàlpito) intr to paw the ground

scalpóre m scene; **fare scalpore** to raise a fuss

scaltrézza f shrewdness, cunning

scaltrire §176 tr to polish, refine; to sharpen the wits of || ref to catch on; to improve

scal·tro -tra adj shrewd, smart

scalzare tr to take the shoes or stockings off of; to undermine || ref to take off one's shoes or stockings

scal·zo -za adj barefoot

scambiare §287 tr to exchange; to mistake || ref to exchange (presents)

scambiévole adj mutual

scàm·bio m (-bi) exchange; (rr) switch;

libero scambio free trade; **scambio di persona** mistaken identity

scamicia·to -ta adj in shirt sleeves; extremist || m extremist; tunic, waist

scamoscia·to -ta adj chamois, suede

scampagnata f excursion, outing

scampanare intr to peal, chime; to flare (said of a garment)

scampanellare (scampanèllo) intr to ring loud and clear

scampani·o m (-ì) toll, peal

scampare tr to save, rescue; **scamparla bella** to have a narrow escape || intr (ESSERE)—**scampare a** to escape from; to take refuge in

scampo m escape; safety; (zool) Norway lobster; **non c'è scampo** there is no way out

scàmpolo m remnant; **scampoli di tempo** free moments

scanalare tr to channel, groove, rabbet || intr to overflow

scanalatura f channel, groove, rabbet

scandagliare §280 tr to sound

scandà·glio m (-gli) sounding lead; **fare uno scandaglio** to make a sounding or survey

scandalismo m scandalmongering, yellow journalism

scandalizzare [ddzz] tr to scandalize, shock || ref to be scandalized

scàndalo m scandal

scandaló·so -sa [s] adj scandalous

scandina·vo -va adj & mf Scandinavian

scandire §176 tr to scan; to syllabize; (telv) to scan

scàndola f wood shingle

scannare tr to slaughter, butcher

scanna·tóio m (-tói) slaughterhouse; gyp joint

scanno m bench; seat; sand bar

scansafati·che mf (-che) loafer

scansare tr to move; to avoid || ref to get out of the way

scansìa f shelf; bookcase

scansióne f scansion; (telv) scanning

scanso m—**a scanso di** in order to avoid

scantinare intr to make a blunder; (mus) to be out of tune

scantinato m basement

scantonare (scantóno) tr to round (a corner) || intr to duck around the corner

scanzona·to -ta adj flippant; unconventional

scapaccióne m clout; **dare uno scapaccione a** to clout, slap

scapa·to -ta adj scatterbrained || m scatterbrain

scapestra·to -ta adj & m libertine

scapigliare §280 tr to dishevel || ref to be disheveled

scapiglia·to -ta adj disheveled; libertine; unconventional; free and easy

scapitare (scàpito) intr to lose

scàpito m damage; loss; **a scapito di** to the detriment of

scàpola f shoulder blade

scapolare m scapular || v (scàpolo) tr (coll) to escape, avoid || intr—**scapolare da** to get out of (danger)

scàpo·lo -la *adj* unmarried || *m* bachelor || *f* see **scapola**

scappaménto *m* escapement (*of watch, of piano*); (aut) exhaust

scappare *tr*—**scapparla bella** to have a narrow escape || *intr* (ESSERE) to flee; to abscond; to run; to get away; to escape; to stick out; to burst out (*said, e.g., of sun*); **far scappare la pazienza a qlcu** to make s.o. lose his patience, to tax s.o.'s patience; **scappare a gambe levate** to run away, beat it; **scappare da** to burst out, e.g., **gli è scappato da ridere** he burst out laughing; **scappar detto di** to blurt out that, e.g., **gli scappò detto di non poterne più** he blurted out that he could not hold out; **scappare di mente** to escape one's mind; **scappar fuori con** to come out with

scappata *f* excursion; sally; escapade; bolt (*of horse*); **fare una scappata** to take a run; **scappata spiritosa** witticism

scappatóia *f* subterfuge; loophole

scappellare (scappèllo) *ref* to tip one's hat

scappellòtto *m* smack, slap (on the head); **entrare a scappellotto** (coll) to squeeze in; **passare a scappellotto** (coll) to squeeze through with influence

scapricciare §128 *tr* to satisfy the whims of

scarabèo *m* beetle; scarab (*stone*); **scarabeo sacro** scarab; **scarabeo stercorario** dung beetle

scarabocchiare §287 (**scarabòcchio**) *tr* to scribble; to blot (*with ink*)

scarabòc·chio *m* (**-chi**) ink blot; scribble; scrawl

scarafàg·gio *m* (**-gi**) cockroach

scaramanzìa *f* exorcism; **per scaramanzia** to ward off the evil eye, for good luck

scaramazza *adj fem* irregular (*pearl*)

scaramùc·cia *f* (**-ce**) skirmish

scaraventare (scaravènto) *tr* to hurl, chuck; to transfer suddenly

scarcerare (scàrcero) *tr* to release from jail

scardinare (scàrdino) *tr* to unhinge

scàri·ca *f* (**-che**) discharge; volley; evacuation; (elec) discharge; (fig) shower

scaricabarili *m*—**giocare a scaricabarili** (fig) to pass the buck

scaricare §197 (**scàrico**) *tr* to unload; to discharge; to hurl (*insults*); to wreak (*anger*); to free (*from responsibility*) || *ref* to unburden oneself; to flow (*said of a river*); to discharge; to run down (*said of a battery or a watch*)

scaricatóre *m* longshoreman; (elec) lightning arrester

scàri·co -ca *adj* (**-chi -che**) empty, unloaded; discharged; clear (*sky*); free; run-down (*e.g., clock*) || *m* unloading; discharge; exhaust; waste, refuse; **a mio (tuo, etc.) scarico** in my (your, etc.) defense || *f* see **scarica**

scarlattina *f* scarlet fever

scarlat·to -ta *adj & m* scarlet

scarmigliare §280 *tr* to dishevel

scarnificare §197 (**scarnifico**) or **scarnire** §176 *tr* to bone, take the flesh off; to make thin; to wear down to the bone

scarni·to -ta or **scar·no -na** *adj* boned; meager; skinny

scaròla *f* escarole, endive

scarpa *f* shoe; wedge, skid; scarp; **fare le scarpe a** to undercut; **scarpe al sole** violent death; **scarpe da sci** ski boots

scarpata *f* escarp, escarpment; slope (*of embankment*); blow with a shoe; **scarpata continentale** continental slope

scarpétta *f* small shoe; low shoe; **scarpette chiodate** spikes; **scarpette da ginnastica** gym shoes

scarpinare *intr* to trudge

scarpóne *m* heavy boot; clodhopper

scarròc·cio *m* (**-ci**) (aer, naut) leeway

scarrozzare (scarròzzo) *tr* to take for a ride || *intr* to go for a ride; to go for a walk

scarrozzata *f* ride, drive

scarseggiare §290 (**scarséggio**) *intr* (ESSERE) to be scarce, be in short supply; **scarseggiare di** to be short of

scarsèlla *f* pocket; (obs) purse

scarsézza *f* or **scarsi·tà** *f* (**-tà**) scarcity, dearth, lack

scar·so -sa *adj* short; scarce; scanty, scant; weak (*wind*); **scarso a** short of

scartabellare (scartabèllo) *tr* to leaf through (*a book*)

scartafàc·cio *m* (**-ci**) note pad, notebook; poorly-bound copybook

scartaménto *m* (rr) gauge; **a scartamento ridotto** narrow-gauge; smallsize; small-scale

scartare *tr* to unpack, unwrap; to discard (*cards*); to remove; to scrap (*e.g., a machine*); (mil) to reject || *intr* to swerve; to side-step

scartata *f* unwrapping; side step; swerving; (fig) scolding

scartina *f* discard

scarto *m* discard; reject; swerve; (mil) rejected soldier; (sports) difference; **di scarto inferior**

scartocciare §128 (**scartòccio**) *tr* to unwrap; to unfold; to husk (*corn*)

scartòffie *fpl* old papers, trash

scassare *tr* to uncrate; to plow up; (coll) to ruin, bust || *ref* (coll) to break down

scassinare *tr* to pick (*a lock*); to burglarize; to break open

scassina·tóre -trice *mf* burglar; **scassinatore di casseforti** safe-cracker

scasso *m* plowing, tilling; burglary

scatenare (scaténo) *tr* to unchain; to trigger; to excite, stir up || *ref* to break loose

scàtola *f* box; can; **a scatola chiusa** sight unseen; **in scatola** canned; **rompere le scatole a** (vulg) to bug, pester; **scatola armonica** music box; **scatola a sorpresa** jack-in-the-box;

scatola cranica cranium, skull; **scatola del cambio** (aut) transmission, gear box

scatolame *m* boxes; canned food

scatolifi·cio *m* (**-ci**) box factory

scattare *tr* to take (*a picture*) ‖ *intr* (ESSERE & AVERE) to jump, spring; to go off (*said of a trap*); to go up (*said of the cost of living*); to go into action, begin

scatto *m* click (*of camera, gun*); outburst; sprint; automatic increase (*in salary*); shutter release; **a scatti** in jerks; **di scatto** suddenly

scaturire §176 *intr* (ESSERE) to spring; to pour, gush; to stem

scavalcare §197 *tr* to jump over; to pass over; to unsaddle; to skip (*a stitch*) ‖ *intr* (ESSERE) to dismount ‖ *ref* (coll) to rush

scavallare *intr* to caper, cavort

scavare *tr* to dig; to dig up, unearth

scava·tóre -trice *adj* excavating ‖ *m* digger ‖ digger, excavator

scavezzacollo *m* scamp; daredevil; **a scavezzacollo** headlong, at breakneck speed

scavezzare (**scavézzo**) *tr* to lop; to burst; to break; to take the halter off (*a horse*)

scavo *m* digging, excavation

scazzottare (**scazzòtto**) *tr* to beat up

scégliere §244 *tr* to choose; to pick out

sceic·co *m* (**-chi**) sheik

scelleratàggine *f* or **scelleratézza** *f* wickedness, villainy

scellera·to -ta *adj* wicked ‖ *m* villain

scellino *m* shilling

scél·to -ta *adj* choice; selected; (mil) first-class ‖ *f* choice; pick; selection; **di prima scelta** choice

scemare (**scémo**) *tr* to diminish, reduce; to lower the level of ‖ *intr* (ESSERE) & *ref* to lessen, diminish

scemènza *f* foolishness, stupidity

scé·mo -ma *adj* silly, foolish ‖ *mf* simpleton, fool

scempiàggine *f* silliness, foolishness

scém·pio -pia (**-pi -pie**) *adj* simple; single; (lit) wicked ‖ *m* ruination; (lit) slaughter; **fare scempio di** to ruin; (lit) to slaughter

scèna *f* scene; stage; acting; scenery; **esser di scena** (theat) to be on; **mettere in scena** (theat) to stage; **scene di prossima programmazione** (mov) coming attractions

scenà·rio *m* (**-ri**) scenery; scenario, setting

scenari·sta *mf* (**-sti -ste**) scenarist; script writer

scenata *f* scene (*outbreak of anger*)

scéndere §245 *tr* to descend, go down; to bring down ‖ *intr* (ESSERE) to descend, go down; to get off; to come (*to an agreement*); to step (*into the ring*); to put up (*at a hotel*); to check in (*at a hotel*)

scendilèt·to *m* (**-to**) scatter rug; bathrobe

sceneggiare §290 (**scenéggio**) *tr* to write a scenario for; to adapt for the stage

sceneggia·tóre -trice *mf* scenarist

sceneggiatura *f* (mov) screenplay; (rad, telv) continuity

scenètta *f* (theat) sketch

scenògrafo *m* scene designer

scenotècni·ca *f* (**-che**) stagecraft

sceriffo *m* sheriff

scèrnere §246 *tr* to discern; to distinguish; to select

scervellare (**scervèllo**) *ref* to rack one's brains

scervella·to -ta *adj* scatterbrained

scésa [s] *f* discent; slope

scespiria·no -na *adj* Shakesperean

scetticismo *m* skepticism

scètti·co -ca (**-ci -che**) *adj* skeptic(al) ‖ *m* skeptic

scèttro *m* scepter

sceverare (**scévero**) *tr* (lit) to distinguish

scé·vro -vra *adj* (lit) free, exempt

schèda *f* card; slip, form; **scheda elettorale** ballot; **scheda perforata** punch card

schedare (**schèdo**) *tr* to file

schedà·rio *m* (**-ri**) card index, card catalogue; file cabinet

schég·gia *f* (**-ge**) splinter; chip

scheggiare §290 (**schéggio**) *tr* & *ref* to splinter

schelètri·co -ca *adj* (**-ci -che**) skeleton, skeletal; succint

schèletro *m* skeleton

schè·ma *m* (**-mi**) diagram; draft; model; scheme; **schema di montaggio** (electron) hookup

schérma *f* fencing

schermàglia *f* argument

schermare (**schérmo**) *tr* to screen; (elec) to shield

schermire §176 *tr* to protect; (obs) to fence with ‖ *ref*—**schermirsi da** to ward off, parry; to protect oneself from

schermi·tóre -trice *mf* fencer

schérmo *m* screen; protection; (elec) shield; **farsi schermo di** to use as protection; **farsi schermo delle mani** to ward off a blow with one's hands

schernire §176 *tr* to deride

schérno *m* derision, ridicule, mockery

scherzare (**schérzo**) *tr* (coll) to mock ‖ *intr* to play; to joke, trifle

schérzo *m* play; joke, jest; freak (*of nature*); child's play; trick; **neppure per scherzo** under no circumstances; **per scherzo** in jest; **stare allo scherzo** to take a joke

scherzó·so -sa *adj* joking; playful

schiacciaménto *m* crushing; flattening

schiaccianó·ci *m* (**-ci**) nutcracker

schiacciante *adj* crushing

schiacciapata·te *m* (**-te**) ricer

schiacciare §128 *tr* to crush; to take (*a nap*); to squelch (*a rumor*); to subdue (*the details of a painting*); to mash (*potatoes*); to tread on, step on (*s.o.'s foot*); to flatten; to run (*s.o.*) over; to make (*s.o.'s figure*) look squatty; to crack (*nuts*); to flunk; (tennis) to smash

schiacciata *f* hot cake; (tennis) smash

schiaffare *tr* (coll) to fling, clap
schiaffeggiare §290 (**schiafféggio**) *tr* to slap; to buffet
schiaffo *m* slap, box
schiamazzare *intr* to squawk, cackle; to honk; to make a racket
schiamazzo *m* squawking, cackle; honk; hubbub
schiantare *tr* to crush, burst || *intr* (ESSERE) (coll) to burst; (coll) to croak || *ref* to break, crack, split
schianto *m* break, crack; crash; bang; knockout (*extraordinary, attractive person or thing*); **di schianto** all of a sudden; **schianto al cuore** heartache
schiappa *f* splinter; (coll) good-for-nothing
schiarimento *m* elucidation
schiarire §176 *tr* to make clearer; to make (*the hair*) light; to clear; to explain; to elucidate || *intr* (ESSERE) to become light || *ref* to clear up (*said of the weather*); to clear (*one's throat*); to fade || *impers* (ESSERE) —**schiarisce** it is getting light
schiarita *f* clearing (*of weather*); improvement (*in relations*)
schiatta *f* race, stock
schiattare *intr* (ESSERE) to burst
schiavi·sta (-**sti** -**ste**) *adj* slave (*e.g., state*) || *mf* antiabolitionist
schiavi·tù *f* (-**tù**) slavery; bondage
schia·vo -**va** *adj* enslaved || *mf* slave
schiccherare (**schicchero**) *tr* to scribble; to soil; to sketch; to dash off; to blurt out; (coll) to clean out
schidionare (**schidióno**) *tr* to put on the spit
schidióne *m* spit
schièna *f* back; divide; crown (*of road*); **giocare di schiena** to buck
schienale *m* back (*of chair; cut of meat*)
schièra *f* crowd; flock; herd; (mil) rank
schieramento *m* alignment
schierare (**schièro**) *tr* to line up || *ref* to line up; **schierarsi dalla parte di** to side with
schiètto -**ta** *adj* pure; frank, honest
schifare *tr* to loathe; to disgust || *ref*—**schifarsi di** to feel disgusted with
schifa·to -**ta** *adj* disgusted
schifiltó·so -**sa** [s] *adj* fastidious; squeamish
schifo *m* disgust, loathing; skiff; shell; **fare schifo a** to disgust; to make sick
schifó·so -**sa** [s] *adj* disgusting, sickening; (slang) tremendous
schioccare §197 (**schiòcco**) *tr* to snap (*the fingers*); to click (*the tongue*); to smack (*the lips*); to crack (*a whip*) || *intr* to crack
schiòc·co *m* (-**chi**) crack, snap; click; smack
schiodare (**schiòdo**) *tr* to take the nails out of
schioppettata *f* gunshot; earshot
schiòppo *m* gun, shotgun; **a un tiro di schioppo** within earshot
schiùdere §125 *tr & ref* to open
schiuma *f* foam, froth; lather; head (*of beer*); dregs, scum; meerschaum;

avere la schiuma alla bocca to froth at the mouth
schiumaiòla *f* skimmer
schiumare *tr* to scum; to skim || *intr* to foam, froth; to lather
schiumó·so -**sa** [s] *adj* foamy
schivare *tr* to avoid; to avert || *ref* to shy
schi·vo -**va** *adj* averse; bashful, shy
schizzare *tr* to spray; to sprinkle; to ooze (*venom*); to sketch; **schizzare fuoco dagli occhi** to have fire in one's eyes || *intr* (ESSERE) to gush; to squirt; to dart; **gli occhi gli schizzano dall'orbita** his eyes are popping out of his head
schizzétto *m* sprayer; syringe; water pistol
schizzinó·so -**sa** [s] *adj* finicky, fastidious
schizzo *m* spray; splash; sketch; survey (*e.g., of literature*)
sci *m* (**sci**) ski
scia *f* wake; track; trail; **scia di condensazione** contrail
sciàbola *f* saber
sciabordare (**sciabórdo**) *tr* to shake, agitate || *intr* to break (*said of waves*)
sciacallo *m* jackal
sciacquadí·ta *m* (-**ta**) finger bowl
sciacquare (**sciàcquo**) *tr* to rinse
sciacquatura *f* rinse
sciacquí·o *m* (-**i**) splash, dash
sciàcquo *m* rinsing (*of the mouth*); mouthwash
sciagura *f* calamity, misfortune
sciagura·to -**ta** *adj* unfortunate; wretched
scialacquare (**scialàcquo**) *tr* to squander
scialare *tr* to squander || *intr* to be well off; to live it up
scial·bo -**ba** *adj* pale, faded; wan
scialle *m* shawl; **scialle da viaggio** traveling blanket
scialo *m* squandering; opulence; **a scialo** lavishly
scialuppa *f* launch; lifeboat
sciamanna·to -**ta** *adj* slovenly
sciamannó·ne -**na** *mf* slovenly person || *f* slattern
sciamare *intr* (ESSERE & AVERE) to swarm
sciame *m* swarm; flock
sciampagna *f* champagne
scianca·to -**ta** *adj* cripple, lame; wobbly (*table*)
sciangài *m* pick-up-sticks || **Sciangài** *f* Shanghai
sciarada *f* charade
sciare §119 *intr* to ski; to back water
sciarpa *f* scarf; sash (*e.g., of an officer or of a mayor*)
scias·sì *m* (-**sì**) chassis
sciàtica *f* (pathol) sciatica
scia·tóre -**trice** *mf* skier
sciatterìa *f* or **sciattézza** *f* slovenliness
sciat·to -**ta** *adj* slovenly, sloppy
scibile *m* knowledge
sciènte *adj* conscious; knowing
scientìfi·co -**ca** *adj* (-**ci** -**che**) scientific
sciènza *f* science; knowledge

scienzia·to -ta *mf* scientist

scilinguàgnolo *m* frenum (*of tongue*); **avere lo scilinguagnolo sciolto** to have a loose tongue

Scilla *f* Scylla; **fra Scilla e Cariddi** between Scylla and Charibdis

scimitarra *f* scimitar

scimmia *f* monkey; (coll) drunk; **fare la scimmia a** to ape; **scimmia antropomorfa** anthropoid ape

scimmié·sco -sca *adj* (**-schi -sche**) monkeyish; apish

scimmiottare (scimmiòtto) *tr* to ape

scimpan·zé *m* (**-zé**) chimpanzee

scimuni·to -ta *adj* idiotic || *mf* idiot

scìndere §247 *tr* (lit) to split; to separate

scintilla *f* spark; sparkle; (fig) scintilla; **scintilla elettrica** jump spark

scintillare *intr* to spark; to sparkle

scintillì·o *m* (**-ì**) sparkle, brilliance

scioccare §197 *tr* to shock

sciocchézza *f* silliness; trifle

sciòc·co -ca (**-chi -che**) *adj* silly, foolish || *mf* fool, blockhead

sciògliere §127 *tr* to loosen; to release; to unfasten, untie; to solve; to disperse; to dissolve; to limber; to fulfill (*a promise*); to unfurl (*sails*) || *ref* to loosen up; to get loose; to dissolve; to melt (*into tears*)

scioglilìn·gua *m*(**-gue**) tongue twister

sciogliménto *m* melting; dissolution; fulfillment; denouement

sciolìna *f* ski wax

scioltézza *f* nimbleness, agility; freedom (*of movement*); ease

sciòl·to -ta *adj* loose; glib; free; blank (*verse*)

scioperante *adj* striking || *mf* striker

scioperare (sciòpero) *intr* to strike

sciopera·to -ta *adj* loafing; lazy || *m* loafer

sciòpero *m* strike; walkout; **sciopero a singhiozzo** slowdown strike; **sciopero bianco** sit-down strike; **sciopero della fame** hunger strike; **sciopero di solidarietà** sympathy strike; **sciopero pignolo** slowdown

sciorinare *tr* to display; to tell (*lies*); to air (*laundry*)

sciovìa *f* ski lift

sciovinìsmo *m* chauvinism, jingoism

scipì·to -ta *adj* insipid

scippo *m* snatching (*e.g., of a bag*)

sciròc·co *m* (**-chi**) sirocco; southeast

sciròppo *m* syrup

sci·sma *m* (**-smi**) schism

scismàti·co -ca *adj* (**-ci -che**) schismatic

scissióne *f* split; (biol, phys) fission

scìs·so -sa *adj* split, rent

scisto *m* schist

sciupare *tr* to spoil; to wear out; to waste; to rumple || *ref* to wear; to run down (*said of health*); to get rumpled

sciupa·to -ta *adj* ruined; worn out; wasted; run down

sciupì·o *m* (**-ì**) waste

sciupó·ne -na *mf* waster, squanderer

sciu·scià *m* (**-scià**) bootblack; urchin

scìvola *f* chute

scivolare (scìvolo) *intr* (ESSERE & AVERE) to slide, glide; to steal; **scivolare d'ala** (aer) to sideslip

scivolata *f* slide, glide; **scivolata d'ala** (aer) sideslip

scìvolo *m* chute; (aer) slip (*for seaplanes*)

scivolóne *m* slip, slide

scivoló·so -sa [s] *adj* slippery

scoccare §197 (scòcco) *tr* to shoot (*an arrow*); to give (*a buss*); to strike (*the hour*) || *intr* (ESSERE) to dart; to spring; to strike (*said of a clock*); to shoot

scocciare §128 (scòccio) *tr* (coll) to break; (coll) to bother; (naut) to unhook || *ref* to be bored

scoccia·tóre -trice *mf* (coll) nuisance

scocciatura *f* (coll) bother, annoyance

scòc·co *m* (**-chi**) darting; stroke (*e.g., of three*); (naut) hook; **scocco di baci** bussing, kissing

scodèlla *f* bowl; soup plate

scodellare (scodèllo) *tr* to dish out

scodellìno *m* small bowl; (mil) pan (*of musket lock*)

scodinzolare (scodìnzolo) *intr* to wag its tail; to waddle (*said of a woman*)

scoglièra *f* reef (*of rocks*); **scogliera corallina** coral reef

scò·glio *m* (**-gli**) rock; reef; cliff; stumbling block

scoiare §248 *tr* to skin

scoiàttolo *m* squirrel

scolabrò·do *m* (**-do**) colander, strainer

scolafrìt·to *m* (**-to**) strainer

scolapa·sta *m* (**-sta**) (coll) colander

scolare (scólo) *tr* to drain; (fig) to polish off || *intr* (ESSERE) to drip || *ref* to melt

scolaré·sco -sca (**-schi -sche**) *adj* school || *f* schoolchildren; student body

scola·ro -ra *mf* pupil; student

scolàsti·co -ca *adj* (**-ci -che**) school; scholastic || *m* scholastic, schoolman || *f* scholasticism

scola·tóio *m* (**-tói**) drain; strainer

scolatura *f* drip, drippings; dregs

scollaccia·to -ta *adj* low-necked; wearing a low-cut dress; dirty, obscene

scollare (scòllo) *tr* to cut off at the neck; to unglue || *ref* to wear a low-necked dress; to come unglued

scollatura *f* neckline; ungluing; **scollatura a barchetta** low neck; **scollatura a punta** V neck

scòllo *m* neck, neckline

scólo *m* drain; drainage; (slang) clap

scolopèndra *f* centipede

scolorare (scolóro) *tr*, *intr* (ESSERE), & *ref* to fade, discolor; to pale

scolorìre §176 *tr*, *intr* (ESSERE), & *ref* to fade, discolor

scolpare (scólpo) *tr* to excuse

scolpìre §176 *tr* to sculpture; to engrave; to emphasize

scólta *f* (lit) sentry; **fare la scolta to** stand guard

scombaciare §128 *tr* to pull apart, separate

scombinare *tr* to disarrange; to upset

scómbro *m* mackerel

scombù·glio m (-gli) (coll) disorder

scombussolare (scombùssolo) tr to upset

scomméssa f bet, wager

scomméttere §198 tr to bet; to separate

scommetti·tóre -trice mf bettor

scomodare (scòmodo) tr to trouble, disturb || ref to take the trouble

scomodi·tà f (-tà) trouble, inconvenience

scòmo·do -da adj awkward, unwieldy; uncomfortable || m inconvenience

scompaginare (scompàgino) tr to upset; (typ) to pi

scompagna·to -ta adj odd

scomparire §108 intr (ESSERE) to disappear; to make a bad showing

scompar·so -sa adj disappeared; extinct || mf deceased || f disappearance; death

scompartiménto m compartment; partition

scompènso m lack of compensation; imbalance

scompigliare §280 tr to disarray; to trouble, upset

scompi·glio m (-gli) disarray; upset

scompisciare §128 tr (vulg) to piss on || ref (vulg) to wet oneself; **scompisciarsi dalle risa** (coll) to split one's sides laughing

scomplè·to -ta adj incomplete

scompórre §218 tr to decompose, disintegrate; to rumple; to dishevel; to upset; to dismantle, take apart; (typ) to pi || ref to lose one's composure

scompó·sto -sta adj unseemly

scomùni·ca f (-che) excommunication

scomunicare §197 (scomùnico) tr to excommunicate; (joc) to ostracize

sconcertare (sconcèrto) tr to upset; to disconcert || ref to become disconcerted

sconcézza f obscenity, indecency

scón·cio -cia (-ci -ce) adj dirty, filthy, obscene || m obscenity; shame

sconclusiona·to -ta adj inconsequential; incoherent; rambling

sconcordanza f disagreement; (gram) lack of agreement

scondi·to -ta adj unseasoned

sconfessare (sconfèsso) tr to disavow; to retract

sconfessióne f disavowal

sconfiggere §104 tr to defeat, rout; to pull (a nail); to unfasten

sconfinare intr to cross the border; **sconfinare da** to stray from

sconfina·to -ta adj boundless, unlimited

sconfitta f defeat, rout

sconfortante adj discouraging

sconfortare (sconfòrto) tr to discourage; to distress || ref to become discouraged

sconfòrto m depression; distress

scongelare (scongèlo) tr to thaw

scongiurare tr to conjure; to implore

scongiuro m conjuration; entreaty

sconnès·so -sa adj disconnected; incoherent

sconnèttere §107 tr to disconnect; to take apart || intr to be incoherent

sconoscènte adj unappreciative

sconosciu·to -ta adj unknown || mf stranger

sconquassare tr to smash, shatter

sconquassa·to -ta adj broken-down; upset

sconquasso m destruction; confusion; smash-up

sconsacrare tr to desecrate

sconsideratézza f thoughtlessness

sconsidera·to -ta adj inconsiderate

sconsigliare §280 tr to dissuade, discourage

sconsiglia·to -ta adj thoughtless

sconsola·to -ta adj disconsolate

scontare (scónto) tr to expiate; to discount; to serve (time in jail)

scontentare (scontènto) tr to dissatisfy

scontèn·to -ta adj & m discontent

scónto m discount; part payment; (fig) partial remission

scontrare (scóntro) tr to meet; (naut) to turn (the wheel) sharply || ref to clash; to collide; to come to blows

scontrino m check, ticket

scóntro m collision; battle, encounter; clash; ward (of key)

scontró·so -sa [s] adj peevish, cross

sconveniènte adj unfavorable; unseemly, unbecoming; indecent

sconvenire §282 intr (ESSERE) to be unseemly or unbecoming

sconvòlgere §289 tr to upset; to disconcert

sconvolgiménto m upsetting; **sconvolgimento di stomaco** stomach upset; **sconvolgimento tellurico** upheaval

sconvòl·to -ta adj upset; disconcerted; distracted

scópa f broom; **scopa per lavaggio** mop

scopare (scópo) tr to sweep

scopata f sweep

scoperchiare §287 (scopèrchio) tr to uncover; to take the lid off

scopèr·to -ta adj uncovered; open; bare; exposed; unpaid || m open ground; open air; overdraft; (econ) short sale; (com) balance; **allo scoperto** in the open; overdrawn (check); short (sale) || f discovery; **alla scoperta** openly

scòpo m purpose, goal, aim

scoppiare §287 (scòppio) tr to uncouple || intr (ESSERE) to burst; to blow; to explode; to break (said, e.g., of news); (fig) to die (e.g., of overeating); **scoppiare a** to burst out (laughing or crying)

scoppiettare (scoppiétto) intr to crackle

scoppiétti·o m (-i) crackle

scòp·pio m (-pi) burst; explosion; outbreak; outburst; blowout (of tire); **a scoppio** internal-combustion (engine); **scoppio di tuono** clap of thunder

scòppola f drop (of plane in air pocket); (coll) rabbit punch

scopriménto m uncovering; unveiling

scoprire §110 tr to uncover; to unveil; to discover; to expose || ref to take off one's clothes; to take one's hat off; to reveal oneself

scopri·tóre -trice *mf* discoverer
scoraggiaménto *m* discouragement
scoraggiante *adj* discouraging
scoraggiare §290 *tr* to discourage, dishearten ‖ *ref* to be or become discouraged
scoraménto *m* (lit) discouragement
scorbuto *m* scurvy
scorciare §128 (scórcio) *tr* to shorten; to foreshorten ‖ *intr* (ESSERE) to shorten, grow shorter; to look foreshortened ‖ *ref* to shorten, grow shorter
scorciatóla *f* shortcut, cutoff
scór·cio *m* (-ci) foreshortening; end, close (*of a period*); **di scorcio** foreshortened
scordare (scòrdo) *tr* to forget; to put out of tune ‖ *ref* to forget; to get out of tune
scoreg·gia *f* (-ge) (vulg) fart
scoreggiare §290 (scoréggio) *intr* (vulg) to fart
scòrgere §249 *tr* to perceive, to discern
scòria *f* slag, dross; (fig) scum, dregs; **scorie atomiche** atomic waste
scorna·to -ta *adj* humiliated, ridiculed; hornless
scòrno *m* humiliation, ridicule
scorpacciata *f* bellyful; **fare una scorpacciata di** to stuff oneself with
scorpióne *m* scorpion ‖ **Scorpione** *m* (astrol) Scorpio
scorrazzare *tr* to wander over ‖ *intr* to run around; to move about; (fig) to ramble; (mil) to raid
scórrere §139 *tr* to raid; to glance over ‖ *intr* (ESSERE) to flow; to run; to glide
scorrerìa *f* raid, foray, incursion
scorrettézza *f* imprecision; impropriety
scorrèt·to -ta *adj* incorrect; improper
scorrévole *adj* sliding; flowing, fluent ‖ *m* slide (*of slide rule*)
scorribanda *f* raid, foray, incursion
scór·so -sa *adj* past, last ‖ *m* error, slip ‖ *f* glance; short stay
scor·sóio -sóia *adj* (-sói -sóie) slip (*knot*)
scòrta *f* escort; provision, stock; **di scorta** spare (*tire*); **fare di scorta a** to escort; **scorta d'onore** (mil) honor guard; **scorte** (com) stockpile; (com) supplies; **scorte morte** agricultural supplies; **scorte vive** livestock
scortare (scòrto) *tr* to escort; to foreshorten
scortecciare §128 (scortéccio) *tr* to strip the bark from; to peel off; to scrape ‖ *ref* to peel off
scortése *adj* discourteous, impolite
scortesìa *f* discourtesy, impoliteness
scorticare §197 (scórtico) *tr* to skin; to be overdemanding with (*students*); to fleece ‖ *ref* to skin (*e.g., one's arm*)
scòrza *f* bark; skin, hide; (fig) appearance; **scorza di limone** lemon peel
scoscendiménto *m* landslide; cliff
scoscé·so -sa [s] *adj* sloping, steep
scòssa *f* shake; jerk; **scossa di pioggia**

downpour; **scossa di terremoto** earth tremor; **scossa elettrica** electric shock; **scossa tellurica** earthquake
scossóne *m* jolt, jerk
scostaménto *m* removal; separation
scostare (scòsto) *tr* to move away; to try to avoid ‖ *intr* (ESSERE) to stand away ‖ *ref* to step aside; to stray
scostuma·to -ta *adj* dissolute, debauched
scotennare (scoténno) *tr* to scalp; to skin (*an animal*)
scòtta *f* whey; (naut) sheet
scottante *adj* burning (*question*); outrageous (*offense*)
scottare (scòtto) *tr* to burn; to scald; to sear; to boil (*eggs*); (fig) to sting ‖ *intr* to burn; to be hot (*said of stolen goods*) ‖ *ref* to get burnt
scottatura *f* burn; (fig) blow, jolt
scòt·to -ta *adj* overcooked, overdone ‖ *m*—**pagare lo scotto** to foot the bill; **pagare lo scotto di** to expiate ‖ *f* see **scotta**
scoutismo *m* scouting
scovare (scóvo) *tr* to rouse (*game*); to find, discover
scovolino *m* pipe cleaner; (mil) small swab
scóvolo *m* (mil) swab
scòzia *f* (archit) scotia ‖ **la Scozia** Scotland
scozzése [s] *adj* Scotch, Scottish ‖ *m* Scotch, Scottish (*language*); Scotchman ‖ *f* Scotchwoman
scozzonare (scozzóno) *tr* to break in (*a horse*); to train
scranna *f* (hist) seat
screanza·to -ta *adj* ill-mannered, rude
screditare (scrédito) *tr* to discredit
scremare (scrèmo) *tr* to cream
scrematrice *f* cream separator
screpolare (scrèpolo) *tr*, *intr* (ESSERE), & *ref* to crack; to chap
screpolatura *f* crack; chap (*of skin*)
screziare §287 (scrèzio) *tr* to mottle, variegate
scrè·zio *m* (-zi) tiff
scri·ba *m* (-bi) scribe (*Jewish scholar*)
scribacchiare §287 *tr* to scribble, scrawl
scribacchino *m* scribbler; hack
scricchiolare (scrìcchiolo) *intr* to crack, creak
scricchiolìo *m* (-ì) crack, creak
scricciolo *m* wren
scrigno *m* jewel box
scriminatura *f* part (*in hair*)
scrit·to -ta *adj* written ‖ *m* writing ‖ *f* sign; inscription; contract; **scritta luminosa** electric sign
scrit·tóio *m* (-tói) writing desk
scrit·tóre -trice *mf* writer
scrittura *f* handwriting; penmanship; writing; contract; entry; (theat) booking; **Sacra Scrittura** Holy Scripture; **scrittura privata** contract; **scrittura pubblica** deed, indenture; **scrittura a macchina** typing
scritturale *adj* scriptural ‖ *m* clerk; copyist; fundamentalist
scritturare *tr* (theat) to book, engage
scrivanìa *f* desk

scrivano *m* clerk, copyist, typist
scrivere §250 (scròce) *tr* & *intr* to write; **scrivere a macchina** to type
scroccare §197 (scròcco) *tr* to sponge (*a meal*); to manage to get (*a prize*) ‖ *intr* to sponge
scrocca·tóre -trice *mf* sponger
scròc·co *m* (-chi) sponging; creaking; **a scrocco** sponging; spring (*lock*); switchblade (*knife*)
scroccó·ne -na *mf* sponger
scròfa *f* sow; slut
scrollare (scròllo) *tr* to shake; to shrug (*one's shoulders*) ‖ *ref* to get into action; to pull oneself together
scrollata *f* shake; **scrollata di spalle** shrug
scrosciare §128 (scròscio) *intr* (ESSERE & AVERE) to pelt down; (fig) to thunder
scrò·scio *m* (-sci) thunder, roar; **scroscio di pioggia** downpour; **scroscio di tuono** thunderclap
scrostare (scròsto) *tr* to pick (*a scab*); to scrape; to peel off ‖ *ref* to peel off
scrosta·to -ta *adj* peeling; scaly
scròto *m* scrotum
scrùpolo *m* scruple; scrupulousness
scrupoló·so -sa [s] *adj* scrupulous
scrutare *tr* to scan, scrutinize
scruta·tóre -trice *adj* inquisitive ‖ *mf* teller (*of votes*)
scrutina·tóre -trice *mf* teller (*of votes*)
scruti·nio *m* (-nii) poll, vote; evaluation (*of an examination*); count (*of votes*); **scrutinio segreto** secret ballot
scucire §143 *tr* to unstitch; (coll) to cough up ‖ *ref* to come unstitched
scucitura *f* unstitching; rip
scuderia *f* stable
scudétto *m* badge; escutcheon; (sports) badge of victory
scudièro *m* esquire
scudisciare §128 *tr* to whip
scudi·scio *m* (-sci) whip
scudo *m* shield; escutcheon; **far scudo a** to shield
scùffia *f* (coll) load (*intoxication*); **fare scuffia** to capsize; **prendersi una scuffia per** to fall for, to fall in love with
scugnizzo *m* Neapolitan urchin
sculacciare §128 *tr* to spank
sculacciata *f* spank, spanking
sculacció·ne *m* spank, spanking
sculettare (sculétto) *intr* to waddle
scul·tóre -trice *mf* sculptor ‖ *f* sculptress
scultura *f* sculpture
scuòla *f* school; **scuola allievi ufficiali** military academy; officers' candidate school; **scuola dell'obbligo** mandatory education; **scuola di danza** dancing school; **scuola di dressaggio** obedience school (*for dogs*); **scuola di guerra** war college; **scuola di guida** driving school; **scuola di perfezionamento per laureati** postgraduate school; **scuola di taglio** sewing school; **scuola materna** kindergarten; **scuola mista** coeducational school

scuòla·bus *m* (-bus) school bus
scuòtere §251 *tr* to shake; to shake up; **scuotere di dosso** to shake off
scure *f* ax; cleaver
scurire §176 *tr*, *intr* (ESSERE), & *ref* to darken
scu·ro -ra *adj* dark ‖ *m* darkness; dark; shutter; **essere allo scuro** to be in the dark
scurrile *adj* scurrilous
scusa *f* excuse; apology; pretext; **chiedere scusa** to apologize
scusare *tr* to excuse; to pardon; to apologize for; **scusi!** pardon me! ‖ *ref* to apologize; to beg off
sdaziare §287 *tr* to clear through customs
sdebitare (sdébito) *tr* to free from debt ‖ *ref* to become free of debt; **sdebitarsi con** to repay a favor to
sdegnare (sdégno) *tr* to scorn; to arouse, enrage ‖ *ref* to get mad
sdégno *m* indignation, anger; (lit) scorn
sdegnó·so -sa [s] *adj* indignant; haughty
sdenta·to -ta *adj* toothless
sdilinquire §176 *tr* to weaken ‖ *intr* (ESSERE) & *ref* to swoon; to become mawkish
sdoganare *tr* to clear through customs
sdolcina·to -ta *adj* mawkish
sdolcinatura *f* mush, slobber
sdoppiamento *m* splitting
sdoppiare §287 (sdóppio) *tr* & *ref* to split
sdottoreggiare §290 (sdottoréggio) *intr* to pontificate
sdràia *f* chaise longue; deck chair
sdraiare §287 *tr* to lay down ‖ *ref* to stretch out (*e.g., on the ground*)
sdràio *m* (sdrài) stretching out; **mettersi a sdraio** to lie down
sdrucciolare (sdrùcciolo) *intr* (ESSERE & AVERE) to slip, slide
sdrucciolévole *adj* slippery
sdrùccio·lo -la *adj* proparoxytone ‖ *m* slip; slope; proparoxytone
sdruccioló·ni *adv* slipping, sliding
sdrucire (sdrùcio) & §176 *tr* to tear, rend, rip
sdrucitura *f* tear, rend, rip
se *m* (se) if ‖ §5 *pron* ‖ *conj* if; whether; **se mai** in the event; **se no** otherwise; **se non tu** (lui, lei, etc.) nobody else but you (him, her, etc.), e.g., **non puoi essere stato se non tu** it could not have been anyone else but you; **se non altro** at least; **se non che** but; **se pure** even if
sé §5 *pron* himself; herself; itself; yourself; themselves; yourselves; oneself; **di per sé stesso** by itself; **fuori di sé** beside oneself; **rientrare in sé** to come back to one's senses; **uscire di sé** to be beside oneself
sebbène *conj* although, though
sèbo *m* sebum, tallow
séc·ca *f* (-che) sand bank, shoal; drought; **dare in secca** to run aground; **in secca** hard up
seccante *adj* drying; annoying
seccare §197 (sécco) *tr* to dry; to bore;

to bother, annoy || *intr* (ESSERE) to dry up || *ref* to dry up; to be annoyed

secca·tóio *m* (-tói) drying room; squeegee (*to remove water from wet decks*)

secca·tóre -trice *mf* bore, pest

seccatura *f* drying; trouble, nuisance

sécchia *f* bucket, pail; **piovere a secchie** to rain cats and dogs

secchiéllo *m* little bucket

séc·chio *m* (-chi) bucket, pail; bucketful; **secchio dell'immondezza** trash can

séc·co -ca (-chi -che) *adj* dry; lanky; sharp || *m* dryness; dry land; drought; **a secco** dry (*cleaning*); **dare in secco** to run aground; **in secco** hard up; **lavare a secco** to dry-clean || *f* see **secca**

secenté·sco -sca *adj* (-schi -sche) seventeenth-century

secentèsi·mo -ma *adj, m & pron* six hundredth

secèrnere §153 (*pp* secrèto) *tr* to secrete

secessióne *f* secession

séco §5 *prep phrase* (lit) with oneself; along, e.g., **portare seco** to bring along

secolare *adj* secular; century-old; worldly || *m* layman

sècolo *m* century; age; world

secónda *f* second; second-year class; **a seconda** with the wind; **a seconda di** according to; **in seconda** (aut) in second; (mil) second in command

secondare (secóndo) *tr* to second

secondà·rio -ria *adj* (-ri -rie) secondary

secondino *m* prison guard, turnkey

secón·do -da *adj* second; (lit) favorable || *m* second; second course; (nav) executive officer || *f* see **seconda** || *pron* second || **secondo** *prep* according to; **secondo me (te, etc.)** in my (your, etc.) opinion

secondogèni·to -ta *adj* second-born

secrezióne *f* secretion

sèdano *m* celery

sedare (sèdo) *tr* to calm, placate

sedati·vo -va *adj & m* sedative

sède *f* seat; branch; residence; period; (gram) syllable; (rr) right of way; **in separata sede** in private; (law) with change of venue; **Santa Sede** Holy See; **sede centrale** main office, home office

sedentà·rio -ria *adj* (-ri -rie) sedentary || *m* sedentary person

sedére *m* sitting; rear, backside || *v* §252 *intr* (ESSERE) to sit, to be seated; to be in session; to be located || *ref* to sit down

sèdia *f* chair; seat; see; **sedia a braccioli** armchair; **sedia a dondolo** rocking chair; **sedia a pozzetto** bucket seat; **sedia a sdraio** deck chair; **sedia da posta** (hist) mail coach; **sedia di vimini** wicker chair; **sedia elettrica** electric chair; **sedia girevole** swivel chair

sedicènne *adj* sixteen-year-old || *mf* sixteen-year-old person

sedicènte *adj* so-called, self-styled

sedicèsi·mo -ma *adj, m & pron* sixteenth

sédici *adj & pron* sixteen; **le sedici** four P.M. || *m* sixteen; sixteenth (*in dates*)

sedile *m* seat; bench; bottom (*of chair*); (aut) bucket seat

sediménto *m* sediment

sediòlo *m* sulky

sedizióne *f* sedition

sedizió·so -sa [s] *adj* seditious

seducènte *adj* seductive; alluring

sedurre §102 *tr* to seduce; to allure; to lead astray; to charm, captivate

seduta *f* sitting; session, meeting; **seduta fiume** (pol) uninterrupted session; **seduta stante** on the spot

sedut·tóre -trice *adj* seductive; alluring; charming || *mf* seducer

seduzióne *f* seduction; allurement; charm

sefardi·ta (-ti -te) *adj* Sephardic || *mf* Sephardi

sé·ga *f* (-ghe) saw; **a sega** serrated; **sega a nastro** band saw; **sega circolare** buzz saw; **sega da carpentiere** lumberman's saw; **sega intelaiata a lama** bucksaw; **sega meccanica** power saw

ségala *f* rye

segali·gno -gna *adj* rye; lean, wiry

segare §209 (ségo) *tr* to saw; to cut

segatrice *f* power saw; **segatrice a disco** circular saw; **segatrice a nastro** band saw

segatura *f* cutting; sawdust

seggétta *f* commode

sèg·gio *m* (-gi) seat (*e.g., in congress*); **seggio elettorale** voting commission

sèggiola *f* chair; **seggiola a sdraio** deck chair

seggiolino *m* child's chair; stool; bucket seat; **seggiolino elettabile** (aer) ejection seat

seggiolóne *m* highchair; easy chair

seggiovìa *f* chair lift

segherìa *f* sawmill

seghetta·to -ta *adj* serrated

seghétto *m* hacksaw; **seghetto da traforo** coping saw

segménto *m* segment; **segmento elastico** (aut) piston ring

segnaccènto *m* accent mark

segnàcolo *m* (lit) symbol, sign

segnalare *tr* to signal; to point out || *ref* to distinguish oneself

segnalazióne *f* signaling; sign, signal; nomination; recommendation; **dare la segnalazione a** to notify; **fare segnalazioni** to signal; **segnalazioni stradali** road signs

segnale *m* sign; signal; bookmark; **segnale di allarme** (mil) alarm; **segnale di occupato** (telp) busy signal; **segnale di via libera** (telp) dial tone; **segnale orario** (rad, telv) time signal; **segnali stradali** road signs

segnalèti·co -ca *adj* (-ci -che) identification (*mark*) || *f* road signs

segnalibro *m* bookmark

segnaline·e *m* (-e) lineman

segnapósto *m* place card

segnapun·ti *m* (-ti) scorekeeper

segnare (ségno) *tr* to mark; to underscore, underline; to jot down; to say (*e.g., five o'clock, said of a watch*); to brand; (sports) to score; **segnare a dito** to point to || *ref* to cross oneself

segnatas·se *m* (-se) postage-due stamp

segnatura *f* signing; signature; library number; (eccl) chancery; (sports) final score; (typ) signature

segnavèn·to *m* (-to) weather vane

ségno *m* mark; bookmark; symbol; sign; signal; boundary; (mus) signature; **a segno che** so that; **a tal segno** to such a point; **essere fatto segno di** to be the target of; **in segno di** as a token of; **mettere a segno** to check, control; **segno della Croce** sign of the Cross; **segno di croce** cross (*mark*); **segno d'interpunzione**, or **di punteggiatura**, or **grafico** punctuation mark; **segno di riconoscimento** identification mark

ségo *m* tallow, suet

segregare §209 (sègrego) *tr* to segregate; to secrete || *ref* to withdraw

segregazióne *f* segregation; **segregazione cellulare** solitary confinement

segregazioni·sta *mf* (-sti -ste) segregationist

segretariato *m* secretariat

segretà·rio -ria *mf* secretary; clerk

segreterìa *f* secretary's office; secretaryship

segretézza *f* secrecy

segré·to -ta *adj* secret; secretive || *m* secret; secrecy; **segreto d'alcova** boudoir secret; **segreto di Pulcinella** open secret

seguace *mf* follower

seguènte *adj* following, next

segù·gio *m* (-gi) bloodhound; (fig) private eye

seguire (séguo) *tr* to follow; to attend || *intr* (ESSERE) to continue; to follow, ensue; (with *dat*) to follow

seguitare (séguito) *intr*—**seguitare a** + *inf* to keep on + *ger, e.g.,* **seguitare a parlare** to keep on talking; **seguiti!** go ahead!

séguito *m* following; retinue; followers; sequence; sequel; pursuit; **di seguito** in succession; **far seguito a** to refer to; **in seguito** thereafter; **in seguito a** as a consequence of

sèi *adj & pron* six; **le sei** six o'clock || *m* six; sixth (*in dates*)

seicènto *adj, m & pron* six hundred || *f* car with a motor displacing 600 cubic centimeters || **il Seicento** the seventeenth century

seimila *adj, m, & pron* six thousand

sélce *f* silica; flint; (lit) stone; **selci** paving blocks

selciare §128 (sélcio) *tr* to pave

selcia·to -ta *adj* paved || *m* paving

selettì·vo -va *adj* selective

selezionare (selezióno) *tr* to select, sort out

selezióne *f* selection; choice

sèlla *f* saddle

sel·làio *m* (-lài) saddler

sellare (sèllo) *tr* to saddle

sellerìa *f* saddler's shop; saddlery; (aut) upholstery

sélva *f* woods, forest

selvaggina *f* game

selvàg·gio -gia (-gi -ge) *adj* savage; vicious (*horse*) || *m* savage; unsociable person

selvàti·co -ca *adj* (-ci -che) wild

selvicoltura *f* forestry

sèlz *m* (sèlz) seltzer, club soda

semàforo *m* traffic light; semaphore

semànti·co -ca *adj* (-ci -che) semantic || *f* semantics

sembiante *m* (lit) look; **fare sembianti di** to pretend

sembianza *f* look; (lit) similarity

sembrare (sémbro) *intr* (ESSERE) to seem, look, appear || *impers*—**sembra** it seems

séme *m* seed; stone (*of fruit*); (cards) suit

seménta *f* sowing season; (lit) seed

seménte *f* seed

semènza *f* seed; brads (*used in upholstery*)

semenzà·io *m* (-zài) hotbed, seedbed

semestrale *adj* semiannual, semiyearly

semèstre *m* semester; half year

sèmi- *pref adj* semi-, *e.g.,* **semicircolare** semicircular; half-, *e.g.,* **semichiuso** half-closed || *pref mf* semi-, *e.g.,* **semicerchio** semicircle; half, *e.g.,* **semitono** half tone; demi-, *e.g.,* **semidio** demigod

semiapèr·to -ta *adj* half-open; ajar

semiasse *m* (mach) axle (*on each side of differential*)

semicér·chio *m* (-chi) semicircle

semichiu·so -sa [s] *adj* half-closed

semicìngola·to -ta *adj & m* half-track

semicircolo *m* semicircle

semiconduttóre *m* semiconductor

semiconvit·tóre -trice *mf* day student

semicù·pio *m* (-pi) sitz bath

semi·dìo *m* (-dèi) demigod

semidòt·to -ta *adj* semilearned

semifinale *f* semifinal

sémina *f* sowing; sowing season

seminare (sémino) *tr* to sow, seed; to plant; (coll) to leave behind

seminà·rio *m* (-ri) seminary; seminar

semina·ta *adj* sown, seeded || *m* sown land; **uscire dal seminato** to digress

semina·tóre -trice *mf* sower || *f* (mach) seeder, seeding machine

seminterrato *m* basement

seminu·do -da *adj* half-naked

semioscurità *f* partial darkness

semirìgi·do -da *adj* semirigid; inelastic

semirimòr·chio *m* (-chi) semitrailer

semisè·rio -ria [s] *adj* (-ri -rie) seriocomic

semisfèra *f* (geom) hemisphere

semi·ta (-ti -te) *adj* Semitic || *mf* Semite

semitòno *m* (mus) semitone, half tone

semmài *conj* if ever; in the event that

sémola *f* bran; (coll) freckles

semolino *m* semolina

semovènte *adj* self-propelled

sempitèr·no -na *adj* (lit) everlasting
sémplice *adj* simple; single; plain; mere; (mil) private; (nav) ordinary ‖ *m* medicinal herb; **semplici** simple folk
semplició·ne -na *adj* simple ‖ *mf* simpleton
semplici·tà *f* (**-tà**) simplicity
semplificare §197 (**semplifico**) *tr* to simplify ‖ *ref* to become easier or simpler
sèmpre *adv* always; ever; yet; **da sempre** from time immemorial; **di sempre** same, same old; **e poi sempre** ever and ever; **ma sempre** but only; **per sempre** forever; **sempre che** provided; **sempre meglio** better and better; **sempre meno** less and less; **sempre però** but only; **sempre vostro** very truly yours
sempreverde *adj, m & f* evergreen
sènape *f* mustard
senapismo *m* mustard plaster
senato *m* senate
sena·tóre -trice *mf* senator
senése [s] *adj & mf* Sienese
senile *adj* old; of old age
senilismo *m* (pathol) senility
senilità *f* old age
senióre *adj & m* elder, senior
Sènna *f* Seine
sénno *m* wisdom; **far senno** to come back to one's senses; **senno di poi** hindsight; **uscir di senno** to go out of one's mind
séno *m* chest; breast, bosom; cove; (anat) sinus; (math) sine; (fig) heart; **in seno a** within
senonché *or* **se non che** *conj* but
sensale *m* broker; commission merchant
sensa·to -ta *adj* sensible, reasonable, sane
sensazionale *adj* sensational
sensazióne *f* sensation
sensibile *adj* sensible; perceptible; appreciable; sensitive (*e.g.*, *to affection*) ‖ *m* world of the senses
sensibili·tà *f* (**-tà**) sensitivity, sensibility
sensibilizzare [ddzz] *tr* to sensitize
sensiti·vo -va *adj* sensitive ‖ *m* medium
sènso *m* sense; feeling; meaning; aspect; tone, fashion; direction; **ai sensi di legge** according to law; a **senso** free (*translation*); **doppio senso** double entendre; **in senso contrario** in the opposite direction; **perdere i sensi** to lose consciousness; **riprendere i sensi** to come to; **sensi** carnal appetite, flesh; **senso unico** one-way; **senso vietato** no entry, one-way
sensò·rio -ria *adj* (**-ri -rie**) sensory
sensuale *adj* sensual, carnal; sensuous
sensualità *f* sensuality
sentènza *f* sentence; maxim
sentenziare §287 (**sentènzio**) *tr* to pass sentence upon, sentence ‖ *intr* to pontificate
sentenzió·so -sa [s] *adj* sententious
sentièro *m* path, pathway
sentimentale *adj* sentimental; mawkish
sentimentalismo *m* sentimentalism
sentiménto *m* feeling; sentiment; sense;

uscire di sentimento (coll) to go out of one's mind
sentina *f* bilge; sink (*of vice*)
sentinèlla *f* sentry, sentinel
sentire *m* feeling ‖ *v* (**sènto**) *tr* to feel; to hear; to listen to; to consult (*a doctor*); to smell; to taste; **farsi sentire** to make oneself heard ‖ *intr* to feel; to listen; to smell; to taste; **non sentirci di quell'orecchio** to turn a deaf ear; **sentirci bene** to have keen hearing ‖ *ref* to feel; **non sentirsela di** to not have the courage to; **sentirsela** to feel up to it
senti·to -ta *adj* heartfelt
sentóre *m* inkling, feeling; sign; (lit) smell
sènza *prep* without; beyond (*e.g.*, *comparison*); **senza + inf** without + *ger*; **senza che + subj** without + *ger*; **senza di + pron** without + *pron*, *e.g.*, **senza di lui** without him; **senz'altro** without any doubt, of course
senza·dìo *m* (**-dìo**)—**i senzadio** the godless
senzapà·tria *m* (**-tria**) man without a country; renegade
senzatét·to *m* (**-to**) homeless person; **i senzatetto** the homeless
separare *tr & ref* to separate
separazióne *f* separation
sepolcrale *adj* sepulchral
sepolcréto *m* cemetery
sepólcro *m* sepulcher, grave
sepoltura *f* burial; grave
seppellire §253 *tr* to bury
séppia *adj invar* sepia ‖ *f* cuttlefish
seppure *conj* even if
sè·psi *f* (**-psi**) sepsis
sequèla *f* series
sequènza *f* sequence
sequestrare (**sequèstro**) *tr* to seize, confiscate; to kidnap; to confine; to quarantine; (law) to attach, sequester
sequèstro *m* seizure; attachment; **sequestro di persona** unlawful detention
séra *f* evening; night; **da mezza sera** cocktail (*dress*); dark (*suit*); **da sera** evening (gown); formal (*attire*)
serac·co *m* (**-chi**) serac
serafino *m* seraph
serale *adj* evening; night
seralménte *adv* in the evening; every evening
serata *f* evening; soiree, evening party; **serata d'addio** (theat) farewell performance; **di beneficenza** benefit performance
serbare (**sèrbo**) *tr* to keep; to save (*e.g.*, *a place*); to bear (*a grudge*) ‖ *ref* to keep oneself; to stay
serba·tóio *m* (**-tói**) tank; reservoir; cartridge clip
sèr·bo -ba *adj & mf* Serbian ‖ *m*—**in serbo** in store
serbocroa·to -ta *adj & mf* Serbo-Croatian
serenata *f* serenade
serenìssi·mo -ma *adj* Serene (*Highness*)
sereni·tà *f* (**-tà**) serenity

seré·no -na *adj* serene; clear, fair (*weather*)

sergènte *m* sergeant; carpenter's clamp; sergente maggiore first sergeant

sèri·co -ca *adj* (-ci -che) silk

sè·rie *f* (-rie) series; (sports) division; fuori serie (aut) custom-built; in serie (aut) standard; (elec) in series

serietà *f* seriousness; gravity

serigrafia *f* silkscreen process

sè·rio -ria (-ri -rie) *adj* serious; stern; poco serio unreliable (*man*); loose (*woman*) || *m* seriousness; sul serio in earnest; really, e.g., bello sul serio really beautiful

sermonare (sermóno) *tr & intr* (lit) to sermonize

sermóne *m* sermon

sermoneggiare §290 (sermonéggio) *intr* to preach; to lecture

seròti·no -na *adj* late; (lit) evening

sèrpa *f* coach box

sèrpe *f* snake, serpent; a serpe coiled, in a coil; nutrirsi or scaldarsi la serpe in seno to nourish a viper in one's bosom

serpeggiare §290 (serpéggio) *intr* to zigzag; to wind; to creep, spread

serpènte *m* snake, serpent; serpente a sonagli rattlesnake

serpenti·no -na *adj* serpentine || *m* serpentine; coil (*of pipe*) || *f* zigzag, turn (*of winding road*); coil (*of pipe*)

sérqua *f* dozen; lot, large number

sèrra *f* dike, levee; hothouse; sierra; un serra serra a milling crowd

serrafi·la *m* (-le) rear-guard soldier || *f* rear ship (*of convoy*)

serrafilo *m* electrician's pliers; (elec) binding post

serrà·glio *m* (-gli) menagerie; seraglio

serramànico *m*—a serramanico clasp (*knife*); switchblade (*knife*)

serrame *m* lock

serraménto *m* closing, bolting || serra-mén·ti & -ta *fpl* closing devices, doors, windows, and shutters

serranda *f* shutter (*of store*)

serrare (sèrro) *tr* to shut, close; to pursue (*the enemy*); to increase (*tempo*); to furl (*sails*); to lock; to clench (*one's teeth, one's fists*); to shake (*hands*) || *intr* to shut; to be tight || *ref* to be wrenched, e.g., gli si serrò il cuore his heart was wrenched; serrarsi addosso a to press (*the enemy*)

serrata *f* lockout

serrate *m*—serrate finale (sports) finish

serra·to -ta *adj* shut (*e.g., door*); concise (*style*); tight (*game*); rapid (*gallop*); closed (*ranks*); thick (*crowd*) || *f* see serrata

serratura *f* lock

sèrto *m* (poet) crown, wreath

sèrva *f* (pej) maidservant, maid

servènte *adj* (*gentleman*) in waiting || *m* gunner; (obs) servant

servìbile *adj* usable

serviènte *m* (eccl) server

servì·gio *m* (-gi) service; favor

servile *adj* servile; menial; modal (*auxiliary*)

servire (sèrvo) *tr* to serve; to wait on; in che posso servirLa? what can I do for you?; may I help you?; per ser-virLa at your service || *intr* to serve || *intr* (ESSERE & AVERE) to serve; to answer the purpose; to last; (with *dat*) (coll) to need, e.g., gli serve il martello he needs the hammer; non servire a nulla to be of no use; servire da to act as || *ref* to help oneself; servirsi da to patronize, deal with; servirsi di to avail oneself of, use

servitóre *m* servant; tea wagon; servitor suo umilissimo your humble servant

servi·tù *f* (-tù) servitude; captivity; servants, help; servitù di passaggio (law) easement

serviziévole *adj* obliging, accommodating

servì·zio *m* (-zi) service; favor; turn; a mezzo servizio part-time (*domestic help*); di servizio delivery (*entrance*); for hire (*car*); domestic (*help*); in servizio out of commission; in servizio in commission; servizi kitchen and bath; facilities; servizi pubblici public services; public works; servizio attivo active duty; servizio permanente effettivo service in the regular army

sèr·vo -va *adj* (lit) enslaved || *m* slave; servant; servo della gleba serf || *f* see serva

servoassisti·to -ta *adj* servocontrolled

servofréno *m* (aut) power brake

servomotóre *m* servomotor

servostèrzo *m* (aut) power steering

sèsamo *m* sesame; apriti sesamo! open sesame!

sessanta *adj, m & pron* sixty

sessantènne *adj* sixty-year-old || *mf* sixty-year-old person

sessantèsi·mo -ma *adj, m & pron* sixtieth

sessantina *f* about sixty

sessióne *f* session

sèsso *m* sex; il sesso debole the fair sex

sessuale *adj* sexual

sestante *m* sextant

sestétto *m* sextet

sestière *m* district, section

sè·sto -sta *adj & pron* sixth || *m* sixth; curve (*of an arch*); fuori sesto out of sorts; mettere in sesto to arrange; to set in order; sesto acuto (archit) ogive

sèt *m* (sèt) set; set all'aperto (mov) location

séta *f* silk; seta artificiale rayon

setacciare §128 *tr* to sift, sieve

setàc·cio *m* (-ci) sieve

setàce·o -a *adj* silky

séte *f* thirst; aver sete to be thirsty; to lust after; sete di thirst for

seteria *f* silk mill; seterie silk goods

setifi·cio *m* (-ci) silk mill

sétola *f* bristle; (joc) stubble

sètta *f* sect

settanta *adj, m & pron* seventy

settantènne *adj* seventy-year-old || *mf* seventy-year-old person

settantèsi·mo -ma *adj, m & pron* seventieth

settantina f about seventy

settà·rio -ria adj & mf (**-ri -rie**) sectarian

sètte adj & pron seven; **le sette** seven o'clock || m seven; seventh (in dates); V-shaped tear (in clothing)

settecentèsi·mo -ma adj, m & pron seven hundredth

settecènto adj, m & pron seven hundred || **il Settecento** the eighteenth century

settèmbre m September

settennale adj seven-year (e.g., plan)

settènne adj seven-year-old || mf seven-year-old child

settentrionale adj northern || mf northerner

settentrióne m north; (astr) Little Bear

setticemia f septicemia

sètti·co -ca adj (**-ci -che**) septic

settimana f week; week's wages; **settimana corta** five-day week

settimanale adj & m weekly

settimi·no -na adj premature (baby) || m (mus) septet

sètti·mo -ma adj, m & pron seventh

sètto m septum

settóre m sector; section, branch; dissector, anatomist; coroner's pathologist

sevè·ro -ra adj severe, stern

seviziare §287 tr to torture

sevizie fpl cruelty

sezionale adj sectional

sezionare (**sezióno**) tr to cut up; to divide up; to dissect

sezióne f section; dissection; chapter (of club); department (of agency); (geom) cross section

sfaccenda·to -ta adj loafing || mf loafer

sfaccettare (**sfaccétto**) tr to facet

sfacchinare intr (coll) to toil, drudge

sfacchinata f (coll) drudgery, grind

sfacciatàggine f brazenness, impudence

sfaccia·to -ta adj brazen, impudent; loud, gaudy; **fare lo sfacciato** to be fresh

sfacèlo m breakdown, collapse

sfà·glio -glii m (**-gli**) swerve (e.g., of horse); (cards) discard

sfaldare tr to exfoliate; to cut into slices || ref to flake, scale; (fig) to collapse, crumble

sfamare tr to feed (the hungry; the family) || ref to get enough to eat

sfare §173 tr to undo || ref to spoil (said, e.g., of meat)

sfarzo m pomp, display; luxury

sfarzó·so -sa [s] adj sumptuous, luxurious

sfasare tr to throw out of phase; (coll) to depress || intr (ESSERE) (aut) to misfire; (elec) to be out of phase

sfasciare §128 tr to remove the bandage from; to unswathe; to smash, shatter || ref to go to pieces; to lose one's figure

sfatare tr to discredit; to unmask

sfatica·to -ta adj lazy || mf loafer

sfat·to -ta adj overdone; overripe; undone (bed); ravaged (by age)

sfavillare intr to spark, sparkle

sfavóre m disfavor

sfavorévole adj unfavorable

sfebbra·to -ta adj free of fever

sfegata·to -ta adj (coll) rabid, fanatical

sfèra f sphere; (coll) hand (of clock); **a sfera** ball-point (pen); **a sfere** ball (bearing); **sfera di cuoio** (sports) pigskin

sfèri·co -ca adj (**-ci -che**) spherical

sferrare (**sfèrro**) tr to unshoe (a horse); to unchain; to draw (a weapon from a wound); to deliver (a blow) || ref to hurl oneself

sfèrza f whip, scourge

sferzare (**sfèrzo**) tr to whip, scourge

sfiancare §197 tr to break open; to tire out; to fit (clothes) too tight || ref to burst open; to get worn out

sfiatare intr to leak (said, e.g., of a tire) || intr (ESSERE) to leak (said of air or gas) || ref to waste one's breath

sfiata·tóio m (**-tói**) vent

sfibbiare §287 tr to unbuckle, unfasten; to untie (a knot)

sfibrante adj exhausting

sfibrare tr to grind (wood) into fibers; to shred (rags) into fibers; to weaken, wear out

sfida f challenge

sfidare tr to challenge, dare; to brave, defy; to endure (the challenge of time); **sfidare che** to bet that

sfidù·cia f (**-cie**) mistrust; (pol) no confidence

sfiducia·to -ta adj downcast, depressed

sfigurare tr to disfigure || intr to make a bad impression; to lose face

sfilacciare §128 tr & ref to ravel, fray

sfilare tr to unstring; to take off (one's shoes); to count (beads); to unthread; to dull (a blade); to ravel || intr (ESSERE) to march, parade; to follow one another || ref to become unthreaded; to become frayed; to run (said of knitted work); to break one's back

sfilata f parade; row; **sfilata di moda** fashion show

sfilza f row, sequence

sfinge f sphinx

sfiniménto m exhaustion

sfinire §176 tr to exhaust, wear out || ref to be worn out

sfintère m sphincter

sfiorare (**sfióro**) tr to graze; to barely touch (a subject); to skim; (lit) to barely reach

sfioratóre m spillway

sfiorire §176 intr (ESSERE) to wither, fade

sfit·to -ta adj not rented

sfocare §197 (**sfòco**) tr to put out of focus; to blur

sfociare §128 (**sfócio**) tr to dredge (the mouth of a river) || intr (ESSERE) to flow; **sfociare in** (fig) to lead to

sfoderare (**sfòdero**) tr to unsheathe; to show off, sport, display; to take the cover or lining off || intr to be drawn out

sfogare §209 (**sfógo**) tr to vent, give vent to || intr (ESSERE) to flow; to pour out; **sfogare in** to turn into || ref—**sfogarsi a** + inf to have one's fill of + *ger*; **sfogarsi con** to unburden oneself to; **sfogarsi su qlcu** to take it out on s.o.

sfoga·tóio *m* (**-tói**) vent

sfoggiare §290 (**sfòggio**) *tr* to display, sport; to show off

sfòg·gio *m* (**-gi**) display, ostentation

sfòglia *f* foil; skin (*of onion*); layer of puff paste; (*ichth*) sole

sfogliare §280 (**sfòglio**) *tr* to pluck (*a flower*); to defoliate (*a tree*); to leaf through (*a book*); to deal (*cards*); to husk (*corn*); to press (*dough*) into layers || *ref* to shed its leaves; to flake

sfogliata *f* defoliation; puff paste; **dare una sfogliata a** to glance through

sfó·go *m* (**-ghi**) exhaust; outlet; vent; (*coll*) eruption (*of skin*)

sfolgorare (**sfólgoro**) *intr* (ESSERE & AVERE) to shine, blaze

sfolgorì·o *m* (**-i**) glittering, blazing

sfollagèn·te *m* (**-te**) billy

sfollaménto *m* evacuation; layoff

sfollare (**sfòllo**) *tr* to clear; to cut the staff of || *intr* (ESSERE & AVERE) to disperse, evacuate; to cut down the staff

sfolla·to -ta *adj* driven from home || *mf* evacuee

sfoltire §176 *tr* to thin out

sfondare (**sfóndo**) *tr* to stave in; to break through; to be heavy on (*the stomach*) || *intr* to give || *ref* to break open

sfóndo *m* background

sfondóne *m* (coll) blunder, error

sforbiciare §128 (**sfòrbicio**) *tr* to clip, shear

sforbiciata *f* clipping; (sports) scissors; (sports) scissors kick

sformare (**sfórmo**) *tr* to pull out of shape; to take out of the mold || *intr* to get mad

sforma·to -ta *adj* out of shape || *m* pudding

sfornare (**sfórno**) *tr* to take out of the oven

sfornire §176 *tr* to deprive; to strip

sfortuna *f* bad luck, misfortune

sfortuna·to -ta *adj* unsuccessful; unlucky, unfortunate

sforzare (**sfòrzo**) *tr* to strain; to force || *ref* to strive, endeavor

sforza·to -ta *adj* forced, unnatural

sfòrzo *m* effort; strain; stretch (*of imagination*); **senza sforzo** effortlessly

sfóttere *tr* (vulg) to make fun of

sfracassare *tr* to smash, crash

sfracellare (**sfracèllo**) *tr & ref* to shatter, smash

sfrangiare §290 *tr* to ravel

sfrattare *tr* to evict; to deport || *intr* to be evicted

sfratto *m* eviction; notice of eviction

sfrecciare §128 (**sfréccio**) *intr* (ESSERE & AVERE) to speed by

sfregaménto *m* rubbing

sfregare §209 (**sfrégo**) *tr* to rub; to scrape; to strike (*a match*)

sfregiare §290 (**sfrégio & sfrègio**) *tr* to disfigure, slash

sfregia·to -ta *adj* disfigured, slashed || *m* scarface

sfré·gio or **sfrè·gio** *m* (**-gi**) slash, scar, gash; insult

sfrenare (**sfréno & sfrèno**) *tr* to take the brake off; to give free rein to || *ref* to kick over the traces

sfriggere §180 *intr* to sizzle

sfrigolì·o *m* (**-i**) sizzle

sfrondare (**sfróndo**) *tr* to defoliate; to lop off; to trim down || *ref* to lose leaves

sfrontatézza *f* effrontery, impudence

sfronta·to -ta *adj* brazen, impudent

sfrusciare §128 *intr* to rustle

sfruttare *tr* to exploit; to exhaust (*e.g., a mine*); to take advantage of

sfrutta·tóre -trice *mf* exploiter, developer (*e.g., of an invention*)

sfuggènte *adj* fleeting; receding (*forehead*); shifty (*glance*)

sfuggire *tr* to avoid, flee || *intr* (ESSERE) to flee, escape, get away; (with *dat*) to escape, e.g., **nulla gli sfugge** nothing escapes him; to break, e.g., **sfuggì a una promessa** he broke a promise; **lasciarsi sfuggire** to let slip

sfuggita *f*—**di sfuggita** hastily; incidentally; **dare una sfuggita** to run down (*e.g., to the post office*)

sfumare *tr* to shade down; to tone down; to trim (*hair*) || *intr* (ESSERE) to vanish; to shade

sfumatura *f* nuance, shade; razor clipping

sfumino *m* stump (*in drawing*)

sfuriare §287 *tr* to vent (*one's anger*) || *intr* to rave

sfuriata *f* outburst of anger; gust (*of wind*); **fare una sfuriata a** to give a scolding to

sgabèllo *m* stool, footstool

sgabuzzino *m* cubbyhole

sgambettare (**sgambétto**) *tr* to trip || *intr* to toddle; to kick (*said of a baby*); to scamper

sgambétto *m* trip, stumble; **dare lo sgambetto a** to trip

sganasciare §128 *tr* to dislocate the jaw of; to break the jaw of; to tear apart || *intr* to steal right and left || *ref* to break one's jaw; **sganasciarsi dalle risa** to split one's sides laughing

sganciare §128 *tr* to unhook; to lay out money; to drop (*bombs*) || *intr* to drop bombs; (coll) to go away || *ref* to get unhooked; (mil) to disengage oneself; **sganciarsi da** to get rid of

sgangherare (**sgànghero**) *tr* to unhinge; to burst || *ref*—**sgangherarsi dalle risa** to split one's sides laughing

sganghera·to -ta *adj* unhinged; broken down; rickety; coarse (*laughter*)

sgarbatéz·za *f* rudeness, incivility; clumsiness

sgarba·to -ta *adj* rude; clumsy

sgarberìa *f* var of **sgarbatezza**

sgarbo *m*—**fare uno sgarbo a** to be rude to

sgargiante *adj* loud, flashy, showy

sgarrare *intr* to go wrong

sgattaiolare (**sgattàiolo**) *intr* (ESSERE) to slip away; to wriggle out

sgelare (sgèlo) *tr & intr* to thaw, melt
sgèlo *m* thaw
sghém·bo -ba *adj* crooked; **a sghembo** askew ‖ **sghembo** *adv* askew; sideways
sghèrro *m* hired assassin; gendarme
sghiacciare §128 *tr* to thaw
sghignazzare *intr* to guffaw
sghignazzata *f* guffaw
sghimbè·scio -scia *adj*—**a** or **di sghimbescio** askew, crooked
sghiribizzo [ddzz] *m* whim, fancy
sgobbare (sgòbbo) *intr* to drudge, plod, plug
sgobbó·ne -na *mf* plugger, plodder, drudge
sgocciolare (sgócciolo) *tr* to let drip ‖ *intr* to drip (*said of container*) ‖ *intr* (ESSERE) to drip (*said of liquid*)
sgocciola·tóio *m* (**-tói**) dish rack; drip pan
sgocciolatura *f* dripping; drippings
sgócciolo *m* last drop; **essere agli sgoccioli** to be coming to an end
sgolare (sgólo) *ref* to shout oneself hoarse
sgomberare (sgómbero) *tr & intr* var of sgombrare
sgómbero *m* moving
sgombrané·ve *m* (**-ve**) snowplow (*truck*)
sgombrare (sgómbro) *tr* to clear; to vacate ‖ *intr* to move, vacate
sgóm·bro -bra *adj* clear ‖ *m* moving; (*ichth*) mackerel
sgomentare (sgoménto) *tr* to frighten; to dismay
sgomén·to -ta *adj* dismayed ‖ *m* dismay; **rimanere di sgomento** to be dismayed
sgominare (sgòmino) *tr* to rout
sgomma·to -ta *adj* unglued; without tires; with poor tires
sgonfiare §287 (sgónfio) *tr* to deflate; to damn with faint praise (*e.g., a play*); (coll) to bore ‖ *intr* (ESSERE) to boast; to balloon ‖ *ref* to go down (*said of swelling*); to go flat (*said of a tire*); (fig) to collapse
sgón·fio -fia *adj* deflated, flat
sgonfiòtto *m* jelly doughnut; puff (*in clothing*)
sgórbia *f* (carp) gouge
sgorbiare §287 (sgòrbio) *tr* to scribble; (carp) to gouge
sgòr·bio *m* (**-bi**) ink spot; scribble, scrawl
sgorgare §209 (sgórgo) *tr* to unclog ‖ *intr* (ESSERE) to gush
sgottare (sgótto) *tr* to bail out (*a boat*)
sgozzare (sgózzo) *tr* to slaughter; to slit the throat of; (fig) to bleed, fleece
sgradévole *adj* disagreeable, unpleasant
sgradire §176 *tr* to refuse ‖ *intr* to be displeasing
sgradi·to -ta *adj* unpleasant; unwelcome
sgraffignare *tr* to snitch, snatch
sgrammatica·to -ta *adj* ungrammatical
sgranare *tr* to shell (*e.g., peas*); to count (*one's beads*); to seed (*grapes*); to open (*one's eyes*) wide; (mach) to disengage ‖ *ref* to crumble; to scratch oneself

sgranchire §176 *tr* to stretch (*e.g., one's legs*)
sgranocchiare §287 (sgranòcchio) *tr* to crunch, munch
sgrassare *tr* to remove the grease from; to skim (*broth*); to scour (*wool*)
sgravare *tr* to relieve, lighten ‖ *ref* to be relieved; to give birth
sgrà·vio *m* (**-vi**) lightening, lessening; **a sgravio di coscienza** to ease one's conscience
sgrazia·to -ta *adj* gawky, clumsy
sgretolare (sgrétolo) *tr & ref* to crumble
sgretola·to -ta *adj* crumbling, falling down
sgridare *tr* to scold, chide
sgridata *f* scolding, reprimand
sgrondare (sgróndo) *tr* to cause to drip ‖ *intr* to drip, trickle
sgroppare (sgròppo) *tr* to wear (*a horse*) out ‖ *intr* to buck (*said of a horse*)
sgroppare (sgróppo) *tr* to untie
sgrossare (sgròsso) *tr* to rough-hew; (fig) to refine
sgrovigliare §280 *tr* to untangle
sgualataggine *f* uncouthness
sguaia·to -ta *adj* crude, vulgar; uncouth ‖ *mf* vulgar person; uncouth person
sguainare *tr* to unsheathe; to show (*one's nails*)
sgualcire §176 *tr* to crumple ‖ *ref* to become crumpled
sgualdrina *f* trollop, strumpet
sguardo *m* glance, look; eyes
sguarnire §176 *tr* to untrim; (mil) to strip, dismantle
sguàtte·ro -ra *mf* dishwasher, scullion ‖ *f* kitchenmaid, scullery maid
sguazzare *tr* to waste, squander ‖ *intr* to splash; to wallow; to be lost (*in shoes too big or clothes too loose*)
sguinzagliare §280 *tr* to unleash, let loose
sgusciare §128 *tr* to shell, hull ‖ *intr* (ESSERE) to slip; **sgusciare di soppiatto** to slip away
shòp·ping *m* (**-ping**) shopping; shopping bag; **fare lo shopping** to go shopping
shràpnel *m* (shràpnel) shrapnel
si *m* (**-si**) (mus) si ‖ §5 *pron*
sì *m* (**sì**) yes; yea; **stare tra il sì e il no** to not be able to make up one's mind; **un . . . sì e l'altro no** every other (*e.g., day*)
sìa *conj* see essere
siamése [s] *adj & mf* Siamese
siberia·no -na *adj & mf* Siberian
sibilante *adj & f* sibilant
sibilare (sìbilo) *intr* to hiss
sibilla *f* sibyl
sìbilo *m* hiss, hissing
sicà·rio *m* (**-ri**) hired assassin
sicché *conj* so that
siccità *f* drought
siccóme *adv* as ‖ *conj* since; as; how
Sicilia, la Sicily
sicilia·no -na *adj & mf* Sicilian
sicomòro *m* sycamore
sicumèra *f* cocksureness, overconfidence
sicura *f* safety lock (*on gun*)

sicurézza *f* security; assurance; safety; certainty; reliability; **di sicurezza** safety; **sicurezza sociale** social security

sicu·ro -ra *adj* sure; safe; steady; **di sicuro** certainly || *m* safety; **camminare sul sicuro** to take no chances || **sicuro** *adv* certainly || *f* see **sicura**

sicur·tà *f* (**-tà**) insurance

siderale *adj* sidereal

sidère·o -a *adj* sidereal

siderùrgi·co -ca (**-ci -che**) *adj* iron-and-steel || *m* iron-and-steel worker

sidro *m* cider, hard cider

sièpe *f* hedge; (fig) wall

sièro *m* serum

sièsta *f* siesta; **fare la siesta** to take a nap, take a siesta

siffat·to -ta *adj* such

sifìlide *f* syphilis

sifóne *m* siphon; siphon bottle; trap

siga·ràio -ràia (**-rài -ràie**) *mf* cigar maker || *m* (ent) grape hopper; || *f* cigarette girl

sigarétta *f* cigarette

sìgaro *m* cigar

sigillare *tr* to seal

sigillo *m* seal; **avere il sigillo alle labbra** to have one's lips sealed; **sigillo sacramentale** seal of confession

sigla *f* acronym; initials; abbreviation; letterword; **sigla musicale** theme song

siglare *tr* to initial

significare §197 (**signìfico**) *tr* to mean; to signify; **significare qlco a qlcu** to inform s.o. of s.th

significati·vo -va *adj* significant; meaningful

significato *m* meaning; **senza significato** meaningless

signóra *f* Madam, Mrs.; lady; mistress, owner; wife || **Nostra Signora** Our Lady

signóre *m* sir, Mr.; gentleman; rich man; lord, master, owner; man; **il signore desidera?** what is your pleasure?; **per signori** stag || **Signore** *m* Lord

signoreggiare §290 (**signoréggio**) *tr* to rule over; to master; to tower over; to overshadow || *intr* to be the master

signoria *f* seigniory; rule; **La Signoria Vostra** your Honor; **Sua Signoria** his Lordship; your Lordship

signorile *adj* seigniorial; gentlemanly; ladylike; elegant, refined

signorina *f* miss; Miss; young lady; spinster

signorino *m* master, young gentleman

signornò *adv* no, Sir

signoró·ne -na *mf* (coll) rich person

signoròtto *m* lordling

signorsì *adv* yes, Sir

silenziatóre *m* silencer (of firearm); (aut) muffler

silèn·zio *m* (**-zi**) silence; (mil) taps; **fare silenzio** to be silent; **ridurre al silenzio** (mil) to silence

silenzió·so -sa [s] *adj* silent; noiseless

silfide *f* sylphid

silfo *m* sylph

silhouèt·te *f* (**-te**) silhouette

sìlice *f* silica

silìcio *m* silicon

silicóne *m* silicone

siliquastro *m* redbud

sìllaba *f* syllable

sillabare (**sìllabo**) *tr* to syllabify; **to spell**

sillabà·rio *m* (**-ri**) reader, primer

sìllabo *m* syllabus

silo *m* silo

silòfono *m* xylophone

siluétta *f* silhouette

silurante *adj* torpedoing, torpedo || *f* destroyer; torpedo boat

silurare *tr* to torpedo; (fig) to fire, dismiss; (fig) to undermine

siluro *m* torpedo

silva·no -na *adj* sylvan

silvèstre *adj* (lit) sylvan; (lit) wild; (lit) hard, arduous

simboleggiare §290 (**simboléggio**) *tr* to symbolize

simbòli·co -ca *adj* (**-ci -che**) symbolic

simbolismo *m* symbolism

sìmbolo *m* symbol

similari·tà *f* (**-tà**) similarity

sìmile *adj* similar; such || *m* like; **i propri simili** fellow men

similòro *m* tombac

simmetrìa *f* symmetry

simmètri·co -ca *adj* (**-ci -che**) symmetrical

simonìa *f* simony

simpamina *f* benzedrine

simpatèti·co -ca *adj* (**-ci -che**) sympathetic

simpatìa *f* like, liking; **cattivarsi la simpatia di** to make oneself well liked by

simpàti·co -ca *adj* (**-ci -che**) *adj* nice, pleasant, congenial || *m* (anat) sympathetic system

simpatizzante [ddzz] *adj* sympathizing || *mf* sympathizer

simpatizzare [ddzz] *intr* to sympathize; to become friends

simpò·sio *m* (**-si**) symposium

simulare (**sìmulo**) *tr* to simulate

simula·tóre -trice *mf* faker, impostor || *m* simulator

simultàne·o -a *adj* simultaneous

sin- *pref adj* syn-, e.g., **sinonimo** synonymous || *pref* *m* & *f* syn-, e.g., **sinonimo** synonym

sin *adv*—**sin da** ever since

sinagò·ga *f* (**-ghe**) synagogue

sincerare (**sincèro**) *tr* (lit) to convince || *ref*—**sincerarsi di** to ascertain

sincè·ro -ra *adj* sincere; pure

sinché *conj* until

sìncope *f* fainting spell; (phonet) syncope; (mus) syncopation

sincronismo *m* syncronism; **sincronismo orrizzontale** (telv) horizontal hold; **sincronismo verticale** (telv) vertical hold

sincronizzare [ddzz] *tr* to syncronize

sincro·no -na *adj* syncronous

sindacale *adj* mayoral; union

sindacalismo *m* trade unionism

sindacali·sta *mf* (**-sti -ste**) union member; union leader

sindacare §197 (sìndaco) *tr* to criticize; to scrutinize

sindaca·to -ta *adj* controlled, scrutinized || *m* control; labor union; syndicate; **sindacato giallo** company union

sìnda·co *m* (-ci) mayor; controller; auditor

sinecura *f* sinecure

sinfonìa *f* symphony; (*of an opera*) overture; (coll) racket (*noise*)

sinfòni·co -ca *adj* (-ci -che) symphonic

singhiozzare (singhiòzzo) *intr* to sob; to hiccup; to jerk

singhiòzzo *m* sob; hiccups; **a singhiozzo** in jerks; by fits and spurts

singolare *adj* singular || *m* singular; (tennis) singles

sìngo·lo -la *adj* single || *m* individual; shell for one oarsman; (rr) roomette; (telp) private line; (tennis) singles

singulto *m* hiccups; sob

sinistra *f* left hand; left

sinistrare *tr* to ruin; to damage

sinistra·to -ta *adj* injured, damaged, ruined || *mf* victim (*of bombing or flood*)

sinistrismo *m* leftism

sinistrì·sta *adj* (-sti -ste) leftish, leftist

sinì·stro -stra *adj* left; sinister || *m* accident; (boxing) left || *f* see **sinistra**

sinistròìde *adj* & *mf* leftist

sino *adv* var of **fino**

sinologìa *f* Sinology

sinòni·mo -ma *adj* synonymous || *m* synonym

sinò·psi *f* (-psi) (mov) synopsis

sinóra *adv* var of **finora**

sinòs·si *f* (-si) synopsis

sinòtti·co -ca *adj* (-ci -che) synoptic(al)

sintas·si *f* (-si) syntax

sìnte·si *f* (-si) synthesis

sintèti·co -ca *adj* (-ci -che) synthetic(al); concise

sintetizzare [ddzz] *tr* to synthesize

sintogram·ma *m* (-mi) (rad) dial

sìntomo *m* symptom

sintonìa *f* harmony; (rad) tuning

sintonizzare [ddzz] *tr* (rad) to tune

sintonizzatóre [ddzz] *m* (rad) tuner

sinuó·so -sa [s] *adj* sinuous, winding

sionismo *m* Zionism

sipà·rio *m* (-ri) curtain; **sipario di ferro** iron curtain

sirèna *f* siren; mermaid; **sirena da nebbia** foghorn

Sìria, la Syria

siria·no -na *adj* & *mf* Syrian

sirìn·ga *f* (-ghe) panpipe; syringe; catheter; grease gun; (orn) syrinx

siringare §209 *tr* to catheterize

siròcchia *f* (obs) sister

sì·sma *m* (-smi) earthquake

sismògrafo *m* seismograph

sismologìa *f* seismology

sissignóre *adv* yes, Sir!

sistè·ma *m* (-mi) system

sistemare (sistèmo) *tr* to arrange; to put in order; to systematize; to settle; to find a job for; to find a husband for; (coll) to fix || *ref* to settle; to get married

sistemazióne *f* arrangement; settlement; job, position

sìstole *f* systole

sitibón·do -da *adj* (lit) thirsty

sì·to -ta *adj* (lit) located || *m* (lit) site, spot, location; (mil) sight; (coll) musty odor

situare (sìtuo) *tr* to locate, place, situate

situazióne *f* situation; condition

slabbrare *tr* to chip; to open (*a wound*) || *intr* to overflow || *ref* to become chipped; to reopen (*said of a cut*)

slacciare §128 *tr* to untie; to unfasten; to unbutton || *ref* to get undone; to get unbuttoned

sladinare *tr* (sports) to train; (mach) to run in, break in

slanciare §128 *tr* to hurl, throw || *ref* to hurl oneself; to rise (*said, e.g., of a tower*)

slancia·to -ta *adj* slender; soaring

slàn·cio *m* (-ci) leap; outburst (*of feeling*); momentum; **di slancio** with a rush; **prendere lo slancio** to get a running start

slargare §209 *tr* to widen; to warm (*the heart*) || *ref* to widen, spread out

slattare *tr* to wean

slava·to -ta *adj* pale, washed out

sla·vo -va *adj* Slav, Slavic || *mf* Slav || *m* Slavic (*language*)

sleale *adj* disloyal; unfair (*competition*)

slealtà *f* (-tà) disloyalty

slegare §209 (slégo) *tr* to untie

slega·to -ta *adj* untied; disconnected

slip *m* (slip) briefs; tank suit, bathing suit (*for men*)

slitta *f* sled, sleigh; (mach) carriage

slittaménto *m* skid; slide

slittare *intr* to sled; to skid; to slide

slogare §209 (slògo) *tr* to dislocate || *ref* to become dislocated; to dislocate (*e.g., an arm*)

slogatura *f* dislocation

sloggiare §290 (slòggio) *tr* to dislodge; to evict || *intr* to vacate

slòg·gio *m* (-gi) moving; eviction

slovac·co -ca *adj* & *mf* (-chi -che) Slovak

smacchiare §287 *tr* to clean; to deforest

smacchia·tóre -trice *mf* cleaner || *m* cleaning fluid; spot remover

smac·co *m* (-chi) letdown; slap in the face

smagliante *adj* dazzling, shining

smagliare §280 *tr* to break the links of; to undo the meshes of; to remove (*a fish*) from the net || *intr* to shine, dazzle || *ref* to run (*said, e.g., of knitted fabric*); to free itself from the net

smagliatura *f* run (*in stockings*); (fig) break

smagrire §176 *tr* to impoverish || *intr* (ESSERE) & *ref* to become thin or lean

smaliziare §287 *tr* to make wiser || *ref* to get wiser

smaltare *tr* to enamel; to glaze

smaltire §176 *tr* to digest; to sleep off (*a drunk*); to swallow (*an offense*);

to sell off; to get rid of; to drain off (*water*)

smaltì·tóio *m* (**-tói**) drain, sewer

smalto *m* enamel; **smalto per le unghie** nail polish

smancerìe *fpl* affectation; mawkishness

smanceró·so -sa [s] *adj* prissy

smangiare §290 *tr* to erode, eat away ‖ *ref* to be consumed (*e.g., by hatred*)

smània *f* frenzy; craze, yearning; **dare in smanie** to be in a frenzy

smaniare §287 *intr* to be delirious; to yearn, crave

smanió·so -sa [s] *adj* eager; disturbing

smantellare (**smantèllo**) *tr* to dismantle; to demolish; to disable (*a ship*)

smargias·so -sa *mf* braggart, boaster

smarrimento *m* loss; bewilderment; discouragement

smarrire §176 *tr* to lose ‖ *ref* to get lost; to get discouraged

smascellare (**smascèllo**) *ref*—**smascellarsi dalle risa** to split one's sides laughing

smascherare (**smàschero**) *tr* & *ref* to unmask

smazzata *f* (cards) deal; (cards) hand

smembramento *m* dismemberment

smembrare (**smèmbro**) *tr* to dismember

smemorataggine *f* forgetfulness

smemora·to -ta *adj* absent-minded; forgetful ‖ *mf* absent-minded or forgetful person

smentire §176 *tr* to belie; to refute; to retract; to be untrue to ‖ *ref* to not be consistent; to contradict oneself

smentita *f* denial; retraction

smeraldo *m* emerald

smerciare §128 (**smèrcio**) *tr* to sell, sell out

smèr·cio *m* (**-ci**) sale

smèr·go *m* (**-ghi**) (zool) merganser

smerigliare §280 *tr* to grind, polish; to sand

smeriglia·to -ta *adj* polished; sand (*paper*); emery (*cloth*); frosted (*glass*)

smerì·glio *m* (**-gli**) emery; (orn) merlin; (ichth) porbeagle

smerlare (**smèrlo**) *tr* to scallop

smèrlo *m* scallop (*along the edge of a garment*)

smés·so -sa *adj* hand-me-down, castoff

sméttere §198 *tr* to stop; to stop wearing; to break up (*housekeeping*); **smettere di** to cut it out ‖ *intr*—**smettere di** + *inf* to stop + *ger*

smezzare [ddzz] (**smèzzo**) *tr* to halve

smidollare (**smidóllo**) *tr* to remove the marrow from; (fig) to emasculate

smilitarizzare [ddzz] *tr* to demilitarize

smil·zo -za *adj* slender; poor, worthless

sminare *tr* to remove mines from

sminuire §176 *tr* to belittle

sminuzzare *tr* to crumble; to mince; to expatiate on ‖ *ref* to crumble

smistamento *m* sorting (*of mail*); (rr) shunting, shifting

smistare *tr* to sort; (rr) to shift; (soccer) to pass; (rad) to unscramble

smisura·to -ta *adj* immense, huge

smitizzante [ddzz] *adj* debunking, demythologizing

smitizzare [ddzz] *tr* to debunk; to demythologize

smobiliare §287 *tr* to remove the furniture from

smobilitare (**smobìlito**) *tr* to demobilize

smobilitazióne *f* demobilization

smoccolare (**smòccolo** & **smóccolo**) *tr* to snuff (*a candle*) ‖ *intr* (slang) to swear, curse

smoda·to -ta *adj* excessive, immoderate

smòg *m* smog

smóking *m* (**smóking**) dinner jacket, tuxedo

smontàbile *adj* dismountable

smontàg·gio *m* (**-gi**) disassembling, dismantling

smontare (**smónto**) *tr* to take apart; to dismantle; to cause (*e.g., whipped cream*) to fall; to take (*a precious stone*) out of its setting; to dishearten; to dissuade; to drop (*s.o.*) off; **smontare la guardia** to come off guard duty ‖ *intr* (ESSERE) to dismount; to get off or out (*of a conveyance*); to fade; to drop (*said, e.g., of beaten eggs*) ‖ *ref* to become downcast

smòrfia *f* grimace; mawkishness; **fare le smorfie** to make faces at

smorfió·so -sa [s] *adj* mawkish, prissy

smòr·to -ta *adj* pale, wan; faded

smorzare (**smòrzo**) *tr* to attenuate; to lessen; to tone down; to turn off (*light*); (phys) to dampen

smorzatóre *m* (mus) damper

smòs·so -sa *adj* moved; loose

smottamento *m* mud slide

smozzicare §197 (**smózzico**) *tr* to crumble; to mince; to clip, mince (*one's words*)

smun·to -ta *adj* emaciated, pale, wan

smuòvere §202 *tr* to budge; to till; (fig) to move ‖ *ref* to budge; to move away; **smuoviti!** get going!

smussare *tr* to blunt; to bevel; (fig) to soften

snaturalizzare [ddzz] *tr* to denaturalize; to denationalize

snaturare *tr* to change the nature of; to distort, misrepresent

snatura·to -ta *adj* distorted; monstrous, unnatural

snebbiare §287 (**snébbio**) *tr* to drive the fog from; to clear (*e.g., one's mind*)

snellézza *f* slenderness; nimbleness

snellire §176 *tr* & *ref* to slenderize

snèl·lo -la *adj* slender; nimble; lively

snervante *adj* enervating

snervare (**snèrvo**) *tr* to enervate, prostrate ‖ *ref* to become enervated

snidare *tr* to drive out, flush

snòb *adj invar* snobbish ‖ *mf* (**snòb**) snob

snobbare (**snòbbo**) *tr* to snub, slight

snobismo *m* snobbishness, snobbery

snobìsti·co -ca *adj* (**-ci -che**) snobbish

snocciolare (**snòcciolo**) *tr* to spill (*a secret*); to peel off (*sums of money*); to pit, stone (*fruit*)

snodare (**snòdo**) *tr* to untie; to limber up; to exercise; to loosen up (*e.g.,* *s.o.'s tongue*) || *ref* to become loose; to wind (*said, e.g., of a road*)

snòdo *m* (mach) joint; **a snodo** flexible

soave *adj* sweet, gentle

sobbalzare *intr* to jerk, jolt

sobbalzo *m* jerk, jolt; **di sobbalzo** with a jolt

sobbarcare §197 *tr* to overburden || *ref* **—sobbarcarsi a** to take it upon oneself to

sobbór·go *m* (**-ghi**) suburb

sobillare *tr* to instigate, stir up

sobilla·tóre -trice *mf* instigator

sobrietà *f* sobriety, temperance

sò·brio -bria *adj* sober, temperate; plain

socchiùdere §125 *tr* to half-shut; to leave ajar

socchiu·so -sa [s] *adj* ajar

soccómbere §186 *intr* to succumb

soccórrere §139 *tr* to help || *intr* (lit) to occur

soccórso *m* help, succor; **mancato soccorso** failure to render assistance; hit-and-run driving

sociale *adj* social; company (*e.g., outing*)

socialismo *m* socialism

sociali·sta (**-sti -ste**) *adj* socialistic || *mf* socialist

sociali·tà *f* (**-tà**) gregariousness; social responsibility

socie·tà *f* (**-tà**) society; company; **in società** in partnership; **società anonima** corporation; **società a responsabilità limitata** limited company; **Società delle Nazioni** League of Nations; **società finanziaria** holding company; **società in accomandita** limited partnership; **società per azioni** corporation

sociévole *adj* sociable; gregarious

sò·cio *m* (**-ci**) member; cardholder; partner; shareholder; **socio fondatore** charter member; **socio sostenitore** patron, sustaining member

sociologia *f* sociology

sociòlo·go -ga *mf* (**-gi -ghe**) sociologist

sòda *f* soda

sodali·zio *m* (**-zi**) society; brotherhood, fraternity; friendship

soddisfacènte *adj* satisfying, satisfactory

soddisfare §173 (*2d sg pres ind* **soddisfài** *or* **soddisfi;** *3d pl pres* **soddisfanno** *or* **soddisfano;** *1st, 2d & 3d sg pres subj* **soddisfaccia** *or* **soddisfi;** *3d pl pres subj* **soddisfàcciano** *or* **soddisfino**) *tr* to satisfy || *intr* (with *dat*) to satisfy || *ref* to be satisfied

soddisfat·to -ta *adj* satisfied

soddisfazióne *f* satisfaction

sòdi·co -ca *adj* (**-ci -che**) sodium

sòdio *m* sodium

sò·do -da *adj* hard; hard-boiled; stubborn; solid; **prenderle sode** to get a good thrashing || *m* hard ground; untilled soil; solid foundation; **venire al sodo** to come to the point; **mettere in sodo** to ascertain || *f* see **soda** || **sodo** *adv* hard

sodomìa *f* sodomy

so·fà *m* (**-fà**) couch, sofa; **sofà a letto** sofa bed

sofferènte *adj* sickly, ailing; (lit) long-suffering

sofferènza *f* suffering, pain; bad debt; **in sofferenza** overdue

soffermare (**sofférmo**) *tr* —**soffermare il passo** to come to a stop || *ref* to linger, pause

soffiare §287 (**sóffio**) *tr* to blow; to whisper; (checkers) to huff; (coll) to steal || *intr* to blow; to bellow; (slang) to squeal (*about somebody's offense*); **soffiare sul fuoco** to stir up trouble || *ref* to blow (*one's nose*)

soffia·to -ta *adj* blown || *m* soufflé || *f* (slang) squealing, darsi una **soffiata di naso** to blow one's nose

soffiatóre *m* glass blower

sòffice *adj* soft

soffierìa *f* glass factory; blower

soffiétto *m* bellows; hood (*of carriage*); (journ) puff, ballyhoo

sóf·fio *m* (**-fi**) blow; breath; **in un soffio** in a jiffy; **soffio al cuore** heart murmur

soffióne *m* blowpipe; fumarole; (bot) dandelion; (coll) spy

soffitta *f* attic, garret

soffitto *m* ceiling

soffocaménto *m* choking

soffocante *adj* stifling; oppressive

soffocare §197 (**sòffoco**) *tr* to choke; to stifle; to suffocate; to smother; to repress

sòffo·co *m* (**-chi**) sultriness

soffóndere §178 *tr* (lit) to suffuse

soffregare §209 (**soffrégo**) *tr* to rub lightly

soffrìggere §180 *tr* to fry lightly || *intr* to mutter

soffrire §207 *tr* to suffer; to endure; **non poter soffrire** to not be able to stand || *intr* to suffer; to ail; **soffrire di** to be troubled with

soffritto *m* fried onions and bacon

sofistica·to -ta *adj* adulterated; sophisticated, studied

sofisti·co -ca *adj* (**-ci -che**) sophistic; faultfinding || *f* sophistry

soggetti·sta *mf* (**-sti -ste**) scriptwriter

soggetti·vo -va *adj* subjective

soggèt·to -ta *adj* subject || *m* subject; (coll) character; (law) person; **cattivo soggetto** hoodlum; **recitare a soggetto** to improvise

soggezióne *f* subjection; awe, embarrassment; **mettere a soggezione** to awe

sogghignare *intr* to sneer

sogghigno *m* sneer

soggiacére §181 *intr* (ESSERE & AVERE) to be subject; to succumb

soggiogare §209 (**soggiógo**) *tr* to subjugate, subdue

soggiornare (**soggiórno**) *intr* to sojourn, stay

soggiórno *m* sojourn, stay; living room; sitting room (*in hotel*)

soggiùngere §183 *tr* to add

soggólo *m* wimple (*of nun*); throatlatch (*on horse*); (mil) chin strap

sòglia *f* doorsill; threshhold

sògliola *f* sole

sognare (**sógno**) *tr* to dream of || *intr*

to dream; **sognare ad occhi aperti** to daydream

sogna·tóre -trice *adj* dreaming ‖ *mf* dreamer

sógno *m* dream; **nemmeno per sogno** (coll) by no means

sòia *f* (bot) soy

sòl *m* (sòl) (mus) sol

so·làio *m* (-lài) attic, loft; (agr) crib

solare *adj* solar; bright; clear ‖ *v* §257 *tr* to sole

solàr·rio *m* (-ri) solarium

solatí·o -a (-i -e) *adj* sunny ‖ *m*—**a solatio** with a southern exposure

solcare §197 (sólco) *tr* to furrow; to plow (*the waves*)

sól·co *m* (-chi) furrow; rut; groove (*of phonograph record*); (fig) path; (naut) wake

solcòmetro *m* (naut) log

soldaté·sco -sca (-schi -sche) *adj* soldier ‖ *f* soldiery; soldiers; undisciplined troops

soldatino *m* toy soldier

soldato *m* soldier; **andare soldato** to enlist; **soldato di ventura** soldier of fortune; **soldato scelto** private first class; **soldato semplice** private

sòldo *m* soldo (*Italian coin*); coin; money; (mil) pay; (fig) penny; **a soldo a soldo** a penny at a time; **al soldo di** in the pay of; **tirare al soldo** to be a tightwad

sóle *m* sun; sunshine; (fig) day, daytime; **sole artificiale** sun lamp; **sole a scacchi** (joc) hoosegow, calaboose

soleggia·to -ta *adj* sunny

solènne *adj* solemn; (joc) first-class

solenni·tà *f* (-tà) solemnity

solennizzare [ddzz] *tr* to solemnize

solére §255 *intr* (ESSERE) + *inf* to be accustomed to + *inf*, e.g., **suole arrivare alle sette** he is accustomed to arrive at seven ‖ *impers* (ESSERE) —**suole** + *inf* it generally + *3d sg ind*, e.g., **suole nevicare** it generally snows

solèrte *adj* (lit) diligent, industrious

solèrzia *f* (lit) diligence

solét·to -ta *adj* (lit) alone, lonely ‖ *f* sole; inner sole; (archit) slab, cement slab

sòlfa *f* (mus) solfeggio; **la solita solfa** the same old story

solfanèllo *m* var of **zofanello**

solfara *f* sulfur mine

solfato *m* sulfate

solfeggiare §290 (solféggio) *tr* to sol-fa

solfiè·ro -ra [*dzz*] *adj* sulfur

solfito *m* sulfite

sólfo *m* var of **zolfo**

solfòri·co -ca *adj* (-ci -che) sulfuric

solforó·so -sa [s] *adj* sulfurous

solfuro *m* sulfide

solidale *adj* solidary; (law) joint; (law) jointly responsible; (mach) built-in; **solidale con** integral with

solidarie·tà *f* (-tà) solidarity; (law) joint liability

solidarizzare [ddzz] *intr* to make common cause, become united

solidificare §197 (solidìfico) *tr* to solidify; to settle

solidi·tà *f* (-tà) solidity; (fig) soundness

sòli·do -da *adj* solid; (law) joint ‖ *m* solid; **in solido** jointly

solilò·quio *m* (-qui) soliloquy

solin·go -ga *adj* (-ghi -ghe) (lit) lonely; (lit) solitary (*enjoying solitude*)

solino *m* detachable collar; **solino duro** stiff collar

soli·sta *mf* (-sti -ste) soloist

solità·rio -ria (-ri -rie) *adj* solitary, lonely ‖ *m* solitaire; solitary

sòli·to -ta *adj* usual, customary; **esser solito** to be accustomed to ‖ *m* habit, custom; **come il solito** as usual; **di solito** usually

solitùdine *f* solitude, loneliness

sollazzare *tr* to amuse ‖ *ref* to have a good time, amuse oneself

sollazzo *m* (lit) amusement; **essere il sollazzo di** to be the laughingstock of

sollecitare (solléci*to*) *tr* to solicit; to urge; to induce; (mach) to stress ‖ *intr & ref* to hasten

sollecitazióne *f* solicitation; urging; (mach) stress

solléci·to -ta *adj* quick, prompt; diligent; solicitous, anxious ‖ *m* (com) solicitation, urging

sollecitùdine *f* solicitude; promptness; diligence; **cortese sollecitudine** (com) prompt attention

solleóne *m* dog days

solleticare §197 (solléti*co*) *tr* to tickle; (fig) to flatter

solléti·co *m* (-chi) tickling; stimulation; **fare il solletico a** to tickle

sollevaménto *m* lifting; **sollevamento di pesi** weight lifting

sollevare (sollèvo) *tr* to lift; to relieve; to pick up; to raise (*e.g., a question*); to excite; to elevate ‖ *ref* to rise; to lift oneself; to pick up (*said of courage or health*)

sollevazióne *f* uprising

sollièvo *m* relief

sollùchero *m*—**andare in solluchero** to become ecstatic; **mandare in solluchero** to thrill

só·lo -la *adj* lone, lonely, alone; only; single; **fare da solo** to operate all by oneself; **solo soletto** all by myself (yourself, himself, etc.); within oneself; **un solo** only one ‖ *m* (mus) solo ‖ *solo adv* only ‖ *solo conj* only; **solo che** provided that

solstì·zio *m* (-zi) solstice

soltanto *adv* only

solùbile *adj* soluble

soluzióne *f* solution; installment; **soluzione di comodo** compromise; **soluzione provvisoria** stopgap

solvènte *adj* & *m* solvent

solvènza *f* solvency

solvìbile *adj* collectable; solvent

sòma *f* burden, load

Somàlia, la Somaliland

sòma·lo -la *adj* & *mf* Somali

soma·ro -ra *mf* donkey, ass

someggia·to -ta *adj* carried by pack animal; carried on mule back

somigliante *adj* similar; **essere somigliante a** to look like ‖ *m* same thing

somiglianza *f* similarity, resemblance

somigliare §280 *tr* to resemble; (lit) to compare ‖ *intr* (ESSERE & AVERE) (with *dat*) to resemble; to seem to be ‖ *ref* to resemble each other

sómma *f* addition; sum; summary

sommare (sómmo) *tr* to add; to consider; **tutto sommato** all in all ‖ *intr* to amount

sommà·rio -ria (-ri -rie) *adj* summary ‖ *m* summary; abstract; (journ) subheading

sommèrgere §162 *tr* to submerge; (fig) to plunge; (fig) to flood (*with insults*) ‖ *ref* to submerge

sommergibile *adj* & *m* submarine

sommés·so -sa *adj* submissive; subdued (*voice*)

somministrare *tr* to administer; to provide; to deliver (*a blow*); to adduce (*proof*)

somministrazióne *f* administration; provision

sommi·tà *f* (-tà) summit

sóm·mo -ma *adj* highest; supreme ‖ *m* top; peak, summit ‖ *f* see **somma**

sommòssa *f* insurrection, riot

sommoviménto *m* tremor (*of earth*); arousal (*of passions*); riot

sommozzatóre *m* skin diver; (nav) frogman

sommuòvere §202 *tr* (lit) to agitate; (lit) to stir up, excite

sonaglièra *f* collar with bells

sonà·glio *m* (-gli) bell; rattle; raindrop; pitter-patter (*of the rain*)

sonante *adj* ringing, sounding; ready (*cash*)

sonare §257 *tr* to sound; to play; to strike (*the hour*); to ring (*a bell*); (coll) to dupe, cheat; (coll) to give a sound thrashing to; **sonare le campane a distesa** to ring a full peal ‖ *intr* (ESSERE & AVERE) to play; to ring (*said of a bell*); to sound; (lit) to spread (*said of reputation*)

sona·to -ta *adj* played; past, e.g., **le tre sonate** past three o'clock; **cinquant'anni sonati** past fifty years of age ‖ *f* ring (*of bell*); (mus) sonata; (coll) thrashing; (coll) cheating

sona·tóre -trice *mf* (mus) player

sónda *f* sound; probe; drill

sondàg·gio *m* (-gi) sounding; probe; drilling; **sondaggio d'opinioni** opinion survey, public opinion poll

sondare (sóndo) *tr* to sound; to probe; to drill; to survey (*public opinion*)

sonería *f* alarm (*of clock*)

sonétto *m* sonnet

sonnacchió·so -sa [s] *adj* sleepy, drowsy

sonnàmbu·lo -la *mf* sleepwalker

sonnecchiare §287 (sonnécchio) *intr* to drowse, take a nap; to nap, nod

sonnellino *m* nap

sonnìfe·ro -ra *adj* soporific; narcotic ‖ *m* sleeping medicine; narcotic

sónno *m* sleep; (lit) dream; **aver sonno** to be sleepy; **far venir sonno a** to bore; **prender sonno** to fall asleep

sonnolèn·to -ta *adj* sleepy; lazy

sonnolènza *f* drowsiness; laziness

sonori·tà *f* (-tà) sonority; acoustics

sonorizzare [ddzz] *tr* to voice; (mov) to dub ‖ *ref* to voice

sonò·ro -ra *adj* sound (*wave*); sonorous; (phonet) sonant, voiced

sontuó·so -sa [s] *adj* sumptuous

sopèr·chio -chia *adj* & *m* (-chi -chie) var of **soverchio**

sopire §176 *tr* to appease, calm

sopóre *m* drowsiness

soporìfe·ro -ra *adj* soporific

soppanno *m* interlining; lining (*of shoes*)

sopperire §176 *intr*—**sopperire a** to provide for; to make up for

soppesare [s] (soppéso) *tr* to heft; (fig) to weigh

soppiantare *tr* to supplant by scheming; to kick out; to replace; to trick

soppiatto *m*—**di soppiatto** stealthily

sopportàbile *adj* bearable, tolerable

sopportare (soppòrto) *tr* to bear, support; to suffer, endure

sopportazióne *f* forbearance, endurance

soppressióne *f* suppression, abolition

sopprìmere §131 *tr* to suppress, do away with

sópra *adj invar* upper; above, preceding ‖ *m* upper, upper part; **al di sopra** above; **al di sopra di** above, over; beyond; **di sopra** upper ‖ *adv* above; up; on top ‖ *prep* on; upon; on top of; over; beyond; above; versus; **sopra pensiero** absorbed in thought

sopràbito *m* overcoat, topcoat

sopraccàri·co -ca (-chi -che) *adj* overburdened ‖ *m* overload; overweight; (naut) supercargo

sopraccenna·to -ta *adj* above-mentioned

sopracci·glio *m* (-gli & -glia *fpl*) brow, eyebrow; window frame

sopraccita·to -ta *adj* above-mentioned

sopraccopèrta *f* bedspread; book jacket, dust jacket ‖ *adv* (naut) on deck

sopraddét·to -ta *adj* above-mentioned

sopraffare §173 *tr* to overcome, overpower

sopraffazióne *f* overpowering; abuse

sopraffinèstra *f* transom window

sopraffi·no -na *adj* first-class; superfine

sopraggitto *m* (sew) overcasting

sopraggiùngere §183 *intr* (ESSERE) to arrive; to happen

sopraintèndere §270 *tr* var of **soprintendere**

soprallùo·go *m* (-ghi) inspection, investigation on the spot

sopralzo *m* var of **soprelevazione**

soprammercato *m*—**per soprammercato** in addition, to boot

soprammòbile *m* knickknack

soprannaturale *adj* & *m* supernatural

soprannóme *m* nickname

soprannominare (soprannòmino) *tr* to nickname

soprannùmero *adj invar* in excess; overtime ‖ *m*—**in soprannumero** extra; in excess

sopra·no -na *adj* upper; (lit) supreme

‖ **sopra·no** *mf* (**-ni -ne**) soprano (*person*) ‖ *m* soprano (*voice*)

soprappensièro *adj invar & adv* immersed in thought

soprappéso [s] *m*—**per soprappeso** besides, into the bargain

soprap·più *m* (**-più**) plus, extra; **in soprappiù** besides, into the bargain

sopraprèzzo *m* extra charge, surcharge

soprascarpa *f* overshoe

soprascrit·to -ta *adj* written above ‖ *f* address

soprassalto *m* start, jump; **di soprassalto** with a start

soprassedére §252 *intr* (ESSERE) to wait; (with *dat*) to postpone

soprassòldo *m* extra pay; (mil) war-zone indemnity

soprastare §263 *intr* (ESSERE) to be the boss

soprattac·co *m* (**-chi**) rubber heel

soprattassa *f* surtax; surcharge

soprattutto *adv* above all, especially

sopravanzare *tr* to overcome ‖ *intr* (ESSERE) to be left over

sopravanzo *m* surplus

sopravvalutare *tr* to overrate

sopravvenire §282 *tr* (lit) to overrun ‖ *intr* (ESSERE) to arrive; to happen, occur; (with *dat*) to befall

sopravvènto *m* windward; **avere il sopravvento** to have the upper hand ‖ *adv* windward

sopravvissu·to -ta *adj* surviving ‖ *mf* survivor

sopravvivènza *f* survival

sopravvivere §286 *intr* (ESSERE) to survive; (with *dat*) to survive, to outlive

soprelevare (**soprelèvo**) *tr* to elevate (*e.g., a railroad*); to increase the height of (*building*)

soprelevazióne *f* elevation; addition of one or more floors

soprintendènte *m* superintendent

soprintendènza *f* superintendency

soprintèndere §270 *tr* to oversee

sopròsso *m* (coll) bony outgrowth

sopruso *m* abuse of power

soqquadro *m*—**a soqquadro** upside down, topsy-turvy

sòrba *f* sorb apple; (coll) hit, blow

sorbettièra *f* ice-cream freezer

sorbétto *m* ice cream; sherbet

sorbire §176 *tr* to sip; (fig) to swallow, endure

sòrbo *m* sorb; service tree

sór·cio *m* (**-ci**) mouse

sòrdi·do -da *adj* sordid; dirty

sordina *f* (mus) sordino, mute; (mus) soft pedal; **in sordina** quietly; stealthily; **mettere in sordina** (mus) to muffle

sór·do -da *adj* deaf; dull (*pain*); deep-seated (*hatred*); hollow (*sound*); (phonet) surd, voiceless; **sordo come una campana** stone-deaf ‖ *mf* deaf person

sordomu·to -ta *adj* deaf and dumb ‖ *mf* deafmute

sorèlla *f* sister

sorellastra *f* stepsister

sorgènte *adj* rising ‖ *f* spring; well (*of oil*); (fig) source; **sorgente del fiume** riverhead

sórgere §258 *intr* (ESSERE) to rise; to arise; to spring forth; **sorgere su un'ancora** (naut) to lie at anchor

sorgi·vo -va *adj* spring (*water*)

sór·go *m* (**-ghi**) sorghum

sormontare (**sormónto**) *tr* to surmount; to overcome ‖ *intr* to fit

sornió·ne -na *adj* cunning, sly ‖ *m* sneak

sorpassare *tr* to get ahead of; to surpass; to overstep; to go above

sorpasso *m* (aut) passing

sorprendènte *adj* surprising, astonishing

sorprèndere §220 *tr* to surprise; to catch; **sorprendere la buona fede di** to take advantage of ‖ *ref* to be surprised

sorprésa [s] *f* surprise; surprise investigation; **di sorpresa** suddenly; unprepared; by surprise

sorrèggere §226 *tr* to sustain, support; to bolster

sorrìdere §231 *tr* (lit) to say with a smile ‖ *intr* to smile; **sorridere a** to appeal to, e.g., **le sorride l'idea di questa gita** the idea of this trip appeals to her; to smile upon, e.g., **gli sorrideva la vita** life was smiling upon him

sorriso [s] *m* smile

sorsata *f* gulp, draught

sorseggiare §290 (**sorséggio**) *tr* to sip

sórso *m* sip; **a sorso a sorso** sipping

sòrta *f* kind, sort

sòrte *f* luck, lot, fate; chance; kind; (com) principal; **per sorte** of each kind; by chance; **tirare a sorte** to cast lots

sorteggiare §290 (**sortéggio**) *tr* to choose by lot; to raffle; **sorteggiare un premio** to draw a prize

sortég·gio *m* (**-gi**) drawing

sortilè·gio *m* (**-gi**) sortilege; sorcery, magic

sortire §176 *tr* (lit) to get by lot; (lit) to have (*results*); (lit) to allot ‖ (**sòrto**) *intr* (ESSERE) to come out (*said, e.g., of a newspaper*); (coll) to be drawn (*by lot*); (coll) to go out; (mil) to make a sally

sortita *f* witticism; (mil) sally, sortie; (theat) appearance

sorvegliante *adj* watchful ‖ *mf* overseer, caretaker; guardian ‖ *m* watchman; foreman

sorveglianza *f* surveillance; supervision

sorvegliare §280 (**sorvéglio**) *tr* to oversee, watch over; to check, control

sorvolare (**sorvólo**) *tr* to fly over; to overfly; (fig) to avoid, skip

sorvólo *m* overflight

sò·sia *m* (**-sia**) double, counterpart

sospèndere §259 *tr* to hang; to suspend; (chem) to prepare a suspension of; (law) to stay

sospensióne *f* suspension; suspense; (law) stay; **sospensione cardanica** gimbals

sospensò·rio m (-ri) jockstrap, supporter

sospé·so -sa [s] adj suspended; suspension (bridge); **in sospeso** in suspense; in abeyance ‖ m employee who has been disciplined by suspension; (com) pending item

sospettare (sospètto) tr to suspect ‖ intr—**sospettare di** to suspect; to fear

sospèt·to -ta adj suspected; suspicious ‖ m dash; suspicion

sospettó·so -sa [s] adj suspicious

sospìngere §126 tr (fig) to drive; (lit) to push

sospirare tr to long for, crave; **fare sospirare** to keep waiting ‖ intr to sigh

sospiro m sigh; longing; (lit) breath; **a sospiri** little by little

sossópra adv upside down

sòsta f stop; reprieve; (rr) demurrage

sostanti·vo -va adj & m substantive

sostanza f substance; **sostanza grigia** gray matter

sostanziale adj substantial

sostanzió·so -sa [s] adj substantial

sostare (sòsto) intr to stop, pause

sostégno m prop; (fig) support

sostenére §271 tr to support; to sustain; to take (an examination); to defend (a thesis); to prop up; to stand (alcohol); to play (a role) ‖ ref to support oneself; to hold up (said, e.g., of a theory); to take nourishment

sosteni·tóre -trice mf backer, supporter

sostentaménto m sustenance, support

sostentare (sostènto) tr to support, keep ‖ ref to feed, eat

sostenu·to -ta adj reserved, austere; rising (prices); bullish (market); starchy (manner)

sostituìbile adj replaceable

sostituire §176 tr to replace, substitute for, take the place of; **sostituire** (qlco or qlcu) **a** to substitute (s.th or s.o.) for

sostitu·to -ta adj acting; associate, assistant ‖ m replacement, substitute

sostituzióne f replacement, substitution

sostrato m substratum

sottàbito m slip

sottacére §268 tr (lit) to withhold

sottacéto adj invar pickled ‖ **sottaceti** mpl pickles

sott'àcqua adv underwater

sotta·no -na adj lower (town) ‖ f skirt; petticoat; (eccl) cassock; **gettare la sottana alle ortiche** to doff the cassock

sottécchi adv—**di sottecchi** stealthily, secretly; **guardare di sottecchi** to peep, look furtively (at)

sottentrare (sottèntro) intr (ESSERE) (with dat) to replace

sotterfù·gio m (-gi) subterfuge

sottèrra adv underground

sotterràne·o -a adj subterranean, underground; secret, clandestine ‖ m cave, vault; dungeon; underground passage ‖ f (rr) subway, underground

sotterrare (sottèrro) tr to bury

sottigliézza f thinness; subtlety

sottile adj thin; subtle; (naut) lightweight ‖ m—**guardare troppo per il sottile** to split hairs

sottilizzare [ddzz] intr to quibble

sottintèndere §270 tr to understand ‖ ref to be understood, be implied

sottinté·so -sa [s] adj understood, implied ‖ m innuendo

sótto adj invar lower ‖ m lower part ‖ adv under; underneath; **al di sotto** below; **al di sotto di** under, below; **di sotto** lower; underneath; downstairs; **di sotto a** under, below; **farsi sotto** to sneak up; **metter sotto** to run over (with a vehicle); **sotto a** under; **sotto di** under ‖ prep under; beneath; below; just before; **prendere sotto gamba** to underestimate; **sotto braccio** arm in arm; **sotto carico** (naut) being loaded; **sotto i baffi** up one's sleeve; **sotto le armi** in the service; **sotto mano** within reach; **sotto voce** under one's breath, sotto-voce

sottoascèl·la m (-la) underarm pad

sottobanco adv under the counter

sottobicchière m coaster

sottobò·sco m (-schi) underbrush, thicket

sottobràccio adv arm in arm

sottòcchio adv under one's eyes

sottoccupa·to -ta adj underemployed

sottochiave adv under lock and key

sottocó·da m (-da) crupper

sottocommissióne f subcommittee

sottocopèrta adv (naut) below decks

sottocòp·pa m (-pa) mat; coaster; (aut) oil pan

sottocòsto adj invar & adv below cost

sottocutàne·o -a adj subcutaneous

sottofà·scia m (-scia) wrapper; **spedire sottofascia** to mail (a newspaper) in a wrapper ‖ f (-sce) wrapper (for cigars)

sottogamba adv lightly; **prendere sottogamba** to underestimate

sottogó·la m & f (-la) chin strap; throatlatch (of harness)

sottolineare (sottolìneo) tr to underline, underscore; to emphasize

sott'òlio adv in oil

sottomano m writing pad ‖ adv underhand; within reach

sottomari·no -na adj & m submarine

sottomés·so -sa adj conquered; subdued; submissive

sottométtere §198 tr to subdue, crush; to defer, postpone; to present (a bill); to subject ‖ ref to submit, yield

sottomissióne f submission

sottopan·cia m (-cia) bellyband, girth

sottopassàg·gio m (-gi) underpass; lower level (of highway)

sottopiatto m saucer

sottopórre §218 tr to subject; to submit ‖ ref to submit; **sottoporsi a** to submit to; to undergo (e.g., an operation)

sottopó·sto -sta adj subject; exposed ‖ m subordinate

sottoprèzzo *adj invar* cut-rate || *adv* at a cut rate

sottoprodótto *m* by-product

sottórdine *m* suborder; **in sottórdine** secondary

sottosca·la *m* (**-la**) space under the stairs; closet under the stairs

sottoscrit·to -ta *adj* & *mf* undersigned

sottoscrit·tóre -trice *mf* subscriber

sottoscrìvere §250 *tr* to subscribe; to sign, undersign; to underwrite || *intr* to subscribe

sottoscrizióne *f* subscription

sottosegretà·rio *m* (**-ri**) undersecretary

sottosópra *adj invar* upset; **mettere sottosopra** to upset; **to turn upside down** || *m* confusion, disorder || *adv* upside down

sottostante *adj* lower; subordinate || *m* subordinate

sottostare §263 *intr* (ESSERE) to be located below; to be subject; to yield, submit; (with *dat*) to undergo (*e.g.*, *an examination*)

sottosuòlo *m* subsoil; cellar

sottosviluppa·to -ta *adj* underdeveloped

sottotenènte *m* second lieutenant; **sottotenènte di vascello** (nav) lieutenant j.g.

sottotèr·ra *m* (**-ra**) basement || *adv* underground

sottotétto *m* attic, garret

sottotìtolo *m* subtitle; (mov) caption

sottovalutare *tr* to underrate

sottovènto *m* & *adv* leeward

sottovèste *f* slip (*undergarment*)

sottovóce *adv* sotto voce, under one's breath

sottrarre §273 *tr* to subtract; **sottrarre a** to take away from, steal from || *ref*—**sottrarsi a** to avoid; to escape from

sottrazióne *f* subtraction

sottufficiale *m* noncommissioned officer

sovènte *adv* often

soverchiante *adj* overwhelming

soverchiare §287 (**sovèrchio**) *tr* to overwhelm; to excel; to bully; (lit) to overflow || *intr* to be in excess

soverchia·tóre -trice *adj* overbearing || *mf* overbearing person, oppressor

sovèr·chio -chia (**-chi -chie**) *adj* excessive; overbearing || *m* overbearing action

sovè·scio *m* (**-sci**) plowing under (*of green manure*)

sovièti·co -ca (**-ci -che**) *adj* Soviet || *mf* Soviet citizen

sovrabbondante *adj* superabundant

sovrabbondare (**sovrabbóndo**) *intr* (ESSERE & AVERE) to be superabundant; to go to excesses

sovraccaricare §197 (**sovraccàrico**) *tr* to overload

sovraccàri·co -ca (**-chi -che**) *adj* overburdened || *m* overload; overweight

sovraespó·sto -sta *adj* overexposed

sovraggiùngere §183 *intr* (ESSERE) var of **sopraggiungere**

sovralimentazióne *f* (aut) supercharging

sovrani·tà *f* (**-tà**) sovereignty

sovra·no -na *adj* & *mf* sovereign

sovrappopolare (**sovrappòpolo**) *tr* to overpopulate

sovrappórre §218 *tr* to overlay; to superimpose; **sovrappórre qlco a** to lay s.th on || *ref* to be superimposed; to be added; **sovrappórsi a** to put oneself above

sovrapproduzióne *f* overproduction

sovrastampa *f* overprint

sovrastante *adj* overlooking, overhanging; impending

sovrastare *tr* to tower over; to hang over; to surpass; to excel || *intr* (ESSERE & AVERE)—**sovrastare a** to tower over; to overlook; to hang over; to surpass; to excel

sovratensióne *f* (elec) surge

sovreccitare (**sovrèccito**) *tr* to overexcite

sovrespórre §218 *tr* to overexpose

sovrimpòsta *f* surtax

sovrimpressióne *f* double exposure

sovruma·no -na *adj* superhuman

sovvenire §282 *tr* (lit) to help || *intr* (with *dat*) (lit) to help || *impers* (ESSERE)—**sovviene** (with *dat*) **di** remember, e.g., **gli sovviene spesso dei suoi cari** he often remembers his dear ones || *ref*—**sovvenirsi di** to remember

sovvenzionare (**sovvenzióno**) *tr* to subsidize, grant a subvention to

sovvenzióne *f* subsidy, subvention

sovversi·vo -va *adj* & *m* subversive

sovvertire (**sovvèrto**) *tr* to subvert

sóz·zo -za *adj* dirty, filthy, foul

sozzura *f* dirt, filth

spaccalé·gna *m* (**-gna**) woodcutter

spaccamón·ti *m* (**-ti**) braggart

spaccaòs·sa *m* (**-sa**) butcher's cleaver

spaccare §197 *tr* to break, burst; to crack; to unpack; to chop; to split || *ref* to crack; to break; to split

spacca·to -ta *adj* broken; split; (coll) identical; (coll) true || *f* (sports, theat) splits

spaccatura *f* break; crack; cleavage; split

spacchétto *m* vent (*in jacket*)

spacciare §128 *tr* to sell out; to palm off; to spread (*reports*); to expedite; to abandon (*as hopeless*); (slang) to push (*e.g.*, *dope*) || *ref*—**spacciarsi per** to pretend to be, pass oneself off as

spaccia·to -ta *adj* (coll) cooked, done for; (coll) hopeless

spaccia·tóre -trice *mf* passer (*of bad currency or stolen goods*); **spacciatore di notizie false** gossipmonger

spàc·cio *m* (**-ci**) sale; passing (*of counterfeit money*); spreading (*of false news*); post exchange; tobacco shop

spac·co *m* (**-chi**) break; split; tear; crack; vent (*in jacket*)

spacconata *f* brag, braggadocio

spaccó·ne -na *mf* braggart, braggadocio

spada *f* sword; **a spada tratta** doggedly; **spade** suit of Neapolitan cards corresponding to spades

spadaccino *m* swordsman; swashbuckler

spadóne *m* two-handed sword

spadroneggiare §290 (**spadronéggio**) *intr* to be domineering or bossy

spaesa·to -ta *adj* out-of-place

spaghétto *m* (coll) fear, jitters; **avere lo spaghetto** (coll) to be scared stiff; **spaghetti** spaghetti

Spagna, la Spain

spagnòla *f* Spanish woman; Spanish influenza

spagnolétta *f* espagnolette; spool; (coll) cigarette; (coll) peanut

spagnò·lo -la *adj* Spanish || *m* Spaniard (*individual*); Spanish (*language*); **gli spagnoli** the Spanish || *f* see **spagnola**

spa·go *m* (**-ghi**) string, twine; (coll) fear, jitters

spalare §287 *tr* to break a pair of

spaia·to -ta *adj* unmatched

spalancare §197 *tr* to open wide || *ref* to open up; to gape

spalare *tr* to shovel; to feather (*oar*)

spalla *f* shoulder; back; abutment (*of bridge*); (theat) stooge, straight man; **alle spalle di qlcu** behind s.o.'s back; **a spalla** on one's back; **fare spalla a** to help; **lavorare di spalle** to elbow one's way; (fig) to worm one's way up; **vivere alle spalle di** to sponge on

spallàrm *interj* (mil) shoulder arms!

spallata *f* push with the shoulder; shrug of the shoulders

spalleggiare §290 (**spalléggio**) *tr* to back, support; (mil) to carry on one's back

spallétta *f* parapet, retaining wall; jamb

spallièra *f* back (*of chair*); head (*of bed*); foot (*of bed*); espalier

spallina *f* epaulet; shoulder strap

spallùccia *f*—**fare spallucce** to shrug one's shoulders

spalmare *tr* to spread; to smear

spalto *m* glacis; **spalti** seats (*of a stadium*)

spanare *tr*) to strip the thread of || *ref* to be stripped (*said, e.g., of the thread of a nut*)

spanciare §128 *tr* to disembowel, gut || *intr* to belly-flop; to bulge (*said of a wall*) || *ref*—**spanciarsi dalle risa** to split one's sides laughing

spanciata *f* belly flop; bellyful; **fare una spanciata** to stuff oneself

spàndere §260 *tr* to spread; to spill; to shed (*tears*); to squander || *ref* to spread

spanna *f* span

spannare *tr* to skim (*milk*)

spannocchiare §287 (**spannòcchio**) *tr* to husk (*corn*)

spappolare (**spàppolo**) *tr* to crush, squash || *ref* to become mushy

sparadrappo *m* adhesive tape; (obs) plaster, poultice

sparagnare *tr* (coll) to save

sparare *tr* to gut, disembowel; to shoot; to let go with (*a kick*); to remove

the hangings from; **spararne delle grosse** to tell tall tales

sparato *m* shirt front, dickey

sparatòria *f* shooting

sparecchiare §287 (**sparécchio**) *tr* to clear (*the table*); to clear away (*one's tools*); to eat up

sparég·gio *m* (**-gi**) disparity; deficit; (sports) play-off

spàrgere §261 *tr* to spread; to shed; to spill || *ref* to spread

spargiménto *m* spreading; **spargimento di sangue** bloodshed

spargisa·le [s] *m* (**-le**) salt shaker

sparigliare §280 *tr* to break a pair of; to break (*a set*)

spariglia·to -ta *adj* unmatched

sparire §176 *intr* (ESSERE) to disappear

sparlare *intr* to backbite; **sparlare di** to backbite, slander

sparo *m* shot

sparpagliare §280 *tr* & *intr* to scatter

spar·so -sa *adj* scattered; dotted; speckled; hanging loosely (*e.g., hair*)

sparta·no -na *adj* & *mf* Spartan

spartiàc·que *m* (**-que**) watershed

spartiné·ve *m* (**-ve**) snowplow

spartire §176 *tr* to divide, share; to separate; **non aver nulla da spartire con** to have nothing to do with

spartito *m* (mus) score; (mus) arrangement

spartitràffi·co *m* (**-co**) median strip

spar·to -ta *adj* (lit) spread || *m* esparto grass

sparu·to -ta *adj* lean, wan; meager

sparvière *m* sparrow hawk; mortarboard

spasimante *m* (joc) lover, wooer

spasimare (**spàsimo**) *intr* to writhe; **spasimare per** to long for; to be madly in love with

spàsimo *m* pang; severe pain; longing

spasmo *m* spasm

spasmòdi·co -ca *adj* (**-ci -che**) spasmodic

spassare *tr* to amuse || *ref*—**spassarsela** to have a good time

spassiona·to -ta *adj* dispassionate, unbiased

spasso *m* fun, amusement; walk; (coll) funny guy; **andare a spasso** to go out for a walk; **essere a spasso** to be out of a job; **mandare a spasso** to fire, dismiss; to get rid of; **per spasso** for fun; **portare a spasso** to lead by the nose; **prendersi spasso di** to make fun of

spassó·so -sa [s] *adj* amusing, droll

spàsti·co -ca *adj* & *mf* spastic

spato *m* spar

spatofluòre *m* fluorspar

spàtola *f* spatula; putty knife; slapstick (*of harlequin*)

spauràc·chio *m* (**chi**) scarecrow; bugaboo, bugbear

spaurare *tr* & *ref* (lit) var of **spaurire**

spaurire §176 *tr* to frighten || *ref* to be scared

spaval·do -da *adj* bold, swaggering

spaventapàs·seri *m* (**-ri**) scarecrow

spaventare (spavènto) *tr* to scare, frighten ‖ *ref* to be scared

spaventévole *adj* frightening, dreadful

spavènto *m* fright, fear

spaventó·so -sa [s] *adj* frightful, fearful

spaziale *adj* space

spaziare §287 *tr* (typ) to space ‖ *intr* to soar; to range, rove (*said, e.g., of eye*)

spazia·tóre -trice *adj* spacing ‖ *f* space bar (*of typewriter*)

spaziatura *f* spacing

spazientire §176 *tr* to make (*s.o.*) lose his patience ‖ *intr* (ESSERE) & *ref* to lose patience

spà·zio *m* (-zi) space; (fig) room; **spazio aereo** air space; **spazio cosmico** outer space

spazió·so -sa [s] *adj* spacious, roomy; wide

spazzacamino *m* chimney sweep

spazzami·ne *m* (-ne) mine sweeper

spazzané·ve *m* (-ve) snowplow

spazzare *tr* to sweep; to plow (*snow*); to clean up

spazzata *f*—**dare una spazzata a** to give a lick and a promise to

spazzatrice *f* street sweeper

spazzatura *f* sweeping; sweepings; rubbish, trash

spazzatu·ràio *m* (-rài) or **spazzino** *m* street cleaner; trashman, garbage collector, trash collector

spàzzola *f* brush; **capelli a spazzola** crew cut

spazzolare (spàzzolo) *tr* to brush

spazzolino *m* little brush; (elec) brush; **spazzolino da denti** toothbrush; **spazzolino per le unghie** nailbrush

spazzolóne *m* push broom

specchiare §287 *tr* (lit) to reflect ‖ *ref* to look at oneself (*in a mirror*); to be reflected; **specchiarsi in qlcu** to model oneself on s.o.

specchièra *f* mirror; dressing table; full-length mirror

specchiétto *m* mirror; synopsis; **specchietto retrovisivo** (aut) rear-view mirror

spèc·chio *m* (-chi) mirror; synopsis; shore (*of lake or river*); panel (*of door or window*); sheet (*of water*); (sports) goal line; (sports) board; **specchio di poppa** (naut) transom; **specchio ustorio** burning glass

speciale *adj* special

speciali·sta *mf* (-sti -ste) specialist

speciali·tà *f* (-tà) specialty; (mil) special services; **specialità farmaceutica** patent or proprietary medicine

specializzare [ddzz] *tr* & *ref* to specialize

spè·cie *f* (-cie) species; kind, sort; appearance, semblance; **fare specie** (with *dat*) (coll) to be surprised, e.g., **gli fa specie** he is surprised; **in specie** especially; **sotto specie di** under pretext of

specifi·ca *f* (-che) itemized list; specification

specificare §197 (specìfico) *tr* to specify; to itemize

specìfi·co -ca (-ci -che) *adj* & *m* specific ‖ *f* see **specifica**

specillo *m* (med) probe

speció·so -sa [s] *adj* specious

spè·co *m* (-chi) (lit) cave

spècola *f* observatory

spècolo *m* (med, surg) speculum

speculare (spèculo) *tr* to observe; to meditate on ‖ *intr* to speculate

specula·tóre -trice *adj* speculating ‖ *mf* speculator; **speculatore al rialzo** bull; **speculatore al ribasso** bear

speda·to -ta *adj* footworn

spedire §176 *tr* to expedite; to prepare; to ship, send, forward; (law) to deliver

spedi·to -ta *adj* rapid; free, easy

spedi·tóre -trice *mf* shipper, sender; shipping clerk

spedizióne *f* shipment, shipping; sending, forwarding; expedition; (naut) papers; **di spedizione** expeditionary

spedizionière *m* shipper, forwarder, forwarding agent

spègnere §262 *tr* to extinguish, put out; to turn off; to slake (*lime*); to kill; to mix (*flour*) with water or milk; to quench; to obliterate (*a memory*) ‖ *ref* to burn out; to go out (*said of a light*); to fade, die away; to die

spegni·tóio *m* (-tói) snuffer

spegnitura *f* (theat) blackout

spelacchiare §287 *tr* to strip of hair ‖ *ref* to shed hair or fur

spelacchia·to -ta *adj* mangy; (pej) baldy

spelare (spélo) *tr* to strip of hair; to pluck (*e.g., a chicken*); (fig) to fleece ‖ *ref* to shed hair or fur; to get bald

spellare (spèllo) *tr* to skin; (fig) to skin, fleece

spelón·ca *f* (-che) cave; hovel, den

spème *f* (poet) hope

spendacció·ne -na *mf* spendthrift

spèndere §220 *tr* to spend

spenderéc·cio -cia *adj* (-ci -ce) spendthrift, prodigal

spennacchiare §287 *tr* to pluck; (fig) to fleece ‖ *ref* to lose its feathers

spennare (spènno) *tr* & *ref* var of **spennacchiare**

spennellare (spennèllo) *tr* to dab

spensieratézza *f* thoughtlessness

spensiera·to -ta *adj* thoughtless, careless; carefree, happy-go-lucky

spèn·to -ta *adj* extinguished; turned off; slaked (*lime*); dull (*color*); low (*tone*)

spenzolare [dz] (spènzolo) *tr* & *intr* to hang ‖ *ref*—**spenzolarsi da** to hang out of

speranza *f* hope; prospect, expectation

speranzó·so -sa [s] *adj* hopeful

sperare (spèro) *tr* to candle (*eggs*); to hope for; to expect ‖ *intr* to hope; to trust

spèrdere §212 (lit) to scatter; (lit) to lose (*one's way*) ‖ *ref* to lose one's way, get lost

sperdu·to -ta *adj* lost, astray; godforsaken (*place*)

sperequazióne *f* disproportion; inequality; unjust distribution

spergiurare *tr & intr* to swear falsely; **giurare e spergiurare** to swear over and over again

spergiu•ro -ra *adj* perjured ‖ *mf* perjurer ‖ *m* perjury

spericola•to -ta *adj* reckless, daring

sperimentale *adj* experimental

sperimentare (**speriménto**) *tr* to test, try out; to experience

sperimenta•to -ta *adj* experienced

spèr•ma *m* (**-mi**) sperm

speronare (**speróno**) *tr* (naut) to ram

speróne *m* spur; abutment; (nav) ram

sperperare (**spèrpero**) *tr* to squander

spèrpero *m* squandering

spèr•so -sa *adj* lost, stray

spertica•to -ta *adj* too long; too tall; exaggerated, excessive

spésa [s] *f* expense; shopping; buy, purchase; **fare la spesa** to shop; **fare le spese di** to be the butt of; **lavorare per le spese** to work for one's keep; **pagare le spese** to bear the charges; **spese expenses**; room and board; **spese di manutenzione** upkeep; **spese minute** petty expenses; **spese processuali** (law) costs

spesare [s] (**spéso**) *tr* to support

spesa•to -ta [s] *adj* with all expenses paid

spès•so -sa *adj* thick; many (*times*) ‖ **spesso spesso** often; **spesso spesso** again and again

spessóre *m* thickness

spettàbile *adj* esteemed; **Spettabile Ditta** (com) Gentlemen

spettàcolo *m* spectacle, show; sight; **dar spettacolo di sé** to make a show of oneself; **spettacolo all'aperto** outdoor performance

spettacoló•so -sa [s] *adj* spectacular; (coll) exceptional; (coll) sensational

spettanza *f* concern; pay

spettare (**spètto**) *intr* (ESSERE)—**spettare a** to belong to ‖ *impers* (ESSERE) —**spetta a it** behooves, it is up to

spetta•tóre -trice *mf* spectator, bystander; **spettatori** public, audience

spettegolare (**spettégolo**) *intr* to gossip

spettinare (**spèttino**) *tr* to muss the hair of

spettrale *adj* ghost-like; spectral

spèttro *m* specter, ghost; spectrum

speziale *m* dealer in spices; (coll) pharmacist

spezierìa *f* grocery; (coll) drug store, pharmacy; **spezierìe** spices

spèzie *fpl* spices

spezzare (**spèzzo**) *tr* to break; to smash; to interrupt ‖ *ref* to break

spezzatìno *m* stew; **spezzatìni** change

spezza•to -ta *adj* broken; fragmentary; interrupted ‖ *m* stew; (theat) set piece; **spezzati** change

spezzettare (**spezzétto**) *tr* to mince

spezzóne *m* small aerial bomb; fragmentation bomb; fragment

spìa *f* spy; indication; peephole; (aut) gauge; (aut) pilot light; **fare la spìa** to be an informer

spiaccicare §197 (**spiàccico**) *tr* to squash, crush ‖ *ref* to be squashed

spiacènte *adj* sorry; (lit) disliked

spiacére §214 *intr* (ESSERE) (with *dat*) to dislike, e.g., **queste parole gli spiacciono** he dislikes these words; to mind, e.g., **se non Le spiace** if you don't mind ‖ *ref*—**spiacersi di** to be sorry for ‖ *impers* (ESSERE) (with *dat*)—**gli spiace** he is sorry

spiacévole *adj* unpleasant

spiàg•gia *f* (**-ge**) beach, shore

spianare *tr* to grade (*land*); to roll (*dough*); to pave (*the way*); to iron (*pleats*); to raze, demolish; to level (*a gun*); **spianare la fronte** to smooth one's brow ‖ *intr* (ESSERE) to be level

spianata *f* esplanade; **dare una spianata a** to level

spianatóia *f* board (*for rolling dough*)

spiana•tóio *m* (**-tói**) rolling pin

spianatrice *f* grader

spiano *m* leveling; esplanade; **a tutto spiano** at full blast; continuously

spiantare *tr* to uproot; to raze, level; to ruin (*financially*) ‖ *ref* to ruin oneself

spianta•to -ta *adj* ruined ‖ *m* pauper

spiare §119 *tr* to spy on; to keep an eye on

spiattellare (**spiattèllo**) *tr* to blurt out

spiazzo *m* square; plain; clearing

spiccare §197 *tr* to detach; to pick; to enunciate; to begin; to draw up (*a commercial paper*); to issue (*a warrant*); **spiccare il volo** (aer) to take off ‖ *intr* to stand out ‖ *ref* to separate (*said, e.g., of the stone of a peach*)

spicca•to -ta *adj* clear, distinct; typical; outstanding

spic•chio *m* (**-chi**) section (*of fruit*); clove (*of garlic*); slice (*e.g., of apple*); arm (*of cross*)

spicciare §128 *tr* to clear up; to wait on; to dispatch (*business*) ‖ *intr* (ESSERE) to flow forth, gush out ‖ *ref* to hurry up, make haste

spicciati•vo -va *adj* expeditious, quick; straightforward; gruff

spiccicare §197 (**spìccico**) *tr* to unglue; to enunciate; to utter ‖ *ref* to come unglued; **spiccicarsi di** to get rid of

spìc•cio -cia (**-ci -ce**) *adj* expeditious, quick; unhampered; small (*change*) ‖ **spicci** *mpl* change

spicciolata *adj* *fem*—**alla spicciolata** little by little; a few at a time

spìccio•lo -la *adj* small (change); (coll) plain ‖ **spìccioli** *mpl* small change

spìc•co -ca (**-chi -che**) *adj* freestone (*e.g., peach*) ‖ *m*—**fare spicco** to stand out

spidocchiare §287 (**spidòcchio**) *tr* to delouse

spièdo *m* spit; **allo spiedo** barbecued

spiegàbile *adj* explainable

spiegaménto *m* (mil) array; (mil) deployment

spiegare §209 (**spiègo**) *tr* to unfold; to let go (*with one's voice*); to unfurl; to spread (*wings*); to deploy (*troops*); to explain; to show, demonstrate; **spiegare il volo** (aer) to take off ‖ *ref* to become unfurled or unfolded;

to make oneself understood; to come to an understanding; to realize

spiega·to -ta *adj* open; full (*voice*)

spiegazióne *f* explanation

spiegazzare *tr* to crumple, rumple

spieta·to -ta *adj* pitiless, ruthless

spifferare (spìffero) *tr* (coll) to blurt out || *intr* to blow in (*said of wind*)

spìffero *m* (coll) draft

spi·ga *f* (**ghe**) panicle (*of oats*); (bot) ear, spike; **a spiga** herringbone

spiga·to -ta *adj* herringbone

spighétta *f* braid; (bot) spikelet

spigionare (spigióno) *ref* to be or become vacant

spiglia·to -ta *adj* easy, free and easy

spi·go *m* (**-ghi**) lavender

spigolare (spìgolo) *tr* to glean

spigola·tóre -trice *mf* gleaner

spigolo *m* corner; edge; (archit) arris

spilla *f* brooch, pin; **spilla da cravatta** tiepin; **spilla di sicurezza** safety pin

spillare *tr* to draw off, tap; to wheedle, worm (*money*) || *intr* to leak (*said of container*) || *intr* (ESSERE) to leak (*said of liquid*)

spillàti·co *m* (**-ci**) (law) pin money (*for one's wife*)

spillo *m* pin; gimlet; trifle; **a spillo** spikelike; **spillo da balia** or **di sicurezza** safety pin

spillóne *m* hatpin; bodkin

spilluzzicare §197 (spillùzzico) *tr* to pick at, nibble; to scrape together

spilorcería *f* stinginess

spilòr·cio -cia (**-ci -ce**) *adj* stingy || *mf* miser, tightwad

spilungó·ne -na *mf* lanky person

spina *f* thorn; quill, spine (*of porcupine*); bone (*of fish*); (fig) preoccupation, worry; **alla spina** (*beer*) on tap; **a spina di pesce** herringbone (*fabric*); **con una spina nel cuore** sick at heart; **essere sulle spine** to be on pins and needles; **spina della botte** tap; bunghole; **spina dorsale** spinal column; (fig) backbone; **spina elettrica** plug

spinà·cio -cio (**-ci**) spinach (*plant*); **spinaci** spinach (*as food*)

spinapésce *m*—**a spinapesce** herringbone

spina·to -ta *adj* barbed (*wire*); herringbone (*fabric*)

spingere §126 *tr* to push, press; to prod, goad || *ref* to push; to reach

spi·no -na *adj* thorny || *m* thorn || *f* see **spina**

spinóne *m* griffon

spinó·so -sa [s] *adj* thorny

spinòtto *m* wrist pin

spinta *f* push; pressure; poke, prod; stress

spinterògeno *m* (aut) distributor unit, ignition system

spin·to -ta *adj* pushed; bent, inclined; (coll) risqué; (coll) far-out, offbeat || *f* see **spinta**

spintóne *m* (coll) push, shove

spionàg·gio *m* (**-gi**) espionage, spying

spioncino *m* peephole

spió·ne -na *mf* spy, stool pigeon

spiovènte *adj* drooping; sloping; falling || *m* slope; drainage area (*of a mountain*)

spiòvere §216 *intr* to fall, to hang down (*said, e.g., of hair*); to flow down || *impers* (ESSERE)—**è spiovuto** it stopped raining

spira *f* turn (*of a coil*); coil (*of serpent*); **a spire** spiral

spirà·glio *m* (**-gli**) small opening; gleam (*of light or hope*)

spirale *adj* spiral || *f* spiral; hairspring; wreath (*of smoke*); **spirale di fumo** smoke ring

spirare *tr* to send forth; (lit) to inspire, infuse; (lit) to show (*kindness*) || *intr* to blow; to emanate; to die; to expire

spirita·to -ta *adj* possessed; wild, mad

spirìti·co -ca *adj* (**-ci -che**) spiritual; spiritualistic

spiritismo *m* spiritualism

spirito *m* spirit; wit; mind; spirits, alcohol; sprite; **bello spirito** wit (*person*); **fare dello spirito** to be witty; to crack jokes; **l'ultimo spirito** (lit) one's last breath; **spirito di corpo** esprit de corps; **spirito di parte** partisanship; **spirito sportivo** sportsmanship

spiritosàggine [s] *f* witticism

spiritó·so -sa [s] *adj* witty; alcoholic

spirituale *adj* spiritual

spizzi·co *m* (**-chi**)—**a spizzico** or **a spizzichi** little by little; **a little at a time**

splendènte *adj* resplendent, shining

splèndere §281 *intr* (ESSERE & AVERE) to shine

splèndi·do -da *adj* splendid; gorgeous; bright || *m*—**fare lo splendido** to be a big spender

splendóre *m* splendor; brightness; beauty

splène *m* (anat) spleen

spòcchia *f* haughtiness

spodestare (spodèsto) *tr* to dispossess; to dethrone; to oust

spoetizzare [ddzz] *tr* to disillusion

spòglia *f* slough (*of snake*); skin (*of onion*); husk (*of corn*); (lit) body; (lit) outer garment; **sotto mentite spoglie** under false pretense; **spoglie** spoils

spogliare §280 (spòglio) *tr* to undress, strip; to strip of armor; to defraud, deprive; to free; to check, examine; to husk (*corn*); to go through (*e.g., correspondence*) || *ref* to undress; to slough (*said, e.g., of a snake*); **spogliarsi di** to get rid of; to divest oneself of; to shake (*a habit*)

spogliarelli·sta *f* (**-ste**) stripteaser

spogliarèllo *m* striptease

spoglia·tóio *m* (**-tói**) dressing room; locker room

spò·glio -glia (**-gli -glie**) *adj* stripped, bare; free || *m* cast-off clothing; sorting; scrutiny; counting (*of votes*); **di spoglio** second-hand (*material*) || *f* see **spoglia**

spòla *f* bobbin; shuttle; **fare la spola** to shuttle

spolétta *f* bobbin, spool; (mil) fuse

spolmonare (**spolmóno**) *ref* (coll) to talk, sing, or shout oneself hoarse

spolpare (**spólpo**) *tr* to gnaw (*a bone*); to eat up (*fruit*); (fig) to fleece

spolverare (**spólvero**) *tr* to dust off, whisk; to powder, dust; to pounce

spolveratura *f* dusting; powdering; sprinkling, smattering (*of knowledge*); **dare una spolveratura a** to brush up on

spolverina *f* (coll) duster

spolverino *m* duster, smock; powder-sugar duster; pounce; (coll) whisk broom

spolverizzaménto [ddzz] *m* sprinkling (*with powder*)

spolverizzare [ddzz] *tr* to dust, powder, pounce

spólvero *m* dusting; powdering; pounce; smattering, sprinkling (*of knowledge*); display

spónda *f* bank (*of river*); side; cushion (*of billiard table*)

sponsale *adj* (lit) wedding || **sponsali** *mpl* (lit) wedding

spontàne·o -a *adj* spontaneous; artless

spopolare (**spòpolo**) *tr* to depopulate || *intr* to be a hit; to become depopulated or deserted

spoppare (**spóppo**) *tr* to wean

sporàdi·co -ca *adj* (**-ci -che**) sporadic

sporcacció·ne -na *adj* filthy || *mf* filthy person; (fig) dirty mouth

sporcare §197 (**spòrco**) *tr* to dirty; to soil || *ref* to get dirty; to soil oneself; **sporcarsi la fedina** (coll) to get a black mark on one's record

sporcìzia *f* dirt, filth

spòr·co -ca (**-chi -che**) *adj* dirty, filthy; foul; **farla sporca** to pull a dirty trick || *m* dirt, filth

sporgènte *adj* leaning; protruding; beetle (*brow*)

sporgènza *f* prominence, projection

spòrgere §217 *tr* to stick out; to stretch out; to lodge (*a complaint*) || *intr* (ESSERE) to project, jut out || *ref* to lean out

spòrt *m* (**spòrt**) sport; game; **per sport** for fun, for pleasure

spòrta *f* shopping bag; bagful; basket; basketful; shopping; **a sporta** wide-brimmed (*hat*)

sportèllo *m* door; panel; window (*in bank, station, etc.*); wicket; branch (*of a bank*); (theat) box office

sportivi·tà *f* (**-tà**) sportsmanship

sporti·vo -va *adj* sporting; sportsman-like; athletic || *m* sportsman

spòr·to -ta *adj* projecting; jutting out || *m* projection; removable shutter (*on store door or window*) || *f* see **sporta**

spòsa *f* bride; wife; **andare in sposa a** to get married to; **sposa promessa** fiancée

sposalì·zio -zia (**-zi -zie**) *adj* (lit) nuptial || *m* wedding

sposare (**spòso**) *tr* to marry; to unite; to embrace (*a cause*); to fit perfectly; to give in marriage || *ref* to get married, marry

spòso *m* bridegroom; **sposi** newlyweds

spossare (**spòsso**) *tr* to exhaust || *ref* to become worn out

spossatézza *f* exhaustion

spostaménto *m* shift; movement; displacement; change

spostare (**spòsto**) *tr* to move; to change, shift; to upset || *ref* to move; to shift; to get out of place; to be upset

sposta·to -ta *adj* ill-adjusted, out of place || *mf* misfit

spran·ga *f* (**-ghe**) bar, crossbar

sprangare §209 *tr* to bar, bolt

sprazzo *m* spray; flash; burst

sprecare §197 (**sprèco**) *tr* to waste; to miss (*an opportunity*) || *ref* to waste one's efforts

sprè·co *m* (**-chi**) waste; squandering

sprecó·ne -na *adj & mf* spendthrift

spregévole *adj* contemptible, despicable

spregiare §290 (**sprègio**) *tr* to despise

sprè·gio *m* (**-gi**) contempt, scorn

spregiudica·to -ta *adj* open-minded, unbiased || *m* open-minded person

sprèmere §123 *tr* to squeeze, press; **spremere le lacrime a** to move to tears || *ref*—**spremersi il cervello** to rack one's brain

spremifrut·ta *m* (**-ta**) squeezer

spremilimó·ni *m* (**-ni**) lemon squeezer

spremuta *f* squeezing; **spremuta d'arancia** orange juice

spretare (**sprèto**) *ref* to doff the cassock

sprezzante *adj* contemptuous, haughty

sprezzare (**sprèzzo**) *tr* (lit) to despise

sprèzzo *m* disdain, contempt

sprigionare (**sprigióno**) *tr* to exhale, emit; to free from prison || *ref* to free oneself; to escape, come forth, issue (*said, e.g., of steam*)

sprimacciare §128 *tr* to beat, fluff (*e.g., a pillow*)

sprizzare *tr* to spout; to sparkle with (*joy, health*) || *intr* (ESSERE) to spurt; to fly (*said of sparks*); to sparkle

sprizzo *m* sprinkle; spurt; spark

sprofondare (**sprofóndo**) *tr* to send to the bottom; to destroy, ruin; to sink || *intr* (ESSERE) to sink; to founder; to cave in; to be sunk (*e.g., in meditation*)

sprolò·quio *m* (**-qui**) long rigmarole

spronare (**spróno**) *tr* to spur, goad

spróne *m* spur; prodding; example; guimpe; buttress; abutment (*of bridge*); **a sprone battuto** at full speed; at once; **dar di sprone a** to spur on; **sprone di cavaliere** (bot) rocket larkspur

sproporziona·to -ta *adj* out of proportion, disproportionate

sproporzióne *f* disproportion

spropòsita·to -ta *adj* out of proportion; excessive; gross (*error*)

spropòsito *m* blunder, error; excessive amount; **a sproposito** out of place; inopportunely

sprovvedu·to -ta *adj* deprived; brainless, witless

sprovvi·sto -sta *adj* deprived; devoid, lacking; **alla sprovvista** suddenly; unawares, off guard

spruzzabianche·rìa *m* (**-rìa**) sprinkler (*to sprinkle clothes*)

spruzzare *tr* to sprinkle, spray; to powder (*sugar*)

spruzzatóre *m* sprayer; (aut) nozzle (*of carburetor*)

spruzzo *m* spray; splash (*of mud*)

spudora·to -ta *adj* shameless; impudent

spugna *f* sponge; **dare un colpo di spugna** to wipe the slate clean; **gettare la spugna** to throw in the towel

spugnare *tr* to sponge; to swab

spugnatura *f* sponge bath

spugnó·so -sa [s] *adj* spongy

spulciare §128 *tr* to pick the fleas off; to scrutinize, examine minutely

spuma *f* foam, froth

spumante *adj* sparkling ‖ *m* sparkling wine; champagne

spumare *intr* to froth

spumeggiante *adj* sparkling; vaporous; foamy

spumeggiare §290 (**spuméggio**) *intr* to foam

spumóne *m* spumoni

spumó·so -sa [s] *adj* foamy, frothy

spunta *f* check; check list; check mark

spuntare *tr* to blunt; to unpin; to overcome; to clip, trim; to check off; **spuntarla** to come out on top; to overcome ‖ *intr* (ESSERE) to appear; to sprout; to rise; to well up (*said of tears*); to pop out; to break through ‖ *ref* to become blunt; to die down

spuntino *m* bite, snack; **fare uno spuntino** to have a bite

spunto *m* sourness (*of wine*); (theat) cue; (sports) sprint; (fig) starting point, origin

spuntóne *m* spike; pike; crag

spurgare §209 *tr* to purge, clear; to clean up ‖ *ref* to expectorate

spur·go *m* (**-ghi**) discharge; reject (*e.g., book*)

spù·rio -ria *adj* (**-ri -rie**) spurious

sputacchiare §287 *tr* to spit upon ‖ *intr* to sputter

sputacchièra *f* spittoon, cuspidor

sputare *tr* to spit; to cough up; (fig) to spew (*venom*); **sputare sangue** to spit blood; (fig) to sweat blood ‖ *intr* to spit

sputasentènze *mf* (**-ze**) wiseacre

sputo *m* spit, sputum; spitting

squadernare (**squadèrno**) *tr* to leaf through; **squadernare qlco a qlcu** to put s.th under the nose of s.o. ‖ *ref* to come apart (*said of a book*)

squadra *f* square (*for measuring right angles*); squad, group; (mil) squadron; (sports) team; **a squadra** at right angles; **fuori squadra** out of kilter; **squadra di pompieri** fire company; **squadra mobile** flying squad

squadrare *tr* to square; (fig) to examine, study

squadriglia *f* (aer, nav) squadron

squadróne *m* squadron (*of cavalry*)

squagliare §280 *tr* to melt ‖ *ref* to melt; **squagliarsela** to take French leave

squalifi·ca *f* (**-che**) disqualification

squalificare §197 (**squalifico**) *tr* to disqualify ‖ *ref* to disqualify oneself; to prove to be unqualified

squàlli·do -da *adj* wretched, dreary, gloomy; faint (*smile*); (lit) emaciated

squallóre *m* wretchedness, dreariness, gloominess

squalo *m* shark

squama *f* scurf (*shed by the skin*); (bot, pathol, zool) scale

squamare *tr & ref* to scale

squamó·so -sa [s] *adj* scaly

squarciagóla *adv*—**a squarciagola** at the top of one's voice

squarciare §128 *tr* to rend, tear apart; to dispel (*a doubt*) ‖ *ref* to become torn; to open

squàr·cio *m* (**-ci**) tear, rip; passage (*of book*)

squartare *tr* to quarter

squartatura *f* quartering

squassare *tr* to shake violently; to wreck

squattrina·to -ta *adj* penniless ‖ *m* pauper

squilibra·to -ta *adj* unbalanced, deranged ‖ *mf* mad or insane person

squili·brio *m* (**-bri**) lack of balance; **squilibrio mentale** insanity; unbalanced mental condition

squillante *adj* ringing, shrill; sharp

squillare *intr* to ring; to ring out; to blare

squillo *m* ring; peal; blare, blast (*of horn*); ‖ *f* call girl

squinternare (**squintèrno**) *tr* to tear (*a book*) to pieces; (fig) to upset

squisi·to -ta *adj* exquisite

squittire §176 *intr* to squeak; to squeal

sradicare §197 (**sràdico**) *tr* to uproot; to eradicate; to pull (*a tooth*)

sragionare (**sragióno**) *intr* to talk nonsense

sregola·to -ta *adj* intemperate; dissolute

srotolare (**sròtolo**) *tr* to unroll

stàb·bio *m* (**-bi**) pen; manure, dung

stabbiòlo *m* pigpen

stàbile *adj* stable; real (*estate*); permanent; stock (*company*) ‖ *m* building

stabiliménto *m* plant, factory; establishment; settlement, colony; conclusion (*of a deal*)

stabilire §176 *tr* to establish; to decide ‖ *ref* to settle

stabili·tà *f* (**-tà**) stability, steadiness

stabilito *m* (law) agreement of sale (*drawn up by a broker*)

stabilizzare [ddzz] *tr & ref* to stabilize

stabilizza·tóre -trice [ddzz] *mf* stabilizing person ‖ *m* (aer) stabilizer; (elec) voltage stabilizer

staccare §197 *tr* to detach; to unhitch; to outdistance; to draw (*a check*); to tear off; to take (*one's eyes*) away; to begin; to enunciate (*words*) ‖ *intr* to stand out; (coll) to stop working ‖ *ref* to come off; **staccarsi da** to come off (*e.g., the wall*); to leave (*one's home; the shore*); (aer) to take off from

stacciare §128 *tr* to sift, sieve

stàc•cio *m* (**-ci**) sieve

staccionata *f* fence; hurdle; stockade

stac•co *m* (**-chi**) tearing off; cut of cloth (*for a suit*); interval; **fare stacco** to stand out

stadèra *f* steelyard; **stadera a ponte** weighbridge

stàdia *f* leveling rod

stà•dio *m* (**-di**) stadium; stage

staffa *f* stirrup; heel (*of sock*); gaiter strap; clamp; (*mach*) bracket; **perdere le staffe** to lose one's nerve

staffétta *f* courier, messenger; pilot (*car*); **a staffetta** relay

staffière *m* groom, footman; servant

staffilare *tr* to whip, belt, lash

staffilata *f* lash

staffile *m* stirrup strap; whip

stàg•gio *m* (**-gi**) stay, upright

stagionale *adj* seasonal ‖ *mf* seasonal worker

stagionare (**stagióno**) *tr* to season, cure

stagiona•to -ta *adj* seasoned, ripe

stagióne *f* season; **da mezza stagione** spring-and-fall (*coat*); **di fine stagione** year-end (*sale*)

stagliare §280 *tr* to hack ‖ *ref* to stand out

staglia•to -ta *adj* sheer (*cliff*)

sta•gnàio *m* (**-gnài**) tinsmith; plumber

stagnante *adj* stagnant

stagnare *tr* to tin; to solder; to stanch ‖ *intr* to stagnate

stagnaro *m* var of **stagnaio**

stagnina *f* tin can

stagnino *m* (*coll*) var of **stagnaio**

sta•gno -gna *adj* watertight; airtight ‖ *m* tin; pond, pool

stagnòla *f* tin foil; tin can

stàio *m* (**stài**) bushel (*container*); **a staio** (*coll*) top (*hat*) ‖ *m* (**stàia** *fpl*) bushel (*measure*); **a staia** in abundance

stalla *f* stable

stallìa *f* (*com*) lay day

stallière *m* stableman, stableboy

stallo *m* seat; stall; (*chess*) stalemate

stallóne *m* stallion

stamane, stamani or **stamattina** *adv* this morning

stambéc•co *m* (**-chi**) ibex

stambèr•ga *f* (**-ghe**) hovel

stambù•gio *m* (**-gi**) hole, hovel

stamburare *tr* to puff up, to boast about ‖ *intr* to drum

stame *m* (*bot*) stamen; thread, yarn

stamigna *f* cheesecloth

stampa *f* printing; print; (*fig*) print; (*fig*) mold; **stampe** printed matter

stampàg•gio *m* (**-gi**) (*mach*) stamping

stampare *tr* to stamp; to print; to impress; to publish ‖ *ref* (*fig*) to be ingraved

stampa•to -ta *adj* printed; impressed ‖ *m* printed form; **stampati** printed matter

stampa•tóre -trice *mf* printer

stampèlla *f* crutch

stamperia *f* print shop

stampìglia *f* rubber stamp; billboard; overprint

stampigliare §280 *tr* to stamp; to overprint

stampinare *tr* to stencil

stampino *m* stencil

stampo *m* mold; stencil; stamp, kind; decoy

stanare *tr* to flush (*game*); (*fig*) to dig up

stancare §197 *tr* to tire, fatigue; to bore ‖ *ref* to tire, weary

stanchézza *f* tiredness, weariness

stan•co -ca *adj* (**-chi -che**) tired; tired out; (*lit*) left (*hand*)

standardizzare [ddzz] *tr* to standardize

stan•ga *f* (**-ghe**) bar; shaft (*of cart*); beam (*of plow*)

stangata *f* blow

stanghétta *f* small bar; bolt (*of lock*); temple (*of spectacles*); (*mus*) bar

stanòtte *adv* tonight; last night

stante *adj* being; standing; **a sé stante** by itself, independent ‖ *prep* because of; **stante che** since

stan•tìo -tìa *adj* (**-tìi; -tìe**) stale; musty

stantuffo *m* piston; plunger

stanza *f* room; stanza; **essere di stanza** (*mil*) to be stationed; **stanza da bagno** bath room; **stanza di compensazione** clearing house; **stanza di soggiorno** living room

stanziare §287 *tr* to allocate; to appropriate; to budget ‖ *ref* to settle

stanzino *m* small room; closet

stappare *tr* to uncork

stare §263 *intr* (ESSERE) to stay; to stand; to live; to be; to be located; to linger; to last; to stick (*e.g., to a rule*); (*poker*) to stand pat; **come sta?** how are you?; **lasciar stare** to leave alone; **lasciar stare che** to leave aside that; **non stare in sé dalla gioia** to be beside oneself with joy; **sta bene!** O.K.!; **starci** to fit, e.g., **ci stanno trecento persone** three hundred people fit there; **stare** + *inf* to be in favor of, e.g., **io ci starei d'andare al cine** I would be in favor of going to the movies; **stare** + *ger* to be + *ger*, e.g., **stava leggendo** he was reading; **stare a** to be up to; to stand on (*ceremony*); to base oneself on; to take (*a joke*); to cost, e.g., **a quanto sta il prosciutto?** how much does the ham cost?; **stare a** + *inf* to keep + *ger*, e.g., **stai sempre a sognare** you always keep dreaming; to take + *inf*, e.g., **stette poco a decidere** he took little time to decide; **stare a cuore** (with *dat*) to deem important, e.g., **gli sta a cuore il lavoro** he deems his work important; **stare a pancia all'aria** to not do a stroke of work; **stare al proprio posto** to keep one's place; **stare a segno** to behave properly; **stare a vedere** to be possible, e.g., **sta a vedere che non viene?** could it be possible that he won't come?; **stare bene** to be well; to be well-off; (with *dat*) to fit, to become, e.g., **questo vestito gli sta**

bene this suit fits him well, this suit becomes him; to serve right, e.g., **gli sta bene!** it serves him right!; **stare comodo** to be at ease; to remain seated; **stare con** (fig) to be on the side of; **starsene** to stay apart, e.g., **se ne sta solo soletto** he stays apart or all alone; **stare fermo** to be quiet; to not move; **stare in forse** to doubt; to be doubtful; **stare sulle proprie** to stand aloof; **stare su** to stand erect; **stare su tardi** to stay up late; **stia comodo!** remain seated!

starna ƒ gray partridge

starnazzare *intr* to flap its wings; to flutter; to cackle

starnutare *intr* to sneeze

starnuto *m* sneeze

stasare [s] *tr* to unplug, unblock

staséra [s] *adv* tonight, this evening

sta·si ƒ (**-si**) (com) stagnation; (pathol) stasis

statale *adj* government; state ‖ *mf* government employee

stàti·co -ca (**-ci -che**) static ‖ ƒ statics

stati·no -na *adj* (coll) migratory ‖ *m* itemized list; (educ) registration form

stati·sta *m* (**-sti**) statesman

statisti·co -ca (**-ci -che**) *adj* statistical ‖ *m* statistician ‖ ƒ statistics; **fare una statistica** (di) to survey; **statistiche statistics** (*data*)

stati·vo -va *adj* nonmigratory; permanent ‖ *m* stand (*of microscope*)

stato *m* state; condition; plight; frame (*of mind*); status; estate (*social class*); **di stato** public (*e.g., school*); **essere in stato di arresto** to be under arrest; **stati** extracts from vital statistics; **Stati Pontifici** Papal States; **Stati Uniti** United States; **stato civile** marital status; vital statistics; **stato confessionale** state under ecclesiastical rule; **stato cuscinetto** buffer state; **stato di preallarme** state of emergency; **stato di previsione** preliminary budget; **stato interessante** pregnancy; **stato maggiore** (mil) general staff

statoreattòre *m* ramjet engine

stàtua ƒ statue

statuà·rio -ria (**-ri -rie**) *adj* statuary; statuesque ‖ *m* sculptor

statunitènse *adj* & *mf* American (*U.S.A.*)

statura ƒ stature; height

statuto *m* statute

stavòlta *adv* (coll) this time

stazionaménto *m* parking; **stazionamento vietato** no parking

stazionare (stazióno) *intr* to park

stazionà·rio -ria *adj* (**-ri -rie**) stationary

stazióne ƒ station; bearing, posture; **stazione balneare** shore resort; **stazione climatica** health resort, spa; **stazione di rifornimento** service station; **stazione di tassametri** cab stand; **stazione estiva** summer resort; **stazione generatrice** power plant; **stazione orbitale** orbiting station; **stazione sanitaria** clinic

stazza ƒ tonnage; (naut) displacement

stazzare *tr* (naut) to gauge; (naut) to displace

stazzonare (stazzóno) *tr* to crumple

steatite ƒ French chalk

stéc·ca ƒ (**-che**) small stick; slat (*of shutter*); rib (*of umbrella*); bone (*of whale*); carton (*of cigarettes*); rail (*of fence*); letter opener; chisel (*of sculptor*); (billiards) cue; (billiards) miscue; (surg) splint; **fare una stecca** (billiards) to miscue; (mus) to sing or play a sour note

steccadèn·ti *m* (**-ti**) (coll) toothpick

steccare §197 (stécco) *tr* to fence; to put in a splint ‖ *intr* to play or sing a sour note; (billiards) to miscue

steccato *m* fence; (racing) inside track

stecchétto *m* small stick; **tenere a stecchetto** to keep on a strict diet; to keep short of money

stecchino *m* toothpick

stecchi·to -ta *adj* stiff; lean, lank; dry (*twig*); dumfounded

stéc·co *m* (**-chi**) stick, twig

stecconata ƒ stockade; fence

stélla ƒ star; rowel (*of spur*); speck of fat (*in soup*); (fig) sky; **a stella** star-shaped; stellar; **montare alle stelle** to be sky-high (*said, e.g., of prices*); **portare alle stelle** to praise to the skies; **stella alpina** edelweiss; **stella cadente** shooting star; **stella di mare** starfish; **stella filante** shooting star; confetti; **stella polare** polestar, lodestar

stellare *adj* stellar; (mach) radial ‖ *v* (stéllo) *tr* to spangle with stars; to stud

stella·to -ta *adj* starry; star-spangled; star-shaped; studded

stellétta ƒ (mil) star; (typ) asterisk; **guadagnarsi le stellette** (mil) to earn a promotion; **portare le stellette** (mil) to be in the service

stellina ƒ starlet

stelloncino *m* (journ) short paragraph

stèlo *m* stem, stalk

stèm·ma *m* (**-mi**) coat of arms; genealogy (*of a manuscript*)

stemperare (stèmpero) *tr* to dilute; to blunt; to untemper; (lit) to waste ‖ *ref* to melt; to become dull or blunt

stendardo *m* banner, standard

stèndere §270 *tr* to stretch; to hang up (*laundry*); to spread; to draw up (*a document*); (mil) to deploy; **stendere a terra** to knock down ‖ *ref* to stretch out

stendibianche·rìa *m* (**-rìa**) clothes rack, clotheshorse

stenodattilògra·fo -fa *mf* shorthand typist

stenografare (stenògrafo) *tr* to take down in shorthand

stenografìa ƒ shorthand, stenography

stenogràfi·co -ca *adj* (**-ci -che**) stenographic, shorthand

stenògra·fo -fa *mf* stenographer

stenòsi ƒ (pathol) stricture

stenotipìa ƒ stenotypy

stentare (stènto) *tr* to eke out (*a living*)

|| *intr* to barely make ends meet; **stentare** *a* to hardly be able to; to find it hard to

stenta·to -ta *adj* hard; stunted; strained (*smile*)

stènto *m* privation; hardship; **a stento** hardly; with difficulty; **senza stento** without any trouble

stèr·co *m* (**-chi**) dung

stereofòni·co -ca *adj* (**-ci -che**) stereo, stereophonic

stereoscòpi·co -ca *adj* (**-ci -che**) stereoscopic

stereoscò·pio *m* (**-pi**) stereoscope

stereotipa·to -ta *adj* stereotyped

sterilizzare [ddzz] *tr* to sterilize

sterlina *f* pound sterling

sterminare (**stèrmino**) *tr* to exterminate

stermina·to -ta *adj* immense, boundless

stermi·nio *m* (**-ni**) extermination; (coll) large amount, lots

stèrno *m* breastbone

sterpàglia *f* brushwood; undergrowth

stèrpo *m* dry twig; bramble

sterrare (**stèrro**) *tr* to excavate

sterratóre *m* digger

sterzare (**stèrzo**) *tr* to diminish by one third; to thin out (*woodland*); (aut) to steer || *intr* to swerve

sterzata *f* swerve

stèrzo *m* handle bar; (aut) steering gear; (aut) steering wheel

stésa [s] *f* coat (*of paint*); string (*of clothes on line*)

stés·so -sa *adj* same, e.g., **lo stesso mese** the same month; very, e.g., **tuo fratello stesso** your very brother; **essere alle stesse** to be just the same; **io stesso** I myself; **lui stesso** he himself, etc.; **per sé stesso** by himself; by itself || *pron* same; same thing; **fa lo stesso** it's all the same, it makes no difference

stesura [s] *f* drawing up (*of a contract*); **prima stesura** first draft

stetoscò·pio *m* (**-pi**) stethoscope

stia *f* chicken coop

Stige *m* Styx

sti·gio -gia *adj* (**-gi -gie**) Stygian

stigmate *fpl* stigmata

stilare *tr* to draft properly

stile *m* style

stilè *adj invar* stylish

stilétto *m* dagger, stiletto

stilizzare [ddzz] *tr* to stylize

stilla *f* (lit) drop, droplet

stillare *tr* to exude; to distill || *intr* (ESSERE) to ooze, drip, exude || *ref*— **stillarsi il cervello** to rack one's brains

stillici·dio *m* (**-di**) dripping; repetition

stilo *m* stylus; arm (*of steelyard*); dagger; gnomon (*of sundial*); (poet) style || *f* (coll) fountain pen

stilogràfi·ca *f* (**-che**) fountain pen

stima *f* appraisal; esteem; (naut) dead reckoning; **a stima d'occhio** more or less

stimare *tr* to estimate; to deem; to esteem || *ref* (coll) to think a lot of oneself

stima·tóre -trice *mf* appraiser; admirer

stimmate *fpl* var of **stigmate**

stimolante *adj & m* stimulant

stimolare (**stimolo**) *tr* to stimulate

stimolo *m* influence; stimulus

stin·co *m* (**-chi**) shinbone; shin; **stinco di santo** saintly person, saint; **rompere gli stinchi a** to annoy

stingere §126 *tr, intr* (ESSERE) & *ref* to fade

stipa *f* kindling wood, brushwood

stipare *tr* & *ref* to crowd, jam

stipendiare §287 (**stipèndio**) *tr* to employ, hire; to pay a salary to

stipendia·to -ta *adj* salaried || *mf* salaried person

stipèn·dio *m* (**-di**) pay, salary

stipétto *m* (naut) closet, cabinet

stipite *m* jamb; stock, family; (bot) trunk (*of palm tree*)

stipo *m* cabinet

stipulare (**stipulo**) *tr* to draw up (*a contract*); to stipulate

stiracchiare §287 *tr* to stretch; to eke out (*a living*); to twist (*a meaning*); to haggle over || *intr* to haggle; to economize || *ref* to stretch out

stirare *tr* to stretch; to iron, press || *intr* to iron || *ref* to stretch out

stira·tóre -trice *mf* ironer, presser

stiratura *f* ironing; stretching

stireria *f* ironing shop

stiro *m*—**ferro da stiro** see **ferro**

stirpe *f* family; birth, origin

stitichézza *f* constipation

stìti·co -ca *adj* (**-ci -che**) constipated; (fig) tight

stiva *f* (naut) hold; (lit) beam (*of plow*)

stivàg·gio *m* (**-gi**) stowage

stivale *m* boot; **dei miei stivali** good-for-nothing; **lustrare gli stivali a qlcu** to lick s.o.'s boots

stivalétto *m* high shoe

stivalóne *m* boot; **stivaloni da equitazione** riding boots; **stivaloni da palude** hip boots

stivare *tr* to stow

stivatóre *m* stevedore

stizza *f* anger; irritation

stizzire §176 *tr* to anger, vex || *ref* to get angry

stizzó·so -sa [s] *adj* peevish, irritable

stoccafisso *m* stockfish

stoccata *f* thrust (*with dagger or rapier*); dig, sarcastic remark; touch (*for money*)

stòc·co *m* (**-chi**) dagger; rapier; stalk (*of corn*)

Stoccólma *f* Stockholm

stòffa *f* cloth, material; (fig) stuff, makings

stoicismo *m* stoicism

stòi·co -ca (**-ci -che**) *adj* stoic, stoical || *m* stoic; Stoic

stolno *m* doormat

stòla *f* stole

stòli·do -da *adj* foolish, silly

stoltézza *f* foolishness, silliness

stól·to -ta *adj* silly || *mf* fool

stomacare §197 (**stòmaco**) *tr* to disgust; to nauseate

stomachévole *adj* disgusting, sickening

stòma·co *m* (**-ci** or **-chi**) stomach; maw (*of animal*); **dare di stomaco** to vomit

stonare (**stòno**) *tr* to sing or play out of tune; to upset || *intr* to sing or play out of tune; to be out of place; to not harmonize

stona·to **-ta** *adj* out-of-tune; upset; clashing (*color*)

stonatura *f* jarring sound; clash (*of colors*); lack of harmony

stóppa *f* tow; oakum; **di stoppa** flaxen; weak, trembling; **stoppa incatramata** oakum

stoppàc·cio *m* (**-ci**) wad

stóppie *fpl* stubble

stoppino *m* wick

stoppó·so -sa [s] *adj* stubby; stringy

stórcere §272 *tr* to twist; to twitch; to wrench (*one's ankle*); to roll (*one's eyes*) || *ref* to twist; to writhe; to bend

stordiménto *m* bewilderment; dizziness

stordire §176 *tr* to bewilder; to daze || *intr* to be bewildered || *ref* to dull one's senses

stordità·ggine *f* carelessness; mistake, blunder

stordi·to -ta *adj* careless; bewildered; amazed; dizzy || *mf* scatterbrain

stòria *f* history; story, tale; fact; **fare storie** to stand on ceremony; **un'altra storia** a horse of another color

stòri·co -ca (**-ci -che**) *adj* historical || *m* historian

storièlla *f* tale, short story; joke

storiografìa *f* historiography

storióne *m* sturgeon

stormire §176 *intr* to rustle

stórmo *m* swarm, flock; (aer) group

stornare (**stórno**) *tr* to ward off; to dissuade; to divert (*funds*); to write off (*as noncollectable*)

stornèllo *m* Italian folksong; (orn) starling

stór·no -na *adj* dapple-gray || *m* (com) transfer; (orn) starling

storpiare §287 (**stòrpio**) *tr* to cripple; to clip (*one's words*)

stòr·pio -pia (**-pi -pie**) *adj* crippled || *m* cripple

stòr·to -ta *adj* twisted; crooked; crippled || *f* twist; dislocation; retort

stoviglie *fpl* dishes; **lavare le stoviglie** to wash the dishes

stra- *pref adj* extra-, e.g., **straordinario** extraordinary; over-, e.g., **stracarico** overloaded

stràbi·co -ca *adj* (**-ci -che**) crosseyed

strabiliante *adj* astonishing, amazing

strabiliare §287 *tr* to amaze || *intr* & *ref* to be amazed

strabismo *m* strabismus, squint

straboccare §197 (**strabócco**) *intr* to overflow

strabocchévole *adj* overflowing

strabuzzare [ddzz] *tr* (coll) to roll (*one's eyes*)

stracàri·co -ca *adj* (**-chi -che**) overloaded, overburdened

stracca *f*—**pigliare una stracca** to be dead tired

straccale *m* breeching (*of harness*); **straccali** (coll) suspenders

straccare §197 *tr* (coll) to tire

stracciaiò·lo -la *mf* ragpicker

stracciare §128 *tr* to tear, rend; to comb (*natural silk*)

stràc·cio -cia (**-ci -ce**) *adj* torn, in rags; waste (*paper*) || *m* rag, tatter; tear, rend; combed silk

stracció·ne -na *mf* tatterdemalion

straccivéndo·lo -la *mf* ragpicker; rag dealer

strac·co -ca *adj* (**-chi -che**) tired; worn-out; **alla stracca** lazily || *f* see stracca

stracòt·to -ta *adj* overcooked, overdone || *m* stew

stracuòcere §144a *tr* to overcook, overdo

strada *f* roadway; street; **da strada** vulgar, common; **divorare la strada** to burn up the road; **essere in mezzo a una strada** to be in a bad way; **fare strada a** to pave the way for; **farsi strada** to make one's way; **prender la strada** to set forth; **strada carrozzàbile** carriage road; **strada dell'orto** easy way out; **strada ferrata** railroad; **strada maestra** main road; **tagliare la strada a** to stand in the way of; (aut) to cut in front of

stradale *adj* road; street; traffic (*e.g., accident*); highway (*police*) || *m* avenue || *f* highway patrol

stradà·rio *m* (**-ri**) street directory

strafalcióne *m* blunder, gross error

strafare §173 *tr* to overdo; to overcook

straföro *m* drilled hole; **di straforo** stealthily

strafottènte *adj* unconcerned, nonchalant; arrogant, impudent

strafottènza *f* nonchalance, unconcern; arrogance, impudence

strage *f* butchery, massacre, carnage; (coll) multitude, lot

stragrande *adj* enormous, huge

stralciare §128 *tr* to prune, trim (*grapevines*); to eliminate, remove; (com) to liquidate

stràl·cio -cia *adj invar* interim; emergency (*e.g., law*); liquidating || *m* (**-ci**) excerpt; clearance sale; **a stralcio** at a bargain

strale *m* (lit) arrow

strallo *m* (naut) stay

stralunare *tr* to roll (*one's eyes*)

straluna·to -ta *adj* upset; wild-eyed

stramazzare *tr* to fell || *intr* (ESSERE) to fall down

stramazzo *m* sluice; (coll) straw mattress

stramberìa *f* eccentricity

stram·bo -ba *adj* odd, queer, eccentric; crooked (*legs*); squint (*eyes*)

strame *m* litter; fodder

strampala·to -ta *adj* strange; preposterous, absurd

stranézza *f* strangeness; oddity

strangolare (**stràngolo**) *tr* to strangle; (naut) to furl

strangola·tóre -trice *mf* strangler

straniare §287 *tr* (lit) to draw away || *ref* to become estranged

straniè·ro -ra *adj* foreign, alien; (lit) strange || *mf* foreigner, alien

stra·no -na *adj* strange, odd; (lit) estranged

straordinà·rio -ria (-ri -rie) *adj* extraordinary; extra || *mf* temporary employee || *m* overtime

strapagare §209 *tr* to overpay; to pay too much for

strapazzare *tr* to rebuke, upbraid; to mishandle; to bungle || *ref* to overwork oneself

strapazza·to -ta *adj* crumpled; bungled; scrambled (*eggs*); overworked || *f* upbraiding, rebuke; fatigue

strapazzo *m* misuse; fatigue; excess; **da strapazzo** working (*clothes*); hackneyed, second-rate

straperdere §212 *tr & intr* to lose hopelessly || *intr* to be wiped out

strapiè·no -na *adj* chock-full

strapiombare (strapiòmbo) *intr* to overhang, jut out

strapiómbo *m* overhang; **a strapiombo** sheer (*cliff*)

strapotènte *adj* overpowering

strappare *tr* to pull; to tear, rend; to wring (*s.o.'s heart*); **strappare le lacrime a qlcu** to move s.o. to tears; **strappare qlco a qlcu** to pry s.th out of s.o.; to snatch s.th from s.o. || *ref* to tear (*e.g., one's hair*)

strappata *f* pull, tug, snatch

strappo *m* pull; tear, rip; infraction, breach; pulling away (*on a bicycle*); patch (*of sky*); **a strappi** in jerks; **strappo muscolare** pulled muscle; sprain

strapuntino *m* folding seat, jump seat; bucket seat; (naut) mattress

straric·co -ca *adj* (**-chi -che**) (coll) immensely rich

straripare *intr* (ESSERE & AVERE) to overflow

strascicare §197 (**stràscico**) *tr* to drag; to shuffle; **strascicare le parole** to drawl

strascichì·o *m* (**-i**) shuffle (*of feet*)

stràsci·co *m* (**-chi**) train (*of skirt*); trail; sequel, aftermath; **a strascico** dragging

strascinare (stràscino) *tr* to drag || *ref* to drag oneself, drag

strascinì·o *m* (**-i**) shuffle

stràscino *m* dragnet, trawl

stratagèm·ma *m* (**-mi**) stratagem

strategia *f* strategy

stratègi·co -ca *adj* (**-ci -che**) strategic

stratè·go *m* (**-ghi**) strategist; general, commander

stratificare §197 (**stratìfico**) *tr* to stratify

strato *m* layer; coat, coating; stratum; (meteor) stratus

stratosfèra *f* stratosphere

strattóne *m* jerk, tug

stravagante *adj* extravagant; whimsical, capricious || *mf* eccentric

stravèc·chio -chia *adj* (**-chi -chie**) aged (*cheese, wine, etc.*); very old

stravincere §285 *tr* to overpower

straviziare §287 *intr* to be intemperate

stravì·zio *m* (**-zi**) intemperance, excess

stravòlgere §289 *tr* to roll (*the eyes*); to distort; to derange

straziante *adj* heartbreaking; excruciating (*pain*); horrible

straziare §287 *tr* to torture; to dismay; to mangle; to murder (*a language*)

strazia·to -ta *adj* torn, stricken

strà·zio *m* (**-zi**) suffering, pain; torture; shame; boredom; **fare strazio di** to squander

stré·ga *f* (**-ghe**) witch; sorceress

stregare §209 (**strégo**) *tr* to bewitch

stregóne *m* sorcerer; witch doctor

stregoneria *f* witchcraft; sorcery

strègua *f* standard, criterion; **alla stregua di** on the basis of

strema·to -ta *adj* exhausted

strènna *f* Christmas gift, New Year's gift; special New Year's issue

strè·nuo -nua *adj* strenuous

strepitare (strèpito) *intr* to make a noise; to shout, make a racket

strèpito *m* noise, racket; **fare strepito** to make a hit

strepitó·so -sa [s] *adj* loud, noisy; resounding (*success*)

streptomicina *f* streptomycin

stressa·to -ta *adj* under stress

strétta *f* grasp, clench; tightening (*of brakes*); hold; press, crush; pang; mountain pass; **mettere alle strette** to drive into a corner; **stretta dei conti** rendering of accounts; **stretta di mano** handshake; **stretta finale** climax

strettézza *f* narrowness; **strettezze** straits, hardship

strét·to -ta *adj* narrow; tight; bare (*necessities*); pure (*e.g., dialect*); strict; clenched (*fist*); heavy (*heart*); minimum (*price*); (phonet) close || *m* straits, narrows || *f* see **stretta** || **stretto** *adv* tightly

strettóia *f* narrow stretch; hardship; bandage

stria *f* stripe, streak

striare §119 *tr* to stripe, streak

stricnina *f* strychnine

stridènte *adj* jarring; clashing (*colors*); strident (*sound*)

stridere §264 *tr* to grit (*one's teeth*) || *intr* to shriek; to squeak; to creak; to clash (*said of colors*); to croak (*said of raven*); to hoot (*said of owl*); to howl (*said of wind*) || *ref* (coll) to be resigned

strido *m* (**-di** & **-da** *fpl*) shriek; squeak

stridóre *m* shriek; creak, squeak; gnashing (*of teeth*)

strìdu·lo -la *adj* shrill

strigare §209 *tr* to disentangle || *ref* to extricate oneself

striglia *f* currycomb

strigliare §280 *tr* to curry; to upbraid || *ref* to groom oneself

strillare *tr* to shout; (coll) to scold; (coll) to hawk (*newspapers*) || *intr* to scream

strillo *m* shriek; shout, scream

strilló·ne -na *mf* loud-mouthed person || *m* newsdealer; newsboy, paperboy

striminzi·to -ta *adj* shrunken; tight; stunted; skinny

strimpellare (strimpèllo) *tr* to thrum; to thrum on

strinare *tr* to singe; to burn (*with a flatiron*)

strin·ga *f* (**-ghe**) lace; shoelace

stringa·to -ta *adj* terse, concise

stringere §265 *tr* to tighten; to grip; to shake, clasp (*a hand*); to drive into a corner; to squeeze; to embrace; to close (*an alliance, a deal*); to wring (*one's heart*); to clench (*the fist*); (lit) to gird (*a sword*); (mus) to accelerate; **stringere d'assedio** to besiege; **stringere i freni** to put the brakes on || *intr* to be tight; **il tempo stringe** time is running short; **stringi, stringi** at the very end, in conclusion || *ref* to squeeze close together; to shrink; to coagulate; to draw close; **stringersi a** to snuggle up to; **stringersi addosso a** to attack; **stringersi nelle spalle** to shrug one's shoulders

stringina·so [s] *m* (**-so**) pince-nez

stri·scia *f* (**-sce**) strip, band; trail; stripe; line; **a strisce** striped; **striscia d'atterramento** airstrip; **striscia di cuoio** strop

strisciante *adj* crawling; (fig) fawning

strisciare §128 *tr* to shuffle (*feet*); to graze; **strisciare una riverenza** to curtsy || *intr* to creep, crawl; to graze by || *ref* to fawn; **strisciarsi a** to rub one's back against

strisciata or **strisciatura** *f* sliding; trail

stri·scio *m* (**-sci**) rubbing; shuffling; **ballare di striscio** to shuffle; **da** or **di striscio** superficial (*wound*)

striscióne *m* festoon; festooned sign; flatterer; **striscione d'arrivo** landing (*in gymnastics*); **striscione del traguardo** (sports) tape

striscióni *adv* crawling

stritolare (stritolo) *tr* to crush, smash

strizzalimó·ni *m*(**-ni**) lemon squeezer

strizzare *tr* to squeeze, press; to wink (*the eye*); **strizzare l'occhio** to wink

strizza·tóio *m* (**-tói**) wringer

strò·fa or **strò·fe** *f* (**-fe**) strophe

strofinàc·cio *m* (**-ci**) dust cloth

strofinare *tr* to rub; to polish || *ref* to rub oneself; to fawn

strofinata *f*—**dare una strofinata a** to give a lick and a promise to

strofinì·o *m* (**-i**) rubbing; wiping

stròla·ga *f* (**-ghe**) (orn) loon

strombatura *f* embrasure

strombazzare *tr* to glorify; **strombazzare i propri meriti** to toot one's own horn || *intr* to blast away on the trumpet

strombazza·tóre -trice *mf* show-off

strombettare (strombétto) *tr* to trumpet, toot

stroncare §197 **(strónco)** *tr* to break off; to break down; to eliminate; (fig) to criticize severely

stroncatura *f* devastating criticism

strònzio *m* strontium

strónzo *m* (vulg) turd

stropicciare §128 *tr* to rub (*hands*); to

drag, shuffle (*feet*); (coll) to crumple || *ref*—**stropicciarsene** (coll) to not give a hoot

stropicci·o *m* (**-i**) rubbing; shuffling

stròzza *f* (coll) gullet, throat

strozzare (stròzzo) *tr* to strangle; to stop up; to fleece, swindle || *ref* to choke; to narrow

strozza·to -ta *adj* choked; choking; strangulated (*hernia*)

strozzatura *f* narrowing

strozzinàg·gio *m* (**-gi**) usury

strozzino *m* usurer, loan shark

struggere §266 *tr* to melt; to consume || *ref* to melt; to pine away; to be upset; **struggersi di** to be consumed by

struggiménto *m* melting; longing; torment

strumentale *adj* instrument (*flying*); capital (*goods*); instructional (*language, in multi-lingual regions*); (gram, mus) instrumental

strumentali·sta *mf* (**-sti -ste**) instrumentalist

strumentalizzare [ddzz] *tr* to use, take advantage of

strumentare (struménto) *tr* to orchestrate

struménto *m* instrument; tool, implement; **strumento a corda** stringed instrument; **strumento a fiato** wind instrument; **strumento di bordo** (aer) flight recorder

strusciare §128 *tr* to rub; to shuffle (*feet*); to crumple; to wear out || *ref*—**strusciarsi a** to fawn on

strutto *m* lard, shortening

struttura *f* structure

strutturare *tr* to organize, structure

struzzo *m* ostrich

stuccare §197 *tr* to putty; to stucco; to surfeit || *ref* to grow weary

stucchévole *adj* sickening

stuc·co -ca (**-chi -che**) *adj* bored; **stucco e ristucco** sick and tired || *m* putty; stucco; plaster of Paris; **rimanere di stucco** to be taken aback

studèn·te -téssa *mf* student

studenté·sco -sca (**-schi -sche**) *adj* student; student-like || *f* student body

studiare §287 *tr* to study; **studiarle tutte** to consider every angle || *intr* to study; to try || *ref* to try; to gaze at oneself

studia·to -ta *adj* affected, studied

stù·dio *m* (**-di**) study; school district; office (*of professional man*); studio; (hist) university; (lit) wish; (mus) étude; **a studio** on purpose; **essere allo studio** to be under consideration

studió·so -sa [s] *adj* studious || *m* scholar

stufa *f* stove, heater; hothouse

stufare *tr* to warm up, heat up; to stew; (coll) to bore

stufato *m* stew

stu·fo -fa *adj* (coll) bored, sick and tired || *f* see **stufa**

stuòia *f* mat; matting

stuòlo *m* throng, crowd; flock; (lit) army

stupefacènte *adj* amazing; habit-forming ‖ *m* dope

stupefare §173 *tr* to amaze, astonish

stupefazióne *f* amazement, astonishment; stupefaction

stupèn·do -da *adj* stupendous

stupidàggine *f* stupidity; silliness; child's play, cinch

stùpi·do -da *adj* stupid; silly; (lit) amazed

stupire §176 *tr* to amaze ‖ *ref* to be amazed

stupóre *m* amazement

stuprare *tr* to rape

stura *f* tapping; uncorking; **dar la stura a** to begin (*a speech*)

sturabottì·glie *m* (-glie) bottle opener

sturalavandì·ni *m* (-ni) plunger (*to open up clogged sink*)

sturare *tr* to uncork; to take the wax out of (*ears*); to open up (*clogged line*)

stuzzicadèn·ti *m* (-ti) toothpick

stuzzicare §197 (**stùzzico**) *tr* to pick (*e.g., one's teeth*); to bother; to excite, arouse; to tease; to sharpen (*appetite*)

su *adv* up; on top; upstairs; **da . . . in su** from . . . on, e.g., **dal mese scorso in su** from last month on; **di su** from upstairs; **in su up;** **metter su** to put on the fire; to instigate; **metter su bottega** to set up shop; **metter su casa** to set up housekeeping; **più su** higher; further up; **su! come on!;** let's go!; **su di on; su e giù** back and forth; up and down; **su per giù** more or less; **tirarsi su** to lift oneself up; to sit up; to get better, recover; **tirar su** to pick up; to grow, raise; **venir su** to grow; to come up ‖ §4 *prep* on, upon; up; towards; over, above; onto; against; at, e.g., **sul far del giorno** at daybreak; on top of; out of, e.g., **due volte su tre** two times out of three; **mettere su superbia** to become proud; **stare sulle sue** to be reserved; **sul serio** in earnest; **su misura** made to order

suaccenna·to -ta *adj* above-mentioned

sub *m* (**sub**) (coll) skindiver

subàcque·o -a *adj* submarine

subaffittare *tr* to sublet

subaffitto *m* subletting, sublet; **prendere in subaffitto** to sublet

subaltèr·no -na *adj* & *m* subaltern; subordinate

subastare *tr* to auction off

sùbbia *f* stonecutter's chisel

subbù·glio *m* (-gli) turmoil, hubbub

subcosciènte *adj* & *m* subconscious

sùbdo·lo -la *adj* treacherous, deceitful

subentrare (**subéntro**) *intr* (ESSERE) (with *dat*) to succeed, follow

subire §176 *tr* to suffer; to undergo

subissare *tr* to ruin; to sink; to overwhelm ‖ *intr* (ESSERE) to sink; to go to rack and ruin

subisso *m* ruin; (coll) lots, plenty

subitàne·o -a *adj* sudden

sùbi·to -ta *adj* (lit) sudden ‖ *m*—**d'un subito** all of a sudden ‖ **subito** *adv* rapidly; immediately; right away; **subito al principio** at the very beginning; **subito dopo** right after; **subito prima** right before ‖ *interj* right away!

sublima·to -ta *adj* sublimated ‖ *m* **sublimato corrosivo** corrosive sublimate

sublime *adj* & *m* sublime

subodorare (**subodóro**) *tr* to suspect; to get wind of

subordinare (**subórdino**) *tr* to subordinate

subordina·to -ta *adj* & *m* subordinate ‖ *f* subordinate clause

subornare (**subórno**) *tr* to bribe

substrato *m* substratum

suburba·no -na *adj* suburban

subùr·bio *m* (-bi) suburb

succedàne·o -a *adj* & *m* substitute

succèdere §132 (*pp* **succeduto** or **succèsso**) *intr* (ESSERE) (with *dat*) to succede, to follow ‖ *ref* to follow one another, follow one after the other ‖ (*pret* **succèssi**; *pp* **succèsso**) *intr* (ESSERE) to happen, to come to pass; (with *dat*) to happen to, to come over, e.g., **che gli è successo?** what happened to him?

successióne *f* succession; **in successione** in succession; in a row

successì·vo -va *adj* successive; next

succèsso *m* success; outcome

successóre *m* successor

successò·rio -ria *adj* (-ri -rie) inheritance (*tax*)

succhiare §287 *tr* to suck

succhièllo *m* gimlet

succhiétto *m* pacifier

sùc·chio *m* (-chi) suck, sucking; (bot) sap; (coll) gimlet

succiaca·pre *m* (-pre) goatsucker, whippoorwill

succin·to -ta *adj* scanty (*clothing*); succinct, concise

suc·co *m* (-chi) juice; (fig) gist

succó·so -sa [s] *adj* juicy; pithy

succursale *f* branch, branch office

sud *m* south

sudafrica·no -na *adj* & *mf* South African

sudamerica·no -na *adj* & *mf* South American

sudàmina *f* prickly heat

sudare *tr* to sweat; to ooze; **sudare il pane** to earn one's living by the sweat of one's brow; **sudare sette camicie** to toil very hard ‖ *intr* to perspire, sweat; to reek

sudà·rio *m* (-ri) shroud

suda·to -ta *adj* wet with perspiration; hard-earned ‖ *f* sweat, sweating

suddét·to -ta *adj* aforesaid, above

sùddi·to -ta *adj* & *mf* subject

suddivìdere §158 *tr* to subdivide

sud-èst *m* southeast

sudiceria *f* filth, filthiness; smut

sùdi·cio -cia (-ci -cie) *adj* dirty, filthy ‖ *m* dirt, filth

sudiciume *m* dirt, filth

sudi·sta *mf* (-sti -ste) Southerner

sudóre *m* sweat, perspiration

sud·òvest *m* southwest
sufficiènte *adj* sufficient, adequate; self-sufficient || *m* sufficient
sufficiènza *f* sufficiency; self-sufficiency; (educ) minimum passing grade
suffisso *m* suffix
suffragare §209 *tr* to support; to pray for
suffragétta *f* suffragette
suffrà·gio *m* (-gi) suffrage
suffumicare §197 (suffùmico) *tr* to fumigate
suffumi·gio *m* (-gi) treatment by inhalation; fumigation
suggellare (suggèllo) *tr* to seal
suggèllo *m* seal
suggeriménto *m* suggestion
suggerire §176 *tr* to suggest; to prompt
suggeri·tóre -trice *mf* prompter || *m* (baseball) coach
suggestionàbile *adj* suggestible
suggestionare (suggestióno) *tr* to influence by suggestion || *ref*—suggestionarsi a + *inf* to talk oneself into + *ger*
suggestióne *f* fascination
suggesti·vo -va *adj* suggestive; fascinating; (law) leading (*question*)
sùghero *m* cork
sugli §4
sugna *f* fat; lard
su·go *m* (-ghi) juice; gravy; gist, pith; **non c'è sugo** it's no fun; there's nothing to it; **senza sugo** pointless, dull
sugó·so -sa [s] *adj* juicy
sui §4
suici·da (-di -de) *adj* suicidal || *mf* suicide (*person*)
suicidare *ref* to commit suicide
suici·dio *m* (-di) suicide (*act*)
sui·no -na *adj* swinish; see **carne** || *m* swine
sul §4
sulfamìdi·co -ca (-ci -che) *adj* sulfa || *m* sulfa drug
sulla §4
sulle §4
sulli §4
sullo §4
sulloda·to -ta *adj* above-mentioned
sultano *m* sultan
summentova·to -ta, **summenziona·to** -ta, **sunnomina·to** -ta *adj* above-mentioned
sunteggiare §290 (suntéggio) *tr* to summarize
sunto *m* résumé, summary
suo sua §6 *adj* & *pron poss* (suòi sue)
suòcera *f* mother-in-law
suòcero *m* father-in-law; **i suoceri** the in-laws
suòla *f* sole (*of shoe*); share (*of plow*); (naut) sliding ways; (rr) flange (*of rail*)
suòlo *m* ground; soil; floor || *m* (suola *fpl*) (coll) layer; (coll) sole (*of shoe*)
suonare (suòno) *tr* & *intr* var of **sonare**
suòno *m* sound; (fig) ring; **a suon di bastonate** with a sound thrashing; **a suon di fischi** with loud boos; **suono armonico** (mus) overtone

suòno·stère·o *m* (-o) stereo tape player
suòra *f* nun, sister
super- *pref adj* & *mf* super-, e.g., **supersonico** supersonic; over-, e.g., **superallenamento** overtraining
superaffollaménto *m* overcrowding
superare (sùpero) *tr* to surpass; to cross; to overcome; to pass; to exceed; (cards) to trump
supera·to -ta *adj* out-of-date, passé
supèrbia *f* pride, haughtiness; **montare in superbia** to get a swelled head
superbió·so -sa [s] *adj* proud, haughty
supèr·bo -ba *adj* proud, haughty; superb; spirited || **i superbi** the haughty ones
supercarburante *m* high-octane gas
supercolòsso *m* supercolossal film
superdònna *f*—**si dà arie di superdonna** she thinks she's hot stuff
supereterodina *f* superheterodyne
superficiale *adj* superficial; surface; cursory, perfunctory || *m* superficial fellow
superfi·cie *f* (-ci & cie) surface; area; **superficie portante** airfoil
supèr·fluo -flua *adj* superfluous || *m* surplus
super·io *m* (-io) superego
superióra *f* (eccl) mother superior
superióre *adj* superior; upper; higher; above; **superiore a** higher than; more than; larger than || *m* superior
superlati·vo -va *adj* & *m* superlative
superlavóro *m* overwork
supermercato *m* supermarket
supersòni·co -ca *adj* (-ci -che) supersonic
supèrstite *adj* surviving; remaining || *mf* survivor
superstizióne *f* superstition
superstizió·so -sa [s] *adj* superstitious
superstrada *f* superhighway
superuòmo *m* superman
supervisióne *f* supervision
supervisóre *m* supervisor; (mov) director
supi·no -na *adj* supine; on one's back
suppellèttile *f* furnishings; equipment; fixtures; fund (*of knowledge*)
supplementare *adj* supplementary
suppleménto *m* supplement; (mil) reinforcement
supplènte *adj* & *mf* substitute
supplènza *f* substitute assignment
suppleti·vo -va *adj* additional; (gram) suppletive
sùppli·ca *f* (-che) supplication; plea; petition
supplicante *mf* supplicant
supplicare §197 (sùpplico) *tr* to beseech; to plead with; to appeal to
supplichévole *adj* beseeching, imploring
supplire §176 *tr* to replace || *intr* (with *dat*) to supplement, make up for
suppliziare §287 *tr* to torture; to execute
suppli·zio *m* (-zi) torture, torment; **estremo supplizio** capital punishment
suppórre §218 *tr* to suppose
suppòrto *m* support, prop
suppositò·rio *m* (-ri) suppository

supposizióne _f_ supposition; presumption

suppó·sto **-sta** _adj_ alleged ‖ _m_ supposition ‖ _f_ suppository

suppurare _intr_ (ESSERE & AVERE) to suppurate

supremazía _f_ supremacy

suprè·mo **-ma** _adj_ supreme

surclassare _tr_ to outclass

surgelare (surgèlo) _tr_ to quick-freeze

surreali·sta _mf_ (-sti -ste) surrealist

surrenale _adj_ adrenal (_gland_)

surrène _m_ (anat) adrenal gland

surriscaldare _tr_ to overheat

surrogare §209 (surrògo) _tr_ to replace

surroga·to **-ta** _adj_ replaceable ‖ _m_ makeshift, ersatz

suscettibile _adj_ susceptible; touchy

suscitare (sùscito) _tr_ to rouse; to give rise to; to provoke

susina _f_ plum

susino _m_ plum tree

susseguènte _adj_ subsequent, following

susseguire (susséguo) _intr_ (ESSERE) (with _dat_) to follow ‖ _ref_ to follow one after the other

sussidiare §287 _tr_ to subsidize

sussidià·rio **-ria** (-ri -rie) _adj_ subsidiary; (nav) auxiliary ‖ _m_ supplementary text book; subsidiary

sussì·dio _m_ (-di) subsidy; assistance, relief; **sussidi audiovisivi** audio-visual aids; **sussidi didattici** teaching aids; **sussidio di disoccupazione** unemployment compensation

sussiè·go _m_ (-ghi) stiffness, haughtiness

sussistènza _f_ substance; subsistence; (mil) quartermaster corps

sussistere §114 _intr_ (ESSERE & AVERE) to subsist; to be, exist

sussultare _intr_ to start, jump; to quake

sussulto _m_ start, jump; **sussulto di terremoto** earth tremor

sussurrare _tr_ to whisper; to murmur, mutter ‖ _intr_ to whisper; to rustle ‖ _ref_—**si sussurra** it is rumored

sussurra··tóre **-trice** _mf_ whisperer; grumbler

sussurrí·o _m_ (-i) whispering; murmur; rustle

sussurro _m_ whisper; murmur

susta _f_ temple (_of_ spectacles); (coll) spring

suvvia _interj_ come!, come on!

svagare §209 _tr_ to entertain; to distract ‖ _ref_ to have a good time; to relax

svaga·to **-ta** _adj_ absent-minded; inattentive

sva·go _m_ (-ghi) entertainment, diversion; avocation, hobby

svaligiare §290 _tr_ to ransack; to rob; to pirate

svaligia·tóre **-trice** _mf_ thief, robber

svalutare (svàluto & svaluto) _tr_ to devaluate; to depreciate; to belittle ‖ _ref_ to depreciate

svalutazióne _f_ depreciation

svanire §176 _intr_ (ESSERE) to evaporate; to vanish

svani·to **-ta** _adj_ faded, evaporated; vanished; enfeebled

svantàg·gio _m_ (-gi) disadvantage

svantaggió·so **-sa** [s] _adj_ disadvantageous

svaporare (svapóro) _intr_ (ESSERE) to evaporate; to vanish

svaria·to **-ta** _adj_ varied; **svaria·ti** **-te** several

svarióne _m_ blunder, gross error

svasare _tr_ to transplant from a pot; to make (_e.g._, a gown) flare

svasa·to **-ta** _adj_ bell-mouthed, flaring

svecchiare §287 (svècchio) _tr_ to renew; to rejuvenate; to modernize

svedése [s] _adj_ Swedish; safety (_match_) ‖ _mf_ Swede ‖ _m_ Swedish

svéglia _f_ awakening; reveille; alarm clock; **dare la sveglia a** to wake up

svegliare §280 _tr_ & _ref_ to wake up

svegliarino _m_ alarm clock; (coll) rebuke

své·glio **-glia** _adj_ (-gli -glie) awake; alert ‖ _f_ see **sveglia**

svelare (svélo) _tr_ to reveal; to unveil ‖ _ref_ to reveal oneself; **svelarsi per** to reveal oneself to be

svèllere §267 _tr_ (lit) to eradicate

sveltézza _f_ quickness; slenderness

sveltire §176 _tr_ to make shrewd; to quicken, accelerate ‖ _ref_ to become smart

svèl·to **-ta** _adj_ quick; slender; brisk; quick-witted; **alla svelta** quickly; **svelto di lingua** loose-tongued; **svelto di mano** light-fingered ‖ **svelto** _interj_ quick!

svenare (svéno) _tr_ to bleed to death; (fig) to bleed ‖ _ref_ to bleed to death; (fig) to bleed oneself white

svéndere §281 _tr_ to sell below cost; to undersell

svéndita _f_ clearance sale

svenévole _adj_ maudlin, mawkish

svenevolézza _f_ maudlinness, mawkishness

sveniménto _m_ faint, swoon

svenire §282 _intr_ (ESSERE) to faint

sventagliare §280 _tr_ to fan; to flash, display

sventagliata _f_ blow with a fan; volley

sventare (svènto) _tr_ to foil, thwart; (naut) to spill (_a sail_)

sventa·to **-ta** _adj_ careless, thoughtless

svèntola _f_ fan (_to kindle fire_); (coll) box, slap; **a sventola** (_ears_) that stick out

sventolare (svèntolo) _tr_ to wave; to fan; to winnow ‖ _intr_ to flutter ‖ _ref_ to fan oneself

sventolì·o _m_ (-i) fluttering, flutter

sventraménto _m_ demolition; disembowelment; hernia

sventrare (svèntro) _tr_ to demolish; to disembowel; to draw (_a fowl_)

sventura _f_ misfortune, mishap; bad luck

sventura·to **-ta** _adj_ unfortunate, unlucky

sverginare (svérgino) _tr_ to deflower

svergognare (svergógno) _tr_ to put to shame; to unmask

svergogna·to **-ta** _adj_ shameless

svergolare (**svérgolo**) *tr & ref* to warp; (mach) to twist

svernare (**svèrno**) *intr* to winter

svérza [dz] *f* big splinter

sverzino [dz] *m* lash, whipcord

svestire (**svèsto**) *tr* to undress; to hull (rice); (fig) to strip || *ref* to undress; **svestirsi di** to shed (e.g., leaves)

svettare (**svétto**) *tr* to pollard, top || *intr* to stand out; to sway (said of a tree)

Svè•vo -va *adj & m* Swabian

Svèzia, la Sweden

svezzaménto *m* weaning

svezzare (**svézzo**) *tr* to wean; **svezzare da** to break (s.o.) of (e.g., a habit)

sviare §119 *tr* to turn aside; to lead astray || *intr & ref* to go astray; to straggle; (rr) to run off the track

svignare *intr* (ESSERE) to slip away || *ref*—**svignarsela** to sneak away

svilire §176 *tr* to devaluate

svillaneggiare §290 (**svillanéggio**) *tr* to insult, abuse

sviluppare *tr* to develop; to cause; (lit) to uncoil || *intr* (ESSERE & AVERE) & *ref* to develop; to break out (said of fire)

sviluppo *m* development; puberty

svincolare (**svìncolo**) *tr* to free; to clear (at customs)

svìncolo *m*—**svincolo autostradale** interchange; **svincolo doganale** customs clearance

svirilizzare [ddzz] *tr* (fig) to emasculate

svisare *tr* to alter, distort

sviscerare (**svìscero**) *tr* to eviscerate; to examine thoroughly || *ref*—**sviscerarsi per** to be crazy about; to bow and scrape to

sviscera•to -ta *adj* ardent, passionate; obsequious

svista *f* slip, error, oversight

svitare *tr* to unscrew

svìzze•ro -ra *adj & mf* Swiss || **la Svizzera** Switzerland

svocia•to -ta *adj* hoarse

svogliatézza *f* laziness; listlessness

svoglia•to -ta *adj* lazy; listless

svolazzare *intr* to flutter, flit

svolazzo *m* flutter; short flight; curlicue, flourish

svòlgere §289 *tr* to unwrap; to unfold; to unwind; to develop; to pursue (an activity); to dissuade || *ref* to unwind; to free oneself; to develop; to take place; to unfold

svolgiménto *m* development; composition

svòlta *f* turn; curve; turning point

svoltare (**svòlto**) *tr* to unwrap || *intr* to turn

svotare §257 or **svuotare** (**svuòto**) *tr* to empty

T

T, t [ti] *m & f* eighteenth letter of the Italian alphabet

tabac•càlo -càia *mf* (**-cài -càie**) tobacconist

tabaccare §197 *intr* to take snuff

tabaccheria *f* cigar store

tabacchièra *f* snuffbox

tabac•co *m* (**-chi**) tobacco; **tabacco da fiuto** snuff

tabarro *m* winter coat; cloak

tabèlla *f* tablet; list; schedule; (coll) clapper, noisemaker; **tabella di marcia** timetable

tabellare *adj* (typ) on wooden blocks; scheduled

tabellóne *m* board; bulletin board; (basketball) backboard

tabernàcolo *m* tabernacle

ta•bù *adj invar & m* (**-bù**) taboo

tàbula *f*—**far tabula rasa di** to make a clean sweep of

tabulare (**tàbulo**) *tr* to tabulate

tabulatóre *m* tabulator

tabulatrice *f* printer (of computer)

tac•ca *f* (**-che**) notch; size; kind; tally; blemish; (typ) nick; **di mezza tacca** middle-sized; mediocre; **tacca di mira** rear sight (of firearm)

tacca•gno -gna *adj* stingy, closefisted || *mf* miser

taccheggia•tóre -trice *mf* shoplifter || *f* prostitute, streetwalker

taccheggiatura *f* or **tacchég•gio** *m* (**-gi**) shoplifting

tacchétto *m* high heel; cleat (on soccer or football shoe)

tacchina *f* turkey hen

tacchino *m* turkey

tàc•cia *f* (**-ce**) notoriety

tacciare §128 *tr*—**tacciare di** to accuse of, charge with

tac•co *m* (**-chi**) heel; block; (typ) underlay; **battere i tacchi** to take to one's heels

taccóne *m* (coll) patch; (coll) hobnail; **battere il taccone** to take to one's heels

taccuino *m* pocketbook; notebook

tacére *m* silence; **mettere a tacere** to silence || §268 *tr* to conceal, withhold; to imply, understand || *intr* to keep quiet; to stop playing; to quiet down; to be silent; **far tacere** to silence; **taci!** (coll) shut up!

tachìmetro *m* tachometer; (aut) speedometer

tacitare (**tàcito**) *tr* to silence, satisfy (a creditor); to pay off

tàci•to -ta *adj* silent; tacit

tacitur•no -na *adj* taciturn

tafano *m* horsefly, gadfly

tafferù•glio *m* (**-gli**) scuffle

taffe•tà *m* (**-tà**) taffeta; **taffetà adesivo**

or **inglese** adhesive plaster, court plaster

tàglia f ransom, reward; size; build; tally; (mach) tackle

tagliabór·se m (-se) pickpocket

tagliabò·schi m (-schi) woodcutter, woodsman

tagliacar·te m (-te) letter opener, paper knife

tagli·àcque m (-àcque) cutwater (of bridge)

tagliaèrba adj invar grass-cutting

tagliafèr·ro m (-ro) cold chisel

taglialé·gna m (-gna) woodcutter

tagliama·re m (-re) cutwater (of ship)

tagliando m coupon

tagliapiè·tre m (-tre) stonecutter

tagliare §280 tr to cut; to cut down; to cut off; to pick (a pocket); to cross (finish line); to tailor (a suit); to blend (wine); to turn off (e.g., water); **tagliare a fette** to slice; **tagliare in due** to split; **tagliare i panni addosso a qlcu** to slander s.o.; **tagliare i ponti con** to sever relations with; **tagliare i viveri a** to cut off supplies from; **tagliare la corda** to run away; **tagliare la strada a** to stand in the way of; (aut) to cut in front of; **tagliare le gambe a** to make wobbly (said of wine); to bite (said of cold); **tagliare per una scorciatoia** to take a shortcut || ref to cut oneself; to tear (said of material)

tagliasìga·ri m (-ri) cigar cutter

tagliata f cut; clearing; (mil) abatis; **tagliata ai capelli** haircut

tagliatèlle fpl noodles

taglia·to -ta adj cut; fashioned; **essere tagliato per** to be cut out for; **tagliato all'antica** old-fashioned; **tagliato con l'accetta** rough-hewn || f see tagliata

taglia·tóre -trice mf cutter

tagliènte adj cutting || m edge

taglière m carving board

taglierina f paper cutter

tà·glio m (-gli) cut; cutting; dressmaking; cutting edge; sharpness; blending (of wines); size; denomination (of paper money); crossing (of t); (bb) fore edge; **a due tagli** double-edged; **a tagli** by the slice; **dare un taglio a** to chop; **di taglio** edgewise; **rifare il taglio a** to sharpen; **taglio cesareo** Caesarean section; **taglio d'abito** suiting; **taglio dei capelli** haircut; **venire in taglio** to come in handy

tagliòla f trap

tagliuzzare tr to shred, cut into shreds

tailandése [s] adj & mf Thai

Tailàndia, la Thailand

tailleur m (tailleur) woman's tailored costume

talal·tro -tra pron indef another, some other

tàlamo m (lit) nuptial bed

talare adj ankle-length || f soutane, cassock

talché conj so that

talco m talcum; talcum powder

tale adj such; such a; that; **il tale** such and such a; **un tale** such a; a certain; **un tal quale** such a; a certain || pron so-and-so; **il tal dei tali** so-and-so; Mr. so-and-so; **il tale** that fellow; that guy; **quel tale** that fellow, that guy; **tale e quale** like; **tali e quali** exactly, word for word; **un tale** someone, a certain person

talèa f (hort) cutting

talènto m talent; inclination; **a proprio talento** gladly, willingly; **di mal talento** grudgingly; **andare a talento a** to suit, e.g., **non gli va a talento nulla** nothing suits him

talismano m talisman

tallire §176 intr (ESSERE & AVERE) to sprout

tallonare (tallóno) tr (sports) to be at the heels of

talloncino m coupon, stub

tallóne m heel; coupon, stub; tang (of knife); **tallone d'Achille** Achilles heel

talménte adv so, so much

talóra adv sometimes

talpa f mole

talu·no -na pron indef some; someone, somebody || **talu·ni -ne** adj & pron indef some

talvòlta adv sometimes

tamarindo m tamarind

tamarice f tamarisk

Tamigi m Thames

tampòco adv—né tampoco (archaic) nor . . . either

tamponaménto m stopping, plugging; rear-end collision

tamponare (tampóno) tr to tampon, plug; to collide with; to hit from the rear; (surg) to tampon

tampóne m plug, tampon; pad; (mus) drumstick; (rr) buffer; (surg) tampon; **tampone di vapore** vapor lock

tana f burrow; den; hole; hovel; base (in children games)

tanàglie fpl var of tenaglie

tan·ca f (-che) can, jerry can; tank

tanfo m musty or stuffy smell

tangènte adj tangent || f tangent; (com) commission

tàngere §269 tr (lit) to touch

Tàngeri f Tangier

tànghero m boor, lout

tangìbile adj tangible

tàni·ca f (-che) var of tanca

tantino m—un tantino a little, e.g., **è un tantino arrabbiato** he is a little angry; a little bit, e.g., **un tantino di dolce** a little bit of cake

tan·to -ta adj & pron such a; so much; as much; **a dir tanto** or **a far tanto** at the most; **ai tanti**

(*del mese*) on such and such a day (*of the month*); **a tanto** to such a point; **to such a level; e tanto** odd, e.g., **mille dollari e tanto** a thousand odd dollars; **è tanto** it has been a long time, e.g., **è tanto che lo conosco** it has been a long time since I made his acquaintance; **fra tanto** meanwhile; **senza tanto chiasso** without any noise; **tan·ti -te** many; so many; as many; a lot, e.g., **grazie tante!** thanks a lot! **tanti . . . che** so many . . . that; **tanti . . . quanti** as many . . . as; **tanto di guadagnato** so much the better || **tanto** *adv* so much; so; only, e.g., **tanto per passare il tempo** only to pass the time; anyhow; anyway; **nè tanto nè quanto** at all; **tant'è** it's the same; **tanto che** so much that, e.g., **mi ha annoiato tanto che l'ho mandato via** he bothered me so much that I dismissed him; **tanto . . . che** both . . . and, e.g., **tanto Maria che Roberto** both Mary and Robert; so much . . . that; **tanto fa** or **vale** it's all the same; **tanto meglio** so much the better; **tanto meno** so much the less; **tanto per cambiare** as usual; **tanto più . . . quanto più** the more . . . the more; **tanto . . . quanto as . . . as** || *s*— **ascoltare con tanto d'orecchie** to be all ears; **di tanto in tanto** from time to time

tapi·no -na *adj* (lit) wretched || *mf* (lit) wretch

tappa *f* stopping place; stop; stage, leg; (sports) lap; **bruciare le tappe** to press on, keep going; **fare tappa** to stop

tappabu·chi *mf* (**-chi**) makeshift, pinch hitter, substitute

tappare *tr* to cork, plug; to shut up tight || *ref* to shut oneself in; to plug (*e.g., one's ears*)

tapparèlla *f* (coll) inside rolling shutter

tappéto *m* rug, carpet; (sports) canvas, mat; **mettere al tappeto** (boxing) to knock out; **tappeto erboso** lawn, green; **tappeto verde** gambling table

tappezzare (**tappèzzo**) *tr* to paper (*a wall*); to upholster

tappezzerìa *f* wallpaper; upholstery; upholsterer's shop; tapestry; wallflower

tappezzière *m* paperhanger; upholsterer

tappo *m* cork, stopper; cap; plug; **tappo a corona** bottle cap; **tappo a vite** screw cap

tara *f* tare

taràntola *f* tarantula

tarare *tr* to tare; to set, adjust

tara·to -ta *adj* net (*weight*); calibrated (*instrument*); sickly, weak

tarchia·to -ta *adj* stocky, sturdy

tardare *tr* to delay || *intr* to delay; to be late

tardi *adv* late; **al più tardi** at the latest; **a più tardi!** so long!; **fare tardi** to be late; **più tardi** later; later on; **sul tardi** in the late afternoon

tardi·vo -va *adj* late; retarded, slow; belated

tar·do -da *adj* slow; late; **di età tarda** of advanced years; **tardo d'ingegno** slow-witted

tardó·ne -na *adj* slow-moving || *mf* slowpoke || *f* old dame, middle-aged vamp

tar·ga *f* (**-ghe**) plate; nameplate; shield; (aut) license plate; (sports) trophy

targare §209 *tr* (aut) to register

targatura *f* (aut) registration

targhétta *f* nameplate

tariffa *f* tariff; rate; rates

tariffà·rio -ria (**-ri -rie**) *adj* tariff; rate || *m* price list; rate book

tarlare *tr* to eat (*said of woodworms or moths*) || *intr* (ESSERE) & *ref* to become worm-eaten; to become moth-eaten

tarlo *m* woodworm; moth; bookworm; (fig) gnawing

tarma *f* moth; clothes moth

tarmare *tr* to eat (*said of moths*) || *intr* (ESSERE) & *ref* to become moth-eaten

tarmici·da (**-di -de**) *adj* moth-repelling || *m* moth repellent

taròc·co *m* (**-chi**) tarot; tarok

tarpare *tr* to clip; **tarpare le ali a** to clip the wings of

tartagliare §280 *tr* & *intr* to stutter, stammer

tàrta·ro -ra *adj* Tartar || *m* tartar; Tartar || **Tartaro** *m* Tartarus

tartaru·ga *f* (**-ghe**) turtle, tortoise; tortoise shell

tartassare *tr* to ill-treat; to harass

tartina *f* slice of bread and butter; canapé

tartufo *m* truffle; (fig) tartuffe, hypocrite

ta·sca *f* (**-sche**) pocket; briefcase; **aver le tasche piene di** to be sick and tired of; **da tasca** pocket; **rompere le tasche a** (vulg) to bother, annoy; **tasca in petto** inside pocket

tascàbile *adj* pocket; vest-pocket

tascapane *m* knapsack, rucksack

tascata *f* pocketful

taschino *m* vest pocket, small pocket

tassa *f* tax; (coll) duty, fee; **tassa complementare** surtax; **tassa di circolazione** road-use tax; **tassa di registro** registration fee; **tassa scolastica** tuition

tassàbile *adj* taxable

tassàmetro *m* taximeter; **tassametro di parcheggio** parking meter

tassare *tr* to tax; to assess || *ref* to pledge money

tassati·vo -va *adj* positive; specific; peremptory

tassazióne *f* taxation; tax

tassèllo *m* dowel; inlay; plug; patch; reinforcement

tas·sì *m* (**-sì**) taxi, taxicab

tassi·sta *m* (**-sti**) taxi driver

tasso *m* stake (*anvil*); yew tree; (com) rate (*e.g., of interest*); (zool) badger; **tasso valutario fluttuante** (econ) fluctuation of currency rate

tastare *tr* to touch; to feel; to probe; **tastare il terreno** (fig) to see how the land lies

tastièra *f* keyboard; manual (*of organ*)

tasto m touch, feeling, feel; plug (e.g., in watermellon); key (of piano or typewriter); sample (in drilling); **tasto bianco** white key, natural; **toccare un tasto falso** to strike a sour note

tastóni adv—**a tastoni** gropingly

tàtti·co -ca (**-ci -che**) adj tactical; tactful ‖ m tactician ‖ f tactics; prudence; tactfulness

tatto m touch; tact

tatuàg·gio m (**-gi**) tattoo

tatuare (**tàtuo**) tr to tattoo

taumatur·go m (**-gi & -ghi**) wonderworker

tauri·no -na adj taurine, bull-like; bull

tavèrna f tavern, inn

tavernière m tavernkeeper

tàvola f board, plank; slab; table; tablet; bookplate; list; **tavola a ribalta** drop-leaf table; **tavola armonica** (mus) sound board; **tavola calda** cafeteria, snack bar; **tavola da stirare** ironing board; **tavola di salvezza** (fig) last recourse, lifesaver; **tavola imbandita** open house; **tavola nera** blackboard; **tavola operatoria** operating table; **tavola pitagorica** multiplication table; **tavola reale** backgammon; **tavole di fondazione** charter (of a charitable institution)

tavolàc·cio m (**-ci**) wooden board (on which soldiers on guard and prisoners used to sleep)

tavolare (**tàvolo**) tr to board up

tavolata f tableful

tavolato m planking; plateau

tavolétta f small table; tablet; bar (e.g., of chocolate)

tavolière m chessboard table; card table; plateau, tableland

tavolino m small table; desk

tàvolo m table; desk; **tavolo di gioco** gambling table; **tavolo d'ufficio** office desk

tavolòzza f palette

tazza f cup; bowl

tazzina f demitasse

tazzóna f mug

te §5 pron pers

tè m (**tè**) tea; **tè danzante** tea dance, thé dansant

tèa adj fem—**rosa tea** tea rose

teatrale adj theatrical

teatro m theater; performance; drama; stage; (fig) scene; **che teatro!** what fun!; **teatro dell'opera** or **teatro lirico** opera house; **teatro di posa** (mov) studio; **teatro di prosa** legitimate theater

teatróne m large theater; (coll) excellent box office

Tèbe f Thebes

tè·ca f (**-che**) case; (eccl) reliquary

tecnicismo m technicality

tècni·co -ca (**-ci -che**) adj technical ‖ m technician; engineer ‖ f technique; technics

téco §5 prep phrase (lit) with you

tedé·sco -sca adj & mf (**-schi -sche**) German

tediare §287 (**tèdio**) tr to bore ‖ ref to get bored

tè·dio m (**-di**) dullness, tedium, boredom; **recare tedio a** to annoy, bother

tedió·so -sa [s] adj dull, tedious

tegame m pan; **al tegame** fried (e.g., eggs)

tegamino m small pan; **uova al tegamino** fried eggs

téglia f pan; baking pan

tégola f tile; (fig) blow

tégolo m tile

teièra f teapot, teakettle

tèk m teak

téla f linen; cloth; material; canvas, oil painting; (fig) plot, trap; (lit) weft; (theat) curtain; **far tela** (coll) to beat it; **tela batista** batiste; **tela cerata** oilcloth; **tela da imballaggio** burlap; **tela di ragno** cobweb; **tela di sacco** sackcloth; **tela greggia** gunny, burlap; **tela smeriglio** emery cloth

te·làio m (**-lài**) loom; frame; embroidery frame; sash; stretcher (for oil painting); (aut) chassis; **telaio di finestra** window sash

teleama·tóre -trice mf TV viewer

telear·ma f (**-mi**) guided missile

telecabina f cable car

telecàmera f TV camera

telecomanda·to -ta adj remote-control

telecomando m remote control

telecommentatóre m TV newscaster

telecròna·ca f (**-che**) TV broadcast; **telecronaca diretta** live broadcast

telecroni·sta mf (**-sti -ste**) TV news announcer, TV newscaster

telediffusióne f TV broadcasting

teledram·ma m (**-mi**) teleplay

telefèri·ca f (**-che**) cableway, telpherage

telefonare (**telèfono**) tr & intr to telephone ‖ ref to call one another

telefonata f telephone call

telefòni·co -ca adj (**-ci -che**) telephone

telefoni·sta mf (**-sti -ste**) telephone operator, central; telephone installer

telèfono m telephone; **telefono a gettone** pay telephone (operated by tokens); **telefono a moneta** pay telephone; **telefono interno** intercommunication system, intercom

telegèni·co -ca adj (**-ci -che**) telegenic, videogenic

telegiornale m TV newscast

telegrafare (**telègrafo**) tr & intr to telegraph

telegràfi·co -ca adj (**-ci -che**) telegraphic

telegrafi·sta mf (**-sti -ste**) telegrapher; telegraph installer

telègrafo m telegraph; **telegrafo di macchina** (naut) engine-room telegraph; **telegrafo ottico** heliograph; wigwag; **telegrafo senza fili** wireless

telegram·ma m (**-mi**) telegram

teleguida f remote control

teleguidare tr to control from a distance, to operate by remote control

Telèmaco m Telemachus

telèmetro m telemeter; range finder

teleobbiettivo m (phot) telephoto lens

telepatìa f telepathy

teleproiètto m guided missile

telericévere §141 tr to receive by TV; to teleview

teleschérmo m television screen

telescò·pio *m* (**-pi**) telescope

telescrivènte *f* teletypewriter; ticker

telescriventi·sta *mf* (**-sti -ste**) teletype operator

teleselezióne *f* (telp) direct distance dialing

telespetta·tóre -trice *mf* televiewer

teletrasméttere §198 *tr* to televise, telecast

teletrasmissióne *f* telecast

televisióne *f* television, TV

televisi·vo -va *adj* television, TV

televisóre *m* television set

tellina *f* sunset shell or clam

télo *m* piece of cloth; yardage, length of material; (mil) side (*of tent*)

tèlo *m* (lit) dart, arrow

telóne *m* canvas; (theat) curtain

tè·ma *m* (**-mi**) theme; (gram) stem

téma *f* (lit) fear; **per tema di** (lit) for fear of

temerarie·tà *f* (**-tà**) recklessness, rashness

temerà·rio -ria *adj* (**-ri -rie**) reckless, rash; ill-founded

temére (**témo & tèmo**) *tr* to fear; to respect ‖ *intr* to fear; **temere di** to be afraid to

temeri·tà *f* (**-tà**) temerity

temìbile *adj* frightening

tèmpera *f* tempera, distemper

temperala·pis *m* (**-pis**) or **temperamatite** *m* (**-te**) pencil sharpener

temperaménto *m* middle course, compromise; temper, temperament

temperante *adj* temperate, moderate

temperanza *f* temperance

temperare (**tèmpero**) *tr* to mitigate; to temper; to sharpen (*a pencil*)

tempera·to -ta *adj* temperate; tempered (*metal*); watered (*wine*)

temperatura *f* temperature; **temperatura ambiente** room temperature

temperino *m* penknife, pocketknife

tempèsta *f* tempest, storm; **tempesta in un bicchier d'acqua** tempest in a teapot

tempestare (**tempèsto**) *tr* to pound; to pepper, pelt; to pester ‖ *intr* to storm

tempesta·to -ta *adj* studded, spangled

tempesti·vo -va *adj* timely

tempestó·so -sa [s] *adj* stormy, tempestuous

tèmpia *f* temple (*side of forehead*); **temple** (lit) head

tempiale *m* temple (*in loom; of spectacles*)

templère *m* Templar

tèm·pio *m* (**-pi & -pli**) temple (*edifice*)

templi·sta *mf* (**-sti -ste**) person or athlete showing good timing; (mus) rhythmist

tèmpo *m* time; weather; age; period, stage; cycle (*of internal-combustion engine*); (gram) tense; (mus) tempo, (mus) movement; (sports) period; (theat, mov) part; **ad un tempo** at the same time; **al tempo che Berta filava** long ago; **a suo tempo** in due time; long ago; **a tempo debito** in due time; **a tempo e luogo** at the opportune time; **a tempo perso** in

one's spare time; **aver fatto il proprio tempo** to be outdated; **c'è sempre tempo** we are still in time; **col tempo** in time; **dare tempo al tempo** to allow time to heal things; **darsi del bel tempo** to have a good time; **da tempo** for a long time; **del tempo di** from the time of; **è scaduto il tempo utile** the time is up; **è tanto tempo** it's been a long time; **fa bel tempo** the weather is fine; **il Tempo** Father Time; **lasciare il tempo che trova** to have no effect; **molto tempo dopo** long afterward; **nel tempo che** while; **per tempo** early; **prima del tempo** formerly; **quanto tempo** how long; **sentire il tempo** to feel the weather in one's bones; **senza por tempo in mezzo** without any delay; **tempi che corrono** present times; **tempo fa** some time ago; **tempo legale** legal time limit; **tempo libero** leisure time; **tempo supplementare** (sports) overtime; **tempo un . . .** within (*e.g., one month*); **un tempo** long ago

temporale *adj* temporal ‖ *m* storm

temporàne·o -a *adj* temporary, provisional

temporeggiare §290 (**temporéggio**) *intr* to temporize

tèmpra *f* (metallurgy) tempering, temper; (mus) timbre; (fig) fiber, timber

temprare (**tèmpro**) *tr* to temper (*metal*); to harden, inure ‖ *ref* to become hardened or inured

tenace *adj* tenacious; tough

tenàcia *f* tenacity

tenaci·tà *f* (**-tà**) strength, resistance; tenacity

tenàglie *fpl* nippers, pincers, pliers; tongs; **a tenaglie** (mil) pincers (*e.g., action*)

tènda *f* curtain; awning; tent

tendènza *f* tendency; trend

tendenzió·so -sa [s] *adj* tendentious

tèn·der *m* (**-der**) (rr) tender

tèndere §270 *tr* to stretch; to tighten; to draw (*a bow*); to cast (*nets*); to lay (*snares*); to reach out (*one's hand*); to prick up (*one's ears*); to draw (*s.o.'s attention*); to set (*sail*) ‖ *intr* to aim; to lean; to tend; to tend to be

tendina *f* curtain, blind

tendine *m* (anat) tendon

tendiscar·pe *m* (**-pe**) shoetree

tenditóre *m* turnbuckle; **tenditore della racchetta** (tennis) press

tendóne *m* big curtain; canvas; tent (*of circus*); (theat) curtain

tendòpo·li *f* (**-li**) tent city

tènebre *fpl* darkness

tenebró·so -sa [s] *adj* dark, gloomy

tenènte *m* lieutenant; (mil) first lieutenant; (nav) lieutenant junior grade; **tenente colonnello** (mil) lieutenant colonel; **tenente di vascello** (nav) lieutenant senior grade

tenére §271 *tr* to hold; to have; to keep; to stand (*e.g., rough sea*); to wear; to make (*a speech*); to follow

(*a course*); **tenere a battesimo** to
stand for, sponsor; **tenere al corrente**
to keep informed; **tenere a memoria**
to remember; **tenere da conto** to hold
in high esteem; to take good care of
(*s.th*); **tenere d'occhio** to keep an eye
on; **tenere la testa** to keep to the
right; **tenere la strada** (aut) to hug
the road; **tenere la testa a partito**
to mend one's ways; **tenere le distanze** to keep aloof; **tenere mano a**
to connive with; **tenere presente** to
bear in mind; **tenere qlco a conto**
to take good care of s.th ‖ *intr* to
hold; to take root; **tenerci che** to be
anxious for, e.g., **ci tengo che vinca
le elezioni** I am anxious for him to
win the elections; **tenere a destra** to
keep to the right; **tenere alle apparenze** to stand on ceremony; to keep
up appearances; **tenere da** to hail
from; to take after; **tenere dietro a**
to follow; to keep abreast of; **tenere
duro** to hold fast; **tenere per** (sports)
to be a fan of ‖ *ref* to hold; to hold
on; to keep; to keep (*e.g., ready*); to
regard oneself; **tenersi a** to adhere to
(*e.g., a treaty*); to hold on to; to
stick to; to follow; **tenersi a galla**
to stay afloat; **tenersi al largo** (naut)
to keep to the open sea; **tenersi al
vento** (naut) to sail to leeward; (fig)
to follow a safe course; **tenersi in
piedi** to stand up; **tenersi per mano**
to hold hands; **tenersi sulle proprie**
to keep aloof

tenerézza *f* tenderness; fondness, en-
dearment

tène·ro -ra *adj* tender ‖ *m* tender portion

tènia *f* tapeworm

teni·tóre -trice *mf* keeper

tènnis *m* tennis; **tennis da tavolo** table
tennis, ping-pong

tennì·sta *mf* (**-sti -ste**) tennis player

tennìsti·co -ca *adj* (**-ci -che**) tennis

tenóne *m* tenon

tenóre *m* character, tone; tenor; alcoholic content; manner (*of living*);
tenore di vita way of life; standard
of living

tensióne *f* tension; **alta tensione** high
tension; **tensione sanguigna** blood
pressure

tentàcolo *m* tentacle

tentare (**tènto**) *tr* to try, attempt; to
assay; to tempt; (lit) to touch

tentativo *m* attempt; **tentativo di furto**
attempted robbery

tenta·tóre -trice *adj* tempting ‖ *m*
tempter ‖ *f* temptress

tentazióne *f* temptation

tentennare (**tenténno**) *tr* to shake; to
rock ‖ *intr* to shake; to wobble; to
hesitate; to stagger

tentóne or **tentóni** *adv* blindly; gropingly; at random

tènue *adj* small (*intestine*); (lit) tenuous, thin

tenu·to -ta *adj* bound, obliged ‖ *f* capacity, volume; estate, farm; uniform; outfit; (sports) endurance,

resistance; **a tenuta d'acqua** watertight; **a tenuta d'aria** airtight; **tenuta
dei libri** bookkeeping; **tenuta di gala**
(mil, nav) full-dress uniform; **tenuta
di servizio** (mil) fatigues; **tenuta di
strada** (aut) roadability

tenzóne *f* combat; poetic contest

teologìa *f* theology

teòlo·go *m* (**-gi**) theologian

teorè·ma *m* (**-mi**) theorem

teorèti·co -ca *adj* (**-ci -che**) theoretic(al)

teorìa *f* theory; (lit) series, row

teòri·co -ca *adj* (**-ci -che**) theoretical ‖
m theoretician

tèpi·do -da *adj* var of **tiepido**

tepóre *m* warmth

téppa *f* underworld, rabble

teppi·sta *m* (**-sti**) hoodlum, hooligan

terapèuti·co -ca *adj* (**-ci -che**) therapeutic ‖ *f* therapeutics

terapìa *f* therapy; **terapia convulsivante**
or **terapia d'urto** shock therapy

Terèsa *f* Theresa

tèrgere §162 *tr* (lit) to wipe

tergicristallo *m* windshield wiper

tergiversare (**tergivèrso**) *intr* to stall;
to beat around the bush

tèr·go *m* (**-ghi**) back (*of a coin*); **a
tergo** on the reverse side ‖ *m* (**-ga**
fpl) (lit) back; **volgere le terga** (lit)
to turn one's back

termale *adj* thermal (*e.g., waters*)

tèrme *fpl* spa, hot spring

tèrmi·co -ca *adj* (**-ci -che**) thermal;
heat, heating

terminale *adj* & *m* terminal

terminare (**tèrmino**) *tr* to border; to
end, terminate ‖ *intr* (ESSERE) to end,
terminate

terminazióne *f* termination; completion; (gram) ending

tèrmine *m* border; marker; term; dead-
line; end; goal; boundary, bounds;
(fig) point; **a termini di legge** according to law; **avere termine** to end;
in altri termini in other words;
mezzo termine half measure; **porre
termine a** to put an end to; **portare
a termine** to put through

terminologìa *f* terminology

termìstore *m* (elec) thermistor

tèrmite *f* termite

termoconvettóre *m* baseboard radiator

termocòppia *f* thermocouple

termodinàmi·co -ca *adj* (**-ci -che**) thermodynamic ‖ *f* thermodynamics

termòforo *m* heating pad

termòmetro *m* thermometer

termonucleare *adj* thermonuclear

tèr·mos *m* (**-mos**) thermos bottle

termosifóne *m* radiator; hot-water
heating system; steam heating system

termòstato *m* thermostat

termovisièra *f* electric defroster

tèrno *m* tern (*in lotto*); **vincere un
terno al lotto** to hit the jackpot

tèrra *f* earth; land; ground; world; city,
town; dirt, soil; clay; **essere a terra**
to be downcast; to be broke; to be
flat (*said of a tire*); **rimanere a terra**
to miss the boat; **sotto terra** underground; **terra bruciata** scorched

earth; **terra di nessuno** no man's land; **terra di Siena** sienna; **terra ferma** terra firma; mainland; **terra** skimming the ground; (naut) close to the shore; (fig) mediocre, second-rate

terracòtta *f* (**terrecòtte**) terra cotta; earthenware

terraférma *f* mainland (*as distinguished from adjacent islands*); terra firma (*dry land, not air or water*)

terràglia *f* crockery; **terraglie** earthenware

terranò·va *m* (**-va**) Newfoundland (*dog*) ‖ **Terranova** *f* Newfoundland

terrapièno *m* embankment

terrazza *f* terrace; **a terrazza** terraced

terrazza·no -na *mf* villager

terrazzo *m* balcony; terrace; ledge, shelf; terrazzo

terremota·to -ta *adj* hit by an earthquake ‖ *mf* earthquake victim

terremòto *m* earthquake

terré·no -na *adj* terrestrial, earthly; ground-floor; first-floor ‖ *m* ground floor; first floor; ground; soil; land, plot of ground; combat zone, terrain; **preparare il terreno** to work the soil; (fig) to pave the way; **scendere sul terreno** to fight a duel; **tastare il terreno** to feel one's way; **terreno di gioco** (sports) field

tèrre·o -a *adj* wan, sallow

terrèstre *adj* terrestrial; ground, land ‖ *m* earthling

terrìbile *adj* terrible; awesome, awful

terric·cio *m* (**-ci**) soil; top soil

terriè·ro -ra *adj* land; landed

terrificare §197 (**terrìfico**) *tr* to terrify

terrina *f* tureen

territò·rio *m* (**-ri**) territory

terróre *m* terror

terrorismo *m* terrorism

terrori·sta *mf* (**-sti -ste**) terrorist

terrorizzare [ddzz] *tr* to terrorize

terró·so -sa [s] *adj* dirty (*e.g., spinach*); dirty-earth (*color*); (chem) rare-earth (*metal*)

tèr·so -sa *adj* clear

tèrza *f* third grade; (aut) third; (eccl) tierce; (rr) third class

terzaforzi·sta (**-sti -ste**) *adj* of the third force ‖ *m* partisan of the third force

terzaròlo *m* (naut) reef

terzétto *m* trio

terzià·rio -ria *adj* (**-ri -rie**) tertiary

terzina *f* tercet

terzino *m* (soccer) back

tèr·zo -za *adj & pron* third ‖ *m* third; third party ‖ *f* see **terza**

terzùlti·mo -ma *adj* third from the end

tésa [s] *f* brim (*of hat*); snare, net

tesare [s] (**téso**) *tr* to pull taut

tè·schio *m* (**-schi**) skull

tè·si *f* (**-si**) thesis; dissertation

té·so -sa [s] *adj* taut, tight; strained; outstretched (*hand*); **con le orecchie tese all ears** ‖ *f* see **tesa**

tesorería *f* treasury; liquid assets

tesorière *m* treasurer

tesòro *m* treasure; treasury; thesaurus; bank vault; **far tesoro di** to treasure, prize; **tesoro mio!** my darling!

Tèspi *m* Thespis

tèssera *f* card; domino (*piece*); tessera (*of mosaic*)

tessera·to -ta *adj* card-carrying; rationed ‖ *mf* card-carrying member; holder of ration card

tèssere *tr* to weave; to spin

tèssile *adj* textile ‖ *m* textile; **tessili** textile workers

tessilsac·co *m* (**-chi**) garment bag

tessi·tóre -trice *mf* weaver

tessitura *f* weaving; spinning mill; (mus) range; (fig) plot

tessuto *m* cloth, fabric; tissue

tèsta *f* head; mind; bulb (*of garlic*); spindle (*of wheel*); warhead (*of torpedo*); row (*of bricks*); **a testa** apiece; per capita; **a testa a testa** neck and neck; **fare di testa propria** to act on one's own; **fare la testa grossa a** to stun; to annoy; **levarsi di testa** to forget about; **mettersi in testa di** to get it into one's head to; **non avere testa di** + *inf* to not feel like + *ger*; **non sapere dove battere la testa** to not know which way to turn; **per una corta testa** by a neck; **rompersi la testa** to rack one's brains; **tenere testa a** to face up to; **testa coda** (aut) spin; **testa di ponte** (mil) bridgehead; **testa di sbarco** beachhead; **testa e croce** head or tails

testaménto *m* will, testament ‖ **Antico** or **Vecchio Testamento** Old Testament; **Nuovo Testamento** New Testament

testardàggine *f* stubbornness

testar·do -da *adj* stubborn

testata *f* headboard (*of bed*); top; end (*e.g., of beam*); heading (*of newspaper*); butt with the head; nose (*of rocket*)

tèste *m* witness

testé *adv* (lit) a short time ago; (lit) presently, in a little while

testìcolo *m* testicle

testièra *f* headboard; crown (*of harness*); battering ram

testimòne *m* witness; **testimone di nozze** best man; **testimone di veduta** or **testimone oculare** eyewitness

testimonianza *f* testimony

testimoniare §287 (**testimònio**) *tr* to attest; to depose, testify; **testimoniare il falso** to bear false witness ‖ *intr* to bear witness

testimò·nio *m* (**-ni**) (coll) witness

testina *f* small head; whimsical person; boiled head of veal; head (*e.g., of tape recorder*)

tèsto *m* text; pie dish; (coll) flower vase; **fare testo** to serve as a model

testó·ne -na *mf* dolt; stubborn person

testuale *adj* textual; word-for-word

testùggine *f* turtle; tortoise

tètano *m* tetanus

tè·tro -tra *adj* (lit) gloomy, dark

tétta *f* (coll) teat

tettarèlla *f* nipple

tétto *m* roof; ceiling price; home; **senza tetto** homeless; **tetto a capanna** gable roof; **tetto a padiglione** hip

roof; **tetto a una falda** lean-to roof; **tetto di paglia** thatched roof
tettóia *f* shed; pillared roof
tettóia-garage *f* (**tettóie-garage**) carport
tettùc·cio *m* (**-ci**) (aut) roof; (aut) top; **tettuccio a bulbo** dome; **tettuccio rigido** (aut) convertible top
ti §5 *pron*
tìbia *f* tibia, shinbone
tic *m* (**tic**) twitch; habit
ticchettì·o *m* (**-i**) click (*of typewriter*); patter (*of rain*); tick (*of clock*)
tìc·chio *m* (**-chi**) whim; tic; viciousness (*of animal*); blemish
tièpi·do -da *adj* tepid, lukewarm
tifo *m* typhus; **fare il tifo per** to root for; to be a fan of
tifoìdea *f* typhoid fever
tifóne *m* typhoon
tifó·so -sa [s] *adj* rooting ‖ *mf* fan, rooter
ti·glio *m* (**-gli**) linden, lime; bast; fiber
tiglió·so -sa [s] *adj* tough, fibrous
tigna *f* ringworm; (coll) tightwad
tignòla *f* clothes moth
tigra·to -ta *adj* striped; tabby
tigre *f* tiger
timballo *m* pie, meat pie; timbale; (lit) drum
timbrare *tr* to stamp; to cancel (*stamps*)
timbro *m* stamp; character (*of a writer*); (mus) timbre; **timbro di gomma** rubber stamp; **timbro postale** postmark
timidézza *f* shyness, bashfulness; timidity
tìmi·do -da *adj* shy, bashful; timid ‖ *mf* shy person
timo *m* (anat) thymus; (bot) thyme
timóne *m* rudder, helm; shaft, pole (*of cart*); **timone di direzione** (aer) rudder; **timone di profondità** (aer) elevator; (nav) diving plane (*of submarine*)
timonièra *f* (naut) pilot house
timonière *m* helmsman, steersman; coxswain
timoniè·ro -ra *adj* rudder; tail (*feather*) ‖ *f* see **timoniera**
timora·to -ta *adj* conscientious; **timorato di Dio** God-fearing
timóre *m* fear; awe; **avere timore di** to fear
timoró·so -sa [s] *adj* timorous
tìmpano *m* (archit) tympanum; (anat) eardrum; (mus) kettledrum; **rompere i timpani a** to deafen
tin·ca *f* (**-che**) (ichth) tench
tinèllo *m* pantry; breakfast room
tìngere §126 *tr* to dye; to dirty, soil; to color ‖ *ref* to dye (*e.g., one's hair*); to put on make-up; to become colored
tino *m* tub, vat
tinòzza *f* tub, washtub
tinta *f* paint; color; dye; shade; stain; **calcare le tinte** to exaggerate; **mezza tinta** halftone, shade; **vedere qlco a fosche tinte** to take a dim view of s.th; **vedere qlco a tinte rosee** to see s.th through rose-colored glasses
tintarèlla *f* (coll) suntan
tinteggiare §290 (**tintéggio**) *tr* to calci-

mine; to whitewash; to tint; to paint (*e.g., a house*)
tintinnare *intr* (ESSERE & AVERE) to jingle; to clink
tintìnni·o *m* (**-i**) jingling; clink
tìn·to -ta *adj* dyed; tinged; soiled; (lit) dark ‖ *f* see **tinta**
tintó·re -ra *mf* dyer; dry cleaner
tintorìa *f* dyeworks; dry cleaning establishment; dyeing
tintura *f* dyeing; dyestuff; tincture; smattering; **tintura di iodio** iodine
tìpi·co -ca *adj* (**-ci -che**) typical
tipificare §197 (**tipìfico**) *tr* to standardize
tipizzare [ddzz] *tr* to standardize
tipo *adj invar* typical, e.g., **famiglia tipo** typical family ‖ *m* type; standard, model; fellow, guy; phylum (*in taxonomy*); **bel tipo** (coll) character, card; **coi tipi di** printed in the shop of; **sul tipo di** similar to; **vero tipo** prototype, epitome
tipografìa *f* typography; print shop
tipogràfi·co -ca *adj* (**-ci -che**) typographical
tipògrafo *m* typographer; owner of print shop, printer
tipòmetro *m* (typ) line gauge
tiptologìa *f* table rapping (*during séance*); tapping in code (*among jailbirds*)
tiraba·ci *m* (**-ci**) (coll) spitcurl
tiràg·gio *m* (**-gi**) draft; **a tiraggio forzato** forced-draft
tiralìne·e *m* (**-e**) ruling pen
tirannìa *f* tyranny
tirànni·co -ca *adj* (**-ci -che**) tyrannical
tiran·no -na *adj* tyrannical ‖ *mf* tyrant
tirante *m* brace; rod; strap; trace (*of harness*); **tirante degli stivali** bootstrap
tirapiè·di *m* (**-di**) hangman's assistant; underling
tirapu·gni *m* (**-gni**) brass knuckles
tirare *tr* to pull; to draw; to tug; to suck; to haul in (*nets*); to deserve (*a slap*); to pluck; to throw; to give (*blows*); to utter (*oaths*); to shoot (*arrows, bullets*); to stretch; to tighten (*one's belt*); to print; to make (*an addition*); (sports) to force (*the pace*); **tirare a lucido** to polish; **tirare a sé** to attract; **tirare a sorte** to draw lots for; **tirare fuori** to draw out; to pull out; to get out; **tirare giù** to lower; to jot down; (coll) to gulp down; **tirare gli orecchi a** to punish by yanking the ears of; **tirare il collo a** to wring the neck of; **tirare in ballo** to bring up (*a subject*); **tirare l'acqua al proprio mulino** to look out for number one; **tirare l'anima coi denti** to be at the end of one's rope; **tirare l'aria** to draw (*said of a chimney*); **tirare le cuoia** (slang) to kick the bucket; **tirare per i capelli** to drag by the hair; to drag in; to push, coerce; **tirare per le lunghe** to stretch out; **tirare su** to lift; to raise (*children*); to pull up ‖ *intr* to be too tight (*said of clothes*); to shoot; to blow (*said of wind*); to

draw (said, e.g., of chimney); **tirare a** to tend toward, lean toward; **tirare a + inf** to try to + inf; **tirare a campare** (coll) to goldbrick; **tirare avanti** to go ahead; to manage to get along; **tirare di boxe** to box; **tirare diritto** to go straight ahead; **tirare di scherma** to fence; **tirare in lungo** to delay, linger; to dillydally; **tirare innanzi** to keep on going; to go ahead; **tirare sul prezzo** to haggle; **tirare via** to hurry along ‖ ref— **tirarsi addosso** (coll) to bring upon oneself; **tirarsi dietro** to drag along; **tirarsi fuori da** to get out of (e.g., trouble); **tirarsi gente in casa** to keep open house; **tirarsi indietro** to move back; **tirarsi in là** to move aside; **tirarsi su** to get up; to recover; to roll up (one's sleeves); **tirarsi un colpo di rivoltella** to shoot oneself

tirastivà·li m (-li) bootjack

tirata f pull; stretch; tirade

tirati·ra m (-ra) (coll) yen; **fare a tiratira per** (coll) to scramble for

tira·to -ta adj taut; forced (smile); drawn (face); tight, closefisted; **tirato con** short of ‖ f see tirata

tira·tóre -trice mf shot; **tiratore scelto** sharpshooter; **franco tiratore** sniper

tiratura f printing

tirchierìa f stinginess

tìr·chio -chia (-chie) adj stingy, closefisted ‖ mf miser

tirèlla f trace (of harness)

tirétto m (coll) drawer

tiritèra f rigmarole

tiro m pull; pair, brace (e.g., of oxen); throw; fire, shot; trick; **a tiro** within reach; **a un tiro di schioppo** within gunshot; **da tiro** draft; **fuori del tiro dell'orecchio** out of earshot; **tiro alla fune** tug of war; **tiro al piattello** trapshooting; **tiro a quattro** four-in-hand; **tiro a segno** rifle range; shooting gallery

tirocì·nio m (-nì) apprenticeship; internship; **tirocinio didattico** practice teaching

tiròide f thyroid

tirolése [s] adj & mf Tyroìean

tirrèni·co -ca adj (-ci -che) Tyrrhenian

Tirrèno m Tyrrhenian Sea

tisana f tea, infusion

tisi f consumption, tuberculosis

tìsi·co -ca (-ci -che) adj consumptive; stunted ‖ mf consumptive

titàni·co -ca adj (-ci -che) titanic

titànio m titanium

titillare tr to tickle

titolare adj titular; regular, full-time ‖ m owner, boss; incumbent ‖ v (tìtolo) tr to name, call

tìtolo m title; heading; name; caption; entry (in dictionary); grade; fineness (of gold); (chem) titer; (educ) credit; **avere titolo a** to have a right to; **a titolo di** as, by way of; **titoli di testa** (mov) credits; **titolo al portatore** security payable to bearer; **titolo azionario** share; **titolo corrente** subtitle; **titolo di credito** instrument of credit; certificate; deed; conveyance; **titolo di studio** degree, diploma; credits; **titolo di trasporto** travel document

titubare (tìtubo) intr to hesitate; to waver

tiziané·sco -sca adj (-schi -sche) titian; Titian

tì·zio m (-zi) fellow, guy

tizzo or tizzóne m brand, firebrand

to' interj here!; well!

tobò·ga m (-ga) toboggan

toccafèrro m tag (game)

toccamano m handshake (to close a deal); bribe, under-the-table tip

toccante adj touching, moving

toccare §197 (tócco) tr to touch; to reach; to concern; to push (a button); to play (an instrument); to feel; to hit (the target); to border on (e.g., the age of forty); **toccare con mano** to make sure of; **toccare il cielo col dito** to be in seventh heaven; **toccare nel vivo** to touch to the quick; **toccare terra** to land; **toccarne molte** to get a good thrashing; **toccato!** touché! ‖ intr (ESSERE) to be touching; **toccare a** to be up to, e.g., **tocca a lui** it's up to him; to have to, e.g., **le tocca partire domani** she has to leave tomorrow; to deserve, e.g., **gli è toccato il premio** he deserved the prize ‖ ref to meet, e.g., **gli estremi si toccano** extremes meet

toccasà·na [s] m (-na) cure-all, panacea

tocca·to -ta adj touché; touched in the head, nutty; **già toccato** abovementioned ‖ f (mus) toccata

tóc·co -ca (-chi -che) adj touched, nutty; spoiled (fruit) ‖ m touch; knock; one o'clock (P.M.); (coll) stroke

tòc·co m (-chi) chunk, piece; mortarboard; toque; **un bel tocco di ragazza** a buxom lass

tò·ga f (-ghe) gown, academic gown; (hist) toga

tògliere §127 tr to remove, take away; to take; to cut (telephone connection); to deduct; to take off; to preclude, prevent; **togliere a** to take away from; **togliere al cielo** (lit) to praise to the skies; **togliere di mezzo** to remove; to do away with; **togliere la parola a** to take the floor from; **togliere l'onore a** to dishonor; **togliere una spina dal cuore a** to relieve the heart and mind of ‖ intr— **tolga Dio!** God forbid! ‖ ref to take off (e.g., one's coat); to have (e.g., a tooth) pulled; to satisfy (a whim); **togliersi di mezzo** to get out of the way; **togliersi la vita** to take one's life; **togliersi qlcu dai piedi** to get rid of s.o.

tòlda f (naut) deck

tolemài·co -ca adj (-ci -che) Ptolemaic

tolétta f dressing table; dressing room; toilet, washroom; dress, gown; **fare toletta** or **farsi la toletta** to make one's toilet

tolleràbile adj tolerable

tollerante *adj* tolerant; liberal

tolleranza *f* tolerance; leeway

tollerare (**tòllero**) *tr* to tolerate; to bear, stand

tòl·to -ta *adj* taken; except, leaving out, e.g., **tolta sua figlia** leaving his daughter out ‖ *m*—**il mal tolto** ill-gotten goods

to·màio *m* (**-mài** & **-màia** *fpl*) or **to·màia** *f* (**-màie**) upper (*of shoe*)

tómba *f* tomb, grave

tombale *adj* grave (*e.g., stone*)

tombino *m* sewer inlet

tómbola *f* bingo; (coll) tumble

tombolare (**tómbolo**) *tr* (coll) to tumble down (*the steps*) ‖ *intr* (ESSERE) to fall headlong; (coll) to go to rack and ruin; (aer) to tumble

tómbolo *m* fall, tumble; bolster; lace pillow; (coll) fatso; **fare un tombolo** to go to rack and ruin; to lose one's position

Tommaso *m* Thomas

tòmo *m* volume; (coll) character

tòna·ca *f* (**-che**) (eccl) frock; (eccl) soutane; **gettare la tonaca alle ortiche** to doff the cassock

tonare §257 *intr* to peal; to thunder ‖ *impers* (ESSERE & AVERE)—**tuona** it is thundering

tondeggiante *adj* round; rounded; chubby; curvaceous

tondino *m* coaster; iron rod (*for re-inforced concrete*); (archit) molding (*at top or bottom of column*); (archit) astragal

tón·do -da *adj* round; (typ) roman ‖ *m* round; circle; plate, dish; (typ) roman; **in tondo** around

tónfo *m* splash; thump

tòni·co -ca (**-ci -che**) *adj* tonic ‖ *m* tonic (*medicine*) ‖ *f* (mus) tonic

tonificare §197 (**tonìfico**) *tr* to invigorate

tonnara *f* tuna nets

tonnellàg·gio *m* (**-gi**) tonnage

tonnellata *f* ton; **tonnellata di stazza** displacement ton

tónno *m* tuna

tòno *m* tone; tune; hue; style; (mus) pitch; (mus) key; **darsi tono** to put on airs; **di tono** stylish; **fuori di tono** out of tune

tonsilla *f* tonsil

tonsura *f* tonsure

tón·to -ta *adj* (coll) dumb, stupid

topàia *f* rat's nest; hovel

topà·zio *m* (**-zi**) topaz

tòpi·co -ca (**-ci -che**) *adj* topical ‖ *f* topic; (coll) blunder

tòpo *m* mouse; rat; **topo campagnolo** field mouse; **topo d'acqua** water rat; **topo d'albergo** hotel thief; **topo d'auto** car thief; **topo di biblioteca** bookworm

topografia *f* topography

topolino *m* little mouse ‖ **Topolino** *m* Mickey Mouse

toporagno *m* shrew

tòppa *f* patch; keyhole

tòppo *m* stump; headstock (*of lathe*)

torace *m* thorax

tórba *f* peat

tórbi·do -da *adj* cloudy; murky ‖ *m* trouble; **pescare nel torbido** to fish in troubled waters; **torbidi** disorder

torbièra *f* peatbog

tòrcere §272 *tr* to twist; to wring; to bend, curve; to curl (*the lips*); to lead astray ‖ *intr* (ESSERE) to bend, curve ‖ *ref* to writhe; to bend over; **torcersi dalle risa** to split with laughter

torchiare §287 (**tòrchio**) *tr* to press

tòr·chio *m* (**-chi**) press; printing press

tòr·cia *f* (**-ce**) torch

torcicòllo *m* stiff neck; (orn) wryneck

torcinaso [s] *m* (vet) twitch

tórdo *m* thrush; simpleton

torèllo *m* young bull; (naut) garboard

torèro *m* bullfighter

tórlo *m* yolk

tórma *f* crowd, throng; herd

torménta *f* blizzard

tormentare (**torménto**) *tr* to torture, torment; to pester, nag ‖ *ref* to worry

torménto *m* torture, torment; pang; bore, pest, annoyance

tornacónto *m* interest, advantage

tornante *m* curve

tornare (**tórno**) *tr* (lit) to restore; (obs) to turn ‖ *intr* (ESSERE) to return; to go back; (coll) to jibe, agree, square; **tornare a** to be profitable to; **tornare a** + *inf* verb + again, e.g., **tornare a essere** to become again; **tornare a fare** to do again; **tornare a bomba** to return to the point; **tornare a galla** to come back to the surface; **tornare a gola** to repeat (*said of food*); **tornare a onore** o **a gieu** to do credit to s.o.; **tornare a pennello** to fit to a T; **tornare in sé** to come to; **tornare opportuno** or **utile a** to suit, e.g., **non gli tornò opportuno vendere la casa** it did not suit him to sell the house; **tornare utile** to come in handy; **tornare sulle proprie decisioni** to change one's mind

tornasóle *m* litmus

tornèllo *m* turnstile

tornèo *m* tournament, tourney

tór·nio *m* (**-ni**) lathe

tornire §176 *tr* to turn, turn up (*on a lathe*); to polish

tornitóre *m* lathe operator

tórno *m* turn; period (*of time*); **levarsi di torno** to get rid of; **torno torno** all around

tòro *m* bull; (archit, geom) torus; (lit) marital bed ‖ **Toro** *m* (astrol) Taurus

torpèdine *f* torpedo

torpedinièra *f* destroyer escort; torpedo-boat destroyer

torpè·do *f* (**-do**) (aut) touring car

torpedóne *m* bus, motor coach

tòrpi·do -da *adj* torpid, sluggish; numb

torpóre *m* torpor, sluggishness; numbness

tórre *f* tower; (chess) castle; (nav) turret; **torre campanaria** bell tower; **torre d'avorio** ivory tower; **torre di**

lancio (rok) gantry; **torre pendente** leaning tower
torrefare §173 *tr* to roast (*coffee*)
torreggiante *adj* towering
torreggiare §290 (**torréggio**) *intr* to tower
torrènte *m* torrent
torrenziale *adj* torrential
torrétta *f* turret; (nav) conning tower (*of submarine*); (archit) bartizan
tòrri·do -da *adj* torrid
torrióne *m* donjon; (nav) conning tower (*of battleship*)
torróne *m* nougat
torsióne *f* torsion
tórso *m* stalk; core (*of fruit*); torso, trunk; **a torso nudo** bare-chested
tórsolo *m* core; stalk; stem; **non vale un torsolo** it's not worth a fig
tórta *f* pie; cake, tart; **torta di mele** apple pie
tòrta *f* twist
tortièra *f* baking pan
tòr·to -ta *adj* twisted; crooked; gloomy (*face*) ‖ *m* wrong; **a torto** unjustly; **avere torto** to be wrong; **avere torto marcio** to be dead wrong; **dar torto a** to lay the blame on; **fare torto a** to wrong, e.g., **fece torto al proprio fratello** he wronged his own brother; to bring discredit upon ‖ *f* see **tòrta** ‖ **torto** *adv* askance
tórtora *f* turtledove
tortuó·so -sa [s] *adj* winding; ambiguous; (fig) devious
tortura *f* torture
torturare *tr* to torture; to pester ‖ *ref* to torment oneself; **torturarsi il cervello** to rack one's brain
tosare (tóso) *tr* to clip, crop; to shear; (fig) to fleece
tosa·tóre -trice *mf* clipper, shearer ‖ *f* clippers; lawn mower
tosatura *f* sheepshearing; clip (*of wool*)
tosca·no -na *adj* & *mf* Tuscan ‖ *m* stogy ‖ **Toscana, la** Tuscany
tósse *f* cough; **tosse asinina** or **canina** whooping cough
tòssi·co -ca (**-ci -che**) *adj* toxic ‖ *m* (archaic) poison
tossicòmane *mf* drug addict
tossicomania *f* drug addiction
tossina *f* toxin
tossire (tósso) & §176 *intr* to cough
tostapa·ne *m* (**-ne**) toaster
tostare (tòsto) *tr* to toast; to roast (*e.g., coffee*)
tò·sto -sta *adj* (lit) prompt; (lit) impudent; (lit) brazen (*face*) ‖ **tosto** *adv* (lit) soon; **ben tosto** (lit) very soon; **tosto che** (lit) as soon as
tòt *adj pl invar* so many, that many ‖ *pron invar* so much, that much
totale *adj* & *m* total
totalità·rio -ria *adj* (**-ri -rie**) total, complete; totalitarian
totalizzare [ddzz] *tr* to add up; to make (*so many points*)
totalizzatóre [ddzz] *m* pari-mutuel; betting window; (mach) totalizator
tòtano *m* squid; (orn) tattler
totocàlcio *m* soccer pool

tovàglia *f* tablecloth
tovagliòlo *m* napkin
tòz·zo -za *adj* stubby, stocky ‖ *m* piece (*of fresh bread*); crust (*of bread*)
tra *prep* among; between
trabàccolo *m* small fishing boat
traballare *intr* to shake; to totter; to wobble; to stagger; to toddle
trabìcolo *m* frame for bedwarmer; jalopy; hulk
traboccante *adj* overflowing
traboccare §197 (**trabócco**) *tr* to knock down ‖ *intr* to overflow (*said of container*) ‖ *intr* (ESSERE) to overflow (*said of liquid*) ‖ *intr* (ESSERE & AVERE) to tip (*said of scales*); **far traboccare** to make (*the scales*) tip
trabocchétto *m* pitfall; trapdoor
trabóc·co *m* (**-chi**)—**trabocco di sangue** internal hemorrhage
tracagnòt·to -ta *adj* stubby, stocky ‖ *mf* stocky person
tracannare *tr* to gulp down
tracchég·gio *m* (**-gi**) delay; (fencing) feint
tràc·cia *f* (**-ce**) track; trace, clue; trail; outline, plan; (lit) trace, row; **buona traccia** right track; **fare la traccia a** to open the way for; **in** or **sotto traccia** concealed (*e.g., wiring*); **tracce** tinge; (chem) traces
tracciante *adj* tracer (*bullet*)
tracciare §128 *tr* to trace; to pave (*the way*); to outline; (lit) to track
tracciato *m* tracing, drawing; outline; map; layout
trachèa *f* trachea, windpipe
tracòlla *f* baldric; shoulder strap; **a tracolla** slung across the shoulders
tracòllo *m* collapse, debacle
tracotanza *f* arrogance
tradiménto *m* treason; treachery; **a tradimento** unawares, unexpectedly; treacherously
tradire §176 *tr* to betray; to fail (*a person; said of memory*) ‖ *ref* to give oneself away
tradi·tóre -trice *adj* charming, seductive; treacherous; deceitful, faithless ‖ *mf* traitor; betrayer ‖ *f* traitress
tradizionale *adj* traditional
tradizióne *f* tradition
tradótta *f* military train
tradurre §102 *tr* to translate
tradut·tóre -trice *mf* translator
traduzióne *f* translation
traènte *mf* (com) drawer
trafela·to -ta *adj* breathless, out of breath
traferro *m* (elec) air gap; (elec) spark gap
trafficante *m* dealer, trader; trafficker
trafficare §197 (**tràffico**) *tr* to sell; to traffic in ‖ *intr* to trade, deal; to hustle
tràffi·co *m* (**-ci**) traffic
trafficó·ne *na mf* hustler
trafiggere §104 *tr* to pierce, stab, transfix; to wound
trafila *f* routine; red tape; (mach) drawplate
trafilare *tr* to wiredraw

trafilétto *m* (journ) short feature, special item; (journ) notice

trafitta *f* stab wound; shooting pain

trafittura *f* stab; shooting pain

traforare (**tràfóro** & **trafóro**) *tr* to bore; to pierce; to carve (*wood*); to pink (*leather*); to embroider with open work

trafóro *m* boring; tunnel; open work

trafugare §209 *tr* to purloin; to sneak off with

tragèdia *f* tragedy; **far tragedie** (coll) to make a fuss

traghettare (**traghétto**) *tr* to ferry

traghétto *m* ferry; **traghetto spaziale** space shuttle

tràgi·co -ca (**-ci -che**) *adj* tragic ‖ *m* tragedian; **il tragico** (fig) the tragic

tragitto *m* journey; (obs) ferry

traguardo *m* sight; aim; goal; finish line; (phot) viewfinder; (sports) tape

traiettòria *f* trajectory; path

tràina *f* towline; **pescare alla traina** to troll

trainare (**tràino**) *tr* to drag, tug, pull

tràino *m* drag; load; trailer

tralasciare §128 *tr* to interrupt; to omit; **non tralasciare di** to not fail to

tràl·cio *m* (**-ci**) stem (*of vine*)

tralíc·cio *m* (**-ci**) ticking, bedtick; trellis; tower (*of high-tension line*)

tralice *m*—**in tralice** askance

tralignare *intr* (ESSERE & AVERE) to degenerate

tram *m* (tram) streetcar

trama *f* woof, weft; plot (*of play*); texture (*of cloth*)

tramà·glio *m* (**-gli**) trammel net

tramandare *tr* to hand down

tramare *tr* & *intr* to weave; to plot

trambusto *m* bustle

tramestí·o *m* (**-i**) bustle, confusion

tramèzza [ddzz] *f* partition

tramezzare (**tramèzzo**) [ddzz] *tr* to interpose; to partition

tramezzino [ddzz] *m* small partition; sandwich; sandwich man

tramèzzo [ddzz] *m* partition; side dish; (sew) insertion ‖ *adv* in between; **tramezzo a** among

tràmite *m* intermediary; (lit) pass; **per tramite di** through ‖ *prep* (coll) by; by means of

tramòg·gia *f* (**-ge**) hopper

tramontana *f* north wind; **perdere la tramontana** to lose one's bearings

tramontare (**tramónto**) *intr* (ESSERE) to set (*said, e.g., of sun*); to end

tramónto *m* setting; sunset; decline

tramortire §176 *tr* to stun ‖ *intr* (ESSERE) to faint, swoon

trampolière *m* wading bird; (orn) stilt

tràmpoli *mpl* stilts

trampolino *m* diving board; springboard; ski jump; (fig) springboard

tramutare *tr* to transfer; to transform

tràn·cia *f* (**-ce**) slice; (mach) shears

tranèllo *m* trap, snare

trangugiare §290 *tr* to swallow; to gulp down

tranne *prep* except, save; **tranne che** unless

tranquillante *m* tranquilizer

tranquillare *tr* & *ref* (lit) to tranquilize; to calm down

tranquilli·tà *f* (**-tà**) tranquillity

tranquillizzare [ddzz] *tr* to tranquilize; to reassure ‖ *ref* to become reassured

tranquíl·lo -la *adj* tranquil, calm; clear (*conscience*)

transatlànti·co -ca *adj* & *m* (**-ci -che**) transatlantic

transazióne *f* compromise

transènna *f* bar, barrier

transètto *m* (archit) transept

trànsfu·ga *m* (**-ghi**) (lit) deserter

transigere §165 *tr* to settle ‖ *intr* to compromise

transistóre *m* transistor

transitàbile *adj* passable

transitare (**trànsito**) *intr* to move; to walk

transiti·vo -va *adj* transitive

trànsito *m* passage; traffic; (lit) passing; **di transito** transient

transitò·rio -ria *adj* (**-ri -rie**) temporary; transitory; transitional

transizióne *f* transition

transoceàni·co -ca *adj* (**-ci -che**) transoceanic

transòni·co -ca *adj* (**-ci -che**) transonic

transunto *m* abstract, summary (*of a document*)

trantràn *m* routine

tran·vài *m* (**-vài**) (coll) streetcar

tranvía *f* streetcar line

tranvià·rio -ria *adj* (**-ri -rie**) streetcar

tranvière *m* streetcar conductor; motorman

trapanare (**tràpano**) *tr* to drill; (surg) to trephine

tràpano *m* drill; (surg) trephine; **trapano a vite** automatic drill

trapassare *tr* to pierce; (fig) to grieve; (poet) to cross; (lit) to pass, spend ‖ *intr* (ESSERE) to go through; to pass (*said of an inheritance*); (lit) to pass away; **trapassare da, per** or **al di là di** to come through (*said, e.g., of a nail, light*)

trapassato *m* (lit) deceased; **trapassato prossimo** past perfect

trapasso *m* crossing; transfer; transition; (lit) passing, death

trapelare (**trapélo**) *intr* (ESSERE) to ooze; to trickle out; to leak through; (fig) to leak out

trapè·zio *m* (**-zi**) trapeze; (geom) trapezoid

trapezòide *adj* trapezoidal ‖ *m* trapezoid

trapiantare *tr* to transplant ‖ *ref* to transfer

trapianto *m* transplantation; transplant; **trapianto cardiaco** heart transplant

tràppola *f* trap; (coll) gadget; (fig) lie; **trappola esplosiva** booby trap

trapunta *f* quilt

trapuntare *tr* to quilt; to embroider

trapun·to -ta *adj* quilted; embroidered; studded ‖ *m* embroidery ‖ *f* see trapunta

trarre §273 *tr* to pull; to drag; to draw; to bring; to deduct; to lead; to unsheathe (*a sword*); to heave (*a sigh*); to spin (*silk, wool*, etc.); **il dado è tratto the die is cast; trarre dalla prigione** to free from prison; **trarre d'impaccio** to get (*s.o.*) out of trouble; **trarre fuori** to extract; **trarre in inganno** to deceive; **trarre in rovina** to ruin; **trarre per mano** to lead by the hand || *intr* to kick (*said of a mule*); (lit) to run; (lit) to blow (*said of the wind*) || *ref* to take off (*e.g., one's hat*); **trarsi d'impaccio** to get out of trouble; **trarsi indietro** to pull back; **trarsi in disparte** to move aside

trasalire [s] §176 *intr* (ESSERE & AVERE) to start, jump

trasanda·to -ta *adj* untidy, slovenly

trasbordare (trasbórdo) *tr* to transfer, transship

trasbórdo *m* transfer, transshipment

trascéndere §245 *tr* to transcend || *intr* (ESSERE) to go to excesses

trascinare *tr* to drag; to stir; to enthrall; to lead astray; **trascinare la vita** to barely make ends meet || *ref* to drag oneself; to drag on

trascolorare (trascolóro) *tr* to discolor; to change the color of || *intr* (ESSERE) & *ref* to discolor; to change color

trascórrere §139 *tr* to pass (*time*); to skim through (*e.g., a book*); (lit) to go through || *intr* to go to excesses || *intr* (ESSERE) to elapse, pass

trascórso *m* slip (*e.g., of pen*); peccadillo

trascrivere §250 *tr* to transcribe

trascrizióne *f* transcription; registration (*e.g., of a deed*)

trascuràbile *adj* negligible

trascurare *tr* to neglect; to fail; to disregard || *ref* to not take care of oneself

trascuratézza *f* negligence, neglect; carelessness; slovenliness

trascura·to -ta *adj* neglected; careless; slovenly

trasecolare (trasècolo) [s] *intr* (ESSERE & AVERE) to marvel, be astonished

trasferìbile *adj* transferable

trasferiménto *m* transfer; conveyance

trasferire §176 *tr* to transfer; to assign, convey || *ref* to move

trasfèrta *f* business trip; traveling expenses, per diem

trasfigurare *tr* to transfigure; to distort (*the truth*) || *ref* to be transfigured; to change countenance

trasfocatóre *m* (phot) zoom lens

trasfóndere §178 *tr* to transfuse; (fig) to instill

trasformàbile *adj* transformable; (aut) convertible

trasformare (trasfórmo) *tr* to transform; to alter || *ref* to transform oneself; to be converted

trasformati·vo -va *adj* (gram) transformational

trasformatóre *m* transformer

trasformazióne *f* transformation

trasformi·sta *mf* (-sti -ste) quick-change artist

trasfusióne *f* transfusion

trasgredire §176 *tr* & *intr* to transgress

trasgressióne *f* transgression

trasgressóre *m* transgressor

trasla·to -ta *adj* figurative; metaphorical; (lit) transferred || *m* figure of speech; metaphor

traslitterare (traslìttero) *tr* to transliterate

traslocare §197 (traslòco) *tr* to transfer; to move || *intr* & *ref* to move

traslò·co *m* (-chi) moving

traslùci·do -da *adj* translucent

trasméttere §198 *tr* to transmit; (rad) to broadcast

trasmetti·tóre -trice *mf* transmitter || *m* (naut) engine-room telegraph; (telg) sender

trasmigrare *intr* (ESSERE & AVERE) to transmigrate || *intr* (ESSERE) to pass, pass on

trasmissióne *f* transmission; conveyance; broadcast; telecast; **trasmissione del pensiero** thought transference

trasmittènte *adj* transmitting; broadcasting || *f* broadcasting station

trasmutare *tr* to transmute; to change

trasogna·to -ta [s] *adj* dreamy; daydreaming; dazed

trasparènte *adj* transparent || *m* transparency

trasparènza *f* transparence; **in trasparenza** against the light

trasparire §108 *intr* (ESSERE) to appear; to shine; to show through; to show, be revealed (*said of feelings*); **far trasparire** to reveal

traspirare *intr* to perspire || *intr* (ESSERE) to show, be revealed

traspirazióne *f* perspiration

traspórre §218 *tr* to transpose

trasportare (traspòrto) *tr* to transport; to carry away; to transfer; to translate; to postpone; (mus) to transpose; **lasciarsi trasportare** to be carried away || *ref* to move; (fig) to go back

trasporta·tóre -trice *mf* carrier || *m* (mach) conveyor belt; (phot) sprocket

traspòrto *m* transportation; transport; transfer; eagerness; moving; (mus) transposition; **trasporto funebre** funeral procession

trasposi·tóre -trice *mf* (mus) transposer

trassa·to -ta *adj* paying || *m* drawee

trastullare *tr* to amuse; to entice || *ref* to have a good time; to loiter

trastullo *m* play, game; fun; plaything

trasudare [s] *tr* to ooze; (fig) to exude || *intr* to ooze (*said of a wall*) || *intr* (ESSERE) to drip (*said of perspiration*)

trasversale *adj* transverse, cross || *f* crossroad

trasvèr·so -sa *adj* transverse || *m* transverse beam

trasvolare (trasvólo) *tr* to fly over, cross by air || *intr*—**trasvolare su** to skip over

trasvolata *f* non-stop flight

tratta *f* tug, pull; (rr) stretch; (com)

draft; (lit) crowd; **tratta dei neri** slave trade; **tratta delle bianche** white slavery

trattàbile adj negotiable; friendly, sociable

trattaménto m treatment; working conditions; food, spread; reception, welcome; **trattamento di favore** special treatment; **trattamento di quiescenza** retirement benefits

trattare tr to treat; to deal with; to transact; to wield; to play (an instrument); to work (e.g., iron); to deal in; **trattare qlcu da bugiardo** to call s.o. a liar; **trattare da cane** to treat like a dog ‖ intr to bargain; **trattare di** to deal with; to take care of; to treat, handle ‖ ref to take good care of oneself ‖ impers (ESSERE) **si tratta di** it's question of

trattà·rio -ria mf (-**ri -rie**) drawee

trattativa f negotiation

trattato m treatise; treaty

trattazióne f treatment

tratteggiare §290 (**trattéggio**) tr to sketch; to outline; to hatch

trattég·gio m (-**gi**) hatching

trattenére §271 tr to keep; to entertain; to withhold; to hold back; to detain ‖ ref to stop; to refrain; to remain

tratteniménto m entertainment, party; delay

trattenuta f withholding; checkoff

trattino m dash; hyphen

trat·to -ta adj drawn, extracted ‖ m stretch; span; passage; tract; gesture; throw (of dice); stroke (of pen); bearing; section; (chess) move; **a larghi tratti** in broad outline; **a tratti** from time to time; **a un tratto** all of a sudden; at the same time; **dare un tratto alla bilancia** to tip the scales; **tratti** features; **tratti del volto** features; **tratto di corda** strappado; **tratto di unione** hyphen; **tutto d'un tratto** all of a sudden; **un bel tratto** quite a while

trat·tóre -trice mf innkeeper; restaurateur ‖ m tractor; **trattore a cingoli** caterpillar tractor ‖ f tractor (vehicle)

trattoria f inn, restaurant

tratturo m cow path

traumatizzare [ddzz] tr to traumatize

travagliare §280 tr to torment; to molest ‖ intr & ref to toil, labor

travà·glio m (-**gli**) suffering; toil; trave (to inhibit horse being shod); **travaglio di parto** labor pains; **travaglio di stomaco** upset stomach

travasare tr to pour off; to decant; to transfer ‖ ref to spill

travaso m pouring off; transfer; **travaso di bile** gall bladder attack; **travaso di sangue** hemorrhage

travatura f roof timbers; **travatura maestra** ridgepole

trave f beam; joist; **fare una trave d'un fuscello** to make a mountain out of a molehill

travedére §279 tr to glimpse ‖ intr to be mistaken

travéggole fpl—**avere le traveggole** to see things; to see one thing for another

travèrsa f crossbar; crossroad; crosspiece; rung; bar (of goalpost); dam; rail (of fence); transom; slat (to hold bedspring); rubber pad; (rr) tie

traversare (travèrso) tr to cross

traversata f passage, crossing

traversìa f strong wind; **traversìe** misfortunes

traversina f (rr) tie

travèr·so -sa adj cross; devious ‖ m width; crossbar; (naut) beam; (naut) side; **a traverso** (naut) on the beam; **capire a traverso** to misunderstand; **di traverso** askance; crosswise; the wrong way ‖ f see **traversa**

traversóne m large crossbar; westerly gale; side blow with saber

travestiménto m disguise; travesty

travestire (travèsto) tr to disguise; to travesty, parody ‖ ref to disguise oneself

traviare §119 tr to lead astray ‖ intr & ref to go astray

travicèllo m joist

travisare tr to distort

travolgènte adj impetuous; fascinating; sweeping

travòlgere §289 tr to overwhelm; to overturn; to sweep away

trazióne f traction

tre [e] adj & pron three; **le tre** three o'clock ‖ m three; third (in dates)

trébbia f thresher; threshing

trebbiare §287 (**trébbio**) tr & intr to thresh

trebbiatrice f thresher, threshing machine

trebbiatura f threshing

tréc·cia f (-**ce**) plait; braid; **treccia a ciambella** bun, knot

trecentèsi·mo -ma adj, m & pron three hundredth

trecènto adj, m & pron three hundred ‖ **il Trecento** the fourteenth century

tredicèsi·mo -ma adj, m & pron thirteenth ‖ f Xmas bonus

trédici adj & pron thirteen; **le tredici** one P.M. ‖ m thirteen; thirteenth (in dates)

trégua f truce; respite; **tregua atomica** nuclear test ban; **senza tregua** without letup

tremare (trèmo) intr to shake, tremble; to quiver; **far tremare** to shake

tremarèlla f—**avere la tremarella** (coll) to shake in one's boots

tremebón·do -da adj (lit) shaky

tremèn·do -da adj tremendous

trementina f turpentine

tremila adj, m & pron three thousand

trèmito m trembling; quivering

tremolare (trèmolo) intr to shake; to quiver; to flicker

trèmo·lo -la adj tremulous ‖ m (bot) aspen; (mus) tremolo

trèno m train; quarter (of animal); set (of tires); threnody, lamentation; **treno accelerato** local; **treno di lusso** Pullman train; **treno direttissimo** express; **treno di vita** mode of life; mode of living; **treno merci** freight train; **treno stradale** tractor-trailer

trenodìa *f* threnody

trénta *adj & pron* thirty || *m* thirty; thirtieth (*in dates*)

trentèsi·mo -ma *adj, m & pron* thirtieth

trentina *f* about thirty

Trènto *f* Trent

trepidare (trèpido) *intr* to fear; to worry

trepidazióne *f* fear, trepidation

treppiède *m* tripod; trivet

tré·sca *f* (-sche) intrigue; liaison

tréspolo *m* stool; pedestal; stand, perch; (coll) jalopy

triàngolo *m* triangle; **triangolo rettangolo** right triangle

tribolare (trìbolo) *tr* to torment, afflict || *intr* to suffer

tribolazióne *f* tribulation, ordeal

tribórdo *m* (naut) starboard

tri·bù *f* (-bù) tribe

tribuna *f* rostrum, platform; (sports) grandstand; **tribuna stampa** press box

tribunale *m* court, tribunal; courthouse; **tribunale dei minorenni** juvenile court; **tribunale di prima istanza** court of first instance

tributare *tr* to bestow

tributà·rio -ria (-ri -rie) *adj* tributary; tax || *m* tributary

tributo *m* tribute; tax

trichè·co *m* (-chi) walrus

triciclo *m* tricycle

tricolóre *adj & m* tricolor

tricòrno *m* cocked hat, tricorn

tricromìa *f* three-color printing; three-color print

tridènte *m* trident

trifase *adj* three-phase

trifocale *adj* trifocal

trifò·glio *m* (-gli) clover; three-leaf clover

trìfola *f* (coll) truffle

trìglia *f* red mullet

trigonometrìa *f* trigonometry

trillóne *m* trillion

trillare *intr* to trill; to vibrate

trillo *m* trill; ringing

trilogìa *f* trilogy

trimestrale *adj* quarterly

trimèstre *m* quarter; quarterly dues; quarterly payment; (educ) quarter, trimester

trimotóre *m* three-engine plane

trina *f* lace

trin·ca *f* (-che) (naut) gammoning; **di trinca** clearly, cleanly; **nuovo di trinca** brand-new

trincare §197 *tr* (coll) to gulp down, swill

trincèa *f* trench

trincerare (trincèro) *tr* to dig trenches in || *ref* to entrench oneself

trincétto *m* shoemaker's blade

trinchétto *m* (naut) foremast; (naut) foresail

trinciante *adj* cutting || *m* carving knife

trinciapóllo *m* meat shears

trinciare §128 *tr* to carve; to shred; to advance (*rash opinions*); to cut up

trinciato *m* smoking tobacco

trinciatrice *f* shredder; slicer

Trinità *f* Trinity

trionfale *adj* triumphal

trionfante *adj* triumphant

trionfare (triónfo) *intr* to triumph

triónfo *m* triumph; center piece; tidbit dish with three or four tiers; trump (*in game of tarot*)

triparti·to -ta *adj* tripartite

triplicare §197 **(trìplico)** *tr & ref* to triple

trìplice *adj* threefold

tri·plo -pla *adj & m* triple

tripode *m* tripod

trippa *f* tripe; (coll) belly

tripudiare §287 *intr* to exult

tripù·dio *m* (-di) exultation

tris *m* (tris) (poker) three of a kind

trisàvola *f* great-great-grandmother

trisàvolo *m* great-great-grandfather; **trisavoli** great-great-grandparents

trisma *m* lockjaw

triste *adj* sad; gloomy, bleak

tristézza *f* sadness

tri·sto -sta *adj* wicked; wretched; poor (*figure*); (lit) sad

tritacar·ne *m* (-ne) meat grinder

tritaghiàc·cio *m* (-cio) ice crusher

tritare *tr* to chop; to grind; to mince, hash; to pound

tri·to -ta *adj* minced, hashed; worn, trite

tritòlo *m* T.N.T.

tritóne *m* (zool) newt; (fig) merman || **Tritone** *m* Triton

trìtti·co *m* (-ci) triptych; export document in triplicate; trilogy

trittòn·go *m* (-ghi) triphthong

triturare *tr* to mince, hash

trivèlla *f* auger, drill; post-hole digger

trivellare (trivèllo) *tr* to drill, bore

triviale *adj* vulgar

trivialì·tà *f* (-tà) vulgarity

trì·vio *m* (-vi) crossroads; trivium; **da trivio** vulgar

trofèo *m* trophy; (mil) insignia (*on headpiece*)

trògolo *m* trough

tròia *f* sow; slut || **Troia** *f* Troy

troia·no -na *adj & m* Trojan

trómba *f* trumpet; bugle, clarion; trunk (*of elephant*); leg (*of boot*); (anat) tube; (aut, rad) horn; **con le trombe nel sacco** crestfallen, dejected; **tromba d'aria** whirlwind; tornado; **tromba marina** waterspout; **tromba delle scale** stairwell

trombétta *f* trumpet

trombettière *m* (mil) trumpeter

trombetti·sta *m* (-sti) trumpet player

trombóne *m* trombone; blunderbuss

trombò·si *f* (-si) thrombosis

troncare §197 **(trónco)** *tr* to chop; to cut off; to clip (*words*); to break, sever; to block (*s.o.'s progress*); to apocopate

tronchése [s] *m* wire cutter

trón·co -ca (-chi -che) *adj* truncate; oxytone; apocopated; exhausted, dead-tired; incomplete; **in tronco** in the middle; (*dismissal*) on the spot || *m* trunk; stub (*of receipt book*);

section (*of highway*); log; strain (*of a family*); (rr) branch; **tronco di cono** truncated cone; **tronco maggiore** (naut) lower mast

troncóne *m* stump

troneggiare §290 (tronéggio) *intr* to tower; to hold forth; **troneggiare su** to lord it over

trón·fio -fia *adj* (-fi -fie) haughty; bombastic

tròno *m* throne

tropicale *adj* tropical

tròpi·co *m* (-ci) tropic

troposfèra *f* troposphere

tròp·po -pa *adj & pron* too much; **trop·pi -pe** too many ‖ *m* too much; **questo è troppo!** enough is enough! ‖ **troppo** *adv* too; too much; **essere di troppo** to be in the way

tròta *f* trout

trottare (tròtto) *intr* to trot

trotterellare (trotterèllo) *intr* to trot along; to toddle

tròtto *m* trot; **piccolo trotto** jog trot

tròttola *f* top

trovare (tròvo) *tr* to find; to visit; **trovare a** or **da ridire** (su) to find fault (with); **trovi?** don't you think so? ‖ *ref* to find oneself; to meet; to be; to be located; to happen, e.g., **mi trovai a passare di fronte a casa sua** I happened to pass in front of his house

trovarò·be *m* (-be) (theat) property man ‖ *f* (theat) dresser

trovata *f* find; trick, gimmick

trovatèl·lo -la *mf* foundling, waif

trovatóre *m* troubadour

trovièro *m* trouvère

truccare §197 *tr* to make up; to falsify; (aut) to soup up ‖ *ref* to put on make-up

truccatura *f* make-up; trick, gimmick

truc·co *m* (-chi) make-up; trick, gimmick

truce *adj* fierce, cruel; menacing

trucidare (trùcido) *tr* to massacre

trùciolo *m* chip, shaving

truculènto *adj* truculent

truffa *f* cheat, fraud, swindle; **truffa all'americana** confidence game

truffare *tr* to cheat, swindle

truffa·tóre -trice *mf* cheat, swindler

truismo *m* truism

truògolo *m* var of **trogolo**

truppa *f* troop; soldiers; **di truppa** (mil) enlisted (*man or woman*); **in truppa** in a flock

tu §5 *pron pers*; **a tu per tu** face to face; **dare del tu a** to address in the familiar form

tuba *f* tuba; (hist) horn, trumpet; (joc) top hat, stovepipe; (anat) tube

tubare *intr* to coo

tubatura *f* piping, tubing; pipe, tube; pipeline

tubazióne *f* tubes, pipes

tubèrcolo *m* tubercle

tubercolosà·rio [s] *m* (-ri) tuberculosis sanitarium

tubercolò·si *f* (-si) tuberculosis

tubercoló·so -sa [s] *adj* tuberculous ‖ *mf* T.B. patient

tùbero *m* tuber

tubétto *m* tube (*for pills or toothpaste*); spool

tubíno *m* small tube; derby (hat)

tubo *m* tube; pipe; (anat) canal, duct; **a tubo** tubular; **tubo di scarico** exhaust pipe; **tubo di troppopieno** overflow; **tubo di ventilazione** air shaft

tubolare *adj* tubular ‖ *m* tire (*for racing bicycle*)

tuffare *tr* to dip; to plunge ‖ *ref* to plunge; to dive

tuffa·tóre -trice *mf* diver ‖ *m* dive bomber

tuffétto *m* (orn) dabchick, grebe

tuffo *m* dive; plunge; throb; **a tuffo** (aer) diving; **scendere a tuffo** (aer) to dive; **tuffo ad angelo** (sports) swan dive; **tuffo d'acqua** downpour

tufo *m* tufa

tu·ga *f* (-ghe) (naut) deckhouse

tugù·rio *m* (-ri) hovel

tulipano *m* tulip

tumefare §173 *tr & ref* to swell

tumefazióne *f* swelling

tùmi·do -da *adj* tumid

tumóre *m* tumor

tùmulo *m* tomb; tumulus

tumulto *m* tumult, riot; commotion

tumultuó·so -sa [s] *adj* tumultuous

tungstèno *m* tungsten

tùni·ca *f* (-che) tunic

Tùnisi *f* Tunis

Tunisìa, la Tunisia

tunisi·no -na *adj & mf* Tunisian

tuo tua §6 *adj & pron poss* (**tuòi tue**)

tuòno *m* thunder

tuòrlo *m* yolk

turàcciolo *m* cork, stopper

turare *tr* to plug, stop; to cork

turba *f* crowd; mob; (pathol) upset

turbaménto *m* commotion, perturbation; disturbance, breach (*of law and order*)

turbante *m* turban

turbare *tr* to muddy; to disturb; to upset ‖ *ref* to become cloudy; to become upset

turba·to -ta *adj* upset; disturbed; distracted

tùrbi·do -da *adj* turbid

turbina *f* turbine

turbinare (tùrbino) *tr* to separate in a centrifuge ‖ *intr* to whirl

tùrbine *m* whirlwind; swarm; tumult

turbinó·so -sa [s] *adj* whirling; tumultuous

turboèli·ca *m* (-ca) turboprop

turbogètto *m* turbojet

turbolèn·to -ta *adj* turbulent

turbolènza *f* turbulence

turbomotrice *f* (rr) turbine engine

turboreattóre *m* turbojet

turcasso *m* quiver

turchése [s] *m* turquoise

Turchìa, la Turkey

turchinétto *m* bluing

turchi·no -na *adj* dark-blue ‖ *m* dark blue

tur·co -ca (-chi -che) *adj* Turkish; **sedere alla turca** to sit cross-legged ‖ *mf* Turk ‖ *m* Turkish (*language*); **bestemmiare come un turco** to swear like a trooper; **fumare come un turco** to smoke like a steam engine

tùrgi·do -da *adj* turgid

turibolo *m* thurible, censer

turismo *m* tourism

turi·sta *mf* (-sti -ste) tourist

turìsti·co -ca *adj* (-ci -che) tourist; travel (e.g., bureau); traveler's (check)

turlupinare *tr* to hoodwink, swindle

turlupinatura *f* swindle, confidence game

turno *m* turn; shift; **a turno** in turn; **di turno** on duty; **fare a turno** to take turns

turpe *adj* base, abject; (lit) ugly

turpilò·quio *m* (-qui) foul language

turpitùdine *f* turpitude

tuta *f* overalls; **tuta antigravità** anti-G suit; **tuta da bambini** jumpers; **tuta spaziale** spacesuit

tutèla *f* guardianship; defense, protection

tutelare *adj* tutelary ‖ *v* (**tutèlo**) *tr* to protect, defend

tùtolo *m* corncob

tu·tóre -trice *mf* guardian; protector

tuttavìa *adv* yet, nevertheless; (lit) always, continuously

tut·to -ta *adj* whole; all; full; **con tutto** in spite of, e.g., **con tutto quello che ho fatto per lui** in spite of all I have done for him; **del tutto** fully, completely; **è tutt'uno** it's all the same; **tutt'altro** completely different; on the contrary; **tutt'altro che** anything but; **tutti** every, e.g., **tutti gli scolari** every pupil; **tutti e due** both ‖ *m* everything; whole; **con tutto che** although; **fare di tutto** to do everything possible; **in tutto** altogether ‖ *pron* **tut·ti -te** all, everybody (of a group); **tutti** everybody ‖ **tutto** *adv* quite; **tutt'a un tratto** all of a sudden; **tutto al contrario** quite the opposite

tuttofa·re *adj invar* of all trades; of all work ‖ *m* factotum, jack-of-all-trades ‖ *f* (-re) maid of all work

tuttóra *adv* yet, still

tzìga·no -na *adj* & *mf* var of **zigano**

U

U, u [u] *m* & *f* nineteenth letter of the Italian alphabet

ubbìa *f* prejudice, bias; complex; whim

ubbidiènte *adj* obedient

ubbidire §176 *tr* to obey ‖ *intr* to obey; to respond (said of a car); (with dat) to obey, e.g., **gli ubbedì** he obeyed him

ubertó·so -sa [s] *adj* fruitful; fertile

ubicazióne *f* location

ubiquità *f* ubiquity; **non ho il dono dell'ubiquità** I can't be everywhere at the same time

ubì·quo -qua *adj* ubiquitous

ubriacare §197 *tr* to make drunk, intoxicate ‖ *ref* to get drunk

ubriacatura or **ubriachézza** *f* drunkenness, intoxication

ubrìa·co -ca (-chi -che) *adj* drunk; **ubriaco fradicio** dead drunk ‖ *mf* drunkard

ubriacó·ne -na *mf* drunkard

uccellare (**uccèllo**) *tr* to take in, cajole ‖ *intr* to snare; to fowl; to hunt birds

uccèllo *m* bird; **uccello di bosco** fugitive; **uccello di galera** gallows bird; **uccello di passo** bird of passage

uccella·tóre -trice *mf* live-bird catcher

uccellièra *f* aviary; large birdcage

uccìdere §274 *tr* to kill ‖ *ref* to kill oneself; to get killed; to kill one another

-àccio -àccia (-ucci -ucce) *suf adj* not very, e.g., **calduccio** not very hot; rather, e.g., **magruccio** rather thin; poor little, e.g., **caruccio** poor little darling ‖ *suf m* & *f* small e.g., **cappelluccio** small hat

uccisióne *f* killing; murder

ucci·so -sa *adj* killed ‖ *mf* victim

ucci·sóre -dìtrice *mf* killer

ucraì·no -na *adj* & *mf* Ukrainian ‖ **l'Ucraina** *f* the Ukraine

udìbile *adj* audible

udiènza *f* audience; hearing; **l'udienza è aperta!** the court is now in session!

udire §275 *tr* to hear; to listen to

udìto *m* hearing

uditòfono *m* hearing aid

udi·tóre -trice *adj* hearing ‖ *mf* (educ) auditor ‖ *m* magistrate

uditò·rio -ria (-ri -rie) *adj* auditory ‖ *m* audience

ufficiale *adj* official ‖ *m* official; officer; **primo ufficiale** (naut) first officer, mate; **ufficiale di giornata** (mil) officer of the day; **ufficiale di rotta** (aer, naut) navigator; **ufficiale giudiziario** clerk of the court; process server, bailiff; **ufficiale medico** (mil) medical officer

ufficiare §128 *tr* to officiate

uffì·cio *m* (-ci) duty; office; bureau; department (of agency); ex-officio; public, e.g., **avvocato d'ufficio** public defender; **ufficio di collocamento** placement bureau; **ufficio di compensazione** clearing house; **uffìcio d'igiene** board of health

uffició·so -sa [s] *adj* unofficial; kindly; white (lie)

uffì·zio *m* (-zi) (eccl) office

ufo *m*—**a ufo** gratis, without paying

ugèllo *m* nozzle

ùg·gia *f* (-ge) darkness; gloom; dislike; **avere in uggia** to dislike

uggiolare (**ùggiolo**) *intr* to whine (said of a dog)

uggió·so -sa [s] *adj* gloomy; boring

ugnare *tr* to bevel; to miter

ugnatura *f* bevel; miter
ùgola *f* uvula; **bagnarsi l'ugola** (coll) to wet one's whistle
ugonòtto *m* Huguenot
uguaglianza *f* equality
uguagliare §280 *tr* to equal; to make equal; to equalize; to level; to compare || *ref* to compare oneself; to be equal; to be compared
uguale *adj* equal; same; even; level; **per me è uguale** it's the same to me || *m* equal; (math) equal sign
ùlcera *f* ulcer; sore
ulcerare (**ùlcero**) *tr* & *ref* to ulcerate
uliva *f* var of **oliva**
ulterióre *adj* further, subsequent, ulterior
ùltima *f* latest news; last straw
ultimare (**ùltimo**) *tr* to complete, finish
ultimato *m* ultimatum
ultimissima *f* latest edition (*of newspaper*); **ultimissime** late news
ùlti·mo·ma *adj* last; final; latest; latter; farthest; ultimate; least; top (*floor*); **all'ultimo, dall'ultimo, nell'ultimo** or **sull'ultimo** lately; finally, at the end || *f* see **ultima**
ultimogèni·to -ta *adj* last-born || *mf* last-born child
ultra- *pref adj* and *m* & *f* ultra-, e.g., **ultraelevato** ultrahigh; super-, e.g., **ultrasonico** supersonic (*speed*)
ultracór·to -ta *adj* ultrashort
ultraròs·so -sa *adj* & *m* infrared
ultraterré·no -na *adj* ultramundane; unearthly
ultraviolét·to -ta *adj* & *m* ultraviolet
ululare (**ùlulo**) *intr* to howl
ululato *m* howl
umanésimo *m* humanism
umani·sta *mf* (-**sti** -**ste**) humanist
umani·tà *f* (-**tà**) humanity; **umanità** *fpl* humanities
umanità·rio -ria *adj* & *mf* (-**ri** -**rie**) humanitarian
uma·no -na *adj* human; humane || *m* human nature; **umani** human beings
um·bro -bra *adj* & *m* Umbrian
umettare (**umétto**) *tr* to moisten, dampen
umidìc·cio -cia *adj* (-**ci** -**ce**) dampish
umidi·tà *f* (-**tà**) humidity, dampness
ùmi·do -da *adj* humid, damp || *m* humidity, dampness; **in umido** stewed (*e.g., meat*)
ùmile *adj* humble || **gli umili** *mpl* the meek
umiliare §287 *tr* to humiliate, humble || *ref* to humble oneself
umiliazióne *f* humiliation
umiltà *f* humility
umóre *m* humor, mood, temper; whim; (bot) sap; **un bell'umore** (coll) quite a character
umorismo *m* humor
umori·sta *mf* (-**sti** -**ste**) humorist
umorìsti·co -ca *adj* (-**ci** -**che**) humorous; amusing, comic, funny
un (apocopated form of **uno**) §9 *indef art* a, an || §9 *numeral adj* one || §12 *reciprocal indef pron*—**l'un l'altro** each other, one another

unànime *adj* unanimous
unanimità *f* unanimity
unàni·mo -ma *adj* unanimous
uncinare *tr* to hook, grapple
uncinétto *m* small hook; crochet hook
uncino *m* hook; grapnel; clasp; pothook; (fig) pretext; **a uncino** hooked
undicèsi·mo -ma *adj*, *m* & *pron* eleventh
ùndici *adj* & *pron* eleven; **le undici** eleven o'clock || *m* eleven; eleventh (*in dates*); (soccer) squad
ùngere §183 *tr* to grease; to oil; to smear; to anoint; to flatter || *ref* to smear oneself
Ungherìa, l' *f* Hungary
ungherése [s] *adj* & *mf* Hungarian
ànghia *f* nail; fingernail; claw; hoof; fluke (*of anchor*); (fig) hairbreadth; **avere le unghie lunghe** to be lightfingered; **unghia del piede** toenail; **unghie** (fig) clutches
unghiata *f* nail scratch
unguènto *m* unguent, ointment
ùni·co -ca *adj* (-**ci** -**che**) only, sole; unique; single (*copy*); complete (*text*) || *f*—**l'unica** the only solution
unicòrno *m* unicorn
unificare §197 (**unìfico**) *tr* to unify; to standardize
unificazióne *f* unification; standardization
uniformare (**unifórmo**) *tr* to make uniform, standardize || *ref*—**uniformarsi a** to conform to; to comply with
unifórme *adj* uniform; standard || *f* uniform; **alta uniforme** (mil) full dress
unilaterale *adj* unilateral
unióne *f* union; agreement; **unione libera** free love
unire §176 *tr* & *ref* to unite
unìsono [s] *m* unison; **all'unisono** in unison
uni·tà *f* (-**tà**) unity; unit; **unità di misura** unit of measurement
unità·rio -ria (-**ri** -**rie**) *adj* unit (*e.g., price*); united || *m* Unitarian
uni·to -ta *adj* united; joined; compact; plain (*color*); consolidated
universale *adj* universal; last (*judgment*)
universi·tà *f* (-**tà**) university
università·rio -ria (-**ri** -**rie**) *adj* university; college || *mf* university or college student; university or college professor
univer·so -sa *adj* universal || *m* universe
unno *m* Hun
u·no -na §9 *indef art* a, an || §9 *numeral adj* one || *m* one || §10 *pron indef* one; **le una, la una**, or **l'una** one o'clock; **l'uno e l'altro** both; **l'uno o l'altro** either, either one; **per uno** in single file; **uno per uno** one by one; each other || §11 *correlative pron* one
un·to -ta *adj* greasy || *m* grease, fat; flattery; anointed one
untuosità [s] *f* greasiness; unction, unctuousness
untuó·so -sa [s] *adj* greasy; unctuous

unzióne *f* unction

uò·mo *m* (**-mini**) man; **come un sol uomo** to a man; **uomo d'affari** businessman; **uomo del giorno** man of the hour; **uomo della strada** man of the street; **uomo di chiesa** churchman; **uomo di fatica** laborer; **uomo di fiducia** trusted man; **uomo di mare** seaman; **uomo di paglia** straw man; **uomo di parola** man of his word; **uomo in mare!** man overboard!; **uomo meccanico** automaton; **uomo morto** (rr) deadman brake; **uomo nuovo** nouveau riche; **uomo rana** frogman

uòpo *m*—**all'uopo** if need be; **essere d'uopo** (lit) to be necessary

uòse [s] *fpl* leggings

uò·vo *m* (**-va** *fpl*) egg; **meglio un uovo oggi che una gallina domani** a bird in a hand is worth two in the bush; **rompere le uova nel paniere a qlcu** to spoil s.o.'s plans; **uovo affogato** poached egg; **uovo alla coque** soft-boiled egg; **uovo all'occhio di bue** fried egg; **uovo da tè** tea ball; **uovo strapazzato** scrambled egg

uragano *m* hurricane; storm (*of applause*); **uragano di neve** blizzard

Urali *mpl* Ural Mountains

uranìfe·ro -ra *adj* uranium-bearing

urànio *m* uranium

urbanésimo *m* urbanization, migration toward the cities

urbanìsti·co -ca (**-ci -che**) *adj* city-planning ‖ *f* city planning

urbani·tà *f* (**-tà**) urbanity, civility; city population

urbanizzare [ddzz] *tr* to urbanize

urba·no -na *adj* urban; urbane

urètra *f* urethra

urgènte *adj* urgent, pressing

urgènza *f* urgency; **d'urgenza** urgent; emergency (*e.g., operation*); **fare urgenza a** to urge

ùrgere §276 *tr* to urge, press ‖ *intr* to be urgent

urina *f* urine

urinà·rio -ria *adj* (**-ri -rie**) urinary

urlare *tr* to shout; to shout down ‖ *intr* to howl; to shout, yell

urla·tóre -trice *adj* screaming ‖ *mf* screamer; loud singer

ur·lo *m* howl ‖ *m* (**-la** *fpl*) yell, scream

urna *f* urn; ballot box; (poet) grave; **urne** polls

-uro *suf m* (chem) -ide, e.g., **cloruro** chloride

urologìa *f* urology

urrà *interj* hurrah!

ursóne *m* Canada porcupine

urtare *tr* to hit; to bump; to annoy ‖ *intr*—**urtare contro** to hit, strike against; **urtare in** to hit; to stumble into ‖ *ref* to get annoyed; to clash; to bump into one another

urto *m* hit; bump; collision; onslaught; clash, disagreement; **urto di nervi** huff

Uruguai, l' *m* Uruguay

uruguaia·no -na *adj & mf* Uruguayan

usanza *f* usage, custom; habit, practice

usare *tr* to use, employ; to wear out; (lit) to frequent; **usare** + *inf* to be accustomed to + *ger* ‖ *intr* to be fashionable; **usare di** to use, employ ‖ *ref* to become accustomed; **si usa** + *inf* it is customary to + *inf*

usa·to -ta *adj* used, second-hand; worn; worn-out; (lit) usual ‖ *m* usage, custom; norm; second-hand goods

usbèr·go *m* (**-ghi**) hauberk; (fig) shield, protection

uscènte *adj* ending, terminating; retiring

uscière *m* receptionist; office boy, errand boy; (coll) court clerk; (coll) bailiff; (coll) tipstaff

ù·scio *m* (**-sci**) door; **infilar l'uscio** to take French leave; **metter tra l'uscio e il muro** (fig) to corner

uscire §277 *intr* (ESSERE) to go out, leave; to come out; to flow out; to escape; to turn out, ensue; **essere uscito** to be out; **uscire da** to leave; to run off (*the track*); **uscire dai gangheri** to get mad; **uscire dal comune** to be out of the ordinary; **uscire dal segno** to go too far; **uscire dal seminato** to go astray; **uscire di mente** a to escape one's mind, e.g., **gli è uscito di mente** it escaped his mind; **uscire di sentimento** to pass out; **uscire di vita** to die; **uscire in** to lead into; **uscire per il rotto della cuffia** to barely make it

uscita *f* exit; outlay; quip, sally; gate (*e.g., in an airport*); (gram) ending; **all'uscita** on the way out; **buona uscita** severance pay; bonus; **libera uscita** day off (*of servant*); (mil) pass; **uscita di sicurezza** emergency exit

usignòlo *m* nightingale

u·so -sa *adj* (lit) accustomed ‖ *m* practice; usage; use; wear; faculty; power (*e.g., of hearing*); (lit) intimate relations; **all'uso di** in the fashion of; **avere per uso di** to be wont to; **come d'uso** as usual; **farci l'uso** to get used to it!; **fuori d'uso** worn-out, out of commission; **uso esterno!** (pharm) not to be taken internally!

ustionare (**ustióno**) *tr* to burn, scorch

ustióne *f* burn

usuale *adj* usual; ordinary, common

usufruire §176 *intr*—**usufruire di** to have the use of; to enjoy

usura *f* usury; (mach) wear and tear; **ad usura** abundantly

usu·ràio -ràia (**-rài -ràie**) *adj* usurious ‖ *mf* usurer, loanshark

usurpare *tr* to usurp

utensile *adj* tool, e.g., **macchina utensile** machine tool ‖ *m* utensil; tool

utènte *m* user; customer, consumer

ùtero *m* uterus, womb

ùtile *adj* useful; usable; workable; legal, prescribed (*e.g., time*); **essere utile a** to help; **venire utile** to come in handy ‖ *m* usefulness; profit, gain

utili·tà *f* (**-tà**) utility, usefulness; profit, gain

utilitària *f* economy car, compact

utilizzare [ddzz] *tr* to utilize

utopìa *f* utopia
utopì·sta *mf* (-stì -ste) utopian
utopìsti·co -ca *adj* (-ci -che) utopian
uva *f* grapes; **un grano di uva passa a raisin; uva passa raisins**

uxorici·da *m* (-di) uxoricide ‖ *f* (-de) murderer of one's husband
uxorici·dio *m* (-di) uxoricide; murder of one's husband
ùzzolo [ddzz] *m* whim, fancy, caprice

V

V, v [vu] *m & f* twentieth letter of the Italian alphabet
V. *abbr* (vostro) your
vacante *adj* vacant
vacanza *f* vacancy; vacation; **fare vacanza** to be on vacation; **vacanze** vacation
vacanzière *m* vacationer
vac·ca *f* (-che) cow
vac·càio *m* (-cài) cowboy; stable boy
vaccheria *f* dairy farm
vacchétta *f* cowhide
vaccina *f* cow manure; cow
vaccinare *tr* to vaccinate
vaccinazióne *f* vaccination
vacci·no -na *adj* cow; bovine ‖ *m* vaccine ‖ *f* see **vaccina**
vacillante *adj* vacillating
vacillare *intr* to totter; to vacillate; to shake; to flicker; to fail, e.g., **la memoria gli vacilla** his memory is failing; **far vacillare** to rock
vacui·tà *f* (-tà) vacuity
và·cuo -cua *adj* empty ‖ *m* vacuum
vademè·cum *m* (-cum) almanac, ready-reference handbook
vagabondàg·gio *m* (-gi) vagrancy; wandering; rambling
vagabondare (vagabóndo) *intr* to wander, rove
vagabón·do -da *adj* wandering; vagabond ‖ *mf* vagrant, bum; tramp; rover
vagare §209 *intr* to wander, ramble, rove
vagheggiare §290 (vaghéggio) *tr* to gaze fondly at; to cherish
vagire §176 *intr* to cry, whimper
vagito *m* cry, whimper
và·glia *m* (-glia) money order ‖ *f—di* **vaglia** worthy, capable
vagliare §280 *tr* to sift, bolt
và·glio *m* (-gli) sieve; **mettere al vaglio** to scrutinize
va·go -ga (-ghi -ghe) *adj* vague; vacant (stare); (lit) beautiful; (lit) roving; (poet) desirous ‖ *m* vagueness; (lit) rover; (anat) vagus
vagonata *f* carload
vagóne *m* (rr) car; **vagone frigorifero** (rr) refrigerator car; **vagone letto** (rr) sleeping car, sleeper; **vagone ristorante** (rr) dining car; **vagone volante** (aer) flying boxcar
vàio vàia (vài vàie) *adj* dark-grey ‖ *m* dark grey; (heral) vair; (zool) Siberian squirrel
vaiòlo *m* smallpox
valan·ga *f* (-ghe) avalanche
valènte *adj* capable, skillful; clever
valentìa *f* skill; cleverness

valentino *m* Valentine (sweetheart)
valènza *f* (chem) valence
valére §278 *tr* to win, get (e.g., an honor for s.o.); **che vale?** what's the use?; **valere la pena** to be worthwhile; **valere un Perù** to be worth a king's ransom ‖ *intr* (ESSERE & AVERE) to be worth; to be of avail; to be valid; to mean; to be the equivalent; **far valere** to enforce; **farsi valere** to assert oneself; **tanto vale** it's all the same; **vale a dire** that is to say; **valere meglio** to be better ‖ *ref—***valersi di** to avail oneself of; to play on; to employ
valévole *adj* valid, good
valicare §197 (vàlico) *tr* to cross, pass
vàli·co *m* (-chi) mountain pass; passage; opening (in a hedge)
validi·tà *f* (-tà) validity
vàli·do -da *adj* valid; able, able-bodied; strong
valigeria *f* luggage; luggage store
valigétta *f* valise; **valigetta diplomatica** attaché case
vali·gia *f* (-ge) suitcase; traveling bag; **fare le valige** to pack one's bags; **valigia diplomatica** diplomatic pouch; attaché case; **valigia per abiti** suit carrier
valiata *f* valley
valle *f* valley; **a valle** downhill; downstream
vallétta *f* (telv) assistant
vallétto *m* valet; page; (telv) assistant
valló·ne -na *adj & mf* Walloon ‖ *m* narrow valley
valóre *m* value; valor, bravery; force; (fig) jewel; (math) variable; **mettere in valore** to raise the value of; **valore di mercato** market value; **valore facciale** face value; **valore locativo** rental value; **valori** valuables; securities; **valori mobiliari** securities
valorizzare [ddzz] *tr* to enhance the value of
valoró·so -sa [s] *adj* brave, valiant
valuta *f* currency; (com) effective date; (com) value (of promissory note)
valutare *tr* to estimate, appraise; to value, prize; to count, reckon; to take into consideration
valutazióne *f* estimation, appraisal; evaluation
valva *f* (bot, zool) valve
vàlvola *f* (anat, mach) valve; (elec) fuse; (rad, telv) tube, valve; **valvola a galleggiante** ball cock; **valvola di sicurezza** safety valve; **valvola in testa** overhead valve
vàl·zer *m* (-zer) waltz

vamp f (vamp) vamp
vampa f flame; blaze; flash; flush
vampata f burst (of heat); blast (of hot air); flash, flush
vampiro m vampire
vanàdio m vanadium
vanaglòria f vainglory, boastfulness
vanaglorió·so -sa [s] adj vainglorious
vandalismo m vandalism
vànda·lo -la adj & m vandal || **Vandalo** m Vandal
vaneggiare §290 (vanéggio) intr to rave; to be delirious; (lit) to open, yawn
vanè·sio -sia adj (-si -sie) vain
van·ga f (-ghe) spade
vangare §209 tr to spade up; to dig with a spade
vangelo m gospel || **Vangelo** m Gospel
vanghétto m spud
vaniglia f vanilla
vanilò·quio m (-qui) empty talk
vani·tà f (-tà) vanity
vanitó·so -sa [s] adj vain, conceited
va·no -na adj vain; (lit) empty, hollow; **in vano** in vain || m empty space; room
vantàg·gio m (-gi) advantage; profit; odds, handicap; discount; (coll) extra; (typ) galley; **a vantaggio di** on behalf of
vantaggió·so -sa [s] adj advantageous
vantare tr to boast of; to set up (a claim) || ref to boast; **vantarsi di** to brag about, vaunt
vanteria f brag, boast, vaunt
vanto m brag, boast; **aver vanto su** (lit) to overcome
vànvera f—**a vanvera** at random
vapóre m vapor; steam; locomotive; steamship; **a tutto vapore** at full speed
vaporétto m small river boat; vaporetto (in Venice)
vaporizzare [ddzz] tr to vaporize; to spray || intr (ESSERE) & ref to evaporate
vaporizzatóre [ddzz] m vaporizer; sprayer
vaporó·so -sa [s] adj vaporous
varaménto m assemblage (of prefab pieces)
varano m monitor lizard
varare tr to launch; to pass (a law); (coll) to back, promote (a candidate)
varcare §197 tr to cross || intr (poet) to pass (said of time)
var·co m (-chi) opening; mountain pass; breach; **attendere al varco** to lie in wait for; **cogliere al varco** to catch unawares; **fare varco in** to breach
varechina f (laundry) bleach
variàbile adj & f variable
variante f variant; detour; (aut) model
variare §287 tr & intr (ESSERE & AVERE) to vary
variazióne f variation
varicèlla f chicken pox
varicó·so -sa [s] adj varicose
varlega·to -ta adj variegated
varie·tà m (-tà) (theat) vaudeville || f variety

và·rio -ria (-ri -rie) adj varied; various; variable; different; **va·ri -rie** several || m variety || **varie** fpl miscellanies || **va·ri -rie** pron indef several
variopin·to -ta adj multicolored
varo m (naut) launch
vas m (vas) subchaser
va·sàio m (-sài) pott
va·sca f (-sche) tub, basin; pool; **vasca da bagno** bathtub; **vasca dei pesci** aquarium; **vasca navale** (naut) basin
vascèllo m vessel, ship
vaselina or **vasellina** f vaseline
vasellame m dishes; set of dishes; **vasellame da cucina** kitchen ware; **vasellame d'argento** silverware; **vasellame di porcellana** chinaware
vasèllo m (lit) vessel
vasi·stas [s] m (-stas) transom
vaso m vase; vessel; jar, pot; nave (of church); hall (of building); (naut) shipway; (poet) cup; **vasi vinari** wine containers; **vaso da fiori** flowerpot; **vaso da notte** chamber pot; **vaso d'elezione** (eccl) chosen vessel (viz., Saint Paul)
vassallo m vassal; (obs) helper
vas·sóio m (-sói) tray; mortarboard
vasti·tà f (-tà) vastness
va·sto -sta adj spacious; vast; (fig) deep
vate m (lit) prophet, poet
vatica·no -na adj Vatican || **Vaticano** m Vatican
vaticinare (vatìcino & vaticìno) tr to prophesy
vatici·nio m (-ni) prophecy
ve §5 pron
V.E. abbr (Vostra Eccellenza) Your Excellency
vècchia f old woman
vecchiàia f old age
vecchiézza f old age
vèc·chio -chia (-chi -chie) adj old; elder; **vecchio come il cucco** as old as the hills || m old man; **vecchi** old people; **vecchio del mestiere** old hand || f see **vecchia**
véc·cia f (-ce) vetch
véce f stead, e.g., **in vece mia** in my stead; (lit) vicissitude; **fare le veci di** to act for or as
vedére m seeing; looks; view, opinion || §279 tr to see; to review; to look over; **chi s'è visto s'è visto!** good-by and good luck!; **dare a vedere** to make believe; **stare a vedere** to watch; observe; **non poter vedere** to not be able to stand; **non vedere l'ora di** to be hardly able to wait for; **vedere male** qlcu to be ill-disposed toward s.o. || intr—**stare a vedere** to wait and see; **vederci bene** to see (e.g., in the dark); **vederci chiaro** to look into it; **vedere di** to try to || ref to see oneself; to see each other; **vedersela brutta** to anticipate trouble
vedétta f lookout; (nav) vedette
védova f widow
vedovanza f widowhood
vedovile adj widow's; widower's || m dower

védo·vo -va adj widowed ‖ m widower ‖ f see **vedova**

veduta f view; (lit) eyesight; **di corte vedute** narrowminded; **di larghe vedute** broadminded

veemènte adj vehement; violent; impassioned

veemènza f vehemence; violence

vegetale adj vegetable ‖ m plant, vegetable

vegetare (vègeto) intr to vegetate

vegetaria·no -na adj & mf vegetarian

vegetazióne f vegetation

vège·to -ta adj vigorous, spry

veggènte adj (obs) seeing ‖ mf fortuneteller ‖ m seer, prophet; **i veggenti** people having eyesight ‖ f seeress, prophetess

véglia f vigil, watch; wakefulness; evening party, soirée; party, crowd; **a veglia** unbelievable (tale); **veglia danzante** dance; **veglia funebre** wake

vegliardo m old man

vegliare §280 (véglio) tr to keep watch over ‖ intr to stay awake; to keep watch; to stay up

veglióne m masked ball

veìcolo m vehicle; carrier (of disease)

véla f sail; sailing; **alzare le vele** to set sail; **ammainare le vele** to take in sail; **a vela** under sail; **far vela** to set sail; **vela aurica** lugsail; **vela bermudiana** or **Marconi** jib; **vela maestra** mainsail

ve·làio m (-lài) sailmaker

velare adj & f (phonet) velar ‖ v (vélo) tr to veil; to cover; to muffle (sound); to attenuate, reduce (a shock); to dim, cloud; to conceal; (phot) to fog ‖ ref to cover oneself with a veil; to take the veil; to get dim, e.g., **gli si è velata la vista** his eyesight got dim

velà·rio m (-ri) (hist) velarium; (theat) curtain

vela·to -ta adj veiled; sheer (hosiery)

velatura f coating; (aer) airfoil; (naut) sails

veleggiare §290 (veléggio) tr (lit) to sail over (the sea) ‖ intr to sail; (aer) to glide

veleggiatóre m sailboat; (aer) glider

veléno m poison; (fig) venom

velenó·so -sa [s] adj poisonous; (fig) venomous

velétta f veil; (naut) topgallant

vèli·co -ca adj (-ci -che) sail, sailing

velièro m sailing ship

veli·no -na adj thin (paper) ‖ f carbon copy; onionskin; slant (given to a news item)

velìvo·lo -la adj (lit) gliding; (lit) sailing ‖ m (lit) airplane, aircraft

velleì·tà f (-tà) wild ambition, dream

vellicare §197 (vèllico) tr to tickle

vèllo m (lit) fleece; **vello d'oro** Golden Fleece

velló·so -sa [s] adj hairy

velluta·to -ta adj velvety

vellutino m thin velvet; velvet ribbon; **vellutino di cotone** velveteen

vellu·to -ta adj (lit) hairy ‖ m velvet; **velluto a coste** corduroy

vélo m veil; coating; film; skin (e.g., of onion); (anat, bot) velum; (fig) body; **fare velo a** to becloud; to fog

velóce adj speedy, quick, fast; fleeting

velocipedastro m poor or reckless bicycle rider

veloci·sta mf (-sti -ste) (sports) sprinter

veloci·tà f (-tà) velocity; speed; (aut) speed; **a grande velocità** by express; **a piccola velocità** by freight; **velocità di crociera** cruising speed; **velocità di fuga** (rok) escape velocity

velòdromo m bicycle ring or track

véna f vein; grain (in wood or stone); mood; streak (of madness); **di vena** willingly; **essere in vena di** to be in the mood to

venale adj venal

venare (véno) tr to vein

vena·to -ta adj veined; streaked; suffused; **venato di sangue** bloodshot

venatura f veining; (fig) streak

vendémmia f vintage

vendemmiare §287 (vendémmio) tr to harvest (grapes) ‖ intr to gather grapes; (fig) to make a killing

vendemmia·tóre -trice mf vintager

véndere §281 tr to sell; **da vendere** plenty, more than enough; **vendere allo scoperto** (fin) to sell short; **vendere fumo** to peddle influence ‖ intr to sell; **vendere allo scoperto** (fin) to sell short ‖ ref to sell; **si vende** for sale

vendétta f vengeance; revenge; **gridare vendetta** to cry out for retribution

vendicare §197 (véndico) tr to avenge ‖ ref to get revenge

vendicati·vo -va adj vengeful, vindictive

vendica·tóre -trice adj avenging ‖ mf avenger

vendifu·mo mf (-mo) influence peddler

véndita f sale; shop; **in vendita** for sale; **vendita allo scoperto** (fin) short sale; **vendita per corrispondenza** catalogue sale

vendi·tóre -trice mf seller; clerk (in store) ‖ m salesman; **venditore ambulante** peddler; **venditore di fumo** influence peddler ‖ f saleslady

venefì·cio m (-ci) poisoning

venèfi·co -ca (-ci -che) adj poisonous; unhealthy ‖ m (lit) poisonmaker

veneràbile or **venerando** adj venerable

venerare (vènero) tr to venerate, revere; to worship

venerazióne f (veneration); worship

vener·dì m (-dì) Friday ‖ **Venerdì Santo** Good Friday

Vènere m (astr) Venus ‖ f (mythol & fig) Venus

venè·reo -rea adj (-rei -ree) venereal

Venèzia f Venice; Venetia (province)

venezia·no -na adj & mf Venetian ‖ f Venetian blind

venezola·no -na adj & mf Venezuelan

vènia f (lit) forgiveness, pardon

venire §282 intr (ESSERE) to come; to turn out (well or badly); to turn out to be; **che viene** next, e.g., **il mese che viene** next month; **come viene** as it is; **far venire** to send for; to give, cause; **un va e vieni** a backward-and-forward motion; **venire + ger** to keep + ger; **venire + pp** to be + pp, e.g., **il portone viene aperto alle tre** the gate is opened at three; **venire a capo di** to solve; **venire ai ferri corti** to come into open conflict; **venire al dunque** or **al fatto** to come to the point; **venire alle corte** to get down to brass tacks; **venire alle mani** or **alle prese** to come to blows; **venire a parole** to have words; **venire a patti con** to come to terms with; **venire a proposito** to come in handy; **venire incontro a** to go to meet; **venire in possesso di** to come into possession of (s.th.); to come into the hands of (s.o.); **venire meno** to faint; **venir meno a** to fail to keep (one's word); **venir su** to grow, come up; **venire via** to give way || ref—**venirsene** to stroll along || impers (with dat)—**viene da** feel the urge to, e.g., **gli venne da starnutire** he felt the urge to sneeze; **gli è venuto da ridere** he felt the urge to laugh; **viene detto** blurt out, e.g., **gli è venuto detto che non gli piaceva quel tipo** he blurted out that he did not like that fellow; **viene fatto di**+inf succeed in+ger, e.g., **le venne fatto di convincerli** she succeeded in convincing them; happen to + inf, e.g., **gli venne fatto di incontrarmi per istrada** he happened to meet me on the way

ventà·glio m (-gli) fan; (fig) spread; **a ventaglio** fanlike; **diramarsi a ventaglio** to fan out

ventaròla f weather vane

ventata f gust of wind; (fig) wave

ventènne adj twenty-year-old || mf twenty-year-old person

ventèsi·mo -ma adj, m & pron twentieth

vénti adj & pron twenty; **le venti** eight P.M. || m twenty; twentieth (in dates)

ventídue adj & pron twenty-two **le ventidue** ten P.M. || m twenty-two; twenty-second (in dates)

ventilare (**vèntilo**) tr to air, ventilate; to winnow (grain); to discuss minutely; to air (a subject); to broach (a subject); to unfurl (a flag) || ref to fan oneself

ventilatóre m fan, ventilator, vent; (min) ventilation shaft; (naut) funnel

ventilazióne f ventilation; winnowing

ventina f score; **una ventina (di)** twenty, about twenty

ventino m twenty-cent coin

ventiquattro adj & pron twenty-four; **le ventiquattro** twelve P.M. || m twenty-four; twenty-fourth (in dates)

ventiquattró·re f (-re) overnight bag; twenty-four-hour race; **ventiquattrore** fpl period of twenty-four hours

ventitré adj & pron twenty-three; **le ventitré** eleven P.M.; **portare il cappello alle ventitré** to wear one's hat cocked || m twenty-three; twenty-third (in dates)

vènto m wind; air; guy wire; **presentarsi al vento** to sail into the wind; **farsi vento** to fan oneself; **a vento** windproof; wind-propelled; **col vento in prora** downwind; **col vento in poppa** upwind; favorably, famously

vèntola f fireside fan; lampshade; candle sconce; blade (of fan)

ventó·so -sa [s] adj windy || f cupping glass; suction cup; (zool) sucker

vèntre m belly; **a ventre a terra** on one's belly; on one's face; at full speed (said of a horse)

ventrìcolo m ventricle

ventrièra f abdominal band or belt

ventrilòquia f ventriloquism

ventrìlo·quo -qua mf ventriloquist

ventuno adj & pron twenty-one; **le ventuno** nine P.M. || m twenty-one; twenty-first (in dates); (cards) blackjack

ventu·ro -ra adj next || f (lit) luck, fortune; (lit) good fortune; **alla ventura** at random, at a venture; **di ventura** of fortune, e.g., **soldato di ventura** soldier of fortune

venustà f (lit) pulchritude

venu·to -ta mf—**nuovo venuto** newcomer; **primo venuto** firstcomer || f coming, arrival

véra f curbstone (of well); (coll) wedding ring

verace adj true; truthful, veracious

veraci·tà f (-tà) veracity, truthfulness

veranda f veranda; porch

verbale adj verbal || m minutes; ticket (given by a policeman); **mettere a verbale** to enter into the record

verbèna f verbena

vèrbo m verb; (lit) word || **Verbo** m (theol) Word

verbosità [s] f verbiage, verbosity

verbó·so -sa [s] adj windy, longwinded, verbose

verda·stro -stra adj greenish

vérde adj green; young, youthful || m green; **al verde** (coll) broke, penniless; **nel verde degli anni** in the prime of life

verdeggiante adj verdant

verderame m blue vitriol; verdigris

verdé·to -ta adj greenish || m verdict

verdógno·lo -la adj greenish; sallow (face)

verdura f vegetables

verecóndia f modesty, bashfulness

verecón·do -da adj modest, bashful

vér·ga f (-ghe) switch; rod; ingot, bar; pole; penis; (eccl) staff, crosier; (naut) yard; **tremare a verga a verga** to shake like a leaf

vergare §209 (**vérgo**) tr to switch; to rule (paper); to stripe; to write

vergati·no -na adj thin (paper) || m striped cloth

verga·to -ta adj striped; watermarked with stripes || m (obs) serge

verginale adj maidenly, virginal

vérgine adj & f virgin || **Vergine** f (eccl) Virgin; (astr) Virgo

verginità f virginity, maidenhood

vergógna f shame; **aver vergogna** to be

ashamed; **vergogne** privates || *interj* for shame!

vergognare (vergógno) *ref* to be ashamed; to feel cheap; **vergognati!** shame on you!

vergognó·so -sa [s] *adj* ashamed; bashful; shameful

veridici·tà *f* (-**tà**) veracity

verídi·co -ca *adj* (-**ci -che**) veracious

verifi·ca *f* (-**che**) verification; control; **verifica fiscale** auditing (*of tax return*)

verificare §197 (verífico) *tr* to verify; to control, check; to audit || *ref* to come true; to happen

verifica·tóre -trice *mf* checker, inspector

verismo *m* verism (*as developed in Italy*)

veri·sta *adj* & *mf* (-**sti -ste**) verist

veri·tà *f* (-**tà**) truth; **in verità** truthfully, verily

veritiè·ro -ra *adj* truthful

vèrme *m* worm; (mach) thread; **verme solitario** tapeworm

vermi·glio -glia (-**gli -glie**) *adj* vermilion; ruby (*lips*) || *m* vermilion

vèr·mut *m* (-**mut**) vermouth

vernàcolo *m* vernacular

vernice *f* varnish; paint; polish; patina; (painting) private viewing; (fig) veneer; **scarpe di vernice** patent-leather shoes; **vernice a olio** oil paint; **vernice a spruzzo** spray paint; **vernice da scarpe** shoe polish

verniciare §128 *tr* to varnish; to paint

vé·ro -ra *adj* true; real; right; pure; **non è vero?** isn't that so? La traduzione precedente è generalmente rimpiazzata da molte altre frasi. Se la prima espressione è negativa, la domanda equivalente a **non è vero?** sarà affermativa, per esempio, **Lei non lavora, non è vero?** You are not working, are you? Se la prima espressione è affermativa, la domanda sarà negativa, per esempio, **Lei lavora, non è vero?** You are working, are you not? or aren't you? Se la prima espressione contiene un ausiliare, la domanda conterrà l'ausiliare stesso senza infinito o senza participio passato, per esempio, **Arriveranno domani, non è vero?** They will arrive tomorrow, won't they? **Ha finito il compito, non è vero?** He has finished his homework, hasn't he? Se la prima espressione non contiene né un ausiliare, né una delle forme del verbo "to be" in funzione di copula, la domanda conterrà l'ausiliare "do" o "did" senza l'infinito del verbo, per esempio, **Lei è vissuto a Milano, non è vero?** You lived in Milano, did you not? **Lei non va mai al parco, non è vero?** You never go to the park, do you?; **non mi par vero** it seems unbelievable || *m* truth; actuality; **a dire il vero** to tell the truth, as a matter of fact; **dal vero** from nature; **salvo il vero** if I am not mistaken || *f* see **vera**

veróne *m* (lit) balcony

verosimiglianza *f* verisimilitude; probability, likelihood

verosìmile *adj* verisimilar; probable, likely

verricèllo *m* winch, windlass

vèrro *m* boar

verru·ca *f* (-**che**) wart

versaménto *m* spilling; payment; deposit

versante *m* depositor; slope, side

versare (vèrso) *tr* to pour; to spill; to shed; to pay; to deposit || *intr* to overflow; **versare in gravi condizioni** to be in a bad way || *ref* to spill; to pour (*said of people*); to empty (*said of a river*)

versàtile *adj* versatile; fickle

versa·to -ta *adj* versed; gifted; fully subscribed to (e.g., stock of a corporation)

verseggia·tóre -trice *mf* verse writer

versétto *m* verse (*of Bible*)

versificare §197 (versífico) *tr* & *intr* to versify

versificazióne *f* versification

versióne *f* version; translation

vèrso *adj invar*—**pollice verso** (hist) thumbs down || *m* verse; local accent; voice, cry; reverse (*of coin*); verso (*of page*); line (*of poetry*); singsong; gesture; direction, way, manner; respect; **andare a verso** (with *dat*) to suit, e.g., **le sue maniere non gli vanno a verso** her manners do not suit him; **a verso** properly; **contro verso** against the grain; **fare un verso** to make faces; **per un verso** on one hand; **rifare il verso** (with *dat*) to mimick; **senza verso** without rhyme or reason; **verso sciolto** blank verse || *prep* toward; near, around; about; for, toward; upon, in return for; as compared with; **verso di** toward

vèrtebra *f* vertebra

vertebrale *adj* vertebral; spinal

vertebra·to -ta *adj* & *m* vertebrate

vertènza *f* quarrel, dispute; **vertenza sindacale** labor dispute

vèrtere §283 *intr*—**vertere su** to deal with, to turn on

verticale *adj* & *f* vertical

vèrtice *m* top, summit; vertex; summit conference

vertìgine *f* vertigo, dizziness; **avere le vertigini** to feel dizzy

vertiginó·so -sa [s] *adj* dizzy; breathtaking

vérza [dz] *f* cabbage

verzière [dz] *m* (lit) fruit, vegetable, and flower garden; (coll) produce market

verzura [dz] *f* verdure

vesci·ca *f* (-**che**) bladder; blister; **vescica di vento** (fig) windbag; **vescica gonfiata** swellhead; **vescica natatoria** air bladder

vescichétta *f* blister; vescicle; **vescichetta biliare** gall bladder

vescìcola *f* blister

vescovado *m* bishopric

véscovo *m* bishop

vè·spa *f* wasp, yellowjacket ‖ *f* (-spe & -spa) motor scooter

ve·spàio *m* (-spài) wasp's nest; (fig) hornet's nest

vespasiano *m* public urinal

Vèspero *m* Vesper

vesperti·no -na *adj* (lit) evening

vèspro *m* (eccl) vespers; (lit) vespertide

vessare (vèsso) *tr* (lit) to oppress

vessatò·rio -ria *adj* (-ri -rie) vexatious

vessazióne *f* oppression

vessillo *m* flag

vestàglia *f* negligee, dressing gown; **vestaglia da bagno** bathrobe

vèste *f* dress; cover; (lit) body; **in veste di** in the quality of; as; in the guise of; **veste da camera** negligee, dressing gown; bathrobe; **veste talare** (eccl) long vestment; **vesti** clothes

vestià·rio *m* (-ri) wardrobe

vestìbolo *m* vestibule, lobby

vestì·gio *m* (-gi & -gia *fpl*) vestige, trace; (lit) footprint

vestire (vèsto) *tr* to dress; to don; to wear; to clothe; to cover, bedeck ‖ *intr* to dress; to fit ‖ *ref* to get dressed; to dress; to dress oneself; to buy one's own clothes

vestì·to -ta *adj* dressed; covered ‖ *m* dress; suit; clothing; **vestiti** clothes; **vestito da donna** dress; **vestito da festa** Sunday best; **vestito da sera** evening clothes, formal suit; evening gown; **vestito da uomo** suit

Vesùvio, il Vesuvius

vetera·no -na *adj* & *mf* veteran

veterinà·rio -ria (-ri -rie) *adj* veterinary ‖ *m* veterinarian ‖ *f* veterinary medicine

vèto *m* veto; **porre il veto a** to veto

ve·tràio *m* (-trài) glass manufacturer; glass dealer; glass blower

vetra·to -ta *adj* glass, glass-enclosed; sand (*paper*) ‖ *m* glare ice, glaze ‖ *f* glass door; glass window; glass enclosure; **vetrata a colori** or **vetrata istoriata** stained-glass window

vetrerìa *f* glassworks; **vetrerie** glassware

vetria·to -ta *adj* glassy; glass-covered

vetrificare §197 (vetrìfico) *tr* to vitrify ‖ *ref* to become vitrified

vetrina *f* show window; showcase, glass cabinet; **mettersi in vetrina** to show off; **vetrine** (coll) eyeglasses

vetrini·sta *mf* (-sti -ste) window dresser

vetri·no -na *adj* glass-like; brittle, fragile ‖ *m* slide (*of microscope*) ‖ *f* see **vetrina**

vetriòlo *m* vitriol

vétro *m* glass; glassware; window pane; piece of glass; **vetro aderente** contact lens; **vetro infrangibile** (aut) safety glass; **vetro smerigliato** ground glass, frosted glass

vetrorèsina *f* fiberglass

vetró·so -sa [s] *adj* vitreous, glassy

vétta *f* peak; top, tip; limb (*of tree*); (naut) end (*of hawser*); **tremare come una vetta** to shake like a leaf

vet·tóre -trice *adj* leading, guiding; spreading, carrying ‖ *m* carrier; (math, phys) vector

vettovagliare §280 *tr* to supply with food

vettovàglie *fpl* victuals, food; supplies

vettura *f* forwarding; coach; car; freight; in vettura! (rr) all aboard!; **prendere in vettura** to hire (*a conveyance*); **vettura belvedere** (rr) observation car; **vettura da turismo** (aut) pleasure car; **vettura di piazza** hack, hackney; **vettura letto** (rr) sleeping car; **vettura ristorante** (rr) diner

vetturétta *f* economy car, compact

vetturino *m* hackman, cab driver

vetu·sto -sta *adj* old, ancient

vezzeggiare §290 (vezzéggio) *tr* to coddle ‖ *intr* (lit) to strut

vezzeggiatì·vo -va *adj* endearing ‖ *m* endearing expression; diminutive

vézzo *m* habit; caress; necklace; bad habit; **vezzi** fondling, petting; mawkish behavior; charms

vezzó·so -sa [s] *adj* graceful, charming; affected, mincing

vi §5

via *m* (via) starting signal; **dare il via a** to give the go-ahead to ‖ *f* street; road, way; route; career; **dare la via a** to open the way to; **in via confidenziale** in confidence; **in via eccezionale** as an exception; **per via di** via, through; (coll) because of; **per via gerarchica** through administrative channels; **per via orale** orally; **per via rettale** rectally; **prendere la via** to be on one's way; **venire a vie di fatto** to come to blows; **Via Crucis** Way of the Cross; **via d'acqua** waterway; **via di scampo** (fig) way out; **via d'uscita** way out; **Via Lattea** Milky Way; **vie di fatto** assault and battery; **vie legali** legal steps ‖ *adv* away; (math) times, by; **e così via** and so on; **e via dicendo** and so on; **tirar via** to hurry along; **via via che** as ‖ *prep* via, by way of

viadótto *m* viaduct

viaggiare §290 *intr* to travel; (com) to deal

viaggia·tóre -trice *adj* traveling; homing (*pigeon*) ‖ *mf* traveler ‖ *m* traveling salesman

viàg·gio *m* (-gi) travel; journey, trip; **buon viaggio!** bon voyage!; **viaggio d'andata e ritorno** round trip; **viaggio di prova** (naut) trial run, shakedown cruise

viale *m* boulevard

viandante *mf* (lit) wayfarer

vià·rio -ria *adj* (-ri -rie) road, highway

viàti·co *m* (-ci) viaticum

viavài *m* coming and going; hustle and bustle

vibrante *adj* vibrant; wiry; (phonet) vibrant ‖ *f* (phonet) trill, vibrant

vibrare *tr* to jar; to deliver (*a blow*); to vibrate; (lit) to hurl ‖ *intr* to vibrate

vibra·to -ta *adj* vibrant; resolute, vigorous ‖ *m* vibrating sound

vibrazióne *f* vibration

vicariato *m* vicarage

vicà·rio *m* (-ri) vicar

vice- *pref adj* vice-, e.g., **vicereale** viceroyal || *pref m & f* vice-, e.g., **viceammiraglio** vice-admiral; assistant, e.g., **vicegovernatore** assistant governor; deputy, e.g., **vicesindaco** deputy mayor

vicediret·tóre -trice *mf* assistant manager

vicènda *f* vicissitude; rotation (*of crops*); **a vicenda** in turn

vicendévole *adj* mutual, reciprocal

vicepresidènte [s] *mf* vice president

vice·ré *m* (-ré) viceroy

vicevèrsa *adv* vice versa; (coll) instead, on the contrary

vichin·go -ga *adj & mf* (-ghi -ghe) Viking

vicinanza *f* nearness; **in vicinanza di** in the neighborhood of; **vicinanze** vicinity, neighborhood

vicinato *m* neighborhood

vici·no -na *adj* near; neighboring; next; close (*relative*) || *mf* neighbor || **vicino** *adv* nearby, near; **da vicino** closely; at close quarters; **vicino a** near; next to, close to

vicissitùdine *f* vicissitude

vi·co *m* (-chi) alley, lane; village; (lit) region

vìcolo *m* alley, court, place; **vicolo cieco** blind alley, dead end

videocassétta *f* video cassette

vidimare (**vìdimo**) *tr* to validate, visa; to sign

vidimazióne *f* validation, visa; signature

viennése [s] *adj & mf* Viennese

viepiù *adv* (lit) more and more

vietare (**vièto**) *tr* to forbid, prohibit

vieta·to -ta *adj* forbidden; **senso vietato** one way; **sosta vietata** no parking; no stopping; **vietato fumare** no smoking

Vietnam, il Vietnam

vietnami·ta *adj & mf* (-ti -te) Vietnamese

viè·to -ta *adj* (lit) old-fashioned; (coll) musty-smelling, rancid

vigènte *adj* current, in force

vìgere §284 *intr* to be in force

vigèsi·mo -ma *adj* twentieth

vigilante *adj* watchful, vigilant || *m* watchman

vigilanza *f* vigilance; surveillance

vigilare (**vigilo**) *tr* to watch; to watch over; to police || *intr* to watch; **vigilare che** to see to it that

vigila·tóre -trice *mf* inspector || *f* camp counselor; **vigilatrice sanitaria** child health inspector

vìgile *adj* (lit) watchful || *m* watch; **vigile del fuoco** fireman; **vigile urbano** policeman

vigìlia *f* fast; vigil; **la vigilia di** on the eve of, the night before

vigliacchería *f* cowardice

vigliac·co -ca (-chi -che) *adj* cowardly || *m* coward

vigna *f* vineyard

vignaiòlo *m* vine dresser

vignéto *m* vineyard

vignétta *f* vignette; **vignetta umoristica** cartoon

vignetti·sta *mf* (-sti -ste) cartoonist

vigógna *f* vicuña

vigóre *m* vigor; **in vigore** in force

vigoría *f* vigor

vigoró·so -sa [s] *adj* vigorous

vile *adj* cowardly; vile, low, cheap; base (*metal*)

vilificare §197 (**vilifico**) *tr* to vilify

vilipèndere §148 *tr* to despise; to show scorn for

villa *f* villa; country house; one-family detached house; (lit) country

villàg·gio *m* (-gi) village; **villaggio del fanciullo** boys' town

villanata *f* boorishness

villanía *f* boorishness, rudeness; insult

villa·no -na *adj* rude, churlish || *mf* boor, churl; (lit) peasant

villanzó·ne -na *mf* boor, uncouth person

villeggiante *mf* vacationist

villeggiare §290 (**villéggio**) *intr* to vacation

villeggiatura *f* vacation, summer vacation

villétta *f* or **villino** *m* bungalow

villó·so -sa [s] *adj* hairy

vil·tà *f* (-tà) baseness; cowardice

viluppo *m* tangle, twist

vìmine *m* withe, wicker, osier

vinàcce *fpl* pressed grapes

vi·nàio *m* (-nài) wine merchant

vincènte *adj* winning || *mf* winner

vincere §285 *tr* to overcome; to win; to convince; to check; to defeat; **vincere per un pelo** to nose out; **vincerla** to come out on top || *ref* to control oneself

vincetòssi·co -co *m* (-ci) swallowwort, tame poison

vincipèr·di *m* (-di) giveaway

vìncita *f* gain; winnings

vinci·tóre -trice *adj* conquering, victorious || *mf* winner; conqueror; victor

vincolare *adj* binding; bound || *v* (**vìncolo**) *tr* to tie; to bind, obligate; to restrict the use of (*real-estate property*)

vìncolo *m* tie, bond; (law) entail; (law) restriction (*in a real-estate deed*)

vinìco·lo -la *adj* wine, wine-producing

vinile *m* vinyl

vino *m* wine; **vin caldo** mulled wine; **vino da pasto** table wine; **vino di marca** vintage wine; **vino di mele** cider

vin·to -ta *adj* vanquished, overcome, defeated; victorious (*battle*); **averla vinta su** to overcome; **darla vinta a** qlcu to let s.o. get away with murder; **darsi per vinto** to give in, yield || *m* vanquished person; **i vinti** the vanquished

viò·la *adj invar* violet || *m* (-la) violet (*color*) || *f* violet; (mus) viola; **viola del pensiero** pansy; **viola mammola** sweet violet

violacciòc·ca *f* (-che) (bot) wallflower

violà·ceo -cea *adj* violet

violare (**vìolo**) *tr* to violate; to run (*a blockade*)

violazióne *f* violation; **violazione di**

domicilio housebreaking, burglary; **violazione di proprietà** trespass

violentare (violènto) *tr* to violate, force; to do violence to; to rape

violèn·to -ta *adj* violent ‖ *m* violent person

violènza *f* violence; **violenza carnale** rape

violét·to -ta *adj & m* violet ‖ *f* (bot) violet

violini·sta *mf* (-sti -ste) violinist

violino *m* violin; **primo violino** concertmaster

violoncelli·sta *mf* (-sti -ste) violoncellist

violoncèllo *m* violoncello, cello

viòttolo *m* path

vipera *f* viper, adder

viràg·gio *m* (-gi) turn; (aer) banking; (naut) tacking; (phot) toning

virare *tr* to veer; to turn (*a winch*); (aer) to bank; (phot) to tone ‖ *intr* to veer, steer; **virare di bordo** (naut) to put about; (naut) to tack

virata *f* turn, veer; (aer) banking; (naut) tacking

virginale *adj* var of **verginale**

virgi·nia *m* (-nia) Virginia tobacco ‖ *f* (-nia) Virginia cigarette

virgola *f* comma; (*used in Italian to set off the decimal fraction from the integer*) decimal point; **doppia virgola** quotation mark

virgolétta *f* quotation mark

virgulto *m* (lit) shoot; (lit) shrub

virile *adj* virile

virilità *f* virility

viròla *f* (mach) male piece

virologia *f* virology

vir·tù *f* (-tù) virtue; (lit) valor

virtuale *adj* virtual

virtualménte *adv* virtually, to all intents and purposes

virtuosismo [s] *m* virtuosity; showing off

virtuosità [s] *f* virtuosity

virtuó·so -sa [s] *adj* virtuous ‖ *mf* virtuoso

virulèn·to -ta *adj* virulent

virulènza *f* virulence

vi·rus *m* (-rus) virus

visce·re *m* (-ri) internal organ; **visceri** entrails, viscera ‖ **viscere** *fpl* entrails, viscera; (fig) heart, feeling; (fig) bowels (*of the earth*)

vi·schio *m* (-schi) mistletoe; birdlime; (fig) trap

vischió·so -sa [s] *adj* sticky, viscous; (com) steady

visci·do -da *adj* viscid; clammy; (fig) unctuous

visciola *f* sour cherry

visciolo *m* sour cherry tree

viscónte *m* viscount

viscontéssa *f* viscountess

viscó·so -sa [s] *adj* viscous, sticky ‖ *f* viscose

visétto *m* small face; baby face

visìbile *adj* visible; obvious

visibì·lio *m* (-li) (coll) crowd; (coll) bunch; **andare in visibilio** to become ecstatic; **mandare in visibilio** to throw into ecstasy, enrapture

visibilità *f* visibility

visièra *f* visor; fencing mask; eyeshade; **visiera termica** (aut) electric defroster

visigò·to -ta *adj* Visigothic ‖ *mf* Visigoth

visionà·rio -ria *adj & mf* (-ri -rie) visionary

visióne *f* vision; sight; (mov, telv) showing; **in visione gratuita** for free examination; **mandare qlco a qlcu in visione** to send s.th to s.o. for his (or her) opinion; **prendere visione di** to examine; to peruse

vi·sìr *m* (-sìr) vizier

vìsita *f* visit; visitation; **fare una visita** to pay a visit; **marcare visita** (mil) to report sick; **visita doganale** customs inspection

visitare (vìsito) *tr* to visit; to inspect

visita·tóre -trice *mf* visitor ‖ *f* social worker

visitazióne *f* visitation

visi·vo -va *adj* visual

viso *m* face; **far buon viso a cattivo gioco** to grin and bear it

visóne *m* mink

visóre *m* (phot) viewer; (phot) viewfinder

vi·spo -spa *adj* brisk, lively

vissu·to -ta *adj* wordly-wise

vista *f* sight, eyesight; view; vista; glance; (poet) window; **a vista** exposed, visible; **a vista d'occhio** as far as the eye can see; **essere in vista** to be expected; to be imminent; to be in the limelight; **far vista di** to pretend to; **in vista di** in view of; **mettere in vista** to show off; **vista a volo d'uccello** bird's-eye view; **vista corta** poor eyesight

vistare *tr* to validate, visa

vi·sto -sta *adj*—**visto che** seeing that, inasmuch as ‖ *m* visa; approval ‖ *f* see **vista**

vistó·so -sa [s] *adj* showy, flashy; (fig) considerable

visuale *adj* visual ‖ *f* view; line of sight

visualizzare [ddzz] *tr* to visualize

vita *f* life; livelihood; living; waist; **avere breve vita** to be short-lived; **fare la vita** to be a prostitute; **vita natural durante** for life; during one's lifetime

vitaiòlo *m* man about town; playboy, bon vivant

vitale *adj* vital

vitalità *f* vitality

vitali·zio -zia (-zi -zie) *adj* life, life-time ‖ *m* life annuity

vitamina *f* vitamin

vite *f* (bot) grapevine; (mach) screw; **a vite** threaded; (aer) in a tailspin; **vite autofilettante** self-tapping screw; **vite del Canadà** woodbine, Virginia creeper; **vite per legno** wood screw; **vite per metallo** machine screw; **vite perpetua** (mach) endless screw, worm gear; **vite prigioniera** stud bolt

vitèllo *m* calf; veal

vitic·cio *m* (-ci) tendril

vìtre·o -a *adj* vitreous; glassy (*eyes*)

vittima *f* victim

vitto *m* food; diet; **vitto e alloggio** room and board

vittòria *f* victory; **cantar vittoria** to crow; to crow too soon

vittorió·so -sa [s] *adj* victorious

vituperare (vitùpero) *tr* to vituperate

vituperévole *adj* contemptible, shameful

vitupè·rio *m* (-ri) shame, infamy; insult; (lit) blame

viuzza *f* narrow street, lane

viva *interj* long live!

vivacchiare §287 *intr* (coll) to get along ‖ *ref*—**si vivacchia** (coll) so, so

vivace *adj* lively, brisk; brilliant; vivacious

vivacità *f* liveliness, briskness; brilliancy, brightness; vivacity

vivaddìo *interj* yes, of course!; by Jove!

vivagno *m* selvage; edge

vi·vàio *m* (-vài) fishpond; fish tank; tree nursery; (fig) seedbed

vivanda *f* food

vivandiè·re -ra *mf* (mil) sutler

vìvere *m* life; living; cost of living; **viveri** food, provisions; allowance ‖ §286 *tr* to live; **vivere un brutto momento** to spend an uncomfortable moment ‖ *intr* (ESSERE) to live; **vive** (typ) stet; **vivere alla giornata** to live from hand to mouth

vivézza *f* liveliness

vìvi·do -da *adj* vivid, lively

vivificare §197 (vivìfico) *tr* to vivify

vivisezionare (vivisezióno) *tr* to vivisect; to scrutinize

vivisezióne *f* vivisection

vì·vo -va *adj* alive; living; live, vivacious; lively; vivid; high (*flame*); bright (*light*); raw (*flesh*); sharp, acute (*pain*); hearty (*thanks*); outright (*expense*); gross (*weight*); brute (*strength*); modern (*language*); kinetic (*energy*); running (*water*) ‖ *m* living being; heart (*of a question*); **al vivo** lively; lifelike; **i vivi e i morti** the quick and the dead; **toccare nel vivo** to sting to the quick ‖ **viva** *interj* see **viva**

viziare §287 *tr* to spoil; to ruin; (law) to vitiate ‖ *ref* to become spoiled

vizia·to -ta *adj* spoiled; ruined; stale (*air*)

vì·zio *m* (-zi) vice; defect; flaw; (law) vitiation

vizió·so -sa [s] *adj* vicious; defective ‖ *mf* profligate

viz·zo -za *adj* withered

vocabolà·rio *m* (-ri) dictionary; vocabulary

vocàbolo *m* word

vocale *adj* vocal; (lit) sonorous ‖ *f* vowel

vocalizzare [ddzz] *tr & ref* to vocalize

vocativo *m* vocative

vocazióne *f* vocation

vóce *f* voice; noise, roar; word; rumor; entry; tone; **ad alta voce** aloud; **a bassa voce** in a low voice; **a viva voce** by word of mouth; **a voce** orally; **dare una voce a** (coll) to call; **dare sulla voce a** to rebuke; to con-tradict; **fare la voce grossa** to raise one's voice; **non avere voce in capitolo** to have no say; **schiarirsi la voce** to clear one's throat; **senza voce** hoarse; **sotto voce** in a low tone; **voce bianca** child's voice (*in singing*)

vociare *m* bawl ‖ §128 (vócio) *intr* to bawl

vociferare (vocìfero) *intr* to vociferate, shout ‖ *ref*—**si vocifera** it is rumored

vó·ga *f* (-ghe) fashion, vogue; energy, enthusiasm; rowing

vogare §209 (vógo) *tr & intr* to row

voga·tóre -trice *mf* rower ‖ *m* oarsman; rowing machine

vòglia *f* wish; whim, fancy; willingness; birthmark; **aver voglia di** to feel like, have a notion to; **di buona voglia** willingly; **di mala voglia** unwillingly

voglió·so -sa [s] *adj* fanciful; (lit) desirous

vói §5 *pron pers* you; **voi altri** you, e.g., **voi altri americani** you Americans

voialtri -tre *pron pl* you, e.g., **voialtri americani** you Americans

volano *m* shuttlecock; (mach) flywheel

volante *adj* flying; loose (*sheet*); free (*agent*) ‖ *m* steering wheel; (mach) hand wheel; shuttlecock

volantino *m* leaflet; fringe; (mach) hand wheel

volare (vólo) *tr* (soccer) to overthrow ‖ *intr* (ESSERE & AVERE) to fly

volata *f* flight; sprint; run; mouth (*of gun*); (tennis) volley; **di volata in a** hurry

volàtile *adj* volatile; flying (*animal*) ‖ **volatili** *mpl* birds

volatilizzare [ddzz] *tr & intr* (ESSERE) to volatilize

volènte *adj*—**Dio volente** God willing; **volente o nolente** willy-nilly

volentièri *adv* gladly, willingly

volére *m* will, wish; **al volere di** at the bidding of ‖ §288 *tr* to will; to want, desire; (lit) to believe, affirm; **l'hai voluto tu** it's your fault; **non vuol dire!** never mind!; **qui ti voglio** here's the rub, that's the trouble; **senza volere** without meaning to; **voglia Dio!** may God grant!; **voler bene** (with *dat*) to like; **volerci** to take, e.g., **ci vorranno due anni per finire questo palazzo** it will take two years to complete this building; **ce ne vogliono ancora tre** it takes three more of them; **voler dire** to mean; to try, e.g., **vuole piovere** it is trying to rain; **volere che** + *subj* to want + *inf*, e.g., **vuole che vengano** he wants them to come; **volere piuttosto** to prefer; **volere è potere** where there is a will there is a way; **voler male** (with *dat*) to dislike; **volerne a** to bear a grudge against; **vorrei** I should like, I'd like; **vuoi . . . vuoi** either . . . or

volgare *adj* vernacular, popular, common; vulgar ‖ *m* vernacular

volgari·tà *f* (-tà) vulgarity

volgarizzare [ddzz] *tr* to popularize

vòlgere §289 *tr* to turn; (lit) to translate ‖ *intr* to turn; (lit) to go by; volgere a to turn toward; to draw near, to approach; volgere in fuga to take to flight ‖ *ref* to turn; to devote oneself

vól·go *m* (-ghi) (lit) crowd, mob

volièra *f* aviary

voliti·vo -va *adj* volitional; strong-minded, strong-willed

vólo *m* flight; fall; al volo on the spot; on the wing; a volo d'uccello as the crow flies; bird's-eye (*e.g.*, *view*); di volo at top speed, immediately; in volo aloft, in the air; prendere il volo to take flight; volo a vela or volo planato gliding; volo strumentale instrument flying; volo veleggiato gliding

volon·tà *f* (-tà) will; di spontanea volontà of one's own volition; pieno di buona volontà eager to please; ultime volontà last will and testament

volontariato *m* volunteer work; apprenticeship without pay; (mil) volunteer service

volontà·rio -ria (-ri -rie) *adj* voluntary ‖ *m* volunteer

volonteró·so -sa [s] *adj* willing, well-disposed

volpacchiòtto *m* fox cub; (fig) sly fox

vólpe *f* fox; (agr) smut; volpe argentata silver fox

volpi·no -na *adj* fox; fox-colored; foxy ‖ *m* Pomeranian

volpó·ne -na *mf* sly fox

vòlt *m* (vòlt) (elec) volt

vòl·ta *m* (-ta) (elec) volt ‖ *f* turn; time; vault; roof (*of mouth*); alla volta di toward; a volta di corriere by return mail; a volte sometimes; c'era una volta once upon a time there was; certe volte sometimes; dare di volta il cervello to go crazy, e.g., gli ha dato di volta il cervello he went crazy; dar la volta to turn sour (*said of wine*); due volte twice; molte volte often; per una volta tanto only once; poche volte seldom; tante volte often; tutto in una volta at one swoop, at one stroke; in one gulp, in one swallow; una volta once; una volta che (coll) inasmuch as; una volta per sempre once and for all; una volta tanto for once; volta a crociera cross vault; volta per volta little by little; volte (math) times, e.g., cinque volte cinque five times five

voltafàc·cia *m* (-cia) volte-face; fare voltafaccia to wheel around (*said of a horse*)

voltagabbà·na *mf* (-na) turncoat

voltàg·gio *m* (-gi) voltage

voltài·co -ca *adj* (-ci -che) voltaic

voltare (vòlto) *tr, intr & ref* to turn

voltastòma·co *m* (-chi) (coll) nausea; fare venire il voltastomaco a qlcu (coll) to turn s.o.'s stomach

voltata *f* turn; curve

volteggiare §290 (voltéggio) *tr* to put (*a horse*) through its paces ‖ *intr* to hover; to flit, flutter; (sports) to vault (*e.g.*, *on horseback or trapeze*)

voltég·gio *m* (-gi) (sports) vaulting

vòltmetro *m* voltmeter

vólto *m* (lit) face

voltura *f* (com, law) transfer

volùbile *adj* fickle

volubilità *f* fickleness

volume *m* volume; bulk; mass

voluminó·so -sa [s] *adj* voluminous, bulky

volu·to -ta *adj* desired; intentional ‖ *f* (archit) volute, scroll

volut·tà *f* (-tà) pleasure, enjoyment; voluptuousness

voluttuà·rio -ria *adj* (-ri -rie) luxury (*goods*)

voluttuó·so -sa [s] *adj* voluptuous, sensuous

vòmere *m* plowshare; trail spade (*of gun*)

vòmi·co -ca *adj* (-ci -che) emetic

vomitare (vòmito) *tr & intr* to vomit

vomitati·vo -va *adj & m* emetic

vòmito *m* vomit

vóngola *f* clam

vorace *adj* voracious

voraci·tà *f* (-tà) voracity

voràgine *f* chasm, gulf, abyss

vòrtice *m* vortex, whirlpool; whirlwind

vorticó·so -sa [s] *adj* whirling, swirling

vò·stro -stra §6 *adj & pron poss*

votare (vóto) *tr* to devote; to vote ‖ *intr* to vote ‖ *ref* to devote oneself

votazióne *f* vote, voting, poll; (educ) grades

voti·vo -va *adj* votive

vóto *m* vow; wish; votive offering; vote, ballot; grade, mark; a pieni voti with highest honors; fare un voto to make a vow; pronunciare i voti to take vows; voto di fiducia vote of confidence; voto preferenziale write-in vote; preferential ballot

vudù *m* voodoo

vuduì·sta *mf* (-sti -ste) voodoo (*person*)

vulcàni·co -ca *adj* (-ci -che) volcanic

vulcanizzare [ddzz] *tr* to vulcanize

vulcano *m* volcano

vulga·to -ta *adj* disseminated ‖ Vulgata *f* Vulgate

vulneràbile *adj* vulnerable

vuotare (vuòto) *tr* to empty; vuotare il sacco to speak one's mind, unburden oneself ‖ *ref* to empty

vuò·to -ta *adj* empty; devoid ‖ *m* vacuum; emptiness; empty space; empty seat; empty feeling; empty (*e.g.*, *container*); a vuoto in vain; wide of the mark; (check) without sufficient funds; andare a vuoto to fail; (mach) to idle; cadere nel vuoto to fall on deaf ears; mandare a vuoto to thwart; sotto vuoto in a vacuum; vuoto d'aria (aer) air pocket; vuoto di cassa deficit; vuoto di potere power vacuum

W

W, w ['doppjo 'vu] *m & f*
wà·fer *m* (**-fer**) wafer
water-clòset *m* (**-clòset**) flush toilet
watt *m* (**watt**) watt

watt·óra *m* (**-óra**) watt-hour
wèstern *m* (**wèstern**) (mov) western
whisky *m* (**whisky**) whiskey
wìgwam *m* (**wìgwam**) wigwam

X

X, x [ɪks] *m & f*
xèno *m* xenon
xenòfo·bo -ba *mf* xenophobe

xè·res *m* (**-res**) sherry
xerografìa *f* xerography
xeròfito *m* xerophyte

Y

Y, y ['ɪpsɪlon] *m & f*
yacht *m* (**yachts**) yacht
yak *m* (**yak**) yak

yànkee *m* (**yànkees**) Yankee
yìddish *adj invar & m* Yiddish

Z

Z, z ['dzɛta] *m & f* twenty-first letter of the Italian alphabet
zabalóne [dz] *m* eggnog
zàcchera *f* splash of mud
zaffare *tr* to plug; to bung
zaffata *f* unpleasant whiff, stench; gust
zafferano [dz] *m* saffron
zaffiro [dz] *m* sapphire
zaffo *m* plug; bung; tampon
zàgara [dz] *f* orange blossom
zàino [dz] *m* knapsack; (mil) pack
zampa *f* paw; (culin) leg; **a quattro zampe** on all fours; **zampa di gallina** crow's-foot; illegible scrawl; **zampa di porco** crowbar
zampare *intr* to paw; to stamp
zampettare (**zampétto**) *intr* to toddle; to scamper
zampillare *intr* (ESSERE & AVERE) to spurt, gush, spring
zampillo *m* spurt, gush, spring
zampino *m* little paw; **metterci lo zampino** to put one's finger in the pie
zampiróne *m* slow-burning mosquito repellent; foul-smelling cigarette
zampógna *f* bagpipe
zampognare (**zampógno**) *intr* to pipe, play the bagpipe
zampóne *m* Modena salami (*stuffed forepaw of a hog*)
zanèlla *f* gully
zàngola *f* butter churn
zanna *f* tusk; fang; **mostrare le zanne** to show one's teeth
zanzara [dz] [dz] *f* mosquito
zanzarièra [dz] [dz] *f* mosquito net; window screen
zappa *f* hoe; **darsi la zappa sui piedi**

to cut one's nose off to spite one's face
zappare *tr* to hoe
zappatóre *m* hoer, digger; (mil) sapper
zar *m* (**zar**) czar
zàttera *f* raft; **zattera di salvataggio** life raft
zatterière *m* log driver
zavòrra [dz] *f* ballast; (fig) deadwood
zavorrare [dz] (**zavòrro**) *tr* to ballast
zàzzera *f* mop (*of hair*)
zèbra [dz] *f* zebra; **zebre** zebra crossing
zebra·to -ta [dz] *adj* zebra-striped
ze·bù [dz] *m* (**-bù**) zebu
zéc·ca *f* (**-che**) mint; (ent) tick; **nuovo di zecca** brand-new
zecchino *m* sequin, gold coin
zèfiro [dz] *m* zephyr
zelante [dz] *adj* zealous; studious ‖ *mf* zealot; eager beaver
zèlo [dz] *m* zeal; **zelo pubblico** public spirit
zènit [dz] *m* zenith
zénzero [dz] [dz] *m* ginger
zép·po -pa *adj* crammed, jammed ‖ *f* wedge; (fig) padding
zerbino [dz] *m* doormat; dandy
zerbinòtto [dz] *m* dandy, sporty fellow
zèro [dz] *m* zero
zìa *f* aunt
zibaldóne [dz] *m* notebook; collection of thoughts; (pej) hodgepodge
zibellino [dz] *m* sable
zibétto [dz] *m* civet cat; civet (*substance used in perfumery*)
zibibbo [dz] *m* raisin
zìga·no -na *adj & mf* gypsy
zìgomo [dz] *m* cheekbone

zigrinare [dz] *tr* to grain (*leather*); to mill, knurl (*metal*)

zigrina·to -ta [dz] *adj* shagreened, grained (*leather*); knurled

zigzàg [dz] [dz] *m* (zigzàg) zigzag; andare a zigzag to zigzag

zigzagare §209 [dz] [dz] *intr* to zigzag

zimarra [dz] *f* cassock; (obs) overcoat

zimbèllo *m* decoy (*bird*); laughingstock

zincare §197 *tr* to zinc

zinco *m* zinc

zingaré·sco -sca (-schi -sche) *adj* & *mf* gypsy

zinga·ro -ra *mf* gypsy

zinnia [dz] *f* zinnia

zio *m* uncle; zio d'America rich uncle

zìpolo *m* peg, bung

zircóne [dz] *m* zircon

zircònio [dz] *m* zirconium

zirlare *intr* to warble; to squeak (*said of mouse*)

zitèlla *f* old maid

zittire §176 *tr* & *intr* to hoot, hiss

zit·to -ta *adj* silent; far stare zitto to hush up; stare zitto to keep quiet || *m* whisper || zitto *interj* quiet!; hush!; shut up!

zizzània [dz] [ddzz] *f* (bot) darnel; seminar zizzania to sow discord

zòccolo *m* clog, sabot; clump, clod; clodhopper; base (*of column*); pedestal; wide baseboard; (zool) hoof

zodìaco [dz] *m* zodiac

zolfanèllo *m* sulfur match

zolfara *f* var of solfara

zólfo *m* sulfur

zòlla *f* clod, clump; turf; lump, cube (*of sugar*)

zollétta *f* lump, cube (*of sugar*)

zòna [dz] *f* zone; area; girdle; band, stripe; ticker tape; (pathol) shingles; (telg) tape; zona glaciale frigid zone; zona tropicale tropics, tropical zone

zónzo [dz] [dz] *m*—andare a zonzo to stroll, loiter along

zoòfito [dz] *m* zoophite

zoologìa [dz] *f* zoology

zoològi·co -ca [dz] *adj* (-ci -che) zoological

zoòlo·go -ga [dz] *mf* (-gi -ghe) zoologist

zootecnìa [dz] *f* animal husbandry

zootècni·co -ca [dz] (-ci -che) *adj* livestock || *m* livestock specialist

zoppicante *adj* limping; halting; shaky

zoppicare §197 (zòppico) *intr* to limp; to be shaky (*in one's studies*); to wobble

zoppicatura *f* limp; wobble

zòp·po -pa *adj* crippled; lame; wobbly || *mf* cripple; lame person

zòti·co -ca [dz] (-ci -che) *adj* uncouth, boorish || *m* churl, boor

zuc·ca *f* (-che) pumpkin; (joc) pate; (coll) empty head

zuccata *f* bump with the head

zuccherare (zùcchero) *tr* to sweeten, sugar

zuccherièra *f* sugar bowl

zuccherifì·cio *m* (-ci) sugar refinery

zuccheri·no -na *adj* sugary || *m* candy; sugar plum; sugar-coated pill

zùcchero *m* sugar; zucchero filato cotton candy; zucchero in polvere powdered sugar

zuccheró·so -sa [s] *adj* sugary

zucchétto *m* scull cap; zucchetto

zucchi·no -na *m* & *f* zucchini

zuccó·ne -na *mf* dunce, dumbbell

zuffa *f* brawl, fight

zufolare (zùfolo) *tr* & *intr* to whistle

zùfolo *m* (mus) whistle, pipe

zu·lù (-lù) [dz] *adj* & *mf* Zulu

zumare [dz] *tr* & *intr* (mov, telv) to zoom

zumata [dz] *f* (mov, telv) zoom

zuppa *f* soup; (fig) mess; zuppa inglese cake with brandy and whipped cream; zuppa pavese consommé with toast and eggs

zuppièra *f* tureen

zup·po -pa *adj* drenched, soaked || *f* see zuppa

Zurigo *f* Zurich

zuzzurullò·ne -na [dz] [ddzz] *mf* overgrown child, just a big kid

PART TWO

Inglese-Italiano

Contents

Indice

	page
La pronunzia dell'inglese	3
La pronunzia delle parole composte	5
La pronunzia dei participi passati	5
English-Italian Vocabulary – *Vocabolario Inglese-Italiano*	7–355

La pronunzia dell'inglese

I simboli seguenti rappresentano approssimativamente tutti i suoni della lingua inglese.

VOCALI

SIMBOLO	SUONO	ESEMPIO
[æ]	Più chiuso della a in caso.	hat [hæt]
[ɑ]	Come la a in basso.	father ['fɑðər] proper ['prɑpər]
[ɛ]	Come la e in sella.	met [mɛt]
[e]	Più chiuso della e in ché. Specialmente in posizione finale, si pronunzia come se fosse seguita da [ɪ].	fate [fet] they [ðe]
[ə]	Come la seconda e nella parola francese gouvernement.	heaven ['hɛvən] pardon ['pɑrdən]
[i]	Come la i in nido.	she [ʃi] machine [məˈʃin]
[ɪ]	Come la i in ritto.	fit [fɪt] beer [bɪr]
[o]	Più chiuso della o in sole. Specialmente in posizione finale, si pronunzia come se fosse seguito da [ʊ].	nose [noz] road [rod] row [ro]
[ɔ]	Meno chiuso della o in torre.	bought [bɔt] law [lɔ]
[ʌ]	Piuttosto simile alla eu nella parola francese peur	cup [kʌp] come [kʌm] mother ['mʌðər]
[ʊ]	Meno chiuso della u in insulto.	pull [pʊl] book [bʊk] wolf [wʊlf]
[u]	Come la u in acuto.	rude [rud] move [muv] tomb [tum]

DITTONGHI

SIMBOLO	SUONO	ESEMPIO
[aɪ]	Come ai in laico.	night [naɪt] eye [aɪ]
[aʊ]	Come au in causa.	found [faʊnd] cow [kaʊ]
[ɔɪ]	Come oi in poi.	voice [vɔis] oil [ɔɪl]

3

SIMBOLO	SUONO	ESEMPIO
[b]	Come la **b** in **bambino**. Suono bilabiale occlusivo sonoro.	**bed** [bɛd] **robber** [ˈrabər]
[d]	Come la **d** in **caldo**. Suono dentale occlusivo sonoro.	**dead** [dɛd] **add** [æd]
[dʒ]	Come la **g** in **gente**. Suono palatale affricato sonoro.	**gem** [dʒɛm] **jail** [dʒel]
[ð]	Come la **d** nella pronuncia castigliana di **nada**. Suono interdentale fricativo sonoro.	**this** [ðɪs] **father** [ˈfaðər]
[f]	Come la **f** in **fare**. Suono labiodentale fricativo sordo.	**face** [fes] **phone** [fon]
[g]	Come la **g** in **gatto**. Suono velare occlusivo sonoro.	**go** [go] **get** [gɛt]
[h]	Come la **c** aspirata nella pronuncia toscana di **casa**.	**hot** [hɔt] **alcohol** [ˈælkə ˌhɔl]
[j]	Come la **i** in **ieri** o la **y** in **yo-yo**. Semiconsonante di suono palatale sonoro.	**yes** [jɛs] **unit** [ˈjunɪt]
[k]	Come la **c** in **casa** ma accompagnato da un'aspirazione. Suono velare occlusivo sordo.	**cat** [kæt] **chord** [kɔrd] **kill** [kɪl]
[l]	Come la **l** in **latino**. Suono alveolare fricativo laterale sonoro.	**late** [let] **allow** [əˈlau]
[m]	Come la **m** in **madre**. Suono bilabiale nasale sonoro.	**more** [mor] **command** [kəˈmænd]
[n]	Come la **n** in **notte**. Suono alveolare nasale sonoro.	**nest** [nɛst] **manner** [ˈmænər]
[ŋ]	Come la **n** in **manca**. Suono velare nasale sonoro.	**king** [kɪŋ] **conquer** [ˈkaŋkər]
[p]	Come la **p** in **patto** ma accompagnato da un'aspirazione. Suono bilabiale occlusivo sordo.	**pen** [pɛn] **cap** [kæp]
[r]	La **r** più comune in molte parti dell'Inghilterra e nella maggior parte degli Stati Uniti e del Canadà è un suono semivocalico articolato con la punta della lingua elevata verso la volta del palato. Questa consonante è debolissima in posizione intervocalica o alla fine di una sillaba, e può appena percepirsi. L'articolazione di questa consonante ha la tendenza di influenzare il suono delle vocali contigue. La **r**, preceduta dai suoni [ʌ] o [ə], dà il proprio colorito a questi suoni e sparisce completamente come suono consonantico.	**run** [rʌn] **far** [far] **art** [ɑrt] **carry** [ˈkæri] **burn** [bʌrn] **learn** [lʌrn] **weather** [ˈwɛðər]
[s]	Come la **s** in **sette**. Suono alveolare fricativo sordo.	**send** [sɛnd] **cellar** [ˈsɛlər]
[ʃ]	Come **sce** in **lasciare**. Suono palatale fricativo sordo.	**shall** [ʃæl] **machine** [məˈʃin]
[t]	Come la **t** in **tavolo** ma accompagnato da un'aspirazione. Suono dentale occlusivo sordo.	**ten** [tɛn] **dropped** [drɑpt]
[tʃ]	Come **c** in **cibo**. Suono palatale affricato sordo.	**child** [tʃaɪld] **much** [mʌtʃ] **nature** [ˈnetʃər]
[θ]	Come la **z** castigliana in **zapato**. Suono interdentale fricativo sordo.	**think** [θɪŋk] **truth** [truθ]
[v]	Come la **v** in **vento**. Suono labiodentale fricativo sonoro.	**vest** [vɛst] **over** [ˈovər] **of** [ɑv]

4

SIMBOLO	SUONO	ESEMPIO
[w]	Come la **u** in **quadro**. Suono labiovelare fricativo sonoro.	**work** [wʌrk] **tweed** [twid] **queen** [kwin]
[z]	Come la **s** in **asilo**. Suono alveolare fricativo sonoro.	**zeal** [zil] **busy** ['bɪzi] **his** [hɪz]
[ʒ]	Come la seconda **g** nella parola francese **garage**. Suono palatale fricativo sonoro.	**azure** ['eʒər] **measure** ['meʒər]

ACCENTO

L'accento tonico principale, indicato col segno grafico ', e l'accento secondario, indicato col segno grafico „ precedono la sillaba sulla quale cadono, per es., **fascinate** ['fæsɪ ˌnet].

La pronunzia delle parole composte

Nella parte inglese-italiano di questo Dizionario la pronunzia figurata di tutte le parole inglesi semplici è indicata in parentesi quadre che seguono immediatamente l'esponente, secondo un nuovo adattamento dell'alfabeto fonetico internazionale.

Vi sono tre generi di parole composte in inglese: (1) le parole in cui gli elementi componenti si sono uniti per formare una parola solida, come per es., **steamboat** vapore; (2) la parole in cui gli elementi componenti sono uniti da un trattino, come per es., **high'-grade'** di qualità superiore; (3) le parole in cui gli elementi componenti rimangono graficamente indipendenti gli uni da gli altri, per es., **post card** cartolina postale. La pronunzia delle parole inglesi composte non è indicata in questo Dizionario qualora gli elementi componenti appaiono come esponenti indipendenti nella loro normale posizione alfabetica e mostrano quindi la loro pronunzia figurata. Solo gli accenti principali e secondari di tali parole sono indicati, come per es., **steam'boat'**, **high'-grade'**, **post' card'**. Se i due membri di una parola composta inglese solida non sono separati da un accento grafico, si usa un punto leggermente elevato sopra il rigo per indicarne la divisione, come per es., **la'dy·like'**.

Nei nomi in cui l'accento secondario cade sul membro **-man** o **-men**, le vocali di tali membri si pronunziano come nelle parole semplici **man** e **men**, come per es., **mailman** ['mel ˌmæn] e **mailmen** ['mel ˌmen]. Nei nomi in cui tali membri componenti non sono accentati, le loro vocali si pronunziano come se fossero un'e muta francese, come per es., **policeman** [pə'lismən] e **policemen** [pə'lismən]. In questo Dizionario la trascrizione fonetica di tali nomi non è stata indicata qualora il primo membro componente appaia come esponente con la sua pronunzia in alfabeto fonetico internazionale. Gli accenti sono ciò nondimeno indicati:

mail'man' s (-men')
police'man s (-men)

La pronunzia dei participi passati

La pronunzia di una parola la cui desinenza è **-ed** (o **-d** dopo una e muta) non è indicata nel presente Dizionario, purché la pronunzia della parola stessa senza tale suffisso appaia con il suo esponente nella sua posizione alfabetica. In tale caso la pronunzia segue le regole indicate qui sotto. Si osservi che il raddoppiamento della vocale finale dopo una semplice vocale tonica non muta la pronunzia del suffisso **-ed**, per es.: **batted** ['bætɪd], **dropped** [drɑpt], **robbed** [rɑbd].

La desinenza **-ed** (o **-d** dopo una e muta) del preterito, del participio passato e di certi aggettivi ha tre pronunzie differenti, che dipendono dal suono in cui il tema termina:

1) Se il tema termina in suono consonantico sonoro (che non sia [d]), cioè [b], [g], [l], [m], [n], [ŋ], [r], [v], [z], [ð], [ʒ] o [dʒ] o in un suono vocalico, l'**-ed** è pronunziato [d]:

SUONO IN CUI TERMINA IL TEMA	INFINITO	PRETERITO E PARTICIPIO PASSATO
[b]	**ebb** [eb] **rob** [rɑb] **robe** [rob]	**ebbed** [ebd] **robbed** [rɑbd] **robed** [robd]

SUONO IN CUI TERMINA IL TEMA	INFINITO	PRETERITO E PARTICIPIO PASSATO
[g]	**egg** [eg] **sag** [sæg]	**egged** [ɛgd] **sagged** [sægd]
[l]	**mail** [mel] **scale** [skel]	**mailed** [meld] **scaled** [skeld]
[m]	**storm** [stɔrm] **bomb** [bɑm] **name** [nem]	**stormed** [stɔrmd] **bombed** [bɑmd] **named** [nemd]
[n]	**tan** [tæn] **sign** [saɪn] **mine** [maɪn]	**tanned** [tænd] **signed** [saɪnd] **mined** [maɪnd]
[ŋ]	**hang** [hæŋ]	**hanged** [hæŋd]
[r]	**fear** [fɪr] **care** [ker]	**feared** [fɪrd] **cared** [kerd]
[v]	**rev** [rɛv] **save** [sev]	**revved** [rɛvd] **saved** [sevd]
[z]	**buzz** [bʌz] **fuze** [fjuz]	**buzzed** [bʌzd] **fuzed** [fjuzd]
[ð]	**smooth** [smuð] **bathe** [beð]	**smoothed** [smuðd] **bathed** [beðd]
[ʒ]	**massage** [mə'sɑʒ]	**massaged** [mə'sɑʒd]
[dʒ]	**page** [pedʒ]	**paged** [pedʒd]
suono vocalico	**key** [ki] **sigh** [saɪ] **paw** [pɔ]	**keyed** [kid] **sighed** [saɪd] **pawed** [pɔd]

2) Se il tema termina in un suono consonantico sordo (che non sia [t]), cioè [f], [k], [p], [s], [θ], [ʃ] o [tʃ], l'-ed si pronunzia [t]:

SUONO IN CUI TERMINA IL TEMA	INFINITO	PRETERITO E PARTICIPIO PASSATO
[f]	**loaf** [lof] **knife** [naɪf]	**loafed** [loft] **knifed** [naɪft]
[k]	**back** [bæk] **bake** [bek]	**backed** [bækt] **baked** [bekt]
[p]	**cap** [kæp] **wipe** [waɪp]	**capped** [kæpt] **wiped** [waɪpt]
[s]	**hiss** [hɪs] **mix** [mɪks]	**hissed** [hɪst] **mixed** [mɪkst]
[θ]	**lath** [læθ]	**lathed** [læθt]
[ʃ]	**mash** [mæʃ]	**mashed** [mæʃt]
[tʃ]	**match** [mætʃ]	**matched** [mætʃt]

3) Se il tema termina in un suono dentale, cioè [t] o [d], l'-ed si pronunzia [ɪd] o [əd]:

SUONO IN CUI TERMINA IL TEMA	INFINITO	PRETERITO E PARTICIPIO PASSATO
[t]	**wait** [wet] **mate** [met]	**waited** ['wetɪd] **mated** ['metɪd]
[d]	**mend** [mend] **wade** [wed]	**mended** ['mendɪd] **waded** ['wedɪd]

L'-ed di alcuni aggettivi aggiunto ad un tema che termina in suono consonantico (oltre a quelli che terminano in [d] o [t]), è ciò nonostante talvolta pronunziato [ɪd] e tale fenomeno è idicato con la piena pronunzia della parola in simboli dell'alfabeto fonetico internazionale, per es., **blessed** ['blɛsɪd], **crabbed** ['kræbɪd].

6

A

A, a [e] *s* prima lettera dell'alfabeto inglese

a [e] *art indef* un, uno, una, un'

aback [ə'bæk] *adv* all'indietro; **taken aback** colto alla sprovvista, sconcertato

aba·cus ['æbəkəs] *s* (**-cuses** or **-ci** [ˌsaɪ]) pallottoliere *m;* (*archit*) abaco

abaft [ə'bæft] or [ə'bɑft] *adv* a poppa ‖ *prep* dietro a

abandon [ə'bændən] *s* disinvoltura ‖ *tr* abbandonare

abase [ə'bes] *tr* umiliare, degradare

abash [ə'bæʃ] *tr* imbarazzare; sconcertare

abate [ə'bet] *tr* ridurre; omettere; (*law*) terminare ‖ *intr* diminuire, calmarsi

aba·tis ['æbətɪs] or [ə'bætɪs] *s* (**-tis** or **-tises**) (*mil*) tagliata

abattoir [ˌæbə'twar] *s* macello

abba·cy ['æbəsi] *s* (**-cies**) abbazia

abbess ['æbɪs] *s* badessa

abbey ['æbɪ] *s* badia, abbazia

abbot ['æbət] *s* abate *m*

abbreviate [ə'brivɪˌet] *tr* abbreviare, raccorciare

abbreviation [əˌbrivɪ'eʃən] *s* (*abbreviated form*) abbreviazione; (*shortening*) abbreviamento

A B C [ˌeˌbi'si] *s* (*letterword*) abbicci *m;* **A B C's** abbecedario

abdicate ['æbdɪˌket] *tr* abdicare a ‖ *intr* abdicare

abdomen ['æbdəmən] or [æb'domən] *s* addome *m*

abduct [æb'dʌkt] *tr* rapire

abed [ə'bed] *adv* a letto

abet [ə'bet] *v* (*pret & pp* **abetted;** *ger* **abetting**) *tr* favoreggiare

abeyance [ə'be·əns] *s* sospensione; **in abeyance** in sospeso

ab·hor [æb'hɔr] *v* (*pret & pp* **-horred;** *ger* **-horring**) *tr* aborrire

abhorrent [æb'hɑrənt] or [æb'hɔrənt] *adj* detestabile

abide [ə'baɪd] *v* (*pret & pp* **abode** or **abided**) *tr* aspettare; tollerare ‖ *intr* —**to abide by** attenersi a; rimanere fedele a

abili·ty [ə'bɪlɪti] *s* (**-ties**) abilità *f*, bravura

abject ['æbdʒekt] or [æb'dʒekt] *adj* abietto, turpe

abjure [æb'dʒur] *tr* abiurare

ablative ['æblətɪv] *adj & s* ablativo

ablaut ['æblaut] *s* apofonia

ablaze [ə'blez] *adj* in fiamme; risplendente

able ['ebəl] *adj* abile, esperto; **to be able to** + *inf* potere + *inf*

able-bodied ['ebəl'badɪd] *adj* sano; forte

abloom [ə'blum] *adj & adv* in fiore

abnormal [æb'nɔrməl] *adj* anormale

aboard [ə'bord] *adv* a bordo; **all aboard!** (rr) signori, in vettura!; **to go aboard** imbarcarsi; **to take aboard** imbarcare ‖ *prep* a bordo di; (*a bus, train, etc.*) in, su

abode [ə'bod] *s* abitazione, dimora

abolish [ə'bɑlɪʃ] *tr* abolire

A-bomb ['eˌbam] *s* bomba atomica

abominable [ə'bamənəbəl] *adj* abominevole

abomination [əˌbamɪ'neʃən] *s* abominazione

aborigines [ˌæbə'rɪdʒɪˌniz] *spl* aborigeni *mpl*

abort [ə'bɔrt] *tr* terminare prematuramente; provocare un aborto in ‖ *intr* abortire

abortion [ə'bɔrʃən] *s* aborto

abound [ə'baund] *intr* abbondare; **to abound in** or **with** abbondare di

about [ə'baut] *adv* circa, press'a poco; qua intorno; qua e là; in direzione opposta; (coll) quasi; **to be about to** star sul punto di ‖ *prep* intorno a; circa a; addosso a; tutt'intorno a; riguardo a

about'-face' *interj* (mil) dietro front!

about'-face' or **about'-face'** *s* voltafaccia; (mil) dietro front *m* ‖ **about'-face'** *intr* fare dietro front

above [ə'bʌv] *adj* soprammenzionato; superiore ‖ *s*—**from above** dal cielo; dall'alto ‖ *adv* in alto; su; più sopra ‖ *prep* sopra, sopra a; più di; al di là di, oltre; **above all** soprattutto

above-mentioned [ə'bʌv'menʃənd] *adj* summenzionato, sunnominato

abrasive [ə'bresɪv] or [ə'brezɪv] *adj & s* abrasivo

abreast [ə'brest] *adj & adv* in fila, in linea; **to keep abreast of** tenersi alla pari con; essere al corrente di

abridge [ə'brɪdʒ] *tr* compendiare; ridurre

abroad [ə'brɔd] *adv* all'estero; all'aria aperta; **to be abroad** (*said of news*) circolare

abrupt [ə'brʌpt] *adj* brusco, improvviso; (*very steep*) scosceso

abscess ['æbses] *s* ascesso

abscond [æb'skɑnd] *intr* scappare; **to abscond with** svignarsela con

absence ['æbsəns] *s* assenza; **in the absence of** in mancanza di

absent ['æbsənt] *adj* assente ‖ [æbˌsent] *tr*—**to absent oneself** assentarsi

absentee [ˌæbsən'ti] *s* assente *mf*

absent-minded ['æbsənt'maɪndɪd] *adj* distratto, assente

absinth ['æbsɪnθ] *s* assenzio

absolute ['æbsəˌlut] *adj & s* assoluto

absolutely ['æbsəˌlutlɪ] *adv* assolutamente, certamente ‖ [ˌæbsə'lutlɪ] *interj* certamente!

absolve [æb'salv] *tr* assolvere

absorb [æb'sɔrb] *tr* assorbire; **to be** or **become absorbed** essere assorto

absorbent [æb'sɔrbənt] *adj* assorbente; (*cotton*) idrofilo ‖ *s* sostanza assorbente

absorbing [æb'sɔrbɪŋ] *adj* interessantissimo

abstain [æb'sten] *intr* astenersi

abstemious [æb'stimɪ·əs] *adj* astemio

abstention [æb'stenʃən] *s* astensione; astenuto (*vote withheld*)

abstinent ['æbstɪnənt] *adj* astinente
abstract ['æbstrækt] *adj* astratto ‖ *s* compendio, sommario ‖ *tr* compendiare ‖ (æb'strækt) *tr* astrarre; (*to steal*) sottrarre
abstruse [æb'strus] *adj* astruso
absurd [æb'sʌrd] *or* [æb'zʌrd] *adj* assurdo
absurdi·ty [æb'sʌrdɪti] *or* [æb'zʌrdɪti] *s* (**-ties**) assurdità *f*
abundant [ə'bʌndənt] *adj* abbondante
abuse [ə'bjus] *s* (*misuse*) abuso; maltrattamento; insulto ‖ [ə'bjuz] *tr* (*to misuse, take unfair advantage of*) abusare di; maltrattare; insultare
abusive [ə'bjusɪv] *adj* abusivo; insultante
abut [ə'bʌt] *v* (*pret & pp* **abutted;** *ger* **abutting**) *intr*—**to abut on** confinare con
abutment [ə'bʌtmənt] *s* rinfianco; (*at either end of bridge*) spalla; (*of buttresses of bridge*) sprone *m*
abysmal [ə'bɪzməl] *adj* abissale; (*e.g., ignorance*) spropositato
abyss [ə'bɪs] *s* abisso
academic [,ækə'demɪk] *adj* accademico
ac'ademic cos'tume *s* toga accademica
academician [ə,kædə'mɪʃən] *s* accademico
ac'adem'ic year' *s* anno scolastico
acade·my [ə'kædəmi] *s* (**-mies**) accademia
accede [æk'sid] *intr* accedere; **to accede to** salire a; accedere a
accelerate [æk'selə,ret] *tr & intr* accelerare
accelerator [æk'selə,retər] *s* acceleratore *m*
accent ['æksɛnt] *s* accento ‖ ['æksɛnt] *or* [æk'sɛnt] *tr* accentare; (*to accentuate*) accentuare
ac'cent mark' *s* segnaccento, accento grafico
accentuate [æk'sɛntʃʊ,et] *tr* accentuare
accept [æk'sɛpt] *tr* accettare
acceptable [æk'sɛptəbəl] *adj* accettabile
acceptance [æk'sɛptəns] *s* accettazione
access ['æksɛs] *s* accesso
accessible [æk'sɛsɪbəl] *adj* accessibile; (*person*) abbordabile
accession [æk'sɛʃən] *s* accessione, acquisto; (*e.g., to the throne*) adito
accesso·ry [æk'sɛsəri] *adj* accessorio ‖ *s* (**-ries**) accessorio; (*to a crime*) complice *m*
accident ['æksɪdənt] *s* accidente *m;* **by accident** accidentalmente, per caso
accidental [,æksɪ'dɛntəl] *adj* accidentale ‖ *s* (mus) accidente *m*
acclaim [ə'klem] *s* acclamazione, applauso ‖ *tr & intr* acclamare, applaudire
acclimate [ə'klaɪ,met] *tr* acclimatare ‖ *intr* acclimatarsi
accolade [,ækə'led] *s* accollata; (fig) elogio
accommodate [ə'kɑmə,det] *tr* (*to adjust, make fit*) accomodare; (*to pro-*

vide with a loan) venire incontro a; (*to supply with lodging*) alloggiare; (*to oblige*) favorire; (*to have room for*) aver posto per
accommodating [ə'kɑmə,detɪŋ] *adj* servizievole, compiacente
accommodation [ə,kɑmə'deʃən] *s* (*favor*) favore *m;* (*loan*) prestito; (*adaptation*) adattamento; (*reconciliation*) conciliazione; (*compromise*) accomodamento; **accommodations** (*traveling space*) posto; (*in a hotel*) alloggio
accommoda'tion train' *s* treno accelerato
accompaniment [ə'kʌmpənɪmənt] *s* accompagnamento
accompanist [ə'kʌmpənɪst] *s* accompagnatore *m*
accompa·ny [ə'kʌmpəni] *v* (*pret & pp* **-nied**) *tr* accompagnare
accomplice [ə'kɑmplɪs] *s* complice *mf*
accomplish [ə'kɑmplɪʃ] *tr* compiere
accomplished [ə'kɑmplɪʃt] *adj* (*completed*) compiuto, terminato; (*skilled*) finito, compiuto
accomplishment [ə'kɑmplɪʃmənt] *s* (*completion*) esecuzione, realizzazione; (*something accomplished*) opera; (*acquired ability*) talento; (*military achievement*) prodezza; (*social skill*) compitezza
accord [ə'kɔrd] *s* accordo; **in accord with** in conformità con; **of one's own accord** spontaneamente; **with one accord** di comune accordo ‖ *tr* concedere ‖ *intr* accordarsi
accordance [ə'kɔrdəns] *s* accordo; **in accordance with** in conformità con
according [ə'kɔrdɪŋ] *adv*—**according as** a seconda che; **according to** secondo, a seconda di
accordingly [ə'kɔrdɪŋli] *adv* per conseguenza, perciò; in conformità
accordion [ə'kɔrdɪ·ən] *s* fisarmonica
accost [ə'kɔst] *or* [ə'kɑst] *tr* accostare, abbordare
accouchement [ə'kuʃmənt] *s* parto
account [ə'kaʊnt] *s* (*explanation*) versione; (*report*) resoconto; conto; (*statement*) estratto conto; **by all accounts** secondo la voce comune; **of account** d'importanza; **of no account** senza importanza; **on account** in acconto; **on account of** a causa di; per l'amor di; **on all accounts** in ogni modo; **on no account** in nessuna maniera; **to call to account** chiedere conto di; **to give a good account of oneself** comportarsi bene; **to take account of** prendere in considerazione; **to turn to account** trarre profitto da ‖ *intr*—**to account for** render conto di; essere responsabile per
accountable [ə'kaʊntəbəl] *adj* responsabile; (*explainable*) spiegabile
accountant [ə'kaʊntənt] *s* contabile *mf*, ragioniere *m*
accounting [ə'kaʊntɪŋ] *s* contabilità *f*, ragioneria
accouterments [ə'kutərmənts] *spl* (mil)

buffetterie *fpl; (trappings)* ornamenti *mpl*

accredit [ə'krɛdɪt] *tr* accreditare; **to accredit s.o. with s.th** ascrivere qlco a credito di qlcu

accrue [ə'kru] *intr* accumularsi; *(said of interest)* maturare

acculturation [ə,kʌltʃə'reʃən] *s* acculturazione

accumulate [ə'kjumjə,let] *tr* accumulare || *intr* accumularsi

accuracy ['ækjərəsi] *s* esattezza, precisione; fedeltà *f*

accurate ['ækjərɪt] *adj* esatto, preciso; fedele

accursed [ə'kʌrsɪd] *or* [ə'kʌrst] *adj* maledetto

accusation [,ækjə'zeʃən] *s* accusa

accusative [ə'kjuzətɪv] *adj & s* accusativo

accuse [ə'kjuz] *tr* accusare

accustom [ə'kʌstəm] *tr* abituare

ace [es] *s* asso; **to be within an ace of** essere quasi sul punto di

ace' in the hole' *s* asso nella manica

acetate ['æsɪ,tet] *s* acetato

ace'tic ac'id [ə'sitɪk] *s* acido acetico

aceti•fy [ə'sɛtɪ,faɪ] *v (pret & pp -fied) tr* acetificare || *intr* acetificarsi

acetone ['æsɪ,ton] *s* acetone *m*

acetylene [ə'sɛtɪ,lin] *s* acetilene *m*

acet'ylene torch' *s* cannello ossiacetilenico

ache [ek] *s* dolore *m* || *intr* dolere, e.g., **my tooth aches** mi duole il dente

Acheron ['ækə,ran] *s* Acheronte *m*

achieve [ə'tʃiv] *tr* compiere, conseguire

achievement [ə'tʃivmənt] *s* compimento; successo; *(exploit)* impresa, prodezza

Achil'les heel' [ə'kɪliz] *s* tallone *m* d'Achille

acid ['æsɪd] *adj & s* acido

acidi•fy [ə'sɪdɪ,faɪ] *v (pret & pp -fied) tr & intr* acidificare

acidity [ə'sɪdɪti] *s* acidità *f*

acid' test' *s* prova del fuoco

ack-ack ['æk'æk] *s (slang)* cannone antiaereo

acknowledge [æk'nɑlɪdʒ] *tr* riconoscere; *(receipt of a letter)* accusare; *(a claim)* ammettere; mostrare la gratitudine per; *(law)* certificare

acknowledgment [æk'nɑlɪdʒmənt] *s* riconoscimento; *(of receipt of a letter)* accusa, cenno

acme ['ækmi] *s* acme *f*

acolyte ['ækə,laɪt] *s* accolito

acorn ['ekɔrn] *or* ['ekɑrn] *s* ghianda

acoustic [ə'kustɪk] *adj* acustico || **acoustics** *s* acustica

acquaint [ə'kwent] *tr* mettere al corrente; **to be acquainted with** conoscere; essere al corrente di; **to become acquainted** *(with each other)* conoscersi

acquaintance [ə'kwentəns] *s* conoscenza; *(person)* conoscente *mf*, conoscenza

acquiesce [,ækwɪ'ɛs] *intr* acconsentire, accondiscendere

acquiescence [,ækwɪ'ɛsəns] *s* accondiscendenza

acquire [ə'kwaɪr] *tr* acquistare

acquisition [,ækwɪ'zɪʃən] *s* acquisto

acquit [ə'kwɪt] *v (pret & pp acquitted; ger acquitting) tr (to pay)* ripagare; *(to declare not guilty)* assolvere; **to acquit oneself** condursi

acquittal [ə'kwɪtəl] *s* assoluzione

acre ['ekər] *s* acro

acrid ['ækrɪd] *adj* acrido, pungente

acrobat ['ækrə,bæt] *s* acrobata *mf*

acrobatic [,ækrə'bætɪk] *adj* acrobatico || **acrobatics** *ssg (e.g., of a stunt pilot)* acrobazie *fpl;* **acrobatics** *spl (gymnastics)* acrobatica

acronym ['ækrənɪm] *s* acronimo, parola macedonia

acropolis [ə'krɑpəlɪs] *s* acropoli *f*

across [ə'krɔs] *or* [ə'krɑs] *adv* dall'altra parte; **to get an idea across to** farsi capire da || *prep* attraverso; *(on the other side of)* al di là di, dall'altra parte di; **to come across** *(a person)* imbattersi in; **to go across** attraversare

across'-the-board' *adj* generale

act [ækt] *s* atto; legge *f;* rappresentazione; **in the act** in flagrante || *tr (a drama)* rappresentare; *(a role)* recitare || *intr (on the stage)* recitare; *(to behave)* comportarsi; *(to perform special duties; to reach a decision)* agire; *(to have an effect)* reagire; **to act as** fungere da; **to act for** rimpiazzare; **to act on** eseguire; **to act up** (coll) fare il matto; non funzionare bene *(said, e.g., of a motor)*; **to act up to** (coll) fare festa a

acting ['æktɪŋ] *adj* facente funzione, interino || *s* recita

action ['ækʃən] *s* azione; *(moving parts)* meccanismo; **to take action** iniziare azione; *(law)* intentare causa

activate ['æktɪ,vet] *tr* attivare

active ['æktɪv] *adj & s* attivo

activi•ty [æk'tɪvɪti] *s (-ties)* attività *f*

act' of God' *s* forza maggiore

actor ['æktər] *s* attore *m*

actress ['æktrɪs] *s* attrice *f*

actual ['æktʃu-əl] *adj* reale

actually ['æktʃu-əli] *adv* realmente, in realtà

actuar•y ['æktʃu,ɛri] *s (-ies)* attuario

actuate ['æktʃu,et] *tr* attuare, mettere in azione; *(to motivate)* stimulare

acuity [ə'kju-ɪti] *s* acuità *f*

acumen [ə'kjumən] *s* acume *m*

acupuncture ['ækju,pʌŋktʃər] *s* agopuntura

acute [ə'kjut] *adj* acuto

ad [æd] *s* (coll) inserzione pubblicitaria

Adam ['ædəm] *s* Adamo; **not to know from Adam** non conoscere affatto

adamant ['ædəmənt] *adj* saldo, inflessibile

Ad'am's ap'ple *s* pomo d'Adamo

adapt [ə'dæpt] *tr* adattare

adaptation [,ædæp'teʃən] *s* adattamento; *(e.g., of a play)* rifacimento

add [æd] *tr* aggiung, e; *(numbers)*

sommare ‖ *intr* aggiungere; far di conto; **to add up to** ammontare a; (coll) voler dire

adder ['ædər] *s* vipera

addict ['ædɪkt] *s* (*to drugs*) tossicomane *mf*; (*to a sport*) tifoso ‖ [ə'dɪkt] *tr* abituare; rendere propenso alla tossicomania; **to addict oneself to** darsi a, abbandonarsi a

addiction [ə'dɪk/ən] *s* dedizione; (*to drugs*) tossicomania; (*to sports*) tifo

add'ing machine' *s* calcolatrice *f*

addition [ə'dɪ/ən] *s* addizione; (*building*) annessi *mpl*; **in addition** inoltre, per di più; **in addition to** oltre a

additive ['ædɪtɪv] *adj & s* additivo

address [ə'drɛs] or ['ædrɛs] *s* (*speech*) discorso; (*place and destination of mail*) indirizzo; (*skill*) destrezza; (*formal request*) petizione; **to deliver an address** pronunciare un discorso ‖ [ə'drɛs] *tr* indirizzare; (*to speak to*) rivolgere la parola a

addressee [,ædrɛ'si] *s* destinatario

address'ing machine' *s* macchina per indirizzi

adduce [ə'djus] or [ə'dus] *tr* addurre

adenoids ['ædə,nɔɪdz] *spl* vegetazioni *fpl* adenoidi, adenoidi *fpl*

adept [ə'dɛpt] *adj & s* esperto

adequate ['ædɪkwɪt] *adj* sufficiente; (*suitable*) conveniente

adhere [æd'hɪr] *intr* aderire

adherence [æd'hɪrəns] *s* aderenza

adherent [æd'hɪrənt] *adj & s* aderente *m*

adhesion [æd'hiʒən] *s* adesione; (*pathol*) aderenza

adhesive [æd'hisɪv] or [æd'hizɪv] *adj & s* adesivo

adhe'sive tape' *s* tela adesiva, cerotto

adieu [ə'dju] or [ə'du] *s* (**adieus** or **adieux**) addio ‖ *interj* addio!

adjacent [ə'dʒesənt] *adj* adiacente

adjective ['ædʒɪktɪv] *adj* aggettivale; accessorio, secondario ‖ *s* aggettivo

adjoin [ə'dʒɔɪn] *tr* confinare con ‖ *intr* essere confinanti

adjoining [ə'dʒɔɪnɪŋ] *adj* confinante; vicino, attiguo

adjourn [ə'dʒʌrn] *tr* aggiornare, rinviare ‖ *intr* rinviarsi

adjournment [ə'dʒʌrnmənt] *s* aggiornamento, rinvio

adjust [ə'dʒʌst] *tr* accomodare; regolare; (*ins*) liquidare ‖ *intr* abituarsi

adjustable [ə'dʒʌstəbəl] *adj* regolabile

adjustment [ə'dʒʌstmənt] *s* aggiustamento; accomodamento; (*ins*) liquidazione del danno

adjutant ['ædʒətənt] *s* aiutante *mf*

ad-lib [,æd'lɪb] *v* (*pret & pp* **-libbed;** *ger* **-libbing**) *tr & intr* improvvisare

administer [æd'mɪnɪstər] *tr* amministrare; (*medicine*) somministrare; (*an oath*) dare ‖ *intr*—**to administer to** ministrare, prestare aiuto a

administrator [æd'mɪnɪs,tretər] *s* amministratore *m*

admirable ['ædmɪrəbəl] *adj* ammirabile, ammirevole

admiral ['ædmɪrəl] *s* ammiraglio

admiral·ty ['ædmɪrəlti] *s* (**-ties**) ammiragliato

admire [æd'maɪr] *tr* ammirare

admirer [æd'maɪrər] *s* ammiratore *m*

admissible [æd'mɪsɪbəl] *adj* ammissibile

admission [æd'mɪ/ən] *s* ammissione; confessione; (*entrance fee*) prezzo d'ingresso; **to gain admission** arrivare a entrare

ad·mit [æd'mɪt] *v* (*pret & pp* **-mitted;** *ger* **-mitting**) *tr* ammettere; confessare ‖ *intr* dare l'ingresso; **to admit of** permettere, ammettere; consentire

admittance [æd'mɪtəns] *s* ammissione; permesso di entrare; **no admittance** divieto d'ingresso

admonish [æd'mɑnɪ/] *tr* ammonire

ado [ə'du] *s* confusione, trambusto; **much ado about nothing** molto rumore per nulla; **to make a big ado** fare cerimonie

adobe [ə'dobi] *s* mattone crudo

adolescence [,ædə'lɛsəns] *s* adolescenza

adolescent [,ædə'lɛsənt] *adj & s* adolescente *mf*

adopt [ə'dɑpt] *tr* adottare

adoption [ə'dɑp/ən] *s* adozione

adorable [ə'dorəbəl] *adj* adorabile

adore [ə'dor] *tr* adorare

adorn [ə'dɔrn] *tr* adornare

adornment [ə'dɔrnmənt] *s* ornamento

adre'nal gland' [æd'rinəl] *s* glandola surrenale

Adriatic [,edri'ætɪk] or [,ædri'ætɪk] *adj* adriatico ‖ *adj & s* Adriatico

adrift [ə'drɪft] *adj & adv* alla deriva

adroit [ə'drɔɪt] *adj* destro

adult [ə'dʌlt] or ['ædʌlt] *adj & s* adulto

adulterate [ə'dʌltə,ret] *tr* adulterare

adulterer [ə'dʌltərər] *s* adultero

adulteress [ə'dʌltərɪs] *s* adultera

adulter·y [ə'dʌltəri] *s* (**-ies**) adulterio

advance [æd'væns] or [æd'vɑns] *adj* avanzato ‖ *s* avanzata; (*increase in price*) aumento; (*of money*) anticipo; **advances** approcci *mpl*; **in advance** in anticipo ‖ *tr* avanzare; aumentare; (*to make earlier*) anticipare; (*money*) anticipare; (*a clock*) mettere avanti ‖ *intr* avanzare; (*said, e.g., of prices*) aumentare

advanced [æd'vænst] or [æd'vɑnst] *adj* avanzato, progredito

advanced' stand'ing *s* trasferimento di voti scolastici

advancement [æd'vænsmənt] or [æd'vɑnsmənt] *s* progresso; promozione; (*mil*) avanzata

advance' public'ity *s* pubblicità *f* di lancio

advantage [æd'væntɪdʒ] or [æd'vɑntɪdʒ] *s* vantaggio; **to advantage** in maniera favorevole; **to take advantage of** approfittarsi di; abusare di ‖ *tr* avantaggiare

advantageous [,ædvən'tedʒəs] *adj* vantaggioso

advent ['ædvɛnt] *s* avvento

adventure [æd'vɛntʃər] *s* avventura || *tr* avventurare || *intr* avventurarsi

adventurer [æd'vɛntʃərər] *s* avventuriero

adventuresome [æd'vɛntʃərsəm] *adj* avventuroso

adventuress [æd'vɛntʃərɪs] *s* avventuriera

adventurous [æd'vɛntʃərəs] *adj* avventuroso

adverb ['ædvʌrb] *s* avverbio

adversar·y ['ædvər ˌsɛri] *s* (-ies) avversario

adverse [æd'vʌrs] or ['ædvʌrs] *adj* avverso, contrario

adversi·ty [æd'vʌrsɪti] *s* (-ties) avversità *f*

advertise ['ædvər ˌtaɪz] or [ˌædvər'taɪz] *tr* propagandare; reclamizzare || *intr* fare la pubblicità; inserire un annunzio; inserzionare

advertisement [ˌædvər'taɪzmənt] or [æd'vʌrtɪsmənt] *s* annuncio pubblicitario, inserzione

advertiser ['ædvər ˌtaɪzər] or [ˌædvər'taɪzər] *s* inserzionista *mf*

advertising ['ædvər ˌtaɪzɪŋ] *s* pubblicità *f*, pubblicismo

ad'vertising a'gent *s* pubblicista *mf*

ad'vertising campaign' *s* campagna pubblicitaria

ad'vertising man' *s* agente *m* di pubblicità, reclamista *m*

advice [æd'vaɪs] *s* consiglio; **a piece of advice** un consiglio

advisable [æd'vaɪzəbəl] *adj* consigliabile

advise [æd'vaɪz] *tr* consigliare; informare || *intr*—**to advise with** chiedere il consiglio di; avere una conferenza con

advisement [æd'vaɪzmənt] *s* considerazione; **to take under advisement** prendere in considerazione

adviser [æd'vaɪzər] *s* consigliere *m*

advisory [æd'vaɪzəri] *adj* consultivo

advocate ['ædvə ˌket] *s* difensore *m*; (*lawyer*) avvocato || *tr* sostenere, propugnare

adze [ædz] *s* ascia

Aege'an Sea' [ɪ'dʒi·ən] *s* mare Egeo

aegis ['idʒɪs] *s* egida

Aeneid ['i·nɪ·ɪd] *s* Eneide *f*

aerate ['eret] or ['e·ə ˌret] *tr* aerare

aerial ['ɛrɪ·əl] or [e'ɪrɪ·əl] *adj* aereo || ['ɛrɪ·əl] *s* (rad & telv) antenna

aer'ial pho'tograph *s* aerofotogramma *m*

aerodrome ['ɛrə ˌdrom] *s* aerodromo

aerodynamic [ˌɛrodaɪ'næmɪk] *adj* aerodinamico || **aerodynamics** *ssg* aerodinamica

aeronaut ['ɛrə ˌnɔt] *s* aeronauta *m*

aeronautic [ˌɛrə'nɔtɪk] *adj* aeronautico || **aeronautics** *ssg* aeronautica

aerosol ['ɛrə ˌsol] *s* aerosol *m*

aerospace ['ɛro ˌspes] *adj* aerospaziale || *s* aerospazio

Aesop ['isɑp] *s* Esopo

aesthete ['ɛsθit] *s* esteta *mf*

aesthetic [ɛs'θɛtɪk] *adj* estetico || **aesthetics** *ssg* estetica

afar [ə'fɑr] *adv* lontano; **from afar** da lontano

affable ['æfəbəl] *adj* affabile

affair [ə'fɛr] *s* affare *m*; (*romance*) relazione amorosa

affect [ə'fɛkt] *tr* influenzare; (*to touch the heart of*) commuovere; (*to pretend to have*) affettare

affectation [ˌæfɛk'teʃən] *s* affettazione

affected [ə'fɛktɪd] *adj* affettato

affection [ə'fɛkʃən] *s* affezione

affectionate [ə'fɛkʃənɪt] *adj* affettuoso, affezionato

affidavit [ˌæfɪ'devɪt] *s* affidavit *m*, dichiarazione sotto giuramento

affiliate [ə'fɪlɪ ˌet] *adj & s* affiliato || *tr* affiliare || *intr* affiliarsi

affini·ty [ə'fɪnɪti] *s* (-ties) affinità *f*

affirm [ə'fʌrm] *tr* affermare; confermare

affirmative [ə'fʌrmətɪv] *adj* affermativo || *s* affermativa

affix ['æfɪks] *s* affisso || [ə'fɪks] *tr* affiggere; (*a signature*) apporre; (*e.g., blame*) attribuire

afflict [ə'flɪkt] *tr* affliggere

affliction [ə'flɪkʃən] *s* afflizione

affluence ['æflʊ·əns] *s* opulenza, abbondanza

affluent ['æflʊ·ənt] *adj* opulento, abbondante; ricco || *s* affluente *m*

afford [ə'fɔrd] *tr* permettersi il lusso di; (*to furnish*) provvedere; (*to give*) dare

affray [ə'fre] *s* rissa

affront [ə'frʌnt] *s* affronto || *tr* fare un affronto a

afghan ['æfgən] or ['æfgæn] *s* coperta di lana all'uncinetto || **Afghan** *adj & s* afgano

afield [ə'fild] *adv* sul campo; **far afield** lontano

afire [ə'faɪr] *adj* ardente; in fuoco, in fiamme

aflame [ə'flem] *adj* in fiamme

afloat [ə'flot] *adj & adv* a galla; a bordo; (*drifting*) alla deriva; (*said of a rumor*) in circolazione

afoot [ə'fʊt] *adj & adv* a piedi; in movimento, in moto

aforementioned [ə'for ˌmɛnʃənd] or **aforesaid** [ə'for ˌsɛd] *adj* suddetto

afoul [ə'faʊl] *adj & adv* in collisione; **to run afoul of** finire nelle mani di, impigliarsi con

afraid [ə'fred] *adj* impaurito, spaventato; **to be afraid (of)** aver paura (di)

African ['æfrɪkən] *adj & s* africano

aft [æft] or [ɑft] *adv* a poppa; indietro

after ['æftər] or ['ɑftər] *adj* seguente; di poppa || *adv* dopo; (*behind*) dietro || *prep* dopo; dopo di; (*in the manner of*) secondo; **to run after** correre dietro a || *conj* dopo che

afterburner ['æftər ˌbʌrnər] or ['ɑftər ˌbʌrnər] *s* (aer) postbruciatore *m*

aftereffect ['æftərɪ ˌfɛkt] or ['ɑftərɪ ˌfɛkt] *s* conseguenza

af'ter-hours' *adj* dopo le ore di ufficio

af'ter-life' *s* aldilà *m*; vita susseguente

aftermath ['æftər ,mæθ] or ['aftər- ,mæθ] s conseguenze fpl; gravi conseguenze fpl

af'ter-noon' adj pomeridiano || s pomeriggio

after-shaving ['æftər ,ʃevɪŋ] or ['aftər- ,ʃevɪŋ] adj dopobarba

af'ter-taste' s retrosapore m

af'ter-thought' s pensiero tardivo

afterward ['æftərwərd] or ['aftərwərd] adv dopo; **long afterward** molto tempo dopo

af'ter-while' adv fra un po'

again [ə'gen] adv di nuovo; ancora; un'altra volta; **again and again** ripetutamente; **as much again** due volte tanto, altrettanto; **to** + inf + **again** tornare a + inf, e.g., **to cook again** tornare a cuocere

against [ə'genst] prep contro; (opposite) in faccia a; **to be against** opporsi a; **to go against the grain** ripugnare

agape [ə'gep] adj & adv a bocca aperta

age [edʒ] s età f; (old age) vecchiaia; (full term of life) vita; (historical or geological period) evo; generazione; **of age** maggiorenne; **to come of age** diventare maggiorenne; **under age** minorenne || tr & intr invecchiare

aged [edʒd] adj dell'età di || ['edʒɪd] adj vecchio, invecchiato

ageless ['edʒlɪs] adj eternamente giovane, che non invecchia mai

agen·cy ['edʒənsɪ] s (-cies) azione; agenzia; mediazione; (of government) ente m

agenda [ə'dʒendə] s agenda, ordine m del giorno

agent ['edʒənt] s agente m; (coll) commesso viaggiatore, agente m di commercio; (rr) gestore m

Age' of Enligh'tenment s illuminismo

agglomeration [ə ,glamə're/ʃən] s agglomerazione

aggrandizement [ə'grændɪzmənt] s aumento, innalzamento

aggravate ['ægrə ,vet] tr aggravare; (coll) irritare, esasperare

aggregate ['ægrɪ ,get] adj & s aggregato, totale m; **in the aggregate** nel complesso || tr aggregare; ammontare a

aggression [ə'gre/ʃən] s aggressione

aggressive [ə'gresɪv] adj aggressivo, attivo

aggressor [ə'gresər] s aggressore m

aggrieve [ə'griv] tr affliggere

aghast [ə'gæst] or [ə'gɑst] adj atterrito

agile ['ædʒɪl] adj agile

agitate ['ædʒɪ ,tet] tr agitare || intr agitarsi

agitator ['ædʒɪ ,tetər] s agitatore m

aglow [ə'glo] adj splendente

agnostic [æg'nɑstɪk] adj & s agnostico

ago [ə'go] adv fa, e.g., **a year ago** un anno fa; **long ago** molto tempo fa

agog [ə'gɑg] adj & adv ansioso; **to set agog** riempire di ansietà

agonize ['ægə ,naɪz] intr soffrire straziantemente; (to struggle) dibattersi

ago·ny ['ægənɪ] s (-nies) agonia

agrarian [ə'grerɪ·ən] adj agrario || s membro del partito agrario

agree [ə'gri] intr aderire, andar d'accordo; (to consent) acconsentire; (gram) concordare; **to agree with** confarsi a, e.g., **eggs do not agree with him** le uova non gli si confanno

agreeable [ə'gri·əbəl] adj gentile; gradevole; (willing to agree) consenziente

agreement [ə'grimənt] s accordo; **in agreement** d'accordo

agriculture ['ægrɪ ,kʌlt/ər] s agricoltura

agriculturist [,ægrɪ'kʌlt/ərɪst] s (farmer) agricoltore m; perito in agricoltura, agronomo

agronomy [ə'grɑnəmɪ] s agronomia

aground [ə'graund] adv alla riva; **to run aground** andare or dare in secca

ague ['egju] s (chill) brivido; febbre f

ahead [ə'hed] adv davanti, avanti; **to get ahead** (coll) andare avanti, aver successo; **to get ahead of** sorpassare; **to go ahead** avanzare; continuare

ahoy [ə'hɔɪ] interj—**ship ahoy!** ehi della barca!

aid [ed] s aiuto; assistente m; (mil) aiutante m di campo || tr aiutare; **to aid and abet** essere complice di

aide [ed] s assistente m

aide-de-camp ['eddə'kæmp] s (aides-de-camp) aiutante m di campo

ail [el] tr affliggere; **what ails you?** che ha? || intr soffrire, essere malato

aileron ['elə ,rɑn] s alerone m

ailing ['elɪŋ] adj ammalato

ailment ['elmənt] s malattia, indisposizione; (chronic) acciacco

aim [em] s mira, intento || tr (a gun) puntare; (words) dirigere || intr mirare; **to aim to** cercare di, aver l'intenzione di

air [er] adj (e.g., pocket) d'aria; (e.g., show) aeronautico || s aria; **by air** per via aerea; **in the open air** all'aria aperta; **to be in the air** circolare; **to be on the air** (rad, telv) essere in onda; **to go on the air** (rad, telv) andare in onda; **to put on airs** darsi delle arie; **to take the air** andar fuori; **up in the air** incerto; (slang) arrabbiato || tr aerare, ventilare

airborne ['er ,bɔrn] or ['er ,born] adj aerosostentato; aerotrasportato

air' brake' s freno ad aria compressa

air' cas'tle s castello in aria

air'-condi'tion tr climatizzare

air' condi'tioner s condizionatore m

air' condi'tioning s aria condizionata, climatizzazione

air-'cool' tr raffreddare con aria

air' corps' s aviazione, arma aeronautica

air'craft' s (-craft) aeromobile m

air'craft car'rier s portaerei f

airdrome ['er ,drom] s aerodromo

air'drop' tr paracadutare

air'field' s campo d'aviazione

air'foil' s superficie f portante, velatura

air' force' s forza aerea

air' gap' s (elec) intraferro

airing ['erɪŋ] s aerazione; passeggiata all'aria aperta; pubblica discussione

air' jack'et s (aer, naut) giubbotto salvagente

air' lane' s aerovia

air'lift' s ponte aereo, aerotrasporto || tr aerotrasportare

air'line' s linea aerea; tubo dell'aria

air' mail' s posta aerea

air'-mail' adj per via aerea || s lettera per posta aerea || adv per posta aerea || tr spedire per posta aerea

air'-mail let'ter s lettera per posta aerea

air'-mail stamp' s francobollo posta aerea

air'man s (-men) aviatore m, aviere m

air' mat'tress s materassino pneumatico

air'plane' s aeroplano, aereo

air'plane car'rier s portaerei f

air' pock'et s vuoto d'aria

air' pollu'tion s contaminazione atmosferica, inquinamento atmosferico

air' port' s aeroporto

air' pump' s pompa pneumatica

air' raid' s incursione aerea

air'-raid shel'ter s rifugio antiaereo

air'-raid warn'ing s allerta

air' ri'fle s fucile m ad aria compressa

air' serv'ice s aeroservizio

air' shaft' s tubo di ventilazione

air'ship' s aeronave f

airsickness ['er,sɪknɪs] s male m d'aria

air' sleeve' s manica a vento

airspace ['er,spes] s aerospazio

air'strip' s aviopista

air' ter'minal s aerostazione

air'tight' adj impermeabile all'aria, ermetico

air'waves' spl onde fpl, radioonde fpl

air'way' s aerovia; **airways** (rad) onda, onde fpl

air·y ['erɪ] adj (-ier; -iest) arioso; leggero; aereo

aisle [aɪl] s (between rows of seats) corsia; (of a church) navata laterale; (theat) canale m

ajar [ə'dʒɑr] adj socchiuso; in disaccordo

akimbo [ə'kɪmbo] adj & adv—with arms akimbo con le mani sui fianchi

akin [ə'kɪn] adj affine; congiunto

alabaster ['ælə,bæstər] or ['ælə,bɑstər] s alabastro

à la carte [,ɑlə'kɑrt] adv alla carta

à la mode [,ɑlə'mod] or [,ælə'mod] adv alla moda; servito con gelato

alarm [ə'lɑrm] s allarme m || tr allarmare

alarm' clock' s sveglia

alas [ə'læs] or [ə'lɑs] interj ahimé!; povero me!

Albanian [æl'benɪ·ən] adj & s albanese mf

albatross ['ælbə,trɔs] or ['ælbə,trɑs] s albatro, diomedea

album ['ælbəm] s album m

albumen [æl'bjumən] s albume m

alchemy ['ælkəmi] s alchimia

alcohol ['ælkə,hɔl] or ['ælkə,hɑl] s alcole m

alcoholic [,ælkə'hɔlɪk] or [,ælkə'hɑlɪk] adj alcolico || s alcolizzato

alcove ['ælkov] s (recess) alcova; (in a garden) chiosco, padiglione m; cameretta attigua

alder ['ɔldər] s ontano, alno

al'der·man s (-men) assessore m municipale, consigliere m municipale

ale [el] s birra amara

alembic [ə'lembɪk] s alambicco

alert [ə'lʌrt] adj attento; vispo || s allerta; **to be on the alert** stare allerta || tr dare l'allerta a

Aleu'tian Is'lands [ə'luʃən] spl Isole Aleutine

Alexander [,ælɪg'zændər] or [,ælɪg-'zandər] s Alessandro

Alexan'der the Great' s Alessandro Magno

Alexandrine [,ælɪg'zændrɪn] adj & s alessandrino

alfalfa [æl'fælfə] s (bot) erba medica

algae ['ældʒi] spl alghe fpl

algebra ['ældʒɪbrə] s algebra

algebraic [,ældʒɪ'bre·ɪk] adj algebrico

Algeria [æl'dʒɪrɪ·ə] s l'Algeria

Algerian [æl'dʒɪrɪ·ən] adj & s algerino

Algiers [æl'dʒɪrz] s Algeri f

alias ['elɪ·əs] s pseudonimo || adv alias

ali·bi ['ælɪ,baɪ] s (-bis) alibi m

alien ['eljən] or ['elɪ·ən] adj straniero; (strange) strano || s straniero; (outsider) estraneo

alienate ['eljə,net] or ['elɪ·ə,net] tr alienare

alight [ə'laɪt] v (pret & pp alighted or alit [ə'lɪt]) intr scendere; **to alight on** or **upon** posarsi su

align [ə'laɪn] tr allineare || intr allinearsi

alike [ə'laɪk] adj uguali; **to look alike** assomigliarsi || adv nello stesso modo

alimen'tary canal' [,ælɪ'mentəri] s tubo digestivo

alimony ['ælɪ,moni] s alimonia

alive [ə'laɪv] adj vivo, in vita; (lively) vivace; **alive to** conscio di; **alive with** brulicante di, pieno zeppo di; **look alive!** fa presto!

alka·li ['ælkə,laɪ] s (-lis or -lies) alcali m

alkaline ['ælkə,laɪn] or ['ælkəlɪn] adj alcalino

all [ɔl] adj indef tutto, tutto il, ogni || s tutto || pron tutto; tutti; **all of** tutti || adv completamente; **all but** quasi; **all in** (slang) stanco morto; **all in all** tutto considerato; **all the better** tanto meglio; **all the worse** tanto peggio; **far all that** per quello che, e; **for all that I know** per quello che io ne sappia; **in all** tutto contato; **it's all right!** va bene!; **not at all** niente affatto; prego

allay [ə'le] tr calmare, mitigare

all' clear' s fine f dell'allarme, cessato allarme

allegation [,ælɪ'geʃən] s asserzione, affermazione

allege [ə'ledʒ] tr asserire, affermare; addurre

allegiance [ə'lidʒəns] s fedeltà f, lealtà f

allegoric(al) [ˌælɪˈɡɑrɪk(əl)] or [ˌælɪ-ˈɡɔrɪk(əl)] *adj* allegorico
allego·ry [ˈælɪˌɡɔri] *s* (**-ries**) allegoria
aller·gy [ˈælərdʒi] *s* (**-gies**) allergia
alleviate [əˈliviˌet] *tr* alleviare
alley [ˈæli] *s* vicolo, calle *f*; (*for bowling*) pista; (*tennis*) corridoio
All' Fools' Day' *s* primo d'aprile
all' fours' *spl*—**on all fours** a quattro gambe
alliance [əˈlaɪəns] *s* alleanza
alligator [ˈælɪˌɡetər] *s* alligatore *m*
alliteration [əˌlɪtəˈreʃən] *s* allitterazione
all-knowing [ˈɔlˈnoɪŋ] *adj* onnisciente
allocate [ˈæləˌket] *tr* assegnare; (*funds*) stanziare; (*to fix the place of*) allogare
allot [əˈlɑt] *v* (*pret & pp* **allotted**; *ger* **allotting**) *tr* distribuire, assegnare
all'-out' *adj* completo; (*ruthless*) acerrimo
allow [əˈlaʊ] *tr* permettere; ammettere; concedere ‖ *intr* **to allow for** prendere in considerazione
allowance [əˈlaʊ·əns] *s* (*limited share*) assegno; concessione; (*reduction in price*) sconto; tolleranza; **to make allowance for** prendere in considerazione
alloy [ˈælɔɪ] or [əˈlɔɪ] *s* lega; impurezza ‖ [əˈlɔɪ] *tr* far lega di, legare; adulterare
all-powerful [ˈɔlˈpaʊ·ərfəl] *adj* onnipotente
all' right' *adj* esatto; bene; in buona salute; (*slang*) dabbene
All' Saints' Day' *s* Ognissanti *m*
All' Souls'' Day' *s* giorno dei morti
all'spice' *s* pimento, pepe *m* della Giamaica
all'-star game' *s* partita sportiva in cui tutti i giocatori sono scelti fra i migliori
allude [əˈlud] *intr* alludere
allure [əˈlʊr] *s* fascino, incanto ‖ *tr* affascinare, incantare
alluring [əˈlʊrɪŋ] *adj* affascinante, seducente
allusion [əˈlu·ʒən] *s* allusione
al·ly [ˈælaɪ] or [əˈlaɪ] *s* (**-lies**) alleato ‖ [əˈlaɪ] *v* (*pret & pp* **-lied**) *tr* allearе; associare; **to become allied** allearsi; imparentarsi ‖ *intr* allearsi
almanac [ˈɔlməˌnæk] *s* almanacco
almighty [ɔlˈmaɪti] *adj* onnipotente
almond [ˈɑmənd] or [ˈæmənd] *s* (*nut*) mandorla; (*tree*) mandorlo
al'mond brittle' *s* croccante *m*
almost [ˈɔlmost] or [ɔlˈmost] *adv* quasi
alms [ɑmz] *s* elemosina
aloe [ˈælo] *s* aloe *m*
aloft [əˈlɔft] or [əˈlɑft] *adv* in alto, sopra; (*aer*) in volo; (*naut*) nell'alberatura
alone [əˈlon] *adj* solo; **let alone** non menzionare; **to leave alone** non disturbare ‖ *adv* solo, unicamente
along [əˈlɔŋ] or [əˈlɑŋ] *adv* (*lengthwise*) per il lungo; (*onward*) avanti; **all along** tutto il tempo; **along with**

con; **to get along** andar d'accordo; andarsene; avanzare; aver successo; **to take along** prendere con sè ‖ *prep* lungo
along'side' *adv* a lato; **alongside of** a lato di ‖ *prep* a lato di, vicino a
aloof [əˈluf] *adj* riservato, freddo; **to keep** or **stand aloof from** tenersi a distanza da ‖ *adv* lontano; da solo
aloud [əˈlaʊd] *adv* ad alta voce
alphabet [ˈælfəˌbet] *s* alfabeto
alpine [ˈælpaɪn] *adj* alpino
Alps [ælps] *spl* Alpi *fpl*
already [ɔlˈredi] *adv* già
Alsace [ælˈses] or [ˈælsæs] *s* l'Alsazia
Alsatian [ælˈseʃən] *adj & s* alsaziano
also [ˈɔlso] *adv* anche
altar [ˈɔltər] *s* altare *m*
al'tar boy' *s* accolito, chierico
al'tar-piece' *s* pala d'altare
alter [ˈɔltər] *tr* alterare; (*a male animal*) castrare ‖ *intr* diventare differente, cambiare
alteration [ˌɔltəˈreʃən] *s* alterazione, modifica
alternate [ˈɔltərnɪt] or [ˈæltərnɪt] *s* sostituto, supplente *mf* ‖ [ˈɔltərˌnet] or [ˈæltərˌnet] *tr* alternare ‖ *intr* alternarsi, avvicendarsi
al'ternating cur'rent *s* corrente alternata
alternator [ˈɔltərˌnetər] or [ˈæltərˌnetər] *s* alternatore *m*
although [ɔlˈðo] *conj* benchè, per quanto, malgrado
altimeter [ælˈtɪmɪtər] or [ˈæltəˌmitər] *s* altimetro
altitude [ˈæltɪˌtjud] or [ˈæltɪˌtud] *s* altitudine *f*
al·to [ˈælto] *s* (**-tos**) contralto
altogether [ˌɔltəˈɡeðər] *adv* completamente, affatto, tutt'insieme
altruist [ˈæltru·ɪst] *s* altruista *mf*
altruistic [ˌæltruˈɪstɪk] *adj* altruistico
alum [ˈæləm] *s* allume *m*
aluminum [əˈlumɪnəm] *s* alluminio
alum·na [əˈlʌmnə] *s* (**-nae** [ni]) diplomata, laureata
alum·nus [əˈlʌmnəs] *s* (**-ni** [naɪ]) diplomato, laureato
alveo·lus [ælˈvi·ələs] *s* (**-li** [ˌlaɪ]) alveolo
always [ˈɔlwɪz] or [ˈɔlwez] *adv* sempre
amalgam [əˈmælɡəm] *s* amalgama *m*
amalgamate [əˈmælɡəˌmet] *tr* amalgamare ‖ *intr* amalgamarsi
amass [əˈmæs] *tr* ammassare
amateur [ˈæmətˌər] *adj* da dilettante ‖ *s* amatore *m*, dilettante *mf*
amaze [əˈmez] *tr* stupire, meravigliare
amazing [əˈmezɪŋ] *adj* straordinario
Amazon [ˈæməˌzɑn] or [ˈæməzən] *s* rio delle Amazzoni; (*myth*) Amazzone *f*
ambassador [æmˈbæsədər] *s* ambasciatore *m*
ambassadress [æmˈbæsədrɪs] *s* ambasciatrice *f*
amber [ˈæmbər] *s* ambra *f*
ambigui·ty [ˌæmbɪˈɡju·ɪti] *s* (**-ties**) ambiguità *f*
ambiguous [æmˈbɪɡju·əs] *adj* ambiguo

ambition [æm'bɪʃən] *s* ambizione
ambitious [æm'bɪʃəs] *adj* ambizioso
amble ['æmbəl] *s* ambio || *intr* ambiare
ambulance ['æmbjələns] *s* ambulanza
ambush ['æmbuʃ] *s* imboscata; **to lie in ambush** tendere un'imboscata || *tr* appostare || *intr* appostarsi
amelioration [ə‚miljə're/ən] *s* miglioramento
amen ['e'men] or ['ɑ'men] *s* amen *m* || *interj* amen!
amenable [ə'minəbəl] or [ə'menəbəl] *adj* docile, aperto; (*accountable*) responsabile
amend [ə'mend] *tr* emendare || **amends** *spl* ammenda, contravvenzione; **to make amends for** fare ammenda per
amendment [ə'mendmənt] *s* emendamento
ameni·ty [ə'minɪti] or [ə'menɪti] *s* (**-ties**) amenità *f*
American [ə'merɪkən] *adj* & *s* americano
Americanize [ə'merɪkə‚naɪz] *tr* americanizzare
amethyst ['æmɪθɪst] *s* ametista
amiable ['emɪ-əbəl] *adj* amabile
amicable ['æmɪkəbəl] *adj* amichevole
amid [ə'mɪd] *prep* in mezzo a, fra, tra
amidship [ə'mɪd/ɪp] *adv* a mezzanave
amiss [ə'mɪs] *adj* erroneo, sbagliato || *adv* erroneamente; **to take amiss** offendersi, prendere in mala parte
ami·ty ['æmɪti] *s* (**-ties**) amicizia
ammeter ['æm‚mitər] *s* amperometro
ammonia [ə'monɪ-ə] *s* ammoniaca; acqua ammoniacale
ammunition [‚æmjə'nɪ/ən] *s* munizione, munizioni *fpl*
amnes·ty ['æmnɪs ti] *s* (**-ties**) amnistia || *v* (*pret* & *pp* **-tied**) *tr* amnistiare
amoeba [ə'mibə] *s* ameba
among [ə'mʌŋ] *prep* fra, tra, in mezzo a
amorous ['æmərəs] *adj* amoroso; erotico
amortize ['æmər‚taɪz] *tr* ammortare
amount [ə'maunt] *s* ammontare *m* || *intr*—**to amount to** ammontare a
ampere ['æmpɪr] *s* ampere *m*
am'pere-hour' *s* amperora *m*
amphibious [æm'fɪbɪ-əs] *adj* anfibio
amphitheater ['æmfɪ‚θi-ətər] *s* anfiteatro
ample ['æmpəl] *adj* ampio
amplifier ['æmplɪ‚faɪ-ər] *s* amplificatore *m*
ampli·fy ['æmplɪ‚faɪ] *v* (*pret* & *pp* **-fied**) *tr* amplificare
amplitude ['æmplɪ‚tjud] or ['æmplɪ‚tud] *s* ampiezza
am'plitude modula'tion *s* modulazione d'ampiezza
amputate ['æmpjə‚tet] *tr* amputare
amputee [‚æmpjə'ti] *s* chi ha subito l'amputazione di un arto
amuck [ə'mʌk] *adv* freneticamente; **to run amuck** dare in un accesso di pazzia; attaccare alla cieca
amulet ['æmjəlɪt] *s* amuleto
amuse [ə'mjuz] *tr* divertire

amusement [ə'mjuzmənt] *s* divertimento
amuse'ment park' *s* parco dei divertimenti, luna park *m*
amusing [ə'mjuzɪŋ] *adj* divertente
an [æn] or [ən] *art indef* var of **a**, used before words beginning with vowel or mute *h*
anachronism [ə'nækrə‚nɪzəm] *s* anacronismo
anaemia [ə'nimɪ-ə] *s* var of **anemia**
anaesthesia [‚ænɪs'θiʒə] *s* anestesia
anaesthetic [‚ænɪs'θetɪk] *adj* & *s* anestetico
anaesthetize [æ'nesθɪ‚taɪz] *tr* anestetizzare
analogous [ə'næləgəs] *adj* analogo
analo·gy [ə'nælədʒɪ] *s* (**-gies**) analogia
analy·sis [ə'nælɪsɪs] *s* (**-ses** [‚siz]) analisi *f*
analyst ['ænəlɪst] *s* analista *mf*
analytic(al) [‚ænə'lɪtɪk(əl)] *adj* analitico
analyze ['ænə‚laɪz] *tr* analizzare
anarchist ['ænərkɪst] *s* anarchico
anarchy ['ænərki] *s* anarchia
anathema [ə'næθɪmə] *s* anatema *m*
anatomic(al) [‚ænə'tɑmɪk(əl)] *adj* anatomico
anato·my [ə'nætəmi] *s* (**-mies**) anatomia
ancestor ['ænsestər] *s* antenato
ances·try ['ænsestri] *s* (**-tries**) lignaggio, prosapia
anchor ['æŋkər] *s* ancora; **to cast anchor** gettare l'ancora; **to ride at anchor** stare all'ancora; **to weigh anchor** salpare l'ancora, salpare || *tr* ancorare || *intr* ancorarsi, stare all'ancora
ancho·vy ['ænt/ovi] *s* (**-vies**) acciuga
ancient ['en/ənt] *adj* antico || *s* vecchio, anziano; **the ancients** gli antichi
ancillary ['ænsɪ‚leri] *adj* dipendente; ausiliario, ausiliare
and [ænd] or [ənd] *conj* e, ed; **and so on,** and so forth e così via
Andean [æn'di-ən] or ['ændɪ-ən] *adj* andino || *s* abitante *mf* della regione andina
Andes ['ændiz] *spl* Ande *fpl*
andiron ['ænd‚aɪ-ərn] *s* alare *m*
anecdote ['ænɪk‚dot] *s* aneddoto
anemia [ə'nimɪ-ə] *s* anemia
anemic [ə'nimɪk] *adj* anemico
an'eroid barom'eter ['ænə‚rɔɪd] *s* barometro aneroide
anesthesia [‚ænɪs'θiʒə] *s* anestesia
anesthetic [‚ænɪs'θetɪk] *adj* & *s* anestetico
anesthetize [æ'nesθɪ‚taɪz] *tr* anestetizzare
aneurysm ['ænjə‚rɪzəm] *s* aneurisma *m*
anew [ə'nju] or [ə'nu] *adv* di nuovo, nuovamente
angel ['endʒəl] *s* angelo; (*financial backer*) finanziatore *m*
angelic(al) [æn'dʒelɪk(əl)] *adj* angelico
anger ['æŋgər] *s* ira, collera || *tr* adirare || *intr* adirarsi, incollerirsi
angle ['æŋgəl] *s* angolo; punto di vista

|| *intr* intrigare; **to angle for** darsi da fare per

an'gle i'ron *s* cantonale *m*, angolare *m*

angler ['æŋglər] *s* pescatore *m* alla lenza; (fig) intrigante m

Anglo-Saxon ['æŋglo'sæksən] *adj & s* anglosassone *mf*

an·gry ['æŋgri] *adj* (-grier; -griest) arrabbiato; (pathol) infiammato; **to become angry at** incollerirsi per; **to become angry with** adirarsi con

anguish ['æŋgwɪʃ] *s* angoscia, pena

angular ['æŋgjələr] *adj* angolare

anhydrous [æn'haɪdrəs] *adj* anidro

aniline ['ænɪlɪn] or ['ænɪ,laɪn] *s* anilina

animal ['ænɪməl] *adj & s* animale *m*

an'imated cartoon' ['ænɪ,metɪd] *s* cartone animato

animation [,ænɪ'meʃən] *s* animazione

animosi·ty [,ænɪ'masɪti] *s* (**-ties**) animosità *f*

animus ['ænɪməs] *s* odio, malanimo

anion ['æn,aɪ·ən] *s* anione *m*

anise ['ænɪs] *s* anice *f*

anisette [,ænɪ'zɛt] *s* anisetta

ankle ['æŋkəl] *s* caviglia

an'kle·bone' *s* malleolo

an'kle support' *s* cavigliera

anklet ['æŋklɪt] *s* calzino corto; bracciale *m* da caviglia

annals ['ænəlz] *spl* annali *mpl*

annex ['ænɛks] *s* annesso, dipendenza || [ə'nɛks] *tr* annettere, appropriarsi di

annihilate [ə'naɪ·ɪ,let] *tr* annientare

anniversa·ry [,ænɪ'vʌrsəri] *adj* anniversario || *s* (**-ries**) anniversario

annotate ['ænə,tet] *tr* annotare

announce [ə'naʊns] *tr* annunciare

announcement [ə'naʊnsmənt] *s* annuncio, partecipazione

announcer [ə'naʊnsər] *s* annunziatore *m*

annoy [ə'nɔɪ] *tr* annoiare, seccare

annoyance [ə'nɔɪ·əns] *s* fastidio, seccatura

annoying [ə'nɔɪ·ɪŋ] *adj* noioso

annual ['ænjʊ·əl] *adj* annuale || *s* annuario; pianta annuale

annui·ty [ə'nju·ɪti] or [ə'nu·ɪti] *s* (**-ties**) annualità *f*; (*for life*) vitalizio

an·nul [ə'nʌl] *v* (*pret & pp* -**nulled**; *ger* -**nulling**) *tr* annullare, cassare

annunciation [ə,nʌnsɪ'eʃən] *s* annunzio || **Annunciation** *s* Annunciazione

anode ['ænod] *s* anodo

anoint [ə'nɔɪnt] *tr* ungere

anomalous [ə'namələs] *adj* anomalo

anoma·ly [ə'naməli] *s* (**-lies**) anomalia

anonymi·ty [,ænə'nɪmɪti] *s* (**-ties**) anonimia; **to preserve one's anonymity** serbare l'anonimo

anonymous [ə'nanɪməs] *adj* anonimo

another [ə'nʌðər] *adj & pron indef* un altro

answer ['ænsər] or ['ɑnsər] *s* risposta; (*to a problem*) soluzione || *tr* rispondere a; **this will answer your purpose** questo fa per Lei; **to answer back** (slang) dare una rispostaccia; **to answer the door** andare a rispondere

|| *intr* rispondere; corrispondere; essere responsabile; **to answer back** (slang) dare una rispostaccia

ant [ænt] *s* formica

antagonism [æn'tægə,nɪzəm] *s* antagonismo

antagonize [æn'tægə,naɪz] *tr* opporsi a; creare antagonismo in

antarctic [ænt'ɑrktɪk] *adj* antartico || **the Antarctic** la regione antartica

anteater ['ænt,itər] *s* formichiere *m*

antecedent [,æntɪ'sidənt] *adj & s* antecedente *m*; **antecedents** antenati *mpl*

antechamber ['æntɪ,tʃembər] *s* anticamera

antedate ['æntɪ,det] *tr* antidatare; (*to happen before*) antecedere

antelope ['æntɪ,lop] *s* antilope *f*

anten·na [æn'tɛnə] *s* (**-nae** [ni]) (*of insect*) antenna || *s* (**-nas**) (rad, telv) antenna

antepenult [,æntɪ'pinʌlt] *s* terzultima sillaba

anteroom ['æntɪ,rum] or ['æntɪ,rʊm] *s* anticamera, sala d'aspetto

anthem ['ænθəm] *s* inno

ant'hill' *s* formicaio

antholo·gy [æn'θɑlədʒi] *s* (**-gies**) antologia

anthracite ['ænθrə,saɪt] *s* antracite *f*

anthrax ['ænθræks] *s* antrace *m*

anthropoid ['ænθrə,pɔɪd] *adj* antropoide, antropomorfo

anthropology [,ænθrə'pɑlədʒi] *s* antropologia

antiaircraft [,æntɪ'ɛr,kræft] or [,æntɪ'ɛr,krɑft] *adj* antiaereo

antibiotic [,æntɪbaɪ'ɑtɪk] *adj & s* antibiotico

antibod·y ['æntɪ,bɑdi] *s* (**-ies**) anticorpo

anticipate [æn'tɪsɪ,pet] *tr* anticipare, prevedere; ripromettersi

anticipation [æn,tɪsɪ'peʃən] *s* anticipazione, previsione

antics ['æntɪks] *spl* pagliacciate *fpl*, buffonate *fpl*

antidote ['æntɪ,dot] *s* antidoto

antifreeze ['æntɪ,friz] *s* anticongelante *m*

antiglare [,æntɪ'glɛr] *adj* antiabbagliante

anti-G' suit' *s* tuta antigravità

antiknock [,æntɪ'nɑk] *adj* antidetonante

antimissile [,æntɪ'mɪsɪl] *adj* antimissile

antimony ['æntɪ,moni] *s* antimonio

antinoise [,æntɪ'nɔɪz] *adj* antirumore

antipa·thy [æn'tɪpəθi] *s* (**-thies**) antipatia

antipersonnel [,æntɪ,pʌrsə'nɛl] *adj* (*e.g., mine*) antiuomo

antiquarian [,æntɪ'kwɛrɪ·ən] *adj & s* antiquario

antiquar·y ['æntɪ,kwɛri] *s* (**-ies**) antiquario

antiquated ['æntɪ,kwetɪd] *adj* antiquato

antique [æn'tik] *adj* antico, vecchio; antiquato || *s* oggetto d'epoca, antichità *f*

antique' deal'er *s* antiquario
antique' store' *s* negozio d'antiquariato
antiqui·ty [æn'tıkwıtı] *s* (**-ties**) antichità *f*
anti-Semitic [,æntısı'mıtık] *adj* antisemita
antiseptic [,æntı'septık] *adj* & *s* antisettico
antislavery [,æntı'slevərı] *adj* antischiavista
antitank [,æntı'tæŋk] *adj* anticarro
antitheft [,æntı'θeft] *adj* antifurto
antithe·sis [æn'tıθısıs] *s* (**-ses** [,sız]) antitesi *f*
antitoxin [,æntı'taksın] *s* antitossina
antitrust [,æntı'trʌst] *adj* antitrust
antler ['æntlər] *s* corno di cervo
antonym ['æntənım] *s* antonimo
Antwerp ['æntwərp] *s* Anversa
anvil ['ænvıl] *s* incudine *m*
anxie·ty [æŋ'zaı·ətı] *s* (**-ties**) ansietà *f*; (*psychol*) angoscia
anxious ['æŋk/əs] *adj* ansioso; **anxious about** sollecito di; **anxious for** desideroso di
any ['enı] *adj indef* ogni, qualunque, qualsiasi; qualche, e.g., **do you know any boy who could help me?** conosce qualche ragazzo che possa aiutarmi?; *di* + *art*, e.g., **do you want any cheese?** vuole del formaggio?; **not . . . any** non . . . nessuno, e.g., **he does not read any newspaper** non legge nessun giornale || *adv* un po', e.g., **do you want any?** ne vuole un po'?; **not . . . any longer** non . . . più; **not . . . any more** non . . . più || *pron* ne, e.g., **do you want any?** ne vuole?
an'y·bod'y *pron indef* chiunque; (*in interrogatory sentences*) qualcuno; **not . . . anybody** non . . . nessuno
an'y·how' *adv* in qualunque modo, comunque; in ogni caso; (*haphazardly*) alla rinfusa
an'y·one' *pron indef* chiunque; (*in interrogatory sentences*) qualcuno; **not . . . anyone** non . . . nessuno
an'y·thing' *s* qualunque cosa || *pron indef* qualcosa; qualunque cosa; tutto quanto; checchessia; **anything at all** qualunque cosa; **not . . . anything** non . . . niente; **not . . . anything at all** non . . . niente affatto, non . . . nulla; **not . . . anything else** non . . . nient'altro
an'y·way' *adv* in qualunque modo, comunque; in ogni caso; (*haphazardly*) alla rinfusa
an'y·where' *adv* dovunque, in qualsiasi luogo; **not . . . anywhere** non . . . in nessun luogo
apace [ə'pes] *adv* presto, rapidamente
apart [ə'part] *adv* a parte, a pezzi; separatamente; **apart from** a parte da; oltre a; **to come apart** andare a pezzi, cadere a pezzi; **to set apart** mettere in disparte; **to take apart** smontare; **to tear apart** fare a pezzi; **to tell apart** distinguere
apartment [ə'partmənt] *s* appartamento; (*single room*) stanza

apart'ment house' *s* casa d'appartamenti
apathetic [,æpə'θetık] *adj* apatico
apathy ['æpəθı] *s* apatia
ape [ep] *s* scimmia antropomorfa; scimmia || *tr* imitare, scimmiottare
Apennines ['æpə,naınz] *spl* Appennini *mpl*
aperture ['æpərt/ər] *s* apertura
apex ['epeks] *s* (**apexes** or **apices** ['æpı,sız]) apice *m*
apheresis [ə'ferısıs] *s* aferesi *f*
aphorism ['æfə,rızəm] *s* aforisma *m*
aphrodisiac [,æfrə'dızı,æk] *adj* & *s* afrodisiaco
apiar·y ['epı,erı] *s* (**-ies**) apiario
apiece [ə'pis] *adv* a testa, per persona; ciascuno
apish ['epı/] *adj* scimmiesco; da scimmia
aplomb [ə'plam] *s* disinvoltura, baldanza
apocalypse [ə'pakə,lıps] *s* apocalisse *f*
apogee ['æpə,dʒı] *s* apogeo
apologetic [ə,palə'dʒetık] *adj* pieno di scuse
apologize [ə'palə,dʒaız] *intr* chiedere scusa, scusarsi
apolo·gy [ə'palədʒı] *s* (**-gies**) scusa; (*makeshift*) surrogato
apoplectic [,æpə'plektık] *adj* & *s* apoplettico
apoplexy ['æpə,pleksı] *s* apoplessia
apostle [ə'pasəl] *s* apostolo
apostrophe [ə'pastrəfı] *s* (*mark*) apostrofo; (*rhet*) apostrofe *f*
apothecar·y [ə'paθı,kerı] *s* (**-ies**) farmacista *mf*
appall [ə'pɔl] *tr* sgomentare, sbigottire
appalling [ə'pɔlıŋ] *adj* sconcertante
appara·tus [,æpə'retəs] *or* [,æpə'rætəs] *s* (**-tus** *or* **-tuses**) apparato
apparel [ə'pærəl] *s* confezioni *fpl*, vestiario
apparent [ə'pærənt] *or* [ə'perənt] *adj* apparente; chiaramente visibile
apparition [,æpə'rı/ən] *s* apparizione
appeal [ə'pil] *s* appello; (*attraction*) attrattiva, fascino || *tr* (*a sentence*) appellare contro || *intr* dare nell'occhio; **to appeal from** (law) appellarsi contro; **to appeal to** supplicare, pregare; piacere a, e.g., **his idea appeals to me** la sua idea mi piace
appear [ə'pır] *intr* apparire; (*to seem*) sembrare; (*said of a book*) uscire; (*before the public*) presentarsi; (law) comparire
appearance [ə'pırəns] *s* apparizione; (*of a book*) pubblicazione; (*outward look*) apparenza; (law) comparizione; **to keep up appearances** salvare le apparenze
appease [ə'piz] *tr* pacificare, placare; (*a desire*) soddisfare
appeasement [ə'pizmənt] *s* pacificazione, tranquillizzazione
appel'late court' [ə'pelıt] *s* corte *f* d'appello
appellation [,æpə'le/ən] *s* denominazione, nome *m*
append [ə'pend] *tr* allegare, aggiungere

appendage [ə'pendɪdʒ] s appendice f
appendicitis [ə,pendɪ'saɪtɪs] s appendicite f
appen·dix [ə'pendɪks] s (**-dixes** or **-dices** [dɪ,siz]) appendice f
appertain [,æpər'ten] intr spettare, riferirsi
appetite ['æpɪ,taɪt] s appetito
appetizer ['æpɪ,taɪzər] s (drink) aperitivo; (food) stimulante m dell'appetito
appetizing ['æpɪ,taɪzɪŋ] adj appetitoso
applaud tr applaudire, applaudire (with dat) || intr applaudire
applause [ə'plɔz] s applauso, applausi mpl
apple ['æpəl] s mela, pomo; (tree) melo, pomo
ap'plejack' s acquavite f di mele
ap'ple of dis'cord s pomo della discordia
ap'ple of one's eye' s pupilla degli occhi di qlcu, beniamino di qlcu
ap'ple pie' s torta di mele
ap'ple pol'isher s leccapiedi mf
ap'ple-sauce' s marmellata di mele; (slang) scemenza
appliance [ə'plaɪ·əns] s apparecchio, apparato; (complicated instrument) congegno; (for domestic chores) utensile m; (act of applying) applicazione
applicant ['æplɪkənt] s postulante mf, aspirante m, candidato
application [,æplɪ'keʃən] s applicazione; uso; richiesta, domanda
ap·ply [ə'plaɪ] v (pret & pp **-plied**) tr applicare; (the brakes) mettere; (e.g., a nickname) affibbiare || intr (said of a rule) essere applicabile; fare richiesta; **to apply for** sollecitare
appoint [ə'pɔɪnt] tr nominare; assegnare; (to furnish) ammobiliare
appointee [,æpɔɪn'ti] s persona nominata a una carica
appointive [ə'pɔɪntɪv] adj a nomina
appointment [ə'pɔɪntmənt] s nomina; (position) ufficio; (agreement to meet) appuntamento; **appointments** mobilia, arredamento; **by appointment** previo appuntamento
apportion [ə'pɔrʃən] tr spartire, dividere proporzionatamente
appraisal [ə'prezəl] s stima, valutazione; (of real estate) estimo
appraise [ə'prez] tr stimare, valutare
appreciable [ə'priʃɪ·əbəl] adj apprezzabile, notevole
appreciate [ə'priʃɪ,et] tr apprezzare, valutare; (to be grateful for) gradire; (to be aware of) rendersi conto di; (to raise in value) valorizzare || intr aumentare di valore
appreciation [ə,priʃɪ'eʃən] s apprezzamento, valutazione; (grateful recognition) gradimento, riconoscenza; valorizzazione
appreciative [ə'priʃɪ,etɪv] adj grato, riconoscente
apprehend [,æprɪ'hend] tr (to fear) temere; (to understand) comprendere; (to arrest) arrestare

apprehension [,æprɪ'henʃən] s timore m, apprensione; comprensione; arresto
apprehensive [,æprɪ'hensɪv] adj apprensivo
apprentice [ə'prentɪs] s apprendista mf, novizio || tr mettere in apprendistato; accettare in apprendistato
apprenticeship [ə'prentɪs,ʃɪp] s apprendistato, carovana
apprise or **apprize** [ə'praɪz] tr avvertire, avvisare; stimare, valutare
approach [ə'protʃ] s (a coming near) avvicinamento; (of night) avvicinarsi m, far m; approssimazione; (access) via d'accesso; (to a problem) impostazione; **approaches** approcci mpl || tr avvicinarsi a, avvicinare; fare approcci con || intr avvicinarsi, approssimarsi
approbation [,æprə'beʃən] s approvazione
appropriate [ə'proprɪ·ɪt] adj appropriato, acconcio || [ə'proprɪ,et] tr (to take) appropriarsi di; (to set aside for some specific use) stanziare
approval [ə'pruvəl] s approvazione; consenso; **on approval** in prova
approve [ə'pruv] tr & intr approvare
approximate [ə'praksɪmɪt] adj approssimato, approssimativo || [ə'praksɪ,met] tr approssimarsi a || intr approssimarsi
apricot ['eprɪ,kat] or ['æprɪ,kat] adj color albicocca || s (fruit) albicocca; (tree) albicocco
April ['eprɪl] s aprile m
A'pril fool' s pesce m d'aprile
A'pril Fools'' Day' s primo d'aprile
apron ['eprən] s grembiale m, grembiule m; **tied to the apron strings of** attaccato alle sottane di
apropos [,æprə'po] adj opportuno || adv—**apropos of** a proposito di
apse [æps] s abside f
apt [æpt] adj atto, appropriato; (quick) pronto; **to be apt to** essere propenso a, portato a
aptitude ['æptɪ,tjud] or ['æptɪ,tud] s attitudine f
ap'titude test' s esame m attitudinale
Apulia [ə'pjulɪ·ə] s la Puglia
aqualung ['ækwə,lʌŋ] s autorespiratore m
aquamarine [,ækwəmə'rin] s acquamarina
aquaplane ['ækwə,plen] s acquaplano || intr andare in acquaplano
aquari·um [ə'kwerɪ·əm] s (**-ums** or **-a** [ə]) acquario, vasca dei pesci
Aquarius [ə'kwerɪ·əs] s (astr) Acquario
aquatic [ə'kwætɪk] or [ə'kwatɪk] adj acquatico || s animale acquatico; pianta acquatica; **aquatics** sport acquatici
aqueduct ['ækwə,dʌkt] s acquedotto
aqueous ['ekwɪ·əs] or ['ækwɪ·əs] adj acquoso
aq'uiline nose' ['ækwɪ,laɪn] s naso aquilino
Arab ['ærəb] adj & s arabo
Arabic ['ærəbɪk] adj & s arabo

arbiter [ˈɑrbɪtər] s arbitro

arbitrary [ˈɑrbɪˌtreri] adj arbitrario

arbitrate [ˈɑrbɪˌtret] tr arbitrare || intr fare l'arbitro

arbitration [ˌɑrbɪˈtreʃən] s arbitrato

arbitrator [ˈɑrbɪˌtretər] s arbitro

arbor [ˈɑrbər] s pergola, pergolato; (mach) albero, asse m

arbore·tum [ˌɑrbəˈritəm] s (-tums or -ta [tə]) arboreto

arbutus [ɑrˈbjutəs] s (Arbutus unedo) corbezzolo

arc [ɑrk] s arco; (elec) arco voltaico || intr (elec) formare un arco

arcade [ɑrˈked] s arcata, portico

arch [ɑrtʃ] adj malizioso || s arco; (anat) arco del piede || tr attraversare; arcuare || intr inarcarsi

archaeology [ˌɑrkɪˈɑlədʒi] s archeologia

archaic [ɑrˈke·ɪk] adj arcaico

archaism [ˈɑrkeˌɪzəm] or [ˈɑrkiˌɪzəm] s arcaismo

archangel [ˈɑrkˌendʒəl] s arcangelo

archbishop [ˈɑrtʃˈbɪʃəp] s arcivescovo

archduke [ˈɑrtʃˈdjuk] or [ˈɑrtʃˈduk] s arciduca m

archene·my [ˈɑrtʃˈɛnɪmi] s (-mies) nemico giurato

archer [ˈɑrtʃər] s arciere m

archery [ˈɑrtʃəri] s tiro con l'arco

archetype [ˈɑrkɪˌtaɪp] s archetipo, prototipo

archipela·go [ˌɑrkɪˈpɛləgo] s (-gos or -goes) arcipelago

architect [ˈɑrkɪˌtɛkt] s architetto

architectural [ˌɑrkɪˈtɛktʃərəl] adj architetturale, architettonico

architecture [ˈɑrkɪˌtɛktʃər] s architettura

archives [ˈɑrkaɪvz] spl archivio

arch'way' s arcata

arc' lamp' s lampada ad arco

arctic [ˈɑrktɪk] adj artico || the Arctic la regione artica

arc' weld'ing s saldatura ad arco

ardent [ˈɑrdənt] adj ardente

ardor [ˈɑrdər] s ardore m

arduous [ˈɑrdʒʊ·əs] or [ˈɑrdju·əs] adj arduo

area [ˈɛrɪ·ə] s area

ar'ea code' s prefisso

Argentina [ˌɑrdʒənˈtinə] s l'Argentina

Argentine [ˈɑrdʒənˌtin] or [ˈɑrdʒənˌtaɪn] adj & s argentino || the Argentine l'Argentina

Argonaut [ˈɑrgəˌnɔt] s argonauta m

argue [ˈɑrgju] tr dibattere; (to indicate) indicare, provare; to argue out of dissuadere da; to argue s.o. into s.th persuadere qlcu di qlco || intr argomentare, discutere

argument [ˈɑrgjəmənt] s discussione, argomentazione; (theme) argomento

argumentative [ˌɑrgjəˈmɛntətɪv] adj litigioso

aria [ˈɑrɪ·ə] or [ˈɛrɪ·ə] s aria

arid [ˈærɪd] adj arido

aridity [əˈrɪdɪti] s aridità f

Aries [ˈɛriz] or [ˈɛriˌiz] s (astr) Ariete m

aright [əˈraɪt] adv correttamente; to set aright rettificare

arise [əˈraɪz] v (pret arose [əˈroz]; pp arisen [əˈrɪzən]) intr alzarsi; (to originate) provenire, trarre origine; (to occur) succedere, avvenire; (to be raised, as objections) avanzarsi

aristocra·cy [ˌærɪsˈtɑkrəsi] s (-cies) aristocrazia

aristocrat [əˈrɪstəˌkræt] s aristocratico

aristocratic [əˌrɪstəˈkrætɪk] adj aristocratico

Aristotelian [ˌærɪstəˈtili·ən] adj & s aristotelico

Aristotle [ˈærɪˌstɑtəl] s Aristotele m

arithmetic [əˈrɪθmətɪk] s aritmetica

arithmetical [ˌærɪθˈmɛtɪkəl] adj aritmetico

arithmetician [ˌærɪθməˈtɪʃən] or [əˌrɪθməˈtɪʃən] s aritmetico

ark [ɑrk] s arca

ark' of the cov'enant s arca dell'alleanza

arm [ɑrm] s braccio; (e.g., of a bear) zampa; (of a chair) bracciolo; (weapon) arma; arm in arm a braccetto; to be up in arms essere in armi; essere indignato; to lay down one's arms deporre le armi; to rise up in arms levarsi in armi; with open arms a braccia aperte || tr armare || intr armarsi

armament [ˈɑrməmənt] s armamento

armature [ˈɑrməˌtʃər] s (of an animal) corazza; (of motor or dynamo) indotto; (of a buzzer or electric bell) ancora

arm'chair' s poltrona

Armenian [ɑrˈmini·ən] adj & s armeno

armful [ˈɑrmˌful] s bracciata

arm'hole' s giro manica

armistice [ˈɑrmɪstɪs] s armistizio

armlet [ˈɑrmlɪt] s bracciale m

armor [ˈɑrmər] s armatura, corazza || tr corazzare, blindare

ar'mored car' s carro armato

ar'mor plate' s lamiera di corazza

armor·y [ˈɑrməri] s (-ies) armeria; arsenale m

arm'pit' s ascella

arm'rest' s bracciolo

ar·my [ˈɑrmi] adj dell'esercito, militare || s (-mies) esercito; (two or more army corps) armata

ar'my corps' s corpo d'armata

aromatic [ˌærəˈmætɪk] adj aromatico

around [əˈraʊnd] adv intorno; all'intorno; dappertutto; to turn around voltarsi || prep intorno a; (coll) vicino a; (approximately) (coll) circa

arouse [əˈraʊz] tr eccitare, incitare; svegliare

arpeg·gio [ɑrˈpɛdʒo] s (-gios) arpeggio

arraign [əˈren] tr citare, portare in giudizio; accusare

arrange [əˈrendʒ] tr disporre, sistemare; (a dispute) comporre, accomodare; (mus) ridurre, arrangiare

arrangement [əˈrendʒmənt] s disposizione, sistemazione; composizione, accomodamento; (mus) riduzione, arrangiamento; **arrangements** preparazione, preparativi *mpl*

array [ə're] *s* ordine *m*; (*clothes*) abbigliamento; (mil) spiegamento, schiera ‖ *tr* disporre; abbigliare, adornare; (mil) spiegare, schierare

arrears [ə'rɪrz] *spl* arretrati *mpl*; **in arrears** in arretrato

arrest [ə'rest] *s* arresto; **under arrest** in arresto ‖ *tr* arrestare; (*the attention*) attrarre

arresting [ə'restɪŋ] *adj* interessante, che fa colpo

arrival [ə'raɪvəl] *s* arrivo; persona arrivata

arrive [ə'raɪv] *intr* arrivare

arrogance ['ærəgəns] *s* arroganza

arrogant ['ærəgənt] *adj* arrogante

arrogate ['ærə ͵get] *tr* (*to take without right*) arrogare per sé, arrogarsi; (*to claim for another*) attribuire ingiustamente

arrow ['æro] *s* freccia, saetta

ar'row·head' *s* punta di freccia; (bot) sagittaria

arsenal ['ɑrsənəl] *s* arsenale *m*

arsenic ['ɑrsɪnɪk] *s* arsenico

arson ['ɑrsən] *s* incendio doloso

art [ɑrt] *s* arte *f*

arter·y ['ɑrtəri] *s* (**-ies**) arteria

artful ['ɑrtfəl] *adj* artificioso; (*clever*) destro; (*crafty*) astuto

arthritic [ɑr'θrɪtɪk] *adj & s* artritico

arthritis [ɑr'θraɪtɪs] *s* artrite *f*

artichoke ['ɑrtɪ ͵tʃok] *s* carciofo

article ['ɑrtɪkəl] *s* articolo

articulate [ɑr'tɪkjəlɪt] *adj* articolato; facile di parola ‖ ['ɑrtɪkjə ͵let] *tr* articolare ‖ *intr* pronunziare in modo articolato

articulation [ɑr ͵tɪkjə'leʃən] *s* articolazione

artifact ['ɑrtɪ ͵fækt] *s* manufatto

artifice ['ɑrtɪfɪs] *s* artificio

artificial [͵ɑrtɪ'fɪʃəl] *adj* artificiale

artillery [ɑr'tɪləri] *s* artiglieria

artil'lery·man *s* (**-men**) artigliere *m*, cannoniere *m*

artisan ['ɑrtɪzən] *s* artigiano

artist ['ɑrtɪst] *s* artista *mf*

artistic [ɑr'tɪstɪk] *adj* artistico

artistry ['ɑrtɪstri] *s* abilità artistica

artless ['ɑrtlɪs] *adj* ingenuo, naturale; ignorante; (*clumsy*) grossolano

arts' and crafts' *spl* arti *fpl* e mestieri *mpl*

art·y ['ɑrti] *adj* (**-ier; -iest**) (coll) interessato nell'arte con ostentazione

Aryan ['ɛrɪ·ən] *or* ['ɑrjən] *adj & s* ariano

as [æz] *or* [əz] *pron rel* che; **the same as** lo stesso che ‖ *adv* come; per esempio; **as . . . as** così . . . come; **as far as** fino a; **as far as I know** per quanto mi consta; **as for** in quanto a, per quanto concerne; **as is** (slang) com'è, nelle condizioni in cui si trova; **as long as** tanto che, mentre che; **as per** secondo; **as soon as** appena, non appena, non appena che; **as to** per quanto concerne; **as well** pure, anche; **as yet** ancora ‖ *prep* come; da; **as a rule** come regola ‖

conj come; mentre; dato che; per quanto; **as if** come se; **as it were** per così dire; **as though** come se

asbestos [æs'bestəs] *s* asbesto, amianto

ascend [ə'send] *tr* ascendere, scalare ‖ *intr* ascendere, salire

ascension [ə'senʃən] *s* ascensione, scalata ‖ **Ascension** *s* Ascensione

ascent [ə'sent] *s* scalata; salita; (*slope*) erta

ascertain [͵æsər'ten] *tr* sincerarsi di, verificare

ascertainable [͵æsər'tenəbəl] *adj* verificabile

ascetic [ə'setɪk] *adj* ascetico ‖ *s* asceta *m*

ascor'bic ac'id [ə'skɔrbɪk] *s* acido ascorbico

ascribe [ə'skraɪb] *tr* attribuire, imputare

aseptic [ə'septɪk] *or* [e'septɪk] *adj* asettico

ash [æʃ] *s* cenere *f*; (bot) frassino

ashamed [ə'ʃemd] *adj* vergognoso; **to be or feel ashamed** vergognarsi

ash'can' *s* pattumiera; (coll) bomba antisommergibile

ashen ['æʃən] *adj* cinereo

ashlar ['æʃlər] *s* bugna, bugnato

ashore [ə'ʃor] *adv* a terra; **to come ashore** andare a terra, sbarcare; **to run ashore** arenarsi

ash'tray' *s* portacenere *m*

Ash' Wednes'day *s* le Ceneri

Asia ['eʒə] *or* ['eʃə] *s* l'Asia *f*

A'sia Mi'nor *s* l'Asia *f* Minore

Asian ['eʒən] *or* ['eʃən] *or* **Asiatic** [͵eʒɪ'ætɪk] *or* [͵eʃɪ'ætɪk] *adj & s* asiatico

aside [ə'saɪd] *s* parola detta a parte; (theat) a parte *m* ‖ *adv* da parte; a parte; **aside from** (coll) eccetto; separato da; **to step aside** farsi da un lato

asinine ['æsɪnaɪn] *adj* (*like an ass*) asinino; (*stupid*) asinesco

ask [æsk] *or* [ɑsk] *tr* chiedere (with *dat*), domandare (with *dat*); invitare; (*a question*) fare; **to ask s.o. for s.th** chiedere or domandare qlco a qlcu; **to ask s.o. to** + *inf* chiedere a qlcu di + *inf* ‖ *intr* chiedere; **to ask about** chiedere informazioni di; **to ask for** chiedere, domandare; **to ask for it** (coll) andare in cerca di disgrazie; (coll) volerlo, e.g., **he asked for it** l'ha voluto

askance [ə'skæns] *adv* di traverso, di sbieco; (fig) con sospetto

asleep [ə'slip] *adj* addormentato; **to fall asleep** addormentarsi

asp [æsp] *s* aspide *m*

asparagus [ə'spærəgəs] *s* asparago; (as *food*) asparagi *mpl*

aspect ['æspekt] *s* aspetto; (*direction anything faces*) esposizione

aspen ['æspən] *s* pioppo tremolo, tremolo

aspersion [ə'spʌrʒən] *or* [ə'spʌrʃən] *s* diffamazione, calunnia; (eccl) aspersione

asphalt ['æsfɔlt] *or* ['æsfælt] *s* asfalto ‖ *tr* asfaltare

asphyxiate [æsˈfɪksɪ ˌet] *tr* asfissiare
aspirant [əˈspaɪrənt] or [ˈæspɪrənt] *s* aspirante *mf*
aspire [əˈspaɪr] *intr* aspirare
aspirin [ˈæspɪrɪn] *s* aspirina
ass [æs] *s* asino
assail [əˈsel] *tr* assalire, assaltare
assassin [əˈsæsɪn] *s* assassino
assassinate [əˈsæsɪ ˌnet] *tr* assassinare
assassination [ə ˌsæsɪˈneʃən] *s* assassinio
assault [əˈsɔlt] *s* assalto ‖ *tr* assaltare
assault' and bat'tery *s* vie *fpl* di fatto
assay [əˈse] or [ˈæse] *s* saggio, esame *m* ‖ [əˈse] *tr* saggiare
assemblage [əˈsemblɪdʒ] *s* assemblea; (mach) montaggio
assemble [əˈsembəl] *tr* riunire; (mach) montare, mettere insieme ‖ *intr* assembrarsi, riunirsi
assembler [əˈsemblər] *s* montatore *m*
assem•bly [əˈsemblɪ] *s* (-blies) assemblea, riunione; (mach) montaggio
assem'bly hall' *s* sala di riunioni
assem'bly line' *s* catena di montaggio
assem'bly•man *s* (-men) membro dell'assemblea legislativa
assent [əˈsent] *s* assenso ‖ *intr* assentire
assert [əˈsʌrt] *tr* asserire; **to assert oneself** far valere i propri diritti
assertion [əˈsʌrʃən] *s* asserzione
assess [əˈses] *tr* stimare, valutare; (*for taxation or fine*) tassare
assessment [əˈsesmənt] *s* valutazione; tassazione
assessor [əˈsesər] *s* agente *m* delle tasse
asset [ˈæset] *s* vantaggio; persona di valore; **assets** (com) attivo; (law) beni *mpl*
assiduous [əˈsɪdʒu-əs] or [əˈsɪdju-əs] *adj* assiduo
assign [əˈsaɪn] *s* cessionario ‖ *tr* assegnare; (*e.g., a date*) fissare; (*a right*) trasferire
assignation [ˌæsɪgˈneʃən] *s* assegnazione; trasferimento; (*date*) appuntamento amoroso
assignment [əˈsaɪnmənt] *s* assegnamento; (*of rights*) trasferimento; (*schoolwork*) compito
assimilate [əˈsɪmɪ ˌlet] *tr* assimilare ‖ *intr* essere assimilato; assimilarsi
assist [əˈsɪst] *s* aiuto ‖ *tr* aiutare, assistere
assistance [əˈsɪstəns] *s* assistenza, aiuto
assistant [əˈsɪstənt] *adj* & *s* assistente *m*
associate [əˈsoʃɪ-ɪt] or [əˈsoʃɪ ˌet] *adj* associato ‖ *s* associato; membro limitato ‖ [əˈsoʃɪ ˌet] *tr* associare ‖ *intr* associarsi
association [ə ˌsoʃɪˈeʃən] *s* associazione
assort [əˈsɔrt] *tr* assortire ‖ *intr* associarsi
assortment [əˈsɔrtmənt] *s* assortimento
assuage [əˈswedʒ] *tr* alleviare
assume [əˈsum] or [əˈsjum] *tr* assumere; (*to appropriate*) usurpare; (*to pretend*) fingere; (*to suppose*) supporre
assumed [əˈsumd] or [əˈsjumd] *adj* supposto, immaginario

assumption [əˈsʌmpʃən] *s* (*arrogance*) aria, arroganza; (*thing taken for granted*) supposizione; (*of an undertaking*) assunzione
assurance [əˈʃurəns] *s* assicurazione, certezza; baldanza, fiducia in sè; (*too much boldness*) sicumera
assure [əˈʃur] *tr* assicurare
assuredly [əˈʃurɪdlɪ] *adv* sicuramente
astatine [ˈæstə ˌtin] *s* astato
asterisk [ˈæstə ˌrɪsk] *s* asterisco, stelloncino
astern [əˈstʌrn] *adv* a poppa, a poppavia
asthma [ˈæzmə] or [ˈæsmə] *s* asma
astonish [əˈstanɪʃ] *tr* meravigliare, stupefare
astonishing [əˈstanɪʃɪŋ] *adj* stupefacente, sorprendente
astound [əˈstaund] *tr* stupefare, sbalordire
astounding [əˈstaundɪŋ] *adj* stupefacente
astraddle [əˈstrædəl] *adv* a cavaliere, a cavalcioni
astray [əˈstre] *adv* sulla cattiva via; **to go astray** traviarsi; **to lead astray** traviare
astride [əˈstraɪd] *adj* & *adv* a cavaliere; (*said of a person*) a cavalcioni ‖ *prep* a cavaliere di; a cavalcioni di
astrology [əˈstralədʒɪ] *s* astrologia
astronaut [ˈæstrə ˌnɔt] *s* astronauta *mf*
astronautic [ˌæstrəˈnɔtɪk] *adj* astronautico ‖ **astronautics** *ssg* astronautica
astronomer [əˈstranəmər] *s* astronomo
astronomic(al) [ˌæstrəˈnamɪk(əl)] *adj* astronomico
astronomy [əˈstranəmɪ] *s* astronomia
astute [əˈstjut] or [əˈstut] *adj* astuto
asunder [əˈsʌndər] *adv* a pezzi; **to tear asunder** separare, fare a pezzi
asylum [əˈsaɪləm] *s* asilo
asymmetry [eˈsɪmɪtrɪ] *s* asimmetria
at [æt] or [ət] *prep* a; in; a casa di, e.g., **at John's** a casa di Giovanni; da, e.g., **at Mary's** da Maria; di, e.g., **to be surprised at** essere sorpreso di; **to laugh at** ridersi di
atheist [ˈeθi-ɪst] *s* ateista *mf*
Athenian [əˈθini-ən] *adj* & *s* ateniese *mf*
Athens [ˈæθɪnz] *s* Atene *f*
athirst [əˈθʌrst] *adj* assetato
athlete [ˈæθlit] *s* atleta *mf*
athletic [æθˈletɪk] *adj* atletico ‖ **athletics** *ssg* & *spl* atletica
Atlantic [ætˈlæntɪk] *adj* atlantico ‖ *adj* & *s* Atlantico
atlas [ˈætləs] *s* atlante *m* ‖ **Atlas** *s* Atlante *m*
atmosphere [ˈætməs ˌfɪr] *s* atmosfera
atmospheric [ˌætməsˈferɪk] *adj* atmosferico ‖ **atmospherics** *spl* disturbi atmosferici
atom [ˈætəm] *s* atomo
at'om bomb' *s* bomba atomica
atomic [əˈtamɪk] *adj* atomico
atom'ic age' *s* era atomica
atom'ic sub'marine *s* sommergibile *m* nucleare
atomize [ˈætə ˌmaɪz] *tr* atomizzare

atomizer [ˈætəˌmaɪzər] s nebulizzatore *m*

at'om smash'er s acceleratore *m* di particelle

atone [əˈton] *intr*—**to atone for** espiare

atonement [əˈtonmənt] s riparazione; espiazione

atop [əˈtɑp] *adv* in cima || *prep* in cima a

atrocious [əˈtroʃəs] *adj* atroce

atroci·ty [əˈtrɑsɪti] s (**-ties**) atrocità *f*

atro·phy [ˈætrəfi] s atrofia || *v* (*pret & pp* -**phied**) *tr* atrofizzare || *intr* atrofizzarsi

attach [əˈtætʃ] *tr* attaccare; (*to affix*) apporre; (*to attribute*) attribuire; (*law*) sequestrare; **to be attached to** essere legato a; fare parte di || *intr*—**to attach to** essere pertinente a

attaché [ˌætəˈʃe] or [əˈtæʃe] s attaché *m.*, addetto

attaché' case' s valigetta diplomatica

attachment [əˈtætʃmənt] s attacco, unione; affezione; (mach) accessorio; (law) sequestro

attack [əˈtæk] s attacco || *tr & intr* attaccare

attain [əˈten] *tr* raggiungere || *intr*—**to attain to** raggiungere, conseguire

attainder [əˈtendər] s morte *f* civile

attainment [əˈtenmənt] s raggiungimento, realizzazione; (*accomplishment*) dote *f*

attempt [əˈtempt] s tentativo; (*attack*) attentato || *tr* tentare; (*s.o.'s life*) attentare a

attend [əˈtend] *tr* (*to be present at*) presenziare, presenziare a, assistere a; (*to accompany*) accompagnare; (*to take care of;* to pay attention to) assistere || *intr*—**to attend to** occuparsi di, attendere a

attendance [əˈtendəns] s (*attending*) presenza; (*company present*) concorso; **to dance attendance** essere al servizio completo

attendant [əˈtendənt] *adj* assistente; (*accompanying*) concomitante || s (*servant*) inserviente *mf*; presente *m*

attention [əˈtenʃən] s attenzione; (mil) attenti *m*; **attentions** attenzioni *fpl*; **to call s.o.'s attention to s.th** fare presente qlco a qlcu; **to stand at attention** stare sull'attenti || *interj* attenti!

attentive [əˈtentɪv] *adj* attento, premuroso

attenuate [əˈtenjuˌet] *tr* attenuare

attest [əˈtest] *tr* attestare || *intr*—**to attest to** attestare, testimoniare

attic [ˈætɪk] s attico, solaio || **Attic** *adj & s* attico

attire [əˈtaɪr] s vestiti *mpl*, vestiario || *tr* vestire

attitude [ˈætɪˌtjud] or [ˈætɪˌtud] s atteggiamento, attitudine *f*; **to strike an attitude** atteggiarsi

attorney [əˈtʌrni] s avvocato; (*proxy*) procuratore *m*

attor'ney gen'eral s (**attor'neys gen'eral** or **attor'ney gen'erals**) procuratore

m generale || **Attorney General** s (U.S.A.) ministro di grazia e giustizia

attract [əˈtrækt] *tr* attrarre; (*attention*) chiamare

attraction [əˈtrækʃən] s attrazione

attractive [əˈtræktɪv] *adj* attrattivo

attribute [ˈætrɪˌbjut] s attributo || [əˈtrɪbjut] *tr* attribuire

attrition [əˈtrɪʃən] s attrito; diminuzione di numero

auburn [ˈɔbərn] *adj & s* biondo fulvo, rosso tizianesco

auction [ˈɔkʃən] s asta, incanto || *tr* vendere all'asta

auctioneer [ˌɔkʃəˈnɪr] s banditore *m* || *tr & intr* vendere all'asta

audacious [ɔˈdeʃəs] *adj* audace

audaci·ty [ɔˈdæsɪti] s (**-ties**) audacia

audience [ˈɔdɪ·əns] s (*hearing*) udienza; uditorio, pubblico

au'dio fre'quency [ˈɔdɪˌo] s audiofrequenza

au'dio-vis'ual aids' *spl* sussidi audiovisivi

audit [ˈɔdɪt] s verifica or esame *m* dei conti || *tr* esaminare i conti di; (*a class*) assistere a, come uditore || *intr* assistere a una classe come uditore

audition [ɔˈdɪʃən] s audizione || *tr* dare un'audizione a

auditor [ˈɔdɪtər] s revisore *m* dei conti; (educ) uditore *m*

auditorium [ˌɔdɪˈtorɪ·əm] s auditorio

auger [ˈɔgər] s succhiello, trivella

aught [ɔt] s zero; **for aught I know** per quanto ne so || *adv* affatto

augment [ɔgˈment] *tr & intr* aumentare

augur [ˈɔgər] s augure *m* || *tr & intr* vaticinare

augu·ry [ˈɔgəri] s (**-ries**) augurio

august [ɔˈgʌst] *adj* augusto || **August** [ˈɔgəst] s agosto

aunt [ænt] or [ɑnt] s zia

aurora [əˈrorə] s aurora

auspice [ˈɔspɪs] s auspicio; **under the auspices of** sotto gli auspici di

austere [ɔsˈtɪr] *adj* austero

Australia [ɔˈstreljə] s l'Australia *f*

Australian [ɔˈstreljən] *adj & s* australiano

Austria [ˈɔstrɪ·ə] s l'Austria *f*

Austrian [ˈɔstrɪ·ən] *adj & s* austriaco

authentic [ɔˈθentɪk] *adj* autentico

authenticate [ɔˈθentɪˌket] *tr* autenticare

author [ˈɔθər] s autore *m*

authoress [ˈɔθərɪs] s autrice *f*

authoritarian [əˌθɑrɪˈterɪ·ən] or [əˌθɔrɪˈterɪ·ən] *adj* autoritario || s persona autoritaria

authoritative [əˈθɑrɪˌtetɪv] or [əˈθɔrɪˌtetɪv] *adj* autorevole; autoritario

authori·ty [əˈθɑrɪti] or [əˈθɔrɪti] s (**-ties**) autorità *f*; **on good authority** da buona fonte, da fonte autorevole

authorize [ˈɔθəˌraɪz] *tr* autorizzare

authorship [ˈɔθərˌʃɪp] s paternità letteraria

au·to [ˈɔto] s (**-tos**) (coll) auto *f*

autobiogra·phy [ˌɔtobaɪˈɑgrəfi] or [ˌɔtobɪˈɑgrəfi] s (**-phies**) autobiografia

autobus ['ɔto ,bʌs] s autobus m
autocratic(al) [,ɔtə'krætɪk(əl)] adj autocratico
autograph ['ɔtə ,græf] or ['ɔtə ,grɑf] adj & s autografo ‖ tr porre l'autografo su, firmare con firma autografa
automat ['ɔtə ,mæt] s ristorante m self-service a distribuzione automatica
automate ['ɔtə ,met] tr automatizzare
automatic [,ɔtə'mætɪk] adj automatico ‖ s pistola automatica
automat'ic transmis'sion s trasmissione automatica
automation [,ɔtə'meʃən] s automazione
automa·ton [ɔ'tɑmə ,tɑn] s (-tons or -ta [tə]) automa m
automobile [,ɔtəmo'bil] or [,ɔtə'mo-bil] adj & s automobile f
automobile' show' s salone m dell'automobile
automotive [,ɔtə'motɪv] adj (self-propelled) automotore; automobilistico
autonomous [ɔ'tɑnəməs] adj autonomo
autonomy [ɔ'tɑnəmi] s autonomia
autop·sy ['ɔtɑpsi] s (-sies) autopsia
au'to trans'port rig' s autotreno per trasporto di automobili
autumn ['ɔtəm] s autunno
autumnal [ɔ'tʌmnəl] adj autunnale
auxilia·ry [ɔg'zɪljəri] adj & s (-ries) ausiliare m
avail [ə'vel] s utilità f; **of no avail** che non serve a nulla ‖ tr servire (with dat); **to avail oneself of** servirsi di; approfittare di ‖ intr servire
available [ə'veləbəl] adj disponibile; **to make available to** mettere alla disposizione di
avalanche ['ævə ,læntʃ] or ['ævə ,lɑntʃ] s valanga
avant-garde [əvɑ̃'gard] adj d'avanguardia
avant-gardism [ə'vɑ̃'gardizəm] s avanguardismo
avarice ['ævərɪs] s avarizia
avaricious [,ævə'rɪʃəs] adj avaro
avenge [ə'vɛndʒ] tr vendicare; **to avenge oneself on** vendicarsi di
avenue ['ævə ,nju] or ['ævənu] s viale m, corso
aver [ə'vʌr] v (pret & pp averred; ger averring) tr asserire, affermare
average ['ævərɪdʒ] adj medio ‖ s media; (naut) avaria; (e.g., of goals) (sports) quoziente m; **on the average** di media ‖ tr fare la media di; fare . . . di media, e.g., **he averages one hundred dollars a week** fa cento dollari di media alla settimana
averse [ə'vʌrs] adj avverso
aversion [ə'vʌrʒən] s avversione
avert [ə'vʌrt] tr (to ward off) evitare; (to turn away) distogliere
aviar·y ['əvi ,ɛri] s (-ies) aviario, voliera
aviation [,evi'eʃən] s aviazione
aviator ['evi ,etər] s aviatore m
avid ['ævɪd] adj avido
avidity [ə'vɪdɪti] s avidità f

avocation [,ævə'keʃən] s svago, passatempo
avoid [ə'vɔɪd] tr evitare
avoidable [ə'vɔɪdəbəl] adj evitabile
avow [ə'vau] tr confessare, ammettere
avowal [ə'vau·əl] s confessione, ammissione
await [ə'wet] tr aspettare, attendere
awake [ə'wek] adj sveglio ‖ v (pret & pp awoke [ə'wok] or awaked) tr svegliare ‖ intr svegliarsi
awaken [ə'wekən] tr svegliare ‖ intr svegliarsi
awakening [ə'wekənɪŋ] s risveglio
award [ə'wɔrd] s (prize) premio; (decision by judge) sentenza ‖ tr aggiudicare
aware [ə'wɛr] adj conscio, consapevole; **to become aware of** rendersi conto di
awareness [ə'wɛrnɪs] s coscienza
awash [ə'wɑʃ] or [ə'wɔʃ] adj & adv a fior d'acqua
away [ə'we] adj distante, assente ‖ adv lontano; via; continuamente; **away back** (coll) molto tempo fa; **away from** lontano da; **to do away with** disfarsi di, sopprimere; **to get away** scappare, sfuggire; **to go away** andarsene; **to run away** fuggire; **to send away** mandar via; **to take away** portar via
awe [ɔ] s estremo rispetto; sacro timore ‖ tr infondere rispetto a; infondere un sacro timore a
aweigh [ə'we] adj (anchor) levato
awesome ['ɔsəm] adj grandioso, imponente
awestruck ['ɔ ,strʌk] adj pieno di sacro timore
awful ['ɔfəl] adj terribile; imponente ‖ adv (coll) terribilmente
awfully ['ɔfəli] adv tremendamente, terribilmente; (coll) molto
awhile [ə'hwaɪl] adv un po', un po' di tempo
awkward ['ɔkwərd] adj (clumsy) goffo, maldestro; (unwieldly) scomodo; (embarrassing) imbarazzante
awl [ɔl] s punteruolo
awning ['ɔnɪŋ] s tenda; (in front of a store) tendone m
A.W.O.L. ['ewɔl] (acronym) or ['e-'dɑbəl ,ju'o'el] (letterword) adj (mil) assente al contrappello
awry [ə'raɪ] adv—**to go awry** andare a capovescio; **to look awry** guardare di sbieco
ax or **axe** [æks] s scure f; **to have an axe to grind** (coll) avere un interesse speciale
axiom ['æksɪ·əm] s assioma m
axiomatic [,æksɪ·ə'mætɪk] adj assiomatico
axis ['æksɪs] s (axes ['æksiz]) asse m
axle ['æksəl] s assale m, asse m
ax'le·tree' s assale m
ay [aɪ] s & adv sì m
Azores [ə'zorz] or ['ezorz] spl Azzorre fpl
azure ['æʒər] or ['eʒər] adj & s azzurro, blu m

B

B, b [bi] *s* seconda lettera dell'alfabeto inglese

baa [bɑ] *s* belato || *intr* belare

babble ['bæbəl] *s* (*murmuring sound*) mormorio; (*senseless prattle*) balbettio || *tr* (*e.g., a secret*) divulgare || *intr* mormorare; balbettare; (*to talk idly*) parlare a vanvera

babe [beb] *s* bebè *m*, bambino; persona inesperta; (*slang*) ragazza

baboon [bæ'bun] *s* babbuino

ba·by ['bebi] *s* (*-bies*) bebè *m*, neonato; bambino; (*the youngest child*) piccolo || *v* (*pret & pp -bied*) *tr* coccolare, ninnare

ba'by car'riage *s* carrozzella

ba'by grand' *s* piano a mezza coda

babyhood ['bebi,hʊd] *s* infanzia

babyish ['bebi·ɪʃ] *adj* infantile

Babylon ['bæbɪlən] *or* ['bæbɪ,lɑn] *s* Babilonia

ba'by sit'ter *s* bambinaia ad ore

ba'by teeth' *spl* denti *mpl* di latte

baccalaureate [,bækə'lɔrɪ·ɪt] *s* baccalaureato; servizio religioso prima del baccalaureato

bacchanal ['bækənəl] *adj* bacchico || *s* baccanale *m*; (*person*) ubriacone *m*, bisboccione *m*

bachelor ['bætʃələr] *s* (*unmarried man*) scapolo, celibe *m*; (*holder of bachelor's degree*) diplomato; (*apprentice knight*) baccelliere *m*

bachelorhood ['bætʃələr,hʊd] *s* celibato

bacil·lus [bə'sɪləs] *s* (*-li* [laɪ]) bacillo

back [bæk] *adj* di dietro, posteriore; arretrato; contrario || *s* dorso, schiena; parte *f* posteriore, didietro; (*of a sheet or coin*) tergo; (*of a knife*) costola; (*of a room*) fondo; (*of a book*) fine *f*; (*of a chair*) schienale *m*; **behind one's back** dietro le spalle di uno; **to turn one's back on** volgere la schiena a || *adv* dietro; indietro; **a few weeks back** alcune settimane fa; **as far back as** sino da; **back of** dietro, dietro a; **to go back on one's word** mancare di parola; **to go back to** ritornare a; **to pay back** ripagare; **to send back** restituire || *tr* appoggiare; far indietreggiare || *intr* indietreggiare; rinculare; **to back down** rinunciarci; **to back off** *or* **out** ritirarsi; **to back up** (*said of a car*) fare marcia indietro

back'ache' *s* mal *m* di schiena

back'bite' *v* (*pret* **-bit**; *pp* **-bitten** *or* **-bit**) *tr* sparlare di || *intr* sparlare

back'bit'er *s* maldicente *mf*

back'board' *s* (*basketball*) tabellone *m*

back'bone' *s* spina dorsale; (*of a book*) costola, dorso; (*fig*) fermezza

back'break'ing *adj* sfiancante

back'door' *adj* segreto, clandestino

back' door' *s* porta di dietro; (*fig*) mezzo clandestino

back'drop' *s* (*theat*) fondale *m*

backer ['bækər] *s* sostenitore *m*, difensore *m*; (*com*) finanziatore *m*

back'fire' *s* (*for firefighting*) controfuoco; (*aut*) ritorno di fiamma || *intr* (*aut*) avere un ritorno di fiamma; (*fig*) raggiungere l'effetto opposto

back'ground' *s* fondo, sfondo; precedenti *mpl*; origine *f*

back'ground mu'sic *s* musica di fondo

backhand ['bæk,hænd] *adj* obliquo || *s* scrittura inclinata a sinistra; (*tennis*) rovescio

back'hand'ed *adj* obliquo; sarcastico; insincero

backing ['bækɪŋ] *s* appoggio; sostegno; (*bb*) dorso

back'ing light' *s* (*aut*) faro retromarcia; (*theat*) luce *f* per il fondale

back'lash' *s* reazione; contraccolpo; (*mach*) gioco

back'log' *s* ceppo; (*fig*) riserva

back' num'ber *s* numero arretrato; (*coll*) persona all'antica

back' pay' *s* paga arretrata, arretrati *mpl*

back' scratch'er *s* manina per grattare la schiena; (*coll*) leccapiedi *m*

back' seat' *s* (*aut*) sedile *m* posteriore; (*fig*) posizione secondaria

back'side' *s* dorso; didietro

back'slide' *v* (*pret & pp -slid* [,slɪd]) *intr* ricadere

back'spac'er *s* tasto ritorno

back'spin' *s* effetto

back'stage' *adj* dietro alle quinte || *s* retroscena *m* || *adv* a retroscena, dietro alle quinte

back'stairs' *adj* indiretto, segreto

back' stairs' *spl* scala di servizio

back'stitch' *s* impuntura || *tr & intr* impunturare

back'stroke' *s* (*swimming*) bracciata sul dorso

back'swept wing' *s* ala a freccia

back' talk' *s* risposta impertinente

back'track' *intr* ritornare sulle proprie tracce; (*fig*) fare macchina indietro

back'up light' *s* (*aut*) faro retromarcia

backward ['bækwərd] *adj* ritroso; poco progredito, retrogrado || *adv* a ritroso, all'indietro; verso il passato; alla rovescia; **backward and forward** (*coll*) completamente, perfettamente; **to go backward and forward** andare avanti e indietro

back'wash' *s* risacca

back'wa'ter *s* gora, ristagno; (*fig*) eremo

back'woods' *spl* zona boscosa lontana dai centri popolati

back'yard' *s* cortile *m* posteriore

bacon ['bekən] *s* pancetta

bacteria [bæk'tɪrɪ·ə] *spl* batteri *mpl*

bacterial [bæk'tɪrɪ·əl] *adj* batterico

bacteriologist [bæk,tɪrɪ'ɑlədʒɪst] *s* batteriologo

bacteriology [bæk,tɪrɪ'ɑlədʒi] *s* batteriologia

bad [bæd] *adj* (**worse** [wʌrs]; **worst** [wʌrst]) cattivo; (*coin*) falso; (*weather*) brutto; (*debt*) insolvibile; severo || *s* male *m*; **from bad to**

worse da male in peggio ‖ *adv* male;
to be too bad essere peccato; **to feel
bad** esser spiacente; sentirsi male; **to
look bad** aver brutta cera
bad' breath' *s* fiato cattivo
bad' egg' *s* (slang) cattivo soggetto
badge [bædʒ] *s* divisa; decorazione;
simbolo, placca
badger ['bædʒər] *s* tasso ‖ *tr* molestare
badly ['bædlɪ] *adv* male; gravemente;
molto
bad'ly off' *adj* in cattive condizioni
badminton ['bædmɪntən] *s* badminton *m*
baffle ['bæfəl] *s* (mach) deflettore *m*;
(rad) schermo acustico ‖ *tr* frustrare,
confondere
baffling ['bæflɪŋ] *adj* sconcertante
bag [bæg] *s* sacco; borsetta; (*of a
marsupial*) borsa; (hunt) presa; **bag
and baggage** con armi e bagagli; **to
be in the bag** (slang) averlo nel sacco;
to be left holding the bag (coll) essere piantato in asso ‖ *v* (*pret & pp*
bagged; *ger* **bagging**) *tr* insaccare;
(hunt) pigliare ‖ *intr* (*to hang
loosely*) far pieghe
baggage ['bægɪdʒ] *s* bagaglio
bag'gage car' *s* bagagliaio
bag'gage check' *s* scontrino del bagaglio
bag'gage room' *s* deposito bagagli
bag-gy ['bægi] *adj* (**-gier; -giest**) come
un sacco
bag'pipe' *s* cornamusa, zampogna
bag'pip'er *s* zampognaro
bail [bel] *s* cauzione; libertà provvisoria sotto cauzione; (*bucket*) sassola
‖ *tr* liberare sotto cauzione; **to bail
out** (*a boat*) sgottare ‖ *intr*—**to bail
out** (aer) gettarsi col paracadute
bailiwick ['belɪwɪk] *s* (fig) sfera di
competenza
bait [bet] *s* esca; (fig) allettamento ‖ *tr*
adescare; (fig) allettare
baize [bez] *s* panno verde
bake [bek] *tr* cuocere al forno ‖ *intr*
cuocersi al forno; abbrustolirsi
bakelite ['bekə,laɪt] *s* bachelite *f*
baker ['bekər] *s* fornaio, panettiere *m*
bak'er's doz'en *s* tredici per ogni dozzina
baker-y ['bekəri] *s* (**-ies**) panetteria
bak'ing pan' ['bekɪŋ] *s* tortiera
bak'ing pow'der *s* lievito in polvere
bak'ing so'da *s* bicarbonato di soda
balance ['bæləns] *s* (*scales*) bilancia;
equilibrio; armonia; (*of watch*) bilanciere *m*; (*remainder; amount due*)
resto; (*of budget*) pareggio; **in the
balance** in bilico; **to lose one's balance** perdere l'equilibrio; **to strike a
balance** fare il bilancio ‖ *tr* bilanciare, pesare; (com) bilanciare, pareggiare ‖ *intr* bilanciarsi
bal'ance of pay'ments *s* bilancia dei
pagamenti
bal'ance of pow'er *s* equilibrio politico
bal'ance of trade' *s* bilancia commerciale
bal'ance sheet' *s* bilancio
balco-ny ['bælkəni] *s* (**-nies**) balcone
m; (theat) galleria

bald [bɔld] *adj* calvo; (*bare*) nudo;
(*unadorned*) semplice
bald' ea'gle *s* aquila col capo bianco
dell'America del Nord
baldness ['bɔldnɪs] *s* calvizie *f*
baldric ['bɔldrɪk] *s* tracolla
bale [bel] *s* balla; collo ‖ *tr* imballare
baleful ['belfəl] *adj* minaccioso, funesto
balk [bɔk] *tr* ostacolare ‖ *intr* inte-
starsi, impuntarsi
Balkan ['bɔlkən] *adj* balcanico ‖ **the
Balkans** i Balcani
balk-y ['bɔki] *adj* (**-ier; -iest**) caparbio,
ostinato
ball [bɔl] *s* palla; pallone *m*; sfera; (*of
the thumb*) polpastrello; (*of wool*)
gomitolo; (*projectile*) palla, pallottola; (*dance*) ballo; **on the ball**
(slang) capace, efficiente; (slang) in
gamba; **to play ball** giocare alla
palla; **to play ball with** essere in
cooperazione con ‖ *tr*—**to ball up**
(slang) confondere
ballad ['bæləd] *s* ballata
ball' and chain' *s* palla di piombo;
(fig) impedimento; (slang) moglie *f*
ball'-and-sock'et joint' ['bɔlən'sɑkɪt] *s*
giunto a sfera
ballast ['bæləst] *s* zavorra; (rr) pietrisco ‖ *tr* zavorrare
ball' bear'ing *s* cuscinetto a sfere
ballet ['bæle] *s* balletto
ballistic [bə'lɪstɪk] *adj* balistico ‖ **bal-
listics** *ssg* balistica
balloon [bə'lun] *s* pallone *m*; (*for children*) palloncino; (*in comic strip*)
fumetto
ballot ['bælət] *s* scheda elettorale; voto
‖ *intr* votare, ballottare
bal'lot box' *s* bussola, urna
ball'play'er *s* giocatore *m* di palla, giocatore *m* di baseball
ball'room' *s* salone *m* da ballo
ballyhoo ['bæli,hu] *s* chiasso; montatura ‖ *tr* far chiasso a favore di
balm [bɑm] *s* balsamo
balm-y ['bɑmi] *adj* (**-ier; -iest**) bal-
samico; salubre; (slang) pazzo
balsam ['bɔlsəm] *s* balsamo; (*plant*)
balsamina
Baltic ['bɔltɪk] *adj* baltico
baluster ['bæləstər] *s* balaustro
balustrade [,bæləs'tred] *s* balaustrata
bamboo [bæm'bu] *s* bambù *m*
bamboozle [bæm'buzəl] *tr* ingannare,
raggirare
bamboozler [bæm'buzlər] *s* raggira-
tore *m*
ban [bæn] *s* bando; (*of marriage*) pubblicazione matrimoniale; (eccl) inter-
detto, scomunica ‖ *v* (*pret & pp*
banned; *ger* **banning**) *tr* proibire
banal ['benəl] *or* [bə'næl] *adj* banale
banana [bə'nænə] *s* banana, (*tree*)
banano
band [bænd] *s* banda, striscia; (*of thin
cloth*) benda; (*of metal, rubber*) fascia, nastro; (*of hat*) nastro; (mus)
banda, fanfara; **to beat the band**
fortemente; abbondantemente ‖ *tr*
unire ‖ *intr*—**to band together** unirsi

bandage ['bændɪdʒ] s benda, bendaggio || tr fasciare

bandanna [bæn'dænə] s fazzolettone colorato

band'box' s cappelliera

bandit ['bændɪt] s bandito

band'mas'ter s capomusica m

bandoleer [,bændə'lɪr] s bandoliera

band' saw' s sega a nastro

band'stand' s chiosco della banda

band'wag'on s carrozzone m da circo; **to jump on the bandwagon** prendere le parti del vincitore

baneful ['benfəl] adj nocivo; funesto

bang [bæŋ] s rumore m, scoppio; (coll) energia; (pleasure) (slang) piacere m, eccitazione; **bangs** frangetta || adv tutto d'un colpo || tr sbattere || intr rimbombare || interj bum!

bang'-up' adj (slang) eccellente, di prim'ordine

banish ['bænɪʃ] tr sbandire, mettere al bando

banishment ['bænɪʃmənt] s bando, esilio

banister ['bænɪstər] s balaustra; **banisters** balaustrata

bank [bæŋk] s (of fish; of fog) banco; (of a river) sponda; (for coins) salvadanaio; (financial institution) banca, banco; (of earth, snow) mucchio, banco; (of clouds) cumulo; (aer) inclinazione laterale; (billiards) sponda || tr (a fire) coprire di cenere; (to pile up) ammonticchiare; (a curve) soprelevare; (money) depositare || intr depositare denaro; (aer) inclinarsi lateralmente; **to bank on** (coll) contare su (di)

bank'book' s libretto bancario, libretto di deposito

banker ['bæŋkər] s banchiere m

banking ['bæŋkɪŋ] adj bancario || s attività bancaria; professione di banchiere

bank' note' s biglietto di banca

bank'roll' s rotolo di carta moneta; soldi mpl || tr (slang) finanziare

bankrupt ['bæŋkrʌpt] adj & s fallito; **to go bankrupt** andare in fallimento || tr dichiarare in fallimento; far fallire

bankrupt•cy ['bæŋkrʌptsi] s (-cies) fallimento

banner ['bænər] adj importante || s bandiera, stendardo; (journ) titolo in grassetto

banns [bænz] spl bandi mpl matrimoniali

banquet ['bæŋkwɪt] s banchetto || tr dar un banchetto a || intr banchettare

bantam ['bæntəm] adj piccolo || s pollo nano

ban'tam-weight' s peso gallo, bantam m

banter ['bæntər] s scherzo, facezia || intr scherzare, celiare

baptism ['bæptɪzəm] s battesimo

baptismal [bæp'tɪzməl] adj battesimale; (certificate) di battesimo

Baptist ['bæptɪst] adj & s battista mf

baptister•y ['bæptɪstəri] s (-ies) battistero

baptize [bæp'taɪz] or ['bæptaɪz] tr battezzare

bar [bɑr] s barra; sbarra; (of soap) saponetta; (of chocolate) tavoletta; (of sand) banco; (obstacle) barriera; bar m; (of public opinion) tribunale m; (legal profession) avvocatura; (of door or window) spranga; (of lead) (typ) lingotto; (mus) battuta; **behind bars** in guardina; **to be admitted to the bar** diventare avvocato; **to tend bar** fare il barista || prep eccetto, salvo; **bar none** senza eccezione || v (pret & pp barred; ger barring) tr sbarrare; sprangare; bloccare; escludere

bar' associa'tion s associazione dell'ordine degli avvocati

barb [bɑrb] s (of arrow) barbiglio

barbarian [bɑr'berɪ-ən] s barbaro

barbaric [bɑr'bærɪk] adj barbaro

barbarism ['bɑrbə,rɪzəm] s barbarismo

barbari•ty [bɑr'bærɪti] s (-ties) barbarie f

barbarous ['bɑrbərəs] adj barbaro, crudele

Bar'bary ape' ['bɑrbəri] s bertuccia

barbecue ['bɑrbɪ,kju] s arrosto allo spiedo || tr arrostire allo spiedo

barbed [bɑrbd] adj irto di punte; mordace, pungente

barbed' wire' s filo spinato

barber ['bɑrbər] s barbiere m; (who cuts and styles hair) parrucchiere m

bar'ber-shop' s barbieria, negozio di barbiere; negozio di parrucchiere

barbiturate [bɑr'bɪtʃə,ret] s barbiturato, barbiturico

bard [bɑrd] s bardo, poeta m

bare [ber] adj nudo; (head) a capo scoperto; (unconcealed) palese; (empty) vuoto; (wire) senza isolante; (unadorned) semplice; **to lay bare** mettere a nudo || tr denudare, scoprire

bare'back' adj & adv senza sella

barefaced ['ber,fest] adj impudente, sfacciato, spudorato

bare'foot' adj scalzo

barehanded ['ber,hændɪd] adj & adv a mani nude

bareheaded ['ber,hedɪd] adj a capo scoperto

barelegged ['ber,legɪd] adj a gambe nude

barely ['berli] adv appena, soltanto

bargain ['bɑrgɪn] s affare m, buon affare m; contrattazione; **at a bargain** a buon prezzo; **into the bargain** in soprappiù || tr—**to bargain away** vendere a buonissimo prezzo || intr contrattare, mercanteggiare; **to bargain for** aspettarsi

bar'gain sale' s vendita sottoprezzo

barge [bɑrdʒ] s barcone m, chiatta || intr—**to barge in** entrare senza chiedere permesso

baritone ['beri,ton] adj di baritono || s baritono m

barium ['berɪ-əm] s bario

bark [bɑrk] s corteccia, scorza; (of dog) abbaiamento, latrato || tr (e.g., *insults*) lanciare ‖ *intr* abbaiare, latrare

bar'keep'er *s* barista *mf*

barker ['barkər] *s* banditore *m*, imbonitore *m*

barley ['barlı] *s* orzo

bar' mag'net *s* calamita a forma di barra allungata

bar'maid' *s* barista *f*

bar'man *s* (-men) barista *m*

barn [barn] *s* granaio; (*for hay*) fienile *m*; (*for livestock*) stalla

barnacle ['barnəkəl] *s* cirripede *m*

barn' owl' *s* civetta

barn'yard' *s* bassacorte *f*, aia

barn'yard fowl' *s* animale *m* da cortile ‖ *spl* animali *mpl* da cortile

barometer [bə'ramıtər] *s* barometro

baron ['bærən] *s* barone *m*; (*industrialist*) cavaliere *m* d'industria

baroness ['bærənıs] *s* baronessa

baroque [bə'rok] *adj* & *s* barocco

bar'rack-room' *adj* da caserma ‖ *s* camerata

barracks ['bærəks] *spl* caserma; camerata

barrage [bə'raʒ] *s* (mil) fuoco di sbarramento

barrel ['bærəl] *s* barile *m*, botte *f*; (*of gun*) canna; (mach) cilindro

bar'rel or'gan *s* organetto di Barberia

barren ['bærən] *adj* sterile; (*without vegetation*) brullo

barricade [,bærı'ked] *s* barricata ‖ *tr* barricare

barrier ['bærı-ər] *s* barriera

bar'rier reef' *s* barriera corallina

barring ['barıŋ] *prep* eccetto, salvo

barrister ['bærıstər] *s* (Brit) avvocato

bar'room' *s* bar *m*, cantina, mescita

bar'tend'er *s* barista *mf*, barman *m*

barter ['bartər] *s* baratto ‖ *tr* & *intr* barattare, permutare

basalt [bə'sɔlt] *s* basalto

base [bes] *adj* basale; basso; servile; (*morally low*) turpe; (*metal*) vile, non prezioso ‖ *s* base *f*; (*in children's games*) tana; (*of a word*) radice *f* basale ‖ *tr* basare

base'ball' *s* baseball *m*, pallabase *f*

base'board' *s* basamento; (*of wall*) zoccolo

Basel ['bazəl] *s* Basilea

baseless ['beslıs] *adj* infondato

basement ['besmənt] *s* scantinato, piano interrato

bashful ['bæʃfəl] *adj* timido

basic ['besık] *adj* fondamentale; (chem) basico

ba'sic commod'ities *spl* articoli *mpl* di prima necessità

basilica [bə'sılıkə] *s* basilica

basin ['besın] *s* catino; vasca; (*of balance*) piatto; (*of river*) bacino; (*of harbor*) darsena

ba·sis ['besıs] *s* (-ses [siz]) base *f*

bask [bæsk] or [bask] *intr* crogiolarsi

basket ['bæskıt] or ['baskıt] *s* cesta; (sports) cesto

bas'ket-ball' *s* pallacanestro *f*

Basque [bæsk] *adj* & *s* basco

bas-relief [,barı'lif] or [,bærı'lif] *s* bassorilievo

bass [bes] *adj* & *s* (mus) basso ‖ [bæs] *s* (ichth) pesce persico

bass' drum' *s* grancassa

bass' horn' *s* bassotuba *m*

bassinet ['bæsə,net] or [,bæsə'net] *s* culla a forma di cesto; carrozzina a forma di cesto

bas·so ['bæso] or ['baso] *s* (-sos or -si [si]) basso

bassoon [bə'sun] *s* fagotto

bass' vi'ol ['vaı-əl] *s* contrabbasso

bastard ['bæstərd] *adj* & *s* bastardo

baste [best] *tr* (*to sew*) imbastire; (*meat*) inumidire con acqua o grasso

bastion ['bæstʃən] or ['bæstı-ən] *s* bastione *m*

bat [bæt] *s* mazza; (*in cricket*) maglio; (coll) colpo; (zool) pipistrello ‖ *v* (*pret* & *pp* **batted**; *ger* **batting**) *tr* colpire con la mazza; **without batting an eye** (coll) senza batter ciglio

batch [bætʃ] *s* (*of bread*) infornata; gruppo, numero

bath [bæθ] or [baθ] *s* bagno; **to take a bath** fare il bagno

bathe [beð] *tr* bagnare, lavare ‖ *intr* bagnarsi, fare il bagno

bather ['beðər] *s* bagnante *mf*

bath'house' *s* (*individual*) cabina; spogliatoio

bath'ing beau'ty *s* bellezza in costume da bagno

bath'ing cap' *s* cuffia da bagno

bath'ing resort' *s* stazione balneare

bath'ing suit' *s* costume *m* da bagno

bath'ing trunks' *spl* mutandine *fpl* da bagno

bath'robe' *s* accappatoio

bath'room' *s* stanza da bagno

bath' salts' *spl* sali *mpl* da bagno

bath'tub' *s* bagno, vasca da bagno

baton [bæ'tan] or ['bætən] *s* bastone *m*; (mus) bacchetta

battalion [bə'tæljən] *s* battaglione *m*

batten ['bætən] *s* assicella; piccola traversa; (naut) bietta ‖ *tr*—**to batten down the hatches** chiudere ermeticamente i boccaporti

batter ['bætər] *s* pasta, farina pastosa; (baseball) battitore *m* ‖ *tr* battere, tempestare di colpi; (*to wear out*) logorare

bat'tering ram' *s* ariete *m*

batter·y ['bætərı] *s* (-ies) (*primary cell*) pila; (*secondary cell*) accumulatore *m*; (*group of batteries*) batteria; (law) assalto; (mil & mus) batteria

battle ['bætəl] *s* battaglia; **to do battle** dar battaglia ‖ *tr* combattere contro ‖ *intr* combattere

bat'tle cry' *s* grido di guerra

battledore ['bætəl,dor] *s* racchetta; **battledore and shuttlecock** gioco del volano

bat'tle-field' *s* campo di battaglia

bat'tle-front' *s* fronte *m* di combattimento

battlement ['bætəlmənt] *s* merlatura

bat'tle roy'al *s* baruffa generale, zuffa generale

bat'tle-ship' *s* corazzata

battue [bæ'tu] or [bæ'tju] *s* (hunt) battuta

bat·ty ['bæti] *adj* (-tier; -tiest) (slang) pazzo, eccentrico

bauble ['bɔbəl] *s* bazzecola, gingillo

Bavaria [bə'vɛrɪə] *s* la Baviera

Bavarian [bə'vɛrɪən] *adj* & *s* bavarese *mf*

bawd [bɔd] *s* ruffiano; ruffiana

bawd·y ['bɔdi] *adj* (-ier; -iest) indecente, osceno

bawd'y-house' *s* casa di malaffare

bawl [bɔl] *s* grido; (coll) pianto || *tr*—**to bawl out** (slang) fare una ramanzina a || *intr* strillare; (coll) piangere

bay [be] *adj* baio || *s* baia; vano, alcova; (*recess in wall*) apertura nel muro; finestra sporgente; (*of dog*) latrato; cavallo baio; (bot) lauro; **at bay** in una posizione disperata || *intr* latrare

bayonet ['be·ənɪt] *s* baionetta || *tr* dare baionettate a || *intr* dare baionettate

bay' win'dow *s* finestra sporgente; (slang) pancia

bazooka [bə'zukə] *s* bazooka *m*

be [bi] *v* (*pres* **am** [æm], **is** [ɪz], **are** [ɑr]; *pret* **was** [wɑz] *or* [wʌz], **were** [wʌr]; *pp* **been** [bɪn]) *intr* essere; fare, e.g., **to be a mason** fare il muratore; fare, e.g., **3 times 3 is 9** tre volte tre fa nove; **be as it may be** comunque sia; **here is** *or* **here are** ecco; **there are** ci sono; **there is** c'è; **to be** futuro, e.g., **my wife to be** la mia futura sposa; **to be ashamed** aver vergogna; **to be cold** aver freddo; **to be hot** aver caldo; **to be hungry** aver fame; **to be in** stare a casa; **to be in a hurry** aver fretta; **to be in with** (coll) essere amico intimo di; **to be off** andarsene; **to be out** essere fuori; **to be out of** (coll) non aver più; **to be right** aver ragione; **to be sleepy** aver sonno; **to be thirsty** avere sete; **to be up** essere alzato; **to be up to** essere all'altezza di; toccare, e.g., **it's up to you** tocca a Lei; **to be warm** avere caldo; **to be wrong** aver torto; sbagliarsi; **to be . . . years old** avere . . . anni || *aux* stare, e.g., **to be waiting** stare aspettando; essere, e.g., **the murder has been committed** l'omicidio è stato commesso; dovere, e.g., **he is to clean the stables tomorrow** domani deve pulire la stalla || *impers* essere, e.g., **it is necessary** è necessario; fare, e.g., **it is cold** fa freddo; **it is hot** fa caldo

beach [bitʃ] *s* spiaggia || *tr* (*a boat*) arenare || *intr* arenarsi

beach'comb' *intr* raccogliere relitti sulla spiaggia

beach'comb'er *s* girellone *m* di spiaggia

beach'head' *s* testa di sbarco

beach' robe' *s* accappatoio

beach' shoe' *s* sandalo da spiaggia

beach' umbrel'la *s* ombrellone *m* da spiaggia

beacon ['bikən] *s* faro || *tr* rischiarare; fare da guida a || *intr* brillare

bead [bid] *s* perlina; grano, chicco; (*drop*) goccia; **beads** (*in a necklace or rosary*) conterie *fpl*; **to count one's beads** recitare il rosario

beagle ['bigəl] *s* segugio, bracco

beak [bik] *s* becco; promontorio

beam [bim] *s* trave *f*; (*of balance*) braccio; (*of light*) raggio; (*ship's breadth*) larghezza; (*smile*) sorriso; (*radio signal*) fascio direttore; (*course indicated by radio beam*) aerovia; (naut) traverso || *tr* (*a radio signal*) dirigere; (e.g., *light*) irraggiare || *intr* raggiare

bean [bin] *s* fagiolo; (*of coffee*) chicco; (slang) testa

bean·er·y ['binəri] *s* (-ies) (slang) gargotta, taverna di secondo ordine

bean'pole' *s* puntello per i fagioli; (coll) palo del telegrafo

bear [bɛr] *s* orso; (astr) orsa; (com) ribassista *m*, giocatore *m* al ribasso || *v* (*pret* **bore** [bor]; *pp* **borne** [born]) *tr* (*to carry*) portare; (*to give birth to*) partorire; (*to sustain*) sostenere; (*to withstand*) sopportare; (*a grudge*) serbare; (*in mind*) tenere; (*interest*) produrre; (*to pay*) pagare; **to bear the date** aver la data; **to bear out** confermare; **to bear witness** testimoniare || *intr* (*to be productive*) fruttificare; (*to move*) dirigersi; (*to be oppressive*) fare pressione; **to bear down on** fare pressione su; avvicinarsi a; **to bear up** resistere; **to bear with** tollerare

bearable ['bɛrəbəl] *adj* tollerabile

beard [bɪrd] *s* barba; (e.g., *in wheat*) arista

bearded *adj* barbuto

beardless ['bɪrdlɪs] *adj* imberbe

bearer ['bɛrər] *s* portatore *m*

bearing ['bɛrɪŋ] *s* portamento; relazione; importanza; (mach) bronzina, cuscinetto; **bearings** orientamento; **to lose one's bearings** perdere la bussola; perdere l'orientamento

bearish ['bɛrɪʃ] *adj* (*like a bear*) orsino; (e.g., *prices*) in ribasso; (*market*) al ribasso; (*speculator*) ribassista

bear'skin' *s* pelle *f* dell'orso; (mil) colbacco

beast [bist] *s* bestia

beast·ly ['bistli] *adj* (-lier; -liest) bestiale || *adv* (coll) malissimo

beast' of bur'den *s* bestia da soma

beast' of prey' *s* animale *m* da rapina

beat [bit] *s* (*of heart*) battito; (*of policeman*) ronda; (*stroke*) colpo; (*habitual route*) cammino battuto; (mus) tempo; (phys) battimento || *v* (*pret* **beat;** *pp* **beat** *or* **beaten**) *tr* battere; percuotere; (*eggs*) frullare; (*to whip*) frustare; (coll) confondere; **beat it!** (slang) vattene!; **to beat a retreat** battere in ritirata; **to beat back** respingere; **to beat down** sopprimere; **to beat off** respingere; **to beat up** (*eggs*) frullare; (*people*) dargliene a || *intr* battere; pulsare; **to beat around the bush** (coll) menare il can per l'aia

beat'en path' ['bitən] *s* cammino battuto

beater ['bitər] *s* frullino

beati·fy [bɪ'ætɪ,faɪ] *v* (*pret* & *pp* **-fied**) *tr* beatificare

beating ['bitɪŋ] s battitura; (*whipping*) frustatura; (*throbbing*) pulsazione, battito; (*defeat*) sconfitta

beau [bo] s (**beaus** or **beaux** [boz]) (*dandy*) bellimbusto; (*girl's sweetheart*) spasimante m

beautician [bju'tɪʃən] s estetista mf

beautiful ['bjutɪfəl] adj bello

beauti-fy ['bjutɪ‚faɪ] v (pret & pp -**fied**) tr abbellire

beau-ty ['bjuti] s (-**ties**) bellezza

beau'ty con'test s concorso di bellezza

beau'ty par'lor s istituto di bellezza

beau'ty sleep' s primo sonno

beau'ty spot' s neo; posto pittoresco

beaver ['bivər] s castoro; pelle f di castoro; cappello a cilindro

because [bɪ'kɔz] conj perchè; **because of** a causa di

beck [bɛk] s gesto; **at the beck and call of** agli ordini di

beckon ['bɛkən] s gesto || tr fare gesto a || intr fare gesto

becloud [bɪ'klaud] tr annebbiare; oscurare

be-come [bɪ'kʌm] v (pret -**came**; pp -**come**) tr convenire a; stare bene a, e.g., **this hat becomes you** questo cappello Le sta bene || intr diventare; farsi; convertirsi, e.g., **water became wine** l'acqua si convertì in vino; succedere, e.g., **what became of my coat?** che è successo del mio pastrano?; essere, e.g., **what will become of me?** che sarà di me?; **to become accustomed** abituarsi; **to become angry** entrare in collera; **to become crazy** impazzire; **to become ill** ammalarsi

becoming [bɪ'kʌmɪŋ] adj conveniente; appropriato; acconcio; **this is very becoming to you** questo Le sta molto bene

bed [bɛd] s letto; (*layer*) strato; giacimento; **to go to bed** andare a letto; **to take to one's bed** mettersi a letto

bed' and board' s vitto e alloggio; pensione completa

bed'bug' s cimice f

bed'clothes' spl lenzuola fpl e coperte fpl, biancheria da letto

bed'cov'er s coperta da letto

bedding ['bɛdɪŋ] s lenzuola fpl e coperte fpl; (*litter*) lettiera; (*foundation*) fondamenta fpl

bedeck [bɪ'dɛk] tr ornare, adornare

bedev-il [bɪ'dɛvɪl] v (pret & pp -**iled** or -**illed**; ger -**iling** or -**illing**) tr tormentare diabolicamente; confondere

bed'fast' adj confinato a letto

bed'fel'low s compagno di letto; compagno di stanza; compagno

bedlam ['bɛdləm] s manicomio; pandemonio

bed' lin'en s biancheria da letto

bed'pan' s padella

bedridden ['bɛd‚rɪdən] adj degente a letto

bed'room' s stanza da letto, camera da letto

bed'room slip'per s babbuccia, pantofola

bed'side' s capezzale m

bed'side man'ner s maniera di fare coi pazienti

bed'sore' s piaga da decubito

bed'spread' s coperta da letto

bed'spring' s rete f del letto; molla del letto

bed'stead' s fusto del letto

bed'tick' s traliccio

bed'time' s ora di coricarsi

bed'warm'er s scaldaletto

bee [bi] s ape f

beech [bitʃ] s faggio

beech'nut' s faggiola

beef [bif] s bue m, manzo; carne f di manzo; (*coll*) forza; (*slang*) lamentela || intr—**to beef up** (*coll*) rinforzare || intr (*slang*) lamentarsi

beef' cat'tle s manzi mpl da carne

beef'steak' s bistecca

beef' stew' s stufato di manzo

bee'hive' s alveare m

bee'keep'er s apicoltore m

bee'line' s—**to make a beeline for** (*coll*) andare direttamente verso

beer [bɪr] s birra

beer' saloon' s birreria

beeswax ['biz‚wæks] s cera d'api

beet [bit] s barbabietola

beetle ['bitəl] adj sporgente, folto || s scarafaggio

bee'tle-browed' adj dalle sopracciglia folte

beet' su'gar s zucchero di barbabietola

be-fall [bɪ'fɔl] v (pret -**fell** ['fɛl]; pp -**fallen** ['fɔlən]) tr succedere a || intr succedere

befitting [bɪ'fɪtɪŋ] adj appropriato

before [bɪ'for] adv prima, prima d'ora || prep (*in time*) prima di; (*in place*) dinnanzi a, davanti a; **before Christ** avanti Cristo || conj prima che

before'hand' adv in anticipo; precedentemente

befriend [bɪ'frɛnd] tr diventare amico di, proteggere, favorire; aiutare

befuddle [bɪ'fʌdəl] tr confondere

beg [bɛg] v (pret & pp **begged**; ger **begging**) tr chiedere; implorare; (*alms*) mendicare; **I beg your pardon** Le chiedo scusa; **to beg s.o. for s.th** chiedere qlco a qlcu || intr chiedere la carità; **to beg for** sollecitare; **beg off** scusarsi; **to go begging** rimanere invenduto

be-get [bɪ'gɛt] v (pret -**got** ['gɑt]; pp -**gotten** or -**got;** ger -**getting**) tr generare

beggar ['bɛgər] s accattone m, mendicante m

be-gin [bɪ'gɪn] v (pret -**gan** ['gæn]; pp -**gun** ['gʌn]; ger -**ginning**) tr & intr cominciare, iniziare; **beginning with** a partire da; **to begin with** per cominciare

beginner [bɪ'gɪnər] s principiante mf

beginning [bɪ'gɪnɪŋ] s inizio, origine f, principio, esordio

begrudge [bɪ'grʌdʒ] tr invidiare; concedere con riluttanza

beguile [bɪ'gaɪl] tr ingannare; sedurre; (*to delight*) divertire

behalf [bɪ'hæf] or [bɪ'hɑf] s—**on behalf of** nell'interesse di; a nome di

behave [bɪˈhev] *intr* comportarsi; comportarsi bene

behavior [bɪˈhevjər] *s* comportamento, condotta; funzionamento

behead [bɪˈhed] *tr* decapitare

behest [bɪˈhest] *s* ordine *m*, comando

behind [bɪˈhaɪnd] *s* didietro; (slang) sedere *m* || *adv* dietro; (*in arrears*) in arretrato; **from behind** dal didietro || *prep* dietro a, dietro di; **behind time** in ritardo

be·hold [bɪˈhold] *v* (*pret & pp* **-held** [ˈheld]) *tr* contemplare; ammirare || *interj* guarda!

behoove [bɪˈhuv] *impers*—**it behooves him to** gli conviene di

being [ˈbiɪŋ] *adj* esistente; **for the time being** per ora || *s* essere *m*, ente *m*

belabor [bɪˈlebər] *tr* attaccare; (fig) ribattere, confutare; (fig) insistere su

belated [bɪˈletɪd] *adj* tardivo

belch [beltʃ] *s* rutto || *tr* eruttare, vomitare || *intr* ruttare

beleaguer [bɪˈligər] *tr* assediare

bel·fry [ˈbelfrɪ] *s* (**-fries**) (*tower*) campanile *m*; (*site of bell*) cella campanaria; (slang) testa

Belgian [ˈbeldʒən] *adj & s* belga *mf*

Belgium [ˈbeldʒəm] *s* il Belgio

be·lie [bɪˈlaɪ] *v* (*pret & pp* **-lied** [ˈlaɪd]; *ger* **-lying** [ˈlaɪˌɪŋ]) *tr* (*to misrepresent*) tradire; (*to prove false*) smentire

belief [bɪˈlif] *s* fede *f*, credenza

believable [bɪˈlivəbəl] *adj* credibile

believe [bɪˈliv] *tr* credere || *intr* credere, aver fede; **to believe in** credere in

believer [bɪˈlivər] *s* credente *mf*

belittle [bɪˈlɪtəl] *tr* menomare

bell [bel] *s* campana; (*for a door*) campanello; (*sound*) rintocco; (*on cattle*) campanaccio; (*of deer*) bramito || *intr* bramire

belladonna [ˌbeləˈdɑnə] *s* belladonna

bell'-bot'tom *adj* a campana

bell'boy' *s* cameriere *m*, ragazzo

belle [bel] *s* bella

belles-lettres [ˌbelˈletrə] *spl* belle lettere

bell' glass' *s* campana di vetro

bell'hop' *s* cameriere *m*, ragazzo

bellicose [ˈbelɪˌkos] *adj* bellicoso

belligerent [bəˈlɪdʒərənt] *adj & s* belligerante *m*

bellow [ˈbelo] *s* muggito; **bellows** mantice *m*; (*of camera*) soffietto || *tr* gridare || *intr* muggire

bell' ring'er [ˈrɪŋər] *s* campanaro

bellwether [ˈbelˌweðər] *s* pecora guida

bel·ly [ˈbelɪ] *s* (**-lies**) ventre *m*, pancia || *v* (*pret & pp* **-lied**) *intr* far pancia

bel'ly·ache' *s* (coll) mal *m* di pancia || *intr* (slang) lamentarsi

bel'ly·but'ton *s* (coll) ombelico

bel'ly dance' *s* (coll) danza del ventre

bel'ly flop' *s* panciata

bellyful [ˈbelɪˌful] *s*—**to have a bellyful** (slang) averne fino agli occhi

bel'ly·land' *intr* (aer) atterrare sul ventre

belong [bɪˈlɔŋ] *or* [bɪˈlɑŋ] *intr* appartenere; stare bene, e.g., **this chair belongs in this room** questa sedia sta bene in questa stanza

belongings [bɪˈlɔŋɪŋz] *or* [bɪˈlɑŋɪŋz] *spl* effetti *mpl* personali

beloved [bɪˈlʌvɪd] *or* [bɪˈlʌvd] *adj & s* diletto, amato

below [bɪˈlo] *adv* sotto; più sotto; sotto zero, e.g., **ten below** dieci gradi sotto zero || *prep* sotto, sotto di

belt [belt] *s* cintura, cinghia; (mach) nastro; (mil) cinturone *m*; (geog) fascia, zona; **to tighten one's belt** far cintura || *tr* cingere; (slang) staffilare

belt'ed tire' *s* copertone cinturato

belt' line' *s* linea di circonvallazione

beltway [ˈbeltˌwe] *s* raccordo anulare

bemoan [bɪˈmon] *tr* lamentare; compiangere

bench [bentʃ] *s* banco, panca; tribunale *m*; (mach) banco di prova; **to be on the bench** (law) essere giudice

bend [bend] *s* curva; (*e.g., of pipe*) gomito, angolo || *v* (*pret & pp* **bent** [bent]) *tr* curvare; piegare; far piegare || *intr* deviare; piegare, piegarsi; **to bend over** inchinarsi

beneath [bɪˈniθ] *adv* sotto; più sotto || *prep* sotto, sotto di

benediction [ˌbenɪˈdɪkʃən] *s* benedizione

benefactor [ˈbenɪˌfæktər] *or* [ˌbenɪˈfæktər] *s* benefattore *m*

benefactress [ˈbenɪˌfæktrɪs] *or* [ˌbenɪˈfæktrɪs] *s* benefattrice *f*

beneficence [bɪˈnefɪsəns] *s* beneficenza

beneficent [bɪˈnefɪsənt] *adj* caritatevole; benefico

beneficial [ˌbenɪˈfɪʃəl] *adj* benefico

beneficiar·y [ˌbenɪˈfɪʃɪˌerɪ] *s* (**-ies**) beneficiario

benefit [ˈbenɪfɪt] *s* beneficio; festa di beneficenza; **for the benefit of** a beneficio di || *tr & intr* beneficiare

ben'efit perfor'mance *s* beneficiata

benevolence [bɪˈnevələns] *s* benevolenza; carità *f*

benevolent [bɪˈnevələnt] *adj* benevolo; (*institution*) benefico

benign [bɪˈnaɪn] *adj* benigno

bent [bent] *adj* curvo; **bent on** deciso a || *s* curva; tendenza, propensità *f*

Benzedrine [ˈbenzɪˌdrin] (trademark) *s* benzedrina

benzene [ˈbenzin] *s* benzolo

benzine [benˈzin] *s* benzina

bequeath [bɪˈkwiθ] *or* [bɪˈkwið] *tr* legare, lasciare in eredità

bequest [bɪˈkwest] *s* legato, lascito

berate [bɪˈret] *tr* redarguire

be·reave [bɪˈriv] *v* (*pret & pp* **-reaved** *or* **-reft** [ˈreft]) *tr* spogliare

bereavement [bɪˈrivmənt] *s* lutto, perdita

beret [bəˈre] *or* [ˈbere] *s* berretto

Berlin [bərˈlɪn] *adj* berlinese || *s* Berlino

Berliner [bərˈlɪnər] *s* berlinese *mf*

Bermuda [bərˈmjudə] *s* le Bermude

ber·ry [ˈberɪ] *s* (**-ries**) (*dry seed*) chicco; (*fruit*) bacca

berserk [bʌr'sʌrk] *adj* infuriato ‖ *adv*
—**to go berserk** impazzire
berth [bʌrθ] *s* (*for a ship*) posto di
ormeggio; (*bed*) cuccetta; (*coll*)
posto
beryllium [bə'rɪlɪ·əm] *s* berillio
be·seech [bɪ'sitʃ] *v* (*pret & pp -sought*
['sɔt] or **-seeched**) *tr* supplicare
be·set [bɪ'sɛt] *v* (*pret & pp -set*; *ger*
-setting) *tr* assediare, circondare;
(*e.g., with problems*) assillare
beside [bɪ'saɪd] *adv* oltre, inoltre ‖
prep vicino a; in confronto di; oltre
a; **beside oneself** fuori di sé; **beside
the point** fuori del seminato
besides [bɪ'saɪdz] *adv* inoltre; d'altronde ‖ *prep* oltre a
besiege [bɪ'sidʒ] *tr* assediare; (*with
questions*) bombardare
besmear [bɪ'smɪr] *tr* imbrattare, sgorbiare; sporcare
besmirch [bɪ'smʌrtʃ] *tr* insudiciare
bespatter [bɪ'spætər] *tr* inzaccherare
be·speak [bɪ'spik] *v* (**-spoke** ['spok];
-spoken) *tr* chiedere anticipatamente
a; (*to show*) dimostrare
best [bɛst] *adj super* (il) migliore; ottimo ‖ *s* meglio; **at best** nella miglior
delle ipotesi; **to do one's best** fare
del proprio meglio; **to get the best of**
avere la meglio di; **to make the best
of** adattarsi a ‖ *adv super* meglio;
had best, e.g., **I had best** dovrei ‖ *tr*
battere, riuscire superiore a
bestial ['bɛstjəl] or ['bɛstʃəl] *adj* bestiale
be·stir [bɪ'stʌr] *v* (*pret & pp -stirred*;
ger **-stirring**) *tr* eccitare; **to bestir
oneself** darsi da fare
best' man' *s* testimone *m* di nozze
bestow [bɪ'sto] *tr* accordare; conferire
best' sell'er *s* best-seller *m*
bet [bɛt] *s* scommessa ‖ *v* (*pret & pp*
bet or **betted**; *ger* **betting**) *tr & intr*
scommettere; **I bet** ci scommetto;
you bet (*coll*) evidentemente
be·take [bɪ'tek] *v* (*pret -took* ['tuk];
pp -taken) *tr*—**to betake oneself**
andare, dirigersi
be·think [bɪ'θɪŋk] *v* (*pret & pp*
-thought ['θɔt]) *tr* **to bethink oneself**
pensare; ricordarsi
Bethlehem ['bɛθlɪ·əm] or ['bɛθlɪ,hɛm]
s Betlemme *f*
betide [bɪ'taɪd] *tr* accadere a ‖ *intr*
accadere
betoken [bɪ'tokən] *tr* indicare, presagire
betray [bɪ'tre] *tr* tradire, ingannare;
(*to reveal*) rivelare
betroth [bɪ'troθ] or [bɪ'troθ] *tr* promettere in matrimonio a
betrothal [bɪ'troθəl] or [bɪ'troθəl] *s*
fidanzamento
betrothed [bɪ'troθd] or [bɪ'troθt] *adj*
fidanzato ‖ *s* promesso sposo, fidanzato
better ['bɛtər] *adj comp* migliore; **to
grow better** migliorare ‖ *s*—**betters**
superiori *mpl*; ottimati *mpl*; **to get
the better of** avere la meglio di ‖ *adv*
meglio; **had better** dovere, e.g., **I had**

better dovrei; **to be better off** stare
meglio; **to think better of** riconsiderare; **you ought to know better** dovrebbe vergognarsi ‖ *tr* sorpassare;
migliorare; **to better oneself** migliorare la propria situazione
bet'ter half' *s* metà *f*
betterment ['bɛtərmənt] *s* miglioramento
bettor ['bɛtər] *s* scommettitore *m*
between [bɪ'twin] *adv* in mezzo; **in between** in mezzo, fra i piedi ‖ *prep*
fra, tra
between'-decks' *s* interponte *m*
bev·el ['bɛvəl] *s* (*instrument*) falsa
squadra; (*sloping part*) augnatura ‖
v (*pret & pp -eled* or **-elled**; *ger* **-eling**
or **-elling**) *tr* augnare
beverage ['bɛvərɪdʒ] *s* bevanda
bev·y ['bɛvɪ] *s* (**-ies**) (*of women*)
gruppo; (*of birds*) stormo
bewail [bɪ'wel] *tr* lamentare
beware [bɪ'wer] *tr* fare attenzione a,
guardarsi da ‖ *intr* fare attenzione,
guardarsi
bewilder [bɪ'wɪldər] *tr* lasciar perplesso, confondere, disorientare
bewilderment [bɪ'wɪldərmənt] *s* perplessità *f*, disorientamento
bewitch [bɪ'wɪtʃ] *tr* stregare
beyond [bɪ'jand] *adv* più lontano ‖ *s*—**the beyond** l'aldilà *m* ‖ *adv* più lontano ‖ *prep* al
di là di; oltre a; più tardi di; **beyond
a doubt** fuori dubbio; **beyond repair**
irreparabile
bias ['baɪ·əs] *s* linea diagonale; pregiudizio; **on the bias** diagonalmente
‖ *tr* prevenire
bib [bɪb] *s* bavaglino
Bible ['baɪbəl] *s* Bibbia
Biblical ['bɪblɪkəl] *adj* biblico
bibliogra·phy [,bɪblɪ'agrəfɪ] *s* (**-phies**)
bibliografia
bibliophile ['bɪblɪ·ə,faɪl] *s* bibliofilo
bicarbonate [baɪ'karbə,net] *s* bicarbonato
biceps ['baɪsɛps] *s* bicipite *m*
bicker ['bɪkər] *s* bisticcio, disputa ‖
intr bisticciare, disputare
bicycle ['baɪsɪkəl] *s* bicicletta
bid [bɪd] *s* offerta; (*cards*) dichiarazione; (*coll*) invito ‖ *v* (*pret* **bade**
[bæd] or **bid**; *pp* **bidden** ['bɪdən] or
bid; *ger* **bidding**) *tr & intr* offrire;
comandare; (*cards*) dichiarare
bidder ['bɪdər] *s* offerente *mf*; (*cards*)
dichiarante *mf*; **the highest bidder** il
miglior offerente
bidding ['bɪdɪŋ] *s* ordine *m*; offerte
fpl; (*cards*) dichiarazione
bide [baɪd] *tr*—**to bide one's time** attendere l'ora propizia
biennial [baɪ'ɛnɪ·əl] *adj* biennale
bier [bɪr] *s* catafalco
bifocal [baɪ'fokəl] *adj* bifocale ‖ **bifo-
cals** *spl* occhiali *mpl* bifocali
big [bɪg] *adj* (**bigger**; **biggest**) grande;
(*coll*) importante; (*coll*) stravagante;
big with child incinta ‖ *adv*—**to talk
big** (*coll*) parlare con iattanza
bigamist ['bɪgəmɪst] *s* bigamo
bigamous ['bɪgəməs] *adj* bigamo

big-bellied ['bɪg,belid] *adj* panciuto
Big' Dip'per *s* Gran Carro
big' game' *s* caccia grossa
big-hearted ['bɪg,hɑrtɪd] *adj* magnanimo, generoso
big' mouth' *s* (slang) sbraitone *m*
bigot ['bɪgət] *s* bigotto, bacchettone *m*
bigoted ['bɪgətɪd] *adj* (*in religion*) bigotto; intransigente
bigot•ry ['bɪgətri] *s* (-ries) bigottismo; intransigenza
big' shot' *s* (slang) pezzo grosso, (un) qualcuno
big' slam' *s* (bridge) grande slam *m*
big'-time op'erator *s* (slang) grosso trafficante
big' toe' *s* alluce *m*
big' wheel' *s* (slang) pezzo grosso
bike [baɪk] *s* (coll) bicicletta
bile [baɪl] *s* bile *f*
bilge [bɪldʒ] *s* sentina; (*of barrel*) ventre *m*
bilge'ways *spl* parati *mpl*
bilingual [baɪˈlɪŋgwəl] *adj* bilingue
bilious ['bɪljəs] *adj* bilioso
bilk [bɪlk] *tr* defraudare
bill [bɪl] *s* (*of bird*) becco; (*statement of charges*) conto; (*e.g., for electricity*) bolletta; (*menu*) lista; (*money*) biglietto; (*proposed law*) disegno di legge; (*handbill*) annunzio; (law) atto; (theat) cartellone *m*; **to fill the bill** (coll) riempire i requisiti; **to foot the bill** (coll) pagare lo scotto || *tr* fare una lista di; mettere in conto a || *intr* (*said of doves*) beccuzzarsi; (*said of lovers*) baciucchiarsi
bill'board' *s* cartellone *m*; (rad, telv) titolo di testa
billet ['bɪlɪt] *s* (mil) alloggiamento; (mil) ordine *m* d'alloggiamento || *tr* (mil) alloggiare, accasermare
bill'fold' *s* portafoglio
bill'head' *s* intestazione di fattura
billiards ['bɪljərdz] *s* bigliardo
bil'ling clerk' *s* fatturista *mf*
billion ['bɪljən] *s* (U.S.A.) miliardo; (Brit) bilione *m*
bill' of exchange' *s* tratta
bill' of fare' *s* menu *m*, lista delle vivande
bill' of lad'ing ['ledɪŋ] *s* polizza di carico
bill' of rights' *s* dichiarazione dei diritti
bill' of sale' *s* atto di vendita
billow ['bɪlo] *s* ondata, cavallone *m*
bill'post'er *s* attacchino
bil•ly ['bɪli] *s* (-lies) manganello
bil'ly goat' *s* capro, caprone *m*
bimonthly [baɪˈmʌnθli] *adj* (*occurring every two months*) bimestrale; (*occurring twice a month*) bimensile
bin [bɪn] *s* cassone *m*; (*for bread*) madia; (*e.g., for coal*) deposito
binaural [baɪˈnorəl] *adj* biauricolare
bind [baɪnd] *v* (*pret & pp* **bound** [baʊnd]) *tr* legare; allacciare; (*to bandage*) fasciare; (*to constipate*) costipare; (*a book*) rilegare; (*to oblige*) obbligare; (mach) grippare
binder ['baɪndər] *s* rilegatore *m*; (*cover*) cartella

binder•y ['baɪndəri] *s* (-ies) rilegatoria
binding ['baɪndɪŋ] *adj* obbligatorio || *s* (*of book*) rilegatura; legatura; fasciatura
bind'ing post' *s* (elec) capocorda; (*e.g., of battery*) (elec) serrafilo
binge [bɪndʒ] *s*—**to go on a binge** (coll) far baldoria
bingo ['bɪngo] *s* tombola
binnacle ['bɪnəkəl] *s* abitacolo
binoculars [bɪˈnɑkjələrz] or [baɪˈnɑkjələrz] *spl* binocolo
biochemical [,baɪ-əˈkemɪkəl] *adj* biochimico
biochemist [,baɪ-əˈkemɪst] *s* biochimico
biochemistry [,baɪ-əˈkemɪstri] *s* biochimica
biodegradable [,baɪ-odɪˈgredəbəl] *adj* biodegradabile
biographer [baɪˈɑgrəfər] *s* biografo
biographic(al) [,baɪ-əˈgræfɪk(əl)] *adj* biografico
biogra•phy [baɪˈɑgrəfi] *s* (-phies) biografia
biologist [baɪˈɑlədʒɪst] *s* biologo
biology [baɪˈɑlədʒi] *s* biologia
biophysics [,baɪ-əˈfɪzɪks] *s* biofisica
biop•sy ['baɪ,ɑpsi] *s* (-sies) biopsia
bipartisan [baɪˈpɑrtɪzən] *adj* (*system*) bipartitico; (*government*) bipartito
biped ['baɪped] *adj & s* bipede *m*
birch [bʌrtʃ] *s* betulla || *tr* scudisciare
bird [bʌrd] *s* uccello; **a bird in the hand is worth two in the bush** un uovo oggi vale meglio di una gallina domani; **birds of a feather** gente *f* della stessa risma; **to kill two birds with one stone** pigliare due piccioni con una fava
bird' cage' *s* gabbia
bird' call' *s* richiamo
birdie ['bʌrdi] *s* uccellino; (golf) giocata di un colpo sotto la media
bird'lime' *s* pania
bird' of pas'sage *s* uccello di passo
bird' of prey' *s* uccello da preda
bird'seed' *s* becchime *m*
bird's'-eye view' *s* vista a volo d'uccello
bird' shot' *s* pallini *mpl* da caccia
birth [bʌrθ] *s* nascita; **to give birth to** dare i natali a; mettere alla luce
birth' certif'icate *s* certificato di nascita
birth' control' *s* limitazione delle nascite
birth'day' *s* natalizio, compleanno; (*of an event*) anniversario
birth'mark' *s* voglia
birth'place' *s* patria; (*e.g., city*) luogo di nascita; **to be the birthplace of** dare i natali a
birth' rate' *s* natalità *f*
birth'right' *s* diritto acquisito sin dalla nascita
biscuit ['bɪskɪt] *s* panino soffice; (Brit) biscotto
bisect [baɪˈsekt] *tr* bisecare || *intr* (*said of roads*) incrociarsi
bisection [baɪˈsekʃən] *s* bisezione
bishop ['bɪʃəp] *s* vescovo; (chess) alfiere *m*
bishopric ['bɪʃəprɪk] *s* vescovado

bismuth [ˈbɪzməθ] *s* bismuto
bison [ˈbaɪsən] or [ˈbaɪzən] *s* bisonte *m*
bisulfate [baɪˈsʌlfet] *s* bisolfato
bisulfite [baɪˈsʌlfaɪt] *s* bisolfito
bit [bɪt] *s* (*of bridle*) morso; (*of key*) mappa; (*tool*) punta, trivella; (*small piece*) briciolo; **a bit** un po'; (coll) un momento; **a good bit** una buona quantità; **bit by bit** poco a poco; **to blow to bits** fare a pezzi; **to champ the bit** mordere il freno; **two bits** (slang) quarto di dollaro, cinque soldi
bitch [bɪtʃ] *s* cagna; (vulg) donnaccia ‖ *intr* (slang) lamentarsi
bite [baɪt] *s* morso; (*mouthful*) boccone *m*; **to take a bite** fare uno spuntino; mangiare un boccone ‖ *v* (*pret* **bit** [bɪt]; *pp* **bit** or **bitten** [ˈbɪtən]) *tr* mordere, addentare; pungere; (*the dust*) baciare ‖ *intr* mordere; (*said of insects*) pungere; (*said of fish*) abboccare
biting [ˈbaɪtɪŋ] *adj* mordace; pungente
bitter [ˈbɪtər] *adj* amaro; (*e.g., fight*) accanito; (*cold*) pungente ‖ *s* amaro; **bitters** amaro
bit'ter end' *s*—**to the bitter end** fino alla fine; fino alla morte
bit'ter·en'der *s* (coll) intransigente *mf*
bitterness [ˈbɪtərnɪs] *s* amarezza
bit'ter·sweet' *adj* dolceamaro; (fig) agrodolce ‖ *s* dulcamara
bitumen [bɪˈtjumən] or [bɪˈtumən] *s* bitume *m*
bivou·ac [ˈbɪvuˌæk] or [ˈbɪvwæk] *s* bivacco ‖ *v* (*pret & pp* **-acked**; *ger* **-acking**) *intr* bivaccare
biweekly [baɪˈwikli] *adj* bisettimanale; quindicinale ‖ *adv* ogni due settimane
biyearly [baɪˈjɪrli] *adj* semestrale ‖ *adv* semestralmente
bizarre [bɪˈzɑr] *adj* bizzarro
blab [blæb] *s* chiacchierone *m* ‖ *v* (*pret & pp* **blabbed**; *ger* **blabbing**) *tr* rivelare ‖ *intr* chiacchierare
black [blæk] *adj* nero; (*without light*) buio ‖ *s* nero; **to wear black** vestire a lutto, vestire di nero ‖ *intr*—**to black out** perdere i sensi
black'-and-blue' *adj* livido e pesto
black'-and-white' *adj* in bianco e nero
black'ball' *s* palla nera, voto contrario ‖ *tr* dare la palla nera a
black'ber'ry *s* (*-ries*) mora
black'bird' *s* merlo
black'board' *s* lavagna, tavola nera
black'cap' *s* capinera
black'damp' *s* putizza
Black' Death' *s* peste bubbonica
blacken [ˈblækən] *tr* annerire; (*shoes*) lucidare; (*reputation*) sporcare
black' eye' *s* occhio pesto; (fig) cattiva reputazione
blackguard [ˈblægɑrd] *s* canaglia
black'head' *s* comedone *m*
blackish [ˈblækɪʃ] *adj* nerastro
black'jack' *s* randello; (cards) ventuno ‖ *tr* randellare
black' mag'ic *s* magia nera

black'mail' *s* ricatto ‖ *tr* ricattare
blackmailer [ˈblækˌmelər] *s* ricattatore *m*
Black' Mari'a [məˈraɪə] *s* (coll) furgone *m* cellulare
black' mar'ket *s* borsa nera
black' marketeer' [ˌmɑrkɪˈtɪr] *s* borsanerista *mf*
blackness [ˈblæknɪs] *s* nerezza
black'out' *s* oscuramento; (theat) spegnitura; (pathol) svenimento passeggero
black' sheep' *s* (fig) pecora nera
black'smith' *s* fabbro
black' tie' *s* cravatta da smoking; smoking *m*
bladder [ˈblædər] *s* vescica
blade [bled] *s* (*of a leaf*) pagina; (*of grass*) stelo, filo; (*of oar*) pala; (*of turbine*) paletta; (*of fan*) ventola; (*of knife*) lama; (coll) caposcarico
blame [blem] *s* colpa; **to be to blame for** aver la colpa di; **to put the blame on s.o. for s.th** attribuire a qlcu la colpa di qlco; **you are to blame** è colpa Sua ‖ *tr* biasimare, incolpare
blameless [ˈblemlɪs] *adj* innocente, senza colpa
blanch [blæntʃ] or [blɑntʃ] *tr* bianchire ‖ *intr* impallidire
bland [blænd] *adj* blando; (*weather*) mite
blandish [ˈblændɪʃ] *tr* blandire
blank [blæŋk] *adj* (*not written on*) in bianco; (*e.g., stare*) vuoto; (*utter*) completo ‖ *s* (*printed form*) modulo; (*cartridge*) cartuccia a salve; (*of the mind*) lacuna; **to draw a blank** (coll) non avere alcun successo ‖ *tr*—**to blank out** cancellare
blank' check' *s* assegno in bianco; (fig) carta bianca
blanket [ˈblæŋkɪt] *adj* generale, combinato ‖ *s* coperta; (*of snow*) cappa ‖ *tr* coprire con una coperta; oscurare
blank' verse' *s* verso sciolto
blare [bler] *s* squillo ‖ *tr* proclamare; fare echeggiare ‖ *intr* squillare; echeggiare
blaspheme [blæsˈfim] *tr & intr* bestemmiare
blasphemous [ˈblæsfɪməs] *adj* bestemmiatore
blasphe·my [ˈblæsfɪmi] *s* (*-mies*) bestemmia
blast [blæst] or [blɑst] *s* (*of air*) raffica; (*of a horn*) squillo; (*blight*) rovina; scoppio, esplosione; **at full blast** a piena velocità ‖ *tr* rovinare; fare scoppiare, far saltare ‖ *intr*—**to blast off** (rok) lanciarsi
blast' fur'nace *s* altoforno
blast'off' *s* lancio di missile o di nave spaziale
blatant [ˈbletənt] *adj* (*noisy*) rumoroso; (*obtrusive*) palmare; (*flashy*) chiassoso
blaze [blez] *s* fiammata; splendore *m*; (*on a horse's head*) stella; **in a blaze** in fiamme ‖ *tr* proclamare; **to blaze a**

trail marcare il cammino || *intr* divampare

bleach [blitʃ] *s* candeggio, candeggina || *tr* imbiancare, candeggiare

bleachers ['blitʃərz] *spl* posti *mpl* allo scoperto or di gradinata

bleak [blik] *adj* nudo, deserto; (*cold*) freddo; (*gloomy*) triste

blear·y ['blɪri] *adj* (*-ler; lest*) (*sight*) cisposo; confuso; offuscato

bleat [blit] *s* belato || *intr* belare

bleed [blid] *v* (*pret & pp* **bled** [bled]) *tr* (*to draw blood from*) salassare; (*a tree*) estrare linfa da; (*coll*) sfruttare || *intr* sanguinare; (*said of a tree*) dar linfa; **to bleed to death** morire dissanguato

blemish ['blɛmɪʃ] *s* difetto; macchia || *tr* danneggiare; macchiare

blend [blɛnd] *s* mescolanza, miscuglio; (*of gasoline*) miscela || *v* (*pret & pp* **blended** or **blent** [blɛnt]) *tr* mescolare, miscelare || *intr* mescolarsi, miscelarsi; armonizzare; fondersi

bless [blɛs] *tr* benedire; (*to endow*) dotare; (*to make happy*) allietare

blessed ['blɛsɪd] *adj* benedetto; beato; fortunato; dotato

bless'ed event' *s* lieto evento

blessing ['blɛsɪŋ] *s* benedizione

blight [blaɪt] *s* (*insect; disease*) piaga; rovina; (*fungus*) ruggine *f* || *tr* rovinare, guastare

blimp [blɪmp] *s* piccolo dirigibile

blind [blaɪnd] *adj* cieco; (*slang*) ubriaco || *s* persiana; tendina; (*decoy*) mascheratura; pretesto || *adv* alla cieca || *tr* accecare

blind' al'ley *s* vicolo cieco

blinder ['blaɪndər] *s* paraocchi *m*

blind' fly'ing *s* (aer) volo senza visibilità

blind'fold' *adj* bendato, cogli occhi bendati || *s* benda || *tr* bendare gli occhi a

blindly ['blaɪndli] *adv* alla cieca

blind' man' *s* cieco

blind'man's buff' *s* mosca cieca

blindness ['blaɪndnɪs] *s* cecità *f*

blind' spot' *s* (anat) punto cieco; (rad) zona di silenzio; (fig) debole *m*

blink [blɪŋk] *s* batter *m* di ciglio; (*glimpse*) occhiata; (*glimmer*) barlume *m*; **on the blink** (slang) fuori servizio || *tr*—**to blink one's eyes** batter il ciglio || *intr* occhieggiare; (*to wink*) ammiccare; (*to flash on and off*) lampeggiare; **to blink at** ignorare; far finta di non vedere

blinker ['blɪŋkər] *s* (*at a crossing*) luce *f* intermittente; (*on a horse*) paraocchi *m*

blip [blɪp] *s* guizzo sullo schermo radar

bliss [blɪs] *s* beatitudine *f*, felicità *f*

blissful ['blɪsfəl] *adj* beato, felice

blister ['blɪstər] *s* vescica, bolla || *tr* coprire di vesciche; (fig) bollare || *intr* coprirsi di vesciche

blithe [blaɪð] *adj* gaio, giocondo

blitzkrieg ['blɪts ‚krig] *s* guerra lampo

blizzard ['blɪzərd] *s* tormenta, ventoneve *m*

bloat [blot] *tr* gonfiare || *intr* gonfiarsi

blob [blɑb] *s* (*lump*) zolla; (*of liquid*) macchia

block [blɑk] *s* (*e.g., of wood*) blocco; (*for chopping*) ceppo; (*pulley*) puleggia; ostacolo; (*of houses*) isolato; (typ) cliché *m* || *tr* bloccare; (*a hat*) mettere in forma; **to block up** tappare

blockade [blɑ'ked] *s* blocco; **to run a blockade** forzare il blocco || *tr* bloccare

block' and tack'le *s* bozzello

block'bust'er *s* (coll) superbomba

block'head' *s* imbecille *mf*

block' let'ter *s* carattere *m* stampatello

block' sig'nal *s* (rr) segnale di blocco

blond [blɑnd] *adj* & *s* biondo

blonde [blɑnd] *s* bionda

blood [blʌd] *s* sangue *m*; **in cold blood** a sangue freddo; **to draw blood** ferire, fare sanguinare

blood' bank' *s* emoteca

bloodcurdling ['blʌd ‚kʌrdlɪŋ] *adj* orripilante

blood' do'nor *s* donatore *m* di sangue

blood'hound' *s* segugio

bloodless ['blʌdlɪs] *adj* esangue; (*e.g., revolution*) senza effusione di sangue

blood'mobile' [mo ‚bil] *s* autoemoteca

blood' poi'soning *s* avvelenamento del sangue

blood' pres'sure *s* pressione sanguigna

blood' rela'tion *s* consanguineo

blood'shed' *s* spargimento di sangue, carneficina

blood'shot' *adj* iniettato di sangue

blood'stained' *adj* macchiato di sangue

blood'stream' *s* circolazione sanguigna

blood'suck'er *s* sanguisuga

blood' test' *s* esame *m* del sangue

blood'thirst'y *adj* assetato di sangue

blood' transfu'sion *s* trasfusione di sangue

blood' type' *s* gruppo sanguigno

blood' ves'sel *s* vaso sanguigno

blood·y ['blʌdi] *adj* (*-ler; -lest*) sanguinoso; (*bloodthirsty*) avido di sangue || *v* (*pret & pp* -**led**) *tr* macchiare di sangue

bloom [blum] *s* fiore *m*; (*state of having open buds*) sboccio; (*youthful glow*) incarnato || *intr* fiorire; sbocciare

bloomers ['blumərz] *spl* pantaloni *mpl* femminili larghi fermati sotto il ginocchio

blossom ['blɑsəm] *s* fiore *m*; sboccio || *intr* sbocciare

blot [blɑt] *s* macchia || *v* (*pret & pp* **blotted;** *ger* **blotting**) *tr* macchiare; (*with blotting paper*) asciugare; **to blot out** cancellare; oscurare || *intr* macchiarsi; (*to be absorbent*) essere assorbente; (*said of a pen*) fare macchie

blotch [blɑtʃ] *s* chiazza, macchia || *tr* chiazzare

blotter ['blɑtər] *s* carta asciugante, carta assorbente; (*book*) registro

blouse [blaʊs] *s* blusa

blow [blo] *s* colpo; (*blast*) folata; (*of*

horn) squillo; (*sudden reverse*) batosta; **at one blow** d'un sol colpo; **to come to blows** venire alle mani; **without striking a blow** senza colpo ferire ‖ *v* (*pret* **blew** [blu]; *pp* **blown**) *tr* soffiare, soffiare su; (*an instrument*) suonare; (*one's nose*) soffiarsi; **to blow in** sfondare; **to blow one's brains out** bruciarsi le cervella; **to blow open** aprire completamente; **to blow out** (*e.g., a candle*) spegnere; (*a fuse*) fondere; **to blow up** (*e.g., a mine*) far brillare; (phot) ingrandire ‖ *intr* soffiare; (*to pant*) ansimare; (*with an instrument*) suonare; (*to puff*) sbuffare; (slang) andarsene; **to blow hot and cold** cambiare d'opinione ogni cinque minuti; **to blow in** (coll) arrivare inaspettatamente; **to blow out** (said, e.g., of a candle) spegnersi; (*said of a fuse*) saltare, fondersi; (*said of a tire*) scoppiare; **to blow over** passare; **to blow up** saltar per aria; (*said of a storm*) scoppiare; (coll) perdere la pazienza, scoppiare d'ira

blow'out' *s* scoppio di un pneumatico
blow'pipe' *s* (*tube*) soffione *m*; (*peashooter*) cerbottana
blow'torch' *s* saldatrice *f* a benzina
blubber ['blʌbər] *s* grasso di balena ‖ *intr* piangere, lamentarsi
bludgeon ['blʌdʒən] *s* randello ‖ *tr* randellare
blue [blu] *adj* blu, azzurro; (*gloomy*) triste; (*e.g., laws*) puritanico ‖ *s* blu *m*, azzurro; **out of the blue** inaspettatamente; **the blues** la malinconia; (mus) blues *m*; **to have the blues** essere giù di morale ‖ *tr* tingere di azzurro; (*a metal*) brunire
blue'ber'ry *s* (-ries) mirtillo
blue'bird' *s* uccello azzurro
blue' blood' *s* sangue *m* blu
blue' cheese' *s* gorgonzola americano
blue' chip' *s* (fin) azione di prim'ordine
blue' jay' *s* ghiandaia azzurra
blue' moon' *s*—**once in a blue moon** ad ogni morte di papa
blue'-pen'cil *v* (*pret & pp* **-ciled** *or* **-cilled**; *ger* **-ciling** *or* **-cilling**) *tr* correggere col lapis blu
blue'print' *s* riproduzione cianografica; (*plan*) piano ‖ *tr* riprodurre in cianografia; preparare dettagliatamente
blue'stock'ing *s* saccente *f*, sapientona
blue' streak' *s*—**like a blue streak** (coll) come un razzo
bluff [blʌf] *adj* scosceso; brusco, burbero ‖ *s* promontorio scosceso; bluff *m*; bluffatore *m* ‖ *intr* bluffare
bluing ['bluɪŋ] *s* turchinetto
bluish ['bluːɪʃ] *adj* bluastro
blunder ['blʌndər] *s* errore *m* madornale ‖ *intr* pigliare un granchio
blunt [blʌnt] *adj* ottuso; (*plain-spoken*) franco ‖ *tr* rendere ottuso
bluntness ['blʌntnɪs] *s* ottusità *f*; franchezza
blur [blʌr] *s* macchia; offuscamento; confusione ‖ *v* (*pret & pp* **blurred**;

ger **blurring**) *tr* macchiare; (*the view*) offuscare
blurb [blʌrb] *s* annuncio pubblicitario
blurt [blʌrt] *tr*—**to blurt out** prorompere a dire, lasciarsi sfuggire
blush [blʌʃ] *s* rossore *m*; (*pinkish natural tinge*) incarnato ‖ *intr* arrossire; **to blush at** vergognarsi di
bluster ['blʌstər] *s* frastuono; (fig) boria ‖ *intr* (*said of the wind*) infuriare; fare il bravaccio
blustery ['blʌstəri] *adj* tempestuoso; violento; (*swaggering*) borioso
boar [bor] *s* verro; (*wild hog*) porco selvatico, cinghiale *m*
board [bord] *s* asse *m*; (*notice*) cartello; (*pasteboard*) cartone *m*; (*table*) tavola; (*meals*) vitto; (*group of administrators*) consiglio; (naut) bordo; **above board** franco; **in boards** rilegato; **on board** a bordo; (rr) in vettura; **to go by the board** andare in rovina; **to tread the boards** fare l'attore ‖ *tr* chiudere con assi; (*to provide with meals*) dare pensione a, tenere a dozzina; (*a ship*) salire a bordo di; (*a train*) salire su; (naut) abbordare ‖ *intr* essere a pensione
board' and lodg'ing *s* pensione completa
boarder ['bordər] *s* pensionante *mf*
board'ing house' *s* pensione di famiglia
board'ing school' *s* collegio di pensionanti
board' of direc'tors *s* consiglio d'amministrazione
board' of health' *s* ufficio d'igiene
board' of trade' *s* camera di commercio
board'walk' *s* passeggiata a mare
boast [bost] *s* millanteria, vanteria ‖ *intr* vantarsi
boastful ['bostfəl] *adj* millantatore
boat [bot] *s* nave *f*, battello; (*small ship*) barca, imbarcazione; (*dish*) salsiera; **in the same boat** nella stessa situazione
boat' hook' *s* alighiero
boat'house' *s* capannone *m* per i canotti
boating ['botɪŋ] *s* escursione in barca
boat'man *s* (-men) barcaiolo
boat' race' *s* regata
boatswain ['bosən] *or* ['bot,swen] *s* nostromo
bob [bɑb] *s* (*plumb*) piombino; (*short haircut*) taglio alla bebè; coda mozza (di cavallo); (*jerky motion*) strattone *m*; (*on pendulum of clock*) lente *f*; (*on fishing line*) sughero ‖ *v* (*pret & pp* **bobbed**; *ger* **bobbing**) *tr* tagliare alla bebè; far muòvere a scatti ‖ *intr* muoversi a scatti; fare mossa; **to bob up** apparire
bobbin ['bɑbɪn] *s* bobina
bob'by pin' ['bɑbi] *s* forcina
bob'by-socks' *spl* (coll) calzini *mpl* da ragazza
bobbysoxer ['bɑbɪˌsɑksər] *s* (coll) ragazzina
bobolink ['bɑbəˌlɪŋk] *s* dolicònice *m*
bob'sled' *s* guidoslitta
bode [bod] *tr & intr* presagire
bodice ['bɑdɪs] *s* giubbetto, copribusto

bodily ['bɑdɪlɪ] *adj* fisico, corporeo ‖ *adv* fisicamente, corporeamente; di persona; in massa

bodkin ['bɑdkɪn] *s* punteruolo; (*for lady's hair*) spillone *m*

bod·y ['bɑdi] *s* (*-ies*) corpo; (*corpse*) cadavere *m*; (*of water*) massa; (*of people*) gruppo; (*of a liquid*) sostanza; (*of truck*) cassone *m*; (*of car*) carrozzeria; (*of tree*) tronco; (*coll*) persona; **in a body** in massa

bod'y·guard' *s* (*of a high official*) guardia del corpo; (*e.g., of a movie star*) guardaspalle *m*

bod'y suit' *s* calzamaglia

bog [bɑg] *s* pantano, palude *m* ‖ (*pret & pp* **bogged**; *ger* **bogging**) *intr*—to **bog down** impelagarsi

bogey·man ['bogɪ,mæn] *s* (**-men** [mɛn]) babau *m*

bogus ['bogəs] *adj* (*coll*) falso, finto

Bohemian [bo'himɪ·ən] *adj* boemo; da bohémien ‖ *s* boemo; (*fig*) bohémien *m*

boil [bɔɪl] *s* bollore *m*, ebollizione; (*pathol*) foruncolo; **to come to a boil** cominciare a bollire ‖ *tr* bollire; **to boil down** condensare ‖ *intr* bollire; **to boil away** evaporare completamente; **to boil down** condensarsi; **to boil over** andare per il fuoco

boiled' ham' *s* prosciutto cotto

boiler ['bɔɪlər] *s* caldaia; (*for cooking*) caldaio

boil'er·mak'er *s* calderaio

boiling ['bɔɪlɪŋ] *adj* bollente ‖ *s* bollore *m*, ebollizione

boisterous ['bɔɪstərəs] *adj* (*storm*) violento; (*loud*) rumoroso

bold [bold] *adj* (*daring*) coraggioso; (*impudent*) sfacciato; (*steep*) scosceso; (*clear, sharp*) netto

bold'face' *s* (*typ*) neretto, grassetto

boldness ['boldnɪs] *s* coraggio, audacia; sfacciataggine *f*, impudenza

boll' wee'vil [bol] *s* antonomo del cotone

bologna [bə'lonə] or [bə'lonjə] *s* mortadella

Bolshevik ['bɑlʃəvɪk] or ['bolʃəvɪk] *adj & mf* bolscevico

bolster ['bolstər] *s* cuscino; cuscinetto; (*support*) sostegno ‖ *tr* sorreggere; **to bolster up** sostenere

bolt [bolt] *s* (*arrow*) freccia; (*of lightning*) fulmine *m*; (*sliding bar*) chiavistello; (*threaded rod*) bullone *m*; (*of paper or cloth*) pezza, rotolo ‖ *adv*—**bolt upright** dritto come un fuso ‖ *tr* (*to swallow hurriedly*) ingollare; (*to fasten, e.g., a door*) sprangare; (*to fasten, e.g., two metal parts*) bullonare; (*e.g., a political party*) abbandonare ‖ *intr* (*said of people*) spiccare un salto; (*said of a horse*) prendere la mano; precipitarsi

bolt' from the blue' *s* fulmine *m* a ciel sereno

bomb [bɑm] *s* bomba; (*e.g., for spraying*) bombola ‖ *tr* bombardare

bombard [bɑm'bɑrd] *tr* bombardare; (*with questions*) bersagliare

bombardment [bɑm'bɑrdmənt] *s* bombardamento

bombast ['bɑmbæst] *s* ampollosità *f*

bombastic [bɑm'bæstɪk] *adj* ampolloso

bomb' cra'ter *s* cratere *m*

bomber ['bɑmər] *s* bombardiere *m*

bomb'proof' *adj* a prova di bomba

bomb'shell' *s* bomba; (fig) colpo di bomba, colpo di sorpresa

bomb' shel'ter *s* rifugio antiaereo

bomb'sight' *s* traguardo aereo

bona fide ['bonə ,faɪdə] *adj* sincero ‖ *adv* in buona fede

bonanza [bə'nænzə] *s* (min) ricca vena; (coll) fortuna

bond [bɑnd] *s* legame *m*, vincolo; (*contractual obligation*) obbligazione; (*interest-bearing certificate*) buono, obbligazione; (*surety*) cauzione; **bonds** catene *fpl*; **in bond** sotto cauzione; (*said of goods*) in punto franco ‖ *tr* unire, connettere

bondage ['bɑndɪdʒ] *s* schiavitù *f*

bond'ed ware'house *s* deposito in punto franco

bond'hold'er *s* obbligazionista *mf*

bonds'man *s* (**-men**) garante *m*

bone [bon] *s* osso; (*of fish*) spina; (*of whale*) stecca; **bones** ossa *fpl*; **to have a bone to pick with** avere un conto da regolare con; **to make no bones about** (coll) ammettere; (coll) parlare esplicitamente ‖ *tr* disossare, cavare le spine a ‖ *intr*—to **bone up on** (coll) ripassare

bone'head' *s* (coll) testa dura

boneless ['bonlɪs] *adj* senz'osso; (*fish*) senza spine

boner ['bonər] *s* (slang) errore *m* madornale

bonfire ['bɑn,faɪr] *s* falò *m*

bonnet ['bɑnɪt] *s* cappello da donna; (*of child*) berrettino

bonus ['bonəs] *s* gratifica; indennità *f*; (*to an outgoing employee*) buonuscita

bon·y ['boni] *adj* (*-ier; -iest*) (*having bones*) osseo; (*emaciated*) scarno; (*fish*) spinoso

boo [bu] *s* fischio, urlaccio ‖ *tr & intr* fischiare, disapprovare

boo·by ['bubi] *s* (**-bies**) stupido

boo'by hatch' *s* (naut) portello; (slang) manicomio; (slang) prigione *f*

boo'by prize' *s* premio dato al peggior giocatore

boo'by trap' *s* (mil) trappola esplosiva; (fig) tranello

boogie-woogie ['bugɪ'wugɪ] *s* bughi-bughi *m*

book [bʊk] *s* libro; (*e.g., of matches*) pacchetto; (*mus*) libretto; (fig) regole *fpl*; **the Book** la Bibbia; **to be in one's book** essere nelle grazie di; **to bring s.o. to book** fare una ramanzina a ‖ *tr* registrare; (*e.g., on a horse*) allibrare; (*e.g., a room*) prenotare; (*an actor*) scritturare

book'bind'er *s* rilegatore *m*

book'bind'er·y *s* (**-ies**) rilegatoria

book'bind'ing *s* rilegatura

book'case' *s* scaffale *m*

book' end' *s* reggilibri *m*

bookie ['buki] *s* (coll) allibratore *m*
booking ['bukɪŋ] *s* (*of a trip*) prenotazione; (*of an actor*) scrittura
book'ing clerk' *s* impiegato alla biglietteria
bookish ['bukɪʃ] *adj* studioso; libresco
book'keep'er *s* contabile *mf*
booklet ['buklɪt] *s* libretto; (*pamphlet*) opuscolo
book'keep'ing *s* contabilità *f*
book'mak'er *s* (*one who accepts bets*) allibratore *m*
book'mark' *s* segnalibro
bookmobile ['bukmo,bil] *s* bibliobus *m*
book'plate' *s* ex libris *m*
book' review' *s* rassegna, recensione
book'sell'er *s* libraio
book'shelf' *s* (-shelves) scaffale *m*
book'stand' *s* (*rack*) scansia; (*stall*) edicola
book'store' *s* libreria
book'worm' *s* (zool) tarlo dei libri; (fig) topo da biblioteca
boom [bum] *s* (*of crane*) braccio; (*barrier*) barriera galleggiante; (*noise*) bum *m*; (fin) boom *m*; (naut) boma; (mov, telv) giraffa ‖ *intr* rimbombare; essere in condizioni floride
boomerang ['bumə,ræŋ] *s* bumerang *m*
boom' town' *s* città *f* fungo
boon [bun] *s* fortuna, benedizione
boon' compan'ion *s* compagnone *m*
boor [bur] *s* bifolco, zotico
boorish ['burɪʃ] *adj* grossolano
boost [bust] *s* aumento; (coll) spinta ‖ *tr* spingere in su; sostenere; (*prices*) alzare; parlare a favore di
booster ['bustər] *s* (*backer*) sostenitore *m*; propulsore *m* a razzo; (rok) propulsore *m* del primo stadio; (med) seconda iniezione
boot [but] *s* stivale *m*; (*kick*) calcio; (*patch*) (aut) pezza; **the boot is on the other foot** la situazione è rovesciata; **to be in the boots of** essere nella pelle di; **to boot** per di più; **to get the boot** (coll) essere messo sulla strada; **to lick the boots of** leccare i piedi a; **to wipe one's boots on** trattare come una pezza da piedi ‖ *tr* dare un calcio a; **to boot out** (slang) buttar fuori
boot'black' *s* lustrascarpe *m*
booth [buθ] *s* (*stall*) banco da mercato; (*for telephoning, voting*) cabina
boot'jack' *s* tirastivali *m*
boot'leg' *adj* di contrabbando ‖ *s* liquore *m* di contrabbando ‖ *v* (pret & pp -legged; ger -legging) *tr* vendere di contrabbando ‖ *intr* vendere alcol di contrabbando
bootlegger ['but,lɛgər] *s* contrabbandiere *m* di liquori
boot'lick'er [,lɪkər] *s* (coll) leccapiedi *mf*
boot'strap' *s* tirante *m* degli stivali
boo·ty ['buti] *s* (-ties) bottino
booze [buz] *s* (coll) bevanda alcolica ‖ *intr* (coll) ubriacarsi
borax ['boræks] *s* borace *m*
border ['bɔrdər] *adj* confinario, con-

finante ‖ *s* bordo, margine *m*; (*between two countries*) confine *m* ‖ *tr* bordare; confinare con ‖ *intr* confinare
bor'der clash' *s* incidente *m* ai confini
bor'der-line' *adj* incerto ‖ *s* frontiera
bore [bor] *s* (*drill hole*) buco, foro; (*hollow part of gun*) anima; (*caliber*) calibro; (*dull person*) seccatore *m*; (*annoyance*) seccatura; (mach) alesaggio ‖ *tr* bucare, forare; seccare; (mach) alesare
boredom ['bordəm] *s* noia, tedio
boring ['borɪŋ] *adj* noioso ‖ *s* trivellazione
born [bɔrn] *adj* nato, partorito; **to be born** nascere; **to be born again** rinascere; **to be born with a silver spoon in one's mouth** nascere con la camicia
borough ['bʌro] *s* borgata, comune *m*
borrow ['baro] or ['bɔro] *tr* chiedere a or in prestito; prendere a or in prestito; ricevere a or in prestito; (*to adopt*) adottare; **to borrow trouble** preoccuparsi per nulla
borrower ['baro·ər] or ['bɔro·ər] *s* chi riceve a prestito; (law) comodatario, prestatario
borrowing ['baro·ɪŋ] or ['bɔro·ɪŋ] *s* prestito; prestito linguistico, forestierismo
bosom ['buzəm] *s* petto, seno; (*e.g., of the family*) grembo, seno; (*of shirt*) pettorina
bos'om friend' *s* amico del cuore
Bosporus ['baspərəs] *s* Bosforo
boss [bɔs] or [bas] *s* (coll) padrone *m*; (coll) direttore *m*; (coll) capintesta *m*; (coll) principale *m*; (archit) bugna, bozza ‖ *tr* fare da padrone a ‖ *intr* fare da padrone
boss·y ['bɔsi] or ['basi] *adj* (-ier; -iest) autoritario
botanical [bə'tænɪkəl] *adj* botanico
botanist ['batənɪst] *s* botanico
botany ['batəni] *s* botanica
botch [batʃ] *s* abborracciatura ‖ *tr* abborracciare
both [boθ] *adj* entrambi i, tutti e due i ‖ *pron* entrambi, tutti e due ‖ *conj* del pari, al medesimo tempo; **both . . . and** tanto . . . quanto
bother ['baðər] *s* (*worry*) noia, seccatura; (*person*) seccatore *m* ‖ *tr* dar noia a, seccare ‖ *intr* preoccuparsi; **to bother about** or **with** occuparsi di; **to bother to -| inf** molestarsi di + *inf*
bothersome ['baðərsəm] *adj* incomodo
bottle ['batəl] *s* bottiglia, fiasco ‖ *tr* imbottigliare; **to bottle up** imbottigliare
bot'tle cap' *s* tappo a corona
bot'tle-neck' *s* collo di bottiglia; (*of traffic*) congestione, imbottigliamento
bot'tle o'pener ['opənər] *s* apribottiglie *m*
bottom ['batəm] *adj* basso; (*price, dollar*) ultimo; infimo ‖ *s* fondo; (*of chair*) sedile *m*; base *f*; (*of bottle*) culo; (*of ship*) scafo; **at bottom** in realtà; **to begin at the bottom** comin-

ciare dalla gavetta; **to get at the bottom of** andare a fondo di; **to go to the bottom** andare a picco

bottomless ['bɑtəmlɪs] *adj* senza fondo

boudoir [bu'dwɑr] *s* gabinetto di toletta (da signora)

bough [baʊ] *s* ramo

bouillon ['bʊjɑn] *s* brodo schietto

boulder ['boldər] *s* masso, roccia

boulevard ['bʊlə,vɑrd] *s* corso

bounce [baʊns] *s* balzo; salto; elasticità *f*; (*of boat or plane*) piastrellamento; (fig) spirito; **to get the bounce** (slang) essere licenziato || *tr* far balzare; (slang) buttar fuori || *intr* rimbalzare; saltare; (aer, naut) piastrellare

bouncer ['baʊnsər] *s* (*in night club*) (slang) buttafuori *m*

bouncing ['baʊnsɪŋ] *adj* forte, vigoroso; grande, rumoroso

bound [baʊnd] *adj* legato; collegato; obbligato; (bb) rilegato; (coll) risoluto; **bound for** destinato a, diretto per; **bound up in** or **with** in strette relazioni con; assorto in || *s* salto; rimbalzo; limite *m*; **bounds** zona limitrofa; **out of bounds** fuori limiti; al di là delle convenienze || *tr* delimitare

bound·a·ry ['baʊndəri] *s* (-ries) confine *m*, limite *m*

bound'ary stone' *s* pietra di confine

boundless ['baʊndlɪs] *adj* illimitato, sconfinato

bountiful ['baʊntɪfəl] *adj* generoso; abbondante

boun·ty ['baʊnti] *s* (-ties) dono generoso; generosità *f*, abbondanza; (*reward*) premio

bouquet [bu'ke] or [bo'ke] *s* mazzo, mazzolino; profumo, aroma *m*

bourgeois ['bʊrʒwa] *adj* & *s* borghese *mf*

bourgeoisie [,bʊrʒwa'zi] *s* borghesia

bout [baʊt] *s* lotta, contesa; (*of illness*) attacco

bow [baʊ] *s* inchino, riverenza; (naut) prua; **to take a bow** ricevere gli applausi || *tr* chinare, piegare || *intr* inchinarsi; sottomettersi; **to bow and scrape** fare riverenza || [bo] *s* (*weapon*) arco; (*knot*) nodo; (mus) archetto; (*stroke of bow*) (mus) arcata || *tr* & *intr* (mus) suonare con l'archetto

bowdlerize ['baʊdlə,raɪz] *tr* espurgare

bowel ['baʊ·əl] *s* budello; **bowels** viscere *fpl*

bow'el move'ment *s* evacuazione; **to have a bowel movement** andar di corpo

bower ['baʊ·ər] *s* pergolato

bowery ['baʊ·əri] *adj* frondoso

bowknot ['bo,nɑt] *s* nodo scorsoio

bowl [bol] *s* (*dish*) ciotola, tazza; (*of pipe*) fornello; (*basin*) catino; (*amphitheater*) arena; (*ball*) boccia; (*delivery of ball*) bocciata; **bowls** bocce *fpl* || *tr* bocciare; **to bowl down** or **over** abbattere || *intr* giocare alle bocce

bowlegged ['bo,legd] or ['bo,legɪd] *adj* con le gambe storte

bowler ['bolər] *s* giocatore *m* di bocce

bowling ['bolɪŋ] *s* bocce *fpl*; bowling *m*, birilli *mpl*

bowl'ing al'ley *s* pista per il bowling; bowling *m*

bowl'ing green' *s* campo di bocce erboso

bowshot ['bo,ʃɑt] *s* tiro d'arco

bowsprit ['baʊsprɪt] or ['bosprɪt] *s* (naut) bompresso

bow' tie' [bo] *s* cravatta a farfalla

bowwow ['baʊ,waʊ] *interj* bau bau!

box [bɑks] *s* scatola; cassa; (*for jury*) banco; (*for sentry*) garitta; (*on coach*) cassetta; (*in stable*) posta; (*slap*) ceffone *m*; (*with fist*) pugno; (bot) bosso; (theat) palco, barcaccia; (baseball) posto del battitore; (typ) riquadratura || *tr* mettere in scatola; (*to slap*) schiaffeggiare; (*to hit with fist*) fare a pugilato con; **to box in** or **up** rinchiudere || *intr* fare a pugni; combattere

box'car' *s* vagone *m* merci coperto

boxer ['bɑksər] *s* pugile *m*

box'hold'er *s* palchettista *mf*

boxing ['bɑksɪŋ] *s* pugilato

box'ing gloves' *spl* guantoni *mpl* da pugilato

box' of'fice *s* sportello, biglietteria; (theat) incasso; (theat) successo

box'-of'fice hit' *s* grande successo

box' pleat' *s* (*of skirt*) cannone *m*

box' seat' *s* posto in palco

box'wood' *s* bosso

boy [bɔɪ] *s* ragazzo, giovane *m* || *interj* accidempoli!

boycott ['bɔɪkɑt] *s* boicottaggio || *tr* boicottare

boy'friend' *s* innamorato, amico

boyhood ['bɔɪhʊd] *s* fanciullezza

boyish ['bɔɪ·ɪʃ] *adj* giovanile

boy' scout' *s* giovane esploratore *m*

bra [brɑ] *s* (coll) reggiseno

brace [bres] *s* (*couple*) paio; (*device for maintaining tension*) tirante *m*; (*prop*) sostegno; (*tool*) trapano; (typ) graffa; **braces** (Brit) bretelle *fpl* || *tr* legare; serrare; puntellare; sostenere; invigorare; **to brace oneself** pigliare animo || *intr*—**to brace up** (coll) pigliare animo

brace' and bit' *s* menarola, trapano

bracelet ['breslɪt] *s* braccialetto

bracer ['bresər] *s* (coll) bicchierino

bracket ['brækɪt] *s* mensola; (*for lamp*) braccio; angolo; classifica; (typ) parentesi quadra || *tr* sostenere con mensola; mettere tra parentesi quadra; classificare

brackish ['brækɪʃ] *adj* salmastro

brad [bræd] *s* chiodino, punta

brag [bræg] *s* vanto || *v* (*pret* & *pp* **bragged;** *ger* **bragging**) *intr* vantare

braggart ['brægərt] *s* millantatore *m*

Brah·man ['brɑmən] *s* (-mans) bramino

braid [bred] *s* treccia; (*strip of cloth*) spighetta; (mil) cordellina || *tr* intrecciare; decorare con spighette

brain [bren] *s* cervello; **brains** cervello, intelligenza; **to rack one's brains** rompersi la testa ‖ *tr* far saltare le cervella di

brain'child' *s* (coll) parto dell'ingegno, idea geniale

brain' drain' *s* (coll) fuga di cervelli

brainless ['brenlɪs] *adj* senza testa

brain' pow'er *s* intelligenza

brain'storm' *s* (coll) ispirazione

brain' trust' *s* consiglio d'esperti

brain'wash'ing *s* lavaggio del cervello

brain' wave' *s* onda encefalica; (coll) idea geniale

brain'work' *s* lavoro intellettuale

brain•y ['breni] *adj* (-i•er; -i•est) intelligente

braise [brez] *tr* (culin) brasare

brake [brek] *s* freno; (*thicket*) macchia ‖ *tr & intr* frenare

brake' drum' *s* tamburo del freno

brake' lin'ing *s* ferodo

brake'man *s* (-men) frenatore *m*

brake' shoe' *s* ganascia

bramble ['bræmbəl] *s* rovo

bran [bræn] *s* crusca

branch [bræntʃ] *s* (*of tree*) branca, ramo; (*of river*) braccio; (*of a family*) ramo; (*of business*) filiale *f*; (rr) diramazione ‖ *intr* biforcarsi; **to branch off** or **out** ramificarsi, diramarsi

branch' line' *s* ferrovia di diramazione

branch' of'fice *s* succursale *f*

brand [brænd] *s* (*burning stick*) tizzone *m*; (*mark; stigma*) marchio; (*label; make*) marca ‖ *tr* (*to mark with a brand*) marchiare; (*to put a stigma on*) bollare; **to brand as** tacciare di

brandied ['brændid] *adj* conservato in acquavite

brand'ing i'ron *s* ferro da marchio

brandish ['brændɪʃ] *tr* brandire

brand'-new' *adj* nuovo fiammante

bran•dy ['brændi] *s* (-dies) cognac *m*, acquavite *f*

brash [bræʃ] *adj* (*too hasty*) avventato; (*insolent*) impudente ‖ *s* frammenti *mpl*; attacco (di malattia), indigestione

brass [bræs] or [brɑs] *s* ottone *m*; (coll) faccia tosta; (slang) alti ufficiali; **brasses** (mus) ottoni *mpl*

brass' band' *s* fanfara

brassiere [brə'zɪr] *s* reggiseno

brass' knuck'les *spl* tirapugni *m*

brass' tack' *s* chiodino or borchia d'ottone; **to get down to brass tacks** (coll) venire al sodo

brass•y ['bræsi] or ['brɑsi] *adj* (-i•er; -i•est) fatto d'ottone; sfacciato, impudente

brat [bræt] *s* marmocchio, monello

brava•do [brə'vado] *s* (-does or -dos) bravata

brave [brev] *adj* coraggioso ‖ *s* persona coraggiosa; guerriero indiano ‖ *tr* (*to defy*) sfidare; (*to meet with courage*) affrontare

bravery ['brevəri] *s* coraggio

bra•vo ['bravo] *s* (-vos) bravo; applauso ‖ *interj* bravo!

brawl [brɔl] *s* zuffa, rissa ‖ *intr* azzuffarsi, rissare

brawn [brɔn] *s* forza muscolare

brawn•y ['brɔni] *adj* (-i•er; -i•est) muscoloso

bray [bre] *s* raglio ‖ *intr* ragliare

braze [brez] *s* brasatura ‖ *tr* brasare

brazen ['brezən] *adj* d'ottone; (*shameless*) sfrontato; (*sound*) penetrante ‖ *tr*—**to brazen out** or **through** affrontare sfacciatamente

brazier ['breʒər] *s* caldano, braciere *m*; (*workman*) ottonaio

Brazil [brə'zɪl] *s* il Brasile

Brazilian [brə'zɪljən] *adj & s* brasiliano

Brazil' nut' *s* noce *f* del Brasile

breach [britʃ] *s* (*gap*) breccia; (*failure to observe a law*) infrazione ‖ *tr* fare breccia su, fare varco in

breach' of faith' *s* abuso di confidenza

breach' of prom'ise *s* rottura di promessa di matrimonio

breach' of the peace' *s* violazione dell'ordine pubblico

bread [bred] *s* pane *m*; **to break bread with** sedersi a tavola con ‖ *tr* impannare

bread' and but'ter *s* pane *m* e burro; (coll) pane quotidiano

bread' crumbs' *spl* pangrattato

breaded ['brɛdɪd] *adj* impannato

bread' knife' *s* coltello da pane

bread' line' *s* coda del pane

bread' stick' *s* grissino

breadth [brɛdθ] *s* (*width*) larghezza; (*scope*) ampiezza

bread'win'ner *s* sostegno della famiglia

break [brek] *s* interruzione; intervallo; omissione; (*breaking*) rottura; (*of bones*) frattura; (*of day*) fare *m*, spuntare *m*; (*sudden change*) mutamento; (*from jail*) evasione; (*luck*) (coll) fortuna; **to give s.o. a break** dare a qlcu l'opportunità ‖ *v* (*pret* broke [brok]; *pp* broken) *tr* (*to smash*) rompere, spezzare; (*to tame*) domare; (*to demote*) destituire; (*a record*) superare; (*to violate*) violare; (*to make bankrupt*) mandare al fallimento; (*to interrupt*) interrompere; (*to reduce the effects of*) attutire; (*to disclose*) rivelare; (*to bring to an end by force*) battere; (*a banknote*) cambiare; (*one's word*) mancare (with *dat*); (*a law*) rompere; **to break asunder** separare; **to break down** analizzare; **to break in** forzare; **to break open** forzare, scassinare; **to break up** dissolvere ‖ *intr* (*to divide*) rompersi; (*to burst*) scoppiare; (*said of voice of youngster*) cambiare; (*said of voice*) indebolirsi; (*said of a crowd*) disperdersi; (*said of weather*) rischiararsi; (*said of prices*) ribassare; (*to come into being*) scoppiare; (boxing) separarsi; **to break asunder** separarsi; **to break away** scappare; **to break down** abbattersi; (aut) essere or rimanere in panna; **to break even** fare patta; **to break in** irrompere; interrompere; **to break into** forzare; **to break into a run** incominciare a correre; **to break loose** liberarsi; (said of a storm) scatenarsi; **to break off** interrompere; **to break out** (said of the skin) avere un'eruzione; (said, e.g., of war) scoppiare; **to break through** aprirsi il varco; **to break up** disperdersi; **to break with** rompere le relazioni con

breakable ['brekəbəl] adj fragile

breakage ['brekɪdʒ] s rottura

break'down' s (in negotiations) rottura; (aut) panna; (chem) analisi f; (pathol) colasso

breaker ['brekər] s (wave) frangente m

breakfast ['brekfəst] s prima colazione || intr fare prima colazione

break'neck' adj pericoloso; **at breakneck speed** a rotta di collo, a rompicollo

break' of day' s alba

break'through' s (mil) penetrazione; (fig) scoperta sensazionale

break'up' s dispersione; dissoluzione; (of a friendship) rottura

break'wa'ter s diga, frangiflutti m

breast [brest] s petto; (of female) seno; (source of emotions) animo; **to make a clean breast of** fare una piena confessione di

breast'bone' s sterno

breast' drill' s trapano da petto

breast'feed' v (pret & pp -fed [fed]) tr allattare

breast'pin' s spilla

breast'stroke' s bracciata a rana

breath [brɛθ] s respiro, respirazione; (odor) alito; (breeze) soffio; (whisper) sussurro; (fig) vita; **out of breath** ansimante; **short of breath** corto di respiro; **to gasp for breath** respirare affannosamente; **under one's breath** sottovoce

breathe [brið] tr respirare; (to whisper) sussurrare; **to breathe one's last** esalare l'ultimo sospiro; **to not breathe a word** non dire una parola || intr respirare; **to breathe in** inspirare; **to breathe out** espirare

breath'ing spell' s attimo di respiro

breathless ['brɛθlɪs] adj senza fiato, ansimante; soffocante

breath'tak'ing s emozionante, commovente

breech [britʃ] s (buttocks) natiche fpl; (rear part) parte f posteriore; (of gun) culatta; **breeches** ['brɪtʃɪz] pantaloni mpl al ginocchio; pantaloni mpl da cavallo; **to wear the breeches** (coll) portare le brache

breed [brid] s razza; tipo; (stock) origine f || v (pret & pp bred [bred]) tr produrre; (to raise) allevare

breeder ['bridər] s allevatore m; riproduttore m

breeding ['bridɪŋ] s (e.g., of livestock) allevamento; educazione

breeze [briz] s brezza

breez•y ['brizi] adj (-ier; -iest) ventilato; (brisk) vivace, brioso

brethren ['brɛðrɪn] spl fratelli mpl

brevi•ty ['brɛvɪti] s (-ties) brevità f

brew [bru] s pozione; bevanda || tr (beer) fabbricare; (to steep) preparare; (to plot) complottare || intr (said of beer) fermentare; (said of a storm) prepararsi

brewer ['bru·ər] s birraio

brew'er's yeast' s lievito di birra

brewer•y ['bru·əri] s (-ies) birreria, fabbrica di birra

bribe [braɪb] s subornazione, bustarella || tr subornare, dare la bustarella a

briber•y ['braɪbəri] s (-ies) subornazione, corruzione

bric-a-brac ['brɪkə‚bræk] s bric-a-brac m, cianfrusaglia, cianfrusaglie fpl

brick [brɪk] s mattone m || tr mattonare

brick'bat' s pezzo di mattone; (coll) insulto

brick'kiln' s fornace f per mattoni

bricklayer ['brɪk‚le·ər] s muratore m

brick'yard' s deposito di mattoni

bridal ['braɪdəl] adj nuziale, da sposa

brid'al wreath' s serto nuziale

bride [braɪd] s sposa

bride'groom' s sposo

bridesmaid ['braɪdz‚med] s damigella d'onore

bridge [brɪdʒ] s ponte m; (of violin) ponticello; (on a ship) ponte m di comando || tr gettare un ponte su; congiungere; **to bridge a gap** colmare una lacuna

bridge'head' s testa di ponte

bridle ['braɪdəl] s briglia || tr mettere la briglia a; (fig) frenare || intr drizzare il capo, insuperbirsi

bri'dle path' s strada cavalcabile

brief [brif] adj breve || s sommario; (law) esposto; (eccl) breve m; **briefs** slip m || tr dare istruzioni a, mettere al corrente

brief' case' s cartella, borsa d'avvocato

brier ['braɪ·ər] s radica; pipa di radica

brig [brɪg] s (naut) brigantino; (naut) prigione

brigade [brɪ'ged] s brigata

brigadier [‚brɪgə'dir] s (coll) brigadier generale m, generale m di brigata

brigand ['brɪgənd] s brigante m

brigantine ['brɪgən‚tin] or ['brɪgən‚taɪn] s (naut) brigantino goletta

bright [braɪt] adj (shining) lucido; (light) brillante; (lively) vivo; intelligente; famoso; (idea) luminoso

brighten ['braɪtən] tr illuminare; ravvivare || intr illuminarsi; ravvivarsi; rischiararsi

bright' lights' spl luci fpl abbaglianti; (aut) fari mpl abbaglianti

brilliance ['brɪljəns] or **brilliancy** ['brɪljənsi] s splendore m, scintillio

brilliant ['brɪljənt] adj brillante

brim [brɪm] s (e.g., of cup) orlo, bordo; (of hat) ala, tesa || v (pret & pp brimmed; ger brimming) intr essere pieno sino all'orlo

brim'stone' s zolfo

brine [braɪn] s salamoia; acqua di mare

bring [brɪŋ] v (pret & pp brought

[brɔt]) *tr* far venire; provocare; (*to carry along*) portare con sè; **to bring about** causare; **to bring around** persuadere; **to bring back** restituire; **to bring down** far abbassare; (fig) umiliare; **to bring forth** dare alla luce; **to bring forward** (*an excuse*) addurre; (math) riportare; **to bring in** introdurre; far entrare; **to bring off** compiere; **to bring on** causare; **to bring oneself** to rassegnarsi a; **to bring out** (*to expose*) rivelare; (*to offer to the public*) presentare al pubblico; (*a book*) far uscire; **to bring to** far rinvenire; (*a ship*) fermare; **to bring together** riunire; **to bring up** (*children*) allevare, tirar su; (*to introduce*) allegare; (*to cough up*) rigettare

bringing-up ['brɪŋɪŋ'ʌp] *s* educazione
brink [brɪŋk] *s* orlo
briquet [brɪ'kɛt] *s* bricchetta
brisk [brɪsk] *adj* (*quick*) svelto; (*sharp*) acuto; (*invigorating*) frizzante; (*gunfire*) nutrito
bristle ['brɪsəl] *s* setola || *intr* (*to be stiff*) irrigidirsi; (*said of hair*) rizzarsi; (*with anger*) adirarsi
bris·tly ['brɪslɪ] *adj* (*-tlier; -tliest*) irto di setole
British ['brɪtɪʃ] *adj* britannico || **the British** i britannici, gl'inglesi
Britisher ['brɪtɪʃər] *s* britannico
Briton ['brɪtən] *s* britannico
Brittany ['brɪtənɪ] *s* la Bretagna
brittle ['brɪtəl] *adj* fragile, friabile; (*crisp*) croccante
broach [brotʃ] *s* (*pin*) spilla; (*spit*) spiedo; (mach) alesatore *m* || *tr* perforare; (*a subject*) intavolare
broad [brɔd] *adj* largo; tollerante, liberale; (*daylight*) pieno; (*story*) grossolano; (*extensive*) lato; (*accent*) pronunciato
broad'cast' *s* disseminazione; (rad) radiodiffusione || *v* (*pret & pp* -cast) *tr* disseminare, diffondere || (*pret & pp* -cast *or* -casted) *tr* radiodiffondere
broad'cast'ing sta'tion *s* stazione radiotrasmittente
broad'cloth' *s* (*wool*) panno di lana; (*cotton*) popeline *f*
broaden ['brɔdən] *tr* allargare, estendere || *intr* allargarsi, estendersi
broad' jump' *s* salto in lunghezza
broadloom ['brɔd,lum] *adj* tessuto su telaio largo
broad-minded ['brɔd'maɪndɪd] *adj* di ampie vedute, liberale
broad-shouldered ['brɔd'ʃoldərd] *adj* largo di spalle
broad'side' *s* (nav) bordo; (nav) bordata; (*verbal criticism*) (coll) sfuriata; (*written criticism*) (coll) attacco violento
broad'sword' *s* spada da taglio
brocade [bro'ked] *s* broccato
broccoli ['brakəlɪ] *s* broccolo; (*as food*) broccoli *mpl*
brochure [bro'ʃur] *s* opuscolo, libriccino

brogue [brog] *s* accento irlandese; scarpa forte e comoda
broil [brɔɪl] *s* cottura alla graticola; carne *f* cotta alla graticola; (*quarrel*) rissa, zuffa || *tr* cucinare alla graticola; bruciare || *intr* cucinare alla graticola; (*to quarrel*) rissare, azzuffarsi
broiler ['brɔɪlər] *s* graticola, gratella; (*chicken*) pollo da cucinare alla gratella *or* allo spiedo
broke [brok] *adj* (coll) al verde
broken ['brokən] *adj* rotto; fratturato; (*e.g., English*) parlato male; (*tamed*) domato
bro'ken-down' *adj* avvilito; rovinato
broken-hearted ['brokən'hartɪd] *adj* affranto
broker ['brokər] *s* sensale *m*; (*on the stock exchange*) agente *m* di cambio
brokerage ['brokərɪdʒ] *s* mediazione
bromide ['bromaɪd] *s* bromuro; (coll) banalità *f*
bromine ['bromin] *s* bromo
bronchitis [braŋ'kaɪtɪs] *s* bronchite *f*
bron·co ['braŋko] *s* (-cos) puledro brado
broncobuster ['braŋko,bʌstər] *s* domatore *m* di puledri bradi
bronze [branz] *adj* bronzeo || *s* bronzo || *tr* bronzare || *intr* abbronzarsi
brooch [brotʃ] *or* [brutʃ] *s* spilla
brood [brud] *s* covata, nidiata || *tr* covare || *intr* chiocciare; meditare; **to brood on** *or* **over** meditare con tristezza (su)
brook [bruk] *s* ruscello || *tr*—**to brook no** non sopportare
broom [brum] *or* [brum] *s* scopa; (*shrub*) saggina
broom'corn' *s* sorgo
broom'stick' *s* manico di scopa
broth [brɔθ] *or* [braθ] *s* brodo
brothel ['braθəl] *or* ['braðəl] *s* postribolo, bordello
brother ['brʌðər] *s* fratello
brotherhood ['brʌðər,hud] *s* fratellanza; (*association*) confraternita
broth'er-in-law' *s* (**brothers-in-law**) cognato
brotherly ['brʌðərlɪ] *adj* fraterno || *adv* fraternamente
brow [brau] *s* ciglio; (*forehead*) fronte *f*; **to knit one's brow** aggrottare la fronte
brow'beat' *v* (*pret* -beat; *pp* -beaten) *tr* intimidire, intimorire
brown [braun] *adj* bruno; (*tanned*) abbronzato || *s* color bruno || *tr* colorare di bruno; abbronzare; (*metal*) brunire; (culin) dorare || *intr* colorarsi di bruno; abbronzarsi; brunirsi; (culin) dorarsi
brownish ['braunɪʃ] *adj* brunastro
brown' stud'y *s*—**In a brown study** assorto in fantasticherie
brown' sug'ar *s* zucchero greggio
browse [brauz] *intr* (*said of cattle*) brucare; sfogliare; **to browse around** curiosare
bruise [bruz] *s* ammaccatura, contu-

sione ‖ *tr* ammaccare ‖ *intr* ammaccarsi

brunet [bru'nɛt] *adj* bruno

brunette [bru'nɛt] *adj & s* bruna

brunt [brʌnt] *s* forza; scontro; peso

brush [brʌʃ] *s* pennello; spazzola; (*stroke*) pennellata; (*light touch*) tocco; (*brushwood*) macchia; (*brief encounter*) scaramuccia; (*elec*) spazzola ‖ *tr* spazzolare; pennellare; **to brush aside** rigettare; **to brush up** ritoccare ‖ *intr*—**to brush by** passar vicino; **to brush up on** ripassare

brush'-off' *s* (*slang*) scortesia; **to give the brush-off to** (*slang*) snobbare

brush'wood' *s* macchia, fratta

brusque [brʌsk] *adj* brusco

brusqueness ['brʌsknɪs] *s* bruschezza

Brussels ['brʌsəlz] *s* Bruxelles *f*

Brus'sels sprouts' *spl* cavolini *mpl*

brutal ['brutəl] *adj* brutale

brutali•ty [bru'tælɪti] *s* (-**ties**) brutalità *f*

brute [brut] *adj & s* bruto

brutish ['brutɪʃ] *adj* bruto

bubble ['bʌbəl] *s* bolla; (*fig*) chimera ‖ *intr* bollire; (*to make a bubbling sound*) barbugliare; **to bubble over** traboccare

bub'ble bath' *s* bagno di schiuma

buccaneer [ˌbʌkə'nɪr] *s* bucaniere *m*

buck [bʌk] *s* (*deer*) cervo; (*goat*) caprone *m*; (*sawhorse*) cavalletto; (*rabbit*) coniglio maschio; (*bucking*) groppata; (*dandy*) damerino; (*slang*) dollaro; **to pass the buck** (*coll*) giocare a scaricabarile ‖ *tr* resistere accanitamente a ‖ *intr* (*said of a horse*) fare salti da caprone; **to buck for** (*slang*) cercare di ottenere; **to buck up** (*coll*) rianimarsi, prender animo

bucket ['bʌkɪt] *s* secchio; bigoncia; (*e.g., of dredge*) benna; **to kick the bucket** (*slang*) tirare le cuoia

buck'et seat' *s* sedile *m*, strapuntino

buckle ['bʌkəl] *s* (*clasp*) fibbia, boccola; piega ‖ *tr* affibbiare ‖ *intr* piegarsi, curvarsi; **to buckle down to** (*coll*) mettersi di buzzo buono a

buck' pri'vate *s* (*slang*) soldato semplice

buckram ['bʌkrəm] *s* tela da fusto

buck'saw' *s* cavalletto

buck'shot' *s* pallini *mpl* da caccia

buck'tooth' *s* (-**teeth**) dente *m* in fuori, dente *m* sporgente

buck'wheat' *s* grano saraceno

bud [bʌd] *s* bocciolo, gemma; **to nip in the bud** troncare sul nascere ‖ *v* (*pret & pp* **budded**; *ger* **budding**) *intr* sbocciare; nascere

Buddhism ['budɪzəm] *s* buddismo

bud•dy ['bʌdi] *s* (-**dies**) (*coll*) amico, compare *m*

budge [bʌdʒ] *tr* smuovere ‖ *intr* muoversi

budget ['bʌdʒɪt] *s* bilancio ‖ *tr* stanziare, preventivare; (*to schedule*) anticipare; (*time*) calcolare in anticipo

budgetary ['bʌdʒɪˌtɛri] *adj* preventivo, di bilancio

buff [bʌf] *adj* bruno giallastro; di pelle ‖ *s* (*leather*) pelle gialla; dilet-

tante *m*; (*mil*) giacca di pelle gialla; (*coll*) pelle nuda ‖ *tr* lucidare; (*to reduce the force of*) ammortizzare

buffa•lo ['bʌfəˌlo] *s* (-**loes** or -**los**) bufalo ‖ *tr* (*coll*) intimidire

buffer ['bʌfər] *s* ammortizzatore *m*; cuscinetto; (*worker*) lucidatore *m*; (*mach*) lucidatrice *f*; (rr) respingente *m*

buff'er state' *s* stato cuscinetto

buffet [bu'fe] *s* (*piece of furniture*) credenza; (*counter*) buffet *m* ‖ ['bʌfɪt] *s* pugno; schiaffo ‖ *tr* dar pugni a; schiaffeggiare; lottare con; (*to push about*) sballottare

buffet' car' [bu'fe] *s* vagone *m* ristorante

buffoon [bə'fun] *s* buffone *m*

buffoon•er•y [bə'funəri] *s* (-**ies**) buffoneria

bug [bʌg] *s* insetto; (*coll*) germe *m*; (*in motor*) (*slang*) noia; (*slang*) pazzo; **to put a bug in the ear of** mettere una pulce nell'orecchio di ‖ *v* (*pret & pp* **bugged**; *ger* **bugging**) *tr* (*slang*) installare un sistema d'ascolto nel telefono di; (*to annoy*) (*slang*) seccare ‖ *intr*—**to bug out** (*slang*) andarsene

bug'bear' *s* spauracchio

bug•gy ['bʌgi] *adj* (-**gier**; -**giest**) pieno di cimici; (*slang*) pazzo ‖ *s* (-**gies**) carrozzino

bug'house' *adj* (*slang*) pazzo ‖ *s* (*slang*) manicomio

bugle ['bjugəl] *s* tromba, cornetta

bugler ['bjuglər] *s* trombettiere *m*

build [bɪld] *v* (*pret & pp* **built** [bɪlt]) *tr* costruire, edificare; fondare, basare; **to build up** sviluppare

builder ['bɪldər] *s* costruttore *m*; costruttore *m* edile

building ['bɪldɪŋ] *s* edificio, stabile *m*; costruzione; edilizia

build'ing and loan' *association* *s* società *f* di credito fondiario

build'ing lot' *s* (*coll*) terreno da costruzioni

build'ing trades' *spl* edilizia

build'-up' *s* concentrazione; sviluppo; processo di preparazione; propaganda favorevole

built'-in' *adj* (*in a wall*) murato; (*in a cabinet*) incassato, incorporato

built'-in clos'et *s* armadio a muro

built'-up' *adj* armato; popolato

bulb [bʌlb] *s* bulbo; (*lamp*) lampadina; (*of a lamp*) globo, cipolla

Bulgarian [bʌl'gɛri•ən] *adj & s* bulgaro

bulge [bʌldʒ] *s* protuberanza, sporgenza ‖ *intr* sporgere, gonfiarsi

bulk [bʌlk] *s* volume *m*, massa; **in bulk** in blocco; sciolto ‖ *intr* avere importanza; aumentare d'importanza

bulk'head' *s* diga; (*naut*) paratia

bulk•y ['bʌlki] *adj* (-**ier**; -**iest**) voluminoso

bull [bul] *s* toro; (*in the stockmarket*) rialzista *mf*; (*slang*) scemenza; (*eccl*) bulla ‖ *tr*—**to bull the market** giocare al rialzo

bull'dog' *s* molosso

bulldoze ['bul,doz] *tr* intimidire; (*land*) livellare

bulldozer ['bul,dozər] *s* livellatrice *f*, apripista *m*

bullet ['bulɪt] *s* palla, pallottola

bulletin ['bulətɪn] *s* bollettino; (*of a school*) albo; (journ) comunicato

bul'letin board' *s* tabellone *m*

bul'let-proof' *adj* blindato

bull'fight' *s* corrida

bull'fight'er *s* torero

bull'finch' *s* (orn) ciuffolotto

bull'frog' *s* rana americana

bull-headed ['bul,hedɪd] *adj* testardo

bullion ['buljən] *s* lingotti *mpl* d'oro or d'argento; frangia d'oro; (*on an Italian general's hat*) greca

bullish ['bulɪʃ] *adj* ostinato; (*market*) al rialzo; (*speculator*) rialzista

bullock ['bulək] *s* manzo

bull'ring' *s* arena

bull's-eye ['bulz,aɪ] *s* centro, tiro in pieno sul bersaglio; **to hit the bull's-eye** fare centro

bul-ly ['buli] *adj* (coll) eccellente || *s* (-lies) bravaccio || *v* (pret & pp -lied) *tr* intimidire

bulrush ['bul,rʌʃ] *s* giunco; (Bibl) papiro

bulwark ['bulwərk] *s* baluardo; protezione || *tr* proteggere

bum [bʌm] *adj* (slang) pessimo || *s* (slang) vagabondo; **on the bum** (slang) rotto, fuori servizio || *v* (pret & pp bummed; ger bumming) *tr* (slang) scroccare || *intr* (slang) oziare; (slang) vivere d'elemosina; (slang) fare lo scroccatore

bumble ['bʌmbəl] *tr* abborracciare || *intr* abborracciare; (*to stagger*) barcollare; (*to stumble*) balbettare; (*said of a bee*) ronzare

bum'blebee' *s* calabrone *m*

bump [bʌmp] *s* botta, botto; (*collision*) colpo, urto; (*swelling*) bernoccolo || *tr* urtare; **to bump off** (slang) uccidere || *intr* urtare, cozzare; **to bump into** incontrarsi con; cozzare contro

bumper ['bʌmpər] *adj* (coll) abbondante || *s* bicchiere pieno fino all'orlo; (aut) paraurti *m;* (rr) respingente *m*

bumpkin ['bʌmpkɪn] *s* beota *m*

bumptious ['bʌmpʃəs] *adj* vanitoso, presuntuoso

bump-y ['bʌmpi] *adj* (-ier; -iest) (*road*) irregolare, ondulato; (*air*) agitato

bun [bʌn] *s* panino; (*of hair*) crocchia, treccia a ciambella

bunch [bʌntʃ] *s* (*of grapes*) grappolo; (*of keys*) mazzo; (*of grass*) ciuffo; (*of people*) gruppo; (*of twigs*) fastello; (*of animals*) branco || *tr* (*things*) ammonticchiare; (*people*) raggruppare || *intr* raggrupparsi

bundle ['bʌndəl] *s* fascio, fastello; (*package*) pacco; (*large package*) collo; (*bunch*) mucchio || *tr* affastellare; impacchettare; ammucchiare; **to bundle off** or **out** cacciare precipitosamente; **to bundle up** infagottare || *intr*—**to bundle up** infagottarsi

bung [bʌŋ] *s* spina, cannella

bungalow ['bʌŋgə,lo] *s* casetta, villino, bungalow *m*

bung'hole' *s* spina, foro della botte

bungle ['bʌŋgəl] *s* abborracciatura || *tr* abborracciare || *intr* lavorare alla carlona

bungler ['bʌŋglər] *s* abborraccione *m*

bungling ['bʌŋglɪŋ] *adj* goffo; mal fatto || *s* abborracciatura

bunion ['bʌnjən] *s* gonfiore *m* dell'alluce

bunk [bʌŋk] *s* letto a castello; (nav) cuccetta; (slang) sciocchezza || *intr* dormire in cuccetta

bunk' bed' *s* letto a castello

bunker ['bʌŋkər] *s* (*bin*) carbonile *m;* (mil) casamatta; (golf) ostacolo

bun-ny ['bʌni] *s* (-nies) coniglietto

bunting ['bʌntɪŋ] *s* ornamento di bandiere; (nav) gala; (orn) zigolo

buoy [bɔɪ] or ['bu·i] *s* boa; (*life preserver*) salvagente *m* || *tr*—**to buoy up** tenere a galla; (fig) rincuorare

buoyancy ['bɔɪ·ənsi] or ['bujənsi] *s* galleggiabilità *f;* (*cheerfulness*) allegria, esuberanza

buoyant ['bɔɪ·ənt] or ['bujənt] *adj* galleggiante; allegro, esuberante

bur [bʌr] *s* riccio, aculeo

burble ['bʌrbəl] *s* gorgoglio || *intr* gorgogliare

burden ['bʌrdən] *s* carico, peso, fardello; (*of a speech*) tema *m;* (*chorus*) ritornello; (naut) portata || *tr* caricare

bur'den of proof' *s* onere *m* della prova

burdensome ['bʌrdənsəm] *adj* oneroso

burdock ['bʌrdɑk] *s* lappa, lappola

bureau ['bjuro] *s* comò *m;* (*agency*) ufficio, servizio

bureaucra-cy [bju'rɑkrəsi] *s* (-cies) burocrazia

bureaucrat ['bjurə,kræt] *s* burocrate *m*

burglar ['bʌrglər] *s* scassinatore *m*

bur'glar alarm' *s* campanello antifurto

burglarize ['bʌrglə,raɪz] *tr* scassinare

bur'glar-proof' *adj* a prova di furto

burgla-ry ['bʌrgləri] *s* (-ries) furto con scasso, scassinatura

Burgundy ['bʌrgəndi] *s* la Borgogna; (*wine*) borgogna *m*

burial ['berɪ·əl] *s* sepoltura

bur'ial ground' *s* cimitero

burin ['bjurɪn] *s* burino, cesello

burlap ['bʌrlæp] *s* tela di iuta

burlesque [bʌr'lesk] *adj* burlesco || *s* farsa, burlesque *m* || *tr* parodiare

burlesque' show' *s* spettacolo di varietà, music-hall *m*

bur-ly ['bʌrli] *adj* (-lier; -liest) membruto, robusto

Burma ['bʌrmə] *s* la Birmania

burn [bʌrn] *s* bruciatura, scottatura || *v* (pret & pp burned or burnt [bʌrnt]) *tr* bruciare; (*to set on fire*) dar fuoco a; (*bricks*) cuocere; **to burn down** radere al suolo; **to burn up** consumare; (*the road*) divorare; (coll) fare arrabbiare || *intr* bruciare, bruciarsi; (*said of lights*) essere acceso, e.g., **the lights were burning** la luce era accesa; **to burn out** (*said of an electric bulb or a fuse*) bruciarsi;

to burn to (fig) agognare di; **to burn up** (coll) essere arrabiato; **to burn with** (e.g., envy) ardere di

burner [ˈbʌrnər] s (of gas fixture or lamp) becco; (of furnace) bruciatore m

burning [ˈbʌrnɪŋ] adj bruciante, scottante || s incendio; (ceramic) cottura finale

burn'ing ques'tion s questione di attualità palpitante

burnish [ˈbʌrnɪʃ] s lucidatura || tr brunire

burnt' al'mond [bʌrnt] s mandorla tostata

burp [bʌrp] s (coll) rutto || intr (coll) ruttare

burr [bʌr] s riccio, aculeo; (rough edge) bava; (dentist's drill) fresa

burrow [ˈbʌro] s tana, buca || intr imbucarsi, rintanarsi

bursar [ˈbʌrsər] s tesoriere universitario

burst [bʌrst] s esplosione; (e.g., of machine gun) raffica; (break) crepa; (of passion) accesso; (of speed) slancio || tr far scoppiare || intr scoppiare, esplodere; **to burst into** (e.g., a room) irrompere in; (e.g., angry words) esplodere in; **to burst out crying** scoppiare in lacrime; **to burst with laughter** scoppiare dalle risa

bur·y [ˈberi] v (pret & pp -ied) tr sotterrare; **to be buried in thought** essere immerso nel pensiero; **to bury the hatchet** fare la pace

bus [bʌs] s (buses or busses) bus m, autobus m || v (pret & pp bused or bussed) ger busing or bussing) tr trasportare con autobus

bus'boy' s secondo cameriere

bus·by [ˈbʌzbi] s (-bies) colbacco

bus' driv'er s conducente mf di autobus

bush [buʃ] s cespuglio, arbusto; **to beat around the bush** menare il can per l'aia

bushed [buʃt] adj (coll) stanco morto

bushel [ˈbuʃəl] s staio

bushing [ˈbuʃɪŋ] s (mach) bronzina

bush·y [ˈbuʃi] adj (-ier; -iest) ricco di arbusti; (face) barbuto

business [ˈbɪznɪs] adj commerciale || s occupazione; commercio; affare m, negozio; faccenda; impiego; **it is not your business** non è affare Suo; **to know one's business** sapere il fatto proprio; **to make it one's business to** proporsi di; **to mean business** (coll) farla sul serio; **to mind one's own business** impicciarsi degli affari propri

businesslike [ˈbɪznɪsˌlaɪk] adj metodico; serio; efficace

busi'ness·man' s (-men') commerciante m, uomo d'affari

busi'ness suit' s abito da passeggio

busi'ness·wom'an s (wom'en) commerciante f

bus'man s (-men) guidatore m d'autobus

buss [bʌs] s (coll) bacione sonoro || tr (coll) baciare sonoramente

bus' stop' s fermata degli autobus

bust [bʌst] s busto; petto; (slang) fallimento; (slang) pugno || tr (slang) rompere; (slang) far fallire; (slang) colpire, dare pugni a; (mil) degradare

buster [ˈbʌstər] s (coll) ragazzo; (coll) rompitore m

bustle [ˈbʌsəl] s (on a dress) guardinfante m; attività f || intr affrettarsi

bus·y [ˈbɪzi] adj (-ier; -iest) occupato || v (pret & pp -ied) tr occupare, tenere occupato; **to busy oneself with** occuparsi di

bus'y·bod'y s (-ies) ficcanaso

bus'y sig'nal s (telp) segnale m d'occupato

but [bʌt] s ma m || adv solo, solamente; **but for** se non . . . per || prep eccetto, ad eccezione di, meno, se non; **all but** quasi || conj ma; che non, e.g., **I never go out in the rain but I catch a cold** non esco mai con la pioggia che non mi pigli un raffreddore

butcher [ˈbutʃər] s macellaio || tr macellare; massacrare

butch'er knife' s coltello da cucina, coltella

butch'er shop' s macelleria

butcher·y [ˈbutʃəri] s (-ies) macello; carneficina

butler [ˈbʌtlər] s cantiniere m, credenziere m

butt [bʌt] s (butting) cornata; (of rifle or gun) calcio; (of cigar) mozzicone m; (target) bersaglio; (end) estremità f; (of ridicule) zimbello; (cask) botte f || tr dare cornate a; cozzare contro || intr—**to butt into** (slang) intromettersi in

butter [ˈbʌtər] s burro || tr imburrare; **to butter up** (coll) adulare

but'ter·cup' s (bot) bottone m d'oro, ranuncolo

but'ter dish' s piattino per il burro, burriera

but'ter·fat' s grasso nel latte

but'ter·fly' s (-flies) farfalla

but'ter knife' s coltello per il burro

but'ter·milk' s latticello

but'ter sauce' s burro fuso

but'ter·scotch' s caramella al burro

buttocks [ˈbʌtəks] spl chiappe fpl, natiche fpl

button [ˈbʌtən] s bottone m || tr abbottonare

but'ton·hole' s occhiello, asola || tr attaccare un bottone a

but'ton·hook' s allacciabottoni m

buttress [ˈbʌtrɪs] s contrafforte m; piedritto || tr rinforzare

buxom [ˈbʌksəm] adj avvenente, procace

buy [baɪ] s compra || v (pret & pp bought [bɔt]) tr comprare; **to buy off** corrompere; **to buy out** comprare la parte di

buyer [ˈbaɪər] s compratore m

buzz [bʌz] s brusio, ronzio || tr volare a bassa quota sopra; (coll) fare una telefonata a || intr ronzare

buzzard [ˈbʌzərd] s (hawk) poiana; avvoltoio americano

buzzer [ˈbʌzər] s suoneria ronzante

buzz′ saw′ *s* sega circolare, segatrice *f* a disco

by [baɪ] *adv* oltre, e.g., **to speed by** correre velocemente oltre; **by and by** fra poco; **by and large** generalmente ‖ *prep* vicino a; di, durante, e.g., **by night** di notte, durante la notte; a, e.g., **they work by the hour** lavorano all'ora; (*not later than, through*) per; (*past*) in fronte a; (*through the agency of*) da; (*according to*) secondo; (math) per, volte; **by far** di molto; **by the way** a proposito

bygone [ˈbaɪ ˌɡɔn] *or* [ˈbaɪ ˌɡɑn] *adj & s* passato; **to let bygones be bygones** dimenticare il passato

bylaw [ˈbaɪ ˌlɔ] *s* legge *f* locale, regolamento di una società

by′-line′ *s* (journ) firma

by′pass′ *s* linea secondaria; (*detour*) deviazione ‖ *tr* fare una deviazione oltre a; (*a difficulty*) evitare

by′path′ *s* sentiero secondario; sentiero privato

by′prod′uct *s* sottoprodotto

bystander [ˈbaɪ ˌstændər] *s* astante *m*, spettatore *m*

byway [ˈbaɪ ˌwe] *s* via traversa

byword [ˈbaɪ ˌwʌrd] *s* proverbio; oggetto di obbrobrio

Byzantium [bɪˈzænʃɪ-əm] *or* [bɪˈzæntɪ-əm] *s* Bisanzio

C

C, c [si] *s* terza lettera dell'alfabeto inglese

cab [kæb] *s* vettura di piazza; tassì *m*; (*of truck or locomotive*) cabina

cabbage [ˈkæbɪdʒ] *s* cavolo, verza

cab′ driv′er *s* autista *m* di piazza; (*of horse-drawn cab*) vetturino

cabin [ˈkæbɪn] *s* (*shed*) capanna; (*hut*) baracca; (aer, naut) cabina

cab′in boy′ *s* mozzo

cabinet [ˈkæbɪnɪt] *s* (*piece of furniture*) vetrina; (*for a radio*) armadietto; (*small room; ministry of a government*) gabinetto

cab′inet-mak′er *s* ebanista *m*

cab′inet-mak′ing *s* ebanisteria

cable [ˈkebəl] *s* cavo; cablogramma; (elec) cablaggio ‖ *tr* cablare, mandare un cablogramma a

ca′ble address′ *s* indirizzo telegrafico

ca′ble car′ *s* funicolare *f*, teleferica

cablegram [ˈkebel ˌɡræm] *s* cablogramma *m*

caboose [kəˈbus] *s* (rr) vagone *m* di coda

cab′stand′ *s* stazione di tassametri

cache [kæʃ] *s* nascondiglio ‖ *tr* mettere in un nascondiglio

cachet [kæˈʃe] *s* sigillo; (*distinguishing feature*) impronta

cackle [ˈkækəl] *s* (*of chickens*) coccodè *m*; (*of people*) chiacchierio ‖ *intr* fare coccodè; ciarlare

cac·tus [ˈkæktəs] *s* (*-tuses or -ti* [taɪ]) cactus *m*

cad [kæd] *s* mascalzone *m*

cadaver [kəˈdævər] *s* cadavere *m*

cadaverous [kəˈdævərəs] *adj* cadaverico

caddie [ˈkædi] *s* portamazze *m*

cadence [ˈkedəns] *s* cadenza

cadet [kəˈdet] *s* cadetto

cadmium [ˈkædmɪ-əm] *s* cadmio

cadres [ˈkædriz] *spl* (mil) quadri *mpl*

Caesar′ean sec′tion [sɪˈzɛrɪ-ən] *s* taglio cesareo

café [kæˈfe] *s* caffè *m*, bar *m*, ristorante *m*

ca′fé soci′ety *s* bel mondo

cafeteria [ˌkæfəˈtɪrɪ-ə] *s* mensa, tavola calda, caffetteria

caffeine [kæˈfin] *or* [ˈkæfi-ɪn] *s* caffeina

cage [kedʒ] *s* gabbia; (*of elevator*) cabina ‖ *tr* ingabbiare

ca·gey [ˈkedʒi] *adj* (*-gier; -giest*) (coll) astuto, cauto

cahoots [kəˈhuts] *s*—**to be in cahoots** (slang) far lega, essere in combutta; **to go cahoots** (slang) dividere in parti eguali

Cain [ken] *s* Caino; **to raise Cain** (slang) arrabbiarsi; (slang) fare una sfuriata

Cairo [ˈkaɪro] *s* il Cairo

caisson [ˈkesən] *s* cassone *m*; (archit) cassettone *m*

cajole [kəˈdʒol] *tr* lusingare; persuadere con lusinghe

cajoler·y [kəˈdʒoləri] *s* (*-ies*) lusinga

cake [kek] *s* dolce *m*; torta, pasta; (*with bread-like dough*) focaccia; (*of soap*) saponetta; (*of earth*) zolla; **to take the cake** (coll) essere il colmo ‖ *tr* incrostare ‖ *intr* indurirsi; incrostarsi

calabash [ˈkælə ˌbæʃ] *s* zucca a fiasca

calaboose [ˈkælə ˌbus] *s* (coll) gattabuia

calamitous [kəˈlæmɪtəs] *adj* calamitoso

calami·ty [kəˈlæmɪti] *s* (*-ties*) calamità *f*

calci·fy [ˈkælsɪ ˌfaɪ] *v* (*pret & pp -fied*) *tr* calcificare ‖ *intr* calcificarsi

calcium [ˈkælsɪ-əm] *s* calcio

calculate [ˈkælkjə ˌlet] *tr* calcolare ‖ *intr* calcolare; **to calculate on** contare su

cal′culating machine′ *s* (macchina) calcolatrice

calcu·lus [ˈkælkjələs] *s* (*-luses or -li* [ˌlaɪ]) (math, pathol) calcolo

calendar [ˈkæləndər] *s* calendario; (*agenda*) ordine *m* del giorno

calf [kæf] *or* [kɑf] *s* (*calves* [kævz] *or* [kɑvz]) vitello; (*of shoes or binding*) pelle *f* di vitello; (*of the leg*) polpaccio

calf′skin′ *s* pelle *f* di vitello

caliber ['kælɪbər] s calibro

calibrate ['kælɪ,bret] tr calibrare

cali·co ['kælɪ,ko] s (-coes or -cos) cotone stampato, calico

California [,kælɪ'fɔrnɪ-ə] s la California

calipers ['kælɪpərz] spl compasso a grossezze, calibro

caliph ['kelɪf] or ['kælɪf] s califfo

calisthenic [,kælɪs'θɛnɪk] adj ginnastico || **calisthenics** spl ginnastica a corpo libero

calk [kɔk] tr var of **caulk**

call [kɔl] s chiamata; visita; (shout) grido, richiamo; (of bugle) squillo; (of telephone) colpo; (of ship) scalo; obbligo; vocazione; (com) richiesta; **on call** disponibile; **within call** a portata di voce || tr chiamare; convocare; (to awaken) svegliare; **to call back** richiamare; **to call in** (e.g., an expert) fare venire; (e.g., currency) domandare, esigere; **to call off** annullare; **to call out** chiamare; **to call together** convocare; **to call up** chiamare per telefono || intr chiamare; visitare; **to call at** passare per la casa di; (naut) fare scalo a; **to call for** venire a prendere; **to call out** gridare; **to go calling** andare a fare visite

cal'la lil'y ['kælə] s (Zantedeschia aethiopica) calla dei fioristi

call'boy' s (in a hotel) fattorino; (theat) buttafuori m

caller ['kɔlər] s visitatore m

call' girl' s ragazza squillo

calling ['kɔlɪŋ] s appello; professione

call'ing card' s biglietto da visita

call' num'ber s numero telefonico; numero di biblioteca

callous ['kæləs] adj calloso; insensibile

callow ['kælo] adj inesperto, immaturo

call' to arms' s chiamata alle armi

call' to the col'ors s chiamata sotto la bandiera

callus ['kæləs] s callo

calm [kɑm] adj calmo, tranquillo || s calma || tr calmare, tranquillizzare || intr—**to calm down** calmarsi; (said of weather) abbonacciarsi

calmness ['kɑmnɪs] s calma, placidità f, tranquillità f

calomel ['kælə,mɛl] s calomelano

calorie ['kælərɪ] s caloria

calum·ny ['kæləmnɪ] s (-nies) calunnia

Calvary ['kælvərɪ] s (Bib) Calvario

cam [kæm] s camma

camber ['kæmbər] s curvatura; convessità f || tr arcuare || intr curvarsi

cambric ['kæmbrɪk] s cambrì m

camel ['kæməl] s cammello

came·o ['kæmɪ,o] s (-os) cammeo

camera ['kæmərə] s macchina fotografica; (mov) cinepresa

cam'era-man' s (-men') operatore m

camomile ['kæmə,maɪl] s camomilla

camouflage ['kæmə,flɑʒ] s mascheramento || tr mascherare, camuffare

camp [kæmp] s accampamento, campo || intr accamparsi

campaign [kæm'pen] s campagna || intr fare una campagna

campaigner [kæm'penər] s veterano; (pol) propagandista mf

camp' bed' s letto da campo, branda

camper ['kæmpər] s campeggiatore m, campeggista mf

camp'fire' s fuoco di accampamento

camp'ground' s terreno per campeggio

camphor ['kæmfər] s canfora

camp'stool' s seggiolino pieghevole

campus ['kæmpəs] s campo, terreno dell'università

cam'shaft' s albero di distribuzione, albero a camme

can [kæn] s lattina, barattolo; (of gasoline or oil) bidone m || v (pret & pp **canned**; ger **canning**) tr inscatolare; (slang) licenziare || v (pret & cond **could**) aux **I can speak** English so parlare inglese; **can he go now?** se ne può andare ora?

Canada ['kænədə] s il Canadà

Canadian [kə'nedɪ-ən] adj & s canadese mf

canal [kə'næl] s canale m

canar·y [kə'nerɪ] s (-ies) canarino || **Canaries** spl Canarie fpl

can·cel ['kænsəl] v (pret & pp -celed or -celled; ger -celing or -celling) tr cancellare; annullare; revocare; (stamps) timbrare, annullare

cancellation [,kænsə'leʃən] s cancellazione, annullamento; cassazione; (of a stamp) bollo

cancer ['kænsər] s cancro || **Cancer** s Cancro

cancerous ['kænsərəs] adj canceroso

candela·brum [,kændə'lɑbrəm] s (-bra [brə] or -brums) candelabro

candid ['kændɪd] adj candido; sincero, franco

candida·cy ['kændɪdəsɪ] s (-cies) candidatura

candidate ['kændɪ,det] s candidato; (for a degree) laureando

can'did cam'era s camera fotografica indiscreta

candied ['kændɪd] adj candito

candle ['kændəl] s candela || tr (eggs) sperare

can'dle-hold'er s var of **candlestick**

can'dle-light' s luce f or lume m di candela

can'dle-pow'er s (phys) candela

can'dle-stick' s (ornate) candeliere m; (plain) bugia

candor ['kændər] s candore m; ingenuità f

can·dy ['kændɪ] s (-dies) dolciumi mpl; **a piece of candy** un bombon || v (pret & pp -died) tr candire

can'dy box' s bomboniera

can'dy dish' s bomboniera; (three-tier-high) alzata

can'dy store' s confetteria

cane [ken] s canna, giunco; (for walking) bastone m || tr bastonare; (chairs) impagliare

cane' seat' s sedia impagliata

cane' sug'ar s zucchero di canna

canine ['kenaɪn] adj canino || s (tooth) canino; (dog) cane m

canister ['kænɪstər] s barattolo

canned' goods' *spl* conserve *fpl* alimentari; prodotti *mpl* in scatola

canned' mu'sic *s* (slang) musica su dischi

canner·y ['kænəri] *s* (**-ies**) fabbrica di conserve alimentari

cannibal ['kænɪbəl] *adj* & *s* cannibale *mf*, antropofago

canning ['kænɪŋ] *s* conservazione

cannon ['kænən] *s* cannone *m*

cannonade [,kænə'ned] *s* cannonata || *tr* cannoneggiare

can'non·ball' *s* palla da cannone

can'non fod'der *s* carne *f* da cannone

can·ny ['kæni] *adj* (**-nier; -niest**) astuto, fino; malizioso

canoe [kə'nu] *s* canoa, piroga

canon ['kænən] *s* canone *m*; (*priest*) canonico

canonical [kə'nɑnɪkəl] *adj* canonico ||

canonicals *spl* paramenti liturgici

canonize [,kænə,naɪz] *tr* canonizzare

can'on law' *s* diritto canonico

canon·ry ['kænənri] *s* (**-ries**) canonicato

can' o'pener ['opənər] *s* apriscatole *m*

cano·py ['kænəpi] *s* (**-pies**) tenda; baldacchino; (*of sky*) (fig) volta

cant [kænt] *adj* ipocrita || *s* linguaggio ipocrita; gergo; (*slope*) inclinazione

cantaloupe ['kæntə,lop] *s* melone *m*

cantankerous [kæn'tæŋkərəs] *adj* bisbetico, attaccabrighe

canteen [kæn'tin] *s* cantina, spaccio; (*metal bottle*) borraccia

canter ['kæntər] *s* piccolo galoppo || *intr* andare al piccolo galoppo

cantiliver ['kæntɪ,lɪvər] *adj* a cantiliver || *s* trave *f* a sbalzo; (archit) trave *f* a mensola

cantle ['kæntəl] *s* arcione *m* posteriore

canton [kæn'tɑn] *s* cantone *m*; regione || *tr* accantonare

cantonment [kæn'tɑnmənt] *s* accantonamento

cantor ['kæntər] or ['kæntɔr] *s* cantore *m*

canvas ['kænvəs] *s* (*cloth*) olona; (*e.g. on open truck*) copertone *m*; (*painting*) tela; (naut) vela; **under canvas** (naut) a vele spiegate

canvass ['kænvəs] *s* discussione; dibattito; (pol) sollecitazione di voti || *tr* discutere; (*votes*) sollecitare; (*to investigate*) indagare; (com) fare la piazza a || *intr* discutere; sollecitare voti; indagare; (com) fare la piazza

canyon ['kænjən] *s* cañon *m*

cap [kæp] *s* berretto; cuffia; (*of academic costume*) berrettone *m*; (*of bottle*) tappo, capsula; (*e.g., of fountain pen*) cappuccio || *v* (*pret* & *pp* **capped**; *ger* **capping**) *tr* (*a person*) coprire il capo di; (*s.o.'s head*) coprire con il berretto; (*a bottle*) mettere il tappo a; terminare; **to cap the climax** essere al colmo

capabili·ty [,kepə'bɪlɪti] *s* (**-ties**) capacità *f*, abilità *f*

capable ['kepəbəl] *adj* capace, abile

capacious [kə'peʃəs] *adj* ampio, capace

capaci·ty [kə'pæsɪti] *s* (**-ties**) capacità *f*; **filled to capacity** pieno zeppo; **in the capacity of** in veste di

cap' and bells' *spl* berretto a sonagli; scettro di buffone

cap' and gown' *s* costume accademico, toga e tocco

caparison [kə'pærɪsən] *s* bardatura || *tr* bardare

cape [kep] *s* cappa, mantello; (mil) mantella; (geog) capo

Cape' of Good' Hope' *s* Capo di Buona Speranza

caper ['kepər] *s* capriola; (bot) cappero; **to cut capers** far capriole; (fig) fare monellerie || *intr* fare capriole; saltellare

Cape' Town' *s* Città *f* del Capo

capital ['kæpɪtəl] *adj* capitale || *s* (*money*) capitale *m*; (*city*) capitale *f*; (*of column*) capitello

cap'ital expen'ditures *spl* spese *fpl* d'impianto

cap'ital goods' *spl* beni *mpl* strumentali

capitalism ['kæpɪtə,lɪzəm] *s* capitalismo

capitalize ['kæpɪtə,laɪz] *tr* capitalizzare; scrivere con la maiuscola || *intr*—**to capitalize on** approfittare di

cap'ital let'ter *s* lettera maiuscola

cap'ital pun'ishment *s* pena capitale

cap'ital stock' *s* capitale *m* sociale

capitol ['kæpɪtəl] *s* campidoglio

capitulate [kə'pɪtʃə,let] *intr* capitolare

capon ['kepən] *s* cappone *m*

caprice [kə'pris] *s* capriccio, ghiribizzo

capricious [kə'prɪʃəs] *adj* capriccioso, estroso

Capricorn ['kæprɪ,kɔrn] *s* Capricorno

capsize ['kæpsaɪz] *tr* capovolgere || *intr* capovolgersi

capstan ['kæpstən] *s* argano

cap'stone' *s* (archit) coronamento

capsule ['kæpsəl] *adj* in miniatura; riassuntivo || *s* capsula

captain ['kæptən] *s* capitano; (naut) comandante *m*; || *tr* capitanare

caption ['kæpʃən] *s* titolo; (mov) didascalia; (journ) leggenda

captivate ['kæptɪ,vet] *tr* cattivare, affascinare

captive ['kæptɪv] *adj* & *s* prigioniero

captivi·ty ['kæp'tɪvɪti] *s* (**-ties**) cattività *f*, prigionia

captor ['kæptər] *s* persona che cattura

capture ['kæptʃər] *s* cattura, presa; (*person*) prigioniero; (*thing*) bottino || *tr* catturare; prendere

car [kɑr] *s* (*of train*) vagone *m*, vettura; (*automobile*) automobile *m* & *f*, macchina, vettura; (*of elevator*) cabina; (*of balloon*) navicella; (*for narrow-gauge track*) carrello

carafe [kə'ræf] *s* caraffa

caramel ['kærəməl] or ['kɑrməl] *s* (*burnt sugar*) caramello; (*candy*) caramella appiccicaticcia

carat ['kærət] *s* carato

caravan ['kærə,væn] *s* carovana; (*covered vehicle*) furgone *m*

caravansa·ry [,kærə'vænsəri] *s* (**-ries**) caravanserraglio

caraway ['kærə,we] *s* cumino

car'barn' *s* rimessa del tram

carbide ['kɑrbaɪd] *s* carburo
carbine ['kɑrbaɪn] *s* carabina
carbol'ic ac'id [kɑr'bɑlɪk] *s* acido fenico
carbon ['kɑrbən] *s* (*in arc light, battery, auto cylinder*) carbone *m*; carta carbone; (*chem*) carbonio
car'bon cop'y *s* copia a carbone, velina
car'bon diox'ide *s* anidride carbonica
car'bon monox'ide *s* ossido di carbonio, monossido di carbonio
car'bon pa'per *s* carta carbone
carbuncle ['kɑrbʌŋkəl] *s* (*stone; boil*) carbonchio; (*boil*) foruncolo
carburetor ['kɑrbə‚retər] or ['kɑrbjə‚retər] *s* carburatore *m*
carcass ['kɑrkəs] *s* carcassa; (*in state of decay*) carogna
card [kɑrd] *s* (*file*) scheda; (*post card*) cartolina; (*personal card*) biglietto; (*announcement*) partecipazione; (*playing card*) carta da gioco; (*coll*) tipo divertente, bel tipo
card'board' *s* cartone *m*
card'-car'rying mem'ber *s* tesserato
card' case' *s* portatessere *m*
card' cat'alogue *s* schedario
card'hold'er *s* socio, tesserato
cardiac ['kɑrdɪ‚æk] *adj* & *s* cardiaco
cardigan ['kɑrdɪgən] *s* panciotto a maglia
cardinal ['kɑrdɪnəl] *adj* cardinale, fondamentale ‖ *s* cardinale *m*
card' in'dex *s* schedario
cardiogram ['kɑrdɪ‚o‚græm] *s* cardiogramma *m*
card' par'ty *s* riunione per giocare a carte
card'sharp' *s* baro
card' ta'ble *s* tavoliere *m*, tavolino da gioco
card' trick' *s* gioco di prestigio colle carte
care [ker] *s* cura, custodia; inquietudine *f*, preoccupazione; cautela; **care of** presso, e.g., **R. Smith care of Jones** R. Smith presso Jones; **to take care** fare attenzione; **to take care of** prendersi cura di, badare a; **to take care of oneself** badare alla salute ‖ *intr* curarsi, badare; **I don't care** non m'importa; **to care about** preoccuparsi di; **to care for** voler bene a; curarsi di; **to care to** volere
careen [kə'rin] *s* carenaggio ‖ *intr* sbandare
career [kə'rir] *adj* di carriera ‖ *s* carriera
care'free' *adj* spensierato
careful ['kerfəl] *adj* attento; diligente; premuroso; **careful!** faccia attenzione!
careless ['kerlɪs] *adj* trascurato; imprudente; indifferente
carelessness ['kerlɪsnɪs] *s* trascuratezza; imprudenza; indifferenza
caress [kə'res] *s* carezza ‖ *tr* carezzare, accarezzare
caretaker ['ker‚tekər] *adj* interinale, provvisorio ‖ *s* custode *m*; guardiano; (*of school*) bidello
care'taker gov'ernment *s* governo interinale

care'worn' *adj* accasciato dalle preoccupazioni
car'fare' *s* passaggio, denaro per il tram; (*small sum of money*) spiccioli *mpl*
car·go ['kɑrgo] *s* (-**goes** or -**gos**) carico mercantile
car'go boat' *s* battello da carico
Caribbean [‚kærɪ'bi·ən] or [kə'rɪbɪ·ən] *s* Mare *m* dei Caraibi
caricature ['kærɪkət‚ʃər] *s* caricatura ‖ *tr* mettere in caricatura
carillon ['kærɪ‚lɑn] or [kə'rɪljən] *s* carillon *m* ‖ *intr* suonare il carillon
car'load' *s* vagone completo, vagonata
carnage ['kɑrnɪdʒ] *s* carnaio, carneficina
carnal ['kɑrnəl] *adj* carnale
carnation [kɑr'neʃən] *adj* incarnato ‖ *s* garofano; (*color*) incarnato
carnival ['kɑrnɪvəl] *adj* carnevalesco ‖ *s* carnevale *m*; festa, spettacolo all'aperto
carob ['kærəb] *s* (*fruit*) carruba; (*tree*) carrubo
car·ol ['kærəl] *s* canzone *f* popolare; pastorella di Natale ‖ *v* (*pret & pp* -**oled** or -**olled**) *ger* -**oling** or -**olling**) *tr* cantare
carom ['kærəm] *s* carambola ‖ *intr* carambolare
carousal [kə'rauzəl] *s* baldoria, gozzoviglia
carouse [kə'rauz] *intr* fare baldoria, gozzovigliare
carousel [‚kærə'zel] or [‚kæru'zel] *s* giostra, carosello
carp ['kɑrp] *s* carpa ‖ *intr* lagnarsi, criticare
carpenter ['kɑrpəntər] *s* falegname *m*
carpentry ['kɑrpəntri] *s* falegnameria
carpet ['kɑrpɪt] *s* tappeto ‖ *tr* coprire con un tappeto, tappetare
carpetbagger ['kɑrpɪt‚bægər] *s* avventuriero; (*hist*) politicante *m*
car'pet sweep'er *s* spazzolone elettrico per tappeti
car'port' *s* tettoia-garage *f*
car'-ren'tal serv'ice *s* servizio di autonoleggi
carriage ['kærɪdʒ] *s* carrozza; (*of gun*) affusto; (*of typewriter*) carrello; (*bearing*) portamento; (*mach*) slitta
carrier ['kærɪ·ər] *s* portatore *m*; (*person or organization in business of carrying goods*) spedizioniere *m*; (*of mail*) postino; (*e.g., on top of station wagon*) portabagagli *m*; (*of a disease*) veicolo
car'rier pig'eon *s* piccione *m* viaggiatore
car'rier wave' *s* (rad) onda portante
carrion ['kærɪ·ən] *s* carogne *fpl*
carrot ['kærət] *s* carota
car·ry ['kæri] *v* (*pret & pp* -**ried**) *tr* portare; trasportare; (*a burden*) sopportare; (*an election*) guadagnare; (*to keep in stock*) avere in assortimento; **to carry along** portare con sé; **to carry away** trasportare; entusiasmare; **to carry forward** riportare; **to carry out** eseguire; **to carry**

through completare; **to carry weight** aver importanza ‖ *intr* avere la portata (di), e.g., **this gun carries two miles** questo cannone ha la portata di due miglia; **to carry on** continuare; (coll) fare baccano

cart [kɑrt] *s* carro, carretto; (*for shopping*) carrello; **to put the cart before the horse** mettere il carro davanti ai buoi ‖ *tr* trasportare col carro

carte blanche ['kɑrt'blɑnʃ] *s* carta bianca

cartel [kɑr'tel] *s* cartello

Carthage ['kɑrθɪdʒ] *s* Cartagine *f*

cart' horse' *s* cavallo da tiro

cartilage ['kɑrtɪlɪdʒ] *s* cartilagine *f*

carton ['kɑrtən] *s* cartone *m;* scatola di cartone; (*of cigarettes*) stecca

cartoon [kɑr'tun] *s* disegno; caricatura; (*comic strip*) fumetto; (mov) disegno animato ‖ *tr* fare caricature di

cartoonist [kɑr'tunɪst] *s* disegnatore *m;* caricaturista *mf*

cartridge ['kɑrtrɪdʒ] *s* cartuccia; (*e.g., of camera*) caricatore *m*

car'tridge belt' *s* cartucciera; (mil) giberna

car'tridge clip' *s* serbatoio

cart'wheel' *s* ruota di carro; **to turn cartwheels** fare la ruota

carve [kɑrv] *tr* (*meats*) trinciare; scolpire, intagliare

carv'ing knife' *s* trinciante *m*

car' wash'er *s* lavamacchine *m*

cascade [kæs'ked] *s* cascata ‖ *intr* cadere a mo' di cascata

case [kes] *s* box; cassetta; (*of watch*) calotta; (*outer covering*) astuccio; (*instance*) caso; (gram) caso; (law) causa; (typ) cassa; **in case** in caso, nel caso; **in no case** in nessun modo ‖ *tr* rinchiudere; (*to package*) impaccare; (slang) ispezionare

casement ['kesmənt] *s* telaio di finestra; finestra a gangheri

case' stud'y *s* casistica

cash [kæʃ] *s* contante *m; * **cash on delivery** spedizione contro assegno; **for cash** in contanti; **a pronta cassa** ‖ *tr* (*a check*) cambiare, incassare ‖ *intr* —**to cash in on** (coll) trarre profitto da

cash' box' *s* cassa

cashew ['kæʃu] *s* (*tree*) anacardio; (*nut*) mandorla indiana

cashier [kæ'ʃɪr] *s* cassiere *m* ‖ *tr* (*to dismiss*) silurare

cashier's' check' *s* assegno circolare

cash' reg'ister *s* registratore *m* cassa

casing ['kesɪŋ] *s* rivestimento; tubo di rivestimento; (*for salami*) budello; (*of tire*) copertone *m*

cask [kæsk] or [kɑsk] *s* barile *m*, botte *f*

casket ['kæskɪt] or ['kɑskɪt] *s* scrigno, cofanetto; (*coffin*) bara, cassa da morto

casserole ['kæsə,rol] *s* tegame *m* di terracotta or vetro; (*food*) pasticcio, timballo

cassette [kə'set] *s* (mus) musicassetta; (mus & phot) caricatore *m*

cassock ['kæsək] *s* sottana, tonaca; **to doff the cassock** gettar la tonaca alle ortiche

cast [kæst] or [kɑst] *s* getto; lancio; forma; (mach) pezzo fuso; (surg) gesso; (theat) complesso artistico, cast *m* ‖ *v* (*pret & pp* **cast**) *tr* gettare; fondere; (*a ballot*) dare; (*the roles*) distribuire; (*actors*) scegliere; **to cast aside** abbandonare; **to cast down** deprimere; **to cast lots** tirare a sorte; **to cast off** abbandonare; **to cast out** buttar fuori ‖ *intr* tirare i dadi; **to cast off** (naut) mollare gli ormeggi

castanets [,kæstə'nets] *spl* nacchere *fpl*

cast'a•way' *adj & s* naufrago; (fig) reprobo

caste [kæst] or [kɑst] *s* casta; **to lose caste** perdere prestigio

caster ['kæstər] or ['kɑstər] *s* ampollina, saliera, pepaiola; (*roller*) rotella per i mobili

castigate ['kæstɪ,get] *tr* castigare, punire; correggere

Castile [kæs'til] *s* (la) Castiglia

Castilian [kæs'tɪljən] *adj & s* castigliano

casting ['kæstɪŋ] or ['kɑstɪŋ] *s* getto, getto fuso; (*in fishing*) pesca a getto

cast' i'ron *s* ghisa

cast'-i'ron *adj* fatto di ghisa; (*e.g., stomach*) fatto d'acciaio, di struzzo

castle ['kæsəl] or ['kɑsəl] *s* castello; (chess) torre *f* ‖ *tr & intr* (chess) arroccare

cas'tle in Spain' or **cas'tle in the air'** *s* castello in aria

cast'off' *adj* abbandonato ‖ *s* rigetto; persona abbandonata; (typ) stima

cas'tor oil' ['kæstər] or ['kɑstər] *s* olio di ricino

castrate ['kæstret] *tr* castrare

casual ['kæʒʊ·əl] *adj* casuale, fortuito; (*clothing*) semplice, sportivo

casually ['kæʒʊ·əli] *adv* con disinvoltura; (*by chance*) fortuitamente

casual•ty ['kæʒʊ·əlti] *s* (-ties) accidente *m*, disastro; vittima; **casualties** (*in war*) perdite *fpl*

casuist•ry ['kæʒʊ·ɪstri] *s* (-ries) (*specious reasoning*) speciosità *f;* (philos) casistica

cat [kæt] *s* gatto; donna perfida; **to let the cat out of the bag** lasciarsi scappare il segreto

cataclysm ['kætə,klɪzəm] *s* cataclisma *m*

catacomb ['kætə,kom] *s* catacomba

catalogue ['kætə,lɔg] or ['kætə,lɑg] *s* catalogo ‖ *tr* catalogare

cat'alogue sale' *s* vendita per corrispondenza

catalyst ['kætəlɪst] *s* catalizzatore *m*

catapult ['kætə,pʌlt] *s* catapulta ‖ *tr* catapultare

cataract ['kætə,rækt] *s* cataratta

catarrh [kə'tɑr] *s* catarro

catastrophe [kə'tæstrəfi] *s* catastrofe *f*, disastro

cat'call' *s* urlo di disapprovazione
catch [kætʃ] *s* presa; cattura; *(of door)* paletto; *(in marriage)* partito; *(trick)* inganno; *(of fish)* pesca; (mach) nottolino ‖ *v (pret & pp* **caught** [kɔt]) *tr* prendere, acchiappare; *(a cold)* pigliare, buscarsi; **to catch hold of** afferrare; **to catch it** (coll) prendersele; **to catch oneself** contenersi; **to catch up** sorprendere sul fatto ‖ *intr* agganciarsi; *(said of a disease)* trasmettersi; **to catch on** capire l'antifona; **to catch up** mettersi al corrente; **to catch up with** raggiungere
catch'-as-catch'-can' *s* lotta libera americana
catch' ba'sin *s* ricettacolo di fogna
catcher ['kætʃər] *s* ricevitore *m*, catcher *m*
catching ['kætʃɪŋ] *adj (alluring)* seducente; *(infectious)* contagioso
catch'word' *s* slogan *m*; (typ) chiamata; (typ) esponente *m* in testa di pagina
catch·y ['kætʃi] *adj* (-ier; -iest) attraente, vivo; *(tricky)* insidioso
catechism ['kætɪˌkɪzəm] *s* catechismo
catego·ry ['kætɪˌɡɔri] *s* (-ries) categoria
cater ['ketər] *intr* provvedere cibo; **to cater to** servire
cater-cornered ['kætərˌkɔrnərd] *adj* diagonale ‖ *adv* diagonalmente
caterer ['ketərər] *s* provveditore *m*
caterpillar ['kætərˌpɪlər] *s* bruco
cat'erpillar trac'tor *s* trattore *m* a cingoli
cat'fish' *s* pesce *m* gatto
cat'gut' *s* (mus) corda di minugia; (surg) catgut *m*, cattegù *m*
cathartic [kə'θɑrtɪk] *adj & s* catartico
cathedral [kə'θidrəl] *s* cattedrale *f*
catheter ['kæθɪtər] *s* catetere *m*
catheterize ['kæθɪtəˌraɪz] *tr* cateterizzare
cathode ['kæθod] *s* catodo
catholic ['kæθəlɪk] *adj* cattolico; *(e.g., mind)* liberale ‖ **Catholic** *adj & s* cattolico
catkin ['kætkɪn] *s* (bot) amento, gattino
cat'nap' *s* corta siesta, sonnellino
cat-o'-nine-tails [ˌkætə'naɪnˌtelz] *s* gatto a nove code
cat's'-paw' *s* gonzo; *(breeze)* brezzolina
catsup ['kætsəp] or ['ketʃəp] *s* salsa piccante di pomodoro, ketchup *m*
cat'tail' *s* stiancia
cattle ['kætəl] *s* bestiame grosso
cat'tle-man *s* (-men) allevatore *m* di bestiame
cat·ty ['kæti] *adj* (-tier; -tiest) malizioso, maligno; felino, gattesco
cat'walk' *s* passerella, ballatoio
Caucasian [kɔ'keʒən] or [kɔ'keʃən] *adj & s* caucasico
caucus ['kɔkəs] *s* comitato elettorale; conciliabolo politico
cauldron ['kɔldrən] *s* calderone *m*
cauliflower ['kɔlɪˌflauˌər] *s* cavolfiore *m*
caulk [kɔk] *tr* calafatare, stoppare
cause [kɔz] *s* causa, cagione ‖ *tr* causare, cagionare; **to cause to** + *inf*

fare + *inf*, e.g., **she caused him to fall** l'ha fatto cadere
cause'way' *s* strada rialzata, scarpata
caustic ['kɔstɪk] *adj* caustico
cauterize ['kɔtəˌraɪz] *tr* cauterizzare
caution ['kɔʃən] *s* cautela, prudenza; ammonizione ‖ *tr* ammonire
cautious ['kɔʃəs] *adj* prudente
cavalcade ['kævəlˌked] or [ˌkævəl-'ked] *s* cavalcata
cavalier [ˌkævə'lɪr] or ['kævəˌlɪr] *adj* altero, sdegnoso; disinvolto ‖ *s* cavaliere *m*
caval·ry ['kævəlri] *s* (-ries) cavalleria
cav'alry·man or **cav'alry·man** *s* (-men' or -men) cavalleggero, soldato di cavalleria
cave [kev] *s* caverna, grotta ‖ *intr*— **to cave in** sprofondarsi; *(to give in)* (coll) cedere; *(to become exhausted)* (coll) diventare spossato
cave'-in' *s* sprofondamento
cave' man' *s* troglodita *m*
cavern ['kævərn] *s* caverna
caviar ['kævɪˌɑr] or [ˌkævɪ'ɑr] *s* caviale *m*
cav·il ['kævɪl] *v (pret & pp* -iled or -illed; *ger* -iling or -illing) *intr* cavillare
cavi·ty ['kævɪti] *s* (-ties) cavità *f*; *(in tooth)* carie *f*
cavort [kə'vɔrt] *intr* far capriole
caw [kɔ] *s* gracchiamento ‖ *intr* gracchiare
cease [sis] *tr* cessare, interrompere ‖ *intr* cessare, interrompersi; **to cease** + *ger* cessare di + *inf*
cease'-fire' *s* sospensione delle ostilità
ceaseless ['sislɪs] *adj* incessante
cedar ['sidər] *s* cedro; legno di cedro
cede [sid] *tr* cedere, trasferire
ceiling ['silɪŋ] *s* soffitto; (aer) altezza massima; **to hit the ceiling** (slang) uscire dai gangheri
ceil'ing price' *s* calmiere *m*, tetto
celebrate ['sɛlɪˌbret] *tr* celebrare ‖ *intr* celebrare; far festa
celebrated ['sɛlɪˌbretɪd] *adj* celebre, famoso
celebration [ˌsɛlɪ'breʃən] *s* celebrazione
celebri·ty [sɪ'lɛbrɪti] *s* (-ties) celebrità *f*
celery ['sɛləri] *s* sedano
celestial [sɪ'lɛstʃəl] *adj* celestiale, celeste
celibacy ['sɛləbəsi] *s* celibato
celibate ['sɛləˌbet] or ['sɛləbɪt] *adj & s* celibe *m*; nubile *f*
cell [sɛl] *s* (e.g., *of jail*) cella; *(of electric battery)* elemento; (biol, phys, pol) cellula
cellar ['sɛlər] *s* cantina; *(partly above ground)* seminterrato
cellist or **'cellist** ['tʃɛlɪst] *s* violoncellista *mf*
cel·lo or **'cel·lo** ['tʃɛlo] *s* (-los) violoncello
cellophane ['sɛləˌfen] *s* cellofan *m*
celluloid ['sɛljəˌlɔɪd] *s* celluloide *f*
Celtic ['sɛltɪk] or ['kɛltɪk] *adj* celtico ‖ *s* lingua celtica

cement [sɪ'mɛnt] *s* cemento ‖ *tr* cementare

cemete·ry ['sɛmɪ ˌtɛri] *s* (**-ries**) cimitero

censer ['sɛnsər] *s* turibolo

censor ['sɛnsər] *s* censore *m* ‖ *tr* censurare

censure ['sɛnʃər] *s* censura, critica ‖ *tr* censurare, criticare

census ['sɛnsəs] *s* censo, censimento

cent [sɛnt] *s* centesimo di dollaro, cent *m;* **not to have a red cent to one's name** non avere il becco di un quattrino

centaur ['sɛntɔr] *s* centauro

centennial [sɛn'tɛnɪ-əl] *adj & s* centenario

center ['sɛntər] *s* centro ‖ *tr* centrare, concentrare ‖ *intr*—**to center on** concentrarsi su

cen'ter·board' *s* chiglia mobile

cen'ter·piece' *s* centro tavola

cen'ter punch' *s* punzone *m,* punteruolo

centigrade ['sɛntɪ ˌgrɛd] *adj* centigrado

centimeter ['sɛntɪ ˌmitər] *s* centimetro

centipede ['sɛntɪ ˌpid] *s* centopiedi *m*

cento ['sɛnto] *s* centone *m*

central ['sɛntrəl] *adj* centrale ‖ *s* centrale *f,* centrale telefonica; (*operator*) telefonista *mf*

Cen'tral Amer'ica *s* l'America Centrale

centralize ['sɛntrə ˌlaɪz] *tr* centralizzare ‖ *intr* centralizzarsi

centu·ry ['sɛntʃəri] *s* (**-ries**) secolo

ceramic [sɪ'ræmɪk] *adj* ceramico ‖ **ceramics** *ssg* ceramica; *spl* oggetti *mpl* di ceramica

cereal ['sɪrɪ-əl] *adj* cerealicolo ‖ *s* (*grain*) cereale *m;* (*uncooked breakfast food, e.g., cornflakes*) fiocchi *mpl;* (*breakfast food to be cooked*) farina

cerebral ['sɛrɪbrəl] *adj* cerebrale

ceremonious [ˌsɛrɪ'monɪ-əs] *adj* cerimonioso

ceremo·ny ['sɛrɪ ˌmoni] *s* (**-nies**) cerimonia; **to stand on ceremony** fare cerimonie

certain ['sʌrtən] *adj* certo; **for certain** di or per certo; **to be certain to** + *inf* non mancare di + *inf*

certainly ['sʌrtənli] *adv* certamente; (*gladly*) con piacere

certain·ty ['sʌrtənti] *s* (**-ties**) certezza

certificate [sər'tɪfɪkɪt] *s* certificato; (*com*) titolo ‖ [sər'tɪfɪ ˌket] *tr* certificare

cer'tified check' *s* assegno a copertura garantita

cer'tified cop'y *s* estratto; (*as a formula on a document*) per copia conforme

cer'tified pub'lic account'ant *s* esperto contabile

certi·fy ['sʌrtɪ ˌfaɪ] *v* (*pret & pp* **-fied**) *tr* certificare, garantire

cervix ['sʌrvɪks] *s* (**cervices** (sər'vaɪsɪz] *cervice f*

cessation [sɛ'seʃən] *s* cessazione

cesspool ['sɛs ˌpul] *s* pozzo nero

Ceylo·nese [ˌsilə'niz] *adj & s* (**-nese**) singalese *mf*

chafe [tʃef] *s* irritazione ‖ *tr* (*the hands*) strofinare; irritare; (*to wear away*) logorare ‖ *intr* irritarsi; logorarsi

chaff [tʃæf] *or* [tʃɑf] *s* lolla; pula; (*joke*) burla; (*fig*) loppa

chaf'ing dish' *s* fornello a spirito

cha·grin [ʃə'grɪn] *s* cruccio, dispiacere *m* ‖ *v* (*pret* **-grined** *or* **-grinned;** *ger* **-grining** *or* **-grinning**) *tr* crucciare, affliggere

chain [tʃen] *s* catena; (*e.g., for necklace*) catenella ‖ *tr* incatenare

chain' gang' *s* catena di forzati

chain' reac'tion *s* reazione a catena

chain' saw' *s* motosega

chain'-smoke' *intr* fumare come un turco

chain' store' *s* negozio a catena

chair [tʃɛr] *s* sedia, seggiola; (*of important person*) seggio; (*at a university*) cattedra; (*chairman*) presidente *m,* presidenza; **to take the chair** cominciare una riunione ‖ *tr* (*a meeting*) presiedere

chair' lift' *s* seggiovia

chair'man *s* (**-men**) presidente *m*

chair'man·ship' *s* presidenza

chair'wom'an *s* (**-wom'en**) presidentessa

chalice ['tʃælɪs] *s* calice *m*

chalk [tʃɔk] *s* gesso ‖ *tr* marcare *or* scrivere col gesso; **to chalk up** prendere appunti di; attribuire

chalk' talk' *s* conferenza illustrata

chalk·y ['tʃɔki] *adj* (**-ier; -iest**) gessoso

challenge ['tʃælɪndʒ] *s* sfida; (*law*) ricusazione; (*mil*) chi va là *m* ‖ *tr* sfidare; (*a juror*) (*law*) ricusare; (*mil*) dare il chi va là a

chamber ['tʃembər] *s* camera, stanza; (*of a palace*) aula; (*of a judge*) gabinetto

chamberlain ['tʃembərlɪn] *s* ciambellano

cham'ber·maid' *s* cameriera

cham'ber of com'merce *s* camera di commercio

cham'ber pot' *s* orinale *m*

chameleon [kə'milɪ-ən] *s* camaleonte *m*

cham·ois ['ʃæmi] *s* (**-ois**) camoscio

champ [tʃæmp] *s* (*slang*) campione *m* ‖ *tr* masticare rumorosamente; (*the bit*) mordere ‖ *intr* masticare rumorosamente

champagne [ʃæm'pen] *s* champagne *m,* spumante *m*

champion ['tʃæmpɪ-ən] *s* campione *m* ‖ *tr* difendere; farsi paladino di

championship ['tʃæmpɪ-ən ˌʃɪp] *s* campionato

chance [tʃæns] *or* [tʃɑns] *adj* casuale, fortuito ‖ *s* occasione; caso; probabilità *f;* rischio; biglietto di lotteria; **by chance** per caso; **not to stand a chance** non avere la probabilità di riuscita; **to take one's chances** arrischiarsi; **to take a chance** attendere l'opportunità ‖ *intr* succedere; **to chance upon** imbattersi in

chancel ['tʃænsəl] *or* ['tʃɑnsəl] *s* presbiterio, coro

chanceller·y ['tʃænsələri] *or* ['tʃɑnsələri] *s* (**-ies**) cancelleria

chancellor ['tʃænsələr] or ['tʃansələr] s cancelliere m
chandelier [ˌʃændə'lir] s lampadario
change [tʃendʒ] s cambiamento; (of clothes) muta; (of currency) cambio; (coins) spiccioli mpl; **for a change** tanto per cambiare; **to keep the change** tenere il resto || tr cambiare, rimpiazzare; (clothes) cambiare, cambiarsi di || intr cambiare, mutare
changeable ['tʃendʒəbəl] adj mutevole, variabile, incostante
change' of heart' s pentimento, conversione
change' of life' s menopausa
chan·nel ['tʃænl] s canale m; tubo, passaggio; stretto; (of river) alveo; (groove) solco; (rad, telv) canale m; **through channels** per via gerarchica || v (pret & pp -neled or -nelled; ger -neling or -nelling) tr incanalare; (a river) incassare || **the Channel** il Canale della Manica
chant [tʃænt] or [tʃant] s canto; salmodia; canzone f || tr & intr cantare
chanticleer ['tʃæntɪˌklɪr] s il gallo
chaos ['ke·as] s caos m
chaotic [ke'atɪk] adj caotico
chap [tʃæp] s (fellow) individuo, tipo; (of skin) screpolatura; **chaps** pantaloni mpl di cuoio || v (pret & pp chapped; ger chapping) tr screpolare || intr screpolarsi
chapel ['tʃæpəl] s cappella
chaperon or **chaperone** ['ʃæpəˌron] s accompagnatrice f (di signorina) || tr accompagnare
chaplain ['tʃæplɪn] s cappellano
chaplet ['tʃæplɪt] s (wreath) corona, ghirlanda; rosario
chapter ['tʃæptər] s capitolo; (of a club) sezione
chap'ter and verse' s—**to give chapter and verse** citare le autorità
char [tʃar] v (pret & pp charred; ger charring) tr carbonizzare; bruciare
character ['kærɪktər] s carattere m; lettera, scrittura; indole f; (theat) personaggio; (coll) tipo; **in character** caratteristico di lui (lei, loro, etc.)
char'acter ac'tor s caratterista m
char'acter ac'tress s caratterista f
char'acter assassina'tion s linciaggio morale
characteristic [ˌkærɪktə'rɪstɪk] adj caratteristico || s caratteristica
characterize ['kærɪktəˌraɪz] tr caratterizzare
char'coal' s carbone m di legna, carbone m dolce; (for sketching) carboncino; (sketch) disegno al carboncino
charge [tʃardʒ] s carica; incarico; responsibilità f; (indictment) accusa; costo; prezzo; debito; **in charge in** comando; **in charge of** a cura di; **to take charge of** prendersi cura di || tr caricare; comandare; accusare; (a price) fare pagare; mettere in conto; **to charge s.o. with s.th** addebitare qlco a qlcu; accusare qlcu di qlco || intr fare una carica

charge' account' s conto corrente
chargé d'affaires [ʃar'ʒe də'fer] s (chargés d'affaires) incaricato d'affari
charger ['tʃardʒər] s cavallo di battaglia; (of a battery) caricatore m
chariot ['tʃærɪ·ət] s cocchio
charioteer [ˌtʃærɪ·ə'tɪr] s auriga m
charis·ma [kə'rɪzmə] s (-mata [mətə]) fascino personale; (theol) carisma m
charitable ['tʃærɪtəbəl] adj (person) caritatevole; (institution) caritativo
chari·ty ['tʃærɪti] s (-ties) carità f; associazione di beneficenza
charlatan ['ʃarlətən] s ciarlatano
charlatanism ['ʃarlətənˌɪzəm] s ciarlataneria
Charlemagne ['ʃarləˌmen] s Carlomagno
Charles [tʃarlz] s Carlo
char'ley horse' ['tʃarli] s (coll) crampo
charlotte ['ʃarlət] s charlotte f || **Char·lotte** s Carlotta
charm [tʃarm] s fascino; amuleto; portafortuna m || tr incantare, stregare
charming ['tʃarmɪŋ] adj affascinante
charnel ['tʃarnəl] adj orribile || s ossario
chart [tʃart] s carta geografica; lista; diagramma m || tr tracciare
charter ['tʃartər] s statuto; privilegio || tr (a company) fondare; (a conveyance) noleggiare
char'ter mem'ber s socio fondatore
char'wom'an s (-wom'en) domestica per la pulizia
chase [tʃes] s inseguimento; caccia; (typ) telaio || tr inseguire; cacciare; (to chisel) cesellare; **to chase away** scacciare || intr—**to chase after** inseguire
chaser ['tʃesər] s cacciatore m; (coll) bibita da bersi dopo un liquore
chasm ['kæzəm] s abisso, baratro
chas·sis ['tʃæsi] s (-sis [siz]) telaio
chaste [tʃest] adj casto
chasten ['tʃesən] tr castigare
chastise [tʃæs'taɪz] tr castigare
chastity ['tʃæstɪti] s castità f
chat [tʃæt] s chiacchierata || v (pret & pp chatted; ger chatting) intr chiacchierare
chatelaine ['ʃætəˌlen] s castellana
chattels ['tʃætəlz] spl beni mpl mobili
chatter ['tʃætər] s cicaleccio; balbettio; (of teeth) battito || intr cicalare; balbettare; (said of teeth) battere
chat'ter·box' s chiacchierone m
chauffeur ['ʃofər] or [ʃo'fʌr] s autista mf || intr fare l'autista
cheap [tʃip] adj a buon mercato, economico; (of poor quality) scadente; **to feel cheap** vergognarsi || adv a buon mercato
cheapen ['tʃipən] tr deprezzare; avvilire; rendere di cattivo gusto
cheapness ['tʃipnəs] s buon mercato, prezzo basso
cheat [tʃit] s truffa; truffatore m || tr imbrogliare, truffare || intr truffare; (at cards) barare
check [tʃɛk] s arresto, pausa; ostacolo;

esame *m;* verifica, controllo; (*of bank*) assegno; (*for baggage*) tagliando, scontrino; (*square pattern*) quadretto; (*fabric in squares*) tessuto a scacchi; (*in a restaurant*) conto; **in check** controllato, sotto controllo; (chess) sotto scacco ‖ *tr* fermare; confrontare; ispezionare; marcare; (*e.g., a coat*) depositare; disegnare a quadretti; (chess) dare scacco a; **to check off** controllare marcando; **to check on** controllare, verificare ‖ *intr* fermarsi; corrispondere perfettamente; **to check in** scendere (a un albergo); **to check out** andar via; pagare il conto; **to check up on** controllare

check'book' *s* libretto d'assegni

checker ['tʃɛkər] *s* ispettore *m;* quadretto; (*in game of checkers*) pedina; **checkers** dama ‖ *tr* variegare; marcare a quadretti

check'er-board' *s* scacchiera

check'ered *adj* (*e.g., career*) pieno di vicissitudini; (*marked with squares*) a scacchi; (*in color*) variegato

check'ing account' *s* conto corrente

check'mate' *s* scacco matto ‖ *tr* dare scacco matto a ‖ *interj* scacco matto!

check'off' dues' *spl* trattenute *fpl* sindacali

check'-out' *s* (*from hotel room*) partenza; (*time*) ora della partenza; (*examination*) esame *m* di controllo; (*in a supermarket*) cassa

check'point' *s* punto di ispezione

check'room' *s* guardaroba *m*

check'up' *s* (*of car*) ispezione; (*of patient*) esame *m* (fisico)

cheek [tʃik] *s* guancia, gota; (coll) faccia tosta

cheek'bone' *s* zigomo

cheek-y ['tʃiki] *adj* (**-ier; -iest**) (coll) impudente, sfacciato

cheer [tʃɪr] *s* gioia, allegria; applauso; **of good cheer** di buon umore ‖ *tr* riempire di gioia, rallegrare; (applaudire; ricevere con applausi ‖ *intr* rallegrarsi; **cheer up!** animo!, coraggio!

cheerful ['tʃɪrfəl] *adj* allegro, di buon umore; (*willing*) volonteroso

cheerless ['tʃɪrlɪs] *adj* tetro, triste

cheese [tʃiz] *s* formaggio ‖ *intr—* **cheese it!** (slang) scappa via!

cheese' cake' *s* torta di formaggio; (slang) pin-up girl *f*

cheese'cloth' *s* etamine *f*, stamigna

chees-y ['tʃizi] *adj* (**-ier; -iest**) di formaggio; come il formaggio; (slang) meschino, di cattiva qualità

chef [ʃɛf] *s* chef *m*, capocuoco

chemical ['kɛmɪkəl] *adj* chimico ‖ *s* prodotto chimico

chemise [ʃə'miz] *s* sottoveste *f*

chemist ['kɛmɪst] *s* chimico

chemistry ['kɛmɪstri] *s* chimica

cherish ['tʃɛrɪʃ] *tr* accarezzare; (*a memory*) custodire; (*a hope*) nutrire

cher·ry ['tʃɛri] *s* (**-ries**) (*tree*) ciliegio; (*fruit*) ciliegia

cher·ub ['tʃɛrəb] *s* (**-ubim** [əbɪm] & **-ubs**) cherubino

chess [tʃɛs] *s* scacchi *mpl*

chess'board' *s* scacchiera

chess'man' or **chess'man** *s* (**-men'** or **-men**) scacco

chest [tʃɛst] *s* petto; (*box*) cassapanca; (*furniture with drawers*) cassettone *m;* (*for money*) forziere *m*

chestnut ['tʃɛsnət] *s* (*tree, wood, color*) castagno; (*nut*) castagna

chest' of drawers' *s* cassettone *m*

cheval' glass' [ʃə'væl] *s* psiche *f*

chevalier [ˌʃɛvə'lɪr] *s* cavaliere *m*

chevron ['ʃɛvrən] *s* gallone *m*

chew [tʃu] *tr* masticare; **to chew the cud** ruminare; **to chew the rag** (slang) chiacchierare ‖ *intr* masticare

chew'ing gum' *s* gomma da masticare

chic [ʃik] *adj* & *s* chic

chicaner·y [ʃɪ'kenəri] *s* (**-ies**) trucco, rigiro

chick [tʃɪk] *s* pulcino; (slang) ragazza

chicken ['tʃɪkən] *s* pollo, pollastro; (coll) giovane *mf;* **to be chicken** (slang) avere la fifa ‖ *intr—*to **chicken out** (coll) indietreggiare

chick'en coop' *s* pollaio

chick'en feed' *s* (slang) spiccioli *mpl*

chicken-hearted ['tʃɪkən ˌhɑrtɪd] *adj* timido, fifone

chick'en pox' *s* varicella

chick'en store' *s* polleria

chick'en wire' *s* rete metallica esagonale

chick'pea' *s* cece *m*

chico·ry ['tʃɪkəri] *s* (**-ries**) cicoria

chide [tʃaɪd] *v* (*pret* **chided** or **chid** [tʃɪd];* pp* **chided, chid,** or **chidden** ['tʃɪdən]) *tr* & *intr* rimproverare, correggere

chief [tʃif] *adj* principale, sommo, supremo ‖ *s* capo, comandante supremo; (slang) padrone *m*

chief' exec'utive *s* capo del governo

chief' jus'tice *s* presidente *m* di una corte; presidente *m* della corte suprema

chiefly ['tʃifli] *adv* principalmente

chief' of staff' *s* capo di stato maggiore

chief' of state' *s* capo dello stato

chieftain ['tʃiftən] *s* capo

chiffon [ʃɪ'fɑn] *s* velo trasparente, chiffon *m;* **chiffons** trine *fpl*

chiffonier [ˌʃɪfə'nɪr] *s* mobile *m* a cassettini, chiffonier *m*

chilblain ['tʃɪl ˌblen] *s* gelone *m*

child [tʃaɪld] *s* (**children** ['tʃɪldrən]) bebè *mf,* bambino; figlio; discendente *mf;* **with child** incinta

child'birth' *s* parto

childhood ['tʃaɪldhʊd] *s* infanzia

childish ['tʃaɪldɪʃ] *adj* infantile

childishness ['tʃaɪldɪʃnɪs] *s* puerilità *f,* infanzia

child' la'bor *s* lavoro dei minorenni

childless ['tʃaɪldlɪs] *adj* senza figli

child'like' *adj* infantile, innocente

child's' play' *s* un gioco

child' wel'fare *s* protezione dell'infanzia

Chile ['tʃɪli] *s* il Cile

Chilean ['tʃɪlɪən] *adj* cileno

chil'i sauce' ['t∫ɪlɪ] *s* salsa di pomodoro con peperoni

chill [t∫ɪl] *adj* freddo ‖ *s* freddo; brivido di freddo; freddezza; (*depression*) abbattimento ‖ *tr* raffreddare; (*a metal*) temprare; (fig) scoraggiare ‖ *intr* raffreddarsi

chill·y ['t∫ɪlɪ] *adj* (**-ier; -iest**) fresco, freddiccio; (*reception*) freddo

chime [t∫aɪm] *s* scampanio; **chimes** campanello ‖ *intr* scampanare; **to chime in** cominciare a cantare all'unisono; (coll) intromettersi

chime' clock' *s* orologio con carillon

chimney ['t∫ɪmnɪ] *s* camino; (*of factory*) ciminiera; **to smoke like a chimney** fumare come un turco

chim'ney flue' *s* tubo di stufa, canna del camino

chim'ney pot' *s* testa della canna fumaria, comignolo

chim'ney sweep' *s* spazzacamino

chimpanzee [t∫ɪm'pænzi] *or* [,t∫ɪmpæn'zi] *s* scimpanzé *m*

chin [t∫ɪn] *s* mento; **to keep one's chin up** (coll) non perdersi di coraggio; **to take it on the chin** (slang) subire una sconfitta ‖ *v* (*pret & pp* **chinned**; *ger* **chinning**) *tr*—**to chin oneself** sollevarsi fino al mento (ai manubri) ‖ *intr* (slang) chiacchierare

china ['t∫aɪnə] *s* porcellana ‖ **China** *s* la Cina

chi'na clos'et *s* armadio per le stoviglie

chi'na·ware' *s* porcellana, stoviglie *fpl*

Chi·nese [t∫aɪ'niz] *adj* cinese ‖ *s* (**-nese**) cinese *mf*

Chi'nese lan'tern *s* lampioncino alla veneziana

Chi'nese puz'zle *s* rebus *m*

chink [t∫ɪŋk] *s* fessura

chin' strap' *s* sottogola

chintz [t∫ɪnts] *s* chintz *m*

chip [t∫ɪp] *s* scheggia; frammento; (*in card games*) gettone *m*; (*of wood*) truciolo; **chip off the old block** vero figlio di suo padre (di sua madre); **chip on one's shoulder** propensità *f* a attaccar brighe ‖ *v* (*pret & pp* **chipped**; *ger* **chipping**) *tr* scheggiare; **to chip in** contribuire ‖ *intr* scheggiarsi

chipmunk ['t∫ɪp,mʌŋk] *s* tamia

chipper ['t∫ɪpər] *adj* (coll) allegro, vivo

chiropodist [kaɪ'rapədɪst] *or* [kɪ'rapədɪst] *s* callista *mf*, pedicure *mf*

chiropractic ['kaɪrə,præktɪs] *s* chiropratica

chirp [t∫ʌrp] *s* (*of birds*) cinguettio; (*of crickets*) cri cri *m* ‖ *intr* cinguettare; fare cri cri

chis·el ['t∫ɪzəl] *s* (*for wood and metal*) scalpello; (*for metal*) cesello ‖ *v* (*pret & pp* **-eled** *or* **-elled**; *ger* **-eling** *or* **-elling**) *tr* scalpellare; cesellare; (slang) imbrogliare ‖ *intr* (slang) imbrogliare, fare l'imbroglione

chiseler ['t∫ɪzələr] *s* scalpellino; cesellatore *m*; (slang) imbroglione *m*

chit-chat ['t∫ɪt,t∫æt] *s* chiacchierata

chivalrous ['∫ɪvəlrəs] *adj* cavalleresco

chivalry ['∫ɪvəlrɪ] *s* cavalleria

chive [t∫aɪv] *s* cipolla porraia

chloride ['klɔraɪd] *s* cloruro

chlorine ['klɔriñ] *s* cloro

chloroform ['klɔrə,fɔrm] *s* cloroformio ‖ *tr* cloroformizzare

chlorophyll ['klɔrəfɪl] *s* clorofilla

chock [t∫ak] *s* (*wedge*) bietta, cuneo

chock-full ['t∫ak'fʊl] *adj* colmo, pieno zeppo

chocolate ['t∫ɔkəlɪt] *or* ['t∫akəlɪt] *s* (*candy*) cioccolato; (*drink*) cioccolata

choc'olate bar' *s* barretta di cioccolato

choice [t∫ɔɪs] *adj* di prima scelta, superiore ‖ *s* scelta; (*variety*) assortimento

choir [kwaɪr] *s* coro

choir'boy' *s* ragazzo cantore

choir' loft' *s* coro

choir'mas'ter *s* maestro di cappella

choke [t∫ok] *s* strozzatura; (aut) farfalla del carburatore ‖ *tr* strozzare; ostruire; (*an internal-combustion engine*) arricchire la miscela di; **to choke back** trattenere; **to choke up** tappare, ostruire ‖ *intr* soffocarsi; **to choke up** tapparsi; (coll) soffocarsi

choker ['t∫okər] *s* (*necklace*) (coll) collana; (*scarf*) (coll) foulard *m*

cholera ['kalərə] *s* colera *m*

choleric ['kalərɪk] *adj* collerico

cholesterol [kə'lɛstə,rol] *or* [kə'lɛstə,ral] *s* colesterina

choose [t∫uz] *v* (*pret* **chose** [t∫oz]; *pp* **chosen** ['t∫ozən]) *tr* scegliere ‖ *intr* —**to choose to** decidere di

choos·y ['t∫uzi] *adj* (**-ier; -iest**) (coll) di difficile contentatura

chop [t∫ap] *s* colpo; (*of meat*) cotoletta; **chops** labbra *fpl*, bocca ‖ *v* (*pret & pp* **chopped**; *ger* **chopping**) *tr* tagliare; (*meat*) tritare; **to chop off** troncare; **to chop up** sminuzzare

chopper ['t∫apər] *s* (*man*) tagliatore *m*; interruttore automatico; coltello da macellaio; (slang) elicottero; **choppers** (slang) i denti

chop'ping block' *s* tagliere *m*

chop·py ['t∫apɪ] *adj* (**-ier; -iest**) (*wind*) variabile; (*sea*) agitato; (*style*) instabile

choral ['kɔrəl] *adj* & *s* corale *m*

chorale [ko'ral] *s* corale *m*

chord [kɔrd] *s* corda; (mus) accordo

chore [t∫or] *s* lavoro; lavoro spiacevole; **chores** faccende domestiche

choreography [,kɔrɪ'agrəfɪ] *s* coreografia

chorine [ko'rin] *s* (slang) ballerina

chorus ['kɔrəs] *s* coro; (*group of dancers*) corpo di ballo; (*of a song*) ritornello

cho'rus girl' *s* ballerina

cho'rus man' *s* (men') corista *m*

chow [t∫aʊ] *s* (*dog*) chow chow *m*; (slang) cibo, pappa

chowder ['t∫aʊdər] *s* zuppa di vongole; zuppa di pesce

Christ [kraɪst] *s* Cristo

christen ['krɪsən] *tr* battezzare

Christendom ['krɪsəndəm] *s* cristianità *f*

christening ['krɪsənɪŋ] s battesimo
Christian ['krɪstʃən] adj & s cristiano
Christianity [ˌkrɪstʃɪ'ænɪtɪ] s (Christendom) cristianità f; (religion) cristianesimo
Chris'tian name' s nome m di battesimo
Christmas ['krɪsməs] adj natalizio ‖ s Natale m; **Merry Christmas!** Buon Natale!
Christ'mas card' s cartoncino natalizio
Christ'mas car'ol s pastorella di Natale
Christ'mas Eve' s vigilia di Natale
Christ'mas gift' s strenna natalizia
Christ'mas tree' s albero di Natale
chrome [krom] adj cromato ‖ s cromo ‖ tr cromare
chromium ['kromɪ-əm] s cromo
chromosome ['kromə,som] s cromosoma m
chronic ['krɑnɪk] adj cronico
chronicle ['krɑnɪkəl] s cronaca ‖ tr fare la storia di
chronicler ['krɑnɪklər] s cronista mf
chronolo·gy [krə'nɑlədʒɪ] s (-gies) cronologia
chronometer [krə'nɑmɪtər] s cronometro
chrysanthemum [krɪ'sænθɪməm] s crisantemo
chub·by ['tʃʌbɪ] adj (-bier; -biest) paffuto
chuck [tʃʌk] s buffetto sotto il mento; (cut of meat) reale m; (of lathe) coppaia ‖ tr accarezzare sotto il mento; (to throw) (coll) gettare
chuckle ['tʃʌkəl] s risatina ‖ intr ridacchiare
chum [tʃʌm] s (coll) amico intimo; (coll) compagno di stanza ‖ v (pret & pp **chummed**) ger **chumming**) intr (coll) essere amico intimo; essere compagno di stanza
chum·my ['tʃʌmɪ] adj (-mier; -miest) (coll) intimo, amicone
chump [tʃʌmp] s ciocco, ceppo; (coll) sciocco
chunk [tʃʌŋk] s grosso pezzo
church [tʃʌrtʃ] s chiesa
churchgoer ['tʃʌrtʃ,go·ər] s praticante mf
church'man s (-men) parrocchiano; (clergyman) sacerdote m
Church' of Eng'land s chiesa anglicana
church'yard' s camposanto
churl [tʃʌrl] s zotico, villano
churlish ['tʃʌrlɪʃ] adj villano
churn [tʃʌrn] s zangola ‖ tr agitare violentemente, sbattere ‖ intr (said of water) ribollire
chute [ʃut] s piano inclinato, canna; (in a river) cascata, rapida; paracadute m; (into a swimming pool) toboga m
Cicero ['sɪsə,ro] s Cicerone m
cider ['saɪdər] s sidro
cigar [sɪ'gɑr] s sigaro
cigar' case' s portasigari m
cigar' cut'ter s tagliasigari m
cigarette [ˌsɪgə'rɛt] s sigaretta
cigarette' butt' s cicca
cigarette' case' s portasigarette m
cigarette' hold'er s bocchino

cigarette' light'er s accendisigaro, accendino
cigarette' pa'per s cartina da sigarette
cigar' store' s tabaccheria, rivendita di sali e tabacchi
cinch [sɪntʃ] s (on a horse) sottopancia m; (hold) (coll) presa; (slang) giochetto ‖ tr legare con una cinghia; (slang) agguantare
cinder ['sɪndər] s tizzone m; (slag) scoria; **cinders** cenere f
cin'der block' s concio di scoria
Cinderella [ˌsɪndə'rɛlə] s (la) Cenerentola
cinema ['sɪnəmə] s cine m, cinema m
cinnabar ['sɪnə,bɑr] s cinabro
cinnamon ['sɪnəmən] s cannella
cipher ['saɪfər] s zero; cifra; codice m; monogramma m ‖ tr calcolare; (to write in code) cifrare
circle ['sʌrkəl] s cerchio; (of theater) prima galleria; (of friends) cerchia ‖ tr cerchiare, compiere una rotazione intorno a
circuit ['sʌrkɪt] s circuito; (district) circoscrizione
cir'cuit break'er s salvamotore m, interruttore automatico
circuitous [sər'kju·ɪtəs] adj tortuoso
circuitry ['sʌrkɪtrɪ] s (plan) schema m di montaggio; (components) elementi mpl di un circuito
circular ['sʌrkjələr] adj & s circolare f
circulate ['sʌrkjə,let] tr mettere in circolazione, diffondere ‖ intr circolare
cir'culating li'brary s biblioteca circolante
circulation [ˌsʌrkjə'leʃən] s circolazione; (of newspaper) diffusione
circumcise ['sʌrkəm,saɪz] tr circoncidere
circumference [sər'kʌmfərəns] s circonferenza
circumflex ['sʌrkəm,flɛks] adj circonflesso ‖ s accento circonflesso
circumscribe [ˌsʌrkəm'skraɪb] tr circoscrivere
circumspect ['sʌrkəm,spɛkt] adj circospetto
circumstance ['sʌrkəm,stæns] s circostanza; (fact) dettaglio; solennità f; **circumstances** condizioni fpl; dettagli mpl; condizioni economiche; **under no circumstances** a nessuna condizione; **under the circumstances** le cose essendo come sono
circumstantial [ˌsʌrkəm'stænʃəl] adj circostanziale, indiziario; (incidental) secondario; (complete) circostanziato
cir'cumstan'tial ev'idence s prova indiziaria
circumstantiate [ˌsʌrkəm'stænʃɪ,et] tr (to support with particulars) comprovare; (to describe in detail) circonstanziare
circumvent [ˌsʌrkəm'vɛnt] tr (to surround) accerchiare; (to outwit) circuire; (a difficulty) eludere, scansare
circus ['sʌrkəs] s circo equestre
cistern ['sɪstərn] s cisterna, serbatoio
citadel ['sɪtədəl] s cittadella
citation [saɪ'teʃən] s citazione

cite [saɪt] *tr* citare

cither ['sɪðər] *s* cetra

citizen ['sɪtɪzən] *s* cittadino; *(civilian)* civile *mf*

citizenship ['sɪtɪzən‚ʃɪp] *s* cittadinanza

citric ['sɪtrɪk] *adj* citrico

citron ['sɪtrən] *s* cedro; cedro candito

cit'rus fruit' ['sɪtrəs] *s* agrumi *mpl*

cit·y ['sɪti] *s* (-ies) città *f*

cit'y counc'il *s* consiglio municipale

cit'y ed'itor *s* capocronista *m*

cit'y fa'thers *spl* maggiorenti *mpl*; consiglieri *mpl* municipali

cit'y hall' *s* municipio

cit'y plan'ning *s* urbanistica

cit'y room' *s* (journ) redazione

civic ['sɪvɪk] *adj* civico ‖ **civics** *s* educazione civica

civil ['sɪvɪl] *adj* civile

civ'il engineer'ing *s* genio civile

civilian [sɪ'vɪljən] *adj* & *s* civile *mf*, borghese *mf*

civili·ty [sɪ'vɪlɪti] *s* (-ties) cortesia; **civilities** ossequi *mpl*

civilization [‚sɪvɪlɪ'zeʃən] *s* civilizzazione, civiltà *f*

civilize ['sɪvɪ‚laɪz] *tr* civilizzare

civ'il law' *s* diritto civile

civ'il serv'ant *s* impiegato statale

civ'il war' *s* guerra civile ‖ **Civil War** *s* *(of the U.S.A.)* guerra di secessione

claim [klem] *s* pretesa; richiesta; (min) concessione ‖ *tr (one's rights)* rivendicare; *(one's property)* richiedere; dichiarare; **to claim to be** pretendere d'essere

claim' check' *s* tagliando

clairvoyance [kler'vɔɪ·əns] *s* chiaroveggenza

clairvoyant [kler'vɔɪ·ənt] *adj* chiaroveggente ‖ *s* veggente *mf*, chiaroveggente *mf*

clam [klæm] *s* vongola ‖ *intr*—**to clam up** (coll) essere muto come un pesce

clamber ['klæmər] *intr* arrampicarsi

clam·my ['klæmi] *adj* (-mier; -miest) coperto di sudore freddo; morbido

clamor ['klæmər] *s* clamore *m* ‖ *intr* fare clamore

clamorous ['klæmərəs] *adj* clamoroso

clamp [klæmp] *s* graffa, morsetto; *(e.g., to hold a hose)* fascetta ‖ *tr* assicurare con graffa, aggrappare; *(a tool)* montare ‖ *intr*—**to clamp down on** (coll) fare pressione su, mettere i freni a

clan [klæn] *s* clan *m*

clandestine [klæn'destɪn] *adj* clandestino

clang [klæŋ] *s* clangore *m* ‖ *intr* risonare con clangore

clannish ['klænɪʃ] *adj* esclusivista, partigiano

clap [klæp] *s* applauso; *(of thunder)* scoppio ‖ *v* (*pret* & *pp* **clapped**) *ger* **clapping**) *tr* *(the hands)* battere; *(e.g., in jail)* schiaffare; **to clap shut** sbattere ‖ *intr* applaudire

clapper ['klæpər] *s* applauditore *m*; *(of bell)* batacchio

clap'trap' *s* imbonimento

claret ['klærɪt] *adj* & *s* chiaretto

clari·fy ['klærɪ‚faɪ] *v* (*pret* & *pp* **-fied**) *tr* chiarificare, chiarire

clarinet [‚klærɪ'net] *s* clarinetto

clarion ['klærɪ·ən] *adj* chiaro e metallico ‖ *s* tromba, clarino

clash [klæʃ] *s* cozzo, urto; conflitto di opinioni ‖ *intr* cozzare, urtarsi; essere in conflitto

clasp [klæsp] *or* [klɑsp] *s* gancio, fermaglio; *(hold)* presa; *(grip)* stretta ‖ *tr* agganciare; *(to hold in the arms)* abbracciare; *(to grip)* stringere

class [klæs] *or* [klɑs] *s* classe *f* ‖ *tr* classificare

class'book' *s* registro

classic ['klæsɪk] *adj* & *s* classico

classical ['klæsɪkəl] *adj* classico

classicism ['klæsɪ‚sɪzəm] *s* classicismo

classicist ['klæsɪsɪst] *s* classicista *mf*

classified ['klæsɪ‚faɪd] *adj* segreto

clas'sified ad' *s* annunzio economico

classi·fy ['klæsɪ‚faɪ] *v* (*pret* & *pp* **-fied**) *tr* classificare

class'mate' *s* compagno di scuola

class'room' *s* aula scolastica

class' strug'gle *s* lotta di classe

class·y ['klæsi] *adj* (-ier; -iest) (slang) di lusso, di prim'ordine

clatter ['klætər] *s* *(of dishes)* acciottolio; vocio, schiamazzo ‖ *tr* acciottolare ‖ *intr* fare schiamazzo

clause [klɔz] *s* clausola; (gram) proposizione

clavicle ['klævɪkəl] *s* clavicola

claw [klɔ] *s* artiglio; *(of lobster)* pinza; *(tool)* raffio; *(of hammer)* granchio; (coll) dita *fpl* ‖ *tr* aggraffiare; artigliare

claw' ham'mer *s* levachiodi *m*

clay [kle] *s* argilla, creta

clay' pipe' *s* pipa di terracotta

clean [klin] *adj* pulito; *(precise)* netto; *(e.g., break)* completo ‖ *adv* completamente ‖ *tr* pulire; **to clean out** pulire, fare repulisti di; (slang) ripulire; **to clean up** pulire completamente; mettere in ordine ‖ *intr* pulirsi, fare pulizia

clean' bill' of health' *s* patente sanitaria; (fig) esonero completo

clean'-cut' *adj* ben delineato, deciso

cleaner ['klinər] *s* pulitore *m*, smacchiatore *m*; *(machine)* pulitrice *f*, smacchiatrice *f*; **to send to the cleaners** (slang) spolpare

clean'ing fluid' *s* smacchiatore *m*

clean'ing wom'an *s* donna di servizio per fare la pulizia

clean·ly ['klenli] *adj* (-lier; -liest) pulito, netto

cleanse [klenz] *tr* pulire; detergere; purificare

cleanser ['klenzər] *s* detergente *m*

clean'-sha'ven *adj* sbarbato di fresco

clean'up' *s* pulizia; (slang) guadagno enorme

clear [klɪr] *adj* chiaro; evidente; completo; innocente; *(profit)* netto; **clear of** libero da ‖ *s* posto libero; **in the clear** libero; esonerato; non in codice ‖ *adv* chiaramente; completamente ‖ *tr* (e.g., *trees*) rischiarare; *(e.g., peo-*

ple) sgombrare; (*the table*) sparecchiare; (*an obstacle*) superare; (*from guilt*) discolpare; (*a profit*) guadagnare; (*goods at customs*) svincolare; (*a ship through customs*) dichiarare il carico di; (*checks*) compensare; **to clear away** or **off** liberare; **to clear out** sgomberare, sbarazzare; **to clear up** spiegare; (*a doubt*) dissipare || *intr* rasserenarsi; (*said of a ship*) partire; **to clear away** or **off** sparire; **to clear out** (coll) andarsene; **to clear up** rasserenarsi

clearance ['klɪrəns] *s* liberazione; (*of a ship*) partenza; (*of goods through customs*) sdoganamento; (*of checks*) compensazione; (*of goods*) liquidazione; (mach) gioco

clear'ance sale' *s* liquidazione

clear'-cut' *adj* chiaro, distinto

clearing ['klɪrɪŋ] *s* (*open space*) radura; (*of checks*) compensazione

clear'ing house' *s* stanza di compensazione

cleat [klit] *s* bietta, cuneo; (*on the sole of shoe*) tacchetto; (naut) galloccia

cleavage ['klivɪdʒ] *s* divisione; fessura

cleave [kliv] *v* (*pret & pp* **cleft** [klɛft] or **cleaved**) *tr* dividere, fendere || *intr* aderire, essere fedele

cleaver ['klivər] *s* scure *f*, accetta; (*of butcher*) spaccaossa *m*, fenditoio

clef [klɛf] *s* (mus) chiave *f*

cleft [klɛft] *adj* diviso, fesso || *s* fessura, crepaccio

cleft' pal'ate *s* palato spaccato, gola lupina

clematis ['klɛmətɪs] *s* clematide *f*

clemen·cy ['klɛmənsɪ] *s* (-cies) clemenza

clement ['klɛmənt] *adj* clemente

clench [klɛntʃ] *s* stretta || *tr* stringere; afferrare

clergy ['klɜrdʒɪ] *s* clero

cler'gy·man *s* (-men) ecclesiastico

cleric ['klɛrɪk] *s* ecclesiastico, sacerdote *m*

clerical ['klɛrɪkəl] *adj* da impiegato; (*error*) burocratico; (*of clergy*) clericale || *s* ecclesiastico; **clericals** abiti ecclesiastici

cler'ical work' *s* lavoro d'ufficio

clerk [klɑrk] *s* impiegato, commesso; (*accountant*) contabile *mf*; (e.g., in a record office*) ufficiale *m*; cancelliere *m*; (*copyist, typist*) scrivano

clever ['klɛvər] *adj* intelligente; bravo, abile; destro

cleverness ['klɛvərnɪs] *s* intelligenza; bravura, abilità *f*

clew [klu] *s* indizio, traccia; (*of yarn*) gomitolo; (naut) bugna

cliché [kli'ʃe] *s* cliché *m*, luogo comune

click [klɪk] *s* (*of camera or gun*) scatto; (*of typewriter*) battito, ticchettio || *tr* (*the tongue*) schioccare; (*the heels*) battere || *intr* ticchettare; (slang) andare d'accordo; (slang) avere fortuna

client ['klaɪ·ənt] *s* cliente *mf*

clientele [,klaɪ·ən'tɛl] *s* clientela

cliff [klɪf] *s* rupe *f*, precipizio

climate ['klaɪmɪt] *s* clima *m*

climax ['klaɪmæks] *s* apice *m*; (*acute phase*) parossismo

climb [klaɪm] *s* salita; (*of a mountain*) scalata, ascensione || *tr* (*the stairs*) salire; (*a mountain*) scalare, ascendere || *intr* salire, arrampicarsi; **to climb down** discendere a carponi; (coll) ritirarsi

climber ['klaɪmər] *s* scalatore *m*; pianta rampicante; (*ambitious person*) (coll) arrampicatore *m*

clinch [klɪntʃ] *s* stretta, presa; (*boxing*) corpo a corpo *m* || *tr* (*nails*) ribattere, ribadire

clincher ['klɪntʃər] *s* chiodo per ribaditura; argomento decisivo

cling [klɪŋ] *v* (*pret & pp* **clung** [klʌŋ]) *intr* avviticchiare, attaccarsi; aderire, rimanere attaccato

cling'stone' peach' *s* pesca duracino

clinic ['klɪnɪk] *s* clinica

clinical ['klɪnɪkəl] *adj* clinico

clinician [klɪ'nɪʃən] *s* clinico

clink [klɪŋk] *s* tintinnio; (slang) gattabuia || *tr* (*glasses*) toccare || *intr* tintinnare

clinker ['klɪŋkər] *s* clinker *m*; mattone vetrificato; (slang) sbaglio

clip [klɪp] *s* (*of hair*) taglio; (*of wool*) tosatura; (*speed*) passo rapido; clip *f*, fermaglio; (*large clip*) fermacarte *m*; (*for cartridges*) caricatore *m*; (coll) colpo || *v* (*pret & pp* **clipped;** *ger* **clipping**) *tr* tagliare, tosare; (*words*) mangiare, storpiare; (*paper*) ritagliare; ritenere; (coll) battere || *intr* andare di buon passo

clipper ['klɪpər] *s* tagliatore *m*; (aer, naut) clipper *m*; **clippers** (*for hair*) tosatrice *f*; (*for nails*) pinze *fpl* per le unghie

clipping ['klɪpɪŋ] *s* taglio; (*from newspaper*) ritaglio

clique [klik] *s* cricca, chiesuola

cloak [klok] *s* mantello, manto; (fig) velo, maschera || *tr* ammantare, velare

cloak'-and-dag'ger *adj* d'avventura

cloak'-and-sword' *adj* di cappa e spada

cloak'room' *s* guardaroba *m*

clock [klɑk] *s* orologio; (*with pendulum*) pendolo, pendola; (*on stocking*) freccia || *tr* registrare, cronometrare

clock'mak'er *s* orologiaio

clock' tow'er *s* torre *f* dell'orologio

clock'wise' *adj & adv* nella direzione delle lancette dell'orologio

clock'work' *s* movimento d'orologeria; **like clockwork** come un orologio

clod [klɑd] *s* zolla; (fig) tonto

clod'hop'per *s* (*shoe*) scarpone *m*; (fig) villano, bifolco

clog [klɑg] *s* intoppo; (*to impede movement*) pastoia; scarpone *m*, zoccolo || *v* (*pret & pp* **clogged;** *ger* **clogging**) *tr* intoppare; (*to hold back*) impastoiare || *intr* otturarsi, ostruirsi

cloister ['klɔɪstər] *s* chiostro || *tr* rinchiudere in un chiostro

close [klos] *adj* vicino; (*translation*)

fedele; *(air in room)* male arieggiato; *(weather)* soffocante; *(stingy)* avaro; limitato, senza gioco; *(haircut)* corto; *(friend)* intimo; *(hit)* preciso; *(enclosed)* chiuso; *(narrow)* stretto || *adv* da vicino; **close to** vicino a || [kloz] *s* fine *f*, conclusione; **to bring to a close** concludere || *tr* chiudere; otturare; concludere; **to·close down** chiudere completamente; **to close out** vendere in liquidazione; **to close up** bloccare || *intr* chiudersi; serrarsi; **to close down** chiudersi completamente; **to close in on** venire alle prese con; **to close up** bloccarsi; *(said of a wound)* rimarginarsi

close' call' [klos] *s* rischio scampato per miracolo

closed' chap'ter *s* affare chiuso

closed' cir'cuit *s* circuito chiuso

closed' sea'son *s* periodo di caccia o pesca vietata

closefisted ['klos'fɪstɪd] *adj* taccagno

close'-fit'ing [klos] *adj* attillato

close-lipped ['klos'lɪpt] *adj* riservato

closely ['kloslɪ] *adv* da vicino; strettamente; fedelmente; attentamente

close' quar'ters [klos] *spl (cramped space)* pigia pigia *m;* **at close quarters** a corpo a corpo

close' quote' [kloz] *s* fine *f* della citazione

close' shave' [klos] *s—***to have a close shave** farsi fare la barba a contropelo; *(coll)* scamparla per un pelo

closet ['klazɪt] *s* armadio a muro; *(small private room)* gabinetto; *(for keeping clothing)* ripostiglio || *tr*— **to be closeted with** essere in conciliabolo con

close'-up' [klos] *s (mov)* primo piano

closing ['klozɪŋ] *s* fine *f*, conclusione

clos'ing price' *s* ultimo corso

clot [klɑt] *s* grumo, coagulo || *v (pret & pp* **clotted;** *ger* **clotting)** *intr* raggrumarsi, coagularsi

cloth [klɔθ] *or* [klɑθ] *s* panno, tessuto, stoffa; abito; *(for binding books)* tela; **the cloth** il clero

clothe [kloð] *v (pret & pp* **clothed** *or* **clad** [klæd]) *tr* vestire, rivestire, coprire

clothes [kloz] *or* [kloðz] *spl* vestiti *mpl*, abiti *mpl; (for a bed)* coltre *f;* **to change clothes** cambiarsi

clothes'bas'ket *s* cesto della biancheria

clothes'brush' *s* spazzola per vestiti

clothes' dry'er *s* asciugatrice *f*

clothes' hang'er *s* attaccapanni *m*

clothes'horse' *s* cavalletto per stendere il bucato; elegantone *m*

clothes'line' *s* corda per stendere il bucato

clothes' moth' *s* tarma, tignola

clothes'pin' *s* molletta

clothes' tree' *s* attaccapanni *m*

clothier ['kloðjər] *s* negoziante *m* di confezioni; mercante *m* di panno

clothing ['kloðɪŋ] *s* vestiti *mpl*, vestiario

cloud [klaud] *s* nuvola, nube *f; (great number)* nuvolo; macchia; sospetto

|| *tr* annuvolare; offuscare || *intr* annuvolarsi; offuscarsi

cloud' bank' *s* banco di nubi

cloud'burst' *s* acquazzone *m*, nubifragio

cloud'-capped' *adj* coperto di nubi

cloudless ['klaudlɪs] *adj* senza nubi

cloud·y ['klaudi] *adj* (-ier; -iest) nuvoloso, annuvolato; confuso; tenebroso

clout [klaut] *s (coll)* schiaffo || *tr* (coll) schiaffeggiare

clove [klov] *s* chiodo di garofano; *(of garlic)* spicchio

cloven-hoofed ['klovən'huft] *adj* dal piede biforcuto; demoniaco

clover ['klovər] *s* trifoglio; **in clover** come un papa

clo'ver·leaf' *s* (-leaves [ˌlivz]) foglia di trifoglio; incrocio stradale a quadrifoglio

clown [klaun] *s* pagliaccio, buffone *m* || *intr* fare il pagliaccio

clownish ['klaunɪʃ] *adj* buffonesco, clownesco, claunesco

cloy [klɔɪ] *tr* saziare fino alla nausea

club [klʌb] *s* bastone *m;* circolo, società *f; (playing card)* fiore *m* || *v (pret & pp* **clubbed;** *ger* **clubbing)** *tr* bastonare || *intr*—**to club together** unirsi

club' car' *s* vagone *m* con servizio di buffet

club'house' *s* sede *f* di un circolo

club'man' *s* (-men') frequentatore *m* di circoli

club'room' *s* sala delle riunioni

club' sand'wich *s* sandwich *m* a tre fette di pane con insalata

club'wom'an *s* (-wom'en) frequentatrice *f* di circoli

cluck [klʌk] *s* (il) chiocciare || *intr* chiocciare

clue [klu] *s* traccia, indizio

clump [klʌmp] *s* gruppo, massa; *(of earth)* zolla || *intr* camminare con passo pesante

clum·sy ['klʌmzi] *adj* (-sier; -siest) goffo, malaccorto, sgraziato

cluster ['klʌstər] *s* gruppo; *(of grapes)* grappolo; *(of bees)* sciame *m; (of stars)* ammasso; *(of people)* folla || *tr* raggruppare || *intr* raggrupparsi

clutch [klʌtʃ] *s* presa; *(claw)* grinfia; *(of chickens)* covata; *(mach)* innesto; *(aut)* frizione; **clutches** grinfie *fpl;* **to throw the clutch in** innestare la marcia; **to throw the clutch out** disinnestare la marcia || *tr* afferrare, aggrappare || *intr*—**to clutch at** aggrapparsi a

clutter ['klʌtər] *tr*—**to clutter up** ingombrare alla rinfusa

coach [kotʃ] *s* carrozza, vettura; vagone *m; (automobile)* berlina; autobus *m; (trainer)* allenatore *m; (teacher)* ripetitore *m* || *tr* allenare; preparare

coach' house' *s* rimessa

coaching ['kotʃɪŋ] *s* suggerimento; *(in school)* ripetizione; *(sports)* allenamento

coach'man *s* (-men) cocchiere *m*

coagulate [ko'ægjə,let] *tr* coagulare || *intr* coagularsi

coal [kol] *s* carbone *m*; (*piece of burning wood*) tizzone *m*; **to call** or **haul over the coals** rimproverare || *tr* rifornire di carbone || *intr* rifornirsi di carbone; (naut) fare carbone

coal'bin' *s* carbonaia

coal' deal'er *s* (*wholesale*) negoziante *m* di carbone; (*retail*) carbonaio

coal' field' *s* bacino carbonifero

coal' gas' *s* gas *m* illuminante

coalition [,ko·ə'lɪʃən] *s* coalizione

coal' mine' *s* miniera di carbone

coal' oil' *s* cherosene *m*

coal' scut'tle *s* secchio del carbone

coal' tar' *s* catrame *m*

coal' yard' *s* carbonaia, carboniera

coarse [kors] *adj* (*manners*) volgare, ordinario; (*unrefined*) greggio; (*lacking refinement in manners*) rozzo, grossolano

coast [kost] *s* costa; discesa a ruota libera; **the coast is clear** la via è libera || *tr* costeggiare || *intr* costeggiare; scendere a ruota libera

coastal ['kostəl] *adj* costiero

coaster ['kostər] *s* nave *f* di cabotaggio; (*amusement*) otto volante, montagna russa; (*small tray*) sottobicchiere *m*

coast'er brake' *s* freno a contropedale

coast' guard' *s* guardacoste *m*

coast'-guard cut'ter *s* guardacoste *m*

coast'ing trade' *s* cabotaggio

coast'land' *s* costa

coast'line' *s* linea costiera, litorale *m*

coast'wise' *adv* lungo la costa

coat [kot] *s* soprabito; cappotto; (*jacket*) giacca; (*hide of man and animals*) mantello; (*of paint*) mano *f*; (*layer*) strato || *tr* vestire, proteggere; ricoprire, coprire

coat'ed ['kotɪd] *adj* rivestito; (*tongue*) patinato

coat' hang'er *s* attaccapanni *m*

coating ['kotɪŋ] *s* rivestimento; (*of paint*) mano *f*; (*of cement*) strato; (*cloth*) tessuto per abiti

coat' of arms' *s* scudo, stemma *m*

coat'room' *s* guardaroba *m*

coat'tail' *s* falda

coax [koks] *tr* blandire; ottenere con lusinghe

cob [kab] *s* spiga di granturco; (*horse*) cavallo da tiro; (*swan*) cigno maschio

cobalt ['kobɔlt] *s* cobalto

cobble ['kabəl] *s* ciottolo || *tr* acciottolare; (*to mend*) raccomodare, riparare

cobbler ['kablər] *s* calzolaio, ciabattino; (*pie*) torta di frutta

cob'ble·stone' *s* ciottolo

cob'web' *s* tela di ragno, ragnatela

cocaine [ko'ken] *s* cocaina

cock [kak] *s* gallo; (*faucet*) rubinetto; (*of gun*) cane *m*; (*of the eye*) ammicco; (*of nose*) angolo (del naso) rivolto all'insù; (*of hay*) covone *m* || *tr* (*a gun*) armare; (*the head*) drizzare

cockade [ka'ked] *s* coccarda

cock-a-doodle-doo ['kakə,dudəl'du] *s* chicchirichì *m*

cock'-and-bull' sto'ry *s* racconto incredibile

cocked' hat' *s* tricorno, cappello tricorno; **to knock into a cocked hat** (slang) distruggere completamente

cockeyed ['kak,aid] *adj* strabico; (slang) sbilenco; (slang) sciocco, scemo

cockle ['kakəl] *s* (*mollusk*) cardio; (*weed*) loglio; (*boat*) barchetta; (*wrinkle*) grinza; **to warm the cockles of one's heart** far bene al cuore || *intr* raggrinzirsi

cock' of the walk' *s* gallo del pollaio

cock'pit' *s* (*of boat*) cabina; (aer) carlinga; (naut) cassero di poppa

cock'roach' *s* scarafaggio, blatta

cocks'comb' *s* cresta di gallo; berretto da buffone

cock'sure' *adj* ostinato; troppo sicuro di sé stesso

cock'tail' *s* cocktail *m*

cock'tail par'ty *s* cocktail *m*

cock·y ['kaki] *adj* (-ier; -iest) impudente, presuntuoso

cocoa ['koko] *s* (*bean*) cacao; (*drink*) cioccolata; (*tree*) cocco

coconut ['kokə,nʌt] *s* noce *f* di cocco

co'conut palm' or **tree'** *s* cocco

cocoon [kə'kun] *s* bozzolo

cod [kad] *s* merluzzo

C.O.D. ['si'o'di] *s* (letterword) **(Collect on Delivery)** contro assegno

coddle ['kadəl] *tr* vezzeggiare

code [kod] *s* codice *m*, cifra; **in code** in codice, in cifra || *tr* mettere in codice or in cifra; cifrare

codex ['kodeks] *s* (**codices** ['kodɪ,siz] or ['kadɪ,siz]) codice *m*

cod'fish' *s* merluzzo

codger ['kadʒər] *s*—**old codger** (coll) vecchietto

codicil ['kadɪsɪl] *s* codicillo

codi·fy ['kadɪ,faɪ] or ['kodɪ,faɪ] *v* (*pret & pp* -fied) *tr* codificare

cod'-liver oil' *s* olio di fegato di merluzzo

coed ['co,ed] *s* studentessa di scuola mista

coeducation [,ko,edʒə'keʃən] *s* coeducazione

co'educa'tional school' [,ko·edʒə'keʃənəl] *s* scuola mista

coefficient [,ko·ɪ'fɪʃənt] *s* coefficiente

coerce [ko'ʌrs] *tr* forzare, costringere

coercion [ko'ʌrʃən] *s* coercizione

coexist [,ko·ɪg'zɪst] *intr* coesistere

coffee ['kɔfi] or ['kafi] *s* caffè *m*; **ground coffee** caffè macinato; **roasted coffee** caffè torrefatto

cof'fee bean' *s* chicco di caffè

cof'fee·cake' *s* pasticcino (da mangiarsi con il caffè)

cof'fee grind'er *s* macinino da caffè, macinacaffè *m*

cof'fee grounds' *spl* fondi *mpl* di caffè

cof'fee house' *s* caffè *m*

cof'fee mak'er *s* macchinetta del caffè

cof'fee mill' *s* macinino del caffè, macinacaffè *m*

cof'fee•pot' *s* caffettiera

cof'fee shop' *s* caffè *m*

coffer ['kɔfər] or ['kɑfər] *s* forziere *m;* (*ceiling*) soffitto a cassettoni; (*archit*) cassettone *m;* **coffers** tesoro

coffin ['kɔfɪn] or ['kɑfɪn] *s* bara

cog [kɑg] *s* dente *m* d'ingranaggio; ruota dentata; **to slip a cog** fare un errore

cogent ['kodʒənt] *adj* convincente, persuasivo

cogitate ['kɑdʒɪ‚tet] *tr & intr* cogitare, ponzare

cognac ['kɔnjæk] or ['kɑnjæk] *s* cognac *m*

cognate ['kɑgnet] *adj* consanguineo, parente, affine ‖ *s* parola dello stesso ceppo linguistico; consanguineo, parente *mf*

cognizance ['kɑgnɪzəns] or ['kɑnɪzəns] *s* conoscenza; **to take cognizance of** prendere conoscenza di

cognizant ['kɑgnɪzənt] or ['kɑnɪzənt] *adj* informato, al corrente

cog'wheel' *s* ruota dentata

cohabit [ko'hæbɪt] *intr* convivere; (*archaic*) coabitare

coheir [ko'ɛr] *s* coerede *mf*

cohere [ko'hɪr] *intr* aderire; (fig) avere nesso

coherent [ko'hɪrənt] *adj* coerente

coiffeur [kwɑ'fʌr] *s* parrucchiere *m* per signora; (Brit) parrucchiere *m*

coiffure [kwɑ'fjur] *s* pettinatura ‖ *tr* pettinare

coil [kɔɪl] *s* (*of rope*) rotolo; (*of pipe*) serpentino; (*of wire*) bobina, avvolgimento ‖ *tr* arrotolare ‖ *intr* arrotolarsi

coil' spring' *s* molla a spirale, molla elicoidale

coin [kɔɪn] *s* moneta; **to pay back in one's own coin** pagare della stessa moneta; **to toss a coin** giocare a testa o croce ‖ *tr* (*money*) coniare, battere; (*words*) inventare, creare; **to coin money** battere moneta; (coll) fare soldoni

coincide [‚ko‧ɪn'saɪd] *intr* coincidere

coincidence [ko'ɪnsɪdəns] *s* coincidenza

coke [kok] *s* coke *m*, carbone *m* coke

colander ['kʌləndər] or ['kɑləndər] *s* colabrodo, colapasta *m*

cold [kold] *adj* freddo; **it is cold** (*said of weather*) fa freddo; **to be cold** (*said of a person*) avere freddo ‖ *s* freddo; (*ailment*) raffreddore *m;* **out in the cold** solo soletto; **to catch cold** pigliare freddo, pigliarsi un raffreddore

cold' blood' *s*—**in cold blood** a sangue freddo

cold'-blood'ed *adj* insensibile; (*sensitive to cold*) freddoloso; (*animal*) a sangue freddo

cold' chis'el *s* tagliaferro

cold' com'fort *s* magra consolazione

cold' cream' *s* crema emolliente

cold' cuts' *spl* salumi *mpl*, affettato

cold' feet' *spl*—**to get cold feet** (coll) perdersi d'animo

cold'-heart'ed *adj*—**to be coldhearted** avere il cuore duro

coldness ['koldnɪs] *s* freddezza

cold' shoul'der *s*—**to get the cold shoulder** (coll) essere trattato con freddezza; **to turn a cold shoulder on** (coll) trattare con freddezza

cold' snap' *s* freddo breve e improvviso

cold' stor'age *s* conservazione a freddo

cold' war' *s* guerra fredda

cold' wave' *s* ondata di freddo

coleslaw ['kol‚slɔ] *s* insalata di cavolo cappuccio

colic ['kɑlɪk] *adj* colico ‖ *s* colica

coliseum [‚kɑlɪ'si‧əm] *s* stadio, arena ‖ **Coliseum** *s* Colosseo

collaborate [kə'læbə‚ret] *intr* collaborare

collaborationist [kə‚læbə're∫ənɪst] *s* collaborazionista *mf*

collaborator [kə'læbə‚retər] *s* collaboratore *m*

collapse [kə'læps] *s* (*of business*) fallimento; (*e.g., of a roof*) caduta; (*of a person*) collasso ‖ *tr* piegare ‖ *intr* (*to shrink*) restringersi, sgonfiarsi; (*said of a business*) fallire; (*said of health*) venir meno; (*said, e.g., of a roof*) cadere, crollare

collapsible [kə'læpsɪbəl] *adj* pieghevole, smontabile

collar ['kɑlər] *s* (*of shirt*) colletto; (*for dog or horse*) collare *m;* (*ring*) anello; (*short piece of pipe*) manicotto ‖ *tr* afferrare per il collo, catturare

col'lar•band' *s* cinturino della camicia

col'lar•bone' *s* clavicola

collate [kə'let] or ['kɑlet] *tr* collazionare, confrontare

collateral [kə'lætərəl] *adj* collaterale; accessorio, addizionale ‖ *s* collaterale *m*

colleague ['kɑlig] *s* collega *mf*

collect ['kɑlekt] *s* (eccl) colletta ‖ [kə'lekt] *adv* contro assegno; (telp) pagamento all'abbonato chiamato ‖ *tr* raccogliere, riunire; (*e.g., stamps*) collezionare; (*mail*) levare; (*bills*) incassare; (*ideas*) coordinare; (*thoughts*) riordinare; (*e.g., classroom papers*) raccogliere; (*taxes*) riscuotere; **to collect oneself** riprendersi, riprendere il controllo di sé stesso ‖ *intr* (*for the poor*) fare la colletta; riunirsi, raccogliersi

collected [kə'lektɪd] *adj* raccolto; equilibrato, padrone di sè

collection [kə'lek∫ən] *s* collezione; (*for the poor*) colletta; (*of mail*) levata; (*heap*) deposito; (*of taxes*) esazione; (*of bills*) riscossione

collec'tion a'gency *s* agenzia di riscossione

collective [kə'lektɪv] *adj* collettivo

collector [kə'lektər] *s* (*of stamps*) collezionista *mf;* (*of taxes*) esattore *m;* (*of tickets*) controllore *m*

college ['kɑlɪdʒ] *s* scuola superiore,

università *f; (e.g., of medicine)* facoltà *f; (electoral)* collegio
collide [kə'laɪd] *intr* collidere, scontrarsi
collie ['kɑli] *s* collie *m*
collier ['kɑljər] *s (ship)* carboniera; *(min)* minatore *m* di carbone
collier•y ['kɑljəri] *s (-ies)* miniera di carbone
collision [kə'lɪʒən] *s* collisione
colloid ['kɑlɔɪd] *adj* colloidale ‖ *s* colloide *m*
colloquial [kə'lokwɪ-əl] *adj* familiare, colloquiale
colloquialism [kə'lokwɪ-ə,lɪzəm] *s* espressione familiare
collo•quy ['kɑləkwi] *s (-quies)* colloquio
collusion [kə'luʒən] *s* collusione; **to be in collusion with** essere d'intelligenza con
cologne [kə'lon] *s* acqua di colonia, colonia ‖ **Cologne** *s* Colonia
colon ['kolən] *s (anat)* colon *m; (gram)* due punti *mpl*
colonel ['kʌrnəl] *s* colonnello
colonist ['kɑlənɪst] *s* colono, coloniale *m*
colonize ['kɑlə,naɪz] *tr & intr* colonizzare
colonnade [,kɑlə'ned] *s* colonnato
colo•ny ['kɑləni] *s (-nies)* colonia
color ['kʌlər] *s* colore *m; off color* sbiadito, scolorito; *(slang)* sporco, volgare; **the colors** i colori, la bandiera; **to call to the colors** chiamare in servizio militare; **to change color** cambiar colore; arrossire; impallidire; **to give or lend color to** far parere probabile; **to lose color** impallidire; **to show one's colors** mostrarsi come si è; **under color of** sotto il pretesto di ‖ *tr* colorare; *(fig)* colorire ‖ *intr* arrossire
col'or-blind' *adj* daltonico
colored ['kʌlərd] *adj* colorato; *(person)* di colore; esagerato
colorful ['kʌlərfəl] *adj* colorito, espressivo
col'or guard' *s* guardia d'onore alla bandiera
coloring ['kʌlərɪŋ] *s* colorazione; colore *m;* pigmento; *(fig)* specie *f*
colorless ['kʌlərlɪs] *adj* incolore, incoloro
col'or photog'raphy *s* fotografia a colori
col'or ser'geant *s* sergente *m* portabandiera
col'or tel'evision *s* televisione a colori
colossal [kə'lɑsəl] *adj* colossale
colossus [kə'lɑsəs] *s* colosso
colt [kolt] *s* puledro
Columbus [kə'lʌmbəs] *s* Colombo
column ['kɑləm] *s* colonna
columnist ['kɑləmnɪst] *s* giornalista incaricato di una colonna speciale; articolista *m*
coma ['komə] *s* coma *m*
comb [kom] *s* pettine *m; (for horse)* striglia; *(of hen or wave)* cresta; *(honeycomb)* favo ‖ *tr* pettinare;

(fig) esaminare minuziosamente ‖ *intr (said of waves)* frangersi
com•bat ['kɑmbæt] *s* combattimento ‖ ['kɑmbæt] *or* [kəm'bæt] *v (pret & pp* -bated *or* -batted; *ger* -bating *or* -batting) *tr & intr* combattere
combatant ['kɑmbətənt] *s* combattente *mf*
com'bat du'ty *s* servizio in zona di guerra
combination [,kɑmbɪ'neʃən] *s* combinazione
combine ['kɑmbaɪn] *s* consorzio; *(pol)* coalizione; mieto-trebbiatrice *f* ‖ [kəm'baɪn] *tr* combinare ‖ *intr* combinarsi
combin'ing form' *s* membro di parola composta
combo ['kɑmbo] *s* orchestrina
combustible [kəm'bʌstɪbəl] *adj & s* combustibile *m*
combustion [kəm'bʌstʃən] *s* combustione
come [kʌm] *v (pret* came [kem]; *pp* come) *intr* venire; arrivare; *(to become)* diventare; *(to amount)* ammontare; **come!** macchè!; **come along!** andiamo!; **come in!** avanti!, entri!; **come on!** andiamo!, avanti!, coraggio!; **to come about** accadere, succedere; **to come across** incontrarsi con; *(slang)* pagare; **to come around** cedere; mettersi d'accordo; *(said of health)* rimettersi; **to come at** raggiungere; *(to attack)* attaccare; **to come back** ritornare; **to come between** mettersi fra; **to come by** ottenere; **to come down** scendere; decadere; essere trasmesso; **to come down with** ammalarsi di; **to come forward** farsi avanti; **to come in** entrare, passare; **to come in for** ricevere; **to come into** ricevere; ereditare; **to come off** succedere; riuscire; **to come on** mostrarsi; migliorare; incontrarsi; **to come out** uscire; debuttare in società; andare a finire; **to come out with** uscire con; mostrare; **to come over** succedere a, *e.g., what came over him?* che gli è successo?; **to come through** riuscire; **to come to** riprendere i sensi; **to come under** essere di competenza di; appartenere a; **to come up** salire; **to come up to** salire fino a; avvicinarsi a; **to come up with** raggiungere; produrre, fornire; proporre
come'back' *s (coll)* ritorno; *(slang)* pronta risposta; **to stage a comeback** *(coll)* ritornare in auge
comedian [kə'midɪ-ən] *s* attore comico; *(author)* commediografo; *(amusing person)* commediante *mf*
comedienne [kə,midɪ'ɛn] *s* attrice comica
come'down' *s (coll)* rovescio di fortuna
come•dy ['kɑmədi] *s (-dies)* commedia
come•ly ['kʌmli] *adj (-lier; -liest)* bello, grazioso
comet ['kɑmɪt] *s* cometa
comfort ['kʌmfərt] *s* conforto, sollievo;

(ease) benessere *m* || *tr* confortare, alleviare

comfortable ['kʌmfərtəbəl] *adj* comodo, agiato; *(e.g., income)* (coll) bastante || *s* coltre *f*

comforter ['kʌmfərtər] *s* consolatore *m*; *(bedcover)* coltre *f*; sciarpa di lana || **the Comforter** lo Spirito Santo, lo Spirito Consolatore

comforting ['kʌmfərtɪŋ] *adj* confortante

com'fort sta'tion *s* latrina pubblica

comic ['kamɪk] *adj* comico || *s (actor)* comico; comicità *f*; **comics** fumetti *mpl*

comical ['kamɪkəl] *adj* comico

com'ic book' *s* libretto a fumetti

com'ic op'era *s* opera buffa

com'ic strip' *s* racconto umoristico a fumetti

coming ['kʌmɪŋ] *adj* venturo, prossimo; promettente || *s* venuta

com'ing out' *s* debutto in società; *(e.g., of stock)* emissione

comma ['kamə] *s* virgola

command [kə'mænd] *or* [kə'mand] *s* comando; *(e.g., of a language)* padronanza || *tr* comandare, ordinare; *(to overlook)* dominare; *(to be able to have)* disporre di || *intr* avere il comando

commandant [,kamən'dænt] *or* [,kamən'dant] *s* comandante *m*

commandeer [,kamən'dɪr] *tr* requisire

commander [kə'mændər] *or* [kə'mandər] *s (of knighthood)* commendatore *m*; (mil) comandante *m*; (nav) capitano di vascello

command'er in chief' *s* comandante *m* in capo

command'ing of'ficer *s* comandante *m*

commandment [kə'mændmənt] *or* [kə'mandmənt] *s* comandamento

command' mod'ule *s* (rok) modulo di comando

commando [kə'mændo] *s* guastatore *m*

commemorate [kə'mɛmə,ret] *tr* commemorare, celebrare

commence [kə'mɛns] *tr & intr* cominciare

commencement [kə'mɛnsmənt] *s* inizio, esordio; *(in a school)* cerimonia per la distribuzione dei diplomi

commend [kə'mɛnd] *tr* lodare; *(to entrust)* raccomandare, affidare

commendable [kə'mɛndəbəl] *adj (person)* lodevole; *(act)* commendevole

commendation [,kamən'defən] *s* lode *f*; raccomandazione; (mil) citazione

comment ['kament] *s* commento || *tr* commentare || *intr* fare commenti; **to comment on** fare commenti su

commentary ['kamən,teri] *s (-ies)* commentario

commentator ['kamən,tetər] *s* commentatore *m*

commerce ['kamərs] *s* commercio

commercial [kə'mɛr/əl] *adj* commerciale || *s* (rad, telv) programma *m* di pubblicità; (rad, telv) annunzio pubblicitario

commiserate [kə'mɪzə,ret] *intr*—**to**

commiserate with commiserare, compiangere

commissar ['kamɪ,sar] *or* [,kamɪ'sar] *s* commissario del popolo

commissary ['kamɪ,sɛri] *s (-ies)* *(store)* economato; *(deputy)* commissario; *(in army)* intendente *m*

commission [kə'mɪ/ən] *s* commissione; *(e.g., in army)* nomina, brevetto; autorità *f*; *(of a crime)* perpetrazione; (il) fare; **in commission** in servizio, in uso; **out of commission** fuori servizio || *tr* nominare, dare un brevetto a; autorizzare; *(a ship)* armare

commis'sioned of'ficer *s* (mil, nav) ufficiale *m*

commissioner [kə'mɪ/ənər] *s* commissario; membro di una commissione

commis'sion mer'chant *s* sensale *m*

com·mit [kə'mɪt] *v (pret & pp -mitted; ger -mitting)* *tr* commettere, perpetrare; *(to deliver)* affidare, consegnare; *(to imprison)* mandare in prigione; *(an insane person)* internare; *(to refer)* rinviare; *(to involve)* comprometterse; **to commit oneself** compromettersi; **to commit to memory** imparare a memoria; **to commit to writing** mettere in iscritto

commitment [kə'mɪtmənt] *s (act of committing)* commissione; *(to an asylum)* internamento; promessa; (law) mandato

committal [kə'mɪtəl] *s* consegna; promessa

committee [kə'mɪti] *s* comitato, commissione

commode [kə'mod] *s (chest of drawers)* cassettone *m*; *(washstand)* lavabo; seggetta, comoda

commodious [kə'modi-əs] *adj* spazioso; conveniente

commodity [kə'madti] *s (-ties)* merce *f*; articolo di prima necessità

commod'ity exchange' *s* borsa merci

common ['kamən] *adj* comune || *s* fondo comunale; pascolo comune; **commons** gente *f* non nobile; refettorio; **in common** in comune || **the Commons** la Camera dei Comuni

com'mon car'rier *s* impresa di trasporti pubblici

commoner ['kamənər] *s* plebeo, borghese *m*; membro della Camera dei Comuni

com'mon law' *s* consuetudine *f*, diritto consuetudinario

com'mon-law mar'riage *s* matrimonio basato sulla mera convivenza

commonly ['kamənli] *adv* generalmente

com'mon·place' *adj* banale, ordinario || *s* banalità *f*, cosa ordinaria

com'mon sense' *s* senso comune

com'mon-sense' *adj* giudizioso

com'mon stock' *s* azione ordinaria; azioni ordinarie

commonweal ['kamən,wil] *s* bene pubblico

com'mon·wealth' *s (citizens of a state)* cittadinanza; repubblica; *(one of the*

50 states of the U.S.A.) stato; comunità *f*, federazione

commotion [kə'moʃən] *s* agitazione

commune [kə'mjun] *s* comune *m* || *intr* confabulare; (eccl) comunicarsi

communicate [kə'mjunɪ,ket] *tr & intr* comunicare

communicating [kə'mjunɪ,ketɪŋ] *adj* comunicante

communication [kə,mjunɪ'keʃən] *s* comunicazione; **communications** sistema *m* di comunicazione; mezzi *mpl* di comunicazione

communicative [kə'mjunɪ,ketɪv] *adj* comunicativo

Communion [kə'mjunjən] *s* Comunione; **to take Communion** comunicarsi

communiqué [kə,mjunɪ'ke] or [kə-'mjunɪ,ke] *s* comunicato

communism ['kɑmjə,nɪzəm] *s* comunismo

communist ['kɑmjənɪst] *s* comunista *mf*

communi·ty [kə'mjunɪti] *s* (-ties) *(people living together)* comunità *f*; *(sharing together)* comunanza; *(neighborhood)* circondario

commu'nity cen'ter *s* centro sociale

commu'nity chest' *s* fondo di beneficenza

commuta'tion tick'et [,kɑmjə'teʃən] *s* biglietto d'abbonamento

commutator ['kɑmjə,tetər] *s* *(switch)* commutatore *m*; *(of dynamo or motor)* collettore *m*

commute [kə'mjut] *tr* commutare || *intr* commutare; fare il pendolare

commuter [kə'mjutər] *s* pendolare *mf*

compact [kəm'pækt] *adj* compatto || ['kɑmpækt] *s* *(small case for face powder)* portacipria *m*; *(agreement)* accordo; *(small car)* utilitaria

companion [kəm'pænjən] *s* compagno; *(one of two items)* pendant *m*; *(lady)* dama di compagnia

compan'ion·ship' *s* cameratismo

compan'ion·way' *s* (naut) scaletta per andare sottocoperta

compa·ny ['kʌmpəni] *s* (-nies) compagnia; (coll) ospite *m* or ospiti *mpl*; (naut) equipaggio; **to bear company** accompagnare; **to be good company** essere simpatico; **to keep company** *(said of a couple)* andare insieme; **to keep company with** accompagnare; (coll) fare la corte a; **to part company** separarsi

comparable ['kɑmpərəbəl] *adj* comparabile, paragonabile

comparative [kəm'pærətɪv] *adj* comparativo; *(e.g., anatomy)* comparato || *s* (gram) comparativo

compare [kəm'per] *s*—**beyond compare** incomparabile || *tr* confrontare; **compared to** a confronto di, in confronto a

comparison [kəm'pærɪsən] *s* confronto; (gram) comparazione; **in comparison with** in confronto a, a confronto di

compartment [kəm'pɑrtmənt] *s* compartimento; (naut) compartimento stagno; (rr) compartimento

compass ['kʌmpəs] *s* *(instrument for showing direction)* bussola; *(boundary)* limite *m*; *(range)* ambito; *(range of voice)* portata; *(of a wall)* cerchia; *(circuit)* circuito; *(drawing instrument)* compasso; **compasses** *(drawing instrument)* compasso || *tr* girare intorno a; comprendere; **to compass about** accerchiare

com'pass card' *s* rosa dei venti

compassion [kəm'pæʃən] *s* compassione

compassionate [kəm'pæʃənɪt] *adj* compassionevole

com'pass saw' *s* gattuccio

com·pel [kəm'pel] *v* (*pret & pp* -**pelled;** *ger* -**pelling**) *tr* forzare, obbligare

compelling [kəm'pelɪŋ] *adj* imperioso, coercitivo

compendious [kəm'pendɪ·əs] *adj* compendioso, conciso

compensate ['kɑmpən,set] *tr & intr* compensare

compensation [,kɑmpən'seʃən] *s* compensazione; *(pay)* pagamento; *(something given to offset a loss)* risarcimento, indennità *f*

compete [kəm'pit] *intr* competere

competence ['kɑmpɪtəns] or **competency** ['kɑmpɪtənsi] *s* *(fitness)* abilità *f*; *(money)* agiatezza; *(authority)* competenza

competent ['kɑmpɪtənt] *adj* abile; competente

competition [,kɑmpɪ'tɪʃən] *s* competizione, gara; *(in business)* concorrenza

competitive [kəm'petɪtɪv] *adj* competitivo; *(based on competition)* di concorso

compet'itive pric'es *spl* prezzi *mpl* di concorrenza

competitor [kəm'petɪtər] *s* competitore *m*, concorrente *mf*; rivale *mf*

compilation [,kɑmpɪ'leʃən] *s* compilazione

compile [kəm'paɪl] *tr* compilare

complacence [kəm'plesəns] or **complacency** [kəm'plesənsi] *s* compiacenza; compiacenza di sé stesso

complacent [kəm'plesənt] *adj* compiaciuto or soddisfatto con sé stesso

complain [kəm'plen] *intr* lagnarsi

complainant [kəm'plenənt] *s* (law) querelante *mf*

complaint [kəm'plent] *s* lagnanza, reclamo; *(sickness)* malattia; (law) querela

complaisance [kəm'plezəns] or ['kɑmplɪ,zæns] *s* compiacenza

complaisant [kəm'plezənt] or ['kɑmplɪ,zænt] *adj* compiacente, cortese

complement ['kɑmplɪmənt] *s* complemento; (naut) equipaggio || ['kɑmplɪ,ment] *tr* completare

complete [kəm'plit] *adj* completo; *(done)* finito || *tr* completare, finire

completion [kəm'pliʃən] *s* completamento, compimento

complex [kəm'pleks] or ['kɑmpleks]

adj complesso, complicato || ['kam-pleks] *s* complesso

complexion [kəm'plekʃən] *s* (*of skin*) carnagione; (*appearance*) aspetto; (*viewpoint*) punto di vista

compliance [kəm'plaɪ·əns] *s* condiscendenza, arrendevolezza; **in compliance with** in conformità di

complicate ['kamplɪ‚ket] *tr* complicare

complicated ['kamplɪ‚ketɪd] *adj* complicato

complici‧ty [kəm'plɪsɪti] *s* (**-ties**) complicità *f*

compliment ['kamplɪmənt] *s* complimento, omaggio || ['kamplɪ‚ment] *tr*—**to compliment s.o. on s.th** felicitarsi con qlcu per qlco; **to compliment s.o. with s.th** regalare qlco a qlcu

complimentary [‚kamplɪ'mentəri] *adj* complimentoso, lusinghiero; (*free*) in omaggio, gratis; (*ticket*) di favore

com‧ply [kəm'plaɪ] *v* (*pret & pp* **-plied**) *intr* acconsentire, accondiscendere; **to comply with** accedere a

component [kəm'ponənt] *adj* componente, costituente || *s* (*component part*) componente *m*; (*force*) componente *f*

compose [kəm'poz] *tr* comporre; **to be composed of** essere composto di; **to compose oneself** calmarsi

composed [kəm'pozd] *adj* calmo, tranquillo

composer [kəm'pozər] *s* (*peacemaker*) conciliatore *m*; (*mus*) compositore *m*

compos'ing stick' *s* (*typ*) compositoio

composite [kəm'pazɪt] *adj & s* composto, composito

composition [‚kampə'zɪʃən] *s* composizione; (*agreement*) compromesso

compositor [kəm'pazɪtər] *s* compositore *m*

compost ['kampost] *s* concime *m* naturale

composure [kəm'pozər] *s* calma

compote ['kampot] *s* (*stewed fruit*) composta; (*dish*) compostiera

compound ['kampaʊnd] *adj* composto; (*fracture*) complesso; (*archit, bot*) composito || *s* composto; parola composta; (*yard*) recinto || [kam'paʊnd] *tr* (*to mix*) combinare; (*to settle*) comporre; (*interest*) capitalizzare

comprehend [‚kamprɪ'hend] *tr* comprendere

comprehensible [‚kamprɪ'hensɪbəl] *adj* comprensibile

comprehension [‚kamprɪ'henʃən] *s* comprensione

comprehensive [‚kamprɪ'hensɪv] *adj* comprensivo

compress ['kampres] *s* compressa || [kəm'pres] *tr* comprimere

compressed' air' *s* aria compressa

compression [kəm'preʃən] *s* compressione

comprise [kəm'praɪz] *tr* comprendere, includere; **to be comprised of** consistere di

compromise ['kamprə‚maɪz] *s* compromesso || *tr* (*a dispute*) transigere, comporre; (*to put in danger*) compromettere || *intr* transigere, fare un compromesso

comptroller [kən'trolər] *s* economo, amministratore *m*, controllore *m*

compulsive [kəm'pʌlsɪv] *adj* obbligatorio, coercitivo; (psychol) compulsivo

compulsory [kəm'pʌlsəri] *adj* obbligatorio

compute [kəm'pjut] *tr & intr* computare, calcolare

computer [kəm'pjutər] *s* calcolatore *m*; elaboratore *m*

comrade ['kamræd] *or* ['kamrɪd] *s* camerata *m*, compagno

com'rade in arms' *s* compagno d'armi

con [kan] *s* contro || *v* (*pret & pp* **conned**) *ger* **conning**) *tr* imparare a memoria; (slang) imbrogliare

concave ['kankev] *or* [kan'kev] *adj* concavo

conceal [kən'sil] *tr* nascondere; (*to keep secret*) celare

concealment [kən'silmənt] *s* occultamento; (*place*) nascondiglio

concede [kən'sid] *tr* concedere

conceit [kən'sit] *s* (*high opinion of oneself*) presunzione; (*fanciful notion*) concetto sottile

conceited [kən'sitɪd] *adj* vanitoso

conceivable [kən'sivəbəl] *adj* concepibile

conceive [kən'siv] *tr & intr* concepire

concentrate ['kansən‚tret] *s* concentrato || *tr* concentrare || *intr* concentrarsi; **to concentrate on** concentrarsi in

concentra'tion camp' [‚kansən'treʃən] *s* campo di concentrazione

concept ['kansept] *s* concetto

conception [kən'sepʃən] *s* concezione

concern [kən'sʌrn] *s* interesse *m*; (*worry*) ansietà *f*; (*firm*) ditta, compagnia; **of concern** d'interesse || *tr* concernere; **as concerns** circa; **to concern oneself** interessarsi; **to whom it may concern** a chiunque possa averne interesse

concerning [kən'sʌrnɪŋ] *prep* riguardo a

concert ['kansərt] *s* concerto || [kən'sʌrt] *tr & intr* concertare

con'cert‧mas'ter *s* primo violino

concer‧to [kən'tʃɛrto] *s* (**-tos** *or* **-ti** [ti]) concerto

concession [kən'seʃən] *s* concessione

conciliate [kən'sɪlɪ‚et] *tr* conciliare, conciliarsi con

concise [kən'saɪs] *adj* conciso

conclude [kən'klud] *tr* concludere || *intr* concludersi, terminare

conclusion [kən'kluʒən] *s* conclusione; **in conclusion** per finire; **to try conclusions with** misurarsi con

conclusive [kən'klusɪv] *adj* decisivo, convincente

concoct [kən'kakt] *tr* preparare, confezionare; (*a story*) inventare

concoction [kan'kakʃən] *s* preparazione, mescolanza; (*unpleasant in taste*) intruglio

concomitant [kən'kɑmɪtənt] *adj* concomitante || *s* fatto or sintomo concomitante

concord ['kɑŋkɔrd] *s* concordia, armonia; (*treaty*) accordo; (gram) concordanza

concourse ['kɑŋkors] *s* confluenza; (*crowd*) affluenza, concorso; (*boulevard*) viale *m*; (rr) salone *m* principale

concrete ['kɑnkrit] or [kɑn'krit] *adj* concreto; fatto di cemento; solido || *s* cemento, calcestruzzo || *tr* (e.g., *a sidewalk*) cementare

con'crete mix'er *s* betoniera

con·cur [kən'kʌr] *v* (*pret & pp* **-curred;** *ger* **-curring**) *intr* (*to work together*) concorrere; (*to agree*) essere d'accordo, aderire

concurrence [kən'kʌrəns] *s* concorso; (*agreement*) accordo

concurrent [kən'kʌrənt] *adj* concomitante, simultaneo; cooperante; armonioso

concussion [kən'kʌʃən] *s* scossa, urto; (*of brain*) commozione cerebrale

condemn [kən'dem] *tr* condannare; (*to take for public use*) espropriare

condemnation [,kɑndem'neʃən] *s* condanna

condense [kən'dens] *tr* condensare || *intr* condensarsi

condescend [,kɑndɪ'send] *intr* condiscendere, degnarsi

condescending [,kɑndɪ'sendɪŋ] *adj* condiscendente

condescension [,kɑndɪ'senʃən] *s* condiscendenza, degnazione

condiment ['kɑndɪmənt] *s* condimento

condition [kən'dɪʃən] *s* condizione; clausola; **on condition that** a condizione che || *tr* condizionare; mettere in buone condizioni fisiche

conditional [kən'dɪʃənəl] *adj & s* condizionale *m*

condole [kən'dol] *intr* condolersi

condolence [kən'doləns] *s* condoglianza

condone [kən'don] *tr* condonare

conduce [kən'djus] or [kən'dus] *intr* contribuire, indurre

conducive [kən'djusɪv] or [kən'dusɪv] *adj* contribuente

conduct ['kɑndʌkt] *s* condotta; direzione || [kən'dʌkt] *tr* condurre; (*an orchestra*) dirigere; **to conduct oneself** condursi, comportarsi || *intr* dirigere

conductor [kən'dʌktər] '*s* direttore *m*; (*of a streetcar*) fattorino, conduttore *m*; (phys) conduttore *m*; (rr) capotreno

conduit ['kɑndɪt] or ['kɑndu·ɪt] *s* condotto

cone [kon] *s* cono; (bot) pigna

Con'estoga wag'on ['kɑnɪ'stogə] *s* carriaggio coperto

confectioner [kən'fekʃənər] *s* confettiere *m*, pasticcere *m*

confec'tioners' sug'ar *s* zucchero in polvere finissimo

confectioner·y [kən'fekʃə,neri] *s* (**-ies**) confetteria, pasticceria; (*candies*) confetture *fpl*

confedera·cy [kən'fedərəsi] *s* (**-cies**) confederazione; lega

confederate [kən'fedərɪt] *s* alleato; (*in crime*) complice *mf* || [kən'fedə,ret] *tr* confederare || *intr* confederarsi

con·fer [kən'fʌr] *v* (*pret & pp* **-ferred;** *ger* **-ferring**) *tr* conferire || *intr* conferire, abboccarsi

conference ['kɑnfərəns] *s* conferenza

confess [kən'fes] *tr* confessare, ammettere || *intr* confessare, confessarsi

confession [kən'feʃən] *s* confessione

confessional [kən'feʃənəl] *s* confessionale *m*

confes'sion of faith' *s* professione di fede

confessor [kən'fesər] *s* confessore *m*

confetti [kən'feti] *s* coriandoli *mpl*

confide [kən'faɪd] *tr* confidare; (*to entrust*) affidare || *intr* confidarsi

confidence ['kɑnfɪdəns] *s* fiducia; sicurezza di sé; (*boldness*) baldanza; (*secrecy*) confidenza

confident ['kɑnfɪdənt] *adj* fiducioso; baldanzoso || *s* confidente *mf*

confidential [,kɑnfɪ'denʃəl] *adj* confidenziale

confine ['kɑnfaɪn] *s* confine *m* || [kən'faɪn] *tr* limitare; confinare; **to be confined** essere in altro stato; **to be confined to bed** dover stare a letto

confinement [kən'faɪnmənt] *s* confino; (*childbirth*) parto; (*imprisonment*) prigionia

confirm [kən'fʌrm] *tr* confermare; (eccl) cresimare

confirmed [kən'fʌrmd] *adj* (e.g., *piece of news*) confermato; (*bachelor; drunkard*) impenitente; inveterato; (e.g., *invalid*) cronico

confiscate ['kɑnfɪs,ket] *tr* confiscare

conflagration [,kɑnflə'greʃən] *s* conflagrazione

conflict ['kɑnflɪkt] *s* conflitto || [kən-'flɪkt] *intr* lottare; essere in conflitto

conflicting [kən'flɪktɪŋ] *adj* contrastante; contraddittorio

confluence ['kɑnflu·əns] *s* confluenza

conform [kən'fɔrm] *tr* conformare || *intr* conformarsi

conformi·ty [kən'fɔrmɪti] *s* (**-ties**) conformità *f*; **in conformity with** in conformità di

confound [kɑn'faʊnd] *tr* confondere || ['kɑn'faʊnd] *tr* maledire; **confound it!** accidenti!

confounded [kɑn'faʊndɪd] or ['kɑn-'faʊndɪd] *adj* maledetto; (*hateful*) odioso

confront [kən'frʌnt] *tr* affrontare, opporsi a; (*to bring face to face*) raffrontare; (*to compare*) confrontare

confrontation [,kɑnfrən'teʃən] *s* contestazione

confuse [kən'fjuz] *tr* confondere; **to get confused** confondersi

confusion [kən'fjuʒən] *s* confusione

congeal [kən'dʒil] *tr* congelare; coagulare || *intr* congelarsi; (*said, e.g., of blood*) coagularsi

congenial [kən'dʒinjəl] *adj* (*agreeable*) simpatico; (*having similar tastes*) affine; (*suited to one's needs or tastes*) congeniale

congenital [kən'dʒenɪtəl] *adj* congenito

con'ger eel' ['kɑŋgər] *s* grongo

congest [kən'dʒest] *tr* congestionare || *intr* essere congestionato

congestion [kən'dʒest/ən] *s* congestione

conglomerate [kən'glɑmərɪt] *adj & s* conglomerato || [kən'glɑmə,ret] *tr* conglomerare || *intr* conglomerarsi

congratulate [kən'græt/ə,let] *tr* congratularsi con

congratulation [kən,grætʃə'leʃən] *s* congratulazione, felicitazione

congregate ['kɑŋgrɪ,get] *intr* congregarsi

congregation [,kɑŋgrɪ'geʃən] *s* congregazione; fedeli *mpl* di una chiesa

congress ['kɑŋgrɪs] *s* parlamento; congresso

con'gress•man *s* (**-men**) deputato al congresso degli S.U.

con'gress•wom'un *s* (**-wom'en**) deputatessa al congresso degli S.U.

conical ['kɑnɪkəl] *adj* conico

conjecture [kən'dʒektʃər] *s* congettura || *tr & intr* congetturare

conjugate ['kɑndʒə,get] *tr* coniugare

conjugation [,kɑndʒə'geʃən] *s* coniugazione

conjunction [kən'dʒʌŋkʃən] *s* congiunzione

conjure [kən'dʒur] *tr* (*to entreat*) scongiurare || ['kɑndʒər] or ['kʌndʒər] *tr* evocare, stregare; **to conjure up** evocare || *intr* fare delle stregonerie

conk [kɑŋk] *intr*—**to conk out** (slang) essere in panna; (slang) svenire

connect [kə'nekt] *tr* connettere, unire || *intr* connettersi, essere associato; (*said of public conveyances*) operare in coincidenza

connect'ing rod' [kə'nektɪŋ] *s* (mach) biella

connection [kə'nekʃən] *s* connessione; unione, associazione; (*of trains*) coincidenza; (*relative*) parente *mf*; (*e.g., of a water pipe*) allacciamento; **in connection with** rispetto a

con'ning tow'er ['kɑnɪŋ] *s* (nav) torretta

conniption [kə'nɪpʃən] *s* (slang) attacco di rabbia

connive [kə'naɪv] *intr* essere connivente; **to connive at** chiudere un occhio su

connote [kə'not] *tr* indicare, suggerire

conquer ['kɑŋkər] *tr & intr* conquistare

conqueror ['kɑŋkərər] *s* conquistatore *m*

conquest ['kɑŋkwest] *s* conquista

conscience ['kɑnʃəns] *s* coscienza; **in all conscience** a prezzo onesto; certamente

conscientious [,kɑnʃɪ'enʃəs] *adj* coscienzoso

conscientious objec'tor [ɑb'dʒektər] *s* obiettore *m* di coscienza

conscious ['kɑnʃəs] *adj* (*aware of one's existence*) cosciente; (*aware*) conscio, consapevole; (*lie*) consapevole; **to become conscious** riprendere i sensi

consciousness ['kɑnʃəsnɪs] *s* coscienza, conoscenza; **to lose consciousness** perdere la conoscenza

conscript ['kɑnskrɪpt] *s* coscritto || [kən'skrɪpt] *tr* coscrivere, arruolare

conscription [kən'skrɪpʃən] *s* coscrizione

consecrate ['kɑnsɪ,kret] *tr* consacrare

consecutive [kən'sekjʊtɪv] *adj* consecutivo; di seguito

consensus [kən'sensəs] *s* consenso

consent [kən'sent] *s* consenso; **by common consent** per comune consenso || *intr* consentire

consequence ['kɑnsɪ,kwens] *s* conseguenza

consequential [,kɑnsɪ'kwenʃəl] *adj* conseguente; importante, d'importanza; pomposo, pieno di sé

consequently ['kɑnsɪ,kwentli] *adv* conseguentemente, per conseguenza

conservation [,kɑnsər'veʃən] *s* conservazione; preservazione delle foreste

conservatism [kən'sʌrvə,tɪzəm] *s* conservatorismo

conservative [kən'sʌrvətɪv] *adj* conservatore; (*cautious*) cauto; (*preserving*) conservativo; (*free from fads*) tradizionale || *s* conservatore *m*

conservato•ry [kən'sʌrvə,tori] *s* (**-ries**) (*greenhouse*) serra; (mus) conservatorio

conserve [kən'sʌrv] *tr* conservare

consider [kən'sɪdər] *tr* considerare

considerable [kən'sɪdərəbəl] *adj* (*fairly large*) considerevole; (*worth thinking about*) considerabile

considerate [kən'sɪdərɪt] *adj* riguardoso, premuroso

consideration [kən,sɪdə'reʃən] *s* considerazione; (*reason*) motivo; (*money*) pagamento; **in consideration of** a cagione di; in cambio di; **on no consideration** in nessuna maniera, mai; **under consideration** in considerazione, sotto esame; **without due consideration** senza riflessione, alla leggera

considering [kən'sɪdərɪŋ] *adv* tutto considerato || *prep* per, visto || *conj* considerando che, visto che

consign [kən'saɪn] *tr* consegnare; (*to send*) inviare; (*to set apart*) assegnare

consignee [,kɑnsaɪ'ni] *s* consegnatario

consignment [kən'saɪnmənt] *s* consegna; **on consignment** in consegna

consist [kən'sɪst] *intr*—**to consist in** consistere in; **to consist of** consistere in, constare di

consisten•cy [kən'sɪstənsi] *s* (**-cies**) (*firmness, amount of firmness*) consistenza; (*logical connection*) coerenza

consistent [kən'sɪstənt] *adj* (*holding firmly together*) consistente; (*agree-*

ing with itself or oneself) conseguente, coerente; compatibile

consolation [,kɑnsə'leʃən] *s* consolazione

console ['kɑnsol] *s* (*table*) console *f*; (*rad, telv*) mobile *m;* (*mus*) console *f* ‖ [kən'sol] *tr* consolare

consonant ['kɑnsənənt] *adj* consonante, armonioso; (*gram*) consonantico ‖ *s* consonante *f*

consort ['kɑnsɔrt] *s* consorte *mf* ‖ [kən'sɔrt] *intr* associarsi; (*to agree*) concordarsi

conspicuous [kən'spɪkjuːəs] *adj* visibile, manifesto; notevole; (*too noticeable*) appariscente; **to make oneself conspicuous** farsi notare

conspira•cy [kən'spɪrəsi] *s* (*-cies*) cospirazione, congiura

conspire [kən'spaɪr] *intr* cospirare, congiurare; (*to act together*) cooperare

constable ['kɑnstəbəl] *or* ['kʌnstəbəl] *s* poliziotto; (*keeper of a castle*) conestabile *m*

constancy ['kɑnstənsi] *s* costanza

constant ['kɑnstənt] *adj & s* costante *f*

constellation [,kɑnstə'leʃən] *s* costellazione

constipate ['kɑnstɪ,pet] *tr* costipare

constipation [,kɑnstɪ'peʃən] *s* costipazione

constituen•cy [kən'stɪtʃuːənsi] *s* (*-cies*) (*voters*) elettorato; (*district*) circoscrizione elettorale

constituent [kən'stɪtʃuːənt] *adj* costituente ‖ *s* (*component*) parte *f* costituente; (*voter*) elettore *m;* (*of a chemical substance*) costituente *m*

constitute ['kɑnstɪ,tjut] *or* ['kɑnstɪ,tut] *tr* costituire

constitution [,kɑnstɪ'tjuʃən] *or* [,kɑnstɪ'tuʃən] *s* costituzione

constrain [kən'stren] *tr* (*to force*) costringere; (*to restrain*) restringere, comprimere

constrict [kən'strɪkt] *tr* stringere, comprimere

construct [kən'strʌkt] *tr* costruire

construction [kən'strʌkʃən] *s* costruzione; (*meaning*) interpretazione

construe [kən'stru] *tr* (*to interpret*) interpretare; (*to translate*) tradurre; (*gram*) analizzare

consul ['kɑnsəl] *s* console *m*

consular ['kɑnsələr] *or* ['kɑnsjələr] *adj* consolare

consulate ['kɑnsəlɪt] *or* ['kɑnsjəlɪt] *s* consolato

consult [kən'sʌlt] *tr* consultare ‖ *intr* consultarsi

consultation [,kɑnsəl'teʃən] *s* consultazione, conferenza

consume [kən'sum] *or* [kən'sjum] *tr* consumare; distruggere; **consumed with** (*passion*) arso di; (*curiosity*) assorbito da

consumer [kən'sumər] *or* [kən'sjumər] *s* consumatore *m*

consum'er goods' *spl* beni *mpl* di consumo

consumerism [kən'sumər,ɪzem] *s* consumismo

consummate [kən'sʌmɪt] *adj* consumato ‖ ['kɑnsə,met] *tr* consumare

consumption [kən'sʌmpʃən] *s* (*decay*) consunzione; (*using up*) consumo; (*pathol*) consunzione

consumptive [kən'sʌmptɪv] *adj* tubercolotico, tisico; (*wasteful*) logorante ‖ *s* tisico, etico

contact ['kɑntækt] *s* contatto; (*elec*) contatto; (*elec*) presa di corrente ‖ *tr* mettersi in contatto con ‖ *intr* (*coll*) mettersi in contatto

con'tact break'er *s* ruttore *m*

con'tact lens' *s* lente *f* a contatto

contagion [kən'tedʒən] *s* contagio

contagious [kən'tedʒəs] *adj* contagioso

contain [kən'ten] *tr* contenere; **to contain oneself** frenarsi

container [kən'tenər] *s* recipiente *m*, contenitore *m*

contaminate [kən'tæmɪ,net] *tr* contaminare

contamination [kən,tæmɪ'neʃən] *s* contaminazione

contemplate ['kɑntəm,plet] *tr* contemplare; (*to think about*) meditare; (*to have in mind*) progettare, avere in mente ‖ *intr* meditare

contemplation [,kɑntəm'pleʃən] *s* contemplazione; (*intention*) intenzione

contemporaneous [kən,tempə'renɪ-əs] *adj* contemporaneo, coevo

contemporar•y [kən'tempə,reri] *adj* contemporaneo, coevo ‖ *s* (*-ies*) contemporaneo

contempt [kən'tempt] *s* (*despising*) disprezzo; (*condition of being despised*) dispregio; (*of the law*) disprezzo

contemptible [kən'temptɪbəl] *adj* disprezzabile, spregevole

contempt' of court' *s* (*law*) offesa alla magistratura, oltraggio al tribunale

contemptuous [kən'temptʃuːəs] *adj* sprezzante, sdegnoso

contend [kən'tend] *tr* dichiarare ‖ *intr* (*to argue*) disputare, contendere; (*to fight*) lottare

contender [kən'tendər] *s* competitore *m*, concorrente *m*

content [kən'tent] *adj* contento; (*willing*) pronto ‖ *s* contentezza ‖ ['kɑntent] *s* contenuto; **contents** contenuto ‖ [kən'tent] *tr* contentare

contented [kən'tentɪd] *adj* soddisfatto

contention [kən'tenʃən] *s* disputa, litigio; contenzione

contentious [kən'tenʃəs] *adj* litigioso

contentment [kən'tentmənt] *s* contentezza

contest ['kɑntest] *s* contesa, controversia; (*game*) gara ‖ [kən'test] *tr* disputare, contestare ‖ *intr* combattere, fare resistenza

contestant [kən'testənt] *s* concorrente *m;* (*law*) contendente *m*

context ['kɑntekst] *s* contesto

contiguous [kən'tɪgjuːəs] *adj* contiguo

continence ['kɑntɪnəns] *s* continenza

continent ['kɑntɪnənt] *adj & s* continente *m;* **on the Continent** nel continente europeo

continental [,kɑntɪ'nentəl] *adj & s* continentale *mf*

contingen·cy [kən'tɪndʒənsɪ] *s* (**-cies**) contingenza, congiuntura; (*chance*) eventualità *f*

contingent [kən'tɪndʒənt] *adj* eventuale; imprevisto; (*philos*) contingente; **to be contingent upon** dipendere da

continual [kən'tɪnjʊ·əl] *adj* continuo

continuance [kən'tɪnjʊəns] *s* continuazione; (*in office*) permanenza; (*law*) rinvio

continue [kən'tɪnju] *tr* continuare; (*to cause to remain*) mantenere; (*law*) rinviare ‖ *intr* continuare; rimanere

continui·ty [,kɑntɪ'nju·ɪtɪ] *or* [,kɑntɪ'nu·ɪtɪ] *s* (**-ties**) continuità *f;* (*mov & telv*) sceneggiatura; (*rad*) copione *m*

continuous [kən'tɪnjʊ·əs] *adj* continuo

contin'uous show'ing *s* (*mov*) spettacolo permanente

contortion [kən'tɔrʃən] *s* contorsione; (*of facts*) distorsione

contour ['kɑntʊr] *s* contorno

con'tour line' *s* curva di livello, isoipsa

contraband ['kɑntrə‚bænd] *adj* di contrabbando ‖ *s* contrabbando

contrabass ['kɑntrə‚bes] *s* contrabbasso

contraceptive [,kɑntrə'septɪv] *adj & s* antifecondativo

contract ['kɑntrækt] *s* contratto ‖ ['kɑntrækt] *or* [kən'trækt] *tr* (*a business deal*) contrattare; (*marriage*) contrarre ‖ *intr* (*to shrink*) contrarsi; **to contract for** contrattare, appaltare

contraction [kən'trækʃən] *s* contrazione

contractor [kən'træktər] *s* (*person who makes a contract*) contraente *m;* (*person who contracts to supply material*) appaltatore *m,* imprenditore *m;* (*in building*) capomastro

contradict [,kɑntrə'dɪkt] *tr* contraddire

contradiction [,kɑntrə'dɪkʃən] *s* contraddizione

contradictory [,kɑntrə'dɪktərɪ] *adj* contraddittorio

contrail ['kɑn‚trel] *s* (*aer*) scia di condensazione

contral·to [kən'trælto] *s* (**-tos**) (*person*) contralto *mf;* (*voice*) contralto *m*

contraption [kən'træpʃən] *s* (*coll*) aggeggio

contra·ry ['kɑntrerɪ] *adj* contrario ‖ [kən'trerɪ] *adj* ostinato, caparbio ‖ ['kɑntrerɪ] *s* (**-ries**) contrario; **on the contrary** al contrario ‖ *adv* contrariamente

contrast ['kɑntræst] *s* contrasto ‖ [kən'træst] *tr* confrontare ‖ *intr* contrastare

contravene [,kɑntrə'vin] *tr* contraddire; (*a law*) contravvenire (with *dat*)

contribute [kən'trɪbjut] *tr* contribuire ‖ *intr* contribuire; (*to a newspaper*) collaborare

contribution [,kɑntrɪ'bjuʃən] *s* contribuzione; (*to a newspaper*) collaborazione

contributor [kən'trɪbjutər] *s* contributore *m;* (*to a newspaper*) collaboratore *m*

contrite [kən'traɪt] *adj* contrito

contrition [kən'trɪʃən] *s* contrizione

contrivance [kən'traɪvəns] *s* dispositivo, congegno; (*faculty*) invenzione; (*scheme*) artificio, piano

contrive [kən'traɪv] *tr* inventare; (*to scheme up*) macchinare; (*to bring about*) effettuare; **to contrive to** trovare il modo di

con·trol [kən'trol] *s* controllo; (*check*) freno; **controls** comandi *mpl;* **to get under control** riuscire a controllare ‖ *v* (*pret & pp* **-trolled;** *ger* **-trolling**) *tr* controllare

controller [kən'trolər] *s* controllore *m;* analista *mf* di gestione; economo; (*mach*) regolatore *m;* (*elec*) interruttore *m* di linea

control'ling in'terest *s* maggioranza delle azioni

control' stick' *s* leva di comando

controversial [,kɑntrə'vʌrʃəl] *adj* controverso, polemico, discusso

controver·sy ['kɑntrə‚vʌrsɪ] *s* (**-sies**) controversia

controvert ['kɑntrə‚vʌrt] *or* [,kɑntrə'vʌrt] *tr* contraddire

contumacious [,kɑntju'meʃəs] *or* [,kɑntu'meʃəs] *adj* ribelle, contumace

contuma·cy ['kɑntjuməsɪ] *or* ['kɑntuməsɪ] *s* (**-cies**) contumacia

contusion [kən'tjuʒən] *or* [kən'tuʒən] *s* contusione

conundrum [kə'nʌndrəm] *s* indovinello

convalesce [,kɑnvə'les] *intr* essere convalescente

convalescence [,kɑnvə'lesəns] *s* convalescenza

convalescent [,kɑnvə'lesənt] *adj & s* convalescente *mf*

con'vales'cent home' *s* convalescenziario

convene [kən'vin] *tr* convocare ‖ *intr* convenire

convenience [kən'vinjəns] *s* convenienza; (*comfort*) agio; (*anything that saves work*) conforto; **at your earliest convenience** quanto prima

convenient [kən'vinjənt] *adj* conveniente, adatto; comodo; **convenient to** (*near*) (coll) vicino a

convent ['kɑnvent] *s* convento di religiose

convention [kən'venʃən] *s* convenzione, assemblea; **conventions** (*customs*) convenzioni *fpl*

conventional [kən'venʃənəl] *adj* convenzionale

converge [kən'vʌrdʒ] *intr* convergere

conversant [kən'vʌrsənt] *adj* versato, esperto, dotto

conversation [,kɑnvər'seʃən] *s* conversazione

converse ['kɑnvʌrs] *adj & s* contrario ‖ [kən'vʌrs] *intr* conversare

conversion [kən'vɑrʒən] *s* conversione; (*unlawful appropriation*) malversazione

convert ['kɑnvɑrt] *s* convertito || [kən'vɑrt] *tr* convertire; misappropriare || *intr* convertirsi

convertible [kən'vɑrtɪbəl] *adj & s* convertibile *f*; (*aut*) trasformabile *f*, decappottabile *f*

convex ['kɑnveks] *or* [kɑn'veks] *adj* convesso

convey [kən've] *tr* (*to carry*) trasportare; (*liquids*) convogliare; (*sounds*) trasmettere; (*to express*) esprimere; (*e.g., property*) trasferire

conveyance [kən've·əns] *s* trasporto; veicolo; comunicazione; (*of property*) trasferimento; (*deed*) titolo di proprietà

convey'or belt' [kən've·ər] *s* trasportatore *m*

convict ['kɑnvɪkt] *s* condannato || [kən'vɪkt] *tr* convincere, condannare

conviction [kən'vɪk/ən] *s* condanna; (*belief*) convinzione, convincimento

convince [kən'vɪns] *tr* convincere

convincing [kən'vɪnsɪŋ] *adj* convincente

convivial [kən'vɪvɪ·əl] *adj* (*festive*) conviviale; gioviale, bonaccione

convocation [ˌkɑnvə'ke/ən] *s* convocazione, assemblea

convoke [kən'vok] *tr* convocare

convoy ['kɑnvɔɪ] *s* (*of ships*) convoglio; (*of vehicles*) carovana || *tr* convogliare

convulse [kən'vɑls] *tr* (*to shake*) scuotere; (*to throw into convulsions*) mettere in convulsioni; (*to cause to shake with laughter*) far torcere dalle risa

coo [ku] *intr* tubare, gemere

cook [kʊk] *s* cuoco || *tr* cuocere; **to cook up** (coll) preparare, macchinare || *intr* (*said of food*) cuocere; (*said of a person*) farsi il fuoco

cook'book' *s* libro di cucina

cookie ['kʊki] *s var of* **cooky**

cooking ['kʊkɪŋ] *s* culinaria

cook'out' *s* picnic *m*, spuntino all'aperto

cook'stove' *s* cucina economica

cook·y ['kʊki] *s* (**-ies**) pasticcino, biscotto

cool [kul] *adj* fresco; calmo; (*not cordial*) freddo; (*bold*) sfacciato || *s* fresco || *tr* rinfrescare; **to cool one's heels** fare anticamera || *intr* rinfrescarsi; **to cool off** rinfrescarsi; calmarsi

coolant ['kulənt] *s* miscela refrigerante

cooler ['kulər] *s* ghiacciaia; (slang) prigione

cool'-head'ed *adj* calmo, imperturbabile

coolish ['kulɪ/] *adj* freschetto

coon [kun] *s* procione *m*

coop [kʊp] *s* pollaio; (slang) coniglierà; **to fly the coop** (slang) scapparsene || *tr*— **to coop up** rinchiudere tra quattro mura

cooper ['kupər] *s* bottaio

cooperate [ko'ɑpə ˌret] *intr* cooperare

cooperation [ko ˌɑpə're/ən] *s* cooperazione

cooperative [ko'ɑpə ˌretɪv] *adj* cooperativo || *s* cooperativa

coordinate [ko'ɔrdɪnɪt] *adj* coordinato; (*gram*) coordinativo || *s* (*math*) coordinata || [ko'ɔrdɪˌnet] *tr & intr* coordinare

coot [kut] *s* (*zool*) folaga; (slang) vecchio pazzo

cootie ['kuti] *s* (slang) pidocchio

cop [kɑp] *s* (slang) poliziotto || *v* (*pret & pp* **copped**; *ger* **copping**) *tr* (slang) rubare

copartner [ko'pɑrtnər] *s* consocio, socio

cope [kop] *intr*—**to cope with** tener testa a

cope'stone' *s* pietra da cimasa

copier ['kɑpɪ·ər] *s* (*person*) copista *mf*; imitatore *m*; (*machine*) duplicatore *m*

copilot ['ko ˌpaɪlət] *s* copilota *mf*

coping ['kopɪŋ] *s* coronamento, cimasa

cop'ing saw' *s* seghetto da traforo

copious ['kopɪ·əs] *adj* copioso

copper ['kɑpˈər] *s* rame *m*; (*coin*) soldo; (*boiler*) calderone *m*; (slang) poliziotto

cop'per·head' *s* vipera (*Ancistrodon contortrix*)

cop'per·smith' *s* battirame *m*, calderaio

coppice ['kɑpɪs] *or* **copse** [kɑps] *s* boschetto

copulate ['kɑpjə ˌlet] *intr* copularsi, congiungersi carnalmente

cop·y ['kɑpi] *s* (**-ies**) copia; modello; manoscritto || *v* (*pret & pp* **-ied**) *tr* copiare, imitare || *intr* copiare; **to copy after** imitare

cop'y·book' *s* quaderno

copyist ['kɑpɪ·ɪst] *s* copista *mf*; imitatore *m*

cop'y·right' *s* copyright *m*, diritto di proprietà letteraria || *tr* registrare; proteggere con copyright

cop'y·writ'er *s* copy-writer *m*, redattore *m* pubblicitario

coquet·ry ['kokətrɪ] *or* [ko'ketrɪ] *s* (**-ries**) civetteria

coquette [ko'ket] *s* civetta

coquettish [ko'ketɪ/] *adj* civettuolo

coral ['kɑrəl] *or* ['kɔrəl] *adj* corallino || *s* corallo

cor'al reef' *s* banco di coralli

cord [kɔrd] *s* corda, fune *f*; (*corduroy*) tessuto cordonato; (*elec*) cordone *m* || *tr* legare con corda

cordial ['kɔrdʒəl] *adj & s* cordiale *m*

corduroy ['kɔrdə ˌrɔɪ] *s* velluto a coste; **corduroys** pantaloni *mpl* alla cacciatora

core [kor] *s* (*of fruit*) torsolo; (*central part*) centro; (*of problem*) nocciolo; (*of earth*) barisfera, nucleo centrale; (*phys*) nucleo; **rotten to the core** guasto nelle ossa

corespondent [ˌkorɪs'pɑndənt] *s* coimputato in un processo di divorzio

cork [kɔrk] *s* (*bark*) sughero; (*stopper*) tappo, tappo di sughero || *tr* tappare

cork' oak' *s* sughero

cork′screw′ *s* cavatappi *m*
cormorant [′kɔrmərənt] *s* cormorano
corn [kɔrn] *s* granturco, mais *m;* (*kernel*) chicco; (*thickening of skin*) callo; (*whiskey*) whisky *m* di granturco; (Brit) grano; (Scot) avena; (slang) banalità *f*
corn′ bread′ *s* pane *m* di farina gialla
corn′ cake′ *s* omelette *f* di granturco
corn′cob′ *s* tutolo
corn′cob pipe′ *s* pipa fatta di un tutolo di pannocchia
corn′crib′ *s* granaio per le pannocchie
corn′ cure′ *s* callifugo
cornea [′kɔrnɪ·ə] *s* cornea
corner [′kɔrnər] *s* angolo; (*of street*) cantonata; situazione difficile; (*of the eye*) coda dell'occhio; (com) accaparramento, incetta, bagarinaggio; **to cut corners** tagliare le spese; **to turn the corner** passare il punto più pericoloso ‖ *tr* mettere in una situazione difficile; (*the market*) incettare, accaparrare
cor′ner cup′board *s* cantoniera, armadio d'angolo
cor′ner stone′ *s* pietra angolare; (*of new building*) prima pietra
cornet [kɔr′nɛt] *s* cornetta
corn′ exchange′ *s* borsa dei cereali
corn′field′ *s* (*in U.S.A.*) campo di granturco; (*in England*) campo di grano; (*in Scotland*) campo di avena
corn′flakes′ *spl* fiocchi *mpl* di granturco
corn′ flour′ *s* farina di granturco
corn′flow′er *s* fiordaliso
corn′husk′ *s* brattea, cartoccio
cornice [′kɔrnɪs] *s* (*of house*) cornicione *m;* (*of room*) cornice *f*
corn′ liq′uor *s* whisky *m* di granturco
corn′ meal′ *s* farina di granturco
corn′ on the cob′ *s* granturco servito in pannocchia
corn′ plas′ter *s* cerotto per i calli
corn′ silk′ *s* barba del granturco
corn′stalk′ *s* fusto di granturco
corn′starch′ *s* amido di granturco
corn·y [′kɔrnɪ] *adj* (**-ier; -iest**) (slang) banale, trito, triviale
coronation [,kɔrə′neʃən] or [,kɔrə′neʃən] *s* incoronazione
coroner [′kɔrənər] or [′kɔrənər] *s* magistrato inquirente
cor′oner's in′quest *s* inchiesta giudiziaria dinanzi a giuria
coronet [′kɔrə,nɛt] or [′kɔrə,nɛt] *s* corona (non reale); diadema *m*
corporal [′kɔrpərəl] *adj* caporalesco ‖ *s* caporale *m*
corporation [,kɔrpə′reʃən] *s* società anonima
corps [kor] *s* (**corps** [korz]) corpo
corps′ de bal′let *s* corpo di ballo
corpse [kɔrps] *s* cadavere *m*
corpulent [′kɔrpjələnt] *adj* corpulento
corpuscle [′kɔrpəsəl] *s* (anat) globulo; (phys) corpuscolo
cor·ral [kə′ræl] *s* recinto per bestiame ‖ *v* (*pret & pp* **-ralled;** *ger* **-ralling**) *tr* mettere in un recinto; catturare
correct [kə′rɛkt] *adj* corretto ‖ *tr* correggere
correction [kə′rɛkʃən] *s* correzione

corrective [kə′rɛktɪv] *adj & s* correttivo
correctness [kə′rɛktnɪs] *s* correttezza
correlate [′kɔrə,let] or [′kɔrə,let] *tr* correlare ‖ *intr* essere in correlazione
correlation [,kɔrə′leʃən] or [,kɔrə′leʃən] *s* correlazione
correspond [,kɑrɪ′spɑnd] or [,kɔrɪ′spɑnd] *intr* corrispondere
correspondence [,kɑrɪ′spɑndəns] or [,kɔrɪ′spɑndəns] *s* corrispondenza
correspond′ence school′ *s* scuola per corrispondenza
correspondent [,kɑrɪ′spɑndənt] or [,kɔrɪ′spɑndənt] *adj & s* corrispondente *mf*
corridor [′kɑrɪdər] or [′kɔrɪdər] *s* corridoio
corroborate [kə′rɑbə,ret] *tr* corroborare
corrode [kə′rod] *tr* corrodere ‖ *intr* corrodersi
corrosion [kə′roʒən] *s* corrosione
corrosive [kə′rosɪv] *adj & s* corrosivo
corrugated [′kɔrə,getɪd] or [′kɔrə,getɪd] *adj* ondulato
corrupt [kə′rʌpt] *adj* corrotto ‖ *tr* corrompere; (*a language*) imbarbarire ‖ *intr* corrompersi
corruption [kə′rʌpʃən] *s* corruzione
corsage [kɔr′sɑʒ] *s* (*bodice*) corpetto; (*bouquet*) mazzolino di fiori da appuntarsi al vestito
corsair [′kɔr,sɛr] *s* corsaro
corset [′kɔrsɪt] *s* corsetto
Corsican [′kɔrsɪkən] *adj & s* corso
cortege [kɔr′tɛʒ] *s* corteggio
cor·tex [′kɔr,tɛks] *s* (**-tices** [tɪ,siz]) cortice *f*
cortisone [′kɔrtɪ,son] *s* cortisone *m*
corvette [kɔr′vɛt] *s* corvetta
cosmetic [kaz′mɛtɪk] *adj & s* cosmetico
cosmic [′kazmɪk] *adj* cosmico
cosmonaut [′kazmə,nɔt] *s* cosmonauta *mf*
cosmopolitan [,kazmə′pɑlɪtən] *adj & s* cosmopolita *mf*
cosmos [′kazməs] *s* cosmo
cost [kɔst] or [kast] *s* costo, prezzo; **at all costs** or **at any cost** ad ogni costo; **costs** (law) spese *fpl* processuali ‖ *v* (*pret & pp* **cost**) *intr* costare
cost·ly [′kɔstlɪ] or [′kastlɪ] *adj* (**-lier; -liest**) costoso; (*sumptuous*) lussuoso
cost′ of liv′ing *s* costo della vita
costume [′kastjum] or [′kastum] *s* costume *m*
cos′tume ball′ *s* ballo in costume
cos′tume jew′elry *s* gioielli falsi
cot [kat] *s* (*narrow bed*) branda; (*cottage*) capanna, cabina
coterie [′kotərɪ] *s* gruppo; (*clique*) chiesuola
cottage [′katɪdʒ] *s* casetta, villino
cot′tage cheese′ *s* ricotta americana
cot′ter pin′ [′katər] *s* copiglia, coppiglia
cotton [′katən] *s* cotone *m* ‖ *intr*—**to cotton up to** (coll) cominciare a provare della simpatia per; (coll) andare d'accordo con
cot′ton can′dy *s* zucchero filato

cot'ton gin' *s* sgranatrice *f*

cot'ton pick'er ['pɪkər] *s* chi raccoglie il cotone; macchina che raccoglie il cotone

cot'tonseed oil' *s* olio di semi di cotone

cot'ton waste' *s* cascame *m* di cotone

cot'ton·wood' *s* pioppo deltoide

couch [kautʃ] *s* canapè *m*, sofà *m*, divano || *tr* esprimere

couch' grass' *s* gramigna

cougar ['kugər] *s* puma *m*

cough [kɔf] *or* [kɑf] *s* tosse *f* || *tr*—**to cough up** sputare, sputare tossendo; (slang) dare, pagare || *intr* tossire

cough' drop' *s* pastiglia per la tosse

cough' syr'up *s* sciroppo per la tosse

could [kud] *v aux*—**I could not come yesterday** non ho potuto venire ieri; **I could not see you tomorrow** non potrei vederLa domani; **it could not be so** non potrebbe essere così

council ['kaunsəl] *s* consiglio; (eccl) concilio

coun'cil·man *s* (-men) consigliere *m* or assessore *m* municipale

coun·sel ['kaunsəl] *s* consiglio; (lawyer) avvocato; **to keep one's counsel** essere riservato; **to take counsel with** consultarsi con || *v* (*pret & pp* -seled or -selled) *ger* -seling or -selling) *tr* consigliare || *intr* consigliare; consigliarsi

counselor ['kaunsələr] *s* consigliere *m*; avvocato

count [kaunt] *s* conto; (nobleman) conte *m*; (law) capo d'accusa || *tr* contare; **to count off by** (twos, threes) contare per (due, tre); **to count out** escludere; (boxing) contare || *intr* contare; (to be worth) valere; **to count on** contare su

count'down' *s* conteggio alla rovescia

countenance ['kauntɪnəns] *s* espressione; (face) faccia; (approval) approvazione || *tr* approvare, incoraggiare

counter ['kauntər] *adj* contrario || *s* contatore *m*; (token) gettone *m*; (table in store) banco; (opposite) contrario || *adv* contro, contrariamente || *tr* contrariare, opporre || *intr* (boxing) rispondere

coun'ter·act' *tr* contrariare, neutralizzare

coun'ter·attack' *s* contrattacco || **coun'ter·attack'** *tr & intr* contrattaccare

coun'ter·bal'ance *s* contrappeso || **coun'ter·bal'ance** *tr* controbilanciare

coun'ter·clock'wise' *adj* antiorario || *adv* in senso antiorario

coun'ter·es'pionage' *s* controspionaggio

counterfeit ['kauntərfɪt] *adj* contraffatto || *s* contraffazione; moneta falsa || *tr & intr* contraffare

counterfeiter ['kauntər‚fɪtər] *s* contraffattore *m*

coun'ter·feit mon'ey *s* moneta falsa

countermand ['kauntər‚mænd] *or* ['kauntər‚mand] *tr* (troops) dare un contrordine a; (an order; a payment) cancellare

coun'ter·march' *s* contromarcia || *intr* fare contromarcia

coun'ter·offen'sive *s* controffensiva

coun'ter·pane' *s* sopraccoperta

coun'ter·part' *s* copia; (person) sosia

coun'ter·point' *s* (mus) contrappunto; (mus) controcanto

Coun'ter Reforma'tion *s* controriforma

coun'ter·rev'olu'tion **s** controrivoluzione

coun'ter·sign' *s* (password) parola d'ordine; (signature) controfirma || *tr* controfirmare

coun'ter·sink' *v* (*pret & pp* -sunk) *tr* incassare, accecare

coun'ter·spy' *s* (-spies) membro del controspionaggio

coun'ter·stroke' *s* contraccolpo

coun'ter·weight' *s* contrappeso

countess ['kauntɪs] *s* contessa

countless ['kauntlɪs] *adj* innumerevole

countrified ['kʌntrɪ‚faɪd] *adj* rustico, rurale

coun·try ['kʌntri] *s* (-tries) (land) terreno; (nation) paese *m*; (land of one's birth) patria; (rural region) campagna

coun'try club' *s* circolo privato sportivo situato nei sobborghi

coun'try cous'in *s* campagnolo

coun'try estate' *s* tenuta

coun'try·folk' *s* campagnoli *mpl*

coun'try gen'tleman *s* proprietario terriero, signorotto di campagna

coun'try house' *s* casa di campagna

coun'try jake' *s* (coll) zoticone *m*

coun'try life' *s* vita rustica

coun'try·man *s* (-men) paesano, compaesano

coun'try·peo'ple *s* gente *f* di campagna

coun'try·side' *s* campagna

coun'try·wide' *adj* nazionale

coun'try·wom'an *s* (-wom'en) *s* paesana, compaesana

coun·ty ['kaunti] *s* (-ties) contea, distretto

coun'ty seat' *s* capoluogo di contea

coup [ku] *s* colpo; colpo di stato

coup de grâce [ku də 'grɑs] *s* colpo di grazia

coup d'état [ku de'ta] *s* colpo di stato

coupe [kup] *or* **coupé** [ku'pe] *s* coupé *m*

couple ['kʌpəl] *s* (of people or animals) paio, coppia; (of things) paio; (link) unione || *tr* accoppiare; (to link) unire, agganciare || *intr* accoppiarsi

couplet ['kʌplɪt] *s* coppia di versi; (mus) couplet *m*

coupling ['kʌplɪŋ] *s* unione; (mach) giunto

coupon ['kupɑn] *or* ['kjupɑn] *s* coupon *m*, tagliando

courage ['kʌrɪdʒ] *s* coraggio; **to have the courage of one's convictions** avere il coraggio delle proprie opinioni

courageous [kə'redʒəs] *adj* coraggioso

courier ['kʌrɪ·ər] *or* ['kurɪ·ər] *s* corriere *m*

course [kors] *s* corso; (part of meal) portata; (place for games) campo;

(row) fila; **in due course** a tempo debito; **in the course of** durante, nel corso di; **of course** certamente, senza dubbio

court [kort] *s (uncovered place surrounded by walls)* corte *f*, cortile *m*; *(royal residence; courtship)* corte *f*; *(short street)* vicolo; *(playing area)* campo; *(law)* corte *f* ‖ *tr* corteggiare; *(e.g., disaster)* andare in cerca di

courteous ['kʌrtɪ‧əs] *adj* cortese

courtesan ['kʌrtɪzən] or ['kortɪzən] *s* cortigiana, meretrice *f*

courte‧sy ['kʌrtɪsɪ] *s* (-sies) cortesia, gentilezza; **through the courtesy of** con il gentile permesso di

court'house' *s* palazzo di giustizia

courtier ['kortɪ‧ər] *s* cortigiano

court' jest'er *s* buffone *m* di corte

court‧ly ['kortlɪ] *adj* (-lier; -liest) cortese, cortigiano; ossequioso

court'-mar'tial *s* (courts-martial) corte *f* marziale ‖ *v* (*pret* & *pp* -tialed or -tialled; *ger* -tialing or -tialling) *tr* sottomettere a corte marziale

court' plas'ter *s* taffettà *m*

court'room' *s* aula di giustizia

courtship ['kort/ɪp] *s* corte *f*, corteggiamento

court'yard' *s* corte *f*, cortile *m*

cousin ['kʌzɪn] *s* cugino

cove [kov] *s* piccola baia, cala

covenant ['kʌvənənt] *s* convenzione, patto ‖ *tr* promettere solennemente

cover ['kʌvər] *s (lid)* coperchio; *(tablecloth; shelter)* coperto; *(of book)* copertina; **to take cover** nascondersi; **under cover** in segreto, segretamente; **under cover of** sotto la protezione di; **under separate cover** in busta a parte, in plico a parte ‖ *tr* coprire; puntare un'arma verso; (journ) riferire, riportare; **to cover up** coprire completamente ‖ *intr (said of paint)* spandersi

coverage ['kʌvərɪdʒ] *s* copertura; (journ) servizio giornalistico; (rad, telv) raggio di udibilità

coveralls ['kʌvər‧ɔlz] *spl* tuta

cov'er charge' *s* coperto

cov'ered wag'on *s* carro coperto da tendone

cov'er girl' *s* ragazza-copertina

covering ['kʌvərɪŋ] *s* copertura; involucro

covert ['kʌvərt] *adj* nascosto, segreto

cov'er-up' *s* dissimulazione; sotterfugio

covet ['kʌvɪt] *tr* desiderare, agognare

covetous ['kʌvɪtəs] *adj* cupido

covey ['kʌvɪ] *s* covata

cow [kau] *s* vacca; *(of seal, elephant, etc.)* femmina *f* ‖ *tr* spaventare, intimidire

coward ['kau‧ərd] *s* codardo, vile *m*

cowardice ['kau‧ərdɪs] *s* codardia, viltà *f*

cowardly ['kau‧ərdlɪ] *adj* codardo, vile ‖ *adv* vilmente

cow'bell' *s* campano, campanaccio

cow'boy' *s* cowboy *m*

cow'catch'er *s* (rr) cacciapietre *m*

cower ['kau‧ər] *intr* rannicchiarsi

cow'herd' *s* guardiano d'armenti

cow'hide' *s* pelle *f* di vacca

cowl [kaul] *s (hood)* cappuccio; *(monk's cloak)* cappa; *(of car)* sostegno del cofano; *(of chimney)* cappello; (aer) cappottatura

cow'lick' *s* ritrosa

cow'pox' *s* (vet) vaiolo bovino

coxcomb ['kaks‧kom] *s* zerbinotto

coxwain ['kaksən] or ['kak‧swen] *s* timoniere *m*

coy [kɔɪ] *adj* timido, ritroso

co‧zy ['kozɪ] *adj* (-zier; -ziest) comodo ‖ *s* (-zies) copriteiera *m*

C.P.A. ['si'pi'e] *s* (letterword) (certified public accountant) esperto contabile

crab [kræb] *s* granchio; (aer) scarroccio; *(complaining person)* (coll) scontroso ‖ *v* (*pret* & *pp* **crabbed**; *ger* **crabbing**) *intr* (coll) lamentarsi

crab' apple' *s* mela selvatica; *(tree)* melo selvatico

crabbed ['kræbɪd] *adj* sgarbato; *(handwriting)* da gallina; *(style)* oscuro, ermetico

crab' louse' *s* piattola

crab‧by ['kræbɪ] *adj* (-bier; -biest) scontroso, sgarbato

crack [kræk] *adj* (slang) di prim'ordine, eccellente ‖ *s (noise)* schiocco; *(break)* rottura, screpolatura, crepa; *(opening)* fessura; (slang) tentativo; (slang) barzelletta ‖ *tr (e.g., a whip)* schioccare; *(to break)* rompere, screpolare; *(oil)* ridurre con distillazione; (coll) risolvere; *(a safe)* (slang) forzare; *(a joke)* (slang) dire; **cracked up to be** (slang) avendo fama di ‖ *intr (to make a noise)* scricchiolare; *(to break)* rompersi, screpolarsi; *(said of voice)* diventare fesso; (slang) avere un esaurimento nervoso; **to crack down** (slang) essere severo; **to crack up** (slang) andare a pezzi

cracked [krækt] *adj* rotto, spezzato; *(voice)* fesso; (coll) pazzo

cracker ['krækər] *s* cracker *m*, galletta

crack'er-bar'rel *adj* in piccolo, alla buona

crack'er-jack' *adj* (slang) di prim'ordine ‖ *s* (slang) persona di prim'ordine

cracking ['krækɪŋ] *s* piroscissione

crackle ['krækəl] *s* crepitio, crepito ‖ *intr* crepitare

crack'pot' *adj* & *s* (coll) mattoide *mf*

crack'-up' *s* accidente *m*; collisione; *(breakdown in health or in relations)* (coll) colasso; (aer) accidente *m* d'atterraggio

cradle ['kredəl] *s* culla; *(of handset)* forcella ‖ *tr* cullare

crad'le‧song' *s* ninnananna

craft [kræft] or [krɑft] *s (skill)* abilità *f*; *(trade)* mestiere *m*; *(guile)* astuzia, furberia; *(ship)* nave *f*; aeronave

craftiness ['kræftɪnɪs] or ['krɑftɪnɪs] *s* astuzia, furberia

crafts'man *s* (-men) operaio specializzato, artigiano

craft' un'ion *s* artigianato, sindacato artigiano

craft·y ['kræfti] or ['krɑfti] *adj* (**-ier;** **-iest**) astuto, furbo

crag [kræg] *s* roccia scoscesa, rupe *f*

cram [kræm] *v* (*pret & pp* **crammed;** *ger* **cramming**) *tr* (*to pack full*) riempire fino all'orlo; (*to stuff with food*) rimpinzare || *intr* rimpinzarsi; (coll) preparare un esame alla svelta

cramp [kræmp] *s* (*painful contraction*) crampo; (*bar with hooks*) grappa; (fig) ostacolo || *tr* ostacolare, restringere

cranber·ry ['kræn͵bɛri] *s* (**-ries**) mirtillo

crane [kren] *s* (orn, mach) gru *f;* (*boom*) (telv, mov) giraffa || *tr* (*one's neck*) allungare || *intr* allungare il collo

crani·um ['kreni·əm] *s* (**-a** [ə]) cranio

crank [kræŋk] *s* manovella; (aut) alzacristalli *m;* (coll) eccentrico || *tr* girare con la manovella; mettere in moto con la manovella

crank'case' *s* coppa dell'olio, carter *m*

crank'shaft' *s* albero a gomito

crank·y ['kræŋki] *adj* (**-ier;** **-iest**) irritabile; eccentrico

cran·ny ['kræni] *s* (**-nies**) (*crevice*) crepaccio; (*crack*) fessura

crape [krep] *s* crespo

crape'hang'er *s* (slang) pessimista uggioso, guastafeste *mf*

craps [kræps] *s* gioco dei dadi; **to shoot craps** giocare ai dadi

crash [kræʃ] *adj* (coll) d'emergenza || *s* (*noise*) scoppio. schianto; accidente *m;* (*collapse of business*) crac *m*, rovescio; (*bad landing*) atterraggio senza carrello || *tr* fracassare; **to crash the gate** (coll) entrare senza invito || *intr* fracassarsi; (com) fallire; **to cash into** investire, cozzare contro; **to cash through** sfondare

crash' dive' *s* immersione rapida di un sottomarino

crash' hel'met *s* casco

crass [kræs] *adj* crasso

crate [kret] *s* gabbia d'imballaggio || *tr* imballare in una gabbia

crater ['kretər] *s* cratere *m*

cravat [krə'væt] *s* cravatta

crave [krev] *tr* anelare; (*to beg*) implorare || *intr*—**to crave for** desiderare ardentemente

craven ['krevən] *adj & s* codardo

craving ['kreviŋ] *s* anelito, desiderio

craw [krɔ] *s* gozzo

crawl [krɔl] *s* strisciamento, avanzata striscioni; (sports) crawl *m* || *intr* strisciare, avanzare striscioni; (*said of worms*) brulicare; (*said of insects*) formicolare; (*to feel creepy*) sentirsi il formicolio

crayfish ['krefiʃ] *s* (*Palinurus vulgaris*) aragosta; (*Astacus; Cambarus*) gambero

crayon ['kre·ən] *s* pastello; disegno a pastello || *tr* disegnare a pastello

craze [krez] *s* mania, moda || *tr* fare impazzire

cra·zy ['krezi] *adj* (**-zier;** **-ziest**) pazzo, matto; **to be crazy about** (coll) esser matto per; **to drive crazy** fare impazzire

cra'zy bone' *s* osso rabbioso (del gomito)

creak [krik] *s* scricchiolio, cigolio || *intr* scricchiolare, cigolare

creak·y ['kriki] *adj* (**-ier;** **-iest**) stridente, cigolante

cream [krim] *s* crema, panna; (*finest part*) fior fiore *m* || *tr* rendere di consistenza cremosa; (*to remove cream from*) scremare; prendere il meglio di

creamer·y ['krimər·i] *s* (**-ies**) (*factory*) caseificio; (*store*) cremeria

cream' puff' *s* bignè *m*

cream·y ['krimi] *adj* (**-ier;** **-iest**) cremoso; butirroso

crease [kris] *s* piega, grinza || *tr* piegare, raggrinzire || *intr* piegarsi, raggrinzirsi, far pieghe

crease'-resis'tant *adj* antipiega

create [kri'et] *tr* creare

creation [kri'e/ən] *s* creazione; **the Creation** il creato

creative [kri'etiv] *adj* creativo

creator [kri'etər] *s* creatore *m*

creature ['kritʃər] *s* creatura

credence ['kridəns] *s* credenza

credentials [kri'dɛn/əlz] *spl* lettere *fpl* credenziali; documento d'autorizzazione

credible ['krɛdɪbəl] *adj* credibile

credit ['krɛdɪt] *s* credito; (*in a school*) unità *f* di promozione; (com) avere *m;* **credits** (mov, telv) titoli *mpl* di testa || *tr* accreditare; **to credit s.o. with s.th** attribuire qlco a qlcu

creditable ['krɛdɪtəbəl] *adj* lodevole

cred'it card' *s* carta di credito

creditor ['krɛdɪtər] *s* creditore *m*

cre·do ['krido] or ['kredo] *s* (**-dos**) credo

credulous ['krɛdʒələs] *adj* credulo

creed [krid] *s* credo

creek [krik] *s* fiumicello

creep [krip] *v* (*pret & pp* **crept** [krɛpt]) *intr* strisciare, avanzare striscioni; (*to grow along a wall*) arrampicarsi; (*to feel creepy*) sentirsi il formicolio

creeper ['kripər] *s* strisciante *m;* (*plant*) rampicante *f*

creeping ['kripiŋ] *adj* lento; (*plant*) rampicante

cremate ['krimet] *tr* cremare

cremato·ry ['krimə͵tori] *adj* crematorio || *s* (**-ries**) forno crematorio

Creole ['kri·ol] *adj & s* creolo

crescent ['krɛsənt] *s* (*of Islam*) mezzaluna; (*of moon*) crescente *m;* (*roll*) cornetto

cress [krɛs] *s* crescione *m*

crest [krɛst] *s* cresta; (heral) stemma *m*, insegna

crestfallen ['krɛst͵fɔlən] *adj* depresso

Cretan ['kritən] *adj & s* cretese *mf*

cretin ['kritən] *s* cretino

crevice ['krɛvis] *s* fessura, fenditura

crew [kru] *s* (*group working together*) personale *m;* (*group of workmen;*

mob) ciurma; (*of a ship or racing boat*) equipaggio; (*sports*) canottaggio

crew' cut' *s* capelli *mpl* a spazzola

crib [krɪb] *s* (*bed*) lettino; (*rack*) rastrelliera; (*building*) capanna, granaio; (*coll*) bigino ‖ *v* (*pret & pp* **cribbed;** *ger* **cribbing**) *tr* (*coll*) usare un bigino in ‖ *intr* (*coll*) usare un bigino; (*coll*) commettere un plagio

cricket [ˈkrɪkɪt] *s* grillo; (*sports*) cricket *m*, palla a spatola

crier [ˈkraɪ·ər] *s* banditore *m*

crime [kraɪm] *s* delitto, crimine *m*

criminal [ˈkrɪmɪnəl] *adj* criminale; (*code*) penale ‖ *s* delinquente *mf*

crimp [krɪmp] *s* piega, pieghettatura; **to put a crimp in** (slang) mettere i bastoni fra le ruote a ‖ *tr* pieghettare; (*the hair*) arricciare

crimson [ˈkrɪmzən] *adj & s* cremisi *m* ‖ *intr* imporporarsi

cringe [krɪndʒ] *intr* rannicchiarsi; (*to fawn*) umiliarsi

crinkle [ˈkrɪŋkəl] *tr* arricciare ‖ *intr* (*to rustle*) sfrusciare

cripple [ˈkrɪpəl] *s* zoppo, sciancato ‖ *tr* storpiare; (*e.g., business*) paralizzare

cri·sis [ˈkraɪsɪs] *s* (**-ses** [siz]) crisi *f*

crisp [krɪsp] *adj* (*brittle*) croccante, friabile; (*air*) frizzante; (*sharp and clear*) acuto

criteri·on [kraɪˈtɪrɪ·ən] *s* (**-a** [ə] or **-ons**) criterio

critic [ˈkrɪtɪk] *s* critico

critical [ˈkrɪtɪkəl] *adj* critico

criticism [ˈkrɪtɪˌsɪzəm] *s* critica

criticize [ˈkrɪtɪˌsaɪz] *tr & intr* criticare

critique [krɪˈtik] *s* critica

croak [krok] *s* (*of frogs*) gracidio; (*of crows*) gracchiamento ‖ *intr* gracidare; gracchiare; (slang) crepare

Croat [ˈkro·æt] *s* croato

Croatian [kroˈeʃən] *adj & s* croato

cro·chet [kroˈʃe] *s* lavoro all'uncinetto ‖ *v* (*pret & pp* **-cheted** [ˈʃed]; *ger* **-cheting** [ˈʃe·ɪŋ]) *tr & intr* lavorare all'uncinetto

crock [krak] *s* vaso di terracotta, giara, orcio

crockery [ˈkrakəri] *s* vasellame *m* di terracotta, terracotta

crocodile [ˈkrakəˌdaɪl] *s* coccodrillo

croc'odile tears' *spl* lacrime *fpl* di coccodrillo

crocus [ˈkrokəs] *s* croco

crone [kron] *s* vecchia incartapecorita

cro·ny [ˈkroni] *s* (**-nies**) amicone *m*, compare *m*

crook [kruk] *s* (*hook*) uncino; (*staff*) pastorale *m*; (*bend*) curva; (*bend of pipe*) gomito; (*coll*) imbroglione *m* ‖ *tr* piegare ‖ *intr* piegarsi

crooked [ˈkrukɪd] *adj* uncinato; curvo, piegato; (*coll*) disonesto

croon [krun] *intr* canterellare; cantare in modo sentimentale

crop [krap] *s* (*of bird*) gozzo; (*agricultural product, growing or harvested*) messe *f*; (*agricultural product harvested*) raccolto; (*riding whip*) fru-

stino; (*hair cut close*) capelli **corti;** gruppo ‖ *v* (*pret & pp* **cropped;** *ger* **cropping**) *tr* (*to cut the ends off of*) spuntare; (*to reap*) raccogliere; (*to cut short*) tosare ‖ *intr*—**to crop out** or **up** apparire inaspettatamente

crop'-dust'ing *s* fumigazione aerea

cropper [ˈkrapər] *s* mietitore *m*; (*sharecropper*) mezzadro; **to come a cropper** (*coll*) fare una cascataccia; (*coll*) andare in rovina

croquet [kroˈke] *s* croquet *m*, pallamaglio *m & f*

croquette [kroˈket] *s* crocchetta

crosier [ˈkroʒər] *s* pastorale *m*

cross [krɔs] or [kras] *adj* trasversale, contrario, obliquo; (*irritable*) bisbetico, di cattivo umore; (*of mixed breed*) incrociato ‖ *s* croce *f*; (*crossing of breeds*) incrocio; **to take the cross** farsi crociato ‖ *tr* crociare, segnare con una croce; (*the street*) attraversare; (*e.g., the legs*) incrociare; (*to draw a line across*) barrare; (*to thwart*) ostacolare; **to cross oneself** farsi il segno della croce; **to cross one's mind** venire in mente a uno; **to cross out** cancellare ‖ *intr* incrociarsi

cross'bones' *spl* teschio e tibie incrociate (*simbolo della morte*)

cross'bow' *s* balestra

cross'breed' *v* (*pret & pp* **-bred** [ˌbred]) *tr* incrociare, ibridare

cross'-coun'try *adj* campestre; attraverso il paese

cross'-exam'ina'tion *s* (law) confronto, interrogatorio in contraddittorio

cross-eyed [ˈkrɔsˌaɪd] or [ˈkrasˌaɪd] *adj* guercio, strabico

crossing [ˈkrɔsɪŋ] or [ˈkrasɪŋ] *s* incrocio; ostacolo; (*of the sea*) traversata; (*of a river*) guado; (rr) passaggio **a** livello

cross'patch' *s* (coll) bisbetico

cross'piece' *s* traversa

cross' ref'erence *s* richiamo, rimando

cross'road' *s* strada trasversale; **at the crossroads** al bivio; **crossroads** crocicchio

cross' sec'tion *s* sezione trasversale

cross' street' *s* traversa

cross' talk' *s* conversazione; (telp) **dia**fonia

cross'word puz'zle *s* cruciverba *m*, parole incrociate

crotch [kratʃ] *s* inforcatura; (*of pants*) cavallo

crotchety [ˈkratʃɪti] *adj* bisbetico

crouch [krautʃ] *intr* accoccolarsi

croup [krup] *s* (pathol) crup *m*

crouton [ˈkrutan] *s* crostino

crow [kro] *s* corvo, cornacchia; (*cry of rooster*) chicchirichì *m;* **as the crow flies** in linea retta, a volo d'uccello; **to eat crow** (coll) mangiarsi le parole ‖ *intr* fare chicchirichì; **to crow over** vantarsi di, esultare per

crow'bar' *s* bastone *m* a leva

crowd [kraud] *s* folla; (*common people*) masse *fpl*; (coll) gruppo ‖ *tr* affollare; (*to push*) spingere ‖ *intr* affollarsi; (*to press forward*) spingersi

crowded ['kraudɪd] *adj* affollato

crown [kraun] *s* corona; (*of hat*) cupola; (*highest point*) sommo ‖ *tr* coronare; (*checkers*) damare; **to crown s.o.** (coll) battere qlcu sulla testa

crown' prince' *s* principe ereditario

crown' prin'cess *s* principessa ereditaria

crow's'-foot' *s* (-feet) zampa di gallina

crow's'-nest' *s* coffa, gabbia

crucial ['kruʃəl] *adj* cruciale, critico

crucible ['krusɪbəl] *s* crogiolo

crucifix ['krusɪfɪks] *s* crocefisso

crucifixion [,krusɪ'fɪkʃən] *s* crocifissione

cruci•fy ['krusɪ,faɪ] *v* (*pret & pp* -fied) *tr* crocifiggere

crude [krud] *adj* (*raw*) grezzo; (*unripe*) acerbo; (*roughly made; uncultured*) rozzo

crudi•ty ['krudɪtɪ] *s* (-ties) rozzezza

cruel ['kruəl] *adj* crudele

cruel•ty ['kru•əltɪ] *s* (-ties) crudeltà *f*

cruet ['kru•ɪt] *s* oliera

cruise [kruz] *s* crociera ‖ *tr* navigare ‖ *intr* andare in crociera; andare avanti e indietro

cruiser ['kruzər] *s* (nav) incrociatore *m*

cruising ['kruzɪŋ] *adj* di crociera

cruis'ing ra'dius *s* autonomia di crociera

cruller ['krʌlər] *s* frittella

crumb [krʌm] *s* briciola ‖ *tr* sbriciolare; (*e.g., a cutlet*) impannare ‖ *intr* sbriciolarsi

crumble ['krʌmbəl] *tr* sbriciolare, polverizzare ‖ *intr* andare a pezzi, polverizzarsi, sbriciolarsi

crum•my ['krʌmɪ] *adj* (-mier; -miest) (slang) sporco; (*miserable*) (slang) schifoso; (*e.g., joke*) (slang) povero

crumple ['krʌmpəl] *tr* sgualcire, spiegazzare; **to crumple into a ball** appallottolare ‖ *intr* spiegazzarsi

crunch [krʌntʃ] *s* crocchio; (coll) stretta, morsa ‖ *tr* sgranocchiare ‖ *intr* crocchiare

crusade [kru'sed] *s* crociata ‖ *intr* crociarsi; (*to take up a cause*) farsi paladino

crusader [kru'sedər] *s* crociato; (*of a cause*) paladino

crush [krʌʃ] *s* pigiatura, schiacciatura; (*crowd*) calca; (coll) infatuazione ‖ *tr* schiacciare; (*to grind*) frantumare; (*to subdue*) sottomettere; (*to extract by squeezing*) pigiare

crust [krʌst] *s* crosta; (slang) faccia tosta ‖ *tr* incrostare ‖ *intr* incrostare, incrostarsi

crustacean [krʌs'teʃən] *s* crostaceo

crust•y ['krʌstɪ] *adj* (-ier; -iest) crostoso; (fig) tosto; rude

crutch [krʌtʃ] *s* gruccia, stampella; (fig) sostegno

crux [krʌks] *s* difficoltà *f*, busillis *m*; (*crucial point*) punto cruciale

cry [kraɪ] *s* (**cries**) (*shout*) grido; (*fit of weeping*) pianto; (*entreaty*) richiamo; (*of animal*) urlo; **a far cry** ben lontano, ben distinto; **to have a good cry** sfogarsi, piangere a calde lacrime ‖ *tr* gridare; (*to proclaim*) bandire; **to cry down** disprezzare; **to cry one's heart out** piangere a calde lacrime; **to cry out** proclamare; **to cry up** elogiare ‖ *intr* gridare, urlare; piangere; **to cry for** implorare

cry'ba'by *s* (-bies) piagnucolone *m*

crypt [krɪpt] *s* cripta

cryptic(al) ['krɪptɪk(əl)] *adj* segreto, occulto, misterioso

crystal ['krɪstəl] *s* cristallo

crys'tal ball' *s* globo di cristallo

crystalline ['krɪstəlɪn] *or* ['krɪstə,laɪn] *adj* cristallino

crystallize ['krɪstə,laɪz] *tr* cristallizzare ‖ *intr* cristallizzarsi

cub [kʌb] *s* cucciolo; (*of lion*) leoncino; (*of fox*) volpicino, volpacchiotto

cubbyhole ['kʌbɪ,hol] *s* sgabuzzino, bugigattolo

cube [kjub] *adj* cubico ‖ *s* cubo; (*of sugar*) zolla ‖ *tr* elevare al cubo; (*to shape*) tagliare in quadretti

cubic ['kjubɪk] *adj* cubico

cub' report'er *s* giornalista novello

cuckold ['kʌkəld] *adj & s* cornuto, becco ‖ *tr* cornificare

cuckoo ['kuku] *adj* (slang) pazzo ‖ *s* cuculo

cuck'oo clock' *s* orologio a cucù

cucumber ['kjukʌmbər] *s* cetriolo

cud [kʌd] *s* mangime masticato; **to chew the cud** ruminare

cuddle ['kʌdəl] *tr* abbracciare affettuosamente ‖ *intr* (*to lie close*) giacere vicino; (*to curl up*) rannicchiarsi, raggomitolarsi

cudg•el ['kʌdʒəl] *s* manganello, randello; **to take up the cudgels for** farsi paladino di ‖ *v* (*pret & pp* -eled *or* -elled; *ger* -eling *or* -elling) *tr* bastonare, randellare; **to cudgel one's brains** rompersi la testa

cue [kju] *s* suggerimento, imbeccata; (*billiards*) stecca; **to miss a cue** (theat) mancare la battuta; (coll) non capire l'antifona ‖ *tr*—**to cue s.o. (in) on** (coll) dare a qlcu informazioni su

cuff [kʌf] *s* (*of shirt*) polsino; (*of trousers*) risvolto; (*slap*) schiaffo ‖ *tr* schiaffeggiare

cuff' links' *spl* bottoni doppi, gemelli *mpl*

cuirass [kwɪ'ræs] *s* corazza

cuisine [kwɪ'zin] *s* cucina

culinary ['kjulɪ,nerɪ] *adj* culinario

cull [kʌl] *s* scarto ‖ *tr* (*to gather, pluck*) cogliere; selezionare, scegliere

culminate ['kʌlmɪ,net] *intr* culminare

culottes [ku'lɑts] *spl* gonna pantaloni

culpable ['kʌlpəbəl] *adj* colpevole

culprit ['kʌlprɪt] *s* colpevole *m*, imputato

cult [kʌlt] *s* culto

cultivate ['kʌltɪ,vet] *tr* coltivare

cultivated [ˈkʌltɪ ˌvetɪd] *adj* colto, coltivato

cultivation [ˌkʌltɪˈveʃən] *s* coltivazione, cultura

culture [ˈkʌltʃər] *s* cultura

cultured [ˈkʌltʃərd] *adj* colto

cul'tured pearl' *s* perla coltivata

culvert [ˈkʌlvərt] *s* chiavica

cumbersome [ˈkʌmbərsəm] *adj* ingombrante, incomodo; (*clumsy*) goffo

cumulative [ˈkjumjə ˌletɪv] *adj* cumulativo

cunning [ˈkʌnɪŋ] *adj* (*sly*) astuto; (*skillful*) abile; (*pretty*) bello; (*created with skill*) ben fatto, fine || *s* astuzia; abilità *f*, destrezza

cup [kʌp] *s* tazza; (*mach, sports*) coppa; (*eccl*) calice *m*; **in one's cups** ubriaco || *v* (*pret & pp* **cupped;** *ger* **cupping**) *tr* mettere ventose a; **to cup one's hands** foggiare le mani a mo' di conca

cupboard [ˈkʌbərd] *s* armadio a muro, dispensa; (*buffet*) credenza

Cupid [ˈkjupɪd] *s* Cupido

cupidity [kjuˈpɪdɪti] *s* cupidigia

cup' of tea' *s* tazza di tè; (coll) forte *m*, e.g., **physics is not my cup of tea** la fisica non è il mio forte

cupola [ˈkjupələ] *s* cupola

cur [kʌr] *s* cane bastardo; (*despicable fellow*) canaglia, gaglioffo

curate [ˈkjurɪt] *s* curato

curative [ˈkjurətɪv] *adj* curativo

curator [kjuˈretər] *s* conservatore *m*

curb [kʌrb] *s* (*of bit*) barbazzale *m*; (*of pavement*) orlo del marciapiede; (*check*) freno || *tr* frenare

curb'stone' *s* cordone *m*; (*of well*) sponda del pozzo

curd [kʌrd] *s* cagliata || *tr* cagliare || *intr* cagliarsi

curdle [ˈkʌrdəl] *tr* cagliare; (*the blood*) far gelare || *intr* cagliarsi; (*said of custard*) impazzare

cure [kjur] *s* cura || *tr* curare; (*e.g., meat*) conservare; (*wood*) stagionare

cure'-all' *s* panacea

curfew [ˈkʌrfju] *s* coprifuoco

curl·o [ˈkʌrl ˌo] *s* (**-os**) curiosità *f*

curiosi·ty [ˌkjurɪˈɑsɪti] *s* (**-ties**) curiosità *f*

curious [ˈkjurɪ·əs] *adj* curioso

curl [kʌrl] *s* (*of hair*) ricciolo; (*anything curled*) rotolo, spirale *f* || *tr* arricciare; arrotolare; (*the lips*) torcere || *intr* arricciarsi; arrotolarsi; **to curl up** raggomitolarsi

curlicue [ˈkʌrlɪ ˌkju] *s* ghirigoro

curl'ing i'ron *s* ferro da arricciare

curl'pa'per *s* bigodino

curl·y [ˈkʌrli] *adj* (**-ier; -iest**) ricciuto

curmudgeon [kərˈmʌdʒən] *s* bisbetico

currant [ˈkʌrənt] *s* (*seedless raisin*) uva passa di Corinto, uva sultanina; (*shrub and berry of genus Ribes*) ribes *m*

curren·cy [ˈkʌrənsi] *s* (**-cies**) (*circulation*) circolazione; (*money*) denaro circolante; (*general use*) corso

current [ˈkʌrənt] *adj & s* corrente *f*

cur'rent account' *s* conto corrente

cur'rent events' *spl* attualità *fpl*, eventi *mpl* correnti

curricu·lum [kəˈrɪkjələm] *s* (**-lums** or **-la** [lə]) programma *m*; piano educativo

cur·ry [ˈkʌri] *s* (**-ries**) (*spice*) curry *m* || *v* (*pret & pp* **-ried**) *tr* (*a horse*) strigliare; (*leather*) conciare; **to curry favor** cercare di compiacere

cur'ry·comb' *s* striglia || *tr* strigliare

curse [kʌrs] *s* maledizione; bestemmia || *tr* maledire || *intr* imprecare, bestemmiare

cursed [ˈkʌrsɪd] or [kʌrst] *adj* maledetto; (*hateful*) odiato

cursive [ˈkʌrsɪv] *adj & s* corsivo

cursory [ˈkʌrsəri] *adj* rapido, superficiale

curt [kʌrt] *adj* (*rude*) brusco, sgarbato; (*short*) breve, conciso

curtail [kərˈtel] *tr* ridurre, restringere

curtain [ˈkʌrtən] *s* (*in front of stage*) sipario; (*for window*) tendina; (fig) cortina || *tr* coprire con tenda; separare con tenda; coprire, nascondere

cur'tain call' *s* (theat) chiamata

cur'tain rais'er [ˈrezər] *s* (theat) avanspettacolo; (sports) incontro preliminare

cur'tain ring' *s* campanella

cur'tain rod' *s* bastone *m* su cui si fissano le tende

curt·sy [ˈkʌrtsi] *s* (**-sies**) riverenza, inchino || *v* (*pret & pp* **-sied**) *intr* fare la riverenza, inchinarsi

curve [kʌrv] *s* curva || *tr* curvare || *intr* curvarsi

curved [kʌrvd] *adj* curvo, curvato

cushion [ˈkuʃən] *s* cuscino; (*of billiard table*) mattonella || *tr* proteggere, ammortizzare, attutire

cuspidor [ˈkʌspɪ ˌdɔr] *s* sputacchiera

cuss [kʌs] *s* (coll) bestemmia; (coll) tipo perverso || *tr* maledire || *intr* bestemmiare

custard [ˈkʌstərd] *s* crema

custodian [kəsˈtodɪ·ən] *s* (*caretaker*) custode *m*, guardiano *m*; (*person who is entrusted with s.th*) conservatore *m*; (*janitor of school*) bidello

custo·dy [ˈkʌstədi] *s* (**-dies**) custodia; (*imprisonment*) arresto; **in custody** in prigione; **to take into custody** arrestare

custom [ˈkʌstəm] *s* costume *m*; (*customers*) clientela; **customs** dogana; diritti *mpl* doganali

customary [ˈkʌstə ˌmeri] *adj* consueto, abituale

custom-built [ˈkʌstəmˈbɪlt] *adj* fatto su misura; (*car*) fuori serie

customer [ˈkʌstəmər] *s* cliente *mf*

cus'tom·house' *adj* doganale || *s* dogana

custom-made [ˈkʌstəmˈmed] *adj* fatto su misura

cus'toms inspec'tion *s* visita doganale

cus'toms of'ficer *s* doganiere *m*

cus'tom work' *s* lavoro fatto su misura

cut [kʌt] *adj* (*prices*) ridotto; **to be cut out for** essere tagliato per || *s* taglio; (*reduction*) ribasso; (*typ*) cliché *m*;

(*snub*) (coll) affronto; (coll) assenza non autorizzata; (coll) parte *f*; **a cut above** (coll) un po' meglio di ‖ *tr* tagliare; (*cards*) alzare; (*prices*) ridurre; (coll) far finta di non riconoscere; (coll) marinare; **cut it out!** basta!; **to cut back** ridurre; **to cut off** tagliare; diseredare; (surg) amputare; **to cut short** interrompere; **to cut teeth** fare i denti; **to cut up** sminuzzare; criticare ‖ *intr* tagliare, tagliarsi; **to cut across** attraversare; **to cut in** interrompere; **to cut under** vendere sottoprezzo; **to cut up** (slang) fare il pagliaccio

cut-and-dried [ˈkʌtənˈdraɪd] *adj* monotono, stantio; bell'e fatto, fatto in anticipo

cutaneous [kjuˈteɪnɪ-əs] *adj* cutaneo

cut'away' coat' [ˈkʌtəˌwe] *s* marsina da giorno

cut'back' *s* riduzione; eliminazione; (mov) ritorno dell'azione a un'epoca anteriore

cute [kjut] *adj* (coll) carino, grazioso; (*shrewd*) (coll) furbo

cut' glass' *s* cristallo intagliato

cuticle [ˈkjutɪkəl] *s* cuticola

cutlass [ˈkʌtləs] *s* sciabola

cutler [ˈkʌtlər] *s* coltellinaio

cutlery [ˈkʌtləri] *s* coltelleria

cutlet [ˈkʌtlɪt] *s* cotoletta; (*flat croquette*) polpetta

cut'off' *s* taglio; (*road*) scorciatoia; (*of cylinder*) otturatore *m*, chiusura dell'ammissione; (*of river*) braccio diretto

cut'out' *s* ritaglio; (aut) valvola di scappamento libero

cut'-rate' *adj* a prezzo ridotto

cutter [ˈkʌtər] *s* tagliatore *m*; (naut) cutter *m*

cut'throat' *adj* spietato; (*relentless*) senza posa ‖ *s* assassino

cutting [ˈkʌtɪŋ] *adj* tagliente ‖ *s* taglio; (*from a newspaper*) ritaglio;

(*e.g., of prices*) riduzione; (hort) talea

cut'ting board' *s* tagliere *m*; (*of dishwasher*) piano d'appoggio

cut'ting edge' *s* taglio

cuttlefish [ˈkʌtəlˌfɪʃ] *s* seppia

cut'wat'er *s* (*of bridge*) tagliacque *m*; (*of boat*) tagliamare *m*

cyanamide [saɪˈænə ˌmaɪd] *s* cianamide *f*; cianamide *f* di calcio

cyanide [ˈsaɪ-əˌnaɪd] *s* cianuro

cycle [ˈsaɪkəl] *s* ciclo; bicicletta; (*of internal combustion engine*) tempo; (phys) periodo ‖ *intr* andare in bicicletta

cyclic(al) [ˈsaɪklɪk(əl)] or [ˈsɪklɪk(əl)] *adj* ciclico

cyclone [ˈsaɪklon] *s* ciclone *m*

cyclops [ˈsaɪklɑps] *s* ciclope *m*

cyclotron [ˈsaɪklo ˌtrɑn] or [ˈsɪklo ˌtrɑn] *s* ciclotrone *m*

cylinder [ˈsɪlɪndər] *s* cilindro; (*container*) bombola

cyl'inder block' *s* monoblocco

cyl'inder bore' *s* alesaggio

cyl'inder head' *s* testa

cylindric(al) [sɪˈlɪndrɪk(əl)] *adj* cilindrico

cymbals [ˈsɪmbəls] *spl* piatti *mpl*

cynic [ˈsɪnɪk] *adj & s* cinico

cynical [ˈsɪnɪkəl] *adj* cinico

cynicism [ˈsɪnɪ ˌsɪzəm] *s* cinismo

cynosure [ˈsaɪnə ˌʃʊr] or [ˈsɪnə ˌʃʊr] *s* centro dell'attenzione

cypress [ˈsaɪprəs] *s* cipresso

Cyprus [ˈsaɪprəs] *s* Cipro

Cyrus [ˈsaɪrəs] *s* Ciro

cyst [sɪst] *s* ciste *f*, cisti *f*

czar [zɑr] *s* zar *m*

czarina [zɑˈrinə] *s* zarina

Czech [tʃɛk] *adj & s* ceco

Czecho-Slovak [ˈtʃɛkoˈslovæk] *adj & s* cecoslovacco

Czecho-Slovakia [ˌtʃɛkosloˈvækɪ-ə] *s* la Cecoslovacchia

D

D, d [di] *s* quarta lettera dell'alfabeto inglese

dab [dæb] *s* tocco; (*of mud*) schizzo; (*e.g., of butter*) spalmata ‖ *v* (*pret & pp* **dabbed;** *ger* **dabbing**) *tr* toccare leggermente; (*to apply a substance to*) spennellare

dabble [ˈdæbəl] *tr* spruzzare ‖ *intr* diguazzare; **to dabble in** occuparsi di; (*stocks*) speculare in

dad [dæd] *s* (coll) papà *m*

dad·dy [ˈdædi] *s* (**-dies**) (coll) papà *m*

daffodil [ˈdæfədɪl] *s* trombone *m*

daff·y [ˈdæfi] *adj* (**-ier; -iest**) (coll) pazzo

dagger [ˈdæɡər] *s* daga, pugnale *m*; (typ) croce *f*; **to look daggers at** fulminare con lo sguardo

dahlia [ˈdæljə] *s* dalia

dai·ly [ˈdeli] *adj* quotidiano, diurno ‖ *s* (**-lies**) quotidiano ‖ *adv* giornalmente

dai'ly dou'ble *s* duplice *f*, accoppiata

dain·ty [ˈdenti] *adj* (**-tier; -tiest**) delicato ‖ *s* (**-ties**) manicaretto

dair·y [ˈderi] *s* (**-ies**) (*store*) latteria; (*factory*) caseificio

dair'y farm' *s* vaccheria

dair'y·man *s* (**-men**) lattaio

dais [ˈde·ɪs] *s* predella

dai·sy [ˈdezi] *s* (**-sies**) margherita

dal·ly [ˈdæli] *v* (*pret & pp* **-lied**) *intr* (*to loiter*) bighellonare; (*to trifle*) scherzare

dam [dæm] *s* diga; (*for fishing*) pescaia; (zool) fattrice *f* ‖ *v* (*pret & pp* **dammed;** *ger* **damming**) *tr* arginare; ostruire; tappare

damage ['dæmɪdʒ] *s* danno, scapito; (fig) menomazione; (com) avaria; **damages** danni *mpl* ‖ *tr* danneggiare, ledere; sinistrare

damascene ['dæmə,sin] or [,dæmə-'sin] *adj* damasceno ‖ *s* damaschinatura ‖ *tr* damaschinare

dame [dem] *s* dama, signora; (slang) donna

damn [dæm] *s*—**I don't give a damn** (slang) me ne impipo; **that's not worth a damn** (slang) non vale un fico ‖ *tr* dannare, condannare ‖ *intr* maledire ‖ *interj* maledizione!

damnation [dæm'ne/ən] *s* dannazione; (theol) condanna

damned [dæmd] *adj* dannato, maledetto ‖ **the damned** i dannati ‖ *adv* maledettamente

damp [dæmp] *adj* umido ‖ *s* umidità *f*; (firedamp) grisou *m* ‖ *tr* inumidire; umettare; (to muffle) smorzare; (waves) (elec) smorzare; **to damp s.o.'s enthusiasm** raffreddare gli spiriti di qlcu; scoraggiare qlcu

dampen ['dæmpən] *tr* inumidire; umettare; smorzare; (s.o.'s enthusiasm) raffreddare

damper ['dæmpər] *s* (of chimney) valvola di tiraggio; (fig) doccia fredda; (mus) smorzatore *m*; (mus) sordina

damsel ['dæmzəl] *s* damigella

dance [dæns] or [dɑns] *s* ballo, danza ‖ *tr & intr* ballare, danzare

dance' band' *s* orchestrina

dance' floor' *s* pista da ballo

dance' hall' *s* sala da ballo

dancer ['dænsər] or ['dɑnsər] *s* danzatore *m*; (expert or professional) ballerino

danc'ing part'ner *s* cavaliere *m*; dama

danc'ing par'ty *s* festa da ballo

dandelion ['dændɪ,laɪən] *s* dente *m* di leone, soffione *m*

dandruff ['dændrəf] *s* forfora

dan-dy ['dændɪ] *adj* (-dier; -diest) (coll) eccellente, magnifico ‖ *s* (-dies) damerino, elegantone *m*

Dane [den] *s* danese *mf*

danger ['dendʒər] *s* pericolo

dangerous ['dendʒərəs] *adj* pericoloso

dangle ['dæŋgəl] *tr* dondolare ‖ *intr* penzolare, ciondolare

Danish ['denɪʃ] *adj & s* danese *m*

dank [dæŋk] *adj* umido

Danube ['dænjub] *s* Danubio

dapper ['dæpər] *adj* azzimato

dapple ['dæpəl] *adj* pezzato ‖ *tr* chiazzare

dap'ple-gray' *adj* storno

dare [der] *s* sfida ‖ *tr* sfidare ‖ *intr* osare; **I dare say** oserei dire; forse, e.g., **I dare say we will be done at seven** forse avremo finito alle sette; **to dare to** (to have the courage to) osare di, fidarsi a

dare'dev'il *s* scavezzacollo

daring ['derɪŋ] *adj* temerario, spericolato ‖ *s* audacia, temerarietà *f*

dark [dɑrk] *adj* scuro; (complexion) bruno; oscuro, segreto; (gloomy) tetro, fosco ‖ *s* oscurità *f*, scuro; tenebre *fpl*; **in the dark** al buio

Dark' Ag'es *spl* alto medio evo

dark-complexioned ['dɑrkkəm'plɛk-ʃənd] *adj* bruno

darken ['dɑrkən] *tr* scurire, oscurare ‖ *intr* scurirsi, oscurarsi

dark' horse' *s* vincitore improvviso, outsider *m*

darkly ['dɑrklɪ] *adv* oscuramente; segretamente

dark' meat' *s* gamba o anca (di pollo o tacchino)

darkness ['dɑrknɪs] *s* oscurità *f*

dark'room' *s* camera oscura

darling ['dɑrlɪŋ] *adj & s* caro, amato

darn [dɑrn] *s* rammendo ‖ *tr* rammendare ‖ *interj* (coll) accidenti!

darned [dɑrnd] *adj* (coll) maledetto ‖ *adv* maledettamente; (coll) tremendamente

darnel ['dɑrnəl] *s* zizzania

darning ['dɑrnɪŋ] *s* rammendo

darn'ing nee'dle *s* ago da rammendo

dart [dɑrt] *s* freccia, dardo; (game) frecciolo ‖ *intr* dardeggiare; lanciarsi, precipitarsi

dash [dæʃ] *s* sciacquio; piccola quantità, sospetto; (spirit) brio; (typ, telg) trattino, lineetta ‖ *tr* lanciare; mescolare; (s.o.'s hopes) frustrare; deprimere; **to dash off** gettar giù; **to dash to pieces** fare a pezzi ‖ *intr* precipitarsi; **to dash against** gettarsi contro; **to dash by** passare a gran velocità; **to dash in** entrare come un razzo; **to dash off** or **out** andarsene in fretta; lanciarsi fuori

dash'board' *s* cruscotto; (in an open carriage) parafango

dashing ['dæʃɪŋ] *adj* impetuoso; vistoso ‖ *s* (of waves) sciacquio

dastard ['dæstərd] *adj & s* vile *mf*, codardo

da'ta proc'essing *s* elaborazione

date [det] *s* (time) data; (palm) palma da datteri; (fruit) dattero; (appointment) (coll) appuntamento; **out of date** fuori moda; **to date** sinora; **up to date** a giorno ‖ *tr* datare; (coll) avere un appuntamento con ‖ *intr*—**to date from** partire da

date' line' *s* linea del cambiamento di data

dative ['detɪv] *adj & s* dativo

datum ['detəm] or ['dætəm] *s* (**data** ['detə] or ['dætə]) dato

daub [dɔb] *s* imbratto ‖ *tr* imbrattare

daughter ['dɔtər] *s* figlia, figliola

daughter-in-law ['dɔtərɪn,lɔ] *s* (**daughters-in-law**) nuora

daunt [dɔnt] *tr* spaventare; intimidire

dauntless ['dɔntlɪs] *adj* intrepido

dauphin ['dɔfɪn] *s* delfino

davenport ['dævən,pɔrt] *s* sofà *m*, sofà *m* letto

davit ['dævɪt] *s* gru *f* per lancia

daw [dɔ] *s* cornacchia

dawdle ['dɔdəl] *intr* bighellonare

dawn [dɔn] *s* alba ‖ *intr* (said of the day) farsi, nascere, spuntare; **to dawn on** cominciare a apparire nella mente di

day [de] *adj* diurno; (student) esterno ‖ *s* giorno; (of travel, work, etc.)

giornata; **a few days ago** giorni fa; **any day now** da un giorno all'altro; **by day** di giorno; **the day after** il giorno dopo; **the day after tomorrow** dopodomani; **the day before yesterday** ieri l'altro; **to call it a day** (coll) finire di lavorare

day′ bed′ *s* sofà *m* letto
day′book′ *s* brogliaccio
day′break′ *s* far *m* del giorno
day′dream′ *s* fantasticheria ‖ *intr* fantasticare
day′ la′borer *s* giornaliero
day′light′ *s* luce *f* del giorno; alba; **in broad daylight** alla luce del sole; **to see daylight** comprendere; vedere la fine
day′light-sav′ing time′ *s* ora legale, ora estiva
day′ nurs′ery *s* asilo infantile
day′ off′ *s* giorno di vacanza; (*of servant*) libera uscita
day′ of reck′oning *s* giorno di rendiconto; (*last judgment*) giorno del giudizio
day′ shift′ *s* turno diurno
day′time′ *adj* diurno ‖ *s* giornata
daze [dez] *s* stordimento; **in a daze** stordito ‖ *tr* stordire
dazzle [′dæzəl] *s* abbagliamento ‖ *tr* abbagliare
dazzling [′dæzlɪŋ] *adj* abbagliante
deacon [′dikən] *s* diacono
dead [dɛd] *adj* morto ‖ *s*—**in the dead of** (*e.g., night*) nel pieno di; **the dead** i morti ‖ *adv* (coll) completamente; (*abruptly*) (coll) di colpo
dead′ beat′ *adj* (coll) stanco morto
dead′beat′ *s* (coll) scroccone *m*
dead′ cen′ter *s* punto morto
dead′drunk′ *adj* ubriaco fradicio
deaden [′dɛdən] *tr* attutire; (*e.g., s.o.'s senses*) ottundere
dead′ end′ *s* vicolo cieco
dead′ let′ter *s* lettera morta; lettera non reclamata
dead′line′ *s* termine *m*
dead′lock′ *s* punto morto ‖ *tr* portare al punto morto ‖ *intr* giungere al punto morto
dead·ly [′dɛdli] *adj* (-lier; -liest) mortale; insopportabile
dead′ pan′ *s* (slang) faccia senza espressione
dead′pan′ *adj* senza espressione
dead′ reck′oning *s* (naut) stima
dead′wood′ *s* legna secca; (fig) zavorra
deaf [dɛf] *adj* sordo; **to turn a deaf ear** fare orecchio di mercante
deaf′-and-dumb′ *adj* sordomuto
deafen [′dɛfən] *tr* assordare, intronare
deafening [′dɛfənɪŋ] *adj* assordante
deaf′-mute′ *s* sordomuto
deafness [′dɛfnɪs] *s* sordità *f*
deal [dil] *s* accordo; quantità *f*; (cards) mano, girata; (coll) affare *m*; (coll) trattamento; **a good deal (of)** or **a great deal (of)** moltissimo ‖ *v* (*pret & pp* **dealt** [dɛlt]) *tr* (*a blow*) menare; (cards) fare, sfogliare; **to deal s.o. in** (coll) includere ‖ *intr* mercanteggiare, commerciare; fare le

carte; **to deal with** trattare con; trattare di
dealer [′dilər] *s* commerciante *mf*, esercente *mf*; (cards) mazziere *m*
dean [din] *s* decano
dear [dir] *adj* (*beloved; expensive*) caro; **dear me!** povero me!; **Dear Sir** egregio Signore ‖ *s* caro
dearie [′dɪri] *s* (coll) caro
dearth [dʌrθ] *s* scarsezza; insufficienza
death [dɛθ] *s* morte *f*; **to bleed to death** morire dissanguato; **to burn to death** morire bruciato; **to choke to death** morire di soffocazione; **to freeze to death** morire di gelo; **to put to death** dare la morte a; **to shoot to death** uccidere a fucilate; **to stab to death** scannare; **to starve to death** far morire di fame; morire di fame
death′bed′ *s* letto di morte
death′blow′ *s* colpo mortale
deathless [′dɛθlɪs] *adj* immortale, eterno
deathly [′dɛθli] *adj* mortale ‖ *adv* mortalmente; assolutamente
death′ pen′alty *s* pena di morte
death′ rate′ *s* mortalità *f*
death′ rat′tle *s* rantolo della morte
death′ ray′ *s* raggio della morte
death′ sen′tence *s* pena di morte
death′ war′rant *s* pena di morte; fine *f* di ogni speranza
death′watch′ *s* veglia mortuaria; (zool) orologio della morte
debacle [de′bakəl] *s* disastro; (*downfall*) tracollo; (*in a river*) sgelo repentino
de·bar [dɪ′bɑr] *v* (*pret & pp* **-barred;** *ger* **-barring**) *tr* escludere; proibire (with *dat*)
debark [dɪ′bɑrk] *tr & intr* sbarcare
debarkation [,dibɑr′ke/ən] *s* sbarco
debase [dɪ′bes] *tr* degradare; adulterare
debatable [dɪ′betəbəl] *adj* discutibile
debate [dɪ′bet] *s* discussione ‖ *tr & intr* discutere
debauch [dɪ′bɔtʃ] *s* dissolutezza, corruzione ‖ *tr* corrompere
debauchee [,dɛbə′ʃi] or [,dɛbə′tʃi] *s* degenerato, vizioso
debaucher·y [dɪ′bɔtʃəri] *s* (-ies) dissolutezza, corruzione
debenture [dɪ′bɛntʃər] *s* (bond) obbligazione; (*voucher*) buono
debilitate [dɪ′bɪlɪ,tet] *tr* debilitare
debili·ty [dɪ′bɪlɪti] *s* (-ties) debolezza
debit [′dɛbɪt] *s* debito; (*debit side*) (com) dare *m* ‖ *tr* addebitare
debonair [,dɛbə′nɛr] *adj* gioviale; cortese
debris [de′bri] *s* detrito, rottami *mpl*
debt [dɛt] *s* debito; **to run into debt** indebitarsi
debtor [′dɛtər] *s* debitore *m*
debut [de′bju] or [′dɛbju] *s* debutto; **to make one's debut** debuttare ‖ *intr* debuttare
debutante [,dɛbju′tɑnt] or [′dɛbjə-,tænt] *s* debuttante *f*, esordiente *f*
decade [′dɛked] *s* decennio
decadence [dɪ′kedəns] *s* decadenza

decadent [dɪ'kedənt] *adj & s* decadente *mf*

decanter [dɪ'kæntər] *s* boccia

decapitate [dɪ'kæpɪ,tet] *tr* decapitare

decay [dɪ'ke] *s (decline)* decadimento; *(rotting)* marciume *m*, putredine *f*; *(of teeth)* carie *f* ‖ *tr* imputridire ‖ *intr* imputridire, marcire; *(said of teeth)* cariarsi

decease [dɪ'sis] *s* decesso ‖ *intr* decedere

deceased [dɪ'sist] *adj & s* defunto

deceit [dɪ'sit] *s* inganno, frode *f*

deceitful [dɪ'sitfəl] *adj* ingannatore, menzognero, subdolo

deceive [dɪ'siv] *tr & intr* ingannare

decelerate [dɪ'selə,ret] *tr & intr* decelerare

December [dɪ'sembər] *s* dicembre *m*

decen·cy ['disənsɪ] *s* (-cies) decenza, pudore *m*; **decencies** convenienze *fpl*

decent ['disənt] *adj* decente; *(proper)* conveniente

decentralize [dɪ'sentrə,laɪz] *tr* decentrare

deception [dɪ'sepʃən] *s* inganno

deceptive [dɪ'septɪv] *adj* ingannevole

decide [dɪ'saɪd] *tr* decidere ‖ *intr* decidere, decidersi

decimal ['desɪməl] *adj & s* decimale *m*

dec'imal point' *s (in Italian the comma is used to separate the decimal fraction from the integer)* virgola

decimate ['desɪ,met] *tr* decimare

decipher [dɪ'saɪfər] *tr* decifrare

decision [dɪ'sɪʒən] *s* decisione

decisive [dɪ'saɪsɪv] *adj* decisivo; *(resolute)* fermo

deck [dek] *s (of cards)* mazzo; *(naut)* coperta, tolda, ponte *m*; **on deck** (coll) pronto; (coll) prossimo ‖ *tr*—**to deck out** adornare; *(with flags)* imbandierare

deck' chair' *s* sedia a sdraio

deck' hand' *s* marinaio di coperta

deck'house' *s* (naut) tuga

deck'le edge' ['dekəl] *s* sbavatura

declaim [dɪ'klem] *tr & intr* declamare

declaration [,deklə'reʃən] *s* dichiarazione

declarative [dɪ'klærətɪv] *adj* declaratorio; (gram) enunciativo

declare [dɪ'kler] *tr* dichiarare ‖ *intr* dichiararsi

declension [dɪ'klenʃən] *s* declinazione

declination [,deklɪ'neʃən] *s* declinazione

decline [dɪ'klaɪn] *s* decadenza; *(in prices)* ribasso; *(in health)* deperimento; *(of sun)* tramonto ‖ *tr* declinare ‖ *intr* declinare; decadere, scadere

declivi·ty [dɪ'klɪvɪtɪ] *s* (-ties) declivio, pendice *f*

decode [di'kod] *tr* decifrare

décolleté [,dekal'te] *adj* scollato

decompose [,dɪkəm'poz] *tr* decomporre ‖ *intr* decomporsi

decomposition [,dikampə'zɪʃən] *s* decomposizione

décor [de'kɔr] *s* decorazione; *(of a room)* stile *m*; (theat) scenario

decorate ['dekə,ret] *tr* decorare

decoration [,dekə'reʃən] *s* decorazione

decorator ['dekə,retər] *s* decoratore *m*

decorous ['dekərəs] or [dɪ'korəs] *adj* corretto, decoroso

decorum [dɪ'korəm] *s* decoro, correttezza

decoy [dɪ'kɔɪ] or ['dikɔɪ] *s* richiamo; *(for birds)* zimbello; *(person)* adescatore *m* ‖ *tr (to lure)* adescare; *(to deceive)* abbindolare

decrease ['dikris] or [dɪ'kris] *s* diminuzione; *(of salary)* decurtazione ‖ [dɪ'kris] *tr* decurtare ‖ *intr* diminuire

decree [dɪ'kri] *s* decreto ‖ *tr* decretare

de·cry [dɪ'kraɪ] *v (pret & pp -cried) tr* denigrare, screditare

dedicate ['dedɪ,ket] *tr* dedicare

dedication [,dedɪ'keʃən] *s* dedizione; *(inscription in a book)* dedica

deduce [dɪ'djus] or [dɪ'dus] *tr* dedurre

deduct [dɪ'dʌkt] *tr* dedurre, defalcare

deductible [dɪ'dʌktɪbəl] *adj* defalcabile ‖ *s* (ins) franchigia

deduction [dɪ'dʌkʃən] *s* deduzione

deed [did] *s* fatto; *(exploit)* prodezza; (law) titolo ‖ *tr* trasferire legalmente

deem [dim] *tr & intr* credere, giudicare

deep [dip] *adj* profondo; basso; *(woods)* folto; *(friendship)* intimo; **deep in debt** carico di debiti; **deep in thought** assorto in pensieri ‖ *adv* profondamente; **deep into the night** a notte fatta; **to go deep into** approfondirsi in

deepen ['dipən] *tr* approfondire ‖ *intr* approfondirsi

deep'-freeze' *tr (pret -froze [froz]; pp -frozen [frozən]) tr* surgelare

deep-laid ['dip,led] *adj* preparato astutamente

deep' mourn'ing *s* lutto stretto

deep-rooted ['dip,rutɪd] *adj* profondo

deep'-sea' fish'ing *s* pesca d'alto mare or d'altura

deep-seated ['dip,sitɪd] *adj* profondo, connaturato

Deep' South' *s* Profondo Sud

deer [dɪr] *s* cervo

deer'skin' *s* pelle *f* di daino

deface [dɪ'fes] *tr* sfigurare

defamation [,defə'meʃən] or [,difə'meʃən] *s* diffamazione

defame [dɪ'fem] *tr* diffamare

default [dɪ'fɔlt] *s* mancanza; *(failure to act)* inadempienza; **in default of** per mancanza di; **to lose by default** dichiarare forfeit ‖ *tr* essere inadempiente a ‖ *intr* essere inadempiente; (sports) dichiarare forfeit

defeat [dɪ'fit] *s* sconfitta, disfatta ‖ *tr* sconfiggere, vincere

defeatism [dɪ'fitɪzəm] *s* disfattismo

defeatist [dɪ'fitɪst] *adj & s* disfattista *mf*

defecate ['defɪ,ket] *intr* defecare

defect ['difekt] or [dɪ'fekt] *s* vizio, difetto ‖ [dɪ'fekt] *intr* defezionare

defection [dɪ'fekʃən] *s* defezione

defective [dɪ'fektɪv] *adj* difettivo, difettoso

defend [dɪ'fɛnd] *tr* difendere, proteggere

defendant [dɪ'fɛndənt] *s* (law) imputato, querelato

defender [dɪ'fɛndər] *s* difensore *m*

defense [dɪ'fɛns] *s* difesa

defenseless [dɪ'fɛnslɪs] *adj* indifeso

defensive [dɪ'fɛnsɪv] *adj* difensivo ‖ *s* difensiva

de·fer [dɪ'fʌr] *v* (*pret & pp* **-ferred**; *ger* **-ferring**) *tr* differire, rinviare ‖ *intr* rimettersi

deference ['dɛfərəns] *s* deferenza

deferential [ˌdɛfə'rɛn/əl] *adj* deferente

deferment [dɪ'fʌrmənt] *s* differimento

defiance [dɪ'faɪ·əns] *s* opposizione; sfida; **in defiance of** a dispetto di

defiant [dɪ'faɪ·ənt] *adj* provocante, ostile

deficien·cy [dɪ'fɪ/ənsi] *s* (**-cies**) deficienza; (com) ammanco

deficient [dɪ'fɪ/ənt] *adj* deficiente

deficit ['dɛfɪsɪt] *adj* deficitario ‖ *s* deficit *m*, disavanzo

defile [dɪ'faɪl] *or* ['difaɪl] *s* gola, passo ‖ [dɪ'faɪl] *tr* profanare ‖ *intr* marciare in fila

define [dɪ'faɪn] *tr* definire

definite ['dɛfɪnɪt] *adj* definito; (gram) determinativo, determinato

definition [ˌdɛfɪ'nɪ/ən] *s* definizione

definitive [dɪ'fɪnɪtɪv] *adj* definitivo

deflate [dɪ'flet] *tr* sgonfiare; (*s.o.'s hopes*) deprimere; (*e.g., currency*) deflazionare

deflation [dɪ'fle/ən] *s* sgonfiamento; (*of prices*) deflazione

deflect [dɪ'flɛkt] *tr* far deflettere ‖ *intr* deflettere

deflower [dɪ'flaʊ·ər] *tr* privare dei fiori; (*a woman*) deflorare

deforest [di'fɔrɛst] *or* [di'fɑrɛst] *tr* disboscare, smacchiare

deform [dɪ'fɔrm] *tr* deformare

deformed [dɪ'fɔrmd] *adj* deforme

deformi·ty [dɪ'fɔrmɪti] *s* (**-ties**) deformità *f*

defraud [dɪ'frɔd] *tr* defraudare

defray [dɪ'fre] *tr* pagare

defrost [di'frɔst] *or* [di'frɑst] *tr* sgelare, sbrinare

defroster [di'frɔstər] *or* [di'frɑstər] *s* (aut) visiera termica

deft [dɛft] *adj* destro, lesto

defunct [dɪ'fʌŋkt] *adj* defunto

de·fy [dɪ'faɪ] *v* (*pret & pp* **-fied**) *tr* sfidare, provocare

degeneracy [dɪ'dʒɛnərəsi] *s* degenerazione

degenerate [dɪ'dʒɛnərɪt] *adj & s* degenerato ‖ [dɪ'dʒɛnəˌret] *intr* degenerare, tralignare

degrade [dɪ'gred] *tr* degradare

degrading [dɪ'gredɪŋ] *adj* degradante

degree [dɪ'gri] *s* grado; titolo accademico; **by degrees** a grado a grado; **to a degree** fino a un certo punto; troppo; **to take a degree** ricevere un titolo di studio

dehydrate [di'haɪdret] *tr* disidratare

deice [di'aɪs] *tr* sgelare

dei·fy ['di·ɪ ˌfaɪ] *v* (*pret & pp* **-fied**) *tr* deificare

deign [den] *intr* degnarsi

dei·ty ['di·ɪti] *s* (**-ties**) deità *f*; **the Deity** Dio

dejected [dɪ'dʒɛktɪd] *adj* demoralizzato

dejection [dɪ'dʒɛk/ən] *s* (*in spirits*) demoralizzazione; (*evacuation*) deiezione

delay [dɪ'le] *s* ritardo, proroga; dilazione; **without further delay** senza ulteriore indugio ‖ *tr* tardare; (*to put off*) differire ‖ *intr* tardare, ritardare

delayed'-ac'tion *adj* a azione differita

delectable [dɪ'lɛktəbəl] *adj* dilettevole

delegate ['dɛlɪ ˌgɛt] *or* ['dɛlɪgɪt] *s* delegato, incaricato; (*to a convention*) congressista *mf* ‖ ['dɛlɪ ˌgɛt] *tr* delegare, incaricare

delegation [ˌdɛlɪ'ge/ən] *s* delegazione

delete [dɪ'lit] *tr* cancellare, sopprimere

deletion [dɪ'li/ən] *s* cancellazione

deliberate [dɪ'lɪbərɪt] *adj* meditato; (*slow in deciding*) cauto; (*slow in moving*) lento ‖ [dɪ'lɪbəˌret] *tr & intr* deliberare

deliberately [dɪ'lɪbərɪtli] *adv* (*on purpose*) deliberatamente; (*without hurrying*) con ponderatezza

delica·cy ['dɛlɪkəsi] *s* (**-cies**) delicatezza; (*choice food*) leccornia

delicatessen [ˌdɛlɪkə'tɛsən] *s* negozio di salumerie ‖ *spl* salumerie *fpl*, articoli alimentari scelti

delicious [dɪ'lɪ/əs] *adj* delizioso

delight [dɪ'laɪt] *s* gioia, delizia ‖ *tr* dilettare ‖ *intr* dilettarsi

delightful [dɪ'laɪtfəl] *adj* delizioso

delinquen·cy [dɪ'lɪŋkwənsi] *s* (**-cies**) colpa; (*offense*) delinquenza; (*in payment of a debt*) morosità *f*

delinquent [dɪ'lɪŋkwənt] *adj* colpevole; (*in payment*) moroso; non pagato ‖ *s* delinquente *m*; debitore moroso

delirious [dɪ'lɪrɪ·əs] *adj* in delirio

deliri·um [dɪ'lɪrɪ·əm] *s* (**-ums** *or* **-a** [ə]) delirio

deliver [dɪ'lɪvər] *tr* consegnare; (*a blow*) affibbiare; (*a speech*) fare; (*a letter*) recapitare; (*electricity or gas*) erogare; (*said of a pregnant woman*) partorire; (*said of a doctor*) assistere durante il parto

deliver·y [dɪ'lɪvəri] *s* (**-ies**) consegna; (*of mail*) distribuzione; (*of merchandise*) fornitura; (*of a speech*) dizione; (*childbirth*) parto; (sports) lancio

deliv'ery·man' *s* (**-men**) fattorino

deliv'ery room' *s* sala parto

deliv'ery truck' *s* furgoncino

dell [dɛl] *s* valletta

delouse [di'laʊs] *or* [di'laʊz] *tr* spidocchiare

delude [dɪ'lud] *tr* illudere, ingannare

deluge ['dɛljudʒ] *s* diluvio, inondazione ‖ **the Deluge** il diluvio universale ‖ *tr* inondare

delusion [dɪ'luʒən] *s* illusione, inganno; (*psychopath*) allucinazione;

(psychopath) idea fissa; **delusions of grandeur** mania di grandezza

de luxe [dɪ'lʊks] or [dɪ'lʌks] adj di lusso || adv in gran lusso

delve [delv] intr frugare; **to delve into** approfondirsi in

demagnetize [di'mægnɪ,taɪz] tr smagnetizzare

demagogue ['demə,gɑg] s demagogo

demand [dɪ'mænd] or [dɪ'mɑnd] s esigenza; (com) richiesta, domanda; **to be in demand** essere in richiesta || tr esigere

demanding [dɪ'mændɪŋ] or [dɪ'mɑndɪŋ] adj esigente, impegnativo

demarcate [dɪ'mɑrket] or ['dimɑr,ket] tr demarcare

démarche [de'mɑrʃ] s progetto, piano

demean [dɪ'min] tr degradare; **to demean oneself** comportarsi; degradarsi

demeanor [dɪ'minər] s condotta, contegno

demented [dɪ'mentɪd] adj demente

demigod ['demɪ,gɑd] s semidio

demijohn ['demɪ,dʒɑn] s damigiana

demilitarize [di'mɪlɪtə,raɪz] tr smilitarizzare

demimonde ['demɪ,mɑnd] s donne fpl della società equivoca

demise [dɪ'maɪz] s decesso

demitasse ['demɪ,tæs] or ['demi,tɑs] s tazzina da caffè; (contents) caffè nero

demobilize [di'mobɪ,laɪz] tr smobilitare

democra·cy [dɪ'mɑkrəsi] s (-cies) democrazia

democrat ['demə,kræt] s democratico

democratic [,demə'krætɪk] adj democratico

demolish [dɪ'mɑlɪʃ] tr demolire

demolition [,demə'lɪʃən] or [,dimə'lɪʃən] s demolizione

demon ['dimən] s demonio

demoniacal [,dimə'naɪ-əkəl] adj demoniaco

demonstrate ['demən,stret] tr & intr dimostrare

demonstration [,demən'streʃən] s dimostrazione

demonstrative [dɪ'mɑnstrətɪv] adj dimostrativo; (giving open exhibition of emotion) espansivo

demonstrator ['demən,stretər] s (of a product) dimostratore m; (in a public gathering) dimostrante m; (product) prodotto usato da dimostratori

demoralize [dɪ'mɑrə,laɪz] or [dɪ'mɔrə,laɪz] tr demoralizzare

demote [dɪ'mot] tr retrocedere

demotion [dɪ'moʃən] s retrocessione

de·mur [dɪ'mʌr] v (pret & pp -murred; ger -murring) intr sollevare obiezioni

demure [dɪ'mjʊr] adj modesto; sobrio

demurrage [dɪ'mʌrɪdʒ] s (com) controstallie fpl; (rr) sosta

den [den] s (of animals, thieves) tana; (little room) bugigattolo; (little room for studying or writing) studiolo; (of lions) (Bib) fossa

denaturalize [di'nætʃərə,laɪz] tr snaturare; privare della nazionalità

dena'tured al'cohol [di'netʃərd] s alcole denaturato

denial [dɪ'naɪ-əl] s diniego; (disavowal) smentita

denim ['denɪm] s tessuto di cotone per tuta; **denims** tuta; (trousers) jeans mpl

denizen ['denɪzən] s abitante mf

Denmark ['denmɑrk] s la Danimarca

denomination [dɪ,nɑmɪ'neʃən] s denominazione; categoria; (com) taglio; (eccl) confessione

denote [dɪ'not] tr denotare, significare

denouement [denu'mɑ̃] s scioglimento

denounce [dɪ'naʊns] tr denunziare

dense [dens] adj denso; stupido

densi·ty ['densɪti] s (-ties) densità f

dent [dent] s ammaccatura; (in a gearwheel) tacca, dente m; **to make a dent** fare progresso; fare impressione || tr ammaccare; (fig) ferire

dental ['dentəl] adj dentale, dentario || s dentale f

den'tal floss' s filo cerato dentario

dentifrice ['dentɪfrɪs] s dentifricio

dentist ['dentɪst] s dentista mf

dentistry ['dentɪstri] s odontoiatria

denture ['dentʃər] s dentiera

denunciation [dɪ,nʌnsɪ'eʃən] or [dɪ,nʌnʃɪ'eʃən] s denunzia

de·ny [dɪ'naɪ] v (pret & pp -nied) tr (to declare not to be true) negare; (to refuse) rifiutare; **to deny oneself to callers** sottrarsi alle visite || intr negare; rifiutare

deodorant [di'odərənt] adj & s deodorante m

deo'dorant spray' s deodorante m spray

deodorize [di'odə,raɪz] tr deodorare

depart [dɪ'pɑrt] intr partire, andarsene; (to diverge) dipartire

departed [dɪ'pɑrtɪd] adj morto, defunto || **the departed** i defunti

department [dɪ'pɑrtmənt] s dipartimento; (of government) ministero; (e.g., of a hospital) reparto; (of agency) sezione, ufficio

depart'ment store' s grandi magazzini mpl

departure [dɪ'pɑrtʃər] s partenza; divergenza, deviazione

depend [dɪ'pend] intr dipendere; **to depend on** (to rely on) contare su; dipendere da

dependable [dɪ'pendəbəl] adj sicuro, fidato

dependence [dɪ'pendəns] s dipendenza; (trust) fiducia

dependen·cy [dɪ'pendənsi] s (-cies) dipendenza; (territory) possessione

dependent [dɪ'pendənt] adj dipendente; a carico; **to be dependent on** dipendere da || s persona a carico

depend'ent clause' s proposizione subordinata

depict [dɪ'pɪkt] tr descrivere, dipingere

deplete [dɪ'plit] tr esaurire

depletion [dɪ'pliʃən] s esaurimento

deplorable [dɪ'plorəbəl] adj deplorevole

deplore [dɪ'plor] tr deplorare

deploy [dɪ'plɔɪ] tr (mil) spiegare, stendere

deployment [dɪ'plɔɪmənt] s (mil) dispositivo, spiegamento

depolarize [di'pola ,raɪz] tr depolarizzare

depopulate [di'papjə ,let] tr spopolare

deport [dɪ'port] tr deportare; **to deport oneself** comportarsi

deportation [,dipor'te/ən] s deportazione

deportee [,dipor'ti] s deportato

deportment [dɪ'portmənt] s condotta, comportamento

depose [dɪ'poz] tr & intr deporre

deposit [dɪ'pazɪt] s deposito; (down payment) caparra || tr depositare || intr depositarsi

depos'it account' s conto corrente

depositor [dɪ'pazɪtər] s versante mf; (to the credit of an established account) correntista mf

deposi•to•ry [dɪ'pazɪ ,tori] s (-ries) deposito; (person) depositario

depos'it slip' s distinta di versamento

depot ['dipo] or ['depo] s magazzino; (mil) deposito; (rr) stazione

depraved [dɪ'prevd] adj depravato

depravi•ty [dɪ'prævɪti] s (-ties) depravazione

deprecate ['deprɪ ,ket] tr deprecare

depreciate [dɪ'pri/ɪ ,et] tr svalutare, deprezzare || intr deprezzarsi

depreciation [dɪ ,pri/ɪ'e/ən] s (drop in value) deprezzamento; (disparagement) disprezzo

depredation [,deprɪ'de/ən] s depredazione

depress [dɪ'pres] tr deprimere; avvilire; (prices) far abbassare

depression [dɪ'pre/ən] s depressione; (gloom) sconforto; (slump) crisi ƒ

deprive [dɪ'praɪv] tr privare; **to deprive oneself** espropriarsi

depth [depθ] s profondità ƒ; (of a house or room) lunghezza; (of sea) fondale m; (fig) vastità ƒ; **in the depth of** nel cuor di; **to go beyond one's depth** non toccare più; (fig) andare oltre le proprie possibilità

depth' bomb' s (aer) bomba antisommergibile

depth' charge' s (nav) granata antisommergibile

depth' of hold' s (naut) puntale m

deputation [,depjə'te/ən] s deputazione

deputize ['depjə ,taɪz] tr deputare

depu•ty ['depjəti] s (-ties) deputato

derail [dɪ'rel] tr far deragliare || intr deragliare, deviare

derailment [dɪ'relmənt] s deragliamento, deviamento

derange [dɪ'rendʒ] tr (to disarrange) dissestare; (to make insane) squilibrare, render pazzo

derangement [dɪ'rendʒmənt] s (disorder) disordine m; (insanity) squilibrio mentale, pazzia

der•by ['dʌrbi] s (-bies) bombetta; (race) derby m

derelict ['derɪlɪkt] adj derelitto; negligente || s derelitto; (naut) relitto

dereliction [,derɪ'lɪk/ən] s (in one's duty) negligenza; (law) derelizione

deride [dɪ'raɪd] tr deridere, schernire, farsi beffe di

derision [dɪ'rɪʒən] s derisione, scherno

derisive [dɪ'raɪsɪv] adj derisorio

derivation [,derɪ've/ən] s derivazione

derivative [dɪ'rɪvətɪv] adj & s derivato

derive [dɪ'raɪv] tr & intr derivare

dermatology [,dʌrmə'talədʒi] s dermatologia

derogatory [dɪ'ragə ,tori] adj dispregiativo

derrick ['derɪk] s gru ƒ; (naut) picco di carico

dervish ['dʌrvɪ/] s dervis m

desalinization [di ,selɪnɪ'ze/ən] s desalazione

desalt [di'sɔlt] tr desalificare

descend [dɪ'send] tr discendere || intr discendere; **to descend on** calare su, gettarsi su

descendant [dɪ'sendənt] adj & s discendente mf

descendent [dɪ'sendənt] adj discendente

descent [dɪ'sent] s (slope) china; (decline) declino; discesa; (lineage) stirpe ƒ, discendenza; (sudden raid) calata

Descent' from the Cross' s Deposizione dalla Croce

describe [dɪ'skraɪb] tr descrivere

description [dɪ'skrɪp/ən] s descrizione

descriptive [dɪ'skrɪptɪv] adj descrittivo

de•scry [dɪ'skraɪ] v (pret & pp **-scried**) tr avvistare

desecrate ['desɪ ,kret] tr profanare, dissacrare

desecration [,desɪ'kre/ən] s profanazione, dissacrazione

desegregate [di'segrɪ ,get] intr sopprimere la segregazione razziale

desegregation [di ,segrɪ'ge/ən] s desegregazione

desensitize [di'sensɪ ,taɪz] tr desensibilizzare

desert ['dezərt] adj & s deserto || [dɪ'zʌrt] s merito; **he received his just deserts** ricevette quanto meritava || tr & intr disertare

deserter [dɪ'zʌrtər] s disertore m

deserted [dɪ'zʌrtɪd] adj (person) abbandonato; (place) deserto

desertion [dɪ'zʌr/ən] s diserzione; abbandono del coniuge

deserve [dɪ'zʌrv] tr & intr meritare

deservedly [dɪ'zʌrvɪdli] adv meritatamente, meritevolmente

design [dɪ'zaɪn] s disegno; (of a play) congegno; **to have designs on** aver mire su || tr disegnare; progettare || intr disegnare; **designed for** destinato a

designate ['dezɪg ,net] tr designare

designer [dɪ'zaɪnər] s disegnatore m

designing [dɪ'zaɪnɪŋ] adj intrigante, macchinatore || s disegnazione

desirable [dɪ'zaɪrəbəl] adj desiderabile

desire [dɪ'zaɪr] s desiderio || tr desiderare

desirous [dɪ'zaɪrəs] adj desideroso

desist [dɪ'zɪst] intr desistere

desk [desk] s scrittoio; tavolo d'ufficio;

(*lectern*) leggio; (*of professor*) cattedra; (*of pupil*) banco; (*com*) cassa

desk'bound' *adj* sedentario; legato al tavolino

desk' pad' *s* blocco da tavolo; blocco per appunti

desolate ['dɛsəlɪt] *adj* desolato, deserto; (*hopeless*) disperato; (*dismal*) lugubre ‖ ['dɛsə͵let] *tr* desolare; devastare

desolation [͵dɛsə'leʃən] *s* desolazione; devastazione

despair [dɪ'spɛr] *s* disperazione; **to be in despair** disperarsi ‖ *intr* disperare, disperarsi

despairing [dɪ'spɛrɪŋ] *adj* disperato

despera-do [͵dɛspə'redo] *or* [͵dɛspə'rado] *s* (**-does** *or* **-dos**) fuorilegge disposto a tutto

desperate ['dɛspərɪt] *adj* disposto a tutto; (*hopeless*) disperato; (*very bad*) atroce, terribile; (*bitter, excessive*) accanito; (*remedy*) estremo

desperation [͵dɛspə'reʃən] *s* disperazione

despicable ['dɛspɪkəbəl] *adj* spregevole, incanaglito

despise [dɪ'spaɪz] *tr* sprezzare, disprezzare, vilipendere

despite [dɪ'spaɪt] *prep* malgrado

despoil [dɪ'spɔɪl] *tr* spogliare

desponden-cy [dɪ'spɑndənsi] *s* (**-cies**) scoraggiamento, abbattimento

despondent [dɪ'spɑndənt] *adj* scoraggiato, abbattuto

despot ['dɛspət] *s* despota *m*

despotic [dɛs'pɑtɪk] *adj* dispotico

despotism ['dɛspə͵tɪzəm] *s* dispotismo

dessert [dɪ'zʌrt] *s* dessert *m*

dessert' spoon' *s* cucchiaio *or* cucchiaino da dessert

destination [͵dɛstɪ'neʃən] *s* destinazione

destine ['dɛstɪn] *tr* destinare

desti-ny ['dɛstɪni] *s* (**-nies**) destino

destitute ['dɛstɪ͵tjut] *or* ['dɛstɪ͵tut] *adj* (*poverty-stricken*) indigente; (*lacking*) privo

destitution [͵dɛstɪ'tjuʃən] *or* [͵dɛstɪ'tuʃən] *s* indigenza, miseria

destroy [dɪ'strɔɪ] *tr* distruggere

destroyer [dɪ'strɔɪ·ər] *s* (nav) cacciatorpediniere *m*

destruction [dɪ'strʌkʃən] *s* distruzione

destructive [dɪ'strʌktɪv] *adj* distruttivo

desultory ['dɛsəl͵tori] *adj*. saltuario, sconnesso

detach [dɪ'tætʃ] *tr* staccare, distaccare; (mil) distaccare

detachable [dɪ'tætʃəbəl] *adj* staccabile; separabile

detached [dɪ'tætʃt] *adj* (*e.g., stub*) staccato; (*e.g., house*) discosto; (*aloof*) riservato, freddo; imparziale

detachment [dɪ'tætʃmənt] *s* distacco; imparzialità *f;* (mil) distaccamento

detail [dɪ'tel] *or* ['ditel] *s* dettaglio, ragguaglio; (mil) distaccamento ‖ [dɪ'tel] *tr* dettagliare; (mil) distaccare

detain [dɪ'ten] *tr* detenere, trattenere

detect [dɪ'tɛkt] *tr* scoprire, discernere; (rad) rivelare

detection [dɪ'tɛkʃən] *s* scoperta; (rad) rivelazione

detective [dɪ'tɛktɪv] *s* detective *m*

detec'tive sto'ry *s* romanzo poliziesco, romanzo giallo

detector [dɪ'tɛktər] *s* (rad) detector *m*, rivelatore *m*

detention [dɪ'tɛnʃən] *s* detenzione

de-ter [dɪ'tʌr] *v* (*pret & pp* **-terred;** *ger* **-terring**) *tr* distogliere, impedire

detergent [dɪ'tʌrdʒənt] *adj & s* detergente *m*

deteriorate [dɪ'tɪrɪ·ə͵ret] *tr* deteriorare ‖ *intr* deteriorarsi, andar giù

determination [dɪ͵tʌrmɪ'neʃən] *s* determinazione

determine [dɪ'tʌrmɪn] *tr* determinare

determined [dɪ'tʌrmɪnd] *adj* determinato, risoluto

deterrent [dɪ'tʌrənt] *s* deterrente *m*

detest [dɪ'tɛst] *tr* detestare, odiare

dethrone [dɪ'θron] *tr* detronizzare

detonate ['dɛtə͵net] *or* ['dɪtə͵net] *tr* far scoppiare ‖ *intr* detonare

detonator ['dɛtə͵netər] *s* innesco

detour ['ditur] *or* [dɪ'tur] *s* deviazione ‖ *tr* far deviare ‖ *intr* deviare

detract [dɪ'trækt] *tr* detrarre ‖ *intr*—**to detract from** diminuire

detractor [dɪ'træktər] *s* detrattore *m*

detriment ['dɛtrɪmənt] *s* detrimento; **to the detriment of a** danno di

detrimental [͵dɛtrɪ'mɛntəl] *adj* pregiudizievole

deuce [djus] *or* [dus] *s* (cards) due *m;* **the deuce!** diavolo!

devaluate [di'væljuˌet] *tr* svalutare

devaluation [di͵væljuˈeʃən] *s* devalutazione, svalutazione

devastate ['dɛvəs͵tet] *tr* devastare

devastating ['dɛvəs͵tetɪŋ] *adj* devastatore, devastante; (*e.g., reply*) schiacciante, annichilante

devastation [͵dɛvəs'teʃən] *s* devastazione

develop [dɪ'vɛləp] *tr* sviluppare; (phot) sviluppare, rivelare ‖ *intr* svilupparsi; manifestarsi

developer [dɪ'vɛləpər] *s* (*e.g., of a new engine*) sfruttatore *m;* (*in real estate*) specialista *mf* in lottizzazione; (phot) sviluppatore *m*, rivelatore *m*

development [dɪ'vɛləpmənt] *s* sviluppo; valorizzazione; sfruttamento; (phot) rivelazione

deviate ['divi͵et] *tr* sviare ‖ *intr* deviare, sviarsi

deviation [͵divi'eʃən] *s* deviazione

deviationism [͵divi'eʃə͵nɪzəm] *s* deviazionismo

deviationist [͵divi'eʃənɪst] *s* deviazionista *mf*

device [dɪ'vaɪs] *s* dispositivo, congegno; (*trick*) stratagemma *m;* (*motto*) divisa, emblema *m;* **to leave s.o. to his own devices** lasciare che qlcu faccia come gli pare e piace

dev-il ['dɛvəl] *s* diavolo; **between the devil and the deep blue sea** fra l'incudine e il martello; **to raise the devil** (slang) fare diavolo a quattro ‖ *v* (*pret & pp* **-iled** *or* **-illed;** *ger*

-iling or **-illing** *tr* condire con spezie or con pepe; (coll) infastidire

devilish ['devəlɪʃ] *adj* diabolico

devilment ['devəlmənt] *s* (*mischief*) diavoleria; (*evil*) cattiveria

devil·try ['devəltri] *s* (**-tries**) malvagità *f*, crudeltà *f*; (*mischief*) diavoleria

devious ['divɪ·əs] *adj* (*tricky*) traverso; (*roundabout*) tortuoso

devise [dɪ'vaɪz] *tr* ideare, inventare; (law) legare, disporre per testamento

devoid [dɪ'vɔɪd] *adj* sprovvisto

devolve [dɪ'valv] *intr*—**to devolve on** ricadere su

devote [dɪ'vot] *tr* dedicare

devoted [dɪ'votɪd] *adj* devoto; dedito, dedicato

devotee [ˌdevə'ti] *s* devoto; (*fan*) fanatico, tifoso, entusiasta *mf*

devotion [dɪ'voʃən] *s* devozione; (*e.g., to work*) dedizione; **devotions** orazioni *mpl*, preghiere *fpl*

devour [dɪ'vaur] *tr* divorare

devout [dɪ'vaut] *adj* devoto; sincero

dew [dju] or [du] *s* rugiada

dew'drop' *s* goccia di rugiada

dew'lap' *s* giogaia

dew·y ['dju·i] or ['du·i] *adj* (**-ier; -iest**) rugiadoso

dexterity [deks'terɪti] *s* destrezza

diabetes [ˌdaɪ·ə'bitɪs] or [ˌdaɪ·ə'bitiz] *s* diabete *m*

diabetic [ˌdaɪ·ə'betɪk] or [ˌdaɪ·ə·'bitɪk] *adj* & *s* diabetico

diabolic(al) [ˌdaɪ·ə·bə'balɪk(əl)] *adj* diabolico

diadem ['daɪ·əˌdem] *s* diadema *m*

diaere·sis [daɪ'erɪsɪs] *s* (**-ses** [ˌsiz]) dieresi *f*

diagnose [ˌdaɪ·əg'nos] or [ˌdaɪ·əg'noz] *tr* diagnosticare

diagno·sis [ˌdaɪ·əg'nosɪs] *s* (**-ses** [siz]) diagnosi *f*

diagonal [daɪ'ægənəl] *adj* & *s* diagonale *f*

dia·gram ['daɪ·əˌgræm] *s* diagramma *m*; (*drawing*) schema *m*; (*plan*) prospetto *m* ‖ *v* (*pret* & *pp* **-gramed** or **-grammed**; *ger* **-graming** or **-gramming**) *tr* diagrammare

dial ['daɪ·əl] *s* (*of watch*) quadrante *m*; (rad) tabella graduata, sintogramma *m*; (telp) disco combinatore ‖ *tr* (rad) sintonizzare; (*a person*) (telp) chiamare; (*a number*) (telp) comporre; (*the phone*) (telp) comporre il numero di ‖ *intr* (telp) comporre il numero

dialect ['daɪ·əˌlekt] *s* dialetto

dialing ['daɪ·əlɪŋ] *s* composizione del numero

dialogue ['daɪ·əˌlɔg] or ['daɪ·əˌlag] *s* dialogo

di'al tel'ephone *s* telefono automatico

di'al tone' *s* (telp) segnale *m* di via libera

diameter [daɪ'æmɪtər] *s* diametro

diametric(al) [ˌdaɪ·ə'metrɪk(əl)] *adj* diametrico, diametrale

diamond ['daɪmənd] *s* diamante *m*; (*figure of a rhombus*) losanga; (baseball) diamante *m*; **diamonds** (cards) quadri *mpl*

diaper ['daɪ·pər] *s* pannolino

diaphanous [daɪ'æfənəs] *adj* diafano

diaphragm ['daɪ·əˌfræm] *s* diaframma *m*; (telp) membrana

diarrhea [ˌdaɪ·ə'ri·ə] *s* diarrea

dia·ry ['daɪ·əri] *s* (**-ries**) diario

diastole [daɪ'æstəli] *s* diastole *f*

diathermy ['daɪ·əˌθɜrmi] *s* diatermia

dice [daɪs] *spl* dadi *mpl*; (*small cubes*) cubetti *mpl*; **no dice** (slang) niente da fare; (slang) risposta a picche

dice' cup' *s* bussolotto

dichloride [daɪ'klorad] *s* bicloruro

dichoto·my [daɪ'katəmi] *s* (**-mies**) dicotomia

dickey ['dɪki] *s* camiciola; (*starched insert*) sparato; (bib) bavaglino

dictaphone ['dɪktəˌfon] *s* dittafono

dictate ['dɪktet] *s* dettato ‖ ['dɪktet] or [dɪk'tet] *tr* dettare

dictation [dɪk'teʃən] *s* dettato; (*act of ordering*) ordine *m*; **to take dictation** scrivere sotto dettatura

dictator ['dɪktetər] or [dɪk'tetər] *s* dittatore *m*

dictatorship ['dɪktetərˌʃɪp] or [dɪk'tetərʃɪp] *s* dittatura

diction ['dɪkʃən] *s* dizione

dictionar·y ['dɪkʃənˌɛri] *s* (**-ies**) dizionario, vocabolario

dic·tum ['dɪktəm] *s* (**-ta** [tə]) detto, sentenza

didactic(al) [daɪ'dæktɪk(əl)] or [dɪ'dæktɪk(əl)] *adj* didattico

die [daɪ] *s* (**dice** [daɪs]) dado; **the die is cast** il dado è tratto ‖ *s* (**dies**) (*for stamping coins, medals,* etc.) stampo; (*for cutting threads*) filiera ‖ *v* (*pret* & *pp* **died**; *ger* **dying**) *intr* morire; **to die hard** morire lentamente; morire lottando; **to die laughing** morire dalle risa; **to die off** morire uno per uno

die'-hard' *adj* & *s* intransigente *m*

die'sel oil' ['dizəl] *s* nafta, gasolio

die'stock' *s* girafiliera

diet ['daɪ·ət] *s* dieta, regime *m* ‖ *intr* stare a dieta

dietetic [ˌdaɪ·ə'tetɪk] *adj* dietetico ‖ **dietetics** *ssg* dietetica

dietitian [ˌdaɪ·ə'tɪʃən] *s* dietista *mf*

differ ['dɪfər] *intr* (*to be different*) differire, differenziarsi; **to differ with** dissentire da

difference ['dɪfərəns] *s* differenza; **to make no difference** fare lo stesso; **to split the difference** dividere la differenza; (fig) venire a un compromesso

different ['dɪfərənt] *adj* differente

differential [ˌdɪfə'renʃəl] *adj* & *s* differenziale *m*

differentiate [ˌdɪfə'renʃɪˌet] *tr* differenziare ‖ *intr* differenziarsi

difficult ['dɪfɪˌkʌlt] *adj* difficile

difficul·ty ['dɪfɪˌkʌlti] *s* (**-ties**) difficoltà *f*

diffident ['dɪfɪdənt] *adj* timido, imbarazzato

diffuse [dɪ'fjus] *adj* diffuso ‖ [dɪ'fjuz] *tr* diffondere ‖ *intr* diffondersi

dig [dɪg] *s* (*poke*) botta, spintone *m*; (*jibe*) stoccata, fiancata ‖ *v* (*pret* & *pp* **dug** [dʌg]; *ger* **digging**) *tr* scavare, sterrare; **to dig up** dissodare; (*to uncover*) dissotterrare ‖ *intr* scavare; **to dig in** (mil) fortificarsi; **to dig into** (coll) sprofondarsi in

digest ['daɪdʒɛst] *s* compendio; (law) digesto ‖ [dɪ'dʒɛst] *or* [daɪ'dʒɛst] *tr & intr* digerire

digestible [dɪ'dʒɛstɪbəl] *or* [daɪ'dʒɛstɪbəl] *adj* digeribile, digestibile

digestion [dɪ'dʒɛstʃən] *or* [daɪ'dʒɛstʃən] *s* digestione

digestive [dɪ'dʒɛstɪv] *or* [daɪ'dʒɛstɪv] *adj* (*tube*) digerente ‖ *s* digestivo

digit ['dɪdʒɪt] *s* cifra, unità *f*; (*finger*) dito; (*toe*) dito del piede

dig'ital clock' *s* orologio a scatto

digitalis [ˌdɪdʒɪ'tælɪs] *or* [ˌdɪdʒɪ'telɪs] *s* (bot) digitale *f*; (pharm) digitalina

dignified ['dɪgnɪˌfaɪd] *adj* dignitoso, fiero, contegnoso

digni-fy ['dɪgnɪˌfaɪ] *v* (*pret & pp* -**fied**) *tr* (*to ennoble*) nobilitare; onorare, esaltare; dare la dignità a

dignitar-y ['dɪgnɪˌtɛri] *s* (-**ies**) dignitario; **dignitaries** dignità *fpl*

digni-ty ['dɪgnɪti] *s* (-**ties**) dignità *f*, decoro; **to stand on one's dignity** mantenere la propria dignità

digress [dɪ'grɛs] *or* [daɪ'grɛs] *intr* digredire, divagare

digression [dɪ'grɛʃən] *or* [daɪ'grɛʃən] *s* digressione, divagazione

dike [daɪk] *s* diga; (*in a river*) argine *m*; (*ditch*) fosso; scarpata

dilapidated [dɪ'læpɪˌdetɪd] *adj* dilapidato, decrepito

dilate [daɪ'let] *tr* dilatare ‖ *intr* dilatarsi

dilatory ['dɪləˌtori] *adj* lento, tardivo; (*e.g., strategy*) dilatorio

dilemma [dɪ'lɛmə] *s* dilemma *m*

dilettan-te [ˌdɪlə'tænti] *adj* dilettantesco ‖ *s* (-**tes** *or* -**ti** [ti]) dilettante *mf*

diligence ['dɪlɪdʒəns] *s* diligenza

diligent ['dɪlɪdʒənt] *adj* diligente

dill [dɪl] *s* (bot) aneto

dillydal-ly ['dɪliˌdæli] *v* (*pret & pp* -**lied**) *intr* farla lunga

dilute [dɪ'lut] *or* [daɪ'lut] *adj* diluito ‖ [dɪ'lut] *tr* diluire ‖ *intr* diluirsi

dilution [dɪ'luʃən] *s* diluizione

dim [dɪm] *adj* (**dimmer**; **dimmest**) (*light*) fioco; (*sight*) debole; (*memory*) vago; (*color*) smorzato; (*sound*) sordo; **to take a dim view of** avere una visione pessimistica di ‖ *v* (*pret & pp* **dimmed**; *ger* **dimming**) *tr* (*lights*) smorzare; **to dim the headlights** abbassare i fari

dime [daɪm] *s* moneta di dieci centesimi di dollaro

dimension [dɪ'mɛnʃən] *s* dimensione

diminish [dɪ'mɪnɪʃ] *tr & intr* diminuire, scemare

diminutive [dɪ'mɪnjətɪv] *adj* (*tiny*) minuscolo; (gram) diminutivo ‖ *s* diminutivo

dimly ['dɪmli] *adv* indistintamente

dimmer ['dɪmər] *s* smorzatore *m*; (aut) luce *f* di incrocio; **dimmers** fari *mpl* antiabbaglianti

dimple ['dɪmpəl] *s* fossetta

dimwit ['dɪmˌwɪt] *s* (slang) stupido, cretino

din [dɪn] *s* fragore *m*, frastuono ‖ *v* (*pret & pp* **dinned**) *ger* **dinning**) *tr* assordare; **to din s.th into s.o.'s ears** rintronare qlco nelle orecchie di qlcu

dine [daɪn] *tr* offrire un pranzo a; offire una cena a ‖ *intr* pasteggiare; cenare; **to dine out** mangiare fuori di casa

diner ['daɪnər] *s* commensale *m*; (rr) vettura ristorante; (U.S.A.) ristorante *m* a forma di vagone

ding-dong ['dɪŋˌdɔŋ] *or* ['dɪŋˌdɑŋ] *s* dindon *m*

din-gy ['dɪndʒi] *adj* (-**gier**; -**giest**) sporco, sbiadito

din'ing car' *s* vagone *m* ristorante

din'ing room' *s* sala da pranzo

dinner ['dɪnər] *s* cena; pranzo; (*formal meal*) banchetto

din'ner coat' *or* **jack'et** *s* smoking *m*

din'ner knife' *s* coltello da tavola

din'ner set' *s* servizio da tavola

din'ner ta'ble *s* desco

din'ner time' *s* ora di pranzo or di cena

dinosaur ['daɪnəˌsɔr] *s* dinosauro

dint [dɪnt] *s* tacca, ammaccatura; **by dint of** a forza di ‖ *tr* ammaccare

diocese ['daɪəˌsis] *or* ['daɪəsɪs] *s* diocesi *f*

diode ['daɪod] *s* diodo

dioxide [daɪ'ɑksaɪd] *s* biossido

dip [dɪp] *s* immersione; (*brief swim*) tuffo, nuotata; (*in a road*) depressione; inclinazione magnetica ‖ *v* (*pret & pp* **dipped**; *ger* **dipping**) *tr* immergere, tuffare; (*the flag*) abbassare; (*bread*) inzuppare ‖ *intr* immergersi, tuffarsi; inclinarsi; (*to drop down*) sparire subitamente; **to dip into** (*a book*) sfogliare; (*business*) mettersi in; (*a container of liquids*) intingere; **to dip into one's purse** spendere soldi

diphtheria [dɪf'θɪrɪə] *s* difterite *f*

diphthong ['dɪfθɔŋ] *or* ['dɪfθɑŋ] *s* dittongo

diphthongize ['dɪfθɔŋˌgaɪz] *or* ['dɪfθɑŋˌgaɪz] *tr & intr* dittongare

diploma [dɪ'plomə] *s* diploma *m*

diploma-cy [dɪ'ploməsi] *s* (-**cies**) diplomazia

diplomat ['dɪpləˌmæt] *s* diplomatico

diplomatic [ˌdɪplə'mætɪk] *adj* diplomatico

dip'lomat'ic pouch' *s* valigia diplomatica

dipper ['dɪpər] *s* mestolo

dip'stick' *s* asta di livello

dire [daɪr] *adj* terribile, orrendo

direct [dɪ'rɛkt] *or* [daɪ'rɛkt] *adj* diretto; sincero ‖ *tr* dirigere; ordinare

direct' cur'rent *s* corrente continua

direct' dis'course *s* discorso diretto

direct' dis'tance di'aling *s* (telp) teleselezione *f*

direct' hit' *s* colpo centrato

direction [dɪ'rɛkʃən] *or* [daɪ'rɛkʃən] *s* direzione; **directions** istruzioni *fpl*; (*for use*) indicazioni *fpl* per l'uso

directional [dɪˈrekʃənəl] or [daɪˈrekʃənəl] *adj* direzionale

directive [dɪˈrektɪv] or [daɪˈrektɪv] *s* direttiva

direct' ob'ject *s* (gram) complemento diretto, complemento oggetto

director [dɪˈrektər] or [daɪˈrektər] *s* direttore *m*, gerente *m*; (*member of a governing body*) consigliere *m*

directorship [dɪˈrektərˌʃɪp] or [daɪˈrektərˌʃɪp] *s* direzione; amministrazione

directo·ry [dɪˈrektərɪ] or [daɪˈrektərɪ] *s* (**-ries**) (*board of directors*) direzione, direttorio; (*list of names and addresses*) rubrica, elenco; (telp) elenco dei telefoni, guida telefonica

dirge [dʌrdʒ] *s* canto funebre

dirigible [ˈdɪrɪdʒɪbəl] *adj* & *s* dirigibile *m*

dirt [dʌrt] *s* (*soil*) terra, suolo; (*dust*) polvere *m*; (*mud*) fango; (*accumulation of dirt*) sudiciume *m*, lerciume *m*; (*moral filth*) porcheria, sozzura; (*gossip*) pettegolezzi *mpl*; **to do s.o. dirt** (slang) calunniare qlcu

dirt'-cheap' *adj* a prezzo bassissimo

dirt' road' *s* strada di terra battuta

dirt·y [ˈdʌrtɪ] *adj* (**-ier; -iest**) sporco, sudicio; fangoso; polveroso; (*e.g.*, spinach) terroso; (*obscene*) sconcio, lurido; immondo ‖ *v* (*pret* & *pp* **-ied**) *tr* sporcare, insudiciare, imbrattare

dir'ty lin'en *s* roba sporca; **to air one's dirty linen in public** mettere i panni al sole

dir'ty trick' *s* brutto tiro

disabili·ty [ˌdɪsəˈbɪlɪtɪ] *s* (**-ties**) incapacità *f*, invalidità *f*

disabil'ity insur'ance *s* assicurazione invalidità

disable [dɪsˈebəl] *tr* mutilare, storpiare; (*a ship*) smantellare; (law) invalidare

disabuse [ˌdɪsəˈbjuz] *tr* disingannare

disadvantage [ˌdɪsədˈvæntɪdʒ] or [ˌdɪsədˈvɑntɪdʒ] *s* svantaggio

disadvantageous [dɪsˌædvənˈtedʒəs] *adj* svantaggioso

disagree [ˌdɪsəˈgri] *intr* discordare, disconvenire; (*to quarrel*) litigare, altercare; **to disagree with** non essere del parere di

disagreeable [ˌdɪsəˈgri·əbəl] *adj* sgradevole

disagreement [ˌdɪsəˈgrimənt] *s* sconcordanza, dissidio, dissenso

disallow [ˌdɪsəˈlaʊ] *tr* non permettere, rifiutare

disappear [ˌdɪsəˈpɪr] *intr* sparire, scomparire

disappearance [ˌdɪsəˈpɪrəns] *s* scomparsa

disappoint [ˌdɪsəˈpɔɪnt] *tr* deludere, disilludere; **to be disappointed** rimanere deluso

disappointment [ˌdɪsəˈpɔɪntmənt] *s* delusione, disinganno, disappunto

disapproval [ˌdɪsəˈpruvəl] *s* disapprovazione, riprova

disapprove [ˌdɪsəˈpruv] *tr* & *intr* disapprovare

disarm [dɪsˈɑrm] *tr* disarmare ‖ *intr* disarmare, disarmarsi

disarmament [dɪsˈɑrməmənt] *s* disarmo

disarming [dɪsˈɑrmɪŋ] *adj* ingraziante, simpatico

disarray [ˌdɪsəˈre] *s* disordine *m*, scompiglio; (*of apparel*) sciatteria ‖ *tr* scomporre, scompigliare

disassemble [ˌdɪsəˈsembəl] *tr* smontare, sconnettere

disassociate [ˌdɪsəˈsoʃɪˌet] *tr* dissociare, disassociare

disaster [dɪˈzæstər] or [dɪˈzɑstər] *s* disastro, sinistro

disastrous [dɪˈzæstrəs] or [dɪˈzɑstrəs] *adj* disastroso

disavow [ˌdɪsəˈvaʊ] *tr* sconfessare

disavowal [ˌdɪsəˈvaʊ·əl] *s* sconfessione

disband [dɪsˈbænd] *tr* (*an assembly*) sciogliere; (*troops*) congedare; (*any group*) sbandare ‖ *intr* sbandarsi

dis·bar [dɪsˈbɑr] *v* (*pret* & *pp* **-barred**; *ger* **-barring**) *tr* (law) radiare dall'albo degli avvocati

disbelief [ˌdɪsbɪˈlif] *s* incredulità *f*

disbelieve [ˌdɪsbɪˈliv] *tr* rifiutarsi di credere a ‖ *intr* rifiutarsi di credere

disburse [dɪsˈbʌrs] *tr* sborsare

disbursement [dɪsˈbʌrsmənt] *s* sborso, disborso

discard [dɪsˈkɑrd] *s* scarto, scartina; **to put into the discard** scartare ‖ *tr* scartare

discern [dɪˈzʌrn] or [dɪˈsʌrn] *tr* scernere, discernere, sceverare

discernible [dɪˈzʌrnɪbəl] or [dɪˈsʌrnɪbəl] *adj* discernibile

discerning [dɪˈzʌrnɪŋ] or [dɪˈsʌrnɪŋ] *adj* perspicace, oculato

discernment [dɪˈzʌrnmənt] or [dɪˈsʌrnmənt] *s* discernimento

discharge [dɪsˈtʃɑrdʒ] *s* (*of a load*) scarico; (*of a gun; of electricity*) scarica; (*of a prisoner*) liberazione; (*of a duty*) adempimento; (*of a debt*) pagamento; (*from a job*) licenziamento; (mil) foglio di congedo; (pathol) spurgo ‖ *tr* scaricare; (*a duty*) adempiere; (*a prisoner*) liberare; (*a debt*) pagare; (*an employee*) licenziare; (*a patient*) lasciar uscire; (*a passenger from a ship*) sbarcare; (*a battery*) scaricare; (mil) congedare ‖ *intr* (said, e.g., *of a liquid*) sboccare; (*said of a gun or a battery*) scaricarsi

disciple [dɪˈsaɪpəl] *s* discepolo

disciplinarian [ˌdɪsɪplɪˈnerɪ·ən] *s* disciplinatore *m*; partigiano di una forte disciplina

disciplinary [ˈdɪsɪplɪˌnerɪ] *adj* disciplinare

discipline [ˈdɪsɪplɪn] *s* disciplina; castigo ‖ *tr* disciplinare; castigare

disclaim [dɪsˈklem] *tr* non riconoscere, negare

disclose [dɪsˈkloz] *tr* rivelare, scoprire

disclosure [dɪsˈkloʒər] *s* rivelazione, scoperta; divulgazione

discolor [dɪsˈkʌlər] *tr* scolorare, scolorire ‖ *intr* scolorirsi

discoloration [dɪsˌkʌləˈreʃən] *s* discolorazione

discomfit [dɪsˈkʌmfɪt] *tr* sconcertare, turbare; frustrare, battere, mettere in fuga

discomfiture [dɪsˈkʌmfɪtʃər] *s* sconcerto, turbamento; frustrazione; disfatta

discomfort [dɪsˈkʌmfərt] *s* disagio || *tr* incomodare

disconcert [ˌdɪskənˈsʌrt] *tr* sconcertare

disconnect [ˌdɪskəˈnekt] *tr* sconnettere; (elec) disinserire

disconsolate [dɪsˈkɑnsəlɪt] *adj* sconsolato, desolato

discontent [ˌdɪskənˈtent] *adj & s* scontento || *tr* scontentare

discontented [ˌdɪskənˈtentɪd] *adj* scontento

discontinue [ˌdɪskənˈtɪnju] *tr* cessare, interrompere

discord [ˈdɪskɔrd] *s* discordia, dissidio

discordance [dɪsˈkɔrdəns] *s* discordanza

discotheque [ˌdɪskoˈtɛk] *s* discoteca

discount [ˈdɪskaunt] *s* sconto || [ˈdɪskaunt] *or* [dɪsˈkaunt] *tr* scontare; (news) fare la tara a

dis'count rate' *s* tasso di sconto

discourage [dɪsˈkʌrɪdʒ] *tr* scoraggiare, sconfortare; (to dissuade) sconsigliare

discouragement [dɪsˈkʌrɪdʒmənt] *s* scoraggiamento; disapprovazione

discourse [ˈdɪskɔrs] *or* [dɪsˈkɔrs] *s* discorso || [dɪsˈkɔrs] *intr* discorrere

discourteous [dɪsˈkʌrtɪ·əs] *adj* scortese

discourte·sy [dɪsˈkʌrtəsi] *s* (-sies) scortesia

discover [dɪsˈkʌvər] *tr* scoprire

discoverer [dɪsˈkʌvərər] *s* scopritore m

discover·y [dɪsˈkʌvəri] *s* (-ies) scoperta

discredit [dɪsˈkredɪt] *s* discredito || *tr* screditare

discreditable [dɪsˈkredɪtəbəl] *adj* indegno, disonorevole

discreet [dɪsˈkrit] *adj* discreto

discrepan·cy [dɪsˈkrepənsi] *s* (-cies) discrepanza, divario

discretion [dɪsˈkreʃən] *s* discrezione

discriminate [dɪsˈkrɪmɪˌnet] *tr* discriminare || *intr*—**to discriminate against** fare delle discriminazioni contro

discrimination [dɪsˌkrɪmɪˈneʃən] *s* discriminazione

discriminatory [dɪsˈkrɪmɪnəˌtori] *adj* discriminante

discuss [dɪsˈkʌs] *tr & intr* discutere

discussion [dɪsˈkʌʃən] *s* discussione

discus thrower [ˈdɪskəs ˈθro·ər] *s* discobolo m

disdain [dɪsˈden] *s* disdegno || *tr* disdegnare, sdegnare

disdainful [dɪsˈdenfəl] *adj* sdegnoso

disease [dɪˈziz] *s* malattia

diseased [dɪˈzizd] *adj* malato

disembark [ˌdɪsemˈbɑrk] *tr & intr* sbarcare

disembarkation [dɪsˌembɑrˈkeʃən] *s* sbarco

disembowel [ˌdɪsemˈbau·əl] *tr* sbudellare, sventrare

disenchant [ˌdɪsenˈtʃænt] *or* [ˌdɪsenˈtʃɑnt] *tr* disincantare

disenchantment [ˌdɪsenˈtʃæntmənt] *or* [ˌdɪsenˈtʃɑntmənt] *s* disinganno

disengage [ˌdɪsenˈgedʒ] *tr* (from a pledge) svincolare; (to disconnect) sgranare, disinnestare; (mil) sganciare

disengagement [ˌdɪsenˈgedʒmənt] *s* liberazione; disinnesto; svincolamento

disentangle [ˌdɪsenˈtæŋgəl] *tr* disincagliare, districare

disentanglement [ˌdɪsenˈtæŋgəlmənt] *s* districamento

disestablish [ˌdɪsesˈtæblɪʃ] *tr* (the Church) separare dallo Stato

disfavor [dɪsˈfevər] *s* disfavore m

disfigure [dɪsˈfɪgjər] *tr* sfigurare, deturpare

disfigurement [dɪsˈfɪgjərmənt] *s* deturpazione

disfranchise [dɪsˈfræntʃaɪz] *tr* privare dei diritti civili

disgorge [dɪsˈgɔrdʒ] *tr* vomitare; (something illicitly obtained) restituire; (said of a river) scaricare || *intr* vomitare; scaricarsi

disgrace [dɪsˈgres] *s* vergogna; disgrazia || *tr* disonorare; privare del favore

disgraceful [dɪsˈgresfəl] *adj* infamante, disonorante

disgruntle [dɪsˈgrʌntəl] *tr* scontentare, irritare

disgruntled [dɪsˈgrʌntəld] *adj* irritato, di cattivo umore

disguise [dɪsˈgaɪz] *s* travestimento || *tr* travestire, dissimulare

disgust [dɪsˈgʌst] *s* disgusto, schifo || *tr* disgustare, fare schifo a

disgusting [dɪsˈgʌstɪŋ] *adj* disgustoso, schifoso

dish [dɪʃ] *s* piatto, **dishes** vasellame m; **to wash the dishes** fare i piatti || *tr* scodellare; (to defeat) (slang) sconfiggere; **to dish out** (slang) distribuire

dish'cloth' *s* canovaccio, strofinaccio

dishearten [dɪsˈhɑrtən] *tr* scoraggiare, disanimare, desolare

dishev·el [dɪˈʃevəl] *v* (pret & pp -eled or -elled; ger -eling or -elling) *tr* scomporre, scarmigliare, scapigliare

dishonest [dɪsˈɑnɪst] *adj* disonesto

dishones·ty [dɪsˈɑnɪsti] *s* (-ties) disonestà *f*

dishonor [dɪsˈɑnər] *s* disonore m || *tr* disonorare; (com) rifiutare di pagare

dishonorable [dɪsˈɑnərəbəl] *adj* disonorevole, disonorante

dish'pan' *s* bacinella per lavare i piatti

dish'rack' *s* portapiatti m, sgocciolatoio

dish'rag' *s* canovaccio, strofinaccio

dish'tow'el *s* canovaccio per le stoviglie

dish'wash'er *s* (person) sguattero, lavapiatti m; (machine) lavastoviglie m & f

dish'wa'ter *s* lavatura di piatti

disillusion [ˌdɪsɪˈluʒən] *s* disillusione || *tr* disilludere

disillusionment [ˌdɪsɪˈluʒənmənt] *s* disillusione

disinclination [dɪsˌɪnklɪˈneʃən] *s* riluttanza, avversione

disinclined [ˌdɪsɪnˈklaɪnd] *adj* riluttante, avverso

disinfect [,dısın'fekt] *tr* disinfettare
disinfectant [,dısın'fektənt] *adj & s* disinfettante *m*
disingenuous [,dısın'dʒenju·əs] *adj* poco schietto, insincero
disinherit [,dısın'herıt] *tr* diseredare
disintegrate [dıs'ıntı ,gret] *tr* disintegrare, disgregare || *intr* disintegrarsi, disgregarsi
disintegration [dıs ,ıntı'greʃən] *s* disintegrazione, disgregamento
disin·ter [,dısın'tʌr] *v* (*pret & pp -terred; ger -terring*) *tr* dissotterrare
disinterested [dıs'ıntə ,restıd] or [dıs-'ıntrıstıd] *adj* disinteressato
disjunctive [dıs'dʒʌŋktıv] *adj* disgiuntivo
disk [dısk] *s* disco; (*of ski pole*) rotella
disk' jock'ey *s* presentatore *m* di un programma radiodiffuso di dischi
dislike [dıs'laık] *s* antipatia, avversione; **to take a dislike for** prendere in uggia || *tr* non piacere (*with dat*), e.g., **he dislikes wine** non gli piace il vino
dislocate [dıslo ,ket] *tr* spostare, mettere fuori posto; (*a bone*) slogare
dislodge [dıs'lɑdʒ] *tr* sloggiare
disloyal [dıs'lɔɪ·əl] *adj* sleale
disloyal·ty [dıs'lɔɪ·əltı] *s* (*-ties*) slealtà *f*
dismal ['dızməl] *adj* tetro, triste; cattivo, orribile
dismantle [dıs'mæntəl] *tr* smontare, smantellare; (*a fortress*) sguarnire
dismay [dıs'me] *s* costernazione || *tr* costernare
dismember [dıs'membər] *tr* smembrare
dismiss [dıs'mıs] *tr* congedare; (*to fire*) licenziare; (*a subject*) scartare; (*from the mind*) scacciare
dismissal [dıs'mısəl] *s* congedo; licenziamento
dismount [dıs'maunt] *tr* disarcionare || *intr* scendere, smontare
disobedience [,dısə'bidı·əns] *s* disubbidienza
disobedient [,dısə'bidı·ənt] *adj* disubbidiente
disobey [,dısə'be] *tr* disubbidire (*with dat*) || *intr* disubbidire
disorder [dıs'ɔrdər] *s* disordine *m* || *tr* disordinare, confondere
disorderly [dıs'ɔrdərlı] *adj* disordinato, confuso; (*unruly*) turbolento
disor'derly con'duct *s* contegno contrario all'ordine pubblico
disor'derly house' *s* bordello, lupanare *m*
disorganize [dıs'ɔrgə ,naız] *tr* disorganizzare
disoriented [dıs'ɔrı ,entıd] *adj* disorientato
disown [dıs'on] *tr* disconoscere
disparage [dıs'pærıdʒ] *tr* svilire, deprezzare
disparagement [dıs'pærıdʒmənt] *s* discredito, deprezzamento
disparate ['dıspərıt] *adj* disparato
dispari·ty [dıs'pærıtı] *s* (*-ties*) disparità *f*, spareggio
dispassionate [dıs'pæʃənıt] *adj* spassionato

dispatch [dıs'pætʃ] *s* dispaccio || *tr* spedire; (*to dismiss*) congedare; uccidere; (*a meal*) (coll) liquidare
dis·pel [dıs'pel] *v* (*pret & pp -pelled; ger -pelling*) *tr* dissipare
dispensa·ry [dıs'pensərı] *s* (*-ries*) dispensario
dispensation [,dıspen'seʃən] *s* (*dispensing*) distribuzione, dispensa; (*exemption*) dispensa
dispense [dıs'pens] *tr* (*medicines*) distribuire; (*justice*) amministrare; (*to distribute*) dispensare; (*to exempt*) esimere || *intr*—**to dispense with** fare a meno di; esimersi da
dispenser [dı'spensər] *s* dispensatore *m*; (*automatic*) distributore *m*
disperse [dıs'pʌrs] *tr* disperdere || *intr* disperdersi
dispersion [dı'spʌrʒən] or [dı'spɜrʃən] *s* dispersione
dispersive [dı'spʌrsıv] *adj* dispersivo
dispirit [dı'spırıt] *tr* scoraggiare
displace [dıs'ples] *tr* muovere; costringere a lasciare il proprio paese; (*to supplant*) rimpiazzare; (naut) dislocare
displaced' per'son *s* rifugiato politico
displacement [dıs'plesmənt] *s* spostamento; sostituzione; (*of a piston*) cilindrata; (naut) dislocamento
display [dıs'ple] *s* sfoggio, mostra || *tr* mostrare; (*e.g., in a store window*) mettere in mostra; (*to unfold*) spiegare; (*to show ostentatiously*) sfoggiare, ostentare; (*ignorance*) rivelare
display' cab'inet *s* bacheca
display' win'dow *s* mostra, vetrina
displease [dıs'pliz] *tr* dispiacere (*with dat*)
displeasing [dıs'plizıŋ] *adj* spiacevole
displeasure [dıs'pleʒər] *s* dispiacere *m*; sfavore *m*
disposable [dıs'pozəbəl] *adj* (*available*) disponibile; (*made to be thrown away after use*) scartabile, da gettarsi via, usa e getta
disposal [dıs'pozəl] *s* disposizione; eliminazione; **to have at one's disposal** disporre di
dispose [dıs'poz] *tr* disporre; **to dispose of** disporre di; (*to get rid of*) sbarazzarsi di; vendere
disposed [dı'spozd] *adj*—**to be disposed to** essere disposto a
disposition [,dıspə'zıʃən] *s* disposizione; (*mental outlook*) indole *f*; tendenza; (mil) ordinamento
dispossess [,dıspə'zes] *tr* spodestare, bandire; (*to evict*) sfrattare
disproof [dıs'pruf] *s* confutazione
disproportionate [,dısprə'porʃənıt] *adj* sproporzionato
disprove [dıs'pruv] *tr* confutare
dispute [dıs'pjut] *s* disputa; **beyond dispute** incontestabile; **in dispute** in discussione || *tr & intr* disputare
disquali·fy [dıs'kwɑlı ,faı] *v* (*pret & pp -fied*) *tr* squalificare
disquiet [dıs'kwaı·ət] *s* inquietudine *f* || *tr* inquietare, turbare
disquisition [,dıskwı'zıʃən] *s* disquisizione

disregard [ˌdɪsrɪ'gɑrd] *s (of a rule)* inosservanza; *(of danger)* disprezzo, noncuranza || *tr* non fare attenzione a

disrepair [ˌdɪsrɪ'per] *s* cattivo stato, rovina

disreputable [dɪs'repjətəbəl] *adj* malfamato; disonorevole; *(in bad condition)* raso, logoro

disrepute [ˌdɪsrɪ'pjut] *s* cattiva fama; **to bring into disrepute** rovinare la reputazione di

disrespect [ˌdɪsrɪ'spekt] *s* mancanza di rispetto || *tr* mancare di rispetto a

disrespectful [ˌdɪsrɪ'spektfəl] *adj* non rispettoso, irriverente

disrobe [dɪs'rob] *tr* svestire || *intr* svestirsi, spogliarsi

disrupt [dɪs'rʌpt] *tr* disorganizzare; interrompere

disruption [dɪs'rʌpʃən] *s* rottura; disorganizzazione

dissatisfaction [ˌdɪssætɪs'fækʃən] *s* scontento, malcontento

dissatisfied [dɪs'sætɪs,faɪd] *adj* scontento, malcontento; insoddisfatto

dissatis•fy [dɪs'sætɪs,faɪ] *v (pret & pp -fied) tr* scontentare

dissect [dɪ'sɛkt] *tr* sezionare

dissemble [dɪ'sɛmbəl] *tr & intr* dissimulare

disseminate [dɪ'sɛmɪ,net] *tr* disseminare, divulgare

dissension [dɪ'sɛnʃən] *s* dissensione

dissent [dɪ'sɛnt] *s* dissenso; *(nonconformity)* dissidio || *intr* dissentire

dissenter [dɪ'sɛntər] *s* dissenziente *m*

dissertation [ˌdɪsər'teʃən] *s* dissertazione

disservice [dɪ'sʌrvɪs] *s* danno; cattivo servizio

dissidence ['dɪsɪdəns] *s* dissidenza

dissident ['dɪsɪdənt] *adj & s* dissidente *m*

dissimilar [dɪ'sɪmɪlər] *adj* dissimile

dissimilate [dɪ'sɪmɪ,let] *tr* dissimilare || *intr* dissimilarsi

dissimulate [dɪ'sɪmjə,let] *tr & intr* dissimulare

dissipate ['dɪsɪ,pet] *tr* dissipare || *intr* dissiparsi; *(to indulge oneself)* darsi alla dissipatezza

dissipated ['dɪsɪ,petɪd] *adj* dissipato

dissipation [ˌdɪsɪ'peʃən] *s* dissipazione

dissociate [dɪ'soʃɪ,et] *tr* dissociare || *intr* dissociarsi

dissolute ['dɪsə,lut] *adj* dissoluto

dissolution [ˌdɪsə'luʃən] *s* dissoluzione

dissolve [dɪ'zɑlv] *tr* sciogliere, disciogliere || *intr* sciogliersi, disciogliersi

dissonance ['dɪsənəns] *s* dissonanza

dissuade [dɪ'swed] *tr* dissuadere

dissyllabic [ˌdɪsɪ'læbɪk] *adj* disillabo

dissyllable [dɪ'sɪləbəl] *s* disillabo

distaff ['dɪstæf] or ['dɪstɑf] *s* rocca

dis'taff side' *s* ramo femminile di una famiglia

distance ['dɪstəns] *s* distanza; **a long distance** (fig) moltissimo; **in the distance** in lontananza; **to keep at a distance** or **to keep one's distance** mantenere le distanze || *tr* distanziare

distant ['dɪstənt] *adj* distante; *(relative)* lontano; *(aloof)* freddo, riservato

distaste [dɪs'test] *s* ripugnanza

distasteful [dɪs'testfəl] *adj* ripugnante, sgradevole

distemper [dɪs'tɛmpər] *s* cimurro; *(painting)* tempera || *tr* dipingere a tempera

distend [dɪs'tɛnd] *tr* stendere, distendere; gonfiare || *intr* stendersi, distendersi; gonfiarsi

distension [dɪs'tɛnʃən] *s* distensione; gonfiamento

distill [dɪs'tɪl] *tr* distillare

distillation [ˌdɪstɪ'leʃən] *s* distillazione

distiller•y [dɪs'tɪləri] *s (-ies)* distilleria

distinct [dɪs'tɪŋkt] *adj* distinto, chiaro; *(not blurred)* nitido

distinction [dɪs'tɪŋkʃən] *s* distinzione

distinctive [dɪs'tɪŋktɪv] *adj* distintivo

distinguish [dɪs'tɪŋwɪʃ] *tr* distinguere

distinguished [dɪs'tɪŋwɪʃt] *adj* distinto

distort [dɪs'tɔrt] *tr* distorcere; *(the truth)* svisare, snaturare

distortion [dɪs'tɔrʃən] *s* deformazione; *(of the truth)* alterazione, svisamento; (rad) distorsione

distract [dɪs'trækt] *tr* distrarre

distracted [dɪs'træktɪd] *adj* distratto; *(irrational)* turbato, sconvolto

distraction [dɪs'trækʃən] *s* distrazione

distraught [dɪs'trɔt] *adj* turbato, stordito

distress [dɪs'trɛs] *s* pena, dispiacere *m*; pericolo; (naut) difficoltà *f* || *tr* sconfortare, affliggere

distressing [dɪs'trɛsɪŋ] *adj* penoso

distress' mer'chandise *s* merce *f* sotto costo

distress' sig'nal *s* segnale *m* di soccorso

distribute [dɪs'trɪbjut] *tr* distribuire

distribution [ˌdɪstrɪ'bjuʃən] *s* distribuzione, erogazione

distributor [dɪs'trɪbjətər] *s* distributore *m*; (aut) distributore *m* d'accensione

district ['dɪstrɪkt] *s* regione; *(of a city)* rione *m*, quartiere *m*; *(administrative division)* distretto || *tr* dividere in distretti

dis'trict attor'ney *s* procuratore *m* generale

distrust [dɪs'trʌst] *s* diffidenza || *tr* diffidare di

distrustful [dɪs'trʌstfəl] *adj* diffidente

disturb [dɪs'tʌrb] *tr* disturbare, turbare; disordinare

disturbance [dɪs'tʌrbəns] *s* disturbo, turbamento, perturbazione; disordine *m*

disuse [dɪs'jus] *s* disuso

ditch [dɪtʃ] *s* fossa, fossato || *tr* scavare un fosso in; (rr) far deragliare; (slang) piantare in asso || *intr* fare un ammaraggio forzato

dither ['dɪðər] *s* agitazione; **to be in a dither** (coll) essere agitato

dit•to ['dɪto] *s (-tos)* lo stesso; *(ditto symbol)* virgolette *fpl* || *adv* ugualmente, idem || *tr* copiare, duplicare

dit'to marks' *spl* virgolette *fpl*

dit·ty ['dɪti] s (-ties) canzonetta

diva ['divə] s (mus) diva

divan ['daɪvæn] or [dɪ'væn] s divano

dive [daɪv] s tuffo; (of a submarine) immersione; (aer) picchiata; (coll) taverna; (com) discesa || v (pret & pp **dived** or **dove** [dov]) intr tuffarsi; (said of submarine) immergersi; (to plunge) lanciarsi; (aer) scendere in picchiata; **to dive for** (e.g., pearls) pescare

dive'-bomb' tr bombardare in picchiata || intr scendere a tuffo

dive' bomb'ing s bombardamento in picchiata

diver ['daɪvər] s tuffatore m; (person who works under water) palombaro; (orn) tuffetto

diverge [dɪ'vʌrdʒ] or [daɪ'vʌrdʒ] intr divergere

divers ['daɪvərz] adj diversi, vari

diverse [dɪ'vʌrs], [daɪ'vʌrs] or ['daɪvʌrs] adj (different) diverso; (of various kinds) multiforme

diversification [dɪ ,vʌrsɪfɪ'keʃən] or [daɪ ,vʌrsɪfɪ'keʃən] s diversificazione

diversi·fy [dɪ'vʌrsɪ ,faɪ] or [daɪ'vʌrsɪ ,faɪ] v (pret & pp **-fied**) tr diversificare || intr diversificarsi

diversion [dɪ'vʌrʒən] or [daɪ'vʌrʒən] s diversione; (pastime) svago

diversi·ty [dɪ'vʌrsɪtɪ] or [daɪ'vʌrsɪtɪ] s (-ties) diversità f

divert [dɪ'vʌrt] or [daɪ'vʌrt] tr deviare; (to entertain) divertire; (money) stornare, distrarre

diverting [dɪ'vʌrtɪŋ] or [daɪ'vʌrtɪŋ] adj divertente

divest [dɪ'vest] or [daɪ'vest] tr spogliare; spossessare; **to divest oneself of** spogliarsi di, espropriarsi di

divide [dɪ'vaɪd] s spartiacque m || tr dividere || intr dividersi

dividend ['dɪvɪ ,dend] s dividendo

dividers [dɪ'vaɪdərz] spl compasso a punte fisse

divination [,dɪvɪ'neʃən] s divinazione

divine [dɪ'vaɪn] adj divino || s sacerdote m, prete m || tr divinare

diviner [dɪ'vaɪnər] s divinatore m

diving ['daɪvɪŋ] s tuffo, immersione

div'ing bell' s campana da palombaro

div'ing board' s trampolino

div'ing suit' s scafandro

divin'ing rod' [dɪ'vaɪnɪŋ] s bacchetta rabdomantica

divini·ty [dɪ'vɪnɪtɪ] s (-ties) divinità f; teologia; **the Divinity** Dio

divisible [dɪ'vɪsɪbəl] adj divisibile

division [dɪ'vɪʒən] s divisione

divisor [dɪ'vaɪzər] s divisore m

divorce [dɪ'vors] s divorzio; **to get a divorce** divorziare || tr (a married couple) divorziare; (one's spouse) divorziare da || intr divorziare

divorcé [dɪvor'se] s divorziato

divorcee [dɪvor'si] s divorziata

divulge [dɪ'vʌldʒ] tr divulgare

dizziness ['dɪzɪnɪs] s vertigine f, stordimento; confusione

diz·zy ['dɪzɪ] adj (-zier; -ziest) (causing dizziness) vertiginoso; (suffering dizziness) preso da vertigine, stordito; (coll) stupido

do [du] v (3rd pers **does** [dʌz]; pret **did** [dɪd]; pp **done** [dʌn]; ger **doing** ['du·ɪŋ]) tr fare; (a problem) risolvere; (a distance) percorrere; (to study) studiare; (to explore) attraversare; (to tire) stancare; **to do one's best** fare del proprio meglio; **to do over** tornare a fare; ripetere; **to do right by** trattare bene; **to do s.o. out of s.th** (coll) portare via qlco a qlcu; **to do to death** mettere a morte; **to do up** (coll) impacchettare; stancare; (one's hair) farsi; vestire; (a shirt) lavare e stirare; **to have done far fare** || intr fare; agire; comportarsi; servire; bastare; stare; succedere; **how do you do?** come sta?; **that will do** basta; è sufficiente; **to have done with** non aver più nulla a che fare con; **to have nothing to do with** non aver nulla a che vedere con; **to have to do with** aver a che fare con, trattarsi di; **to do away with** togliere di mezzo; **to do for** servire da; **to do well** crescere bene; **to do without** fare a meno di || v aux used 1) in interrogative sentences: **Do you speak Italian?** Parla italiano?; 2) in negative sentences: **I do not speak Italian** Non parlo italiano; 3) to avoid repetition of a verb or full verbal expression: **Did you go to church this morning? Yes, I did.** È stato in chiesa questa mattina? Sì, ci sono stato; 4) to lend emphasis to a principal verb: **I do believe what you told me** Ci credo a quello che mi ha detto; 5) in inverted constructions after certain adverbs: **Seldom does he come to see me** Mi viene a vedere di raro; 6) in a supplicating tone with imperatives: **Do come in** entri per favore

docile ['dɑsɪl] adj docile

dock [dɑk] s (wharf) molo; (waterway between two piers) darsena; (area including piers and waterways) scalo portuario; (law) gabbia degli imputati || tr (to deduct from the wages of) fare una deduzione a; (to deduct s.o.'s salary) dedurre da; (an animal) scodare; (naut) attraccare || intr (aer) agganciarsi; (naut) attraccare

dockage ['dɑkɪdʒ] s attracco; (charges) diritti mpl di porto

docket ['dɑkɪt] s ordine m del giorno; (law) ruolo delle sentenze; **on the docket** (coll) pendente, in sospeso

dock' hand' s portuale m

docking ['dɑkɪŋ] s (aer) aggancio; (naut) attracco

dock'yard' s cantiere m navale

doctor ['dɑktər] s dottore m; (physician) medico || tr curare; aggiustare; falsificare; adulterare || intr esercitare la medicina; (coll) curarsi, prendere medicine

doctorate ['dɑktərɪt] s dottorato

doctrine ['dɑktrɪn] s dottrina

document ['dɑkjəmənt] s documento || ['dɑkjə ,ment] tr documentare

documenta·ry [,dɑkjə'mentəri] *adj* & *s* (**-ries**) documentario
documentation [,dɑkəmen'teʃən] *s* documentazione
doddering ['dɑdərɪŋ] *adj* tremante, rimbambito
dodge [dɑdʒ] *s* scarto, schivata; (fig) stratagemma *m* ǁ *tr* schivare, evitare ǁ *intr* schivarsi; (fig) rispondere evasivamente; **to dodge around the corner** scantonare
do·do ['dodo] *s* (**-dos** or **-does**) (coll) rimbecillito
doe [do] *s* (*of deer*) cerva; (*of goat*) capretta; (*of rabbit*) coniglia
doeskin ['do ,skɪn] *s* pelle *f* di daino, pelle *f* di dante; lana finissima
doff [dɑf] or [dɔf] *tr* (*one's hat*) togliersi; (*clothing*) deporre
dog [dɔg] or [dɑg] *s* cane *m;* **to go to the dogs** (coll) andare in malora; **to put on the dog** (coll) darsi delle arie ǁ *v* (*pret* & *pp* **dogged;** *ger* **dogging**) *tr* seguire; perseguitare
dog'catch'er *s* accalappiacani *m*
dog' days' *s* solleone *m*, canicola
doge [dodʒ] *s* doge *m*
dog'-ear' *s* orecchia, orecchio
dog'fight' *s* duello aereo
dogged ['dɔgɪd] or ['dɑgɪd] *adj* accanito
doggerel ['dɔgərəl] or ['dɑgərəl] *s* versi *mpl* da colascione
dog·gy ['dɔgi] or ['dɑgi] *adj* (**-gier; -giest**) vistoso; canino ǁ *s* (**-gies**) cagnolino
dog'house' *s* canile *m;* **to be in the doghouse** (slang) essere in disgrazia
dog' Lat'in *s* latino maccheronico
dogma ['dɔgmə] or ['dɑgmə] *s* dogma *m*
dogmatic [dɔg'mætɪk] or [dɑg'mætɪk] *adj* dogmatico
dog' rac'ing *s* corse *fpl* dei cani
dog' show' *s* mostra canina
dog's' life' *s* vita da cani
Dog' Star' *s* canicola
dog' tag' *s* (mil) piastrina, piastrino
dog'-tired' *adj* (coll) stanco morto
dog'tooth' *s* (**-teeth** [,tiθ]) canino
dog' track' *s* cinodromo
dog'watch' *s* (naut) quarto di solo due ore, gaettone *m*
dog'wood' *s* corniolo
doi·ly ['dɔɪli] *s* (**-lies**) centrino
doings ['du·ɪŋz] *spl* azioni *fpl*, fatti *mpl*
do'-it-your-self' *s* il fare tutto da sé
doldrums ['dɑldrəmz] *spl* calma equatoriale; inattività *f;* depressione
dole [dol] *s* elemosina; (*to the jobless*) sussidio di disoccupazione ǁ *tr*—**to dole out** distribuire parsimoniosamente
doleful ['dolfəl] *adj* lugubre, triste
doll [dɑl] *s* bambola ǁ *intr*—**to doll up** (slang) agghindarsi
dollar ['dɑlər] *s* dollaro
dol'lar-wise' *adv* in termini finanziari
dol·ly ['dɑli] *s* (**-lies**) pupattola; (*low, wheeled frame for moving heavy loads*) carrello; (mov, telv) carrello

ǁ *v* (*pret* & *pp* **-lied**) *intr* (mov, telv) carrellare
dol'ly shot' *s* (mov, telv) carrellata
dolphin ['dɑlfɪn] *s* delfino
dolt [dolt] *s* gonzo, balordo
doltish ['doltɪʃ] *adj* gonzo, balordo
domain [do'men] *s* dominio; (law) proprietà *f;* (fig) campo, orbita
dome [dom] *s* cupola
dome' light' *s* lampadario
domestic [də'mestɪk] *adj* & *s* domestico
domesticate [də'mestɪ ,ket] *tr* domesticare
domicile ['dɑmɪsɪl] or ['dɑmɪ ,saɪl] *s* domicilio ǁ *tr* domiciliare
dominance ['dɑmɪnəns] *s* dominio
dominant ['dɑmɪnənt] *adj* & *s* dominante *f*
dominate ['dɑmɪ ,net] *tr* & *intr* dominare
domination [,dɑmɪ'neʃən] *s* dominazione
domineer [,dɑmɪ'nɪr] *intr* spadroneggiare
domineering [,dɑmɪ'nɪrɪŋ] *adj* dispotico, tirannico
Dominican [də'mɪnɪkən] *adj* & *s* domenicano; (eccl) domenicano
dominion [də'mɪnjən] *s* dominio
domi·no ['dɑmɪ ,no] *s* (**-noes** or **-nos**) (*costume and person*) domino; (*piece*) tessera di domino; **dominoes** (*game*) domino
don [dɑn] *s* signore *m;* don *m;* membro di un collegio universitario inglese ǁ *v* (*pret* & *pp* **donned;** *ger* **donning**) *tr* (*clothes*) mettersi, vestire
donate ['donet] *tr* donare, dare
donation [do'neʃən] *s* donazione
done [dʌn] *adj* fatto; finito; stanco; (culin) ben cotto, ben rosolato
done' for' *adj* (coll) stanco morto; (coll) rovinato; (coll) fuori combattimento; (coll) morto
donjon ['dʌndʒən] or ['dɑndʒən] *s* torrione *m*, maschio
Don Juan [dɑn 'wɑn] or [dɔn 'hwɑn] *s* Don Giovanni
donkey ['dɑŋki] or ['dʌŋki] *s* asino, somaro
donnish ['dɑnɪʃ] *adj* pedante
donor ['donər] *s* donatore *m*
doodle ['dudəl] *tr* & *intr* scarabocchiare, riempire di ghirigori
doom [dum] *s* destino; morte *f*, rovina; sentenza di morte; giudizio finale ǁ *tr* destinare; condannare; condannare a morte
doomsday ['dumz ,de] *s* giorno del giudizio
door [dor] *s* porta; (*of a carriage or automobile*) portiera, sportello; (*one part of a double door*) battente *m;* **behind closed doors** a porte chiuse; **to see to the door** accompagnare alla porta; **to show s.o. the door** mettere qlcu alla porta
door'bell' *s* campanello della porta
door' check' *s* chiusura automatica di porta, scontro
door'frame' *s* cornice *f*

door'head' s architrave m
door'jamb' s stipite m
door'keep'er s portinaio
door'knob' s maniglia della porta
door' knock'er s battente m
door' latch' s paletto
door'man' s (-men') portiere m, portinaio; (of large apartment house) guardaportone m
door'mat' s stoino, zerbino
door'nail' s borchione m; **dead as a doornail** morto e ben morto
door'post' s stipite m
door' scrap'er s raschietto
door'sill' s soglia
door'step' s gradino davanti la porta
door'stop' s paracolpi m
door'-to-door' adj (shipment) diretto; (selling) di porta in porta
door'way' s vano della porta; porta
dope [dop] s lubrificante m; (aer) vernice f; (slang) stupido, scemo; (slang) informazioni fpl; (slang) narcotico ‖ tr (slang) narcotizzare; **to dope out** (slang) indovinare, decifrare, immaginare
dope' fiend' s (slang) tossicomane mf
dope'sheet' s giornaletto con le previsioni delle corse ippiche
dormant ['dɔrmənt] adj dormente; latente
dor'mer win'dow ['dɔrmər] s abbaino
dormito·ry ['dɔrmɪˌtori] s (-ries) dormitorio
dor·mouse ['dɔrˌmaʊs] s (-mice [ˌmaɪs]) ghiro
dosage ['dosɪdʒ] s dosatura
dose [dos] s dose f; (coll) boccone amaro ‖ tr dosare; somministrare
dossier ['dɑsɪˌe] s incartamento
dot [dɑt] s punto; **on the dot** (coll) in punto ‖ v (pret & pp **dotted;** ger **dotting**) tr punteggiare; **to dot one's i's** mettere i punti sulle i
dotage ['dotɪdʒ] s rimbecillimento; **to be in one's dotage** essere rimbambito
dotard ['dotərd] s vecchio rimbambito
dote [dot] intr rimbambirsi; **to dote on** essere pazzo per
doting ['dotɪŋ] adj che ama alla follia; (from old age) rimbambito, rimbecillito
dots' and dash'es spl (telg) punti mpl e tratti mpl
dot'ted line' s linea punteggiata; **to sign on the dotted line** firmare inconsideratamente
double ['dʌbəl] adj doppio ‖ s doppio; (bridge) contre m; **doubles** (tennis) doppio ‖ tr raddoppiare; (bridge) contrare ‖ intr raddoppiarsi; (bridge) contrare; (mov, theat) sostenere due ruoli; (mov) doppiare; **to double up** (said of two people) dividere la stessa camera, dividere lo stesso letto; piegarsi in due
double-barreled ['dʌbəl'bærəld] adj a due canne; (fig) a doppio fine
dou'ble bass' s contrabbasso
dou'ble bed' s letto matrimoniale
dou'ble boil'er s bagnomaria m

double-breasted ['dʌbəl'brestɪd] adj a doppio petto, doppiopetto
dou'ble chin' s pappagorgia
dou'ble-cross' tr (coll) tradire
dou'ble date' s (coll) appuntamento amoroso di due coppie
dou'ble-deal'ing adj doppio
dou'ble-deck'er s (bed) letto a castello; (sandwich) tramezzino doppio; autobus m a due piani; (naut) nave f due ponti; (aer) aereo due ponti
double-edged ['dʌbəl'edʒd] adj a due tagli, a doppio taglio
dou'ble en'try s (com) partita doppia
dou'ble fea'ture s (mov) programma m di due lungometraggio
double-header ['dʌbəl'hedər] s treno con due locomotive; due partite di baseball giocate successivamente
double-jointed ['dʌbəl'dʒɔɪntɪd] adj snodato
dou'ble-park' tr & intr parcheggiare in doppia fila
dou'ble-quick' adj & adv a passo di carica
dou'ble stand'ard s—**to have a double standard** usare due pesi e due misure
doublet ['dʌblɪt] s (close-fitting jacket) farsetto; (philol) doppione m
dou'ble-talk' s discorso incomprensibile; **to give s.o. double-talk** parlare evasivamente a qlcu ‖ intr parlare evasivamente
dou'ble time' s paga doppia; (mil) passo di carica
doubleton ['dʌbəltən] s doppio
doubly ['dʌblɪ] adv doppiamente
doubt [daʊt] s dubbio; **beyond doubt** senza dubbio; **if in doubt** in caso di dubbio; **no doubt** senza dubbio ‖ tr dubitare di ‖ intr dubitare
doubter ['daʊtər] s incredulo
doubtful ['daʊtfəl] adj incerto; dubbioso
doubtless ['daʊtlɪs] adj indubitabile ‖ adv senza dubbio; probabilmente
douche [duʃ] s irrigazione f; (instrument) irrigatore m ‖ tr irrigare ‖ intr fare irrigazioni
dough [do] s pasta di pane; (money) (slang) soldi mpl, quattrini mpl
dough'boy' s fantaccino americano
dough'nut' s ciambella; (with filling) sgonfiotto
dough·ty ['daʊti] adj (-tier; -tiest) forte, coraggioso
dough·y ['do·i] adj (-ier; -iest) pastoso, molle
dour [daʊr] or [dʊr] adj triste, severo
douse [daʊs] tr immergere; bagnare; (the light) (coll) spegnere
dove [dʌv] s colomba, tortora
dovecote ['dʌvˌkot] s piccionaia
dove'tail' s coda di rondine ‖ tr calettare a coda di rondine; (to make fit) adattare, far combaciare ‖ intr (to fit) combaciare; corrispondere
dowager ['daʊ·ədʒər] s vedova titolata; vecchia signora austera; **queen dowager** regina madre
dow·dy ['daʊdi] adj (-dier; -diest) trasandato

dow•el ['dauəl] *s* caviglia, tassello ‖ *v* (*pret & pp* **-eled** or **-elled;** *ger* **-eling** or **-elling**) *tr* tassellare

dower ['dauər] *s* (*widow's portion*) legittima, vedovile *m;* (*marriage portion; natural gift*) dote *f* ‖ *tr* dotare; assegnare un vedovile a

down [daun] *adj* che discende; basso; (*train*) che va al centro; depresso; finito; (*money, payment*) anticipato; (*storage battery*) esaurito ‖ *s* (*of fruit and human body*) lanugine *f;* (*of birds*) piumino; (*upset*) rovescio; discesa; (*sandhill*) duna ‖ *adv* giù; all'ingiù, in giù; dabbasso; a terra; al sud; (*in cash*) a contanti; **down and out** rovinato; senza una soldo; **down from de; down on one's knees** in ginocchio; **down to** fino a; **down under** agli antipodi; **down with . . . !** abasso . . . !; **to get down to work** mettersi seriamente al lavoro; **to go down** scendere; **to lie down** sdraiarsi; andare a letto; **to sit down** sedersi ‖ *prep* giù per; **down the river** a valle; **down the street** giù per la strada ‖ *tr* abbattere; (*coll*) buttar giù, tracannare

down'cast' *adj* mogio, sfiduciato

down'fall' *s* rovina, rovescio

down'grade' *adj & adv* in declivio, a valle ‖ *s* discesa; **to be on the downgrade** essere in declino ‖ *tr* attribuire minor importanza a; degradare

downhearted ['daun,hartɪd] *adj* scoraggiato, abbattuto

down'hill' *adj & adv* in declivio; **to go downhill** declinare

down' pay'ment *s* acconto

down'pour' *s* acquazzone *m,* rovescio

down'right' *adj* assoluto; completo; franco, diretto ‖ *adv* completamente

down'stairs' *adj* del piano di sotto ‖ *s* il piano di sotto; i piani di sotto ‖ *adv* dabbasso, di sotto, giù

down'stream' *adv* a valle

down'stroke' *s* corsa discendente

down'town' *adj* centrale ‖ *s* centro della città ‖ *adv* al centro della città

down' train' *s* treno discendente, treno che va al centro

down'trend' *s* tendenza al ribasso

downtrodden ['daun,tradən] *adj* calpestato, oppresso

downward ['daunwərd] *adj & adv* all'ingiù

down•y ['dauni] *adj* (**-ier; -iest**) piumoso, lanuginoso; (*soft*) molle, morbido

dow•ry ['dauri] *s* (**-ries**) dote *f*

doze [doz] *s* pisolo ‖ *intr* dormicchiare; **to doze off** appisolarsi

dozen ['dazən] *s* dozzina

dozy ['dozi] *adj* sonnolento

drab [dræb] *adj* (**drabber; drabbest**) grigiastro; (*dull*) scialbo ‖ *s* colore grigiastro; (*fabric*) tela naturale; donna di malaffare

drach•ma ['drækmə] *s* (**-mas** or **-mae** [mi]) dramma

draft [dræft] or [draft] *s* corrente *f* d'aria; (*pulling*) tiro; (*in a chimney*)

tiraggio; (*sketch, outline*) schizzo; (*first form of a writing*) prima stesura; (*drink*) sorso, bicchiere *m;* (*com*) tratta, lettera di credito; (*law*) progetto, disegno; (*naut*) pesca; (*mil*) coscrizione *f,* leva; **on draft** alla spina ‖ *tr* disegnare; fare uno schizzo di; (*a document*) stendere; (*mil*) coscrivere; **to be drafted** essere di leva, andar coscritto

draft' age' *s* età *f* di leva

draft' beer' *s* birra alla spina

draft' board' *s* consiglio di leva

draft' dodg'er ['dadʒər] *s* renitente *m* alla leva, imboscato

draftee [,dræf'ti] or [,draf'ti] *s* coscritto

draft' horse' *s* cavallo da tiro

drafts'man *s* (**-men**) disegnatore *m;* (*man who draws up documents*) redattore *m*

draft' trea'ty *s* progetto di trattato

draft•y ['dræfti] or ['drafti] *adj* (**-ier; -iest**) pieno di correnti d'aria

drag [dræg] *s* (*sledge for conveying heavy bodies*) traino, treggia; (*on a cigarette*) boccata; (*aer*) resistenza aerodinamica; (*naut*) pressione idrostatica; (*naut*) draga; (*fig*) noia; (*influence*) (*slang*) aderenze *fpl;* (*a bore*) (*slang*) rompiscatole *m* ‖ *v* (*pret & pp* **dragged;** *ger* **dragging**) *tr* strascinare, strascicare; (*naut*) rastrellare ‖ *intr* strascicare, strascicarsi; dilungarsi; **to drag on** andare per le lunghe

drag'net' *s* paranza; (*fig*) retata

dragon ['drægən] *s* drago, dragone *m*

drag'on-fly' *s* (**-flies**) libellula

dragoon [drə'gun] *s* (*mil*) dragone *m* ‖ *tr* forzare, costringere

drain [dren] *s* scolo; prosciugamento; (*geog*) spiovente *m;* (*surg*) drenaggio; (*fig*) salasso ‖ *tr* (*a liquid*) scolare; prosciugare; (*humid land; a wound*) drenare ‖ *intr* scolare; prosciugarsi; (*geog*) defluire

drainage ['drenidʒ] *s* drenaggio; (*geog*) displuvio, spartiacque *m*

drain'board' *s* scolatoio per le stoviglie

drain' cock' *s* rubinetto di scarico

drain'pipe' *s* tubo di scarico

drake [drek] *s* anatra maschio

dram [dræm] *s* dramma; bicchierino di liquore

drama ['dramə] or ['dræmə] *s* dramma *m;* (*art and genre*) drammatica

dramatic [drə'mætɪk] *adj* drammatico ‖ **dramatics** *ssg* drammatica; *spl* rappresentazione dilettantesca; comportamento drammatico

dramatist ['dræmətɪst] *s* drammaturgo

dramatize ['dræmə,taɪz] *tr* drammatizzare

drape [drep] *s* tenda, cortina; (*of a curtain*) drappeggio; (*of a skirt*) taglio ‖ *tr* drappeggiare

draper•y ['drepəri] *s* (**-ies**) drapperia; negozio di tessuti; **draperies** tendaggi *mpl*

drastic ['dræstɪk] *adj* drastico

draught [dræft] or [draft] s & tr var of **draft**

draught' beer' s birra alla spina

draw [drɔ] s (in a game) patta; (in a lottery) sorteggio; (act of drawing) tiro; (of chimney) tiraggio; (attraction) attrazione; (of a drawbridge) ala || v (pret **drew** [dru]; pp **drawn** [drɔn]) tr (a line) tirare; (to attract) richiamare; (butter) fondere; (a sword) sguainare; (a nail) estrarre; (people) attrarre; (a sigh) emettere; (a curtain) far scorrere; (a salary) pigliare; (a prize) ricevere; (a game) impattare; (in card games) pescare; (a drawbridge) sollevare; (said of a ship) pescare; (a comparison) fare; (a profit) ricavare; (a chicken) sventrare; (e.g., a picture) disegnare, ritrarre; (to sketch in words) descrivere; (a contract) stipulare; (interest) ricevere; (com) spiccare, staccare; **to draw forth** far uscire; **to draw off** estrarre; (a liquid) spillare; **to draw** (shoes) **on** mettersi; **to draw** (money) **on** ritirare da; **to draw** (a draft) **on** domiciliare presso; **to draw oneself up** raddrizzarsi; **to draw out** (to persuade to talk) far parlare, tirar fuori le parole a; **to draw up** (a document) estendere; (mil) schierare || intr (said of chimney) tirare; impattare; sorteggiare un premio; aver attrazione; disegnare; **to draw aside** scostarsi; **to draw back** retrocedere, ritirarsi; **to draw near** avvicinarsi; volgere a; **to draw to a close** essere quasi finito; **to draw together** unirsi

draw'back' s inconveniente m

draw'bridge' s ponte levatoio

drawee [‚drɔ'i] v trattario, trassato

drawer ['drɔ·ər] s disegnatore m; (com) traente m || [drɔr] s cassetto; **drawers** mutande fpl

drawing ['drɔ·ɪŋ] s disegno; (in a lottery) sorteggio

draw'ing board' s tavolo da disegno

draw'ing card' s attrazione

draw'ing room' s salotto, salottino

draw'knife' s (-knives [‚naɪvz]) coltello a petto

drawl [drɔl] s accento strascicato || tr dire con accento strascicato || intr strascicare le parole

drawn' but'ter s burro fuso

drawn' work' s lavoro a giorno

dray [dre] s carro pesante; slitta, treggia; autocarro

drayage ['dre·ɪdʒ] s carreggio

dray'man s (-men) carrettiere m

dread [dred] adj spaventoso, terribile || s spavento, terrore m || tr & intr temere

dreadful ['dredfəl] adj spaventevole, terribile; (coll) orribile

dread'nought' s corazzata

dream [drim] s sogno; illusione, fantasticheria; **dream come true** sogno fatto realtà || v (pret & pp **dreamed** or **dreamt** [dremt]) tr sognare; **to dream up** (coll) immaginare, fantasticare || intr sognare

dreamer ['drimər] s sognatore m

dream'land' s paese m dei sogni

dream·y ['drimi] adj (-ier; -iest) sognante; (visionary) trasognato; vago

drear·y ['drɪri] adj (-ier; -iest) squallido; triste; (boring) noioso

dredge [dredʒ] s draga || tr dragare; (culin) infarinare

dredger ['dredʒər] s (boat) draga; (container) spolverino

dredging ['dredʒɪŋ] s dragaggio

dregs [dregz] spl feccia

drench [drentʃ] tr infradiciare, inzuppare

dress [dres] s vestito; vestiti mpl; vestito da donna; abito; abito da cerimonia; (of a bird) piumaggio || tr vestire; adornare, decorare; (hair) pettinare; (a wound) medicare; (leather) conciare; (food) condire; (a boat) pavesare; **to dress down** (coll) rimproverare; **to get dressed** vestirsi || intr vestire; vestirsi; (mil) schierarsi; **to dress up** vestirsi da sera; farsi bello, mettersi in gala

dress' ball' s ballo di gala

dress' coat' s frac m

dresser ['dresər] s toletta; (sideboard) credenza; **to be a good dresser** vestire con eleganza

dress' goods' spl stoffa per abiti

dressing ['dresɪŋ] s ornamento; (for food) condimento; sugo; (stuffing for fowl) ripieno; (fertilizer) concime m; (for a wound) medicazione

dress'ing down' s ramanzina

dress'ing gown' s vestaglia

dress'ing room' s spogliatoio, toletta; (theat) camerino

dress'ing sta'tion s posto di pronto soccorso

dress'ing ta'ble s toletta, specchiera

dress'mak'er s sarta, sarto per donna

dress'mak'ing s taglio, sartoria

dress' rehears'al s prova generale

dress' shirt' s camicia inamidata

dress' suit' s marsina

dress' u'niform s (mil) alta uniforme

dress·y ['dresi] adj (-ier; iest) (coll) elegante, ricercato

dribble ['drɪbəl] s goccia || tr (sports) palleggiare, dribblare || intr gocciolare; (at the mouth) sbavare; (sports) dribblare

driblet ['drɪblɪt] s piccola quantità; **in driblets** col contagocce

dried' beef' [draɪd] s carne seccata

dried' fruit' s frutta secca

drier ['draɪ·ər] s (for hair) asciugacapelli m; (for clothes) asciugatrice f

drift [drɪft] s movimento; (of sand, snow, etc.) cumulo; (snowdrift) neve accumulata dal vento; tendenza, corrente f; intenzione; (aer, naut) deriva; (rad, telv) deviazione || intr andare alla deriva; (said of snow) accumularsi; (aer, naut) derivare, scadere

drift' ice' s ghiaccio alla deriva

drift'pin' s (mach) mandrino

drift'wood' s legname andato alla deriva

drill [drɪl] *s* esercizio; (*fabric*) tela cruda; (*agr*) seminatrice *f;* (*mach*) trapano, trivella; (*mil*) esercitazioni *fpl* militari ‖ *tr* trivellare; istruire; (*mil*) insegnare gli esercizi militari a ‖ *intr* addestrarsi; (*mil*) fare gli esercizi militari

drill′mas′ter *s* istruttore *m*

drill′ press′ *s* trapano a colonna

drink [drɪŋk] *s* bevanda; **the drinks are on the house!** paga il proprietario! ‖ *v* (*pret* **drank** [dræŋk]; *pp* **drunk** [drʌŋk]) *tr* bere; assorbire; **to drink down** tracannare; **to drink in** bere, assorbire; (*air*) aspirare ‖ *intr* bere; **to drink out of** bere da; **to drink to the health of** bere alla salute di

drinkable ['drɪŋkəbəl] *adj* bevibile, potabile

drinker ['drɪŋkər] *s* bevitore *m*

drinking ['drɪŋkɪŋ] *s* (il) bere

drink′ing foun′tain *s* fontanella pubblica

drink′ing song′ *s* canzone bacchica

drink′ing straw′ *s* cannuccia

drink′ing trough′ *s* abbeveratoio

drink′ing wa′ter *s* acqua potabile

drip [drɪp] *s* sgocciolo, sgocciolatura ‖ *v* (*pret & pp* **dripped**; *ger* **dripping**) *intr* sgocciolare, stillare; (*said of perspiration*) trasudare

drip′ cof′fee *s* caffè fatto con la macchinetta

drip′-dry′ *adj* non-stiro

drip′ pan′ *s* (culin) ghiotta; (mach) coppa

dripping ['drɪpɪŋ] *s* gocciolio; **drippings** grasso che cola dall'arrosto

drive [draɪv] *s* scarrozzata; strada; passeggiata; impulso; forza, iniziativa; urgenza; spinta; campagna; (aut) trazione; (mach) trasmissione ‖ *v* (*pret* **drove** [drov]; *ger* **driven** ['drɪvən]) *tr* (*a nail*) ficcare, piantare; (*e.g., cattle*) condurre, parare; (*s.o. in a carriage or auto*) condurre, portare; spingere; stimulare; forzare; spingere a lavorare; (*sports*) colpire molto forte; **to drive away** scacciare; **to drive back** respingere; **to drive mad** far impazzire; **to drive out** scacciare ‖ *intr* fare una scarrozzata; **to drive at** parare a; voler dire; **to drive hard** lavorare sodo; **to drive in** entrare in automobile; (*a place*) entrare in automobile in; **to drive on the right** guidare a destra; **to drive out** uscire in macchina; **to drive up** arrivare in macchina

drive′-in′ mov′ie the′ater *s* cineparco

drive′-in′ res′taurant *s* ristorante *m* con servizio alla portiera

driv•el ['drɪvəl] *s* (*slobber*) bava; (*nonsense*) scemenza ‖ *v* (*pret* **-eled** or **-elled**; *ger* **-eling** or **-elling**) *intr* sbavare; dire scemenze

driver ['draɪvər] *s* guidatore *m;* (*of a carriage*) cocchiere *m;* (*of a locomotive*) macchinista *m;* (*of pack animals*) carrettiere *m,* mulattiere *m*

driv′er's li′cense *s* patente automobilistica

driv′er's seat′ *s* posto di guida

drive′ shaft′ *s* albero motore

drive′way′ *s* strada privata d'accesso; carrozzabile *f*

drive′ wheel′ *s* ruota motrice

driv′ing school′ ['draɪvɪŋ] *s* autoscuola, scuola guida

drizzle ['drɪzəl] *s* pioviggine *f* ‖ *intr* piovigginare

droll [drol] *adj* buffo, spassoso

dromedar•y ['dromə,deri] *s* (**-ies**) dromedario

drone [dron] *s* fuco, pecchione *m;* (*hum*) ronzio; (*of bagpipe*) bordone *m;* areoplano teleguidato ‖ *tr* dire in tono monotono ‖ *intr* (*to live in idleness*) fare il fannullone; (*to buzz, hum*) ronzare

drool [drul] *s* (*slobber*) bava; (*slang*) scemenza ‖ *intr* sbavare; (*slang*) dire scemenze

droop [drup] *s* accasciamento ‖ *intr* (*to sag*) pendere; (*to lose spirit*) accasciarsi; (*said, e.g., of wheat*) avvizzire

drooping ['drupɪŋ] *adj* (*eyelid*) abbassato; (*shoulder*) spiovente; (fig) accasciato

drop [drɑp] *s* goccia; (*slope*) pendenza; (*earring*) pendente *m;* (*in temperature*) discesa; (*from an airplane*) lancio; (*trap door*) botola; (*gallows*) trabocchetto della forca; (*lozenge*) pastiglia; (*slit for letters*) buca; (*curtain*) tela; (*in prices*) calo; **a drop in the bucket** una goccia nell'oceano ‖ *v* (*pret & pp* **dropped**; *ger* **dropping**) *tr* lasciar cadere; (*a letter*) imbucare; (*a curtain*) abbassare; (*a remark*) lasciar scappare; (*a note*) scrivere; omettere; abbandonare; (*anchor*) gettare; (*from an airplane*) lanciare; (*from an automobile*) lasciare; (*from a list*) cancellare ‖ *intr* cadere; lasciarsi cadere; terminare; **to drop dead** cader morto; **to drop in** entrare un momento; **to drop off** sparire; addormentarsi; morire improvvisamente; **to drop out** scomparire; ritirarsi; dare le dimissioni

drop′ cur′tain *s* telone *m*

drop′ ham′mer *s* maglio

drop′-leaf′ ta′ble *s* tavola a ribalta

drop′light′ *s* lampada sospesa

drop′out′ *s* studente *m* che abbandona permanentemente la scuola media

dropper ['drɑpər] *s* contagocce *m*

dropsical ['drɑpsɪkəl] *adj* idropico

dropsy ['drɑpsi] *s* idropisia

dross [drɑs] or [drɔs] *s* scoria; (fig) feccia

drought [draʊt] *s* siccità *f;* (*shortage*) mancanza

drove [drov] *s* branco; folla; **in droves** in massa

drover ['drovər] *s* mandriano

drown [draʊn] *tr & intr* affogare, annegare

drowse [draʊz] *intr* sonnecchiare

drow•sy ['draʊzi] *adj* (**-sier; -siest**) sonnolento, insonnolito

drub [drʌb] *v* (*pret & pp* **drubbed**; *ger* **drubbing**) *tr* bastonare; battere

drudge [drʌdʒ] *s* sgobbone *m* || *intr* sgobbare, sfacchinare
drudger·y ['drʌdʒəri] *s* (*-ies*) lavoro ingrato, sfacchinata
drug [drʌg] *s* droga, medicina; narcotico; **drug on the market** merce *f* invendibile || *v* (*pret & pp* **drugged;** *ger* **drugging**) *tr* drogare, narcotizzare *m*
drug' ad'dict *s* tossicomane *mf*
drug' addic'tion *s* tossicomania
druggist ['drʌgɪst] *s* farmacista *mf*
drug' hab'it *s* tossicomania
drug'store' *s* farmacia
drug' traf'fic *s* traffico in stupefacenti
druid ['druːɪd] *s* druida *m*
drum [drʌm] *s* (*cylinder; instrument*) tamburo; (*container*) fusto || *v* (*pret & pp* **drummed;** *ger* **drumming**) *tr* stamburare; **to drum up** (*customers*) farsi; (*enthusiasm*) creare || *intr* tambureggiare; (*with the fingers*) tamburellare
drum'beat' *s* rullo di tamburi
drum' corps' *s* banda di tamburi
drum'fire' *s* fuoco nutrito
drum'head' *s* membrana del tamburo
drum' ma'jor *s* tamburo maggiore
drummer ['drʌmər] *s* (*salesman*) agente *m* viaggiatore; (*mus*) tamburo; (*mil*) tamburino
drum'stick' *s* bacchetta del tamburo; (*of cooked fowl*) coscia
drunk [drʌŋk] *adj* ubriaco; **to get drunk** ubriacarsi || *s* ubriaco; (*spree*) sbornia; **to go on a drunk** (*coll*) ubriacarsi
drunkard ['drʌŋkərd] *s* ubriacone *m*
drunken ['drʌŋkən] *adj* ubriaco
drunk'en driv'ing—**to be arrested for drunken driving** esser arrestato per aver guidato in stato di ubriachezza
drunkenness ['drʌŋkənnɪs] *s* ubriachezza, ebbrezza
dry [draɪ] *adj* (**drier; driest**) secco; (*boring*) arido; **to be dry** aver sete || *s* (**drys**) abolizionista *mf* || *v* (*pret & pp* **dried**) *tr* seccare; (*to wipe dry*) asciugare || *intr* seccarsi; **to dry up** prosciugarsi, essiccarsi; (*slang*) star zitto
dry' bat'tery *s* pila a secco; (*group of dry cells*) batteria a secco
dry' cell' *s* pila a secco
dry'-clean' *tr* lavare a secco, pulire a secco
dry' clean'er *s* tintore *m*
dry' clean'ing *s* lavaggio a secco, pulitura a secco
dry'-clean'ing estab'lishment *s* tintoria
dry' dock' *s* bacino di carenaggio
dryer ['draɪ·ər] *s* var of **drier**
dry'-eyed' *adj* a occhi asciutti
dry' farm'ing *s* coltivazione di terreno arido
dry' goods' *spl* tessuti *mpl*; aridi *mpl*
dry'-goods store' *s* drapperia, negozio di tessuti
dry' ice' *s* neve carbonica, ghiaccio secco
dry' law' *s* legge *f* proibizionista
dry' meas'ure *s* misura per solidi
dryness ['draɪnɪs] *s* siccità *f*; (*e.g., of a speaker*) aridità *f*

dry' nurse' *s* balia asciutta
dry' run' *s* esercizio di prova; (**mil**) esercitazione senza munizioni
dry' sea'son *s* stagione arida
dry' wash' *s* roba lavata e asciugata ma non stirata
dual ['djuː·əl] *or* ['duː·əl] *adj & s* duale *m*
duali·ty [dju'ælɪti] *or* [du'ælɪti] *s* (**-ties**) dualità *f*
dub [dʌb] *s* (*slang*) giocatore inesperto || *v* (*pret & pp* **dubbed;** *ger* **dubbing**) *tr* chiamare, affibbiare il nome di; (*a knight*) armare; (*mov*) doppiare
dubbing ['dʌbɪŋ] *s* doppiaggio
dubious ['djuːbɪ·əs] *or* ['duːbɪ·əs] *adj* dubbioso; incerto
ducat ['dʌkət] *s* ducato
duchess ['dʌtʃɪs] *s* duchessa
duch·y ['dʌtʃi] *s* (**-ies**) ducato
duck [dʌk] *s* anatra; mossa rapida; (*in the water*) tuffo; (*dodge*) schivata; **ducks** pantaloni *mpl* di tela cruda || *tr* (*one's head*) abbassare rapidamente; (*in water*) tuffare; (*a blow*) schivare || *intr* tuffarsi; **to duck out** (*coll*) svignarsela
duckling ['dʌklɪŋ] *s* anatroccolo
ducks' and drakes' *s*—**to play ducks and drakes with** buttar via, sperperare
duck' soup' *s* (*slang*) cosa facilissima
duct [dʌkt] *s* tubo, condotto
ductile ['dʌktɪl] *adj* duttile
duct'less gland' ['dʌktlɪs] *s* ghiandola a secrezione interna
duct'work' *s* condotto, canalizzazione
dud [dʌd] *s* (*slang*) bomba inesplosa; (*person*) (*slang*) fallito; (*enterprise*) (*slang*) fallimento; **duds** (*coll*) vestito; roba
dude [djud] *or* [dud] *s* elegantone *m*
due [dju] *or* [du] *adj* dovuto; atteso, debito; pagabile; **due to** dovuto a; **to fall due** scadere; **when is the train due?** a che ora arriva il treno? || *s* spettanza; debito; **dues** (*of a member*) quota sociale; **to get one's due** ricevere quanto uno merita; **to give the devil his due** trattare ognuno con giustizia || *adv* in direzione, e.g., **due north** in direzione nord
duel ['djuː·əl] *or* ['duː·əl] *s* duello; **to fight a duel** battersi a duello || *v* (*pret & pp* **dueled** *or* **duelled;** *ger* **dueling** *or* **duelling**) *intr* duellare
duelist *or* **duellist** ['djuː·əlɪst] *or* ['duː·əlɪst] *s* duellante *mf*
dues-paying ['djuz,pe·ɪŋ] *or* ['duz,pe·ɪŋ] *adj* regolare, effettivo
duet [dju'ɛt] *or* [du'ɛt] *s* duetto
duf'fel bag' ['dʌfəl] *s* sacca da viaggio
duke [djuk] *or* [duk] *s* duca *m*
dukedom ['djukdəm] *or* ['dukdəm] *s* ducato
dull [dʌl] *adj* (*not sharp*) spuntato, senza filo; (*color*) spento, sbiadito; (*sound, mind*) sordo; (*stupid*) ebete, tonto; (*business*) inattivo; (*boring*) noioso, melenso; (*flat*) opaco, appannato || *tr* spuntare; sbiadire; inebetire; ottundere; (*enthusiasm*) raffreddare; (*pain*) alleviare || *intr*

spuntarsi; sbiadirsi; inebetirsi; raffreddarsi

dullard ['dʌlərd] s stupido

duly ['djuli] or ['duli] adv debitamente

dumb [dʌm] adj (lacking the power to speak) muto; (coll) tonto, stupido

dumb'bell' s manubrio; (slang) zuccone m, stupido

dumb' crea'ture s animale m, bruto

dumb' show' s pantomima

dumb'wai'ter s montavivande m

dumfound [,dʌm'faund] tr interdire, lasciare esterrefatto

dum•my ['dʌmi] adj copiato; falso ‖ s (-mies) (dress form) manichino; (in card games) morto; (figurehead) uomo di paglia, prestanome m; (skeleton copy of a book) menabò m; copia; (slang) stupido, tonto

dump [dʌmp] s immondezzaio; mucchio di spazzature; (mil) deposito munizioni; (min) montagnetta di scarico; **to be down in the dumps** (coll) avere le paturnie ‖ tr scaricare; (to tip over) rovesciare; (com) scaricare sul mercato; (com) vendere sottocosto

dumping ['dʌmpɪŋ] s scarico; (com) dumping m

dumpling ['dʌmplɪŋ] s gnocco

dump' truck' s ribaltabile m

dump•y ['dʌmpi] adj (-ier; -iest) grassoccio, tarchiato

dun [dʌn] adj bruno grigiastro ‖ s creditore importuno; (demand for payment) sollecitazione di pagamento ‖ v (pret & pp dunned; ger dunning) tr sollecitare

dunce [dʌns] s ignorante mf, zuccone m

dunce' cap' s berretto d'asino

dune [djun] or [dun] s duna

dung [dʌŋ] s sterco, letame m ‖ tr concimare con il letame

dungarees [,dʌŋgə'riz] spl tuta di cotone blu

dungeon ['dʌndʒən] s carcere sotterraneo; (fortified tower) torrione m, maschio

dung'hill' s letamaio

dunk [dʌŋk] tr inzuppare

du•o ['dju•o] or ['du•o] s (-os) duo

duode•num [,dju•ə'dinəm] or [,du•ə'dinəm] s (-na [nə]) duodeno

dupe [djup] or [dup] s gonzo ‖ tr gabbare, ingannare

du'plex house' ['djupleks] or ['dupleks] s casa di due appartamenti

duplicate ['djuplɪkɪt] or ['duplɪkɪt] adj & s duplicato ‖ ['djuplɪ,ket] or ['duplɪ,ket] tr duplicare

du'plicating machine' s duplicatore m

duplici•ty [dju'plɪsɪti] or [du'plɪsɪti] s (-ties) duplicità f, doppiezza

durable ['djurəbəl] or ['durəbəl] adj durabile, duraturo

du'rable goods' spl beni mpl durevoli

duration [dju're/ən] or [du're/ən] s durata

during ['djurɪŋ] or ['durɪŋ] prep durante

du'rum wheat' ['djurəm] or ['durəm] s grano duro

dusk [dʌsk] s crepuscolo

dust [dʌst] s polvere f ‖ tr (to free of dust) spolverare; (to sprinkle with dust) spolverizzare; **to dust off** (slang) rimettere in uso; (slang) spolverare le spalle a

dust' bowl' s regione polverosissima

dust'cloth' s strofinaccio

dust' cloud' s polverone m

duster ['dʌstər] s (cloth) cencio; (light overgarment) spolverino

dust' jack'et s sopraccoperta

dust'pan' s pattumiera

dust' rag' s strofinaccio

dust•y ['dʌsti] adj (-ier; -iest) polveroso; grigiastro

Dutch [dʌt/] adj olandese; (slang) tedesco ‖ s (language) olandese m; (language) tedesco; **in Dutch** (slang) in disgrazia; (slang) nei pasticci; **the Dutch** gli olandesi; (slang) i tedeschi; **to go Dutch** (coll) pagare alla romana

Dutch'man s (-men) olandese m; (slang) tedesco

Dutch' treat' s invito alla romana

dutiable ['djuti-əbəl] or ['duti-əbəl] adj soggetto a dogana

dutiful ['djutɪfəl] or ['dutɪfəl] adj obbediente, doveroso

du•ty ['djuti] or ['duti] s (-ties) dovere m; (task) funzione; dazio, dogana; **off duty** libero; in libera uscita; **on duty** in servizio; di guardia; **to do one's duty** fare il proprio dovere; **to take up one's duties** entrare in servizio

du'ty-free' adj esente da dogana

dwarf [dwɔrf] adj & s nano ‖ tr rimpiccolire ‖ intr rimpiccolire; apparire più piccolo

dwarfish ['dwɔrfɪ/] adj nano, da nano

dwell [dwel] v (pret & pp dwelled or dwelt [dwelt]) intr dimorare, abitare; **to dwell on** or **upon** intrattenersi su

dwelling ['dwelɪŋ] s abitazione, residenza

dwell'ing house' s casa d'abitazione

dwindle ['dwɪndəl] intr diminuire; restringersi, consumarsi

dye [daɪ] s tinta, colore m ‖ v (pret & pp dyed; ger dyeing) tr tingere

dyed-in-the-wool ['daɪdɪnðə,wul] adj tinto prima della tessitura; completo, intransigente

dyeing ['daɪ-ɪŋ] s tintura

dyer ['daɪ-ər] s tintore m

dye'stuff' s tintura, materia colorante

dying ['daɪ-ɪŋ] adj morente

dynamic [daɪ'næmɪk] or [dɪ'næmɪk] adj dinamico

dynamite ['daɪnə,maɪt] s dinamite f ‖ tr far saltare con la dinamite

dyna•mo ['daɪnə,mo] s (-mos) dinamo f

dynast ['daɪnæst] s dinasta m

dynas•ty ['daɪnəsti] s (-ties) dinastia

dysentery ['dɪsən,teri] s dissenteria

dyspepsia [dɪs'pɛpsɪ-ə] or [dɪs'pɛp/ə] s dispepsia

E

E, e [i] *s* quinta lettera dell'alfabeto inglese

each [it∫] *adj indef* ogni ‖ *pron indef* ognuno, ciascuno; **each other** ci; vi; si; l'un l'altro ‖ *adv* l'uno; a testa

eager ['igər] *adj (enthusiastic)* ardente; **eager for** avido di; **eager to** + *inf* desideroso di + *inf*

ea'ger bea'ver *s* zelante *mf*

eagerness ['igərnıs] *s* ardore *m;* brama

eagle ['igəl] *s* aquila

ea'gle owl' *s* gufo reale

eaglet ['iglıt] *s* aquilotto

ear [ir] *s* orecchio; *(of corn)* pannocchia; *(of wheat)* spiga; **to be all ears** essere tutt'orecchi; **to prick up one's ears** tendere l'orecchio; **to turn a deaf ear** far l'orecchio di mercante

ear'ache' *s* mal *m* d'orecchi

ear'drop' *s* pendente *m*

ear'drum' *s* timpano

ear'flap' *s* paraorecchi *m*

earl [ʌrl] *s* conte *m*

earldom ['ʌrldəm] *s* contea

ear-ly ['ʌrli] **(-lier; -liest)** *adj (occurring before customary time)* di buon'ora; *(first in a series)* primo; *(far back in time)* remoto, antico; *(occurring in near future)* prossimo ‖ *adv* presto; per tempo, di buon'ora; **as early as** *(a certain time of day)* già a; *(a certain time or date)* fin da, già in; **as early as possible** quanto prima possibile; **early in** (e.g., *the month*) all'inizio di; **early in the morning** di mattina presto, di buon mattino; **early in the year** all'inizio dell'anno

ear'ly bird' *s* persona mattiniera

ear'ly mass' *s* prima messa

ear'ly ris'er *s* persona mattiniera

ear'mark' *s* contrassegno ‖ *tr* contrassegnare; assegnare a scopo speciale

ear'muff' *s* paraorecchi *m*

earn [ʌrn] *tr* guadagnare, guadagnarsi; *(to get one's due)* meritarsi; *(interest)* (com) produrre ‖ *intr* trarre profitto, rendere

earnest ['ʌrnıst] *adj* serio; fervente; **in earnest** sul serio ‖ *s* caparra

ear'nest mon'ey *s* caparra

earnings ['ʌrnıŋz] *s* guadagno; salario

ear'phone' *s (of sonar)* orecchiale *m;* (rad, telp) cuffia

ear'piece' *s (of eyeglasses)* susta; (telp) ricevitore *m*

ear'ring' *s* orecchino

ear'shot' *s* tiro dell'orecchio; **within earshot** a portata di voce

ear'split'ting *adj* assordante

earth [ʌrθ] *s* terra; **to come back to** or **down to earth** scendere dalle nuvole

earthen ['ʌrθən] *adj* di terra; di terracotta

ear'then·ware' *s* coccio, terraglie *fpl,* terracotta

earthling ['ʌrθlıŋ] *s* terrestre *mf*

earthly ['ʌrθli] *adj* terreno, terrestre;

to be of no earthly use non servire assolutamente a niente

earthmover ['ʌrθ‚muvər] *s* ruspa

earth'quake' *s* terremoto

earth'work' *s* terrapieno

earth'worm' *s* lombrico

earth·y ['ʌrθi] *adj* **(-ier; -iest)** terroso; *(coarse)* rozzo; pratico; sincero, diretto

ear' trum'pet *s* corno acustico

ear'wax' *s* cerume *m*

ease [iz] *s* facilità *f; (naturalness)* spigliatezza, disinvoltura; *(comfort)* benestare *m;* tranquillità *f;* **at ease!** (mil) riposo!; **with ease** con facilità ‖ *tr* facilitare; *(a burden)* alleggerire; *(to let up on)* rallentare; mitigare; **to ease out** licenziare con le buone maniere ‖ *intr* alleviarsi, mitigarsi, diminuire; rallentare

easel ['izəl] *s* cavalletto

easement ['izmənt] *s* attenuamento; (law) servitù *f*

easily ['izıli] *adv* facilmente; senza dubbio; probabilmente

easiness ['izınıs] *s* facilità *f;* disinvoltura; grazia, agilità *f;* indifferenza

east [ist] *adj* orientale, dell'est ‖ *s est m* ‖ *adv* verso l'est

Easter ['istər] *s* Pasqua

East'er egg' *s* uovo di Pasqua

East'er Mon'day *s* lunedì *m* di Pasqua

eastern ['istərn] *adj* orientale

East'er·tide' *s* tempo pasquale

eastward ['istwərd] *adv* verso l'est

eas·y ['izi] *adj* **(-ier; -iest)** facile; *(conducive to ease)* comodo, agiato; *(free from worry)* tranquillo; *(easygoing)* disinvolto, spigliato; *(not tight)* ampio; *(not hurried)* lento, moderato ‖ *adv* (coll) facilmente; (coll) tranquillamente; **to take it easy** (coll) riposarsi; (coll) non prendersela; (coll) andar piano

eas'y chair' *s* poltrona

eas'y·go'ing *adj (person)* comodone; *(horse)* sciolto nell'andatura

eas'y mark' *s* (coll) gonzo

eas'y mon'ey *s* denaro fatto senza fatica; soldi rubati

eas'y terms' *spl* facilitazioni *fpl* di pagamento

eat [it] *v* **(pret ate** [et]; **pp eaten** ['itən])** *tr* mangiare; **to eat away** smangiare; **to eat up** mangiarsi ‖ *intr* mangiare

eatable ['itəbəl] *adj* mangiabile ‖ **eatables** *spl* commestibili *mpl*

eaves [ivz] *spl* gronda

eaves'drop' *v* **(pret & pp -dropped; ger -dropping)** *intr* origliare

ebb [eb] *s* riflusso; decadenza ‖ *intr (said of the tide)* ritirarsi; decadere

ebb' and flow' *s* flusso e riflusso

ebb' tide' *s* riflusso, deflusso

ebon·y ['ebəni] *s* **(-ies)** ebano

ebullient [ı'bʌljənt] *adj* bollente

eccentric [ek'sentrık] *adj & s* eccentrico

eccentrici·ty [ˌɛksɛn'trɪsɪti] s (-ties) eccentricità f, originalità f
ecclesiastic [ɪˌklizɪ'æstɪk] adj & s ecclesiastico
echelon ['ɛʃəˌlɑn] s scaglione m; (mil) scaglione m || tr scaglionare
ech·o ['ɛko] s (-oes) eco || tr far eco a || intr echeggiare, riecheggiare
éclair [e'kler] s dolce ripieno di crema
eclectic [ɛk'lɛktɪk] adj & s eclettico
eclipse [ɪ'klɪps] s eclisse f, eclissi f || tr eclissare
eclogue ['ɛklɔg] or ['ɛklɑg] s egloga
ecology [ɪ'kɑlədʒi] s ecologia
economic(al) [ˌikə'nɑmɪk(əl)] or [ˌɛkə'nɑmɪk(əl)] adj economico
economics [ˌikə'nɑmɪks] or [ˌɛkə'nɑmɪks] s economia (politica)
economist [ɪ'kɑnəmɪst] s economista mf
economize [ɪ'kɑnəˌmaɪz] tr & intr economizzare
econo·my [ɪ'kɑnəmi] s (-mies) economia
ecosystem ['ɛkoˌsɪstəm] s ecosistema m
ecsta·sy ['ɛkstəsi] s (-sies) estasi f
ecstatic [ɛk'stætɪk] adj estatico
ecumenic(al) [ˌɛkjə'mɛnɪk(əl)] adj ecumenico
eczema ['ɛksɪmə] or [ɛg'zimə] s eczema m
ed·dy ['ɛdi] s (-dies) turbine m || v (pret & pp -died) tr & intr turbinare
edelweiss ['ɛdəlˌvaɪs] s stella alpina
edge [ɛdʒ] s (of knife, sword, etc) filo, tagliente m; (border at which a surface terminates) orlo, bordo; (of a wound) labbro, margine m; (of a book) taglio; (of a tumbler) giro; (of clothing) vivagno; (of a table) spigolo; (slang) vantaggio; **on edge** nervoso; **to have the edge on** (coll) avere il vantaggio su; **to set the teeth on edge** far allegare i denti || tr affilare, aguzzare; orlare, bordare; **to edge out** riuscire ad eliminare || intr avanzare lentamente
edgeways ['ɛdʒˌwez] adv di taglio; **to not let s.o. get a word in edgeways** non lasciar dire una parola a qlcu
edging ['ɛdʒɪŋ] s orlo, bordo
edg·y ['ɛdʒi] adj (-ier; -iest) acuto, angolare; nervoso, ansioso
edible ['ɛdɪbəl] adj mangereccio, mangiabile || **edibles** spl commestibili mpl
edict ['idɪkt] s editto
edification [ˌɛdɪfɪ'keʃən] s edificazione
edifice ['ɛdɪfɪs] s edificio
edi·fy ['ɛdɪˌfaɪ] v (pret & pp -fied) tr edificare
edifying ['ɛdɪˌfaɪ·ɪŋ] adj edificante
edit ['ɛdɪt] tr redigere; (e.g., a manuscript) correggere; (an edition) curare; (a newspaper) dirigere; (mov) montare
edition [ɪ'dɪʃən] s edizione
editor ['ɛdɪtər] s (of a newspaper or magazine) direttore m, gerente mf; (of an editorial) redattore m, cronista mf; (of a critical edition) editore m; (of a manuscript) revisore m

editorial [ˌɛdɪ'torɪ·əl] adj editoriale || s capocronaca m, articolo di fondo
ed'ito'rial staff s redazione
ed'itor in chief' s gerente mf responsabile
educate ['ɛdʒuˌket] tr educare, erudire
education [ˌɛdʒu'keʃən] s educazione; istruzione, insegnamento
educational [ˌɛdʒu'keʃənəl] adj educativo
educa'tional institu'tion s istituto di magistero
educator ['ɛdʒuˌketər] s educatore m
eel [il] s anguilla; **to be as slippery as an eel** guizzare di mano come un'anguilla
ee·rie or **ee·ry** ['ɪri] adj (-rier; -riest) spettrale, pauroso
efface [ɪ'fes] tr cancellare; **to efface oneself** eclissarsi, mettersi in disparte
effect [ɪ'fɛkt] s effetto; (main idea) tenore m; **in effect** in vigore; in realtà; **to go into effect** or **to take effect** andare in vigore; **to put into effect** mandare ad effetto || tr effettuare
effective [ɪ'fɛktɪv] adj efficace; (actually in effect) effettivo; (striking) che colpisce; **to become effective** entrare in vigore
effectual [ɪ'fɛkt/u·əl] adj efficace
effectuate [ɪ'fɛkt/u ˌet] tr effettuare
effeminacy [ɪ'fɛmɪnəsi] s effeminatezza
effeminate [ɪ'fɛmɪnɪt] adj effeminato
effervesce [ˌɛfər'vɛs] intr essere in effervescenza
effervescence [ˌɛfər'vɛsəns] s effervescenza
effervescent [ˌɛfər'vɛsənt] adj effervescente
effete [ɪ'fit] adj esausto, sterile
efficacious [ˌɛfɪ'keʃəs] adj efficace
effica·cy ['ɛfɪkəsi] s (-cies) efficacia
efficien·cy [ɪ'fɪʃənsi] s (-cies) efficienza; (mech) rendimento, efficienza
effi'ciency engineer' s analista mf tempi e metodi
efficient [ɪ'fɪʃənt] adj efficiente; (person) abile; (mech) efficiente
effi·gy ['ɛfɪdʒi] s (-gies) effigie f
effort ['ɛfərt] s sforzo
effronter·y [ɪ'frʌntəri] s (-ies) sfrontatezza, sfacciataggine f
effusion [ɪ'fjuʒən] s effusione
effusive [ɪ'fjusɪv] adj espansivo
egg [ɛg] s uovo; (slang) bravo ragazzo || tr—**to egg on** incitare
egg'beat'er s frullino, sbattiuova m
egg'cup' s portauovo
egg'head' s (coll) intellettuale mf
eggnog ['ɛgˌnɑg] s zabaione m
egg'plant' s melanzana, petonciano
egg'shell' s guscio d'uovo
egoism ['ɛgoˌɪzəm] or ['igoˌɪzəm] s egoismo
egoist ['ɛgo·ɪst] or ['igo·ɪst] s egoista mf
egotism ['ɛgoˌtɪzəm] or ['igoˌtɪzəm] s egotismo
egotist ['ɛgotɪst] or ['igotɪst] s egotista mf

egregious [ɪ'griːdʒəs] *adj* gigantesco, tremendo, marchiano

egress ['iːgres] *s* uscita

Egypt ['iːdʒɪpt] *s* l'Egitto

Egyptian [ɪ'dʒɪp/ən] *adj & s* egiziano

ei'der down' ['aɪdər] *s* piumino

ei'der duck' *s* edredone *m*

eight [et] *adj & pron* otto || *s* otto; **eight o'clock** le otto

eighteen ['et'tiːn] *adj, s & pron* diciotto

eighteenth ['et'tiːnθ] *adj, s & pron* diciottesimo || *s* (*in dates*) diciotto

eighth [etθ] *adj & s* ottavo || *s* (*in dates*) otto

eight' hun'dred *adj, s & pron* ottocento

eightieth ['etɪ·ɪθ] *adj, s & pron* ottantesimo

eight·y ['eti] *adj & pron* ottanta || *s* (*-ies*) ottanta *m; the* **eighties** gli anni ottanta

either ['iːðər] *or* ['aɪðər] *adj* l'uno o l'altro; l'uno e l'altro; ciascuno; entrambi i, tutti e due i || *pron* l'uno o l'altro; l'uno e l'altro; entrambi || *adv—not either* nemmeno || *conj—either . . . or* o . . . o

ejaculate [ɪ'dʒækjə‚let] *tr* esclamare; (*physiol*) emettere || *intr* esclamare; (*physiol*) avere un'eiaculazione

eject [ɪ'dʒekt] *tr* espellere, gettar fuori; (*to evict*) sfrattare

ejection [ɪ'dʒek/ən] *s* espulsione; (*of a tenant*) sfratto

ejec'tion seat' *s* sedile *m* eiettabile

eke [iːk] *tr—to eke out a living** sbarcare il lunario

elaborate [ɪ'læbərɪt] *adj* (*done with great care*) elaborato; (*detailed*) minuzioso; (*ornate*) ornato || [ɪ'læbə‚ret] *tr* elaborare || *intr—to elaborate on* or **upon** circonstanziare, particolareggiare

elapse [ɪ'læps] *intr* passare, trascorrere

elastic [ɪ'læstɪk] *adj & s* elastico

elasticity [ɪ‚læs'tɪsɪti] *or* [‚iːlæs'tɪsɪti] *s* elasticità *f*

elated [ɪ'letɪd] *adj* esultante, gongolante

elation [ɪ'leʃən] *s* esultanza, gaudio

elbow ['elbo] *s* gomito; (*in a river*) ansa; (*of a chair*) braccio; **at one's elbow** sotto mano; **out at the elbows** coi gomiti logori; **to crook the elbow** alzare il gomito; **to rub elbows** stare gomito a gomito; **up to the elbows** fino al collo || *tr—to elbow one's way* aprirsi il passo a gomitate || *intr* dar gomitate

el'bow grease' *s* (coll) olio di gomiti

el'bow patch' *s* toppa al gomito

el'bow rest' *s* bracciolo

el'bow-room' *s* spazio sufficiente; libertà *f* d'azione

elder ['eldər] *adj* seniore, maggiore || *s* (bot) sambuco; (eccl) maggiore *m*

el'der·ber'ry *s* (*-ries*) sambuco; (*fruit*) bacca del sambuco

elderly ['eldərli] *adj* attempato, anziano

eld'er states'man *s* uomo di stato esperto

eldest ['eldɪst] *adj* (il) maggiore; (il) più vecchio

elect [ɪ'lekt] *adj & s* eletto; **the elect** gli eletti || *tr* eleggere

election [ɪ'lek/ən] *s* elezione

electioneer [ɪ‚lek/ə'nɪr] *intr* fare una campagna elettorale

elective [ɪ'lektɪv] *adj* elettivo || *s* corso facoltativo

electorate [ɪ'lektərɪt] *s* elettorato

electric(al) [ɪ'lektrɪk(əl)] *adj* elettrico

elec'tric blend'er *s* frullatore *m*

elec'tric chair' *s* sedia elettrica

elec'tric cord' *s* piattina, filo elettrico

elec'tric eel' *s* gimnoto

elec'tric eye' *s* occhio elettrico

electrician [ɪ‚lek'trɪ/ən] *or* [‚elek-'trɪ/ən] *s* elettricista *m*

electricity [ɪ‚lek'trɪsɪti] *or* [‚elek-'trɪsɪti] *s* elettricità *f*

elec'tric me'ter *s* contatore *m* della luce

elec'tric per'cola'tor *s* caffettiera elettrica

elec'tric shav'er *s* rasoio elettrico

elec'tric shock' *s* scossa elettrica, elettroquasso

elec'tric tape' *s* nastro isolante

elec'tric train' *s* elettrotreno

electri·fy [ɪ'lektrɪ‚faɪ] *v* (*pret & pp* **-fied**) *tr* (*to provide with electric power*) elettrificare; (*to communicate electricity to; to thrill*) elettrizzare

electrocute [ɪ'lektrə‚kjut] *tr* fulminare con la corrente; far morire sulla sedia elettrica

electrode [ɪ'lektrod] *s* elettrodo

electrolysis [ɪ‚lek'tralɪsɪs] *or* [‚elek-'tralɪsɪs] *s* elettrolisi *f*

electrolyte [ɪ'lektrə‚laɪt] *s* elettrolito

electromagnet [ɪ‚lektrə'mægnɪt] *s* elettrocalamita

electromagnetic [ɪ‚lektrəmæg'netɪk] *adj* elettromagnetico

electromotive [ɪ‚lektrə'motɪv] *adj* elettromotore

electron [ɪ'lektran] *s* elettrone *m*

electronic [ɪ‚lek'tranɪk] *or* [‚elek-'tranɪk] *adj* elettronico || **electronics** *s* elettronica

electroplating [ɪ'lektrə‚pletɪŋ] *s* galvanostegia

electrostatic [ɪ‚lektrə'stætɪk] *adj* elettrostatico

electrotype [ɪ'lektrə‚taɪp] *s* stereotipia || *tr* stereotipare

eleemosynary [‚elɪ'masɪ‚nerɪ] *adj* caritatevole, di beneficenza

elegance ['elɪgəns] *s* eleganza

elegant ['elɪgənt] *adj* elegante

elegiac [‚elɪ'dʒaɪ·æk] *adj* elegiaco

ele·gy ['elɪdʒɪ] *s* (*-gies*) elegia

element ['elɪmənt] *s* elemento; **to be out of one's element** essere fuori del proprio ambiente

elementary [‚elɪ'mentəri] *adj* elementare

elephant ['elɪfənt] *s* elefante *m*

elevate ['elɪ‚vet] *tr* elevare, innalzare

elevated ['elɪ‚vetɪd] *adj* elevato || *s* ferrovia soprelevata, metropolitana soprelevata

elevation [‚elɪ'veʃən] *s* elevazione; (surv) quota

elevator ['elɪ‚vetər] *s* ascensore *m;*

(for freight) montacarichi m; (for hoisting grain) elevatore m di grano; (warehouse for storing grain) deposito granaglie; (aer) timone m di profondità

eleven [ɪ'levən] adj & pron undici || s undici m; **eleven o'clock** le undici

eleventh [ɪ'levənθ] adj, s & pron undicesimo || s (in dates) undici m

elev'enth hour' s ultimo momento

elf [elf] s (elves [ɛlvz]) elfo

elicit [ɪ'lɪsɪt] tr cavare, sottrarre

elide [ɪ'laɪd] tr elidere

eligible ['elɪdʒɪbəl] adj eleggibile; accettabile

eliminate [ɪ'lɪmɪ,net] tr eliminare

elision [ɪ'lɪʒən] s elisione

elite [e'lit] adj eletto, scelto || s—the **elite** l'élite f

elk [elk] s alce m

ellipse [ɪ'lɪps] s (geom) ellisse f

ellip·sis [ɪ'lɪpsɪs] s (-ses [siz]) (gram) ellissi f

elliptic(al) [ɪ'lɪptɪk(əl)] adj ellittico

elm [elm] s olmo

elongate [ɪ'lɔŋget] or [ɪ'laŋget] tr allungare, prolungare

elope [ɪ'lop] intr fuggire con un amante

elopement [ɪ'lopmənt] s fuga con un amante

eloquence ['ɛləkwəns] s eloquenza

eloquent ['ɛləkwənt] adj eloquente

else [ɛls] adj—**nobody else** nessun altro; **nothing else** nient'altro; **somebody else** qualcun altro; **something else** qualcosa d'altro; **what else** che altro; **who else** chi altro; **whose else** di che altra persona || adv—**how else** in che altra maniera; **or else** se no; altrimenti; **when else** in che altro momento; in che altro periodo; **where else** dove mai, da che parte

else'where' adv altrove

elucidate [ɪ'lusɪ,det] tr dilucidare

elude [ɪ'lud] tr eludere

elusive [ɪ'lusɪv] adj elusivo; (evasive) fugace, sfuggente

emaciated [ɪ'meʃɪ,etɪd] adj smunto, emaciato, macilento

emanate ['ɛmə,net] tr & intr emanare

emancipate [ɪ'mænsɪ,pet] tr emancipare

embalm [ɛm'bam] tr imbalsamare

embankment [ɛm'bæŋkmənt] s terrapieno

embar·go [ɛm'bargo] s (-goes) embargo || tr mettere l'embargo a

embark [ɛm'bark] intr imbarcarsi

embarkation [,ɛmbar'keʃən] s imbarco

embarrass [ɛm'bærəs] tr imbarazzare, mettere a disagio; (to impede) imbarazzare, impacciare; mettere in difficoltà economiche

embarrassing [ɛm'bærəsɪŋ] adj sconcertante; imbarazzante

embarrassment [ɛm'bærəsmənt] s imbarazzo, disagio, confusione; impaccio; difficoltà finanziaria, dissesto

embas·sy ['ɛmbəsi] s (-sies) ambasciata

em·bed [ɛm'bed] s (pret & pp -bedded; ger -bedding) tr incastrare, incassare

embellish [ɛm'belɪʃ] tr imbellire

embellishment [ɛm'belɪʃmənt] s abbellimento; (fig) fioretto

ember ['ɛmbər] s brace f; **embers** braci fpl

Em'ber days' spl tempora fpl

embezzle [ɛm'bezəl] tr appropriare, malversare || intr appropriarsi

embezzlement [ɛm'bezəlmənt] s appropriazione indebita, malversazione; (of public funds) peculato

embezzler [ɛm'bezlər] s malversatore m

embitter [ɛm'bɪtər] tr amareggiare

emblazon [ɛm'blezən] tr blasonare; celebrare

emblem ['ɛmbləm] s emblema m

emblematic(al) [,ɛmblə'mætɪk(əl)] adj emblematico

embodiment [ɛm'badɪmənt] s incarnazione, personificazione

embod·y [ɛm'badɪ] v (pret & pp -ied) tr incarnare, personificare; incorporare

embolden [ɛm'boldən] tr imbaldanzire

embolism ['ɛmbə,lɪzəm] s embolia

emboss [ɛm'bɔs] or [ɛm'bas] tr (metal) sbalzare; (paper) goffrare

embrace [ɛm'bres] s abbraccio || tr abbracciare || intr abbracciarsi

embrasure [ɛm'breʒər] s (archit) strombatura; (mil) feritoia

embroider [ɛm'brɔɪdər] tr ricamare, trapuntare

embroider·y [ɛm'brɔɪdərɪ] s (-ies) ricamo, trapunto

embroil [ɛm'brɔɪl] tr ingarbugliare; (to involve in contention) coinvolgere

embroilment [ɛm'brɔɪlmənt] s imbroglio; (in contention) disaccordo

embry·o ['ɛmbrɪ,o] s (-os) embrione m

embryology [,ɛmbrɪ'alədʒɪ] s embriologia

embryonic [,ɛmbrɪ'anɪk] adj embrionale

emcee ['ɛm'si] s presentatore m || tr presentare

emend [ɪ'mɛnd] tr emendare

emendation [,imen'deʃən] s emendamento

emerald ['ɛmərəld] s smeraldo

emerge [ɪ'mʌrdʒ] intr emergere

emergence [ɪ'mʌrdʒəns] s emergenza

emergen·cy [ɪ'mʌrdʒənsɪ] s (-cies) emergenza

emer'gency brake' s freno a mano

emer'gency ex'it s uscita di sicurezza

emer'gency land'ing s atterraggio di fortuna

emer'gency ward' s sala d'urgenza

emeritus [ɪ'mɛrɪtəs] adj emerito

emersion [ɪ'mʌrʒən] or [ɪ'mʌrʃən] s emersione

emery ['ɛmərɪ] s smeriglio

em'ery cloth' s tela smeriglio

em'ery wheel' s mola a smeriglio

emetic [ɪ'mɛtɪk] adj & s emetico

emigrant ['ɛmɪgrənt] adj & s emigrante mf

emigrate ['ɛmɪ,gret] intr emigrare

émigré [emi'gre] or ['ɛmɪ,gre] s emigrato

eminence [ˈɛmɪnəns] *s* eminenza; (eccl) Eminenza

eminent [ˈɛmɪnənt] *adj* eminente

emissar·y [ˈɛmɪˌsɛri] *s* (**-ies**) emissario

emission [ɪˈmɪʃən] *s* emissione

emit [ɪˈmɪt] *v* (*pret & pp* **emitted;** *ger* **emitting**) *tr* emettere

emolument [ɪˈmɑljəmənt] *s* emolumento

emotion [ɪˈmoʃən] *s* emozione

emotional [ɪˈmoʃənəl] *adj* emotivo

emperor [ˈɛmpərər] *s* imperatore *m*

empha·sis [ˈɛmfəsɪs] *s* (**-ses** [ˌsiz]) enfasi *f*, risalto

emphasize [ˈɛmfəˌsaɪz] *tr* dar rilievo a, sottolineare

emphatic [ɛmˈfætɪk] *adj* enfatico

emphysema [ˌɛmfɪˈsimə] *s* enfisema *m*

empire [ˈɛmpaɪr] *s* impero

empiric(al) [ɛmˈpɪrɪk(əl)] *adj* empirico

empiricist [ɛmˈpɪrɪsɪst] *s* empirista *mf*

emplacement [ɛmˈplɛsmənt] *s* piazzola, postazione

employ [ɛmˈplɔɪ] *s* impiego || *tr* impiegare, usare; valersi di

employee [ɛmˈplɔɪ-i] or [ˌɛmplɔɪˈi] *s* impiegato, dipendente *mf*

employer [ɛmˈplɔɪ-ər] *s* dirigente *mf*, datore *m* di lavoro

employment [ɛmˈplɔɪmənt] *s* impiego, occupazione

employ′ment a′gency *s* agenzia di collocamento

empower [ɛmˈpau-ər] *tr* autorizzare; permettere

empress [ˈɛmprɪs] *s* imperatrice *f*

emptiness [ˈɛmptɪnɪs] *s* vuoto

emp·ty [ˈɛmpti] *adj* (**-tier; -tiest**) vuoto; (*gun*) scarico; (*hungry*) (coll) digiuno; (fig) esausto || *v* (*pret & pp* **-tied**) *tr* vuotare || *intr* vuotarsi

empty-handed [ˈɛmptiˈhændɪd] *adj* a mani vuote

empty-headed [ˈɛmptiˈhɛdɪd] *adj* dalla testa vuota, balordo

empyrean [ˌɛmpɪˈri-ən] *adj & s* empireo

emulate [ˈɛmjəˌlɛt] *tr* emulare

emulator [ˈɛmjəˌlɛtər] *s* emulo

emulous [ˈɛmjələs] *adj* emulo

emulsi·fy [ɪˈmʌlsɪˌfaɪ] *v* (*pret & pp* **-fied**) *tr* emulsionare

emulsion [ɪˈmʌlʃən] *s* emulsione

enable [ɛnˈebəl] *tr* abilitare; permettere (*with dat*)

enact [ɛnˈækt] *tr* decretare; (*a role*) rappresentare

enactment [ɛnˈæktmənt] *s* legge *f*; (*of a law*) promulgazione; (*of a play*) rappresentazione

enam·el [ɪnˈæməl] *s* smalto || *v* (*pret & pp* **-eled** or **-elled;** *ger* **-eling** or **-elling**) *tr* smaltare

enam′el·ware′ *s* utensili *mpl* di cucina di ferro smaltato

enamor [ɛnˈæmər] *tr* innamorare; **to become enamored of** innamorarsi di

encamp [ɛnˈkæmp] *tr* accampare || *intr* accamparsi

encampment [ɛnˈkæmpmənt] *s* campeggio; (mil) accampamento

encase [ɛnˈkes] *tr* incassare

encephalitis [ɛnˌsɛfəˈlaɪtɪs] *s* encefalite *f*

enchain [ɛnˈtʃen] *tr* incatenare

enchant [ɛnˈtʃænt] or [ɛnˈtʃɑnt] *tr* incantare

enchantment [ɛnˈtʃæntmənt] or [ɛnˈtʃɑntmənt] *s* incanto, malìa

enchanting [ɛnˈtʃæntɪŋ] or [ɛnˈtʃɑntɪŋ] *adj* incantatore, incantevole

enchantress [ɛnˈtʃæntrɪs] or [ɛnˈtʃɑntrɪs] *s* incantatrice *f*, maliarda

enchase [ɛnˈtʃes] *tr* incastonare

encircle [ɛnˈsʌrkəl] *tr* rigirare, girare intorno a; (mil) circondare

enclave [ˈɛnklev] *s* enclave *f*

enclitic [ɛnˈklɪtɪk] *adj* enclitico || *s* enclitica

enclose [ɛnˈkloz] *tr* rinchiudere; (*in a letter*) accludere, includere; **to enclose herewith** accludere alla presente

enclosure [ɛnˈkloʒər] *s* (*land surrounded by fence*) recinto, chiuso; (*e.g., letter*) allegato

encomi·um [ɛnˈkomi-əm] *s* (**-ums** or **-a** [ə]) encomio, elogio

encompass [ɛnˈkʌmpəs] *tr* circondare; racchiudere, contenere

encore [ˈɑŋkor] *s* bis *m* || *tr* (*a performance*) chiedere il bis di; (*a performer*) chiedere il bis a || *interj* bis!

encounter [ɛnˈkauntər] *s* (*casual meeting*) incontro; (*combat*) scontro || *tr* incontrare || *intr* scontrarsi

encourage [ɛnˈkʌrɪdʒ] *tr* incoraggiare; (*to foster*) favorire

encouragement [ɛnˈkʌrɪdʒmənt] *s* incoraggiamento; favoreggiamento

encroach [ɛnˈkrotʃ] *intr*—**to encroach on** or **upon** invadere; usurpare; occupare il territorio di

encumber [ɛnˈkʌmbər] *tr* imbarazzare, ingombrare; (*to load with debts, etc*) gravare

encumbrance [ɛnˈkʌmbrəns] *s* imbarazzo; ingombro; gravame *m*

encyclical [ɛnˈsɪklɪkəl] or [ɛnˈsaɪklɪkəl] *s* enciclica

encyclopedia [ɛnˌsaɪkləˈpidɪ-ə] *s* enciclopedia

encyclopedic [ɛnˌsaɪkləˈpidɪk] *adj* enciclopedico

end [ɛnd] *s* (*extremity; concluding part*) fine *f*; (*e.g., of the week*) fine *f*; (*purpose*) fine *m*; (*part adjacent to an extremity*) lembo; (*small piece*) pezza, avanzo; (*of a beam*) testata; (sports) estrema; **at the end of** in capo a; in fondo a; **in the end** alla fine, all'ultimo; **no end** (coll) moltissimo; **no end of** (coll) un mucchio di; **to make both ends meet** sbarcare il lunario; **to no end** senza effetto; **to stand on end** mettere in piedi, drizzare; mettersi diritto; (*said of hair*) drizzarsi; **to the end that** affinché || *tr* finire, terminare; **to end up** andare a finire || *intr* finire, terminare; **to end up** finire

endanger [ɛnˈdendʒər] *tr* mettere in pericolo

endear [ɛn'dɪr] *tr* affezionare; **to endear oneself to** rendersi caro a

endeavor [ɛn'dɛvər] *s* tentativo, sforzo ‖ *intr* tentare, sforzarsi

endemic [ɛn'dɛmɪk] *adj* endemico ‖ *s* endemia

ending ['ɛndɪŋ] *s* fine *f*, conclusione; (gram) terminazione, desinenza

endive ['ɛndaɪv] *s* indivia

endless ['ɛndlɪs] *adj* interminabile; sterminato; (mach) senza fine

end'most' *adj* estremo, ultimo

endorse [ɛn'dɔrs] *tr* girare; (fig) approvare, confermare

endorsee [,ɛndɔr'si] *s* giratario

endorsement [ɛn'dɔrsmənt] *s* girata; approvazione, conferma

endorser [ɛn'dɔrsər] *s* girante *mf*

endow [ɛn'dau] *tr* dotare

endowment [ɛn'daumənt] *adj* dotale ‖ *s* (*of an institution*) dotazione; (*gift, talent*) dote *f*

end' pap'er *s* risguardo

endurance [ɛn'djurəns] or [ɛn'durəns] *-s* sopportazione, tolleranza; (*ability to hold out*) resistenza, forza; (*lasting time*) durata

endure [ɛn'djur] or [ɛn'dur] *tr* sopportare, tollerare; resistere (with *dat*) ‖ *intr* durare, resistere

enduring [ɛn'djurɪŋ] or [ɛn'durɪŋ] *adj* duraturo, durevole; paziente

enema ['ɛnəmə] *s* clistere *m*

ene·my ['ɛnəmi] *adj* nemico ‖ *s* (**-mies**) nemico

en'emy al'ien *s* straniero nemico

energetic [,ɛnər'dʒɛtɪk] *adj* energetico, vigoroso

ener·gy ['ɛnərdʒi] *s* (**-gies**) energia

enervate ['ɛnər‚vɛt] *tr* snervare

enfeeble [ɛn'fibəl] *tr* indebolire

enfold [ɛn'fold] *tr* avvolgere; abbracciare

enforce [ɛn'fɔrs] *tr* far osservare; ottenere per forza; (*e.g., obedience*) imporre; (*an argument*) far valere

enforcement [ɛn'fɔrsmənt] *s* imposizione; (*of a law*) esecuzione

enfranchise [ɛn'fræntʃaɪz] *tr* liberare; concedere il diritto di voto a

engage [ɛn'gedʒ] *tr* occupare; riservare; (*s.o.'s attention*) attrarre; (*a gear*) ingranare; (*the enemy*) ingaggiare; (*to hire*) assumere; (theat) scritturare; **to be engaged, to be engaged to be married** essere fidanzato; **to engage s.o. in conversation** intavolare una conversazione con qlcu ‖ *intr* essere occupato; essere impiegato; assumere un'obbligazione; (mil) impegnarsi; (mach) ingranare, incastrarsi

engaged [ɛn'gedʒd] *adj* fidanzato; occupato, impegnato; (*column*) murato

engagement [ɛn'gedʒmənt] *s* accordo; fidanzamento; impegno, contratto; (*appointment*) appuntamento; (mil) azione; (mach) innesto

engage'ment ring' *s* anello di fidanzamento

engaging [ɛn'gedʒɪŋ] *adj* attrattivo

engender [ɛn'dʒɛndər] *tr* ingenerare

engine ['ɛndʒɪn] *s* macchina; (aut) motore *m*; (rr) locomotiva, motrice *f*

engineer [,ɛndʒə'nɪr] *s* ingegnere *m*; (rr) macchinista *m*; (mil) zappatore *m*, geniere *m* ‖ *tr* costruire; progettare

engineering [,ɛndʒə'nɪrɪŋ] *s* ingegneria

en'gine house' *s* stazione dei pompieri

en'gine·man' *s* (**-men**) (rr) macchinista *m*

en'gine room' *s* sala macchine

en'gine-room' tel'egraph *s* (naut) telegrafo di macchina, trasmettitore *m*

England ['ɪŋglənd] *s* l'Inghilterra

Englander ['ɪŋgləndər] *s* nativo dell'Inghilterra

English ['ɪŋglɪʃ] *adj* inglese ‖ *s* inglese *m*; (billiards) effetto; **the English** gli inglesi

Eng'lish Chan'nel *s* Canale *m* della Manica

Eng'lish dai'sy *s* margherita

Eng'lish horn' *s* (mus) corno inglese

Eng'lish·man *s* (**-men**) inglese *m*

Eng'lish-speak'ing *adj* di lingua inglese, anglofono

Eng'lish·wom'an *s* (**-wom'en**) inglese *f*

engraft [ɛn'græft] or [ɛn'grɑft] *tr* (hort) innestare; (fig) inculcare

engrave [ɛn'grev] *tr* incidere

engraver [ɛn'grevər] *s* incisore *m*

engraving [ɛn'grevɪŋ] *s* incisione

engross [ɛn'gros] *tr* preoccupare, assorbire; redigere ufficialmente, scrivere a grandi caratteri; monopolizzare

engrossing [ɛn'grosɪŋ] *adj* assorbente

engulf [ɛn'gʌlf] *tr* sommergere, inondare

enhance [ɛn'hæns] or [ɛn'hɑns] *tr* valorizzare; far risaltare

enigma [ɪ'nɪgmə] *s* enigma *m*

enigmatic(al) [,ɪnɪg'mætɪk(əl)] *adj* enigmatico

enjambment [ɛn'dʒæmmənt] or [ɛn'dʒæmbmənt] *s* inarcatura

enjoin [ɛn'dʒɔɪn] *tr* ingiungere, intimare

enjoy [ɛn'dʒɔɪ] *tr* godere; **to enjoy +** *ger* provar piacere in + *inf*; **to enjoy oneself** divertirsi

enjoyable [ɛn'dʒɔɪ‚əbəl] *adj* gradevole

enjoyment [ɛn'dʒɔɪmənt] *s* (*pleasure*) piacere *m*; (*pleasurable use*) godimento

enkindle [ɛn'kɪndəl] *tr* infiammare

enlarge [ɛn'lɑrdʒ] *tr* aumentare; ingrossare; (phot) ingrandire ‖ *intr* aumentare; **to enlarge on** or **upon** dilungarsi su

enlargement [ɛn'lɑrdʒmənt] *s* aumento; ingrossamento; (phot) ingrandimento

enlighten [ɛn'laɪtən] *tr* illustrare, illuminare

enlightenment [ɛn'laɪtənmənt] *s* spiegazione, schiarimento ‖ **Enlightenment** *s* illuminismo

enlist [ɛn'lɪst] *tr* (*e.g., s.o.'s favor*) guadagnarsi; (*the help of a person*) ottenere; (mil) ingaggiare ‖ *intr* (mil) ingaggiarsi, arruolarsi; **to enlist**

in (*a cause*) dare il proprio appoggio a

enlistment [en'lɪstmənt] *s* arruolamento, ingaggio

enliven [en'laɪvən] *tr* ravvivare

enmesh [en'mɛʃ] *tr* irretire

enmi•ty ['enmɪti] *s* (**-ties**) inimicizia

ennoble [en'nobəl] *tr* nobilitare

ennui ['ɑnwi] *s* noia, tedio

enormous [ɪ'nɔrməs] *adj* enorme

enormously [ɪ'nɔrməsli] *adv* enormemente

enough [ɪ'nʌf] *adj* abbastanza || *s* il sufficiente || *adv* abbastanza || *interj* basta!

enounce [ɪ'naʊns] *tr* enunciare; (*to declare*) affermare

enrage [en'redʒ] *tr* infuriare, irritare

enrapture [en'ræptʃər] *tr* mandare in visibilio, estasiare

enrich [en'rɪtʃ] *tr* arricchire

enroll [en'rol] *tr* arruolare, ingaggiare; (*a student*) iscrivere || *intr* arruolarsi, ingaggiarsi; (*said of a student*) iscriversi

enrollment [en'rolmənt] *s* arruolamento, ingaggio; (*of a student*) iscrizione

en route [ɑn 'rut] *adv* in cammino; **en route to** in via per

ensconce [en'skɑns] *tr* nascondere; **to esconce oneself** rannicchiarsi, istallarsi comodamente

ensemble [ɑn'sɑmbəl] *s* insieme *m*; (*mus*) concertato

ensign ['ensaɪn] *s* (*standard*) bandiera, insegna; (*badge*) distintivo || ['ensən] *or* ['ensaɪn] *s* guardamarina *m*

ensilage ['ensɪlɪdʒ] *s* (*preservation of fodder*) insilamento; (*preserved fodder*) insilato

ensile ['ensaɪl] *or* [en'saɪl] *tr* insilare

enslave [en'slev] *tr* fare schiavo, asservire

enslavement [en'slevmənt] *s* asservimento

ensnare [en'sner] *tr* irretire

ensue [en'su] *or* [en'sju] *intr* risultare; seguire, conseguire

ensuing [en'su-ɪŋ] *or* [en'sju-ɪŋ] *adj* risultante, conseguente; seguente

ensure [en'ʃur] *tr* assicurare, garantire

entail [en'tel] *s* (*law*) obbligo || *tr* provocare, comportare; (*law*) obbligare

entangle [en'tæŋgəl] *tr* intricare, imbrogliare, impigliare

entanglement [en'tæŋgəlmənt] *s* groviglio, garbuglio

enter ['entər] *tr* (*a house*) entrare in; (*in the customhouse*) dichiarare; (*to make a record of*) registrare; (*a student*) iscrivere; iscriversi a; fare membro; (*to undertake*) intraprendere; **to enter s.o.'s head** passare per la testa a qlcu || *intr* entrare; (*theat*) entrare in scena; **to enter into** entrare in; (*a contract*) impegnarsi in; **to enter on** *or* **upon** intraprendere

enterprise ['entər ˌpraɪz] *s* (*undertak-

ing*) impresa; (*spirit, push*) intraprendenza

enterprising ['entər ˌpraɪzɪŋ] *adj* intraprendente

entertain [ˌentər'ten] *tr* divertire, intrattenere; (*guests*) ospitare; (*a hope*) accarezzare; (*a proposal*) considerare || *intr* ricevere

entertainer [ˌentər'tenər] *s* (*host*) ospite *mf*; (*in public*) attore *m*, cantante *mf*, fine dicitore *m*

entertaining [ˌentər'tenɪŋ] *adj* divertente

entertainment [ˌentər'tenmənt] *s* trattenimento, svago; spettacolo, attrazione; buon trattamento

enthrall [en'θrɔl] *tr* affascinare, incantare; (*to subjugate*) asservire, soggiogare

enthrone [en'θron] *tr* mettere sul trono, intronizzare; esaltare, innalzare

enthuse [en'θuz] *or* [en'θjuz] *tr* (*coll*) entusiasmare || *intr* (*coll*) entusiasmarsi

enthusiasm [en'θuzɪ ˌæzəm] *or* [en-'θjuzɪ ˌæzəm] *s* entusiasmo

enthusiast [en'θuzɪ ˌæst] *or* [en'θjuzɪ-ˌæst] *s* entusiasta *mf*, maniaco

enthusiastic [en ˌθuzɪ'æstɪk] *or* [en-ˌθjuzɪ'æstɪk] *adj* entusiastico

entice [en'taɪs] *tr* attrarre, provocare; tentare

enticement [en'taɪsmənt] *s* attrazione, provocazione; tentazione

entire [en'taɪr] *adj* intero

entirely [en'taɪrli] *adv* interamente; (*solely*) solamente

entire•ty [en'taɪrti] *s* (**-ties**) interezza; totalità *f*

entitle [en'taɪtəl] *tr* dar diritto a; (*to give a name to*) intitolare

enti•ty ['entɪti] *s* (**-ties**) (*something real; organization, institution*) ente *m*; (*existence*) entità *f*

entomb [en'tum] *tr* seppellire

entombment [en'tummənt] *s* sepoltura

entomology [ˌentə'mɑlədʒi] *s* entomologia

entourage [ˌɑntu'rɑʒ] *s* seguito

entrails ['entrelz] *or* ['entrəlz] *spl* visceri *mpl*

entrain [en'tren] *tr* far salire sul treno || *intr* imbarcarsi sul treno

entrance ['entrəns] *s* entrata, ingresso || [en'træns] *or* [en'trɑns] *tr* ipnotizzare, incantare

en'trance exam'ina'tion *s* esame *m* d'ammissione

entrancing [en'trænsɪŋ] *or* [en'trɑns-ɪŋ] *adj* incantatore

entrant ['entrənt] *s* nuovo membro; (*sports*) concorrente *mf*

en•trap [en'træp] *v* (*pret & pp* **-trapped;** *ger* **-trapping**) *tr* intrappolare, irretire

entreat [en'trit] *tr* implorare

entreat•y [en'triti] *s* (**-ies**) implorazione, supplica

entree ['ɑntre] *s* entrata, ingresso; (*culin*) prima portata

entrench [en'trentʃ] *tr* trincerare || *intr*
—**to entrench on** *or* **upon** violare

entrust [en'trʌst] *tr* affidare, confidare

en•try ['entri] *s* (**-tries**) entrata; *(item)* partita, registrazione; *(in a dictionary)* lemma, esponente *m; (sports)* concorrente *mf*

entwine [en'twaɪn] *tr* intrecciare ‖ *intr* intrecciarsi

enumerate [ɪ'njumə,ret] or [ɪ'numə,ret] *tr* enumerare

enunciate [ɪ'nʌnsɪ,et] or [ɪ'nʌnʃɪ,et] *tr* enunciare, staccare

envelop [en'vɛləp] *tr* involgere

envelope ['envə,lop] or ['anvə,lop] *s (for a letter)* busta; *(wrapper)* involucro

envenom [en'venəm] *tr* avvelenare

enviable ['envɪ·əbəl] *adj* invidiabile

envious ['envɪ·əs] *adj* invidioso

environment [en'vaɪrənmənt] *s* ambiente *m;* condizioni *fpl* ambientali

environs [en'vaɪrənz] *spl* dintorni *mpl,* sobborghi *mpl*

envisage [en'vɪzɪdʒ] *tr* considerare, immaginare

envoi ['envɔɪ] *s* (pros) congedo

envoy ['envɔɪ] *s* inviato; *(mil)* parlamentare *m;* (pros) congedo

en•vy ['envɪ] *s* (**-vies**) invidia ‖ *v (pret & pp* **-vied**) *tr* invidiare

enzyme ['enzaɪm] or ['enzɪm] *s* enzima *m*

epaulet or **epaulette** ['epə,let] *s* spallina

epenthe•sis [ɛ'penθɪsɪs] *s* (**-ses** [,siz]) epentesi *f*

ephemeral [ɪ'femərəl] *adj* effimero

epic ['epɪk] *adj* epico ‖ *s* epica

epicure ['epɪ,kjur] *s* epicureo

epicurean [,epɪkju'ri·ən] *adj & s* epicureo

epidemic [,epɪ'demɪk] *adj* epidemico ‖ *s* epidemia

epidermis [,epɪ'dʌrmɪs] *s* epidermide *f*

epiglottis [,epɪ'glɑtɪs] *s* epiglottide *f*

epigram ['epɪ,græm] *s* epigramma *m*

epilepsy ['epɪ,lepsɪ] *s* epilessia

epileptic [,epɪ'leptɪk] *adj & s* epilettico

epilogue ['epɪ,lɔg] or ['epɪ,lɑg] *s* epilogo

Epiphany [ɪ'pɪfənɪ] *s* Epifania

Episcopalian [ɪ,pɪskə'peli·ən] *adj & s* episcopaliano

episode ['epɪ,sod] *s* episodio

epistle [ɪ'pɪsəl] *s* epistola

epitaph ['epɪ,tæf] *s* epitaffio

epithet ['epɪ,θet] *s* epiteto

epitome [ɪ'pɪtəmi] *s* epitome *f;* (fig) prototipo, personificazione

epitomize [ɪ'pɪtə,maɪz] *tr* epitomare; (fig) incarnare, personificare

epoch ['epək] or ['ipɑk] *s* epoca

epochal ['epəkəl] *adj* memorabile

ep'och-mak'ing *adj*—**to be epoch-making** fare epoca

Ep'som salt' ['epsəm] *s* sale *m* inglese

equable ['ekwəbəl] or ['ikwəbəl] *adj* uniforme; tranquillo

equal ['ikwəl] *adj* uguale; **equal to** pari a, all'altezza di ‖ *s* uguale *m* ‖ *v (pret & pp* **equaled** or **equalled;** *ger* **equaling** or **equalling**) *tr* uguagliare

equali•ty [ɪ'kwɑlɪtɪ] *s* (**-ties**) uguaglianza

equalize ['ikwə,laɪz] *tr* uguagliare; *(to make uniform)* perequare, pareggiare

equally ['ikwəlɪ] *adv* ugualmente

equanimity [,ikwə'nɪmɪtɪ] *s* equanimità *f*

equate [i'kwet] *tr* mettere in forma di equazione; considerare uguale or uguali

equation [i'kweʒən] or [i'kweʃən] *s* equazione

equator [i'kwetər] *s* equatore *m*

equatorial [,ikwə'tori·əl] *adj* equatoriale

equer•ry ['ekwəri] or [ɪ'kweri] *s* (**-ries**) scudiero

equestrian [ɪ'kwestrɪ·ən] *adj* equestre ‖ *s* cavallerizzo

equilateral [,ikwɪ'lætərəl] *adj* equilatero

equilibrium [,ikwɪ'lɪbrɪ·əm] *s* equilibrio

equinoctial [,ikwɪ'nɑkʃəl] *adj* equinoziale

equinox ['ikwɪ,nɑks] *s* equinozio

equip [ɪ'kwɪp] *v (pret & pp* **equipped;** *ger* **equipping**) *tr* equipaggiare; **to equip** (*e.g., a ship*) **with** munire di

equipment [ɪ'kwɪpmənt] *s* equipaggiamento; *(skill)* attitudine *f,* capacità *f*

equipoise ['ikwɪ,pɔɪz] or ['ekwɪ,pɔɪz] *s* equilibrio ‖ *tr* equilibrare

equitable ['ekwɪtəbəl] *adj* equo

equi•ty ['ekwɪtɪ] *s* (**-ties**) *(fairness)* equità *f;* valore *m* al netto; *(in a corporation)* interessenza azionaria

equivalent [ɪ'kwɪvələnt] *adj* equivalente ‖ *s* equivalente *m;* (com) controvalore *m*

equivocal [ɪ'kwɪvəkəl] *adj* equivoco

equivocate [ɪ'kwɪvə,ket] *intr* giocare sulle parole, parlare in maniera equivoca

equivocation [ɪ,kwɪvə'keʃən] *s* equivocità *f;* equivoco

era ['ɪrə] or ['irə] *s* era, evo

eradicate [ɪ'rædɪ,ket] *tr* sradicare

erase [ɪ'res] *tr* cancellare

eraser [ɪ'resər] *s* gomma da cancellare; *(for blackboard)* spugna

erasure [ɪ'reʃər] or [ɪ'reʒər] *s* cancellatura; *(of a tape)* cancellazione

ere [er] *prep* (lit) prima di ‖ *conj* (lit) prima che

erect [ɪ'rekt] *adj* dritto, eretto; *(hair)* irto ‖ *tr (to set in upright position)* drizzare; *(a building)* erigere, costruire; *(a machine)* montare

erection [ɪ'rekʃən] *s* erezione

ermine ['ʌrmɪn] *s* ermellino; (fig) carica di giudice, toga, magistratura

erode [ɪ'rod] *tr* erodere ‖ *intr* corrodersi, consumarsi

erosion [ɪ'roʒən] *s* erosione

erotic [ɪ'rɑtɪk] *adj* erotico

err [ʌr] *intr* errare; *(to be incorrect)* sbagliarsi

errand ['erənd] *s* corsa, commissione; **to run an errand** fare una commissione

er'rand boy' *s* fattorino, galoppino

erratic [ɪ'rætɪk] *adj* erratico; strano, eccentrico

erra·tum [ɪ'retəm] or [ɪ'rɑtəm] *s* (**-ta** [tə]) errore *m* di stampa

erroneous [ɪ'ronɪ-əs] *adj* erroneo

error ['ɛrər] *s* errore *m*, sbaglio

erudite ['ɛrʊ ˌdaɪt] or ['ɛrjʊ ˌdaɪt] *adj* erudito, dotto

erudition [ˌɛrʊ'dɪʃən] or [ˌɛrjʊ'dɪʃən] *s* erudizione

erupt [ɪ'rʌpt] *intr* (*said of a volcano*) eruttare; (*said of a skin rash*) fiorire; (*said of a tooth*) spuntare; (*fig*) erompere

eruption [ɪ'rʌpʃən] *s* eruzione

escalate ['ɛskə ˌlet] *tr & intr* aumentare

escalation [ˌɛskə'leʃən] *s* aumento

escalator ['ɛskə ˌletər] *s* scala mobile

escallop [ɛs'kæləp] *s* (*on edge of cloth*) dentellatura, festone *m;* (*mollusk*) pettine *m* || *tr* cuocere in conchiglia; cuocere al forno con salsa e pane grattugiato

escapade [ˌɛskə'ped] *s* scappatella

escape [ɛs'kep] *s* (*getaway*) fuga; (*from responsibility, duties, etc.*) scampo || *tr* sottrarsi a, eludere; **to escape s.o.** scappare da qlcu; scappar di mente a qlcu || *intr* scappare; sprigionarsi; **to escape from** (*a person*) sfuggire a; (*jail*) evadere da

escapee [ˌɛskə'pi] *s* evaso

escape' lit'erature' *s* letteratura di evasione

escapement [ɛs'kepmənt] *s* scappamento

escape' veloc'ity *s* (rok) velocità *f* di fuga

escarpment [ɛs'kɑrpmənt] *s* scarpata

eschew [ɛs't'fu] *tr* evitare, rifuggire da

escort ['ɛskɔrt] *s* scorta; (*of a woman or girl*) compagno, cavaliere *m* || [ɛs'kɔrt] *tr* scortare

escutcheon [ɛs'kʌtʃən] *s* scudo; (*plate in front of lock on door*) bocchetta

Eski·mo ['ɛskɪ ˌmo] *adj* eschimese || *s* (**-mos** or **-mo**) eschimese *mf*

esopha·gus [ɪ'sɑfəgəs] *s* (**-gi** [ˌdʒaɪ]) esofago

espalier [ɛs'pæljər] *s* spalliera

especial [ɛs'pɛʃəl] *adj* speciale

espionage ['ɛspɪ-ənɪdʒ] or [ˌɛspɪ-ə-'nɑʒ] *s* spionaggio

esplanade [ˌɛsplə'ned] or [ˌɛsplə'nɑd] *s* spianata, piazzale *m*

espousal [ɛs'pauzəl] *s* sposalizio; (*of a cause*) adozione

espouse [ɛs'pauz] *tr* sposare; (*to advocate*) abbracciare, adottare

esquire [ɛs'kwaɪr] or ['ɛskwaɪr] *s* scudiero || **Esquire** *s* titolo di cortesia usato generalmente con persone di riguardo

essay ['ɛse] *s* saggio

essayist ['ɛse-ɪst] *s* saggista *mf*

essence ['ɛsəns] *s* essenza

essential [ɛ'sɛnʃəl] *adj & s* essenziale *m*

establish [ɛs'tæblɪʃ] *tr* stabilire

establishment [ɛs'tæblɪʃmənt] *s* stabilimento; fondazione; **the Establishment** l'autorità costituita

estate [ɛs'tet] *s* stato; condizione sociale; (*landed property*) tenuta; (*a*

person's possessions) patrimonio; (*left by a decedent*) massa ereditaria

esteem [ɛs'tim] *s* stima || *tr* stimare

esthete ['ɛsθit] *s* esteta *mf*

esthetic [ɛs'θɛtɪk] *adj* estetico || **esthetics** *ssg* estetica

estimable ['ɛstɪməbəl] *adj* stimabile

estimate ['ɛstɪ ˌmet] or ['ɛstɪmɪt] *s* stima, valutazione; (*statement of cost of work to be done*) preventivo || ['ɛstɪ ˌmet] *tr* stimare, valutare; preventivare

estimation [ˌɛstɪ'meʃən] *s* stima; **in my estimation** a mio parere

estimator ['ɛstɪ ˌmetər] *s* preventivista *mf*

estrangement [ɛs'trendʒmənt] *s* alienazione, disaffezione

estuar·y ['ɛstʃʊ ˌɛri] *s* (**-ies**) estuario

etch [ɛtʃ] *tr & intr* incidere all'acquaforte

etcher ['ɛtʃər] *s* acquafortista *mf*

etching ['ɛtʃɪŋ] *s* acquaforte *f*

eternal [ɪ'tʌrnəl] *adj* eterno

eterni·ty [ɪ'tʌrnɪti] *s* (**-ties**) eternità *f*

ether ['iθər] *s* etere *m*

ethereal [ɪ'θɪrɪ-əl] *adj* etereo

ethical ['ɛθɪkəl] *adj* etico

ethics ['ɛθɪks] *ssg* etica

Ethiopian [ˌiθɪ'opɪ-ən] *adj & s* etiope *mf*

ethnic(al) ['ɛθnɪk(əl)] *adj* etnico

ethnography [ɛθ'nɑgrəfɪ] *s* etnografia

ethnology [ɛθ'nɑlədʒɪ] *s* etnologia

ethyl ['ɛθɪl] *s* etile *m*

ethylene ['ɛθɪ ˌlin] *s* etilene *m*

etiquette ['ɛtɪ ˌkɛt] *s* etichetta

étude [e'tjud] *s* (mus) studio

etymology [ˌɛtɪ'mɑlədʒɪ] *s* etimologia

ety·mon ['ɛtɪ ˌmɑn] *s* (**-mons** or **-ma** [mə]) etimo

eucalyp·tus [ˌjukə'lɪptəs] *s* (**-tuses** or **-ti** [taɪ]) eucalipto

Eucharist ['jukərɪst] *s* Eucaristia

eugenics [jʊ'dʒɛnɪks] *ssg* eugenetica

eulogistic [ˌjulə'dʒɪstɪk] *adj* elogiativo

eulogize ['julə ˌdʒaɪz] *tr* elogiare

eulo·gy ['julədʒɪ] *s* (**-gies**) elogio; elogio funebre

eunuch ['junək] *s* eunuco

euphemism ['jufɪ ˌmɪzəm] *s* eufemismo

euphemistic [ˌjufɪ'mɪstɪk] *adj* eufemistico

euphonic [jʊ'fɑnɪk] *adj* eufonico

eupho·ny ['jufənɪ] *s* (**-nies**) eufonia

euphoria [jʊ'forɪ-ə] *s* euforia

euphuism ['jufju ˌɪzəm] *s* eufuismo

Europe ['jurəp] *s* l'Europa

European [ˌjurə'pi-ən] *adj & s* europeo

euthanasia [ˌjuθə'neʒə] *s* eutanasia

evacuate [ɪ'vækju ˌet] *tr & intr* evacuare

evacuation [ɪ ˌvækju'eʃən] *s* evacuazione

evacuee [ɪ'vækju ˌi] or [ɪ ˌvækju'i] *s* sfollato

evade [ɪ'ved] *tr* eludere || *intr* evadere

evaluate [ɪ'væljʊ ˌet] *tr* valutare

evaluation [ɪ ˌvæljʊ'eʃən] *s* valutazione

Evangel [ɪ'vændʒəl] *s* Vangelo

evangelic(al) [ˌivæn'dʒɛlɪk(əl)] or [ˌɛvən'dʒɛlɪk(əl)] *adj* evangelico

Evangelist [ɪ'vændʒəlɪst] s evangelista m

evaporate [ɪ'væpə,ret] tr & intr evaporare

evasion [ɪ'veʒən] s evasione; (subterfuge) scappatoia

evasive [ɪ'vesɪv] adj evasivo

eve [iv] s vigilia; **on the eve of** la vigilia di

even ['ivən] adj (smooth) piano, regolare; (number) pari; uguale, uniforme; (temperament) calmo, placido; **even with** a livello di; **to be even** mettersi in pari; **to get even** prendersi la rivincita || adv anche; fino, perfino; pure; esattamente; magari; **even as** proprio mentre; **even if** anche se, quando pure; **even so** anche se così; **even though** quantunque; **even when** anche quando; **not even** neppure, nemmeno; **to break even** impattare || tr spianare; **to even up** bilanciare

evening ['ivnɪŋ] adj serale || s sera, serata; **all evening** tutta la sera; **every evening** tutte le sere; **in the evening** la sera

eve′ning clothes′ spl vestito da sera

eve′ning gown′ s vestito da sera da signora

eve′ning star′ s espero

e′ven·song′ s (eccl) vespro

event [ɪ'vent] s avvenimento; (outcome) evenienza; (public function) manifestazione; (sports) prova; **at all events** or **in any event** in ogni caso; **in the event that** in caso che, se mai

eventful [ɪ'ventfəl] adj ricco di avvenimenti; movimentato

eventual [ɪ'ventʃʊ·əl] adj finale

eventuali·ty [ɪ,ventʃʊ'ælɪti] s (-ties) eventualità f, evenienza

eventually [ɪ'ventʃʊ·əli] adv finalmente, alla fine

eventuate [ɪ'ventʃʊ,et] intr risultare; accadere

ever ['evər] adv (at all times) sempre; (at any time) mai; **as ever** come sempre; **as much as ever** tanto come prima; **ever since** (since that time) sin da; da allora in poi; **ever so** molto; **ever so much** moltissimo; **hardly ever** or **scarcely ever** quasi mai; **not . . . ever** non . . . mai

ev′er·glade′ s terreno paludoso coperto di erbe

ev′er·green′ adj & s sempreverde m & f; **evergreens** decorazione di sempreverdi

ev′er·last′ing adj eterno; incessante; (lasting indefinitely) duraturo; (wearisome) noioso || s eternità f; (bot) semprevivo

ev′er·more′ adv eternamente; **for evermore** per sempre

every ['evri] adj tutti i; (each) ogni, ciascuno; (being each in a series) ogni, e.g., **every three days** ogni tre giorni; **every bit** (coll) in tutto e per tutto, e.g., **every bit a man** un uomo in tutto e per tutto; **every now and then** di quando in quando; **every once in a while** una volta ogni tanto;

every other day ogni secondo giorno; **every which way** (coll) da tutte le parti; (coll) in disordine

ev′ery·bod′y pron indef ognuno, tutti

ev′ery·day′ adj di ogni giorno; quotidiano; ordinario

ev′ery·man′ s l'uomo qualunque || pron chiunque

ev′ery·one′ or **ev′ery one′** pron indef ciascuno, tutti

ev′ery·thing′ pron indef tutto, ogni cosa, tutto quanto

ev′ery·where′ adv dappertutto, dovunque

evict [ɪ'vɪkt] tr sfrattare, sloggiare

eviction [ɪ'vɪk/ən] s sfratto, sloggio

evidence ['evɪdəns] s evidenza; (law) prova

evident ['evɪdənt] adj evidente

evil ['ivəl] adj cattivo, malvagio || s male m; disgrazia

evildoer ['ivəl,du·ər] s malfattore m, malvagio

e′vil·do′ing s malafatta, malvagità f

e′vil eye′ s iettatura, malocchio

evil-minded ['ivəl'maɪndɪd] adj malintenzionato

e′vil one′, the il nemico

evince [ɪ'vɪns] tr mostrare, manifestare

evoke [ɪ'vok] tr evocare

evolution [,evə'lu/ən] s evoluzione

evolve [ɪ'vɑlv] tr sviluppare || intr evolversi

ewe [ju] s pecora

ewer ['ju·ər] s brocca

ex [eks] prep includere

exacerbation [ɪg,zæsər'be/ən] s esulcerazione, esacerbazione

exacerbate [ɪg'zæsər,bet] tr esacerbare, esulcerare

exact [eg'zækt] adj esatto || tr esigere

exacting [eg'zæktɪŋ] adj esigente

exaction [eg'zæk/ən] s esazione

exactly [eg'zæktli] adv esattamente; (sharp, on the dot) in punto

exactness [eg'zæktnɪs] s esattezza

exaggerate [eg'zædʒə,ret] tr esagerare

exalt [eg'zɔlt] tr elevare, esaltare

exam [eg'zæm] s (coll) esame m

examination [eg,zæmɪ'ne/ən] s esame m; **to take an examination** sostenere un esame

examine [eg'zæmɪn] tr esaminare

examiner [eg'zæmɪnər] s esaminatore m

example [eg'zæmpəl] or [eg'zɑmpəl] s esempio; (precedent) precedente m; (of mathematics) problema m; **for example** per esempio

exasperate [eg'zæspə,ret] tr esasperare

excavate ['ekskə,vet] tr scavare

exceed [ek'sid] tr eccedere

exceedingly [ek'sidɪŋli] adv estremamente, sommamente

ex·cel [ek'sel] v (pret & pp -celled; ger -celling) tr sorpassare || intr eccellere

excellence ['eksələns] s eccellenza

excellen·cy ['eksələnsi] s (-cies) eccellenza; **Your Excellency** Sua Eccellenza

excelsior [ek'selsɪ·ər] s trucioli mpl per imballaggio

except [ek'sept] prep eccetto; **except**

for tranne, ad eccezione di; **except that** eccetto che ‖ *tr* eccettuare
exception [ɛk'sɛp/ən] *s* eccezione; **to take exception** obiettare; scandalizzarsi; **with the exception of** a esclusione di, eccetto
exceptional [ɛk'sɛp/ənəl] *adj* eccezionale
excerpt ['ɛksʌrpt] or [ɛk'sʌrpt] *s* brano, selezione ‖ [ɛk'sʌrpt] *tr* scegliere, selezionare
excess ['ɛksɛs] or [ɛk'sɛs] *adj* eccedente ‖ [ɛk'sɛs] *s* (*amount or degree by which one thing exceeds another*) eccedente *m*, eccedenza; (*excessive amount; immoderate indulgence; unlawful conduct*) eccesso; **in excess of** più di
ex'cess bag'gage *s* bagaglio eccedente
ex'cess fare' *s* (rr) supplemento
excessive [ɛk'sɛsɪv] *adj* eccessivo
ex'cess-prof'its tax' *s* tassa sui soprapprofitti
exchange [ɛks't/ɛndʒ] *s* scambio; (*place for buying and selling*) borsa; (*transactions in the currencies of two different countries*) cambio; (telp) centrale *f*, centralino; **in exchange for** in cambio di ‖ *tr* scambiare, scambiarsi; **to exchange blows** venire alle mani; **to exchange greetings** salutarsi
exchequer [ɛks't/ɛkər] or ['ɛkst/ɛkər] *s* erario, tesoro
ex'cise tax' [ɛk'saɪz] or ['ɛksaɪz] *s* imposta sul consumo
excitable [ɛk'saɪtəbəl] *adj* eccitabile
excite [ɛk'saɪt] *tr* eccitare
excitement [ɛk'saɪtmənt] *s* eccitazione
exciting [ɛk'saɪtɪŋ] *adj* emozionante; (*stimulating*) eccitante
exclaim [ɛks'klem] *tr & intr* esclamare
exclamation [ˌɛksklə'me/ən] *s* esclamazione
exclama'tion mark' or **point'** *s* punto esclamativo
exclude [ɛks'klud] *tr* escludere
excluding [ɛks'kludɪŋ] *prep* a esclusione di, senza contare
exclusion [ɛks'kluʒən] *s* esclusione; **to the exclusion of** tranne, salvo
exclusive [ɛks'klusɪv] *adj* esclusivo; **exclusive of** escluso, senza contare ‖ *s* (journ) esclusiva
excommunicate [ˌɛkskə'mjunɪ ˌket] *tr* scomunicare
excommunication [ˌɛkskə ˌmjunɪ'ke/ən] *s* scomunica
excoriate [ɛks'korɪ ˌet] *tr* criticare aspramente, vituperare
excrement ['ɛkskrəmənt] *s* escremento
excruciating [ɛks'kru/ɪ ˌetɪŋ] *adj* (*e.g., pleasure*) estremo; (*e.g., pain*) atroce, lancinante, straziante
exculpate ['ɛkskʌl ˌpet] or [ɛks'kʌlpet] *tr* scolpare, scagionare
excursion [ɛks'kʌrʒən] or [ɛks'kʌr/ən] *s* escursione, gita
excursionist [ɛks'kʌrʒənɪst] or [ɛks'kʌr/ənɪst] *s* escursionista *mf*
excusable [ɛks'kjuzəbəl] *adj* scusabile
excuse [ɛks'kjus] *s* scusa ‖ [ɛks'kjuz] *tr* scusare; esentare; (*a debt*) rimettere

execute ['ɛksɪ ˌkjut] *tr* (*to carry out; to produce*) eseguire; (*to put to death*) giustiziare; (law) rendere esecutorio
execution [ˌɛksɪ'kju/ən] *s* esecuzione; (*e.g., of a criminal*) esecuzione capitale
executioner [ˌɛksɪ'kju/ənər] *s* giustiziere *m*, boia *m*, carnefice *m*
executive [ɛg'zɛkjətɪv] *adj* esecutivo ‖ *s* esecutivo; (*of a school, business, etc.*) dirigente *mf*
Exec'utive Man'sion *s* palazzo del governatore; residenza del capo del governo statunitense
executor [ɛg'zɛkjətər] *s* (law) esecutore testamentario
executrix [ɛg'zɛkjətrɪks] *s* (law) esecutrice testamentaria
exemplary [ɛg'zɛmpləri] or ['ɛgzəm ˌplɛri] *adj* esemplare
exempli-fy [ɛg'zɛmplɪ ˌfaɪ] *v* (*pret & pp* **-fied**) *tr* esemplificare
exempt [ɛg'zɛmpt] *adj* esente ‖ *tr* esimere, esentare
exemption [ɛg'zɛmp/ən] *s* esenzione
exercise ['ɛksər ˌsaɪz] *s* esercizio; cerimonia; **to take exercise** fare del moto ‖ *tr* esercitare; (*care*) usare; (*to worry*) preoccupare ‖ *intr* esercitarsi
exert [ɛg'zʌrt] *tr* (*e.g., power*) esercitare; **to exert oneself** sforzarsi
exertion [ɛg'zʌr/ən] *s* sforzo, tentativo; (*active use*) uso, esercizio
exhalation [ˌɛks·hə'le/ən] *s* (*of gas, vapors*) esalazione; (*of air from lungs*) espirazione
exhale [ɛks'hel] or [ɛg'zel] *tr* (*gases, vapors, etc.*) esalare; (*air from lungs*) espirare ‖ *intr* esalare; espirare
exhaust [ɛg'zɔst] *s* scarico, scappamento; tubo di scarico or scappamento ‖ *tr* (*to wear out*) spossare, finire; (*to use up*) esaurire, dar fondo a; vuotare
exhaust' fan' *s* aspiratore *m*
exhaustion [ɛg'zɔst/ən] *s* esaurimento; estenuazione; (sports) cotta
exhaustive [ɛg'zɔstɪv] *adj* esauriente
exhaust' man'ifold *s* collettore *m* di scarico
exhaust' pipe' *s* tubo di scarico
exhaust' valve' *s* valvola di scappamento
exhibit [ɛg'zɪbɪt] *s* esposizione; (law) documento in giudizio ‖ *tr* esibire
exhibition [ˌɛksɪ'bɪ/ən] *s* esibizione
exhibitor [ɛg'zɪbɪtər] *s* espositore *m*
exhilarating [ɛg'zɪlə ˌretɪŋ] *adj* esilarante
exhort [ɛg'zɔrt] *tr* esortare
exhume [ɛks'hjum] or [ɛg'zjum] *tr* esumare, dissotterrare
exigen•cy ['ɛksɪdʒənsi] *s* (**-cies**) esigenza
exigent ['ɛksɪdʒənt] *adj* esigente
exile ['ɛgzaɪl] or ['ɛksaɪl] *s* esilio; (*person*) esule *mf* ‖ *tr* esiliare
exist [ɛg'zɪst] *intr* esistere
existence [ɛg'zɪstəns] *s* esistenza
existing [ɛg'zɪstɪŋ] *adj* esistente
exit ['ɛgzɪt] or ['ɛksɪt] *s* uscita ‖ *intr* uscire

exodus ['ɛksədəs] *s* esodo

exonerate [eg'zɑnə‚ret] *tr* (*from an obligation*) esonerare; (*from blame*) scagionare

exorbitant [eg'zɔrbitənt] *adj* esorbitante

exorcise ['ɛksɔr‚saɪz] *tr* esorcizzare

exotic [eg'zɑtɪk] *adj* esotico

expand [ɛks'pænd] *tr* (*a metal*) dilatare; (*gas*) espandere; (*to enlarge*) allargare, ampliare; (*to unfold*) spiegare; (*math*) svolgere, sviluppare ‖ *intr* dilatarsi; espandersi; allargarsi, ampliarsi; spiegarsi, estendersi

expanse [ɛks'pæns] *s* vastità *f*

expansion [ɛks'pænʃən] *s* espansione

expansive [ɛks'pænsɪv] *adj* espansivo

expatiate [ɛks'peʃɪ‚et] *intr* dilungarsi

expatriate [ɛks'petrɪ‚ɪt] *adj* esiliato ‖ *s* esule *mf* ‖ [ɛks'petri‚et] *tr* esiliare; **to expatriate oneself** espatriare

expect [ɛks'pɛkt] *tr* aspettare, attendere; (*coll*) credere, supporre; **to expect it** aspettarselo, aspettarsela

expectan-cy [ɛks'pɛktənsi] *s* (*-cies*) aspettativa, aspettazione

expect'ant moth'er [ɛks'pɛktənt] *s* futura madre

expectation [‚ɛkspɛk'teʃən] *s* aspettativa

expectorate [ɛks'pɛktə‚ret] *tr & intr* espettorare

expedien-cy [ɛks'pidɪ‚ənsi] *s* (*-cies*) industria, ingegno; opportunismo, vantaggio personale

expedient [ɛks'pidɪ‚ənt] *adj* conveniente; vantaggioso; (*acting with self-interest*) opportunista ‖ *s* espediente *m*

expedite ['ɛkspɪ‚daɪt] *tr* sbrigare, accelerare; (*a document*) dar corso a

expedition [‚ɛkspɪ'dɪʃən] *s* spedizione; (*speed*) celerità *f*

expeditionary [‚ɛkspɪ'dɪʃən‚eri] *adj* (*e.g., corps*) di spedizione

expeditious [‚ɛkspɪ'dɪʃəs] *adj* spicciativo, spiccio

ex-pel [ɛks'pɛl] *v* (*pret & pp* **-pelled;** *ger* **-pelling**) *tr* espellere, scacciare

expend [ɛks'pɛnd] *tr* spendere, consumare

expendable [ɛks'pɛndəbəl] *adj* spendibile; da buttarsi via; (*mil*) da sacrificare

expenditure [ɛks'pɛndɪt(ʃ)ər] *s* spesa

expense [ɛks'pɛns] *s* spesa; **at the expense of** al costo di; **expenses** spese *fpl;* **to meet expenses** far fronte alle spese

expense' account' *s* conto delle spese risarcibili

expensive [ɛks'pɛnsɪv] *adj* caro, costoso

experience [ɛks'pɪrɪ‚əns] *s* esperienza ‖ *tr* sperimentare, provare

experienced [ɛks'pɪrɪ‚ənst] *adj* esperto, sperimentato

experiment [ɛks'pɛrɪmənt] *s* esperimento ‖ [ɛks'pɛrɪ‚mɛnt] *intr* sperimentare

expert ['ɛkspərt] *adj & s* esperto

expertise [‚ɛkspər'tiz] *s* maestria

expiate ['ɛkspɪ‚et] *tr* espiare

expiation [‚ɛkspɪ'eʃən] *s* espiazione

expire [ɛks'paɪr] *tr* espirare ‖ *intr* (*to breathe out*) espirare; (*said of a contract*) scadere; (*to die*) morire

explain [ɛks'plen] *tr* spiegare; **to explain away** giustificare; dar ragione di ‖ *intr* spiegare, spiegarsi

explainable [ɛks'plenəbəl] *adj* spiegabile

explanation [‚ɛksplə'neʃən] *s* spiegazione, delucidazione

explanatory [ɛks'plænə‚tori] *adj* esplicativo

explicit [ɛks'plɪsɪt] *adj* esplicito

explode [ɛks'plod] *tr* far scoppiare; (*a theory*) smontare ‖ *intr* scoppiare

exploit [ɛks'plɔɪt] *or* ['ɛksplɔɪt] *s* impresa, prodezza ‖ [ɛks'plɔɪt] *tr* utilizzare, sfruttare

exploitation [‚ɛksplɔɪ'teʃən] *s* utilizzazione, sfruttamento

exploration [‚ɛksplə'reʃən] *s* esplorazione

explore [ɛks'plor] *tr* esplorare

explorer [ɛks'plorər] *s* esploratore *m*

explosion [ɛks'ploʒən] *s* esplosione, scoppio; (*of a theory*) confutazione

explosive [ɛks'plosɪv] *adj & s* esplosivo

exponent [ɛks'ponənt] *s* esponente *m*

export ['ɛksport] *adj* di esportazione ‖ *s* esportazione, articolo di esportazione ‖ [ɛks'port] *or* ['ɛksport] *tr & intr* esportare

exportation [‚ɛkspor'teʃən] *s* esportazione

exporter ['ɛksportər] *or* [ɛks'portər] *s* esportatore *m*

expose [ɛks'poz] *tr* esporre; (*to unmask*) smascherare

exposé [‚ɛkspo'ze] *s* rivelazione scandalosa, smascheramento

exposition [‚ɛkspə'zɪʃən] *s* esposizione; interpretazione, commento

expostulate [ɛks'pɑstʃə‚let] *intr* protestare; **to expostulate with** lagnarsi con

exposure [ɛks'poʒər] *s* (*disclosure*) rivelazione; (*situation with regard to sunlight*) esposizione; (*phot*) esposizione

expo'sure me'ter *s* (phot) fotometro, esposimetro

expound [ɛks'paʊnd] *tr* esporre

express [ɛks'prɛs] *adj* espresso ‖ *s* (rr) celere *m*, rapido, direttissimo; **by express** per espresso, a grande velocità ‖ *adv* per espresso, a grande velocità ‖ *tr* esprimere; mandare per espresso; (*to squeeze out*) spremere; **to express oneself** esprimersi

ex'press com'pany *s* servizio corriere

expression [ɛks'prɛʃən] *s* espressione

expressive [ɛks'prɛsɪv] *adj* espressivo

expressly [ɛks'prɛsli] *adv* espressamente

express'man *s* (*-men*) fattorino di servizio corriere

express'way' *s* autostrada

expropriate [ɛks'propri‚et] *tr* espropriare

expulsion [ɛks'pʌlʃən] *s* espulsione

expunge [ɛksˈpʌndʒ] *tr* espungere
expurgate [ˈɛkspərˌget] *tr* espurgare
exquisite [ˈɛkskwɪzɪt] or [ɛksˈkwɪzɪt] *adj* squisito; intenso
ex'serv'ice-man' *s* (-men') ex combattente *m*
extant [ˈɛkstənt] or [ɛksˈtænt] *adj* ancora esistente
extemporaneous [ɛks ˌtɛmpəˈrenɪ·əs] *adj* estemporaneo; (*made for the occasion*) improvvisato
extempore [ɛksˈtɛmpəri] *adj* improvvisato || *adv* senza preparazione
extemporize [ɛksˈtɛmpə ˌraɪz] *tr & intr* improvvisare
extend [ɛksˈtɛnd] *tr* allungare; estendere; (*e.g., aid*) offrire; (*payment of a debt*) dilazionare || *intr* estendersi
extended [ɛksˈtɛndɪd] *adj* esteso; prolungato
extension [ɛksˈtɛnʃən] *s* estensione; prolungamento; (com) proroga; (telp) derivazione
exten'sion lad'der *s* scala porta, scala a prolunga
exten'sion ta'ble *s* tavola allungabile
exten'sion tel'ephone' *s* telefono interno
extensive [ɛksˈtɛnsɪv] *adj* (*wide*) vasto; (*lengthy*) lungo; (*characterized by extention*) estensivo
extent [ɛksˈtɛnt] *s* estensione; **to a certain extent** fino a un certo punto; **to a great extent** in larga misura; **to the full extent** all'estremo limite
extenuate [ɛksˈtɛnjuˌet] *tr* (*to make seem less serious*) attenuare; (*to underrate*) sottovalutare
exterior [ɛksˈtɪrɪ·ər] *adj & s* esteriore *m*
exterminate [ɛksˈtʌrmɪˌnet] *tr* sterminare
external [ɛksˈtʌrnəl] *adj* esterno || **externals** *spl* esteriorità *f*, di fuori *m*
extinct [ɛksˈtɪŋkt] *adj* estinto
extinction [ɛksˈtɪŋkʃən] *s* estinzione
extinguish [ɛksˈtɪŋgwɪʃ] *tr* estinguere
extinguisher [ɛksˈtɪŋgwɪʃər] *s* estintore *m*
extirpate [ˈɛkstərˌpet] or [ɛksˈtʌrpet] *tr* estirpare
ex·tol [ɛksˈtol] or [ɛksˈtal] *v* (*pret & pp* -tolled; *ger* -tolling) *tr* inneggiare
extort [ɛksˈtort] *tr* estorcere
extortion [ɛksˈtorʃən] *s* estorsione
extra [ˈɛkstrə] *adj* extra; (*spare*) di scorta || *s* (*of a newspaper*) edizione straordinaria; (*something additional*) soprappiù *m*; (theat) figurante *mf* || *adv* straordinariamente
ex'tra charge' *s* supplemento
extract [ˈɛkstrækt] *s* estratto || [ɛksˈtrækt] *tr* (*to pull out*) estrarre; (*to take from a book*) scegliere, selezionare
extraction [ɛksˈtrækʃən] *s* estrazione
extracurricular [ˌɛkstrəkəˈrɪkjələr] *adj* fuori del programma normale
extradition [ˌɛkstrəˈdɪʃən] *s* estradizione
ex'tra-dry' *adj* molto secco, brut
ex'tra fare' *s* supplemento al biglietto

ex'tra·mar'ital *adj* extraconiugale
extramural [ˌɛkstrəˈmjurəl] *adj* fuori della scuola, interscolastico; fuori delle mura
extraneous [ɛksˈtrenɪ·əs] *adj* estraneo
extraordinary [ˌɛkstrəˈordɪˌnɛri] or [ɛksˈtrordɪˌnɛri] *adj* straordinario
extrapolate [ɛksˈtræpəˌlet] *tr & intr* estrapolare
extrasensory [ˌɛkstrəˈsɛnsəri] *adj* extrasensoriale
extravagance [ɛksˈtrævəgəns] *s* prodigalità *f*; (*wildness, folly*) stravaganza
extravagant [ɛksˈtrævəgənt] *adj* prodigo; (*wild, foolish*) stravagante
extreme [ɛksˈtrim] *adj & s* estremo; **in the extreme** in massimo grado; **to go to extremes** andare agli estremi
extremely [ɛksˈtrimli] *adv* estremamente, in sommo grado
extreme' unc'tion *s* Estrema Unzione
extremist [ɛksˈtrimɪst] *adj & s* estremista *mf*
extremi·ty [ɛksˈtrɛmɪti] *s* (-ties) estremità *f*; (*great want*) estrema necessità; **extremities** estremi *mpl*; (*hands and feet*) estremità *fpl*
extricate [ˈɛkstrɪˌket] *tr* districare
extrinsic [ɛksˈtrɪnsɪk] *adj* estrinseco
extrovert [ˈɛkstrə ˌvʌrt] *s* estroverso
extrude [ɛksˈtrud] *tr* estrudere || *intr* protrudere
exuberant [ɛgˈzubərənt] or [ɛgˈzjubərənt] *adj* esuberante
exude [ɛgˈzud] or [ɛkˈsud] *tr & intr* trasudare, stillare
exult [ɛgˈzʌlt] *intr* esultare, tripudiare
exultant [ɛgˈzʌltənt] *adj* esultante
eye [aɪ] *s* occhio; (*of hook and eye*) occhiello; **to catch one's eye** attirare l'attenzione di qlcu; **to feast one's eyes on** deliziarsi la vista con; **to lay eyes on** riuscire a vedere; **to make eyes at** fare gli occhi dolci a; **to roll one's eyes** stralunare gli occhi; **to see eye to eye** andare perfettamente d'accordo; **to shut one's eyes to** chiudere un occhio a; far finta di non vedere; **without batting an eye** senza batter ciglio || *v* (*pret & pp* **eyed**) *ger* **eying** or **eyeing**) *tr* occhieggiare; **to eye up and down** guardare da capo a piedi
eye'ball' *s* globo oculare
eye'bolt' *s* bullone *m* ad anello
eye'brow' *s* sopracciglio; **to raise one's eyebrows** inarcare le sopracciglia
eye'cup' *s* occhiera
eye'drop'per *s* contagocce *m*
eyeful [ˈaɪ ˌful] *s* vista, colpo d'occhio; (coll) bellezza
eye'glass' *s* (*of optical instrument*) lente *f*, oculare *m*; (*eyecup*) occhiera; **eyeglasses** occhiali *mpl*
eye'lash' *s* ciglio
eyelet [ˈaɪlɪt] *s* occhiello, maglietta, asola; (*hole to look through*) feritoia
eye'lid' *s* palpebra
eye' o'pener [ˈopənər] *s* affare *m* che apre gli occhi; (coll) bicchierino bevuto di mattina presto

eye'piece' s oculare m
eye'shade' s visiera
eye' shad'ow s rimmel m
eye'shot' s—**within eyeshot** a portata di vista
eye'sight' s vista; (range) capacità visiva
eye' sock'et s occhiaia, orbita
eye'sore' s pugno in un occhio

eye'strain' s vista affaticata
eye'-test chart' s tabella optometrica
eye'tooth' s (-teeth) dente canino; **to cut one's eyeteeth** (coll) fare esperienza; **to give one's eyeteeth for** (coll) dare un occhio della testa per
eye'wash' s (flattery) burro, lusinga; (pharm) collirio; (slang) balla
eye' wit'ness s testimone m oculare

F

F, f [ef] s sesta lettera dell'alfabeto inglese
fable ['febəl] s favola
fabric ['fæbrɪk] s stoffa, tessuto; fabbrica, struttura
fabricate ['fæbrɪ‚ket] tr fabbricare
fabrication [‚fæbrɪ'keʃən] s fabbricazione; falsificazione, invenzione
fabulous ['fæbjələs] adj favoloso
façade [fə'sad] s facciata
face [fes] s volto, viso, faccia; (surface) superficie f; (of coin) diritto; (of precious stone) faccetta; (of watch) mostra; (grimace) smorfia; (of building) facciata, (typ) occhio; **in the face of** di fronte a; **to have a long face** fare il muso lungo; **to keep a straight face** contenere le risa; **to show one's face** farsi vedere || tr far fronte a, fronteggiare; (a wall) ricoprire; (a suit) foderare; **facing** di fronte a || intr—**to face about** voltarsi, fare dietro front; **to face on** dare a; **to face up to** guardare in faccia
face' card' s figura
face' lift'ing s plastica facciale
face' pow'der s cipria
facet ['fæsɪt] s faccetta; (fig) faccia
facetious [fə'siʃəs] adj faceto
face' val'ue s valore m facciale
facial ['feʃəl] adj facciale || s massaggio facciale
fa'cial tis'sue s velina detergente
facilitate [fə'sɪlɪ‚tet] tr facilitare
facili·ty [fə'sɪlɪti] s (-ties) facilità f; **facilities** (installations) attrezzature fpl; (for transportation) mezzi mpl; (services) servizi mpl
facing ['fesɪŋ] s rivestimento
facsimile [fæk'sɪmɪli] s facsimile m
fact [fækt] s fatto; **in fact** in realtà; **the fact is that** il fatto si è che
faction ['fækʃən] s fazione; discordia
factional ['fækʃənəl] adj fazioso; (partisan) partigiano
factionalism ['fækʃənə‚lɪzəm] s partigianeria; parzialità f
factor ['fæktər] s fattore m || tr scomporre in fattori
facto·ry ['fæktəri] s (-ries) fabbrica
factual ['fæktʃʊ‐əl] adj effettivo, reale
facul·ty ['fækəlti] s (-ties) facoltà f
fad [fæd] s moda passeggera
fade [fed] tr stingere || intr (said of colors) stingersi, sbiadire; (said of

sounds, sight, radio signals, memory, etc.) svanire, affievolirsi; (said of beauty) sfiorire
fade'-out' s affievolimento, affievolirsi m; (mov) chiusura in dissolvenza; (rad, telv) evanescenza
fading ['fedɪŋ] s affievolimento; (mov) dissolvenza; (rad, telv) evanescenza
fag [fæg] s schiavo del lavoro; (coll) sigaretta || tr—**to fag out** stancare
fagot ['fægət] s fascina, fastello
fail [fel] s—**without fail** senza meno || tr mancare (with dat); (a student) riprovare; (an examination) farsi bocciare in || intr fallire, venire a meno; (said of a student) farsi riprovare; (said of a motor) rompersi, fermarsi; (com) cadere in fallimento; **to fail to** mancare di
failure ['feljər] s insuccesso; insufficienza; (student) bocciato; (com) fallimento
faint [fent] adj debole; **to feel faint** sentirsi mancare || s svenimento || intr svenire
faint-hearted ['fent'hartɪd] adj codardo, timido
fair [fer] adj giusto, onesto; (moderately large) discreto; (even) liscio; (civil) gentile; (hair) biondo; (complexion) chiaro; (sky, weather) sereno || s (exhibition) fiera; (carnival) sagra || adv direttamente; **to play fair** agire onestamente
fair'ground' s terreno dell'esposizione, campo della fiera
fairly ['ferli] adv giustamente, imparzialmente; discretamente, abbastanza; completamente
fair-minded ['fer'maɪndɪd] adj equanime, equo, giusto
fairness ['fernɪs] s giustizia, imparzialità f; bellezza; (of complexion) bianchezza
fair' play' s comportamento leale
fair' sex' s bel sesso
fair'-weath'er adj—**a fair-weather friend** un amico del tempo felice
fair·y ['feri] adj fatato || s (-ies) fata; (slang) finocchio
fair'y god'mother s buona fata
fair'y·land' s terra delle fate
fair'y tale' s fiaba, racconto delle fate
faith [feθ] s fede f; **to break faith with** venir meno alla parola data a; **to keep faith with** tener fede alla parola

data a; **to pin one's faith on** porre tutte le proprie speranze su; **upon my faith!** in fede mia!

faithful ['feθfəl] *adj* fedele || **the faithful** i fedeli

faithless ['feθlɪs] *adj* infedele, sleale

fake [fek] *adj* falso, finto || *s* contraffazione; *(person)* imbroglione *m* || *tr & intr* contraffare, falsificare

faker ['fekər] *s* (coll) imbroglione *m*

falcon ['fɔkən] *or* ['fɔlkən] *s* falcone *m*

falconer ['fɔkənər] *or* ['fɔlkənər] *s* falconiere *m*

falconry ['fɔkənri] *or* ['fɔlkənri] *s* falconeria

fall [fɔl] *adj* autunnale || *s* caduta; *(of water)* cataratta, cascata; *(of prices)* ribasso; *(autumn)* autunno; **falls** cataratta, cascate *fpl* || *v* *(pret* **fell** [fel]; *pp* **fallen** ['fɔlən)* *intr* cadere; discendere; **to fall apart** farsi a pezzi; **to fall back** (mil) ripiegare; **to fall behind** rimanere indietro; **to fall down** cadere; stramazzare; **to fall due** scadere; **to fall flat** stramazzare; essere un insuccesso; **to fall for** (slang) lasciarsi abbindolare da; (slang) innamorarsi di; **to fall in** *(said of a building)* crollare; (mil) allinearsi; **to fall in with** imbattersi in; mettersi d'accordo con; **to fall off** ritirarsi; diminuire; **to fall out** accadere; essere in disaccordo; (mil) rompere i ranghi; **to fall out of** cadere da; **to fall out with** inimicarsi con; **to fall over** cadere; (coll) adulare; **to fall through** fallire; **to fall to** cominciare; (coll) cominciare a mangiare; *(said, e.g., of an inheritance)* ricadere su; **to fall under** rientrare in

fallacious [fə'leʃəs] *adj* fallace

falla·cy ['fæləsi] *s* (-cies) fallacia

fall' guy' *s* (slang) testa di turco

fallible ['fælɪbəl] *adj* fallibile

fall'ing star' *s* stella cadente

fall'out' *s* pulviscolo radioattivo

fall'out shel'ter *s* rifugio antiatomico

fallow ['fælo] *adj* incolto; **to lie fallow** rimanere incolto || *s* maggese *m* || *tr* maggesare

false [fɔls] *adj* falso; *(hair, teeth, etc.)* posticcio, finto || *adv* falsamente; **to play false** tradire

false' bot'tom *s* doppio fondo

false' col'ors *spl* apparenze mentite

false' face' *s* maschera; *(ugly false face)* mascherone *m*

false'-heart'ed ['fɔls'hɑrtɪd] *adj* perfido

falsehood ['fɔls·hʊd] *s* falsità *f*, falso

false' pretens'es *spl* falso, impostura; **under false pretenses** allegando ragioni false

falset·to [fɔl'seto] *s* (-tos) *(voice)* falsetto; *(person)* cantante *m* in falsetto

falsi·fy ['fɔlsɪ,faɪ] *v* *(pret & pp* **-fied)** *tr* falsificare; *(to disprove)* smentire || *intr* mentire

falsi·ty ['fɔlsɪti] *s* (-ties) falsità *f*

falter ['fɔltər] *s* vacillamento; *(in*

speech) balbettio || *intr* vacillare; balbettare

fame [fem] *s* fama

famed [femd] *adj* famoso

familiar [fə'mɪljər] *adj* familiare; intimo; **to be familiar with** *(people)* aver pratica con; *(things)* aver pratica di

familiari·ty [fə,mɪlɪ'ærɪti] *s* (-ties) familiarità *f*, dimestichezza

familiarize [fə'mɪljə,raɪz] *tr* far conoscere

fami·ly ['fæmɪli] *adj* familiare; **in the family way** (coll) in altro stato || *s* (-lies) famiglia

fam'ily man' *s* (men') padre *m* di famiglia

fam'ily name' *s* cognome *m*

fam'ily tree' *s* albero genealogico

famine ['fæmɪn] *s* carestia

famished ['fæmɪ/t] *adj* famelico; **to be famished** avere una fame da lupo

famous ['feməs] *adj* famoso; (coll) eccellente

fan [fæn] *s* ventaglio; (elec) ventilatore *m*; (coll) tifoso, patito || *v* *(pret & pp* **fanned)** *ger* **fanning)** *tr* sventagliare; *(to winnow)* vagliare; *(fire, passions)* attizzare || *intr* sventagliarsi; **to fan out** *(said of a road)* diramarsi a ventaglio

fanatic [fə'nætɪk] *adj & s* fanatico

fanatical [fə'nætɪkəl] *adj* fanatico

fanaticism [fə'nætɪ,sɪzəm] *s* fanatismo

fan' belt' *s* (aut) cinghia del ventilatore

fancied ['fænsɪd] *adj* immaginario

fancier ['fænsɪ·ər] *s* maniaco, tifoso; *(of animals)* conoscitore *m*, allevatore *m*

fanciful ['fænsɪfəl] *adj* fantasioso, estroso; immaginario

fan·cy ['fænsi] *adj* (-cier; -ciest) immaginario; immaginativo; ornamentale; di lusso; fantasioso, estroso || *s* fantasia; *(whim)* grillo, estro; **to take a fancy to** prendere una passione per || *v* *(pret & pp* **-cied)** *tr* immaginare

fan'cy ball' *s* ballo in costume

fan'cy dress' *s* costume *m*

fan'cy foods' *spl* cibi *mpl* di lusso

fan'cy-free' *adj* libero dai lacci dell'amore

fan'cy skat'ing *s* pattinaggio artistico

fan'cy-work' *s* (sew) ricamo ornamentale

fanfare ['fænfer] *s* fanfara

fang [fæŋ] *s* zanna; *(of reptile)* dente velenoso

fan'light' *s* lunetta

fantastic(al) [fæn'tæstɪk(əl)] *adj* fantastico

fanta·sy ['fæntəzi] *or* ['fæntəsi] *s* (-sies) fantasia

far [fɑr] *adj* distante; **on the far side of** dall'altra parte || *adv* lontano; **as far as** fino a; **as far as I am concerned** per quanto mi riguardi; **as far as I know** per quanto io sappia; **by far** di gran lunga; **far and near** in lungo e in largo; **far away** molto lontano; **far be it from me** Dio me ne scampi e liberi; **far better** molto meglio; molto migliore; **far different** molto differente; **far from** lontano da; **far from it** tutto al contrario; **far into** fino al fondo di; **far into the night** fino a tarda ora; **far more** molto più; **far off** lontanissimo; **how far** quanto lontano; **how far is it?** a che distanza è da qui?; **in so far as** in quanto; **thus far** sinora; **to go far towards** contribuire molto a

faraway ['farǝ,we] *adj* distante, lontano; distratto

farce [fars] *s* farsa

farcical ['farsɪkǝl] *adj* farsesco

fare [fer] *s* prezzo della corsa; passeggero; *(food)* vitto ‖ *intr* andare, e.g., **how did you fare?** come Le è andata?

Far' East' *s* Estremo Oriente

fare'well' *s* congedo, commiato; **to bid farewell to** or **to take farewell of** prender commiato da ‖ *interj* addio!

far-fetched ['far'fetʃt] *adj* peregrino, campato in aria

far-flung ['far'flʌŋ] *adj* ampio; d'ampia distribuzione

farm [farm] *adj* agricolo ‖ *s* fattoria, tenuta ‖ *tr (land)* coltivare ‖ *intr* fare l'agricoltore or l'allevatore

farmer ['farmǝr] *s* agricoltore *m*, contadino

farm'hand' *s* bracciante *m*

farm'house' *s* casa colonica, masseria

farming ['farmɪŋ] *s* agricoltura, coltivazione

farm'yard' *s* aia

far'-off' *adj* lontano

far-reaching ['far'ritʃɪŋ] *adj* di grande portata

far-sighted ['far'saɪtɪd] *adj* lungimirante; perspicace; presbite

farther ['farðǝr] *adj* più lontano; addizionale ‖ *adv* più lontano, più in là; inoltre; **farther on** più oltre

farthest ['farðɪst] *adj* (il) più lontano; ultimo ‖ *adv* al massimo

farthing ['farðɪŋ] *s* (Brit) quarto di centesimo

Far' West' *s* (U.S.A.) lontano Occidente

fascinate ['fæsɪ,net] *tr* affascinare

fascinating ['fæsɪ,netɪŋ] *adj* incantatore, affascinante

fascism ['fæsɪzǝm] *s* fascismo

fascist ['fæsɪst] *adj & s* fascista *mf*

fashion ['fæʃǝn] *s* voga, moda; foggia, maniera; alta società; **after a fashion** in certo modo; **in fashion** di moda; **out of fashion** fuori moda; **to go out of fashion** passare di moda ‖ *tr* fare, foggiare

fashionable ['fæʃǝnǝbǝl] *adj* elegante, alla moda

fash'ion design'ing *s* alta moda

fash'ion plate' *s* figurino

fash'ion show' *s* sfilata di moda

fast [fæst] or [fast] *adj* veloce; *(clock)* che corre, in anticipo; dissoluto; ben legato; *(color)* solido; *(friend)* fedele ‖ *s* digiuno; **to break fast** rompere il digiuno ‖ *adv* rapidamente, fortemente; *(asleep)* profondamente; **to hold fast** tenersi saldo; **to live fast** condurre una vita dissoluta ‖ *intr* digiunare, fare vigilia

fast' day' *s* giorno di magro

fasten ['fæsǝn] or ['fasǝn] *tr* fissare; attaccare; *(a door)* sbarrare; *(a nickname; blows)* affibbiare; *(a dress)* allacciarsi ‖ *intr* attaccarsi

fastener ['fæsǝnǝr] or ['fasǝnǝr] *s* legaccio, laccio; *(snap, clasp)* fermaglio; *(for papers)* fermacarte *m*

fastidious [fæs'tɪdɪ-ǝs] *adj* schizzinoso; meticoloso

fasting ['fæstɪŋ] or ['fastɪŋ] *s* digiuno

fat [fæt] *adj* **(fatter; fattest)** grasso; *(productive)* forte, ricco, pingue; **to get fat** ingrassare ‖ *s* grasso, unto; *(of pork)* sugna

fatal ['fetǝl] *adj* fatale

fatalism ['fetǝ,lɪzǝm] *s* fatalismo

fatalist ['fetǝlɪst] *s* fatalista *mf*

fatali•ty [fǝ'tælɪti] *s* **(-ties)** *(in an accident)* morte *f*; accidente *m* mortale; fatalità *f*

fate [fet] *s* fato; **the Fates** le Parche ‖ *tr* predestinare

fated ['fetɪd] *adj* destinato

fateful ['fetfǝl] *adj* fatidico, fatale

fat'head' *s* (coll) zuccone *m*

father ['faðǝr] *s* padre *m*; *(male ancestor)* antenato ‖ *tr* procreare; creare; assumere la paternità di

fatherhood ['faðǝr,hʊd] *s* paternità *f*

fa'ther-in-law' *s* **(fathers-in-law)** suocero

fa'ther-land' *s* patria

fatherless ['faðǝrlɪs] *adj* orfano di padre; senza padre

fatherly ['faðǝrli] *adj* paterno

Fa'ther's Day' *s* festa del papà

Fa'ther Time' *s* il Tempo

fathom ['fæðǝm] *s* braccio ‖ *tr* sondare

fathomless ['fæðǝmlɪs] *adj* senza fondo; imponderabile

fatigue [fǝ'tig] *s* fatica, strapazzo; (mil) comandata ‖ *tr* stancare, affaticare

fatigue' clothes' *spl* (mil) tenuta di servizio, tenuta di fatica

fatten ['fætǝn] *tr & intr* ingrassare

fat•ty ['fæti] *adj* **(-tier; -tiest)** grasso; (pathol) adiposo ‖ *s* **(-ties)** (coll) tombolo

fatuous ['fætʃʊ-ǝs] *adj* fatuo

faucet ['fɔsɪt] *s* rubinetto

fault [fɔlt] *s* *(misdeed, blame)* colpa; *(defect)* difetto, magagna; (geol) faglia; (sports) fallo; **it's your fault** è colpa Sua; **to a fault** all'eccesso; **to find fault with** trovare a ridire sul conto di

fault'find'er *s* ipercritico, criticone *m*

fault'find'ing *adj* criticone ‖ *s* ipercritica

faultless ['fɔltlɪs] *adj* perfetto, inappuntabile

fault•y ['fɔlti] *adj* **(-ier; -iest)** manchevole, difettoso

faun [fɔn] *s* fauno

fauna ['fɔnǝ] *s* fauna

favor ['fevǝr] *s* favore *m*; *(letter)* pregiata; **do me the favor to** mi faccia il piacere di; **by your favor** col Suo permesso; **favors** regali *mpl* di festa; **to be in favor with** essere nelle grazie di; **to be out of favor** cadere in disgrazia ‖ *tr* favorire; (coll) assomigliare (with *dat*)

favorable ['fevǝrǝbǝl] *adj* favorevole

favorite ['fevǝrɪt] *adj & s* favorito

favoritism ['fevǝrɪ,tɪzǝm] *s* favoritismo

fawn [fɔn] *s* cerbiatto ‖ *intr*—**to fawn on** adulare, strusciarsi a

faze [fez] *tr* (coll) perturbare

fear [fɪr] *s* paura; **for fear of** per paura di; **for fear that** per paura che; **no fear** non c'è pericolo; **to be in fear of** aver timore di ‖ *tr & intr* temere

fearful ['fɪrfǝl] *adj* pauroso, timorato; (coll) spaventoso

fearless ['fɪrlɪs] *adj* impavido

feasible ['fizɪbǝl] *adj* fattibile, possibile

feast [fist] *s* festa; (*sumptuous meal*) festino, banchetto ‖ *tr* intrattenere ‖ *intr* banchettare; **to feast on** rallegrarsi alla vista di

feat [fit] *s* fatto, prodezza

feather ['fɛðǝr] *s* penna; (*soft and fluffy structure covering bird*) piuma; (*type*) qualità *f*, conio; (*tuft*) pennacchio; **in fine feather** di buon umore; **in buona salute** ‖ *tr* impennare; coprire di piume; (naut) spalare; (aer) bandierare; **to feather one's nest** arricchirsi

feath'er bed' *s* letto di piume

feath'er-bed'ding *s* impiego di mano d'opera non necessaria richiesto da un sindacato operaio

feath'er-brain' *s* cervello di gallina

feath'er-edge' *s* (*of board*) augnatura; (*of sharpened tool*) filo morto

feath'er-weight' *s* peso piuma

feathery ['fɛðǝri] *adj* piumato; leggero

feature ['fit/ǝr] *s* fattezza; caratteristica; (journ) articolo principale; (mov) attrazione; **features** fattezze *fpl* ‖ *tr* caratterizzare; mettere in evidenza; (coll) immaginare

fea'ture film' *s* lungometraggio

fea'ture sto'ry *s* articolo di spalla

February ['fɛbru ,ɛri] *s* febbraio

feces ['fisiz] *spl* feci *fpl*

feckless ['fɛklɪs] *adj* debole; inetto

federal ['fɛdǝrǝl] *adj* federale ‖ *s* federalista *mf*

federate ['fɛdǝ ,ret] *adj* federato ‖ *tr* federare ‖ *intr* federarsi

federation [,fɛdǝ'reʃǝn] *s* federazione

federative ['fɛdǝ ,retɪv] or ['fɛdǝrǝtɪv] *adj* federativo

fedora [fɪ'dorǝ] *s* cappello floscio di feltro

fed' up' [fɛd] *adj* stanco e stufo; **to be fed up with** averne fin sopra gli occhi di

fee [fi] *s* onorario; (*charge allowed by law*) diritto; (*tip*) mancia; (*for tuition*) tassa; (*for admission*) ingresso ‖ *tr* pagare

feeble ['fibǝl] *adj* debole, fievole

feeble-minded ['fibǝl'maɪndɪd] *adj* rimbecillito; debole, vacillante

feed [fid] *s* mangime *m;* (coll) mangiata; (mach) dispositivo d'alimentazione ‖ *v* (*pret & pp* **fed** [fɛd]) *tr* nutrire; (*a machine*) alimentare; (*cattle*) pascere; (theat) imbeccare ‖ *intr* mangiare; **to feed upon** nutrirsi di

feed'back' *s* (*of a computer*) ritorno d'informazioni; (electron) reazione

feed' bag' *s* musetta

feed' pump' *s* pompa di alimentazione

feed' trough' *s* (*for cattle*) vasca; (*for hogs*) trogolo

feed' wire' *s* cavo di alimentazione

feel [fil] *s* sensazione; (*touch*) tocco; (*vague mental impression*) senso ‖ *v* (*pret & pp* **felt** [fɛlt]) *tr* sentire; (*e.g., with the hands*) palpare, toccare; (*s.o.'s pulse*) tastare ‖ *intr* (*sick, tired, etc.*) sentirsi; **to feel bad** sentirsi male; (*to be unhappy*) essere spiacente; **to feel cheap** vergognarsi; **to feel comfortable** sentirsi a proprio agio; **to feel for** cercare di toccare; avere compassione per; **to feel like** aver voglia di; **to feel safe** sentirsi al sicuro; **to feel sorry** essere spiacente; **to feel sorry for** aver compassione di; pentirsi di

feeler ['filǝr] *s* (*hint*) sondaggio; **feelers** (*of insect*) antenne *fpl;* (*of mollusk*) tentacoli *mpl;* **to put out feelers** (fig) tastare il terreno

feeling ['filɪŋ] *s* (*with senses*) senso; (*impression, emotion*) sentimento, sensazione; opinione

feign [fen] *tr* fingere; inventare; imitare ‖ *intr* far finta; **to feign to be** fingersi

feint [fent] *s* finta ‖ *intr* fare una finta

feldspar ['fɛld ,spar] *s* feldspato

felicitate [fǝ'lɪsɪ ,tet] *tr* felicitarsi con

felicitous [fǝ'lɪsɪtǝs] *adj* felice, indovinato; eloquente

fell [fɛl] *adj* crudele, mortale ‖ *tr* (*trees*) abbattere

felloe ['fɛlo] *s* cerchione *m;* (*part of the rim*) gavello

fellow ['fɛlo] *s* compagno; collega *m;* (*of a society*) membro, socio; (*holder of fellowship*) borsista *mf;* (coll) tipo, tizio; (coll) innamorato; **good fellow** buon diavolo; galantuomo

fel'low cit'izen *s* concittadino

fel'low coun'try·man *s* (-men) concittadino

fel'low crea'ture *s* prossimo

fel'low-man' *s* (-men') prossimo

fel'low mem'ber *s* consocio

fellowship ['fɛlo ,ʃɪp] *s* compagnia; (*for study*) borsa di studio

fel'low trav'eler *s* simpatizzante *mf;* criptocomunista *mf;* compagno di viaggio

felon ['fɛlǝn] *s* criminale *mf;* (pathol) patereccio, giradito

felo·ny ['fɛlǝni] *s* (-nies) delitto doloso

felt [fɛlt] *s* feltro

felt' board' *s* lavagna di panno

felt'-tip pen' *s* pennarello

female ['fimel] *adj* (*sex*) femminile;

(*animal, plant, piece of a device*) femmina ‖ *s* femmina

feminine [ˈfemɪnɪn] *adj* & *s* femminile *m*

feminism [ˈfemɪ ˌnɪzəm] *s* femminismo

fence [fens] *s* steccato, staccionata; (*for stolen goods*) ricettatore *m;* (*carp*) squadra di guida; (*sports*) scherma; **on the fence** (*coll*) indeciso ‖ *tr* recingere ‖ *intr* tirare di scherma

fencing [ˈfensɪŋ] *s* scherma; (*fig*) schermaglia

fenc'ing mask' *s* visiera

fend [fend] *tr*—**to fend off** parare ‖ *intr*—**to fend for oneself** (*coll*) badare a sé stesso

fender [ˈfendər] *s* (*of trolley car*) salvagente *m;* (*of fireplace*) parafuoco; (*aut*) parafango; (*naut*) parabordo

fennel [ˈfenəl] *s* finocchio

ferment [ˈfʌrment] *s* fermento ‖ [fərˈment] *tr* & *intr* fermentare

fern [fʌrn] *s* felce *f*

ferocious [fəˈroʃəs] *adj* feroce

ferocity [fəˈrɑsɪti] *s* ferocia

ferret [ˈferɪt] *s* furetto ‖ *tr*—**to ferret out** scovare ‖ *intr* indagare

Fer'ris wheel' [ˈferɪs] *s* ruota (del parco dei divertimenti)

fer-ry [ˈferi] *s* (*-ries*) traghetto; nave *f* traghetto ‖ *v* (*pret* & *pp* **-ried**) *tr* traghettare ‖ *intr* attraversare

fer'ry-boat' *s* nave *f* traghetto, ferryboat *m*

fertile [ˈfʌrtɪl] *adj* fertile

fertilize [ˈfʌrtɪ ˌlaɪz] *tr* fertilizzare; (*to impregnate*) fecondare

fertilizer [ˈfʌrtɪ ˌlaɪzər] *s* fertilizzante *m;* (*e.g., of flowers*) fecondatore *m*

fervent [ˈfʌrvənt] *adj* fervente, fervido

fervid [ˈfʌrvɪd] *adj* fervido

fervor [ˈfʌrvər] *s* fervore *m*

fester [ˈfestər] *s* ulcera, piaga ‖ *tr* corrompere ‖ *intr* suppurare; (*fig*) corrompersi

festival [ˈfestɪvəl] *adj* festivo ‖ *s* festa; (*of music*) festival *m*

festive [ˈfestɪv] *adj* festivo

festivi-ty [fesˈtɪvɪti] *s* (*-ties*) festività *f*

festoon [fesˈtun] *s* festone *m* ‖ *tr* ornare di festoni

fetch [fetʃ] *tr* andare a prendere; (*a price*) fruttare, vendersi per

fetching [ˈfetʃɪŋ] *adj* (*coll*) cattivante, attraente

fete [fet] *s* festa ‖ *tr* festeggiare

fetid [ˈfetɪd] *or* [ˈfitɪd] *adj* fetido

fetish [ˈfitɪʃ] *or* [ˈfetɪʃ] *s* feticcio

fetlock [ˈfetlɑk] *s* nocca; (*tuft of hair*) barbetta

fetter [ˈfetər] *s* ceppo, catena ‖ *tr* mettere ai ceppi, incatenare

fettle [ˈfetəl] *s* stato, condizione; **in fine fettle** in buone condizioni

fetus [ˈfitəs] *s* feto

feud [fjud] *s* antagonismo; odio ereditario ‖ *intr* essere in lotta

feudal [ˈfjudəl] *adj* feudale

feudalism [ˈfjudə ˌlɪzəm] *s* feudalismo

fever [ˈfivər] *s* febbre *f*

feverish [ˈfivərɪʃ] *adj* febbrile

few [fju] *adj* & *pron* pochi; **a few** alcuni; **quite a few** molti

fiancé [ˌfi·ɑnˈse] *s* fidanzato

fiancée [ˌfi·ɑnˈse] *s* fidanzata

fias-co [fiˈæsko] *s* (*-cos* or *-coes*) fiasco

fib [fɪb] *s* menzogna, frottola ‖ *v* (*pret* & *pp* **fibbed;** *ger* **fibbing**) *intr* raccontar frottole

fiber [ˈfaɪbər] *s* fibra; (*fig*) tempra

fi'ber-glass' *s* vetroresina

fibrous [ˈfaɪbrəs] *adj* fibroso

fickle [ˈfɪkəl] *adj* volubile, incostante, mobile

fiction [ˈfɪkʃən] *s* (*invention*) finzione; (*branch of literature*) novellistica

fictional [ˈfɪkʃənəl] *adj* immaginario

fictionalize [ˈfɪkʃənə ˌlaɪz] *tr* romanzare

fictitious [fɪkˈtɪʃəs] *adj* fittizio

fiddle [ˈfɪdəl] *s* violino; **fit as a fiddle** in perfetta salute ‖ *tr* (*coll*) suonare sul violino; **to fiddle away** (*coll*) sprecare ‖ *intr* (*coll*) suonare il violino; **to fiddle with** (*coll*) giocherellare con

fiddler [ˈfɪdlər] *s* (*coll*) violinista *mf*

fiddling [ˈfɪdlɪŋ] *adj* triviale, futile, insignificante

fideli-ty [faɪˈdelɪti] *or* [fɪˈdelɪti] *s* (*-ties*) fedeltà *f*

fidget [ˈfɪdʒɪt] *intr* agitarsi; **to fidget with** giocherellare con

fidgety [ˈfɪdʒɪti] *adj* irrequieto

fiduciar-y [fɪˈdjuʃɪ ˌeri] *or* [fɪˈduʃɪ ˌeri] *adj* fiduciario ‖ *s* (*-ies*) fiduciario

fie [faɪ] *interj* vergogna!

fief [fif] *s* feudo

field [fild] *adj* (*mil*) da campagna ‖ *s* campo; (*sports*) terreno; (*min*) giacimento; (*of motor or dynamo*) (*elec*) induttore *m;* (*phys*) campo

fielder [ˈfildər] *s* (*outfielder*) giocatore *m* del campo esterno

field' glass'es *spl* binocolo

field' hock'ey *s* hockey *m* su prato

field' mag'net *s* induttore *m*, calamita induttrice

field' mar'shal *s* (*mil*) maresciallo di campo

field' mouse' *s* topo di campagna

field'piece' *s* pezzo da campagna

fiend [find] *s* diavolo; (*coll*) addetto, tifoso

fiendish [ˈfindɪʃ] *adj* diabolico

fierce [fɪrs] *adj* fiero, feroce; (*wind*) furioso; (*coll*) maledetto

fierceness [ˈfɪrsnɪs] *s* ferocia

fier-y [ˈfaɪri] *or* [ˈfaɪ·əri] *adj* (*-ier; -iest*) ardente, focoso

fife [faɪf] *s* piffero

fifteen [ˈfɪfˈtin] *adj, s* & *pron* quindici *m*

fifteenth [ˈfɪfˈtinθ] *adj, s* & *pron* quindicesimo ‖ *s* (*in dates*) quindici *m*

fifth [fɪfθ] *adj, s* & *pron* quinto ‖ *s* (*in dates*) cinque *m*

fifth' col'umn *s* quinta colonna

fiftieth [ˈfɪftɪ·ɪθ] *adj, s* & *pron* cinquantesimo

fif-ty [ˈfɪfti] *adj* & *pron* cinquanta ‖ *s* (*-ties*) cinquanta *m;* **the fifties** gli anni cinquanta

fif'ty-fif'ty *adv*—**to go fifty-fifty** fare a metà

fig [frg] *s* fico

fight [fart] *s* lotta; baruffa; combattimento; spirito combattivo; (*sports*) incontro; **to pick a fight with** attaccar briga con || *v* (*pret & pp* **fought** [fɔt]) *tr* lottare con; combattere contro; opporsi a || *intr* lottare; combattere; **to fight shy of** cercar di evitare

fighter ['fartər] *s* lottatore *m*; (*warrior*) combattente *m*; (aer) caccia *m*

fig' leaf' *s* foglia di fico

figment ['frgmənt] *s* finzione

figurative ['frgjərətɪv] *adj* (fa) figurativo; (rhet) figurato

figure ['frgjər] *s* figura; numero; prezzo; **to be good at figures** far bene di conto; **to cut a figure** fare una buona figura; **to keep one's figure** conservare la linea || *tr* figurare; immaginare; raffigurare; supporre, calcolare; **to figure out** calcolare; decifrare || *intr* apparire; **to figure on** (coll) contare su

fig'ure-head' *s* uomo di paglia, prestanome *m*; (naut) polena

fig'ure of speech' *s* figura retorica

fig'ure skat'ing *s* pattinaggio artistico

figurine [ˌfrgjəˈrin] *s* figurina

filament ['frləmənt] *s* filamento

filbert ['frlbərt] *s* (*tree*) nocciolo, avellano; (*nut*) nocciola, avellana

filch [frltʃ] *tr* rubacchiare

file [faɪl] *s* (*row*) fila; (*tool*) lima; (*folder*) filza; (*room*) archivio; (*of cards*) schedario || *tr* mettere in fila; limare; archiviare, schedare; (journ) trasmettere || *intr* sfilare; **to file for** fare domanda di

file' clerk' *s* schedarista *mf*

filet [fɪˈle] or ['frle] *s* filetto || *tr* tagliare in filetti

filial ['frlɪ-əl] or ['frljəl] *adj* filiale

filiation [ˌfrlɪˈeʃən] *s* filiazione

filibuster ['frlɪˌbʌstər] *s* (*tactics*) ostruzionismo; (*speech*) discorso ostruzionista; (*person making such a speech*) ostruzionista *mf*; (*buccaneer*) filibustiere *m* || *tr* fare ostruzionismo contro || *intr* fare dell'ostruzionismo

filigree ['frlɪˌgri] *adj* filigranato || *s* filigrana || *tr* lavorare in filigrana

filing ['faɪlɪŋ] *s* (*of documents*) schedatura; limatura; **filings** limatura

fil'ing cab'inet *s* schedario

fil'ing card' *s* cartellino, scheda

fill [frl] *s* sazietà *f*; (*place filled with earth*) terrapieno; **to have or get one's fill** mangiare a sazietà || *tr* riempire; (*an order*) eseguire; (*a hole*) otturare; (*a tooth*) piombare; (*a tire*) gonfiare; (*a place*) occupare; (*with sand*) interrare; **to fill out** (*a form*) riempire; **to fill up** (aut) fare il pieno di || *intr* riempirsi; **to fill in** prendere il posto; **to fill up** riempirsi

filler ['frlər] *s* ripieno; (*person*) riempitore *m*; (*painting*) mestica; (journ) articolo riempitivo

fillet ['frlɪt] *s* nastro, fascia; (*for hair*) nastro; (archit) listello || *tr* filettare

|| ['frle] or ['frlɪt] *s* (*of meat or fish*) filetto || *tr* tagliare a filetti

filling ['frlɪŋ] *s* (*of a tooth*) impiombatura; (*of turkey*) ripieno

fill'ing sta'tion *s* stazione di rifornimento

fillip ['frlɪp] *s* stimolo; colpetto col dito || *tr* dare un colpetto col dito a; (fig) stimolare

fil·ly ['frli] *s* (**-lies**) puledra

film [frlm] *s* pellicola; (mov, phot) pellicola, film *m* || *tr* filmare

film' li'brary *s* cineteca, filmoteca

film'strip' *s* film

film·y ['frlmi] *adj* (**-ier; -iest**) sottile, delicato; (*look*) annebbiato

filter ['frltər] *s* filtro || *tr & intr* filtrare

filtering ['frltərɪŋ] *s* filtrazione

fil'ter pa'per *s* carta da filtro

fil'ter tip' *s* filtro, bocchino filtro

filth [frlθ] *s* sporco, sporcizia

filth·y ['frlθi] *adj* (**-ier; -iest**) sporco, sudicio

filth'y lu'cre ['lukər] *s* il vile metallo

filtrate ['frltret] *s* liquido filtrato || *tr & intr* filtrare

fin [frn] *s* pinna; (slang) biglietto da cinque dollari

final ['faɪnəl] *adj* finale; (*last in a series*) ultimo; definitivo, insindacabile || *s* esame *m* finale; **finals** (sports) finale *f*

finale [fɪˈnɑli] *s* (mus) finale *m*

finalist ['faɪnəlɪst] *s* finalista *mf*

finally ['faɪnəli] *adv* finalmente

finance [fɪˈnæns] or [ˈfaɪnæns] *s* finanza; **finances** finanze *fpl* || *tr* finanziare

financial [fɪˈnænʃəl] or [faɪˈnænʃəl] *adj* finanziario

financier [ˌfɪnənˈsɪr] or [ˌfaɪnənˈsɪr] *s* finanziere *m*

financing [fɪˈnænsɪŋ] or [ˈfaɪnænsɪŋ] *s* finanziamento

finch [frntʃ] *s* fringuello

find [faɪnd] *s* trovata || *v* (*pret & pp* **found** [faʊnd]) *tr* trovare; rinvenire; (*s.o. innocent or guilty*) dichiarare; **to find out** venire a sapere || *intr* (law) sentenziare; **to find out about** informarsi su

finder ['faɪndər] *s* (phot) mirino; (astr) cannochiale cercatore

finding ['faɪndɪŋ] *s* scoperta; (law) sentenza

fine [faɪn] *adj* buono; bello, fino, fine || *s* multa || *adv* (coll) benissimo; **to feel fine** (coll) sentirsi benissimo || *tr* multare

fine' arts' *spl* belle arti

fineness ['faɪnnɪs] *s* finezza; (*of metal*) titolo

fine' print' *s* testo in caratteri minuti

finer·y ['faɪnəri] *s* (**-ies**) ornamenti *mpl*, fronzoli *mpl*; abito vistoso

fine-spun ['faɪnˌspʌn] *adj* sottile

finesse [fɪˈnes] *s* finezza; (bridge) impasse *f* || *tr* fare l'impasse a || *intr* fare l'impasse

fine'-tooth comb' *s* pettine fitto; **to go over with a fine-tooth comb** esaminare minuziosamente

finger [ˈfɪŋgər] s dito; **to have a finger in the pie** avere le mani in pasta; **to put one's finger on the spot** mettere il dito nella piaga; **to slip between the fingers** sfuggire di tra le dita; **to snap one's fingers at** infischiarsi di; **to twist around one's little finger** fare ciò che si vuole di ‖ tr toccare con le dita; (to pilfer) rubacchiare; (slang) mostrare a dito

fin'ger board' s (mus) tastiera

fin'ger bowl' s sciacquadita m

fingering [ˈfɪŋgərɪŋ] s palpeggiamento; (mus) diteggiatura

fin'ger mark' s ditata

fin'ger-nail' s unghia

fin'ger-print' s impronta digitale ‖ tr prendere le impronte digitali di

fin'ger-tip' s polpastrello; **to have at one's fingertips** avere sulla punta delle dita, sapere a menadito

finical [ˈfɪnɪkəl] or **finicky** [ˈfɪnɪkɪ] adj pignolo, schizzinoso

finish [ˈfɪnɪʃ] s fine f; finitura; (sports) finale m ‖ tr finire; **to finish off** distruggere ‖ intr finire; **to finish +** ger finire di + inf; **to finish by +** ger finire per + inf

fin'ishing school' s scuola di perfezionamento per signorine

fin'ishing touch' s ultimo tocco

finite [ˈfaɪnaɪt] adj finito

Finland [ˈfɪnlənd] s la Finlandia

Finlander [ˈfɪnləndər] s finlandese mf

Finn [fɪn] s (member of a Finnish-speaking group of people) finnico; (native or inhabitant of Finland) finlandese mf

Finnic [ˈfɪnɪk] adj & s finnico

Finnish [ˈfɪnɪʃ] adj finlandese ‖ s (language) finlandese m

fir [fʌr] s abete m

fire [faɪr] s fuoco; (destructive burning) incendio; **to be on fire** ardere; **to be under enemy fire** essere sotto tiro nemico; **to catch fire** infiammarsi; **to hang fire** essere in sospeso; **to open fire** aprire il fuoco; **to set on fire, to set fire to** dar fuoco a; **under fire** sotto fuoco nemico; accusato ‖ tr accendere; (an oven) scaldare; (bricks) cuocere; (a weapon) sparare; (the imagination) riscaldare; (an employee) (coll) licenziare ‖ intr accendersi; **to fire on** far fuoco su; **to fire up** attivare una caldaia

fire' alarm' s avvisatore m d'incendio

fire'arm' s arma da fuoco

fire'ball' s palla da cannone esplosiva; (lightning) lampo a forma di globo infocato; meteorite m a forma di globo infocato; globo infocato

fire'boat' s lancia dei pompieri

fire'box' s (of a boiler) fornello; (to give alarm) stazione d'allarme

fire'brand' s tizzone m; (fig) fiaccola della discordia

fire'brick' s mattone refrattario

fire' brigade' s corpo di pompieri volontari

fire'bug' s (coll) incendiario

fire' com'pany s corpo dei pompieri;

compagnia d'assicurazioni contro gli incendi

fire'crack'er s mortaretto

fire'damp' s grisou m

fire' depart'ment s corpo dei pompieri

fire'dog' s alare m

fire' drill' s esercitazione in caso d'incendio

fire' en'gine s autopompa

fire' escape' s scala di sicurezza

fire' extin'guisher s estintore m

fire'fly' s (-flies) lucciola

fire'guard' s parafuoco

fire' hose' s manichetta

fire'house' s caserma dei pompieri

fire' hy'drant s bocca d'incendi

fire' insur'ance s assicurazione contro gli incendi

fire' i'rons spl arnesi mpl del camino

fire'man s (-men) (man who extinguishes fires) pompiere m, vigile m del fuoco; (stoker) fochista m

fire'place' s camino

fire'plug' s bocca da incendio, idrante m

fire'proof' adj incombustibile ‖ tr rendere incombustibile

fire' sale' s vendita di merce avariata dal fuoco

fire'screen' s parafuoco

fire' ship' s brulotto

fire'side' s focolare m

fire'trap' s edificio senza mezzi adeguati per combattere incendi

fire' wall' s paratia antincendio

fire' wa'ter s (coll) acquavite f

fire'wood' s legna

fire'works' spl fuochi mpl artificiali

firing [ˈfaɪrɪŋ] s (of furnace) alimentazione; (of bricks) cottura; (of a gun) sparo; (of soldiers) tiro; (of an internal-combustion engine) accensione; (of an employee) (coll) licenziamento

fir'ing line' s linea del fuoco

fir'ing or'der s (aut) ordine m d'accensione

fir'ing pin' s percussore m

fir'ing squad' s (for saluting at a burial) plotone m d'onore; (for executing) plotone m d'esecuzione

firm [fʌrm] adj forte, fermo ‖ s ditta, compagnia

firmament [ˈfʌrməmənt] s firmamento

firm' name' s ragione f sociale

firmness [ˈfʌrmnɪs] s fermezza

first [fʌrst] adj primo ‖ s primo; (aut) prima; (mus) voce f principale; **at first** sulle prime; **from the first** da bel principio ‖ adv prima; **first of all** per prima cosa

first' aid' s pronto soccorso

first'-aid' kit' s cassetta farmaceutica d'urgenza

first'-aid' sta'tion s posto di pronto soccorso

first'-born' adj & s primogenito

first'-class' adj di prim'ordine, sopraffino ‖ adv in prima classe

first' cous'in s cugino primo

first'-day cov'er s busta primo giorno

first' draft' s brutta copia

first' fin'ger *s* dito indice
first' floor' *s* pianoterra *m*
first' fruits' *spl* primizie *fpl*
first' lieuten'ant *s* tenente *m*
firstly [ˈfʌrstli] *adv* in primo luogo
first' mate' *s* (naut) primo ufficiale, comandante *m* in seconda, secondo
first' name' *s* nome *m* di battesimo
first' night' *s* (theat) prima
first' of'ficer *s* (naut) primo ufficiale, comandante *m* in seconda, secondo
first'-rate' *adj* di prima forza; eccellente || *adv* (coll) benissimo
first'-run' *adj* di prima visione
fiscal [ˈfɪskəl] *adj* (*pertaining to public treasury*) fiscale; finanziario || *s* avvocato fiscale
fis'cal year' *s* esercizio finanziario
fish [fɪʃ] *s* pesce *m*; **to be like a fish out of water** essere come un pesce fuor d'acqua; **to be neither fish nor fowl** non essere né carne né pesce; **to drink like a fish** bere come una spugna || *tr* pescare || *intr* pescare; **to fish for compliments** cercare di farsi fare dei complimenti; **to go fishing** andare alla pesca; **to take fishing** portare con sé alla pesca
fish'bone' *s* lisca, spina di pesce
fish'bowl' *s* vaschetta per i pesci rossi
fisher [ˈfɪʃər] *s* pescatore *m*; (zool) martora canadese
fish'er·man *s* (**-men**) pescatore *m*; (*boat*) peschereccio
fish·er·y [ˈfɪʃəri] *s* (**-ies**) (*activity*) pesca; (*business*) pescheria; (*grounds*) riserva di pesca, luogo dove si pesca
fish' glue' *s* colla di pesce
fish'hook' *s* amo
fishing [ˈfɪʃɪŋ] *adj* da pesca || *s* pesca
fish'ing reel' *s* mulinello
fish'ing rod' *s* canna da pesca
fish'ing tack'le *s* attrezzatura da pesca
fish'line' *s* lenza
fish' mar'ket *s* pescheria
fish'pool' *s* peschiera
fish' spear' *s* fiocina
fish' sto'ry *s* (coll) fandonia; **to tell fish stories** sparare grosse
fish'tail' *s* (aut) imbardata (aer) spedalata || *intr* (aut) imbardare; (aer) compiere una spedalata
fish'wife' *s* (**-wives'**) pescivendola; (*foul-mouthed woman*) ciana
fish'worm' *s* lombrico
fish·y [ˈfɪʃi] *adj* (**-ier; -iest**) che sa di pesce; (coll) dubbioso, inverosimile
fission [ˈfɪʃən] *s* (biol) scissione; (phys) fissione
fissionable [ˈfɪʃənəbəl] *adj* fissionabile
fissure [ˈfɪʃər] *s* fenditura; (*in rock*) crepaccio
fist [fɪst] *s* pugno; (typ) indice *m*; **to shake one's fist at** mostrare i pugni a
fist'fight' *s* scontro a pugni
fist'ful' *s* pugno, manciata
fisticuff [ˈfɪstɪˌkʌf] *s* pugno; **fisticuffs** scontro a pugni
fit [fɪt] *adj* (**fitter; fittest**) indicato; idoneo, adatto; in buona salute; **fit to be tied** (coll) infuriato, arrabbia-

tissimo; **fit to eat** mangiabile; **to feel fit** sentirsi in buona salute; **to see fit** giudicare conveniente || *s* equipaggiamento; (*of a suit*) taglio; (*of one piece with another*) incastro; (*of coughing*) accesso; (*of anger*) attacco; **by fits and starts** a pezzi e a bocconi || *v* (*pret & pp* **fitted;** *ger* **fitting**) *tr* adattare; quadrare a; andar bene a; equipaggiare; preparare; servire a; esser d'accordo con; **to fit out** or **up** attrezzare, equipaggiare || *intr* stare; incastrare; (*said of clothes*) cascare; entrare; **to fit in** entrarci
fitful [ˈfɪtfəl] *adj* capriccioso; incostante, irregolare
fitness [ˈfɪtnɪs] *s* convenienza; idoneità *f*; buona salute
fitter [ˈfɪtər] *s* aggiustatore *m*; (*of machinery*) montatore *m*; (*of clothing*) sarto che mette in prova
fitting [ˈfɪtɪŋ] *adj* appropriato, adatto, conveniente || *s* adattamento; (*of a garment*) prova; tubo adattabile; (carp) incastro; **fittings** accessori *mpl*; utensili *mpl*; (*iron trimmings*) ferramenta *fpl*
five [faɪv] *adj & pron* cinque || *s* cinque *m*; **five o' clock** le cinque
five' hun'dred *adj*, *s & pron* cinquecento
five'-year plan' *s* piano quinquennale
fix [fɪks] *s*—**in a tight fix** (coll) nei pasticci; **to be in a fix** (coll) star fresco, essere nei guai || *tr* riparare; fissare; (*a meal*) preparare; (*a bayonet*) inastare; (*attention*) attrarre, fermare; (*hair*) mettere a posto; (coll) arrangiare || *intr* fissarsi, stabilirsi; **to fix on** scegliere
fixed [fɪkst] *adj* fisso; (time) improrogabile; (coll) arrangiato
fixing [ˈfɪksɪŋ] *adj* fissativo || *s* (*fastening*) attacco; (phot) fissaggio; **with all the fixings** (coll) con tutti i contorni
fix'ing bath' *s* bagno di fissaggio
fixture [ˈfɪkstʃər] *s* infisso; accessorio; (*of a lamp*) guarnizione; **fixtures** (*e.g., of a store*) suppellettili *fpl*
fizz [fɪz] *s* effervescenza; gazosa; (Brit) spumante *m* || *intr* frizzare
fizzle [ˈfɪzəl] *s* (coll) fiasco || *intr* crepitare; (coll) fare fiasco
flabbergast [ˈflæbərˌɡæst] *tr* (coll) sbalordire, lasciare stupefatto
flab·by [ˈflæbi] *adj* (**-bier; -biest**) floscio, flaccido, cascante
flag [flæɡ] *s* bandiera || *v* (*pret & pp* **flagged;** *ger* **flagging**) *tr* imbandierare; segnalare; (rr) far fermare || *intr* ammosciarsi, afflosciarsi
flageolet [ˌflædʒəˈlɛt] *s* flautino
flag'man *s* (**-men**) (rr) manovratore *m*
flag' of truce' *s* bandiera parlamentaria
flag'pole' *s* pennone *m*
flagrant [ˈfleɡrənt] *adj* flagrante; scandaloso
flag'ship' *s* nave ammiraglia
flag'staff' *s* pennone *m*
flag' sta'tion *s* (rr) stazione facoltativa
flag'stone' *s* lastra di pietra

flag′ stop′ s (rr) fermata facoltativa
flail [flel] s correggiato ‖ tr battere col correggiato; battere
flair [fler] s fiuto, istinto
flak [flæk] s fuoco antiaereo
flake [flek] s falda; (of snow) fiocco, falda; (of cereal) fiocco; ‖ tr sfaldare; (fish) scagliare ‖ intr sfaldarsi
flak·y ['fleki] adj (-ier; -iest) a falde, faldoso
flamboyant [flæm'bɔɪ-ənt] adj sgargiante; (archit) fiammeggiante
flame [flem] s fiamma ‖ tr & intr fiammeggiare
flamethrower ['flem,θro-ər] s lanciafiamme m
flaming ['flemɪŋ] adj fiammeggiante; appassionato; (culin) alla fiamma
flamin·go [flə'mɪŋgo] s (-gos or -goes) fenicottero, fiammingo
flammable ['flæməbəl] adj infiammabile
Flanders ['flændərz] s le Fiandre
flange [flændʒ] s (e.g., on a pipe) flangia; (on I beam) bordo; (of a wheel) cerchione m
flank [flæŋk] s fianco ‖ tr fiancheggiare
flannel ['flænəl] s flanella
flap [flæp] s (in clothing) falda; (of hat) tesa; (of book) risvolto; (of pocket) patta; (of shoe) linguetta; (blow) colpo; (of a table) pannello; (of the counter in a store) ribalta; (of wings) alata ‖ v (pret & pp flapped; ger flapping) tr battere, sbattere; (to move violently) sbatacchiare ‖ intr penzolare
flare [fler] s vampa; scintillio; (of a dress) svasatura; (mil) fuoco di segnalazione; flares (trousers) calzoni mpl a zampe d'elefante ‖ tr svasare ‖ intr scintillare; (said of a garment) scampanare; to flare up divampare; (said of an illness) aggravarsi, infiammarsi
flare′-up′ s vampa, fiammata; (of an illness) recrudescenza; scoppio d'ira, accesso di collera
flash [flæʃ] s (of light) sprazzo; (of lightning) lampo, baleno; (of hope) raggio; (of joy) accesso; (journ, phot) flash m; (fig) lampo; flash in the pan fuoco di paglia ‖ tr (powder) accendere; (a sword) brandire; (journ) diffondere; (e.g., money) (coll) ostentare ‖ intr lampeggiare, balenare, folgorare; to flash by passare come un lampo
flash′back′ s flashback m
flash′ bulb′ s lampada lampo
flash′ cube′ s cuboflash m
flash′ flood′ s inondazione torrenziale
flashing ['flæʃɪŋ] s metallo per coprire la conversa; commessura metallica fra tetto e comignolo
flash′light′ s lampadina tascabile; (of a lighthouse) luce f intermittente; (phot) fotolampo, lampeggiatore m
flash′light bulb′ s lampada per fotolampo
flash·y ['flæʃi] adj (-ier; -iest) sgargiante, chiassoso, vistoso

flask [flæsk] or [flɑsk] s fiasco, fiasca; (for laboratory use) beuta
flat [flæt] adj (flatter; flattest) piano; (nose) camuso; (boat) a fondo piatto; (surface) liscio; (beer) svanito; (tire) sgonfio; (denial) deciso; (mus) bemolle; (coll) al verde ‖ s (flat surface) piatto; (flat area) piano; (apartment) appartamento; (mus) bemolle m; (coll) gomma a terra ‖ adv—to fall flat fallire
flat′boat′ s chiatta
flat′car′ s (rr) pianale m
flat-footed ['flæt,futɪd] adj dai piedi piatti; (coll) inflessibile
flat′head′ s (of a bolt) testa piatta; (coll) testa di legno
flat′i′ron s ferro da stiro
flat′ race′ s corsa piana
flatten ['flætən] tr schiacciare; distendere ‖ intr appiattirsi; indebolirsi; to flatten out appiattirsi; (aer) porsi in linea orizzontale di volo
flatter ['flætər] tr adulare, lusingare; (to make seem more attractive) favorire ‖ intr adulare
flatterer ['flætərər] s adulatore m, lusingatore m
flattering ['flætərɪŋ] adj lusinghiero
flatter·y ['flætəri] s (-ies) lusinga
flat′ tire′ s gomma a terra
flat′top′ s portaerei f
flatulence ['flætʃələns] s flatulenza
flat′ware′ s argenteria, vasellame m
flaunt [flɔnt] or (flɑnt] tr sfoggiare, ostentare
flautist ['flɔtɪst] s flautista mf
flavor ['flevər] s sapore m, gusto; condimento ‖ tr insaporire; condire; aromatizzare, profumare
flavoring ['flevərɪŋ] s condimento, sapore m
flaw [flɔ] s difetto, menda, fallo; (crack) incrinatura
flawless ['flɔlɪs] adj senza difetti
flax [flæks] s lino
flaxen ['flæksən] adj di lino; biondo
flax′seed′ s linosa
flay [fle] tr scorticare, scoiare
flea [fli] s pulce f
flea′bite′ s morso di pulce; (fig) inezia, seccatura secondaria
fleck [flɛk] s macchia; efelide f ‖ tr chiazzare, macchiare
fledgling ['flɛdʒlɪŋ] s uccellino appena nato; (fig) pivello
flee [fli] v (pret & pp fled [flɛd]) tr & intr fuggire, sfuggire
fleece [flis] s vello; (e.g., of clouds) bioccolo ‖ tr tosare; (fig) pelare
fleec·y ['flisi] adj (-ier; -iest) lanoso; (sky) a pecorelle
fleet [flit] adj rapido ‖ s flotta
fleeting ['flitɪŋ] adj fugace, passeggero
Fleming ['flemɪŋ] s fiammingo
Flemish ['flemɪʃ] adj & s fiammingo
flesh [flɛʃ] s carne f; (of fruit) polpa; in the flesh in carne ed ossa; to lose flesh dimagrire; to put on flesh ingrassare
flesh′ and blood′ s (relatives) carne f della carne, i miei, i suoi, etc.; il corpo umano

flesh-colored [ˈfleʃ ˌkʌlərd] *adj* color carne

fleshiness [ˈfleʃɪnɪs] *s* carnosità *f*

fleshless [ˈfleʃlɪs] *adj* scarno

flesh'pot' *s* piatto di carne; locale *m* di dissoluzione; **fleshpots** vita dissoluta

flesh' wound' *s* ferita superficiale

flesh·y [ˈfleʃi] *adj* (**-ier; -iest**) carnoso; polposo

flex [flɛks] *tr* piegare || *intr* piegarsi

flexible [ˈflɛksɪbəl] *adj* flessibile; (*joint*) a snodo

flick [flɪk] *s* schiocco; (slang) pellicola cinematografica || *tr* schioccare

flicker [ˈflɪkər] *s* fiamma tremolante; (*of eyelids*) battito; (*of hope*) bagliore *m* || *intr* tremolare; vacillare

flier [ˈflaɪ·ər] *s* aviatore *m*; (*venture*) (coll) impresa rischiosa; (coll) foglio volante

flight [flaɪt] *s* fuga; (*of an airplane*) volo; (*of birds*) stormo; (*of stairs*) rampa; (*of fancy*) slancio; **to put to flight** mettere in fuga; **to take flight** prendere la fuga

flight' deck' *s* ponte *m* di volo

flight·y [ˈflaɪti] *adj* (**-ier; -iest**) frivolo; volubile

flim-flam [ˈflɪm ˌflæm] *s* (coll) imbroglio, truffa || *v* (*pret & pp* **-flammed; ger -flamming**) *tr* (coll) imbrogliare, truffare

flim·sy [ˈflɪmzi] *adj* (**-sier; -siest**) leggero; (*material*) di scarsa consistenza; (*excuse*) inconsistente

flinch [flɪntʃ] *intr* indietreggiare; **without flinching** senza scomporsi

fling [flɪŋ] *s* tiro; ballo scozzese; **to go on a fling** darsi alla pazza gioia; **to have a fling** al tentare di fare; **to have one's fling** correre la cavallina || *v* (*pret & pp* **flung** [flʌŋ]) *tr* sbattere, scagliare; (*e.g., in jail*) schiaffare; **to fling open** spalancare; **to fling shut** chiudere improvvisamente

flint [flɪnt] *s* selce *f*, pietra focaia

flint'lock' *s* fucile *m* a pietra focaia

flint·y [ˈflɪnti] *adj* (**-ier; -iest**) pietroso; (*unmerciful*) spietato; duro come un macigno

flip [flɪp] *adj* (**flipper; flippest**) impertinente || *s* buffetto; salto mortale || *v* (*pret & pp* **flipped; ger flipping**) *tr* sbattere in aria; muovere d'un tratto **to flip a coin** giocare a testa e croce; **to flip shut** (*e.g., a fan*) chiudere improvvisamente

flippancy [ˈflɪpənsi] *s* leggerezza

flippant [ˈflɪpənt] *adj* scanzonato, leggero

flirt [flʌrt] *s* (*woman*) civetta; (*man*) vagheggino || *intr* (*said of a woman*) civettare; (*said of a man*) fare il damerino; **to flirt with** flirtare con; (*an idea*) accarezzare; (*death*) giocare con

flit [flɪt] *v* (*pret & pp* **flitted; ger flitting**) *intr* svolazzare, volteggiare; passare rapidamente, volare

flitch [flɪtʃ] *s* fetta di pancetta

float [flot] *s* (*raft*) galleggiante *m*; (*of mason*) cazzuola; carro allegorico || *tr* far galleggiare; (*a business*) lanciare; (*stocks, bonds*) emettere || *intr* galleggiare, tenersi a galla

floating [ˈflotɪŋ] *adj* galleggiante

flock [flɑk] *s* (*of birds*) stormo; (*of sheep*) gregge *m*; (*of people*) stuolo; (*of wool*) fiocco; (fig) mucchio || *intr* affollarsi, riunirsi, radunarsi

floe [flo] *s* tavola di ghiaccio

flog [flɑg] *v* (*pret & pp* **flogged; ger flogging**) *tr* battere, fustigare

flood [flʌd] *s* (*caused by rain*) diluvio; (*sudden rise of river*) piena, fiumana; (*of tide*) flusso || *tr* inondare; (aut) ingolfare || *intr* straripare; (aut) ingolfarsi || **the Flood** il diluvio universale

flood'gate' *s* (*of a canal*) chiusa; (*of a dam*) saracinesca

flood'light' *s* riflettore *m*

flood' tide' *s* flusso

floor [flor] *s* (*inside bottom surface of room*) pavimento; (*story of building*) piano; (*of the sea, a swimming pool, etc.*) fondo; (*of the exchange*) recinto delle grida; (*of an assembly hall*) emiciclo; (naut) madiere *m*; **to ask for the floor** chiedere la parola; **to have the floor** avere la parola; **to take the floor** prendere la parola || *tr* pavimentare; abbattere, gettare al suolo; (coll) confondere; (coll) vincere

flooring [ˈflorɪŋ] *s* palco, impiantito

floor' mop' *s* redazza

floor' plan' *s* pianta

floor' show' *s* spettacolo di caffè concerto

floor'walk'er *s* direttore *m* di sezione

floor' wax' *s* cera da pavimenti

flop [flɑp] *s* (coll) fiasco || *v* (*pret & pp* **flopped; ger flopping**) *tr* lasciar cadere; sbattere || *intr* lasciarsi cadere; (coll) fare fiasco; **to flop over** (*to change sides*) cambiare casacca

flora [ˈflorə] *s* flora

floral [ˈflorəl] *adj* floreale

Florence [ˈflorəns] *or* [ˈflɑrəns] *s* Firenze *f*

Florentine [ˈflɑrən ˌtin] *or* [ˈflorən ˌtin] *adj & s* fiorentino

florescence [floˈrɛsəns] *s* inflorescenza

florid [ˈflorɪd] *or* [ˈflɑrɪd] *adj* florido

florist [ˈflorɪst] *s* fiorista *mf*, fioraio

floss [flɔs] *or* [flɑs] *s* ianugine *f*; (*of corn*) barba

floss·y [ˈflɔsi] *or* [ˈflɑsi] *adj* (**-ier; -iest**) serico; (*downy*) lanuginoso; (coll) vistoso

flotsam [ˈflɑtsəm] *s* relitti gettati a mare

flot'sam and jet'sam *s* relitti *mpl* di naufragio; (*trifles*) cianfrusaglie *fpl*; gentaglia, vagabondi *mpl*

flounce [flaʊns] *s* balza, falda, falpalà *m* || *tr* ornare di falpalà || *intr*—**to flounce out** andarsene irosamente

flounder [ˈflaʊndər] *s* (ichth) passera || *intr* dibattersi

flour [flaʊr] *adj* farinoso || *s* farina || *tr* infarinare

flourish [ˈflʌrɪʃ] *s* (*with the sword*) mulinello; (*with the pen*) ghirigoro; (*as part of signature*) svolazzo; (mus) fioritura || *tr* (*one's sword*) roteare || *intr* rifiorire, prosperare

flourishing ['flʌrɪ/ɪŋ] *adj* prosperoso

flour' mill' *s* mulino per grano

floury ['flauri] *adj* farinoso; infarinato

flout [flaut] *tr* burlarsi di || *intr* burlare, motteggiare

flow [flo] *s* flusso; (*of a river*) regime *m* || *intr* fluire; (*said of tide*) montare; (*said of hair in the air*) ondeggiare; **to flow into** gettarsi in, sfociare in; **to flow over** traboccare; **to flow with** abbondare di

flower ['flau·ər] *s* fiore *m* || *tr* infiorare || *intr* fiorire

flow'er bed' *s* aiola fiorita

flow'er gar'den *s* giardino

flow'er girl' *s* fioraia; (*at a wedding*) damigella d'onore

flow'er·pot' *s* vaso da fiori

flow'er shop' *s* negozio di fiori

flow'er show' *s* esposizione di fiori

flow'er·stand' *s* portafiori *m*

flowery ['flau·əri] *adj* fiorito

flowing ['flo·ɪŋ] *adj* (*water*) corrente; (*language*) scorrevole; (*e.g., hair*) fluente; (*e.g., lines of a dress*) filante

flu [flu] *s* influenza

fluctuate ['flʌktʃu‚et] *intr* fluttuare, ondeggiare; (*said of prices*) oscillare

flue [flu] *s* gola, fumaiolo

fluency ['flu·ənsɪ] *s* facilità *f* di parola

fluent ['flu·ənt] *adj* (*speaker*) facondo; (*style*) fluido

fluently ['flu·əntli] *adv* correntemente

fluff [flʌf] *s* lanugine *f*; vaporosità *f*; (*of an actor*) papera || *tr* sprimacciare || *intr* sprimacciarsi; (coll) impaperarsi

fluff·y ['flʌfi] *adj* (**-ier; -iest**) lanuginoso; vaporoso

fluid ['flu·ɪd] *adj & s* fluido

flu'id drive' *s* trasmissione idraulica

fluidity [flu'ɪdɪtɪ] *s* fluidità *f*

fluke [fluk] *s* (*of anchor*) marra, dente *m*; (*in billiards*) colpo fortunato; (ichth) passera

flume [flum] *s* gora; condotta forzata

flunk [flʌŋk] *s* (coll) bocciatura || *tr* (coll) bocciare; (*a course*) (coll) farsi bocciare in || *intr* (coll) fare fiasco; **to flunk out** (coll) farsi bocciare

flunk·y ['flʌŋki] *s* (**-ies**) valletto; parassita *m*

fluor ['flu·ɔr] *s* fluorite *f*

fluorescence [‚flu·ə'rɛsəns] *s* fluorescenza

fluorescent [‚flu·ə'rɛsənt] *adj* fluorescente

fluoridation [‚flu·ərɪ'deʃən] *s* fluorizzazione

fluoride ['flu·ə‚raɪd] *s* fluoruro

fluorine ['flu·ə‚rin] *s* fluoro

fluoroscope ['flu·ərə‚skop] *s* schermo fluorescente

fluorspar ['flu·er‚spɑr] *s* spatofluore *m*

flur·ry ['flʌri] *s* (**-ries**) agitazione; (*of wind*) raffica; (*of rain*) acquazzone *m*; (*of snow*) turbine *m* || *v* (*pret & pp* **-ried**) *tr* agitare

flush [flʌʃ] *adj* livellato; contiguo; prospero, ben provvisto; abbondante; vigoroso; (*full to overflowing*) rigurgitante; arrossito; **flush with** allo stesso livello che || *s* (*of water*) flusso improvviso; (*in the cheeks*) caldana, scalmana; (*of spring*) germogliare *m*; (*of joy*) ebbrezza; (*of youth*) rigoglio; (*in poker*) colore *m* || *adv* rasente, raso || *tr* (*to cause to blush*) far arrossire; lavare con un getto d'acqua; (*e.g., a rabbit*) snidare || *intr* essere accaldato; (*to blush*) arrossire; (*to gush*) zampillare

flush' tank' *s* sciacquone *m*

flush' toi'let *s* gabinetto a sciacquone

fluster ['flʌstər] *s* nervosismo, eccitazione || *tr* innervosire, eccitare

flute [flut] *s* (*of a column*) scanalatura; (mus) flauto || *tr* scanalare

flutist ['flutɪst] *s* flautista *mf*

flutter ['flʌtər] *s* svolazzo; agitazione; sensazione || *intr* frullare; svolazzare; agitarsi; (*said of the heart*) palpitare; (*said of the heartbeat*) essere irregolare

flux [flʌks] *s* (*flow*) flusso; (*for fusing metals*) fondente *m*

fly [flaɪ] *s* (*flies*) mosca; (*of trousers*) finta; (*for fishing*) mosca artificiale || *v* (*pret* **flew** [flu]; *pp* **flown** [flon]) *tr* (*an airplane*) pilotare, far volare; trasportare a volo; (*e.g., an ocean*) trasvolare; (*a flag*) battere || *intr* volare; fugare, scappare; (*said of a flag*) ondeggiare; **to fly away** involarsi; **to fly into a rage** andare in eccessi; **to fly off** volare via; scappare; **to fly over** trasvolare; **to fly shut** chiudersi improvvisamente

fly'blow' *s* uovo di mosca

fly'-by-night' *adj* poco raccomandabile; di breve durata

fly'catch'er *s* (orn) pigliamosche *m*

flyer ['flaɪ·ər] *s* var of **flier**

fly'-fish' *intr* pescare con le mosche artificiali

flying ['flaɪ·ɪŋ] *adj* volante; rapido; **in fuga**; (*start*) lanciato || *s* volo

fly'ing boat' *s* idrovolante *m* a scafo centrale

fly'ing but'tress *s* contrafforte *m*

fly'ing col'ors *spl* successo; **with flying colors** a bandiere spiegate

fly'ing field' *s* campo d'aviazione

fly'ing sau'cer *s* disco volante

fly'ing sick'ness *s* male *m* d'aria

fly'ing squad' *s* squadra mobile

fly'ing time' *s* ore *fpl* di volo

fly'leaf' *s* (**-leaves'**) (bb) guardia

fly' net' *s* (*for a bed*) moschettiera; (*for a horse*) scacciamosche *m*

fly'pa'per *s* carta moschicida

fly'speck' *s* macchia di mosca; macchiolina

fly' swat'ter ['swɑtər] *s* scacciamosche *m*

fly'trap' *s* pigliamosche *m*

fly'wheel' *s* volano

foal [fol] *s* puledro || *intr* (*said of a mare*) figliare

foam [fom] *s* schiuma || *intr* schiumare

foam' rub'ber *s* gommapiuma

foam·y ['fomɪ] *adj* (-ier; -iest) spumoso, schiumeggiante

fob [fɑb] *s* taschino per l'orologio; (*chain*) catenina per l'orologio ‖ *v* (*pret & pp* **fobbed**) *ger* **fobbing**) *tr*— **to fob off s.th on s.o.** rifilare qlco a qlcu

f.o.b. or **F.O.B.** [,ef ,o 'bi] *adv* (letter-word) (**free on board**) franco

focal ['fokəl] *adj* focale

fo·cus ['fokəs] *s* (-**cuses** or -**ci** [saɪ]) fuoco; (*of a disease*) focolaio ‖ *v* (*pret & pp* -**cused** or -**cussed**; *ger* -**cusing** or -**cussing**) *tr* mettere a fuoco; (*attention*) concentrare ‖ *intr* convergere

fodder ['fɑdər] *s* foraggio

foe [fo] *s* nemico

fog [fɑg] or [fɔg] *s* nebbia; (phot) velo ‖ *v* (*pret & pp* **fogged**) *ger* **fogging**) *tr* annebbiare; (phot) velare ‖ *intr* annebbiarsi; (phot) velarsi

fog' bank' *s* banco di nebbia

fog'bound' *adj* avvolto nella nebbia

fog·gy ['fɑgɪ] or ['fɔgɪ] *adj* (-gier; -giest) annebbiato; nebbioso; (*idea*) vago; (phot) velato; **it is foggy** fa nebbia

fog'horn' *s* sirena da nebbia

foible ['fɔɪbəl] *s* debolezza, debole *m*

foil [fɔɪl] *s* (*thin sheet of metal*) foglia; (*of mirror*) argentatura; contrasto, risalto; (*sword*) fioretto ‖ *tr* sventare; (*a mirror*) argentare

foist [fɔɪst] *tr*— **to foist s.th on s.o.** rifilare qlco a qlcu

fold [fold] *s* piega; drappeggio; (*for sheep*) ovile *m*; (*of sheep; of the faithful*) gregge *m*; (geol) corrugamento ‖ *tr* piegare; (*the arms*) incrociare; **to fold up** ripiegare ‖ *intr* piegarsi; **to fold up** (coll) fare fallimento

folder ['foldər] *s* (*pamphlet*) pieghevole *m*; (*cover*) portacarte *m*

folding ['foldɪŋ] *adj* pieghevole

fold'ing cam'era *s* macchina fotografica a soffietto

fold'ing chair' *s* sedia pieghevole

fold'ing cot' *s* branda

fold'ing door' *s* porta a libro

fold'ing seat' *s* strapuntino

foliage ['folɪ·ɪdʒ] *s* fogliame *m*

foli·o ['folɪ ,o] *adj* in-folio ‖ *s* (-os) foglio; (*book*) in-folio ‖ *tr* numerare

folk [fok] *adj* popolare ‖ *s* (**folk** or **folks**) gente *f*; **your folks** i Suoi

folk'lore' *s* folclore *m*

folk' mu'sic *s* musica folcloristica

folk' song' *s* canzone *f* tradizionale

folk·sy ['foksɪ] *adj* (-sier; -siest) socievole; alla buona, alla mano

folk'ways' *spl* costumi *mpl* tradizionali

follicle ['fɑlɪkəl] *s* follicolo

follow ['fɑlo] *tr* seguire; (*to keep up with*) interessarsi di; **to follow suit** seguire l'esempio; (cards) rispondere al colore ‖ *intr* seguire; derivare; **as follows** come segue; **it follows** ne risulta

follower ['fɑlo·ər] *s* seguace *m*; discepolo; partigiano

following ['fɑlo·ɪŋ] *adj* susseguente ‖ *s* seguito; aderenti *mpl*

fol'low-up' *adj* susseguente; ricordativo; da continuarsi ‖ *s* prosecuzione; lettera ricordativa

fol·ly ['fɑlɪ] *s* (-lies) follia; **follies** rivista di varietà

foment [fo'ment] *tr* fomentare

fond [fɑnd] *adj* appassionato; (*of food*) ghiotto; **to become fond of** appassionarsi di

fondle ['fɑndəl] *tr* accarezzare, vezzeggiare

fondness ['fɑndnɪs] *s* tenerezza; passione

font [fɑnt] *s* acquasantiera, pila; fonte *f* battesimale; (typ) fondita

food [fud] *adj* alimentare ‖ *s* cibo, vitto; (*for animals*) mangiare *m*; **food for thought** materia di che pensare

food' store' *s* negozio di commestibili

food'stuffs' *spl* commestibili *mpl*

fool [ful] *s* scemo, sciocco; (*jester*) buffone *m*; (*person imposed on*) vittima, zimbello; **to make a fool of** beffarsi di; **to play the fool** fare lo stupido ‖ *tr* infinocchiare, ingannare; **to fool away** sprecare ‖ *intr* giocare, fare per gioco; **to fool around** perdere il proprio tempo; **to fool with** giocherellare con

fooler·y ['fulərɪ] *s* (-ies) pazzia, buffonata

fool'har'dy ['ful,hɑrdɪ] *adj* (-dier; -diest) temerario

fooling ['fulɪŋ] *s* scherzo; **no fooling** senza scherzi, parlando sul serio

foolish ['fulɪʃ] *adj* sciocco; matto

fool'proof' *adj* a tutta prova; infallibile

fools'cap' *s* berretto a sonagli; carta formato protocollo

fool's' er'rand *s* impresa inutile

fool's' par'adise *s* felicità immaginaria

foot [fut] *s* (**feet** [fit]) piede *m*; (*of an animal*) zampa; (*of horse*) zoccolo; **to drag one's feet** procedere a passo di lumaca; **to put one's best foot forward** fare del proprio meglio; **to put one's foot down** farsi valere, imporsi; **to put one's foot in it** (coll) fare una topica; **to stand on one's own two feet** agire indipendentemente; **to tread under foot** calcare ‖ *tr* (*the bill*) pagare; **to foot it** andare a piedi; ballare

footage ['futɪdʒ] *s* distanza or lunghezza in piedi; (*of film measured in meters*) metraggio

foot'-and-mouth' disease' *s* (vet) afta epizootica

foot'ball' *s* (*ball*) pallone *m*; (*game*) pallovale *f*; (*soccer*) calcio, football *m*

foot'board' *s* (*support for foot*) predellino; (*of bed*) spalliera

foot' brake' *s* freno a pedale

foot'bridge' *s* passerella, ponte riservato ai pedoni

foot'fall' *s* passo

foot'hill' *s* collina ai piedi di una montagna

foot'hold' s stabilità f; **to gain a foothold** prender piede

footing ['futɪŋ] s piede m, e.g., **he lost his footing** perse piede; **on a friendly footing** in relazioni amichevoli; **on an equal footing** su un piede di parità; **on a war footing** su un piede di guerra

foot'lights' spl luci fpl della ribalta; (fig) ribalta, scena

foot'loose' adj completamente libero

foot'man s (-men) staffiere m

foot'mark' s orma

foot'note' s rimando, rinvio

foot'path' s sentiero

foot'print' s orma, pesta

foot' race' s corsa podistica

foot'rest' s pedana

foot' rule' s regolo di un piede

foot' soldier' s fante m, fantaccino

foot'sore' adj coi piedi stanchi

foot'step' s passo; **to follow in the footsteps of** seguire le orme di

foot'stone' s pietra tombale a piè di un sepolcro; (archit) pietra di sostegno

foot'stool' s sgabello

foot' warm'er s scaldino

foot'wear' s calzature fpl

foot'work' s allenamento delle gambe; (fig) manovra delicata

foot'worn' adj (road) battuto; (person) spedato

foozle ['fuzəl] s schiappinata || tr & intr mancare completamente

fop [fɑp] s bellimbusto, gagà m

for [fɔr] prep per; malgrado, e.g., **for all his wealth** malgrado tutta la sua ricchezza; come, e.g., **he uses his house for an office** adopera la casa come ufficio; di, e.g., **time for bed** ora di andare a letto; da, e.g., **he has been here for three days** è qui da tre giorni; per amor di; **to go for a walk** andare a fare una passeggiata || conj perchè, poichè

forage ['fɑrɪdʒ] or ['fɔrɪdʒ] s foraggero || s foraggio || tr foraggiare || intr andare in cerca di foraggio

foray ['fɔre] or ['fɔre] s razzia, scorreria || intr razziare

for·bear' ['bɛr] v (pret -bore ['bor]; pp -borne ['born]) tr astenersi da || intr essere longanime

forbearance [fɔr'bɛrəns] s longanimità f, tolleranza; astensione

for·bid' [fɔr'bɪd] v (pret -bade ['bæd] or -bad ['bæd]; pp -bidden ['bɪdən]; ger -bidding) tr proibire, vietare || intr—**God forbid!** Dío ci scampi!

forbidding [fɔr'bɪdɪŋ] adj severo, sinistro

force [fɔrs] s forza; (staff of workers) forza, personale m; (phys) forza; **by force of** a forza di; **by main force** con tutte le sue forze; **in force** vigente; in gran numero; **to join forces** allearsi || tr forzare; obbligare; **to force back** respingere; **to force open** forzare; **to force s.th on s.o.** obbligare qlcu a accettare qlco

forced [fɔrst] adj forzato; studiato

forced' air' s aria sotto pressione

forced' draft' s tiraggio forzato

forced' land'ing s atterraggio forzato

forced' march' s marcia forzata

forceful ['fɔrsfəl] adj vigoroso, energico

for·ceps ['fɔrsəps] s (-ceps or -cipes [sɪ ,piz]) (dent, surg) pinze fpl; (obstet) forcipe m

force' pump' s pompa premente

forcible ['fɔrsɪbəl] adj impetuoso, energico; efficace

ford [ford] s guado || tr guadare

fore [for] adj davanti; (naut) prodiero || s davanti m; (naut) prua; **to the fore** alla ribalta; d'attualità || adv prima; (naut) a proravia || interj attenzione!

fore' and aft' adv a poppa e a prua

fore'arm' s avambraccio || **fore·arm'** tr premunire; prevenire

fore'bears' spl antenati mpl

forebode [for'bod] tr (to portend) preannunziare; (to have a presentiment of) presentire

foreboding [for'bodɪŋ] s preannunzio; presentimento

fore'cast' s pronostico || v (pret & pp -cast or -casted) tr pronosticare

forecastle ['foksəl], ['fɔr,kæsəl] or ['fɔr,kɑsəl] s castello, pozzetto

fore·close' tr escludere, precludere; (a mortgage) (law) precludere il riscatto di

fore·doom' tr condannare all'insuccesso

fore' edge' s (bb) taglio

fore'fa'ther s antenato

fore'fin'ger s dito indice

fore'front' s—**in the forefront** all'avanguardia

fore·go' v (pret -went'; pp -gone') tr & intr precedere

fore·go'ing adj precedente, anteriore

fore'gone' conclu'sion s conclusione inevitabile; decisione già scontata

fore'ground' s primo piano

forehanded ['for,hændɪd] adj previdente; (thrifty) risparmiatore

forehead ['fɑrɪd] or ['fɔrɪd] s fronte f

foreign ['fɑrɪn] or ['fɔrɪn] adj straniero; (product; affairs) estero; **foreign to** estraneo a

for'eign affairs' spl affari esteri

for'eign-born' adj nato all'estero

foreigner ['fɑrɪnər] or ['fɔrɪnər] s straniero, forestiero

for'eign exchange' s divise fpl; (money) valuta

for'eign min'ister s ministro degli affari esteri

for'eign of'fice s ministero degli affari esteri

for'eign serv'ice s servizio diplomatico e consolare; (Brit) servizio militare in paesi d'oltremare

fore'leg' s zampa anteriore

fore'lock' s ciuffo sulla fronte; **to take time by the forelock** acchiappare l'occasione

fore'man s (-men) sorvegliante m, capomastro; presidente m dei giurati

foremast ['formast], ['fɔr,mæst] or ['fɔr,mɑst] s trinchetto

foremost ['fɔr,most] adj primo, principale, più importante

fore'noon' adj mattinale || s mattina
fore'part' s parte f anteriore; prima parte
fore'paw' s zampa anteriore
fore'quar'ter s quarto anteriore
fore'run'ner s precursore m, predecessore m, foriero
fore·sail ['fɔrsəl] or ['fɔr‚sel] s trinchetto
fore·see' v (pret -saw'; pp -seen') tr prevedere
foreseeable [for'si·əbəl] adj prevedibile
fore·shad'ow tr presagire
fore·short'en tr scorciare
fore'sight' s (prudence) previdenza; (foreknowledge) previsione
fore'sight'ed adj previdente
fore'skin' s prepuzio
forest ['fɑrɪst] or ['fɔrɪst] adj forestale || s foresta, bosco
fore·stall' tr prevenire; anticipare; (to buy up) accaparrare
for'est rang'er ['rendʒər] s guardaboschi m, guardia forestale
forestry ['fɑrɪstri] or ['fɔrɪstri] s selvicoltura
fore'taste' s pregustazione || tr pregustare
fore·tell' v (pret & pp -told') tr predire, presagire, preannunziare
fore'thought' s premeditazione; previdenza
forever [fɔr'ɛvər] adv per sempre; continuamente
fore·warn' tr prevenire, preavvertire
fore'word' s avvertenza, prefazione
forfeit ['fɔrfɪt] adj perduto || s perdita, confisca; multa; (article deposited) pegno; **forfeits** (game) pegni mpl || tr decadere da
forfeiture ['fɔrfɪt/ər] s perdita di un pegno
forgather [fɔr'gæðər] intr riunirsi; incontrarsi
forge [fɔrdʒ] s fucina, forgia || tr forgiare; (a lie) inventare; (e.g., handwriting) falsificare || intr forgiare; commettere un falso; **to forge ahead** farsi strada
forger·y ['fɔrdʒəri] s (-ies) falsificazione, falso, contraffazione
for·get [fɔr'gɛt] v (pret -got ['gɑt]; pp -got or -gotten ['gɑtən]) tr dimenticare; **forget it!** non si preoccupi!; **to forget oneself** venir meno alla propria dignità; **to forget to** passare di mente a (qlcu) di, e.g., **he forgot to turn off the lights** gli è passato di mente di spegnere la luce
forgetful [fɔr'gɛtfəl] adj (apt to forget) smemorato; (neglectful) dimentico, immemore
forgetfulness [fɔr'gɛtfəlnɪs] s (inability to recall) smemorataggine f; (neglectfulness) dimenticanza
for·get'-me-not' s nontiscordardimé m
forgivable [fɔr'gɪvəbəl] adj perdonabile
for·give [fɔr'gɪv] v (pret -gave'; pp -giv'en) tr perdonare
forgiveness [fɔr'gɪvnɪs] s perdono
forgiving [fɔr'gɪvɪŋ] adj clemente
for·go [fɔr'go] v (pret -went; pp -gone) tr rinunciare (with dat)

fork [fɔrk] s (pitchfork) forca, forcone m; (of a bicycle) forcella; (for eating) forchetta; (of a tree or road) biforcazione, diramazione || tr muovere col forcone; inforcare; **to fork out** (slang) cacciar fuori || intr biforcarsi, diramarsi
forked [fɔrkt] adj biforcuto
fork'-lift truck' s carrello elevatore a forca
forlorn [fɔr'lɔrn] adj abbandonato; disperato; miserabile
forlorn' hope' s impresa disperata
form [fɔrm] s forma; (paper to be filled out) formulario; (construction to give shape to cement) cassaforma || tr formare || intr formarsi
formal ['fɔrməl] adj formale; di gala, da sera, da etichetta
for'mal attire' s vestito da cerimonia
for'mal call' s visita di prammatica
formali·ty [fɔr'mælɪti] s (-ties) formalità f; (excessive adherence to rules) formalismo
for'mal par'ty s ricevimento di gala
for'mal speech' s discorso ufficiale
format ['fɔrmæt] s formato
formation [fɔr'me/ən] s formazione
former ['fɔrmər] adj (preceding) anteriore; (long past) passato, antico; (having once been) già, ex; (of two) primo; **the former** quello
formerly ['fɔrmərli] adv già, prima, in tempi passati
form'fit'ting adj aderente al corpo
formidable ['fɔrmɪdəbəl] adj formidabile
formless ['fɔrmlɪs] adj informe
form' let'ter s lettera a formulario, stampato
formu·la ['fɔrmjələ] s (-las or -lae [‚li]) formula
formulate ['fɔrmjə‚let] tr formulare
for·sake [fɔr'sek] v (pret -sook ['suk]; pp -saken ['sekən]) tr abbandonare
fort [fɔrt] s forte m, fortezza
forte [fɔrt] s forte m
forth [fɔrθ] adv avanti; **and so forth** e così via; **from this day forth** da oggi in poi; **to go forth** uscire
forth'com'ing adj prossimo; immediatamente disponibile
forth'right' adj diretto || adv direttamente; senza ambagi; immediatamente
forth'with' adv immediatamente
fortieth ['fɔrtɪ·ɪθ] adj, s & pron quarantesimo
fortification [‚fɔrtɪfɪ'ke/ən] s fortificazione
forti·fy ['fɔrtɪ‚faɪ] v (pret & pp -fied) tr fortificare; aumentare il livello alcolico di
fortitude ['fɔrtɪ‚tjud] or ['fɔrtɪ‚tud] s fortezza, fermezza
fortnight ['fɔrtnaɪt] or ['fɔrtnɪt] s quindicina, due settimane
fortress ['fɔrtrɪs] s fortezza, forte m
fortuitous [fɔr'tju·ɪtəs] or [fɔr'tu·ɪtəs] adj fortuito, occasionale
fortunate ['fɔrt/ənɪt] adj fortunato
fortune ['fɔrt/ən] s fortuna; **to make a fortune** farsi un patrimonio; **to tell**

s.o. his fortune leggere il futuro a qlcu

for'tune hunt'er *s* cacciatore *m* di dote

for'tune-tel'ler *s* indovino, cartomante *mf*

for·ty ['fɔrtɪ] *adj & pron* quaranta ‖ *s* (-ties) quaranta *m*; **the forties** gli anni quaranta

fo·rum ['forəm] *s* (-rums or -ra [rə]) foro

forward ['fɔrwərd] *adj* avanzato; precoce; impertinente ‖ *s* (soccer) avanti *m* ‖ *adv* avanti; **to bring forward** mettere in luce; riportare; **to come forward** avanzare; **to look forward to** anticipare il piacere di ‖ *tr* inoltrare, trasmettere; promuovere

fossil ['fɑsɪl] *adj & s* fossile *m*

foster ['fɑstər] or ['fɔstər] *adj* adottivo; di latte ‖ *tr* allevare; promuovere

fos'ter home' *s* famiglia adottiva

foul [faul] *adj* sporco; (air) viziato; (wind) contrario; (weather; breath) cattivo; (baseball) fuori linea di gioco ‖ *s* (of boats) urto, collisione; (baseball) palla colpita fuori linea di gioco; (boxing) colpo basso; (sports) fallo ‖ *adv* slealmente; (baseball) fuori linea di gioco; **to fall foul of** entrare in collisione con; urtarsi con; **to run foul of** avere una controversia con ‖ *tr* sporcare; otturare; (baseball) colpire fuori linea di gioco ‖ *intr* (said of two boats) entrare in collisione; (said, e.g., of a rope) imbrogliarsi

foul-mouthed ['faul'mauðd] or ['faul-'mauθt] *adj* sboccato, osceno

foul' play' *s* reato; (sports) gioco sleale

found [faund] *tr* fondare; (to melt, to cast) fondere

foundation [faun'deʃən] *s* fondazione; (endowment) dotazione; (charitable) patronato; (masonry support) platea, fondamenta *fpl*; (make-up) fondo tinta; (fig) fondatezza

founder ['faundər] *s* fondatore *m*; (of family) capostipite *m*; (of metals) fonditore *m* ‖ *intr* (said of a ship) affondare; (said of a horse) azzopparsi; (to fail) fare fiasco

foundling ['faundlɪŋ] *s* trovatello

found'ling hos'pital *s* brefotrofio

found·ry ['faundrɪ] *s* (-ries) fonderia

found'ry·man [-mən] *s* fonditore *m*

fount [faunt] *s* fonte *f*

fountain ['fauntən] *s* fonte *f*, fontana; (of knowledge) pozzo

foun'tain-head' *s* sorgente *f*

foun'tain pen' *s* penna stilografica

foun'tain syringe' *s* clistere *m* a pera

four [for] *adj & pron* quattro ‖ *s* quattro; **four o'clock** le quattro; **on all fours** gattoni, carponi

four'-cy'cle *adj* a quattro tempi

four'-cyl'inder *adj* a quattro cilindri

four'-flush' *intr* (coll) millantarsi

fourflusher ['for‚flʌʃər] *s* (coll) millantatore *m*

four-footed ['for'futɪd] *adj* quadrupede

four' hun'dred *adj, s & pron* quattro-

cento ‖ **the Four Hundred** l'alta società

four'-in-hand' *s* cravatta a cappio; tiro a quattro

four'-lane' *adj* a quattro corsie

four'-leaf clo'ver *s* quadrifoglio

four-legged ['for'legɪd] or ['for'legd] *adj* a quattro zampe; (schooner) (coll) a quattro alberi

four'-letter word' *s* parolaccia di quattro lettere

four'-mo'tor plane' *s* quadrimotore *m*

four'-o'clock' *s* (bot) bella di notte

four' of a kind' *s* (cards) poker *m*

four'post'er *s* letto a baldacchino

four'score' *adj* ottanta

foursome ['forsəm] *s* gruppo di quattro giocatori

fourteen ['for'tin] *adj, s & pron* quattordici *m*

fourteenth ['for'tinθ] *adj, s & pron* quattordicesimo ‖ *s* (in dates) quattordici *m*

fourth [forθ] *adj, s & pron* quarto ‖ *s* (in dates) quattro

fourth' estate' *s* quarto potere

four'-way' *adj* a quattro orifizi; **fra quattro persone**; quadruplice

fowl [faul] *s* pollo ‖ *intr* uccellare

fowl'ing piece' *s* fucile *m* da caccia

fox [fɑks] *s* volpe *f* ‖ *tr* (coll) ingannare

fox'glove' *s* digitale *f*

fox'hole' *s* buca ricovero

fox'hound' *s* segugio

fox' hunt' *s* caccia alla volpe

fox' ter'rier *s* fox-terrier *m*

fox'-trot' *s* (of a horse) piccolo trotto; (dance) fox-trot *m*

fox·y ['fɑksɪ] *adj* (-ier; -iest) volpino, astuto

foyer ['fɔɪ·ər] *s* (of a private house) ingresso, vestibolo; (theat) ridotto

fracas ['frekəs] *s* lite *f*, tumulto

fraction ['frækʃən] *s* frazione; frammento

fractional ['frækʃənəl] *adj* frazionario; insignificante

fractious ['frækʃəs] *adj* litigioso, permaloso; indisciplinato

fracture ['fræktʃər] *s* frattura ‖ *tr* fratturare; (e.g., an arm) fratturarsi, rompersi ‖ *intr* fratturarsi

fragile ['frædʒɪl] *adj* fragile

fragment ['frægmənt] *s* frammento; (e.g., of a movie) spezzone *m* ‖ *tr* frammentare, spezzare

fragmenta'tion bomb' [‚frægmən'te-ʃən] *s* bomba dirompente

fragrant ['fregrənt] *adj* fragrante

frail [frel] *adj* (not robust) gracile; (easily broken) fragile; (morally weak) debole ‖ *s* canestro di giunco

frail·ty ['freltɪ] *s* (-ties) fragilità *f*; (of a person) debolezza

frame [frem] *s* (of picture) cornice *f*; (of glasses) montatura; (structure) ossatura; (of a building) ingabbiatura, impalcatura; (for embroidering) telaio; (of a window) intelaiatura; (of mind) stato; (of government) sistema *m*; (mov) inquadratura; (phot) fotogramma *m*; (aer) ordinata;

(naut) costa ‖ *tr* (*to put in a frame*) incorniciare; montare; costruire; inventare; esprimere; (slang) architettare un' accusa contro

frame' house' *s* casa con l'ossatura di legno

frame'-up' *s* (slang) complotto per incriminare un innocente

frame'work' *s* intelaiatura, impalcatura; palificazione

franc [fræŋk] *s* franco

France [fræns] or [frɑns] *s* la Francia

Frances ['frænsɪs] or ['frɑnsɪs] *s* Francesca

franchise ['fræntʃaɪz] *s* diritto di voto; concessione; (*privilege*) franchigia

Francis ['frænsɪs] or ['frɑnsɪs] *s* Francesco

Franciscan [fræn'sɪskən] *adj* & *s* francescano

frank [fræŋk] *adj* sincero, schietto ‖ *s* affrancatura postale; lettera affrancata; (*franking privilege*) franchigia postale ‖ *tr* affrancare ‖ **Frank** *s* (*member of Frankish tribe*) franco; (*masculine name*) Franco

frankfurter ['fræŋkfərtər] *s* salsiccia di Francoforte, Frankfurter *m*

frankincense ['fræŋkɪn͵sens] *s* olibano

Frankish ['fræŋkɪʃ] *adj* & *s* franco

frankness ['fræŋknɪs] *s* franchezza

frantic ['fræntɪk] *adj* frenetico

frappé [fræ'pe] *adj* & *s* frappé *m*

frat [fræt] *s* (slang) associazione di studenti

fraternal [frə'tʌrnəl] *adj* fraterno

fraterni·ty [frə'tʌrnɪti] *s* (**-ties**) (*brotherliness*) fraternità *f*; sodalizio; (eccl) confraternita; (U.S.A.) associazione di studenti

fraternize ['frætər͵naɪz] *intr* fraternizzare

fraud [frɔd] *s* truffa, frode *f*; (*person*) (coll) truffatore *m*

fraudulent ['frɔdjələnt] *adj* fraudolento; (*conversion*) indebito

fraught [frɔt] *adj*—**fraught with** carico di, gravido di

fray [fre] *s* zuffa, rissa, lotta ‖ *intr* sfilacciarsi, logorarsi

freak [frik] *s* (*sudden fancy*) capriccio, ticchio; (*person, animal*) fenomeno

freakish ['frikɪʃ] *adj* capriccioso; strano, grottesco

freckle ['frekəl] *s* lentiggine *f*, efelide *f*

freckle-faced ['frekəl͵fest] *adj* lentigginoso

freckly ['frekli] *adj* lentigginoso

Frederick ['fredərɪk] *s* Federico

free [fri] *adj* (**freer** ['fri·ər]; **freest** ['fri·ɪst]) libero; gratis; franco; sciolto; esente; generoso; **to be free with** essere prodigo di; **to set free** liberare ‖ *adv* liberamente; in libertà; gratis ‖ *v* (*pret* & *pp* **freed** [frid]; *ger* **freeing** ['fri·ɪŋ]) *tr* liberare; (*from customs*) svincolare; esimere

freebooter ['fri͵butər] *s* pirata *m*

free'born' *adj* nato in libertà; proprio di un popolo libero

freedom ['fridəm] *s* libertà *f*

free'dom of speech' *s* libertà *f* di parola

free'dom of the press' *s* libertà *f* di stampa

free'dom of the seas' *s* libertà *f* di navigazione

free'dom of wor'ship *s* libertà religiosa

free' en'terprise *s* economia libera

free'-for-all' *s* rissa, tafferuglio

free' hand' *s* libertà assoluta

free'-hand' *adj* a mano libera

freehanded ['fri'hændɪd] *adj* liberale, generoso

free' lance' *s* giornalista *mf* pubblicista; scrittore *m* che lavora senza contratto; soldato di ventura

free'load'er ['fri͵lodər] *s* (coll) mangiatore *m* a sbafo

free'man *s* (**-men**) uomo libero; cittadino

Free'ma'son *s* frammassone *m*

Free'ma'sonry *s* frammassoneria

free' of charge' *adj* gratis, senza spese

free' port' *s* porto franco

free' serv'ice *s* manutenzione gratuita

free'-spo'ken *adj* franco, aperto

free'stone' *adj* spiccagnolo ‖ *s* pesca spicca

free'think'er *s* libero pensatore

free' thought' *s* libero pensiero

free' trade' *s* libero scambio

free'trad'er *s* liberoscambista *mf*

free'way' *s* autostrada

free' will' *s* libero arbitrio

freeze [friz] *s* gelo, gelata; (*e.g., of prices*) blocco ‖ *v* (*pret* **froze** [froz]; *pp* **frozen**) *tr* gelare; (*credits, rentals, etc.*) bloccare ‖ *intr* gelarsi; (*said of brakes*) inchiodarsi; morire assiderato; (*to become immobilized*) irrigidirsi

freeze'-dry' *v* (*pret* & *pp* **-dried'**) *tr* liofilizzare

freezer ['frizər] *s* congelatore *m*; (*for making ice cream*) sorbettiera

freight [fret] *s* carico; (*charge*) porto; (naut) nolo; **by freight** come carico mercantile; (rr) a piccola velocità ‖ *tr* spedire come carico

freight' car' *s* vagone *m* or carro merci

freighter ['fretər] *s* speditore *m*; nave *f* da carico

freight' plat'form *s* (rr) banchina adibita al traffico merci

freight' sta'tion *s* (rr) stazione merci

freight' train' *s* treno merci, merci *m*

freight' yard' *s* (rr) scalo merci

French [frentʃ] *adj* & *s* francese *m; the* **French** i francesi

French' bread' *s* pane *m* a bastone

French' chalk' *s* pietra da sarto

French' door' *s* porta a vetri

French' dress'ing *s* salsa verde con aceto

French' fried' pota'toes *spl* patate fritte affettate

French' horn' *s* (mus) corno

French' leave' *s*—**to take French leave** andarsene all'inglese, filare all'inglese

French'man *s* (**-men**) francese *m*

French' tel'ephone *s* microtelefono

French' toast' *s* pane dorato al salto

French' win'dow *s* portafinestra

French'wom'an *s* (**-wom'en**) francese *f*

frenzied ['frenzɪd] *adj* frenetico

fren·zy ['frenzɪ] *s* (-zies) frenesia

frequen·cy ['frikwənsɪ] *s* (-cies) frequenza

fre'quency modula'tion *s* modulazione di frequenza

frequent ['frikwənt] *adj* frequente || [frɪ'kwent] or ['frikwənt] *tr* frequentare, praticare

frequently ['frikwəntlɪ] *adv* frequentemente

fres·co ['fresko] *s* (-coes or -cos) affresco || *tr* affrescare

fresh [freʃ] *adj* fresco; (*water*) dolce; (*new*) nuovo; (*wind*) moderato; (*inexperienced*) novizio; (*cheeky*) (slang) sfacciato; **fresh in** (coll) appena arrivato; **fresh out** (coll) appena esaurito, di recente;

freshen ['freʃən] *tr* rinfrescare || *intr* rinfrescarsi

freshet ['freʃɪt] *s* piena, crescita

fresh'man *s* (-men) (*newcomer*) novizio; (educ) matricola

freshness ['freʃnɪs] *s* freschezza; (*of air*) frescura; (*cheek*) (slang) sfacciataggine *f*

fresh'-wa'ter *adj* d'acqua dolce; poco conosciuto; piccolo

fret [fret] *s* (*interlaced design*) fregio, greca; irritazione; (mus) tasto || *v* (*pret* & *pp* **fretted;** *ger* **fretting**) *tr* fregiare || *intr* fremere, trepidare, agitarsi

fretful ['fretfəl] *adj* irritabile, permaloso

fret'work' *s* greca

Freudianism ['frɔɪdɪ-ə,nɪzəm] *s* freudismo

friar ['fraɪ-ər] *s* frate *m*

friar·y ['fraɪ-ərɪ] *s* (-ies) convento di frati

fricassee [,frɪkə'si] *s* fricassea

friction ['frɪkʃən] *s* frizione; disaccordo, dissenso

fric'tion tape' *s* nastro isolante

Friday ['fraɪdɪ] *s* venerdì *m*

fried [fraɪd] *adj* fritto

fried' egg' *s* uovo al tegame, uovo occhio di manzo

friend [frend] *s* amico; **to be friends with** essere amico di; **to make friends** allacciare amicizie; **to make friends with** fare l'amicizia di

friend·ly ['frendlɪ] *adj* (-lier; -liest) amico, amichevole

friendship ['frendʃɪp] *s* amicizia

frieze [friz] *s* (archit) fregio

frigate ['frɪgɪt] *s* fregata

fright [fraɪt] *s* spavento; **to take fright at** spaventarsi di

frighten ['fraɪtən] *tr* intimorire, spaventare; **to frighten away** mettere in fuga, sgomentare || *intr* spaventarsi

frightful ['fraɪtfəl] *adj* spaventevole, orribile; (coll) enorme

frightfulness ['fraɪtfəlnɪs] *s* spavento; terrorismo

frigid ['frɪdʒɪd] *adj* freddo; (*zone*) glaciale

frigidity [frɪ'dʒɪdɪtɪ] *s* (fig) frigidezza; (pathol) frigidità *f*

frill [frɪl] *s* pieghettatura; (*of birds and other animals*) collarino; (*in dress, speech, etc.*) affettazione

fringe [frɪndʒ] *s* frangia; (*in dressmaking*) volantino; (*on curtains*) balza; **on the fringe of** all'orlo di || *tr* orlare

fringe' ben'efits *spl* assegni *mpl*, benefici *mpl* marginali

fripper·y ['frɪpərɪ] *s* (-ies) (*finery*) fronzoli *mpl*; ostentazione; (*trifles*) cianfrusaglie *fpl*

frisk [frɪsk] *tr* perquisire; (slang) derubare || *intr* fare capriole

frisk·y ['frɪskɪ] *adj* (-ier; -iest) gaio, vivace

fritter ['frɪtər] *s* frittella; frammento || *tr*—**to fritter away** sprecare

frivolous ['frɪvələs] *adj* frivolo

friz [frɪz] *s* (**frizzes**) ricciolo || *v* (*pret* & *pp* **frizzed;** *ger* **frizzing**) *tr* arricciare

frizzle ['frɪzəl] *s* ricciolo || *tr* arricciare || *intr* arricciarsi

friz·zly ['frɪzlɪ] *adj* (-zlier; -zliest) crespo, riccio

fro [fro] *adv*—**to and fro** avanti e indietro; **to go to and fro** andare e venire

frock [frɑk] *s* gabbano; (*smock*) grembiule *m*; blusa; (*of priest*) tonaca

frock' coat' *s* finanziera

frog [frɑg] or [frɔg] *s* rana; (*button and loop on a garment*) alamaro; (*in throat*) raschio

frog'man' *s* (-men') sommozzatore *m*, uomo rana

frol·ic ['frɑlɪk] *s* scherzo, monelleria || *v* (*pret* & *pp* **-icked;** *ger* **-icking**) *intr* scherzare, folleggiare

frolicsome ['frɑlɪksəm] *adj* scherzoso

from [frʌm], [frɑm] or [frəm] *prep* da; di, e.g., **I am from New York** sono di New York; da parte di; a, e.g., **to take s.th away from s.o.** portar via qlco a qlcu

front [frʌnt] *adj* frontale, anteriore; di fronte || *s* fronte *m* & *f*; (*of a building*) prospetto; (*of a book*) principio; (*of a shirt*) sparato; (*e.g., of wealth*) apparenza; (theat) boccascena *m*; (mil) fronte *m*; **in front of** dinanzi a; **to put on a front** (coll) fare ostentazione; **to put up a bold front** (coll) farsi coraggio || *tr* (*to face*) fronteggiare; (*to confront*) affrontare; (*to supply with a front*) coprire; servire da facciata a || *intr*—**to front on** dare su

frontage ['frʌntɪdʒ] *s* facciata, veduta; terreno di fronte alla casa

front' door' *s* porta d'entrata

front' drive' *s* (aut) trazione anteriore

frontier [frʌn'tɪr] *adj* limitrofo || *s* frontiera

fron'tiers'man *s* (-men) pioniere *m*

frontispiece ['frʌntɪs,pis] *s* (*of book*) pagina illustrata di fronte al frontispizio; (*of building*) facciata

front' mat'ter *s* (*of book*) parte *f* preliminare

front'-page' *tr* stampare in prima pagina

front' porch' *s* porticato

front' room' s stanza con vista sulla strada
front' row' s prima fila
front' seat' s posto in una delle file davanti; (aut) sedile m anteriore
front' steps' spl scalinata d'ingresso
front' view' s vista sulla strada
frost [frɔst] or [frɑst] s gelo, brina, gelata; (fig) freddezza; (slang) fiasco || tr agghiacciare; (with sugar) glassare; (glass) smerigliare
frost'bite' s congelamento
frost'ed glass' s vetro smerigliato
frosting ['frɔstɪŋ] or ['frɑstɪŋ] s glassatura; (of glass) smerigliatura
frost·y ['frɔstɪ] or ['frɑstɪ] adj (-ier; -iest) brinato; (hair) canuto; (fig) gelido
froth [frɔθ] or [frɑθ] s schiuma; (fig) frivolezza || intr schiumare; (at the mouth) avere la schiuma
froth·y ['frɔθɪ] or ['frɑθɪ] adj (-ier; -iest) spumoso; frivolo
froward ['frowərd] adj indocile
frown [fraun] s aggrottare m delle ciglia; (of disapproval) cipiglio || intr aggrottare le ciglia; **to frown at or on** disapprovare
frows·y or **frowz·y** ['frauzɪ] adj (-ier; -iest) sporco; puzzolente
fro'zen foods' ['frozən] spl cibi congelati; cibi surgelati
frugal ['frugəl] adj parsimonioso; (in food and drink) frugale
fruit [frut] adj (tree) fruttifero; (dish) da frutta || s (such as apple) frutto; (collectively) frutta, e.g., **I like fruit** mi piace la frutta; (fig) frutto
fruit' cake' s torta con noci e canditi
fruit' cup' s macedonia di frutta
fruit' dish' s fruttiera, portafrutta m
fruit' fly' s moscerino del vino
fruitful ['frutfəl] adj fruttuoso
fruition [fru'ɪʃən] s realizzazione; **to come to fruition** giungere a buon fine
fruit' jar' s vaso da frutta
fruit' juice' s sugo or spremuta di frutta
fruitless ['frutlɪs] adj infruttuoso
fruit' sal'ad s macedonia di frutta
fruit' stand' s bancarella da fruttivendolo
fruit' store' s negozio di frutta
frumpish ['frʌmpɪʃ] adj trasandato
frustrate ['frʌstret] tr frustrare
fry [fraɪ] s (fries) fritto || v (pret & pp fried) tr & intr friggere
fry'ing pan' s padella; **out of the frying pan into the fire** dalla padella nella brace
fudge [fʌdʒ] s dolce m di cioccolato
fuel ['fju·əl] s combustibile m; (fig) cibo || v (pret & pp fueled or fuelled; ger fueling or fuelling) tr rifornire di carburante || intr rifornirsi di carburante
fuel' cell' s cellula elettrogena
fu'el oil' s nafta, olio pesante
fu'el tank' s serbatoio del carburante
fugitive ['fjudʒɪtɪv] adj & s fuggiasco, fuggitivo
fugue [fjug] s (mus) fuga
ful·crum ['fʌlkrəm] s (-crums or -cra [krə]) fulcro

fulfill [ful'fɪl] tr (to carry out) eseguire; (an obligation) mantenere; (to bring to an end) completare
fulfillment [ful'fɪlmənt] s adempimento; realizzazione
full [ful] adj pieno; (speed) tutto; (garment) ampio; (voice) spiegato; (of food) sazio; (member) effettivo; **full of aches and pains** pieno d'acciacchi; **full of fun** divertentissimo; **full of play** pieno di vita || s pieno; colmo; **in full** per esteso, in pieno; **to the full** completamente || adv completamente; **full many (a)** moltissimi; **full well** perfettamente || tr follare
full-blooded ['ful'blʌdɪd] adj vigoroso; purosangue
full-blown ['ful'blon] adj completamente sbocciato; maturo
full-bodied ['ful'badɪd] adj forte, ricco
full' dress' s vestito da sera; (mil) tenuta di gala, alta uniforme
full-faced ['ful'fest] adj paffuto; (view) intero; (typ) grassetto
full-fledged ['ful'fledʒd] adj completamente sviluppato; vero, autentico
full-grown ['ful'gron] adj completamente sviluppato, adulto
full' house' s (theat) piena; (poker) full m
full'-length' adj a mezzo specchiera
full'-length mo'vie s lungometraggio
full' moon' s luna piena
full' name' s nome m e cognome m
full'-page' adj di tutta una pagina
full' pow'ers spl pieni poteri
full' sail' adv a vele spiegate
full'-scale' adj in grandezza naturale; completo
full-sized ['ful'saɪzd] adj in grandezza naturale
full' speed' adv a tutta velocità
full' stop' s fermata; (gram) punto
full' swing' s piena attività
full' tilt' adv a tutta forza
full'-time' adj a orario completo
fully ['fulɪ] or ['fulɪ] adv completamente, del tutto
fulsome ['fulsəm] or ['fʌlsəm] adj basso, volgare; nauseante
fumble ['fʌmbəl] tr (a ball) lasciar cadere || intr titubare; andare a tentoni; (in one's pocket) cercare alla cieca
fume [fjum] s fumo, vapore m, esalazione || tr affumicare || intr fumare, esalare fumo; (to show anger) irritarsi
fumigate ['fjumɪ‚get] tr fumigare
fumigation [‚fjumɪ'geʃən] s fumigazione
fun [fʌn] s divertimento, spasso; **to be fun** essere divertente; **to have fun** divertirsi; **to make fun of** prendersi gioco di
function ['fʌŋkʃən] s funzione || intr funzionare, marciare, camminare
functional ['fʌŋkʃənəl] adj funzionale
functionalism ['fʌŋkʃənəl‚ɪzəm] s funzionalismo
functionar·y ['fʌŋkʃə‚nerɪ] s (-ies) funzionario

fund [fʌnd] s fondo; (of knowledge) suppellettile f ‖ tr (debts) consolidare

fundamental [ˌfʌndə'mentəl] adj fondamentale ‖ s fondamento

fundamentalist [ˌfʌndə'mentəlɪst] adj & s scritturale m

funeral ['fjunərəl] adj funebre, funerario ‖ s funerale m, trasporto funebre; **it's not my funeral** (slang) non sono affari miei

fu'neral direc'tor s imprenditore m di pompe funebri

fu'neral home' or **par'lor** s impresa di pompe funebri

fu'neral serv'ice s ufficio dei defunti

funereal [fju'nɪrɪ·əl] adj funebre

fungous ['fʌŋgəs] adj fungoso

fungus ['fʌŋgəs] s (**funguses** or **fungi** ['fʌndʒaɪ]) fungo

funicular [fju'nɪkjələr] adj & s funicolare f

funk [fʌŋk] s (coll) paura; (coll) codardo; **in a funk** (coll) con una paura matta

fun·nel ['fʌnəl] s imbuto; (smokestack) fumaiolo; (for ventilation) manica a vento ‖ v (pret & pp -neled or -nelled; ger -neling or -nelling) tr incanalare

funnies ['fʌniz] spl pagine fpl fumetti

fun·ny ['fʌni] adj (-nier; -niest) comico, buffo; (coll) strano; **to strike as funny** parere strano or buffo a

fun'ny bone' s osso rabbioso (del gomito); **to strike s.o.'s funny bone** far ridere qlcu

fur [fʌr] s pelo; (garment) pelliccia; (on the tongue) patina

furbelow ['fʌrbəˌlo] s falpalà m

furbish ['fʌrbɪʃ] tr lustrare; mettere a nuovo; **to furbish up** rinfrescare

furious ['fjʊrɪ·əs] adj furioso

furl [fʌrl] tr (a flag) incazzottare; (naut) raccogliere, strangolare

fur-lined ['fʌrˌlaɪnd] adj foderato di pelliccia

furlong ['fʌrlɔŋ] or ['fʌrlɑŋ] s un ottavo di miglio terrestre

furlough ['fʌrlo] s licenza ‖ tr licenziare

furnace ['fʌrnɪs] s fornace f; (to heat a house) caldaia del calorifero

furnish ['fʌrnɪʃ] tr fornire; ammobiliare

furnishings ['fʌrnɪʃɪŋz] spl mobilia; (things to wear) accessori mpl da uomo

furniture ['fʌrnɪtʃər] s mobili mpl, mobilia; (naut) attrezzatura; **a piece of furniture** un mobile

fur'ni·ture deal'er s mobiliere m

furor ['fjʊrər] s furore m

furrier ['fʌrɪ·ər] s pellicciaio

furrier·y ['fʌrɪ·əri] s (-ies) pellicceria

furrow ['fʌro] s solco ‖ tr solcare

further ['fʌrðər] adj più lontano; ulteriore ‖ adv oltre; più; inoltre ‖ tr favorire, incoraggiare

furtherance ['fʌrðərəns] s avanzamento, incoraggiamento

furthermore ['fʌrðərˌmor] adv inoltre

furthest ['fʌrðɪst] adj (il) più lontano ‖ adv al massimo

furtive ['fʌrtɪv] adj furtivo

fu·ry ['fjʊri] s (-ries) furia

furze [fʌrz] s ginestra spinosa

fuse [fjuz] s (for igniting an explosive) miccia; (for detonating an explosive) spoletta; (elec) fusibile m; **to burn out a fuse** bruciare un fusibile ‖ tr fondere ‖ intr fondersi; (elec) saltare

fuse' box' s valvoliera

fuselage ['fjuzəˌlɪdʒ] or [ˌfjuzə'lɑʒ] s fusoliera

fusible ['fjuzɪbəl] adj fusibile

fusillade [ˌfjuzɪ'led] s fucileria; (fig) gragnola ‖ tr attaccare con fuoco di fucileria

fusion ['fjuʒən] s fusione

fuss [fʌs] s agitazione inutile; (coll) alterco per nulla; **to make a fuss** accogliere festosamente; fare molte storie; **to make a fuss over** aver un alterco su ‖ tr disturbare ‖ intr agitarsi per un nonnulla

fuss·y ['fʌsi] adj (-ier; -iest) (person) pignolo, meticoloso; (object) carico di fronzoli; (writing) complicato

fustian ['fʌstʃən] s fustagno; (fig) verbosità f, magniloquenza

fust·y ['fʌsti] adj (-ier; -iest) ammuffito, che sa di muffa; antico, sorpassato

futile ['fjutɪl] adj (unproductive) sterile; (unimportant) futile

futili·ty [fju'tɪlɪti] s (-ties) sterilità f; futilità f

future ['fjutʃər] adj futuro ‖ s futuro; **futures** contratto con consegna a termine; **in the near future** nel prossimo avvenire

fuze [fjuz] s (for igniting an explosive) miccia; (for detonating an explosive) spoletta; (elec) fusibile m ‖ tr innestare la spoletta a

fuzz [fʌz] s lanugine f, peluria; (in corners) polvere f; (slang) poliziotto; (slang) polizia

fuzz·y ['fʌzi] adj (-ier; -iest) lanuginoso; coperto di polvere; (indistinct) confuso

G

G, g [dʒi] s settima lettera dell'alfabeto inglese

gab [gæb] s (coll) parlantina ‖ v (pret & pp **gabbed;** ger **gabbing**) intr (coll) chiacchierare

gabardine ['gæbərˌdin] s gabardine f

gabble ['gæbəl] s barbugliamento ‖ intr barbugliare

gable ['gebəl] s (archit) timpano

ga'ble roof' s tetto a due falde, tetto a capanna

gad [gæd] v (pret & pp **gadded;** ger **gadding**) intr bighellonare

gad'about' adj ozioso ‖ s vagabondo, bighellone m; fannullone m

gad'fly' s (-flies) tafano, moscone m

gadget ['gædʒɪt] *s* congegno, dispositivo, macchinetta

Gaelic ['gelɪk] *adj & s* gaelico

gaff [gæf] *s* arpione *m*; (naut) picco; **to stand the gaff** (slang) aver pazienza

gag [gæg] *s* bavaglio; (*joke*) barzelletta; (theat) battuta improvvisata || *v* (*pret & pp* **gagged**; *ger* **gagging**) *tr* imbavagliare; soffocare || *intr* sentirsi venire la nausea

gage [gedʒ] *s* (*pledge*) pegno; (*challenge*) sfida

gaie·ty ['ge·ɪti] *s* (**-ties**) gaiezza

gaily ['geli] *adv* allegramente

gain [gen] *s* profitto; (*increase*) aumento || *tr* guadagnare; (*to reach*) raggiungere; (*altitude*) prendere || *intr* (*said of a patient*) migliorare; (*said of a watch*) correre; **to gain on** guadagnare terreno su; sorpassare

gainful ['genfəl] *adj* rimunerativo

gain'say' *v* (*pret & pp* **-said** [,sed] or [,sɛd]) *tr* disdire, misconoscere; negare

gait [get] *s* portamento, andatura

gaiter ['getər] *s* ghetta

gala ['gælə] or ['gelə] *adj* di gala || *s* gala *m & f*, festa

galax·y ['gælɪksi] *s* (**-ies**) galassia

gale [gel] *s* (*of wind*) bufera; (*of laughter*) scoppio; **to weather the gale** resistere alla tempesta

gall [gɔl] *s* fiele *m*; bile *f*; cistifellea; scorticatura; (*gallnut*) galla; (*audacity*) (coll) faccia tosta || *tr* irritare || *intr* irritarsi; (naut) logorarsi

gallant ['gælənt] or [gə'lænt] *adj* galante || ['gælənt] *adj* (*brave*) valoroso; (*grand*) magnifico; (*showy*) festivo || *s* prode *m*; (*man attentive to women*) galante *m*

gallant·ry ['gæləntri] *s* (**-ries**) galanteria; valore *m*

gall' blad'der *s* vescichetta biliare

gall'-blad'der attack' *s* travaso di bile

galleon ['gælɪ·ən] *s* galeone *m*

galler·y ['gæləri] *s* (**-ies**) galleria; tribuna; (*cheapest seats in theater*) loggione *m*

galley ['gæli] *s* (*vessel*) galera; (*kitchen*) (aer) cucina; (*kitchen*) (naut) cambusa; (*galley proof*) (typ) bozza in colonna; (*tray*) (typ) vantaggio

gal'ley proof' *s* bozza in colonna

gal'ley slave' *s* galeotto

Gallic ['gælɪk] *adj* gallo, gallico

galling ['gɔlɪŋ] *adj* irritante

gallivant ['gælɪ,vænt] *intr* andare a spasso; fare il galante

gall'nut' *s* galla

gallon ['gælən] *s* gallone *m*

galloon [gə'lun] *s* gallone *m*, nastro

gallop ['gæləp] *s* galoppo; **at a gallop** al galoppo || *tr* far galoppare || *intr* galoppare

gal·lows ['gæloz] *s* (**-lows** or **-lowses**) forca; (min) castelletto

gal'lows bird' *s* (coll) remo di galera, pendaglio da forca

gall'stone' *s* calcolo biliare

galore [gə'lor] *adv* in abbondanza

galosh [gə'lɑʃ] *s* stivaletto di gomma

galvanize ['gælvə,naɪz] *tr* galvanizzare

gal'vanized i'ron *s* ferro zincato

gambit ['gæmbɪt] *s* gambetto

gamble ['gæmbəl] *s* azzardo; (*game*) gioco d'azzardo || *tr* giocare; **to gamble away** giocarsi || *intr* giocare d'azzardo; (com) speculare

gambler ['gæmblər] *s* giocatore *m*; speculatore *m*

gambling ['gæmblɪŋ] *s* gioco (d'azzardo)

gam'bling den' *s* bisca

gam'bling house' *s* casa da gioco

gam·bol ['gæmbəl] *s* salto, capriola || *v* (*pret & pp* **-boled** or **-bolled**; *ger* **-boling** or **-bolling**) *intr* saltare, far capriole

gambrel ['gæmbrəl] *s* garretto

gam'brel roof' *s* tetto a mansarda

game [gem] *adj* da caccia, coraggioso; (leg) (coll) zoppo; (coll) pronto || *s* (*amusement*) gioco; (*contest*) partita; (*any sport*) sport *m*; (*wild animals hunted*) selvaggina; (*any pursuit*) attività *f*; (*object of pursuit*) bersaglio; (bridge) manche *f*; **the game is up** il gioco è fallito; **to make game of** farsi gioco di; **to play the game** giocare onestamente

game' bag' *s* carniere *m*

game'cock' *s* gallo da combattimento

game'keep'er *s* guardacaccia *m*

game' of chance' *s* gioco d'azzardo

game' preserve' *s* bandita di caccia

game' war'den *s* guardacaccia *m*

gamut ['gæmət] *s* (mus, fig) gamma

gam·y ['gemi] *adj* (**-ier**; **-iest**) coraggioso; (culin) che sa di selvatico

gander ['gændər] *s* papero, oca

gang [gæŋ] *adj* multiplo || *s* (*of workers*) ganga; (*of thugs*) cricca || *intr*—**to gang up** riunirsi; **to gang up against** or **on** (coll) gettarsi insieme contro

gangling ['gæŋglɪŋ] *adj* dinoccolato

gangli·on ['gæŋglɪ·ən] *s* (**-ons** or **-a** [ə]) ganglio

gang'plank' *s* palanca, plancia

gangrene ['gæŋgrin] *s* cancrena || *tr* far andare in cancrena || *intr* andare in cancrena

gangster ['gæŋstər] *s* gangster *m*

gang'way' *s* (*passageway*) corridoio; (*gangplank*) passerella, scalandrone *m*; (*in ship's side*) barcarizzo || *interj* lasciar passare!

gan·try ['gæntri] *s* (**-tries**) (*of crane*) cavalletto; (rr) ponte *m* delle segnalazioni; (rok) piattaforma verticale, torre *f* di lancio

gap [gæp] *s* (*pass*) passo; (*in a wall*) breccia; (*interval*) lacuna; (*between two points of view*) abisso; (mach) gioco

gape [gep] or [gæp] *s* apertura; (*yawn*) sbadiglio; sguardo di meraviglia || *intr* stare a bocca aperta; **to gape at** guardare a bocca aperta

garage [gə'rɑʒ] *s* rimessa

garb [gɑrb] *s* veste *f* || *tr* vestire

garbage ['gɑrbɪdʒ] *s* pattume *m*, immondizia, immondizie *fpl*

gar'bage can' *s* portaimmondizie *m*

gar'bage collec'tor *s* spazzaturaio, spazzino, netturbino

garble ['garbəl] *tr* falsare, mutilare

garden ['gardən] *s* (*of vegetables*) orto; (*of flowers*) giardino

gardener ['gardnər] *s* (*of vegetables*) ortolano; (*of flowers*) giardiniere *m*

gardenia [gar'dinɪ·ə] *s* gardenia

gardening ['gardnɪŋ] *s* orticoltura; giardinaggio

gar'den par'ty *s* trattenimento in giardino

gargle ['gargəl] *s* gargarismo || *intr* gargarizzare

gargoyle ['gargɔɪl] *s* doccione *m*, gargolla

garish ['gerɪʃ] or ['gærɪʃ] *adj* apariscente; abbagliante

garland ['garlənd] *s* ghirlanda || *tr* inghirlandare

garlic ['garlɪk] *s* aglio

garment ['garmənt] *s* capo di vestiario

gar'ment bag' *s* tessilsacco

garner ['garnər] *tr* mettere in granaio; (*to get*) acquistarsi; (*to hoard*) incettare

garnet ['garnɪt] *adj & s* granata

garnish ['garnɪʃ] *s* guarnizione; || *tr* guarnire; (*law*) sequestrare

garret ['gærɪt] *s* sottotetto, soffitta

garrison ['gærɪsən] *s* guarnigione, presidio || *tr* presidiare

garrote [gə'rat] or [gə'rot] *s* strangolamento; garrotta || *tr* strangolare; giustiziare con la garrotta

garrulous ['gærələs] or ['gærjələs] *adj* garrulo, loquace

garter ['gartər] *s* giarrettiera

gas [gæs] *s* gas *m*; (coll) benzina; (slang) successo; (slang) chiacchiere *fpl* || *v* (*pret & pp* **gassed**) *ger* **gassing**) *tr* fornire di gas; (mil) gassare; (slang) divertire || *intr* emettere gas; (slang) chiacchierare; **to gas up** fare il pieno

gas'bag' *s* involucro per il gas; (coll) chiacchierone *m*

gas' burn'er *s* becco a gas; (*on a stove*) fornello a gas

Gascony ['gæskəni] *s* la Guascogna

gaseous ['gæsɪ·əs] *adj* gassoso

gas' fit'ter *s* gassista *m*

gash [gæʃ] *s* sfregio || *tr* sfregiare

gas' heat' *s* calefazione a gas

gas'hold'er *s* gassometro

gasi•fy ['gæsɪ‚faɪ] *v* (*pret & pp* **-fied**) *tr* gassificare || *intr* gassificarsi

gas' jet' *s* fornello a gas; fiamma

gasket ['gæskɪt] *s* guarnizione

gas'light' *s* luce *f* del gas

gas' main' *s* tubatura principale del gas

gas' mask' *s* maschera antigas

gas' me'ter *s* contatore *m* del gas

gasoline ['gæsə‚lin] or [‚gæsə'lin] *s* benzina

gas'oline' deal'er *s* benzinaio

gas'oline' pump' *s* colonnetta, distributore *m* di benzina

gasp [gæsp] or [gɑsp] *s* respirazione affannosa; (*of death*) rantolo || *tr* dire affannosamente || *intr* boccheggiare

gas' range' *s* cucina a gas, fornello a gas

gas'-sta'tion attend'ant *s* benzinaio

gas' stove' *s* cucina a gas

gas' tank' *s* gassometro; (aut) serbatoio di benzina

gastric ['gæstrɪk] *adj* gastrico

gastronomy [gæs'tranəmi] *s* gastronomia

gas' works' *s* officina del gas

gate [get] *s* porta; (*in fence or wall*) cancello; (*of sluice*) saracinesca; (*in an airport or station*) uscita, (rr) barriera; (sports, theat) incasso totale; **to crash the gate** (coll) fare il portoghese

gate'keep'er *s* portiere *m*; (rr) guardiabarriere *m*

gate'way' *s* passaggio, entrata

gather ['gæðər] *tr* raccogliere, cogliere; (*news*) raccapezzare; (*dust*) coprirsi di; (*e.g., a shawl*) avvolgere; (*speed*) aumentare (di); concludere, dedurre; (*signatures*) (bb) riunire; (sew) increspare || *intr* riunirsi; raccogliersi; accumularsi

gathering ['gæðərɪŋ] *s* riunione; (bb) raccolta e piegatura; (pathol) ascesso; (sew) pieghettatura

gaud•y ['gɔdi] *adj* (-ier; -iest) chiassoso, vistoso

gauge [gedʒ] *s* misura; calibro; (*for liquids*) indicatore *m* di livello; (*of carpenter*) graffietto; indice *m*; diametro; (aut) spia; (rr) scartamento || *tr* misurare; calibrare; (naut) stazzare

Gaul [gɔl] *s* gallo

gaunt [gɔnt] or [gɑnt] *adj* magro, emaciato; (*e.g., landscape*) desolato

gauntlet ['gɔntlɪt] or ['gɑntlɪt] *s* guanto; guanto di ferro; guantone *m*, manopola; **to run the gauntlet** (fig) esporsi alla critica; **to take up the gauntlet** raccogliere il guanto; **to throw down the gauntlet** gettare il guanto

gauze [gɔz] *s* garza

gavel ['gævəl] *s* martello, martelletto

gavotte [gə'vat] *s* gavotta

gawk [gɔk] *s* sciocco || *intr* guardare a bocca aperta

gawk•y ['gɔki] *adj* (-ier; -iest) sgraziato, goffo

gay [ge] *adj* gaio; brillante; dissipato; (slang) omosessuale

gaye•ty ['ge·ɪti] *s* (-ties) gaiezza

gaze [gez] *s* sguardo fisso || *intr* fissare lo sguardo

gazelle [gə'zɛl] *s* gazzella

gazette [gə'zɛt] *s* gazzetta

gazetteer [‚gæzə'tɪr] *s* dizionario geografico

gear [gɪr] *s* utensili *mpl*, attrezzi *mpl*; (*mechanism*) meccanismo, dispositivo; (aut) marcia; (mach) ingranaggio **out of gear** disingranato; (fig) disturbato; **to throw into gear** ingranare; **to throw out of gear** disingranare; (fig) disturbare || *tr* adattare || *intr* adattarsi

gear' box' *s* scatola del cambio

gear'shift' *s* cambio di velocità

gear'shift lev'er s leva del cambio
gear'wheel' s ruota dentata
gee [dʒi] *interj* oh!; che bellezza!; **gee up!** (*command to a draft animal*) arri!
Gei'ger count'er ['gaigər] s contatore m Geiger
gel [dʒel] s gel m || v (*pret & pp* **gelled;** *ger* **gelling**) *intr* gelatinizzarsi
gelatine ['dʒelətɪn] s gelatina
geld [geld] v (*pret & pp* **gelded** or **gelt** [gelt]) *tr* castrare
gem [dʒem] s gemma, gioia
Gemini ['dʒemɪ ,naɪ] *spl* i Gemelli
gender ['dʒendər] s (gram) genere m; (coll) sesso
gene [dʒin] s (biol) gene m
genealo·gy [,dʒenɪ'ælədʒi] or [,dʒini-'ælədʒi] s (**-gies**) genealogia
general ['dʒenərəl] *adj & s* generale m
gen'eral deliv'ery s fermo in posta, fermo posta m
generalissi·mo [,dʒenərə'lɪsɪmo] s (**-mos**) generalissimo
generali·ty [,dʒenə'rælɪti] s (**-ties**) generalità f
generalize ['dʒenərə ,laɪz] *tr & intr* generalizzare
generally ['dʒenərəli] *adv* in genere, generalmente
gen'eral part'ner s accomandatario
gen'eral practi'tioner s medico generico
generalship ['dʒenərəl ,ʃɪp] s generalato; strategia, abilità f militare; abilità amministrativa
gen'eral staff' s stato maggiore
generate ['dʒenə ,ret] *tr* (*offspring; electricity*) generare; (math) originare
gen'erat'ing sta'tion s centrale elettrica
generation [,dʒenə'reʃən] s generazione
generative ['dʒenə ,retɪv] *adj* generativo
gen'erative gram'mar s grammatica generativa
generator ['dʒenə ,retər] s generatore m; (elec) generatrice f
generic [dʒɪ'nerɪk] *adj* generico
generous ['dʒenərəs] *adj* generoso; abbondante, copioso
gene·sis ['dʒenɪsɪs] s (**-ses** [,siz]) genesi f || **Genesis** s (Bib) Genesi m
genetic [dʒɪ'netɪk] *adj* genetico || **genetics** *ssg* genetica
Geneva [dʒɪ'nivə] s Ginevra
Genevan [dʒɪ'nivən] *adj & s* ginevrino
genial ['dʒini·əl] *adj* affabile, geniale
genie ['dʒini] s genio
genital ['dʒenɪtəl] *adj* genitale || **genitals** *spl* genitali *mpl*
genitive ['dʒenɪtɪv] *adj & s* genitivo
genius ['dʒinjəs] or ['dʒini·əs] s (**geniuses**) genio || s (**genii**) ['dʒini-,aɪ] (*spirit; deity*) genio
Genoa ['dʒeno·ə] s Genova
genocide ['dʒenə ,saɪd] s (*act*) genocidio; (*person*) genocida *mf*
Geno·ese [,dʒeno'iz] *adj* genovese || s (**-ese**) genovese *mf*
genre ['ʒɑnrə] *adj* (e.g., *painting*) di genere || s genere m

genteel [dʒen'til] *adj* (*well-bred*) beneducato; (*affectedly polite*) manieroso, manierato
gentian ['dʒenʃən] s genziana
gentile ['dʒentɪl] or ['dʒentaɪl] *adj* gentilizio || ['dʒentaɪl] *adj & s* non circonciso; non ebreo; cristiano; (*pagan*) gentile
gentili·ty [dʒen'tɪlɪti] s (**-ties**) distinzione, raffinatezza
gentle ['dʒentəl] *adj* (e.g., *manner*) gentile; (e.g., *wind*) dolce, soave; (*wellborn*) bennato; (*tap*) leggero
gen'tle·folk' s gente f per bene
gen'tle·man s (**-men**) signore m; (*attendant to a person of high rank*) gentiluomo; (*well-mannered man*) gentleman m
gen'tleman in wait'ing s gentiluomo di camera
gentlemanly ['dʒentəlmənli] *adj* signorile
gen'tlemen of the road' s brigante m; vagabondo
gen'tlemen's agree'ment s accordo fondato sulla buona fede
gen'tle sex' s gentil sesso
gentry ['dʒentri] s gente f per bene
genuine ['dʒenju·ɪn] *adj* genuino
genus ['dʒinəs] s (**genera** ['dʒenərə] or **genuses**) genere m
geographer [dʒi'ɑgrəfər] s geografo
geographic(al) [,dʒi·ə'græfɪk(əl)] *adj* geografico
geogra·phy [dʒi'ɑgrəfi] s (**-phies**) geografia
geologic(al) [,dʒi·ə'lɑdʒɪk(əl)] *adj* geologico
geologist [dʒi'ɑlədʒɪst] s geologo
geolo·gy [dʒi'ɑlədʒi] s (**-gies**) geologia
geometric(al) [,dʒi·ə'metrɪk(əl)] *adj* geometrico
geometrician [dʒi ,ɑmɪ'trɪʃən] s geometra *mf*
geome·try [dʒi'ɑmɪtri] s (**-tries**) geometria
George [dʒɔrdʒ] s Giorgio
geranium [dʒɪ'reni·əm] s geranio
geriatrics [,dʒeri'ætrɪks] *ssg* geriatria
germ [dʒʌrm] s germe m
German ['dʒʌrmən] *adj & s* tedesco
germane [dʒər'men] *adj* pertinente
Germanize ['dʒʌrmə ,naɪz] *tr* germanizzare
Ger'man mea'sles s rosolia, rubeola
Ger'man sil'ver s alpacca
Germany ['dʒʌrməni] s la Germania
germ' car'rier s portatore m di germi
germ' cell' s cellula germinale
germicidal [,dʒʌrmɪ'saɪdəl] *adj* germicida
germicide ['dʒʌrmɪ ,saɪd] s germicida m
germinate ['dʒʌrmɪ ,net] *intr* germinare
germ' war'fare s guerra batteriologica
gerontology [,dʒerən'tɑlədʒi] s gerontologia
gerund ['dʒerənd] s gerundio
gestation [dʒes'teʃən] s gestazione
gesticulate [dʒes'tɪkjə ,let] *intr* gesticolare

gesticulation [dʒɛs ˌtɪkjə'leʃən] s gesticolazione

gesture ['dʒɛstʃər] s gesto ǁ intr gestire, gesticolare

get [gɛt] v (pret got [gɑt]; pp got or gotten ['gɑtən]; ger getting) tr ottenere; ricevere; prendere; andare a comprare; procacciare; riportare; procurarsi; riscuotere; guadagnare; to get across far capire; to get back riacquistare; to get down staccare; (to swallow) tranguigiare; to get off togliere, cavare; to get s.o. to + inf indurre che qlcu + subj; to get done far fare; to get up (coll) avere; to have got to + inf (coll) dovere + inf ǁ intr (to become) diventare, farsi; (to arrive) arrivare, venire; to get out (said of a convalescent) alzarsi; to get along andarsene; andare avanti; tirare avanti, giostrare, aver successo; to get along in years essere avanti con gli anni; to get along with andare d'accordo con; to get angry arrabbiarsi; to get around uscire; divulgarsi; rigirare; to get away scappare, darsela a gambe; to get away with s.th scappare con qlco; (coll) farla franca; to get back ritornare; ricuperare; to get back at (coll) vendicarsi di; to get behind rimanere indietro; (to support) appoggiare, patrocinare; to get better migliorare; to get by passare oltre; (to succeed) arrivare a farcela; passare inosservato; to get even with rifarsi con, prendersi la rivincita con; to get going mettersi in moto; to get in entrare; rientrare; arrivare; to get in deeper and deeper cacciarsi nei pasticci; to get in with diventare amico di; to get married sposarsi to get off andarsene; smontare da; to get old invecchiare; to get on andare avanti; andare d'accordo; to get out uscire; propagarsi; to get out of (a car) uscire da; (trouble) trarsi di; to get out of the way togliersi di mezzo; to get run over essere investito; to get through finire; arrivare; farsi capire; to get to be finire per essere; to get under way mettersi in cammino; to get up alzarsi; to not get over it (coll) non arrivare a rassegnarsi

get'a•way' s fuga; (sports) partenza

get'-to-geth'er s riunione, crocchio

get'up' s (coll) stile m, presentazione; (coll) costume m, abbigliamento

gewgaw ['gjugɔ] s cianfrusaglia

geyser ['gaɪzər] s geyser m

ghast•ly ['gæstli] or ['gɑstli] adj (-lier; -liest) orribile, orrendo; spettrale

gherkin ['gʌrkɪn] s cetriolino

ghet•to ['geto] s (-tos or -toes) ghetto

ghost [gost] s spettro, fantasma m; not a ghost of nemmeno l'ombra di; to give up the ghost rendere l'anima

ghost•ly ['gostli] adj (-lier; -liest) spettrale, fantomatico

ghost' sto'ry s storia di fantasmi

ghost' town' s città morta

ghost' writ'er s collaboratore anonimo

ghoul [gul] s spirito necrofago; ladro di tombe

ghoulish ['gulɪʃ] adj demoniaco, macabro

GI ['dʒi'aɪ] (letterword) (General Issue) s (GI's) soldato degli Stati Uniti

giant ['dʒaɪ•ənt] adj & s gigante m

giantess ['dʒaɪ•əntɪs] s gigantessa

gibberish ['dʒɪbərɪʃ] or ['gɪbərɪʃ] s linguaggio inintelligibile

gibbet ['dʒɪbɪt] s forca ǁ tr impiccare sulla forca; (to hold up to scorn) mettere alla berlina

gibe [dʒaɪb] s scherno, frecciata ǁ intr schernire; to gibe at beffarsi di

giblets ['dʒɪblɪts] spl rigaglie fpl

giddiness ['gɪdɪnɪs] s vertigine f; frivolezza

gid•dy ['gɪdi] adj (-dier; -diest) vertiginoso; preso dalle vertigini; frivolo

gift [gɪft] s regalo; (natural ability) dono, dote f; (for Christmas) strenna

gifted ['gɪftɪd] adj dotato

gift' horse' s—never look a gift horse in the mouth a caval donato non si guarda in bocca

gift' of gab' s (coll) facondia; to have the gift of gab (coll) avere la lingua sciolta

gift' pack'age s pacco-dono

gift' shop' s negozio di regali

gift'-wrap' v (pret & pp -wrapped; ger -wrapping) tr incartare in carta speciale per regali

gigantic [dʒaɪ'gæntɪk] adj gigantesco

giggle ['gɪgəl] s risolino ǁ intr ridere scioccamente, ridacchiare

gigo•lo ['dʒɪgə ˌlo] s (-los) gigolo

gild [gɪld] v (pret & pp gilded or gilt [gɪlt]) tr dorare, indorare

gilding ['gɪldɪŋ] s doratura

gill [gɪl] s (of fish) branchia ǁ [dʒɪl] s quarto di pinta

gilt [gɪlt] adj & s dorato

gilt-edged ['gɪlt ˌedʒd] adj a bordo dorato; di primissima qualità

gimcrack ['dʒɪm ˌkræk] adj di nessun valore ǁ s cianfrusaglia

gimlet ['gɪmlɪt] s succhiello

gimmick ['gɪmɪk] s (slang) trucco

gin [dʒɪn] s (liquor) gin m; (trap) trappola; (mach) arganello; (tex) sgranatrice f di cotone ǁ v (pret & pp ginned; ger ginning) tr ginnare, sgranare

ginger ['dʒɪndʒər] s zenzero; (coll) energia, vivacità f

gin'ger ale' s gazosa allo zenzero

gin'ger•bread' s pan di zenzero; ornamento di cattivo gusto

gingerly ['dʒɪndʒərli] adj cauto ǁ adv con cautela

gin'ger•snap' s biscotto allo zenzero

gingham ['gɪŋəm] s rigatino

giraffe [dʒɪ'ræf] or [dʒɪ'rɑf] s giraffa

girandole ['dʒɪrən ˌdol] s girandola

gird [gʌrd] v (pret & pp girt [gʌrt] or girded) tr cingere; (to equip) dotare; (to prepare) preparare; (to surround) circondare

girder ['gʌrdər] s longherina

girdle ['gʌrdəl] s reggicalze m, zona, fascetta || tr fasciare; circondare

girl [gʌrl] s fanciulla; ragazza

girl' friend' s amica, innamorata

girlhood ['gʌrlhud] s adolescenza, giovinezza

girlish ['gʌrlɪʃ] adj fanciullesco; da ragazza

girl' scout' s giovane esploratrice f

girth [gʌrθ] s circonferenza; fascia; (to hold a saddle) sottopancia m

gist [dʒɪst] s sugo, nocciolo, essenza

give [gɪv] s elasticità f || v (pret gave [gev]; pp given ['gɪvən]) tr dare; (trouble) causare; (a play) rappresentare; (a speech; fruit; a sigh) fare; **to give away** distribuire gratuitamente; (to reveal) lasciarsi sfuggire; (a bride) accompagnare all'altare; (coll) tradire; **to give back** restituire; **to give forth** (odors) emettere; **to give oneself up** darsi; **to give up** cedere; (a position) abbandonare || intr dare; cedere; (said, e.g., of a rope) rompersi; **to give in** cedere; darsi per vinto; **to give out** esaurirsi; venir meno; **to give up** darsi per vinto

give'-and-take' s compromesso; conversazione briosa

give'a-way' s premio gratuito; rivelazione involontaria; (game) vinciperdi m; (rad, telv) programma m a premi

given ['gɪvən] adj dato; **given that** dato che, concesso che

giv'en name' s nome m di battesimo

giver ['gɪvər] s donatore m; dispensatore m

gizzard ['gɪzərd] s magone m

glacial ['gleʃəl] adj glaciale

glacier ['gleʃər] s ghiacciaio

glad [glæd] adj (gladder; gladdest) felice, lieto, contento; **to be glad (to)** essere felice (di)

gladden ['glædən] tr rallegrare

glade [gled] s radura

glad' hand' s (coll) accoglienza calorosa

gladiator ['glædɪ‚etər] s gladiatore m

gladiola [‚glædɪ'olə] or [glə'daɪ-ələ] s gladiolo

gladly ['glædlɪ] adv volentieri, di buon grado

gladness ['glædnɪs] s contentezza

glad' rags' s (coll) panni mpl da festa; (coll) vestito da sera

glamorous ['glæmərəs] adj affascinante, attraente

glamour ['glæmər] s fascino, malia

glam'our girl' s ragazza sci-sci

glance [glæns] or [glɑns] s occhiata, guardata; **at first glance** a prima vista || intr lanciare uno sguardo; **to glance at** dare un'occhiata a; **to glance off** sorvolare su; deviare da; **to glance over** dare una scorsa a

gland [glænd] s ghiandola

glanders ['glændərz] spl morva

glare [gler] s splendore m, luce f abbagliante; sguardo minaccioso || intr risplendere; lanciare occhiatacce; **to glare at** fare la faccia feroce a

glare' ice' s vetrato

glaring ['glerɪŋ] adj risplendente, abbagliante; (look) torvo; evidente

glass [glæs] or [glɑs] s vetro; (tumbler) bicchiere m; (mirror) specchio; (glassware) cristalleria; **glasses** occhiali mpl

glass' blow'er ['blo-ər] s vetraio

glass' case' s vetrinetta

glass' cut'ter s tagliatore m di cristallo; (tool) diamante m tagliavetro

glass' door' s porta a vetri

glassful ['glæsful] or ['glɑsful] s bicchiere m

glass'house' s vetreria; (fig) casa di vetro

glass'ware' s vetreria, cristalleria

glass' wool' s vetro filato

glass'work'er s vetraio

glass'works' s vetreria, cristalleria

glass-y ['glæsi] or ['glɑsi] adj (-ier; -iest) vetriato, vetroso

glaze [glez] s vernice vitrea; smalto; (of ice) superficie invetriata; (culin) glassa || tr smaltare; invetriare; (culin) glassare

glazier ['gleʒər] s vetraio

gleam [glim] s barlume m, raggio || intr baluginare

glean [glin] tr spigolare, racimolare; (to gather facts) raccogliere

glee [gli] s gioia, esultanza

glee' club' s società f corale

glib [glɪb] adj (glibber; glibbest) loquace; (tongue) facile, sciolto

glide [glaɪd] s scivolata; (aer) volo a vela, volo planato; (mus) legamento || intr scivolare; (aer) librarsi, planare; **to glide away** scorrere

glider ['glaɪdər] s (aer) libratore m, veleggiatore m

glimmer ['glɪmər] s barlume m || intr brillare, luccicare; tralucere

glimmering ['glɪmərɪŋ] adj tenue, tremulo || s luce fioca; barlume m

glimpse [glɪmps] s occhiata; **to catch a glimpse of** intravedere || tr travedere

glint [glɪnt] s scintillio || intr scintillare

glisten ['glɪsən] s scintillio, luccichio || intr scintillare, luccicare

glitter ['glɪtər] s luccichio || intr rilucere, sfolgorare

gloaming ['glomɪŋ] s crepuscolo (vespertino)

gloat [glot] intr guardare con maligna soddisfazione; **to gloat over** godere di

global ['globəl] adj globale; universale; globulare

globe [glob] s globo; (with map of earth) mappamondo

globe-trotter ['glob‚trɑtər] s giramondo

globule ['glɑbjul] s globulo

glockenspiel ['glɑkən‚spil] s vibrafono

gloom [glum] s oscurità f; malinconia, uggia

gloom-y ['glumi] adj (-ier; -iest) lugubre, triste, tetro

glori•fy ['glɔrɪ‚faɪ] v (pret & pp -fied) tr glorificare; (to enhance) esaltare

glorious ['glɔrɪ·əs] *adj* glorioso; magnifico, splendido

glo·ry ['glɔrɪ] *s* (**-ries**) gloria; **to go to glory** morire ‖ *v* (*pret & pp* **-ried**) *intr* gloriarsi

gloss [glɔs] *or* [glɑs] *s* lucentezza, patina; (*commentary*) glossa ‖ *tr* satinare, patinare; (*to annotate*) glossare; **to gloss over** nascondere, discolpare

glossa·ry ['glɑsərɪ] *s* (**-ries**) glossario

gloss·y ['glɔsi] *or* ['glɑsi] *adj* (**-ier; -iest**) lucido; (*paper*) satinato

glottal ['glɑtəl] *adj* articolato alla glottide

glottis ['glɑtɪs] *s* glottide *f*

glove [glʌv] *s* guanto

glove' compart'ment *s* cassetto portaoggetti

glow [glo] *s* fuoco, incandescenza; splendore *m*, scintillio; calore *m*; colorito acceso ‖ *intr* essere incandescente; (*said of cheeks*) avvampare; (*said of cat's eyes*) fosforeggiare

glower ['glau·ər] *s* sguardo torvo ‖ *intr* guardare col viso torvo

glowing ['glo·ɪŋ] *adj* incandescente; acceso; entusiasta, entusiastico

glow'worm' *s* lucciola; lampiride *m*

glucose ['glukos] *s* glucosio

glue [glu] *s* colla, mastice *m* ‖ *tr* incollare, ingommare

glue'pot' *s* pentolino per la colla

gluey ['glu·i] *adj* (**gluier; gluiest**) attaccaticcio; (*smeared with glue*) incollato

glum [glʌm] *adj* (**glummer; glummest**) tetro, accigliato

glut [glʌt] *s* abbondanza; eccesso; **there is a glut on the market** il mercato è saturo ‖ *v* (*pret & pp* **glutted; ger glutting**) *tr* saziare; (*the market*) saturare; (*a channel*) otturare

glutton ['glʌtən] *adj & s* ghiottone *m*

gluttonous ['glʌtənəs] *adj* ghiotto

glutton·y ['glʌtənɪ] *s* (**-ies**) ghiottoneria, golosità *f*

glycerine ['glɪsərɪn] *s* glicerina

G'-man' *s* (**-men'**) agente *m* federale

gnarl [nɑrl] *s* nodo ‖ *tr* torcere ‖ *intr* ringhiare

gnarled [nɑrld] *adj* nodoso; (*wrinkled*) grinzoso

gnash [næʃ] *tr* digrignare ‖ *intr* digrignare i denti

gnat [næt] *s* moscerino, pappataci *m*

gnaw [nɔ] *tr* rosicchiare, rodere ‖ *intr* —**to gnaw at** (fig) rimordere

gnome [nom] *s* gnomo

go [go] *s* (**goes**) andata; energia; (*for traffic*) via libera; **it's a go** è un affare fatto; **it's all the go** (coll) è all'ultimo grido; **it's no go** (coll) è impossibile; **on the go** in continuo andare e venire; **to make a go of** (coll) aver successo con ‖ *v* (*pret* **went** [wɛnt]; *pp* **gone** [gɔn] *or* [gɑn]) *tr* (coll) sopportare; (coll) scommettere; (coll) pagare; **to go it alone** fare da sé ‖ *intr* andare; (*to operate*) camminare, funzionare; (*e.g., mad*) diventare; (*said of numbers*) entrare; **gone!** vendutol; **so it goes** così va il mondo; **to**

be going to + *inf* andare a + *inf*, e.g., **I am going to New York to see him** vado a New York a vederlo; (*to express futurity*) use *fut ind*, e.g., **I am going to stay home today** starò a casa oggi; **to be gone** essere andato; esser morto; **to go against** opporsi a; **to go ahead** andar avanti; tirare avanti; **to go around** andare in giro; **to go away** andarsene; **to go back** tornare; **to go by** passare per; regolarsi su; (*said of time*) passare; **to go down** discendere; (*said of a boat*) affondare; **to go fishing** andare a pescare; **to go for** vendersi per; andare a pigliare; attaccare; favorire; **to go get** andare a pigliare; **to go house hunting** andare in cerca di una casa; **to go hunting** andare a caccia; **to go in** entrare in; (*to fit in*) starci in; **to go in for** dedicarsi a; **to go into** investigare; darsi a, dedicarsi a; (*gear*) (aut) ingranare; **to go in with** associarsi con; **to go off** andarsene; aver luogo; (*said of a bomb*) esplodere; (*said of a rifle*) sparare; (*said of a trap*) scattare; **to go on** continuare, protrarsi; **to go on** + *ger* continuare a + *inf*; **to go out** uscire; passare di moda; (*said, e.g., of fire*) spegnersi; (*to strike*) mettersi in sciopero; **to go over** aver successo; leggere; esaminare; **to go over to** passare ai ranghi di; **to go skiing** andare a sciare; **to go swimming** andare a nuotare, andare al bagno; **to go through** esperimentare; (*to examine carefully*) rovistare; (*said, e.g., of a plan or a project*) aver successo; (*a fortune*) dissipare; **to go through a red light** passare la strada col semaforo rosso; **to go with** andare accompagnare; (*a girl*) essere l'amico di; **to go without** fare a meno di

goad [god] *s* pungolo ‖ *tr* pungolare; (fig) spronare

go'-ahead' *s* intraprendente ‖ *s* via *m*

goal [gol] *s* meta; (football) gol *m*

goalie ['goli] *s* portiere *m*

goal'keep'er *s* portiere *m*

goal' line' *s* linea di porta

goal' post' *s* montante *m*

goat [got] *s* capra; (*male*) becco; (coll) capro espiatorio; **to get the goat of** (coll) irritare

goatee [go'ti] *s* barbetta, pizzo

goat'herd' *s* capraio

goat'skin' *s* pelle *f* di capra

goat'suck'er *s* caprimulgo

gob [gɑb] *s* massa informe; **gobs** (coll) mucchio, quantità *f* enorme

gobble ['gɑbəl] *s* gloglottio ‖ *tr* ingozzare; **to gobble up** (coll) trangugiare; (coll) impadronirsi di ‖ *intr* trangugiare; (*said of a turkey*) gloglottare

gobbledegook ['gɑbəldɪ͵guk] *s* linguaggio oscuro

go'-between' *s* intermediario; (*pander*) mezzano; (poet) pronubo

goblet ['gɑblɪt] *s* coppa

goblin ['gɑblɪn] *s* folletto

go'-by' *s*—**to give s.o. the go-by** (coll) schivare qlcu

go'-cart' *s* carrettino; (*walker*) girello

god [gad] *s* dio; **God forbid** Dio ci scampi; **God grant** voglia Dio; **God willing** se Dio vuole
god'child' *s* (-chil'dren) figlioccio
god'daugh'ter *s* figlioccia
goddess ['gadɪs] *s* dea, diva
god'fa'ther *s* padrino
God'-fear'ing *adj* timorato di Dio
God'for•sak'en *adj* miserabile; (*place*) sperduto, fuori di mano
god'head' *s* deità *f* || **Godhead** *s* Ente Supremo, Dio
godless ['gadlɪs] *adj* ateo; malvagio || **the godless** i senza Dio
god•ly ['gadlɪ] *adj* (-li•er; -liest) devoto, pio
god'moth'er *s* madrina
God's' a'cre *s* camposanto
god'send' *s* manna, provvidenza
god'son' *s* figlioccio
God'speed' *s* successo, buona fortuna
go-getter ['go ˌgɛtər] *s* (coll) persona intraprendente
goggle ['gagəl] *intr* stralunare gli occhi
goggle-eyed ['gagəl ˌaɪd] *adj* dagli occhi sporgenti
goggles ['gagəlz] *spl* occhiali *mpl* da protezione
going ['go•ɪŋ] *adj* in moto, in funzione; **going on** quasi, e.g., **it is going on seven o'clock** sono quasi le sette || *s* andata; progresso
go'ings on' *s* (coll) comportamento, contegno; (coll) avvenimenti *mpl*
goiter ['gɔɪtər] *s* gozzo
gold [gold] *adj* aureo, d'oro || *s* oro
gold'beat'er *s* battiloro
gold'brick' *s* imitazione, frode *f*; (slang) fannullone *m*
gold' dig'ger ['dɪgər] *s* cercatore *m* d'oro; (coll) donna unicamente interessata nel denaro
golden ['goldən] *adj* aureo, d'oro; (*gilt*) dorato; (fig) splendido
gold'en age' *s* età *f* dell'oro
gold'en calf' *s* vitello d'oro
Gold'en Fleece' *s* vello d'oro
gold'en mean' *s* aurea mediocrità
gold'en-rod' *s* (bot) verga d'oro
gold'en rule' *s* regola della carità cristiana
gold'en wed'ding *s* nozze *fpl* d'oro
gold-filled ['gold ˌfɪld] *adj* otturato in oro
gold'finch' *s* cardellino
gold'fish' *s* pesce rosso
goldilocks ['gɔldɪ ˌlaks] *s* bionda; (bot) ranuncolo
gold' leaf' *s* oro in foglia
gold' mine' *s* miniera d'oro
gold' plate' *s* vasellame *m* d'oro
gold'-plate' *tr* dorare
gold' rush' *s* febbre *f* dell'oro
gold'smith' *s* orefice *m*
gold' stand'ard *s* regime aureo
golf [gɑlf] *s* golf *m* || *intr* giocare a golf
golf' cart' *s* mini-auto *f* per campi da golf
golf' club' *s* mazza; associazione di giocatori di golf
golfer ['gɑlfər] *s* giocatore *m* di golf
golf' links' *spl* campo di golf

Golgotha ['gɑlgəθə] *s* il Golgota
gondola ['gɑndələ] *s* gondola
gondolier [ˌgɑndə'lɪr] *s* gondoliere *m*
gone [gɔn] *or* [gɑn] *adj* partito; rovináto; andato; morto; **gone on** (coll) innamorato di
gong [gɔŋ] *or* [gɑŋ] *s* gong *m*
goo [gu] *s* (coll) sostanza appiccicaticcia
good [gud] *adj* (**better; best**) buono; **good and . . .** (coll) molto, e.g., **good and cheap** molto a buon mercato; **good for** buono per; responsabile per; (*equivalent*) valido per; **to be good at** esser bravo a; **to be no good** (coll) non servire a nulla; (coll) essere un perdigiorno; **to make good** avere successo; (*one's promise*) mantenere; (*a debt*) pagare; (*damages*) indennizzare || *s* bene *m*; utile *m*, profitto; **for good** per sempre; **for good and all** una volta per sempre; **goods** merce *f*, mercanzia; **the good** il bene; **i buoni**; **to catch with the goods** (coll) cogliere in flagrante; **to deliver the goods** (slang) mantenere le promesse; **to do good** fare del bene; **to the good** come profitto; come attivo; **what is the good of . . . ?** a che serve . . . ?
good' afternoon' *s* buon pomeriggio
good'-by' [ˌgud'baɪ] *s* addio || *interj* addio!; arrivederci!
good' day' *s* buon giorno
good' deed' *s* buona azione
good' egg' *s* (slang) bonaccione *m*, gran brava persona
good' eve'ning *s* buona sera; buona notte
good' fel'low *s* buon ragazzo
good'-fel'low•ship' *s* cameratismo
good'-for-noth'ing *adj* inutile, senza valore || *s* pelandrone *m*, inetto
Good' Fri'day *s* Venerdì Santo
good' grac'es *spl* buone grazie
good-hearted ['gud 'hɑrtɪd] *adj* di buon cuore
good'-hum'ored *adj* di buon umore
good'-look'ing *adj* bello
good' looks' *s* bellezza
good•ly ['gudlɪ] *adj* (-li•er; -liest) bello; di buona qualità; ampio, considerevole
good' morn'ing *s* buon giorno
good-natured ['gud 'net/ərd] *adj* bonaccione, affabile
goodness ['gudnɪs] *s* bontà *f*; **for goodness sake!** per amor di Dio!; **goodness knows!** chi sa mai! || *interj* Dio mio!
good' night' *s* buona notte
good'-sized' *adj* piuttosto grande
good' speed' *s* buona fortuna
good'-tem'pered *adj* di carattere mite, gioviale
good' time' *s* periodo gradevole; **to have a good time** divertirsi; **to make good time** andare di buon passo
good' turn' *s* favore *m*, servizio
good' will' *s* buona volontà; (coll) reputazione; (com) clientela
good•y ['gudi] *adj* (coll) troppo buono || *s* (-ies) (coll) s±ᴜ፤ᴄᴜᴇllo; **goodies**

(coll) ghiottonerie *fpl* || *interj* (coll) bene!, benissimo!

gooey ['gu·i] *adj* (**gooier; gooiest**) (slang) attaccaticcio

goof [guf] *s* (slang) sciocco || *tr* (slang) rovinare; **to goof up** (*an opportunity*) (slang) mancare || *intr* (slang) pigliare un granchio; **to goof off** (slang) battere la fiacca; **to goof up** (slang) farla grossa

goof·y ['gufi] *adj* (**-ier; -iest**) (slang) sciocco

goon [gun] *s* (slang) scemo; (coll) crumiro, gaglioffo, terrorista *m*

goose [gus] *s* (**geese** [gis]) oca; **the goose hangs high** tutto va per il meglio; **to cook one's goose** rompere le uova nel paniere di qlcu; **to kill the goose that lays the golden eggs** uccidere la gallina delle uova d'oro || *s* (**gooses**) ferro da stiro per sarto

goose'ber'ry *s* (**-ries**) uva spina; (*berry*) bacca d'uva spina

goose' egg' *s* (slang) zero; (*lump on the head*) (coll) bernoccolo

goose' flesh' *s* pelle *f* d'oca

goose'neck' *s* collo d'oca

goose' pim'ples *spl* pelle *f* d'oca

goose' step' *s* passo dell'oca

gopher ['gofər] *s* scoiattolo di terra, citillo

gore [gor] *s* sangue coagulato; (*in a garment*) gherone *m* || *tr* (*with a horn*) incornare; inserire gheroni in

gorge [gɔrdʒ] *s* gola, burrone *m*; (*meal*) mangiata || *tr* rimpinzare || *intr* rimpinzarsi

gorgeous ['gɔrdʒəs] *adj* splendido, magnifico

gorilla [gə'rɪlə] *s* gorilla *m*

gorse [gɔrs] *s* gineprone *m*

gor·y ['gori] *adj* (**-ier; -iest**) sanguinolento

gosh [gaʃ] *interj* perbacco!

goshawk ['gas‚hɔk] *s* sparviere *m*, astore *m*

gospel ['gaspəl] *s* vangelo || **Gospel** *s* Vangelo

gos'pel truth' *s* santissima verità

gossamer ['gasəmər] *s* ragnatela; (*variety of gauze*) garza finissima; tessuto impermeabile finissimo

gossip ['gasɪp] *s* maldicenza; (*person*) pettegolo; **piece of gossip** maldicenza || *intr* spettegolare

gossipy ['gasɪpi] *adj* pettegolo

Goth [gaθ] *s* Goto

Gothic ['gaθɪk] *adj* & *s* gotico

gouge [gaudʒ] *s* (*cut made with a gouge*) scanalatura; (*tool*) sgorbia; (coll) truffa || *tr* sgorbiare; (coll) truffare

goulash ['gulaʃ] *s* gulasch *m*

gourd [gord] *or* [gurd] *s* zucca

gourmand ['gurmənd] *s* ghiottone *m*

gourmet ['gurme] *s* buongustaio

gout [gaut] *s* gotta, podagra

gout·y ['gauti] *adj* (**-ier; -iest**) gottoso

govern ['gʌvərn] *tr* governare; (gram) reggere

governess ['gʌvərnɪs] *s* governante *f*, istitutrice *f*

government ['gʌvərnmənt] *s* governo; (gram) reggenza

governmental [‚gʌvərn'mentəl] *adj* governativo

governor ['gʌvərnər] *s* governatore *m*; (mach) regolatore *m*

governorship ['gʌvərnər‚ʃɪp] *s* governatorato

gown [gaun] *s* (*of a woman*) vestito; (*academic*) toga; (*of a physician or patient*) gabbanella; (*of a priest*) veste *f* talare

grab [græb] *s* presa; **up for grabs** (coll) pronto a esser pigliato || *v* (*pret* & *pp* **grabbed;** *ger* **grabbing**) *tr* pigliare, afferrare

grace [gres] *s* (*charm; favor*) grazia; (*pardon*) mercé *f*; (*prayer*) benedicite *m*; (com) dilazione; **to say grace** recitare il benedicite; **with good grace** di buona voglia || *tr* adornare

graceful ['gresfəl] *adj* grazioso, vezzoso, leggiadro

grace' note' *s* (mus) appoggiatura

gracious ['greʃəs] *adj* grazioso; misericordioso || *interj* Dio buono!

gradation [gre'deʃən] *s* gradazione; (*step in a series*) passo

grade [gred] *s* grado; (*slope*) pendenza; (*mark in school*) voto; **to make the grade** raggiungere la meta || *tr* selezionare; (*a student*) dare un voto a; (*land*) spianare

grade' cros'sing *s* (rr) passaggio a livello

grade' school' *s* scuola elementare

gradient ['gredɪ·ənt] *adj* in pendenza || *s* pendenza; (phys) gradiente *m*

gradual ['grædʒʊ·əl] *adj* graduale

graduate ['grædʒʊ·ɪt] *adj* graduato; superiore; (*student*) laureato; (*candidate for degree*) laureando || ['grædʒʊ‚et] *tr* graduare; laureare, diplomare || *intr* laurearsi, diplomarsi

grad'uate school' *s* facoltà *f* di studi avanzati

graduation [‚grædʒʊ'eʃən] *s* graduazione; laurea; cerimonia della consegna delle lauree

graft [græft] *or* [graft] *s* (hort) innesto; (surg) trapianto; (coll) prevaricazione || *tr* (hort) innestare; (surg) trapiantare || *intr* (coll) prevaricare

gra'ham bread' ['gre·əm] *s* pane *m* integrale

grain [gren] *s* chicco; (*of sand*) granello; (*cereal seeds*) granaglie *fpl*; (*in wood*) venatura; (*in stone*) grana; **against the grain** di cattivo verso || *tr* granulare; (*leather*) zigrinare; (*metal*) granire

grain' el'evator *s* elevatore *m* di grano; (*building*) deposito di cereali

graining ['grenɪŋ] *s* venatura

gram [græm] *s* grammo

grammar ['græmər] *s* grammatica

grammarian [grə'merɪ·ən] *s* grammatico

gram'mar school' *s* scuola elementare

grammatical [grə'mætɪkəl] *adj* grammatico

gramophone ['græmə‚fon] s (trademark) grammofono

grana·ry ['grænəri] s (-ries) granaio

grand [grænd] adj grandioso; grande, famoso

grand'aunt' s prozia

grand'child' s (-chil'dren) nipote mf

grand'daugh'ter s nipote f

grand' duch'ess s granduchessa

grand' duke' s granduca m

grandee [græn'di] s grande m

grandeur ['grænd‚ər] or ['grænd‚ʒur] s grande m, grandiosità f

grand'fa'ther s nonno; (forefather) antenato

grand'father's clock' s grande orologio a pendolo

grandiose ['grændɪ‚os] adj grandioso

grand' ju'ry s giuria investigativa

grand' lar'ceny s furto importante

grand' lodge' s grande oriente m

grandma ['grænd‚ma], ['græm‚ma] or ['græmə] s (coll) nonna

grand'moth'er s nonna

grand'neph'ew s pronipote m

grand'niece' s pronipote f

grand' op'era s opera, opera lirica

grandpa ['grænd‚pa], ['græn‚pa] or ['græmpə] s (coll) nonno

grand'par'ent s nonno, nonna

grand' pian'o s pianoforte m a coda

grand'son' s nipote m

grand'stand' s tribuna

grand' to'tal s somma totale; importo globale

grand'un'cle s prozio

grand' vizier' s gran visir m

grange [grendʒ] s (farm) fattoria; (organization of farmers) sindacato di agricoltori

granite ['grænɪt] s granito

grant [grænt] or [grɑnt] s concessione; (sum of money) sovvenzione; trapasso di proprietà || tr concedere; (a wish) esaudire; (a permit) rilasciare; (law) trasferire; **to take for granted** ammettere come vero; trattare con indifferenza

grantee [græn'ti] or [grɑn'ti] s concessionario; beneficiario

grant'-in-aid' s (grants'-in-aid') sussidio governativo a un ente pubblico; borsa di studio

grantor [græn'tɔr] or [grɑn'tɔr] s concedente m, concessore m

granular ['grænjələr] adj granulare

granulate ['grænjə‚let] tr granulare || intr diventare granulato

gran'ulated sug'ar s zucchero cristallizzato

granule ['grænjul] s granulo

grape [grep] s chicco d'uva; (vine) vite f; **grapes** uva

grape' ar'bor s pergolato

grape'fruit' s pompelmo

grape' juice' s succo d'uva

grape'shot' s mitraglia

grape'vine' s vite f; **by the grapevine** di bocca in bocca; (mil) attraverso la radio fante

graph [græf] or [grɑf] s (diagram) grafico; (gram) segno grafico

graphic(al) ['græfɪk(əl)] adj grafico

graphite ['græfaɪt] s grafite f

graph' pa'per s carta millimetrata

grapnel ['græpnəl] s uncino; (anchor) grappino

grapple ['græpəl] s uncino; lotta corpo a corpo || tr uncinare || intr combattere; **to grapple with** lottare con

grap'pling i'ron s raffio, grappino

grasp [græsp] or [grɑsp] s impugnatura; (power) possesso; **to have a good grasp of** sapere a fondo; **within the grasp of** nei limiti della comprensione di || tr (with hand) impugnare; (to get control of) impadronirsi di; (fig) capire || intr—**to grasp at** cercare di afferrare

grasping ['græspɪŋ] or ['grɑspɪŋ] adj tenace; avido, cupido

grass [græs] or [grɑs] s erba; (pasture land) pastura; (lawn) tappeto erboso; **to go to grass** (said of cattle) andare al pascolo; andare in vacanza; ritirarsi; andare in rovina; morire; **to not let the grass grow under one's feet** non dormire in piuma

grass' court' s campo da tennis d'erba

grass'hop'per s cavalletta

grass'-roots' adj popolare

grass' seed' s semente f d'erba

grass' wid'ow s donna separata dal marito

grass·y ['græsi] or ['grɑsi] adj (-ier; -iest) erboso

grate [gret] s (for cooking) griglia; (at a window) grata || tr mettere una grata a; (one's teeth) digrignare; (e.g., cheese) grattugiare || intr stridere, cigolare; **to grate on one's nerves** dare sui nervi di qlcu

grateful ['gretfəl] adj riconoscente; (pleasing) piacevole, gradito

grater ['gretər] s grattugia

grati·fy ['grætɪ‚faɪ] v (pret & pp -fied) tr gratificare, soddisfare

gratifying ['grætɪ‚faɪ·ɪŋ] adj soddisfacente, piacevole

grating ['gretɪŋ] adj irritante; (sound) stridente || s inferriata

gratis ['gretɪs] or ['grætɪs] adj gratuito || adv gratis

gratitude ['grætɪ‚tjud] or ['grætɪ‚tud] s gratitudine f, riconoscenza

gratuitous [grə'tju·ɪtəs] or [grə'tu·ɪtəs] adj gratuito

gratui·ty [grə'tju·ɪti] or [grə'tu·ɪti] s (-ties) mancia, regalia

grave [grev] adj grave || s tomba, sepolcro, fossa

gravedigger ['grev‚dɪgər] s becchino

gravel ['grævəl] s ghiaia; (pathol) renella

grav'en im'age ['grevən] s idolo

grave'stone' s pietra tombale

grave'yard' s cimitero, camposanto

gravitate ['grævɪ‚tet] intr gravitare

gravitation [‚grævɪ'teʃən] s gravitazione

gravi·ty ['grævɪti] s (-ties) gravità f

gravure [grə'vjur] or ['grevjur] s fotoincisione

gra·vy ['grevi] s (-vies) (juice from

cooking meat) sugo; (*sauce made with it*) salsa, intingolo; (slang) guadagni *mpl* facili

gra'vy boat' *s* salsiera

gra'vy train' *s* (slang) greppia, mangiatoia

gray [gre] *adj* grigio; (*gray-haired*) canuto ‖ *s* grigio; cavallo grigio ‖ *intr* incanutire

gray'beard' *s* vecchio

gray-haired ['gre ,herd] *adj* canuto

gray'hound' *s* levriere *m*

grayish ['gre·ɪʃ] *adj* grigiastro

gray' mat'ter *s* materia grigia

graze [grez] *tr* (*to touch lightly*) sfiorare; (*to scratch lightly*) scalfire; (*grass*) brucare; (*cattle*) pascere, pascolare ‖ *intr* pascere, brucare

grease [gris] *s* grasso, unto ‖ [gris] or [griz] *tr* ingrassare, ungere

grease' cup' [gris] *s* coppa dell'olio

grease' gun' [gris] *s* ingrassatore *m*

grease' lift' [gris] *s* piattaforma di lubrificazione

grease' paint' [gris] *s* cerone *m*

grease' pit' [gris] *s* fossa di riparazione

greas·y ['grisi] or ['grizi] *adj* (-ier; -iest) grasso, unto, untuoso

great [gret] *adj* grande; (coll) eccellente ‖ **the great** i grandi

great'-aunt' *s* prozia

Great' Bear' *s* Orsa Maggiore

Great' Brit'ain ['brɪtən] *s* la Gran Bretagna

Great' Dane' *s* danese *m*, alano

Great'er New York' *s* Nuova York e i suoi sobborghi

great'-grand'child' *s* (-chil'dren) pronipote *mf*

great'-grand'daught'er *s* pronipote *f*

great'-grand'fa'ther *s* bisnonno

great'-grand'moth'er *s* bisnonna

great'-grand'par'ent *s* bisnonno, bisnonna

great'-grand'son' *s* pronipote *m*

greatly ['gretli] *adj* molto

great'-neph'ew *s* pronipote *m*

greatness ['gretnɪs] *s* grandezza

great'-niece' *s* pronipote *f*

great'-un'cle *s* prozio

Grecian ['griʃən] *adj* & *s* greco

Greece [gris] *s* la Grecia

greed [grid] *s* avarizia, avidità *f*

greediness ['gridɪnɪs] *s* bramosia

greed·y ['gridi] *adj* (-ier; -iest) avaro; ingordo, bramoso

Greek [grik] *adj* & *s* greco

green [grin] *adj* verde; (fig) verde, inesperto ‖ *s* verde *m*; (*lawn*) tappeto erboso; **greens** verdura, insalata

green'back' *s* (U.S.A.) biglietto di banca

green' earth' *s* verdaccio

greener·y ['grinəri] *s* (-ies) (*foliage*) vegetazione; (*hothouse*) serra

green'-eyed' *adj* dagli occhi verdi; (coll) geloso

green'gage' *s* regina claudia

green'horn' *s* (slang) pivello, sempliciotto

green'house' *s* serra

greenish ['grinɪʃ] *adj* verdastro

Greenland ['grinlənd] *s* la Groenlandia

green' light' *s* semaforo verde; (coll) via *m*

greenness ['grinnɪs] *s* verdore *m*, verdezza; inesperienza

green' pep'per *s* peperone *m* verde

greensward ['grin ,sword] *s* tappeto erboso

green' thumb' *s* abilità *f* speciale per il giardinaggio

green' veg'etables *spl* verdura

green'wood' *s* bosco verde

greet [grit] *tr* salutare; ricevere; (*e.g., one's ears*) offrirsi a

greeting ['gritɪŋ] *s* saluto; accoglienza ‖ **greetings** *interj* saluti!

greet'ing card' *s* cartolina d'auguri

gregarious [grɪ'gɛrɪ·əs] *adj* (*living in the midst of others*) gregario; (*sociable*) sociale

Gregorian [grɪ'gorɪ·ən] *adj* gregoriano

grenade [grɪ'ned] *s* granata

grenadier [,grɛnə'dɪr] *s* granatiere *m*

grenadine [,grɛnə'din] *s* granatina

grey [gre] *adj*, *s* & *intr* var of **gray**

grid [grɪd] *s* (*network*) rete *f*; (*on map*) reticolato; (electron) griglia

griddle ['grɪdəl] *s* tegame *m*

grid'dle·cake' *s* frittella cotta in teglia, crêpe *m*

grid'i'ron *s* griglia; campo di football; (theat) graticcia

grief [grif] *s* affanno, dolore *m*; disgrazia; **to come to grief** andare in rovina

grievance ['grivəns] *s* lagnanza; motivo di lagnanza

grieve [griv] *tr* affliggere ‖ *intr* affliggersi, dolersi; **to grieve over** soffrire per

grievous ['grivəs] *adj* doloroso, penoso; (*error*) grave; (*deplorable*) deplorevole

griffin ['grɪfɪn] *s* grifo, grifone *m*

grill [grɪl] *s* griglia ‖ *tr* mettere alla griglia; (coll) interrogare insistentemente

grille [grɪl] *s* inferriata; (aut) mascherina, calandra

grill'room' *s* grill-room *m*, rosticceria

grim [grɪm] *adj* (grimmer; grimmest) (*stern*) accigliato; (*fierce*) feroce; (*sinister*) sinistro; (*unyielding*) implacabile

grimace ['grɪməs] or [grɪ'mes] *s* smorfia, sberleffo ‖ *intr* fare le boccacce

grime [graɪm] *s* sporco; (*soot*) fuliggine *f*

grim·y ['graɪmi] *adj* (-ier; -iest) sporco; fuligginoso

grin [grɪn] *s* sorriso; (*malicious in intent*) ghigno ‖ *v* (*pret* & *pp* grinned; *ger* grinning) *intr* sorridere; ghignare

grind [graɪnd] *s* macinata; (*laborious work*) (coll) macina; (slang) sgobbone *m* ‖ *v* (*pret* & *pp* ground [graʊnd]) *tr* macinare; (*to sharpen*) molare; (*lenses*) smerigliare; (*meat*) tritare; opprimere; (*a crank*) girare; (mach) rettificare ‖ *intr* macinare; frantumarsi; cigolare; (coll) sgobbare

grinder ['graɪndər] *s* (*to sharpen tools*) mola; (*to grind coffee*) macinino;

(*back tooth*) molare *m*; (*person*) molatore *m*

grind'stone' *s* mola; **to keep one's nose to the grindstone** lavorare senza posa

grin·go ['grɪŋgo] *s* (**-gos**) (*disparaging*) gringo

grip [grɪp] *s* (*grasp*) presa; (*with hand*) stretta; (*handle*) impugnatura; **to come to grips** venire alle prese ‖ *v* (*pret & pp* **gripped;** *ger* **gripping**) *tr* stringere; impugnare; attirare l'attenzione di

gripe [graɪp] *s* (coll) lamentela; (naut) rizza; **gripes** colica ‖ *intr* (coll) lamentarsi, brontolare

grippe [grɪp] *s* influenza

gripping ['grɪpɪŋ] *adj* interessantissimo, affascinante

gris·ly ['grɪzli] *adj* (**-lier; -liest**) orribile, spaventoso

grist [grɪst] *s* (*grain to be ground*) macinata; (*ground grain*) farina; (coll) mucchio; **to be grist to the mill of** (coll) fare comodo a

gristle ['grɪsəl] *s* cartilagine *f*

gris·tly ['grɪsli] *adj* (**-tlier; -tliest**) cartilaginoso

grist'mill' *s* mulino

grit [grɪt] *s* sabbia, arenaria; (fig) forza d'animo ‖ *v* (*pret & pp* **gritted;** *ger* **gritting**) *tr* (*one's teeth*) far stridere, digrignare

grit·ty ['grɪti] *adj* (**-tier; -tiest**) sabbioso, granuloso; (fig) forte, coraggioso

griz·zly ['grɪzli] *adj* (**-zlier; -zliest**) brizzolato, canuto ‖ *s* (**-zlies**) orso grigio

groan [gron] *s* gemito ‖ *intr* gemere; (*to be overburdened*) essere sovraccarico

grocer ['grosər] *s* droghiere *m*; pizzicagnolo; proprietario di negozio di generi alimentari

grocer·y ['grosəri] *s* (**-ies**) (*store selling spices, soap, etc.*) drogheria; (*store selling cheese, cold cuts, etc.*) negozio di pizzicagnolo; negozio di generi alimentari; **groceries** generi *mpl* alimentari, commestibili *mpl*

grog [grɑg] *s* grog *m*

grog·gy ['grɑgi] *adj* (**-gier; -giest**) (coll) groggy, intontito

groin [grɔɪn] *s* (anat) inguine *m*; (archit) costolone *m*

groom [grum] *s* mozzo di stalla; (*bridegroom*) sposo ‖ *tr* rassettare; (*horses*) rigovernare; (pol) preparare per le elezioni

grooms'man *s* (**-men**) compare *m* di nozze

groove [gruv] *s* scanalatura; (*of a pulley*) gola; (*of a phonograph record*) solco; (fig) routine *f* ‖ *tr* scanalare, incavare

grope [grop] *intr* brancicare; (*for words*) cercare; **to grope for** cercare a tastoni

gropingly ['gropɪŋli] *adv* a tastoni

gross [gros] *adj* (*thick*) spesso; (*coarse*) volgare; (*fat*) grosso; (*error*) mar-

chiano; (*without deductions*) lordo ‖ *s* grossa ‖ *tr* fare un incasso lordo di

grossly ['grosli] *adv* approssimativamente; totalmente

gross' na'tional prod'uct *s* reddito nazionale

grotesque [gro'tesk] *adj & s* grottesco

grot·to ['grɑto] *s* (**-toes** or **-tos**) grotta

grouch [graut/] *s* (coll) malumore *m*; (coll) persona stizzosa ‖ *intr* (coll) brontolare

grouch·y ['graut/i] *adj* (**-ier; -iest**) (coll) stizzoso, brontolone

ground [graund] *s* (*earth, soil, land*) terra; (*piece of land*) terreno; (basis) causa, fondatezza; (elec) terra, massa; (fig) occasione, motivo; **grounds** giardini *mpl*, terreno; (*of coffee*) fondi *mpl*; **on the ground of** per motivo di; **to break ground** dare la prima palata; (fig) mettere la prima pietra; **to fall to the ground** cadere al suolo; (fig) fallire; **to gain ground** guadagnar terreno; **to give ground** ceder terreno; **to lose ground** perder terreno; **to stand one's ground** non indietreggiare ‖ *tr* fondare; (elec) mettere a massa; **to be grounded** (*said of an airplane*) essere forzato di rimanere a terra; **to be well grounded** essere bene al corrente ‖ *intr* incagliarsi

ground' connec'tion *s* messa a terra

ground' crew' *s* (aer) personale *m* di servizio

ground' floor' *s* pianterreno

ground' glass' *s* vetro smerigliato

ground' hog' *s* marmotta americana

ground' lead' [lid] *s* (elec) collegamento a massa

groundless ['graundlɪs] *adj* infondato

ground' meat' *s* carne tritata

ground' plan' *s* progetto, pianta

ground' swell' *s* mareggiata

ground' wire' *s* filo di terra, filo di massa

ground'work' *s* fondamento, base *f*

group [grup] *adj* collettivo ‖ *s* gruppo; (aer) stormo ‖ *tr* raggruppare ‖ *intr* raggrupparsi

grouse [graus] *s* gallo cedrone; (slang) brontolio ‖ *intr* (slang) brontolare

grout [graut] *s* stucco ‖ *tr* stuccare

grove [grov] *s* boschetto

grov·el ['grʌvəl] or ['grɑvəl] *v* (*pret & pp* **-eled** or **-elled;** *ger* **-eling** or **-elling**) *intr* umiliarsi

grow [gro] *v* (*pret* **grew** [gru]; *pp* **grown** [gron]) *tr* (*plants*) coltivare; (*animals*) allevare; (*a beard*) farsi crescere ‖ *intr* crescere; svilupparsi; nascere; venir su; (*to become*) diventare; farsi; **to grow angry** arrabbiarsi; **to grow old** invecchiare; **to grow out of** (*fashion*) passare di; originare da; **to grow up** svilupparsi

growing ['gro·ɪŋ] *adj* crescente; (*pains*) di crescenza; (*child*) in crescita

growl [graul] *s* ringhio; brontolio ‖ *intr* (*said of animals*) ringhiare; brontolare

grown'-up' *adj* adulto, grande ‖ *s* **(grown-ups)** adulto

growth [groθ] *s* crescita, sviluppo; aumento; (pathol) escrescenza

growth' stock' *s* azione *f* che promette di aumentare di valore

grub [grʌb] *s* (*drudge*) sgobbone *m*; larva di coleottero; (coll) mangiare *m* ‖ *v* (*pret & pp* **grubbed;** *ger* **grubbing**) *tr* scavare, zappare, dissodare ‖ *intr* cercare assiduamente; scavare; sgobbare

grub-by [ˈgrʌbi] *adj* (**-bier; -biest**) sporco; bacato; infestato di larve

grudge [grʌdʒ] *s* rancore *m*; **to have a grudge against** nutrire rancore contro ‖ *tr* (*to spend unwillingly*) lesinare; invidiare

grudgingly [ˈgrʌdʒɪŋli] *adv* di cattiva voglia

gru-el [ˈgru-əl] *s* farinata d'avena ‖ *v* (*pret & pp* **-eled** *or* **-elled;** *ger* **-eling** *or* **-elling**) *tr* estenuare

gruesome [ˈgrusəm] *adj* raccapricciante

gruff [grʌf] *adj* brusco, burbero; (*voice*) rauco, roco

grumble [ˈgrʌmbəl] *s* brontolio ‖ *intr* brontolare, borbottare

grump-y [ˈgrʌmpi] *adj* (**-ier; -iest**) di cattivo umore, scontroso

grunt [grʌnt] *s* grugnito ‖ *intr* grugnire

G-string [ˈdʒiˌstrɪŋ] *s* (*loincloth*) perizoma *m*; (*worn by a female entertainer*) triangolino di stoffa; (mus) corda di sol

guarantee [ˌgærənˈti] *s* garanzia; (*guarantor*) garante *mf* ‖ *tr* garantire

guarantor [ˈgærənˌtɔr] *s* garante *mf*

guaran-ty [ˈgærənti] *s* (**-ties**) garanzia ‖ *v* (*pret & pp* **-tied**) *tr* garantire

guard [gɑrd] *s* guardia; (*safeguard*) protezione; (*in a prison*) guardia carceraria; (*of a sword*) guardamano; (football) mediano; **off guard** alla sprovvista; **on guard** in guardia; di fazione; **to mount a guard** montare la guardia; **under guard** ben custodito ‖ *tr* guardare ‖ *intr* fare la sentinella; **to guard against** guardarsi da

guarded [ˈgɑrdɪd] *adj* (*remark*) prudente

guard'house' *s* locale *m* di detenzione; (mil) corpo di guardia

guardian [ˈgɑrdɪ-ən] *adj* tutelare ‖ *s* guardiano; (law) tutore *m*

guard'ian an'gel *s* angelo custode

guardianship [ˈgɑrdɪ-ənˌʃɪp] *s* protezione; (law) tutela

guard'rail' *s* guardavia *m*; (naut) parapetto

guard'room' *s* (mil) corpo di guardia

guards'man *s* (**-men**) guardia

guerrilla [gəˈrɪlə] *s* guerrigliero

guerril'la war'fare *s* guerriglia

guess [ges] *s* congettura, supposizione ‖ *tr & intr* congetturare, supporre; (*to estimate correctly*) indovinare; (coll) credere; **I guess so** credo di sì

guess'work' *s* congettura

guest [gest] *s* invitato, ospite *m*; (*of a hotel*) cliente *mf*; (*of a boarding house*) pensionante *mf*

guest' book' *s* albo d'onore; (*in a hotel*) registro

guffaw [gəˈfɔ] *s* sghignazzata ‖ *intr* sghignazzare

Guiana [gɪˈɑnə] *or* [gɪˈænə] *s* la Guayana

guidance [ˈgaɪdəns] *s* guida, governo; **for your guidance** per Sua norma

guide [gaɪd] *s* guida ‖ *tr* guidare

guide'board' *s* indicatore *m* stradale

guide'book' *s* guida

guid'ed mis'sile [ˈgaɪdɪd] *s* telearma, teleproietto, missile teleguidato

guide' dog' *s* cane *m* conduttore di un cieco

guide'line' *s* falsariga; corda fissa; linea di condotta, direttiva

guide'post' *s* indicatore *m* stradale

guide' word' *s* esponente *m* in testa di pagina

guidon [ˈgaɪdən] *s* guidone *m*

guild [gɪld] *s* associazione mutua; (hist) gilda

guild'hall' *s* palazzo delle corporazioni

guile [gaɪl] *s* astuzia, frode *f*

guileful [ˈgaɪlfəl] *adj* astuto, insidioso

guileless [ˈgaɪllɪs] *adj* sincero, innocente

guillotine [ˈgɪləˌtin] *s* ghigliottina ‖ [ˌgɪləˈtin] *tr* ghigliottinare

guilt [gɪlt] *s* colpa, reità *f*

guiltless [ˈgɪltlɪs] *adj* innocente

guilt-y [ˈgɪlti] *adj* (**-ier; -iest**) colpevole, reo

guimpe [gɪmp] *or* [gæmp] *s* sprone *m*

guinea [ˈgɪni] *s* ghinea; gallina faraona ‖ **Guinea** *s* la Guinea

guin'ea fowl' *s* gallina faraona

guin'ea pig' *s* porcellino d'India, cavia; (fig) cavia

guise [gaɪz] *s* aspetto; veste *f*; **under the guise of** in guisa di

guitar [gɪˈtɑr] *s* chitarra

guitarist [gɪˈtɑrɪst] *s* chitarrista *mf*

gulch [gʌltʃ] *s* burrone *m*

gulf [gʌlf] *s* golfo; abisso

Gulf' Stream' *s* corrente *f* del Golfo

gull [gʌl] *s* gabbiano; (coll) credulone *m* ‖ *tr* darla a bere a

gullet [ˈgʌlɪt] *s* gargarozzo; esofago

gullible [ˈgʌlɪbəl] *adj* credulone

gul-ly [ˈgʌli] *s* (**-lies**) borro, zanella

gulp [gʌlp] *s* sorsata ‖ *tr*—**to gulp down** (*food*) ingoiare; (*drink*) tracannare; (fig) ingoiare, tranguigiare

gum [gʌm] *s* gomma; (*mucus on eyelids*) cispa; gamma (anat) gengive *fpl* ‖ *v* (*pret & pp* **gummed;** *ger* **gumming**) *tr* ingommare; **to gum up** (slang) guastare ‖ *intr* secernere gomma

gum' ar'abic *s* gomma arabica

gum'boil' *s* flemmone *m* gengivale

gum'boot' *s* stivale *m* da palude

gum'drop' *s* caramella alla gelatina di frutta, pasticca di gomma, drop *m*

gum-my [ˈgʌmi] *adj* (**-mier; -miest**) gommoso, vischioso; (*eyelid*) cisposo

gumption [ˈgʌmpʃən] *s* (coll) iniziativa; (coll) coraggio, fegato

gum'shoe' *s* caloscia; (slang) poliziotto ‖ *v* (*pret & pp* **-shoed;** *ger* **-shoeing**)

intr (slang) camminare silenziosamente

gun [gʌn] s (*rifle*) fucile m; (*revolver*) revolver m; (*pistol*) rivoltella; (*e.g., for spraying*) rivoltella; **to stick to one's guns** tener duro || v (*pret & pp* **gunned;** *ger* **gunning**) *tr* far fuoco su, freddare; (*a motor*) (slang) accelerare rapidamente || *intr* andare a caccia; sparare; **to gun for** andare a caccia di

gun'boat' s cannoniera, esploratore m

gun' car'riage s affusto

gun'cot'ton s fulmicotone m

gun'fire' s fuoco, tiro

gun'man s (**-men**) bandito, sicario

gun' met'al s bronzo da cannoni; acciaio brunito

gunnel ['gʌnəl] s (naut) frisata

gunner ['gʌnər] s artigliere m, servente m

gunnery ['gʌnəri] s artiglieria, tiro

gunnysack ['gʌni,sæk] s sacco di tela greggia

gunpoint ['gʌn,pɔɪnt] s mirino; **at gunpoint** a mano armata, e.g., **he was held up at gunpoint** subì una rapina a mano armata

gun'pow'der s polvere nera or pirica

gun'run'ner s contrabbandiere m di armi da fuoco

gun'shot' s schioppettata; revolverata; **within gunshot** a tiro di schioppo

gun'shot' wound' s schioppettata

gun'smith' s armaiolo

gun'stock' s cassa del fucile

gunwale ['gʌnəl] s frisata

gup·py ['gʌpi] s (**-pies**) lebiste m

gurgle ['gʌrgəl] s gorgoglio, borboglio || *intr* gorgogliare, borbogliare; (*said of a human being*) barbugliare

gush [gʌʃ] s getto, fiotto || *intr* zampillare, sgorgare; (coll) dare in effusioni

gusher ['gʌʃər] s pozzo di petrolio; (coll) persona espansiva

gushing ['gʌʃɪŋ] adj zampillante, sgorgante; (coll) espansivo || s zampillio; (coll) espansione, effusione

gush·y ['gʌʃi] adj (**-ier; -iest**) (coll) espansivo, effusivo

gusset ['gʌsɪt] s gherone m

gust [gʌst] s (*of wind*) raffica; (*of smoke*) ondata, zaffata; (*of noise*) esplosione; (*of anger*) sfuriata

gusto ['gʌsto] s gusto; entusiasmo

gust·y ['gʌsti] adj (**-ier; -iest**) a raffiche, burrascoso

gut [gʌt] s budello; **guts** budello; (slang) fegato, coraggio || v (*pret & pp* **gutted;** *ger* **gutting**) *tr* sparare, spanciare; distruggere l'interno di

gutta-percha ['gʌtə'pʌrtʃə] s guttaperca

gutter ['gʌtər] s (*on side of road*) cunetta; (*in street*) rigagnolo; (*of roof*) doccia, grondaia; (fig) bassifondi mpl

gut'ter·snipe' s monello

guttural ['gʌtərəl] adj & s gutturale f

guy [gaɪ] s cavo di sicurezza; (coll) tipo, tizio || *tr* burlarsi di

guzzle ['gʌzəl] *tr & intr* trincare, bere a garganella

guzzler ['gʌzlər] s ubriacone m

gym [dʒɪm] s (coll) palestra

gymnasi·um [dʒɪm'nezɪ·əm] s (**-ums** or **-a** [ə]) palestra

gymnast ['dʒɪmnæst] s ginnasta mf

gymnastic [dʒɪm'næstɪk] adj ginnastico || **gymnastics** spl ginnastica

gynecologist [,gaɪnə'kɑlədʒɪst], [,dʒaɪnə'kɑlədʒɪst] or [,dʒɪnə'kɑlədʒɪst] s ginecologo

gyp [dʒɪp] s (coll) imbroglio; (*person*) (coll) imbroglione m || v (*pret & pp* **gypped;** *ger* **gypping**) *tr* imbrogliare

gypsum ['dʒɪpsəm] s gesso

gyp·sy ['dʒɪpsi] adj zingaresco, zingaro || s (**-sies**) zingaro || **Gypsy** s (*language*) zingaresco

gypsyish ['dʒɪpsi·ɪʃ] adj zingaresco

gyrate ['dʒaɪret] *intr* turbinare

gyrocompass ['dʒaɪro,kʌmpəs] s girobussola

gyroscope ['dʒaɪrə,skop] s giroscopio

H

H, h [etʃ] s ottava lettera dell'alfabeto inglese

haberdasher ['hæbər,dæʃər] s camiciaio; (*dealer in notions*) merciaio

haberdasher·y ['hæbər,dæʃəri] s (**-ies**) camiceria; merceria

habit ['hæbɪt] s abitudine f; (*addiction*) vizio; (*garb*) saio; **to be in the habit of** aver l'usanza di

habitat ['hæbɪ,tæt] s habitat m

habitation [,hæbɪ'teʃən] s abitazione

habit-forming ['hæbɪt,fɔrmɪŋ] adj (*e.g., drugs*) stupefacente; (*e.g., T.V.*) assuefacente, che fa venire il vizio

habitual [hə'bɪtʃu·əl] adj abituale

habitué [hə,bɪtʃu'e] s habitué m

hack [hæk] s (*cut*) taglio; (*notch*) tacca; (*cough*) tosse secca; cavallo da nolo; vettura di piazza; (*nag*) ronzino; (*poor writer*) scribacchino || *tr* tagliare; stagliare

hack'man s (**-men**) vetturino

hackney ['hækni] s cavallo da sella; vettura di piazza

hackneyed ['hæknid] adj banale, trito

hack'saw' s seghetto per metalli

haddock ['hædək] s eglefino

haft [hæft] or [hɑft] s impugnatura

hag [hæg] s (*ugly old woman*) megera; (*witch*) strega

haggard ['hægərd] adj sparuto, macilento; (*wild-looking*) stralunato

haggle ['hægəl] *intr* mercanteggiare

hagiographer [,hægɪ'ɑgrəfər] or [,hedʒi'ɑgrəfər] *s* agiografo

hagiography [,hægɪ'ɑgrəfi] or [,hedʒi-'ɑgrəfi] *s* agiografia

Hague, The [heg] *s* L'Aia *f*

hail [hel] *s* (*precipitation*) grandine *f*; (*greeting*) saluto; **within hail a** portata di voce || *tr* salutare; accogliere; chiamare; (*e.g., blows*) far cadere || *intr* grandinare; **to hail from** venire da || *interj* salute!; salve!

hail'-fel'low *adj* gioviale

Hail' Mar'y *s* Ave Maria, avemaria

hail'stone' *s* chicco di grandine

hail'storm' *s* grandinata

hair [her] *s* capelli *mpl*; (*of animals*) pelame *m* or pelo; **a hair** (*a single filament*) un capello or un pelo; **to a hair** a perfezione; **to get in one's hair** (slang) dare sui nervi a qlcu; **to let one's hair down** (slang) parlare francamente; (slang) comportarsi alla buona; **to make one's hair stand on end** far rizzare i capelli a qlcu; **to not turn a hair** non scomporsi; **to split hairs** cercare il pelo nell'uovo

hair'breadth' *s* spessore *m* di un capello; **to escape by a hairbreadth** scamparla per un pelo

hair'brush' *s* spazzola per i capelli

hair'cloth' *s* cilicio

hair'cut' *s* taglio dei capelli; **to get a haircut** farsi tagliare i capelli

hair'do' *s* (**-dos**) acconciatura

hair'dress'er *s* parrucchiere *m* per signora; pettinatrice *f*

hair' dri'er *s* asciugacapelli *m*

hair' dye' *s* tintura per i capelli

hairless ['herlɪs] *adj* pelato, calvo

hair' net' *s* rete *f* per i capelli

hair'pin' *s* forcella, forcina, molletta

hair-raising ['her ,rezɪŋ] *adj* orripilante

hair' re-mov'er *s* depilatorio

hair' restor'er [rɪ'storər] *s* rigeneratore *m* per i capelli

hair' rib'bon *s* nastro per i capelli

hairsplitting ['her ,splɪtɪŋ] *adj* meticoloso, pignolo

hair'spring' *s* spirale *f*

hair' styl'ing *s* pettinatura per signora

hair-y ['herɪ] *adj* (**-ier; -iest**) peloso, villoso, irsuto

hake [hek] *s* merluzzo, nasello

halberd ['hælbərd] *s* alabarda

halberdier [,hælbər'dɪr] *s* alabardiere *m*

halcyon ['hælsɪ-ən] *adj* calmo, pacifico

hale [hel] *adj* sano, robusto || *tr* trascinare a viva forza

half [hæf] or [hɑf] *adj* mezzo; **a half** or **half a** mezzo; **half the** la metà di || *s* (**halves** [hævz] or [hɑvz]) metà *f*; (*arith*) mezzo; **in half** a metà; **to go halves** fare a metà || *adv* mezzo, e.g., **half asleep** mezzo addormentato; a metà, e.g., **half finished** a metà finito; **half past** e mezzo or e mezza, e.g., **half past three** le tre e mezzo or le tre e mezza; **half . . . half** metà . . . metà

half'-and-half' *adj* mezzo e mezzo || *s* mezza crema e mezzo latte; mezza

birra chiara e mezza scura || *adv* a metà, in parti uguali

half'back' *s* (football) mediano; (soccer) laterale *m*

half-baked ['hæf ,bekt] or ['hɑf ,bekt] *adj* mezzo cotto; (*ideas*) infondato, inesperto

half' bind'ing *s* rilegatura in mezza pelle

half'-blood' *s* meticcio; fratellastro; sorellastra

half'-breed' *s* meticcio

half' broth'er *s* fratellastro

half-cocked ['hæf ,kɑkt] or ['hɑf ,kɑkt] *adj* immaturo, precipitato || *adv* (coll) precipitatamente

half' fare' *s* mezza corsa

half'-full' *adj* mezzo pieno

half-hearted ['hæf ,hɑrtɪd] or ['hɑf-,hɑrtɪd] *adj* indifferente, freddo

half'-hol'iday *s* mezza festa

half' hose' *s* calzini *mpl* corti

half'-hour' *s* mezz'ora; **on the half-hour** ogni trenta minuti allo scoccare dell'ora e della mezz'ora

half'-length' *adj* a mezzo busto || *s* ritratto a mezzo busto

half'life' *s* (phys) vita media

half'-mast' *s*—**at half-mast** a mezz'asta

half'-moon' *s* mezzaluna

half' mourn'ing *s* mezzo lutto

half' note' *s* (mus) minima

half' pay' *s* mezza paga

halfpen-ny ['hepəni] or ['hepni] *s* (**-nies**) mezzo penny

half' pint' *s* mezza pinta; (slang) mezza cartuccia, mezza calzetta

half'-seas o'ver *adj*—**to be half-seas over** (slang) essere sbronzato

half' shell' *s*—**on the half shell** in conchiglia

half' sis'ter *s* sorellastra

half' sole' *s* mezza suola

half'-sole' *tr* mettere la mezza suola a

half'-staff' *s*—**at half-staff** a mezz'asta

half-timbered ['hæf ,tɪmbərd] or ['hɑf-,tɪmbərd] *adj* in legno e muratura

half' ti'tle *s* occhiello, occhietto

half'tone' *s* mezzatinta

half'-track' *s* semicingolato

half'truth' *s* mezza verità, mezza bugia

half'way' *adj* a metà strada; parziale, mezzo || *adv* a metà strada; **halfway through** nel mezzo di; **to meet halfway** fare concessioni mutue

half-witted ['hæf ,wɪtɪd] or ['hɑf-,wɪtɪd] *adj* mezzo scemo

halibut ['hælɪbət] *s* ippoglosso

halide ['hælaɪd] or ['helaɪd] *s* alogenuro

halitosis [,hælɪ'tosɪs] *s* alito cattivo, fiato puzzolente

hall [hɔl] *s* (*passageway*) corridoio; (*entranceway*) vestibolo; (*large meeting room*) salone *m*; (*assembly room of a university*) aula magna; (*building of a university*) edificio

halleluiah or **hallelujah** [,hælɪ'lujə] *s* alleluia *m* || *interj* alleluia!

hall'mark' *s* punzone *m* di garanzia; (fig) contrassegno, caratteristica

hal-lo [hə'lo] *s* (**-los**) grido || *interj* ehi!

hallow ['hælo] *tr* santificare

hallowed ['hælod] *adj* consacrato
Halloween or **Hallowe'en** [,hælo'in] *s* vigilia di Ognissanti
hallucination [hə,lusi'neʃən] *s* allucinazione
hall'way' *s* corridoio; entrata
ha·lo ['helo] *s* (**-los** or **-loes**) alone *m*
halogen ['hælədʒən] *s* alogeno
halt [hɔlt] *adj* zoppicante || *s* fermata; **to call a halt** dare ordine di fermarsi; **to come to a halt** fermarsi || *tr* fermare || *intr* fermarsi, esitare || *interj* altolà!
halter ['hɔltər] *s* (*for leading horse*) cavezza; (*noose*) capestro; (*hanging*) impiccagione; corpino bagno di sole
halting ['hɔltɪŋ] *adj* zoppicante; esitante
halve [hæv] or [hɑv] *tr* dimezzare
halyard ['hæljərd] *s* (naut) drizza
ham [hæm] *s* (*part of leg behind knee*) polpaccio; (*thigh and buttock*) coscia; (*cured meat from hog's hind leg*) prosciutto; (slang) istrione *m*; (slang) radioamatore *m*; **hams** natiche *fpl*
ham' and eggs' *spl* uova *fpl* col prosciutto
hamburger ['hæm,bʌrgər] *s* hamburger *m*
hamlet ['hæmlɪt] *s* frazione, paese *m* ||
Hamlet *s* Amleto
hammer ['hæmər] *s* martello; (*of gun*) cane *m*; (*of piano*) martelletto; **under the hammer** all'asta pubblica || *tr* martellare; **to hammer out** battere; portare a fine faticosamente || *intr* martellare; **to hammer away** lavorare accanitamente
hammock ['hæmək] *s* amaca
hamper ['hæmpər] *s* cesta || *tr* imbarazzare, intralciare
hamster ['hæmstər] *s* criceto
ham·string ['hæm,strɪŋ] *v* (*pret & pp* **-strung**) *tr* azzoppare; tagliare i garretti a; (fig) impastoiare
hand [hænd] *adj* manuale; fatto a mano || *s* mano *f*; (*workman*) garzone *m*, operaio; (*way of writing*) scrittura; (*signature*) firma; (*clapping of hands*) applauso; (*of clock or watch*) lancetta; (*all the cards in one's hand*) gioco; (*a round of play*) smazzata, mano *f*; (*player*) giocatore *m*; (*skill*) destrezza; (*side*) lato; **all hands** (naut) tutto l'equipaggio; (coll) tutti *mpl*; **at first hand** direttamente; **at hand** a portata di mano; **hand in glove** in perfetta unione; **hand in hand** tenendosi per mano; **hands up!** le mani in alto!; **hand to hand** corpo a corpo; **in hand** tra le mani; **in his own hand** di proprio pugno; **on hand** disponibile; **on hands and knees** (*crawling*) a gattoni; (*beseeching*) in ginocchio; **on the one hand** da un canto; **on the other hand** per contro; **to change hands** cambiare di mano; **to clap hands** battere le mani; **to eat out of one's hand** essere sottomesso a qlcu; **to get out of hand** diventare incontrollabile; **to have a hand in** prender parte a; **to have one's hands**

full essere occupatissimo; **to hold hands** tenersi per mano; **to hold up one's hands** (*as a sign of surrender*) alzare le mani; **to join hands** darsi la mano; **to keep one's hands off** non mettere il naso in; **to lend a hand** dare una mano; **to live from hand to mouth** vivere alla giornata; **to not lift a hand** non alzare un dito; **to play into the hands of** fare il gioco di; **to shake hands** darsi la mano; **to show one's hand** scoprire il proprio gioco; **to take in hand** prendere in mano; (*a matter*) prendere in esame; **to throw up one's hands** darsi per vinto; **to try one's hand** mettere la propria abilità alla prova; **to turn one's hand** to dedicarsi a; **to wash one's hands of** lavarsi le mani di; **under my hand** di mia firma autografa; **under the hand and seal of** firmato di pugno da || *tr* dare, porgere; **to hand down** tramandare; **to hand in** consegnare; **to hand on** trasmettere; **to hand out** distribuire
hand'bag' *s* borsetta
hand' bag'gage *s* valigie *fpl* a mano
hand'ball' *s* palla a mano
hand'bill' *s* manifestino, foglio volante
hand'book' *s* manuale *m*; guida; (*of a particular field*) prontuario
hand'breadth' *s* palmo
hand'car' *s* (rr) carrello a mano
hand'cart' *s* carretto a mano
hand'cuffs' *spl* manette *fpl* || *tr* mettere le manette a
handful ['hænd,ful] *s* manata, manciata
hand' glass' *s* lente *f* di ingrandimento; specchietto
hand' grenade' *s* bomba a mano
handi·cap ['hændɪ,kæp] *s* svantaggio; (sports) handicap *m* || *v* (*pret & pp* **-capped**; *ger* **-capping**) *tr* andicappare
handicraft ['hændɪ,kræft] or ['hændɪ,krɑft] *s* destrezza manuale; artigianato
handiwork ['hændɪ,wʌrk] *s* lavoro fatto a mano; opera, lavoro
handkerchief ['hæŋkərt/ɪf] or ['hæŋkər ,tʃɪf] *s* fazzoletto
handle ['hændəl] *s* manico; (*of a sword*) impugnatura; (*of a door*) maniglia; (*of a drawer*) pomolo; (*of a hand organ*) manovella; espediente *m*; **to fly off the handle** (slang) uscire dai gangheri || *tr* maneggiare; manovrare, dirigere; commerciare in || *intr* comportarsi
handle'bar' *s* manubrio
handler ['hændlər] *s* (sports) allenatore *m*
hand'made' *adj* fatto a mano
hand'maid' or **hand'maid'en** *s* domestica, serva; (fig) ancella
hand'-me-down' *adj* smesso || *s* vestito smesso or di seconda mano
hand' or'gan *s* organetto, organino, organetto di Barberia
hand'out' *s* elemosina di cibo; articolo distribuito gratis; comunicato stampa
hand-picked ['hænd ,pɪkt] *adj* colto a mano; scelto specialmente

hand'rail' *s* guardamano, passamano
hand'saw' *s* sega a mano
hand'set' *s* microtelefono
hand'shake' *s* stretta di mano
handsome ['hænsəm] *adj* bello; considerevole; generoso
hand'spring' *s* capriola, salto mortale fatto toccando il terreno con le mani
hand'-to-hand' *adj* corpo a corpo
hand'-to-mouth' *adj* precario, da un giorno all'altro
hand'work' *s* lavoro fatto a mano
hand'writ'ing *s* scrittura
hand'wrought' *adj* lavorato a mano
hand-y ['hændi] *adj* (-ier; -iest) (*easy to handle*) maneggevole; (*within easy reach*) vicino; (*skillful*) destro, abile; **to come in handy** tornare utile
hand'y-man' *s* (-men') factotum *m*
hang [hæŋ] *s* maniera di cadere; **to get the hang of** (coll) imparare a adoperare; **to not give a hang** (coll) non importare un fico a || *v* (*pret & pp* **hung** [hʌŋ]) *tr* sospendere; (*laundry*) stendere; (*to attach*) attaccare; (*a door or window*) mettere sui cardini; (*one's head*) abbassare; **hang it!** (coll) al diavolo!; **to hang up** appendere; sospendere il progresso di || *intr* pendere, penzolare; esitare; essere sospeso; essere attaccato; **to hang around** ciondolare, oziare, gironzolare; **to hang on** essere sospeso a; dipendere da; persistere; (*s.o.'s words*) pendere; **to hang out** sporgersi; (slang) raccogliersi; (slang) vivere; **to hang over** esser sospeso; (*to threaten*) minacciare; **to hang together** mantenersi uniti; **to hang up** (telp) riattaccare || *v* (*pret* **hanged** or **hung**) *tr* (*to execute*) impiccare || *intr* impiccarsi
hangar ['hæŋər] or ['hæŋgar] *s* rimessa; (aer) aviorimessa, hangar *m*
hanger ['hæŋər] *s* gancio, uncino; (*for clothes*) attaccapanni *m*
hang'er-on' *s* (hangers-on) seguace *mf*; seccatore *m*; (*sponger*) parassita *m*
hanging ['hæŋɪŋ] *adj* pendente, pensile || *s* impiccagione; **hangings** parati *mpl*
hang'man *s* (-men) boia *m*
hang'nail' *s* pipita delle unghie
hang'out' *s* (coll) ritrovo abituale
hang'o'ver *s* mal *m* di testa dopo una sbornia
hank [hæŋk] *s* matassa
hanker ['hæŋkər] *intr* agognare
Hannibal ['hænɪbəl] *s* Annibale *m*
haphazard [,hæp'hæzərd] *adj* fortuito, a caso || *adv* a caso; alla carlona
hapless ['hæplɪs] *adj* sfortunato
happen ['hæpən] *intr* succedere; to **happen along** sopravvenire; **to happen on** incontrarsi per caso con; **to happen to** + *inf* per caso + *ind*, e.g., I **happened to see her at the theater** l'ho incontrata per caso a teatro
happening ['hæpənɪŋ] *s* avvenimento, fatto
happily ['hæpɪli] *adv* felicemente; fortunatamente

happiness ['hæpɪnɪs] *s* felicità *f*; gioia, piacere *m*
hap-py ['hæpi] *adj* (-pier; -piest) lieto, felice, contento; **to be happy to** avere il piacere di
hap'py-go-luck'y *adj* spensierato
hap'py me'dium *s* giusto mezzo
Hap'py New Year' *interj* buon anno!, felice anno nuovo!
harangue [hə'ræŋ] *s* arringa, concione || *tr & intr* arringare
harass ['hærəs] or [hə'ræs] *tr* bersagliare; tartassare, tormentare
harbinger ['harbɪndʒər] *s* foriero; annunzio || *tr* annunziare
harbor ['harbər] *adj* di porto, portuario || *s* porto || *tr* albergare; (*love or hatred*) nutrire; (*e.g., a criminal*) dare ricetto a
har'bor mas'ter *s* capitano di porto
hard [hard] *adj* duro; (*difficult*) difficile; (*work*) improbo; (*solder*) forte; (*hearing or breathing*) grosso; (*drinker*) impenitente; (*liquor*) fortemente alcolico; **to be hard on** essere severo con; (*to wear out fast*) logorare rapidamente || *adv* duro; forte; molto; **hard upon** subito dopo
hard'-and-fast' *adj* inflessibile
hard-bitten ['hard'bɪtən] *adj* duro, incallito
hard-boiled ['hard'bɔɪld] *adj* (*egg*) sodo; (coll) duro
hard' can'dy *s* caramelle *fpl*; **piece of hard candy** caramella
hard' cash' *s* denaro contante
hard' ci'der *s* sidro fermentato
hard' coal' *s* antracite *f*
hard'-earned' *adj* guadagnato a stento
harden ['hardən] *tr* indurire || *intr* indurirsi
hardening ['hardənɪŋ] *s* indurimento; (metallurgy) tempra
hard' facts' *spl* realtà *f*
hard-fought ['hard'fɔt] *adj* accanito
hard-headed ['hard'hedɪd] *adj* astuto; ostinato, caparbio
hard-hearted ['hard'hartɪd] *adj* dal cuore duro
hardihood ['hardɪ,hud] *s* forza, coraggio; insolenza
hardiness ['hardɪnɪs] *s* ardire *m*; vigore *m*, robustezza fisica
hard' la'bor *s* lavori forzati
hard' luck' *s* mala sorte
hard'-luck' sto'ry *s* storia delle proprie disgrazie
hardly ['hardli] *adv* appena, quasi no; (*with great difficulty*) a malapena, a fatica; **hardly ever** quasi mai
hardness ['hardnɪs] *s* durezza
hard'-of-hear'ing *adj* duro d'orecchio
hard-pressed ['hard'prest] *adj* oppresso; **to be hard-pressed for** essere a corto di
hard' rub'ber *s* ebanite *f*
hard' sauce' *s* miscela di burro e zucchero
hard'-shell crab' *s* granchio con la corazza
hardship ['hardʃɪp] *s* pena, privazione; **hardships** privazioni *fpl*, strettezze *fpl*

hard'tack' s galletta
hard' times' spl strettezze fpl
hard' to please' adj di difficile contentatura
hard' up' adj (coll) in urgente bisogno; to be hard up for (coll) essere a corto di
hard'ware' s ferramenta fpl; macchinario
hard'ware store' s negozio di ferramenta
hard-won ['hard ,wʌn] adj (victory, battle) conquistato con molti sforzi; (money) acquistato con molti sforzi
hard'wood' s legno forte
hard'wood floor' s pavimento di legno, parquet m
har·dy ['hardi] adj (-dier; -diest) forte, resistente; (rash) temerario; (hort) resistente al freddo
hare [her] s lepre f
harebrained ['her ,brend] adj scervellato, sventato
hare'lip' s labbro leporino
harem ['herəm] s arem m
hark [hark] intr ascoltare; to hark back (said of hounds) ritornare sulla pista; riandare col pensiero || interj ascolta!
harken ['harkən] intr ascoltare
harlequin ['harləkwin] s arlecchino
harlot ['harlət] s meretrice f, baldracca
harm [harm] s danno || tr rovinare; nuocere (with dat), fare del male (with dat)
harmful ['harmfəl] adj nocivo
harmless ['harmlis] adj innocuo
harmonic [har'manik] adj armonico || s (phys) armonica || harmonics ssg armonica; spl suoni armonici
harmonica [har'manikə] s armonica a bocca
harmonious [har'moni-əs] adj armonioso
harmonize ['harmə,naiz] tr intonare; (mus) armonizzare || intr intonarsi; (mus) cantare all'unisono
harmo·ny ['harməni] s (-nies) armonia
harness ['harnis] s bardatura, finimenti mpl; (fig) routine f; to die in the harness morire sulla breccia || tr bardare, imbrigliare; (a waterfall) captare
har'ness mak'er s sellaio
har'ness race' s corsa al trotto, corsa di cavalli col sulky
harp [harp] s arpa || intr—to harp on ripetere ostinatamente
harpist ['harpist] s arpista mf
harpoon [har'pun] s rampone m || tr & intr arpionare
harpsichord ['harpsi,kərd] s arpicordo, clavicembalo
har·py ['harpi] s (-pies) arpia
harrow ['hæro] s erpice m || tr (agr) erpicare; (fig) tormentare
harrowing ['hæro·iŋ] adj straziante
har·ry ['hæri] v (pret & pp -ried) tr saccheggiare; tormentare
harsh [harʃ] adj (to touch) ruvido; (to taste or hearing) aspro; inclemente

harshness ['harʃnis] s ruvidezza; asprezza; inclemenza
hart [hart] s cervo
harum-scarum ['herəm'skerəm] adj & s scervellato
harvest ['harvist] s raccolta, mietitura || tr raccogliere, mietere
harvester ['harvistər] s (person) mietitore m; (machine) mietitrice f
har'vest home' s fine f della mietitura; festa dei mietitori; canzone f dei mietitori
har'vest moon' s luna di settembre
has-been ['hæz ,bin] s (person) fallito; (thing) anticaglia
hash [hæʃ] s polpettone m || tr tritare
hash' house' s osteria di terz'ordine
hashish ['hæʃiʃ] s ascisc m
hasp [hæsp] or [hasp] s boncinello
hassle ['hæsəl] s (coll) rissa, disputa
hassock ['hæsək] s cuscino poggiapiedi
haste [hest] s premura; in haste di premura; to make haste fare presto
hasten ['hesən] tr affrettare || intr affrettarsi
hast·y ['hesti] adj (-ier; -iest) frettoloso; precipitato
hat [hæt] s cappello; to keep under one's hat (coll) mantenere il segreto su; to throw one's hat in the ring (coll) dichiarare la propria candidatura
hat'band' s nastro del cappello
hat' block' s forma da cappelli
hat'box' s cappelliera
hatch [hætʃ] s (brood) nidiata; (shading line) tratteggio; (trap door) porta a ribalta; (lower half of door) mezza porta; (naut) boccaporto || tr (eggs) covare; (a drawing) tratteggiare; complottare, tramare || intr schiudersi
hat'check' girl' s guardarobiera
hatchet ['hætʃit] s accetta; to bury the hatchet fare la pace
hatch'way' s (trap door) porta a ribalta; (naut) boccaporto
hate [het] s odio || tr & intr odiare
hateful ['hetfəl] adj odioso
hat'pin' s spillone m
hat'rack' s attaccapanni m
hatred ['hetrid] s odio, livore m
hatter ['hætər] s cappellaio
haughtiness ['hotinis] s superbia
haugh·ty ['hoti] adj (-tier; -tiest) superbo, sprezzante
haul [hol] s (tug) tiro; (amount caught) retata; (distance transported) percorso, pezzo || tr trasportare; tirare; (naut) alare
haunch [hontʃ] or [hantʃ] s fianco; anca; (hind quarter of an animal) coscia; (same used for food) cosciotto
haunt [hont] or [hant] s ritrovo, nido || tr frequentare assiduamente; perseguitare
haunt'ed house' s casa frequentata dai fantasmi
haute couture [ot ku'tyr] s alta moda
have [hæv] s—the haves and the have-nots gli abbienti e i nullatenenti || v

(*pret & pp* had [hæd]) *tr* avere; (*a dream*) fare; (*to get, take*) prendere, ottenere, ricevere; **to have got** (coll) avere; **to have got to** + *inf* (coll) dovere + *inf*; **to have it in for** (coll) serbar rancore per; **to have it out with** avere a che dire con; **to have on** portare; **to have** (s.th) **to do with** avere (qlco) a che fare con, e.g., **I don't want to have anything to do with him** non voglio aver nulla a che fare con lui; **to have** + *inf* fare + *inf*, e.g., **I had him pay the bill** gli ho fatto pagare il conto; **to have** + *pp* fare + *inf*, e.g., **I had my watch repaired** ho fatto aggiustare l'orologio ‖ *intr*—**to have at** attaccare, mettersi di buzzo buono con; **to have to** + *inf* dovere + *inf*; **to have to do with** avere a che fare con; trattare di, e.g., **this book has to do with superstition** questo libro tratta di superstizione ‖ *v aux* avere, e.g., **he has studied his lesson** ha studiato la sua lezione

havelock ['hævlɑk] *s* coprinuca *m*

haven ['hevən] *s* porto; asilo

haversack ['hævər,sæk] *s* bisaccia; (mil) zaino

havoc ['hævək] *s* rovina; **to play havoc with** rovinare; scompigliare

haw [hɔ] *s* (*of hawthorn*) bacca; (*in speech*) esitazione ‖ *intr* voltare a sinistra ‖ *interj* voltare a sinistra!

hawk [hɔk] *s* falco; (*mortarboard*) sparviere *m*; (coll) persona rapace ‖ *tr* imbonire; (*newspapers*) strillare; **to hawk up** sputare raschiandosi la gola ‖ *intr* fare il merciaiolo ambulante; schiarirsi la gola

hawker ['hɔkər] *s* merciaiolo ambulante

hawse [hɔz] *s* (naut) cubia; (*hole*) (naut) occhio di cubia; (naut) altezza di cubia

hawse'hole' *s* occhio di cubia

hawser ['hɔzər] *s* cavo, gomena

haw'thorn' *s* biancospino

hay [he] *s* fieno; **to hit the hay** (slang) andare a letto; **to make hay while the sun shines** battere il ferro fin ch'è caldo

hay' fe'ver *s* febbre *f* da fieno, raffreddore *m* da fieno

hay'field' *s* prato seminato a fieno

hay'fork' *s* forcone *m;* (mach) rastrello

hay'loft' *s* fienile *m*

haymow ['he ,mau] *s* fienile *m*

hay'rack' *s* rastrelliera

hay'ride' *s* gita notturna in carro di fieno

hay'seed' *s* semente *f* d'erba; (coll) semplicione *m*, campagnolo

hay'stack' *s* meta, pagliaio

hay'wire' *adj* (coll) disordinato, in confusione; (coll) impazzito ‖ *s* filo per legare il fieno

hazard ['hæzərd] *s* pericolo; (*chance*) rischio; (golf) ostacolo ‖ *tr* rischiare; (*an opinion*) arrischiare

hazardous ['hæzərdəs] *adj* pericoloso

haze [hez] *s* foschia; (fig) confusione ‖ *tr* far la matricola a

hazel ['hezəl] *adj* nocciola ‖ *s* (*tree*) nocciolo; (*fruit*) nocciola

ha'zel·nut' *s* nocciola

hazing ['hezɪŋ] *s* vessazione, angheria; (*at university*) matricola

ha·zy ['hezi] *adj* (**-zier; -ziest**) nebbioso; confuso

H-bomb ['etʃ ,bɑm] *s* bomba H

he [hi] *s* (**hes**) maschio ‖ *pron pers* (**they**) lui, egli, esso

head [hɛd] *s* testa, capo; (*of bed*) testiera; (*caption*) testata; (*of a nail*) cappello; (*on a glass of beer*) schiuma; (*of a boil*) punta purulenta; (*e.g., of cattle*) capo; **at the head of** a capo di; **from head to foot** da capo a piedi; **head over heels** a gambe levate; completamente; **heads or tails** testa o croce; **over one's head** al di sopra della capacità intellettuale di qlcu; (*going to a higher authority*) al di sopra di qlcu; **to be out of one's head** (coll) esser matto; **to bring to a head** far giungere alla crisi; **to come into one's head** passar per la mente a qlcu; **to go to one's head** dare al cervello a qlcu; **to keep one's head** non perdere la testa; **to keep one's head above water** arrivare a sbarcare il lunario; **to not make head or tail of** non riuscire a raccappezzarsi su ‖ *tr* dirigere, comandare; essere alla testa di ‖ *intr*—**to head towards** dirigersi verso

head'ache' *s* mal di capo, emicrania

head'band' *s* fascia sul capo; (bb) capitello; (typ) filetto

head'board' *s* testiera del letto

head' cheese' *s* salame *m* di testa

head'dress' *s* acconciatura

header ['hɛdər] *s*—**to take a header** (coll) gettarsi a capofitto

head'first' *adv* a capofitto

head'gear' *s* copricapo; (*for protection*) casco

head'hunt'er *s* cacciatore *m* di teste

heading ['hɛdɪŋ] *s* intestazione; (*of a chapter of a book*) titolo; (journ) testata, capopagina *m*

headland ['hɛdlənd] *s* promontorio

headless ['hɛdlɪs] *adj* senza testa

head'light' *s* (naut, rr) fanale *m;* (aut) faro

head'line' *s* (*of a page of a book*) titolo; (journ) testata ‖ *tr* intestare; fare pubblicità a

head'lin'er *s* (slang) attrazione principale

head'long' *adj* precipitoso ‖ *adv* a precipizio; a capofitto

head'man' *s* (**-men**) capo; giustiziere *m*

head'mas'ter *s* direttore *m* di un collegio per ragazzi

head'most' *adj* primo, più avanzato

head' of'fice *s* sede *f* centrale

head' of hair' *s* capigliatura

head'-on' *adj* frontale ‖ *adv* di fronte, frontalmente

head'phones' *spl* cuffia

head'piece' *s* (*any covering for the head*) copricapo; (*helmet*) elmo; (*brains, judgment*) testa; (*of bed*) spalliera; (*headset*) cuffia; (typ) testata

head′quar′ters *s* sede *f* centrale, direzione; (mil) quartier *m* generale

head′rest′ *s* poggiatesta *m*, testiera

head′set′ *s* cuffia

head′ship′ *s* direzione

head′stone′ *s* pietra angolare; (*on a grave*) pietra tombale

head′stream′ *s* affluente *m* principale

head′strong′ *adj* testardo, ostinato

head′wait′er *s* capocameriere *m*

head′wa′ters *spl* fonti *fpl* or sorgenti *fpl* d'un fiume

head′way′ *s* progresso; **to make headway** progredire

head′wear′ *s* copricapo

head′wind′ *s* vento di prua

head′work′ *s* lavoro intellettuale

head·y [′hɛdi] *adj* (*-ier; -iest*) eccitante; impetuoso; violento; (*clever*) astuto; intossicante

heal [hil] *tr* sanare, guarire; purificare || *intr* risanarsi, guarire; (*said of a wound*) rimarginare

healer [′hilər] *s* guaritore *m*

health [hɛlθ] *s* salute *f;* **to radiate health** sprizzare salute da tutti i pori; **to your health!** alla Sua salute!

health′ depart′ment *s* sanità *f*

healthful [′hɛlθfəl] *adj* salutare

health′ insur′ance *s* assicurazione malattia

health·y [′hɛlθi] *adj* (*-ier; -iest*) sano; salubre

heap [hip] *s* mucchio; (coll) insalata, mare *m* || *tr* ammucchiare; **to heap s.th upon s.o.** colmare qlcu di qlco; **to heap with** colmare di

hear [hɪr] *v* (*pret & pp* **heard** [hʌrd]) *tr* udire; **to hear it said** sentirlo dire || *intr* udire; **hear!, hear!** bravo!; **to hear about** sentir parlare di; **to hear from** aver notizie di; **to hear of** sentir parlare di; **to hear that** sentir dire che

hearer [′hɪrər] *s* ascoltatore *m*

hearing [′hɪrɪŋ] *s* (*sense*) udito, orecchio; (*act*) udienza; **in the hearing of** in presenza di; **within hearing** a portata d'orecchio

hear′ing aid′ *s* uditofono

hear′say′ *s* diceria; **by hearsay** per sentito dire

hearse [hʌrs] *s* carro, carrozzone *m*, or furgone *m* funebre

heart [hɑrt] *s* cuore *m*; (*e.g., of lettuce*) grumolo; **after one's heart** di gusto di qlcu; **by heart** a memoria; **heart and soul** di tutto cuore; **to break the heart of** spezzare il cuore di; **to die of a broken heart** morire di crepacuore; **to eat one's heart out** piangere silenziosamente; **to get to the heart of** sviscerare il nocciolo di; **to have one's heart in one's work** lavorare di buzzo buono; **to have one's heart in the right place** avere buone intenzioni; **to lose heart** scoraggiarsi; **to open one's heart to** aprire il cuore a; **to take heart** prender coraggio; **to take to heart** prendersi a cuore; **to**

wear one's heart on one's sleeve parlare a cuore aperto; **with one's heart in one's mouth** col cuore in bocca

heart′ache′ *s* angustia, angoscia

heart′ attack′ *s* attacco cardiaco

heart′beat′ *s* battito del cuore

heart′break′ *s* angoscia straziante

heart′break′er *s* rubacuori *m*

heartbroken [′hɑrt‚brokən] *adj* col cuore spezzato

heart′burn′ *s* bruciore *m* di stomaco

heart′ disease′ *s* mal *m* di cuore

hearten [′hɑrtən] *tr* rincuorare

heart′ fail′ure *s* (*death*) arresto cardiaco; collasso cardiaco

heartfelt [′hɑrt‚fɛlt] *adj* sentito

hearth [hɑrθ] *s* focolare *m*

hearth′stone′ *s* pietra del focolare

heartily [′hɑrtɪli] *adv* di cuore, cordialmente; saporitamente

heartless [′hɑrtlɪs] *adj* senza cuore, insensibile

heart′ mur′mur *s* soffio al cuore

heart-rending [′hɑrt‚rɛndɪŋ] *adj* da far male al cuore

heart′sick′ *adj* afflitto, sconsolato

heart′strings′ *spl* precordi *mpl*

heart′-to-heart′ *adj* cuore a cuore

heart′ trans′plant *s* trapianto cardiaco

heart′wood′ *s* cuore *m* del legno

heart·y [′hɑrti] *adj* (*-ier; -iest*) cordiale, di cuore; abbondante; (*eater*) grande

heat [hit] *adj* termico || *s* calore *m*; (*of room, house, etc.*) riscaldamento; (zool) fregola; (sports) batteria; (fig) fervore *m*; **in heat** (zool) in amore || *tr* scaldare, riscaldare; (fig) eccitare || *intr* riscaldarsi; (fig) accalorarsi

heated [′hitɪd] *adj* accalorato

heater [′hitər] *s* riscaldatore *m*; (*for central heating*) calorifero; (*to heat hands or bed*) scaldino; (*to heat water in tub*) scaldabagno

heath [hiθ] *s* (*shrub*) brugo, erica; (*tract of land*) brughiera

hea·then [′hiðən] *adj* pagano; irreligioso || *s* (*-then* or *-thens*) pagano

heathendom [′hiðəndəm] *s* (*worship*) paganesimo; (*land*) pagania

heather [′hɛðər] *s* erica, brugo

heating [′hitɪŋ] *adj* di riscaldamento || *s* riscaldamento

heat′ing pad′ *s* termoforo

heat′ light′ning *s* lampo di caldo

heat′ shield′ *s* (rok) scudo termico

heat′stroke′ *s* colpo di calore

heat′ wave′ *s* ondata di caldo

heave [hiv] *s* sollevamento, sforzo; **heaves** (vet) bolsaggine *f* || *v* (*pret & pp* **heaved** or **hove** [hov]) *tr* sollevare, alzare; rigettare; (*a sigh*) emettere || *intr* alzarsi e abbassarsi; (*said of one's chest*) palpitare; avere conati di vomito

heaven [′hɛvən] *s* cielo; **for heaven's sake!** or **good heavens!** per amor del cielo!; **heavens** (*firmament*) cielo || **Heaven** *s* cielo

heavenly [′hɛvənli] *adj* celeste

heav′enly bod′y *s* corpo celeste

heav·y [′hɛvi] *adj* (*-ier; -iest*) (*of great*

weight) pesante; *(liquid)* denso; *(cloth, sea)* grosso; *(traffic)* forte; *(serious)* grave; *(crop)* abbondante; *(rain)* dirotto; *(features)* grossolano; *(heart)* stretto; *(ponderous)* macchinoso; *(industry)* grande; *(stock market)* abbattuto ‖ *adv* (coll) pesantemente; **to hang heavy** *(said of time)* passar lentamente

heav'y-du'ty *adj* extraforte

heavy-hearted ['hɛvɪ'hɑrtɪd] *adj* afflitto, triste

heav'y·set' *adj* forte, corpulento

heav'y·weight' *s* peso massimo

Hebrew ['hibru] *adj & s* ebreo; *(language)* ebraico

hecatomb ['hɛkə ,tom] or ['hɛkə ,tum] *s* ecatombe *f*

heckle ['hɛkəl] *tr* interrompere con domande imbarazzanti

hectic ['hɛktɪk] *adj* febbrile

hedge [hɛdʒ] *s* barriera; *(of bushes)* siepe *f*; *(in stock market)* operazione controbilanciante ‖ *tr* circondare con siepe; **to hedge in** circondare ‖ *intr* evitare di compromettersi; (com) coprirsi

hedge'hog' *s* (zool) riccio; *(porcupine)* (zool) porcospino

hedge'hop' *v (pret & pp* -**hopped;** *ger* **hopping)** *intr* volare a volo radente

hedgehopping ['hɛdʒ ,hɑpɪŋ] *s* volo radente

hedge'row' [ro] *s* siepe *f*

heed [hid] *s* attenzione; **to take heed** fare attenzione ‖ *tr* badare a ‖ *intr* fare attenzione, badare

heedless [hidlɪs] *adj* sbadato

heehaw ['hi ,hɔ] *s (of donkey)* raglio d'asino; risata ‖ *intr* ragliare; ridere fragorosamente

heel [hil] *s (of shoe, of foot)* calcagno, tallone *m*; *(of stocking or shoe)* tallone *m*; *(raised part of shoe below heel)* tacco; (coll) farabutto; **down at the heel** mal ridotto; **to cool one's heels** aspettare a lungo; **to kick up one's heels** darsi alla pazza gioia; **to show a clean pair of heels** or **to take to one's heels** battere i tacchi

heeler ['hilər] *s* politicante *mf*

heft·y ['hɛfti] *adj* (-ier; -iest) *(heavy)* pesante; *(strong)* forte

hegemon·y [hɪ'dʒɛməni] or ['hɛdʒɪ ,moni] *s* (-ies) egemonia

hegira [hɪ'dʒaɪrə] or ['hɛdʒɪrə] *s* fuga

heifer ['hɛfər] *s* manza, giovenca

height [haɪt] *s* altezza; *(of a person)* altezza, statura; *(e.g., of folly)* colmo

heighten ['haɪtən] *tr* innalzare; *(to increase the amount of)* accrescere, aumentare ‖ *intr* aumentare

heinous ['henəs] *adj* nefando, odioso

heir [ɛr] *s* erede *m*

heir' appar'ent *s* **(heirs' appar'ent)** erede necessario

heirdom ['ɛrdəm] *s* eredità *f*

heiress ['ɛrɪs] *s* ereditaria, erede *f*

heirloom ['ɛr ,lum] *s* cimelio di famiglia

Helen ['hɛlən] *s* Elena

helicopter ['hɛlɪ ,kɑptər] *s* elicottero

heliport ['hɛlɪ ,port] *s* eliporto

helium ['hilɪ·əm] *s* elio

helix ['hiliks] *s* **(helixes** or **helices** ['hɛlɪ ,siz])** spirale *f*; (geom) elica

hell [hɛl] *s* inferno

hell-bent ['hɛl'bɛnt] *adj* (coll) risoluto; **to be hell-bent on** (coll) avere un chiodo in testa di

hell'cat' *s* arpia, megera

hellebore ['hɛlɪ ,bor] *s* elleboro

Hellene ['hɛlin] *s* greco

Hellenic [hɛ'lɛnɪk] or [hɛ'linɪk] *adj* ellenico

hell'fire' *s* fuoco dell'inferno

hellish ['hɛlɪʃ] *adj* infernale

hel·lo [hɛ'lo] *s* saluto ‖ *interj* ciao!; *(on telephone)* pronto!

helm [hɛlm] *s* barra del timone; ruota del timone; timone *m* ‖ *tr* dirigere

helmet ['hɛlmɪt] *s* (mil) elmetto; (sports) casco; (hist) elmo

helms'man *s* (-men) timoniere *m*

help [hɛlp] *s* aiuto; *(relief)* rimedio, e.g., **there's no help for it** non c'è rimedio; servitù *f*; impiegati *mpl*; operai *mpl*; **to come to the help of** venire in aiuto di ‖ *tr* aiutare; soccorrere, mitigare; *(to wait on)* servire; **it can't be helped** non c'è rimedio; **so help me God!** Dio mi sia testimonio!; **to help down** aiutare a scendere; **to help s.o. with his coat** aiutare qlcu a mettersi il cappotto; **to help oneself** servirsi da solo; **to help up** aiutare a salire; aiutare ad alzarsi; **to not be able to** *+inf*, e.g., **he can't help laughing** non può fare a meno di ridere ‖ *intr* aiutare ‖ *interj* aiuto!

helper ['hɛlpər] *s* aiutante *m*; *(in a shop)* garzone *m*, lavorante *m*

helpful ['hɛlpfəl] *adj* utile, servizievole

helping ['hɛlpɪŋ] *s (of food)* razione

helpless ['hɛlplɪs] *adj (weak)* debole; *(powerless)* impotente; senza risorse; *(confused)* perplesso; *(situation)* irrimediabile

help'mate' *s* compagno; *(wife)* compagna

helter-skelter ['hɛltər'skɛltər] *adj & adv* in fretta e furia; alla rinfusa

hem [hɛm] *s (any edge)* orlo; *(of skirt)* basta, pedana; *(of suit)* falda ‖ *v (pret & pp* **hemmed;** *ger* **hemming)** *tr* orlare, bordare; **to hem in** insaccare ‖ *intr* esitare; **to hem and haw** esitare; essere evasivo

hemisphere ['hɛmɪ ,sfɪr] *s* emisfero

hemistich ['hɛmɪ ,stɪk] *s* emistichio

hem'line' *s* orlo della gonna

hem'lock' *s (herb and poison)* cicuta; *(Tsuga canadensis)* abete *m* del Canada

hemoglobin [,hɛmə'globɪn] or [,himə'globɪn] *s* emoglobina

hemophilia [,hɛmə'fɪlɪ·ə] or [,himə'fɪlɪ·ə] *s* emofilia

hemorrhage ['hɛmərɪdʒ] *s* emorragia

hemorrhoids ['hɛmə ,rɔɪdz] *spl* emorroidi *fpl*

hemostat ['hɛmə ,stæt] or ['himə ,stæt] *s* pinza emostatica

hemp [hɛmp] *s* canapa

hemstitch ['hɛm,stɪtʃ] s orlo a giorno ‖ tr & intr orlare a giorno

hen [hɛn] s gallina

hence [hɛns] adv di qui; da ora; quindi; di qui a, e.g., **three weeks hence** di qui a tre settimane

hence'forth' adv d'ora innanzi

hench·man ['hɛntʃmən] s (-men [mən]) accolito; politicante m

hen'house' s pollaio

henna ['hɛnə] s henna ‖ tr tingere con la henna

hen'peck' tr (a husband) trovare a ridire con

hen'pecked' hus'band s marito dominato dalla moglie

her [hʌr] adj poss suo, il suo ‖ pron pers la, lei; **to her** le, a lei

herald ['hɛrəld] s araldo; annunziatore m ‖ tr annunziare

heraldic [hɛ'rældɪk] adj araldico

herald·ry ['hɛrəldri] s (-ries) (office) consulta araldica; (science) araldica; (coat of arms) blasone m

herb [ʌrb] or [hʌrb] s erba; erba medicinale

herbaceous [hʌr'beʃəs] adj erbaceo

herbage ['ʌrbɪdʒ] or ['hʌrbɪdʒ] s erba; (law) erbatico

herbalist ['hʌrbəlɪst] or ['ʌrbəlɪst] s erborista mf

herbari·um [hʌr'bɛrɪ·əm] s (-ums or -a [ə]) erbario

herb' doc'tor s erborista mf

herculean [hʌr'kjulɪ·ən] or [,hʌrkju-'li·ən] adj erculeo

herd [hʌrd] s (of sheep) gregge m; (of cattle) mandria; (of men) torma ‖ tr & intr imbrancare

herds'man s (-men) (of cattle) mandriano, vaccaio; (of sheep) pastore m

here [hɪr] adj presente ‖ s—the **here and the hereafter** la vita presente e l'aldilà ‖ adv qui, qua; **here and there** qua e là; **here is** or **here are** ecco; **that's neither here not there** ciò non ha nulla a che vedere ‖ interj presente!

hereabouts ['hɪrə,bauts] adv qua vicino

here·af'ter s aldilà m ‖ adv d'ora innanzi; nel futuro

here·by' adv con la presente

hereditary [hɪ'rɛdɪ,tɛri] adj ereditario

heredi·ty [hɪ'rɛdɪti] s (-ties) eredità f

here·in' adv qui; in questo posto

here·of' adv di questo

here·on' adv su questo; su questo

here·sy ['hɛrəsi] s (-sies) eresia

heretic ['hɛrətɪk] adj & s eretico

heretical [hɪ'rɛtɪkəl] adj eretico

heretofore [,hɪrtu'for] adv sinora

here·u·pon' adv su questo; in questo; immediatamente dopo

here·with' adv accluso; con la presente

heritage ['hɛrɪtɪdʒ] s eredità f

hermetic(al) [hʌr'mɛtɪk(əl)] adj ermetico

hermit ['hʌrmɪt] s eremita m

hermitage ['hʌrmɪtɪdʒ] s eremitaggio

herni·a ['hʌrnɪ·ə] s (-as or -ae [,i]) ernia

he·ro ['hɪro] s (-roes) eroe m

heroic [hɪ'ro·ɪk] adj eroico ‖ **heroics** spl linguaggio altisonante

heroin ['hɛro·ɪn] s (pharm) eroina

heroine ['hɛro·ɪn] s eroina

heroism ['hɛro,ɪzəm] s eroismo

heron ['hɛrən] s airone m

herring ['hɛrɪŋ] s aringa

her'ring-bone' s (in fabrics) spina di pesce; (in hardwood floors) spiga

hers [hʌrz] pron poss il suo; **of hers** suo

herself [hʌr'sɛlf] pron pers lei stessa; sé stessa; si, e.g., **she enjoyed herself** si divertì; **with herself** con sé

hertz [hʌrts] s hertz m

hesitan·cy ['hɛzɪtənsi] s (-cies) titubanza, esitanza

hesitant ['hɛzɪtənt] adj esitante

hesitate ['hɛzɪ,tet] intr esitare, titubare; (to stutter) balbettare

hesitation [,hɛzɪ'teʃən] s esitazione

heterodox ['hɛtərə,dɑks] adj eterodosso

heterodyne ['hɛtərə,daɪn] s eterodina

heterogeneous [,hɛtərə'dʒɪnɪ·əs] adj eterogeneo

hew [hju] v (pret hewed; pp hewed or hewn) tr tagliare; (a passage) aprirsi; (a statue) abbozzare; **to hew down** abbattere ‖ intr—**to hew close to the line** (coll) filare diritto

hex [hɛks] s strega; incantesimo ‖ tr stregare, incantare

hexameter [hɛks'æmɪtər] s esametro

hey [he] interj ehi!

hey'day' s apogeo

hia·tus [haɪ'etəs] s (-tuses or -tus) (gap) lacuna; (gram) iato

hibernate ['haɪbər,net] intr ibernare; (said of people) svernare

hibiscus [hɪ'bɪskəs] or [haɪ'bɪskəs] s ibisco

hic·cup ['hɪkəp] s singhiozzo ‖ v (pret & pp -cuped or -cupped; ger -cuping or -cupping) intr singhiozzare

hick [hɪk] adj & s (coll) rustico

hicko·ry ['hɪkəri] s (-ries) hickory m

hidden ['hɪdən] adj nascosto

hide [haɪd] s cuoio, pelle f; **hides** cuoio; **neither hide nor hair** nemmeno una traccia; **to tan s.o.'s hide** (coll) dargliele sode a qlcu ‖ v (pret hid [hɪd]; pp hid or hidden ['hɪdən]) tr nascondere ‖ intr nascondersi; **to hide out** (coll) rintanarsi

hide'-and-seek' s rimpiattino; **to play hide-and-seek** giocare a rimpiattino or a nascondino

hide'bound' adj retrogrado, conservatore

hideous ['hɪdɪ·əs] adj orribile, brutto

hide'out' s nascondiglio

hiding ['haɪdɪŋ] s nascondere m; (place) nascondiglio; **in hiding** nascosto

hid'ing place' s nascondiglio

hie [haɪ] v (pret & pp hied; ger hieing or hying) tr—**hie thee home** affrettati a tornare a casa ‖ intr affrettarsi

hierar·chy ['haɪ·ə,rɑrki] s (-chies) gerarchia

hieroglyphic [,haɪ·ərə'glɪfɪk] adj & s geroglifico

hi-fi [ˈhaɪˈfaɪ] *adj* di alta fedeltà ‖ *s* alta fedeltà

higgledy-piggledy [ˈhɪgəldiˈpɪgəldi] *adj* confuso ‖ *adv* alla rinfusa

high [haɪ] *adj* alto; (*color*) forte; (*merry*) allegro; (*luxurious*) lussuoso; (coll) ubriaco; (culin) frollo; **high and dry** abbandonato; **high and mighty** (coll) arrogante ‖ *adv* molto; riccamente; **to aim high** mirare in alto; **to come high** essere caro ‖ *s* (aut) quarta, diretta; **on high** in cielo

high' al'tar *s* altare *m* maggiore

high'ball' *s* whiskey con ghiaccio e gazosa ‖ *intr* (slang) andare di carriera

high' blood' pres'sure *s* ipertensione

high'born' *adj* di nobile lignaggio

high'boy' *s* cassettone alto

high'brow' *s* intellettuale *mf*; (coll) intellettualoide *mf*

high'chair' *s* seggiolino per bambini

high' command' *s* comando supremo

high' cost' of liv'ing *s* carovita *m*, caroviveri *m*

high'er educa'tion *s* insegnamento universitario, istruzione superiore

higher-up [ˌhaɪ·ərˈʌp] *s* (coll) superiore *m*

high' explo'sive *s* esplosivo ad alta potenza

highfalutin [ˌhaɪfəˈlutən] *adj* (coll) pomposo, pretenzioso

high' fidel'ity *s* high fidelity, alta fedeltà

high'-fre'quency *adj* ad alta frequenza

high' gear' *s* (aut) presa diretta

high'-grade' *adj* di qualità superiore

high-handed [ˈhaɪˈhændɪd] *adj* arbitrario

high' hat' *s* cappello a cilindro

high'-hat' (coll) snob *m* ‖ *v* (*pret & pp* **-hatted;** *ger* **-hatting**) *tr* (coll) snobbare

high'-heeled' shoe' [ˈhaɪ ˌhild] *s* scarpa coi tacchi alti

high' horse' *s* comportamento arrogante; **to get up on one's high horse** darsi delle grandi arie

high' jinks' [dʒɪŋks] *s* (slang) pagliacciata, gazzarra

high' jump' *s* salto in altezza

highland [ˈhaɪlənd] *adj* montagnoso ‖ **highlands** *spl* regione montagnosa

high' life' *s* high-life *f*, alta società

high'light' *s* punto culminante ‖ *tr* mettere in risalto

highly [ˈhaɪli] *adv* altamente, molto; (*paid*) profumatamente; **to speak highly of** parlar molto bene di

High' Mass' *s* messa cantata

high-minded [ˈhaɪˈmaɪndɪd] *adj* magnanimo

highness [ˈhaɪnɪs] *s* altezza ‖ **Highness** *s* Altezza

high' noon' *s* mezzogiorno in punto; (fig) sommo

high-pitched [ˈhaɪˈpɪtʃt] *adj* acuto; intenso, emozionante

high-powered [ˈhaɪˈpau·ərd] *adj* ad alta potenza; (*binoculars*) ad alto ingrandimento

high'pres'sure *adj* ad alta pressione ‖ *tr* sollecitare con insistenza

high-priced [ˈhaɪˈpraɪst] *adj* caro, di alto prezzo

high' priest' *s* sommo sacerdote

high' rise' *s* edificio di molti piani

high'road' *s* strada principale

high'school' *s* scuola media; (*in Italy*) liceo

high' sea' *s* alto mare; **high seas** alto mare

high' soci'ety *s* l'alta società

high'-sound'ing *adj* altisonante

high'-speed' *adj* ad alta velocità

high-spirited [ˈhaɪˈspɪrɪtɪd] *adj* fiero, vivace, focoso

high' spir'its *spl* allegria, vivacità *f*

high-strung [ˈhaɪˈstrʌŋ] *adj* teso, nervoso

high'-test' fuel' *s* supercarburante *m*

high' tide' *s* alta marea; punto culminante

high' time' *s* ora, e.g., **it is high time for you to go** è proprio ora che Lei se ne vada; (coll) baldoria

high' trea'son *s* (*against the sovereign*) lesa maestà; (*against the state*) alto tradimento

high' wa'ter *s* alta marea; (*in a river*) straripamento

high'way' *adj* autostradale ‖ *s* autostrada

high'way'man *s* (**-men**) grassatore *m*

hijack [ˈhaɪˌdʒæk] *tr* rubare; (*e.g., an airplane*) dirottare ‖ *intr* effettuare un dirottamento

hijacker [ˈhaɪˌdʒækər] *s* ladro a mano armata; (*e.g., of an airplane*) dirottatore *m*

hijacking [ˈhaɪˌdʒækɪŋ] *s* furto a mano armata; dirottamento

hike [haɪk] *s* (*for pleasure*) gita, camminata; (*increase*) aumento; (mil) marcia ‖ *tr* tirar su; aumentare ‖ *intr* fare una gita; (mil) fare una marcia

hiker [ˈhaɪkər] *s* camminatore *m*

hilarious [hɪˈlɛrɪ·əs] *or* [haɪˈlɛrɪ·əs] *adj* ilare; (*e.g., joke*) allegro, divertente

hill [hɪl] *s* collina ‖ *tr* rincalzare

hillbil·ly [ˈhɪlˌbɪli] *s* (**-lies**) (coll) montanaro rustico

hillock [ˈhɪlək] *s* poggio, collinetta

hill'side' *s* pendio

hill'top' *s* cima

hill·y [ˈhɪli] *adj* (**-ier; -iest**) collinoso; ripido

hilt [hɪlt] *s* impugnatura, elsa; **up to the hilt** completamente

him [hɪm] *pron pers* lo; lui; **to him** gli, a lui

himself [hɪmˈsɛlf] *pron pers* lui stesso; sé stesso; si, e.g., **he enjoyed himself** si è divertito; **with himself** con sé

hind [haɪnd] *adj* posteriore, di dietro ‖ *s* cerva

hinder [ˈhɪndər] *tr* ostacolare, impedire

hindmost [ˈhaɪnd ˌmost] *adj* ultimo

hind'quar'ter *s* quarto posteriore

hindrance [ˈhɪndrəns] *s* ostacolo, impedimento

hind'sight' s senno di poi

Hindu ['hɪndu] adj & s indù mf

hinge [hɪndʒ] s cardine m; (bb) cerniera; (philately) listello gommato; punto principale ‖ tr munire di cardini ‖ intr—**to hinge on** dipendere da

hin•ny ['hɪni] s (-nies) bardotto

hint [hɪnt] s insinuazione; **to take the hint** capire l'antifona ‖ tr & intr insinuare; **to hint at** alludere a

hinterland ['hɪntər,lænd] s retroterra m, entroterra m

hip [hɪp] adj—**to be hip to** (slang) essere al corrente di ‖ s anca, fianco; (of a roof) spigolo

hip'bone' s ileo, osso iliaco

hipped [hɪpt] adj (livestock) zoppicante; (roof) a padiglione; **hipped on** (coll) ossessionato per

hippie ['hɪpi] s capellone m

hip•po ['hɪpo] s (-pos) (coll) ippopotamo

hippodrome ['hɪpə,drom] s ippodromo

hippopota•mus [,hɪpə'pɑtəməs] s (-muses or -mi [,maɪ]) ippopotamo

hip' roof' s tetto a padiglione

hire [haɪr] s paga, salario; nolo; **for hire** a nolo ‖ tr (help) impiegare; (a conveyance) noleggiare ‖ intr—**to hire out** mettersi a servizio

hired' girl' s lavorante f di campagna

hired' hand' s lavorante mf

hired' man' s (men') lavorante m di campagna

hireling ['haɪrlɪŋ] adj venale ‖ s persona prezzolata

his [hɪz] adj poss suo, il suo ‖ pron poss il suo

Hispanic [hɪs'pænɪk] adj ispano

Hispanist ['hɪspənɪst] s ispanista mf

hiss [hɪs] s (of fire, wind, serpent, etc.) sibilo; (of disapproval) fischio, zittio ‖ tr zittire ‖ intr zittire; sibilare; (said of a kettle) fischiare

histology [hɪs'tɑlədʒi] s istologia

historian [hɪs'torɪ-ən] s storico

historic(al) [hɪs'tarɪk(əl)] or [hɪs-'tɔrɪk(əl)] adj storico

histo•ry ['hɪstəri] s (-ries) storia

histrionic [,hɪstrɪ'ɑnɪk] adj teatrale; (artificial, affected) istrionico, teatrale ‖ **histrionics** s istrionismo, teatralità f

hit [hɪt] s colpo; successo; (sarcastic remark) frecciata; **to be a hit** far furore; **to make a hit with** fare ottima impressione con ‖ v (pret & pp hit; ger hitting) tr colpire; (to bump) cozzare; (the target) toccare, imbroccare, infilare; (with a car) metter sotto; (a certain speed) andare a ‖ intr battere; **to hit on** (s.th new) imbroccare; **to hit out at** attaccare

hit'-and-run' adj (driver) colpevole di mancato soccorso

hit'-and-run' driv'er s pirata m della strada

hitch [hɪtʃ] s (jerk) strattone m; (knot) nodo; difficoltà f, ostacolo; ‖ tr (to tie) attaccare; (oxen) aggiogare; (slang) sposare

hitch'hike' intr fare l'autostop

hitch'hik'er s autostoppista mf

hitch'ing post' s palo per attaccare un cavallo

hither ['hɪðər] adv qua, qui; **hither and thither** qua e là

hith'er•to' adv sinora

hit'-or-miss' adj fatto alla carlona

hit' rec'ord s disco di grande successo

hive [haɪv] s (box for bees) alveare m; (swarm) sciame m; **hives** orticaria ‖ tr (bees) raccogliere

hoard [hord] s cumulo; (of money) gruzzolo ‖ tr & intr custodire gelosamente; tesaurizzare

hoarding ['hordɪŋ] s ammassamento, tesaurizzazione

hoarfrost ['hor,frɔst] s brina

hoarse [hors] adj rauco, svociato

hoarseness ['horsnɪs] s raucedine f

hoar•y ['hori] adj (-ier; -iest) canuto, incanutito

hoax [hoks] s mistificazione ‖ tr mistificare

hob [hɑb] s mensola del focolare; **to play hob with** (coll) mettere a soqquadro

hobble ['hɑbəl] s zoppicamento; (to tie legs of animal) pastoia ‖ tr far zoppicare; imbarazzare; mettere le pastoie a ‖ intr zoppicare

hob•by ['hɑbi] s (-bies) svago, passatempo; **to ride a hobby** dedicarsi troppo alla propria occupazione favorita

hob'by-horse' s cavallo a dondolo

hob'gob'lin s folletto

hob'nail' s brocca, bulletta

hob•nob ['hɑb,nɑb] v (pret & pp -nobbed; ger -nobbing) intr essere amiconi; **to hobnob with** essere intimo di

ho•bo ['hobo] s (-bos or -boes) girovago, vagabondo

Hob'son's choice' ['hɑbsənz] s scelta fra quanto viene offerto o niente

hock [hɑk] s garretto; (coll) pegno; **in hock** (coll) impegnato, al monte di pietà ‖ tr tagliare i garretti a; (coll) impegnare

hockey ['hɑki] s hockey m

hock'ey play'er s hockeista m, discatore m

hock'shop' s (coll) negozio di prestiti su pegno

hocus-pocus ['hokəs'pokəs] s (meaningless formula) abracadabra m; gherminella

hod [hɑd] s vassoio; secchio per il carbone

hod' car'rier s manovale m

hodgepodge ['hɑdʒ,pɑdʒ] s farragine f

hoe [ho] s marra, zappa ‖ tr & intr zappare

hog [hɑg] or [hɔg] s suino, porco, maiale m ‖ v (pret & pp hogged; ger hogging) tr (slang) mangiarsi il meglio di

hoggish ['hɑgɪʃ] or ['hɔgɪʃ] adj maialesco; egoista

hogs'head' s barilozzo di sessantatré galloni

hog'wash' s broda da maiali

hoist [hɔɪst] *s* montacarichi *m*; *(lift)* spinta || *tr* alzare, rizzare; *(a flag)* inastare; (naut) issare

hoity-toity ['hɔɪtɪ'tɔɪtɪ] *adj* arrogante, altezzoso

hokum ['hokəm] *s* (coll) fandonie *fpl*; (coll) sentimentalismo volgare

hold [hold] *s* presa, piglio; *(handle)* impugnatura; autorità *f*, ascendente *m*; (wrestling) presa; (mus) corona; (naut) cabina bagagli; (mus) corona; (naut) cala, stiva; **to take hold of** afferare; impossessarsi di || *v* (*pret & pp* **held** [held]) *tr* tenere; *(to hold up)* sostenere; *(e.g., with a pin)* assicurare; *(a rank)* rivestire; contenere; *(a meeting)* avere; *(a note)* (mus) filare; **to hold back** trattenere; **to hold in** trattenere; **to hold one's own** non perdere terreno; **to hold over** differire; **to hold up** reggere, sostenere; *(to rob)* (coll) derubare, rapinare || *intr* stare; *(to cling)* reggere; restare valido; **hold on!** un momento!; **to hold back** frenarsi; **to hold forth** fare un discorso; **to hold off** astenersi; mantenersi a distanza; **to hold on** continuare; **to hold on to** attaccarsi a; **to hold out** tener duro, resistere; **to hold out for** mantenersi fermo per

holder ['holdər] *s* possessore *m*, detentore *m*; *(e.g., for a cigar)* bocchino; *(e.g., for a pot)* manico, impugnatura

holding ['holdɪŋ] *s* possesso; **holdings** valori *mpl*, patrimonio

hold'ing com'pany *s* società finanziaria

hold'up' *s* *(delay)* interruzione; (coll) rapina a mano armata; (fig) furto

hold'up man' *s* grassatore *m*

hole [hol] *s* buco; *(in cheese)* occhio; *(in a road)* buca; *(den)* tana; *(burrow)* fossa; **in a hole** in grane, in difficoltà; **to burn a hole in one's pocket** *(said of money)* scorrere attraverso le mani bucate di qlcu; **to pick holes in** trovare a ridire su || *intr*—**to hole up** (coll) imbucarsi

holiday ['halɪ‚de] *s* giorno festivo, festa; vacanza

holiness ['holɪnɪs] *s* santità *f*; **his Holiness** sua Santità

Holland ['haland] *s* l'Olanda *f*

Hollander ['haləndər] *s* olandese *mf*

hollow ['halo] *adj* vuoto; *(sound)* sordo; *(eyes, cheeks)* infossato; vano, futile || *s* buca, cavità *f*; *(small valley)* valletta || *adv*—**to beat all hollow** (coll) battere completamente || *tr* scavare

hol•ly ['halɪ] *s* (-lies) agrifoglio

holly'hock' *s* altea, malvone *m*

holm' oak' [hom] *s* leccio

holocaust ['halə‚kɔst] *s* olocausto

holster ['holstər] *s* fondina

ho•ly ['holɪ] *adj* (-lier; -liest) santo; *(writing)* sacro; *(water)* benedetto

Ho'ly Ghost' *s* Spirito Santo

ho'ly or'ders *spl* ordini sacri; **to take holy orders** entrare in un ordine religioso

Ho'ly Rood' [rud] *s* Santa Croce

Ho'ly Scrip'ture *s* Sacra Scrittura

Ho'ly See' *s* Santa Sede

Ho'ly Sep'ulcher *s* Santo Sepolcro

Ho'ly Thurs'day *s* l'Ascensione; il giovedì santo

ho'ly wa'ter *s* acqua benedetta, acquasanta

Ho'ly Writ' *s* Sacra Scrittura

homage ['hamɪdʒ] *or* ['amɪdʒ] *s* omaggio

homburg ['hambʌrg] *s* lobbia *m & f*

home [hom] *adj* casalingo, domestico; nazionale || *s* casa, dimora; *(fatherland)* patria; *(for the sick, aged, etc.)* ricovero; (sports) meta, traguardo; **at home** a casa; *(at ease)* a proprio agio; (sports) nel proprio campo; **away from home** fuori di casa; **make yourself at home** stia comodo; **to be at home** *(to receive callers)* ricevere || *adv* a casa; **to see home** accompagnare a casa; **to strike home** toccare nel vivo

home'bod'y *s* (-ies) persona casalinga

homebred ['hom‚bred] *adj* domestico; rozzo; semplice

home'brew' *s* bevanda fatta in casa

home-coming ['hom‚kʌmɪŋ] *s* ritorno a casa

home' coun'try *s* paese *m* natale

home' deliv'ery *s* trasporto a domicilio

home' front' *s* fronte domestico

home'land' *s* paese natio

homeless ['homlɪs] *adj* senza tetto

home' life' *s* vita familiare

home-loving ['hom‚lʌvɪŋ] *adj* casalingo

home•ly ['homlɪ] *adj* (-lier; -liest) *(not goodlooking)* brutto; *(not elegant)* semplice, scialbo

homemade ['hom'med] *adj* fatto in casa

homemaker ['hom‚mekər] *s* casalinga

home' of'fice *s* sede *f* centrale || **Home Office** *s* (Brit) ministero degli interni

homeopath ['homɪ‚ə‚pæθ] *or* ['hamɪ‚ə‚pæθ] *s* omeopatico

home' plate' *s* casa base

home' port' *s* porto d'iscrizione (nel registro marittimo)

home' rule' *s* autogoverno

home' run' *s* colpo che permette al battitore di percorrere tutte le basi del diamante fino alla casa base

home'sick' *adj* nostalgico; **to be homesick for** sentire la nostalgia per

home'sick'ness *s* nostalgia

homespun ['hom‚spʌn] *adj* filato a casa; semplice

home'stead *s* casa e terreno

home'stretch' *s* (sports) dirittura d'arrivo; (fig) fase *f* finale

home'town' *s* città *f* natale

homeward ['homwərd] *adj* di ritorno || *adv* verso casa; verso la patria

home'work' *s* lavoro a domicilio; *(of a student)* dovere *m*, esercizio

homey ['homi] *adj* (homier; homiest) intimo, comodo

homicidal [‚hamɪ'saɪdəl] *adj* omicida

homicide ['hamɪ‚saɪd] *s* (act) omicidio; *(person)* omicida *mf*

homi•ly ['hamɪli] *s* (-lies) omelia

homing ['homɪŋ] *adj* (*pigeon*) viaggiatore; (*weapon*) cercatore del bersaglio

hominy ['hɑmɪnɪ] *s* granturco macinato

homogenei·ty [ˌhomədʒɪ'niˌɪtɪ] or [ˌhɑmədʒɪ'niˌɪtɪ] *s* (*-ties*) omogeneità *f*

homogeneous [ˌhomə'dʒɪnɪ·əs] or [ˌhɑmə'dʒɪnɪ·əs] *adj* omogeneo

homogenize [hə'mɑdʒəˌnaɪz] *tr* omogeneizzare

homonym ['hɑmənɪm] *s* omonimo

homonymous [hə'mɑnɪməs] *adj* omonimo

homosexual [ˌhomə'sekʃʊ·əl] *adj* & *s* omosessuale *mf*

hone [hon] *s* cote *f* ‖ *tr* affilare

honest ['ɑnɪst] *adj* onesto; guadagnato onestamente; integro, schietto

honesty ['ɑnɪstɪ] *s* onestà *f*; (bot) lunaria

hon·ey ['hʌnɪ] *adj* melato, dolce ‖ *s* miele *m*; nettare *m*; (coll) caro ‖ *v* (*pret* & *pp* **-eyed** or **-ied**) *tr* dire parole melate a

hon'ey·bee' *s* ape domestica

hon'ey·comb' *s* favo ‖ *tr* crivellare

honeyed ['hʌnɪd] *adj* melato

hon'eydew' mel'on *s* melone *m* dolce dalla scorza liscia

hon'ey lo'cust *s* acacia a tre spine

hon'ey·moon' *s* luna di miele ‖ *intr* andare in viaggio di nozze

honeysuckle ['hʌnɪˌsʌkəl] *s* caprifoglio

honk [haŋk] or [hɔŋk] *s* (*of wild goose*) schiamazzo; (*of automobile horn*) suono del clacson ‖ *tr* (aut) suonare ‖ *intr* schiamazzare; (aut) suonare

honkytonk ['haŋkɪˌtaŋk] or ['hɔŋkɪˌtɔŋk] *s* (coll) locale notturno rumoroso

honor ['ɑnər] *s* onore *m* ‖ *tr* onorare; (com) accettare e pagare

honorable ['ɑnərəbəl] *adj* (*upright*) onorato; (*bringing honor; worthy of honor*) onorevole

honorari·um [ˌɑnə'rerɪ·əm] *s* (*-ums* or **-a** [ə]) onorario

honorary ['ɑnəˌrerɪ] *adj* onorario

honorific [ˌɑnə'rɪfɪk] *adj* onorifico ‖ *s* titolo onorifico; formula di gentilezza

hon'or sys'tem *s* sistema scolastico basato sulla parola d'onore

hood [hʊd] *s* cappuccio; cappuccio di toga universitaria; (*of carriage*) soffietto; (aut) cofano; (slang) gangster *m* ‖ *tr* incappucciare

hoodlum ['hudləm] *s* (slang) facinoroso, gangster *m*, teppista *m*

hoodoo ['hudu] *s* (*body of primitive rites*) vuduismo; (*bad luck*) iettatura; (*person who brings bad luck*) iettatore *m* ‖ *tr* iettare

hood'wink' *tr* turlupinare, imbrogliare

hooey ['hu·ɪ] *s* (coll) sciocchezze *fpl*

hoof [hʊf] or [huf] *s* zoccolo, unghia; **on the hoof** (*cattle*) vivo ‖ *tr*—**to hoof it** (slang) camminare; ballare

hoof'beat' *s* rumore *m* degli zoccoli

hook [hʊk] *s* gancio; (*for fishing*) amo;

(*to join two things*) agganciamento; (*for pulling*) raffio, rampino; (*curve*) curva; (*of hook and eye*) uncinello; (boxing) hook *m*, gancio; **by hook or by crook** di riffa o di raffa; **to swallow the hook** abboccare all'amo ‖ *tr* agganciare; (*to bend*) curvare; (*fish*) pigliare; (*to wound with the horns*) incornare; **to hook up** agganciare; (*e.g., a loudspeaking system*) montare ‖ *intr* agganciarsi; curvarsi

hookah ['hʊkə] *s* narghilè *m*

hook' and eye' *s* uncinello e occhiello

hook' and lad'der *s* autoscala

hooked' rug' *s* tappeto fatto all'uncinetto

hook'nose' *s* naso gobbo

hook'up' *s* (electron) diagramma *m*, schema *m* di montaggio; (rad, telv) rete *f*

hook'worm' *s* anchilostoma *m*

hooky ['hʊkɪ] *s*—**to play hooky** marinare la scuola

hooligan ['hulɪgən] *s* teppista *m*

hooliganism ['hulɪgənˌɪzəm] *s* teppismo

hoop [hup] or [hʊp] *s* cerchio ‖ *tr* cerchiare

hoop' skirt' *s* crinolina

hoot [hut] *s* grido della civetta; grido di derisione ‖ *tr* zittire ‖ *intr* stridere; **to hoot at** fischiare

hoot' owl' *s* allocco

hop [hap] *s* salto, saltello; (aer) breve volo; (bot) luppolo; (coll) corsa; **hops** (*dried flowers of hop vine*) luppolo ‖ *v* (*pret* & *pp* **hopped**; *ger* **hopping**) *tr* saltare su; (aer) trasvolare ‖ *intr* saltellare; saltellare su un piede; **to hop over** saltare su; fare una corsa a

hope [hop] *s* speranza ‖ *tr* & *intr* sperare; **to hope for** sperare

hope' chest' *s* corredo da sposa

hopeful ['hopfəl] *adj* (*feeling hope*) fiducioso; (*giving hope*) promettente

hopeless ['hoplɪs] *adj* disperato

hopper ['hapər] *s* tramoggia

hop'scotch' *s* gioco del mondo

horde [hord] *s* orda

horehound ['horˌhaund] *s* marrubio; pastiglie *fpl* per la tosse al marrubio

horizon [hə'raɪzən] *s* orizzonte *m*

horizontal [ˌhɑrɪ'zantəl] or [ˌhɔrɪ'zantəl] *adj* & *s* orizzontale *f*

hormone ['hɔrmon] *s* ormone *m*

horn [hɔrn] *s* corno; (aut) clacson *m*, avvisatore acustico; (mus) corno; (*trumpet*) (slang) tromba; **to blow one's horn** cantare le proprie lodi; **to lock horns** lottare, disputare; **to pull in one's horns** battere in ritirata ‖ *intr*—**to horn in** (slang) intromettersi (in)

horned' owl' *s* allocco

hornet ['hɔrnɪt] *s* calabrone *m*

hor'net's nest' *s* vespaio; **to stir up a hornet's nest** suscitare un vespaio

horn' of plen'ty *s* corno dell'abbondanza

horn'pipe' *s* clarinetto contadinesco inglese fatto di corno di bue

horn'-rimmed glass'es ['hɔrn'rımd] spl occhiali cerchiati di corno or con la montatura di corno

horn•y ['hɔrni] adj (-ier; -iest) corneo; (callous) calloso; (having hornlike projections) cornuto; (slang) preso da desiderio lussurioso

horoscope ['hɔrə,skop] or ['hɑrə,skop] s oroscopo

horrible ['hɔrıbəl] or ['hɑrıbəl] adj orrendo, orribile

horrid ['hɑrıd] or ['hɔrıd] adj orrido, orribile

horri•fy ['hɑrı,faı] or ['hɔrı,faı] v (pret & pp -fied) tr inorridire

horror ['hɑrər] or ['hɔrər] s orrore m; **to have a horror of** provare orrore per

hors d'oeuvre [ɔr 'dʌrv] s (hors d'oeuvres [ɔr 'dʌrvz]) s antipasto

horse [hɔrs] s cavallo; (of carpenter) cavalletto; **hold your horses!** (coll) aspetti un momento!; **to back the wrong horse** (coll) puntare sul perdente; **to be a horse of another color** (coll) essere un altro paio di maniche || intr—**to horse around** (slang) giocherellare; (slang) fare tiri burloni

horse'back' s—**on horseback** a cavallo || adv—**to ride horseback** montare a cavallo

horse' block' s montatoio

horse'break'er s domatore m di cavalli

horse'car' s tram m a cavalli

horse' chest'nut s (tree) ippocastano; (nut) castagna d'India

horse' deal'er s mercante m di cavalli

horse' doc'tor s veterinario

horse'fly' s (-flies) tafano

horse'hair' s crine m di cavallo; (fabric) cilicio

horse'hide' s cuoio di cavallo

horse'laugh' s risataccia

horse'man s (-men) cavallerizzo

horsemanship ['hɔrsmən,ʃɪp] s equitazione, maneggio

horse' meat' s carne equina

horse' op'era s western m

horse' pis'tol s pistola da sella

horse'play' s gioco violento, tiro burlone

horse'pow'er s cavallo vapore inglese

horse' race' s corsa ippica

horse'rad'ish s cren m, barbaforte m

horse' sense' s (coll) senso comune

horse'shoe' s ferro di cavallo

horse'shoe mag'net s calamita a ferro di cavallo

horse'shoe nail' s chiodo da cavallo

horse' show' s concorso ippico

horse' thief' s ladro di cavalli

horse'-trade' intr trafficare

horse'whip' s staffile m || v (pret & pp -whipped) ger -whipping) tr staffilare

horse'wom'an s (-wom'en) amazzone f

hors•y ['hɔrsi] adj (-ier; -iest) equestre; (interested in horses) appassionato ai cavalli; (coll) goffo

horticulture ['hɔrtı,kʌltʃər] s orticoltura

horticulturist [,hɔrtı'kʌltʃ/ərɪst] s orticoltore m

hose [hoz] s (stocking) calza; (sock) calzino corto; (flexible tube) manica || **hose** spl calze fpl

hosier ['hoʒər] s calzettaio

hosiery ['hoʒəri] s calze fpl; calzificio

hospice ['haspɪs] s ospizio

hospitable ['haspıtəbəl] or [has'pıtəbəl] adj ospitale

hospital ['haspıtəl] s ospedale m

hospitali•ty [,haspı'tælıti] s (-ties) ospitalità f

hospitalize ['haspıtə,laız] tr ospedalizzare

host [host] s ospite m; (at an inn) oste m; (army) milizia; (crowd) folla || **Host** s (eccl) ostia

hostage ['hastıdʒ] s ostaggio

hostel ['hastəl] s ostello della gioventù

hostel•ry ['hastəlrı] s (-ries) albergo

hostess ['hostıs] s ospite f, padrona di casa; (e.g., on a bus) accompagnatrice f, guida f; (aer) assistente f di volo

hostile ['hastıl] adj ostile

hostili•ty [has'tılıti] s (-ties) ostilità f

hostler ['haslər] or ['aslər] s stalliere m

hot [hat] adj (hotter; hottest) caldo; (reception) caloroso; (e.g., pepper) piccante; (fresh) fresco; (pursuit) impetuoso; (in rut) in calore; (coll) radioattivo; **to be hot** (said of a person) aver caldo; (said of the weather) fare caldo; **to make it hot for** (coll) dare del filo da torcere a

hot' air' s aria calda; (slang) fumo

hot'-air fur'nace s impianto di riscaldamento ad aria calda

hot' baths' spl terme fpl

hot'bed' s (e.g., of revolt) focolaio; (hort) semenzaio, letto caldo

hot'-blood'ed adj ardente; impetuoso

hot' cake' s frittella; **to sell like hot cakes** vendersi come se fosse regalato

hot' dog' s Frankfurter m, Würstel m

hotel [ho'tel] adj alberghiero || s albergo

ho•tel'keep'er s albergatore m

hot'head' s testa calda

hotheaded ['hat,hedıd] adj esaltato, scalmanato

hot'house' s serra

hot' plate' s fornello elettrico, scaldavivande m

hot' springs' spl terme fpl

hot-tempered ['hat'tempərd] adj impulsivo, irascibile

hot' wa'ter s—**to be in hot water** (coll) essere nei guai

hot'-wa'ter boil'er s caldaia del termosifone

hot'-wa'ter bot'tle s borsa dell'acqua calda

hot'-wa'ter heat'er s scaldabagno

hot'-wa'ter heat'ing s riscaldamento a circolazione di acqua calda

hound [haund] s bracco; **to follow the hounds** or **to ride to hounds** andare a caccia alla volpe || tr perseguitare

hour [aur] s ora; **by the hour** a ore; **in an evil hour** in un brutto momento; **on the hour** ogni ora al suonar del-

l'ora; **to keep late hours** andare a
letto tardi
hour'glass' *s* clessidra
hour' hand' *s* lancetta delle ore
hourly ['aurlɪ] *adj* orario || *adv* ogni
ora; spesso
house [haus] *s* (**houses** ['hauzɪz])
casa; (*legislative body*) camera; (*size
of audience*) concorso di pubblico;
teatro; **to keep house** fare le faccende domestiche; **to put one's house
in order** migliorare il proprio comportamento; accomodare le proprie
faccende || [hauz] *tr* allogare
house' arrest' *s* arresto a domicilio
house'boat' *s* casa galleggiante
house'break'er *s* scassinatore *m*
housebreaking ['haus,brekɪŋ] *s* violazione di domicilio, scasso
housebroken ['haus,brokən] *adj* (*e.g.,
cat*) che è stato addestrato a tenersi
pulito
house'clean'ing *s* pulizia della casa;
(*fig*) pulizia, impulsiti *m*
house'coat' *s* vestaglia da casa
house' cur'rent *s* corrente *f* di rete
house'fly' *s* (-**flies**) mosca domestica
houseful ['haus,ful] *s* casa piena
house' fur'nishings *spl* arredi domestici
house'hold' *adj* domestico || *s* famiglia
house'hold'er *s* capo della famiglia
house'-hunt' *intr*—**to go house-hunting**
andare in cerca di casa
house'keep'er *s* governante *f*
house'keep'ing *s* faccende domestiche;
to set up housekeeping metter su
casa
house'keeping apart'ment *s* apparta-
mentino
house'maid' *s* domestica
house' me'ter *s* contatore domestico
house'moth'er *s* maestra in pensionato
per studenti
house' of cards' *s* castello di carte
house' of ill' repute' *s* casa di malaffare
house' paint'er *s* imbianchino
house' physi'cian *s* medico residente
house'top' *s* tetto; **to shout from the
housetops** proclamare ai quattro
venti
housewarming ['haus,wormɪŋ] *s* festa
per l'inaugurazione di una casa
house'wife' *s* (-**wives'**) donna di casa
house'work' *s* faccende domestiche
housing ['hauzɪŋ] *s* (*of a horse*) gualdrappa; (*dwelling*) abitazioni *fpl*;
(*carp*) alloggiamento; (*mach*) gabbia,
custodia; (*aut*) coppa; (*of transmission*) (aut) scatola
hous'ing short'age *s* crisi *f* degli alloggi
hovel ['hʌvəl] or ['havəl] *s* catapec-
chia, stamberga; (*shed*) baracca
hover ['hʌvər] or ['havər] *intr* librarsi;
(*on the lips*) trapelare; (*fig*) ondeggiare, esitare
how [hau] *adv* come; (*at what price*)
a quanto; **how early** quando, a che
ora; **how else** in che altro modo; **how
far** fino a dove; quanto, e.g., **how far
is it to the station?** quanto c'è da qui
alla stazione?; **how long** quanto
tempo; **how many** quanti; **how much**

quanto; **how often** quante volte; **how
old are you?** quanti anni ha?; **how
soon** quando, a che ora; **how + adj**
quanto + *adj*, e.g., **how beautiful she
is!** quanto è bella!
how·ev'er *adv* comunque; in qualunque
modo; per quanto . . . , e.g., **however
wrong he may be** per quanto torto
possa avere || *conj* come, e.g., **do it
however you want** lo faccia come
vuole
howitzer ['hau·ɪtsər] *s* obice *m*
howl [haul] *s* ululato, urlo; scoppio di
risa || *tr* gridare; **to howl down**
sopraffare a grida; || *intr* ululare,
urlare
howler ['haulər] *s* urlatore *m*; (coll)
strafalcione *m*, topica
hoyden ['hɔɪdən] *s* ragazzaccia
hub [hʌb] *s* mozzo; (fig) centro
hubbub ['hʌbəb] *s* putiferio, fracasso
hub'cap' *s* (aut) calotta della ruota
huckleber·ry ['hʌkəl,berɪ] *s* (-**ries**)
mirtillo
huckster ['hʌkstər] *s* venditore *m* ambulante; trafficante *m*
huddle ['hʌdəl] *s* conferenza segreta ||
intr affollarsi, accalcarsi
hue [hju] *s* tono, tinta; **hue and cry**
grido d'indignazione
huff [hʌf] *s* stizza; **in a huff** di cattivo
umore || *tr* (checkers) buffare
hug [hʌg] *s* abbraccio || *v* (*pret & pp*
hugged; *ger* **hugging**) *tr* abbracciare;
(*e.g., a wall*) costeggiare || *intr* ab-
bracciarsi
huge [hjudʒ] *adj* smisurato, immane
huh [hʌ] *interj* eh!
hulk [hʌlk] *s* scafo, carcassa; (*unwieldy object*) trabiccolo
hulking ['hʌlkɪŋ] *adj* grosso e goffo
hull [hʌl] *s* (*of ship or hydroplane*)
scafo; (*of dirigible*) intelaiatura; (*of
airplane*) fusoliera; (*e.g., of a nut*)
guscio || *tr* sgusciare; (*rice*) brillare
hullabaloo ['hʌləbə,lu] or [,hʌləbə'lu]
s fracasso, baccano
hum [hʌm] *s* canterellio; (*of bee, ma-
chine, etc.*) ronzio || *v* (*pret & pp*
hummed; *ger* **humming**) *tr* canterel-
lare || *intr* canterellare; (*to buzz*)
ronzare; (coll) vibrare, essere attivo
human ['hjumən] *adj* umano
hu'man be'ing *s* essere umano
humane [hju'men] *adj* umano; compassionevole
humanist ['hjumənɪst] *adj* umanistico
|| *s* umanista *mf*
humanitarian [hju,mænɪ'terɪ·ən] *adj & *
s umanitario
humani·ty [hju'mænɪtɪ] *s* (-**ties**) umanità *f*; **humanities** (*of Greece and
Rome*) studi umanistici; (*literature,
art, philosophy*) scienze umanistiche
hu'man·kind' *s* genere umano
humble ['hʌmbəl] or ['ʌmbəl] *adj*
umile || *tr* umiliare
hum'ble pie' *s*—**to eat humble pie** accettare un'umiliazione
hum'bug' *s* frottola; (*person*) impostore
m || *v* (*pret & pp* -**bugged**; *ger*

-bugging) *tr* imbrogliare ‖ *intr* fare l'imbroglione

hum'drum' *adj* noioso, monotono

humer·us ['hjumərəs] *s* (-i [,aı]) omero

humid ['hjumıd] *adj* umido

humidifier [hju'mıdı ,faı-ər] *s* evaporatore *m*

humidi·fy [hju'mıdı ,faı] *v* (*pret & pp* -**fied**) *tr* inumidire

humidity [hju'mıdıtı] *s* umidità *f*

humiliate [hju'mılı ,et] *tr* umiliare

humiliating [hju'mılı ,etıŋ] *adj* umiliante

humility [hju'mılıtı] *s* umiltà *f*

hummingbird ['hʌmıŋ ,bʌrd] *s* colibrì *m*

humor ['hjumər] or ['jumər] *s* umore *m*; umorismo; **out of humor** di cattivo umore ‖ *tr* adattarsi alle fisime di, assecondare

humorist ['hjumərıst] or ['jumərıst] *s* umorista *mf*

humorous ['hjumərəs] or ['jumərəs] *adj* umoristico

hump [hʌmp] *s* gobba; (*in the ground*) monticello

hump'back' *s* gobba; (*person*) gobbo

humus ['hjuməs] *s* humus *m*

hunch [hʌntʃ] *s* gobba; (*premonition*) (coll) sospetto ‖ *tr* piegare ‖ *intr* accovacciarsi

hunch'back' *s* gobba; (*person*) gobbo

hundred ['hʌndrəd] *adj, s & pron* cento; **a hundred** or **one hundred** cento; **by the hundreds** a centinaia

hundredth ['hʌndrədθ] *adj, s & pron* centesimo

hun'dred·weight' *s* cento libbre

Hungarian [hʌŋ'gerı-ən] *adj & s* ungherese *mf*

Hungary ['hʌŋgərı] *s* l'Ungheria *f*

hunger ['hʌŋgər] *s* fame *f* ‖ *intr* aver fame; **to hunger for** aver un desiderio ardente di, agognare

hun'ger strike' *s* sciopero della fame

hungry ['hʌŋgrı] *adj* (-**grier; -griest**) affamato; **to be hungry** aver fame; **to go hungry** andare digiuno

hunk [hʌŋk] *s* (coll) bel pezzo

hunt [hʌnt] *s* caccia; **on the hunt for** a caccia di ‖ *tr* cacciare; (*to look for*) cercare ‖ *intr* andare a caccia; cercare; **to go hunting** andare a caccia; **to hunt for** cercare

hunter ['hʌntər] *s* cacciatore *m*; (*dog*) cane *m* da caccia

hunting ['hʌntıŋ] *adj* da caccia ‖ *s* caccia

hunt'ing box' *s* capanno

hunt'ing dog' *s* cane *m* da caccia

hunt'ing ground' *s* terreno di caccia

hunt'ing horn' *s* corno da caccia

hunt'ing jack'et *s* cacciatora

hunt'ing lodge' *s* (*hut*) capanno; villino da caccia

hunt'ing sea'son *s* stagione della caccia

huntress ['hʌntrıs] *s* cacciatrice *f*

hunts'man *s* (-**men**) cacciatore *m*

hurdle ['hʌrdəl] *s* (*hedge*) siepe *f*; (*wooden frame*) barriera; (sports, fig) ostacolo; **hurdles** corsa ad ostacoli ‖ *tr* saltare, superare

hur'dle race' *s* corsa agli ostacoli

hurl [hʌrl] *s* lancio ‖ *tr* lanciare; **to hurl back** respingere

hurrah [hʊ'ra] or **hurray** [hʊ're] *s* viva *m* ‖ *tr* applaudire ‖ *intr* gridare urrà ‖ *interj* evviva!, urrà!; **hurrah for . . . !** viva . . . !

hurricane ['hʌrı ,ken] *s* uragano

hurried ['hʌrid] *adj* frettoloso

hur·ry ['hʌri] *s* (-**ries**) fretta; **to be in a hurry** avere fretta ‖ *v* (*pret & pp* -**ried**) *tr* affrettare, sollecitare ‖ *intr* affrettarsi; **to hurry after** correr dietro a; **to hurry away** andarsene di furia; **to hurry back** ritornare presto; **to hurry up** spicciarsi

hurt [hʌrt] *adj* (*injured*) ferito; (*offended*) risentito ‖ *s* (*harm*) danno; (*injury*) ferita; (*pain*) dolore *m* ‖ *v* (*pret & pp* **hurt**) *tr* (*to harm*) fare male a; (*to injure*) ferire; (*to offend*) offendere; (*to pain*) dolere (**with** *dat*) ‖ *intr* fare male, dolere; aver male, e.g., **my head hurts** ho male alla testa

hurtle ['hʌrtəl] *intr* sferrarsi, scagliarsi, precipitarsi

husband ['hʌzbənd] *s* marito ‖ *tr* amministrare con economia

hus'band·man *s* (-**men**) agricoltore *m*

husbandry ['hʌzbəndrı] *s* agricoltura; (*management of domestic affairs*) governo, economia domestica

hush [hʌʃ] *s* silenzio ‖ *tr* far tacere; **to hush up** (*a scandal*) soffocare ‖ *intr* tacere ‖ *interj* zittol

hushaby ['hʌʃə ,baı] *interj* fa' la nanna!

hush'-hush' *adj* segretissimo

hush' mon'ey *s* prezzo del silenzio

husk [hʌsk] *s* guscio; (*of corn*) spoglia ‖ *tr* sgusciare; (*rice*) brillare; (*corn*) scartocciare, spogliare

husk·y ['hʌskı] *adj* (-**ier; -iest**) forte; (*voice*) rauco

hus·sy ['hʌzı] or ['hʌsı] *s* (-**sies**) poca di buono; ragazza impudente

hustle ['hʌsəl] *s* vigore *m*; (slang) traffico ‖ *tr* forzare, spingere ‖ *intr* affrettarsi, scalmanarsi; (slang) trafficare; (*said of a prostitute*) (slang) accostare un cliente

hustler ['hʌslər] *s* (*go-getter*) persona intraprendente; (slang) trafficone *m*, imbroglione *m*; (slang) passeggiatrice *f*

hut [hʌt] *s* casolare *m*, casupola

hyacinth ['haı-əsınθ] *s* giacinto

hybrid ['haıbrıd] *adj & s* ibrido

hybridize ['haıbrı ,daız] *tr & intr* ibridare

hy·dra ['haıdrə] *s* (-**dras** or -**drae** [drı]) idra

hydrant ['haıdrənt] *s* idrante *m*; (*water faucet*) rubinetto

hydrate ['haıdret] *s* idrato ‖ *tr* idratare ‖ *intr* idratarsi

hydraulic [haı'drɔlık] *adj* idraulico ‖ **hydraulics** *s* idraulica

hydrau'lic ram' *s* pompa idraulica

hydriodic [,haıdrı'ɑdık] *adj* iodidrico

hydrobromic [,haıdrə'bromık] *adj* bromidrico

hydrocarbon [ˌhaɪdrəˈkɑrbən] s idrocarburo
hydrochloric [ˌhaɪdrəˈklɔrɪk] adj clo-
ridrico
hydroelectric [ˌhaɪdro·ɪˈlektrɪk] adj
idroelettrico
hydrofluoric [ˌhaɪdrəfluˈɑrɪk] or
[ˌhaɪdrəfluˈɔrɪk] adj fluoridrico
hydrofoil [ˈhaɪdrəˌfɔɪl] s superficie
idrodinamica; (winglike member)
aletta idrodinamica; (vessel) aliscafo, idroplano
hydrogen [ˈhaɪdrədʒən] s idrogeno
hy'drogen bomb' s bomba all'idrogeno
hy'drogen perox'ide s perossido d'idrogeno, acqua ossigenata
hy'drogen sul'fide s solfuro d'idrogeno
hydrometer [haɪˈdrɑmɪtər] s areome-
tro
hydrophobia [ˌhaɪdrəˈfobɪ·ə] s idro-
fobia
hydroplane [ˈhaɪdrəˌplen] s (aer) idrovolante m; (naut) idroscivolante m,
idroplano
hydroxide [haɪˈdrɑksaɪd] s idrossido
hyena [haɪˈinə] s iena
hygiene [ˈhaɪdʒin] or [ˈhaɪdʒɪˌin] s
igiene f
hygienic [ˌhaɪdʒɪˈenɪk] or [haɪ-
ˈdʒinɪk] adj igienico
hymn [hɪm] s inno
hymnal [ˈhɪmnəl] s innario
hyperacidity [ˌhaɪpərəˈsɪdɪti] s iperacidità f
hyperbola [haɪˈpʌrbələ] s (geom) iper-
bole f
hyperbole [haɪˈpʌrbəli] s (rhet) iper-
bole f

hyperbolic [ˌhaɪpərˈbɑlɪk] adj iper-
bolico
hypersensitive [ˌhaɪpərˈsensɪtɪv] adj
ipersensibile
hypertension [ˌhaɪpərˈtenʃən] s ipertensione
hyphen [ˈhaɪfən] s trattino
hyphenate [ˈhaɪfəˌnet] tr unire con
trattino; scrivere con trattino
hypno·sis [hɪpˈnosɪs] s (-ses [siz])
ipnosi f
hypnotic [hɪpˈnɑtɪk] adj & s ipnotico
hypnotism [ˈhɪpnəˌtɪzəm] s ipnotismo
hypnotize [ˈhɪpnəˌtaɪz] tr ipnotizzare
hypochondriac [ˌhaɪpəˈkɑndrɪˌæk] or
[ˌhɪpəˈkɑndrɪˌæk] s ipocondriaco
hypocri·sy [hɪˈpɑkrəsi] s (-sies) ipo-
crisia
hypocrite [ˈhɪpəkrɪt] s ipocrita mf
hypocritical [ˌhɪpəˈkrɪtɪkəl] adj ipocrita
hypodermic [ˌhaɪpəˈdʌrmɪk] adj ipo-
dermico
hyposulfite [ˌhaɪpəˈsʌlfaɪt] s iposolfito
hypotenuse [haɪˈpɑtɪˌnus] or [haɪ-
ˈpɑtɪˌnjus] s ipotenusa
hypothesis [haɪˈpɑθɪsɪs] s (-ses [ˌsiz])
ipotesi f
hypothesize [haɪˈpɑθɪˌsaɪz] tr ipotizzare
hypothetic(al) [ˌhaɪpəˈθetɪk(əl)] adj
ipotetico
hyssop [ˈhɪsəp] s issopo
hysteria [hɪsˈtɪrɪ·ə] s isterismo
hysteric [hɪsˈterɪk] adj isterico ‖ **hysterics** s isterismo
hysterical [hɪsˈterɪkəl] adj isterico

I

I, i [aɪ] s nona lettera dell'alfabeto
inglese
I [aɪ] pron pers (we [wi]) io; **it is I**
sono io
iambic [aɪˈæmbɪk] adj giambico
iam·bus [aɪˈæmbəs] s (-bi [baɪ])
giambo
I'-beam' s putrella
Iberian [aɪˈbɪrɪ·ən] adj iberico ‖ s abitante mf dell'Iberia; lingua iberica
ibex [ˈaɪbeks] s (ibexes or ibices [ˈɪbɪ-
ˌsiz]) stambecco
ice [aɪs] s ghiaccio; **to break the ice**
rompere il ghiaccio; **to cut no ice**
(coll) non avere importanza; **to skate
on thin ice** cacciarsi in una situazione
delicata ‖ tr gelare; (to cover with
icing) glassare ‖ intr gelarsi
ice' age' s epoca glaciale
ice' bag' s borsa di ghiaccio
iceberg [ˈaɪsˌbʌrg] s borgognone m,
montagna di ghiaccio
ice'boat' s slitta a vela; (icebreaker)
rompighiaccio
icebound [ˈaɪsˌbaund] adj chiuso dal
ghiaccio
ice'box' s ghiacciaia
ice'break'er s rompighiaccio

ice' buck'et s secchiello da ghiaccio
ice'cap' s calotta glaciale
ice'-cold' adj gelido, ghiacciato
ice' cream' s gelato, sorbetto
ice'-cream cone' s cono gelato
ice'-cream freez'er s gelatiera
ice'-cream par'lor s gelateria
ice' cube' s cubetto di ghiaccio
ice' hock'ey s hockey m su ghiaccio
Iceland [ˈaɪslənd] s l'Islanda f
Icelander [ˈaɪsˌlændər] or [ˈaɪsləndər]
s islandese mf
Icelandic [aɪsˈlændɪk] adj islandese ‖
s (language) islandese m
ice'man' s (-men') venditore m di
ghiaccio
ice' pack' s banco di ghiaccio; (ice
bag) borsa di ghiaccio
ice' pick' s rompighiaccio
ice' shelf' s tavolato di ghiaccio
ice' skate' s pattino da ghiaccio
ice' wa'ter s acqua gelata
ichthyology [ˌɪkθɪˈɑlədʒi] s ittiologia
icicle [ˈaɪsɪkəl] s ghiacciolo
icing [ˈaɪsɪŋ] s glassa; (meteor) gelo
iconoclast [aɪˈkɑnəˌklæst] s icono-
clasta mf

iconoscope [aɪ'kɑnə,skop] *s* (trademark) iconoscopio

icy ['aɪsi] *adj* (**icier**; **iciest**) ghiacciato; (*e.g.*, *wind*, *hands*) gelido; (fig) glaciale

idea [aɪ'di·ə] *s* idea

ideal [aɪ'di·əl] *adj & s* ideale *m*

idealist [aɪ'di·əlɪst] *adj & s* idealista *mf*

idealistic [aɪ,di·əl'ɪstɪk] *adj* idealistico

idealize [aɪ'di·ə,laɪz] *tr* idealizzare

identic(al) [aɪ'dɛntɪk(-əl)] *adj* identico

identification [aɪ,dɛntɪfɪ'ke/ən] *s* identificazione, riconoscimento

identifica'tion card' *s* carta d'identità

identifica'tion tag' *s* piastrina

identi·fy [aɪ'dɛntɪ,faɪ] *v* (*pret & pp* **-fied**) *tr* identificare

identi·ty [aɪ'dɛntɪti] *s* (**-ties**) identità *f*

ideolo·gy [,aɪdɪ'ɑlədʒi] *or* [,ɪdɪ'ɑlədʒi] *s* (**-gies**) ideologia

ides [aɪdz] *spl* idi *mpl & fpl*

idio·cy ['ɪdɪ·əsi] *s* (**-cies**) idiozia

idiom ['ɪdɪ·əm] *s* (*expression that is contrary to the usual patterns of the language*) locuzione idiomatica, idiotismo; (*style of language*) lingua, idioma *m*; (*style of an author*) stile *m*; (*character of a language*) indole *f*

idiomatic [,ɪdɪ·ə'mætɪk] *adj* idiomatico

idiosyncra·sy [,ɪdɪ·ə'sɪnkrəsi] *s* (**-sies**) eccentricità *f*, originalità *f*; (med) idiosincrasia

idiot ['ɪdɪ·ət] *s* idiota *mf*

idiotic [,ɪdɪ'ɑtɪk] *adj* idiota

idle ['aɪdəl] *adj* (*unemployed*) disoccupato; (*machine*) fermo; (*capital*) giacente; (*time*) perso; (*talk*) vano; (*lazy*) fannullone, ozioso; **to run idle** girare a vuoto || *tr*—**to idle away** (*time*) sprecare || *intr* poltrire, fare il fannullone; (aut) girare al minimo

idleness ['aɪdəlnɪs] *s* ozio

idler ['aɪdlər] *s* fannullone *m*

idling ['aɪdlɪŋ] *s* (*of motor*) minimo

idol ['aɪdəl] *s* idolo

idola·try [aɪ'dɑlətri] *s* (**-tries**) idolatria

idolize ['aɪdə,laɪz] *tr* idolatrare

idyll ['aɪdəl] *s* idillio

idyllic [aɪ'dɪlɪk] *adj* idilliaco

if [ɪf] *conj* se; **as if** come se; **even if** anche se; **if so** se è così; **if true** se è vero

ignis fatuus ['ɪgnɪs'fæt/u·əs] *s* (**ignes fatui** ['ɪgniz'fæt/u,aɪ]) fuoco fatuo

ignite [ɪg'naɪt] *tr* infiammare || *intr* infiammarsi

ignition [ɪg'nɪ/ən] *s* ignizione; (aut) accensione

igni'tion switch' *s* (aut) chiavetta dell'accensione

igni'tion sys'tem *s* (aut) apparecchiatura d'accensione

ignoble [ɪg'nobəl] *adj* ignobile

ignominious [,ɪgnə'mɪnɪ·əs] *adj* ignominioso

ignoramus [,ɪgnə'reməs] *s* ignorante *mf*

ignorance ['ɪgnərəns] *s* ignoranza

ignorant ['ɪgnərənt] *adj* ignorante; **to be ignorant of** ignorare

ignore [ɪg'nor] *tr* (*a person; a person's kindness*) ignorare

ill [ɪl] *adj* (*worse* [wʌrs]; *worst* [wʌrst]) malato; **to take ill** cadere malato || *adv* male; **to take ill** prendere in mala parte

ill-advised ['ɪləd'vaɪzd] *adj* inconsulto, sconsiderato

ill'-at-ease' *adj* imbarazzato, spaesato

ill-bred ['ɪl'brɛd] *adj* maleducato

ill-considered ['ɪlkən'sɪdərd] *adj* sconsiderato

ill-disposed ['ɪldɪs'pozd] *adj* maldisposto, malintenzionato

illegal [ɪ'ligəl] *adj* illegale

illegible [ɪ'lɛdʒɪbəl] *adj* illeggibile

illegitimate [,ɪlɪ'dʒɪtɪmɪt] *adj* illegittimo

ill' fame' *s* pessima fama

ill-fated ['ɪl'fetɪd] *adj* infausto

ill-gotten ['ɪl'gɑtən] *adj* male acquistato

ill-humored ['ɪl'hjumərd] *adj* di cattivo umore

illicit [ɪ'lɪsɪt] *adj* illecito

illitera·cy [ɪ'lɪtərəsi] *s* (**-cies**) analfabetismo; (*mistake*) solecismo; ignoranza

illiterate [ɪ'lɪtərɪt] *adj* (*uneducated*) illetterato; (*unable to read or write*) analfabeta || *s* analfabeta *mf*

ill-mannered ['ɪl'mænərd] *adj* screanzato, ineducato

illness ['ɪlnɪs] *s* malattia

illogical [ɪ'lɑdʒɪkəl] *adj* illogico

ill-spent ['ɪl'spɛnt] *adj* sprecato

ill-starred ['ɪl'stɑrd] *adj* nato sotto una cattiva stella; sfortunato, funesto

ill-tempered ['ɪl'tɛmpərd] *adj* di cattivo umore

ill-timed ['ɪl'taɪmd] *adj* inopportuno

ill'-treat' *tr* maltrattare, tartassare

illuminate [ɪ'lumɪ,net] *tr* illuminare; (*a manuscript*) miniare

illumination [ɪ,lumɪ'ne/ən] *s* illuminazione; (*in manuscript*) miniatura

illusion [ɪ'luʒən] *s* illusione

illusive [ɪ'lusɪv] *adj* illusorio

illusory [ɪ'lusəri] *adj* illusorio

illustrate ['ɪləs,tret] *or* [ɪ'lʌstret] *tr* illustrare

illustration [,ɪləs'tre/ən] *s* illustrazione

illustrator ['ɪləs,tretər] *s* illustratore *m*

illustrious [ɪ'lʌstrɪ·əs] *adj* illustre

ill' will' *s* astio, ruggine *f*, malevolenza

image ['ɪmɪdʒ] *s* immagine *f*; **the very image of** il ritratto parlante di

image·ry ['ɪmɪdʒri] *or* ['ɪmɪdʒəri] *s* (**-ries**) (*mental images*) fantasia; (*images collectively*) immagini *fpl*; (rhet) linguaggio figurato

imaginary [ɪ'mædʒɪ,nɛri] *adj* immaginario

imagination [ɪ,mædʒɪ'ne/ən] *s* immaginazione

imagine [ɪ'mædʒɪn] *tr & intr* immaginare; (*to conjecture*) immaginarsi; **imagine!** si figuri!

imbalance [ɪm'bæləns] *s* scompenso

imbecile ['ɪmbɪsɪl] *adj & s* imbecille *mf*

imbecili·ty [ˌɪmbɪˈsɪlɪti] s (-ties) imbecillità f, imbecillaggine f

imbibe [ɪmˈbaɪb] tr (to drink) bere; assorbire || intr bere

imbue [ɪmˈbju] tr imbevere

imitate [ˈɪmɪˌtet] tr imitare

imitation [ˌɪmɪˈteʃən] adj (e.g., jewelry) falso || s imitazione

imitator [ˈɪmɪˌtetər] s imitatore m

immaculate [ɪˈmækjəlɪt] adj immacolato

immaterial [ˌɪməˈtɪrɪ·əl] adj immateriale; poco importante; **it's immaterial to me** a me fa lo stesso

immature [ˌɪməˈtjur] or [ˌɪməˈtur] adj immaturo

immeasurable [ɪˈmeʒərəbəl] adj incommensurabile, smisurato

immediacy [ɪˈmidɪ·əsi] s immediatezza

immediate [ɪˈmidɪ·ɪt] adj immediato

immediately [ɪˈmidɪ·ɪtli] adv immediatamente

immemorial [ˌɪmɪˈmorɪ·əl] adj immemorabile

immense [ɪˈmens] adj immenso

immerge [ɪˈmʌrdʒ] intr sommergersi

immerse [ɪˈmʌrs] tr immergere

immersion [ɪˈmʌrʃən] or [ɪˈmʌrʒən] s immersione

immigrant [ˈɪmɪɡrənt] adj & s immigrante mf

immigrate [ˈɪmɪˌɡret] intr immigrare

immigration [ˌɪmɪˈɡreʃən] s immigrazione

imminent [ˈɪmɪnənt] adj imminente

immobile [ɪˈmobɪl] or [ɪˈmobɪl] adj immobile

immobilize [ɪˈmobɪˌlaɪz] tr immobilizzare

immoderate [ɪˈmadərɪt] adj smodato, sregolato

immodest [ɪˈmadɪst] adj immodesto

immoral [ɪˈmarəl] or [ɪˈmorəl] adj immorale

immortal [ɪˈmortəl] adj & s immortale mf

immortalize [ɪˈmortəˌlaɪz] tr eternare, immortalare

immune [ɪˈmjun] adj immune

immunize [ˈɪmjəˌnaɪz] or [ɪˈmjunaɪz] tr immunizzare

imp [ɪmp] s diavoletto; (child) frugolo

impact [ˈɪmpækt] s impatto

impair [ɪmˈper] tr danneggiare; (to weaken) indebolire

impan·el [ɪmˈpænəl] v (pret & pp -eled or -elled; ger -eling or -elling) tr iscrivere nella lista dei giurati; (a jury) selezionare

impart [ɪmˈpart] tr (a secret) far conoscere; (knowledge) impartire; (motion) imprimere

impartial [ɪmˈparʃəl] adj imparziale

impassable [ɪmˈpæsəbəl] or [ɪmˈpasəbəl] adj impraticabile, intransitabile

impasse [ɪmˈpæs] or [ˈɪmpæs] s vicolo cieco, impasse f

impassible [ɪmˈpæsɪbəl] adj impassibile

impassioned [ɪmˈpæʃənd] adj caloroso, veemente

impassive [ɪmˈpæsɪv] adj impassibile

impatience [ɪmˈpeʃəns] s impazienza

impatient [ɪmˈpeʃənt] adj impaziente

impeach [ɪmˈpitʃ] tr accusare; (a public official) sottoporre a un'inchiesta; (a statement) mettere in dubbio

impeachment [ɪmˈpitʃmənt] s accusa; inchiesta

impeccable [ɪmˈpekəbəl] adj impeccabile

impecunious [ˌɪmpɪˈkjunɪ·əs] adj indigente

impedance [ɪmˈpidəns] s impedenza

impede [ɪmˈpid] tr impedire, intralciare

impediment [ɪmˈpedɪmənt] s impedimento; ostacolo

im·pel [ɪmˈpel] v (pret & pp -peled or -pelled; ger -peling or -pelling) tr spingere, forzare

impending [ɪmˈpendɪŋ] adj imminente, incombente

impenetrable [ɪmˈpenətrəbəl] adj impenetrabile

impenitent [ɪmˈpenɪtənt] adj impenitente || s persona impenitente

imperative [ɪmˈperɪtɪv] adj (commanding) imperativo; (urgent) imperioso || s imperativo

imperceptible [ˌɪmpərˈseptɪbəl] adj impercettibile

imperfect [ɪmˈpʌrfɪkt] adj & s imperfetto

imperfection [ˌɪmpərˈfɛkʃən] s imperfezione

imperial [ɪmˈpɪrɪ·əl] adj imperiale || s (goatee) barbetta, mosca; (top of coach) imperiale m

imperialist [ɪmˈpɪrɪ·əlɪst] adj & s imperialista mf

imper·il [ɪmˈperɪl] v (pret & pp -iled or -illed; ger -iling or -illing) tr mettere in pericolo

imperious [ɪmˈpɪrɪ·əs] adj imperioso

imperishable [ɪmˈperɪʃəbəl] adj imperituro, duraturo

impersonate [ɪmˈpʌrsəˌnet] tr (to pretend to be) spacciarsi per; (on the stage) impersonare

impertinence [ɪmˈpʌrtɪnəns] s impertinenza

impertinent [ɪmˈpʌrtɪnənt] adj impertinente

impetuous [ɪmˈpetʃʊ·əs] adj impetuoso

impetus [ˈɪmpɪtəs] s impeto, foga

impie·ty [ɪmˈpaɪ·əti] s (-ties) empietà f

impinge [ɪmˈpɪndʒ] intr—**to impinge on** or **upon** violare; (said, e.g., of the sun) ferire; (the imagination) colpire

impious [ˈɪmpɪ·əs] adj empio

impish [ˈɪmpɪʃ] adj indiavolato

implant [ɪmˈplænt] tr innestare; instillare, istillare

implement [ˈɪmplɪmənt] s utensile m, strumento || [ˈɪmplɪˌment] tr completare, mettere in opera; (to provide with implements) attrezzare

implicate [ˈɪmplɪˌket] tr implicare

implicit [ɪmˈplɪsɪt] adj implicito; (unquestioning) assoluto, cieco

implied [ɪmˈplaɪd] adj implicito

implore [ɪmˈplor] tr (a person; pardon)

implorare; **(to entreat)** raccomandarsi a

im·ply [ɪmˈplaɪ] v (pret & pp **-plied**) tr voler dire, significare; implicare, sottintendere

impolite [ˌɪmpəˈlaɪt] adj scortese

import [ˈɪmport] s importazione; articolo d'importazione; importanza ‖ [ɪmˈport] or [ˈɪmport] tr importare; significare ‖ intr importare

importance [ɪmˈportəns] s importanza

important [ɪmˈportənt] adj importante

importation [ˌɪmporˈteʃən] s importazione

importer [ɪmˈportər] s importatore m

importunate [ɪmˈportʃənɪt] adj importuno

importune [ˌɪmporˈtjun] or [ˌɪmporˈtun] tr importunare

impose [ɪmˈpoz] tr imporre ‖ intr—to impose on or upon abusare di; abusare della gentilezza di

imposing [ɪmˈpozɪŋ] adj imponente

imposition [ˌɪmpəˈzɪʃən] s imposizione; abuso; abuso della gentilezza; inganno

impossible [ɪmˈpɑsɪbəl] adj impossibile

impostor [ɪmˈpɑstər] s impostore m

imposture [ɪmˈpɑstʃər] s impostura

impotence [ˈɪmpətəns] s impotenza

impotent [ˈɪmpətənt] adj impotente

impound [ɪmˈpaʊnd] tr rinchiudere, recintare; **(water)** raccogliere; **(law)** sequestrare, confiscare

impoverish [ɪmˈpɑvərɪʃ] tr impoverire

impracticable [ɪmˈpræktɪkəbəl] adj impraticabile; **(intractable)** intrattabile

impractical [ɪmˈpræktɪkəl] adj poco pratico

impregnable [ɪmˈprɛgnəbəl] adj inespugnabile, imprendibile

impregnate [ɪmˈprɛgnet] tr impregnare

impresari·o [ˌɪmprɪˈsɑri ˌo] s (**-os**) impresario

impress [ɪmˈprɛs] tr **(to affect in mind or feelings)** impressionare; **(to produce by pressure; to fix on s.o.'s mind)** imprimere; **(mil)** arruolare

impression [ɪmˈprɛʃən] s impressione

impressionable [ɪmˈprɛʃənəbəl] adj impressionabile

impressive [ɪmˈprɛsɪv] adj impressionante, imponente

imprint [ˈɪmprɪnt] s impronta; **(typ)** indicazione dell'editore ‖ [ɪmˈprɪnt] tr imprimere

imprison [ɪmˈprɪzən] tr imprigionare

imprisonment [ɪmˈprɪzənmənt] s prigione, prigionia

improbable [ɪmˈprɑbəbəl] adj improbabile

impromptu [ɪmˈprɑmptju] or [ɪmˈprɑmptu] adj improvvisato ‖ s improvvisazione; **(mus)** impromptu m ‖ adv all'improvviso

improper [ɪmˈprɑpər] adj **(erroneous)** improprio; **(inappropriate; unseemly)** scorretto; **(math)** improprio

improve [ɪmˈpruv] tr migliorare; **(an opportunity)** approfittare di ‖ intr migliorare; **to improve on** or **upon** perfezionare

improvement [ɪmˈpruvmənt] s miglioramento, perfezionamento; **(in real estate)** miglioria; **(e.g., of time)** buon uso

improvident [ɪmˈprɑvɪdənt] adj improvvido, imprevidente

improvise [ˈɪmprəˌvaɪz] tr & intr improvvisare

imprudence [ɪmˈprudəns] s imprudenza

imprudent [ɪmˈprudənt] adj imprudente

impudence [ˈɪmpjədəns] s impudenza, sfrontatezza, sfacciataggine f

impudent [ˈɪmpjədənt] adj sfrontato, sfacciato, spudorato

impugn [ɪmˈpjun] tr impugnare

impulse [ˈɪmpʌls] s impulso

impulsive [ɪmˈpʌlsɪv] adj impulsivo

impunity [ɪmˈpjunɪti] s impunità f

impure [ɪmˈpjʊr] adj impuro

impuri·ty [ɪmˈpjʊrɪti] s (**-ties**) impurità f

impute [ɪmˈpjut] tr imputare

in [ɪn] adj interno; **(coll)** moderno, alla moda ‖ s relazione; **the ins and outs** tutti i dettagli ‖ adv dentro; a casa; in ufficio; **in here** qui dentro; **in there** lì dentro; **to be in** essere a casa; **to be in for** essere destinato a; **to be in with** essere in intimità con ‖ prep in; **(within)** dentro a; **(over, through)** per; di, e.g., **the best in the class** il migliore della classe; **dressed in** vestito di; **in so far as** per quanto; **in that** per quanto, dato che

inability [ˌɪnəˈbɪlɪti] s inabilità f

inaccessible [ˌɪnækˈsɛsɪbəl] adj inaccessibile

inaccura·cy [ɪnˈækjərəsi] s (**-cies**) inesattezza, imprecisione

inaccurate [ɪnˈækjərɪt] adj inesatto

inaction [ɪnˈækʃən] s inazione

inactive [ɪnˈæktɪv] adj inattivo

inadequate [ɪnˈædɪkwɪt] adj inadeguato, inadatto

inadvertent [ˌɪnədˈvʌrtənt] adj disattento; inavvertito

inadvisable [ˌɪnədˈvaɪzəbəl] adj poco consigliabile

inane [ɪnˈen] adj insensato, assurdo

inanimate [ɪnˈænɪmɪt] adj inanimato

inappreciable [ˌɪnəˈpriʃɪ·əbəl] adj inapprezzabile

inappropriate [ˌɪnəˈpropri·ɪt] adj non appropriato, improprio

inarticulate [ˌɪnɑrˈtɪkjəlɪt] adj **(sounds, words)** inarticolato; **(person)** incapace di esprimersi

inasmuch as [ˌɪnəsˈmʌtʃ ˌæz] conj dato che, visto che, in quanto che

inattentive [ˌɪnəˈtɛntɪv] adj disattento

inaugural [ɪnˈɔgjərəl] adj inaugurale ‖ s discorso inaugurale

inaugurate [ɪnˈɔgjəˌret] tr inaugurare

inauguration [ɪnˌɔgjəˈreʃən] s inaugurazione; **(investiture of a head of government)** assunzione dei poteri

inborn [ˈɪnˈbɔrn] adj innato, ingenito

inbreeding [ˈɪnˌbridɪŋ] s incrocio fra animali o piante affini

incandescent [ˌɪnkənˈdɛsənt] adj incandescente

incapable [ɪn'kepəbəl] *adj* incapace
incapacitate [ˌɪnkə'pæsɪˌtet] *tr* inabilitare; (*law*) interdire
incapaci·ty [ˌɪnkə'pæsɪti] *s* (**-ties**) incapacità *f*
incarcerate [ɪn'kɑrsəˌret] *tr* incarcerare
incarnate [ɪn'kɑrnɪt] or [ɪn'kɑrnet] *adj* incarnato || [ɪn'kɑrnet] *tr* incarnare
incarnation [ˌɪnkɑr'neʃən] *s* incarnazione
incendiarism [ɪn'sɛndɪ·əˌrɪzəm] *s* incendio doloso; (*agitation*) sobillazione
incendiar·y [ɪn'sɛndɪˌeri] *adj* incendiario || *s* (**-ies**) incendiario; (fig) sobillatore *m*
incense ['ɪnsɛns] *s* incenso || *tr* (*to burn incense for*) incensare || [ɪn'sɛns] *tr* irritare, esasperare
in'cense burn'er *s* (*person*) incensatore *m;* (*vessel*) incensiere *m*
incentive [ɪn'sɛntɪv] *adj* & *s* incentivo
inception [ɪn'sɛpʃən] *s* principio
incertitude [ɪn'sʌrtɪˌtjud] or [ɪn'sʌrtɪˌtud] *s* incertezza
incest ['ɪnsɛst] *s* incesto
incestuous [ɪn'sɛstʃʊ·əs] *adj* incestuoso
inch [ɪntʃ] *s* pollice *m;* **to be within an inch of** essere a due dita da || *intr—* **to inch ahead** spingersi avanti poco a poco
incidence ['ɪnsɪdəns] *s* incidenza
incident ['ɪnsɪdənt] *adj* incidente, incidentale || *s* incidente *m*
incidental [ˌɪnsɪ'dɛntəl] *adj* incidentale || *s* elemento incidentale; **incidentals** piccole spese
incidentally [ˌɪnsɪ'dɛntəli] *adv* incidentalmente, per inciso; a proposito
incinerator [ɪn'sɪnəˌretər] *s* inceneritore *m*
incision [ɪn'sɪʒən] *s* incisione
incisive [ɪn'saɪsɪv] *adj* incisivo
incite [ɪn'saɪt] *tr* incitare, stimulare
inclemen·cy [ɪn'klɛmənsi] *s* (**-cies**) inclemenza
inclination [ˌɪnklɪ'neʃən] *s* inclinazione
incline ['ɪnklaɪn] or [ɪn'klaɪn] *s* declivio || [ɪn'klaɪn] *tr* inclinare || *intr* inclinarsi
inclose [ɪn'kloz] *tr* includere, accludere; **to inclose herewith** accludere alla presente
inclosure [ɪn'kloʒər] *s* (*land surrounded by fence*) recinto; (*e.g., letter*) allegato
include [ɪn'klud] *tr* includere; **including** incluso, e.g., **three books including the grammar** tre libri inclusa la grammatica
inclusive [ɪn'klusɪv] *adj* incluso, e.g., **until next Friday inclusive** fino a venerdì prossimo incluso; **inclusive of** inclusivo di, e.g., **price inclusive of freight** prezzo inclusivo delle spese di trasporto
incogni·to [ɪn'kɑgnɪˌto] *adj* incognito || *s* (**-tos**) incognito || *adv* in incognito

incoherent [ˌɪnko'hɪrənt] *adj* incoerente
incombustible [ˌɪnkəm'bʌstɪbəl] *adj* incombustibile
income ['ɪnkʌm] *s* reddito, provento
in'come tax' *s* imposta sul reddito
incoming ['ɪnˌkʌmɪŋ] *adj* entrante; futuro; (*tide*) ascendente || *s* entrata
incomparable [ɪn'kɑmpərəbəl] *adj* incomparabile, impareggiabile
incompatible [ˌɪnkəm'pætɪbəl] *adj* incompatibile
incomplete [ˌɪnkəm'plit] *adj* incompleto, tronco, scompleto
incomprehensible [ˌɪnkɑmprɪ'hɛnsɪbəl] *adj* incomprensibile
inconceivable [ˌɪnkən'sivəbəl] *adj* inconcepibile
inconclusive [ˌɪnkən'klusɪv] *adj* inconcludente
incongruous [ɪn'kɑŋgru·əs] *adj* incongruo
inconsequential [ɪnˌkɑnsɪ'kwɛnʃəl] *adj* (*lacking proper sequence of thought or speech*) inconseguente; (*trivial*) di poca importanza
inconsiderate [ˌɪnkən'sɪdərɪt] *adj* inconsiderato, sconsiderato
inconsisten·cy [ˌɪnkən'sɪstənsi] *s* (**-cies**) inconsistenza
inconsistent [ˌɪnkən'sɪstənt] *adj* inconsistente, inconseguente
inconsolable [ˌɪnkən'soləbəl] *adj* inconsolabile, sconsolato
inconspicuous [ˌɪnkən'spɪkju·əs] *adj* poco appariscente, poco apparente
inconstant [ɪn'kɑnstənt] *adj* incostante
incontinence [ɪn'kɑntɪnəns] *s* incontinenza
incontrovertible [ˌɪnkɑntrə'vʌrtɪbəl] *adj* incontrovertibile
inconvenience [ˌɪnkən'vini·əns] *s* scomodo, incomodo || *tr* scomodare
inconvenient [ˌɪnkən'vini·ənt] *adj* incomodo, inconveniente
incorporate [ɪn'kɔrpəˌret] *tr* incorporare; costituire in società anonima || *intr* incorporarsi; costituirsi in società anonima
incorrect [ˌɪnkə'rɛkt] *adj* scorretto
increase ['ɪnkris] *s* aumento; crescita; **to be on the increase** essere in aumento || [ɪn'kris] *tr* aumentare; (*by propagation*) moltiplicare || *intr* aumentare; moltiplicarsi
increasingly [ɪn'krisɪŋlɪ] *adv* sempre più
incredible [ɪn'krɛdɪbəl] *adj* incredibile
incredulous [ɪn'krɛdʒələs] *adj* incredulo
increment ['ɪnkrɪmənt] *s* aumento, incremento
incriminate [ɪn'krɪmɪˌnet] *tr* incriminare
incrust [ɪn'krʌst] *tr* incrostare
incubate ['ɪnkjəˌbet] *tr* incubare || *intr* essere in incubazione; (*said, e.g., of a hen*) covare; (fig) covare
incubator ['ɪnkjəˌbetər] *s* incubatrice *f*
inculcate [ɪn'kʌlket] or ['ɪnkʌlˌket] *tr* inculcare

incumben·cy [ɪn'kʌmbənsi] s (-cies) incombenza

incumbent [ɪn'kʌmbənt] adj—**to be incumbent on** incombere a, spettare a || s titolare mf

incunabula [ˌɪnkjʊ'næbjələ] spl (beginnings) origini fpl; (early printed books) incunaboli mpl

in·cur [ɪn'kʌr] v (pret & pp -curred; ger -curring) tr incorrere in; (a debt) assumere, contrarre

incurable [ɪn'kjurəbəl] adj & s incurabile mf

incursion [ɪn'kʌrʒən] or [ɪn'kʌrʃən] s incursione, scorreria

indebted [ɪn'detɪd] adj indebitato; obbligato

indecen·cy [ɪn'disənsi] s (-cies) indecenza, sconcezza

indecent [ɪn'disənt] adj indecente, sconveniente

indecisive [ˌɪndɪ'saɪsɪv] adj indeciso; (e.g., event) non decisivo

indeed [ɪn'did] adv difatti, infatti || interj davvero!

indefatigable [ˌɪndɪ'fætɪɡəbəl] adj indefesso, infaticabile

indefensible [ˌɪndɪ'fensɪbəl] adj indifendibile, insostenibile

indefinable [ɪndɪ'faɪnəbəl] adj indefinibile

indefinite [ɪn'defɪnɪt] adj indefinito

indelible [ɪn'delɪbəl] adj indelebile

indemnification [ɪnˌdemnɪfɪ'keʃən] s indennità f, indennizzo

indemni·fy [ɪn'demnɪˌfaɪ] v (pret & pp -fied) tr indennizzare

indemni·ty [ɪn'demnɪti] s (-ties) indennità f, indennizzo

indent [ɪn'dent] tr frastagliare, dentellare; (typ) far rientrare

indentation [ˌɪnden'teʃən] s frastaglio, dentellatura; (typ) accapo

indenture [ɪn'dentʃər] s scrittura pubblica; contratto di apprendista || tr obbligare per contratto

independence [ˌɪndɪ'pendəns] s indipendenza

independent [ˌɪndɪ'pendənt] adj & s indipendente mf

indescribable [ˌɪndɪ'skraɪbəbəl] adj indescrivibile

indestructible [ˌɪndɪ'strʌktɪbəl] adj indistruttibile

indeterminate [ˌɪndɪ'tʌrmɪnɪt] adj indeterminato

index ['ɪndeks] s (indexes or indices ['ɪndɪˌsiz]) indice m; (typ) indice m indicatore || tr mettere un indice a; mettere all'indice || **Index** s Indice m

in'dex card' s scheda di catalogo

in'dex fin'ger s dito indice

India ['ɪndɪə] s l'India f

In'dia ink' s inchiostro di china

Indian ['ɪndɪən] adj & s indiano

In'dian club' s clava di ginnastica

In'dian corn' s granoturco

In'dian file' s fila indiana || adv in fila indiana

In'dian O'cean s Oceano Indiano

In'dian sum'mer s estate f di San Martino

In'dian wres'tling s braccio di ferro

In'dia pa'per s carta bibbia, carta d'India

In'dia rub'ber s caucciù m

indicate ['ɪndɪˌket] tr indicare

indication [ˌɪndɪ'keʃən] s indicazione

indicative [ɪn'dɪkətɪv] adj & s indicativo

indicator ['ɪndɪˌketər] s indicatore m, indice m

indict [ɪn'daɪt] tr accusare

indictment [ɪn'daɪtmənt] s accusa, atto d'accusa

indifferent [ɪn'dɪfərənt] adj indifferente; (not particularly good) passabile

indigenous [ɪn'dɪdʒɪnəs] adj indigeno

indigent ['ɪndɪdʒənt] adj indigente || **the indigent** gli indigenti

indigestion [ˌɪndɪ'dʒestʃən] s indigestione

indignant [ɪn'dɪɡnənt] adj indignato

indignation [ˌɪndɪɡ'neʃən] s indignazione

indigni·ty [ɪn'dɪɡnɪti] s (-ties) indignità f

indi·go ['ɪndɪˌɡo] adj indaco || s (-gos or -goes) indaco

indirect [ˌɪndɪ'rekt] or [ˌɪndaɪ'rekt] adj indiretto

in'direct dis'course s discorso indiretto

indiscernible [ˌɪndɪ'zʌrnɪbəl] or [ˌɪndɪ'sʌrnɪbəl] adj indiscernibile

indiscreet [ˌɪndɪs'krit] adj indiscreto

indispensable [ˌɪndɪs'pensəbəl] adj indispensabile, imprescindibile

indispose [ˌɪndɪs'poz] tr indisporre

indisposed [ˌɪndɪs'pozd] adj (disinclined) mal disposto; (slightly ill) indisposto

indissoluble [ˌɪndɪ'saljəbəl] adj indissolubile

indistinct [ˌɪndɪ'stɪŋkt] adj indistinto

indite [ɪn'daɪt] tr redigere

individual [ˌɪndɪ'vɪdʒʊəl] adj individuale || s individuo

individuali·ty [ˌɪndɪˌvɪdʒʊ'ælɪti] s (-ties) individualità f; (person of distinctive character) individuo

Indochina ['ɪndo'tʃaɪnə] s l'Indocina f

Indo-Chi·nese ['ɪndot'faɪ'niz] adj indocinese || s (-nese) indocinese mf

Indo-European ['ɪndoˌjurə'pi·ən] adj & s indoeuropeo

indolent ['ɪndələnt] adj indolente

Indonesia [ˌɪndo'niʒə] or [ˌɪndo'niʒə] s l'Indonesia f

Indonesian [ˌɪndo'niʃən] or [ˌɪndo'niʒən] adj & s indonesiano

indoor ['ɪnˌdor] adj situato in casa; da farsi in casa

indoors ['ɪn'dorz] adv dentro, a casa, al coperto

indorse [ɪn'dors] tr (com) girare; (fig) appoggiare, approvare

indorsee [ˌɪndor'si] s giratario

indorsement [ɪn'dorsmənt] s (com) girata; (fig) appoggio, approvazione

indorser [ɪn'dorsər] s girante mf

induce [ɪn'djus] or [ɪn'dus] tr indurre

inducement [ɪn'djusmənt] or [ɪn'dusmənt] s stimolo, incentivo

induct [ɪn'dʌkt] *tr* installare; iniziare; (mil) arruolare

induction [ɪn'dʌkʃən] *s* iniziazione; (elec & log) induzione; (mil) arruolamento

indulge [ɪn'dʌldʒ] *tr* indulgere (with *dat*) || *intr* cedere, lasciarsi andare; **to indulge** in abbandonarsi a; permettersi il lusso di

indulgence [ɪn'dʌldʒəns] *s* compiacenza; intemperanza, abbandono; (*leniency*) indulgenza

indulgent [ɪn'dʌldʒənt] *adj* indulgente

industrial [ɪn'dʌstrɪ-əl] *adj* industriale

industrialist [ɪn'dʌstrɪ-əlɪst] *s* industriale *m*

industrialize [ɪn'dʌstrɪ-ə‚laɪz] *tr* industrializzare

industrious [ɪn'dʌstrɪ-əs] *adj* industrioso, laborioso

indus·try ['ɪndʌstrɪ] *s* (**-tries**) industria

inebriation [ɪn‚ibrɪ'e/ən] *s* ubriachezza

inedible [ɪn'edɪbəl] *adj* immangiabile

ineffable [ɪn'efəbəl] *adj* ineffabile

ineffective [‚ɪnɪ'fɛktɪv] *adj* inefficace; (*person*) incapace

ineffectual [‚ɪnɪ'fɛktʃʊ-əl] *adj* inefficace

inefficient [‚ɪnɪ'fɪʃənt] *adj* inefficiente

ineligible [ɪn'elɪdʒɪbəl] *adj* ineleggibile

inequali·ty [‚ɪnɪ'kwɑlɪtɪ] *s* (**-ties**) disuguaglianza

inequi·ty [ɪn'ekwɪtɪ] *s* (**-ties**) ingiustizia

ineradicable [‚ɪnɪ'rædɪkəbəl] *adj* inestirpabile

inertia [ɪn'ʌrʃe] *s* inerzia

inescapable [‚ɪnes'kepəbəl] *adj* ineluttabile, inderogabile

inevitable [ɪn'evɪtəbəl] *adj* inevitabile

inexact [‚ɪneg'zækt] *adj* inesatto

inexcusable [‚ɪneks'kjuzəbəl] *adj* inescusabile

inexhaustible [‚ɪneg'zɔstɪbəl] *adj* inesauribile

inexorable [ɪn'eksərəbəl] *adj* inesorabile

inexpedient [‚ɪnek'spidɪ-ənt] *adj* inopportuno

inexpensive [‚ɪnek'spensɪv] *adj* poco costoso, a buon mercato

inexperience [‚ɪnek'spɪrɪ-əns] *s* inesperienza

inexplicable [ɪn'eksplɪkəbəl] *adj* inesplicabile

inexpressible [‚ɪnek'spresɪbəl] *adj* indicibile, inesprimibile

infallible [ɪn'fælɪbəl] *adj* infallibile

infamous ['ɪnfəməs] *adj* infame

infa·my ['ɪnfəmɪ] *s* (**-mies**) infamia

infan·cy ['ɪnfənsɪ] *s* (**-cies**) infanzia

infant ['ɪnfənt] *adj* infantile; (*in the earliest stage*) (fig) nascente || *s* neonato, bebè *m*

infantile ['ɪnfən‚taɪl] or ['ɪnfəntɪl] *adj* infantile

infan·try ['ɪnfəntrɪ] *s* (**-tries**) fanteria

in'fantry·man *s* (**-men**) fante *m*

infatuated [ɪn'fætʃʊ‚etɪd] *adj* infatuato

infect [ɪn'fekt] *tr* infettare

infection [ɪn'fekʃən] *s* infezione

infectious [ɪn'fekʃəs] *adj* infettivo

in·fer [ɪn'fʌr] *v* (*pret & pp* **-ferred;** *ger* **-ferring**) *tr* inferire; (coll) dedurre, supporre

inferior [ɪn'fɪrɪ-ər] *adj & s* inferiore *m*

inferiority [ɪn‚fɪrɪ'ɑrɪtɪ] *s* inferiorità *f*

inferior'ity com'plex *s* complesso di inferiorità

infernal [ɪn'fʌrnəl] *adj* infernale

infest [ɪn'fest] *tr* infestare

infidel ['ɪnfɪdəl] *adj & s* infedele *mf*

infideli·ty [‚ɪnfɪ'delɪtɪ] *s* (**-ties**) infedeltà *f*

in'field' *s* campo interno, diamante *m*

infiltrate [ɪn'fɪltret] or ['ɪnfɪl‚tret] *tr* infiltrarsi in || *intr* infiltrarsi

infinite ['ɪnfɪnɪt] *adj & s* infinito

infinitive [ɪn'fɪnɪtɪv] *adj* infinitivo || *s* infinito

infini·ty [ɪn'fɪnɪtɪ] *s* (**-ties**) infinità *f*; (math) infinito

infirm [ɪn'fʌrm] *adj* infermo; (*not firm*) debole

infirma·ry [ɪn'fʌrmərɪ] *s* (**-ries**) infermeria

infirmi·ty [ɪn'fʌrmɪtɪ] *s* (**-ties**) infermità *f*

inflame [ɪn'flem] *tr* infiammare || *intr* infiammarsi

inflammable [ɪn'flæməbəl] *adj* infiammabile

inflammation [‚ɪnflə'meʃən] *s* infiammazione

inflate [ɪn'flet] *tr* gonfiare; (*currency, prices*) inflazionare || *intr* gonfiarsi

inflation [ɪn'fleʃən] *s* inflazione; (*of a tire*) gonfiatura

inflect [ɪn'flekt] *tr* curvare; (*voice*) modulare; (gram) flettere

inflection [ɪn'flekʃən] *s* inflessione; (gram) flessione

inflexible [ɪn'fleksɪbəl] *adj* inflessibile

inflict [ɪn'flɪkt] *tr* infliggere, inferire

influence ['ɪnflu-əns] *s* influenza || *tr* influire su, influenzare

influential [‚ɪnflu'enʃəl] *adj* influente

influenza [‚ɪnflu'enzə] *s* influenza

inform [ɪn'fɔrm] *tr* informare || *intr* dare informazioni; **to inform on** denunziare, fare la spia contro

informal [ɪn'fɔrməl] *adj* non ufficiale, ufficioso; (*unceremonious*) alla buona, familiare

informant [ɪn'fɔrmənt] *s* informatore *m*; (*informer*) delatore *m*; (ling) fonte *f* orale, informatore *m*

information [‚ɪnfər'meʃən] *s* informazioni *fpl*; conoscenze *fpl*

informational [‚ɪnfər'meʃənəl] *adj* informativo

informed' sour'ces *spl* fonti *fpl* attendibili

informer [ɪn'fɔrmər] *s* (*informant*) informatore *m*; (*spy*) delatore *m*

infraction [ɪn'frækʃən] *s* infrazione

infrared [‚ɪnfrə'red] *adj & s* infrarosso

infrequent [ɪn'frikwənt] *adj* infrequente

infringe [ɪn'frɪndʒ] *tr* violare || *intr*—**to infringe on** or **upon** violare, contravvenire a

infringement [ɪn'frɪndʒmənt] *s* infrazione

infuriate [ɪn'fjʊrɪ ,et] *tr* infuriare

infuse [ɪn'fjuz] *tr* infondere

infusion [ɪn'fjuʒən] *s* infusione

ingenious [ɪn'dʒinjəs] *adj* ingegnoso

ingenui·ty [,ɪndʒɪ'nu·ɪti] *or* [,ɪndʒɪ-'nju·ɪti] *s* (-ties) ingegnosità *f*

ingenuous [ɪn'dʒɛnju·əs] *adj* ingenuo

ingenuousness [ɪn'dʒɛnju·əsnɪs] *s* ingenuità *f*

ingest [ɪn'dʒɛst] *tr* ingerire

ingoing ['ɪn ,goɪŋ] *adj* entrante

ingot ['ɪŋgət] *s* lingotto, massello

ingraft [ɪn'græft] *or* [ɪn'grɑft] *tr* (hort & surg) innestare; (fig) inculcare

ingrate ['ɪngret] *s* ingrato

ingratiate [ɪn'greʃɪ ,et] *tr*—**to ingratiate oneself with** ingraziarsi

ingratiating [ɪn'greʃɪ ,etɪŋ] *adj* attraente, affascinante, insinuante

ingratitude [ɪn'grætɪ ,tjud] *or* [ɪn-'grætɪ ,tud] *s* ingratitudine *f*

ingredient [ɪn'gridɪ·ənt] *s* ingrediente *m*

in'grown nail' ['ɪngron] *s* unghia incarnita

ingulf [ɪn'gʌlf] *tr* sommergere, inondare

inhabit [ɪn'hæbɪt] *tr* abitare, popolare

inhabitant [ɪn'hæbɪtənt] *s* abitante *mf*

inhale [ɪn'hel] *tr & intr* inspirare

inherent [ɪn'hɪrənt] *adj* inerente

inherit [ɪn'herɪt] *tr & intr* ereditare

inheritance [ɪn'herɪtəns] *s* eredità *f*

inheritor [ɪn'herɪtər] *s* erede *mf*

inhibit [ɪn'hɪbɪt] *tr* inibire

inhospitable [ɪn'hɑspɪtəbəl] *or* [,ɪn-hɑs'pɪtəbəl] *adj* inospitale

inhuman [ɪn'hjumən] *adj* inumano

inhumane [,ɪnhju'men] *adj* inumano

inimical [ɪ'nɪmɪkəl] *adj* nemico

iniqui·ty [ɪ'nɪkwɪti] *s* (-ties) iniquità *f*

ini·tial [ɪ'nɪʃəl] *adj & s* iniziale *f* ‖ *v* (pret -tialed *or* -tialled; ger -tialing *or* -tialling) *tr* siglare

initiate [ɪ'nɪʃɪ ,et] *tr* iniziare

initiation [ɪ ,nɪʃɪ'eʃən] *s* iniziazione

initiative [ɪ'nɪʃɪ-ətɪv] *or* [ɪ'nɪʃətɪv] *s* iniziativa

inject [ɪn'dʒɛkt] *tr* iniettare; introdurre

injection [ɪn'dʒɛkʃən] *s* iniezione

injudicious [,ɪndʒu'dɪʃəs] *adj* avventato, sconsiderato

injunction [ɪn'dʒʌŋkʃən] *s* ingiunzione

injure ['ɪndʒər] *tr* (to harm) danneggiare; (to wound) ferire; (to offend) offendere, ingiuriare

injurious [ɪn'dʒʊrɪ·əs] *adj* dannoso; offensivo, ingiurioso

inju·ry ['ɪndʒəri] *s* (-ries) (harm) danno; (wound) ferita, lesione; offesa, ingiuria

injustice [ɪn'dʒʌstɪs] *s* ingiustizia

ink [ɪŋk] *s* inchiostro ‖ *tr* inchiostrare

inkling ['ɪŋklɪŋ] *s* sentore *m*, indizio

ink'stand' *s* (container) calamaio; (stand) calamaiera

ink'well' *s* calamaio

ink·y ['ɪŋki] *adj* (-ier; -iest) nero come l'inchiostro; nero d'inchiostro

inlaid ['ɪn ,led] *or* [,ɪn'led] *adj* intarsiato, incrostato

inland ['ɪnlənd] *adj & s* interno ‖ *adv* verso l'interno

in'-law' *s* affine *mf*

in·lay ['ɪn ,le] *s* intarsio, tassello ‖ [ɪn'le] *or* ['ɪn ,le] *v* (pret & pp -laid) *tr* intarsiare

in'let *s* (of the shore) insenatura; (entrance) ammissione

in'mate' *s* (patient, e.g., in an insane asylum) internato; (in a jail) prigioniero

inn [ɪn] *s* taverna, osteria

innate [ɪ'net] *or* ['ɪnet] *adj* innato

inner ['ɪnər] *adj* interno, interiore; intimo, profondo

in'ner·spring' mat'tress *s* materasso a molle

in'ner tube' *s* camera d'aria

inning ['ɪnɪŋ] *s* (baseball) turno

inn'keep'er *s* locandiere *m*, oste *m*

innocence ['ɪnəsəns] *s* innocenza

innocent ['ɪnəsənt] *adj & s* innocente *mf*

innovate ['ɪnə ,vet] *tr* innovare

innovation [,ɪnə've ʃən] *s* innovazione

innuen·do [,ɪnju'ɛndo] *s* (-does) sottinteso, insinuazione

innumerable [ɪ'njumərəbəl] *or* [ɪ'numərəbəl] *adj* innumerevole

inoculate [ɪn'ɑkjə ,let] *tr* inoculare; (e.g., with hatred) inoculare; permeare

inoculation [ɪn ,ɑkjə'leʃən] *s* inoculazione

inoffensive [,ɪnə'fɛnsɪv] *adj* inoffensivo

inopportune [ɪn ,ɑpər'tjun] *or* [ɪn-,ɑpər'tun] *adj* inopportuno

inordinate [ɪn'ɔrdɪnɪt] *adj* smoderato

inorganic [,ɪnɔr'gænɪk] *adj* inorganico

in'pa'tient *s* degente *mf*

in'put' *s* entrata; (elec, mach) energia immessa

inquest ['ɪnkwɛst] *s* inchiesta

inquire [ɪn'kwaɪr] *tr* domandare, chiedere ‖ *intr*—**to inquire about, after,** *or* **for** chiedere di; **to inquire into** investigare

inquir·y [ɪn'kwaɪri] *or* ['ɪnkwɪri] *s* (-ies) indagine *f*, inchiesta

inquisition [,ɪnkwɪ'zɪʃən] *s* inquisizione

inquisitive [ɪn'kwɪzɪtɪv] *adj* indagatore, curioso

in'road' *s* incursione, invasione

insane [ɪn'sen] *adj* pazzo, matto

insane' asy'lum *s* manicomio

insani·ty [ɪn'sænɪti] *s* (-ties) pazzia, follia, demenza

insatiable [ɪn'seʃəbəl] *adj* insaziabile

inscribe [ɪn'skraɪb] *tr* iscrivere; (a book) dedicare; (geom) inscrivere

inscription [ɪn'skrɪpʃən] *s* scritta, iscrizione; (of a book) dedica

inscrutable [ɪn'skrutəbəl] *adj* imperscrutabile

insect ['ɪnsɛkt] *s* insetto

insecticide [ɪn'sɛktɪ ,saɪd] *adj & s* insetticida *m*

insecure [,ɪnsɪ'kjʊr] *adj* malsicuro

inseparable [ɪn'sɛpərəbəl] *adj* inseparabile

insert ['ɪnsʌrt] s inserzione; (circular) inserto || [ɪn'sʌrt] tr inserire
insertion [ɪn'sʌrʃən] s inserzione; (in lunar orbit) immissione; (of lace) tramezzo
in·set ['ɪn‚set] s intercalazione || [ɪn-'set] or ['ɪn‚set] v (pret & pp -set; ger -setting) tr intercalare
in'shore' adj & adv vicino alla spiaggia
in'side' adj interno; privato, confidenziale || s interno; **insides** (coll) interiora fpl; **to be on the inside** avere informazioni confidenziali || adv dentro; all'interno; **inside of** dentro, dentro a, dentro di; **to turn inside out** rovesciare, voltare il diritto al rovescio || prep dentro, dentro a
in'side flap' s (bb) risvolto
insider [‚ɪn'saɪdər] s persona informata
in'side track' s (racing) steccato; **to have the inside track** (coll) trovarsi in una situazione vantaggiosa
insidious [ɪn'sɪdɪ·əs] adj insidioso
in'sight' s intuito, penetrazione
insigni·a [ɪn'sɪgnɪ·ə] s (-a or -as) distintivo; (distinguishing sign) segno
insignificant [‚ɪnsɪg'nɪfɪkənt] adj insignificante
insincere [‚ɪnsɪn'sɪr] adj insincero
insinuate [ɪn'sɪnju‚et] tr insinuare
insist [ɪn'sɪst] intr insistere
insofar as [‚ɪnso'fɑr‚æz] conj per quanto
insolence ['ɪnsələns] s insolenza
insolent ['ɪnsələnt] adj insolente
insoluble [ɪn'sɑljəbəl] adj insolubile
insolven·cy [ɪn'sɑlvənsi] s (-cies) insolvenza
insomnia [ɪn'sɑmnɪ·ə] s insonnia
insomuch [‚ɪnso'mʌtʃ] adv fino al punto; **insomuch as** giacché, visto che; **insomuch that** fino al punto che
inspect [ɪn'spekt] tr ispezionare
inspection [ɪn'spekʃən] s ispezione
inspector [ɪn'spektər] s ispettore m
inspiration [‚ɪnspɪ're·ʃən] s ispirazione
inspire [ɪn'spaɪr] tr & intr ispirare
install [ɪn'stɔl] tr installare
installment [ɪn'stɔlmənt] s rata; (of a book) dispensa; **in installments** a rate
install'ment plan' s pagamento rateale; **on the installment plan** con facilitazioni di pagamento
instance ['ɪnstəns] s esempio; (law) istanza; **for instance** per esempio
instant ['ɪnstənt] adj istantaneo || s istante m; mese m corrente
instantaneous [‚ɪnstən'tenɪ·əs] adj istantaneo
instantly ['ɪnstəntli] adv immediatamente, istantaneamente
instead [ɪn'sted] adv invece; **instead of** invece di
in'step' s collo del piede
instigate ['ɪnstɪ‚get] tr istigare
instigation [‚ɪnstɪ'geʃən] s istigazione
in·still' tr instillare, istillare
instinct ['ɪnstɪŋkt] s istinto
instinctive [ɪn'stɪŋktɪv] adj istintivo

institute ['ɪnstɪ‚tjut] or ['ɪnstɪ‚tut] s istituto || tr istituire
institution [‚ɪnstɪ'tju/ən] or [‚ɪnstɪ-'tu/ən] s istituzione
institutionalize [‚ɪnstɪ'tju/ənə‚laɪz] or [‚ɪnstɪ'tu/ənə‚laɪz] tr istituzionalizzare
instruct [ɪn'strʌkt] tr istruire
instruction [ɪn'strʌkʃən] s istruzione
instructive [ɪn'strʌktɪv] adj istruttivo
instructor [ɪn'strʌktər] s istruttore m
instrument ['ɪnstrəmənt] s strumento; (law) istrumento || ['ɪnstrə‚ment] tr strumentare
instrumental [‚ɪnstrə'mentəl] adj strumentale; **to be instrumental in** contribuire a
instrumentalist [‚ɪnstrə'mentəlɪst] s strumentista mf
instrumentali·ty [‚ɪnstrəmən'tælɪtɪ] s (-ties) mediazione, aiuto
in'strument fly'ing s volo strumentale
in'strument pan'el s (aut) cruscotto
insubordinate [‚ɪnsə'bɔrdɪnɪt] adj insubordinato
insufferable [ɪn'sʌfərəbəl] adj insoffribile
insufficient [‚ɪnsə'fɪʃənt] adj insufficiente
insular ['ɪnsələr] or ['ɪnsjulər] adj insulare; (e.g., attitude) gretto
insulate ['ɪnsə‚let] tr isolare
in'sulating tape' s ['ɪnsəletɪŋ] s nastro isolante
insulation [‚ɪnsə'leʃən] s isolamento
insulator ['ɪnsə‚letər] s isolatore m
insulin ['ɪnsəlɪn] s insulina
insult ['ɪnsʌlt] s insulto || [ɪn'sʌlt] tr insultare, insolentire
insulting [ɪn'sʌltɪŋ] adj insultante
insurance [ɪn'ʃurəns] s assicurazione
insure [ɪn'ʃur] tr assicurare
insurer [ɪn'ʃurər] s assicuratore m
insurgent [ɪn'sʌrdʒənt] adj & s insorgente mf
insurmountable [‚ɪnsər'mauntəbəl] adj insormontabile
insurrection [‚ɪnsə'rekʃən] s insurrezione
insusceptible [‚ɪnsə'septɪbəl] adj non suscettibile
intact [ɪn'tækt] adj intatto, integro
in'take' s (place of taking in) entrata; (act of taking in) ammissione; (mach) presa, immissione, aspirazione
in'take man'ifold s collettore m d'ammissione
intangible [ɪn'tændʒɪbəl] adj intangibile; (fig) vago, inafferrabile
integer ['ɪntɪdʒər] s numero intero
integral ['ɪntɪgrəl] adj integrale; (part of a whole) integrante || s (math) integrale m
integration [‚ɪntɪ'greʃən] s integrazione
integrity [ɪn'tegrɪtɪ] s integrità f
intellect ['ɪntə‚lekt] s intelletto
intellectual [‚ɪntə'lektʃu·əl] adj & s intellettuale mf
intelligence [ɪn'telɪdʒəns] s intelligenza; informazione, conoscenza

intel'ligence bu'reau s ufficio spionaggi
intel'ligence quo'tient s quoziente m d'intelligenza
intelligent [ɪn'telɪdʒənt] adj intelligente
intelligentsia [ɪn ˌtelɪ'dʒentsɪ-ə] or [ɪn-ˌtelɪ'gentsɪ-ə] s intellighenzia, intellettualità f
intelligible [ɪn'telɪdʒɪbəl] adj intelligibile, comprensibile
intemperance [ɪn'tempərəns] s intemperanza, sregolatezza
intemperate [ɪn'tempərɪt] adj intemperante; (climate) rigoroso
intend [ɪn'tend] tr intendere, prefiggersi; (to mean for a particular purpose) destinare; (to signify) voler dire
intendance [ɪn'tendəns] s intendenza
intendant [ɪn'tendənt] s intendente m
intended [ɪn'tendɪd] adj & s (coll) promesso, promessa
intense [ɪn'tens] adj intenso
intensi·fy [ɪn'tensɪ-faɪ] v (pret & pp **-fied**) tr intensificare, rinforzare; (phot) rinforzare || intr intensificarsi, rinforzarsi
intensi·ty [ɪn'tensɪti] s (**-ties**) intensità f
intensive [ɪn'tensɪv] adj intensivo
intent [ɪn'tent] adj intento, attento; **intent on** deciso a || s (purpose) intento, scopo; (meaning) significato; **to all intents and purposes** virtualmente, in realtà
intention [ɪn'tenʃən] s intenzione
intentional [ɪn'tenʃənəl] adj intenzionale, deliberato
intentionally [ɪn'tenʃənəli] adv apposta, deliberatamente
in·ter [ɪn'tʌr] v (pret & pp **-terred**; ger **-terring**) tr interrare, inumare
interact [ˌɪntər'ækt] intr esercitare un'azione reciproca
interaction [ˌɪntər'ækʃən] s azione reciproca
inter·breed [ˌɪntər'brid] s (pret & pp **-bred** ['bred]) tr incrociare || intr incrociarsi
intercalate [ɪn'tʌrkə ˌlet] tr intercalare
intercede [ˌɪntər'sid] intr intercedere
intercept [ˌɪntər'sept] tr intercettare
interceptor [ˌɪntər'septər] s (person) intercettatore m; (aer) intercettore m
interchange ['ɪntər ˌtʃendʒ] s interscambio; (on a highway) svincolo autostradale || [ˌɪntər't/əndʒ] tr scambiare || intr scambiarsi
intercollegiate [ˌɪntərkə'lidʒɪ-ɪt] adj interscolastico, fra università
intercom ['ɪntər ˌkɑm] s citofono
intercourse ['ɪntər ˌkors] s comunicazione; (of products, ideas, etc.) scambio; (copulation) copula, coito; **to have intercourse** accoppiarsi sessualmente
intercross [ˌɪntər'krɔs] or [ˌɪntər-'krɑs] tr incrociare || intr incrociarsi
interdict ['ɪntər ˌdɪkt] s interdetto || [ˌɪntər'dɪkt] tr interdire; **to interdict s.o. from** + ger interdire a qlcu di + inf
interest ['ɪntərɪst] or ['ɪntrɪst] s in-

teresse m; **the interests** i potenti || ['ɪntərɪst], ['ɪntrɪst] or ['ɪntə ˌrest] tr interessare
interested ['ɪntrɪstɪd] or ['ɪntə ˌrestɪd] adj interessato
interesting ['ɪntrɪstɪŋ] or ['ɪntə- ˌrestɪŋ] adj interessante
interfere [ˌɪntər'fɪr] intr interferire; (sports) ostacolare l'azione; **to interfere with** interferire in
interference [ˌɪntər'fɪrəns] s interferenza
interim ['ɪntərɪm] adj interino || s interim m; **in the interim** frattanto
interior [ɪn'tɪrɪ-ər] adj & s interno
interject [ˌɪntər'dʒekt] tr interporre || intr interporsi
interjection [ˌɪntər'dʒekʃən] s interposizione; esclamazione; (gram) interiezione
interlard [ˌɪntər'lɑrd] tr infiorare, lardellare
interline [ˌɪntər'laɪn] tr scrivere nell'interlinea di; (a garment) foderare con ovattina
interlining ['ɪntər ˌlaɪnɪŋ] s soppanno
interlink [ˌɪntər'lɪŋk] tr concatenare
interlock [ˌɪntər'lɑk] tr connettere || intr connettersi
interlope [ˌɪntər'lop] intr intromettersi; trafficare senza permesso
interloper [ˌɪntər'lopər] s intruso
interlude ['ɪntər ˌlud] s interludio; (theat) intermezzo
intermarriage [ˌɪntər ˌmærɪdʒ] s matrimonio tra consanguinei; matrimonio fra membri di razze diverse
intermediar·y [ˌɪntər'midɪ ˌerɪ] adj intermediario || (**-ies**) s intermediario
intermediate [ˌɪntər'midɪ-ɪt] adj intermedio
interment [ɪn'tʌrmənt] s inumazione
intermingle [ˌɪntər'mɪŋgəl] tr mescolare || intr mescolarsi
intermission [ˌɪntər'mɪʃən] s interruzione; (theat) intervallo
intermittent [ˌɪntər'mɪtənt] adj intermittente
intermix [ˌɪntər'mɪks] tr mescolare || intr mescolarsi
intern ['ɪntʌrn] s interno || [ɪn'tʌrn] tr internare
internal [ɪn'tʌrnəl] adj interno
inter'nal-combus'tion en'gine s motore m a combustione interna, motore m a scoppio
inter'nal rev'enue s fisco
international [ˌɪntər'næʃənəl] adj internazionale
in'terna'tional date' line' s linea del cambiamento di data
internationalize [ˌɪntər'næʃənə ˌlaɪz] tr internazionalizzare
internecine [ˌɪntər'nisɪn] adj micidiale, sanguinario
internee [ˌɪntʌr'ni] s internato
internist [ɪn'tʌrnɪst] s internista mf
internment [ɪn'tʌrnmənt] s internamento
internship ['ɪntʌrn ˌʃɪp] s tirocinio in un ospedale, internato

interpellate [,ɪntər'pelet] or [ɪn'tʌrpɪ-,let] tr interpellare
interplanetary [,ɪntər'plænə,teri] adj interplanetario
interplay ['ɪntər,ple] s azione reciproca
interpolate [ɪn'tʌrpə,let] tr interpolare
interpose [,ɪntər'poz] tr frapporre
interpret [ɪn'tʌrprɪt] tr interpretare
interpreter [ɪn'tʌrprətər] s interprete mf
interrogate [ɪn'terə,get] tr & intr interrogare
interrogation [ɪn,terə'geʃən] s interrogazione
interroga'tion mark' or **point'** s punto interrogativo
interrupt [,ɪntə'rʌpt] tr interrompere
interruption [,ɪntə'rʌpʃən] s interruzione
interscholastic [,ɪntərskə'læstɪk] adj interscolastico
intersect [,ɪntər'sekt] tr intersecare ‖ intr intersecarsi
intersection [,ɪntər'sekʃən] s (of streets, roads, etc.) crocevia m; (geom) intersezione
intersperse [,ɪntər'spʌrs] tr cospargere, inframezzare
interstellar [,ɪntər'stelər] adj interstellare
interstice [ɪn'tʌrstɪs] s interstizio
intertwine [,ɪntər'twaɪn] tr intrecciare ‖ intr intrecciarsi
interval ['ɪntərvəl] s intervallo; **at intervals** a intervalli; di tanto in tanto
intervene [,ɪntər'vin] intr intervenire; (to happen) succedere
intervening [,ɪntər'vinɪŋ] adj—**in the intervening time** nel frattempo
intervention [,ɪntər'venʃən] s intervenzione
interview ['ɪntər,vju] s intervista ‖ tr intervistare
inter·weave [,ɪntər'wiv] v (pret -wove ['wov] or -weaved; pp -wove, -woven or -weaved) tr intessere
intestate [ɪn'testet] or [ɪn'testɪt] adj intestato
intestine [ɪn'testɪn] s intestino
inthrall [ɪn'θrɔl] tr affascinare, incantare; (to subjugate) asservire, soggiogare
inthrone [ɪn'θron] tr mettere sul trono, intronizzare; esaltare, innalzare
intima·cy ['ɪntɪməsi] s (-cies) intimità f
intimate ['ɪntɪmɪt] adj & s intimo ‖ ['ɪntɪ,met] tr insinuare
intimation [,ɪntɪ'meʃən] s insinuazione
intimidate [ɪn'tɪmɪ,det] tr intimidire
into ['ɪntu] or ['ɪntʊ] prep in; verso; contro
intolerant [ɪn'talərənt] adj & s intollerante mf, insofferente mf
intomb [ɪn'tum] tr inumare, seppellire
intombment [ɪn'tummənt] s sepoltura
intonation [,ɪnto'neʃən] s intonazione
intone [ɪn'ton] tr intonare ‖ intr salmodiare
intoxicant [ɪn'taksɪkənt] s bevanda alcoolica

intoxicate [ɪn'taksɪ,ket] tr ubriacare; esilarare; (to poison) avvelenare, intossicare
intoxication [ɪn,taksɪ'keʃən] s ubriachezza; ebbrezza, allegria; (poisoning) avvelenamento, intossicazione
intractable [ɪn'træktəbəl] adj intrattabile
intransigent [ɪn'trænsɪdʒənt] adj & s intransigente mf
intransitive [ɪn'trænsɪtɪv] adj intransitivo
intravenous [,ɪntrə'vinəs] adj intravenoso, endovenoso
intrench [ɪn'trentʃ] tr & intr var of entrench
intrepid [ɪn'trepɪd] adj intrepido
intrepidity [,ɪntrɪ'pɪdɪti] s intrepidezza
intricate ['ɪntrɪkɪt] adj intricato
intrigue [ɪn'trig] or ['ɪntrig] s intrigo; tresca, intrigo amoroso; (theat) intreccio ‖ [ɪn'trig] tr incuriosire ‖ intr intrigare; trescare
intrinsic(al) [ɪn'trɪnsɪk(əl)] adj intrinseco
introduce [,ɪntrə'djus] or [,ɪntrə'dus] tr introdurre; (a product) lanciare; (a person) presentare
introduction [,ɪntrə'dʌkʃən] s introduzione; presentazione
introductory [,ɪntrə'dʌktəri] adj introduttivo
introit ['ɪntro·ɪt] s (eccl) introito
introspective [,ɪntrə'spektɪv] adj introspettivo
introvert ['ɪntrə,vʌrt] adj & s introverso
intrude [ɪn'trud] intr intrudersi, intrufolarsi
intruder [ɪn'trudər] s intruso; importuno
intrusion [ɪn'truʒən] s intrusione
intrusive [ɪn'trusɪv] adj invadente
intrust [ɪn'trʌst] tr affidare, confidare
intuition [,ɪntu'ɪʃən] or [,ɪntju'ɪʃən] s intuizione, intuito
inundate ['ɪnən,det] tr inondare
inundation [,ɪnən'deʃən] s inondazione
inure [ɪn'jʊr] tr indurire, assuefare ‖ intr entrare in vigore; **to inure to** ridondare in favore di
invade [ɪn'ved] tr invadere
invader [ɪn'vedər] s invasore m
invalid [ɪn'vælɪd] adj (non. valid) invalido ‖ ['ɪnvəlɪd] adj (person) invalido; (thing) povero; (diet) per malati ‖ ['ɪnvəlɪd] s invalido
invalidate [ɪn'vælɪ,det] tr invalidare
invalidity [,ɪnvə'lɪdɪti] s invalidità f
invaluable [ɪn'væljʊ·əbəl] adj inestimabile, inapprezzabile
invariable [ɪn'verɪ·əbəl] adj invariabile
invasion [ɪn'veʒən] s invasione
invective [ɪn'vektɪv] s invettiva
inveigh [ɪn've] intr—**to inveigh against** inveire contro
inveigle [ɪn'vegəl] or [ɪn'vigəl] tr sedurre, abbindolare
invent [ɪn'vent] tr inventare
invention [ɪn'venʃən] s invenzione

inventiveness [ɪnˈvɛntɪvnɪs] *s* inventiva

inventor [ɪnˈvɛntər] *s* inventore *m*

invento·ry [ˈɪnvənˌtori] *s* (**-ries**) inventario || *v* (*pret* & *pp* **-ried**) *tr* inventariare

inverse [ɪnˈvʌrs] *adj* & *s* inverso

inversion [ɪnˈvʌrʒən] or [ɪnˈvʌrʃən] *s* inversione

invert [ˈɪnvʌrt] *s* invertito || [ɪnˈvʌrt] *tr* invertire

invertebrate [ɪnˈvʌrtɪ‚bret] or [ɪnˈvʌrtɪbrɪt] *adj* & *s* invertebrato

invest [ɪnˈvɛst] *tr* investire || *intr* fare un investimento; fare investimenti

investigate [ɪnˈvɛstɪ‚ɡet] *tr* investigare

investigation [ɪn‚vɛstɪˈɡeʃən] *s* investigazione

investigator [ɪnˈvɛstɪ‚ɡetər] *s* investigatore *m*

investment [ɪnˈvɛstmənt] *s* (*of money*) investimento; (*e.g.*, *with an office*) investitura; (*siege*) assedio

investor [ɪnˈvɛstər] *s* investitore *m*

inveterate [ɪnˈvɛtərɪt] *adj* inveterato

invidious [ɪnˈvɪdɪ‚əs] *adj* irritante, odioso

invigorate [ɪnˈvɪɡə‚ret] *tr* invigorire

invigorating [ɪnˈvɪɡə‚retɪŋ] *adj* ritemprante, ricostituente, rinforzante

invincible [ɪnˈvɪnsɪbəl] *adj* invincibile

invisible [ɪnˈvɪzɪbəl] *adj* invisibile

invis'ible ink' *s* inchiostro simpatico

invitation [‚ɪnvɪˈteʃən] *s* invito

invite [ɪnˈvaɪt] *tr* invitare

inviting [ɪnˈvaɪtɪŋ] *adj* invitante, attrattivo; (*food*) appetitoso; accogliente

invoice [ˈɪnvɔɪs] *s* fattura; **as per invoice** secondo fattura || *tr* fatturare

invoke [ɪnˈvok] *tr* invocare; (*a spirit*) evocare

involuntary [ɪnˈvɑlən‚teri] *adj* involontario

involve [ɪnˈvɑlv] *tr* involvere, includere; occupare; (*to bring unpleasantness upon*) implicare, coinvolgere; complicare

invulnerable [ɪnˈvʌlnərəbəl] *adj* invulnerabile

inward [ˈɪnwərd] *adj* interno || *adv* al di dentro, verso l'interno

iodide [ˈaɪ‚ə‚daɪd] *s* ioduro

iodine [ˈaɪ‚ə‚dɪn] *s* iodio || [ˈaɪ‚ə‚daɪn] *s* tintura di iodio

ion [ˈaɪ‚ən] or [ˈaɪ‚ɑn] *s* ione *m*

ionize [ˈaɪ‚ə‚naɪz] *tr* ionizzare

IOU [ˈaɪ‚oˈju] *s* (letterword) (**I owe you**) cambiale *f*, pagherò *m*

I.Q. [ˈaɪˈkju] *s* (letterword) (**intelligence quotient**) quoziente *m* d'intelligenza

Iranian [aɪˈreni‚ən] *adj* & *s* iraniano

Ira·qi [ɪˈraki] *adj* iracheno || *s* (**-qis**) iracheno

irate [ˈaɪret] or [aɪˈret] *adj* irato

ire [aɪr] *s* ira, collera

Ireland [ˈaɪrlənd] *s* l'Irlanda *f*

iris [ˈaɪrɪs] *s* iride *f*

I'rish·man *s* (**-men**) irlandese *m*

I'rish stew' *s* stufato all'irlandese

I'rish·wom'an *s* (**-wom'en**) irlandese *f*

irk [ʌrk] *tr* infastidire, annoiare

irksome [ˈʌrksəm] *adj* fastidioso

iron [ˈaɪ‚ərn] *adj* ferreo || *s* ferro; (*to press clothes*) ferro da stiro; **irons** ferri *mpl*; **strike while the iron is hot** batti il ferro fin ch'è caldo || *tr* (*clothes*) stirare; **to iron out** (*a difficulty*) (coll) appianare

i'ron·bound' *adj* ferrato; (*unyielding*) ferreo, inflessibile; (*rock-bound*) roccioso, scabroso

ironclad [ˈaɪ‚ərn‚klæd] *adj* corazzato, blindato; inflessibile, ferreo

i'ron constitu'tion *s* salute *f* di ferro

i'ron cur'tain *s* cortina di ferro

i'ron horse' *s* locomotiva a vapore

ironic(al) [aɪˈrɑnɪk(əl)] *adj* ironico

ironing [ˈaɪ‚ərnɪŋ] *s* stiratura; roba stirata; roba da stirare

i'roning board' *s* tavolo or asse *m* da stiro

i'ron lung' *s* polmone *m* d'acciaio

i'ron·ware' *s* ferrame *m*

i'ron will' *s* volontà *f* di ferro

i'ron·work' *s* lavoro in ferro; **ironworks** *ssg* ferriera

i'ron-work'er *s* ferraio; metalmeccanico, siderurgico

iro·ny [ˈaɪrəni] *s* (**-nies**) ironia

irradiate [ɪˈredɪ‚et] *tr* irradiare || *intr* irradiare, irradiarsi

irrational [ɪˈræʃənəl] *adj* irrazionale

irrecoverable [‚ɪrɪˈkʌvərəbəl] *adj* irrecuperabile

irredeemable [‚ɪrɪˈdiməbəl] *adj* irredimibile

irrefutable [‚ɪrɪˈfjutəbəl] *adj* irrefutabile

irregular [ɪˈrɛɡjələr] *adj* irregolare || *s* (mil) irregolare *m*

irrelevance [ɪˈrɛləvəns] *s* irrilevanza

irrelevant [ɪˈrɛləvənt] *adj* irrilevante

irreligious [‚ɪrɪˈlɪdʒəs] *adj* irreligioso

irremediable [‚ɪrɪˈmidɪ‚əbəl] *adj* irrimediabile

irremovable [‚ɪrɪˈmuvəbəl] *adj* irremovibile, inamovibile

irreplaceable [‚ɪrɪˈplesəbəl] *adj* insostituibile

irrepressible [‚ɪrɪˈprɛsɪbəl] *adj* irreprimibile, incontenibile

irreproachable [‚ɪrɪˈprotʃəbəl] *adj* irreprensibile

irresistible [‚ɪrɪˈzɪstɪbəl] *adj* irresistibile

irrespective [‚ɪrɪˈspɛktɪv] *adj*—**irrespective of** senza riguardo a

irresponsible [‚ɪrɪˈspɑnsɪbəl] *adj* irresponsabile

irretrievable [‚ɪrɪˈtrivəbəl] *adj* irrecuperabile

irreverent [ɪˈrɛvərənt] *adj* irriverente

irrevocable [ɪˈrɛvəkəbəl] *adj* irrevocabile

irrigate [ˈɪrɪ‚ɡet] *tr* irrigare

irrigation [‚ɪrɪˈɡeʃən] *s* irrigazione

irritant [ˈɪrɪtənt] *adj* & *s* irritante *m*

irritate [ˈɪrɪ‚tet] *tr* irritare

irritation [‚ɪrɪˈteʃən] *s* irritazione

irruption [ɪˈrʌpʃən] *s* irruzione

isinglass [ˈaɪzɪn‚ɡlæs] or [ˈaɪzɪŋ‚ɡlɑs] *s* (*gelatine*) colla di pesce; mica

Islam [ˈɪsləm] or [ɪsˈlɑm] *s* l'Islam *m*

island ['aɪlənd] *adj* isolano ‖ *s* isola; *(for safety of pedestrians)* salvagente *m*

islander ['aɪləndər] *s* isolano

isle [aɪl] *s* isoletta

isolate ['aɪsə‚let] or ['ɪsə‚let] *tr* isolare

isolation [‚aɪsə'leʃən] or [‚ɪsə'leʃən] *s* isolamento

isolationist [‚aɪsə'leʃənɪst] or [‚ɪsə'leʃənɪst] *s* isolazionista *mf*

isosceles [aɪ'sɑsə‚liz] *adj* isoscele

isotope ['aɪsə‚top] *s* isotopo

Israel ['ɪzrɪ‚əl] *s* l'Israele *m*

Israe·li [ɪz'reli] *adj* israeliano ‖ *s* (-lis [liz]) israeliano

Israelite ['ɪzrɪ‚ə‚laɪt] *adj* & *s* israelita *mf*

issuance ['ɪʃu‚əns] *s* *(of stamps, stocks, bonds, etc.)* emissione; *(e.g., of clothes)* distribuzione; *(of a law)* emanazione

issue ['ɪʃu] *s* *(outlet)* uscita; distribuzione; *(result)* conseguenza; *(offspring)* prole *f*; *(of a magazine)* puntata, fascicolo; *(of a bond)* emissione; *(yield)* prodotto; *(of a law)* promulgazione; *(pathol)* flusso; **at issue** in discussione; **to face the issue** affrontare la situazione; **to force the issue** forzare la soluzione; **to take issue with** non essere d'accordo con, dissentire da ‖ *tr* *(e.g., a book)* pubblicare; *(bonds, orders)* emettere; *(a communiqué)* diramare; *(e.g., food)* distribuire ‖ *intr* uscire; **to issue from** provenire da

isthmus ['ɪsmɑs] *s* istmo

it [ɪt] *pron pers* esso, essa; lo, la; **it is**

I sono io; **it is raining** piove; **it is four o'clock** sono le quattro

Italian [ɪ'tæljən] *adj* & *s* italiano

Ital'ian-speak'ing *adj* italofono

italic [ɪ'tælɪc] *adj* (typ) corsivo ‖ **italics** *s* (typ) corsivo ‖ **Italic** *adj* italico

italicize [ɪ'tælɪ‚saɪz] *tr* stampare in carattere corsivo; sottolineare

Italy ['ɪtəli] *s* l'Italia *f*

itch [ɪtʃ] *s* prurito; (pathol) rogna; *(eagerness)* (fig) pizzicore *m* ‖ *tr* prudere, e.g., **his foot itches him** gli prude il piede ‖ *intr* *(said of a part of body)* prudere; *(said of a person)* avere il prurito; **to itch to** avere il pizzicore di

itch·y ['ɪtʃi] *adj* (-ier; -iest) che prude; (pathol) rognoso

item ['aɪtəm] *s* articolo; notizia; *(on the agenda)* questione; (slang) notizia scottante

itemize ['aɪtə‚maɪz] *tr* dettagliare, specificare

itinerant [aɪ'tɪnərənt] or [ɪ'tɪnərənt] *adj* itinerante, ambulante ‖ *s* viaggiatore *m*, viandante *m*

itinerar·y [aɪ'tɪnə‚reri] or [ɪ'tɪnə‚reri] *adj* itinerario ‖ *s* (-ies) itinerario

its [ɪts] *adj* & *pron poss* il suo

itself [ɪt'self] *pron pers* sé stesso; si, e.g., **it opened itself** si è aperto

ivied ['aɪvɪd] *adj* coperto di edera

ivo·ry ['aɪvəri] *adj* d'avorio ‖ *s* (-ries) avorio; **ivories** (slang) tasti *mpl* del piano; (slang) palle *fpl* da bigliardo; *(dice)* (slang) dadi *mpl*; (slang) denti *mpl*

i'vory tow'er *s* torre *f* d'avorio

ivy ['aɪvi] *s* (ivies) edera

J

J, j [dʒe] *s* decima lettera dell'alfabeto inglese

jab [dʒæb] *s* puntata; *(prick)* puntura; *(with elbow)* gomitata ‖ *v* (pret & pp **jabbed**; ger **jabbing**) *tr* pugnalare; pungere; dare una gomitata a ‖ *intr* dare colpi

jabber ['dʒæbər] *s* borbottamento, ciarla ‖ *tr* & *intr* borbottare, ciarlare

jack [dʒæk] *s* *(for lifting heavy objects)* cricco, martinetto; *(jackass)* asino; *(device for turning a spit)* girarrosto; *(to remove a boot)* cavastivali *m*; *(cards)* fante *m*; *(bowling)* pallino; *(rad & telv)* jack *m*; *(elec)* presa; (slang) soldi *mpl*; **every man jack** ognuno, tutti *mpl* ‖ **Jack** *s* marinaio; (coll) buonuomo ‖ *tr*—**to jack up** alzare col cricco; *(prices)* (coll) alzare

jackal ['dʒækəl] *s* sciacallo

jack'ass' *s* asino

jack'daw' *s* cornacchia

jacket ['dʒækɪt] *s* giacca; *(of boiled*

potatoes) buccia; *(of book)* soprac-coperta; *(metal casing)* camicia

jack'ham'mer *s* martello perforatore

jack'-in-the-box' *s* scatola a sorpresa

jack'knife' *s* (-knives) coltello a serra-manico; (sports) salto a pesce

jack'-of-all'-trades' *s* factotum *m*

jack-o'-lantern ['dʒækə‚læntərn] *s* lanterna a forma di testa umana fatta con una zucca; fuoco fatuo

jack'pot' *s* monte *m* premi; **to hit the jackpot** (slang) vincere un terno al lotto

jack' rab'bit *s* lepre nordamericana di taglia grande

jack'screw' *s* cricco a verme

jack'-tar' *s* (coll) marinaio

jade [dʒed] *adj* di giada, come la giada ‖ *s* *(ornamental stone)* giada; *(worn-out horse)* ronzino; *(disreputable woman)* donnaccia ‖ *tr* logorare

jad'ed ['dʒedɪd] *adj* logoro, stanco; *(appetite)* stucco

jag [dʒæg] *s* slabbratura; **to have a jag on** (slang) avere la sbornia

jagged ['dʒægɪd] *adj* dentato, slabbrato

jaguar ['dʒægwɑr] *s* giaguaro

jail [dʒel] *s* prigione *f*; **to break jail** evadere dal carcere ‖ *tr* carcerare

jail'bird' *s* galeotto, remo di galera

jail'break' *s* evasione *f* dal carcere

jailer ['dʒelər] *s* carceriere *m*

jalop·y [dʒə'lɑpi] *s* (**-ies**) carcassa, trespolo, trabiccolo

jam [dʒæm] *s* stretta, compressione; (*in traffic*) imbottigliamento; (*preserve*) marmellata, confettura; (*difficult situation*) (coll) pasticcio ‖ *v* (*pret* & *pp* **jammed**; *ger* **jamming**) *tr* stipare; (*e.g., one's finger*) schiacciare, schiacciarsi; (rad) disturbare; **to jam on the brakes** bloccare i freni ‖ *intr* schiacciarsi; (*said of firearms*) incepparsi; (mach) grippare

jamb [dʒæm] *s* stipite *m*

jamboree [ˌdʒæmbə'ri] *s* riunione nazionale di giovani esploratori; (coll) riunione

James [dʒemz] *s* Giacomo

jamming ['dʒæmɪŋ] *s* radiodisturbo

jam-packed ['dʒæm'pækt] *adj* gremito, pieno fino all'orlo

jangle ['dʒæŋɡəl] *s* suono stridente; (*quarrel*) baruffa ‖ *tr* fare suoni stridenti con ‖ *intr* stridere; litigare

janitor ['dʒænɪtər] *s* portiere *m*

janitress ['dʒænɪtrɪs] *s* portinaia

January ['dʒænjuˌeri] *s* gennaio

ja·pan [dʒə'pæn] *s* lacca giapponese; oggetto di lacca ‖ *v* (*pret* & *pp* **-panned**; *ger* **-panning**) *tr* laccare ‖ **Japan** *s* il Giappone

Japa·nese [ˌdʒæpə'niz] *adj* giapponese ‖ *s* (**-nese**) giapponese *mf*

Jap'anese bee'tle *s* scarabeo giapponese

Jap'anese lan'tern *s* lampioncino alla veneziana

Jap'anese persim'mon *s* cachi *m*

jar [dʒɑr] *s* barattolo *m*; (*earthenware container*) orcio, giara; discordanza; (*jolt*) scossa; (fig) brutta sorpresa; **on the jar** (*said of a door*) socchiuso ‖ *v* (*pret* & *pp* **jarred**; *ger* **jarring**) *tr* scuotere; far stridere ‖ *intr* vibrare; stridere; essere in conflitto; **to jar on** irritare

jardiniere [ˌdʒɑrdɪ'nɪr] *s* (*pot*) vaso da fiori; giardiniera

jargon ['dʒɑrɡən] *s* gergo

jasmine ['dʒæsmɪn] *or* ['dʒæzmɪn] *s* gelsomino

jasper ['dʒæspər] *s* diaspro

jaundice ['dʒɔndɪs] *or* ['dʒɑndɪs] *s* itterizia; (fig) invidia

jaundiced ['dʒɔndɪst] *or* ['dʒɑndɪst] *adj* itterico; (fig) invidioso

jaunt [dʒɔnt] *or* [dʒɑnt] *s* passeggiata, gita

jaun·ty ['dʒɔnti] *or* ['dʒɑnti] *adj* (**-tier**; **-tiest**) disinvolto; elegante

Java·nese [ˌdʒævə'niz] *adj* giavanese ‖ *s* (**-nese**) giavanese *m*

javelin ['dʒævlɪn] *or* ['dʒævəlɪn] *s* giavellotto

jaw [dʒɔ] *s* mascella, mandibola; (mach) ganascia; **jaws** fauci *fpl*; gola, stretta ‖ *tr* (slang) rimproverare ‖

intr (slang) chiacchierare; (slang) fare la predica

jaw'bone' *s* mascella, mandibola

jaw'break'er *s* (coll) parola difficile da pronunciare; (coll) caramella durissima; (mach) frantoio a mascelle

jay [dʒe] *s* (orn) ghiandaia; (coll) sempliciotto

jay'walk' *intr* attraversare la strada contro la luce rossa del semaforo

jay'walk'er *s* (coll) pedone distratto che attraversa la strada contro la luce rossa del semaforo

jazz [dʒæz] *s* jazz *m*; (slang) spirito ‖ *tr*—**to jazz up** (slang) dar vita a

jazz' band' *s* orchestra jazz

jealous ['dʒeləs] *adj* geloso; (*envious*) invidioso; vigilante

jealous·y ['dʒeləsi] *s* (**-ies**) gelosia; invidia; vigilanza

jean [dʒin] *s* tela cruda; **jeans** pantaloni *mpl* di tela cruda

jeep [dʒip] *s* gip *f*, jeep *f*

jeer [dʒɪr] *s* beffa ‖ *tr* beffare ‖ *intr* beffarsi; **to jeer at** mottegiare

Jeho'vah's Wit'nesses [dʒɪ'hovəs] *spl* Testimoni *mpl* di Geova

jell [dʒel] *s* gelatina ‖ *intr* (*to congeal*) gelatinizzarsi; (*to become substantial*) cristallizzarsi

jel·ly ['dʒeli] *s* (**-lies**) gelatina ‖ *v* (*pret* & *pp* **-lied**) *tr* gelatinizzare ‖ *intr* gelatinizzarsi

jel'ly·fish' *s* medusa; (*weak person*) (coll) fiaccone *m*

jeopardize ['dʒepərˌdaɪz] *tr* compromettere, mettere a repentaglio

jeopardy ['dʒepərdi] *s* pericolo, repentaglio

jeremiad [ˌdʒerɪ'maɪˌæd] *s* geremiade *f*

Jericho ['dʒerɪˌko] *s* Gerico *f*

jerk [dʒʌrk] *s* strattone *m*, scatto; tic *m*; (*stupid person*) scempio, sciocco; **by jerks** a scatti ‖ *tr* tirare a strattoni; (*meat*) essiccare ‖ *intr* sobbalzare

jerked' beef' *s* fetta di carne di bue essicata

jerkin ['dʒʌrkɪn] *s* giubbetto

jerk'wa'ter *adj* di scarsa importanza

jerk·y ['dʒʌrki] *adj* (**-ier**; **-iest**) sussultante; (*style*) disuguale

Jerome [dʒə'rom] *s* Gerolamo

jersey ['dʒʌrzi] *s* jersey *m*, maglione *m*

Jerusalem [dʒɪ'rusələm] *s* Gerusalemme *f*

jest [dʒest] *s* scherzo, burla; **in jest** per celia ‖ *intr* scherzare

jester ['dʒestər] *s* mottegiatore *m*, burlone *m*; (hist) buffone *m*

Jesuit ['dʒeʒuˌɪt] *or* ['dʒezjuˌɪt] *adj* & *s* gesuita *m*

Jesuitic(al) [ˌdʒeʒuˈɪtɪk(əl)] *or* [ˌdʒezjuˈɪtɪk(əl)] *adj* gesuitico

Jesus ['dʒizəs] *s* Gesù *m*

Je'sus Christ' *s* Gesù *m* e Cristo

jet [dʒet] *s* (of a fountain*) zampillo; (*stream shooting forth from nozzle*) getto; (*mineral; lustrous black*) giaietto; (aer) aereo a getto ‖ *v* (*pret* & *pp* **jetted**; *ger* **jetting**) *tr* spruzzare || *intr* zampillare; volare in aereo a getto

jet' age' *s* era dell'aviogetto

jet'-black' *adj* nero come il carbone

jet' bomb'er *s* bombardiere *m* a reazione

jet' coal' *s* carbone *m* a lunga fiamma

jet' en'gine *s* motore *m* a reazione

jet' fight'er *s* caccia *m* a reazione

jet'lin'er *s* aviogetto da trasporto passeggeri

jet' plane' *s* aviogetto

jet' propul'sion *s* gettopropulsione

jetsam ['dʒɛtsəm] *s* relitto

jet' stream' *s* corrente *f* a getto; scappamento di motore a razzo

jettison ['dʒɛtɪsən] *s* (naut) alleggerimento || *tr* (naut) alleggerirsi di; (fig) disfarsi di

jet·ty ['dʒɛti] *s* (**-ties**) gettata; (*wharf*) molo, imbarcadero

Jew [dʒu] *s* giudeo

jewel ['dʒu·əl] *s* pietra preziosa; (*valuable personal ornament*) gioia, gioiello; (*of a watch*) rubino; (*costume jewelry*) gioia finta; (fig) valore *m*, gioiello

jew'el case' *s* scrigno, portagioie *m*

jeweler *or* **jeweller** ['dʒu·ələr] *s* gioielliere *m*, orefice *m*

jewelry ['dʒu·əlri] *s* gioielli *mpl*

jew'elry shop' *s* gioielleria

Jewess ['dʒu·ɪs] *s* giudea

Jewish ['dʒu·ɪʃ] *adj* giudeo

jews'-harp *or* **jew's-harp** ['dʒuz,harp] *s* scacciapensieri *m*

jib [dʒɪb] *s* (*of a crane*) (mach) braccio (di gru); (naut) fiocco, vela Marconi

jib' boom' *s* asta di fiocco

jibe [dʒaɪb] *s* burla, beffa || *intr* beffarsi; accordarsi; **to jibe at** beffarsi di

jif·fy ['dʒɪfi] *s*—**in a jiffy** (coll) in men che non si dica

jig [dʒɪg] *s* (*dance*) giga; **the jig is up** (slang) tutto è perduto

jigger ['dʒɪgər] *s* bicchierino di liquore d'un'oncia e mezza; (*flea*) pulce *f* tropicale; (*gadget*) (coll) aggeggio; (naut) bozzello; (min) crivello

jiggle ['dʒɪgəl] *s* scossa || *tr* scuotere, agitare || *intr* scuotersi

jig' saw' *s* sega da traforo

jig'saw puz'zle *s* gioco di pazienza, rompicapo

jilt [dʒɪlt] *tr* piantare

jim·my ['dʒɪmi] *s* (**-mies**) piccolo piede di porco || *v* (*pret & pp* **-mied**) *tr* scassinare; **to jimmy open** scassinare

jingle ['dʒɪŋgəl] *s* sonaglio, bubbolo; (*sound*) rumore *m* di sonagliera; cantilena, rima infantile || *tr* far suonare || *intr* tintinnare

jin·go ['dʒɪŋgo] *adj* sciovinista || *s* (**-goes**) sciovinista *mf*; **by jingo!** perbacco!

jingoism ['dʒɪŋgo,ɪzəm] *s* sciovinismo

jinx [dʒɪŋks] *s* iettatura; (*person*) iettatore *m* || *tr* portare la iettatura a

jitters ['dʒɪtərz] *spl* (coll) nervosismo; **to have the jitters** (coll) essere nervoso

jittery ['dʒɪtəri] *adj* nervoso

job [dʒab] *s* (*piece of work*) lavoro;

(*task*) mansione; (*employment*) posto, impiego; (slang) furto; **by the job** a cottimo; **on the job** (slang) attento, sollecito; **to be out of a job** essere disoccupato; **to lie down on the job** (slang) dormire sul lavoro

job' anal'ysis *s* valutazione delle mansioni

jobber ['dʒabər] *s* grossista *mf*; (*pieceworker*) lavoratore *m* a cottimo; funzionario disonesto

job'hold'er *s* impiegato *m*; (*in the government*) burocrate *m*

jobless ['dʒablɪs] *adj* disoccupato

job' lot' *s* (com) saldo

job' print'er *s* piccolo tipografo non specializzato

job' print'ing *s* piccolo lavoro tipografico

jockey ['dʒaki] *s* fantino || *tr* (*a horse*) montare; manovrare; (*to trick*) abbindolare

jockstrap ['dʒak,stræp] *s* sospensorio

jocose [dʒo'kos] *adj* giocoso

jocular ['dʒakjələr] *adj* scherzoso

jog [dʒag] *s* spinta; piccolo trotto || *v* (*pret & pp* **jogged**; *ger* **jogging**) *tr* spingere leggermente; (*the memory*) rinfrescare || *intr* barcollare; **to jog along** continuare col solito tran tran

jog' trot' *s* piccolo trotto; (fig) tran tran *m*

John [dʒan] *s* Giovanni *m*

John' Bull' *s* il tipico inglese; gli inglesi, il popolo inglese

John' Han'cock ['hænkak] *s* (coll) la firma

johnnycake ['dʒani,kek] *s* pane *m* di granturco

John'ny-come'-late'ly *s* (coll) ultimo

John'ny-jump'-up' *s* violetta, viola del pensiero

John'ny-on-the-spot' *s* (coll) persona sempre pronta

John' the Bap'tist *s* San Giovanni Battista

join [dʒɔɪn] *tr* giungere, congiungere; associarsi a; unire; (*e.g., a party*) farsi membro di; (*the army*) arruolarsi in; (*battle*) ingaggiare; (*to empty into*) sfociare in || *intr* congiungersi, unirsi; (*said, e.g., of two rivers*) confluire

joiner ['dʒɔɪnər] *s* falegname *m*; membro di molte società

joint [dʒɔɪnt] *adj* congiunto || *s* (*in a pipe*) giuntura; (*of bones*) giuntura, articolazione; (*hinge of book*) brachetta; (*in woodwork*) incastro, commettitura; (*of meat*) taglio; (mach) snodo; (*gambling den*) (slang) bisca; (elec) innesto; (slang) bettola; **out of joint** slogato; (fig) fuori luogo; **to throw** (*e.g., one's arm*) **out of joint** slogarsi

joint' account' *s* conto in comune

joint' commit'tee *s* commissione mista

jointly ['dʒɔɪntli] *adv* unitamente

joint' own'er *s* condomino

joint'-stock' com'pany *s* società *f* per azioni a responsabilità illimitata

joist [dʒɔɪst] *s* trave *f*

joke [dʒok] *s* burla, barzelletta; (*trifling matter*) cosa da nulla; (*person laughed at*) zimbello; **to tell a joke** raccontare una barzelletta; **to play a joke on** fare uno scherzo a || *tr*—**to joke one's way into** ottenere dicendo barzellette || *intr* burlare, dire storielle; **joking aside** senza scherzi

joker ['dʒokər] *s* burlone *m*, fumista *m*; (*wise guy*) saputello; (*hidden provision*) clausola ingannatrice; (*cards*) matta

jol·ly ['dʒali] *adj* (**-lier; -liest**) allegro, gaio || *adv* (coll) molto || *v* (*pret & pp* **-lied**) *tr* (coll) prendersi gioco di

jolt [dʒolt] *s* scossa || *tr* scuotere || *intr* sobbalzare

Jonah ['dʒonə] *s* Giona; (fig) uccello di mal augurio

jongleur ['dʒaŋglər] *s* giullare *m*

jonquil ['dʒaŋkwɪl] *s* giunchiglia

Jordan ['dʒɔrdən] *s* (*country*) la Giordania; (*river*) Giordano

Jordanian [dʒɔr'denɪ·ən] *adj & s* giordano

josh [dʒaʃ] *tr & intr* (coll) canzonare

jostle ['dʒasəl] *s* spintone *m* || *tr* spingere || *intr* scontrarsi; farsi strada a gomitate

jot [dʒat] *s*—**I don't care a jot for** non mi importa un fico di || *v* (*pret & pp* **jotted;** *ger* **jotting**) *tr*—**to jot down** notare, gettar giù

jounce [dʒauns] *s* scossa || *tr* scuotere || *intr* sobbalzare

journal ['dʒarnəl] *s* (*newspaper*) giornale *m*; (*magazine*) rivista; (*daily record*) diario; (com) giornale *m*; (mach) perno; (naut) giornale *m* di bordo

journalese [ˌdʒarnə'liz] *s* linguaggio giornalistico

journalism ['dʒarnəˌlɪzəm] *s* giornalismo

journalist ['dʒarnəlɪst] *s* giornalista *mf*

journey ['dʒarni] *s* viaggio || *intr* viaggiare

jour'ney·man *s* (**-men**) operaio specializzato

joust [dʒast] or [dʒust] or [dʒaust] *s* giostra || *intr* giostrare

jovial ['dʒovɪ·əl] *adj* gioviale

jowl [dʒaul] *s* (*cheek*) guancia; (*jawbone*) mascella; (*of cattle*) giogaia; (*of fowl*) bargiglio; (*of fat person*) pappagorgia

joy [dʒɔɪ] *s* gioia, allegria; **to leap with joy** ballare dalla gioia

joyful ['dʒɔɪfəl] *adj* gioioso, festoso; **joyful over** lieto di

joyless ['dʒɔɪlɪs] *adj* senza gioia

joyous ['dʒɔɪ·əs] *adj* gioioso

joy' ride' *s* (coll) gita in auto; (coll) gita all'impazzata in auto

jubilant ['dʒubɪlənt] *adj* esultante

jubilation [ˌdʒubɪ'leʃən] *s* giubilo

jubilee ['dʒubɪˌli] *s* (*jubilation*) giubilo; (eccl) giubileo

Judaism ['dʒudeˌɪzəm] *s* giudaismo

judge [dʒadʒ] *s* giudice *m* || *tr & intr* giudicare; **judging by** a giudicare da

judge' ad'vocate *s* avvocato militare; avvocato della marina da guerra

judgeship ['dʒadʒʃɪp] *s* carica di giudice

judgment ['dʒadʒmənt] *s* giudizio; (*legal decision*) sentenza

judg'ment day' *s* giorno del giudizio

judg'ment seat' *s* banco dei giudici; tribunale *m*

judicature ['dʒudɪkət/ər] *s* carica di giudice

judicial [dʒu'dɪʃəl] *adj* giudiziario; (*becoming a judge*) giudizioso

judiciar·y [dʒu'dɪʃɪˌɛri] *adj* giudiziario || *s* (**-ies**) (*judges collectively*) magistratura; (*judicial branch*) potere giudiziario

judicious [dʒu'dɪʃəs] *adj* giudizioso

jug [dʒag] *s* brocca, boccale *m*; (*narrow-necked vessel*) orcio; (*jail*) (slang) prigione

juggle ['dʒagəl] *s* gioco di prestigio || *tr* fare il giocoliere con; (*documents, facts*) alterare frodolentemente; **to juggle away** ghermire, trafugare || *intr* fare il giocoliere; fare l'imbroglione

juggler ['dʒaglər] *s* giocoliere *m*, prestigiatore *m*; impostore *m*

juggling ['dʒaglɪŋ] *s* giochi *mpl* di prestigio

Jugoslav ['jugo'slav] *adj & s* iugoslavo, jugoslavo

Jugoslavia ['jugo'slavɪ·ə] *s* la Iugoslavia, la Jugoslavia

jugular ['dʒagjələr] or ['dʒugjələr] *adj & s* giugulare *f*

juice [dʒus] *s* sugo; (*natural fluid of an animal body*) succo; (slang) elettricità *f*; (slang) benzina; **to stew in one's own juice** (coll) annegarsi nel proprio sugo

juic·y ['dʒusi] *adj* (**-ier; -iest**) sugoso, succoso; (*spicy*) piccante

jukebox ['dʒuk ˌbaks] *s* grammofono a gettone, juke-box *m*

julep ['dʒulɪp] *s* bibita di menta col ghiaccio; (pharm) giulebbe *m*

julienne [ˌdʒulɪ'ɛn] *s* giuliana

July [dʒu'laɪ] *s* luglio

jumble ['dʒambəl] *s* intrico, garbuglio || *tr* ingarbugliare

jum·bo ['dʒambo] *adj* (coll) enorme || *s* (**-bos**) (*person*) (coll) elefante *m*; (*thing*) (coll) oggetto enorme

jump [dʒamp] *s* salto; (*in a parachute*) lancio; (*of prices*) sbalzo; (*start*) soprassalto; **on the jump** in moto; **to get or to have the jump on** (coll) avere il vantaggio su || *tr* saltare; (*a horse*) far saltare; (*prices*) alzare; uscire da, saltare, **the train jumped the track** il treno uscì dalle rotaie; (*to attack*) (coll) balzare su; (checkers) suffiare || *intr* saltare; (*from surprise*) trasalire; (*said of prices*) salire; (*in a parachute*) lanciarsi; **to jump at** (*e.g., an offer*) afferrare; **to jump on** saltare su; (coll) sgridare, arrabbiarsi con; **to jump over** oltrepassare; (*a page*) saltare; **to jump to a conclusion** arrivare precipitosamente a una conclusione

jumper ['dʒampər] *s* saltatore *m*; camiciotto; **jumpers** tuta da bambini

jump'ing jack' ['dʒʌmpɪŋ] *s* marionetta

jump'ing-off' place' *s* fine *f* del mondo; (fig) trampolino, punto di partenza

jump' seat' *s* strapuntino

jump' spark' *s* scintilla elettrica; (*of induction coil*) (elec) scintilla d'intraferro

jump' wire' *s* filo elettrico di contatto

jump•y ['dʒʌmpi] *adj* (**-ier; -iest**) nervoso, eccitato

junction ['dʒʌŋkt/ən] *s* congiunzione; (*of two rivers*) confluenza; (carp) commettitura; (rr) raccordo ferroviario

juncture ['dʒʌŋkt/ər] *s* giuntura; (*occasion*) congiuntura; (*moment*) momento

June [dʒun] *s* giugno

jungle ['dʒʌŋgəl] *s* giungla

junglegym ['dʒʌŋgəl,dʒɪm] *s* (trademark) castello

junior ['dʒunjər] *adj* minore, di minore età; giovane; (*in American university*) del penultimo anno; figlio, e.g., **John H. Smith, Junior** Giovanni H. Smith, figlio || *s* minore *m*; socio secondario; studente *m* del penultimo anno

jun'ior col'lege *s* scuola universitaria unicamente di primo biennio

jun'ior high' school' *s* scuola media; ginnasio

juniper ['dʒunɪpər] *s* ginepro

ju'niper ber'ry *s* coccola di ginepro

junk [dʒʌŋk] *s* roba vecchia, ferro vecchio; (*Chinese ship*) giunca; (naut) carne salata || *tr* (slang) gettar via

junk' deal'er *s* robivecchi *m*

junket ['dʒʌŋkɪt] *s* budino di giuncata; (*outing*) viaggio di piacere; viaggio pagato a spese del tesoro || *intr* far un viaggio di piacere; far un viaggio a spese del tesoro

junk'man' *s* (**-men'**) ferravecchio; rigattiere *m*

junk' room' *s* ripostiglio

junk' shop' *s* negozio di robivecchi

junk'yard' *s* cantiere *m* di ferravecchio

juridical [dʒu'rɪdɪkəl] *adj* giuridico

jurisdiction [,dʒurɪs'dɪk/ən] *s* giurisdizione

jurisprudence [,dʒurɪs'prudəns] *s* giurisprudenza

jurist ['dʒurɪst] *s* giurista *mf*

juror ['dʒurər] *s* giurato

ju•ry ['dʒuri] *s* (**-ries**) giuria

ju'ry box' *s* banco della giuria

ju'ry•man *s* (**-men**) giurato

just [dʒʌst] *adj* giusto || *adv* giustamente, giusto; appena; proprio; **just as** come, proprio come; **just beyond** un po' più in là (di); **just now** poco fa, or ora; **just out** appena uscito, appena pubblicato

justice ['dʒʌstɪs] *s* giustizia; (*judge*) giudice *m;* **to bring to justice** arrestare e condannare; **to do justice to** render giustizia a; apprezzare bastantemente

jus'tice of the peace' *s* giudice *m* conciliatore

justifiable ['dʒʌstɪ,faɪ·əbəl] *adj* giustificabile

justi•fy ['dʒʌstɪ,faɪ] *v* (*pret & pp* **-fied**) *tr* giustificare; (typ) giustificare

justly ['dʒʌstli] *adj* giustamente

jut [dʒʌt] *v* (*pret & pp* **jutted;** *ger* **jutting**) *intr*—**to jut out** strapiombare, sporgere

jute [dʒut] *s* iuta || **Jute** *s* Juto

juvenile ['dʒuvənɪl] or ['dʒuvə,naɪl] *adj* giovanile; minorile || *s* giovane *mf;* libro per la gioventù; (theat) amoroso

ju'venile court' *s* tribunale *m* per i minorenni

ju'venile delin'quency *s* delinquenza minorile

juvenilia [,dʒuvə'nɪlɪ·ə] *spl* opere *fpl* giovanili; libri *mpl* per ragazzi

juxtapose [,dʒʌkstə'poz] *tr* giustapporre

K

K, k [ke] *s* undicesima lettera dell'alfabeto inglese

kale [kel] *s* verza; (slang) cocuzza, soldi *mpl*

kaleidoscope [kə'laɪdə,skop] *s* caleidoscopio

kangaroo [,kæŋgə'ru] *s* canguro

katydid ['ketɪdɪd] *s* grossa cavalletta verde nordamericana

kedge [kedʒ] *s* (naut) ancorotto

keel [kil] *s* chiglia || *intr*—**to keel over** (naut) abbattersi in carena, capovolgersi; (fig) svenire

keelson ['kelsən] or ['kɪlsən] *s* (naut) controchiglia

keen [kin] *adj* (*sharpened*) affilato; (*wind; wit*) tagliente, mordente; (*eyes*) penetrante; (*ears; mind*) acuto,

fine; (*eager*) entusiasta; intenso, vivo; (slang) meraviglioso; **to be keen on** essere appassionato per

keep [kip] *s* mantenimento; (*of medieval castle*) torrione *m*, maschio; **for keeps** (coll) seriamente; (coll) per sempre; **to earn one's keep** guadagnarsi la vita || *v* (*pret & pp* **kept** [kept]) *tr* mantenere; (*watch*) fare; (*one's word*) mantenere; (*to withhold*) trattenere; (*accounts*) tenere; (*servants, guests*) avere; (*a garden*) coltivare; (*a business*) esercitare; (*a holiday*) festeggiare; (*to support*) sostentare; (*a secret; one's seat*) serbare; (*to decide to purchase*) prendere **to keep away** tener lontano; **to keep back** trattenere; (*a secret*) man tenere; **to keep down** reprimere; (*expenses*) ridurre al minimo; **to keep s.o. from** + *ger* impedire a qlcu di + *inf*; **to keep in** tener chiuso; **to keep off** tenere a distanza; (*e.g., moisture*) non lasciar penetrare; **to keep s.o. informed about s.th** tenere qlcu al corrente di qlco; **to keep s.o. waiting** fare aspettare qlcu; **to keep up** mantenere, sostenere ‖ *intr* **to keep** + *ger* continuare a + *inf*; **to keep away** tenersi lontano; **to keep from** + *ger* evitare di + *inf*; **to keep informed (about)** tenersi al corrente (di); **to keep in with** (coll) stare nelle buone grazie di; **to keep off** stare lontano (da); (*the grass*) non calpestare; **to keep on** + *ger* seguitare a + *inf*; **to keep out** star fuori, non entrare; **to keep out of** non entrare in; (*danger*) stare lontano da; non immischiarsi in; **to keep quiet** stare tranquillo; **to keep to** (*left or right*) tenere; **to keep to oneself** stare in disparte; **to keep up** continuare; **to keep up with** stare alla pari con; (*e.g., the news*) tenersi al corrente di

keeper ['kipər] *s* (*of a shop*) tenitore *m*; guardiano; (*of a game preserve*) guardacaccia *m*; (*of a magnet*) ancora

keeping ['kipɪŋ] *s* custodia; (*of a holiday*) celebrazione; **in keeping with** in armonia con; **in safe keeping** in luogo sicuro; **out of keeping with** in cattivo accordo con

keep'sake' *s* ricordo
keg [keg] *s* barilotto, botticella
ken [ken] *s* portata; **beyond the ken of** al di là dell'ambito di
kennel ['kenəl] *s* canile *m*
kep-i ['kepi] or ['kepi] *s* (-**is**) chepì *m*
kept' wo'man [kept] *s* (**wom'en**) mantenuta
kerchief ['kʌrtʃɪf] *s* fisciù *m*
kernel ['kʌrnəl] *s* (*of a nut*) gheriglio; (*of wheat*) chicco; (fig) nucleo
kerosene ['kɛrə,sin] or [,kɛrə'sin] *s* cherosene *m*, petrolio da illuminazione
kerplunk [kər'plʌŋk] *interj* patapum!
ketchup ['ketʃəp] *s* salsa piccante di pomodoro, ketchup *m*
kettle ['ketəl] *s* marmitta, paiolo; (*tea-kettle*) bricco, teiera
ket'tle-drum' *s* timpano
key [ki] *adj* a chiave; chiave ‖ *s* chiave *f*; (*of piano, typewriter, etc.*) tasto; (*cotter pin*) chiavetta, coppiglia; (*reef*) isolotto; (*tone of voice*) tono; (fig, mus) chiave *f*; (bot) samara; (telg) tasto trasmettitore, manipolatore *m*; **off key** stonato ‖ *tr* aggiustare; inchiavardare; **to key up** eccitare, portare al parossismo
key'board' *s* tastiera
key'hole' *s* toppa, buco della serratura; (*of a clock*) buco della chiave
key'note' *s* (mus) tono; (fig) principio informatore
key'note address' *s* discorso d'apertura
key'punch op'era'tor *s* perforatore *m*
key' ring' *s* portachiavi

key'stone' *s* chiave *f* di volta
key' word' *s* parola chiave
kha-ki ['kɑki] or ['kæki] *adj* cachi ‖ *s* (-**kis**) cachi *m*
khedive [kə'div] *s* kedivè *m*
kibitz ['kɪbɪts] *intr* (coll) dare consigli non richiesti
kibitzer ['kɪbɪtsər] *s* (*at a card game*) (coll) consigliere *m* importuno; (coll) ficcanaso *mf*
kibosh ['kaɪbɑʃ] or [kɪ'bɑʃ] *s* (coll) sciocchezza; **to put the kibosh on** (coll) impossibilitare
kick [kɪk] *s* calcio, pedata; (*of a gun*) rinculo; (*complaint*) (slang) protesta; (*of liquor*) (slang) forza; **to get a kick out of** (slang) pigliar piacere da ‖ *tr* prendere a calci; (*a ball*) calciare; (*one's feet*) battere; **to kick out** (coll) sbatter fuori a pedate; **to kick up a row** scatenare un putiferio ‖ *intr* calciare; (*said of an animal*) scalciare, trarre; (*said of a firearm*) rinculare; (coll) lamentarsi; **to kick against the pricks** dar calci al vento; **to kick off** (football) dare il calcio d'inizio
kick'back' *s* (coll) contraccolpo; (coll) intrallazzo, bustarella
kick'off' *s* calcio d'inizio
kid [kɪd] *s* capretto; (coll) piccolo; **kids** guanti *mpl* or scarpe *fpl* di capretto ‖ *v* (*pret & pp* **kidded**; *ger* **kidding**) *tr* (coll) prendere in giro; **to kid oneself** (coll) farsi illusioni ‖ *intr* (coll) dirlo per scherzo
kidder ['kɪdər] *s* (coll) burlone *m*
kid' gloves' *spl* guanti *mpl* di capretto; **to handle with kid gloves** trattare con la massima cautela
kid'nap' *v* (*pret & pp* **-naped** or **-napped**; *ger* **-naping** or **-napping**) *tr* rapire, sequestrare
kidnaper or **kidnapper** ['kɪd,næpər] *s* rapitore *m* a scopo d'estorsione
kidnaping or **kidnapping** ['kɪd,næpɪŋ] *s* rapimento a scopo di estorsione
kidney ['kɪdni] *s* rene *m*; (culin) rognone *m*; (*temperament*) carattere *m*; (*kind*) tipo
kid'ney bean' *s* fagiolo
kid'ney stone' *s* calcolo renale
kill [kɪl] *s* uccisione; (*game killed*) cacciagione; (coll) fiumicello; **for the kill** per il colpo finale ‖ *tr* uccidere; eliminare; (*a bill*) bocciare; (fig) opprimere
killer ['kɪlər] *s* uccisore *m*
kill'er whale' *s* orca
killing ['kɪlɪŋ] *adj* mortale; (*exhausting*) opprimente; (coll) molto divertente ‖ *s* uccisione; (*game killed*) cacciagione; (coll) fortuna; **to make a killing** (coll) fare una fortuna da un giorno all'altro
kill'-joy' *s* guastafeste *mf*
kiln [kɪl] or [kɪln] *s* forno, fornace *f*
kil-o ['kɪlo] or ['kilo] *s* (-**os**) chilogrammo; chilometro
kilocycle ['kɪlə,saɪkəl] *s* chilociclo
kilogram ['kɪlə,græm] *s* chilogrammo
kilo-hertz ['kɪlə,hʌrts] *s* (-**hertz**) chilohertz

kilometer ['kɪlə ,mitər] or [kɪ'lɑmɪtər] s chilometro

kilowatt ['kɪlə ,wɑt] s kilowatt m, chilowatt m

kilowatt-hour ['kɪlə ,wɑt'aʊr] s (**kilowatt-hours**) chilowattora m

kilt [kɪlt] s gonnellino

kilter ['kɪltər] s—**to be out of kilter** (coll) essere fuori squadra

kimo·no [kɪ'monə] or [kɪ'mono] s (**-nos**) chimono

kin [kɪn] s (*family relationship*) parentela; (*relatives*) parenti mpl; **of kin** parente, affine; **the next of kin** il parente più prossimo, i parenti più prossimi

kind [kaɪnd] adj gentile; **kind to** buono con || s genere m, specie f; **a kind of** una specie di; **all kinds of** (coll) ogni sorta di; **in kind** in natura; **kind of** (coll) quasi, piuttosto; **of a kind** dello stesso stampo; (*mediocre*) di poco valore

kindergarten ['kɪndər ,gɑrtən] s scuola materna, giardino d'infanzia

kindergartner ['kɪndər ,gɑrtnər] s allievo della scuola d'infanzia; (*teacher*) maestra giardiniera

kind-hearted ['kaɪnd'hɑrtɪd] adj gentile, di buon cuore

kindle ['kɪndəl] tr accendere || intr accendersi

kindling ['kɪndlɪŋ] s accensione; legna minuta

kin'dling wood' s legna minuta per accendere il fuoco

kind-ly ['kaɪndli] adj (**-lier; -liest**) gentile; (*climate*) benigno; favorevole || adv gentilmente; cordialmente; per gentilezza; **to not take kindly to** non accettare di buon grado

kindness ['kaɪndnɪs] s gentilezza; **have the kindness to** abbia la bontà di

kindred ['kɪndrɪd] adj imparentato; affine || s parentela; affinità f

kinescope ['kɪnɪ ,skop] s (trademark) cinescopio

kinetic [kɪ'nɛtɪk] or [kaɪ'nɛtɪk] adj cinetico || **kinetics** s cinetica

kinet'ic en'ergy s forza viva, energia cinetica

king [kɪŋ] s re m; (checkers) dama; (cards, chess) re m

king'bolt' s perno

kingdom ['kɪŋdəm] s regno

king'fish'er s martin pescatore m

king-ly ['kɪŋli] adj (**-lier; -liest**) reale; (*stately*) maestoso || adv regalmente

king'pin' s birillo centrale; (aut) perno dello sterzo; (fig) figura principale

king' post' s (archit) ometto, monaco

king's' e'vil s scrofola

kingship ['kɪŋʃɪp] s regalità f

king'-size adj extra-grande

king's' ran'som s ricchezza di Creso

kink [kɪŋk] s (*in a rope*) arricciatura; (*in hair*) crespatura; (*soreness in neck*) torcicollo; (*flaw*) ostacolo; (*mental twist*) ghiribizzo || tr attorcigliare || intr attorcigliarsi

kink-y ['kɪŋki] adj (**-ier; -iest**) attorcigliato; (*hair*) crespo

kinsfolk ['kɪnz ,fok] s parentado

kinship ['kɪnʃɪp] s parentela; affinità f

kins'man s (**-men**) parente m

kins'wom'an s (**-wom'en**) parente f

kipper ['kɪpər] s aringa affumicata || tr (*herring or salmon*) affumicare

kiss [kɪs] s bacio; (*billiards*) rimpallo leggerissimo; (*confection*) meringa || tr baciare; **to kiss away** (*tears*) asciugare con baci || intr baciare, baciarsi; (*billiards*) rimpallare leggermente

kit [kɪt] s (*case*) cassetta dei ferri; (*tools*) ferri mpl del mestiere; (*set of supplies*) corredo; (*of small tools*) astuccio; (*of a traveler*) borsa da viaggio; (*pail*) secchio; **the whole kit and caboodle** (coll) tutti quanti

kitchen ['kɪtʃən] s cucina

kitchenette [,kɪtʃə'nɛt] s cucinetta

kitch'en gar'den s orto

kitch'en-maid' s sguattera

kitch'en police' s (mil) corvè f di cucina

kitch'en range' s cucina economica

kitch'en sink' s acquaio

kitch'en-ware' s utensili mpl di cucina

kite [kaɪt] s cervo volante, aquilone m; (orn) nibbio

kith' and kin' [kɪθ] spl amici mpl e parenti mpl

kitten ['kɪtən] s gattino

kittenish ['kɪtənɪʃ] adj giocattolone; civettuolo

kit·ty ['kɪti] s (**-ties**) gattino; (cards) piatto || interj micio!

kleptomaniac [,klɛptə'menɪ ,æk] s cleptomane mf

knack [næk] s abilità f, destrezza

knapsack ['næp ,sæk] s zaino

knave [nev] s furfante m; (cards) fante m

knavery ['nevəri] s (**-ies**) furfanteria

knead [nid] tr maneggiare, intridere; (*a muscle*) massaggiare

knee [ni] s ginocchio; (*of trousers*) ginocchiera; (mach) gomito; **to bring s.o. to his knees** ridurre qlcu all'obbedienza; **to go down on one's knees (to)** gettarsi in ginocchio (davanti a)

knee' breech'es [,brɪtʃɪz] spl calzoni mpl al ginocchio

knee'cap' s rotula, patella; (*protective covering*) ginocchiera

knee'-deep' adj fino al ginocchio

knee'-high' adj fino al ginocchio

knee' jerk' s riflesso patellare

kneel [nil] v (pret & pp knelt [nɛlt] or kneeled) intr inginocchiarsi

knee'pad' s ginocchiera

knee'pan' s rotula, patella

knell [nɛl] s rintocco funebre, campana a morto; **to toll the knell of** annunciare la morte di || intr suonare a morte

knickers ['nɪkərz] spl knickerbockers mpl, calzoni mpl alla zuava

knickknack ['nɪk ,næk] s soprammobile m; gingillo, ninnolo

knife [naɪf] s (**knives** [naɪvz]) coltello; (*of a paper cutter*) mannaia; (*of a milling machine*) fresa; **to go under the knife** essere sulla tavola operatoria || tr accoltellare; mettere il coltello nella schiena di

knife' sharp'ener s affilatoio

knife' switch' *s* (elec) coltella

knight [naɪt] *s* cavaliere *m;* (chess) cavallo || *tr* armare cavaliere

knight-errant ['naɪt'ɛrənt] *s* (**knights-errant**) cavaliere *m* errante

knighthood ['naɪt·hʊd] *s* cavalleria

knightly ['naɪtli] *adj* cavalleresco

knit [nɪt] *v* (*pret & pp* **knitted** or **knit;** *ger* **knitting**) *tr* lavorare a maglia; (*to join*) unire; (e.g., *the brow*) corrugare || *intr* lavorare a maglia; fare la calza; unirsi; (*said of a bone*) saldarsi

knitting ['nɪtɪŋ] *s* maglia, lavoro a maglia

knit'ting machine' *s* macchina per maglieria

knit'ting mill' *s* maglieria

knit'ting nee'dle *s* ferro da calza

knit'wear *s* maglieria

knit'wear store' *s* maglieria

knob [nɑb] *s* (*lump*) bozza, protuberanza; (*of a door*) maniglia; (*on furniture*) pomolo; (*hill*) collinetta rotondeggiante; (rad, telv) manopola, pulsante *m*

knock [nɑk] *s* colpo; (*on a door*) tocco; (slang) attacco, critica || *tr* battere; (*repeatedly*) sbatacchiare; (slang) attaccare, criticare; **to knock down** (*with a punch*) stendere a terra; (*a wall*) diroccare; (*to the highest bidder*) aggiudicare; (e.g., *a machine*) smontare; **to knock off** (*work*) (slang) sospendere; (slang) terminare; (slang) uccidere; **to knock out** mettere fuori combattimento || *intr* battere; (aut) battere in testa; (slang) criticare; **to knock about** (slang) gironzolare; **to knock against** urtare contro; **to knock at** (e.g., *a door*) battere a, bussare a; **to knock off** (slang) cessare di lavorare

knock'down' *adj* (*blow*) knock down, che atterra; (*dismountable*) smontabile || *s* (*blow*) colpo che atterra; (*discount*) sconto

knocker ['nɑkər] *s* (*on a door*) battaglio, bussatoio; (coll) criticone *m*

knock-kneed ['nɑk,nid] *adj* con le gambe a X [iks]

knock'out' *s* pugno che mette fuori combattimento; fuori combattimento; (coll) pezzo di giovane

knock'out drops' *spl* (slang) narcotico

knoll [nol] *s* poggio, rialzo

knot [nɑt] *s* nodo; (*worn as an ornament*) fiocco; (*in wood*) nocchio; gruppo; protuberanza; (*tie*) nodo;

(naut) nodo; **to tie the knot** (coll) sposarsi || *v* (*pret & pp* **knotted;** *ger* **knotting**) *tr* annodare; (*the brow*) corrugare || *intr* annodarsi

knot'hole' *s* buco lasciato da un nodo (nel legno)

knot-ty ['nɑti] *adj* (-**tier;** -**tiest**) nodoso; (fig) spinoso

know [no] *s*—**to be in the know** (coll) essere al corrente || *v* (*pret* **knew** [nju] or [nu]; *pp* **known**) *tr & intr* (*by reasoning or learning*) sapere; (*by the senses or by perception; through acquaintance or recognition*) conoscere; **as far as I know** per quanto io ne sappia; **to know about** essere al corrente di; **to know best** essere il miglior giudice; **to know how to** + *inf* sapere + *inf;* **to know it all** (coll) sapere tutto; **to know what's what** (coll) saperla lunga; **you ought to know better** dovresti vergognarti

knowable ['no·əbəl] *adj* conoscibile

know'-how' *s* sapere *m,* abilità *f*

knowingly ['no·ɪŋli] *adv* con conoscenza di causa; (*on purpose*) apposta

know'-it-all' *adj & s* (coll) saputello

knowledge ['nɑlɪdʒ] *s* (*faculty*) scibile *m,* sapere *m,* sapienza; (*awareness, acquaintance, familiarity*) conoscenza; **to have a thorough knowledge of** conoscere a fondo; **to my knowledge** per quanto io ne sappia; **with full knowledge** con conoscenza di causa; **without my knowledge** a mia insaputa

knowledgeable ['nɑlɪdʒəbəl] *adj* intelligente, bene informato

knuckle ['nʌkəl] *s* nocca; foro del cardine, cardine *m;* **knuckles** pugno di ferro || *intr*—**to knuckle down** (coll) lavorare di impegno; **to knuckle under** (coll) darsi per vinto

knurl [nʌrl] *s* granitura || *tr* godranare, zigrinare

Koran [koˈrɑn] or [koˈræn] *s* Corano

Korea [koˈri·ə] *s* la Corea

Korean [koˈri·ən] *adj & s* coreano

kosher ['koʃər] *adj* kasher, casher, puro secondo la legge giudaica; (coll) autentico

kowtow ['kauˈtau] or ['koˈtau] *intr* inchinarsi servilmente

Kremlin ['kremlɪn] *s* Cremlino

Kremlinology [,kremlɪˈnɑlədʒi] *s* Cremlinologia

kudos ['kjudɑs] or ['kudɑs] *s* (coll) gloria, fama, approvazione

ɪ

L, l [ɛl] *s* dodicesima lettera dell'alfabeto inglese

la-bel ['lebəl] *s* marca, etichetta; (*descriptive word*) qualifica || *v* (*pret & pp* -**beled** or -**belled;** *ger* -**beling** or -**belling**) *tr* etichettare; qualificare

labial ['lebɪ·əl] *adj & s* labiale *f*

labor ['lebər] *adj* operaio || *s* lavoro; (*toil*) fatica; (*childbirth*) parto; (*body of wage earners*) manodopera; (*class as contrasted with management*) prestatori *mpl* d'opera, lavoro; **labors** fatiche *fpl;* **to be in labor** avere le doglie || *intr* lavorare; (*to exert one-*

self) travagliare; (*said of a ship*) rollare e beccheggiare; **to labor for** lottare per; **to labor under** soffrire di

laborato·ry ['læbərə,tori] s (**-ries**) laboratorio

la'bor dispute' s vertenza sindacale

labored ['lebərd] *adj* elaborato, artificiale; penoso, difficile

laborer ['lebərər] s lavoratore *m*; (*unskilled worker*) bracciante *m*, manovale *m*, uomo di fatica

laborious [lə'borɪ·əs] *adj* laborioso

la'bor un'ion s sindacato

Labourite ['lebə,raɪt] s laburista *mf*

labyrinth ['læbɪrɪnθ] s labirinto

lace [les] s (*cord or string*) stringa; (*netlike ornament*) trina, merletto; (*braid*) gallone *m* ‖ *tr* stringare; merlettare; (coll) fustigare

lace'work' s trina, merletto, pizzo

lachrymose ['lækrɪ,mos] *adj* lacrimoso

lacing ['lesɪŋ] s stringa, cordone *m*; gallone *m*; (coll) battuta, frustata

lack [læk] s mancanza, scarsezza, difetto ‖ *tr* mancare di, scarseggiare di ‖ *intr* mancare, scarseggiare, difettare

lackadaisical [,lækə'dezɪkəl] *adj* letargico, indifferente

lackey ['læki] s lacchè *m*

lacking ['lækɪŋ] *prep* privo di

lack'lus'ter *adj* smorto, spento

laconic [lə'kɑnɪk] *adj* laconico

lacquer ['lækər] s lacca ‖ *tr* laccare

lac'quer spray' s lacca spray

lac'quer ware' s oggetti *mpl* laccati

lacu·na [le'kjunə] s (**-nas** or **-nae** [ni]) lacuna

lac·y ['lesi] *adj* (**-ier; -iest**) simile al merletto

lad [læd] s ragazzo, fanciullo

ladder ['lædər] s scala; (*stepladder hinged on top*) scaleo; (*stepping stone*) (fig) scalino

lad'der truck' s autocarro di pompieri munito di scale

la'dies' man' s beato fra le donne

la'dies' room' s gabinetto per signore

ladle ['ledəl] s ramaiolo, mestolo; (*of tinsmith*) cucchiaio ‖ *tr* scodellare

la·dy ['ledi] s (**-dies**) signora, dama

la'dy·bug' s coccinella

la'dy·fin'ger s savoiardo, lingua di gatto

la'dy-in-wait'ing s (**ladies-in-waiting**) dama di corte

la'dy·kil'ler s rubacuori *m*

la'dy·like' *adj* signorile; **to be ladylike** comportarsi come una signora

la'dy·love' s amata

la'dy of the house' s padrona di casa

ladyship ['ledi,ʃɪp] s signoria

la'dy's maid' s cameriera personale della signora

lag [læg] s ritardo ‖ *v* (*pret & pp* **lagged;** *ger* **lagging**) *intr* ritardare; **to lag behind** rimanere indietro

la'ger beer' s birra invecchiata

laggard ['lægərd] s tardo, pigro

lagoon [lə'gun] s laguna

laid' pa'per [led] s carta vergata

laid' up' *adj* messo da parte; (naut) disarmato; (coll) costretto a letto

lair [ler] s tana, covo

laity ['le·ɪti] s laicato

lake [lek] *adj* lacustre ‖ s lago

lamb [læm] s agnello

lambaste [læm'best] *tr* (*to thrash*) sferzare; (*to reprimand*) riprovare

lamb' chop' s cotoletta d'agnello

lambkin ['læmkɪn] s agnellino; (fig) innocente *mf*

lamb'skin' s (*leather*) pelle *f* d'agnello; (*skin with its wool*) agnello

lame [lem] *adj* zoppo; difettoso; (*disabled*) invalido; (*excuse*) debole ‖ *tr* azzoppare

lament [lə'ment] s lamento; lamento funebre ‖ *tr* lamentare ‖ *intr* lamentarsi

lamentable ['læmǝntǝbǝl] or [lǝ'mentǝbǝl] *adj* lamentevole

lamentation [,læmǝn'teʃǝn] s lamentazione

laminate ['læmɪ,net] *tr* laminare

lamp [læmp] s lampada

lamp'black' s nerofumo

lamp' chim'ney s tubo di vetro di lampada a petrolio

lamp'light' s luce *f* di lampada

lamp'light'er s lampionaio

lampoon [læm'pun] s satira ‖ *tr* satireggiare

lamp'post' s colonna del lampione

lamp'shade' s paralume *m*, ventola

lamp'wick' s lucignolo

lance [læns] or [lɑns] s lancia; (surg) lancetta ‖ *tr* (*with an oxygen lance*) tagliare col cannello ossidrico; (surg) sbrigliare, incidere col bisturi

lance' rest' s resta

lancet ['lænsɪt] or ['lɑnsɪt] s (surg) lancetta

land [lænd] *adj* terrestre; (*wind*) di terra ‖ s terra; **on land, on sea, and in the air** per mare, per terra e nel cielo; **to make land** toccare terra; **to see how the land lies** tastare terreno ‖ *tr* sbarcare; (aer) fare atterrare; (coll) pigliare ‖ *intr* sbarcare; (*to come to rest*) andare a finire; (naut) toccar terra; (aer) atterrare; **to land on one's feet** cadere in piedi; **to land on one's head** andare a gambe all'aria; **to land on the moon** allunare; **to land on the water** ammarare

land' breeze' s vento di terra

landed ['lændɪd] *adj* (*owning land*) terriero; (*real estate*) immobile

land'fall' s (*sighting land*) avvistamento; terra avvistata; (*landslide*) frana

land' grant' s terreno ricevuto in dono dallo stato

land'hold'er s proprietario terriero

landing ['lændɪŋ] s (*of passengers*) sbarco; (*place where passengers and goods are landed*) imbarcadero; (*of stairway*) pianerottolo; (aer, naut) atterraggio

land'ing bea'con s radiofaro d'atterraggio

land'ing card' s cartoncino di sbarco

land'ing craft' s imbarcazione da sbarco

land'ing field' s campo d'atterraggio

land'ing flap' s (aer) ipususostentatore m

land'ing gear' s (aer) carrello d'atterraggio

land'ing strip' s (aer) pista d'atterraggio

land'la•dy s (-dies) (of an apartment) padrona di casa; (of a lodging house) affittacamere f; (of an inn) ostessa

landlocked ['lænd,lɑkt] adj circondato da terra

land'lord' s (of an apartment) padrone m di casa; (of a lodging house) affittacamere m; (of an inn) oste m

land•lubber ['lænd,lʌbər] s marinaio d'acqua dolce

land'mark' s (boundary stone) pietra di confine; (distinguishing landscape feature) punto di riferimento; (fig) pietra miliare

land' of'fice s ufficio del catasto

land'-office busi'ness s (coll) sacco d'affari

land'own'er s proprietario terriero

landscape ['lænd,skep] s paesaggio ‖ tr abbellire

land'scape gar'dener s giardiniere m ornamentale

land'scape paint'er s paesista mf

landscapist ['lænd,skepɪst] s paesista mf

land'slide' s frana; (fig) vittoria strepitosa

landward ['lændwərd] adv verso terra, verso la costa

land' wind' s vento di terra

lane [len] s (narrow street) vicolo, viuzza; (of a highway) corsia; (naut) rotta; (aer) corridoio

langsyne [,læŋ'saɪn] s (Scotch) tempo passato ‖ adv (Scotch) molto tempo fa

language ['læŋgwɪdʒ] s lingua; (style of language) linguaggio; (of a special group of people) gergo

lan'guage lab'oratory s laboratorio linguistico

languid ['læŋgwɪd] adj languido

languish ['læŋgwɪ/] intr languire; affettare languore

languor ['læŋgər] s languore m

languorous ['læŋgərəs] adj languido; (causing languor) snervante

lank [læŋk] adj scarnito, sparuto

lank•y ['læŋki] adj (-ier; -iest) scarnito, sparuto

lantern ['læntərn] s lanterna

lan'tern slide' s diapositiva

lanyard ['lænjərd] s (naut) drizza; (mil) agghetto, cordellina

lap [læp] s (of human body or clothing) grembo; (with the tongue) leccata; (of the waves) sciacquio; (sports) giro, tappa; **in the lap of** in mezzo a, e.g., **in the lap of luxury** in mezzo alle delicatezze ‖ v (pret & pp lapped; ger lapping) tr lappare; (said, e.g., of waves) lambire; (to fold) piegare; (to overlap); sovrapporre; **to lap up** lappare; (coll) accettare con entusiasmo ‖ intr sovrapporsi; **to lap against** (said of the waves) lambire; **to lap over** traboccare

lap'board' s tavolino da lavoro da tenersi sulle ginocchia

lap' dissolve' s (mov) dissolvenza incrociata

lap' dog' s cagnolino da salotto

lapel [lə'pel] s risvolto

Lap'land' s la Lapponia

Laplander ['læp,lændər] s lappone mf

Lapp [læp] s lappone mf; (language) lappone m

lap' robe' s coperta da viaggio

lapse [læps] s (interval) spazio di tempo; (fall, decline) caduta; (of memory) perdita; errore m; (ins) risoluzione; (law) decadenza ‖ intr cadere, ricadere; cadere in disuso; (said of time) passare; (ins) risolversi; (law) decadere

lap'wing' s pavoncella

larce•ny ['lɑrsəni] s (-nies) furto

larch [lɑrt/] s larice m

lard [lɑrd] s strutto ‖ tr lardellare

larder ['lɑrdər] s dispensa

large [lɑrdʒ] adj grande, grosso ‖ s— **at large** in libertà

large' intes'tine s intestino crasso

largely ['lɑrdʒli] adv in gran parte

large'-scale' adj su larga scala

lariat ['lærɪ•ət] s lazo, laccio

lark [lɑrk] s allodola; (coll) burla; **to go on a lark** (coll) far festa

lark'spur' s (rocket larkspur) sprone m di cavaliere; (field larkspur) consolida reale

lar•va ['lɑrvə] s (-vae [vi]) larva

laryngitis [,lærɪn'dʒaɪtɪs] s laringite f

laryngoscope [lə'rɪŋgə,skop] s laringoscopio

larynx ['lærɪŋks] s (larynxes or larynges [lə'rɪndʒiz]) laringe f

lascivious [lə'sɪvɪ•əs] adj lascivo

lasciviousness [lə'sɪvɪ•əsnɪs] s lascivia

laser ['lesər] s (acronym) (light amplification by stimulated emission of radiation) laser m

lash [læ/] s (cord on end of whip) sverzino; (blow with whip; scolding) staffilata; (of animal's tail) colpo; (eyelash) ciglio; (fig) assalto ‖ tr (to whip) frustare; (to bind) legare; (to shake) agitare; (to attack with words) staffilare ‖ intr lanciarsi; **to lash out** at attaccare violentemente

lashing ['læ/ɪŋ] s legatura; (severe scolding) staffilata; (fastening with a rope) (naut) rizza

lass [læs] s ragazza, giovane f; innamorata

las•so ['læso] s (-sos or -soes) lasso, lazo ‖ tr pigliare col lasso

last [læst] or [lɑst] adj ultimo, passato; (most recent) scorso; **before last** ierlaltro, e.g., **the night before last** ierlaltro notte; **every last one** tutti senza eccezione; **last but one** penultimo ‖ s ultima persona; ultima cosa; fine f; (for holding shoes) forma; **at last** alla fine; **at long last!** finalmente!; **stick to your last!** fa' il mestiere tuo!; **the last of the month** alla fine del mese; **to breathe one's last** dare l'ultimo sospiro; **to see the last of s.o.** vedere qlcu per l'ultima volta; **to the last** fino alla fine ‖ *adv* ultimo, per ultimo, alla fine ‖ *intr* durare, continuare

lasting ['læstɪŋ] *or* ['lɑstɪŋ] *adj* duraturo, durevole

lastly ['læstli] *or* ['lɑstli] *adv* finalmente, in conclusione

last'-min'ute news' *s* notizie *fpl* dell'ultima ora

last' name' *s* cognome *m*

last' night' *adv* ieri sera; la notte scorsa

last' quar'ter *s* ultimo quarto

last' sleep' *s* ultimo sonno

last' straw' *s* ultima, colmo

Last' Sup'per *s* Ultima Cena

last will' and tes'tament *s* ultime volontà *fpl*

last' word' *s* ultima parola; (*latest style*) ultima novità, ultimo grido

latch [lætʃ] *s* saliscendi *m*; (*wooden*) nottola ‖ *tr* chiudere col saliscendi

latch'key' *s* chiave *f* per saliscendi

latch'string' *s—***the latchstring is out** faccia come fosse a casa Sua

late [let] *adj* (*happening after the usual time*) tardo; (*person*) in ritardo; (*hour of the night*) avanzato; (*news*) dell'ultima ora, recente; (*incumbent of an office*) predecessore, ex, passato; (*coming toward the end of a period*) tardivo; (*deceased*) defunto, fu; **in the late 30's, 40's, etc.** verso la fine del decennio che va dal 1930, 1940, etc. al 1940, 1950, etc.; **of late** recentemente; **to be late in +** *ger* essere in ritardo a + *inf*; **to grow late** farsi tardi; **to keep late hours** fare le ore piccole ‖ *adv* tardi; in ritardo; **late in** (*the week, the month, etc.*) alla fine di; **late in life** a un'età avanzata

latecomer ['let ˌkʌmər] *s* ritardatario

lateen' sail' [læ'tin] *s* vela latina

lately ['letli] *adv* recentemente

latent ['letənt] *adj* latente

later ['letər] *adj comp* più tardi; (*event*) susseguente; **later than** posteriore a ‖ *adv comp* più tardi; **later on** più tardi; **see you later** (coll) arrivederci, a ben presto

lateral ['lætərəl] *adj* laterale

lath [læθ] *or* [lɑθ] *s* listello, striscia di legno ‖ *tr* mettere listelli su

lathe [leð] *s* tornio

lather ['læðər] *s* schiuma di sapone; schiuma ‖ *tr* insaponare; (coll) bastonare ‖ *intr* schiumare

lathery ['læðəri] *adj* schiumoso

lathing ['læθɪŋ] *or* ['lɑθɪŋ] *s* costruzione con listelli

Latin ['lætɪn] *or* ['lætən] *adj & s* latino

Lat'in-Amer'ica *s* l'America latina

Lat'in-Amer'ican *adj* dell'America latina

Lat'in Amer'ican *s* abitante *mf* dell'America latina

latitude ['lætɪ ˌtjud] *or* ['lætɪ ˌtud] *s* latitudine *f*

latrine [lə'trin] *s* latrina militare

latter ['lætər] *adj* (*more recent*) posteriore; (*of two*) secondo; **the latter** questo; **the latter part of** la fine di

lattice ['lætɪs] *s* graticcio ‖ *tr* munire di graticcio, graticciare

lat'tice gird'er *s* trave *f* a traliccio

lat'tice-work' *s* graticcio, traliccio

Latvia ['lætvɪ·ə] *s* la Lettonia

laud [lɔd] *tr* lodare

laudable ['lɔdəbəl] *adj* lodevole

laudanum ['lɔdənəm] *or* ['lɔdnəm] *s* laudano

laudatory ['lɔdə ˌtori] *adj* lodativo

laugh [læf] *or* [lɑf] *s* riso ‖ *tr*—**to laugh away** dissipare ridendo; **to laugh off** prendere sotto gamba, non dare importanza a ‖ *intr* ridere, ridersi; **to laugh at** ridersi di; **to laugh up one's sleeve** ridere sotto i baffi

laughable ['læfəbəl] *or* ['lɑfəbəl] *adj* risibile

laughing ['læfɪŋ] *or* ['lɑfɪŋ] *adj* che ride; **to be no laughing matter** non esserci niente da ridere ‖ *s* riso

laugh'ing gas' *s* gas *m* esilarante

laugh'ing-stock' *s* ludibrio, zimbello

laughter ['læftər] *or* ['lɑftər] *s* riso

launch [lɔntʃ] *or* [lɑntʃ] *s* (*of a ship*) varo; (*of a rocket*) lancio; (naut) lancia, scialuppa ‖ *tr* (*to throw; to send forth*) lanciare; (naut) varare ‖ *intr* lanciarsi

launching ['lɔntʃɪŋ] *or* ['lɑntʃɪŋ] *s* lancio; (*of a ship*) varo

launch'ing pad' *s* piattaforma di lancio

launder ['lɔndər] *or* ['lɑndər] *tr* lavare e stirare ‖ *intr* riuscire dopo il lavaggio

launderer ['lɔndərər] *or* ['lɑndərər] *s* lavandaio stiratore *m*

laundress ['lɔndrɪs] *or* ['lɑndrɪs] *s* lavandaia stiratrice *f*

laundromat ['lɔndrə ˌmæt] *or* ['lɑndrə ˌmæt] *s* (trademark) lavanderia a gettone

laun-dry ['lɔndri] *or* ['lɑndri] *s* (-dries) lavanderia; (*clothing*) bucato

laun'dry-man' *s* (-men') lavandaio

laun'dry-wom'an *s* (-wom'en) lavandaia

laureate ['lɔrɪ·ɪt] *adj* laureato ‖ *s* laureato; poeta laureato

lau-rel ['lɔrəl] *or* ['lɑrəl] *s* lauro, alloro; **laurels** (fig) alloro; **to rest or sleep on one's laurels** dormire sugli allori ‖ *v* (*pret & pp* -reled *or* -relled; *ger* -reling *or* -relling) *tr* laureare

lava ['lɑvə] *or* ['lævə] *s* lava

lavato-ry ['lævə ˌtori] *s* (-ries) (*room*) gabinetto da bagno; (*bowl*) lavabo; (*toilet*) gabinetto di decenza, cesso

lavender ['lævəndər] *s* lavanda

lavish ['lævɪʃ] *adj* prodigo ‖ *tr* prodigare, profondere

law [lɔ] *s* (*of man, of nature, of science*) legge *f*; (*study, profession of law*) diritto; **to enter the law** farsi avvocato; **to go to law** ricorrere alla legge; **to lay down the law** dettar legge; **to maintain law and order** mantenere la pace interna; **to practice law** far l'avvocato

law-abiding ['lɔ·ə ˌbaɪdɪŋ] *adj* osservante della legge

law'break'er *s* violatore *m* della legge

law' court' s tribunale m di giustizia
lawful ['lɔfəl] adj legale, legittimo
lawless ['lɔlɪs] adj illegale; (unbridled) sfrenato
law'mak'er s legislatore m
lawn [lɔn] s tappeto erboso; (fabric) batista
lawn' mow'er s tosatrice f
law' of'fice s ufficio d'avvocato
law' of na'tions s diritto delle genti
law' of the jun'gle s legge f della giungla
law' stu'dent s studente m di legge
law'suit' s causa, lite f, processo
lawyer ['lɔjər] s avvocato, legale m
lax [læks] adj (in morals) lasso, rilassato; (rope) lento; (negligent) trascurato; vago, indeterminato
laxative ['læksətɪv] adj purgativo ‖ s purga, purgante m
lay [le] adj (not belonging to the clergy) laico; (not having special training) non dotto, profano ‖ s configurazione, disposizione ‖ v (pret & pp laid [led]) tr mettere, collocare; (snares) tendere; (one's eyes; a stone) porre; (blame) dare, gettare; (a bet) fare; (for consideration) presentare; (the table) imbandire; (said of a hen) deporre; (plans) impostare; (to locate) disporre; **to be laid in** (said of a scene) aver luogo in; **to lay aside** mettere da parte; **to lay down** dichiarare; (one's life) dare; (one's arms) deporre; **to lay low** abbattere; uccidere; **to lay off** (workers) licenziare; (to measure) marcare; (slang) lasciare in pace; **to lay open** rivelare; (to a danger) esporre; **to lay out** estendere; preparare, disporre; (a corpse) comporre; (money) (coll) sborsare; **to lay over** posporre; **to lay up** mettere da parte; obbligare a letto; (naut) disarmare ‖ intr (said of a hen) fare le uova; **to lay about** dar botte da orbi; **to lay for** (slang) attendere al varco; **to lay off** (coll) cessare di lavorare; **to lay over** trattenersi, fermarsi; **to lay to** (naut) navigare alla cappa
lay' broth'er s frate m secolare; converso
lay' day' s (com) stallia
layer ['le·ər] s (of paint) mano f; (of bricks) testa; (e.g., of rocks) strato, falda; (anat) pannicolo; (hort) propaggine f ‖ tr (hort) propagginare
lay'er cake' s dolce m a strati
layette [le'et] s corredino
lay' fig'ure s manichino
laying ['le·ɪŋ] s posa; (of eggs) deporre m; (of a wire) tendere m
lay'man s (-men) (member of the laity) laico, secolare m; (not a member of a special profession) laico, profano
lay'off' s (dismissal of workers) licenziamento; (period of unemployment) disoccupazione
lay' of the land' s andamento generale
lay'out' s piano; (sketch) tracciato; (of tools) armamentario; (coll) residenza; (typ) menabò m; (coll) banchetto, festino

lay'o'ver s fermata in un viaggio
lay' sis'ter s suora al secolo; conversa
laziness ['lezɪnɪs] s pigrizia
la·zy ['lezi] adj (-zier; -ziest) pigro
la'zy·bones' s (coll) poltrone m
lea [li] s (fallow land) maggese m; (meadow) prato
lead [led] adj piombeo ‖ s piombo; (of lead pencil) mina; (for sounding depth) (naut) scandaglio; (typ) interlinea ‖ [led] v (pret & pp leaded; ger leading) tr impiombare; (typ) interlineare ‖ [lid] s (foremost place) primato; (guidance) guida, direzione; (leash) guinzaglio; (journ) testata; (cards) mano f, prima mano; (elec) conduttore m; (mach) passo; (min) filone m; (rad, telv) filo d'entrata; (theat) ruolo principale; (theat) primo attore; (theat) prima attrice; **to take the lead** prendere il comando ‖ [lid] v (pret & pp led [led]) tr condurre, portare; (to command) comandare, essere alla testa di; (an orchestra) dirigere; (a good or bad life) fare; (s.o. into vice) trascinare; (cards) cominciare a giocare; (elec, mach) anticipare; **to lead astray** forviare ‖ intr essere in testa, guidare; prendere l'offensiva; (said of a road) condurre; (cards) cominciare a giocare; **to lead to** risultare in; **to lead up to** andare a condurre a
leaden ['ledən] adj (of lead; like lead) plumbeo; (sluggish) tardo; (with sleep) carico; triste
leader ['lidər] s capo, comandante m; (ringleader) capobanda m; (of an orchestra) direttore m; (among animals) guidaiolo; (in a dance) ballerino guidaiolo; (sports) capintesta m; (journ) articolo di fondo
lead'er dog' s cane m guida di ciechi
leadership ['lidər,ʃɪp] s comando, direzione; doti fpl di comando
leading ['lidɪŋ] adj principale; primo; dirigente, preeminente
lead'ing ar'ticle s articolo di fondo
lead'ing edge' s (aer) bordo d'attacco
lead'ing la'dy s prima attrice
lead'ing man' s (men) primo attore
lead'ing ques'tion s domanda suggestiva, domanda orientatrice
lead'ing strings' spl dande fpl
lead'-in wire' ['lid,ɪn] s filo d'antenna
lead' pen'cil [led] s lapis m, matita
leaf [lif] s (leaves [livz]) (of plant) foglia; (of vine) pampino; (of paper) foglio; (of double door) battente m; (of table) asse m a ribalta; **to turn over a new leaf** ricominciare una nuova vita ‖ intr fogliare; **to leaf through** sfogliare
leafless ['liflɪs] adj senza foglie
leaflet ['liflɪt] s manifestino, volantino; (of plant) foglietta
leaf' spring' s molla a balestra
leaf'stalk' s picciolo
leaf·y ['lifi] adj (-ier; -iest) foglioso, frondoso
league [lig] s lega ‖ tr associare ‖ intr associarsi

League' of Na'tions s Società f delle Nazioni

leak [lik] s (in a roof) stillicidio; (in a ship) falla; (of water, gas, steam) fuga; (of electricity) dispersione; buco, fessura; (of news) filtrazione; **to spring a leak** avere una perdita; (naut) cominciare a far acqua || tr (gas, liquids) perdere, lasciar scappare; (news) lasciar trapelare || intr (said of water, gas etc.,) perdere, scappare; (said of a barrel) spillare; (naut) fare acqua; **to leak away** (said of money) andarsene; **to leak out** (said of news) trapelare

leakage ['likɪdʒ] s perdita, fuoruscita, fuga; (elec) dispersione; (com) colaggio

leak·y ['liki] adj (-ier; -iest) che perde; (naut) che fa acqua; (coll) indiscreto

lean [lin] adj magro, secco; (gasoline mixture) povero || v (pret & pp leaned or leant [lɛnt]) tr inclinare; appoggiare || intr pendere, inclinarsi; (fig) inclinare, tendere; **to lean against** appoggiarsi a, addossarsi a; **to lean back** sdraiarsi; **to lean on** appoggiarsi su; **to lean out (of)** sporgersi (da); **to lean over backwards** fare di tutto; **to lean toward** (fig) tendere a, avere un'inclinazione per

leaning ['linɪŋ] adj inclinato, pendente || s inclinazione

lean'ing tow'er s torre f pendente

lean'-to' s (-tos) tetto a una falda

leap [lip] s salto, balzo; **by leaps and bounds** a passi da gigante; **leap in the dark** salto nel vuoto || v (pret & pp leaped or leapt [lɛpt]) tr saltare || intr saltare; (said of one's heart) balzare

leap'frog' s cavallina; **to play leapfrog** giocare alla cavallina

leap' year' s anno bisestile

learn [lʌrn] s (pret & pp learned or learnt [lʌrnt]) tr imparare; imparare a memoria; (news) apprendere || intr istruirsi, apprendere

learned ['lʌrnɪd] adj dotto; (word) colto

learn'ed jour'nal s rivista scientifica

learn'ed soci'ety s associazione di eruditi

learn'ed word' s parola dotta

learn'ed world' s mondo di dotti

learner ['lʌrnər] s apprendista mf; studente m; (beginner) principiante mf

learning ['lʌrnɪŋ] s istruzione; (scholarship) erudizione

lease [lis] s locazione, contratto d'affitto; **a new lease on life** nuove prospettive di felicità; vita nuova (dopo una malattia) || tr locare; prendere in affitto || intr affittare

lease'hold' adj affittato || s beni mpl sotto locazione

leash [liʃ] s guinzaglio; **to strain at the leash** mordere il freno || tr frenare, controllare

least [list] adj minore, menomo, minimo || s (il) meno; **at least or at the least** per lo meno, quanto meno;

not in the least nient'affatto || adv meno

leather ['lɛðər] s cuoio

leath'er·back' tur'tle s tartaruga di mare

leath'er goods' store' s pelletteria

leathery ['lɛðəri] adj coriaceo

leave [liv] s (permission) permesso; (permission to be absent) licenza; (farewell) commiato; **on leave** in licenza; **to take French leave** andarsene all'inglese; **to take leave (of)** prender congedo (da) || v (pret & pp left [lɛft]) tr (to go away from) lasciare, uscire da; (to let stay) lasciare; (to bequeath) lasciare in testamento; **leave it to me!** lasciami fare!; **to be left** restare, e.g., **the door was left open** la porta restò aperta; esserci, e.g., **there is no bread left** non c'è più pane; **to leave alone** lasciare in pace; **to leave no stone unturned** cercare ogni possibilità; **to leave off** abbandonare, lasciare; **to leave out** omettere; **to leave things as they are** lasciar stare le cose || intr andarsene; (said of a conveyance) partire

leaven ['lɛvən] s lievito || tr lievitare; (fig) impregnare, permeare

leavening ['lɛvənɪŋ] s lievito

leave'-tak'ing s commiato

leavings ['livɪŋz] spl rifiuti mpl

Leba·nese [ˌlɛbə'niz] adj libanese || s (-nese) libanese mf

Lebanon ['lɛbənən] s il Libano

lecher ['lɛtʃər] s libertino

lecherous ['lɛtʃərəs] adj libidinoso

lechery ['lɛtʃəri] s lussuria

lectern ['lɛktərn] s leggio

lecture ['lɛktʃər] s conferenza; (tedious reprimand) pistolotto || tr dare una conferenza a; sermoneggiare || intr fare una conferenza; sermoneggiare

lecturer ['lɛktʃərər] s conferenziere m

ledge [lɛdʒ] s cornice f, cornicione m

ledger ['lɛdʒər] s (com) libro mastro

ledg'er line' s (mus) rigo supplementare

lee [li] s (shelter) rifugio; (naut) parte f sottovento; **lees** feccia

leech [litʃ] s mignatta, sanguisuga; **to stick like a leech** attaccarsi come una sanguisuga

leek [lik] s porro

leer [lɪr] s occhiata lussuriosa or maligna || intr—**to leer** at guardare di sbieco, sbirciare

leer·y ['lɪri] adj (-ier; -iest) sospettoso

leeward ['liwərd] or ['lu·ərd] adj di sottovento || s sottovento, poggia || adv sottovento

lee'way' s (aer, naut) deriva, scarroccio; (in time) (coll) tolleranza; (coll) libertà f d'azione

left [lɛft] adj sinistro; (pol) di sinistra || s sinistra; (boxing) sinistro || adv alla sinistra

left' field' s fuoricampo di sinistra

left'-hand' drive' s guida a sinistra

left-handed ['lɛft'hændɪd] adj (individual) mancino; (awkward) goffo;

(compliment) ambiguo; *(mach)* sinistrorso

leftish [ˈleftɪʃ] *adj* sinistrista

leftist [ˈleftɪst] *adj* di sinistra ‖ *s* membro della sinistra

left'o'ver *adj & s* rimanente *m*; **leftovers** resti *mpl*

left'-wing' *adj* di sinistra

left-winger [ˈleftˈwɪŋər] *s* (coll) membro dell'estrema sinistra; (coll) membro della sinistra

leg [leg] *s* (of man, animal, table, chair; of trousers) gamba; (of fowl; of lamb) coscia; (of boot) gambale *m*; (of a journey) tappa; **to be on one's last legs** essere agli estremi, essere ridotto alla disperazione; **to not have a leg to stand on** (coll) non avere la minima giustificazione; **to pull the leg of** (coll) prendere in giro, burlarsi di; **to shake a leg** (coll) affrettarsi; *(to dance)* (coll) ballare; **to stretch one's legs** sgranchirsi le gambe

lega·cy [ˈlegəsi] *s* (-cies) legato

legal [ˈligəl] *adj* legale

legali·ty [lɪˈgælɪti] *s* (-ties) legalità *f*

legalize [ˈligəˌlaɪz] *tr* legalizzare

le'gal ten'der *s* denaro a corso legale

legate [ˈlegɪt] *s* legato

legatee [ˌlegəˈti] *s* legatario

legation [lɪˈgeʃən] *s* legazione

legend [ˈlɛdʒənd] *s* leggenda

legendary [ˈlɛdʒənˌdɛri] *adj* leggendario

legerdemain [ˌlɛdʒərdɪˈmen] *s* gioco di prestigio; *(trickery)* imbroglio

legging [ˈlɛgɪŋ] *s* gambale *m*

leg·gy [ˈlegi] *adj* (-gier; -giest) dalle gambe lunghe

leg'horn' *s* cappello di paglia di Firenze; gallina bianca livornese ‖ **Leghorn** *s* Livorno

legible [ˈlɛdʒɪbəl] *adj* leggibile

legion [ˈlidʒən] *s* legione *f*

legislate [ˈlɛdʒɪsˌlet] *tr* ordinare per mezzo di legge ‖ *intr* legiferare

legislation [ˌlɛdʒɪsˈleʃən] *s* legislazione

legislative [ˈlɛdʒɪsˌletɪv] *adj* legislativo

legislator [ˈlɛdʒɪsˌletər] *s* legislatore *m*

legislature [ˈlɛdʒɪsˌletʃər] *s* legislatura; corpo legislativo

legitimacy [lɪˈdʒɪtɪməsi] *s* legittimità *f*

legitimate [lɪˈdʒɪtɪmɪt] *adj* legittimo ‖ [lɪˈdʒɪtɪˌmet] *tr* legittimare

legitimize [lɪˈdʒɪtɪˌmaɪz] *tr* legittimare

leg' of lamb' *s* cosciotto d'agnello

legume [ˈlegjum] or [lɪˈgjum] *s* (pod) legume *m*; *(table vegetables)* legumi *mpl*; (bot) leguminose *fpl*

leg'work' *s* lavoro che involve molto cammino

leisure [ˈliʒər] or [ˈlɛʒər] *s* ozio; **at leisure** senza fretta; disoccupato; **at one's leisure** quando si abbia un po' di tempo libero

lei'sure class' *s* gente agiata

lei'sure hours' *spl* ore *fpl* d'ozio

leisurely [ˈliʒərli] or [ˈlɛʒərli] *adj* lento ‖ *adv* lentamente, a tempo perso

lei'sure time' *s* tempo libero

lemon [ˈlɛmən] *s* limone *m*; *(car)* (coll) catorcio

lemonade [ˌlɛməˈned] *s* limonata

lem'on squeez'er *s* spremilimoni *m*

lend [lɛnd] *s* (pret & pp lent [lɛnt]) *tr* prestare; *(a hand)* dare

lender [ˈlɛndər] *s* prestatore *m*

lend'ing li'brary *s* biblioteca circolante

length [lɛŋθ] *s* lunghezza; *(of time)* durata; **at length** finalmente; **to go to any lengths** fare quanto è possibile; essere disposto a tutto; **to keep at arm's length** *(someone else)* tenere a distanza (qlcu); *(said of oneself)* tenere la distanza

lengthen [ˈlɛŋθən] *tr* allungare ‖ *intr* allungarsi

length'wise' *adj* longitudinale ‖ *adv* per il lungo

length·y [ˈlɛŋθi] *adj* (-ier; -iest) lungo, prolungato

lenien·cy [ˈliniˌənsi] *s* (-cies) indulgenza

lenient [ˈliniˌənt] *adj* indulgente, clemente

lens [lɛnz] *s* lente *f*; *(of the eye)* cristallino

Lent [lɛnt] *s* quaresima

Lenten [ˈlɛntən] *adj* quaresimale

lentil [ˈlɛntəl] *s* lenticchia

Leo [ˈli·o] *s* (astr) il Leone

leopard [ˈlɛpərd] *s* leopardo

leotard [ˈli·əˌtɑrd] *s* calzamaglia

leper [ˈlɛpər] *s* lebbroso

leprosy [ˈlɛprəsi] *s* lebbra

leprous [ˈlɛprəs] *adj* lebbroso; *(of an animal or plant)* squamoso

Lesbian [ˈlɛzbɪˌən] *adj* lesbico ‖ *s* lesbico; *(female homosexual)* lesbica

lesbianism [ˈlɛzbɪˌəˌnɪzəm] *s* lesbismo

lese majesty [ˈlizˈmædʒɪsti] *s* delitto di lesa maestà

lesion [ˈliʒən] *s* lesione

less [lɛs] *adj* minore ‖ *adv* meno; **less and less** sempre meno; **less than** meno che; *(followed by numeral or personal pron)* meno di; *(followed by verb)* meno di quanto ‖ *s* meno

lessee [lɛsˈi] *s* locatario; *(of business establishment)* concessionario

lessen [ˈlɛsən] *tr* diminuire, ridurre ‖ *intr* diminuire, ridursi

lesser [ˈlɛsər] *adj comp* minore

lesson [ˈlɛsən] *s* lezione

lessor [ˈlɛsər] *s* locatore *m*

lest [lɛst] *conj* per paura che

let [lɛt] *v* (pret & pp let; ger letting) *tr* permettere; *(to rent)* affittare; **let + inf** che + subj, e.g., **let him go** che vada; **let alone** tanto meno; senza menzionare; **let good enough alone** essere contento dell'onesto; **let us + inf = 1st pl impv**, e.g., **let us sing** cantiamo; **to let da affittare**; **to let alone** lasciare in pace; **to let be** lasciar stare; **to let by** lasciar passare; **to let down** far scendere; deludere; tradire; abbandonare; **to let fly** *(insults)* lanciare; **to let go** lasciar libero; vendere; **to let in** fare entrare; **to let it go at that** non parlarne più; **to let know** far sapere; **to**

let loose sciogliere; **to let out** lasciar uscire; *(a secret)* divulgare; *(a scream)* lasciarsi scappare; *(to enlarge)* allargare; affittare; **to let through** lasciar passare; **to let up** lasciar salire; lasciar alzare ‖ *intr* affittare; **to let down** diminuire gli sforzi; **to let go of** disfarsi di; **to let on** (coll) fare finta; **to not let on** (coll) non lasciar trapelare; **to let out** *(said, e.g., of school)* terminare; **to let up** (coll) cessare; (coll) diminuire

let'down' *s* diminuzione; smacco, umiliazione; delusione

lethal ['liθəl] *adj* letale

lethargic [lɪ'θɑrdʒɪk] *adj* letargico

lethar·gy ['lɛθərdʒi] *s* (**-gies**) letargo

Lett [lɛt] *s* lettone *mf*; *(language)* lettone *m*

letter ['lɛtər] *s* lettera; **letters** *(literature)* lettere *fpl*, letteratura; **to the letter** alla lettera ‖ *tr* marcare con lettere

let'ter box' *s* cassetta delle lettere

let'ter car'rier *s* postino

let'ter drop' *s* buca delle lettere

let'ter-head' *s* capolettera *m*; *(paper with printed heading)* carta da lettera intestata

lettering ['lɛtərɪŋ] *s* iscrizione; lettere *fpl*

let'ter of cred'it *s* lettera di credito

let'ter o'pener ['opənər] *s* tagliacarte *m*

let'ter pa'per *s* carta da lettere

let'ter-per'fect *adj* alla lettera; che sa alla perfezione

let'ter-press' *s* stampato in tipografia ‖ *adv* a stampa tipografica

let'ter scales' *spl* pesalettere *m*

let'ter-word' *s* sigla

Lettish ['lɛtɪʃ] *adj & s* lettone *m*

lettuce ['lɛtɪs] *s* lattuga

let'up' *s* (coll) pausa, sosta; (coll) tregua; **without letup** (coll) senza posa

leucorrhea [,lukə'ri·ə] *s* leucorrea

leukemia [lu'kimi·ə] *s* leucemia

Levant [lɪ'vænt] *s* levante *m*

levee ['lɛvi] *s* *(embankment)* argine *m*; *(reception)* ricevimento

lev·el ['lɛvəl] *adj* piano; livellato; equilibrato; **level with** a livello di; **one's level best** (coll) il proprio meglio ‖ *s* *(instrument)* livella; *(degree of elevation)* livello; *(flat surface)* spianata, pianura; **on the level** (slang) onesto; onestamente; **to find one's level** trovare il proprio ambiente ‖ *v* *(pret & pp* **-eled** *or* **-elled;** *ger* **-eling** *or* **-elling)** *tr* livellare; *(to flatten out)* spianare; *(e.g., prices)* pareggiare, ragguagliare; *(a gun)* puntare; (coll) gettare a terra; (fig) dirigere ‖ *intr*— **to level off** (aer) volare orizzontalmente

level-headed ['lɛvəl'hɛdɪd] *adj* equilibrato

lev'eling rod' *s* stadia

lever ['livər] *or* ['lɛvər] *s* leva ‖ *tr* far leva su ‖ *intr* far leva

leverage ['livərɪdʒ] *or* ['lɛvərɪdʒ] *s* azione di una leva; (fig) potere *m*

leviathan [lɪ'vaɪ·əθən] *s* leviatano

levitation [,lɛvɪ'teʃən] *s* levitazione

levi·ty ['lɛvɪti] *s* (**-ties**) leggerezza

lev·y ['lɛvi] *s* (**-ies**) *(of taxes)* esazione; *(of money)* tributo; *(of troops)* leva ‖ *v* *(pret & pp* **-ied)** *tr* *(a tax)* imporre; *(soldiers)* reclutare; *(war)* fare

lewd [lud] *adj* *(lustful)* lascivo; osceno

lexical ['lɛksɪkəl] *adj* lessicale

lexicographer [,lɛksɪ'kɑgrəfər] *s* lessicografo

lexicographic(al) [,lɛksɪko'græfɪk(əl)] *adj* lessicografico

lexicography [,lɛksɪ'kɑgrəfi] *s* lessicografia

lexicology [,lɛksɪ'kɑlədʒi] *s* lessicologia

lexicon ['lɛksɪkən] *s* lessico

liabili·ty [,laɪ·ə'bɪlɪti] *s* (**-ties**) svantaggio; responsabilità *f*; *(e.g., to disease)* tendenza; (com) passivo; **liabilities** debiti *mpl*; (com) passivo

liabil'ity insur'ance *s* assicurazione sulla responsabilità civile

liable ['laɪ·əbəl] *adj* *(e.g., to disease; e.g., to make mistakes)* soggetto; responsabile; probabile; *(e.g., to a fine)* passibile

liaison ['li·ə,zɑn] *or* [li'ezɑn] *s* legame *m*; relazione illecita; (mil, nav) collegamento; (phonet) legamento

li'aison of'ficer *s* ufficiale *m* di collegamento

liar ['laɪ·ər] *s* bugiardo, mentitore *m*

libation [laɪ'beʃən] *s* (joc) libazione, bevuta

li·bel ['laɪbəl] *s* diffamazione; *(defamatory writing)* libello ‖ *v* *(pret & pp* **-beled** *or* **-belled;** *ger* **-beling** *or* **-belling)** *tr* diffamare

libelous ['laɪbələs] *adj* diffamatorio

liberal ['lɪbərəl] *adj* liberale; *(translation)* libero ‖ *s* liberale *mf*

liberali·ty [,lɪbə'rælɪti] *s* (**-ties**) liberalità *f*; *(breadth of mind)* ampiezza di vedute

liberal-minded ['lɪbərəl'maɪndɪd] *adj* liberale, tollerante

liberate ['lɪbə,ret] *tr* liberare

liberation [,lɪbə're/ən] *s* liberazione

liberator ['lɪbə,retər] *s* liberatore *m*

libertine ['lɪbər,tin] *adj & s* libertino

liber·ty ['lɪbərti] *s* (**-ties**) libertà *f*; **to take the liberty to** permettersi di

liberty-loving ['lɪbərti'lavɪŋ] *adj* amante della libertà

libidinous [lɪ'bɪdɪnəs] *adj* libidinoso

libido [lɪ'bido] *or* [lɪ'baɪdo] *s* libidine *f*; (psychoanal) libido *f*

Libra ['lɪbrə] *or* ['laɪbrə] *s* (astr) Bilancia

librarian [laɪ'brɛrɪ·ən] *s* bibliotecario

librar·y ['laɪ,brɛri] *or* ['laɪbrəri] *s* (**-ies**) biblioteca; *(room in a house; collection of books)* libreria

li'brary num'ber *s* segnatura

li'brary sci'ence *s* biblioteconomia

libret·to [lɪ'brɛto] *s* (**-tos**) (mus) libretto

Libya ['lɪbɪ·ə] *s* la Libia

license ['laɪsəns] *s* licenza; (aut) patente *f* ‖ *tr* dare la licenza a

li'cense num'ber *s* numero di targa di circolazione

li'cense plate' *or* **tag'** *s* targa di circolazione

licentious [laɪ'sen/əs] *adj* licenzioso

lichen ['laɪkən] *s* lichene *m*

lick [lɪk] *s* leccata, leccatura; (coll) esplosione di energia; (coll) velocità *f*; (coll) battitura; (coll) ripulita; **to give a lick and a promise to** (coll) fare rapidamente e con poca attenzione || *tr* leccare; (*said of waves, flames, etc.*) lambire; (*to defeat*) (coll) battere, vincere; (*e.g., with a stick*) (coll) bastonare

licorice ['lɪkərɪs] *s* liquirizia

lid [lɪd] *s* coperchio; (*eyelid*) palpebra; (*curb*) (coll) restrizione, freno; (*hat*) (slang) cappello

lie [laɪ] *s* menzogna; **to catch in a lie** pigliare in castagna; **to give the lie to** smentire || *v* (*pret & pp* **lied**; *ger* **lying**) *tr*—**to lie oneself out of** *or* **to lie one's way out of** trarsi fuori da (*un impaccio*) con una menzogna || *intr* mentire || *v* (*pret* **lay** [le]; *pp* **lain** [len]; *ger* **lying**) *intr* essere sdraiato; trovarsi; (*in the grave*) giacere; **to lie down** sdraiarsi

lie' detec'tor *s* macchina della verità

lien [lin] *or* ['li·ən] *s* diritto di pegno, diritto di garanzia

lieu [lu] *s*—**in lieu of** in luogo di

lieutenant [lu'tenənt] *s* luogotenente *m*; (mil) tenente *m*; (nav) tenente *m* di vascello

lieuten'ant colo'nel *s* (mil) tenente *m* colonnello

lieuten'ant command'er *s* (nav) capitano di corvetta

lieuten'ant gen'eral *s* (mil) generale *m* di corpo d'armata

lieuten'ant gov'ernor *s* (USA) vicegovernatore *m*

lieuten'ant jun'ior grade' *s* (nav) sottotenente *m* di vascello

life [laɪf] *adj* (*animate*) vitale; (*lifelong*) perpetuo; (*annuity*) vitalizio; (*working from nature*) dal vero || *s* (**lives** [laɪvz]) vita; (*of an insurance policy*) forza; **for life** a vita; **for the life of me** per quanto io provi; **the life and soul of** (*e.g., the party*) l'anima di; **to come to life** tornare a sé; riprender vita; **to depart this life** passar a miglior vita; **to run for one's life** scappare a tutta corsa

life' annu'ity *s* rendita vitalizia

life' belt' *s* cintura di salvataggio

life'boat' *s* imbarcazione di salvataggio, lancia di salvataggio

life' buoy' *s* salvagente *m*

life' float' *s* zattera di salvataggio

life'guard' *s* bagnino

life' impris'onment *s* ergastolo

life' insur'ance *s* assicurazione sulla vita

life' jack'et *s* cintura *or* giubbotto di salvataggio

lifeless ['laɪflɪs] *adj* inanimato; (*in a faint*) esanime; senza vita

life'like' *adj* (*e.g., portrait*) parlante; naturale

life' line' *s* sagola di salvataggio; (fig) linea di comunicazioni vitale

life'long' *adj* perpetuo, a vita

life' of Ri'ley ['raɪli] *s* vita del michelaccio

life' of the par'ty *s* anima della festa

life' preserv'er [prɪ'zɑrvər] *s* salvagente *m*

lifer ['laɪfər] *s* (slang) ergastolano

life' raft' *s* zattera di salvataggio

life'sav'er *s* salvatore *m* della vita; (*something that saves from a predicament*) ancora di salvezza

life' sen'tence *s* condanna all'ergastolo

life'-size' *adj* in grandezza naturale

life'time' *adj* vitalizio || *s* corso della vita

life' vest' *s* (air, naut) giubbotto salvagente *or* di salvataggio

life'work' *s* lavoro di tutta una vita

lift [lɪft] *s* sollevamento; (*act of helping*) aiuto; (*ride*) passaggio; (*apparatus*) elevatore *m*; (aer) portanza || *tr* sollevare, alzare; (*one's hat*) levarsi; rimuovere; (coll) plagiare; (coll) rubare; (*fire*) (mil) sospendere || *intr* sollevare, sollevarsi; (*said, e.g., of fog*) dissiparsi

lift'-off' *s* (aer) decollo verticale

lift' truck' *s* carrello elevatore

ligament ['lɪgəmənt] *s* legamento

ligature ['lɪgət/ər] *s* legatura

light [laɪt] *adj* (*in weight*) leggero; (*hair*) biondo; (*complexion*) chiaro; (*oil*) fluido; (naut) con poco carico; (*room*) chiaro, illuminato; (*beer*) chiaro; **light in the head** (dizzy) allegro; (*silly*) scimunito; **to make light of** prendere sotto gamba || *s* luce *f*; (*to light a cigarette*) fuoco; (*to control traffic*) segnale *m*; (*shining example*) luminare *m*; (*lighthouse*) faro; (*window*) luce *f*; **according to one's lights** secondo l'intelligenza che il buon Dio gii (le) ha dato; **against the light** controluce; **in this light** sotto questo punto di vista; **lights** esempio; (*of sheep*) polmone *m*; **to come to light** venire alla luce; **to shed** *or* **throw light on** mettere in luce; **to strike a light** accendere un fiammifero || *v* (*pret & pp* **lighted** *or* **lit** [lɪt]) *tr* (*to furnish with illumination*) illuminare; (*to ignite*) accendere; **to light up** illuminare || *intr* illuminarsi; accendersi; (*said, e.g., of a bird*) posarsi; (*from a car*) scendere; **to light into** (coll) gettarsi contro; **to light out** (slang) darsela a gambe; **to light upon** imbattersi in || *adv* senza bagagli; senza carico

light' bulb' *s* lampadina

light-complexioned ['laɪtkəm'plek/ənd] *adj* dal colorito chiaro

lighten ['laɪtən] *tr* alleggerire, sgravare; illuminare; (*to cheer up*) rallegrare || *intr* alleggerirsi; (*to become less dark*) illuminarsi; (*to give off flashes of lightning*) lampeggiare

lighter ['laɪtər] *s* accenditore *m*; (naut) burchio

light-fingered ['laɪt'fɪŋgərd] *adj* svelto di mano, con le mani lunghe

light-footed [ˈlaɪtˈfʊtɪd] *adj* agile

light-headed [ˈlaɪtˈhedɪd] *adj* (*dizzy*) allegro; (*simple*) scemo

light-hearted [ˈlaɪtˈhɑrtɪd] *adj* allegro

light'house' *s* faro

lighting [ˈlaɪtɪŋ] *s* illuminazione

lightly [ˈlaɪtli] *adv* alla leggera

light' me'ter *s* esposimetro

lightness [ˈlaɪtnɪs] *s* (*in weight*) leggerezza; (*in illumination*) chiarezza

light·ning [ˈlaɪtnɪŋ] *s* lampo, fulmine *m* ‖ *v* (*ger* **-ning**) *intr* lampeggiare

light'ning arrest'er [əˈrɛstər] *s* scaricatore *m*

light'ning bug' *s* lucciola

light'ning rod' *s* parafulmine *m*

light' op'era *s* operetta

light'ship' *s* battello faro

light-struck [ˈlaɪtˌstrʌk] *adj* che ha preso luce

light'weight' *adj* leggero; da mezza stagione, e.g., **lightweight coat** cappotto da mezza stagione

light'-year' *s* anno luce

likable [ˈlaɪkəbəl] *adj* simpatico

like [laɪk] *adj* uguale, simile; uguale a, simile a, e.g., **this hat is like mine** questo cappello è simile al mio; (elec) di segno uguale; **like father like son** tale il padre quale il figlio; **to feel like** + *ger* aver voglia di + *inf*; **to look like** assomigliare a; sembrare, e.g., **it looks like rain** sembra che pioverà ‖ *s* (*liking*) preferenza; (*fellow man*) simile *m*; **and the like e** cose dello stesso genere; **to give like for like** rendere pane per focaccia ‖ *adv* come; **like enough** (coll) probabilmente ‖ *prep* come ‖ *conj* (coll) come; come se; (coll) che, e.g., **it seems like he is afraid** sembra che abbia paura ‖ *tr* volere bene (with *dat*), e.g., **I like her very much le** voglio molto bene; trovar piacere in, e.g., **I like music** trovo piacere nella musica; piacere (with *dat*), e.g., **John likes apples** le mele piacciono a Giovanni; **to like best** or **better** preferire; **to like it in** trovarsi a proprio agio in; **to like to** + *inf* piacere (with *dat*) + *inf*, e.g., **she likes to dance le** piace ballare; gradire che + *subj*, e.g., **I should like him to pay a visit to my parents** gradirei che facesse una visita ai miei genitori ‖ *intr* volere, desiderare, e.g., **as you like** come desidera; **if you like** se vuole

likelihood [ˈlaɪklɪˌhʊd] *s* probabilità *f*

like-ly [ˈlaɪkli] *adj* (**-lier; -liest**) probabile; verosimile; a proposito; promettente; **to be likely to** + *inf* essere probabile + *fut*, e.g., **Mary is likely to get married in the spring** è probabile che Maria si sposerà in primavera ‖ *adv* probabilmente

like-minded [ˈlaɪkˈmaɪndɪd] *adj* dello stesso parere, della stessa opinione

liken [ˈlaɪkən] *tr* paragonare

likeness [ˈlaɪknɪs] *s* (*picture*) ritratto; (*similarity*) rassomiglianza; apparenza

like'wise' *adv* ugualmente; inoltre; **to do likewise** fare lo stesso

liking [ˈlaɪkɪŋ] *s* simpatia; **to be to the liking of** essere di gusto di; **to have a liking for** (*things*) prendere gusto per; (*people*) affezionarsi a

lilac [ˈlaɪlək] *adj* & *s* lilla *m*

Lilliputian [ˌlɪlɪˈpjuʃən] *adj* & *s* lillipuziano

lilt [lɪlt] *s* canzone *f* a cadenza; movimento a cadenza; (*in verse*) cadenza

lil·y [ˈlɪli] *s* (**-ies**) giglio; **to gild the lily** cercare di migliorare quanto è già perfetto

lil'y of the val'ley *s* mughetto

li'ma bean' [ˈlaɪmə] *s* fagiolo bianco

limb [lɪm] *s* (*of body*) membro, arto; (*of tree*) ramo; (*of cross*) braccio; **to be out on a limb** (coll) essere nei guai

limber [ˈlɪmbər] *adj* agile ‖ *intr*—**to limber up** sciogliersi i muscoli, sgranchirsi le gambe

lim·bo [ˈlɪmbo] *s* (**-bos**) esilio; dimenticatoio; (theol) limbo

lime [laɪm] *s* (*calcium oxide*) calce *f*; (*Citrus aurantifolia*) limetta agra; (*linden tree*) tiglio ‖ *tr* gessare

lime'kiln' *s* fornace *f* da calce

lime'light' *s*—**to be in the limelight** essere in vista

limerick [ˈlɪmərɪk] *s* canzoncina umoristica di cinque versi

lime'stone' *s* calcare *m*

limit [ˈlɪmɪt] *s* limite *m*; (coll) colmo; **to go to the limit** andare agli estremi ‖ *tr* limitare

limitation [ˌlɪmɪˈteʃən] *s* limitazione

lim'ited-ac'cess high'way [ˈlɪmɪtɪd] *s* autostrada, strada con corsia d'accesso

lim'ited com'pany *s* società *f* a responsabilità limitata

lim'ited mon'archy *s* monarchia costituzionale

limitless [ˈlɪmɪtlɪs] *adj* illimitato

limousine [ˈlɪməˌzin] or [ˌlɪməˈzin] *s* berlina

limp [lɪmp] *adj* floscio; debole ‖ *s* zoppicatura ‖ *intr* zoppicare

limpid [ˈlɪmpɪd] *adj* limpido

linage [ˈlaɪnɪdʒ] *s* (typ) numero di linee

linchpin [ˈlɪntʃˌpɪn] *s* acciarino

linden [ˈlɪndən] *s* tiglio

line [laɪn] *s* linea; (*e.g., of people*) fila; (*of trees*) filare *m*; (*for fishing*) lenza; (*written or printed*) rigo, riga; (*wrinkle*) ruga; (*of goods*) ramo; (naut) gherlino; **all along the line** su tutta la linea; **in line** allineato; sotto controllo; **in line with** secondo; **out of line** fuori d'allineamento; (slang) in disaccordo; **to bring into line** far filare; **to draw the line at** fermarsi a; stabilire il limite a; **to fall in line** conformarsi; allinearsi; **to have a line on** (coll) aver informazioni su; **to read between the lines** leggere fra le righe; **to stand in line** fare la coda; **to toe the line** filare diritto; **to wait in line** fare la fila ‖ *tr* rigare; (*e.g., the street*) schierare lungo; (*a suit*) foderare; (*a brake*) rivestire; **to line up** allineare; trovare, scovare ‖ *intr*

—**to line up** mettersi in fila; fare la coda

lineage ['lını·ıdʒ] s lignaggio

lineaments ['lını·əmənts] spl lineamenti mpl

linear ['lını·ər] adj lineare

line'man s (-men) (elec) guardafili m; (sports) guardalinee m; (surv) assistente geometra m

linen ['lınən] adj di tela di lino || s (fabric) tela di lino, lino; (yarn) filo di lino; biancheria

lin'en clos'et s guardaroba m per la biancheria

line' of fire' s (mil) linea di tiro

line' of least' resist'ance s principio del minimo sforzo; **to follow the line of least resistance** prendere la via più facile

line' of sight' s visuale f; (mil) linea di mira

liner ['laınər] s transatlantico

line'-up' s disposizione; (of prisoners) allineamento; (sports) formazione

linger ['lıŋgər] intr indugiare, soffermarsi; (to be tardy) tardare; rimanere in vita; **to linger over** contemplare

lingerie [ˌlænʒəˈri] s biancheria intima

lingering ['lıŋgərıŋ] adj prolungato

lingual ['lıŋgwəl] adj linguale || s suono linguale

linguist ['lıŋgwıst] s poliglotto; (specialist in linguistics) glottologo

linguistic [lıŋˈgwıstık] adj linguistico || **linguistics** s linguistica, glottologia

lining ['laınıŋ] s (of a coat) fodera; (of auto brake) guarnizione; (of a furnace) rivestimento interno; (of wall) rivestimento

link [lıŋk] s anello, maglia; unione; (of sausage) nocco; **links** corso di golf || tr connettere || intr connettersi

linnet ['lınıt] s fanello

linotype ['laınəˌtaıp] s linotype f || tr comporre in linotipia

lin'otype op'erator s linotipista mf

linseed ['lınˌsid] s linosa

lin'seed oil' s olio di lino

lint [lınt] s peluria, sfilacciatura; (for dressing wounds) filaccia

lintel ['lıntəl] s architrave m

lion ['laı·ən] s leone m; celebrità f; **to beard the lion in his den** affrontare l'avversario a casa sua; **to put one's head in the lion's mouth** cacciarsi nei pericoli

lioness ['laı·ənıs] s leonessa

lion-hearted ['laı·ənˌhɑrtıd] adj cuor di leone, coraggioso

lionize ['laı·əˌnaız] tr festeggiare come una celebrità

li'ons' den' s fossa dei leoni

li'on's share' s parte f del leone

lip [lıp] s labbro; (of a jar) beccuccio; (slang) linguaggio insolente; **to smack one's lips** leccarsi le labbra

lip'read' v (pret & pp -read [ˌred]) tr leggere le labbra di || intr leggere le labbra

lip' read'ing s labiolettura

lip' serv'ice s omaggio non sentito

lip'stick' s rossetto per le labbra, matita per le labbra

lique·fy ['lıkwıˌfaı] v (pret & pp -fied) tr & intr liquefare

liqueur [lıˈkʌr] s liquore m

liquid ['lıkwıd] adj liquido || s liquido; (phonet) liquida

liquidate ['lıkwıˌdet] tr & intr liquidare

liquidity [lıˈkwıdıti] s liquidità f

liq'uid meas'ure s misura di capacità per liquidi

liquor ['lıkər] s distillato alcolico, bevanda alcolica; (broth) brodo

Lisbon ['lızbən] s Lisbona

lisp [lısp] s pronuncia blesa || intr parlare bleso

lissome ['lısəm] adj flessibile, agile

list [lıst] s lista, elenco; (border) orlo; (selvage) cimossa, vivagno; (naut) sbandamento; **lists** lizza; **to enter the lists** entrare in lizza || tr elencare, listare || intr (naut) sbandare, andare alla banda

listen ['lısən] intr ascoltare; obbedire; **to listen in** ascoltare una conversazione; (rad) captare una comunicazione; **to listen to** ascoltare; obbedire a, prestare attenzione a; **to listen to reason** intendere ragione

listener ['lısənər] s ascoltatore m; radioascoltatore m

lis'tening post' s (mil) posto di ascolto

listless ['lıstlıs] adj svogliato

list' price' s prezzo di catalogo

lita·ny ['lıtəni] s (-nies) litania

liter ['litər] s litro

literacy ['lıtərəsi] s abilità f di leggere e scrivere; istruzione

literal ['lıtərəl] adj letterale

literary ['lıtəˌreri] adj letterario; (individual) letterato

literate ['lıtərıt] adj che sa leggere e scrivere; (educated) istruito; (wellread) letterato || s persona che sa leggere e scrivere; letterato

literature ['lıtərət/ər] s letteratura; (printed matter) opuscoli pubblicitari

lithe [laıθ] adj flessibile, agile

lithium ['lıθı·əm] s litio

lithograph ['lıθəˌgræf] or ['lıθəˌgrɑf] s litografia || tr litografare

lithographer [lıˈθɑgrəfər] s litografo

lithography [lıˈθɑgrəfi] s litografia

Lithuania [ˌlıθuˈenı·ə] s la Lituania

Lithuanian [ˌlıθuˈenı·ən] adj & s lituano

litigant ['lıtıgənt] adj & s litigante mf

litigate ['lıtıˌget] tr & intr litigare

litigation [ˌlıtıˈgeʃən] s litigio; (lawsuit) lite f, causa

litmus ['lıtməs] s tornasole m

lit'mus pa'per s cartina al tornasole

litter ['lıtər] s disordine m; (scattered rubbish) pattume m; (young brought forth at one birth) figliata; (of puppies) cucciolata; (bedding for animals) strame m; (stretcher; bed carried by men or animals) lettiga, portantina || tr mettere in disordine; spargere rifiuti per; coprire di strame || intr partorire

lit'ter·bug' s sparpagliatore m di rifiuti

littering ['lɪtərɪŋ] s—no littering vietato gettare rifiuti

little ['lɪtəl] adj (in size) piccolo; (in amount) poco, e.g., little salt poco sale; a little un po' di, e.g., a little salt un po' di sale; the little ones i piccini ‖ s poco; a little un po'; to make little of farsi gioco di; non pigliar sul serio; to think little of non tener di conto ‖ adv poco; little by little poco a poco, mano a mano

Lit'tle Bear' s Orsa minore

Lit'tle Dip'per s Piccolo Carro

lit'tle fin'ger s mignolo; to twist around one's little finger maneggiare come un fantoccio

lit'tle·neck' s piccola vongola (Venus mercenaria)

lit'tle owl' s civetta

lit'tle peo'ple spl fate fpl; folletti mpl

Lit'tle Red Rid'inghood' ['raɪdɪŋ ˌhud] s Cappuccetto Rosso

lit'tle slam' s (bridge) piccolo slam

liturgic(al) [lɪ'tʌrdʒɪk(əl)] adj liturgico

litur·gy ['lɪtərdʒi] s (-gies) liturgia

livable ['lɪvəbəl] adj abitabile; socievole; tollerabile

live [laɪv] adj vivo; (flame) ardente; di attualità; (elec) sotto tensione; (telv) in diretta ‖ [lɪv] tr vivere; to live down (one's past) far dimenticare; to live it up (coll) darsi alla bella vita, scialare; to live out (e.g., a war) sopravvivere (with dat) ‖ intr vivere; to live from hand to mouth vivere alla giornata; to live high darsi alla bella vita; to live on continuare a vivere; (e.g., vegetables) vivere di; vivere alle spalle di; to live up to (one's promises) compiere; (one's earnings) spendere

live' coal' [laɪv] s brace f

livelihood ['laɪvlɪ ˌhud] s vita; to earn one's livelihood guadagnarsi la vita

livelong ['lɪv ˌlɔŋ] or ['lɪv ˌlɑŋ] adj—all the livelong day tutto il santo giorno

live·ly ['laɪvli] adj (-lier; -liest) vivo, vivace; (color) vivido; (resilient) elastico; (tune) brioso

liven ['laɪvən] tr animare ‖ intr animarsi, rianimarsi

liver ['lɪvər] s abitante mf; (anat) fegato

liver·y ['lɪvəri] s (-ies) livrea

liv'ery·man s (-men) stalliere m

liv'ery sta'ble s stallaggio

livestock ['laɪv ˌstɑk] adj zootecnico ‖ s bestiame m

live' wire' [laɪv] s (elec) filo carico di corrente; (slang) persona energica

livid ['lɪvɪd] adj livido; (with anger) incollerito

living ['lɪvɪŋ] adj vivo; (conditions) abitativo ‖ s vivere m; to earn a living guadagnarsi la vita

liv'ing quar'ters spl abitazione, alloggio

liv'ing room' s stanza di soggiorno

liv'ing wage' s salario sufficiente per vivere

lizard ['lɪzərd] s lucertola

load [lod] s peso, carico; loads of (coll) un mucchio di; to get a load of (slang) stare a vedere; (slang) stare a sentire; to have a load on (slang) essere ubriaco ‖ tr caricare ‖ intr caricarsi

loaded ['lodɪd] adj caricato; (slang) ubriaco fradicio; (slang) ricchissimo

load'ed dice' spl dadi truccati

load'stone' s magnetite f; (fig) calamita

loaf [lof] s (loaves [lovz]) pane m; (molded mass) forma; (of sugar) pane m; (long and thin loaf) filone m ‖ intr batter fiacca, oziare

loafer ['lofər] s fannullone m

loam [lom] s ricca argilla sabbiosa; terra da fonderia

loan [lon] s prestito; to hit for a loan (coll) dare una stoccata a ‖ tr prestare

loan' shark' s (coll) strozzino

loan' word' s (ling) prestito

loath [loθ] adj poco disposto; nothing loath molto volentieri

loathe [loð] tr detestare, aborrire

loathsome ['loðsəm] adj abominevole, disgustoso

lob [lɑb] s (tennis) pallonetto ‖ v (pret & pp lobbed) ger lobbing) tr (tennis) dare un pallonetto a

lob·by ['lɑbi] s (-bies) anticamera, vestibolo; sollecitazione di voti ‖ v (pret & pp -bied) intr sollecitare voti, influenzare il voto dietro le quinte

lobbyist ['lɑbɪ·ɪst] s politicante m che cerca di influenzare il voto dietro le quinte

lobe [lob] s lobo

lobster ['lɑbstər] s (Palinurus vulgaris) aragosta; (Hommarus vulgaris) astice m

lob'ster pot' s nassa per aragoste

local ['lokəl] adj locale ‖ s treno accelerato; notizia di interesse locale; (of a union) sezione

locale [lo'kæl] s località f

locali·ty [lo'kælɪti] s (-ties) località f

localize ['lokə ˌlaɪz] tr localizzare

lo'cal op'tion s referendum m locale sulla vendita di alcolici

locate [lo'ket] or ['loket] tr (to discover the location of) localizzare; (to place, settle) situare, stabilire; (to ascribe a location to) individuare ‖ intr stabilirsi

location [lo'keʃən] s localizzazione; posizione; sito; on location (mov) in esterno

lock [lɑk] s serratura; (of a canal) chiusa; (of hair) ciocca; (of a firearm) percussore m; (mach) freno; lock, stock, and barrel (coll) completamente; under lock and key sotto chiave ‖ tr chiudere a chiave; serrare; (a boat) far passare per una chiusa; unire; abbracciare; to lock in chiudere sotto chiave; to lock out chiudere fuori; (workers) sbarrare dal lavoro; to lock up chiudere a chiave; incarcerare

locker ['lɑkər] s armadietto a chiave; (in the form of a chest) bauletto

lock'er room' s spogliatoio
locket ['lakɪt] s medaglione m
lock'jaw' s tetano, trisma m
lock' nut' s controdado
lock'out' s serrata
lock'smith' s magnano, fabbro
lock' step' s—**to march in lock step** marciare a passo serrato
lock' stitch' s punto a filo doppio
lock' ten'der s guardiano di chiusa
lock'up' s prigione; (typ) messa in forma
lock' wash'er s rondella di sicurezza
locomotive [,lokə'motɪv] s locomotiva
lo·cus ['lokəs] s (-ci [saɪ]) luogo
locust ['lokəst] s (ent) locusta; (cicada) (ent) cicala; (bot) robinia
lode [lod] s filone m, vena
lode'star' s stella polare; guida
lodge [ladʒ] s casetta; padiglione m da caccia; albergo; (e.g., of Masons) loggia || tr alloggiare, ospitare; depositare; contenere; (a complaint) sporgere || intr alloggiare; essere contenuto, trovarsi; andar a finire
lodger ['ladʒər] s inquilino
lodging ['ladʒɪŋ] s alloggio
loft [lɔft] or [laft] s (attic) solaio; (hayloft) fienile m; (in theater or church) galleria
loft·y ['lɔfti] or ['lafti] adj (-ier; -iest) alto, elevato; (haughty) orgoglioso
log [lɔg] or [lag] s ceppo, ciocco; (naut) solcometro; (aer, naut) giornale m di bordo; **to sleep like a log** dormire della grossa || v (pret & pp logged; ger logging) tr registrare; (a speed) fare; (a distance) percorrere
logarithm ['lɔgə,rɪðəm] or ['lagə,rɪðəm] s logaritmo
log'book' s (aer, naut) libro di bordo
log' cab'in s capanna di tronchi
log' chip' s (naut) barchetta
log' driv'er s zatteriere m
log' driv'ing ['draɪvɪŋ] s fluitazione
logger ['lɔgər] or ['lagər] s taglialegna m; trattore m per trasporto tronchi
log'ger·head' s testone m; **at loggerheads** in lite
loggia ['lodʒə] s loggia
logic ['ladʒɪk] s logica
logical ['ladʒɪkəl] adj logico
logician [lo'dʒɪʃən] s logico
logistic(al) [lo'dʒɪstɪk(əl)] adj logistico
logistics [lo'dʒɪstɪks] s logistica
log'jam' s ingorgo fluviale dovuto a ammasso di tronchi; (fig) ristagno
log' line' s (naut) sagola
log'roll' intr barattare favori politici
log'wood' s campeggio
loin [lɔɪn] s lombo; **to gird up one's loins** prepararsi per l'azione
loin'cloth' s perizoma m, copripudende m
loiter ['lɔɪtər] tr—**to loiter away** (time) sprecare in ozio || intr bighellonare, trastullarsi
loiterer ['lɔɪtərər] s perdigiorno
loll [lal] intr sdraiarsi pigramente, adagiarsi pigramente; pendere
lollipop ['lalɪ,pap] s caramella sullo stecchetto, lecca-lecca m

Lombard ['lambərd] or ['lambərd] adj & s lombardo; (hist) longobardo
Lom'bardy pop'lar s pioppo italico
London ['lʌndən] adj londinese || s Londra
Londoner ['lʌndənər] s londinese mf
lone [lon] adj solo; solitario
loneliness ['lonlinɪs] s solitudine f
lone·ly ['lonli] adj (-lier; -liest) solingo, solo, solitario
lonesome ['lonsəm] adj solitario
lone' wolf' s (coll) orso, solitario
long [lɔŋ] or [laŋ] adj (longer ['lɔŋgər] or ['laŋgər]; longest ['lɔŋgɪst] or ['laŋgɪst]) adj lungo; **three meters long** lungo tre metri || adv molto, molto tempo; **as long as** mentre; (provided) fin tanto che; (inasmuch as) dato che; **before long** fra poco; **how long?** quanto?; **long ago** molto tempo fa; **long before** molto prima; **long since** molto tempo fa; **no longer** non più; **so long!** (coll) ciao!, arrivederci!; **so long as** fino a che, finché || intr anelare; **to long for** sviscerarsi per, sospirare per
long'boat' s (naut) lancia
long'-dis'tance adj (telp) interurbano, intercomunale; (sports) di fondo; (aer) a distanza
long'-drawn'-out' adj prolungato
longeron ['landʒərən] s longherone m
longevity [lan'dʒevɪti] s longevità f
long' face' s (coll) faccia triste, muso lungo
long'hair' adj & s (coll) intellettuale mf; (coll) musicomane mf
long'hand' s (scritto) a mano || s scrittura a mano; **in longhand** scritto a mano
longing ['lɔŋɪŋ] or ['laŋɪŋ] adj bramoso, anelante || s brama, anelito
longitude ['landʒɪ,tjud] or ['landʒɪ,tud] s longitudine f
long·lived ['lɔŋ'laɪvd], ['lɔŋ'lɪvd], ['laŋ'laɪvd] or ['laŋ'lɪvd] adj (person) longevo, di lunga vita; (e.g., rumor) di lunga durata
long'-play'ing rec'ord s disco di grande durata
long'-range' adj a lunga portata
long'shore'man s (-men) portuale m, scaricatore m
long'stand'ing adj vecchio, che esiste da lungo tempo
long'-suf'fering adj paziente, longanime
long' suit' s (cards) serie lunga; (fig) forte m
long'-term' adj a lunga scadenza
long'-wind'ed adj verboso; (speech) chilometrico
look [lʊk] s (appearance) aspetto; (glance) sguardo; (search) ricerca; **looks** aspetto, apparenza; **to take a look at** dare un'occhiata a || tr guardare; (one's age) mostrare; **to look daggers at** fulminare con lo sguardo; **to look up** (e.g., in a dictionary) cercare; andare a visitare; venire a visitare || intr guardare; cercare; parere; **look out!** attenzione!; **to look after** badare a; occuparsi di; **to look at** guardare; **to look back** riguardare;

(fig) guardare al passato; **to look down on s.o.** guardare qlcu dall'alto in basso; **to look for** cercare; aspettarsi; **to look forward to** anticipare il piacere di; **to look ill** avere una brutta cera; **to look in on** passare per la casa di; **to look into** esaminare a fondo; **to look like** sembrare, parere; **to look out** fare attenzione; **to look out for** aver cura di; **to look out of** guardare da; **to look out on** dare su; **to look through** guardare per; (*a book*) sfogliare; **to look toward** dare su; **to look up to** ammirare, guardare con ammirazione; **to look well** avere una buona cera; fare figura

looker-on [ˌlʊkərˈɑn] or [ˌlʊkərˈɔn] *s* (**lookers-on**) astante *m*

look'ing glass' [ˈlʊkɪŋ] *s* specchio

look'out' *s* guardia; (*person; watch kept; place from which a watch is kept*) vedetta; (*concern*) (coll) affare *m*; **to be on the lookout** stare in guardia; **to be on the lookout for** essere in cerca di

loom [lum] *s* telaio ‖ *intr* apparire indistintamente; pararsi dinanzi; apparire

loon [lun] *s* scemo; fannullone *m*; (orn) (*Gavia*) strolaga

loon·y [ˈluni] *adj* (**-ier; -iest**) (slang) pazzo ‖ *s* (**-ies**) (slang) pazzo

loop [lup] *s* cappio; (*e.g., of a road*) tortuosità *f*; (*for fastening a button*) occhiello; (*aer*) cerchio or giro della morte; (phys) ventre *m*; ‖ *tr* fare cappi in; annodare; **to loop the loop** (aer) fare il giro della morte ‖ *intr* avanzare tortuosamente, girare

loop'hole' *s* (*narrow opening*) feritoia; (*means of evasion*) scappatoia

loose [lus] *adj* libero, sciolto; (*available*) disponibile; (*not firm*) rilasciato; (*tooth*) che balla; (*unchaste*) facile; (*garment*) ampio; (*soil*) smosso; (*translation*) libero; (*rein*) lento; **to become loose** sciogliersi; **to break loose** mettersi in libertà; **to have loose bowels** avere la diarrea; **to turn loose** liberare ‖ *s*—**to be on the loose** (coll) essere in libertà; (coll) correre la cavallina ‖ *tr* sciogliere; slegare; lanciare

loose' change' *s* spiccioli *mpl*

loose' end' *s* capo sciolto; **at loose ends** indeciso; disoccupato, senza nulla da fare

loose'-leaf' *adj* a fogli mobili

loosen [ˈlusən] *tr* snodare; rilasciare; smuovere; allentare; (*the bowels*) liberare dalla stitichezza ‖ *intr* snodarsi; rilasciarsi; smuoversi; allentarsi

looseness [ˈlusnɪs] *s* scioltezza; (*in morals*) sregolatezza

loose-tongued [ˈlusˈtʌŋd] *adj* sciolto di lingua; linguacciuto, maldicente

loot [lut] *s* bottino ‖ *tr* saccheggiare

lop [lɑp] *v* (*pret & pp* **lopped**; *ger* **lopping**) *tr* lasciar cadere, lasciar penzolare; **to lop off** mozzare; (*a tree*) potare; (*a vine*) stralciare ‖ *intr* penzolare

lopsided [ˈlɑpˈsaɪdɪd] *adj* che pende da una parte; asimmetrico, sproporzionato

loquacious [loˈkweʃəs] *adj* loquace

lord [lɔrd] *s* signore *m*; (Brit) lord *m* ‖ *tr*—**to lord it over** signoreggiare su

lord·ly [ˈlɔrdli] *adj* (**-lier; -liest**) signorile, magnifico; altero, disdegnoso, arrogante

Lord's' Day', **the** la domenica, il giorno del Signore

lordship [ˈlɔrdʃɪp] *s* signoria

Lord's' Prayer' *s* paternostro

Lord's' Sup'per *s* Eucarestia; Ultima Cena

lore [lor] *s* tradizioni *fpl* popolari; cognizioni *fpl*

lorgnette [lɔrnˈjɛt] *s* occhialetto, lorgnette *f*; binocolo da teatro col manico

lor·ry [ˈlɑri] or [ˈlɔri] *s* (**-ries**) (rr) vagoncino; (Brit) camion *m*

lose [luz] *v* (*pret & pp* **lost** [lɑst] or [lɔst]) *tr* perdere; (*said of a physician*) non riuscire a salvare; **to lose heart** perdersi d'animo; **to lose oneself** perdersi, smarrirsi ‖ *intr* perdere; (*said of a watch*) ritardare; **to lose out** rimetterci

loser [ˈluzər] *s* perdente *mf*

losing [ˈluzɪŋ] *adj* perdente ‖ **losings** *spl* perdite *fpl*

loss [lɔs] or [lɑs] *s* perdita; **to be at a loss** essere perplesso; **to be at a loss to** + *inf* non saper come + *inf*; **to sell at a loss** vendere in perdita

loss' of face' *s* perdita di faccia

lost [lɔst] or [lɑst] *adj* perduto; **lost in thought** assorto in sé stesso; **lost to** perso per; insensibile a

lost'-and-found' depart'ment *s* ufficio degli oggetti smarriti

lost' sheep' *s* percorella smarrita

lot [lɑt] *s* (*for building*) lotto; (*fate*) sorte *f*; (*parcel, portion*) partita; (*of people*) gruppo; (coll) grande quantità *f*; (coll) tipo, soggetto; **a lot (of)** or **lots of** (coll) molto, molti; **to cast** or **to throw in one's lot with** condividere la sorte di; **to draw** or **to cast lots** tirare a sorte

lotion [ˈloʃən] *s* lozione

lotter·y [ˈlɑtəri] *s* (**-ies**) lotteria, riffa

lotto [ˈlɑto] *s* tombola, lotto

lotus [ˈlotəs] *s* loto

loud [laʊd] *adj* forte; (*noisy*) rumoroso; (*voice*) alto; (*garish*) sgargiante, chiassoso, appariscente; (*foul-smelling*) puzzolente ‖ *adv* a voce alta; rumorosamente

loud-mouthed [ˈlaʊdˌmaʊθt] or [ˈlaʊdˌmaʊðd] *adj* chiassone

loud'speak'er *s* altoparlante *m*

lounge [laʊndʒ] *s* divano, sofà *m*; sala soggiorno; ridotto ‖ *intr* oziare, star senza far niente; bighellonare; **to lounge around** bighellonare

lounge' liz'ard *s* (slang) damerino, bellimbusto, gagà *m*

louse [laʊs] *s* (**lice** [laɪs]) pidocchio ‖ *tr*—**to louse up** (slang) rovinare

lous·y [ˈlaʊzi] *adj* (**-ier; -iest**) pidocchioso; (*mean; bungling*) (coll) schifoso; (*filthy*) (coll) sporco; **lousy with** (*e.g., money*) (slang) pieno di

lout [laut] *s* gaglioffo, tanghero

louver ['luvər] *s* sportello girevole di persiana; (aut) feritoia per ventilazione

lovable ['lʌvəbəl] *adj* amabile

love [lʌv] *s* amore *m;* (tennis) zero; **not for love nor money** a nessun prezzo; **to be in love (with)** essere innamorato (di); **to make love to** fare l'amore con ‖ *tr* amare; voler bene a; piacere (with *dat*), e.g., **she loves short skirts** le piacciono le sottane corte

love' affair' *s* passione, amori *mpl*

love'bird' *s* (orn) inseparabile *m;* **love-birds** (slang) amanti appassionati

love' child' *s* figlio naturale

love' feast' *s* agape *f*

loveless ['lʌvlɪs] *adj* senza amore

lovelorn ['lʌv,lɔrn] *adj* abbandonato dalla persona amata

love·ly ['lʌvli] *adj* (-lier; -liest) bello; (coll) delizioso

love' match' *s* matrimonio d'amore

love' po'tion *s* filtro d'amore

lover ['lʌvər] *s* amante *m;* (*e.g., of music*) amico, appassionato

love' seat' *s* amorino

love'sick' *adj* malato d'amore

love'sick'ness *s* mal *m* d'amore

love' song' *s* canzone *f* d'amore

loving ['lʌvɪŋ] *adj* affezionato, amoroso; **your loving son** il vostro affezionato figlio

lov'ing-kind'ness *s* tenera sollecitudine

low [lo] *adj* basso; (*deep*) profondo; (*diet*) magro; (*visibility*) cattivo; (*dress*) scollato; (*dejected*) abbattuto; (*fire*) lento; (*flame; speed*) piccolo; **to lay low** ammazzare; abbattere; **to lie low** rimanere nascosto; attendere ‖ *s* punto basso; prezzo minimo; (*of cow*) muggito; (aut) prima velocità; (meteor) depressione ‖ *adv* basso, a basso, in basso ‖ *intr* (*said of a cow*) muggire

low'born' *adj* di umili origini

low'boy' *s* cassettone basso con le gambe corte

low'brow' *adj & s* (coll) ignorante *mf*

low'-cost hous'ing *s* case *fpl* popolari

Low' Coun'tries, the i Paesi Bassi

low'-down' *adj* (coll) basso, vile ‖ **low'-down'** *s* (coll) semplice verità *f,* notizie *fpl* confidenziali

lower ['lo-ər] *adj* inferiore, disotto ‖ *tr* abbassare; (*prices*) ribassare ‖ *intr* diminuire; discendere ‖ ['lau-ər] *intr* aggrottare le ciglia; (*said of the weather*) imbronciarsi

low'er berth' ['lo-ər] *s* cuccetta inferiore

low'er case' ['lo-ər] *s* (typ) cassa inferiore

lower-case ['lo-ər,kes] *adj* (typ) minuscolo

low'er mid'dle class' ['lo-ər] *s* piccola borghesia

lowermost ['lo-ər,most] *adj* (il) più basso, (l') infimo

low'-fre'quency *adj* a bassa frequenza

low' gear' *s* prima velocità, prima

lowland ['loland] *s* pianura ‖ **Lowlands** *spl* Scozia meridionale, bassa Scozia

low·ly ['loli] *adj* (-lier; -liest) umile

Low' Mass' *s* messa bassa

low-minded ['lo'maɪndɪd] *adj* vile, basso

low-necked ['lo'nɛkt] *adj* scollato

low-pitched ['lo'pɪt/t] *adj* (*sound*) basso, grave; (*roof*) poco inclinato

low'-pres'sure *adj* a bassa pressione

low-priced ['lo'praɪst] *adj* a buon mercato, a basso prezzo

low' shoe' *s* scarpa bassa

low'-speed' *adj* di piccola velocità

low-spirited ['lo'spɪrɪtɪd] *adj* depresso

low' tide' *s* bassa marea; (fig) punto più basso

low' visibil'ity *s* scarsa visibilità

low' wa'ter *s* (low tide) bassa marea; (*of a river*) magra

loyal ['lɔɪ-əl] *adj* leale

loyalist ['lɔɪ-əlɪst] *s* lealista *mf*

loyal·ty ['lɔɪ-əlti] *s* (-ties) lealtà *f*

lozenge ['lazɪndʒ] *s* losanga; (*candy cough drop*) pasticca, pastiglia

LP ['ɛl'pi] *s* (letterword) (trademark) disco di grande durata

lubricant ['lubrɪkənt] *adj & s* lubrificante *m*

lubricate ['lubrɪ,ket] *tr* lubrificare; (*e.g., one's hands*) ungersi

lubrication [,lubrɪ'keʃən] *s* lubrificazione

lubricous ['lubrɪkəs] *adj* lubrico; incerto, incostante

lucerne [lu'sʌrn] *s* erba medica

lucid ['lusɪd] *adj* lucido

Lucifer ['lusɪfər] *s* Lucifero

luck [lʌk] *s* (good or bad) sorte *f;* (good) sorte *f,* fortuna; **down on one's luck** in cattive condizioni; **in luck** fortunato; **out of luck** sfortunato; **to bring luck** portare (buona) fortuna; **to try one's luck** tentare la sorte; **worse luck** disgraziatamente

luckily ['lʌkɪli] *adv* fortunatamente

luckless ['lʌklɪs] *adj* sfortunato

luck·y ['lʌki] *adj* (-ier; -iest) fortunato; (*supposed to bring luck*) portafortuna; (*foretelling good luck*) di buon augurio; **to be lucky** aver fortuna

luck'y hit' *s* (coll) colpo di fortuna

lucrative ['lukrətɪv] *adj* lucrativo

ludicrous ['ludɪkrəs] *adj* ridicolo

lug [lʌg] *s* manico; (pull) tiro; **to put the lug on s.o.** (slang) batter cassa a qlcu ‖ *v* (pret & pp **lugged**; ger **lugging**) *tr* tirarsi dietro; (coll) introdurre a sproposito

luggage ['lʌgɪdʒ] *s* (used in traveling) bagaglio; (*found in a store*) valigeria

lug'gage store' *s* valigeria

lugubrious [lu'gubrɪ-əs] or [lu'gjubrɪ-əs] *adj* lugubre

lukewarm ['luk,wɔrm] *adj* tiepido

lull [lʌl] *s* momento di calma, calma ‖ *tr* calmare, pacificare; addormentare

lulla·by ['lʌlə,baɪ] *s* (-bies) ninnananna

lumbago [lʌm'bego] *s* lombaggine *f*

lumber ['lʌmbər] *s* legname *m*, legno da costruzione; cianfrusaglie *fpl* ‖ *intr* muoversi pesantemente
lum'ber·jack' *s* boscaiolo
lum'ber jack'et *s* giaccone *m*
lum'ber·man *s* (**-men**) (*dealer*) commerciante *m* in legname; (*man who cuts down lumber*) boscaiolo
lum'ber room' *s* ripostiglio
lum'ber·yard' *s* deposito legnami
luminar·y ['lumɪ ˌnɛri] *s* (**-ies**) luminare *m*
luminous ['lumɪnəs] *adj* luminoso
lummox ['lʌməks] *s* (coll) scimunito
lump [lʌmp] *s* grumo; mucchio; cumulo; (*swelling*) bernoccolo; (*of sugar*) zolletta; (*in one's throat*) groppo; (coll) stupidone *m*; **in the lump** in blocco; nell'insieme ‖ *tr* mescolare; (*to make into lumps*) raggrumare; **to lump it** (coll) mandarla giù
lumpish ['lʌmpɪʃ] *adj* grumoso; goffo; balordo
lump' sum' *s* ammontare unico, somma globale
lump·y ['lʌmpi] *adj* (**-ier; -iest**) grumoso; (*person*) pesante, ottuso; (*sea*) agitato
luna·cy ['lunəsi] *s* (**-cies**) pazzia
lunar ['lunər] *adj* lunare
lu'nar land'ing *s* allunaggio
lu'nar mod'ule *s* modulo lunare
lu'nar rov'er *s* auto *f* lunare
lunatic ['lunətɪk] *adj* & *s* demente *mf*
lu'natic asy'lum *s* manicomio
lu'natic fringe' *s* estremisti *mpl* fanatici
lunch [lʌntʃ] *s* (*regular midday meal*) seconda colazione; (*light meal*) spuntino, merenda ‖ *intr* fare colazione; fare uno spuntino
lunch' bas'ket *s* portavivande *m*
luncheon ['lʌntʃən] *s* seconda colazione; pranzo ufficiale
luncheonette [ˌlʌntʃə'nɛt] *s* tavola calda
lunch'eon meat' *s* insaccati *mpl*
lunch'room' *s* tavola calda
lung [lʌŋ] *s* polmone *m*
lunge [lʌndʒ] *s* slancio; (*fencing*) affondo ‖ *intr* slanciarsi
lurch [lʌrtʃ] *s* barcollamento; (*at close of a game*) cappotto; (naut) sbandata; **to leave in the lurch** piantare

in asso ‖ *intr* barcollare; (naut) sbandare
lure [lʊr] *s* esca; (fig) insidie *fpl* ‖ *tr* adescare; **to lure away** distogliere, sviare
lurid ['lʊrɪd] *adj* (*fiery*) ardente, acceso; sensazionale; (*gruesome*) orripilante
lurk [lʌrk] *intr* stare in agguato, nascondersi; (fig) essere latente
luscious ['lʌ/əs] *adj* delizioso; lussuoso, lussureggiante; voluttuoso
lush [lʌʃ] *adj* lussureggiante, lussuoso
lust [lʌst] *s* desiderio sfrenato; libidine *f*, lussuria ‖ *intr*—**to lust after or for** aver sete di
luster ['lʌstər] *s* (*gloss*) lustro, lucentezza; (*glory*) lustro, onore *m*
lus'ter·ware' *s* ceramiche smaltate
lustful ['lʌstfəl] *adj* lussurioso
lustrous ['lʌstrəs] *adj* lucido
lust·y ['lʌsti] *adj* (**-ier; -iest**) vigoroso, gagliardo
lute [lut] *s* (mus) liuto; (chem) luto
Lutheran ['luθərən] *adj* & *s* luterano
luxuriance [lʌg'ʒʊrɪ·əns] *s* rigoglio
luxuriant [lʌg'ʒʊrɪ·ənt] *adj* lussureggiante; (*imagery*) ridondante
luxuriate [lʌg'ʒʊrɪ ˌet] or [lʌk'ʃʊrɪ ˌet] *intr* lussureggiare; trovare piacere
luxurious [lʌg'ʒʊrɪ·əs] or [lʌk'ʃʊrɪ·əs] *adj* lussuoso, fastoso
luxu·ry ['lʌk/əri] or ['lʌgʒəri] *s* (**-ries**) lusso, sfarzo
lye [laɪ] *s* ranno, lisciviva
lying ['laɪ·ɪŋ] *adj* menzognero ‖ *s* il mentire
ly'ing-in' hos'pital *s* clinica ostetrica, maternità *f*
lymph [lɪmf] *s* linfa
lymphatic [lɪm'fætɪk] *adj* linfatico
lynch [lɪntʃ] *tr* linciare
lynching ['lɪntʃɪŋ] *s* linciaggio
lynx [lɪŋks] *s* lince *f*
lynx-eyed ['lɪŋks ˌaɪd] *adj* dagli occhi di lince
lyonnaise [ˌlaɪ·ə'nez] *adj* (culin) alla maniera di Lione
lyre [laɪr] *s* lira
lyric ['lɪrɪk] *adj* lirico ‖ *s* lirica; (*words of a song*) parole *fpl*
lyrical ['lɪrɪkəl] *adj* lirico
lyricism ['lɪrɪ ˌsɪzəm] *s* lirismo
lyricist ['lɪrɪsɪst] *s* (*writer of words for songs*) paroliere *m*; (*poet*) lirico

M

M, m [ɛm] *s* tredicesima lettera dell'alfabeto inglese
ma'am [mæm] or [mɑm] *s* (coll) signora
macadam [mə'kædəm] *s* macadàm *m*
macadamize [mə'kædə ˌmaɪz] *tr* macadamizzare
macaroni [ˌmækə'roni] *s* maccheroni *mpl*
macaroon [ˌmækə'run] *s* amaretto
macaw [mə'kɔ] *s* ara

mace [mes] *s* mazza; (*spice*) macis *m* & *f*
mace' bear'er *s* mazziere *m*
machination [ˌmækɪ'neʃən] *s* macchinazione, macchina
machine [mə'ʃin] *s* macchina ‖ *tr* fare a macchina
machine' gun' *s* mitragliatrice *f*
machine'-gun' *v* (*pret & pp* **-gunned; ger -gunning**) *tr* mitragliare
machine'-made' *adj* fatto a macchina

machiner·y [məˈʃinəri] s (-ies) macchinario, meccanismo
machine' screw' s vite f per metallo
machine' shop' s officina meccanica
machine' tool' s macchina utensile
machinist [məˈʃinist] s meccanico; (nav) secondo macchinista
mackerel [ˈmækərəl] s maccarello
mack'erel sky' s cielo a pecorelle
mackintosh [ˈmækin ˌtaʃ] s impermeabile m
mad [mæd] adj (madder; maddest) (angry; rabid) arrabbiato; (insane; foolish) pazzo, folle; furioso; **to be mad about** (coll) andar pazzo per; **to drive mad** far impazzire; **to go mad** impazzire; (said of a dog) diventare idrofobo
madam [ˈmædəm] s signora
mad'cap' s mattoide m, rompicollo
madden [ˈmædən] tr (to make angry) inferocire; (to make insane) fare impazzire
made-to-order [ˈmedtəˈɔrdər] adj fatto apposta; (clothing) fatto su misura
made'-up' adj inventato; (using cosmetics) truccato
mad'house' s manicomio
mad'man' s (-men') pazzo
madness [ˈmædnis] s rabbia; pazzia
Madonna lily [məˈdɑnə] s giglio
maelstrom [ˈmelstrəm] s vortice m
magazine [ˈmægə ˌzin] or [ˌmægəˈzin] s (periodical) rivista, giornale m; (warehouse) magazzino; (for cartridges) caricatore m; (for powder) polveriera; (naut) santabarbara; (phot) magazzino
maggot [ˈmægət] s larva di dittero
Magi [ˈmedʒaɪ] spl Re Magi
magic [ˈmædʒik] adj magico ‖ s magia; illusionismo; **as if by magic** come per incanto
magician [məˈdʒiʃən] s (entertainer) illusionista mf; (sorcerer) mago
magistrate [ˈmædʒis ˌtret] s magistrato
magnanimous [mægˈnænɪməs] adj magnanimo
magnesium [mægˈniʃɪ/ɪ-əm] or [mægˈniʒɪ-əm] s magnesio
magnet [ˈmægnit] s calamita, magnete m
magnetic [mægˈnetik] adj magnetico
magnetism [ˈmægnɪ ˌtizəm] s magnetismo
magnetize [ˈmægnɪ ˌtaɪz] tr calamitare, magnetizzare
magne·to [mægˈnito] s (-tos) magnete m
magnificent [mægˈnɪfɪsənt] adj magnifico
magni·fy [ˈmægnɪ ˌfaɪ] v (pret & pp -fied) tr ingrandire; (to exaggerate) magnificare
mag'nifying glass' s lente f d'ingrandimento
magnitude [ˈmægnɪ ˌtjud] or [ˈmægnɪ ˌtud] s grandezza
magpie [ˈmæg ˌpaɪ] s gazza
mahlstick [ˈmɑl ˌstɪk] or [ˈmɔl ˌstɪk] s appoggiamano
mahoga·ny [məˈhɑgəni] s (-nies) mogano

Mahomet [məˈhɑmɪt] s Maometto
maid [med] s (girl) ragazza; (servant) cameriera, domestica
maiden [ˈmedən] s pulzella
maid'en·hair' s (bot) capelvenere m
maid'en·head' s imene m
maidenhood [ˈmedən ˌhʊd] s verginità f
maid'en la'dy s zitella
maid'en name' s nome m da signorina
maid'en voy'age s viaggio inaugurale
maid'-in-waiting s (maids-in-waiting) (of a princess) damigella d'onore; (of a queen) dama d'onore
maid' of hon'or s (attendant at a wedding; attendant of a princess) damigella d'onore; (attendant of a queen) dama d'onore
maid'serv'ant s domestica, ancella
mail [mel] s posta; (of armor) maglia; **by return mail** a volta di corriere ‖ tr impostare
mail'bag' s sacco postale
mail'boat' s battello postale
mail'box' s cassetta or buca delle lettere
mail' car' s vagone m postale
mail' car'rier s postino, portalettere m
mail'ing list' s indirizzario
mail'ing per'mit s abbonamento postale
mail'man' s (-men') portalettere m
mail' or'der s ordinazione per corrispondenza
mail'-order house' s ditta che fa affari unicamente per corrispondenza
mail'plane' s areoplano postale
mail' train' s treno postale
maim [mem] tr mutilare
main [men] adj principale, maggiore ‖ s condotta principale; **in the main** principalmente, per lo più
main' clause' s proposizione principale
main' course' s piatto forte
main' deck' s ponte m principale
mainland [ˈmen ˌlænd] or [ˈmenlənd] s terra ferma, continente m
main' line' s (rr) linea principale
mainly [ˈmenli] adv principalmente
mainmast [ˈmenmæst], [ˈmen ˌmæst] or [ˈmen ˌmast] s albero maestro
mainsail [ˈmensəl] or [ˈmen ˌsel] s vela maestra
main'spring' s molla motrice; (fig) molla
main'stay' s (naut) strallo di maestra; (fig) cardine m
main' street' s strada principale
maintain [menˈten] tr mantenere
maintenance [ˈmentɪnəns] s mantenimento; (upkeep) manutenzione
maître d'hôtel [ˌmetər doˈtɛl] s (butler) maggiordomo; (headwaiter) capocameriere m
maize [mez] s mais m
majestic [məˈdʒestik] adj maestoso
majes·ty [ˈmædʒisti] s (-ties) maestà f
major [ˈmedʒər] adj maggiore ‖ s (educ) specializzazione; (mil) maggiore m ‖ intr (educ) specializzarsi
major·do·mo [ˌmedʒərˈdomo] s (-mos) maggiordomo
ma'jor gen'eral s generale m di divisione

majori·ty [məˈdʒɑrɪti] or [məˈdʒɔrɪti] *adj* maggioritario ǁ *s* (**-ties**) (*being of full age*) maggiore età *f*; (*larger number or part*) maggioranza; (mil) grado di maggiore

make [mek] *s* (*brand*) marca; (*form*) stile *m*; produzione; **on the make** (slang) tirando l'acqua al proprio mulino ǁ *v* (*pret & pp* **made** [med]) *tr* fare; (*a train*) pigliare; (*a circuit*) chiudere; essere, e.g., **she will make a good typist** sarà una buona dattilografa; **to make** + *inf* fare + *inf*, e.g., **she made him study** lo fece studiare; **to make into** trasformare in; **to make known** far sapere; **to make of** pensare di; **to make oneself known** darsi a conoscere; **to make out** decifrare; (*a prescription*) scrivere, preparare; (*a check*) riempire; **to make over** convertire; (com) trasferire; **to make up** preparare, comporre; (*a story*) inventare; (*lost time*) riguadagnare; (typ) impaginare; (theat) truccare ǁ *intr* essere fatto; **to make away with** rubare; disfarsi di; **to make believe** that + *inf* far finta di + *inf*, e.g., **he made believe (that) he was sleeping** fece finta di dormire; **to make for** avvicinarsi a; attaccare; (*better relations*) contribuire a cementare; **to make much of** (coll) fare le feste a; **to make off** andarsene; **to make off with** svignarsela con; **to make out** (coll) farcela; **to make toward** incamminarsi verso; **to make up** truccarsi; fare la pace; **to make up for** compensare per, supplire a; **to make up to** (coll) ingraziarsi; (coll) fare la corte a

make'-be·lieve' *adj* immaginario ǁ *s* finzione, sembianza

maker [ˈmekər] *s* fabbricante *mf*, costruttore *m* ǁ **Maker** *s* Fattore *m*

make'shift' *adj* improvvisato, di fortuna ǁ *s* espediente *m*, ripiego; (*person*) tappabuchi *mf*

make'-up' *s* composizione, costituzione; truccatura, cosmetico; (typ) impaginazione; (journ) caratteristica

make'-up man' *s* truccatore *m*

make'-up test' *s* esame *m* di riparazione

make'weight' *s* giunta, contentino; (fig) supplemento, di più *m*

making [ˈmekɪŋ] *s* fabbricazione; costituzione; causa del successo; **makings** materiale *m*; (*potential*) stoffa

maladjusted [ˌmæləˈdʒʌstɪd] *adj* spostato

mala·dy [ˈmælədi] *s* (**-dies**) malattia

malaise [mæˈlez] *s* malessere *m*

malapropos [ˌmæləprəˈpo] *adj* inopportuno ǁ *adv* a sproposito

malaria [məˈlɛrɪə] *s* malaria

Malay [ˈmele] or [məˈle] *adj & s* malese *mf*

malcontent [ˈmælkənˌtɛnt] *adj & s* malcontento

male [mel] *adj & s* maschio

malediction [ˌmælɪˈdɪkʃən] *s* maledizione

malefactor [ˈmælɪˌfæktər] *s* malfattore *m*

male' nurse' *s* infermiere *m*

malevolent [məˈlɛvələnt] *adj* malevolo

malfeasance [mælˈfizəns] *s* reato di pubblico funzionario

malice [ˈmælɪs] *s* malizia; (law) dolo; **to bear malice** serbar rancore; **with malice prepense** (law) con premeditazione

malicious [məˈlɪʃəs] *adj* malizioso, maligno

malign [məˈlaɪn] *adj* maligno ǁ *tr* calunniare

malignan·cy [məˈlɪgnənsi] *s* (**-cies**) malignità *f*; (pathol) malignità *f*

malignant [məˈlɪgnənt] *adj* maligno

maligni·ty [məˈlɪgnɪti] *s* (**-ties**) malignità *f*

malinger [məˈlɪŋgər] *intr* fingersi ammalato, darsi malato (per sottrarsi al proprio dovere)

mall [mɔl] or [mæl] *s* viale *m*; (*strip of land in a boulevard*) aiola

mallet [ˈmælɪt] *s* maglio; (*of a stone cutter*) mazzuolo

mallow [ˈmælo] *s* malva

malnutrition [ˌmælnjuˈtrɪʃən] or [ˌmælnuˈtrɪʃən] *s* malnutrizione

malodorous [mælˈodərəs] *adj* puzzolente

malpractice [mælˈpræktɪs] *s* incuria, negligenza; (*of physician or lawyer*) negligenza colposa

malt [mɔlt] *s* malto

maltreat [mælˈtrit] *tr* maltrattare

mamma [ˈmɑmə] or [məˈmɑ] *s* (coll) mamma

mammal [ˈmæməl] *s* mammifero

mammalian [mæˈmelɪən] *adj & s* mammifero

mammoth [ˈmæməθ] *adj* mastodontico ǁ *s* mammut *m*

man [mæn] *s* (**men** [mɛn]) uomo; (*in chess*) pedina; (*in checkers*) pezzo; **a man** uno, e.g., **a man can get lost in this town** uno può perdersi in questa città; **as one man** come un sol uomo; **man alive!** accidenti!; **man and wife** marito e moglie; **to be one's own man** essere completamente indipendente ǁ *v* (*pret & pp* **manned**; *ger* **manning**) *tr* (*a boat*) equipaggiare; (*a fortress*) guarnire; (*a cannon*) maneggiare

man' about town' *s* vitaiolo

manacle [ˈmænəkəl] *s*—**manacles** manette *fpl* ǁ *tr* ammanettare

manage [ˈmænɪdʒ] *tr* (*a business*) gestire; (*e.g., a tool*) maneggiare ǁ *intr* sbrogliarsela; **to manage to** fare in modo di; ingegnarsi a; **to manage to get along** barcamenarsi

manageable [ˈmænɪdʒəbəl] *adj* maneggevole

management [ˈmænɪdʒmənt] *s* direzione, gestione; (*executives collectively*) classe *f* dirigente; direzione; (*college course*) economia aziendale

manager [ˈmænədʒər] *s* direttore *m*, gerente *mf*; (theat) impresario; (sports) procuratore *m*, manager *m*

managerial [ˌmænəˈdʒɪrɪəl] *adj* direttoriale, imprenditoriale

man'aging ed'itor s gerente m responsabile, redattore m in capo

mandate ['mændet] s mandato ‖ tr dare in mandato a

mandatory ['mændə,tori] adj obbligatorio

mandolin ['mændəlin] s mandolino

mandrake ['mændrek] s mandragola

mandrel ['mændrəl] s (mach) mandrino

mane [men] s criniera

maneuver [mə'nuvər] s manovra ‖ tr manovrare ‖ intr manovrare; (aer, nav) evoluire; (fig) intrigare

manful ['mænful] adj maschile, risoluto

manganese ['mæŋgə,nis] or ['mæŋgə,niz] s manganese m

mange [mendʒ] s rogna

manger ['mendʒər] s presepio

mangle ['mæŋgəl] tr straziare, lacerare

man·gy ['mendʒi] adj (-gier; -giest) rognoso; (squalid) misero

man'han'dle tr malmenare, maltrattare

man'hole' s passo d'uomo, pozzetto

manhood ['mænhud] s virilità f; uomini mpl, umanità f

man'hunt' s caccia all'uomo

mania ['meni·ə] s mania

maniac ['meni,æk] adj & s maniaco

manicure ['mæni,kjur] s (treatment) manicure f; (manicurist) manicure mf ‖ tr (a person) curare le mani di; (the hands) curare

manicurist ['mæni,kjurist] s manicurista mf, manicure mf

manifest ['mæni,fest] adj manifesto ‖ s (naut) manifesto di carico ‖ tr manifestare

manifes·to [,mæni'festo] s (-toes) manifesto

manifold ['mæni,fold] adj molteplice ‖ s copia; carta velina; (aut, mach) collettore m

manikin ['mænikin] s manichino; (dwarf) nano

man' in the moon' s faccia di uomo che appare nella luna piena

man' in the street' s uomo qualunque, uomo della strada

manipulate [mə'nipjə,let] tr manipolare

man'kind' s genere umano ‖ **man'kind'** s il sesso maschile

manliness ['mænlinis] s virilità f

man·ly ['mænli] adj (-lier; -liest) maschio, virile

manned' space'ship s astronave pilotata

mannequin ['mænikin] s (figure) manichino; (person) indossatrice f

manner ['mænər] s maniera; **by all manner of means** in tutti i modi; **in a manner of speaking** in una certa maniera; **in the manner of** alla moda di; **manners** maniere, fpl, educazione; **to the manner born** avvezzo sin dalla nascita

mannish ['mæniʃ] adj maschile; (woman) mascolino

man' of God' s santo; profeta m; (priest) uomo al servizio di Dio

man' of let'ters s letterato

man' of means' s uomo danaroso

man' of parts' s uomo di talento

man' of straw' s uomo di paglia

man' of the world' s uomo di mondo

man-of-war [,mænəv'wɔr] s (men-of-war [,menəv'wɔr]) nave f da guerra

manor ['mænər] s maniero; feudo

man'or house' s maniero, palazzo

man' o'verboard interj uomo in mare!

man'pow'er s manodopera; (mil) effettivo

mansard ['mænsɑrd] s mansarda

man'serv'ant s (men'serv'ants) servo, servitore m

mansion ['mænʃən] s palazzo, palazzina; (manor house) maniero

man'slaugh'ter s omicidio colposo

mantel ['mæntəl] s parte f anteriore dei pilastri del camino; (shelf above it) mensola

man'tel·piece' s mensola del camino

man'tis shrimp' ['mæntis] s canocchia

mantle ['mæntəl] s mantello, cappa ‖ tr ammantare; (to conceal) nascondere ‖ intr (to blush) arrossire

manual ['mænju·əl] adj manuale ‖ s (book) manuale m; (mil) esercizio; (mus) tastiera d'organo

man'ual train'ing s istruzione nelle arti e mestieri

manufacture [,mænjə'fæktʃər] s fabbricazione; (thing manufactured) manufatto ‖ tr fabbricare

manufacturer [,mænjə'fæktʃərər] s fabbricante mf, industriale m

manure [mə'njur] or [mə'nur] s letame m ‖ tr concimare

manuscript ['mænjə,skript] adj & s manoscritto

many ['meni] adj & pron molti; **a good many** or **a great many** un buon numero; **as many . . . as** tanti . . . quanti; **as many as** fino a, e.g., **they sell as many as five thousand dozen** vendono fino a cinquemila dozzine; **how many** quanti; **many a** molti, e.g., **many a day** molti giorni; **many another** molti altri; **many more** molti di più; **so many** tanti; **too many** troppi; **twice as many** altrettanti, il doppio

many-sided ['meni,saidid] adj multilaterale; versatile

map [mæp] s mappa; (of a city) piano ‖ v (pret & pp mapped; ger mapping) tr tracciare la mappa di; mostrare sulla mappa; **to map out** fare il piano di

maple ['mepəl] s acero

maquette [mɑ'ket] s plastico

mar [mɑr] v (pret & pp marred; ger marring) tr deturpare, sfigurare

maraud [mə'rɔd] tr & intr predare

marauder [mə'rɔdər] s predone m

marble ['mɑrbəl] adj marmoreo ‖ s marmo; (little ball of glass) bilia; **marbles** bilie fpl; **to lose one's marbles** (slang) mancare una rotella a qlcu ‖ tr marmorizzare

march [mɑrtʃ] s marcia; (hist) marca; **to steal a march on** guadagnare il vantaggio su ‖ *tr* far marciare ‖ *intr* marciare ‖ **March** *s* marzo

marchioness ['mɑrʃənɪs] *s* marchesa

mare [mer] *s* (*female horse*) cavalla; (*female donkey*) asina

margarine ['mɑrdʒərɪn] *s* margarina

margin ['mɑrdʒɪn] *s* margine *m*; (econ) scoperto

mar'gin stop' *s* marginatore *m*

marigold ['mærɪ ˌgold] *s* fiorrancio

marihuana or **marijuana** [ˌmɑrɪ-'hwɑnə] *s* marijuana

marina [mə'rinə] *s* porto turistico di imbarcazioni, porticciolo turistico

marinate ['mærɪ ˌnet] *tr* marinare

marine [mə'rin] *adj* marino, marittimo ‖ *s* marina; soldato di fanteria da sbarco; **marines** fanteria da sbarco; **tell that to the marines!** (coll) va a raccontarlo ai frati!

mariner ['mærɪnər] *s* marinaio

marionette [ˌmærɪ-ə'nɛt] *s* marionetta

mar'ital sta'tus ['mærɪtəl] *s* stato civile

maritime ['mærɪ ˌtaɪm] *adj* marittimo

marjoram ['mɑrdʒərəm] *s* origano; (*sweet marjoram*) maggiorana

mark [mɑrk] *s* segno; (*brand*) marca; (*of punctuation*) punto; (*in an examination*) voto; (*sign made by illiterate person*) croce *f*; (*landmark*) segnale *m*; (*target*) bersaglio; (*spot*) macchia; (*starting point in a race*) linea di partenza; (*of confidence*) voto; (*coin*) marco; impronta; **to be beside the mark** essere fuori del seminato; **to hit the mark** colpire il bersaglio; **to leave one's mark** lasciare la propria impronta; **to make one's mark** raggiungere il successo; **to miss the mark** fallire il colpo; **to toe the mark** mettersi in fila; filare diritto ‖ *tr* marcare, segnare, contrassegnare; (*a student*) dar il voto a; (*a test*) esaminare; improntare; notare, avvertire; **to mark down** mettere in iscritto; ribassare il prezzo di

mark'down' *s* riduzione di prezzo

market ['mɑrkɪt] *s* mercato; **to bear the market** giocare al ribasso; **to bull the market** giocare al rialzo; **to play the market** giocare in borsa; **to put on the market** lanciare sul mercato ‖ *tr* mettere sul mercato

marketable ['mɑrkɪtəbəl] *adj* commerciabile, vendibile

marketing ['mɑrkɪtɪŋ] *s* compravendita; marketing *m*

mar'ket-place' *s* piazza del mercato

mar'ket price' *s* prezzo corrente

mark'ing gauge' ['mɑrkɪŋ] *s* graffietto

marks'man *s* (-**men**) tiratore *m*; **a good marksman** un tiratore scelto

marksmanship ['mɑrksmən ˌʃɪp] *s* qualità *f* di tiratore scelto

mark'up' *s* margine *m* di rivendita

marl [mɑrl] *s* marna ‖ *tr* marnare

marmalade ['mɑrmə ˌled] *s* marmellata d'arance

marmot ['mɑrmət] *s* marmotta

maroon [mə'run] *adj* & *s* marrone *m* ‖ *tr* abbandonare (*in un luogo deserto*)

marquee [mɑr'ki] *s* pensilina

marquess ['mɑrkwɪs] *s* marchese *m*

marque-try ['mɑrkətri] *s* (-**tries**) intarsio

marquis ['mɑrkwɪs] *s* marchese *m*

marquise [mɑr'kiz] *s* marchesa; (Brit) pensilina

marriage ['mærɪdʒ] *s* matrimonio

marriageable ['mærɪdʒəbəl] *adj* adatto al matrimonio; (*woman*) nubile

mar'riage por'tion *s* dote *f*

mar'riage rate' *s* nuzialità *f*

mar'ried life' *s* vita coniugale

marrow ['mæro] *s* midollo

mar·ry ['mæri] *v* (*pret* & *pp* -**ried**) *tr* sposare; **to get married to** sposarsi con ‖ *intr* sposarsi; **to marry into** (*e.g., a noble family*) imparentarsi con; **to marry the second time** risposarsi

Mars [mɑrz] *s* Marte *m*

Marseilles [mɑr'selz] *s* Marsiglia

marsh [mɑrʃ] *s* palude *f*, lama

mar·shal ['mɑrʃəl] *s* direttore *m* di una sfilata; maestro di cerimonie; (mil) maresciallo; (U.S.A.) ufficiale *m* di giustizia ‖ *v* (*pret* & *pp* -**shaled** or -**shalled**; *ger* -**shaling** or -**shalling**) *tr* introdurre cerimoniosamente; mettere in buon ordine

marsh' mal'low *s* (bot) altea

marsh'mal'low *s* dolce *m* di gelatina e zucchero

marsh·y ['mɑrʃi] *adj* (-**ier**; -**iest**) paludoso, palustre

marten ['mɑrtən] *s* (*Martes martes*) martora; (*Martes zibellina*) zibellino

martial ['mɑrʃəl] *adj* marziale

mar'tial law' *s* legge *f* marziale

Martian ['mɑrʃən] *adj* & *s* marziano

martin ['mɑrtɪn] *s* rondicchio

martinet [ˌmɑrtɪ'nɛt] or ['mɑrtɪ ˌnɛt] *s* pignolo

martyr ['mɑrtər] *s* martire *mf*

martyrdom ['mɑrtərdəm] *s* martirio

mar·vel ['mɑrvəl] *s* meraviglia ‖ *v* (*pret* & *pp* -**veled** or -**velled**; *ger* -**veling** or -**velling**) *intr* meravigliarsi; **to marvel at** stupirsi di, meravigliarsi di

marvelous ['mɑrvələs] *adj* meraviglioso

Marxist ['mɑrksɪst] *adj* & *s* marxista *mf*

mascara [mæs'kærə] *s* bistro, rimmel *m*

mascot ['mæskət] *s* mascotte *f*

masculine ['mæskjəlɪn] *adj* & *s* maschile *m*

mash [mæʃ] *s* (*crushed mass*) poltiglia; (*to form wort*) decotto d'orzo germinato; (*e.g., for poultry*) intriso ‖ *tr* schiacciare; impastare

mashed' pota'toes *spl* purè *m* di patate

masher ['mæʃər] *s* utensile *m* per schiacciare; (slang) pappagallo

mask [mæsk] or [mɑsk] *s* maschera; (phot) mascherina ‖ *tr* mascherare; (phot) mettere una mascherina a ‖ *intr* mascherarsi

masked' ball' *s* ballo in maschera

mason ['mesən] *s* muratore *m* ‖ **Mason** *s* massone *m*

mason·ry ['mesənri] *s* (-**ries**) arte *f* del

muratore; muratura || **Masonry** *s* massoneria

masquerade [,mæskə'red] or [,mɑskə-'red] *s* mascherata; (*disguise*) maschera; (*pretense*) finzione || *intr* mascherarsi; **to masquerade as** mascherarsi da; farsi passare per

mass [mæs] *s* massa; (*celebration of the Eucharist*) messa; **in the mass** nell'insieme; **the masses** le masse || *tr* ammassare || *intr* ammassarsi, accumularsi

massacre ['mæsəkər] *s* massacro, strage *f* || *tr* massacrare, trucidare

massage [mə'sɑʒ] *s* massaggio || *tr* massaggiare

masseur [mæ'sœr] *s* massaggiatore *m*

masseuse [mæ'sœz] *s* massaggiatrice *f*

massive ['mæsɪv] *adj* massiccio; (*e.g., dose*) massivo; solido

mass' me'dia ['midɪ·ə] *s* mezzi *mpl* di comunicazione di massa

mass' meet'ing *s* assemblea popolare; adunanza in massa

mass' produc'tion *s* produzione in serie

mast [mæst] or [mɑst] *s* (*post*) palo; (*agr*) ghiande *fpl*, faggiole *fpl*; (*naut*) albero; **before the mast** come marinaio semplice

master ['mæstər] or ['mɑstər] *s* (*employer*) padrone *m*; (*male head of household*) capo di casa; (*man who possesses some special skill*) maestro; (*title of respect for a boy*) signorino; (*naut*) capitano || *tr* dominare; (*a language*) possedere

mas'ter bed'room *s* camera da letto padronale

mas'ter blade' *s* foglia maestra (di una balestra)

mas'ter build'er *s* capomastro

masterful ['mæstərfəl] or ['mɑstərfəl] *adj* autoritario; provetto, magistrale

mas'ter key' *s* chiave maestra

masterly ['mæstərlɪ] or ['mɑstərlɪ] *adj* magistrale || *adv* magistralmente

mas'ter mechan'ic *s* mastro meccanico

mas'ter-mind' *s* mente direttiva || *tr* organizzare, dirigere

mas'ter of cer'emonies *s* maestro di cerimonia; (*in a night club, radio, etc.*) presentatore *m*

mas'ter-piece' *s* capolavoro

mas'ter ser'geant *s* (mil) sergente *m* maggiore

mas'ter stroke' *s* colpo da maestro

mas'ter-work' *s* capolavoro

master-y ['mæstərɪ] or ['mɑstərɪ] *s* (-**ies**) (*command of a subject*) dominio; (*skill*) maestria

mast'head' *s* (journ) titolo; (naut) testa d'albero

masticate ['mæstɪ ,ket] *tr* masticare

mastiff ['mæstɪf] or ['mɑstɪf] *s* mastino

masturbate ['mæstər ,bet] *tr* masturbare || *intr* masturbarsi

mat [mæt] *s* (*for floor*) tappeto, stuoia; (*under a dish*) tondo, sottocoppa, centrino; (*before a door*) stoino, zerbino; (*around a picture*) bordo di cartone; (sports) materas-

sino; (typ) flan *m*; flano || *v* (*pret & pp* **matted**; *ger* **matting**) *tr* coprire di stuoie; arruffare || *intr* arruffarsi

match [mætʃ] *s* (*counterpart*) uguale *m*; (*suitably associated pair*) paio; (*light*) fiammifero; (*wick*) miccia; (*prospective mate*) partito; (sports) partita, gara; **to be a match for** essere pari a, fare fronte a; **to meet one's match** trovare un degno rivale || *tr* uguagliare, pareggiare; (*colors*) combinare; (*in pairs*) appaiare; giocarsi, e.g., **to match s.o. for the drinks** giocarsi le bevande con qlcu || *intr* corrispondersi, fare il paio

match'box' *s* scatola di fiammiferi; (*of wax matches*) scatola di cerini

matchless ['mætʃlɪs] *adj* incomparabile, senza pari

match'mak'er *s* paraninfo

mate [met] *s* compagno; (*husband or wife*) consorte *mf*; (*to a female*) maschio; (*to a male*) femmina; (chess) scacco matto; (naut) primo ufficiale || *tr* appaiare; (chess) dar scacco matto a; **to be well mated** esser ben appaiato || *intr* accoppiarsi

material [mə'tɪrɪ·əl] *adj* materiale; importante || *s* materiale *m*, materia; (*cloth, fabric*) tela, stoffa; **materials** occorrente *m*

materialist [mə'tɪrɪ·əlɪst] *s* materialista *mf*

materialize [mə'tɪrɪ·ə ,laɪz] *intr* materializzarsi

matériel [mə ,tɪrɪ'el] *s* materiale *m*; materiale bellico

maternal [mə'tʌrnəl] *adj* materno

maternity [mə'tʌrnɪti] *s* maternità *f*

mater'nity ward' *s* maternità *f*

mathematical [,mæθɪ'mætɪkəl] *adj* matematico

mathematician [,mæθɪmə'tɪʃən] *s* matematico

mathematics [,mæθɪ'mætɪks] *s* matematica

matinée [,mætɪ'ne] *s* mattinata, diurna

mat'ing sea'son *s* calore *m*

matins ['mætɪnz] *spl* mattutino

matriarch ['metrɪ ,ɑrk] *s* matrona dignitosa; donna che possiede l'autorità matriarcale

matricidal [,mætrɪ'saɪdəl] or [,mætrɪ-'saɪdəl] *adj* matricida

matricide ['mætrɪ ,saɪd] or ['mætrɪ- ,saɪd] *s* (*act*) matricidio; (*person*) matricida *mf*

matriculate [mə'trɪkjə ,let] *tr* immatricolare || *intr* immatricolarsi

matriculation [mə ,trɪkjə'leʃən] *s* immatricolazione, iscrizione

matrimonial [,mætrɪ'monɪ·əl] *adj* matrimoniale

matrimo·ny ['mætrɪ ,moni] *s* (-**nies**) matrimonio

ma·trix ['metrɪks] or ['mætrɪks] *s* (-**trices** [trɪ ,siz] or -**trixes**) matrice *f*

matron ['metrən] *s* matrona; direttrice *f*; guardiana

matronly ['metrənlɪ] *adj* matronale

matter ['mætər] *s* (*physical substance*) materia; (*pus*) materia; (*affair, busi-*

ness) faccenda; (*material of a book*) contenuto; (*reason*) motivo; (*copy for printer*) manoscritto; (*printed material*) stampati *mpl*; **a matter of** un caso di; **for that matter** per quanto riguarda ciò; **in the matter** al soggetto; **no matter** non importa; **no matter how** non importa come; **no matter when** non importa quando; **no matter where** non importa dove; **what is the matter?** cosa succede?; **what is the matter with you?** cosa ha? || *intr* importare

mat'ter of course' *s*—as **a matter of course** come se nulla fosse, come se fosse una cosa naturale

mat'ter of fact' *s*—as **a matter of fact** in realtà, a onor del vero

matter-of-fact ['mætərəv ,fækt] *adj* prosaico, pratico

mattock ['mætək] *s* piccone *m*

mattress ['mætrɪs] *s* materasso

mature [mə't/ʊr] *or* [mə'tʊr] *adj* maturo; (*due*) scaduto || *tr* maturare || *intr* maturare; (*com*) scadere

maturity [mə't/ʊrɪti] *or* [mə'tʊrɪti] *s* maturità *f*; (*com*) scadenza

maudlin ['mɔdlɪn] *adj* sentimentale, lagrimoso; piagnucoloso e ubriaco

maul [mɔl] *tr* maltrattare, bistrattare

maulstick ['mɔl ,stɪk] *s* appoggiamano

maundy ['mɔndi] *s* lavanda

Maun'dy Thurs'day *s* giovedì santo

mausole-um [,mɔsə'li-əm] *s* (**-ums** *or* **-a** [ə]) mausoleo

maw [mɔ] *s* (*e.g., of a hog*) stomaco; (*of carnivorous mammal*) fauci *fpl*; (*of fowl*) gozzo; (*fig*) bocca, fauci *fpl*

mawkish ['mɔkɪʃ] *adj* (*sickening*) nauseante; (*sentimental*) svenevole

maxim ['mæksɪm] *s* massima

maximum ['mæksɪməm] *adj* & *s* massimo

may [me] *v aux*—**it may be** può essere; **may I come in?** si può?; **may you be happy!** possa tu essere felice! || **May** *s* maggio

maybe ['mebi] *adv* forse

May' Day' *s* primo maggio; festa della primavera; (*hist*) calendimaggio (*in Florence*)

mayhem ['mehɛm] *or* ['me-əm] *s* mutilazione dolosa

mayonnaise [,me-ə'nez] *s* maionese *f*

mayor ['me-ər] *or* [mer] *s* sindaco

mayoress ['me-ərɪs] *or* ['merɪs] *s* donna sindaco

May'pole *s* maio, maggio, palo per le danze di calendimaggio

May'pole dance' *s* ballo figurato con nastri per la festa di primavera

May' queen' *s* reginetta di maggio

maze [mez] *s* dedalo, labirinto

me [mi] *pron* me; mi; **to me** mi; **a me** mi

meadow ['mɛdo] *s* prato

mead'ow-land' *s* prateria

meager ['migər] *adj* magro

meal [mil] *s* (*food*) pasto; (*unbolted grain*) farina

meal'time' *s* ora del pasto

mean [min] *adj* (*intermediate*) medio;

(*low in rank*) basso, umile; (*shabby*) misero; (*of poor quality*) inferiore; (*stingy*) taccagno; (*nasty*) villano; (*vicious, as a horse*) intrattabile; (*coll*) indisposto; (*coll*) vergognoso; (*slang*) splendido; **no mean** eccellente || *s* media, termine medio; **by all means** certamente, senza dubbio; **by means of** per mezzo di; **by no means** in nessuna maniera; **means** beni *mpl*; (*agency*) mezzo, maniera; **to live on one's means** vivere di rendita || *v* (*pret* & *pp* **meant** [mɛnt]) *tr* significare, voler dire; **to mean to** pensare || *intr*—**to mean well** aver buone intenzioni

meander [mɪ'ændər] *s* meandro || *intr* serpeggiare, vagare

meaning ['minɪŋ] *s* senso, significato

meaningful ['minɪŋfəl] *adj* significativo

meaningless ['minɪŋlɪs] *adj* senza senso, senza significato

meanness ['minnɪs] *s* viltà *f*, bassezza; (*stinginess*) meschinità *f*; (*lowliness*) umiltà *f*, povertà *f*

mean'time' *s*—**in the meantime** nel frattempo || *adv* frattanto, intanto

mean'while' *s* & *adv* var of **meantime**

measles ['mizəlz] *s* morbillo; (*German measles*) rosolia

mea-sly ['mizli] *adj* (**-slier; -sliest**) col morbillo; (*coll*) miserabile

measurable ['mɛʒərəbəl] *adj* misurabile

measure ['mɛʒər] *s* misura; (*legislative bill*) progetto di legge; (*mus*) battuta; **in a measure** in un certo senso; **to take the measure of** prendere le misure di; giudicare accuratamente || *tr* misurare; (*a distance*) percorrere; **to measure out** somministrare || *intr* misurare; **to measure up to** essere all'altezza di

measurement ['mɛʒərmənt] *s* misura; **to take s.o.'s measurements** prendere le misure di qlcu

meas'uring cup' *s* vetro graduato

meat [mit] *s* carne *f*; (*food in general*) cibo; (*of nut*) gheriglio; (*fig*) sostanza, midollo

meat'ball' *s* polpetta

meat' grind'er *s* tritacarne *m*

meat' loaf' *s* polpettone *m*

meat' mar'ket *s* macelleria

meat-y ['miti] *adj* (**-ier; -iest**) carnoso, polputo; (*fig*) sostanzioso

Mecca ['mɛkə] *s* la Mecca; **the Mecca** (*fig*) la Mecca

mechanic [mɪ'kænɪk] *s* meccanico; (*aut*) motorista *m*

mechanical [mɪ'kænɪkəl] *adj* meccanico; (*machinelike*) (*fig*) macchinale

mechan'ical engineer'ing *s* ingegneria meccanica

mechan'ical pen'cil *s* matita automatica

mechanics [mɪ'kænɪks] *s* meccanica

mechanism ['mɛkə ,nɪzəm] *s* meccanismo, congegno

mechanize ['mɛkə ,naɪz] *tr* meccanizzare

medal ['mɛdəl] *s* medaglia

medallion [mɪ'dæljən] *s* medaglione *m*

meddle ['mɛdəl] *intr* intromettersi

meddler ['mɛdlər] *s* ficcanaso

meddlesome ['mɛdəlsəm] *adj* invadente, indiscreto

median ['midɪ·ən] *adj* medio, mediano || *s* punto medio, numero medio

me'dian strip' *s* spartitraffico

mediate ['midɪ‚et] *tr (a dispute)* comporre; *(parties)* pacificare || *intr (to be in the middle)* mediare; fare da paciere

mediation [‚midɪ'eʃən] *s* mediazione

mediator ['midɪ‚etər] *s* mediatore *m*

medical ['mɛdɪkəl] *adj* medico; *(student)* di medicina

medicinal [mə'dɪsɪnəl] *adj* medicinale

medicine ['mɛdɪsɪn] *s* medicina

med'icine cab'inet *s* armadietto farmaceutico

med'icine kit' *s* cassetta farmaceutica

med'icine man' *s* (men') stregone indiano

medieval [‚midɪ'ivəl] *or* [‚mɛdɪ'ivəl] *adj* medievale

medievalist [‚midɪ'ivəlɪst] *or* [‚mɛdɪ'ivəlɪst] *s* medievalista *mf*

mediocre ['midɪ‚okər] *or* [‚midɪ'okər] *adj* mediocre

mediocri·ty [‚midɪ'ɑkrɪtɪ] *s* (-ties) mediocrità *f*

meditate ['mɛdɪ‚tet] *tr & intr* meditare

meditation [‚mɛdɪ'teʃən] *s* meditazione

Mediterranean [‚mɛdɪtə'renɪ·ən] *adj & s* Mediterraneo

medi·um ['midɪ·əm] *adj* medio; *(heat)* moderato; *(meat)* cotto moderatamente || *s* (-ums *or* -a [ə]) *(middle state; mean)* media; mezzo; *(in spiritualism)* medium *m*; media *(of communication)* media *mpl*; through the medium of per mezzo di

medlar ['mɛdlər] *s (tree)* nespolo; *(fruit)* nespola

medley ['mɛdlɪ] *s* farragine *f*, mescolanza; *(mus)* pot-pourri *m*

medul·la [mɪ'dʌlə] *s* (-lae [li]) midollo

meek [mik] *adj* mansueto, umile

meekness ['miknɪs] *s* mansuetudine *f*

meerschaum ['mɪrʃəm] *or* ['mɪrʃɔm] *s* schiuma; pipa di schiuma

meet [mit] *adj* conveniente || *s* incontro || *v (pret & pp* met [mɛt]) *tr* incontrare, incontrarsi con; *(to become acquainted with)* fare la conoscenza di; riunirsi con; *(to cope with)* sopperire a; *(said of a public carrier)* fare coincidenza con; andar incontro a; *(one's obligations)* far fronte a; *(bad luck)* avere; to meet the eyes of presentarsi agli occhi di || *intr* incontrarsi; riunirsi; conoscersi; till we meet again arrivederci; to meet with incontrare, incontrarsi con; *(an accident)* avere; *(said of a public carrier)* fare coincidenza con

meeting ['mitɪŋ] *s* riunione, ritrovo; seduta, convegno; *(political)* comizio; *(e.g., of two rivers)* confluenza; duello

meet'ing of the minds' *s* accordo, consonanza di voleri

meet'ing place' *s* luogo di riunione

megacycle ['mɛgə‚saɪkəl] *s* megaciclo

megaphone ['mɛgə‚fon] *s* megafono, portavoce *m*

megohm ['mɛg‚om] *s* megaohm *m*

melancholia [‚mɛlən'kolɪ·ə] *s* melanconia, malinconia

melanchol·y ['mɛlən‚kɑlɪ] *adj* malinconico || *s* (-ies) malinconia

melee ['mele] *or* ['mɛle] *s (fight)* mischia; confusione

mellow ['mɛlo] *adj (fruit)* maturo; *(wine)* pastoso; *(voice)* soave, melodioso || *tr* raddolcire || *intr* raddolcirsi

melodic [mɪ'lɑdɪk] *adj* melodico

melodious [mɪ'lodɪ·əs] *adj* melodioso

melodramatic [‚mɛlədrə'mætɪk] *adj* melodrammatico

melo·dy ['mɛlədɪ] *s* (-dies) melodia

melon ['mɛlən] *s* melone *m*, popone *m*

melt [mɛlt] *tr* sciogliere; *(metals)* fondere; *(fig)* intenerire || *intr* sciogliersi; fondersi; *(fig)* intenerirsi; to melt away svanire; to melt into convertirsi in, diventare; *(tears)* struggersi in

melt'ing pot' *s* crogiolo

member ['mɛmbər] *s* membro

membership ['mɛmbər‚ʃɪp] *s* associazione; numero di membri

membrane ['mɛmbren] *s* membrana

memen·to [mɪ'mɛnto] *s* (-tos *or* -toes) oggetto ricordo

mem·o ['mɛmo] *s* (-os) (coll) memorandum *m*

memoir ['mɛmwɑr] *s* memoria, memoriale *m*; biografia; memoirs memorie *fpl*

memoran·dum [‚mɛmə'rændəm] *s* (-dums *or* -da [də]) memorandum *m*

memorial [mɪ'morɪ·əl] *adj* commemorativo || *s* sacrario; *(petition)* memoriale *m*

Memo'rial Day' *s* giorno dei caduti

memorialize [mɪ'morɪ·ə‚laɪz] *tr* commemorare

memorize ['mɛmə‚raɪz] *tr* imparare a memoria

memo·ry ['mɛmərɪ] *s* (-ries) memoria; to commit to memory imparare a memoria

menace ['mɛnɪs] *s* minaccia || *tr & intr* minacciare

ménage [me'nɑʒ] *s* casa; *(housekeeping)* economia domestica

menagerie [mə'næʒərɪ] *or* [mə'nædʒərɪ] *s* serraglio

mend [mɛnd] *s* riparo; to be on the mend migliorare || *tr (to repair)* raccomodare, riparare; *(to patch)* rammendare; *(fig)* correggere || *intr* correggersi

mendacious [mɛn'deʃəs] *adj* mendace

mendicant ['mɛndɪkənt] *adj & s* mendicante *mf*

menfolk ['mɛn‚fok] *spl* uomini *mpl*

menial ['minɪ·əl] *adj* basso, servile || *s* servitore *m*, servo

menses ['mɛnsiz] *spl* mestruazione, mestrui *mpl*

men's' fur'nishings *spl* articoli *mpl* d'abbigliamento maschile

men's' room' *s* gabinetto per signori

menstruate ['mɛnstrʊ ,et] *intr* avere le mestruazioni

men'tal arith'metic ['mɛntəl] *s* calcolo mentale

men'tal hos'pital *s* manicomio

men'tal ill'ness *s* malattia mentale

men'tal reserva'tion *s* riserva mentale

men'tal test' *s* test *m* mentale

mention ['mɛnʃən] *s* menzione || *tr* menzionare; **don't mention it** non c'è di che

menu ['mɛnju] or ['menju] *s* menu *m*, lista

meow [mɪ'aʊ] *s* miagolio || *intr* miagolare

Mephistophelian [,mɛfɪstə'fili·ən] *adj* mefistofelico

mercantile ['mʌrkən ,til] or ['mʌrkən- ,taɪl] *adj* mercantile

mercenar-y ['mʌrsə ,neri] *adj* mercenario || *s* (-ies) mercenario

merchandise ['mʌrtʃən ,daɪz] *s* mercanzia, merce *f*

merchant ['mʌrtʃənt] *adj* mercantile || *s* mercante *m*, commerciante *mf*

mer'chant·man *s* (-men) mercantile *m*

mer'chant marine' *s* marina mercantile

merciful ['mʌrsɪfəl] *adj* misericordioso

merciless ['mʌrsɪlɪs] *adj* spietato

mercu·ry ['mʌrkjəri] *s* (-ries) mercurio || **Mercury** *s* Mercurio

mer·cy ['mʌrsi] *s* (-cies) misericordia; **at the mercy of** alla mercé di

mere [mɪr] *adj* mero, puro

meretricious [,mɛrɪ'trɪʃəs] *adj* vistoso, chiassoso, sgargiante; artificiale, falso, finto

merge [mʌrdʒ] *tr* fondere || *intr* fondersi; (*said of two roads*) convergere; **to merge into** convertirsi lentamente in

merger ['mʌrdʒər] *s* fusione

meridian [mə'rɪdɪ·ən] *adj* meridiano; culminante || *s* meridiano; apogeo

meringue [mə'ræŋ] *s* meringa

merit ['mɛrɪt] *s* merito || *tr* meritare

meritorious [,mɛrɪ'tori·əs] *adj* meritorio

merlon ['mʌrlən] *s* merlo

mermaid ['mʌr ,med] *s* sirena

mer'man' *s* (-men') tritone *m*

merriment ['mɛrɪmənt] *s* allegria

mer·ry ['mɛri] *adj* (-rier; -riest) allegro, giocondo; **to make merry** divertirsi

Mer'ry Christ'mas *interj* Buon Natale!

mer'ry-go-round' *s* giostra, carosello; (*of parties*) serie ininterrotta

mer'ry·mak'er *s* festaiolo

mesh [mɛʃ] *s* (*network*) rete *f*; (*each open space of net*) maglia; (*mach*) ingranaggio; **meshes** rete *f* || *tr* irretire; (*mach*) ingranare || *intr* irretirsi; (*mach*) ingranarsi

mess [mɛs] *s* (*dirty condition*) disordine *m*; (*meal for a group of people*) mensa, rancio; porzione; **to get into a mess** mettersi nei pasticci; **to make a mess of** rovinare || *tr* sporcare; disordinare; rovinare || *intr* mangiare in comune; **to mess around** (coll) perdersi in cose inutili

message ['mɛsɪdʒ] *s* messaggio

messenger ['mɛsəndʒər] *s* messaggero; (*person who goes on an errand*) fattorino; (mil) portaordini *m*

mess' hall' *s* mensa

Messiah [mə'saɪ·ə] *s* Messia *m*

mess' kit' *s* gavetta, gamella

mess'mate' *s* compagno di rancio

mess' of pot'tage ['pɑtɪdʒ] *s* (Bib & fig) piatto di lenticchie

Messrs. ['mɛsərz] *pl of* Mr.

mess·y ['mɛsi] *adj* (-ier; -iest) disordinato; sporco

metal ['mɛtəl] *adj* metallico || *s* metallo

metallic [mɪ'tælɪk] *adj* metallico

metallurgy ['mɛtə ,lʌrdʒi] *s* metallurgia

met'al pol'ish *s* lucido per metalli

met'al·work' *s* lavoro di metallo

metamorpho·sis [,mɛtə'mɔrfəsɪs] *s* -ses [,siz]) metamorfosi *f*

metaphony [mə'tæfəni] *s* metafonia, metafonesi *f*

metaphor ['mɛtəfər] or ['mɛtə ,fɔr] *s* metafora

metaphorical [,mɛtə'fɑrɪkəl] or [,mɛtə'fɔrɪkəl] *adj* metaforico

metathe·sis [mɪ'tæθɪsɪs] *s* (-ses [,siz]) metatesi *f*

mete [mit] *tr*—**to mete out** distribuire

meteor ['miti·ər] *s* meteora

meteoric [,miti'ɑrɪk] or [,miti'ɔrɪk] *adj* meteorico; (fig) rapidissimo, folgorante

meteorite ['miti·ə ,raɪt] *s* meteorite *m* & *f*

meteorology [,miti·ə'rɑlədʒi] *s* meteorologia

meter ['mitər] *s* (*unit of length; verse*) metro; (*instrument for measuring gas, water, etc.*) contatore *m*; (mus) tempo || *tr* misurare col contatore

me'ter read'er *s* lettore *m*, letturista *m*

methane ['mɛθen] *s* metano

method ['mɛθəd] *s* metodo

methodic(al) [mɪ'θɑdɪk(əl)] *adj* metodico

Methodist ['mɛθədɪst] *adj* & *s* metodista *mf*

Methuselah [mɪ'θuzələ] *s* Matusalemme *m*

meticulous [mɪ'tɪkjələs] *adj* meticoloso

metric(al) ['mɛtrɪk(əl)] *adj* metrico

metronome ['mɛtrə ,nom] *s* metronomo

metropolis [mɪ'trɑpəlɪs] *s* metropoli *f*

metropolitan [,mɛtrə'pɑlɪtən] *adj* & *s* metropolitano

mettle ['mɛtəl] *s* disposizione, temperamento; brio, animo; **to be on one's mettle** impegnarsi a fondo

mettlesome ['mɛtəlsəm] *adj* brioso

mew [mju] *s* miagolio; (orn) gabbiano; **mews** scuderie *fpl*

Mexican ['mɛksɪkən] *adj* & *s* messicano

Mexico ['mɛksɪ ,ko] *s* il Messico

mezzanine ['mɛzə ,nin] *s* mezzanino

mica ['maɪkə] *s* mica

microbe ['maɪkrob] *s* microbo

microbiology [,maɪkrəbaɪ'alədʒi] *s* microbiologia

microcard ['maɪkrə ,kɑrd] *s* microscheda

microfarad [ˌmaɪkrəˈfæræd] *s* microfarad *m*

microfilm [ˈmaɪkrəˌfɪlm] *s* microfilm *m* ‖ *tr* microfilmare

microgroove [ˈmaɪkrəˌgruv] *adj* microsolco ‖ *s* microsolco; disco microsolco

microphone [ˈmaɪkrəˌfon] *s* microfono

microscope [ˈmaɪkrəˌskop] *s* microscopio

microscopic [ˌmaɪkrəˈskɑpɪk] *adj* microscopico

microwave [ˈmaɪkrəˌwev] *s* microonda

mid [mɪd] *adj* mezzo, la metà di, e.g., **mid October** la metà di ottobre

mid'day' *adj* di mezzogiorno ‖ *s* mezzogiorno

middle [ˈmɪdəl] *adj* medio, mezzo ‖ *s* mezzo, metà *f*; *(of human body)* cintura; **about the middle of** verso la metà di; **in the middle of** nel mezzo di

mid'dle age' *s* mezza età ‖ **Middle Ages** *spl* Medio Evo

mid'dle class' *s* ceto medio, borghesia

Mid'dle East' *s* Medio Oriente

Mid'dle Eng'lish *s* inglese *m* medievale parlato fra il 1150 e il 1500

mid'dle fin'ger *s* dito medio

mid'dle-man' *s* (**-men'**) intermediario

middling [ˈmɪdlɪŋ] *adj* mediocre, passabile ‖ *s* *(coarsely ground wheat)* farina grossa integrale; **middlings** articoli *mpl* di qualità mediocre ‖ *adv* moderatamente

mid-dy [ˈmɪdi] *s* (**-dies**) aspirante *m* di marina

mid'dy blouse' *s* marinara

midget [ˈmɪdʒɪt] *s* nano

midland [ˈmɪdlənd] *adj* centrale, interno ‖ *s* regione centrale

mid'night' *adj* di mezzanotte; **to burn the midnight oil** studiare a lume di candela ‖ *s* mezzanotte *f*

midriff [ˈmɪdrɪf] *s* diaframma *m; (middle part of body)* cintura, vita

mid'ship'man *s* (**-men**) aspirante *m* di marina

midst [mɪdst] *s* mezzo, centro; **in the midst of** in mezzo a

mid'stream' *s*—**in midstream** in mezzo al fiume

mid'sum'mer *s* cuore *m* dell'estate

mid'way' *adj* situato a metà strada ‖ *s* metà strada; viale *m* principale di un' esposizione ‖ *adv* a metà strada

mid'week' *s* mezzo della settimana

mid'wife' *s* (**-wives'**) levatrice *f*

mid'win'ter *s* cuore *m* dell'inverno

mid'year' *adj* nel mezzo dell'anno ‖ *s* mezzo dell'anno; **midyears** (coll) esami *mpl* nel mezzo dell'anno scolastico

mien [min] *s* aspetto, portamento

miff [mɪf] *s* (coll) battibecco ‖ *tr* (coll) offendere

might [maɪt] *s* forza, potenza; **with might and main** a tutta forza ‖ *v aux* used to form the potential, e.g., **he might change his mind** è possibile che cambi opinione

might-y [ˈmaɪti] *adj* (**-ier; -iest**) potente; *(huge)* grandissimo ‖ *adv* (coll) moltissimo, grandemente

migraine [ˈmaɪgren] *s* emicrania

migrate [ˈmaɪgret] *intr* migrare

migratory [ˈmaɪgrəˌtori] *adj* migratore

milch [mɪltʃ] *adj* lattifero

mild [maɪld] *adj* dolce, mite, gentile; *(disease)* leggero

mildew [ˈmɪlˌdju] or [ˈmɪlˌdu] *s* *(mold)* muffa; *(plant disease)* peronospora

mile [maɪl] *s* miglio terrestre; miglio marino

mileage [ˈmaɪlɪdʒ] *s* distanza in miglia

mile'age tick'et *s* biglietto calcolato in miglia simile al biglietto chilometraggio

mile'post' *s* colonnina miliare

mile'stone' *s* pietra miliare

milieu [mɪlˈju] *s* ambiente *m*

militancy [ˈmɪlɪtənsi] *s* bellicismo; spirito militante

militant [ˈmɪlɪtənt] *adj & s* militante *mf*

militarism [ˈmɪlɪtəˌrɪzəm] *s* militarismo

militarist [ˈmɪlɪtərɪst] *adj & s* militarista *mf*

militarize [ˈmɪlɪtəˌraɪz] *tr* militarizzare

military [ˈmɪlɪˌteri] *adj* militare ‖ *s*— **the military** le forze armate

mil'itary acad'emy *s* scuola allievi ufficiali, accademia militare

mil'itary police' *s* polizia militare

militate [ˈmɪlɪˌtet] *intr* militare

militia [mɪˈlɪʃə] *s* milizia

mili'tia-man *s* (**-men**) miliziano

milk [mɪlk] *adj* lattifero; di latte; **al latte** ‖ *s* latte *m* ‖ *tr* mungere; (fig) spillare ‖ *intr* dare latte

milk' can' *s* bidone *m* per il latte

milk' choc'olate *s* cioccolato al latte

milk' diet' *s* regime latteo

milking [ˈmɪlkɪŋ] *s* mungitura

milk'maid' *s* lattaia

milk'man' *s* (**-men'**) lattaio

milk' of hu'man kind'ness *s* grande compassione

milk' pail' *s* secchio da latte

milk' shake' *s* frappé *m* or frullato di latte

milk'sop' *s* effeminato

milk'weed' *s* vincetossico

milk-y [ˈmɪlki] *adj* (**-ier; -iest**) latteo; *(whitish)* lattiginoso

Milk'y Way' *s* Via Lattea

mill [mɪl] *s* *(for grinding grain)* mulino; *(for making fabrics)* filanda; *(for cutting wood)* segheria; *(for refining sugar)* zuccherificio; *(for producing steel)* acciaieria; *(to grind coffee)* macinino; *(part of a dollar)* millesimo; **to put through the mill** mettere a dura prova ‖ *tr* *(grains)* macinare; *(coins)* zigrinare; *(steel)* laminare; *(ore)* frantumare; *(with a milling machine)* fresare; *(chocolate)* frullare ‖ *intr*—**to mill about** or **around** girare intorno

millennial [mɪˈlɛnɪˌəl] *adj* millenario

milleni·um [mɪ'lɛnɪ·əm] s (-ums or -a [ə]) millennio

miller ['mɪlər] s mugnaio; (ent) tignola notturna

millet ['mɪlɪt] s panico, miglio

milliampere [,mɪlɪ'æmpɪr] s milliampere m

milliard ['mɪljərd] or ['mɪljɑrd] s (Brit) miliardo, bilione m

milligram ['mɪlɪ,græm] s milligrammo

millimeter ['mɪlɪ,mitər] s millimetro

milliner ['mɪlɪnər] s modista

milliner·y ['mɪlɪ,nɛri] or ['mɪlɪnəri] s (-ies) cappelli mpl per signora; modisteria; articoli mpl di modisteria

mil'linery shop' s modisteria

milling ['mɪlɪŋ] s (of grain) macinatura; (of coins) granitura; (mach) fresatura

mill'ing machine' s fresatrice f

million ['mɪljən] adj milione di, milioni di || s milione m

millionaire [,mɪljən'ɛr] s milionario

millionth ['mɪljənθ] adj, s & pron milionesimo

millivolt ['mɪlɪ,volt] s millivolt m

mill'pond' s gora

mill'race' s corrente f che aziona il mulino; canale m di presa

mill'stone' s mola, macina, palmento; (fig) peso, gravame m

mill' wheel' s ruota del mulino

mill'work' s lavoro di falegnameria; lavoro di falegnameria fatto a macchina

mime [maɪm] s mimo || tr mimare

mimeograph ['mɪmɪ·ə,græf] or ['mɪmɪə,grɑf] s (trademark) ciclostile m || tr ciclostilare

mim·ic ['mɪmɪk] s mimo, imitatore m || v (pret & pp -icked; ger -icking) tr imitare, scimmiottare

mimic·ry ['mɪmɪkri] s (-ries) mimica; (biol) mimetismo

minaret [,mɪnə'rɛt] or ['mɪnə,rɛt] s minareto

mince [mɪns] tr tagliuzzare, triturare; (words) pronunziare con affettazione; **to not mince one's words** non aver peli sulla lingua

mince'meat' s carne tritata; **to make mincemeat of** annientare completamente

mince' pie' s torta di frutta secca e carne tritata

mind [maɪnd] s mente f; opinione; to bear in mind tener presente; to be not in one's right mind essere fuori di senno; to be of one mind essere d'accordo; to be out of one's mind essere impazzito; to change one's mind cambiare d'opinione; to go out of one's mind impazzire; to have a mind to aver voglia di; to have in mind to pensare a; to have on one's mind avere in mente; to lose one's mind uscire di mente; to make up one's mind decidersi; to my mind a mio modo di vedere; to say whatever comes to one's mind dire quanto salta in testa, e.g., John always says whatever comes to his mind Gio-

vanni dice sempre quanto gli salta in testa; to set one's mind on risolversi a; to slip one's mind scappare di mente (with dat), e.g., it slipped his mind gli è scappato di mente; to speak one's mind dire la propria opinione; with one mind unanimamente || tr (to take care of) occuparsi di; obbedire (with dat); do you mind the smoke? Le disturba il fumo?; mind your own business si occupi degli affari Suoi || intr osservare, fare attenzione; rincrescere, e.g., do you mind if I go? Le rincresce se vado?; never mind non si preoccupi

mindful ['maɪndfəl] adj memore

mind' read'er s lettore m del pensiero

mind' read'ing s lettura del pensiero

mine [maɪn] s (e.g., of coal) miniera; (mil & nav) mina || pron poss il mio; mio || tr minare; (earth) scavare; (ore) estrarre || intr lavorare una miniera; (mil & nav) minare

mine' detec'tor s rivelatore m di mine

mine'field' s campo minato

mine'lay'er s posamine m

miner ['maɪnər] s minatore m

mineral ['mɪnərəl] adj & s minerale m

mineralogy [,mɪnə'rælədʒi] s mineralogia

min'eral wool' s cotone m or lana minerale

mine' sweep'er s dragamine m

mingle ['mɪŋgəl] tr mescolare; unire || intr mescolarsi, associarsi

miniature ['mɪnɪ·ət/ər] or ['mɪnɪt/ər] s miniatura; to paint in miniature miniare, dipingere in miniatura

min'iature golf' s minigolf m

miniaturization [,mɪnɪ·ət/ərɪ'ze/ən] or [,mɪnɪt/ərɪ'ze/ən] s miniaturizzazione

minimal ['mɪnɪməl] adj minimo

minimize ['mɪnɪ,maɪz] tr minimizzare

minimum ['mɪnɪməm] adj & s minimo

min'imum wage' s salario minimo

mining ['maɪnɪŋ] adj minerario || s estrazione di minerali; (nav) posa di mine

minion ['mɪnjən] s servo; favorito, beniamino

min'ion of the law' s poliziotto

miniskirt ['mɪnə,skʌrt] s minigonna

minister ['mɪnɪstər] s ministro; pastore m protestante || tr & intr ministrare

ministerial [,mɪnɪs'tɪrɪ·əl] adj ministeriale

minis·try ['mɪnɪstri] s (-tries) ministero; sacerdozio

mink [mɪŋk] s visone m

minnow ['mɪno] s pesciolino; (ichth) ciprino

minor ['maɪnər] adj minore || s minore m, minorenne mf; (educ) corso secondario

minori·ty [mɪ'nɑrɪti] or [mɪ'nɔrɪti] adj minoritario || s (-ties) (smaller number or part; group differing in race, etc., from majority) minoranza; (under legal age) minorità f

minstrel ['mɪnstrəl] s (hist) menestrello; (U.S.A.) comico vestito da nero

minstrel·sy ['mɪnstrəlsi] s (-sies) giulleria; poesia giullaresca

mint [mɪnt] s zecca; (plant) menta; (losenge) mentina; (fig) miniera d'oro ‖ tr coniare

minuet [,mɪnjuʹet] s minuetto

minus ['maɪnəs] adj meno ‖ s meno, perdita ‖ prep meno, senza

minute [maɪʹnjut] or [maɪʹnut] adj minuto ‖ ['mɪnɪt] adj fatto in un minuto ‖ s minuto; momento; **minutes** processo verbale; **to write up the minutes** tenere i verbali; **up to the minute** al corrente; dell'ultima ora

min'ute hand' ['mɪnɪt] s sfera or lancetta dei minuti

minutiae [mɪʹnjuʃɪ,i] or [mɪʹnuʃɪ,i] spl minuzie fpl

minx [mɪŋks] s sfacciata, civetta

miracle ['mɪrəkəl] s miracolo

mir'acle play' s sacra rappresentazione

miraculous [mɪʹrækjələs] adj miracoloso

mirage [mɪʹrɑʒ] s miraggio

mire [maɪr] s limo, mota

mirror ['mɪrər] s specchio ‖ tr specchiare, riflettere

mirth [mʌrθ] s allegria, gioia

mir·y ['maɪri] adj (-ier; -iest) fangoso, limaccioso

misadventure [,mɪsədʹventʃər] s disavventura, contrattempo

misanthrope ['mɪsən,θrop] s misantropo

misanthropy [mɪsʹænθrəpi] s misantropia

misapprehension [,mɪsæprɪʹhenʃən] s malinteso

misappropriation [,mɪsə,proprɪʹeʃən] s malversazione

misbehave [,mɪsbɪʹhev] intr comportarsi male

misbehavior [,mɪsbɪʹhevɪ·ər] s cattiva condotta

miscalculation [,mɪskælkjəʹleʃən] s calcolo errato

miscarriage [mɪsʹkærɪdʒ] s (of justice) errore m; (of a letter) disguido; (pathol) aborto

miscar·ry [mɪsʹkæri] v (pret & pp -ried) intr (said of a project) fallire; (said of a letter) smarrirsi; (pathol) abortire

miscellaneous [,mɪsəʹlenɪ·əs] adj miscellaneo

miscella·ny ['mɪsə,leni] s (-nies) miscellanea

mischief ['mɪstʃɪf] s (harm) danno; (disposition to annoy) malizia; (prankishness) birichinata

mischievous ['mɪstʃɪvəs] adj dannoso; malizioso; birichino

misconception [,mɪskənʹsepʃən] s concetto erroneo, fraintendimento

misconduct [mɪsʹkɑndəkt] s cattiva condotta; (of a public official) malgoverno ‖ [,mɪskənʹdʌkt] tr male amministrare; **to misconduct oneself** comportarsi male

misconstrue [,mɪskənʹstru] or [mɪsʹkɑnstru] tr fraintendere

miscount [mɪsʹkaunt] s conteggio erroneo ‖ tr & intr contare male

miscue [mɪsʹkju] s sbaglio; (in billiards) stecca ‖ intr steccare; (theat) sbagliarsi di battuta

mis·deal ['mɪs,dil] s distribuzione sbagliata ‖ [mɪsʹdil] v (pret & pp -dealt [delt]) tr & intr distribuire erroneamente

misdeed [mɪsʹdid] or ['mɪs,did] s misfatto, malfatto

misdemeanor [,mɪsdɪʹminər] s cattiva condotta; (law) delitto colposo

misdirect [,mɪsdɪʹrekt] or [,mɪsdaɪʹrekt] tr dare un indirizzo sbagliato a; (a letter) mettere un indirizzo sbagliato su

misdoing [mɪsʹdu·ɪŋ] s misfatto

miser ['maɪzər] s avaro, spilorcio

miserable ['mɪzərəbəl] adj miserabile, miserevole; (coll) malissimo; (coll) schifoso

miserly ['maɪzərli] adj spilorcio

miser·y ['mɪzəri] s (-ies) miseria

misfeasance [mɪsʹfizəns] s infrazione della legge; abuso di autorità commesso da pubblico funzionario

misfire [mɪsʹfaɪr] s difetto di esplosione; (aut) difetto d'accensione ‖ intr (said of a gun) fare cilecca; (aut) dare accensione irregolare; (fig) fallire

mis·fit ['mɪs,fɪt] s vestito che non va bene; (person) spostato, pesce m fuor d'acqua ‖ [mɪsʹfɪt] v (pret & pp -fitted; ger -fitting) intr andar male

misfortune [mɪsʹfortʃən] s disgrazia

misgiving [mɪsʹgɪvɪŋ] s dubbio, timore m, cattivo presentimento

misgovern [mɪsʹgʌvərn] tr amministrare male

misguided [mɪsʹgaɪdɪd] adj fuorviato; (e.g., kindness) sconsigliato

mishap ['mɪshæp] or [mɪsʹhæp] s accidente m, infortunio

misinform [,mɪsɪnʹform] tr dare informazioni errate a

misinterpret [,mɪsɪnʹterprɪt] tr interpretare male, trasfigurare

misjudge [mɪsʹdʒʌdʒ] tr & intr giudicare male

mis·lay [mɪsʹle] v (pret & pp -laid [,led]) tr (e.g., tile) applicare in maniera sbagliata; (e.g., papers) smarrire, mettere al posto sbagliato

mis·lead [mɪsʹlid] v (pret & pp -led [,led]) tr sviare, traviare

misleading [mɪsʹlidɪŋ] adj ingannatore

mismanagement [mɪsʹmænɪdʒmənt] s malgoverno

misnomer [mɪsʹnomər] s termine improprio

misplace [mɪsʹples] tr mettere fuori di posto; (trust) riporre erroneamente

misprint ['mɪs,prɪnt] s errore m di stampa, refuso ‖ [mɪsʹprɪnt] tr stampare erroneamente

mispronounce [,mɪsprəʹnauns] tr pronunciare in modo erroneo

mispronunciation [,mɪsprə,nʌnsɪ-

'e/ən] or [ˌmɪsprə ˌnʌnʃɪ'e/ən] *s* errore *m* di pronuncia

misquote [mɪs'kwot] *tr* citare incorrettamente

misrepresent [ˌmɪsreprɪ'zent] *tr* travisare, snaturare; (pol) rappresentare slealmente

miss [mɪs] *s* sbaglio, omissione; tiro fuori bersaglio; signorina ‖ *tr* (*a train, an opportunity*) perdere; (*the target*) fallire; (*an appointment*) mancare; (*the point*) non vedere, non capire; per poco, e.g., **the car missed hitting him** l'automobile non l'ha investito per poco ‖ *intr* sbagliare, fallire; mancare il bersaglio ‖ **Miss** *s* signorina, la signorina

missal ['mɪsəl] *s* messale *m*

misshapen [mɪs'/epən] *adj* deforme, malfatto

missile ['mɪsɪl] *adj* missilistico ‖ *s* missile *m*

mis'sile launch'er *s* lanciamissili *m*

missing ['mɪsɪŋ] *adj* mancante; assente; (*in action*) disperso

mis'sing link' *s* anello di congiunzione

miss'ing per'son *s* disperso

mission ['mɪ/ən] *s* missione

missionar·y ['mɪ/ən ˌeri] *adj* missionario ‖ *s* (-ies) (eccl) missionario; (dipl) incaricato in missione

missive ['mɪsɪv] *s* missiva

mis·spell [mɪs'spel] *v* (*pret & pp* **-spelled** or **-spelt** ['spelt]) *tr & intr* scrivere male

misspelling [mɪs'spelɪŋ] *s* errore *m* di ortografia

misspent [mɪs'spent] *adj* sprecato

misstatement [mɪs'stetmənt] *s* dichiarazione inesatta

misstep [mɪs'step] *s* passo falso

miss·y ['mɪsi] *s* (-ies) (coll) signorina

mist [mɪst] *s* caligine *f*, foschia; (*of tears*) velo; (*of smoke, vapors, etc.*) nuvola

mis·take [mɪs'tek] *s* errore *m*, sbaglio; **and no mistake** (coll) di sicuro; **by mistake** per sbaglio; **to make a mistake** sbagliarsi ‖ *v* (*pret* **-took** ['tʊk]; *pp* **-taken**) *tr* fraintendere; **to be mistaken for** essere preso per; **to mistake for** pigliare per

mistaken [mɪs'tekən] *adj* errato, sbagliato; **to be mistaken** essere in errore, sbagliarsi

mister ['mɪstər] *s* (mil, nav) signore *m*; (coll) marito ‖ *interj* (coll) signore!; (coll) Lei!; (coll) buonuomo! ‖ **Mister** *s* Signore *m*

mistletoe ['mɪsəl ˌto] *s* vischio

mistreat [mɪs'trit] *tr* maltrattare

mistreatment [mɪs'tritmənt] *s* maltrattamento

mistress ['mɪstrɪs] *s* (*of a household*) signora, padrona; (*paramour*) amante *f*, ganza; (Brit) maestra di scuola

mistrial [mɪs'traɪ·əl] *s* processo viziato da errore giudiziario

mistrust [mɪs'trʌst] *s* diffidenza ‖ *tr* diffidare di ‖ *intr* diffidarsi

mistrustful [mɪs'trʌstfəl] *adj* diffidente

mist·y ['mɪsti] *adj* (-ier; -iest) fosco, brumoso; (fig) vago, confuso

misunder·stand [ˌmɪsʌndər'stænd] *v* (*pret & pp* **-stood** ['stʊd]) *tr* fraintendere, equivocare

misunderstanding [ˌmɪsʌndər'stændɪŋ] *s* malinteso

misuse [mɪs'jus] *s* abuso; (*of funds*) malversazione ‖ [mɪs'juz] *tr* abusare di; (*funds*) malversare

misword [mɪs'wʌrd] *tr* comporre male

mite [maɪt] *s* obolo; (ent) acaro

miter ['maɪtər] *s* (carp) ugnatura; (carp) giunto a quartabuono; (eccl) mitra ‖ *tr* tagliare a quartabuono, ugnare; giungere a quartabuono

mi'ter box' *s* cassetta per ugnature

mi'ter joint' *s* giunto a quartabuono

mitigate ['mɪtɪ ˌget] *tr* mitigare

mitten ['mɪtən] *s* manopola, muffola

mix [mɪks] *tr* mescolare; (*colors*) mesticare; (*dough*) impastare; (*salad*) condire; **to mix up** confondere ‖ *intr* confondersi, mescolarsi

mixed [mɪkst] *adj* misto; (*candy*) assortito; (coll) confuso

mixed' com'pany *s* riunione *f* di ambo i sessi

mixed' drink' *s* miscela di liquori diversi

mixed' feel'ing *s* sentimento ambivalente

mixed' met'aphor *s* metafora incongruente

mixer ['mɪksər] *s* (mach) mescolatrice *f*; **to be a good mixer** essere socievole

mixture ['mɪkst/ər] *s* mistura, mescolanza; (aut) miscela, carburazione

mix'-up' *s* confusione; (coll) baruffa

mizzen ['mɪzən] *s* mezzana

moan [mon] *s* gemito ‖ *intr* gemere

moat [mot] *s* fosso, fossato

mob [mɑb] *s* turba ‖ *v* (*pret & pp* **mobbed**; *ger* **mobbing**) *tr* assaltare; affollarsi intorno a; (*a place*) affollare

mobile ['mobɪl] or ['mobil] *adj* mobile

mo'bile home' *s* caravan *m*, roulotte *f*

mobility [mo'bɪlɪti] *s* mobilità *f*

mobilization [ˌmobɪlɪ'ze/ən] *s* mobilitazione

mobilize ['mobɪ ˌlaɪz] *tr & intr* mobilitare

mob' rule' *s* legge *f* della teppa

mobster ['mɑbstər] *s* gangster *m*

moccasin ['mɑkəsɪn] *s* mocassino

Mo'cha cof'fee ['mokə] *s* caffè *m* moca

mock [mɑk] *adj* finto, imitato ‖ *s* dileggio, burla ‖ *tr* deridere, canzonare; ingannare ‖ *intr* motteggiare; **to mock at** farsi gioco di

mocker·y ['mɑkəri] *s* (-ies) dileggio, scherno; (*subject of derision*) zimbello; (*poor imitation*) contraffazione

mock'-hero'ic *adj* eroicomico

mockingbird ['mɑkɪŋ ˌbʌrd] *s* mimo

mock' or'ange *s* gelsomino selvatico

mock' tur'tle soup' *s* finto brodo di tartaruga

mock'-up' *s* modello dimostrativo

mode [mod] *s* modo, maniera; (*fashion*) moda; (gram) modo

mod·el ['mɑdəl] *adj* modello, e.g., **model student** studente modello ‖ *s* modello; (woman serving as subject for artists) modello f; (woman wearing clothes at fashion show) indossatrice f || v (pret & pp -eled or -elled; ger -eling or -elling) tr modellare || intr modellarsi; fare il manichino

mod'el air'plane s aeromodello

mo'del-air'plane build'er s aeromodellista mf

mod'eling clay' s plastilina

moderate ['mɑdərɪt] adj moderato || ['mɑdə,ret] tr moderare; (a meeting) presiedere a || intr moderarsi

moderator ['mɑdə,retər] s moderatore m; (mediator) arbitro; (phys) moderatore m

modern ['mɑdərn] adj moderno

modernize ['mɑdər,naɪz] tr modernizzare, rimodernare

modest ['mɑdɪst] adj modesto

modes•ty ['mɑdɪsti] s (-ties) modestia

modicum ['mɑdɪkəm] s piccola quantità

modi•fy ['mɑdɪ,faɪ] v (pret & pp -fied) tr modificare; (gram) determinare

modish ['mɑdɪʃ] adj alla moda

modulate ['mɑdʒə,let] tr & intr modulare

modulation [,mɑdʒə'leʃən] s modulazione

mohair ['mo,her] s mohair m

Mohammedan [mo'hæmɪdən] adj & s maomettano

Mohammedanism [mo'hæmɪdə,nɪzəm] s maomettismo

moist [mɔɪst] adj umido; lacrimoso

moisten ['mɔɪsən] tr inumidire || intr inumidirsi

moisture ['mɔɪstʃər] s umidità f

molar ['molər] s molare m

molasses [mə'læsɪz] s melassa

mold [mold] s stampo, forma; (fungus) muffa; humus m; (fig) indole f || tr plasmare, conformare; (to make moldy) fare ammuffire || intr ammuffire

molder ['moldər] s modellatore m || intr sgretolarsi; polverizzarsi

molding ['moldɪŋ] s modellato; (archit, carp) modanatura

mold•y ['moldi] adj (-ier; -iest) ammuffito

mole [mol] s (pier) molo; (harbor) darsena; (spot on skin) neo; (small mammal) talpa

molecule ['mɑlɪ,kjul] s molecola

mole'hill' s mucchio di terra sopra la tana di talpe

mole'skin' s pelle f di talpa; (fabric) fustagno di prima qualità

molest [mə'lest] tr molestare; fare proposte disoneste a

moll [mɑl] s (slang) ragazza della malavita; (slang) puttana

molli•fy ['mɑlɪ,faɪ] v (pret & pp -fied) tr pacificare, placare

mollusk ['mɑləsk] s mollusco

mollycoddle ['mɑlɪ,kɑdəl] s effeminato || tr viziare, coccolare

Mo'lotov cock'tail ['mɑlə,tɔf] s bottiglia Molotov

molt [molt] s muda || intr andare in muda

molten ['moltən] adj fuso

molybdenum [mə'lɪbdɪnəm] or [,mɑlɪb'dinəm] s molibdeno

moment ['momənt] s momento; **at any moment** da un momento all'altro

momentary ['momən,teri] adj momentaneo

momentous [mo'mentəs] adj grave, importante

momen•tum [mo'mentəm] s (-tums or -ta [tə]) slancio; (mech) momento

monarch ['mɑnərk] s monarca m

monarchic(al) [mə'nɑrkɪk(əl)] adj monarchico

monarchist ['mɑnərkɪst] adj & s monarchico

monar•chy ['mɑnərki] s (-chies) monarchia

monastic [mə'næstɪk] adj monastico, monacale

monasticism [mə'næstɪ,sɪzəm] s monachesimo

Monday ['mʌndi] s lunedì m

monetary ['mɑnɪ,teri] adj monetario; pecuniario

money ['mʌni] s denaro; **to be in the money** esser carico di soldi; **to make money** far quattrini

mon'ey-bag' s borsa per denaro; **moneybags** (coll) riccone sfondato

moneychanger ['mʌnɪ,tʃendʒər] s cambiavalute m

moneyed ['mʌnid] adj danaroso

moneylender ['mʌni,lendər] s prestatore m di denaro

mon'ey-mak'er s capitalista mf; affare vantaggioso

mon'ey or'der s vaglia m

Mongolian [mɑŋ'golɪ·ən] adj & s mongolo

mon•goose ['mɑŋgus] s (-gooses) mangusta

mongrel ['mʌŋgrəl] or ['mɑŋgrəl] adj ibrido || s ibrido; cane bastardo

monitor ['mɑnɪtər] s (educ) capoclasse mf; (rad, telv) monitore m || tr osservare; (a signal) controllare; (a broadcast) ascoltare

monk [mʌŋk] s monaco

monkey ['mʌŋki] s scimmia; **to make a monkey of** farsi gioco di || intr—**to monkey around** (coll) oziare; **to monkey around with** (coll) giocherellare con

mon'key-shines' spl (slang) monellerie fpl, pagliacciate fpl

mon'key wrench' s chiave f inglese

monkhood ['mʌŋkhud] s monacato

monkshood ['mʌŋks,hud] s (bot) aconito

monocle ['mɑnəkəl] s monocolo

monogamy [mə'nɑgəmi] s monogamia

monogram ['mɑnə,græm] s monogramma m

monograph ['mɑnə,græf] or ['mɑnə,grɑf] s monografia

monolithic [,mɑnə'lɪθɪk] adj monolitico

monologue ['monə,log] or ['monə-,lag] s monologo

monomania [,monə'menɪ-ə] s monomania

monomial [mə'nomɪ-əl] s monomio

monopolize [mə'napə,laɪz] tr monopolizzare, accaparrare

monopo·ly [mə'napəlɪ] s (-lies) monopolio, privativa

monorail ['monə,rel] s monorotaia

monosyllable ['monə,sɪləbəl] s monosillabo

monotheist ['monə,θi-ɪst] adj & s monoteista mf

monotonous [mə'natənəs] adj monotono

monotype ['monə,taɪp] s (method) monotipia; (typ) monotipo

monoxide [mə'naksaɪd] s monossido

monseigneur [,mansen'jœr] s monsignore m

monsignor [man'sinjər] s (-monsignors or monsignori [,monsi'njori]) (eccl) monsignore m

monsoon [man'sun] s monsone m

monster ['manstər] adj mostruoso || s mostro

monstrance ['manstrəns] s ostensorio

monstrosi·ty [man'strasɪtɪ] s (-ties) mostruosità f

monstrous ['manstrəs] adj mostruoso

month [mʌnθ] s mese m

month·ly ['mʌnθlɪ] adj mensile || s (-lies) rivista mensile; **monthlies** (coll) mestruazione || adv mensilmente

monument ['manjəmənt] s monumento

moo [mu] s muggito || intr muggire

mood [mud] s umore m, vena; (gram) modo; **moods** luna, malumore m

mood·y ['mudɪ] adj (-ier; -iest) triste, malinconico; lunatico, capriccioso

moon [mun] s luna; **once in a blue moon** ad ogni morte di papa || tr— **to moon away** (time) (coll) sprecare || intr—**to moon about** (coll) gingillarsi, baloccarsi; (to daydream about) (coll) sognarsi di

moon'beam' s raggio di luna

moon'light' s chiaro m di luna

moon'light'ing s secondo lavoro notturno

moon'shine' s chiaro di luna; (coll) chiacchiere fpl, balle fpl; (coll) whisky m distillato illegalmente

moon'shot' s lancio alla luna

moon'stone' s lunaria

moor [mur] s brughiera, landa || tr ormeggiare || intr ormeggiarsi || **Moor** s moro

Moorish ['murɪʃ] adj moresco

moor'land' s brughiera, landa

moose [mus] s (moose) alce americano

moot [mut] adj controverso, discutibile

mop [map] s scopa di filacce; (naut) redazza; (of hair) zazzera || v (pret & pp mopped; ger mopping) tr (a floor) pulire, asciugare; (one's brow) asciugarsi; **to mop up** rastrellare

mope [mop] intr andare rattristato

mopish ['mopɪʃ] adj triste, avvilito

moral ['marəl] or ['morəl] adj morale || s (of a fable) morale f; **morals** (ethics) morale f; (modes of conduct) costumi mpl

morale [mə'ræl] or [mə'ral] s morale m

morali·ty [mə'rælɪtɪ] s (-ties) moralità f

mor'als charge' s accusa di oltraggio al pudore

morass [mə'ræs] s palude f

moratori·um [,morə'torɪ-əm] or [,marə'torɪ-əm] s (-ums or -a [ə]) moratoria

morbid ['morbɪd] adj (gruesome) orribile; (feelings; curiosity; pertaining to disease; pathologic) morboso

mordacious [mor'deʃəs] adj mordace

mordant ['mordənt] adj & s mordente m

more [mor] adj & s più m || adv più; **more and more** sempre più; **more than** più di; (followed by verb) più di quanto; **the more . . . the less** tanto più . . . quanto meno

more·o'er adv per di più, inoltre

Moresque [mo'resk] adj moresco

morgue [morg] s deposito, obitorio; (journ) archivio di un giornale, frigorifero

moribund ['morɪ,bʌnd] or ['marɪ,bʌnd] adj moribondo

morning ['mornɪŋ] adj mattiniero || s mattina, mattino; **good morning** buon giorno; **in the morning** di mattina

morn'ing coat' s giacca nera a code

morn'ing-glo'ry s (-ries) convolvolo; (Ipomea) campanella; (Convolvulus tricolor) bella di giorno

morn'ing sick'ness s vomito di gravidanza

morn'ing star' s Lucifero, stella del mattino

Moroccan [mə'rakən] adj & s maroc- chino

morocco [mə'rako] s (leather) maroc- chino || **Morocco** s il Marocco

moron ['moran] s deficiente mf

morose [mə'ros] adj tetro, imbronciato

morphine ['morfin] s morfina

morphology [mor'falədʒɪ] s morfologia

morrow ['moro] or ['maro] s—**on the morrow** l'indomani, il giorno se- guente; domani

morsel ['morsəl] s boccone m, boccon- cino; pezzetto

mortal ['mortəl] adj & s mortale m

mortality [mor'tælɪtɪ] s mortalità f; (death or destruction on a large scale) moria

mortar ['mortər] s (mixture of lime or cement) malta, calcina; (bowl) mortaio; (mil) mortaio, lanciabombe m

mor'tar·board' s sparviere m; (cap) tocco accademico

mortgage ['morgɪdʒ] s ipoteca || tr ipotecare

mortgagee [,morgɪ'dʒi] s creditore m ipotecario

mortgagor ['morgɪdʒər] s debitore m ipotecario

mortician [mɔr'tɪʃən] s impresario di pompe funebri

morti-fy ['mɔrtɪ ,faɪ] v (pret & pp -fied) tr mortificare; **to be mortified** vergognarsi

mortise ['mɔrtɪs] s intaccatura, incastro || tr incassare, incastrare

mor'tise lock' s serratura incastrata

mortuar-y ['mɔrtʃʊ ,ɛri] adj mortuario || s (-ies) camera mortuaria

mosaic [mo'ze-ɪk] s mosaico

Moscow ['maskaʊ] or ['masko] s Mosca

Moses ['mozɪz] or ['mozɪs] s Mosè m

Mos-lem ['mɑzləm] or ['mɑsləm] adj musulmano || s (-lems or -lem) musulmano

mosque [mɑsk] s moschea

mosqui-to [məs'kito] s (-toes or -tos) zanzara

mosqui'to net' s zanzariera

moss [mɔs] or [mɑs] s musco

moss'back' s (coll) ultraconservatore m, fossile m

moss-y ['mɔsi] or ['mɑsi] adj (-ier; -iest) muscoso

most [most] adj il più di, la maggior parte di || s la maggioranza, i più; **most of** la maggior parte di; **to make the most of** trarre il massimo da || adv più, maggiormente, al massimo

mostly ['mostli] adv per lo più, maggiormente, al massimo

motel [mo'tɛl] s motel m, autostello

moth [mɔθ] or [mɑθ] s falena; (clothes moth) tarma

moth'ball' s pallina antitarmica

moth-eaten ['mɔθ ,itən] or ['mɑθ ,itən] adj tarmato; antiquato

mother ['mʌðər] adj (love, tongue) materno; (country) natio; (church, company) madre || s madre f; (elderly woman) (coll) zia || tr fare da madre a; creare; procreare; assumere la maternità di

moth'er coun'try s madrepatria

Moth'er Goose' s supposta autrice di una raccolta di favole infantili

motherhood ['mʌðər ,hʊd] s maternità f

moth'er-in-law' s (moth'ers-in-law') suocera

moth'er-land' s madrepatria

motherless ['mʌðərlɪs] adj orfano di madre, senza madre

mother-of-pearl ['mʌðərəv'pɑrl] adj madreperlaceo || s madreperla

motherly ['mʌðərli] adj materno

Moth'er's Day' s giorno della madre, festa della mamma

moth'er supe'rior s madre superiora

moth'er tongue' s madrelingua; (language from which another language is derived) lingua madre

moth'er wit' s intelligenza nativa

moth' hole' s tarlatura

moth-y ['mɔθi] or ['mɑθi] adj (-ier; -iest) tarmato

motif [mo'tif] s motivo

motion ['moʃən] s movimento; (e.g., of a dancer) movenza, mossa; (in parliamentary procedure) mozione; **in motion** in moto || intr fare cenno

motionless ['moʃənlɪs] adj immobile

mo'tion pic'ture s pellicola cinematografica; **motion pictures** cinematografia

mo'tion-picture' adj cinematografico

motivate ['moti ,vet] tr animare, incitare

motive ['motɪv] adj motivo; (producing motion) motore || s motivo; (incentive) movente m

mo'tive pow'er s forza motrice; impianto motore; (rr) insieme m di locomotive

motley ['mɑtli] adj eterogeneo; variato, variopinto

motor ['motər] adj motore; (operated by motor) motorizzato; (pertaining to motor vehicles) motoristico || s motore m; (aut) macchina || intr viaggiare in macchina

mo'tor-boat' s motobarca, motoscafo

mo'tor-bus' s torpedone m; autobus m

motorcade ['motər ,ked] s carovana di automobili

mo'tor-car' s automobile f

mo'tor-cy'le s motociclette

motorist ['motərɪst] s automobilista mf

motorize ['motə ,raɪz] tr motorizzare

mo'torman s (-men) guidatore m di tram; guidatore m di locomotive

mo'tor sail'er s motoveliero

mo'tor scoot'er s motoretta

mot'or ship' s motonave f

mo'tor truck' s autocarro, camion m

mo'tor ve'hicle s motoveicolo

mottle ['mɑtəl] tr chiazzare, screziare

mot-to ['mɑto] s (-toes or -tos) motto, divisa

mould [mold] s, tr, & intr var of **mold**

mound [maʊnd] s monticello, collinetta

mount [maʊnt] s monte m, montagna; (horse for riding) cavalcatura, monta; (setting for a jewel) montatura; supporto; (for a picture) incorniciatura || tr montare; (a wall) scalare; (theat) allestire || intr montare; (to climb) salire

mountain ['maʊntən] s montagna; **to make a mountain out of a molehill** fare di un bruscolo una trave, fare d'una mosca un elefante

moun'tain climb'ing s alpinismo

mountaineer [,maʊntə'nɪr] s montanaro

mountainous ['maʊntənəs] adj montagnoso

moun'tain rail'road s ferrovia a dentiera

moun'tain range' s catena di montagne

moun'tain sick'ness s mal m di montagna

mountebank ['maʊntɪ ,bæŋk] s ciarlatano

mounting ['maʊntɪŋ] s (act) il montare, montaggio; (setting) montatura; (mach) supporto

mourn [morn] tr (the loss of s.o.) piangere; (a misfortune) lamentare || intr piangere; vestire a lutto

mourner ['mornər] s persona in lutto; (penitent sinner) penitente mf;

(woman hired to attend a funeral or funerals) prefica

mourn′er′s bench′ *s* banco dei penitenti

mournful ['mɔrnfəl] *adj* luttuoso, funesto; *(gloomy)* lugubre

mourning ['mɔrnɪŋ] *s* lutto; **to be in mourning** portare il lutto

mourn′ing band′ *s* bracciale *m* a lutto

mouse [maʊs] *s* (**mice** [maɪs]) topo, sorcio

mouse′hole′ *s* topaia; piccolo buco

mouser ['maʊzər] *s* cacciatore *m* di topi

mouse′trap′ *s* trappola per topi

moustache [məs'tæʃ] *or* [məs'tɑʃ] *s* baffi *mpl*, mustacchi *mpl*

mouth [maʊθ] *s* (**mouths** [maʊðz]) bocca; **by mouth** per via orale; **to be born with a silver spoon in one's mouth** essere nato con la camicia; **to make one's mouth water** fare venire a qlcu l'acquolina in bocca

mouthful ['maʊθ͵fʊl] *s* boccata

mouth′ or′gan *s* armonica a bocca

mouth′piece′ *s* *(of wind instrument)* bocchetta; *(of bridle)* imboccatura; *(of megaphone)* boccaglio; *(of cigarette)* bocchino; *(of telephone)* imboccatura; *(spokesman)* portavoce *m*

mouth′wash′ *s* sciacquo, risciacquo

movable ['muvəbəl] *adj* mobile, movibile; *(law)* mobiliare

move [muv] *s* movimento; *(change of residence)* trasloco; *(step)* passo; *(e.g., in chess)* mossa; **on the move in** moto, in movimento; **to get a move on** (coll) affrettarsi ‖ *tr* muovere; *(the bowels)* provocare l'evacuazione di; *(to prompt)* spingere; *(to stir the feelings of)* emozionare, commuovere; *(law)* proporre; *(com)* svendere; **to move up** *(a date)* anticipare ‖ *intr* muoversi; passare; *(to another house)* traslocare; *(to another city)* trasferirsi; *(said of goods)* avere una vendita; *(said of the bowels)* evacuare; procedere; *(law)* presentare una mozione; *(coll)* andarsene; **to move away** andarsene; trasferirsi; **to move back** tirarsi indietro; **to move in** avanzare; *(society)* frequentare; **to move off** allontanarsi

movement ['muvmənt] *s* movimento; *(of a watch)* meccanismo; *(of the bowels)* evacuazione; *(mus)* movimento, tempo

movie ['muvi] *s* (coll) film *m*, pellicola

movie·goer ['muvi͵go·ər] *s* frequentatore *m* del cinema

mov′ie house′ *s* (coll) cinematografo

mov′ie·land′ *s* (coll) cinelandia

moving ['muvɪŋ] *adj* commovente, emozionante ‖ *s* trasporto; *(from one house to another)* trasloco

mov′ing pic′ture *s* film *m*, pellicola

mov′ing stair′case′ *s* scala mobile

mow [mo] *v* (*pret* **mowed**; *pp* **mowed** *or* **mown**) *tr & intr* falciare

mower ['mo·ər] *s* falciatore *m*; *(mach)* falciatrice *f*

Mr. ['mɪstər] *s* (**Messrs.** ['mesərz]) Signore *m*

Mrs. ['mɪsɪz] *s* Signora

much [mʌtʃ] *adj & pron* molto; **as much . . . as** tanto . . . quanto; **too much** troppo ‖ *adv* molto; **however much** per quanto; **how much** quanto; **too much** troppo; **very much** moltissimo

mucilage ['mjusɪlɪdʒ] *s* colla; *(gummy secretion in plants)* mucillagine *f*

muck [mʌk] *s* letame *m*; *(dirt)* sudiciume *m*; *(min)* materiale *m* di scoria

muck′rake′ *intr* (coll) sollevare scandali

mucous ['mjukəs] *adj* mucoso

mucus ['mjukəs] *s* muco

mud [mʌd] *s* fango, melma, limo; **to sling mud at** calunniare

muddle ['mʌdəl] *s* confusione, guazzabuglio ‖ *tr* confondere, intorbidire ‖ *intr*—**to muddle through** arrangiarsi; cavarsela alla meno peggio in

mud′dle·head′ *s* (coll) semplicione *m*

mud·dy ['mʌdi] *adj* (-**dier**; -**diest**) fangoso, melmoso; *(obscure)* torbido ‖ *v* (*pret & pp* -**died**) *tr* turbare, intorbidare; *(to soil with mud)* infangare

mud′guard′ *s* parafango

mud′hole′ *s* pozzanghera, fangaia

mud′ slide′ *s* smottamento

mudslinger ['mʌd͵slɪŋgər] *s* calunniatore *m*

muff [mʌf] *s* manicotto ‖ *tr* (coll) mancare; *(to handle badly)* (coll) abborracciare; *(sports)* mancare di pigliare

muffin ['mʌfɪn] *s* panino soffice

muffle ['mʌfəl] *tr* infagottare, imbacuccare; *(a sound)* velare, smorzare

muffler ['mʌflər] *s* sciarpa; *(aut)* silenziatore *m*, marmitta

mufti ['mʌfti] *s*—**in mufti** in borghese

mug [mʌg] *s* tazzona; *(slang)* muso, grugno ‖ *v* (*pret & pp* -**mugged**) *ger* **mugging**) *tr* (slang) fotografare; *(slang)* attaccare proditoriamente ‖ *intr* fare le smorfie

mug·gy ['mʌgi] *adj* (-**gier**; -**giest**) afoso, opprimente

mulat·to [mju'læto] *or* [mə'læto] *s* (-**toes**) mulatto

mulber·ry ['mʌl͵beri] *s* (-**ries**) *(tree)* gelso; *(fruit)* mora di gelso

mulct [mʌlkt] *tr* defraudare

mule [mjul] *s* mulo; *(slipper)* pianella

muleteer [͵mjulə'tɪr] *s* mulattiere *m*

mulish ['mjulɪʃ] *adj* testardo

mull [mʌl] *tr* (wine) scaldare aggiungendo spezie ‖ *intr*—**to mull over** pensarci sopra, rinvangare

mulled′ wine′ *s* vino caldo

mullion ['mʌljən] *s* colonnina che divide una bifora

multigraph ['mʌltɪ͵græf] *or* ['mʌltɪ͵grɑf] *s* (trademark) poligrafo ‖ *tr* poligrafare

multilateral [͵mʌltɪ'lætərəl] *adj* multilaterale

multimotor [͵mʌltɪ'motər] *s* plurimotore *m*

multiple ['mʌltɪpəl] *adj & s* multiplo

multiplici·ty [͵mʌltɪ'plɪsɪti] *s* (-**ties**) molteplicità *f*

multi·ply ['mʌltɪ͵plaɪ] *v* (*pret & pp* -**plied**) *tr* moltiplicare ‖ *intr* moltiplicarsi

multistage ['mʌltɪ ˌstedʒ] *adj* (rok) pluristadio

multitude ['mʌltɪ ˌtjud] *or* ['mʌltɪ ˌtud] *s* moltitudine *f*

mum [mʌm] *adj* zitto; **mum's the word!** acqua in bocca!; **to keep mum** stare zitto || *interj* zitto!

mumble ['mʌmbəl] *tr* biascicare || *intr* farfugliare

mummer·y ['mʌməri] *s* (-ies) buffonata, mascherata

mum·my ['mʌmi] *s* (-mies) mummia

mumps [mʌmps] *s* orecchioni *mpl*

munch [mʌntʃ] *tr* sgranocchiare

mundane ['mʌnden] *adj* mondano

municipal [mju'nɪsɪpəl] *adj* municipale

municipal·ity [mju ˌnɪsɪ'pælɪti] *s* (-ties) municipio

munificent [mju'nɪfɪsənt] *adj* munifico

munition [mju'nɪʃən] *s* munizione || *tr* fornire di munizioni

muni'tion dump' *s* deposito munizioni

mural ['mjurəl] *adj* murale || *s* pittura murale

murder ['mʌrdər] *s* omicidio || *tr* assassinare

murderer ['mʌrdərər] *s* omicida *m*

murderess ['mʌrdərɪs] *s* omicida *f*

murderous ['mʌrdərəs] *adj* omicida, crudele, sanguinario

murk·y ['mʌrki] *adj* (-ier; -iest) fosco, tenebroso; brumoso, nebbioso

murmur ['mʌrmər] *s* mormorio || *tr & intr* mormorare

Mur'phy bed' ['mʌrfi] *s* letto a scomparsa

muscle ['mʌsəl] *s* muscolo

muscular ['mʌskjələr] *adj* muscolare; (*having well-developed muscles*) muscoloso

muse [mjuz] *s* musa; **the Muses** le Muse || *intr* meditare, rimuginare

museum [mju'zi·əm] *s* museo

mush [mʌʃ] *s* pappa, polentina; (fig) leziosaggine *f*, sdolcinatura

mush'room *s* fungo || *intr* venir su come i funghi; **to mushroom into** diventare rapidamente

mush'room cloud' *s* fungo atomico

mush·y ['mʌʃi] *adj* (-ier; -iest) polposo, spappolato; (fig) sdolcinato, sentimentale

music ['mjuzɪk] *s* musica; **to face the music** (coll) affrontare le conseguenze; **to set to music** mettere in musica

musical ['mjuzɪkəl] *adj* musicale

mu'sical com'edy *s* operetta, commedia musicale

musicale [ˌmjuzɪ'kæl] *s* serata musicale

mu'sic box' *s* scatola armonica

mu'sic cab'inet *s* scaffaletto per la musica

mu'sic hall' *s* salone *m* da concerti; (Brit) teatro di varietà, music-hall *m*

musician [mju'zɪʃən] *s* musicista *mf*

musicianship [mju'zɪʃən ˌʃɪp] *s* abilità *f* musicale, virtuosismo

musicologist [ˌmjuzɪ'kɑlədʒɪst] *s* musicologo

musicology [ˌmjuzɪ'kɑlədʒi] *s* musicologia

mu'sic stand' *s* portamusica *m*

musk [mʌsk] *s* muschio

musk' deer' *s* mosco

musket ['mʌskɪt] *s* moschetto

musketeer [ˌmʌskɪ'tɪr] *s* moschettiere *m*

musk'mel'on *s* melone *m*

musk' ox' *s* bue muschiato

musk'rat' *s* ondatra, topo muschiato

muslin ['mʌzlɪn] *s* mussolina

muss [mʌs] *tr* (*the hair*) scompigliare, arruffare; (*clothing*) (coll) sciupare

mussel ['mʌsəl] *s* mussolo

Mussulman ['mʌsəlmən] *adj & s* musulmano

muss·y ['mʌsi] *adj* (-ier; -iest) (coll) arruffato, scompigliato

must [mʌst] *s* (*new wine*) mosto; (*mold*) muffa; (coll) cosa assolutamente indispensabile || *v aux*—**I must go now** devo andarmene ora; **it must be Ann** deve essere Anna; **she must be ill** dev'essere malata; **they must have known it** devono averlo saputo

mustache [məs'tæʃ], [məs'tɑʃ] *or* ['mʌstæʃ] *s* baffi *mpl*, mustacchi *mpl*

mustard ['mʌstərd] *s* mostarda

mus'tard plas'ter *s* senapismo

muster ['mʌstər] *s* adunata, rivista; **to pass muster** passar ispezione || *tr* chiamare a raccolta; riunire; **to muster in** arruolare; **to muster out** congedare; **to muster up courage** prendere coraggio a quattro mani

mus'ter roll' *s* ruolo; (naut) appello

mus·ty ['mʌsti] *adj* (-ier; -iest) (*moldy*) ammuffito; (*stale*) stantio; (fig) ammuffito, stantio

mutation [mju'teʃən] *s* mutazione

mute [mjut] *adj & s* muto || *tr* mettere la sordina a

mutilate ['mjutɪ ˌlet] *tr* mutilare

mutineer [ˌmjutɪ'nɪr] *s* ammutinato

mutinous ['mjutɪnəs] *adj* ammutinato

muti·ny ['mjutɪni] *s* (-nies) ammutinamento || *v* (*pret & pp* -nied) *intr* ammutinarsi

mutt [mʌt] *s* (slang) cane bastardo; (slang) scemo

mutter ['mʌtər] *tr & intr* borbottare

mutton ['mʌtən] *s* montone *m*

mut'ton chop' *s* cotoletta di montone

mutual ['mutʃu·əl] *adj* mutuo, vicendevole

mu'tual aid' *s* mutualità *f*

mu'tual fund' *s* fondo comune di investimento

muzzle ['mʌzəl] *s* (*of animal*) muso; (*device to keep animal from biting*) museruola; (*of firearm*) bocca || *tr* mettere la museruola a; (fig) imbavagliare

my [maɪ] *adj poss* mio, il mio || *interj* (coll) corbezzoli!

myriad ['mɪrɪ·əd] *s* miriade *f*

myrrh [mʌr] *s* mirra

myrtle ['mʌrtəl] *s* mirto, mortella

myself [maɪ'sɛlf] *pron pers* io stesso; me, me stesso; mi, e.g., **I hurt myself** mi sono fatto male

mysterious [mɪsˈtɪrɪ·əs] *adj* misterioso
myster·y [ˈmɪstəri] *s* (-ies) mistero
mystic [ˈmɪstɪk] *adj & s* mistico
mystical [ˈmɪstɪkəl] *adj* mistico
mysticism [ˈmɪstɪˌsɪzəm] *s* misticismo
mystification [ˌmɪstɪfɪˈkeʃən] *s* mistificazione
mysti·fy [ˈmɪstɪˌfaɪ] *v* (*pret & pp* -fied) *tr* avvolgere nel mistero; (*to hoax*) mistificare
myth [mɪθ] *s* mito
mythical [ˈmɪθɪkəl] *adj* mitico
mythological [ˌmɪθəˈlɑdʒɪkəl] *adj* mitologico
mytholo·gy [mɪˈθɑlədʒɪ] *s* (-gies) mitologia

N

N, n [ɛn] *s* quattordicesima lettera dell'alfabeto inglese
nab [næb] *v* (*pret & pp* nabbed; *ger* nabbing) *tr* (slang) afferrare, agguantare
nag [næg] *s* ronzino ǁ *v* (*pret & pp* nagged; *ger* nagging) *tr & intr* tormentare, infastidire
naiad [ˈne·æd] or [ˈnaɪ·æd] *s* naiade *f*
nail [nel] *s* (*of finger or toe*) unghia; (*of metal*) chiodo; **to hit the nail on the head** cogliere nel giusto ǁ *tr* inchiodare
nail'brush' spazzolino per le unghie
nail' file' *s* lima per le unghie
nail' pol'ish *s* smalto per le unghie
nail' set' *s* punzone *m*
naïve [nɑˈiv] *adj* candido, ingenuo
naked [ˈnekɪd] *adj* nudo, ignudo; **to strip naked** denudare; denudarsi; **with the naked eye** a occhio nudo
name [nem] *s* nome *m*; (*first name*) nome *m*; (*last name*) cognome *m*; fama, reputazione; titolo; lignaggio; **in the name of** nel nome di; **to call s.o. names** coprire qlco di ingiurie; **to go by the name of** essere conosciuto sotto il nome di; **to make a name for oneself** farsi un nome; **what is your name?** come si chiama Lei? ǁ *tr* nominare; menzionare; battezzare; (*a price*) fissare
name' day' *s* onomastico
nameless [ˈnemlɪs] *adj* senza nome, anonimo
namely [ˈnemli] *adv* cioè, vale a dire
name'plate' *s* targa, targhetta
namesake [ˈnem‚sek] *s* omonimo; persona chiamata in onore di qualcun altro
nan'ny goat' [ˈnæni] *s* capra
nap [næp] *s* lanugine *f*; (*pile*) pelo; pisolino, sonnellino; **to take a nap** schiacciare un sonnellino ǁ *v* (*pret & pp* napped; *ger* napping) *intr* sonnecchiare; **to catch napping** cogliere alla sprovvista
napalm [ˈnepɑm] *s* napalm *m*
nape [nep] *s* nuca
naphtha [ˈnæfθə] *s* nafta
napkin [ˈnæpkɪn] *s* tovagliolo
nap'kin ring' *s* portatovagliolo
Naples [ˈnepləz] *s* Napoli *f*
Napoleonic [nəˌpoliˈɑnɪk] *adj* napoleonico
narcissus [nɑrˈsɪsəs] *s* narciso
narcotic [nɑrˈkɑtɪk] *adj & s* narcotico
narrate [næˈret] *tr* narrare

narration [næˈreʃən] *s* narrazione
narrative [ˈnærətɪv] *adj* narrativo ǁ *s* narrazione; (*genre*) narrativa
narrator [næˈretər] *s* narratore *m*
narrow [ˈnæro] *adj* stretto; limitato; (*illiberal*) meschino, ristretto ǁ **narrows** *spl* stretti *mpl* ǁ *tr* limitare, restringere ǁ *intr* limitarsi, restringersi
nar'row escape' *s*—**to have a narrow escape** scamparla bella
nar'row-gauge' *adj* a scartamento ridotto
narrow-minded [ˈnæroˈmaɪndɪd] *adj* gretto, ristretto d'idee
nasal [ˈnezal] *adj & s* nasale *f*
nasturtium [nəˈstʌrʃəm] *s* nasturzio
nas·ty [ˈnæsti] or [ˈnɑsti] *adj* (-tier; -tiest) brutto, cattivo; sgradevole, orribile; sudicio; (*foul*) perfido
natatorium [ˌnetəˈtorɪ·əm] *s* piscina
nation [ˈneʃən] *s* nazione
national [ˈnæʃənəl] *adj & s* nazionale *mf*
na'tional an'them *s* inno nazionale
na'tional debt' *s* debito pubblico
na'tional hol'iday *s* festa nazionale
nationalism [ˈnæʃənˌælɪti] *s* nazionalismo
nationali·ty [ˌnæʃənˈælɪti] *s* (-ties) nazionalità *f*
nationalize [ˈnæʃənəˌlaɪz] *tr* nazionalizzare
na'tion-wide' *adj* su scala nazionale
native [ˈnetɪv] *adj* nativo, indigeno, oriundo; (*language*) materno ǁ *s* indigeno, nativo
na'tive land' *s* patria, paese natio
nativi·ty [nəˈtɪvɪti] *s* (-ties) nascita, natività *f* ǁ **Nativity** *s* Natività *f*
Nato [ˈneto] *s* (acronym) (**North Atlantic Treaty Organization**) la N.A.T.O.
nat·ty [ˈnæti] *adj* (-tier; -tiest) accurato, elegante
natural [ˈnætʃərəl] *adj* naturale ǁ *s* imbecille *mf*; (mus) bequadro; (mus) tono naturale; (mus) tasto bianco; **a natural** (coll) proprio quello che ci vuole
naturalism [ˈnætʃərəˌlɪzəm] *s* naturalismo
naturalist [ˈnætʃərəlɪst] *s* naturalista *mf*
naturalization [ˌnætʃərəlɪˈzeʃən] *s* naturalizzazione
nat'uraliza'tion pa'pers *spl* documenti *mpl* di naturalizzazione

naturalize ['næt/ərə,laız] *tr* naturalizzare

naturally ['næt/ərəli] *adv* naturalmente

nature ['net/ər] *s* natura; **from nature** dal vero

naught [nɔt] *s* niente *m;* zero; **to come to naught** ridursi al nulla; **to set at naught** disprezzare

naugh·ty ['nɔti] *adj* (**-tier; -tiest**) cattivo, disubbidiente; (*joke*) di cattivo genere

nausea ['nɔ∫ɪ·ə] *or* ['nɔsɪ·ə] *s* nausea

nauseate ['nɔ∫ɪ,et] *or* ['nɔsɪ,et] *tr* nauseare ‖ *intr* essere nauseato

nauseating ['nɔ∫ɪ,etɪŋ] *or* ['nɔsɪ,etɪŋ] *adj* nauseabondo, stomachevole

nauseous ['nɔ∫ɪ·əs] *or* ['nɔsɪ·əs] *adj* nauseabondo

nautical ['nɔtɪkəl] *adj* nautico, marittimo, marino

naval ['nevəl] *adj* navale

na'val acad'emy *s* accademia navale

na'val of'ficer *s* ufficiale *m* di marina

na'val sta'tion *s* base *f* navale

nave [nev] *s* navata centrale; (*of a wheel*) mozzo

navel ['nevəl] *s* ombelico

na'vel or'ange *s* arancia (con depressione alla sommità)

navigability [,nævɪgə'bɪlɪti] *s* navigabilità *f;* (*of a ship*) manovrabilità *f*

navigable ['nævɪgəbəl] *adj* (*river*) navigabile; (*ship*) manovrabile

navigate ['nævɪ,get] *tr & intr* navigare

navigation [,nævɪ'ge∫ən] *s* navigazione

navigator ['nævɪ,getər] *s* navigatore *m;* (*in charge of navigating ship or plane*) ufficiale *m* di rotta

na·vy ['nevi] *adj* blu marino ‖ *s* (**-vies**) marina (da guerra)

na'vy bean' *s* fagiolo secco

na'vy blue' *s* blu marino

na'vy yard' *s* arsenale *m*

nay [ne] *s* no; voto negativo ‖ *adv* no; anzi

Nazarene [,næzə'rin] *adj & s* nazzareno; **the Nazarene** il Nazzareno

Nazi ['nɑtsi] *or* ['nætsi] *adj & s* nazista *mf*

N-bomb ['ɛn,bɑm] *s* bomba al neutrone

Neapolitan [,ni·ə'pɑlɪtən] *adj & s* napoletano

neap' tide' [nip] *s* marea di quadratura

near [nɪr] *adj* vicino, prossimo; intimo; esatto ‖ *adv* vicino, da vicino ‖ *prep* vicino a, accanto a; **to come near** avvicinarsi a ‖ *tr* avvicinarsi a ‖ *intr* avvicinarsi

nearby ['nɪr,baɪ] *adj* vicino ‖ *adv* vicino, qui vicino

Near' East' *s* Medio Oriente

nearly ['nɪrli] *adv* quasi; (*a little more or less*) press'a poco; per poco non, e.g., **he nearly died** per poco non morì

near-sighted ['nɪr'saɪtɪd] *adj* miope

near'-sight'ed·ness *s* miopia

neat [nit] *adj* netto, pulito; elegante, accurato; puro

neat's'-foot oil' *s* olio di piede di bue

Nebuchadnezzar [,nɛbjəkəd'nɛzər] *s* Nabucodonosor *m*

nebu·la ['nɛbjələ] *s* (**-lae** [,li] *or* **-las**) nebulosa

nebular ['nɛbjələr] *adj* nebulare

nebulous ['nɛbjələs] *adj* nebuloso

necessary ['nɛsɪ,sɛri] *adj* necessario

necessitate [nɪ'sɛsɪ,tet] *tr* necessitare, esigere

necessitous [nɪ'sɛsɪtəs] *adj* bisognoso

necessi·ty [nɪ'sɛsɪti] *s* (**-ties**) necessità *f*

neck [nɛk] *s* collo; (*of a horse*) incollatura; (*of violin*) manico; (*of mountain*) gola, passo; **neck and neck** testa a testa; **to stick one's neck out** (coll) esporsi al pericolo; **to win by a neck** vincere per una corta testa ‖ *intr* (slang) abbracciarsi, sbaciucchiarsi

neck'band' *s* colletto

neckerchief ['nɛkər,t∫ɪf] *s* fazzoletto da collo

necklace ['nɛklɪs] *s* collana

neck'line' *s* giro collo, scollatura

necktie ['nɛk,taɪ] *s* cravatta

neck'tie pin' *s* spilla da cravatta

necrolo·gy [nɛ'krɑlədʒi] *s* (**-gies**) necrologia

necromancy ['nɛkrə,mænsi] *s* necromanzia

nectar ['nɛktər] *s* nettare *m*

née *or* **nee** [ne] *adj* nata

need [nid] *s* necessità *f,* bisogno; povertà *f;* **if need be** se ci fosse bisogno; **in need** in strettezze ‖ *tr* aver bisogno di ‖ *intr* necessitare, essere in necessità ‖ *v aux*—**to need (to) +** *inf* dovere + *inf*

needful ['nidfəl] *adj* necessario

needle ['nidəl] *s* ago; (*of phonograph*) puntina; **to look for a needle in a haystack** cercare l'ago nel pagliaio ‖ *tr* cucire; (fig) aguzzare, eccitare

nee'dle bath' *s* bagno a doccia filiforme

nee'dle·case' *s* agoraio

nee'dle·point' *s* merletto; ricamo su canovaccio

needless ['nidlɪs] *adj* inutile

nee'dle·work' *s* lavoro di cucito; (*embroidery*) ricamo; (*needlepoint*) merletto

needs [nidz] *adv* necessariamente; **it must needs be** dev'essere proprio così

need·y ['nidi] *adj* (**-ier; -iest**) bisognoso, indigente ‖ **the needy** i bisognosi

ne'er-do-well ['nɛrdu,wɛl] *adj & s* buono a nulla

negate ['nɛget] *or* [nɪ'get] *tr* invalidare; negare

negation [nɪ'ge∫ən] *s* negazione

negative ['nɛgətɪv] *adj* negativo ‖ *s* negativa; (elec) polo negativo; (gram) negazione ‖ *tr* respingere, votare contro; neutralizzare

neglect [nɪ'glɛkt] *s* negligenza, trascuratezza ‖ *tr* trascurare; **to neglect to** trascurare di; dimenticarsi di

neglectful [nɪ'glɛktfəl] *adj* negligente, trascurato

négligée *or* **negligee** [,nɛglɪ'ʒe] *s* vesto *f* da camera *or* vestaglia per signora

negligence ['nɛglɪdʒəns] *s* negligenza, trascuratezza

negligent [ˈnɛɡlɪdʒənt] *adj* negligente, trascurato

negligible [ˈnɛɡlɪdʒɪbəl] *adj* trascurabile, insignificante

negotiable [nɪˈgoʊ/ɪ·əbəl] *adj* negoziabile; (*security*) al portatore; (*road*) transitabile

negotiate [nɪˈgoʊ/ɪ‚et] *tr* negoziare; (*to overcome*) superare ‖ *intr* negoziare

negotiation [nɪ‚goʊ/ɪˈeʃən] *s* negoziazione, negoziato

Ne·gro [ˈnigro] *adj* negro ‖ *s* (**-groes**) negro, nero

neigh [ne] *s* nitrito ‖ *intr* nitrire

neighbor [ˈnebər] *adj* vicino, adiacente ‖ *s* vicino; (*fellow man*) prossimo ‖ *tr* essere vicino a ‖ *intr* essere vicino

neighborhood [ˈnebər‚hʊd] *s* vicinanza, vicinato; **in the neighborhood of** nei pressi di; (coll) a un dipresso, all'incirca

neighboring [ˈnebərɪŋ] *adj* vicino, attiguo; (*country*) limitrofo

neighborly [ˈnebərli] *adj* da buon vicino, socievole

neither [ˈniðər] or [ˈnaɪðər] *adj indef* nessuno dei due, e.g., **neither boy** nessuno dei due ragazzi ‖ *pron indef* nessuno dei due, nè l'uno nè l'altro ‖ *conj* neppure, nemmeno, e.g., **neither do I** nemmeno io; **neither . . . nor** nè . . . nè

neme·sis [ˈnɛmɪsɪs] *s* (**-ses** [‚siz]) nemesi *f* ‖ **Nemesis** *s* Nemesi *f*

neologism [niˈɑlə‚dʒɪzəm] *s* neologismo

neomycin [‚ni·əˈmaɪsɪn] *s* neomicina

ne'on lamp' [ˈni·ɑn] *s* lampada al neon

neophyte [ˈni·ə‚faɪt] *s* neofita *mf*

nepenthe [nɪˈpɛnθi] *s* nepente *f*

nephew [ˈnɛfju] or [ˈnɛvju] *s* nipote *m*

Nepos [ˈnipəs] or [ˈnɛpəs] *s* Nipote *m*

Neptune [ˈnɛpt/un] or [ˈnɛptjun] *s* Nettuno

neptunium [nɛpˈt/uni·əm] or [nɛpˈtjuni·əm] *s* (chem) nettunio

Nero [ˈnɪro] *s* Nerone *m*

nerve [nʌrv] *adj* nervoso ‖ *s* nervo; (*courage*) coraggio; (*boldness*) (coll) faccia tosta; **to get on one's nerves** dare ai nervi di qlcu; **to lose one's nerve** perdere le staffe

nerve'-racking [ˈnʌrv‚rækɪŋ] *adj* irritante, esasperante

nervous [ˈnʌrvəs] *adj* nervoso

nerv'ous break'down *s* esaurimento nervoso

nervousness [ˈnʌrvəsnɪs] *s* nervosismo

nerv·y [ˈnʌrvi] *adj* (**-ier; -iest**) (*strong*) forte, vigoroso; audace; (coll) insolente, sfacciato

nest [nɛst] *s* nido; (*of hen*) cova; (*retreat*) rifugio; (*hangout*) tana; (*brood*) nidiata; **to feather one's nest** farsi il gruzzolo ‖ *tr* (e.g., *tables*) mettere l'uno nell'altro ‖ *intr* nidificare

nest' egg' *s* endice *m*; (fig) gruzzolo

nestle [ˈnɛsəl] *tr* annidare ‖ *intr* annidarsi, nidificare; (*to cuddle up*) rannicchiarsi

net [nɛt] *adj* netto ‖ *s* rete *f*; (*snare*) laccio, trappola; guadagno netto ‖

tr prendere con la rete; (*a sum of money*) fare un guadagno netto di

nether [ˈnɛðər] *adj* inferiore, infero

Netherlander [ˈnɛðər‚lændər] or [ˈnɛðˈərləndər] *s* olandese *mf*

Netherlands, The [ˈnɛðərləndz] *spl* i Paesi Bassi

netting [ˈnɛtɪŋ] *s* rete *f*

nettle [ˈnɛtəl] *s* ortica ‖ *tr* irritare, provocare

net'work' *s* rete *f*

neuralgia [njuˈrældʒə] or [nuˈrældʒə] *s* nevralgia

neurology [njuˈrɑlədʒi] or [nuˈrɑlədʒi] *s* neurologia

neuro·sis [njuˈrosɪs] or [nuˈrosɪs] (**-ses** [siz]) *s* neurosi *f*

neurotic [njuˈrɑtɪk] or [nuˈrɑtɪk] *adj* & *s* neurotico

neuter [ˈnjutər] or [ˈnutər] *adj* neutro ‖ *s* genere neutro

neutral [ˈnjutrəl] or [ˈnutrəl] *adj* neutro; (*not aligned*) neutrale ‖ *s* neutrale *m*; (mach) folle *m*

neutralist [ˈnjutrəlɪst] or [ˈnutrəlɪst] *adj* & *s* neutralista *mf*

neutrality [njuˈtrælɪti] or [nuˈtrælɪti] *s* neutralità *f*

neutralize [ˈnjutrə‚laɪz] or [ˈnutrə‚laɪz] *tr* neutralizzare

neutron [ˈnjutrɑn] or [ˈnutrɑn] *s* neutrone *m*

neu'tron bomb' *s* bomba al neutrone

never [ˈnɛvər] *adv* mai, giammai; non . . . mai; **never mind** non importa

nev'er·more' *adv* mai più

nevertheless [‚nɛvərðəˈlɛs] *adv* ciò nonostante, ciò nondimeno, tuttavia

new [nju] or [nu] *adj* nuovo; **what's new?** che c'è di nuovo?

new' arri'val *s* nuovo venuto; (*baby*) neonato

new'born' *adj* neonato; (e.g., *faith*) rinato

New'cas'tle *s*—**to carry coals to Newcastle** portare l'acqua al mare, portare vasi a Samo

newcomer [ˈnju‚kʌmər] or [ˈnu‚kʌmər] *s* nuovo venuto

New' Eng'land *s* la Nuova Inghilterra

newfangled [ˈnju‚fæŋgəld] or [ˈnu‚fæŋgəld] *adj* all'ultima moda; di nuovo conio, di nuova invenzione

Newfoundland [ˈnjufənd‚lænd] or [ˈnufənd‚lænd] *s* la Terranova ‖ [njuˈfaʊndlənd] or [nuˈfaʊndlənd] *s* (*dog*) terranova *m*

newly [ˈnjuli] or [ˈnuli] *adv* di recente, di fresco

new'ly·wed' *s* sposino or sposina; **the newlyweds** gli sposi

new' moon' *s* luna nuova, novilunio

news [njuz] or [nuz] *s* notizie *fpl*; **a news item** una notizia; **a piece of news** una notizia

news' a'gency *s* agenzia d'informazioni

news'beat' *s* colpo giornalistico

news'boy' *s* strillone *m*

news'cast' *s* notiziario

news'cast'er *s* annunziatore *m*, radiocommentatore *m*, telecommentatore *m*

news' con'ference *s* conferenza stampa

news' cov'erage s reportaggio

news'deal'er s venditore m di giornali

news'man' s (-men') (*reporter*) giornalista m; giornalaio

newsmonger ['njuz,mʌŋgər] or ['nuz,mʌŋgər] s persona pettegola, gazzettino

news'pa'per adj giornalistico ‖ s giornale m

news'pa'per·man' s (-men') giornalista m

news'print' s carta da giornale

news'reel' s cinegiornale m

news'stand' s chiosco, edicola

news'week'ly s (-lies) settimanale m d'informazione

news'wor'thy adj degno d'essere pubblicato, di viva attualità

news·y ['njuzi] or ['nuzi] adj (-ier; -iest) (coll) informativo

New' Tes'tament s Nuovo Testamento

New' Year's' card' s cartolina d'auguri di capodanno

New' Year's' Day' s il capo d'anno, il capodanno

New' Year's' Eve' s la vigilia di capodanno, la sera di San Silvestro

New' York' [jɔrk] adj nuovayorchese ‖ s New York f, Nuova York

New' York'er ['jɔrkər] s nuovayorchese mf

New' Zea'land ['zilənd] adj neozelandese ‖ s la Nuova Zelanda

New' Zea'lander ['ziləndər] s neozelandese mf

next [nekst] adj prossimo, seguente; (*month*) prossimo, entrante ‖ adv la prossima volta; dopo, in seguito; **next to** vicino a; **next to nothing** quasi nulla; **to come next** essere il prossimo

next'-door' adj della casa vicina ‖ **next'-door'** adv nella casa vicina

next' of kin' s (**next' of kin'**) parente più prossimo

niacin ['naɪ·əsɪn] s niacina

Niag'ara Falls' [naɪ'ægərə] spl le Cascate del Niagara

nib [nɪb] s becco; punta; **his nibs** (slang & pej) sua eccellenza

nibble ['nɪbəl] s piccolo morso ‖ tr & intr mordicchiare, sbocconcellare; (*said of a fish*) abboccare

nice [naɪs] adj (*pleasant*) simpatico, gentile; (*requiring skill*) buono, bello; (*fine*) sottile; (*refined*) raffinato, per bene; (*fussy*) esigente, difficile; rispettabile; (*weather*) bello; (*attractive*) bello; **nice . . . and** (coll) bello, e.g., **it is nice and warm** fa un bel caldo

nice-looking ['naɪs'lʊkɪŋ] adj bello, attraente

nicely ['naɪsli] adv precisamente, esattamente; (coll) benissimo

nice·ty ['naɪsəti] s (-ties) esattezza, precisione; **to a nicety** con la massima precisione

niche [nɪtʃ] s nicchia

Nicholas ['nɪkələs] s Nicola m

nick [nɪk] s intaccatura; (*of a dish*) slabbratura; **in the nick of time** al

momento giusto ‖ tr intaccare; (*to cut*) tagliare; (*a dish*) slabbrare

nickel ['nɪkəl] s nichel m; moneta americana di cinque cents ‖ tr nichelare

nick'el plate' s nichelatura

nick'el-plate' tr nichelare

nicknack ['nɪk,næk] s soprammobile m; gingillo, ninnolo

nick'name' s nomignolo, soprannome m ‖ tr soprannominare

nicotine ['nɪkə,tin] s nicotina

niece [nis] s nipote f

nif·ty ['nɪfti] adj (-tier; -tiest) (coll) elegante; (coll) eccellente

niggard ['nɪgərd] adj & s spilorcio

night [naɪt] adj notturno ‖ s notte f; **at or by night** di notte; **the night before last** l'altra notte; **to make a night of it** (coll) fare le ore piccole

night'cap' s berretto da notte; bicchierino di liquore che si beve prima di coricarsi

night' club' s night-club m

night' driv'ing s il guidare di notte

night'fall' s crepuscolo; **at nightfall** sul cader della notte, all'imbrunire

night'gown' s camicia da notte

nightingale ['naɪtən,gel] s usignolo

night' latch' s serratura a molla

night' let'ter s telegramma notturno

night'long' adj di tutta la notte ‖ adv tutta la notte

nightly ['naɪtli] adj di notte; di ogni notte ‖ adv di notte; ogni notte

night'mare' s incubo

nightmarish ['naɪt,merɪʃ] adj raccapricciante

night' owl' s (coll) nottambulo

night' school' s scuola serale

night'shirt' s camicia da notte

night'time' s notte f

night'walk'er s nottambulo; vagabondo notturno; (*prostitute*) passeggiatrice f

night' watch' s guardia notturna

night' watch'man s (-men) guardiano notturno

nihilist ['naɪ·ɪlɪst] s nichilista mf

nil [nɪl] s nulla m, niente m

Nile [naɪl] s Nilo

nimble ['nɪmbəl] adj agile, svelto

Nimrod ['nɪmrɑd] s Nembrod m

nincompoop ['nɪnkəm,pup] s babbeo, tonto, semplicione m

nine [naɪn] adj & pron nove ‖ s nove m; **nine o' clock** le nove

nine' hun'dred adj, s & pron novecento

nineteen ['naɪn'tin] adj, s & pron diciannove m

nineteenth ['naɪn'tinθ] adj & s diciannovesimo; (*century*) decimonono ‖ s (*in dates*) diciannove m ‖ pron diciannovesimo

ninetieth ['naɪntɪ·ɪθ] adj, s & pron novantesimo

nine·ty ['naɪnti] adj & pron novanta ‖ s (-ties) novanta m; **the gay nineties** il decennio scapestrato dal 1890 al 1900

ninth [naɪnθ] adj, s & pron nono ‖ s (*in dates*) nove m

nip [nɪp] s morso, pizzicotto; freddo pungente; (*of liquor*) bicchierino,

sorso; **nip and tuck** testa a testa ‖ *v*
(*pret & pp* **nipped; *ger* nipping**) *tr*
pizzicare, mordere; (*to squeeze*) spremere; (*to freeze*) gelare; (*liquor*) sorseggiare; **to nip in the bud** arrestare
di bel principio ‖ *intr* bere a sorsi
nipple ['nɪpəl] *s* capezzolo; (*of rubber*)
tettarella; (*mach*) corto tubo filettato a entrambe le estremità, manicotto, cappuccio
Nippon [nɪ'pɑn] or ['nɪpɑn] *s* il Giappone
Nippon·ese [ˌnɪpə'niz] *adj* nipponico
‖ *s* (**-ese**) Giapponese *mf*
nip·py ['nɪpɪ] *adj* (**-pier; -piest**) mordente, pizzicante; gelato
nirvana [nɪr'vɑnə] *s* il nirvana
nit [nɪt] *s* lendine *m;* pidocchio
niter ['naɪtər] *s* nitro
nit'-pick' *intr* (coll) cercare il pelo nell'uovo
nitrate ['naɪtret] *s* nitrato; (agr) nitrato di soda; (agr) nitrato di potassio
ni'tric ac'id ['naɪtrɪk] *s* acido nitrico
nitride ['naɪtraɪd] *s* azoturo, nitruro
nitrogen ['naɪtrədʒən] *s* azoto
nitroglycerin [ˌnaɪtrə'glɪsərɪn] *s* nitroglicerina
ni'trous ox'ide ['naɪtrəs] *s* ossidulo di
azoto
nitwit ['nɪt ˌwɪt] *s* (slang) baggiano
no [no] *adj* nessuno; **no admittance**
vietato l'ingresso; **no doubt** senza
dubbio; **no matter** non importa; **no
parking** divieto di sosta; **no smoking**
vietato fumare; **no thoroughfare** divieto di transito; **no use** inutilmente;
with no senza ‖ *s* no; voto negativo
‖ *adv* no; non; **no longer** non . . .
più; **no sooner** non appena
Noah ['no·ə] *s* Noè *m*
nob·by ['nɑbi] *adj* (**-bier; -biest**)
(slang) elegante; (slang) eccellente
nobili·ty [no'bɪlɪtɪ] *s* (**-ties**) nobiltà *f*
noble ['nobəl] *adj & s* nobile *m*
no'ble·man *s* (**-men**) nobile *m*, nobiluomo
no'ble·wom'an *s* (**-wom'en**) nobile *f*,
nobildonna
nobod·y ['no ˌbɑdi] or ['nobədi] *s*
(**-ies**) nessuno, illustre sconosciuto ‖
pron indef nessuno; **nobody but** nessun altro che; **nobody else** nessun
altro
nocturnal [nɑk'tʌrnəl] *adj* notturno
nod [nɑd] *s* cenno d'assenso, cenno
del capo; (*of person going to sleep*)
crollo del capo ‖ *v* (*pret & pp*
nodded; *ger* nodding) *tr* (*one's head*)
inclinare; **to nod assent** fare cenno
di sì ‖ *intr* inclinare il capo; (*to
drowse*) assopirsi
node [nod] *s* nodo; protuberanza;
(phys) nodo
no'-good' *adj & s* (coll) buono a nulla
nohow ['no ˌhaʊ] *adv* (coll) in nessuna
maniera
noise [nɔɪz] *s* rumore *m* ‖ *tr* divulgare
noiseless ['nɔɪzlɪs] *adj* silenzioso
nois·y ['nɔɪzi] *adj* (**-ier; -iest**) rumoroso, chiassoso

nomad ['nomæd] *adj & s* nomade *m*
no' man's' land' *s* terra di nessuno
nominal ['nɑmɪnəl] *adj* nominale; simbolico
nominate ['nɑmɪ ˌnet] *tr* presentare la
candidatura di; (*to appoint*) nominare, designare
nomination [ˌnɑmɪ'neʃən] *s* candidatura; nomina
nominative ['nɑmɪnətɪv] *adj & s* nominativo
nominee [ˌnɑmɪ'ni] *s* candidato designato
nonbelligerent [ˌnɑnbə'lɪdʒərənt] *adj
& s* non belligerante *m*
nonbreakable [nɑn'brekəbəl] *adj* infrangibile
nonce [nɑns] *s*—**for the nonce** per
l'occasione
nonchalance ['nɑnʃələns] or [ˌnɑnʃə'lɑns] *s* disinvoltura, indifferenza
nonchalant ['nɑnʃələnt] or [ˌnɑnʃə'lɑnt] *adj* disinvolto, indifferente
noncom ['nɑn ˌkɑm] *s* (coll) sottufficiale *m*
noncombatant [nɑn'kɑmbətənt] *adj*
non combattente ‖ *s* persona non
combattente
non'commis'sioned of'ficer [ˌnɑnkə'mɪʃ/ənd] *s* sottufficiale *m*
noncommittal [ˌnɑnkə'mɪtəl] *adj* ambiguo, evasivo
non compos mentis ['nɑn 'kɑmpəs 'mentɪs] *adj* pazzo; (law) incapace
nonconformist [ˌnɑnkən'fɔrmɪst] *s*
anticonformista *mf*, nonconformista
mf
nondelivery [ˌnɑndɪ'lɪvəri] *s* mancata
consegna
nondescript ['nɑndɪ ˌskrɪpt] *adj* indefinibile, inclassificabile
none [nʌn] *pron indef* nessuno; **none
of** nessuno di; **none other** nessun
altro ‖ *adv* non; affatto, niente affatto; **none the less** ciò nonostante,
nondimeno
nonenti·ty [nɑn'entɪti] *s* (**-ties**) inesistenza; (*person*) nullità *f*
nonfiction [nɑn'fɪkʃən] *s* letteratura
non romanzesca
nonfulfillment [ˌnɑnfʊl'fɪlmənt] *s*
mancanza di esecuzione
nonintervention [ˌnɑnɪntər'venʃən] *s*
non intervento
nonmetal ['nɑn ˌmetəl] *s* metalloide *m*
nonpayment [nɑn'pemənt] *s* mancato
pagamento
non·plus ['nɑnplʌs] or [nɑn'plʌs] *s*
perplessità *f* ‖ *v* (*pret & pp* **-plussed**
or **plused;** *ger* **-plussing** or **-plusing**)
tr lasciare perplesso
nonprofit [nɑn'prɑfɪt] *adj* senza scopo
lucrativo
nonrefillable [ˌnɑnri'fɪləbəl] *adj* (*prescription*) non ripetibile; (*e.g., bottle*) non ricaricabile
nonresident [nɑn'rezɪdənt] *s* persona
di passaggio, non residente *mf*
nonresidential [nɑn ˌrezi'denʃəl] *adj*
commerciale, non residenziale
nonscientific [nɑn ˌsaɪ·ən'tɪfɪk] *adj* non
scientifico

nonsectarian [ˌnɑnsɛk'tɛrɪ·ən] *adj* che non segue nessuna confessione religiosa

nonsense ['nɑnsɛns] *s* sciocchezza, assurdità *f*, nonsenso

nonsensical [nɑn'sɛnsɪkəl] *adj* sciocco, assurdo, illogico

nonskid ['nɑn'skɪd] *adj* antiderapante

nonstop ['nɑn'stɑp] *adj & adv* senza scalo

nonsupport [ˌnɑnsə'pɔrt] *s* mancato pagamento degli alimenti

noodle ['nudəl] *s* (slang) scemo; (slang) testa; **noodles** tagliatelle *fpl*

noo'dle soup' *s* tagliatelle *fpl* in brodo

nook [nʊk] *s* angolo, cantuccio

noon [nun] *s* mezzogiorno; **at high noon** a mezzogiorno in punto

no one or **no-one** ['no ˌwʌn] *pron indef* nessuno; **no one else** nessun altro

noontime ['nun ˌtaɪm] *s* mezzogiorno

noose [nus] *s* laccio, nodo scorsoio

nor [nɔr] *conj* nè

Nordic ['nɔrdɪk] *adj* nordico

norm [nɔrm] *s* norma, media, tipo

normal ['nɔrməl] *adj* normale ‖ *s* condizione normale; norma; (geom) normale *f*

Norman ['nɔrmən] *adj & s* normanno

Normandy ['nɔrməndɪ] *s* la Normandia

Norse [nɔrs] *adj* norvegese; scandinavo ‖ *s* (*ancient Scandinavian language*) scandinavo; (*language of Norway*) norvegese *m*; **the Norse** gli scandinavi; i norvegesi

Norse'man *s* (**-men**) normanno

north [nɔrθ] *adj* del nord, settentrionale ‖ *s* nord *m* ‖ *adv* al nord, verso il nord

North' Amer'ica *s* l'America del Nord

North' Amer'ican *adj & s* nordamericano

north'east' *adj* di nord-est ‖ *s* nord-est *m* ‖ *adv* al nord-est

north'east'er *s* vento di nord-est

northern ['nɔrðərn] *adj* settentrionale; (*Hemisphere*) boreale

North' Kore'a *s* la Corea del Nord

North' Pole' *s* polo nord

northward ['nɔrθwərd] *adv* verso il nord

north'west' *adj* di nord-ovest ‖ *s* nord-ovest *m* ‖ *adv* al nord-ovest

north' wind' *s* vento del nord, aquilone *m*

Norway ['nɔrwe] *s* la Norvegia

Norwegian [nɔr'widʒən] *adj & s* norvegese *mf* ‖ *s* (*language*) norvegese *m*

nose [noz] *s* naso; (*of missile*) testata; **to blow one's nose** soffiarsi il naso; **to count noses** contare il numero dei presenti; **to follow one's nose** andare a lume di naso; **to lead by the nose** menare per il naso; **to look down one's nose at** (coll) guardare dall'alto in basso; **to pay through the nose** pagare un occhio della testa; **to pick one's nose** mettersi le dita nel naso; **to speak through the nose** parlare nel naso; **to thumb one's nose at** fare marameo a; **to turn up one's nose at** guardare dall'alto in basso, guardare

con disprezzo ‖ *tr* fiutare; **to nose out** vincere per un pelo ‖ *intr* fiutare; **to nose about** curiosare

nose' bag' *s* musetta

nose'band' *s* museruola di cavallo

nose'bleed' *s* sangue *m* dal naso

nose' cone' *s* ogiva

nose' dive' *s* (*of prices*) subita discesa; (aer) discesa in picchiata

nose'-dive' *intr* discendere in picchiata

nosegay ['noz ˌge] *s* mazzolino di fiori

nose' glass'es *spl* occhiali *mpl* a stringinaso

nose' ring' *s* nasiera

nose'wheel' *s* (aer) ruota del carrello anteriore

no'-show' *s* (coll) passeggero che si è prenotato e non parte

nostalgia [nɑ'stældʒə] *s* nostalgia

nostalgic [nɑ'stældʒɪk] *adj* nostalgico

nostril ['nɑstrɪl] *s* narice *f*

nos·y ['nozi] *adj* (**-ier; -iest**) (coll) curioso

not [nɑt] *adv* no; non; **not at all** niente affatto; **not yet** non ancora; **to think not** credere di no; **why not?** come no?

notable ['notəbəl] *adj* notevole, notabile ‖ *s* notabile *m*

notarize ['notə ˌraɪz] *tr* munire di fede notarile

nota·ry ['notəri] *s* (**-ries**) notaio

notch [nɑtʃ] *s* tacca; (*in mountain*) passo; (coll) tantino; **notches** (coll) di gran lunga, e.g., **notches above** di gran lunga migliore ‖ *tr* intaccare

note [not] *s* nota, annotazione; (*currency*) banconota; (*communication*) memorandum *m*; (*of bird*) canto; (*tone of voice*) tono; (*reputation*) riguardo; (*short letter*) biglietto, letterina; (mus) nota; (com) cambiale *f* ‖ *tr* notare, annotare; osservare

note'book' *s* (*for school*) quaderno; taccuino, notes *m*

noted ['notɪd] *adj* ben noto, eminente

note' pa'per *s* carta da lettera

note'wor'thy *adj* notevole

nothing ['nʌθɪŋ] *s* niente *m*, nulla; **for nothing** gratis; inutilmente; **next to nothing** quasi niente ‖ *pron indef* niente, nulla, non . . . niente, non . . . nulla; **nothing else** nient'altro; **to make nothing of** it non farne caso ‖ *adv* per nulla; **nothing less** non meno

notice ['notɪs] *s* attenzione; notizia, notifica; annunzio, preavviso; (*in newspaper*) trafiletto; (law) disdetta; **on short notice** senza preavviso; (com) a breve scadenza; **to escape the notice of** passare inavvertito a; **to serve notice to** far sapere a, far constatare a ‖ *tr* osservare, notare, prendere nota di

noticeable ['notɪsəbəl] *adj* notevole; (*e.g., difference*) percettibile

noti·fy ['notɪ ˌfaɪ] *v* (*pret & pp* **-fied**) *tr* informare, far sapere

notion ['noʃən] *s* nozione; (*whim*) capriccio; **notions** mercerie *fpl*; **to have a notion to** aver voglia di

notorie·ty [ˌnotə'raɪ·ɪtɪ] *s* (**-ties**) (*state*

of being well known) notorietà *f;* cattiva fama

notorious [no'tori·əs] *adj (generally known)* notorio; *(unfavorably known)* notorio

no'-trump' *adj & s* senza atout *m*

notwithstanding [ˌnɑtwɪð'stændɪŋ] or [ˌnɑtwɪθ'stændɪŋ] *adv* ciò nonostante || *prep* malgrado || *conj* sebbene

nougat ['nugət] *s* torrone *m*

noun [naʊn] *s* nome *m*, sostantivo

nourish ['nʌrɪʃ] *tr* nutrire

nourishing ['nʌrɪʃɪŋ] *adj* nutriente

nourishment ['nʌrɪʃmənt] *s* nutrimento

novel ['nɑvəl] *adj* nuovo, novello, insolito, originale || *s* romanzo

novelist ['nɑvəlɪst] *s* romanziere *m*

novel·ty ['nɑvəlti] *s* (**-ties**) novità *f;* **novelties** chincaglierie *fpl*

November [no'vɛmbər] *s* novembre *m*

novice ['nɑvɪs] *s* novizio

novitiate [no'vɪʃɪ·ɪt] *s* noviziato

novocaine ['novə‚ken] *s* novocaina

now [naʊ] *s* presente *m* || *adv* adesso; **from now on** d'ora in poi; **just now** un momento fa; **now and then** di tempo in tempo; **now that** visto che || *conj* visto che, dato che

nowadays ['naʊ·ə‚dez] *adv* al giorno d'oggi, oggidì

no'way' *adv* in nessun modo; nient'affatto

no'where' *adv* da nessuna parte; **nowhere else** da nessun'altra parte, in nessun altro luogo

noxious ['nɑkʃəs] *adj* nocivo

nozzle ['nɑzəl] *s (of hose or pipe)* boccaglio; *(of tea pot, gas burner)* becco; *(of gun)* bocca; *(of sprinkling can)* bocchetta; (aut, mach) becco; (slang) naso

nth [ɛnθ] *adj* ennesimo; **to the nth degree** all'ennesima potenza

nuance [nju'ɑns] or ['nju·ɑns] *s* sfumatura

nub [nʌb] *s* protuberanza; *(of coal)* pezzo; (coll) nocciolo, cuore *m*

nuclear ['njuklɪ·ər] or ['nuklɪ·ər] *adj* nucleare

nu'clear fis'sion *s* fissione nucleare

nu'clear fu'sion *s* fusione nucleare

nu'clear test' ban' *s* accordo per la tregua atomica

nucle·us ['njuklɪ·əs] or ['nuklɪ·əs] *s* (**-i** [‚aɪ] or **-uses**) nucleo

nude [njud] or [nud] *adj* nudo || *s*—**in the nude** nudo

nudge [nʌdʒ] *s* gomitatina || *tr* dare di gomito a

nudist ['njudɪst] or ['nudɪst] *adj & s* nudista *mf*

nudi·ty ['njudɪti] or ['nudɪti] *s* (**-ties**) nudità *f*

nugget ['nʌgɪt] *s* pepita

nuisance ['njusəns] or ['nusəns] *s* noia, seccatura; *(person)* seccatore *m*, pittima *mf*

null [nʌl] *adj* nullo; **null and void** invalido

nulli·fy ['nʌlɪ‚faɪ] *v* (*pret & pp* **-fied**) *tr* annullare, invalidare

nulli·ty ['nʌlɪti] *s* (**-ties**) nullità *f*

numb [nʌm] *adj* intorpidito; *(from cold)* intirizzito; **to become numb** intorpidirsi || *tr* intorpidire

number ['nʌmbər] *s* numero; *(for sale)* articolo di vendita; *(publication)* fascicolo; *(of a serial)* dispensa, puntata; **a number of** parecchi; **beyond or without number** senza numero, infiniti || *tr* numerare, contare; **his days are numbered** i suoi giorni sono contati || *intr*—**to number among** essere tra

numberless ['nʌmbərlɪs] *adj* innumerevole

numeral ['njumərəl] or ['numərəl] *adj* numerale || *s* numero

numerical [nju'mɛrɪkəl] or [nu'mɛrɪkəl] *adj* numerico

numerous ['njumərəs] or ['numərəs] *adj* numeroso

numskull ['nʌm‚skʌl] *s* (coll) stupido

nun [nʌn] *s* monaca, religiosa

nuptial ['nʌpʃəl] *adj* nuziale || **nuptials** *spl* nozze *fpl*

nurse [nʌrs] *s* infermiera; *(to suckle a child)* nutrice *f; (to take care of a child)* bambinaia || *tr (to minister to)* curare; allattare; allevare; *(e.g., hatred)* covare || *intr* fare l'infermiera

nurser·y ['nʌrsəri] *s* (**-ies**) stanza dei bambini; *(shelter for children)* asilo infantile; (hort) vivaio

nurs'ery·man *s* (**-men**) orticoltore *m*

nurs'ery rhyme' *s* canzoncina per i più piccini

nurs'ery school' *s* scuola materna

nursing ['nʌrsɪŋ] *adj* infermieristico || *s* allattamento; professione d'infermiera

nurs'ing bot'tle *s* biberon *m*, poppatoio

nurs'ing home' *s* convalescenziario; ospizio dei vecchi, gerontocomio

nurture ['nʌrtʃər] *s* allevamento; nutrimento || *tr* allevare; alimentare; *(e.g., hope)* accarezzare

nut [nʌt] *s* noce *f; (eccentric)* (slang) esaltato, pazzoide *m;* (mus) capotasto; (mach) madrevite *f*, dado; **a hard nut to crack** un osso duro da rodere; **to be nuts for** (coll) essere pazzo per

nut'crack'er *s* schiaccianoci *m*

nutmeg ['nʌt‚mɛg] *s* noce moscata

nutrition [nju'trɪʃən] or [nu'trɪʃən] *s (process)* nutrizione; *(food)* nutrimento

nutritious [nju'trɪʃəs] or [nu'trɪʃəs] *adj* nutriente

nut'shell' *s* guscio di noce; **in a nutshell** in breve, in poche parole

nut·ty ['nʌti] *adj* (**-tier; -tiest**) che sa di noci; (slang) pazzo; **nutty about** (slang) pazzo per

nuzzle ['nʌzəl] *tr* toccare col muso, ammusare || *intr (said of swine)* grufolare; *(said of other animals)* stare muso a muso, ammusare; *(to snuggle)* rannicchiarsi

nylon ['naɪlɑn] *s* nailon *m*

nymph [nɪmf] *s* ninfa

O

O, o [o] *s* quindicesima lettera dell'alfabeto inglese

O *interj* o!, oh!

oaf [of] *s* balordo, scemo, imbecille *mf*

oak [ok] *s* quercia

oaken ['okən] *adj* di quercia, quercino

oakum ['okəm] *s* stoppa incatramata

oar [or] *s* remo; **to lie** or **rest on one's oars** dormire sugli allori; non lavorare più ‖ *tr* spingere coi remi ‖ *intr* remare

oar'lock' *s* scalmo

oars'man *s* (**-men**) rematore *m*

oa·sis [o'esɪs] *s* (**-ses** [siz]) oasi *f*

oat [ot] *s* avena; **oats** (*seeds*) avena; **to feel one's oats** (coll) essere pieno di vita; (coll) sentirsi importante; **to sow one's wild oats** correre la cavallina

oath [oθ] *s* giuramento; **on oath** sotto giuramento; **to take an oath** giurare, prestar giuramento

oat'meal' *s* (*breakfast food*) fiocchi *mpl* d'avena; farina d'avena

obdurate ['abdjʊrɪt] *adj* indurito, inesorabile; impenitente, incallito

obedience [o'bidɪ·əns] *s* obbedienza, ubbidienza

obedient [o'bidɪ·ənt] *adj* ubbidiente

obeisance [o'besəns] or [o'bisəns] *s* saluto rispettoso; omaggio

obelisk ['abəlɪsk] *s* obelisco

obese [o'bis] *adj* obeso

obesity [o'bisɪti] *s* obesità *f*

obey ['obe] *tr* ubbidire (with *dat*), ubbidire ‖ *intr* ubbidire

obfuscate [ab'fʌsket] or ['abfəs‚ket] *tr* offuscare

obituar·y [o'bɪtʃʊ‚ɛri] *adj* necrologico ‖ *s* (**-ies**) necrologia

object ['abdʒɪkt] *s* oggetto ‖ [ab'dʒɛkt] *tr* obiettare ‖ *intr* fare obiezioni, obiettare

objection [ab'dʒɛkʃən] *s* obiezione

objectionable [ab'dʒɛkʃənəbəl] *adj* reprensibile; (*e.g., odor*) sgradevole; offensivo

objective [ab'dʒɛktɪv] *adj* & *s* obiettivo

obligate ['ablɪ‚get] *tr* obbligare

obligation [‚ablɪ'geʃən] *s* obbligo, obbligazione

oblige [ə'blaɪdʒ] *tr* obbligare; favorire; **much obliged** obbligatissimo

obliging [ə'blaɪdʒɪŋ] *adj* compiacente, accomodante, servizievole

oblique [ə'blik] *adj* obliquo; indiretto

obliterate [ə'blɪtə‚ret] *tr* obliterare; spegnere, distruggere

oblivion [ə'blɪvɪ·ən] *s* oblio

oblivious [ə'blɪvɪ·əs] *adj* (*forgetful*) dimentico; (*unaware*) ignaro

oblong ['ablɔŋ] or ['ablaŋ] *adj* oblungo

obnoxious [əb'nakʃəs] *adj* detestabile

oboe ['obo] *s* oboe *m*

oboist ['obo·ɪst] *s* oboista *mf*

obscene [ab'sin] *adj* osceno

obsceni·ty [ab'senɪti] or [ab'sinɪti] *s* (**-ties**) oscenità *f*, sconcezza

obscure [əb'skjʊr] *adj* oscuro ‖ *tr* oscurare

obscuri·ty [əb'skjʊrɪti] *s* (**-ties**) oscurità *f*

obsequies ['absɪkwiz] *spl* esequie *fpl*

obsequious [əb'sikwɪ·əs] *adj* ossequioso, servile

observance [əb'zʌrvəns] *s* osservanza; **observances** pratiche *fpl*; cerimonie *fpl*

observation [‚abzər've/ən] *s* osservazione; osservanza

observa'tion car' *s* (rr) vettura belvedere

observato·ry [əb'zʌrvə‚tori] *s* (**-ries**) osservatorio

observe [əb'zʌrv] *tr* osservare

observer [əb'zʌrvər] *s* osservatore *m*

obsess [əb'sɛs] *tr* ossessionare

obsession [əb'se/ən] *s* ossessione

obsolescent [‚absə'lɛsənt] *adj* che sta cadendo in disuso

obsolete ['absə‚lit] *adj* disusato

obstacle ['abstəkəl] *s* ostacolo

obstetrical [ab'stɛtrɪkəl] *adj* ostetrico

obstetrics [ab'stɛtrɪks] *s* ostetricia

obstina·cy ['abstɪnasi] *s* (**-cies**) ostinazione

obstinate ['abstɪnɪt] *adj* ostinato

obstreperous [ab'strɛpərəs] *adj* turbolento; rumoroso

obstruct [əb'strʌkt] *tr* ostruire

obstruction [əb'strʌkʃən] *s* ostruzione

obtain [əb'ten] *tr* ottenere ‖ *intr* prevalere, essere in voga

obtrusive [əb'trusɪv] *adj* intruso, importuno; sporgente

obtuse [əb'tjus] or [əb'tus] *adj* ottuso

obviate ['abvɪ‚et] *tr* ovviare (with *dat*)

obvious ['abvɪ·əs] *adj* ovvio, palmare

occasion [ə'keʒən] *s* occasione; **on occasion** di quando in quando ‖ *tr* occasionare

occasional [ə'keʒənəl] *adj* saltuario; (*e.g., verses*) d'occasione

occasionally [ə'keʒənəli] *adv* occasionalmente, di tanto in tanto

occident ['aksɪdənt] *s* occidente *m*

occidental [‚aksɪ'dɛntəl] *adj* & *s* occidentale *mf*

occlud'ed front' [ə'kludɪd] *s* fronte occluso

occlusion [ə'kluʒən] *s* occlusione

occlusive [ə'klusɪv] *adj* occlusivo ‖ *s* occlusiva

occult [ə'kʌlt] or ['akʌlt] *adj* occulto

occupancy ['akjəpənsi] *s* occupazione, presa di possesso; (*tenancy*) locazione

occupant ['akjəpənt] *s* occupante *m*; (*tenant*) inquilino

occupation [‚akjə'peʃən] *s* occupazione

occupational [‚akjə'peʃənəl] *adj* occupazionale; (*e.g., disease*) professionale, del lavoro

occu·py ['akjə‚paɪ] *v* (*pret* & *pp* **-pied**) *tr* occupare; (*to dwell in*) abitare

oc·cur [ə'kʌr] *v* (*pret* & *pp* **-curred;**

ger **-curring**) *intr* accadere, succedere; incontrarsi; (*to come to mind*) venir in mente, e.g., **it occurs to me** mi viene in mente

occurrence [ə'kʌrəns] *s* evento, avvenimento; apparizione

ocean ['oʃən] *s* oceano

o'cean lin'er *s* transatlantico

o'clock [ə'klak] *adv* secondo l'orologio; **it is one o'clock** è la una; **it is two o'clock** sono le due

octane ['akten] *adj* ottanico ‖ *s* ottano

octave ['aktɪv] or ['aktev] *s* ottava

Octavian [ak'tevɪən] *s* Ottaviano

October [ak'tobər] *s* ottobre *m*

octo·pus ['aktəpəs] *s* (**-puses** or **-pi** [,paɪ]) (*small*) polpo; (*large*) piovra; (fig) piovra

ocular ['akjələr] *adj & s* oculare *m*

oculist ['akjəlɪst] *s* oculista *mf*

odd [ad] *adj* (*number*) dispari, strambo, bizzarro; (*not matching*) scompagnato, spaiato; strano; e rotti, e.g., **three hundred odd** tre cento e rotti ‖ **odds** *ssg* or *spl* probabilità *f*; (*advantage*) vantaggio, superiorità *f*; **at odds** in disaccordo; **by all odds** senza dubbio; **it makes no odds** fa lo stesso; **the odds are** la quota è; **to set at odds** seminare zizzania fra

oddi·ty ['adɪtɪ] *s* (**-ties**) stranezza

odd' jobs' *spl* lavori saltuari

odd' lot' *s* (fin) compravendita di meno di cento unità

odds' and ends' *spl* un po' di tutto

odious ['odɪ·əs] *adj* odioso

odor ['odər] *s* odore *m*; **to be in bad odor** aver cattiva fama

odorless ['odərlɪs] *adj* inodoro

odorous ['odərəs] *adj* odoroso

Odysseus [o'dɪsjus] or [o'dɪsɪ·əs] *s* Odisseo

Odyssey ['adɪsɪ] *s* Odissea

Oedipus ['edɪpəs] or ['idɪpəs] *s* Edipo

of [ʌv] or [əv] *prep* di, e.g., **the lead of the pencil** la mina della matita; a, e.g., **to think of** pensare a; meno, e.g., **a quarter of ten** le dieci meno un quarto

off [ɔf] or [af] *adj* (*wrong*) sbagliato; (*slightly abnormal*) matto, pazzo; inferiore; (*electricity*) tagliato; (*agreement*) sospeso; libero, in libertà; distante; destro; (*season*) morto ‖ *adv* via; fuori, lontano, distante; **to be off** mettersi in marcia ‖ *prep* da; fuori da; al disotto di; lontano da; distolto da, e.g., **his eyes were off the target** i suoi occhi erano distolti dal bersaglio; (naut) al largo di

offal ['afəl] or ['ɔfəl] *s* (*of butchered animal*) frattaglie *fpl*; rifiuti *mpl*

off' and on' *adv* di tempo in tempo

off'beat' *adj* insolito, originale

off' chance' *s* possibilità remota

off'-col'or *adj* scolorito; indisposto; (*joke*) di dubbio gusto

offend [ə'fɛnd] *tr & intr* offendere

offender [ə'fɛndər] *s* offensore *m*

offense [ə'fɛns] *s* offesa; **to take offense** (at) offendersi (di)

offensive [ə'fɛnsɪv] *adj* offensivo ‖ *s* offensiva

offer ['ɔfər] or ['afər] *s* offerta ‖ *tr* offrire; (*thanks*) porgere; (*resistance*) opporre ‖ *intr* offrirsi

offering ['ɔfərɪŋ] or ['afərɪŋ] *s* offerta

off'hand' *adj* fatto all'improvviso; sbrigativo, alla buona ‖ *adv* all'improvviso; bruscamente

office ['ɔfɪs] or ['afɪs] *s* ufficio; funzione, incombenza; (*of a doctor*) gabinetto; (*of a lawyer*) studio; (eccl) uffizio; **through the good offices of** per tramite di

of'fice boy' *s* fattorino

of'fice-hold'er *s* pubblico funzionario

of'fice hours' *spl* orario d'ufficio

officer ['ɔfɪsər] or ['afɪsər] *s* (*in a corporation*) funzionario; (*policeman*) agente *m*; (mil, nav, naut) ufficiale *m*; **officer of the day** (mil) ufficiale *m* di giornata

of'fice seek'er *s* ['sikər] *s* aspirante *m* a un ufficio pubblico

of'fice supplies' *spl* articoli *mpl* di cancelleria

official [ə'fɪʃəl] *adj* ufficiale ‖ *s* funzionario, ufficiale *m*

officiate [ə'fɪʃɪ,et] *intr* ufficiare

officious [ə'fɪʃəs] *adj* invadente, inframettente; **to be officious** essere un impiccione

offing ['ɔfɪŋ] or ['afɪŋ] *s*—**in the offing** al largo; (fig) in preparazione, probabile

off'-lim'its *adj* proibito; **off-limits to** ingresso proibito a

off'-peak' heat'er *s* (elec) scaldabagno azionato unicamente in periodi di consumo minimo

off'-peak' load' *s* (elec) carico di consumo minimo

off'print' *s* estratto

off'set' *s* compensazione; (typ) offset *m* ‖ **off'set'** *v* (*pret & pp* **-set**; *ger* **-setting**) *tr* compensare; stampare in offset

off'shoot' *s* (*of plant*) germoglio; (*of family or race*) discendente *mf*; (*branch*) ramo; (fig) conseguenza

off'shore' *adj* (*wind*) di terra; (*fishing*) vicino alla costa; (*island*) costiero ‖ *adv* al largo

off'side' *adv* (sports) fuori gioco

off'spring' *s* discendente *m*; prole *f*; figlio; figli *mpl*

off'stage' *adv* tra le quinte

off'-the-rec'ord *adj* confidenziale ‖ *adv* confidenzialmente

often ['ɔfən] or ['afən] *adv* sovente, spesso; **how often?** quante volte?; **once too often** una volta di troppo

ogive ['odʒaɪv] or [o'dʒaɪv] *s* ogiva

ogle ['ogəl] *tr* adocchiare, occhieggiare

ogre ['ogər] *s* orco

ohm [om] *s* ohm *m*

oil [ɔɪl] *adj* (*pertaining to edible oil*) oleario; (*e.g., well*) di petrolio; (*e.g., lamp*) a olio; (*tanker*) petroliero; (*field*) petrolifero ‖ *s* olio; petrolio; **to burn the midnight oil** studiare a lume di candela; **to pour oil on troubled waters** pacificare; **to strike oil** trovare petrolio ‖ *tr* oliare; lubrifi-

care; ungere ‖ *intr* (*said of a motorship*) fare petrolio
oil' burn'er *s* bruciatore *m* a gasolio
oil'can' *s* oliatore *m*
oil'cloth' *s* incerata, tela cerata
oil' field' *s* giacimento petrolifero
oil' lamp' *s* lampada a petrolio
oil'man *s* (**-men**) (*retailer*) mercante *m* di petrolio; (*operator*) petroliere *m*
oil' paint'ing *s* quadro a olio
oil' slick' *s* macchia d'olio
oil' tank'er *s* petroliera
oil' well' *s* pozzo di petrolio
oil·y [ˈɔɪli] *adj* (**-ier; -iest**) oleoso; untuoso
ointment [ˈɔɪntmənt] *s* unguento
O.K. [ˈoˈke] *adj* (coll) corretto ‖ *s* (coll) approvazione ‖ *adv* (coll) benissimo, d'accordo ‖ *v* (*pret & pp* **O.K.'d;** *ger* **O.K.'ing**) *tr* (coll) dare l'approvazione a ‖ *interj* benissimo!
okra [ˈokrə] *s* (bot) ibisco esculento; (bot) baccello dell'ibisco esculento
old [old] *adj* vecchio; antico, vetusto; **how old is . . . ?** quanti anni ha . . .?; **of old** anticamente; **to be . . . years old** avere . . . anni
old' age' *s* vecchiaia
old' boy' *s* vecchietto arzillo; (Brit) vecchio mio
old'-clothes'man' *s* (**-men'**) rigattiere *m*
old' coun'try *s* madre patria
old-fashioned [ˈoldˈfæʃənd] *adj* all'antica; fuori moda
old' fo'gey *or* **old' fo'gy** [ˈfogi] *s* (**-gies**) uomo di idee antiquate, reazionario
Old' Glo'ry *s* la bandiera degli Stati Uniti
Old' Guard' *s* (U.S.A.) parte *f* più conservatrice di un partito
old' hand' *s* vecchio del mestiere
old' maid' *s* zitella
old' mas'ter *s* grande maestro; quadro di un gran maestro
old' moon' *s* luna calante
old' salt' *s* lupo di mare
old' school' *s* gente *f* all'antica
old' school' tie' *s* (Brit) cravatta coi colori della propria scuola; (fig) tradizionalismo
Old' Tes'tament *s* Antico Testamento
old'-time' *adj* all'antica; del tempo antico
old-timer [ˈoldˈtaɪmər] *s* (coll) veterano; (coll) vecchio
old' wives' tale' *s* superstizione da donnicciole; racconto di vecchie comari
Old' World' *s* mondo antico
oleander [ˌoliˈændər] *s* oleandro
oligar·chy [ˈɑlɪˌgɑrki] *s* (**-chies**) oligarchia
olive [ˈɑlɪv] *adj* oleario; (*color*) olivastro ‖ *s* (*tree*) olivo; (*fruit*) oliva
ol'ive branch' *s* ramoscello d'olivo
ol'ive grove' *s* oliveto
ol'ive oil' *s* olio d'oliva
Oliver [ˈɑlɪvər] *s* Oliviero
ol'ive tree' *s* olivo
Olympiad [oˈlɪmpɪˌæd] *s* olimpiade *f*
Olympian [oˈlɪmpɪˌən] *adj* olimpico ‖ *s* deità olimpica; giocatore olimpico

Olympic [oˈlɪmpɪk] *adj* olimpico, olimpionico
omelet *or* **omelette** [ˈɑməlɪt] *or* [ˈɑmlɪt] *s* frittata, omelette *f*
omen [ˈomən] *s* augurio
ominous [ˈɑmɪnəs] *adj* infausto, ominoso
omission [oˈmɪʃən] *s* omissione
omit [oˈmɪt] *v* (*pret & pp* **omitted;** *ger* **omitting**) *tr* omettere
omnibus [ˈɑmnɪˌbʌs] *or* [ˈɑmnɪbəs] *adj* di interesse generale ‖ *s* bus *m*; volume collettivo
omnipotent [ɑmˈnɪpətənt] *adj* onnipotente
omniscient [ɑmˈnɪʃənt] *adj* onnisciente
omnivorous [ɑmˈnɪvərəs] *adj* onnivoro
on [ɑn] *or* [ɔn] *adj* addosso, e.g., **with his hat on** col cappello addosso; in uso, in funzione; (*light*) acceso; (*deal*) fatto, concluso; (*e.g., game*) già cominciato; **what is on at the theater?** che cosa si dà al teatro? ‖ *adv* su; avanti; dietro, e.g., **to drag on** tirarsi dietro; **and so on** e così via; **come on!** va via!; **farther on** più in là; **later on** più tardi; **to be on to s.o.** (coll) scoprire il gioco di qlcu; **to have on** avere addosso; **to . . . on** continuare a, e.g., **the band played on** la banda continuò a suonare; **to put on** mettersi ‖ *prep* su, sopra; a, e.g., **on foot** a piedi; **on his arrival** al suo arrivo; sotto, e.g., **on my responsibility** sotto la mia responsabilità; contro, e.g., **an attack on the government** un attacco contro il governo; da, e.g., **on good authority** da buona fonte; **on all sides** da tutte le parti; verso, e.g., **to march on the capital** marciare verso la capitale; dopo, e.g., **victory on victory** vittoria dopo vittoria
on' and on' *adv* senza cessa
once [wʌns] *s* una volta; volta, e.g., **this once** questa volta ‖ *adv* una volta; mai, e.g., **if this once becomes known** se questo si risapesse mai; **all at once** repentinamente; **at once** subito; allo stesso tempo; **for once** almeno una volta; **once and again** ripetutamente; **once in a blue moon** ad ogni morte di papa; **once in a while** di tanto in tanto; **once upon a time there was** c'era una volta ‖ *conj* se appena; una volta che
once'-o'ver *s* (coll) occhiata rapida; **to give s.th the once-over** (coll) esaminare qlco rapidamente; (coll) pulire qlco superficialmente
one [wʌn] *adj* uno; un certo, e.g., **one Smith** un certo Smith; unico e.g., **one price** prezzo unico ‖ *s* uno ‖ *pron* uno, e.g., **how can one live here?** come è possibile che uno viva qui?; sì, e.g., **how does one go to the museum?** come si va al museo?; **I for one** per lo meno io; **it's all one and the same to me** per me fa lo stesso; **my little one** piccolo mio; **one and all** tutti; **one another** sì, e.g., **they wrote one another** sì scrissero;

l'un(o) l'altro, e.g., **they looked at one another** si guardarono l'un l'altro; **one o'clock** la una; **one's** il suo, il proprio; **the blue hat and the red one** il cappello blu e quello rosso; **the one and only** l'unico; **the one that** chi, quello che; **this one** questo; **that one** quello; **to make one** unire

one'-eyed' adj monocolo

one'-horse' adj a un solo cavallo; (coll) da nulla, poco importante

one'-man' show' s personale f

onerous ['anərəs] adj oneroso

one-self' pron sé stesso; se; si; **to be oneself** essere normale; comportarsi normalmente

one-sided ['wʌn'saɪdɪd] adj unilaterale; ingiusto, parziale

one'-track' adj a un solo binario; (coll) unilaterale, limitato

one'-way' adj a senso unico; (ticket) semplice, d'andata

onion ['ʌnjən] s cipolla; **to know one's onions** (coll) conoscere i propri polli

on'ion-skin' s carta pelle aglio, carta velina

on'look'er s presente m, spettatore m

only ['onlɪ] adj solo, unico ‖ adv solo, soltanto, non . . . più di; **not only . . . but also** non solo . . . ma anche ‖ conj ma; se non che

on'set' s attacco; (beginning) inizio; **at the onset** dapprincipio

onslaught ['an,slɔt] or ['ɔn,slɔt] s attacco

on'to prep su, sopra a; **to be onto** (coll) rendersi conto del gioco di

onward ['anwərd] or **onwards** ['an-wərdz] adv avanti, più avanti

onyx ['anɪks] s onice m

ooze [uz] s trasudazione; liquido per concia ‖ tr sudare ‖ intr trasudare; (said, e.g., of blood) stillare; (said, e.g., of air) filtrare; (fig) trapelare

opal ['opəl] s opale m

opaque [o'pek] adj opaco; (writer's style) oscuro; stupido

open ['opən] adj aperto, scoperto; (job) vacante; (time) libero; (hunting season) legale; indeciso; manifesto; (hand) liberale; (needlework) a giorno; **to break** or **to crack open** forzare; **to throw open** aprire completamente ‖ s apertura; (in the woods) radura; **in the open** all'aperto; all'aria aperta; in alto mare; apertamente ‖ tr aprire; (an account) impostare; **to open up** spalancare; (one's eyes) sbarrare ‖ intr aprire, aprirsi; (theat) esordire; **to open into** sboccare in; **to open on** dare su; **to open up** sbottonarsi

o'pen-air' adj all'aria aperta

open-eyed ['opən,aɪd] adj con gli occhi aperti; meravigliato; fatto con piena conoscenza

open-handed ['opən'hændɪd] adj generoso, liberale

open-hearted ['opən'hartɪd] adj franco, sincero; gentile

o'pen house' s tavola imbandita; **to keep open house** aver sempre ospiti

opening ['opənɪŋ] s apertura; (of dress) giro collo; (e.g., of sewer) imbocco; (in the woods) radura; (vacancy) posto vacante; (beginning) inizio; (chance to say something) occasione

o'pening night' s debutto, prima

o'pening num'ber s primo numero

o'pening price' s prezzo d'apertura

open-minded ['opən'maɪndɪd] adj di larghe vedute; imparziale

o'pen se'cret s segreto di Pulcinella

o'pen shop' s officina che impiega chi non è membro del sindacato

o'pen-work' s traforo

opera ['apərə] s opera

op'era glass'es ['apərə] s binocolo da teatro

op'era hat' s gibus m

op'era house' s teatro dell'opera

operate ['apə,ret] tr (a machine) far funzionare; (a shop) gestire; operare ‖ intr funzionare; operare; **to operate on** (surg) operare

operatic [,apə'rætɪk] adj operistico

op'erating expens'es spl spese fpl di ordinaria amministrazione

op'erating room' s sala operatoria

op'erating ta'ble s tavola operatoria

operation [,apə're'ʃən] s operazione; funzionamento, marcia

opera'tions research' s ricerca operativa

operator ['apə,retər] s operatore m; (of a conveyance) conduttore m, conducente mf; (com) gestore m; (telp) telefonista mf; (surg) chirurgo operatore; (slang) faccendiere m

opiate ['opɪ·ɪt] or ['opɪ,et] adj & s oppiato

opinion [ə'pɪnjən] s opinione; **in my opinion** a mio modo di vedere; **to have a high opinion of** avere una grande stima di

opinionated [ə'pɪnjə,netɪd] adj ostinato, testardo, dogmatico

opium ['opɪ·əm] s oppio

o'pium den' s fumeria d'oppio

opossum [ə'pasəm] s opossum m

opponent [ə'ponənt] s avversario

opportune [,apər'tjun] or [,apər'tun] adj opportuno

opportunist [,apər'tjunɪst] or [,apər-'tunɪst] s opportunista mf

opportuni-ty [,apər'tjunɪti] or [,apər-'tunɪti] s (-ties) opportunità f, occasione

oppose [ə'poz] tr opporsi a

opposite ['apəsɪt] adj opposto; di rimpetto, e.g., **the house opposite** la casa di rimpetto ‖ s contrario ‖ prep di faccia a, di rimpetto a

op'posite num'ber s persona di grado corrispondente

opposition [,apə'zɪʃən] s opposizione

oppress [ə'pres] tr opprimere

oppressive [ə'presɪv] adj oppressivo; opprimente, soffocante

oppressor [ə'presər] s oppressore m

opprobrious [ə'probrɪ·əs] adj obbrobrioso

opprobrium [ə'probrɪ·əm] s obbrobrio
optic ['aptɪk] adj ottico ‖ **optics** ssg ottica
optical ['aptɪkəl] adj ottico
optician [ap'tɪʃən] s ottico, occhialaio
optimism ['aptɪ‚mɪzəm] s ottimismo
optimist ['aptɪmɪst] s ottimista mf
optimistic [‚aptɪ'mɪstɪk] adj ottimistico
option ['apʃən] s opzione
optional ['apʃənəl] adj facoltativo
optometrist [ap'tamɪtrɪst] s optometrista mf
opulent ['apjələnt] adj opulento
or [ɔr] conj o; (or else) oppure
oracle ['arəkəl] or ['ɔrəkəl] s oracolo
oracular [o'rækjələr] adj profetico; ambiguo; misterioso; sentenzioso
oral ['ɔrəl] adj orale
orange ['arɪndʒ] or ['ɔrɪndʒ] adj di arance; arancio ‖ s arancia; arancio m
orangeade [‚arɪndʒ'ed] or [‚ɔrɪndʒ-'ed] s aranciata
or'ange blos'som s zagara
or'ange grove' s araneeto
or'ange juice' s sugo d'arancia
or'ange squeez'er s spremiagrumi m
or'ange tree' s arancio
orang-outang [o'ræŋu‚tæŋ] s orango
oration [o'reʃən] s orazione, discorso
orator ['arətər] or ['ɔrətər] s oratore m
oratorical [‚arə'tarɪkəl] or [‚ɔrə'tarɪ-kəl] adj oratorio
oratori·o [‚arə'torɪ‚o] or [‚ɔrə'torɪ‚o] s (-os) (mus) oratorio
orato·ry ['arə‚torɪ] or ['ɔrə‚torɪ] s (-ries) oratoria; (eccl) oratorio
orb [ɔrb] s orbe m
orbit ['ɔrbɪt] s orbita; **to go into orbit** entrare in orbita ‖ tr mettere in orbita; orbitare intorno a ‖ intr orbitare
or'biting sta'tion s stazione orbitale
orchard ['ɔrtʃərd] s frutteto
orchestra ['ɔrkɪstrə] s orchestra; (parquet) platea
orchestral [ɔr'kɛstrəl] adj orchestrale
or'chestra pit' s golfo mistico
or'chestra seat' s poltrona di platea
orchestrate ['ɔrkɪs‚tret] tr orchestrare
orchid ['ɔrkɪd] s orchidea
ordain [ɔr'den] tr predestinare; decretare; (eccl) ordinare
ordeal [ɔr'dil] or [ɔr'di·əl] s sfacchinata; (hist) ordalia
order ['ɔrdər] s ordine m; compito, e.g., **a big order** un compito difficile; (com) commessa, ordinazione; (mil) consegna; **in order that** affinché; **in order to** + inf per + inf; **made to order** fatto su misura; **to get out of order** guastarsi; **to give an order** dare un ordine; (com) fare una commessa ‖ tr (e.g., a drink) ordinare; (a person) ordinare (with dat); (e.g., a suit of clothes) far fare; **to order around** mandare attorno; **to order s.o. away** mandar via qlcu
or'der blank' s cedola d'ordinazione
order·ly ['ɔrdərlɪ] adj ordinato; disciplinato ‖ s (-lies) (in a hospital) in-

serviente mf; (mil) ordinanza, attendente m
ordinal ['ɔrdɪnəl] adj & s ordinale m
ordinance ['ɔrdɪnəns] s ordinanza
ordinary ['ɔrdɪ‚nerɪ] adj ordinario
ordnance ['ɔrdnəns] s artiglieria; bocche fpl da fuoco; munizionamento
ore [or] s minerale m (metallifero)
organ ['ɔrgən] s organo
organ·dy ['ɔrgəndɪ] s (-dies) organdì m
or'gan grind'er s suonatore m d'organetto
organic [ɔr'gænɪk] adj organico
organism ['ɔrgə‚nɪzəm] s organismo
organist ['ɔrgənɪst] s organista mf
organization [‚ɔrgənɪ'zeʃən] s organizzazione
organize ['ɔrgə‚naɪz] tr organizzare
organizer ['ɔrgə‚naɪzər] s organizzatore m
or'gan loft' s palco, galleria per l'organo
orgasm ['ɔrgæzəm] s orgasmo
or·gy ['ɔrdʒɪ] s (-gies) orgia
orient ['orɪ·ənt] s oriente m ‖ **Orient** s Oriente m ‖ **orient** ['orɪ‚ent] tr orientare, orizzontare
oriental [‚orɪ'entəl] adj orientale ‖ **Oriental** s orientale mf
orifice ['arɪfɪs] or ['ɔrɪfɪs] s orifizio
origin ['arɪdʒɪn] or ['ɔrɪdʒɪn] s origine f, provenienza
original [ə'rɪdʒɪnəl] adj & s originale mf
originate [ə'rɪdʒɪ‚net] tr originare ‖ intr originare, originarsi
oriole ['orɪ‚ol] s oriolo, rigogolo
Ork'ney Is'lands ['ɔrknɪ] spl Orcadi fpl
ormolu ['ɔrmə‚lu] s (alloy) similoro; (gold powder) polvere f d'oro; (gilded metal) bronzo dorato
ornament ['ɔrnəmənt] s ornamento ‖ ['ɔrnə‚ment] tr ornamentare
ornamental [‚ɔrnə'mentəl] adj ornamentale
ornate [ɔr'net] or ['ɔrnet] adj ornato; (style) elaborato
ornithologist [‚ɔrnɪ'θalədʒɪst] s ornitologo
orphan ['ɔrfən] adj & s orfano ‖ tr rendere orfano
orphanage ['ɔrfənɪdʒ] s (institution) orfanotrofio; (condition) orfanezza
Orpheus ['ɔrfjus] or ['ɔrfɪ·əs] s Orfeo
orthodox ['ɔrθə‚daks] adj ortodosso
orthogra·phy [ɔr'θagrəfɪ] s (-phies) ortografia
oscillate ['asɪ‚let] intr oscillare
osier ['oʒər] s vimine m; (bot) vinco
osmosis [az'mosɪs] or [as'mosɪs] s osmosi f
osprey ['asprɪ] s falco pescatore
ossi·fy ['asɪ‚faɪ] v (pret & pp -fied) tr ossificare ‖ intr ossificarsi
ostensible [as'tensɪbəl] adj apparente, preteso
ostentatious [‚asten'teʃəs] adj ostentato
osteopathy [‚astɪ'apəθɪ] s osteopatia
ostracism ['astrə‚sɪzəm] s ostracismo

ostracize ['astrə,saɪz] *tr* dare l'ostra-cismo a, ostracizzare

ostrich ['astrɪtʃ] *s* struzzo

Othello [o'θelo] *or* [ə'θelo] *s* Otello

other ['ʌðər] *adj* & *pron indef* altro ‖ *adv*—**other than** diversamente che

otherwise ['ʌðər,waɪz] *adv* altrimenti; differentemente

otter ['atər] *s* lontra

ottoman ['atəmən] *s* (*fabric*) otto-mano; (*sofa*) ottomana; cuscino per i piedi ‖ **Ottoman** *adj* & *s* ottomano

ouch [autʃ] *interj* ahi!

ought [ɔt] *s* qualcosa; zero; **for ought I know** per quanto io sappia ‖ *v aux* is rendered in Italian by the condi-tional of *dovere*, e.g., **you ought to be ashamed** dovresti vergognarti

ounce [auns] *s* oncia

our [aur] *adj poss* nostro, il nostro

ours [aurz] *pron poss* il nostro

ourselves [aur'selvz] *pron pers* noi stessi; ci, e.g., **we enjoyed ourselves** ci siamo divertiti

oust [aust] *tr* espellere; (*a tenant*) sfrattare

out [aut] *adj* erroneo; esterno; fuori pratica; svenuto; ubriaco; finito; (*book*) pubblicato; (*lights*) spento; fuori moda; introvabile; palmare; di permesso, e.g., **my night out** la mia serata di permesso; (*e.g., at the knees*) frusto; (*sports*) fuori gioco ‖ *s* via d'uscita; **to be on the outs** *or* **at outs with** (coll) essere in disac-cordo con ‖ *adv* fuori, all'infuori; all'aria libera; **out for** in cerca di; **out of** fuori, fuori di; di; da; (*e.g., money*) a corto di, senza; su, e.g., **two students out of three** due stu-denti su tre ‖ *prep* fuori di; per, lungo ‖ *interj* fuori!

out' and away' *adv* di gran lunga

out'-and-out' *adj* perfetto, completo ‖ *adv* perfettamente, completamente

out'bid' *v* (*pret* **-bid**; *pp* **-bid** *or* **-bidden**; *ger* **-bidding**) *tr* fare un'of-ferta migliore di; (bridge) fare una dichiarazione più alta di

out'board mo'tor *s* fuoribordo, motore *m* fuoribordo

out'break' *s* insurrezione; (*of hives*) eruzione; (*of anger; of war*) scoppio

out'build'ing *s* dipendenza

out'burst' *s* (*of tears; of laughter*) scop-pio; (*of energy*) impeto, slancio

out'cast' *s* vagabondo reietto

out'come' *s* risultato

out'cry' *s* (**-cries**) grido, chiasso

out'dat'ed *adj* fuori moda

out'dis'tance *tr* distanziare

out'do' *v* (*pret* **-did**; *pp* **-done**) *tr* sor-passare; **to outdo oneself** sorpassare sé stesso

out'door' *adj* all'aria aperta

out'doors' *s* aria libera, aperta cam-pagna ‖ *adv* all'aria aperta, fuori di casa

out'er space' ['autər] *s* spazio cosmico

out'field' *s* (baseball) campo esterno

out'field'er *s* (baseball) esterno

out'fit' *s* equipaggiamento; (*female cos-*

tume) insieme *m*; (*of bride*) corredo; (*group*) (coll) corpo; (*com*) compa-gnia ‖ *v* (*pret* & *pp* **-fitted**; *ger* **-fitting**) *tr* equipaggiare

out'flow' *s* efflusso

out'go'ing *adj* in partenza; (*tide*) de-crescente; (*character*) espansivo ‖ *s* efflusso

out'grow' *v* (*pret* **-grew**; *pp* **-grown**) *tr* essere troppo grande per; sorpassare in statura; perdere l'interesse per ‖ *intr* protrudere

out'growth' *s* risultato, conseguenza; crescita

outing ['autɪŋ] *s* gita, scampagnata

outlandish [aut'lændɪʃ] *adj* strano, bizzarro; dall'aspetto straniero; (*re-mote, far away*) in capo al mondo

out'last' *tr* sopravvivere (with *dat*)

out'law' *s* fuorilegge *mf* ‖ *tr* proscri-vere; dichiarare illegale

out'lay' *s* disborso ‖ **out·lay'** *v* (*pret* & *pp* **-laid**) *tr* sborsare

out'let *s* uscita; (*e.g., of river*) sbocco; (*com*) mercato; (*elec*) presa di cor-rente; (fig) sfogo

out'line' *s* contorno; traccia, tracciato; sagoma, profilo; prospetto ‖ *tr* de-lineare; tracciare, tratteggiare; sago-mare, profilare; prospettare

out'live' *tr* sopravvivere (with *dat*)

out'look' *s* prospettiva; (*watch*) guar-dia; (*mental view*) modo di vedere, opinione

out'ly'ing *adj* lontano, fuori di mano; periferico

outmoded [,aut'modɪd] *adj* fuori moda, antiquato

out'num'ber *tr* superare in numero

out'-of-date' *adj* fuori moda

out'-of-door' *adj* all'aria aperta

out'-of-doors' *adj* all'aria aperta ‖ *s* aria aperta ‖ *adv* all'aria aperta; fuori di casa

out'-of-print' *adj* esaurito

out'-of-the-way' *adj* appartato, fuori mano; inusitato, strano

out' of tune' *adj* stonato ‖ *adv* fuori di tono

out' of work' *adj* disoccupato

out'pa'tient *s* paziente *mf* esterno

out'post' *s* (mil) posto avanzato

out'put' *s* produzione; (elec) uscita; (mach) rendimento, potenza utile

out'rage *s* oltraggio, indecenza ‖ *tr* oltraggiare; (*a woman*) violare

outrageous [aut'redʒəs] *adj* oltrag-gioso; (*excessive*) eccessivo; atroce, feroce

out'rank' *tr* superare in grado

out'rid'er *s* battistrada *m*

out'right' *adj* completo, intero ‖ *adv* completamente; apertamente; sul colpo; sull'istante

out'set' *s* inizio, principio

out'side' *adj* esterno; (*unlikely*) impro-babile; (*price*) massimo ‖ *s* esterno, di fuori *m*; aspetto esteriore; vita fuori del carcere ‖ *adv* fuori, di fuori; **outside of** fuori di ‖ *prep* fuori di; (coll) all'infuori di

outsider [‚aut'saɪdər] *s* estraneo, intruso; (sports) outsider *m*
out'skirts' *spl* sobborghi *mpl*, periferia
out'spo'ken *adj* franco, esplicito
out'stand'ing *adj* saliente, eminente; (*debt*) arretrato, non pagato
outward ['autwərd] *adj* esterno, superficiale || *adv* al di fuori
out'weigh' *tr* pesare più di; eccedere in importanza
out'wit' *v* (*pret* & *pp* **-witted;** *ger* **-witting**) *tr* farla in barba di; (*a pursuer*) far perdere la traccia or la pista a
oval ['ovəl] *adj* & *s* ovale *m*
ova·ry ['ovəri] *s* (**-ries**) ovaia
ovation [o've/ən] *s* ovazione
oven ['ʌvən] *s* forno
over ['ovər] *adj* superiore; esterno; finito, concluso || *adv* su, sopra; dall'altra parte; dall'altra sponda; al rovescio; di nuovo; (*at the bottom of a page*) continua; qui, e.g., **hand over the money** dammi qui il denaro; **over again** di nuovo; **over against** contro; **over and over** ripetutamente; **over here** qui; **over there** là || *prep* su, sopra; dall'altra parte di; attraverso, per; (*a certain number*) più di; a causa di; **over and above** in eccesso di
o'ver·all' *adj* completo, totale || **over·alls** *spl* tuta
o'ver·bear'ing *adj* arrogante, prepotente
o'ver·board' *adv* in acqua; **man overboard!** uomo in mare!; **to go overboard** andare agli estremi
o'ver·cast' *adj* annuvolato || *s* cielo annuvolato || *v* (*pret* & *pp* **-cast**) *tr* coprire, annuvolare
o'ver·charge' *s* prezzo eccessivo; sovraccarico; (elec) carica eccessiva || **o'ver·charge'** *tr* far pagare eccessivamente; sovraccaricare
o'ver·coat' *s* soprabito, pastrano
o'ver·come' *v* (*pret* **-came;** *pp* **-come**) *tr* vincere, sopraffare; (*e.g., passions*) frenare; opprimere
o'ver·con'fidence *s* sicumera
o'ver·crowd' *tr* gremire
o'ver·do' *v* (*pret* **-did;** *pp* **-done**) *tr* esagerare; strafare; esaurire; (*meat*) stracuocere || *intr* esaurirsi
o'ver·dose' *s* dose eccessiva
o'ver·draft' *s* assegno allo scoperto
o'ver·draw' *v* (*pret* **-drew;** *pp* **-drawn**) *tr* emettere allo scoperto; (*a check*) emettere allo scoperto; (*a character*) esagerare la descrizione di
o'ver·due' *adj* in ritardo; (com) in sofferenza, scaduto
o'ver·eat' *v* (*pret* **-ate;** *pp* **-eaten**) *tr* & *intr* mangiare troppo
o'ver·exer'tion *s* sforzo eccessivo
o'ver·expose' *tr* sovresporre
o'ver·expo'sure *s* sovresposizione
o'ver·flow' *s* (*of a river*) piena, straripamento; (*excess*) sovrabbondanza; (*e.g., of a fountain*) trabocco; (*outlet*) tubo di troppopieno || **o'ver·flow'** *intr* (*said of a river*) straripare; (*said of a container*) traboccare

o'ver·fly' *v* (*pret* **-flew;** *pp* **-flown**) *tr* sorvolare; (*a target*) oltrepassare
o'ver·grown' *adj* cresciuto troppo; coperto, denso
o'ver·hang' *s* strapiombo || **o'ver·hang'** *v* (*pret* & *pp* **-hung**) *tr* sovrastare (with *dat*); sovrastare; (*to threaten*) minacciare; pervadere, permeare || *intr* sovrastare, strapiombare
o'ver·haul' *s* riparazione; esame *m*, revisione || *tr* riparare; esaminare, ripassare, rivedere; raggiungere, mettersi alla pari con
o'ver·head' *adj* in alto, sopra la testa; aereo; elevato, pensile; generale || **o'ver·head'** *adv* in alto, di sopra || **o'ver·head'** *s* spese *fpl* generali
o'ver·head projec'tor *s* lavagna luminosa
o'ver·head valve' *s* valvola in testa
o'ver·hear' *v* (*pret* & *pp* **-heard**) *tr* sentire per caso, udire per caso
o'ver·heat' *tr* surriscaldare || *intr* surriscaldarsi; eccitarsi
overjoyed [‚ovər'dʒɔɪd] *adj* felicissimo; **to be overjoyed** non stare in sé dalla contentezza
overland ['ovər‚lænd] or ['ovərlənd] *adj* & *adv* per via di terra
o'ver·lap' *v* (*pret* & *pp* **-lapped;** *ger* **-lapping**) *tr* sovrapporre, estendersi sopra || *intr* sovrapporsi, estendersi; coincidere parzialmente
o'ver·load' *s* sovraccarico || **o'ver·load'** *tr* sovraccaricare, stracaricare
o'ver·look' *tr* sovrastare su, dominare; ispezionare, sorvegliare; passare sopra, trascurare; dare su, e.g., **the window overlooks the street** la finestra dà sulla strada
o'ver·lord' *s* dominatore *m* || *tr* dominare despoticamente
overly ['ovərli] *adv* eccessivamente
o'ver·night' *adj* per la notte, per solo una notte || **o'ver·night'** *adv* durante la notte; la notte prima
o'vernight bag' *s* astuccio di toletta per la notte
o'ver·pass' *s* cavalcavia, viadotto
o'ver·pop'ulate *tr* sovrappopolare
o'ver·pow'er *tr* sopraffare
o'ver·pow'ering *adj* schiacciante
o'ver·produc'tion *s* sovrapproduzione
o'ver·rate' *tr* sopravvalutare
o'ver·run' *v* (*pret* **-ran;** *pp* **-run;** *ger* **-running**) *tr* invadere, infestare; inondare; (*one's time*) oltrepassare, eccedere
o'ver·sea' or **o'ver·seas'** *adj* di oltremare || **o'ver·sea'** or **o'ver·seas'** *adv* oltremare, al di là dei mari
o'ver·see' *v* (*pret* **-saw;** *pp* **-seen**) *tr* sorvegliare
o'ver·seer' *s* sorvegliante *mf*
o'ver·shad'ow *tr* oscurare, eclissare
o'ver·shoe' *s* soprascarpa
o'ver·shoot' *v* (*pret* & *pp* **-shot**) *tr* (*the target*) oltrepassare; (*said of water*) scorrere sopra; **to overshoot oneself** andare troppo in là || *intr* (aer) atterrare lungo e richiamare
o'ver·sight' *s* sbadataggine *f*, svista; sorveglianza, supervisione

o'ver·sleep' v (pret & pp **-slept**) tr (a certain hour) dormire oltre || intr dormire troppo a lungo

o'ver·step' v (pret & pp **-stepped**; ger **-stepping**) tr eccedere, oltrepassare

o'ver·stock' tr riempire eccessivamente

o'ver·sup·ply' s (**-plies**) fornitura superiore alla richiesta || **o'ver·sup·ply'** v (pret & pp **-plied**) tr fornire in quantità superiore alla richiesta

overt ['ovʌrt] or [o'vʌrt] adj palmare, chiaro, manifesto

o'ver·take' v (pret **-took**; pp **-taken**) tr raggiungere, sorpassare; sorprendere

o'ver-the-count'er (securities) venduto direttamente al compratore

o'ver·throw' s rovesciamento; disfatta || **o'ver·throw'** s (pret **-threw**; pp **-thrown**) tr rovesciare, sconfiggere

o'ver·time' adj supplementare, fuori orario || s straordinario; (sports) tempo supplementare || adv fuori orario

o'ver·tone' s (mus) suono armonico; (fig) sottinteso

o'ver·trump' s taglio con atout più alto || **o'ver·trump'** tr & intr tagliare con atout più alto

overture ['ovʌrtʃər] s apertura; (mus) preludio, sinfonia

o'ver·turn' s rovesciamento || **o'ver·turn'** tr rovesciare, travolgere || intr rovesciarsi, ribaltarsi

overweening [,ovʌr'winɪŋ] adj presuntuoso, vanitoso; esagerato, eccessivo

o'ver·weight' adj troppo grasso; oltrepassante i limiti di peso || **o'ver·weight'** s sovraccarico; preponderanza; eccesso di peso

overwhelm [,ovʌr'hwɛlm] tr schiacciare, debellare; coprire; (e.g., with kindness) colmare, ricolmare

o'ver·work' s lavoro straordinario; superlavoro || **o'ver·work'** tr far lavorare eccessivamente || intr lavorare eccessivamente

Ovid ['avɪd] s Ovidio

ow [au] interj ahi!

owe [o] tr dovere || intr essere in debito

owing ['o·ɪŋ] adj dovuto; **owing to** a causa di

owl [aul] s gufo, barbagianni m

own [on] adj proprio, e.g., **my own brother** il mio proprio fratello || s il proprio; **on one's own** (coll) per proprio conto; (without anybody's advice) di testa propria; **to come into one's own** entrare in possesso del proprio; essere riconosciuto per quanto si vale; **to hold one's own** non perdere terreno; essere pari || tr possedere; riconoscere || intr—**to own up to** confessare

owner ['onər] s padrone m, proprietario, titolare m

ownership ['onər‚ʃɪp] s proprietà f

own'er's li'cence s permesso di circolazione

ox [aks] s (**oxen** ['aksən]) bue m

ox'cart' s carro tirato da buoi

oxide ['aksaɪd] s ossido

oxidize ['aksɪ‚daɪz] tr ossidare || intr ossidarsi

oxygen ['aksɪdʒən] s ossigeno

ox'ygen mask' s maschera respiratoria

ox'ygen tent' s tenda ad ossigeno

oxytone ['aksɪ‚ton] adj tronco, ossitono || s ossitono

oyster ['ɔɪstər] adj di ostriche || s ostrica

oys'ter bed' s ostricaio, banco di ostriche

oys'ter cock'tail s ostriche fpl servite in valva

oys'ter fork' s forchettina da ostriche

oys'ter·house' s ristorante m per la vendita delle ostriche

oys'ter·knife' s coltello per aprire le ostriche

oys'ter·man s (**-men**) ostricaio

oys'ter shell' s conchiglia d'ostrica

oys'ter stew' s brodetto d'ostriche

ozone ['ozon] s ozono

P

P, p [pi] s sedicesima lettera dell'alfabeto inglese

pace [pes] s passo, andatura; (of a horse) ambio; **to keep pace with** andare di pari passo con; **to put s.o. through his paces** mettere qlcu a dura prova; **to set the pace for** fare l'andatura per; dare l'esempio a || tr misurare a passi, percorrere; **to pace the floor** andare avanti e indietro per la stanza || intr camminare lentamente; andare al passo; (said of a horse) ambiare

pace'mak'er s battistrada m; (in races) chi stabilisce il passo; (med) pacemaker m

pacific [pə'sɪfɪk] adj pacifico || **Pacific** adj & s Pacifico

pacifier ['pæsɪ‚faɪ·ər] s paciere m; (teething ring) succhietto, tettarella

pacifism ['pæsɪ‚fɪzəm] s pacifismo

pacifist ['pæsɪfɪst] adj & s pacifista mf

paci·fy ['pæsɪ‚faɪ] v (pret & pp **-fied**) tr pacificare

pack [pæk] s fardello, pacco; (of merchandise) balla; (of lies) mucchio; (of cards) mazzo; (of thieves) banda; (of dogs) muta; (of animals) branco; (of birds) stormo; (of cigarettes) pacchetto; (of ice) banchiglia; (of people) turba || tr affardellare, impaccare; (to wrap) imballare; ammucchiare; (in cans) mettere in conserva; (people) stipare; (a trunk) fare; **to pack in** stipare; **to pack off** mandare via || intr ammucchiarsi, pigiarsi, accalcarsi; **to pack up** fare il baule

package ['pækɪdʒ] *s* pacco, collo; (*small*) pacchetto ‖ *tr* impacchettare

pack' an'imal *s* bestia da soma

packer ['pækər] *s* imballatore *m*; (*of canned goods*) proprietario (di fabbrica di conserve alimentari)

packet ['pækɪt] *s* pacchetto; (*boat*) vapore *m* postale

packing ['pækɪŋ] *s* imballaggio; (*on shoulders of suit*) spallina; (*mach*) stoppa; (*ring*) (mach) guarnizione

pack'ing box' or **case'** *s* cassa d'imballaggio

pack'ing house' *s* fabbrica di conserve alimentari; fabbrica di carne in conserva

pack'ing slip' *s* foglio d'imballaggio

pack'sad'dle *s* basto

pack'thread' *s* spago d'imballaggio

pack'train' *s* fila di animali da soma

pact [pækt] *s* patto

pad [pæd] *s* cuscinetto, tampone *m*; imbottitura; (*of writing paper*) blocco da annotazioni; (*of an animal*) superficie *f* plantare, zampa; (*of a water lily*) foglia, (rok) piattaforma ‖ *v* (*pret & pp* **padded**; *ger* **padding**) *tr* imbottire, ovattare; (*e.g., a speech*) infarcire ‖ *intr* camminare pesantemente

pad'ding *s* imbottitura

paddle ['pædəl] *s* pagaia; (*of waterwheel*) pala ‖ *tr* remare; (*to spank*) bastonare ‖ *intr* remare; (*to splash*) diguazzare

pad'dle wheel' *s* ruota a pale

paddock ['pædək] *s* prato d'allenamento, paddock *m*

pad'lock' *s* lucchetto ‖ *tr* chiudere col lucchetto

pagan ['pegən] *adj & s* pagano

paganism ['pegə‚nɪzəm] *s* paganesimo

page [pedʒ] *s* (*of a book*) pagina; (*at court*) paggio; (*in hotels*) fattorino, valletto ‖ *tr* impaginare; (*in hotels*) chiamare, far chiamare

pageant ['pædʒənt] *s* parata, corteo, spettacolo

pageant·ry ['pædʒəntri] *s* (**-ries**) pompa, fasto

paginate ['pædʒɪ‚net] *tr* impaginare

pail [pel] *s* secchio

pain [pen] *s* dolore *m*; **on pain of** sotto pena di; **to take pains** to prendersi cura di; **to take pains not to** guardarsi da ‖ *tr & intr* dolere

painful ['penfəl] *adj* doloroso, penoso

pain'kill'er *s* (coll) analgesico

painless ['penlɪs] *adj* indolore

painstaking ['penz‚tekɪŋ] *adj* meticoloso

paint [pent] *s* (*for pictures*) colore *m*; (*for a house*) vernice *f*; (*make-up*) trucco ‖ *tr* dipingere; (*a house*) verniciare, tinteggiare ‖ *intr* (*with make-up*) dipingersi; essere pittore

paint'box' *s* scatola da colori

paint'brush' *s* pennello

painter ['pentər] *s* (*of pictures*) pittore *m*; (*of a house*) verniciatore *m*; (naut) barbetta

painting ['pentɪŋ] *s* pittura, dipinto

paint' remov'er [rɪ'muvər] *s* solvente *m* per levar la vernice

paint' thin'ner *s* diluente *m*

pair [per] *s* paio; (*of people*) coppia ‖ *tr* appaiare, accoppiare ‖ *intr* appaiarsi, accoppiarsi

pair' of scis'sors *s* forbici *fpl*

pair' of trou'sers *s* calzoni *mpl*

pajamas [pə'dʒɑməz] or [pə'dʒæməz] *spl* pigiama *m*

Pakistan [‚pɑkɪ'stɑn] *s* il Pakistan

Pakistani [‚pɑkɪ'stɑni] *adj & s* pachistano

pal [pæl] *s* (coll) compagno ‖ *v* (*pret & pp* **palled**; *ger* **palling**) *intr* (coll) essere compagni

palace ['pælɪs] *s* palazzo

palatable ['pælətəbəl] *adj* gustoso, appetitoso; accettabile

palatal ['pælətəl] *adj & s* palatale *f*

palate ['pælɪt] *s* palato

pale [pel] *adj* pallido ‖ *s* palo; (*enclosure*) recinto; (fig) ambito ‖ *intr* impallidire

pale'face' *s* faccia pallida

palette ['pælɪt] *s* tavolozza

palfrey ['pɔlfri] *s* palafreno

palisade [‚pælɪ'sed] *s* palizzata; (*line of cliffs*) dirupo

pall [pɔl] *s* panno mortuario; (*of smoke*) cappa ‖ *tr* saziare, infastidire ‖ *intr* saziarsi, perdere l'appetito

pall'bear'er *s* chi accompagna il feretro; chi porta il feretro

palliate ['pælɪ‚et] *tr* attenuare, alleviare

pallid ['pælɪd] *adj* pallido

pallor ['pælər] *s* pallore *m*

palm [pɑm] *s* (*tree and leaf*) palma; (*of hand; measure*) palmo; **to carry off the palm** riportare la palma; **to grease the palm of** ungere le ruote a ‖ *tr* far sparire nella mano; nascondere; **to palm off s.th on s.o.** rifilare qlco a qlcu

palmet·to [pæl'meto] *s* (**-tos** or **-toes**) palmeto

palmist ['pɑmɪst] *s* chiromante *mf*

palmistry ['pɑmɪstri] *s* chiromanzia

palm' leaf' *s* palma, foglia di palma

palm' oil' *s* olio di palma

Palm' Sun'day *s* Domenica delle Palme

palpable ['pælpəbəl] *adj* palpabile

palpitate ['pælpɪ‚tet] *intr* palpitare

pal·sy ['pɔlzi] *s* (**-sies**) paralisi *f* ‖ *v* (*pret & pp* **-sied**) *tr* paralizzare

pal·try ['pɔltri] *adj* (**-trier; -triest**) vile, meschino, irrisorio

pamper ['pæmpər] *tr* viziare; (*the appetite*) saziare

pamphlet ['pæmflɪt] *s* opuscolo, libello

pan [pæn] *s* padella, casseruola; (*of a balance*) coppa, piatto; (phot) bacinella ‖ *v* (*pret & pp* **panned**; *ger* **panning**) *tr* friggere; (*gold*) vagliare in padella; (*salt*) estrarre in salina; (coll) criticare ‖ *intr* essere estratto; **to pan out** (coll) riuscire ‖ **Pan** *s* Pan *m*

panace·a [‚pænə'si·ə] *s* panacea

Pan'ama Canal' ['pænə‚mɑ] *s* Canale *m* di Panama

Pan'ama hat' *s* panama *m*
Panamanian [,pænə'menɪ·ən] or [,pænə'manɪ·ən] *adj* & *s* panamegno
pan'cake' *s* frittella ‖ *intr* (aer) atterrare a piatto
pan'cake land'ing *s* atterraggio a piatto
pancreas ['pænkrɪ·əs] *s* pancreas *m*
pander ['pændər] *s* mezzano ‖ *intr* ruffianeggiare; **to pander to** favorire, assecondare i desideri di
pane [pen] *s* pannello, vetro di finestra
pan·el ['pænəl] *s* pannello; gruppo che discute in faccia al pubblico, telequiz *m*; discussione pubblica; (*of door or window*) specchio; (law) lista di giurati ‖ *v* (*pret* & *pp* **-eled** or **-elled**; *ger* **-eling** or **-elling**) *tr* coprire di pannelli
pan'el discus'sion *s* colloquio di esperti in faccia al pubblico
panelist ['pænəlɪst] *s* partecipante *mf* a una discussione in faccia al pubblico
pan'el lights' *spl* luci *fpl* del cruscotto
pan'el truck' *s* camioncino
pang [pæŋ] *s* (*sharp pain*) spasimo; (*of remorse*) tormento
pan'han'dle *s* manico della padella ‖ *intr* accattare, mendicare
pan·ic ['pænɪk] *adj* & *s* panico ‖ *v* (*pret* & *pp* **-icked**; *ger* **-icking**) *tr* riempire di panico ‖ *intr* essere colto dal panico
pan'ic-strick'en *adj* morto di paura, in preda al panico
pano·ply ['pænəplɪ] *s* (**-plies**) panoplia; abbigliamento in pompa magna
panorama [,pænə'ræmə] or [,pænə'ramə] *s* panorama *m*
pan·sy ['pænzɪ] *s* (**-sies**) viola del pensiero
pant [pænt] *s* anelito, affanno; **pants** pantaloni *mpl*, calzoni *mpl*; **to wear the pants** portare i calzoni ‖ *intr* ansare; (*said of heart*) palpitare
pantheism ['pænθɪ,izəm] *s* panteismo
pantheon ['pænθɪ,ɑn] or ['pænθɪ·ən] *s* panteon *m*, pantheon *m*
panther ['pænθər] *s* pantera
panties ['pæntiz] *spl* mutandine *fpl*
pantomime ['pæntə,maim] *s* pantomima
pan·try ['pæntri] *s* (**-tries**) dispensa
pap [pæp] *s* pappa
papa·cy ['pepəsi] *s* (**-cies**) papato
Pa'pal States' ['pepəl] *spl* Stati *mpl* pontifici
paper ['pepər] *adj* di carta, cartaceo ‖ *s* carta; (*newspaper*) giornale *m*; (*of a student*) tema *m*, saggio; (*of a scholar*) dissertazione; **on paper** per iscritto ‖ *tr* (*a wall*) tappezzare
pa'per·back' *s* libro in brossura
pa'per·boy' *s* giornalaio, strillone *m*
pa'per clip' *s* fermaglio per le carte, clip *m*
pa'per cone' *s* cartoccio
pa'per cut'ter *s* rifilatrice *f*
pa'per doll' *s* pupazzetto di carta
pa'per·hang'er *s* tappezziere *m*
pa'per knife' *s* tagliacarte *m*
pa'per mill' *s* cartiera
pa'per mon'ey *s* carta moneta

pa'per prof'its *spl* guadagni *mpl* non realizzati su valori non venduti
pa'per tape' *s* (*of teletype*) nastro di carta; (*of computer*) nastro perforato
pa'per·weight' *s* fermacarte *m*
pa'per work' *s* lavoro a tavolino
papier-mâché [,pepərmə'ʃe] *s* cartapesta
paprika [pæ'prikə] or ['pæprɪkə] *s* paprica
papy·rus [pə'paɪrəs] *s* (**-ri** [raɪ]) papiro
par [pɑr] *adj* alla pari, nominale; normale ‖ *s* parità *f*, valore *m* nominale; **at par** alla pari
parable ['pærəbəl] *s* parabola
parabola [pə'ræbələ] *s* parabola
parachute ['pærə,ʃut] *s* paracadute *m* ‖ *intr* lanciarsi col paracadute
par'a-chute jump' *s* lancio col paracadute
parachutist ['pærə,ʃutɪst] *s* paracadutista *mf*
parade [pə'red] *s* parata, sfilata; ostentazione, sfoggio ‖ *tr* ostentare, sfoggiare; disporre in parata ‖ *intr* fare mostra di sé; (mil) sfilare
paradise ['pærə,daɪs] *s* paradiso
paradox ['pærə,dɑks] *s* paradosso
paradoxical [,pærə'dɑksɪkəl] *adj* paradossale
paraffin ['pærəfɪn] *s* paraffina
paragon ['pærə,gɑn] *s* paragone *m*
paragraph ['pærə,græf] or ['pærə,grɑf] *s* paragrafo, capoverso; (*in a newspaper*) trafiletto; (*of law*) comma *m*
parakeet ['pærə,kit] *s* parrocchetto
paral·lel ['pærə,lel] *adj* parallelo ‖ *s* (geog, fig) parallelo; (geom) parallela; **parallels** (typ) sbarrette *fpl* verticali ‖ *v* (*pret* & *pp* **-leled** or **-lelled**; *ger* **-leling** or **-lelling**) *tr* collocare parallelamente; correre parallelo a; confrontare
par'allel bars' *spl* parallele *fpl*
paraly·sis [pə'rælɪsɪs] *s* (**-ses** [,siz]) paralisi *f*
paralytic [,pærə'lɪtɪk] *adj* & *s* paralitico
paralyze ['pærə,laɪz] *tr* paralizzare
paramount ['pærə,maunt] *adj* capitale, supremo
paramour ['pærə,mur] *s* amante *mf*
paranoiac [,pærə'nɔɪ·æk] *adj* & *s* paranoico
parapet ['pærə,pet] *s* parapetto
paraphernalia [,pærəfər'nelɪ·ə] *spl* roba, cose *fpl*; attrezzi *mpl*, aggeggi *mpl*
parasite ['pærə,saɪt] *s* parassita *m*
parasitic(al) [,pærə'sɪtɪk(əl)] *adj* parassitico, parassitario
parasol ['pærə,sɔl] or ['pærə,sɑl] *s* parasole *m*, ombrellino da sole
par'a-troop'er *s* paracadutista *m*
par'a-troops' *spl* truppe *fpl* paracadutiste
parboil ['pɑr,bɔɪl] *tr* bollire parzialmente; (fig) far bollire
parcel ['pɑrsəl] *s* pacchetto; (*of land*) appezzamento ‖ *v* (*pret* & *pp* **-celed** or **-celled**; *ger* **-celing** or **-celling**) *tr*

impacchettare; **to parcel out** dividere, distribuire

par'cel post' s servizio pacchi postali

parch [part∫] tr bruciare; (*land*) inaridire; (*e.g., beans*) essiccare; **to be parched** bruciare dalla sete ‖ *intr* arrostirsi; inaridire

parchment ['part∫mənt] s pergamena

pardon ['pardən] s perdono, grazia; **I beg your pardon** scusi ‖ tr perdonare; (*an offense*) graziare

pardonable ['pardənəbəl] adj perdonabile, veniale

par'don board' s ufficio per la decisione delle grazie

pare [per] tr (*fruit, potatoes*) sbucciare, pelare; (*nails*) tagliare; (*expenses*) ridurre

parent ['perənt] adj madre, principale ‖ s genitore m or genitrice f; (fig) origine f; **parents** genitori mpl

parentage ['perəntɪdʒ] s discendenza, lignaggio

parenthesis [pə'renθɪsɪs] s (**-ses** [,siz]) parentesi f; **in parenthesis** tra parentesi

parenthetically [,pærən'θetɪkəli] adv tra parentesi

parenthood ['perənt,hud] s paternità f or maternità f

pariah [pə'raɪə] or ['parɪə] s paria m

pari-mutuel ['pærɪ'mjut∫ʊəl] s totalizzatore m

par'ing knife' ['perɪŋ] s coltello per sbucciare

Paris ['pærɪs] s Parigi f

parish ['pærɪ∫] s parrocchia

parishioner [pə'rɪ∫ənər] s parrocchiano

Parisian [pə'rɪʒən] adj & s parigino

parity ['pærɪti] s parità f

park [park] s parco ‖ tr parcare, parcheggiare ‖ *intr* parcare, parcheggiare, stazionare

parking ['parkɪŋ] s posteggio, parcheggio; **no parking** divieto di parcheggio

park'ing lights' spl luci fpl di posizione

park'ing lot' s posteggio, parcheggio

park'ing me'ter s parchimetro

park'ing tick'et s contravvenzione per parcheggio abusivo

park'way' s boulevard m

parlay ['parli] or [par'le] tr rigiocare

parley ['parli] s trattativa, conferenza ‖ *intr* parlamentare

parliament ['parlɪmənt] s parlamento

parlor ['parlər] s salotto; (*of beautician or undertaker*) salone m; (*of convent*) parlatorio

par'lor car' s vettura salone

par'lor game' s gioco di società

par'lor pol'itics s politica da caffè

Parmesan [,parmɪ'zæn] adj & s parmigiano

Parnassus [par'næsəs] s (*poetry; poets*) parnaso; il Parnaso

parochial [pə'rokɪəl] adj parrocchiale; ristretto, limitato; (*school*) confessionale

paro·dy ['pærədi] s (**-dies**) parodia ‖ v (*pret & pp* **-died**) tr parodiare

parole [pə'rol] s parola d'onore; libertà f condizionale, condizionale f ‖ tr mettere in libertà condizionale

paroxytone [pær'aksɪ,ton] adj parossitono ‖ s parola parossitona

par·quet [par'ke] s pavimento di legno tassellato, tassellato; (theat) platea ‖ v (*pret & pp* **-queted** ['ked]; ger **-queting** ['ke·ɪŋ]) tr pavimentare in legno tassellato

par'quet cir'cle s poltroncine fpl

parricide ['pærɪ,saɪd] s (*act*) patricidio, parricidio; (*person*) patricida mf, parricida mf

parrot ['pærət] s pappagallo ‖ tr scimmiottare, fare il pappagallo a

par·ry ['pæri] s (**-ries**) parata ‖ v (*pret & pp* **-ried**) tr parare; (fig) evitare

parse [pars] tr (gram) analizzare grammaticalmente

parsimonious [,parsɪ'monɪ·əs] adj parsimonioso

parsley ['parsli] s prezzemolo

parsnip ['parsnɪp] s pastinaca

parson ['parsən] s parroco; pastore m protestante

part [part] s parte f; (*of a machine*) pezzo, organo; (*of hair*) riga; **for my part** per parte mia; **on the part of** da parte di; **part and parcel** parte f integrante; **parts** abilità f, dote f; regione f, paesi mpl; **to do one's part** fare il proprio dovere ‖ adv parzialmente, in part ‖ tr dividere, separare; **to part company** separarsi; **to part one's hair** farsi la riga ‖ *intr* separarsi; **to part from** separarsi da, dividersi da; **to part with** rinunciare a

par·take [par'tek] v (*pret* **-took** ['tuk]; *pp* **-taken**) tr condividere ‖ *intr*—**to partake in** partecipare a; **to partake of** condividere

parterre [par'ter] s aiola; (theat) platea

Parthenon ['parθɪ,nan] s Partenone m

partial ['par∫əl] adj parziale

participate [par'tɪsɪ,pet] *intr* partecipare; **to participate in** partecipare a

participation [par,tɪsɪ'pe∫ən] s partecipazione

participle ['partɪ,sɪpəl] s participio

particle ['partɪkəl] s particella

particular [pər'tɪkjələr] adj (*belonging to a single person*) particolare; (*exacting*) esigente, fastidioso ‖ s particolare m; **in particular** specialmente, particolarmente

part'ing adj (*words*) di commiato; (*last*) ultimo ‖ s commiato; separazione

partisan ['partɪzən] adj & s partigiano

partition [par'tɪ∫ən] s partizione, divisione; (*or house*) tramezzo ‖ tr dividere; tramezzare

partner ['partnər] s (*in sports*) compagno; (*in dancing*) cavaliere m, dama; (*husband or wife*) consorte mf; (com) socio

partnership ['partnər,∫ɪp] s associazione; (com) società f

part' of speech' s parte f del discorso

partridge ['partrɪdʒ] s pernice f

part' time' adj a orario ridotto, a ore

par·ty ['parti] adj comune; di gala ‖ s (**-ties**) festa, ricevimento, trattenimento; (*of people*) gruppo; (*indi-*

vidual) persona; (pol) partito; (law) contraente *mf*; (mil) distaccamento; **to be a party to** prendere parte a; essere complice di

par'ty girl' *s* ragazza che fa la vita

par'ty-go'er *s* frequentatore *m* di trattenimenti

part'y line' *s (boundary)* linea di confine; *(of Communist party)* politica del partito; (telp) linea in coutenza

pass [pæs] *or* [pɑs] *s* passaggio; *(state)* stato, situazione; *(free ticket)* ingresso gratuito; *(leave of absence given to a soldier)* congedo, permesso; *(of a hypnotist)* gesto; *(between mountains)* passo; (slang) tentativo d'abbraccio; **a pretty pass** (coll) un bell'affare || *tr (a course in school)* passare; *(to promote)* promuovere; *(a law)* approvare; *(a sentence)* pronunciare; *(an opinion)* esprimere, avanzare; *(to excrete)* evacuare; far muovere; **to pass by** non fare attenzione a; **to pass off** (e.g., *bogus money)* azzeccare; **to pass on** trasmettere; **to pass out** distribuire; **to pass over** omettere || *intr (to go)* passare; *(said of a law)* essere approvato; *(said of a student)* essere promosso; *(to be accepted)* farsi passare; *(said, e.g., of two trains)* incrociarsi; **to come to pass** accadere, succedere; **to pass as** passare per; **to pass away** morire; **to pass out** (slang) svenire; **to pass over or through** attraversare, passare per

passable ['pæsəbəl] *or* ['pɑsəbəl] *adj* praticabile; *(by boat)* navigabile; *(adequate)* passabile; *(law)* promulgabile

passage ['pæsɪdʒ] *s* passaggio; *(of a law)* approvazione; *(ticket)* biglietto di passaggio; *(of the bowels)* evacuazione

pass'book' *s* libretto di banca; libretto della cassa di risparmio

passenger ['pæsəndʒər] *s* passeggero

passer-by ['pæsər'baɪ] *or* ['pɑsər'baɪ] *s* **(passers-by)** passante *mf*

passing ['pæsɪŋ] *or* ['pɑsɪŋ] *adj (fleeting)* fuggente; *(casual)* incidentale; *(grade)* che concede la promozione || *s* passaggio; *(death)* morte *f;* promozione

passion ['pæʃən] *s* passione

passionate ['pæʃənɪt] *adj* appassionato; *(hot-tempered)* collerico, veemente, ardente

passive ['pæsɪv] *adj & s* passivo

pass'key' *s* chiave maestra; *(for use of hotel help)* comunella

Pass'o'ver *s* Pasqua ebraica

pass'port' *s* passaporto

pass'word' *s* parola d'ordine

past [pæst] *or* [pɑst] *adj* passato, scorso; **ex,** e.g., **past president** ex presidente || *s* passato || *adv* oltre; al di fuori; al di là || *prep* oltre; al di là di; dopo (di); **past belief** incredibile; **past cure** incurabile; **past hope** senza speranza; **past recovery** incurabile; **past three o'clock** le tre passate

paste [pest] *s (dough)* pasta; *(adhesive)* colla; diamante *m* artificiale || *tr* incollare; (slang) dare pugni a

paste'board' *s* cartone *m*

pastel [pæs'tɛl] *adj & s* pastello

pasteurize ['pæstə,raɪz] *tr* pastorizzare

pastime ['pæs,taɪm] *or* ['pɑs,taɪm] *s* diversione, passatempo

pastor ['pæstər] *or* ['pɑstər] *s* pastore *m,* sacerdote *m*

pastoral ['pæstərəl] *or* ['pɑstərəl] *adj* pastorale || *s (poem, letter)* pastorale *f; (crosier)* pastorale *m*

pas·try ['pestri] *s* **(-tries)** pasticceria

pas'try cook' *s* pasticciere *m*

pas'try shop' *s* pasticceria

pasture ['pæstʃər] *or* ['pɑstʃər] *s* pastura, pascolo || *tr* condurre al pascolo || *intr* brucare

past·y ['pesti] *adj* **(-ier; -iest)** pastoso; flaccido

pat [pæt] *s* colpetto; *(of butter)* panetto || *v (pret & pp* **patted;** *ger* **patting)** *tr* accarezzare leggermente; battere leggermente; **to pat on the back** elogiare, incoraggiare battendo sulla spalla

patch [pætʃ] *s (on a suit or shoes)* toppa; *(in a tire)* pezza; *(on wound)* benda; *(of ground)* appezzamento; *(small area)* tomba || *tr* rammendare; **to patch up** *(an argument)* comporre; *(to produce crudely)* raffazzonare

patent ['petənt] *adj* patente, palmare || ['pætənt] *adj* brevettato || *s (of invention)* brevetto; *(sole right)* privativa || *tr* brevettare

pat'ent leath'er ['pætənt] *s* copale *m & f,* pelle *f* di vernice

pat'ent med'icine ['pætənt] *s* specialità *f* medicinale

pat'ent right' ['pætənt] *s* proprietà brevettata

paternal [pə'tʌrnəl] *adj* paterno

paternity [pə'tʌrnɪti] *s* paternità *f*

path [pæθ] *or* [pɑθ] *s* via battuta, sentiero; (fig) via

pathetic [pə'θɛtɪk] *adj* patetico

path'find'er *s* esploratore *m*

pathology [pə'θɑlədʒi] *s* patologia

pathos ['peθɑs] *s* patos *m,* pathos *m*

path'way' *s* sentiero, cammino

patience ['peʃəns] *s* pazienza

patient ['peʃənt] *adj & s* paziente *mf*

patriarch ['petrɪ,ɑrk] *s* patriarca *m*

patrician [pə'trɪʃən] *adj & s* patrizio

patricide ['pætrɪ,saɪd] *s (act)* patricidio; *(person)* parricida *mf*

Patrick ['pætrɪk] *s* Patrizio

patrimo·ny ['pætrɪ,moni] *s* **(-nies)** patrimonio

patriot ['petrɪ,ət] *or* ['pætrɪ,ət] *s* patriota *m*

patriotic [,petrɪ'ɑtɪk] *or* [,pætrɪ'ɑtɪk] *adj* patriottico

patriotism ['petrɪ,ə,tɪzəm] *or* ['pætrɪ,ə,tɪzəm] *s* patriottismo

pa·trol [pə'trol] *s (group)* pattuglia; *(individual)* soldato *or* agente *m* di pattuglia || *v (pret & pp* **-trolled;** *ger* **-trolling)** *tr & intr* pattugliare

patrol'man *s* **(-men)** agente *m,* poliziotto

patrol' wag'on s carrozzone m cellulare, cellulare m

patron ['petrən] or ['pætrən] s patrono, sostenitore m; (customer) cliente mf

patronize ['petrə‚naɪz] or ['pætrə‚naɪz] tr (to support) sostenere; trattare con condiscendenza; essere cliente abituale di

pa'tron saint' s patrono

patter ['pætər] s (e.g., of rain) battito; (of feet) scalpiccio; (speech) chiacchierio ‖ intr battere, picchiettare; chiaccherare

pattern ['pætərn] s modello; disegno; (of flight) procedura ‖ tr modellare

pat·ty ['pæti] s (-ties) pasticcino; (meat cake) polpetta

paucity ['pɔsɪti] s pochezza, scarsità f, insufficienza

Paul [pɔl] s Paolo

paunch [pɔntʃ] s pancia

paunch·y ['pɔntʃi] adj (-ier; -iest) panciuto

pauper ['pɔpər] s povero, indigente mf

pause [pɔz] s pausa; (of a tape recorder) arresto momentaneo; **to give pause (to)** dar di che pensare (a) ‖ intr far pausa, fermarsi; (to hesitate) esitare, vacillare

pave [pev] tr pavimentare, lastricare; **to pave the way (for)** aprire il cammino (a)

pavement ['pevmənt] s pavimentazione, lastricato; (sidewalk) marciapiede m

pavilion [pə'vɪljən] s padiglione m; (of circus) tendone m

paw [pɔ] s zampa ‖ tr (to touch with paws) dar zampate a; (to handle clumsily) maneggiare goffamente; (coll) palpeggiare ‖ intr zampare

pawn [pɔn] s (security) pegno; (tool of another person) pedina; (chess) pedina, pedone m; (fig) ostaggio ‖ tr dare in pegno, impegnare

pawn'bro'ker s prestatore m su pegno

pawn'shop' s agenzia di prestiti su pegno, monte m di pietà

pawn' tick'et s ricevuta di pegno, polizza del monte di pietà

pay [pe] s pagamento; (wages) paga, salario; (mil) soldo ‖ v (pret & pp **paid** [ped]) tr pagare; (wages) conguagliare; (one's respects) presentare; (a visit) fare; (a bill) saldare; (attention) fare, presentare; **to pay back** ripagare; (fig) pagare pan per focaccia a; **to pay for** pagare; **to pay off** liquidare; (in order to discharge) pagare e licenziare; **to pay up** saldare ‖ intr pagare; valere la pena; **pay as you enter** pagare all'ingresso; **pay as you go** pagare le tasse per trattenuta; **pay as you leave** pagare all'uscita

payable ['pe‐əbəl] adj pagabile

pay' boost' s aumento di salario

pay'check' s assegno in pagamento del salario; salario, paga

pay'day' s giorno di paga

payee [pe'i] s beneficiario

pay' en'velope s bustapaga

payer ['pe‐ər] s pagatore m

pay'load' s peso utile

pay'mas'ter s ufficiale m pagatore

payment ['pemənt] s pagamento

pay'off' s pagamento, regolamento; (coll) conclusione

pay' phone' s telefono a moneta

pay'roll' s lista degli impiegati; libro paga

pay' sta'tion s telefono pubblico

pea [pi] s pisello

peace [pis] s pace f; **to hold one's peace** tacere, stare zitto

peaceable ['pisəbəl] adj pacifico

peaceful ['pisfəl] adj pacifico

peace'mak'er s paciere m

peace' of mind' s serenità f d'animo

peace' pipe' s calumet m della pace

peach [pitʃ] s pesca; (coll) persona or cosa stupenda

peach' tree' s pesco

peach·y ['pitʃi] adj (-ier; -iest) (coll) stupendo

pea'cock' s pavone m

peak [pik] s picco; (of traffic) punta; (of one's career) sommo

peak' hour' s ora di punta

peak' load' s carico delle ore di punta, carico massimo

peal [pil] s (of bells) squillo; (of gun) rombo; (of laughter) scoppio; (of thunder) scroscio ‖ intr scampanare, squillare

pea'nut' s nocciolina americana; (plant) arachide f

pea'nut but'ter s pasta d'arachidi

pear [per] s (fruit) pera; (tree) pero

pearl [pʌrl] s perla; (mother-of-pearl) madreperla; colore perlaceo

pearl' oys'ter s ostrica perlifera

pear' tree' s pero

peasant ['pezənt] adj & s contadino

pea'shoot'er s cerbottana

pea' soup' s minestra di piselli; (coll) nebbione m

peat [pit] s torba

pebble ['pebəl] s ciottolo

peck [pek] s beccata; misura di due galloni; a peck of trouble un mare di guai ‖ tr beccare ‖ intr beccare; **to peck at** beccucciare

peculation [‚pekjə'leʃən] s malversazione, peculato

peculiar [pɪ'kjuljər] adj peculiare; (odd) strano

pedagogue ['pedə‚gɑg] s pedagogo

pedagogy ['pedə‚godʒi] or ['pedə‚gɑdʒi] s pedagogia

ped·al ['pedəl] s pedale m ‖ v (pret & pp **-aled** or **-alled**; ger **-aling** or **-alling**) tr spingere coi pedali ‖ intr pedalare

pedant ['pedənt] s pedante mf

pedantic [pɪ'dæntɪk] adj pedantesco

pedant·ry ['pedəntri] s (-ries) pedanteria

peddle ['pedəl] tr vendere di porta in porta ‖ intr fare il venditore ambulante

peddler ['pedlər] s venditore m or merciaiolo ambulante

pedestal ['pedɪstəl] *s* piedistallo
pedestrian [pɪ'destrɪ-ən] *adj* pedestre ‖ *s* pedone *m*
pediatrics [ˌpidɪ'ætrɪks] *or* [ˌpedɪ-'ætrɪks] *s* pediatria
pedigree ['pedɪˌgri] *s* albero genealogico; discendenza, lignaggio
pediment ['pedɪmənt] *s* frontone *m*
peek [pik] *s* sbirciata ‖ *intr* sbirciare
peel [pil] *s* scorza, buccia; *(of baker)* pala ‖ *tr* sbucciare; **to keep one's eyes peeled** (slang) tenere gli occhi aperti ‖ *intr* pelarsi
peep [pip] *s* sbirciata; *(sound)* pigolio ‖ *intr* guardare attraverso una fessura; *(said of birds)* pigolare; *(to begin to appear)* fare capolino
peep'hole' *s* spioncino
Peep'ing Tom' *s* guardone *m*
peep' show' *s* cosmorama *m*
peer [pɪr] *s* pari *m*, uguale *m*; *(Brit)* pari *m* ‖ *intr* guardare da vicino
peerless ['pɪrlɪs] *adj* senza pari
peeve [piv] *s* (coll) seccatura, irritazione ‖ *tr* (coll) seccare, irritare
peevish ['pivɪʃ] *adj* irritabile
peg [peg] *s* (*to plug holes*) zipolo; *(pin)* cavicchio; *(mus)* bischero; (coll) grado; **to take down a peg** (coll) fare abbassare la testa a ‖ *v* (*pret & pp* **pegged**; *ger* **pegging**) *tr* fissare con cavicchi; *(prices)* stabilizzare ‖ *intr*—**to peg away** lavorare di lena
peg' leg' *s* gamba di legno
Peking ['pi'kɪŋ] *s* Pechino *f*
Peking·ese [ˌpikɪ'niz] *adj* pechinese ‖ *s* (*-ese*) pechinese *mf*
pelf [pelf] *s* (pej) denaro rubacchiato, maltolto
pelican ['pelɪkən] *s* pellicano
pellet ['pelɪt] *s* pallottola; *(for shotgun)* pallino; *(pill)* pillola
pell-mell ['pel'mel] *adj* confuso, disordinato ‖ *adv* alla rinfusa
Peloponnesian [ˌpeləpə'niʃən] *adj & s* peloponnesiaco
pelt [pelt] *s* pelle grezza; *(blow)* colpo ‖ *tr* scagliare contro; *(to beat)* battere violentemente ‖ *intr* battere, scrosciare
pen [pen] *s* *(enclosure)* recinto; *(for writing)* penna; *(pen point)* pennino ‖ *v* (*pret & pp* **penned**; *ger* **penning**) *tr* scrivere a penna; *(to compose)* redigere ‖ *v* (*pret & pp* **penned** *or* **pent**; *ger* **penning**) *tr* recintare
penalize ['pinəˌlaɪz] *tr* punire; (sports) penalizzare
penal·ty ['penəlti] *s* (*-ties*) punizione; *(fine)* multa; *(for late payment)* penale *f*; **under penalty of** sotto pena di
pen'alty goal' *s* calcio di rigore
penance ['penəns] *s* penitenza
penchant ['pen/ənt] *s* propensione
pen·cil ['pensɪl] *s* matita; *(of rays)* fascio ‖ *v* (*pret & pp* **-ciled** *or* **-cilled**; *ger* **-ciling** *or* **-cilling**) *tr* scrivere a matita; (med) pennellare
pen'cil sharp'ener *s* temperalapis *m*
pendent ['pendənt] *adj* pendente, sospeso ‖ *s* pendente *m*, ciondolo

pending ['pendɪŋ] *adj* imminente; **in sospeso** ‖ *prep* durante; fino a
pendulum ['pendʒələm] *s* pendolo
pen'dulum bob' *s* lente *f*
penetrate ['peniˌtret] *tr & intr* penetrare
penguin ['pengwɪn] *s* pinguino
pen'hold'er *s* portapenne *m*
penicillin [ˌpenɪ'sɪlɪn] *s* penicillina
peninsula [pə'nɪnsələ] *s* penisola
peninsular [pə'nɪnsələr] *adj & s* peninsulare
penitence ['penɪtəns] *s* penitenza
penitent ['penɪtənt] *adj & s* penitente *mf*
pen'knife' *s* (*-knives*) temperino
penmanship ['penmənˌʃɪp] *s* calligrafia
pen' name' *s* nome *m* di penna, pseudonimo
pennant ['penənt] *s* pennone *m*
penniless ['penɪlɪs] *adj* povero **in canna**, senza un soldo
pennon ['penən] *s* pennone *m*
pen·ny ['peni] *s* (*-nies*) (U.S.A.) centesimo ‖ *s* (**pence** [pens]) (Brit) penny *m*
pen'ny pinch'er ['pɪntʃər] *s* spilorcio
pen' pal' *s* amico corrispondente
pen'point' *s* pennino; *(of ball-point pen)* punta
pension ['penʃən] *s* pensione ‖ *tr* pensionare, mettere in pensione
pensioner ['penʃənər] *s* pensionato
pensive ['pensɪv] *adj* pensieroso
Pentecost ['pentɪˌkɔst] *or* ['pentɪˌkɑst] *s* la Pentecoste
penthouse ['pentˌhaus] *s* appartamento di lusso sul tetto; tettoia
pent-up ['pentˌʌp] *adj* represso
penult ['pinʌlt] *s* penultima
penum·bra [pɪ'nʌmbrə] *s* (*-brae* [bri] *or* *-bras*) penombra
penurious [pɪ'nurɪ-əs] *adj* taccagno, meschino; indigente
penury ['penjəri] *s* taccagneria; estrema povertà, miseria
pen'wip'er *s* nettapenne *m*
people ['pipəl] *spl* popolo, gente *f*; *(relatives)* famiglia; gente *f* del popolo; si, e.g., **people say** si dice ‖ *ssg* (**peoples**) nazione, popolazione ‖ *tr* popolare
pep [pep] *s* (coll) animo, brio ‖ *v* (*pret & pp* **pepped**; *ger* **pepping**) *tr*—**to pep up** (coll) dar animo a
pepper ['pepər] *s* pepe *m* ‖ *tr* pepare; *(to pelt)* tempestare
pep'per·box' *s* pepaiola
pep'per·mint' *s* menta piperita
per [pʌr] *prep* per; *(for each)* il, e.g., **three dollars per meter** tre dollari il metro; **as per** secondo
perambulator [pər'æmbjəˌletər] *s* carrozzella, carrozzino
per capita [pər 'kæpɪtə] per persona, **a testa**
perceive [pər'siv] *tr* percepire
percent [pər'sent] *s* percento, per cento
percentage [pər'sentɪdʒ] *s* percento, percentuale *f*; (coll) vantaggio
perception [pər'sepʃən] *s* percezione

perch [pʌrtʃ] *s* (*roost*) posatoio; (*horizontal rod*) ballatoio; (ichth) pesce persico ‖ *intr* appollaiarsi

percolator ['pʌrkə,letər] *s* caffettiera filtro a circolazione

percus'sion cap' [pər'kʌʃən] *s* capsula di percussione

per diem [pər 'daɪ·əm] *s* assegno giornaliero

perdition [pər'dɪʃən] *s* perdizione

perennial [pə'rɛnɪ·əl] *adj* perenne ‖ *s* pianta perenne

perfect ['pʌrfɪkt] *adj & s* perfetto ‖ [pər'fɛkt] *tr* perfezionare

perfidious [pər'fɪdɪ·əs] *adj* perfido

perfi·dy ['pʌrfɪdɪ] *s* (-dies) perfidia

perforate ['pʌrfə,ret] *tr* perforare

perforation [,pʌrfə're/ən] *s* perforazione; (*of postage stamp*) dentellatura

perforce [pər'fors] *adv* per forza, necessariamente

perform [pər'form] *tr* (*a task*) eseguire; (*a promise*) adempiere; (*to enact*) rappresentare ‖ *intr* recitare; (*said, e.g., of a machine*) funzionare

performance [pər'formans] *s* esecuzione; (*of a machine*) funzionamento; (*deed*) atto di prodezza; (theat) rappresentazione

performer [pər'formər] *s* esecutore *m*; attore *m*; acrobata *mf*

perform'ing arts' *spl* arti *fpl* dello spettacolo

perfume ['pʌrfjum] *s* profumo ‖ [pər'fjum] *tr* profumare

perfumer·y [pər'fjuməri] *s* (-ies) profumeria

perfunctory [pər'fʌŋktəri] *adj* superficiale, pro forma; indifferente

perhaps [pər'hæps] *adv* forse

per·il ['pɛrəl] *s* pericolo ‖ *v* (*pret & pp* -iled or -illed; *ger* -iling or -illing) *tr* mettere in pericolo

perilous ['pɛrɪləs] *adj* pericoloso

period ['pɪrɪ·əd] *s* periodo; mestruazione; (*in school*) ora; (sports) tempo; (gram) punto

pe'riod cos'tume *s* costume *m* dell'epoca

periodic [,pɪrɪ'ɑdɪk] *adj* periodico

periodical [,pɪrɪ'ɑdɪkəl] *adj & s* periodico

periphery [pə'rɪfəri] *s* (-ies) periferia

periscope ['pɛrɪ,skop] *s* periscopio

perish ['pɛrɪʃ] *intr* perire

perishable ['pɛrɪʃəbəl] *adj* deteriorabile

periwig ['pɛrɪ,wɪg] *s* parrucca

perjure ['pʌrdʒər] *tr*—**to perjure oneself** spergiurare, giurare il falso

perju·ry ['pʌrdʒəri] *s* (-ies) spergiuro

perk [pʌrk] *tr* (*the head, the ears*) alzare; **to perk oneself up** agghindarsi ‖ *intr*—**to perk up** ringalluzzirsi

permanence ['pʌrmənəns] *s* permanenza

permanen·cy ['pʌrmənənsi] *s* (-cies) permanenza

permanent ['pʌrmənənt] *adj* permanente ‖ *s* permanente *f*, ondulazione permanente

per'manent fix'ture *s* cosa or persona permanente

per'manent ten'ure *s* inamovibilità *f*

per'manent way' *s* (rr) sede *f* stradale ed armamento

permeate ['pʌrmɪ,et] *tr* permeare ‖ *intr* permearsi

permissible [pər'mɪsɪbəl] *adj* permissibile

permission [pər'mɪʃən] *s* permesso

per·mit ['pʌrmɪt] *s* permesso; patente *f*, licenza ‖ [pər'mɪt] *v* (*pret & pp* -mitted; *ger* -mitting) *tr* permettere

permute [pər'mjut] *tr* permutare

pernicious [pər'nɪʃəs] *adj* pernicioso

pernickety [pər'nɪkɪti] *adj* (coll) incontentabile, meticoloso

perorate ['pɛrə,ret] *intr* perorare

peroxide [pər'ɑksaɪd] *s* perossido; perossido d'idrogeno

perox'ide blonde' *s* bionda ossigenata

perpendicular [,pʌrpən'dɪkjələr] *adj & s* perpendicolare *f*

perpetrate ['pʌrpɪ,tret] *tr* (*a crime*) perpetrare; (*a blunder*) commettere

perpetual [pər'pɛt/ʊ·əl] *adj* perpetuo

perpetuate [pər'pɛt/ʊ,et] *tr* perpetuare

perplex [pər'plɛks] *tr* lasciare perplesso

perplexed [pər'plɛkst] *adj* perplesso

perplexi·ty [pər'plɛksɪti] *s* (-ties) perplessità *f*

per se [pər 'si] di per sé

persecute ['pʌrsɪ,kjut] *tr* perseguitare

persevere [,pʌrsɪ'vɪr] *intr* perseverare

Persian ['pʌrʒən] *adj & s* persiano

Per'sian Gulf' *s* Golfo Persico

persimmon [pər'sɪmən] *s* diospiro virginiano; cachi *m*

persist [pər'sɪst] or [pər'zɪst] *intr* persistere

persistent [pər'sɪstənt] or [pər'zɪstənt] *adj* persistente

person ['pʌrsən] *s* persona; **no person** nessuno

personage ['pʌrsənɪdʒ] *s* personaggio; persona

personal ['pʌrsənəl] *adj* personale; (*goods*) mobile ‖ *s* inserzione personale; trafiletto di società

personali·ty [,pʌrsə'nælɪti] *s* (-ties) personalità *f*; offesa personale

personal'ity cult' *s* culto della personalità

per'sonal prop'erty *s* beni *mpl* mobili

personi·fy [pər'sɑnɪ,faɪ] *v* (*pret & pp* -fied) *tr* personificare

personnel [,pʌrsə'nɛl] *s* personale *m*

per'son-to-per'son call' *s* (telp) chiamata con preavviso

perspective [pər'spɛktɪv] *s* prospettiva

perspicacious [,pʌrspɪ'ke/əs] *adj* perspicace

perspire [pər'spaɪr] *intr* sudare

persuade [pər'swed] *tr* persuadere

persuasion [pər'sweʒən] *s* persuasione; fede religiosa

pert [pʌrt] *adj* impertinente, sfacciato; vivace

pertain [pər'ten] *intr* appartenere; (*to have reference*) riferirsi

pertinacious [,pʌrtɪ'ne/əs] *adj* pertinace

pertinent ['pʌrtɪnənt] *adj* pertinente
perturb [pər'tʌrb] *tr* perturbare
Peru [pə'ru] *s* il Perù
perusal [pə'ruzəl] *s* attenta lettura
peruse [pə'ruz] *tr* leggere attentamente
pervade [pər'ved] *tr* pervadere
perverse [pər'vʌrs] *adj* perverso; (*obstinate*) ostinato
perversion [pər'vʌrʒən] *s* perversione
perversi·ty [pər'vʌrsɪti] *s* (-ties) perversità *f;* contrarietà *f*
pervert ['pʌrvərt] *s* pervertito, degenerato || [pər'vʌrt] *tr* pervertire, degenerare
pes·ky ['peski] *adj* (-kier; -kiest) (coll) noioso, molesto
pessimism ['pɛsɪ mɪzəm] *s* pessimismo
pessimist ['pesɪmɪst] *s* pessimista *mf*
pessimistic [pesɪ'mɪstɪk] *adj* pessimistico
pest [pest] *s* peste *f*, pestilenza; insetto; animale nocivo; (*person*) peste *f*, seccatore *m*
pester ['pestər] *tr* seccare, annoiare
pest'house' *s* lazzaretto
pesticide ['pestɪ saɪd] *s* insetticida *m*
pestiferous [pest'tɪfərəs] *adj* pestifero
pestilence ['pestɪləns] *s* pestilenza
pestle ['pesəl] *s* pestello
pet [pet] *s* animale favorito; beniamino || *v* (*pret & pp* petted; *ger* petting) *tr* accarezzare || *intr* (coll) pomiciare
petal ['petəl] *s* petalo
petard [pɪ'tard] *s* petardo
pet'cock' *s* chiavetta
Peter ['pitər] *s* Pietro; **to rob Peter to pay Paul** fare un buco per tappare un altro || *intr*—**to peter out** (coll) affievolirsi
petition [pɪ'tɪ/ən] *s* petizione || *tr* rivolgere un'istanza a
pet' name' *s* nomignolo vezzeggiativo
Petrarch ['pitrark] *s* Petrarca *m*
petri·fy ['petrɪ faɪ] *v* (*pret & pp* -fied) *tr* pietrificare || *intr* pietrificarsi
petrol ['petrəl] *s* (Brit) benzina
petroleum [pɪ'trolɪ·əm] *s* petrolio
pet' shop' *s* negozio di animali domestici
petticoat ['petɪ kot] *s* sottoveste *f;* (coll) sottana, gonnella
pet·ty ['peti] *adj* (-tier; -tiest) insignificante, minore; meschino
pet'ty cash' *s* cassa delle piccole spese
pet'ty lar'ceny *s* furterello
pet'ty of'ficer *s* (nav) sottufficiale *m* di marina
petulant ['petjələnt] *adj* stizzoso, irritabile
pew [pju] *s* banco di chiesa
pewter ['pjutər] *s* peltro; oggetti *mpl* di peltro
phalanx ['felæŋks] *or* ['fælæŋks] *s* falange *f*
phantasm ['fæntæzəm] *s* fantasma *m*
phantom ['fæntəm] *s* fantasma *m*
Pharaoh ['fero] *s* Faraone *m*
pharisee ['færɪ si] *s* fariseo || **Pharisee** *s* fariseo
pharmaceutical [farmə'sutɪkəl] *adj* farmaceutico

pharmacist ['farməsɪst] *s* farmacista *mf*
pharma·cy ['farməsi] *s* (-cies) farmacia
pharynx ['færɪŋks] *s* faringe *f*
phase [fez] *s* fase *f* || *tr* mettere in fase; sincronizzare; **to phase in** mettere in operazione gradualmente; **to phase out** eliminare gradualmente
pheasant ['fezənt] *s* fagiano
phenobarbital [fino'barbɪ tæl] *s* acido fenil-etilbarbiturico, barbiturato
phenomenal [fɪ'namɪnəl] *adj* fenomenale
phenome·non [fɪ'namɪ nan] *s* (-na [nə]) fenomeno
phial ['faɪ·əl] *s* fiala
philanderer [fɪ'lændərər] *s* donnaiolo
philanthropist [fɪ'lænθrəpɪst] *s* filantropo
philanthro·py [fɪ'lænθrəpi] *s* (-pies) filantropia
philatelist [fɪ'lætəlɪst] *s* filatelico
philately [fɪ'lætəli] *s* filatelia
Philip ['fɪlɪp] *s* Filippo
Philippine ['fɪlɪ pin] *adj* filippino || **Philippines** *spl* isole *fpl* Filippine
Philistine [fɪ'lɪstɪn], ['fɪlɪ stin] *or* ['fɪlɪ staɪn] *adj & s* filisteo
philologist [fɪ'lalədʒɪst] *s* filologo
philology [fɪ'lalədʒi] *s* filologia
philosopher [fɪ'lasəfər] *s* filosofo
philosophic(al) [fɪlə'safɪk(əl)] *adj* filosofico
philoso·phy [fɪ'lasəfi] *s* (-phies) filosofia
philter ['fɪltər] *s* filtro
phlebitis [flɪ'baɪtɪs] *s* flebite *f*
phlegm [flɛm] *s* (*secretion*) muco, catarro; (*self-possession*) flemma; apatia
phlegmatic(al) [flɛg'mætɪk(əl)] *adj* flemmatico
Phoebus ['fibəs] *s* Febo
Phoenician [fɪ'nɪ/ən] *or* [fɪ'ni/ən] *adj & s* fenicio
phoenix ['finɪks] *s* fenice *f*
phone [fon] *s* (coll) telefono || *tr & intr* (coll) telefonare
phone' call' *s* chiamata telefonica
phonetic [fo'netɪk] *adj* fonetico || **phonetics** *s* fonetica
phonograph ['fonə græf] *or* ['fonə graf] *s* fonografo
phonology [fə'nalədʒi] *s* fonologia
pho·ny ['foni] *adj* (-nier; -niest) (coll) falso || *s* (-nies) (coll) frode *f;* (*person*) (coll) impostore *m*
phosphate ['fasfet] *s* fosfato
phosphorescent [fasfə'resənt] *adj* fosforescente
phospho·rus ['fasfərəs] *s* (-ri [raɪ]) fosforo
pho·to ['foto] *s* (-tos) (coll) foto *f*
photo·cop·y ['fotə kapi] *s* (-ies) fotocopia || *tr* fotocopiare
pho'toelec'tric cell' [foto·ɪ'lɛktrɪk] *s* cellula fotoelettrica
photoengraving [foto·en'grevɪŋ] *s* fotoincisione
pho'to fin'ish *s* photofinish *m*, arrivo con fotografia

photogenic [ˌfotoˈdʒenɪk] *adj* fotogenico

photograph [ˈfotəˌgræf] *or* [ˈfotəˌgrɑf] *s* fotografia ‖ *tr* fotografare ‖ *intr*—**to photograph well** riuscire in fotografia

photographer [fəˈtɑgrəfər] *s* fotografo

photography [fəˈtɑgrəfi] *s* fotografia

photojournalism [ˌfotəˈdʒʌrnəˌlɪzəm] *s* giornalismo fotografico

pho'to·play' *s* dramma adattato per il cinematografo

photostat [ˈfotəˌstæt] *s* (trademark) copia fotostatica ‖ *tr* riprodurre fotostaticamente

phototube [ˈfotəˌtjub] *or* [ˈfotəˌtub] *s* fototubo

phrase [frez] *s* (gram) locuzione; (mus) frase *f* ‖ *tr* esprimere, formulare ‖ *intr* (mus) fraseggiare

phrenology [frɪˈnɑlədʒi] *s* frenologia

Phyllis [ˈfɪlɪs] *s* Fillide *f*

phy·lum [ˈfaɪləm] *s* (-la [lə]) phylum *m*, tipo

phys·ic [ˈfɪzɪk] *s* purgante *m* ‖ *v* (pret & pp -icked; ger -icking) *tr* dare il purgante a, purgare

physical [ˈfɪzɪkəl] *adj* fisico

physician [fɪˈzɪʃən] *s* medico

physicist [ˈfɪzɪsɪst] *s* fisico

physics [ˈfɪzɪks] *s* fisica

physiognomy [ˌfɪziˈɑgnəmi] *or* [ˌfɪziˈɑnəmi] *s* fisionomia

physiological [ˌfɪziəˈlɑdʒɪkəl] *adj* fisiologico

physiology [ˌfɪziˈɑlədʒi] *s* fisiologia

physique [fɪˈzik] *s* fisico

pi [paɪ] *s* (math) pi greco; (typ) tipi scartati ‖ *v* (pret & pp pied; ger piing) *tr* (typ) scompaginare, scomporre

pian·o [pɪˈæno] *s* (-os) piano

picaresque [ˌpɪkəˈrɛsk] *adj* picaresco

picayune [ˌpɪkəˈjun] *adj* meschino, minore, di poca importanza

picco·lo [ˈpɪkəˌlo] *s* (-los) ottavino

pick [pɪk] *s* (tool) piccone *m*; (choice) scelta; (the best) fiore *m*; (mus) plettro ‖ *tr* scavare; (to scratch at) grattare; (to gather) cogliere; (to pluck) spennare; (to pull apart) separare; (one's teeth) stuzzicarsi; (a bone) rosicchiare; (to choose) scegliere; (a lock) scassinare; (a pocket) tagliare, rubare; (mus) pizzicare; **to pick a fight** attaccare briga; **to pick faults** trovare a ridire; **to pick out** scegliere; distinguere; discriminare; **to pick s.o. to pieces** (coll) tagliare i panni addosso a qlcu; **to pick up** sollevare; (to find) trovare; (to learn) arrivare a sapere; (a radio signal) captare; (speed) acquistare ‖ *intr* usare il piccone; **to pick at** (food) spilluzzicare; (coll) criticare; **to pick on** (coll) scegliere; (coll) criticare; **to pick up** (coll) migliorarsi

pick'ax' *s* piccone *m*

picket [ˈpɪkɪt] *s* picchetto ‖ *tr* rinchiudere con palizzata; (to hitch) legare; (to post) (mil) mettere di picchetto; (e.g., a factory) picchettare

pick'et fence' *s* steccato

pick'et line' *s* corteo di scioperanti; corteo di dimostranti

pickle [ˈpɪkəl] *s* salamoia, sottaceto; (cucumber) cetriolo sottaceto; **to get into a pickle** (coll) cacciarsi in un imbroglio ‖ *tr* mettere sottaceto; (metallurgy) decapare

pick-me-up [ˈpɪkmiˌʌp] *s* (coll) spuntino; (coll) bevanda stimulante

pick'pock'et *s* borseggiatore *m*, borsaiolo

pick'up' *s* sollevamento; (in speed) accelerazione; (of phonograph) pick-up *m*, fonorivelatore *m*; (aut) camioncino; (coll) persona conosciuta per caso; (coll) miglioramento

pick'-up-sticks' *spl* sciangai *m*

pic·nic [ˈpɪknɪk] *s* picnic *m* ‖ *v* (pret & pp -nicked; ger -nicking) *intr* fare merenda all'aperto

pictorial [pɪkˈtoriəl] *adj* pittorico; illustrato; vivido ‖ *s* rivista illustrata

picture [ˈpɪktʃər] *s* illustrazione, disegno; (painting) quadro, dipinto; (of a person) ritratto; fotografia; film *m*, pellicola ‖ *tr* fare il ritratto di; disegnare; dipingere; fotografare; descrivere; immaginare, immaginarsi

pic'ture frame' *s* cornice *f*

pic'ture gal'lery *s* pinacoteca, galleria di quadri, quadreria

pic'ture post' card' *s* cartolina illustrata

pic'ture show' *s* cinematografo; mostra di quadri

picturesque [ˌpɪktʃəˈrɛsk] *adj* pittoresco

pic'ture tube' *s* tubo televisivo

pic'ture win'dow *s* finestra panoramica

piddling [ˈpɪdlɪŋ] *adj* insignificante

pie [paɪ] *s* (with fruit) torta; (with meat) timballo; (orn) pica ‖ *v* (pret & pp pied; ger pieing) *tr* (typ) scompaginare, scomporre

piece [pis] *s* pezzo; (e.g., of cloth) pezza; **a piece of advice** un consiglio; **a piece of baggage** un collo; **a piece of furniture** un mobile *m*; **a piece of news** una notizia; **by the piece** a cottimo; **to break to pieces** frantumare; frantumarsi; **to cut to pieces** fare a pezzi; **to fall to pieces** cadere a pezzi; **to fly to pieces** rompersi in mille pezzi; **to give s.o. a piece of one's mind** dirne a qlcu di tutti i colori; **to go to pieces** perdere il controllo di sé stesso; **to take to pieces** confutare punto per punto ‖ *tr* rappezzare, mettere insieme ‖ *intr* (coll) mangiucchiare

piece'meal' *adv* poco a poco

piece'work' *s* lavoro a cottimo

piece'work'er *s* cottimista *mf*

pier [pɪr] *s* (of a bridge) pila; (over water) molo; (archit) pilastro, pilone *m*

pierce [pɪrs] *tr* forare, bucare; penetrare; (to stab) trapassare ‖ *intr* penetrare

piercing [ˈpɪrsɪŋ] *adj* acuto; (eyes) penetrante; (pain) lancinante

pier' glass' *s* specchiera

pie-ty ['paɪ-əti] *s* (-**ties**) pietà *f*

piffle ['pɪfəl] *s* (coll) fesserie *fpl*

pig [pɪg] *s* maiale *m*, porco; (metallurgy) lingotto, massello; **to buy a pig in the poke** comprare il gatto nel sacco

pigeon ['pɪdʒən] *s* piccione *m*

pi'geon-hole' *s* nicchia nella piccionaia; (*for filing*) casella ‖ *tr* (*to lay aside for later time*) archiviare; (*to shelve, e.g., an application*) insabbiare

pi'geon house' *s* colombaia, piccionaia

piggish ['pɪgɪʃ] *adj* porcino, maialesco

pig'gy-back' ['pɪgɪ,bæk] *adv* sulle spalle, sulla schiena; (rr) su carrello stradale per trasporto carri

pig'head'ed *adj* ostinato, cocciuto

pig' i'ron *s* ghisa, ferro grezzo

pigment ['pɪgmənt] *s* pigmento ‖ *tr* pigmentare ‖ *intr* pigmentarsi

pig'pen' *s* porcile *m*

pig'skin' *s* pelle *f* di maiale; (coll) pallone *m* da football, sfera di cuoio

pig'sty' *s* (-**sties**) porcile *m*

pig'tail' *s* codino; (*of girl*) treccia; treccia di tabacco

pike [paɪk] *s* (*weapon*) picca; (*road*) autostrada; (ichth) luccio

piker ['paɪkər] *s* (coll) uomo pidocchioso

pile [paɪl] *s* (*heap*) pila; (*for burning a corpse*) pira; (*large building*) mole *f*; (*beam*) palo; (*of carpet*) pelo; (*of money*) (slang) gruzzolo; (coll) mucchio; **piles** emorroidi *fpl* ‖ *tr* ammucchiare, accumulare; **to pile up** ammonticchiare ‖ *intr* accumularsi; **to pile into** pigiarsi in; **to pile up** accumularsi

pile' driv'er *s* battipalo, berta

pilfer ['pɪlfər] *tr* & *intr* rubacchiare

pilgrim ['pɪlgrɪm] *s* pellegrino

pilgrimage ['pɪlgrɪmɪdʒ] *s* pellegrinaggio

pill [pɪl] *s* pillola; amara pillola; (coll) rompiscatole *mf*; **to sugar-coat the pill** addolcire la pillola

pillage ['pɪlɪdʒ] *s* saccheggio, rapina ‖ *tr* & *intr* saccheggiare, rapinare

pillar ['pɪlər] *s* pilastro, colonna; **from pillar to post** da Erode a Pilato

pill'box' *s* scatoletta per le pillole; (mil) casamatta

pillo-ry ['pɪləri] *s* (-**ries**) gogna, berlina ‖ *v* (*pret* & *pp* -**ried**) *tr* mettere alla berlina

pillow ['pɪlo] *s* cuscino, guanciale *m*

pil'low-case' *s* federa

pilot ['paɪlət] *adj* pilota ‖ *s* pilota *m*; (*of locomotive*) respingente *m* ‖ *tr* pilotare

pi'lot light' *s* fiammella automatica

pimp [pɪmp] *s* ruffiano, lenone *m*

pimple ['pɪmpəl] *s* bitorzolo

pim-ply ['pɪmpli] *adj* (-**plier**; -**pliest**) bitorzoluto

pin [pɪn] *s* (*of metal*) spillo; (*peg*) caviglia; (*adornment*) spilla; (*linchpin*) acciarino; (*of key*) mappa; (*clothespin*) molletta; (*bowling pin*) birillo; **to be on pins and needles** stare sulle spine ‖ *tr* appuntare; (*to hold*) immobilizzare; **to pin s.o. down** forzare qlcu a rivelare i propri piani **to pin s.th on s.o.** (coll) dare la colpa a qlcu per qlco

pinafore ['pɪnə,for] *s* grembiulino

pinaster [paɪ'næstər] *s* pino marittimo

pin'ball machine' *s* biliardino

pince-nez ['pæns,ne] *s* occhiali *mpl* a stringinaso

pincers ['pɪnsərz] *ssg or spl* tenaglie *fpl*; (zool) pinze *fpl*

pinch [pɪntʃ] *s* (*squeeze*) pizzicotto; (*of tobacco*) presa; (*of salt*) pizzico; (*hardship*) strettoia; **in a pinch** in caso di necessità ‖ *tr* stringere, pizzicare; (*to press*) comprimere; ridurre alle strettezze; (slang) rubare; (slang) arrestare ‖ *intr* stringere; (*to be stingy*) fare l'avaro

pin'cush'ion *s* puntaspilli *m*

pine [paɪn] *s* pino ‖ *intr*—**to pine away** struggersi; **to pine for** spasimare per

pine'ap'ple *s* ananas *m*

pine' cone' *s* pigna

pine' nee'dle *s* ago del pino

ping [pɪŋ] *s* rumore secco; rumore metallico ‖ *intr* fare un rumore secco or metallico

pin'head' *s* capocchia di spillo; (slang) testa quadra

pin'hole' *s* forellino

pink [pɪŋk] *adj* rosa ‖ *s* color *m* rosa; condizione perfetta; (bot) garofano ‖ *tr* orlare a zig-zag; (*to stab*) perforare

pin' mon'ey *s* denaro per le piccole spese

pinnacle ['pɪnəkəl] *s* pinnacolo

pin'point' *adj* di precisione ‖ *s* punta di spillo ‖ *tr* mettere in rilievo

pin'prick' *s* puntura di spillo

pint [paɪnt] *s* pinta

pintle ['pɪntəl] *s* maschietto

pin'up' *s* pin-up-girl *f*

pioneer [,paɪə'nɪr] *s* pioniere *m* ‖ *tr* aprire la via a ‖ *intr* fare il pioniere

pioneering [,paɪə'nɪrɪŋ] *adj* pionieristico

pious ['paɪ-əs] *adj* pio, devoto

pip [pɪp] *s* (*seed*) seme *m*; (vet) pipita

pipe [paɪp] *s* tubo, canna; (*of stove*) cannone *m*; (*for smoking*) pipa; (mus) legno; (mus) cornamusa ‖ *tr* suonare; cantare ad alta voce; fischiare; condurre in una tubatura; munire di tubatura ‖ *intr* suonare la zampogna; **to pipe down** (slang) stare zitto

pipe' clean'er *s* scovolino

pipe' dream' *s* castello in aria

pipe' line' *s* oleodotto; (fig) fonte *f* (d'informazioni)

pipe' or'gan *s* organo a canne

piper ['paɪpər] *s* zampognaro; **to pay the piper** pagare lo scotto

pipe' wrench' *s* chiave *f* per tubi

piping ['paɪpɪŋ] *adj* (voice) acuto; (*sound*) di cornamusa ‖ *s* tubatura; suono di cornamuse; suono acuto; (*on cakes*) fregio; (*on garments*) cor-

doncino ornamentale || *adv*—**piping
hot** scottante, bollente

pippin ['pɪpɪn] *s* mela renetta; (*seed*)
seme *m*; (fig) gran brava persona

piquant ['pikənt] *adj* piccante

pique [pik] *s* picca, ripicco || *tr* offendere, eccitare

pira·cy ['paɪrəsi] *s* (**-cies**) pirateria

pirate ['paɪrɪt] *s* pirata *mf* || *tr* derubare; (*a book*) svaligiare, pubblicare illegalmente || *intr* pirateggiare

pirouette [,pɪru'et] *s* piroetta || *intr* piroettare

Pisces ['paɪsiz] or ['pɪsiz] *s* (astr) Pesci *mpl*

pistol ['pɪstəl] *s* pistola

piston ['pɪstən] *s* pistone *m*

pis'ton displace'ment *s* cilindrata

pis'ton ring' *s* segmento elastico

pis'ton rod' *s* (*of a steam engine*) biella d'accoppiamento; (*of a motor*) asta del pistone, biella

pis'ton stroke' *s* corsa dello stantuffo

pit [pɪt] *s* (*in the ground*) buca; (*trap*) trappola; (*of fruit*) nocciolo; (*of stomach*) bocca; (*scar*) buttero; (*in exchange*) recinto delle grida; (*for fights*) arena; (theat) platea; (min) miniera; (aut) fossa di riparazione || *v* (*pret & pp* **pitted**; *ger* **pitting**) *tr* infossare; butterare; opporre; (*to remove pits from*) snocciolare

pitch [pɪtʃ] *s* (*black sticky substance*) pece *f*; (*throw*) lancio; (*of a roof*) pendenza, inclinazione; (*of a boat*) beccheggio; (*of a screw*) passo; (*of sound*) altezza || *tr* lanciare; (*a tent*) rizzare || *intr* beccheggiare; **to pitch in** (coll) mettersi al lavoro; (coll) cominciare a mangiare

pitch' ac'cent *s* accento di altezza

pitch' at'titude *s* assetto longitudinale

pitch'-dark' *adj* nero come la pece

pitched' bat'tle *s* battaglia campale

pitcher ['pɪtʃər] *s* brocca; (baseball) lanciatore *m*

pitch'fork' *s* forca, tridente *m*; **to rain pitchforks** (coll) piovere a dirotto

pitch' pipe' *s* (mus) corista *m*

pit'fall' *s* trappola, trabocchetto

pith [pɪθ] *s* midollo; (*strength*) (fig) forza; (fig) succo, essenza

pith·y ['pɪθi] *adj* (**-ier; -iest**) midolloso; succoso, essenziale

pitiful ['pɪtɪfəl] *adj* pietoso

pitiless ['pɪtɪlɪs] *adj* spietato

pit·y ['pɪti] *s* (**-ies**) pietà *f*; **it is a pity that** è un peccato che; **what a pity!** che peccato! || *v* (*pret & pp* **-ied**) *tr* aver pietà di

Pius ['paɪ·əs] *s* Pio

pivot ['pɪvət] *s* asse *m*, perno; (fig) asse *m* || *tr* imperniare || *intr* imperniarsi; **to pivot on** fare perno su; dipendere da

placard ['plækɑrd] *s* manifesto, affisso || *tr* affiggere

place [ples] *s* luogo; locale *m*; (*court*) piazzetta; (*short street*) vicolo; residenza; sito, luogo, località *f*; (*point*) punto; (*space occupied*) posto; (*office*) posto, impiego; **in no place**

da nessuna parte; **in place** a posto; **in place of** al posto di, invece di; **in the first place** in primo luogo; **in the next place** in secondo luogo; **to know one's place** saper stare al proprio posto; **to take place** aver luogo || *tr* piazzare, mettere; (*to find employment for*) collocare; (*to identify*) ravvisare || *intr* (sports) piazzarsi

place·bo [plə'sibo] *s* (**-bos** or **-boes**) rimedio fittizio

place' card' *s* segnaposto

placement ['plesmənt] *s* (*e.g., of furniture*) collocazione; (*employment*) collocamento

place' name' *s* toponimo

place' of busi'ness *s* ufficio, negozio

placid ['plæsɪd] *adj* placido

plagiarism ['pledʒə ,rɪzəm] *s* plagio

plagiarize ['pledʒə ,raɪz] *tr* plagiare

plague [pleg] *s* peste bubbonica; (*widespread affliction*) piaga, flagello || *tr* infestare, appestare; tormentare

plaid [plæd] *s* tessuto scozzese

plain [plen] *adj* piano; aperto; evidente, esplicito; semplice; (*undyed*) naturale; comune, ordinario; **in plain English** senz'ambagi; **in plain view** di fronte a tutti || *s* pianura

plain'-clothes' man' *s* (**-men'**) agente *m* in borghese

plains'man *s* (**-men**) abitante *m* della pianura

plaintiff ['plentɪf] *s* querelante *mf*

plaintive ['plentɪv] *adj* lamentevole

plan [plæn] *s* piano, progetto || *v* (*pret & pp* **planned**; *ger* **planning**) *tr & intr* progettare

plane [plen] *adj* piano || *m* piano; (*tool*) pialla; (aer) aeroplano; (aer) ala d'aeroplano; (bot) platano || *tr* piallare || *intr* andare in aeroplano

plane' sick'ness *s* male *m* d'aria

planet ['plænɪt] *s* pianeta *m*

plane' tree' *s* platano

plan'ing mill' *s* officina di piallatura

plank [plæŋk] *s* tavola, asse *m*; (*of political party*) piattaforma || *tr* coprire d'assi; cucinare sulla graticola e servire sul tagliere; **to plank down** (*e.g., money*) (coll) snocciolare

plant [plænt] or [plɑnt] *s* (*factory*) impianto, stabilimento; (*e.g., of a college*) complesso di edifici; (bot) pianta; (mach) apparato motore; (slang) trappola || *tr* (*e.g., a tree*) piantare; (*seeds*) seminare; (*to stock*) fornire

plantation [plæn'teʃən] *s* piantagione

planter ['plæntər] *s* piantatore *m*; (mach) piantatrice *f*

plaster ['plæstər] or ['plɑstər] *s* (*gypsum*) gesso; (*mixture to cover walls*) intonaco, malta; (*poultice*) impiastro || *tr* ingessare; intonacare; impiastrare; (*with posters*) affiggere, ricoprire

plas'ter·board' *s* cartone *m* di gesso

plas'ter cast' *s* (sculp) gesso; (surg) ingessatura

plas'ter of Par'is *s* gesso, stucco

plastic ['plæstɪk] *adj & s* plastico

plate 237 **plug**

plate [plet] s (*dish*) piatto; (*sheet of metal*) placca, piastra; (*thin sheet of metal*) lamina; (*of vacuum tube*) placca; (*of auto license*) targa; (*of condenser*) armatura; (*tableware*) vasellame m d'argento, vasellame m d'oro; dentiera; (baseball) casa base; (phot) lastra; (typ) cliché m ‖ tr (*with gold or silver*) placcare; (*with armor*) blindare, corazzare

plateau [plæ'to] s altipiano

plate' glass' s lastrone m

platen ['plætən] s rullo

platform ['plæt‚form] s piattaforma; (*for speaker*) tribuna, palco; (*for passengers*) (rr) marciapiede m; (*at end of car*) (rr) piattaforma

plat'form car' s (rr) pianale m

platinum ['plætɪnəm] s platino

plat'inum blonde' s bionda platinata

platitude ['plætɪ‚tjud] or ['plætɪ‚tud] s trivialità f, banalità f

Plato ['pleto] s Platone m

platoon [pla'tun] s plotone m

platter ['plætər] s piatto di portata; (slang) disco di grammofono

plausible ['plɔzɪbəl] adj plausibile; (*person*) credibile, attendibile

play [ple] s gioco; libertà f d'azione; recreazione; turno, volta; (*mach*) gioco m; dramma m; (mach) gioco ‖ tr giocare; giocare contro; causare, produrre; (*a drama*) rappresentare; (*a character*) fare la parte di; (*to wield*) esercitare; (mus) suonare; **to play back** (*e.g., a tape*) riprodurre; **to play down** diminuire l'importanza di; **to play one off against another** mettere uno contro l'altro; **to play up** dare importanza a ‖ intr giocare; (*to act*) giocare, comportarsi; (theat) recitare; (mus) suonare; (mach) aver gioco; **to play on** continuare a giocare; continuare a suonare; valersi di; **to play safe** non prendere rischi; **to play sick** fare il malato; **to play up to** fare la corte a

play'back' s riproduzione; apparechiatura di riproduzione

play'bill' s (theat) programma m

play'boy' s playboy m. gaudente m

player ['ple-ər] s giocatore m; (theat) attore m; (mus) suonatore m

play'er pian'o s pianola

playful ['plefəl] adj giocoso

playgoer ['ple‚go-ər] s frequentatore m del teatro

play'ground' s parco di ricreazione; (*resort*) posto di villeggiatura

play'house' s teatro; casa di bambole

play'ing card' ['ple-ɪŋ] s carta da gioco

play'ing field' s campo da gioco

play'mate' s compagno di gioco

play'-off' s (sports) spareggio

play'pen' s recinto, box m

play'thing' s giocattolo

play'time' s ricreazione

playwright ['ple‚raɪt] s drammaturgo, commediografo

play'writ'ing s drammaturgia

plaza ['plæzə] or ['plɑzə] s piazzale m

plea [pli] s scusa; richiesta, domanda; (law) dichiarazione

plead [plid] v (pret & pp **pleaded** or **pled** [pled]) tr (*ignorance*) dichiarare; (*a case*) perorare ‖ intr supplicare; argomentare; **to plead guilty** dichiararsi colpevole

pleasant ['plezənt] adj piacevole; (*person*) simpatico

pleasant·ry ['plezəntri] s (-ries) facezia, motto

please [pliz] tr piacere (with *dat*) ‖ intr piacere; **as you please** come vuole; **if you please** per favore; **please** per cortesia; **to be pleased to** avere il piacere di; **to be pleased with** essere soddisfatto con; **to do as one pleases** fare come par e piace

pleasing ['plizɪŋ] adj piacevole

pleasure ['pleʒər] s piacere m; desiderio; **what is your pleasure?** cosa desidera?

pleas'ure car' s vettura da turismo

pleat [plit] s piega ‖ tr piegare, pieghettare

plebeian [plɪ'bi-ən] adj & s plebeo

plebiscite ['plebɪ‚saɪt] s plebiscito

pledge [pledʒ] s pegno; promessa; voto; (*person*) ostaggio; (*toast*) brindisi m; **as a pledge** in pegno; **to take the pledge** giurare d'astenersi dal bere ‖ tr dare in pegno; (*to bind*) far promettere a

plentiful ['plentɪfəl] adj abbondante

plenty ['plenti] s abbondanza ‖ adv (coll) abbastanza

pleurisy ['plurɪsi] s pleurite f

pliable ['plaɪ-əbəl] adj flessibile, pieghevole; docile

pliers ['plaɪ-ərz] ssg or spl pinze fpl

plight [plaɪt] s condizione o situazione precaria ‖ tr—**to plight one's troth** fidanzarsi

plod [plad] v (pret & pp **plodded;** ger **plodding**) tr percorrere pesantemente ‖ intr camminare pesantemente; (*to drudge*) sgobbare

plot [plat] s (*of ground*) appezzamento; (*of a play*) trama, intreccio; (*evil scheme*) cospirazione, trama ‖ v (pret & pp **plotted;** ger **plotting**) tr fare il piano di; macchinare; preparare la trama di; (aer, naut) fare il punto di ‖ intr tramare, cospirare

plover ['plʌvər] or ['plovər] s piviere m

plow [plau] s aratro; (*for snow*) spazzaneve m ‖ tr arare; (*e.g., water*) solcare; (*snow*) spazzare; **to plow back** reinvestire ‖ intr arare; aprirsi la via; camminare pesantemente

plow'man s (-men) aratore m; contadino

plow'share' s vomere m

pluck [plʌk] s strattone m; coraggio; (*giblets*) frattaglie fpl ‖ tr (*to snatch*) tirare; (*e.g., fruit*) svellere; (*a fowl*) spennare; (mus) pizzicare ‖ intr tirare; **to pluck up** farsi coraggio

pluck·y ['plʌki] adj (-ier; -iest) coraggioso

plug [plʌg] s tappo, zaffo; tavoletta di

tabacco; bocca da incendi; (elec) spina; (*horse*) (slang) ronzino; (slang) raccomandazione ‖ *v* (*pret & pp* **plugged**) *ger* **plugging**) *tr* tappare, otturare; colpire; inserire; (slang) fare la pubblicità di; **to plug in** (elec) innestare, connettere ‖ *intr* (coll) sgobbare

plum [plʌm] *s* (*fruit*) susina; (*tree*) susino; (slang) cosa bellissima; (slang) colpo di fortuna

plumage ['plumɪdʒ] *s* piumaggio

plumb [plʌm] *adj* appiombo ‖ *s* piombino ‖ *adv* appiombo; (coll) completamente ‖ *tr* determinare la verticale col piombino; assodare

plumb' bob' *s* piombino

plumber ['plʌmər] *s* installatore *m*, idraulico

plumbing ['plʌmɪŋ] *s* impianto idraulico; mestiere *m* d'idraulico; sondaggio

plumb'ing fix'tures *spl* rubinetteria, impianti *mpl* sanitari

plumb' line' *s* filo a piombo

plum' cake' *s* panfrutto

plume [plum] *s* piuma; (*tuft of feathers*) pennacchio ‖ *tr* coprire di piume; **to plume oneself on** piccarsi di; **to plume one's feathers** pulirsi le penne

plummet ['plʌmɪt] *s* piombino ‖ *intr* cadere a piombo

plump [plʌmp] *adj* grassoccio, paffuto; franco ‖ *s* caduta ‖ *adv* francamente ‖ *intr* cadere a piombo

plum' pud'ding *s* budino con uva passa

plum' tree' *s* susino

plunder ['plʌndər] *s* (*act*) saccheggio; (*loot*) bottino ‖ *tr & intr* saccheggiare

plunge [plʌndʒ] *s* (*fall*) caduta; (*dive*) nuotata, tuffo ‖ *tr* gettare; tuffare; (*e.g.*, *a knife*) configgere ‖ *intr* (*to rush*) precipitarsi; (*to gamble*) (coll) darsi al gioco; (fig) ripiombare

plunger ['plʌndʒər] *s* tuffatore *m*; (*for clearing clogged drains*) sturalavandini *m*; (*mach*) stantuffo; (coll) giocatore temerario

plunk [plʌŋk] *adv* (coll) proprio; (coll) con un colpo secco ‖ *tr* (coll) gettare; lasciar cadere; (mus) pizzicare ‖ *intr* (coll) lasciarsi cadere

plural ['plurəl] *adj & s* plurale *m*

plus [plʌs] *adj* superiore; (elec) positivo; (coll) con lode ‖ *s* più *m*; soprappiù *m* ‖ *prep* più

plush [plʌʃ] *adj* di lusso ‖ *s* peluche *f*, felpa

Plutarch ['plutɑrk] *s* Plutarco

Pluto ['pluto] *s* Plutone *m*

plutonium [plu'tonɪ·əm] *s* plutonio

ply [plaɪ] *s* (**plies**) spessore *m*; (*layer*) strato; (*of rope*) legnolo ‖ *v* (*pret & pp* **plied**) *tr* (*a trade*) esercitare; (*a tool*) maneggiare; (*to assail*) premere, incalzare ‖ *intr* lavorare assiduamente; **to ply between** fare la spola tra

ply'wood' *s* legno compensato

pneumatic [nju'mætɪk] or [nu'mætɪk] *adj* pneumatico

pneumat'ic drill' *s* martello perforatore or pneumatico

pneumonia [nju'monɪ·ə] or [nu'monɪ·ə] *s* polmonite *f*

poach [potʃ] *tr* (*eggs*) affogare ‖ *intr* cacciare or pescare di frodo

poacher ['potʃər] *s* bracconiere *m*; pescatore *m* di frodo

pock [pɑk] *s* buttero

pocket ['pɑkɪt] *adj* tascabile ‖ *s* tasca; (billiards) buca; (aer) vuoto; (min) deposito ‖ *tr* intascare; (*e.g.*, *one's pride*) ingoiare

pock'et-book' *s* portafoglio; (*woman's purse*) borsetta

pock'et book' *s* libro tascabile

pock'et-hand'kerchief *s* fazzoletto

pock'et-knife' *s* (-knives) temperino

pock'et mon'ey *s* spiccioli *mpl*

pock'mark' *s* buttero

pod [pɑd] *s* baccello; (aer) contenitore *m*

poem ['po·ɪm] *s* poesia; (*of some length*) poema *m*

poet ['po·ɪt] *s* poeta *m*

poetess ['po·ɪtɪs] *s* poetessa

poetic [po'ɛtɪk] *adj* poetico ‖ **poetics** *ssg* poetica

poetry ['po·ɪtri] *s* poesia

pogrom ['pogrəm] *s* pogrom *m*

poignancy ['pɔɪnjənsi] or ['pɔɪnənsi] *s* strazio; intensità *f*

poignant ['pɔɪnjənt] or ['pɔɪnənt] *adj* straziante; intenso

point [pɔɪnt] *s* (*sharp end*) punta; (*something essential*) essenziale *m*; (*hint*) suggerimento; (*dot, decimal point, spot, degree, instant, position of compass*) punto; (coll) costrutto; **beside the point** fuori del seminato; **in point of** per quanto concerne; **to come to the point** venire al sodo; **to get the point** capire l'antifona; **to make a point of** dar importanza a; insistere di; **to stretch a point** fare un'eccezione, fare uno strappo alla regola; **to the point** a proposito ‖ *tr* (*e.g.*, *a weapon*) puntare; (*to sharpen*) aguzzare; (*to dot*) punteggiare; (*to give force to*) dare enfasi a; (*with mortar*) rinzaffare ‖ *intr* puntare; **to point at** puntare il dito a; **to point to** mostrare a dito

point'blank' *adj & adv* a bruciapelo

pointed ['pɔɪntɪd] *adj* appuntito; personale, diretto, acuto

pointer ['pɔɪntər] *s* (*rod*) bacchetta; indice *m*, indicatore *m*; cane *m* da punta, pointer *m*; (coll) direttiva

poise [pɔɪz] *s* equilibrio, stabilità *f*; dignità *f* ‖ *tr* equilibrare ‖ *intr* equilibrarsi, stare in equilibrio

poison ['pɔɪzən] *s* veleno ‖ *tr* avvelenare

poi'son i'vy *s* edera del Canada, tossicodendro

poisonous ['pɔɪzənəs] *adj* velenoso

poke [pok] *s* spinta, urto; (*with elbow*) gomitata; (slang) polentone *m* ‖ *tr* (*to prod*) spingere, urtare; (*the head*) sporgere; (*the fire*) attizzare; **to poke fun at** burlarsi di; **to poke one's nose into** ficcare il naso in ‖ *intr* (*to jab*) urtare; (*to thrust oneself*) ficcarsi; (*to pry*) ficcare il naso; **to poke around** gironzolare; **to poke out** spuntare, protrudere

poker ['pokər] *s* (*game*) poker *m*; (*bar*) attizzatoio

pok'er face' *s* faccia impassibile

pok·y ['poki] *adj* (**-ier; -iest**) (coll) lento; (coll) meschino, modesto ‖ (**-ies**) *s* (slang) gattabuia

Poland ['polənd] *s* la Polonia

po'lar bear' ['polər] *s* orso bianco

polarize ['polə‚raɪz] *tr* polarizzare

pole [pol] *s* palo; (*long rod*) pertica; (*of wagon*) timone *m*; (*for jumping*) asta; (astr, biol, elec, geog, math) polo ‖ *tr* (*a boat*) spingere con un palo ‖ *intr* spingere una barca con un palo ‖ **Pole** *s* polacco

pole'cat' *s* puzzola

pole' lamp' *s* lampada a stelo

pole'star' *s* stella polare

pole' vault' *s* salto coll'asta

police [pə'lis] *s* polizia ‖ *tr* vigilare, proteggere; (mil) pulire

police'man *s* (**-men**) agente *m* di polizia, vigile urbano

police' state' *s* governo poliziesco

police' sta'tion *s* commissariato di polizia

poli·cy ['palisi] *s* (**-cies**) politica; (ins) polizza

polio ['polɪ‚o] *s* (coll) polio *f*

polish ['palɪʃ] *s* lustro, lucentezza; (*for shoes or furniture*) cera; (fig) raffinatezza, eleganza ‖ *tr* pulire; (*e.g., a stone*) levigare; **to polish off** (slang) finire; **to polish up** (slang) migliorare ‖ *intr* pulirsi, diventar lucido ‖ **Polish** ['polɪʃ] *adj* & *s* polacco

polisher ['palɪʃər] *s* lucidatore *m*; (mach) lucidatrice *f*

polite [pə'laɪt] *adj* raffinato, cortese

politeness [pə'laɪtnɪs] *s* cortesia

politic ['palɪtɪk] *adj* prudente; (*expedient*) diplomatico

political [pə'lɪtɪkəl] *adj* politico

politician [‚palɪ'tɪʃən] *s* politico; (pej) politicante *m*, politicastro

politics ['palɪtɪks] *ssg* or *spl* politica

poll [pol] *s* votazione; (*registering of votes*) scrutinio; (*analysis of public opinion*) referendum *m*, sondaggio; (*head*) testa; **to go to the polls** andare alle urne; **to take a poll** fare un'inchiesta ‖ *tr* ricevere i voti di; contare i voti di; (*a tree*) potare; fare un'inchiesta di

pollen ['palən] *s* polline *m*

pollinate ['palɪ‚net] *tr* fecondare col polline

poll'ing booth' ['polɪŋ] *s* cabina elettorale

polliwog ['palɪ‚wag] *s* girino

poll' tax' *s* capitazione

pollute [pə'lut] *tr* insudiciare; (*to defile*) desecrare, profanare; (*e.g., the environment*) inquinare, contaminare

pollution [pə'luʃən] *s* inquinamento, contaminazione

poll' watch'er *s* rappresentante *m* di lista

polo ['polo] *s* polo

po'lo play'er *s* giocatore *m* di polo, polista *m*

po'lo shirt' *s* maglietta, polo

polygamist [pə'lɪgəmɪst] *s* poligamo

polygamous [pə'lɪgəməs] *adj* poligamo

polyglot ['palɪ‚glat] *adj* & *s* poliglotto

polygon ['palɪ‚gan] *s* poligono

polynomial [‚palɪ'nomɪ‚əl] *adj* polinomiale ‖ *s* polinomio

polyp ['palɪp] *s* (pathol, zool) polipo

polytheist ['palɪθi‚ɪst] *s* politeista *mf*

polytheistic [‚palɪθi'ɪstɪk] *adj* politeistico

pomade [pə'med] or [pə'mad] *s* pomata

pomegranate ['pam‚grænɪt] *s* (*shrub*) melograno; (*fruit*) melagrana

pom·mel ['pʌməl] or ['paməl] *s* (*of sword*) pomello; (*of saddle*) arcione *m* ‖ *v* (*pret & pp* **-meled** or **-melled**; *ger* **-meling** or **-melling**) *tr* prendere a pugni

pomp [pamp] *s* pompa

pompadour ['pampə‚dor] or ['pampə‚dur] *s* acconciatura a ciuffo

pompous ['pampəs] *adj* pomposo

pon·cho ['pant/o] *s* (**-chos**) poncho

pond [pand] *s* stagno

ponder ['pandər] *tr* & *intr* ponderare; **to ponder over** pensare sopra

ponderous ['pandərəs] *adj* ponderoso

poniard ['panjərd] *s* pugnale *m*

pontiff ['pantɪf] *s* pontefice *m*

pontifical [pan'tɪfɪkəl] *adj* pontificale

pontoon [pan'tun] *s* (*boat*) chiatta, pontone *m*; (aer) galleggiante *m*

po·ny ['poni] *s* (**-nies**) pony *m*; (*glass and drink*) bicchierino; (*for cheating*) (slang) bigino

poodle ['pudəl] *s* barbone *m*, cane *m* barbone

pool [pul] *s* (*pond*) stagno; (*puddle*) pozza; (*for swimming*) piscina; (*game*) biliardo; (com) cartello, consorzio; (com) fondo comune ‖ *tr* mettere in un fondo comune ‖ *intr* formare un cartello or un consorzio

pool'room' *s* sala da biliardo

pool' ta'ble *s* tavolo da biliardo

poop [pup] *s* poppa; (deck) casseretto

poor [pur] *adj* povero; (*inferior*) scadente ‖ **the poor** *spl* i poveri

poor' box' *s* cassetta per l'elemosina

poor'house' *s* asilo dei poveri

poorly ['purli] *adv* male

pop [pap] *s* scoppio; (*soda*) gazzosa ‖ *v* (*pret & pp* **popped**; *ger* **popping**) *tr* far scoppiare; **to pop the question** (coll) fare la domanda di matrimonio ‖ *intr* esplodere con fragore; **to pop in** fare una capatina; entrare all'improvviso

pop'corn' *s* pop-corn *m*

pope [pop] *s* papa *m*

popeyed ['pap‚aɪd] *adj* con gli occhi sporgenti; con gli occhi fuori dalle orbite

pop'gun' *s* fucile *m* ad aria compressa

poplar ['paplər] *s* pioppo

pop·py ['papi] *s* (**-pies**) papavero

pop'py·cock' *s* (coll) scemenza

popsicle ['pɑpsɪkəl] *s* (trademark) gelato da passeggio

populace ['pɑpjəlɪs] *s* gente *f*, popolino

popular ['pɑpjələr] *adj* popolare

popularize ['pɑpjələ ‚raɪz] *tr* divulgare, volgarizzare

populate ['pɑpjə ‚let] *tr* popolare

population [‚pɑpjə'leʃən] *s* popolazione

populous ['pɑpjələs] *adj* popoloso

porcelain ['pɔrsəlɪn] *or* ['pɔrslɪn] *s* porcellana

porch [pɔrtʃ] *s* portico

porcupine ['pɔrkjə‚paɪn] *s* (*Hystrix cristata*) istrice *m* & *f*, porcospino; (*Erethizon dorsatum*) ursone *m*, porcospino americano

pore [por] *s* poro ‖ *intr*—**to pore over** studiare minutamente

pork [pork] *s* carne *f* di maiale

pork' butch'er shop' *s* salumeria

pork'chop' *s* cotoletta di maiale

porous ['porəs] *adj* poroso

po'rous plas'ter *s* cataplasma *m*

porphy-ry ['pɔrfɪri] *s* (**-ries**) porfido

porpoise ['pɔrpəs] *s* focena; (*dolphin*) delfino

porridge ['pɑrɪdʒ] *or* ['pɔrɪdʒ] *s* pappa, farinata

port [port] *adj* portuario ‖ *s* (*harbor*; *wine*) porto; (*naut*) babordo, sinistra; (*opening in side of ship*) portello; (*round opening*) (naut) oblò *m*

portable ['portəbəl] *adj* portabile

portal ['portəl] *s* portale *m*

portend [por'tend] *tr* presagire

portent ['portent] *s* presagio

portentous [por'tentəs] *adj* sinistro, funesto, premonitore; (*amazing*) portentoso

porter ['portər] *s* (*doorman*) portiere *m*; (*man who carries luggage*) facchino; (*of a sleeper*) conduttore *m*; (*in a store*) inserviente *mf*; (*beverage*) birra scura e amara

portfoli-o [port'foli ‚o] *s* (**-os**) cartella; (*office; holdings*) portafoglio

port'hole' *s* (*opening in side of ship*) portello; (*round opening*) (naut) oblò *m*

porti-co ['pɔrtɪ ‚ko] *s* (**-cos** *or* **-coes**) portico

portion ['porʃən] *s* porzione; (*dowry*) dote *f* ‖ *tr*—**to portion out** dividere, ripartire

port-ly ['portli] *adj* (**-lier; -liest**) obeso, corpulento

port' of call' *s* scalo

portrait ['portret] *or* ['portrɪt] *s* ritratto

portray [por'tre] *tr* ritrarre

portrayal [por'tre‚əl] *s* delineazione, ritratto

Portugal ['portʃəgəl] *s* il Portogallo

Portu-guese ['portʃə ‚giz] *adj* portoghese ‖ *s* (**-guese**) portoghese *mf*

pose [poz] *s* posa ‖ *tr* (*a question*) avanzare; (*a model*) mettere in posa ‖ *intr* posare; **to pose as** posare a, atteggiarsi a

posh [pɑʃ] *adj* (coll) di lusso

position [pə'zɪʃən] *s* posizione; rango;

impiego, posto; **to be in a position to** essere in grado di

positive ['pɑzɪtɪv] *adj* positivo ‖ *s* positivo; (phot) positiva

possess [pə'zes] *tr* possedere

possession [pə'zeʃən] *s* possedimento; (*of mental faculties*) possesso; **possessions** (*wealth*) beni *mpl*

possessive [pə'zesɪv] *adj* possessivo; (*e.g., mother*) opprimente, soffocante

possible ['pɑsɪbəl] *adj* possibile

possum ['pɑsəm] *s* opossum *m*; **to play possum** (coll) fare il morto

post [post] *s* (*mail*) posta; (*pole*) palo; (*in horse racing*) linea di partenza; posizione, rango; (*job*) posto; (mil) presidio ‖ *tr* mettere in una lista; impostare; tenere al corrente; **post no bills** divieto d'affissione

postage ['postɪdʒ] *s* affrancatura

post'age me'ter *s* affrancatrice *f*

post'age stamp' *s* francobollo

postal ['postəl] *adj* postale

post'al card' *s* cartolina postale

pos'tal per'mit *s* abbonamento postale

post'al sav'ings bank' *s* cassa di risparmio postale

post'al scale' *s* pesalettere *m*

post' card' *s* cartolina illustrata; cartolina postale

post'date' *tr* postdatare

poster ['postər] *s* cartellone *m*, manifesto pubblicitario

posterity [pɑs'terɪti] *s* posterità *f*

postern ['postərn] *adj* posteriore ‖ *s* postierla

post' exchange' *s* spaccio militare

post'haste' *adv* al più presto possibile

posthumous ['pɑstʃuməs] *adj* postumo

post'man *s* (**-men**) portalettere *m*

post'mark' *s* bollo, timbro postale ‖ *tr* bollare, timbrare

post'mas'ter *s* ricevitore *m* postale

post'master gen'eral *s* (**postmasters general**) ministro delle poste

post-mortem ['post'mortəm] *adj* postumo ‖ *s* autopsia

post' of'fice *s* ufficio postale

post'-office box' *s* casella postale

postpaid ['post ‚ped] *adj* franco di porto

postpone [post'pon] *tr* differire, posporre

postscript ['post ‚skrɪpt] *s* poscritto

postulant ['postʃələnt] *s* postulatore *m*, postulante *mf*

posture ['pɑstʃər] *s* portamento; posa ‖ *intr* posare

post'war' *adj* del dopoguerra

po-sy ['pozi] *s* (**-sies**) fiore *m*; (*nosegay*) mazzolino di fiori

pot [pɑt] *s* pentola, pignatta; pitale *m*, orinale *m*; (*in gambling*) (coll) piatto; **to go to pot** andare a gambe all'aria

potash ['pɑt ‚æʃ] *s* potassa

potassium [pə'tæsɪ‚əm] *s* potassio

pota-to [pə'teto] *s* (**-toes**) patata

pota'to om'elet *s* omelette *f* con patate

potbellied ['pɑt ‚belɪd] *adj* panciuto

poten-cy ['potənsi] *s* (**-cies**) potenza

potent ['potənt] *adj* potente

potentate ['potən ˌtet] s potentato
potential [pə'tenʃəl] adj & s potenziale m
pot'hold'er s patta, presa
pot'hook' s uncino
potion ['poʃən] s pozione
pot'luck' s—**to take potluck** mangiare quello che passa il convento
pot' shot' s colpo sparato a casaccio
potter ['patər] s vasaio
pot'ter's clay' s argilla per stoviglie
pot'ter's field' s cimitero dei poveri
potter-y ['patəri] s (**-ies**) vasellame m; fabbrica di vasellame; ceramica
pouch [pautʃ] s sacchetto, borsa; (of kangaroo) borsa
poultice ['poltis] s cataplasma m
poultry ['poltri] s pollame m
poul'try-man s (**-men**) pollivendolo
pounce [pauns] intr—**to pounce on** balzare su
pound ['paund] s libbra; lira sterlina; (for stray animals) recinto || tr battere, picchiare; tempestare di colpi; (to crush) polverizzare || intr battere
pound' cake' s dolce m fatto con una libbra di burro, una di zucchero ed una di farina
pound' ster'ling s lira sterlina
pour [por] tr versare; (e.g., tea) servire; (wine) mescere; (stones upon an enemy) far piovere || intr fluire; (to rain) diluviare; **to pour in** affluire; **to pour out** uscire in massa
pout [paut] s broncio || intr tenere il broncio
poverty ['pavərti] s povertà f
POW ['pi'o'dʌbl ju] s (letterword) (prisoner of war) prigioniero di guerra
powder ['paudər] s polvere f; (for the face) cipria; (med) polverina || tr incipriare; (to sprinkle with powder) spolverizzare
pow'dered sug'ar s zucchero in polvere
pow'der puff' s piumino
pow'der room' s toletta
powdery ['paudəri] adj polveroso; fragile; (snow) farinoso
power ['pau·ər] s (ability, authority) potere m; forza, energia; (nation) potenza; (math, phys) potenza; **in power** al potere; **the powers that be** i potenti || tr azionare
pow'er-boat' s barca a motore
pow'er brake' s (aut) servofreno
pow'er com'pany s compagnia di elettricità
pow'er drive' s picchiata
powerful ['pau·ərfəl] adj poderoso
pow'er-house' s centrale elettrica
powerless ['pau·ərlis] adj impotente
pow'er line' s elettrodotto
pow'er mow'er s motofalciatrice f
pow'er of attor'ney s procura legale
pow'er plant' s stazione f generatrice; (aut) gruppo motore
pow'er steer'ing s servosterzo
pow'er tool' s apparecchiatura a motore
pow'er vac'uum s vuoto di potere
practical ['præktikəl] adj pratico

prac'tical joke' s scherzo da prete
practically ['præktikəli] adv (in a practical manner; virtually, really) praticamente; più o meno, quasi
practice ['præktis] s pratica; (of a profession) esercizio; (e.g., of a doctor) clientela; (process of doing something) prassi f; (habitual performance) abitudine f || tr praticare, esercitare || intr esercitarsi, praticare; (to be active in a profession) esercitare; **to practice as** esercitare la professione di
practitioner [præk'tiʃənər] s professionista mf
Prague [prag] or [preg] s Praga
prairie ['preri] s prateria
prai'rie dog' s cinomio
prai'rie wolf' s coyote m
praise [prez] s lode f, elogio || tr lodare, elogiare; **to praise to the skies** levare alle stelle
praise'wor'thy adj lodevole
pram [præm] s (coll) carrozzella
prance [præns] or [prans] s caracollo || intr caracollare; (to caper) ballonzolare
prank [præŋk] s burla, tiro
prate [pret] intr cianciare
prattle ['prætəl] s ciancia, chiacchierio || intr cianciare, parlare a vanvera
pray [pre] tr & intr pregare
prayer [prer] s preghiera
prayer' book' s libro di preghiere
preach [pritʃ] tr & intr predicare
preacher ['pritʃər] s predicatore m
preamble ['pri ˌæmbəl] s preambolo
precarious [pri'keri·əs] adj precario
precaution [pri'koʃən] s precauzione
precede [pri'sid] tr & intr precedere
precedent ['presidənt] s precedente m
precept ['prisept] s precetto
precinct ['prisiŋkt] s distretto; circoscrizione elettorale; **precincts** dintorni mpl
precious ['preʃəs] adj prezioso || adv—**precious little** (coll) molto poco
precipice ['presipis] s precipizio
precipitate [pri'sipi ˌtet] adj precipitoso || s precipitato || tr & intr precipitare
precipitous [pri'sipitəs] adj precipitoso, a precipizio
precise [pri'sais] adj preciso
precision [pri'siʒən] s precisione
preclude [pri'klud] tr precludere; escludere
precocious [pri'koʃəs] adj precoce
predatory ['predə ˌtori] adj da preda, predatore
predicament [pri'dikəmənt] s situazione critica or imbarazzante
predict [pri'dikt] tr predire
prediction [pri'dikʃən] s predizione
predispose [ˌpridis'poz] tr predisporre
predominant [pri'daminənt] adj predominante
preeminent [pri'eminənt] adj preminente
preempt [pri'empt] tr occupare or acquistare in precedenza
preen [prin] tr (feathers, fur) lisciarsi;

to preen oneself agghindarsi, attillarsi

prefabricate [pri'fæbri‚ket] *tr* prefabbricare

preface ['prefis] *s* prefazione || *tr* prefazionare; essere la prefazione di

pre-fer [pri'fʌr] *v* (*pret & pp* **-ferred;** *ger* **-ferring**) *tr* preferire; (*to advance*) promuovere; (*law*) presentare, avanzare

preferable ['prefərəbəl] *adj* preferibile

preference ['prefərəns] *s* preferenza

preferred' stock' *s* azioni *fpl* privilegiate

prefix ['prifiks] *s* prefisso || *tr* prefiggere

pregnan·cy ['pregnənsi] *s* (**-cies**) gravidanza

pregnant ['pregnənt] *adj* incinta, gravida; (fig) gravido

prehistoric [‚prihis'tarik] or [‚prihis'tɔrik] *adj* preistorico

prejudice ['predʒədis] *s* pregiudizio; preconcetto; **without prejudice** senza detrimento || *tr* (*to harm*) pregiudicare; predisporre; **to prejudice against** prevenire contro

prejudicial ['predʒə'diʃəl] *adj* pregiudizievole

prelate ['prelit] *s* prelato

prelimi·nar·y [pri'limi‚neri] *adj* preliminare || *s* (**-ies**) preliminare *m*

prelude ['preljud] or ['prilud] *s* preludio || *tr* preludere a || *intr* preludere

premeditate [pri'medi‚tet] *tr* premeditare

premier [pri'mir] or ['primi·ər] *s* primo ministro, presidente *m* del consiglio

premiere [prə'mjer or [pri'mir] *s* prima; prima attrice

premise ['premis] *s* premessa; **on the premises** nella proprietà, sul luogo; **premises** proprietà *f*

premium ['primi·əm] *s* premio; **at a premium** in gran richiesta; a prezzo altissimo

premonition [‚primə'niʃən] *s* presentimento; indizio

preoccupation [pri‚akjə'peʃən] *s* preoccupazione

preoccu·py [pri'akjə‚pai] *v* (*pret & pp* **-pied**) *tr* preoccupare; (*to occupy beforehand*) occupare prima

prepaid [pri'ped] *adj* pagato in anticipo; franco di porto

preparation [‚prepə'reʃən] *s* preparazione; (*for a trip*) preparativo; (pharm) preparato

preparatory [pri'pærə‚tori] *adj* preparatorio

prepare [pri'per] *tr* preparare || *intr* prepararsi

preparedness [pri'peridnəs] or [pri-'perdnis] *s* preparazione; preparazione militare

pre·pay [pri'pe] *v* (*pret & pp* **-paid**) *tr* pagare anticipatamente

preponderant [pri'pandərənt] *adj* preponderante

preposition [‚prepə'ziʃən] *s* preposizione

prepossessing [‚pripə'zesiŋ] *adj* simpatico, attraente, piacevole

preposterous [pri'pastərəs] *adj* assurdo, ridicolo

prep' school' [prep] *s* (coll) scuola preparatoria

prerecorded [‚prirɪ'kɔrdɪd] *adj* (rad & telv) a registrazione differita

prerequisite [pri'rekwizit] *s* requisito

prerogative [pri'ragətiv] *s* prerogativa

presage ['presidʒ] *s* presagio || [pri-'sedʒ] *tr* presagire

Presbyterian [‚prezbi'tiri·ən] *adj & s* presbiteriano; Presbiteriano

prescribe [pri'skraib] *tr & intr* prescrivere

prescription [pri'skripʃən] *s* prescrizione; (pharm) ricetta

presence ['prezəns] *s* presenza; **in the presence of** alla presenza di

present ['prezənt] *adj* presente || *s* presente *m*, regalo || [pri'zent] *tr* presentare; **present arms!** presentat'arm!; **to present s.o. with s.th** regalare qlco a qlcu

presentable [pri'zentəbəl] *adj* presentabile

presentation [‚prezən'teʃən] or [‚prizən'teʃən] *s* presentazione; (theat) rappresentazione

presenta'tion cop'y *s* copia d'omaggio

presentiment [pri'zentimənt] *s* presentimento

presently ['prezəntli] *adv* fra poco; attualmente

preserve [pri'zʌrv] *s* (*for hunting*) riserva; preserves conserva, marmellata || *tr* preservare; conservare

preserved' fruit' *s* frutta in conserva

preside [pri'zaid] *intr* presiedere; **to preside over** presiedere, presiedere a

presiden·cy ['prezidənsi] *s* (**-cies**) presidenza

president ['prezidənt] *s* presidente *m*; (*of a university*) rettore *m*

press [pres] *s* pressione; (*crowd*) folla; (*closet*) armadio; (mach) pressa; (typ) stampa; **to go to press** andare in macchina || *tr* (*to push*) spingere, premere; (*to squeeze*) spremere; (*to embrace*) abbracciare; forzare; costringere, urgere, sollecitare; (*to iron*) stirare || *intr* premere; avanzare

press' a'gent *s* agente pubblicitario

press' con'ference *s* conferenza stampa

pressing ['presiŋ] *adj* pressante, urgente || *s* (*of records*) incisione

press' release' *s* comunicato stampa

pressure ['preʃər] *s* pressione; tensione, urgenza || *tr* pressare, incalzare con insistenza

pres'sure cook'er ['kukər] *s* pentola a pressione

pressurize ['preʃə‚raiz] *tr* pressurizzare

prestige [pres'tiʒ] or ['prestidʒ] *s* prestigio

prestigious [pres'tidʒi·əs] or [pre-'stidʒəs] *adj* onorato, stimato

presumably [pri'zuməbli] or [pri'zjuməbli] *adv* presumibilmente

presume [pri'zum] or [pri'zjum] *tr* presumere; **to presume to** prendersi la libertà di ‖ *intr* assumere; **to presume on** or **upon** abusare di

presumption [prɪˈzʌmp/ən] *s* presunzione; supposizione

presumptuous [prɪˈzʌmptʃʊ-əs] *adj* presuntuoso

presuppose [ˌprisə'poz] *tr* presupporre

pretend [prɪˈtɛnd] *tr* fingere, fare finta di ‖ *intr* fingere; **to pretend to** (*e.g., the throne*) pretendere a

pretender ǀprɪˈtɛndər ǀ *s* pretendente *mf;* impostore *m*

pretense [prɪˈtɛns] or [ˈpritɛns] *s* pretesa; finzione; **under false pretenses** allegando ragioni false; **under pretense of** sotto l'apparenza di

pretentious [prɪˈtɛn/əs] *adj* pretenzioso

preterit ǀˈprɛtərɪtǀ *adj* passato, preterito ‖ *s* passato remoto, preterito

pretext ǀˈpritɛkstǀ *s* pretesto

pretonic ǀpriˈtɑnɪkǀ *adj* pretonico

pret·ty ǀˈprɪtiǀ *adj* (**-tier; -tiest**) grazioso, carino; (*e.g., sum of money*) (coll) bello ‖ *adv* abbastanza; molto; **sitting pretty** (slang) ben messo

prevail [prɪˈvel] *intr* prevalere; **to prevail on** or **upon** persuadere

prevailing [prɪˈvelɪŋ] *adj* prevalente

prevalent ǀˈprɛvələntǀ *adj* comune

prevaricate [prɪˈværɪˌket] *intr* mentire

prevent [prɪˈvɛnt] *tr* impedire; **to prevent from** + *ger* impedire (with *dat*) di + *inf* or che + *subj*

prevention [prɪˈvɛn/ən] *s* prevenzione

preventive [prɪˈvɛntɪv] *adj* preventivo ‖ *s* rimedio preventivo

preview [ˈpriˌvju] *s* indizio; (*private showing*) (mov) anteprima; (*showing of brief scenes for advertising*) (mov) scene *fpl* di prossima programmazione

previous [ˈprivɪ-əs] *adj* previo, precedente ‖ *adv* precedentemente; **previous to** prima di

prewar [ˈpriˌwɔr] *adj* anteguerra

prey [pre] *s* preda; **to be prey to** essere preda di ‖ *intr* predare; **to prey on** or **upon** predare, sfruttare; preoccupare

price [praɪs] *s* prezzo; **at any price** a qualunque costo ‖ *tr* chiedere il prezzo di; fissare il prezzo di

price' control' *s* calmiere *m*

price' cut'ting *s* riduzione di prezzo

price' fix'ing *s* regolamento dei prezzi

price' freez'ing *s* congelamento dei prezzi

priceless [ˈpraɪslɪs] *adj* inestimabile; (coll) molto divertente

price' list' *s* listino prezzi

price' tag' *s* cartellino del prezzo

price' war' *s* guerra dei prezzi

prick [prɪk] *s* punta; puntura; **to kick against the pricks** tirare calci al vento ‖ *tr* bucare, forare; pungere; (*to goad*) spronare; (*the ears*) ergere; (*said, e.g., of the conscience*) rimordere (with *dat*)

prick·ly [ˈprɪkli] *adj* (**-lier; -liest**) spinoso, pungente

prick'ly heat' *s* sudamina

prick'ly pear' *s* ficodindia *m*

pride [praɪd] *s* orgoglio; arroganza; **the**

pride of il fiore di ‖ *tr*—**to pride oneself on** or **upon** inorgoglirsi di

priest [prist] *s* prete *m*, sacerdote *m*

priesthood [ˈpristˌhʊd] *s* sacerdozio

priest·ly [ˈpristli] *adj* (**-lier; -liest**) sacerdotale

prig [prɪg] *s* pedante *mf*, moralista *mf*

prim [prɪm] *adj* (**primmer; primmest**) formale, corretto, compito

prima·ry [ˈpraɪˌmɛri] or [ˈpraɪməri] *adj* primario ‖ *s* (**-ries**) elezione preferenziale; (elec) bobina primaria; (elec) primario

prime [praɪm] *adj* primo; originale; di prima qualità ‖ *s* (*earliest part*) inizio; (*best period*) fiore *m*; (*choicest part*) fior fiore *m*; (math) numero primo; (*mark*) (math) primo ‖ *tr* preparare; (*a pump*) adescare; (*a firearm*) innescare; (*a canvas*) mesticare; (*a wall*) dare la prima mano a; (*to supply with information*) istruire

prime' min'ister *s* primo ministro

primer [ˈprɪmər] *s* sillabario, abbecedario ‖ [ˈpraɪmər] *s* innesco, detonatore *m*

primeval [praɪˈmivəl] *adj* primordiale

primitive [ˈprɪmɪtɪv] *adj* primitivo

primp [prɪmp] *tr* agghindare ‖ *intr* agghindarsi

prim'rose' *s* primula

prim'rose path' *s* sentiero dei piaceri

prince [prɪns] *s* principe *m*; **to live like a prince** vivere da principe

prince' roy'al *s* principe ereditario

princess [ˈprɪnsɪs] *s* principessa

principal [ˈprɪnsɪpəl] *adj* principale ‖ *s* (*chief*) padrone *m*, principale *m*; (*of school*) direttore *m*, preside *m*; (actor) primo attore; (com) capitale *m*; (law) mandante *mf*

principle [ˈprɪnsɪpəl] *s* principio; **on principle** per principio

print [prɪnt] *s* stampa; (*cloth*) tessuto stampato; (*printed matter*) stampato; (*newsprint*) giornale *m*; (*mark made by one's thumb*) impronta; (phot) positiva; **in print** stampato; disponibile; **out of print** esaurito ‖ *tr* stampare, tirare; (*to write in print*) scrivere in stampatello; (*in the memory*) imprimere

print'ed cir'cuit *s* circuito stampato

print'ed mat'ter *s* stampati *mpl*

printer [ˈprɪntər] *s* stampatore *m*; (*of computer*) tabulatrice *f*

print'er's dev'il *s* apprendista *m* tipografo

print'er's ink' *s* inchiostro da stampa

printing [ˈprɪntɪŋ] *s* stampa; stampato; tiratura, edizione; (*writing in printed letters*) stampatello

prior [ˈpraɪ-ər] *adj* anteriore, precedente ‖ *s* priore *m* ‖ *adv* prima; **prior to** prima di

prior·i·ty [praɪˈɑrɪti] or [praɪˈɔrɪti] *s* (**-ties**) priorità *f*

prism [ˈprɪzəm] *s* prisma *m*

prison [ˈprɪzən] *s* prigione, carcere *m*

prisoner [ˈprɪzənər] or [ˈprɪznər] *s* prigioniero

pris'on van' *s* furgone *m* cellulare

pris·sy ['prɪsi] *adj* (**-sier; -siest**) smanceroso, smorfioso

priva·cy ['praɪvəsi] *s* (**-cies**) ritiro; segreto; **to have no privacy** non esser mai lasciato in pace

private ['praɪvɪt] *adj* privato, personale || *s* soldato semplice; **in private** privatamente; **privates** pudende *fpl*

pri'vate eye' *s* poliziotto privato

pri'vate first' class' *s* soldato scelto

pri'vate hos'pital *s* clinica

priv'ate view'ing *s* (mov) anteprima; (painting) vernice *f*

privet ['prɪvɪt] *s* ligustro

privilege ['prɪvɪlɪdʒ] *s* privilegio

priv·y ['prɪvi] *adj* privato; **privy to** segretamente a conoscenza di || *s* (**-ies**) latrina

prize [praɪz] *s* premio; (nav) preda || *tr* valutare, stimare

prize' fight' *s* incontro di pugilato

prize' fight'er *s* pugile *m*, pugilista *m*

prize' ring' *s* ring *m*, quadrato

pro [pro] *s* (**pros**) pro; voto favorevole; argomento favorevole; (coll) professionista *m*; **the pros and the cons** il pro e il contro

probabil·i·ty [,prabə'bɪlɪti] *s* (**-ties**) probabilità *f*

probable ['prabəbəl] *adj* probabile

probate ['probet] *s* omologazione di un testamento; copia autentica di un testamento || *tr* (*a will*) omologare

probation [pro'beʃən] *s* prova; periodo di prova; (law) condizionale *f*, libertà vigilata; (educ) provvedimento disciplinare

probe [prob] *s* inchiesta; (surg) sonda || *tr* indagare; sondare

problem ['prabləm] *s* problema *m*

procedure [pro'sidʒər] *s* procedura

proceed [pro'sid] *s*—**proceeds** provento || [pro'sid] *intr* procedere

proceeding [pro'sidɪŋ] *s* procedimento; **proceedings** atti *mpl*; (law) procedimenti *mpl*

process ['proses] *s* processo; **in the process of time** in processo di tempo || *tr* trattare

procession [pro'sɛʃən] *s* processione

proc'ess serv'er *s* ufficiale giudiziario

proclaim [pro'klem] *tr* proclamare

proclitic [pro'klɪtɪk] *adj* proclitico || *s* parola proclitica

procrastinate [pro'kræstɪ,net] *tr & intr* procrastinare

procure [pro'kjur] *tr* ottenere || *intr* ruffianeggiare

prod [prad] *s* pungolo, stimolo || *v* (*pret & pp* **prodded**; *ger* **prodding**) *tr* stimulare, pungolare, incitare

prodigal ['pradɪgəl] *adj & s* prodigo

prodigious [pro'dɪdʒəs] *adj* prodigioso

prodi·gy ['pradɪdʒi] *s* (**-gies**) prodigio

produce ['prodjus] *or* ['produs] *s* produzione; prodotti *mpl* agricoli || [pro'djus] *or* [pro'dus] *tr* produrre; (theat) presentare

producer [pro'djusər] *or* [pro'dusər] *s* produttore *m*; (*of a play*) impresario; (mov) produttore *m*

product ['pradʌkt] *s* prodotto

production [pro'dʌkʃən] *s* produzione

profane [pro'fen] *adj* profano; blasfemo || *tr* profanare

profani·ty [pro'fænɪti] *s* (**-ties**) bestemmia

profess [pro'fɛs] *tr & intr* professare

profession [pro'fɛʃən] *s* professione

professor [pro'fɛsər] *s* professore *m*

proffer ['prafər] *s* offerta || *tr* offrire

proficient [pro'fɪʃənt] *adj* abile, competente

profile ['profaɪl] *s* profilo || *tr* profilare

profit ['prafɪt] *s* profitto; vantaggio; **at a profit** con guadagno || *tr* avvantaggiare; giovare (with *dat*) || *intr* avvantaggiarsi; **to profit by** approfittare di

profitable ['prafɪtəbəl] *adj* vantaggioso

prof'it and loss' *s* profitti *mpl* e perdite *fpl*

profiteer [,prafɪ'tɪr] *s* profittatore *m* || *intr* fare il profittatore

prof'it shar'ing *s* cointeressenza, partecipazione agli utili

prof'it tak'ing *s* realizzo

profligate ['praflɪgɪt] *adj & s* dissoluto; prodigo

pro for'ma in'voice ['fɔrmə] *s* fattura fittizia

profound [pro'faund] *adj* profondo

profuse [pro'fjus] *adj* profuso, abbondante; **profuse in** prodigo di

proge·ny ['pradʒəni] *s* (**-nies**) prole *f*

progno·sis [prag'nosɪs] *s* (**-ses** [siz]) prognosi *f*

prognostic [prag'nastɪk] *s* pronostico

prognosticate [prag'nastɪ,ket] *tr* pronosticare

pro·gram ['progræm] *s* programma *m* || *v* (*pret & pp* **-gramed** *or* **-grammed**; *ger* **-graming** *or* **-gramming**) *tr* programmare

programmer ['progræmər] *s* pannellista *mf*, programmatore *m*

progress ['progres] *s* progresso; **in progress** in corso; **to make progress** fare dei progressi || [prə'grɛs] *intr* progredire; migliorare

progressive [prə'grɛsɪv] *adj* (*proceeding step by step*) progressivo; (*progressista*) || *s* progressista *mf*

prohibit [pro'hɪbɪt] *tr* proibire

prohibition [,pro·ə'bɪʃən] *s* proibizione; (hist) proibizionismo

project ['pradʒɛkt] *s* progetto || [prə'dʒɛkt] *tr* (*to propose, plan*) progettare; (*light, a shadow, etc.*) proiettare || *intr* sporgere, protrudere

projectile [prə'dʒɛktɪl] *s* proiettile *m*

projection [prə'dʒɛkʃən] *s* proiezione, sporgenza

projector [prə'dʒɛktər] *s* (*apparatus*) proiettore *m*; (*person*) progettista *mf*

proletarian [,prolɪ'tɛrɪ·ən] *adj & s* proletario

proliferate [prə'lɪfə,ret] *intr* proliferare

prolific [prə'lɪfɪk] *adj* prolifico

prolix ['prolɪks] *or* [pro'lɪks] *adj* prolisso

prologue ['prolɔg] *or* ['prolag] *s* prologo

prolong [proˈlɒŋ] or proˈlɑŋ] tr prolungare
promenade [ˌprɑmɪˈned] or [ˌprɑmɪˈnɑd] s passeggiata; ballo di gala ‖ tr & intr passeggiare
promenade′ deck′ s ponte m passeggiata
prominent [ˈprɑmɪnənt] adj prominente
promise [ˈprɑmɪs] s promessa ‖ tr & intr promettere
prom′ising young′ man′ s giovane m di belle speranze
prom′issory note′ [ˈprɑmɪˌsori] s cambiale f, pagherò m
promonto·ry [ˈprɑmənˌtori] s (-ries) promontorio
promote [prəˈmot] tr promuovere
promotion [prəˈmoʃən] s promozione
prompt [prɑmpt] adj pronto ‖ tr incitare, istigare; (theat) suggerire
prompter [ˈprɑmptər] s suggeritore m, rammentatore m
prompt′er′s box′ s buca del suggeritore
promptness [ˈprɑmptnɪs] s prontezza
promulgate [ˈprɑməlˌget] or [proˈmʌlget] tr promulgare
prone [pron] adj prono
prong [prɒŋ] or [prɑŋ] s punta; (of fork) dente m; (of pitchfork) rebbio
pronoun [ˈpronaʊn] s pronome m
pronounce [prəˈnaʊns] tr pronunziare
pronounced [prəˈnaʊnst] adj pronunziato, marcato
pronouncement [prəˈnaʊnsmənt] s dichiarazione ufficiale
pronunciamen·to [prəˌnʌnsɪəˈmento] s (-tos) pronunciamento
pronunciation [prəˌnʌnsɪˈeʃən] or [prəˌnʌnʃɪˈeʃən] s pronunzia
proof [pruf] adj—**proof against** a prova di ‖ s prova; (of alcoholic beverages) gradazione; (typ) bozza
proof′read′er s correttore m di bozze
prop [prɑp] s sostegno, puntello; (pole) palo; **props** attrezzi mpl teatrali ‖ v (pret & pp **propped**; ger **propping**) tr sostenere, puntellare
propaganda [ˌprɑpəˈɡændə] s propaganda
propagate [ˈprɑpəˌget] tr propagare ‖ intr propagarsi
pro·pel [prəˈpel] v (pret & pp **-pelled**; ger **-pelling**) tr propulsare, spingere, azionare; (a rocket) propellere
propeller [prəˈpelər] s elica
propensi·ty [prəˈpensɪti] s (-ties) propensione
proper [ˈprɑpər] adj appropriato, corretto; decente, convenevole; (gram) proprio; **proper to** proprio di
proper·ty [ˈprɑpərti] s (-ties) proprietà f; **properties** attrezzi mpl teatrali
prop′erty man′ s trovarobe m, attrezzista m
prop′erty own′er s proprietario fondiario
prophe·cy [ˈprɑfɪsi] s (-cies) profezia
prophe·sy [ˈprɑfɪˌsaɪ] v (pret & pp **-sied**) tr profetizzare
prophet [ˈprɑfɪt] s profeta m
prophetess [ˈprɑfɪtɪs] s profetessa

prophylactic [ˌprɒfɪˈlæktɪk] adj profilattico ‖ s rimedio profilattico; preservativo
propitiate [prəˈpɪʃɪˌet] tr propiziare
propitious [prəˈpɪʃəs] adj propizio
prop′jet′ s turboelica m
proportion [prəˈporʃən] s proporzione; **in proportion as** a misura che; **in proportion to** in proporzione a; **out of proportion** sproporzionato ‖ tr proporzionare, commensurare
proportionate [prəˈporʃənɪt] adj proporzionato
proposal [prəˈpozəl] s proposta; proposta di matrimonio
propose [prəˈpoz] tr proporre ‖ intr fare una proposta di matrimonio; **to propose to** chiedere la mano di; proporsi di + inf
proposition [ˌprɑpəˈzɪʃən] s proposizione, proposta; (coll) progetto ‖ tr fare delle proposte indecenti a
propound [prəˈpaʊnd] tr proporre
proprietary [prəˈpraɪəˌteri] adj padronale; esclusivo, patentato
proprietor [prəˈpraɪətər] s proprietario
proprietress [prəˈpraɪətrɪs] s proprietaria
proprie·ty [prəˈpraɪəti] s (-ties) correttezza, decoro; **proprieties** convenzioni fpl sociali
propulsion [prəˈpʌlʃən] s propulsione
prorate [proˈret] tr rateizzare
prosaic [proˈze·ɪk] adj prosaico
proscribe [proˈskraɪb] tr proscrivere
prose [proz] adj prosaico ‖ s prosa
prosecute [ˈprɑsɪˌkjut] tr eseguire; (law) processare
prosecutor [ˈprɑsɪˌkjutər] s esecutore m; (law) querelante m; (law) avvocato d'accusa
proselyte [ˈprɑsɪˌlaɪt] s proselito
prose′ writ′er s prosatore m
prosody [ˈprɑsədi] s prosodia, metrica
prospect [ˈprɑspekt] s vista; prospettiva; candidato; probabile cliente m; **prospects** speranze fpl ‖ intr fare il cercatore; **to prospect for** fare il cercatore di
prospectus [prəˈspektəs] s prospetto
prosper [ˈprɑspər] tr & intr prosperare
prosperi·ty [prɑsˈperɪti] s (-ties) prosperità f, benessere m
prosperous [ˈprɑspərəs] adj prospero
prostitute [ˈprɑstɪˌtjut] or [ˈprɑstɪˌtut] s prostituta ‖ tr prostituire
prostrate [ˈprɑstret] adj prostrato ‖ tr prostrare
prostration [prɑsˈtreʃən] s prostrazione
protagonist [proˈtæɡənɪst] s protagonista mf
protect [prəˈtekt] tr proteggere
protection [prəˈtekʃən] s protezione
protégé [ˈprotəˌʒe] s protetto, favorito
protégée [ˈprotəˌʒe] s protetta, favorita
protein [ˈproti·ɪn] or [ˈprotin] s proteina
pro tempore [proˈtempəˌri] adj provvisorio, interinale
protest [ˈprotɛst] s protesta; (com)

protesto || [pro'test] *tr & intr* protestare

Protestant ['pratɪstənt] *adj & s* protestante *mf*

protester [prə'testər] *s* protestatario

prothonotar·y [pro'θɑnə,teri] *s* (**-ies**) (law) cancelliere *m* capo

protocol ['protə,kɑl] *s* protocollo

protoplasm ['protə,plæzəm] *s* protoplasma *m*

prototype | 'protə,taɪp] *s* prototipo

proto·zoon [,protə'zo·ɑn] *s* (**-zoa** ['zo·ə]) protozoo

protract [pro'trækt] *tr* prolungare

protractor [pro'træktər] *s* rapportatore *m*

protrude [pro'trud| *intr* sporgere

proud [praʊd] *adj* fiero; arrogante; maestoso, magnifico

proud' flesh' *s* tessuto di granulazione

prove [pruv] *v* (*pret* **proved**; *pp* **proved** or **proven**) *tr* provare; (*ore*) analizzare; (law) omologare; (math) fare la prova di || *intr* risultare

proverb ['provərb] *s* proverbio

provide [prə'vaɪd] *tr* provvedere || *intr*—**to provide for** provvedere a; (*to be ready for*) prepararsi a

provided |prə'vaɪdɪd] *conj* a condizione che, purché; **provided that** a condizione che, purché

providence ['provɪdəns] *s* provvidenza

providential [,provɪ'dɛn/əl] *adj* provvidenziale

providing [prə'vaɪdɪŋ] *conj* var of **provided**

province ['provɪns] *s* provincia; (fig) pertinenza, competenza

provision [prə'vɪ/ən] *s* provvedimento; clausola; **provisions** *viveri mpl*

provi·so [prə'vaɪzo] *s* (**-sos** or **-soes**) stipulazione, clausola

provoke [prə'vok] *tr* provocare; contrariare, irritare

prow [praʊ] *s* prora, prua

prowess ['praʊ·ɪs] *s* prodezza; maestria

prowl [praʊl] *intr* andare in cerca di preda; vagabondare

prowler ['praʊlər] *s* vagabondo; ladro

proximity [prɑk'sɪmɪti] *s* prossimità *f*

prox·y ['prɑksi] *s* (**-ies**) procura; (*person*) procuratore *m*

prude [prud] *s* pudibondo

prudence ['prudəns] *s* prudenza

prudent ['prudənt] *adj* prudente

pruder·y ['prudəri] *s* (**-ies**) attitudine pudibonda

prudish ['prudɪ/] *adj* pudibondo

prune [prun] *s* prugna secca || *tr* potare

pry [praɪ] *v* (*pret & pp* **pried**) *tr*—**to pry open** forzare con una leva; **to pry s.th out of s.o.** strappare qlco a qlcu || *intr* intromettersi, cacciarsi

psalm [sɑm] *s* salmo

pseudo ['sudo] or ['sjudo] *adj* falso, finto, sedicente

pseudonym ['sudənɪm] or ['sjudənɪm] *s* pseudonimo

psychiatrist [saɪ'kaɪ·ətrɪst] *s* psichiatra *mf*

psychiatry [saɪ'kaɪ·ətri] *s* psichiatria

psychic ['saɪkɪk] *adj* psichico || *s* medium *mf*

psychoanalysis [,saɪko·ə'nælɪsɪs] *s* psicanalisi *f*

psychoanalyze [,saɪko'ænə,laɪz] *tr* psicanalizzare

psychologic(al) [,saɪko'lɑdʒɪk(əl)] *adj* psicologico

psychologist [saɪ'kɑlədʒɪst] *s* psicologo

psycholo·gy [saɪ'kɑlədʒi] *s* (**-gies**) psicologia

psychopath ['saɪkə,pæθ] *s* psicopatico

psycho·sis [saɪ'kosɪs] *s* (**-ses** [siz]) psicosi *f*

psychotic [saɪ'kɑtɪk] *adj* psicotico

pub [pʌb] *s* (Brit) taverna, bar *m*

puberty | 'pjubərti] *s* pubertà *f*

public ['pʌblɪk] *adj & s* pubblico

pub'lic-address' sys'tem *s* sistema *m* d'amplificazione per discorsi in pubblico

publication [,pʌblɪ'ke/ən] *s* pubblicazione

pub'lic convey'ance *s* veicolo di servizi pubblici

publicity [pʌb'lɪsɪti] *s* pubblicità *f*

publicize ['pʌblɪ,saɪz] *tr* pubblicare, divulgare

pub'lic li'brary *s* biblioteca comunale

pub'lic-opin'ion poll' *s* sondaggio d'opinioni

pub'lic pros'ecutor *s* pubblico ministero

pub'lic school' *s* (U.S.A.) scuola dell'obbligo; (Brit) scuola privata, collegio

pub'lic serv'ant *s* funzionario pubblico

pub'lic speak'ing *s* oratoria

pub'lic spir'it *s* civismo

pub'lic toi'let *s* gabinetto pubblico

pub'lic util'ity *s* impresa di servizio pubblico; **public utilities** azioni emesse da imprese di servizi pubblici

publish ['pʌblɪ/] *tr* pubblicare

publisher ['pʌblɪ/ər] *s* editore *m*; (journ) direttore *m* responsabile

pub'lishing house' *s* casa editrice

pucker ['pʌkər] *s* grinza || *tr* raggrinzire || *intr* raggrinzirsi

pudding ['pʊdɪŋ] *s* budino, torta

puddle ['pʌdəl] *s* pozza, pozzanghera || *intr* diguazzare

pudg·y ['pʌdʒi] *adj* (**-ier; -iest**) grassoccio

puerile ['pju·əril] *adj* puerile

Puerto Rican ['pwerto'rikən] *adj & s* portoricano

puff [pʌf] *s* soffio, sbuffo; (*e.g., of cigar*) boccata; (*pad*) piumino; (*exaggerated praise*) pistolotto; (culin) bignè *m* || *tr* sbuffare; gonfiare; adulare || *intr* soffiare, sbuffare; (*to breathe heavily*) ansimare, ansare; gonfiarsi; tirare boccate

puff' paste' *s* pasta sfoglia

pugilist ['pjudʒɪlɪst] *s* pugile *m*

pug-nosed ['pʌg,nozd] *adj* camuso

puke [pjuk] *tr & intr* (slang) vomitare

pull [pʊl] *s* tiro; (*act of drawing in*) tirata; (*handle*) tirante *m*; (slang) influenza, appoggi *mpl* || *tr* tirare; (*a tooth*) cavare; (*a muscle*) strappare;

(a punch) (coll) limitare la forza di; **to pull apart** fare a pezzi; **to pull down** abbattere; degradare; **to pull on** *(e.g., one's pants)* infilarsi; **to pull oneself together** ricomporsi; **to pull s.o.'s leg** beffarsi di qlcu || *intr* tirare; **to pull apart** andare a pezzi; **to pull at** tirare; **to pull away** andarsene; **to pull off** (coll) fare il tifo per; **to pull in** *(said of a train)* arrivare, entrare in stazione; **to pull out** *(said of a train)* partire; **to pull through** guarire, riuscire a cavarsela; **to pull up to** avanzare fino a

pullet ['pulɪt] *s* pollastra

pulley ['pulɪ] *s* puleggia, carrucola

pulp [pʌlp] *s* polpa; *(for making paper)* pasta

pulpit ['pulpɪt] *s* pulpito

pulsate ['pʌlset] *intr* pulsare

pulsation [pʌl'seʃən] *s* pulsazione

pulse [pʌls] *s* polso; **to feel** or **take the pulse of** tastare il polso a

pulverize ['pʌlvə‚raɪz] *tr* polverizzare

pum'ice stone' *s* ['pʌmɪs] *s* pomice *f*, pietra pomice

pum-mel ['pʌməl] *v (pret & pp -meled* or *-melled)* or *(ger -meling* or *-melling) tr* prendere a pugni

pump [pʌmp] *s* pompa; *(slipper)* scarpina || *tr* pompare; (coll) cavare un segreto a; **to pump up** pompare

pumpkin ['pʌmpkɪn] or ['puŋkɪn] *s* zucca

pump-priming ['pʌmp‚praɪmɪŋ] *s* stimolo governativo per sostenere l'economia

pun [pʌn] *s* gioco di parole || *v (pret & pp punned; ger punning) intr* fare giochi di parole

punch [pʌntʃ] *s* pugno; *(tool)* puntaruolo, punzone *m*; *(drink)* ponce *m*; (coll) forza || *tr* dare un pugno a; *(metal)* punzonare; *(a ticket)* perforare || **Punch** *s* Pulcinella *m*; **pleased as Punch** soddisfattissimo

punch' bowl' *s* vaso per il ponce

punch' card' *s* scheda perforata

punch' clock' *s* orologio di controllo

punch'-drunk' *adj* stordito

punched' tape' *s* nastro perforato

punch'ing bag' *s* sacco

punch' line' *s* perfinire *m*, motto finale

punctilious [pʌŋk'tɪlɪ-əs] *adj* cerimonioso, pignolo

punctual ['pʌŋktʃu-əl] *adj* puntuale

punctuate ['pʌŋktʃu‚et] *tr* punteggiare

punctuation [‚pʌŋktʃu'eʃən] *s* punteggiatura

punctua'tion mark' *s* segno d'interpunzione

puncture ['pʌŋktʃər] *s* puntura; *(hole)* bucatura; **to have a puncture** avere una gomma a terra || *tr* bucare, perforare || *intr* essere bucato

punct'ure-proof' *adj* antiperforante

pundit ['pʌndɪt] *s* esperto, autorità *f*

pungent ['pʌndʒənt] *adj* pungente

punish ['pʌnɪʃ] *tr* punire

punishment ['pʌnɪʃmənt] *s* punizione, castigo

punk [pʌŋk] *adj* (slang) di pessima

qualità || *s* esca; *(decayed wood)* legno marcio; (slang) malandrino

punster ['pʌnstər] *s* freddurista *mf*

punt [pʌnt] *s* (football) calcio dato al pallone prima che tocchi il terreno

pu-ny ['pjuni] *adj (-nier; -niest)* insignificante, meschino; *(weak)* debole

pup [pʌp] *s* cucciolo

pupil ['pjupəl] *s* allievo, scolaro; (anat) pupilla

puppet ['pʌpɪt] *s* marionetta, burattino; (fig) fantoccio

puppeteer [‚pʌpɪ'tɪr] *s* burattinaio

pup'pet gov'ernment *s* governo fantoccio or pupazzo

pup'pet show' *s* spettacolo di marionette

pup-py ['pʌpɪ] *s (-pies)* cucciolo

pup'py love' *s* amore *m* giovanile

purchase ['pʌrtʃəs] *s* compra, acquisto; *(grip)* presa, leva || *tr* comprare, acquistare

pur'chasing pow'er *s* potere *m* d'acquisto

pure [pjur] *adj* puro

purgative ['pʌrgətɪv] *adj* purgativo || *s* purga

purge [pʌrdʒ] *s* purga || *tr* purgare

puri-fy ['pjurɪ‚faɪ] *v (pret & pp -fied) tr* purificare || *intr* purificarsi

puritan ['pjurɪtən] *adj & s* puritano || **Puritan** *adj & s* puritano

purity ['pjurɪti] *s* purezza

purloin [pər'lɔɪn] *tr & intr* rubare

purple ['pʌrpəl] *adj* purpureo || *s* porpora

purport ['pʌrport] *s* senso, significato || [pər'port] *tr* significare; **to purport to** + *inf* pretendere di + *inf*

purpose ['pʌrpəs] *s* scopo, fine *m*; **on purpose** apposta; **to good purpose** con buoni risultati; **to no purpose** inutilmente; **to serve one's purpose** fare al caso proprio

purposely ['pʌrpəslɪ] *adv* a bella posta, apposta

purr [pʌr] *s* ronfare *m* || *intr* fare le fusa

purse [pʌrs] *s* borsa; *(woman's handbag)* borsetta; *(for men)* borsetto || *tr (one's lips)* arricciare

purser ['pʌrsər] *s* commissario di bordo

purse' snatch'er ['snætʃər] *s* borsaiolo

purse' strings' *spl* cordini *mpl* della borsa; **to hold the purse strings** controllare le spese

purslane ['pʌrslen] or ['pʌrslɪn] *s* (bot) porcellana

pursue [pər'su] or [pər'sju] *tr* perseguire; *(to harass)* perseguitare; *(a career)* proseguire

pursuit [pər'sut] or [pər'sjut] *s* inseguimento, caccia; occupazione, esercizio

pursuit' plane' *s* caccia *m*

purvey [pər've] *tr* provvedere, fornire

pus [pʌs] *s* pus *m*

push [puʃ] *s* spinta; *(advance)* avanzata; (coll) impulso, energia || *tr* premere, spingere; *(a product)* promuovere la vendita di; dare impulso a; *(narcotics)* (slang) spacciare; **to**

push around (coll) dare spintoni a; (fig) fare pressione su; **to push back** ricacciare || *intr* spingere; **to push ahead** avanzarsi a spintoni, avanzarsi; **to push on** avanzare

push' but'ton *s* pulsante *m*, bottone *m*

push'-button con'trol *s* controllo a pulsanti

push'cart' *s* carretto a mano

pusher ['puʃər] *adj* spingente; (aer) propulsivo || *s* spingitore *m*; (aer) aeroplano a elica propulsiva; (slang) spacciatore *m* di stupefacenti

pushing ['puʃɪŋ] *adj* aggressivo, intraprendente

puss [pus] *s* micio

puss' in the cor'ner *s* gioco dei quattro cantoni

puss·y ['pusi] *s* (**-ies**) micio

puss'y wil'low *s* salice americano a gattini

pustule ['pʌstʃul] *s* pustola

put [put] *v* (*pret* & *pp* **put**; *ger* **putting**) *tr* mettere; (*to estimate*) stimare; (*a question*) rivolgere; (*to throw*) lanciare; imporre; **to put across** (slang) far accettare; **to put aside, away** or **by** mettere da parte; **to put down** annotare; (*to suppress*) reprimere; **to put off** differire; evadere; **to put on** (*clothes*) mettersi; (*a brake*) azionare; (*to assume*) fingere; (*airs*) darsi; **to put out** spegnere; imbarazzare; incomodare; deludere; annoiare, irritare; (*of a game*) espellere; **to put it over on s.o.** farla a qlcu; **to put off** rinviare; **to put over** mandare ad effetto; **to put to flight** mettere in fuga; **to put to shame** svergognare; **to put through** portare a termine; **to put up** offrire; mettere in conserva; alloggiare; costruire; (*money*) contribuire; (coll) incitare || *intr* dirigersi; **to put to sea** mettersi in mare; **to put up** prendere alloggio; **to put up with** tollerare

put'-out' *adj* sconcertato, seccato

putrid ['pjutrɪd] *adj* putrido

Putsch [putʃ] *s* tentativo di sollevazione, sollevazione

putter ['pʌtər] *intr* occuparsi di inezie; **to putter about** andare avanti e indietro

put·ty ['pʌti] *s* (**-ties**) stucco, mastice *m* || *v* (*pret* & *pp* **-tied**) *tr* stuccare

put'ty knife' *s* spatola

put'-up' *adj* (coll) complottato

puzzle ['pʌzəl] *s* enigma *m*; (toy) indovinello || *tr* rendere perplesso, confondere; **to puzzle out** decifrare || *intr* essere perplesso

puzzler ['pʌzlər] *s* enigma *m*

puzzling ['pʌzlɪŋ] *adj* enigmatico

pyg·my ['pɪgmi] *s* (**-mies**) pigmeo

pylon *s* pilone *m*

pyramid ['pɪrəmɪd] *s* piramide *f* || *tr* (*e.g., costs*) aumentare gradualmente; (*one's money*) aumentare giocando in margine

pyre [paɪr] *s* pira

Pyrenees ['pɪrɪ ,niz] *spl* Pirenei *mpl*

pyrites [paɪ'raɪtiz] or ['paɪraɪts] *s* pirite *f*

pyrotechnics [,paɪrə'tɛknɪks] *spl* pirotecnica

python ['paɪθən] or ['paɪθən] *s* pitone *m*

pythoness ['paɪθənɪs] *s* pitonessa

pyx [pɪks] *s* (eccl) pisside *f*

Q

Q, q [kju] *s* diciassettesima lettera dell'alfabeto inglese

quack [kwæk] *adj* falso || *s* medicastro; ciarlatano; qua qua *m* || *intr* (said *of a duck*) fare qua qua

quacker·y ['kwækəri] *s* (**-ies**) ciarlataneria

quadrangle ['kwɑd ,ræŋgəl] *s* quadrangolo

quadrant ['kwɑdrənt] *s* quadrante *m*

quadruped ['kwɑdru ,ped] *adj* & *s* quadrupede *m*

quadruple ['kwɑdrupəl] or [kwɑ'drupəl] *adj* quadruplo; (*alliance*) quadruplice || *s* quadruplo || *tr* quadruplicare || *intr* quadruplicarsi

quaff [kwɑf] or [kwæf] *s* lungo sorso || *tr* & *intr* bere a lunghi sorsi

quail [kwel] *s* quaglia || *intr* sgomentarsi

quaint [kwent] *adj* strano, strambo, originale; all'antica ma bello

quake [kwek] *s* terremoto || *intr* tremare, sussultare

Quaker ['kwekər] *adj* & *s* quacchero, quacquero

Quak'er meet'ing *s* riunione di quaccheri; (coll) riunione in cui si parla poco

quali·fy ['kwɑlɪ ,faɪ] *v* (*pret* & *pp* **-fied**) *tr* qualificare; (*for a profession*) abilitare || *intr* qualificarsi; abilitarsi

quali·ty ['kwɑlɪti] *s* (**-ties**) qualità *f*; (*of a sound*) timbro

qualm [kwɑm] *s* scrupolo di coscienza; preoccupazione; nausea

quanda·ry ['kwɑndəri] *s* (**-ries**) incertezza, perplessità *f*

quanti·ty ['kwɑntɪti] *s* (**-ties**) quantità *f*

quan·tum ['kwɑntəm] *adj* quantistico || *s* (**-ta** [tə]) quanto

quarantine ['kwɑrən ,tin] or ['kwɔrən-,tin] *s* quarantena || *tr* mettere in quarantena

quar·rel ['kwɑrəl] or ['kwɔrəl] *s* litigio, diverbio; **to have no quarrel with** non essere in disaccordo con; **to pick a quarrel with** venire a diverbio con || *v* (*pret* & *pp* **-reled** or **-relled**; *ger* **-reling** or **-relling**) *intr* litigare

quarrelsome ['kwɑrəlsəm] or ['kwɔrəlsəm] *adj* litigioso, rissoso

quar·ry ['kwɑri] or ['kwɔri] *s* (-**ries**) cava; (*game*) selvaggina, cacciagione ‖ *v* (*pret & pp* -**ried**) *tr* cavare

quart [kwɔrt] *s* quarto di gallone

quarter ['kwɔrtər] *adj* quarto ‖ *s* quarto; moneta di un quarto di dollaro; (*three months*) trimestre *m*; (*of town*) quartiere *m*; **a quarter after one** l'una e un quarto; **a quarter of an hour** un quarto d'ora; **a quarter to one** l'una meno un quarto; **at close quarters** corpo a corpo; **quarters** quartiere *m* ‖ *tr* squartare; (*soldiers*) accasermare

quar'ter-deck' *s* cassero

quar'ter-hour' *s* quarto d'ora; **on the quarter-hour** ogni quindici minuti allo scoccare del quarto d'ora

quarter·ly ['kwɔrtərli] *adj* trimestrale ‖ *s* (-**lies**) pubblicazione trimestrale ‖ *adv* trimestralmente

quar'ter-mas'ter *s* (mil) intendente *m* militare; (nav) secondo capo

quartet [kwɔr'tɛt] *s* quartetto

quartz [kwɔrts] *s* quarzo

quasar ['kwesɑr] *s* (astr) radiostella

quash [kwɑʃ] *tr* sopprimere; annullare

quaver ['kwevər] *s* tremito; (mus) tremolo; (mus) croma ‖ *intr* tremare

quay [ki] *s* molo

queen [kwin] *s* regina; (*in cards*) donna; (chess) regina

queen' bee' *s* ape regina; (fig) basilessa

queen' dow'ager *s* regina vedova

queen·ly ['kwinli] *adj* (-**lier**; -**liest**) da regina; regio

queen' moth'er *s* regina madre

queen' post' *s* monaco

queen's' Eng'lish *s* inglese corretto

queer [kwɪr] *adj* strano, curioso; poco bene, indisposto; falso; (slang) omosessuale ‖ *s* (slang) finocchio ‖ *tr* rovinare, mettere in pericolo

quell [kwɛl] *tr* soffocare, domare; (*pain*) calmare

quench [kwɛntʃ] *tr* (*fire, thirst*) spegnere, estinguere; (*rebellion*) soffocare; (elec) ammortizzare

que·ry ['kwɪri] *s* (-**ries**) domanda; punto interrogativo; dubbio ‖ *v* (*pret & pp* -**ried**) *tr* interrogare; (typ) apporre punto interrogativo a

quest [kwɛst] *s* ricerca; **in quest of** in cerca di

question ['kwɛstʃən] *s* domanda; problema *m*, quesito; (*matter*) questione; **beyond question** senza dubbio; **out of the question** impossibile; **this is beside the question** questo non c'entra; **to ask a question** fare una domanda; **to be a question of** trattarsi di; **to call in** or **into question** mettere in dubbio; **without question** senza dubbio ‖ *tr* interrogare; mettere in dubbio; (pol) interpellare

questionable ['kwɛstʃənəbəl] *adj* discutibile

ques'tion mark' *s* punto interrogativo

questionnaire [,kwɛstʃən'ɛr] *s* questionario

queue [kju] *s* (*of hair*) codino; (*of people*) coda ‖ *intr* fare la coda

quibble ['kwɪbəl] *intr* sottilizzare

quick [kwɪk] *adj* pronto, sollecito; sbrigativo; veloce, rapido; vivo ‖ *s*— **the quick and the dead** i vivi e i morti; **to cut to the quick** toccare nel vivo

quicken ['kwɪkən] *tr* sveltire; animare; ravvivare

quick'lime' *s* calce viva

quick' lunch' *s* tavola calda

quickly ['kwɪkli] *adv* svelto, alla svelta; presto

quick'sand' *s* sabbia mobile

quick'-set'ting *adj* a presa rapida

quick'sil'ver *s* argento vivo

quick'work' *s* (naut) opera viva

quiet ['kwaɪ·ət] *adj* quieto; silenzioso; (com) calmo; **to keep quiet** stare zitto ‖ *s* quiete *f*, tranquillità *f*; pace *f*, calma ‖ *tr* quietare; calmare ‖ *intr*— **to quiet down** quietarsi, calmarsi

quill [kwɪl] *s* penna d'oca; (*basal part of feather*) calamo; (*e.g., of porcupine*) aculeo

quilt [kwɪlt] *s* trapunta, imbottita ‖ *tr* trapuntare

quince [kwɪns] *s* cotogna; (*tree*) cotogno

quinine ['kwaɪnaɪn] *s* (*alkaloid*) chinina; (*salt of the alkaloid*) chinino

quinsy ['kwɪnzi] *s* angina

quintessence [kwɪn'tɛsəns] *s* quintessenza

quintet [kwɪn'tɛt] *s* quintetto

quintuplet [kwɪn'tjuplet] or [kwɪn'tuplet] *s* gemello nato da un parto quintuplice

quip [kwɪp] *s* frizzo, uscita ‖ *v* (*pret & pp* **quipped**; *ger* **quipping**) *tr & intr* uscire a dire, dire come battuta

quire [kwaɪr] *s* ventiquattro fogli; (bb) quinterno

quirk [kwʌrk] *s* stranezza, manierismo; (*quibble*) cavillo; (*sudden turn*) mutamento improvviso

quit [kwɪt] *adj* libero; **to be quits** esser pari; **to call it quits** finirla, farla finita ‖ *v* (*pret & pp* **quit** or **quitted**; *ger* **quitting**) *tr* abbandonare ‖ *intr* andarsene; abbandonare l'impiego; smettere (di + *inf*)

quite [kwaɪt] *adv* completamente; molto, del tutto

quitter ['kwɪtər] *s* persona che abbandona facilmente

quiver ['kwɪvər] *s* fremito; (*to hold arrows*) faretra, turcasso ‖ *intr* fremere, tremare

quixotic [kwɪks'ɑtɪk] *adj* donchisciottesco

quiz [kwɪz] *s* (**quizzes**) esame *m*; interrogatorio ‖ *v* (*pret & pp* **quizzed**; *ger* **quizzing**) *tr* esaminare; interrogare

quiz' game' *s* quiz *m*

quiz' pro'gram *s* programma *m* di quiz

quiz' sec'tion *s* (educ) classe *f* a base di esercizi (e non di conferenze)

quizzical ['kwɪzɪkəl] *adj* strano, curioso; (*derisive*) canzonatore

quoin [kɔɪn] or [kwɔɪn] *s* cantone *m*,

pietra angolare; (*piece of wood*) zeppa; (typ) serraforme *m* ‖ *tr* fissare con serraforme

quoit [kwɔɪt] *or* [kɔɪt] *s* anello di corda o di metallo da lanciarsi come gioco; **quoits** *ssg* gioco consistente nel lancio di anelli su di un piolo

quondam [ˈkwɑndæm] *adj* quondam

quorum [ˈkwɔrəm] *s* quorum *m*

quota [ˈkwotə] *s* (*share*) quota; (*of*

imports) contingentamento; (*of persons*) contingente *m*

quotation [kwoˈteʃən] *s* (*from a book*) citazione; (*of prices*) quotazione

quota'tion mark' *s* doppia virgola, virgoletta

quote [kwot] *s* citazione, richiamo ‖ *tr & intr* citare, richiamare; (com) quotare; **quote** cito

quotient [ˈkwoʃənt] *s* quoziente *m*

R

R, r [ɑr] *s* diciottesima lettera dell'alfabeto inglese

rabbet [ˈræbɪt] *s* scanalatura, incastro ‖ *tr* scanalare, incastrare

rab·bi [ˈræbaɪ] *s* (**-bis**) rabbino

rabbit [ˈræbɪt] *s* coniglio

rab'bit ears' *spl* (telv) doppia antenna a stilo

rabble [ˈræbəl] *s* gentaglia, marmaglia

rab'ble-rous'er [ˈrauzər] *s* arruffapopoli *m*

rabies [ˈrebiz] *or* [ˈrebɪˌiz] *s* rabbia

raccoon [ræˈkun] *s* procione *m*

race [res] *s* (*branch of human stock*) razza; (*contest in speed*) corsa; (*contest of any kind*) gara; (*channel*) canale *m* di adduzione ‖ *tr* far correre; gareggiare (in velocità) con; (*a motor*) imballare ‖ *intr* correre; fare le corse; (*said of a motor*) imballarsi; (naut) fare le regate

race' horse' *s* cavallo da corsa

race' ri'ot *s* contestazione di razza

race' track' *s* pista

racial [ˈreʃəl] *adj* razziale

rac'ing car' *s* automobile *f* da corsa

rack [ræk] *s* (*to hang clothes*) attaccapanni *m*; (*framework to hold fodder, baggage, guns, etc.*) rastrelliera; (mach) cremagliera; **to go to rack and ruin** andare a rotoli ‖ *tr* tormentare, torturare; **to rack off** (*wine*) travasare; **to rack one's brains** rompersi il capo, lambiccarsi il cervello

racket [ˈrækɪt] *s* racchetta; (*noise*) chiasso, gazzarra; (coll) racket *m*; **to raise a racket** fare gazzarra

racketeer [ˌrækɪˈtɪr] *s* chi è nel racket; (*engaged in extortion*) ricattatore *m* ‖ *intr* essere nel racket; fare il ricattatore

rack' rail'way *s* ferrovia a cremagliera

rac·y [ˈresi] *adj* (**-ier; -iest**) pungente, vigoroso; piccante

radar [ˈredɑr] *s* radar *m*

radiant [ˈrediˌənt] *adj* raggiante, radioso

radiate [ˈrediˌet] *tr* irradiare ‖ *intr* irradiarsi

radiation [ˌrediˈeʃən] *s* radiazione

radia'tion sick'ness *s* malattia causata da radiazione atomica

radiator [ˈrediˌetər] *s* radiatore *m*

ra'diator cap' *s* tappo del radiatore

radical [ˈrædɪkəl] *adj* radicale ‖ *s*

radicale *mf*; (chem, math) radicale *m*

radi·o [ˈrediˌo] *s* (**-os**) radio *f*; radiogramma *m* ‖ *tr* radiotrasmettere

radioactive [ˌrediˈoˈæktɪv] *adj* radioattivo

ra'dio am'ateur *s* radioamatore *m*

ra'dio announc'er *s* radioannunciatore *m*

ra'dio bea'con *s* radiofaro

ra'dio-broad'cast *s* radiodiffusione ‖ *tr* radiodiffondere

ra'dio com'pass *s* radiobussola

ra'dio-fre'quency *s* radiofrequenza

ra'dio lis'tener *s* radioascoltatore *m*

radiology [ˌrediˈɑlədʒi] *s* radiologia

ra'dio net'work *s* rete *f*

ra'dio news'caster *s* radiocronista *mf*

ra'dio-pho'to *s* (**-tos**) (coll) radiofoto *f*

ra'dio set' *s* radioricevente *f*

ra'dio sta'tion *s* stazione radio

radish [ˈrædɪʃ] *s* ravanello

radium [ˈrediˌəm] *s* radio

radi·us [ˈrediˌəs] *s* (**-i** [ˌaɪ] *or* **-uses**) (anat) radio; (fig, geom) raggio; **within a radius of** entro un raggio di

raffle [ˈræfəl] *s* riffa ‖ *tr* sorteggiare

raft [ræft] *or* [rɑft] *s* zattera; (coll) mucchio

rafter [ˈræftər] *or* [ˈrɑftər] *s* puntone *m*

rag [ræg] *s* straccio; **to chew the rag** (slang) chiacchierare

ragamuffin [ˈrægəˌmʌfɪn] *s* straccione *m*

rag' doll' *s* bambola di pezza

rage [redʒ] *s* rabbia; **to be all the rage** furoreggiare; **to fly into a rage** montare in bestia ‖ *intr* infuriare

ragged [ˈrægɪd] *adj* cencioso; (*torn*) stracciato; (*edge*) rozzo, scabroso

ragpicker [ˈrægˌpɪkər] *s* cenciaiolo, straccivendolo

rag'weed' *s* (bot) ambrosia

raid [red] *s* irruzione, razzia ‖ *tr* scorrere ‖ *intr* scorrazzare

rail [rel] *s* (*of fence*) stecca, traversa; (*fence*) stecconata; (*railing*) ringhiera; (rr) rotaia; **by rail** per ferrovia; **rails** titoli *mpl* ferroviari ‖ *intr* inveire; **to rail at** inveire contro

rail'car' *s* automotrice *f*

rail' fence' *s* stecconata fatta di traverse piallate alla buona

rail'head' s fine f della linea ferroviaria
railing ['reliŋ] s ringhiera
rail'road' adj ferroviario || s ferrovia || tr trasportare in ferrovia; (a bill) far passare precipitosamente; (coll) imprigionare falsamente
rail'road cros'sing s passaggio a livello
rail'road'er s ferroviere m
rail'way' s ferrovia, strada ferrata
raiment ['remənt] s (lit) abbigliamento
rain [ren] s pioggia; **rain or shine** con qualunque tempo || tr fare piovere; (lit) piovere; **to rain cats and dogs** piovere a catinelle; **to rain out** far sospendere per via della pioggia || intr piovere
rainbow ['ren ,bo] s arcobaleno
rain'coat' s impermeabile m
rain'fall' s acquazzone m; piovosità f
rain·y ['reni] adj (-ier; -iest) piovoso, piovano
rain'y day' s giorno piovoso; (fig) tempi mpl difficili
raise [rez] s aumento || tr levare, rialzare; (children, animals) allevare; (to build) tirare su; (a question) sollevare; (the dead) risollevare; (to increase) aumentare; (money) raccogliere; (a siege) togliere; (at cards) rilanciare; (anchor) salpare; (math) elevare
raisin ['rezən] s grano d'uva passa, grano d'uva secca; **raisins** uva passa, uva secca
rake [rek] s rastrello; (person) porcaccione m, libertino || tr rastrellare; **to rake in money** far soldini
rake'-off' s (coll) compenso illecito, bustarella; (coll) sconto
rakish ['rekɪʃ] adj libertino; brioso, vivace; **to wear one's hat at a rakish angle** portare il cappello sulle ventitré
ral·ly ['ræli] s (-lies) riunione, comizio; adunata; ricupero || v (pret & pp -lied) tr riunire, chiamare a raccolta; rianimare || intr riunirsi; rianimarsi; (said of stock prices) rialzarsi; rimettersi in forze; **to rally to the side of** correre all'aiuto di
ram [ræm] s (male sheep) montone m; (mil) ariete m; (nav) sperone m; (mach) maglio del battipalo || v (pret & pp rammed; ger ramming) tr battere, sbattere contro; cacciare, conficcare; forzare; (nav) speronare || intr—**to ram into** sbattere contro
ramble ['ræmbəl] s girata || intr (to wander around) gironzolare; vagare; (said of a vine) crescere disordinatamente; (said, e.g., of a river) serpeggiare; (fig) scorrazzare, divagare
rami·fy ['ræmɪ,faɪ] v (pret & pp -fied) tr ramificare || intr ramificarsi
ram'jet en'gine s statoreattore m
ramp [ræmp] s rampa
rampage ['ræmpedʒ] s stato d'eccitazione; **to go on a rampage** infierire, comportarsi furiosamente
rampart ['ræmpart] s baluardo, muraglione m

ram'rod' s (for ramming) (mil) bacchetta; (for cleaning) (mil) scovolo
ram'shack'le adj cadente, in rovina
ranch [ræntʃ] s fattoria agricola
rancid ['rænsɪd] adj rancido
rancor ['ræŋkər] s rancore m
random ['rændəm] adj fortuito; **at random** alla rinfusa, a casaccio
range [rendʒ] s (row) fila; (rank) classe f; (distance) portata; campo di tiro a segno; raggio d'azione; (scope) gamma; (for grazing) pascolo; (stove) fornello, cucina economica; **within range of** alla portata di || tr allineare; ordinare; passare attraverso; mandare al pascolo || intr variare, fluttuare; estendersi; trovarsi; (mil) portare; **to range over** percorrere; (fig) trattare
range' find'er s telemetro
rank [ræŋk] adj esuberante; grossolano; denso, spesso; puzzolente; eccessivo; completo, assoluto || s rango, grado; (row) fila, schiera; **ranks** truppe fpl, ranghi mpl || tr arrangiare, allineare; classificare; avere rango superiore a || intr avere il massimo rango; **to rank high** avere un'alta posizione; **to rank low** avere una posizione bassa; **to rank with** essere allo stesso livello di
rank' and file' s truppa; massa
rankle ['ræŋkəl] tr irritare || intr inasprirsi
ransack ['rænsak] tr (to search thoroughly) frugare, rovistare; (to pillage) svaligiare, saccheggiare
ransom ['rænsəm] s taglia, riscatto || tr riscattare
rant [rænt] intr farneticare, parlare a vanvera
rap [ræp] s colpo, colpetto; **I don't care a rap** non m'importa un fico; **to take the rap** (slang) prendersi la colpa || v (pret & pp rapped; ger rapping) tr dare colpi a; battere; **to rap out** (e.g., a command) lanciare || intr dare colpi, bussare
rapacious [rə'peʃəs] adj rapace
rape [rep] s rapimento; (of a woman) stupro; (bot) ravizzone m || tr rapire; forzare, violentare
rapid ['ræpɪd] adj rapido || **rapids** spl rapide fpl
rap'id-fire' adj a tiro rapido
rapidity [rə'pɪdəti] s rapidità f
rapier ['repɪ·ər] s spada, stocco
rapt [ræpt] adj assorto; estatico
rapture ['ræptʃər] s rapimento, estasi f
rare [rer] adj raro; (thinly distributed) rado; (gas) rarefatto; (meat) al sangue; (gem) prezioso
rare'-earth' met'al s metallo delle terre rare
rare·fy ['rerɪ,faɪ] v (pret & pp -fied) tr rarefare || intr rarefarsi
rarely ['rerli] adv di rado, raramente
rascal ['ræskəl] s briccone m, birbante m
rash [ræʃ] adj temerario, precipitato || s eruzione; (fig) mucchio
rasp [ræsp] or [rɑsp] s raspa; rumore

m di raspa || *tr* raspare; irritare; dire con voce roca || *intr* fare rumore raspante

rasp·ber·ry ['ræz‚beri] or ['rɑz‚beri] *s* (-ries) lampone *m*; (slang) pernacchia

rat [ræt] *s* ratto; *(to give fullness to hair)* posticcio; (slang) traditore *m*; **to smell a rat** (coll) subodorare un inganno

ratchet ['rætʃɪt] *s* nottolino

rate [ret] *s* *(of interest)* saggio, tasso; prezzo; costo; velocità *f*; *(degree of action)* ragione; tariffa; **at any rate** ad ogni modo; **at the rate of** in ragione di || *tr* valutare, classificare || *intr* essere considerato; essere classificato

rate' of exchange' *s* corso del cambio

rather ['ræðər] or ['rɑðər] *adv* piuttosto; a preferenza; per meglio dire; bensì; discretamente; **rather than** piuttosto di || *interj* e come!

rati·fy ['rætɪ‚faɪ] *v* (*pret & pp* **-fied**) *tr* ratificare, sancire

rating ['retɪŋ] *s* classifica; (nav) grado; (com) valutazione

ra·tio ['reʃo] or ['reʃɪ‚o] *s* (-tios) ragione, rapporto; proporzione

ration ['reʃən] or ['ræʃən] *s* razione || *tr* razionare

rational ['ræʃənəl] *adj* razionale

ra'tion bool' *s* tessera di razionamento

rat' poi'son *s* veleno per i topi

rat' race' *s* (coll) corsa dei barberi

rattle ['rætəl] *s* *(sharp sounds)* fracasso; *(child's toy)* sonaglio; *(noise-making device)* raganella; *(in throat)* rantolo || *tr* scuotere; *(to confuse)* sconcertare; **to rattle off** dire rapidamente, snocciolare || *intr* risuonare; scuotersi; cianciare

rat'tle·snake' *s* serpente *m* a sonagli

rat'trap' *s* trappola per topi; *(hovel)* topaia; *(jam)* (fig) frangente *m*

raucous ['rɔkəs] *adj* rauco

ravage ['rævɪdʒ] *s* distruzione; **ravages** *(of time)* oltraggio || *tr* distruggere, disfare

rave [rev] *intr* farneticare, delirare; infuriare; andare in estasi; **to rave about** levare alle stelle

raven ['revən] *s* corvo

ravenous ['rævənəs] *adj* famelico

ravine [rə'vin] *s* canalone *m*, burrone *m*

ravish ['rævɪʃ] *tr* incantare, entusiasmare; rapire; *(a woman)* stuprare

raw [rɔ] *adj* crudo; *(e.g., silk)* grezzo; *(flesh)* vivo; inesperto

raw' deal' *s* trattamento brutale e ingiusto

raw'hide' *s* pelle greggia

raw' mate'rial *s* materia prima

ray [re] *s* raggio; *(fish)* razza

rayon ['re·ɑn] *s* raion *m*

raze [rez] *tr* radere al suolo

razor ['rezər] *s* rasoio

ra'zor blade' *s* lametta

ra'zor strop' *s* coramella

razz [ræz] *s* (slang) pernacchia || *tr* (slang) prendere in giro

reach [ritʃ] *s* portata; estensione; **out**

of reach (of) fuori della portata (di); oltre alle possibilità (di); fuori tiro (di); **within reach of** alla portata di || *tr* raggiungere; toccare; *(customers)* guadagnare || *intr* estendere la mano; **to reach for** cercare di raggiungere

react [rɪ'ækt] *intr* reagire

reaction [rɪ'ækʃən] *s* reazione

reactionar·y [rɪ'ækʃə‚neri] *adj* reazionario || *s* (-ies) reazionario

reactor [rɪ'æktər] *s* reattore *m*

read [rid] *v* (*pret & pp* **read** [red]) *tr* leggere; *(s.o.'s thoughts)* leggere in; **to read over** ripassare || *intr* leggere; saper leggere; essere concepito, e.g., **your cable reads thus** il vostro telegramma è concepito così; leggersi, e.g., **this books reads easily** questo libro si legge facilmente; **to read on** continuare a leggere

reader ['ridər] *s* lettore *m*; libro di lettura, sillabo

readily ['redɪli] *adv* velocemente; facilmente; di buona voglia

reading ['ridɪŋ] *s* lettura; dizione

read'ing desk' *s* leggio

read'ing glass' *s* lente *f* d'ingrandimento; **reading glasses** occhiali *mpl* per la lettura

read'ing lamp' *s* lampada da scrittoio

read'ing room' *s* sala di lettura

read·y ['redi] *adj* (-ier; -iest) pronto; disponibile; **to make ready** prepararsi; **preparasi** || *v* (*pret & pp* **-ied**) *tr* preparare || *intr* prepararsi

read'y cash' *s* denaro contante

read'y-made cloth'ing *s* confezioni *fpl*

read'y-made suit' *s* vestito già fatto

reaffirm [‚ri·ə'fʌrm] *tr* riaffermare

reagent [rɪ'edʒənt] *s* reagente *m*

real ['ri·əl] *adj* effettivo, reale

re'al estate' *s* beni *mpl* immobili, proprietà *f* immobiliare

re'al-estate' *adj* immobiliare, fondiario

realism ['ri·ə‚lɪzəm] *s* realismo

realist ['ri·əlɪst] *s* realista *mf*

realistic [‚ri·ə'lɪstɪk] *adj* realistico

reali·ty [rɪ'ælɪti] *s* (-ties) realtà *f*

realize ['ri·ə‚laɪz] *tr* rendersi conto di; concretare; realizzare || *intr* convertire proprietà in contanti

realm [rɛlm] *s* regno

realtor ['ri·əl‚tɔr] or ['ri·əltər] *s* (trademark) agente *m* d'immobili; membro dell'associazione nazionale

realty ['ri·əlti] *s* proprietà *f* immobiliare

ream [rim] *s* risma; **reams** pagine *fpl* e pagine || *tr* alesare

reamer ['rimər] *s* (mach) alesatore *m*; (dentistry) fresa

reap [rip] *tr & intr* *(to cut)* mietere; *(to gather)* raccogliere

reaper ['ripər] *s* *(person)* mietitore *m*; (mach) mietitrice *f*

reappear [‚ri·ə'pɪr] *intr* ricomparire, riapparire

reappearance [‚ri·ə'pɪrəns] *s* riapparizione, ricomparsa

reapportionment [‚ri·ə'porʃənmənt] *s* ridistribuzione

rear [rɪr] *adj* posteriore, di dietro || *s*

retro, di dietro; posteriore *m;* (mil) retroguardia ‖ *tr* alzare, elevare; allevare, educare ‖ *intr* (*said of a horse*) impennarsi

rear' ad'miral *s* contrammiraglio

rear' drive' *s* trazione posteriore

rear' end' *s* retro, di dietro; (coll) posteriore *m;* (aut) retrotreno

rearmament [rɪ'ɑrməmənt] *s* riarmo

rear'-view mir'ror *s* specchietto retrovisivo

rear' win'dow *s* (aut) lunetta posteriore

reason ['rizən] *s* ragione; **by reason of** per causa di; **to bring s.o. to reason** indurre qlcu alla ragione; **to stand to reason** esser logico ‖ *tr & intr* ragionare

reasonable ['rizənəbəl] *adj* ragionevole

reassessment [,ri·ə'sɛsmənt] *s* rivalutazione

reassure [,ri·ə'ʃʊr] *tr* rassicurare, riassicurare

reawaken [,ri·ə'wekən] *tr* risvegliare ‖ *intr* risvegliarsi

rebate ['ribet] *or* [rɪ'bet] *s* ribasso ‖ *tr* ribassare

rebel ['rɛbəl] *adj & s* ribelle *mf* ‖ **re·bel** [rɪ'bɛl] *v* (*pret & pp* **-belled;** *ger* **-belling**) *intr* ribellarsi

rebellion [rɪ'bɛljən] *s* ribellione

rebellious [rɪ'bɛljəs] *adj* ribelle

re·bind [ri'baɪnd] *v* (*pret & pp-* **bound** ['baʊnd]) *tr* rifasciare; (bb) rilegare

rebirth ['rɪbʌrθ] *or* [rɪ'bʌrθ] *s* rinascita

rebore [ri'bor] *tr* rialesare, rettificare

rebound ['rɪ,baʊnd] *or* [rɪ'baʊnd] *s* rimbalzo ‖ [ri'baʊnd] *intr* rimbalzare

rebroad'casting sta'tion *s* stazione ripetitrice

rebuff [rɪ'bʌf] *s* rifiuto ‖ *tr* respingere, rifiutare

rebuild [ri'bɪld] *v* (*pret & pp* **-built** ['bɪlt]) *tr* ricostruire, riedificare

rebuke [rɪ'bjuk] *s* rabbuffo ‖ *tr* rabbuffare

re·but [rɪ'bʌt] *v* (*pret & pp* **-butted;** *ger* **-butting**) *tr* confutare

rebuttal [rɪ'bʌtəl] *s* confutazione

recall [rɪ'kɔl] *or* ['rikɔl] *s* richiamo; revoca ‖ [rɪ'kɔl] *tr* richiamare; ricordare, ricordarsi di; richiamare alla memoria

recant [rɪ'kænt] *tr* ritrattare ‖ *intr* ritrattarsi

re·cap ['ri,kæp] *or* [ri'kæp] *v* (*pret & pp* **-capped;** *ger* **-capping**) *tr* ricapitolare, riepilogare; (*a tire*) rifare il battistrada a

recapitulation [,rikə,pɪtʃə'leʃən] *s* ricapitolazione, riepilogo

re·cast ['ri,kæst] *or* ['ri,kɑst] *s* rifusione ‖ [ri'kæst] *or* [ri'kɑst] *v* (*pret & pp* **-cast**) *tr* rifondere

recede [rɪ'sid] *intr* ritirarsi, allontanarsi; recedere, retrocedere; (*said, e.g., of chin*) sfuggire

receipt [rɪ'sit] *s* ricevimento; (*acknowledgment of payment*) ricevuta; (*recipe*) ricetta; **receipts** incasso, introito ‖ *tr* quietanzare

receive [rɪ'siv] *tr* ricevere; (*stolen goods*) ricettare; (*to have inflicted upon one*) subire ‖ *intr* ricevere

receiver [rɪ'sivər] *s* ricevitore *m;* ricettatore *m;* (law) curatore *m* fallimentare; (telp) auricolare *m*

receiv'ing set' *s* apparecchio radioricevente

receiv'ing tell'er *s* cassiere *m* incaricato delle riscossioni

recent ['risənt] *adj* recente

recently ['risəntli] *adv* recentemente, di recente

receptacle [rɪ'sɛptəkəl] *s* recipiente *m;* (elec) presa

reception [rɪ'sɛpʃən] *s* accoglienza; (*function*) ricevimento

recep'tion desk' *s* ufficio informazioni, bureau *m*

receptionist [rɪ'sɛpʃənɪst] *s* accoglitrice *f;* (*male*) usciere *m*

receptive [rɪ'sɛptɪv] *adj* ricettivo

recess [rɪ'sɛs] *or* ['rɪses] *s* intermezzo, interludio; ora di ricreazione; (*in a line*) rientranza; (*in a wall*) nicchia, alcova; (fig) recesso ‖ [rɪ'sɛs] *tr* aggiornare, dare vacanza a; incassare, mettere in una nicchia ‖ *intr* aggiornarsi, prendersi vacanza

recession [rɪ'sɛʃən] *s* ritirata; processione finale; (com) recessione

recipe ['rɛsɪ,pi] *s* ricetta

reciprocal [rɪ'sɪprəkəl] *adj* reciproco

reciprocity [,rɛsɪ'prɑsɪti] *s* reciprocità *f*

recital [rɪ'saɪtəl] *s* narrazione; (*of music or poetry*) recital *m*

recite [rɪ'saɪt] *tr* raccontare; (*music or poetry*) recitare

reckless ['rɛklɪs] *adj* temerario, spericolato

reckon ['rɛkən] *tr* calcolare; considerare; (coll) supporre ‖ *intr* contare; **to reckon with** prevedere, tener conto di

reclaim [rɪ'klem] *tr* (*land*) sanare, prosciugare; (*substances*) rigenerare; (fig) rigenerare

recline [rɪ'klaɪn] *tr* reclinare ‖ *intr* reclinarsi, adagiarsi

recluse [rɪ'klus] *or* ['rɛklus] *adj & s* recluso

recognition [,rɛkəg'nɪʃən] *s* riconoscimento

recognize ['rɛkəg,naɪz] *tr* riconoscere

recoil [rɪ'kɔɪl] *s* indietreggiamento; (*of a firearm*) rinculo ‖ *intr* indietreggiare; rinculare

recollect [,rɛkə'lɛkt] *tr & intr* ricordare

recollection [,rɛkə'lɛkʃən] *s* ricordo

recommend [,rɛkə'mɛnd] *tr* raccomandare

recompense ['rɛkəm,pɛns] *s* ricompensa ‖ *tr* ricompensare

reconcile ['rɛkən,saɪl] *tr* riconciliare; **to reconcile oneself** rassegnarsi

reconnaissance [rɪ'kɑnɪsəns] *s* ricognizione

reconnoiter [,rɛkə'nɔɪtər] *or* [,rikə'nɔɪtər] *tr & intr* perlustrare

reconsider [,rikən'sɪdər] *tr* riconsiderare

reconstruct [ˌrikən'strʌkt] *tr* ricostruire

reconversion [ˌrikən'vʌrʒən] *s* riconversione

record ['rekərd] *s* registrazione; annotazione; (*official report*) verbale *m*, protocollo; (*criminal*) fedina sporca; (*of a phonograph*) disco; (*educ*) documenti *mpl* scolastici; (sports) record *m*, primato; **off the record** confidenziale; confidenzialmente; **records** annali *mpl*, documenti *mpl*; **to break a record** battere un record ‖ [rɪ'kɔrd] *tr* registrare; mettere a verbale; (*e.g., a song*) incidere

rec'ord break'er *s* (sports) primatista *mf*

rec'ord chang'er ['tʃendʒər] *s* cambiadischi *m*

recorder [rɪ'kɔrdər] *s* (*apparatus*) registratore *m*; (law) cancelliere *m*; (mus) flauto a imboccatura a tubo

rec'ord hold'er *s* (sports) primatista *mf*

recording [rɪ'kɔrdɪŋ] *s* registrazione; (*of a record*) incisione; (*record*) disco

record'ing sec'retary *s* cancelliere *m*

rec'ord play'er *s* giradischi *m*

recount ['ri ˌkaunt] *s* nuovo conteggio ‖ [ri'kaunt] *tr* (*to count again*) ricontare ‖ [rɪ'kaunt] *tr* (*to narrate*) raccontare

recourse [rɪ'kors] or ['rikors] *s* ricorso; (com) rivalsa; **to have recourse to** ricorrere a

recover [rɪ'kʌvər] *tr* ricuperare, riacquistare; (*a substance*) rigenerare; **to recover consciousness** riaversi, riprendere conoscenza ‖ *intr* rimettersi; guadagnare una causa

recover·y [rɪ'kʌvəri] *s* (-**ies**) ricupero; guarigione; **past recovery** incurabile

recreant ['rekri·ənt] *adj & s* codardo; traditore *m*

recreation [ˌrekri'eʃən] *s* ricreazione

recruit [rɪ'krut] *s* recluta ‖ *tr & intr* reclutare

rectangle ['rek ˌtæŋgəl] *s* rettangolo

rectifier ['rektə ˌfaɪ·ər] *s* rettificatore *m*; (elec) raddrizzatore *m*

recti·fy ['rektɪ ˌfaɪ] *v* (*pret & pp* -**fied**) *tr* rettificare; (elec) raddrizzare

rectitude ['rektɪ ˌtud] or ['rektɪ ˌtjud] *s* rettitudine *f*

rec·tum ['rektəm] *s* (-**tums** or -**ta** [tə]) retto

recumbent [rɪ'kʌmbənt] *adj* sdraiato

recuperate [rɪ'kjupə ˌret] *tr* ricuperare ‖ *intr* ristabilirsi, rimettersi

re·cur [rɪ'kʌr] *v* (*pret & pp* -**curred**; *ger* -**curring**) *intr* ricorrere; ritornare; tornare a mente

recurrent [rɪ'kʌrənt] *adj* ricorrente

recycle [ri'saɪkəl] *tr* riconvertire; (*e.g., in chemical industry*) riciclare

red [red] *adj* (**redder; reddest**) rosso ‖ *s* rosso; **in the red** in debito, in rosso ‖ **Red** *adj & s* (*Communist*) rosso

red'bait' *tr* dare del comunista a

red'bird' *s* cardinale *m*

red-blooded ['red ˌblʌdɪd] *adj* sanguigno; vigoroso

red'breast' *s* pettirosso

red'bud' *s* siliquastro

red'cap' *s* (Brit) poliziotto militare; (U.S.A.) facchino

red' cell' *s* globulo rosso

red' cent' *s*—**to not have a red cent** (coll) non avere il becco di un quattrino

Red' Cross' *s* Croce Rossa

redden ['redən] *tr* arrossare ‖ *intr* arrossire

redeem [rɪ'dim] *tr* redimere; (*a promise*) disimpegnare

redeemer [rɪ'dimər] *s* redentore *m*

redemption [rɪ'dempʃən] *s* redenzione; disimpegno

red-handed ['red'hændɪd] *adj*—**to be caught red-handed** esser colto sul fatto or con le mani nel sacco

red'head' *s* persona dai capelli rossi

red' her'ring *s* argomento usato per sviare l'attenzione; aringa affumicata

red-hot' *adj* rovente, incandescente; fresco fresco, appena uscito

rediscover [ˌridɪs'kʌvər] *tr* riscoprire

red-let'ter *adj* memorabile

red'-light' dis'trict *s* quartiere *m* delle case di tolleranza

red' man' *s* pellerossa *m*

re-do ['ri'du] *v* (*pret* -**did** ['dɪd]; *pp* -**done** ['dʌn]) *tr* rifare

redolent ['redələnt] *adj* fragrante, profumato; **redolent of** che sa di

redoubt [rɪ'daut] *s* (mil) ridotta

redound [rɪ'daund] *intr* ridondare

red' pep'per *s* pepe *m* di Caienna

redress [rɪ'dres] or ['ridres] *s* riparazione, risarcimento ‖ [rɪ'dres] *tr* riparare, risarcire

red'skin' *s* pellerossa *mf*

red' tape' *s* trafila, burocrazia

reduce [rɪ'djus] or [rɪ'dus] *tr* ridurre; diluire; (mil) retrocedere; (*a hernia*) (surg) sbrigliare ‖ *intr* ridursi; (*to lose weight*) dimagrire

reducing [rɪ'djusɪŋ] or [rɪ'dusɪŋ] *adj* dimagrante; (chem) riducente

reduction [rɪ'dʌkʃən] *s* riduzione

redundant [rɪ'dʌndənt] *adj* ridondante

red'wood' *s* sequoia

reed [rid] *s* (*stalk*) calamo; (*plant*) canna; (mus) linguetta; (mus) strumento a linguetta

reedit [ri'edɪt] *tr* rifondere

reef [rif] *s* scoglio, barriera; (naut) terzarolo; (min) vena, filone *m* ‖ *tr* (*sail*) imbrogliare

reefer ['rifər] *s* giacchetta a doppio petto; (slang) sigaretta di marijuana

reek [rik] *intr* puzzare; sudare, evaporare, fumare

reel [ril] *s* (*spool*) bobina; (*sway*) vacillamento; (*for fishing*) mulinello; **off the reel** senza esitazione ‖ *tr* bobinare; **to reel off** rifilare ‖ *intr* barcollare

reelection [ˌri·ɪ'lekʃən] *s* rielezione

reenlist [ˌri·en'lɪst] *tr* arruolare di nuovo ‖ *intr* arruolarsi di nuovo

reen·try [rɪ'entri] *s* (-**tries**) rientro

reexamination [ˌri·eg ˌzæmɪ'neʃən] *s* riesame *m*

re·fer [rɪ'fʌr] v (pret & pp **-ferred**; ger **-ferring**) tr riferire || intr riferirsi

referee [ˌrefə'ri] s arbitro || tr & intr arbitrare

reference ['refərəns] s riferimento; (testimonial) referenza; (e.g., in a book) rinvio, rimando

ref'erence book' s libro di consultazione

referen·dum [ˌrefə'rendəm] s (-dums or -da [də]) referendum m

refill ['rifɪl] s ricambio || [rɪ'fɪl] tr riempire di nuovo

refine [rɪ'faɪn] tr raffinare

refinement [rɪ'faɪnmənt] s raffinatezza; (of oil) raffinatura

refiner·y [rɪ'faɪnəri] s (-ies) raffineria

reflect [rɪ'flɛkt] tr riflettere || intr riflettere, riflettersi

reflection [rɪ'flɛk/ən] s riflessione

reflex ['riflɛks] adj riflesso || s riflesso; (camera) reflex m

reflexive [rɪ'flɛksɪv] adj riflessivo

reforestation [ˌrifɔrɪs'te/ən] or [ˌrifɔrɪs'te/ən] s rimboschimento

reform [rɪ'fɔrm] s riforma || tr riformare || intr correggersi

reformation [ˌrefər'me/ən] s riforma || **Reformation** s—**the Reformation** la Riforma

reformato·ry [rɪ'fɔrmə,tori] adj riformativo || s (-ries) riformatorio

reformer [rɪ'fɔrmər] s riformatore m

reform' school' s riformatorio

refraction [rɪ'fræk/ən] s rifrazione

refrain [rɪ'fren] s ritornello, intercalare m || intr astenersi

refresh [rɪ'frɛ/] tr rinfrescare; ristorare || intr ristorarsi

refreshing [rɪ'frɛ/ɪŋ] adj rinfrescante; ristoratore; ricreativo

refreshment [rɪ'frɛ/mənt] s rinfresco

refrigerate [rɪ'frɪdʒə,ret] tr refrigerare

refrigerator [rɪ'frɪdʒə,retər] s refrigerante m, frigorifero

refrig'erator car' s vagone frigorifero

re·fuel [rɪ'fjul] v (pret & pp **-fueled** or **-fuelled**; ger **-fueling** or **-fuelling**) tr rifornire di carburante || intr rifornirsi di carburante

refuge ['refjudʒ] s rifugio; scampo; **to take refuge (in)** rifugiarsi (in)

refugee [ˌrefju'dʒi] s rifugiato

refund [rɪ'fʌnd] s rifusione || [rɪ'fʌnd] tr (to repay) rifondere || [ri'fʌnd] tr (bonds) consolidare; (to fund anew) rifondere

refurnish [rɪ'fʌrnɪ/] tr riammobiliare

refusal [rɪ'fjuzəl] s rifiuto

refuse ['refjus] s rifiuto, spazzatura || [rɪ'fjuz] tr rifiutare; **to refuse to** rifiutarsi di

refute [rɪ'fjut] tr smentire, confutare

regain [rɪ'gen] tr riguadagnare; **to regain consciousness** tornare in sé

regal ['rigəl] adj reale, regale

regale [rɪ'gel] tr intrattenere, rallegrare

regalia [rɪ'geli·ə] spl (of royalty) prerogative fpl reali; alta uniforme

regard [rɪ'gard] s riguardo; (look)

sguardo; (esteem) rispetto; **in regard to** rispetto a; **regards** rispetti mpl; **warm regards** cordiali saluti mpl; **without regard to** senza considerare || tr considerare; osservare; concernere; **as regards** per quanto concerne

regarding [rɪ'gardɪŋ] prep per quanto concerne

regardless [rɪ'gardlɪs] adj incurante || adv ciò nonostante; costi quello che costi; **regardless of** malgrado

regatta [rɪ'gætə] s regata

regen·cy ['ridʒənsi] s (-cies) reggenza

regenerate [rɪ'dʒɛnə,ret] tr rigenerare || intr rigenerarsi

regent ['ridʒənt] s reggente mf

regicide ['redʒɪ,saɪd] s (act) regicidio; (person) regicida mf

regiment ['redʒɪmənt] s reggimento || ['redʒɪ,ment] tr irregimentare

regimental [ˌredʒɪ'mentəl] adj reggimentale || **regimentals** spl uniforme f reggimentale

region ['ridʒən] s regione

register ['redʒɪstər] s registro; (for controlling the flow of air) regolatore m dell'aria || tr registrare; (e.g., a student) iscrivere; (e.g., anger) dimostrare; (a letter) raccomandare || intr registrarsi; iscriversi; fare impressione

reg'istered let'ter s raccomandata

reg'istered nurse' s infermiera diplomata

registrar ['redʒɪs,trar] s registratore m, archivista mf; (of deeds) ricevitore m

registration [ˌredʒɪs'tre/ən] s registrazione; (e.g., of a student) iscrizione; (of mail) raccomandazione

registra'tion fee' s diritto di segreteria

re·gret [rɪ'gret] s pentimento, rammarico; **regrets** scuse fpl || v (pret & pp **-gretted**; ger **-gretting**) tr rimpiangere; **to regret** to essere spiacente di

regrettable [rɪ'gretəbəl] adj deplorevole

regular ['regjələr] adj regolare; (life) regolato; (coll) vero || s cliente m abituale; (mil) effettivo

regularity [ˌregju'lærɪti] s regolarità f

regularize ['regjələ,raɪz] tr regolarizzare

regulate ['regjə,let] tr regolare

regulation [ˌregjə'le/ən] s regolazione; (rule) regolamento

rehabilitate [ˌrihə'bɪlɪ,tet] tr riabilitare

rehearsal [rɪ'hʌrsəl] s prova

rehearse [rɪ'hʌrs] tr provare || intr fare le prove

rehiring [ri'haɪrɪŋ] s riassunzione

reign [ren] s regno || intr regnare

reimburse [ˌri·ɪm'bʌrs] tr rimborsare

rein [ren] s redine f; **to give full rein to** dare briglia sciolta a || tr guidare con le redini; frenare

reincarnation [ˌri·ɪnkar'ne/ən] s reincarnazione

reindeer ['ren,dɪr] s renna

reinforce [ˌri·ɪn'fors] tr rinforzare; (a wall) armare

re'inforced con'crete s cemento armato

reinforcement [ˌri·ɪn·ˈforsmənt] *s* rinforzo

reinstate [ˌri·ɪn·ˈstet] *tr* reintegrare

reiterate [ri·ˈɪtə ˌret] *tr* reiterare

reject [ˈridʒɛkt] *s* rigetto, rifiuto; **rejects** scarti *mpl* || [rɪ·ˈdʒɛkt] *tr* rigettare; (*to refuse*) rifiutare

rejection [rɪ·ˈdʒɛkʃən] *s* rigetto; rifiuto

rejoice [rɪ·ˈdʒɔɪs] *intr* rallegrarsi

rejoin [ri·ˈdʒɔɪn] *tr* raggiungere; (*to reunite*) riunire; (*to reply*) rispondere

rejoinder [rɪ·ˈdʒɔɪndər] *s* risposta; (*law*) controreplica

rejuvenation [rɪ ˌdʒuvɪ ˈneʃən] *s* ringiovanimento

rekindle [ri·ˈkɪndəl] *tr* riaccendere

relapse [rɪ·ˈlæps] *s* ricaduta || *intr* ricadere

relate [rɪ·ˈlet] *tr* mettere in relazione; (*to tell*) narrare

relation [rɪ·ˈleʃən] *s* relazione; (*account*) resoconto; (*relative*) parente *mf*; (*kinship*) parentela; **in relation to or with** in relazione a

relationship [rɪ·ˈleʃən ˌʃɪp] *s* rapporto, relazione; (*kinship*) parentela

relative [ˈrɛlətɪv] *adj* relativo || *s* congiunto, parente *mf*

relativity [ˌrɛləˈtɪvɪti] *s* relatività *f*

relax [rɪ·ˈlæks] *tr* rilasciare, rilassare || *intr* rilasciarsi, rilassarsi

relaxation [ˌrilæksˈeʃən] *s* distensione; (*entertainment*) ricreazione

relaxa'tion of ten'sion *s* distensione

relaxing [rɪ·ˈlæksɪŋ] *adj* rilassante; divertente

relay [ˈrile] or [rɪ·ˈle] *s* (elec) relè *m*; (rad) ripetitore *m*; (mil, sports) staffetta; (sports) corsa a staffetta || *v* (*pret & pp* -layed) *tr* trasmettere, ritrasmettere || [rɪ·ˈle] *v* (*pret & pp* -laid) *tr* rimettere, porre di nuovo

re'lay race' *s* corsa a staffetta

release [rɪ·ˈlis] *s* (*e.g., from jail*) liberazione; (*from obligation*) disimpegno; (*for publication*) autorizzazione; (*mov*) distribuzione; (*journ*) comunicato; (*aer*) lancio; (*mach*) scappamento || *tr* liberare; disimpegnare; autorizzare la pubblicazione di; (*mov*) distribuire; (*a bomb*) (aer) lanciare; **to release s.o. from a debt** rimettere un debito a qlcu

relent [rɪ·ˈlent] *intr* placarsi

relentless [ri·ˈlentlɪs] *adj* implacabile

relevant [ˈrɛlɪvənt] *adj* pertinente

reliable [rɪ·ˈlaɪ·əbəl] *adj* (*person*) fidato; (*source*) attendibile

reliance [rɪ·ˈlaɪ·əns] *s* fiducia, fede *f*

relic [ˈrɛlɪk] *s* reliquia

relief [rɪ·ˈlif] *s* sollievo; sussidio; (*prominence; projection*) rilievo; (mil) cambio; **in relief** in rilievo; **on relief** sotto sussidio

relieve [rɪ·ˈliv] *tr* (*e.g., pain*) alleviare; (*e.g., a load*) sgravare; (mil) rilevare

religion [rɪ·ˈlɪdʒən] *s* religione

religious [rɪ·ˈlɪdʒəs] *adj* religioso

relinquish [ri·ˈlɪŋkwɪʃ] *tr* abbandonare

relish [ˈrɛlɪʃ] *s* piacere *m*, gusto; sapore *m*, aroma *m*; (culin) condimento || *tr* gustare, apprezzare; dare gusto a

reluctance [rɪ·ˈlʌktəns] *s* riluttanza

reluctant [rɪ·ˈlʌktənt] *adj* riluttante

re·ly [rɪ·ˈlaɪ] *v* (*pret & pp* -lied) *intr* fare assegnamento; **to rely on** fidarsi di, fondarsi su

remain [rɪ·ˈmen] *s*—**remains** resti *mpl*; resti *mpl* mortali || *intr* restare, rimanere

remainder [rɪ·ˈmendər] *s* resto, restante *m*; (*unsold books*) fondi *mpl* di libreria || *tr* vendere come rimanenza

re·make [ri·ˈmek] *v* (*pret & pp* -made [ˈmed]) *tr* rifare

remark [rɪ·ˈmark] *s* osservazione, rimarco || *tr & intr* osservare; **to remark on** fare osservazioni su

remarkable [rɪ·ˈmarkəbəl] *adj* notevole

remar·ry [ri·ˈmæri] *v* (*pret & pp* -ried) *intr* riprendere moglie, risposarsi

reme·dy [ˈrɛmɪdi] *s* (-dies) rimedio || *v* (*pret & pp* -died) *tr* rimediare (with *dat*)

remember [rɪ·ˈmembər] *tr* ricordarsi di; (*to send greetings to*) ricordare || *intr* ricordare, ricordarsi

remembrance [rɪ·ˈmembrəns] *s* rimembranza, ricordo

remind [rɪ·ˈmaɪnd] *tr* rammentare

reminder [rɪ·ˈmaɪndər] *s* promemoria

reminisce [ˌrɛmɪ·ˈnɪs] *intr* ricordare il passato

reminiscence [ˌrɛmɪ·ˈnɪsəns] *s* reminiscenza

remiss [rɪ·ˈmɪs] *adj* negligente

re·mit [rɪ·ˈmɪt] *v* (*pret & pp* -mitted; *ger* -mitting) *tr* rimettere; (*to a lower court*) (law) rinviare

remittance [rɪ·ˈmɪtəns] *s* rimessa

remnant [ˈrɛmnənt] *s* (*remaining quantity*) rimanente *m*; (*of cloth*) scampolo; vestigio; **remnants** (*of merchandise*) rimanenze *fpl*, fondi *mpl* di magazzino

remod·el [ri·ˈmadəl] *v* (*pret & pp* -eled or -elled; *ger* -eling or -elling) *tr* rimodellare; ricostruire

remonstrance [rɪ·ˈmanstrəns] *s* rimostranza

remonstrate [rɪ·ˈmanstret] *intr* protestare, rimostrare; **to remonstrate with** rimostrare a

remorse [rɪ·ˈmɔrs] *s* rimorso

remorseful [rɪ·ˈmɔrsfəl] *adj* tormentato dal rimorso, pentito

remote [rɪ·ˈmot] *adj* remoto

remote' control' *s* telecomando

removable [rɪ·ˈmuvəbəl] *adj* amovibile

removal [rɪ·ˈmuvəl] *s* rimozione; trasferimento; (*dismissal*) destituzione

remove [rɪ·ˈmuv] *tr* rimuovere; (*one's jacket*) togliersi, cavarsi; (*from office*) destituire; eliminare || *intr* trasferirsi; andarsene

remuneration [rɪ ˌmjunə·ˈreʃən] *s* rimunerazione

renaissance [ˌrenəˈsans] or [rɪ·ˈnesəns] *s* rinascimento, rinascita || **Renaissance** *s* Rinascimento

rend [rend] *v* (*pret & pp* rent [rent]) *tr* (*to tear*) stracciare; (*to split*) fendere, squarciare

render [ˈrendər] *tr* (*justice*) rendere;

(a service) fare; *(aid)* prestare; *(a bill)* presentare; *(to translate)* tradurre; *(a piece of music)* interpretare; *(e.g., fat)* struggere

rendez·vous ['rɑndə‚vu] *s* (-**vous** [‚vuz]) appuntamento; *(in space)* incontro ‖ *v (pret & pp* -**voused** [‚vud]; *ger* -**vousing** [‚vu·ɪŋ]) *intr* incontrarsi

rendition [ren'dɪʃən] *s* restituzione, resa; traduzione; interpretazione

renege [rɪ'nɪg] *s* rifiuto ‖ *intr* rifiutare; (coll) venire meno

renew [rɪ'nju] or [rɪ'nu] *tr* rinnovare ‖ *intr* rinnovarsi

renewal [rɪ'nju·əl] or [rɪ'nu·əl] *s* rinnovo, rinnovamento

renounce [rɪ'nauns] *tr* rinunziare (with *dat*); ripudiare

renovate ['renə‚vet] *tr* rinnovare; *(a building)* restaurare; *(a room)* rimettere a nuovo

renown [rɪ'naun] *s* rinomanza

renowned [rɪ'naund] *adj* rinomato

rent [rent] *adj* scisso ‖ *s* fitto, pigione; *(tear)* squarcio ‖ *tr* locare, dare a pigione ‖ *intr* prendere a pigione

rental ['rentəl] *s* affitto

renter ['rentər] *s* affittuario, locatario

renunciation [rɪ‚nʌnsɪ'eʃən] or [rɪ‚nʌnʃɪ'eʃən] *s* rinunzia

reopen [ri'opən] *tr* riaprire ‖ *intr* riaprirsi

reopening [ri'opənɪŋ] *s* riapertura

reorganize [ri'ɔrgə‚naɪz] *tr* riorganizzare ‖ *intr* riorganizzarsi

repair [rɪ'per] *s* riparazione; **in good repair** in buono stato ‖ *tr* riparare ‖ *intr* riparare, dirigersi

repair'man' *s* (-**men'**) aggiustatore *m*

repaper [ri'pepər] *tr* ritappezzare

reparation [‚repə'reʃən] *s* riparazione

repartee [‚repɑr'ti] *s* replica arguta, rimando

repast [rɪ'pæst] or [rɪ'pɑst] *s* pasto

repatriate [ri'petrɪ‚et] *tr* rimpatriare

re-pay [rɪ'pe] *v (pret & pp* -**paid** ['ped]) *tr* ripagare

repayment [rɪ'pemənt] *s* rimborso; risarcimento, compensazione

repeal [rɪ'pil] *s* revoca, abrogazione ‖ *tr* revocare, abrogare

repeat [rɪ'pit] *s* ripetizione ‖ *tr* ripetere ‖ *intr* ripetere; *(said of food)* tornare a gola

re-pel [rɪ'pel] *v (pret & pp* -**pelled**; *ger* -**pelling**) *tr* respingere, ricacciare; ripugnare (with *dat*)

repent [rɪ'pent] *tr* pentirsi di ‖ *intr* pentirsi, ravvedersi

repentance [rɪ'pentəns] *s* pentimento

repentant [rɪ'pentənt] *adj* pentito

repercussion [‚rɪpər'kʌʃən] *s* ripercussione

reperto·ry ['repər‚tori] *s* (-**ries**) (com) magazzino; (theat) repertorio

repetition [‚repɪ'tɪʃən] *s* ripetizione

repine [rɪ'paɪn] *intr* lamentarsi

replace [rɪ'ples] *tr (to put back)* rimettere; *(to take the place of)* rimpiazzare

replaceable [rɪ'plesəbəl] *adj* sostituibile

replacement [rɪ'plesmənt] *s* rimpiazzo, sostituzione; **as a replacement for** al posto di

replenish [rɪ'plenɪʃ] *tr* rifornire

replete [rɪ'plit] *adj* pieno zeppo

replica ['replɪkə] *s* replica

re·ply [rɪ'plaɪ] *s* (-**plies**) risposta ‖ *v (pret & pp* -**plied**) *tr & intr* rispondere

report [rɪ'port] *s* rapporto, informazione; voce *f*, rumore *m*; *(of a physician)* responso; *(of a firearm)* detonazione ‖ *tr* riportare, rapportare; denunziare ‖ *intr* fare un rapporto; fare il cronista; presentarsi; **to report sick** (mil) marcare visita

report' card' *s* pagella

reportedly [rɪ'portɪdli] *adv* secondo la voce comune

reporter [rɪ'portər] *s* cronista *mf*, reporter *m*

reporting [rɪ'portɪŋ] *s* reportage *m*

repose [rɪ'poz] *s* riposo ‖ *tr* posare, riporre ‖ *intr* riposare

reprehend [‚reprɪ'hend] *tr* riprovare, rimproverare

represent [‚reprɪ'zent] *tr* rappresentare

representation [‚reprɪzen'teʃən] *s* rappresentazione; protesta; **representations** dichiarazioni *fpl*

representative [‚reprɪ'zentətɪv] *adj* rappresentativo ‖ *s* rappresentante *mf*; (pol) deputato

repress [rɪ'pres] *tr* reprimere

repression [rɪ'preʃən] *s* repressione

reprieve [rɪ'priv] *s* tregua temporanea; sospensione della pena capitale ‖ *tr* accordare una tregua a; sospendere l'esecuzione di

reprimand ['reprɪ‚mænd] or ['reprɪ‚mɑnd] *s* sgridata, ramanzina ‖ *tr* sgridare, rimproverare

reprint ['ri‚prɪnt] *s* ristampa; *(offprint)* estratto ‖ [ri'prɪnt] *tr* ristampare

reprisal [rɪ'praɪzəl] *s* rappresaglia

reproach [rɪ'protʃ] *s* rimprovero; vituperio ‖ *tr* rimproverare; **to reproach s.o. for s.th** rimproverare qlcu di qlco, rimproverare qlco a qlcu

reproduce [‚riprə'djus] or [‚riprə'dus] *tr* riprodurre ‖ *intr* riprodursi

reproduction [‚riprə'dʌkʃən] *s* riproduzione

reproof [rɪ'pruf] *s* rimprovero

reprove [rɪ'pruv] *tr* rimproverare; disapprovare

reptile ['reptɪl] *s* rettile *m*

republic [rɪ'pʌblɪk] *s* repubblica

republican [rɪ'pʌblɪkən] *adj & s* repubblicano

repudiate [rɪ'pjudɪ‚et] *tr* ripudiare; rinnegare

repugnant [rɪ'pʌgnənt] *adj* ripugnante

repulse [rɪ'pʌls] *s* rifiuto; sconfitta ‖ *tr* rifiutare; *(e.g., an enemy)* sconfiggere

repulsive [rɪ'pʌlsɪv] *adj* ripulsivo

reputation [‚repjə'teʃən] *s* reputazione

repute [rɪ'pjut] *s* reputazione, fama ‖ *tr* reputare

reputedly [rɪ'pjutɪdlɪ] *adv* secondo l'opinione corrente

request [rɪ'kwɛst] *s* domanda, richiesta; **at the request of** su domanda di ‖ *tr* richiedere

Requiem ['rikwɪ ,ɛm] or ['rɛkwɪ ,ɛm] *adj* di Requiem ‖ *s* Requiem *m & f*; Messa di Requiem

require [rɪ'kwaɪr] *tr* richiedere

requirement [rɪ'kwaɪrmənt] *s* requisito; richiesta, fabbisogno

requisite ['rɛkwɪzɪt] *adj* requisito, richiesto ‖ *s* requisito

requisition [,rɛkwɪ'zɪʃən] *s* requisizione

requital [rɪ'kwaɪtəl] *s* contraccambio

requite [rɪ'kwaɪt] *tr* (*e.g., an injury*) contraccambiare; (*a person*) contraccambiare (with *dat*)

re-read [ri'rid] *v* (*pret & pp* -read ['rɛd]) *tr* rileggere

resale ['ri ,sel] or [ri'sel] *s* rivendita

rescind [rɪ'sɪnd] *tr* annullare, cancellare; (law) rescindere

rescue ['rɛskju] *s* salvataggio, liberazione; **to go to the rescue of** andare al soccorso di ‖ *tr* salvare, liberare, soccorrere

research [rɪ'sʌrtʃ] or ['risʌrtʃ] *s* ricerca, indagine *f* ‖ *intr* investigare

re-sell [ri'sɛl] *v* (*pret & pp* -sold ['sold]) *tr* rivendere

resemblance [rɪ'zɛmbləns] *s* somiglianza

resemble [rɪ'zɛmbəl] *tr* somigliare (with *dat*), rassomigliare (with *dat*); **to resemble one another** rassomigliarsi

resent [rɪ'zɛnt] *tr* (*a remark*) risentirsi per; (*a person*) risentirsi con

resentful [rɪ'zɛntfəl] *adj* risentito

resentment [rɪ'zɛntmənt] *s* risentimento

reservation [,rɛzər've ʃən] *s* riserva; (*e.g., for a room*) prenotazione

reserve [rɪ'zʌrv] *s* riserva; (*self-restraint*) riserbo, contegno ‖ *tr* riservare; prenotare

reservist [rɪ'zʌrvɪst] *s* riservista *m*

reservoir ['rɛzər ,vwɑr] *s* serbatoio, cisterna; (*large storage place for supplying community with water*) bacino di riserva; (fig) pozzo

re-set [ri'sɛt] *v* (*pret & pp* -set; *ger* -setting) *tr* rimettere a posto; (*a watch*) regolare; (*a gem*) incastonare di nuovo; (*a machine*) rimontare

re-ship [ri'ʃɪp] *v* (*pret & pp* -shipped; *ger* -shipping) *tr* rispedire; (*on a ship*) reimbarcare ‖ *intr* reimbarcarsi

reshipment [ri'ʃɪpmənt] *s* rispedizione; (*on a ship*) reimbarco

reside [rɪ'zaɪd] *intr* risiedere

residence ['rɛzɪdəns] *s* residenza

resident ['rɛzɪdənt] *adj & s* residente *mf*

residential [,rɛzɪ'dɛnʃəl] *adj* residenziale

residue ['rɛzɪ ,dju] or ['rɛsɪ ,du] *s* residuo

resign [rɪ'zaɪn] *tr* rassegnare, abbandonare; **to be resigned to** rassegnarsi a ‖ *intr* dimettersi, rassegnare le dimissioni

resignation [,rɛzɪg'neʃən] *s* (*from a job*) dimissione; (*submission*) rassegnazione

resin ['rɛzɪn] *s* resina

resist [rɪ'zɪst] *tr* resistere (with *dat*) ‖ *intr* resistere

resistance [rɪ'zɪstəns] *s* resistenza

resole [ri'sol] *tr* risolare

resolute ['rɛzə ,lut] *adj* risoluto

resolution [,rɛzə'luʃən] *s* risoluzione; **good resolutions** buoni propositi

resolve [rɪ'zɒlv] *s* risoluzione ‖ *tr* risolvere ‖ *intr* risolversi

resonance ['rɛzənəns] *s* risonanza

resort [rɪ'zɒrt] *s* (appeal) ricorso; (*for vacation*) centro di villeggiatura ‖ *intr* ricorrere

resound [rɪ'zaʊnd] *intr* risonare

resounding [rɪ'zaʊndɪŋ] *adj* risonante; (*success*) strepitoso

resource [rɪ'sɔrs] or ['risɔrs] *s* risorsa

resourceful [rɪ'sɔrsfəl] *adj* ingegnoso

respect [rɪ'spɛkt] *s* rispetto; **respects** rispetti *mpl*, ossequi *mpl*; **with respect to** rispetto a ‖ *tr* rispettare

respectable [rɪ'spɛktəbəl] *adj* rispettabile; onesto, per bene

respectful [rɪ'spɛktfəl] *adj* rispettoso

respecting [rɪ'spɛktɪŋ] *prep* rispetto a

respective [rɪ'spɛktɪv] *adj* rispettivo

respiratory ['rɛspɪrə ,tori] or [rɪ'spaɪrə ,tori] *adj* respiratorio

respire [rɪ'spaɪr] *tr & intr* respirare

respite ['rɛspɪt] *s* tregua, requie *f*; (*reprieve*) proroga, dilazione

resplendent [rɪ'splɛndənt] *adj* risplendente

respond [rɪ'spɒnd] *intr* rispondere

response [rɪ'spɒns] *s* risposta

responsibili·ty [rɪ ,spɒnsɪ'bɪlɪtɪ] *s* (-ties) responsabilità *f*

responsible [rɪ'spɒnsɪbəl] *adj* responsabile; (*job*) di fiducia; **responsible for** responsabile di

responsive [rɪ'spɒnsɪv] *adj* rispondente; (*e.g., to affection*) sensibile; (*e.g., motor*) che risponde

rest [rɛst] *s* riposo; (*what remains*) resto; (mus) pausa; **at rest** in riposo; tranquillo, in pace; (*dead*) morto; **the rest** il resto, gli altri; **to come to rest** andare a finire; **to lay to rest** sotterrare ‖ *tr* riposare; (*to direct one's eyes*) dirigere; (*faith*) porre ‖ *intr* riposarsi, riposare; appoggiarsi; **to rest assured (that)** esser sicuro (che); **to rest on** aver fiducia in; basarsi su; (*one's laurels*) dormire su

restaurant ['rɛstərənt] or ['rɛstə ,rɑnt] *s* ristorante *m*

restful ['rɛstfəl] *adj* riposante, tranquillo

rest' home' *s* casa di riposo

rest'ing place' *s* luogo di riposo; (*of a staircase*) pianerottolo; (*of the dead*) ultima dimora

restitution [,rɛstɪ'tjuʃən] or [,rɛstɪ'tuʃən] *s* restituzione

restive [ˈrestɪv] *adj* irrequieto; (*e.g.*, *horse*) recalcitrante

restless [ˈrestlɪs] *adj* irrequieto; (*night*) insonne, in bianco

restock [riˈstɑk] *tr* rifornire; (*e.g.*, *with fish*) ripopolare

restoration [ˌrɛstəˈreʃən] *s* restaurazione

restore [rɪˈstor] *tr* restaurare, ripristinare

restrain [rɪˈstren] *tr* ritenere, frenare; limitare

restraint [rɪˈstrent] *s* restrizione; controllo, ritegno; detenzione

restrict [rɪˈstrɪkt] *tr* restingere, limitare

restriction [rɪˈstrɪkʃən] *s* restrizione

rest' room' *s* toletta; gabinetto di decenza

restructuring [rɪˈstrʌktʃərɪŋ] *s* ristrutturazione

result [rɪˈzʌlt] *s* risultato || *intr* risultare; **to result in** risolversi in, concludersi con

resume [rɪˈzum] or [rɪˈzjum] *tr* riprendere || *intr* ricominciare

résumé [ˌrezuˈme] or [ˌrezjuˈme] *s* sunto, riassunto

resumption [rɪˈzʌmpʃən] *s* ripresa

resurface [riˈsʌrfɪs] *tr* mettere copertura nuova a || *intr* riemergere

resurrect [ˌrezəˈrekt] *tr* & *intr* risuscitare

resurrection [ˌrezəˈrekʃən] *s* risurrezione

resuscitate [rɪˈsʌsɪˌtet] *tr* rendere alla vita

retail [ˈritel] *adj* & *adv* al dettaglio, al minuto || *s* dettaglio || *tr* dettagliare, vendere al minuto || *intr* vendere or vendersi al minuto

retailer [ˈritelər] *s* dettagliante *mf*

retain [rɪˈten] *tr* ritenere; (*a lawyer*) assicurarsi i servizi di

retaliate [rɪˈtælɪˌet] *intr* fare rappresaglie; **to retaliate for** ricambiare

retaliation [rɪˌtælɪˈeʃən] *s* rappresaglia

retard [rɪˈtard] *s* ritardo || *tr* ritardare

retch [retʃ] *intr* avere sforzi di vomito

reticence [ˈretɪsəns] *s* riservatezza

reticent [ˈretɪsənt] *adj* riservato, taciturno

retina [ˈretɪnə] *s* retina

retinue [ˈretɪˌnju] or [ˈretɪˌnu] *s* seguito, corteggio

retire [rɪˈtaɪr] *tr* ritirare; (*an employee*) giubilare, mettere a riposo || *intr* ritirarsi; andare a riposo; (*to go to bed*) andare a letto

retired [rɪˈtaɪrd] *adj* (*employee*) in pensione; (*officer*) a riposo

retirement [rɪˈtaɪrmənt] *s* ritiro; (*of an employee*) pensionamento, quiescenza

retort [rɪˈtort] *s* risposta per le rime; controreplica; (chem) storta || *tr* rispondere per le rime a || *intr* rispondere per le rime

retouch [riˈtʌtʃ] *tr* ritoccare

retrace [riˈtres] *tr* ripercorrere; **to retrace one's steps** ritornare sui propri passi

retract [rɪˈtrækt] *tr* ritrattare, disdire || *intr* disdirsi

re·tread [ˈri ˌtred] *s* pneumatico col copertone ricostruito || [riˈtred] *v* (*pret & pp* -**treaded**) *tr* ricostruire il copertone di || *v* (*pret* -**trod** [ˈtrad]; *pp* -**trod** or -**trodden**) *tr* ripercorrere || *intr* rimettere il piede

retreat [rɪˈtrit] *s* (*seclusion*) ritiro; (mil) ritirata; (eccl) esercizio spirituale; **to beat a retreat** battere in ritirata || *intr* ritirarsi

retrench [rɪˈtrentʃ] *tr* ridurre, tagliare; (mil) trincerare || *intr* ridurre le spese; (mil) trincerarsi

retribution [ˌretrɪˈbjuən] *s* ricompensa; (theol) giudizio finale

retributive [rɪˈtrɪbjətɪv] *adj* retributivo

retrieve [rɪˈtriv] *tr* riguadagnare, riconquistare; (*to repair*) risarcire; (hunt) riportare || *intr* riportare la presa

retriever [rɪˈtrivər] *s* cane *m* da presa

retroactive [ˌretroˈæktɪv] *adj* retroattivo

retrofiring [ˌretroˈfaɪrɪŋ] *s* accensione dei retrorazzi

retrogress [ˌretrəˈgres] *intr* regredire; retrocedere

retrorocket [ˌretroˈrɑkɪt] *s* retrorazzo

retrospect [ˈretrəˌspekt] *s* esame retrospettivo; **in retrospect** retrospettivamente

retrospective [ˌretrəˈspektɪv] *adj* retrospettivo

re·try [riˈtraɪ] *v* (*pret & pp* -**tried**) *tr* (*a person*) riprocessare; (*a case*) ritentare

return [rɪˈtʌrn] *adj* di ritorno; ripetuto || *s* restituzione; ritorno; profitto; (*of income tax*) dichiarazione; risposta; rapporto ufficiale; (*of an election*) responso; (sports) rimando, rimessa; **in return** (for) in cambio (di); **many happy returns of the day!** cento di questi giorni!; **returns** (*of an election*) responso, risultato || *tr* tornare, ritornare restituire; (*a favor*) contraccambiare; (*a profit*) dare; (*thanks; a decision*) rendere; (sports) ribattere || *intr* tornare; rispondere

return' ad'dress *s* indirizzo del mittente

return' bout' *s* (boxing) rivincita

return' mail' *s*—**by return mail** a volta di corriere, a giro di posta

return' tick'et *s* biglietto di ritorno; (Brit) biglietto di andata e ritorno

reunification [riˌjunɪfɪˈkeʃən] *s* riunione, unificazione

reunion [riˈjunjən] *s* riunione

reunite [ˌrijuˈnaɪt] *tr* riunire || *intr* riunirsi

rev [rev] *s* (coll) giro || *v* (*pret & pp* **revved;** *ger* **revving**) *tr*—**to rev up** (coll) imballare || *intr* (coll) accelerare, imballarsi

revamp [riˈvæmp] *tr* rinnovare, rappezzare

reveal [rɪˈvil] *tr* rivelare, svelare

reveille [ˈrevəli] *s* sveglia, levata

rev·el [ˈrevəl] *s* baldoria || *v* (*pret &*

pp **-eled** or **-elled; ger -eling** or **-elling** *intr* gozzovigliare; bearsi

revelation [ˌrevəˈleʃən] *s* rivelazione ‖ **Revelation** *s* (Bib) Apocalisse *f*

revel·ry [ˈrevəlri] *s* (**-ries**) baldoria

revenge [rɪˈvendʒ] *s* vendetta ‖ *tr* vendicare

revengeful [rɪˈvendʒfəl] *adj* vendicativo

revenue [ˈrevəˌnju] or [ˈrevəˌnu] *s* entrata, profitto; (*government income*) entrate *fpl* erariali

rev'enue cut'ter *s* motobarca della guardia di finanza

rev'enue stamp' *s* marca da bollo

reverberate [rɪˈvʌrbəˌret] *intr* riverberarsi; (*said, e.g., of sound*) ripercuotersi, risonare; (*said of an echo*) rimbalzare

revere [rɪˈvɪr] *tr* venerare, riverire

reverence [ˈrevərəns] *s* riverenza ‖ *tr* ossequiare

reverend [ˈrevərənd] *adj & s* reverendo

reverent [ˈrevərənt] *adj* reverente

reverie [ˈrevəri] *s* sogno, fantasticheria

reversal [rɪˈvʌrsəl] *s* inversione, cambio; (law) annullamento

reverse [rɪˈvʌrs] *adj* rovescio, contrario; (mach) di retromarcia ‖ *s* contrario; (*rear*) dietro; (*misfortune, side of a coin not bearing principal design*) rovescio; (mach) retromarcia ‖ *tr* invertire; rovesciare; mettere in marcia indietro; **to reverse oneself** cambiare d'opinione; **to reverse the charges** far pagare al destinatario; (telp) far pagare al numero chiamato ‖ *intr* invertirsi

revert [rɪˈvʌrt] *intr* ritornare

review [rɪˈvju] *s* (*critical article*) recensione; (*magazine*) rivista; (educ) ripasso, ripetizione; (mil) rivista ‖ *tr* recensire; rivedere; (*a lesson*) ripassare; (mil) passare in rassegna

revile [rɪˈvaɪl] *tr* insultare, offendere

revise [rɪˈvaɪz] *s* revisione; (typ) seconda bozza ‖ *tr* rivedere; correggere

revision [rɪˈvɪʒən] *s* revisione

revisionism [rɪˈvɪʒəˌnɪzəm] *s* revisionismo

revival [rɪˈvaɪvəl] *s* ripresa delle forze; (*restoration*) ripristino; (*of learning*) rinascimento; risveglio religioso; (theat, mov) ripresa

revive [rɪˈvaɪv] *tr* ravvivare; (*a custom*) ripristinare; (theat) dare la ripresa di ‖ *intr* ravvivarsi; risorgere

revoke [rɪˈvok] *tr* revocare

revolt [rɪˈvolt] *s* rivolta ‖ *tr* rivoltare ‖ *intr* rivoltarsi

revolting [rɪˈvoltɪŋ] *adj* rivoltante

revolution [ˌrevəˈluʃən] *s* rivoluzione

revolutionar·y [ˌrevəˈluʃəˌneri] *adj* rivoluzionario ‖ *s* (**-ies**) rivoluzionario

revolve [rɪˈvalv] *tr* far rotare; (*in one's mind*) rivolgere ‖ *intr* girare, rotare

revolver [rɪˈvalvər] *s* rivoltella

revolv'ing book'case *s* scaffale *m* girevole

revolv'ing cred'it *s* credito rotativo

revolv'ing door' *s* porta girevole

revolv'ing fund' *s* fondo rotativo

revue [rɪˈvju] *s* rivista

revulsion [rɪˈvʌlʃən] *s* ripugnanza, avversione; (med) revulsione

reward [rɪˈwərd] *s* premio, ricompensa; (*money offered for capture*) taglia; (*for return of articles lost*) mancia competente ‖ *tr* premiare, ricompensare

rewarding [rɪˈwərdɪŋ] *adj* rimunerativo; gradevole

re-wind [rɪˈwaɪnd] *s* (*of a tape*) ribobinazione ‖ *v* (*pret & pp* **-wound** [waund]) *tr* ribobinare

re-write [rɪˈraɪt] *v* (*pret* **-wrote** [ˈrot]; *pp* **-written** [ˈrɪtən]) *tr* riscrivere; (*news*) rimaneggiare, correggere

rhapso·dy [ˈræpsədi] *s* (**-dies**) rapsodia

rheostat [ˈriˌstæt] *s* reostato

rhesus [ˈrisəs] *s* reso

rhetoric [ˈretərɪk] *s* retorica

rhetorical [rɪˈtɑrɪkəl] or [rɪˈtɔrɪkəl] *adj* retorico

rheumatic [ruˈmætɪk] *adj & s* reumatico

rheumatism [ˈruməˌtɪzəm] *s* reumatismo

Rhine [raɪn] *s* Reno

Rhineland [ˈraɪnˌlænd] *s* la Renania

rhine'stone' *s* gemma artificiale

rhinoceros [raɪˈnɑsərəs] *s* rinoceronte *m*

Rhodes [rodz] *s* Rodi *f*

Rhone [ron] *s* Rodano

rhubarb [ˈrubarb] *s* rabarbaro; (slang) baruffa

rhyme [raɪm] *s* rima; **without rhyme or reason** senza capo né coda ‖ *tr & intr* rimare

rhythm [ˈrɪðəm] *s* ritmo

rhythmic(al) [ˈrɪðmɪk(əl)] *adj* ritmico

rial·to [rɪˈælto] *s* (**-tos**) mercato ‖ **the Rialto** il ponte di Rialto; il centro teatrale di New York

rib [rɪb] *s* costola; (*cut of meat*) costata; (*of umbrella*) stecca; (*of leaf*) nervatura; (aer, archit) centina; (naut) costa ‖ *v* (*pret & pp* **ribbed; *ger* ribbing**) *tr* (slang) prendersi gioco di

ribald [ˈrɪbəld] *adj* volgare, indecente

ribbon [ˈrɪbən] *s* nastro; (*decoration*) nastrino; **ribbons** (*shreds*) brandelli *mpl*

rice [raɪs] *s* riso

rich [rɪtʃ] *adj* ricco; (*food*) nutrito, grasso; (*voice*) generoso; (*voice*) caldo; (*color*) vivo; (*odor*) forte; (coll) divertente; (coll) assurdo; **to strike it rich** trovare la miniera d'oro ‖ **riches** *spl* ricchezze *fpl*; **the rich i** ricchi

rickets [ˈrɪkɪts] *s* rachitismo

rickety [ˈrɪkɪti] *adj* (*object*) sgangherato; (*person*) vacillante; (*suffering from rickets*) rachitico

rid [rɪd] *v* (*pret & pp* **rid; *ger* ridding**) *tr* liberare, sbarazzare; **to get rid of** liberarsi di, sbarazzarsi di

riddance [ˈrɪdəns] *s* liberazione; **good riddance!** che sollievo!

riddle [ˈrɪdəl] *s* enigma *m*, indovi-

nello; (*sieve*) crivello ‖ *tr* crivellare; (*to sift*) vagliare; (*s.o.'s reputation*) rovinare; **to riddle with** crivellare di
ride [raɪd] *s* scarrozzata; cavalcata; gita ‖ *v* (*pret* **rode** [rod]; *pp* **ridden** [ˈrɪdən]) *tr* cavalcare, montare, montare su; (*e.g., a bus*) andare in; (*the waves*) galleggiare su; attraversare; tiranneggiare; farsi gioco di; **to ride down** travolgere; sorpassare; **to ride out** uscire felicemente da la ‖ *intr* cavalcare; fare una passeggiata, fare una gita; (*to float*) galleggiare; **to let ride** lasciar correre; **to ride on** dipendere da
rider [ˈraɪdər] *s* cavallerizzo; ciclista *mf*; viaggiatore *m*, passeggero
ridge [rɪdʒ] *s* (*of mountains*) crinale *m*, dorsale *f*; (*of roof*) displuvio; (*agr*) porca
ridge'pole' *s* trave maestra, colmo
ridicule [ˈrɪdɪˌkjul] *s* ridicolo; **to expose to ridicule** porre in ridicolo ‖ *tr* ridicolizzare
ridiculous [rɪˈdɪkjələs] *adj* ridicolo
rid'ing boot' *s* stivalone *m* d'equitazione
rid'ing school' *s* maneggio
rife [raɪf] *adj* comune, prevalente; **rife with** pieno di
riffraff [ˈrɪfˌræf] *s* gentaglia
rifle [ˈraɪfəl] *s* fucile *m*; cannone rigato ‖ *tr* (*a place*) svaligiare; (*a person*) derubare; (*a gun*) rigare
rifle' range' *s* tiro a segno
rift [rɪft] *s* crepa, fessura; disaccordo
rig [rɪg] *s* attrezzatura, equipaggio; impianto di sondaggio (per il petrolio); (*outfit*) tenuta ‖ *v* (*pret* & *pp* **rigged**; *ger* **rigging**) *tr* attrezzare, equipaggiare; guarnire; abbigliare in maniera strana
rigging [ˈrɪgɪŋ] *s* (naut) padiglione *m*; (*tackle*) (naut) rizza; (coll) vestiti *mpl*
right [raɪt] *adj* giusto; corretto; (*mind*) sano; destro, diritto; (geom) retto; (geom) perpendicolare; **right or wrong** a torto o a ragione; **to be all right** star bene di salute; **to be right** aver ragione ‖ *s* diritto; quanto è giusto, (il) giusto; (*in a company*) interessenza; (*right hand*) destra; (*turn*) giro a destra; (boxing) diritto; (tex) dritto; (pol) destra; **by right** in giustizia; **on the right** alla destra; **to be in the right** aver ragione ‖ *adv* direttamente; completamente; immediatamente; proprio, precisamente, correttamente, giustamente; bene; alla destra; (coll) molto; **all right** benissimo ‖ *tr* drizzare; correggere; rimettere a posto ‖ *intr* drizzarsi
righteous [ˈraɪtʃəs] *adj* retto; virtuoso
right' field' *s* (baseball) campo destro
rightful [ˈraɪtfəl] *adj* giusto; legittimo
right'-hand drive' *s* guida a destra
right-handed [ˈraɪtˈhændɪd] *adj* che usa la destra; destrorso
right'-hand man' *s* braccio destro
rightist [ˈraɪtɪst] *adj* conservatore ‖ *s* conservatore *m*, membro della destra

rightly [ˈraɪtli] *adv* correttamente; giustamente; **rightly or wrongly** a torto o a ragione
right' mind' s—in one's right mind nel pieno possesso delle proprie facoltà, con la testa a posto
right' of way' *s* precedenza; (law) servitù *f* di passaggio; (rr) sede *f*
rights' of man' *s* diritti *mpl* dell'uomo
right'-wing' *adj* della destra
right-winger [ˈraɪtˈwɪŋər] *s* membro della destra, conservatore *m*
rigid [ˈrɪdʒɪd] *adj* rigido
rigmarole [ˈrɪgməˌrol] *s* sproloquio
rigorous [ˈrɪgərəs] *adj* rigoroso
rile [raɪl] *tr* irritare, esasperare
rill [rɪl] *s* rigagnolo
rim [rɪm] *s* orlo, bordo; (*of a wheel*) cerchione *m*
rime [raɪm] *s* brina; (*in verse*) rima ‖ *tr* brinare; rimare ‖ *intr* rimare
rind [raɪnd] *s* (*of animals*) cotenna; (*of fruit or cheese*) scorza
ring [rɪŋ] *s* (*for finger*) anello; (*anything round*) cerchio; (*circular course*) pista; (*of people*) crocchio; (*of evildoers*) combriccola; (*of anchor*) anello; (*sound of bell*) squillo; (*loud sound of bell*) scampanellata; (*of small bell; of glassware*) tintinnio; (*act of ringing*) sonata; (fig) chiamata; (fig) suono; (boxing) quadrato; (mach) ghiera; (fig, taur) arena; **to run rings around** essere molto migliore di ‖ *v* (*pret* & *pp* **ringed**) *tr* accerchiare; mettere un anello a ‖ *intr* formare cerchi ‖ *v* (*pret* **rang** [ræŋ]; *pp* **rung** [rʌŋ]) *tr* sonare; squillare; tintinnare; chiamare al telefono; **to ring up** chiamare al telefono; (*a sale*) battere sul registratore di cassa ‖ *intr* sonare; squillare; tintinnare; chiamare; (*said of one's ears*) fischiare; **to ring for** chiamare col campanello; **to ring off** terminare una conversazione telefonica; **to ring up** chiamare al telefono
ring-around-a-rosy [ˈrɪŋəˌraʊndəˈrozi] *s* girotondo
ringing [ˈrɪŋɪŋ] *adj* alto, sonoro ‖ *s* accerchiamento; squillo; tintinnio; (*in the ears*) fischio
ring'lead'er *s* capobanda *m*
ringlet [ˈrɪŋlɪt] *s* anellino
ring'mas'ter *s* direttore *m* di circo equestre
ring'side' *s* posto vicino al quadrato
ring'worm' *s* tigna
rink [rɪŋk] *s* pattinatoio
rinse [rɪns] *s* risciacquatura ‖ *tr* risciacquare
riot [ˈraɪət] *s* sommossa, tumulto; profusione; **to be a riot** (coll) essere divertentissimo; **to run riot** sfrenarsi; (*said of plants*) crescere disordinatamente ‖ *intr* tumultuare; darsi alle gozzoviglie
rioter [ˈraɪətər] *s* rivoltoso
rip [rɪp] *s* sdrucitura; (*open seam*) scucitura ‖ *v* (*pret* & *pp* **ripped**; *ger* **ripping**) *tr* sdrucire; (*to open the*

seam *of*) scucire || *intr* sdrucirsi; scucirsi; **to rip out with insults** (coll) prorompere in improperi

ripe [raɪp] *adj* maturo; (*lips*) turgido; (*cheese*) stagionato; pronto

ripen ['raɪpən] *tr* & *intr* maturare

ripple ['rɪpəl] *s* increspatura; (*sound*) mormorio || *tr* increspare || *intr* incresparsi; mormorare

rise [raɪz] *s* (*of prices, temperature*) aumento; (*of a road*) salita; (*of ground*) elevazione; (*of a heavenly body*) levata; (*in rank*) ascesa; (*of a step*) alzata; (*of a stream*) sorgente *f*; (*of water*) crescita; **to get a rise out of** (coll) farsi rispondere per le rime da; **to give rise to** dar origine a || *v* (*pret* **rose** [roz]; *pp* **risen** ['rɪzən]) *intr* (*said of the sun*) sorgere; rialzarsi; (*said of plants*) crescere; (*said of the wind*) alzarsi; (*said of a building*) ergersi; (*to return from the dead*) risorgere; (*to increase*) aumentare; **to rise above** alzarsi al di sopra di; essere al di sopra di; **to rise to** sorgere all'altezza di

riser ['raɪzər] *s* (*of step*) alzata; (*upright*) montante *m*; **early riser** persona mattiniera; **late riser** dormiglione *m*

risk [rɪsk] *s* rischio; **to run or take a risk** correre un rischio || *tr* rischiare

risk·y ['rɪski] *adj* (**-ier; -iest**) rischioso

risqué [rɪs'ke] *adj* audace, spinto

rite [raɪt] *s* rito; **last rites** riti *mpl* funebri

ritual ['rɪtʃʊ·əl] *adj* & *s* rituale *m*

ri·val ['raɪvəl] *s* rivale *mf* || *v* (*pret* & *pp* **-valed** *or* **-valled**; *ger* **-valing** *or* **-valling**) *tr* rivaleggiare con

rival·ry ['raɪvəlri] *s* (**-ries**) rivalità *f*

river ['rɪvər] *s* fiume *m*; **down the river** a valle; **up the river** a monte

riv'er ba'sin *s* bacino fluviale

riv'er·bed' *s* letto di fiume

riv'er front' *s* riva di fiume

riv'er·head' *s* sorgente *f* di fiume

riv'er·side' *adj* rivierasco || *s* riva del fiume

rivet ['rɪvɪt] *s* ribattino; (*of scissors*) perno || *tr* ribadire; (*s.o.'s attention*) concentrare

roach [rotʃ] *s* scarafaggio

road [rod] *adj* stradale || *s* strada; via; (naut) rada; **to be in the road of** ostacolare il cammino a; **to burn up the road** divorare la strada; **to get out of the road** togliersi di mezzo

roadability [ˌrodə'bɪlɪti] *s* tenuta di strada

road'bed' *s* (*of highway*) piattaforma; (rr) massicciata, infrastruttura

road'block' *s* (mil) barricata; (fig) impedimento

road'house' *s* taverna su autostrada

road' la'borer *s* cantoniere *m*

road' map' *s* carta stradale

road' roll'er *s* compressore *m* stradale, rullo compressore

road' serv'ice *s* servizio di assistenza stradale

road'side' *s* bordo della strada

road'side inn' *s* taverna posta su autostrada

road' sign' *s* indicatore *m* stradale

road'stead' *s* rada

road'way' *s* carreggiata; strada

roam [rom] *s* vagabondaggio || *intr* girovagare per || *intr* girovagare

roar [ror] *s* ruggito, muggito; boato, fragore *m* || *intr* muggire; **to roar with laughter** fare una risata

roast [rost] *s* arrosto; torrefazione || *tr* arrostire; (*coffee*) tostare, torrefare; (coll) farsi beffe di || *intr* arrostirsi

roast' beef' *s* rosbif *m*

roast'ed pea'nut *s* nocciolina americana abbrustolita

roast' pork' *s* arrosto di maiale

rob [rɑb] *v* (*pret* & *pp* **robbed;** *ger* **robbing**) *tr* & *intr* derubare

robber ['rɑbər] *s* ladro, malandrino

robber·y ['rɑbəri] *s* (**-ies**) furto

robe [rob] *s* (*of a woman*) vestito; (*of a professor*) toga; (*of a priest*) abito talare; (*dressing gown*) vestaglia; (*for lap*) coperta da viaggio; **robes** vestiti *mpl* || *tr* vestire || *intr* vestirsi

robin ['rɑbɪn] *s* pettirosso

robot ['robɑt] *s* robot *m*

robust [ro'bʌst] *adj* robusto

rock [rɑk] *s* roccia; (*any stone*) pietra; (*sticking out of water*) scoglio; (*one that is thrown*) sasso; (*hill*) rocca; (slang) pietra preziosa; **on the rocks** (coll) in rovina; (coll) al verde; (*said, e.g., of whiskey*) sul ghiaccio || *tr* far vacillare; dondolare || *intr* vacillare; dondolare

rock'-bot'tom *adj* (l') ultimo; (il) minimo

rock' can'dy *s* zucchero candito

rock' crys'tal *s* cristallo di rocca

rocker ['rɑkər] *s* (*curved piece at bottom of rocking chair*) dondolo; sedia a dondolo; (mach) bilanciere *m*; **off one's rocker** (slang) matto

rocket ['rɑkɪt] *s* razzo || *intr* partire come un razzo

rock'et launch'er ['lɔntʃər] *or* ['lɑntʃər] *s* lanciarazzo

rock' gar'den *s* giardino piantato fra le rocce

rock'ing chair' *s* sedia a dondolo

rock'ing horse' *s* cavallo a dondolo

rock' salt' *s* salgemma *m*

rock' wool' *s* cotone *m* or lana minerale

rock·y ['rɑki] *adj* (**-ier; -iest**) roccioso; traballante; (coll) debole

rod [rɑd] *s* verga, bacchetta; scettro; punizione; (*bar*) asta; (*for fishing*) canna da pesca; (anat, biol) bastoncino; (mach) biella; (surv) biffa; (Bib) razza, tribù *f*; (slang) pistola; **spare the rod and spoil the child** la madre pietosa fa la piaga cancrenosa

rodent ['rodənt] *adj* & *s* roditore *m*

rod'man *s* (**-men**) *s* aiutante *m* geometra

roe [ro] *s* capriolo; (*of fish*) uova *fpl*

rogue [rog] *s* furfante *m*; (*scamp*) pícaro

rogues'' gal'lery s collezione di fotografie di malviventi

rôle or **role** [rol] s ruolo, parte f; **to play a role** fare la parte

roll [rol] s (of film, paper, etc.) rotolo, bobina; (of fat) strato; (roller) rotella; (of bread) panino; (ondulazione; (noise) rullio, rullo; (of a boat) rollio; (of thunder) rombo; (list) ruolo; (of money) (slang) fascio; **to call the roll** fare la chiama || tr far rotolare; (one's r's) arrotare; (one's eyes) stralunare; (e.g., dough) spianare; (steel) laminare; (to wrap) arrotolare; (a drum) rullare; **to roll back** (prices) ridurre; **to roll out** spianare; srotolare; **to roll up** (one's sleeves) arrotolarsi; accumulare; aumentare || intr rotolare; rullare; arrotolarsi; raggomitolarsi; **to roll on** passare; **to roll out** srotolarsi; (to get out of bed) (slang) alzarsi

roll' call' s chiama, appello

roller ['rolər] s rotella; (for hair) bigodino; rotolo; (wave) ondata lunga

roll'er bear'ing s cuscinetto a rotolamento

roll'er coast'er s montagne russe

roll'er skate' s pattino a rotelle

roll'er-skate' intr pattinare coi pattini a rotelle

roll'er tow'el s bandinella

roll'ing mill' ['rolɪŋ] s laminatoio

roll'ing pin' s matterello

roll'ing stock' s (rr) materiale m rotabile

roll'-top desk' s scrivania a piano scorrevole

roly-poly ['roli'poli] adj grassoccio

roman ['romən] adj (typ) romano, tondo || s (typ) carattere romano, tondo || **Roman** adj & s romano

Ro'man can'dle s candela romana

Ro'man Cath'olic Church' s Chiesa Cattolica Apostolica Romana

romance [ro'mæns] or ['romæns] s romanzo; sentimentalità f; idillio, intrigo amoroso; (mus) romanza || [ro'mæns] intr scrivere romanzi; raccontare romanzi; fare il romantico || **Romance** ['romæns] or [ro-'mæns] adj romanzo, neolatino

Ro'man Em'pire s Impero Romano

romanesque [,romən'esk] adj romantico || **Romanesque** adj & s romanico

Ro'man nose' s naso aquilino

romantic [ro'mæntɪk] adj romantico

romanticism [ro'mæntɪ,sɪzəm] s romanticismo

romanticist [ro'mæntɪsɪst] s romantico

romp [ramp] intr ruzzare

rompers ['rampərz] spl pagliaccetto

roof [ruf] or [rʊf] s (of house) tetto; (of heaven) volta; (of car) tetto, padiglione m; **to hit the roof** (slang) andare fuori dai gangheri; **to raise the roof** (slang) fare molto chiasso; (slang) protestare violentemente || tr ricoprire con tetto

roofer ['rufər] or ['rʊfər] s conciatetti m

roof' gar'den s giardino pensile

rook [rʊk] s (bird) cornacchia; (in chess) torre f || tr truffare

rookie ['rʊki] s novizio; (mil) recluta

room [rum] or [rʊm] s stanza, camera; vano, locale m; posto, spazio; opportunità f; **to make room** far luogo || intr alloggiare

room' and board' s vitto e alloggio

room' clerk' s impiegato d'albergo assegnato alle prenotazioni

roomer ['rumər] or ['rʊmər] s inquilino

room'ing house' s casa con camere d'affittare

room'mate' s compagno di stanza

room-y ['rumi] or ['rʊmi] adj (-ier; -iest) ampio, spazioso

roost [rust] s (perch) ballatoio; (house for chickens) pollaio; (place for resting) posto di riposo; **to rule the roost** essere il gallo del pollaio || intr appollaiarsi; andare a dormire

rooster ['rustər] s gallo

root [rut] or [rʊt] s radice f; **to get to the root of** andare al fondo di; **to take root** metter radici || tr inchiodare, piantare || intr radicare; (said of swine) grufolare; **to root for** fare il tifo per

rooter ['rutər] or ['rʊtər] s tifoso

rope [rop] s fune f, corda; (of a hangman) capestro; laccio, lasso; **to know the ropes** (coll) conoscere la faccenda a fondo, saperla lunga || tr legare con fune; prendere al laccio; **to rope in** (slang) imbrogliare

rope'danc'er or **rope'walk'er** s funambolo

rosa·ry ['rozəri] s (-ries) rosario

rose [roz] adj & s rosa

rose'bud' s bottoncino di rosa

rose'bush' s rosaio

rose'-col'ored adj color di rosa

rose'-colored glass'es spl occhiali mpl rosa

rose' gar'den s roseto

rosemar·y ['roz,meri] s (-ies) rosmarino

rose' of Shar'on ['ʃɛrən] s altea

rosette [ro'zet] s rosetta; (archit) rosone m

rose' win'dow s rosone m

rose'wood' s palissandro

rosin ['razɪn] s colofonia

roster ['rastər] s ruolino; orario scolastico

rostrum ['rastrəm] s tribuna

ros·y ['rozi] adj (-ier; -iest) rosa, roseo

rot [rat] s marcio; (coll) stupidaggine f || v (pret & pp **rotted**; ger **rotting**) tr & intr imputridire

ro'tary en'gine ['rotəri] s motore rotativo

ro'tary press' s rotativa

rotate ['rotet] or [ro'tet] tr & intr rotare

rotation [ro'teʃən] s rotazione f; **in rotation** in successione, a turno

rote [rot] s ripetizione macchinale; **by rote** a memoria

rot'gut' s (slang) acquavite f di infima qualità

rotisserie [ro'tɪsəri] *s* girarrosto a motore

rotten ['rɑtən] *adj* marcio, fradicio; corrotto

rotund [ro'tʌnd] *adj* (*plump*) rotondetto; (*voice*) profondo; (*speech*) enfatico

rouge [ruʒ] *s* belletto, rossetto ‖ *tr* dare il belletto a ‖ *intr* darsi il belletto

rough [rʌf] *adj* scabroso; (*sea*) agitato; (*crude*) rozzo, rude; (*road*) accidentato; approssimativo ‖ *tr*—**to rough it** vivere primitivamente; **to rough up** malmenare

rough'cast' *s* intonaco; modello disgrossato ‖ *v* (*pret & pp* **-cast**) *tr* (*a wall*) intonacare; disgrossare, dirozzare

rough' cop'y *s* brutta copia

rough-hew ['rʌf'hju] *tr* digrossare, dirozzare

roughly ['rʌfli] *adv* aspramente; rozzamente; approssimativamente

round [raund] *adj* rotondo ‖ *s* tondo; (*of applause; of guns*) salva; (*of a single gun*) colpo, tiro; (*of a chair*) piolo; (*of a doctor*) giro; (*of a policeman*) ronda; serie *f;* (*of golf*) partita; (*e.g., of bridge*) mano *f;* (*boxing*) ripresa ‖ *adv* intorno; dal principio alla fine ‖ *prep* intorno a; attraverso ‖ *tr* (*to make round*) arrotondare; circondare; (*a corner*) scantonare; **to round off** arrotondare; completare, perfezionare; **to round up** raccogliere; (*cattle*) condurre

roundabout ['raundə,baut] *adj* indiretto ‖ *s* giacca attillata; via traversa; giro di parole; (Brit) giostra; (Brit) anello stradale

round'house' *s* rimessa per locomotive

round-shouldered ['raund'ʃoldərd] *adj* dalle spalle spioventi

round'-trip tick'et *s* biglietto d'andata e ritorno

round'up' *s* (*of cattle*) riunione; (*of criminals*) retata; (*of facts*) riassunto

rouse [rauz] *tr* svegliare; suscitare; (*game*) scovare ‖ *intr* svegliarsi

rout [raut] *s* sconfitta, rotta ‖ *tr* sconfiggere, mettere in rotta ‖ *intr* grufolare

route [rut] *or* [raut] *s* via, rotta; itinerario ‖ *tr* istradare

routine [ru'tin] *adj* ordinario ‖ *s* trafila, routine *f*

rove [rov] *intr* vagabondare, vagare

rover ['rovər] *s* vagabondo

row [rau] *s* piazzata, scenata; (*clamor*) (coll) baccano; **to raise a row** (coll) fare baccano ‖ [ro] *s* fila; (*of figures*) finca; (*e.g., of trees*) filare *m;* **in a row** in continuazione, di seguito ‖ *tr* vogare ‖ *intr* remare, vogare

rowboat ['ro,bot] *s* barca a remi

row·dy ['raudi] *adj* (**-dier; -diest**) turbolento ‖ *s* (**-dies**) attaccabrighe *mf*

rower ['ro·ər] *s* rematore *m*

rowing ['ro·ɪŋ] *s* (*action*) voga; (*sport*) canottaggio

royal ['rɔɪ·əl] *adj* reale, regio

royalist ['rɔɪ·əlɪst] *adj* sostenitore del re ‖ *s* realista *mf*

royal·ty ['rɔɪ·əlti] *s* (**-ties**) regalità *f;* membro della famiglia reale; nobiltà *f;* diritto d'autore; diritto d'inventore; percentuale *f* sugli utili

rub [rʌb] *s* frizione; difficile *m;* **here's the rub** qui sta il bussillis ‖ *v* (*pret & pp* **rubbed**; *ger* **rubbing**) *tr* fregare; **to rub elbows with** stare giunto a gomiti con; **to rub out** cancellare con la gomma; (slang) togliere di mezzo ‖ *intr* sfregare; **to rub off** venir via sfregando; cancellarsi

rubber ['rʌbər] *s* gomma, caucciù *m;* gomma da cancellare; (*overshoe*) caloscia; (*in cards*) rubber *m;* (sports) bella

rub'ber band' *s* elastico

rub'ber·neck' *s* (coll) ficcanaso; (coll) turista curioso ‖ *intr* (coll) allungare il collo

rub'ber plant' *s* albero del caucciù

rub'ber stamp' *s* timbro di gomma; (coll) persona che approva inconsultamente

rub'ber-stamp' *tr* timbrare; (coll) approvare inconsultamente

rubbish ['rʌbɪʃ] *s* spazzatura; immondizia; (fig) detrito; (coll) sciocchezza

rubble ['rʌbəl] *s* (*broken stone*) pietrisco; (*masonry*) mistura di malta e pietrame; (*broken bits*) calcinacci *mpl*

rub'down' *s* fregagione

rube [rub] *s* (slang) contadino gonzo

ru·by ['rubi] *adj* vermiglio ‖ (**-bies**) *s* rubino

rudder ['rʌdər] *s* timone *m;* (aer) timone *m* di direzione

rud·dy ['rʌdi] *adj* (**-dier; -diest**) rubicondo

rude [rud] *adj* rude, sgarbato

rudiment ['rudɪmənt] *s* rudimento

rue [ru] *tr* lamentare, rimpiangere

rueful ['rufəl] *adj* lamentevole; triste

ruffian ['rʌfɪ·ən] *s* ribaldo

ruffle ['rʌfəl] *s* increspatura; (*of drum*) rullo; (sew) gala, crespa ‖ *tr* increspare; arruffare; irritare; (*a drum*) far rullare; (sew) guarnire di gala or crespa

rug [rʌg] *s* tappeto

rugged ['rʌgɪd] *adj* aspro, irregolare; rugoso; rozzo; forte; tempestuoso

ruin ['ru·ɪn] *s* rovina ‖ *tr* rovinare, mandare in rovina

rule [rul] *s* regola; dominazione; (*reign*) regno; (*law*) ordinanza; (typ) filetto; **as a rule** in generale ‖ *tr* governare; dominare; (*with lines*) rigare; (*law*) deliberare; **to rule out** escludere ‖ *intr* governare; regnare; **to rule over** governare

rule' of thumb' *s* regola basata sull'esperienza; **by rule of thumb** secondo la propria esperienza

ruler ['rulər] *s* governante *m*, dominatore *m;* (*for ruling lines*) riga, regolo

ruling ['rulɪŋ] *adj* dirigente ‖ *s* (*ruled lines*) rigatura; (law) decisione

rum [rʌm] *s* rum *m;* (*any alcoholic drink*) acquavite *f*

Rumanian [ruˈmɛnɪ·ən] *adj & s* rumeno

rumble [ˈrʌmbəl] *s* rimbombo; *(of the intestines)* gorgoglio; *(slang)* rissa fra ganghe rivali ‖ *intr* rimbombare; gorgogliare

ruminate [ˈrumɪ ˌnet] *tr & intr* ruminare

rummage [ˈrʌmɪdʒ] *tr & intr* rovistare, frugare

rum'mage sale' *s* vendita di cianfrusaglie

rumor [ˈrumər] *s* voce *f*, diceria ‖ *tr* vociferare; **it is rumored that** corre voce che

rump [rʌmp] *s* anca; posteriore *m; (of beef)* quarto posteriore

rumple [ˈrʌmpəl] *s* piega ‖ *tr* spiegazzare, sgualcire ‖ *intr* sgualcirsi

rumpus [ˈrʌmpəs] *s* tumulto; rissa; **to raise a rumpus** fare baccano

run [rʌn] *s* corsa; percorso; produzione; *(e.g., in a stocking)* smagliatura; direzione; *(spell)* serie *f; (in cards)* scala; *(of goods)* richiesta; *(on a bank)* afflusso; **in the long run** a lungo andare; **on the run** (coll) di corsa; in fuga; **the common run of men** la media della gente; **to give s.o. a run for his money** dare a qlcu del filo da torcere; essere denaro ben speso per qlcu, e.g., **that sweater gave me a run for my money** quello sweater è stato denaro ben speso per me; **to have a long run** tenere il cartellone per lungo tempo; **to have the run of** avere la libertà di andare e venire per ‖ *v (pret* ran [ræn]; *pp* **run;** *ger* **running)** *tr* muovere; *(a horse)* far correre; *(the street)* vivere liberamente in; *(game)* inseguire; trasportare; *(a machine)* far camminare; *(a store)* esercire; *(a candidate)* portare; *(a risk)* correre; *(a blockade)* violare; mettere, ficcare; *(a line)* tirare; **to run down** cacciare; esaminare; trovare; *(a pedestrian)* investire; denigrare, criticare; **to run in** *(a machine)* rodare; (slang) schiaffare in prigione; **to run off** creare di getto; cacciare; *(typ)* tirare; **to run up** ammassare ‖ *intr* correre; scappare; *(in a race)* arrivare; *(said of a candidate)* portarsi; passare; *(said of knitted material)* smagliarsi; *(said of a liquid)* scorrere; *(said of a color)* sbavare; *(said of fish)* migrare; funzionare; *(to become)* diventare; *(to be worded)* essere del tenore; *(com)* decorrere; *(theat, mov)* durare in cartellone; **to run across** imbattersi in; **to run aground** incagliarsi in; **to run away** fuggire; *(said of a horse)* prendere la mano; **to run down** *(said of a liquid)* scorrere; *(said of a battery, a watch)* scaricarsi; *(in health)* sciuparsi; **to run for** presentarsi candidato per; **to run in the family** essere una caratteristica familiare; **to run into** imbattersi in; ammontare a; *(to follow)* succedersi a; **to run off the track** (rr) uscire dalle rotaie; **to run out** aver termine; scadere; esaurirsi;

to run out of rimanere senza; **to run over** oltrepassare; *(e.g., with a car)* investire; **to run through** trapassare; *(a fortune)* dilapidare; esaminare rapidamente

run'a·way' *adj* fuggiasco; *(horse)* che ha preso la mano ‖ *s* fuggiasco; cavallo che ha preso la mano; fuga

run'-down' *adj* esausto; negletto, cadente; *(watch, battery)* scarico

rung [rʌŋ] *s (of chair or ladder)* piolo

runner [ˈrʌnər] *s* corridore *m;* messaggero; fattorino, messo; *(of sleigh)* pattino; *(of ice skate)* lama; *(rug)* guida; *(on a table)* striscia di pizzo; *(in stocking)* smagliatura

run'ner-up' *s* (**runners-up**) finalista *mf* secondo

running [ˈrʌnɪŋ] *adj* in corsa; da corsa; *(water)* corrente; *(vine)* rampicante; *(knot)* scorsoio; *(sore)* purulento; *(writing)* corsivo; consecutivo; *(start)* (sports) lanciato ‖ *s* corsa; *(of a business)* esercizio; direzione; funzionamento; **to be in the running** avere possibilità di vittoria

run'ning board' *s* (aut) pedana

run'ning head' *s* titolo corrente

run·ny [ˈrʌnɪ] *adj* (-nier; -niest) *(liquid)* scorrevole; *(color)* sbavante; **to have a runny nose** avere la goccia al naso

run'off' *s* ballottaggio

run-of-the-mill [ˈrʌnəvðəˈmɪl] *adj* ordinario, corrente

run'proof' *adj* indemagliabile

runt [rʌnt] *s* nanerottolo; animale deperito

run'way' *s* pista; *(of a stream)* letto; *(for animals)* chiusa; (aut) corsia

rupture [ˈrʌptʃər] *s* rottura; (pathol) ernia ‖ *tr* rompere; causare un'ernia a ‖ *intr* rompersi; soffrire di ernia

ru'ral free' deliv'ery [ˈrurəl] *s* distribuzione postale campestre

ruse [ruz] *s* astuzia, stratagemma *m*

rush [rʌʃ] *adj* urgente ‖ *s* fretta; slancio, corsa; *(of blood)* ondata; *(rushing of persons to a new mine)* febbre *f;* (bot) giunco; **in a rush** in fretta e furia ‖ *tr* affrettare; portare di fretta; spingere; (coll) fare la corte a; **to rush through** fare di fretta; *(e.g., a bill through Congress)* far approvare di fretta ‖ *intr* lanciarsi; affrettarsi; passare velocemente; **to rush through** *(a book)* leggere velocemente; *(one's work)* fare in fretta; *(a town)* attraversare velocemente

rush'-bot'tomed chair' *s* sedia di giunchi

rush' can'dle *s* lumicino con lo stoppino fatto di midollo di giunco

rush' hour' *s* ora di punta

russet [ˈrʌsɪt] *adj* color cannella

Russia [ˈrʌʃə] *s* la Russia

Russian [ˈrʌʃən] *adj & s* russo

rust [rʌst] *s* ruggine *f;* (fig) torpore *m* ‖ *tr* arrugginire ‖ *intr* arrugginirsi

rustic [ˈrʌstɪk] *adj & s* rustico

rustle [ˈrʌsəl] *s* fruscio· *(of leaves)* stormire *m* ‖ *tr* far frusciare; far stormire; (cattle) (coll) rubare ‖ intr frusciare; stormire; (coll) lavorare di buzzo buono

rust•y ['rʌstɪ] adj (-ier; -iest) rugginoso; color ruggine; fuori pratica

rut [rʌt] s (track) solco, carrareccia; (of animals) fregola; (il) solito tran tran

ruthless ['ruθlɪs] adj spietato

rye [raɪ] s segala; whiskey m di segala

S

S, s [es] s diciannovesima lettera dell'alfabeto inglese

Sabbath ['sæbəθ] s (of Jews) sabato; (of Christians) domenica; **to keep the Sabbath** osservare il riposo domenicale

sabbat'ical year' [sə'bætɪkəl] s anno di congedo; (Bib) anno sabbatico

saber ['sebər] s sciabola

sa'ber rat'tling s minacce fpl di guerra

sable ['sebəl] adj nero ‖ s zibellino; **sables** vestiti di lutto

sabotage ['sæbə,taʒ] s sabotaggio ‖ tr & intr sabotare

saccharin ['sækərɪn] s saccarina

sachet ['sæʃe] or [sæ'ʃe] s sacchetto profumato (per la biancheria)

sack [sæk] s sacco; (of an employee) (slang) licenziamento; (slang) letto ‖ tr insaccare; (to lay waste) saccheggiare, mettere a sacco; (slang) licenziare

sack'cloth' s tela di sacco; (for penitence) sacco, cilicio; **in sackcloth and ashes** pentito e contrito

sacrament ['sækrəmənt] s sacramento

sacramental [,sækrə'mentəl] adj sacramentale

sacred ['sekrəd] adj sacro

sacrifice ['sækrɪ,faɪs] s sacrificio; **at a sacrifice** in perdita ‖ tr sacrificare; (com) svendere

sacrilege ['sækrɪlɪdʒ] s sacrilegio

sacrilegious [,sækrɪ'lɪdʒəs] or [,sækrɪ'lidʒəs] adj sacrilego

sacristan ['sækrɪstən] s sagrestano

sacris•ty ['sækrɪstɪ] s (-ties) sagrestia

sad [sæd] adj (sadder; saddest) triste; (bad) cattivo; (color) tetro

sadden ['sædən] tr rattristare ‖ intr rattristarsi

saddle ['sædəl] s sella ‖ tr insellare; **to saddle with** gravare di

saddle'bag' s fonda

saddlebow ['sædəl,bo] s arcione m anteriore

sad'dle-cloth' s gualdrappa

saddler ['sædlər] s sellaio

sad'dle-tree' s arcione m

sadist ['sædɪst] or ['sedɪst] s sadico

sadistic [sæ'dɪstɪk] or [se'dɪstɪk] adj sadico

sadness ['sædnɪs] s tristezza

sad' sack' s (coll) marmittone m

safe [sef] adj sicuro; cauto; (distance) rispettoso; **safe and sound** sano e salvo ‖ s cassaforte f

safe'-con'duct s salvacondotto

safe'-depos'it box' s cassetta di sicurezza

safe'guard' s salvaguardia ‖ tr salvaguardare

safe•ty ['sefti] adj di sicurezza ‖ s (-ties) sicurezza; (of a gun) sicura; **to reach safety** mettersi in salvo

safe'ty belt' s (of a worker) imbraca; (aer, aut) cintura di sicurezza; (naut) cintura di salvataggio

safe'ty glass' s vetro infrangibile

safe'ty is'land s salvagente m

safe'ty match' s fiammifero svedese

safe'ty pin' s spillo di sicurezza

safe'ty ra'zor s rasoio di sicurezza

safe'ty valve' s valvola di sicurezza

saffron ['sæfrən] s zafferano

sag [sæg] s cedimento; depressione; (of a rope) allentamento ‖ v (pret & pp sagged; ger sagging) intr curvarsi; cedere, afflosciarsi; allentarsi; (said of prices) calare

sagacious [sə'geʃəs] adj sagace

sage [sedʒ] adj saggio, savio ‖ s saggio, savio; (bot) salvia

sage'brush' s artemisia

Sagittarius [,sædʒɪ'teri•əs] s Sagittario

sail [sel] s vela; (of windmill) ala; gita a vela; **to set sail** far vela; **under full sail** a piena velatura ‖ tr veleggiare, navigare; (a boat) far navigare ‖ intr veleggiare, navigare; far vela; volare; (said of a vessel) partire; **to sail into** (coll) attaccare

sail'boat' s nave f a vela, veliero

sail'cloth' s tela di olona

sailing ['selɪŋ] adj in partenza ‖ s partenza; navigazione; navigazione a vela

sail'ing ship' s veliero

sail'mak'er s velaio

sailor ['selər] s marinaio

saint [sent] adj & s santo ‖ tr santificare, canonizzare

saint'hood's santità f

saintliness ['sentlɪnɪs] s santità f

Saint' Vi'tus's dance' ['vaɪtəsəz] s (pathol) ballo di San Vito

sake [sek] s causa, interesse m; **for the sake of** per il bene di, per l'amor di

salaam [sə'lɑm] s salamelecco ‖ tr fare salamelecchi

salable ['seləbəl] adj vendibile

salacious [sə'leʃəs] adj salace

salad ['sæləd] s insalata

sal'ad bowl' s insalatiera

sal'ad oil' s olio da tavola

sala•ry ['sæləri] s (-ries) stipendio

sale [sel] s vendita; (at reduced prices) svendita, saldo; **for sale** in vendita; si vende, si vendono

sales'clerk' s commesso, impiegato

sales'la'dy s (**-dies**) commessa, impiegata

sales'man s (**-men**) venditore m; commesso; (*traveling*) piazzista m

sales'man·ship' s arte f di vendere

sales' promo'tion s promozione delle vendite, promotion f

sales'room' s sala di esposizione; sala vendite

sales' talk' s discorso da venditore; (*e.g., of a barker*) imbonimento

sales' tax' s imposta sulle vendite

saliva [səˈlaɪvə] s saliva

sallow [ˈsælo] adj giallastro, olivastro

sal·ly [ˈsæli] s (**-lies**) escursione, gita; (*outburst*) esplosione; (*witty remark*) uscita; (mil) sortita || v pret & pp **-lied**) intr fare una sortita; **to sally forth** balzar fuori

salmon [ˈsæmən] s salmone m

salon [sæˈlɑn] s salone m

saloon [səˈlun] s taverna; (*on a passenger vessel*) salone m

saloon' keep'er s taverniere m

salt [sɔlt] s sale m; **to be worth one's salt** valere il pane che si mangia || tr salare; (*cattle*) dare sale a; **to salt away** (coll) metter via, conservare

salt' bed' s salina

salt'cel'lar s saliera

saltine [sɔlˈtin] s galletta salata

saltish [ˈsɔltɪʃ] adj salmastro

salt'pe'ter s (*potassium nitrate*) salnitro; (*sodium nitrate*) nitro del Cile

salt' shak'er s saliera

salt·y [ˈsɔlti] adj (**-ier; -iest**) salato

salubrious [səˈlubrɪ·əs] adj salubre

salutation [ˌsæljəˈte/ən] s saluto

salute [səˈlut] s saluto || tr salutare

salvage [ˈsælvɪdʒ] s ricupero || tr ricuperare

salvation [sælˈve/ən] s salvezza

Salva'tion Ar'my s Esercito della Salvezza

salve [sæv] or [sɑv] s unguento || tr lenire, alleviare

sal·vo [ˈsælvo] s (**-vos** or **-voes**) salva

Samaritan [səˈmærɪtən] adj & s samaritano

same [sem] adj & pron indef medesimo, stesso; **it's all the same to me** a me fa lo stesso; **just the same** lo stesso, ugualmente; ciò nonostante; **same . . .** as lo stesso . . . che

sameness [ˈsemnɪs] s uniformità f; monotonia

sample [ˈsæmpəl] s campione m, saggio || tr (*to take a sample of*) campionare; (*to taste*) assaggiare, provare

sam'ple cop'y s esemplare m di campione

sancti·fy [ˈsæŋktɪ ˌfaɪ] v (pret & pp **-fied**) tr santificare

sanctimonious [ˌsæŋktɪˈmonɪ·əs] adj che affetta devozione ipocrita

sanction [ˈsæŋk/ən] s sanzione || tr sanzionare

sanctuar·y [ˈsæŋkt/ʊ ˌeri] s (**-ies**) santuario; **to take sanctuary** prendere asilo, rifugiarsi

sand [sænd] s sabbia || tr insabbiare;

(*to polish*) smerigliare; cospergere di sabbia

sandal [ˈsændəl] s sandalo

san'dal·wood' s sandalo

sand'bag' s sacchetto a terra

sand'bank' s banco di sabbia

sand' bar' s cordone m litorale, banco di sabbia

sand'blast' s sabbiatura || tr pulire con sabbiatura, sabbiare

sand'box' s cassone m pieno di sabbia; (rr) sabbiera

sand'glass' s orologio a polvere or a sabbia

sand'pa'per s carta vetrata || tr pulire con carta vetrata

sand'stone' s arenaria

sandwich [ˈsændwɪt/] s panino imbottito, tramezzino || tr inserire

sand'wich man' s tramezzino, uomo sandwich

sand·y [ˈsændi] adj (**-ier; -iest**) sabbioso; (*hair*) biondo rossiccio

sane [sen] adj sensato

sanguinary [ˈsæŋgwɪn ˌeri] adj sanguinario

sanguine [ˈsæŋgwɪn] adj fiducioso; (*complexion*) sanguigno

sanitary [ˈsænɪ ˌteri] adj sanitario

san'itary nap'kin s pannolino igienico

sanitation [ˌsænɪˈte/ən] s sanità f

sanity [ˈsænɪti] s sanità f di mente

Santa Claus [ˈsæntə ˌkloz] s Babbo Natale

sap [sæp] s linfa, succhio; (mil) trincea; (coll) scemo || v (pret & pp **sapped**; ger **sapping**) tr scavare; insidiare, minare; (*to weaken*) indebolire

sapling [ˈsæplɪŋ] s alberello; (*youth*) giovanetto

sapphire [ˈsæfaɪr] s zaffiro

Saracen [ˈsærəsən] adj & s saraceno

sarcasm [ˈsɑrkæzəm] s sarcasmo

sarcastic [sɑrˈkæstɪk] adj sarcastico

sardine [sɑrˈdin] s sardina; **packed in like sardines** pigiati come le acciughe

Sardinia [sɑrˈdɪnɪ·ə] s la Sardegna

Sardinian [sɑrˈdɪnɪ·ən] adj & s sardo

sarsaparilla [ˌsɑrsəpəˈrɪlə] s salsapariglia

sash [sæ/] s sciarpa; (*around one's waist*) fusciacca; (*of window*) telaio

sash' win'dow s finestra a ghigliottina

sas·sy [ˈsæsi] adj (**-sier; -siest**) (coll) impertinente; (pert) (coll) vivace

satchel [ˈsæt/əl] s sacca; (*of schoolboy*) cartella

sateen [sæˈtin] s satin m

satellite [ˈsætə ˌlaɪt] s satellite m

satiate [ˈse/ɪ ˌet] tr saziare

satin [ˈsætən] s raso

satire [ˈsætaɪr] s satira

satiric(al) [səˈtɪrɪk(əl)] adj satirico

satirist [ˈsætɪrɪst] s satirico

satirize [ˈsætɪ ˌraɪz] tr satireggiare

satisfaction [ˌsætɪsˈfæk/ən] s soddisfazione

satisfactory [ˌsætɪsˈfæktəri] adj soddisfacente

satis·fy [ˈsætɪs ˌfaɪ] v (pret & pp **-fied**) tr & intr soddisfare

saturate [ˈsæt/ə ˌret] tr saturare

Saturday ['sætərdɪ] s sabato

Saturn ['sætərn] s (astr) Saturno

sauce [sɔs] s salsa; (of fruit) conserva; (of chocolate) crema; (coll) insolenza, impertinenza || tr condire; rendere piccante || [sɔs] or [sæs] tr (coll) rispondere con impertinenza a

sauce'pan' s casseruola

saucer ['sɔsər] s piattino

sau•cy ['sɔsɪ] adj (-cier; -ciest) impertinente; (pert) vivace

sauerkraut ['saʊr,kraʊt] s sarcraùti mpl, crauti mpl

saunter ['sɔntər] s giro, bighellonata || intr girandolare, bighellonare

sausage ['sɔsɪdʒ] s salsiccia

savage ['sævɪdʒ] adj & s selvaggio

savant ['sævənt] s erudito

save [sev] prep tranne, salvo || tr salvare; (money) risparmiare; (to save apart) serbare; **to save face** salvare le apparenze || intr fare economia

saving ['sevɪŋ] adj economico; che redime || **savings** spl risparmi mpl, economie fpl || **saving** prep eccetto, salvo

sav'ings account' s conto di risparmio

sav'ings and loan' associa'tion s cassa di risparmio che concede mutui

sav'ings bank' s cassa di risparmio

savior ['sevjər] s salvatore m

Saviour ['sevjər] s Salvatore m

savor ['sevər] s sapore m || tr assaporare; (to flavor) saporire || intr odorare; **to savor of** sapere di; odorare di

savor•y ['sevərɪ] adj (-ier; -iest) saporoso; piccante; delizioso || s (-ies) (bot) santoreggia

saw [sɔ] s (tool) sega; detto, proverbio || tr segare

saw'buck' s cavalletto

saw'dust' s segatura

saw'horse' s cavalletto

saw'mill' s segheria

Saxon ['sæksən] adj & s sassone m

saxophone ['sæksə,fon] s sassofono

say [se] s dire m; **to have no say** non aver voce in capitolo; **to have one's say** esprimere la propria opinione; **to have the say** avere l'ultima parola || v (pret & pp said [sɛd]) tr dire; **I should say so!** certamente!; **it is said** si dice; **no sooner said than done** detto fatto; **that is to say** vale a dire; **to go without saying** essere ovvio

saying ['se•ɪŋ] s detto, proverbio

scab [skæb] s crosta; (strikebreaker) crumiro

scabbard ['skæbərd] s guaina, fodero

scab•by ['skæbɪ] adj (-bier; -biest) crostoso; (animal) rognoso; (slang) vile

scabrous ['skæbrəs] adj scabroso

scads [skædz] spl (slang) un mucchio

scaffold ['skæfəld] s impalcatura; (to execute a criminal) patibolo

scaffolding ['skæfəldɪŋ] s incastellatura, ponteggio

scald [skɔld] tr scottare; (e.g., milk) cuocere al disotto del punto d'ebollizione

scale [skel] s (e.g., of map) scala;

piatto della bilancia; (of fish) squama; **on a large scale** in grande scala; **scales** bilancia; **to tip the scales** far inclinare la bilancia || tr squamare; (to incrust) incrostare; (to weigh) pesare; scalare; graduare; ridurre a scala || intr squamarsi; scrostarsi

scallion ['skæljən] s scalogno

scallop ['skɑləp] or ['skæləp] s (for cooking) conchiglia; (mollusk) pettine m; (slice of meat) scaloppina; (on edge of cloth) dentello, smerlo || tr (fish) cuocere in conchiglia; dentellare, smerlare

scalp [skælp] s cuoio capelluto || tr scotennare; (tickets) fare il bagarinaggio di

scalpel ['skælpəl] s scalpello

scalper ['skælpər] s bagarino

scal•y ['skelɪ] adj (-ier; -iest) squamoso; scrostato

scamp [skæmp] s cattivo soggetto, briccone m

scamper ['skæmpər] intr sgambettare; **to scamper away** darsela a gambe

scan [skæn] v (pret & pp scanned; ger scanning) tr scrutare; dare un'occhiata a; (verse) scandire; (telv) analizzare, scandire, esplorare

scandal ['skændəl] s scandalo

scandalize ['skændə,laɪz] tr scandalizzare

scandalous ['skændələs] adj scandaloso

Scandinavian [,skændɪ'nevɪ-ən] adj & s scandinavo

scanning ['skænɪŋ] s (telv) esplorazione

scan'ning line' s (telv) riga di analisi

scant [skænt] adj scarso; corto || tr diminuire; lesinare

scant•y ['skæntɪ] adj (-ier; -iest) appena sufficiente; povero, magro; (clothing) succinto

scapegoat ['skep,got] s capro espiatorio

scar [skɑr] s cicatrice f; (fig) sfregio || v (pret & pp scarred; ger scarring) tr segnare, marcare; sfregiare || intr cicatrizzarsi

scarce [skɛrs] adj scarso, raro; **to make oneself scarce** (coll) non farsi vedere

scarcely ['skɛrslɪ] adv appena; a mala pena; non . . . affatto; **scarcely ever** raramente; non . . . affatto

scarci•ty ['skɛrsɪtɪ] s (-ties) scarsità f, scarsezza; carestia

scare [skɛr] s spavento || tr spaventare, impaurire; **to scare away** fare scappare per lo spavento; **to scare up** (money) (coll) metter insieme

scare'crow' s spaventapasseri m

scarf [skɑrf] s (scarfs or scarves [skɑrvz]) sciarpa; cravattone m; (cover for table) centro, striscia

scarf'pin' s spilla da cravatta

scarlet ['skɑrlɪt] adj scarlatto

scar'let fe'ver s scarlattina

scar•y ['skɛrɪ] adj (-ier; -iest) (timid) (coll) fifone m; (causing fright) (coll) spaventevole

scathing [ˈskeðɪŋ] *adj* severo, bruciante

scatter [ˈskætər] *tr* disperdere, sparpagliare || *intr* disperdersi, sparpagliarsi

scatterbrained [ˈskætərˌbrend] *adj* scervellato, stordito

scenari·o [sɪˈnɛrɪˌo] or [sɪˈnɑrɪˌo] *s* (-os) scenario

scenarist [sɪˈnɛrɪst] or [sɪˈnɑrɪst] *s* scenarista *mf*, sceneggiatore *m*

scene [sin] *s* (*view*) paesaggio; (*place*) scena; (theat) scena, quadro; **behind the scenes** dietro le quinte; **to make a scene** fare una scenata

scener·y [ˈsinəri] *s* (-ies) paesaggio; (theat) scenario

scenic [ˈsinɪk] or [ˈsɛnɪk] *adj* pittoresco; (*pertaining to the stage*) scenico

scent [sɛnt] *s* odore *m*; profumo; (*sense of smell*) fiuto, odorato; (*trail*) traccia, pista || *tr* profumare; (*to detect*) fiutare, annusare

scepter [ˈsɛptər] *s* scettro

sceptic [ˈskɛptɪk] *adj* & *s* scettico

sceptical [ˈskɛptɪkəl] *adj* scettico

scepticism [ˈskɛptɪˌsɪzəm] *s* scetticismo

schedule [ˈskɛdjʊl] *s* lista; programma *m*; (*of trains, planes, etc.*) orario || *tr* programmare; mettere in orario

scheme [skim] *s* schema *m*; piano, progetto; (*plot*) trama || *tr* progettare; tramare

schemer [ˈskimər] *s* progettista *mf*; (*underhanded*) manipolatore *m*, concertatore *m*

scheming [ˈskimɪŋ] *adj* intrigante, scaltro

schism [ˈsɪzəm] *s* scisma *m*

schist [ʃɪst] *s* scisto

scholar [ˈskɑlər] *s* (*pupil*) alunno; detentore *m* di una borsa di studio; (*learned person*) dotto, studioso

scholarly [ˈskɑlərli] *adj* erudito, studioso

scholarship [ˈskɑlərˌʃɪp] *s* erudizione; (*money*) borsa di studio

scholasticism [skəˈlæstɪˌsɪzəm] *s* scolastica

school [skul] *s* scuola; (*of a university*) facoltà *f*; (*of fish*) banco || *tr* istruire, insegnare

school′ age′ *s* età scolastica

school′bag′ *s* cartella

school′ board′ *s* comitato scolastico

school′boy′ *s* alunno, scolaro

school′ bus′ *s* scuolabus *m*

school′ day′ *s* giorno di scuola; durata della giornata scolastica

school′girl′ *s* alunna, scolara

school′house′ *s* scuola, edificio scolastico

schooling [ˈskulɪŋ] *s* istruzione

school′mas′ter *s* maestro di scuola; direttore scolastico

school′mate′ *s* compagno di scuola, condiscepolo

school′room′ *s* aula scolastica

school′teach′er *s* maestro

school′ year′ *s* anno scolastico

schooner [ˈskunər] *s* goletta

sciatica [saɪˈætɪkə] *s* (pathol) sciatica

science [ˈsaɪəns] *s* scienza

sci′ence fic′tion *s* fantascienza

sci′ence-fic′tion *adj* fantascientifico

scientific [ˌsaɪənˈtɪfɪk] *adj* scientifico

scientist [ˈsaɪəntɪst] *s* scienziato

scimitar [ˈsɪmɪtər] *s* scimitarra

scintillate [ˈsɪntɪˌlet] *intr* scintillare

scion [ˈsaɪən] *s* rampollo, discendente *m*

scissors [ˈsɪzərz] *ssg* or *spl* forbici *fpl*

scoff [skɔf] or [skɑf] *s* dileggio, beffa || *intr* burlarsi; **to scoff at** burlarsi di, dileggiare

scold [skold] *s* megera || *tr* & *intr* sgridare, rimproverare

scoop [skup] *s* (*ladlelike utensil*) paletta; (*kitchen utensil*) cucchiaio, cucchiaione *m*; cucchiaiata; palettata; (*of dredge*) benna; (*hollow*) buco; (naut) gottazza; (journ) primizia, esclusiva; (coll) colpo || *tr* vuotare a cucchiaiate; (journ) battere; (naut) gottare; **to scoop out** (*e.g., sand*) scavare; (*soup*) scodellare

scoot [skut] *s* (coll) corsa || *intr* (coll) correre precipitosamente

scooter [ˈskutər] *s* monopattino

scope [skop] *s* ampiezza; lunghezza; **to give full scope to** dare piena libertà d'azione a

scorch [skɔrtʃ] *s* scottatura || *tr* bruciacchiare; bruciare, inaridire; (fig) ferire || *intr* bruciarsi

scorching [ˈskɔrtʃɪŋ] *adj* bruciante

score [skor] *s* (*in a game*) punteggio; (*in an examination*) nota; linea, segno, marca; (*twenty*) ventina; (mus) partitura; **scores** un mucchio; **to keep score** segnare il punteggio; **to settle a score** (fig) saldare un conto || *tr* raggiungere il punteggio di, fare; marcare; guadagnare; (*to censure*) sgridare, rimproverare; (mus) orchestrare

score′board′ *s* quadro del punteggio

score′keep′er *s* segnapunti *m*

scorn [skɔrn] *s* disdegno, disprezzo || *tr* & *intr* disdegnare, disprezzare

scornful [ˈskɔrnfəl] *adj* disdegnoso

Scorpio [ˈskɔrpɪˌo] *s* Scorpione *m*

scorpion [ˈskɔrpɪən] *s* scorpione *m*

Scot [skɑt] *s* scozzese *mf*

Scotch [skɑtʃ] *adj* scozzese || *s* scozzese *m*; whisky *m* scozzese; **the Scotch** gli scozzesi

Scotch′man *s* (-men) scozzese *m*

Scotch′ pine′ *s* pino silvestre

Scotch′ tape′ *s* (trademark) nastro autoadesivo Scotch

scot′-free′ *adj* impune; **to get off scot-free** farla franca

Scotland [ˈskɑtlənd] *s* la Scozia

Scottish [ˈskɑtɪʃ] *adj* scozzese || *s* scozzese *mf*; **the Scottish** gli scozzesi

scoundrel [ˈskaʊndrəl] *s* birbante *m*, farabutto, manigoldo

scour [skaʊr] *tr* sgrassare fregando, pulire fregando; (*the countryside*) battere

scourge [skʌrdʒ] *s* sferza; (fig) flagello || *tr* sferzare

scout [skaʊt] *s* esplorazione; giovane esploratore *m;* giovane esploratrice *f;* (mil) ricognitore *m;* (nav) esploratore *m;* (slang) tipo ‖ *tr* esplorare, riconoscere; cercar di trovare; disdegnare

scouting ['skaʊtɪŋ] *s* scoutismo

scowl [skaʊl] *s* cipiglio ‖ *intr* aggrottare le ciglia; guardare torvamente

scram [skræm] *v* (*pret & pp* **scrammed;** *ger* **scramming**) *intr* (coll) tagliare la corda; **scram!** (coll) vattene!, (coll) escimi di tra i piedi!

scramble ['skræmbəl] *s* ruffa, gara ‖ *tr* (*to grab up*) arraffare; confondere, mescolare; (*eggs*) strapazzare ‖ *intr* arrampicarsi; (*to struggle*) azzuffarsi

scram'bled eggs' *spl* uova strapazzate

scrap [skræp] *s* pezzetto, frammento; ritaglio, rottame *m;* (coll) baruffa; **scraps** avanzi *mpl;* ‖ *v* (*pret & pp* **scrapped;** *ger* **scrapping**) *tr* scartare ‖ *intr* (coll) fare baruffa

scrap'book' *s* album *m* di ritagli (di giornale o fotografie)

scrape [skrep] *s* impiccio, imbroglio; baruffa ‖ *tr* raschiare, graffiare; **to scrape together** racimolare ‖ *intr* raschiare; **to scrape along** vivacchiare; **to scrape through** passare per il rotto della cuffia

scraper ['skrepər] *s* raschietto

scrap' i'ron *s* rottami *mpl* di ferro

scrap' pa'per *s* carta straccia; carta da appunti

scratch [skrætʃ] *s* graffio, scalfittura; scarabocchio; (billiards) punto perduto; (sports) linea di partenza; **from scratch** da bel principio; dal niente; **up to scratch** soddisfacente ‖ *tr* graffiare, grattare; (*e.g.. a horse*) cancellare ‖ *intr* graffiare; (*said of a chicken*) raspare; (*said of a pen*) grattare

scratch' pad' *s* quaderno per appunti

scratch' pa'per *s* carta da appunti

scrawl [skrɔl] *s* scarabocchio ‖ *tr & intr* scarabocchiare

scraw·ny ['skrɔni] *adj* (-nier; -niest) ossuto, scarno

scream [skrim] *s* grido, strillo; cosa divertentissima; persona divertentissima ‖ *intr* gridare, strillare

screech [skritʃ] *s* stridio ‖ *intr* stridere

screech' owl' *s* gufo; (*barn owl*) barbagianni *m*

screen [skrin] *s* (*movable partition*) paravento; (*in front of fire*) parafuoco; rete metallica; (*sieve*) vaglio; (mov; phys) schermo; (telv) teleschermo ‖ *tr* schermare; riparare, proteggere; (*to sieve*) vagliare; (*a film*) proiettare; (*to adapt*) (mov) sceneggiare

screen' grid' *s* (rad, telv) griglia schermo

screen' test' *s* provino

screw [skru] *s* vite *f;* giro di vite; (*of a boat*) elica; **to have a screw loose** (slang) avere una rotella fuori di posto; **to put the screws on** far pressione su ‖ *tr* avvitare; (*to twist*)

torcere; **to screw up** (slang) rovinare; **to screw up one's courage** prendere il coraggio a quattro mani ‖ *intr* avvitarsi

screw'ball' *s* (slang) pazzoide *m,* svitato

screw'driv'er *s* cacciavite *m*

screw' eye' *s* occhiello a vite

screw' jack' *s* martinetto a vite

screw' propel'ler *s* elica

screw·y ['skru·i] *adj* (-ier; -iest) (slang) pazzo; (slang) fuori di posto, strano

scribble ['skrɪbəl] *s* scarabocchio ‖ *tr & intr* scarabocchiare

scribe [skraɪb] *s* (*Jewish scholar*) scriba *m;* copista *mf* ‖ *tr* tracciare, incidere

scrimmage ['skrɪmɪdʒ] *s* ruffa; (*football*) azione

scrimp [skrɪmp] *tr & intr* lesinare

script [skrɪpt] *s* scrittura, scrittura a mano; manoscritto; testo; (*e.g., of a play*) copione *m;* (typ) carattere *m* inglese

scriptural ['skrɪptʃərəl] *adj* scritturale, biblico

scripture ['skrɪptʃər] *s* scrittura ‖ **Scripture** *s* Scrittura

script'writ'er *s* soggettista *mf*

scrofula ['skrɑfjələ] *s* scrofola

scroll [skrol] *s* rotolo di carta, rotolo di pergamena; (*of violin*) riccio; (archit) voluta, cartoccio

scroll'work' *s* ornamentazione a voluta

scro·tum ['skrotəm] *s* (-ta [tə] or -tums) scroto

scrub [skrʌb] *s* boscaglia; alberelli *mpl;* animale bastardo; persona di poco conto; (*act of scrubbing*) fregata; (sports) giocatore *m* di riserva ‖ *v* (*pret & pp* **scrubbed;** *ger* **scrubbing**) *tr* pulire, fregare

scrub' oak' *s* rovere basso

scrub'wom'an *s* (-wom'en) lavatrice *f,* donna a giornata

scruff [skrʌf] *s* nuca, collottola

scruple ['skrupəl] *s* scrupolo

scrupulous ['skrupjələs] *adj* scrupoloso

scrutinize ['skrutɪ‚naɪz] *tr* scrutare, disaminare

scruti·ny ['skrutɪni] *s* (-nies) attento esame, disamina

scuff [skʌf] *s* graffio, logorio ‖ *tr* logorare, graffiare

scuffle ['skʌfəl] *s* zuffa, rissa ‖ *intr* azzuffarsi, colluttare

scull [skʌl] *s* (*oar*) remo a bratto; (*boat*) canotto ‖ *tr* spingere a bratto ‖ *intr* vogare a bratto

sculler·y ['skʌləri] *s* (-ies) retrocucina

scul'lery maid' *s* sguattera

scullion ['skʌljən] *s* sguattero

sculptor ['skʌlptər] *s* scultore *m*

sculptress ['skʌlptrɪs] *s* scultrice *f*

sculpture ['skʌlptʃər] *s* scultura ‖ *tr & intr* scolpire

scum [skʌm] *s* schiuma; (*slag*) scoria; (*rabble*) feccia, gentaglia ‖ *v* (*pret & pp* **scummed;** *ger* **scumming**) *tr & intr* schiumare

scum·my ['skʌmi] *adj* (-mier; -miest) spumoso; (coll) vile, schifoso

scurf [skʌrf] *s* (*shed by the skin*) squama; incrostazione

scurrilous ['skʌrɪləs] *adj* scurrile

scur·ry ['skʌri] *v* (*pret & pp* -ried) *intr* affrettarsi; **to scurry around** dimenarsi

scur·vy ['skʌrvi] *adj* (-vier; -viest) spregevole, meschino || *s* scorbuto

scuttle ['skʌtəl] *s* (*for coal*) secchio; (*trap door*) botola; corsa, fuga; (naut) boccaporto || *tr* aprire una falla in, affondare || *intr* affrettarsi, darsi alla corsa

scut'tle-butt' *s* (naut) barilozzo dell'acqua; (coll) rumore *m*, diceria

scuttling ['skʌtlɪŋ] *s* autoaffondamento

Scylla ['sɪlə] *s* Scilla; **between Scylla and Charybdis** fra Scilla e Cariddi

scythe [saɪð] *s* falce *f*

sea [si] *s* mare *m*; (*wave*) maroso; **at sea** in alto mare; **by the sea** a mare, sulla costa; **to follow the sea** farsi marinaio; **to put to sea** prendere il largo

sea'board' *adj* costiero || *s* litorale *m*

sea' breeze' *s* brezza marina

sea'coast' *s* costa, litorale *m*

sea' dog' *s* (*seal*) foca; (*sailor*) lupo di mare

seafarer ['si,ferər] *s* marinaio; viaggiatore marittimo

sea'food' *s* pesce *m*; (*shellfish*) frutti *mpl* di mare

seagoing ['si,go·ɪŋ] *adj* di alto mare

sea' gull' *s* gabbiano

seal [sil] *s* sigillo; (*sea animal*) foca; (fig) suggello || *tr* sigillare, apporre i sigilli a; (fig) suggellare

sea' legs' *spl*—**to have good sea legs** avere piede marino

sea' lev'el *s* livello del mare

seal'ing wax' *s* ceralacca

seal'skin' *s* pelle *f* di foca

seam [sim] *s* (*abutting of edges*) giuntura; (*stitches*) costura, cucitura; (*scar*) cicatrice *f*; (*wrinkle*) ruga; (in *metal*) commettitura; (min) filone *m*, vena

sea'man *s* (-men) marinaio

sea' mile' *s* miglio marino

seamless ['simlɪs] *adj* senza giuntura; (*stockings*) senza cucitura

seamstress ['simstrɪs] *s* cucitrice *f*

seam·y ['simi] *adj* (-ier; -iest) pieno di cuciture; basso, sordido; (*unpleasant*) spiacevole

séance ['se·ɑns] *s* seduta spiritica

sea'plane' *s* idrovolante *m*

sea'port' *s* porto di mare

sea' pow'er *s* potenza navale

sear [sɪr] *adj* secco || *s* scottatura || *tr* scottare, bruciare; (*to brand*) marcare a fuoco; inaridire; (fig) indurire

search [sʌrtʃ] *s* ricerca, investigazione; (*frisking a person*) perquisizione; **in search of** in cerca di || *tr* cercare, investigare; perquisire, frugare || *intr* investigare; **to search for** cercare; **to search into** investigare

searching ['sʌrtʃ/ɪŋ] *adj* (*e.g., inspec-*

tion) profondo; (*e.g., glance*) indagatore, penetrante

search'light' *s* proiettore *m*, riflettore *m*; (mil) fotoelettrica

search' war'rant *s* mandato di perquisizione

sea'scape' *s* vista del mare; (*painting*) marina

sea' shell' *s* conchiglia

sea'shore' *s* costa, marina, mare *m*

sea'sick' *adj*—**to be seasick** aver mal di mare

sea'sick'ness *s* mal *m* di mare

sea'side' *s* costa, riviera, marina

season ['sizən] *s* stagione; **in season** di stagione; **in season and out of season** sempre, continuamente; **out of season** fuori stagione || *tr* (*food*) condire; (*to mature*) stagionare; (*e.g., wood*) stagionare

seasonal ['sizənəl] *adj* stagionale

seasoning ['sizənɪŋ] *s* condimento; (*of wood*) stagionamento

sea'son's greet'ings *spl* migliori auguri *mpl* per le feste natalizie

sea'son tick'et *s* biglietto d'abbonamento

seat [sit] *s* sedia; (*part of chair*) sedile *m*; (*of human body*) sedere *m*; (*of pants*) fondo; sito, posto; (*e.g., of government*) sede *f*; (*in parliament*) seggio; (*e.g., of learning*) centro; (tr, theat) posto || *tr* far sedere; aver posti per; (*a chair*) mettere il sedile a; (*pants*) mettere il fondo a; (*an official*) insediare; (mach) installare; **to be seated** essere seduto; **to seat oneself** sedersi

seat' belt' *s* cintura di sicurezza

seat' cov'er *s* guaina, foderina

seat'ing room' *s* posti *mpl* a sedere

sea' wall' *s* diga

sea'way' *s* via marittima; alto mare; mare grosso; rotta percorsa; via di fiume accessibile a navi da trasporto

sea'weed' *s* alga marina; pianta marina

sea'wor'thy *adj* atto a tenere il mare

secede [sɪ'sid] *intr* separarsi, distaccarsi

secession [sɪ'sɛʃən] *s* secessione

seclude [sɪ'klud] *tr* appartare; isolare

seclusion [sɪ'kluʒən] *s* reclusione; solitudine *f*, intimità *f*

second ['sɛkənd] *adj & pron* secondo; **to be second to none** non cederla a nessuno || *s* secondo; (*in a duel*) padrino; (*in dates*) due *m*; (aut, mus) seconda; **seconds** (com) articoli *mpl* di seconda qualità; **to have seconds on** servirsi una seconda volta di || *tr* assecondare; (*a motion*) appoggiare || *adv* in secondo luogo

secondar·y ['sɛkən,dɛri] *adj* secondario || *s* (-ies) (elec) secondario

sec'ond-best' *adj* (il) migliore dopo il primo; **to come off second-best** arrivare secondo

sec'ond-class' *adj* di seconda qualità; (aer, naut, rr) di seconda classe

sec'ond hand' *s* lancetta dei secondi

sec'ond-hand' *adj* di seconda mano, d'occasione

sec'ond lieuten'ant s sottotenente m

sec'ond-rate' adj di seconda categoria; (inferior) da strapazzo

sec'ond sight' s chiaroveggenza

sec'ond wind' [wɪnd] s—**to get one's second wind** riprendere fiato

secre•cy ['sikrəsi] s (-cies) segretezza; **in secrecy** in segreto

secret ['sikrɪt] adj & s segreto; **in secret** in segreto

secretar•y ['sɛkrɪ,teri] s (-ies) segretario; (desk) scrittoio

se'cret bal'lot s scrutinio segreto

secrete [sɪ'krit] tr nascondere; (physiol) secernere

secretive ['sikrɪtɪv] or [sɪ'kritɪv] adj riservato, poco comunicativo

sect [sɛkt] s setta

sectarian [sɛk'tɛrɪ-ən] adj & s settario

section ['sɛktʃən] s sezione; (of city) rione m; (of fruit) spicchio; (of highway) tronco; (rr) tratta ‖ tr sezionare

sectional ['sɛkʃənəl] adj (e.g., bookcase) componibile; sezionale; locale, regionale

secular ['sɛkjələr] adj & s secolare m

secularism ['sɛkjələ,rɪzəm] s laicismo

secure [sɪ'kjur] adj salvo, sicuro ‖ tr ottenere; assicurare; fissare; (law) garantire

securi•ty [sɪ'kjurɪti] s (-ties) sicurezza; protezione; garanzia; (person) garante m; **securities** valori mpl, titoli mpl

sedan [sɪ'dæn] s (aut) berlina

sedan' chair' s bussola, portantina

sedate [sɪ'det] adj calmo, posato

sedation [sɪ'deʃən] s ritorno alla calma; stato di calma mentale

sedative ['sɛdətɪv] adj & s sedativo

sedentary ['sɛdən,teri] adj sedentario

sedge [sɛdʒ] s carice m

sediment ['sɛdɪmənt] s sedimento

sedition [sɪ'dɪʃən] s sedizione

seditious [sɪ'dɪʃəs] adj sedizioso

seduce [sɪ'djus] or [sɪ'dus] tr sedurre

seducer [sɪ'djusər] or [sɪ'dusər] s seduttore m, corruttore m

seduction [sɪ'dʌkʃən] s seduzione

seductive [sɪ'dʌktɪv] adj seduttore

sedulous ['sɛdʒələs] adj diligente

see [si] s (eccl) sede f ‖ v (pret saw [sɔ]; pp seen [sin]) tr vedere; **to see off** andare ad accompagnare; **to see through** portare a termine ‖ intr vedere; **see here!** faccia attenzione!; **to see after** prender cura di; **to see through** conoscere il gioco di

seed [sid] s seme m, semenza; **to go to seed** andare in semenza; deteriorarsi ‖ tr seminare; (fruit) togliere i semi da ‖ intr seminare; produrre semi

seed'bed' s semenzaio; (fig) vivaio

seeder ['sidər] s (person) seminatore m; (machine) seminatrice f

seedling ['sidlɪŋ] s piantina da trapianto

seed•y ['sidi] adj (-ier; -iest) pieno di semi; (unkempt) malmesso, malvestito

seeing ['si·ɪŋ] conj visto che, dato che

See'ing Eye' dog' s cane m guida per ciechi'

seek [sik] v (pret & pp sought [sɔt]) tr cercare, ricercare; **to be sought after** essere ricercato; **to seek to** cercare di

seem [sim] intr parere, sembrare

seemingly ['simɪŋli] adv apparentemente

seem•ly ['simli] adj (-lier; -liest) decoroso; appropriato

seep [sip] intr colare, filtrare

seer [sɪr] s profeta m, veggente m

see'saw' s altalena; (motion) viavai m ‖ intr altalenare

seethe [sið] intr bollire

segment ['sɛgmənt] s segmento

segregate ['sɛgrɪ,get] tr segregare

segregation [,sɛgrɪ'geʃən] s segregazione

segregationist [,sɛgrɪ'geʃənɪst] s segregazionista mf

Seine [sɛn] s Senna

seismograph ['saɪzmə,græf] or ['saɪzmə,grɑf] s sismografo

seismology [saɪz'mɑlədʒi] s sismologia

seize [siz] tr afferrare; impossessarsi di; (with one's clenched fist) impugnare; comprendere; (law) sequestrare, confiscare

seizure ['siʒər] s conquista, cattura; (of an illness) attacco; (law) sequestro, pignoramento

seldom ['sɛldəm] adj di raro, raramente

select [sɪ'lɛkt] adj scelto, selezionato ‖ tr prescegliere, selezionare

selectee [sɪ,lɛk'ti] s (mil) recluta

selection [sɪ'lɛkʃən] s selezione, scelta

selective [sɪ'lɛktɪv] adj selettivo

self [sɛlf] adj stesso ‖ s (selves [sɛlvz]) sé stesso; io, personalità f; **all by one's self** senza aiuto altrui ‖ pron sé stesso

self'-abuse' s abuso delle proprie forze; masturbazione

self'-addressed' adj col nome e l'indirizzo del mittente

self'-cen'tered adj egocentrico

self'-con'scious adj imbarazzato, vergognoso, timido

self'-control' s padronanza di sé stesso, autocontrollo

self'-defense' s autodifesa; **in self-defense** in legittima difesa

self'-deni'al s abnegazione

self'-deter'mina'tion s autodeterminazione

self'-dis'cipline s autodisciplina

self'-ed'ucat'ed adj autodidatta

self'-employed' adj che lavora in proprio

self'-ev'i•dent adj evidente, lampante

self'-ex•plan'a•tor'y adj ovvio, che si spiega da sé

self'-gov'ernment s autogoverno; controllo sopra sé stesso

self'-im•por'tant adj presuntuoso

self'-in•dul'gence s intemperanza

self'-in'terest s egoismo, interesse m

selfish ['sɛlfɪʃ] adj egoista

selfishness ['sɛlfɪʃnɪs] s egoismo

selfless ['sɛlflɪs] *adj* disinteressato; altruista

self'-liq'ul-dat'ing *adj* autoammortizzabile

self'-love' *s* amor proprio

self'-made' *adj* che si è fatto da sé

self'-por'trait *s* autoritratto

self'-pos-sessed' *adj* calmo, padrone di sé

self'-pres'er-va'tion *s* conservazione

self'-pro-pelled' *adj* semovente

self'-re-li'ant *adj* pieno di fiducia in sé stesso

self'-re-spect' *s* rispetto di sé stesso

self'-right'eous *adj* che si considera più morale degli altri, ipocrita

self'-sac'ri-fice' *s* sacrificio di sé, spirito di sacrificio

self'-same' *adj* stesso e medesimo

self'-sat'is-fied' *adj* contento di sé

self'-seek'ing *adj* egoista || *s* egoismo

self'-serv'ice *s* autoservizio

self'-start'er *s* motorino d'avviamento

self'-styled' *adj* sedicente

self'-support' *s* indipendenza economica

self'-tap'ping screw' *s* vite *f* autofilettante

self'-taught' *adj* autodidatta

self-threading ['sɛlf'θrɛdɪŋ] *adj* autofilettante

self'-willed' *adj* ostinato, caparbio

self'-wind'ing *adj* a carica automatica

sell [sɛl] *v* (*pret* & *pp* **sold** [sold]) *tr* vendere; (*an idea*) fare accettare; **to sell off** svendere, liquidare; **to sell out** smerciare; vendere a stralcio; (coll) tradire || *intr* vendere, vendersi; fare il venditore; **to sell off** (*said of the stock market*) essere in ribasso; **to sell out** vendere a stralcio; vendersi

seller ['sɛlər] *s* venditore *m*

Selt'zer wa'ter ['sɛltsər] *s* selz *m*

selvage ['sɛlvɪdʒ] *s* cimosa, vivagno

semantic [sɪ'mæntɪk] *adj* semantico || **semantics** *s* semantica

semaphore ['sɛmə,for] *s* semaforo

semblance ['sɛmbləns] *s* apparenza, specie *f*; apparizione

semen ['simɛn] *s* sperma *m*

semester [sɪ'mɛstər] *adj* semestrale || *s* semestre *m*

semicircle ['sɛmɪ,sʌrkəl] *s* semicircolo

semicolon ['sɛmɪ,kolən] *s* punto e virgola

semiconductor [,sɛmikən'dʌktər] *s* semiconduttore *m*

semiconscious [,sɛmi'kɑnʃəs] *adj* mezzo cosciente

semifinal [,sɛmi'faɪnəl] *s* semifinale *f*

semilearned [,sɛmi'lʌrnɪd] *adj* semidotto

semimonth-ly [,sɛmi'mʌnθli] or [,sɛmai'mʌnθli] *adj* quindicinale || *s* (-**lies**) rivista quindicinale

seminar ['sɛmɪ,nɑr] or [,sɛmɪ'nɑr] *s* seminario

seminar-y ['sɛmɪ,nɛri] *s* (-**ies**) seminario

Semite ['sɛmaɪt] or ['simaɪt] *s* semita *mf*

Semitic [sɪ'mɪtɪk] *adj* semitico || *s* lingua semitica; (*family of languages*) semitico

semitrailer ['sɛmɪ,trelər] *s* semirimorchio

semiweek-ly [,sɛmi'wikli] or [,sɛmai-'wikli] *adj* bisettimanale || *s* (-**lies**) periodico bisettimanale

semiyearly [,sɛmi'jɪrli] or [,sɛmai-'jɪrli] *adj* semestrale || *adv* due volte all'anno

senate ['sɛnɪt] *s* senato

senator ['sɛnətər] *s* senatore *m*

send [sɛnd] *v* (*pret* & *pp* **sent** [sɛnt]) *tr* inviare, mandare; spedire; (*e.g., a punch*) lanciare; **to send back** rimandare; **to send forth** emettere; **to send packing** licenziare su due piedi || *intr* (rad) trasmettere; **to send for** mandare a chiamare, far venire

sender ['sɛndər] *s* speditore *m*, mittente *m*; (telg) trasmettitore *m*

send'-off' *s* (coll) addio affettuoso; (coll) lancio

senility [sɪ'nɪlɪti] *s* (pathol) senilismo

senior ['sinjər] *adj* maggiore, più anziano; seniore, di grado più elevato; dell'ultimo anno, laureando; senior, il vecchio || *s* maggiore *m*; seniore *m*, persona di grado più elevato; studente *m* dell'ultimo anno, laureando

sen'ior cit'izen *s* vecchio, pensionato

seniority [sin'jɑrɪti] or [sin'jɔrɪti] *s* anzianità *f*

sensation [sɛn'seʃən] *s* sensazione

sensational [sɛn'seʃənəl] *adj* sensazionale

sense [sɛns] *s* senso; **in a sense** in un certo senso; **to come to one's senses** riprendere il giudizio; **to make sense out of** arrivare a capire; **to take leave of one's senses** perdere il ben dell'intelletto || *tr* intuire; comprendere

senseless ['sɛnslɪs] *adj* (*unconscious*) privo di sensi; (*meaningless*) insensato, privo di senso

sense' or'gan *s* organo di senso

sensibili-ty [,sɛnsɪ'bɪlɪti] *s* (-**ties**) sensibilità *f*; **sensibilities** suscettibilità *f*

sensible ['sɛnsɪbəl] *adj* sensato; (*keenly aware*) sensibile; cosciente

sensitive ['sɛnsɪtɪv] *adj* sensitivo, sensibile; delicato

sensitize ['sɛnsɪ,taɪz] *tr* sensibilizzare

sensory ['sɛnsəri] *adj* sensorio

sensual ['sɛnʃʊ-əl] *adj* sensuale

sensuous ['sɛnʃʊ-əs] *adj* sensuale

sentence ['sɛntəns] *s* (gram) frase; (law) sentenza, condanna || *tr* sentenziare, condannare

sentiment ['sɛntɪmənt] *s* sentimento

sentimental [,sɛntɪ'mɛntəl] *adj* sentimentale

sentimentalism [,sɛntɪ'mɛntəl,ɪzəm] *s* sentimentalismo

sentinel ['sɛntɪnəl] *s* sentinella; **to stand sentinel** montare di sentinella

sen-try ['sɛntri] *s* (-**tries**) sentinella

sen'try box' *s* garitta, casotto

separate ['sɛpərɪt] *adj* separato ||

['sepə ,ret] *tr* separare || *intr* separarsi

separation [,sepə're∫ən] *s* separazione

Sephardic [sı'fɑrdık] *adj* sefardita

September [sep'tembər] *s* settembre *m*

septic ['septık] *adj* settico

sep'tic tank' *s* fossa settica

sepulcher ['sepəlkər] *s* sepolcro

sequel ['sikwəl] *s* seguito

sequence ['sikwəns] *s* serie *f*, sequenza, successione; conseguenza; (cards, eccl, mov) sequenza; (gram) correlazione

sequester [sı'kwestər] *tr* isolare, appartare; (law) sequestrare

sequin ['sikwın] *s* lustrino

ser·aph ['serəf] *s* (**-aphs** or **-aphim** [əfım]) serafino

Serbian ['sʌrbı·ən] *adj & s* serbo

Serbo-Croatian [,sʌrbokro'e∫ən] *adj & s* serbocroato

sere [sır] *adj* secco, appassito

serenade [,serə'ned] *s* serenata || *tr* fare la serenata a || *intr* fare la serenata

serene [sı'rin] *adj* sereno

serenity [sı'renıti] *s* serenità *f*

serf [sʌrf] *s* servo della gleba

serfdom ['sʌrfdəm] *s* servitù *f* della gleba

serge [sʌrdʒ] *s* saia

sergeant ['sɑrdʒənt] *s* sergente *m*

ser'geant at arms' *s* (**ser'geants at arms'**) ufficiale *m* delegato a mantenerè l'ordine

ser'geant ma'jor *s* (**sergeants major** or **sergeant majors**) (in U.S. Army) sergente *m* maggiore; (in Italian Army) maresciallo

serial ['sırı·əl] *adj* a puntate, a dispense || *s* periodico; romanzo a puntate; programma *m* a serie

se'rial num'ber *s* matricola *f* (of a book) segnatura; (aut) matricola di telaio

se·ries ['sıriz] *s* (**-ries**) serie *f*; (works dealing with the same topic) collana; **in series** (elec) in serie

serious ['sırı·əs] *adj* serio

seriousness ['sırı·əsnıs] *s* serietà *f*; **in all seriousness** molto sul serio

sermon ['sʌrmən] *s* sermone *m*

sermonize ['sʌrmə ,naız] *tr & intr* sermonare

serpent ['sʌrpənt] *s* serpente *m*

se·rum ['sırəm] *s* (**-rums** or **-ra** [rə]) siero

servant ['sʌrvənt] *s* servo, domestico; (civil servant) funzionario; (fig) servitore *m*

serv'ant girl' *s* serva, domestica

serv'ant prob'lem *s* crisi *f* ancillare

serve [sʌrv] *s* (in tennis) servizio || *tr* servire; (a sentence) espiare; (to suffice) bastare (with dat); (a writ) notificare; **to serve s.o. right** stare bene (with dat), e.g., **it serves him right** gli sta bene || *intr* servire; **to serve as** fare da

service ['sʌrvıs] *s* servizio; (of a writ) notifica; (branch of the armed forces) arma; **at your service** per servirLa || *tr* rifornire, riparare

serviceable ['sʌrvısəbəl] *adj* utile; durevole; pratico; riparabile

serv'ice club' *s* casa del soldato

serv'ice·man' *s* (**-men'**) militare *m;* riparatore *m*, aggiustatore *m*

serv'ice mod'ule *s* modulo di servizio

serv'ice rec'ord *s* stato di servizio

serv'ice sta'tion *s* stazione di servizio or di rifornimento

serv'ice-sta'tion attend'ant *s* benzinaio

serv'ice stripe' *s* gallone *m*

servile ['sʌrvıl] *adj* servile

servitude ['sʌrvı ,tjud] or ['sʌrvı ,tud] *s* servitù *f*; lavori forzati

sesame ['sesəmi] *s* sesamo; **open sesame** apriti sesamo

session ['se∫ən] *s* sessione *f*, seduta

set [set] *adj* determinato, preordinato; abituale; fisso, rigido; (ready) pronto; meditato, studiato || *s* (e.g., of books) collezione, serie *f*; (e.g., of chess) gioco; set *m*, insieme *m*, completo; (of tires) treno; (of horses) pariglia; (of tennis) partita; (of dishes) servizio; (of kitchen utensils) batteria; posizione, atteggiamento; (of a garment) linea; (e.g., of cement) presa; (of people) gruppo; (of thieves) genia; (of sails) muta; (of lines) (geom) fascio; (rad, telv) apparato; (theat, mov) set *m* || *v* (pret & pp set; ger setting) *tr* porre, deporre; mettere; (fire) dare; (the table) imbandire; (a watch) regolare; (s.o. a certain number of tricks) far cadere di; (a price) fissare; (a gem) incastonare; (a fracture) mettere a posto; (a saw) allicciare; (a trap) tendere; (hair) acconciare; stabilire; insediare; (to plant) piantare; (a sail) tendere; (e.g., milk) rapprendere; calibrare, tarare; (cement) solidificare; (typ) comporre; **to set back** ritardare; (a clock) mettere indietro; **to set forth** descrivere; **to set one's heart on** desiderare ardentemente; **to set store by** tenere in gran conto; **to set up** metter su; impiantare; (drinks) (slang) pagare || *intr* (said, e.g., of the sun) tramontare; (said of a liquid) solidificarsi; (said of cement) fare presa; (said of milk) rapprendersi; (said of a hen) covare; (said of a garment) cascare; (said of hair) prendere la piega; **to set about** mettersi a; **to set out** porsi in cammino; **to set out to** mettersi a; **to set to work** mettersi a lavorare; **to set upon** attaccare

set'back' *s* rovescio, contrarietà *f*

set'screw' *s* vite *f* di pressione

setting ['setıŋ] *s* (environment) ambiente *m;* (of a gem) montatura; (of cement) presa; (e.g., of the sun) tramonto; (theat) scenario; (mus) arrangiamento

set'ting-up' ex'ercises *spl* ginnastica da camera

settle ['setəl] *tr* determinare, risolvere; sistemare, regolare; (a bill) saldare; installarsi in, colonizzare; calmare; (a liquid) far depositare; (law) conciliare ‖ *intr* mettersi d'accordo; saldare un conto; stanziarsi, domiciliarsi; fermarsi, posare; (*said of a liquid*) depositare, calmarsi; solidificarsi; **to settle down to work** mettersi a lavorare di buzzo buono; **to settle on** scegliere, fissare

settlement ['sɛtəlmənt] *s* stabilimento; sistemazione, regolamento; colonia, comunità *f;* (*of a building*) infossamento; agenzia di beneficenza

settler ['sɛtlər] *s* fondatore *m;* colono; conciliatore *m*

set'up' *s* portamento; (*e.g., of tools*) disposizione; quanto è necessario per mescolare una bibita alcolica; (coll) incontro truccato

seven ['sɛvən] *adj & pron* sette ‖ *s* sette *m;* **seven o'clock** le sette

sev'en hun'dred *adj, s & pron* settecento

seventeen ['sɛvən'tin] *adj, s & pron* diciassette *m*

seventeenth ['sɛvən'tinθ] *adj, s & pron* diciassettesimo ‖ *s* (*in dates*) diciassette *m*

seventh ['sɛvənθ] *adj, s & pron* settimo ‖ *s* (*in dates*) sette *m*

seventieth ['sɛvəntɪ·ɪθ] *adj, s & pron* settantesimo

seven·ty ['sɛvəntɪ] *adj & pron* settanta ‖ *s* (**-ties**) settanta *m;* **the seventies** gli anni settanta

sever ['sɛvər] *tr* tagliare, mozzare; (*relations*) troncare ‖ *intr* separarsi

several ['sɛvərəl] *adj* parecchi, vari; rispettivi ‖ *spl* parecchi *mpl*

sev'erance pay' ['sɛvərəns] *s* buonuscita, indennità *f* di licenziamento

severe [sɪ'vɪr] *adj* severo; (*weather*) rigido; (*pain*) acuto; (*illness*) grave

sew [so] *v* (*pret* **sewed**; *pp* **sewed** or **sewn**) *tr & intr* cucire

sewage ['su·ɪdʒ] or ['sju·ɪdʒ] *s* acque *fpl* di scolo o di rifiuto

sewer ['su·ər] or ['sju·ər] *s* fogna, chiavica

sewerage ['su·ərɪdʒ] or ['sju·ərɪdʒ] *s* fognatura; drenaggio, rimozione delle acque di rifiuto

sew'ing machine' ['so·ɪŋ] *s* macchina da cucire

sex [sɛks] *s* sesso

sex' appeal' *s* attrattiva fisica, sex appeal *m*

sextant ['sɛkstənt] *s* sestante *m*

sextet [sɛks'tɛt] *s* sestetto

sexton ['sɛkstən] *s* sagrestano

sexual ['sɛk/ʊ·əl] *adj* sessuale

sex·y ['sɛksɪ] *adj* (**-ier; -iest**) (coll) erotico; (coll) procace

shab·by ['/æbɪ] *adj* (**-bier; -biest**) (*clothes*) frusto; (*house*) malandato; (*person*) malvestito; (*deal*) cattivo

shack [/æk] *s* baracca

shackle ['/ækəl] *s* ceppo; (*to tie an animal*) pastoia; (fig) ostacolo; **shackles** ceppi *mpl*, manette *fpl* ‖ *tr* mettere in ceppi; (fig) inceppare

shad [/æd] *s* alosa

shade [/ed] *s* ombra; (*of lamp*) paralume *m;* (*of window*) tendina; (*for*

the eyes) visiera; (*hue*) tinta, sfumatura; **a shade of** un po' di; **shades** tenebre *fpl;* ombre *fpl* ‖ *tr* ombreggiare; sfumare, digradare; (*a price*) ribassare leggermente

shadow ['/ædo] *s* ombra ‖ *tr* ombreggiare; (*to follow*) pedinare; **to shadow forth** adombrare, preannunciare

shadowy ['/ædo·ɪ] *adj* ombroso, ombreggiato; illusorio, chimerico

shad·y ['/edɪ] *adj* (**-ier; -iest**) ombroso; spettrale; (coll) losco; **to keep shady** (slang) starsene lontano

shaft [/æft] or [/ɑft] *s* (*of arrow*) asta; (*of feather*) rachide *f;* (*of light*) raggio; (*handle*) manico; (*of wagon*) stanga, timone *m;* (*of motor*) albero; (*of column*) fusto; (*of elevator*) pozzo; (*in a mountain*) camino; (min) fornello; (fig) frecciata

shag·gy ['/ægɪ] *adj* (**-gier; -giest**) peloso, irsuto; (*unkempt*) trasandato; (*cloth*) ruvido

shag'gy dog' sto'ry *s* storiella senza capo né coda

shake [/ek] *s* scossa; stretta di mano; momento, istante *m;* **the shakes** la tremarella ‖ *v* (*pret* **shook** [/ʊk]; *pp* **shaken**) *tr* scuotere; scrollare; (*s.o.'s hands*) serrare; (*e.g., with a mixer*) sbattere; agitare, perturbare; eludere, disfarsi di ‖ *intr* tremare; (*to totter*) traballare, tentennare; scuotere; darsi la mano

shake'down' *s* estorsione, concussione; (*bed*) lettuccio di fortuna

shake'down' cruise' *s* (naut) viaggio di prova

shaker ['/ekər] *s* (*e.g., for sugar*) spolverino; (*for cocktails*) sbattighiaccio, shaker *m*

shake'-up' *s* cambiamento completo, riorganizzazione, rimaneggiamento

shak·y ['/ekɪ] *adj* (**-ier; -iest**) tremebondo; traballante, zoppicante

shall [/æl] *v* (*cond* **should** [/ʊd]) *v aux* si usa per formare (1) il futuro dell'indicativo, per es., **I shall do it** lo farò; (2) il futuro perfetto dell'indicativo, per es., **I shall have done it** l'avrò fatto; (3) espressioni di obbligo o necessità, per es., **what shall I do?** che devo fare?, che vuole che faccia?

shallow ['/ælo] *adj* basso, poco profondo; leggero, superficiale

sham [/æm] *adj* falso, finto ‖ *s* frode *f*, contraffazione ‖ *v* (*pret & pp* **shammed**; *ger* **shamming**) *tr & intr* fingere

sham' bat'tle *s* finta battaglia

shambles ['/æmbəlz] *s* macello; confusione, disordine

shame [/em] *s* vergogna; **shame on you!** vergogna!; **what a shame!** che peccato! ‖ *tr* svergognare, disonorare

shame'faced' *adj* timido, vergognoso

shameful ['/emfəl] *adj* vergognoso

shameless ['/emlɪs] *adj* sfrontato, impudente, svergognato

shampoo [ʃæm'pu] *s* shampoo *m* ‖ *tr* fare lo shampoo a

shamrock ['ʃæmrɑk] *s* trifoglio irlandese

shanghai ['ʃæŋhaɪ] *or* [ʃæŋ'haɪ] *tr* imbarcare a viva forza ‖ **Shanghai** *s* Sciangai *f*

shank [ʃæŋk] *s* fusto; (*of tool*) codolo; (*stem*) gambo; (*of bird*) zampa; (*of anchor*) fuso; (*coll*) principio; (*coll*) fine *f*; **to ride shank's mare** andare col cavallo di San Francesco

shan·ty ['ʃænti] *s* (**-ties**) bicocca

shan'ty·town' *s* bidonville *f*

shape [ʃep] *s* forma; **in bad shape** in cattive condizioni; **out of shape** sformato ‖ *tr* formare, foggiare; plasmare, conformare ‖ *intr* formarsi; **to take shape** prender forma

shapeless ['ʃeplɪs] *adj* informe

shape·ly ['ʃepli] *adj* (**-lier; -liest**) ben fatto, formoso

share [ʃɛr] *s* parte *f*; interesse *m*; (*of stock*) azione *f*; (*of plow*) suola; **to go shares** dividere in parti eguali ‖ *tr* (*to enjoy jointly*) condividere; (*to apportion*) ripartire ‖ *intr* partecipare, prender parte

sharecropper ['ʃɛr ˌkrɑpər] *s* mezzadro

share'hold'er *s* azionista *mf*

shark [ʃɑrk] *s* pescecane *m*; (*schemer*) piovra; (*slang*) esperto

sharp [ʃɑrp] *adj* affilato, acuto; angoloso; (*e.g., curve*) forte; distinto, ben delineato; (*taste*) pungente, salato; (*pain*) vivo; (*words*) mordace; (*slang*) elegante ‖ *s* (*mus*) diesis *m* ‖ *adv* acutamente; in punto, e.g., **at seven o'clock sharp** alle sette in punto

sharpen ['ʃɑrpən] *tr* affilare; (*a pencil*) fare la punta a ‖ *intr* affilarsi

sharpener ['ʃɑrpənər] *s* (*person*) affilatore *m*; (*machine*) affilatrice *f*

sharper ['ʃɑrpər] *s* gabbamondo

sharp'shoot'er *s* tiratore scelto

shatter ['ʃætər] *tr* frantumare; sfracellare; (*health*) rovinare; (*nerves*) sconvolgere; distruggere ‖ *intr* frantumarsi, andare in pezzi

shat'ter·proof' *adj* infrangibile

shave [ʃev] *s* rasatura; **to have a close shave** scapparla *or* scamparla bella ‖ *tr* (*the face*) radere, sbarbare; (*wood*) piallare; (*to scrape*) sfiorare; (*prices*) ridurre; (*a lawn*) tosare ‖ *intr* rasarsi

shaving ['ʃevɪŋ] *adj* da barba, per barba, e.g., **shaving cream** crema da or per barba ‖ *s* rasatura; **shavings** trucioli *mpl*

shav'ing brush' *s* pennello da barba

shav'ing soap' *s* sapone *m* per la barba

shawl [ʃɔl] *s* scialle *m*

she [ʃi] *s* (**shes**) femmina ‖ *pron pers* (**they**) essa, lei

sheaf [ʃif] *s* (**sheaves** [ʃivz]) covone *m*; (*of paper*) fascio

shear [ʃɪr] *s* lama di cesoia; tagliatura; **shears** cesoie *fpl* ‖ *v* (*pret* **sheared**; *pp* **sheared** *or* **shorn** [ʃɔrn]) *tr* (*sheep*) tosare; (*cloth*) tagliare; **to shear s.o. of** privare qlcu di

sheath [ʃiθ] *s* (**sheaths** [ʃiðz]) guaina, coperta; (*of a sword*) fodero

sheathe [ʃið] *tr* rinfoderare, inguainare

shed [ʃɛd] *s* portico, tettoia; (geog) spartiacque *m*, versante *m* ‖ *v* (*pret & pp* **shed;** *ger* **shedding**) *tr* (*e.g., blood*) spargere, versare; (*light*) dare, fare; (*feathers*) spogliarsi di, lasciar cadere

sheen [ʃin] *s* lucentezza

sheep [ʃip] *s* (**sheep**) pecora; **sheep's eyes** occhio di triglia; **to separate the sheep from the goats** separare i buoni dai cattivi

sheep'dog' *s* cane *m* da pastore

sheepish ['ʃipɪʃ] *adj* timido, goffo; pecoresco, pedissequo

sheep'skin' *s* pelle *f* di pecora; (*parchment*) cartapecora; (bb) bazzana; (coll) diploma *m*

sheer [ʃɪr] *adj* trasparente, fino, velato; puro; (*cliff*) stagliato ‖ *adv* completamente ‖ *intr* deviare

sheet [ʃit] *s* (*for bed*) lenzuolo; (*of paper*) foglio; (*of metal*) lamina; (*of water*) specchio; (naut) scotta

sheet' light'ning *s* lampeggio all'orizzonte

sheet' met'al *s* lamiera

sheet' mu'sic *s* spartito non rilegato

sheik [ʃik] *s* sceicco; (*great lover*) (slang) rubacuori *m*

shelf [ʃɛlf] *s* (**shelves** [ʃɛlvz]) scaffale *m*, scansia; (*ledge*) terrazzo, ripiano; banco di sabbia; **on the shelf** in disparte, dimenticato

shell [ʃɛl] *s* (*of egg or crustacean*) guscio; (*of mollusk*) conchiglia; (*of vegetable*) baccello; proietto, proiettile *m*; (*cartridge*) cartuccia; (*of a cartridge*) bossolo; (*framework*) armatura; (*of boiler*) involucro; imbarcazione da regata, schifo, iole *f* ‖ *tr* (*vegetables*) sgranare; bombardare, cannoneggiare; **to shell out** (slang) tirar fuori

shel·lac [ʃə'læk] *s* gomma lacca ‖ *v* (*pret & pp* **-lacked;** *ger* **-lacking**) *tr* verniciare con gomma lacca; (slang) dare una batosta a

shell'fish' *ssg* (**-fish**) frutto di mare; crostaceo; *spl* frutti *mpl* di mare; crostacei *mpl*

shell' hole' *s* cratere *m*

shell' shock' *s* psicosi traumatica bellica

shelter ['ʃɛltər] *s* rifugio, ricovero; **to take shelter** rifugiarsi ‖ *tr* raccogliere, ospitare, dare rifugio a

shelve [ʃɛlv] *tr* mettere sullo scaffale; (*a bill*) insabbiare; mettere a riposo

shepherd ['ʃɛpərd] *s* pastore *m* ‖ *tr* guardare, curarsi di

shep'herd dog' *s* cane *m* da pastore

shepherdess ['ʃɛpərdɪs] *s* pastora

sherbet ['ʃʌrbət] *s* sorbetto

sheriff ['ʃɛrɪf] *s* sceriffo

sher·ry ['ʃɛri] *s* (**-ries**) xeres *m*

shield [ʃild] *s* scudo; (*for armpit*) sottoascella *m*; (*badge*) scudetto; (elec) schermo ‖ *tr* proteggere; (elec) schermare

shift [ʃɪft] *s* cambio, cambiamento;

(period of work) turno; **(group of workmen)** operai *mpl* di turno, squadra di lavoro; espediente *m*, sotterfugio || *tr* cambiare; spostare; **(blame)** riversare; || *intr* cambiare; spostarsi; fare da sé; vivere di espedienti; **(rr)** manovrare; **(aut)** cambiare marcia

shift' key' *s* tasto maiuscole

shift·less ['∫ɪftlɪs] *adj* pigro, ozioso

shift·y ['∫ɪftɪ] *adj* (-ier; -iest) astuto; evasivo; pieno d'espedienti; **(glance)** sfuggente

shilling ['∫ɪlɪŋ] *s* scellino

shimmer ['∫ɪmər] *s* luccichio || *intr* luccicare, mandare bagliori

shim·my ['∫ɪmi] *s* (-mies) **(dance)** shimmy *m*; **(aut)** farfallamento delle ruote, shimmy *m* || *intr* ballare lo shimmy; vibrare

shin [∫ɪn] *s* stinco; **(of cattle)** cannone *m* || *v* (pret & pp **shinned**; ger **shinning**) *tr* arrampicarsi su || *intr* arrampicarsi

shin'bone' *s* stinco, tibia

shine [∫aɪn] *s* splendore *m*; luce *f*; bel tempo; lucidatura, lucido; **to take a shine to** **(coll)** prender simpatia per || *v* (pret & pp **shined**) *tr* pulire, lucidare || *v* (pret & pp **shone** [∫on]) *tr* **(e.g., a flashlight)** dirigere i raggi di || *intr* brillare, luccicare, risplendere; **(to excel)** essere brillante, eccellere

shiner ['∫aɪnər] *s* **(slang)** occhio pesto

shingle ['∫ɪŋgəl] *s* assicella di copertura; **(to cover a wall)** mattoncino di rivestimento; **(Brit)** greto ciottoloso; **(coll)** capelli *mpl* alla bebé; **shingles** **(pathol)** erpete *m*, zona; **to hang out one's shingle** **(coll)** aprire un ufficio professionale || *tr* coprire di assicelle o mattoncini; **(hair)** tagliare alla bebé

shining ['∫aɪnɪŋ] *adj* brillante, lucente

shin·y ['∫aɪni] *adj* (-ier; -iest) lucente, lucido; **(paper)** patinato

ship [∫ɪp] *s* nave *f*, bastimento; aeronave *f*; aeroplano; **(crew)** equipaggio || *v* (pret & pp **shipped**; ger **shipping**) *tr* imbarcare; mandare, spedire; **(oars)** disarmare; **(water)** imbarcare || *intr* imbarcarsi

ship'board'—on shipboard a bordo

ship'build'er *s* costruttore *m* navale

ship'build'ing *s* architettura navale

ship'mate' *s* compagno di bordo

shipment ['∫ɪpmənt] *s* invio, spedizione

ship'own'er *s* armatore *m*

shipper ['∫ɪpər] *s* speditore *m*, spedizioniere *m*, mittente *m*

shipping ['∫ɪpɪŋ] *s* imbarco; spedizione; **(naut)** trasporto marittimo

ship'ping clerk' *s* speditore *m*

ship'ping room' *s* ufficio impaccatura

ship'shape' *adj & adv* in perfette condizioni

ship'side' *s* molo

ship's' pa'pers *spl* documenti *mpl* di bordo

ship'wreck' *s* naufragio; **(remains)** relitto || *tr* far naufragare || *intr* naufragare

ship'yard' *s* cantiere *m* navale

shirk [∫ʌrk] *tr* **(work)** evitare; **(responsibility)** sottrarsi a || *intr* imboscarsi

shirt [∫ʌrt] *s* camicia; **to keep one's shirt on** **(slang)** non perdere la calma; **to lose one's shirt** **(slang)** perdere la camicia

shirt' front' *s* sparato

shirt' sleeve' *s* manica di camicia

shirt'tail' *s* falda della camicia

shirt'waist' *s* blusa da donna

shiver ['∫ɪvər] *s* brivido || *intr* rabbrividire, battere i denti

shoal [∫ol] *s* secca, banco di sabbia

shock [∫ɑk] *s* urto, collisione; scossa; scossa elettrica; **(pathol)** shock *m* || *tr* scuotere; **(to strike against)** urtare; scandalizzare, indignare; dare la scossa elettrica a; **(fig)** scioccare

shock' absorb'er [æb'sɔrbər] *s* ammortizzatore *m* di colpi

shocking ['∫ɑkɪŋ] *adj* disgustoso, scandalizzante

shock' ther'apy *s* terapia d'urto

shock' troops' *spl* truppe *fpl* d'assalto

shod·dy ['∫ɑdi] *adj* (-dier; -diest) scadente, falso

shoe [∫u] *s* scarpa; **(horseshoe)** ferro da cavallo; **(of a tire)** copertone *m*; **(of brake)** ganascia, ceppo || *v* (pret & pp **shod** [∫ɑd]) *tr* calzare; **(a horse)** ferrare

shoe'black' *s* lustrascarpe *m*

shoe'horn' *s* corno da scarpe, calzatoio

shoe'lace' *s* laccio delle scarpe

shoe'mak'er *s* calzolaio

shoe' pol'ish *s* crema or cera da scarpe

shoe'shine' *s* lucidatura, lustramento di scarpe

shoe' store' *s* calzoleria

shoe'string' *s* laccio delle scarpe; **on a shoestring** con quattro soldi

shoe'tree' *s* tendiscarpe *m*

shoo [∫u] *intr* fare sció a || *intr* fare sció

shoot [∫ut] *s* **(e.g., with a firearm)** tiro; gara di tiro; **(chute)** scivolo; **(rok)** lancio; **(bot)** getto, virgulto || *v* (pret & pp **shot** [∫ɑt]) *tr* **(any missile)** tirare; **(a bullet)** sparare; **(to execute with a bullet)** fucilare; **(to fling)** lanciare; **(the sun)** prendere l'altezza di; **(dice)** gettare; **(mov, telv)** girare, riprendere; **to shoot down** **(a plane)** abbattere; **to shoot up** **(coll)** terrorizzare sparando a casaccio || *intr* tirare, sparare; passare rapidamente; nascere; **(said of pain)** dare fitte; **(mov)** cinematografare; **to shoot at** tirare a; **(coll)** cercar di ottenere

shoot'ing gal'lery *s* tiro a segno

shoot'ing match' *s* gara di tiro a segno; **(slang)** tutto, ogni cosa

shoot'ing star' *s* stella cadente

shop [∫ɑp] *s* **(store)** negozio, rivendita; **(workshop)** officina; **to talk shop** parlare del proprio lavoro || *v* (pret & pp **shopped**; ger **shopping**) *intr* fare la spesa; **to go shopping** andare a fare la spesa; **to shop around** cercare un'occasione di negozio in negozio

shop'girl' *s* venditrice *f*

shop'keep'er *s* negoziante *mf*
shoplifter ['ʃap‚lɪftər] *s* taccheggiatore *m*
shopper ['ʃapər] *s* compratore *m*
shopping ['ʃapɪŋ] *s* compra; (*purchases*) compre *fpl*, shopping *m*
shop'ping bag' *s* sporta, shopping *m*
shop'ping cen'ter *s* centro d'acquisto, ipermercato
shop'ping dis'trict *s* zona commerciale
shop'win'dow *s* vetrina
shop'worn' *adj* sciupato, usato
shore [ʃor] *s* costa, riva; spiaggia, lido; (fig) regione; (*support*) sostegno, puntello ‖ *tr* puntellare
shore' din'ner *s* pranzo di pesce
shore' leave' *s* (naut) franchigia
shore'line' *s* frangia costiera
shore' patrol' *s* polizia della marina
short [ʃort] *adj* (*in stature*) piccolo, basso; (*in space, time*) breve; (*scanty*) scarso; succinto; (*in quantity*) poco, piccolo; (*rude*) brusco; **in a short time** in breve; **in short** per farla breve; **on short notice** senza preavviso; **short of breath** corto di fiato; **to be short of** scarseggiare di ‖ *s* (elec) cortocircuito; (mov) cortometraggio; **shorts** (*underwear*) mutande *fpl*; (*sports attire*) calzoncini *mpl*, shorts *mpl* ‖ *adv* brevemente; bruscamente; (com) allo scoperto, e.g., **to sell short** vendere allo scoperto; **to run short of** essere a corto di; **to stop short** fermarsi di colpo ‖ *tr* (elec) causare un cortocircuito in ‖ *intr* (elec) andare in cortocircuito
shortage ['ʃortɪdʒ] *s* mancanza; (*of food*) carestia; (*from pilfering*) ammanco
short'cake' *s* torta di pasta frolla; torta ricoperta di frutta fresca
short'-change' *tr* non dare il cambio giusto a; (coll) imbrogliare
short'cir'cuit *s* (elec) cortocircuito
short'-cir'cuit *tr* mandare in cortocircuito; (coll) rovinare ‖ *intr* andare in cortocircuito
short'com'ing *s* difetto, manchevolezza
short'cut' *s* scorciatoia
shorten ['ʃortən] *tr* raccorciare, abbreviare ‖ *intr* raccorciarsi, abbreviarsi
shortening ['ʃortənɪŋ] *s* raccorciamento; (culin) grasso, strutto
short'hand' *adj* stenografico ‖ *s* stenografia; **to take shorthand** stenografare
short'hand' typ'ist *s* stenodattilografo
short-lived ['ʃort'laɪvd] or ['ʃort'lɪvd] *adj* effimero, di breve vita
shortly ['ʃortli] *adv* in breve, brevemente; fra poco; bruscamente; **shortly after** poco dopo
short'-range' *adj* di corta portata
short' sale' *s* vendita allo scoperto
short-sighted ['ʃort'saɪtɪd] *adj* miope; (fig) miope
short'stop' *s* (baseball) interbase *m*
short' sto'ry *s* novella
short-tempered ['ʃort'tempərd] *adj* irascibile
short'-term' *adj* a breve scadenza

short'wave' *adj* alle onde corte ‖ *s* onda corta
short' weight' *s*—**to give short weight** rubare sul peso
shot [ʃat] *s* tiro, sparo; (*cartridge*) cartuccia; (*for cannon*) palla; (*pellets of lead*) pallini *mpl*; (*person*) tiratore *m*; (*hypodermic injection*) iniezione; (*of liquor*) bicchierino; (phot) istantanea; (sports) peso; (mov) inquadratura; **not by a long shot** nemmeno a pensarci; **to start like a shot** partire come una palla da cannone; **to take a shot at** tirare un colpo a; (*to attempt to*) provarsi a
shot'gun' *s* schioppo, fucile *m* da caccia
shot' put' *s* lancio del peso
should [ʃʊd] *v aux* si usa nelle seguenti situazioni: 1) per formare il condizionale presente, per es., **if I should wait for him, I should miss the train** se lo aspettassi, perderei il treno; 2) per formare il perfetto del condizionale, per es., **if I had waited for him, I should have missed the train** se lo avessi aspettato, avrei perso il treno; 3) per indicare la necessità di un'azione, per es., **he should go at once** dovrebbe andare immediatamente; **he should have gone immediately** sarebbe dovuto andare immediatamente
shoulder ['ʃoldər] *s* spalla; (*of highway*) banchina; **across the shoulder** a bandoliera; **to put one's shoulders to the wheel** mettersi a lavorare di buzzo buono; **to turn a cold shoulder to** volgere le spalle a ‖ *tr* portare sulle spalle; (*a responsibility*) addossarsi; spingere con le spalle
shoul'der blade' *s* scapola
shoul'der strap' *s* spallina; (mil) tracolla
shout [ʃaʊt] *s* urlo, grido ‖ *tr* urlare, gridare; **to shout down** far tacere a forza di strilli ‖ *intr* gridare
shove [ʃʌv] *s* spintone *m* ‖ *tr* spingere ‖ *intr* spingere, dare spintoni; **to shove off** allontanarsi dalla riva; (slang) andarsene
shov-el ['ʃʌvəl] *s* pala ‖ *v* (*pret & pp* -eled or -elled; *ger* -eling or -elling) *tr* spalare ‖ *intr* lavorare di pala
show [ʃo] *s* mostra; apparenza; traccia; ostentazione; (mov, telv, theat) spettacolo; **to make a show of** dar spettacolo di; **to steal the show from** ricevere tutti gli applausi invece di ‖ *tr* mostrare, esporre; (*a movie*) presentare; dimostrare, insegnare; provare; (*to register*) segnare; (*one's feelings*) manifestare; (*to the door*) accompagnare; **to show in** fare entrare; **to show off** mettere in mostra ‖ *intr* mostrarsi; presentarsi, apparire; (*said of a horse*) (sports) arrivare terzo, piazzarsi; **to show off** mettersi in mostra; **to show up** (coll) mostrarsi; (coll) farsi vedere
show' bill' *s* cartellone *m*
show'boat' *s* battello per spettacoli teatrali

show' busi'ness s industria dello spettacolo

show'case' s bacheca, vetrina

show'down' s carte scoperte; chiarificazione

shower ['ʃauˑər] s (of rain) acquazzone m; (shower bath) doccia; (e.g., for a bride) ricevimento cui i partecipanti devono portare un regalo; (fig) pioggia || tr inaffiare; **to shower with** colmare di || intr diluviare; fare la doccia

show'er bath' s doccia

show' girl' s ballerina, girl f

show'man s (-men) impresario teatrale; persona che ha molta scena

show'-off' s reclamista m, strombazzatore m

show'piece' s capolavoro, oggetto d'arte

show'place' s luogo celebre; **to be a showplace** (said, e.g., of a house) essere arredato perfettamente

show'room' s sala di mostra

show' win'dow s vetrina

show·y ['ʃoˑi] adj (-ier; -iest) vistoso, sgargiante

shrapnel ['ʃræpnəl] s shrapnel m

shred [ʃrɛd] s brano, brandello; ritaglio; (fig) granello; **to cut to shreds** fare a brandelli || v (pret & pp **shredded** or **shred;** ger **shredding**) tr fare a brandelli; (paper) tagliuzzare

shrew [ʃru] s (woman) bisbetica; (animal) toporagno

shrewd [ʃrud] adj astuto, scaltro

shriek [ʃrik] s strido; strillo; risata stridula || intr stridere; strillare

shrill [ʃrɪl] adj stridulo, squillante

shrimp [ʃrɪmp] s gamberetto; (person) omiciattolo, nanerottolo

shrine [ʃraɪn] s santuario, sacrario

shrink [ʃrɪŋk] v (pret **shrank** [ʃræŋk] or **shrunk** [ʃrʌŋk]; pp **shrunk** or **shrunken**) tr contrarre, restringere || intr contrarsi, restringersi; ritirarsi

shrinkage ['ʃrɪŋkɪdʒ] s restringimento; (in weight) calo

shriv·el ['ʃrɪvəl] v (pret & pp -eled or -elled; ger -eling or -elling) tr raggrinzire; (from heat) raccartocciare; (to wither) avvizzire || intr raggrinzirsi; accartocciarsi; avvizzire; **to shrivel up** incartapecorire

shroud [ʃraud] s sudario, lenzuolo funebre; (fig) cappa || tr avvolgere

Shrove' Tues'day [ʃrov] s martedì grasso

shrub [ʃrʌb] s arbusto

shrubber·y ['ʃrʌbəri] s (-ies) arbusti mpl, cespugli mpl

shrug [ʃrʌg] s scrollata di spalle || v (pret & pp **shrugged;** ger **shrugging**) tr scrollare; **to shrug one's shoulders** scrollare le spalle || intr fare spallucce

shudder ['ʃʌdər] s brivido, fremito || intr rabbrividire, fremere

shuffle ['ʃʌfəl] s (of cards) mescolata; turno di fare il mazzo; (of feet) strascichio; evasione || tr mescolare; strisciare, strascicare || intr fare il

mazzo; scalpicciare; ballare di striscio; **to shuffle off** strascicarsi, scalpicciare; **to shuffle out of** evadere da

shun [ʃʌn] v (pret & pp **shunned;** ger **shunning**) tr evitare, schivare

shunt [ʃʌnt] tr sviare; (elec) shuntare; (rr) deviare

shut [ʃʌt] adj chiuso || v (pret & pp **shut;** ger **shutting**) tr chiudere, serrare; **to shut in** rinchiudere; **to shut off** (e.g., gas) tagliare; **to shut up** tappare; imprigionare; (coll) fare star zitto || intr chiudersi; **to shut up** (coll) stare zitto, tacere

shut'down' s chiusura

shutter ['ʃʌtər] s (outside a window) persiana, gelosia; (outside a store window) serranda, saracinesca; (phot) otturatore m

shuttle ['ʃʌtəl] s spola, navetta || intr fare la spola

shut'tle-cock' s volano, volante m

shut'tle train' s treno che fa la spola fra due stazioni

shy [ʃaɪ] adj (shyer or shier; shyest or shiest) timido; (fearful) schivo, ritroso; corto, a corto, e.g., **he is shy of funds** è a corto di denaro || v (pret & pp shied) intr ritirarsi; schivarsi; (said of a horse) adombrarsi; **to shy away** tenersi discosto

shyster ['ʃaɪstər] s (coll) azzeccagarbugli m

Si·a·mese [ˌsaɪˑəˈmiz] adj siamese || s (-mese) siamese mf

Si'amese twins' spl fratelli mpl siamesi

Siberian [saɪˈbɪrɪˑən] adj & s siberiano

sibilant ['sɪbɪlənt] adj & s sibilante f

sibyl ['sɪbɪl] s sibilla

sic [sɪk] adv sic || [sɪk] v (pret & pp sicked; ger sicking) tr aizzare; **sick 'em!** va!; **to sick on** aizzare contro

Sicilian [sɪˈsɪljən] adj & s siciliano

Sicily ['sɪsɪli] s la Sicilia

sick [sɪk] adj ammalato; nauseato; (bored) stucco; **sick at heart** con una spina nel cuore; **to be sick and tired** averne sin sopra i capelli; **to be sick at one's stomach** avere la nausea; **to take sick** cader malato || tr (a dog) aizzare

sick'bed' s letto d'ammalato

sicken ['sɪkən] tr ammalare; disgustare || intr ammalarsi

sickening ['sɪkənɪŋ] adj stomachevole

sick' head'ache s emicrania accompagnata da nausea

sickle ['sɪkəl] s falce messoria, falcetto

sick' leave' s congedo per motivi di salute

sick·ly ['sɪkli] adj (-lier; -liest) cagionevole, malaticcio

sickness ['sɪknɪs] s malattia; nausea

side [saɪd] adj laterale || s parte f, lato; (e.g., of a coin) faccia; (slope) versante m; (of human body, of a ship) fianco; **to take sides** parteggiare || intr parteggiare; **to side with** schierarsi dalla parte di

side'board' s credenza

side'burns' spl basette fpl, favoriti mpl

side'car' s motocarrozzetta; carrozzino laterale (di motocarrozzetta)

side' dish' s portata extra

side' door' s porta laterale

side' effect' s effetto secondario

side'-glance' s occhiata di sbieco

side' is'sue s questione secondaria

side'line' s linea laterale; impiego secondario; attività secondaria

sidereal [saɪˈdɪrɪ-əl] adj siderale

side'sad'dle adv all'amazzone

side' show' s spettacolo secondario di baraccone; affare secondario

side'slip' intr (aer) scivolare d'ala

side'split'ting adj che fa sbellicare dalle risa

side' step' s passo laterale, scartata

side'-step' v (pret & pp -stepped; ger -stepping) tr evitare || intr farsi da parte; fare una scartata

side'track' s binario morto di smistamento || tr sviare; (rr) smistare

side' view' s vista di profilo

side'walk' s marciapiede m

side'walk café' s caffè m con tavolini all'aperto

sideward [ˈsaɪdwərd] adj obliquo, a sghembo || adv verso un lato; di sghembo

side'ways' adj sghembo || adv di sghembo; di fianco

side' whisk'ers spl favoriti mpl

siding [ˈsaɪdɪŋ] s (rr) diramazione, binario morto, raccordo ferroviario

sidle [ˈsaɪdəl] intr andare al lato; muoversi furtivamente

siege [sidʒ] s assedio; (of illness) ricorrenza d'attacchi; **to lay siege to** cingere d'assedio, assediare

siesta [siˈɛstə] s siesta; **to take a siesta** fare la siesta

sieve [sɪv] s vaglio, setaccio || tr vagliare, setacciare

sift [sɪft] tr (flour) abburattare; setacciare; (to scatter with a sieve) spolverare; (fig) vagliare

sigh [saɪ] s sospiro || tr mormorare sospirando || intr sospirare; **to sigh for** sospirare

sight [saɪt] s vista, visione; spettacolo, veduta; (opt) mira, traguardo; (mil) mirino, tacca di mira; (coll) mucchio; **a sight of** (coll) molto; **at first sight** a prima vista; **at sight** ad apertura di libro; (com) a vista; **out of sight** fuori di vista; lontano dagli occhi; (prices) astronomico; **sights** luoghi mpl interessanti; **sight unseen** senza averlo visto prima, a occhi chiusi; **to be a sight** (coll) essere un orrore; **to catch sight of** arrivare a intravedere; **to know by sight** conoscere di vista; **to not be able to stand the sight of s.o.** not poter vedere qlcu nemmeno dipinto || tr avvistare; (a weapon) mirare || intr mirare, prendere di mira; osservare attentamente

sight' draft' s (com) tratta a vista

sight'-read' v (pret & pp -read [ˌred]) tr & intr leggere a libro aperto

sight'see'ing adj turistico || s turismo; visite fpl turistiche

sightseer [ˈsaɪtˌsi-ər] s turista mf

sign [saɪn] s segno; segnale m; (e.g., on a store) insegna, cartello; **signs** tracce fpl || tr firmare; ingaggiare; indicare, segnalare || intr firmare; fare segno; **to sign off** (rad, telv) terminare la trasmissione; **to sign up** iscriversi

sig·nal [ˈsɪgnəl] adj insigne, segnalato || s segnale m || v (pret & pp -naled or -nalled; ger -naling or -nalling) tr segnalare || intr fare segnalazioni

sig'nal corps' s (mil) armi fpl di trasmissione

sig'nal tow'er s (rr) posto di blocco

signato·ry [ˈsɪgnəˌtori] s (-ries) firmatario

signature [ˈsɪgnətʃər] s firma; segno musicale; (typ) segnatura

sign'board' s cartellone m

signer [ˈsaɪnər] s firmatario

sig'net ring' [ˈsɪgnɪt] s anello col sigillo

significance [sɪgˈnɪfɪkəns] s importanza; (meaning) significato

significant [sɪgˈnɪfɪkənt] adj importante

signi·fy [ˈsɪgnɪˌfaɪ] v (pret & pp -fied) tr significare

sign'post' s palo indicatore

silence [ˈsaɪləns] s silenzio || tr far tacere; (mil) ridurre al silenzio

silent [ˈsaɪlənt] adj silenzioso, tacito

si'lent mov'ie s cinema muto

silhouette [ˌsɪluˈet] s silhouette f, siluetta

silicon [ˈsɪlɪkən] s silicio

silicone [ˈsɪlɪˌkon] s silicone m

silk [sɪlk] adj di seta || s seta; **to hit the silk** (slang) gettarsi col paracadute

silken [ˈsɪlkən] adj serico, di seta

silk' hat' s cappello a cilindro

silk'screen proc'ess s serigrafia

silk'-stock'ing adj & s aristocratico

silk'worm' s baco da seta, filugello

silk·y [ˈsɪlki] adj (-ier; -iest) di seta; come la seta

sill [sɪl] s basamento; (of a door) soglia; (of a window) davanzale m

sil·ly [ˈsɪli] adj (-lier; -liest) sciocco, scemo

si·lo [ˈsaɪlo] s (-los) silo || tr insilare

silt [sɪlt] s sedimento

silver [ˈsɪlvər] adj d'argento; (voice) argentino; (plated with silver) argentato || s argento || tr inargentare

sil'ver·fish' s (ent) lepisma

sil'ver foil' s foglia d'argento

sil'ver fox' s volpe argentata

sil'ver lin'ing s spiraglio di speranza

sil'ver plate' s vasellame m d'argento; argentatura

sil'ver screen' s (mov) schermo

sil'ver·smith' s argentiere m

sil'ver spoon' s ricchezza ereditata; **to be born with a silver spoon in one's mouth** esser nato con la camicia

sil'ver·ware' s argenteria

sil'ver·ware' chest' s portaposate m

similar [ˈsɪmɪlər] adj simile

similari·ty [ˌsɪmɪˈlærɪti] s (-ties) similarità f, somiglianza

simile [ˈsɪmɪli] s similitudine f

simmer ['sɪmər] *tr* cuocere a fuoco lento || *intr* cuocere a fuoco lento; (fig) ribollire; **to simmer down** (slang) calmarsi

simper ['sɪmpər] *s* sorriso scemo || *intr* fare un sorriso scemo

simple ['sɪmpəl] *adj* semplice

simple-minded ['sɪmpəl'maɪndɪd] *adj* semplicione, scemo

simpleton ['sɪmpəltən] *s* semplicione *m*

simulate ['sɪmjə ,let] *tr* simulare

simultaneous [,saɪməl'tenɪ·əs] or [,sɪməl'tenɪ·əs] *adj* simultaneo

sin [sɪn] *s* peccato || *v* (*pret & pp* **sinned;** *ger* **sinning**) *intr* peccare

since [sɪns] *adv* da allora, da allora in poi; da tempo fa || *prep* da || *conj* dacché; poiché, dato che

sincere [sɪn'sɪr] *adj* sincero

sincerity [sɪn'sɛrɪti] *s* sincerità *f*

sine [saɪn] *s* (math) seno

sinecure ['saɪnɪ ,kjur] or ['sɪnɪ ,kjur] *s* sinecura

sinew ['sɪnju] *s* tendine *m;* (fig) nerbo

sinful ['sɪnfəl] *adj* (*person*) peccatore; (*act, intention, etc.*) peccaminoso

sing [sɪŋ] *v* (*pret* **sang** [sæŋ] or **sung** [sʌŋ]; *pp* **sung**) *tr* cantare; **to sing to sleep** ninnare || *intr* cantare; (*said, e.g., of the ears*) fischiare

singe [sɪndʒ] *v* (*ger* **singeing**) *tr* strinare, bruciacchiare

singer ['sɪŋər] *s* cantante *mf;* (*in night club*) canzonettista *mf*

single ['sɪŋgəl] *adj* unico, solo; (*room*) a un letto; (*bed*) a una piazza; (*man*) celibe; (*woman*) nubile; (*combat*) corpo a corpo; semplice, sincero || **singles** *ssg* singolare *m* || *tr* scegliere; **to single out** individuare

single-breasted ['sɪŋgəl'brɛstɪd] *adj* a un petto, monopetto

sin'gle entry' *s* partita semplice

sin'gle file' *s* fila indiana

single-handed ['sɪŋgəl'hændɪd] *adj* da solo, senza aiuto altrui

sin'gle-phase' *adj* (elec) monofase

sin'gle room' *s* camera a un letto

sin'gle-track' *adj* (rr) a binario semplice; (fig) di corte vedute

sing'song' *adj* monotono || *s* cantilena

singular ['sɪŋgjələr] *adj & s* singolare *m*

sinister ['sɪnɪstər] *adj* sinistro

sink [sɪŋk] *s* acquaio; (*sewer*) scolo, fogna; (fig) sentina || *v* (*pret* **sank** [sæŋk] or **sunk** [sʌŋk]; *pp* **sunk**) *tr* sprofondare; infiggere; (*a well*) scavare; (*in tone*) abbassare; (*a boat*) mandare a picco; rovinare; investire; perdere || *intr* sprofondarsi; abbassarsi; (*said, of the sun, prices, etc.*) calare; andare a picco; lasciarsi cadere; (*in vice*) impantanarsi; (*said of one's cheeks*) infossarsi; (*in thought*) perdersi; **to sink down** sedersi; **to sink in** penetrare

sink'ing fund' *s* fondo d'ammortamento

sinner ['sɪnər] *s* peccatore *m*

Sinology [sɪ'nɑlədʒi] *s* sinologia

sinuous ['sɪnju·əs] *adj* sinuoso

sinus ['saɪnəs] *s* seno

sip [sɪp] *s* sorso || *v* (*pret & pp* **sipped;** *ger* **sipping**) *tr* sorbire, sorseggiare

siphon ['saɪfən] *s* sifone *m* || *tr* travasare con un sifone

si'phon bot'tle *s* sifone *m*

sir [sʌr] *s* signore *m;* (Brit) sir *m;* **Dear Sir** Illustrissimo signore; (com) Egregio signore

sire [saɪr] *s* (*king*) sire *m;* padre *m,* stallone *m* || *tr* generare

siren ['saɪrən] *s* sirena

sirloin ['sʌrlɔɪn] *s* lombata, lombo

sirup ['sɪrəp] or ['sʌrəp] *tr* sciroppo

sis·sy ['sɪsi] *s* (-sies) effemminato

sister ['sɪstər] *adj* (*ship*) gemello; (*language*) sorella; (*corporation*) consorella || *s* sorella; (*nun*) suora, monaca

sis'ter-in-law' *s* (**sis'ters-in-law'**) cognata

Sis'tine Chap'el ['sɪstin] *s* Cappella Sistina

sit [sɪt] *v* (*pret & pp* **sat** [sæt]; *ger* **sitting**) *intr* sedere; posare; (*said of a hen*) covare; (*said of a jacket*) stare; essere in sessione; **to sit down** sedersi; **to sit in on** partecipare a; assistere a; **to sit still** state tranquillo; **to sit up** alzarsi; (coll) essere sorpreso

sit'-down strike' *s* sciopero bianco

site [saɪt] *s* sito, luogo, posizione

sitting ['sɪtɪŋ] *s* seduta; (*of a court*) sessione; (*of a hen*) covata; (*serving of a meal*) turno

sit'ting duck' *s* (slang) facile bersaglio

sit'ting room' *s* soggiorno

situate ['sɪtʃu ,et] *tr* situare

situation [,sɪtʃu'eʃən] *s* situazione, posizione; posto

sitz' bath' [sɪts] *s* semicupio

six [sɪks] *adj & pron* sei || *s* sei *m;* **at sixes and sevens** in disordine; **six o'clock** le sei

six' hun'dred *adj, s & pron* seicento

sixteen ['sɪks'tin] *adj, s & pron* sedici *m*

sixteenth ['sɪks'tinθ] *adj, s & pron* sedicesimo || *s* (*in dates*) sedici *m*

sixth [sɪksθ] *adj, s & pron* sesto || *s* (*in dates*) sei *m*

sixtieth ['sɪkstɪ·ɪθ] *adj, s & pron* sessantesimo

six·ty ['sɪksti] *adj & pron* sessanta || *s* (-ies) sessanta *m;* **the sixties** gli anni sessanta

sizable ['saɪzəbəl] *adj* considerevole

size [saɪz] *s* grandezza; quantità *f;* (*of person or garment*) taglia; (*of shoes*) numero; (*of hat*) giro; (*of a pipe*) diametro; (*for gilding*) colla; (fig) situazione || *tr* misurare, classificare secondo grandezza; incollare; **to size up** (coll) stimare, giudicare

sizzle ['sɪzəl] *s* sfrigolio || *intr* sfriggere

skate [sket] *s* pattino; (slang) tipo || *intr* pattinare; **to skate on thin ice** andare in cerca di disgrazie

skat'ing rink' *s* pattinatoio

skein [sken] *s* gomitolo, matassa

skeleton ['skɛlɪtən] *adj* scheletrico || *s* scheletro

skel'eton key' *s* chiave maestra

skeptic ['skɛptɪk] *adj & s* scettico

skeptical ['skeptɪkəl] *adj* scettico
sketch [sketʃ] *s* schizzo, disegno; abbozzo, bozzetto; (theat) scenetta ‖ *tr* schizzare, disegnare; abbozzare
sketch'book' *s* album *m* di schizzi; quaderno per abbozzi
skew [skju] *adj* obliquo ‖ *s* movimento obliquo; (*chisel*) scalpello a taglio obliquo ‖ *tr* tagliare di sghembo ‖ *intr* (*to swerve*) deviare; (*to look obliquely*) guardare di sghembo
skew' chis'el *s* scalpello a taglio obliquo
skewer ['skju·ər] *s* spiedino ‖ *tr* mettere allo spiedo
ski [ski] *s* (**skis** or **ski**) sci *m* ‖ *intr* sciare
ski' boot' *s* scarpa da sci
skid [skɪd] *s* (*device to check a wheel*) scarpa; (*skidding forward*) slittamento; (*skidding sideway*) sbandamento; (aer, mach) pattino ‖ *v* (*pret & pp* **skidded;** *ger* **skidding**) *tr* frenare ‖ *intr* (*forward*) slittare; (*sideways*) sbandare
skid' row' [ro] *s* quartiere malfamato
skier ['ski·ər] *s* sciatore *m*
skiff [skɪf] *s* skiff *m*, singolo
skiing ['ski·ɪŋ] *s* sci *m*
ski' jump' *s* salto con gli sci; trampolino di salto
ski' lift' *s* sciovia
skill [skɪl] *s* destrezza, perizia
skilled [skɪld] *adj* abile, esperto
skilled' la'bor *s* manodopera qualificata
skillet ['skɪlɪt] *s* padella
skillful ['skɪlfəl] *adj* destro, abile
skim [skɪm] *v* (*pret & pp* **skimmed;** *ger* **skimming**) *tr* (*milk*) scremare; (e.g., *broth*) sgrassare; (*to graze*) sfiorare; (*the ground*) radere; (a *page*) trascorrere ‖ *intr* sfiorare; **to skim over** scorrere
ski' mask' *s* passamontagna *m*
skimmer ['skɪmər] *s* schiumaiola; (*hat*) canottiera
skim' milk' *s* latte scremato or magro
skimp [skɪmp] *tr* lesinare ‖ *intr* economizzare, risparmiare
skimp·y ['skɪmpi] *adj* (**-ier; -iest**) corto, scarso; taccagno
skin [skɪn] *s* pelle *f*; (*rind*) scorza; (*of onion*) spoglia; **by the skin of one's teeth** (coll) per il rotto della cuffia; **soaked to the skin** bagnato fino alle ossa; **to have a thin skin** offendersi facilmente ‖ *v* (*pret & pp* **skinned;** *ger* **skinning**) *tr* pelare, spellare; (e.g., *one's knee*) spellarsi; (slang) tosare; **to skin alive** (slang) scotennare; (slang) battere in pieno
skin'-deep' *adj* a fior di pelle
skin'-div'er *s* nuotatore subacqueo, sub *m*; (mil) sommozzatore *m*
skin'flint' *s* avaro
skin' game' *s* truffa
skin·ny ['skɪni] *adj* (**-nier; -niest**) magro, scarno
skin' test' *s* cutireazione
skip [skɪp] *s* salto ‖ *v* (*pret & pp*

skipped; *ger* **skipping**) *tr* (a *fence; a meal*) saltare; (a *subject*) sorvolare; (*school*) (coll) marinare ‖ *intr* saltare, salterellare; (*said of typewriter*) saltare uno spazio; (coll) svignarsela
ski' pole' *s* racchetta da sci
skipper ['skɪpər] *s* capitano, comandante *m*
skirmish ['skʌrmɪʃ] *s* scaramuccia ‖ *intr* battersi in una scaramuccia
skirt [skʌrt] *s* sottana, gonna; (*edge*) orlo; (*woman*) (slang) gonnella ‖ *tr* orlare; costeggiare; (a *subject*) evitare
ski' run' *s* pista da sci
skit [skɪt] *s* (theat) quadretto comico
skittish ['skɪtɪʃ] *adj* bizzarro, balzano; timido; (*horse*) ombroso
skulduggery [skʌl'dʌgəri] *s* trucco disonesto
skull [skʌl] *s* cranio, teschio
skull' and cross'bones *s* due tibie incrociate ed un teschio
skull'cap' *s* papalina
skunk [skʌŋk] *s* puzzola, moffetta; (coll) puzzone *m*
sky [skaɪ] *s* (**skies**) cielo; firmamento; **to praise to the skies** portare al cielo
sky'div'er *s* paracadutista *mf*
sky'jack'er *s* pirata *m* dell'aria
sky'lark' *s* allodola ‖ *intr* (coll) darsi alla pazza gioia
sky'light' *s* lucernario
sky'line' *s* linea dell'orizzonte; (*of city*) profilo
sky'rock'et *s* razzo ‖ *intr* salire come un razzo
sky'scrap'er *s* grattacielo
sky'writ'ing *s* scrittura pubblicitaria aerea
slab [slæb] *s* (*of stone*) lastra, lastrone *m*; (*of wood*) tavola; (*slice*) fetta
slack [slæk] *adj* lento, allentato; negligente, indolente; (fig) fiacco, morto ‖ *s* lentezza; negligenza; stagione morta, inattività *f*; **slacks** pantaloni *mpl* da donna; pantaloni sciolti ‖ *tr* allentare; trascurare; (*lime*) spegnere ‖ *intr* rilasciarsi; essere negligente; **to slack up** rallentare
slacker ['slækər] *s* fannullone *m*; (mil) imboscato
slag [slæg] *s* scoria
slake [slek] *tr* spegnere
slalom ['slaləm] *s* slalom *m*
slam [slæm] *s* colpo; (*of door*) sbatacchiamento; (*in cards*) cappotto; (coll) strapazzata ‖ *v* (*pret & pp* **slammed;** *ger* **slamming**) *tr* sbattere, sbatacchiare; (coll) strapazzare ‖ *intr* sbattere, sbatacchiare
slam'bang' *adv* (coll) con gran rumore, precipitosamente
slander ['slændər] *s* calunnia, maldicenza ‖ *tr* calunniare, diffamare
slanderous ['slændərəs] *adj* calunnioso, diffamatorio
slang [slæŋ] *s* gergo
slant [slænt] *s* inclinazione; punto di vista ‖ *tr* inclinare; (*news*) snaturare ‖ *intr* inclinarsi; deviare

slap [slæp] *s* manata; *(in the face)* schiaffo, ceffone *m; (noise)* rumore *m;* insulto ‖ *v (pret & pp* **slapped;** *ger* **slapping)** *tr* dare una manata a; schiaffeggiare

slap'dash' *adj* raffazzonato, fatto a casaccio ‖ *adv* a casaccio

slap'hap'py *adj (punch-drunk)* stordito; *(giddy)* allegro, festante

slap'stick' *adj* buffonesco ‖ *s* bastone *m* d'Arlecchino; buffonata

slash [slæʃ] *s* sfregio; *(of prices)* riduzione ‖ *tr* sfregiare; *(cloth)* tagliare; *(prices)* ridurre

slat [slæt] *s* travicello, regolo; *(for bed)* traversa; *(of shutter)* stecca

slate [slet] *s* ardesia, lavagna; lista elettorale; **clean slate** buon certificato ‖ *tr* coprire con tegole d'ardesia; proporre la nomina di; *(to schedule)* mettere in cantiere

slate' roof' *s* tetto d'ardesia

slattern ['slætərn] *s (slovenly woman)* sciamannona; *(harlot)* puttana

slaughter ['slɔtər] *s* eccidio, carneficina ‖ *tr* sgozzare, scannare

slaugh'ter-house' *s* macello, scannatoio

Slav [slɑv] *or* [slæv] *adj & s* slavo

slave [slev] *adj & s* schiavo ‖ *intr* lavorare come uno schiavo

slave' driv'er *s* negriere *m*

slavery ['slevəri] *s* schiavitù *f*

slave' trade' *s* tratta degli schiavi

Slavic ['slɑvɪk] *or* ['slævɪk] *adj & s* slavo

slay [sle] *v (pret* **slew** [slu]; *pp* **slain** [slen]) *tr* scannare, uccidere

slayer ['sle·ər] *s* uccisore *m*

sled [slɛd] *s* slittino, slitta ‖ *v (pret & pp* **sledded;** *ger* **sledding)** *intr* slittare

sledge' ham'mer *s* [slɛdʒ] *s* mazza

sleek [slik] *adj* liscio, lustro; elegante ‖ *tr* lisciare, ammorbidire

sleep [slip] *s* sonno; **to go to sleep** addormentarsi; **to put to sleep** addormentare; uccidere con un anestetico ‖ *v (pret & pp* **slept** [slept]) *tr* dormire; aver posto a dormire per; **to sleep it over** dormirci sopra; **to sleep off a hangover** smaltire una sbornia dormendo ‖ *intr* dormire; **to sleep in** dormire fino a tardi; passare la notte a casa; **to sleep out** passare la notte fuori di casa

sleeper ['slipər] *s (person)* dormiente *mf; (beam, timber)* trave *f*

sleep'ing bag' *s* sacco a pelo

sleep'ing car' *s* vettura letto

sleep'ing pill' *s* sonnifero

sleepless ['sliplɪs] *adj* insonne; *(night)* bianco

sleep'walk'er *s* sonnambulo

sleep·y ['slipi] *adj* (**-ier; -iest**) insonnolito, sonnolento; **to be sleepy** aver sonno

sleep'y-head' *s* dormiglione *m*

sleet [slit] *s* nevischio ‖ *impers* **it is sleeting** cade il nevischio

sleeve [sliv] *s* manica; *(of phonograph record)* busta; *(mach)* manicotto; **to laugh in** *or* **up one's sleeve** ridere sotto i baffi

sleigh [sle] *s* slitta ‖ *intr* andare in slitta

sleigh' bells' *spl* bubboli *mpl* da slitta, sonagliera da slitta

sleigh' ride' *s* passeggiata in slitta

sleight' of hand' [slaɪt] *s.* gioco di prestigio

slender ['slendər] *adj* smilzo, snello; esiguo, esile

sleuth [sluθ] *s* segugio

slew [slu] *s* (coll) mucchio

slice [slaɪs] *s* fetta; *(of an orange)* spicchio ‖ *tr* tagliare a fette; *(fig)* fendere

slick [slɪk] *adj* liscio, lustro; scivoloso; astuto; (slang) ottimo ‖ *s* posto scivoloso; (coll) rivista stampata su carta patinata ‖ *tr* lisciare, lustrare; **to slick up** (coll) acconciare

slicker ['slɪkər] *s* impermeabile *m* di tela cerata; (coll) furbo di tre cotte

slide [slaɪd] *s* scivolata, scivolone *m; (chute)* scivolo; *(landslide)* frana; *(for projection)* diapositiva; *(of a microscope)* vetrino; *(mach)* guida; *(of a slide rule)* (mach) cursore *m* ‖ *v (pret & pp* **slid** [slɪd]) *tr* far scivolare ‖ *intr* sdrucciolare, scivolare; *(said of a car)* pattinare, slittare; **to let slide** lasciar correre

slide' fas'tener *s* chiusura lampo

slide' projec'tor *s* diascopio

slide' rule' *s* regolo calcolatore

slide' valve' *s* (mach) cassetto di distribuzione

slid'ing door' *s* porta scorrevole

slid'ing scale' *s* scala mobile

slight [slaɪt] *adj* leggero, lieve; delicato ‖ *s* noncuranza, disattenzione; affronto ‖ *tr* fare con negligenza; *(to snub)* trattare con noncuranza, snobbare

slim [slɪm] *adj* (**slimmer; slimmest**) sottile; magro

slime [slaɪm] *s* melma; *(e.g., of a snail)* bava

slim·y ['slaɪmi] *adj* (**-ier; -iest**) melmoso; bavoso; sudicio

sling [slɪŋ] *s (to shoot stones)* fionda; *(naut)* braca; **in a sling** *(arm)* al collo ‖ *v (pret & pp* **slung** [slʌŋ]) *tr* gettare; lanciare; *(freight)* imbracare; sospendere; mettere a bandoliera

sling'shot' *s* fionda

slink [slɪŋk] *v (pret & pp* **slunk** [slʌŋk]) *intr* andare furtivamente; **to slink away** eclissarsi

slip [slɪp] *s* scivolone *m;* svista, errore *m; (in prices)* discesa; *(underdress)* sottoveste *f; (pillowcase)* federa; *(of paper)* pezzo; *(space between two wharves)* darsena, imbarcatoio; *(form)* modulo; personcina; *(inclined plane)* (naut) scalo d'alaggio; (bot) innesto; **to give the slip to** eludere ‖ *v (pret & pp* **slipped;** *ger* **slipping)** *tr* infilare; liberare; liberarsi da; omettere; **to slip off** togliersi; **to slip on** mettersi; **to slip one's mind** dimenticarsi di, e.g., **it slipped my mind** me ne sono dimenticato ‖ *intr* scivolare, scorrere; sdrucciolare; sbagliare; peggiorare; **to let slip** lasciarsi sfuggire; **to slip away** svignarsela; **to slip by** (*said of time*) passare, fuggire; **to slip out of s.o.'s hands** sguSciare dalle mani di qlcu; **to slip up** sbagliarsi

slip'cov'er s fodera

slip'knot' s nodo scorsoio

slip' of the tongue' s errore m nel parlare

slipper [´slɪpər] s pantofola

slippery [´slɪpəri] adj sdrucciolevole, scivoloso; evasivo; incerto

slip'shod' adj trasandato, mal fatto

slip'-up' s (coll) sbaglio

slit [slɪt] s taglio, fenditura || v (pret & pp **slit;** ger **slitting**) tr tagliare, fendere; **to slit the throat of** sgozzare

slob [slɑb] s (slang) rozzo, villanzone m

slobber [´slɑbər] s bava; sdolcinatura || intr sbavare; parlare sdolcinatamente

sloe [slo] s (*shrub*) prugnolo; (*fruit*) prugnola

slogan [´slogən] s slogan m

sloop [slup] s cutter m

slop [slɑp] s pastone m; (slang) sbobba || v (pret & pp **slopped;** ger **slopping**) tr versare, imbrodare || intr rovesciarsi, scorrere; (slang) perdersi in smancerie

slope [slop] s costa, pendice f; (*of mountain or roof*) spiovente m || tr inclinare || intr digradare, scendere

slop-py [´slɑpi] adj (-pier; -piest) fangoso; bagnato; (*slovenly*) sciatto; (*done badly*) abborracciato

slot [slɑt] s scanalatura; (*for letters*) buca; (*e.g., on a broadcasting schedule*) posizione

sloth [sloθ] or [slɔθ] s pigrizia; (zool) bradipo, poltrone m

slot' machine' s macchina a gettone

slouch [slautʃ] s postura goffa; persona goffa; (coll) poltrone m || intr muoversi goffamente; **to slouch in a chair** sdraiarsi

slouch' hat' s cappello floscio

slough [slau] s pantano; (fig) abisso || [slʌf] s (*of snake*) spoglia; (pathol) crosta || tr—**to slough off** spogliarsi di || intr sbucciarsi, cadere

Slovak [´slovæk] or [slo´væk] adj & s slovacco

sloven-ly [´slʌvənli] adj (-lier; -liest) sciatto, trasandato

slow [slo] adj lento; (*sluggish*) tardo; (*clock*) indietro, in ritardo; (*in understanding*) tardivo || adv piano || tr rallentare || intr rallentarsi; (*said of a watch*) ritardare

slow'down' s sciopero pignolo

slow' mo'tion s—**in slow motion** al rallentatore m

slow'-motion projec'tor s rallentatore m

slow'poke' s (coll) poltrone m

slug [slʌg] s (*heavy piece of metal*) lingotto; (*metal disk*) gettone m; (fig) poltrone m; (zool) lumaca; (coll) colpo, mazzata || v (pret & pp

slugged; ger **slugging**) tr picchiare sodo

sluggard [´slʌgərd] s poltrone m

sluggish [´slʌgɪʃ] adj pigro, indolente; lento, fiacco

sluice [slus] s canale m; stramazzo

sluice' gate' s paratoia

slum [slʌm] s bassifondi mpl || v (pret & pp **slummed;** ger **slumming**) intr visitare i bassifondi

slumber [´slʌmbər] s dormiveglia m, sonnellino || intr dormire, dormicchiare

slump [slʌmp] s depressione, crisi f; (*in prices*) ribasso, calo || intr impantanarsi; peggiorare; (*said of prices*) ribassare, calare

slur [slʌr] s insulto, macchia; critica; (mus) legatura f || v (pret & pp **slurred;** ger **slurring**) tr pronunziare indistintamente; (*a subject*) sorvolare; insultare, calunniare; (mus) legare

slush [slʌʃ] s poltiglia di neve; fanghiglia; (fig) sdolcinatezza

slut [slʌt] s cagna; (*slovenly woman*) sciamannona; troia, puttana

sly [slai] adj (slyer or slier; slyest or sliest) furbo; insidioso; (*hiding one's true feelings*) sornione; **on the sly** furtivamente

smack [smæk] s schiaffo; (*of whip or lips*) schiocco; (*taste*) traccia, sapore m; (coll) bacio collo schiocco || adv di colpo, direttamente || tr dare uno schiaffo a; colpire; (*the whip or one's lips*) schioccare; schioccare un bacio a || intr—**to smack of** sapere di

small [smɔl] adj piccolo; povero; basso, umile; (*change*) spicciolo; (typ) minuscolo

small' arms' s armi fpl portatili

small' busi'ness s piccolo commercio

small' cap'ital s (typ) maiuscoletto

small' change' s spiccioli mpl

small' fry' s minutaglia; bambini mpl; gente f di poca importanza

small' hours' spl ore fpl piccole

small' intes'tine s intestino tenue

small-minded [´smɔl´maɪndɪd] adj di corte vedute, gretto

small' of the back' s fine f della schiena, reni fpl

smallpox [´smɔl‚pɑks] s vaiolo

small' talk' s conversazione futile

small'-time' adj di poca importanza

small'-town' adj di provincia

smart [smɑrt] adj intelligente; scaltro, furbo; (*pain*) acuto; (*in appearance*) elegante; (*pert*) impertinente; (coll) grande, abbondante || s dolore acuto, sofferenza || intr bruciare; dolere; soffrire

smart' al'eck [´ælɪk] s saputello

smart' set' s bel mondo

smash [smæʃ] s sconquasso; colpo; collisione; rovina, fallimento; (tennis) smash m, schiacciata || tr sconquassare; sfracellare; rovinare; (tennis) schiacciare || intr sconquassarsi; sfracellarsi; andare in rovina; **to smash into** scontrarsi con

smash' hit' s successone m

smash'-up' *s* sconquasso

smattering ['smætərɪŋ] *s* infarinatura, spolvero

smear [smɪr] *s* macchia, imbrattatura; calunnia; (bact) striscio || *tr* imbrattare; spalmare; calunniare

smear' campaign' *s* campagna di vilipendio

smell [smɛl] *s* odore *m; (sense)* olfatto, odorato; profumo || *v (pret & pp* **smelled** or **smelt**) *tr* fiutare, odorare || *intr* odorare; *(to stink)* puzzare; profumare; **to smell of** odorare di; puzzare di

smell'ing salts' *spl* sali aromatici

smell·y ['smɛli] *adj* (-ier; -iest) puzzolente

smelt [smɛlt] *s* (ichth) eperlano || *tr & intr* fondere

smile [smaɪl] *s* sorriso || *intr* sorridere

smiling ['smaɪlɪŋ] *adj* sorridente

smirk [smʌrk] *s* ghigno || *intr* ghignare

smite [smaɪt] *v (pret* **smote** [smot]; *pp* **smitten** ['smɪtən] or **smit** [smɪt]) *tr* colpire; percuotere; affliggere, castigare

smith [smɪθ] *s* fabbro

smith·y ['smɪθi] *s* (-ies) fucina

smit'ten *adj* afflitto; innamorato

smock [smak] *s* camice *m; (of mechanic)* camiciotto

smock' frock' *s* blusa da lavoro

smog [smag] *s* foschia, smog *m*

smoke [smok] *s* fumo; **to go up in smoke** andare in cenere || *tr* affumicare; *(tobacco)* fumare; **to smoke out** cacciare col fumo; scoprire || *intr* fumare; *(said, e.g., of the earth)* fumigare

smoke'-filled room' *s* stanza da riunioni piena di fumo

smoke'less pow'der ['smoklɪs] *s* polvere *f* senza fumo

smoker ['smokər] *s* fumatore *m;* salone *m* fumatori; (rr) vagone *m* fumatori

smoke' rings' *spl* anelli *mpl* di fumo

smoke' screen' *s* cortina di fumo

smoke'stack' *s* fumaiolo

smoking ['smokɪŋ] *s* (il) fumare; **no smoking** vietato fumare

smok'ing car' *s* vagone *m* fumatori

smok'ing jack'et *s* giacca da casa

smok'ing room' *s* stanza per fumatori

smok·y ['smoki] *adj* (-ier; -iest) fumoso

smolder ['smoldər] *s* fumo derivante da fuoco che cova || *intr (said of fire or passion)* covare; *(said of s.o.'s eyes)* ardere

smooch [smutʃ] *intr* (coll) baciarsi, baciucchiarsi

smooth [smuð] *adj* liscio, levigato; *(face)* glabro; di consistenza uniforme; *(flat)* piano; senza interruzioni; tranquillo; elegante; *(sound)* armonioso; *(taste)* gradevole; *(wine)* abboccato; *(sea)* calmo; *(style)* fluido || *tr* lisciare, levigare; appianare, facilitare; calmare; **to smooth away** appianare

smooth-faced ['smuð‚fest] *adj (beardless)* glabro; liscio

smooth-spoken ['smuð‚spokən] *adj* mellifluo

smooth·y ['smuði] *s* (-ies) galante *m*

smother ['smʌðər] *tr* affogare, soffocare

smudge [smʌdʒ] *s* macchia, imbrattatura || *tr* macchiare, imbrattare; *(a garden)* affumicare

smudge' pot' *s* apparecchiatura per affumicare

smug [smʌg] *adj* (**smugger; smuggest**) pieno di sé stesso; liscio, lisciato

smuggle ['smʌgəl] *tr* contrabbandare || *intr* praticare il contrabbando

smuggler ['smʌglər] *s* contrabbandiere *m*

smuggling ['smʌglɪŋ] *s* contrabbando

smut [smʌt] *s* sudiciume *m;* oscenità *f;* (agr) volpe *f,* golpe *f*

smut·ty ['smʌti] *adj* (-tier; -tiest) sudicio; osceno; (agr) malato di volpe

snack [snæk] *s* spuntino, merenda; porzione

snack' bar' *s* tavola calda

snag [snæg] *s* tronco sommerso; protuberanza, sporgenza; *(tooth)* dente rotto; (fig) intoppo, ostacolo; **to hit a snag** incontrare un ostacolo || *v (pret & pp* **snagged**; *ger* **snagging**) *tr* fare uno straccio a; (fig) ostacolare

snail [snel] *s* chiocciola, lumaca; **at a snail's pace** come una lumaca

snake [snek] *s* serpente *m; (nonvenomous)* biscia

snake' in the grass' *s* pericolo nascosto; *(person)* serpe *f* in seno

snap [snæp] *s (sharp sound)* schiocco; *(bite)* morso; *(fastener)* bottone automatico; *(of cold weather)* breve periodo; *(manner of speaking)* tono tagliente; (phot) istantanea; (coll) vigore *m;* (coll) cosa da nulla || *v (pret & pp* **snapped**; *ger* **snapping**) *tr* schioccare; chiudere di colpo; spezzare di colpo; *(a picture)* scattare; **to snap one's fingers at** infischiarsi di; **to snap up** afferrare; *(a person)* tagliare la parola a || *intr* schioccare; *(to crack)* rompersi di colpo; **to snap at** cercare di mordere; *(a bargain)* cercare di afferrare; **to snap out of it** (coll) riprendersi; **to snap shut** chiudersi di colpo

snap'drag'on *s* (bot) bocca di leone

snap' fas'tener *s* bottone automatico

snap' judg'ment *s* decisione presa senza riflessione

snap·py ['snæpi] *adj* (-pier; -piest) mordente, mordace; (coll) vivo, vivace; (coll) elegante; **to make it snappy** (slang) sbrigarsi

snap'shot' *s* istantanea

snare [snɛr] *s* laccio, lacciolo; *(of a drum)* corda

snare' drum' *s* cassa rullante

snarl [snɑrl] *s (of a dog)* ringhio; groviglio; *(of traffic)* ingorgo; (fig) confusione || *tr* urlare con un ringhio; *(to tangle)* aggrovigliare; complicare || *intr* ringhiare; aggrovigliarsi; complicarsi

snatch [snætʃ] *s* strappo, strappone *m;* presa; pezzetto; momentino || *tr &*

intr strappare; **to snatch at** cercare di afferrare; **to snatch from** strappare a

sneak [snik] *s* furfante *m* ‖ *tr* mettere di nascosto; pigliare di nascosto ‖ *intr*—**to sneak in** entrare di nascosto; **to sneak out** svignarsela

sneaker ['snikər] *s* furfante *m;* scarpetta da ginnastica

sneak' thief' *s* ladro, topo

sneak·y ['sniki] *adj* (**-ier; -iest**) furtivo

sneer [snɪr] *s* ghigno ‖ *intr* sogghignare; **to sneer at** beffarsi si

sneeze [sniz] *s* starnuto ‖ *intr* starnutare; **not to be sneezed at** (coll) non essere disprezzabile

snicker ['snɪkər] *s* risatina ‖ *intr* fare una risatina

snide [snaɪd] *adj* malizioso

sniff [snɪf] *s* fiuto, fiutata; (*scent*) odore *m* ‖ *tr* fiutare ‖ *intr* aspirare rumorosamente; (*with emotion*) moccicare; **to sniff at** annusare; mostrare disprezzo per

sniffle ['snɪfəl] *s* moccio; **to have the sniffles** moccicare ‖ *intr* moccicare

snip [snɪp] *s* taglio; pezzetto; (*person*) (coll) mezza cartuccia ‖ *v* (*pret & pp* **snipped;** *ger* **snipping**) *tr* tagliuzzare

snipe [snaɪp] *s* tiro di nascosto; (orn) beccaccino ‖ *intr* sparare in appostamento; attaccare da lontano

sniper ['snaɪpər] *s* franco tiratore, cecchino

snippet ['snɪpɪt] *s* ritaglio, frammento; (fig) mezza cartuccia

snip·py ['snɪpi] *adj* (**-pier; -piest**) frammentario; (coll) corto, brusco; (coll) arrogante

snitch [snɪtʃ] *tr & intr* (coll) graffignare, sgraffignare

sniv·el ['snɪvəl] *s* moccio; singhiozzo, piagnisteo; falsa commozione ‖ *v* (*pret & pp* **-eled** or **-elled;** *ger* **-eling** or **-elling**) *intr* singhiozzare, piagnucolare; (*to have a runny nose*) moccicare, avere il moccio

snob [snɑb] *s* snob *mf*

snobbery ['snɑbəri] *s* snobismo

snobbish ['snɑbɪʃ] *adj* snobistico

snoop [snup] *s* (coll) ficcanaso ‖ *intr* (coll) ficcare il naso

snoop·y ['snupi] *adj* (**-ier; -iest**) (coll) curioso, invadente

snoot [snut] *s* (slang) naso

snoot·y ['snuti] *adj* (**-ier; -iest**) (coll) snobistico

snooze [snuz] *s* (coll) sonnellino ‖ *intr* (coll) fare un sonnellino

snore [snor] *s* russamento ‖ *intr* russare

snort [snɔrt] *s* sbuffo ‖ *intr* sbuffare

snot [snɑt] *s* (slang) moccio

snot·ty ['snɑti] *adj* (**-tier; -tiest**) (coll) snobistico; (coll) arrogante; (slang) moccioso

snout [snaut] *s* muso; (*of pig*) grugno; (*of person*) muso, grugno

snow [sno] *s* neve *f* ‖ *intr* nevicare

snow'ball' *s* palla di neve ‖ *tr* gettare palle di neve a ‖ *intr* aumentare come una palla di neve

snow'blind' *adj* accecato dalla neve

snow'bound' *adj* prigioniero della neve

snow-capped ['sno,kæpt] *adj* coperto di neve

snow'drift' *s* banco di neve

snow'fall' *s* nevicata

snow' fence' *s* barriera contro la neve

snow'flake' *s* fiocco di neve

snow' flur'ry *s* neve portata da raffiche

snow' line' *s* limite *m* delle nevi perenni

snow'man' *s* (**-men'**) uomo di neve

snow'plow' *s* spazzaneve *m*

snow'shoe' *s* racchetta da neve

snow'slide' *s* valanga

snow'storm' *s* bufera di neve

snow' tire' *s* gomma da neve, pneumatico da neve

snow'-white' *adj* bianco come la neve

snow·y ['sno·i] *adj* (**-ier; -iest**) nevoso

snub [snʌb] *s* affronto ‖ *v* (*pret & pp* **snubbed;** *ger* **snubbing**) *tr* snobbare

snub·by ['snʌbi] *adj* (**-bier; -biest**) camuso, rincagnato

snuff [snʌf] *s* fiutata; tabacco da fiuto; (*of a candlewick*) moccolo; **up to snuff** (coll) soddisfacente; (coll) bene ‖ *tr* fiutare; tabaccare; (*a candle*) smoccolare; **to snuff out** spegnere; (fig) soffocare

snuff'box' *s* tabacchiera

snuffers ['snʌfərz] *spl* smoccolatoio

smug [snʌg] *adj* (**snugger; snuggest**) comodo; (*dress*) attillato; compatto; (*well-off*) agiato; (*sum*) discreto; (*sheltered*) ben protetto; (*well-hidden*) nascosto

snuggle ['snʌgəl] *intr* rannicchiarsi; **to snuggle up to** stringersi a

so [so] *adv* così; così or tanto + *adj* or *adv;* per quanto; and so certamente; pure; **and so on** e così via; **or so** più o meno; **to think so** credere di sì; **so as to** + *inf* per + *inf;* **so far** sinora, finora; **so long!** arrivederci!; **so many** tanti; **so much** tanto; **so so** così così; **so that** in maniera che, di modo che; **so to speak** per così dire ‖ *conj* cosicché ‖ *interj* bene!; basta!; così!

soak [sok] *s* bagnata; (*toper*) (slang) ubriacone *m* ‖ *tr* bagnare, inzuppare; imbevere; (coll) ubriacare; (slang) far pagare un prezzo esorbitante a; **to soak up** assorbire; **soaked to the skin** bagnato fino alle ossa ‖ *intr* stare a molle, macerare; inzupparsi

so'-and-so' *s* (**-sos**) tal *m* dei tali; tal cosa

soap [sop] *s* sapone *m* ‖ *tr* insaponare

soap'box' *s* cassa di sapone; tribuna improvvisata

soap'box or'ator *s* oratore *m* che parla da una tribuna improvvisata

soap' bub'ble *s* bolla di sapone

soap' dish' *s* portasapone *m*

soap' flakes' *spl* sapone *m* a scaglie

soap' op'era *s* (coll) trasmissione radiofonica o televisiva lacrimogena

soap' pow'der *s* sapone *m* in polvere

soap'stone' *s* pietra da sarto

soap'suds' *spl* saponata

soap·y ['sopi] *adj* (**-ier; -iest**) saponoso

soar [sor] *intr* spaziare, slanciarsi; (aer) librarsi

sob [sɑb] *s* singhiozzo || *v* (*pret & pp* **sobbed**; *ger* **sobbing**) *tr* dire a singhiozzi || *intr* singhiozzare

sober ['sobər] *adj* sobrio; non ubriaco || *intr* smaltire la sbornia; **to sober down** calmarsi; **to sober up** smaltire la sbornia

sobriety [so'braɪəti] *s* sobrietà *f*

sobriquet ['sobrɪ,ke] *s* nomignolo

sob' sis'ter *s* giornalista lacrimogeno

sob' sto'ry *s* storia lacrimogena

so'-called' *adj* cosiddetto

soccer ['sɑkər] *s* calcio, football *m*

sociable ['soʃəbəl] *adj* sociale, socievole

social ['soʃəl] *adj* sociale || *s* riunione sociale

so'cial climb'er ['klaɪmər] *s* arrampicatore *m* sociale

so'cial con'tract *s* patto sociale

socialism ['soʃə,lɪzəm] *s* socialismo

socialist ['soʃəlɪst] *s* socialista *mf*

socialite ['soʃə,laɪt] *s* persona che appartiene all'alta società

So'cial Reg'ister *s* (trademark) annuario dell'alta società

so'cial secu'rity *s* sicurezza sociale

so'cial work'er *s* visitatrice *f*, assistente *mf* sociale

socie·ty [sə'saɪəti] *s* (**-ties**) società *f*; (*companionship or company*) compagnia

soci'ety ed'itor *s* cronista mondano

sociology [,sosɪ'ɑlədʒi] *or* [,soʃɪ-'ɑlədʒi] *s* sociologia

sock [sɑk] *s* calzino; (slang) colpo forte; (slang) attore *m* di prim'ordine; (slang) spettacolo eccezionale || *tr* (slang) dare un forte colpo a

socket ['sɑkɪt] *s* (*of eye*) occhiaia; (*of tooth*) alveolo; (*of candlestick*) bocciolo; (*wall socket*) (elec) presa di corrente; (elec) portalampada *m*

sock'et wrench' *s* chiave *f* a tubo

sod [sɑd] *s* zolla; terreno erboso || *v* (*pret & pp* **sodded**; *ger* **sodding**) *tr* piotare

soda ['sodə] *s* soda

so'da crack'er *s* galletta fatta al bicarbonato

so'da wa'ter *s* soda, gazosa

sodium ['sodɪəm] *adj* sodico || *s* sodio

sofa ['sofə] *s* sofà *m*, divano

so'fa bed' *s* sofà *m* letto

soft [sɔft] *or* [sɑft] *adj* molle; (*smooth*) morbido; (*iron*) dolce; (*hat*) floscio; (*person*) rammollito; (coll) facile

soft'-boiled' egg' ['sɔft'bɔɪld] *or* ['sɑft'bɔɪld] *s* uovo alla coque

soft' coal' *s* carbone bituminoso

soft' drink' *s* bibita

soften ['sɔfən] *or* ['sɑfən] *tr* mollificare, rammollire; (fig) intenerire || *intr* intenerirsi

softener ['sɔfənər] *or* ['sɑfənər] *s* ammorbidente *m*

soft' land'ing *s* allunaggio morbido

soft'-ped'al *v* (*pret & pp* **-aled** *or*

-alled; *ger* **-aling** *or* **-alling**) *tr* mettere in sordina; (coll) moderare

soft'-shell crab' *s* mollecca

soft' soap' *s* sapone *m* molle; (coll) adulazione

soft'-soap' *tr* (coll) insaponare

sog·gy ['sɑgi] *adj* (**-gier**; **-giest**) rammollito, inzuppato

soil [sɔɪl] *s* suolo, terreno; territorio; (*spot*) macchia; (*filth*) porcheria, lordura || *tr* sporcare, macchiare || *intr* sporcarsi, macchiarsi

soil' pipe' *s* tubo di scarico

soiree *or* **soirée** [swɑ're] *s* serata

sojourn ['sodʒʌrn] *s* soggiorno || ['sodʒʌrn] *or* [so'dʒʌrn] *intr* soggiornare

solace ['sɑlɪs] *s* conforto || *tr* confortare, consolare

solar ['solər] *adj* solare

so'lar bat'tery *s* batteria solare

solder ['sɑdər] *s* saldatura; lega per saldatura || *tr* saldare

sol'dering i'ron *s* saldatoio

soldier ['soldʒər] *s* (*man of rank and file*) soldato; (*man in military service*) militare *m* || *intr* fare il soldato

sol'dier of for'tune *s* soldato di ventura

soldier·y ['soldʒəri] *s* (**-ies**) soldatesca

sold-out ['sold,aut] *adj* esaurito; (*e.g., theater*) completo

sole [sol] *adj* solo, unico; esclusivo || *s* (*of foot*) pianta; (*of stocking*) soletta; (*of shoe*) suola; (*fish*) sfoglia || *tr* solare

solely ['solli] *adv* solamente

solemn ['sɑləm] *adj* solenne

solicit [sə'lɪsɪt] *tr* sollecitare; adescare, accostare

solicitor [sə'lɪsɪtər] *s* sollecitatore *m*; agente *m*; (law) procuratore *m*

solicitous [sə'lɪsɪtəs] *adj* sollecito

solicitude [sə'lɪsɪ,tjud] *or* [sə'lɪsɪ,tud] *s* sollecitudine *f*

solid ['sɑlɪd] *adj* solido; (*not hollow*) sodo; (*e.g., clouds*) denso; (*wall*) pieno, massiccio; (*word*) con grafia unita; intero; unanime, solidale; (*good*) buono; (*e.g., gold*) puro, massiccio

solidity [sə'lɪdɪti] *s* solidità *f*

sol'id-state' *adj* transistorizzato, senza valvole

solilo·quy [sə'lɪləkwi] *s* (**-quies**) soliloquio

solitaire ['sɑlɪ,ter] *s* solitario

solitar·y ['sɑlɪ,teri] *adj* solitario; unico || *s* (**-ies**) persona solitaria

sol'itary confine'ment *s* segregazione cellulare

solitude ['sɑlɪ,tjud] *or* ['sɑlɪ,tud] *s* solitudine *f*

so·lo ['solo] *adj* solo, solitario; (mus) solista || *s* (**-los**) (mus) solo

soloist ['solo·ɪst] *s* solista *mf*

so' long' *interj* (coll) ciao!; (coll) addio!; (coll) arrivederci!

solstice ['sɑlstɪs] *s* solstizio

soluble ['sɑljəbəl] *adj* solubile

solution [sə'luʃən] *s* soluzione

solvable ['sɑlvəbəl] *adj* risolvibile

solve [sɑlv] *tr* risolvere, sciogliere

solvency ['salvənsi] s solvenza

solvent ['salvənt] adj & s solvente m

somber ['sambər] adj tetro

some [sʌm] adj indef qualche; di + art, e.g., **some apples** delle mele; (coll) forte, grande ‖ pron indef alcuni, taluni; ne, e.g., **I have some** ne ho

some'bod'y pron indef taluno, qualcuno; **somebody else** qualcun altro ‖ s (-ies) (coll) qualcuno

some'day' adv qualche giorno

some'how' adv in qualche modo; **somehow or other** in un modo o nell'altro

some'one' pron indef qualcuno, taluno; **someone else** qualcun altro

somersault ['sʌmər,səlt] s salto mortale ‖ intr fare un salto mortale

something ['sʌmθɪŋ] pron indef qualcosa; **something else** qualcos'altro ‖ adv un po'; (coll) molto, moltissimo

some'time' adj antico, di un tempo ‖ adv un giorno o l'altro, uno di questi giorni

some'times' adv talora, talvolta

some'way' adv in qualche modo

some'what' s qualcosa ‖ adv piuttosto, un po'

some'where' adv in qualche luogo, da qualche parte; a qualche momento; **somewhere else** altrove

somnambulist [sam'næmbjəlɪst] s sonnambulo

somnolent ['samnələnt] adj sonnolento

son [sʌn] s figlio

sonar ['sonar] s ecogoniometro, sonar m

song [sɔŋ] or [saŋ] s canto, canzone f; **for a song** per un soldo

song'bird' s uccello canoro

Song' of Songs' s Cantico dei Cantici

songster ['sɔŋstər] s cantante m, canzonettista m

songstress ['sɔŋstrɪs] s cantante f, canzonettista f

song'writ'er s canzoniere m

son'ic boom' ['sanɪk] s boato sonico

son'-in-law' s (sons'-in-law') genero

sonnet ['sanɪt] s sonetto

son·ny ['sʌni] s (-nies) figliolo

sonori·ty [sə'narɪti] or [sə'nɔrɪti] s (-ties) sonorità f

soon [sun] adv in breve, ben presto; subito, presto; **as soon as** non appena, quanto prima; **as soon as possible** quanto prima; **I had sooner** preferirei; **how soon?** quando?; **soon after** poco dopo; **sooner or later** prima o poi, tosto o tardi

soot [sut] or [sut] s fuliggine f

soothe [suð] tr calmare, lenire

soothsayer ['suθ,se·ər] s indovino

soot·y ['suti] or ['suti] adj (-ier; -iest) fuligginoso

sop [sap] s (soaked food) zuppa; (bribe) dono, offa ‖ v (pret & pp sopped; ger sopping) tr intingere, inzuppare; **to sop up** assorbire

sophisticated [sə'fɪstɪ,ketɪd] adj sofisticato, smaliziato

sophistication [sə,fɪstɪ'ke/ən] s eccessiva ricercatezza; gusti mpl raffinati

sophomore ['safə,mor] s studente m del secondo anno, fagiolo

sophomoric [,safə'mɔrɪk] adj saputello, presuntuoso; ingenuo, imberbe

sopping ['sapɪŋ] adv—**sopping wet** inzuppato

sopran·o [sə'præno] or [sə'prano] adj per soprano, da soprano ‖ s (-os) soprano mf

sorcerer ['sɔrsərər] s mago, stregone m

sorceress ['sɔrsərɪs] s maga, strega

sorcer·y ['sɔrsəri] s (-ies) stregoneria

sordid ['sɔrdɪd] adj sordido

sore [sor] adj irritato; indolenzito; estremo, grave; **to be sore at** (coll) aversela con ‖ s piaga, ulcera; dolore m, afflizione; **to open an old sore** riaprire una ferita

sorely ['sorli] adv penosamente; gravemente, urgentemente

soreness ['sornɪs] s dolore m, afflizione

sore' spot' s (fig) piaga

sore' throat' s mal m di gola

sorori·ty [sə'rarɪti] or [sə'rɔrɪti] s (-ties) associazione femminile universitaria

sorrel ['sarəl] or ['sɔrəl] s sauro

sorrow ['saro] or ['sɔro] s dolore m, cordoglio ‖ intr affliggersi, provar cordoglio; **to sorrow for** rimpiangere

sorrowful ['sarəful] or ['sɔrəfəl] adj doloroso

sor·ry ['sari] or ['sɔri] adj (-rier; -riest) spiacente, desolato, dolente; povero, cattivo; **to be sorry** dolersi; dispiacere a, e.g., **he is sorry** gli dispiace ‖ interj mi dispiace!, scusi!

sort [sɔrt] s tipo, specie f; maniera; **a sort of** una specie di; **out of sorts** depresso; ammalato; di mal umore; **sort of** (coll) piuttosto; (coll) un certo, e.g., **sort of a headache** un certo mal di testa ‖ tr assortire; (mail) smistare

so'-so' adj passabile ‖ adv così così

sot [sat] s ubriacone m

soubrette [su'brεt] s (theat) soubrette f

soul [sol] s anima; **upon my soul!** sulla mia parola!

sound [saʊnd] adj sano; solido, forte; valido, buono; (sleep) profondo; valido, legale; onesto ‖ s suono; rumore m; (of an animal) verso; (passage of water) stretto; (surg) sonda; (ichth) vescica natatoria; **within sound of** alla portata di ‖ adv profondamente ‖ tr (an instrument) sonare; pronunciare; (e.g., s.o.'s chest) auscultare; (praises) cantare; (to measure) sondare ‖ intr sonare; parere, sembrare; fare uno scandaglio; **to sound like** avere il suono di; dare l'impressione di, parere

sound' bar'rier s muro del suono

sound' film' s pellicola sonora

soundly ['saʊndli] adv solidamente; profondamente; completamente

sound'proof' adj a prova di suono ‖ tr insonorizzare

sound' track' s (mov) sonoro, colonna sonora

sound' truck' s autoveicolo con impianto sonoro

sound' wave' s onda sonora

soup [sup] s zuppa, minestra

soup' dish' s piatto fondo

soup' kitch'en s asilo dei poveri che serve zuppa gratuitamente

soup'spoon' s cucchiaio (da minestra)

sour [saur] adj acido; (fruit) acerbo ‖ tr inacidire ‖ intr inacidirsi

source [sors] s fonte f, sorgente f

source' lan'guage s lingua di partenza

source' mate'rial s fonti fpl originali

sour' cher'ry s (fruit) amarena; (tree) amareno

sour' grapes' interj l'uva è verde!

south [sauθ] adj meridionale, del sud ‖ s sud m, meridione m ‖ adv verso il sud

South' Amer'ica s l'America f del Sud

South' Amer'ican adj & s sudamericano

southeast [ˌsauθ'ist] adj di sud-est ‖ s sud-est ‖ adv al sud-est

southern [ˈsʌðərn] adj meridionale

South'ern Cross' s Croce f del Sud

southerner [ˈsʌðərnər] s meridionale mf

South' Kore'a s la Corea del Sud

south'paw' adj & s (coll) mancino

South' Pole' s Polo sud

South' Vietnam·ese' [vɪˌetnəˈmiz] adj vietnamita del sud ‖ s (-ese) vietnamita mf del sud

southward [ˈsauθwərd] adv verso il sud

south'west' adj di sud-ovest ‖ s sud-ovest m ‖ adv al sud-ovest

souvenir [ˌsuvəˈnɪr] or [ˈsuvəˌnɪr] s ricordo, memoria

sovereign [ˈsavrɪn] or [ˈsʌvrɪn] adj sovrano ‖ s (king) sovrano; (queen; coin) sovrana

sovereign·ty [ˈsavrɪnti] or [ˈsʌvrɪnti] s (-ties) sovranità f

soviet [ˈsovɪˌet] or [ˌsovɪˈet] adj sovietico ‖ s soviet m

So'viet Rus'sia s la Russia Sovietica

sow [sau] s porca, troia ‖ [so] v (pret sowed; pp sown or sowed) tr seminare

soybean [ˈsɔɪˌbin] s soia; seme m di soia

spa [spa] s terme fpl

space [spes] adj spaziale ‖ s spazio; periodo; **after a space** dopo un po' ‖ tr spaziare; **to space out** diradare

space' bar' s barra spaziatrice, spaziatrice f

space' cen'ter s cosmodromo

space'craft' s astronave f

space' flight' s volo spaziale

space'man' s (-men') navigatore m spaziale

spacer [ˈspesər] s spaziatrice f, barra spaziatrice

space'ship' s astronave f

space'suit' s scafandro astronautico, tuta spaziale

spacious [ˈspeʃəs] adj spazioso

spade [sped] s vanga; (cards) picca; **to call a spade a spade** dire pane al pane, vino al vino ‖ tr vangare

spade'work' s lavoro preliminare

spaghetti [spəˈgɛti] s spaghetti mpl

Spain [spen] s la Spagna

span [spæn] s (of the hand) spanna; (of time) tratto; (of a bridge) campata, luce f; (of horses) paio; (aer) apertura ‖ v (pret & pp spanned; ger spanning) tr misurare a spanne; attraversare, oltrepassare; (said of time) abbracciare

spangle [ˈspæŋgəl] s lustrino ‖ tr tempestare di lustrini; (with bright objects) stellare ‖ intr brillare

Spaniard [ˈspænjərd] s spagnolo

Spanish [ˈspænɪʃ] adj & s spagnolo; **the Spanish** gli spagnoli

Span'ish-Amer'ican adj & s ispanoamericano

Span'ish broom' s ginestra

Span'ish fly' s mosca cantaride

Span'ish om'elet s frittata di pomodori, cipolle e peperoni

Span'ish-speak'ing adj di lingua spagnola

spank [spæŋk] tr sculacciare

spanking [ˈspæŋkɪŋ] adj rapido; forte; (coll) eccellente, straordinario ‖ s sculacciata

spar [spar] s (mineral) spato; (naut) asta, pennone m; (aer) longherone m ‖ v (pret & pp sparred; ger sparring) intr fare la box

spare [sper] adj di riserva; libero, in eccesso; (e.g., diet) frugale; (lean) magro ‖ tr salvare, risparmiare; perdonare; (to do without) fare a meno di, privarsi di; **to have . . . to spare** aver . . . d'avanzo; **to spare oneself** risparmiarsi

spare' parts' s pezzi mpl di ricambio

spare' room' s camera per gli ospiti

spare' tire' s ruota di scorta, pneumatico di scorta

spare' wheel' s ruota di scorta

sparing [ˈsperɪŋ] adj economico; (scanty) scarso

spark [spark] s scintilla; traccia ‖ tr (coll) rianimare; (coll) corteggiare ‖ intr scintillare

spark' coil' s bobina d'accensione

spark' gap' s (elec) traferro, intraferro

sparkle [ˈsparkəl] s scintilla; (luster) scintillio; allegria, vivacità f ‖ intr scintillare; (said, e.g., of eyes) brillare, luccicare; (said of wine) frizzare, spumeggiare

sparkling [ˈsparklɪŋ] adj scintillante; (wine) frizzante, spumeggiante; (water) gassoso

spark' plug' s candela

sparrow [ˈspæro] s passero

sparse [spars] adj rado

Spartan [ˈspartən] adj & s spartano

spasm [ˈspæzəm] s spasmo; sprazzo d'energia

spasmodic [spæzˈmadɪk] adj spasmodico; intermittente, a sprazzi

spastic [ˈspæstɪk] adj & s spastico

spat [spæt] s litigio, battibecco; **spats**

ghette *fpl* ‖ *v* (*pret* & *pp* **spatted; ger spatting**) *intr* avere un battibecco

spatial [ˈspeʃəl] *adj* spaziale

spatter [ˈspætər] *tr* schizzare, spruzzare ‖ *intr* gocciolare

spatula [ˈspætʃələ] *s* spatola

spawn [spɔn] *s* prole *f*, progenie *f*; risultato ‖ *tr* produrre, generare ‖ *intr* (ichth) deporre le uova

spay [spe] *tr* asportare le ovaie a

speak [spik] *v* (*pret* **spoke** [spok]; *pp* **spoken**) *tr* (*a language*) parlare; (*the truth*) dire ‖ *intr* parlare; **so to speak** per così dire; **speaking!** al telefono!; **to speak of** importante, che valga parlarne; **to speak out** dire la propria opinione

speak'-eas'y *s* (**-ies**) bar clandestino

speaker [ˈspikər] *s* conferenziere *m*, oratore *m*; (*of a language*) parlante *mf*; (pol) presidente *m*; (rad) altoparlante *m*

speaking [ˈspikɪŋ] *adj* parlante; **to be on speaking terms** parlarsi ‖ *s* parlare *m*, discorso

speak'ing tube' *s* tubo acustico

spear [spɪr] *s* lancia; (*for fishing*) arpione *m*; (*of grass*) stelo ‖ *tr* trafiggere con la lancia

spear' gun' *s* fucile subacqueo

spear'head' *s* punta di lancia ‖ *tr* condurre, dirigere

spear'mint' *s* menta romana spicata

special [ˈspeʃəl] *adj* speciale ‖ *s* prezzo speciale; treno speciale

spe'cial deliv'ery *s* espresso

spe'cial draw'ing rights' *spl* (econ) diritti *mpl* speciali di prelievo

specialist [ˈspeʃəlɪst] *s* specialista *mf*

specialize [ˈspeʃə ˌlaɪz] *tr* specializzare ‖ *intr* specializzarsi

spe'cial part'ner *s* accomandante *mf*

special·ty [ˈspeʃəlti] *s* (**-ties**) specialità *f*

spe·cies [ˈspisiz] *s* (**-cies**) specie *f*

specific [spɪˈsɪfɪk] *adj* & *s* specifico

specification [ˌspesɪfɪˈkeʃən] *s* specifica; (com) capitolato

specif'ic grav'ity *s* peso specifico

speci·fy [ˈspesɪ ˌfaɪ] *v* (*pret* & *pp* **-fied**) *tr* specificare

specimen [ˈspesɪmən] *s* esemplare *m*; (coll) tipo

specious [ˈspiʃəs] *adj* specioso

speck [spek] *s* macchiolina; (*of dust*) granello; (*of hope*) filo ‖ *tr* macchiettare

speckle [ˈspekəl] *s* macchiolina ‖ *tr* macchiettare, picchiettare

spectacle [ˈspektəkəl] *s* spettacolo; **spectacles** occhiali *mpl*

spectator [ˈspektetər] or [spekˈtetər] *s* spettatore *m*

specter [ˈspektər] *s* spettro

spec·trum [ˈspektrəm] *s* (**-tra** [trə] or **-trums**) spettro; (fig) gamma

speculate [ˈspekjə ˌlet] *intr* speculare

speech [spitʃ] *s* parola, parlata; (*before an audience*) discorso; (*of an actor*) elocuzione; **in speech** oralmente

speech' clin'ic *s* clinica per la correzione dei difetti del linguaggio

speechless [ˈspitʃlɪs] *adj* senza parole, muto

speed [spid] *s* velocità *f*; (aut) marcia ‖ *tr* accelerare, affrettare ‖ *intr* accelerare, affrettarsi; guidare oltre la velocità massima

speed'boat' *s* motoscafo da corsa

speeding [ˈspidɪŋ] *s* eccesso di velocità

speed' king' *s* asso del volante

speed' lim'it *s* limite *m* di velocità

speedometer [spiˈdɑmɪtər] *s* tachimetro; (*to record the distance covered*) contachilometri *m*

speed'-up' *s* accelerazione

speed'way' *s* (*highway*) autostrada; (*for races*) pista

speed·y [ˈspidi] *adj* (**-ier; -iest**) veloce, rapido

spell [spel] *s* malia, incantesimo; fascino; turno; attacco; periodo di tempo; **to cast a spell on** incantare ‖ *v* (*pret* & *pp* **spelled** or **spelt** [spelt]) *tr* compitare; scrivere in tutte lettere; voler dire; **to spell out** (coll) spiegare dettagliatamente ‖ *intr* scrivere, sillabare ‖ *v* (*pret* & *pp* **spelled**) *tr* rimpiazzare

spell'bind' *v* (*pret* & *pp* **-bound**) *tr* affascinare

spell'bind'er *s* oratore *m* abbagliante

spelling [ˈspelɪŋ] *adj* ortografico ‖ *s* (*act*) compitazione; (*way a word is spelled*) grafia; (*subject of study*) ortografia

spell'ing bee' *s* gara di ortografia

spelunker [spɪˈlʌŋkər] *s* esploratore *m* di caverne

spend [spend] *v* (*pret* & *pp* **spent** [spent]) *tr* spendere; (*time*) passare

spender [ˈspendər] *s* spenditore *m*

spend'ing mon'ey *s* denaro per le piccole spese personali

spend'thrift' *s* sprecone *m*, spendaccione *m*

sperm [spʌrm] *s* sperma *m*

sperm' whale' *s* capodoglio

spew [spju] *tr* & *intr* vomitare

sphere [sfɪr] *s* sfera

spherical [ˈsferɪkəl] *adj* sferico

sphinx [sfɪŋks] *s* (**sphinxes** or **sphinges** [ˈsfɪndʒiz]) sfinge *f*

spice [spaɪs] *s* droga; spezie *fpl*; (fig) gusto, sapore *m* ‖ *tr* drogare; dare gusto a, rendere piccante

spick-and-span [ˈspɪkəndˈspæn] *adj* ordinato e pulito

spic·y [ˈspaɪsi] *adj* (**-ier; -iest**) drogato; piccante

spider [ˈspaɪdər] *s* ragno

spi'der·web' *s* ragnatela

spiff·y [ˈspɪfi] *adj* (**-ier; -iest**) (slang) elegante, bello

spigot [ˈspɪgət] *s* (*peg*) zipolo; (*faucet*) rubinetto

spike [spaɪk] *s* chiodo, chiodone *m*; (*sharp-pointed piece*) spuntone *m*; (rr) arpione *m*; (bot) spiga ‖ *tr* inchiodare; mettere chiodi a; (*a rumor*) porre fine a; (coll) alcolizzare

spill [spɪl] *s* rovesciamento; liquido rovesciato; (coll) caduta ‖ *v* (*pret* & *pp* **spilled** or **spilt** [spɪlt]) *tr* rovesciare, spandere; versare; (naut) sventare; (coll) far cadere; (slang) snocciolare || *intr* rovesciarsi; versarsi

spill'way' *s* sfioratore *m.* stramazzo

spin [spɪn] *s* giro; (*twirl*) mulinello; corsa; **to go into a spin** (aer) cadere a vite || *v* (*pret & pp* **spun** [spʌn]; *ger* **spinning**) *tr* far girare; (*e.g., thread*) filare; **to spin out** prolungare; **to spin a yarn** raccontare una storia || *intr* girare; (*said of a top*) prillare; filare

spinach ['spɪnɪt/] or ['spɪnɪdʒ] *s* spinacio; (*leaves used as food*) spinaci *mpl*

spi'nal col'umn ['spaɪnəl] *s* spina dorsale, colonna vertebrale

spi'nal cord' *s* midollo spinale

spindle ['spɪndəl] *s* (*rounded rod*) fuso; (*shaft, axle*) asse *m;* balaustro

spine [spaɪn] *s* spina; spina dorsale; (bb) costola; (fig) forza, carattere *m*

spineless ['spaɪnlɪs] *adj* senza spine; senza carattere

spinet ['spɪnɪt] *s* spinetta

spinner ['spɪnər] *s* filatore *m; (machine)* filatrice *f*

spinning ['spɪnɪŋ] *adj* filante || *s* filatura; rotazione

spin'ning mill' *s* filanda

spin'ning wheel' *s* filatoio

spinster ['spɪnstər] *s* zitella

spi·ral ['spaɪrəl] *adj & s* spirale *f* || *v* (*pret & pp* **-raled** or **-ralled;** *ger* **-raling** or **-ralling**) *intr* muoversi lungo una spirale

spi'ral stair'case *s* scala a chiocciola

spire [spaɪr] *s* (*of a steeple*) guglia, freccia; (*of grass*) foglia; (*spiral*) spirale *f*

spirit ['spɪrɪt] *s* spirito; valore *m,* vigore *m;* bevanda spiritosa; **out of spirits** giù di morale || *tr*—**to spirit away** portar via misteriosamente

spirited ['spɪrɪtɪd] *adj* brioso; (*horse*) superbo, vivace

spir'it lamp' *s* lampada a spirito

spiritless ['spɪrɪtlɪs] *adj* senza anima, senza vita

spir'it lev'el *s* livella a bolla d'aria

spiritual ['spɪrɪt/u·əl] *adj* spirituale; (*séance*) spiritico

spiritualism ['spɪrɪt/uə,lɪzəm] *s* spiritismo; (philos) spiritualismo

spiritualist ['spɪrɪt/uə·lɪst] *s* spiritista *mf;* (philos) spiritualista *mf*

spirituous ['spɪrɪt/u·əs] *adj* alcolico

spit [spɪt] *s* sputo; (*for roasting*) spiedo, schidione *m;* punta; **the spit and image of** (coll) il ritratto parlante di || *v* (*pret & pp* **spat** [spæt] or **spit;** *ger* **spitting**) *tr & intr* sputare

spite [spaɪt] *s* dispetto, ripicco; **in spite of** a dispetto di, a onta di; **out of spite** per picca || *tr* far dispetto a; offendere; contrariare

spiteful ['spaɪtfəl] *adj* dispettoso

spit'fire' *s* persona collerica; (*woman*) bisbetica

spit'ting im'age *s* (coll) ritratto parlante

spittoon [spɪ'tun] *s* sputacchiera

splash [splæ/] *s* schizzo, spruzzo; (*of mud*) zacchera; (*sound*) tonfo; **to make a splash** fare molto sci-sci || *tr & intr* sguazzare

splash'down' *s* (rok) ammaraggio, urto on l'acqua

spleen [splin] *s* cattivo umore, bile *f;* (anat) milza, splene *m*

splendid ['splɛndɪd] *adj* splendido; ottimo, magnifico

splendor ['splɛndər] *s* splendore *m*

splice [splaɪs] *s* giuntura || *tr* giuntare

splint [splɪnt] *s* stecca || *tr* steccare

splinter ['splɪntər] *s* scheggia || *tr* scheggiare || *intr* scheggiarsi

splin'ter group' *s* gruppo dissidente

split [splɪt] *adj* spaccato; diviso || *s* spaccatura; fessura; rottura, divisione; **splits** (sports) spaccato || *v* (*pret & pp* **split;** *ger* **splitting**) *tr* spaccare; dividere; **to split one's sides with laughter** scoppiare dalle risa || *intr* scindersi, dividersi; **to split up** separarsi

split' personal'ity *s* sdoppiamento della personalità

splitting ['splɪtɪŋ] *adj* che fende; che si fende; violento, fortissimo || *s*— **splittings** frammenti *mpl*

splotch [splat/] *s* macchia, chiazza || *tr* macchiare, chiazzare

splurge [splʌrdʒ] *s* ostentazione || *intr* fare ostentazione; fare una spesa matta

splutter ['splʌtər] *s* crepitio; (*utterance*) barbugliamento || *tr* barbugliare || *intr* crepitare; barbugliare

spoil [spɔɪl] *s* spoglia, bottino; **spoils** (mil) spoglie *fpl;* (pol) profitto, vantaggio || *v* (*pret & pp* **spoiled** or **spoilt** [spɔɪlt]) *tr* rovinare, sciupare; (*a child*) viziare; (*food*) deteriorare || *intr* guastarsi, andare a male

spoilage ['spɔɪlɪdʒ] *s* deterioramento

spoiled [spɔɪld] *adj* (*child*) viziato; (*food*) andato a male, passato

spoils' sys'tem *s* sistema politico secondo il quale le cariche vanno al partito vincitore

spoke [spok] *s* (*of a wheel*) raggio; (*of a ladder*) piolo

spokes'man *s* (**-men**) portavoce *m*

sponge [spʌndʒ] *s* spugna; **to throw in the sponge** (slang) gettare la spugna || *tr* pulire con spugna; assorbire; (coll) scroccare || *intr* assorbire; **to sponge off** (coll) vivere alle spalle di

sponge' bath' *s* spugnatura

sponge' cake' *s* pan *m* di Spagna

sponger ['spʌndʒər] *s* scroccatore *m*

sponge' rub'ber *s* gommapiuma

spon·gy ['spʌndʒi] *adj* (**-gier; -giest**) spugnoso

sponsor ['spansər] *s* patrocinatore *m; (of a charitable institution)* patrono; (*godfather*) padrino; (*godmother*) madrina || *tr* patrocinare; (rad, telv) offrire

sponsorship ['spansər,/ɪp] *s* patrocinio

spontaneous [span'teni·əs] *adj* spontaneo

spoof [spuf] *s* mistificazione; parodia ‖ *tr* mistificare; parodiare ‖ *intr* mistificare; fare una parodia

spook [spuk] *s* (coll) spettro

spook·y ['spuki] *adj* (-ier; -iest) (coll) spettrale; *(horse)* (coll) nervoso

spool [spul] *s* spola, rocchetto

spoon [spun] *s* cucchiaio; *(lure)* cucchiaino; **born with a silver spoon in one's mouth** nato con la camicia ‖ *tr* servire col cucchiaino ‖ *intr* (coll) limonare

spoonerism ['spunə ‚rızəm] *s* papera

spoon'-feed' *v* *(pret & pp -fed) tr* nutrire col cucchiaino; (fig) coccolare

spoonful ['spun ‚ful] *s* cucchiaiata

spoon·y ['spuni] *adj* (-ier; -iest) (coll) svenevole

sporadic(al) [spə'rædɪk(əl)] *adj* sporadico

spore [spor] *s* spora

sport [sport] *adj* sportivo ‖ *s* sport *m;* gioco; *(laughingstock)* zimbello; *(gambler)* (coll) giocatore *m; (person who behaves in a sportsmanlike manner)* (coll) spirito sportivo; *(flashy fellow)* (coll) tipo fino; (biol) mutazione; **to make sport of** farsi gioco di ‖ *tr* (coll) sfoggiare; **to sport away** dissipare ‖ *intr* divertirsi; giocare; farsi beffe

sport' clothes' *spl* vestiti *mpl* sport

sport'ing chance' *s* pari opportunità *f* di vincere

sport'ing goods' *spl* articoli *mpl* sportivi

sport'ing house' *s* (coll) bordello

sports'cast'er *s* annunziatore sportivo

sports' fan' *s* appassionato agli spettacoli sportivi, tifoso

sports'man *s* (-men) sportivo

sports'man·ship' *s* sportività *f,* spirito sportivo

sports' news' *s* notiziario sportivo

sports'wear' *s* articoli *mpl* d'abbigliamento sportivo

sports'writ'er *s* cronista sportivo

sport·y ['sporti] *adj* (-ier; -iest) (coll) elegante; (coll) sportivo; (coll) appariscente

spot [spat] *s* macchia; luogo, punto, posto; *(e.g., of tea)* goccia; **spots** locali *mpl;* **on the spot** sul posto; *(right now)* seduta stante; (slang) in difficoltà; **to hit the spot** (slang) soddisfare completamente ‖ *v* *(pret & pp spotted) ger spotting) tr* macchiare; spargere; (coll) riconoscere ‖ *intr* macchiare; macchiarsi

spot' cash' *s* pronta cassa

spot'-check' *tr* fare un breve sondaggio di; controllare rapidamente

spot' check' *s* breve sondaggio; rapido controllo

spotless ['spatlɪs] *adj* immacolato, senza macchia

spot'light' *s* riflettore *m;* (aut) proiettore *m;* **to be in the spotlight** (fig) essere il centro d'attenzione

spot' remov'er [rɪ'muvər] *s* smacchiatore *m*

spot' weld'ing *s* saldatura per punti

spouse [spauz] *or* [spaus] *s* consorte *mf*

spout [spaut] *s* *(to carry water from roof)* doccia; *(of jar, pitcher, etc.)* becco, beccuccio; *(jet)* zampillo, getto ‖ *tr & intr* sprizzare, zampillare; (coll) declamare

sprain [spren] *s* distorsione ‖ *tr* distorcere, distorcersi

sprawl [sprɔl] *intr* sdraiarsi

spray [spre] *s* spruzzo; *(of the sea)* schiuma; *(device)* spruzzatore *m; (twig)* ramoscello ‖ *tr & intr* spruzzare

sprayer ['spre·ər] *s* spruzzatore *m,* schizzetto, vaporizzatore *m;* (hort) irroratrice *f*

spray' gun' *s* pistola a spruzzo; (hort) irroratrice *f*

spray' paint' *s* vernice *f* a spruzzo

spread [spred] *s* espansione; diffusione; differenza; tappeto, coperta; elasticità *f; (of the wings of bird or airplane)* apertura; cibo da spalmare; (coll) festino; (journ) articolo di fondo *or* pubblicitario su varie colonne ‖ *v* *(pret & pp spread) tr* tendere, estendere; *(one's legs)* divaricare; *(wings)* spiegare; spargere; *(the table)* preparare; *(butter)* spalmare; diffondere ‖ *intr* estendersi; spiegarsi; spargersi; spalmarsi; diffondersi

spree [spri] *s* baldoria, bisboccia; **to go on a spree** darsi alla pazza gioia

sprig [sprɪg] *s* ramoscello

spright·ly ['spraɪtli] *adj* (-ier; -iest) brioso, vivace

spring [sprɪŋ] *adj* primaverile; sorgivo; a molla ‖ *s* *(season)* primavera; *(issue of water from earth)* fonte *f,* polla; *(elastic device)* molla; elasticità *f; (leap)* salto; *(crack)* fenditura; (aut) balestra ‖ *v* *(pret* **sprang** [spræŋ] *or* **sprung** [sprʌŋ]; *pp* **sprung**) *tr (e.g., a lock)* far scattare; *(a leak)* aprire; *(a mine)* far brillare ‖ *intr* saltare; *(said of a metal spring)* scattare; scaturire, zampillare; nascere, derivare; esplodere; **to spring forth** *or* **up** sorgere

spring'board' *s* pedana, trampolino

spring' chick'en *s* pollo giovanissimo; (slang) ragazzina

spring' fe'ver *s* indolenza primaverile

spring' mat'tress *s* materasso a molle

spring' tide' *s* marea di sizigia

spring'time' *s* primavera

sprinkle ['sprɪŋkəl] *s* spruzzo, spruzzatina; *(small amount)* pizzico ‖ *tr* spruzzare; *(e.g., sugar)* spolverizzare ‖ *intr* sprizzare; piovigginare

sprinkler ['sprɪŋklər] *s* annaffiatoio; *(person)* annaffiatore *m*

sprinkling ['sprɪŋklɪŋ] *s* sprizzo, spruzzo; *(with holy water)* aspersione; *(with powder)* spolverizzamento; *(e.g., of knowledge)* spolvero, spolveratura; *(of people)* piccolo numero

sprin'kling can' *s* annaffiatoio

sprint [sprɪnt] *s* (sports) scatto, volata ‖ *intr* (sports) scattare

sprite [spraɪt] *s* spirito folletto

sprocket ['sprɑkɪt] *s* moltiplica; (phot) trasportatore *m*

sprout [spraut] *s* germoglio ‖ *intr* germogliare; crescere rapidamente

spruce [sprus] *adj* elegante, attillato ‖ *s* abete rosso ‖ *tr* attillare, azzimare ‖ *intr* attillarsi, azzimarsi

spry [spraɪ] *adj* (**spryer** or **sprier; spryest** or **spriest**) vegeto

spud [spʌd] *s* vanghetto, tagliaradici *m*; (coll) patata

spun' glass' *s* lana di vetro

spunk [spʌŋk] *s* (coll) coraggio, fegato

spur [spʌr] *s* sperone *m*; (rr) raccordo ferroviario; (fig) pungolo; **on the spur of the moment** lì per lì ‖ *v* (*pret & pp* **spurred;** *ger* **spurring**) *tr* spronare; **to spur on** spronare, incitare

spurious ['spjurɪəs] *adj* spurio

spurn [spʌrn] *s* disprezzo, sdegno; rifiuto ‖ *tr* disprezzare, sdegnare; rifiutare

spurt [spʌrt] *s* spruzzo, zampillo; (*sudden burst*) scatto repentino ‖ *intr* sprizzare, zampillare; scattare

sputter ['spʌtər] *s* barbugliamento; (*sizzling*) crepitio ‖ *tr* barbugliare ‖ *intr* barbugliare; crepitare

spu•tum ['spjutəm] *s* (**-ta** [tə]) sputo

spy [spaɪ] *s* (**spies**) spia ‖ *v* (*pret & pp* **spied**) *tr* spiare; osservare ‖ *intr* fare la spia; **to spy on** spiare

spy'glass' *s* cannocchiale *m*

spying ['spaɪ·ɪŋ] *s* spionaggio

squabble ['skwɑbəl] *s* battibecco ‖ *intr* litigare

squad [skwɑd] *s* squadra

squadron ['skwɑdrən] *s* (*of cavalry*) squadrone *m*; (aer, nav) squadriglia; (mil) squadra

squalid ['skwɑlɪd] *adj* sordido; squallido, misero

squall [skwɔl] *s* groppo, turbine *m*; urlo ‖ *intr* gridare, urlare

squalor ['skwɑlər] *s* sordidezza; squallore *m*, miseria

squander ['skwɑndər] *tr* scialacquare, dilapidare, sperperare

square [skwɛr] *adj* quadrato, e.g., **two square miles** due miglia quadrate; di . . . di lato, e.g., **two miles square** di due miglia di lato; ad angolo retto; solido; saldato; (coll) onesto; (coll) diretto; (coll) sostanzioso; (slang) all'antica; **to get square with** (coll) fargliela pagare a ‖ *s* quadrato; (*small square, e.g., of checkerboard*) quadretto; (*city block*) isolato; (*open area in city*) piazza, piazzale *m*; (*of carpenter*) squadra; **on the square** ad angolo retto; (coll) onesto ‖ *adv* ad angolo retto; (coll) onestamente ‖ *tr* squadrare; dividere in quadretti; elevare al quadrato; quadrare; (*a debt*) saldare; **to square with** adattare a ‖ *intr* quadrare; **to square off** prepararsi, mettersi in posizione difensiva

square' dance' *s* danza figurata americana

square' meal' *s* (coll) pasto abbondante

square' root' *s* radice quadrata

square' shoot'er ['ʃutər] *s* (coll) persona onesta

squash [skwɑʃ] *s* spappolamento; (bot) zucca; (sports) squash *m* ‖ *tr* spappolare; spiaccicare; (*e.g., a rumor*) sopprimere; (*a person*) (coll) ridurre al silenzio ‖ *intr* spiaccicarsi

squash•y ['skwɑʃi] *adj* (**-ier; -iest**) tenero; (*ground*) fangoso, pantanoso; (*fruit*) maturo

squat [skwɑt] *adj* tozzo ‖ *v* (*pret & pp* **squatted;** *ger* **squatting**) *intr* accoccolarsi; stabilirsi illegalmente su territorio altrui; stabilirsi su terreno pubblico per ottenerne titolo

squatter ['skwɑtər] *s* intruso

squaw [skwɔ] *s* squaw *f*; (coll) donna

squawk [skwɔk] *s* schiamazzo; (slang) lamento stridulo ‖ *intr* schiamazzare; (slang) lamentarsi strillando

squaw' man' *s* bianco sposato con una pellerossa

squeak [skwik] *s* strido; cigolio ‖ *intr* stridere; cigolare; (*said of a mouse*) squittire; **to squeak through** farcela per il rotto della cuffia

squeal [skwil] *s* strido ‖ *intr* stridere; (slang) cantare, fare il delatore

squealer ['skwilər] *s* (slang) delatore *m*

squeamish ['skwimɪʃ] *adj* pudibondo; scrupoloso; (*easily nauseated*) schifiltoso, schizzinoso

squeeze [skwiz] *s* spremuta; stretta, abbraccio; **to put the squeeze on** (coll) far pressione su ‖ *tr* premere; spremere, pigiare; stringere ‖ *intr* stringere; **to squeeze through** aprirsi il passo attraverso; (fig) farcela a pena

squeezer ['skwizər] *s* spremifrutta *m*

squelch [skwɛltʃ] *s* osservazione schiacciante ‖ *tr* schiacciare

squid [skwɪd] *s* calamaro, totano

squint [skwɪnt] *s* tendenza losca; (coll) occhiata; (pathol) strabismo ‖ *tr* (*one's eyes*) socchiudere ‖ *intr* socchiudere gli occhi; guardare furtivamente

squint-eyed ['skwɪnt‚aɪd] *adj* guercio, losco; malevolo

squire [skwaɪr] *s* (*of a lady*) cavalier *m* servente; (Brit) proprietario terriero; (U.S.A.) giudice *m* conciliatore ‖ *tr* (*a woman*) accompagnare

squirm [skwʌrm] *s* contorsione ‖ *intr* contorcersi; mostrare imbarazzo; **to squirm out of** cavarsela da

squirrel ['skwʌrəl] *s* scoiattolo

squirt [skwʌrt] *s* schizzo; (*instrument*) schizzetto; (coll) saputello ‖ *tr & intr* schizzare

stab [stæb] *s* pugnalata; (*of pain*) fitta; **to make a stab at** (coll) provare ‖ *v* (*pret & pp* **stabbed**) *tr* pugnalare, trafiggere ‖ *intr* pugnalare

stabilize ['stebəl‚aɪz] *tr* stabilizzare

stab' in the back' *s* pugnalata nella schiena or alle spalle

stable ['stebəl] *adj* stabile ‖ *s* stalla; (*of race horses*) scuderia

sta'ble-boy' *s* stalliere *m*

stack [stæk] *s* pila; (*of hay or straw*) pagliaio; (*of firewood*) catasta; (*of books*) scaffale *m;* camino; (coll) mucchio, sacco ‖ *tr* ammonticchiare, accatastare

stadi-um ['stedɪ-əm] *s* (**-ums** or **-a** [ə]) stadio

staff [stæf] or [stɑf] *s* bastone *m;* asta, albero; personale *m,* corpo; (mil) stato maggiore; (mus) rigo, pentagramma *m* ‖ *tr* dotare di personale

staff' of'ficer *s* ufficiale *m* di stato maggiore

stag [stæg] *adj* per signori soli ‖ *s* (*deer*) cervo; maschio; (coll) signore *m* ‖ *adv* senza compagna

stage [stedʒ] *s* fase *f*, stadio; tappa, giornata; (*coach*) diligenza; teatro; piattaforma; (*of microscope*) piatto portaoggetti; (theat) scena, palcoscenico; **by easy stages** poco a poco; **to go on the stage** diventare attore ‖ *tr* mettere in scena; organizzare

stage'coach' *s* diligenza

stage'craft' *s* scenotecnica

stage' door' *s* (theat) ingresso degli artisti

stage' fright' *s* tremarella

stage'hand' *s* macchinista *m*

stage' left' *s* (theat) la sinistra della scena guardando il pubblico

stage' man'ager *s* direttore *m* di scena

stage' right' *s* (theat) la destra della scena guardando il pubblico

stage'-struck' *adj* innamorato del teatro

stage' whis'per *s* a parte *m*

stagger ['stægər] *tr* far traballare; impressionare; (*troops; hours*) scaglionare ‖ *intr* traballare

stag'gering *adj* traballante; impressionante, stupefacente

staging ['stedʒɪŋ] *s* impalcatura; (theat) messa in scena

stagnant ['stægnənt] *adj* stagnante

staid [sted] *adj* serio, grave

stain [sten] *s* macchia; tinta; colorante *m* ‖ *tr* macchiare; tingere; colorare ‖ *intr* macchiarsi

stained' glass' *s* vetro colorato

stained'-glass win'dow' *s* vetrata a colori

stainless ['stenlɪs] *adj* immacolato; (*steel*) inossidabile

stair [ster] *s* scala

stair'case' *s* scala

stair'way' *s* scala

stair'well' *s* tromba delle scale

stake [stek] *s* picchetto; (*e.g., of cart*) staggio; (*to support a plant*) puntello; (*in gambling*) puglia, giocata; **at stake** in gioco; **to die at the stake** morire sul rogo; **to pull up stakes** (coll) andarsene, traslocare ‖ *tr* picchettare; puntellare; attaccare a un palo; attraversare; (coll) aiutare; **to stake out** picchettare; (slang) tenere sotto sorveglianza; **to stake out a claim** avanzare una pretesa

stale [stel] *adj* stantio; (*air*) viziato; (fig) ritrito

stale'mate' *s* (chess) stallo; **to reach a** stalemate essere in una posizione di stallo ‖ *tr* mettere in una posizione di stallo

stalk [stɔk] *s* stelo; (*of corn*) stocco; (*of salad*) piede *m* ‖ *tr* braccare ‖ *intr* avanzare furtivamente; camminare con andatura maestosa

stall [stɔl] *s* (*in a stable*) posta; (*booth in a market*) bancarella; (*seat*) stallo; (*space in a parking lot*) spazio per il parcheggio ‖ *tr* (*an animal*) stallare; (*a car*) parcheggiare; (*a motor*) far fermare; **to stall off** eludere, tenere a bada ‖ *intr* impantanarsi; stare nella posta; (*said of a motor*) fermarsi; (*to temporize*) menare il can per l'aia

stallion ['stæljən] *s* stallone *m*

stalwart ['stɔlwərt] *adj* forte, gagliardo ‖ *s* sostenitore *m*

stamen ['stemən] *s* stame *m*

stamina ['stæmɪnə] *s* forza, vigore *m*

stammer ['stæmər] *s* balbuzie *f* ‖ *tr &* *intr* balbettare

stammerer ['stæmərər] *s* balbuziente *mf*

stamp [stæmp] *s* (*postage stamp*) francobollo; (*device to show that a fee has been paid*) timbro, bollo; impressione; carattere *m;* sigillo; (*tool for stamping coins*) conio; (*tool for crushing ore*) maglio ‖ *tr* timbrare, stampigliare, bollare; sigillare; coniare; (*one's foot*) battere, pestare; imprimere; caratterizzare; (mach) stampare; **to stamp out** spegnere; sopprimere ‖ *intr* battere il piede; (*said of a horse*) zampare

stampede [stæm'pid] *s* fuga precipitosa ‖ *tr* precipitarsi verso; far fuggire precipitosamente ‖ *intr* precipitarsi

stamp'ing ground' *s* (coll) luogo di ritrovo abituale

stamp' pad' *s* tampone *m*

stamp'-vend'ing machine' *s* distributore automatico di francobolli

stance [stæns] *s* posizione

stanch [stɑntʃ] *adj* leale; forte; a tenuta d'acqua ‖ *s* chiusa ‖ *tr* arrestare il flusso da; (*blood*) stagnare

stand [stænd] *s* posizione; resistenza, difesa; tribuna, palco; sostegno, supporto; (*booth in market*) posteggio; posto di sosta ‖ *v* (*pret & pp* **stood** [stud]) *tr* mettere in piedi; reggere, sostenere; sopportare, tollerare; (*one's ground*) mantenere; (*a chance*) avere; (*watch*) fare; (coll) pagare; **to stand off** tenere a distanza ‖ *intr* stare; essere alto; fermarsi; stare in piedi; trovarsi; aver forza; essere; (*e.g., apart*) tenersi; **to stand back of** spalleggiare; **to stand by** appoggiare; **to stand for** rappresentare, voler dire; appoggiare, favorire; tenere a battesimo; (coll) tollerare; **to stand in line** fare la fila or la coda; **to stand in with** (coll) essere nelle buone grazie di; **to stand out** stagliarsi, distaccarsi, risaltare; **to stand up** tenersi in piedi; resistere, durare; **to stand up to** affrontare

standard ['stændərd] *adj* (*usual*) normale; uniforme, standard; (*language*) corretto, preferito || *s* standard *m*; (*model*) modello, campione *m*; (*flag*) stendardo

stand'ard·bear'er *s* portabandiera *m*

standardize ['stændər‚daɪz] *tr* standardizzare

stand'ard of liv'ing *s* tenore *m* di vita

stand'ard time' *s* ora ufficiale, ora legale

standee [stæn'di] *s* passeggero in piedi; spettatore *m* in piedi

stand'-in' *s* (mov) controfigura; **to have a stand-in with** (coll) essere nelle buone grazie di

standing ['stændɪŋ] *adj* (*jump*) da fermo; in piedi; fermo; (*water*) stagnante; vigente, permanente; (*idle*) fuori uso || *s* posizione, rango, situazione; classifica; **in good standing** riconosciuto da tutti; **of long standing** vecchio, da lungo tempo

stand'ing ar'my *s* esercito permanente

stand'ing room' *s* posto in piedi

standpatter ['stænd‚pætər] *s* (coll) seguace *mf* dell'immobilismo

stand'point' *s* punto di vista

stand'still' *s* fermata; riposo; **to come to a standstill** fermarsi

stanza ['stænzə] *s* stanza

staple ['stepəl] *adj* principale || *s* articolo di prima necessità; elemento indispensabile; (*e.g., to hold wire*) cavallottino, cambretta; (*to fasten papers*) grappetta; fibra tessile || *tr* aggraffare

stapler ['steplər] *s* cucitrice *f* a grappe

star [stɑr] *s* (*any heavenly body, except the moon, appearing in the sky*) astro; (*heavenly body radiating self-produced energy*) stella; (*actor*) divo; (*actress*) diva, stella (*athlete*) asso; (fig, mov) stella; (typ) stelletta; **to thank one's lucky stars** ringraziare la propria stella || *v* (*pret & pp* **starred**) *ger* **starring**) *tr* costellare, stellare; presentare come stella; (typ) marcare con stelletta || *intr* primeggiare

starboard ['stɑrbərd] *or* ['stɑr‚bɔrd] *adj* di dritta, di tribordo || *s* dritta, tribordo || *adv* a dritta, a tribordo

starch [stɑrtʃ] *s* amido, fecola; (*in laundering*) salda; (coll) forza || *tr* inamidare

starch·y ['stɑrtʃi] *adj* (-ier; -iest) amidaceo; (*e.g., collar*) inamidato; (*manner*) sostenuto, contegnoso

star' dust' *s* polveri *fpl* meteoriche; (fig) polvere *f* di stelle

stare [ster] *s* sguardo fisso || *intr* rimirare; **to stare at** fissare gli occhi addosso a

star'fish' *s* stella di mare

star'gaze' *intr* guardare le stelle; sognare ad occhi aperti

stark [stɑrk] *adj* completo; desolato; severo, serio; duro, rigido || *adv* completamente

stark'-na'ked *adj* nudo e crudo

starlet ['stɑrlɪt] *s* stellina, divetta

star'light' *s* lume *f* delle stelle

starling ['stɑrlɪŋ] *s* storno, stornello

Stars' and Stripes' *s* bandiera stellata

Star'-Spangled Ban'ner *s* bandiera stellata

star' sys'tem *s* (mov) divismo

start [stɑrt] *s* inizio, principio; partenza; linea di partenza; (*sudden jerk*) sussulto, soprassalto; (*advantage*) vantaggio; (*spurt*) scatto || *tr* iniziare, principiare; mettere in moto; dare il via a; (*a conversation*) intavolare; (*game*) stanare || *intr* iniziare, principiare; mettersi in moto; incamminarsi; (*to be startled*) trasalire, sussultare; **to start + ger** mettersi a + *inf*; **to start + ger + again** rimettersi a + *inf*; **to start after** andare in cerca di

starter ['stɑrtər] *s* (*of a venture*) iniziatore *m*; partente *m*; (aut) motorino d'avviamento; (sports) mossiere *m*

starting ['stɑrtɪŋ] *adj* di partenza || *s* messa in marcia

start'ing crank' *s* manovella d'avviamento

start'ing point' *s* punto di partenza

startle ['stɑrtəl] *tr* far trasalire || *intr* trasalire, sussultare

startling ['stɑrtlɪŋ] *adj* allarmante, sorprendente

starvation [stɑr've/ən] *s* fame *f*, inedia, inanizione

starva'tion wag'es *spl* paga da fame

starve [stɑrv] *tr* affamare; far morire di fame; **to starve out** prendere per fame || *intr* essere affamato; morire di fame

starving ['stɑrvɪŋ] *adj* famelico

state [stet] *adj* statale; ufficiale; di gala, di lusso || *s* condizione; stato; gala, pompa; **to lie in state** essere esposto in camera ardente; **to live in state** vivere sfarzosamente || *tr* dichiarare, affermare; (*a problem*) impostare

stateless ['stetlɪs] *adj* apolide

state·ly ['stetli] *adj* (-lier; -liest) maestoso, imponente

statement ['stetmənt] *s* dichiarazione, affermazione; comunicazione; (com) estratto conto

state' of mind' *s* stato d'animo

state'room' *s* cabina; (rr) compartimento privato

states'man *s* (-men) statista *m*, uomo di stato

static ['stætɪk] *adj* statico; (rad) atmosferico || *s* disturbi *mpl* atmosferici

station ['ste/ən] *s* stazione; rango, condizione || *tr* stazionare

sta'tion a'gent *s* capostazione *m*

stationary ['ste/ən‚eri] *adj* stazionario

sta'tion break' *s* (rad, telv) intervallo

stationer ['ste/ənər] *s* cartolaio

stationery ['ste/ən‚eri] *s* (*writing paper*) carta da lettere; (*writing materials*) cancelleria

sta'tionery store' *s* cartoleria

sta'tion house' *s* posto di polizia

sta'tion·mas'ter *s* capostazione *m*

sta'tion wag'on *s* giardinetta

statistical [stə'tɪstɪkəl] *adj* statistico

statistician [‚stætɪs'tɪ/ən] *s* statistico

statistics [stə'tıstıks] *ssg* (*science*) statistica; *spl* (*data*) statistiche *fpl*

statue ['stæt/ʊ] *s* statua

statuesque [ˌstæt/ʊ'esk] *adj* statuario

stature ['stæt/ər] *s* statura

status ['stetəs] *s* stato, condizione; condizione sociale

sta'tus sym'bol *s* simbolo della posizione sociale

statute ['stæt/ʊt] *s* legge *f*; regolamento

stat'ute of limita'tions *s* legge *f* che governa la prescrizione

statutory ['stæt/ʊˌtori] *adj* legale

staunch [stɔnt/] or [stɑnt/] *adj, s & tr* var of **stanch**

stave [stev] *s* (*of barrel*) doga; (*of ladder*) piolo; (*mus*) rigo, pentagramma *m* ‖ *v* (*pret & pp* **staved** or **stove** [stov]) *tr* bucare; (*to smash*) sfondare; **to stave off** tenere a bada

stay [ste] *s* permanenza, soggiorno; (*brace*) staggio; (*of corset*) stecca di balena; sostegno; (*law*) sospensione; (*naut*) strallo ‖ *tr* fermare; sospendere; poner freno a ‖ *intr* stare; mantenersi; restare, rimanere; (*at a hotel*) sostare; **to stay up** stare alzato

stay'-at-home' *adj* casalingo ‖ *s* persona casalinga

stead [sted] *s* posto; **in his stead** in suo luogo; **to stand in good stead** esser utile

stead'fast' *adj* fermo, risoluto

stead·y ['stedi] *adj* (**-ier; -iest**) stabile, fermo; regolare, costante; abituale; calmo, sicuro ‖ *v* (*pret & pp* **-ied**) *tr* rinforzare; calmare ‖ *intr* rinforzarsi; calmarsi

steak [stek] *s* bistecca

steal [stil] *s* (coll) furto ‖ *v* (*pret* **stole** [stol]; *pp* **stolen**) *tr* rubare; involare; (*the attention*) cattivare ‖ *intr* rubare; **to steal away** svignarsela; **to steal out** uscire di soppiatto; **to steal upon** approssimarsi silenziosamente a

stealth [stelθ] *s* clandestinità *f*; **by stealth** di straforo, di soppiatto

steam [stim] *adj* a vapore ‖ *s* vapore *m*; fumo; **to get up steam** aumentare la pressione; **to let off steam** scaricare la pressione; (slang) sfogarsi ‖ *tr* (*a steamship*) guidare; esalare; esporre al vapore; (*e.g., glasses*) appannare ‖ *intr* dar vapore, fumigare; bollire; (*to become clouded*) appannarsi; andare a vapore; **to steam ahead** avanzare a tutto vapore

steam'boat' *s* vapore *m*

steam' en'gine *s* macchina a vapore

steamer ['stimər] *s* vapore *m*

steam'er rug' *s* coperta da viaggio

steam'er trunk' *s* bauletto da cabina

steam' heat' *s* riscaldamento a vapore

steam' roll'er *s* rullo compressore; (fig) rullo compressore

steam'ship' *s* piroscafo, vapore *m*

steam' shov'el *s* escavatore m a vapore

steam' ta'ble *s* tavola riscaldata a vapore per mantenere calde le vivande

steed [stid] *s* destriere *m*

steel [stil] *adj* d'acciaio; (*industry*) siderurgico ‖ *s* acciaio; (*bar*) stecca d'acciaio; (*for sharpening knives*) affilacoltelli *m*; (fig) spada, brando ‖ *tr* acciaiare; **to steel oneself** corazzarsi, indurirsi; armarsi di coraggio

steel' wool' *s* paglia di ferro

steel'works' *spl* acciaieria

steelyard ['stilˌjɑrd] or ['stiljərd] *s* stadera

steep [stip] *adj* erto, scosceso, ripido; (*price*) alto ‖ *tr* immergere, saturare, imbevere

steeple ['stipəl] *s* campanile *m*; (*spire*) cuspide *f*, guglia

stee'ple·chase' *s* corsa ad ostacoli

stee'ple·jack' *s* aggiustatore *m* di campanili

steer [stɪr] *s* bue *m*, manzo ‖ *tr* governare, guidare; (aer) pilotare ‖ *intr* governare; **to steer clear of** evitare

steerage ['stɪrɪdʒ] *s* (naut) alloggio passeggeri di terza classe

steer'ing wheel' *s* (aut) volante *m*, sterzo; (naut) ruota del timone

stellar ['stelər] *adj* stellare; (*role*) da stella

stem [stem] *s* (*of pipe, of key*) cannello; (*of goblet*) gambo; (*of column*) fusto; (*of spoon*) manico; (*of watch*) corona; (*of a word*) tema *m*; (*of note*) (mus) gamba; (bot) peduncolo, stelo; (bot) gambo; **from stem to stern** da poppa a prua ‖ *v* (*pret & pp* **stemmed**; *ger* **stemming**) *tr* togliere il gambo a; (*to check*) arrestare; (*to dam up*) arginare; (*to plug*) otturare; (*the tide*) risalire, andare contro ‖ *intr* originare, derivare

stem'-win'der *s* orologio a corona

stench [stent/] *s* tanfo, fetore *m*

sten·cil ['stensəl] *s* stampo, stampino; parole *fpl* a stampo ‖ *v* (*pret & pp* **-ciled** or **-cilled**; *ger* **-ciling** or **-cilling**) *tr* stampinare

stenographer [stə'nɑgrəfər] *s* stenografo

stenography [stə'nɑgrəfi] *s* stenografia

step [step] *s* passo; (*footprint*) orma, impronta; (*of ladder*) piolo; (*of staircase*) gradino; (*of carriage*) montatoio; **step by step** passo passo; **to watch one's step** fare molta attenzione ‖ *v* (*pret & pp* **stepped**; *ger* **stepping**) *tr* scaglionare; **to step off** misurare a passi ‖ *intr* camminare, andare a passi; mettere il piede; **to step aside** scostarsi; **to step back** indietreggiare; **to step on it** (slang) fare presto; **to step on the gas** (coll) accelerare; **to step on the starter** avviare il motore

step'broth'er *s* fratellastro, fratello consanguineo

step'child' *s* (**-children** [ˌt/ɪldrən]) figliastro

step'daugh'ter *s* figliastra

step'fa'ther *s* patrigno

step'lad'der *s* scala a gradini or a libretto

step'moth'er *s* matrigna

steppe [step] *s* steppa

step'ping stone' *s* passatoio, pietra per guadare; (fig) gradino

step'sis'ter *s* sorellastra

step'son' *s* figliastro

stere•o ['stɛrɪ ,o] or ['stɪrɪ ,o] *adj* stereofonico; stereoscopico ‖ *s* (-os) musica stereofonica; sistema stereofonico; fotografia stereoscopica

stereotyped ['stɛrɪ-ə,taɪpt] or ['stɪrɪ-ə-,taɪpt] *adj* stereotipato

sterile ['stɛrɪl] *adj* sterile

sterilize ['stɛrɪ ,laɪz] *tr* sterilizzare

sterling ['stʌrlɪŋ] *adj* di lira sterlina; d'argento; puro; eccellente ‖ *s* argento .925; vasellame *m* d'argento puro

stern [stʌrn] *adj* severo ‖ *s* poppa

stet [stet] *v* (*pret & pp* **stetted;** *ger* **stetting**) *tr* marcare con la parola "vive"

stethoscope ['stɛθə ,skop] *s* stetoscopio

stevedore ['stivə ,dor] *s* stivatore *m*

stew [stju] or [stu] *s* stufato, guazzetto ‖ *tr* stufare ‖ *intr* cuocere a fuoco lento; (coll) preoccuparsi

steward ['stju•ərd] or ['stu•ərd] *s* amministratore *m*, agente *m*; maggiordomo; (aer, naut) cambusiere *m*, cameriere *m*

stewardess ['stju•ərdɪs] or ['stu•ərdɪs] *s* (naut) cameriera; (aer) hostess *f*, assistente *f* di volo

stewed' fruit' *s* composta di frutta

stewed' toma'toes *spl* pomodori *mpl* in umido

stick [stɪk] *s* stecco; legno; bacchetta; bastone *m*; (*e.g., of candy*) cannello; (naut) albero; (typ) compositoio; **in the sticks** (coll) in casa del diavolo ‖ *v* (*pret & pp* **stuck** [stʌk]) *tr* pungere; ficcare, infiggere; attaccare; confondere; **to be stuck** essere insabbiato; essere attaccato; (fig) essere confuso; **to stick out** (*the head*) sporgere; (*the tongue*) cacciare; **to stick up** (slang) assaltare a mano armata, rapinare ‖ *intr* rimanere attaccato; persistere; (*said of glue*) appiccicarsi; (*to one opinion*) tenersi; stare; **to stick out** sporgere; **to stick together** rimanere uniti; **to stick up** risaltare; (*said, e.g., of quills*) rizzarsi; **to stick up for** (coll) stare dalla parte di

sticker ['stɪkər] *s* etichetta gommata; spina; persona zelante; (coll) busillis *m*

stick'ing plas'ter *s* cerotto

stick'pin' *s* spilla da cravatta

stick'up' *s* (slang) grassazione

stick•y ['stɪki] *adj* (-ier; -iest) attaccaticcio; vischioso; (*weather*) afoso, soffocante; (fig) difficile

stiff [stɪf] *adj* rigido, duro; forte; (*price*) alto; denso ‖ *s* (slang) cadavere *m*; **poor stiff** (slang) povero diavolo

stiff' col'lar *s* colletto duro

stiffen ['stɪfən] *tr* irrigidire ‖ *intr* irrigidirsi

stiff' neck' *s* torcicollo; ostinazione

stiff'-necked' *adj* testardo

stiff' shirt' *s* camicia inamidata

stifle ['staɪfəl] *tr* soffocare

stigma ['stɪgmə] *s* (-mas or -mata [mətə]) stigma *m*

stigmatize ['stɪgmə ,taɪz] *tr* stigmatizzare

still [stɪl] *adj* fermo, tranquillo; silenzioso; (*wine*) non spumante ‖ *s* calma; distillatore *m;* distilleria; (phot) fotografia singola ‖ *adv* ancora; tuttora ‖ *conj* tuttavia ‖ *tr* calmare ‖ *intr* calmarsi

still'birth' *s* parto di infante nato morto

still'born' *adj* nato morto

still' life' *s* (lifes') natura morta

stilt [stɪlt] *s* trampolo; (*in water*) palafitta; (orn) trampoliere *m*

stilted ['stɪltɪd] *adj* elevato; pomposo

stimulant ['stɪmjələnt] *adj & s* stimulante *m*, eccitante *m*

stimulate ['stɪmjə ,let] *tr* stimulare

stimu•lus ['stɪmjələs] *s* (-li [,laɪ]) stimolo

sting [stɪŋ] *s* puntura; (*of insect*) pungiglione; (fig) scottatura ‖ *v* (*pret & pp* **stung** [stʌŋ]) *tr & intr* pungere

stin•gy ['stɪndʒi] *adj* (-gier; -giest) tirchio, taccagno

stink [stɪŋk] *s* puzza ‖ *v* (*pret* **stank** [stæŋk] or **stunk** [stʌŋk]; *pp* **stunk**) *tr* far puzzare ‖ *intr* puzzare; **to stink of money** (slang) aver soldi a palate

stinker ['stɪŋkər] *s* (slang) puzzone *m*

stint [stɪnt] *s* limite *m;* lavoro assegnato, compito ‖ *intr* lesinarsi

stipend ['staɪpənd] *s* stipendio; assegno di studio, presalario

stipulate ['stɪpjə ,let] *tr* stipulare

stir [stʌr] *s* agitazione, movimento; (*poke*) spinta; **to create a stir** creare una sensazione ‖ *v* (*pret & pp* **stirred;** *ger* **stirring**) *tr* mescolare; muovere; (*fire*) ravvivare; (*pity*) fare; **to stir up** eccitare, svegliare; (*to rebellion*) sommuovere ‖ *intr* muoversi, agitarsi

stirring ['stʌrɪŋ] *adj* commovente

stirrup ['stʌrəp] or ['stɪrəp] *s* staffa

stitch [stɪtʃ] *s* punto; maglia; (*pain*) fitta; (*bit*) poco, po' *m;* **to be in stitches** (coll) sbellicarsi dalle risa ‖ *tr* cucire; aggraffare ‖ *intr* cucire

stock [stɑk] *s* regolare, comune; banale, ordinario; di bestiame; borsistico; azionario; (aut) di serie; (theat) stabile ‖ *s* provvista, scorta; capitale *m* sociale; azione *f;* azioni *fpl*, titoli *mpl;* (*of tree*) tronco; (*of family; of anchor; of anvil*) ceppo; razza, famiglia; materia prima; (*of rifle*) cassa; (*broth*) brodo; (*handle*) manico; (*livestock*) bestiame *m;* (theat) compagnia stabile; **in stock** in magazzino, disponibile; **out of stock** esaurito; **stocks** gogna, berlina; **to take stock** fare l'inventario; **to take stock in** (coll) aver fede in ‖ *tr* fornire; fornire di bestiame; fornire di pesci ‖ *intr*—**to stock up** fare rifornimenti

stockade [stɑ'ked] *s* staccionata

stock'breed'er *s* allevatore *m* di bestiame

stock'bro'ker *s* agente *m* di cambio
stock' car' *s* automobile *f* di serie; (rr) carro bestiame
stock' com'pany *s* (theat) compagnia stabile; (com) società anonima
stock' div'idend *s* dividendo pagato in azioni
stock' exchange' *s* borsa valori
stock'fish' *s* stoccafisso
stock'hold'er *s* azionista *mf*
stock'holder of rec'ord *s* azionista *mf* registrato nei libri della compagnia
Stockholm ['stakhom] *s* Stoccolma
stocking ['stakıŋ] *s* calza
stock' in trade' *s* stock *m;* ferri *mpl* del mestiere
stock' mar'ket *s* borsa valori
stock'pile' *s* riserva, scorta ‖ *tr* mettere in riserva ‖ *intr* mettere in riserva materie prime
stock' rais'ing *s* allevamento bestiame
stock'room' *s* magazzino, deposito
stock•y ['staki] *adj* (**-ier; -iest**) tozzo, tarchiato
stock'yard' *s* chiuso per il bestiame
stoic ['sto·ık] *adj* & *s* stoico
stoicism ['sto·ı ,sızəm] *s* stoicismo
stoke [stok] *tr* (*fire*) attizzare; (*a furnace*) caricare
stoker ['stokər] *s* fochista *m*
stolid ['stalıd] *adj* impassibile
stomach ['stʌmək] *s* stomaco ‖ *tr* (fig) digerire
stone [ston] *s* sasso, pietra; (*of fruit*) osso; (pathol) calcolo ‖ *tr* lapidare; affilare con la pietra; (*fruit*) snocciolare
stone'-broke' *adj* (coll) senza un soldo, senza il becco di un quattrino
stone'-deaf' *adj* sordo come una campana
stone'ma'son *s* tagliapietra *m*
stone' quar'ry *s* cava di pietra
stone's' throw' *s* tiro di sasso; **within a stone's throw** a un tiro di schioppo
ston•y ['stoni] *adj* (**-ier; -iest**) di sasso, sassoso, pietroso
stooge [studʒ] *s* (theat) spalla; (slang) complice *mf*
stool [stul] *s* sgabello, seggiolino; gabinetto; (*mass evacuated*) feci *fpl*
stool' pi'geon *s* piccione *m* di richiamo; (slang) spia
stoop [stup] *s* curvatura, inclinazione; scalini *mpl* d'ingresso ‖ *intr* inclinarsi, piegarsi; degnarsi, umiliarsi
stoop-shouldered ['stup'ʃoldərd] *adj* con le spalle cadenti
stop [stap] *s* fermata, sosta; arresto; otturazione, blocco; cessazione; ostacolo; (*of a check*) fermo; (*restraint*) freno; (*of organ*) registro; **to come to a stop** fermarsi; cessare; **to put a stop to** metter fine a ‖ *v* (*pret & pp* **stopped;** *ger* **stopping**) *tr* fermare, cessare; arrestare, sospendere; tappare, otturare; (*a check*) mettere il fermo a; **to stop up** tappare, otturare ‖ *intr* fermarsi; arrestarsi; (*said of a ship*) fare scalo; (*at an hotel*) scendere; **to stop** + *ger* smettere di or cessare di + *inf*

stop'cock' *s* rubinetto di arresto
stop'gap' *adj* provvisorio ‖ *s* soluzione provvisoria; (*person*) tappabuchi *m*
stop'light' *s* (*traffic light*) semaforo; (aut) luce *f* di stop
stop'o'ver *s* fermata intermedia
stoppage ['stapıdʒ] *s* fermata, arresto; (*of work, wages, etc.*) sospensione
stopper ['stapər] *s* tappo, turacciolo
stop' sign' *s* segnale *m* di fermata
stop'watch' *s* cronometro a scatto
storage ['storıdʒ] *s* magazzinaggio; (*place for storing*) magazzino; (*of a computer*) memoria
stor'age bat'tery *s* (elec) accumulatore *m*
store [stor] *s* negozio; magazzino; (*supply*) scorta; **in store** in serbo; **to set store by** dare molta importanza a ‖ *tr* immagazzinare; **to store away** accumulare
store'house' *s* magazzino, deposito; (*of knowledge*) miniera
store'keep'er *s* negoziante *m*
store'room' *s* magazzino; (naut) dispensa
stork [stork] *s* cicogna
storm [storm] *s* tempesta, temporale *m;* (*on the Beaufort scale*) burrasca; (mil) assalto; (fig) scoppio ‖ *tr* assaltare ‖ *intr* tempestare; imperversare; (mil) andare all'attacco
storm' cloud' *s* nuvolone *m*
storm' door' *s* controporta
storm' sash' *s* controfinestra
storm' troops' *spl* truppe *fpl* d'assalto
storm' win'dow *s* controfinestra
storm•y ['stormi] *adj* (**-ier; -iest**) tempestoso, burrascoso; (fig) inquieto, violento
sto•ry ['stori] *s* (**-ries**) storia, racconto, romanzo; (*plot*) trama; (*level*) piano; (coll) storia, menzogna ‖ *v* (*pret & pp* **-ried**) *tr* istoriare
sto'ry-tell'er *s* narratore *m*, novelliere *m;* (coll) mentitore *m*
stoup [stup] *s* (eccl) acquasantiera
stout [staut] *adj* grasso, obeso; forte, robusto; leale; coraggioso ‖ *s* birra nera forte
stout-hearted ['staut ,hartıd] *adj* coraggioso
stove [stov] *s* (*for warmth*) stufa; (*for cooking*) fornello, cucina economica
stove'pipe' *s* tubo della stufa, cannone *m;* (*hat*) (coll) tuba
stow [sto] *tr* mettere in riserva; riempire; (naut) stivare ‖ *intr*—**to stow away** imbarcarsi clandestinamente
stowage ['sto·ıdʒ] *s* stivaggio; (*place*) stiva
stow'a·way' *s* passeggero clandestino
straddle ['strædəl] *s* divaricamento ‖ *tr* (*a horse*) cavalcare; (*the legs*) divaricare; favorire entrambe le parti in ‖ *intr* cavalcare; stare a gambe divaricate; (coll) tenere il piede tra due staffe
strafe [straf] or [stref] *s* attacco violento ‖ *tr* attaccare violentemente con fuoco aereo; bombardare violentemente; (slang) punire

straggle ['strægəl] *intr* sbandarsi, sviarsi; sparpagliarsi, essere sparpagliato

straggler ['stræglər] *s* ritardatario

straight [stret] *adj* diritto, ritto; (*e.g., shoulders*) quadro; candido, franco; (*honest, upright*) retto; inalterato; (*hair; whiskey*) liscio; **to set s.o. straight** mettere qlcu sulla retta via; mostrare la verità a qlcu || *s* rettilinea; (*cards*) scala || *adv* dritto; sinceramente; rettamente; **straight ahead** sempre diritto; **straight away** immediatamente; **to go straight** vivere onestamente

straighten ['stretən] *tr* ordinare; raddrizzare || *intr* raddrizzarsi

straight' face' *s* faccia seria

straight' flush' *s* (*cards*) scala reale

straight'for'ward *adj* diretto; onesto

straight' man' *s* (theat) spalla

straight' ra'zor *s* rasoio a mano libera

straight'way' *adv* immediatamente

strain [stren] *s* sforzo; fatica eccessiva; tensione, pressione; strappo muscolare; tono, stile *m*; (*family*) famiglia; tendenza, vena; (coll) lavoro severo; (mus) aria, melodia || *tr* passare, colare; (*e.g., a rope*) tirare al massimo; (*one's ear*) tendere; (*a muscle*) strappare; (*the ankle*) slogare; (*e.g., words*) storcere, forzare || *intr* colare, filtrare; tendersi, tirare; sforzarsi; fare resistenza; **to strain at** tirare; resistere a

strained [strend] *adj* (*smile*) stentato; (*relations*) teso

strainer ['strenər] *s* scolatoio

strait [stret] *s* stretto; **straits** stretto; (fig) strettezze *fpl*; **to be in dire straits** essere nei frangenti

strait' jack'et *s* camicia di forza

strait'-laced' *adj* puritano, pudibondo

strand [strænd] *s* sponda, lido; (of *metal cable*) trefolo; (of *rope*) legnolo; (of *pearls*) filo || *tr* sfilare; (*e.g., a rope*) ritorcere, intrecciare; (*e.g., a boat*) lasciare incagliato; **to be stranded** trovarsi incagliato

stranded ['strændɪd] *adj* (*ship*) incagliato, arenato; (*e.g., rope*) ritorto, intrecciato

strange [strendʒ] *adj* strano; straniero; non abituato; inusitato

stranger ['strendʒər] *s* forestiero; nuovo venuto, intruso

strangle ['stræŋgəl] *tr* strangolare; soffocare || *intr* strangolarsi; soffocarsi

strap [stræp] *s* (of *leather*) correggia; (*for holding things together*) tirante *m*; (*shoulder strap*) bretella; (*for passengers to hold on to*) manopola; (*to hold a sandal*) guiggia; (*to hold a baby*) falda; (*strop*) coramella || *v* (*pret & pp* **strapped**; *ger* **strapping**) *tr* legare con correggia or tirante; (*a razor*) affilare

strap'hang'er *s* (coll) passeggero senza posto a sedere

strapping ['stræpɪŋ] *adj* robusto; (coll) grande, enorme

stratagem ['strætedʒəm] *s* stratagemma *m*

strategic(al) [strə'tidʒɪk(əl)] *adj* strategico

strategist ['strætɪdʒɪst] *s* stratego

strate·gy ['strætɪdʒɪ] *s* (-**gies**) strategia

strati·fy ['strætɪ,faɪ] *v* (*pret & pp* -**fied**) *tr* stratificare || *intr* stratificarsi

stratosphere ['strætə,sfɪr] or ['stretə,sfɪr] *s* stratosfera

stra·tum ['stretəm] or ['strætəm] *s* (-**ta** [tə] or -**tums**) strato

straw [strɔ] *adj* di paglia; di nessun valore; falso, fittizio || *s* paglia; (*for drinking*) cannuccia; **I don't care a straw** non mi importa un fico; **to be the last straw** essere il colmo

straw'ber·ry *s* (-**ries**) fragola

straw'hat' *s* cappello di paglia; (*with hard crown*) paglietta

straw' man' *s* (*figurehead*) uomo di paglia; (*scarecrow*) spaventapasseri *m*

straw' mat'tress *s* pagliericcio

straw' vote' *s* votazione esplorativa

stray [stre] *adj* sbandato, randagio; casuale, fortuito || *s* animale randagio || *intr* sviarsi; (fig) sbandarsi

streak [strik] *s* stria; (of *light*) raggio; (of *madness*) ramo, vena; (of *luck*) (coll) periodo; **like a streak** (coll) come un lampo || *tr* striare, venare || *intr* striarsi, venarsi; andare come un lampo

stream [strim] *s* corrente *f*; (of *light*) raggio; (of *people*) fiumana, torrente *m*; (of *cars*) fila || *intr* colare; filtrare, penetrare; (*said of a flag*) fluttuare

streamer ['strimər] *s* pennone *m*; nastro; raggio di luce

streamlined ['strim,laɪnd] *adj* aerodinamico; (aer) carenato

stream'lin'er *s* treno dal profilo aerodinamico

street [strit] *adj* stradale || *s* via, strada

street'car' *s* tram *m*

street' clean'er *s* spazzino; (mach) spazzatrice *f*

street' clothes' *spl* vestiti *mpl* da passeggio; vestito da passeggio

street' floor' *s* pianterreno

street'light' *s* lampione *m*

street' map' *s* pianta della città; stradario

street' sign' *s* segnale *m* stradale

street' sprin'kler *s* carro annaffiatoio

street' walk'er *s* passeggiatrice *f*

strength [streŋθ] *s* forza; resistenza; (of *spirituous liquors*) gradazione; (com) tendenza al rialzo; (mil) numero; **on the strength of** basandosi su

strengthen ['streŋθən] *tr* rinforzare; (fig) convalidare, rinsaldare || *intr* rinforzarsi, ingagliardirsi

strenuous ['strenju·əs] *adj* vigoroso; strenuo

stress [stres] *s* enfasi *f*, importanza; spinta; tensione, preoccupazione; accento; (mech) sollecitazione; **to lay**

stress on mettere in rilievo ‖ tr (a word) accentare, accentuare; (to emphasize) accentuare; (mech) sollecitare

stress' ac'cent s accento di intensità

stretch [stretʃ] s tiro, tirata; (in time or space) periodo; (of road) tratto, percorrenza; (of imagination) sforzo; (rr) tratta; (slang) periodo di detenzione; **at a stretch** di un tiro ‖ tr tirare; tendere, distendere; (the imagination) forzare; (facts) esagerare; (money) stiracchiare; (one's legs) sgranchirsi; (the truth) esagerare; **to stretch oneself** sdraiarsi ‖ intr estendersi; stiracchiarsi; distendersi; **to stretch out** sdraiarsi

stretcher ['stretʃər] s (for a painting) telaio; (tool) tenditore m. tenditoio; (to carry wounded) barella, lettiga

stretch'er-bear'er s portantino

strew [stru] v (pret **strewed;** pp **strewed** or **strewn**) tr spargere, cospargere; disseminare

stricken ['strɪkən] adj afflitto; ferito; danneggiato

strict [strɪkt] adj stretto, severo

stricture ['strɪktʃər] s aspra critica; (pathol) stenosi f

stride [straɪd] s passo; andatura; **rapid strides** grandi passi mpl; **to hit one's stride** avanzare a andatura regolare; **to take s.th in one's stride** fare qlco senza sforzi ‖ v (pret **strode** [strod]; pp **stridden** ['strɪdən]) tr attraversare a grandi passi; attraversare di un salto ‖ intr camminare a grandi passi; (majestically) incedere

strident ['straɪdənt] adj stridente

strife [straɪf] s discordia; concorrenza

strike [straɪk] s (blow) colpo; (stopping of work) sciopero; (discovery of oil, ore, etc.) scoperta; (of fish) abboccatura; colpo di fortuna ‖ v (pret & pp **struck** [strʌk]) tr colpire, percuotere; infiggere; (a match) strofinare; (fire) accendere; fare impressione su; incontrare improvvisamente; (e.g., ore) scoprire; (roots) mettere; (a coin) coniare; andare in sciopero contro; arrivare a; (a posture) prendere; (the hour) scoccare; cancellare, eliminare; (sails) calare; (attention) richiamare; **to strike it rich** scoprire una miniera; avere un colpo di fortuna ‖ intr dare un colpo; cadere; (said of a bell) suonare; accendersi; scioperare; (mil) attaccare; **to strike out** mettersi in marcia; (to fail) (fig) fallire, venir meno

strike'break'er s crumiro

striker ['straɪkər] s battitore m; (clapper in clock) martelletto; (worker) scioperante m

striking ['straɪkɪŋ] adj impressionante, sorprendente; notevole; scioperante

strik'ing pow'er s potere m d'assalto

string [strɪŋ] s spago, cordicella; (e.g., of apron) laccio; (of pearls) filo; (of onions; of lies) filza; (row) fila, infilata; (mus) corda; **no strings attached** (coll) senza condizioni;

strings strumenti mpl a corda; (coll) condizioni fpl; **to pull strings** usare influenza ‖ v (pret & pp **strung** [strʌŋ]) tr legare; allacciare; infilare; infilzare; (a racket) munire di corde; (to stretch) tendere; (a musical instrument) mettere le corde a; (slang) ingannare; **to string along** (slang) menare per il naso; **to string up** impiccare ‖ intr—**to string along with** (slang) andare d'accordo con

string' bean' s fagiolino

stringed' in'strument s strumento a corda

stringent ['strɪndʒənt] adj stringente; urgente; severo

string' quartet' s quartetto d'archi

strip [strɪp] s striscia; (of metal) lamina; (of land) lingua ‖ v (pret & pp **stripped**) ger **stripping**) tr spogliare; denudare; (a fruit) pelare; (a ship) sguarnire; (tobacco) togliere le nervature da; scortecciare; (thread) spanare; **to strip of** spogliare di ‖ intr spogliarsi; denudarsi; fare lo spogliarello

stripe [straɪp] s stria, striscia, riga, lista; tipo, qualità f; (mil) gallone m ‖ tr striare, filettare, rigare

strip' min'ing s sfruttamento minerario a cielo aperto

strip'tease' s spogliarello

stripteaser ['strɪp,tizər] s spogliarellista

strive [straɪv] v (pret **strove** [strov]; pp **striven** ['strɪvən]) intr sforzarsi; lottare; **to strive to** sforzarsi di

stroke [strok] s colpo; (of bell or clock) rintocco; (of pen) tratto, frego; (of brush) pennellata; (of arms in swimming) bracciata; colpo apoplettico; (caress) carezza; (with oar) vogata; (of oar or paddle) palata; (of a master) tocco; (of a piston) corsa; (keystroke) battuta; (of genius) lampo; (of the hour) scocco; **to not do a stroke of work** non muovere un dito ‖ tr accarezzare

stroll [strol] s passeggiata; **to take a stroll** fare una passeggiata ‖ intr fare una passeggiata, andare a zonzo; errare

stroller ['strolər] s girovago; carrozzella; (itinerant performer) (theat) guitto

strong [strɔŋ] or [strɑŋ] adj forte, vigoroso; valido; acceso, zelante; (butter) rancido; (cheese) piccante; (com) sostenuto

strong'box' s cassaforte f

strong' drink' s bevanda alcolica

strong'hold' s piazzaforte f

strong' man' s (in a circus) maciste m; (leader) anima; dittatore m

strong-minded ['strɔŋ,maɪndɪd] or ['strɑŋ,maɪndɪd] adj volitivo

strong'point' s luogo fortificato

strontium ['strɑnʃi·əm] s stronzio

strop [strɑp] s coramella, affilarasoio ‖ v (pret & pp **stropped;** ger **stropping**) tr affilare

strophe ['strofi] s strofa, strofe f

struc'tural steel' [ˈstrʌkt/ərəl] s profilato di acciaio

structure [ˈstrʌkt/ər] s struttura; edificio ‖ tr strutturare

struggle [ˈstrʌgəl] s lotta; sforzo ‖ intr lottare; sforzare, dibattersi

strum [strʌm] v (pret & pp **strummed; ger strummed**) tr & intr strimpellare

strumpet [ˈstrʌmpɪt] s sgualdrina, puttana

strut [strʌt] s controvento, puntello, saettone m; incedere impettito; (aer) montante ‖ v (pret & pp **strutted; ger strutting**) intr pavoneggiarsi, fare la ruota

strychnine [ˈstrɪknaɪn] or [ˈstrɪknɪn] s stricnina

stub [stʌb] s (of tree) coppo; (e.g., of cigar) mozzicone m; (of a check) matrice f, madre f ‖ v (pret & pp **stubbed; ger stubbing**) tr sradicare; **to stub one's toe** inciampare

stubble [ˈstʌbəl] s (of beard) pelo ispido; **stubbles** stoppie fpl

stubborn [ˈstʌbərn] adj (headstrong) testardo; (resolute) accanito; (e.g., resistance) ostinato; (e.g., illness) ribelle; (soil) ingrato

stucco [ˈstʌko] s (-coes or -cos) stucco ‖ tr stuccare

stuck [stʌk] adj infisso; attaccato; (glued) incollato; (unable to continue) in panna; **stuck on** (slang) invaghito di

stuck'-up' adj (coll) presuntuoso, arrogante

stud [stʌd] s (in upholstery) borchia; bottone m da sparato; (of walls) montante m; (stallion) stallone m; (for mares) monta; (archit) bugna, bugnato ‖ v (pret & pp **studded; ger studding**) tr cospergere; (with stars) costellare; (with jewels) incastonare, ingioiellare

stud' bolt' s prigioniero

stud'book' s registro della genealogia

student [ˈstjudənt] or [ˈstudənt] adj studentesco ‖ s studente m; scolaro; (investigator) studioso

stu'dent bod'y s scolaresca

stud'horse' s stallone m

studied [ˈstʌdɪd] adj premeditato; (affected) studiato

studi·o [ˈstudɪˌo] or [ˈstjudɪˌo] s (-os) studio

studious [ˈstjudɪ·əs] or [ˈstudɪ·əs] adj studioso; assiduo, zelante

stud·y [ˈstʌdi] s (-ies) studio ‖ v (pret & pp **-ied**) tr & intr studiare

stuff [stʌf] s roba, cosa; stoffa; materiale m; (nonsense) scemenze fpl; medicina; (coll) mestiere m ‖ tr riempire, inzeppare; (one's stomach) rimpinzare; (e.g., poultry) farcire; (e.g., salami) insaccare; (a dead animal) impagliare; **to stuff up** intasare ‖ intr rimpinzarsi

stuffed' shirt' s persona altezzosa

stuffing [ˈstʌfɪŋ] s ripieno

stuff·y [ˈstʌfi] adj (-ier; -iest) soffocante, opprimente; (nose) chiuso; pedante

stumble [ˈstʌmbəl] intr incespicare, inciampare; sbagliare, impaperarsi; **to stumble on** or **upon** intopparsi in

stum'bling block' s inciampo, scoglio

stump [stʌmp] s (of tree) toppo, ceppo; (e.g., of arm) moncherino, moncone m; (of cigar, candle) mozzicone m; dente rotto; tribuna popolare; (for drawing) sfumino; **up a stump** (coll) completamente perplesso ‖ tr mozzare; lasciare perplesso; (coll) fare discorsi politici in

stump' speech' s discorso politico

stun [stʌn] v (pret & pp **stunned; ger stunning**) tr tramortire; (fig) sbalordire

stunning [ˈstʌnɪŋ] adj (blow) che stordisce; sbalorditivo, magnifico

stunt [stʌnt] s atrofia; creatura striminzita; bravata, prodezza; (for publicity) montatura ‖ tr striminzire; arrestare la crescita di ‖ intr fare delle acrobazie

stunt'ed adj striminzito

stunt' fly'ing s acrobazia aerea

stunt' man' s (mov) controfigura

stupe·fy [ˈstjupɪˌfaɪ] or [ˈstupɪˌfaɪ] v (pret & pp **-fied**) tr istupidire, intontire

stupendous [stjuˈpendəs] or [stuˈpendəs] adj stupendo

stupid [ˈstjupɪd] or [ˈstupɪd] adj stupido, ebete, scemo

stupor [ˈstjupər] or [ˈstupər] s torpore m. stupore m

stur·dy [ˈstʌrdi] adj (-dier; -diest) forte; (robust) tarchiato; risoluto

sturgeon [ˈstʌrdʒən] s storione m

stutter [ˈstʌtər] s tartagliamento ‖ tr & intr tartagliare

sty [staɪ] s (sties) porcile m; (pathol) orzaiolo

style [staɪl] s stile m; tono; (mode of living) treno ‖ tr chiamare col nome di

stylish [ˈstaɪlɪʃ] adj alla moda, di tono

sty·mie [ˈstaɪmi] v (pret & pp **-mied; ger -mieing**) tr ostacolare, contrastare

styp'tic pen'cil [ˈstɪptɪk] s matita emostatica

Styx [stɪks] s Stige m

suave [swɑv] or [swev] adj soave

subaltern [səbˈɔltərn] adj & s subalterno

subcommittee [ˈsʌbkəˌmɪti] s sottocommissione

subconscious [sʌbˈkɑnʃəs] adj & s subcosciente m

subconsciousness [sʌbˈkɑnʃəsnɪs] s subcosciente m, subcoscienza

sub'deb' s (coll) signorina più giovane di una debuttante

subdivide [ˌsʌbdɪˈvaɪd] or [ˌsʌbdɪˈvaɪd] tr suddividere ‖ intr suddividersi

subdue [səbˈdju] or [səbˈdu] tr soggiogare, sottomettere; (color, voice) attenuare

subdued [səbˈdjud] or [səbˈdud] adj (voice) sommesso; (light) tenue

subheading ['sʌb,hediŋ] s sottotitolo; (journ) sommario

subject ['sʌbdʒikt] adj soggetto; **subject to** (e.g., a cold) soggetto a; (e.g., a fine) passibile di || s soggetto, materia, proposito; (of a ruler) suddito; (gram, med, philos) soggetto || [səb-'dʒekt] tr sottomettere

sub'ject cat'alogue s catalogo per materie

sub'ject in'dex s indice m per materie

subjection [səb'dʒekʃən] s soggezione

subjective [səb'dʒektɪv] adj soggettivo

sub'ject mat'ter s soggetto

subjugate ['sʌbdʒəˌget] tr soggiogare

subjunctive [səb'dʒʌŋktɪv] adj & s congiuntivo

sublease ['sʌb,lis] s subaffitto || [,sʌb-'lis] tr subaffittare

sub-let [sʌb'let] or ['sʌb,let] v (pret & pp -let; ger -letting) tr subaffittare

sub-machine' gun' [,sʌbmə'ʃin] s mitra m

submarine ['sʌbməˌrin] adj & s sottomarino

sub'marine chas'er ['tʃesər] s cacciasommergibili m

submerge [səb'mʌrdʒ] tr sommergere || intr sommergersi

submersion [səb'mʌrʒən] or [səb-'mʌrʃən] s sommersione

submission [səb'mɪʃən] s sottomissione

submissive [səb'mɪsɪv] adj sottomesso

sub-mit [səb'mɪt] v (pret & pp -mitted; ger -mitting) tr sottomettere; presentare, deferire; osservare rispettosamente || intr sottomettersi

subordinate [səb'ɔrdɪnɪt] adj & s subordinato || [səb'ɔrdɪˌnet] tr subordinare

suborna'tion of per'jury [,sʌbər'neʃən] s subornazione

subplot ['sʌb,plɑt] s intreccio secondario

subpoena or **subpena** [sʌb'pinə] or [sə-'pinə] s mandato di comparizione || tr citare

sub rosa [sʌb'rozə] adv in segreto

subscribe [səb'skraɪb] tr sottoscrivere || intr sottoscrivere; **to subscribe to** sottoscrivere a; (a magazine) abbonarsi a; (an opinion) approvare

subscriber [səb'skraɪbər] s sottoscrittore m; abbonato

subscription [sʌb'skrɪpʃən] s sottoscrizione; (e.g., to a newspaper) abbonamento; (e.g., to club) quota

subsequent ['sʌbsɪkwənt] adj susseguente, posteriore

subservient [səb'sʌrvɪ-ənt] adj subordinato; ossequioso; servile

subside [səb'saɪd] intr calmarsi; (said of water) decrescere

subsidiar-y ['sʌbsɪdɪˌɛri] adj sussidiario || s (-ies) sussidiario

subsidize ['sʌbsɪˌdaɪz] tr sussidiare, sovvenzionare; (by bribery) subornare

subsi-dy ['sʌbsɪdi] s (-dies) sussidio, sovvenzione

subsist [səb'sɪst] intr sussistere

subsistence [səb'sɪstəns] s sussistenza

subsoil ['sʌb,sɔɪl] s sottosuolo

substance ['sʌbstəns] s sostanza

substandard [sʌb'stændərd] adj inferiore al livello normale

substantial [səb'stænʃəl] adj considerevole; ricco, influente; (food) sostanzioso; (e.g., reason) sostanziale

substantiate [səb'stænʃɪˌet] tr provare, verificare; dare prova di, sostanziare

substantive ['sʌbstəntɪv] adj & s sostantivo

substation ['sʌb,steʃən] s ufficio postale secondario; (elec) sottostazione

substitute ['sʌbstɪˌtjut] or ['sʌbstɪˌtut] adj provvisorio, interino || s (thing) sostituto, surrogato; (person) sostituto, supplente m; **beware of substitutes** guardarsi dalle contraffazioni || tr—**to substitute for** sostituire (qlco or qlcu) a || intr—**to substitute for** sostituire, rimpiazzare, e.g., **he substituted for the teacher** sostituì il maestro

substitution [,sʌbstɪ'tjuʃən] or [,sʌbstɪ'tuʃən] s sostituzione; (by fraud) contraffazione

substra-tum [sʌb'stretəm] s (-ta [tə]) sostrato, substrato

subterfuge ['sʌbtərˌfjudʒ] s sotterfugio

subterranean [,sʌbtə'renɪ-ən] adj & s sotterraneo

subtitle ['sʌb,taɪtəl] s sottotitolo; (journ) titolo corrente; (mov) didascalia || tr dare una didascalia a

subtle ['sʌtəl] adj sottile

subtle-ty ['sʌtəlti] s (-ties) sottigliezza

subtract [səb'trækt] tr sottrarre

subtraction [sʌb'trækʃən] s sottrazione

suburb ['sʌbʌrb] s suburbio, sobborgo; **the suburbs** la periferia

suburban [sə'bʌrbən] adj suburbano

suburbanite [sə'bʌrbəˌnaɪt] s abitante mf dei suburbi

subvention [səb'venʃən] s sovvenzione || tr sovvenzionare

subversive [səb'vʌrsɪv] adj & s sovversivo

subvert [səb'vʌrt] tr sovvertire

subway ['sʌb,we] s sotterranea, metropolitana, metrovia; sottopassaggio

sub'way sta'tion s stazione della metropolitana

succeed [sək'sid] tr succedere (with dat), subentrare (with dat) || intr riuscire; **to succeed to** (the throne) succedere a

success [sək'sɛs] s successo, riuscita

successful [sək'sɛsfəl] adj felice, fortunato; che ha avuto successo

succession [sək'sɛʃən] s successione; **in succession** in seguito, uno dopo l'altro

successive [sək'sɛsɪv] adj successivo

succor ['sʌkər] s soccorso || tr soccorrere

succotash ['sʌkəˌtæʃ] s verdura di fagioli e granturco

succumb [sə'kʌm] intr soccombere

such [sʌtʃ] adj & pron indef tale, simile; **such** a un simile, un tale; **such**

a + *adj* tanto + *adj*, e.g., **such a beautiful story** una storia tanto bella; **such as** tale quale, come

suck [sʌk] *s* succhio || *tr* succhiare; *(air)* aspirare; **to suck in** (slang) ingannare

sucker ['sʌkər] *s* lattante *mf;* (bot) succhione *m;* (mach) pistone *m;* (coll) fesso, pollo, minchione *m*

suckle ['sʌkəl] *tr* allattare; nutrire || *intr* poppare

suck'ling pig' ['sʌklɪŋ] *s* maiale *m* di latte

suction ['sʌkʃən] *s* aspirazione

suc'tion cup' *s* ventosa

suc'tion pump' *s* pompa aspirante

sudden ['sʌdən] *adj* subito, improvviso; **all of a sudden** all'improvviso

suddenly ['sʌdənli] *adv* all'improvviso

suds [sʌdz] *spl* saponata; schiuma; (coll) birra

sue [su] or [sju] *tr* querelare || *intr* querelarsi; **to sue for damages** chiedere i danni; **to sue for peace** chiedere la pace

suede [swed] *s* pelle scamosciata

suet ['su·ɪt] or ['sju·ɪt] *s* grasso, sego

suffer ['sʌfər] *tr* soffrire; *(e.g., heavy losses)* subire || *intr* soffrire, patire

sufferance ['sʌfərəns] *s* tolleranza

suffering ['sʌfərɪŋ] *adj* sofferente || *s* sofferenza, strazio, patimento

suffice [sə'faɪs] *intr* bastare

sufficient [sə'fɪʃənt] *adj* sufficiente

suffix | ['sʌfɪks] *s* suffisso

suffocate ['sʌfə‚ket] *tr & intr* soffocare

suffrage ['sʌfrɪdʒ] *s* suffragio

suffragette [‚sʌfrə'dʒɛt] *s* suffragetta

suffuse [sə'fjuz] *tr* soffondere

sugar ['ʃugər] *adj* *(water)* zuccherato; *(industry)* zuccheriero || *s* zucchero || *tr* zuccherare

sug'ar beet' *s* barbabietola da zucchero

sug'ar bowl' *s* zuccheriera

sug'ar cane' *s* canna da zucchero

sug'ar-coat' *tr* inzuccherare; *(e.g., the pill)* addolcire

sug'ar ma'ple *s* acero

sug'ar-plum' *s* zuccherino

sug'ar spoon' *s* cucchiaino per lo zucchero

sug'ar tongs' *spl* mollette *fpl* per lo zucchero

sugary ['ʃugəri] *adj* zuccherino, zuccheroso

suggest [səg'dʒɛst] *tr* suggerire

suggestion [səg'dʒɛstʃən] *s* suggerimento; (psychol) suggestione; ombra, traccia

suggestive [səg'dʒɛstɪv] *adj* suggestivo; *(risqué)* scabroso

suicidal [‚su·ɪ'saɪdəl] or [‚sju·ɪ'saɪdəl] *adj* suicida

suicide ['su·ɪ‚saɪd] or ['sju·ɪ‚saɪd] *s* *(person)* suicida *mf;* *(act)* suicidio; **to commit suicide** suicidarsi

suit [sut] or [sjut] *s* vestito da uomo; *(of a lady)* tailleur *m;* *(of cards)* seme *m,* colore *m;* *(for bathing)* costume *m;* corte *f,* corteggiamento; domanda, supplica; (law) causa; **to follow suit** seguire l'esempio; (cards)

rispondere a colore || *tr* adattarsi (with *dat*); convenire (with *dat*); **suit yourself** faccia come vuole || *intr* convenire, andare a proposito

suitable ['sutəbəl] or ['sjutəbəl] *adj* indicato, conveniente

suit'case' *s* valigia

suite [swit] *s* gruppo, serie *f;* serie *f* di stanze; *(of furniture)* mobilia; *(retinue)* seguito; (mus) suite *f*

suiting ['sutɪŋ] or ['sjutɪŋ] *s* taglio d'abito

suit' of clothes' *s* completo maschile

suitor ['sutər] or ['sjutər] *s* pretendente *m;* (law) querelante *mf*

sul'fa drugs' ['sʌlfə] *spl* sulfamidici *mpl*

sulfate ['sʌlfet] *s* solfato

sulfide ['sʌlfaɪd] *s* solfuro

sulfite ['sʌlfaɪt] *s* solfito

sulfur ['sʌlfər] *adj* solfiero || *s* zolfo; color *m* zolfo

sulfuric [sʌl'fjurɪk] *adj* solforico

sul'fur mine' *s* solfara

sulfurous ['sʌlfərəs] *adj* solforoso

sulk [sʌlk] *s* broncio || *intr* imbronciarsi

sulk·y ['sʌlki] *adj* (-ier; -iest) imbronciato || *s* (-ies) *(in horse racing)* sediolo, sulky *m*

sullen ['sʌlən] *adj* bieco, triste, tetro

sul·ly ['sʌli] *v* *(pret & pp* -lied) *tr* insudiciare, insozzare

sulphur ['sʌlfər] *adj & s* var of **sulfur**

sultan ['sʌltən] *s* sultano

sul·try ['sʌltri] *adj* (-trier; -triest) soffocante; infocato, appassionato

sum [sʌm] *s* somma; sommario; problema *m* di aritmetica || *v* *(pret & pp* summed; *ger* summing) *tr* sommare; **to sum up** riepilogare

sumac or **sumach** ['ʃumæk] or ['sumæk] *s* sommacco

summarize ['sʌmə‚raɪz] *tr* riassumere

summa·ry ['sʌməri] *adj* sommario || *s* (-ries) sommario, sunto

summer ['sʌmər] *adj* estivo || *s* estate *f* || *intr* passare l'estate

sum'mer resort' *s* stazione estiva

summersault ['sʌmər‚sɔlt] *s & intr* var of **somersault**

sum'mer school' *s* scuola estiva

summery ['sʌməri] *adj* estivo

summit ['sʌmɪt] *s* sommità *f*

sum'mit con'ference *s* riunione al vertice

summon ['sʌmən] *tr* convocare, invitare; evocare; (law) compulsare

summons ['sʌmənz] *s* ordine *m,* comando; (law) citazione || *tr* (law) citare

sumptuous ['sʌmptʃu·əs] *adj* sontuoso

sun [sʌn] *s* sole *m;* **place in the sun** posto al sole || *v* *(pret & pp* sunned; *ger* sunning) *tr* esporre al sole || *intr* prendere il sole

sun' bath' *s* bagno di sole

sun'beam' *s* raggio di sole

sun'burn' *s* abbronzatura || *v* *(pret & pp* -burned or -burnt) *tr* abbronzare || *intr* abbronzarsi

sundae ['sʌndi] s gelato con sciroppo, frutta o noci

Sunday ['sʌndi] adj domenicale ‖ s domenica

Sun'day best' s (coll) vestito da festa

Sun'day's child' s bambino nato con la camicia

Sun'day school' s scuola domenicale della dottrina

sunder ['sʌndər] tr separare

sun'di'al s meridiana

sun'down' s tramonto

sundries ['sʌndriz] spl generi mpl diversi

sundry ['sʌndri] adj vari, diversi

sun'fish' s pesce m mola, pesce m luna

sun'flow'er s girasole m

sun'glass'es spl occhiali mpl da sole

sunken ['sʌŋkən] adj affondato, sommerso; (hollow) incavato

sun' lamp' s sole m artificiale

sun'light' s luce f del sole

sun'lit' adj illuminato dal sole

sun·ny ['sʌni] adj (-nier; -niest) solatio, soleggiato; allegro, ridente; **it is sunny** fa sole

sun'ny side' s parte soleggiata; lato buono; **on the sunny side of** (e.g., thirty) al disotto dei . . . anni

sun' porch' s veranda a solatìo

sun'rise' s sorgere m del sole; **from sunrise to sunset** dall'alba al tramonto

sun'set' s tramonto

sun'shade' s tenda; parasole m

sun'shine' s sole m, luce f del sole; **in the sunshine** al sole

sun'spot' s macchia solare

sun'stroke' s insolazione

sun' tan' s tintarella

sun'tan lo'tion s pomata antisole, abbronzante m

sun'up' s sorgere m, levare m del sole

sun' vi'sor s (aut) aletta parasole, parasole m

sup [sʌp] v (pret & pp **supped**; ger **supping**) intr cenare

super ['supər] adj (coll) superficiale; (coll) di prim'ordine, super ‖ s (coll) sovrintendente m; (coll) articolo di prim'ordine, super m

superabundant [,supərə'bʌndənt] adj sovrabbondante

superannuated [,super'ænju ,etid] adj giubilato, pensionato; messo a riposo per limiti di età; antiquato

superb [su'pʌrb] or [sə'pʌrb] adj superbo

supercar·go ['supər ,kargo] s (-goes) (naut) sopraccarico

supercharge [,supər't/ard3] tr sovralimentare

supercilious [,supər'sıli·əs] adj altero, arrogante

superficial [,supər'fı/əl] adj superficiale

superfluous [su'pʌrflu·əs] adj superfluo

su'per·high'way s autostrada

superhuman [,supər'hjumən] adj sovrumano

superimpose [,supərim'poz] tr sovrapporre

superintendent [,supərin'tendənt] s soprintendente m; (of schools) provveditore m

superior [sə'pırı·ər] or [su'pırı·ər] adj superiore; di superiorità; (typ) esponente ‖ s superiore m

superiority [sə'pırı'arıti] or [su ,pırı'arıti] s superiorità f

superlative [sə'pʌrlətıv] or [su'pʌrlətıv] adj & s superlativo

su'per·man' s (-men') superuomo

supermarket ['supər ,markıt] s supermercato

supernatural [,supər'næt/ərəl] adj soprannaturale

superpose [,supər'poz] tr sovrapporre

supersede [,supər'sid] tr rimpiazzare, sostituire

supersensitive [,supər'sensıtıv] adj ipersensibile

supersonic [,supər'sanık] adj supersonico

superstition [,supər'stı/ən] s superstizione

superstitious [,supər'stı/əs] adj superstizioso

supervene [,supər'vin] intr sopravvenire

supervise ['supər ,vaiz] tr sorvegliare, dirigere

supervision [,supər'vı/ən] s supervisione, sorveglianza, direzione

supervisor ['supər ,vaizər] s supervisore m, sorvegliante mf; ispettore m

supper ['sʌpər] s cena

sup'per·time' s ora di cena

supplant [sə'plænt] tr rimpiazzare

supple ['sʌpəl] adj flessibile; docile

supplement ['sʌplımənt] s supplemento ‖ ['sʌplı ,ment] tr completare, supplire (with dat)

suppliant ['sʌplı·ənt] adj & s supplicante mf

supplicant ['sʌplıkənt] s supplicante mf

supplication [,sʌplı'ke/ən] s supplica

supplier [sʌ'plaı·ər] s fornitore m

sup·ply [sə'plaı] s (-plies) rifornimento, fornitura; provvista, scorta; (com) offerta; **supplies** riforniminenti mpl, vettovaglie fpl ‖ v (pret & pp **-plied**) tr fornire, provvedere; (food) vettovagliare

supply' and demand' s domanda ed offerta

support [sə'port] s sostegno, appoggio; puntello, rincalzo; mantenimento ‖ tr sostenere, appoggiare; puntellare; (a cause) caldeggiare; mantenere

supporter [sə'portər] s fautore m, sostenitore m; (jockstrap) sospensorio; giarrettiera; fascia elastica

suppose [sə'poz] tr supporre; ammettere; **suppose we take a walk?** che ne dice se facessimo una passeggiata?; **to be supposed to** aver fama di essere; **to suppose so** credere di sì

supposed [sə'pozd] adj presunto

supposition [,sʌpə'zı/ən] s supposizione

supposito·ry [sə'pazı ,tori] s (-ries) suppositorio, supposta

suppress [sə'pres] tr sopprimere

suppression [sə'prɛʃən] *s* soppressione

suppurate ['sʌpjə,ret] *intr* suppurare

supreme [sə'prim] *or* [su'prim] *adj* supremo, sommo

Supreme' Court' *s (in Italy)* Corte *f* di Cassazione; *(in U.S.A.)* tribunale *m* di ultima istanza

surcharge ['sʌr,tʃardʒ] *s* soprapprezzo; soprattassa; sovraccarico; (philately) sovrastampa || [,sʌr-'tʃardʒ] *or* ['sʌr,tʃardʒ] *tr* sovraccaricare

sure [ʃur] *adj* sicuro; **to be sure!** certamente!, senza dubbio! || *interj* (coll) certamente!; **sure enough!** (coll) difatti

sure-footed ['sjur'futɪd] *adj* dal piede sicuro

sure' thing' *s* (coll) successo garantito || *adv* (coll) certamente || *interj* (coll) di sicuro!

sure-ty ['ʃurtɪ] *or* ['ʃurɪtɪ] *s* (**-ties**) malleveria

surf [sʌrf] *s* frangente *m*

surface ['sʌrfɪs] *adj* superficiale || *s* superficie *f* || *tr* rifinire; spianare; ricoprire || *intr* emergere

sur'face mail' *s* posta ordinaria

surf'board' *s* tavola per il surfing

surfeit ['sʌrfɪt] *s* eccesso; sazietà *f* || *tr* saziare, rimpinzare || *intr* saziarsi, rimpinzarsi

surf'ing *s* surfing *m*

surge [sʌrdʒ] *s* ondata; fiotto; (elec) sovratensione || *intr* ondeggiare, fluttuare; *(said, e.g., of a crowd)* affluire

surgeon ['sʌrdʒən] *s* (medico) chirurgo

surger-y ['sʌrdʒərɪ] *s* (**-ies**) chirurgia; sala operatoria

surgical ['sʌrdʒɪkəl] *adj* chirurgico

sur-ly ['sʌrlɪ] *adj* (**-lier; -liest**) arcigno, imbronciato

surmise [sər'maɪz] *or* ['sʌrmaɪz] *s* congettura, supposizione || [sər-'maɪz] *tr & intr* congetturare, supporre

surmount [sər'maunt] *tr* sormontare; coronare

surname ['sʌr,nem] *s* cognome *m*; *(added name)* soprannome *m* || *tr* dare il cognome a; soprannominare

surpass [sər'pæs] *or* [sər'pas] *tr* sorpassare, superare

surplice ['sʌrplɪs] *s* cotta

surplus ['sʌrplʌs] *adj* eccedente || *s* sopravvanzo, eccedenza

surprise [sər'praɪz] *adj* insperato, improvviso || *s* sorpresa || *tr* sorprendere

surprise' par'ty *s* improvvisata

surprising [sər'praɪzɪŋ] *adj* sorprendente

surrender [sə'rɛndər] *s* resa || *tr* arrendere || *intr* arrendersi

surren'der val'ue *s* (ins) valore *m* di riscatto

surreptitious [,sʌrep'tɪʃəs] *adj* clandestino, nascosto, furtivo

surround [sə'raund] *tr* circondare, contornare; (mil) aggirare

surrounding [sə'raundɪŋ] *adj* circostante, circonvicino || **surroundings** *spl* dintorni *mpl;* ambiente *m*

surtax ['sʌr,tæks] *s* sovrimposta, soprattassa; imposta complementare

surveillance [sər'veləns] *or* [sər-'veljəns] *s* sorveglianza, vigilanza

survey ['sʌrve] *s* quadro generale, schizzo; indagine *f; (of opinion)* sondaggio; rapporto; rilievo topografico; perizia || [sʌr've] *or* ['sʌrve] *tr* fare un'indagine di; sondare; rilevare; misurare || *intr* fare un rilievo

sur'vey course' *s* corso di rassegna generale

surveyor [sər've-ər] *s* livellatore *m*, geometra *m*

survival [sər'vaɪvəl] *s* sopravvivenza

survive [sər'vaɪv] *tr* sopravvivere (**with** *dat*) || *intr* sopravvivere

surviving [sər'vaɪvɪŋ] *adj* superstite

survivor [sər'vaɪvər] *s* sopravvissuto, superstite *mf*

survivorship [sər'vaɪvər,ʃɪp] *s* (law) sopravvivenza

susceptible [sə'sɛptɪbəl] *adj* suscettibile, ricettivo; impressionabile; **susceptible to** *(e.g., colds)* soggetto a

suspect ['sʌspekt] *or* [səs'pekt] *adj* sospetto || ['sʌspekt] *s* sospetto || [səs'pekt] *tr* sospettare

suspend [səs'pend] *tr* sospendere || *intr* essere sospeso; fermarsi; fermare i pagamenti

suspenders [səs'pendərz] *spl* bretelle *fpl*

suspense [səs'pens] *s* sospensione; sospeso; **in suspense** in sospeso

suspen'sion bridge' [səs'penʃən] *s* ponte sospeso

suspicion [səs'pɪʃən] *s* sospetto

suspicious [səs'pɪʃəs] *adj (subject to suspicion)* sospetto; *(inclined to suspect)* sospettoso

sustain [səs'ten] *tr* sostenere, sorreggere; *(with food)* sostentare; *(a conversation)* mantenere; *(a loss)* soffrire; (law) confermare

sustenance ['sʌstɪnəns] *s* sostentamento

sutler ['sʌtlər] *s* (mil) vivandiere *m*

swab [swab] *s* (mil) scovolo; (naut) redazza; (surg) batuffolo di cotone || *v (pret & pp* **swabbed;** *ger* **swabbing)** *tr* pulire con la redazza; spugnare; assorbire col cotone

swaddle ['swadəl] *tr* fasciare

swad'dling clothes' *spl* fasce *fpl* del neonato

swagger ['swægər] *s* spavalderia || *intr* fare lo spavaldo

swain [swen] *s* innamorato; *(lad)* contadinotto

swallow ['swalo] *s (of liquid)* sorso; *(of food)* boccone *m; (*orn) rondine *f* || *tr & intr* tranguglare, inghiottire

swal'low-tailed' coat' ['swalo,teld] *s* frac *m*, marsina, abito a coda di rondine

swal'low-wort' *s* vincetossico

swamp [swamp] *s* pantano, palude *f* || *tr* inondare, sommergere

swamp-y ['swampɪ] *adj* (**-ier; -iest**) paludoso, pantanoso

swan [swan] *s* cigno

swan' dive' *s* volo dell'angelo

swank [swæŋk] *adj* (coll) elegante, vistoso ‖ *s* (coll) eleganza vistosa

swan's-down ['swɑnz,daʊn] *s* piuma di cigno, piumino; mollettone *m*

swan' song' *s* canto del cigno

swap [swɑp] *s* scambio, baratto ‖ *v* (*pret* & *pp* **swapped**; *ger* **swapping**) *tr* & *intr* scambiare, barattare

swarm [swɔrm] *s* sciame *m* ‖ *intr* sciamare; (fig) formicolare

swarth·y ['swɔrði] *or* ['swɔrθi] *adj* (-ier; -iest) olivastro, abbronzato

swashbuckler ['swɑʃ,bʌklər] *s* spadaccino, rodomonte *m*

swat [swɑt] *s* colpo ‖ *v* (*pret* & *pp* **swatted**; *ger* **swatting**) *tr* colpire; (*a fly*) schiacciare

sway [swe] *s* dondolio, ondeggiamento; dominio ‖ *tr* dondolare, fare oscillare; influenzare; dominare ‖ *intr* dondolarsi, ondulare; oscillare

swear [swɛr] *v* (*pret* **swore** [swor]; *pp* **sworn** [sworn]) *tr* giurare; (*to secrecy*) fare giurare; **to swear in** fare prestar giuramento a; **to swear off** giurare di rinunziare a; **to swear out a warrant** ottenere un atto di accusa sotto giuramento ‖ *intr* giurare; (*to blaspheme*) bestemmiare; **to swear at** maledire; **to swear by** giurare su, avere certezza di; **to swear to** dichiarare sotto giuramento; giurare di + *inf*

swear'word' *s* bestemmia, parolaccia

sweat [swɛt] *s* sudata; sudore *m* ‖ *v* (*pret* & *pp* **sweat** *or* **sweated**) *tr* sudare; far sudare; **to sweat it out** (slang) farcela fino alla fine; **to sweat off** (*weight*) perdere sudando ‖ *intr* sudare

sweater ['swɛtər] *s* maglione *m*, golf *m*, sweater *m*

sweat' shirt' *s* maglione *m* da ginnastica

sweat·y ['swɛti] *adj* (-ier; -iest) sudato; che fa sudare

Swede [swid] *s* svedese *mf*

Sweden ['swidən] *s* la Svezia

Swedish ['swidɪʃ] *adj* & *s* svedese *m*

sweep [swip] *s* scopata; movimento circolare; estensione; curva; (*of wind*) soffio; (*of well*) mazzacavallo; **to make a clean sweep of** far piazza pulita di ‖ *v* (*pret* & *pp* **swept** [swept]) *tr* spazzare, scopare; percorrere con lo sguardo; (*eyes*) dirigere; travolgere ‖ *intr* scopare; passare; estendersi; dragare

sweeper ['swipər] *s* spazzino; (*machine*) spazzatrice *f*; (nav) dragamine *m*

sweeping ['swipɪŋ] *adj* esteso; travolgente, decisivo ‖ **sweepings** *spl* spazzatura

sweep'-sec'ond *s* lancetta dei secondi a perno centrale

sweep'stakes' *ssg or spl* lotteria abbinata alle corse dei cavalli

sweet [swit] *adj* dolce; (*butter*) senza sale; (*cider*) analcolico; **to be sweet on** (coll) essere innamorato di ‖

sweets *spl* dolci *mpl*; (coll) patate *fpl* dolci ‖ *adv* dolcemente; **to smell sweet** saper di buono

sweet'bread' *s* animella

sweet'bri'er *s* eglantina

sweeten ['switən] *tr* inzuccherare; raddolcire; purificare ‖ *intr* raddolcirsi; purificarsi

sweet'heart' *s* innamorato; innamorata; caro, amore *m*

sweet' mar'joram *s* maggiorana

sweet'meats' *spl* dolci *mpl*, confetti *mpl*

sweet' pea' *s* pisello odoroso

sweet' pota'to *s* batata, patata americana; (mus) ocarina

sweet-scented ['swit,sɛntɪd] *adj* odoroso, profumato

sweet' tooth' *s* debole *m* per i dolci

sweet-toothed ['swit,tuθt] *adj* goloso

sweet' wil'liam *s* garofano barbuto

swell [swɛl] *adj* (slang) elegante; (slang) eccellente, di prim'ordine ‖ *s* gonfiore *m*; onda, ondata; aumento; (mus) crescendo; (slang) elegantone *m* ‖ *v* (*pret* & *pp* **swelled**; *pp* **swelled** *or* **swollen** ['swolən]) *tr* gonfiare, ingrossare; aumentare ‖ *intr* gonfiare, ingrossarsi; aumentare; (*said of the sea*) alzarsi; (*with pride*) montarsi

swelled' head' *s* borioso; **to have a swelled head** montarsi, essere pieno di sé

swelter ['swɛltər] *intr* soffocare dal caldo

swept'back wing' *s* ala a freccia

swerve [swʌrv] *s* scarto, sbandamento ‖ *tr* sviare ‖ *intr* scartare, sbandare

swift [swɪft] *adj* rapido ‖ *s* rondone *m* ‖ *adv* rapidamente

swig [swɪg] *s* (coll) sorso ‖ *v* (*pret* & *pp* **swigged**; *ger* **swigging**) *tr* & *intr* (coll) bere a grandi sorsi

swill [swɪl] *s* imbratto; risciacquatura ‖ *tr* tracannare, trincare ‖ *intr* bere a lunghi sorsi

swim [swɪm] *s* nuoto; **the swim** (*in social activities*) la corrente ‖ *v* (*pret* **swam** [swæm]; *pp* **swum** [swʌm]; *ger* **swimming**) *tr* traversare a nuoto ‖ *intr* nuotare; essere inondato; (*said of one's head*) girare, e.g., **her head is swimming** le gira la testa

swimmer ['swɪmər] *s* nuotatore *m*

swimming ['swɪmɪŋ] *s* nuoto

swim'ming pool' *s* piscina

swim'ming trunks' *spl* mutandine *fpl* da bagno

swim'suit' *s* costume *m* da bagno

swindle ['swɪndəl] *s* truffa, imbroglio ‖ *tr* truffare, imbrogliare

swine [swaɪn] *s* suino, maiale *m*, porco; **swine** *spl* suini *mpl*

swing [swɪŋ] *s* oscillazione *s*; dondolio; curva; (*suspended seat*) altalena; alternarsi *m*; piena attività; (boxing) sventola; (mus) swing *m*; **free swing** libertà *f* d'azione; **in full swing** (coll) in piena attività ‖ *v* (*pret* & *pp* **swung** [swʌŋ]) *tr* (*e.g., one's arms*) dondolare, oscillare; *(a weapon)* brandire; *(e.g., a club)* rotare; far girare; appendere; *(a deal)* (coll) riuscire ad ottenere || *intr* dondolare, dondolarsi, oscillare; girare; essere sospeso; cambiare; (boxing) dare una sventola; **to swing open** aprirsi al colpo

swing'ing door' ['swɪŋɪŋ] *s* porta oscillante

swinish ['swaɪnɪʃ] *adj* porcino

swipe [swaɪp] *s* (coll) colpo forte || *tr* (coll) dare un forte colpo a; (slang) portare via, rubare

swirl [swʌrl] *s* turbine *m*, vortice *m* || *tr* far girare || *intr* turbinare

swirling ['swʌrlɪŋ] *adj* vorticoso

swish [swɪʃ] *s (of whip)* schiocco; *(of silk)* fruscio || *tr (a whip)* schioccare; || *intr* schioccare; frusciare

Swiss [swɪs] *adj* svizzero || *s* svizzero; **the Swiss** gli svizzeri

Swiss' chard' [tʃɑrd] *s* bietola

Swiss' cheese' *s* groviera

Swiss' Guards' *spl* guardie *fpl* svizzere

switch [swɪtʃ] *s* verga; vergata; *(false hair)* posticcio; cambio, trapasso; (elec) interruttore *m*; (rr) scambio || *tr* battere, frustare; (elec) commutare; (rr) deviare; (fig) girare; **to switch off** *(light, radio, etc.)* spegnere; **to switch on** *(light, radio, etc.)* accendere || *intr* fustigare; cambiare; (rr) deviare

switch'back' *s* strada a zigzag; (rr) tracciato a zigzag

switch'blade knife' *s* coltello a serramanico

switch'board' *s* quadro

switch'board op'erator *s* centralinista *mf*

switch'ing en'gine *s* locomotiva da manovra

switch'man *s* (-men) deviatore *m*

switch'yard' *s* stazione smistamento

Switzerland ['swɪtsərlənd] *s* la Svizzera

swiv•el ['swɪvəl] *s* perno, gancio girevole || *v (pret & pp* -eled ór -elled; *ger* -eling or -elling) *intr* girare

swiv'el chair' *s* sedia girevole

swoon [swun] *s* deliquio, svenimento || *intr* svenire

swoop [swup] *s* calata a piombo || *intr* calare a piombo, piombare

sword [sord] *s* spada; **at swords' points** pronti a incrociare le spade; **to put to the sword** passare a fil di spada

sword' belt' *s* cinturone *m*

sword' cane' *s* bastone animato

sword'fish' *s* pesce *m* spada

swords'man *s* (-men) spadaccino

sword' swal'lower ['swɑlo•ər] *s* giocoliere *m* che ingoia spade

sword' thrust' *s* stoccata

sworn [sworn] *adj* giurato

sycophant ['sɪkəfənt] *s* adulatore *m*; parassita *mf*

syllable ['sɪləbəl] *s* sillaba

sylla•bus ['sɪləbəs] *s* (-bi [ˌbaɪ]) sillabo, sommario scolastico

syllogism ['sɪlə‚dʒɪzəm] *s* sillogismo

sylph [sɪlf] *s* silfo; silfide *f*; (fig) silfide *f*

sylvan ['sɪlvən] *adj* silvano

symbol ['sɪmbəl] *s* simbolo

symbolic(al) [sɪm'bɑlɪk(əl)] *adj* simbolico

symbolism ['sɪmbə‚lɪzəm] *s* simbolismo

symbolize ['sɪmbə‚laɪz] *tr* simboleggiare

symmetric(al) [sɪ'metrɪk(əl)] *adj* simmetrico

symme•try ['sɪmɪtri] *s* (-tries) simmetria

sympathetic [ˌsɪmpə'θetɪk] *adj* simpatetico; ben disposto

sympathi•ze ['sɪmpə‚θaɪz] *intr*—**to sympathize with** aver compassione di; mostrar comprensione per; *(to be in accord with)* simpatizzare con

sympa•thy ['sɪmpəθi] *s* (-thies) compassione, commiserazione; **to be in sympathy with** essere d'accordo con; **to extend one's sympathy to** fare le condoglianze a

sym'pathy strike' *s* sciopero di solidarietà

symphonic [sɪm'fɑnɪk] *adj* sinfonico

sympho•ny ['sɪmfəni] *s* (-nies) sinfonia

symposi•um [sɪm'pozɪ•əm] *s* (-a [ə]) simposio, colloquio

symptom ['sɪmptəm] *s* sintomo

synagogue ['sɪnə‚gɔg] or ['sɪnə‚gɑg] *s* sinagoga

synchronize ['sɪŋkrə‚naɪz] *tr & intr* sincronizzare

synchronous ['sɪŋkrənəs] *adj* sincrono

sincopation [ˌsɪŋkə'peʃən] *s* sincope *f*

syncope ['sɪŋkə‚pi] *s* (phonet) sincope *f*

syndicate ['sɪndɪkɪt] *s* sindacato || ['sɪndɪ‚ket] *tr* organizzare in un sindacato

synonym ['sɪnənɪm] *s* sinonimo

synonymous [sɪ'nɑnɪməs] *adj* sinonimo

synop•sis [sɪ'nɑpsɪs] *s* (-ses [siz]) sinossi *f*; (mov) sinopsi *f*

synoptic(al) [sɪ'nɑptɪk(əl)] *adj* sinottico

syntax ['sɪntæks] *s* sintassi *f*

synthe•sis ['sɪnθɪsɪs] *s* (-ses [ˌsiz]) sintesi *f*

synthesize ['sɪnθɪ‚saɪz] *tr* sintetizzare

synthetic(al) [sɪn'θetɪk(əl)] *adj* sintetico

syphilis ['sɪfɪlɪs] *s* sifilide *f*

Syria ['sɪrɪ•ə] *s* la Siria

Syrian ['sɪrɪ•ən] *adj & s* siriano

syringe [sɪ'rɪndʒ] or ['sɪrɪndʒ] *s (fountain syringe)* schizzetto; *(for hypodermic injections)* siringa || *tr* schizzettare; iniettare

syrup ['sɪrəp] or ['sʌrəp] *s* sciroppo

system ['sɪstəm] *s* sistema *m*

systematic(al) [ˌsɪstə'mætɪk(əl)] *adj* sistematico

systematize ['sɪstəmə‚taɪz] *tr* ridurre a sistema

systole ['sɪstəli] *s* sistole *f*

T

T, t [ti] *s* ventesima lettera dell'alfabeto inglese; **to fit to a T** calzare come un guanto

tab [tæb] *s* (*strap*) linguetta; (*of a pocket*) patta; targa; (*label*) etichetta; **to keep tabs on** (coll) sorvegliare; **to pick up the tab** (coll) pagare il conto

tab·by ['tæbɪ] *s* (**-bies**) gatto tigrato; gatta; (*spinster*) zitella; vecchia pettegola

tabernacle ['tæbər‚nækəl] *s* tabernacolo

table ['tebəl] *s* tavola; (*food*) mensa; (*people at a table*) tavolata; (*synopsis*) quadro, prospetto; (*list or catalogue*) indice *m*; **to turn the tables** rovesciare la posizione; **under the table** ubriaco fradicio ‖ *tr* aggiornare, rinviare

tab·leau ['tæblo] *s* (**-leaus** or **-leaux** [loz]) quadro vivente

ta'ble-cloth' *s* tovaglia

table d'hôte ['tabəl'dot] *s* pasto a prezzo fisso

tableful ['tebəl‚ful] *s* (*persons*) tavolata; (*food*) tavola apparecchiata

ta'ble-land' *s* tavoliere *m*

ta'ble lin'en *s* biancheria da tavola

ta'ble man'ners *spl* maniere *fpl* a tavola

ta'ble of con'tents *s* indice *m* delle materie

ta'ble-spoon' *s* cucchiaio

tablespoonful ['tebəl‚spun‚ful] *s* cucchiaiata

tablet ['tæblɪt] *s* (*writing pad*) blocco; (*slab*) lapide *f*; (*flat rigid sheet*) tabella, tavoletta; (pharm) disco, pastiglia

ta'ble talk' *s* conversazione familiare a tavola

ta'ble ten'nis *s* ping-pong *m*, tennis *m* da tavolo

ta'ble-ware' *s* servizio da tavola

ta'ble wine' *s* vino da pasto

tabloid ['tæblɔɪd] *s* giornale *m* a carattere sensazionale

taboo [tə'bu] *adj & s* tabù *m* ‖ *tr* proibire assolutamente

tabulate ['tæbjə‚let] *tr* tabulare

tabulator ['tæbjə‚letər] *s* tabulatore *m*, incolonnatore *m*

tachometer [tə'kɑmɪtər] *s* tachimetro

tacit ['tæsɪt] *adj* tacito

taciturn ['tæsɪ‚tʌrn] *adj* taciturno

tack [tæk] *s* bulletta; cambio di direzione; (naut) virata; (sew) imbastitura ‖ *tr* imbullettare; attaccare; (naut) bordeggiare; (sew) imbastire ‖ *intr* virare; mutare di direzione

tackle ['tækəl] *s* attrezzatura; (mach) taglia, paranco; (gear) (naut) padiglione *m* ‖ *tr* attaccare, affrontare; (sports) placcare, bloccare

tack·y ['tæki] *adj* (**-ier; -iest**) appiccicaticcio; (coll) trasandato

tact [tækt] *s* tatto

tactful ['tæktfəl] *adj* pieno di tatto

tactical ['tæktɪkəl] *adj* tattico

tactician [tæk'tɪʃən] *s* tattico

tactics ['tæktɪks] *ssg* (mil) tattica ‖ *spl* tattica

tactless ['tæktlɪs] *adj* che non ha tatto, indiscreto

tadpole ['tæd‚pol] *s* girino

taffeta ['tæfɪtə] *s* taffettà *m*

taffy ['tæfi] *s* caramella, zucchero d'orzo; (coll) lisciata

tag [tæg] *s* etichetta; (*on a shoelace*) punta dell'aghetto; conclusione; (*last words of speech*) pistolotto finale; epiteto; frase fatta; (*of hair*) ciocca; (*in writing*) ghirigoro; (*game*) toccaferro ‖ *v* (*pret & pp* **tagged; ger tagging**) *tr* etichettare; (*to fine*) multare; aggiungere; soprannominare; accusare; stabilire il prezzo di; (coll) pedinare ‖ *intr* seguire da presso

tag' end' *s* (*e.g., of day*) fine *f*; estremità logorata; avanzo

tail [tel] *adj* di coda ‖ *s* coda; fine *f*; (*of coin*) croce *f*; **tails** falde *fpl*, frac *m*; **to turn tails** darsela a gambe ‖ *tr* attaccare; finire; (coll) pedinare

tail' assem'bly *s* (aer) impennaggio

tail' end' *s* coda, fine *f*

tail'light' *s* fanale *m* di coda

tailor ['telər] *s* sarto ‖ *tr* (*a suit*) tagliare, confezionare; (*one's conduct*) adattare ‖ *intr* fare il sarto

tailoring ['telərɪŋ] *s* sartoria

tai'lor-made' *adj* fatto su misura

tai'lor shop' *s* sartoria

tail'piece' *s* coda, estremità *f*; (mus) cordiera; (typ) fusello finale

tail'race' *s* canale *m* di scarico

tail'spin' *s* avvitamento

tail'wind' *s* (aer) vento di coda; (naut) vento in poppa

taint [tent] *s* macchia; infezione ‖ *tr* macchiare, infettare, corrompere

take [tek] *s* presa; (*of fish*) retata; (mov) presa; ripresa; (slang) incasso ‖ *v* (*pret* **took** [tuk]; *pp* **taken**) *tr* prendere, pigliare; ricevere, accettare; portare; (*to get by force*) portar via; (*a nap*) schiacciare; (*a bath*) fare; (*a joke*) stare a; (*an examination*) sostenere; (*one's own life*) togliersi; (*to deduct*) cavare; (*a purchase*) comprare; (*to convey*) portare; (*time*) impiegare; (*a step, a walk*) fare; (*a subject*) studiare; (*responsibility, role, etc.*) assumere; (*an oath*) prestare; (*root*) mettere; (*exception*) sollevare; credere; (*e.g., a photograph*) fare, scattare; (slang) fregare; **it takes** ci vuole, ci vogliono; **to take amiss** prendere a male; **to take apart** scomporre; smontare; **to take back** riprendere; **to take down** abbassare; smontare; prender nota di; **to take for** prendere per; **to take from** portar via a; **to take in** (*to admit*) ammettere, ricevere; (*to encompass*) includere; (*a dress*) restringere; (*to cheat*) ingannare; (*water*) fare; (*a point of inter-*

est) visitare; **to take it** accettare, ammettere; (slang) resistere; **to take off** (*e.g., one's coat*) togliersi; portar via; scontare, defalcare; (slang) imitare; **to take on** ingaggiare; assumere; intraprendere; accettare la sfida di; **to take out** cavare, togliere; (*e.g., a girl*) portar fuori; (*e.g., a patent*) ottenere; **to take over** rilevare; (slang) imbrogliare; **to take place** aver luogo; **to take s.o.'s eye** attrarre l'attenzione di qlcu; **to take the place of** sottentrare a; **to take up** cominciare a studiare; sollevare, tirar su; (*a duty*) assumere; (*time, space*) occupare || *intr* prendere; scattare; darsi; diventare; **to take after** rassomigliare a; **to take off** (coll) partire, andarsene; (aer) decollare, involare; **to take up with** (coll) fare amicizia con; (coll) vivere con; **to take well** riuscire bene in fotografia

take'off' *s* parodia; (aer) decollaggio; (mach) presa di forza

tal'cum pow'der [ˈtælkəm] *s* talco

tale [tel] *s* storia, racconto; favola, fiaba; (*lie*) bugia, frottola; (*piece of gossip*) maldicenza

tale'bear'er *s* pettegolo

talent [ˈtælənt] *s* talento; persona di talento; gente *f* di talento

talented [ˈtæləntɪd] *adj* dotato di talento, dotato d'ingegno

tal'ent scout' *s* scopritore *m* di talenti

talk [tɔk] *s* chiacchierata; discorso, conferenza; (*language*) parlata; (*gossip*) pettegolezzo; **to cause talk** originare pettegolezzi || *tr* parlare; convincere parlando; **to talk up** elogiare || *intr* parlare; discutere; **to talk on** discutere; continuare a parlare; **to talk up** parlare apertamente

talkative [ˈtɔkətɪv] *adj* loquace

talker [ˈtɔkər] *s* parlatore *m*

talkie [ˈtɔki] *s* (coll) parlato

talk'ing machine' *s* grammofono

talk'ing pic'ture *s* film parlato

tall [tɔl] *adj* alto; (coll) stravagante, esagerato

tallow [ˈtælo] *s* sego

tal·ly [ˈtæli] *s* (-lies) tacca, taglia || *v* (*pret & pp* -lied) *tr* contare, registrare || *intr* riscontrare

tal'ly sheet' *s* foglio di spunta

talon [ˈtælən] *s* artiglio

tambourine [ˌtæmbəˈrin] *s* tamburello

tame [tem] *adj* addomesticato; docile, mansueto; mite || *tr* addomesticare; domare; (*water power*) captare

tamp [tæmp] *tr* pigiare, comprimere; (*e.g., ground*) costipare

tamper [ˈtæmpər] *s* (*person*) pigiatore *m*; (*tool*) mazzeranga || *intr* intrigare; **to tamper with** (*a lock*) forzare; (*a document*) manomettere; (*a witness*) corrompere

tampon [ˈtæmpɑn] *s* (surg) tampone *m* || *tr* (surg) tamponare

tan [tæn] *adj* marrone; (*by sun*) abbronzato || *v* (*pret & pp* **tanned;** *ger* **tanning**) *tr* (*leather*) conciare; abbronzare; (coll) picchiare, sculacciare

tandem [ˈtændəm] *adj & adv* in tandem || *s* tandem *m*

tang [tæŋ] *s* sapore *m* piccante; odore *m* forte; traccia; (*of knife*) tallone *m*; (*sound*) tintinnio

tangent [ˈtændʒənt] *adj* tangente || *s* tangente *f*; **to fly off at a tangent** cambiare improvvisamente d'idea

tangerine [ˌtændʒəˈrin] *s* mandarino

tangible [ˈtændʒɪbəl] *adj* tangibile

Tangier [tænˈdʒɪr] *s* Tangeri *f*

tangle [ˈtæŋɡəl] *s* intrico; (coll) litigio || *tr* intricare || *intr* intricarsi; (coll) litigare

tank [tæŋk] *s* conserva, serbatoio; (mil) carro armato

tankard [ˈtæŋkərd] *s* boccale *m*

tank' car' *s* (rr) carro botte

tanker [ˈtæŋkər] *s* petroliera; (aer) aerocisterna

tank' farm'ing *s* idroponica

tank' truck' *s* autocisterna

tanner [ˈtænər] *s* conciapelli *m*

tanner·y [ˈtænəri] *s* (-ies) conceria

tantalize [ˈtæntəˌlaɪz] *tr* stuzzicare con vane promesse

tantamount [ˈtæntəˌmaunt] *adj* equivalente

tantrum [ˈtæntrəm] *s* bizze *fpl*

tap [tæp] *s* colpetto, buffetto; (*in a keg*) spina, cannella; (*faucet*) rubinetto; (elec) presa; (mach) maschio; **on tap** alla spina; (coll) disponibile; **taps** (mil) silenzio || *v* (*pret & pp* **tapped;** *ger* **tapping**) *tr* battere; picchiare, picchiettare; (*from a barrel*) spillare; mettere il cannello a; (*resources*) usare; (*a telephone*) intercettare; (*water, electricity*) derivare; (mach) maschiare || *intr* picchiare

tap' dance' *s* tip tap *m*

tap'-dance' *intr* ballare il tip tap

tape [tep] *s* nastro; (sports) striscione *m* del traguardo || *tr* legare con nastro; misurare col metro a nastro; registrare su nastro magnetico

tape' meas'ure *s* metro a nastro; nastro per misurare

tape' play'er *s* riproduttore *m* a nastro magnetico

taper [ˈtepər] *s* cerino || *tr* affusolare || *intr* affusolarsi; **to taper off** rastremarsi; diminuire in intensità; diminuire a poco a poco

tape'-re·cord' *tr* registrare su nastro magnetico

tape' record'er *s* magnetofono, registratore *m* a nastro

tapes·try [ˈtæpɪstri] *s* (-tries) tappezzeria || *v* (*pret & pp* **-tried**) *tr* tappezzare

tape'worm' *s* verme solitario, tenia

tappet [ˈtæpɪt] *s* (aut) punteria

tap'room' *s* taverna, osteria

tap'root' *s* radice *f* a fittone

tap' wa'ter *s* acqua corrente

tap' wrench' *s* giramaschio

tar [tɑr] *s* catrame *m* || *v* (*pret & pp* **tarred;** *ger* **tarring**) *tr* incatramare

tar·dy ['tardi] *adj* (**-dier; -diest**) in ritardo; lento

tare [ter] *s* tara || *tr* tarare

target ['targɪt] *s* segno, bersaglio

tar'get date' *s* data progettata

tar'get lan'guage *s* lingua obbiettivo, lingua di arrivo

tar'get prac'tice *s* esercizio di tiro a segno

tariff ['tærɪf] *s* (*duties*) tariffa doganale; (*charge or fare*) tariffa

tarnish ['tarnɪʃ] *s* ossidazione; (fig) macchia || *tr* appannare || *intr* appannarsi, perdere il lustro

tar' pa'per *s* carta catramata

tarpaulin [tar'pɔlɪn] *s* telone *m* impermeabile incatramato

tarragon ['tærəgɑn] *s* dragoncello

tar·ry ['tɑri] *adj* incatramato || ['tæri] *v* (*pret & pp* **-ried**) *intr* rimanere; ritardare

tart [tart] *adj* acido, pungente || *s* torta; (slang) puttana

tartar ['tartər] *s* tartaro; cremore *m* di tartaro; (*shrew*) megera; **to catch a tartar** imbattersi in un muso duro

Tartarus ['tartərəs] *s* Tartaro

task [tæsk] *or* [tɑsk] *s* compito, incarico; **to take to task** rimproverare

task' force' *s* gruppo formato per una missione speciale

task'mas'ter *s* sorvegliante *m*; sorvegliante severo

tassel ['tæsəl] *s* nappa; (bot) ciuffo

taste [test] *s* gusto, sapore *m*; buon gusto; (*sampling, e.g., of wine*) assaggio; esperienza; **to one's taste** a genio di qlcu || *tr* gustare, assaggiare || *intr* sentire, sapere; **to taste of** degustare; sapere di

tasteless ['testlɪs] *adj* insipido; di cattivo gusto

tast·y ['testi] *adj* (**-ier; -iest**) saporito; (coll) di buon gusto

tatter ['tætər] *s* brandello, sbrendolo || *tr* sbrindellare

tattered ['tætərd] *adj* sbrindellato

tattle ['tætəl] *s* chiacchiera; (*gossip*) pettegolezzo || *intr* chiacchierare; spettegolare

tat'fle·tale' *adj* rivelatore || *s* gazzetta, chiacchierone *m*

tattoo [tæ'tu] *s* tatuaggio; (mil) ritirata || *tr* tatuare

taunt [tɔnt] *or* [tɑnt] *s* rimprovero sarcastico, insulto || *tr* rimproverare sarcasticamente, insultare

Taurus ['tɔrəs] *s* (astr) Toro

taut [tɔt] *adj* teso, tirato

tavern ['tævərn] *s* osteria

taw·dry ['tɔdri] *adj* (**-drier; -driest**) vistoso, sgargiante, pacchiano

taw·ny ['tɔni] *adj* (**-nier; -niest**) falbo, fulvo

tax [tæks] *s* tassa, imposta || *tr* tassare; (*s.o.'s patience*) mettere a dura prova

taxable ['tæksəbəl] *adj* tassabile

tax'able in'come *s* imponibile *m*

taxation [tæk'seʃən] *s* imposizione, tassazione, contribuzione

tax' collec'tor *s* esattore *m* delle imposte

tax' deduc'tion *s* detrazione

tax'-ex·empt' *adj* esente da tasse

tax' evad'er [ɪ'vedər] *s* evasore *m*

tax·i ['tæksi] *s* (**-is**) tassì *m* || *v* (*pret & pp* **-ied**; *ger* **-ling** *or* **-ying**) *tr* far rullare || *intr* andare in tassì; (aer) rullare

tax'i·cab' *s* tassì *m*

tax'i driv'er *s* tassista *m*

tax'i·plane' *s* aeroplano da noleggio, aerotassì *m*

taxi' stand' *s* posteggio di tassì

tax'pay'er *s* contribuente *mf*

tax' rate' *s* imponibilità *f*

tea [ti] *s* tè *m*; (*medicinal infusion*) tisana; (*beef broth*) brodo di carne

tea' bag' *s* sacchetto di tè

tea' ball' *s* uovo da tè

tea'cart' *s* servitore *m*

teach [titʃ] *v* (*pret & pp* **taught** [tɔt]) *tr & intr* insegnare

teacher ['titʃər] *s* maestro, insegnante *mf*

teach'ers col'lege *s* scuola magistrale

teach'er's pet' *s* beniamino del maestro

teaching ['titʃɪŋ] *adj* insegnante || *s* insegnamento, dottrina

teach'ing aids' *spl* sussidi *mpl* didattici

teach'ing staff' *s* corpo insegnante

tea'cup' *s* tazza da tè

tea' dance' *s* tè *m* danzante

teak [tik] *s* tek *m*

tea'ket'tle *s* bricco del tè

team [tim] *s* (*e.g., of horses*) pariglia; (sports) squadra, equipaggio || *tr* apparigliare; tirare o trasportare con pariglia || *intr*—**to team up** unirsi, associarsi

team'mate' *s* compagno di squadra

teamster ['timstər] *s* (*of horses*) carrettiere *m*; (*of truck*) camionista *m*, autotrenista *m*

team'work' *s* affiatamento, collaborazione

tea'pot' *s* teiera

tear [tɪr] *s* lacrima; **to hold back one's tears** ingoiare le lacrime; **to laugh away one's tears** cambiare dal pianto al riso || [ter] *s* strappo || [ter] *v* (*pret* **tore** [tor]; *pp* **torn** [tɔrn]) *tr* strappare; stracciare; (*one's heart*) squarciare; (*to wound*) sbranare; (*one's hair*) strapparsi; **to tear apart** rompere in due; separare; **to tear down** demolire; (*a piece of equipment*) smontare; **to tear off** staccare; **to tear to pieces** dilaniare; fare a pezzi; **to tear up** (*a piece of paper*) stracciare; (*a street*) scavare || *intr* strapparsi, stracciarsi; **to tear along** precipitarsi; correre all'impazzata

tear' bomb' [tɪr] *s* bomba lacrimogena

tearful ['tɪrfəl] *adj* lacrimoso

tear' gas' [tɪr] *s* gas lacrimogeno

tear-jerker ['tɪr ˌdʒʌrkər] *s* (coll) storia lacrimogena

tear-off ['ter ˌɔf] *adj* da staccarsi, perforato

tea'room' *s* sala da tè

tear' sheet' [ter] *s* copia di annuncio pubblicitario

tease [tiz] *tr* stuzzicare, molestare;

(*hair*) accotonare; (*e.g., wool*) cardare

tea'spoon' *s* cucchiaino

teaspoonful ['ti ,spun ,ful] *s* cucchiaino

teat [tit] *s* capezzolo

tea'time' *s* l'ora del tè

tea' wag'on *s* servitore *m*

technical ['teknıkəl] *adj* tecnico

technicali•ty [,teknı'kælıti] *s* (**-ties**) tecnicismo; dettaglio tecnico

technician [tek'nıʃən] *s* tecnico

technics ['teknıks] *ssg or spl* tecnica

technique [tek'nik] *s* tecnica

ted'dy bear' ['tedi] *s* orsacchiotto

tedious ['tidı•əs] *or* ['tidʒəs] *adj* tedioso, noioso

tee [ti] *adj* fatto a T ‖ *s* giunto a tre vie; (*golf*) piazzola di partenza ‖ *tr*—**to tee off** (slang) cominciare ‖ *intr*—**to be teed off** (slang) essere arrabbiato; **to tee off** (golf) colpire la palla dalla piazzola di partenza; **to tee off on** (slang) rimproverare severamente

teem [tim] *intr* brulicare; piovere a dirotto; **to teem with** abbondare di

teeming ['timıŋ] *adj* brulicante; (*rain*) torrenziale

teen-ager ['tin ,edʒər] *s* giovane *mf* dai 13 ai 19 anni

teens [tinz] *spl* numeri inglesi che finiscono in **-teen** (dal 13 al 19); **to be in one's teens** avere dai 13 ai 19 anni

tee-ny ['tini] *adj* (**-nier; -niest**) (coll) piccolo, piccolissimo

teeter ['titər] *s* altalena, dondolio ‖ *intr* dondolarsi, oscillare

teethe [tið] *intr* mettere i denti

teething ['tiðıŋ] *s* dentizione

teeth'ing ring' *s* dentaruolo

teetotaler [ti'totələr] *s* astemio

tele•cast ['telı ,kæst] *or* ['telı ,kast] *s* teletrasmissione ‖ *v* (*pret & pp* **-cast** *or* **-casted**) *tr & intr* teletrasmettere

telegram ['telı ,græm] *s* telegramma *m*

telegraph ['telı ,græf] *or* ['telı ,graf] *s* telegrafo ‖ *tr & intr* telegrafare

tel'egraph pole' *s* palo del telegrafo

Telemachus [tı'leməkəs] *s* Telemaco

telemeter [tı'lemıtər] *s* telemetro ‖ *tr* misurare col telemetro

telepathy [tı'lepəθi] *s* telepatia

telephone ['telı ,fon] *s* telefono ‖ *tr & intr* telefonare

tel'ephone book' *s* elenco *or* guida dei telefoni

tel'ephone booth' *s* cabina telefonica

tel'ephone call' *s* chiamata telefonica, colpo di telefono

tel'ephone direc'tory *s* elenco *or* guida dei telefoni

tel'ephone exchange' *s* centrale telefonica

tel'ephone op'erator *s* centralinista *mf*, telefonista *mf*

tel'ephone receiv'er *s* ricevitore *m*

tel'ephoto lens' ['telı ,foto] *s* teleobbiettivo

teleplay ['telı ,ple] *s* teledramma *m*

teleprinter ['telı ,prıntər] *s* telescrivente *f*

telescope ['telı ,skop] *s* telescopio ‖ *tr*

snodare; condensare ‖ *intr* essere snodabile; (*in a collision*) incastrarsi

teletype ['telı ,taıp] *s* telescrivente *f* ‖ *tr & intr* trasmettere per telescrivente

teleview ['telı ,vju] *tr* telericevere

televiewer ['telı ,vju•ər] *s* telespettatore *m*

televise ['telı ,vaız] *tr* teletrasmettere

television ['telı ,vıʃən] *adj* televisivo ‖ *s* televisione

tel'evision screen' *s* teleschermo

tel'evision set' *s* televisore *m*

tell [tel] *v* (*pret & pp* **told** [told]) *tr* dire; (*to narrate*) raccontare; (*to count*) contare; distinguere; **I told you so!** te l'avevo detto!; **to tell off** (coll) dire il fatto suo a ‖ *intr* dire; prevedere; avere effetto; **to tell on** (*s.o.'s health*) pesare a, e.g., **age was telling on his health** l'età pesava alla sua salute; (coll) denunciare

teller ['telər] *s* narratore *m*; (*of bank*) cassiere *m*; (*of votes*) scrutatore *m*

temper ['tempər] *s* indole *f*, temperamento; umore *m*; calma; (metallurgy) tempra; **to keep one's temper** mantenersi calmo; **to lose one's temper** perdere la pazienza ‖ *tr* temprare ‖ *intr* temprarsi

temperament ['tempərəmənt] *s* indole *f*, temperamento, carattere *m*

temperamental [,tempərə'mentəl] *adj* emotivo, capriccioso

temperance ['tempərəns] *s* (*self-restraint in action*) temperanza; (*abstinence from alcoholic beverages*) sobrietà *f*

temperate ['tempərıt] *adj* temperato

temperature ['tempərətʃər] *s* temperatura

tempest ['tempıst] *s* tempesta; **tempest in a teapot** tempesta in un bicchier d'acqua

tempestuous [tem'pestʃu•əs] *adj* tempestoso

temple ['tempəl] *s* (*place of worship*) tempio; (*of spectacles*) susta, stanghetta; (anat) tempia

tem•po ['tempo] *s* (**-pos** *or* **-pi** [pi]) (mus) tempo; (fig) ritmo

temporal ['tempərəl] *adj* temporale

temporary ['tempə ,reri] *adj* temporaneo, provvisorio, transitorio, interino

temporize ['tempə ,raız] *intr* temporeggiare

tempt [tempt] *tr* tentare

temptation [temp'teʃən] *s* tentazione

tempter ['temptər] *s* tentatore *m*

tempting ['temptıŋ] *adj* tentatore

ten [ten] *adj & pron* dieci ‖ *s* dieci *m*; **ten o'clock** le dieci

tenable ['tenəbəl] *adj* difendibile

tenacious [tı'neʃəs] *adj* tenace

tenant ['tenənt] *s* inquilino, pigionante *mf*; (*of land*) fittavolo

tend [tend] *tr* riguardare, governare; accudire (with *dat*), e.g., **he tends the fire** accudisce al fuoco ‖ *intr* tendere; **to tend to** propendere verso; **to tend to**, e.g., **one's own business** attendere a; **to tend to** + *inf* tendere a + *inf*

tenden•cy ['tendənsi] *s* (**-cies**) tendenza, propensione

tender ['tɛndər] *adj* tenero; sensibile, dolorante ‖ *s* offerta; (naut) nave *f* rifornimento; (naut) lancia; (rr) carboniera ‖ *tr* offrire

tender-hearted ['tɛndər ,hɑrtɪd] *adj* dal cuore tenero

ten'der·loin' *s* filetto ‖ **Tenderloin** *s* rione *m* della mala vita

tenderness ['tɛndərnɪs] *s* tenerezza

tendon ['tɛndən] *s* tendine *m*

tendril ['tɛndrɪl] *s* viticcio

tenement ['tɛnɪmənt] *s* appartamento; casa; casamento

ten'ement house' *s* casamento

tenet ['tɛnɪt] *s* dogma *m*, dottrina

tennis ['tɛnɪs] *s* tennis *m*

ten'nis court' *s* campo da tennis

ten'nis play'er *s* tennista *mf*

tenor ['tɛnər] *s* tenore *m*

tense [tɛns] *adj* teso ‖ *s* (gram) tempo

tension ['tɛnʃən] *s* tensione

tent [tɛnt] *s* tenda; (*of circus*) tendone *m*

tentacle ['tɛntəkəl] *s* tentacolo

tentative ['tɛntətɪv] *adj* a titolo di prova; (*smile*) esile

tenth [tɛnθ] *adj, s & pron* decimo ‖ *s* (*in dates*) dieci *m*

tenuous ['tɛnjʊ·əs] *adj* tenue

tenure ['tɛnjər] *s* (*in office*) raffermo; (*permanency of employment*) inamovibilità *f*; (law) possesso

tepid ['tɛpɪd] *adj* tiepido

tercet ['tʌrsɪt] *s* terzina

term [tʌrm] *s* vocabolo, voce *f*; periodo, durata; termine *m*; (com) scadenza; **terms** condizioni *fpl*; **to be on good terms** essere in buone relazioni; **to come to terms** venire a patti ‖ *tr* chiamare, definire

termagant ['tʌrməgənt] *s* megera

terminal ['tʌrmɪnəl] *adj* terminale ‖ *s* (*end or extremity*) terminale *m*; (elec) morsetto; (rr) capolinea *m*

terminate ['tʌrmɪ ,net] *tr & intr* terminare

terminus ['tʌrmɪnəs] *s* termine *m*, fine *m*; (rr) capolinea *m*

termite ['tʌrmaɪt] *s* termite *f*

terrace ['tɛrəs] *s* terrazza, terrazzo; (agr) gradino, scaglione *m*

terra firma ['tɛrə 'fʌrmə] *s* terra ferma

terrain [tɛ'ren] *s* terreno

terrestrial [tə'rɛstrɪ·əl] *adj* terrestre

terrific [tə'rɪfɪk] *adj* terrificante; (coll) tremendo

terri·fy ['tɛrɪ ,faɪ] *v* (*pret & pp* **-fied**) *tr* terrificare, inorridire

territo·ry ['tɛrɪ ,tori] *s* (**-ries**) territorio

terror ['tɛrər] *s* terrore *m*

terrorize ['tɛrə ,raɪz] *tr* terrorizzare; dominare col terrore

ter'ry cloth' ['tɛri] *s* tessuto a spugna

terse [tʌrs] *adj* conciso, terso

tertiary ['tʌr/ɪ ,ɛri] *or* ['tʌr/əri] *adj* terziario

test [tɛst] *s* prova, saggio; esame *m* ‖ *tr* provare, saggiare; esaminare; (*e.g., a machine*) collaudare

testament ['tɛstəmənt] *s* testamento ‖ **Testament** *s* Testamento Nuovo

test' ban' *s* interdizione degli esperimenti nucleari

test' flight' *s* volo di prova

testicle ['tɛstɪkəl] *s* testicolo

testi·fy ['tɛstɪ ,faɪ] *v* (*pret & pp* **-fied**) *tr & intr* testimoniare

testimonial [,tɛstɪ'monɪ·əl] *s* (*certificate*) benservito, referenza; (*expression of esteem*) segno di gratitudine

testimo·ny ['tɛstɪ ,moni] *s* (**-nies**) testimonianza

test' pat'tern *s* (telv) monoscopio

test' pi'lot *s* pilota *m* collaudatore

test' tube' *s* provetta

tetanus ['tɛtənəs] *s* tetano

tether ['tɛðər] *s* cavezza, pastoia; **at the end of one's tether** al limite delle proprie risorse ‖ *tr* legare; incavezzare, impastoiare

tetter ['tɛtər] *s* eczema *m*, impetigine *f*

text [tɛkst] *s* testo; tema *m*

text'book' *s* libro di testo

textile ['tɛkstɪl] *or* ['tɛkstaɪl] *adj & s* tessile *m*

textual ['tɛkstʃʊ·əl] *adj* testuale

texture ['tɛkstʃər] *s* (*of cloth*) trama, caratteristica, proprietà *f*

Thai ['tɑ·i] *or* ['taɪ] *adj & s* tailandese *mf*

Thailand ['taɪlənd] *s* la Tailandia

Thames [tɛmz] *s* Tamigi *m*

than [ðæn] *conj* di, e.g., **he is faster than you** è più veloce di te; (*before a verb*) di quanto, e.g., **he is smarter than I thought** è più intelligente di quanto pensavo; che, e.g., **he had barely begun to eat than it was time to leave** non aveva appena cominciato a mangiare che era ora di andarsene

thank [θæŋk] *s*—**thanks** ringraziamenti *mpl*; **thanks to** grazie a, in grazia di ‖ *tr* ringraziare ‖ **thanks** *interj* grazie!

thankful ['θæŋkfəl] *adj* grato

thankless ['θæŋklɪs] *adj* ingrato

Thanksgiv'ing Day' [,θæŋks'gɪvɪŋ] *s* giorno del Ringraziamento

that [ðæt] *adj dem* (**those**) quel; codesto; **that one** quello, quello là ‖ *pron dem* (**those**) quello; codesto ‖ *pron rel* che, quello che, il quale; **that is** cioè; **that's that** (coll) ecco fatto, ecco tutto ‖ *adv* (coll) tanto, così; **that far** così lontano; **that many** tanti; **that much** tanto ‖ *conj* che

thatch [θætʃ] *s* paglia, copertura di paglia; (*hair*) capigliatura ‖ *tr* coprire di paglia

thaw [θɔ] *s* sgelo ‖ *tr* sgelare ‖ *intr* sgelarsi

the [ðə], [ðɪ], *or* [ði] *art def* il; al, e.g., **one dollar the dozen** un dollaro alla dozzina ‖ *adv*—**so much the worse for him** tanto peggio per lui; **the more . . . the more** quanto più . . . tanto più

theater ['θi·ətər] *s* teatro

the'ater·go'er *s* frequentatore *m* abituale del teatro

the'ater news' *s* cronaca teatrale

theatrical [θɪ'ætrɪkəl] *adj* teatrale

Thebes [θibz] *s* Tebe *f*

thee [ði] *pron pers* (Bib; poet) ti; te

theft [θɛft] *s* furto, ruberia

their [ðer] *adj poss* il loro, loro
theirs [ðerz] *pron poss* il loro
them [ðem] *pron pers* li; loro; **to them** loro
theme [θim] *s* tema *m*, soggetto; saggio; (mus) tema *m*
theme' song' *s* (mus) tema *m* centrale; (rad) sigla musicale
them-selves' *pron pers* essi stessi, loro stessi; si, e.g., **they enjoyed themselves** si divertirono
then [ðen] *adj* allora, di allora ‖ *s* quel tempo; **by then** a quell'epoca; **from then on** da quel giorno in poi ‖ *adv* allora; indi, poi; **then and there** a quel momento
thence [ðens] *adv* indi, quindi; da lì; da allora in poi
thence'forth' *adv* da allora in poi
theolo·gy [θi'ɑlədʒi] *s* (-gies) telogia
theorem [θi·ərəm] *s* teorema *m*
theoretical [ˌθi·ə'rɛtɪkəl] *adj* teoretico
theo·ry [θi·əri] *s* (-ries) teoria
therapeutic [ˌθɛrə'pjutɪk] *adj* terapeutico ‖ **therapeutics** *ssg* terapeutica
thera·py [θɛrəpi] *s* (-pies) terapia
there [ðer] *adv* lì, là; **there are** ci sono; **there is** c'è; ecco, e.g., **there it is** eccolo
there'abouts' *adv* circa, approssimativamente, giù di lì
there'af'ter *adv* in seguito, dipoi
there'by' *adv* quindi, perciò, così
therefore [ðerfor] *adv* per questo, quindi, dunque
there'in' *adv* lì; in quel rispetto
there'of' *adv* di ciò, da ciò
Theresa [tə'risə] *or* [tə'resə] *s* Teresa
there'upon' *adv* su questo; a quel momento; come conseguenza
thermal [θʌrməl] *adj* (water) termale; (capacity) termico
thermistor [θər'mɪstər] *s* (elec) termistore *m*
thermocouple [θʌrmo,kʌpəl] *s* termocoppia
thermodynamic [ˌθʌrmodaɪ'næmɪk] *adj* termodinamico ‖ **thermodynamics** *ssg* termodinamica
thermometer [θər'mɑmɪtər] *s* termometro
thermonuclear [ˌθʌrmo'njuklɪ·ər] *or* [ˌθʌrmo'nuklɪ·ər] *adj* termonucleare
ther'mos bot'tle [θʌrməs] *s* termos *m*
thermostat [θʌrmə,stæt] *s* termostato
thesau·rus [θɪ'sɔrəs] *s* (-ri [raɪ] *or* -ruses) tesoro, lessico, compendio
these [ðiz] *pl of* **this**
the·sis [θisɪs] *s* (-ses [siz]) tesi *f*
Thespis [θɛspɪs] *s* Tespi *m*
they [ðe] *pron pers* essi, loro
thick [θɪk] *adj* spesso, grosso; folto, denso; pieno, coperto; viscoso; stupido; (coll) intimo ‖ *s* spessore *m*; **in the thick of** nel folto di; **through thick and thin** nei tempi buoni e cattivi
thicken [θɪkən] *tr* ispessire; ingrossare; infoltire ‖ *intr* ispessirsi; ingrossarsi; (said of a plot) complicarsi
thicket [θɪkɪt] *s* boscaglia, macchia
thick-headed [θɪk,hɛdɪd] *adj* indietro, stupido

thick'set' *adj* tarchiato; (hedge) fitto, denso
thief [θif] *s* (thieves [θivz]) ladro
thieve [θiv] *intr* rubare
thiever·y [θivəri] *s* (-ies) furto
thigh [θaɪ] *s* coscia
thigh'bone' *s* femore *m*
thimble [θɪmbəl] *s* ditale *m*
thin [θɪn] *adj* (thinner; thinnest) (paper, ice) sottile; (lean) magro, smilzo; (e.g., hair) rado; (air) fine; (excuse) tenue; (voice) esile; (wine) leggero, annacquato ‖ *v* (pret & pp thinned; ger thinning) *tr* assottigliare; (paint) diluire ‖ *intr* assottigliarsi; **to thin out** (said of a crowd; one's hair) diradarsi
thine [ðaɪn] *adj & pron poss* (Bib & poet) tuo, il tuo
thing [θɪŋ] *s* cosa; **not to get a thing out of** non riuscire a capire; non cavare un briciolo d'informazione da; **of all things!** che cosa!; che sorpresa!; **the thing** l'ultima moda; **things** roba; **to see things** avere allucinazioni
think [θɪŋk] *v* (pret & pp thought [θɔt]) *tr* pensare; credere; **to think it over** ripensarci; **to think nothing of it** non darci la minima importanza; **to think of** (to have as an opinion of) pensare di, e.g., **what do you think of that doctor?** cosa ne pensa di quel medico?; **to think out** decifrare; **to think up** immaginare ‖ *intr* pensare; **to think not** credere di no; **to think of** (to turn one's thoughts to) pensare a, e.g., **he is thinking of the future** pensa al futuro; (to imagine) immaginare; **to think so** credere di sì; **to think well of** avere una buona opinione di
thinkable [θɪŋkəbəl] *adj* pensabile
thinker [θɪŋkər] *s* pensatore *m*
third [θʌrd] *adj, s & pron* terzo ‖ *s* terzo; (in dates) tre *m*; (aut) terza
third' degree' *s* interrogatorio di terzo grado
third' rail' *s* (rr) rotaia elettrificata di contatto
third'-rate' *adj* di terz'ordine
Third' World' *s* Terzo Mondo
thirst [θʌrst] *s* sete *f* ‖ *intr* aver sete; **to thirst for** aver sete di
thirst·y [θʌrsti] *adj* (-ier; -iest) assetato, sitibondo; **to be thirsty** avere sete
thirteen [θʌr'tin] *adj, s & pron* tredici *m*
thirteenth [θʌr'tinθ] *adj, s & pron* tredicesimo ‖ *s* (in dates) tredici *m*
thirtieth [θʌrtɪ·ɪθ] *adj, s & pron* trentesimo ‖ *s* (in dates) trenta *m*
thir·ty [θʌrti] *adj & pron* trenta ‖ *s* (-ties) trenta *m*; **the thirties** gli anni trenta
this [ðɪs] *adj dem* (these) questo; **this one** questo, questo qui ‖ *pron dem* (these) questo, questo qui ‖ *adv* (coll) tanto, così
thistle [θɪsəl] *s* cardo
thither [θɪðər] *or* [θɪðər] *adv* là, da quella parte

Thomas ['tɑməs] s Tommaso

thong [θɒŋ] or [θɑŋ] s coreggia

thorax ['θoræks] s (-raxes or -races [rə,siz]) torace m

thorn [θɔrn] s spina

thorn·y ['θorni] adj (-ier; -iest) spinoso

thorough ['θʌro] adj completo, esauriente

thor'ough·bred' adj di razza; (horse) purosangue ‖ s individuo di razza; (horse) purosangue mf

thor'ough·fare' s passaggio; **no thoroughfare** divieto di passaggio

thor'ough·go'ing adj completo, esauriente

thoroughly ['θʌroli] adv a fondo

those [ðoz] pl of **that**

thou [ðaʊ] pron pers (Bib; poet) tu ‖ tr dare del tu a

though [ðo] adv tuttavia ‖ conj malgrado, sebbene; **as though** come se

thought [θɔt] s pensiero; **perish the thought!** (coll) nemmeno a pensarci!

thoughtful ['θɔtfəl] adj pensieroso, riflessivo; (considerate) sollecito

thoughtless ['θɔtlɪs] adj irriflessivo; sconsiderato; (reckless) incurante

thought' trans'fer'ence s trasmissione del pensiero

thousand ['θaʊzənd] adj, s & pron mille m; **a thousand** or **one thousand** mille m

thousandth ['θaʊzəndθ] adj, s & pron millesimo

thralldom ['θrɔldəm] s schiavitù f

thrash [θræʃ] tr battere; (agr) trebbiare; **to thrash out** discutere a fondo ‖ intr agitarsi, dibattersi

thread [θrɛd] s filo; (mach) filetto, verme m; **to lose the thread of** perdere il filo di ‖ tr infilare; (fig) pervadere; (mach) filettare, impanare; **to thread one's way through** aprirsi il passaggio attraverso

thread'bare' adj frusto, logoro

threat [θrɛt] s minaccia

threaten ['θrɛtən] tr & intr minacciare

threatening ['θrɛtənɪŋ] adj minaccioso; (e.g., letter) minatorio

three [θri] adj & pron tre ‖ s tre m; **three o'clock** le tre

three'-cor'nered adj triangolare; (hat) a tre punte

three' hun'dred adj, s & pron trecento

threepenny ['θrɛpəni] or ['θrɪpəni] adj del valore di tre penny; di nessun valore

three'-phase' adj trifase

three'-ply' adj a tre spessori

three' R's' [ɑrz] spl lettura, scrittura e aritmetica

three'score' adj sessanta

three' thou'sand adj, s & pron tre mila mpl

threno·dy ['θrɛnədi] s (-dies) trenodia

thresh [θrɛʃ] tr (agr) trebbiare; **to thresh out** discutere a fondo ‖ intr trebbiare; battere

thresh'ing machine' s trebbiatrice f

threshold ['θrɛʃold] s soglia

thrice [θraɪs] adv tre volte; molto

thrift [θrɪft] s economia

thrift·y ['θrɪfti] adj (-ier; -iest) eco-

nomo, economico; vigoroso; prospero

thrill [θrɪl] s fremito d'emozione; esperienza emozionante ‖ tr emozionare ‖ intr emozionarsi; vibrare

thriller ['θrɪlər] s (coll) thrilling m

thrilling ['θrɪlɪŋ] adj emozionante, thrilling

thrive [θraɪv] v (pret **thrived** or **throve** [θrov]; pp **thrived** or **thriven** ['θrɪvən]) intr prosperare, fiorire

throat [θrot] s gola; **to clear one's throat** schiarirsi la voce

throb [θrɑb] s battito, palpito, tuffo ‖ v (pret & pp **throbbed;** ger **throbbing**) intr palpitare, pulsare

throe [θro] s agonia, travaglio, spasimo; **in the throes of** nel travaglio di; (e.g., battle) nel momento più penoso di

throne [θron] s trono

throng [θrɒŋ] or [θrɑŋ] s folla, stuolo ‖ intr affollarsi

throttle ['θrɑtəl] s (of locomotive) leva di comando; (of motorcycle) manetta; (of car) acceleratore m; (mach) valvola di controllo ‖ tr soffocare; (mach) regolare

through [θru] adj diretto, senza fermate; **to be through** aver finito; **to be through with** farla finita con ‖ adv attraverso; da una parte all'altra; completamente; ‖ prep attraverso, per; durante; fino alla fine di; per mezzo di

through·out' adv completamente, da un capo all'altro; dappertutto ‖ prep durante tutto, e.g., **throughout the afternoon** durante tutto il pomeriggio; per tutto, e.g., **throughout the house** per tutta la casa

throw [θro] s getto, tiro, lancio; gettata; coperta leggera ‖ v (pret **threw** [θru]; pp **thrown**) tr gettare, tirare, lanciare; (a shadow) proiettare; (the current) connettere; (said of a horse) disarcionare; (wrestling) gettare a terra; (a game) (coll) perdere intenzionalmente; (coll) stupire; **to throw away** gettar via; perdere; **to throw back** rigettare; ritardare; **to throw in** (the clutch) innestare; (coll) aggiungere; **to throw oneself into** darsi a; **to throw out** sbatter fuori; (the clutch) disinnestare; **to throw over** abbandonare ‖ intr gettare, tirare, lanciare; **to throw up** vomitare

thrum [θrʌm] v (pret & pp **thrummed;** ger **thrumming**) intr tambureggiare; (mus) far scorrere la mano sulle corde di uno strumento

thrush [θrʌʃ] s tordo

thrust [θrʌst] s (push) spinta; botta; (with dagger) pugnalata; (with sword) stoccata ‖ v (pret & pp **thrust**) tr spingere; conficcare, configgere; **to thrust oneself** (e.g., into a conversation) ficcarsi

thru'way' s autostrada

thud [θʌd] s tonfo ‖ v (pret & pp **thudded;** ger **thudding**) intr fare un rumore sordo

thug [θʌg] s fascinoroso

thumb [θʌm] *s* pollice *m;* **all thumbs** maldestro, goffo; **thumbs down** pollice verso; **to twiddle one's thumbs** girare i pollici, essere ozioso; **under the thumb of** sotto l'influenza di || *tr* sporcare con le dita; (*a book*) sfogliare; **to thumb a ride** chiedere l'autostop; **to thumb one's nose** (at) fare marameo (a)

thumb' in'dex *s* margine *m* a scaletta

thumb'nail' *adj* breve, conciso || *s* unghia del pollice

thumb'screw' *s* vite *f* ad aletta

thumb'tack' *s* puntina

thump [θʌmp] *s* tonfo || *tr* battere, percuotere || *intr* battere; cadere con un tonfo; camminare a passi pesanti; (*said of the heart*) palpitare violentemente

thumping ['θʌmpɪŋ] *adj* (coll) straordinario, eccezionale; (coll) grande

thunder ['θʌndər] *s* tuono; (*of applause*) scroscio; (*of a cannon*) rombo || *tr* lanciare || *intr* tonare, rombare; (fig) scrosciare

thun'der·bolt' *s* folgore *f*, fulmine *m*

thun'der·clap' *s* scroscio di tuono

thunderous ['θʌndərəs] *adj* fragoroso

thun'der·show'er *s* acquazzone *m* accompagnato da tuoni

thun'der·storm' *s* temporale *m*

thun'der·struck' *adj* attonito

Thursday ['θʌrsdi] *s* giovedì *m*

thus [ðʌs] *adv* così; **thus far** sino qui

thwack [θwæk] *s* colpo || *tr* colpire

thwart [θwɔrt] *adj* obliquo || *adv* di traverso || *tr* contrariare, sventare

thy [ðaɪ] *adj poss* (Bib; poet) tuo, il tuo

thyme [taɪm] *s* timo

thy'roid gland' ['θaɪrɔɪd] *s* tiroide *f*

thyself [ðaɪ'sɛlf] *pron* (Bib; poet) te stesso; te, ti

tiara [taɪ'ɑrə] or [taɪ'ɛrə] *s* (*female adornment*) diadema *m;* (eccl) tiara

tick [tɪk] *s* (*of pillow*) fodera; (*of mattress*) guscio; (*of clock*) ticchettio; (*dot*) punto; (ent) zecca; **on tick** (coll) a credito || *intr* fare ticchettio; **to make s.o. tick** mandare avanti qlcu

ticker ['tɪkər] *s* telescrivente *f;* (slang) orologio; (slang) cuore *m*

tick'er tape' *s* nastro della telescrivente

ticket ['tɪkɪt] *s* biglietto; (*e.g., of pawnbroker*) polizza; (*slip of paper or identifying tag*) bolletta, bollettino; (*summons*) verbale *m;* (*e.g., to indicate price*) etichetta; lista dei candidati; **that's the ticket** (coll) questo è quello che fa

tick'et a'gent *s* bigliettaio

tick'et of'fice *s* biglietteria

tick'et scalp'er ['skælpər] *s* bagarino

tick'et win'dow *s* sportello

ticking ['tɪkɪŋ] *s* traliccio

tickle ['tɪkəl] *s* solletico || *tr* solleticare; divertire || *intr* avere il solletico

ticklish ['tɪklɪʃ] *adj* sensibile al solletico; delicato; permaloso; **to be ticklish** soffrire il solletico

tick-tock ['tɪk ˌtɑk] *s* tic tac *m*

tid'al wave' ['taɪdəl] *s* onda di marea; (fig) ondata

tidbit ['tɪd ˌbɪt] *s* bocconcino

tiddlywinks ['tɪdli ˌwɪŋks] *s* gioco della pulce

tide [taɪd] *s* marea; **to go against the tide** andare contro la corrente; **to stem the tide** fermare la corrente || *tr* portare sulla cresta delle onde; **to tide over** aiutare; (*a difficulty*) sormontare

tide'wa'ter *s* marea; costa marina

tidings ['taɪdɪŋz] *spl* notizie *fpl*

ti·dy ['taɪdi] *adj* (**-dier; -diest**) pulito, ordinato || *s* (**-dies**) cofanetto, astuccio; appoggiacapo || *v* (*pret & pp* **-died**) *tr* rassettare, mettere in ordine || *intr* rassettarsi

tie [taɪ] *s* laccio, nodo, vincolo; (*in games*) patta; (*necktie*) cravatta; (archit) traversa; (rr) traversina; (mus) legatura || *v* (*pret & pp* **tied;** *ger* **tying**) *tr* allacciare, annodare; legare; confinare; (*a game*) impattare; (*a person*) impattarla con; **to be tied up** essere occupato; **to tie down** confinare, limitare; **to tie up** legare; impedire; (*e.g., traffic*) intasare || *intr* allacciarsi; (*in games*) impattare

tie' beam' *s* catena

tie'pin' *s* spilla da cravatta

tier [tɪr] *s* gradinata; ordine *m*, livello

tiff [tɪf] *s* screzio, litigio

tiger ['taɪgər] *s* tigre *f*

ti'ger lil'y *s* giglio cinese

tight [taɪt] *adj* teso; stretto; compatto; impermeabile; ermetico; pieno; (*game*) (coll) serrato; (coll) tirato; (slang) ubriaco || **tights** *spl* calzamaglia || *adv* strettamente; **to hold tight** tenere stretto

tighten ['taɪtən] *tr* (*e.g., one's belt*) tirare; (*e.g., a screw*) stringere || *intr* tirarsi; stringersi

tight-fisted ['taɪt'fɪstɪd] *adj* taccagno

tight'-fit'ting *adj* attillato

tight'rope' *s* corda tesa

tight' squeeze' *s*—**to be in a tight squeeze** (coll) essere alle strette

tight'wad' *s* (coll) spilorcio

tigress ['taɪgrɪs] *s* tigre femmina

tile [taɪl] *s* mattonella; (*for floor*) piastrella; (*for roof*) tegola, coppo || *tr* coprire di mattonelle; coprire di piastrelle; coprire di coppi

tile' roof' *s* tetto di tegole

till [tɪl] *s* cassetto dei soldi || *prep* fino a || *conj* fino a che . . . non, fino a che, sinché . . . non, sinché || *tr* lavorare, coltivare

tilt [tɪlt] *s* inclinazione; giostra, torneo; **full tilt** di gran carriera; a tutta forza || *tr* inclinare; (*a lance*) mettere in resta; attaccare || *intr* inclinarsi; giostrare; **to tilt at** combattere con

timber ['tɪmbər] *s* legno, legname *m* da costruzione; alberi *mpl;* (fig) tempra

tim'ber·land' *s* bosco destinato a produrre legname

tim'ber line' *s* linea della vegetazione

timbre ['tɪmbər] s (phonet & phys) timbro

time [taɪm] s tempo; ora, e.g., **what time is it?** che ora è?; volta, e.g., **three times** tre volte; giorni mpl, e.g., **in our time** ai giorni nostri; momento; ultima ora; ore fpl lavorative; periodo, e.g., **Xmas time** periodo natalizio; **for a long time** da lungo; **for the time being** per ora, per il momento; **in time** presto; col tempo; **on time** a tempo; a rate; (said, e.g., of a bus) in orario; **times** volte, e.g., **seven times seven** sette volte sette; **to bide one's time** aspettare l'ora propizia; **to do time** (coll) essere in prigione; **to have a good time** divertirsi; **to have no time for** non poter sopportare; **to lose time** (said of a watch) ritardare; **to make time** avanzare rapidamente; guadagnare terreno; **to pass the time of day** fare una chiacchierata; salutarsi; **to take one's time** fare le cose senza fretta; **to tell time** leggere l'orologio ‖ tr fissare il momento di; calcolare il tempo di; (sports) cronometrare

time′ bomb′ s bomba a orologeria
time′card′ s cartellino di presenza
time′ clock′ s orologio di controllo (delle presenze)
time′ expo′sure s (phot) posa
time′ fuse′ s spoletta a tempo
time′keep′er s marcatempo; orologio; (sports) cronometrista mf
timeless ['taɪmlɪs] adj senza fine, eterno
time·ly ['taɪmli] adj (-lier; -liest) opportuno, tempestivo
time′piece′ s orologio; cronometro
time′ sig′nal s segnale orario
time′ta′ble s orario; tabella di marcia
time′work′ s lavoro a ore
time′worn′ adj logorato dal tempo
time′ zone′ s fuso orario
timid ['tɪmɪd] adj timido, pavido
tim′ing gears′ ['taɪmɪŋ] spl ingranaggi mpl di distribuzione
timorous ['tɪmərəs] adj timoroso
tin [tɪn] s (element) stagno; (tin plate; can) latta ‖ v (pret & pp tinned; ger tinning) tr stagnare
tin′ can′ s latta
tincture ['tɪŋkt/ər] s tintura
tin′ cup′ s tazzina metallica
tinder ['tɪndər] s esca
tin′der·box′ s cassetta con l'esca e l'acciarino; persona eccitabile; (fig) polveriera
tin′ foil′ s stagnola
ting-a-ling ['tɪŋə‚lɪŋ] s dindìn m
tinge [tɪndʒ] s sfumatura; pizzico, punta ‖ v (ger tingeing or tinging) tr sfumare; dare una traccia di sapore a
tingle ['tɪŋɡəl] s formicolio, pizzicore m ‖ intr informicolirsi, pizzicare; (said of the ears) ronzare; (with enthusiasm) fremere
tin′ hat′ s (slang) elmetto
tinker ['tɪŋkər] s calderaio, ramaio ‖ intr armeggiare
tinkle ['tɪŋkəl] s tintinnio ‖ tr far tintinnare ‖ intr tintinnare

tin′ plate′ s latta
tin′ roof′ s tetto di lamiera di latta
tinsel ['tɪnsəl] s orpello, lustrino
tin′smith′ s lattoniere m, stagnino
tin′ sol′dier s soldatino di piombo
tint [tɪnt] s tinta, sfumatura ‖ tr tinteggiare
tin′ware′ s articoli mpl di latta
ti·ny ['taɪni] adj (-nier; -niest) piccino
tip [tɪp] s punta; (of mountain) vetta; (of umbrella) gorbia; (of shoe) mascherina; (of cigarette) bocchino; (of shoestring) aghetto; colpetto; (fee) mancia; informazione confidenziale; inclinazione ‖ v (pret & pp tipped; ger tipping) tr mettere la punta a; inclinare, rovesciare; (one's hat) levarsi; dare la mancia a; toccare, battere; (the scales) far traboccare; **to tip in** (bb) inserire fuori testo; **to tip off** (coll) dare informazioni confidenziali a ‖ intr inclinarsi; dare la mancia
tip′cart′ s carro ribaltabile
tip′-off′ s (coll) avvertimento confidenziale
tipped′-in′ adj (bb) fuori testo
tipple ['tɪpəl] intr sbevucchiare
tip′staff′ s usciere m
tip·sy ['tɪpsi] adj (-sier; -siest) brillo
tip′toe′ s punta di piedi ‖ v (pret & pp -toed; ger -toeing) intr camminare in punta di piedi
tirade ['taɪred] s tirata
tire [taɪr] s gomma, pneumatico; (of metal) cerchione m ‖ tr stancare ‖ intr stancarsi; infastidirsi
tire′ chain′ s catena antineve
tired [taɪrd] adj stanco, stracco
tire′ gauge′ s manometro della pressione delle gomme
tireless ['taɪrlɪs] adj infaticabile
tire′ pres′sure s pressione (delle gomme)
tire′ pump′ s pompa (per i pneumatici)
tiresome ['taɪrsəm] adj faticoso; (boring) noioso
tissue ['tɪʃu] s tessuto; tessuto finissimo, velina
tis′sue pa′per s carta velina
titanium [tai'teni·əm] or [tɪ'teni·əm] s titanio
tithe [taɪð] s decima ‖ tr imporre la decima su; pagare la decima di
Titian ['tɪʃən] adj tizianesco ‖ s Tiziano
title ['taɪtəl] s titolo; (sports) campionato ‖ tr intitolare
ti′tle deed′ s titolo di proprietà
ti′tle·hold′er s campione m, primatista mf
ti′tle page′ s frontespizio
ti′tle role′ s (theat) ruolo principale
tit′mouse′ s (-mice) (orn) cincia
titter ['tɪtər] s risatina ‖ intr ridacchiare
titular ['tɪt/ələr] adj titolare
TNT ['ti‚ɛn'ti] s (letterword) tritolo
to [tu], [tʊ] or [tə] adv—**to and fro** da una parte all'altra, avanti e indietro; **to come to** tornare in sè ‖ prep a, e.g., **he is going to Rome** va a Roma; **he gave a kiss to his mother**

diede un bacio a sua madre; **she is learning to sew** impara a cucire; per, e.g., **he has been a true friend to me** è stato un vero amico per me; da, e.g., **there is still a lot of work to do** c'è ancora molto lavoro da fare; con, e.g., **she was very kind to me** è stata molto gentile con me; in, e.g., **we went to church** siamo andati in chiesa; fino a, e.g., **to see s.o. to the station** accompagnare qlcu fino alla stazione; in confronto di, e.g., **the accounts are nothing to what really happened** le storie non sono nulla, in confronto di quanto è realmente successo; meno, e.g., **ten minutes to seven** le sette meno dieci

toad [tod] *s* rospo

toad'stool' *s* agarico, fungo velenoso

to-and-fro [tu-ənd'fro] *adj* avanti e indietro

toast [tost] *s* pane tostato; (*drink to s.o.'s health*) brindisi *m*; **a piece of toast** una fetta di pane tostato || *tr* tostare; brindare alla salute di || *intr* tostarsi; brindare

toaster ['tostər] *s* (*of bread*) tostapane *m*; persona che fa un brindisi

toast'mas'ter *s* persona che annuncia i brindisi, maestro di cerimonie

tobac·co [tə'bæko] *s* (**-cos**) tabacco

tobacconist [tə'bækənɪst] *s* tabaccaio

tobac'co pouch' *s* borsa da tabacco

toboggan [tə'bɑgən] *s* toboga *m*

tocsin ['tɑksɪn] *s* campana a martello; scampanata d'allarme

today [tu'de] *s & adv* oggi *m*

toddle ['tɑdəl] *s* passo vacillante || *intr* traballare, trotterellare

tod·dy ['tɑdi] *s* (**-dies**) ponce *m*

to-do [tə'du] *s* (**-dos**) (coll) daffare *m*, rumore *m*

toe [to] *s* dito del piede; (*of shoe*) punta || *v* (*pret & pp* **toed**; *ger* **toe-ing**) *tr*—**to toe the line** filare diritto

toe'nail' *s* unghia del piede

together [tu'geðər] *adv* insieme; **to bring together** riunire; riconciliare; **to call together** chiamare a raccolta; **to stick together** (coll) rimanere uniti, stare insieme

togs [tɑgz] *spl* vestiti *mpl*

toil [tɔɪl] *s* travaglio, sfacchinata; **toils** reti *fpl*, lacci *mpl* || *intr* travagliare, sfacchinare

toilet ['tɔɪlɪt] *s* toletta; gabinetto, ritirata; **to make one's toilet** farsi la toletta

toi'let pa'per *s* carta igienica

toi'let pow'der *s* polvere *f* di talco

toi'let soap' *s* sapone *m* da toletta

toi'let wa'ter *s* acqua da toletta

token ['tokən] *s* segno, marca; ricordo; (*used as money*) gettone *m*; **by the same token** per di più; **in token of** in segno di, come prova di

tolerance ['tɑlərəns] *s* tolleranza

tolerate ['tɑlə‚ret] *tr* tollerare

toll [tol] *s* (*of bell*) rintocco; (*e.g., for passage over bridge*) pedaggio; (*tax*) dazio; (*compensation for grinding grains*) molenda; (*number of victims*) perdite *fpl*; (telp) tariffa inter-

urbana || *tr* (*a bell*) sonare a morto; (*the faithful*) chiamare a raccolta || *intr* sonare a morto

toll' bridge' *s* ponte *m* a pedaggio

toll' call' *s* (telp) chiamata interurbana

toll'gate' *s* barriera di pedaggio; (*in a turnpike*) casello

toma·to [tə'meto] *or* [tə'mɑto] *s* (**-toes**) pomodoro

toma'to juice' *s* sugo di pomodoro

tomb [tum] *s* tomba

tomboy ['tɑm‚bɔɪ] *s* maschietta

tomb'stone' *s* pietra tombale, lapide *f*

tomcat ['tɑm‚kæt] *s* gatto maschio

tome [tom] *s* tomo

tomorrow [tu'mɑro] *or* [tu'mɔro] *s* domani *m*; **the day after tomorrow** dopodomani *m* || *adv* domani

tom-tom ['tɑm ‚tɑm] *s* tam-tam *m*

ton [tʌn] *s* tonnellata; **tons** (coll) montagne *fpl*

tone [ton] *s* tono; (fig) tenore *m* || *tr* intonare; **to tone down** (*colors*) smorzare; (*sounds*) sfumare || *intr* intonarsi; **to tone down** moderarsi; **to tone up** rinforzarsi

tone' po'em *s* poema sinfonico

tongs [tɔŋz] *spl* [tɑŋz] *spl* tenaglie *fpl*; (*e.g., for sugar*) molle *fpl*

tongue [tʌŋ] *s* (*language*) lingua; (*of bell*) battaglio; (*of shoe*) linguetta; (*of wagon*) timone *m*; (anat) lingua; (carp) maschio; **tongue in cheek** poco sinceramente; **to hold one's tongue** mordersi la lingua; **to speak with forked tongue** essere di due lingue

tongue' depres'sor *s* abbassalingua *m*

tongue'-lash'ing *s* sgridata

tongue' twist'er *s* scioglilingua *m*

tonic ['tɑnɪk] *adj & s* tonico

tonight [tu'naɪt] *s* questa sera, questa notte || *adv* stasera; stanotte

tonnage ['tʌnɪdʒ] *s* tonnellaggio, stazza

tonsil ['tʌnsəl] *s* tonsilla

ton·y ['toni] *adj* (**-ier; -iest**) (slang) elegante, di lusso

too [tu] *adv* (*also*) anche, pure; (*more than enough*) troppo; **too bad!** peccato!; **too many** troppi; **too much** troppo

tool [tul] *s* utensile *m*, attrezzo; (*person*) strumento; (*of lathe*) punta || *tr* lavorare; (bb) decorare

tool' bag' *s* borsa degli attrezzi

tool'box' *s* cassetta attrezzi

tool'mak'er *s* attrezzista *m*

tool'shed' *s* barchessa

toot [tut] *s* (*of horn*) suono; (*of locomotive*) fischio; (*of car's horn*) colpo; (coll) gazzarra || *tr* strombettare; **to toot one's own horn** strombazzare i propri meriti || *intr* strombettare

tooth [tuθ] *s* (**teeth** [tiθ]) dente *m*

tooth'ache' *s* mal *m* di denti

tooth'brush' *s* spazzolino da denti

toothless ['tuθlɪs] *adj* sdentato

tooth'paste' *s* pasta dentifricia

tooth'pick' *s* stuzzicadenti *m*

tooth' pow'der *s* polvere dentifricia

top [tɑp] *s* cima, sommo, vertice *m*; (*upper part of anything*) disopra *m*;

(*of mountain, tree*) vetta; (*of box*) coperchio; (*beginning*) principio; (*of bottle*) imboccatura; (*of a bridge*) testata; (*of wagon*) mantice *m*; (*of car*) tetto; (*of wall*) coronamento; (*toy*) trottola; (*naut*) gabbia; **at the top of one's voice** a perdifiato; **from top to bottom** daccapo a piedi, dal principio alla fine; **on top of** in cima di; subito dopo; **the tops** (coll) il migliore, il fiore; **to blow one's top** (slang) dare in escandescenze; **to sleep like a top** dormire come un ghiro || *v* (*pret & pp* **topped**); *ger* **topping**) *tr* (*a tree*) svettare; coronare; superare

topaz ['topæz] *s* topazio

top' bil'ling *s*—**to get top billing** essere artista di cartello; (journ) ricevere il posto più importante

top' boot' *s* stivale *m* a tromba

top'coat' *s* soprabito di mezza stagione

toper ['topər] *s* ubriacone *m*

topgal'lant sail' [,top'gælənt] *s* (naut) pappafico, veletta

top' hat' *s* cappello a staio o a cilindro

top'-heav'y *adj* troppo pesante in cima, sovraccarico in cima

topic ['topɪk] *s* topica, tema *m*

top'knot' *s* crocchia

topless ['toplɪs] *adj* (*mountain*) di cui non si vede la vetta, eccelso; (*bathing suit*) topless

top'mast' *s* (naut) alberetto

top'most' *adj* il più alto

topogra·phy [tə'pɑgrəfi] *s* (-phies) topografia

topple ['topəl] *tr* abbattere, rovesciare || *intr* rovesciarsi, cadere

top' prior'ity *s* priorità massima

topsail ['topsəl] or ['top,sel] *s* (naut) gabbia

top'-se'cret *adj* segretissimo

top'soil' *s* strato superiore del terreno

topsy-turvy ['topsi'tʌrvi] *adj* rovesciato; confuso || *s* soqquadro || *adv* a soqquadro

torch [tortʃ] *s* fiaccola, torcia; **to carry the torch for** (slang) amare disperatamente

torch'bear'er *s* portatore *m* di fiaccola; (fig) capo, guida *m*

torch'light' *s* luce *f* di fiaccola

torch' song' *s* canzone *f* triste d'amore non corrisposto

torment ['torment] *s* tormento || [tor'ment] *tr* tormentare

torna·do [tor'nedo] *s* (-dos or -does) tornado, tromba d'aria

torpe·do [tor'pido] *s* (-does) siluro || *tr* silurare

torpe'do boat' *s* motosilurante *f*

torpe'do-boat destroy'er *s* torpediniera

torrent ['torənt] or ['tɔrənt] *s* torrente *m*

torrid ['torɪd] or ['tɔrɪd] *adj* torrido

torsion ['torʃən] *s* torsione

tor'sion bar' *s* barra di torsione

tor·so ['torso] *s* (-sos) torso

tortoise ['tortəs] *s* tartaruga

tor'toise shell' *s* tartaruga

torture ['tortʃər] *s* tortura || *tr* torturare

toss [tos] or [tas] *s* lancio, getto || *tr* lanciare, gettare; (*to fling about*) sballottare; (*one's head*) alzare sdegnosamente; agitare; rivoltare; (*an opinion*) avventare; **to toss off** fare rapidamente; (*e.g., a drink*) buttar giù; **to toss up** (*a coin*) gettar in aria, gettare a testa o croce; (coll) rigettare || *intr* agitarsi, dimenarsi; **to toss and turn** (*in bed*) girarsi; **to toss up** giocare a testa o croce

toss'up' *s* testa e croce; (coll) eguale probabilità *f*

tot [tat] *s* bambino, piccolo

to·tal ['totəl] *adj* totale; (*e.g., loss*) completo || *s* totale *m* || *v* (*pret & pp* **-taled** or **-talled**; *ger* **-taling** or **-talling**) *tr* ammontare a; (*to make a total of*) sommare

totalitarian [to ,tælɪ'terɪ·ən] *adj* totalitario || *s* aderente *mf* al totalitarismo

totter ['totər] *s* vacillamento || *intr* vacillare

touch [tʌtʃ] *s* (*act*) tocco; (*sense*) tatto; (*of an illness*) leggero attacco; (*slight amount*) punta; (*for money*) (slang) stoccata; **to get in touch with** mettersi in contatto con; **to lose one's touch** perdere il tocco personale || *tr* toccare; raggiungere; riguardare; (*for a loan*) (slang) dare una stoccata a; **to touch on** menzionare; **to touch up** ritoccare || *intr* toccare; **to touch down** (aer) atterrare

touching ['tʌtʃɪŋ] *adj* toccante, commovente || *prep* riguardo a

touch'stone' *s* pietra di paragone

touch' type'writing *s* dattilografia a tatto

touch·y ['tʌtʃi] *adj* (-ier; -iest) suscettibile, permaloso; delicato, precario, rischioso

tough [tʌf] *adj* duro; forte; (*luck*) cattivo; violento || *s* malvivente *m*

toughen ['tʌfən] *tr* indurire || *intr* indurirsi

tough' luck' *s* disdetta, sfortuna

tour [tur] *s* gita, viaggio; (sports) giro; (mil) turno; (theat) tournée *f* || *tr* girare; (theat) portare in tournée || *intr* girare; (theat) andare in tournée

tour'ing car' ['turɪŋ] *s* automobile *f* da turismo

tourist ['turɪst] *adj* turistico || *s* turista *mf*

tournament ['turnəmənt] or ['tʌrnə·mənt] *s* torneo

tourney ['turni] or ['tʌrni] *s* torneo || *intr* giostrare

tourniquet ['turnɪ,ket] or ['tʌrnɪ,ke] *s* laccio emostatico

tousle ['tauzəl] *tr* spettinare

tow [to] *s* rimorchio; (*e.g., of hemp*) stoppa; **to take in tow** prendere a rimorchio ||*tr* rimorchiare

toward(s) [tord(z)] or [tə'word(z)] *prep* (*in the direction of*) verso; (*in respect to*) per; (*near*) vicino a; (*a certain hour*) su, verso

tow'boat' *s* rimorchiatore *m*

tow' car' *s* rimorchiatore *m*

tow·el ['tau·əl] *s* asciugamano; (*of paper*) salvietta; **to throw in the**

towel (slang) gettare la spugna ‖ v (*pret & pp* -**eled** or -**elled;** *ger* -**eling** or -**elling**) *tr* asciugare

tow'el rack' *s* portaasciugamani *m*

tower ['taʊ‧ər] *s* torre *f* ‖ *intr* torreggiare

towering ['taʊ‧ərɪŋ] *adj* torreggiante; gigantesco; eccessivo

towline ['to‧ˌlaɪn] *s* cavo di rimorchio

town [taʊn] *s* città *f;* (*townspeople*) cittadinanza; **in town** in città

town' clerk' *s* segretario municipale

town' coun'cil *s* consiglio comunale

town' cri'er *s* banditore *m* municipale

town' hall' *s* municipio

township ['taʊn‧ʃɪp] *s* suddivisione di contea

towns'man *s* (-**men**) cittadino; concittadino

towns'peo'ple *spl* cittadini *mpl;* gente *f* di città

town' talk' *s* dicerie *fpl,* pettegolezzi *mpl*

tow'path' *s* strada d'alaggio

tow'rope' *s* corda da rimorchio

tow' truck' *s* autogru *f*

toxic ['tɑksɪk] *adj & s* tossico

toy [tɔɪ] *adj* giocattolo; di giocattoli ‖ *s* giocattolo; (*trifle*) nonnulla *m;* (*trinket*) gingillo ‖ *intr* giocare; **to toy with** (*to play with*) giocare con; (*to trifle, e.g., with food*) baloccarsi con; (*an idea*) accarezzare; (*to flirt with*) flirtare con

toy' bank' *s* salvadanaio

toy' sol'dier *s* soldatino di piombo

trace [tres] *s* traccia, vestigio; (*tracing*) tracciato; (*of harness*) tirella; (fig) ombra ‖ *tr* tracciare; (*e.g., s.o.'s ancestry*) rintracciare; (*a pattern*) lucidare

trac'er bul'let ['tresər] *s* pallottola tracciante

trache·a ['treki‧ə] *s* (-**ae** [‧ˌi]) trachea

tracing ['tresɪŋ] *s* tracciato

track [træk] *s* (*of foot*) traccia, pesta; (*rut*) solco, rotaia; (*of boat*) scia; corso; (*course followed by boat*) rotta; (*of tape recorder*) pista; (*of tractor*) cingolo; (*of ideas*) successione; (*width of a vehicle measured from wheel to wheel*) (aut) carreggiata; (rr) binario; (*track and field*) (sports) atletica leggera; (*for horses*) (sports) galoppatoio; (*for running*) (sports) pista, corsia; **to keep track of** non perder di vista; **to lose track of** perder di vista; **to make tracks** (coll) affrettarsi; **to stop in one's tracks** (coll) fermarsi di colpo ‖ *tr* rintracciare, seguire le tracce di; lasciare tracce su; **to track down** rintracciare

track'ing sta'tion ['trækɪŋ] *s* (rok) stazione di avvistamento

track'less trol'ley ['træklɪs] *s* filobus *m*

track' meet' *s* incontro di atletica leggera

track'walk'er *s* (rr) guardialinee *m*

tract [trækt] *s* tratto, opuscolo, trattatello; (anat) tubo, canale *m*

traction ['træk/ən] *s* trazione

trac'tion com'pany *s* società *f* di trasporti urbani

tractor ['træktər] *s* trattore *m;* (*of a tractor-trailer*) motrice *f*

trac'tor-trail'er *s* treno stradale

trade [tred] *s* commercio; affare *m;* occupazione, mestiere *m;* (*people*) commercianti *mpl,* professionisti *mpl;* mercato; (*customers*) clientela; (*in slaves*) tratta ‖ *tr* mercanteggiare; cambiare; **to trade in** dare come pagamento parziale ‖ *intr* trafficare, commerciare; comprare; **to trade in** lavorare in; **to trade on** approfittarsi di

trade'mark' *s* marca or marchio di fabbrica

trade' name' *s* ragione sociale

trader ['tredər] *s* trafficante *m*

trade' school' *s* scuola d'avviamento professionale, scuola d'arti e mestieri

trades'man *s* (-**men**) commerciante *m;* artigiano

trade' un'ion *s* sindacato di lavoratori

trade' un'ionist *s* sindacalista *mf*

trade' winds' *spl* alisei *mpl*

trad'ing post' *s* centro di scambi commerciali; (*in stock exchange*) posto delle compravendite

trad'ing stamp' *s* buono premio

tradition [trə'dɪʃən] *s* tradizione

traditional [trə'dɪʃənəl] *adj* tradizionale

traduce [trə'djus] or [trə'dus] *tr* calunniare

traf·fic ['træfɪk] *s* traffico, circolazione; commercio; comunicazione ‖ v (*pret & pp* -**ficked**) *ger* -**ficking**) *intr* trafficare

traf'fic cir'cle *s* raccordo a circolazione rotatoria

traf'fic court' *s* tribunale *m* della polizia stradale

traf'fic is'land *s* isola spartitraffico

traf'fic jam' *s* intralcio del traffico, ingorgo stradale

traf'fic light' *s* semaforo

traf'fic man'ager *s* dirigente *m* del traffico; (rr) gestore *m* di stazione

traf'fic sign' *s* segnale *m* di circolazione stradale, cartello indicatore

traf'fic tick'et *s* contravvenzione per violazione del traffico

tragedian [trə'dʒidɪ‧ən] *s* tragico

trage·dy ['trædʒɪdɪ] *s* (-**dies**) tragedia

tragic ['trædʒɪk] *adj* tragico

trail [trel] *s* sentiero; (*track*) traccia, pista; (*of robe*) strascico, coda; (*of smoke*) pennacchio; (*left by an airplane*) striscia; (*of people*) codazzo ‖ *tr* strascicare; essere sulla fatta di; (*e.g., dust on the road*) sollevare; (*mud*) lasciar cadere ‖ *intr* strascicare; (*said, e.g., of a snake*) strisciare; (*said of a plant*) arrampicarsi; **to trail off** mutare; (*to weaken*) affievolirsi

trailer ['trelər] *s* traino; (*to haul freight*) semirimorchio; (*for living*) carovana, roulotte *f;* (bot) rampicante *m*

train [tren] *s* (*of vehicles*) convoglio; (*of robe*) strascico; (*of thought*) ordine *m*; (*of people*) coda; (rr) treno ‖ *tr* addestrare, impratichire; (*a weapon*) puntare, rivolgere; (*a horse*) scozzonare; (*e.g., a dog*) ammaestrare; (*a plant*) far crescere; (sports) allenare ‖ *intr* addestrarsi; ammaestrarsi; (sports) allenarsi

trained' nurse' *s* infermiera diplomata

trainer ['trenər] *s* allenatore *m*

training ['trenɪŋ] *s* esercizio, esercitazione; (sports) allenamento

train'ing camp' *s* campo addestramento

train'ing school' *s* scuola di addestramento professionale; riformatorio

train'ing ship' *s* nave *f* scuola

trait [tret] *s* tratto, caratteristica

traitor ['tretər] *s* traditore *m*

traitress ['tretrɪs] *s* traditrice *f*

trajecto·ry [trə'dʒɛktəri] *s* (**-ries**) traiettoria

tramp [træmp] *s* lunga camminata; vagabondo; (*hussy*) sgualdrina ‖ *tr* attraversare; calpestare ‖ *intr* camminare a passi fermi; fare il vagabondo

trample ['træmpəl] *tr* calpestare; (fig) conculcare ‖ *intr*—**to trample on** or **upon** calpestare

trampoline ['træmpə,lin] *s* trampolino di olona per salti mortali

tramp' steam'er *s* carretta

trance [træns] or [trɑns] *s* trance *f*; (*dazed condition*) estasi *f*

tranquil ['træŋkwɪl] *adj* tranquillo

tranquilize ['træŋkwɪ,laɪz] *tr* tranquillizzare ‖ *intr* tranquillizzarsi

tranquilizer ['træŋkwɪ,laɪzər] *s* tranquillante *m*

tranquillity [træn'kwɪlɪti] *s* tranquillità *f*

transact [træn'zækt] or [træns'ækt] *tr* sbrigare, trattare

transaction [træn'zæk/ən] or [træns'æk/ən] *s* disbrigo, operazione

transatlantic [,trænsət'læntɪk] *adj & s* transatlantico

transcend [træn'sɛnd] *tr* trascendere, sorpassare ‖ *intr* eccellere

transcribe [træn'skraɪb] *tr* trascrivere

transcript ['trænskrɪpt] *s* copia; traduzione; (educ) copia ufficiale del certificato di studi

transcription [træn'skrɪp/ən] *s* trascrizione

transept ['trænsɛpt] *s* transetto

trans·fer ['trænsfər] *s* trasferimento; passaggio; (*pattern*) rapporto; (*of funds*) giro; (*of real estate*) compravendita; (law) voltura ‖ [træns'fʌr] or ['trænsfər] *v* (*pret & pp* **-ferred;** *ger* **-ferring**) *tr* trasferire, trasportare; (*funds*) stornare; (*a design*) rapportare; (*real estate*) compravendere ‖ *intr* trasferirsi; cambiare di treno

trans'fer tax' *s* tassa di successione; tassa sulla compravendita

transfix [træns'fɪks] *tr* trafiggere; paralizzare, inchiodare

transform [træns'fɔrm] *tr* trasformare; (elec) trasformare ‖ *intr* trasformarsi

transforma'tional gram'mar [,trænsfər-

'me/ənəl] *s* grammatica trasformativa

transformer [træns'fɔrmər] *s* trasformatore *m*

transfusion [træns'fju/ən] *s* trasfusione

transgress [træns'grɛs] *tr* trasgredire; (*a limit or boundry*) oltrepassare ‖ *intr* peccare

transgression [træns'grɛ/ən] *s* trasgressione; peccato

transient ['træn/ənt] *adj* passeggero, temporaneo; di passaggio ‖ *s* ospite *mf* di passaggio

transistor [træn'zɪstər] *s* transistore *m*

transit ['trænsɪt] or ['trænzɪt] *s* transito

transition [træn'zɪ/ən] *s* transizione

transitional [træn'zɪ/ənəl] *adj* di transizione

transitive ['trænsɪtɪv] *adj* transitivo ‖ *s* verbo transitivo

transitory ['trænsɪ,tori] *adj* transitorio

translate [træns'let] or ['trænslet] *tr* tradurre; convertire; (*to transfer*) trasportare ‖ *intr* tradursi

translation [træns'le/ən] *s* traduzione; trasformazione; (telg) ritrasmissione

translator [træns'letər] *s* traduttore *m*

transliterate [træns'lɪtə,ret] *tr* traslitterare

translucent [træns'lusənt] *adj* traslucido; (fig) chiaro

transmission [træns'mɪ/ən] *s* trasmissione; (aut) trasmissione

trans·mit [træns'mɪt] *v* (*pret & pp* **-mitted;** *ger* **-mitting**) *tr & intr* trasmettere

transmitter [træns'mɪtər] *s* trasmettitore *m*

transmit'ting set' *s* emittente *f*

transmit'ting sta'tion *s* stazione trasmettitrice

transmute [træns'mjut] *tr & intr* trasmutare

transom ['trænsəm] *s* (*crosspiece*) traversa; (*window over door*) vasistas *m*; (naut) specchio di poppa

transparen·cy ['træns'pɛrənsi] *s* (**-cies**) trasparenza; (*design on a translucent substance*) trasparente *m*; (phot) diapositiva

transparent [træns'pɛrənt] *adj* trasparente

transpire [træns'paɪr] *intr* (*to happen*) avvenire; (*to perspire*) traspirare; (*to become known*) trapelare

transplant [træns'plænt] or [træns'plɑnt] *tr* trapiantare ‖ *intr* trapiantarsi

transport ['trænsport] *s* trasporto; mezzo di trasporto ‖ [træns'port] *tr* trasportare

transportation [,trænspor'te/ən] *s* trasporto; trasporti *mpl*, locomozione; biglietto di trasporto

trans'port work'er *s* ferrotranviere *m*

transpose [træns'poz] *tr* trasporre; (mus) trasportare

trans·ship [træns'/ɪp] *v* (*pret & pp* **-shipped;** *ger* **-shipping**) *tr* trasbordare

trap [træp] *s* trappola, tranello;

(*double-curved pipe*) sifone *m;* (slang) bocca; (sports) congegno lanciapiattelli || *v* (*pret & pp* **trapped; ger trapping**) *tr* intrappolare, accalappiare

trap' door' *s* trabocchetto, botola; (theat) ribalta

trapeze [trə'piz] *s* (sports) trapezio

trapezoid ['træpɪˌzɔɪd] *s* (geom) trapezio, trapezoide *m*

trapper ['træpər] *s* cacciatore *m* di animali da pelliccia con trappole

trappings ['træpɪŋz] *spl* ornamenti *mpl;* (*for a horse*) gualdrappa

trap'shoot'ing *s* tiro al piattello

trash [træʃ] *s* immondizia, spazzatura; (*nonsense*) sciocchezze *fpl;* (*junk*) ciarpame *m;* (*worthless people*) gentaglia

trash' can' *s* portaimmondizie *m*

travail ['trævəl] or [trə'vel] *s* travaglio; travaglio di parto

trav-el ['trævəl] *s* viaggio; traffico; (mach) corsa || *v* (*pret & pp* **-eled** or **-elled; ger -eling** or **-elling**) *tr* viaggiare per, percorrere || *intr* viaggiare; muoversi; (coll) andare

trav'el a'gency *s* ufficio turistico

traveler ['trævələr] *s* viaggiatore *m*

trav'eler's check' *s* assegno viaggiatori

trav'eling bag' *s* sacca da viaggio

trav'eling expens'es *spl* spese *fpl* di viaggio; (*per diem*) trasferta

trav'eling sales'man *s* (**-men**) commesso viaggiatore

traverse ['trævərs] or [trə'vʌrs] *tr* attraversare

traves-ty ['trævɪstɪ] *s* (**-ties**) parodia || *v* (*pret & pp* **-tied**) *tr* parodiare

trawl [trɔl] *s* (*fishing net*) rete *f* a strascico; (*fishing line*) lenza al traino || *tr & intr* pescare con la rete a strascico; pescare con la lenza al traino

trawling ['trɔlɪŋ] *s* pesca con la rete a strascico; pesca con la lenza al traino

tray [tre] *s* guantiera, vassoio; (chem, phot) bacinella

treacherous ['tretʃərəs] *adj* traditore, subdolo; incerto, pericoloso

treacher-y ['tretʃərɪ] *s* (**-ies**) tradimento

tread [tred] *s* (*step*) passo; (*of shoe*) suola; (*of tire*) battistrada *m;* (*of stairs*) pedata || *v* (*pret* **trod** [trɑd]; *pp* **trodden** ['trɑdən] or **trod**) *tr* calpestare; (*the boards*) calcare; accoppiarsi con || *intr* camminare; **to tread on** calpestare

treadle ['tredəl] *s* pedale *m*

tread'mill' *s* ruota azionata col camminare; (fig) lavoro ingrato

treason ['trizən] *s* tradimento

treasonable ['trizənəbəl] *adj* traditore

treasure ['treʒər] *s* tesoro || *tr* far tesoro di

treasurer ['treʒərər] *s* tesoriere *m*

treas'ure hunt' *s* caccia al tesoro

treasur-y ['treʒərɪ] *s* (**-ies**) tesoreria; tesoro, erario

treat [trit] *s* trattenimento; (*something affording pleasure*) piacere *m,* diletto || *tr* trattare; (*to cure*) curare, medi-

care; offrire un trattenimento a || *intr* trattare; pagare per il trattenimento

treatise ['tritɪs] *s* trattato

treatment ['tritmənt] *s* trattamento; (*of a theme*) trattazione

trea-ty ['tritɪ] *s* (**-ties**) trattato

treble ['trebəl] *adj* (*threefold*) triplo; (mus) soprano || *s* (*person*) soprano *mf;* (*voice*) soprano || *tr* triplicare || *intr* triplicarsi

tree [tri] *s* albero

tree' farm' *s* bosco ceduo

tree' frog' *s* raganella

treeless ['trilɪs] *adj* spoglio, **senza** alberi

tree'top' *s* cima dell'albero

trellis ['trelɪs] *s* traliccio, graticcio

tremble ['trembəl] *s* tremito || *intr* tremare

tremendous [trɪ'mendəs] *adj* tremendo

tremor ['tremər] or ['trimər] *s* tremito; (*of earth*) scossa

trench [trentʃ] *s* fosso, canale *m;* (mil) trincea

trenchant ['trentʃənt] *adj* mordace, caustico; vigoroso; incisivo

trench' coat' *s* trench *m*

trench' mor'tar *s* lanciabombe *m*

trend [trend] *s* tendenza, orientamento || *intr* tendere, dirigersi

Trent [trent] *s* Trento *f*

trespass ['trespəs] *s* (law) intrusione, violazione di proprietà || *intr* entrare senza diritto, intrudersi; peccare; **no trespassing** divieto di passaggio; **to trespass against** peccare contro; **to trespass on** entrare abusivamente in; (*e.g., s.o.'s time*) abusare di; violare

tress [tres] *s* treccia

trestle ['tresəl] *s* cavalletto; viadotto **a** cavalletti; ponte *m* a cavalletti

trial ['traɪ·əl] *s* tentativo, prova; tribolazione, croce *f;* (law) giudizio, processo; **on trial** in prova; (law) sotto processo; **to bring to trial** sottoporre a processo

tri'al and er'ror *s* metodo per tentativo; **by trial and error** a tastoni

tri'al balloon' *s* pallone *m* sonda

tri'al by ju'ry *s* processo con giuria

tri'al ju'ry *s* giuria civile o processuale

tri'al or'der *s* (com) ordine *m* di prova

tri'al run' *s* viaggio di prova

triangle ['traɪˌæŋgəl] *s* triangolo; (*in drafting*) quartabuono

tribe [traɪb] *s* tribù *f*

tribunal [trɪ'bjunəl] or [traɪ'bjunəl] *s* tribunale *m*

tribune ['trɪbjun] *s* tribuna

tributar-y ['trɪbjəˌterɪ] *adj* tributario || *s* (**-ies**) tributario

tribute ['trɪbjut] *s* tributo; **to pay trib-ute to** (*e.g., beauty*) rendere omaggio a

trice [traɪs] *s* momento, istante *m;* **in a trice** in un batter d'occhio

trick [trɪk] *s* gherminella, inganno; trucco, tiro, scherzo; (*knack*) abilità *f;* (*feat*) atto; (*set of cards won*) presa; turno; (coll) piccola; **to be up to one's old tricks** farne una delle sue; **to play a dirty trick on** fare un brutto tiro a‖ *tr* giocare, ingannare

tricker•y ['trɪkərɪ] *s* (**-ies**) gherminella, inganno

trickle ['trɪkəl] *s* gocciolio, filo ‖ *intr* gocciolare; (*said of people*) andare or venire alla spicciolata; (*said of news*) trapelare

trickster ['trɪkstər] *s* imbroglione *m*

trick•y ['trɪkɪ] *adj* (**-ier; -iest**) ingannatore; (*machine*) complicato; (*ticklish to deal with*) delicato

tried [traɪd] *adj* fedele, provato

trifle ['traɪfəl] *s* bazzecola, bagattella; (*small amount of money*) piccolezza, miseria; **a trifle** un po'‖ *tr*—**to trifle away** sprecare ‖ *intr* gingillarsi; **to trifle with** giocherellare con; scherzare con; divertirsi con

trifling ['traɪflɪŋ] *adj* futile; insignificante, trascurabile

trifocal [traɪˈfokəl] *adj* trifocale ‖ **trifocals** *spl* occhiali *mpl* trifocali

trigger ['trɪgər] *s* (*of a firearm*) grilletto; (*of any device*) leva di sgancio ‖ *tr* (*a gun*) far sparare; (fig) scatenare

trigonometry [ˌtrɪgəˈnɑmɪtrɪ] *s* trigonometria

trill [trɪl] *s* trillo, gorgheggio; vibrazione; (*speech sound*) (phonet) vibrante *f* ‖ *tr* gorgheggiare; pronunziare con vibrazione ‖ *intr* trillare, gorgheggiare

trillion ['trɪljən] *s* trilione *m*

trilo•gy ['trɪlədʒɪ] *s* (**-gies**) trilogia

trim [trɪm] *adj* (**trimmer; trimmest**) lindo, azzimato ‖ *s* condizione; buona condizione; (*dress*) vestito; (*of hair*) taglio, sfumatura; decorazione, ornamento; (*of sails*) orientamento; (aut) attrezzatura della carrozzeria ‖ *v* (*pret & pp* **trimmed;** *ger* **trimming**) *tr* tagliare; (*an edge*) rifilare; adattare; arrangiare; (*Christmas tree*) decorare; (*hair*) sfumare; (*a tree*) potare; ordinare, assettare; (*a sail*) orientare; (aer) equilibrare; (mach) sbavare; (coll) rimproverare; (coll) bastonare; (*to defeat* (coll) battere, vincere

trimming ['trɪmɪŋ] *s* ornamento, guarnizione; (coll) battitura, batosta; **trimmings** guarnizioni *mpl*; (mach) sbavatura; (mach) rifilatura

trini•ty ['trɪnɪtɪ] *s* (**-ties**) (*group of three*) triade *f* ‖ **Trinity** *s* Trinità *f*

trinket ['trɪŋkɪt] *s* (*small ornament*) ninnolo, gingillo; **trinkets** (*trivial objects*) paccottiglia

tri•o ['tri-o] *s* (**-os**) terzetto

trip [trɪp] *s* viaggio; corsa; (*stumble*) inciampata; (*act of causing s.o. to stumble*) sgambetto; (*error*) passo falso; passo agile ‖ *v* (*pret & pp* **tripped;** *ger* **tripping**) *tr* far inciampare, far cadere; fare lo sgambetto a; cogliere in fallo; (mach) far scattare ‖ *intr* inciampare; fare un passo falso; avanzare saltellando, saltellare; **to trip over** inciampare in

tripartite [traɪˈpɑrtaɪt] *adj* tripartito

tripe [traɪp] *s* trippa; (slang) sciocchezze *fpl*

trip'ham'mer *s* maglio meccanico

triphthong ['trɪfθɔŋ] or ['trɪfθɑŋ] *s* trittongo

triple ['trɪpəl] *adj & s* triplo ‖ *tr* triplicare ‖ *intr* triplicarsi

triplet ['trɪplɪt] *s* (*offspring*) nato da un parto trigemino; (mus, poet) terzina

triplicate ['trɪplɪkɪt] *adj* triplicato ‖ *s* triplice copia ‖ ['trɪplɪˌket] *tr* triplicare

tripod ['traɪpɑd] *s* (*e.g., for a camera*) treppiede *m*; (*stool with three legs*) tripode *m*

triptych ['trɪptɪk] *s* trittico

trite [traɪt] *adj* trito, ritrito

triumph ['traɪ-əmf] *s* trionfo ‖ *intr* trionfare

trium'phal arch' [traɪˈʌmfəl] *s* arco trionfale

trivia ['trɪvɪ-ə] *spl* banalità *f*, futilità *f*

trivial ['trɪvɪ-əl] *adj* insignificante, futile, banale

Trojan ['trodʒən] *adj & s* troiano

Tro'jan Horse' *s* cavallo di Troia

Tro'jan War' *s* guerra troiana

troll [trol] *tr & intr* pescare con la lenza al trono, pescare con il cucchiaino

trolley ['trɑlɪ] *s* asta di presa, trolley *m*; carrozza tranviaria, tram *m*

trol'ley bus' *s* filobus *m*

trol'ley car' *s* vettura tranviaria, tram *m*

trol'ley pole' *s* trolley *m*

trollop ['trɑləp] *s* (*slovenly woman*) sciattona; (*hussy*) sgualdrina

trombone ['trɑmbon] *s* trombone *m*

troop [trup] *s* truppa, gruppo; (*of animals*) branco; (*of cavalry*) squadrone *m*; **troops** soldati *mpl* ‖ *intr* raggrupparsi; marciare insieme

trooper ['trupər] *s* soldato di cavalleria; poliziotto a cavallo; **to swear like a trooper** bestemmiare come un turco

tro•phy ['trofɪ] *s* (**-phies**) trofeo; (*any memento*) ricordo

tropic ['trɑpɪk] *adj* tropicale ‖ *s* tropico; **tropics** zona tropicale

tropical ['trɑpɪkəl] *adj* tropicale

troposphere ['trɑpəˌsfɪr] *s* troposfera

trot [trɑt] *s* trotto ‖ *v* (*pret & pp* **trotted;** *ger* **trotting**) *tr* far trottare; **to trot out** (coll) squadernare, esibire ‖ *intr* trottare

troth [troθ] or [troθ] *s* promessa di matrimonio; **by my troth** affé di Dio; **in troth** in verità; **to plight one's troth** impegnarsi; dare la parola

troubadour ['trubəˌdor] or ['trubəˌdur] *s* trovatore *m*

trouble ['trʌbəl] *s* disturbo, fastidio; inconveniente *m*, grattacapo; disordine *m*, conflitto; (*of a mechanical nature*) panna, guasto; **not to be worth the trouble** non valere la pena; **that's the trouble** questo è il male; **the trouble is that** il guaio è che; **to be in trouble** essere nei guai; **to be**

looking for trouble andare a cercarsi le grane; **to get into trouble** mettersi nei pasticci; **to have trouble in** + *ger* durar fatica a + *inf*; **to take the trouble** incomodarsi ‖ *tr* molestare, disturbare; (*e.g., water*) intorbidare; dar del filo da torcere a; **to be troubled with** soffrire di; **to trouble oneself** scomodarsi

trouble' light' *s* lampada di soccorso

trou'ble·mak'er *s* mettimale *mf*

troubleshooter [ˈtrʌbəlˌʃutər] *s* localizzatore *m* di guasti; (*in disputes*) paciere *m*, conciliatore *m*

troubleshooting [ˈtrʌbəlˌʃutɪŋ] *s* localizzazione dei guasti; (*of disputes*) composizione

troublesome [ˈtrʌbəlsəm] *adj* molesto; difficile

trouble' spot' *s* luogo di disordini, polveriera

trough [trɔf] *or* [trɔf] *s* (*to knead bread*) madia; (*for feeding pigs*) trogolo; (*for feeding animals*) mangiatoia; (*for watering animals*) abbeveratoio; (*gutter*) doccia; (*between two waves*) cavo

troupe [trup] *s* troupe *f*

trouper [ˈtrupər] *s* membro della troupe; vecchio attore; tipo di cui ci si può fidare

trousers [ˈtrauzərz] *spl* pantaloni *mpl*

trousseau [truˈso] *or* [ˈtruso] *s* (**-seaux** *or* **-seaus**) corredo da sposa

trout [traut] *s* trota

trouvère [truˈvɛr] *s* troviero

trowel [ˈtrau·əl] *s* cazzuola, mestola

Troy [trɔɪ] *s* Troia

truant [ˈtru·ənt] *s* fannullone *m*; **to play truant** marinare la scuola

truce [trus] *s* tregua

truck [trʌk] *s* autocarro, camion *m*; (*tractor-trailer*) autotreno; (*van*) furgone *m*; (*to be moved by hand*) carretto; verdura per il mercato; (*mach, rr*) carrello; (*coll*) robaccia; (*coll*) relazioni *fpl* ‖ *tr* trasportare per autocarro, autotrasportare

truck'driv'er *s* camionista *m*

truck' farm' *s* fattoria agricola per la produzione degli ortaggi

truculent [ˈtrʌkjələnt] *or* [ˈtrukjələnt] *adj* truculento

trudge [trʌdʒ] *intr* camminare; **to trudge along** camminare laboriosamente, scarpinare

true [tru] *adj* vero; esatto, conforme; legittimo; infallibile; a livello; **to come true** verificarsi; **true to life** conforme alla realtà

true' cop'y *s* copia conforme

true-hearted [ˈtru ˌhɑrtɪd] *adj* fedele

true'love knot' *s* nodo d'amore

truffle [ˈtrʌfəl] *or* [ˈtrufəl] *s* tartufo

truism [ˈtru·ɪzəm] *s* truismo

truly [ˈtruli] *adv* veramente, correttamente; **yours truly** distinti saluti

trump [trʌmp] *s* (*cards*) atout *m*; (Italian cards) briscola; **no trump** senza atout ‖ *tr* superare; (*cards*) pigliare con un atout o con una briscola; **to**

trump up inventare, fabbricare ‖ *intr* giocare un atout o una briscola

trumpet [ˈtrʌmpɪt] *s* tromba; (*toy*) trombetta; **to blow one's own trumpet** cantar le proprie lodi ‖ *tr* strombazzare ‖ *intr* sonar la tromba; strombazzare; (*said of an elephant*) barrire

truncheon [ˈtrʌntʃən] *s* bastone *m* del comando; (Brit) manganello

trunk [trʌŋk] *s* (*of living body, tree, family, railroad*) tronco; (*for clothes*) baule *m*; (*of elephant*) tromba; (aut) bagagliaio; (archit) fusto; (telp) linea principale; **trunks** pantaloncini *mpl*

trunk' hose' *s* (hist) brache *fpl*

truss [trʌs] *s* (*to support a roof*) capriata, incavallatura; (*based on cantilever system*) intralicciatura; (*for reducing a hernia*) cinto, brachiere *m*; (bot) infiorescenza ‖ *tr* legare, assicurare

trust [trʌst] *s* fede *f*; speranza; fiducia, custodia; (com) trust *m*, cartello; (law) fedecommesso; **in trust** in deposito; come fedecommesso; **on trust** a credito ‖ *tr* fidarsi di; credere (with *dat*); (*to entrust*) dare in deposito a; dare a credito a ‖ *intr* credere; fidarsi, prestar fede; **to trust in** (*e.g., a friend*) fidarsi di; (*God*) aver fede in

trust' com'pany *s* compagnia fedecommissaria; banca di deposito

trustee [trʌsˈti] *s* amministratore *m*; fiduciario; (*of a university*) curatore *m*; (*of an estate*) fedecommissario

trusteeship [trʌsˈtiʃɪp] *s* amministrazione; (law) fedecommesso; (pol) amministrazione fiduciaria

trustful [ˈtrʌstfəl] *adj* fiducioso

trust'wor'thy *adj* fidato, di fiducia

trust·y [ˈtrʌsti] *adj* (**-ier; -iest**) fidato ‖ *s* (**-ies**) carcerato degno di fiducia

truth [truθ] *s* verità *f*; **in truth** in verità

truthful [ˈtruθfəl] *adj* verace, veritiero

try [traɪ] *s* (**tries**) tentativo, prova ‖ *v* (*pret & pp* **tried**) *tr* provare; (*s.o.'s patience*) mettere a dura prova; (*a person*) (law) processare; (*a case*) (law) giudicare; **to try on** (*clothes*) provare; **to try out** provare; esperimentare ‖ *intr* cercare, tentare; **to try out for** cercare di ottenere il posto di; (sports) cercare di farsi accettare in; **to try to** cercare di

trying [ˈtraɪɪŋ] *adj* duro, penoso, difficile

tryst [trɪst] *or* [traɪst] *s* appuntamento

T'-shirt' *s* maglietta

tub [tʌb] *s* tino, bigoncia; vasca da bagno; (*clumsy boat*) (slang) carretta; (*fat person*) (slang) bombolo

tube [tjub] *or* [tub] *s* tubo; (*e.g., for toothpaste*) tubetto; (*of tire*) camera d'aria; (anat) tuba, tromba; (coll) ferrovia sotterranea

tuber [ˈtjubər] *or* [ˈtubər] *s* tubero

tubercle [ˈtjubərkəl] *or* [ˈtubərkəl] *s* tubercolo

tuberculosis [tju͵bɑrkjəˈloʊsɪs] or [tu͵-bɑrkjəˈloʊsɪs] *s* tubercolosi *f*

tuck [tʌk] *s* basta || *tr* ripiegare; **to tuck away** nascondere; (slang) fare una scorpacciata di; **to tuck in** rincalzare; **to tuck up** rimboccare

tucker [ˈtʌkər] *s* collarino di merletto || *tr*—**to tucker out** (coll) stancare *m*

Tuesday [ˈtjuzdi] or [ˈtuzdi] *s* martedì *m*

tuft [tʌft] *s* (*of feathers*) pennacchio; (*of hair*) cernecchio; (*of flowers*) cespo; (*fluffy threads*) fiocco, nappa || *tr* impuntire; adornare di fiocchi || *intr* crescere a cernecchi

tug [tʌg] *s* strattone *m*, strappata; (*struggle*) lotta; (*boat*) rimorchiatore *m* || *v* (*pret & pp* **tugged;** *ger* **tugging**) *tr* tirare; (*a boat*) rimorchiare || *intr* tirare con forza; lottare

tug'boat' *s* rimorchiatore *m*

tug' of war' *s* tiro alla fune

tuition [tjuˈɪʃən] or [tuˈɪʃən] *s* (*instruction*) insegnamento; tassa scolastica

tulip [ˈtjulɪp] or [ˈtulɪp] *s* tulipano

tumble [ˈtʌmbəl] *s* rotolone *m*, ruzzolone *m*; (*somersault*) salto mortale; caduta; disordine *m*, confusione; (*confused heap*) mucchio || *intr* rotolare, ruzzolare; cadere, capitombolare; gettarsi; rigirarsi; **to tumble down** cadere in rovina; **to tumble to** (coll) rendersi conto di

tum'ble-down' *adj* dilapidato

tumbler [ˈtʌmblər] *s* (*acrobat*) saltimbanco; (*glass*) bicchiere *m*; (*in a lock*) levetta; (*toy*) misirizzi *m*

tumor [ˈtjumər] or [ˈtumər] *s* tumore *m*

tumult [ˈtjumʌlt] or [ˈtumʌlt] *s* tumulto

tun [tʌn] *s* botte *f*, barile *m*

tuna [ˈtunə] *s* tonno

tune [tjun] or [tun] *s* (*air*) aria; (*manner of speaking*) tono; **in tune** intonato; **out of tune** stonato; **to change one's tune** cambiare di tono || *tr* intonare; **to tune in** (rad) sintonizzare; **to tune out** (rad) interrompere la sintonizzazione di; **to tune up** (*a motor*) mettere a punto; (mus) intonare

tuner [ˈtunər] or [ˈtjunər] *s* (rad) sintonizzatore *m*; (mus) accordatore *m*

tungsten [ˈtʌŋstən] *s* tungsteno

tunic [ˈtjunɪk] or [ˈtunɪk] *s* tunica

tun'ing coil' [ˈtunɪŋ] or [ˈtjunɪŋ] *s* bobina di sintonia

tun'ing fork' *s* diapason *m*, corista *m*

Tunis [ˈtjunɪs] or [ˈtunɪs] *s* Tunisi *f*

Tunisia [tjuˈnɪʒə] or [tuˈnɪʒə] *s* la Tunisia

Tunisian [tjuˈnɪʒən] or [tuˈnɪʒən] *adj & s* tunisino

tunnel [ˈtʌnəl] *s* tunnel *m*, traforo, galleria; (min) galleria || *v* (*pret & pp* **-neled** or **-nelled;** *ger* **-neling** or **-nelling**) *tr* costruire un passaggio attraverso o sotto a

turban [ˈtʌrbən] *s* turbante *m*

turbid [ˈtʌrbɪd] *adj* turbido

turbine [ˈtʌrbɪn] or [ˈtʌrbaɪn] *s* turbina

turbojet [ˈtʌrboˌdʒɛt] *s* turboreattore *m*

turboprop [ˈtʌrboˌprɑp] *s* turboelica *m*

turbulent [ˈtʌrbjələnt] *adj* turbolento

tureen [tuˈrin] or [tjuˈrin] *s* terrina

turf [tʌrf] *s* zolla erbosa; (*peat*) torba; **the turf** il campo delle corse; le corse, il turf

turf'man *s* (**-men**) amatore *m* delle corse ippiche

Turk [tʌrk] *s* turco

turkey [ˈtʌrki] *s* tacchino || **Turkey** *s* la Turchia

turk'ey vul'ture *s* (*Cathartes aura*) avvoltoio americano

Turkish [ˈtʌrkɪʃ] *adj & s* turco

Turk'ish tow'el *s* asciugamano spugna

turmoil [ˈtʌrmɔɪl] *s* subbuglio

turn [tʌrn] *s* giro; (*time for action*) turno, volta; (*change of direction*) voltata; (*bend*) svolta, curva; (*of events*) piega; servizio; inclinazione, attitudine *f*; (*of key*) mandata; (*of coil*) spira; (coll) colpo, sussulto; (aer, naut) virata; **at every turn** a ogni piè sospinto; **in turn** a tua (Sua, vostra, etc.) volta; **to be one's turn** toccare a qlcu, e.g., **it's your turn** tocca a Lei; **to take turns** fare a turno || *tr* girare, voltare; (*soil*) rovesciare; cambiare; (*to make sour*) coagulare; (*to translate*) tradurre; (*e.g., ten years*) raggiungere; (*e.g., one's eyes*) volgere; (*on a lathe*) tornire; (*e.g., a coat*) rivoltare; (*to twist*) torcere; (*the wheel*) (aut) sterzare; **to turn against** mettere su contro; **to turn around** rigirare; (*s.o.'s words*) ritorcere; **to turn aside** sviare; **to turn away** cacciare via; **to turn back** ricacciare; restituire; (*the clock*) ritardare; **to turn down** ripiegare; (*the light*) abbassare; (*an offer*) rifiutare; **to turn in** ripiegare; denunziare; rassegnare; **to turn off** (*e.g., light*) spegnere, smorzare; (*gas, water, etc.*) tagliare; (*e.g., a faucet*) chiudere; **to turn on** (*e.g., light, radio, etc.*) accendere; (*e.g., a faucet*) aprire; **to turn out** mettere alla porta; (*animals*) fare uscire dalla stalla; rivoltare; (*light*) spegnere; produrre, fabbricare; **to turn up** ripiegare in su, rimboccare; (*on a lathe*) tornire; tirar su; (*a card*) scoprire; trovare; (*e.g., the radio*) alzare || *intr* girare; svoltare, e.g., **turn left at the corner** svolti a sinistra all'angolo; girarsi; cambiare; fermentare; cambiare di colore; diventare; (naut) virare; **to turn against** voltarsi contro; inimicarsi con; **to turn around** fare una giravolta; **to turn aside** or **away** sviarsi; **to turn back** ritornare; retrocedere; **to turn down** piegarsi in giù; rovesciarsi; **to turn in** piegarsi, ripiegarsi; tornare a casa; (coll) andare a dormire; **to turn into** sfogare in; trasformarsi in; **to turn on** voltarsi contro; girarsi su; dipendere da; occuparsi di; **to turn**

out riuscire; **to turn out to be** manifestarsi; riuscire ad essere; **to turn over** rotolarsi; rovesciarsi; **to turn up** voltarsi all'insù; alzarsi; apparire, farsi vedere

turn'buck'le s tenditore m

turn'coat' s voltagabbana mf; **to become a turncoat** voltar gabbano

turn'down' adj (collar) rovesciato || s rifiuto

turn'ing point' s punto decisivo

turnip ['tʌrnɪp] s rapa

turn'key' s secondino, carceriere m

turn' of life' s menopausa

turn' of mind' s disposizione naturale

turn'out' s (gathering of people) concorso; (crowd) folla; produzione; (outfit) vestito; stile m, moda; (in a road) slargo, piazzola; (horse and carriage) equipaggio; (rr) binario laterale

turn'over' s (upset) rovesciamento, ribaltamento; (of customers) movimento di clienti; (of business) giro d'affari; rotazione di lavoratori; (com) ciclo operativo

turn'pike' s autostrada a pedaggio

turn' sig'nal s (aut) indicatore m di direzione, lampeggiatore m

turnstile ['tʌrn‚staɪl] s tornello

turn'ta'ble s (of phonograph) piatto rotante; (rr) piattaforma girevole

turpentine ['tʌrpən‚taɪn] s trementina

turpitude ['tʌrpɪ‚tjud] or ['tʌrpɪ‚tud] s turpitudine f

turquoise ['tʌrkɔɪz] or ['tʌrkwɔɪz] s turchese m

turret ['tʌrɪt] s torretta

turtle ['tʌrtəl] s tartaruga; **to turn turtle** rovesciarsi, capovolgersi

tur'tle-dove' s tortora

Tuscan ['tʌskən] adj & s toscano

Tuscany ['tʌskəni] s la Toscana

tusk [tʌsk] s zanna

tussle ['tʌsəl] s lotta, zuffa || intr lottare, azzuffarsi

tutor ['tjutər] or ['tutər] s istitutore privato, ripetitore m; (guardian) tutore m || tr dare ripetizione a || intr dare ripetizioni; studiare con un ripetitore

tuxe·do [tʌk'sido] s (-dos) smoking m

twaddle ['twɑdəl] s sciocchezze fpl || intr dire sciocchezze

twang [twæŋ] s (of musical instrument) suono vibrato; (of voice) timbro nasale || tr pizzicare; dire con un timbro nasale || intr parlare con voce nasale

twang·y ['twæŋi] adj (-ier; -iest) (tone) metallico; (voice) nasale

tweed [twid] s tweed m; **tweeds** abito di tweed

tweet [twit] s pigolio || intr pigolare

tweeter ['twitər] s altoparlante m per alte audiofrequenze, tweeter m

tweezers ['twizərz] spl pinzette fpl

twelfth [twelfθ] adj, s & pron dodicesimo || s (in dates) dodici m

Twelfth'-night' s vigilia dell'Epifania; sera dell'Epifania

twelve [twelv] adj & pron dodici || s dodici m; **twelve o'clock** le dodici

twentieth ['twentɪ·ɪθ] adj, s & pron ventesimo || s (in dates) venti m

twen·ty ['twenti] adj & pron venti || s (-ties) venti m; **the twenties** gli anni venti

twice [twaɪs] adv due volte

twice'-told' adj detto più di una volta; detto e ridetto

twiddle ['twɪdəl] tr—**to twiddle one's thumbs** rigirare i pollici, oziare

twig [twɪg] s ramoscello; **twigs** sterpi mpl

twilight ['twaɪ‚laɪt] adj crepuscolare || s crepuscolo

twill [twɪl] s diagonale m || tr tessere in diagonale

twin [twɪn] adj & s gemello

twine [twaɪn] s spago || tr intrecciare || intr intrecciarsi

twinge [twɪndʒ] s punta, dolore acuto

twinkle ['twɪŋkəl] s scintillio; batter m d'occhio || intr scintillare

twin'-screw' adj a due eliche

twirl [twʌrl] s giro, mulinello || tr girare; (slang) lanciare || intr girare rapidamente, frullare

twist [twɪst] s curva; giro; viluppo, intreccio; tendenza, inclinazione; (yarn) ritorno; (e.g., of lemon) fettina; (dance) twist m || tr intrecciare; torcere; (e.g., the face) contorcere; (the meaning) stravolgere, stiracchiare; girare || intr intrecciarsi; torcersi, divincolarsi; girare; serpeggiare; **to twist and turn** (in bed) girarsi e rigirarsi

twister ['twɪstər] s (coll) tromba d'aria

twit [twɪt] v (pret & pp **twitted;** ger **twitting**) tr ridicolizzare

twitch [twɪtʃ] s tic m; (jerk) strattone m; (to restrain a horse) torcinaso || intr contrarsi; tremare; **to twitch at** tirare

twitter ['twɪtər] s garrito, cinguettio; (chatter) chiacchierio; ansia, agitazione || intr garrire, cinguettare; chiacchierare; tremare d'ansia

two [tu] adj & pron due || s due m; **to put two and two together** arrivare alle logiche conclusioni; **two o'clock** le due

two'-cy'cle adj a due tempi

two'-cyl'inder adj a due cilindri

two'-edged' ['tu ‚edʒd] adj a doppio filo

two'fold' adj duplice, doppio

two' hun'dred adj, s & pron duecento

twosome ['tusəm] s coppia

two'-time' tr (slang) fare le corna a

two'-way ra'dio s ricetrasmettitore m

tycoon [taɪ'kun] s magnate m

type [taɪp] s tipo; (typ) carattere m; (pieces collectively) (typ) caratteri mpl || tr scrivere a macchina; simbolizzare || intr scrivere a macchina

type'face' s stile m di carattere

type'script' s dattiloscritto

typesetter ['taɪp ‚setər] s (person) compositore m; (machine) compositrice f

type′write′ v (pret -wrote; pp -written) tr & intr dattilografare, scrivere a macchina
type′writ′er s (machine) macchina da scrivere; (typist) dattilografo
type′writ′ing s dattilografia, scrittura a macchina; lavoro battuto a macchina
ty′phoid fe′ver [′taifɔid] s febbre f tifoide
typhoon [tai′fun] s tifone m
typical [′tipikəl] adj tipico
typi·fy [′tipi ,fai] v (pret & pp -fied) tr simbolizzare

typist [′taipist] s dattilografo
typographic(al) [,taipə′græfik(əl)] adj tipografico
typograph′ical er′ror s errore m di stampa
typography [tai′pɑgrəfi] s tipografia
tyrannic(al) [ti′rænik(əl)] or [tai-′ræník(əl)] adj tirannico
tyrannous [′tirənəs] adj tiranno
tyrant [′tairənt] s tiranno
ty·ro [′tairo] s (-ros) principiante m
Tyrrhe′nian Sea′ [ti′rini·ən] s Mare Tirreno

U

U, u [ju] s ventunesima lettera dell'alfabeto inglese
ubiquitous [ju′bikwitəs] adj ubiquo
udder [′ʌdər] s mammella
ugliness [′ʌglinis] s bruttezza
ug·ly [′ʌgli] adj (-lier; -liest) brutto
Ukraine, the [′jukren] or [ju′kren] s l'Ucraina f
Ukrainian [ju′kreni·ən] adj & s ucraino
ulcer [′ʌlsər] s piaga, ulcera; (corrupting element) (fig) piaga
ulcerate [′ʌlsə ,ret] tr ulcerare ‖ intr ulcerarsi
ulterior [ʌl′tiri·ər] adj ulteriore; (motive) nascosto, secondo
ultimate [′ʌltimit] adj ultimo
ultima·tum [,ʌlti′metəm] s (-tums or -ta [tə]) ultimato
ultimo [′ʌlti ,mo] adv del mese scorso
ul′tra-high fre′quency [′ʌltrə′hai] s frequenza ultraelevata
ultrashort [,ʌltrə′ʃɔrt] adj ultracorto
ultraviolet [,ʌltrə′vai·əlit] adj & s ultravioletto
umbil′ical cord′ [ʌm′bilikəl] s cordone m ombelicale
umbrage [′ʌmbridʒ] s—to take umbrage at adombrarsi per
umbrella [ʌm′brelə] s ombrello, paracqua m; (mil) ombrello
umbrel′la stand′ s portaombrelli m
Umbrian [′ʌmbri·ən] adj & s umbro
umlaut [′umlaut] s metafonesi f; (mark) dieresi f ‖ tr cambiare il timbro di; scrivere con dieresi
umpire [′ʌmpair] s arbitro ‖ tr arbitrare ‖ intr fare l'arbitro
UN [′ju′en] s (letterword) (United Nations) ONU f
unable [ʌn′ebəl] adj incapace; to be unable to essere impossibilitato a, non potere
unabridged [,ʌnə′bridʒd] adj integrale, non abbreviato
unaccented [ʌn′æksentid] or [,ʌnæk-′sentid] adj non accentato, atono
unacceptable [,ʌnək′septəbəl] adj inaccettabile
unaccountable [,ʌnə′kauntəbəl] adj irresponsabile; inesplicabile
unaccounted-for [,ʌnə′kauntid ,fər]

adj (e.g., failure) inesplicato; (e.g., soldier) irreperibile, mancante
unaccustomed [,ʌnə′kʌstəmd] adj (unusual) insolito; non abituato
unafraid [,ʌnə′fred] adj impavido
unaligned [ʌnə′laind] adj non impegnato
unanimity [,junə′nimiti] s unanimità f
unanimous [ju′næniməs] adj unanime
unanswerable [ʌn′ænsərəbəl] adj per cui non vi è risposta; (argument) irrefutabile, incontestabile
unappreciative [,ʌnə′priʃi ,etiv] adj sconoscente, ingrato
unapproachable [,ʌnə′protʃəbəl] adj inabbordabile; incomparabile
unarmed [ʌn′ɑrmd] adj disarmato, inerme
unascertainable [ʌn ,æsər′tenəbəl] adj non verificabile
unassailable [,ʌnə′seləbəl] adj inattaccabile
unassembled [,ʌnə′sembəld] adj smontato
unassuming [,ʌnə′sumiŋ] or [,ʌnə-′sjumiŋ] adj modesto, semplice
unattached [,ʌnə′tæt/t] adj indipendente; (loose) sciolto; non sposato; non fidanzato
unattainable [,ʌnə′tenəbəl] adj inarrivabile, irraggiungibile
unattractive [,ʌnə′træktiv] adj poco attraente
unavailable [,ʌnə′veləbəl] adj non disponibile
unavailing [,ʌnə′veliŋ] adj futile
unavoidable [,ʌnə′vɔidəbəl] adj inevitabile, ineluttabile
unaware [,ʌnə′wer] adj inconsapevole, ignaro ‖ adv inaspettatamente; (unknowingly) inavvertitamente
unawares [,ʌnə′werz] adv inaspettatamente; (unknowingly) inavvertitamente
unbalanced [ʌn′bælənst] adj sbilanciato, squilibrato
unbandage [ʌn′bændidʒ] tr sbendare
un·bar [ʌn′bɑr] v (pret & pp -barred; ger -barring) tr disserrare il chiavistello di
unbearable [ʌn′berəbəl] adj insopportabile, insostenibile

unbeatable [ʌn'bitəbəl] *adj* imbattibile

unbecoming [ˌʌnbɪ'kʌmɪŋ] *adj* sconveniente, indegno; *(e.g., hat)* disadatto, che non sta bene

unbelievable [ˌʌnbɪ'livəbəl] *adj* incredibile

unbeliever [ˌʌnbɪ'livər] *s* miscredente *mf*

unbending [ʌn'bendɪŋ] *adj* inflessibile

unbiased [ʌn'baɪəst] *adj* imparziale, spassionato

un-bind [ʌn'baɪnd] *v* (*pret & pp* **-bound** ['baund]) *tr* slegare

unbleached [ʌn'blitʃt] *adj* non candeggiato, al colore naturale

unbolt [ʌn'bolt] *tr* (*a door*) togliere il chiavistello a; sbullonare

unborn [ʌn'bɔrn] *adj* nascituro

unbosom [ʌn'buzəm] *tr* (*a secret*) rivelare; **to unbosom oneself** aprire il proprio animo, sfogarsi

unbound [ʌn'baund] *adj* sciolto, libero; (*book*) non rilegato

unbreakable [ʌn'brekəbəl] *adj* infrangibile

unbridle [ʌn'braɪdəl] *tr* sbrigliare

unbuckle [ʌn'bʌkəl] *tr* sfibbiare

unburden [ʌn'bʌrdən] *tr* scaricare; **to unburden oneself (of)** vuotare il sacco (di)

unburied [ʌn'berid] *adj* insepolto

unbutton [ʌn'bʌtən] *tr* sbottonare

uncalled-for [ʌn'kɔld ˌfɔr] *adj* superfluo, gratuito; fuori di posto, sconveniente

uncanny [ʌn'kæni] *adj* misterioso, straordinario

uncared-for [ʌn'kerd ˌfɔr] *adj* negletto, trascurato

unceasing [ʌn'sisɪŋ] *adj* incessante

unceremonious [ˌʌnserɪ'moni-əs] *adj* senza cerimonie

uncertain [ʌn'sʌrtən] *adj* incerto

uncertain-ty [ʌn'sʌrtənti] *s* (**-ties**) incertezza

unchain [ʌn'tʃen] *tr* scatenare, sferrare

unchangeable [ʌn'tʃendʒəbəl] *adj* immutabile

uncharted [ʌn'tʃɑrtid] *adj* inesplorato

unchecked [ʌn'tʃekt] *adj* incontrollato

uncivilized [ʌn'sɪvɪ ˌlaɪzd] *adj* incivile

unclad [ʌn'klæd] *adj* svestito

unclaimed [ʌn'klemd] *adj* non reclamato; (*letter*) giacente

unclasp [ʌn'klæsp] or [ʌn'klɑsp] *tr* sfibbiare

unclassified [ʌn'klæsɪ ˌfaɪd] *adj* non classificato; non secreto

uncle ['ʌŋkəl] *s* zio

unclean [ʌn'klin] *adj* immondo

un-clog [ʌn'klɑg] *v* (*pret & pp* **-clogged**; *ger* **-clogging**) *tr* disintasare

unclouded [ʌn'klaudid] *adj* sereno, senza nubi

uncollectible [ˌʌnkə'lektɪbəl] *adj* inesigibile

uncomfortable [ʌn'kʌmfərtəbəl] *adj* scomodo, disagevole

uncommitted [ˌʌnkə'mɪtɪd] *adj* non impegnato

uncommon [ʌn'kɑmən] *adj* raro, straordinario

uncompromising [ʌn'kɑmprə ˌmaɪzɪŋ] *adj* intransigente

unconcerned [ˌʌnkən'sʌrnd] *adj* indifferente, noncurante

unconditional [ˌʌnkən'dɪʃənəl] *adj* incondizionato

uncongenial [ˌʌnkən'dʒini-əl] *adj* antipatico, sgradito

unconquerable [ʌn'kɑŋkərəbəl] *adj* inconquistabile, inespugnabile

unconscionable [ʌn'kɑn/ənəbəl] *adj* senza scrupoli; eccessivo

unconscious [ʌn'kɑn/əs] *adj* (*without awareness*) inconscio, inconsapevole; (*temporarily devoid of consciousness*) incosciente; (*unintentional*) involontario

unconsciousness [ʌn'kɑn/əsnɪs] *s* incoscienza

unconstitutional [ˌʌnkɑnstɪ'tju/ənəl] or [ˌʌnkɑnstɪ'tu/ənəl] *adj* incostituzionale

uncontrollable [ˌʌnkən'troləbəl] *adj* incontrollabile, ingovernabile

unconventional [ˌʌnkən'ven/ənəl] *adj* non convenzionale, anticonformista

uncork [ʌn'kɔrk] *tr* stappare

uncouple [ʌn'kʌpəl] *tr* sganciare, disconnettere

uncouth [ʌn'kuθ] *adj* zotico, incivile, pacchiano

uncover [ʌn'kʌvər] *tr* scoprire

unction ['ʌŋk/ən] *s* unzione; (fig) untuosità *f*

unctuous ['ʌŋkt/u-əs] *adj* untuoso

uncultivated [ʌn'kʌltɪ ˌvetɪd] *adj* incolto

uncultured [ʌn'kʌlt/ərd] *adj* incolto, rozzo

uncut [ʌn'kʌt] *adj* non tagliato; (*book*) intonso

undamaged [ʌn'dæmɪdʒd] *adj* indenne, illeso

undaunted [ʌn'dɔntid] *adj* imperterrito, impavido

undeceive [ˌʌndɪ'siv] *tr* disingannare

undecided [ˌʌndɪ'saɪdɪd] *adj* indeciso

undefeated [ˌʌndɪ'fitɪd] *adj* invitto

undefended [ˌʌndɪ'fendɪd] *adj* indifeso

undefensible [ˌʌndɪ'fensɪbəl] *adj* insostenibile

undefiled [ˌʌndɪ'faɪld] *adj* puro, immacolato

undeniable [ˌʌndɪ'naɪ-əbəl] *adj* innegabile, indubitato

under ['ʌndər] *adj* di sotto; (*lower*) inferiore; (*clothing*) intimo, personale ‖ *adv* sotto; più sotto; **to go under** affondare; cedere; (coll) fallire ‖ *prep* sotto; sotto a; (*e.g., 20 years old*) meno di; **under full sail** a vele spiegate; **under lock and key** sotto chiave; **under oath** sotto giuramento; **under penalty of death** sotto pena di morte; **under sail** a vela; **under separate cover** in plico separato; **under steam** sotto pressione; **under the hand and seal of** firmato di pugno di; **under the weather** (coll) un po' indisposto; **under way** già iniziato

un'der·age' *adj* minorenne

un'der-arm' pad' *s* sottoascella *m*

un'der·bid' v (pret & pp **-bid;** ger **-bidding**) tr fare un'offerta inferiore a quella di

un'der·brush' s sottobosco

un'der·car'riage s (aut) telaio; (aer) carrello d'atterraggio

un'der·clothes' spl biancheria intima

un'der·consump'tion s sottoconsumo

un'der·cov'er adj segreto

un'der·cur'rent s (of water) corrente subacquea; (of air) corrente f inferiore; (fig) controcorrente f

underdeveloped [ˌʌndərdɪ'veləpt] adj sottosviluppato

un'der·dog' s chi è destinato ad avere la peggio; vittima; **the underdogs** i diseredati

un'der·done' adj non cotto abbastanza

un'der·es'timate' tr sottovalutare

un'der·gar'ment s indumento intimo

un'der·go' v (pret **-went;** pp **-gone**) tr (a test) passare, sottostare (with dat); (surgery) subire, sottoporsi a; soffrire

un'der·grad'uate adj (student) non ancora laureato; (course) per studenti non ancora laureati ‖ s studente universitario che non ha ancora ricevuto il primo diploma

un'der·ground' adj sotterraneo; segreto ‖ s regione sotterranea; macchia, resistenza ‖ adv sottoterra; alla macchia, segretamente

un'der·growth' s sterpaglia

underhanded ['ʌndər'hændəd] adj subdolo, di sottomano

un'der·line' or **un'der·line'** tr sottolineare

underling ['ʌndərlɪŋ] s tirapiedi m

un'der·mine' tr scalzare, minare

underneath [ˌʌndər'niθ] adj inferiore ‖ s disotto ‖ adv sotto, di sotto ‖ prep sotto a, sotto

undernourished [ˌʌndər'nʌrɪʃt] adj denutrito, malnutrito

un'der·pass' s sottopassaggio

un'der·pay' s (pret & pp **-paid**) tr & intr pagare insufficientemente

un'der·pin' v (pret & pp **-pinned;** ger **-pinning**) tr rincalzare

underprivileged [ˌʌndər'prɪvɪlɪdʒd] adj derelitto, diseredato

un'der·rate' tr sottovalutare

un'der·score' tr sottolineare

un'der·sea' adj sottomarino ‖ adv sotto il mare

un'der·seas' adv sotto il mare

un'der·sec'retar'y s (-ies) sottosegretario

un'der·sell' v (pret & pp **-sold**) tr vendere a prezzo minore di; (to sell for less than actual value) svendere

un'der·shirt' s camiciola, canottiera

undersigned ['ʌndər,saɪnd] adj sottoscritto

un'der·skirt' s sottogonna

un'der·stand' v (pret & pp **-stood**) tr capire, comprendere; sottintendere; (to accept as true) constare, e.g., **he understands that you are wrong** gli consta che Lei ha torto ‖ intr capire, comprendere

understandable [ˌʌndər'stændəbəl] adj comprensibile

understanding [ˌʌndər'stændɪŋ] adj comprensivo, tollerante ‖ s (mind) intelletto; (knowledge) conoscenza; comprensione, intendimento; (agreement) intesa, accordo

understatement [ˌʌndər'stetmənt] s sottovalutazione

un'der·stud'y s (-ies) (theat) doppio, sostituto ‖ v (-ied) tr (an actor) fare il doppio di

un'der·take' v (pret **-took;** ger **-taken**) tr intraprendere; (to promise) promettere

undertaker [ˌʌndər'tekər] or ['ʌndər,tekər] s impresario ‖ ['ʌndər,tekər] s impresario di pompe funebri

undertaking [ˌʌndər'tekɪŋ] s (task) impresa; (promise) promessa ‖ ['ʌndər,tekɪŋ] s impresa di pompe funebri

un'der·tone' s bassa voce; (background sound) ronzio di fondo; tono; colore smorzato

un'der·tow' s (on the beach) risacca; (countercurrent below surface) controcorrente f

un'der·wa'ter adj subacqueo ‖ adv sottacqua

un'der·wear' s biancheria intima

un'der·world' s (criminal world) malavita, teppa; (abode of spirits) ade m, averno; mondo sotterraneo; mondo sottomarino; antipodi mpl

un'der·write' v (pret **-wrote;** pp **-written**) tr sottoscrivere; (to insure) assicurare

un'der·writ'er s sottoscrittore m; (ins) assicuratore m

undeserved [ˌʌndɪ'zʌrvd] adj immeritato

undesirable [ˌʌndɪ'zaɪrəbəl] adj & s indesiderabile mf

undetachable [ˌʌndɪ'tætʃəbəl] adj non movibile

undeveloped [ˌʌndɪ'veləpt] adj (land) non sfruttato; (country) sottosviluppato

undigested [ˌʌndɪ'dʒestɪd] adj non digerito

undignified [ʌn'dɪgnɪ,faɪd] adj poco decoroso

undiscernible [ˌʌndɪ'zʌrnɪbəl] or [ˌʌndɪ'sʌrnɪbəl] adj impercettibile

undisputed [ˌʌndɪ'spjutəd] adj indiscusso, incontrastato

un·do [ʌn'du] v (pret **-did;** pp **-done**) tr sfare, disfare; rovinare; (a package) aprire; (a knot) sciogliere

undoing [ʌn'du·ɪŋ] s rovina

undone [ʌn'dʌn] adj non finito; **to come undone** disfarsi; **to leave nothing undone** non tralasciare di fare nulla

undoubtedly [ʌn'daʊtɪdli] adv indubbiamente, senza dubbio

undress ['ʌn,dres] or [ʌn'dres] s vestaglia; vestito da ogni giorno ‖ [ʌn'dres] tr spogliare, svestire; (a *wound*) sbendare ‖ *intr* spogliarsi, svestirsi

undrinkable [ʌn'drɪŋkəbəl] *adj* imbevibile, non potabile

undue [ʌn'dju] or [ʌn'du] *adj* indebito; immeritato; eccessivo

undulate ['ʌndjə ˌlet] *intr* ondulare

unduly [ʌn'djuli] or [ʌn'duli] *adv* indebitamente, eccessivamente

unearned [ʌn'ʌrnd] *adj* non guadagnato col lavoro; immeritato; non ancora guadagnato

un'earned in'crement *s* plusvalenza

unearth [ʌn'ʌrθ] *tr* dissotterrare

unearthly [ʌn'ʌrθli] *adj* ultraterreno; spettrale; impossibile, straordinario

uneasy [ʌn'izi] *adj* (*worried*) preoccupato; (*constrained*) scomodo; (*not conducive to ease*) inquietante, a disagio

uneatable [ʌn'itəbəl] *adj* immangiabile

uneconomic(al) [ˌʌnikə'nɑmɪk(əl)] or [ˌʌnekə'nɑmɪk(əl)] *adj* antieconomico

uneducated [ʌn'edʒə ˌketɪd] *adj* ineducato

unemployed [ˌʌnem'plɔɪd] *adj* disoccupato, incollocato; improduttivo ‖ **the unemployed** i disoccupati

unemployment [ˌʌnem'plɔɪmənt] *s* disimpiego, disoccupazione

unemploy'ment compensa'tion *s* sussidio di disoccupazione

unending [ʌn'endɪŋ] *adj* interminabile

unequal [ʌn'ikwəl] *adj* disuguale, impari; **to be unequal to** (*a task*) non essere all'altezza di

unequaled or **unequalled** [ʌn'ikwəld] *adj* ineguagliato

unerring [ʌn'ʌrɪŋ] or [ʌn'ɛrɪŋ] *adj* infallibile; corretto, preciso

unessential [ˌʌne'senʃəl] *adj* non essenziale

uneven [ʌn'ivən] *adj* disuguale, ineguale; (*number*) dispari

uneventful [ˌʌnɪ'ventfəl] *adj* senza avvenimenti importanti; (*life*) tranquillo

unexceptionable [ˌʌnek'sepʃənəbəl] *adj* ineccepibile, irreprensibile

unexpected [ˌʌnek'spektɪd] *adj* inaspettato, imprevisto

unexplained [ˌʌnek'splend] *adj* inesplicato

unexplored [ˌʌnek'splord] *adj* inesplorato

unexposed [ˌʌnek'spozd] *adj* (phot) non esposto alla luce

unfading [ʌn'fedɪŋ] *adj* immarcescibile; imperituro

unfailing [ʌn'felɪŋ] *adj* immancabile, infallibile; (*inexhaustible*) inesauribile; (*dependable*) sicuro

unfair [ʌn'fer] *adj* ingiusto; disonesto, sleale

unfaithful [ʌn'feθfəl] *adj* infedele

unfamiliar [ˌʌnfə'mɪljər] *adj* poco pratico; poco abituale, strano; non conosciuto

unfasten [ʌn'fæsən] or [ʌn'fɑsən] *tr* sfibbiare, sciogliere

unfathomable [ʌn'fæðəməbəl] *adj* insondabile

unfavorable [ʌn'fevərəbəl] *adj* sfavorevole

unfeeling [ʌn'filɪŋ] *adj* insensibile

unfetter [ʌn'fetər] *tr* sciogliere dalle catene

unfinished [ʌn'fɪnɪʃt] *adj* incompiuto; grezzo, non rifinito; (*business*) inevaso

unfit [ʌn'fɪt] *adj* disadatto; inabile

unfledged [ʌn'fledʒd] *adj* implume

unfold [ʌn'fold] *tr* schiudere; (*e.g., a newspaper*) spiegare ‖ *intr* schiudersi; svolgersi

unforeseeable [ˌʌnfor'si-əbəl] *adj* imprevedibile

unforeseen [ˌʌnfor'sin] *adj* imprevisto

unforgettable [ˌʌnfər'getəbəl] *adj* indimenticabile

unforgivable [ˌʌnfər'gɪvəbəl] *adj* imperdonabile

unfortunate [ʌn'fɔrtʃənɪt] *adj & s* disgraziato, sfortunato

unfounded [ʌn'faundɪd] *adj* infondato

un-freeze [ʌn'friz] *v* (*pret* **-froze**; *pp* **-frozen**) *tr* disgelare; (*credit*) sbloccare

unfriend·ly [ʌn'frendli] *adj* (**-lier**; **-liest**) *adj* mal disposto, ostile; sfavorevole

unfruitful [ʌn'frutfəl] *adj* infruttuoso

unfulfilled [ˌʌnfəl'fɪld] *adj* incompiuto

unfurl [ʌn'fʌrl] *tr* spiegare, dispiegare

unfurnished [ʌn'fʌrnɪʃt] *adj* smobiliato

ungainly [ʌn'genli] *adj* sgraziato, maldestro

ungentlemanly [ʌn'dʒentəlmənli] *adj* indegno di un gentleman

ungird [ʌn'gʌrd] *tr* discingere

ungodly [ʌn'gɑdli] *adj* irreligioso, empio; (*dreadful*) (coll) atroce

ungracious [ʌn'greʃəs] *adj* rude, scortese; (*task*) sgradevole

ungrammatical [ˌʌngrə'mætɪkəl] *adj* sgrammaticato

ungrateful [ʌn'gretfəl] *adj* ingrato

ungrudgingly [ʌn'grʌdʒɪŋli] *adv* di buon grado, volentieri

unguarded [ʌn'gɑrdɪd] *adj* incustodito, indifeso; incauto, imprudente

unguent ['ʌŋgwənt] *s* unguento

unhappiness [ʌn'hæpɪnɪs] *s* infelicità *f*

unhap·py [ʌn'hæpi] *adj* (**-pier**; **-piest**) infelice, sfortunato

unharmed [ʌn'hɑrmd] *adj* illeso

unharness [ʌn'hɑrnɪs] *tr* togliere i finimenti a

unhealth·y [ʌn'helθi] *adj* (**-ier**; **-iest**) malsano

unheard-of [ʌn'hʌrd ˌɑv] *adj* (*unknown*) sconosciuto; inaudito

unhinge [ʌn'hɪndʒ] *tr* sgangherare; (fig) sconvolgere

unhitch [ʌn'hɪtʃ] *tr* sganciare; (*a horse*) staccare

unho·ly [ʌn'holi] *adj* (**-lier**; **-liest**) empio; terribile, atroce

unhook [ʌn'huk] *tr* sganciare

unhoped-for [ʌn'hopt ˌfor] *adj* insperato

unhorse [ʌn'hɔrs] *tr* disarcionare

unhurt [ʌn'hʌrt] *adj* incolume, illeso

unicorn ['junɪ‚kɔrn] *s* unicorno

unification [‚junɪfɪ'keʃən] *s* unificazione

uniform ['junɪ‚fɔrm] *adj & s* uniforme *f* || *tr* uniformare

uni•fy ['junɪ‚faɪ] *v* (*pret & pp* **-fied**) *tr* unificare

unilateral [‚junɪ'lætərəl] *adj* unilaterale

unimpeachable [‚ʌnɪm'pitʃəbəl] *adj* irrefutabile; irreprensibile

unimportant [‚ʌnɪm'pɔrtənt] *adj* poco importante

uninhabited [‚ʌnɪn'hæbɪtɪd] *adj* inabitato, disabitato

uninspired [‚ʌnɪn'spaɪrd] *adj* senza ispirazione, prosaico

unintelligent [‚ʌnɪn'telɪdʒənt] *adj* non intelligente; stupido

unintelligible [‚ʌnɪn'telɪdʒɪbəl] *adj* inintelligibile

uninterested [ʌn'ɪntrɪstɪd] or [ʌn-'ɪntə‚restɪd] *adj* non interessato

uninteresting [ʌn'ɪntrɪstɪŋ] or [ʌn-'ɪntə‚restɪŋ] *adj* poco interessante

uninterrupted [‚ʌnɪntə'rʌptɪd] *adj* ininterrotto

union ['junjən] *s* unione; unione matrimoniale; (*of workers*) sindacato

unionize ['junjə‚naɪz] *tr* organizzare in un sindacato || *intr* organizzarsi in un sindacato

un'ion shop' *s* fabbrica che assume solo sindacalisti

un'ion suit' *s* combinazione

unique [ju'nik] *adj* unico

unison ['junɪsən] or ['junɪzən] *s* unisono; **in unison** all'unisono

unit ['junɪt] *adj* unitario || *s* unità *f*; (mach, elec) gruppo

unite [ju'naɪt] *tr* unire || *intr* unirsi

united [ju'naɪtɪd] *adj* unito

Unit'ed King'dom *s* Regno Unito

Unit'ed Na'tions *spl* Organizzazione delle Nazioni Unite

Unit'ed States' *adj* statunitense || **the United States** *ssg* gli Stati Uniti

uni•ty ['junɪti] *s* (-ties) unità *f*

universal [‚junɪ'vʌrsəl] *adj* universale

u'niver'sal joint' *s* giunto cardanico

universe ['junɪ‚vʌrs] *s* universo

universi•ty [‚junɪ'vʌrsɪti] *adj* universitario || *s* (-ties) università *f*

unjust [ʌn'dʒʌst] *adj* ingiusto

unjustified [ʌn'dʒʌstɪ‚faɪd] *adj* ingiustificato

unkempt [ʌn'kempt] *adj* spettinato; trascurato

unkind [ʌn'kaɪnd] *adj* scortese; duro, crudele

unknowable [ʌn'no‚əbəl] *adj* inconoscibile

unknowingly [ʌn'no‚ɪŋli] *adv* inconsapevolmente

unknown [ʌn'non] *adj* sconosciuto || *s* incognito; (math) incognita

Un'known Sol'dier *s* Milite Ignoto

unlace [ʌn'les] *tr* slacciare

unlatch [ʌn'lætʃ] *tr* tirare il saliscendi a

unlawful [ʌn'lɔfəl] *adj* illegale

unleash [ʌn'liʃ] *tr* sguinzagliare; (fig) scatenare

unleavened [ʌn'levənd] *adj* azzimo

unless [ʌn'les] *conj* se non che, salvo che

unlettered [ʌn'letərd] *adj* ignorante; (*illiterate*) analfabeta

unlike [ʌn'laɪk] *adj* dissimile, differente; dissimile da, e.g., **a copy unlike the original** una copia dissimile dall'originale; (elec) di segno contrario || *prep* diversamente da, a differenza di; **it was unlike him to arrive late** non era cosa normale per lui arrivare in ritardo

unlikely [ʌn'laɪkli] *adj* improbabile

unlimber [ʌn'lɪmbər] *tr* mettere in batteria || *intr* prepararsi a fare fuoco; (fig) prepararsi

unlimited [ʌn'lɪmɪtɪd] *adj* illimitato

unlined [ʌn'laɪnd] *adj* (e.g., *coat*) non foderato; (*paper*) non rigato

unload [ʌn'lod] *tr* scaricare; (*passengers*) sbarcare; (*to get rid of*) liberarsi di || *intr* scaricare; sbarcare

unloading [ʌn'lodɪŋ] *s* discarica; sbarco

unlock [ʌn'lɑk] *tr* aprire

unloose [ʌn'lus] *tr* rilasciare; sciogliere

unloved [ʌn'lʌvd] *adj* poco amato

unlovely [ʌn'lʌvli] *adj* poco attraente

unluck•y [ʌn'lʌki] *adj* (-ier; -iest) sfortunato, disgraziato

un•make [ʌn'mek] *v* (*pret & pp* **-made** ['med]) *tr* disfare; deporre

unmanageable [ʌn'mænɪdʒəbəl] *adj* incontrollabile

unmanly [ʌn'mænli] *adj* non virile, effeminato; codardo

unmannerly [ʌn'mænərli] *adj* scortese

unmarketable [ʌn'mɑrkɪtəbəl] *adj* invendibile

unmarriageable [ʌn'mærɪdʒəbəl] *adj* che non si può sposare; non adatto al matrimonio

unmarried [ʌn'mærid] *adj* scapolo; (*female*) nubile

unmask [ʌn'mæsk] or [ʌn'mɑsk] *tr* smascherare || *intr* smascherarsi

unmatchable [ʌn'mætʃəbəl] *adj* impareggiabile

unmatched [ʌn'mætʃd] *adj* impareggiabile; (*unpaired*) spaiato

unmentionable [ʌn'menʃənəbəl] *adj* innominabile

unmerciful [ʌn'mʌrsɪfəl] *adj* spietato

unmesh [ʌn'meʃ] *tr* disingranare || *intr* disingranarsi

unmindful [ʌn'maɪndfəl] *adj* immemore; incurante

unmistakable [‚ʌnmɪs'tekəbəl] *adj* inconfondibile

unmitigated [ʌn'mɪtɪ‚getɪd] *adj* completo; assoluto, perfetto

unmixed [ʌn'mɪkst] *adj* puro

unmoor [ʌn'mur] *tr* disormeggiare

unmoved [ʌn'muvd] *adj* immoto; fisso, immobile; (fig) impassibile

unmuzzle [ʌn'mʌzəl] *tr* togliere la museruola a

unnamed [ʌn'nemd] *adj* innominato

unnatural [ʌn'nætʃərəl] *adj* contro natura, snaturato; innaturale; affettato

unnecessary [ʌn'nesə ˌseri] *adj* inutile

unnerve [ʌn'nʌrv] *tr* snervare

unnoticeable [ʌn'notɪsəbəl] *adj* impercettibile

unnoticed [ʌn'notɪst] *adj* inosservato

unobserved [ˌʌnəb'zʌrvd] *adj* inosservato

unobtainable [ˌʌnəb'tenəbəl] *adj* non ottenibile, irraggiungibile

unobtrusive [ˌʌnəb'trusɪv] *adj* discreto, riservato

unoccupied [ʌn'ɑkjə ˌpaɪd] *adj* libero, disponibile; (*not busy*) disoccupato

unofficial [ˌʌnə'fɪʃəl] *adj* non ufficiale, ufficioso

unopened [ʌn'opənd] *adj* non aperto, chiuso; (*letter*) non dissuggellato; (*book*) intonso

unorthodox [ʌn'ɔrθə ˌdɑks] *adj* non ortodosso

unpack [ʌn'pæk] *tr* spaccare, sballare

unpalatable [ʌn'pælətəbəl] *adj* di gusto spiacevole

unparalleled [ʌn'pærə ˌlɛld] *adj* incomparabile, senza pari

unpardonable [ʌn'pardənəbəl] *adj* imperdonabile

unpatriotic [ˌʌnpetrɪ'ɑtɪk] or [ˌʌnpætrɪ'ɑtɪk] *adj* antipatriottico

unperceived [ˌʌnpər'sivd] *adj* inosservato

unperturbable [ˌʌnpər'tʌrbəbəl] *adj* imperterrito, imperturbato

unpleasant [ʌn'plɛsənt] *adj* spiacevole; (*person*) antipatico

unpopular [ʌn'pɑpjələr] *adj* impopolare

unpopularity [ʌn ˌpɑpjə'lærɪti] *s* impopolarità *f*

unprecedented [ʌn'presɪ ˌdɛntɪd] *adj* senza precedenti, inaudito

unprejudiced [ʌn'predʒədɪst] *adj* senza pregiudizio, imparziale

unpremeditated [ˌʌnprɪ'medɪ ˌtetɪd] *adj* impremeditato

unprepared [ˌʌnprɪ'perd] *adj* impreparato

unprepossessing [ˌʌnpripə'zesɪŋ] *adj* poco attraente, antipatico

unpresentable [ˌʌnprɪ'zentəbəl] *adj* impresentabile

unpretentious [ˌʌnprɪ'tenʃəs] *adj* modesto, senza pretese

unprincipled [ʌn'prɪnsɪpəld] *adj* senza principi

unproductive [ˌʌnprə'dʌktɪv] *adj* improduttivo

unprofitable [ʌn'prɑfɪtəbəl] *adj* infruttuoso

unpronounceable [ˌʌnprə'naʊnsəbəl] *adj* impronunziabile

unpropitious [ˌʌnprə'pɪʃəs] *adj* inauspicato

unpublished [ʌn'pʌblɪʃt] *adj* inedito

unpunished [ʌn'pʌnɪʃt] *adj* impunito

unqualified [ʌn'kwɑlɪ ˌfaɪd] *adj* inabile, inidoneo; assoluto, completo

unquenchable [ʌn'kwentʃəbəl] *adj* inappagabile, inestinguibile

unquestionable [ʌn'kwestʃənəbəl] *adj* indiscutibile

unravel [ʌn'rævəl] *v* (*pret & pp* -eled

or -elled; *ger* -eling or -elling) *tr* dipanare ‖ *intr* districarsi; chiarirsi

unreachable [ʌn'ritʃəbəl] *adj* irraggiungibile

unreal [ʌn'ri-əl] *adj* irreale

unreality [ˌʌnrɪ'ælɪti] *s* (-ties) irrealità *f*

unreasonable [ʌn'rizənəbəl] *adj* irragionevole

unrecognizable [ʌn'rekəg ˌnaɪzəbəl] *adj* irriconoscibile

unreel [ʌn'ril] *tr* svolgere, srotolare ‖ *intr* srotolarsi

unrefined [ˌʌnrɪ'faɪnd] *adj* non raffinato, greggio; volgare, ordinario

unrelenting [ˌʌnrɪ'lentɪŋ] *adj* inesorabile, inflessibile; indefesso

unreliable [ˌʌnrɪ'laɪ-əbəl] *adj* malfido; (*news*) inattendibile

unremitting [ˌʌnrɪ'mɪtɪŋ] *adj* incessante, costante

unrented [ʌn'rentɪd] *adj* da affittare

unrepeatable [ˌʌnrɪpitəbəl] *adj* irripetibile

unrepentant [ˌʌnrɪ'pentənt] *adj* impenitente

un'requit'ed love' [ˌʌnrɪ'kwaɪtɪd] *s* amore non corrisposto

unresponsive [ˌʌnrɪ'spɑnsɪv] *adj* apatico, insensibile

unrest [ʌn'rest] *s* agitazione

un-rig [ʌn'rɪg] *v* (*pret & pp* -rigged; *ger* -rigging) *tr* (naut) disarmare

unrighteous [ʌn'raɪtʃəs] *adj* ingiusto

unripe [ʌn'raɪp] *adj* immaturo

unrivaled or **unrivalled** [ʌn'raɪvəld] *adj* senza pari

unroll [ʌn'rol] *tr* srotolare

unromantic [ˌʌnro'mæntɪk] *adj* poco romantico

unruffled [ʌn'rʌfəld] *adj* calmo, imperturbabile

unruly [ʌn'ruli] *adj* turbolento; indisciplinato, insubordinato

unsaddle [ʌn'sædəl] *tr* (*a horse*) dissellare; (*a rider*) scavalcare

unsafe [ʌn'sef] *adj* malsicuro, pericolante

unsaid [ʌn'sed] *adj* non detto, taciuto; **to leave unsaid** passare sotto silenzio

unsalable [ʌn'seləbəl] *adj* invendibile

unsanitary [ʌn'sænɪ ˌteri] *adj* antigienico

unsatisfactory [ʌn ˌsætɪs'fæktəri] *adj* poco soddisfacente

unsatisfied [ʌn'sætɪs ˌfaɪd] *adj* insoddisfatto, inappagato

unsavory [ʌn'sevəri] *adj* insipido; (fig) disgustoso, nauseabondo

un-say [ʌn'se] *v* (*pret & pp* -said [sed']) *tr* disdire

unscathed [ʌn'skeðd] *adj* incolume

unscheduled [ʌn'skedʒʊld] *adj* non in elenco; (*event*) fuori programma; (*e.g., flight*) fuori orario; (*phase of production*) non programmato

unscientific [ˌʌnsaɪ-ən'tɪfɪk] *adj* poco scientifico

unscrew [ʌn'skru] *tr* svitare ‖ *intr* svitarsi

unscrupulous [ʌn'skrupjələs] *adj* senza scrupoli

unseal [ʌn'sil] *tr* dissigillare

unseasonable [ʌnˈsizənəbəl] *adj* fuori stagione; inopportuno

unseasoned [ʌnˈsizənd] *adj* scondito; (*crop*) immaturo; (*crew*) inesperto

unseat [ʌnˈsit] *tr* (*a rider*) scavalcare, disarcionare; (*e.g., a congressman*) far perdere il seggio a, defenestrare

unseemly [ʌnˈsimli] *adj* disdicevole, sconveniente

unseen [ʌnˈsin] *adj* non visto, inosservato; nascosto, occulto; invisibile

unselfish [ʌnˈsɛlfɪʃ] *adj* disinteressato

unsettled [ʌnˈsetəld] *adj* disabitato; disorganizzato; disordinato, erratico; indeciso; (*bill*) da pagare

unshackle [ʌnˈʃækəl] *tr* liberare

unshaken [ʌnˈʃekən] *adj* inconcusso

unshapely [ʌnˈʃepli] *adj* senza forma, deforme

unshaven [ʌnˈʃevən] *adj* non rasato

unshatterable [ʌnˈʃætərəbəl] *adj* infrangibile

unsheathe [ʌnˈʃið] *tr* sguainare

unshod [ʌnˈʃɑd] *adj* scalzo; (*horse*) sferrato

unshrinkable [ʌnˈʃrɪŋkəbəl] *adj* irrestringibile

unsightly [ʌnˈsaɪtli] *adj* ripugnante, brutto

unsinkable [ʌnˈsɪŋkəbəl] *adj* insommergibile

unskilled [ʌnˈskɪld] *adj* inesperto

un′skilled la′bor *s* lavoro manuale; mano d'opera non specializzata

unskillful [ʌnˈskɪlfəl] *adj* maldestro

unsnarl [ʌnˈsnɑrl] *tr* sbrogliare

unsociable [ʌnˈsoʃəbəl] *adj* insocievole

unsold [ʌnˈsold] *adj* invenduto

unsolder [ʌnˈsɑdər] *tr* dissaldare

unsophisticated [ˌʌnsəˈfɪstɪˌketɪd] *adj* semplice, puro

unsound [ʌnˈsaund] *adj* malsano, malato; (*decayed*) guasto, imputridito; falso, fallace; (*sleep*) leggero

unsown [ʌnˈson] *adj* incolto, non seminato

unspeakable [ʌnˈspikəbəl] *adj* indicibile; (*atrocious*) innominabile, inqualificabile

unsportsmanlike [ʌnˈspɔrtsmənˌlaɪk] *adj* antisportivo

unstable [ʌnˈstebəl] *adj* instabile

unsteady [ʌnˈstedi] *adj* malfermo; incostante; irregolare

unstinted [ʌnˈstɪntɪd] *adj* generoso, senza limiti

unstitch [ʌnˈstɪtʃ] *tr* scucire

un-stop [ʌnˈstɑp] *v* (*pret & pp* -**stopped**; *ger* -**stopping**) *tr* stasare

unstressed [ʌnˈstrest] *adj* non accentuato; (*e.g., syllable*) non accentato

unstrung [ʌnˈstrʌŋ] *adj* (*beads*) sfilato; (*instrument*) allentato; (*person*) snervato

unsuccessful [ˌʌnsəkˈsesfəl] *adj* (*person*) sfortunato; (*deal*) mancato; **to be unsuccessful** fallire

unsuitable [ʌnˈsutəbəl] or [ʌnˈsjutəbəl] *adj* inappropriato

unsurpassable [ˌʌnsərˈpæsəbəl] or [ˌʌnsərˈpɑsəbəl] *adj* insuperabile

unsuspected [ˌʌnsəˈspɛktɪd] *adj* insospettato

unswerving [ʌnˈswʌrvɪŋ] *adj* diritto, fermo, costante

unsympathetic [ˌʌnsɪmpəˈθetɪk] *adj* indifferente, che non mostra comprensione

unsystematic(al) [ˌʌnsɪstəˈmætɪk(əl)] *adj* senza sistema

untactful [ʌnˈtæktfəl] *adj* senza tatto

untamed [ʌnˈtemd] *adj* indomito

untangle [ʌnˈtæŋgəl] *tr* sgrovigliare

unteachable [ʌnˈtitʃəbəl] *adj* indocile; refrattario agli studi

untenable [ʌnˈtɛnəbəl] *adj* insostenibile

unthankful [ʌnˈθæŋkfəl] *adj* ingrato

unthinkable [ʌnˈθɪŋkəbəl] *adj* impensabile

unthinking [ʌnˈθɪŋkɪŋ] *adj* irriflessivo

untidy [ʌnˈtaɪdi] *adj* disordinato

un-tie [ʌnˈtaɪ] *v* (*pret & pp* -**tied;** *ger* -**tying**) *tr* sciogliere; (*a knot*) slacciare, snodare ‖ *intr* sciogliersi

until [ʌnˈtɪl] *prep* fino, fino a ‖ *conj* fino a che, finché

untillable [ʌnˈtɪləbəl] *adj* incoltivabile

untimely [ʌnˈtaɪmli] *adj* intempestivo; (*death*) prematuro

untiring [ʌnˈtaɪrɪŋ] *adj* instancabile

untold [ʌnˈtold] *adj* non detto, non raccontato; incalcolabile; (*inexpressable*) indicibile

untouchable [ʌnˈtʌtʃəbəl] *adj & s* intoccabile *mf*

untouched [ʌnˈtʌtʃt] *adj* intatto, insensibile; non menzionato

untoward [ʌnˈtord] *adj* sfavorevole; sconveniente, disdicevole

untrammeled or **untrammelled** [ʌnˈtræməld] *adj* non inceppato

untried [ʌnˈtraɪd] *adj* non provato

untroubled [ʌnˈtrʌbləd] *adj* tranquillo

untrue [ʌnˈtru] *adj* falso

untrustworthy [ʌnˈtrʌstˌwʌrði] *adj* infido, malfido

untruth [ʌnˈtruθ] *s* falsità *f*, menzogna

untruthful [ʌnˈtruθfəl] *adj* falso, menzognero

untwist [ʌnˈtwɪst] *tr* districare ‖ *intr* districarsi

unusable [ʌnˈjuzəbəl] *adj* inservibile

unused [ʌnˈjuzd] *adj* inutilizzato; **unused to** [ʌnˈjustu] disavvezzo a

unusual [ʌnˈjuʒʊəl] *adj* insolito

unutterable [ʌnˈʌtərəbəl] *adj* impronunciabile; indicibile

unvanquished [ʌnˈvæŋkwɪʃt] *adj* invitto

unvarnished [ʌnˈvɑrnɪʃt] *adj* non verniciato; puro, semplice

unveil [ʌnˈvel] *tr* svelare; (*a statue*) scoprire, inaugurare ‖ *intr* scoprirsi

unveiling [ʌnˈvelɪŋ] *s* scoprimento

unvoiced [ʌnˈvɔɪst] *adj* non espresso; (*phonet*) sordo

unwanted [ʌnˈwɑntɪd] *adj* non desiderato

unwarranted [ʌnˈwɑrəntɪd] *adj* ingiustificato

unwary [ʌnˈweri] *adj* incauto

unwavering [ʌnˈwevərɪŋ] *adj* fermo, incrollabile

unwelcome [ʌnˈwelkəm] *adj* malaccetto, sgradito

unwell [ʌnˈwel] *adj* poco bene; **to be**

unwell *(said of a woman)* (coll) avere le mestruazioni

unwholesome [ʌn'holsəm] *adj* malsano

unwieldy [ʌn'wildi] *adj* ingombrante

unwilling [ʌn'wiliŋ] *adj* riluttante

unwillingly [ʌn'wiliŋli] *adv* a malincuore, a controvoglia

un-wind [ʌn'waind] *v (pret & pp -wound* ['waund]) *tr* svolgere ‖ *intr* svolgersi; *(said of a watch)* scaricarsi; *(said of a person)* rilasciarsi

unwise [ʌn'waiz] *adj* malaccorto

unwished-for [ʌn'wiʃt,fɔr] *adj* indesiderato, non augurato

unwitting [ʌn'witiŋ] *adj* involontario

unwonted [ʌn'wʌntid] *adj* insolito

unworldly [ʌn'wʌrdli] *adj (not of this world)* non terrestre; *(not interested in things of this world)* non mondano; *(naive)* semplice

unworthy [ʌn'wʌrði] *adj* indegno

un-wrap [ʌn'ræp] *v (pret & pp -wrapped; ger -wrapping) tr* scartare, svolgere, scartocciare

unwrinkled [ʌn'riŋkəld] *adj* senza una grinza

unwritten [ʌn'ritən] *adj* orale; non scritto; *(blank)* in bianco

unyielding [ʌn'jildiŋ] *adj* inflessibile

unyoke [ʌn'yok] *tr* liberare dal giogo

up [ʌp] *adj* che va verso la città; diretto al nord; al corrente; finito, terminato; alto; su; *(sports)* pari; **to be up and about** essere in piedi ‖ *s* salita; vantaggio; aumento; **ups and downs** alti e bassi *mpl* ‖ *adv* su; in alto; alla pari; **to be up** essere alzato; *(in sports or games)* essere avanti; **to be up in arms** essere in armi; essere indignato; **to be up to a person** toccare a una persona; **to get up** alzarsi; **to go up** salire; **to keep up** mantenere; continuare; **to keep up with** mantenersi alla pari con; **up above** lassù; **up against** (coll) contro; **up against it** (coll) in una strettoia; **up to** fino a; *(capable of)* (coll) all'altezza di; *(scheming)* (coll) tramando; **what's up?** che succede? ‖ *prep* su; sopra; fino a; **to go up a river** risalire un fiume

up-and-coming ['ʌpən'kʌmiŋ] *adj* promettente

up-and-doing ['ʌpən'du·iŋ] *adj* (coll) intraprendente; (coll) attivo

up-and-up ['ʌpən'ʌp] *s—on the up-and-up* (coll) aperto; (coll) apertamente; (coll) in ascesa

up-braid' *tr* rimproverare, strapazzare

upbringing ['ʌp,briŋiŋ] *s* educazione

up'coun'try *adj* all'interno ‖ *s* interno ‖ *adv* verso l'interno

up-date' *tr* aggiornare

upheaval [ʌp'hivəl] *s* sommovimento; (geol) sconvolgimento tellurico

up'hill' *adj* erto, scosceso; arduo, faticoso ‖ *adv* in salita, all'insù

up-hold' *v (pret & pp -held) tr* alzare; sostenere; difendere

upholster [ʌp'holstər] *tr* tappezzare

upholsterer [ʌp'holstərər] *s* tappezziere *m*

upholster·y [ʌp'holstəri] *s* (-ies) tap-

pezzeria; *(e.g., of cushions)* imbottitura; (aut) selleria

up'keep' *s* manutenzione; spese *fpl* di manutenzione

upland ['ʌplənd] *or* ['ʌplænd] *adj* alto, elevato ‖ *s* terreno elevato

up'lift' *s* elevazione; miglioramento sociale; edificazione ‖ **up'lift'** *tr* elevare

upon [ʌ'pʌn] *prep* su, sopra, in; **upon + ger** non appena + *pp*, e.g., **upon arising** non appena alzato; **upon my word!** sulla mia parola!

upper ['ʌpər] *adj* superiore, disopra; *(town)* soprano; *(river)* alto ‖ *s* disopra *m; (of shoe)* tomaia; (rr) (coll) cuccetta; **on one's uppers** ridotto al verde

up'per berth' *s* cuccetta superiore

up'per case' *s* (typ) cassa delle maiuscole, cassa superiore

up'per-case' *adj* (typ) maiuscolo

up'per classes' *spl* classi *fpl* elevate

up'per hand' *s* vantaggio; **to have the upper hand** prendere il disopra

up'per·most' *adj* (il) più alto; principale ‖ *adv* principalmente, in primo luogo

uppish ['ʌpiʃ] *adj* (coll) arrogante, snob

up-raise' *tr* alzare, tirare su

up'right' *adj* ritto, verticale; dabbene, onesto ‖ *s* staggio, montante *m* ‖ *adv* verticalmente

uprising [ʌp'raiziŋ] *or* ['ʌp,raiziŋ] *s* sollevazione, insurrezione

up'roar' *s* gazzarra, cagnara, fracasso

uproarious [ʌp'rori·əs] *adj* tumultuoso; *(noisy)* rumoroso; *(funny)* comico

up-root' *tr* sradicare

up-set' *adj* rovesciato; scompigliato; *(emotionally)* scombussolato; *(stomach)* imbarazzato ‖ **up'set'** *s (overturn)* rovesciamento; *(defeat)* rovescio; *(disorder)* scompiglio; *(illness)* imbarazzo, disturbo ‖ **up-set'** *v (pret & pp -set; ger -setting) tr* rovesciare; scompigliare; indisporre ‖ *intr* rovesciarsi, ribaltarsi

upset' price' *s* prezzo minimo di vendita di un oggetto all'asta

upsetting [ʌp'setiŋ] *adj* sconcertante

up'shot' *s* conclusione; essenziale *m*

up'side' *s* disopra *m*

up'side down' *adv* alla rovescia; **a gambe all'aria;** a soqquadro

up'stage' *adj* al fondo della scena; altiero, arrogante ‖ *adv* al fondo della scena ‖ *tr* trattare altezzosamente; (theat) rubare la scena a

up'stairs' *adj* del piano di sopra ‖ *s* piano di sopra ‖ *adv* su, al piano di sopra

upstanding [ʌp'stændiŋ] *adj* diritto; forte; onorevole

up'start' *s* arrivato, nuovo ricco

up'stream' *adv* a monte, controcorrente

up'stroke' *s (in handwriting)* tratto ascendente; (mach) corsa ascendente

up'swing' *s (in prices)* ascesa; miglioramento; **to be on the upswing** migliorare

up'-to-date' *adj* recentissimo; moderno; dell'ultima ora

up'town' *adj* della parte più alta della città ‖ *adv* nella parte più alta della città

up'trend' *s* tendenza al rialzo

up'turn' *s* rivolta; (com) rialzo

upturned [' ʌp'tʌrnd] *adj* rivolto all'insù; (*upside down*) capovolto

upward ['ʌpwərd] *adj* ascendente ‖ *adv* all'insù; **upward of** più di

U'ral Moun'tains ['jurəl] *spl* Urali *mpl*

uranium [ju'renɪ·əm] *s* uranio

urban ['ʌrbən] *adj* urbano

urbane [ʌr'ben] *adj* urbano

urbanite ['ʌrbə‚naɪt] *s* abitante *mf* di una città

urbanity [ʌr'bænɪti] *s* urbanità *f*

urbanize ['ʌrbə‚naɪz] *tr* urbanizzare

ur'ban renew'al *s* ricostruzione urbanistica

urchin ['ʌrtʃɪn] *s* monello, birichino

ure·thra [ju'riθrə] *s* (**-thras** or **-thrae** [θri]) uretra

urge [ʌrdʒ] *s* stimolo ‖ *tr* urgere, sollecitare, spronare; (*to endeavor to persuade*) esortare; (*an enterprise*) accelerare ‖ *intr*—**to urge against** opporsi a

urgen·cy ['ʌrdʒənsi] *s* (**-cies**) urgenza

urgent ['ʌrdʒənt] *adj* urgente; (*desire*) prepotente

urinal ['jurɪnəl] *s* (*receptacle*) orinale *m*; (*for a bedridden person*) pappagallo; (*place*) orinatoio, vespasiano

urinary ['jurɪ‚neri] *adj* urinario

urinate ['jurɪ‚net] *tr & intr* orinare

urine ['jurɪn] *s* urina

urn [ʌrn] *s* urna; (*for making coffee*) caffettiera; (*for making tea*) samovar *m*

urology [ju'rɑlədʒi] *s* urologia

Uruguay ['jurə‚gwe] or ['jurə‚gwaɪ] *s* l'Uruguai *m*

Uruguayan [‚jurə'gwe·ən] or [‚jurə'gwaɪ·ən] *adj & s* uruguaiano

us [ʌs] *pron pers* ci; noi; **to us** ci, a noi, per noi

U.S.A. ['ju'es'e] *s* (letterword) (**United States of America**) S.U.A. *mpl*

usable ['juzəbəl] *adj* servibile, adoperabile

usage ['jusɪdʒ] or ['juzɪdʒ] *s* uso, usanza; (*of a language*) uso

use [jus] *s* uso, impiego, usanza; **in use** in uso, in servizio; **it's no use** non giova; **out of use** disusato; **to be of no use** non servire a nulla; **to have**

no use for non aver bisogno di; non poter soffrire; **to make use of** servirsi di; **what's the use?** a che pro? ‖ [juz] *tr* usare, impiegare, servirsi di; **to use badly** maltrattare; **to use up** consumare, esaurire ‖ *intr*—**used to** translated in Italian in three ways: (1) by the imperfect indicative, e.g., **he used to go to church at seven o'clock** andava in chiesa alle sette; (2) by the imperfect indicative of **solere**, e.g., **he used to smoke all day** soleva fumare tutto il giorno; (3) by the imperfect indicative of **avere l'abitudine di**, e.g., **he used to go to the shore** aveva l'abitudine di andare alla spiaggia

used [juzd] *adj* uso, usato; **to get used to** ['juzdtu] or ['justu] fare la mano a, abituarsi a

useful ['jusfəl] *adj* utile

usefulness ['jusfəlnɪs] *s* utilità *f*

useless ['juslɪs] *adj* inutile, inservibile

user ['juzər] *s* utente *mf*

usher ['ʌʃər] *s* (*doorkeeper*) portiere *m*; (hist) cerimoniere *m*; (theat) maschera; (mov) lucciola ‖ *tr* introdurre; **to usher in** annunciare, introdurre

U.S.S.R. ['ju'es'es'ɑr] *s* (letterword) (**Union of Soviet Socialist Republics**) U.R.S.S. *f*

usual ['juʒu·əl] *adj* usuale, abituale; **as usual** come il solito

usually ['juʒu·əli] *adj* usualmente

usurp [ju'zʌrp] *tr* usurpare

usu·ry [juʒəri] *s* (**-ries**) usura

utensil [ju'tensɪl] *s* utensile *m*

uter·us ['jutərəs] *s* (**-i** [‚aɪ]) utero

utilitarian [‚jutɪlɪ'teri·ən] *adj* utilitario

utili·ty [ju'tɪlɪti] *s* (**-ties**) utilità *f*; compagnia di servizi pubblici

utilize ['jutɪ‚laɪz] *tr* utilizzare

utmost ['ʌt‚most] *adj* sommo; estremo; massimo ‖ *s*—**the utmost** il massimo; **to do one's utmost** fare tutto il possibile; **to the utmost** al massimo limite

utopia [ju'topɪ·ə] *s* utopia

utopian [ju'topɪ·ən] *adj* utopistico ‖ *s* utopista *mf*

utter ['ʌtər] *adj* completo, totale ‖ *tr* proferire, pronunziare; (*a sigh*) dare, fare

utterly ['ʌtərli] *adj* completamente

uxoricide [ʌk'sorɪ‚saɪd] *s* (*husband*) uxoricida *m*; (*act*) uxoricidio

uxorious [ʌk'sorɪ·əs] *adj* eccessivamente innamorato della propria moglie; dominato dalla moglie

V

V, v [vi] *s* ventiduesima lettera dell'alfabeto inglese

vacan·cy ['vekənsi] *s* (**-cies**) (*emptiness*) vuoto; (*unfilled position*) vacanza; (*unfilled job*) posto vacante; (*in a building*) appartamento libero;

(*in a hotel*) camera libera; **no vacancy** completo

vacant ['vekənt] *adj* (*empty*) vuoto; (*position*) vacante; (*expression of the face*) vago

vacate ['veket] *tr* sgombrare; (*a posi-*

tion) ritirarsi da; (law) annullare; **to vacate one's mind of worries** liberarsi dalle preoccupazioni || *intr* sloggiare; (coll) andarsene

vacation [veˈkeʃən] *s* vacanza, villeggiatura; vacanze *fpl* || *intr* estivare, villeggiare

vacationer [veˈkeʃənər] *s* villeggiante *mf*, vacanziere *m*

vacationist [veˈkeʃənɪst] *s* villeggiante *mf*, vacanziere *m*

vaca′tion with pay′ *s* vacanze *fpl* pagate

vaccinate [ˈvæksɪ ˌnet] *tr* vaccinare

vaccination [ˌvæksɪˈneʃən] *s* vaccinazione

vaccine [vækˈsin] *s* vaccino

vacillate [ˈvæsɪ ˌlet] *intr* vacillare

vacillating [ˈvæsɪ ˌletɪŋ] *adj* vacillante

vacui•ty [vəˈkjuˌɪti] *s* (**-ties**) vacuità *f*

vacu•um [ˈvækjuˌəm] *s* (**-ums** or **-a** [ə]) vuoto; **in a vacuum** sotto vuoto || *tr* pulire con l'aspirapolvere

vac′uum clean′er *s* aspirapolvere *m*

vac′uum-pack′ed *adj* confezionato sotto vuoto

vac′uum tube′ *s* tubo elettronico

vagabond [ˈvægə ˌbɑnd] *adj & s* vagabondo

vagar•y [vəˈgɛri] *s* (**-ies**) capriccio

vagran•cy [ˈvegrənsi] *s* (**-cies**) vagabondaggio

vagrant [ˈvegrənt] *adj & s* vagabondo

vague [veg] *adj* vago

va′gus nerve′ [ˈvegəs] *s* (anat) vago

vain [ven] *adj* vano; (*conceited*) vanitoso; **in vain** in vano

vainglorious [venˈglɔriˌəs] *adj* vanaglorioso

valance [ˈvæləns] *s* balza, mantovana

vale [vel] *s* valle *f*

valedictorian [ˌvælɪdɪkˈtɔriˌən] *s* studente *m* che pronuncia il discorso di commiato

valence [ˈveləns] *s* (chem) valenza

valentine [ˈvælən ˌtaɪn] *s* (*sweetheart*) valentino; (*card*) cartolina di San Valentino

valet [ˈvælɪt] or [ˈvæle] *s* valletto

valiant [ˈvæljənt] *adj* valoroso

valid [ˈvælɪd] *adj* valido

validate [ˈvælɪ ˌdet] *tr* convalidare, vidimare; (sports) omologare

validation [ˌvælɪˈdeʃən] *s* convalida, vidimazione; (sports) omologazione

validi•ty [vəˈlɪdɪti] *s* (**-ties**) validità *f*

valise [vəˈlis] *s* valigetta

valley [ˈvæli] *s* valle *f*, vallata; (*of roof*) linea di compluvio

valor [ˈvælər] *s* valore *m*, coraggio

valorous [ˈvælərəs] *adj* valoroso

valuable [ˈvæljuˌəbəl] or [ˈvæljəbəl] *adj* (*having monetary worth*) prezioso; pregevole, pregiato || **valuables** *spl* valori *mpl*

value [ˈvælju] *s* valore *m*; importanza; (com) valuta, valore *m*; **an excellent value** un acquisto eccellente || *tr* stimare, valutare

value′-added tax′ *s* imposta sul valore aggiunto

valueless [ˈvæljuˌlɪs] *adj* senza valore

valve [vælv] *s* (anat, mach, rad, telv)

valvola; (bot, zool) valva; (mus) pistone *m*

valve′ gears′ *spl* meccanismo di distribuzione

valve′-in-head′ en′gine *s* motore *m* a valvole in testa

valve′ lift′er [ˈlɪftər] *s* alzavalvole *m*

valve′ seat′ *s* sede *f* della valvola

valve′ spring′ *s* molla di valvola

valve′ stem′ *s* stelo di comando della valvola

vamp [væmp] *s* parte *f* anteriore della tomaia; (*patchwork*) rabberciatura; (*female*) vamp *f* || *tr* (*a shoe*) rimontare; rabberciare; (*to concoct*) inventare, raffazzonare; (*an accompaniment*) improvvisare; (*said of a female*) sedurre

vampire [ˈvæmpaɪr] *s* vampiro; (*female*) vamp *f*

van [væn] *s* camionetta, autofurgone *m*; (mil & fig) avanguardia

vanadium [vəˈnedi̇ˌəm] *s* vanadio

vandal [ˈvændəl] *adj & s* vandalo || **Vandal** *adj & s* Vandalo

vandalism [ˈvændə ˌlɪzəm] *s* vandalismo

vane [ven] *s* (*weathervane*) banderuola; (*of windmill, of turbine*) pala; (*of feather*) barba

vanguard [ˈvæn ˌgɑrd] *s* avanguardia; **in the vanguard** all'avanguardia

vanilla [vəˈnɪlə] *s* vaniglia

vanish [ˈvænɪʃ] *intr* svanire

van′ishing cream′ [ˈvænɪʃɪŋ] *s* crema evanescente

vani•ty [ˈvænɪti] *s* (**-ties**) vanità *f*; (*table*) toletta; (*case*) astuccio di toletta

vanquish [ˈvæŋkwɪʃ] *tr* superare, vincere

van′tage ground′ [ˈvæntɪdʒ] *s* posizione favorevole

vapid [ˈvæpɪd] *adj* insipido

vapor [ˈvepər] *s* vapore *m*; (*visible vapor*) vapori *mpl*

vaporize [ˈvepə ˌraɪz] *tr* vaporizzare || *intr* vaporizzarsi

va′por lock′ *s* tampone *m* di vapore

vaporous [ˈvepərəs] *adj* vaporoso

va′por trail′ *s* scia di condensazione

variable [ˈvɛrɪˌəbəl] *adj & s* variabile *f*

variance [ˈvɛrɪˌəns] *s* divario, differenza; **at variance with** (*a thing*) differente da; differentemente da; (*a person*) in disaccordo con

variant [ˈvɛrɪˌənt] *adj & s* variante *f*

variation [ˌvɛrɪˈeʃən] *s* variazione

varicose [ˈvɛrɪ ˌkos] *adj* varicoso

varied [ˈvɛrid] *adj* vario, svariato

variegated [ˈvɛrɪˌəˌgetɪd] or [ˈvɛrɪˌgetɪd] *adj* variegato, screziato

varie•ty [vəˈraɪˌɪti] *s* (**-ties**) varietà *f*

vari′ety show′ *s* spettacolo di varietà

varnish [ˈvɑrnɪʃ] *s* vernice *f* || *tr* verniciare; (fig) dare la vernice a

variola [vəˈraɪˌələ] *s* (pathol) vaiolo

various [ˈvɛrɪˌəs] *adj* vari; (*varicolored*) vario, variegato

varsi•ty [ˈvɑrsɪti] *adj* (sports) universitario || *s* (**-ties**) (sports) squadra numero uno

var·y ['veri] v (pret & pp **-ied**) tr & intr variare

vase [ves] or [vez] s vaso

vaseline ['væsə,lin] s (trademark) vaselina

vassal ['væsəl] adj & s vassallo

vast [væst] or [vɑst] adj vasto

vastly ['væstlı] or ['vɑstlı] adv enormemente

vastness ['væstnıs] or ['vɑstnıs] s vastità f

vat [væt] s tino, bigoncia

Vatican ['vætıkən] adj vaticano ‖ s Vaticano

Vat'ican Cit'y s Città f del Vaticano

vaudeville ['vodvıl] or ['vɔdəvıl] s spettacolo di varietà; (theatrical piece) vaudeville m, commedia musicale

vault [vɔlt] s volta; (underground chamber) cantina; (of a bank) camera di sicurezza; (burial chamber) cripta; (of heaven) cappa; (leap) salto ‖ tr formare a mo' di volta; saltare ‖ intr saltare

vaunt [vɔnt] or [vɑnt] s vanto, vanteria ‖ tr vantarsi di ‖ intr vantarsi

veal [vil] s vitello

veal' chop' s scaloppa, cotoletta di vitello

veal' cut'let s scaloppina

vedette [vɪ'dɛt] s (nav) vedetta; (mil) sentinella avanzata

veer [vɪr] s virata ‖ tr far cambiare di direzione a ‖ intr virare; (said of the wind) cambiare di direzione

vegetable ['vedʒɪtəbəl] adj vegetale ‖ s (plant) vegetale m; (edible plant) ortaggio; **vegetables** verdura, erbe fpl, erbaggi mpl, ortaggi mpl

veg'etable gar'den s orto

veg'etable soup' s minestra di verdura

vegetarian [,vedʒɪ'terɪ-ən] adj & s vegetariano

vegetate ['vedʒɪ,tet] intr vegetare

vehemence ['vi-ıməns] s veemenza

vehement ['vi-ımənt] adj veemente

vehicle ['vi-ıkəl] s veicolo

vehic'ular traf'fic [vɪ'hıkjələr] s circolazione stradale

veil [vel] s velo; **to take the veil** prendere il velo ‖ tr velare

vein [ven] s vena; (streak) venatura; (of ore) filone m ‖ tr venare

velar ['vilar] adj & s velare f

vellum ['veləm] s pergamena

veloci·ty [vɪ'lɑsıti] s (-ties) velocità f

velvet ['velvıt] adj di velluto ‖ s velluto; (slang) guadagno al gioco; (coll) situazione all'acqua di rose

velveteen [,velvɪ'tin] s vellutino di cotone

velvety ['velvıti] adj vellutato

vend [vend] tr vendere; (to peddle) fare il venditore ambulante di

vend'ing machine' s distributore automatico

vendor ['vendər] s venditore m

veneer [və'nır] s impiallacciatura, piallaccio; (fig) vernice f ‖ tr impiallacciare

venerable ['venərəbəl] adj venerabile

venerate ['venə,ret] tr venerare

venereal [vɪ'nırı-əl] adj venereo

Venetia [vɪ'nı/ı-ə] or [vɪ'nı/ə] s (province) Venezia

Venetian [vɪ'nı/ən] adj & s veneziano

Vene'tian blind' s veneziana, persiana avvolgibile

Venezuelan [,venı'zwilən] adj & s venezolano

vengeance ['vendʒəns] s vendetta; **with a vengeance** violentemente; eccessivamente

vengeful ['vendʒfəl] adj vendicativo

Venice ['venıs] s Venezia

venire·man [vɪ'naırımən] s (-men) membro di un collegio di giurati

venison ['venısən] or ['venızən] s carne f di cervo

venom ['venəm] s veleno

venomous ['venəməs] adj velenoso

vent [vent] s sfiatatoio; (of jacket) spacco; **to give vent to** dare sfogo a ‖ tr sfogare, sfuriare; mettere uno sfiatatoio a; **to vent one's spleen** sfogare la bile

vent' hole' s apertura di sfogo

ventilate ['ventı,let] tr ventilare

ventilator ['ventı,letər] s ventilatore m

ventricle ['ventrıkəl] s ventricolo

ventriloquist [ven'trıləkwıst] s ventriloquo

venture ['vent/ər] s azzardo, avventura rischiosa; **at a venture** alla ventura ‖ tr avventurare ‖ intr avventurarsi, arrischiarsi

venturesome ['vent/ərsəm] adj (risky) rischioso; (daring) avventuroso

venturous ['vent/ərəs] adj avventuroso

vent' win'dow s (aut) deflettore m

venue ['venju] s (law) posto dove ha avuto luogo il reato; (law) luogo dove si riunisce la corte; **change of venue** cambio di giurisdizione

Venus ['vinəs] s (very beautiful woman) venere f; (astr) Venere m; (myth) Venere f

veracious [vɪ're/əs] adj verace

veraci·ty [vɪ'ræsıti] s (-ties) veridicità f

veranda or **verandah** [və'rændə] s veranda

verb [vʌrb] adj verbale ‖ s verbo

verbalize ['vʌrbə,laız] tr esprimere con parole; (gram) convertire in forma verbale ‖ intr essere verboso

verbatim [vər'betım] adj letterale ‖ adv parola per parola, testualmente

verbena [vər'binə] s (bot) verbena

verbiage ['vʌrbı-ıdʒ] s verbosità f; (style of wording) espressione

verbose [vər'bos] adj verboso

verdant ['vʌrdənt] adj verde, verdeggiante

verdict ['vʌrdıkt] s verdetto

verdigris ['vʌrdı,gris] s verderame m

verdure ['vʌrdʒər] s verde m

verge [vʌrdʒ] s orlo, limite m; bordo; (of a column) fusto; **on the verge of** al punto di; all'orlo di ‖ intr—**to verge on** costeggiare, rasentare

verification [,verıfı'ke/ən] s verifica

veri·fy ['vɛrɪ ˌfaɪ] v (pret & pp **-fied**) tr verificare, confermare

verily ['vɛrɪlɪ] adv in verità

veritable ['vɛrɪtəbəl] adj vero

vermilion [vər'mɪljən] adj & s vermiglio

vermin ['vʌrmɪn] ssg (person) persona abominevole || spl (animals or persons) insetti mpl

vermouth [vər'muθ] or ['vʌrmuθ] s vermut m

vernacular [vər'nækjələr] adj volgare || s volgare m, vernacolo; (language peculiar to a class or profession) gergo

versatile ['vʌrsətɪl] adj (person) versatile; (tool or device) a vari usi

verse [vʌrs] s verso; (Bib) versetto

versed [vʌrst] adj versato

versification [ˌvʌrsɪfɪ'keʃən] s versificazione

versi·fy ['vʌrsɪ ˌfaɪ] v (pret & pp **-fied**) tr & intr versificare

version ['vʌrʒən] s versione

ver·so ['vʌrso] s (**-sos**) (of coin) rovescio; (of page) verso

versus ['vʌrsəs] prep contro; in confronto a

verte·bra ['vʌrtɪbrə] s (**-brae** [ˌbri] or **-bras**) vertebra

vertebrate ['vʌrtə ˌbret] adj & s vertebrato

ver·tex ['vʌrtɛks] s (**-texes** or **-tices** [tɪ ˌsiz]) vertice m

vertical ['vʌrtɪkəl] adj & s verticale f

ver'tical hold' s (telv) regolatore m del sincronismo verticale

ver'tical sta'bilizer s (aer) deriva

verti·go ['vʌrtɪ ˌgo] s (**-goes** or **-gos**) vertigine f

verve [vʌrv] s verve f, brio

very ['vɛrɪ] adj (utter) grande, completo; (precise) vero e proprio; (mere) stesso, e.g., **his very brother** suo fratello stesso || adv molto, e.g., **to be very rich** essere molto ricco

vesicle ['vɛsɪkəl] s vescichetta

vesper ['vɛspər] s vespro; **vespers** vespri mpl || **Vesper** s Vespero

ves'per bell' s campana a vespro

vessel ['vɛsəl] s (ship) nave f, vascello; (container) vaso; (anat) vaso; (fig) vasello

vest [vɛst] s (of man's suit) panciotto, gilè m; (of woman's garment) corpino || tr vestire; **to vest** (authority) **in** concedere a; **to vest with** investire di || intr vestirsi; **to vest in** passare a

vest'ed in'terest s interesse acquisito

vestibule ['vɛstɪ ˌbjul] s vestibolo

vestige ['vɛstɪdʒ] s vestigio

vestment ['vɛstmənt] s (eccl) paramento

vest'-pock'et adj da tasca, tascabile

ves·try ['vɛstrɪ] s (**-tries**) sagrestia; (chapel) cappella; giunta esecutiva della chiesa episcopaliana

ves'try·man s (**-men**) membro della giunta esecutiva della chiesa episcopaliana

Vesuvius [vɪ'suvɪ·əs] or [vɪ'sjuvɪ·əs] s il Vesuvio

vetch [vɛtʃ] s veccia; (grass pea) cicerchia

veteran ['vɛtərən] adj & s veterano

veterinarian [ˌvɛtərɪ'nɛrɪ·ən] s veterinario

veterinar·y ['vɛtərɪ ˌnɛri] adj veterinario || s (**-ies**) veterinario

ve·to ['vito] s (**-toes**) veto || tr porre il veto a

vex [vɛks] tr irritare, tormentare

vexation [vɛk'seʃən] s fastidio, contrarietà f

vexatious [vɛk'seʃəs] adj irritante, fastidioso; (law) vessatorio

vexing ['vɛksɪŋ] adj noioso, fastidioso, irritante

via ['vaɪ·ə] prep via, per via di

viaduct ['vaɪ·ə ˌdʌkt] s viadotto

vial ['vaɪ·əl] s fiala, boccetta

viand ['vaɪ·ənd] s vivanda, manicaretto

viati·cum [vaɪ'ætɪkəm] s (**-cums** or **-ca** [kə]) (eccl) viatico

vibrate ['vaɪbret] tr & intr vibrare

vibration [vaɪ'breʃən] s vibrazione

vicar ['vɪkər] s vicario

vicarage ['vɪkərɪdʒ] s residenza del vicario; (office; duties) vicariato

vicarious [vaɪ'kɛrɪ·əs] or [vɪ'kɛrɪ·əs] adj sostituto; (punishment) ricevuto in vece di altra persona; (power) delegato; (enjoyment) di riflesso

vice [vaɪs] s vizio

vice'-ad'miral s viceammiraglio, ammiraglio di squadra

vice'-pres'ident s vicepresidente m

viceroy ['vaɪsrɔɪ] s viceré m

vice versa ['vaɪsi 'vʌrsə] or ['vaɪsə 'vʌrsə] adv viceversa

vicini·ty [vɪ'sɪnɪtɪ] s (**-ties**) vicinanze fpl, paraggi mpl

vicious ['vɪʃəs] adj vizioso; maligno, malvagio; (dog) cattivo, che morde; (horse) selvaggio; (headache) tremendo; (reasoning; circle) vizioso

victim ['vɪktɪm] s vittima

victimize ['vɪktɪ ˌmaɪz] tr fare una vittima di; ingannare; (hist) sacrificare

victor ['vɪktər] s vincitore m

victorious [vɪk'torɪ·əs] adj vittorioso

victo·ry ['vɪktərɪ] s (**-ries**) vittoria

victuals ['vɪtəlz] spl vettovaglie fpl

vid'eo cassette' ['vɪdɪ ˌo] s videocassetta

vid'eo sig'nal s segnale m video

vid'eo tape' s nastro televisivo

vie [vaɪ] v (pret & pp **vied**; ger **vying**) intr gareggiare; **to vie for** disputarsi

Vien·nese [ˌvi·ə'niz] adj viennese || s (**-nese**) viennese mf

Vietnam [ˌviet'nɑm] s il Vietnam

Vietnam·ese [vɪ ˌetnə'miz] adj vietnamita || s (**-ese**) vietnamita mf; (language) vietnamita m

view [vju] s vista; (picture) veduta; prospetto; esame m; punto di vista; **to be on view** (said of a corpse) essere esposto; **to keep in view** non perdere di vista; **to take a dim view of** avere un'opinione scettica di; **with a view to** con lo scopo di || tr guardare, osservare; considerare

viewer ['vju·ər] *s* spettatore *m;* (telv) telespettatore *m;* (phot) visore *m;* (phot) proiettore *m* di diapositive

view'find'er *s* (phot) traguardo, visore *m*

view'point' *s* punto di vista

vigil ['vɪdʒɪl] *s* vigilia; **to keep vigil** vegliare

vigilance ['vɪdʒɪləns] *s* vigilanza

vigilant ['vɪdʒɪlənt] *adj* vigilante

vignette [vɪn'jet] *s* vignetta

vigor ['vɪgər] *s* vigore *m,* gagliardia

vigorous ['vɪgərəs] *adj* vigoroso

Viking ['vaɪkɪŋ] *s* vichingo

vile [vaɪl] *adj* vile, malvagio; *(wretchedly bad)* orribile; disgustoso, ripugnante; *(filthy)* sporco; *(poor)* povero, basso

vili·fy ['vɪlɪ,faɪ] *v* (*pret & pp* **-fied**) *tr* vilificare

villa ['vɪlə] *s* villa

village ['vɪlɪdʒ] *s* villaggio, paese *m*

villager ['vɪlɪdʒər] *s* paesano

villain ['vɪlən] *s* scellerato; *(of a play)* cattivo, anima nera

villainous ['vɪlənəs] *adj* vile, infame

villain·y ['vɪləni] *s* (**-ies**) scelleratezza, malvagità *f*

vim [vɪm] *s* vigore *m,* brio

vinaigrette [,vɪnə'gret] *s* boccetta dell'aceto aromatico

vinaigrette' sauce' *s* salsa verde

vindicate ['vɪndɪ,ket] *tr* scolpare; difendere, sostenere; *(e.g., a claim)* rivendicare

vindictive [vɪn'dɪktɪv] *adj* vendicativo

vine [vaɪn] *s* *(climber)* rampicante *f;* *(grape plant)* vite *f*

vine'dress'er *s* vignaiolo

vinegar ['vɪnɪgər] *s* aceto

vinegarish ['vɪnɪgərɪʃ] *adj* acetoso; (fig) acre, mordace

vinegary ['vɪnɪgəri] *adj* acetoso; (fig) irritabile, irascibile

vineyard ['vɪnjərd] *s* vigna, vigneto

vintage ['vɪntɪdʒ] *s* vendemmia; vino di annata eccezionale; (fig) edizione

vintager ['vɪntɪdʒər] *s* vendemmiatore *m*

vin'tage wine' *s* vino di marca

vin'tage year' *s* buona annata

vintner ['vɪntnər] *s* produttore *m* di vino; vinaio

vinyl ['vaɪnɪl] or ['vɪnɪl] *s* vinile *m*

violate ['vaɪ·ə,let] *tr* violare

violation [,vaɪ·ə'leʃən] *s* violazione

violence ['vaɪ·ələns] *s* violenza

violent ['vaɪ·ələnt] *adj* violento

violet ['vaɪ,əlɪt] *adj* violetto || *s* *(color)* violetto, viola; (bot) violetta; *(Viola odorata)* viola mammola

violin [,vaɪ·ə'lɪn] *s* violino

violinist [,vaɪ·ə'lɪnɪst] *s* violinista *mf*

violoncellist [,vaɪ·ələn't'felɪst] or [,vi·ələn't'felɪst] *s* violoncellista *mf*

violoncel·lo [,vaɪ·ələn't'felo] or [,vi·ələn't'felo] *s* (**-los**) violoncello

VIP ['vi'aɪ'pi] *s* (letterword) (**Very Important Person**) persona di maggiore riguardo

viper ['vaɪpər] *s* vipera; *(any snake)* serpe *f;* *(spiteful person)* vipera

vira·go [vɪ'rego] *s* (**-goes** or **-gos**) megera, donna dal caratteraccio impossibile

virgin ['vʌrdʒɪn] *adj & s* vergine *f* || **Virgin** *s* Vergine *f*

vir'gin birth' *s* parto verginale della Madonna; (zool) partenogenesi *f*

Virgin'ia creep'er [vər'dʒɪnɪ·ə] *s* vite *f* del Canada

virginity [vər'dʒɪnɪti] *s* virginità *f*

Virgo ['vʌrgo] *s* (astr) Vergine *f*

virility [vɪ'rɪlɪti] *s* virilità *f*

virology [vaɪ'rɑlədʒi] *s* virologia

virtual ['vʌrtʃʊ·əl] *adj* virtuale

virtue ['vʌrtʃu] *s* virtù *f*

virtuosi·ty [,vʌrtʃʊ'ɑsɪti] *s* (**-ties**) virtuosità *f,* virtuosismo

virtuo·so [,vʌrtʃʊ'oso] *s* (**-sos** or **-si** [si]) virtuoso

virtuous ['vʌrtʃʊ·əs] *adj* virtuoso

virulence ['vɪrjələns] *s* virulenza

virulent ['vɪrjələnt] *adj* virulento

virus ['vaɪrəs] *s* virus *m*

visa ['vizə] *s* visto || *tr* vistare

visage ['vɪzɪdʒ] *s* faccia; apparenza

vis-à-vis [,vizə'vi] *adj* l'uno di fronte all'altro || *adv* vis-à-vis || *prep* di fronte a

viscera ['vɪsərə] *spl* visceri *mpl,* viscere *fpl*

viscount ['vaɪkaunt] *s* visconte *m*

viscountess ['vaɪkauntɪs] *s* viscontessa

viscous ['vɪskəs] *adj* viscoso

vise [vaɪs] *s* morsa

visé ['vize] or [vi'ze] *s & tr* var of **visa**

visible ['vɪzɪbəl] *adj* visibile

Visigoth ['vɪzɪ,gɑθ] *s* visigoto

vision ['vɪʒən] *s* visione; *(sense)* vista

visionar·y ['vɪʒə,nɛri] *adj* visionario || *s* (**-ies**) visionario

visit ['vɪzɪt] *s* visitare; affliggere, colpire; *(a punishment)* far ricadere || *intr* visitare; *(to chat)* fare un chiacchierata

visitation [,vɪzɪ'teʃən] *s* visitazione; punizione divina, visita del Signore

vis'iting card' *s* biglietto da visita

vis'iting hours' *spl* orario delle visite

vis'iting nurse' *s* infermiera che visita i pazienti a domicilio

visitor ['vɪzɪtər] *s* visitatore *m*

visor ['vaɪzər] *s* visiera; (fig) maschera

vista ['vɪstə] *s* vista, prospettiva

visual ['vɪʒu·əl] *adj* visivo, visuale

vis'ual acu'ity *s* acutezza visiva

visualize ['vɪʒu·ə,laɪz] *tr* formare l'immagine mentale di; *(to make visible)* visualizzare

vital ['vaɪtəl] *adj* vitale; *(deadly)* mortale || **vitals** *spl* organi vitali

vitality [vaɪ'tælɪti] *s* vitalità *f*

vitalize ['vaɪtə,laɪz] *tr* animare, infondere vita a

vi'tal statis'tics *spl* statistiche *fpl* anagrafiche

vitamin ['vaɪtəmɪn] *s* vitamina

vitiate ['vɪʃɪ,et] *tr* viziare

vitreous ['vɪtrɪ·əs] *adj* vitreo, vetroso

vitriolic [,vɪtrɪ'ɑlɪk] *adj* di vetriolo; (fig) caustico

vituperate [vaɪ'tupə,ret] or [vaɪ'tjupə,ret] *tr* vituperare

viva ['vivə] s evviva ‖ *interj* vival
vivacious [vɪ'veʃəs] or [vaɪ've/əs] *adj* vivace
vivaci·ty [vɪ'væsɪti] or [vaɪ'væsɪti] s (-ties) vivacità *f*, gaiezza
viva voce ['vaɪvə 'vosi] *adv* a viva voce
vivid ['vɪvɪd] *adj* vivido
vivi·fy ['vɪvɪ ,faɪ] *v* (*pret & pp* -fied) *tr* vivificare
vivisection [,vɪvɪ'sɛk/ən] s vivisezione
vixen ['vɪksən] s volpe femmina; (*ill-tempered woman*) megera
vizier [vɪ'zɪr] or ['vɪzjər] s visir *m*
vocabular·y [vo'kæbjə ,lɛri] s (-ies) vocabolario
vocal ['vokəl] *adj* vocale; (*inclined to express oneself freely*) che si fa sentire, loquace; (*e.g., outburst*) verbale
vocalist ['vokəlɪst] s cantante *mf*; (*of jazz*) vocalist *mf*
vocalize ['voke/ən] *tr* vocalizzare ‖ *intr* vocalizzarsi
vocation [vo'ke/ən] s vocazione; professione, impiego
voca'tional educa'tion s istruzione professionale
vocative ['vakətɪv] *adj* vocativo
vociferate [vo'sɪfə ,ret] *intr* vociferare
vociferous [vo'sɪfərəs] *adj* rumoroso, vociferante
vogue [vog] s voga, moda; **in vogue** in voga, di moda
voice [vɔɪs] s voce *f*; (*of animals*) verso; **in a loud voice** a voce alta; **in a low voice** a voce bassa; **to give voice to** esprimere; **with one voice** con una sola voce ‖ *tr* esprimere; (*phonet*) sonorizzare ‖ *intr* sonorizzarsi
voiced [vɔɪst] *adj* (phonet) sonoro
voiceless ['vɔɪslɪs] *adj* senza voce; muto; (phonet) sordo, duro
void [vɔɪd] *adj* (*useless*) inutile; (*empty*) vuoto; (law) invalido, nullo; **void of** sprovvisto di ‖ s vuoto; (*gap*) buco ‖ *tr* vuotare; (*the bowels*) evacuare; annullare ‖ *intr* andare di corpo
volatile ['valətɪl] *adj* volatile; instabile; (*disposition*) volubile, incostante
volatilize ['valətɪ ,laɪz] *tr* volatilizzare ‖ *intr* volatilizzarsi
volcanic [val'kænɪk] *adj* vulcanico
volca·no [val'keno] s (-noes or -nos) vulcano
volition [və'lɪ/ən] s volontà *f*; **of one's own volition** di propria volontà
volley ['vali] s (*e.g., of bullets*) scarica, sventagliata; (tennis) volata ‖ *tr* colpire a volo ‖ *intr* colpire la palla a volo
vol'ley-ball' s pallavolo *f*
volplane ['val ,plen] s planata ‖ *intr* planare
volt [volt] s volt *m*
voltage ['voltɪdʒ] s voltaggio
volt'age divid'er [dɪ'vaɪdər] s divisore *m* del voltaggio
voltaic [val'te·ɪk] *adj* voltaico
volte-face [volt'fas] s voltafaccia *m*

volt'me'ter s voltmetro
voluble ['valjəbəl] *adj* locuace
volume ['valjəm] s volume *m*; **to speak volumes** avere molta importanza; essere molto espressivo
voluminous [və'lumɪnəs] *adj* voluminoso
voluntar·y ['valən ,tɛri] *adj* volontario ‖ s (-ies) assolo di organo
volunteer [,valən'tɪr] *adj & s* volontario ‖ *tr* dare or dire volontariamente ‖ *intr* offrirsi; arruolarsi come volontario; **to volunteer to** + *inf* offrirsi di + *inf*
voluptuar·y [və'lʌpt/ʊ ,ɛri] *adj* voluttuoso ‖ s (-ies) sibarita *m*, epicureo
voluptuous [və'lʌpt/ʊ·əs] *adj* voluttuoso
volute [və'lut] s voluta
vomit ['vamɪt] s vomito ‖ *tr & intr* vomitare, rigettare
voodoo ['vudu] *adj* di vudù ‖ s (*practice*) vudù *m*; (*person*) vuduista *mf*
voracious [və're/əs] *adj* vorace
voracity [və'ræsɪti] s voracità *f*
vor·tex ['vɔrtəks] s (-texes or -tices [tɪ ,siz]) vortice *m*
vota·ry ['votəri] s (-ries) persona legata da un voto; amante *mf*, appassionato
vote [vot] s voto; **to put to the vote** mettere ai voti; **to tally the votes** procedere allo scrutinio dei voti ‖ *tr* votare; dichiarare; **to vote down** respingere; **to vote in** eleggere; **to vote out** scacciare ‖ *intr* votare
vote' get'ter ['gɛtər] s accaparratore *m* di voti; slogan *m* che conquista voti
voter ['votər] s elettore *m*
vot'ing machine' ['votɪŋ] s macchina per registrare lo scrutinio dei voti
votive ['votɪv] *adj* votivo
vo'tive of'fering s voto, ex voto, offerta votiva
vouch [vaut/] *tr* garantire ‖ *intr*—**to vouch for** (*s.th*) garantire; (*s.o.*) rendersi garante per, garantire per
voucher ['vaut/ər] s garante *mf*; (*certificate*) ricevuta, pezza d'appoggio
vouch·safe' *tr* concedere,. accordare ‖ *intr*—**to vouchsafe to** + *inf* degnarsi di + *inf*
voussoir [vu'swar] s cuneo
vow [vau] s voto; **to take vows** pronunciare i voti ‖ *tr* promettere; (*vengeance*) giurare ‖ *intr* fare un voto
vowel ['vau·əl] s vocale *f*
voyage ['vɔɪ·ɪdʒ] s viaggio; (*by sea*) traversata ‖ *tr* attraversare ‖ *intr* viaggiare
voyager ['vɔɪ·ɪdʒər] s viaggiatore *m*, passeggero
vulcanize ['vʌlkə ,naɪz] *tr* vulcanizzare
vulgar ['vʌlgər] *adj* volgare; comune, popolare
vulgari·ty [vʌl'gærɪti] s (-ties) volgarità *f*
Vul'gar Lat'in s latino volgare
Vulgate ['vʌlget] s Vulgata
vulnerable ['vʌlnərəbəl] *adj* vulnerabile
vulture ['vʌlt/ər] s avvoltoio

W

W, w ['dʌbəl ,ju] *s* ventitreesima lettera dell'alfabeto inglese

wad [wɑd] *s* (*of cotton*) batuffolo, bioccolo; (*of money*) mazzetta, rotolo; (*of tobacco*) pallottola; (*in a gun*) stoppaccio ‖ *v* (*pret & pp* **wadded;** *ger* **wadding**) *tr* arrotolare; (*shot*) comprimere; (*fig*) imbottire

waddle ['wɑdəl] *s* andatura a mo' di anitra ‖ *intr* sculettare

wade [wed] *tr* guadare ‖ *intr* guadare; avanzare faticosamente; sguazzare; **to wade into** (coll) attaccare violentemente; **to wade through** procedere a stento per; leggere con difficoltà

wad'ing bird' ['wedɪŋ] *s* trampoliere *m*

wafer ['wefər] *s* disco adesivo di carta per chiudere lettere; (*cake*) wafer *m*, cialda; (eccl, med) ostia

waffle ['wɑfəl] *s* cialda

waf'fle i'ron *s* schiacce *fpl*

waft [wæft] *or* [wɑft] *tr* portare leggermente *or* a volo ‖ *intr* librarsi, spandersi

wag [wæg] *s* (*of head*) cenno; (*of tail*) scodinzolio; (*person*) burlone *m* ‖ *v* (*pret & pp* **wagged;** *ger* **wagging**) *tr* (*the head*) scuotere; (*the tail*) dimenare ‖ *intr* scodinzolare

wage [wedʒ] *s* salario, paga; **wages** salario, paga; ricompensa; prezzo, e.g., **the wages of sin is death** la morte è il prezzo del peccato ‖ *tr* (*war*) fare

wage' earn'er ['ʌrnər] *s* salariato

wager ['wedʒər] *s* scommessa; **to lay a wager** fare una scommessa ‖ *tr & intr* scommettere

wage'work'er *s* lavoratore salariato

waggish ['wægɪʃ] *adj* scherzoso, comico, burlone

Wagnerian [vɑg'nɪrɪ-ən] *adj & s* wagneriano

wagon ['wægən] *s* carro, carretto; (*e.g., Conestoga wagon*) carriaggio; furgone *m*; carrozzone *m*; **to be on the wagon** (slang) astenersi dal bere; **to hitch one's wagon to a star** avere altissime ambizioni

wag'tail' *s* (orn) ballerina, cutrettola

waif [wef] *s* (*foundling*) trovatello; abbandonato; animale smarrito

wail [wel] *s* gemito, lamento ‖ *intr* gemere, lamentarsi

wain·scot ['wenskət] *or* ['wenskɑt] *s* pannello per rivestimenti ‖ *v* (*pret & pp* **-scoted** *or* **-scotted;** *ger* **-scoting** *or* **-scotting**) *tr* rivestire di pannelli di legno

waist [west] *s* vita, cintura; blusa, camicetta, corpetto

waist'band' *s* cintola

waist'cloth' *s* perizoma *m*

waistcoat ['west ,kot] *or* ['westkət] *s* corpetto, gilè *m*

waist'line' *s* vita, cintura; **to keep** *or* **watch one's waistline** conservare la linea

wait [wet] *s* attesa; **to lie in wait** attendere al varco ‖ *tr* (*one's turn*) attendere ‖ *intr* attendere, aspettare; **to wait for** attendere, aspettare; **to wait on** servire; **to wait up for** (coll) aspettare alzato

wait'-and-see' pol'icy *s* attendismo

waiter ['wetər] *s* cameriere *m*; (*tray*) vassoio

wait'ing list' *s* lista di aspettativa

wait'ing room' *s* sala d'aspetto

waitress ['wetrɪs] *s* cameriera

waive [wev] *tr* (*one's rights*) rinunciare (with *dat*); differire; mettere da parte

waiver ['wevər] *s* rinuncia

wake [wek] *s* (*any watch*) veglia; (*watch by a dead body*) veglia funebre; (*of a boat*) solco, scia; **in the wake of** come risultato di; nelle orme di ‖ *v* (*pret* **waked** *or* **woke** [wok]; *pp* **waked**) *tr* svegliare ‖ *intr* svegliarsi; **to wake to** darsi conto di; **to wake up** svegliarsi

wakeful ['wekfəl] *adj* sveglio; insonne

waken ['wekən] *tr* svegliare ‖ *intr* svegliarsi

wale [wel] *s* segno lasciato da una frustata, vescica; (*in fabric*) riga, costa

Wales [welz] *s* la Galles

walk [wok] *s* (*act*) camminata; (*distance*) cammino; (*for pleasure*) passeggiata; (*gait*) andatura; (*line of work*) attività *f*, mestiere *m*; (*sidewalk*) marciapiede *m*; (*in a garden*) sentiero; (*yard for domestic animals to exercise in*) recinto; (sports) marcia; **to go for a walk** andare a fare una passeggiata ‖ *tr* (*a street*) percorrere; (*a horse*) passeggiare; (*a patient*) far camminare; (*a heavy piece of furniture*) abbambinare; **to walk off** (*a headache*) far passare camminando ‖ *intr* camminare; passeggiare; (*said of a horse*) andare al passo; (sports) marciare; **to walk away from** andarsene a piedi da; **to walk off with** rubare; vincere con facilità; **to walk out** uscire in segno di protesta; (coll) mettersi in sciopero; **to walk out on** (coll) piantare in asso

walkaway ['wokə ,we] *s* facile vittoria

walker ['wokər] *s* camminatore *m*; (*to teach a baby to walk*) girello

walkie-talkie ['wokɪ'tokɪ] *s* trasmettitore-ricevitore *m* portatile

walk'ing pa'pers *spl*—**to give s.o. his walking papers** (coll) dare gli otto giorni a qlcu

walk'-in refrig'erator *s* cella frigorifera

walk'ing stick' *s* bastone *m* da passeggio

walk'·on' *s* (*actor*) figurante *m*, comparsa; (*role*) particina

walk'out' *s* sciopero

walk'o'ver *s* facile vittoria, passeggiata

wall [wol] *s* muro; (*between rooms; of a vein*) parete *f*; (*rampart*) muraglia; **to drive to the wall** ridurre alla disperazione; **to go to the wall** perdere; fare fallimento ‖ *tr* murare; **to wall up** circondare con muro

wall'board' *s* pannello da costruzione

wallet ['wɑlɪt] *s* portafoglio

wall'flow'er *s* violacciocca gialla; **to be a wallflower** fare tappezzeria

Walloon [wɑ'lun] *adj & s* vallone *mf*

wallop ['wɑləp] *s* (coll) colpo violento; (coll) effetto ‖ *tr* (coll) dare un colpo violento a; (coll) battere completamente

wallow ['wɑlo] *s* diguazzamento; (*place*) brago, pantano ‖ *intr* diguazzare; (*in wealth*) nuotare

wall'pa'per *s* tappezzeria ‖ *tr* tappezzare

walnut ['wɔlnət] *s* (*tree; wood*) noce *m;* (*fruit*) noce *f*

walrus ['wɔlrəs] or ['wɑlrəs] *s* tricheco

Walter ['wɔltər] *s* Gualtiero

waltz [wɔlts] *s* valzer *m* ‖ *tr* ballare il valzer con; (coll) condurre con disinvoltura ‖ *intr* ballare il valzer

wan [wɑn] *adj* (**wanner; wannest**) (*face*) smunto, sparuto, smorto; (*light*) debole

wand [wɑnd] *s* bacchetta

wander ['wɑndər] *tr* vagare per ‖ *intr* vagare, vagabondare; errare

wanderer ['wɑndərər] *s* vagabondo; pellegrino

Wan'dering Jew' *s* ebreo errante

wan'der-lust' *s* passione del vagabondaggio

wane [wen] *s* decadenza, declino; calare *m* della luna; **on the wane** in declino; (*moon*) calante ‖ *intr* decadere, declinare; (*said of the moon*) calare

wangle ['wæŋgəl] *tr* (coll) ottenere con l'astuzia, rimediare; (coll) falsificare; **to wangle one's way out of** (coll) tirarsi fuori da . . . con l'astuzia ‖ *intr* (coll) arrangiarsi

want [wɑnt] or [wɔnt] *s* bisogno, necessità *f;* domanda; miseria; **for want of** a causa della mancanza di; **to be in want** essere in miseria; **to be in want of** aver bisogno di ‖ *tr* volere, desiderare; mancare; aver bisogno di ‖ *intr* desiderare; **to be wanting** mancare, e.g., **three cards are wanting** mancano tre carte; **to want for** aver bisogno di

want' ad' *s* annunzio economico

wanton ['wɑntən] *adj* di proposito, deliberato; arbitrario; licenzioso, sfrenato; (*archaic*) lussureggiante

war [wɔr] *s* guerra; **to go to war** entrare in guerra; (*said of a soldier*) andare in guerra; **to wage war** fare la guerra ‖ *v* (*pret & pp* **warred;** *ger* **warring**) *intr* guerreggiare; **to war on** fare la guerra a

warble ['wɔrbəl] *s* gorgheggio ‖ *intr* gorgheggiare

warbler ['wɔrblər] *s* canterino; uccello canoro; (orn) beccafico

war' cloud' *s* minaccia di guerra

ward [wɔrd] *s* (*of city*) distretto; (*division of hospital*) corsia; (*separate building in hospital*) padiglione *m;*

(*guardianship*) tutela; (*minor*) pupillo; (*of lock*) scontro ‖ *tr*—**to ward off** stornare, schermirsi da

warden ['wɔrdən] *s* guardiano; (*of jail*) direttore *m;* (*in wartime*) capofabbricato

ward' heel'er *s* politicantuccio

ward'robe *s* guardaroba *m*

ward'robe trunk' *s* baule *m* armadio

ward'room' *s* (nav) quadrato

ware [wer] *s* vasellame *m;* **wares** merce *f*

war' ef'fort *s* sforzo bellico

ware'house' *s* deposito, magazzino

ware'house'man *s* (**-men**) magazziniere *m*

war'fare' *s* guerra

war'head' *s* (mil) testa

war'horse' *s* cavallo di battaglia; (coll) veterano

warily ['werɪlɪ] *adv* con cautela

wariness ['werɪnɪs] *s* cautela

war'like' *adj* guerresco, guerriero

war' loan' *s* prestito di guerra

war' lord' *s* generalissimo

warm [wɔrm] *adj* caldo; (*lukewarm*) tiepido; (*clothes*) che tiene caldo; (*with anger*) acceso; **to be warm** (*said of a person*) avere caldo; (*said of the weather*) fare caldo ‖ *tr* scaldare, riscaldare; (*s.o.'s heart*) slargare; **to warm up** riscaldare ‖ *intr* scaldarsi, riscaldarsi; **to warm up** (*said, e.g., of a room*) riscaldarsi; (*with emotion*) eccitarsi, accalorarsi; **to warm up to** prender simpatia per

warm-blooded ['wɔrm'blʌdɪd] *adj* (*animal*) a sangue caldo; impetuoso, ardente

war' memo'rial *s* monumento ai caduti

warmer ['wɔrmər] *s* scaldino

warm-hearted ['wɔrm'hɑrtɪd] *adj* caloroso, cordiale

warm'ing pan' *s* scaldaletto

warmonger ['wɔr,mʌŋgər] *s* guerrafondaio

war' moth'er *s* madrina di guerra

warmth [wɔrmθ] *s* calore *m,* tepore *m;* foga, entusiasmo

warm'up' *s* preparazione; (*of radio, engine, etc.*) riscaldamento

warn [wɔrn] *tr* avvertire, mettere in guardia; (*to admonish*) ammonire; informare; **to warn off** intimare di allontanarsi (da)

warn'ing *adj* di avvertimento ‖ *s* avvertimento, ammonimento; (law) diffida

war' nose' *s* acciarino, testa

war' of nerves' *s* guerra dei nervi

War' of the Roses' *s* Guerra delle due Rose

warp [wɔrp] *s* (*of a fabric*) ordito; (*of a board*) svergolamento, curvatura; aberrazione mentale; (naut) gherlino ‖ *tr* curvare, svergolare; (*a fabric*) ordire; falsare, alterare; (naut) tirare col gherlino ‖ *intr* curvarsi; falsarsi, alterarsi; (naut) agire

war'path' *s*—**to be on the warpath** essere sul sentiero della guerra, prepararsi alla guerra; (*to be angry*) essere arrabiato, essere di cattivo umore

war'plane' *s* aeroplano da guerra

war' prof'iteer *s* pescecane *m*

warrant ['wɑrənt] or ['wɔrənt] *s* garanzia; certificato; ricevuta; (com) nota di pegno; (law) ordine *m*, mandato ‖ *tr* garantire; autorizzare

warrantable ['wɑrəntəbəl] or ['wɔrəntəbəl] *adj* giustificabile, legittimo

war'rant of'ficer *s* sottufficiale *m*

warran•ty ['wɑrənti] or ['wɔrənti] *s* (**-ties**) garanzia; autorizzazione

warren ['wɑrən] or ['wɔrən] *s* conigliera; (fig) formicaio

warrior ['wɔrjər] or ['wɑrjər] *s* guerriero

Warsaw ['wɔrsɔ] *s* Varsavia

war'ship' *s* nave *f* da guerra

wart [wɔrt] *s* verruca

war'time' *s* tempo di guerra

war'-torn' *adj* devastato dalla guerra

war' to the death' *s* guerra a morte

war•y ['weri] *adj* (**-ier; -iest**) guardingo

wash [wɑʃ] or [wɔʃ] *s* lavata; (*clothes washed or to be washed*) bucato; (*rushing movement of water*) sciacquio; (*dirty water*) lavatura; (*painting*) mano *f* di colore; (aer, naut) scia ‖ *tr* lavare; (*dishes*) rigovernare; (*said of sea or river*) bagnare; **to be washed up** essere finito; **to wash away** (*soil of river bank*) dilavare; portar via ‖ *intr* lavarsi; fare il bucato; essere lavabile; (*said of waves*) battere

washable ['wɑʃəbəl] or ['wɔʃəbəl] *adj* lavabile

wash'-and-wear' *adj* non-stiro

wash'ba'sin *s* conca, catinella

wash'bas'ket *s* cesto del bucato

wash'board' *s* asse *m* da lavanda; (*baseboard*) battiscopa *m*

wash'bowl' *s* conca, catinella

wash'cloth' *s* pezzuola per lavarsi

wash'day' *s* giorno del bucato

washed-out ['wɑʃt‚aʊt] or ['wɔʃt‚aʊt] *adj* slavato; (coll) stanco; (coll) abbattuto, accasciato

washed-up ['wɑʃt'ʌp] or ['wɔʃt'ʌp] *adj* (coll) finito

washer ['wɑʃər] or ['wɔʃər] *s* (*person*) lavatore *m*; (*machine*) lavatrice *f*; (*under head of bolt*) rondella, rosetta; (*ring to prevent leakage*) guarnizione

wash'er-man *s* (**-men**) lavatore *m*

wash'er-wom'an *s* (**-wom'en**) lavatrice *f*, lavandaia

wash' goods' *spl* tessuti *mpl* lavabili

washing ['wɑʃɪŋ] or ['wɔʃɪŋ] *s* lavata, lavaggio, lavanda; (*of clothes*) bucato; **washings** lavaggio

wash'ing machine' *s* lavabiancheria, lavatrice *f*

wash'ing so'da *s* soda da lavare

wash'out' *s* erosione; (aer) svergolamento negativo; (coll) rovina completa

wash'rag' *s* pezzuola per lavarsi; straccio di cucina

wash'room' *s* gabinetto, toletta

wash'stand' *s* lavabo, lavamano

wash'tub' *s* mastello, lavatoio

wash' wa'ter *s* lavatura

wasp [wɑsp] *s* vespa

waste [west] *s* spreco; (*refuse*) scarico, rifiuto; (*desolate country*) landa; (*excess material*) scarto; (*for wiping machinery*) cascame *m* di cotone; **to go to waste** essere sciupato; **to lay waste** devastare ‖ *tr* perdere, sciupare, sprecare ‖ *intr*—**to waste away** intristire, consumarsi

waste'bas'ket *s* cestino della carta straccia

wasteful ['westfəl] *adj* dispendioso; distruttivo

waste'pa'per *s* cartastraccia

waste' pipe' *s* tubo di scarico

waste' prod'uct *s* scarto; (*body excretion*) escremento

wastrel ['westrəl] *s* sciupone *m*; spendaccione *m*, prodigo

watch [wɑtʃ] *s* orologio; (*lookout*) guardia; (mil) guardia; (naut) turno; **to be on the watch for** essere all'erta per; **to keep watch over** vegliare su ‖ *tr* (*to look at*) osservare; (*to oversee*) vigilare; guardare; fare attenzione a ‖ *intr* guardare; (*to keep awake*) vegliare; **to watch for** fare attenzione a; **to watch out** fare attenzione; **to watch out for** fare attenzione a; essere all'erta per; **to watch over** sorvegliare; **watch out!** attenzione!

watch'band' *s* cinturino dell'orologio

watch'case' *s* cassa dell'orologio

watch' charm' *s* ciondolo dell'orologio

watch' crys'tal *s* cristallo dell'orologio

watch'dog' *s* cane *m* da guardia; (fig) guardiano

watch'dog' commit'tee *s* comitato di sorveglianza

watchful ['wɑtʃfəl] *adj* vigile

watchfulness ['wɑtʃfəlnɪs] *s* vigilanza

watch'mak'er *s* orologiaio

watch'man *s* (**-men**) guardiano, sorvegliante *m*; (*at night*) guardia notturna, metronotte *m*

watch' night' *s* notte *f* di San Silvestro; ufficio religioso della vigilia di Capodanno

watch' pock'et *s* taschino dell'orologio

watch'tow'er *s* torre *f* d'osservazione

watch'word' *s* parola d'ordine, consegna; slogan *m*

water ['wɔtər] or ['wɑtər] *s* acqua; **of the first water** di prim'ordine; (*e.g., a thief*) della più bell'acqua; **to back water** retrocedere; **to be in deep water** essere in cattive acque; **to fish in troubled waters** pescare nel torbido; **to hold water** aver fondamento; **to keep above water** (fig) tenersi a galla; **to make water** (*to urinate*) urinare; (naut) fare acqua; **to throw cold water on** scoraggiare ‖ *tr* bagnare; dare acqua a; (*cattle*) abbeverare; (*wine*) annacquare ‖ *intr* abbeverarsi; (*said of the mouth*) aver l'acquolina; (*said, e.g., of a ship*) fare acqua; (*said of the eyes*) lacrimare

wa'ter bug' *s* bacherozzolo
wa'ter car'rier *s* acquaiolo
wa'ter-col'or *s* acquerello
wa'ter-cooled' *adj* a raffreddamento ad acqua
wa'ter-course' *s* corso d'acqua
wa'ter-cress' *s* crescione *m*
wa'ter cure' *s* cura delle acque
wa'ter-fall' *s* cascata
wa'ter-front' *s* riva, banchina
wa'ter gap' *s* gola, passo
wa'ter ham'mer *s* colpo d'ariete
wa'ter heat'er *s* scaldabagno, scaldacqua *m*
wa'ter ice' *s* granita
wa'tering can' *s* annaffiatoio
wa'tering place' *s* stabilimento balneare; stazione termale; *(drinking place)* abbeveratoio
wa'tering pot' *s* annaffiatoio
wa'tering trough' *s* abbeveratoio
wa'ter jack'et *s* camicia d'acqua
wa'ter lil'y *s* nenufaro
wa'ter line' *s* linea di galleggiamento or d'acqua; linea di livello
wa'ter main' *s* tubo di flusso principale
wa'ter-mark' *s* linea di livello massimo; *(in paper)* filigrana
wa'ter-mel'on *s* cocomero, anguria
wa'ter me'ter *s* contatore *m* dell'acqua
wa'ter mill' *s* mulino ad acqua
wa'ter pipe' *s* tubo dell'acqua
wa'ter po'lo *s* pallanuoto *f*
wa'ter pow'er *s* forza idrica
wa'ter-proof' *adj & s* impermeabile *m*
wa'ter-repel'lent *adj* idroripellente
wa'ter-shed' *s* spartiacque *m*, displuvio
wa'ter ski' *s* idrosci *m*
wa'ter sof'tener *s* decalcificatore *m*
wa'ter-spout' *s* *(to carry water from roof)* pluviale *m*; *(meteor)* tromba marina
wa'ter sys'tem *s* *(of a river)* sistema *m* fluviale; *(of city)* conduttura dell'acqua, impianto idrico
wa'ter-tight' *adj* stagno, ermetico; *(fig)* perfetto, inconfutabile
wa'ter tow'er *s* torre *f* serbatoio
wa'ter wag'on *s* *(mil)* carro dell'acqua; **to be on the water wagon** *(slang)* astenersi dal bere
wa'ter-way' *s* via d'acqua, idrovia
wa'ter wheel' *s* ruota or turbina idraulica; *(of steamboat)* ruota a pale
wa'ter wings' *spl* galleggiante *m* per nuotare
wa'ter-works' *s* impianto idrico; *(pumping station)* impianto di pompaggio
watery [ˈwɔtəri] *or* [ˈwɑtəri] *adj* acquoso; lacrimoso; povero, insipido; umido, acquitrinoso
watt [wɑt] *s* watt *m*
watt'-hour' *s* (**-hours**) wattora *m*
wattle [ˈwɑtəl] *s* *(of bird)* bargiglio
watt'me'ter *s* wattmetro
wave [wev] *s* onda; *(of cold; of feeling)* ondata; *(of the hand)* cenno; *(of hair)* onda, ondulazione ‖ *tr (a flag)* sventolare; *(the hair)* ondulare; *(the hand)* fare cenno con; **to wave aside** fare cenno di allontanarsi e; *(e.g., a proposal)* rifiutare ‖ *intr* ondeggiare; fare cenni con la mano
wave'length' *s* lunghezza d'onda
wave' mo'tion *s* movimento ondulatorio
waver [ˈwevər] *intr* ondeggiare, oscillare; *(to hesitate)* titubare, tentennare; *(to totter)* pencolare
wav-y [ˈwevi] *adj* (**-ier; -iest**) *(sea)* ondoso; *(hair)* ondulato
wax [wæks] *s* cera; *(fig)* fantoccio ‖ *tr* incerare; *(a recording)* (coll) registrare ‖ *intr* aumentare; diventare; *(said of the moon)* crescere; **to wax indignant** indignarsi
wax' pa'per *s* carta cerata, carta oleata
wax'works' *s* museo di statue di cera
way [we] *s* maniera, modo; via; condizione; **across the way** di fronte; **a good way** un buon tratto; **all the way** fino alla fine della strada; completamente; **all the way to** fino a; **any way** ad ogni modo; **by the way** a proposito; **in a way** in un certo modo; fino a un certo punto; **in every way** per ogni verso; **in this way** in questa maniera; **one way** senso unico; **on the way to** andando a; **on the way out** uscendo; diminuendo, sparendo; **out of the way** eliminato; fuori mano; strano; irregolare; **that way** in quella direzione; per di lì; in quella maniera; **this way** in questa direzione; per di qui; in questa maniera; **to be in the way** essere d'impaccio; **to feel one's way** avanzare a tentoni; **to force one's way** aprirsi il passo a viva forza; **to get out of the way** togliersi di mezzo; **to give way** *(said of a rope)* rompersi; **to give way to** cedere a, darsi a; **to go out of one's way** darsi da fare, disturbarsi; **to have one's way** vincerla; **to keep out of the way** stare fuori dai piedi; **to know one's way around** conoscere bene la via; *(fig)* sapere il fatto proprio; **to know one's way** to sapere andare a; **to lead the way** guidare, fare da guida; prendere l'iniziativa; **to lose one's way** perdersi; **to make one's way** avanzare; fare carriera; **to make way for** far largo a; **to mend one's ways** mettere la testa a partito; **to not know which way to turn** non sapere a che santo votarsi; **to put out of the way** togliere di mezzo; **to see one's way to** vedere la possibilità di; **to take one's way** andarsene; **to wind one's way through** andare a zig zag lungo; **to wing one's way** andare a volo; **under way** in moto; in cammino, avviato; **way in** entrata; **way out** uscita; **ways** modi *mpl*, maniera *fpl*; (naut) scalo; **which way?** da che parte?; in che modo?, per dove?
way'bill' *s* lettera di vettura
wayfarer [ˈweˌfɛrər] *s* viandante *m*
way'lay' *v* (*pret & pp* **-laid**) *tr* tendere un agguato a; fermare improvvisamente
way' of life' *s* tenore *m* di vita

way'side' *s* bordo della strada; **to fall by the wayside** cadere per istrada; (fig) fare fiasco

way' sta'tion *s* stazione con fermata facoltativa

way' train' *s* treno omnibus

wayward ['wewərd] *adj* indocile, caparbio; irregolare; capriccioso

we [wi] *pron pers* noi; noialtri, e.g., **we Italians** noialtri italiani

weak [wik] *adj* debole

weaken ['wikən] *tr* indebolire, infiacchire || *intr* indebolirsi, infiacchirsi

weakling ['wiklɪŋ] *s* debolino, rammollito

weak-minded ['wik'maɪndɪd] *adj* irresoluto; scemo

weakness ['wiknɪs] *s* debolezza, fiacchezza; (*liking*) debole *m*

wealth [welθ] *s* ricchezza

wealth·y ['welθi] *adj* (-**ier;** -**iest**) ricco

wean [win] *tr* svezzare, slattare; **to wean away from** disavvezzare da

weanling ['winlɪŋ] *adj* appena svezzato || *s* bambino or animale appena svezzato

weapon ['wepən] *s* arma

weaponry ['wepənri] *s* armi *fpl*, armamento

wear [wer] *s* uso, servizio; (*clothing*) vestiti *mpl*, indumenti *mpl*; (*wasting away from use*) consumo, logorio; (*lasting quality*) durata, durabilità *f*; **for everyday wear** per ogni giorno || *v* (*pret* **wore** [wor]; *pp* **worn** [worn]) *tr* portare, avere indosso; (*to cause to deteriorate*) logorare, consumare; (*to tire*) stancare; **to wear out** logorare, strusciare; (*a horse*) sfiancare; (*one's patience*) esaurire; (*s.o.'s hospitality*) abusare di || *intr* logorarsi, consumarsi; **to wear off** diminuire, sparire; **to wear out** logorarsi; stancarsi; esaurirsi; **to wear well** essere di ottima durata

wear' and tear' [ter] *s* logorio

weariness ['wirinɪs] *s* fatica, stanchezza

wear'ing appar'el ['werɪŋ] *s* abbigliamento, articoli *mpl* d'abbigliamento

wearisome ['wirɪsəm] *adj* affaticante, (*tedious*) noioso

wea·ry ['wiri] *adj* (-**rier;** -**riest**) stanco || *v* (*pret & pp* -**ried**) *tr* stancare || *intr* stancarsi

weasel ['wizəl] *s* donnola

wea'sel words' *spl* parole *fpl* ambigue

weather ['weðər] *s* tempo; maltempo; **to be under the weather** (coll) non sentirsi bene; (*to be slightly drunk*) (coll) essere alticcio || *tr* (*lumber*) stagionare; (*adversities*) superare, resistere (*with dat*)

weather-beaten ['weðər,bitən] *adj* segnato dalle intemperie

weath'er bu'reau *s* servizio meteorologico

weath'er-cock' *s* banderuola

weath'er fore'cast *s* previsioni *fpl* del tempo, bollettino meteorologico

weath'er-man' *s* (-**men'**) meteorologo

weath'er report' *s* bollettino meteorologico

weath'er strip'ping ['strɪpɪŋ] *s* guarnizione a nastro per inzeppare

weath'er vane' *s* banderuola, ventarola

weave [wiv] *s* tessitura || *v* (*pret* **wove** [wov] or **weaved** ['wovən]) *tr* tessere; (fig) inserire; **to weave one's way** aprirsi un varco serpeggiando || *intr* tessere; serpeggiare

weaver ['wivər] *s* tessitore *m*

web [web] *s* tessuto; (*of spider*) tela; (*of rail*) anima, gambo; (zool) membrana; (fig) rete *f*, maglia

web-footed ['web,futɪd] *adj* palmipede

wed [wed] *v* (*pret & pp* **wed** or **wedded**; *ger* **wedding**) *tr* sposare; (*said of the groom*) impalmare; (*said of the bride*) andare in sposa a || *intr* sposarsi

wedding ['wedɪŋ] *adj* nuziale || *s* sposalizio, nozze *fpl*, matrimonio

wed'ding cake' *s* torta nuziale

wed'ding day' *s* giorno di nozze

wed'ding invita'tion *s* invito a nozze

wed'ding march' *s* marcia nuziale

wed'ding ring' *s* fede *f*, vera

wedge [wedʒ] *s* cuneo; (*of pie*) spicchio; (*to split wood*) bietta; (*to hold a wheel*) scarpa || *tr* incuneare

wed'lock *s* matrimonio

Wednesday ['wenzdi] *s* mercoledì *m*

wee [wi] *adj* piccolo piccolo

weed [wid] *s* malerba, erbaccia; (coll) sigaretta; (slang) marijuana; **weeds** vestito da lutto, gramaglie *fpl* || *tr* sarchiare, mondare

weeder ['widər] *s* (agr) estirpatore *m*

weed'ing hoe' *s* sarchio, zappa

weed'-kill'er *s* diserbante *m*

week [wik] *s* settimana; **week in, week out** una settimana dopo l'altra

week'day' *s* giorno feriale

week'end' *s* fine-settimana *m*, fine *f* di settimana, week-end *m* || *intr* passare il fine-settimana

week·ly ['wikli] *adj* settimanale || *s* (-**lies**) settimanale *m* || *adv* settimanalmente

weep [wip] *v* (*pret & pp* **wept** [wept]) *tr* piangere; **to weep oneself to sleep** addormentarsi piangendo; **to weep one's eyes out** piangere a calde lacrime || *intr* piangere; **to weep for joy** piangere di gioia

weeper ['wipər] *s* piagnone *m*; (*hired mourner*) prefica

weep'ing wil'low *s* salice *m* piangente

weep·y ['wipi] *adj* (-**ier;** -**iest**) piangente, lacrimoso

weevil ['wivəl] *s* curculione *m*

weft [weft] *s* (*yarns running across warp*) trama; (*fabric*) tela, tessuto

weigh [we] *tr* pesare; (*anchor*) levare; (*to make heavy*) appesantire; (fig) soppesare, ponderare; **to weigh down** piegare || *intr* pesare; gravitare; **to weigh in** (sports) pesarsi; **to weigh upon** gravare a

weigh'bridge' *s* stadera

weight [wet] *s* peso; (fig) peso; **to carry weight** aver del peso; **to lose weight** diminuire di peso; **to put on weight** crescere di peso; **to throw**

one's weight around far sentire la propria importanza || *tr* appesantire; (*statistically*) ponderare, dare un certo peso a

weightless ['wetlɪs] *adj* senza peso, imponderabile

weightlessness ['wetlɪsnɪs] *s* imponderabilità *f*

weight·y ['weti] *adj* (-ier; -iest) pesante; importante

weir [wɪr] *s* sbarramento; (*for catching fish*) pescaia

weird [wɪrd] *adj* soprannaturale, misterioso; strano, bizzarro

welcome ['wɛlkəm] *adj* benvenuto; gradito; **you are welcome** (*i.e., gladly received*) sia il benvenuto; (*in answer to thanks*) prego; **you are welcome to it** è a Sua disposizione; **you are welcome to your opinion** pensi come la vuole || *s* benvenuto || *tr* dare il benvenuto a; accettare; gradire || *interj* benvenuto!

weld [wɛld] *s* saldatura autogena; (bot) guaderella || *tr* saldare || *intr* saldarsi

welder ['wɛldər] *s* saldatore *m*; (*machine*) saldatrice *f*

welding ['wɛldɪŋ] *s* saldatura autogena

wel'fare' *s* benessere *m*; (*effort to improve living conditions*) beneficenza, assistenza; **to be on welfare** ricevere assistenza pubblica

wel'fare state' *s* stato sociale or assistenziale

well [wɛl] *adj* bene; in buona salute || *s* pozzo; (*for ink*) pozzetto, serbatoio; (*spring*) sorgente *f*; (*shaft for stairs*) tromba || *adv* bene; **as well** pure; **as well ... as** tanto ... come; **as well as** tanto come, non meno che || *intr* —**to well up** sgorgare || *interj* beh!; bene!; allora!, dunque!

well-appointed ['wɛlə'pɔɪntɪd] *adj* ben ammobiliato

well-attended ['wɛlə'tɛndɪd] *adj* molto frequentato

well-behaved ['wɛlbɪ'hevd] *adj* beneducato; **to be well-behaved** comportarsi bene

well'-be'ing *s* benessere *m*

well'born' *adj* bennato

well-bred ['wɛl'brɛd] *adj* educato, costumato

well-disposed ['wɛldɪs'pozd] *adj* bendisposto

well-done ['wɛl'dʌn] *adj* benfatto; (*meat*) ben cotto

well-fixed ['wɛl'fɪkst] *adj* (coll) agiato, abbiente

well-formed ['wɛl'fɔrmd] *adj* benfatto

well-founded ['wɛl'faundɪd] *adj* fondato

well-groomed ['wɛl'grumd] *adj* (*person*) curato; (*horse*) ben governato

well-heeled ['wɛl'hild] *adj* (coll) agiato, benestante

well-informed ['wɛlɪn'fɔrmd] *adj* bene informato

well-intentioned ['wɛlɪn'tɛnʃənd] *adj* benintenzionato

well'-kept' *adj* ben conservato; (*person*) benportante; (*secret*) ben mantenuto

well-known ['wɛl'non] *adj* notorio, ben noto

well-meaning ['wɛl'minɪŋ] *adj* benevolo, benintenzionato

well-nigh ['wɛl'naɪ] *adv* quasi

well'-off' *adj* agiato, benestante

well-preserved ['wɛlprɪ'zʌrvd] *adj* ben conservato; (*person*) benportante

well-read ['wɛl'rɛd] *adj* colto, che ha letto molto

well-spoken ['wɛl'spokən] *adj* (*person*) raffinato nel parlare; (*word*) a proposito

well'spring' *s* sorgente *f*

well' sweep' *s* mazzacavallo del pozzo

well-tempered ['wɛl'tɛmpərd] *adj* ben temperato

well-thought-of ['wɛl'θɔt,ʌv] *adj* tenuto in alta considerazione

well-timed ['wɛl'taɪmd] *adj* opportuno

well-to-do ['wɛltə'du] *adj* benestante

well-wisher ['wɛl'wɪʃər] *s* amico, sostenitore *m*

well-worn ['wɛl'worn] *adj* (*clothing*) liso, consunto, trito; (*argument*) logoro, banale; portato con eleganza

welsh [wɛlʃ] *intr* —**to welsh on** (*a promise*) (slang) mancare a; (*a person*) (slang) fregare || **Welsh** *adj & s* gallese *mf*; **the Welsh** i gallesi

Welsh'man *s* (-men) gallese *m*

Welsh' rab'bit or **rare'bit** ['rɛrbɪt] *s* fonduta fatta con la birra servita su pane abbrustolito

welt [wɛlt] *s* (*finish along a seam*) costa; (*of shoe*) guardolo; (*wale from a blow*) riga, sferzata

welter ['wɛltər] *s* guazzabuglio; confusione; (*a tumbling about*) rotolio || *intr* rotolarsi, guazzare

wel'ter-weight' *s* (boxing) peso welter, peso medio-leggero

wench [wɛntʃ] *s* ragazza, giovane *f*

wend [wɛnd] *tr* —**to wend one's way** dirigere i propri passi

werewolf ['wɪr,wulf] *s* lupo mannaro

west [wɛst] *adj* occidentale || *s* ovest *m*, occidente *m* || *adv* verso l'ovest

western ['wɛstərn] *adj* occidentale || *s* western *m*

West' In'dies ['ɪndiz] *spl* Indie *fpl* Occidentali

westward ['wɛstwərd] *adv* verso l'ovest

wet [wɛt] *adj* (wetter; wettest) bagnato; (*paint*) fresco; (*damp*) umido; (*rainy*) piovoso; che permette la vendita delle bevande alcoliche || *s* umidità *f*; antiproibizionista *mf* || *v* (pret & pp wet or wetted; ger wetting) *tr* bagnare || *intr* bagnarsi

wet' blan'ket *s* guastafeste *mf*

wether ['wɛðər] *s* castrone *m*

wet' nurse' *s* nutrice *f*, balia

whack [hwæk] *s* (slang) colpo, percossa; (slang) prova, tentativo || *tr* (slang) percuotere

whale [hwel] *s* balena; **a whale of** (slang) gigantesco, e.g., **a whale of a lie** una bugia gigantesca; enorme, e.g., **a whale of a difference** una differenza enorme || *tr* (coll) battere || *intr* pescare balene

whale'bone' *s* osso di balena, fanone *m*

wharf [hwɔrf] *s* (**wharves** [hwɔrvz] or **wharfs**) molo

what [hwɑt] *adj interr* che; quale || *adj rel* quello . . . che; il . . . che, e.g., **wear what tie you prefer** mettiti la cravatta che preferisci || *pron interr* che; quale; **what else?** che altro?; **what if** . . . ? e se . . . ?; **what of it?** e che me ne importa? || *pron rel* quello che; **what's what** (coll) tutta la situazione || *interj* **what a** . . . ! che . . . !, e.g., **what a beautiful day!** che splendida giornata!

what•ev'er *adj* qualsiasi; qualunque || *pron* quanto; che; quello che

what'not' *s* scaffaletto

wheal [hwil] *s* vescichetta

wheat [hwit] *s* grano, frumento

wheedle ['hwidəl] *tr* adulare; persuadere con lusinghe; (*money*) spillare

wheel [hwil] *s* ruota; (*of cheese*) forma; (coll) bicicletta; **at the wheel** al volante; **in controllo** || *tr* roteare; portare in carrozzella || *intr* girare

wheelbarrow ['hwil ,bæro] *s* carriola

wheel'base' *s* passo

wheel'chair' *s* carrozzella

wheel' col'umn *s* (aut) piantone *m* di guida

wheeler-dealer ['hwilər'dilər] *s* (slang) grande affarista *m*

wheel' horse' *s* cavallo di timone; lavoratore *m* di fiducia

wheelwright ['hwil ,raɪt] *s* carradore *m*

wheeze [hwiz] *s* affanno; (pathol) rantolo || *intr* respirare affannosamente; (pathol) rantolare

whelp [hwelp] *s* cucciolo || *tr & intr* figliare, partorire

when [hwen] *adv & conj* quando

whence [hwens] *adv* donde, di dove || *conj* donde; per che ragione

when•ev'er *conj* ogniqualvolta, qualora

where [hwer] *adv & conj* dove

whereabouts ['hwerə ,baʊts] *s* luogo dove uno si trova || *adv & conj* dove

whereas [hwer'æz] *conj* mentre; visto che, considerato che

where•by' *adv* per cui, col quale

wherever [hwer'evər] *adv* dove mai || *conj* dovunque

wherefore ['hwerfor] *s* perché *m* || *adv* perché || *conj* per cui, percome

where•from' *adv* donde

where•in' *adv* dove; in che modo || *conj* dove; nel quale

where•of' *adv* di che || *conj* di che; del quale

where•upon' *adv* sul che; laonde, dopodiché

wherewithal ['hwerwɪð ,ɔl] *s* mezzi *mpl*

whet [hwet] *v* (*pret & pp* **whetted;** *ger* **whetting**) *tr* affilare; (*the appetite*) aguzzare

whether ['weðər] *conj* se; **whether or no** ad ogni modo, in ogni caso; **whether or not** . . . o che non

whet'stone' *s* pietra da affilare

whey [hwe] *s* scotta

which [hwɪtʃ] *adj interr* quale || *adj rel* il (la, etc.) quale || *pron interr* che; quale; **which is which** qual'è

l'uno e qual'è l'altro || *pron rel* **che;** il quale; quello che

which•ev'er *adj & pron rel,* qualunque

whiff [hwɪf] *s* (*of air*) soffio; fiutata; (*trace of odor*) zaffata; **to get a whiff of** sentire l'odore di || *intr* soffiare; (*said of a smoker*) dare boccate

while [hwaɪl] *s* tempo; **a long while** un bel pezzo; **a while ago** un tratto fa; **to be worth one's while** valere la pena || *conj* mentre || *tr*—**to while away** passare piacevolmente

whim [hwɪm] *s* capriccio, estro

whimper ['hwɪmpər] *s* piagnucolio || *tr & intr* piagnucolare

whimsical ['hwɪmzɪkəl] *adj* capriccioso, estroso, stravagante

whine [hwaɪn] *s* (*of dog*) guaito; (*of person*) piagnucolio || *intr* (*said of a dog*) guaire, uggiolare; (*said of a person*) piagnucolare

whin•ny ['hwɪnɪ] *s* (**-nies**) nitrito || *v* (*pret & pp* **-nied**) *intr* nitrire

whip [hwɪp] *s* frusta; uova *fpl* sbattute con frutta || *v* (*pret & pp* **whipped** or **whipt;** *ger* **whipping**) *tr* frustare, battere; (*eggs*) frullare; (coll) vincere, sconfiggere; **to whip off** (coll) buttar giù; **to whip out** tirar fuori rapidamente; **to whip up** (coll) preparare in quattro e quattr'otto; (coll) eccitare, incitare

whip'cord' *s* cordino della frusta; (*fabric*) saia a diagonale

whip' hand' *s* mano che tiene la frusta; vantaggio, posizione vantaggiosa

whip'lash' *s* scudisciata

whipped' cream' *s* panna montata

whipper-snapper ['hwɪpər ,snæpər] *s* pivello

whippet ['hwɪpɪt] *s* piccolo levriere

whip'ping boy' ['hwɪpɪŋ] *s* testa di turco

whip'ping post' *s* palo per la fustigazione

whippoorwill [,hwɪpər'wɪl] *s* caprimulgo, succiacapre *m*

whir [hwʌr] *s* ronzio || *v* (*pret & pp* **whirred;** *ger* **whirring**) *intr* ronzare; volare ronzando

whirl [hwʌrl] *s* giro improvviso; corsa; mulinello; (fig) successione || *tr & intr* mulinare; **my head whirls** mi gira la testa

whirligig ['hwʌrlɪ ,gɪg] *s* turbine *m;* (*carrousel*) giostra; (*toy*) girandola; (ent) ragno d'acqua

whirl'pool' *s* risucchio, mulinello

whirl'wind' *s* turbine *m*, tromba d'aria

whirlybird ['hwʌrli ,bʌrd] *s* (coll) elicottero

whish [hwɪʃ] *s* fruscio || *intr* frusciare

whisk [hwɪsk] *s* scopatina || *tr* scopare, spolverare; (*eggs*) sbattere; **to whisk out of sight** far sparire || *intr* guizzare

whisk' broom' *s* scopetta per i vestiti, spolverino

whiskers ['hwɪskərz] *spl* barba; (*on side of man's face*) basette *fpl;* (*of cat*) baffi *mpl*

whiskey ['hwɪski] *s* whisky *m*

whisper ['hwɪspər] s sussurro, bisbiglio, mormorio; **in a whisper** in un sussurro ‖ *tr & intr* sussurrare, bisbigliare, mormorare

whisperer ['hwɪspərər] s sussurrone m

whispering ['hwɪspərɪŋ] adj di maldicenze ‖ s sussurro; maldicenza

whistle ['hwɪsəl] s fischio; **to wet one's whistle** (coll) bagnarsi l'ugola ‖ *tr* fischiare ‖ *intr* fischiare, zufolare; **to whistle for** chiamare con un fischio; (money) aspettare in vano

whis'tle stop' s stazioncina, paesetto

whit [hwɪt] s—**not a whit** niente affatto

white [hwaɪt] adj bianco ‖ s bianco; **whites** (pathol) leucorrea

white'cap' s frangente m, cavallone m, onda crespa

white' coal' s carbone bianco

white'-col'lar adj impiegatizio

white' feath'er s—**to show the white feather** mostrarsi vile

white' goods' spl biancheria da casa; articoli mpl di cotone; apparecchi mpl elettrodomestici

white-haired ['hwaɪt,herd] adj dai capelli bianchi; (coll) favorito

white' heat' s calor bianco

white' lead' [led] s biacca

white' lie' s bugia innocente

white' meat' s bianco, carne f del petto

whiten ['hwaɪtən] tr imbiancare, sbiancare ‖ intr imbiancarsi, sbiancarsi; impallidire

whiteness ['hwaɪtnɪs] s bianchezza

white' plague' s tubercolosi f

white' slav'ery s tratta delle bianche

white' tie' s cravatta da frac; marsina, abito da cerimonia

white'wash' s imbiancatura; (fig) copertura ‖ tr imbiancare, intonacare; (fig) coprire

white' wa'ter lil'y s ninfea

whither ['hwɪθər] adv dove, a che luogo ‖ conj dove

whiting ['hwaɪtɪŋ] s (ichth) nasello; (ichth) merlango

whitish ['hwaɪtɪʃ] adj biancastro

whitlow ['hwɪtlo] s patereccio

Whitsuntide ['hwɪtsən,taɪd] s settimana di Pentecoste

whittle ['hwɪtəl] tr digrossare; **to whittle away** or **down** ridurre gradualmente

whiz or **whizz** [hwɪz] s sibilo; (coll) asso ‖ v (pret & pp **whizzed**; ger **whizzing**) intr—**to whiz by** passare sibilando; passare come una freccia

who [hu] pron interr chi; **who else?** chi altri?; **who goes there?** (mil) chi va là?; **who's who** chi è l'uno e chi è l'altro; chi è la gente importante ‖ pron rel chi; il quale

whoa [hwo] or [wo] interj fermo!

who•ev'er pron rel chiunque

whole [hol] adj tutto, intero; sano, intatto; **made out of the whole cloth** completamente immaginario ‖ s tutto; **as a whole** nell'insieme; **on the whole** in generale

wholehearted ['hol,hɑrtɪd] adj molto sincero, generoso

whole' note' s (mus) semibreve f

whole'sale' adj & adv all'ingrosso ‖ s ingrosso ‖ tr vendere all'ingrosso ‖ intr vendersi all'ingrosso

wholesaler ['hol,selər] s grossista mf

wholesome ['holsəm] adj (beneficial) salutare; (in good health) sano

wholly ['holi] adv interamente

whom [hum] pron interr chi ‖ pron rel che; il quale

whom•ev'er pron rel chiunque

whoop [hup] or [hwup] s urlo; (pathol) urlo della pertosse; **to not be worth a whoop** (coll) non valere un fico secco ‖ tr—**to whoop it up** (slang) fare il diavolo a quattro ‖ intr urlare

whoop'ing cough' ['hupɪŋ] or ['hwup-ɪŋ] s pertosse f

whopper ['hwɑpər] s (coll) enormità f; (coll) fandonia, bugia enorme

whopping ['hwɑpɪŋ] adj (coll) enorme

whore [hor] s puttana ‖ intr—**to whore around** puttaneggiare; andare a puttane

whortleber•ry ['hwʌrtəl,beri] s (-ries) mirtillo

whose [huz] pron interr di chi ‖ pron rel di chi; del quale; di cui

why [hwaɪ] s (whys) perché m; **the whys and the wherefores** il perché e il percome ‖ adv perché ‖ interj diamine!; **why, certainly!** certamente!; **why, yes!** evidentemente!

wick [wɪk] s stoppino, lucignolo

wicked ['wɪkɪd] adj malvagio; (mischievous) cattivo; (dreadful) terribile, bestiale

wicker ['wɪkər] adj di vimini ‖ s vimine m

wicket ['wɪkɪt] s (small door) portello; (ticket window) sportello; (of a canal) chiusa; (cricket) porta; (croquet) archetto

wide [waɪd] adj largo; esteso; (eyes) aperto; (sense of a word) lato ‖ adv largamente; completamente; lontano; **wide of the mark** lontano dal bersaglio

wide'-an'gle adj grandangolare

wide'-awake' adj sveglio

widen ['waɪdən] tr slargare, estendere ‖ intr slargarsi, estendersi

wide'-o'pen adj spalancato; (to a gambler) accessibile

wide'-spread' adj (e.g., arms) aperto; diffuso

widow ['wɪdo] s vedova; (cards) morto ‖ tr lasciar vedova

widower ['wɪdo•ər] s vedovo

widowhood ['wɪdo,hud] s vedovanza

wid'ow's mite' s obolo della vedova

wid'ow's weeds' spl gramaglie fpl vedovili

width [wɪdθ] s larghezza

wield [wild] tr (e.g., a sword) brandire; (e.g., a hammer) maneggiare; (power) esercitare

wife [waɪf] s (wives [waɪvz]) moglie f

wig [wɪg] s parrucca

wiggle ['wɪgəl] s dimenio; (of fish)

guizzo || *tr* dimenare || *intr* dimenarsi; guizzare

wig'wag' *s* segnalazione con bandierine || *v* (*pret* & *pp* **-wagged;** *ger* **-wagging**) *tr* & *intr* segnalare con bandierine

wigwam ['wɪgwɑm] *s* tenda a cupola dei pellirosse, wigwam *m*

wild [waɪld] *adj* (*animal*) feroce; (*e.g., berry*) selvatico; (*barbarous*) selvaggio; (*violent*) furioso; (*mad*) pazzo; (*unruly*) discolo, indisciplinato; (*extravagant*) pazzesco; (*shot or throw*) lanciato all'impazzata; **wild about** pazzo per || *s* regione deserta; **the wild** la foresta; **wilds** regioni selvagge || *adv* pazzamente; **to go wild** andare in delirio; **to run wild** crescere all'impazzata; correre senza freno

wild' boar' *s* cinghiale *m*

wild' card' *s* matta

wild'cat' *s* gatto selvatico; lince *f;* impresa arrischiata || *v* (*pret* & *pp* **-catted;** *ger* **-catting**) *tr* & *intr* esplorare per conto proprio

wild'cat strike' *s* sciopero non autorizzato dal sindacato

wilderness ['wɪldərnɪs] *s* deserto

wild-eyed ['waɪld ,aɪd] *adj* stralunato; (*scheme*) pazzesco

wild'fire' *s* fuoco greco; fuoco fatuo; **to spread like wildfire** crescere come la gramigna; (*said of news*) spargersi come il baleno

wild' flow'er *s* fiore *m* di campo

wild' goose' *s* oca selvatica

wild'-goose' chase' *s* ricerca della luna nel pozzo

wild'life' *s* animali *spl* selvatici

wild' oat' *s* avena selvatica; **to sow one's wild oats** correre la cavallina

wild' ol'ive *s* olivastro, oleastro

wile [waɪl] *s* stratagemma *m*, inganno; (*cunning*) astuzia || *tr* allettare; **to wile away** passare piacevolmente

will [wɪl] *s* volontà *f,* volere *m;* (*law*) testamento; **at will** a volontà || *tr* volere; (*law*) legare || *intr* volere; **do as you will** faccia come vuole || *v* (*pret* & *cond* **would**) *aux* **she will leave tomorrow** partirà domani; **a cactus plant will live two months without water** una pianta grassa può vivere due mesi senz'acqua

willful ['wɪlfəl] *adj* volontario; ostinato

willfulness ['wɪlfəlnɪs] *s* volontarietà *f;* ostinatezza

William ['wɪljəm] *s* Guglielmo

willing ['wɪlɪŋ] *adj* volonteroso; **to be willing** essere disposto

willingly ['wɪlɪŋli] *adv* di buon grado, volentieri

willingness ['wɪlɪŋnɪs] *s* buona voglia, propensione

will-o'-the-wisp ['wɪləðə'wɪsp] *s* fuoco fatuo; (*fig*) illusione, chimera

willow ['wɪlo] *s* salice *m*

willowy ['wɪlo·i] *adj* pieghevole; (*slender*) snello; pieno di giunchi

will' pow'er *s* forza di volontà

willy-nilly ['wɪlɪ'nɪli] *adv* volente o nolente

wilt [wɪlt] *tr* far appassire || *intr* appassire, avvizzire

wil·y ['waɪli] *adj* (**-ier; -iest**) astuto, scaltro

wimple ['wɪmpəl] *s* soggolo

win [wɪn] *s* vittoria, vincita || *v* (*pret* & *pp* **won** [wʌn]; *ger* **winning**) *tr* & *intr* guadagnare; **to win out** vincere, aver successo

wince [wɪns] *s* sussulto || *intr* sussultare

winch [wɪntʃ] *s* verricello; (*handle*) manovella; (naut) mollinello

wind [wɪnd] *s* vento; (*gas in intestines*) vento; (*breath*) fiato, tenuta; **to break wind** scoreggiare; **to get wind of** subodorare; **to sail close to the wind** (naut) andare all'orza; **to take the wind out of the sails of** sconcertare; **winds** (mus) fiati *mpl* || *tr* far perdere il fiato a || [waɪnd] *v* (*pret* & *pp* **wound** [waʊnd]) *tr* (*to wrap up*) arrotolare; (*thread, wool*) dipanare, aggomitolare; (*a clock*) caricare; (*a handle*) far girare; **to wind one's way through** serpeggiare per; **to wind up** arrotolare; eccitare; finire, portare a termine || *intr* serpeggiare, snodarsi

windbag ['wɪnd ,bæg] *s* (*of a bagpipe*) otre *m;* (fig) parolaio, otre *m* di vento

windbreak ['wɪnd ,brek] *s* frangivento

wind' cone' [wɪnd] *s* manica a vento

winded ['wɪndɪd] *adj* senza fiato

windfall ['wɪnd ,fɔl] *s* frutta abbattuta dal vento; provvidenza, manna del cielo

wind'ing sheet' ['waɪndɪŋ] *s* lenzuolo funebre

wind'ing stairs' ['waɪndɪŋ] *spl* scala a chiocciola

wind' in'strument [wɪnd] *s* (mus) strumento a fiato

windlass ['wɪndləs] *s* verricello

windmill ['wɪnd ,mɪl] *s* mulino a vento; (*air turbine*) aeromotore *m;* **to tilt at windmills** combattere i mulini a vento

window ['wɪndo] *s* finestra; (*of ticket office*) sportello; (*of car or coach*) finestrino

win'dow dress'er *s* vetrinista *mf*

win'dow dress'ing *s* vetrinistica; (fig) facciata, apparenza

win'dow en'velope *s* busta a finestrella

win'dow frame' *s* intelaiatura della finestra

win'dow-pane' *s* vetro, invetriata

win'dow sash' *s* intelaiatura della finestra

win'dow screen' *s* zanzariera

win'dow shade' *s* tendina avvolgibile

win'dow-shop' *v* (*pret* & *pp* **-shopped;** *ger* **-shopping**) *intr* guardare nelle vetrine senza comprare

win'dow sill' *s* davanzale *m* della finestra

windpipe ['wɪnd ,paɪp] *s* trachea

windproof ['wɪnd ,pruf] *adj* resistente al vento

windshield ['wɪnd ,ʃild] *s* parabrezza *m*

wind'shield wash'er *s* lavacristallo

wind'shield wip'er s tergicristallo
windsock ['wɪnd,sɑk] s (aer) manica a vento
windstorm ['wɪnd,stɔrm] s bufera di vento
wind' tun'nel [wɪnd] s (aer) galleria aerodinamica
wind-up ['waɪnd,ʌp] s conclusione
windward ['wɪndwərd] s orza, sopravvento; **to turn to windward** mettersi al sopravvento
Wind'ward Is'lands spl Isole fpl Sopravvento
wind•y ['wɪndi] adj (-ier; -iest) ventoso; verboso, ampolloso; **it is windy** fa vento
wine [waɪn] s vino || tr offrire vino a || intr bere del vino
wine' cel'lar s cantina
wine'glass' s bicchiere da vino
winegrower ['waɪn,groʊ•ər] s vinificatore m, viticoltore m
wine' press' s torchio per l'uva
winer•y ['waɪnəri] s (-ies) stabilimento vinicolo
wine'shop' s fiaschetteria
wine'skin' s otre m
wine' stew'ard s sommelier m
winetaster ['waɪn,testər] s degustatore m di vini
wing [wɪŋ] s ala; (unit of air force) aerobrigata; (theat) quinta; **to take wing** levarsi a volo; **under one's wing** sotto la protezione di qlcu || tr ferire nell'ala; **to wing one's way** volare, portarsi a volo
wing' chair' s poltrona a orecchioni
wing' col'lar s colletto per marsina
wing' nut' s (mach) galletto
wing'span' s (of airplane) apertura alare
wing'spread' s (of bird) apertura alare
wink [wɪŋk] s ammicco; **in a wink** in un batter d'occhio; **to not sleep a wink** non chiudere occhio; **to take forty winks** (coll) schiacciare un pisolino || tr (the eye) strizzare || intr ammiccare, strizzare l'occhio; (to blink) battere le ciglia; **to wink at** ammiccare a; far finta di non vedere
winner ['wɪnər] s vincitore m
winning ['wɪnɪŋ] adj vincente, vincitore; attraente, simpatico || **winnings** spl vincita
winnow ['wɪno] tr ventilare, brezzare; (fig) vagliare || intr svolazzare
winsome ['wɪnsəm] adj attraente
winter ['wɪntər] adj invernale || s inverno || intr svernare
win'ter-green' s tè m del Canadà; olio di gaulteria
win•try ['wɪntri] adj (-trier; -triest) invernale; freddo
wipe [waɪp] tr forbire, detergere; (to dry) asciugare; **to wipe away** (tears) asciugare; **to wipe off** pulire, forbire; **to wipe out** distruggere completamente; (coll) eliminare
wiper ['waɪpər] s strofinaccio; (mach) camma; (elec) contatto scorrevole
wire [waɪr] s filo metallico; telegramma m; (coll) telegrafo; **to pull wires** manovrare di dietro le quinte

|| tr legare con filo metallico; attrezzare l'elettricità in; (coll) mandare per telegrafo; (coll) telegrafare || intr (coll) telegrafare
wire' cut'ter s pinza tagliafili
wire' entan'glement s reticolato di filo spinato
wire' gauge' s calibro da fili
wire-haired ['waɪr,herd] adj a pelo ruvido
wireless ['waɪrlɪs] adj senza fili || s telegrafo senza fili; telegrafia senza fili
wire' nail' s chiodo da falegname
wirepulling ['waɪr,pʊlɪŋ] s manovra dietro alle quinte
wire' record'er s magnetofono a filo
wire' screen' s rete metallica
wire'tap' v (pret & pp -tapped; ger -tapping) tr (a conversation) intercettare
wiring ['waɪrɪŋ] s sistema m di fili elettrici
wir•y ['waɪri] adj (-ier; -iest) fatto di filo; (hair) ispido; (tone) metallico, vibrante; (sinewy) segaligno
wisdom ['wɪzdəm] s senno, sapienza, saggezza
wis'dom tooth' s dente m del giudizio
wise [waɪz] adj saggio, sapiente; (decision) giudizioso; **to be wise to** (slang) accorgersi del gioco di; **to get wise** (slang) mangiare la foglia; (slang) diventare impertinente || s modo, maniera; **in no wise** in nessun modo || tr—**to wise up** (slang) avvertire || intr—**to wise up** (slang) accorgersi
wiseacre ['waɪz,ekər] s sapientone m
wise'crack' s (coll) spiritosaggine f || intr (coll) dire spiritosaggini
wise' guy' s (slang) sputasentenze m
wish [wɪʃ] s desiderio; augurio; **to make a wish** formulare un desiderio || tr desiderare; augurare; **to wish s.o. a good day** dare il buon giorno a qlcu || intr desiderare; **to wish for** desiderare
wish'bone' s forcella
wishful ['wɪʃfəl] adj desideroso
wish'ful think'ing s pio desiderio
wistful ['wɪstfəl] adj melanconico, pensoso, meditabondo
wit [wɪt] s spirito; (person) bellospirito; (understanding) senso; **to be at one's wits' end** non sapere a che santo votarsi; **to have one's wits about one** avere presenza di spirito; **to live by one's wits** vivere di espedienti
witch [wɪtʃ] s strega
witch'craft' s stregoneria
witch' doc'tor s stregone m
witch'es' Sab'bath s sabba m
witch' ha'zel s (shrub) amamelide f; (liquid) estratto di amamelide
witch' hunt' s caccia alle streghe
with [wɪð] or [wɪθ] prep con; a, e.g., **with open arms** a braccia aperte; di, e.g., **covered with silk** coperto di seta; **to be satisfied with the performance** essere contento della rappresentazione; da, e.g., **with the In-**

dians dagli indiani; **to part with** separarsi da

with-draw' v (pret **-drew**; pp **-drawn**) tr ritirare || intr ritirarsi

withdrawal [wɪð'drɔə-əl] or [wɪθ'drɔ-əl] s ritiro, ritirata; (of funds) prelevamento

wither ['wɪðər] tr intisichire; (with a glance) incenerire || intr avvizzire, intisichire

with-hold' v (pret & pp **-held**) tr trattenere; (information) sottacere; (payment) defalcare; (permission) negare

withhold'ing tax' s imposta trattenuta

with-in' adv dentro, didentro || prep entro, entro di, dentro a, dentro di; fra; in; (a time period) nel giro di

with-out' adv fuori || prep senza; fuori, fuori di; **to do without** fare a meno di; **without + ger** senza + inf, e.g., **without saying a word** senza dire una parola; senza che + subj, e.g., **she fell without helping her** cadde senza che nessuno l'aiutasse

with-stand' v (pret & pp **-stood**) tr resistere (with dat), reggere (with dat)

witness ['wɪtnɪs] s testimone mf; **in witness whereof** in fé di che; **to bear witness** far fede || tr (to be present at) presenziare; (to attest) testimoniare, firmare come testimone

wit'ness stand' s banco dei testimoni

witticism ['wɪtɪ sɪzəm] s motto, battuta spiritosa, spiritosaggine f

wittingly ['wɪtɪŋli] adv consapevolmente

wit-ty ['wɪti] adj (-tier; -tiest) spiritoso, divertente

wizard ['wɪzərd] s mago

wizardry ['wɪzərdri] s magia

wizened ['wɪzənd] adj raggrinzito

woad [wod] s (bot) guado

wobble ['wɑbəl] s oscillazione, dondolio || intr oscillare, dondolare; (said of a chair) zoppicare; (fig) titubare

wob-bly ['wɑbli] adj (-blier; -bliest) oscillante, zoppo, malfermo

woe [wo] s disgrazia, afflizione, sventura; || interj—**woe is me!** ahimè!

woebegone ['wobɪ gɑn] or ['wobɪ gɑn] adj triste, abbattuto

woeful ['wofəl] adj sfortunato, disgraziato; (of poor quality) orribile

wolf [wʊlf] s (wolves [wʊlvz]) lupo; (coll) dongiovanni m; **to cry wolf** gridare al lupo; **to keep the wolf from the door** tener lontana la miseria || tr & intr mangiare come un lupo

wolf'hound' s cane m da pastore alsaziano

wolfram ['wʊlfrəm] s wolframio

wolf's-bane or **wolfsbane** ['wʊlfs ben] s (bot) aconito

wolverine [wʊlvə'rin] s (zool) ghiottone m

woman ['wʊmən] s (women ['wɪmɪn]) donna

womanhood ['wʊmən hʊd] s (quality) femminilità f; (women collectively) donne fpl, sesso femminile

womanish ['wʊmənɪʃ] adj femminile; (effeminate) effeminato

wom'an-kind' s sesso femminile

womanly ['wʊmənli] adj (-lier; -liest) femminile, muliebre

wom'an suf'frage s suffragio alle donne

woman-suffragist ['wʊmən 'sʌfrədʒɪst] s suffragista mf

womb [wum] s utero; (fig) seno

womenfolk ['wɪmɪn fok] spl le donne

wonder ['wʌndər] s (something strange and surprising) meraviglia; (feeling) ammirazione; (miracle) prodigio, miracolo; **for a wonder** cosa strana; **no wonder that** non fa meraviglia che; **to work wonders** fare miracoli || tr—**to wonder that** meravigliarsi che; **to wonder how, if, when, where, who, why** domandarsi or chiedersi come, se, quando, dove, chi, perché || intr meravigliarsi; chiedersi; **to wonder at** ammirare

won'der drug' s medicina miracolosa

wonderful ['wʌndərfəl] adj meraviglioso

won'der-land' s paese m delle meraviglie

wonderment ['wʌndərmənt] s sorpresa, meraviglia, stupore m

won'der-work'er s taumaturgo

wont [wʌnt] or [wɔnt] adj abituato, solito || s abitudine f, costume m

wonted ['wʌntɪd] or ['wɔntɪd] adj solito, abituale

woo [wu] tr (a woman) corteggiare; (to seek to win) allettare; (good or bad consequences) andare in cerca di

wood [wʊd] s legno; (firewood) legna; (keg) barile m; **out of the woods** fuori pericolo; al sicuro; **woods** bosco, selva

woodbine ['wʊd baɪn] s (honeysuckle) abbracciabosco; (Virginia creeper) vite f del Canadà

wood' carv'ing s intaglio in legno, statua in legno

wood'chuck' s marmotta americana

wood'cock' s beccaccia

wood'cut' s silografia

wood'cut'ter s boscaiolo

wooded ['wʊdɪd] adj legnoso, boschivo

wooden ['wʊdən] adj di legno; duro, rigido; inespressivo

wood' engrav'ing s silografia

wooden-headed ['wʊdən hɛdɪd] adj (coll) dalla testa dura

wood'en leg' s gamba di legno

wood'en shoe' s zoccolo

wood' grouse' s gallo cedrone

woodland ['wʊdlənd] adj boschivo || s foresta, bosco

wood'man s (-men) boscaiolo

woodpecker ['wʊd pɛkər] s picchio

wood'pile' s legnaia

wood' screw' s vite f per legno

wood'shed' s legnaia

woods'man s (-men) abitatore m dei boschi; boscaiolo

wood'wind' s strumento a fiato di legno

wood'work' s lavoro in legno; parti fpl di legno

wood'work'er s ebanista m, falegname m

wood'worm' s tarlo

wood-y ['wudi] *adj* (**-ier; -iest**) bo-scoso, alberato; (*like wood*) legnoso

wooer ['wu-ər] *s* corteggiatore *m*

woof [wuf] *s* (*yarns running across warp*) trama; (*fabric*) tessuto

woofer ['wufər] *s* altoparlante *m* per basse audiofrequenze, woofer *m*

wool [wul] *s* lana

woolen ['wulən] *adj* di lana || *s* tessuto di lana; **woolens** laneria

woolgrower ['wul‚gro·ər] *s* allevatore *m* di pecore

wool-ly ['wuli] *adj* (**-ier; -iest**) di lana; lanoso; (*coll*) confuso

word [wʌrd] *s* parola; **by word of mouth** oralmente; **to be as good as one's word** essere di parola; **to have a word with** dire quattro parole a; **to have word from** aver notizie da; **to keep one's word** essere di parola; **to leave word** lasciar detto; **to send word that** mandare a dire che; **words** (*quarrel*) baruffa || *tr* esprimere, formulare || **Word** *s* (theol) Verbo

word' count' *s* conto lessicale

word' forma'tion *s* formazione delle parole

wording ['wʌrdɪŋ] *s* fraseologia, dicitura

word' or'der *s* disposizione delle parole in una frase

word'stock' *s* lessico

word-y ['wʌrdi] *adj* (**-ier; -iest**) verboso, parolaio

work [wʌrk] *s* lavoro; (*of art, fortification, etc.*) opera; **at work** al lavoro, in ufficio; (*in operation*) in servizio; **out of work** sen a lavoro, disoccupato; **to give s.o. the works** (slang) trattare male; (slang) ammazzare; **to shoot the works** (slang) scialare; **works** opificio; meccanismo; (*of clock*) castello || *tr* far funzionare; lavorare, maneggiare; (*e.g., a miracle*) operare; (*e.g., iron*) trattare; **to work up** preparare; stimulare, eccitare || *intr* lavorare; (*said of a machine*) funzionare; (*said of a remedy*) avere effetto; **to work loose** sciogliersi; **to work out** andare a finire; (*said of a problem*) sciogliersi; (*said of a total*) ammontare; (*sports*) allenarsi

workable ['wʌrkəbəl] *adj* (*feasible*) praticabile; (*e.g., iron*) lavorabile

work'bench' *s* banco

work'book' *s* manuale *m* d'istruzioni; (*for students*) quaderno d'esercizi

work'box' *s* cassetta dei ferri del mestiere; (*for needlework*) cestino da lavoro

work'day' *adj* lavorativo; ordinario, di tutti i giorni || *s* (*working day*) giorno feriale, giornata lavorativa

worked-up ['wʌrkt'ʌp] *adj* sovreccitato

worker ['wʌrkər] *s* lavorante *m*, lavoratore *m*, operaio

work' force' *s* mano *f* d'opera

work'horse' *s* cavallo da tiro; (*tireless worker*) lavoratore indefesso

work'house' *s* carcere *m* con lavoro obbligatorio; (Brit) istituto dei poveri

work'ing class' *s* classe operaia

work'ing condi'tions *spl* trattamento, condizioni *fpl* di lavoro

work'ing girl' *s* ragazza lavoratrice

work'ing hours' *spl* orario di lavoro

working'man *s* (**-men**) lavoratore *m*

work'ing or'der *s* buone condizioni, efficienza

work'ing-wom'an *s* (**-wom'en**) operaia, lavoratrice *f*

work'man *s* (**-men**) lavoratore *m;* (*skilled worker*) operaio specializzato

workmanship ['wʌrkmən‚ʃɪp] *s* fattura; (*work executed*) opera

work' of art' *s* opera d'arte

work'out' *s* (sports) esercizio, allenamento

work'room' *s* (*for manual work*) officina; (*study*) gabinetto, laboratorio

work'shop' *s* officina

work' stop'page *s* sospensione del lavoro

world [wʌrld] *adj* mondiale || *s* mondo; **a world of** un monte di; **for all the world** per tutto l'oro del mondo; **in the world** al mondo; **since the world began** da che mondo è mondo; **the other world** l'altro mondo; **to bring into the world** mettere al mondo; **to see the world** conoscere il mondo; **to think the world of** tenere in altissima considerazione

world' affairs' *spl* relazioni *fpl* internazionali

world-ly ['wʌrldi] *adj* (**-ier; -iest**) mondano, secolare

world'ly-wise' *adj* vissuto

world's' fair' *s* esposizione *f* mondiale

world' war' *s* guerra mondiale

world'-wide' *adj* mondiale

worm [wʌrm] *s* verme *m* || *tr* liberare dai vermi; **to worm a secret out of s.o.** carpire un segreto a qlcu; **to worm one's way into** insinuarsi in

worm-eaten ['wʌrm‚itən] *adj* tarlato, ba ato

worm' gear' *s* meccanismo a vite perpetua, ingranaggio elicoidale

worm'wood' *s* assenzio; (fig) amarezza

worm-y ['wʌrmi] *adj* (**-ier; -iest**) verminoso; (*worm-eaten*) bacato; (*groveling*) vile, strascicante

worn [worn] *adj* usato; (*look*) stanco, esausto

worn'-out' *adj* logoro, scalcinato; (*by illness*) consunto; (fig) trito

worrisome ['wʌrisəm] *adj* preoccupante; (*inclined to worry*) preoccupato

wor-ry ['wʌri] *s* (**-ries**) preoccupazione, inquietudine *f;* (*trouble*) fastidio || *v* (*pret & pp* **-ried**) *tr* preoccupare, inquietare; **to be worried** essere impensierito || *intr* preoccuparsi, inquietarsi; **don't worry!** non si preoccupi!

worse [wʌrs] *adj & s* peggiore *m*, peggio || *adv* peggio; **worse and worse** di male in peggio

worsen ['wʌrsən] *tr & intr* peggiorare

wor-ship ['wʌrʃɪp] *s* venerazione, adorazione; servizio religioso; **your Worship** La Signoria Vostra || *v* (*pret &*

pp **-shiped** or **-shipped; ger -shiping**
or **-shipping**) *tr* venerare, adorare

worshiper or **worshipper** ['wʌrʃɪpər] *s*
adoratore *m;* (*in church*) devoto, fedele *m*

worst [wʌrst] *adj* (il) peggiore; pes-
simo ‖ *s* peggio, peggiore *m;* **at worst**
alla peggio; **if worst comes to worst**
alla peggio; **to get the worst** averne
la peggio ‖ *adv* peggio

worsted ['wustɪd] *adj* di lana pettinata
‖ *s* tessuto di lana pettinata

wort [wʌrt] *s* mosto di malto; pianta,
erba

worth [wʌrθ] *adj* che vale, da, e.g.,
worth ten dollars da dieci dollari; **to
be worth** valere; essere di pregio; **to
be worth** + *ger* valere la pena (di) +
inf, e.g., **it is worth reading** vale la
pena (di) leggerlo ‖ *s* pregio, valore
m; **a dollar's worth** un dollaro di

worthless ['wʌrθlɪs] *adj* senza valore;
inutile; inservibile; (*person*) indegno

worth′while′ *adj* meritevole, meritevole
d'attenzione

wor·thy ['wʌrði] *adj* (**-thier; -thiest**)
degno, meritevole ‖ *s* (**-thies**) maggio-
rente *mf*

would [wud] *v aux* **they said they
would come** dissero che sarebbero
venuti; **he would buy it if he had the
money** lo comprerebbe se avesse i
soldi; **would you be so kind to**
avrebbe la cortesia di; **he would
spend every winter in Florida** passava
tutti gli inverni in Florida; **would
that . . . !** oh se . . . !, volesse il cielo
che . . . !, magari . . . !

would′-be′ *adj* preteso, sedicente; (*intended to be*) inteso

wound [wund] *s* ferita ‖ *tr* ferire

wounded ['wundɪd] *adj* ferito ‖ **the
wounded** i feriti

wow [wau] *s* distorsione acustica di
suono riprodotto; (slang) successone
m ‖ *tr* (slang) entusiasmare ‖ *interj*
(coll) accidenti!

wrack [ræk] *s* naufragio; vestigio;
(*seaweed*) alghe marine gettate sulla
spiaggia; **to go to wrack and ruin**
andare completamente in rovina

wraith [reθ] *s* spettro, fantasma *m*

wrangle ['ræŋɡəl] *s* baruffa, alterco ‖
intr altercare, rissare

wrap [ræp] *s* sciarpa; mantello ‖ *v*
(*pret & pp* **wrapped; ger wrapping**) *tr*
involgere; impaccare; **to be wrapped
up in** essere assorto in; **to wrap up**
avvolgere; (*in paper*) incartare; (*in
clothing*) imbaccucare; (coll) concludere ‖ *intr*—**to wrap up** imbacuc-
carsi, avvolgersi

wrapper ['ræpər] *s* veste *f* da camera,
peignoir *m;* (*of newspaper*) fascia,
fascetta; (*of cigars*) involto

wrap′ping pa′per ['ræpɪŋ] *s* carta
d'impacco or d'imballaggio

wrath [ræθ] or [rɑθ] *s* ira; vendetta

wrathful ['ræθfəl] or ['rɑθfəl] *adj* collerico, iracondo

wreak [rik] *tr* (*vengeance*) infliggere;
(*anger*) scaricare

wreath [riθ] *s* (**wreaths** [riðz]) ghirlanda; (*of laurel*) laurea; (*of smoke*)
spirale *f*

wreathe [rið] *tr* inghirlandare; avviluppare; (*a garland*) intessere ‖ *intr*
(*said of smoke*) innalzarsi in spire

wreck [rek] *s* rottame *m,* relitto; naufragio; rovina; catastrofe *f,* disastro;
(fig) rottame *m,* relitto ‖ *tr* far naufragare; distruggere, rovinare; (*a
train*) fare scontrare, fare deragliare;
(*a building*) demolire

wreckage ['rekɪdʒ] *s* rottami *mpl,* relitti *mpl;* rovine *fpl*

wrecker ['rekər] *s* (*tow truck*) autogrù
f; (*housewrecker*) demolitore *m*

wreck′ing ball′ *s* martello demolitore

wreck′ing car′ *s* autogrù *f*

wrecking′ crane′ *s* (rr) carro gru

wren [ren] *s* scricciolo

wrench [rentʃ] *s* chiave *f;* (*pull*) tiro;
(*of a joint*) distorsione ‖ *tr* torcere,
distorcere; (*one's limb*) torcersi, distorcersi

wrest [rest] *tr* strappare, togliere a viva
forza; (*to twist*) torcere

wrestle ['resəl] *s* lotta, combattimento
‖ *intr* fare la lotta, lottare

wrestler ['reslər] *s* lottatore *m*

wrestling ['reslɪŋ] *s* lotta

wretch [retʃ] *s* disgraziato, tapino

wretched ['retʃɪd] *adj* (*pitiable*) misero, disgraziato, tapino; (*poor,
worthless*) miserabile

wriggle ['rɪɡəl] *s* (e.g., *of a snake*)
guizzo; dondolio ‖ *tr* dondolare, dimenare ‖ *intr* guizzare; dimenarsi;
to wriggle out of sgattaiolare da, di-
vincolarsi da

wrig·gly ['rɪɡli] *adj* (**-glier; -gliest**) che
si contorce; (fig) evasivo

wring [rɪŋ] *v* (*pret & pp* **wrung** [rʌŋ])
tr torcere; (*wet clothing*) strizzare;
(*one's heart*) stringersi; (e.g., *one's
hands*) torcersi; **to wring the truth
out of** strappare la verità a ‖

wringer ['rɪŋər] *s* strizzatoio

wrinkle ['rɪŋkəl] *s* (*on skin*) ruga; (*on
fabric*) crespa, grinza; (coll) trovata,
espediente *m* ‖ *tr* corrugare, raggrinzire; (*fabric*) increspare

wrin′kle-proof′ *adj* antipiega, ingualci-
bile

wrin·kly ['rɪŋkli] *adj* (**-klier; -kliest**)
rugoso, grinzoso

wrist [rɪst] *s* polso

wrist′band′ *s* polso

wrist′ pin′ *s* spinotto

wrist′ watch′ *s* orologio da polso

writ [rɪt] *s* scritto; (law) ordine *m*

write [raɪt] *v* (*pret* **wrote** [rot]; *pp*
written ['rɪtən]) *tr* scrivere; **to write
down** mettere in iscritto; (*to disparage*) menomare; **to write off** (*a
debt*) cancellare; (com) stornare; **to
write up** redigere, scrivere in pieno;
(*to ballyhoo*) scrivere le lodi di ‖ *intr*
scrivere; **to write back** rispondere per
lettera

write′-in-vote′ *s* voto per candidato il
cui nome non è nella lista

writer ['raɪtər] *s* scrittore *m*

write'-up' s descrizione scritta, conto; stamburata, elogio; (com) valutazione eccesiva

writhe [raɪð] intr contorcersi, spasimare, dibattersi

writing ['raɪtɪŋ] s lo scrivere; (something written) scritto; (characters written) scrittura; professione di scrittore; **at this writing** scrivendo questa mia; **in one's own writing** di proprio pugno; **to put in writing** mettere in iscritto

writ'ing desk' s scrittoio

writ'ing mate'rials spl l'occorrente m per scrivere, oggetti mpl di cancelleria

writ'ing pa'per s carta da lettere

writ'ten ac'cent ['rɪtən] s accento grafico

wrong [rɔŋ] or [rɑŋ] adj sbagliato, erroneo; (awry) guasto; (step) falso; cattivo, ingiusto; **there is nothing wrong with him** non ha niente; **to be wrong** (mistaken) aver torto; (guilty) aver la colpa || s torto; **to be in the wrong** essere in errore; **to do wrong** fare del male; commettere un'ingiustizia || adv male; (backward) alla rovescia; **to go wrong** andare alla rovescia; andare per la cattiva strada || tr far torto a, offendere, maltrattare

wrongdoer ['rɔŋ ˌdu·ər] or ['rɑŋ ˌdu·ər] s peccatore m, trasgressore m

wrongdoing ['rɔŋ ˌdu·ɪŋ] or ['rɑŋ ˌdu·ɪŋ] s peccato, offesa, trasgressione

wrong' num'ber s (telp) numero sbagliato; **you have the wrong number** Lei si è sbagliato di numero

wrong' side' s rovescio; (of street) altra parte; **to get out of bed on the wrong side** alzarsi di malumore; **wrong side out** alla rovescia

wrought' i'ron [rɔt] s ferro battuto

wrought'-up' adj sovreccitato

wry [raɪ] adj (wrier; wriest) sbieco, storto; pervertito, alterato; ironico

wry'neck' s ʹorn & pathol) torcicollo

X

X, x [ɛks] s ventiquattresima lettera dell'alfabeto inglese

Xanthippe [zæn'tɪpi] s Santippe f

Xavier ['zævɪ·ər] or ['zevɪ·ər] s Saverio

xebec ['zibɛk] s (naut) sciabecco

xenon ['zinɑn] or ['zenɑn] s xeno

xenophobe ['zɛnə ˌfob] s xenofobo

Xenophon ['zɛnəfən] s Senofonte m

xerography [zɪ'rɑgrəfi] s xerografia

xerophyte [zɪrə ˌfaɪt] s xerofito

Xerxes ['zʌrksɪs] s Serse m

Xmas ['krɪsməs] s Natale m

x-ray ['ɛks ˌre] adj radiografico || s raggio X; (photograph) radiogramma m, radiografia || tr radiografare

xylograph ['zaɪlə ˌgræf] or ['zaɪlə ˌgrɑf] s silografia

xylophone ['zaɪlə ˌfon] s silofono

Y

Y, y [waɪ] s venticinquesima lettera dell'alfabeto inglese

yacht [jɑt] s yacht m, panfilo

yacht' club' s club m nautico, associazione velica

yak [jæk] s yak m || v (pret & pp **yakked; ger yakking**) intr (slang) ciarlare, chiacchierare

yam [jæm] s igname m; (sweet potato) patata dolce, batata

yank [jæŋk] s tiro, strattone m || tr dare uno strattone a, tirare || intr dare uno strattone, tirare

Yankee ['jæŋki] adj & s yankee mf

yap [jæp] s guaito; (slang) chiacchierio, ciancia || v (pret & pp **yapped; ger yapping**) intr latrare, guaire; (slang) chiacchierare, ciarlare

yard [jɑrd] s cortile m; recinto; yard m, iarda; (naut) pennone m; (rr) scalo smistamento

yard'arm' s estremità f del pennone

yard' goods' spl tessuti mpl in pezza

yard'mas'ter s (rr) capo dello scalo smistamento

yard'stick' s stecca di una iarda di lunghezza; (fig) metro

yarn [jɑrn] s filo, filato; (coll) storia

yarrow ['jæro] s millefoglie m

yaw [jɔ] s (naut) straorzata; (aer) imbardata || intr (naut) straorzare, guizzare; (aer) imbardare

yawl [jɔl] s barca a remi; (naut) iolla

yawn [jɔn] s sbadiglio || intr sbadigliare; (said, e.g., of a hole) vaneggiare, aprirsi

yea [je] s & adv sì m

yean [jin] intr (said of sheep or goat) partorire

year [jɪr] s anno; **to be . . . years old** avere . . . anni; **year in, year out** un anno dopo l'altro

year'book' s annuario

yearling ['jɪrlɪŋ] adj di un anno di età || s animale m di un anno di età

yearly ['jɪrli] *adj* annuale ‖ *adv* annualmente

yearn [jʌrn] *intr* smaniare, sospirare; **to yearn for** anelare per

yearning ['jʌrnɪŋ] *s* anelo, sospiro ardente

yeast [jist] *s* lievito

yeast' cake' *s* compressa di lievito

yell [jɛl] *s* urlo ‖ *tr* gridare ‖ *intr* urlare

yellow ['jɛlo] *adj* giallo; *(newspaper)* sensazionale; *(cowardly)* (coll) vile ‖ *s* giallo; giallo d'uovo ‖ *intr* ingiallire

yellowish ['jɛlo·ɪʃ] *adj* giallastro

yel'low·jack'et *s* vespa, calabrone *m*

yel'low streak' *s* (coll) vena di codardia

yelp [jɛlp] *s* guaito ‖ *intr* guaire

yeo'man *s* (**-men**) (naut) sottufficiale *m*; (Brit) piccolo proprietario terriero

yeo'man of the guard' *s* guardia del servizio reale

yeo'man's serv'ice *s* lavoro onesto

yes [jɛs] *s* sì *m*; **to say yes** dire di sì ‖ *adv* sì ‖ *v* (*pret & pp* **yessed;** *ger* **yessing**) *tr* dire di sì a ‖ *intr* dire di sì

yes' man' *s* (coll) persona che approva sempre; (coll) leccapiedi *m*

yesterday ['jɛstərdɪ] *or* ['jɛstər,de] *s & adv* ieri *m*

yet [jɛt] *adv* ancora; tuttavia; **as yet** sinora; **nor yet** nemmeno; **not yet** non ancora ‖ *conj* ma, però, pure

yew' tree' [ju] *s* tasso

Yiddish ['jɪdɪʃ] *adj & s* yiddish *m*

yield [jild] *s* rendimento, resa; *(crop)* raccolto; (com) reddito, gettito ‖ *tr* rendere, fruttare ‖ *intr* rendere, fruttare, produrre; *(to surrender)* cedere, arrendersi; sottomettersi; cedere il posto

yodeling *or* **yodelling** ['jodəlɪŋ] *s* tirolesa

yoke [jok] *s* *(contrivance)* giogo; *(pair, e.g., of oxen)* paio; *(of shirt)* sprone *m*; (naut) barra del timone; **to throw**

off the yoke scuotere il giogo ‖ *tr* aggiogare

yokel ['jokəl] *s* zoticone *m*

yolk [jok] *s* tuorlo

yonder ['jandər] *adj* situato lassù; situato laggiù ‖ *adv* lassù; laggiù

yore [jor] *s—of yore* del tempo antico, del tempo in cui Berta filava

you [ju] *pron pers* Lei; tu; Le, La; te, ti; voi; vi; Loro ‖ *pron indef* si, e.g., **you eat at noon** si mangia a mezzogiorno

young [jʌŋ] *adj* (**younger** ['jʌŋɡər]; **youngest** ['jʌŋɡɪst]) giovane ‖ **the young** i giovani

young' hope'ful *s* giovane *m* di belle speranze

young' la'dy *s* giovane *f*; *(married)* giovane signora

young' man' *s* giovane *m*, giovanotto

young' peo'ple *s* i giovani

youngster ['jʌŋstər] *s* giovanetto; *(child)* bambino

your [jur] *adj* Suo, il Suo; tuo, il tuo; vostro, il vostro

yours [jurz] *pron poss* Suo, il Suo; tuo, il tuo; vostro, il vostro; **of yours** Suo; **very truly yours** distinti saluti

your·self [jur'sɛlf] *pron pers* (**-selves** ['sɛlvz]) Lei stesso; sé stesso; si, e.g., **are your enjoying yourself?** si diverte?

youth [juθ] *s* (**youths** [juθs] *or* [juðz]) gioventù *f*, giovinezza; *(person)* giovane *mf*; i giovani

youthful ['juθfəl] *adj* giovane, giovanile

yowl [jaul] *s* urlo ‖ *intr* urlare

Yugoslav ['jugo'slav] *adj & s* iugoslavo

Yugoslavia ['jugo'slavɪ·ə] *s* la Iugoslavia

Yule [jul] *s* il Natale; le feste natalizie

Yule' log' *s* ceppo

Yuletide ['jul,taɪd] *s* le feste natalizie

Z

Z, z [zi] *s* ventiseiesima lettera dell'alfabeto inglese

za·ny ['zeni] *adj* (**-nier; -niest**) comico, buffonesco ‖ *s* (**-nies**) buffone *m*, pagliaccio

zeal [zil] *s* zelo, entusiasmo

zealot ['zɛlət] *s* zelante *mf*, fanatico

zealotry ['zɛlətri] *s* fanatismo

zealous ['zɛləs] *adj* zelante, volenteroso

zebra ['zibrə] *s* zebra

ze'bra cross'ing *s* zebre *fpl*

zebu ['zibju] *s* zebù *m*

zenith ['ziniθ] *s* zenit *m*

zephyr ['zɛfər] *s* zefiro

ze·ro ['ziro] *s* (**-roes**) zero ‖ *tr—to zero in** (mil) aggiustare il mirino di ‖ *intr—to zero in on* (mil) concentrare il fuoco su

ze'ro grav'ity *s* gravità *f* zero

ze'ro hour' *s* ora zero

zest [zɛst] *s* entusiasmo; *(flavor)* aroma *m*, sapore *m*

Zeus [zus] *s* Zeus *m*

zig-zag ['zɪɡ,zæɡ] *adj & adv* a zigzag ‖ *s* zigzag *m*; serpentina ‖ *v* (*pret & pp* **-zagged;** *ger* **-zagging**) *intr* zigzagare; serpeggiare

zinc [zɪŋk] *s* zinco

zinnia ['zɪnɪ·ə] *s* zinnia

Zionism ['zaɪ·ə,nɪzəm] *s* sionismo

zip [zɪp] *s* (coll) sibilo; (coll) energia, vigore *m* ‖ *v* (*pret & pp* **zipped;** *ger* **zipping**) *tr* chiudere con cerniera lampo; aprire con cerniera lampo; (coll) portare rapidamente; **to zip up** (*to add zest to*) dare gusto a ‖ *intr* aprirsi con cerniera lampo; sibilare; (coll) filare, correre; **to zip by** (coll) passare come un lampo

zip' code' s codice m di avviamento postale

zipper ['zɪpər] s cerniera or serratura lampo

zircon ['zʌrkɑn] s zircone m

zirconium [zər'konɪ·əm] s zirconio

zither ['zɪθər] s cetra tirolese

zodiac ['zodɪ‚æk] s zodiaco

zone [zon] s zona; distretto postale || tr dividere in zone

zoo [zu] s giardino zoologico

zoologic(al) [‚zo·ə'lɑdʒɪk(əl)] adj zoologico

zoologist [zo'ɑlədʒɪst] s zoologo

zoology [zo'ɑlədʒi] s zoologia

zoom [zum] s ronzio; (aer) cabrata, impennata; (mov, telv) zumata || tr (aer) far cabrare, fare impennare; (mov, telv) zumare || intr ronzare; (aer) cabrare, impennarsi; (mov, telv) zumare

zoom' lens' s (phot) transfocatore m

zoophite ['zo·ə‚faɪt] s zoofito

Zu·lu ['zulu] adj zulù || s (-lus) zulù mf

Zurich ['zurɪk] s Zurigo f

PART THREE

Appendix – Appendice

Italian Abbreviations
Abbreviazioni italiane

Please note the labels *(BE)* and *(GB)* for British English and British usage respectively.

A

A. *ampere* ampere (amp.); *lettera assicurata* registered letter

a. *anno* year (yr.); *ara* are; *accelerazione* acceleration

AA *Alto Adige* South Tyrol

A.A.M.S. *Azienda Autonoma dei Monopoli di Stato* Board of State Monopolies

A.A.S.S. *Azienda Autonoma Statale della Strada* Independent State Company for the Highway System

A.A.S.T. *Azienda Autonoma di Soggiorno e Turismo* Independent Local Tourist Board

ab. *abitanti* population (pop.)

abb. *abbonamento* subscription

abbr. *abbreviato* abbreviated

A.B.I. *Associazione Bancaria Italiana* Italian Bankers' Association

abl. *ablativo* ablative

abr. *abrogato* repealed

a.br.sc. *a breve scadenza* short-term

A.C. *Azione Cattolica* Catholic Action (C.A.); *Aviazione Civile* civil aviation

a.C. *avanti Cristo* before Christ (B.C.)

a.c. *anno corrente* current year; *a capo* new paragraph (n.p.); *assegno circolare* cashier's check, (*BE*) banker's draft

A.C.A *Associazione Culturale Aeronautica* Aeronautical Cultural Association

acc. *accusativo* accusative (acc.); *acconto* deposit, part payment

ACI *Automobile Club d'Italia* Italian Automobile Club; *Aereo Club d'Italia* Italian Aero Club

A.C.I.S. *Alto Commissariato per l'Igiene e la Sanità* Office of the High Commissioner for Public Health

ACLI *Associazioni Cristiane dei Lavoratori Italiani* Christian Association(s) of Italian workers

a.C.n. *ante Christum natum* before the birth of Christ (B.C.)

a. corr. *anno corrente* this year

A.D. *Anno Domini* Anno Domini (A.D.)

ad. *adagio* adagio, slowly

A.D.S. *Accertamento Diffusione Stampa* Audit Bureau of Circulation

ad. us. (Latin) *ad usum* for use

AELS *Associazione Europea di Libero Scambio* European Free Trade Association (EFTA)

A.E.P *Agenzia Europea della Produttività* European Productivity Board

A.f. *Agricoltura e foreste* Agriculture and forests

a.f. *alta frequenza* high frequency (HF)

Aff.Est. *Affari Esteri* Foreign Affairs; ***Ministero degli Affari Esteri*** State Department

aff.mo *affezionatissimo* very affectionately

AFI *Associazione Internazionale Fiscale* International Fiscal Association (IFA)

AG *Agrigento* Agrigento

Ag *argento* silver

A.G. *Albergo per la Gioventù* Youth Hostel

agg. *aggettivo* adjective

A.G.I. *Associazione Giornalistica Italiana* Association of Italian Journalists

AGIP *Azienda Generale Italiana Petroli* General Italian Oil Company

A.I. *Aeronautica Italiana* Italian Aeronautics

Aia: *Tribunale dell'Aia* International Court of Justice, The Hague (*L'Aia = The Hague*)

A.I.A. *Associazione Italiana Arbitri* Italian Association of Referees

A.I.E. *Associazione Italiana degli Editori* Italian Association of Publishers

A.I.E.A. *Agenzia Internazionale per l'Energia Atomica* International Atomic Energy Agency

A.I.G. *Associazione Italiana Alberghi per la Gioventù* Italian Youth Hostels Association

AL *Alessandria* Alessandria

Al *alluminio* aluminum

alg. *algebra* algebra (alg.)

ALI *Aviolinee Italiane* Italian Airlines

ALITALIA *Aerolinee Italiane Internazionali* International Italian Airlines

all. *allegro* allegro

all., alleg. *allegato* enclosed (encl.), enclosure (encl.)

all.to *allegretto* allegretto

alt. *altitudine* altitude; *altezza* height

A.M. *Aeronautica Militare* Air Force

a.m. *antimeridiano* in the morning (a.m.)

A.M.E. *Accordo Monetario Europeo* European Monetary Agreement (E.M.A.)

AMIG *Associazione Mutilati ed Invalidi di Guerra* Association of Disabled Ex-Servicemen

Amm. *ammiraglio* admiral

amm.ne *amministrazione* administration

AN *Ancona* Ancona

A.N. *Alleanza Nazionale* National Alliance

A.N.A. *Associazione Nazionale Alpini* National Mountain Troops Veterans' Association

A.N.A.A. *Associazione Nazionale Agenti Assicurazione* National Association of Insurance Agents

A.N.A.S. *Azienda Nazionale Autonoma delle Strade* National Highway Authority

and.o *andantino* andantino

A.N.E.A. *Associazione Nazionale fra gli Enti di Assistenza* National Association of Welfare Boards

ang. *angolo* corner

A.N.I.A. *Associazione Nazionale delle Imprese Assicurative* National Association of Insurance Companies and Agencies

A.N.I.C. *Associazione Nazionale dell' Industria Chimica* National Association of Chemical Industries

A.N.I.C.A *Associazione Nazionale Industrie Cinematografiche e Affini* National Association of Cinematographic (= *Film*) and Related Industries

A.N.P.I. *Associazione Nazionale Partigiani d'Italia* National Association of Italian Partisans

A.N.S.A. *Agenzia Nazionale Stampa Associata* National Associated Press Agency

AO *Aosta* Aosta

AP *Ascoli Piceno* Ascoli Piceno

a.p.c. *a pronta cassa* collect on delivery (c.o.d.)

app. *appendice* appendix

AQ *Aquila* Aquila

AR *Arezzo* Arezzo

Arc. *Arcivescovo* Archbishop (Arch.)

A.R.C.E. *Associazione per le Relazioni Culturali con l' Estero* Association for Cultural Relations with Foreign Countries

arch. *architetto* architect

arp. *arpeggio* Arpeggio

art. *articolo* article

As *arsenico* arsenic

A.S.C.I. *Associazione Scoutistica Cattolica Italiana* Association of Italian Catholic Scouts

ass. *associazione* association; *assessore* councilor, member of an administrative council

ASSITALIA *Assicurazioni d'Italia* Italian Insurance Company

A.S.S.T. *Azienda di Stato per i Servizi Telefonici* National Telephone Company

astr. *astronomia* astronomy

AT *Asti* Asti

A.T. *Antico Testamento* Old Testament. (O.T.)

A.T.A. *Associazione Turistica Albergatori* Association of Italian Hotel Keepers

atm. *atmosfera* atmosphere

a.u.c. *ab urbe condita* from the foundation of the city of Rome

aus. *ausiliare* auxiliary

AV *Avellino* Avellino

AVIS *Associazione Volontari Italiani del Sangue* Association of Voluntary Blood-Donors of Italy

avv. *avvocato* lawyer, attorney-at-law

az. *azione* stock, share

B

B. *Barone* baron; *beato* blessed

b. *boreale* northern

BA *Bari* Bari

B.A. *Belle Arti* Fine Arts

banch. *banchiere* banker

Bar. *barone* baron

B.ca, b.ca *banca* bank

B.C.I. *Banca Commerciale Italiana* Italian Commercial Bank

B.E.I. *Banca Europea degli Investimenti* European Investment Bank

b.f. *bassa frequenza* low frequency (LF)

BG *Bergamo* Bergamo

B.I. *Banca d'Italia* Bank of Italy

bibl. *bibliografia* bibliography

b.i.d. (Latin) *bis in die, due volte al giorno* twice a day

bim. *bimestre* two-month period; *bimestrale* bimonthly, every two months; *bimensile* semimonthly, twice a month

biochim. *biochimica* biochemistry

B.I.R.S. *Banca Internazionale di Ricostruzione e Sviluppo* International Bank for Reconstruction and Development

BL *Belluno* Belluno

B.M. *Banca Mondiale* World Bank

b.m. *beata memoria* in blessed memory

B.M.T. *Bollettino Meteorologico Telefonico* telephonic weather forecast

BN *Benevento* Benevento

B.N.L. *Banca Nazionale del Lavoro* National Bank of Labor

BO *Bologna* Bologna

BOT *Buono Ordinario del Tesoro* treasury bill, short-term treasury bond

B.P. *Bassa Pressione* low pressure (L.P.); *Basilica Pontificia* Pontifical Basilica

b.p. *buono per* valid for

BR *Brindisi* Brindisi; *Brigate Rosse* Red Brigades

B.R. *Brigate Rosse* Red Brigades

brev. *brevetto* patent

B.R.I. *Banca dei Regolamenti Internazionali* Bank for International Settlements (B.I.S.)

bross. *in brossura* in paperback binding

BS *Brescia* Brescia

B.ssa *Baronessa* baroness

btg. *battaglione* battalion

B.U. *Bollettino Ufficiale* Official Bulletin

B.V.(M.) *Beata Vergine (Maria)* Blessed Virgin (Mary)

BZ *Bolzano* Bolzano

C

C *grado celsius* Celsius; *centigrado* centigrade; *carbonio* carbon; *grande caloria* kilocalorie (kcal.)

c *piccola caloria* gram calorie (cal.)

C. *codice* code; *Conte* Count, *(BE)* Earl; *capitolo* chapter

CA *Cagliari* Cagliari

ca *circa* about

C.A. *Consorzio Agrario* agricultural cooperative

c.a. *corrente anno* current year; *corrente alternata* alternating current (AC)

C.A.A *Corte d'Assise d'Appello* Criminal Court of Appeal

cad. *cadauno* each (one)

C.A.I. *Club Alpino Italiano* Italian Alpine Club

cal *caloria* calorie

CAMBITAL *Ufficio Italiano Cambi* Italian Bureau of Exchange

C.A.M.E.N *Centro di Applicazioni Militari dell'Energia*

Nucleare Center for Military Applications of Nuclear Energy

can.co. *canonico* canonical

cap. *capitolo* chapter (ch.); *capitano* captain; *caporale* private 1st class, *(GB)* lance corporal

C.A.P. *Codice di Avviamento Postale* zip code

Card. *Cardinale* Cardinal

Cass. *Cassazione* Cassation

cat. *categoria* category; *catalogo* catalog

Cav. *Cavaliere* knight *(title)*

CB *Campobasso* Campobasso

CC *Carabinieri* Carabinieri *(police with military duties)*

cc *centimetri cubici* cubic centimeters

C.C. *Camera di Commercio* Chamber of Commerce; *Carta Costituzionale* Constitutional Charter; *Codice Civile* Civil Code; *Corte dei Conti* Supreme State Audit Court; *Corpo Consolare* Consular Corps

c.c. *conto corrente* current account (a/c, c/o); *corrente continua* direct current (DC)

C.C.I. *Camera di Commercio Internazionale* International Chamber of Commerce

C.C.L. *contratto collettivo di lavoro* collective agreement *(on wages)*

c.c.p *conto corrente postale* postal check account

C.C.T. *Certificato di Credito del Tesoro* treasury bill

CD *Corpo Diplomatico* Diplomatic Corps

C.D. *Comitato Direttivo* steering committee

C.d'A. *Corpo d'Armata* Army Corps; *Corte d'Appello* Court of Appeals; *Corte d'Assise* Court of Assizes, Jury Court

C.d.Co. *Codice di Commercio* Commercial Code

C.d.L. *Camera del Lavoro* Labor Union Center

C.d.S. *Codice della Strada* Road Traffic Regulations, *(BE)* Highway Code

CE *Caserta* Caserta

C.E. *Consiglio d'Europa, Consiglio Europeo* Council of Europe; *Comitato Esecutivo* Executive Committee

CEA *Confederazione Europea dell'Agricoltura* Federation of European Agriculture

CECA *Comunità Europea del Carbone e dell'Acciaio* European Coal and Steel Community (ECSC)

C.E.D. *Comunità Europea di Difesa* European Defence Community (EDC)

C.E.E. *Comunità Economica Europea* European Economic Community (EEC)

C.E.E.A. *Comunità Europea per l'Energia Atomica* European Atomic Energy Community (EAEC)

C.E.N. *Centro di Studi dell'Energia Nucleare* Atomic Energy Research Center

C.E.N.S.I.S. *Centro Studi Investimenti Sociali* Study Center on Social Conditions and Investments

C.E.R.E.S. *Centro di Ricerche e Studi Economici* Center for Economic Studies and Research

C.E.R.N. *Comitato Europeo di Ricerche Nucleari* European Council for Nuclear Research

cf., cfr. *confronta* compare (cf.)

C.G. *Console Generale* Consul General

C.G.I.L. *Confederazione Generale Italiana del Lavoro* General Federation of Italian Labor Unions

CH *Chieti* Chieti

chir. *chirurgia* surgery

C.ia *compagnia* Company

C.I.G. *Corte Internazionale di Giustizia* International Court of Justice

CIGA *Compagnia Italiana dei Grandi Alberghi* Italian Company of Large Hotels

C.I.O. *Comitato Internazionale Olimpico* International Olympic Committee (IOC)

C.I.P. *Comitato Interministeriale dei Prezzi* Interministerial Prices Committee

C.I.S. *Comitato Internazionale degli Scambi* International Trade Committee

C.I.S.A.L. *Confederazione Italiana Sindacati Autonomi dei Lavoratori* Italian Federation of Independent Labor Unions

C.I.S.L. *Confederazione Italiana Sindacati Lavoratori* Italian Federation of Labor Unions

C.I.S.N.A.L. *Confederazione Italiana Sindacati Nazionali Lavoratori* Italian Federation of National Labor Unions

CIT *Compagnia Italiana di Turismo* Italian Tourist Company

CL *Caltanissetta* Caltanissetta

cl *centilitro* centiliter

C.L. *Commissione legislativa* Legislative Committee

cm *centimetro* centimeter

c.m. *corrente mese* instant (inst.)

cmq *centimetro quadrato* square centimeter

CN *Cuneo* Cuneo

c.n. *capitale netto* net capital

C.N.R. *Consiglio Nazionale delle Ricerche* National Council for Scientific Research

CO *Como* Como

cod. *codice* code (of law)

Col. *Colonnello* Colonel (Col.)

Com. *Comandante* Commander

comm. *commercio* trade, commerce

CONFINDUSTRIA *Confederazione Generale dell'Industria Italiana* Federation of Italian Industrial Enterprises

C.O.N.I. *Comitato Olimpico Nazionale Italiano* Italian National Olympic Committee

coniug. *coniugazione* conjugation

contraz. *contrazione* contraction

coop. *cooperativa* cooperative (business); *cooperazione* cooperation

C.P. *Codice Penale* Penal Code; *casella postale* post office box (P.O. box); *Capitaneria di Porto* Port Authorities

c.p. *cartolina postale* postcard, postal card; *casella postale* post office box (P.O. box)

C.P.C. *Codice di Procedura Civile* Code of Civil Procedure

C.P.M. *Codice Penale Militare* Military Penal Code

C.P.P. *Codice di Procedura Penale* Code of Penal Procedure

CR *Cremona* Cremona

c.r. *con riserva* with reservations

C.R.I. *Croce Rossa Italiana* Italian Red Cross

CS *Cosenza* Cosenza

C.S. *Collegio Sindacale* board of directors; *Comando Supremo* Supreme Command; *Corte Suprema* Supreme Court; *Consiglio di Sicurezza* Security Council

c.s. *come sopra* as above

C.so *Corso* Avenue
C.ssa *contessa* countess
CT *Catania* Catania
C.te *conte* count, *(BE)* earl
c.to *conto* account (a/c, c/a)
CV, C.V. *cavallo vapore* horsepower (h.p.)
c.v.d. *come volevasi dimostrare* which was to be proven
C.V.L. *Corpo Volontari della Libertà* Volunteer Corps of
   Fighters for Liberty
CZ *Catanzaro* Catanzaro

D

D *diretto* fast (train) *(faster than local train, slower than
   express or Intercity train)*
d. *diametro* diameter; *dose* dose
D.A. *diritti di autore* copyright
D/A *documenti contro accettazione* documents against
   acceptance
dal *decalitro* decaliter *(= ten liters)*
dam *decametro* decameter *(= ten meters)*
db *decibel* decibel
d.C. *dopo Cristo* anno Domini (A.D.)
d.c. *da capo* repeat from the beginning
d.c.p. *documenti contro pagamento* documents against
   payment (D/P)
D. cr. *divisione corazzata* armored division
DD *direttissimo* fast through train
dd. *datato* dated
D.D.D. *Direzione delle Dogane* Customs Administration
decr. *decrescendo* decrescendo; *decreto* decree, ordinance
deriv. *derivazione* derivation; *derivato* derivative
dett. *dettaglio* detail; *dettagliante* retailer
dev.mo *devotissimo* yours truly *(in letters)*
D.F. *Diritto Finanziario* financial law
dg. *decigrammo* decigram *(= ten grams)*
D.G. *direzione generale* Head Office
dil. *diluito* diluted
dim. *diminuendo* diminuendo

dipl. *diploma* diploma, certificate
Dir. *direzione* management, director's office; *direttore* director
dir. *diritto* straight ahead; *diritto* law
Distr. *Distretto* district
Div. *divisione* department; *divisione* (army) division
dl *decilitro* deciliter *(= ten liters)*
D.L. *decreto legge* ordinance, rule
D.M. *decreto ministeriale* ministerial decree
dmc *decimetro cubo* cubic decimeter
doc. *documento* document
Dott. *Dottore* doctor, Doctor
D.P. *decreto presidenziale* presidential decree
dr. *dottore* doctor, Doctor; *destra* right
dr.ssa *dottoressa* lady doctor; Doctor
D.ssa *Duchessa* duchess
D.T. *direttore tecnico* technical director
dz. *dozzina* dozen; *dizionario* dictionary

E

E *Est* East
E.A. *Ente Autonomo* Independent Board
E.A.M. *Ente Autotrasporti Merci* Freight Transportation Board
E/C *estratto conto* statement (of account)
E.C.A. *Ente Comunale di Assistenza* Municipal Relief Board
Ecc. *Eccellenza* Excellency *(title)*
ecc. *eccetera* et cetera, and so on (etc.)
eccl. *ecclesiastico* ecclesiastic
ECG *elettrocardiogramma* electrocardiogram (ECG)
ed. *edizione* edition; *editore* publisher
EE *Escursionisti Esteri* foreign excursionists *(temporary license plate)*
EEG *elettroencefalogramma* electroencephalogram (EEG)
E.E.P. *Ente Europeo per la Produttività* European Productivity Agency (EPA)
eff. *effetto (= cambiale)* bill, promissory note; *effettivo* effective

E.F.I. *Ente Finanziamenti Industriali* Board of Industrial Financing

Egr. Sig. *Egregio Signore* Dear Sir

E.I. *Esercito Italiano* Italian Army; *Enciclopedia Italiana* Italian Encyclopedia

Em. *Eminenza* Eminence *(title)*

EN *Enna* Enna

ENAL *Ente Nazionale per l'Assistenza dei Lavoratori* National Board for the Assistance of the Workers

ENASARCO *Ente Nazionale di Assistenza agli Agenti e Rappresentanti di Commercio* National Board of Assistance for Commercial Agents and Representatives

ENEL *Ente Nazionale per l'Energia Elettrica* National Electricity Board

ENIT *Ente Nazionale Italiano per il Turismo* Italian State Tourist Board

ENPI *Ente Nazionale per la Prevenzione degli Infortuni* National Board for the Prevention of Industrial Accidents

E.P.T. *Ente Provinciale per il Turismo* District Board of Tourism

eq. *equazione* equation

E.R.P. *Piano di Ricostruzione Europea* European Recovery Program (E.R.P.)

es. *esempio* example

escl. *escluso, esclusa* excluding (excl.); *esclusivo, esclusiva* exclusive; *esclamazione* exclamation

e segg. *e seguenti* and the following (ones)

estr. *estratto* extract

EU *Europa Unita* United Europe

euf. *eufemismo* euphemism

E.U.R. *Esposizione Universale di Roma* Universal Exhibition of the City of Rome

E.V. *Eccellenza Vostra* Your Excellency

e.v. *era volgare* Christian era (C.E.), anno Domini (A.D.)

F *Fahrenheit* Fahrenheit; *farad* farad; *Fiume* river
f *forte* forte; *funzione* function
f. *femminile* feminine; *feriale* weekday
F.A.I. *Federazione Aeronautica Internazionale* International Aeronautical Federation (IAF)
fam. *famiglia* family
farm. *farmacia* pharmacy
fatt. *fattura* invoice (inv.)
f.c. *fuori combattimento* knockout (KO)
FE *Ferrara* Ferrara
FEDERMECCANICA *Federazione Sindacale dell'Industria Metalmeccanica Italiana* Labor Union of the Italian Mechanical Engineering Industries
fem. *femminile* female
f.e.m. *forza elettromotrice* electromotive force (emf, EMF)
ferr. *ferrovia* railroad, railways
ff *fortissimo* very loud
FF. *Fratelli* brothers
FF.AA. *Forze Armate* armed forces
FF.SS. *Ferrovie dello Stato* Italian State Railways
FG *Foggia* Foggia
FI *Firenze* Florence
fil. *filiale* branch
F.I.M. *Federazione Italiana Metalmeccanici* Italian Federation of Mechanical Engineering and Metal Workers
FINMARE *Società Finanziaria Marittima* Maritime Investment Company
fl. *fluido* fluid
F.lli *Fratelli* brothers
F.L.N. *Fronte di Liberazione Nazionale* National Liberation Front
f.m. *fine mese* end of the month
F.M.I. *Fondo Monetario Internazionale* International Monetary Fund (IMF)
FO *Forlì* Forlì
fp. *forte-piano* forte-piano

FR *Frosinone* Frosinone
Fr.f. *franco francese* French franc
Fr.s. *franco svizzero* Swiss franc
F.S. *Ferrovvie dello Stato* Italian State Railways
f.s. *far seguire* please forward
F.S.M. *Federazione Sindacale Mondiale* World Federation
  of Labor Unions
f.to *firmato* signed
fut. *futuro* future

G

g *grammo* gram; *grammi* grams
g. *giorno* day
G.A. *Giunta Amministrativa* Administrative Council
Gazz. Uff. *Gazzetta Ufficiale* Official Gazette
G.d.F. *Guardia di Finanza* Revenue Guard Corps
GE *Genoa*
Gen. *Generale* General
geofis. *geofisica* geophysics
geol. *geologia* geology
ger. *gerundio* gerund
gg. *giorni* days
G.I. *Giudice Istruttore* Committing Magistrate
G.M. *Gran Maestro* Grand Master
G.N. *Genio Navale* Naval Engineers
GO *Gorizia* Gorizia
G.P.A. *Giunta Provinciale Amministrativa* District Admin-
  istrative Council
GR *Grosseto* Grosseto
gr. *grammo* gram; *grammi* grams
G.V. *grande velocità* high speed *(express goods service)*

H

h *ora* hour (H)
H *ospedale* hospital; *Ungheria* Hungary
ha *ettaro* hectare *(= 10,000 m^2)*

Hb *emoglobina* hemoglobin
h.c. *honoris causa* for honor's sake
hg *ettogrammo* hectogram *(= 100 grams)*
hl *ettolitro* hectoliter *(= 100 liters)*
hm *ettometro* hectometer *(= 100 meters)*
Hz *hertz* hertz

I

I *Italia* Italy
I.A.C.P. *Istituto Autonomo Case Popolari* Independent Institution for Public Housing
I.A.E.A. *Agenzia Internazionale dell'Energia Atomica* International Atomic Energy Agency (IAEA)
IATA *Associazione Internazionale Trasporti Aerei* International Air Transport Association
ib., ibid. (Latin) *ibidem* in the same book, chapter, etc. (ib., ibid.)
ICE *Istituto per il Commercio Estero* Institute for the Promotion of Foreign Trade
I.C.S. *Istituto Centrale di Statistica* Central Institute of Statistics
id. (Latin) *idem, lo stesso* idem, the same
id.c.s. (Latin) *idem come sopra* the same as above
I.d.L. *Ispettorato del Lavoro* Inspectorate of Labor
idr. *idraulica* hydraulics; *idraulico* hydraulic
I.F. *Intendenza di Finanza* Internal Revenue Office
I.G.E. *Imposta Generale sull'Entrata* sales tax
Ill.mo: *Illustrissimo Signor (+ name)* Dear Sir, ...
IM *Imperia* Imperia
imp., imper. *imperativo* imperative
imperf. *imperfetto* imperfect, past tense
I.N.A. *Istituto Nazionale delle Assicurazioni* National Insurance Institute
I.N.A.I.L. *Istituto Nazionale per l'Assicurazione contro gli Infortuni sul Lavoro* National Institute for Insurance against Industrial Accidents
I.N.A.M. *Istituto Nazionale per l'Assicurazione contro le malattie* National Institute for Health Insurance

I.N.A.S. *Istituto Nazionale di Assistenza Sociale* National Institute for Social Security

inc. *incaricato* teacher appointed on a yearly basis

indic. *indicativo* indicative

ing. *ingegnere* engineer (eng.)

ing. chim. *ingegnere chimico* chemical engineer; *ingegneria chimica* chemical engineering

ing. civ. *ingegnere civile* civil engineer; *ingegneria civile* civil engineering

I.N.P.S. *Istituto Nazionale di Previdenza Sociale* National Welfare Institute

intr. *intransitivo* intransitive

I.P.L. *Ispettorato Provinciale del Lavoro* District Labor Inspectorate

I.P.S. *Istituto Poligrafico dello Stato* State Printing and Stationery Institute

IRI *Istituto per la Ricostruzione Industriale* Institute for Industrial Reconstruction

I.R.P.E.F. *Imposta sul Reddito delle Persone Fisiche* Personal Income Tax

IS *Isernia* Isernia

ispett. *ispettore* inspector

ISTAT *Istituto Centrale di Statistica* Central Institute of Statistics

ISVEIMER *Istituto per lo Sviluppo Economico dell'Italia Meridionale* Institute for the Economic Development of Southern Italy

I.V.A. *Imposta sul Valore Aggiunto* Value Added Tax (VAT), sales tax

K

kc *chilociclo* kilocycle

kcal *chilocaloria* kilocalorie

kg *chilogrammo* kilogram

kl *chilolitro* kiloliter

km *chilometro* kilometre

km/h *chilometri all'ora* kilometers per hour

kV *chilovolt* kilovolt

kW *chilowatt* kilowatt
kWh *chilowattora* kilowatt-hour

L

l *litro* liter
lab. *laboratorio* laboratory
L.A.I. *Linee Aeree Italiane* Italian Airlines
lat. *latitudine* latitude; *latino* Latin
l.c., l. cit. *luogo citato* in the place cited
LE *Lecce* Lecce
L.E.C.E. *Lega Europea di Cooperazione Economica* European League of Economic Cooperation
leg. *legale* legal; *legato* bound
legg. *leggero* soft
lett. *letterario* literary
LI *Livorno* Livorno
libr. *libraio* bookseller
Lit. *Lire italiane* Italian lire
LL.PP. *Lavori Pubblici* Public Works
l.m. *livello del mare* sea level
loc. cit. (Latin) *loco citato, luogo citato* in the place cited
locuz. *locuzione* phrase, expression
log. *logaritmo* logarithm (log.)
long. *longitudine* longitude
LT *Latina* Latina
LU *Lucca* Lucca
L.V. *lettera di vettura* waybill, bill of lading

M

m *metro* meter; *miglio* mile, *miglia* miles; *massimo* maximum; *minimo* minimum
M.A.E. *Ministero degli Affari Esteri* Ministry of Foreign Affairs, State Department, *(GB)* Foreign Office
mag. *maggio* may
Magg. *Maggiore* Major *(rank)*; *Maggiore* the elder, the older *(after names)*; *Maggiore* bigger, more important

March. *Marchese* marquis, marquess

mar. merc. *marina mercantile* merchant marine

masch. *maschile* masculine (masc.)

Mc *megaciclo* megacycle

mc *metro cubo* cubic meter

m.c. *mese corrente* of this month, instant (inst.)

ME *Messina* Messina

M.E. *Medio Evo* (the) Middle Ages

MEC *Mercato Europeo Comune* European Common Market

mens. *mensile* monthly

M.F. *Ministero delle Finanze* Ministry of Finance, Treasury Department, *(GB)* Treasury

M.F.E. *Movimento Federalista Europeo* European Federalist Movement

mg *milligrammo*

MHz *megahertz*

MI *Milano* Milan

M.I. *Ministero degli Interni* Ministry of the Interior, Department of the Interior, *(GB)* Home Office

M.I.B. *Indice Borsa Milano* Milan Stock Exchange Index

mitt. *mittente* sender

mm *millimetro*

M.M. *Marina Militare* Navy

M.M.M. *Ministero della Marina Mercantile* Ministry of the Merchant Navy

MN *Mantova* Mantova

M/N *motonave* motor vessel (MV)

MO *Modena*

mod. *modello* model

Mons. *Monsignore* Monsignor (Mgr.)

M.P. (Latin) *manu propria* personally

mq *metro quadrato* square meter

M.sa *Marchesa* marchioness

M.se *Marchese* marquis, marquess

M.S.I. *Movimento Sociale Italiano* Italian Social Movement *(right-wing political party)*

MT *Matera* Matera

mus. *musica* music; *musicale* musical

M.V. *Maria Vergine* Virgin Mary

M/V *motoveliero* motor sailer

N

N *azoto* nitrogen; *Nord* North
n. *nato* born; *numero* number (no.)
NA *Napoli* Naples
Na *sodio* sodium
N.B. *nota bene* note well
N.D. *Nobil Donna* noblewoman
N.d.A. *nota dell'autore* author's note
N.d.E. *nota dell'editore* publisher's note
N.d.R. *nota della redazione* editor's note
N.d.T. *nota del traduttore* translator's note
NE *Nord-Est* northeast (NE)
neg. *negativo* negative
neol. *neologismo* neologism
N.N. *niente di nuovo, nessuna novità* nothing new; (Latin) *nescio nomen* name unknown
NO *Nord-Ovest* northwest (NW); *Novara* Novara
no., n.o *numero* number (no.)
N° *numero* number (no.)
nob. *nobile* noble
nom. *nominativo* nominative (nom.)
ns. *nostro* our, ours
N.T. *Nuovo Testamento* New Testament (NT)
NU *Nuoro* Nuoro
N.U. *Nazioni Unite* United Nations (UN); *Nobil Uomo* nobleman

O

O *ossigeno* oxygen; *Ovest* west (W)
OC *onde corte* short wave (SW)
O.C.C. *Organizzazione per la Cooperazione Commerciale* Organization for Trade Cooperation (OTC)
O.C.S.E. *Organizzazione per la Cooperazione e lo Sviluppo Economico* Organization for Economic Cooperation and Development (OECD)
o.d.g., O.d.G. *ordine del giorno* agenda
O.F.M. *Ordine dei Frati Minori* Order of Friars Minor *(Franciscans)*

O.I.L. *Organizzazione Internazionale del Lavoro* International Labor Organization

OL *onde lunghe* long wave (LW)

OM *onde medie* medium wave (MW)

O.M.S. *Organizzazione Mondiale della Sanità* World Health Organization (W.H.O.)

On. *Onorevole* Member of Congress (MC), *(GB)* Member of Parliament

onom. *onomastico* name day

ONU *Organizzazione delle Nazioni Unite* United Nations Organization (UNO)

OO.PP. *Opere Pubbliche* public works

op. *opera* work

O.P. *Ordine dei Predicatori* Order of Preachers *(Dominicans)*

op. cit. (Latin) *opere citato,* (Italian) *opera citata* in the work cited

orch. *orchestra* orchestra

OSA *Organizzazione degli Stati Americani* Organization of American States (OAS)

O.S.SS.A. *Ordine Superiore della Santissima Annunziata* Order of the Annunziata *(i.e. the Virgin Mary)*

ott. *ottobre* October

O.V.N.I. *oggetto volante non identificato* unidentified flying object (UFO)

P

P *parcheggio* parking, parking lot

P. *Padre* Father

p. *pagina* page (p.); *piano* piano, soft(ly)

PA *Palermo*

P.A. *Patto Atlantico* Atlantic Treaty*; posta aerea* airmail

pag. *pagina* page (p.)

par. *par.* paragraph (par.)

pass. *passato* past (tense); *passivo* passive

PC *Piacenza* Piacenza

P.C. *Partito Comunista* Communist Party; *parte civile* co--plaintiff *(in a legal procedure)*

p.c. *per conoscenza* for the attention of (attn.); *per condo-glianze* please accept our/my condolences

P/C *polizza di carico* bill of lading

p.c.c. *per copia conforme* certified copy *(+ signature)*

PD *Padova* Padua

P.D.S. *Partito Democratico della Sinistra* Democratic Party of the Left

PE *Pescara* Pescara

p.e. *per esempio* for example (e.g.)

ped. *pedale* pedal

pers. *personale* personal; *persona* person; *persone* persons

p.f. *per favore* please

PG *Perugia* Perugia

P.G. *Procuratore Generale* District Attorney, Senior Public Prosecutor

PI *Pisa* Pisa

P.I. *Pubblica Istruzione* Public Education

P.L.I. *Partito Liberale Italiano* Italian Liberal Party

P.M. *Polizia Militare* Military Police (M.P.); *Pubblico Mini-stero* Public Prosecutor; *Posta Militare* Military Post; *Pontefice Massimo* Pontifex Maximus *(i.e. the Pope)*

p.m. *pomeridiano* in the afternoon (p.m.)

P.M.I. *punto morto inferiore* bottom dead center (B.D.C.)

P.M.S. *punto morto superiore* top dead center (T.D.C.)

P.N.L., Pnl, pnl *prodotto nazionale lordo* Gross National Product (GNP)

PN *Pordenone* Pordenone

POLFER *Polizia Ferroviaria* Railroad Police

POLSTRADA *Polizia Stradale* Highway Police

PP. *porto pagato* carriage/postage paid

pp. *pianissimo* pianissimo, very soft(ly); *pagine* pages

p.p. *pacco postale* parcel; *per procura* by proxy; *prima parte* first part*; primo piano* second floor, *(GB)* first floor; *posa piano* handle with care

ppa. *per procura* by proxy

P.P.I. *Partito Popolare Italiano* Italian People's Party

PP.TT. *Poste e Telecomunicazioni* postal and telecommunications services

P.Q.M. *per questi motivi* for these reasons

PR *Parma* Parma; *Pubbliche Relazioni* Public Relations

P.R. *Partito Radicale* Radical Party; *Procuratore della Repubblica* (Senior) Public Prosecutor

p.r. *per ringraziamento* with thanks

P.R.A. *Pubblico Registro Automobilistico* Motor Registration Office

pref. *prefazione* preface; *prefisso* prefix

Preg.mo., Pr.mo *Pregiatissimo* Dear ...; *Pr.mo Sig. E. Rossi (on envelope)* E. Rossi, Esq.

Prof. *professore* professor *(title also used for teachers)*

Prof.ssa *professoressa* (lady) professor *(title also used for lady teachers)*

PS *Pesaro* Pesaro

P.S. *Pubblica Sicurezza* Police; (Latin) *postscriptum,* (Italian) *poscritto* postscript; *Previdenza Sociale* Social Security (Insurance)

PT *Pistoia* Pistoia

P.T.P. *Posto Telefonico Pubblico* public telephone

PV *Pavia* Pavia

P.V. *piccola velocità* slow ordinary freight service

p.v. *prossimo venturo* next

PZ *Potenza* Potenza

P.za *Piazza* square (sq.)

P.zle *Piazzale* large square

Q

q *quintale* quintal *(= 100 kg)*

q. *quadrato* square

q.b. *quanto basta* as much as is sufficient, as required

Q.G. *Quartier Generale* Headquarters (H.Q.)

Q.I. *quoziente d'intelligenza* intelligence quotient (IQ)

quad. *quaderno* periodical; number, issue *(of periodical)*

quot. *quotazione* quotation

R

r *raggio* radius *(Mathematics)*

R. *raccomandata* registered (letter); *Reverendo* reverend;

(treno) rapido express (train); *regio* royal; *regina* queen

RA *Ravenna* Ravenna

racc. *raccomandata* registered (letter)

Rag. *ragioniere* accountant

RAI *Radiotelevisione Italiana* (formerly: *Radioaudizioni Italiane*) Italian Broadcasting Corporation

rappr. *rappresentante* representative

R.A.S. *Riunione Adriatica di Sicurtà* United Adriatic Insurance Companies

RAU *Repubblica Araba Unita* United Arab Republic (U.A.R.)

RC *Reggio Calabria* Reggio Calabria

R.C. *Rotary Club* Rotary Club

Rc *radice cubica* cubic root

rd *radiante* radian *(Mathematics)*

R.D. *Regio Decreto* Royal Decree

R.D.T. *Repubblica Democratica Tedesca* German Democratic Republic (GDR)

RE *Reggio Emilia* Reggio Emilia

Rep. *Repubblica* Republic

Rev., rev. *reverendo* reverend

R.F. *radiofrequenza* radio frequency

R.F.T. *Repubblica Federale Tedesca* Federal Republic of Germany (FRG)

RG *Ragusa* Ragusa

Rgt. *reggimento* regiment (Rgt)

RI *Rieti* Rieti

R.I. *Repubblica Italiana* Italian Republic

R.I.Na. *Registro Navale Italiano* Italian Register of Shipping

ripr. viet. *riproduzione vietata* copyright, all rights reserved

R.M. *ricchezza mobile* income *(for taxation)*

R.mo *Reverendissimo* very reverend

RO *Rovigo* Rovigo

RP *risposta pagata* reply paid (RP)

R.P. *Reverendo Padre* Reverend Father; *riservato personale* private and confidential

Rq *radice quadrata* square root

RSM *Repubblica di San Marino* Republic of San Marino

R.T. *radiotelegrafia* radiotelegraphy
R.U. *Regno Unito* United Kingdom (UK)

S

s *secondo* second (sec.)
S *Sud* South
S. *Santo, Santa* Saint
SA *Salerno* Salerno
S.A. *Società Anonima* Corporation (Corp.); *Sua Altezza* His/Her Highness (H.H.); *servizio attivo* active duty
s.a. (Latin) *sine anno,* (Italian) *senza anno* sine anno, no year
sab. *sabato* Saturday
S.Acc. *Società in Accomandita* Limited Partnership
SACE *Sezione Speciale per l'Assicurazione del Credito delle Esportazioni* Export Credit Guarantee Department (E.C.G.D.)
S.a.r.L. *Società a responsabilità limitata* Limited (Liability) Company
s.b.f. *salvo buon fine* with the usual proviso
sc *secante* secant
S.C. *Sede Centrale* head office; *Sacro Collegio* Sacred Committee, Cardinals' Committee; *Stato Civile* marital status
s.c. *secondo consumo* according to consumption; *sopra citato* mentioned above, above-mentioned
S.C.V. *Stato della Città del Vaticano* State of the Vatican City
s.d. *senza data* no date (n.d.)
s.d.l. *senza data e luogo* no place or date
S.d.S. *Segretario di Stato* undersecretary, *(BE)* minister of state
S.E. *Sua Eccellenza* His/Her Excellency
seg. *seguente* following (f., foll.)
segr. *segretario* secretary
S.Em. *Sua Eminenza* His Eminence
Sen. *Senatore* senator
S.E.O. *salvo errori e omissioni* errors and omissions excepted

serg. *sergente* sergeant (Sgt.)

sez. *sezione* section, division, department

S.F.I. *Società Finanziaria Internazionale* International Finance Corporation (IFC)

S.G. *Sua Grazia* His/Her Grace (H.G.)

SI *Siena* Siena

S.I. *Socialisti Italiani* Italian Socialists

S.I.A.E. *Società Italiana Autori ed Editori* Italian Association of Authors and Publishers

sig. *signore* Mr.

sigg. *signori* Messieurs (Messrs.)

sig.na *signorina* Miss

sig.ra *signora* Mrs.

sim. *simile* similar

S.I.M. *Servizio Informazioni Militari* Army Intelligence Service

sist. *sistema* system

s.l.m. *sul livello del mare* above sea level

S.M. *Stato Maggiore* General Staff *(armed forces)*; *Sua Maestà* His/Her Majesty;

S.M.E. *Sistema Monetario Europeo* European Monetary System (EMS)

S.M.I. *Sua Maestà Imperiale* His/Her Imperial Majesty (H.I.M.)

s.n. *senza numero* without number; *senza nome* without name

S.N.D.A. *Società Nazionale Dante Alighieri* National Dante Alighieri Society

SO *Sondrio* Sondrio

Soc. *Società* company, corporation; association; society

SP *La Spezia* La Spezia

sp. *specie* kind

S.P. *Santo Padre* Holy Father

S.P.A. *Società Protettrice degli Animali* Society for the Prevention of Cruelty to Animals

S.p.A. *Società per Azioni* Joint Stock Company

Spett. *spettabile; Spett. ditta ...* Messieurs ... *(on envelope, when addressing firms)*

S.P.M. *sue proprie mani* personal, for the attention of (attn.)

SR *Siracusa*

S.R. *Sacra Rota* Sacred Roman Rota *(Catholic church tri-bunal)*
S.R.C. *Sacra Romana Chiesa* Holy Roman Church
S.R.I. *Sacro Romano Imperio* Holy Roman Empire
S.r.l. *Società a responsabilità limitata* Limited Company
SS *Sassari* Sassari
S.S. *Santa Sede* Holy See; *Sua Santità* His Holiness
SS.PP. *Santi Padri* Holy Fathers
S.Ten. *sottotenente* lieutenant
S.U. *Stati Uniti* United States (U.S.)
SV *Savona* Savona
S.V. *Signoria Vostra* Your Lordship
s.v. *sotto voce* in a low voice, subdued

T

t *tonnellata* ton; *tempo* time; *temperatura* temperature
t. *tomo* tome, volume (vol.)
TA *Taranto* Taranto
tab. *tabella* table
TAC *tomografia assiale computerizzata* computerized axial tomography (CAT)
tang. *tangente* tangent (tan)
TAR *Tribunale Amministrativo Regionale* Regional Administrative Court of Law
TBC, tbc *tubercolosi* tuberculosis (TB)
T.C.I. *Touring Club Italiano* Italian Touring Club
TE *Teramo* Teramo
tel. *telefono* telephone
temp. *temperatura* temperature
ten. *tenente* first lieutenant
TEP *tonnellata equivalente petrolio* oil equivalent ton
T.M.E.C. *Tempo Medio dell'Europa Centrale* Central European Time (CET)
T.M.G. *Tempo Medio di Greenwich* Greenwich Mean Time (GMT)
TN *Trento* Trent, Trento
TO *Torino* Turin
tom. *tomo* tome, volume (vol.)

TOTIP *Totalizzatore Ippico* horse-race pools *(system of public betting on horse races)*

TOTOCALCIO *Totalizzatore Calcistico* football pools *(system of public betting on football teams)*

TP *Trapani* Trapani

TR *Terni* Terni

tr. *tratta* draft

trad. *traduttore* translator; *traduzione* translation

trans. *transitivo* transitive; *transito* transit

trim. *trimestre* quarter, term, period of three months; *trimestrale* quarterly

TS *Trieste* Trieste

T.S.L. *tonnellata di stazza lorda* gross register ton (G.R.T.)

T.S.N. *tonnellata di stazza netta* net ton (N.T.)

T.T. *trasferimento telegrafico* telegraphic transfer

T.U. *Testo Unico* Unified Legal Code

T.U.S. *tasso ufficiale di sconto* bank rate

TV *televisione* television (TV)

T.V.A. *Tassa sul Valore Aggiunto* Value Added Tax (VAT), sales tax

TV *Treviso* Treviso

TVC *televisore a colori* color TV set

U

U *uranio* uranium

U.C. *Ufficio di Collocamento* State/Federal Employment Agency, *(BE)* jobcentre

U.C.E. *unità di conto europea* European unit of account

U.C.I. *Unione Ciclistica Internazionale* International Union of Cyclists

UD *Udine* Udine

U.D.I. *Unione Donne Italiane* Association of Italian Women

U.E. *Unione Europea* European Union (EU)

UEO *Unione Europea Occidentale* Western European Union (WEU)

U.I.L. *Unione Italiana dei Lavoratori* Italian Federation of

Labor Unions; *Ufficio Internazionale del Lavoro* International Labor Office

ult. *ultimo* last

un. *unità* unit; unity

UNESCO *Organizzazione delle Nazioni Unite per l'Educazione, la Scienza e la Cultura* United Nations Educational, Scientific and Cultural Organization

u.p. *ultima parte* last part

U.P.I. *Ufficio Privato Investigativo* Private Detective Agency

U.P.U. *Unione Postale Universale* Universal Postal Union

URSS *Unione delle Repubbliche Socialiste Sovietiche* Union of Sovietic Socialist Republics (U.S.S.R.)

u.s. *ultimo scorso* last *(after date)*

U.S.L. *Unità Sanitaria Locale* Local Health Unit/Center

U.V. *ultravioletto* ultraviolet (UV)

V

V *volt* volt; *volume* volume

v *velocità* velocity

V. *Via* Street

v. *vedi, vedasi* see; *verso* verse

VA *Varese* Varese

V.A. *Vostra Altezza* Your Highness

val. *valuta* currency

var. *variabile* variable (var.); *varietà* variety (var.); *variante* variant (var.)

Vat. *Vaticano* Vatican

vb. *verbo* verb

VC *Vercelli* Vercelli

V.C. *Valore Civile* civil bravery; *Vice Console* Vice Consul

V.d.F. *vigili del fuoco* fire department

VE *Venezia* Venice

V.E. *Vostra Eccellenza* Your Excellency

Ven. *venerabile* venerable

ven. *venerdì* Friday

V.F. *vigili del fuoco* fire department

VI *Vicenza* Vicenza

viv. *vivace* lively
V.le *Viale* Avenue
vol. *volume* volume (vol.)
V.P. *Vice Presidente* Vice President
VR *Verona* Verona
v.r. *vedi retro* please turn over (p.t.o.)
Vs. *Vostro* Yours *(in letters)*
vs. *vostro* your
V.S. *Vostra Santità* Your Holiness; *Vostra Signoria* Your Lordship
v.s. *vedi sopra* see above; *vedi sotto* see below
VT *Viterbo* Viterbo
V.T. *Vecchio Testamento* Old Testament (OT)
V.U. *Vigili Urbani* municipal police

W

W *watt* watt (W)
Wh *wattora* watt-hour (Wh)

X

X. *Cristo* Christ

Y

Y.C.I. *Yacht Club d'Italia* Italian Yacht Club

Z

Z.d.G. *Zona di Guerra* war zone

Notes/Appunti

Notes/Appunti

Notes/Appunti